# Treatise on International Criminal Law

# Treatise on International Criminal Law

## *Volume III: International Criminal Procedure*

Second Edition

KAI AMBOS
*With the assistance of*
ALEXANDER HEINZE
PETER RACKOW
SUSANN ABOUELDAHAB

OXFORD
UNIVERSITY PRESS

OXFORD
UNIVERSITY PRESS

Great Clarendon Street, Oxford, OX2 6DP,
United Kingdom

Oxford University Press is a department of the University of Oxford.
It furthers the University's objective of excellence in research, scholarship,
and education by publishing worldwide. Oxford is a registered trade mark of
Oxford University Press in the UK and in certain other countries



First Edition published in 2016
Second Edition published in 2025



Published in the United States of America by Oxford University Press
198 Madison Avenue, New York, NY 10016, United States of America

British Library Cataloguing in Publication Data

Data available

Library of Congress Control Number: 2024945020

ISBN 978–0–19–286866–4

DOI: 10.1093/law/9780192868664.001.0001

Printed and bound by
CPI Group (UK) Ltd, Croydon, CR0 4YY

MIX
Paper | Supporting
responsible forestry
FSC® C013604

*TO VÂNIA, the best that happened in my life, and their gifts Analu, Lara and Patrick.*

# Preface

The second edition of this third and final volume of my 'Treatise on International Criminal Law' is overdue after about eight years since the first edition was published. As the first edition, this second edition too took me more time than originally anticipated, not only due to other commitments but in particular because of the vast size and technical complexity of its subject matter as well as the well-nigh unmanageable scope of the vast case law. In fact, the sheer amount of material to read, analyse, and write about means that this volume of the trilogy in particular is something of an unfinished business. This is especially true for the chapters with some comparative references (Chapters VII and VIII), where in this edition more jurisdictions have been included, making the selection somewhat more representative, yet still not representative enough.

The second edition maintains the general structure of the first edition, starting, in Chapter I, with an understanding of international criminal procedure (complemented by pre-prosecutorial investigative mechanisms) that is informed by historical precedents, basic procedural concepts, and, above all, fair trial rights. Besides this, any criminal procedure is largely framed and implemented by the trial actors, analysed as 'participants' in Chapter II. International criminal procedure is different from national criminal procedure, however, in that it is implemented by international(ized) criminal tribunals and nowadays even predominantly by a permanent international criminal court whose jurisdiction does not coincide with sovereign territories but is, rather, derived from such territories governed by States. The ensuing jurisdictional principles are analysed in Chapter III, Section A., followed by an explanation of the ICC's jurisdiction; the related questions of the relationship between this international and national jurisdictions (called 'complementarity' under the ICC regime) are investigated in Section B. of the same chapter. We then delve into the actual procedure or proceedings from the preliminary investigation to appeals (Chapters IV to VI) with a special treatment of selected issues (Chapter IV, Section B.) and a specific chapter (V) dedicated to evidence and disclosure in between. Of course, international criminal tribunals are like giants without arms and legs, unable to enforce their law without the support of States. Thus, for some the existence and legitimacy of these tribunals hinges on the cooperation of States (or lack thereof). The relevant regimes therefore require examination in Chapter VII. Last but not least and indeed related to the former, decisions of international criminal tribunals, especially their sentences, must be enforced. This is dealt with in Chapter VIII. Some concluding remarks will then, hopefully, round off the book.

Apart from updating the case law and relevant scholarly literature—an almost unachievable enterprise—we have also added some (sub-)sections, e.g. on the already mentioned non-judicial investigative mechanisms, special forms of digital evidence, the 'submission approach' to material and information, trial management, political elements within the 'interests of justice', etc. In order not to further expand the scope of the book we often refer to the first edition with regard to earlier case law. The note on gender-neutral language is still valid: the use of the male or female forms throughout the whole book, with prevalence of the female form, is rather random; it is not intended to have any substantive implication. As in the other volumes and in the previous edition, there is a general literature list at the end of this volume and more specific bibliographies for each chapter which are available on the

OUP Companion website; in addition, a new documents list has been added at the end of the volume.

It is a truism to say that such a book, indeed this whole three-volume Treatise, could not have been researched and written by one person alone. This is particularly true for this last volume for the reasons set out above. There have been many helping hands on different fronts. At my Göttingen chair, first of all I have to thank Dr. Alexander Heinze, LL.M. who was not only deeply involved in (re-)writing and updating Chapters IV, V, and IX but always served as my first resource person for any substantive or organizational question. I also greatly thank apl. Prof. Dr. Peter Rackow for his substantial updating of Chapters I, III, and VII as well as Susann Aboueldahab for her great support with regard to Chapters II, VIII, and, at a later stage, to Chapters I and III (apart from her last-minute assistance regarding the chapter bibliographies and other issues). Rodolfo Gonzaléz Espinoza assisted in updating Chapter VI, and Inês Freixo updated case law in various chapters. Among the students, Jonathan Stelter assumed a special responsibility, but a number of others (Lea Brockmann, Marius Münkel, Marlene Nebel, Helene Schiffel) provided valuable assistance too. At The Hague, some of my colleagues and friends at the ICC and KSC (Eleni Chaitidou, Rod Rastan) have provided me with relevant information, not only case law, from the Court; special thanks goes to Simon Meisenberg and Inneke Onsea with our wonderful legal team (especially Jennifer Depiazza) at the KSC Appeals Panel, always able and willing to assist me with regard to the ever-expanding case law of the KSC. Last but not least, I also thank Kim Vollrodt from OUP and the copy editors, especially Caroline Valia-Kollery who spotted quite a few errors. The full text was submitted at the beginning of May 2024 and all hyperlinks have been checked around that time; the proofs have been revised and partly updated in September 2024.

Kai Ambos, Göttingen and The Hague, September 2024

# Contents

# Figures

# Table of Cases

## INTERNATIONAL COURTS, TRIBUNALS AND MONITORING MECHANISMS

**European Commission of Human Rights**



**European Court of Human Rights**

**European Court of Justice**

**Extraordinary Chambers in the Courts of Cambodia**



**Human Rights Committee**

**Inter-American Commission on Human Rights**



**Inter-American Court of Human Rights**

**ILO Administrative Tribunal**



**International Court of Justice**

**International Criminal Court**

**International Criminal Tribunal for Rwanda**

**International Criminal Tribunal for the Former Yugoslavia**

**Mechanism for International Criminal Tribunals**

**Special Tribunal for Lebanon**

**US Military Commission, Manila**



**US Nuremberg Military Tribunals**

## NATIONAL CASES

### Colombia



### France



### Germany

CONSTITUTIONAL COURT:



FEDERAL COURT OF JUSTICE:



STATE SUPREME COURTS:



### Kazakhstan



### South Africa



### Switzerland

**United Kingdom**



**United States**

# Table of Legislation

## INTERNATIONAL LEGISLATION

## NATIONAL LEGISLATION

### Argentina



### Australia



### Austria



### Bangladesh

**Netherlands**

# Abbreviations

| Abbreviation | Meaning | |
|---|---|---|
| AALCO | Asian-African Legal Consultative Organization | |
| ABAJ | American Bar Association Journal | |
| AC | Appeals Chamber | |
| ACHR | American Convention on Human Rights | |
| ACHPR | African (Banjul) Charter on Human and Peoples' Rights | |
| | Advisory Committee on Nominations of Judges of the ICC | |
| ADPCP | Anuario de Derecho Penal y Ciencias Penales | |
| AFRC | Armed Forces Revolutionary Council | |
| AfrJICompL | African Journal of International and Comparative Law | |
| AfrJLS | African Journal of Legal Studies | |
| AI | Amnesty International | |
| AIDP | Association International de Droit pénal | |
| AJCL | American Journal of Criminal Law | |
| AJCompL | American Journal of Comparative Law | |
| AJIL | American Journal of International Law | |
| Ala. | Alabama | |
| ALC | Annotated Leading Cases | |
| ALC | Armée de Libération du Congo | |
| ALI | American Law Institute | |
| alic | actio libera in causa | |
| Alt. | Alternative | |
| AltaLR | Alberta Law Review | |
| AmUIntLRev | American University International Law Review | |
| AmUJGender SocPol'y&L | American University Journal of Gender, Social Policy & the Law | |
| AnwBl | Anwaltsblatt | |
| AP | Additional Protocol | |
| APuZ | Aus Politik und Zeitgeschichte | |
| ARIEL | Austrian Review of International & European Law | |
| ArizJICompL | The Arizona Journal of International and Comparative Law | |
| Art. | Article | |
| ASIL | American Society of International Law | |
| ASP | Assembly of State Parties | |
| ASR | African Security Review | |
| AustYBIL | Australian Yearbook of International Law | |
| AVR | Archiv des Völkerrechts | German Law Journal |

| | | |
|---|---|---|
| BCInt'l& CompLRev | Boston College International and Comparative Law Review | |
| BelgianRIL | Belgian Review of International Law | |
| BGBl | Bundesgesetzblatt | German Federal Law Gazette |
| BGH | Bundesgerichtshof | German Federal Court |
| BGHR GG | BGH-Rechtsprechung | Collection of Decisions of the German Federal Court in Constitutional matters |
| BGHSt | Entscheidungen des Bundesgerichtshofs in Strafsachen | Official Collection of Decisions of the German Federal Court in criminal matters |
| BJCrim | British Journal of Criminology | |
| BMJ | Bundesministerium für Justiz | German Federal Ministry of Justice |
| Boletim IBCCrim | Boletim Instituto Brasileiro de Ciências Criminais | |
| BR-Drs. | Bundesrats-Drucksache | Printed Matter of the Federal Council of the German Parliament |
| BuffCLR | Buffalo Criminal Law Review | |
| BUILJ | Boston University International Law Journal | |
| Bull. Crim. | Bulletin des Arrêts de la Cour de Cassation, Chambre Criminelle | Official Collection of Decisions of the French Cour de Cassation in criminal matters |
| BVerfG | Bundesverfassungsgericht | German Constitutional Court |
| BVerfGE | Entscheidungen des Bundesverfassungsgerichts | Official Collection of Decisions of the German Constitutional Court |
| BYbIL | British Yearbook of International Law | |
| C & P | Carrington's & Payne's English Nisi Prius Reports | |
| CalApp | Court of Appeals of California | |
| CalLR | California Law Review | |
| CambLJ | The Cambridge Law Journal | |
| Cambodian PC 1956 | Cambodian Penal Code of 1956 | |
| CanYbIL | Canadian Yearbook of International Law | |
| CappRep | Criminal Appeal Reports | |
| CAR | Central African Republic | |
| CardozoLR | Cardozo Law Review | |
| CardozoJConfRes | Cardozo Journal of Conflict Resolution | |
| CathULR | Catholic University Law Review | |
| CC | Criminal Code | |

| | | |
|---|---|---|
| CCA (2002) | Criminal Code 2002 (Australia) | |
| CCC | Canadian Criminal Cases | |
| CCL | Control Council Law | |
| CCP | Code of Criminal Procedure | |
| CDF | Civil Defence Forces | |
| CDJP | Cuadernos de Doctrina y Jurisprudencia Penal | Argentinean Law Journal |
| CERD | Committee on the Elimination of Racial Discrimination | |
| cf. | confer | |
| Ch | Chapter | |
| ChapmanLR | Chapman Law Review | |
| ChatHouseILDG | Chatham House International Law Discussion Group | |
| ChicJIL | Chicago Journal of International Law | |
| ChiKentJI&CompL | Chicago Kent Journal of International and Comparative Law | |
| ChicKentLR | Chicago Kent Law Review | |
| ChinJIL | Chinese Journal of International Law | |
| CIL | Customary International Law | |
| CISA | Convention Implementing the Schengen Agreement | |
| CJA | Criminal Justice Act (England and Wales) | |
| CJE | Code of Judicial Ethics ICC | |
| Cl & F | Clark & Finnelly's House of Lords Cases | |
| CLF | Criminal Law Forum | |
| CLJ | Cambridge Law Journal | |
| CLP | Current Legal Problems | |
| CLR | Criminal Law Review | |
| CMR | Court-Martial Reports | |
| CoE<br>ColHRLR | Council of Europe<br>Columbia Human Rights Law Review | |
| ColJTransnat'lL | Columbia Journal of Transnational Law | |
| ColLR | Columbia Law Review | |
| conc. | Concurring | |
| ConnJIL | Connecticut Journal of International Law | |
| coord. | Coordinator | |
| CornILJ | Cornell International Law Journal | |
| CP | Code Pénal, Código Penal, Codice Penale | French, Spanish, Portuguese and Italian Criminal Code (France, Spain, Portugal and Italy) |
| CPDIL | Committee on the Progressive Development of International Law and its Codification | |
| CPC | Criminal Procedure Code | |
| CPP | Code de Procédure Penal, Código de Procedimiento Penal, Codice di Procedura Penale, Código de Processo Penal | Code of Criminal Procedure |
| CPT | Committee for the Prevention of Torture (Council of Europe) | |

| | | |
|---|---|---|
| CrLPhil | Criminal Law and Philosophy | |
| Crime Law Soc Change | Crime, Law and Social Change | |
| CrimJust | Criminal Justice | |
| Crit. | Critically | |
| CSS | Counsel Support Section | |
| CWRJIL | Case Western Reserve Journal of International Law | |
| CWRLR | Case Western Reserve Law Review | |
| DAB | Disciplinary Appeals Board ICC | |
| DB | Disciplinary Board ICC | |
| DCC | Document Containing the Charges (ICC) | |
| DCCB | Draft Criminal Code Bill (for England and Wales) | |
| DenvJIL&Pol'y | Denver Journal of International Law and Policy | |
| DePaulLR | DePaul Law Review | |
| DickJIL | Dickinson Journal of International Law | |
| DINA | Dirección de Inteligencia Nacional | Chilean Secret Service |
| DÖV | Die öffentliche Verwaltung | German Law Journal |
| DPAS | Division of Prosecutorial Administrative Services (OTP ICC) | |
| DRC | Democratic Republic of Congo | |
| DStR | Deutsches Strafrecht | German ournal |
| DukeJComp&IL | Duke Journal of Comparative and International Law | |
| DukeLJ | Duke Law Journal | |
| DuqULR | Duquesne University Law Review | |
| EAC Senegal | Extraordinary African Chambers in the Senegalese Courts | |
| ECBA | European Criminal Bar Association | |
| ECCC | Extraordinary Chambers in the Courts of Cambodia | |
| ECCC-Law | Law on the Establishment of the Extraordinary Chambers | |
| ECHR | European Convention on Human Rights | |
| ECJ | Court of Justice of the European Union | |
| ECtHR | European Court of Human Rights | |
| ECtRep | European Court Reports | |
| EEC Treaty | Treaty establishing the European Economic Community | |
| e.g. | Exempli gratia | For example |
| EJCCLCJ | European Journal of Crime, Criminal Law and Criminal Justice | |
| EJCrim | European Journal of Criminology | |
| EJIL | European Journal of International Law | |
| EJLRef | European Journal of Law Reform | |
| Elements | Elements of Crimes | |
| EmoryILR | Emory International Law Review | |
| EOC | Elements of Crimes | |
| Espec. | Especially | |
| EssexHRR | Essex Human Rights Review | |
| Et al. | Et alii | And others |

| | | |
|---|---|---|
| Ethics | Ethics (Chicago Journals) | |
| Ethics&IntAff | Ethics & International Affairs | |
| EU Charter | Charter of the Fundamental Rights of the European Union | |
| EuGRZ | Europäische Grundrechte-Zeitschrift | |
| EULEX | European Union Rule of Law Mission | |
| ExCom | Executive Committee (ICC OTP) | |
| Fallos | Colección Oficial de Fallos de la Corte Suprema de Justicia de la Nación | Official Collection of Argentinean Supreme Court Decisions |
| FARC | Fuerzas Armadas Revolucionarias de Colombia — Ejército del Pueblo | Revolutionary Armed Forces of Colombia — People's Army |
| FAZ | Frankfurter Allgemeine Zeitung | |
| FCP | French Code Pénal | |
| FDLR | Forces Démocratiques de la Libération du Rwanda | |
| FEC | Far Eastern Commission | |
| FedRCrimProc | Federal Rules of Criminal Procedure (US) | |
| FIDH | International Federation for Human Rights | |
| FletcherFWAJ | Fletcher Forum of World Affairs Journal | |
| FletcherJHS | Fletcher Journal of Human Security | |
| FloridaJIL | Florida Journal of International Law | |
| fn. | Footnote, footnotes | |
| FNI | Front des Nationalistes et Intégrationnistes | |
| ForAff | Foreign Affairs | |
| FordhamILJ | Fordham International Law Journal | |
| FordhamLR | Fordham Law Review | |
| FPLC | Forces Patriotiques pour la Libération du Congo | |
| FRPI | Force de Resistence Patriotique en Ituri | |
| FRY | Federal Republic of Yugoslavia | |
| FS | Festschrift | |
| FYbIL | Finnish Yearbook of International Law | |
| GA | Goltdammer's Archiv für Strafrecht | |
| GA Res | UN-General Assembly Resolution | |
| GAOR | GA Official Records | |
| GC | Geneva Convention | |
| GDR | German Democratic Republic | |
| GeorgiaJI&CompL | Georgia Journal of International and Comparative Law | |
| GeoJIL | Georgetown Journal of International Law | |
| GeoJLegalEthics | Georgetown Journal of Legal Ethics | |
| GeoLJ | Georgetown Law Journal | |
| GeoWashILR | George Washington International Law Review | |
| GermanLJ | German Law Journal | |
| Gestapo | Geheime Staatspolizei | Secret State Police of the National Socialists |
| GoJIL | Göttingen Journal of International Law | |
| GP | General Part | |
| GRULAC | Latin American and the Caribbean Group of States | |

| | | |
|---|---|---|
| GS | Gedächtnisschrift | |
| GYbIL | German Yearbook of International Law | |
| HarvHRJ | Harvard Human Rights Journal | |
| HarvILJ | Harvard International Law Journal | |
| HarvLJ | Harvard Law Journal | |
| HarvLR | Harvard Law Review | |
| HoustonJIL | Houston Journal of International Law | |
| HR | Human Ressources | |
| HRC | Human Rights Committee | |
| HRL | Human Rights Law | |
| HRLC | Human Rights Law Commentary | |
| HRLJ | Human Rights Law Journal | |
| HRLR | Human Rights Law Review | |
| HRQ | Human Rights Quarterly | |
| HRW | Human Rights Watch | |
| HuV-I | Humanitäres Völkerrecht- Informationsschriften | |
| i.a. | Inter alia | Among others |
| IAR | International Affairs Review | |
| IACtHR | Inter-American Court of Human Rights | |
| IBAHRI | International Bar Association Human Rights Institute | |
| Ibid | Ibidem | The same place |
| ICC | International Criminal Court | |
| ICCS | Statute of the ICC | |
| ICCPR | International Covenant on Civil and Political Rights | |
| ICG | International Crisis Group | |
| | | |
| ICJ | International Court of Justice | |
| ICL | International Criminal Law | |
| ICLQ | International and Comparative Law Quarterly | |
| ICLR | International Criminal Law Review | |
| ICLRep | International Criminal Law Reports | |
| ICP | Italian Codice Penale | |
| ICRC | International Committee of the Red Cross | |
| ICT | International Crimes Tribunal in Bangladesh | |
| ICTA (1973) | International Crimes (Tribunals) Act 1973 | |
| ICTJ | International Centre for Transitional Justice | |
| ICTR | International Criminal Tribunal for Rwanda | |
| ICTRS | Statute of the ICTR | |
| ICTY | International Criminal Tribunal for the former Yugoslavia | |
| ICTYS | Statute of the ICTY | |
| ID | Investigation Division (ICC OTP) | |
| IDF | International Detention Facility | |
| Id | Idem | The same |
| i.e. | id est | That is |
| IHCC | Iraqi Higher Criminal Court | |
| IHCCS | Law of the Iraqi Higher Criminal Court | |
| IHL | International Humanitarian Law | |

| | | |
|---|---|---|
| IHT | International Herald Tribune | |
| IJEP | International Journal of Evidence and Proof | |
| IJTJ | International Journal of Transitional Justice | |
| IKEMS | Information, Knowledge and Evidence Management Section (ICC-OTP) | |
| ILA | International Law Association | |
| ILC | International Law Commission | |
| ILM | International Legal Materials | |
| ILO | International Labour Organization | |
| ILR | International Law Reports | |
| ILSAJICL | International Law Students Association Journal of International and Comparative Law | |
| IMT | International Military Tribunal | |
| IMTFE | International Military Tribunal for the Far East | |
| IMTFES | International Military Tribunal for the Far East Statute | IMTFE(S) |
| IMTS | International Military Tribunal Statute | |
| IncCLRep | Incorporated Council of Law Reporting | |
| IndianaI&CLR | Indiana International & Comparative Law Review | |
| IndianaLJ | Indiana Law Journal | |
| IndYbILPol'y | Indian Yearbook of International Law and Policy | |
| INEF | Institut für Entwicklung und Frieden | |
| Insight ICC | Insight on the International Criminal Court Newsletter of the NGO Coalition for the ICC | |
| IntAff | International Affairs | |
| InternAbl | Internationales Anwaltsblatt | |
| Interpol | International Criminal Police Organization | |
| IOP | Immediate Office of the Prosecutor (OTP ICC) | |
| IR ECCC | Internal Rules ECCC | |
| IRMCTS | Statute of the International Residual Mechanism for Criminal Tribunals | |
| IRG | Gesetz über die internationale Rechtshilfe in Strafsachen | Act on the Mutual Assistance in Criminal Matters |
| IRRC | International Review of the Red Cross | |
| IRud | Internationales Recht und Diplomatie | |
| ISISC | Instituto Superiore di Scienze Criminali | International Institute of Higher Studies in Criminal Sciences, Siracusa, Italy |
| IsLR | Israel Law Review | |
| IST | Iraqi Special Tribunal | |
| ISTS | Iraqi Special Tribunal Statute | |
| IStGHG | German ICC Cooperation Act (IStGH-Gesetz) | |
| IsYbHR | Israel Yearbook on Human Rights | |
| JA | Juristische Arbeitsblätter | German Law Journal |
| JArmConfL | Journal of Armed Conflict Law | |
| JCCD | Jurisdiction, Complementarity and Co-operation Division (ICC OTP) | |
| JCE | Joint criminal enterprise | |
| JCL | Journal of Criminal Law | |

| | | |
|---|---|---|
| JCL&Crim | Journal of Criminal Law & Criminology | |
| JCompL | Journal of Comparative Law | |
| JCP | Juris-Classeur Périodique/La Semaine Juridique | French Law Journal |
| JCSL | Journal of Conflict and Security Law | |
| JICJ | Journal of International Criminal Justice | |
| JILIR | Journal of International Law & International Relations | |
| JJZG | Jahrbuch der juristischen Zeitgeschichte | German Law Journal |
| JLS | Journal of Legal Studies | |
| JMarshallLR | John Marshall Law Review | |
| JNA | Jugoslovenska narodna armija | Yugoslavian Army |
| JPD | Jueces para la Democracia | Spanish Law Journal |
| JPR | Journal of Peace Research | |
| JR | Juristische Rundschau | German Law Journal |
| JSPTL (NS) | Journal of the Society of Public Teachers of Law (New Series) | |
| JTransnat'lLPol'y | Journal of Transnational Law and Policy | |
| Jura | Juristische Ausbildung | German Law Journal |
| JuS | Juristische Schulung | German Law Journal |
| JZ | Juristenzeitung | German Law Journal |
| K.A. | Kai Ambos | |
| KCLJ | Kings College Law Journal | |
| KJ | Kritische Justiz | German Law Journal |
| KLA | Kosovo Liberation Army | |
| KritV | Kritische Vierteljahresschrift für Gesetzgebung und Rechtswissenschaft | German Law Journal |
| La Ley | La Ley – Revista jurídica española de doctrina, jurisprudencia y bibliografía | |
| Law & Soc Inquiry | Law & Social Inquiry | |
| Law&Soc'yR | Law & Society Review | |
| Loy. L.A. Int'l & Comp. L. Rev | Loyola of Los Angeles International and Comparative Law Review | |
| LCP | Law and Contemporary Problems | |
| LEC | Ley de Enjuciamiento Criminal | Spanish Criminal Procedure Code |
| LG | Landgericht | German district court |
| LJIL | Leiden Journal of International Law | |
| LNOJ | League of Nations Official Journal | |
| LouiLR | Louisiana Law Review | |
| LPICT | Law & Practice of International Courts & Tribunals | |
| LQR | Legal Quarterly Review | |
| LRA | Lord's Resistance Army | |
| LRC | Law Reform Commission (of Canada) | |
| LRTWC | Law Reports of Trials of War Criminals | |
| MaastJECompL | Maastricht Journal of European and Comparative Law | |
| McGeorge L Rev | McGeorge Law Review | |
| MDR | Monatsschrift für deutsches Recht | |
| MelbJIL | Melbourne Journal of International Law | |

| | | |
|---|---|---|
| MelbULR | Melbourne University Law Review | |
| Merkourios UJIEL | Merkourios Utrecht Journal of International and European Law | |
| MichJIL | Michigan Journal of International Law | |
| MichLR | Michigan Law Review | |
| MICT | Mechanisms for International Criminal Tribunals | |
| MilLR | Military Law Review | |
| MinnesotaLR | Minnesota Law Review | |
| MINUSCA | United Nations Multidimensional Integrated Stabilization Mission in the Central African Republic | |
| MLC | Mouvement de Libération du Congo | |
| MLR | Modern Law Review | |
| mn. | Margin number | |
| MONUC | Mission de l'Organisation des Nations Unies en République Démocratique du Congo | Renamed MONUSCO |
| MONUSCO | Mission de l'Organisation des Nations Unies pour la stabilisation en République Démocratique du Congo (United Nations Organization Stabilization Mission in the Democratic Republic of the Congo) | Former MONUC |
| MOU | Memorandum of Understanding | |
| MPC | Model Penal Code | |
| MPEPIL | Max Planck Encyclopedia of Public International Law | |
| MPI | Max Planck Institute | |
| MPYbUNL | Max Planck Yearbook of United Nations Law | |
| MRCDDH | Memoria, revista sobre cultura, democracia y derechos humanos | |
| n./nn. | note / notes | |
| NCJIL&ComReg | North Carolina Journal of International Law & Commercial Regulation | |
| NCLR | New Criminal Law Review | |
| NDC = NVR | National Defence Council = Nationaler Verteidigungsrat der DDR | |
| NDP | Nueva Doctrina Penal | |
| NebraskaLR | Nebraska Law Review | |
| NELR | New England Law Review | |
| Newsletter SupraCrim | Newsletter Supranational Criminology | |
| NGO | Non-Governmental Organisation | |
| NILR | Netherlands International Law Review | |
| NJW | Neue Juristische Wochenschrift | |
| NLR | Nova Law Review | |
| NordJIL | Nordic Journal of International Law | |
| NotreDameLR | Notre Dame Law Review | |
| NQHR | Netherlands Quarterly of Human Rights | |
| NStZ | Neue Zeitschrift für Strafrecht | |
| NStZ-RR | Neue Zeitschrift für Strafrecht-Rechtsprechungsreport | |
| NYbIL | Netherlands Yearbook of International Law | |

| | | |
|---|---|---|
| NYLF | New York Law Forum | |
| NYU JILP | New York University Journal of International Law & Politics | |
| NWJIHR | Northwestern Journal of International Human Rights | |
| NZLR | New Zealand Law Reports | |
| OAS | Organization of American States | |
| OGHBrZ | Oberster Gerichtshof für die Britische Zone in Strafsachen | Supreme Court of the British Zone of Occupation |
| OGHSt | Entscheidungen des Obersten Gerichtshofes für die Britische Zone in Strafsachen | Official Collection of Decisions of the Supreme Court for the British Zone |
| OHCHR | UN Office of the High Commissioner for Human Rights | |
| OJEC | Official Journal of the European Communities | |
| OJ EU | Official Journal of the European Union | |
| OJLS | Oxford Journal of Legal Studies | |
| OLG | Oberlandesgericht | German Higher Regional Court |
| OPCD | Office of Public Counsel for the Defence (ICC) | |
| OPCV | Office of Public Counsel for Victims (ICC) | |
| OregonLR | Oregon Law Review | |
| ÖRiZ | Österreichische Richterzeitung | |
| öStGB | österreichische Strafgesetzbuch | Austrian Criminal Code |
| OTP | Office of the Prosecutor | |
| OTR | On the Record (publication on the travaux of the ICC) | |
| OWiG | Ordnungswidrigkeitengesetz | Law on administrative offences |
| p./pp. | page/pages | |
| PACE | Police and Criminal Evidence Act, 1984 (England and Wales | |
| para./paras. | paragraph/paragraphs | |
| PC | Penal Code | |
| PCIJ | Permanent Court of International Justice | |
| PD | Practice Direction | |
| ProsD | Prosecution Division (ICC OTP) | |
| PennStLR | Penn State Law Review | |
| PILR | Pace International Law Review | |
| PISG | Provisional Institutions of Self-Government | |
| PMC | Private Military Companies | |
| POW | Prisoners of War | |
| PrepCom | ICC-Preparatory Committee | |
| PrepCommis | Preparatory Commission | |
| Proc | Proceedings, Procedure | |
| PTC | Pre-Trial Chamber | |
| PVS | Politische Vierteljahreszeitschrift | |

| | | |
|---|---|---|
| QBD | Queens Bench Division | |
| RabelsZ | Rabels Zeitschrift für ausländisches und internationales Privatrecht | |
| R2P | Responsibility to Protect | |
| RCD | Recueil des Cours de l'Académie de la Haye en ligne | The Hague Academy Collected Courses Online |
| RCP | Revista de Ciencias Penales | Uruguayan Law Journal |
| RDPC | Revista de Derecho Penal y Criminología | Spanish /Belgian Law Journal |
| RDPP | Revista de Derecho y Proceso Penal | Spanish Law Journal |
| Reg | Regulation(s) | |
| RegC | Regulations of the Court (ICC) | |
| RegentULR | Regent University Law Review | |
| RegOTP | Regulations of the Office of the Prosecutor (ICC) | |
| RegR | Regulations of the Registry (ICC) | |
| RegTFV | Regulations of the Trust Fund for Victims | |
| Report ICTR (1995) | Report of the Secretary-General pursuant to paragraphs of Security Council Resolution 955 (1994) | |
| Report ICTY (1993) | Security Council, Report of the Secretary-General Pursuant to Paragraph 2 of Security Council Resolution 808 (1993) | |
| Res | Resolution | |
| RevDPC | Revue de Droit Pénal et de Criminologie | |
| RGBl | Reichsgesetzblatt | Law Gazette of the German Reich |
| RIADP | Revista Iberoamericana de Derecho Procesal | |
| RIADPC | Revista Iberoamericana de Derecho Procesal Constitucional | |
| RIDC | Revue Internationale de Droit Comparé | |
| RIDP | Revue International de Droit Pénal | |
| RIDPP | Rivista Italiana di Diritto e Procedura Penale | |
| RIS | Review of International Studies | |
| RISK | Risk: Health, Safety and Environment | |
| RogWillULR | Roger Williams University Law Review | |
| RP | Revista Penal | |
| RPCC | Revista Portuguesa de Ciencia Criminal | |
| RPE | Rules of Procedure and Evidence | |
| RPE ICC | Rules of Procedure and Evidence ICC, 9 September 2002, last amendment 27 November 2013 (Res. ICC-ASP/12/Res.7) | |
| RSC | Revue de Science Criminelle et de Droit Pénal Comparé | |
| RSCSL Agreement | Agreement Between the United Nations and the Government of Sierra Leone on the Establishment of a Residual Special Court for Sierra Leone | |
| RSCSL Statute | Statute of the Residual Special Court for Sierra Leone | |
| RStGB | Reichsstrafgesetzbuch | Criminal Code of the German Reich |

| | | |
|---|---|---|
| RUF | Revolutionary United Front | |
| RutLJ | Rutgers Law Journal | |
| S + F | Vierteljahresschrift für Sicherheit und Frieden | |
| s. | section | |
| SALTT | Suspects at Large Tracking Team (OTP ICC) | |
| SanDiegoILJ | San Diego International Law Journal | |
| SantaClaraJIL | Santa Clara Journal of International Law | |
| SchwJZ | Schweizerische Juristen-Zeitung | |
| scil. | scilicet | namely |
| SCAP | Supreme Commander of the Allied Powers | |
| SC Law | Law on Specialist Chambers and Specialist Prosecutor's Office (Republic of Kosovo) | |
| SCP | Spanish Código Penal | |
| SCR | Supreme Court Reports (Canada) | |
| SCSL | Special Court for Sierra Leone | |
| SCSLS | Statute of the SCSL | |
| SITF | Special Investigative Task Force (Republic of Kosovo) | |
| SPC | Special Jurisdiction for Peace (Colombia) | |
| SJZ | Süddeutsche Juristenzeitung | |
| SL | Sendero Luminoso | Rebel Group 'Shining Path' |
| SocSciQ | Social Science Quarterly | |
| SoRep 2nd | Southern Reporter, 2nd Series | |
| SAfrJCL&Crim | South African Journal of Criminal Law & Criminology | |
| SAYbIL | South African Yearbook of International Law | |
| SouthwesternJIL | Southwestern Journal of International Law | |
| SPSC | Special Panels for Serious Crimes Dilli (East Timor) | |
| SPD | Special Panels Dilli (East Timor) | |
| SRSG | Special Representative of the Secretary-General | |
| SS | Schutzstaffel of the NSDAP | |
| St.John'sLR | St. John's Law Review | |
| StanfordJIL | Stanford Journal of International Law | |
| StGB | Strafgesetzbuch | German Penal Code |
| StPO | Strafprozessordnung | German Code of Criminal Procedure |
| STL | Special Tribunal for Lebanon | |
| STL Agreement | Agreement between the United Nations and the Lebanese Republic on the Establishment of a Special Tribunal for Lebanon | |
| STLS | STL Statute | |
| StraFo | Strafverteidiger Forum | |
| StV | Strafverteidiger | |
| Subs. | Subsection | |
| Subpara./subparas. | Subparagraph/subparagraphs | |
| Suffolk Transnat'lLR | Suffolk Transnational Law Review | |

| | | |
|---|---|---|
| SwissStGB | schweizerisches Strafgesetzbuch | Swiss Criminal Code |
| SZ | Süddeutsche Zeitung | |
| TC | Trial Chamber | |
| TempleLQ | Temple Law Quarterly | |
| Tex. A&M L. R. | Texas A&M Law Review | |
| TexILJ | Texas International Law Journal | |
| TexTechLR | Texas Tech Law Review | |
| TFEU | Treaty on the Functioning of the European Union | |
| TIL | Theoretical Inquiries in Law | |
| Tilburg ForLR | Tilburg Foreign Law Review | |
| TRC | Truth and Reconciliation Commission | |
| Transnat'lLCP | Transnational Law and Contemporary Problems | |
| TulaneJI&CL | Tulane Journal of International and Comparative Law | |
| TulsaLR | Tulsa Law Review | |
| TFV | Trust Fund for Victims | |
| TWC | Trials of war criminals before the Nuernberg Military Tribunals under Control Council law no. 10 | |
| UCDavisJIL&Pol'y | University of California, Davis, Journal of International Law & Policy | |
| UCDavisLR | University of California, Davis, Law Review | |
| UCLA JIL & ForAff | UCLA Journal of International Law and Foreign Affairs | |
| UDHR | Universal Declaration of Human Rights | |
| UK | United Kingdom | |
| ULR | Utrecht Law Review | |
| UMiamiICompLR | University of Miami International and Comparative Law Review | |
| UMichJLRef | University of Michigan Journal of Law Reform | |
| UN | United Nations | |
| UN Basic Principles and Guidelines | UN Basic Principles and Guidelines on the Right to a Remedy and Reparation for Victims of Gross Violation of International Human Rights Law and Serious Violations of International Humanitarian Law | |
| UN Doc | United Nations Document | |
| UN GA | UN General Assembly | |
| UNSC | UN Security Council | |
| UNCLOS | UN Convention on the Law of the Sea | |
| UNCTOC | UN Convention on Transnational Organized Crime | |
| UNMIL | United Nations Mission in Liberia | |
| UNOCI | United Nations Operation in Côte d'Ivoire | |
| UNTAET | United Nations Mission in East Timor | |
| UNTS | United Nations Treaty Series | |
| UNWCC | UN War Crimes Commission | |
| UN-Yb | Yearbook of the United Nations | |
| UPaLR | University of Pennsylvania Law Review | |
| UPittsbLR | University of Pittsburgh Law Review | |

| | | |
|---|---|---|
| URichLR | University of Richmond Law Review | |
| US-GPO | United States General Printing Office | |
| USSC | US Sentencing Commission | |
| USSG | US Sentencing Guidelines | |
| USSR | Union of Soviet Socialist Republics | |
| UStThomas JL&PubPol'y | University of St. Thomas Journal of Law and Public Policy | |
| VaparaisoULR | Valparaiso University Law Review | |
| VanderbiltJTL | Vanderbilt Journal of Transnational Law | |
| VanderbiltLR | Vanderbilt Law Review | |
| VCDR | Vienna Convention on Diplomatic Relations | |
| VCLT | Vienna Convention on the Law of Treaties | |
| VictUWellLR | Victoria Uni of Wellington Law Review | |
| VirginiaLRev | Virginia Law Review | |
| VirgJIL | Virginia Journal of International Law | |
| VPRS | Victim Participation and Reparation Section | |
| VR | Verwaltungsrundschau: Zeitschrift für Verwaltung in Praxis und Wissenschaft | |
| VRS | Vojska Republike Srpske | Bosnian-Serb Army |
| VStGB | Völkerstrafgesetzbuch | German International Criminal Law Code |
| VWU | Victims and Witnesses Unit (ICC Registry) | |
| WashUGlSLR | Washington University Global Studies Law Review | |
| WashULR | Washington University Law Review | |
| WCRO | War Crimes Research Office | |
| WEOG | Western European and Others Group of States | |
| WGPM | Working Group on Procedural Matters | |
| WhittierLR | Whittier Law Review | |
| WILJ | Wisconsin International Law Journal | |
| Wistra | Zeitschrift für Wirtschafts- und Steuerstrafrecht | |
| Wm & Mary LR | William and Mary Law Review | |
| WW II | World War II | |
| YaleJIL | The Yale Journal of International Law | |
| YaleLJ | The Yale Law Journal | |
| YbIHL | Yearbook of International Humanitarian Law | |
| *YbILC* | Yearbook of the International Law Commission | |
| ZaöRV | Zeitschrift für ausländisches öffentliches Recht und Völkerrecht | |
| ZIS | Zeitschrift für Internationale Strafrechtsdogmatik | |
| ZStrR | Schweizerische Zeitschrift für Strafrecht | |
| ZStW | Zeitschrift für die gesamte Strafrechtswissenschaft | |

# About the Companion Website

www.oup.com/ambosIII (https://global.oup.com/booksites/content/9780192844262/)
Oxford University Press has created a website to accompany **Treatise on International Criminal Law, Vol. III: International Criminal Procedure**. The full bibliographies for each chapter are available here. The reader is encouraged to consult this resource in conjunction with the chapters.

# I

# The Framework of International Criminal Procedure

## Conceptual Foundations, Origins, Goals, and Rights

*The full chapter bibliography can be downloaded from

### A. Conceptual foundations

The debate on international criminal procedure remains to be influenced by the apparent dichotomy between the inquisitorial 'civil law' and the adversarial 'common law' process. Yet, this dichotomy is overstated and ignores the complexities of largely mixed procedural systems[1] which are, in line with a functional or issue-oriented approach already adopted in the first volume of this Treatise,[2] more interested in concrete solutions to specific procedural problems than in grand theoretical designs.[3] In any case, to avoid any terminological and conceptual confusion and explain this book's take on international criminal procedure, some clarifications are necessary.

#### (1) 'Civil law' and 'common law'—The division into legal families

International criminal procedure has traditionally been analysed as a blending of the common law and civil law traditions.[4] Both concepts describe a certain legal system or legal tradition,[5] that is, 'an operating set of legal institutions, procedures and rules'[6] (legal system)

[1] See also Bohlander, *JICJ*, 12 (2014), 493 ('There is no such thing as "the" common or civil law system'); Wheeler, *Right to Be Present* (2019), p. 34 with further references ('there is no longer any true expression of either system'); Ross and Thaman, in Ross and Thaman, *Comparative Criminal Procedure* (2016), p. 13 ('it has become increasingly clear that it is difficult today to neatly classify systems as falling squarely in one camp or the other'); Heinze, in Bergsmo et al., *Power* (2020), p. 173.

[2] Ambos, *Treatise ICL I* (2021), pp. 129–31; previously Ambos, in Bohlander, *International Criminal Justice* (2007), p. 501

[3] cf. in this respect also Langer, in Ross and Thaman, *Comparative Criminal Procedure* (2016) who, while admitting that 'the distinction between adversarial and inquisitorial systems is both old and alive' (p. 523), justifies it on essentially epistemological grounds ('help explain important differences between the criminal processes of different jurisdictions' (p. 523); 'enable researchers to generate hypotheses to explain or account for differences between procedural regulations across jurisdictions' (p. 525); 'enable scholars to discuss a large number of jurisdictions at once' (p. 526)); at the same time, the distinction can have 'negative effects' ('blinding'; 'distracting'; 'blurring' (pp. 526 ff.)).

[4] Tochilovsky, *EJCCLCJ*, 6 (1998), 55 ff.; Findlay, *ICLQ*, 50 (2001), 26 ff.; Meron, *JICJ*, 2 (2004), 521–5; Mundis, *LJIL*, 14 (2001), 367 ff.; Keen, *LJIL*, 17 (2004), 767–814; Schuon, *Procedure* (2010), p. 11; Ohlin, *UCLA JIL & ForAff*, 14 (2009), 81.

[5] Generally Heinze, *Disclosure* (2014), pp. 104 ff.; Billis, *Rolle des Richters* (2015), pp. 14 ff.

[6] Merryman and Pérez-Perdomo, *Civil Law* (2019), p. 1; McGonigle Leyh, *Procedural Justice?* (2011), p. 65.

or 'a set of deeply rooted, historically conditioned attitudes about the nature of law, about the role of law in society and the polity, about the proper organization and operation of a legal system, and about the way law is or should be made, applied, studied, perfected, and taught'[7] (legal tradition). According to more or less reliable estimates, 34 per cent of the world's jurisdictions are based on the civil law model, or civil law systems mixed with others (e.g. indigenous or religious legal ideologies),[8] while approximately 28 per cent of the jurisdictions follow the common law model, including systems compounded with it.[9]

### (a) *Civil law*

The term 'civil law' stems from the Latin words 'ius civile'[10] and is also referred to as Romano-Germanic law or European Continental law.[11] Lawyers with a common law background normally use the term to capture all non-English legal traditions.[12] Generally speaking, there are three connotations associated with the concept: (1) the application of legal principles, normally derived from or based on written law; (2) the search for truth; and (3) a largely inquisitorial approach in proceedings.[13] Typical procedural elements of the civil law tradition are the following:

- 'one case approach';[14]
- existence of an investigating magistrate, its paradigmatic form being the *juge d'instruction*,[15] tasked to investigate the truth; in more 'accusatorial' systems this task is taken over by a State Prosecutor as public official;[16]
- the judge as an active umpire, who is (also) under a legal duty to establish the true facts of a case and to submit the appropriate evidence accordingly;[17] and,
- the victim as a participant with own procedural rights (concept of *partie civile*).[18]

In contrast, civil law's emphasis on written law[19] is less relevant given the increasing reliance on statutes and other written sources in modern common law systems. At any rate, the civil

[7] Merryman and Pérez-Perdomo, *Civil Law* (2019), p. 2; McGonigle Leyh, *Procedural Justice?* (2011), p. 65.
[8] Heinze, *Disclosure* (2014), p. 106.
[9] cf. University of Ottawa, World Legal Systems Research Group internet site, <http://www.juriglobe.ca/eng/index.php>.
[10] Dainow, *AJCompL*, 15 (1966–1967), 420.
[11] Heinze, *Disclosure* (2014), p. 107.
[12] Ibid.
[13] McGonigle Leyh, *Procedural Justice?* (2011), p. 70; Bohlander, *JICJ*, 12 (2014), 494 ff.; on the importance of truth-seeking, see e.g. Boyne, in Ross and Thaman, *Comparative Criminal Procedure* (2016), p. 223 with regard to 'Germany's Inquisitorial System' in comparison to the U.S. adversarial system ('inquisitorial model's conviction that a neutral fact-finder can objectively discover the "truth"'); Desportes and Lazerges-Cousquer, *Traité* (2013), mn. 550; Kühne, *Strafprozessrecht* (2015), mn. 1, 628, 751; Peters, *Strafprozeß* (1985), pp. 16, 82–3; Billis, *Rolle des Richters* (2015), pp. 42 ff.
[14] Where only one case is prepared by a State official who carries out the major part of the investigations, see Ambos, *ICLR*, 3 (2003), 4; Schuon, *Procedure* (2010), p. 4; Langer, *AJCompL*, 53 (2005), 839.
[15] Heinze, *Disclosure* (2014), p. 107; furthermore, see Karnavas, *ICLR*, 20 (2020), 90.
[16] See on the Prosecutor e.g. Weigend, 'Prosecution', in Dressler, *Encyclopedia of Crime and Justice* (2002), pp. 1233–4. This is why the Prosecutor, like the judge, has a duty to gather both inculpatory and exculpatory evidence, see ibid. at p. 1234; Heinze and Fyfe, in Ambos et al., *Core Concepts I* (2020), pp. 346, 366; Sluiter and Tiernan, *JICJ*, 18 (2020), 644.
[17] Schuon, *Procedure* (2010), p. 4; Langer, *AJCompL*, 53 (2005), 840; Heinze, *Disclosure* (2014), p. 108.
[18] On the role of the victim as a *partie civile* in the criminal procedure of France and Italy, respectively, see e.g. Rassat, *Procedure pénale* (2017), pp. 195–231; Lozzi, *Procedura penale* (2020), pp. 128–33. See also Chapter II, E.(4) in this volume.
[19] See Dainow, *AJCompL*, 15 (1966–1967), 424 ('Generally, in civil law jurisdictions the main source or basis of the law is legislation, and large areas are codified in a systematic manner. These codes constitute a very distinctive feature of a Romanist legal system, or the so-called civil law.'); on codifications generally Merryman and Pérez Perdomo, *Civil Law Tradition* (2019), pp. 27 ff.; in more detail, see Heinze, *Disclosure* (2014), p. 108.

law tradition as 'a body of general principles carefully arranged and closely integrated'[20] suggests an ideological element in the history and reality of codification, including elements of legal theory and the sociology of law.[21] Further, the generality of legal rules is high—codes in civil law are said to be rather a collection of abstract principles than specific rules for particular situations or even concrete cases.[22] Finally, since legal certainty and predictability[23] are 'supreme values' and basically 'unquestioned dogmas'[24] in the civil law tradition—think only on its stricter take on the principle of legality (*nullum crimen sine lege*)[25]—it promotes sophisticated methods of interpretation[26] and common definitions and classifications.[27]

### *(b) Common law*

Common law, also often (misleadingly)[28] referred to as 'Anglo-American' law, is characterized by the concept of a dialectical competition between the parties, in which the stronger—and therefore true—version of the case will prevail.[29] Typical procedural elements of this tradition are:

- a party-driven process;[30]
- a 'two cases approach', that is, the parties prepare two cases during the pre-trial stage and present their respective cases subsequently at trial;[31]
- an attitude towards getting the best results for the clients instead of uncovering the truth;[32]
- the judge as a passive umpire whose task is to ensure that the parties abide by the procedural rules;[33]
- complex rules of evidence;[34]
- the jury as a decision maker.[35]

While the civil law tradition emphasizes codification, the chief source of law in common law legal systems is case law of the courts.[36] It is 'both the source and the proof of the law,

[20] Dainow, *AJCompL*, 15 (1966–1967), 424; see also Heinze, *Disclosure* (2014), p. 108 with further references.
[21] Koch, *MichJIL*, 25 (2003–2004), 24.
[22] Sanders, in Borgatta and Montgomery, *Encyclopedia of Sociology III* (2000), p. 1546; see also Dainow, *AJCompL*, 15 (1966–1967), 424; Heinze, *Disclosure* (2014), p. 109; for a German perspective, see Bohlander, *LJIL*, 24 (2011), 402.
[23] Koch, *MichJIL*, 25 (2003–2004), 36.
[24] Merryman and Pérez-Perdomo, *Civil Law* (2019), p. 48.
[25] cf. Ambos, *Treatise ICL I* (2021), pp. 143 ff.
[26] See Koch, *MichJIL*, 25 (2003–2004), 31; Heinze, *Disclosure* (2014), p. 109.
[27] Koch, *MichJIL*, 25 (2003–2004), 33; see also Bohlander, *JICJ*, 12 (2014), 504.
[28] This is misleading, because it ignores—inter alia—(1) the difference between English Law and American Law; (2) the fact that the USA has many legal systems; (3) the relationship of English Law to Scottish or (Northern) Irish Law; see Heinze, *Disclosure* (2014), p. 110.
[29] McGonigle Leyh, *Procedural Justice?* (2011), p. 70, Schuon, *Procedure* (2010), p. 4. See generally Bohlander, *JICJ*, 12 (2014), 493 ff.; Billis, *Rolle des Richters* (2015), pp. 27 ff.
[30] i.e. the matter of what evidence to submit, and in which order, is mainly left to the parties, Schuon, *Procedure* (2010), p. 3; furthermore, see Heinze and Fyfe, in Ambos et al., *Core Concepts I* (2020), p. 366 ('A party in a contest model will carry out investigations to his or her own benefit, but may not collect evidence that diminishes his or her chances of winning the case'); Karnavas, *ICLR*, 20 (2020), 90; Sluiter and Tiernan, *JICJ*, 18 (2020), 643.
[31] Schuon, *Procedure* (2010), p. 3; Karnavas, *ICLR*, 20 (2020), 90 ('the parties ... are expected to advance their respective cases solely and independently').
[32] Kagan, *Adversarial Legalism* (2003), p. 244.
[33] See 'Democracy? Freedom? Justice? Law? What's all this?', *The Economist*, 23 December 1999, <http://www.economist.com/node/346736>.
[34] Heinze, *Disclosure* (2014), p. 111.
[35] Ibid.
[36] Zander, 'Forms and Functions', in Eser and Rabenstein, *Neighbours in Law* (2001), pp. 32, 43; Heinze, *Disclosure* (2014), p. 111.

pronounced in connection with actual cases.'[37] While the civil law tradition rather follows abstract (deductive) reasoning than a casuistic (inductive) approach,[38] common law decisions are reached through confrontation and reasoned debate,[39] that is, by assessing 'the force of arguments' from all sides.[40] Legal certainty is 'not elevated to the level of dogma'[41] as it is often the case in civil law systems.

## (2) Theories of criminal procedure

While legal traditions may categorize the criminal process on an abstract level, there are countless theories that account for the structure of criminal procedure itself. Criminal procedure in that regard means '[t]he rules governing the mechanisms under which crimes are investigated, prosecuted, adjudicated, and punished.'[42] Although 'criminal procedure' has, apart from other differences, a narrower meaning than 'criminal justice', for our purposes both terms can be used synonymously.[43]

### *(a) Adversarial and inquisitorial*

The terms 'adversarial' and 'inquisitorial' are probably the most commonly used concepts to classify procedural systems.[44] Unfortunately, it is often ignored that these terms have not a single meaning, but several,[45] and thus confusion abounds in literature and case law.[46] In a nutshell, these terms can have both a traditional and a historical meaning and may describe a theoretical model, a procedural type, and an ideal of procedure.[47]

Used in their *traditional meaning*, the terms usually describe the actual features of criminal justice within the common law or civil law tradition. 'Adversarial' in this context means nothing more than a criminal process that relies on the assistance of counsel (as an adversary of the prosecution) and follows due process of law[48] —that is, features present in legal systems with both a common law and a civil law tradition.[49] As a *theoretical model*, the terms 'adversarial' and 'inquisitorial' describe the goal of the process, that is, conflict-resolution versus the search for truth.[50] This meaning is congeneric with a third meaning,

[37] Dainow, *AJCompL*, 15 (1966–1967), 425.
[38] Bohlander, *LJIL*, 24 (2011), 402 (fn. omitted).
[39] Peters, *ColLR*, 97 (1997), 358–9 (fn. omitted).
[40] Wolfe and Proszek, *TulsaLR*, 33 (1997), 305.
[41] Merryman and Pérez-Perdomo, *Civil Law* (2019), p. 48.
[42] Garner, *Dictionary* (2019), p. 472.
[43] On the difference in detail, see Section C., note 599 in this chapter and main text; see also Heinze, *Disclosure* (2014), pp. 113 ff.
[44] cf. Heinze, *Disclosure* (2014), p. 117 ff.; Heinze, in Bergsmo et al., *Power* (2020), p. 172; see also Fedorova, *Equality of Arms* (2012), p. 92; Billis, *Rolle des Richters* (2015), pp. 62 ff.; De Meester, *Investigation Phase* (2015), p. 82.
[45] Doran, Jackson, and Seigel, *AJCL*, 23 (1995–1996), 13; Damaška, *UpaLR*, 121 (1973), 507, 513; Illuminati, *NCJIL&ComReg*, 35 (2009–2010), 297 ('concept of an accusatorial system is one of the most difficult to understand and scholars offer very different explanations ... notions of accusatorial and inquisitorial processes are abstractions ... traditional dichotomy alludes to two hypothetical models obtained by making a generalization from some real features of existing and no longer existing systems. It follows that it is not a matter of how the law is interpreted that defines the dichotomy; rather, the concept depends on the choice of an ideologically oriented scale of values.')
[46] For examples, see Heinze, *Disclosure* (2014), pp. 129 ff., 152 ff.
[47] Ibid., p. 118. By contrast, *Fedorova* identifies only three different 'senses' of the term adversarial: a traditional model, a theoretical model, and an ideal model; see Fedorova, *Equality of Arms* (2012), pp. 94–6.
[48] Damaška, in Dressler, *Encyclopedia of Crime and Justice* (2002), p. 25.
[49] Heinze, *Disclosure* (2014), p. 119; in Bergsmo et al., *Power* (2020), pp. 175–6.
[50] Heinze, International Criminal Procedure (2014), p. 119; Fedorova, *Equality of Arms* (2012), p. 95; Damaška, in Dressler, *Encyclopedia of Crime and Justice* (2002), p. 26; also see Langer, in Ackerman et al., *Visions* (2016),

the '*ideal of procedure*', where the terms have a purely normative meaning,[51] as Weberian ideal-types,[52] to demonstrate whether certain procedural elements are closer or farther from the adversarial/inquisitorial ideal.[53] Alexander Heinze exemplifies this approach as follows:

> 'Adversarial' as an ideal of procedure includes—amongst other things—the presumption of innocence, the privilege against self-incrimination and the use of oral testimony, which are then contrasted with counter-tendencies (allegedly) to be found in Continental proceedings ... In the U.S.A., 'inquisitorialism', on the contrary, has always been used as an idealised system against which the courts defined their own system.[54]

In a similar context, the terms 'adversarial' and 'inquisitorial' are also often used as ideal *models of proof*, applying 'to a particular hypothesis of proof'.[55] This variant of the ideal of procedure is very often used to render a certain model of proof effective and therefore preferable over another. The adversarial model of proof, for instance, 'claims that truth is best discovered by powerful statements on both sides of a question', while for the inquisitorial model of proof truth is best achieved 'by an active judge and a strong investigating (state-) agency, which are committed to objectivity'.[56] We will analyse this in more detail in Chapter V when dealing with evidence in international criminal procedure.

Probably the most suitable meaning of 'adversarial' and 'inquisitorial' for comparative purposes is a *procedural* one. This purely descriptive[57] approach categorizes a criminal process as adversarial or inquisitorial by identifying the lowest common denominator. Thus, a procedural element is adversarial when it is found within the process of the majority of common law systems.[58] For instance, the trial by jury or the hearsay rule 'would qualify as features of the adversarial system if all common law jurisdictions included these elements at a certain moment in time'.[59]

Last but not least, the most controversial meaning of 'adversarial' and 'inquisitorial' is the so-called '*historical meaning*'.[60] It describes both concepts in their original appearance and focuses on certain procedural elements that put their mark on the nature of the process, such

p. 279 who, referring to *Damaška*, contrasts the '*conflict-solving* model' with '*policy implementing* models'; furthermore, see Heinze, in Bergsmo et al., *Power* (2020), pp. 176–7 also with reference to *Damaška*.

[51] Jackson, *MLR*, 68 (2005), 742; Illuminati, *NCJIL& ComReg*, 35 (2009–2010), 298 ('The features of the accusatorial system are determined only through contrast to those of the inquisitorial system and vice versa; therefore they represent only ideal models that, in practice, can combine in different ways in relation to several variables.'); Fedorova, *Equality of Arms* (2012), pp. 97 ff.

[52] Langer, *HarvILJ*, 45 (2004), 8 with n. 29. *Tatjana Hörnle* even goes so far as to say that the terms 'adversarial' and 'inquisitorial' cannot be something other than ideal-types; see Hörnle, *ZStW*, 117 (2005), 804. About *Weber's* ideal types, see in more detail Heinze, *Disclosure* (2014), pp. 180 ff., 195 ff. and Ambos and Heinze, in Bergsmo, *Abbreviated Procedures* (2017), pp. 28–32.

[53] Hörnle, *ZStW*, 117 (2005), 804; Langer, *HarvILJ*, 45 (2004), 9.

[54] Heinze, *Disclosure* (2014), p. 121 (fn. omitted).

[55] Ibid., p. 122.

[56] Ibid.; see also Goodpaster, *JCL&Crim*, 78 (1987–1988), 121; Heinze, in Bergsmo et al., *Power* (2020), p. 179.

[57] Heinze, *Disclosure* (2014), p. 120; id., in Bergsmo et al., *Power* (2020), p. 177.

[58] Damaška, 'Adversary System', in Dressler, *Encyclopedia of Crime and Justice* (2002), p. 28; see also Herrmann, *SAfrJCL&Crim*, 2 (1978), 4–6.

[59] Langer, *HarvILJ*, 45 (2004), 7; Heinze, *Disclosure* (2014), p. 120.

[60] Swoboda, *CLF*, 18 (2007), 157; Swoboda, *Verfahrens- und Beweisstrategien* (2013), p. 69; cf. Roberts, *OJLS*, 28 (2008), 370, 375; furthermore, see Langer, in Ackerman et al., *Visions* (2016), p. 274 who raises the historical perspective of 'how the adversarial and the inquisitorial systems and common and civil law became central categories of comparative criminal procedure'.

as questions of which party is given prosecutorial power and whether the judge can initiate proceedings *proprio motu.*[61] Features of adversariness are, for instance, the discretionary power to instigate a prosecution case, the burden of proof on the Prosecutor, the principle of publicity and orality of the trial, or the judge's passive role as the arbitrator of the dispute.[62] In contrast, the elements of the inquisitorial process are, inter alia, 'different forms of intolerable pressure against defendants in order to achieve co-operation, including physical and mental torture', the occurrence of the procedure 'in complete secrecy', or a 'method of rational deduction and forensic enquiry'.[63] Of course, this refers to the pre-enlightment, religiously inspired inquisitorial process of the codes preceding the French revolution and Napoleon's restorative criminal procedure code of 1808.[64]

The five different meanings of 'adversarial' and 'inquisitorial' demonstrate that there is more to this dichotomy than usually suggested by the authors of relevant comparative or international criminal procedure texts. While this surely complicates the classification of criminal procedure models along the lines of these concepts, it does not make them completely redundant. They may still be used as general categories or indicators of a certain procedural structure using the precise definitions and caveats proposed here.

### *(b) Other models of criminal procedure*

Of course, there have always been other attempts to model criminal procedure. The relevant approaches can generally be divided into descriptive and normative models, although not all of them fit into this distinction and many of them seem to have an overlap between a rather descriptive or a rather normative take. The most prominent example of the former category is *Herbert Packer's* Crime Control and Due Process Model. Packer's bifurcated approach focuses, on the one hand, on the efficient suppression of crime and, on the other, on fair trial rights and the concept of limited governmental power.[65] Thus, while under 'crime control' speed, efficiency, and finality are the overriding values and any rule or measure compromising such values is deemed inappropriate,[66] 'due process' aims at the protection of the 'most disadvantaged' and thus demands equal treatment regardless of wealth or social status.[67] Packer's categorization served as a basis for further elaborations, for example, taking into account rehabilitation and societal stability,[68] focusing on cases that never reach the courtroom,[69] emphasizing more strongly the protection of innocents,[70] and the interests of victims.[71]

[61] Illuminati, *NCJIL&ComReg*, 35 (2009–2010), 298. Thus, structural elements of the adversarial method are: '1. The state must be prevented by law from using its power to apply psychological or physical pressure to distort the free testimony of the individual. 2. The state must be prevented by law from using its superior resources to create an unfair trial. 3. The individual must be an active subject of the process and not merely a passive object.'; see Vogler, *Criminal Justice* (2005), p. 130; McDermott, *Fairness* (2016), pp. 10–11.

[62] Illuminati, *NCJIL&ComReg*, 35 (2009–2010), 300.

[63] Vogler, *Criminal Justice* (2005), pp. 19–20; for another description of the historical meaning of inquisitorial, see Illuminati, *NCJIL&ComReg*, 35 (2009–2010), 301 ff.

[64] Roberts and Zuckerman, *Criminal Evidence* (2010), p. 47 with further references.

[65] Packer, *Criminal Sanction* (1969), pp. 149–53; see also the account of McDermott, *Fairness* (2016), pp. 9–10.

[66] cf. Heinze, *Disclosure* (2014), p. 134.

[67] See Packer, *Criminal Sanction* (1969), p. 168.

[68] Griffiths, *YaleLJ*, 79 (1969–1970), 359–417.

[69] Choongh, *BJCrim*, 38 (1998), 625.

[70] Findley, *TexTechLR*, 41 (2008–2009), 133 ff., 141 ff.

[71] Roach, *JCL&Crim*, 89 (1999), 672; Aviram, *Law & Soc Inquiry*, 36 (2011), 241. See more recently Trüg, *ZStW*, 125 (2013), 79, who however neglects existing procedural models which take the role of the victim into consideration.

Among the normative approaches, *Duff et al.*,[72] *Burns*,[73] and *Ashworth and Redmayne*[74] developed perhaps the most influential one, focusing on normative theories of the criminal trial and exploring what *should* happen at trial.[75] Last but not least, *Damaška*, in his seminal *The Faces of Justice*, developed a set of models based on attitudes towards State authority and on concepts of government.[76] Accordingly, the hierarchical and coordinate models describe two structures of State authority that express two 'ideals of officialdom'.[77] *Damaška*'s second pair of procedural models refers to the notions of the State: the 'reactive state' and the 'activist state'.[78] The task of the reactive State is limited to 'providing a supporting framework within which its citizens pursue their chosen goals'.[79] The type of proceeding in a reactive State is 'conflict solving',[80] amounting to a contest between two formally coequal disputants before the State official as the neutral decision maker.[81] In contrast, the nature of proceeding in an activist State is 'policy implementing', that is, the justice system is considered an instrument to implement certain policies.[82]

## B. The history of international criminal procedure

### (1) The origins of international criminal procedure

Volume I of this Treatise presented a historical overview of ICL from the early attempts to prosecute international crimes to the establishment of the ICC.[83] This need not be repeated here but a quick look at this history with a focus on the emerging international criminal procedure and the relevant tribunals provides some important insights to better understand the modern developments.

Although crimes against the basic principles of humanity are nothing new to the history of mankind, their prosecution is a rather recent phenomenon.[84] The proposal of the president of the International Committee of the Red Cross (ICRC), *Gustave Moynier*, to set up an International Criminal Court (ICC) after the German-French War in 1870–1, remained without any political resonance.[85] When, subsequent to the 1919 Preliminary Peace Conference, the first international investigative commission was established and the Versailles Peace Treaty was dictated,[86] Article 227 of this Treaty provided the establishment of a 'special tribunal' that should have five judges, to be appointed by the USA, Great Britain, France, Italy, and Japan. The Allies accused the former German emperor, *William II of Hohenzollern*, of a supreme offence against international morality and the sanctity of the treaties. However, the tribunal was never established[87] since, on the one hand, William

[72] Duff et al., *Trial II* (2006).
[73] Burns, *Trial* (1999).
[74] Ashworth and Redmayne, *Criminal Process* (2010).
[75] See, in more detail, Heinze, *Disclosure* (2014), pp. 141 ff.; also Swart, *JICJ*, 6 (2008), 89 ff.
[76] Damaška, *Faces of Justice* (1986), pp. 8–12.
[77] Ibid., p. 16.
[78] In more detail, Heinze, *Disclosure* (2014), pp. 145 ff.; also see id., in Bergsmo et al., *Power* (2020), p. 157.
[79] Damaška, *Faces of Justice* (1986), p. 73.
[80] Ibid., p. 97.
[81] Ibid., pp. 73–80 and 97–147.
[82] Ibid., pp. 82, 84.
[83] Ambos, *Treatise ICL I* (2021), pp. 1 ff.
[84] Safferling, *International Criminal Procedure* (2001), p. 31.
[85] Ambos, *Treatise ICL I* (2021), p. 2 with further references.
[86] Ibid.
[87] Safferling, *Criminal Procedure* (2012), p. 9.

II found refuge in the Netherlands and was never extradited and, on the other, the German government failed to hand over 896 persons whom the Allies had intended to prosecute.[88]

Germany, which had previously passed a national law to implement Articles 228 and 229 of the Versailles treaty, passed new legislation at the end of 1919[89] to be able to prosecute German suspects before its own Supreme Court (the *Reichsgericht*), sitting at Leipzig.[90] Yet, these trials took place on the basis of the German Code of Criminal Procedure and thus do not represent examples of international criminal procedure.[91]

### *(a) Nuremberg*

It was not before 1945 that procedural rules emerged with the establishment of the International Military Tribunal (IMT) of Nuremberg.[92] The Allies set up the IMT to prosecute twenty-three 'Major War Criminals'.[93] While substantive ICL is normally considered the main achievement of the Nuremberg trials, one must not underestimate the importance of its procedural regime. As US Chief Prosecutor *Robert H. Jackson* put it:

> The very breadth of the offense ... is a most important reason for a trial, for it is highly desirable that there be established and declared by actual decision, after adequate hearing and determination of the facts, the principles of international law applicable to the broad, vicious Nazi enterprise. The application of this law may be novel because the scope of the Nazi activity has been broad and ruthless without precedent. The basic principles to be applied, however, are not novel and all that is needed is a wise application of those principles on a sufficiently comprehensive scale to meet the situation. International law must develop to meet the needs of the times ... not by enunciating new principles but by adapting old ones.[94]

The IMT consisted of four judges, each with an 'alternate';[95] each Signatory State could appoint a Chief Prosecutor.[96] The Chief Prosecutors basically had to conduct the investigations with a view to the preparation of an indictment and the trial.[97] The Committee of Chief Prosecutors was also given the task to draft rules of procedure, to be approved, amended, or rejected by the tribunal.[98] These rules did not necessarily have to be consistent with the Charter.[99] Finally, eleven rules of procedure were adopted by the tribunal on 29 October

88 Ambos, *Treatise ICL I* (2021), p. 3 with further references.

89 'Gesetz zur Verfolgung von Kriegsverbrechen und Kriegsvergehen', 18 December 1919, *RGBl* (1919), 2125–6.

90 For further details, see Ambos, *Treatise ICL I* (2021), p. 3 with further references.

91 In the same vein, Safferling, *Criminal Procedure* (2012), p. 11.

92 cf. Zappalà, in Sluiter et al., *International Criminal Procedure* (2013), p. 44. On its origins in the 'Declaration of London', see Ambos, *Treatise ICL I* (2021), p. 5.

93 For a list of defendants and the final verdicts, see Ambos, *Treatise ICL I* (2021), pp. 5–6. About the seletion of cases at the IMT, see Karstedt, *JICJ* 13 (2015), 724 ff.

94 American Memorandum Presented at San Francisco, 30 April 1945, taken from the Report of Robert H. Jackson, United States Representative to the International Conference on Military Trials, London, 1945, at p. 37. See also May and Wierda, *Evidence* (2002), p. 1.

95 Art. 2 IMTS. 'The alternates shall, so far as they are able, be present at all sessions of the Tribunal. In case of illness of any member of the Tribunal or his incapacity for some other reason to fulfill his functions, his alternate shall take his place.' See also Wald, *CardozoLR*, 27 (2005–2006), 1560.

96 cf. Art. 14 IMTS.

97 cf. Art. 15 IMTS.

98 Arts. 13 and 14 (e) IMTS; see also May and Wierda, *Evidence* (2002), pp. 20–1. The effort to create rules of procedure highlights the difference with national war crimes trials based on national law. On British war crimes trials in Europe and Asia, see Chea and Vormbaum, *LJIL*, 31 (2018), 673.

99 Wallach, *ColJTransnat'lL*, 37 (1998–1999), 861.

1945.[100] Compared to the rules of the modern international criminal tribunals, these rules were rather rudimentary and limited to a few basic statements.[101] A more detailed regime would have made a compromise between the different legal systems of the Allied Powers—the British (incl. Northern Irish) and American on the one hand and the French and the Soviet Union on the other—impossible.[102] Indeed, the disagreements over procedure were 'more numerous and stubborn than those over substantive law'.[103] As *May* and *Wierda* state:

> [i]t was the view of the Russians that the criminality of the Nazi leaders had already been established and that the task of the tribunal would be to mete out individual sentences. The other powers strenuously disagreed with this concept, because it deprived the trial of its essential function, namely, that of independently determining guilt. The Russians conceded this point but disagreement remained on the form that the process should take.[104]

*Jackson* recalls that the four major Allied Powers at the conference 'agreed in principle that no country reasonably could insist that an international trial should be conducted under its own system and that we must borrow from all and devise an amalgamated procedure that would be workable, expeditious and fair'.[105]

In substance, the rules of procedure adopted a rather adversarial approach[106] in the procedural sense explained above.[107] This follows from both the sequence of the trial and the rules of evidence. The trial started with the reading of the indictment in court.[108] After that the defendant was asked whether he or she pleaded 'guilty' or 'not guilty', then the prosecution made an opening statement, followed by the information given by both the defence and the prosecution as to what evidence (if any) they wished to submit to the court and by a ruling of the court upon the admissibility of any such evidence.[109] In fact, as noted by Francis Biddle, US Attorney General during WWII and the US judge at the IMT, '[a]s the trial proceeded it became necessary ... to rule almost daily on questions regarding the admissibility of evidence'.[110]

The right to question witnesses was mainly reserved for the adversaries: it started with the examination of the prosecution witnesses, followed by the examination of the defence

[100] *Nuremberg Trial Proceedings* Vol. 1, Rules of Procedure (29 October 1945), <avalon.law.yale.edu/imt/imtrules.asp>.

[101] Zappalà, in Sluiter et al., *International Criminal Procedure* (2013), p. 46.

[102] Address of Justice Robert Jackson at the School of Advanced International Studies, NYC, 25 August 1948, at 3: 'Also, although the French and Russian systems were both civil law systems derived from Roman law, they each had been shaped by the vastly differing influences of the French school of postrevolutionary political liberalism on the one hand and the doctrine of absolutism which prevailed in Russia on the other.' See also May and Wierda, *Evidence* (2002), p. 19.

[103] Jackson, *TempleLQ*, 22 (1948), 148; furthermore, see Crowe, in Dittrich et al., *Tokyo Tribunal* (2020), pp. 40–1 with further references.

[104] May and Wierda, *Evidence* (2002), p. 19 (fn. omitted).

[105] Jackson, *ABAJ*, 35 (1949), 815. See generally 'Report of Robert H. Jackson, United States Representative to the International Conference on Military Trials', London 1945, <http://www.loc.gov/rr/frd/Military_Law/pdf/jackson-rpt-military-trials.pdf>; 'Justice Jackson's Final Report to the President Concerning the Nürnberg War Crimes Trial' (1946); <http://www.roberthjackson.org/files/thecenter/files/bibliography/1940s/final-report-to-the-president.pdf>; see also Wallach, *ColJTransnat'lL*, 37 (1998–1999), 854.

[106] Safferling, *Criminal Procedure* (2012), p. 14; see also 'Report of Robert H. Jackson, United States Representative to the International Conference on Military Trials', London 1945, pp. 405–15, <http://www.loc.gov/rr/frd/Military_Law/pdf/jackson-rpt-military-trials.pdf>.

[107] See Section A.(2)(a) in this chapter.

[108] Art. 24 (a) IMTS.

[109] Art. 24 (d) and (e) IMTS; see also May and Wierda, *ColJTransnat'lL*, 37 (1998–1999), 738.

[110] Biddle, in Mettraux, *Nuremberg Trial* (2008), p. 202.

witnesses,[111] while each party had a right to 'crossexamine any witnesses and any Defendant who gives testimony'.[112] Only afterwards the court was allowed to 'put any question to any witness and to any defendant, at any time'. Ultimately, after the closing statements by the parties,[113] the defendant was entitled to the 'last word'[114] and the court delivered a judgment and pronounced a sentence.[115]

Last but not least, Article 16 IMTS provided for certain fair trial requirements.[116] Especially the US wanted to make sure that the trial was conceived as fair.[117] In President *Truman's* words, 'the world should be impressed by the fairness of the trial. These German murderers must be punished, but only upon proof of individual guilt at a trial.'[118] *Jackson* famously argued: 'Unless we write the record of this movement with clarity and precision, we cannot blame the future if in days of peace it finds incredible the accusatory generalities uttered during war. We must establish incredible events by credible evidence.'[119]

Pursuant to Article 16 (d) IMTS, '[a] Defendant shall have the right to conduct his own defense before the Tribunal or to have the assistance of Counsel.' This Article is supplemented by Rule 2(d) of the Rules of Procedure, which further substantiates this right.[120] The defense counsel were selected by the defendants themselves and were 'outstanding lawyers at the German Bar—long before the advent of Nazism'.[121] In addition to the stipulation that the trial be 'fair', the IMTS required that it be 'expeditious' and that the tribunal 'take strict measures' to prevent 'unreasonable delay' and rule out 'irrelevant issues and statements'.[122]

Considering the sequence of the trial, it becomes apparent, however, that some features of the adversarial process model are missing:[123] there was—for instance—no trial by jury.[124] Consequently,[125] the IMT was 'not bound by technical rules of evidence',[126] a typical feature

[111] Art. 24 (f) IMTS.

[112] Art. 24 (g) IMTS. This right, however, was rarely invoked, see Kempner, *Ankläger* (1986), p. 248; Kamardi, *Prozessordnung sui generis* (2009), p. 31.

[113] Art. 24 (h), (i) IMTS.

[114] Art. 24 (j) IMTS; see 'Report of Robert H. Jackson, United States Representative to the International Conference on Military Trials', London 1945, pp. 193, 409, <http://www.loc.gov/rr/frd/Military_Law/pdf/jackson-rpt-military-trials.pdf>.

[115] Art. 24 (k) IMTS.

[116] In more detail, see Safferling, *Criminal Procedure* (2012), p. 15.

[117] Wald, *CardozoLR*, 27 (2005–2006), 1574.

[118] Biddle, *In Brief Authority* (1962/1972), p. 372; Wald, *CardozoLR*, 27 (2005–2006), 1574; on the history of the development of Article 17 IMTS, with particular reference to the role of the Soviet representatives, see Schulmeister-André, *Einfluss* (2016), pp. 280 ff.

[119] Taylor, *Nuremberg Trials* (1992), p. 54.

[120] Rule 2(d) of the Rules of Procedure reads: 'Each defendant has the right to conduct his own defense or to have the assistance of counsel. Application for particular counsel shall be filed at once with the General Secretary of the Tribunal at the Palace of Justice, Nuremberg, Germany. The Tribunal will designate counsel for any defendant who fails to apply for particular counsel or, where particular counsel requested is not within ten (10) days to be found or available, unless the defendant elects in writing to conduct his own defense. If a defendant has requested particular counsel who is not immediately to be found or available, such counsel or a counsel of substitute choice may, if found and available before trial be associated with or substituted for counsel designated by the Tribunal, provided that (1) only one counsel shall be permitted to appear at the trial for any defendant, unless by special permission of the Tribunal, and (2) no delay of trial will be allowed for making such substitution or association.'

[121] Dodd, in Mettraux, *Nuremberg Trial* (2008), p. 197; see also Wright, in Mettraux, *Nuremberg Trial* (2008), p. 323.

[122] See Art. 18 IMTS; see also Wright, in Mettraux, *Nuremberg Trial* (2008), p. 333.

[123] See also May and Wierda, *ColJTransnat'lL*, 37 (1998–1999), 729–30.

[124] Safferling, *Criminal Procedure* (2012), p. 14; Rutledge, *RegentULR*, 16 (2003–2004), 156; Minear, *Tokyo Trial* (1971), p. 119.

[125] Note that the connection between the existence of a jury as decision maker and technical rules of evidence is disputed; see the seminal study by Damaška, *Evidence Law Adrift* (1997), pp. 27–37.

[126] Art. 19 IMTS. See also Minear, *Tokyo Trial* (1971), p. 6.

of the ideal-type of an adversarial process,[127] but explicitly rejected by the tribunal's procedural regime.[128] Rather, the tribunal was instructed to 'adopt and apply to the greatest possible extent expeditious and nontechnical procedure, and [to] admit any evidence which it deem[ed] to have probative value'.[129] Thus, strict technical rules, such as hearsay rules, turned out to be more relaxed as evidence needed only be probative to a reasonable person.[130] In this regard, Lord Justice Sir Geoffrey Lawrence, British Judge at the IMT, stated:

> As to the weight which is to be attached to the witness' evidence, that, of course, is a matter which will have to be considered by the Tribunal. It is open to the Defense to give evidence in answer to the evidence of [the witness] and also to comment upon or criticise that evidence, and so far as his evidence consisted of his own conclusions drawn from facts which he had seen or evidence which he had heard, the correctness of those conclusions will be considered by the Tribunal, conclusions being matters for the final decision of the Tribunal.[131]

Moreover, official governmental documents and UN reports could be admitted into the record by notice alone.[132] The parties presented their respective cases in open court and the evidence-testing process had an oral character.[133] Especially the role of the judges departed from what was known as the adversarial ideal: they used a dialectic method in order to determine what evidence was credible and to what extent[134] and admitted a large quantity of documentary materials into evidence.[135] Although the IMTS does not make any reference to affidavit evidence, the tribunal 'displayed an ambivalent attitude towards its admission'[136] and generally allowed a party to admit an affidavit subject to calling the witness for cross-examination.[137] Thousands of documents and affidavits were submitted, while only thirty three witnesses gave evidence for the prosecution, as compared to sixty-one defence witnesses.[138]

To prevent possible Nazi propaganda by the defendants, Article 18 IMTS vested the judges with broad powers to manage the trials, such as to interrogate the defendants, to 'take strict measures to prevent any action which will cause reasonable delay, and rule out irrelevant issues and statements of any kind whatsoever' and to 'deal summarily with any contumacy, imposing appropriate punishment, including exclusion of any Defendant or his Counsel from some or all further proceedings, but without prejudice to the determination of

127 See Section A.(2)(a) in this chapter.

128 Rutledge, *RegentULR*, 16 (2003–2004), 166.

129 Art. 19 IMTS.

130 Wald, *CardozoLR*, 27 (2005–2006), 1580.

131 Lord Justice Sir Geoffrey Lawrence during the morning session of the IMT on 5 February 1946, Nuremberg Trial Proceedings Vol. 7, at p. 14, <http://avalon.law.yale.edu/imt/02-05-46.asp>. Hearsay evidence and affidavits were also widely accepted in CCL No. 10 cases. See e.g. *US v. Flick*, *TWC*, *VI* (1952), p. 1188; *US v. von Weizsäcker (the 'Ministries Case')*, *TWC*, *XIV* (1952), p. 315; *US v. Pohl*, *TWC*, *V* (1952), p. 959; May and Wierda, *ColJTransnat'lL*, 37 (1998–1999), 746.

132 cf. Art. 21 IMTS; see also Wald, *CardozoLR*, 27 (2005–2006), 1580; Dodd, in Mettraux, *Nuremberg Trial* (2008), p. 193: 'Delegations from some fifteen of the United Nations came to Nurnberg as official observers, and in the course of their duties supplied such material to the prosecution.'

133 Zappalà, in Sluiter et al., *International Criminal Procedure* (2013), p. 47.

134 Ibid.

135 Ibid., p. 46; Levi, Hagan, and Dezalay, *LCP*, 79 (2016), 295.

136 May and Wierda, *ColJTransnat'lL*, 37 (1998–1999), 749.

137 Taylor, *Nuremberg Trials* (1992), pp. 241–2; Wallach, *ColJTransnat'lL*, 37 (1998–1999), 875 with n. 95; Dodd, in Mettraux, *Nuremberg Trial* (2008), p. 196.

138 May and Wierda, *ColJTransnat'lL*, 37 (1998–1999), 744.

the charges'.[139] The judges could also require the production of documents or other evidentiary material.[140] Furthermore, the Indictment should include 'full particulars specifying in detail the charges against the Defendants', and the prosecution was supposed to additionally provide 'all the documents lodged with the Indictment',[141] a quite unusual requirement for common law practice.[142] Another compromise was made with regard to testimony: by allowing both sworn testimony and unsworn statement, the judges chose to combine elements from the adversarial and inquisitorial ideal-types.[143]

In sum, the process before the IMT was—with surprisingly little debate[144]—designed along the lines of the adversarial procedure, but with a few exceptions,[145] thus 'blending and balancing of elements from the Continental European inquisitorial system and the Anglo-American adversarial system'.[146] This was 'not necessarily an obvious choice'.[147] In fact, it was the explicit policy goal of the USA to

> expose to public opinion (in particular in that country) the misdeeds committed by the Nazi regime. The objective was to stigmatize not only the aggressive war unleashed by the Third Reich and the crimes against humanity committed against the Jews and other minorities, but also any kind of totalitarian power. This would be done by illustrating the risks associated with totalitarianism while at the same time showing the strength of democracies.[148]

For that reason, the US opted for both an 'international' and at the same time 'military' tribunal. Within a military tribunal judges have a much more active role than their counterparts in other civil or criminal courts, presiding over the entire proceedings,[149] ordering the production of additional evidence and free from technical rules of evidence.[150] In fact, the procedural rules were largely based on American practice before military commissions,[151] as applied in the seminal 1942 *Ex parte Quirin* case against Nazi saboteurs.[152] However, the tribunal's military blend went only that far since *Jackson* issued a 'clarion call' to all the Allies

[139] See also Wallach, *ColJTransnat'lL*, 37 (1998–1999), 861; furthermore, see Schulmeister-André, *Einfluss* (2016), pp. 288–91 (on the Soviet influence on the creation of Art. 18 IMTS).

[140] Art. 17 IMTS; Safferling, *Criminal Procedure* (2012), p. 14; May and Wierda, *ColJTransnat'lL*, 37 (1998–1999), 742.

[141] Art. 16a IMTS.

[142] Kamardi, *Prozessordnung sui generis* (2009), p. 31; Wallach, *ColJTransnat'lL*, 37 (1998–1999), 861 ('a nod to continental practice').

[143] Wald, *CardozoLR*, 27 (2005–2006), 1573; May and Wierda, *ColJTransnat'lL*, 37 (1998–1999), 742; Ordinance No. 7, Art. XI (i).

[144] Rutledge, *RegentULR*, 16 (2003–2004), 166; Minear, *Tokyo Trial* (1971), p. 6. But see Taylor, *Nuremberg Trials* (1992), pp. 63–74. Note also the tension between the normative aspiration and the actual procedural implementation in the courtroom. While, for example, the dossier including all the evidence was uncomfortable for common law lawyers, the entire process of cross-examination was confusing for civil law lawyers (see Taylor, *Nuremberg Trials* (1992), p. 64).

[145] Zappalà, in Sluiter et al., *International Criminal Procedure* (2013), p. 46; Rutledge, *RegentULR*, 16 (2003–2004), 156; Wald, *CardozoLR*, 27 (2005–2006), 1573.

[146] Morris and Scharf, *Guide ICTY I* (1995), pp. 7–8; Wallach, *ColJTransnat'lL*, 37 (1998–1999), 854.

[147] Zappalà, in Sluiter et al., *International Criminal Procedure* (2013), p. 45.

[148] Ibid., pp. 45–6; see also Wald, *CardozoLR*, 27 (2005–2006), 1560.

[149] Rutledge, *RegentULR*, 16 (2003–2004), 166.

[150] Hofstetter, *Verfahrensrecht* (2005), p. 63; Lederer, *Military Courthouse* (1976), p. 14.

[151] *Ex parte Quirin*, 317 US 1, 46 (1942); Cowles, *ABAJ*, 30 (1944), 330 ff.; Glueck, *NebraskaLR*, 24 (1945), 143 ff.; Lauer, *St.John'sLR*, 20 (1945), 18 ff.; Wallach, *ColJTransnat'lL*, 37 (1998–1999), 854.

[152] Wallach, *ColJTransnat'lL*, 37 (1998–1999), 854 with further references.

to appoint respected jurists who would tolerate 'no drumhead court martial, no Moscow-type show trial, no foregone conclusions'.[153]

### (b) *Tokyo*

The Tokyo Trials were based on the Charter for the Far East, or 'Tokyo Charter', which was proclaimed on 19 January 1946 by the Supreme Commander for the Allied Powers (SCAP), General *Douglas MacArthur*, acting on behalf of the Allied Powers.[154] The Charter was, unlike the London Charter, not part of a treaty or an agreement among the Allies but issued by the SCAP by way of general orders.[155] Representatives of the Allied nations which had been involved in the struggle in Asia (the USA, Britain, France, the Soviet Union, Australia, Canada, China, the Netherlands, New Zealand, India, and the Philippines) formed the Far Eastern Commission (FEC), whose main task was to develop a policy of occupation for Japan and to coordinate the Allied policies in the Far East. Part of this policy was the prosecution of the major war criminals.[156] Thus, the International Military Tribunal for the Far East (IMTFE) was established by a special proclamation of the SCAP on the same day its Charter was proclaimed.[157] The role of the Allied forces in the proceedings remained limited,[158] 'partly due to MacArthur's dominating presence in post-war Japan'.[159]

The tribunal consisted 'of not less than six members nor more than eleven members, appointed by the Supreme Commander for the Allied Powers from the names submitted by the Signatories to the Instrument of Surrender, India, and the Commonwealth of the Philippines'.[160] It did not provide for appointment of alternates.[161] Instead, 'the presence of a majority of all members [was] necessary to constitute a quorum'.[162] All decisions and judgments of the IMTFE had to be rendered 'by a majority vote of those Members of the Tribunal present. In case the votes are evenly divided, the vote of the President shall be decisive'.[163] The tribunal was entitled to 'draft and amend rules of procedure consistent with the fundamental provisions of this Charter' (Article 7 IMTFE). It also had coercive powers similar to the Nuremberg Tribunal.[164] The evidentiary rules were laid down in Article 13 IMTFE and 'a synthesis of those contained in the Nuremberg Charter and Rules and those found in the

[153] Taylor, *Nuremberg Trials* (1992), p. 45. *Jackson* had previously announced at an ASIL speech in 1945: 'I am not so troubled as some seem to be over problems of jurisdiction of war criminals or of finding existing and recognized law by which standards of guilt may be determined. But all experience teaches that there are certain things you cannot do under the guise of judicial trial ... You must put no man on trial before anything that is called a court, if you are not prepared to establish his personal guilt ... The ultimate principle is that you must put no man on trial under the forms of judicial proceedings if you are not willing to see him freed if not proven guilty', <http://www.roberthjackson.org/files/thecenter/files/bibliography/1940s/rule-of-law-among-nations.pdf>; see also Wald, *CardozoLR*, 27 (2005–2006), 1560.

[154] 'Proclamation by the Supreme Commander for the Allied Powers' (19 January 1946), reprinted in Prichard and Zaide, *Tokyo I* (1981); see also Ambos, *Treatise ICL I* (2021), pp. 6–8; Minear, *Tokyo Trial* (1971), p. 20; Rutledge, *RegentULR*, 16 (2003–2004), 156; O'Keefe, *ICL* (2015), pp. 90–1.

[155] Ambos, *Treatise ICL I* (2021), p. 6; Wallach, *ColJTransnat'lL*, 37 (1998–1999), 864; O'Keefe, *ICL* (2015), p. 90.

[156] Ambos, *Treatise ICL I* (2021), p. 6. Yet, shortly after the end of the trials a period of clemency began, resulting in the release of the last war criminal in 1958, cf. Wilson, *JICJ*, 13 (2015), 745 ff.

[157] Thus, the IMTFE 'is the only international criminal court to date to have been established and empowered by means of a proclamation issued by a joint organ of several states'; see O'Keefe, *ICL* (2015), p. 89.

[158] Minear, *Tokyo Trial* (1971), p. 20; Rutledge, *RegentULR*, 16 (2003–2004), 156.

[159] Rutledge, *RegentULR*, 16 (2003–2004), 156.

[160] Art. 2 IMTFES.

[161] Wallach, *ColJTransnat'lL*, 37 (1998–1999), 864.

[162] Art. 4 IMTFES.

[163] Art. 4 (b) IMTFES.

[164] Wallach, *ColJTransnat'lL*, 37 (1998–1999), 865.

Royal Warrant issued for trial of war criminals by the United Kingdom'.[165] As it was the case at the Nuremberg Tribunal, the IMTFE was not bound by technical rules of evidence.[166] By law, the tribunal was urged to 'adopt and apply to the greatest possible extent expeditious and non-technical procedure, and shall admit any evidence which it deems to have probative value'.[167] All 'purported admissions or statements of the accused' were admissible.[168] Furthermore, the IMTFES entitled the tribunal to 'require to be informed of the nature of any evidence before it is offered in order to rule upon the relevance'.[169] Article 13 IMTFES also provided for specific types of evidence that were admissible, including documents issued by the government and armed forces, medical reports, affidavits, diaries, and letters, together with copies or other secondary evidence if originals were not available.[170] Thus, the aspiration was obviously to admit as much evidence as possible against the defendants.[171] The tribunal ruled that all cross-examination should be limited to matters arising out of the examination-in-chief.[172] As was the case during the Nuremberg trials, hearsay evidence was readily admitted, both in oral evidence and in the form of affidavits.[173] Justice *Pal* said in his dissenting opinion in the Tokyo Tribunal judgment:

> [W]e admitted much material which normally would have been discarded as hearsay evidence. The exclusion ... of hearsay evidence is not grounded upon its intrinsic lack of probative value. It is ordinarily excluded because the possible infirmities with respect to the observation, memory, narration and veracity of him who utters the offered words remain untested when the deponent is not subjected to cross-examination. These might be so far exposed by cross-examination as to enable the judge fairly to evaluate the utterance. The major part of the evidence given in this case consists of hearsay ... statements taken from persons not produced before us for cross-examination. Much caution will be needed in weighing this evidence.[174]

Article 13(c)(3) of the IMTFES explicitly lists affidavits as admissible evidence and insofar deviates from the IMTS, which omits any such reference.[175] Consequently, a decision to that end was taken at the beginning of the trial, in spite of a defence objection, which was overruled because the tribunal was 'not bound by the rules of evidence or the rules of procedure'.[176] Judge *Pal* remarked in his dissenting opinion that the decision was debated seriously and for a long time, and then accepted with 'a certain amount of misgivings'.[177] As *May* and *Wierda* point out, the tribunal 'recognized that by allowing affidavit evidence, the

[165] See The Royal Warrant, Regulations For The Trial Of War Criminals, 18 June 1945, <http://avalon.law.yale.edu/imt/imtroyal.asp>; Wallach, *ColJTransnat'lL*, 37 (1998–1999), 865.
[166] Art. 13 (a) first sentence IMTFES.
[167] Art. 13 (a) second sentence IMTFES.
[168] Art. 13 (a) third sentence IMTFES.
[169] Art. 13 (b) IMTFES.
[170] Art. 13 (c) IMTFES; May and Wierda, *ColJTransnat'lL*, 37 (1998–1999), 731.
[171] Wallach, *ColJTransnat'lL*, 37 (1998–1999), 866.
[172] Dissenting Opinion of Justice Pal (July 25, 1946), reprinted in Röling, *Tokyo Judgment* (1977), p. 639; May and Wierda, *ColJTransnat'lL*, 37 (1998–1999), 739.
[173] May and Wierda, *ColJTransnat'lL*, 37 (1998–1999), 745.
[174] Dissenting opinion of Justice Pal, reprinted in Röling, *Tokyo Judgment* (1977), p. 630; May and Wierda, *ColJTransnat'lL*, 37 (1998–1999), 745.
[175] May and Wierda, *ColJTransnat'lL*, 37 (1998–1999), 751.
[176] Dissenting opinion of Justice Pal, reprinted in Röling, *Tokyo Judgment* (1977), p. 636; May and Wierda, *ColJTransnat'lL*, 37 (1998–1999), 751.
[177] Dissenting opinion of Justice Pal, reprinted in Röling, *Tokyo Judgment* (1977), p. 636.

rule against leading questions lost all its importance and that the effect of the interrogatory on which an affidavit was based "increases the range but decreases the accuracy of the narration".[178] According to another author

> [a] characteristic feature ... was the large amount of documentary evidence that was introduced by the prosecution to support the charges and specifications and often by the defense to refute them. The defense contested the introduction of affidavits in the first trial but was overruled by the Commission, which pointed out that the protection of the United States Constitution and the Articles of War was not available to the accused as a Japanese citizen and a former belligerent.[179]

The rules of procedure were similarly as few as those of the IMT: while the IMT had eleven rules, the IMTFE only had nine.

### *(c) Post-Nuremberg and post-Tokyo trials*

The Nuremberg and Tokyo Trials were followed by a series of prosecutions of Nazi criminals in the four zones of occupation,[180] pursuant to Control Council Law (CCL) No. 10.[181] The Law comprised five articles and was adopted by the four occupying powers in order to provide a 'uniform legal basis in Germany for the prosecution of war criminals'.[182] In addition, each occupying power promulgated various ordinances to regulate proceedings in their military zones.[183] Thus, for example, proceedings in the US occupation zone were regulated by Ordinance No. 7, which was largely based on the IMTS.[184]

A tribunal composed of US-American judges conducted twelve separate trials of 177 defendants over a period of two and a half years.[185] The US also organized the post-Tokyo Trials.[186] The Supreme Commander of the Allied Powers (SCAP) and the Commanding General of the US Eighth Army promulgated the respective regulations[187] and rules of procedure.[188] They were based on those of the IMT, IMTFE, and Control Council tribunals.[189]

The tribunals in the US occupation zone in Germany were to 'consist of three or more members to be designated by the Military Governor' and possibly alternate members.[190] As a rule, all members and alternates had to be lawyers admitted to practice, for at least five years, in the highest US courts or the US Supreme Court.[191] The course of the proceedings

[178] May and Wierda, *ColJTransnat'lL*, 37 (1998–1999), 751; Dissenting opinion of Justice Pal, reprinted in Röling, *Tokyo Judgment* (1977), p. 636.

[179] Spurlock, *ABAJ*, 36 (1950), 389.

[180] Post-war Germany was divided by the Allied Powers (France, Russia, UK, and USA) into four zones of occupation jointly controlled by the Allied Control Council, but effectively controlled by each respective power.

[181] Heller, *Nuremberg Military Tribunals* (2012), pp. 9 ff.; also Ambos, *Treatise ICL I* (2021), p. 8; Ambos, *Völkerstrafrecht* (2002), pp. 83 ff.; König, *Legitimation* (2003), pp. 97 ff.; Engelhart, *Jura*, 26 (2004), 737; on the problem of retroactivity, de Haan, *JICJ*, 13 (2015), 793–4.

[182] Allied CCL No. 10, Dec. 20, 1945; May and Wierda, *Evidence* (2002), p. 21; O'Keefe, *ICL* (2015), p. 99.

[183] Trials were also held by the British, Australians, Canadians, Polish, Chinese, Dutch, and French; cf. May and Wierda, *Evidence* (2002), p. 21; O'Keefe, *ICL* (2015), p. 100.

[184] May and Wierda, *Evidence* (2002), p. 21.

[185] May and Wierda, *ColJTransnat'lL*, 37 (1998–1999), 732.

[186] May and Wierda, *Evidence* (2002), p. 21.

[187] Regulations promulgated by the Supreme Commander of the Allied Powers, 24 September 1945 (for the famous *Yamashita* trial), 5 December 1945 (regulated the Yokohama trials) (amended in December 1946).

[188] Rules of Procedure, promulgated 5 February 1946.

[189] May and Wierda, *Evidence* (2002), p. 21.

[190] Art. II (b) Ordinance No. 7.

[191] Ibid.

was similar to that at the IMT and IMTFE.[192] The judges possessed, as at the IMT,[193] broad powers to manage the trials.[194] The tribunals 'shall not be bound by technical rules of evidence'.[195] This corresponds to Article 19 IMT, including that the tribunals 'shall adopt and apply to the greatest possible extent expeditious and nontechnical procedure, and shall admit any evidence which they deem to have probative value'. Interestingly, however, Article VII of Ordinance No. 7 goes beyond Article 19 IMT towards the admission of all evidence of any probative value:[196]

> Without limiting the foregoing general rules, the following shall be deemed admissible if they appear to the tribunal to contain information of probative value relating to the charges: affidavits, depositions, interrogations and other statements, diaries, letters, the records, findings, statements and judgments of the military tribunals and the reviewing and confirming authorities of any of the United Nations, and copies of any document or other secondary evidence of the contents of any document, if the original is not readily available or cannot be produced without delay. The tribunal shall afford the opposing party such opportunity to question the authenticity or probative value of such evidence as in the opinion of the tribunal the ends of justice require.

As a consequence, German documents in particular have been 'the principal evidence relied upon by the prosecution in each of the Nuremberg trials'.[197] In the *Balkan Generals* trial[198] the tribunal made clear, however, that Article VII Ordinance No. 7:

> applies to the competency [sic] of evidence only, and does not have the effect of giving weight and credibility to such evidence as a matter of law. It is still within the province of the Tribunal to test it by the usual rules of law governing the evaluation of evidence. Any other interpretation would seriously affect the right of the defendants to a fair and impartial trial. The interpretation thus given and consistently announced throughout the trial by this Tribunal is not an idle gesture to be announced as a theory and ignored in practice; it is a substantive right composing one of the essential elements of a fair and impartial adjudication.[199]

[192] cf. Art. XI Ordinance No. 7: 'The proceedings at the trial shall take the following course: a) The tribunal shall inquire of each defendant whether he has received and had an opportunity to read the indictment against him and whether he pleads "guilty" or "not guilty." b) The prosecution may make an opening statement. c) The prosecution shall produce its evidence subject to the cross examination of its witnesses. d) The defense may make an opening statement. e) The defense shall produce its evidence subject to the cross examination of lts witnesses. f) Such rebutting evidence as may be held by the tribunal to be material may be, produced by either the prosecution or the defense. g) The defense shall address the court. h) The prosecution shall address the court. i) Each defendant may make a statement to the tribunal. j) The tribunal shall deliver judgment and pronounce sentence.'

[193] Art. 18 IMTS.

[194] Art. VI Ordinance No. 7.

[195] Art. VII Ordinance No. 7.

[196] Wallach, *ColJTransnat'lL*, 37 (1998–1999), 863.

[197] See Rules and Practice Concerning Various Types of Evidence, *TWC, XV* (1997), p. 633; May and Wierda, *ColJTransnat'lL*, 37 (1998–1999), 748.

[198] *US v. von List et al.* (Hostage case) (case 7), US GPO, *TWC, XI* (1997) (19 February 1948), pp. 757 ff.; Ambos, *Treatise ICL I* (2021), p. 8.

[199] See *US v. von List et al.* (Hostage case) (case 7), US GPO, *TWC, XI* (1997) (19 February 1948), p. 1258; *TWC, XV* (1997), p. 95. See also *US v. Krupp*, *TWC, XV* (1997), p. 646, in which the tribunal was presented a document without signature and without evidence as to its author or origin. The Presiding Judge, Judge Daly, said: 'The Tribunal's feeling is that this gets to a matter of weight rather than to admissibility, as long as it is conceded that this is a captured document, and that gets also to the question of probative value.' (p. 649). The document was admitted. See generally May and Wierda, *ColJTransnat'lL*, 37 (1998–1999), 755.

In fact, the use of affidavit evidence was as extensive as before the IMT, where the defence invoked this kind of evidence more often than the prosecution did.[200] However, in the *IG-Farben* trial[201] affidavits were held inadmissible, on the ground that 'the right of a defendant who is being tried in a criminal action or proceeding to interrogate witnesses who testify against him is a fundamental right and not merely a rule of evidence'.[202] In the *Einsatzgruppen*,[203] *Ministries*,[204] and *High Command*[205] cases, the tribunals reverted to the earlier practice of allowing such evidence.[206]

As was the case before both the IMT and the IMTFE, fair trial principles played an important role during the Post-Nuremberg and Post-Tokyo Trials, too. Ordinance No. 7 laid down several fair trial rights for the defendant, inter alia, the right to have adequate time for the preparation of his defence,[207] the right to counsel,[208] the right to be present,[209] and the right to present evidence and cross-examine witnesses.[210] Additionally, the following principles were listed in the *Flick et al.* judgment:

- There can be no conviction without proof of personal guilt.
- Such guilt must be proved beyond a reasonable doubt.
- The presumption of innocence follows each defendant throughout the trial.
- The burden of proof is at all times upon the prosecution.
- If from credible evidence two reasonable inferences may be drawn, one of guilt and the other of innocence, the latter must be taken.[211]

[200] May and Wierda, *ColJTransnat'lL*, 37 (1998–1999), 749.

[201] *US v. Krauch et al., TWC, XV* (1997), pp. 880–91. Thereon Jeßberger, *JICJ*, 8 (2010), 783 ff; Ambos, *Treatise ICL I* (2021), p. 8.

[202] *US v. Krauch et al.* (Farben case) (case 6), US GPO, *TWC, XV* (1997) (29 July 1948), p. 891; *TWC, VII* (1997) (29 July 1948); also May and Wierda, *ColJTransnat'lL*, 37 (1998–1999), 761–2.

[203] *US v. Ohlendorf et al.* ('Einsatzgruppen-trial') (case 9), US GPO, *TWC, IV* (1997) (10 April 1948) against twenty-four heads of the task-forces of the *Sicherheitspolizei* (security police) and of the *Sicherheitsdienst* (security service) which joined with the security police in 1939 to form the Reichssicherheitshauptamt), see Streim, in Rückerl, *NS-Prozesse* (1971), p. 65; Ambos, *Treatise ICL I* (2021), p. 8.

[204] *US v. von Weizsäcker et al.* ('Ministries case', 'Wilhelmstraßen-Trial') (case 11), US GPO, *TWC, XIV* (1997) (11 April 1949), against twenty-one ministers, permanent secretaries, *Gauleiter*, high-ranked SS-leaders, and other leading persons; cf. Haensel and Kempner, *Wilhelmstraßenprozeß* (1950), pp. 1 ff.; Ambos, *Treatise ICL I* (2021), pp. 8–9.

[205] *US v. von Leeb et al.* ('High Command Trial') (case 12), US GPO, *TWC, XI* (1997) (28 October 1948), against fourteen high-ranking officers of the German armed forces; cf. Ambos, *Treatise ICL I* (2021), p. 9.

[206] See *TWC, XV* (1997), p. 880 (summarizing); May and Wierda, *ColJTransnat'lL*, 37 (1998–1999), 752.

[207] See Art. IV (a) Ordinance No. 7: 'A defendant shall be furnished, at a reasonable time before his trial, a copy of the indictment and of all documents lodged with the indictment, translated into a language which he understands. The indictment shall state the charges plainly, concisely and with sufficient particulars to inform defendant of the offenses charged.'

[208] See Art. IV (c) Ordinance No. 7: 'A defendant shall have the right to be represented by counsel of his own selection, provided such counsel shall be a person qualified under existing regulations to conduct cases before the courts of defendant's country, or any other person who may be specially authorized by the tribunal. The tribunal shall appoint qualified counsel to represent a defendant who is not represented by counsel of his own selection.'

[209] See Art. IV (d) Ordinance No. 7: 'Every defendant shall be entitled to be present at his trial except that a defendant may be proceeded against during temporary absences if in the opinion of the tribunal defendant's interests will not thereby be impaired, and except further as provided in Art. VI (c). The tribunal may also proceed in the absence of any defendant who has applied for and has been granted permission to be absent.'

[210] See Art. IV (e) Ordinance No. 7: 'A defendant shall have the right through his counsel to present evidence at the trial in support of his defense, and to cross-examine any witness called by the prosecution.'

[211] *US v. Flick, TWC, VI* (1952), p. 1189; see also May and Wierda, *ColJTransnat'lL*, 37 (1998–1999), 754; generally Ambos, *Treatise I* (2021), p. 8.

### *(d) Problems and legacies of the IMT and IMTFE*

As we have seen above, one of the fundamental pillars of the Nuremberg and Tokyo as well as the successor trials has been the fairness and expediency of the proceedings. Many famous statements can be recalled in this context, for example President Truman's words, already quoted above, that 'the world should be impressed by the fairness of the trial'.[212]

Of course, this was not the only purpose of these trials. The tribunals were also established to do justice by punishing the (most) responsible and to contribute to the historical truth. Indeed, in the words of British IMT Judge Geoffrey Lawrence, one wanted to punish 'those who were guilty', to establish 'the supremacy of international law over national law' and to prove 'actual facts, in order to bring home to the German people and to the peoples of the world, the depths of infamy to which the pursuit of total warfare had brought Germany'.[213] And still more explicit with regard to the objective to create an accurate and irrefutable historical record:

> Would anyone have believed, had it not been proved by the evidence and the documents, that the Germans ordered the Polish intelligentsia, the Polish nobility and the Polish clergy to be killed out of hand; that actually before making war on the Soviet Union they ordered all commissars to be killed on capture; that they ordered that the Jews and other prisoners should be gassed if unable to work; and that in accordance with these inhuman orders many millions of human beings had been butchered?[214]

From this perspective, focusing rather on the policy behind Nuremberg and Tokyo than the actual law and its application, the whole enterprise can be considered a success, indeed a milestone in the development of ICL and international accountability for very serious crimes.[215] Indeed, the birth of the 'age of accountability', somewhat euphemistically announced by the UN Secretary General at the ICC's Kampala Review Conference invoking the establishment of the ICTY and ICTR in 1993 and 1994 and the ICC in 1998,[216] would not have been possible without the Nuremberg and Tokyo precedents. The picture is more nuanced, of course, if one takes a closer look at the law and the decisions of the historic tribunals.[217] Here one may draw some important conclusions and learn some important lessons with a view to modern international criminal procedure. In fact, examining the shortcomings of these tribunals more closely, one better understands the challenges of the current international criminal tribunals. Despite the passage of time from Nuremberg to The Hague the difficulties, challenges, and expectations from the different constituencies remain basically the same.

[212] Quoted in Biddle, *In Brief Authority* (1962/1976), p. 372; Wald, *CardozoLR*, 27 (2005–2006), 1574. See also Haensel, *DePaulLR*, 13 (1963–1964), 258.

[213] Lawrence, in Mettraux, *Nuremberg Trial* (2008), p. 292; furthermore, see May and Fyfe, in Hayashi and Bailliet, *Criminal Tribunals* (2017), p. 30 arguing that 'Nuremberg succeded because of the reasonableness of its procedures and the rulings of its judges'.

[214] Lawrence, in Mettraux, *Nuremberg Trial* (2008), p. 293.

[215] Chiam, in Blumenthal and McCormack, *Legacy of Nuremberg* (2008), p. 205; also Wheeler, *Fairness* (2023), p. 27 ('the most purely legal goal of international criminal trials').

[216] UN Secretary General, Address at the ICC's First Review Conference in Kampala, 31 May 2010, <http://www.un.org/sg/STATEMENTS/index.asp?nid=4585>; see also de Serpa Soares, *JICJ*, 13 (2015), 669 ff. (without, however, referring to the historic precedents).

[217] cf. Wright, in Mettraux, *Nuremberg Trial* (2008), p. 325, distinguishing between two kinds of criticisms, those against the decisions and sentences and those directed towards the law.

There are several procedural issues that received attention during and after the post-WWII trials. The first concerns the *judges' independence* which according to the critics was never guaranteed. Three of the Allies' representatives who signed the London Agreement became judges of the IMT—*William Allen Jowitt* for Great Britain, *Robert Falco* for France, and *Iona Timofeevich Nikichenko* for the Soviet Union.[218] *Jackson*, who signed for the USA, became the Chief US-American Prosecutor.[219] The ensuing executive interference with the newly created judiciary is difficult to reconcile with the principle of the separation of powers,[220] although one must not lose sight of the fact that the heavy involvement of the executive branch in the appointment of international judges is common practice until today; indeed, it appears to be one of the root causes of the often, to put it mildly, controversial qualification of many international judges.[221] Be that as it may, the Allied Powers never seriously considered appointing judges from third countries, let alone from Germany, to the bench.[222] The judges also drafted their own procedural rules.[223] Despite ensuing concerns regarding the judges' impartiality, no mechanism was adopted to challenge the judges on these grounds. In fact, Article 3 IMTS explicitly dismisses such a possibility.[224] This means nothing less than that the judges 'had ruled for themselves that they could not be turned down as prejudiced'.[225] Thereby they decided on a question (judicial bias) 'in which the judge, rejected as biased, is normally not allowed to participate in the answer'.[226]

Secondly, there was an apparent *structural inequality* between the prosecution and the defence.[227] At the IMT, for the total of twenty-one accused and six indicted organizations, on the defence side there were twenty-seven defence counsel, fifty-four junior counsel, and sixty-seven secretaries.[228] By contrast, on the prosecution side, there was a large US-American delegation consisting of some 2000 staff, and further 170 British, twenty-four Soviet Prosecutors, and twelve French staff.[229] While the admission of foreign, especially US-American, defence counsel was theoretically possible, in practice it was impossible to find one and bring him to the Court in time.[230] For closing arguments, each defendant

[218] Laternser, in Mettraux, *Nuremberg Trial* (2008), p. 478; Haensel, *DePaulLR*, 13 (1963–1964), 256.

[219] Safferling, *Criminal Procedure* (2012), p. 16.

[220] Safferling and Graebke, *ZStW* 123 (2011), 67.

[221] See the seminal study by Mackenzie et al., *Selecting International Judges* (2010), pp. 2–3, 122 ff., 152 ff.; thereon Ambos, *CLF*, 23 (2012), 223 with further references; see recently also Bohlander, 'Article 36', in Ambos, *Commentary* (2022), mn. 3 ff.

[222] Marrus, *Nuremberg Trial* (1997), p. 251; Kauffmann, *WhittierLR*, 9 (1987–1988), 538 and 550 ff. Other German commentators have expressed their disappointment that no German judge was involved, see Jescheck, *Verantwortlichkeit* (1952), pp. 416 ff.; Safferling, *Criminal Procedure* (2012), p. 16; Safferling and Graebke, *ZStW*, 123 (2011), 67.

[223] Safferling, *Criminal Procedure* (2012), p. 16.

[224] Art. 3 IMTS reads: 'Neither the Tribunal, its members nor their alternates can be challenged by the prosecution, or by the Defendants or their Counsel.' See also Safferling and Graebke, *ZStW* 123 (2011), 67.

[225] Laternser, in Mettraux, *Nuremberg Trial* (2008), p. 478.

[226] Ibid.

[227] Safferling, *Criminal Procedure* (2012), p. 17.

[228] Ibid., p. 16; for a detailed list of counsel, see Safferling and Graebke, *ZStW* 123 (2011), 48 ff.

[229] Safferling, *Criminal Procedure* (2012), p. 17.

[230] Kronstein, *ColLRev*, 53 (1953), 143, mentioning as main obstacles currency and travel problems as well as the time pressure which made it difficult for the judges to wait for such a counsel. In concrete terms *Kronstein* refers (at 143) to Alfried Krupp's attempt 'to find a suitable American lawyer, since he considered it vital that he be defended by an American lawyer before a court composed of American judges. It was only on December 8, 1947, that a formal motion for admission of the law firm of Foley and Carroll of Hayward, California, was filed ... Mr. Carroll was in Germany in connection with other cases. He did not, however, have a military permit which would allow him to stay in Germany for the Krupp trial, and the judges felt that he had deceived the court when he failed to inform all parties to the case of that fact.'

had one-half day but the prosecution three.[231] The financial resources for the defence were limited:[232] Every defence counsel received 9500 *Reichsmark* for the first client and half of it for every other client but this fee—payment of which has often been delayed—also had to serve to pay assistants and cover all other expenses, for example with regard to the acquisition of exculpatory material. Apart from that, the post-war situation with heavy problems of infrastructure made it (financially) difficult if not impossible to transfer defence witnesses to Nuremberg.[233] The overall situation of defence counsel at Nuremberg has been impressively, albeit a bit clumsily, summarized by *Hans Laternser*, then Chief Counsel for the German High Command and the German General Staff:

> The German defense counsel began their activity in October 1945 in the severely bombed city of Nuremberg. They stood there with literally empty hands. To perform their jobs they had, for the time being, a small library room in which not even every defense counsel had his own working place. Later a large library room was placed at the disposal of all of the defenders. There they each had a working table. At that time, however, they did not yet have a single telephone. In the course of the later procedures, every chief defense attorney received a room for himself. But even then the entire defense of the processes running in part simultaneously had only a single telephone connection from which they could make long distance calls. The situation of the prosecuting authority stood in no expressible proportion to this.[234]

Thirdly, at least before some judges, the defence had, in procedural terms, to fight against a kind of *presumption of guilt* entailing a de facto reversal of the burden of proof.[235] As *Goodhart* put it: 'In the first place [the Nuremberg trials] have given the defendants an opportunity of proving, if they could, that they had not taken part in the Nazi conspiracy, or that some other ground of defence was open to them.'[236] Defendants were denied certain defences and could, as we have seen above, be tried in absentia.[237] While the prosecution witnesses were heard directly by the IMT, the defence witnesses were only heard by a military commission and their statements were presented in written form to the bench.[238] In other words, the defence witnesses have never been directly examined by the judges. *Laternser* thus summarizes: '[T]he weapons of the prosecuting authority and defense were extremely unequal at the beginning of the process. Even though this inequality was later modified somewhat, the inequalities could not be compensated, even approximately, at any phase of the processes.'[239]

231 Wald, *CardozoLR*, 27 (2005–2006), 1585.

232 For details, see Safferling and Graebke, *ZStW*, 123 (2011), 75 ff.

233 Kastner, *Von den Siegern* (2001), p. 135; Safferling and Graebke, *ZStW*, 123 (2011), 74.

234 Laternser, *WhittierLR*, 8 (1986–1987), 561.

235 In the same vein, Ehrenfreund, *Nuremberg Legacy* (2007), p. 33.

236 Goodhart, in Mettraux, *Nuremberg Trial* (2008), p. 637.

237 Rutledge, *RegentULR*, 16 (2003–2004), 154. See also with regard to Tokyo, Minear, *Tokyo Trial* (1971), p. 120, listing entire categories of evidence declared inadmissible at the Tokyo trials; for example, evidence showing the Japanese–Chinese relationship at the time and evidence relating to the development and use of nuclear weapons were both forbidden; Fabian, *DePaulLR*, 49 (2000), 982, delineating certain protections and rules used in the post-WW II trials that are no longer deemed acceptable practice. See generally Scharf, *DenvJIL&Pol'y*, 25 (1997), 305 ff., comparing the Nuremberg trial with the ICTY for purposes of showing improvements in policies and rules since the WW II trials.

238 Laternser, in Mettraux, *Nuremberg Trial* (2008), p. 480 ('The chairman of this commission, a British lieutenant colonel, made a report on the entire interrogations; the report was presented to the International Military Tribunal.'). See also Safferling and Graebke, *ZStW* 123 (2011), 74.

239 Laternser, in Mettraux, *Nuremberg Trial* (2008), p. 480.

Fourthly, the IMT faced many *evidentiary problems.* While the tribunal could ask the parties to inform about their evidence beforehand so that it could rule on its relevance,[240] in actual fact it applied this rule only to the defence evidence which had to be explicitly approved.[241] The prosecution was free to produce any evidence it considered relevant. Another problem was the sheer amount of written evidence in the form of thousands of documents and affidavits.[242] At least 90 per cent of the evidence offered in Nuremberg consisted of the Nazis' own written records, in the form of orders, directives, diaries, journals, memoranda, and correspondence.[243] As *Carl Haensel*, associate to defence counsel *Horst Pelckmann*, pointed out: 'The first surprise in Nuremberg in October, 1945, was the enormous quantity and quality of documents which were introduced in evidence by the prosecution. When the United States Army entered German territory, it had specialized military personnel whose duties were to capture and preserve German documents, records and archives.'[244] He added: 'The documents of the Staff Main Office (S.S. Center) alone filled six large railway cars … The hunting for documents resulted in the most complete documentation ever compiled of the history of a single period.'[245] *Telford Taylor*, initially assistant to Chief Prosecutor *Robert H. Jackson* and later his successor, noted that the admission of an overwhelming number of documents was considerably slowed down since it was required that the prosecution read them into the record.[246] As a result, Justice Jackson opined that certain documents did not need to be read into the record.[247] This was criticized as a violation of the principle of oral presentation of evidence,[248] but it was considered in line with or even demanded in general terms by Article 18 IMTS, which required the tribunal to 'confine the Trial strictly to an expeditious hearing'.[249] The admission of a large amount of affidavits, in turn, created problems with the principle of immediacy (*Unmittelbarkeitsgrundsatz*) according to which all evidence must be heard and seen by the deciding judges.[250] In any case, the prosecution wanted to make sure that its evidence was 'foolproof' and therefore withdrew any item whose authenticity was questioned by the defence.[251]

Regrettably, however, the prosecution archives remained closed to the defence.[252] Disclosure, so important before the ICC, and indeed an indispensable prerequisite to achieving equality of arms,[253] did not seem to have been *en vogue*. Sadly enough, the prosecution did not only withhold evidence from the defence but also from the Court.[254]

[240] cf. Art. 20 IMTS stating that '[t]he Tribunal may require to be informed of the nature of any evidence before it is offered so that it may rule upon the relevance thereof.' See also Taylor, *Nuremberg Trials* (1992), p. 319; Wald, *CardozoLR*, 27 (2005–2006), 1583.

[241] Laternser, *WhittierLR*, 8 (1986–1987), 566.

[242] May and Wierda, *ColJTransnat'lL*, 37 (1998–1999), 744.

[243] Dodd, in Mettraux, *Nuremberg Trial* (2008), p. 194.

[244] Haensel, *DePaulLR*, 13 (1963–1964), 255–6.

[245] Ibid., 256.

[246] Taylor, *Nuremberg Trials* (1992), p. 176; Wallach, *ColJTransnat'lL*, 37 (1998–1999), 876 with n. 97.

[247] See also Safferling and Graebke, *ZStW*, 123 (2011), 72.

[248] See generally Bohlander, *German Criminal Procedure* (2021), p. 28.

[249] See also Safferling and Graebke, *ZStW*, 123 (2011), 72.

[250] Ibid. See generally about this principle Bohlander, *German Criminal Procedure* (2021), pp. 28–30 and Chapter V, A.(2)(b) in this volume.

[251] Dodd, in Mettraux, *Nuremberg Trial* (2008), p. 194 ('Of all the thousands of documents offered in evidence, only two items were questioned by the defense on the grounds of authenticity. Both of these items were withdrawn by the prosecution in order to make sure that our evidence was foolproof. This, in itself, is something of a record for litigation.').

[252] Safferling, *Criminal Procedure* (2012), p. 17.

[253] See thereon Section D.(2)(b) in this chapter and Chapter V, B. in this volume. See also Heinze, *Disclosure* (2014), pp. 311 ff.

[254] Laternser, *WhittierLR*, 8 (1986–1987), 561.

Although this practice seems to find support in the Rules of Procedure,[255] it casts a shadow on the presumed fairness of the proceedings. As *Laternser* bitterly remarked:

> At the beginning of the court proceedings in Nuremberg, the prosecuting authority already possessed an extremely extensive mass of evidence ... The defenders could utilize this entire confiscated material only so far as the prosecuting authority decided, in the course of the processes, to submit it to the court as evidence. The defenders themselves had no possibility whatsoever to look through the archives in Washington and London for exonerating evidence. Because of these facts, valuable material for the defense has most certainly not been used.[256]

### (2) The influence of Nuremberg and Tokyo on the procedure of international criminal tribunals

The principles resulting from the IMT proceedings were an important substructure for the upcoming development in the field of ICL,[257] including international criminal procedure. It was further influenced by the Tokyo trial and the numerous trials in the German occupation zones and in other allied jurisdictions.[258] Nuremberg had shown that an international criminal tribunal could work.[259]

While generally the proceedings can be qualified as fair,[260] we have seen above that they were far from perfect.[261] Apart from the many specific problems faced by the IMT, such as the limited independence of judges, the inequality between prosecution and defence, evidentiary problems (including limited disclosure), a more fundamental problem was the marked adversarial tendency of the tribunal alien to the German defendants.[262] Take the following, fairly paradigmatic dialogue between one of the judges and *Alfried Krupp*:

> Judge: 'Mr. Krupp, did someone advise you that these proceedings were to be conducted according to the rules of procedure of an American Court?'
>
> Krupp: 'No, Your Honor stated that these proceedings were carried out according to rules of their own, but at any rate they are rather different from the German rules of procedure, which, although I cannot say that with any authority of course, don't seem to be anything near the American rules of procedure.'[263]

[255] Pursuant to Rule 17 of the Uniform Rules of Procedure, the prosecution could withhold copies of documents to be offered into evidence until twenty-four hours before it desired to offer them. See also May and Wierda, *ColJTransnat'lL*, 37 (1998–1999), 757.

[256] Laternser, *WhittierLR*, 8 (1986–1987), 561–2.

[257] See Ambos, *Treatise ICL I* (2021), p. 11 with further references.

[258] cf. Wright, 'Nuremberg Trial', in Mettraux, *Nuremberg Trial* (2008), p. 352; for a recent insight into the Netherlands' treatment of crimes committed during the German occupation by way of so-called 'extraordinary justice (*bijzondere rechtspleging*)', see Brands, *JICJ*, 13 (2015), 763 ff.

[259] See e.g. Dodd, in Mettraux, *Nuremberg Trial* (2008), p. 198.

[260] Haensel, *DePaulLR*, 13 (1963–1964), 258; Wald, *CardozoLR*, 27 (2005–2006), 1596.

[261] Wald, *CardozoLR*, 27 (2005–2006), 1596–7; Levi, Hagan, and Dezalay, *LCP*, 79 (2016), 297 with further references.

[262] Laternser, *WhittierLR*, 8 (1986–1987), 560; Pannenbecker, *DePaulLR*, 14 (1964–1965), 349; Safferling, *Criminal Procedure* (2012), p. 18.

[263] Cited in Kronstein, *ColLRev*, 53 (1953), 142.

As we have seen above,[264] the common law tradition differs from its civil law counterpart in many ways—not only with regard to certain procedural elements or techniques such as cross-examination, the concept of disclosure, and the principled prohibition of hearsay evidence, but also with respect to the trial participants and their position within the proceedings. For a defence counsel with a civil law background, one of the most important, if not *the* most important, difficulty is the parties' responsibility in the presentation and evaluation of evidence.[265] Of course, this radically different approach of an adversarial as compared to an inquisitorial procedure also affects the other participants with a civil law background. Thus, some argue that one of the reasons for the acquittal of Nazi-journalist *Fritzsche* was the 'disastrous performance' of the Russian Chief Prosecutor *Rudenko* in the coutroom.[266]

It must not be overlooked, however, that the compromise character of the Rules of Procedure entailed the softening of many adversarial features of the common law tradition. As *Kronstein* put it: 'The adoption by the Tribunal of a so-called international standard of procedure only meant a softening of American rules of procedure and evidence worked out in the interest of a "fair trial".' Typical are the 'continuous references by the prosecution to the fact that "even" under American procedure certain methods of presenting evidence were permissible'.[267] With regard to both the IMT and the IMFE, *Wallach* remarks that there were 'improper communications with judges,[268] inconsistent rulings favoring the prosecution,[269] vague and ambiguous indictments under the Tokyo rules, questions regarding the applicability of the Geneva Conventions to defendants, the denial of motions to recuse arguably biased judges'.[270]

Be that as it may, the different procedural approaches and the ensuing problems can be seen as precursors of the problems and difficulties of modern international criminal procedure.

### (a) *The development of procedural rules at the ad hoc tribunals*

In Europe, WWII was followed by a long and stable period of peace that was interrupted by massive violations of IHL and human rights in the Former Yugoslavia beginning in 1991.[271] In reaction to this situation the UN established the 'United Nations Commission of Experts Pursuant to Security Council Resolution 780'.[272] The Commission submitted a first Interim Report on the basis of which the Security Council (SC) decided to establish the International Criminal Tribunal for the Former Yugoslavia (ICTY).[273] The Statute of the ICTY (ICTYS) was annexed to the Expert Report.[274] Apart from articles dealing with questions of substantive law (Articles 2–7, 24 ICTYS) and the organization of the court (Articles

[264] See Section A.(1) in this chapter.

[265] Schuon, *Procedure* (2010), p. 3.

[266] Safferling, *Criminal Procedure* (2012), p. 18; Schäfers, *Nürnberg* (2012), pp. 168–86.

[267] Kronstein, *ColLR*, 53 (1953), 142.

[268] *Taylor* says that Justice *Jackson* himself engaged in *ex parte* communications with Judge *Biddle*, and that in doing so he sent 'the proprieties "by the way" for fair [sic]'. (Taylor, *Nuremberg Trials* (1992), p. 134).

[269] See Röling, *The Tokyo Judgment* (1977), pp. 633–4; Taylor, *Nuremberg Trials* (1992), p. 321.

[270] Wallach, *ColJTransnat'lL*, 37 (1998–1999), 877–8 with further references.

[271] Ambos, *Treatise ICL I* (2021), p. 24.

[272] UN Doc. S/RES/780 (1992); Bassiouni, *AJIL*, 88 (1994), 789 ff.

[273] Resolution 827 of 25 May 1993, UN Doc. S/RES/827 (1993), in *HRLJ* (1993), 197; for further references, see Ambos, *Treatise ICL I* (2021), p. 24.

[274] Last amended by SC Res. 1877, 7 July 2009, where it was decided that the President of the Tribunal may assign to the Appeals Chamber up to four additional permanent judges serving in the Trial Chambers.

11–17, 31–4 ICTYS), the ICTYS also contains some basic provisions on the procedure before the tribunal (Articles 1, 8–10, 18–23, 25–30 ICTYS).[275] These provisions put more emphasis on the rights of the accused and the fairness of the proceedings in general than the Statutes of the IMT and the IMTFE.[276] Nevertheless, the ICTYS resembles its predecessors in Nuremberg and Tokyo as it is aligned with the common law tradition; civil law features have only been integrated through subsequent case law and various reforms of the Rules of Procedure and Evidence (RPE)[277] as will be seen in a moment. The RPE[278] as well as several other additional instruments[279] have been adopted by the judges themselves.[280] For lawyers with a civil law background this is difficult to reconcile with the principle of separation of powers.[281] Originally, the RPE also resembled the adversarial system since the USA submitted the most advanced draft to the judges.[282] However, in the course of their innumerable amendments,[283] several civil law features have been incorporated.[284] As to the great number of amendments, the first president of the tribunal, *Antonio Cassese*, explained to the UN General Assembly:

> [i]t would have been impossible for the first truly international criminal tribunal to have adopted the first ever international criminal procedural and evidentiary code from a first draft dealing perfectly with all the diverse issues with which the Tribunal has to cope ... It would have equally been impossible for the issues ... to have been perfectly anticipated and solved at the beginning of 1994 [before the commencement of the first proceedings].[285]

The second ad hoc tribunal, the International Criminal Tribunal for Rwanda (ICTR), was established by SC Resolution 955 of 8 November 1994.[286] The Statute of the ICTR (ICTRS) resembles largely the ICTYS.[287] Similarly, the RPE ICTR largely resemble the RPE ICTY and have also been amended several times, albeit not as often as the RPE ICTY.[288]

[275] For the wording, cf. Security Council, Report of the Secretary-General Pursuant to Paragraph 2 of Security Council Resolution 808 (1993), UN Doc. S/25707, 3 May 1993 (hereinafter: Report ICTY (1993)), paras. 32 ff., <http://www.icty.org/x/file/Legal%20Library/Statute/statute_re808_1993_en.pdf>; reprinted in *HRLJ* (1996), 211 ff.; see also Ambos, *Treatise ICL I* (2021), p. 26 with further references.

[276] Safferling, *Criminal Procedure* (2012), p. 25.

[277] Ibid.

[278] The Rules were adopted in February 1994, UN IT/32, 14 March 1994.

[279] All these instruments can be found at <http://www.icty.org/en/documents>; for other instruments, see Ambos, *Treatise ICL I* (2021), p. 26 with n. 186.

[280] In more detail, see Terris, Romano, and Swigart, *International Judge* (2007), p. 109.

[281] cf. Merryman and Pérez-Perdomo, *Civil Law* (2019), pp. 23 ff. About the Judge-Legislator in more detail, see previously Ambos, *Treatise ICL I* (2021), p. 45 with n. 343. The same criticism was made vis-à-vis the IMT and IMTFE, see Section B.(1)(d) in this chapter.

[282] cf. Morris and Scharf, *Guide ICTY I* (1995), p. 177; see also Ntanda Nsereko, *CLF*, 5 (1994), 508, stating that the ICTY 'relied heavily on proposals from the US government and from non-governmental organizations such as the US-based Lawyers Committee for Human Rights'; Boas et al., *Procedure* (2011), p. 24.

[283] Latest amendment IT/278 of 22 May 2013; cf. Terris, Romano, and Swigart, *International Judge* (2007), p. 109 (on average more than three times a year); Safferling, *Criminal Procedure* (2012), p. 25 (2.6 times a year).

[284] See, for many, Langer, *AJCompL*, 53 (2005), 836 ff., explaining why and to what extent the ICTY procedure has adopted a 'managerial judging system' (thereon Chapter IV, A.(2)(a) in this volume *in fine*). See also Safferling, *Criminal Procedure* (2012), p. 25; Heinze, *Disclosure* (2014), p. 501; De Meester, *Investigation Phase* (2015), p. 83. We will return to these changes in the following chapters in this volume, see esp. Chapter V, A.(4)(c).

[285] Address of 19 November 1996, United Nations Press Release GA/9166, Bulletin of the International Criminal Tribunal for the Former Yugoslavia 2, no. 13 (1996).

[286] Ambos, *Treatise ICL I* (2021), p. 27 with further references.

[287] Report of the Secretary-General pursuant to paragraphs of SC resolution 955 (1994); UN Doc. S/1995/134, 13 February 1995 (hereinafter: Report ICTR (1995)), para. 18.

[288] Safferling, *Criminal Procedure* (2012), p. 27.

On 22 December 2010, the Security Council established the International Residual Mechanism for Criminal Tribunals (MICT) with two branches for the ICTY and the ICTR.[289] The relevant SC Resolution 1966 (2010) did not only contain the MICT Statute as an annex, but also the so-called 'Transitional Arrangements' (TA).[290] They provide detailed rules on, inter alia, the allocation of competences, that is, which organ of the ICTY/ICTR or MICT is responsible for the completion of ongoing or the commencement of new proceedings.[291] The MICT is a subsidiary organ of the Security Council pursuant to Article 29 of the UN Charter.[292] The ICTY branch started to operate on 1 July 2013, the ICTR branch on 1 July 2012.[293] The resolution scheduled the completion of the ICTY's and ICTR's remaining work rather optimistically as 'no later than 31 December 2014'.[294] In fact, the Appeals Chamber of the ICTR issued its final judgment only on 14 December 2015[295] and closed at the same time, i.e. one year later than expected.[296] The Residual Mechanisms adopted new RPE on 8 June 2012 (corrigendum on 17 August 2012),[297] which draw upon the procedures already in place at the ICTY and ICTR.[298] The MICT conducts review proceedings,[299] supervises the enforcement of sentences, and decides on pardon or commutation of sentences.[300] It also handles trials for contempt of the tribunal and false testimony,[301] and ensures the protection of victims and witnesses.[302]

### *(b) The development of procedural rules at the ICC*

During the 1998 Rome State Conference for the establishment of the ICC[303] the procedural law of the court was the object of deliberations of the Working Group on Procedural Matters (WGPM)[304] but given the technical nature of this law it was a bit overshadowed

[289] SC Res. 1966 (2010).

[290] Transitional Arrangements, Resolution 1966 (2010), S/Res/1966 (2010), Annex 2; pp. 18 ff.

[291] See SC Res. 1966 (2010), p. 2 para. 2 ('*Decides* that the provisions of this resolution and the Statutes of the Mechanism and of the ICTY and ICTR shall be subject to the transitional arrangements set out in Annex 2 to this resolution' (emphasis in the original)). See also Denis, *JICJ*, 9 (2011), 819; McIntyre, *GoJIL*, 3 (2011), 929, 931 ff.; furthermore, see McDermott, *QIL*, 40 (2017), 11 ff. on the adherence to the fair trial principle in the MICT's practice.

[292] O'Keefe, *ICL* (2015), p. 488; see also Soufi and Maurice, *ICLR*, 15 (2015), 547; McDermott, *QIL*, 40 (2017), 39 considers the MICT to be 'a new international criminal tribunal in its own right'.

[293] SC Res. 1966 (2010), p. 2 para. 1, including a Statute of the International Residual Mechanism for Criminal Tribunals; SC, 6463rd meeting (22 December 2010), S/PV.6463. For further references, see Ambos, *Treatise ICL I* (2021), pp. 28–9.

[294] SC Res. 1966 (2010), para. 3.

[295] *Prosecutor v. Nyiramasuhuko et al.*, No. ICTR-98-42-A, Judgment (14 December 2015).

[296] See, for instance, Leithead, 'Rwanda genocide: International Criminal Tribunal closes', *BBC* (14 December 2015).

[297] Rules of Procedure and Evidence, MICT/1 (8 June 2012).

[298] Klamberg, *Evidence* (2013), p. 72; McIntyre, *GoJIL*, 3 (2011), 925. For similarities and differences between the RPE ICTY/ICTR and the RPE MICT, see McIntyre, ibid., 934 ff. For instance, the MICT provides for a common Prosecutor and Registrar for both branches (ICTR and ICTY), Art. 4(b) and (c) MICT Statute, see ibid., at 940–1 and Soufi and Maurice, *ICLR*, 15 (2015), 549–50.

[299] Art. 24 MICT Statute; Arts. 2(1), (2), 3 TA. For more detail, see Denis, *JICJ*, 9 (2011), 828.

[300] Acquaviva, *JICJ*, 9 (2011), 795; Gozani, *Loy. L.A. Int'l & Comp. L. Rev.*, 36 (2015), 339.

[301] Art. 1(4) MICT Statute. See also Gozani, *Loy. L.A. Int'l & Comp. L. Rev.*, 36 (2015), 346. Contrary to the practice at the ICTY and ICTR, these proceedings, however, are dealt with by a Single Judge, see McIntyre, *GoJIL*, 3 (2011), 941–2.

[302] Art. 20 MICT Statute; Art. 5(2) and (4) TA; Denis, *JICJ*, 9 (2011), 830 ff.

[303] For an overview of the negotiating history of the ICC, see Ambos, *Treatise ICL I* (2021), pp. 30 ff.

[304] The WGPM was set up to 'discuss the technical issues of criminal law procedures contained in Parts 5 (Investigation and Prosecution), 6 (The Trial) and 7 (Appeal and Revision) of the Rome Statute'; see Fernández de Gurmendi, in Lee, *ICC* (1999), p. 217.

by politically more controversial issues such as the jurisdiction of the Court, the role of the Prosecutor, and the crimes to be included.[305]

The RPE ICC were finally agreed on in the Preparatory Commission[306] in November 2000[307] and formally adopted by the first Assembly of State Parties (ASP)[308] in September 2002.[309] Thus, the 'Judge-Legislator'[310] model known from the ad hoc tribunals, controversially discussed during the negotiations, was finally overcome.[311] Indeed, while some felt that giving 'legislative power' to the judges 'would promote institutional adaptability', others, probably the majority, believed that this would contradict the rule of law.[312] *Terris*, *Romano*, and *Swigart* suspect 'that the delegates at the Rome conference were concerned by confusions created by the judges' constant tinkering with the rules of procedure of the Yugoslavia tribunal'.[313] Thus, in the end, legal certainty and transparency prevailed over legislative flexibility and judge-made law.[314]

The judges retain, however, the possibility to issue provisional rules—'in urgent cases where the Rules do not provide for a specific situation before the Court'—with a two-thirds majority.[315] Also, the judges later adopted Regulations of the Court[316] which, albeit in a much more limited way, frame the procedural law of the Court.[317] Another legal source is the Agreement on Privileges and Immunities, which grants certain immunities and privileges to the judges, the Prosecutor and its staff, the Registrar and its staff, as well as to counsel, experts, witnesses, or any other person required to be present at the seat of the Court.[318] On 3 March 2006 the Regulations of the Registry were adopted and entered into force on the same day and have been amended twice since then.[319] On 23 April 2009 the Regulations of the OTP were adopted and entered into force on the same day.[320] Other legal sources are, inter alia: the Code of Professional Conduct for Counsel,[321] the Code of Judicial Ethics,[322] the

[305] See also Safferling, *Criminal Procedure* (2012), p. 48, although too strongly stating that the 'procedural law... was not at the centre of discussion'.

[306] This Preparatory Commission was established to agree on additional legal instruments and to prepare the first ASP meeting, see Ambos, *Treatise ICL I* (2021), p. 33.

[307] Report by the Preparatory Commission for the ICC, Addendum, 2 November 2000, PCNICC/2000/1/Add.1.

[308] About the ASP, see Art. 112 ICCS and Ambos, *Treatise ICL I* (2021), pp. 43–4.

[309] RPE ICC, Adopted by the Assembly of States Parties, First session, 3–10 September 2002, Official Records, ICC-ASP/1/3, <https://legal.un.org/icc/asp/1stsession/report/first_report_contents.htm>; Ambos, *Treatise ICL I* (2021), p. 45; Ambos, 3 *ICLR* (2003), 1, 2.

[310] On this term, see Ambos, *Treatise ICL I* (2021), p. 45 with n. 343.

[311] Boas, in Boas and Schabas, *Developments* (2003), pp. 1 ff.

[312] In more detail, see Terris, Romano, and Swigart, *International Judge* (2007), p. 108.

[313] Ibid., p. 108.

[314] cf. also Guariglia, *Concepto* (2005), pp. 1115 ff.; Kreß and Wannek, in Kirsch, *Internationale Strafgerichtshöfe* (2005), pp. 241 ff.

[315] Art. 51 (3) ICCS.

[316] Regulations of the Court, Doc. No. ICC-BD/01–01–04, 26 June 2005, latest version: CC-BD/01-03-11, 2 November 2011.

[317] Take e.g. the highly relevant Reg. 55 RegC to be discussed in Chapter IV, B.(7) in this volume.

[318] cf. Art. 48 ICCS and Agreement on the Privileges and Immunities of the ICC, Adopted by the ASP, First session, New York, 3–10 September 2002, Official Records, ICC-ASP/1/3, <https://www.icc-cpi.int/NR/rdonlyres/23F24FDC-E9C2-4C43-BE19-A19F5DDE8882/140090/Agreement_on_Priv_and_Imm_120704EN.pdf>.

[319] Regulations of the Registry Approved by the Presidency on 6 March 2006, as amended on 25 September 2006 and 4 December 2013, Official documents of the ICC, ICC-BD/03-03-13s <https://www.icc-cpi.int/iccdocs/registry/Regulations-of-the-Registry-Eng.pdf>.

[320] Regulations of the Office of the Prosecutor, ICC-BD/05-01-09a, <https://www.icc-cpi.int/NR/rdonlyres/FFF97111-ECD6-40B5-9CDA-792BCBE1E695/280253/ICCBD050109ENG.pdf>.

[321] Code of Professional Conduct for Counsel, Adopted at the 3rd plenary meeting on 2 December 2005, by consensus, ICC-ASP/4/Res.1, <https://www.icc-cpi.int/NR/rdonlyres/BD397ECF-8CA8-44EF-92C6-AB4BEBD55BE2/140121/ICCASP432Res1_English.pdf>.

[322] Code of Judicial Ethics, ICC-BD/02-01-05, <https://www.icc-cpi.int/NR/rdonlyres/A62EBC0F-D534-438F-A128-D3AC4CFDD644/140141/ICCBD020105_En.pdf>.

Staff Rules,[323] and the Staff Regulations.[324] Last but not least, as we will see in the following chapters, especially the one on evidence, international criminal procedure is largely determined by judicial practice.

The RPE ICC consist of 225 Rules subdivided into twelve chapters.[325] They have to be consistent with the Statute.[326] Moreover, the explanatory note to the final RPE document[327] states that the Rules do not affect the national procedural law or rules.[328] Thus, in a nutshell, the Rules concretize and enhance the norms of the Statute that regulate the Court's competence, organization, and procedure.

### (c) *The development of procedural rules at the 'mixed' tribunals*

As a result of the increasing internationalization of prosecution of international crimes, many so-called 'mixed' or hybrid tribunals have been established in several States.[329] These tribunals are called 'mixed' because they have a mixed national-international legal basis and recruit national and international (foreign) Prosecutors and judges. They are designed partly in response to criticisms of the ICTY and the ICTR and supposed to combine the strengths of the ad hoc tribunals with the benefits of local prosecutions.[330] In contrast to the IMT and the ICC (multilateral treaty among states), the IMTFE (proclamation of a joint organ of states), and the ICTY, ICTR, and MICT (Decision of the UN Security Council under chapter VII of the UN Charter),[331] these tribunals may be either part of a transitional UN administration or of a regional organization (sub-section (i) in this section (2)(c)), or based on a bilateral agreement with the UN or a regional organization (sub-section (ii) in this section (2)(c)), or on legislative provisions adopted by an occupying power or the territorial State itself (sub-section (iii) in this section (2)(c)).

#### (i) Procedural rules at tribunals that are part of a transitional UN administration or a regional organization

This category encompasses the 'United Nations Mission in East Timor' (UNTAET) and the transitional administration in Kosovo (UNMIK- and EULEX-Panels).

[323] Staff Rules of the ICC, as amended, entered into force on 27 July 2015, ICC/AI/2015/004/Cor.1, <https://www.icc-cpi.int/NR/rdonlyres/56F9B14B-B682-4D9C-8762-A25B944FA214/140109/270715AmmedSREng.pdf>.

[324] Staff Regulations, Adopted by the ASP, Second session, New York, 8–12 September 2003, Official Records, ICC-ASP/2/10, <https://www.icc-cpi.int/NR/rdonlyres/3119BD70-DFB6-4B8C-BC17-3019CC1D0E21/140182/Staff_Regulations_120704EN.pdf>.

[325] General provisions (Rules 1–3); composition and administration of the Court (4–43); jurisdiction and admissibility (44–62); provisions relating to various stages of the proceedings (63–103); investigation and prosecution (104–30); trial procedure (131–44); penalties (145–8); appeal and revision (149–61); offences and misconduct against the Court (162–72); compensation to an arrested or convicted person (173–5); international cooperation and judicial assistance (176–97); and enforcement (198–225).

[326] cf. Art. 51 (4) ICCS.

[327] See asterisk on the title page of the RPE, <https://www.icc-cpi.int/iccdocs/PIDS/legal-texts/RulesProcedureEvidenceEng.pdf>.

[328] See also Ambos, *Treatise ICL I* (2021), p. 46.

[329] See generally ibid., pp. 62 ff. with further references. Generally on the category of 'mixed', 'hybrid', or 'internationalized' tribunals, Williams, *JICJ*, 14 (2016), 26–7; Cross, *JICJ*, 14 (2016), 81. Crit. O'Keefe, *ICL* (2015), pp. 86 ff. (rejecting these categories as 'a formal legal category of court' but admitting that 'they may usefully describe the judicial composition, jurisdiction ratione materiae, and applicable law of a criminal court', p. 86). Pleading for 'mixed' as a functional vis-à-vis normative category of international criminal tribunals, Cimiotta, *JICJ*, 14 (2016), 60 ff.

[330] Katzenstein, *HarvHRJ*, 45 (2003), 245 ff.

[331] See, for the same classification, O'Keefe, *ICL* (2015), pp. 89 ff.

*(1) **East Timor (UNTAET)*** In East Timor—in accordance with SC Resolution 1272 (1999) of 25 October 1999—UNTAET had an overall administrative responsibility and was empowered to exercise all legislative and executive authority, including with regard to justice matters.[332] Panels with exclusive jurisdiction over serious criminal offences (Special Panels for Serious Crime—SPSC) were established within the District Court in the capital Dili.[333] Additionally, the Regulation 2000/30 on Transitional Rules of Criminal Procedure[334] was adopted on 25 September 2000.[335] The latter was to remain applicable to the extent that it did not conflict with 'internationally recognized standards' and any UNTAET law.[336] Given the mixed civil and common law features of East Timor's criminal procedure,[337] the newly adopted Procedure Code constitutes a unique model of international criminal procedure, resembling the RPE ICC in some aspects.[338] Most interestingly, section 54.5 makes 'internationally recognized principles' applicable if the Code fails to contain a regulation on a specific issue.[339] In 2005, the mandate of the Serious Crimes Unit expired and its investigative functions were resumed by the Serious Crimes Investigation Team, assisting the Office of the Prosecutor-General of East Timor.[340] On 16 September 2005, the Government of East Timor adopted a 'Criminal Procedure Code' that entered into force on 1 January 2006 and repealed the Transitional UNTAET Code.[341]

*(2) **Kosovo: From UNMIK and EULEX to the Kosovo Specialist Chambers (KSC)***

*1 Origin and development As already set out in Volume I of this Treatise,[342] in Kosovo there are three instances for the adjudication of crimes of international concern. The mandate of the UN administration (UNMIK) to maintain 'civil law and order'[343] resulted in the creation of hybrid judicial panels.[344] After the EU Rule of Law Mission in Kosovo (EULEX) was established in February 2008 and became fully operational in December 2008,[345] EULEX justice staff provided support in Kosovo Courts under its executive mandate until 2018.[346]*

332 Katzenstein, *HarvHRJ*, 45 (2003), 245 ff.

333 cf. primarily UNTAET Reg. 2000/15, in Ambos and Othman, *Approaches* (2003), pp. 231 ff.

334 UNTAET Regulation 2000/30 on Transitional Rules of Criminal Procedure, 25 September 2000, as amended by UNTAET Regulation 2001/25, 14 September 2001.

335 See generally Linton, *MelbULR*, 25 (2001), 174 ff.

336 Sections 2–3 UNTAET Regulation 1999/1 on the Authority of the Transitional Administration in East Timor, 27 November 1999; Section 3 TRCP; Vasiliev, in Sluiter et al., *International Criminal Procedure* (2013), p. 16.

337 Linton, *MelbULR*, 25 (2001), 174.

338 Vasiliev, in Sluiter et al., *International Criminal Procedure* (2013), p. 16.

339 Regulation 2001/25 on the Amendment of UNTAET Regulation No. 2000/11 on the Organization of Courts in East Timor and UNTAET Regulation No. 2000/30 on the Transitional Rules of Criminal Procedure, UNTAET/REG/2001/25, 14 September 2001. Crit. regarding the reliance on Indonesian criminal procedure Vasiliev, in Sluiter et al., *International Criminal Procedure* (2013), p. 16.

340 Ambos, *Treatise ICL I* (2021), p. 71.

341 Decree-Law No. 13/2005, Art. 2(1)(a). Furthermore, see Ambos, *Treatise ICL I* (2021), pp. 70–1 and first edition (2013) pp. 30–1 with further references.

342 Ambos, *Treatise ICL I* (2021), pp. 66–7.

343 SC Res. 1244, 10 June 1999, 11(i).

344 Perriello and Wierda, *Lessons* (2006), pp. 8, 12 ff.

345 Council Joint Action 2008/124/CFSP of 4 February 2008 on the European Union Rule of Law Mission in Kosovo, EULEX KOSOVO, amended by Council Joint Action 2009/445/CFSP of 9 June 2009; Council Decision 2010/322/CFSP of 8 June 2010; Council Decision 2012/291/CFSP of 5 June 2012; Council Decision 2014/349/CFSP of 12 June 2014; Council Decision (CFSP) 2016/947 of 14 June 2016; Council Decision (CSFP) 2018/856 of 8 June 2018; Council Decision (CSFP) 2020/792 of 11 June 2020. In depth on the EULEX mandate, Zupančič and Pejič, *Limits* (2018), pp. 66 ff.; furthermore, see Holvoet, *CLR*, 28 (2017), 40–2; Muharremi, *Int J Transit Justice*, 13 (2019), 298.

346 cf. Council Joint Action 2008/124/CFSP of 4 February 2008, High Representative, 4 June 2018; also see Zupančič and Pejič, *Limits* (2018), pp. 82 ff. With respect to the end of the EULEX executive mandate, see Council

*Even preceding this development, as early as mid-2003, the Special Representative of the Secretary-General (SRSG) had approved a Provisional Criminal Code and, furthermore, a Provisional Criminal Procedure Code for Kosovo; on 1 January 2013 then the new Criminal Procedure Code of 2012, which is more adversarial in nature, entered into force.*[347] *The new law proved to be alien to both civil law trained lawyers in Kosovo and international staff.*[348] *Furthermore, because of the quantity and nature of the changes, the implementation of this legislation has been considered as 'one of the greatest challenges facing the Kosovo criminal justice system'.*[349]

In a parallel development the Kosovo parliament adopted, on 3 August 2015 and based on an agreement between Kosovo and the EU, a constitutional amendment to make the establishment of a Special Court possible, namely the so-called 'Specialist Chambers' and 'Specialist Prosecutor's Office' (SPO).[350] They shall sit in Priština, Kosovo, and—as the so-called Kosovo Relocated Specialist Judicial Institution (KRSJI)—in The Hague, Netherlands;[351] the KSC then became its permanent seat in the former Europol building. According to Article 6-10 of the Law on the Specialist Chambers and Specialist Prosecutor's Office (KSC Law)[352] the Specialist Chambers have jurisdiction over crimes allegedly committed by former members of the Kosovo Liberation Army (KLA) from 1 January 1998 to 31 December 2000.[353] Once all judgments of the Specialist Chambers become final and the Court has fulfilled its mission, a residual mechanism with 'residual Specialist Chambers' may be established, provided that it is fully internationalized and located outside Kosovo.[354] At the time of writing (September 2024), two cases concerning three defendants (Hysni Gucati and Nasim Haradinaj regarding administration of justice offences and Salih Mustafa regarding war crimes) have become final[355] with the respective judgments of the Appeals Panel.[356] There are a few other cases at the (pre-)trial stage, the most important of which is the one against the KLA leadership around former President Thaçi.

of the EU, Press Release, Eulex Kosovo: New role for the EU rule of law mission, 8 June 2018, <https://www.consilium.europa.eu/en/press/press-releases/2018/06/08/eulex-kosovo-new-role-for-the-eu-rule-of-law-mission/>.

347 On these developments, see Ambos, *Treatise ICL I* (2021), pp. 66–7 with further references.

348 Perriello and Wierda, *Lessons* (2006), p. 24.

349 American Bar Association, *Advocacy* (February 2014), p. 22.

350 Law No. 04/L-274 on Ratification of the International Agreement between the Republic of Kosovo and the European Union on the European Rule of Law Mission in Kosovo, 23 April 2014; Amendment to the Constitution of the Republic of Kosovo, Amendment No. 24; Law on Specialist Chambers and Specialist Prosecutor's Office (SC Law), Art. 1(1); on that Ristic, *BalkanInsight* (6 August 2015); see generally Cimiotta, *JICJ*, 14 (2016), 54 ff.; Citroni, *JICJ*, 14 (2016), 126; Cross, *JICJ*, 14 (2016), 80; Yanev, *JICJ*, 14 (2016), 101; Heinze, *JICJ*, 15 (2017), 987; Ambos and Meisenberg, *MPEiPro* (2019), mn. 11-2.

351 cf. Art. 3 (6) SC Law (referring in clause 2 to an international agreement with the host State where the Chamber 'shall also have a seat'). They may also 'sit elsewhere on an exceptional basis if necessary in the interests of proper administration of justice'.

352 <https://www.scp-ks.org/sites/default/files/public/05-1-053_a.pdf>.

353 Arts. 6–10 SC Law. Kersten, *Justice in Conflict* (10 August 2015). Furthermore, see Muharremi, *Int J Transit Justice*, 13 (2019), 295–6 and Ambos, *Treatise ICL I* (2021), p. 68.

354 Art. 60 KSC Law.

355 Given that the KSC structure mirrors the domestic system of Kosovo, defendants have extraordinary remedies before a Supreme Court Chamber and an individual complaint procedure to a Constitutional Court Chamber regarding possible rights violations of the Kosovo Constitution; see below Chapter VI note 3.

356 The AJ in Gucati and Haradinaj was delivered on 2 February 2023, the one in Mustafa on 14 December 2023 (in this case the overall sentence has, on 10 September 2024, been reduced to 15 years following a Supreme Court decision); for an overview of the cases, see <https://www.scp-ks.org/en/cases>; recently Meisenberg, *ZfIStW*, 3 (2024), 11 ff.

2. *Institutional background* The Specialist Chambers consist of two organs: The Chambers and the Registry. The Chambers, mirroring the organization of the court system in Kosovo, include a Basic Court Chamber, a Court of Appeals Chamber, a Supreme Court Chamber, and a Constitutional Court Chamber.[357] They are independent from the Kosovo judiciary and have a roster of independent (exclusively) international judges.[358] The Chambers normally sit in panels of three judges (with a reserve judge at the trial stage),[359] but the KSC Law also explicitly allows for 'individual judges as necessary performing other functions'.[360]

As an independent and distinct institution from the Specialist Chambers, the Specialist Prosecutor's Office (SPO) 'shall be an independent office for the investigation and prosecution of crimes within the jurisdiction of the Specialist Chambers'.[361] The police within the SPO have 'the authority and responsibility to exercise powers given to Kosovo police under Kosovo law'.[362]

3. *The KSC's Rules of Procedure and Evidence* In determining its RPE, the judges were 'guided by the Kosovo Criminal Procedure Code 2012', Law No. 04/L-123.[363] The RPE entered into force on 5 July 2017;[364] they are composed of thirteen chapters and 211 rules and contain a Part II with rules for the Constitutional Court Chamber.[365]

According to Article 35(1) KSC Law the SPO is under an obligation to investigate and prosecute 'persons responsible for the crimes falling within the jurisdiction of the Specialist Chambers'. Rule 43(1) RPE provides that a person is to be treated as a suspect and entitled to at least the rights under Article 38(3) KSC Law if the SPO 'has grounds to believe that the person committed or participated in the commission of a crime within the jurisdiction of the Specialists Chambers'.[366] In the case of an indictment, the SPO shall, pursuant to Rule 86(3)(a) RPE, provide 'a detailed outline demonstrating the relevance of each item of evidentiary material to each allegation, with particular reference to the conduct of the suspect with respect to the alleged crime(s)' with its indictment. In particular, this obligation goes beyond the parallel rules of Rule 47 ICTY/ICTR RPE, which only require the provision of 'supporting material', and also beyond the more demanding

[357] Arts. 3(1), 24(1)(a) KSC Law. See also Ristic, *BalkanInsight* (6 August 2015); Cimiotta, *JICJ*, 14 (2016), 57; Cross, *JICJ*, 14 (2016), 82; Heinze, *JICJ*, 15 (2017), 987; Karnavas, *ICLR*, 20 (2020), 81 ('attachment to each level of the Kosovo judiciary').

[358] Art. 26(1) KSC Law. See more concretely Art. 28 KSC Law. International judges are those 'with nationalities other the Kosovar one': see Cimiotta, *JICJ*, 14 (2016), 58; Muharremi, *ZaöRV*, 76 (2016), 967 ('control by international judges and personal makes the specialist Chambers an international tribunal although it is established by Kosovo law'); id., *Int J Transit Justice*, 13 (2019), 291 ('entirely under international control'). They must 'possess the qualifications required in their respective states' (Art. 27(1) KSC Law) and have an 'established competence and court experience of the judges in criminal law and procedure, international law and constitutional law as appropriate' (Art. 27(1) KSC Law).

[359] Art. 25(1)(b) KSC Law.

[360] Art. 25(1)(f) KSC Law. See also Cimiotta, *JICJ*, 14 (2016), 58 and, furthermore, with regard to functions of the Registry Ambos, *Treatise ICL I* (2021), p. 68 with further references.

[361] Art. 24(2) SC Law. See also Art. 35 SC Law. See Heinze, *JICJ*, 15 (2017), 988–90; Karnavas, *ICLR*, 20 (2020), 78 ('SPO is a continuation of the Special Investigative Task Force'); also Stahn, *ZaöRV*, 77 (2017), 375 and, more generally, Cimiotta, *JICJ*, 14 (2016), 59.

[362] Art. 35(3) SC Law; Heinze, *JICJ*, 15 (2017), 990 ('cannot be overstated'; 'huge advantage over other offices of the prosecutor that lack a police and depend on state responsibility').

[363] Art. 19 (2) KSC Law. In more detail, Cimiotta, *JICJ*, 14 (2016), 63 ff.; Heinze, *JICJ*, 15 (2017), 992 and Ambos, *Treatise ICL I* (2020), p. 69.

[364] In more detail, see Ambos and Meisenberg, *MPEiPro* (2019), mn. 31–4. For the current version, see <https://www.scp-ks.org/en/documents/rules-procedure-and-evidence>.

[365] For a detailed analysis, see Heinze, *JICJ*, 15 (2017), 992 ff.; Karnavas, *ICLR*, 20 (2020), 92 ff.

[366] See Heinze, *JICJ*, 15 (2017), 993.

provisions of the SCSL and the Special Panel for Serious Crime in East Timor.[367] In this regard, it is important to note that Article 19(2) KSC Law, in conjunction with the 2012 Kosovo Criminal Procedure Code, imposes an obligation on the prosecution to investigate exculpatory circumstances.[368]

Rule 94 contains a detailed provision on plea agreements that is absent from other RPEs[369] encouraging them at the early stage of the proceedings ('preferably before the opening of the case'). Once the indictment is confirmed, the Pre-Trial Judge shall order the prosecution to produce a current proofing chart.[370] The RPE also differ from those of other international(ized) courts in that Rule 103 requires the prosecution to disclose exculpatory material to the defence 'immediately' (not just as soon as possible).[371] Once the Pre-Trial Judge declares a case to be ready for trial, a trial panel will be assigned by the KSC President. As to the procedure for taking evidence, Rule 127 provides, in a quite detailed fashion, the parties' right to cross-examine showing an adversarial tendency.[372]

*4. Critical views* The KSC faces multiple criticisms, especially from institutions and persons close to the KLA. While criticism from persons or entities targeted by international criminal tribunals is quite common to all international criminal tribunals, there are some specific problems related to the unique features of the KSC. While the KSC's close relationship with the Kosovar judicial system[373] and its establishment pursuant to a constitutional amendment adopted by the Kosovar parliament[374] make the KSC an internationalized domestic court[375] with, apparently, a greater legitimacy in the region concerned,[376] it cannot be denied that considerable political pressure from the EU and the USA has made it possible in the first place.[377] In addition, it is argued that the 'exclusive control of international judges and personnel makes the KSC' de facto 'an international tribunal' notwithstanding its legal basis in Kosovo law.[378] In this respect it has to be noted that the KSC have an international basis in the above mentioned Kosovo-EU agreement. This agreement delegates 'all necessary powers and mandates to operate the separate Judicial chambers and specialist prosecutor's office' to EULEX.[379] In practical terms this delegation is, pursuant to Article 162 of the Kosovo Constitution and the KSC Law, executed by the KSC which is independent of EULEX. With regard to the subject matter jurisdiction, it is criticized that the SPC was 'tailor made to address specific cases touched upon in the Marty Report and further investigated by the SITF Prosecutor'.[380]

While here is not the place to take issue with these criticisms in detail, it should be noted that the political dynamics surrounding the KSC's establishment must not be attributed to the institution and its concrete fulfilment of its mandate. Insofar as the standard to be

[367] On this, see Heinze, *JICJ*, 15 (2017), 994; also see Karnavas, *ICLR*, 20 (2020), 97 ('obligation to contribute to the establishment of the truth [very much so in the civil law tradition]').
[368] Karnavas, *ICLR*, 20 (2020), 85–6 with n. 28.
[369] See Karnavas, *ICLR*, 20 (2020), 92 with n. 48.
[370] Rule 95(4) and Karnavas, *ICLR*, 20 (2020), 100–3.
[371] Karnavas, *ICLR*, 20 (2020), 92.
[372] Heinze, *JICJ*, 15 (2017), 996–7.
[373] Karnavas, *ICLR*, 20 (2020), 81.
[374] cf. Art. 162 of the Constitution introduced by Amendment No. 24 of 3 August 2015.
[375] Muharremi, *ZaöRV*, 76 (2016), 991.
[376] See Holvoet, *CLR*, 28 (2017), 45.
[377] Ibid., 45–6; Muharremi, *ZaöRV*, 76 (2016), 992.
[378] Muharremi, *ZaöRV*, 76 (2016), 968.
[379] See Law No. 04/L-274, above note 362.
[380] *Vagias*, *LJIL*, 33 (2020), 1042–3.

applied is the expediency and fairness of the proceedings, to which this author can attest based on his personal experience, the KSC's performance certainly deserves praise. In fact, the RPE are an explicit manifestation of the KSC's strong commitment to fair and expedient proceedings and thus there are well-founded hopes that the 'reasonableness of its procedures'[381] will contribute to the KSC's success. As to the KSC's subject matter jurisdiction, it is true that Article 6(1) KSC Law explicitly refers to the 'Council of Europe Assembly Report', i.e. the so-called Marty Report,[382] but this does not mean that the subject matter jurisdiction is confined to the acts mentioned in this Report (i.e. organ trafficking and inhuman treatment). This follows from Article 6(2) KSC Law which extends the jurisdiction to a series of offences of the Kosovo Constitution. In addition, both the Court of Appeals Panel and the Specialist Chamber of the Constitutional Court (SCCC) have made clear that the KSC's jurisdiction is not limited to the allegations contained in the Report and that the charges to be brought against an individual under the KSC legal framework only need to 'be related' to the Report.[383]

**(ii) Procedural rules at tribunals based on a bilateral agreement with the UN or a regional organization**

Within this second category are the Special Court for Sierra Leone (SCSL), including its residual mechanism (Residual Special Court for Sierra Leone, RSCSL), the Extraordinary Chambers in the Court of Cambodia (ECCC), and the Special Tribunal for Lebanon (STL) to be looked at more closely in the following; in addition, on the basis of an agreement between Senegal and the African Union, the Extraordinary African Chambers in the Senegalese Courts (EAC Senegal) have been established in 2012.[384]

***(1) Special Court for Sierra Leone/Residual Special Court for Sierra Leone*** The SCSL was created by an agreement between the UN Secretary General and the government of Sierra Leone on 16 January 2002 to prosecute persons who bear the greatest responsibility for the crimes committed during Sierra Leone's devastating civil war.[385] The Statute of the Court (SCSLS) was annexed to the agreement.[386] The Court's subject matter jurisdiction extends to crimes against humanity, war crimes, and certain other international crimes as well as certain (national) crimes under Sierra Leonean law.[387] The Court has concurrent jurisdiction

[381] May and Fyfe 'Legitimacy', in Hayashi and Bailliet, *Criminal Tribunals* (2017), p. 30 with regard to the Nuremberg Trials, which of course had an incomparably more difficult starting point.

[382] CoE Doc. 12462 of 7 January 2011; thereto see Governa and Paiusco, in Power (2020), pp. 613–15; furthermore, see Mucaj, *ICLR*, 21 (2021), 4 ('hybrid legal mechanism to investigate some of the allegations made in the Marty Report').

[383] KSC, Decision on Appeals Against 'Decision on Motions Challenging the Jurisdiction of the Specialist Chambers', KSC-BC-2020-06 /IA009, F00030, 23 December 2021, paras. 66–7 (also paras. 68–73, 78); KSC, Decision on the Referral of Hashim Thaçi Concerning the Right to an Independent and Impartial Tribunal Established by Law and to a Reasoned Opinion, KSC-CC-2022-15, F00010, 13 June 2022, paras. 73–85. For further details, see Meisenberg, *ZfIStW*, 3 (2024), 11 ff.

[384] Agreement between the Government of the Republic of Senegal and the African Union on the Creation of Extraordinary African Chambers in the Senegalese Courts, 22 August 2012, French original version available at <http://www.chambresafricaines.org/pdf/Accord%20UA-Senegal%20Chambres%20africaines%20extra%20Aout%202012.pdf>; for a detailed analysis, see Williams, *JICJ*, 11 (2013), 1139 ff.; O'Keefe, *ICL* (2015), pp. 103, 397 ff.

[385] See Art. 1 SCSLS and UN SC Res. 1315 (2000), Reprinted in Kelsall, *Culture* (2009), pp. 254 ff. See also Ambos, *Treatise ICL I* (2021), p. 71 with further references.

[386] Reprinted in Kelsall, *Culture* (2009), pp. 259 ff.

[387] See Arts. 2–5 SCSLS. Art. 5 lists crimes regarding the (sexual) abuse and abduction of girls and the wanton destruction of property.

with the national courts but prevails in case of conflict and may at any stage of the procedure request a national court to defer to its competence.[388]

The responsibility to create and amend the RPE rested—as at the ICTY and ICTR—with the judges who 'may be guided' by the 1965 Criminal Procedure Act of Sierra Leone.[389] The Rules addressed, as usual, the finer technical questions not regulated by the Court's Statute,[390] but also introduced some innovations to the existing international criminal procedure, such as the establishment of a Defence Office,[391] an Outreach Office[392] under Rule 33(A), and the Legacy Phase Working Group.[393] The SCSL, like the IMT and the ad hoc tribunals, is not bound by national rules of evidence.[394]

As was the case with the ad hoc tribunals, upon the completion of trials and appeals at the SCSL, the UN and the Government of Sierra Leone on 11 August 2010 concluded an agreement on the establishment of a Residual Special Court for Sierra Leone to maintain international standards and fulfil the SCSL's mandate.[395] According to Article 1(3) RSCSL Agreement '[t]he Residual Special Court shall continue the jurisdiction, functions, rights and obligations of the Special Court subject to the provisions of this Agreement and the Statute'. The Parliament of Sierra Leone ratified the RSCSL Agreement in December 2011.[396] The RSCSL

> shall: maintain, preserve and manage its archives, including the archives of the Special Court; provide for witness and victim protection and support; respond to requests for access to evidence by national prosecution authorities; supervise enforcement of sentences; review convictions and acquittals; conduct contempt of court proceedings; provide defence counsel and legal aid for the conduct of proceedings before the Residual Special Court; respond to requests from national authorities with respect to claims for compensation; and prevent double jeopardy.[397]

Since the SCSL was, as already mentioned, created by an agreement between the UN Secretary General and the government of Sierra Leone and is therefore not a subsidiary organ of the Security Council,[398] the funding of the RSCSL is not provided by the UN but rather 'by voluntary contributions from the international community'.[399]

[388] cf. Art. 8 SCSLS.

[389] cf. Art. 14 (2) SCSLS.

[390] cf. Jalloh, *AfrJICompL*, 15 (2007), 177 ('questions regarding how practically to provide legal aid to the accused in order to ensure fair trials . . . , how to disseminate impartial and accurate information about its work . . . and how to leave a tangible legacy for Sierra Leone that extends well beyond the prosecution of a small number of individuals "bearing greatest responsibility" to include nurturing the rule of law and the country's impoverished justice sector').

[391] Rule 45 RPE SCSL. See, in more detail, Jones et al., *JICJ*, 2 (2004), 211 ff.; Skilbeck, *EssexHRR*, 1 (2004), 66 ff. For a comparative evaluation of the institutional structures of the defence in ad hoc international criminal tribunals, see Schabas, *Criminal Tribunals* (2006), pp. 613–18.

[392] Rule 33A RPE SCSL.

[393] Nmehielle and Jalloh, *Fletcher, FWAJ*, 30 (2) (2006), 110 ff.; generally Jalloh, *AfrJICompL*, 15 (2007), 177 ff.

[394] Rule 89 (A) RPE SCSL.

[395] Agreement Between the United Nations and the Government of Sierra Leone on the Establishment of a Residual Special Court for Sierra Leone, <http://www.rscsl.org/Documents/RSCSL%20Agreement%20and%20Statute.pdf>. About the negotiation process in more detail, see Mphepo, *ICLR*, 14 (2014), 182 ff.

[396] The Residual Special Court for Sierra Leone Agreement (Ratification) Act, 2011, Supplement to the Sierra Leone Gazette Vol. CXLIII, No. 6. See also Donlon, *JICJ*, 11 (2013), 862.

[397] Art. 1(1) RSCSL Statute. See, in more detail, Donlon, *JICJ*, 11 (2013), 864 ff.; Mphepo, *ICLR*, 14 (2014), 186 ff.

[398] See also Donlon, *JICJ*, 11 (2013), 860.

[399] Art. 3 RSCSL Agreement: 'The expenses of the Residual Special Court shall be borne by voluntary contributions from the international community. The Parties and the oversight committee may explore alternative means of financing the Residual Special Court.' See also Donlon, *JICJ*, 11 (2013), 863.

Thus, 'cost and efficiency' highly influenced the RSCSL's structure.[400] The RSCSL, which has not yet attracted the same attention as the MIC,[401] consists of three primary organs: the Chambers, the Office of the Prosecutor, and the Registry.[402] Generally speaking, the RSCSL resembles the SCSL to such an extent that it has already been suggested that 'continuing with a reduced size and more streamlined SCSL might well have been feasible'.[403] This does not only follow from a structural but also from a normative perspective: the RSCSL Statute mirrors the SCSL Statute and the RSCSL even explicitly applies *mutatis mutandis* the RPE SCSL.[404] Consequently, throughout this book both the SCSL Statute and RSCSL Statute are referred to, while the references to the RPE will be reduced to those of the SCSL.

***(2) Extraordinary Chambers in the Court of Cambodia*** The bilateral agreement with the UN 'concerning the prosecution in Cambodian law of crimes committed during the period of democratic Kampuchea', that is, during the period from 17 April 1975 to 6 January 1979, was signed on 6 June 2003.[405] It entered into force on 29 April 2005. In addition, with a view to the national prosecution of these crimes, the 'Law on the Establishment of the Extraordinary Chambers' was adopted on 10 August 2001 and amended on 5 and 27 October 2004 (ECCC-Law).[406] This Law permits the application of both national and international substantive and procedural law at the ECCC.[407] Their subject matter jurisdiction encompasses genocide, crimes against humanity, and grave breaches of the GC as well as certain other enumerated international and national crimes.[408]

As was the case with the ICTY, ICTR, and the SCSL, the judges were entrusted with the power to 'vote on' the procedural rules of the tribunal, the so-called 'Internal Rules'.[409] According to the preamble of these Rules, their purpose was 'to consolidate applicable Cambodian procedure for proceedings before the ECCC and ... to adopt additional rules where these existing procedures do not deal with a particular matter, or if there is uncertainty regarding their interpretation or application, or if there is a question regarding their consistency with international standards'. Challenges to the constitutionality of the Internal Rules or their superiority to the Cambodian Code of Criminal Procedure, which was adopted in August 2007, have been dismissed.[410]

400 For examples, see Mphepo, *ICLR*, 14 (2014), 185 ff.

401 Ibid., 178.

402 Art. 2 RSCSL Statute. See, in more detail, Donlon, *JICJ*, 11 (2013), 858, 864; Mphepo, *ICLR*, 14 (2014), 184.

403 Mphepo, *ICLR*, 14 (2014), 180.

404 Art. 16(1) RSCSL Statute: 'The Rules of Procedure and Evidence of the Special Court for Sierra Leone obtaining at the time of the closure of the Special Court shall apply *mutatis mutandis* to the conduct of the legal proceedings before the Residual Special Court.' See also Mphepo, *ICLR*, 14 (2014), 197.

405 Agreement between the UN and the Royal Government of Cambodia concerning the Prosecution under Cambodian Law of Crimes committed during the period of Democratic Kampuchea, <http://www.eccc.gov.kh/sites/default/files/legal-documents/Agreement_between_UN_and_RGC.pdf>. See generally Ambos, *Treatise ICL I* (2021), p. 73. For details of the negotiations, see Kashyap, 'Framework', in Ambos and Othman, *Approaches* (2003), pp. 191 ff.; see also Beigbeder, *Justice* (2005), pp. 129 ff.; Ambach, *HuV-I*, 18 (2005), 110; Bohlander and Winter, 'Strafgerichte', in Kirsch, *Internationale Strafgerichtshöfe* (2005), pp. 267 ff.; Bantekas and Nash, *ICL* (2010), pp. 455 ff.; Donlon, 'Hybrid', in Schabas and Bernaz, *Routledge Handbook ICL* (2011), pp. 90 ff.

406 'Law on the Establishment of Extraordinary Chambers in the Courts of Cambodia for the Prosecution of Crimes Committed during the Period of Democratic Kampuchea', original version reprinted in Ambos and Othman, *Approaches* (2003), pp. 267 ff. Also <http://www.derechos.org/human-rights/seasia/doc/krlaw.html>.

407 Petit and Ahmed, *NWJIHR*, 8 (2010), 165 ff., para. 8.

408 Arts. 2–8 ECCC-Law. See also Ambos, *Treatise ICL I* (2021), p. 73 and furthermore, pp. 73 ff. with regard to the ECCC's structure and proceedings.

409 cf. Rule 18 of the Internal Rules. About these Rules in more detail, see Linton, *SYBIL*, 11 (2007), 195–259 and esp. Jørgensen, *Chambers* (2018), pp. 48–53 and 110 ff.

410 ECCC, *Prosecutor v. Nuon Chea*, PTC, Decision on Nuon Chea's Appeal Against Order Refusing Request for Annulment, No. 002/19-09-2007-ECCC/OCIJ (PTC 06), 26 August 2008, para. 14; *Prosecutor v. Khieu Samphan*,

According to the 2003 bilateral Agreement '[t]he procedure shall be in accordance with Cambodian law'.[411] Thus, given the inquisitorial procedure embodied in Cambodia's colonial (French) Procedural Code, the ECCC took the same procedural approach.[412] Special features characterizing this system include: (1) the provision for judicial investigation by 'impartial' Co-Investigating Judges;[413] (2) participation of the defendants throughout the judicial investigation;[414] (3) victim participation as 'civil parties' throughout the proceedings;[415] (4) the adoption of the 'free proof principle';[416] (5) the right of the judge to examine witnesses prior to the Co-Prosecutors and all the other parties;[417] and (6) the existence of a case file;[418] mentioned throughout the Internal Rules.[419] Of course, the long-ago events covered by the ECCC's jurisdiction pose a particular challenge in evidentiary terms.[420]

Furthermore, the ECCC are distinct in that they require a supermajority in their three judicial chambers, that is, in the Pre-Trial Chamber, the Trial Chamber, and the Supreme Court Chamber.[421] The Pre-Trial and Trial Chambers are composed of three Cambodian and two international judges,[422] while the Supreme Court Chamber is composed of four Cambodian and three international judges.[423] The term 'supermajority' means an affirmative vote of at least four of the five judges in the Pre-Trial or Trial Chamber, and at least five of the seven judges in the Supreme Court Chamber.[424] The supermajority requirement ensures that for any decision of the Pre-Trial and Trial Chambers, an affirmative vote of at least one

PTC, Decision on Khieu Samphan's Appeal against the Order on Translation Rights and Obligations of the Parties, No. 002/19-09-2007-ECCC/OCIJ (PTC 11), 20 February 2009, para. 2. Crit. see Linton, *SYBIL*, 11 (2007), 195, 237 ff.

411 Agreement between the UN and the Royal Government of Cambodia concerning the Prosecution under Cambodian Law of Crimes committed during the period of Democratic Kampuchea, Art. 12 (1).

412 Petit and Ahmed, *NWJIHR*, 8 (2010), 165 ff., para. 12.

413 Rule 55(5) Internal Rules: 'In the conduct of judicial investigations, the Co-Investigating Judges may take any investigative action conducive to ascertaining the truth. In all cases, they shall conduct their investigation impartially, whether the evidence is inculpatory or exculpatory.' On this, see Sluiter and Tiernan, *JICJ*, 18 (2020), 644–5 and 649–53 and furthermore, see pp. 658–62 regarding the 'Role of the Defence in Investigations'.

414 ECCC, *Prosecutor v. Nuon Chea*, PTC, Decision on Nuon Chea's Appeal Regarding Appointment of An Expert, No. 002/19-09-2007-ECCC/OCIJ (PTC 07), 22 October 2008, paras. 25–7.

415 See Rules 23, *23bis*, *23ter*, *23quarter*, and *23quinquies* Internal Rules.

416 Rule 87(1) Internal Rules: 'Unless provided otherwise in these IRs, all evidence is admissible. The onus is on the Co-Prosecutors to prove the guilt of the accused. In order to convict the accused, the Chamber must be convinced of the guilt of the accused beyond reasonable doubt.'

417 Rule 90 Internal Rules: '1.... The judges have a duty to raise all pertinent questions, whether these would tend to prove or disprove the guilt of the Accused. 2. The Co-Prosecutors and all the other parties and their lawyers shall also have the right to question the Accused. All questions shall be asked with the permission of the President. Except for questions asked by the Co-Prosecutors and the lawyers, all questions shall be asked through the President of the Chamber and in the order as determined by him.' This inquisitorial feature, however, was slightly diluted by the introduction of Rule 91*bis*: 'The President of the Trial Chamber shall determine the order in which the judges, the Co-Prosecutors and all the other parties and their lawyers shall have the right to question the Accused, the witnesses, experts and Civil Parties.'

418 The case file is defined in the Glossary of the Internal Rules: '"Case File" (dossier) refers to all the written records (*procès verbaux*) of investigative action undertaken in the course of a Preliminary Investigation or a Judicial Investigation, together with all applications by parties, written decisions and any attachments thereto at all stages of the proceedings, including the record of proceedings before the Chambers.'

419 See also Petit and Ahmed, *NWJIHR*, 8 (2010), 165 ff., para. 12.

420 cf. McDermott, *JICJ*, 18 (2020), 747–8 ('ECCC's fact-finding role could be described as nothing short of Sisyphean').

421 Petit and Ahmed, *NWJIHR*, 8 (2010), para. 24. On the role of the PTC, see Naidu and Williams, *JICJ*, 18 (2020), 665 ff. and on that of the SCC, see Vasiliev, *JICJ*, 18 (2020), 725 ff.

422 Art. 9(1) ECCC-Law.

423 Art. 9(2) ECCC-Law. See generally Jørgensen and Zahar, in Sluiter et al., *International Criminal Procedure* (2013), p. 1174.

424 Agreement between the UN and the Royal Government of Cambodia concerning the prosecution under Cambodian Law of Crimes committed during the period of Democratic Kampuchea, Art. 4. See generally Sluiter et al., *International Criminal Procedure* (2013), p. 1174.

international judge is required.[425] According to *Petit* and *Ahmed*, '[t]his supermajority formula was the key to the acceptance of the present hybrid nature of the ECCC by the United Nations and the Government of Cambodia.'[426] Despite initial scepticism, the supermajority formula seems to have essentially fulfilled its function.[427]

Generally speaking, it is fair to say that the ECCC jurisprudence has provided important impulses for the law of evidence, taking into account in particular its specific challenges.[428] Thus, the Supreme Court Chamber criticized, on the level of principle and with reference to comparative law considerations,[429] the Trial Chamber's practice of permitting witnesses to review prior statements, but considered it justified in the case at hand given that the ensuing procedural risks had not been that great.[430] As to the admissibility of written evidence (in lieu of oral testimony), the Supreme Court Chamber invoked the principle of freedom of evidence as per Internal Rule 87[431] and further clarified that Internal Rule 84(1) does not contain an 'entirely unfettered right to examine witnesses against the accused'.[432] However, the Chamber then concludes, explicitly following the 'persuasive jurisprudence of the European Court of Human Rights', that 'a conviction may not be based solely or to a decisive degree on evidence by a witness whom the defence has not had an opportunity to examine, unless there are sufficient counterbalancing factors in place, so that an accused is given an effective opportunity to challenge the evidence against him'.[433]

***(3) Special Tribunal for Lebanon (STL)*** Although the STL was ultimately created by a UNSC Resolution, it fits into the category of tribunals 'based on a bilateral agreement with the UN' in light of the rather specific process leading to its establishment: while an agreement has been concluded between the UN and the Lebanese Republic on the STL's

[425] Petit and Ahmed, *NWJIHR*, 8 (2010), 165 ff., para. 24; Jørgensen and Zahar, in Sluiter et al., *International Criminal Procedure* (2013), p. 1174.

[426] Petit and Ahmed, *NWJIHR*, 8 (2010), 165 ff., para. 24; Lobba and Pons, *JICJ*, 18 (2020), 609.

[427] See Lobba and Pons, *JICJ*, 18 (2020), 609–10.

[428] In more detail, see McDermott, *JICJ*, 18 (2020), 750 ff.; furthermore, see ECCC, *Prosecutor v. Nuon Chean and Khieu Samphan*, TC, Trial Judgment, Case 002/02, 16 November 2018, para. 57 ('Considering the significant time that has passed since the DK era, documents recorded contemporaneously with the charged events are some of the most important sources of evidence.').

[429] ECCC, *Prosecutor v. Nuon Chean and Khieu Samphan*, SCC, Appeal Judgment, Case 002/01, F36, 23 November 2016, para. 262 ('in systems following the Romano-Germanic tradition, witness proofing is generally inadmissible'); cf. in general Case 002/1 Jørgensen, *Chambers* (2018), pp. 147–51

[430] ECCC, *Nuon Chean and Khieu Samphan*, SCC, Appeal Judgment, Case 002/01, F 36, 23 November 2016, paras. 267–8 ('actual risks resulting from the review or prior statements in this case were not great. First, at the time of the hearing, spontaneity of trial testimony may have been forgone in any event'; 'practice of exposing witnesses to what they previously said could interfere with or distort their memory, and thus the truth, by reducing the spontaneity with which their evidence is offered in court ... Accordingly, the value of such practices has to be evaluated by weighing the in-court time that would be saved against the risk that the spontaneity of the witness' testimony be jeopardised.'). cf. in general Case 002/1 Jørgensen, *Chambers* (2018), pp. 147–51.

[431] ECCC, *Nuon Chean and Khieu Samphan*, SCC, Appeal Judgment, Case 002/01, F 36, 23 November 2016, para. 284 ; on that, see also McDermott, *JICJ*, 18 (2020), 750–1; furthermore, see ECC, *Nuon Chean and Khieu Samphan*, TC, Trial Judgment, Case 002/02, 16 November 2018, para. 42 ('Unless provided otherwise, all evidence is admissible').

[432] ECCC, *Nuon Chean and Khieu Samphan*, SCC, Appeal Judgment, Case 002/01, F 36, 23 November 2016, para. 286 ('an entirely unfettered right to examine witnesses against the accused would bear the risk of compromising a court's ability to render justice in cases of the size and complexity as the case at hand').

[433] ECCC, *Nuon Chean and Khieu Samphan*, SCC, Appeal Judgment, Case 002/01, F 36, 23 November 2016, para. 296; also see ECCC, *Nuon Chean and Khieu Samphan*, TC, Trial Judgment, Case 002/02, 16 November 2018, para. 69 ('absent the opportunity to examine the source or author of evidence, less weight may be assigned to that evidence').

establishment,[434] the Lebanese parliament never formally voted on this Agreement.[435] Instead, the STL has been established by UN SC Resolution 1757 (30 May 2007), following the urgent request of Lebanon's prime minister, who felt that the Agreement enjoyed the support of a majority of the parliament.[436] It was this parliamentary support that even found its way into the wording of the Resolution.[437] This experience shows that the line between the establishment of a tribunal by the Security Council or by other means is sometimes difficult to draw and the criteria to be taken into account should, in any case, not be too formal.[438]

The STL, which is is neither a subsidiary organ of the UN, nor a part of the Lebanese court system,[439] is unique in that the applicable law according to Article 2(a) STL Statute (STLS) is national in character.[440] Furthermore, the STL is the first UN-assisted tribunal to combine, from the outset, substantial elements of both a common law and a civil law legal tradition:[441] In this respect, the civil law elements of the proceedings before the STL are particularly noticeable in the distinctly strong position of the Pre-Trial Judge, which is essentially geared towards filtering out meritless prosecutions and at the same time ensuring the speedy trial of the parties.[442] In particular, Rule 92(C) of the STL's RPE, which in exceptional cases requires the Pre-Trial Judge to carry out his own investigative activities for the purpose of impartially investigating the case,[443] clearly borrows from civil law. In addition, the far-reaching possibilities for the tribunal to take measures to ensure expeditious hearings and prevent unreasonable delays (Article 21(1) STLS[444]) and in particular the possibility of proceedings in absentia (Article 22 STLS) are rather associated with civil law.[445] At any rate, the STL's lack of national and international support finally led to its closure at the end of July 2022.[446]

[434] Agreement between the United Nations and the Lebanese Republic on the Establishment of a Special Tribunal for Lebanon, UN Doc. S/RES/1757 (2007) (30 May 2007), Annex. In more detail, see Mégret, *LJIL*, 21 (2008), 488 ff.

[435] In more detail, see O'Keefe, *ICL* (2015), pp. 95–6. More concretely, 'parliamentary mechanisms in Lebanon appeared to be blocked because of a refusal by the Speaker of Parliament to convene it', Mégret, *LJIL*, 21 (2008), 492; furthermore, see May and Fyfe, in Hayashi and Bailliet, *Criminal Tribunals* (2017), p. 36.

[436] Letter dated 14 May 2007 from the Prime Minister of Lebanon to the Secretary-General UN Doc. S/2007/281 (16 May 2007), Annex, p. 2, O'Keefe, *ICL* (2015), pp. 95–6; in more detail, see Ambos, Treatise *ICL I* (2021), p. 77

[437] UN SC Res. 1757 (30 May 2007), Preamble '*Recalling also* that the Agreement … was signed by the Government of Lebanon and the United Nations respectively on 23 January and 6 February 2007, *Referring* to the letter of the Prime Minister of Lebanon to the Secretary-General … , which recalled that the parliamentary majority has expressed its support for the Tribunal.' See also Schabas, *LJIL*, 21 (2008), 522.

[438] In the same vein, Schabas, *LJIL*, 21 (2008), 522 with further references.

[439] Report of the Secretary-General on the Establishment of a Special Tribunal for Lebanon, para. 6, UN Doc. S/2006/893 (15 November 2006); for more details, see Ambos, Treatise *ICL I* (2021), p. 78.

[440] ICTY and ICTR, by contrast, are limited to prosecuting crimes in violation of international law (see Art. 1 ICTYS/ICTRS) and the (other) hybrid tribunals prosecute crimes under both domestic and international law; see also Yun, *SantaClaraJIL*, 7 (2010), 181.

[441] Report of the Secretary-General, UN Doc. S/2006/893 (15 November 2006) para. 8 ('more elements of civil law are evident than of common law').

[442] For more details, see Hrdličková, in Sturma, *Rome Statute* (2019), pp. 210–12.

[443] The Pre-Trial Judge may, in exceptional circumstances, himself endeavour to gather evidence by any appropriate means where he considers that the interests of justice, the need for the impartial establishment of truth, and the necessity to ensure a fair and expeditious trial, in particular the need to ensure the equality of arms and to preserve evidence, make it imperative to gather an important piece of evidence, either inculpatory or exculpatory, which the Parties or the victims participating in the proceedings have been unable to collect.

[444] 'The Special Tribunal shall confine the trial, appellate and review proceedings strictly to an expeditious hearing of the issues raised by the charges, or the grounds for appeal or review, respectively. It shall take strict measures to prevent any action that may cause unreasonable delay.'

[445] Report of the Secretary-General on the Establishment of a Special Tribunal for Lebanon, para. 9, UN Doc. S/2006/893 (15 November 2006): 'most notable manifestations of civil law elements'.

[446] For good background analysis, see Blanford et al., *Atlantic Council*, 13 July 2021.

**(iii) Procedural rules at other tribunals**

Within this last category we have the Iraqi Higher Criminal Court (IHCC), the International Crimes Tribunal (ICT) in Bangladesh, and the 'Special Jurisdiction for Peace' (SJP) in Colombia, to be looked at more closely now.

*(1) **Iraqi Higher Criminal Court (IHCC)*** The IHCC was formerly established as the Iraqi Special Tribunal by the US Coalition Provisional Authority, although the validity of the establishment was questioned.[447] Its Statute (ISTS) was issued 10 December 2003 by the Iraqi Governing Council.[448] The Statute was replaced with an amended Statute (Statute of IHCC, hereinafter: IHCCS) in August 2005 and—together with Rules of Procedure and Evidence (hereinafter: RPE IHCC)[449]—approved on 18 October 2005 in Law No. 10 by the first freely elected Parliament.[450] The tribunal's name was then changed to the 'Iraqi Higher Criminal Court'.[451] The Court is considered to fulfil the requirements of an internationalized tribunal, since both the IHCCS and RPE IHCC have not only been influenced by the Iraqi Criminal Procedural Code (Law 23 of 1971)[452] and the Iraqi Penal Code (Law 111 of 1969),[453] but also by the UN ad hoc tribunals and especially the ICC.[454]

The IHCC is not part of the regular Iraqi judicial system but an autonomous organ with its own rules and an own administrative capacity. It is a 'hybrid institution with a hybrid procedural system'.[455] It has jurisdiction over any Iraqi national or resident of Iraq accused of the core crimes (genocide, crimes against humanity, and war crimes)[456] committed since 17 July 1968 (takeover of the Ba'ath Party) and up until and including 1 May 2003 in the territory

[447] See e.g. Bassiouni, *CornILJ*, 38 (2005), 346, 358, 361 ff.; van Esveld, *Anfal Trial* (2009), p. 2; previously Ambos, *Treatise ICL I* (2021), pp. 81 ff. It was also said that the establishment of the tribunal did not meet the requirements of a proper legislative process, see HRW, *Judging Dujail* (19 November 2006), p. 8 with n. 19 ('Draft legislation should normally be referred by the relevant ministry or the Council of Ministers to the State Consultative Council (Majlis Shura al-Dawla) for review before being debated in parliament. In this instance, the Council of Ministers sent the draft statute to the State Consultative Council and the Transitional National Assembly simultaneously. Consequently, in August 2005 parliament debated and adopted a draft law that had not been reviewed by the State Consultative Council. When the error was discovered, the adopted law was sent to the State Consultative Council for review, then re-debated and re-enacted with further amendments in September 2005.').

[448] cf. <http://www.preventgenocide.org/law/domestic/iraqispecialtribunal.htm>; Donlon, in Schabas and Bernaz, *Routledge Handbook ICL* (2011), pp. 99 ff.

[449] The RPE were promulgated as an annex to Law No. 10 of 2005, Rules of Procedure and Gathering of Evidence With Regard to the Iraqi Higher Criminal Court, Official Gazette of the Republic of Iraq, No. 4006, 18 October 2005, English translation available at <https://ihl-databases.icrc.org/applic/ihl/ihl-nat.nsf/0/62dfa419b75d039cc12576a1005fd6c1/$FILE/IST_statute_official_english.pdf>. See generally van Esveld, *Anfal Trial* (2009), p. 2.

[450] Law of the Iraqi Higher Criminal Court (Law No. 10 of 2005), Official Gazette of the Republic of Iraq (18 October 2005). See also Trahan, *MichJIL*, 30 (2009), 308.

[451] cf. ICTJ, *Creation and First Trials of the Supreme Iraqi Criminal Tribunal* (October 2005), pp. 2 ff., <https://www.ictj.org/sites/default/files/ICTJ-Iraq-Creation-Tribunal-2005-English.pdf>; Mettraux, *JICJ*, 5 (2007), 287 ff.

[452] See Art. 16 IHCCS: 'The Tribunal shall follow the rules of procedure provided for in the Criminal Procedure Law 23 of 1971 and the Rules of Procedures and Evidence appended to this Law, of which it shall be considered an integral part.'

[453] van Esveld, *Anfal Trial* (2009), p. 2.

[454] Heller, *CWRJIL*, 39 (2006–2007), 263 ('[I]nsofar as the IHT incorporates many of the best elements of the International Criminal Tribunal for the Former Yugoslavia (ICTY), the International Criminal Tribunal for Rwanda (ICTR), and the International Criminal Court (ICC), the Tribunal's substantive and procedural law represent a significant advance over some of the more problematic aspects of traditional Iraqi criminal justice.'); Scharf, *JICJ*, 5 (2007), 258, 259; also see Ambos, *Treatise ICL I* (2021), p. 81.

[455] cf. Zappalà, *JICJ*, 2 (2004), 855 ff.; ChatHouseILDG, *The Iraqi Tribunal* (4 December 2009), p. 7. Crit. Scharf, *JICJ*, 5 (2007), 258, 259, who does not qualify it as a hybrid internationalized court ('But the IHT is not fully international or even international enough to be dubbed a hybrid court, since its seat is Baghdad, its Prosecutor is Iraqi, it uses the Iraqi Criminal Code to supplement the provisions of its statute and rules, and its bench is composed exclusively of Iraqi judges.').

[456] Arts. 11–13 IHCCS. See also van Esveld, *Anfal Trial* (2009), p. 2.

of the Republic of Iraq, or elsewhere.[457] The IHCC consists of Investigative Judges, one or more Trial Chambers, and an Appeals Chamber.[458] The Investigative Judges are viewed as separate organs of the tribunal, 'may gather evidence from whatever source [they deem] appropriate and to communicate directly with all relevant parties',[459] 'shall initiate investigations on the basis of information obtained from any source',[460] 'have the power to question suspects, victims or their relatives, and witnesses, to collect evidence and to conduct on-site investigations'[461] and are entrusted with the preparation of an indictment.[462] The rights of the accused are defined in Article 19 IHCCS and resemble Article 14 of the International Covenant on Civil and Political Rights.[463] Investigations, in accordance with Article 16 IHCCS, are governed by Criminal Procedure Law 23 of 1971, which echoes the procedural law within the civil law tradition.[464]

*(2)* ***International Crimes Tribunal (ICT) in Bangladesh*** A purely national tribunal for international crimes with a purely national procedure has been created in Bangladesh.[465] Following the enactment of the International Crimes (Tribunals) Act in 1973 (ICTA),[466] and amendments to the Act,[467] the ICT was established in Dhaka. On the basis of Article 6(1) ICTA,[468] the Bangladeshi government established a second tribunal in 2012. The jurisdiction of the Bangladesh Tribunals includes crimes against humanity, crimes against peace, genocide, war crimes, and 'violation of any humanitarian rules applicable in armed conflicts laid down in the Geneva Conventions of 1949', and 'any other crimes under international law'.[469] The tribunals are called 'International Crimes Tribunal-1' and 'International Crimes Tribunal-2'[470] and are 'special criminal tribunals within the judicial system of Bangladesh, staffed entirely by Bangladeshi personnel appointed by the Bangladeshi government'.[471]

Common law and customary international law are treated as primary sources of law.[472] The 1872 Evidence Act and 1898 Criminal Procedure Code (largely based on English

[457] Art. 1 (2) IHCCS; also see Ambos, *Treatise ICL I* (2021), p. 81.
[458] Art. 3 IHCCS.
[459] Art. 8 (5) and (7) IHCCS.
[460] Art. 18 (1) IHCCS.
[461] Art. 18 (2) IHCCS.
[462] Art. 18 (3) IHCCS.
[463] See Sissons and Bassin, *JICJ*, 5 (2007), 272, 273. About the equality of arms before the IHCC, see ibid., 280 ff. Crit. Heller, *CWRJIL*, 39 (2006–2007), 269 ff. About the right to counsel before the IHCC, see HRW, *Iraqi High Tribunal and Representation* (February 2006). About the defence's right to disclosure in the Anfal trial, see Simperingham and Gard, *Prosecution Witness* (2007), pp. 9 ff. About general fair trial issues in the Anfal trial, see Trahan, *MichJIL*, 30 (2009), 315 ff.
[464] In more detail, see HRW, *Judging Dujail* (19 November 2006), pp. 9 ff. There was of course a US influence, see e.g. De Villers, *Doj J. Fed. L. & Prac.*, 19 (2019) 25–6 ('American prosecutors are used to an adversatorial system with citizen jurors ... in other parts of the world, an adversarial system with citizen jurors is extremely rare. Iraq was no exception').
[465] See Linton, *CLF*, 21 (2010), 310; Kay, 'Bangladesh War Crimes Tribunal—A Wolf in Sheep's Clothing?' (Lecture in London), 18 October 2011, <https://mozlum.blogspot.com/2010/11/bangladesh-war-crimes-tribunal-wolf-in.html> <http://www.internationallawbureau.com/blog/?p=1927>; Ambos, *Treatise ICL I* (2021), p. 63.
[466] International Crimes (Tribunals) Act 1973, Act no. XIX of 1973, 20 July 1973; O'Keefe, *ICL* (2015), p. 395; in more detail, see Samad, *CLF*, 27 (2016), 261 ff.
[467] See International Crimes (Tribunals) (Amendment) Acts 2009, 2012, and 2013.
[468] 'For the purpose of section 3, the Government may ... set up one or more Tribunals, each consisting of a Chairman and not less than two and not more than four other members.'
[469] Art. 3(2)(a)–(f) ICTA 1973.
[470] See the Tribunals' website <http://www.ict-bd.org/>.
[471] O'Keefe, *ICL* (2015), p. 396.
[472] Linton, *CLF*, 21 (2010), 221 ff.

statutes) form—at least in part—the procedural framework of the tribunal. Thus, for example, after formal charges have been submitted, the Court decides upon their confirmation (framing) or non-confirmation (discharge).[473] However, both the Act and the Code are not applicable in their entirety.[474] In this regard, Article 19(1) ICTA provides that the '[t]ribunal shall not be bound by any technical rules of evidence',[475] which may be seen as a parallel Article 19 IMTS or Article 13 IMTFES.[476] Furthermore, Article 19(4) ICTA provides for the tribunal to 'take judicial notice of official governmental documents'.[477] Even though Article 6(2)(a)) ICTA (since 2009) itself obliges the Tribunal to provide a fair trial, there are nevertheless certain fairness restrictions.[478]

*(3)* ***Special Jurisdiction for Peace in Colombia*** After over three years of peace negotiations between the Colombian government and the 'Revolutionary Armed Forces of Colombia-People's Army' (FARC-EP) an agreement was achieved on the creation of a 'Special Jurisdiction for Peace' (SJP, *Jurisdicción Especial para la Paz, JEP*),[479] an essentially domestic tribunal with a quite international legal framework.[480] Its genesis and structure has already been explained in the first volume of this Treatise,[481] so that we will focus here on the procedural peculiarities.

The SJP is a separate body within Colombia's justice system[482] with a somewhat complicated structure: it consists of three '*Salas previas*' (kinds of pre-trial chambers)—responsible for fact-finding, amnesties and pardons, and the determination of the legal situation of the respective persons subject to the tribunal—and the more important '*Tribunal para la Paz*' (Tribunal for Peace), which will conduct the main trials.[483] The JEP's jurisdiction *ratione materiae* covers both international and (serious) national crimes. Interestingly, the SJP can resort directly not just to the domestic criminal code but also to international legal instruments as primary sources of law, which, importantly, include the ICC Statute.[484] While the SJP's jurisdiction *ratione personae* in principle covers all parties to the conflict, its jurisdiction *ratione temporis* extends to crimes committed from the beginning of the conflict until 1

[473] See s. 265D and C of the 1898 Criminal Procedure Code, <https://www.unodc.org/tldb/pdf/Bangladesh_Code_of_Criminal_Procedure_1898_Full_text.pdf>.

[474] See Samad, *CLF*, 27 (2016), 286–7.

[475] '[A]nd it shall adopt and apply to the greatest possible extent expeditious and non-technical procedure, and may admit any evidence, including reports and photographs published in newspapers, periodicals and magazines, films and tape-recordings and other materials as may be tendered before it, which it deems to have probative value' (Art. 19(1) ICTA).

[476] Crit. Samad, *CLF*, 27 (2016), 287.

[477] Crit. ibid., 287 ('government documents can be given as status of evidence automatically without any challenge of scrutiny of the content').

[478] See Ambos, *Treatise ICL I* (2021), p. 84 with further references.

[479] The full agreement (Acuerdo sobre las Víctimas del Conflicto) was published on 5 December 2015 and is available at <http://es.presidencia.gov.co/Documents/Punto5.pdf>.

[480] Acuerdo sobre las Víctimas del Conflicto, p. 23.

[481] Ambos, *Treatise ICL I* (2021), pp. 85 ff.

[482] English Summary of the September 23 Government-FARC Communiqué on the Transitional Justice Accord (23 September 2015), <https://colombiapeace.org/english-summary-of-the-september-23-government-farc-communique-on-the-transitional-justice-accord/>.

[483] See Acuerdo sobre las Víctimas del Conflicto, p. 29 para. 45 and p. 35 paras. 52–3; on this, see Rojas Betancorth, in Fabra-Zamora et al., *Special Jurisdiction* (2021), p. 162.

[484] Final Peace Agreement, No. 40; Trans. Art. 5 Legislative Act 01/2017 (4 April 2017) with Colombian Constitutional Court Judgment C-080 (15 August 2018), para. 4.1.5.3.; Art. 23 Statutory Law (6 June 2019). Crit. Tarapués Sandino, in Ambos and Peters, *Transitional Justice* (2022), p. 78–9; on the conformity with the principle of legality, see Ambos and Cote Barco, in Ambos and Peters, *Transitional Justice* (2022), pp. 127–9; for a general overview, see Ambos, *Treatise ICL I* (2021), pp. 87–8.

December 2016.[485] Notwithstanding the fact that the SJP started its work on 15 March 2018, the Procedural Code and the Statutory Law were not approved until July 2018[486] and June 2019[487] respectively.[488]

The SJP's aim is, essentially, to ascertain the criminal accountability of all parties involved in the armed conflict—however, in accordance with international practice, limited to a focus of those primarily responsible[489]—with a dual procedural model: alleged perpetrators who submit to the new jurisdiction voluntarily and fully confess to their acts can expect a maximum—so-called alternative—sanction of up to eight years (see Article 127-8 Statutory Law), while those who refuse to cooperate will be subject to ordinary criminal proceedings which may result in a prison sentence of up to twenty years.[490] All concerned must contribute actively to the ascertainment of the truth, to the reparation of victims, and to guaranteeing the non-repetition of the crimes committed. The SJP's bifurcated approach, by which restorative and retributive justice are to be reconciled,[491] entails a sophisticated procedure: in a first step, the *Sala previa* shall determine the jurisdiction of the SJP and then, in further 'dialogical' proceedings, establish whether an acknowledgment of truth and responsibility is made.[492] If there is no acknowledgement, a normal adversarial trial procedure takes place,[493] following the referral of (only) such cases to the SJP's Investigation and Indictment Unit.[494] Otherwise, the competent *Sala* or the *Tribunal para la Paz* will decide whether to grant amnesty or to apply one of the aforementioned sanctions under Article 127-8 Statutory Law.[495]

The agreement makes a distinction between (political) crimes open to an amnesty and the core crimes under international criminal law, namely genocide, crimes against humanity, and serious war crimes, for which an amnesty is excluded.[496] But an amnesty is not only excluded for the core crimes (albeit with the qualifier 'serious' for war crimes), but also for individual acts such as forced expulsion, forced disappearance, torture, and—very broadly—'sexual violence'.[497]

[485] For details and exceptions, see Ambos, *Treatise ICL I* (2021), pp. 88–9.

[486] Ley No. 1922 of 18 July 2018, Diario Oficial No. 50.658.

[487] Ley No. 1957 of 6 June 1957, Diario Oficial No. 50.976.

[488] See Ambos and Aboueldahab, in Ambos and Peters, *Transitional Justice* (2022), p. 53.

[489] For details, see Tarapués Sandino, in Ambos and Peters, *Transitional Justice* (2022), pp. 66–7; Ambos, *Treatise ICL I* (2021), p. 88 and furthermore, see p. 90 on the JEP's prioritization strategy.

[490] cf. Final Peace Agreement, Nos. 28, 47 and pp. 182 ff. The agreement distinguishes between (political) crimes open to an amnesty and the ICL (core) crimes and certain individual crimes (such as forced expulsion, enforced disappearance, torture, and—very broadly—'sexual violence') for which an amnesty is excluded; cf., in more detail, Ambos, in Fabra-Zamora et al., *Peace Agreement* (2021), pp. 123 ff. and Ambos and Cote, *Amnistía* (2019).

[491] Castro Cuenca, in Ambos and Peters, *Transitional Justice* (2022), pp. 98 ff.; Ambos and Aboueldahab, in Ambos and Peters, *Transitional Justice* (2022), p. 43; Tarapués Sandino, in Ambos and Peters, *Transitional Justice* (2022), p. 77.

[492] Rojas Betancourt, in Fabra-Zamora et al., *Special Jurisdiction* (2021), p. 163; Tarapués Sandino, in Ambos and Peters, *Transitional Justice* (2022), p. 77; on the 'dialogical' procedure as a type of plea bargaining, see González-Ruiz, *EJIL: Talk!*, 27 March 2024.

[493] See Ambos, *Treatise ICL I* (2021), p. 89; on cases of non compliance with the conditions associated with the process of acknowledgement of truth or responsibility (e.g. failure to present the 'monitoring report' or to 'show sufficient commitment to contribute to the truth and to satisfy the victim's rights'), see Ambos and Aboueldahab, in Ambos and Peters, *Transitional Justice* (2022), pp. 49–50; furthermore, see Tarapués Sandino, in Ambos and Peters, *Transitional Justice* (2022), pp. 65–6 ('must fully comply').

[494] Arts. 86, 87 Statutory Law (6 June 2019). See thereon also Tarapués Sandino, in Ambos and Peters, *Transitional Justice* (2022), p. 77.

[495] See Ambos, *Treatise ICL I* (2021), pp. 89–90, also with a view to the enforcement of sanctions pursuant to Arts. 127–8 Statutory Law.

[496] Detailed in Ambos, in Fabra-Zamora et al., *Special Jurisdiction* (2021), pp. 123 ff.

[497] See, in more detail, Ambos, *Treatise ICL I* (2021), pp. 89–90; Ambos, *Opinio Juris* (8 October 2015); Ambos, *El Espectador*, 20 December 2015, p. 46.

### (d) *Intermediate conclusion*

The Nuremberg IMT, beyond representing the first ever trial of major international criminals,[498] also impacted on the development of international criminal procedure.[499] That does not mean, of course, that the IMT's procedural rules have been a perfect role model for subsequent international criminal tribunals. As previously demonstrated, although the main trials before the IMT and IMTFE have generally been considered as fair, both tribunals had many deficiencies. However, to conclude that the RPE of the IMT and other post WWII tribunals 'are not very instructive'[500] certainly goes too far. Quite the opposite is true. When the ICTY and ICTR were established, lessons learned from both the IMT and IMTFE played an important role. In turn, both legacies and shortcomings of the first ad hoc tribunals informed the administration of later tribunals such as the SCSL, the ECCC, the STL, and the Kosovo Courts/KSC.

The establishment of the first permanent International Criminal Court would not have been possible without these previous experiences and, indeed, these experiences, especially the law and practice of ICTY/ICTR, have greatly influenced the procedural regime of the ICC. All these more recent tribunals have addressed at least some of the limitations of the earlier tribunals.[501] They do not only incorporate the right to fair trial with the ensuing concrete rights[502] in a comprehensive manner but also 'place at centre-stage the whole concept of international human rights protection and humanitarian law enforcement in their proceedings'.[503] Of course, comparing the procedural rules of these tribunals, it becomes clear that a cut-and-paste mentality has largely dominated the drafting of their rules;[504] yet, it is also true that there is a process of lessons learnt and thus subsequent rules build on previous rules and often develop them further or complement them. At any rate, previous codifications inform subsequent ones and the ensuing normative build-up runs like a common thread through the history of international criminal procedure up to the creation of the ICC and subsequent tribunals. States and also judicial operators are reluctant to reinvent the wheel and tend to start from existing law and rules. Whether this approach served the good of the course of international criminal justice will be seen at various places in this book.

## (3) Investigating international crimes

In the national context, criminal investigations are dominated by State actors, namely public prosecutors and the police (independent criminal investigations[505] by private individuals

[498] Chiam, in Blumenthal and McCormack, *Legacy of Nuremberg* (2008), p. 205.

[499] Zappalà, *Human Rights* (2005), p. 244 with n. 1 ('it was noted that it was precisely for having respected the right to a fair trial that the Nuremberg trials constituted a milestone in international criminal justice').

[500] La Rosa, *IRRC*, 37 (321) (1997), 636.

[501] Chiam, in Blumenthal and McCormack, *Legacy of Nuremberg* (2008), p. 205.

[502] See Section D. of this chapter.

[503] Hassan-Morlai, *AfrJLS*, 3 (2009), 97.

[504] cf. Terris, Romano, and Swigart, *The International Judge* (2007), p. 110 in relation to international justice.

[505] We understand 'criminal investigation' narrowly, i.e. all fact-finding endeavours done in the context of a formal criminal investigation or examination for violations of ICL; for the purpose of a criminal trial for violations of ICL; and capable of leading to the identification and punishment of those responsible for violations of ICL. For an overview of broader investigation definitions, see Heinze, *NCLR*, 24 (2021), 214–15, with further references.

not being a regular phenomenon).[506] In addition, the (State) investigation procedure is geared towards the possible filing of criminal charges in the domestic courts. By contrast, international or supranational investigations present, as we will see now, a more heterogeneous and complex picture. This is especially due to the fact that there is only a fine line between the monitoring of human rights violations and a criminal investigation in the narrow sense. In the following, we will thus refer to fact-finding, where it is difficult to draw this line.[507]

### (a) *Fact-finding at the UN level*

(Official) fact-finding missions are not a new instrument of international law. Strictly speaking they are, as evidenced by their name ('fact-finding'), geared to collecting *facts* that are then to form the basis for the resolution of interstate conflicts.[508] In Volume I of this Treatise, we have given an overview of measures taken to investigate international crimes: so-called Fact-Finding Missions (FFMs), Commissions of Inquiry (CoIs), and other novel investigative mechanisms,[509] are a field 'very much alive and still evolving' but probably in need of a centralized and permanent support structure.[510]

Thus, in contrast to a more comprehensive Experts Commission such as the one preparing the establishment of the ICTY,[511] fact-finding missions do not, in principle, apply the facts to the law or decide legal questions,[512] although the delimitation between facts and law can obviously become problematic in individual cases.[513] Take for example the 'International, Impartial and Independent Mechanism to Assist in the Investigation and Prosecution of Those Responsible for the Most Serious Crimes under International Law Committed in the Syrian Arab Republic since March 2011' (IIIM), established on 21 December 2016.[514] It has been called a 'completely new and unique form of international criminal investigations'[515] and has the mandate to create or secure the basis for subsequent criminal proceedings.[516]

[506] Two forms of private investigations are a regular phenomenon, though: first, investigations in partnership with or in the interest of a State organ. Partnerships between the police and private security companies are a commen constellation. Secondly, private individuals conducting internal investigations, esp. in the compliance context. In more detail, see Heinze, in Bergsmo and Dittrich, *Integrity* (2020), pp. 631 ff.

[507] For more details on the term 'fact-finding', see Heinze, *NCLR*, 24 (2021), 215 with further references in n. 11.

[508] Jacobs and Harwood, in Bergsmo, *Quality Control* (2020), p. 343; de Vries, J., *Confl. Secur. Law*, 24 (2019), 600 ('a purely factual investigation').

[509] Ambos, *Treatise ICL I* (2021), p. 65.

[510] cf. D'Alessandra, *JICJ*, 21 (2023), 551, 555 ff. (564), 566 ff. (stressing the production of information, 'evidentiary lifecycle'), 569 ff. (advocating a 'permanent UN investigative entity' with an administrative but perhaps also an investigative function).

[511] SC Res. 780, 6 October 1992. Its mandate was to investigate violations of international humanitarian law in (former) Yugoslavia, cf. ibid., para. 2: 'Requests the Secretary-General to establish ... an impartial Commission of Experts to examine and analyse the information submitted ..., together with such further information as the Commission may obtain through its own investigations or through the efforts, of other persons or bodies ... with a view to providing the Secretary-General with its conclusions on the evidence of grave breaches of the Geneva Conventions and other violations of international humanitarian law committed in the territory of the former Yugoslavia.' On this and other UN Commissions, cf. Brunner, *Untersuchungskommissionen* (2022), pp. 554 ff.

[512] Accordingly, the 1907 Hague Convention for the Pacific Settlement of International Disputes limited its inquiries to 'disputes of an international nature involving neither honour nor vital interests, and arising from a difference of opinion on points of facts' (Art. 9). On this, see Jacobs and Harwood, in Bergsmo, *Quality Control* (2020), p. 343 and in depth Brunner, *Untersuchungskommissionen* (2022), pp. 47 ff.

[513] de Vries, J., *Confl. Secur. Law*, 24 (2019), 600.

[514] UN GA Res. 71/248, <https://www.securitycouncilreport.org/atf/cf/%7B65BFCF9B-6D27-4E9C-8CD3-CF6E4FF96FF9%7D/a_res_71_248.pdf>. See Lhotský, in Šturma, *Rome Statute* (2019), p. 150.

[515] Heinze, *ZIS*, 14 (2019), 171; Whiting, *JICJ*, 15 (2017), 232 ('UN General Assembly stepped into the breach'; 'historic'); also see Wenaweser and Cockayne, *JICJ*, 15 (2017), 212–13; D'Alessandra, *JICJ*, 21 (2023), 559–60.

[516] A/RES/71/248, para. 4: 'to collect, consolidate, preserve and analyse evidence of violations of international humanitarian law and human rights violations and abuses and to prepare files in order to facilitate and expedite fair and independent criminal proceedings, in accordance with international law standards, in national, regional

Thus, it amounts, at least, to a 'quasi-prosecuting' body[517] which, however, goes too far for some.[518]

At any rate, the combination of a fact-finding measure and a newly established court or tribunal could establish an effective accountability mechanism—take, for instance, the (not yet established) hybrid court in South Sudan[519] or the already existing Commission of Human Rights in South Sudan.[520]

It goes beyond the scope of this section to address all FFMs, CoIs etc.,[521] but just to name a few: in the second half of 2017, the government of Iraq approached the UN to help investigate or prosecute crimes committed by the so-called Islamic State terrorist group,[522] whereupon the Security Council on 21 September 2017 adopted Resolution 2379,[523] stipulating, amongst other measures, the establishment of:

> an Investigative Team, headed by a Special Adviser, to support domestic efforts to hold ISIL (Da'esh) accountable by collecting, preserving, and storing evidence in Iraq of acts that may amount to war crimes, crimes against humanity and genocide committed by the terrorist group ISIL (Da'esh) ... to ensure the broadest possible use before national courts, and complementing investigations being carried out by the Iraqi authorities, or investigations carried out by authorities in third countries at their request. Due to their exclusive attachment to Iraqi courts or authorities, the Iraqi government enjoys a relatively strong position.[524]

On 27 September 2018, the Human Rights Council (HRC) tasked the 'Independent Investigative Mechanism for Myanmar' (IIMM) with a mission resembling that of the Syria IIIM.[525] Here again the reason for this decision was that the ICC has no jurisdiction

or international courts or tribunals that have or may in the future have jurisdiction over these crimes, in accordance with international law'.

517 See Heinze, *ZIS*, 14 (2019), 172; id, in Bergsmo and Dittrich, *Integrity* (2020), p. 625; D'Alessandra, *JICJ*, 21 (2023), 551, 562 ('pre-prosecutorial'); in more detail, see Wenaweser and Cockayne, *JICJ*, 15 (2017), 224–8.

518 See the Russian complaint (UN Doc. A/71/793, p. 1): 'A number of powers vested in the "mechanism" under resolution 71/248, including those of "analys[ing] evidence" and "prepar[ing] files", are prosecutorial in nature. However, prosecutions, criminal investigations and support of criminal investigations are not among the functions of the General Assembly. It cannot create an organ that has more powers than the Assembly itself.' On this, see Whiting, *JICJ*, 15 (2017), 233–4.

519 The establishment has been delayed but finally on 3 Sept. 2024 the South Sudanese Parliament adopted two TJ laws providing for the establishment, see https://www.hrw.org/news/2024/09/09/south-sudan-parliament-approves-transitional-justice-laws. See generally Akech, *ICTJ*, 14 (2021), 585 ff.; Lavery, *JICJ*, 18 (2020), 278 ff.; Abdelsalam Babiker, *MPEiPro*, October 2022.

520 See <https://www.ohchr.org/en/hr-bodies/hrc/co-h-south-sudan/index>. See also Heinze, in Dittrich and Heinze, *Rome Statute* (2021), pp. 99–100.

521 See, for recent CoIs, Heinze, in Dittrich and Heinze, *Rome Statute* (2021), pp. 99 ff.

522 UN Doc. S/2017/710, p. 2 ('we call on you to ask the international community to provide assistance, so that we can make use of international expertise in our effort to prosecute the terrorist entity ISIL'). See Abad Castelos, *Age Hum. Rights J.*, 16 (2021), 17 on the issue that Iraq did not ratify the Rome Statute, that a UNSC referral did not seem likely, and that the ICC Prosecutor had decided not to open a preliminary examination on the basis of personal jurisdiction (Statement of the Prosecutor of the International Criminal Court, Fatou Bensouda, on the alleged crimes committed by ISIS of 8 April 2015, <https://www.icc-cpi.int/news/statement-prosecutor-international-criminal-court-fatou-bensouda-alleged-crimes-committed-isis>: 'ISIS is a military and political organisation primarily led by nationals of Iraq and Syria. Thus, at this stage, the prospects of my Office investigating and prosecuting those most responsible, within the leadership of ISIS, appear limited.').

523 S/RES/2379 (2017).

524 Abad Castelos, *Age Hum. Rights J.*, 16 (2021), 9–10 and 24 ('subordination to the Iraqi Government'); also see Lhotský, 'Syria', in Šturma, *Rome Statute* (2019), p. 151.

525 A/HRC/RES/39/2, para. 22: 'to collect, consolidate, preserve and analyse evidence of the most serious international crimes and violations of international law committed in Myanmar since 2011, and to prepare files in

over Myanmar (not being a State Party to the Rome Statute) and that the Security Council will not be able, due to a possible Chinese veto, to refer the situation to the ICC.[526]

Similarly, in March 2022, the HRC set up an 'independent international commission of inquiry' to investigate human rights as well as IHL violations 'and related crimes in the context of the aggression against the Ukraine by the Russian Federation', to gather related evidence 'in view of any future legal proceedings', and to 'identify, where possible, those individuals and entities responsible for violations or abuses of human rights or violations of international humanitarian law, or other related crimes, in Ukraine, with a view to ensuring that those responsible are held accountable'.[527]

### (b) *Private criminal investigations in a narrow sense*

In parallel to (official) fact-finding missions and CoIs, the importance of criminal investigations for the prosecution of international crimes cannot be overestimated, as can be illustrated by investigations in the former Yugoslavia and Kosovo, Rwanda, Sierra Leone, and Cambodia.[528] What distinguishes those investigations from any other fact-finding mentioned above is their context: at the time when the material is collected by private individuals, it is not yet clear which institution, tribunal, or court will eventually use it as evidence. Due to technology development and to the spread of information, today there is a plethora of evidence documenting possible ICL violations that domestic investigators in particular rely on. This can range from the manifold initiatives, sometimes even student initiatives, that search social media for hints of core crimes which may have been committed;[529] or more professional entities, such as Caesar, the code name of a former Syrian military photographer who brought over 50,000 photographs out of the country, 28,000 of which show detainees in Syrian prisons killed by torture, outright execution, disease, malnutrition, or other ill-treatment;[530] or Belingcat,[531] which provided crucial intelligence with regard to the investigation, by a Dutch-led JIT, of the shooting down of Malaysia Airlines flight MH17 over Ukraine on 17 July 2014;[532] to professional investigators in the ranks of the Commission for International Justice and Accountability (CIJA).[533] The latter is certainly the most elaborate entity of individuals investigating ICL violations. It was set up by the UK government—against the backdrop of the inability of the UN and the ICC to respond to atrocities in Syria

order to facilitate and expedite fair and independent criminal proceedings, in accordance with international law standards, in national, regional or international courts or tribunals that have or may in the future have jurisdiction over these crimes, in accordance with international law'. See thereto D'Alessandra, *JICJ*, 21 (2023), 560–1, 563.

[526] On this, see Stavrou, *UJIEL*, 36 (2021), 99–100.

[527] A/HRC/RES/49/1, 4 March 2022, para. 11.

[528] Heinze, *ZIS*, 14 (2019), 169–71; id., in Bergsmo and Dittrich, *Integrity* (2020), pp. 619–24.

[529] The Human Rights Center at UC Berkeley and Bellingcat have used open source and social media material in an effort to support the OTP, see Nwadikwa-Jonathan and Ortizi, in Dittrich and Heinze, *Rome Statute* (2021), p. 298; Mehandru and Koenig, *DukeLTR*, 17 (2019), pp. 129 ff.; for a nuanced and differentiated account, weighing advantages and risks of open source information in international fact-finding, see McDermott, Murray, and Koenig, *Opinio Juris* (19 December 2019). The authors are part of a larger team that initiated the project 'Using open source research to transform the discovery and documentation of Human Rights Violations', see OSR4Rights <https://osr4rights.org>.

[530] See Afshar, *The Guardian*, 27 August 2018. About the use of Caesar material by German Courts, see Ritscher, *ZIS*, 14 (2019), 600; Heinze, in Bergsmo and Dittrich, *Integrity* (2020), pp. 628–9.

[531] According to its website, Bellingcat is an 'independent international collective of researchers, investigators and citizen journalists using open source and social media investigation to probe a variety of subjects', see <https://www.bellingcat.com/about/>.

[532] de Hoon, *UJIEL*, 33 (2017), 91 ff.; Heinze, in Bergsmo and Dittrich, *Integrity* (2020), p. 624.

[533] <https://cijaonline.org/>.

and Iraq[534]—as an association of non-State actors[535] which is meanwhile well funded by a number of States, including the UK, USA, Canada, and Germany, as well as the EU.[536]

While such private investigations and/or information may prove to be very useful as the evidentiary starting point of an official investigation[537] and at least CIJA information already seemed to have been used in domestic (German) investigations,[538] the ensuing privatization of criminal investigations raises a number of questions. First of all, there is no ethical (let alone legal) framework for private investigators comparable to that of public prosecutors;[539] in addition, the concept of 'private investigator' is not properly defined.[540] Secondly, the lack of ethical obligations for private investigators could produce further consequences with regard to the admissibility of the collected evidence in court: either the material is inadmissible given that it is considered as tainted from the outset; or it will be admitted notwithstanding, for the simple reason that it is the only available evidence.[541] We will return to this issue below.[542]

## C. Goals of international criminal justice

Numerous goals have been proclaimed to justify the creation of international criminal courts and tribunals.[543] Countless attempts have been made to categorize and analyse these goals, together with the use of different terms such as 'objective', 'ambition', or 'function'.[544] I have argued previously,[545] drawing on the German and Anglo-American philosophical debate and its forerunners, that the overall 'function' of ICL is the protection of fundamental individual and collective legal goods ('Rechtsgüter') and the prevention of harm to these goods, that is, ultimately the protection of human dignity.[546] In this book I will use the

[534] Rankin, *Global Resp. Protect*, 9 (2017), 396–7; also see Kassab, *MichJIL*, 39 (2018), 290; furthermore, see Heinze, *ZIS*, 14 (2019), 171.

[535] In more detail, see Rankin, *Global Resp. Protect*, 9 (2017), 400.

[536] Ibid., 400–1.

[537] See Kassab, *MichJIL*, 39 (2018), 287–9 ('Investigators suggest that the existing evidence that links the Assad regime to war crimes and crimes agaings humanity is more complete and incriminatory than any body of evidence that has been previously gathered during an active conflict' (289) with reference to a *New Yorker* article) with further references.

[538] See Heinze, in Bergsmo and Dittrich, *Integrity* (2020), pp. 629–30; Heinze, *EJIL: Talk!*, 26 February 2019.

[539] Heinze, *ZIS*, 14 (2019), 176–7; id., in Bergsmo and Dittrich, *Integrity* (2020), pp. 634–40 with further references.

[540] Heinze, *ZIS*, 14 (2019), 174–5; id., in Bergsmo and Dittrich, *Integrity* (2020), pp. 631–4 with further references.

[541] Heinze, in Bergsmo and Dittrich, *Integrity* (2020), pp. 616–17 ('Prosecutors of both national courts and ICTs become taciturn when confronted with illegal behaviour by their most important aids'); Heinze, *ZIS*, 14 (2019), 178–9 (pointing to the free admission of evidence).

[542] Chapter V, A.(8)(b).

[543] This is documented in the statutes of the international courts and their preambles, in resolutions adopted by the UN Security Council, in remarks made by members of the Council when adopting these resolutions, in the case law of the ad hoc tribunals, and in other official contexts; see e.g. ICC Statute, Preamble para. 3. See also Damaška, *ChicKentLR*, 83 (2008), 331; Heinze, *Disclosure* (2014), p. 210; De Meester, *Investigation Phase* (2015), pp. 93–4. See a list of goals for the ICTY in Schrag, *JICJ*, 2 (2004), 428. See also Woods, *VirgJIL*, 52 (2011–2012), 639, 656 ('International criminal law has numerous goals—so many that some have questioned whether the regime can realistically achieve them all') (fn. omitted). See generally Swart, *JICJ*, 6 (2008), 100.

[544] See Heinze, in Cullen et al., *Politics* (2020), pp. 38–43 (distinguishing between 'purpose/justification/function' and 'goal/aim/objective', with the latter terms referring to more distant objects [42]).

[545] Ambos, *CrLPhil*, 9 (2015), 319 ff.; Ambos, *Treatise ICL I* (2021), pp. 106 ff., 112–13.

[546] In a similar vein, Heinze, in Cullen et al., *Politics* (2020), p. 45 ('protection of the essential preconditions for communal living (*Rechts*güterschutz) and/or the prevention of harm (harm principle)').

term 'goal'—'[t]he object to which effort or ambition is directed'[547]—instead of 'objective', 'aim', 'ambition', or 'function', since it seems best to fit with regard to international criminal *justice*.[548]

There are differences between the terms 'criminal procedure' and 'criminal justice'. 'Criminal procedure' has already been defined above as '[t]he rules governing the mechanisms under which crimes are investigated, prosecuted, adjudicated, and punished. It includes the protection of accused persons' constitutional rights.'[549] 'Criminal Justice', on the contrary, may be defined as 'society's formal response to crime and is defined more specifically in terms of a series of decisions and actions taken by a number of agencies in response to a specific crime or criminal or crime in general'.[550] In the view of *Davies, Croall, and Tyrer*, the criminal process merely governs 'such matters as the investigation of crime, the arrest and interrogation of suspects, prosecution decisions, bail procedure, trial procedures, rules of evidence and the role of the jury, if there is one'.[551] Thus, criminal 'justice' is the broader concept, of which the criminal process is a part;[552] transferred to the international level this means that international criminal *procedure* is only a 'more specific and subsidiary discipline' of international criminal *justice*.[553]

Taking a closer look at the goals of international criminal justice, one can distinguish between traditional goals, being pursued equally by international and national systems of criminal justice alike, without the transfer of goals originating from the national context being problematic per se,[554] and the more idiosyncratic, specific goals of international criminal tribunals.[555] Of course, some traditional goals of international criminal justice may also

[547] Simpson and Weiner, *Dictionary, VI* (1989), p. 632. Similarly, '*objective*' means 'something aimed at, an object or end' (ibid., p. 644), and 'aim' is 'a thing desired to be effected' or 'an objective' (ibid., p. 276), i.e. all three terms can be used interchangeably. In contrast, 'ambition' is '[t]he object of strong desire or aspiration' (ibid., p. 387), rather describing the attitude of one's own desire to achieve something (cf. Galbraith, *MichJIL*, 31 (2009–2010), 84 ff., who, however, uses the terms 'ambitions', 'goals', and 'objectives' interchangeably). A '*function*' is 'the action of performing', an 'activity', 'the mode of action by which it fulfills its purpose' (Simpson and Weiner, *Dictionary, VI* (1989), p. 262) or 'the manner in which a particular activity is directed toward its particular goal or objective' (Ohlin, in Sluiter et al., *International Criminal Procedure* (2013), p. 55).

[548] In the same vein, Ohlin, in Sluiter et al., *International Criminal Procedure* (2013), p. 55 with n. 40.

[549] Garner, *Dictionary* (2019), p. 472.

[550] Davies, Croall, and Tyrer, *Criminal Justice* (2015), p. 8.

[551] Ibid., p. 9.

[552] Heinze, *Disclosure* (2014), p. 117.

[553] See Ohlin, in Sluiter et al., *International Criminal Procedure* (2013), p. 55; Heinze, in Cullen et al., *Politics* (2020), pp. 34–5; Mertins, *Proceedings* (2022), p. 113. Therefore, even a distinction between goals of international criminal justice and of international criminal procedure (in this vein, see Ohlin, *UCLA JIL & ForAff*, 14 (2009), 83) should not overlook the fact that both types of goals are linked; see, in more detail, De Meester, *Investigation Phase* (2015), pp. 99–103. De Meester's instructive analysis of the goals of international criminal procedure rests on the juxtaposition of the function of national and international criminal procedure, the former being the 'execution of substantive criminal law' vis-à-vis the latter 'surpass[ing] its purely instrumental function' (p. 100). This premise, however, seems questionable, since there have always been voices (other than those supporting De Meester's claim, such as Arzt, in Arnold et al., *Festschrift Eser* (2005), pp. 691–2 with further references) that advocated a meaning and purpose of criminal procedure far beyond being a mere handmaid of substantive criminal law: see e.g. Tulkens, in Delmas-Marty, *Criminal Process and Human Rights* (1995), pp. 6–7; Dripps, *BuffCLR*, 2 (1999), 637.

[554] cf. Neubacher, in Jeßberger and Geneuss, *Punish Perpetrators* (2020), p. 28 ('aims can be transferred … if a few caveats are considered'); conc. Ambos, in Jeßberger and Geneuss, *Punish Perpetrators* (2020), p. 108. In the end, van Sliedregt, *Punish Perpetrators* (2020), pp. 100–2 also arrives at a differentiated view by contrasting the 'domestic analogy of transplant' and the 'domestic analogy proper'.

[555] See also Swart, *JICJ*, 6 (2008), 101; Galbraith, *MichJIL*, 31 (2009–2010), 85 ff.; Olásolo, *International Criminal Law* (2018), p. 7 ('(i) ICL goals related to the maintenance of international peace and security as a collective value protected by international crimes; and (ii) ICL goals that have traditionally been considered by national criminal law as goals of punishment'); Mertins, *Proceedings* (2022), pp. 113, 114 ('[i]mplementation of substantive criminal law and punishment by convicting the guilty and acquitting the innocent' versus '[f]urther goals of criminal procedure').

be taken as specific goals of international criminal justice and vice versa.[556] All the more so, the labels used for the relevant goals—'general', 'special', 'broader', 'official', 'operative'[557]—do not make matters clearer.

### (1) Traditional goals of international criminal justice

As traditional goals of international criminal law and justice, retribution ('just deserts') and prevention are discussed.[558] In classical retribution terms, punishment is to be seen as a fair balance for the wrong of the offence: '*punitur, quia peccatum est*' ('The individual must be punished because he broke the law.'). This is an absolute or even absolutist approach ('absolute theory') since punishment is imposed for the commission of the specific offence alone, even if it fulfils no social or other purpose. While this approach has strong philosophical underpinnings[559] and the idea of retribution finds strong support in the international case law,[560] it cannot conclusively explain the purpose of punishment and the goals of international criminal justice. As I have argued previously,[561] a balance of the suffered wrong, as suggested by an absolute retributivist approach, is plainly unthinkable in case of international mass crimes. In addition, today there exists a widely shared belief among criminal law scholars across different jurisdictions that the imposition of punishment needs more than a mere backward-looking, offence-focused justification since crimes are the result of complex socio-psychological processes and the ensuing criminal sanctions do not only concern the respective perpetrators but society in general.[562] This is all the more true for

[556] Heinze, *Disclosure* (2014), p. 210.

[557] See ibid. with further references.

[558] I draw here on Ambos, *Treatise ICL I* (2021), pp. 115 ff.; furthermore, see Keenan, *MichJIL*, 37 (2016), 448–50.

[559] Think only of Immanuel Kant's famous 'island example' ('*Inselbeispiel*') according to which punishment must be enforced even if the person sentenced remains alone, with no other humans, on an island, i.e. punishment must be preserved at any cost notwithstanding the complete absence of any preventive utility (Kant, *Die Metaphysik der Sitten* (1798), p. 229; English translation in Kant, *The Metaphysics of Morals* (1797), in *The Cambridge Edition of the Works of Immanuel Kant: Practical Philosophy* (1996), pp. 353, 474).

[560] See, more recently, ICTY, *Prosecutor v. Mladić*, TC, Judgment, No. IT-09-92-T, 22 November 2017, para. 5181 ('primary purposes of sentencing are retribution and deterrence'); in the same vein, *Prosecutor v. Karadžić*, TC Judgment, No. IT-95-5/18-T, 24 March 2016, para. 6025; in a recent contempt case the MICT accentuated deterrence, see *Prosecutor v. Nzabonimpa et al.*, Judgment (Single Judge), No. MICT-18-116-T, 25 June 2021, para. 389; KSC, *Prosecutor v. Mustafa*, KSC-CA-2023-02/F00038/RED, AJ, 14 December 2023, para. 451 (deterrence and retribution as 'primary objectives of sentencing', with rehabilitation not playing 'a predominant role'); furthermore, see ECtHR, *Hutchinson v. UK*, No. 57592/08, Grand Chamber Judgment (17 January 2017), para. 19; for earlier case law, see previous edition, p. 46 with note 503. The ICC case law refers to 'retribution' but also to preventive purposes (esp. deterrence), cf. *Prosecutor v. Bemba*, TC, Sentencing Decision, No. ICC-01/05-01/08, 21 June 2016, paras. 10–11 ('retribution and deterrence as the primary objectives'); *Prosecutor v. Al Mahdi*, TC, Judgment, No. ICC-01/12-01/15, 27 September 2016, paras. 66–7; *Prosecutor v. Ntaganda*, TC, Sentencing Judgment, No. ICC-01/04-02/06, 7 November 2019, paras. 9–10; summing up *Prosecutor v. Ongwen*, TC, Sentencing Judgment, No. ICC-02/04-01/15, 6 May 2021, para. 60 ('sentencing regime aimed primarily at retribution for the crimes committed and deterrence (both individual and general); rehabilitation of the sentenced person, albeit to a lesser extent, may also constitute a relevant consideration in this context'). cf. in this respect Burghard and Epik, *ZIS*, 14 (2019), 286, 288–9 (with further examples); in-depth on the penal rationale understanding of jurisprudence by Vasiliev, in Jeßberger and Geneuss, *Punish Perpetrators* (2020), pp. 57 ff.

[561] Ambos, *Treatise ICL I* (2021), pp. 118–19 with reference to Jäger, *KritV*, 76 (1993), 259, 270.

[562] cf. Roxin, in Simester, du Bois-Pedain, and Neumann, *Criminal Theory* (2014), pp. 23 ff. (p. 26: punishment as a 'form of social control'); see also Ashworth and Zedner, in Simester, du Bois-Pedain, and Neumann, *Criminal Theory* (2014), pp. 3, 6–7 (discussing Andrew von Hirsch's approach); Bentham, in von Hirsch, Ashworth, and Roberts, *Sentencing* (2009), pp. 53, 54; Duff, in von Hirsch, Ashworth, and Roberts, *Sentencing* (2009), pp. 126, 128 ff.; Andenaes, *UPaLR*, 114 (1966), 949 ff., 959 ff.

international crimes and thus for the workings of international criminal justice given the fact that the crimes within the subject matter of the international criminal tribunals are additionally complicated by (international) policy implications.

As a consequence, preventive considerations must complement our perspective. Prevention is forward-looking in that it focuses on the social impact of punishment, either in a negative or a positive sense. *Negatively* speaking, prevention is equated to deterrence, that is, it is expected that punishment will prevent offences in the future, that is, it will at least deter the relevant offender: '*punitur, ne peccetur*' ('The individual must be punished so that he and others will no longer break the law.'). In contrast to this special, offender-focused form of deterrence, general deterrence serves to discourage other persons—the society in general—from committing or continuing to commit similar crimes as the punished offender (negative general prevention).[563] Although it seems at least intuitively plausible that the prosecution of international crimes at the international and/or national level (possibly by third states) produces a (general) deterrent effect,[564] general deterrence is difficult to demonstrate and one may be even more sceptical as to its real impact at the international level.[565] In fact, any preventive effect of criminal law, especially deterrence, is of less significance in the macrocriminal context given the unique character and historical context of international offences and offenders;[566] one may even argue that macrocriminals are perfectly socialized since they commit the criminal acts demanded from them by the criminal system they are a part of.[567]

From a *positive* preventive perspective, it is expected or, to put it more realistically, hoped, that the punishment of the offender strengthens society's sense of right and wrong and reaffirms the trust in the law and its validity (positive general prevention).[568] So understood, (international) criminal law and justice fulfil at the same time a didactic, educative function. In the Anglo-American literature, this approach is often discussed under the concept of 'expressivism' focusing on the (possible) communicative function of punishment.[569]

[563] Swart, *JICJ*, 6 (2008), 100; see generally Heinrich, *Strafrecht AT I* (2019), mn. 17; Ambos and Steiner, *JuS*, 41 (2001), 12; Momsen and Rackow, *JA*, 36 (2004), 336–7; Heinze, *Disclosure* (2014), p. 213.

[564] Ambos, *Treatise ICL I* (2021), p. 120, using the example of the *Pinochet* case.

[565] Francis and Francis, in May and Hoskins, *ICL* (2010), pp. 58 ff.; Golash, in May and Hoskins, *ICL* (2010), pp. 201 ff.

[566] See also Ku and Nzelibe, *WashULR*, 84 (2006), 832; see also e.g. Wippman, *Fordham ILJ*, 23 (1999–2000), 474; Galbraith, *MichJIL*, 31 (2009–2010), 94; Olásolo, *International Criminal Law* (2018), p. 8.

[567] See also ICTY, *Prosecutor v. Kunarac et al.*, AC, Judgment, No. IT-96-23 & No. IT-96-23/1 A, 12 June 2002, para. 840; Reuss, *Zivilcourage* (2012), p. 10; Ambos, 'Prosecution of Former Nazi Camp Guards—About Restoring Society's Trust in Law and Participation in a Criminal Enterprise', *EJIL: Talk!*, 20 May 2013, <http://www.ejiltalk.org/prosecution-of-former-nazi-camp-guards-about-restoring-societys-trust-in-law-and-participation-in-a-criminal-enterprise/>.

[568] cf. BVerfGE 45, 187 (256); BVerfGE NJW 2004, 2073 (2075); Ambos and Steiner, *JuS*, 41 (2001), 12; Roxin and Greco, *Strafrecht AT I* (2020), § 3 mn. 26; Momsen and Rackow, *JA*, 36 (2004), 338–9; Heinze, *Disclosure* (2014), p. 214; furthermore, see Neubacher, in Jeßberger and Geneuss, *Punish Perpetrators* (2020), p. 28 ('strengthening faith in the rule of law (a purpose sometimes labelled as "expressionist theory")').

[569] Drumbl, *Atrocity* (2007), pp. 173 ff.; Sloane, *StanfordJIL*, 43 (2007), 44; Fisher, *Accountability* (2012), pp. 51, 56–63, 65; Stahn, *LJIL*, 25 (2012), 279–80; May, *Aggression* (2008), pp. 329 ff.; Sander, *LJIL*, 32 (2019), 853 ('faith in the pedagogical qualities of international criminal courts'); Heinze, in Cullen et al., *Politics* (2020), pp. 32–3; furthermore, see Stahn, *Introduction ICL* (2019), pp. 384–5 and Chouliaras, in Hayashi and Bailliet, *Criminal Tribunals* (2017), pp. 126–8. From a German perspective, see also Günther, in Simester, du Bois-Pedain, and Neumann, *Criminal Theory* (2014), pp. 123 ff. About the communicative function within the (new) retributivist theories, see Pawlik, *FS Rudolphi* (2004), pp. 213, 229, arguing that the difference between retribution and deterrence is not which theory takes into account the society's interests, but *how* these interests are taken into account. According to this approach of a retributivist theory, the purpose of criminal law is to (1) vest the normatively required mutual respect between persons with external stability and (2) reject any lack of respect as irrelevant *in a communicatively unambiguous way* (translation by the author, italics added).

### (2) Special goals of international criminal justice

Beyond the traditional goals of criminal justice, international criminal justice is directed towards certain specific or special goals of its own.[570] Indeed, the criticism has been correctly made that the sheer number of goals to be pursued by international criminal tribunals cannot realistically be achieved even by much better equipped national justice systems.[571] Be that as it may, it is fair to say that there are certain goals that play a more prominent role at the international than at the domestic level.[572] These goals may be labelled 'broader goals'[573] or 'general' goals.[574] We will take a quick look at them now.

#### *(a) Provision of an accurate historical record of events/substantive truth finding*

One of the most prominent special goals of international criminal justice is the creation of an accurate historical record.[575] It was first promoted at the IMT and IMTFE.[576] Despite Soviet and British voices that demanded the execution of the Nazi leaders without further ado, the US representatives opted for the creation of a tribunal to, inter alia, prove 'actual facts, in order to bring home to the German people and to the peoples of the world, the depths of infamy to which the pursuit of total warfare had brought Germany'.[577] As *Karstedt* pointed out, '[t]he prosecutions had revealed a truth that could never be denied again by the majority of the population, and in particular they prepared future elites for shouldering the moral burden'.[578]

570 Some of these special goals may be assigned to the category of 'traditional goals' though, cf. Heinze, *Disclosure* (2014), p. 210. It is therefore somewhat exaggerated to speak of (entirely) 'new goals' (Chouliaras, in Hayashi and Bailliet, *Criminal Tribunals* (2017), p. 124).

571 cf. Damaška, *NCJIL&ComReg*, 36 (2010–2011), 376 ('international criminal tribunals aspire to pursue so many goals that even national law enforcement systems, with their far stronger institutional support and greater enforcement powers, could buckle under the weight of a comparable agenda'). See also Mégret, *UCLA JIL & ForAff*, 14 (2009), 68; furthermore, see Vasiliev, in Jeßberger and Geneuss, *Punish Perpetrators* (2020), p. 79 with regard to the international case law: 'Abstract penal goals provide highly inconclusive guidance for meting out individual punishments. Sentences are neither deduced from, nor informed by, those goals directly.' Yet, this is not detrimental as long as the sentences, which are imposed on the legitimizing foundation of the theory of punishment, are just, fair, and proportionate (Ambos, in Jeßberger and Geneuss, *Punish Perpetrators* (2020), p. 109).

572 See, e.g. Turner, *ChicJIL*, 10 (2009–2010), 689 ('Yet international criminal trials, to a greater degree than domestic trials, serve goals beyond that of determining guilt or innocence according to fair procedures. These goals include providing an authoritative record of the crimes for posterity, giving victims a forum in which to express their grief and outrage, spreading support for human rights, and promoting peace and reconciliation.'); Woods, *VirgJIL*, 52 (2011–2012), 647 ('The international criminal regime differs from domestic criminal regimes in a number of important respects. These include the multiple communities the international regime seeks to serve, the exceptional crimes under its subject matter jurisdiction, and its unique set of goals') (fn. omitted).

573 Turner, *ChicJIL*, 10 (2009–2010), 689; Nicholson, *JICJ*, 17 (2019), 356 ('promote the rule of law and set standards for domestic courts to follow'); Wheeler, *ICLR*, 16 (2016), 528–9 ('goals can be divided into the judicial and the political').

574 See Heinze, *Disclosure* (2014), p. 210 with further references.

575 The Secretary-General has observed that to 'establish ... a record of past events' is an objective of international criminal justice, see Report of the Secretary-General on the Rule of Law and Transitional Justice in Conflict and Post-Conflict Societies, J 38, UN Doc. S/2004/616 (23 August 2004); SCSL, *Prosecutor v. Brima et al.*, TC, Decision on Confidential Motion to Call Evidence in Rebuttal, No. SCSL-04-16-T, 14 November 2006, para. 31; *Prosecutor v. Ntagerura et al.*, TC, Decision on the Prosecutor's Motion for Leave to Call Evidence in Rebuttal Pursuant to Rules 54, 73, and 85 (A)(iii) of the Rules of Procedure and Evidence, No. ICTR-99-46-T, 21 May 2003, para. 34. See Tochilovsky, *Jurisprudence* (2014), p. 644; also Kochhar and Hieramente, *LJIL*, 29 (2016), 231–3.

576 See Section B.(1)(a) and (b) in this chapter.

577 Lawrence, in Mettraux, *Nuremberg Trial* (2008), p. 292.

578 Karstedt, in Blumenthal and McCormack, *Legacy of Nuremberg* (2008), p. 33.

The goal of historical truth-seeking is related to the goal of substantive truth finding.[579] As former ICTY and ICC Judge Jorda pointed out,

> [e]stablishing the truth behind events and preventing all forms of revisionism have always been the underlying objectives of all international criminal justice systems, and in particular the system practised in The Hague. Much has been accomplished on that score. The atrocities committed and the plans that were their inspiration are no longer merely the subject of media accounts or of the descriptions of commissions of experts, which are always vulnerable to polemic. These events have entered into the realm of incontrovertible judicial evidence.[580]

While truth-seeking is also a goal in domestic criminal proceedings, it is limited there to the determination of the facts of the prosecution case with a view to establish the guilt or innocence of the accused.[581] A macrocriminal context or design, linked to an armed or other conflict, which is so characteristic for international criminal proceedings, is conspicuously absent in ordinary domestic proceedings. While there the crime scene is normally easy to reconstruct and the victims are clearly identified, on an international level 'there are inevitably hot disputes about the order of magnitude of the atrocities involved, their causes, and the links between the atrocities and the government or the rebel forces'.[582]

*(b) Restoration of international peace and security*

According to the preamble of the ICC Statute, the commission of international crimes threatens the 'peace, security and well-being of the world'.[583] As a consequence, a violation of these interests affects the 'international community as a whole'[584] and is aimed against mankind as such.[585] Thus, the Statute implies that the Court's contribution to reducing the commission of grave crimes is designed to advance the cause of international peace and security. Thereby a link between the Court and the Security Council's Chapter VII authority[586] is established, turning the maintenance of 'international peace and security' into one of the goals of the ICC as the main proponent of international criminal justice. In this vein, the maintenance and restoration of international peace and security was identified by the Security

[579] Tuinstra, *Defence Counsel in ICL* (2009), p. 123; Ohlin, *UCLA JIL & ForAff*, 14 (2009), 96 ff.; Taylor, *Nuremberg Trials* (1992), p. 54 ('establish incredible events by credible evidence'), also Heinze, *Disclosure* (2014), p. 218.

[580] Statement of Judge Claude Jorda, Statement, UN SCOR, 55th Sess., 4161st mtg, at 3, UN Doc. S/PV.4161 (20 June 2000); in this regard, also see Wheeler, *Fairness* (2023), p. 108 ('it guards against historical revisionism by producing a narrative that is made up of incontrovertible, judicially determined evidence').

[581] Galbraith, *MichJIL*, 31 (2009–2010), 89.

[582] Ibid.

[583] ICCS, Preamble, para. 3.

[584] Preamble, paras. 4 and 9; also Art. 5, para. 1.

[585] See thereon Werle and Jessberger, *Principles ICL* (2020), mn. 106 ff.; Werle, in Grundmann et al., *FS Humboldt* (2009), p. 1220; Triffterer, *ZStW*, 114 (2002), 342; Neubacher, *Grundlagen* (2005), pp. 100 ff.; Ambos, in Neubacher and Klein, *Recht* (2006), pp. 111 ff.; Cryer, *Prosecuting* (2005), p. 4; emphasizing this collective element, Lagodny, *ZStW*, 113 (2001), 803 and Gil Gil, *ZStW*, 112 (2000), 382; in particular on the ICC Preamble, see Triffterer, Bergsmo, and Ambos, in Ambos, *Commentary* (2022), mn. 9.

[586] Chapter VII of the UN Charter permits the UNSC to 'determine the existence of any threat to the peace, breach of the peace, or act of aggression' and take military and non-military action to 'restore international peace and security'. In more detail in our context, see Shany, *Assessing the Effectiveness* (2014), p. 230; Broomhall, *International Justice* (2003), pp. 45–6.

Council as a major purpose of the ICTY and ICTR.[587] The ICTY itself noted that it would work as 'a tool for promoting reconciliation and restoring true peace'.[588] This purpose was heavily bound up with the 'Nuremberg legacy'.[589] Indeed, 'the Allies' political and social agenda behind the Nuremberg Trial and its strategy became the major lesson to be learned by the I[nternational]C[riminal]T[ribunal]s'.[590]

Thus, the existence of international criminal justice is based on the premise that (international) justice is a prerequisite of (international) peace. Indeed, the ICC Prosecutor noted that 'the ICC was created on the premise that justice is an essential component of a stable peace'.[591] In substantive terms, this means that ICL is devoted to preventing harm, pursuant to an *international harm principle*.[592] Beyond that, it is also argued that international criminal tribunals are established for the achievement of transitional justice goals as part of a broader project of stabilization and transformation[593] and thus facilitate societal reconciliation and the creation of the preconditions for a durable peace.[594] In this regard, they starkly differ from ordinary domestic criminal courts. To emphasize this contrast it has been said that domestic criminal law 'simply helps preserve a properly functioning society' while international criminal law aspires to help create one'.[595]

Of course, these are highflying goals which entail the risk of creating over-expectations against the background of which international criminal justice and especially the ICC are, arguably, doomed to failure. It is not the place here to elaborate on this further; it suffices to refer to *Damaška*'s appropriate diagnosis of the growing disparity between declaration and achievement in international criminal justice.[596] In any case, in the course of this book, we will encounter the goal of restoring peace and security in many procedural elements, such as the discretion of the Prosecutor when and whom to charge.[597]

### (c) *Satisfaction of victims—Victim participation*

A third goal within the category of special goals is the satisfaction of the victims of international crimes.[598] This goal is interrelated with the role of victims as legal participants,[599]

[587] See also Bagaric and Morss, *ICLR*, 6 (2006), 242 ff.; Havemann, in Haveman and Olusanya, *Sentencing* (2006), p. 154; Ayat, *ICLR*, 7 (2007), 394 ff.; Henham, *ICLR*, 7 (2007), 449 ff.; Cornacchia, *Pena* (2009), pp. 136 ff.; Safferling, *Internationales Strafrecht* (2011), p. 69 referring to the UN Charter; Futamura, *Tokyo Trial* (2008), pp. 20 ff.

[588] General Assembly, Security Council, 49th Session, A/49/342, S/1994/1007, Annual Report of the International Tribunal for the Prosecution of Persons Responsible for Serious Violations of International Humanitarian Law Committed in the Territory of the former Yugoslavia since 1991 (29 August 1994), para. 16.

[589] Bushnell, *AustYBIL*, 28 (2009), 57, 64 ff.; Futamura, *Tokyo Trial* (2008), pp. 31 ff.

[590] Futamura, *Tokyo Trial* (2008), p. 46.

[591] ICC-OTP, *Interests of Justice* (2007), p. 8.

[592] cf. May, *Aggression* (2008), pp. 80–95; see previously Ambos, *Treatise ICL I* (2021), pp. 106 ff., 112 ff.

[593] Posner and Vermeule, *HarvLR*, 117 (2004), 766–7; Galbraith, *MichJIL*, 31 (2009–2010), 92; de Hoon, *ICLR*, 17 (2017), 596–7.

[594] See e.g. Cassese, *MLR*, 61 (1998), 6; Cryer, in Cryer et al., *ICL* (2019), p. 41.

[595] Galbraith, *MichJIL*, 31 (2009–2010), 92.

[596] Damaška, *ChicKentLR*, 83 (2008), 329 ff., 365.

[597] Danner, *AJIL*, 97 (2003), 520–1; Galbraith, *MichJIL*, 31 (2009–2010), 92–3. *Greenawalt* has observed that had the ICTY made its prosecutorial decisions strictly on the basis of the gravity of the crimes, 'it is conceivable that it would have expended its limited resources prosecuting Serb-perpetrated offenses such as the genocide at Srebrenica and other atrocities, without ever reaching Croat and Muslim crimes that, while often hideously grim, were not as large-scale or, at least in the apparent case of the Bosnian Government, did not involve the same degree of high-level sponsorship and planning.' See Greenawalt, *NYUJIL&Pol'y*, 39 (2007), 648.

[598] Schrag, *JICJ*, 2 (2004), 428; Swart, *JICJ*, 6 (2008), 100; Keenan, *MichJIL*, 37 (2016), 466 ff.; Haslam and Edmunds, *JICJ*, 15 (2017), 933 ('key part of international criminal law's claim to authority and legitimacy'); with a view to compensation commissions and tort law, see Wiessner and Willard, *AJIL*, 93 (1999), 316, 330.

[599] Koller, *NYUJIL&Pol'y*, 40 (2007–2008), 1029; Ohlin, 'Goals', in Sluiter et al., *International Criminal Procedure* (2013), pp. 64 ff.

one of the most controversial aspects of international criminal procedure,[600] to be dealt with in more detail in Chapter II in this volume.[601] We can anticipate here that the ICC Statute contains victims' provisions in a so far unprecedent manner, that is, on victim protection (Articles 68 (1), 57 (3)(c),(e), 64 (2)),[602] victim reparations (Article 75),[603] and victim participation (Article 68 (3)).[604] In addition, an 'Office of Public Counsel for Victims' (OPCV)[605] was created and the victim can choose a legal representative (Rule 90(1)).[606]

These broad participation rights of victims are generally justified by their special interest, as victims are the most and directly affected of international crimes, for justice to be done.[607] In this way, the victims' suffering shall be explicitly recognized given that public acknowledgement of the violations is crucial for victims.[608] This constitutes in itself a kind of reparation in the form of satisfaction, covering a 'wide and varied range of non-monetary measures that may contribute to the broader and longer-term restorative aims of reparation'.[609]

### (3) The goals in context

As we have just seen, international criminal justice pursues multiple goals which in turn refer back to the purposes of ICL.[610] As to the traditional goals of criminal justice it has already

[600] See Friman, in Sluiter and Vasiliev, *International Criminal Procedure* (2009), pp. 205–6; Zappalà, *Human Rights* (2005), p. 222; Stahn, *ZaöRV*, 77 (2017), 398 ('has caused certain problems'); Coleman, *ICLR*, 20 (2020), 379 ff. (on '[C]onflicts between Victim's Rights to Participate and the Presumption of Innocence').

[601] See Chapter II, E. in this volume.

[602] Generally Tochilovsky, *Jurisprudence* (2014), pp. 341 ff.; on the ICC-System, see ICC, *Prosecutor v. Katanga and Ngudjolo Chui*, PTC, Decision on Evidentiary Scope of the Confirmation Hearing, Preventive Relocation and Disclosure under Art. 67(2) of the Statute and Rule 77 of the Rules, No. ICC-01/04-01/07-428-Corr, 18 April 2008, paras. 11 ff.; Safferling, *ZStW*, 122 (2010), 105–6; Bock, *Opfer* (2010), pp. 430 ff. See also Chapter II, E.(5) in this volume.

[603] See generally Dwertmann, *Reparation System* (2010) with further references; see also Bock, *ZStW*, 119 (2007), 678–9; Bock, *Opfer* (2010), pp. 555 ff.; Henzelin, Heiskanen, and Mettraux, *CLF*, 17 (2006), 321 ff.; Zahar and Sluiter, *ICL* (2008), pp. 76 ff.; Zegveld, in Stahn and van den Herik, *Future Perspectives* (2010), pp. 611 ff.; Mundis, *LJIL*, 14 (2001), 861; Greco, *ICLR*, 7 (2007), 531 ff., 545–6; Heikkilä, *International Criminal Tribunals* (2004), pp. 166 ff., 180 ff.; Ambach, in Sieber et al. *Alternative Systems* (2018), pp. 110 ff.; Safferling and Petrossian, *Victims* (2021), pp. 267 ff.; Birkett, *LJIL*, 32 (2019), 592–3. See Chapter II, E.(6) in this volume.

[604] Generally Heikkilä, *International Criminal Tribunals* (2004), pp. 73 ff., 140 ff., 164–5; Bock, *ZStW*, 119 (2007), 670 ff.; Bock, *Opfer* (2010), pp. 210 ff., 371 ff., 440 ff.; Safferling, *ZStW*, 122 (2010), 101 ff., Stahn, Olásolo, and Gibson, *JICJ*, 4 (2006), 225 ff.; Tochilovsky, *Jurisprudence* (2014), pp. 759 ff.; Zahar and Sluiter, *ICL* (2008), pp. 73 ff.; Wheeler, *ICLR*, 16 (2016), 526 ('rights previously unknown in international criminal law'); Safferling and Petrossian, *Victims* (2021), pp. 143–51, 188 ff. See Chapter II, E.(4) in this volume.

[605] About its functions and role, see Chapter II, E.(3) in this volume. See also PTC, *Situation in Uganda*, No. ICC-02/04-101, Decision on Victims' Application for Participation a/0010/06, a/0064/06 to a 0070/06, a/0081/06 to a/0104/06 and a/0111/06 to a/0127/06, paras. 4, 164 (10 August 2007); ICC, *Prosecutor v. Kony et al.*, PTC, Decision on the OPCV's Observations on Victim's Applications on the Prosecution's Objections Thereto, No. ICC-02/04-01/05-243, 17 April 2007; *Lubanga*, TC, Decision on the Role of the Office of Public Counsel for Victims and its Request for Access to Documents, No. ICC-01/04-01/06-1211, 6 March 2008. See also Massidda and Pellet, in Stahn and Sluiter, *Practice* (2009), pp. 691 ff., 706; Bock, *Opfer* (2010), pp. 501 ff.

[606] *Prosecutor v. Kony et al.*, PTC, Decision on Legal Representation, Appointment of Counsel for the Defence, Protective Measures and Time-Limit for Submission of Observations on Applications of Participation etc., No. ICC-02/04-01/05-134, 2 February 2007, para. 7.

[607] Pena, *ILSAJICL*, 16 (2009–2010), 500; but see also, on the victims' contribution to truth, Wheeler, *ICLR*, 16 (2016), 528 (referring to the victims' representative closing statement in *Prosecutor v. Lubanga*, No. ICC-01/04-01/06, Office of Public Counsel for Victim Closing Statement (25 August 2011): 'The main concern, the essential concern of the victims participating in this trial, over and beyond the conviction of the accused, is therefore to contribute to the establishment of the truth').

[608] Redress, 'Implementing Victim's Rights (March 2006)', p. 38, <http://www.redress.org/downloads/publications/Reparation%20Principles.pdf>.

[609] Ibid., p. 38; but also see Wheeler, *Fairness* (2023), p. 130 ('cathartic').

[610] Galbraith, *MichJIL*, 31 (2009–2010), 93; De Meester, *Investigation Phase* (2015), pp. 99–102.

been argued above[611] that a transfer to the international level is not possible without further ado. Indeed, the traditional purposes of punishment (retribution and prevention) face specific problems when applied in the international criminal justice context. It is therefore quite plausible to argue that international criminal justice must abandon any reliance on these traditional goals.[612]

Of course, it is not an easy task to replace the traditional by special goals of international criminal justice. Also, it is hardly possible to meet all the alleged goals or, at least, to meet them simultaneously and completely. Moreover, a closer look reveals that there are tensions between these goals[613] and each goal entails ambitious, indeed sometimes overly ambitious, expectations.

Thus, it is questionable whether international criminal tribunals have the expertise to engage in historical fact-finding.[614] History involves different modes of reasoning[615] and does not use 'the same cognitive lenses' as the criminal justice process.[616] As Richard A. Wilson puts it: While historical analysis 'proceeds through academic discussion and at least in principle, through cooperation between scholars', 'law's epistemology is positivist and realist and it requires falsifiable and verifiable evidence, and typically relies upon a scientific, forensic approach to evidence.'[617] Also, macrocriminal events operate in a different timeframe than ordinary criminal events. Creating a record of these events may take a few months,[618] several years,[619] or even decades and centuries;[620] that is, we are talking of historical, not just judicial periods. In sum, creating a historical record ought rightly to be reserved for historians alone, if only to avoid the overloading of the criminal justice process.[621]

[611] Section C.(1) in this chapter.

[612] See e.g. Drumbl, *Atrocity* (2007), pp. 194–205; see also Blumenson, *ColJTransnat'lL*, 44 (2005–2006), 871–2 ('Notwithstanding the achievements and great potential of the ICC and the other international criminal tribunals, one cannot assume that uniform reliance on prosecution and punishment will always best further the cause of human rights.'). Some go further to argue that international criminal justice should be entirely abandoned in favour of other mechanisms that better promote the historical record and transitional justice aims. See e.g. Rabkin, *CornILJ*, 38 (2005), 775–7.

[613] Damaška, *ChicKentLR*, 83 (2008), 331; De Meester, *Investigation Phase* (2015), pp. 102–3; but also see Wheeler, *Fairness* (2023), p. 4 ('Identifying the goals of international criminal trial is only the first step').

[614] Galbraith, *MichJIL*, 31 (2009–2010), 95.

[615] Wilson, *HRQ*, 27 (2005), 912 ff.; Galbraith, *MichJIL*, 31 (2009–2010), 95.

[616] Damaška, *NCJIL&ComReg*, 36 (2010–2011), 372; Heinze, *Disclosure* (2014), p. 222 with further references.

[617] Wilson, *HRQ*, 27 (2005), 912–13 ('History, on the other hand, is more pluralistic, open, and interpretative in both its methods and conclusions. Courts ultimately must embrace one entire account to the exclusion of all others, whereas historians often accept aspects of competing accounts. Historians live more comfortably with difference of opinion, and they often recognize that their evidence and conclusions are not always falsifiable or verifiable. Law is concerned with context only insofar as it impinges on the guilt or innocence of one individual. In trials, context is heavily circumscribed and is confined to specific persons and their related criminal acts, whereas historians generally look for cultural context, social patterns, and shared public practices and beliefs. Historians often locate individual agency within a wider context, thus diffusing guilt throughout the social fabric.').

[618] As was the case with the UN-appointed Commission of Inquiry on Darfur; see Report of the International Commission of Inquiry on Darfur to the United Nations Secretary-General, 25 January 2005, p. 2 ('In October 2004, the Secretary General ... requested that they report back on their findings within three months.').

[619] See e.g. the three-year South Africa Truth and Reconciliation Commission (TRC) and the four-year Sierra Leone Truth Commission; see United States Institute of Peace, *Truth Commission—Sierra Leone*, <http://www.usip.org/publications/truth-commission-sierra-leone>; *Truth Commission—South Africa*, <http://www.usip.org/publications/truth-commission-south-africa>.

[620] Galbraith, *MichJIL*, 31 (2009–2010), 102–3.

[621] See Robertson, *The Independent*, 28 May 2011 ('[T]here is a problem with prosecutors and judges who think they have a duty to write history rather than to adjudicate specific allegations. They seriously overload their indictments—Milosevic, for example, was charged with responsibility for three separate wars spanning 10 years, when he could have been convicted simply and expeditiously for the ethnic cleansing of Kosovo.'), <http://www.independent.co.uk/voices/commentators/geoffrey-robertson-mistakes-the-mladic-trial-needs-to-avoid-2290229.html>; see also De Meester, *Investigation Phase* (2015), p. 102.

Nevertheless, despite these differences, history and law still have some things, in terms of methods and objectives, in common. Take for example the weighing of information and assessing its facticity, utilizing eyewitness testimony, searching for corroborating evidence, and demonstrating 'sensitivity to the context of individual actions and the individual's social environment'.[622] Furthermore, trial participants usually make their claims in two ways: the narrative mode, where they 'simply tell their stories, performing speech acts of telling, asserting and claiming' and the questioning mode, where the adversary and/or the judge question the witness.[623] It is especially the former mode that proves similarities between methods of history and methods of law, since both judges and historians express facts in a chronological and narrative form.[624] *Dworkin* underlines this argument by comparing decision-making to literature, where judges 'are authors as well as critics'. To that end, he invents an 'artificial genre of literature' that he calls 'chain novel': 'In this enterprise a group of novelists writes a novel seriatim; each novelist in the chain interprets the chapters he has been given in order to write a new chapter, which is then added to what the next novelist receives, and so on.'[625] Thus, there seems to be a similarity between historical and legal methods in so far as 'the parties arrange facts sequentially in order to construct a plausible narrative, and in so doing assert a causality between acts, facts, and events'.[626]

As to apparent tensions, the tension between peace and justice, relevant for the goal of restoring international peace and security, is perhaps the most obvious one. Indeed, the role of (criminal) justice is one of the most controversial questions within the framework of peace negotiations of transitional justice processes. Does an emphasis on justice, including criminal prosecutions, jeopardize the potential success of such negotiations or is it rather a prerequisite for the achievement of a sustainable peace?[627] Some have claimed, for instance, that the ICC's arrest warrants for Ugandan rebel leaders 'are proving a stumbling block in peace negotiations';[628] that international prosecution will 'simply cause parties to conflicts to fight to the last';[629] that amnesties are granted for alleged perpetrators of international crimes in exchange for their cooperation with 'alternative justice' mechanisms that do not entail individual criminal responsibility and punishment (e.g. truth and reconciliation commissions);[630] or, last but not least, that a reduced sentence for a perpetrator's peace-making effort demonstrates the 'unpredictability' of the goal of restoring peace and security.[631] Others

[622] Wilson, *HRQ*, 27 (2005), 913.

[623] Danet, *Law&Soc'yR*, 14 (1979–1980), 514. See also Ewick and Silbey, *Law&Soc'yR*, 29 (1995), 197 ff.

[624] Wilson, *HRQ*, 27 (2005), 918.

[625] Dworkin, *Law's Empire* (1986), p. 229.

[626] Wilson, *HRQ*, 27 (2005), 918.

[627] cf. Damaška, *ChicKentLR*, 83 (2008), 331–2; Balasco, *FletcherJHS*, 28 (2013), 52; Shany, *Assessing the Effectiveness* (2014), p. 230; Olásolo, *International Criminal Law* (2018), p. 11 ('enforcement of ICL on those bearing the greatest responsibility for international crimes would only be possible if they are no longer in power').

[628] See e.g. Minow, *Between Vengeance and Forgiveness* (1998), p. 128; Galbraith, *MichJIL*, 31 (2009–2010), 95.

[629] Anonymous, *HRQ*, 18 (1996), 251 ('What this makes perfectly clear is that there were only two available courses of international action: negotiate a peace or let the parties fight it out.'); Cryer, in Cryer et al., *ICL* (2019), p. 42.

[630] Shany, *Assessing the Effectiveness* (2014), p. 231.

[631] Drumbl, *Atrocity* (2007), p. 62 ('The influence of peace and reconciliation as goals of punishing extraordinary international criminals is unpredictable, perhaps because it is such an ambitious goal. I say unpredictable insofar as another high-profile plea-bargained defendant had received operational discount in the quantum of sentence for her post hoc peace-making efforts.').

regard peace, or at least a sustainable peace, without justice as an illusion. In that regard, Justice *Goldstone* speaks for many when he states:

> If you have peace without justice in countries where millions of people have suffered, where hundreds of thousands of people have been murdered and tens of thousands of women have been raped, do you really expect that by brushing the atrocities committed under the carpet and allowing collective guilt to take hold one will achieve lasting peace? I do not believe so.[632]

In a similar vein, *Akhavan* claims that 'punishing the perpetrators of ethnic cleansing is the only realistic option for achieving peace'.[633] From this perspective then peace and justice are not mutually exclusive but the realization of justice is the prerequisite of the former[634] and, in addition, satisfies legitimate victims demands as expressed in the respective other special goal of satisfaction to victims.[635] The fact that 'reparative justice' may procedurally depend on 'retributive justice' may be seen as a consequence of these correlations.[636]

Similar tensions exist between the goal to establish a historical record and the goal to punish the perpetrators of international crimes. Any concession to truth-seeking by mechanisms of negotiations which make the establishment of the facts part of a bargaining process, especially the notorious charge bargaining,[637] not only hinder the establishment of the procedural truth but are also alien to the idea of an accurate historical record.[638] Of course, a confession product of such a bargaining process ('guilty plea') may contribute to the truth[639] but it always carries the risk of being untrue and often only refers to a part of the events.[640]

[632] Goldstone, *Prosecuting* (1996), p. 19; in the same vein, see Stewart, in Sieber et al., *Alternative Systems* (2018), p. 138.

[633] Akhavan, *HRQ*, 20 (1998), 743. About the view on the peace and justice debate through the lenses of realism and liberalism (or idealism), see Futamura, *Tokyo Trial* (2008), p. 23.

[634] This is also emphasized in para. 3 of the Preamble of the ICCS, see Bergsmo, Triffterer, and Ambos, in Ambos, *Commentary* (2022), mn. 11; Goldstone, *NYUJIL&Pol'y*, 28 (1996), 486 ff.; Williams and Scharf, *Peace with Justice?* (2002), pp. 235 ff.

[635] See also Rothe, Meernik, and Ingadóttir, *Realities* (2013), pp. 302–3, arguing that contrary to the goal of retribution, the ICC's goal to maintain peace and security 'looks at the impact of the crime far more comprehensively, and engages with the consequences for victims as well as the responsibility of perpetrators'.

[636] cf. Stewart, in Sieber et al., *Alternative Systems* (2018), pp. 132–3 (referring to the ICC's reparation proceedings after conviction).

[637] A charge bargain is '[a] plea bargain whereby a Prosecutor agrees to drop some of the counts or reduce the charge to a less serious offense in exchange for a plea of either guilty or no contest from the defendant': Garner, *Dictionary* (2019), p. 1394. See also *Hoskins v. Maricle*, 150 S.W.3d 1 (26 August 2004), at 21: 'A "charge bargain," which dismisses or amends one or more charges in exchange for a guilty plea to the reduced charges, or a "hybrid bargain," which is a charge bargain with an additional agreement with respect to sentencing, can be approved or rejected in discretion of trial court, but trial court must articulate prosecutor's reasons for forming bargain and court's reasons for rejecting it.' For more detailed observations on charge bargaining, see Boss and Angarella, *CrimJust*, 21 (2006), 22 ff.; Davis, *Arbitrary Justice* (2007), pp. 43 ff. We will return to this in Chapter IV, B.(8) in this volume.

[638] See also Damaška, *NCJIL&ComReg*, 36 (2010–2011), 372; ICTY, *Prosecutor v. Momir Nikolić*, TC, Sentencing Judgment, No. IT-02-60/1-S, 2 December 2003, para. 63 ('In cases where factual allegations are withdrawn, the public record established by that case might be incomplete or at least open to question, as the public will not know whether the allegations were withdrawn because of insufficient evidence or because they were simply a "bargaining chip" in the negotiation process.'); Petrig, *ChiKentJIl&Comp*, 8 (2008), 4, 15.

[639] In this sense apparently Ohlin, in Sluiter et al., *International Criminal Procedure* (2013), p. 62, arguing that 'a plea-bargaining defendant may offer evidence to a tribunal that would otherwise remain unavailable, and in so doing improve the historical record'.

[640] This is not to say that an adversarial procedure characterized by a rule-guided discursive, dialogical method is, as a matter of principle, less suitable for contributing to an (objective) truth; cf. Mertins, *Proceedings* (2022), pp. 118–19.

On the other hand, the aim of providing an accurate historical record may conflict with due process rights in that it may entail the imposition of pressure on the defendant to speak (to) the truth. Also, it may cause Prosecutors and judges to consider more evidence than necessary for the conviction of the defendant.[641]

In contrast to criminal justice actors, historians are not restricted by any efficiency demands, at least not the ones typical for a judicial process; instead, they prioritize 'vast reams of quantitative or qualitative data in order to establish context and background, even if such an effort might take scholars years or decades to accomplish'.[642] Fully aware of the difference between a lawyer's and historian's approach, *Hannah Arendt*, herself a philosopher and political scientist, criticized the Prosecutor of the Eichmann trial because of his 'attempt to drag out these hearings forever' by exploring historical questions that seemed to have no relevance for the defendant's guilt or innocence.[643] In her view a criminal trial has a limited criminal justice purpose, namely 'to render justice, and nothing else; even the noblest of ulterior purposes [the creation of a historical record] ... can only detract from the law's main business: to weigh the charges brought against the accused, to render judgment, and to mete out due punishment'.[644] Thus, from the admittedly narrow criminal justice perspective, administering justice must not be confused with the project of writing adequate historical accounts of mass atrocities. Indeed, as rightly observed by May and Wierda, any result achieved in terms of creating a historical record can only be a 'by-product of the trials where the emphasis must necessarily be in determining whether the prosecution has established guilt beyond reasonable doubt'.[645]

There is another reason not to overburden a criminal trial with the goal of historical truth-seeking, that is, the impact that this may have on the compatriots of the defendant and the achievement of a stable peace in the territorial State of the crimes. Thus, Eric A. Posner argues that the Nuremberg trials made the German people 'feel that they were themselves on trial', since the trials 'made clear the vast participation of ordinary citizens in the Nazi extermination machine, even though "[t]hat had never been [chief prosecutor] Jackson's intention. He, like many others, had hoped to prune out Nazism and induce healthy growth in remaining Germany." '[646] Another example is, arguably, the ICTR's dealing with the events that triggered the genocide in Rwanda, that is, the shooting down of the plane carrying Rwanda's president in 1994, and the fear that the revelation of the persons responsible for the attack 'might unsettle Rwanda still further and impede its post conflict transition'.[647] Of course, these and other examples certainly give rise to controversy. After all, if a criminal trial establishes—as a side-effect, as argued above—a part of the historical truth, for example with regard to the perpetrators' peoples' heavy involvement in the crimes, the judges are not

[641] Galbraith, *MichJIL*, 31 (2009–2010), 90.

[642] Ohlin, 'Goals', in Sluiter et al., *International Criminal Procedure* (2013), p. 62.

[643] Arendt, *Eichmann in Jerusalem* (2006), pp. 4–5, 9.

[644] Ibid., p. 253.

[645] May and Wierda, in May et al., *Essays on ICTY Procedure and Evidence* (2001), p. 253; in the same vein, Holtermann, in Hayashi and Bailliet, *Criminal Tribunals* (2017), pp. 217–18 ('the call of Arendt and others is rather a call for moderation of the scope of epistemic ambition of the ICTs'). Challenging this narrow view, Wilson, *HRQ*, 27 (2005), 909, 922 ('Since the state is distant [in international criminal proceedings] and therefore less able to influence or even interfere in trials, one might expect the historical perspectives of international tribunals to differ from the patchy and impoverished documentary record of national trials.'). About the relationship between international criminal tribunals and truth commissions, see Roche, *BJCrim*, 45 (2005), 565 ff.

[646] Posner, *DukeLJ*, 55 (2005–2006), 140 (fn. omitted).

[647] Galbraith, *MichJIL*, 31 (2009–2010), 96.

the cause but only the messenger of the bad news. Ultimately, the society concerned must accept and cope with this truth.

Of course, there are many more instances of conflicting goals but the analysis so far should have shown that the goals of international criminal justice should not be over-emphasized and, clearly, the special goals should certainly not be overstated but rather downplayed. Modesty, not overstatement and unrealistic aspirations, is the wise choice of the day, not least to avoid a further enlargement of the deep rifts between declaration and achievement.[648] On the other hand, we should focus on the 'socio-pedagogical' mission of international criminal justice as 'one of strengthening the public sense of accountability for human rights violations',[649] that is, positive general prevention in the sense explained above.[650]

In any case, the comparison of the historical features of international criminal procedure and the alleged goals of international criminal justice demonstrates their close relationship dating back to the IMT and IMTFE trials. The following chapters will confirm the influence of the historic trials on modern international criminal procedure. Also, they will build on the conceptual clarifications made at the beginning of this chapter and sometimes revert to the goals discussed here.

## D. Rights of the Accused

### (1) Overview

Defendants in international criminal proceedings enjoy the rights generally recognized in universal (cf. Article 14 ICCPR) and regional human rights instruments (Article 6 ECHR and APs, Articles 47, 48 EU Charter,[651] and Articles 8 ACHR and 7 (1) ACHPR[652]).[653] These

648 Damaška, *ChicKentLR*, 83 (2008), 364–5.

649 Ibid., 340, 346 ff.

650 cf. Section C.(1) in this chapter.

651 The Charter of Fundamental Rights of the European Union ('EU Charter') basically draws on the ECHR and will therefore here only be referred to subsidiarily. It applies to the EU Member States as part of its primary law pursuant to the (reformed) EU Treaty, Art. 6 (1). Its interpretation lies within the competence of the Court of Justice of the European Union (CJEU), cf. Ambos, *EurCrL* (2018), pp. 74 and 142 ff. On the importance of the ECtHR's jurisprudence for the ICC, Croquet, *HRLR*, 11 (2011), 91 ff., affirming, somewhat exaggeratedly, a 'deferential attitude' of the ICC (94, 122 ff.).

652 The ACHPR of 1981 contains only a limited number of procedural rights and lacks an effective enforcement mechanism (despite the existence of the African Commission on Human and Peoples' Rights, set up in 1987, and a corresponding court which since July 2004 is part of the African Court of Justice).

653 cf. Keitner, *UCLA JIL & ForAff*, 6 (2001/2002), 226 ('highest standards'); Zappalà, in Cassese, Chiavario, and De Francesco, *Problemi* (2005), pp. 399 ff.; Beresford, in Dolgopol and Gardam, *Challenges of Conflict* (2005), pp. 367 ff.; Tochilovsky, *Jurisprudence* (2014), pp. 437 ff.; Gradoni, in Sluiter et al., *International Criminal Procedure* (2013), pp. 74 ff.; Safferling, *Criminal Procedure* (2012), pp. 58 ff.; Demko, *Verteidigung* (2014), pp. 202 ff.; for an overview of the individual rights, see Calvo-Goller, *Trial Proceedings* (2006), pp. 226 ff.; Friman, in Cryer et al., *ICL* (2019), pp. 415 ff.; Zahar and Sluiter, *ICL* (2008), pp. 63, 292 ff.; von Braun, *Internationalisierte Strafgerichte* (2008), pp. 68 ff., 79 ff.; Weissbrodt and Zinsmaster, in Brown, *Handbook ICL* (2011), pp. 265 ff., 275 ff.; Gless, *Internationales Strafrecht* (2021), mn. 1006; for a crit. view, see Kirsch, *AnwBl*, 16 (2011), 166; with regard to the right to be tried by an independent and impartial tribunal, the *nulla poena sine lege* principle, as well as the right of appeal, see Gradoni, *LJIL*, 19 (2006), 859 ff.; on Art. 20 ICTRS, see Schomburg and Nemitz, in Decaux, Dieng, and Sow, *Human Rights* (2007), pp. 93 ff.; on compensation for accused persons before the Ad hoc Tribunals, cf. Acquaviva, *LJIL*, 20 (2007), 621 ff.; on the obligation to comply with international human rights law in international criminal proceedings, see Gradoni, in Sluiter et al., *International Criminal Procedure* (2013), pp. 80 ff.

rights, which will be analysed in more detail below,[654] can be summarized—with the respective references to the relevant provisions of the ICC, ICTY, ICTR, SCSL, and RSCSL Statutes as well as the KSC Law in brackets—as follows:

a) Presumption of innocence (Article 66 (1) ICCS, Article 21 (3) ICTYS, Article 20 (3) ICTRS, Article 17 (3) SCSLS/RSCSL Statute; Article 21 (3) KSC Law);[655]
b) Prosecutorial onus to prove the guilt of the accused (Article 66 (2) ICCS) and judicial conviction of the accused's guilt beyond reasonable doubt (Article 66 (3) ICC Statute, Rule 87 (A) RPE ICTY/ICTR/SCSL; Article 21 (3) KSC Law);[656]
c) Fair and public hearing in full equality (Article 67 (1) ICCS, Article 21 (2) ICTYS, Article 20 (2) ICTRS, Article 17 (2) SCSLS/RSCSL Statute; Article 21 (2) KSC Law);[657]
d) To be informed promptly and in detail of the nature, cause, and content of the charges in a language which the accused fully understands and speaks (Articles 55 (1)(c), 67 (1)(a) ICCS, Article 21 (4)(a) ICTYS, Article 20 (4)(a) ICTRS, Article 17 (4)(a) SCSLS/RSCSL Statute; Article 21 (4)(a), 38 (3)(a) KSC Law);[658]
e) Adequate time and facilities for the preparation of the defence and communication with counsel of the accused's choosing (Articles 55 (2)(c), 67 (1)(b), (d) ICCS, Articles 18 (3), 21 (4)(b) ICTYS, Articles 17 (3), 20 (4)(b) ICTRS, Article 17 (4)(b) SCSLS/RSCSL Statute; Article 21 (4)(c) KSC Law),[659] including, in principle, a right to self-representation (Article 67 (1)(d) ICCS, Article 14 (3)(d) ICCPR, Article 21 (4)(d)

[654] Sub-section (3) in this section; see also Schabas and McDermott, in Ambos, *Commentary* (2022), mn. 7 ff. (esp. 19 ff.).

[655] cf. Arts. 14 (2) ICCPR, 6 (2) ECHR, 48 (1) EU Charter, 8 (2) cl. 1 ACHR, 7 (1)(b) ACHPR; on Art. 8 ACHR, see Ibañez Rivas, 'Articulo 8', in Steiner and Uribe, *CIDH Comentario* (2019), pp. 290–3. On Art. 66(1) ICCS, see Elberling, in Klamberg, *Commentary* (2023), n. 540. See generally Khan and Alagendra, in Jalloh and Marong, *Promoting Accountability* (2015), pp. 158 ff. On membership liability often displacing the presumption of innocence, see Murphy, in May and Hoskins, *ICL* (2010), pp. 225, 239.

[656] On the proximity to the civil law standard of '*conviction intime*', see Zahar and Sluiter, *ICL* (2008), p. 391; for a crit. view, however, see De Smet, in Stahn and Sluiter, *Practice* (2009), pp. 421, 430–1, who applies the 'beyond reasonable doubt' standard of proof only for the establishment of the defendant's guilt or innocence, but not for the establishment (or not) of the material elements of the crime; in favour of the 'intimate, personal' *conviction intime*, rather than the 'rational' beyond reasonable doubt standard, as the former 'corresponds more to the reality of international decision-making' Jacobs, in Sluiter et al., *International Criminal Procedure* (2013), pp. 1145–6, 1149. See also the nuanced Rule 140 RPE KSC. Thereon in more detail, Chapter V, A.(2)(b) in this volume.

[657] See also Arts. 14 (1) cl. 2 ICCPR, 6 (1) ECHR and 47 EU Charter. According to *Prosecutor v. Šešelj*, AC, Public Redacted Version of Judgment, No. IT-03-67-R77.2-A, 19 May 2010, para. 32, 'the established practice of the Tribunal to publish redacted public versions of documents' or even judgments does not violate the right to a fair and public hearing.

[658] See also Arts. 14 (3)(a) ICCPR, 6 (3)(a) ECHR and 8 (2)(b) ACHR; see also Ibanez Rivas, in Steiner and Uribe, *CIDH Comentario* (2019), pp. 294–6; cf. also Regulation 41 RegOTP and *Prosecutor v. Muhimana*, No. ICTR-95-1B-A, AC Partly Dissenting Opinion of Judge Schomburg on the Interpretation of the Right to be Informed, paras. 1 ff. (21 May 2007); for a comprehensive analysis, see Jordash and Coughlan, in Darcy and Powderly, *Judicial Creativity* (2010), pp. 286 ff.; de Meester, Pitcher, Rastan, and Sluiter, in Sluiter et al., *International Criminal Procedure* (2013), pp. 228 ff.; Elberling and Pérez-León Acevedo, in Klamberg, *Commentary* (2017), n. 546; ICC, *Pre-Trial Practice Manual* (September 2015), p. 6 (meaning 'to be further refined in practice').

[659] See also Arts. 14 (3)(b) ICCPR, 6 (3)(b) and (c) ECHR, 8 (2)(c) and (d) ACHR, and Art. 7 (1)(c) ACHPR; cf. also Ibañez Rivas, 'Articulo 8', in Steiner and Uribe, *CIDH Comentario* (2019), p. 296. See also Rule 42 (A)(i) RPE ICTY/ICTR/SCSL. Rule 42 is based on Art. 14 (3) ICCPR and Art. 6 (3) ECHR, cf. *Prosecutor v. Delalić et al.*, TC, Decision on Zdravko Mucic's Motion for the Exclusion of Evidence, No. IT-96-21-T, 2 September 1997, para. 60. On defence counsel in ICL, see generally Tuinstra, *Defence Counsel in ICL* (2009); De Meester, *Investigation Phase* (2015), pp. 345 ff.; see, in more detail, Chapter II, C. in this volume.

ICTYS, Article 20 (4)(d) ICTRS, Article 17 (4)(d) SCSLS/RSCSL Statute; Article 21 (4)(e) KSC Law);[660]

f) To be tried without undue delay (Article 67 (1)(c) ICCS, Article 21(4)(c) ICTYS, Article 20 (4)(c) ICTRS, Article 17 (4)(c) SCSLS/RSCSL Statute; Article 21 (4)(d) KSC Law),[661] especially in the context of pre-trial detention;[662]

g) To be present, in principle, at the trial,[663] and, when necessary, assignment of legal assistance (Articles 55 (2)(c), (d), 67 (1)(d) ICCS, Articles 18 (3), 21 (4)(d) ICTYS, Articles 17 (3), 20 (4)(d) ICTRS, Article 17 (4)(d) SCSLS/RSCSL Statute; Article 21 (4)(e) KSC Law);[664]

h) To present evidence, especially to obtain the attendance and examination of exculpatory witnesses and to adequately examine the incriminating witnesses (Article 67 (1)(e) ICCS, Article 21 (4)(e) ICTYS, Article 20 (4)(e) ICTRS, Article 17 (4)(e) SCSLS/RSCSL Statute; Article 21 (4)(f) KSC Law); disclosure of exculpatory or mitigating evidence by the Prosecution (Article 67 (2) ICCS, Rule 68 RPE ICTY/ICTR/SCSL, Rules 102-12 RPE KSC);[665]

i) Assistance of a competent interpreter (Articles 55 (1)(c), 67 (1)(f) ICCS, Articles 18 (3), 21(4)(f) ICTYS, Articles 17 (3), 20 (4)(f) ICTRS, Article 17 (4)(f) SCSLS/RSCSL Statute; Article 21 (4)(g), 38(3)(d) KSC Law);[666]

j) Comprehensive right to silence and non-self-incrimination, without such silence being interpreted to the detriment of the accused (Articles 55 (1)(a), (2)(b), 67 (1)(g) ICCS, Article 21 (4)(g) ICTYS, Article 20 (4)(g) ICTRS, Article 17 (4)(g) SCSLS/RSCSL Statute; Articles 21 (4)(h), 38 (3)(b) KSC Law);[667]

660 See also Arts. 14 (3)(d) ICCPR, 6 (3)(c) ECHR, 8 (2)(d) ACHR, and 7 (1)(c) ACHPR; see also Ibañez Rivas, 'Articulo 8', in Steiner and Uribe, *CIDH Comentario* (2019), p. 297. This issue is, of course, controversial, see Chapter II, D.(3) in this volume.

661 See also Arts. 14 (3)(c) ICCPR, 6 (1) cl. 1 ECHR, 47 cl. 2 EU Charter, Art. 8 (1) cl. 1 ACHR and Art. 7 (1)(d) ACHPR; on Art. 8 ACHR, see Ibañez Rivas, 'Articulo 8', in Steiner and Uribe, *CIDH Comentario* (2019), p. 269. cf. also Tochilovsky, *Jurisprudence* (2014), pp. 503 ff.; criticizing the length of the proceedings before the ICC, Kaul, *ZIS*, 2 (2007), 497; similarly McDermott, in Sluiter et al., *International Criminal Procedure* (2013), pp. 796–8 (*Lubanga* and *Katanga* trials); for a nuanced view, see Whiting, *HarvILJ*, 50 (2009), 323 ff.

662 See also Art. 9 (3) ICCPR ('trial within a reasonable time or to release'), Art. 5 (3) ECHR, and Art. 7 (5) ACHR; on Art. 7 ACHR, see Casas, 'Articulo 7', in Steiner and Uribe, *CIDH Comentario* (2019), pp. 247–51. On arrest and pre-trial detention in more detail, see Chapter IV, B.(6) in this volume.

663 See also Art. 14 (3)(d) ICCPR. On the presence requirement and the recent change of the RPE ICC (new Rules 134*bis*, *ter*, and *quater*) by the ASP at its 12th session (November 2013) in light of the Kenya proceedings, see Chapter II, D.(2) in this volume.

664 See also Arts. 14 (3)(d) ICCPR, 6 (3)(c) ECHR, and 8 (2)(e) ACHR; on Art. 8 ACHR, see Ibañez Rivas, 'Articulo 8', in Steiner and Uribe, *CIDH Comentario* (2019), pp. 300–3; cf. also Zappalá, *Human Rights* (2005), pp. 59 ff.

665 See, in more detail on evidence and disclosure, Chapter V in this volume.

666 See also Arts. 14 (3)(f) ICCPR, 6 (3)(e) ECHR, and 8 (2)(a) ACHR; on the latter, see Ibañez Rivas, 'Articulo 8', in Steiner and Uribe, *CIDH Comentario* (2019), pp. 293–4; pursuant to Art. 67 (1)(f) ICCS 'the proceedings of or documents presented to the Court' shall be 'in a language which the accused fully understands and speaks'. See also Rule 42 (A)(ii) RPE ICTY/ICTR/SCSL. However, the ICTY case law dissents explicitly from this standard, where it suffices that one '[understands the language] sufficiently in order to allow for the effective exercise of his right to conduct his defence', see *Prosecutor v. Karadžić*, AC, Decision on Interlocutory Appeal of the Trial Chamber's Decision on Prosecution Motion Seeking Determination that the Accused Understands English, No. IT-95-5/18-AR73.3, 4 June 2009, para. 11; that is consistent with Arts. 14 (3) ICCPR, 6 (3) ECHR, and 8 (2) ACHR; cf. also Ibañez Rivas, 'Articulo 8', in Steiner and Uribe, *CIDH Comentario* (2019), pp. 256 ff; Zappalá, *Human Rights* (2005), pp. 55 ff.

667 See also Art. 14 (3)(g) ICCPR and Art. 8 (2)(g) ACHR; Ibañez Rivas, 'Articulo 8', in Steiner and Uribe, *CIDH Comentario* (2019), pp. 304–5. See also Rules 42 (A)(iii), 63 (B) RPE ICTY/ICTR/SCSL; cf. Safferling and Hartwig, *ZIS*, 4 (2009), 788 ff.; de Meester, Pitcher, Rastan, and Sluiter, in Sluiter et al., *International Criminal Procedure* (2013), pp. 224 ff., 243, 245–7; Boas et al., *Procedure* (2011), pp. 109–10; Safferling and Hartwig,

k) Prohibition of a reversal of the burden of proof or any onus of rebuttal (Article 67 (1) (i) ICCS);[668]
l) Right to review of conviction and sentence by a higher tribunal (implicitly recognized by the existence of appeals procedures in the Statutes);[669]
m) Right not to be tried or punished twice for the same offence (double jeopardy rule, *ne bis in idem*, Article 20 ICCS; Article 17 KSC Law).[670]

## (2) Fair trial and equality of arms

### *(a) Preliminary remarks*

The principle of a fair trial,[671] as explicitly mentioned in the title of Article 6 (1) ECHR and Article 8 (1) ACHR,[672] constitutes a kind of umbrella right describing the essence of procedural rights (the idea of fairness).[673] At the same time, this idea of fairness is expressed in a series of individual rights, which as a whole aim at ensuring a criminal procedure, grounded in the rule of law.[674] These individual rights are partly listed in Article 14 (3) ICCPR, Article 6 (3) ECHR,[675] and Article 8 (2) ACHR, but these provisions are

*International Criminal Procedure* (2012), pp. 289–91; Zappalá, *Human Rights* (2005), pp. 55, 77 ff.; for a detailed comparative analysis, see Damaška, *UPaLR*, 121 (1972–1973), 521 ff.

[668] cf. Zahar and Sluiter, *ICL* (2008), pp. 360 ff.

[669] See also Arts. 14 (5) ICCPR, 2 (1) ECHR AP VII, and Art. 8 (2)(h) ACHR; on the latter, see Ibanez Rivas, 'Articulo 8', in Steiner and Uribe, *CIDH Comentario* (2019), pp. 305–9. For a more detailed analysis, see Chapter VI in this volume.

[670] See also Arts. 14 (7) ICCPR, 4 (1) ECHR AP VII, 50 EU Charter, and 8 (4) ACHR; see also Ibañez Rivas, 'Articulo 8', in Steiner and Uribe, *CIDH Comentario* (2019), pp. 310–12. On the domestic application of this principle, see Arts. 14 (7) ICCPR, 4 AP 7 ECHR, and 8 (4) ACHR; on the application within the EU, see Arts. 50 and 54 EU Charter.

[671] On this principle as a fundamental key aspect of the criminal proceedings, see Weigend, *ZStW*, 113 (2001), 276; McDermott, *Fairness* (2016), pp. 21 ff.; also see Wheeler, *Fairness* (2023), pp. 6 ff.; for earlier references see previous edition p. 61 with note 612.On the impact of legal culture differences on the fairness of the procedure, see Krüßmann, *Transnationales Strafprozessrecht* (2009), pp. 149–64. On the impact of the constituent elements of the right to a fair trial, see Safferling, *Criminal Procedure* (2012), pp. 61–2.

[672] Arts. 14 (1) ICCPR and 47 (2) EU Charter also refer to a 'fair and public hearing', but do not, as Arts. 6 ECHR and 8 ACHR, explicitly carry the umbrella right to a fair trial in the title of the provision. See, in this regard, Walther, *GA*, 150 (2003), 219, arguing, with reference to the original wording of Art. 6 ECHR, that there is a distinction between 'fair trial' in the chapeau of Art. 6 and 'fair hearing' in the first sentence of Art. 6 (1); on the relation between fair trial and fair hearing with regard to the ECtHR case law, see Demko, *Verteidigung* (2014), pp. 220 ff., on the *travaux* to Art. 14 ICCPR, see now Clooney and Webb, *Article 14 of the ICCPR* (2021).

[673] cf. HRCt, *Reid v. Jamaica* (1990) UN Doc. CCPR/C/39/D/250/1987, para. 11.5; more recently *Y.M. v. Russia* (2016) UN Doc. CCPR/C/116/D/2059/2011, paras. 9.2–9; cf. Demko, *Verteidigung* (2014), pp. 236–7 with direct regard to the relation of the principle of fairness to the individual rights in Art. 6 (3) ECHR; Schabas, *CCPR* (2019), Art. 14 mn. 14; in the same vein, McDermott, in Sluiter et al., *International Criminal Procedure* (2013), pp. 773, 805, 807; cf. also Safferling, *Criminal Procedure* (2012), pp. 60–1; Grabenwarter, *ECHR* (2014), Art. 6 mn. 1.

[674] Pache, *NVwZ*, 20 (2001), 1342–3; Grabenwarter and Pabel, *EMRK* (2021), § 24 mn. 66; Gaede, *Fairness* (2007), pp. 159–61; also Rzepka, *Fairness* (2000), pp. 34 ff., 82 ff.; McDermott, in Sluiter et al., *International Criminal Procedure* (2013), pp. 772 ('multifaceted' duty for the proceedings to be carried out fairly and expeditiously), p. 816; furthermore, see Wheeler, *Fairness* (2023), p. 30 ('A state that acts consistently within the rule of law is one that values law and order, ensures the separation of powers between different forms of the government, and guarantees fairness in how the law is applied').

[675] Meyer-Ladewig et al., 'Article 6' in Meyer-Ladewig and Nettesheim, *EMRK* (2017), mn. 90; Gaede, *Fairness* (2007) pp. 159–60; Demko, *Verteidigung* (2014), pp. 230 ff.; see also Safferling, *International Criminal Procedure* (2001), p. 30 ('kaleidoscope of rights'); Rzepka, *Fairness* (2000), pp. 82 ff. See also—albeit less detailed—Arts. 47, 48 EU Charter.

not exhaustive. Rather, some fundamental rights with a more comprehensive character, such as the principle of 'equality of arms', the presumption of innocence, the right to remain silent (in the form of the right to non-self-incrimination, *nemo tenetur se ipsum accusare*),[676] the right to be heard by an impartial and independent tribunal,[677] and, last but not least, the right to be tried within reasonable time, can also be derived from Article 14 (1), (2) ICCPR,[678] Article 6 (1), (2) ECHR,[679] and Article 8 (1) ACHR.[680] In fact, these more general rights often overlap with the more specific rights listed in the subsequent paragraphs.

The importance of the fair trial guarantee as compared to other human rights guarantees cannot be overestimated. If one looks at the European human rights system, as the most active and elaborated one, one quickly discovers that Article 6 ECHR proceedings and violations are in quantitative terms most significant: since its establishment in 1959 up to 2023, the ECtHR has delivered 26,689 judgments; in 2023 in a third (372) of the judgments a violation of the *fair trial* principle was found.[681]

### (b) Equality of arms

One of the key features of the umbrella concept of 'fair trial' is another broad concept: the principle of equality of arms.[682] In its modern understanding, it not only covers the formal

676 This right is contained in Arts. 14(3)(g) IPCPR and 8(2)(g) ACHR, but not explicitly in the ECHR; yet the ECtHR recognizes it as part of a fair trial since *Funke v. France* (1993) 16 EHRR 297. On its historical origin, see Ambos, *LJIL*, 15 (2002), 159.

677 For a more detailed analysis of the qualifiers 'impartial' and 'independent', see Chapter II, A.(4) in this volume.

678 cf. *Fei v. Colombia* (1994) UN Doc. CCPR/C/53/D/514/1992, para. 8.4 ('respect for the principle of equality of arms, of adversary proceedings and of expeditious proceedings'); *Andela v. Cameroon* (2017) UN Doc. CCPR/C/121/D/2764/2016, paras. 7.4–7.5; in the same vein, *Burgoa v. Bolivia* (2018) UN Doc. CCPR/C/122/D/2628/2015, para. 11.8 ('important aspect of the fairness of a hearing is its expeditiousness and that delays that cannot be justified by the complexity of the case or the behaviour of the parties detract from the principle of a fair hearing').

679 Meyer-Ladewig et al., 'Article 6' in Meyer-Ladewig and Nettesheim, *EMRK* (2017), mn. 90; Grabenwarter and Pabel, in Dörr et al., *EMRK/GG I* (2021/2022), ch. 14 mn. 113 ff.

680 Rzepka, *Fairness* (2000), pp. 82 ff.; Demko, *Verteidigung* (2014), pp. 210 ff.

681 ECtHR, *Annual Report 2023* (2023), p. 110 (plus the figures of the 2014 Report). <http://www.echr.coe.int/Documents/Annual_report_2014_ENG.pdf>.

682 ECtHR, *Ofner et al. v. Austria*, Application Nos. 524/59 and 617/59, Committee of Ministers Decision (5 April 1963), para. 1; *Neumeister v. Austria*, Application No. 1936/63, Judgment (27 June 1968), para. 22; *Regner v. Czech Republic*, Application No. 35289/11, Judgment (19 September 2017), para. 146; *Hodžić v. Croatia*, Application No. 28932/14, Judgment (4 April 2019), para. 60 ('one of the elements of the broader concept of fair trial'); *Alexandru-Radu Luca v. Romania*, Application No. 20837/18, Judgment (14 June 2022), para. 58; for further (earlier) case law see previous edition, p. 61 with note 623; for the HRCt, see *Dudko v. Australia* (2007) UN Doc. CCPR/C/90/D/1347/2005, para. 7.4; *Perterer v. Austria* (2004) 8 Selected Decisions of the HRCt 273, para. 9.2. HRCt, 'General Comment 32' (23 August 2007 UN Doc. CCPR/C/GC/32, para. 13; Kazakhstan CCPR/C/KAZ/CO/2 (2016) 37 ('prosecution retains wide powers in the judicial process, in relation to both civil and criminal proceedings, which adversely affects the equality of arms'); see also IACtHR, 'The Right to Information on Consular Assistance in the Framework of the Guarantees of the Due Process of Law', Advisory Opinion, Inter-American Court of Human Rights Series A No. 16 (1 October 1999), para. 117 ('for "the due process of law" a defendant must be able to exercise his rights and defend his interests effectively and in full procedural equality'); Noor Muhammad, in Henkin, *Bill of Rights* (1981), p. 146; Rzepka, *Fairness* (2000), p. 83; Braitsch, *Gerichtssprache* (1991), p. 124; Kohlbacher, *'Waffengleichheit'* (1979), pp. 25–6; Wasek-Wiaderek, *Equality* (2000), p. 23; Barkhuysen et al., in van Dijk et al., *European Convention on Human Rights* (2018), pp. 562 ff.; Satzger, *Internationales Strafrecht* (2020), § 11 mn. 80; Satzger, *ICL* (2018), § 9 mn. 80; Gundel, in Merten and Papier, *Grundrechte, VI/1* (2010), § 146 mn. 105 ff.; generally on the equality of arms, see McDermott, in Sluiter et al., *International Criminal Procedure* (2013), pp. 776–7 (IMT, IMTFE), 788–92 (ICTY, ICTR, SCSL), 798–9 (ICC), 804–5 (STL), 810 ('minimum guarantees "in full equality"'); Zappalá, *Human Rights* (2005), p. 112; Gaede, *Fairness* (2007), pp. 305 ff. (for a critique, see pp. 641 ff.); Demko, *Verteidigung* (2014), pp. 255–6, 30, 356 ff. ('Bedeutung des Rechts ... auf rechtliches Gehör und des Rechtsprinzips der Waffengleichheit als der *"Kernausübungselemente"* des Menschenrechts des Angeklagten auf Verteidigung im Strafverfahren'); Grabenwarter, *ECHR* (2014), Art. 6 mn. 81; Stanziola Vieira, *Paridade de Armas*

procedural equality of the accused with the (public) Prosecutor,[683] but also entails more substantive consequences. Accordingly, in the words of the ECtHR:

> each party must be afforded a reasonable opportunity to present his case ... under conditions that do not place him at a substantial disadvantage vis-à-vis his opponent.[684]

Similarly, the HRCt stated:

> [Equality of arms] means that the same procedural rights are to be provided to all the parties ... The principle of equality between parties ... demands, inter alia, that each side be given the opportunity to contest all the arguments ... by the other party.[685]

Thus, equality of arms presupposes that 'both prosecution and defence must be given the opportunity to have knowledge of and comment on the observations filed and the evidence adduced by the other party'.[686] No party can be granted (additional) rights to the detriment of the other party.[687] Furthermore, an 'increased sensitivity to the fair administration of justice' is required, as well as attaching 'importance to appearances'.[688] The principle does not depend on 'further, quantifiable unfairness'.[689]

(2014), p. 210; Schabas and McDermott, 'Article 67', in Ambos, *Commentary* (2022), mn. 18; from a Polish perspective, see Brodzisz, *ZIS*, 4 (2009), 109.

[683] *Ofner et al. v. Austria*, Application Nos. 524/59 and 617/59, Committee of Ministers Decision (5 April 1963), para. 1 ('procedural equality of the accused with the public prosecutor'); *Dudko v. Australia* (2007) UN Doc. CCPR/C/90/D/1347/2005, para. 7.4 ('an opportunity equal to that of the State party'); cf. Demko, *Verteidigung* (2014), pp. 357 ff. Bringing the victim into the equation IACtHR, *Genie-Lacayo Case*, Series C No. 30, Judgment (29 January 1997), para. 88 (*in casu* the victim's father found 'himself in a clear situation of inferiority in relation to the defendant or the military judges when he appeared as the accusing party before the ... courts'; yet, the Court rejected the application with regard to this point); cf. Medina, *ACHR* (2022), pp. 354–5.

[684] *Dombo Beheer B.V. v. The Netherlands*, Application No. 14448/88, Judgment (27 October 1993), para. 33; for conc. earlier case law see previous edition, p. 62 with note 625; more recently *Avotiņš v. Latvia*, Application No. 17502/07 (23 May 2016), para. 119; *Regner v. Czech Republic*, Application No. 35289/11, Grand Chamber Judgment (19 September 2017), para. 146; *Prebil v. Slovenia*, Application No. 29278/16, Judgment (19 March 2019), para. 42; *Hodžić v. Croatia*, Application No. 28932/14, Judgment (4 April 2019), para. 60. See also Haefliger and Schürmann, *EMRK* (1999), pp. 185, 223; Haefliger and Schürmann, *Die EMRK und die Schweiz* (2014), pp. 38–9; Villiger, *Handbuch EMRK* (2020), p. 311; Merrills, *ECtHR* (1995), p. 166; Harris, O'Boyle, and Warbrick, *Law of the ECHR* (2018), pp. 415–17; Gless, *Internationales Strafrecht* (2021), mn. 78; Gaede, *Fairness* (2007), p. 305; Gut, Kirsch, Mundis, and Taylor, in Sluiter et al., *International Criminal Procedure* (2013), pp. 1270–1, Friman, Brady, Costi, Guariglia, and Stuckenberg, in Sluiter et al., *International Criminal Procedure* (2013), p. 157.

[685] HRCt, 'General Comment 32' (23 August 2007) UN Doc. CCPR/C/GC/32, para. 13; see also *Jansen-Gielen v. The Netherlands* (2001) UN Doc. CCPR/C/71/D/846/1999, para. 8.2; *Äärelä and Näkkäläjärvi v. Finland* (2001) UN Doc. CCPR/C/73/D/779/1997, para. 7.4.

[686] ECtHR, *Öcalan v. Turkey*, Application No. 46221/99, Judgment (12 March 2003), para. 166; more recently *Murtazaliyeva v. Russia*, Application No. 36658/05, Grand Chamber Judgment (18 December 2018), para. 91; *Kikabidze v. Georgia*, Application No. 57642/12, Judgment (16 November 2021), para. 41; *Alexandru-Radu Luca v. Romania*, Application No. 20837/18, Judgment (14 June 2022), para. 58; for further (earlier) case law see previous edition, p. 62 with note 627. On the ICCPR, see *Äärelä and Näkkäläjärvi v. Finland* (2001) UN Doc. CCPR/C/73/D/779/1997, para. 7.4. See also Tochilovsky, *Jurisprudence* (2014), p. 444.

[687] cf. McDermott, in Sluiter et al., *International Criminal Procedure* (2013), pp. 778–80, 789, 805 (arguing that 'the recognition of rights' for other parties 'should not be at the expense of the accused').

[688] See ECtHR, *Bulut v. Austria*, Application No. 17358/90, Judgment (22 February 1996), para. 47; more recently *Kikabidze v. Georgia*, Application No. 57642/12, Judgment (16 November 2021), para. 40; for further (earlier) case law, see previous edition, p. 63 with note 629;

[689] ECtHR, *Bulut v. Austria*, Application No. 17358/90, Judgment (22 February 1996), para. 49; for conc. case law, see previous edition, p. 63 with note 630; more recently *Kliba v. Croatia*, Application No. 30375/16 (18 April 2019), para. 24. On the debate whether the principle of equality of arms also applies to the prosecution, cf. Zappalá, *Human Rights* (2005), pp. 113–14.

### (c) Towards an adversarial procedure?

The ECtHR further reads into the fair trial principle and the ensuing equality of arms the right to an 'adversarial' procedure.[690] While the Court leaves the question of the (better) procedural system explicitly open,[691] its actual interpretation of fair trial and equality of arms in terms of the concrete procedural consequences and requirements shows an adversarial rather than an inquisitorial tendency;[692] arguably, though, this does not mean that the trial proceedings have to be structured in a strictly adversarial, two-case fashion.[693] In any case, the adversarial–inquisitorial dichotomy, already alluded to above,[694] should not be overstated since the alleged theoretical implications are mostly downplayed in the procedural practice.[695] In this sense, the scholarly literature avoids conceptual determinations and calls, instead, for a comprehensive and active participation in the procedure in the sense of an '*audiatur et altera pars*'[696] or—more specifically—for equal opportunities for the parties to make their arguments,[697] also with regard to expert witnesses.[698]

[690] ECtHR, *Brandstetter v. Austria*, Application Nos. 11170/84, 12876/87, and 13468/87, Judgment (28 August 1991), para. 66; *Öcalan v. Turkey*, Application No. 46221/99, Judgment (12 May 2005), para. 146; *Gadirov v. Azerbaijan*, Application No. 24510/06, Judgment (20 June 2013), para. 37; *Avotiņš v. Latvia*, Application No. 17502/07 (23 May 2016), para. 119; *Regner v. Czech Republic*, Application No. 35289/11, Judgment (19 September 2017), para. 146; *Prebil v. Slovenia*, Application No. 29278/16, Judgment (19 March 2019), para. 42 ('Court reiterates that the adversarial principle and the principle of equality of arms, which are closely linked, are fundamental components of the concept of a "fair hearing"'); *Kikabidze v. Georgia*, Application No. 57642/12, Judgment (16 November 2021), para. 41 ('right to an adversarial trial'); *Faysal Pamuk v. Turkey*, Application No. 430/13, Judgment (18 January 2022), para. 47 ('before an accused can be convicted, all evidence against him must normally be produced in his presence at a public hearing with a view to adversarial argument'). In the same vein, Friman, Brady, Costi, Guariglia, and Stuckenberg, in Sluiter et al., *International Criminal Procedure* (2013), p. 480 ('human rights are based on an underlying assumption that criminal proceedings shall be of an adversarial character'); for a nuanced view, also McDermott, in Sluiter et al., *International Criminal Procedure* (2013), p. 811 ('While the notion of equality of arms was typically an offspring of the adversarial procedural tradition, modern continental systems have incorporated the doctrine').

[691] ECtHR, *Öcalan v. Turkey*, Application No. 46221/99, Judgment (12 May 2005), para. 146 ('Various ways are conceivable in which national law may secure that this requirement is met'); *Oao Neftyanaya Kompaniya Yukos v. Russia*, Application No. 14902/04, Judgment (20 September 2011), para. 538; *Murtazaliyeva v. Russia*, Application No. 36658/05, Grand Chamber Judgment (18 December 2018), para. 91; *Alexandru-Radu Luca v. Romania*, Application No. 20837/18, Judgment (14 June 2022), para. 59 ('States enjoy a certain margin of appreciation in this area'). See also Kohlbacher, *'Waffengleichheit'* (1979), pp. 1, 24; Spaniol, *Verteidigerbeistand* (1990), p. 127; McDermott, in Sluiter et al., *International Criminal Procedure* (2013), p. 807.

[692] In a similar vein, Spaniol, *Verteidigerbeistand* (1990), p. 126; Matscher, *ÖRiZ*, 86 (1993), 154; Sommer, in Brüssow et al., *Strafverteidigung* (2007), § 17 mn. 94; Jung, *GA*, 150 (2003), 203; Demko, *Verteidigung* (2014), pp. 348. In favour of an adversarial structure in the pre-trial proceedings ('kontradiktorisch ausbalancierte[s] Ermittlungsverfahren'), Schünemann, in Triffterer, *GS Vogler* (2004), p. 92; in a similar vein, Stanziola Vieira, *Paridade de Armas* (2014), p. 160.

[693] cf. Jackson, *MLR*, 68 (2005), 753 ff., arguing that the ECtHR strives to translate the defence rights of Art. 6 ECHR into a form of adversarialism that is both compatible with the continental *procédure contradictoire* and the common law adversarial trial; conc. Vasiliev, in Sluiter et al., *International Criminal Procedure* (2013), pp. 636–7.

[694] Section A.(2)(a) in this chapter.

[695] For a fundamental analysis, see Trüg, *Lösungskonvergenzen trotz Systemdivergenzen* (2003), pp. 72 ff., 104 ff., 203 ff., 480 ff.; cf. also Jung, *StV*, 10 (1990), 510; Dammer and Albanese, *Comparative Criminal Justice* (2014), p. 149; Jorg, Field, and Brants, in Harding et al., *Criminal Justice in Europe* (1995), p. 41; Tulkens, in Delmas-Marty, *Criminal Process and Human Rights* (1995), pp. 8–9; Sanders and Young, *Criminal Justice* (2021), pp. 11–14; Ambos, *ICLR*, 3 (2003), 2 ff.

[696] Fawcett, *ECHR* (1987), p. 137; Medina, *ACHR* (2022), pp. 353–4.

[697] Esser, *Europäisches Strafverfahrensrecht* (2002), p. 406; Esser, *Europäisches und Internationales Strafrecht* (2023), § 9 mn. 225; Haefliger and Schürmann, *EMRK* (1999), p. 187; Villiger, *Handbuch EMRK* (2020), p. 311; Demko, *Verteidigung* (2014), pp. 243, 334 ff., 363 ff., who speaks of an antithetical participation ('antithetische Teilnahme'). In the same vein on Art. 8 (1) ACHR, seeIbañez Rivas, 'Articulo 8', in Steiner and Uribe, *CIDH Comentario* (2019), pp. 270–82; Medina, *ACHR* (2022), pp. 353–4.

[698] Esser, *Europäisches Strafverfahrensrecht* (2002), pp. 700 ff.; left open by Demko, *Verteidigung* (2014), p. 414. On this, see ECtHR, *Bönisch v. Austria*, Application No. 8658/79, Judgment (6 May 1985), para. 29, and more recently *Constantinides v. Greece*, Application No. 76438/12, Judgment (6 October 2016), para. 37: 'Although the

In any case, some statements of the case law do indeed sound adversarial. Thus, if the Court argues that any tribunal must commence a trial uninfluenced, without a 'preconceived idea',[699] it argues in fact against the existence of any written pre-trial information for the judges in form of a dossier. Similarly, it has been said that the questioning of witnesses should be adversarial.[700]

With regard to the position and role of national prosecutorial authorities, such as the Austrian *Generalprokurator* and the Belgian *Procureur Général*, the Court held, on the one hand, that they turn into adversaries[701] as soon as they express an opinion on the admissibility of the application of the defendant;[702] therefore, the accused has a right to respond since otherwise he would be put at a substantial disadvantage. On the other hand, the Court has explicitly refused to consider the *Procureur* as an adversary.[703] In a similar vein, an adversarial reading of Article 6 (1) ECHR is difficult to reconcile with the existence of a *juge d'instruction*, at least if this judge acts impartially in a truth-seeking manner.[704]

### (d) *Application* ratione temporis

The ECtHR speaks of 'proceedings', thereby making clear that the right to a fair trial does not only apply to the trial, but also to the pre-trial phase.[705] Nothing different follows from

wording of Article 6 § 3 (d) refers to witnesses and not experts, the guarantees in paragraph 3 are inherent aspects of the right to a fair trial enshrined in paragraph 1 of Article 6.'

[699] ECtHR, *Barberà, Messegué and Jabardo v. Spain*, Application No. 10590/83, Judgment (6 December 1988), paras. 76–7; *Gutu v. Moldova*, Application No. 20289/02, Judgment (7 June 2007), para. 46; *Natunen v. Finland*, Application No. 21022/04, Judgment (31 March 2009), para. 53; *Bodet v. Belgium*, Application No. 78480/13, Judgment (5 January 2017), para. 36 ('principe de la présomption d'innocence exige, entre autres, qu'en remplissant leurs fonctions les membres du tribunal ne partent pas de l'idée préconçue'); *SA-Capital Oy v. Finland*, Application No. 5556/10, Judgment (14 February 2019), para. 107; Esser, *Europäisches Strafverfahrensrecht* (2002), pp. 624–5; Esser, *Europäisches und Internationales Strafrecht* (2023), § 9 mn. 213. On the compatibility of military courts with the right to a fair trial, see Bucherer, *Vereinbarkeit* (2005), pp. 37 ff. and on the relevant ECtHR case law, pp. 43 ff.

[700] cf. e.g. ECtHR, *Kostovski v. The Netherlands*, Application No. 11454/85, Judgment (20 November 1989), para. 41; for further case law, see previous edition, p. 64 with note 641; more recently *Alexandru-Radu Luca v. Romania*, Application No. 20837/18, Judgment (14 June 2022), para. 32. See also Esser, *Europäisches Strafverfahrensrecht* (2002), pp. 632 ff.; Peukert, in Strafverteidigervereinigungen, *Reform oder Roll-Back?* (1997), pp. 238–9.

[701] ECtHR, *Borgers v. Belgium*, Application No. 12005/86, Judgment (30 October 1991), paras. 24 ff., 26 ('becomes objectively speaking his ally or his opponent'); *Brandstetter v. Austria*, Application Nos. 11170/84, 12876/87, and 13468/87, Judgment (28 August 1991), para. 67; *Bulut v. Austria*, Application No. 17358/90, Judgment (22 February 1996), para. 48. See also Wasek-Wiaderek, *Equality* (2000), pp. 24 ff.; Esser, *Europäisches Strafverfahrensrecht* (2002), pp. 412 ff.

[702] ECtHR, *Bulut v. Austria*, Application No. 17358/90, Judgment (22 February 1996), para. 48 ('while their objectivity could not be questioned, from the moment they recommended that an appeal be allowed or dismissed their opinion could not be regarded as neutral'); for a contrary view, however, Gaede, *Fairness* (2007), pp. 307–8.

[703] ECtHR, *Delcourt v. Belgium*, Application No. 2689/65, Judgment (17 January 1970), paras. 32–3 ('Nor is the Procureur général at the Court of Cassation the virtual adversary of the accused whose conviction or acquittal may lead to an appeal in cassation; nor does he become their actual adversary when he submits in open court that their arguments should not be accepted.').

[704] ECtHR, *Pandy v. Belgium*, Application No. 13583/02, Judgment (21 September 2006), para. 51, referring to the *juge d'instruction* as an impartial organ of justice ('juge d'instruction, chargé d'instruire tant à charge qu'à décharge, réponde à des critères d'impartialité'); on that subject, see also Kuty, *RevDPC*, 87 (2007), 365 ff.

[705] cf. ECtHR, *García Alva v. Germany*, Application No. 23541/94, Judgment (13 February 2001), para. 39 ('it follows from the wording of Article 6—and particularly from the autonomous meaning to be given to the notion of "criminal charge"—that this provision has some application to pre-trial proceedings'); for conc. further case law, see previous edition, p. 65 with note 646; more recently *Ibrahim et al. v. UK*, Application No. 50541/08 et al., Grand Chamber Judgment (13 September 2016), paras. 249 and 253 ('the guarantees of Article 6 are applicable from the moment that a "criminal charge" exists within the meaning of this Court's case-law (see paragraph 249) and may therefore be relevant during pre-trial proceedings if and in so far as the fairness of the trial is likely to be seriously prejudiced by an initial failure to comply with them'); *Simeonovi v. Bulgaria*, Application

the use of the terms, 'tribunal' and 'charged with a criminal offence' in Article 6 (1) and (3) ECHR[706] since the term 'charge' has to be understood broadly, regardless of its meaning in the domestic systems, that is, it encompasses any form of accusation, be it of a 'criminal' or only administrative, 'non-criminal' nature.[707] As to the application to disciplinary proceedings, the Court focuses on the nature of the offence and the severity of the penalty.[708]

No. 21980/04, Grand Chamber Judgment (12 May 2017), para. 110; *Beuze v. Belgium*, Application No. 71409/10, Grand Chamber Judgment (9 November 2018), para. 119; *Bjarki H. Diego v. Iceland*, Application No. 30965/17, Judgment (22 March 2022), para. 43. See also Commission European Communities, *Green Paper Financial Interests* (2001), p. 44, <http://eur-lex.europa.eu/legal-content/EN/TXT/PDF/?uri=CELEX:52001DC0715&from=EN>, stressing that the defence rights of the ECHR find application already 'at the preparatory stage'. See further Rzepka, *Fairness* (2000), pp. 85–6; Esser, *Europäisches Strafverfahrensrecht* (2002), p. 401; Sommer, in Brüssow et al., *Strafverteidigung* (2007), § 17 mn. 94–5, 101; Gaede, *Fairness* (2007), pp. 191 ff.; Friman, Brady, Costi, Guariglia, and Stuckenberg, in Sluiter et al., *International Criminal Procedure* (2013), pp. 454–5; Demko, *Verteidigung* (2014), pp. 341–2. On the ICCPR, cf. Noor Muhammad, in Henkin, *Bill of Rights* (1981), pp. 151–2; see also Jacobs, 'Article 55', in Ambos, *Commentary* (2022), mn. 4 ff.

[706] ECtHR, *Imbrioscia v. Switzerland*, Application No. 13972/88, Judgment (24 November 1993), para. 36; for further case law, see previous edition, p. 65 with note 647; more recently *Dvorski v. Croatia*, Application No. 25703/11, Judgment (20 October 2015), para. 76 ('even if the primary purpose of Article 6 of the Convention, as far as criminal proceedings are concerned, is to ensure a fair trial by a "tribunal" competent to determine "any criminal charge", it does not follow that the Article has no application to pre-trial proceedings'); *Bjarki H. Diego v. Iceland*, Application No. 30965/17, Judgment (22 March 2022), para. 43 ('"criminal charge", within the autonomous Convention meaning of that term'); furthermore, see above at note 755. See also Gaede, *Fairness* (2007), pp. 191 ff.; Gless, *Internationales Strafrecht* (2021), mn. 71; Gundel, in Merten and Papier, *Grundrechte, VI/1* (2010), § 146 mn. 58; cf. Tiwisina, *Verfahrensdauer* (2010), p. 25. The term 'criminal charge' in Art. 14 ICCPR requires a broad and autonomous interpretation as well; see *Van Duzen v. Canada* (1982) UN Doc. Supp. No. 40 (A/37/40), pp. 150 ff., para. 10.2; *Sayadi and Vinck v. Belgium* (2008), UN Doc. CCPR/C/94/D/1472/2006, para. 10.11; *Osiyuk v. Belarus* (2009) UN Doc. CCPR/C/96/D/1311/2004, para. 7.3 ('the concept of a "criminal charge" bears an autonomous meaning, independent of the categorisations employed by the national legal system'); Schabas, *CCPR* (2019), Art. 14 mn. 17.

[707] cf. Walischewski, *Akteneinsichtsrechts* (1999), pp. 87–8; Rzepka, *Fairness* (2000), pp. 26 ff., 97; Esser, *Europäisches Strafverfahrensrecht* (2002), pp. 51 ff.; Esser, *Europäisches und Internationales Strafrecht* (2023), § 9 mn. 204 ff.; Braitsch, *Gerichtssprache* (1991), p. 128; Meyer-Ladewig, 'Article 6' in Meyer-Ladewig and Nettesheim, *EMRK* (2017), mn. 24–5; Peukert, in Strafverteidigervereinigungen, *Reform oder Roll-Back?* (1997), p. 237; Kadelbach, in Strafverteidigervereinigungen, *Reform oder Roll-Back?* (1997), p. 251; Sommer, in Brüssow et al., *Strafverteidigung* (2007), § 17 mn. 118–20; Gaede, in Gaede, Meyer, and Schlegel, *HRRS-FG Fezer* (2008), p. 24; Satzger, *Internationales Strafrecht* (2020), § 11 mn. 69; Satzger, *ICL* (2018), § 9 mn. 69; Medina, *ACHR* (2022), pp. 322 ff.; esp. with regard to the antitrust fines of the EU, Lorenzmeier, *ZIS*, 3 (2008), 23 ff.; in detail, Gaede, *Fairness* (2007), pp. 79 ff., esp. pp. 98 ff.

[708] cf. ECtHR, *Engel and Others v. The Netherlands*, Application Nos. 5100/71, 5101/71, 5102/71, 5354/72, and 5370/72, Judgment (8 June 1976), para. 82; see also *J.B. v. Switzerland*, Application No. 31827/96, Judgment (3 May 2001), para. 44; more recently *Gestur Jonsson and Ragnar Halldor Hall v. Iceland*, Application Nos. 68273/14 and 68271/14, Judgment (22 December 2020), para. 75; *Ramos Nunes de Carvalho e Sá v. Portugal*, Application Nos. 55391/13, 57728/13, and 74041/13, Grand Chamber Judgment (6 November 2018), para. 122. In *Engel*, the Court denied, however, a violation of Art. 6, since the disciplinary, two days arrest imposed 'was of too short a duration to belong to the "criminal" law'. Also, again see *Ramos Nunes de Carvalho e Sá v. Portugal*, Application Nos. 55391/13, 57728/13, and 74041/13, Grand Chamber Judgment (6 November 2018), para. 123 ('disciplinary proceedings as such cannot be characterised as "criminal"') with further references ultimately also denying a 'criminal charge' ('the Court observes that the statutory provisions authorising the imposition of penalties were not aimed at the public in general but at a specific category, namely judges. Such provisions are designed to protect the profession's honour and reputation and to maintain public trust in the judiciary', at para. 125). On the *Engel* case and the corresponding autonomous interpretation, see Letsas, *EJIL*, 15 (2004), 297; Grabenwarter and Pabel, *EMRK* (2021), § 5 mn. 9–13 with further references; Maffei, *Confrontation* (2006), p. 63; Grabenwarter and Pabel, in Dörr et al., *EMRK/GG I* (2021/2022), ch. 14 mn. 20 ff.; Trechsel, *EMRK* (1974), pp. 16 ff. On taxation proceedings as 'criminal charge' within the meaning of Art. 6, see Morsch, in Müller-Dietz et al., *FS Jung* (2007), pp. 612 ff. On the nature of administrative offences in the sense of the German *Ordnungswidrigkeitengesetz*, see *Öztürk v. Germany*, Application No. 8544/79, Judgment (21 February 1984), paras. 51 ff., where the ECtHR found that such a petty 'offence' is '*criminal in character*' within the meaning of Art. 6 ECHR. These criteria also apply to the determination of a 'criminal charge' within the meaning of Art. 14 ICCPR, see *Perterer v. Austria* (2004) UN Doc. CCPR/C/81/D/1015/2001, para. 9.2; *Osiyuk v. Belarus* (2009) UN Doc. CCPR/C/96/D/1311/2004, para. 7.3; HRCt, 'General Comment 32' (23 August 2007) UN Doc. CCPR/C/GC/32, para. 15; Schabas, *CCPR* (2019), Art. 14 mn. 17–18.

It clearly follows that Article 6 ECHR applies at an early stage of the proceedings, 'even at the stage of the preliminary investigation into an offence by the police'.[709] In other words, once a person becomes a 'suspect', that is, 'a person concerning whom the Prosecutor possesses reliable information which tends to show' that he 'may have committed a crime',[710] the fair trial rights are triggered. The determination of the suspect status does not entirely fall within the discrection of the Prosecutor, but is to be made objectively, taking into account the effective investigative measures against the relevant person.[711] A more restrictive approach, limiting fair trial and equality of arms to the post-confirmation or trial phase, that is, once a person becomes an 'accused',[712] would undermine these rights since the later a suspect is enabled to participate in the proceedings the later he can influence them and their outcome.[713] In other words, without early participation of the suspect the results of the investigation against him will prejudice the whole proceedings.[714] Indeed, this is the reason why it is an old demand of defence counsel to have early defence rights—especially a right to

[709] ECtHR, *Murray v. UK*, Application No. 18731/91, Judgment (8 February 1996), para. 62; for conc. case law, see previous edition, p. 66 with note 650; more recently, *Ibrahim et al. v. UK*, Application No. 50541/08 et al., Grand Chamber Judgment (13 September 2016), para. 253 ('The investigation stage may be of particular importance for the preparation of the criminal proceedings: the evidence obtained during this stage often determines the framework in which the offence charged will be considered at the trial and national laws may attach consequences to the attitude of an accused at the initial stages of police interrogation which are decisive for the prospects of the defence in any subsequent criminal proceedings. An accused may therefore find himself in a particularly vulnerable position at that stage of the proceedings'); *Beuze v. Belgium*, Application No. 71409/10, Grand Chamber Judgment (9 November 2018), paras. 124 ff. with regard to the right of access to a lawyer during police custody. cf. also Frister, *StV*, 18 (1998), 159–60; Wasek-Wiaderek, *Equality* (2000), pp. 20–1; Rzepka, *Fairness* (2000), p. 58; Esser, *Europäisches Strafverfahrensrecht* (2002), p. 453; also Haefliger and Schürmann, *EMRK* (1999), p. 219; Sommer, in Brüssow et al., *Strafverteidigung* (2007), § 17 mn. 70; Toney, *IJEP*, 5 (2001), 46–7; European Criminal Policy Initiative, *ZIS*, 8 (2013), 438; expressing doubts Villiger, *Handbuch EMRK* (2020), pp. 307, 312.

[710] cf. Rule 2 RPE ICTY/ICTR/SCSL. While the term 'suspect' does not appear as such in the ICC law, it is defined in Art. 55 (2) as a person with regard to whom 'grounds to believe' exist that he 'has committed a crime' (cf. Jacobs, 'Article 55', in Ambos, *Commentary* (2022), mn. 11; de Meester, Pitcher, Rastan, and Sluiter, in Sluiter et al., *International Criminal Procedure* (2013), p. 232; Boas et al., *Procedure* (2011), p. 109); De Meester, *Investigation Phase* (2015), pp. 332 ff.).

[711] cf. *Ibrahim et al. v. UK*, Application No. 50541/08 et al., Grand Chamber Judgment (13 September 2016), para. 249 ('A "criminal charge" exists from the moment that an individual is officially notified by the competent authority of an allegation that he has committed a criminal offence, or from the point at which his situation has been substantially affected by actions taken by the authorities as a result of a suspicion against him'); *Simeonovi v. Bulgaria*, Application No. 21980/04, Grand Chamber Judgment (12 May 2017), para. 110; *Beuze v. Belgium*, Application No. 71409/10, Grand Chamber Judgment (9 November 2018), para. 119. In favour of an objective approach, also HRCt, *Márques de Morais v. Angola* (2005) UN Doc. CCPR/C/83/D/1128/2002, para. 5.2; 'General Comment 32' (23 August 2007) UN Doc. CCPR/C/GC/32, para. 31 ('as soon as the person concerned is formally charged with a criminal offence ... or the individual is publicly named as such'); also de Meester, Pitcher, Rastan, and Sluiter, in Sluiter et al., *International Criminal Procedure* (2013), p. 216; Friman, Brady, Costi, Guariglia, and Stuckenberg, in Sluiter et al., *International Criminal Procedure* (2013), p. 454 ('the term should be understood in a substantive rather than formal sense and the question is, whether the person is ... substantially affected by the steps taken against him or her'); for a contrary view, see Noor Muhammad, in Henkin, *Bill of Rights* (1981), p. 145.

[712] cf. Rules 2 RPE ICTY/ICTR/SCSL ('A person against whom one or more counts in an indictment have been confirmed'); see also Rules 47(H)(ii) RPE ICTY/ICTR/SCSL (suspect becomes accused with confirmation of indictment).

[713] In a similar vein, Wasek-Wiaderek, *Equality* (2000), p. 21; Walischewski, *Akteneinsichtsrechts* (1999), p. 87; Braitsch, *Gerichtssprache* (1991), pp. 129–30; cf. also ECtHR, *Murray v. UK*, Application No. 18731/91, Judgment (8 February 1996), para. 66 ('paramount importance'); also Sommer, in Brüssow et al., *Strafverteidigung* (2007), § 17 mn. 94–5; Schleiminger, *Konfrontation* (2001), p. 291; Nack, in Boetticher et al., *Sonderheft Schäfer* (2002), p. 51; Wohlers, *GA*, 152 (2005), 26 ff.; Demko, *Verteidigung* (2014), p. 342 ('sich auf das gesamte Strafverfahren erstreckend—*durchgängig* eine "*Gesamtheit* von *konkret* ausübbaren antithetischen Teilnahmehandlungen" ermöglicht worden ist').

[714] Frister, *StV*, 18 (1998), 160; Schünemann, *StV*, 18 (1998), 394–5; Schünemann, *StV*, 20 (2000), 159; Däubler-Gmelin, *StV*, 21 (2001), 361; Braitsch, *Gerichtssprache* (1991), p. 130; Arquint, in Schindler and Schlauri, *Verfahren* (2001), p. 195.

be present during police interrogation—and why this demand has informed many procedural reforms.[715]

Under the procedural regime of the ICC, this early application of basic defence rights is explicitly provided for by Article 55 ICCS listing the 'rights of persons during an investigation'.[716]

In sum, the right to a fair trial is triggered in any case by 'the official notification' of the alleged criminal offence of a person during the investigation phase,[717] and lasts until the final closure of all appeal proceedings.[718] Furthermore, it is by now acknowledged in the case law of the ECtHR that a '"criminal charge" exists' from the moment the person concerned is 'substantially affected by actions taken by the authorities as a result of a suspicion against him'.[719]

### (3) Concrete rights

#### (a) *Preliminary remarks*

The rights of the accused in Article 14 (3) ICCPR, Article 6 (3) ECHR, and Article 8 (2) ACHR are components of the above discussed broader fair trial principle, laid down in Article 14 (1) ICCPR, Article 6 (1), and Article 8 (2) ACHR,[720] but they are not always clearly distinguishable from that principle. Thus, the ECtHR derives from the (just mentioned) general right to adversarial proceedings, in conjunction with Article 6 (3)(c)–(e) ECHR, the right 'to have knowledge of and comment on the observations filed and the evidence adduced by the other party[721] (especially of the prosecution)', as well as the right to be present at and take part in the (first instance and the appeal) hearing.[722] Article 14 (1) ICCPR

[715] cf. recently Nobis, *StV*, 35 (2015), 59–60.

[716] See also Safferling and Hartwig, *International Criminal Procedure* (2012), p. 286; Zappalá, *Human Rights* (2005), p. 54.

[717] ECtHR, *Deweer v. Belgium*, Application No. 6903/75, Judgment (27 February 1980), para. 46..

[718] Satzger, *Internationales Strafrecht* (2020), § 11 mn. 70; Satzger, *ICL* (2018), § 9 mn. 70; Noor Muhammad, in Henkin, *International Bill of Rights* (1981), p. 146. For the application of the fair trial principle throughout the entire proceedings, cf. also Steiner, *Fairnessprinzip* (1995), p. 150; Rönnau, *Absprache* (1990), p. 208; Eisenberg and Conen, *NJW* (1998), 2248.

[719] Most recently *Bjarki H. Diego v. Iceland*, Application No. 30965/17, Judgment (22 March 2022), para. 43; also, cf. note 761 above. Furthermore, see Directive (EU) 2016/343 of the European Parliament and of the Council (9 March 2016), recital 12 ('Directive should apply to natural persons who are suspects or accused persons in criminal proceedings. It should apply from the moment when a person is suspected or accused of having committed a criminal offence, or an alleged criminal offence, and, therefore, even before that person is made aware by the competent authorities of a Member State, by official notification or otherwise.')

[720] cf. Rzepka, *Fairness* (2000), pp. 25–6, 57; Meyer-Ladewig et al., 'Artikel 6' in Meyer-Ladewig and Nettesheim, *EMRK* (2017), mn. 221, both with case law references; Demko, *Verteidigung* (2014), p. 230. In detail, Gaede, *Fairness* (2007), pp. 159 ff.; Tochilovsky, *Jurisprudence* (2014), pp. 443 ff.; on the ICCPR, see Noor Muhammad, in Henkin, *Bill of Rights* (1981), p. 151; on the ACHR, see Medina, *ACHR* (2022), pp. 310–11, 386; Ibañez Rivas, 'Articulo 8', in Steiner and Uribe, *CIDH Comentario* (2019), pp. 270 ff.; Ùbeda de Torres, in Burgorgue-Larsen and Ùbeda de Torres, *IACtHR* (2011), p. 665.

[721] The accused is also entitled to comment on any evidence submitted by an 'independent member of the national legal service' (ECtHR, *Kress v. France*, Application No. 39594/98, Judgment (7 June 2001), para. 74; *Zhuk v. Ukraine*, Application No. 45783/05, Judgment (21 October 2010), para. 25; see also note 736 above, with references to recent case law.

[722] ECtHR, *Colozza v. Italy*, Application No. 9024/80, Judgment (12 February 1985), para. 27; for further case law, see previous edition, p. 68 with note 662; more recently *Arps v. Croatia*, Application No. 23444/12, Judgment (25 October 2016), para. 28. cf. also Esser, *Europäisches Strafverfahrensrecht* (2002), pp. 406 ff., 410, 415, 458, 721 with further references in nn. 218–19; Esser, *Europäisches und Internationales Strafrecht* (2023), § 9 mn. 217, 249; Haefliger and Schürmann, *EMRK* (1999), pp. 183–4, 186–8; Villiger, *Handbuch EMRK* (2020), pp. 309–10; Meyer-Ladewig et al., 'Artikel 6' in Meyer-Ladewig and Nettesheim, *EMRK* (2017), mn. 99; Peukert, in Strafver

similarly entails the 'fundamental duty of the courts to ensure equality between the parties, including the ability to contest all the argument and evidence adduced by the other party';[723] Article 14 (3)(d) ICCPR provides explicitly for the right to be tried in one's presence, but *in absentia* trials are not prohibited absolutely under Article 14 (3)(d) ICCPR.[724]

Thus, there is a structural similarity between adversarial procedure and equality of arms in that both require the right to personal attendance at the proceedings with the opportunity to comment on and challenge evidence,[725] especially incriminating one.[726] This opportunity must also exist with regard to official declarations of the Court[727] and presupposes, in appeal proceedings, the communication of a draft judgment to both parties, not only to the Prosecutor.[728] Of course, the opportunity to take part in the proceedings presupposes the accused's capability to stand trial.[729]

The individual rights contained in Article 14 (3) ICCPR, Article 6 (3) ECHR, and Article 8 (2) ACHR also partially overlap.[730] They can be summarized under the general right to an effective and adequate defence[731]—which, as a separate right, is listed once again in Article 14 (3)(d) ICCPR, Article 6 (3)(c) ECHR, and Article 8 (2)(d) ACHR—wherein one can distinguish two levels of protection. At the first level, the basic prerequisites of an effective defence are guaranteed by giving the accused the right to be informed of the charges[732] and to have adequate time and facilities for the preparation of the defence.[733] The second level refers to the exercise of defence *stricto sensu*, which encompasses the right to be present,[734] not to be compelled to testify against oneself,[735] the right to confrontation,[736] and to assistance of

teidigervereinigungen, *Reform oder Roll-Back?* (1997), pp. 237–8; Sommer, in Brüssow et al., *Strafverteidigung* (2007), § 17 mn. 97.

[723] See HRCt, *Jansen-Gielen v. The Netherlands* (2001) UN Doc. CCPR/C/71/D/846/1999, para. 8.2; *Näkkäläjärvi v. Finland* (2001) UN Doc. CCPR/C/73/D/779/1997, para. 7.4.

[724] See HRCt, 'General Comment 32' (23 August 2007) UN Doc. CCPR/C/GC/32, para. 36. Generally on the admissibility of *in absentia* trials, see Esser, *Europäisches Strafverfahrensrecht* (2002), pp. 721 ff.; Zappalà, *Human Rights* (2005), pp. 126 ff., arguing that trials *in absentia* are permitted by human rights law, as long as the accused enjoys all guarantees regarding his right to be present during the trial, McDermott, in Sluiter et al., *International Criminal Procedure* (2013), p. 763; Schwarz, *Afr. Hum. Rights Law J.*, 16 (2016), 102 ff.

[725] Esser, *Europäisches Strafverfahrensrecht* (2002), p. 415; also Villiger, *Handbuch EMRK* (2020), pp. 309, 334 (personal participation and questioning).

[726] *Bernard v. France*, Application No. 22885/93, Judgment (23 April 1998), para. 38; more recently *Kaharan v. Turkey*, Application No. 53848/07, Judgment (16 March 2021), para. 37 ('adequate and proper opportunity to challenge and question a witness against him'); also Villiger, *Handbuch EMRK* (2020), p. 314.

[727] Esser, *Europäisches Strafverfahrensrecht* (2002), pp. 417–18; in a similar vein, Schabas, *CCPR* (2019), Art. 14, mn. 32.

[728] cf. Esser, *Europäisches Strafverfahrensrecht* (2002), pp. 418–19.

[729] ECtHR, *Mielke v. Germany*, Application No. 30047/96, Judgment (25 November 1996), para. 36.

[730] cf. also Haefliger and Schürmann, *EMRK* (1999), p. 227 (regarding letters (b) and (c)); Villiger, *Handbuch EMRK* (2020), p. 323 (regarding lit. (a) and (b)). On Art. 14 (3) ICCPR, see Joseph and Castan, *ICCPR* (2013), p. 491 (regarding lit. (d) and (b)).

[731] In favour of Art. 6 (3)(b) as the parent right ('Mutterrecht') encompassing all others, Trechsel, in Schweizer, Burkert, and Gasser, *FS Drucy* (2002), p. 995; cf. also Demko, *Verteidigung* (2014), pp. 236, 238–9.

[732] Arts. 14 (3)(a) ICCPR, 6 (3)(a) ECHR, 8 (2)(b) ACHR; see also Ibañez Rivas, 'Articulo 8', in Steiner and Uribe, *CIDH Comentario* (2019), pp. 294–6; Grabenwarter, *ECHR* (2014), Art. 6 mn. 124.

[733] Arts. 14 (3)(b) ICCPR, 6 (3)(b) ECHR, and 8 (2)(c) ACHR; see also Ibañez Rivas, 'Articulo 8', in Steiner and Uribe, *CIDH Comentario* (2019), p. 296; with regard to the information of the (factual basis of the) charges before the confirmation hearing in view of Art. 67 (1)(b) ICCS and Rule 121 (3) RPE ICC, see ICC, *Pre-Trial Practice Manual* (March 2022), p. 7.

[734] Art. 14 (3)(d) ICCPR.

[735] Arts. 14 (3)(g) ICCPR, and 8 (2)(g) ACHR; see also Ibañez Rivas, 'Articulo 8', in Steiner and Uribe, *CIDH Comentario* (2019), pp. 304–5.

[736] Arts. 14 (3)(e) ICCPR, 6 (3)(e) ECHR, and 8 (2)(f) ACHR; see also Ibañez Rivas, 'Articulo 8', in Steiner and Uribe, *CIDH Comentario* (2019), pp. 303–4.

an interpreter.[737] It should be noted that the list of these procedural rights is not exhaustive but may be expanded by the case law taking recourse to the umbrella rights of a fair trial and equality of arms.[738]

### (b) *Presumption of innocence*

The presumption of innocence is enshrined in Article 14 (2) ICCPR, Article 6 (2) ECHR,[739] and Article 8 (2) cl. 1 ACHR: 'Everyone charged with a criminal offence shall have the right to be presumed innocent until proved guilty according to law.'[740] The presumption of innocence applies only to criminal proceedings and shall ensure that the judge does not commence the trial with a preconceived idea about the guilt of the accused.[741] The principle entails further that the burden of proof lies with the prosecution and cannot be reversed.[742] In addition, the presumption of innocence, together with the standard of proof beyond reasonable doubt, entails that any doubt should benefit the accused (*in dubio pro reo*).[743] The presumption of innocence is binding on all public authorities; accordingly, they should not only refrain from making public statements regarding the guilt of the suspect or accused[744]

[737] Arts. 14 (3)(f) ICCPR, 6 (3)(e) ECHR, and 8 (2)(a) ACHR; see also Ibañez Rivas, 'Articulo 8', in Steiner and Uribe, *CIDH Comentario* (2019), pp. 293–4.

[738] Villiger, *Handbuch EMRK* (2020), p. 322; Demko, *Verteidigung* (2014), pp. 237 ff., 245 ff.; similarly Peukert, in Strafverteidigervereinigungen, *Reform oder Roll-Back?* (1997), p. 243 (wider margin of appreciation); Noor Muhammad, in Henkin, *Bill of Rights* (1981), p. 151; Medina, *ACHR* (2022), pp. 414–15.

[739] See also Art. 48 (1) EU Charter: 'Everyone who has been charged shall be presumed innocent until proved guilty according to law.'

[740] Art. 14 (2) ICCPR.

[741] Barrot, *ZJS*, 3 (2010), 701; Corstens and Pradel, *European Criminal Law* (2002), pp. 412 ff.; McDermott, *Fairness* (2016), pp. 42 ff.; see note 749 in this chapter. The presumption of innocence is related to the right to an impartial tribunal, insofar as it requires the judges to be unbiased towards the accused (see Friman, Brady, Costi, Guariglia, and Stuckenberg, in Sluiter et al., *International Criminal Procedure* (2013), p. 455); see also in general Schabas and McDermott, 'Article 66', in Ambos, *Commentary* (2022), mn. 10 ff.

[742] cf. ECtHR, *Salabiaku v. France*, Application No. 10519/83, Judgment (7 October 1988), para. 28; more recently *Tsvetkova v. Russia*, Application No. 54381/08, Judgment (10 April 2018), para. 192 ('presumption of innocence will be infringed where the burden of proof is shifted from the prosecution to the defence'); furthermore, see *Pasquini v. San Marino*, Application No. 23349/17, Judgment (20 October 2020), para. 32 *Pasquini v. San Marino*, Application No. 23349/17, Judgment (20 October 2020), para. 32; also Satzger, *Internationales Strafrecht* (2020), § 11 mn. 94; Satzger, *ICL* (2018), § 9 mn. 92; HRCt, 'General Comment 32' (23 August 2007) UN Doc. CCPR/C/GC/32, para. 30; Noor Muhammad, in Henkin, *Bill of Rights* (1981), p. 150; Safferling /Hartwig, *International Criminal Procedure* (2012), pp. 287–8; Zappalá, *Human Rights* (2005), pp. 85, 91 ff.; Friman, Brady, Costi, Guariglia, and Stuckenberg, in Sluiter et al., *International Criminal Procedure* (2013), p. 455; Grabenwarter, *ECHR* (2014), Art. 6 mn. 156; Medina, *ACHR* (2022), pp. 386–7; furthermore, see Coleman, *ICLR*, 20 (2020), 375–7 differentiating between a 'procedural and non-procedural' aspect of the presumption of innocence with the latter protecting 'individuals from being treated as if they are guilty without first being convicted of a crime'; see also in general Schabas and McDermott, 'Article 66', in Ambos, *Commentary* (2022), mn. 18 ff.

[743] ECtHR, *Barberà, Messegué and Jabardo v. Spain*, Application No. 10590/83, Judgment (6 December 1988), para. 77; *Natunen v. Finland*, Application No. 21022/04, Judgment (31 March 2009), para. 53; *Ajdaric v. Croatia*, Application No. 20883/09, Judgment (13 December 2011), para. 35; *Tsvetkova v. Russia*, Application No. 54381/08, Judgment (10 April 2018), para. 192 ('any doubt should benefit the accused'); HRCt, 'General Comment 32' (23 August 2007) UN Doc. CCPR/C/GC/32, para. 30; *Khudayberdiev v. Kyrgyzstan* (2020) UN Doc. CCPR/C/127/D/2522/2015, para. 10.2; *Khadzhiyev v. Turkmenistan* (2018) UN Doc. CCPR/C/122/D/2252/2013, para. 7.10 ('guarantees that no guilt can be presumed until the charge has been proved beyond resonable doubt, ensures that the accused has the benefit of doubt and requires that persons accused of a criminal act must be tretaed in accordance with this principle'). See also Friman, Brady, Costi, Guariglia, and Stuckenberg, in Sluiter et al., *International Criminal Procedure* (2013), p. 455. For a fundamental treatment, see Zopfs, *In dubio pro reo* (1999), pp. 328 ff., (pp. 330–1, 334) according to whom the principle constitutes an autonomous decision rule ('*Entscheidungsregel*') based on Roman Law and *the ius commune*, expressing a principle of justice supported by the century-old idea that it is more just not to inflict harm (even if it were right/justified) than to inflict harm without right/justification.

[744] cf. HRCt, 'General Comment 13' (1994) UN Doc. HRI/GEN/1/Rev.1 at 14 (1994), para. 7 ('duty for all public authorities to refrain from prejudging the outcome of a trial') and 'General Comment 32' (23 August 2007) UN Doc. CCPR/C/GC/32, para. 30 ('duty for all public authorities to refrain … from making public

but they are also obliged to intervene to prevent such statements by the media or other parties.[745]

The flip side of the presumption of innocence is the right to silence and non-self-incrimination (*nemo tenetur se ipsum accusare*).[746] For the one who is presumed innocent should not be obliged to contribute to proving the opposite. This right is explicitly guaranteed by Article 14 (3)(g) ICCPR, Article 8 (2)(g) ACHR, and the above-mentioned provisions of the international criminal tribunals.[747] The ECtHR takes it to 'lie at the heart of the notion of a fair procedure'.[748] It is not confined to cases where the suspect/accused had to withstand real coercion, but generally protects his freedom to speak or to remain silent, that is, his right not to contribute substantially to his own conviction.[749] Article 55 (1) (a) ICCS extends the right to non-self incrimination to witnesses;[750] this is supported by a

statements affirming the guilt of the accused'). See also Schabas, *CCPR* (2019), Art. 14 mn. 61; Gundel, in Merten and Papier, *Grundrechte, VI/1* (2010), § 146 mn. 137; Barrot, *ZJS*, 3 (2010), 703 ff.; Peters and Altwicker, *EMRK* (2012), § 21 mn. 6; Kreicker, in Sieber et al., *Europäisches Strafrecht* (2014), § 51 mn. 24; Medina, *ACHR* (2022), pp. 387 ff.; Grabenwarter, *ECHR* (2014), Art. 6 mn. 158.

[745] *Allenet de Ribemont v. France*, Application No. 15175/89, Judgment (10 February 1995), paras. 11, 41; on that, Peters and Altwicker, *EMRK* (2012), § 21 mn. 10; Grabenwarter and Pabel, *EMRK* (2021), § 24 mn. 142–3; *Borovský v. Slovakia*, Application No. 24528/02, Judgment (2 June 2009), para. 46; more recently *Tsvetkova v. Russia*, Application No. 54381/08, Judgment (10 April 2018), para. 192; *Berenson-Mejía Case*, Judgment, Reparations, and Costs, IACtHR Series C No. 119, 24 November 2004, paras. 158–61; *J. vs. Perú Case*, Judgment, Reparations and Costs, IACtHR Serie C No. 275, 27 November 2013, para. 244; thereon Ùbeda de Torres, in Burgorgue-Larsen and Ùbeda de Torres, *Inter-American Court of Human Rights* (2011), pp. 664–5. See also Zappalá, *Human Rights* (2005), pp. 85–6; Grabenwarter, *ECHR* (2014), Art. 6 mn. 160. On the presumption of innocence in German, French, and English criminal procedure, see Gleß, *Beweisrechtsgrundsätze* (2006), pp. 203 ff.

[746] *Krumpholz v. Austria*, Application No. 13201/05, Judgment (18 March 2010), para. 30 ('closely linked'); more recently and more clearly *Pasquini v. San Marino*, Application No. 23349/17, Judgment (20 October 2020), para. 32 ('the presumption of innocence imposes requirements in respect of, *inter alia*, ... the privilege against self-incrimination'); see also de Meester, Pitcher, Rastan, and Sluiter, in Sluiter et al., *International Criminal Procedure* (2013), p. 245 ('closely connected to the presumption of innocence'); Safferling and Hartwig, *International Criminal Procedure* (2012), p. 287 ('closely related'); Zappalá, *Human Rights* (2005), p. 55; Gless, *Internationales Strafrecht* (2021), mn. 92, Ambos, *IsLR*, 42 (2009), 385; Grabenwarter, *ECHR* (2014), Art. 6 mn. 152; for a crit. analysis taking into account, inter alia, the case law of the U.S. Supreme Court, see Ransiek and Winsel, *GA*, 162 (2015), 622 ff.

[747] See note 717 and main text in this chapter.

[748] *Murray v. UK*, Application No. 18731/91, Judgment (8 February 1996), para. 45; for further case law, see previous edition, p. 70 with note 688; more recently *Bajic v. North Macedonia*, Application No. 2833/13, Judgment (10 June 2021), para. 64; cf. also Schabas, *CCPR* (2019), Art. 14 mn. 108 ('essence of a fair trial'); Grabenwarter and Pabel, *EMRK* (2021), § 24 mn. 140, Meyer-Ladewig et al., 'Artikel 6' in Meyer-Ladewig and Nettesheim, *EMRK* (2017), mn. 129; Walter, in Roth, *Europäisierung* (2010), pp. 303–4, de Meester, Pitcher, Rastan, and Sluiter, in Sluiter et al., *International Criminal Procedure* (2013), p. 305; Boas et al., *Procedure* (2011), pp. 109–10; Safferling and Hartwig, *International Criminal Procedure* (2012), p. 287; fundamentally Moscarini, *RIDPP*, 49 (2006), 611 ff. For a crit. view, see Matt, *GA*, 153 (2006), 327–8.

[749] e.g. by giving a sample of his handwriting if this sample together with other evidence would prove the charge against the accused, cf. *Prosecutor v. Delalić et al.*, No. IT-96-21-T, TC, Decision on the Prosecution's Oral Request for the Admission of Exhibit 155 into Evidence and for an Order to Compel the Accused, Zdravko Mucic, to provide a Handwriting Sample, paras. 47–8 (19 January 1998); de Meester, Pitcher, Rastan, and Sluiter, in Sluiter et al., *International Criminal Procedure* (2013), p. 292. On unitary and bifurcated models of criminal procedure and the prohibition of self-incrimination, see Acquaviva, in Sluiter et al., *International Criminal Procedure* (2013), pp. 538–40, arguing, that, although a unitary procedure does not violate the rights of the accused, a bifurcated model of procedure is more protective; on this cf. also Vasiliev, in Sluiter et al., *International Criminal Procedure* (2013), p. 670. On the interplay between the right to silence and the right to self-representation, esp. during the so-called 'negotiated agreements' proceeding (*Verständigung*) of the German criminal procedure (§ 257c StPO), see Spaniol, in Burkhardt et al., *FG Eser* (2015), pp. 432 ff.

[750] See also Rule 74 RPE ICC (assurance of confidentiality by Chamber); de Meester, Pitcher, Rastan, and Sluiter, in Sluiter et al., *International Criminal Procedure* (2013), pp. 267–8, 276, also referring to the ECCC Rules; *contra* Judge McDonald, Dissenting Opinion, ICTY, D. Tadic, TC, 27 November 1996, para. 32 n. 4.

broad interpretation of the relevant human rights guarantees, in particular Article 14 (3) (g) ICCPR.[751] The autonomy of a person under investigation is effectively undermined if adverse inferences are drawn from the silence of the accused.[752] The clear prohibition in this regard by Article 55 (2)(b) ICCS—'without such silence being a consideration in the determination of guilt or innocence'—is therefore to be welcomed.[753] Similarly, it contributes to the effectiveness of this right if the suspect/accused/witness is informed of it prior to questioning,[754] and cautioned that any statement could be used in evidence against him.[755]

Equally, the authorities must not use subterfuge to elicit, from a suspect who has decided to remain silent, confessions or other statements of an incriminatory nature.[756] Nevertheless, such an obtaining of incriminating evidence may not amount to a violation of the *nemo tenetur* principle, if it 'was [not] tainted with the element of coercion or oppression,' and the defendant 'was not detained on remand'.[757] In a similar vein, the *Delalić* ICTY TC did not see an illict inducement in the case of an 'advice' to the accused to confess since this would 'assist in mitigation of punishment'.[758] Regulation 43 (1) RegOTP, however, more strictly prohibits any 'inducement whatsoever ... in exchange for questioning or a statement'.[759] In any case, one has to draw a line between still acceptable techniques of interrogation and oppressive or coercive conduct ('improper compulsion')[760] during interrogation, which turns on the

[751] cf. Ambos, *LJIL*, 15 (2002), 160–2; leaving it open ('unclear'), de Meester, Pitcher, Rastan, and Sluiter, in Sluiter et al., *International Criminal Procedure* (2013), p. 280, but in the result in favour of this right, recommending it as a general principle, at p. 282.

[752] *Delalić et al.*, No. IT-96-21-T, Decision on the Prosecution's Oral Request, paras. 46 ff. (*contra* ECtHR, *Murray v. UK*, Application No. 18731/91, Judgment (8 February 1996) and the Prevention of Terrorism Act 1989 of Northern Ireland). cf. Safferling and Hartwig, *International Criminal Procedure* (2012), pp. 287–8; on the ICCPR, see HRCt, 'Concluding Observations on the United Kingdom' (27 July 1995) UN Doc. CCPR/C/79/Add. 55, para. 17. See also Gaynor, in Sluiter et al., *International Criminal Procedure* (2013), pp. 1124–5, arguing that drawing inferences from the silence of the accused is not incompatible with Art. 6 ECHR per se.

[753] Crit. of the lack of such a clear rule in the law of ICTY, ICTR, and SCSL, de Meester, Pitcher, Rastan, and Sluiter, in Sluiter et al., *International Criminal Procedure* (2013), p. 234; recognizing this as a rule, p. 254.

[754] cf. Reg. 40 (c) RegOTP and Rule 42 (1)(a) RPE KSC; in favour de Meester, Pitcher, Rastan, and Sluiter, in Sluiter et al., *International Criminal Procedure* (2013), p. 282.

[755] Rule 42 (A)(iii) RPE ICTY/ICTR/SCSL. While such a rule does not exist in the ICC law, the prosecution has clarified that it always gives this information to the person concerned, cf. *Prosecutor v. Katanga and Ngudjolo Chui*, No. ICC-01/04-01/07-336, Prosecution's Observations regarding Admission for the Confirmation Hearing of the Transcripts of Interview of Deceased Witness 12 pursuant to Arts. 61 and 69 of the Statute, para. 21 (20 March 2008), ('Although neither the Statute nor Rules so require, the Prosecution has adopted, and consistently applied, a policy of informing all persons questioned—including under Art. 55 (2)—that their evidence may be used in subsequent proceedings' [fn. omitted]); *Prosecutor v. Ali Muhammad Ali Abd-Al-Rahman*, Decision on the Admissibility of Video (DAR-OTP-0216-0119) and Records of Telephone Calls (DAR-OTP-0216-0127, DAR-OTP-0216-0128), ICC-02/05-01/20-876, 17 February 2003, paras. 17, 57.

[756] *Allan v. UK*, Application No. 48539/99, Judgment (5 November 2002), para. 50; more recently *Ibrahim et al. v. UK*, Application No. 50541/08 et al., Grand Chamber Judgment (13 September 2016), para. 267. See also de Meester, Pitcher, Rastan, and Sluiter, in Sluiter et al., *International Criminal Procedure* (2013), p. 224; cf. Boas et al., *Procedure* (2011), pp. 111–12.

[757] ECtHR, *Bykov v. Russia*, Application No. 4378/02, Judgment (10 March 2009), para. 102; more recently *Ibrahim et al. v. UK*, Application No. 50541/08 et al., Grand Chamber Judgment (13 September 2016), para. 267 clarifying that the usage of subterfuge is (in principle) among the 'situations which give rise to concerns as to improper compulsion in breach of Article 6'; furthermore, see *Hasalikova v. Slovakia*, Application No. 39654/15, Judgment (24 June 2021), para. 58. In a similar case, where a conversation was intercepted between a person in pre-trial detention and his wife, the German Federal Court (*Bundesgerichtshof*, BGH) did not refer to the *nemo tenetur* principle, but to the fair trial principle, cf. German *BGHSt* 53, 294 ff.; for a crit. view, see Walter, in Roth, *Europäisierung* (2010), p. 302; Hauck, *NStZ*, 30 (2010), 19 ff.; see also Schabas, *CCPR* (2019), Art. 14 mn. 110.

[758] *Delalić et al.*, No. IT-96-21-T, Decision on Mucic's Motion for Exclusion of Evidence, para. 54.

[759] Similarly, the Rule 21 (3) of the ECCC internal Rules and Rule 42 (1)(b) RPE KSC prohibit all forms of inducement; in favour de Meester, Pitcher, Rastan, and Sluiter, in Sluiter et al., *International Criminal Procedure* (2013), pp. 238, 255.

[760] ECtHR, *Allan v. UK*, Application No. 48539/99, Judgment (5 November 2002), para. 50 (referring in this regard to 'methods of coercion or oppression in defiance of the will of the accused'); more recently *Ibrahim et al.*

voluntariness of a declaration or confession and thus must be considered a violation of the right to silence.[761] Of course, this line cannot be drawn in the abstract, but depends on the circumstances of the concrete case.

Both 'fair trial' and presumption of innocence are intimately interrelated with the *culpability principle*. Although the former is of a procedural and the latter of a substantive nature, in any case the (procedural) presumption of innocence is predicated on the assumption that the (substantive) guilt must and can be proved.[762]

The presumption of innocence may prohibit, further, the imposition of costs and expenses without a formal determination of guilt[763] or the partial shifting of the burden of proof on the accused (something not categorically precluded by the ECtHR).[764] Furthermore, the principle entails that the judicial revocation of the suspension of a prison sentence, on the grounds that the convicted person committed a new criminal offence during the period of probation,[765] is subject to the condition that the new alleged offence has already been tried by the first instance[766] (and the person concerned convicted) or that the person concerned made a confession in presence of his defence counsel.[767] On the other hand, the presumption of innocence does not impede the non-suspension of the remainder of a sentence of

*v. UK*, Application No. 50541/08 et al., Grand Chamber Judgment (13 September 2016), para. 267 ('Court must first consider the nature and degree of compulsion used to obtain the evidence'); furthermore, see *Fariz Ahmadov v. Azerbaijan*, Application No. 40321/07, Judgment (14 January 2021), para. 51 with regard to the right to be assisted by a lawyer.

761 For a discussion and references, see de Meester, Pitcher, Rastan, and Sluiter, in Sluiter et al., *International Criminal Procedure* (2013), pp. 226–8, 243; on deception during questioning from a comparative perspective, see pp. 250–1.

762 In this sense, see also Gollwitzer, *Menschenrechte* (2005), Art. 6 MRK mn. 103, 105; on the culpability principle, see Ambos, *Treatise ICL I* (2021), pp. 150–2 ('optimization requirement').

763 The decisive factor is whether a finding of guilt may be inferred from the reasoning of a decision and/or the language used (cf. *Demjanjuk v. Germany*, Application No. 24247/15, Judgment (24 January 2019), paras. 37–8). Furthermore, see Kreicker, in Sieber et al., *Europäisches Strafrecht* (2014), § 51 mn. 24; Peters and Altwicker, *EMRK* (2012), § 21 mn. 7, both with further case law references.

764 ECtHR, *Salabiaku v. France*, Application No. 10519/83, Judgment (7 October 1988), para. 28 ('the Convention does not prohibit such presumptions in principle. It does, however, require the Contracting State to remain within certain limits in this respect as regards criminal law.'); but also see *Poletan and Azirovik v. Macedonia*, Application Nos. 26711/07, 32786/10, and 34278/10, Judgment (12 May 2016), para. 64 ('presumption of innocence will be infringed where the burden of proof is shifted from the prosecution to the defence') and most recently *Makarashvili and Others v. Georgia*, Application Nos. 23158/20, 31365/20, 32525/20, Judgment (22 September 2023), paras. 61–4; on the ICCPR, see HRCt, 'General Comment 13', para. 7. See also Peters and Altwicker, *EMRK* (2012), § 21 mn. 9; Satzger, *ICL* (2018), § 9 mn. 92; Satzger, *Internationales Strafrecht* (2020), § 11 mn. 94.

765 This scenario has become relevant in two ECtHR cases concerning Germany (see note 816) on the revocation of probation (§ 56 f of the German Criminal Code) and on the revocation of probation in juvenile criminal proceedings (§ 26 German Youth Courts Act). On the current German case law in this regard, which (in accordance with the relevant ECtHR case law) now requires a conviction or a credible, unrevoked confession before a judge, cf., in greater detail, Hubrach, '§ 56 f', in Cirener et al., Leipziger Kommentar—*StGB*, v. (2022), mn. 9–10 with further references. For the (at times) intensive discussion in German literature, cf. the previous edition, p. 73 with notes 706–7.

766 ECtHR, *Böhmer v. Germany*, Application No. 37568/97, Judgment (3 October 2002), para. 65; see also *El Kaada v. Germany*, Application No. 2130/10, Judgment (12 November 2015) para. 57 ('domestic trial courts competent to decide on the new charges had not yet delivered a judgment in the applicant's case in which he had been proved guilty of the new offence at the time of the impugned revocation decisions'); with regard to *El Kaada*, see Esser, *NStZ*, 36 (2016), 697.

767 *ECtHR, Böhmer v. Germany*, Application No. 37568/97, Judgment (3 October 2002), para. 65; *El Kaada v. Germany* concerned a case in which the applicant had withdrawn a confession (*El Kaada v. Germany*, Application No. 2130/10, Judgment (12 November 2015) para. 59 ('the domestic courts could no longer base their conclusion that the applicant committed another offence during the probation period on a valid confession')).

imprisonment after two-thirds has been served since this decision depends on a (positive) prognosis of the future (non-criminal) conduct of the convicted person.[768]

### *(c) Prompt information about nature and cause of the charge*

The right to be informed as early as possible of the 'nature and cause' of the charge or accusation, as laid down in Article 14 (3)(a) ICCPR, Article 6 (3)(a) ECHR, and Article 8 (2)(b) ACHR,[769] protects the accused from being taken by surprise.[770] From the perspective of an effective equality of arms, it is indispensable that the accused be informed comprehensively and truthfully about the charges from the very beginning of the investigation directed against him.[771] Otherwise, he will suffer an irretrievable disadvantage vis-à-vis the Prosecutor.[772] Thus, the duty to provide information arises as soon as a concrete person is investigated, that is, as soon as a concrete suspect exists.[773] A limitation of the right to be informed only at the moment of the filing of the actual charges, as suggested by some case law,[774] is too formalistic and understates the importance of the information right for an effective defence. Of course, information about the 'charges' within the meaning of the respective provisions is only possible if such charges exist, that is, at the earliest at the end of the formal investigation. However, as already argued above, the fair trial and equality of arms principles require that the person investigated is informed as early as possible about the reasons and grounds for the suspicion against her, although this suspicion has still to further mature to turn into a precise charge or charges.[775] Indeed, Rule 42 (A) RPE ICTY/

[768] cf. ECtHR, *M. M. v. Germany*, Application No. 23091/93, Judgment (30 November 1994); *OLG Hamm NStZ*, 24 (2004), 685; *OLG Düsseldorf*, 12 (1992), 287; for a discussion, see Peglau, *ZRP*, 36 (2003), 243 with reference to the *M. M. v. Germany* judgment.

[769] cf. Schabas, *CCPR* (2019), Art. 14 mn. 63–6; also Simon, *Beschuldigtenrechte* (1998), pp. 7 ff.; Rzepka, *Fairness* (2000), pp. 8 ff.; Esser, *Europäisches Strafverfahrensrecht* (2002), pp. 437 ff.; Esser, *Europäisches und Internationales Strafrecht* (2023), § 9 mn. 243; Braitsch, *Gerichtssprache* (1991), pp. 137 ff.; Frister, *StV*, 18 (1998), 159; Villiger, *Handbuch EMRK* (2020), pp. 323–4.; Meyer-Ladewig et al., 'Article 6' in Meyer-Ladewig and Nettesheim, *EMRK* (2017), mn. 223.

[770] Trechsel, *ZStR*, 96 (1979), 343 ('Überraschung und Überrumpelung'); in a similar vein, Villiger, *Handbuch EMRK* (2020), pp. 323 emphasizing the facilitation of effective defence; cf. also Cape et al., *Criminal Defence* (2010), p. 33; de Meester, Pitcher, Rastan, and Sluiter, in Sluiter et al., *International Criminal Procedure* (2013), pp. 228–30 ('ensure privilege against self-incrimination'); Noor Muhammad, in Henkin, *Bill of Rights* (1981), p. 152 ('necessary to enable the accused to prepare his defense adequately'). On the problem of cumulative charges, cf. Zappalá, *Human Rights* (2005), pp. 120 ff.

[771] ECtHR, *Corigliano v. Italy*, Application No. 8304/78, Judgment (10 December 1982), para. 34; *Kravtas v. Lithuania*, Application No. 12717/06, Judgment (18 January 2011), para. 35 (focusing on the interference with the situation of the suspect); *Mulosmani v. Albania*, Application No. 29864/03, Judgment (8 October 2013), para. 123; *Drassich v. Italy*, Application No. 65173/09, Judgment (22 February 2018), para. 66 ('un'informazione precisa e completa delle accuse formulate a carico dell'imputato, e dunque la qualificazione giuridica che il giudice potrebbe adottare nei suoi confronti'); HRCt, 'General Comment 32' (23 August 2007) UN Doc. CCPR/C/GC/32, para. 31; HRCt, General Comment 13, para. 14 (focusing on the moment of 'official suspicion against a specific person'); for a different view, see Medina, *ACHR* (2022), p. 392.

[772] On this understanding of equality of arms, cf. previously Ambos, *NStZ*, 23 (2003), 16; regarding the ad hoc tribunals, see McDermott, in Sluiter et al., *International Criminal Procedure* (2013), pp. 790–1.

[773] Simon, *Beschuldigtenrechte* (1998), pp. 9–10; similarly Frister, *StV*, 18 (1998), 159 ff., 161; Sommer, in Brüssow et al., *Strafverteidigung* (2007), § 17 mn. 61; Villiger, *Handbuch EMRK* (2020), p. 323; for a different view, see Esser, *Europäisches Strafverfahrensrecht* (2002), p. 440.

[774] *Prosecutor v. Delalić et al.*, TC, Decision on the Motion on the Exclusion and Restitution of Evidence and other Material Seized from the Accused Zejnil Delalić, No. IT-96-21-T, 9 October 1996, paras. 10–11; *Prosecutor v. Haraqija and Morina*, TC, Decision on Bajrush Morina's Request for a Declaration of Inadmissibility and Exclusion of Evidence, No. IT-04-84-R77.4, 28 August 2008, paras. 29–30. In a similar vein, de Meester, Pitcher, Rastan, and Sluiter, in Sluiter et al., *International Criminal Procedure* (2013), pp. 229–30, 235, 252, concluding however, at p. 243, that 'most tribunals … require that the suspect is informed' and recognizing, as a rule, at p. 254, a right to be informed 'prior to interrogation' of a suspicion regarding crimes; this rule should become a principle.

[775] In the same vein, Safferling, *International Criminal Procedure* (2003), pp. 119–20; Zappalà, *Human Rights* (2005), pp. 48–50.

ICTR/SCSL as well as Rule 43(2) RPE KSC impose the general duty on the Prosecutor to 'inform the suspect'. Even more explicitly, Article 55 (2) ICCS grants the suspect certain information rights if interrogated by the Prosecutor or national authorities,[776] including the right 'to be informed, prior to being questioned, that there are grounds to believe that he or she has committed a crime',[777] that is, is a suspect.[778] The questioning of a suspect must always be recorded.[779] In any case, the information may not be provided if there are reasonable grounds to fear that the suspect would thwart the investigation in any other way than by exercising his procedural rights.[780]

The right to be informed entails the duty to notify—usually in writing—the person concerned of the contents of the formal indictment,[781] even when the accused was already informed of the nature and cause of the charges.[782] This applies in particular if the indictment contains new legal or factual aspects.[783] In any case, the right to be informed also results from the nature of adversarial proceedings, given that the accusation is the first formal and binding declaration of the opponent or adversary.[784]

Comprehensive information requires 'that the prosecution authorities disclose to the defence all material evidence in their possession for or against the accused';[785] that also includes, for instance, any information on the credibility of an incriminating witness.[786]

[776] Rule 112 RPE ICC on the 'Recording of questioning in particular cases' does not address the national authorities; see de Meester, Pitcher, Rastan, and Sluiter, in Sluiter et al., *International Criminal Procedure* (2013), p. 233.

[777] Art. 55(2)(a) ICCS; in this vein, see also Reg. 41 RegOTP; extending the right to be informed about 'the nature and scope of the investigation' to any person questioned, Reg. 40 (e) RegOTP.

[778] See note 762 in this chapter.

[779] cf. Rule 112 RPE ICC characterizing this as a recording 'in particular cases'; for a more comprehensive provision, see Rule 44 RPE KSC; see also de Meester, Pitcher, Rastan, and Sluiter, in Sluiter et al., *International Criminal Procedure* (2013), pp. 233, 254 (considering it as a rule). In the case of witnesses, Rule 111 RPE ICC applies (cf. ibid., p. 269); in favour of recording in this regard, also (considering it a principle) ibid., p. 281. For a summary of other tribunals, see ibid., pp. 275–6.

[780] cf. Alamuddin, in Khan, *Evidence* (2010), p. 272, arguing that esp. suspected senior government officials may hamper the investigation, conc. de Meester, Pitcher, Rastan, and Sluiter, in Sluiter et al., *International Criminal Procedure* (2013), p. 235; with regard to the ECHR, see Gillmeister, *StraFo*, (1996), 115–16; Simon, *Beschuldigtenrechte* (1998), pp. 10–11; Sommer, in Brüssow et al., *Strafverteidigung* (2007), § 17 mn. 61.

[781] Haefliger and Schürmann, *EMRK* (1999), p. 220; see also *Prosecutor v. Bemba*, TC, Judgment pursuant to Art. 74 of the Statute, No. ICC-01/05-01/08-3343, 21 March 2016, para. 33 with further references; furthermore, see *Prosecutor v. Ongwen*, TC, Decision on Defence Motions Alleging Defects in the Confirmation Decision, No. ICC-02/04-01/15-1476 07-03-2019 1/16 EC T, 7 March 2019, para. 18.

[782] *Kamasinski v. Austria*, Application No. 9783/82, Judgment (19 December 1989), para. 79; also *Bemba*, No. ICC-01/05-01/08-3343; *Prosecutor v. Dominic Ongwen*, AC, Judgment on the appeal of Mr Dominic Ongwen against Trial Chamber IX's 'Decision on Defence Motions Alleging Defects in the Confirmation Decision', No. ICC-02/04-01/15-1562, 17 July 2019, para. 69; *Prosecutor v. Alfred Yekatom and Patrice-Edouard Ngaïssona*, TC, Decision on the 'Prosecution's Urgent Request for Redactions to the Warrant of Arrest for Alfred YEKATOM (ICC-01/14-01/18-1-US-Exp)', No. ICC-01/14-01/18-6-Red2, 8 February 2011, para. 3; *Prosecutor v. Ali Muhammad Ali Abd-Al-Rahman*, PTC, Corrected Version of 'Decision on the confirmation of charges against Ali Muhammad Ali Abd-Al-Rahman ("Ali Kushayb"), ICC-02/05-01/20-433, 9 July 2021', No. ICC-02/05-01/20-433-Corr, 23 November 2021, para. 29.

[783] cf. Simon, *Beschuldigtenrechte* (1998), pp. 5–6; Esser, *Europäisches Strafverfahrensrecht* (2002), pp. 442 ff. On the highly controversial legal re-characterization of charges, see Chapter IV, B.(7) in this volume.

[784] Esser, *Europäisches Strafverfahrensrecht* (2002), p. 443; Kühne, *StV*, 14 (1994), 67.

[785] *Edwards v. UK*, Application No. 13071/87, Judgment (16 December 1992), para. 36; *Rowe and Davis v. UK*, Application No. 28901/95, Judgment (16 February 2000), para. 60; *Natunen v. Finland*, Application No. 21022/04, Judgment (31 March 2009), para. 39; yet also see *Rook v. Germany*, Application No. 1586/15, Judgment (25 July 2019), para. 58; cf. also Esser, *Europäisches Strafverfahrensrecht* (2002), pp. 403 ff.; Sommer, in Brüssow et al., *Strafverteidigung* (2007), § 17 mn. 61; Plowden and Kerrigan, *NLJ*, 151 (2001), 735–6; Wohlers and Schlegel, *NStZ*, 30 (2010), 489–90.

[786] ECtHR, *Jespers v. Belgium*, Application No. 8403/78, European Commission of Human Rights Report (14 December 1981), para. 58.

The *right to disclosure* can be considered a part of the right to adequate facilities for the preparation of the defence.[787] Of course, this right is not absolute but subject to competing interests, in particular reasons of national security or witness protection.[788] In any case, substantial disadvantages caused by non-disclosure to the accused must be 'sufficiently counterbalanced' through procedural safeguards.[789] Disclosure obligations are the typical consequence of an adversarial procedure that seeks to compensate prosecutorial superiority with a view to equality of arms. This is the reason that these obligations apply primarily to the prosecution. In contrast, defence disclosure obligation would violate, in principle, the principle of equality of arms[790] and the prohibition of self-incrimination.[791] We will return to the disclosure regime in international criminal procedure at a later stage.[792]

The 'inquisitorial' counterpart to disclosure is the right to unlimited *access to the case file*.[793] The ECtHR speaks of 'access to the case file'[794] and refers to the inspection of the file as a possible form of that access. While this right is not explicitly set out in Article 14 ICCPR, 6 ECHR, and 8 ACHR, it can be derived from the principle of equality of arms,[795] the right to a legal hearing,[796] and the right to adequately prepare the defence.[797] It also follows from the right to be informed since a broad reading of this right encompasses having full knowledge of the case file. While the jurisprudence has so far not set a fixed point in time by which

[787] Arts. 14 (3)(b) ICCPR, 6 (3)(b) ECHR, 8 (2)(c) ACHR; see also Ibañez Rivas, 'Articulo 8', in Steiner and Uribe, *CIDH Comentario* (2019), pp. 296; cf. HRCt, 'Concluding Observations on Canada', UN Doc. CCPR/C/CAN/CO/5, para. 13; HRCt, 'General Comment 32' (23 August 2007) UN Doc. CCPR/C/GC/32, para. 33); in a similar vein, Tochilovsky, in Sluiter et al., *International Criminal Procedure* (2013), p. 1095; also Grabenwarter, *ECHR* (2014), Art. 6 mn. 85.

[788] *Rowe and Davis v. UK*, Application No. 28901/95, Judgment (16 February 2000), paras. 54, 61; *Leas v. Estonia*, Application No. 59577/08, Judgment (6 March 2012), para. 78; *Donohue v. Ireland*, Application No. 19165/08, Judgment (12 December 2013), para. 74; more recently *Adomaitis v. Lithuania*, Application No. 14833/18, Judgment (18 January 2022), para. 68; *Paci v. Belgium*, Application No. 45597/09, Judgment (17 April 2018), para. 85. On restrictions on the right to disclosure, see also Tochilovsky, in Sluiter et al., *International Criminal Procedure* (2013), p. 1095. On the protection of witnesses in the EU, see Enikö, *RIDP*, 77 (2006), 313 ff. On the right to disclosure in the statutes of the international tribunals, cf. Zappalá, *Human Rights* (2005), pp. 143 ff. (pp. 147 ff. on the ICCS).

[789] ECtHR, *Jasper v. UK*, Application No. 27052/95, Judgment (16 February 2000), para. 52; see also Toney, *IJEP*, 5 (2001), 39, 49 ff.; Tochilovsky, in Sluiter et al., *International Criminal Procedure* (2013), p. 1095.

[790] May and Wierda, *ColJTransnat'lL*, 37 (1998/1999), 760–1; also see Safferling, *International Criminal Procedure* (2003), p. 202.

[791] cf. Brady, in Lee, *ICC* (2001), pp. 403, 414; Klamberg, inSluiter et al., *International Criminal Procedure* (2013), p. 1104 (no obligation to disclose exculpatory evidence to the prosecution).

[792] See Chapter V, B. in this volume.

[793] In detail, Walischewski, *Akteneinsichtsrechts* (1999), pp. 71 ff. and *passim*; Esser, *Europäisches Strafverfahrensrecht* (2002), pp. 424 ff.; Esser, *Europäisches und Internationales Strafrecht* (2023), § 9 mn. 245; Braitsch, *Gerichtssprache* (1991), pp. 152 ff.; Grabenwarter, *ECHR* (2014), Art. 6 mn. 129.

[794] cf. e.g. ECtHR, *Öcalan v. Turkey*, Application No. 46221/99, Judgment (12 March 2003), paras. 158 ff.; more recently *Matanović v. Croatia*, Application No. 2742/12, Judgment (4 April 2017), para. 159 ('Court reiterates that the right to a fair trial also implies the right of access to the case file'); likewise, *Kikabidze v. Georgia*, Application No. 57642/12, Judgment (16 November 2021), para. 42.

[795] In the same vein, ECtHR, *Öcalan v. Turkey*, Application No. 46221/99, Judgment (12 March 2003), para. 159; Esser, *Europäisches Strafverfahrensrecht* (2002), p. 425; see also Wohlers and Schlegel, *NStZ*, 30 (2010), 489; Grabenwarter, *ECHR* (2014), Art. 6 mn. 80. For a crit. view, see Trechsel, in Schweizer, Burkert, and Gasser, *FS Druey* (2002), p. 996.

[796] Haefliger and Schürmann, *EMRK* (1999), p. 188; from the perspective of constitutional law, see Walischewski, *Akteneinsichtsrechts* (1999), pp. 11 ff.; see also Rau, *StraFo*, 13 (2008), 9 ff.

[797] HRCt, 'General Comment 32' (23 August 2007) UN Doc. CCPR/C/GC/32, para. 33; see also ECtHR, *Öcalan v. Turkey*, Application No. 46221/99, Judgment (12 March 2003), para. 163; more recently *Rook v. Germany*, Application No. 1586/15, Judgment (25 July 2019), para. 57. In the same vein, Trechsel, in Schweizer, Burkert, and Gasser, *FS Druey* (2002), p. 994; Simon, *Beschuldigtenrechte* (1998), pp. 29, 30 ff.; Walischewski, *Akteneinsichtsrechts* (1999), p. 86; Villiger, *Handbuch EMRK* (2020), p. 325–6; Sommer, in Brüssow et al., *Strafverteidigung* (2007), § 17 mn. 65; HRCt, 'General Comment 32' (23 August 2007) UN Doc. CCPR/C/GC/32, para. 33.

access must be granted,[798] this right must clearly—equality of arms!—be applicable already at the investigation stage of the proceedings.[799] Indeed, the effective exercise of the specific rights of Article 14 (3) ICCPR, Article 6 (3) ECHR, and Article 8 (2) ACHR presupposes providing timely and adequate information to the suspect, if necessary through access to the case file. On the other hand, the accused is entitled to have access to all pieces of evidence as long as they are available, until the conclusion of the proceedings; this also applies to intercepted telephone calls.[800]

The suspect may personally inspect the case file if there is no defence counsel.[801] In any case, given that this right is primarily a right of the defendant, he should have, in principle, personal access to the evidence and at the latest 'before the hearing'.[802] This is also reasonable in light of the fact that the accused usually knows the facts of the case, and is, therefore, best suited to assess the contents of the case file.[803] This is especially true in the case of high-level accused since they will have the best insight into the structure of their organization. Thus, the ECtHR justified the personal right of Kurdish PKK leader Abdullah Öcalan to access the case file on the grounds that the defendant, due to his leadership position, was the '*best able*' person 'to assess the relevance ... of the substantial body of evidence that had been adduced by the prosecution' and prepare the defence accordingly.[804]

Of course, the right to access to the case file is subject to—similarly to the right to disclosure—some *limitations*. First of all, there may exist an interest in ensuring the confidentiality of the investigation, for instance, for reasons of witness protection, that may justify a limitation of the right to access.[805] Further, the right can be de facto restricted, for example by granting access to an incomplete file not including all relevant documents. This raises the question of the responsible authority for the keeping of case files and its effective control.[806]

[798] Crit. Esser, *Europäisches Strafverfahrensrecht* (2002), p. 430 ff.; on the corresponding right under Art. 14 (3)(b) ICCPR, cf. Schabas, *CCPR* (2019), Art. 14 mn. 69; Noor Muhammad, in Henkin, *Bill of Rights* (1981), pp. 151–2.

[799] cf. also Walischewski, *Akteneinsichtsrechts* (1999), pp. 93–4, 97, 140; Trechsel, in Schweizer, Burkert, and Gasser, *FS Druey* (2002), pp. 1006–8; Esser, *Europäisches Strafverfahrensrecht* (2002), p. 430; Braitsch, *Gerichtssprache* (1991), p. 154; Sommer, in Brüssow et al., *Strafverteidigung* (2007), § 17 mn. 65; Schabas, *CCPR* (2019), Art. 14 mn. 64; Medina, *ACHR* (2022), p. 392 ('a moment preceding the beginning of the oral trial').

[800] ECtHR, *Natunen v. Finland*, Application No. 21022/04, Judgment (31 March 2009), paras. 46 ff.; more recently *Rook v. Germany*, Application No. 1586/15, Judgment (25 July 2019), paras. 67 ff. and esp. (and differentiating) *Sigurður Einarsson* v. *Iceland*, Application No. 39757/15, Judgment (4 June 2019), paras. 88 ff. With regard to summaries of transcripts from intercepted telephone calls, see *BGH StV*, 30 (2010), 238 with concurring commentary from Stuckenberg. For a more restrictive understanding of this right, see HRCt, 'General Comment 32' (23 August 2007), UN Doc. CCPR/C/GC/32, para. 33 ('access must include all materials that the prosecution plans to offer in court against the accused or that are exculpatory').

[801] ECtHR, *Foucher v. France*, Application No. 22209/93, Judgment (18 March 1997), paras. 35–6; Walischewski, *Akteneinsichtsrechts* (1999), pp. 205 ff., 225; also Braitsch, *Gerichtssprache* (1991), pp. 153–4.

[802] ECtHR, *Kremzow v. Austria*, Application No. 12350/86, Judgment (21 September 1993), para. 63; *Öcalan v. Turkey*, Application No. 46221/99, Judgment (12 March 2003), para. 160; *Kikabidze v. Georgia*, Application No. 57642/12, Judgment (16 February 2022), paras. 42, 48–9. For a detailed view, see Walischewski, *Akteneinsichtsrechts* (1999), pp. 144 ff., 189 ff.

[803] Trechsel, in Schweizer, Burkert, and Gasser, *FS Druey* (2002), p. 997; Walischewski, *Akteneinsichtsrechts* (1999), pp. 92, 144.

[804] ECtHR, *Öcalan v. Turkey*, Application No. 46221/99, Judgment (12 March 2003), para. 161. Similarly Trechsel, in Schweizer, Burkert, and Gasser, *FS Druey* (2002), p. 997.

[805] ECtHR, *Foucher v. France*, Application No. 22209/93, Judgment (18 March 1997), para. 35 (*obiter*); *Habran and Dalem v. Belgium*, Application Nos. 43000/11 and 49380/11, Judgment (29 May 2017), paras. 95 ff.; *Rook v. Germany*, Application No. 1586/15, Judgment (25 July 2019), paras. 67–8; *Uab Braitin v. Lithuania*, Application No. 13863/19, Judgment (13 June 2023), para. 58; Esser, *Europäisches Strafverfahrensrecht* (2002), pp. 353, 430.

[806] Thereon Trechsel, in Schweizer, Burkert, and Gasser, *FS Druey* (2002), pp. 998 ff.

Last but not least, the exercise of the right may be restricted to the defence counsel.[807] This may generate problems if this counsel has not been freely chosen by the defendant but assigned to him by court, since then the ensuing relationship may not be one of full confidence. It is also possible that the counsel either does not inform the accused of the contents of the file or does not exercise the right to access at all. From this it follows that an exclusive right of counsel to access the case file is only acceptable if this counsel enjoys the full confidence of the defendant.[808]

Notwithstanding the limitations just mentioned the right to access the case file must apply absolutely in the case of a remedy against detention (*habeas corpus proceedings* pursuant to Article 9 (4) ICCPR, Article 5 (4) ECHR, and Article 7 (6) ACHR).[809] According to the ECtHR case law, the defence counsel must have access to all documents and information in the investigation file, which are necessary to assess the lawfulness of the accused's detention and therefore indispensable 'in order effectively to challenge' it.[810] Legitimate confidentiality interests, albeit to be taken into account, 'cannot be pursued at the expense of substantial restrictions on the rights of the defence'.[811] Apart from that, equality of arms also requires that the arrested person be 'promptly' and fully informed on the reasons for his arrest.[812] The 'benefit of an adversarial procedure' must be granted;[813] that includes, as generally, the presence in hearings[814] and the possibility to reply to the Prosecutor.[815] Accordingly, the ECtHR

[807] cf. ECtHR, *Kamasinski v. Austria*, Application No. 9783/82, Judgment (19 December 1989), para. 88; *Kremzow v. Austria*, Application No. 12350/86, Judgment (21 September 1993), para. 52; *Rook v. Germany*, Application No. 1586/15, Judgment (25 July 2019), paras. 67–8; *Uab Braitin v. Lithuania*, Application No. 13863/19, Judgment (13 June 2023), para. 58; Esser, *Europäisches Strafverfahrensrecht* (2002), pp. 424–5; Haefliger and Schürmann, *EMRK* (1999), p. 225. For a crit. view, see Trechsel, in Schweizer, Burkert, and Gasser, *FS Druey* (2002), p. 997.

[808] In a similar vein, Esser, *Europäisches Strafverfahrensrecht* (2002), pp. 428–9.

[809] See also Simon, *Beschuldigtenrechte* (1998), pp. 31–2, 42–3; Walischewski, *Akteneinsichtsrechts* (1999), pp. 71 ff., 84, 141; Esser, *Europäisches Strafverfahrensrecht* (2002), pp. 351 ff.; Esser, *Europäisches und Internationales Strafrecht* (2023), § 9 mn. 246; Ambos, *NStZ*, 23 (2003), 14; Jung, *GA*, 150 (2003), 201–2; for a crit. view, see Trechsel, in Schweizer, Burkert, and Gasser, *FS Druey* (2002), pp. 1004–5.

[810] ECtHR, *Shishkov v. Bulgaria*, Application No. 38822/97, Judgment (9 January 2003), para. 77; for further case law, see previous edition, p. 78 with note 749; more recently *Yücel v. Turkey*, Application No. 27684/17, Judgment (25 January 2022), para. 105 ('L'égalité des armes n'est pas assurée si l'avocat se voit refuser l'accès aux pièces du dossier qui revêtent une importance essentielle pour une contestation efficace de la légalité de la détention de son client'); see also IACtHR, *Castillo Petruzzi et al.*, Series C No. 52, Judgment (30 May 1999), paras. 138, 140–1, 153 and 155; with direct reference to the principle of equality of arms HRCt, *Jansen-Gielen v. The Netherlands* (2001) UN Doc. CCPR/C/71/D/846/1999, para. 8.2.

[811] *Shishkov v. Bulgaria*, Application No. 38822/97, Judgment (9 January 2003), para. 77; *Podeschi v. San Marino*, Application No. 66357/14, Judgment (13 April 2017) para. 176.

[812] Arts. 9 (2) ICCPR, 5 (2) ECHR, (4) ACHR; see also Casal, 'Articulo 7', in Steiner and Uribe, *CIDH Comentario* (2019), pp. 239–42; cf. Esser, *Europäisches Strafverfahrensrecht* (2002), pp. 342 ff.; on 'equality of arms', see Peukert, in Strafverteidigervereinigungen, *Reform oder Roll-Back?* (1997), p. 235. Sommer, in Brüssow et al., *Strafverteidigung* (2007), § 17 mn. 137, regards the duty to inform pursuant to Art. 6 (3)(a) ECHR as more extensive than the one resulting from Art. 5 (2) ECHR. On the ICCPR, see *Kelly v. Jamaica* (1991) UN Doc. CCPR/C/41/D/253/1987, para. 5.8 f. (where the HRCt, however, wants to limit this right to a person 'formally charged with a criminal offence'); see also *Juan Humberto Sánchez Case*, Judgment, IACtHR Series C No. 102, 23 November 2003, para. 82; *Bulacio Case*, Judgment, IACtHR Series C No. 100, 18 September 2003, para. 128; thereon Medina, *ACHR* (2022), pp. 276–8.

[813] ECtHR, *Sanchez-Reisse v. Switzerland*, Application No. 9862/82, Judgment (21 October 1986), para. 51; for further case law, see previous edition, p. 78 with note 752; *Bokhonko v. Georgia*, Application No. 6739/11, Judgment (22 October 2020), para. 97; *Vorotņikova v. Latvia*, Application No. 68188/13, Judgment (4 February 2021), para. 26. Thereon also Esser, *Europäisches Strafverfahrensrecht* (2002), p. 346; Sommer, in Brüssow et al., *Strafverteidigung* (2007), § 17 mn. 158.

[814] Esser, *Europäisches Strafverfahrensrecht* (2002), p. 349, who sees in the suspect's request to review the detention an implied request for presence in the relevant hearing. See also for the relevance of the right to a hearing for the accused on the one hand, and for the victim and his relatives on the other hand, Medina, *ACHR* (2014), p. 181.

[815] cf. Esser, *Europäisches Strafverfahrensrecht* (2002), pp. 347–8; Esser, *Europäisches und Internationales Strafrecht* (2023), § 9 mn. 223.

found a violation by Austria since only the Prosecutor was present in a hearing discussing the legality of the detention.[816]

In structural terms, it is fair to say that access to the case file, again, depends on the understanding of the principle of equality of arms. If this is understood in an adversarial, formal sense, full access must be granted thereby putting this right on the same footing as the disclosure rules of the adversarial system. If, in contrast, the equality principle is understood in the more substantive sense of the inquisitorial system, full access is only granted in case of detention with regard to the essential information to appeal against this detention.[817]

### (d) *Adequate time and facilities for the preparation of defence*

Article 14 (3)(b) ICCPR, Article 6 (3)(b) ECHR, and Article 8 (2)(c) ACHR ensure for the defendant 'adequate time and facilities for the preparation of his defence' (Article 14 (3) (b) ICCPR).[818] This right is yet another expression of the equality of arms principle in that the defendant should have exactly the same time to prepare his case as the prosecution to prepare the accusation.[819] Thus, the right also applies already at the pre-trial stage.[820] Any change of the prosecution case at a later stage of the proceedings may also call for a suspension to give the defence extra time to adjust to the new situation.[821]

Of course, it is difficult to determine *in abstracto* when time and facilities to prepare the defence are 'adequate', especially since the French version is not even equivalent, speaking of '*facilités nécessaires*'.[822] What is clear is that a (too) brief mock or 'show' trial is unacceptable.[823] Apart from that, the decision depends on the circumstances of the concrete case.[824] For instance, while a period of three weeks for the reply to a forty-nine-page document was considered to be adequate,[825] a period of two weeks for a 17,000-page file (which, in addition, had to be photocopied by the defence counsel themselves),[826] twelve hours before the rendering of the judgment[827] or an hour or three days before the start of a complex trial has been considered inadequate.[828]

816 cf. ECtHR, *Toth v. Austria*, Application No. 11894/85, Judgment (12 December 1991), para. 33; *Kocamış and Kurt v. Turkey*, Application No. 22717/13, Judgment (25 January 2022), para. 24 ('proceedings must be adversarial and must always ensure equality of arms between the parties ... Equality is not ensured if the public prosecutor is allowed to make oral submissions during the review proceedings while the detained person or his lawyer is denied this opportunity'); thereon Esser, *Europäisches Strafverfahrensrecht* (2002), p. 348.

817 Similarly Esser, *Europäisches Strafverfahrensrecht* (2002), pp. 352–3; Grabenwarter, *ECHR* (2014), Art. 6 mn. 130.

818 On the ICCPR, see HRCt, 'General Comment 32' (23 August 2007) UN Doc. CCPR/C/GC/32, para. 32. For a detailed discussion, see Simon, *Beschuldigtenrechte* (1998), pp. 27 ff.; Rzepka, *Fairness* (2000), pp. 60 ff.; Esser, *Europäisches Strafverfahrensrecht* (2002), pp. 447 ff.; Braitsch, *Gerichtssprache* (1991), pp. 146 ff.; Haefliger and Schürmann, *EMRK* (1999), pp. 221 ff.; Villiger, *Handbuch EMRK* (2020), pp. 325–7.

819 HRCt, 'General Comment 32' (23 August 2007) UN Doc. CCPR/C/GC/32, para. 32; *Smith v. Jamaica* (1993) UN Doc. CCPR/C/47/D/282/1988, para. 10.4; see also Braitsch, *Gerichtssprache* (1991), p. 146; Haefliger and Schürmann, *EMRK* (1999), p. 223.

820 Zappalá, *Human Rights* (2005), p. 123 ('at least from the moment of ... arrival at the UN Detention Unit'); see also Rzepka, *Fairness* (2000), p. 60.

821 See e.g. Reg. 55 (2) RegC; for a discussion, see Chapter IV, B.(7) in this volume.

822 See also Trechsel, in Schweizer, Burkert, and Gasser, *FS Druey* (2002), pp. 995–6.

823 Villiger, *Handbuch EMRK* (2020), p. 325.

824 HRCt, *Kelly v. Jamaica* (1991) UN Doc. CCPR/C/41/D/253/1987, para. 5.9; 'General Comment 32' (23 August 2007) UN Doc. CCPR/C/GC/32, para. 32; more recently *Y.M. v. Russia* (2016) UN Doc. CCPR/C/116/D/2059/2011, para. 9.3 ('determination of "adequate time" depends on the circumstances of each case'); Noor Muhammad, in Henkin, *Bill of Rights* (1981), p. 152.

825 ECtHR, *Kremzow v. Austria*, Application No. 12350/86, Judgment (21 September 1993), para. 48.

826 *Öcalan v. Turkey*, Application No. 46221/99, Judgment (12 March 2003), paras. 165, 167.

827 IACtHR, *Castillo Petruzzi et al.*, Series C No. 52, Judgment (30 May 1999), paras. 138, 140–1.

828 cf. ECtHR, *Twalib v. Greece*, Application No. 24294/94, Judgment (9 June 1998), para. 40; *Daud v. Portugal*, Application No. 22600/93, Judgment (21 April 1998), para. 39; furthermore, see e.g. ECtHR, *Nevzlin v. Russia*,

The right to 'facilities' may include the supply of the relevant physical resources (e.g. legal texts, books, computers), particularly in the case of a detained defendant who has no access to these facilities.[829] It may also include, as already stated above,[830] the disclosure of any exonerating evidence.[831]

### (e) *Full and effective defence*

The right to a full and effective defence, as covered by Article 14 (3)(d) ICCPR, Article 6 (3)(b) ECHR,[832] and Article 8 (2)(d), (e) ACHR, protects in fact *three rights*: that is, the right to self-representation, the right to a counsel of the accused's own choosing, and the right to free legal representation.[833] Thus, the right to an effective defence can be exercised by the accused himself or through his defence counsel.[834] This distinction shows that the defence counsel does not replace the defendant, but only assists him.[835] This also explains why the Court can order the defendant's personal attendance at trial.[836] Yet, the said distinction does not preclude that defence counsel and defendant may sometimes be regarded as a unity, in particular if the latter is to be held accountable for the misconduct of his counsel, for instance, if the counsel of his own choosing does not appear at trial[837] or does not file certain motions.[838]

The defence counsel should already be assigned at the investigation phase, because his absence may, given the prejudicial effect of the investigation,[839] entail an irreparable imbalance between the prosecution and the defendant.[840] Concretely speaking, the question is whether

Application No. 26679/08, Judgment (18 January 2022), paras. 149–50 (two weeks to examine a '19,000-page case file involving accusations concerning several episodes of murder and attempted murder'); *Y.M. v. Russia* (2016) UN Doc. CCPR/C/116/D/2059/2011, paras. 7.8 with n. 19 and 9.3 (six weeks to study a casefile comprised of 1,200 pages and three videocassettes); also see Schabas, *CCPR Commentary* (2019), Art. 14 mn. 63.

[829] Villiger, *Handbuch EMRK* (2020), p. 326; Noor Muhammad, in Henkin, *Bill of Rights* (1981), p. 152. It seems, however, that the HRCt, does not consider the provision of physical resources to be a part of the right to adequate facilities, see HRCt, 'General Comment 32' (23 August 2007) UN Doc. CCPR/C/GC/32, para. 33.

[830] Note 783 in this chapter and main text.

[831] HRCt, 'General Comment 32' (23 August 2007) UN Doc. CCPR/C/GC/32, para. 33; also Villiger, *Handbuch EMRK* (2020), p. 326; McDermott, in Sluiter et al., *International Criminal Procedure* (2013), p. 806.

[832] cf. also Art. 47 (2) EU Charter: 'Everyone shall have the possibility of being advised, defended and represented.'

[833] cf. HRCt, 'General Comment 32' (23 August 2007) UN Doc. CCPR/C/GC/32, paras. 36 ff.; *Y.M. v. Russia* (2016) UN Doc. CCPR/C/116/D/2059/2011, para. 9.4 ('right ... not only to choose but also to replace a lawyer'); Rzepka, *Fairness* (2000), pp. 64 ff.; Esser, *Europäisches Strafverfahrensrecht* (2002), pp. 450 ff., 466 ff.; Braitsch, *Gerichtssprache* (1991), pp. 155 ff.; Villiger, *Handbuch EMRK* (2020), pp. 327–32; Demko, *HRRS*, 7 (2006), 250; Grabenwarter, *ECHR* (2014), Art. 6 mn. 131 ff.; see also Commission, *Green Paper—Procedural Safeguards* (2003), pp. 20–6; De Meester, *Investigation Phase* (2015), pp. 345 ff.

[834] cf. Schabas, *CCPR* (2019), Art. 14 mn. 86–7.

[835] cf. HRCt, *Correia de Matos v. Portugal* (2006), UN Doc. CPR/C/86/D/1123/2002/Rev.1, para. 7.3 (speaking of the defence counsel as the '*assistant*' of the accused); on the ACHR, cf. Medina, *ACHR* (2022), p. 394 ('Article 8 (2) allows the accused to either defend himself personally or be assisted by legal counsel').

[836] Haefliger and Schürmann, *EMRK* (1999), p. 228; on the limits of sanctioning the accused's absence from trial without excuse, see Esser, Gaede and Tsambikakis, *NStZ*, 31 (2011), 147–8.

[837] cf. HRCt, 'General Comment 32' (23 August 2007) UN Doc. CCPR/C/GC/32, para. 38; *H.C. v. Jamaica* (1992) UN Doc. CCPR/C/45/D/383/1989, para. 6.3; see also Peukert, 'Artikel 6', in Frowein and Peukert, *EMRK-Kommentar* (2009), mn. 293; conc. Sommer, in Brüssow et al., *Strafverteidigung* (2007), § 17 mn. 67–9.

[838] cf. Spaniol, *Verteidigerbeistand* (1990), pp. 171–2; Esser, *Europäisches Strafverfahrensrecht* (2002), pp. 639 ff.

[839] cf. note 764 and text in this chapter.

[840] cf. Gut, Kirsch, Mundis, and Taylor, in Sluiter et al., *International Criminal Procedure* (2013), pp. 1260–1; Weigend, *StV*, 20 (2000), 385 with n. 24; Esser, *Europäisches Strafverfahrensrecht* (2002), pp. 476–7; Haefliger and Schürmann, *EMRK* (1999), p. 328; Simon, *Beschuldigtenrechte* (1998), pp. 55–6; Meyer-Ladewig et al., 'Artikel 6' in Meyer-Ladewig and Nettesheim, *EMRK* (2017), mn. 91, 230; Wohlers, *GA*, 152 (2005), 35 with n. 174; Commission, *Green Paper—Procedural Safeguards* (2003), pp. 22–3. On the presence of the defence counsel during a police interrogation, see Esser, Gaede and Tsambikakis, *NStZ*, 31 (2011), 144 with case law references.

a specific investigative measure interferes with the defence position of the accused to such a degree that the absence of counsel would lead to an irreparable disadvantage. In the ECtHR's view, this is the case when the accused is deprived of legal assistance 'at the initial stages' of an interrogation by the police or an investigating judge.[841] At appeal proceedings, the right to effective defence arises if a hearing takes place, since that implies that the case is of certain importance and the participation of defence counsel is in the interests of justice.[842]

The right to an effective defence presupposes the participation of the accused and/or of the defence counsel in hearings, and, if necessary, in interrogations as well. This makes clear that this right is rooted in the right to a judicial hearing.[843] Thus, the defendant and/or his counsel are to be summoned to appear at a hearing[844] and notified of any change of the date of the hearing;[845] a hearing is even to be rescheduled if there is an impediment to counsel being present.[846] Otherwise, the defendant would be deprived of his right to legal assistance.[847] The particularly important right to counsel during interrogation, including interpretation, is explicitly laid down in the law of the international criminal tribunals.[848] This entails that the suspect or accused will be informed about the nature and scope of this right and that a—in principle possible—waiver will be made voluntarily, expressly, and fully informed.[849] Under the ICC regime a waiver of the right to be questioned in the presence of counsel 'shall be recorded in writing and, if possible, be audio- or video-recorded'.[850]

Hodgson, in Ross and Thaman, *Comparative Criminal Procedure* (2016), pp. 261–2 (with regard to France) argues that the idea of the need for legal representation by a defence lawyer in the early (police) investigative phase is less clear from an inquisitorial model.

[841] On police interrogation: ECtHR, *Murray v. UK*, Application No. 18731/91, Judgment (8 February 1996), paras. 66 ff., 81 ('the first 48 hours of his police detention'); for conc. case law, see previous edition, p. 81 with note 780; more recently *Ibrahim v. UK*, Application No. 50541/08, Grand Chamber Judgment (13 September 2016), paras. 256 ff. with emphasis on the 'scope for access to legal advice to be, exceptionally, delayed'; furthermore, see *Beuze v. Belgium*, Application No. 71409/10 (9 November 2018), paras. 125–30; on interrogation by an investigating judge, *Quaranta v. Switzerland*, Application No. 12744/87, Judgment (24 May 1991), para. 36; in a similar vein, HRCt, *Aliev v. Ukraine* (2003), UN Doc. CCPR/C/78/D/781/1997, para. 7.2. See also Esser, *Europäisches Strafverfahrensrecht* (2002), pp. 476–8; Villiger, *Handbuch EMRK* (2020), pp. 327–8; de Meester, Pitcher, Rastan, and Sluiter, in Sluiter et al., *International Criminal Procedure* (2013), pp. 244–5.

[842] cf. HRCt, 'General Comment 32' (23 August 2007) UN Doc. CCPR/C/GC/32, para. 38 ('The gravity of the offence is important in deciding whether counsel should be assigned . . . as is the existence of some objective chance of success at the appeals stage'); ECtHR, *Pakelli v. Germany*, Application No. 8398/78, Judgment (25 March 1983), para. 36; *Nikolayenko v. Ukraine*, Application No. 39994/06 (15 November 2012), para. 61; more recently and generally *Mtchedlishvili v. Georgia*, Application No. 894/12 (25 February 2021), paras. 30–3 to 'the application of Article 6 to proceedings before courts of appeal' (30): 'depends on the special features of the proceedings involved'. See thereon Kieschke, *EGMR* (2003), pp. 119 ff.

[843] Fundamentally Spaniol, *Verteidigerbeistand* (1990), pp. 212 ff. (219 ff.); conc. Walther, *GA*, 150 (2003), 222; also Meyer-Ladewig et al., 'Artikel 6' in Meyer-Ladewig and Nettesheim, *EMRK* (2017), mn. 99, 112.

[844] cf. HRCt, 'General Comment 32' (23 August 2007) UN Doc. CCPR/C/GC/32, para. 36; *Mbenge v. Zaire* (1990) UN Doc. CCPR/C/OP/2, paras. 14.1 ff.; see also Esser, *Europäisches Strafverfahrensrecht* (2002), pp. 459 ff.; Meyer-Ladewig et al., 'Artikel 6' in Meyer-Ladewig and Nettesheim, *EMRK* (2017), mn. 126.

[845] ECtHR, *Alimena v. Italy*, Application No. 11910/85, Judgment (19 February 1991), paras. 18 ff.; Simon, *Beschuldigtenrechte* (1998), p. 50; Esser, *Europäisches Strafverfahrensrecht* (2002), p. 462.

[846] Kadelbach, in Strafverteidigervereinigungen, *Reform oder Roll-Back?* (1997), p. 254.

[847] ECtHR, *Alimena v. Italy*, Application No. 11910/85, Judgment (19 February 1991), para. 20; *Ibrahim and Others v. UK*, Application No. 50541/08 (13 September 2016), paras. 249–74; *Beuze v. Belgium*, Application No. 71409/10 (9 November 2018), paras. 119–50.

[848] See note 716 in this chapter.

[849] cf. Rules 42 (b), 63(A) ICTY/ICTR/SCSL; Art. 55 (2)(d) ICCS; Art. 38 (3)(c) KSC Law and Rule 43(3), (4) RPE KSC; see also de Meester, Pitcher, Rastan, and Sluiter, in Sluiter et al., *International Criminal Procedure* (2013), pp. 221–3, 234 (with case law references), 253 (as a principle). While under the law of the ad hoc tribunals the waiver may be withdrawn by the suspect/accused expressing 'a desire to have counsel' again, such a possibility is not explicitly recognized in the ICC law.

[850] Rule 112 (1)(b) RPE ICC; similarly Rule 43 (3) RPE KSC.

The accused and his counsel are entitled to confidential and unrestricted contact already at the pre-trial stage.[851] The confidentiality of the communication—'out of hearing of a third person'—is a fundamental prerequisite of the *practical effectiveness* of the right to defence with a view to its effective preparation.[852] While the extent of the contact is not specified in the relevant provisions and State Parties have a discretion in how to make the right effective, the standard of practical effectiveness is ultimately the decisive criterion of the compliance with the right.[853] Thus, for example, in the highly complex *Öcalan* case the ECtHR has considered insufficient that Öcalan's counsel could meet his client only twice a week for one hour respectively.[854] In the previous *Murray* case, the Court had already held that a forty-eight-hour-long phase of interrogations without access to a lawyer after the arrest of the suspect constituted a breach of Article 6 (3)(c) ECHR.[855] Similarly, the HRCt in the *Gridin* case found a period of five days without contact to a lawyer to be a violation of Article 14 (3)(b) ICCPR.[856]

The right to defence does not cease to exist if the accused chooses to be absent or is at large.[857] If the accused, 'in spite of having been properly summoned, does not appear' without an excuse, the counsel is, in any case, entitled to defend the accused in his absence.[858]

[851] IACtHR, *Castillo Petruzzi et al.*, Series C No. 52, Judgment (30 May 1999), para. 139; *Barreto Leiva Case*, Judgment, Reparations and Costs Serie C No. 206 (17 November 2009), parr. 62; *Cabrera García and Montiel Flores Case*, Judgment, Reparations and Costs Serie C n.º 220 (26 November 2010), parr. 155; *Rodríguez Revolorio et al. Case*, Judgment, Reparations and Costs Serie C No. 387 (14 October 2019), para. 104; *Girón et al. Case*, Judgment, Reparations and Costs Serie C No. 390 (15 October 2019), para. 96; Medina, *ACHR* (2022), pp. 395–6; Simon, *Beschuldigtenrechte* (1998), pp. 30, 53 ff.; Rzepka, *Fairness* (2000), pp. 72–3; Esser, *Europäisches Strafverfahrensrecht* (2002), pp. 501 ff.; Haefliger and Schürmann, *EMRK* (1999), pp. 223–4; Villiger, *Handbuch EMRK* (2020), pp. 333; Meyer-Ladewig et al., 'Artikel 6' in Meyer-Ladewig and Nettesheim, *EMRK* (2017), mn. 235; Braitsch, *Gerichtssprache* (1991), pp. 147–8 (with reference to Art. 6 (3)(b)); Gundel, in Merten and Papier, *Grundrechte, VI*/1 (2010), § 146 mn. 143; on the confidentiality of correspondence, Ambos, *NStZ*, 23 (2003), 15; also Wessing, *Wistra*, 26 (2007), 173–4 (right to deny testimony for counsel).

[852] EctHR, *Öcalan v. Turkey*, Application No. 46221/99, Judgment (12 March 2003), para. 146 with further references; see also on the ICCPR, *Arutyunyan v. Uzbekistan* (2004) UN Doc. CCPR/C/80/D/917/2000, para. 6.3; on the ACHR IACtHR, *Castillo Petruzzi et al.*, Series C No. 52, Judgment (30 May 1999), para. 139; *Cantoral Benavides Case*, Series C No. 69, Judgment (18 August 2000), para. 127; *Bulacio Case*, Series C No. 100, Judgment (18 September 2003), para. 130.

[853] ECtHR, *Öcalan v. Turkey*, Application No. 46221/99, Judgment (12 March 2003), para. 153 with further references; *Ibrahim and Others v. UK*, Application No. 50541/08 (13 September 2016), paras. 249–74; *Beuze v. Belgium*, Application No. 71409/10, (9 November 2018), paras. 119–50.

[854] ECtHR, *Öcalan v. Turkey*, Application No. 46221/99, Judgment (12 March 2003), para. 154; *Ibrahim and Others v. UK*, Application No. 50541/08 (13 September 2016), paras. 249–74; *Beuze v. Belgium*, Application No. 71409/10 (9 November 2018), paras. 119–50. Along the same lines, *BGH StV*, 29 (2009), 566–7, arguing that the right to an effective defence is infringed when the period between the appointment of counsel and the trial is too short to sufficiently prepare the defence; *in casu*, the newly assigned counsel was granted five days by the trial court to become acquainted with the six-file-folders-long case file and develop a defence strategy; thus, in such a case, the trial should be adjourned for additional preparation if counsel makes such request.

[855] ECtHR, *Murray v. UK*, Application No. 18731/91, Judgment (8 February 1996), paras. 63–70 (the accused was suspected of terrorism and therefore prohibited from speaking to his counsel during the first forty-eight hours of the arrest. The ECtHR found also a breach of Art. 6 (3)(d) ECHR because of the possibility to draw inferences from the silence of the accused during the police interrogations); in a similar vein, *Atristain Gorosabel v. Spain*, Application No. 15508/5, Judgment (18 January 2022), para. 41.

[856] HRCt, *Gridin v. Russian Federation* (2000) UN Doc. CCPR/C/69/D/770/1997, para. 8.5.

[857] ECtHR, *Poitrimol v. France*, Application No. 14032/88, Judgment (23 November 1993), paras. 33–5; for further case law, see previous edition, p. 83 with note 796; more recently *Hokkeling v. The Netherlands*, Application No. 30749/12, Judgment (14 February 2017), para. 52; see also Esser, *Europäisches Strafverfahrensrecht* (2002), pp. 463 ff; Sommer, in Brüssow et al., *Strafverteidigung* (2007), §17 mn. 69; Paul, *Art. II Genozidkonvention* (2008), pp. 247 ff. (with further ECtHR case law references).

[858] ECtHR, *Kari-Pekka Pietiläinen v. Finland*, Application No. 13566/06, Judgment (22 September 2009), paras. 31 ff.; *Neziraj v. Germany*, Application No. 30804/07, Judgment (8 November 2012), para. 19; *Frolovs v. Latvia*, Application No. 13289/06, Judgment (15 June 2017), para. 44.

The ECtHR even considers that a State, due to its caretaker position, has a duty to intervene on behalf of the accused who is insufficiently defended.[859] Yet, this seems to go too far and may only be plausible if counsel has been assigned by the public authorities.[860] In any case, the defendant has certain responsibilities, for example, in making sure that his counsel appears at trial and regarding the right defence strategy.[861] A rights violation would only exist if the competent national court would take no action in the face of the obviously insufficient exercise of the duties of defence counsel.[862] In a similar vein, the ICTY held that a Chamber may have to examine if a defendant is adequately and effectively represented.[863]

The accused is entitled to *free legal assistance*, 'if he does not have sufficient means to pay for such assistance', and 'when the interests of justice so require'.[864] The second condition depends on the seriousness of the offence, the complexity of the case, and the personal situation of the accused.[865] Of course, this condition concerns only the free legal

[859] Esser, *Europäisches Strafverfahrensrecht* (2002), pp. 457–8, 472–3, 490–1; Esser, *Europäisches und Internationales Strafrecht* (2318), § 9 mn. 259; Sommer, in Brüssow et al., *Strafverteidigung* (2007), § 17 mn. 104 (derives from the 'fair trial'); Toney, *IJEP*, 5 (2001), 56; cf. also Gaede, in Gaede, Meyer and Schlegel, *HRRS-FG Fezer* (2008), p. 28; rightly crit. in this respect the *BGH* case law, Beulke and Barisch, *StV*, 26 (2006), 569 with references on the case law.

[860] In this vein, see HRCt, 'General Comment 32' (23 August 2007) UN Doc. CCPR/C/GC/32, para. 38; *H.C. v. Jamaica* (1992) UN Doc. CCPR/C/45/D/383/1989, para. 6. 3 (arguing that a State Party is only responsible for failures of counsel publicly assigned to the accused while misbehaviour by a privately instructed counsel has to be attributed to the accused); also see Villiger, *Handbuch EMRK* (2020), p. 331.

[861] cf. Peukert, 'Artikel 6', in Frowein and Peukert, *EMRK-Kommentar* (2009), mn. 293; Sommer, in Brüssow et al., *Strafverteidigung* (2007), § 17 mn. 67–8.

[862] Sommer, in Brüssow et al., *Strafverteidigung* (2007), § 17 mn. 68.

[863] *Prosecutor v. Halilović*, AC, Decision on the Interlocutory Appeal Concerning Admission of Interview of the Accused from the Bar Table, No. IT-01-48-AR73.2, 19 August 2005, paras. 61, 62 (TC, in principle, obliged to assess a lawyer's 'actual competence to adequately represent the interests' of suspect if substantive evidence is adduced to the contrary); conc. *Prosecutor v. Popović et al.*, TC, Decision on the Admissibility of the Borovčanin Interview and the Amendment of the Rule 65ter Exhibit List, No. IT-05-88-T, 25 October 2007, para. 31 ('With regard to the right to be assisted by counsel, a Trial Chamber is obliged to assess a lawyer's "actual competence to adequately represent the interests" of the suspect, but only where substantive evidence is adduced to the contrary'), *Prosecutor v. Hadžić*, TC, Consolidated Decision on the Continuation of Proceedings, No. IT-04-75-T, 26 October 2015, para. 40 ('What is required from an accused to be deemed fit to stand trial is a standard of overall capacity allowing for a meaningful participation in the trial, if he or she is duly represented by counsel'); *Prosecutor v. Kabuga*, AC, Decision on Appeals of Further Decision on Felicien Kabuga's Fitness to Stand Trial, No. MICT-13-38-AR80.3, 7 August 2023, para. 24; *Prosecutor v. Kabuga*, Decision on Felicien Kabuga's Fitness to Stand Trial and to be Transferred to and Detained in Arusha, No. MICT-13-38-PT, 13 June 2022, para. 42; *Prosecutor v. Kabuga*, Decision on an Appeal of a Decision on Felicien Kabuga's Fitness to Stand Trial, No. MICT-13-38-AR80.1, 15 August 2022, para. 12, *Prosecutor v. Kabuga*, Further Decision on Felicien Kabuga's Fitness to Stand Trial, No. MICT-13-38-T, 6 June 2023, para. 28 , *Prosecutor v. Kabuga*, AC, Decision on Appeals of Further Decision on Felicien Kabuga's Fitness to Stand Trial, No. MICT-13-38-AR80.3, 7 August 2023, para. 23; for a discussion, see de Meester, Pitcher, Rastan, and Sluiter, in Sluiter et al., *International Criminal Procedure* (2013), pp. 223–4.

[864] ECtHR, *Pakelli v. Germany*, Application No. 8398/78, Judgment (25 April 1983), para. 31; for further case law, see previous edition p. 84 with note 803 ; in a similar vein, invoking fairness considerations, see IACtHR, 'Exceptions to the Exhaustion of Domestic Remedies (Art. 46 (1), 46 (2)(2), and 46 (2)(b) American Convention on Human Rights), Advisory Opinion, Series A No. 11 (10 August 1990), paras. 25–7; *Ruano Torres Case* Judgment, Reparations and Costs Serie C No. 303 (5 October 2015), paras. 157, 163; *Girón et al. Case* Judgment, Reparations and Costs Serie C No. 390 (15 October 2019), paras. 100–1. See in detail, Esser, *Europäisches Strafverfahrensrecht* (2002), pp. 474 ff.; Simon, *Beschuldigtenrechte* (1998), pp. 48–9, 56 ff.; Haefliger and Schürmann, *EMRK* (1999), pp. 229 ff.; Haefliger and Schürmann, *Die EMRK und die Schweiz* (2014), p. 43; Villiger, *Handbuch EMRK* (2020), pp. 331–2; Sommer, in Brüssow et al., *Strafverteidigung* (2007), § 17 mn. 71–4; Demko, in Gaede, Meyer and Schlegel, *HRRS-FG Fezer* (2008), pp. 1 ff.; Medina, *ACHR* (2022), pp. 397–8; Ibañez Rivas, 'Articulo 8', in Steiner and Uribe, *CIDH Comentario* (2019), pp. 300–3. See also Art. 47 (3) EU Charter: 'Legal aid shall be made available to those who lack sufficient resources in so far as such aid is necessary to ensure effective access to justice.'

[865] ECtHR, *Quaranta v. Switzerland*, Application No. 12744/87, Judgment (24 May 1991), paras. 33–5; *Leka v. Albania*, Application No. 60569/09, Judgment (05 March 2024), para. 92. See also Simon, *Beschuldigtenrechte*

assistance and does not in any way limit the right to counsel of one's own choosing if the accused can afford it.[866] As far as the public assignment of a defence counsel is concerned, 'the national courts must certainly have regard to the defendant's wishes', however 'they can override those wishes when there are relevant and sufficient grounds'.[867] This includes, in principle, the right to self-representation[868] to be discussed in more detail in the next chapter.[869]

### *(f) Right to witness confrontation*

The right to 'examine, or have examined' the witnesses, as laid down in Article 14(3)(e) ICCPR, Article 6 (3)(d) ECHR, and Article 8 (2)(f) ACHR, amounts, in fact, to a right to cross-examine and confront the witnesses and thus is clearly of an adversarial nature.[870] In substance, the rule wants to ensure a 'full equality of arms',[871] requiring 'that the defendant be given [at some point during the proceedings] an adequate and proper opportunity to challenge and question a witness against him',[872] and, in addition, to call witnesses in his

(1998), pp. 57 ff.; Esser, *Europäisches Strafverfahrensrecht* (2002), pp. 477 ff.; in a similar vein, see HRCt, 'General Comment 32' (23 August 2007) UN Doc. CCPR/C/GC/32, para. 38.

866 cf. Schabas, *CCPR* (2019), Art. 14 mn. 87 ff., 90.

867 ECtHR, *Croissant v. Germany*, Application No. 13611/88, Judgment (25 September 1992), para. 29; *Karpyuk and Others v. Ukraine*, Application Nos. 30582/04 32152/04, Judgment (6 October 2015), para. 144; thereon also Simon, *Beschuldigtenrechte* (1998), pp. 59–60; Esser, *Europäisches Strafverfahrensrecht* (2002), pp. 492 ff.; Villiger, *Handbuch EMRK* (2020), p. 331; more restrictively regarding the free choice of counsel, Haefliger and Schürmann, *EMRK* (1999), pp. 226, 232. See also Gut, Kirsch, Mundis, and Taylor, in Sluiter et al., *International Criminal Procedure* (2013), p. 1261.

868 cf. Arts. 67 (1)(d) ICCS, 14 (3)(d) ICCPR, 21 (4)(d) ICTYS, 20 (4)(d) ICTRS; for a more specific and restrictive rule see Art. 21 (5) KSC Law.

869 Chapter II, D.(3) in this volume.

870 See the classic Amendment VI to the US Constitution: 'to be *confronted* with the witnesses against him; to have compulsory process for obtaining witnesses in his favour'. See also Rule 85 (A) RPE ICTY ('Each Party is entitled to call witnesses and present evidence') and more explicitly Art. 21 (4)(f) KSC Law ('to examine, or have examined the witness against him or her') as well as Rule 127 (3) ('A witness called before the Trial Panel shall first be examined by the calling Party, then cross-examined by the opposing Party if it elects to exercise this right. Direct examination and cross-examination shall be allowed in each case'). See also HRCt, 'General Comment 32' (23 August 2007) UN Doc. CCPR/C/GC/32, para. 38. On the antithetical participation, see Demko, *Verteidigung* (2014), pp. 243, 334 ff., 363 ff.; also Haefliger and Schürmann, *EMRK* (1999), p. 239; Simon, *Beschuldigtenrechte* (1998), p. 103; Wasek-Wiaderek, *Equality* (2000), p. 27; Sommer, in Brüssow et al., *Strafverteidigung* (2007), § 17 mn. 77; Beulke, in Hanack et al., *FS Riess* (2002), p. 6 with n. 12; Schleiminger, *Konfrontation* (2001), p. 143; Grabenwarter, *ECHR* (2014), Art. 6 mn. 143.

871 ECtHR, *Engel and Others v. The Netherlands*, Application Nos. 5100/71, 5101/71, 5102/71, 5354/72, 5370/72, Judgment (8 June 1976), para. 91; for further case law, see previous edition, p. 85 with note 810; more recently *Poropat v. Slovenia*, Application No. 21668/12, Judgment (9 May 2017), para. 41. See also Schabas, *CCPR* (2019), Art. 14, mn. 94; Esser, *Europäisches Strafverfahrensrecht* (2002), p. 633; Villiger, *Handbuch EMRK* (2020), p. 334; Braitsch, *Gerichtssprache* (1991), p. 163; Demko, *Verteidigung* (2014), pp. 381–2.

872 *Nevzlin v. Russia*, Application No. 26679/08, Judgment (18 January 2022), para. 173 ('the defendant must be given an adequate and proper opportunity to challenge and question a witness against him or her—either when the statements are made or at a later stage of the proceedings'); *Faysal Pamuk v. Turkey*, Application No. 430/13, Judgment (18 January 2022), para. 47; *Constantinides v. Greece*, Application No. 76438/12, Judgment (6 October 2016), para. 38; see also HRCt, 'General Comment 32' (23 August 2007) UN Doc. CCPR/C/GC/32, para. 39 ('a right to have witnesses admitted that are relevant for the defence, and to be given a proper opportunity to question and challenge witnesses against them at some stage of the proceedings'). See also Krauß, *V-Leute* (1999), pp. 103 ff., 108 ff., 120; Simon, *Beschuldigtenrechte* (1998), p. 106; Rzepka, *Fairness* (2000), pp. 74–5; Villiger, *Handbuch EMRK* (2020), p. 335; Beulke, in Hanack et al., *FS Riess* (2002), pp. 14, 21; Schleiminger, *Konfrontation* (2001), p. 33; Pauly, *StV*, 22 (2002), 291–2; Ambos, *NStZ*, 23 (2003), 16; Wohlers, *ZStrR*, 123 (2005), 164–5; Gaede, *Fairness* (2007), pp. 278 ff.; Velten, *StV*, 27 (2007), 100; Vasiliev, in Sluiter et al., *International Criminal Procedure* (2013), pp. 636–7; Grabenwarter, *ECHR* (2014), Art. 6 mn. 143–4; Demko, *Verteidigung* (2014), pp. 370, 445 ff. This right can be also derived from the right to personal participation in the proceedings, cf. Villiger, *Handbuch EMRK* (2020), p. 334.

favour.[873] The term 'witness' must 'be given an autonomous interpretation';[874] it encompasses any statement which may become relevant with regard to conviction of the accused, independent of whether it is made in open court or somewhere else or whether it is the statement of the co-accused.[875]

Even though the confrontation may take place at any point during the proceedings, the right also applies already at the investigation phase.[876] The wording 'have examined' would seem to imply that the defence counsel could replace the accused; however, as in case of the case file, the normally better factual knowledge of the accused may speak against that, at least against his replacement by counsel.[877] The rule goes beyond a mere right to examine witnesses, granting a true right to 'challenge'[878] and 'confront' the witnesses.[879] As already said above, such a right to confrontation flows directly from a 'full equality of arms'. For such an equality can only exist if the accused can examine the incriminating witnesses thoroughly,[880] including by cross-examination, in the sense of a 'tested evidence'.[881]

The accused must have knowledge of the full witness statement in order to have the 'opportunity to challenge any aspect' of it.[882] If, after the (first) examination of a witness,

[873] Schleiminger, *Konfrontation* (2001), pp. 31 ff.; Braitsch, *Gerichtssprache* (1991), pp. 165–6; on the burden of proof of the accused, cf. ECHR, *Garaudy v. France*, Application No. 65831/01, Judgment (24 June 2003); more recently *Murtazaliyeva v. Russia*, Application No. 36658/05, Judgment (18 December 2018), paras. 140 ff.

[874] ECHR, *Asch v. Austria*, Application No. 12398/86, Judgment (26 April 1991), para. 25; more recently *Constantinides v. Greece*, Application No. 76438/12, Judgment (6 October 2016), para. 37 ('Court reiterates that the notion of "witness" is to be interpreted autonomously from its meaning in the domestic law'); cf. Demko, *Verteidigung* (2014), pp. 414 ff.; Grabenwarter, *ECHR* (2014), Art. 6 mn. 144.

[875] Gaede, ' in Gaede, Meyer and Schlegel, *HRRS-FG Fezer* (2008), p. 24; Gundel, in Merten and Papier, *Grundrechte*, *VI*/1 (2010), § 146 mn. 147.

[876] Simon, *Beschuldigtenrechte* (1998), p. 106; Schleiminger, *Konfrontation* (2001), p. 291; Demko, *Verteidigung* (2014), pp. 430 ff.; probably also Wohlers, *GA*, 152 (2005), 32; confusingly, de Meester, Pitcher, Rastan, and Sluiter, in Sluiter et al., *International Criminal Procedure* (2013), p. 278, stating that the right does not exist during the investigation if the witness can be examined at trial and thus suggesting that this is the normative rule; instead, the provision should be interpreted as providing this right as early as possible; see also Acquaviva and Heikkilä, in Sluiter et al., *International Criminal Procedure* (2013), p. 853, stating with reference to ECtHR case law, that the opportunity to examine the witness at a later stage of the trial is sufficient.

[877] The interpretation is controversial, see, on the one hand, Schleiminger, *Konfrontation* (2001), pp. 291, 320–1 and, on the other, Wohlers, *ZStrR*, 123 (2005), 164.

[878] Walther, *GA*, 150 (2003), 215.

[879] ECHR, *Saïdi v. France*, Application No. 14647/89, Judgment (20 September 1993), para. 44; more recently *Dastan v. Turkey*, Application No. 37272/08, Judgment (10 October 2017), para. 21; Esser, *Europäisches Strafverfahrensrecht* (2002), p. 643; Esser, *Europäisches und Internationales Strafrecht* (2023), § 9 mn. 262; Tochilovsky, *Jurisprudence* (2014), p. 540; Cornelius, *NStZ*, 28 (2008), 244 (247); Demko, *Verteidigung* (2014), pp. 115 ff.; cf. also Jung, *GA*, 156 (2009), 236 as well as Amendment VI to the US Constitution: 'to be *confronted*' (emphasis added).

[880] For the same result, see Walther, *GA*, 150 (2003), 214 ff., 220 ('Prozessgrundrecht allerhöchsten Ranges'); Walther, *JZ*, 59 (2004), 1110 with n. 50; cf. also Schleiminger, *Konfrontation* (2001), p. 17. On the accused's right 'to be confronted with a witness' as 'an essential element of fair criminal proceedings' ('principle of immediacy') see KSC, Judgment on the Referral of the Rules of Procedure and Evidence Adopted by Plenary on 17 March 2017 to the Specialist Chamber of the Constitutional Court Pursuant to Article 19(5) of Law no. 05/L-053 on Specialist Chambers and Specialist Prosecutor's Office, KSC-CC-PR-2017-01, F00004, 26 April 2017, para. 44.

[881] cf. *Prosecutor v. Kordić and Čerkez*, TC, Decision on the Prosecution Application to Admit the Tulica Report and Dossier into Evidence, No. IT-95-14/2, 29 July 1999, para. 23 (the admissibility of written witnesses' statements 'would amount to the wholesale admission of hearsay untested by cross-examination ... and would be of no probative value'); in a similar vein, *Schatschaschwili v. Germany*, Application No. 9154/10, Judgment (15 December 2015), para. 107. See also Beulke, in Hanack et al., *FS Riess* (2002), pp. 15, 21; generally Ambos, *ICLR*, 3 (2003), 23 ff.

[882] ECtHR, *Bricmont v. Belgium*, Application No. 10857/84, Judgment (7 July 1989), para. 81; *Ibrahim and Others v. UK*, Application No. 50541/08 (13 September 2016), paras. 249-74; *Leka v. Albania*, Application No. 60569/09, Judgment (5 March 2024), para. 118; IACtHR *Cantoral Benavides*, Series C No. 69, Judgment (18 August 2000), para. 127; *Amrhein et al. Case*, Judgment, Reparations and Costs Serie C No. 354 (25 April 2018), para. 449, *Álvarez Ramos Case*, Judgment, Reparations and Costs Serie C No. 380 (30 August 2019), para. 157; see also Esser, *Europäisches Strafverfahrensrecht* (2002), p. 644.

that same witness gives new incriminating testimony, the accused must also have a new opportunity—equality of arms!—of further cross-examination.[883] On the other hand, it would probably violate the equality of arms if only one party had the opportunity to conduct an additional cross-examination.[884] The confrontation can take place without the defence counsel if the accused can exercise his rights adequately on his own.[885]

The confrontation right extends, in principle, to all witnesses, including 'independent witnesses', since equality of arms requires access to all evidence.[886] With regard to expert witnesses, the right to confrontation gives the accused the right to comment if the expert report amounts to essential incriminating evidence;[887] yet, the mere fact that an expert witness belongs to a public authority that participates in the proceedings, or has even set the prosecution in motion 'does not [automatically] justify his being regarded ... as a witness for the prosecution'.[888]

The right to confrontation suffers some exceptions or *limitations*.[889] First of all, it must be balanced against justified witness or victim protection interests, with the fairness of the trial determined pursuant to an overall assessment of the proceedings.[890] Concrete exceptions to the confrontation right are recognized in case of unavailable and anonymous witnesses, with strict requirements regarding both unavailability and anonymity.[891] While the ECtHR does not regard statements by anonymous witnesses as inadmissible from the outset, it

[883] Correctly Esser, *Europäisches Strafverfahrensrecht* (2002), p. 646; Beulke, in Hanack et al., *FS Riess* (2002), p. 15; against this view, Schlothauer, *StV*, 21 (2001), 128; regarding § 255a StPO *BGHSt* 48, 268 (271, 274); for a crit. view on that, see Walther, *JZ*, 59 (2004), 1110–11; restrictively also *Entscheidungen des Schweizerischen Bundesgerichts (BGE)* 113 Ia 412 (422).

[884] *Prosecutor v. Delalić et al.*, TC, Decision on the Motion on Presentation of Evidence by the Accused, Esad Landzo, No. IT-96-21-T, 1 May 1997, paras. 28–9; *Prosecutor v. Turinabo et al.*, Decision on Motion for Access to Prosecution Requests for Assistance and Responses Thereto, No. MICT-18-116-PT, 18 April 2019, p. 3; *Prosecutor v. Turinabo et al.*, Decision on Motion to Compel the Prosecution to Provide Information under Rule 71(B) relating to Prosecution Personnel, No. MICT-18-116-PT, 18 April 2019, p. 3; *Prosecutor v. Kabuga*, Decision on Prosecution Motion for Admission of Evidence of Witness KAB004 pursuant to Rule 112, No. MICT-13-38-PT, 26 August 2022, p. 3. See also May and Wierda, *ColJTransnat'lL*, 37 (1998/1999), pp. 739–40.

[885] cf. Esser, *Europäisches Strafverfahrensrecht* (2002), p. 645; Schleiminger, *Konfrontation* (2001), p. 16.

[886] cf. Chand, *NLJ*, 150 (2000), p. 1666.

[887] *Bönisch v. Austria*, Application No. 8658/79, Judgment (6 May 1985), para. 32; *Mantovanelli v. France*, Application No. 21497/93, Judgment (18 March 1997), para. 36 ('real opportunity to comment effectively on it'); cf. also Wasek-Wiaderek, *Equality* (2000), pp. 31–2.

[888] ECtHR, *Brandstetter v. Austria*, Application Nos. 11170/84, 12876/87, and 13468/87, Judgment (28 August 1991), paras. 44 ff.; *Danilov v. Russia*, Application No. 88/05, Judgment (1 December 2020), paras. 109–11; *Tabak v. Croatia*, Application No. 24315/13, Judgment (13 January 2022) para. 60 and Joint Dissenting Opinion of Judges Turković, Paczolay and Felici, paras. 3–5.

[889] See generally Brunhöber, *ZIS*, 5 (2010), 767–8; Vasiliev, in Sluiter et al., *International Criminal Procedure* (2013), pp. 636–7; Demko, *Verteidigung* (2014), pp. 457 ff.

[890] cf. Schabas, *CCPR* (2019), Art. 14 mn. 95 ('courts are ... provided with relatively broad discretion. but 'principles of fairness and "equality of arms"' to be taken into account); Acquaviva and Heikkilä, in Sluiter et al., *International Criminal Procedure* (2013), pp. 852–4; Demko, *Verteidigung* (2014), pp. 457–8, 465 ff.; also Dehne-Niemann, *HRRS*, 11 (2010), 189 ff.; Zöller, *ZJS*, 3 (2010), 441. On the decision not to hear a witness, see Combs, in Sluiter et al., *International Criminal Procedure* (2013), pp. 695–6.

[891] In detail on that, see Esser, *Europäisches Strafverfahrensrecht* (2002), pp. 648 ff., 657 ff., 678; Gaede, *StV*, 26 (2006), 602 ff.; for a crit. view, see Maffei, *Confrontation* (2006), p. 95 ('confrontation is too easily surrendered'); Trechsel, *EMRK* (1974), pp. 314 ff.; Demko, *ZStrR*, 122 (2004), 418 ff.; also KSC-CC-PR-2017-01, F00004, paras. 179–82 ('adequate and sufficient justification', 'measure of last resort', 'strong procedural safegruards ... to ensure that the proceedings ... are fair'). Regarding anonymous witnesses and police officers as witnesses, see Safferling, *NStZ*, 26 (2006), 77 ff.; Gaede, *Fairness* (2007), pp. 281 ff.; Wohlers, *FS Trechsel* (2002), p. 829; on the risks for the police officers when testifying as civilian witnesses, *van Mechelen and Others v. The Netherlands*, Application Nos. 21363/93, 21364/93, 21427/93, and 22056/93), Judgment (23 April 1997), para. 56). On the questioning of ICRC/UN employees and journalists, see Linton, in Sluiter et al., *International Criminal Procedure* (2013), pp. 920 ff.

requires that the defendant be given the opportunity for some sort of confrontation.[892] In this sense, the fact that the accused did not have the opportunity to challenge and question an incriminating witness, due to the latter's refusal to testify in open court, should be taken into consideration in the assessment of the evidence, which, in any case, should 'be treated with extreme care'.[893] In the case of a deposition that has been made by a witness whom the accused had no opportunity to examine, the final assessment depends on the circumstances of the concrete case, in particular whether this deposition has been corroborated by other evidence and whether the court had relied exclusively on it.[894] Thus, in the *Haas* case the ECtHR held that the defence rights were sufficiently respected since the evidence obtained from anonymous intelligence sources was not decisive for the conviction and thoroughly corroborated by further evidence.[895] This line was further accentuated by the ECtHR in the *Sapunarescu* and *Bracci* cases:[896] Even though 'at no point in time' were the accused or their defence counsel 'afforded an opportunity to cross-examine the anonymous main witness for the prosecution in person', the conviction 'cannot be considered to have been based to a decisive extent on the depositions' of the anonymous witness.[897] Yet even if the testimony of the anonymous or absent witness is not decisive for the proceedings, 'the Court still needs to determine whether there existed sufficient factors to counterbalance any handicaps that the admission of that evidence might have entailed for the defence'.[898]

With regard to questioning of witnesses by an investigating judge in the absence of the defendant but with counsel, it suffices if the counsel is 'put in a position to ask the witnesses

[892] ECtHR, *van Mechelen and Others v. The Netherlands*, Application Nos. 21363/93, 21364/93, 21427/93, 22056/93, Judgment (23 April 1997), paras. 56–62 ('direct questioning'); *S. N. v. Sweden*, Application No. 34209/96, Judgment (2 July 2002), para. 44 ('opportunity … to question'); more recently e.g. *Bátěk and Others v. Czech Republic*, Application No. 54146/09, Judgment (12 January 2017), para. 37 ('before an accused can be convicted, all the evidence against him must normally be produced in his presence at a public hearing for the purpose of adversarial argument'); *Asatryan v. Armenia*, Application No. 3571/09, Judgment (12 April 2017), para. 53 ('as a general rule, Article 6 §§ 1 and 3 (d) require that the defendant be given an adequate and proper opportunity to challenge and question a witness against him, either when he makes his statements or at a later stage'); *Dastan v. Turkey*, Application No. 37272/08, Judgment (10 October 2017), para. 33. For a detailed analysis with case law references, see Simon, *Beschuldigtenrechte* (1998), pp. 108 ff.; Esser, *Europäisches Strafverfahrensrecht* (2002), pp. 663 ff., 672; Haefliger and Schürmann, *EMRK* (1999), pp. 182–3, 241; Villiger, *Handbuch EMRK* (2020), pp. 3334–5; Fuchs, *ÖJZ*, (2001), 501–2; Zerbes, in Cottier, Sahlfeld, and Rüetschi, *Information und Recht* (2002), pp. 379, 383–4, 389–90; Sommer, in Brüssow et al., *Strafverteidigung* (2007), § 17 mn. 83–6; summarizing Jung, *GA*, 150 (2003), 200; Renzikowski, *JZ*, 54 (1999), 612.

[893] ECtHR, *Haas v. Germany*, Application No. 73047/01, Decision as to the Admissibility of Application (17 November 2005); also *BGH NStZ*, 24 (2004), 691 (692) and *BGHSt* 46, 93 (106).

[894] ECtHR, *Bracci v. Italy*, Application No. 36822/02, Judgment (13 October 2005), paras. 54 ff.; from an Italian perspective, see Zacchè, *Indice Penale* 9 (2006), 427 ff., see also de Meester, Pitcher, Rastan, and Sluiter, in Sluiter et al., *International Criminal Procedure* (2013), p. 278; Combs, in Sluiter et al., *International Criminal Procedure* (2013), p. 730.

[895] *Haas v. Germany*, Application No. 73047/01, with crit. commentary by Esser, *NStZ*, 27 (2007), 106; cf. also Combs, in Sluiter et al., *International Criminal Procedure* (2013), pp. 714–15.

[896] ECtHR, *Sapunarescu v. Germany*, Application No. 22007/03, Decision as to the Admissibility of Application (11 September 2006), with critical commentary by Sommer, *StraFo*, 2007, 109; *Bracci v. Italy*, Application No. 36822/02, Judgment (13 October 2005), paras. 54 ff.

[897] ECtHR, *Sapunarescu v. Germany*, Application No. 22007/03, paras. 32–3; more recently with regard to a police agent's anonymous testimony, *Batek and Others v. Czech Republik*, Application No.54146/09, Judgment (12 January 2017), para. 50 ('considering the extent and weight of other evidence and bearing in mind the importance ascribed thereto by the national courts, the agent's testimony cannot be tretated as decisive').

[898] *Batek and Others v. Czech Republik*, Application No. 54146/09, Judgment (12 January 2017), para. 50; *Seton v. UK*, Application No. 55287/10 (31 March 2016), para. 64 regarding 'absent-witness evidence'; furthermore, see *Simon Price v. UK*, Application No. 15602/07 (15 September 2016), para. 116 ('the Court should not only review the existence of sufficient counterbalancing factors in cases where the evidence of the absent witness was the sole or the decisive basis for the applicant's conviction'); in the same vein, *Constantinides v. Greece*, Application No. 76438/12 (6 October 2016), para. 39.

whatever questions he considered to be in the interests of the defence'.[899] It does not suffice, however, to carry out the questioning in a purely written form with the questions read out by an investigating officer.[900] It is equally insufficient if the defendant (and his counsel) are physically separated from the investigating judge and the witness and can only ask questions 'via a sound link', for in such a situation they are neither aware of the identity of the witness nor can they test his reliability.[901]

The right to confrontation has been, on the other hand, slightly more relaxed in child abuse cases and with regard to the use of new (video) technologies. Thus, as to the former, it is admissible that the defendant and his counsel watch the examination of the child witness through a one-way mirror and ask questions through the judge.[902] As far as the use of video link testimony is concerned, the ECtHR finds it generally in conformity with the fair trial and the right to confrontation 'in view of the legislative changes providing for alternative ways of giving testimony'.[903] While this is, as such, hardly a convincing argument, the gist of the issue is whether some form of confrontation remains possible.[904]

### (g) *Free assistance of an interpreter*

The right to the free assistance of an interpreter, as set out in Article 14 (3)(f) ICCPR, Article 6 (3)(e) ECHR, and Article 8 (2)(a) ACHR, complements the right to an effective defence during the entire proceedings with a view to all relevant documents or statements.[905] With

[899] ECtHR, *Doorson v. The Netherlands*, Application No. 20524/92, Judgment (26 March 1996), paras. 73–5; *Snijders v. The Netherlands*, Application No. 56440/15, Judgment (06 February 2024), para. 22; Esser, *Europäisches Strafverfahrensrecht* (2002), pp. 666 ff.; Villiger, *Handbuch EMRK* (2020), p. 335.

[900] cf. Simon, *Beschuldigtenrechte* (1998), p. 135; Schleiminger, *Konfrontation* (2001), p. 15 as well as Ambos, *NStZ*, 23 (2003), 16–17 with further references.

[901] ECtHR, *van Mechelen and Others v. The Netherlands*, Application Nos. 21363/93, 21364/93, 21427/93, 22056/93, Judgment (23 April 1997), para. 59; *Snijders v. The Netherlands*, Application No. 56440/15, Judgment (06 February 2024), paras. 22, 56; *Škoberne v. Slovenia*, Application No. 19920/20, Judgment (15 February 2024), para. 99; Esser, *Europäisches Strafverfahrensrecht* (2002), pp. 668 ff.; also Schleiminger, *Konfrontation* (2001), p. 16; Wohlers, in Donatsch, Forster and Schwarzenegger, *FS Trechsel* (2002), p. 816.

[902] cf. ECtHR, *Accardi and Others v. Italy*, Application No. 30598/02, Judgment (20 January 2005); similarly *T.K. v. Lithuania*, Application No. 14000/12, Judgment (12 June 2018), para. 98.

[903] ECtHR, *Ahorugeze v. Sweden*, Application No. 37075/09, Judgment (27 October 2011), para. 123; in the same vein, *S. N. v. Sweden*, Application No. 34209/96, Judgment (2 July 2002), para. 49, arguing that the accused could have requested that the police interview with the child witness be videotaped. Also, *Khodorkovskiy and Lebedev v. Russia* (No. 2) Applications Nos. 51111/07 42757/07, Judgment (14 January 2020), paras. 447, 478 ('Article 6 § 3 (d) leaves it to [The States], again as a general rule, to assess whether it is appropriate to call witnesses; it does not require the attendance and examination of every witness on the accused's behalf: its essential aim, as is indicated by the words "under the same conditions", is a full "equality of arms" in the matter'). The HRCt only held that the judge is obliged to ensure the attendance of witnesses (HRCt, *Lloyd Grant v. Jamaica* (1994) UN Doc. CcPR/C/50/D/353/1988).

[904] cf. Simon, *Beschuldigtenrechte* (1998), pp. 113–14; Esser, *Europäisches Strafverfahrensrecht* (2002), pp. 670–1, 677; Schleiminger, *Konfrontation* (2001), pp. 318–19; Wohlers, *ZStrR*, 123 (2005), 166; Gaede, *Fairness* (2007), p. 282; McDermott, in Sluiter et al., *International Criminal Procedure* (2013), p. 873, also noting that the principle of equality of arms might be violated when only the witnesses of one party are interviewed via video link.

[905] ECtHR, *Kamasinski v. Austria*, Application No. 9783/82, Judgment (19 December 1989), para. 74 ('all those documents or statements in the proceedings instituted against him which is necessary for him to understand or to have rendered into the court's language in order to have the benefit of a fair trial'); in the same vein, *Vizgirda v. Slovenia*, Application No. 59868/08, Judgment (28 August 2018), para. 81 (on the State's positive obligation to provide interpretation: 'it is incumbent on the authorities involved in the proceedings, in particular the domestic courts, to ascertain whether the fairness of the trial requires, or has required, the appointment of an interpreter to assist the defendant'); for a recent analysis of the ECHR's case law on Art. 6 (3)(e) ECHR, see Vogiatzis, *HRLR*, 22 (2022), 9 ff. cf. also Schabas, *CCPR* (2019), Art. 14, mn. 102–4; Medina, *ACHR* (2022), p. 390; Simon, *Beschuldigtenrechte* (1998), pp. 142 ff.; Rzepka, *Fairness* (2000), pp. 80 ff.; Esser, *Europäisches Strafverfahrensrecht* (2002), pp. 508 ff.; Esser, *Europäisches und Internationales Strafrecht* (23), § 9 mn. 269; Kieschke, *EGMR* (2003), pp. 72 ff.; Braitsch, *Gerichtssprache* (1991), pp. 166 ff.; Haefliger and Schürmann, *EMRK* (1999), pp. 188, 234 ff.; Sommer, in Brüssow et al., *Strafverteidigung* (2007), § 17 mn. 87–90; Grabenwarter and Pabel, in Dörr et al., *EMRK/GG I* (2021/2022), ch. 14 mn. 161; De Meester, *Investigation Phase* (2015), pp. 377 ff. On the criteria to determine how much of the proceedings should be interpreted, see Commission, *Green Paper—Procedural Safeguards* (2003), pp. 26–31 (30, Question 10).

this, a comprehensive 'communication right' is guaranteed. It is a right, as in other cases, of the defendant, not his counsel, although one may expect that counsel helps his client to understand the relevant documents; while this should not per se remove the client's right to translation, the counsel's intermediation may be considered sufficient, especially if waiting for a translation may entail a considerable delay.[906]

The right is not, as suggested by the reference to 'the language used in court' (e.g. Article 14 (3)(f) ICCPR), limited to the actual trial but extends to the whole pre-trial phase, including mere preparatory meetings between the defendant and his counsel.[907] The early application of the right explicitly results from the (other) right, previously mentioned above, 'to be informed promptly in a language' which the suspect understands (Article 14 (3)(a) ICCPR).[908]

This right also covers the translation of transcripts of a telecommunication (or any other) interception into the mother tongue of the accused, as long as this is necessary to enable him to fully participate in the proceedings and exercise his rights. It will be necessary if the pertinent documents are relevant for his defence with a view to the overarching fairness principle[909] and if he is not 'completely fluent in the language in ordinary, non-technical conversation'.[910] A different matter is the bearing of the translation costs which should depend on the importance of the translated document and the financial situation of the accused.[911] The interpreter of an international criminal tribunal acts, being an officer of the respective tribunal, as 'an impartial third party in the furtherance of the administration of justice'.[912]

### *(h) Trial without undue delay*

There are mainly two issues concerning this right as set out in Article 14 (3)(c) ICCPR, Article 6 (1) cl. 1 ECHR, and Article 8 (1) cl. 1 ACHR. First, it is practically impossible to determine in the abstract when a procedural delay turns out to be 'undue'.[913] The ECtHR

[906] cf. HRCt, *Harward v. Norway* (1994) UN Doc. CCPR/C/51/D/451/1991, para. 9.5, arguing that an accused has no right to a translation of all the relevant documents, if his counsel is familiar with the language of the proceedings and has access to an interpreter. In a similar vein, KSC, Decision on Haradinaj's Request for Clarification on Appeal Timescale, KSC-CA-2022-01/F00005, 25 May 2022, para. 4 with further references ('in cases before international criminal courts where trial judgments were issued in a language which the accused did not understand, an extension of time for the filing of a notice of appeal was generally not warranted where the convicted person's counsel could work in the language in which the trial judgment was pronounced').

[907] This is now settled; for the earlier controversy, see Peukert, 'Artikel 6', in Frowein and Peukert, *EMRK-Kommentar* (2009), mn. 317; Braitsch, *Gerichtssprache* (1991), p. 183; Haefliger and Schürmann, *EMRK* (1999), p. 235 with n. 81; Sommer, in Brüssow et al., *Strafverteidigung* (2007), § 17 mn. 90; Bernhardt, in Geiger, *Völkerrechtlicher Vertrag* (2000), pp. 147–8; similarly Medina, *ACHR* (2022), p. 392.

[908] See also Arts. 5 (2) and 6 (3)(a) ECHR; see further Haefliger and Schurmann, *EMRK* (1999), pp. 220, 234–5; Villiger, *Handbuch EMRK* (2020), pp. 327–8; Esser, *Europäisches Strafverfahrensrecht* (2002), pp. 511 ff.; Cape et al., *Criminal Defence* (2010), pp. 49–50. On the problems regarding the language of the suspect, cf. Zappalá, *Human Rights* (2005), pp. 56 ff.

[909] cf. Arts. 55 (1)(c) and 67 (1)(f) ICCS ('to meet the requirements of fairness'); *Harward v. Norway* (1994) UN Doc. CCPR/C/51/D/451/1991, paras. 9.4 and 9.5. (linking any limitation to the right of an effective defence).

[910] *Prosecutor v. Katanga and Ngudjolo Chui*, AC, Judgment on the Appeal against the Decision of Pre-Trial Chamber I Entitled 'Decision on the Defence Request Concerning Languages', No. ICC-01/04-01/07-522, 27 May 2008, para. 61.This follows from the high standard of Arts. 55 (1)(c) and 67 (1)(f) ICCS requiring that the suspect/accused 'fully understands and speaks' the language used. Human rights law seems to be less strict, cf. *Kaminski v. Austria*, Application No. 9783/82, Judgment (19 December 1989), para. 77 (general ability to understand sufficient).

[911] See e.g. German Constitutional Court (*Bundesverfassungsgericht, BVerfG*) holding that Art. 6 (3)(e) ECHR only requires the reimbursement of the interpreting costs of the accused, but not the translation costs of wiretap transcripts, cf. *BVerfG, NStZ*, 24 (2004), 274 (275).

[912] *Prosecutor v. Delalić et al.*, TC, Decision on the Motion *Ex Parte* by the Defence of Zdravko Mucic Concerning the Issue of a Supoena to an Interpreter, No. IT-96-21-T, 8 July 1997, para. 10.

[913] cf. Grabenwarter, *ECHR* (2014), Art. 6 mn. 95; McDermott, *Fairness* (2016), pp. 52 ff.; for 'instructive' ICTY, ICTR, and SCSL decisions regarding 'the permissible length of proceedings and what would constitute an

performs a *procedural or factual analysis*, the main aim of which is to establish which delays are to be attributed to domestic authorities[914] given that other delays, especially those caused by the defendant or his defence counsel, are not to be taken into account.[915] The Court does not set an abstract temporal threshold or limit but checks the reasonableness of the length of the proceedings on a case-by-case basis by reference to different criteria such as complexity of the case, conduct of the applicant or authorities, and the importance of what is at stake for the applicant.[916] The IACtHR also takes the same criteria into account.[917] Scholarly opinions also support an overall assessment considering similar factors.[918] At any rate, a total inactivity of the State authorities normally entails a violation of the principle.[919]

The second issue concerns the controversy about the *consequences* of an undue delay.[920] One view holds that it constitutes a procedural obstacle and must therefore necessarily lead to a (anticipated) termination of the proceedings (the so-called *procedural solution*).[921] Another, less radical view wants to compensate for the violation by a mitigation of the final punishment in case of conviction (the so-called *sentencing solution*). The latter view is theoretically inconsistent since it lumps together two issues—procedural delay and adequate punishment—which have nothing to do with each other. Yet, from a practical perspective, mitigation is more convincing than a definitive stay of proceedings given that the latter generates impunity, which, at least in cases of serious crimes, is never a desirable outcome

unreasonable consumption of time', see McDermott, in Sluiter et al., *International Criminal Procedure* (2013), pp. 785–8; furthermore, see Gumpert and Nuzban, *EJIL: Talk!*, 15 November 2019.

[914] cf. Ambos, *EuCrL* (2018), pp. 88–9. The requirement for rapid action applies to the State Party as a whole, i.e. delays caused by all State authorities are to be taken into account.

[915] cf. ECtHR, *Peterke/Lembcke v. Germany*, No. 4290/03, Judgment (3 February 2009); *Nicolae Virgiliu Tănase v. Romania*, Application No. 41720/13, Judgment (25 June 2019), paras. 210–14. For an instructive account of the criteria, cf. Grabenwarter, *ECHR* (2014), Art. 6 mn. 94; cf. also HRCt, *Albert Berry v. Jamaica* (1994) UN Doc. CCPR/C/50/D/330/1988; *Stephens v. Jamaica* (1995) UN Doc. CCPR/C/55/D/373/1989; *Tony Jones v. Jamaica* (29 May 1998) UN Doc. CCPR/C/62/D/585/1994.

[916] For the leading case, see ECtHR, *König v. Germany*, Application No. 6232/73, Judgment (Merits) (28 June 1978), para. 99; see also *Deumeland v. Germany*, Application No. 9384/81, Judgment (29 May 1986), paras. 78 ff.; *Lazariu v. Romania*, Application No. 31973/03, Judgment (Merits) (13 November 2014), para. 147; more recently *Ramiz Jafarov v. Azerbaijan*, Application No. 40424/12, Judgment (16 June 2022), para. 55. In a similar vein, *Prosecutor v. Prosper Mugiraneza*, AC, Decision on Prosper Mugiraneza's Interlocutory Appeal from Trial Chamber II Decision of 2 October 2003 Denying the Motion to Dismiss the Indictment, Demand Speedy Trial and for Appropriate Relief, No. ICTR-99-50-AR73, 27 February 2004 (considering length of the delay, complexity of the proceedings, conduct of the parties and of the relevant authorities, as well as the prejudice to the accused); explicitly stressing the case-by-case approach and listing the relevant factors, *Prosecutor v. Prosper Mugiraneza*, AC Judgment, No. ICTR-99-50-A, 4 February 2013, para. 30; *Prosecutor v. Seselj*, Judgment, No. MICT-16-99-A, 11 April 2018, para. 41; *Prosecutor v. Karadzic*, Judgment, No. MICT-13-55-A, 20 March 2019, para. 89; cf. also McDermott, in Sluiter et al., *International Criminal Procedure* (2013), p. 817.

[917] IACtHR, *Genie Lacayo*, Series C 21, Judgment (29 January 1997), paras. 77 ff.; *Juan Humberto Sánchez*, Series C 99, Judgment (7 June 2003), paras. 129, 132; more recently *Case of Favela Nova Brasilia v. Brasil*, Judgment (16 February 2017), para. 218 ('Court will examine the four pertinent criteria established in its case law: (i) the complexity of the matter; (ii) the procedural activity of the interested parties; (iii) the conduct of the judicial authorities, and (iv) the effects on the legal situation of the person concerned'); on the complexity criterion at para. 227 ('Court notes that the characteristics of the proceedings were not particularly complex, considering that the names of the police officers who took part in the raid, and also of the individuals who they allegedly had to look for or arrest during the incident should have been known'); see also Medina, *ACHR* (2022), pp. 357 ff.

[918] Grabenwarter, *ECHR* (2014), Art. 6 mn. 94–6; Medina, *ACHR* (2022), pp. 357 ff. (stressing the criteria of the seriousness of the consequences for the party (p. 203)); Schabas, *CCPR* (2019), Art. 14 mn. 75 ff., esp. 77.

[919] ECtHR, *G.S. v. Austria*, Application No. 26297/95, Judgment (21 December 1999), paras. 33 ff.

[920] See also Ambos, *EuCrL* (2018), pp. 89–90 with further references.

[921] On that, including further references, cf. Baumanns, *Beschleunigungsgrundsatz* (2011), pp. 307 ff., 311 ff. and Pastor, *Plazo* (2002), pp. 545–6.

of a criminal trial where otherwise the accused's guilt can be proven beyond any reasonable doubt.

The undue delay concept gains particular importance in the context of the principle of complementarity, where 'unjustified delay' is one of the criteria to determine unwillingness of a State with regard of its duty to investigate and prosecute international crimes.[922] We will therefore return to this issue below.[923]

### *(i) Right to judicial review*

The right to judicial review, as contained in Article 2 (1) ECHR AP VII, Article 14 (5) ICCPR, and Article 8 (2)(h) ACHR, grants persons convicted of a crime by a tribunal the right to have the judgment reviewed by a court of higher instance. The ECtHR interprets the term 'criminal offence' in Article 2 (1) ECHR AP VII in the sense of the term 'criminal charge'[924] in Article 6 (1) ECHR.[925] Persons who have been acquitted do not have the right to appeal, regardless of the reasons for the acquittal.[926] Whether the conviction is a decision by a tribunal or not depends on the severity of the sanction.[927] *Ratione temporis*, the right to a judicial review has to be granted before the judgment has become final.[928] The court of higher instance has to be able to quash the judgment or to make significant changes to the judgment or sentence.[929]

It is, however, unclear whether a full review of both the facts (evidence) and the law is required.[930] According to the ECtHR, State Parties enjoy a considerable discretion when implementing this right and may restrict the scope of the review to matters of law.[931] In contrast, the HRCt and the IACtHR seem to follow a broader approach, demanding a *full review* of the conviction and the sentence on matters of evidence, law, and the conduct of the proceedings.[932]

922 Art. 17 (2)(b) ICCS.

923 Chapter III, B.(2)(d)(iii)(2) in this volume.

924 Note 757 and main text in this chapter.

925 ECtHR, *Gurepka v. Ukraine*, Application No. 61406/00, Judgment (6 September 2005), para. 55; *Zaivecs v. Latvia*, Application No. 65022/01, Judgment (31 July 2007), para. 53 ('concept of "criminal offence" … corresponds to that of "criminal charge"'), more recently *Société Oxygene Plus v. France*, Application No. 76959/11, Judgment (17 May 2016), para. 43. See also Flinterman, in van Dijk et al., *ECHR* (2018), p. 972; for the determination of 'criminal charge' see also Grabenwarter, *ECHR* (2014), Art. 6 mn. 18 ff.; furthermore, see Djukić, *Appeal* (2019), p. 63.

926 Grabenwarter, *ECHR* (2014), Protocol 7 Art. 2 mn. 2; Djukić, *Appeal* (2019), pp. 67–8.

927 cf. Harris, O'Boyle, and Warbrick, *ECHR* (2018), p. 960.

928 IACtHR, *Herrera Ulloa v. Costa Rica*, Series C 107, Judgment (2 July 2004), para. 158; *Amrhein et al. Case*, Judgment, Reparations and Costs Serie C No. 354 (25 April 2018), para. 256; *Gorigoitia Case* Judgment, Reparations and Costs Serie C No. 382 (2 September 2019), para. 46; *Rodríguez Revolorio et al. Case* Judgment, Reparations and Costs Serie C No. 387 (14 Octuber 2019), para. 127; *Girón et al. Case* Judgment, Reparations and Costs Serie C No. 390 (15 October 2019), para. 113; on that, see Úbeda de Torres, in Burgorgue-Larsen and Úbeda de Torres, *IACtHR* (2011), pp. 660–1.

929 Grabenwarter, *ECHR* (2014), Protocol 7 Art. 2 mn. 3.

930 Zappalá, *Human Rights* (2005), pp. 158–9; cf. Úbeda de Torres, in Burgorgue-Larsen and Úbeda de Torres, *IACtHR* (2011), p. 661; see also Medina, *ACHR* (22), pp. 404 ff.

931 ECtHR, *Krombach v. France*, Application No. 29731/96, Judgment (13 February 2001), para. 96; cf. Flinterman, in van Dijk et al., *ECHR* (2018), p. 973; furthermore, see Djukić, *Right to Appeal* (2019), pp. 65–7.

932 HRCt, *Perera v. Australia* (1995) UN Doc. CCPR/C/53/D/536/1993, para. 6.4 ('article 14, paragraph 5, does not require that a Court of Appeal proceed to a factual retrial, but … conduct an evaluation of the evidence presented at the trial and of the conduct of the trial'); *Domukovsky et al. v. Georgia* (1998) UN Doc. CCPR/C/62/D/623/1995, CCPR/C/62/D/624/1995, CCPR/C/62/D/626/1995, CCPR/C/62/D/627/1995, para. 18.11. (insufficiency of an appeal limited to matters of law); *Gómez Vázquez v. Spain* (2000) UN Doc. CCPR/C/69/D/701/1996, para. 11.1; in the same vein, *Wade v. Senegal* (2018) UN Doc. CCPR/C/124/D/2783/2016, para. 12.4; cf. Schabas, *CCPR* (2019), Art. 14 mn. 119; Djukić, *Appeal* (2019), pp. 75–6; Medina, *ACHR* (2022), pp. 404 ff.; Grabenwarter, *ECHR* (2014), Art. 6 mn. 85; similar on Art. 2 ECHR AP VII, Flinterman, in van Dijk et al., *ECHR* (2018), pp. 972–4. See also Zappalá, *Human Rights* (2005), pp. 166 ff., arguing for such a broad scope at the appeals stage of the international criminal tribunals.

A 'factual retrial' is, however, not necessary.[933] Courts are, nevertheless, allowed to dismiss an appeal without an oral hearing, after assessing the judgment and the arguments by the appellant, if the appeal will not lead to a reduction of the sentence imposed by the court of first instance.[934]

There is, according to the HRCt, also no 'automatic right to an appeal', 'as long as the examination of an application for leave to appeal entails a full review, ... of the conviction and sentence and as long as the procedure allows for due consideration of the nature of the case'.[935] In contrast, the ECtHR argues that, in analogy to Article 6 (1) ECHR, any such limitation has to 'pursue a legitimate aim and [must] not infringe the very essence of that right'.[936] A convicted person has also to be able to make use of this right 'independent of any discretionary action by the authorities'.[937] The admission and assessment of evidence, which was available to the defence at the trial stage, may be limited at the appeals stage as well.[938]

The right to judicial review only requires the national law to provide for a second instance.[939] However, if the appeals court convicts an accused who was acquitted by the first instance court, such an appeal must be granted.[940] In contrast, as indicated by Article 2 (2) ECHR AP VII,[941] there is no right to a review of the appeals judgment in this case.[942] If a State, nevertheless, provides further instances of appeal, effective access has to be granted.[943]

The reviewing tribunal has to be a *higher* court.[944] Thus, according to the HRCt, Article 14 (5) ICCPR is violated when the trial of first instance takes place before the supreme court of the applicable jurisdiction.[945] However, this does not apply to the right under Article 2 (1) ECHR AP VII, as Article 2 (2) contains an exception for trials of first instance before

933 HRCt, *Perera v. Australia* (1995) UN Doc. CCPR/C/53/D/536/1993, para. 6.4.

934 HRCt, *Bryhn v. Norway* (1999) UN Doc. CCPR/C/67/D/789/1997, para. 7.2.

935 HRCt, *Lumley v. Jamaica* (1999) UN Doc. CCPR/C/65/D/662/1995, para. 7.3; confirmed in *Anderson v. Australia* (2002) UN Doc. CCPR/C/74/D/802/1998, para. 7.5.

936 ECtHR, *Krombach v. France*, Application No. 29731/96, Judgment (13 February 2001), para. 96; *Gurepka v. Ukraine*, Application No. 61406/00, Judgment (6 September 2005), para. 59; more recently *Y.B. v. Russia*, Application No. 71155/17, Judgment (20 July 2021), para. 40; cf. Harris, O'Boyle, and Warbrick, *ECHR* (2018), pp. 959–60.

937 ECtHR, *Gurepka v. Ukraine*, Application No. 61406/00, Judgment (6 September 2005), para. 59.

938 HRCt, *H.T.B. v. Canada* (1993) UN Doc. CCPR/C/49/D/534/1993, para. 4.3.

939 HRCt, *Henry v. Jamaica* (1991) UN Doc. CCPR/C/43/D/230/1987, para. 8.4; HRCt, 'General Comment 32' (23 August 2007) UN Doc. CCPR/C/GC/32, para. 45; Medina, *ACHR* (2022), p. 403.

940 HRCt, 'General Comment 32' (23 August 2007) UN Doc. CCPR/C/GC/32, para. 47; *Gomaríz Valera v. Spain* (2005) UN Doc. CCPR/C/84/D/1095/2002, para. 7.1.

941 The relevant part of Art. 2 (2) ECHR AP VII reads: 'subject to exceptions ... in which the person concerned ... was convicted following an appeal against acquittal'.

942 In this vein, see Boas, Jackson, Roche, and Taylor III, in Sluiter et al., *International Criminal Procedure* (2013), p. 1002 and Grabenwarter, *ECHR* (2014), Protocol 7 Art. 2 mn. 5.

943 HRCt, 'General Comment 32' (23 August 2007) UN Doc. CCPR/C/GC/32, para. 45; also see *Khadzhiyev and Muradova v. Turmenistan* (2018) UN Doc. CCPR/C/122/D/2252/2013, para. 7.11 ('the right to have one's conviction reviewed can only be exercised effectively if the convicted person is entitled to have access to a duly reasoned, written judgment of the trial court').

944 HRCt, *Gelazauskas v. Lithuania* (1997) UN Doc. CCPR/C/77/D/836/1998, paras. 7.2, 7.6; more recently *Spisso v. Venezuela* (2017) UN Doc. CCPR/C/119/D/2481/2014, para. 7.11; Schabas, *CCPR* (2019), Art. 14 mn. 121; on the ACHR, see IACtHR, *Herrera Ulloa v. Costa Rica*, Series C 107, Judgment (2 July 2004), para. 158; *Amrhein et al. v. Costa Rica*, Serie C No. 354, Judgment (25 April 2018), para. 256; *Gorigoitía v. Argentina*, Serie C No. 382, Judgment (2 September 2019), para. 46, *Rodríguez Revolorio et al. v. Guatemala*, Serie C No. 387, Judgment (14 October 2019), para. 127; *Girón v. Guatemala*, Serie C No. 390, Judgment (15 October 2019), para. 113.

945 HRCt, *Spisso v. Venezuela* (2017) UN Doc. CCPR/C/119/D/2481/2014, para. 7.11; *Gelazauskas v. Lithuania* (1997) UN Doc. CCPR/C/77/D/836/1998, paras. 7.2, 7.6; for a detailed assessment, see Gradoni, *LJIL*, 19 (2006), 847, 863 ff., 865, arguing for a general right to judicial review in ICL, and Zappalá, *Human Rights* (2005), pp. 159 ff., arguing against it; cf. also Schabas, *CCPR* (2019), Art. 14 mn. 121.

supreme courts, offences of minor character,[946] and, as just mentioned, convictions following an appeal against acquittal.[947]

### *(j)* Ne bis in idem *(double jeopardy rule)*

The right not to be tried and punished twice for the same offence (*ne*[948] *bis in idem*), as enshrined in Article 14 (7) ICCPR, Article 4 ECHR AP VII, and Article 8 (4) ACHR, clearly applies to *domestic* proceedings, that is, to proceedings within the same jurisdiction.[949] The principle contains three autonomous guarantees, that is, that no one shall be (i) liable to be tried, (ii) actually tried, or (iii) punished.[950] It prohibits any inititation of criminal proceedings. The ensuing questions—what is the same offence (the '*idem*'), what is a 'final' conviction/acquittal, and under what conditions can such a final judgment be revised (lifting the *res judicata* obstacle)[951]—have been partly addressed by the human rights case law.

As to the first question—determining the same offence ('*idem*')—the HRCt refers to 'the same events that had been the basis of his first trial and conviction'.[952] The ECtHR, in interpreting 'same offence' in Article 4 ECHR AP VII, first asked for the same actual conduct,[953] then referred to the 'same essential elements'[954] and now takes a kind of naturalistic approach requiring 'identical facts or facts which are substantially the same'.[955] The object of the accusation also must be substantially identical.[956] On a different note, the IACtHR understands the term 'same cause' in Article 8 (4) ACHR in a broader sense than 'same crime' in other international human rights instruments.[957] It considers that, for the purpose of a possible double prosecution/conviction (double jeopardy), ordinary and military

[946] cf. Harris, O'Boyle, and Warbrick, *ECHR* (2018), pp. 959–60.

[947] cf. Flinterman, in van Dijk et al., *ECHR* (2018), p. 975.

[948] It is, according to the Latin grammatical rule governing prohibitive commands, 'ne', not 'non' (as unfortunately often said and written); see previously Ambos, *ICLR*, 3 (2003), 33 with n. 219; see also Bernard, *JICJ*, 9 (2011), 863 with n. 1.

[949] See also Bernard, *JICJ*, 9 (2011), 864–5.

[950] See regarding Art. 4 ECHR AP VII *Zolotukhin v. Russia*, Application No. 14939/03, Judgment (10 February 2009), para. 110; more recently *A and B v. Norway*, Applications Nos. 24130/11 and 29758/11, Grand Chamber Judgment (15 November 2016), paras. 101 ff.; *Krombach v. France*, Application No. 67521/14, Judgment (20 February 2018), para. 36 on the restriction of Art. 4 ECHR AP VII to 'juridictions du même État'; *Stavila v. Romania*, Application No. 23126/16, Judgment (1 March 2022), paras. 88 ff.

[951] See, on the one hand, Art. 4 (2) AP 7 ECHR and, on the other, Art. 84 ICCS, to be discussed in more detail in Chapter VI, C. in this volume.

[952] HRCt, *Marieta Terán Jijón v. Ecuador* (1992) UN Doc. CCPR/C/44/D/277/1988 at 76, para. 5.4; see also HRCt, *Robert John Fardon v. Australia* (2010) UN Doc. CCPR/C/98/D/1629/2007 and HRCt, *Kenneth Davidson Tillman v. Australia* (2010) UN Doc. CCPR/C/98/D/1635/2007 (prison term because of sex offences and subsequent preventive arrest).

[953] *Gradinger v. Austria*, Application No. 15963/90, Judgment (23 October 1995), para. 55.

[954] *Franz Fischer v. Austria*, Application No. 37950/97, Judgment (29 May 2001), para. 25; reaffirmed in *W. F. v. Austria*, Application No. 38275/97, Judgment (30 May 2002), paras. 25 ff. and *Sailer v. Austria*, Application No. 38237/97, Judgment (6 June 2002), paras. 25 ff.; for an overview of the development, see *Zolotukhin v. Russia*, Application No. 14939/03, Judgment (10 February 2009), paras. 70–1.

[955] *Zolotukhin v. Russia*, Application No. 14939/03, Judgment (10 February 2009), paras. 78–9; for further case law, see previous edition, p. 94 with note 893; more recently *A and B v. Norway*, Application No. 24130/11, Grand Chamber Judgment (15 November 2016), para. 141 ('factual circumstances ... were sufficiently similar'); *Stavila v. Romania*, Application No. 23126/16, Judgment (1 March 2022), para. 89 ('same facts').

[956] *Franz Fischer v. Austria*, Application No. 37950/97, Judgment (29 May 2001), paras. 25 ff.; cf. also *Krombach v. France*, Application No. 29731/96, Judgment (13 February 2001), paras. 25 ff. and *Zolotukhin v. Russia*, Application No. 14939/03, Judgment (10 February 2009), paras. 79 ff.

[957] IACtHR, *Loayza-Tamayo v. Peru*, Judgment (17 September 1997), para. 66; *Rosadio Villavicencio v. Peru*, Judgment (8 October 2020), para. 23 ('State shall not be able to launch new proceedings against the victim for the facts examined in the Judgment, regardless of any domestic law the State might invoke') and before *Rosadio Villavicencio v. Peru*, Judgment (14 October 2019), para. 87 ('la misma base fáctica'). See also Medina, *ACHR* (2022), pp. 410–11.

proceedings are to be treated equally,[958] i.e. a conviction by a military court impedes a second trial/conviction by an ordinary court based on the same facts;[959] only mere disciplinary military proceedings do not impede a second trial before an ordinary court since they pursue a different objective.[960]

As to the meaning of final conviction/acquittal the HRCt requires a decision against which no further judicial review is possible.[961] Similarly, the ECtHR demands a legally binding decision (*res judicata*) that does not allow for any (further) judicial remedy.[962]

As to the third question—possibility of a revision—Article 14 (7) ICCPR and Article 8 (2) (h) ACHR do not provide explicitly for the possibility of reconsidering a case. Only Article 4 (2) ECHR AP VII allows for the revision of a judgment if there is evidence of new facts, or if there has been a fundamental defect in the proceeding.[963] Concretely speaking, the ECtHR considers the grant of amnesty in respect of war crimes as such a fundamental defect.[964]

As said at the beginning of this section, the *ne bis in idem* principle is explicitly limited to the appropriate domestic jurisdiction in the relevant human rights provisions, that is, it does not apply at the interstate or international level. There are two exceptions though. First, the law of the EU has recognized since 1990 with Article 54 of the Convention Implementing the Schengen Agreement (CISA)[965] a transnational *ne bis in idem* for the common space of the EU.[966] This rule has later been confirmed by Article 50 EU-Charter, albeit this provision lacks the enforcement (third) element of Article 54 CISA.[967]

Secondly, the ICC regime recognizes with Article 20 ICCS a partial *ne bis in idem* in the vertical relationship between State Parties and the Court. However, while the rule only offers a full protection against a second prosecution and trial[968] at the domestic level once the relevant suspect has already been convicted or acquitted by the Court (so-called 'downwards'

[958] To the extent, of course, that proceedings before military courts are admissible at all in light of Art. 8(1) ACHR, cf. IACtHR, *Cantoral Benavides v. Peru*, Judgment (18 August 2000), paras. 137–40.

[959] IACtHR, *Loayza-Tamayo v. Peru*, Judgment (17 September 1997), paras. 74–5.

[960] cf. *Rosadio Villavicencio v. Peru*, Judgment (14 October 2019), paras. 116 (stressing the different objectives of ordinary and *disciplinary* military proceedings), 120 (affirming a violation of Art. 8 (4) ACHR regarding ordinary/military proceedings but denying such a violation regarding ordinary/*disciplinary* military proceedings).

[961] HRCt, UN Doc. A/C.3/L.821/Rev.1 (27 November 1959); quoted according to Schabas, *CCPR* (2019), Art. 14 mn. 137 with n. 611.

[962] *Nikitin v. Russia*, Application No. 50178/99, Judgment (20 July 2004), para. 37; the ECtHR desisted from answering the question of whether an amnesty meets the requirements of a final conviction or acquittal (ECtHR *Marguš v. Croatia*, Application No. 4455/10, Judgment (13 November 2012), paras. 66 ff., esp. 99).

[963] Art. 4 (2) ECHR AP VII; see also *Nikitin v. Russia*, Application No. 50178/99, Judgment (20 July 2004), paras. 45 ff. (the 'supervisory review' under Russian law as such an exception); *Xheraj v. Albania*, Application No. 37959/02, Judgment (29 July 2008), paras. 69 ff.; more recently *Sismanidis and Sitaridis*, Application Nos. 66602/09 and 71819/12 (9 June 2016), para. 26; cf. also Schabas, *CCPR* (2019), Art. 14 mn. 140.

[964] *Marguš v. Croatia*, Application No. 4455/10, Judgment (13 November 2012), paras. 72 ff.; more recently *Atesoglu v. Turkey*, Application No. 53645/10, Judgment (20 January 2015), para. 25.

[965] On the so-called Schengen *acquis* (1985/1990) which was incorporated into EU law with the Treaty of Amsterdam of 1997, see Ambos, *EuCrL* (2018), pp. 25–6; Satzger, *ICL* (2018), § 8 mn. 63; Satzger, *Internationales Strafrecht* (2020), § 10 mn. 64.

[966] Art. 54 provides: 'A person whose trial has been finally disposed of in one Contracting Party may not be prosecuted in another Contracting Party for the same acts provided that, if a penalty has been imposed, it has been enforced, is actually in the process of being enforced or can no longer be enforced under the laws of the sentencing Contracting Party.' For a detailed analysis of this provision, see Ambos, *EuCrL* (2018), pp. 147–60; Satzger, *ICL* (2018), § 8 mn. 63–4; Satzger, *Internationales Strafrecht* (2020), § 10 mn. 64 ff.; for a briefer analysis, see Bernard, *JICJ*, 9 (2011), 866.

[967] On the difficult relationship between these two provisions, see CJEU, *Spasic*, C–129/14 PPU (27 May 2014), paras. 51 ff.; see also Ambos, *EuCrL* (2018), p. 158; Satzger, *ICL* (2018), § 8 mn. 65; Satzger, *Internationales Strafrecht* (2020), § 10 mn. 66–9, all three with further references.

[968] Leaving aside the obvious application of the rule for second prosecutions *within* the ICC, cf. Art. 20 (1) ICCS; see thereon Friman, Brady, Costi, Guariglia, and Stuckenberg, in Sluiter et al., *International Criminal Procedure* (2013), p. 442.

*ne bis in idem*),[969] the same is not true for the inverse situation, that is, if the relevant person has first been tried at the domestic level (so-called 'upwards' *ne bis in idem*). In this case, a second prosecution and trial by the ICC is only blocked if the domestic proceedings have been in line with the unwillingness criteria of the ICC's complementarity regime.[970] These criteria, together with the relevant *ne bis in idem* questions, will be analysed in detail in Chapter III in this volume.[971]

### (4) Overall assessment of fair trial

In the European human rights system, not every violation of the above-mentioned rights leads automatically to the overall verdict of a fair trial violation by the relevant State Party. Rather, the ECtHR performs a quite unique—and in the other human rights systems thus far unknown[972]—*two levels test or analysis*:[973] at the first level, it determines whether an individual rights violation has been committed; at the second level, it then carries out an *overall assessment of the entire proceedings*[974] in order to determine whether the violation in question was so serious that these proceedings as a whole have to be considered unfair within the meaning of Article 6 ECHR (the so-called doctrine of overall assessment or examination).[975]

[969] cf. Art. 20 (2) ICCS.

[970] cf. Art. 20 (3) ICCS referring to the unwillingness criteria contained in Art. 17 (2)(a) and (c); see also Friman, Brady, Costi, Guariglia, and Stuckenberg, in Sluiter et al., *International Criminal Procedure* (2013), pp. 442–3.

[971] Chapter III, B.(2)(d)(iii) in this volume.

[972] In the ACHR system, the Court only examines the individual violation, see e.g. *Cantoral Benavides vs Perú*, Judgment (18 August 2000), para. 127 (confidential communication between suspect and his lawyer); for further case law, see previous edition, p. 95 with note 909 ; more recently *Acosta et al. v. Nicaragua*, Judgment, Serie C No. 334 (25 March 2017), para. 165; *Ortiz Hernández et al. v. Venezuela*, Judgment, Serie C No. 338 (22 August 2017), para. 145; *Vereda La Esperanza v. Colombia*, Judgment, Serie C No. 341 (31 August 2017), para. 211; *Carvajal Carvajal et al. v. Colombia*, Judgment, Serie C No. 352 (13 March 2018), para. 126; *Omeara Carrascal et al. v. Colombia*, Judgment, Serie C No. 368 (21 November 2018), para. 253; *Díaz Loreto et al. v. Venezuela*, Judgment, Serie C No. 392 (19 November 2019), para. 122. The same applies to the ICCPR system; see HRCt, *Polay Campos v. Peru* (1997) UN Doc. CCPR/C/61/D/577/1994, para. 8.8 (trial by 'faceless' judges); furthermore, see HRCt, 'General Comment 36' (3 September 2019), UN Doc. CCPR/C/GC/36, para. 41 with regard to violations of the fair trial guarantees pursuant to Art. 14 CCPR resulting in death penalty verdicts. In more recent judgments regarding the military justice system the IACtHR has, however, analysed the overall impact of military proceedings on certain fair trial rights, cf. esp. *Arguelles et al. v. Argentina*, Serie C No. 288, Judgment (20 November 2014), para. 166 looking at the process in its integral form ['de manera integral'], esp. the review of the military court's judgment by an ordinary court and denying a violation of Arts. 8 (1) and 25 (1) ACHR; more recently *Coc Max et al. (Xamán Massacre) v. Guataemala*, Judgment (22 August 2018), para. 84 also denying a violation of Art. 8(1) ACHR as 'it is not evident that the intervention of the military jurisdiction had an impact on the subsequent action of the ordinary jurisdiction'.

[973] On the two-level test instructively, see Krauß, *V-Leute* (1999), pp. 141 ff.; see also Satzger, *Internationales Strafrecht* (2020), § 11 mn. 79; Satzger, *ICL* (2018), § 9 mn. 79.

[974] cf. Haefliger and Schürmann, *EMRK* (1999), pp. 180, 219; Villiger, *Handbuch EMRK* (2020), p. 307; Barkhuysen et al., in van Dijk et al., *ECHR* (2018), p. 561; Rzepka, *Fairness* (2000), pp. 102 ff.; Schleiminger, *Konfrontation* (2001), pp. 8, 21; Meyer-Ladewig et al., 'Artikel 6' in Meyer-Ladewig and Nettesheim, *EMRK* (2017), mn. 92; Demko, *HRRS*, 6 (2005), 283 ff.; Gaede, *Fairness* (2007), pp. 427 ff.; Vogel and Matt, *StV*, 27 (2007), 209 and crit. 211; Gless, *Internationales Strafrecht* (2021), mn. 87–8; Demko, *Verteidigung* (2014), p. 236; crit. Walter, in Roth, *Europäisierung* (2010), p. 306; Vogiatzis, *HRLR*, 22 (2022), 12 ('very problematic approach'); cf. also Hauck, *NStZ*, 30 (2010), 20 ff.; Gaede, *JR*, 81 (2009), 495–6.

[975] cf. for instance *Öcalan v. Turkey*, Application No. 46221/99, Judgment (12 March 2003), paras. 140, 153 ('in the light of the entirety of the proceedings, has deprived the accused of a fair hearing'); *Haas v. Germany*, Application No. 73047/01, Decision as to the Admissibility of Application (17 November 2005); *Zaichenko v. Russia*, Application No. 39660/02, Judgment (18 February 2010), para. 36; *Bandaletov v. Ukraine*, Application No. 23180/06, Judgment (31 October 2013), para. 58; more recently e.g. *Ibrahim et al. v. UK*, Application No. 50541/08 et al., Grand Chamber Judgment (13 September 2016), para. 251 ('fair trial must be examined in each case having regard to the development of the proceedings as a whole and not on the basis of an isolated consideration of one particular aspect'); *Almaši v. Serbia*, Application No. 21388/15, Judgment (8 October 2019), para. 100

Such an overall unfairness may follow from a particularly serious individual violation, for instance, if police agents 'persuade' a fully law-abiding citizen to commit a crime (making the subsequent adjudication unlawful 'right from the outset'),[976] if a confession is obtained by torture,[977] or if the suspect is completely deprived of legal representation while in police custody.[978] If no such flagrant violation affecting the principle of equality of arms[979] or the core of defence rights[980] has taken place, the violation may be remedied at a different procedural phase, for example, a violation at the investigation stage may be remedied at trial or appeal. In fact, the Grand Chamber has confirmed that (even) core rights violations of Art. 6(3) ECHR have to be measured against the overall fairness standard since these rights 'are not aims in themselves'.[981] The ECtHR is particularly 'flexible' with regard to the *admissibility of evidence* obtained by way of a rights violation, for example, by sidestepping the right to confrontation[982] or, going beyond fair trial rights, the right to respect for private and family life (Article 8 ECHR).[983] On the one hand, the Court grants the national legislator, in particular

('The question that must be answered is whether the proceedings as a whole, including the way in which the evidence was obtained, were fair'); *Chernika v. Ukraine*, Application No. 53791/11, Judgment (12 March 2020), para. 51 ('primary concern under Article 6 is to evaluate the overall fairness of criminal proceedings'); furthermore, see *Akbay v. Germany*, Application Nos. 40495/15 and others, Judgment (15 October 2020), para. 109 ('Court, for its part, must acertain whether the proceedings as a whole, including the way in which evidence was taken, were fair'). For a crit. view regarding the overall assessment of the defence rights in the investigation phase, see Gaede, *Fairness* (2007), pp. 455 ff.

[976] ECtHR, *Teixeira de Castro v. Portugal*, Application No. 25829/94, Judgment (9 June 1998), paras. 35–6, 39; for further case law, see previous edition, p. 96 with note 913; more recently *Akbay v. Germany*, Application Nos. 40495/15 and others, Judgment (15 October 2020), para. 123 ('deprived of a fair trial from the onset').

[977] cf. *Gäfgen v. Germany*, Application No. 22978/05, Judgment (30 June 2008), paras. 97 ff. (confirmed by the Grand Chamber, Application No. 22978/05, (1 June 2010)), where, however, no violation of Art. 6 was found by the Court ('only' inhuman treatment, para. 70); reviewed in detail, Esser, *NStZ*, 28 (2008), 657. On confessions extracted by torture under the ICCPR, see HRCt, 'General Comment 32' (23 August 2007) UN Doc. CCPR/C/GC/32, para. 41. On the practice of the international criminal tribunals, see Zappalá, *Human Rights* (2005), pp. 149 ff., crit. the lack of rules on the admission of evidence obtained in violation of the RPE.

[978] *Öcalan v. Turkey*, Application No. 46221/99, Judgment (12 March 2003), paras. 140 ff.; against a restriction of the right to legal representation in general, Spaniol, *Verteidigerbeistand* (1990), pp. 164 ff., 173; conc. Walther, *GA*, 150 (2003), 222.

[979] cf. *De Haes and Gijsels v. Belgium*, Application No. 19983/92, Judgment (24 February 1997), paras. 58–9 ('substantial disadvantage'); Toney, *IJEP*, 5 (2001), 47.

[980] *Magee v. UK*, Application No. 28135/95, Judgment (6 June 2000), paras. 44–5 (defence rights 'irretrievably prejudiced'); *Öcalan v. Turkey*, Application No. 46221/99, Judgment (12 March 2003), para. 143; see also Spaniol, *Verteidigerbeistand* (1990), pp. 164 ff., 173.

[981] cf. *Correia des Matos v. Portugal*, Application No. 56402/12, Grand Chamber Judgment (4 April 2018), para. 120 ('minimum rights listed in Article 6 § 3, which exemplify the requirements of a fair trial in respect of typical procedural situations which arise in criminal cases, are not aims in themselves: their intrinsic aim is always to contribute to ensuring the fairness of the criminal proceedings as a whole'); *Chernika v. Ukraine*, Application No. 53791/11, Judgment (12 March 2020), para. 52 ('Compliance with the requirements of a fair trial must be examined in each case having regard to the proceedings as a whole and not on the basis of an isolated consideration of one particular aspect or one particular incident'); but for a different emphasis apparently, *Ibrahim et al. v. UK*, Application No. 50541/08 et al., Grand Chamber Judgment (13 September 2016), para. 251 ('it cannot be excluded that a specific factor may be so decisive as to enable the fairness of the trial to be assessed at an earlier stage in the proceedings').

[982] In depth and with further references, see Ambos, *Beweisverwertungsverbote* (2010), pp. 102 ff. On the developments in the case law, see Lubig and Sprenger, *ZIS*, 3 (2008), 433.

[983] *Bykov v. Russia*, Application No. 4378/02, Judgment (10 March 2009), para. 91 ('As regards, in particular, the examination of the nature of the Convention violation found, the Court observes that … it found the use of covert listening devices to be in breach of Art. 8 since recourse to such devices lacked a legal basis in domestic law and the interferences with those applicants' right to respect for their private life were not "in accordance with the law". Nonetheless, the admission in evidence of information obtained thereby did not in the circumstances of the cases conflict with the requirements of fairness guaranteed by Art. 6 § 1'); also see *Akhlyustin v. Russia*, Application No. 21200/05, Judgment (7 November 2017), para. 52 with further references ('The Court has already found in several cases where the use of covert listening devices was not "in accordance with the law" and therefore in breach

with regard to the law of evidence, a wide *margin of appreciation* and limits its judicial control to cases of blatant abuse.[984] On the other hand, such (unlawfully obtained) evidence can, though with 'extreme care', still be used;[985] an overall fair trial violation would come only then into consideration if the conviction was 'based either *solely or to a decisive extent*' on this tainted evidence, if the proceedings were not conducted with thorough scrutiny and without 'sufficient counterbalancing factors'.[986] Thus, the ensuing 'sole or decisive rule'[987] is not absolute[988] given that a thorough conduct of the proceedings and 'sufficient counterbalancing factors' may ultimately rule out an overall fair trial violation. Concretely speaking, for example, a transcript of a declaration of a witness who invokes his right to refuse testimony

of Article 8 that the admission in evidence of information obtained thereby did not, in the circumstances of the cases, conflict with the requirements of fairness guaranteed by Article 6 § 1') and *López Ribalda et al. v. Spain*, Application Nos. 1874/13 and 8567/13, Grand Chamber Judgment (17 October 2019), para. 151 ('while the use of evidence secured as a result of a measure found to be in breach of Article 3 always raises serious issues as to the fairness of the proceedings . . . , the question whether the use in evidence of information obtained in violation of Article 8 or of domestic law rendered a trial as a whole unfair, contrary to Article 6, has to be determined with regard to all the circumstances of the case'). For a crit. view, see Jung, *GA*, 156 (2009), 655; Gaede, *JR*, 81 (2009), 500.

[984] cf. e.g. ECtHR, *S. N. v. Sweden*, Application No. 34209/96, Judgment (2 July 2002), para. 44; for further case law, see previous edition, p. 97 with note 920; more recently *Murtazaliyeva v. Russia*, Application No. 36658/05, Grand Judgment (18 December 2018), para. 139 ('admissibility of evidence is primarily a matter for regulation by national law'). See also Jung, in Callies, *Herausforderungen* (2015), pp. 976–7 (defining the margin of apprreciation as a 'strategy of discharge' ['*Entlastungsstrategie*'] and calling the ECtHR a guarantor of justice on a case-by-case basis, p. 981); see also Sommer, in Brüssow et al., *Strafverteidigung* (2007), § 17 mn. 78, 102. On the general 'margin of appreciation' doctrine in this respect, see Tulkens and Donnay, *RSC*, (2006), 3 ff.; Klamberg, in Sluiter et al., *International Criminal Procedure* (2013), p. 1037.

[985] ECtHR, *Doorson v. The Netherlands*, Application No. 20524/92, Judgment (26 March 1996), para. 76; for further case law, see previous edition, p. 97 with note 921; more recently *Strassenmeyer v. Germany*, Application No. 57818/18, Judgment (2 May 2023), para. 69 ('most careful scrutiny').

[986] ECtHR, *Al-Kawaja and Tahery v. UK*, Application Nos. 26766/05 and 22228/06, Judgment (15 December 2011), para. 147 ('At the same time where a conviction is based solely or decisively on the evidence of absent witnesses, the Court must subject the proceedings to the most searching scrutiny . . . the admission of such evidence . . . would require sufficient counterbalancing factors, including the existence of strong procedural safeguards. The question in each case is whether there are sufficient counterbalancing factors in place, including measures that permit a fair and proper assessment of the reliability of that evidence to take place. This would permit a conviction to be based on such evidence only if it is sufficiently reliable given its importance in the case'); *Karparenko v. Russia*, Application No. 5605/04, Judgment (13 March 2013), para. 61; *Matytsina v. Russia*, Application No. 58428/10, Judgment (27 March 2014), para. 152; more recently *Ibrahim et al. v. UK*, Application No. 50541/08 et al., Grand Chamber Judgment (13 September 2016), para. 274 provided a 'non-exhaustive list of factors, drawn from the Court's case-law', that may be used on a discretionary basis ('where appropriate') 'to assess the impact of procedural failings at the pre-trial stage on the overall fairness of the criminal proceedings' including inter alia '[w]hether the applicant had the opportunity to challenge the authenticity of the evidence and oppose its use'; '[t]he quality of the evidence and whether the circumstances in which it was obtained cast doubt on its reliability or accuracy'; 'whether the evidence formed an integral or significant part of the probative evidence upon which the conviction was based, and the strength of the other evidence in the case'; '[o]ther relevant procedural safeguards afforded by domestic law and practice'; furthermore, see *Al Alo v. Slovakia*, Application No. 32084/19, Judgment (10 February 2022), para. 43 with regard to the important group of cases of the use of the testimony of a witness who does not testify in person. See also Gaynor, in Sluiter et al., *International Criminal Procedure* (2013), pp. 1071–2. For the earlier ECtHR jurisprudence, see previous edition, p. 97 with note 922 *in fine*.

[987] See also ECtHR, *Al-Kawaja and Tahery v. UK*, Application Nos. 26766/05 and 22228/06, Judgment (15 December 2011), para. 119 ('when a conviction is based solely or to a decisive degree on depositions that have been made by a person whom the accused has had no opportunity to examine or to have examined, whether during the investigation or at the trial, the rights of the defence may be restricted to an extent that is incompatible with the guarantees provided by Art. 6 (the so-called "sole or decisive rule")'); more recently *Al Alo v. Slovakia*, Application No. 32084/19, Judgment (10 February 2022), paras. 43 ff.; *Chernika v. Ukraine*, Application No. 53791/11, Judgment (12 March 2020), para. 40.

[988] See also ECtHR, *Al-Kawaja*, op. cit., para. 119 ('Court will examine below whether the latter rule is to be considered as an absolute rule the breach of which automatically leads to a finding that the proceedings have not been fair'); *Alo v. Slovakia*, Application No. 32084/19, Judgment (10 February 2022), para. 43 ('question of whether there was a good reason for admitting the evidence'); *Chernika v. Ukraine*, Application No. 53791/11, Judgment (12 March 2020), para. 41.

in open court is admissible if that written declaration is corroborated by further evidence and does not constitute the only evidentiary basis of the judicial decision.[989]

In sum, a (overall) fair trial violation on the ground of unlawfully obtained or regularly inadmissible evidence may be prevented by taking recourse to other (incriminating) evidence, which corroborates this evidence or generally supports the prosecution case. Thus, the overall assessment doctrine may undermine the fair trial performance of domestic courts given that individual rights violations have no immediate consequences and may, at any rate, be compensated by other procedural measures.[990] In fact, the doctrine turns thereby into a mere *balancing exercise* weighing fair trial rights with prosecutorial or public order interests but without providing for precise contours.[991]

Notwitstanding those serious concerns, it must not be overlooked that the overall assessment doctrine may also operate in favour of the accused. On the one hand, it takes into account all the developments during the entire proceedings, including further violations, which may then aggravate the overall fair trial violation. On the other hand, it has a transnational, cross-border potential of fair trial protection since it includes in the fair trial analysis all investigatory activities, independent of their geographical location or temporal point of reference, as long as they concern the proceedings object of the human rights litigation. Ultimately, it must be determined on a case-by-case-basis whether the individual fair trial restrictions taken all together amount to an overall unfair trial.

[989] ECtHR, *Asch v. Austria*, Application No. 12398/86, Judgment (26 April 1991), paras. 28–31; cf. also Esser, *Europäisches Strafverfahrensrecht* (2002), pp. 652 ff.

[990] For a crit. view, see also Esser, *Europäisches Strafverfahrensrecht* (2002), pp. 404, 468; Esser, *Europäisches und Internationales Strafrecht* (2023), § 9 mn. 219–20; Beulke, in Hanack et al., *FS Riess* (2002), p. 9; Schleiminger, *Konfrontation* (2001), pp. 8 ff.

[991] In a similar vein, Walther, *GA*, 150 (2003), 218; previously Ambos, *NStZ*, (2003), 16; for a different view, see Wohlers, *GA*, 152 (2005), 26.

# II
# Role and Status of Legal Participants

*The full chapter bibliography can be downloaded from

## A. Judges and Chambers

### (1) Position

The question of the position of the judge in a domestic criminal system is usually, leaving cultural factors aside, a question of the choice of model of criminal procedure. What role a judge is called to play in criminal proceedings is fundamentally a systemic issue, determined by the system in force and determining at the same time the character of the whole system.[1] However, there is no such determining system in force at an international court like the ICC, where elements from the adversarial and the inquisitorial models are taken to create a unique procedural system[2] which, in addition, has no proper history of its own comparable to that of ancient national systems. Thus, to understand the role of judges in such a 'modern' system, one has to pursue an inductive rather than a deductive approach, that is, one cannot infer the judicial powers and functions 'from above' (from the system), rather, one has to analyse the specific rules 'from below'.

From the perspective of the normative design, ICC judges are 'more interventionist'[3] and 'more active … in establishing the truth'[4] than their counterparts at the ad hoc tribunals. The trial judges 'confer with the parties and adopt such procedures as are necessary to facilitate the fair and expeditious conduct of the proceedings',[5] deciding on 'any issue concerning the conduct of the proceedings'.[6] They may request 'for the determination of the truth' the submission of all evidence, like 'the attendance and testimony of witnesses and production of documents', either prior to the trial or during the course of the trial.[7] Furthermore, they are in the position to 'order the production of evidence *in addition* to that already collected

[1] cf. Friman, in Cryer et al., *ICL* (2019), p. 406; De Smet, in Stahn and Sluiter, *Practice* (2009), p. 408 ('Two fundamental choices any system of criminal procedure has to make … the question of judicial fact-finding and the role of judges in the different procedural phases'); Billis, *Rolle des Richters* (2015), p. 73 ('Rolle des Richters … als zentrales modelltrennendes Charakteristikum'), 82.

[2] Friman, 'Procedures', in Cryer et al., *ICL* (2019), pp. 409–10 with n. 31; De Smet, 'Structural Analysis', in Stahn and Sluiter, *Practice* (2009), p. 418 ('do not adhere to any neat theoretical categories'); Kreß, *JICJ*, 1 (2003), 604–5; Zappalà, in Sluiter et al., *International Criminal Procedure* (2013), p. 50; Billis, *Rolle des Richters* (2015), p. 447.

[3] Friman, 'Procedures', in Cryer et al., *ICL* (2012), p. 430 (p. 410 in 4th edn, 2019).

[4] Safferling, *Criminal Procedure* (2012), p. 131; Orie, 'Accusatorial v. Inquisitorial', in Cassese et al., *Rome Statute II* (2002), p. 1475; De Smet, 'Structural Analysis', in Stahn and Sluiter, *Practice* (2009), pp. 419 ff.

[5] Art. 64 (3)(a) ICCS; Klamberg, 'Article 64', in Klamberg et al., *Commentary ICC II* (2023), p. 198.

[6] Rule 134 (1) RPE ICC. See also Bitti, 'Article 64', in Ambos, *Commentary* (2022), mn. 21–7; Schabas, *ICC Commentary* (2016), pp. 978–80; Boas et al., *International Criminal Procedure* (2011), p. 265.

[7] Arts. 64 (6)(b) and 69 (3) ICCS. For a comparative analysis of witness summonses to obtain additional evidence before the ICTR, ICTY, SCSL, and the ICC, see Pichou, *ICLR*, 17 (2017), 135. See also Piragoff and Clarke, 'Article 69', in Ambos, *Commentary* (2022), mn. 4–6; Schabas, *ICC Commentary* (2016), pp. 1086–7; Orie, in Cassese et al., *Rome Statute II* (2002), pp. 1476–7; Billis, *Rolle des Richters* (2015), pp. 432–3.

prior to the trial or presented during the trial by the parties',[8] to 'question a witness before or after a witness is questioned by a participant'.[9] Yet, notwithstanding that 'judges may potentially play a significant role'[10] in the truth-finding process, they are not obliged to do so and may instead leave the control over 'the order and manner in which the evidence shall be submitted' to the Prosecutor and the defence.[11] In contrast, the role of the judges during the criminal investigation is limited.[12] We will return to this at later stages in this book.[13]

Yet, if the Prosecutor fails to make a request with regard to a 'unique investigative opportunity'[14] the PTC may request such a measure, upon consultation with the Prosecutor, 'on its own initiative' in order 'to preserve evidence that it deems would be essential for the defence at trial'.[15] Furthermore, the PTC can take similar measures 'upon the request of a person who has been arrested or has appeared pursuant to a summons under article 58', even if there is no unique investigative opportunity and without consulting the Prosecutor.[16] These limited investigative powers do not, of course, turn the PTC into an 'investigative judge'.[17] In fact, these powers of the PTC are to be interpreted restrictively taking into consideration its role during the pre-trial proceedings, that is, to safeguard the rights of the suspect/accused and to assist the defence in the collection of evidence.[18]

### (2) Composition of Chambers

The second organ of the ICC is the Judicial Division consisting of the Appeals, Trial, and Pre-Trial Divisions,[19] carrying out the judicial functions of the Court.[20] The eighteen judges of the Court are assigned to divisions 'in such a way that each division', 'based on the nature of the functions to be performed by [it] and the qualifications and experience of the judges elected to the Court', 'shall contain an appropriate combination of expertise in criminal law

[8] Art. 64 (6)(d) ICCS (emphasis added).

[9] Rule 140 (2)(c) RPE ICC. See also Orie, in Cassese et al., *Rome Statute II* (2002), p. 1475; De Smet, in Stahn and Sluiter, *Practice* (2009), pp. 419–20; Schabas, *ICC Commentary* (2016), pp. 983–5; Combs, in Sluiter et al., *International Criminal Procedure* (2013), pp. 693, 702; Boas et al., *International Criminal Procedure* (2011), pp. 263–6.

[10] Cassese and Gaeta, *ICL* (2013), p. 378.

[11] Rule 140 (1) RPE ICC. See also Cassese and Gaeta, *ICL* (2013), p. 378; Orie, in Cassese et al., *Rome Statute II* (2002), pp. 1476–7; Safferling, *Criminal Procedure* (2012), p. 131; De Smet, in Stahn and Sluiter, *Practice* (2009), pp. 419–20; Kirsch, *ICLR*, 6 (2006), 279.

[12] Friman, in Cryer et al., *ICL* (2019), p. 410.

[13] cf. in particular Chapter V, A.(1) and (3)(a) in this volume.

[14] See generally Orie, in Cassese et al., *Rome Statute II* (2002), pp. 1475–6; Guariglia and Hochmayr, 'Article 56', in Ambos, *Commentary* (2022), mn. 11.

[15] Art. 56 (3)(a) ICCS. See also Guariglia and Hochmayr, 'Article 56', in Ambos, *Commentary* (2022), mn. 23–9; Schabas, *ICC Commentary* (2016), pp. 874–5; de Meester et al., in Sluiter et al., *International Criminal Procedure* (2013), p. 188.

[16] Art. 57 (3)(b) ICCS. See also Orie, 'Accusatorial v. Inquisitorial', in Cassese et al., *Rome Statute II* (2002), p. 1476; Guariglia and Hochmayr, 'Article 57', in Ambos, *Commentary* (2022), mn. 18 ff., esp. 25; Klamberg, 'Article 57', in Klamberg et al., *Commentary ICC II* (2023), p. 86.

[17] Friman, 'Procedures', in Cryer et al., *ICL* (2019), p. 411; on the introduction of an investigating judge for speeding up the trial, see Safferling, *Criminal Procedure* (2012), p. 137; see also de Meester et al., in Sluiter et al., *International Criminal Procedure* (2013), pp. 187–8; De Smet, in Stahn and Sluiter, *Practice* (2009), pp. 422–3; in favour of an investigating judge in the ICC, de Hemptinne, *JICJ*, 5 (2007), 402 ff.; see also Higgins, *JICJ*, 5 (2007), 396 ff., proposing an independent investigative commission, in favour of increased judicial intervention in the pre-trial proceedings.

[18] Friman, in Cryer et al., *ICL* (2019), p. 410; Orie, in Cassese et al., *Rome Statute II* (2002), p. 1476; Guariglia and Hochmayr, 'Article 57', in Ambos, *Commentary* (2022), mn. 17–18; Klamberg, 'Article 56', in Klamberg et al., *Commentary ICC II* (2023), pp. 77–9.

[19] Art. 34 (b) ICCS.

[20] Art. 39 (2)(a) ICCS.

and procedure and in international law'.[21] The judges' assignment to the divisions in general and with regard to concrete situations and cases is to be decided by the Presidency.[22] Indeed, this constitutes its most important judicial function[23] and confirms its prominent role in the institutional framework of the Court.[24]

### *(a) Pre-Trial Chamber*

The functions of the PTC, laid down in Article 57 ICCS, 'shall be carried out either by three judges of the Pre-Trial Division or by a single judge of that division',[25] with predominantly criminal trial experience.[26] Normally, the (at least) six judges[27] of the Pre-Trial Division are divided into one or more PTCs established pursuant to Article 39 (2)(c) ICCS and Reg. 46 RegC. Notwithstanding the, perhaps, misleading wording of Article 39 (2)(b)(iii) ICCS ('single judge of that division'), a Single Judge does not constitute a PTC.[28] Rather, some of the functions of the PTC can be exercised by a Single Judge;[29] that would happen for reasons of 'the distribution of work within the Chamber and the proper management and efficiency in the handling of cases'[30] or, when necessary, due to the 'issues involved and the circumstances of the proceedings before the Chamber'.[31] Proceedings for offences against the administration of justice (Article 70 ICCS) are the exception to the rule, where pursuant to the (amended) Rule 165 (2) RPE ICC and Reg. 66*bis* (1) RegC, '[a] Chamber composed of one judge from the Pre-Trial Division shall exercise the functions and powers of the Pre-Trial Chamber'.[32] Whenever a 'decision by the full Chamber is not expressly provided for

[21] Art. 39 (1) ICCS. See also McDermott, 'Article 39', in Klamberg et al., *Commentary ICC I* (2023), pp. 956–7. For the civil or common law background of the (previous) judges see Powderly, *Judges* (2020), p. 53 (finding a 'dominance of the civil law tradition' to be 'more pronounced on the ICC bench, with 26 of the 47 seats (approximately 55.3%)').

[22] cf. Rule 4*bis* (2) RPE ICC; see also Arts. 35 (3), 39 (4) ICCS, Reg. 12 RegC. On the most recent assignment of six newly elected judges to the three judicial divisions (pre-trial, trial, and appeal) and Chambers, see ICC-Pres-01/24, Presidency Decision assigning judges to divisions and recomposing Chambers (12 March 2024), <https://www.icc-cpi.int/news/icc-presidency-assigns-judges-judicial-divisions-and-chambers-2>. The Presidency also constituted, recomposed, and dissolved a number of Chambers where it considered necessary.

[23] cf. Ambach and Rackwitz, *LCP*, 76 nos. 3 & 4 (2013), 131–3.

[24] cf. ibid., 127 ff. On the Presidency's role with regard to the review of administrative decision, see Chapter VI, D.(2) in this volume.

[25] Art. 39 (2)(b)(iii) ICCS.

[26] Art. 39 (1) ICCS. On the importance of judges with criminal trial experience, see also Ambach and Rackwitz, *LCP*, 76 nos. 3 & 4 (2013), 132.

[27] cf. Art. 39 (1) ICCS second sentence ('not less than six judges'). At the time of writing (September 2024) there have been six judges: <https://www.icc-cpi.int/judges/judicial-division?f[0]=division:581> but in addition Judge Guillou from the Trial Division has been assigned to PTC I dealing with the Palestine situation <https://www.icc-cpi.int/judges/judicial-divisions/chambers/786>.

[28] cf. Rule 7 RPE ICC and Reg. 47 RegC. See also Deschênes and Staker, 'Article 39', in Triffterer, *Commentary* (2008), mn. 4; Abtahi and Young, 'Article 39', in Ambos, *Commentary* (2022), mn. 6.

[29] cf. Arts. 57 (2)(b) and 39 (2)(b)(iii) ICCS and Reg, 47 RegC. cf. also McDermott, 'Article 39', in Klamberg et al., *Commentary ICC I* (2023), pp. 961–2; Klamberg, 'Article 57', in Klamberg et al., *Commentary ICC II* (2023), p. 85.

[30] cf. *Situation in the Central African Republic II*, PTC II Decision on the Designation of a Single Judge, No. ICC-01/14-01/21, 17 March 2021, paras. 9, 10, designating a Single Judge responsible for 'carrying out the functions of the Chamber'; *Situation in the Central African Republic*, PTC II Decision Designating Single Judges, No. ICC-01/05-24, 23 March 2009, para. 5, designating the same Single Judge 'responsible for all victims' issues in relation to the proceedings of the situation in the Central African Republic.' Likewise, the Presidency can replace judges following their request to be excused from their exercise of function in a respective PTC on the basis of workload, see ICC-Pres-01/23, Presidency Decision Replacing a Judge in Pre-Trial Chamber II (21 February 2023).

[31] *Situation in the Central African Republic II*, No. ICC-01/14-01/21, paras. 9, 10 and *Prosecutor v. Gaddafi and Al-Senussi*, PTC I Decision Designating a Single Judge, No. ICC-01/11-01/11-511, 13 February 2014, para. 4, 'to ensure the proper management, expeditiousness and efficiency of the proceedings.' See also *Situation in the Central African Republic II*, PTC II Decision Designating a Single Judge, No. ICC-01/14-23-US-Exp, 9 November 2018, para. 3.

[32] See ICC, *Report Provisional Amendments Rules* (2016).

in the Statute or the Rules' the designated Single Judge can make the decision.[33] Such a decision by the full PTC is required[34] for the authorization of a *proprio motu* investigation of the Prosecutor,[35] for challenges to the admissibility of a case and to the jurisdiction of the Court,[36] for investigations by the Prosecutor on the territory of a State,[37] for the confirmation of the charges hearing[38] and for the protection of national security information.[39] Furthermore, the decision of the Prosecutor not to proceed with an investigation[40] should be reviewed by the full PTC.[41] The same applies to the decision concerning a unique investigative opportunity under Article 56 ICCS.[42]

*(b) Trial Chamber*

A Trial Chamber consists of three judges of the Trial Division.[43] The wording that 'the functions of the Trial Chamber shall be carried out by three judges of the Trial Division'[44] implies that there are no permanent Trial Chambers, but that a TC shall be formed for each case, while more than one Chamber can coexist,[45] that is, a judge can be a member of more than one TC.

Judges assigned to the Pre-Trial Division can be temporarily attached to the Trial Division and vice versa when 'the efficient management of the Court's workload so requires'.[46] That is, however, the last similarity with the PTCs. Unlike the PTCs, there is no designation of a Single Judge at the TC level,[47] except in the just mentioned case of proceedings for offences against the administration of justice (Article 70 ICCS).[48] Generally, 'all the judges of the Trial Chamber shall be present at each stage of the trial and throughout their deliberations'.[49]

The functions of the TC are contained in Article 64 ICCS. Its main duties are to 'ensure that a trial is fair and expeditious and is conducted with full respect for the rights of the accused and due regard for the protection of victims and witnesses'.[50] The trial ends with a decision on the innocence or guilt of the accused, and on a possible sentence.[51]

33 Rule 7 (2) RPE ICC.
34 cf. Art. 57 (2) ICCS.
35 Art. 15 ICCS.
36 Arts. 18 and 19 ICCS.
37 Art. 54 (2) ICCS.
38 Art. 61 (7) ICCS.
39 Art. 72 ICCS.
40 Art. 53 (3)(a) and (b) ICCS.
41 Rules 108 (1) and 110 (1) RPE ICC.
42 Rule 114 (2) RPE ICC. See also Safferling, *Criminal Procedure* (2012), pp.140–1; Guariglia and Hochmayr, 'Article 57', in Ambos, *Commentary* (2022), mn. 8; Schabas, *ICC Commentary* (2016), pp. 878–85.
43 Safferling, *Criminal Procedure* (2012), pp. 142–5; Abtahi and Young, 'Article 39', in Ambos, *Commentary* (2022), mn. 5; Schabas, *ICC Commentary* (2016), p. 718.
44 Art. 39 (2)(b)(ii) ICCS.
45 Art. 39 (2)(c) ICCS.
46 Art. 39 (4) ICCS.
47 *Prosecutor v. Lubanga*, TC Decision on Whether Two Judges Alone May Hold a Hearing, No. ICC-01/04-01/06-1349, 22 May 2008, para. 12 ('the presiding judge cannot adopt an analogous role to that of the single judge of the Pre-Trial Chamber'); see also Schabas, *ICC Commentary* (2016), pp. 1129–35; Triffterer and Kiss, 'Article 74', in Ambos, *Commentary* (2022), mn. 12–25; Nignan, 'Article 74', in Fernandez et al., *Statut* (2019), 1972–3; on the power of the presiding judge throughout the proceedings, cf. Bitti, 'Article 64', in Ambos, *Commentary* (2022), mn. 57–64; Vasiliev, 'Article 74', in Klamberg et al., *Commentary ICC II* (2023), pp. 419–22; Klamberg, 'Article 64', in Klamberg et al., *Commentary ICC II* (2023), pp. 214, 217.
48 cf. Rule 165 (2) RPE ICC and Reg. 66*bis* (2) RegC according to which '[a] Chamber composed of one judge shall exercise the functions and powers of the Trial Chamber'.
49 Art. 74 (1) ICCS. Thereon, cf. also Vasiliev, 'Article 74', in Klamberg et al., *Commentary ICC II* (2023), pp. 419–22.
50 Art. 64 (2) ICCS.
51 Safferling, *Criminal Procedure* (2012), p. 145; Schabas, *ICC Commentary* (2016), pp. 976 ff.; Bitti, 'Article 64', in Ambos, *Commentary* (2022), mn. 8; Röben, *MPYbUNL*, 7 (2003), 516.

### (c) *Appeals Chamber*

The Appeals Chamber consists of all five judges of the Appeals Division, including the President of the Court.[52] ICTY and ICTR have a common AC;[53] the KSC has a 'Court of Appeals Panel' composed of three judges.[54] The judges of the ICC's AC 'decide on a presiding Judge for each appeal'.[55] A judge assigned to the Appeals Division must not serve in any other division.[56] Judges assigned to the other two Divisions, however, can be assigned temporarily to every other Division.[57]

The functions of the Appeals Division as instances of appeal and revision[58] are dealt with in Chapter VI in this volume. The AC exercises 'original jurisdiction'[59] with regard to 'any question as to the disqualification of the Prosecutor or a Deputy Prosecutor'[60] and the reduction of sentence.[61]

## (3) Selection

Courts are only as good as the people sitting on the bench. This is true for national as well as international courts, with the caveat that the legal officers/clerks of national supreme or international courts may compensate to some extent for the limited competence of the judges for whom they work. This does not mean, though, that the qualification of the judges should in any way be compromised by political considerations. Unfortunately, as everyone with some experience in the national or international judiciary knows, the reality is different. Even in States with consolidated democracy and high regard for their judiciary and jurisprudence,[62] party affiliation and politics influence the election of judges to the national supreme courts, let alone on the international level, where 'politicization ... is endemic'.[63]

[52] Art. 39 (2)(b)(i) ICCS. Exception to this rule are, again, the proceedings pursuant to Art. 70 ICCS, where Rule 165 (2) RPE ICC and Reg. 66*bis* (2) RegC provide for a panel of three judges to decide appeals.

[53] cf. Art. 13 (4) ICTRS according to which the members of the ICTY AC shall also serve as members of the ICTR AC.

[54] Art. 25 (1)(c) KSC Law. Currently the Panel consists of four judges three of which are interchangeably assigned to specific cases.

[55] Reg. 13 RegC.

[56] Art. 39 (4) ICCS.

[57] cf. ibid. (cross-assignment between Trial and Pre-Trial Division) and Reg. 12 RegC (from the Trial and Pre Trial Division to the Appeals Division). See also Abtahi and Young, 'Article 39', in Ambos, *Commentary* (2022), mn. 13; Schabas, *ICC Commentary* (2016), p. 719; Safferling, *Criminal Procedure* (2012), p. 145; on cross-assignment among Divisions, see also McDermott, 'Article 39', in Klamberg et al., *Commentary ICC I* (2023), pp. 959, 966 (crit. at 964 on 'contaminated' judges who have served at the PTC or TC (or both) and are later assigned to the AC).

[58] Arts. 81–4 ICCS.

[59] Schabas, *ICC Commentary* (2016), p. 718.

[60] cf. Art. 42 (8) ICCS and Rule 34 (3) RPE ICC.

[61] cf. Art. 110 ICCS and Rule 224 (3) and (4) RPE ICC.

[62] Take, for example, the case of Germany, where party affiliation is an important, sometimes indispensable requirement to become a supreme or constitutional court judge or Federal Prosecutor-General; for an empirical study, see Bohlander and Latour, *German Judiciary* (1998), p. 45, concluding that there exists 'a rather sinister picture of the influence political parties exert over the elections to the BGH [German Supreme Court]'; see also Bohlander, in Bohlander, *International Criminal Justice* (2007), pp. 357–8; recently Bohlander, *JCompL*, 19 (2024), 459 . As the Spanish example shows, however, at least formal party affiliation could be prohibited for judges. Art. 395 of the Spanish Law of the Organization of the Judiciary (*Ley Organica del Poder Judicial*) provides that judges must not belong to political parties or trade unions or work for these ('No podrán los jueces o magistrados pertenecer a partidos políticos o sindicatos o tener empleo al servicio de los mismos'). Some criticize, however, the undermining of this rule by the Associations of Judges, which are close to the political parties ('*Asociación Profesional de la Magistratura*' of a conservative tendency and '*Jueces para la Democracía*' of a left-wing orientation).

[63] Mackenzie et al., *Selecting International Judges* (2010), p. 135; in addition, more subtle forms of politicization may exist, e.g. rewarding of submissive and accommodating behaviour, contrary to a democratic and independent judiciary.

Both the nomination and the election processes of the international courts,[64] especially of the ICJ and ICC, are criticized for having a high degree of politicization, and lacking in transparency and minimum standards, which would guarantee a minimum qualification of the judges so elected.[65]

Trying to address some of those issues, at least in the selection of judges, the ICCS provides for formally strict selection rules.[66] The candidates shall be of 'high moral character, impartiality and integrity'[67] and 'possess the qualifications of their national law for appointment to the highest judicial offices'.[68] They shall also 'have established competence in criminal law and procedure, and the necessary relevant experience, whether as judge, Prosecutor, advocate or in other similar capacity, in criminal proceedings'[69] or 'competence in relevant areas of international law such as international humanitarian law and the law of human rights, and extensive experience in a professional legal capacity which is of relevance to the judicial work of the Court'[70] and 'have an excellent knowledge of and be fluent in at least one of the working languages of the Court', that is, English or French.[71]

In addition, the ASP adopted a resolution on 10 September 2004 on the 'Procedure for the nomination and election of judges, the Prosecutor and Deputy Prosecutors of the International Criminal Court',[72] which contains precise rules for the nomination and election of the judges and which was amended in December 2019.[73] Prior to this, at its tenth session in 2011,[74] the ASP had set up an Advisory Committee on Nominations of Judges of the ICC (ACN).[75] In a parallel move, the CICC established a committee of distinguished jurists whose task is to rate the candidates as (un)qualified based on available (public)

[64] For a brief account on the ICC electoral procedure, see Safferling, *Criminal Procedure* (2012), pp. 129–30.

[65] See Mackenzie et al., *Selecting International Judges* (2010), p. 173 ('nomination practices are fragmented, lacking in transparency', [only] 'a few candidates emerge following a transparent and formal consultative process that focuses on merit', 'it is not unusual for individuals to be selected as a result of overtly political considerations or even nepotism. Whatever form of nomination process is adopted, all nominated candidates must work their way through a highly politicized election process'); in the same vein, see *Cesare Romano* who refers quite bluntly in his preface to a 'troubling lack of transparency and the absence of common or minimum standards in the process ... the endemic and almost total absence of public scrutiny or political accountability that raises alarm bells' (Mackenzie et al., *Selecting International Judges* (2010), p. ix); Boas et al., *International Criminal Procedure* (2011), pp. 252 ff. (p. 255, 'former diplomats, government bureaucrats, parliamentarians and other domestic politicians, and academics, thereby diluting the number of judges with experience'); on the ICTY judges, see also Bohlander, in Bohlander, *International Criminal Justice* (2007), pp. 326–30; less critical but equally demanding improvements, Mettraux et al., *Expert Initiative Effectiveness ICC* (2014), pp. 224–7 (paras. 27–35).

[66] For a detailed analysis, see Bohlander, 'Article 36', in Ambos, *Commentary* (2022), mn. 3–12; Kovács, 'Article 36', in Fernandez et al., *Statut I* (2019), pp. 1217 ff.; Nimigan, *EJIL*, 33 (2022), 967–73.

[67] Art. 36 (3)(a) ICCS. On independence and impartiality of judges, see Bohlander, in Bohlander, *International Criminal Justice* (2007), pp. 362–8.

[68] On the 'huge difference between the criteria in the individual domestic systems as far as the requirements for the highest judicial offices are concerned', see Bohlander, in Bohlander, *International Criminal Justice* (2007), pp. 357–62; for a crit. view, see also Ambos, *LJIL*, 21 (2008), 915 with n. 21.

[69] Art. 36 (3)(b)(i) ICCS.

[70] Art. 36 (3)(b)(ii) ICCS. See also McDermott, 'Article 36', in Klamberg et al., *Commentary ICC I* (2023), p. 933 (arguing that there is a 'slightly higher value ... given to competence in criminal law over international law').

[71] Art. 36 (3)(c) ICCS; on the question of command of languages, see Bohlander, 'Article 36', in Ambos, *Commentary* (2022), mn. 7.

[72] ICC-ASP/3/Res.6—Consolidated version, <https://asp.icc-cpi.int/iccdocs/asp_docs/Resolutions/ICC-ASP-ASP3-Res-06-ENG.pdf>. For a good explanation of the complicated election procedure, see ICC-ASP/16/INF.2, 'Informal Guide and Commentary to the Procedure for the Nomination and Election of Judges of the International Criminal Court'.

[73] ICC-ASP/18/Res.4, 'Resolution on the Review of the Procedure for the Nomination and Election of Judges', <https://asp.icc-cpi.int/sites/asp/files/asp_docs/ASP18/ICC-ASP-18-Res4-ENG.pdf>.

[74] Resolution ICC-ASP/10/Res.5.

[75] cf. Art. 36 (4)(c) ICCS. Welcoming this move Mettraux et al., *Expert Initiative Effectiveness ICC* (2014), p. 225 (para. 29).

information.[76] The ACN is, according to its terms of reference,[77] composed of nine members, 'designated by the ASP by consensus', 'reflecting the principal legal systems of the world and an equitable geographical representation, as well as a fair representation of both genders', with 'established competence and experience in criminal or international law'. It prepares 'information and analysis, of a technical character, strictly on the suitability of the candidates' which is then presented to the ASP in order 'to facilitate that the highest-qualified individuals are appointed as judges of the ICC'.[78]

Yet, notwithstanding this stricter *selection* frame, the *nomination* practice of the ICC, with regard to nominations through national procedures, is criticized for having 'fragmented, inconsistent and highly variable' results, as the selection is not based on merits.[79] In fact, the candidates' merit is often a secondary factor[80] and State Parties have not succeeded in reaching a more objective, rational, and less politicized ICC nomination and election procedure. Especially diplomats or former politicians without any or relevant judicial experience are not suited for a court whose main work is that of a criminal trial court.[81]

Of course, 'soft factors' such as a more or less equal geographical representation of all parts of the world on the bench[82] and the gender aspect must certainly be taken into account in international courts. Yet the qualification of the candidates should never be compromised, and 'talented outsiders' should also have the possibility of getting nominated and elected. After all, the world courts (ICJ and ICC), unlike the European regional courts,[83] are under no obligation to have judges from all State Parties on the bench.[84]

It is also striking that there is a certain rotation of judges among the international criminal tribunals, for example, from an ad hoc tribunal to the ICC or vice versa. While this may have

[76] See on this 'Independent Panel on ICC Judicial Elections', <https://citeseerx.ist.psu.edu/document?repid=rep1&type=pdf&doi=a020b19bbb2b004893bfd6761a1ac23cadd73f86>.

[77] ICC-ASP/10/36—Annex, 'Report of the Bureau on the Establishment of an Advisory Committee on Nominations of Judges of the International Criminal Court'.

[78] See e.g. ICC-ASP, *ACN Report* (2020); Schmitt, *FS Werle* (2022), pp. 279 ff., 290 (welcoming this Report for being 'significantly bolder' in its assessment of the candidates than in the past). For the most recent report, see ICC-ASP, *ACN Report* (2023).

[79] Mackenzie et al., *Selecting International Judges* (2010), p. 98 ('some candidates may be selected through a transparent and consultative process that focuses on merit, whilst their competitors may have emerged because they were the best friend of the minister, or they were the minister him or herself'); Bohlander, 'Article 36', in Ambos, *Commentary* (2022), mn. 3 ff.

[80] A recent example is from the 2023 Judges' election (https://asp.icc-cpi.int/elections/judges/2023/Results): The candidate from Mongolia (E. Damdin, List A) was elected in the first round (!) with 81 votes (two thirds of the 114 valid ones) although he only received a 'formally qualified' by the ACN Report (ICC-ASP/22/4, p. 11 para. 7), while other more qualified candidates (e.g. U. Hohoff from Germany ['well qualified', ibid., p. 13 para. 7] or A. Parmas from Estonia ['highly qualified', ibid., p. 17 para. 7]) have not been elected at all or only in a later round (most remarkably K. Paek, another candidate from the Asean group, being 'highly qualified' [ibid., p. 16 para 7], was only elected in the eleventh round with 83 votes). There is no rational explanation for such an outcome.

[81] See also Terris, Romano, and Swigart, *International Judge* (2007); Bohlander, *NCLR*, 12 (2009), 529, arguing in particular that diplomats, government officials, and academics are not suited for judicial tasks since they lack practical experience which, in turn, should be the main reason to recruit practitioners; but on the merits of 'academia', see Mackenzie et al., *Selecting International Judges* (2010), pp. 52–3. The former US Federal and ICTY Judge P. M. Wald also calls for better qualified judges; cf. Wald, *ICLR*, 11 (2011), 402, criticizing the fact that 'judges were appointed who had neither any prior experience nor even much knowledge about the criminal law process'. With regard to the ICTY and ICTR, see Safferling, *Criminal Procedure* (2012), p. 130; see further Creamer and Godzimirska, *LJIL*, 30 (2017), 947–66, analysing how governments use their power of judicial nomination and appointment in the context of the ICJ.

[82] Mackenzie et al., *Selecting International Judges* (2010), p. 175, although this may entail a particularly strong link to specific State interests ('selecting ambassadors' at p. 60). See further McAuliffe, *ICLR*, 11 (2011), 361, 'universal acceptance of the utility of the general principle of geographical representation'.

[83] For the ECtHR, cf. Arts. 20, 22 ECHR; for the EU Court, see Art. 19 (2) cl. 1 EU Treaty.

[84] On the contrary, the Inter-American Court of Human Rights (IACtHR) is only composed of seven judges (Art. 52 ACHR) to be selected from the twenty-five State Parties, <http://www.oas.org/dil/treaties_B-32_American_Convention_on_Human_Rights.htm>.

a positive effect in terms of an accumulated competence and experience ('epistemic community'),[85] it also entails the risk of creating a kind of closed shop to which outsiders cannot get access easily or at all. Such a consequence would be regrettable, for new experienced judges from domestic systems may bring in new ideas and approaches which may enrich the ICC and other international criminal tribunals.

Given the strong politicization of the national nomination procedures, quality control can occur only at the international level via the nomination and election procedures of the international courts themselves. Such hearings can be most helpful since they might at least prevent the least qualified candidates from becoming judges. In this regard, the NGO Coalition for the ICC makes an important contribution in presenting and screening the ICC candidates.[86] In addition, the role of the ACN should be strengthened and its evaluation of the candidates should be binding, i.e. a candidate who is not at least 'well qualified' should not be eligible.[87]

It is clear that the legitimacy of the international courts depends to a large degree on the legitimacy of the selection procedure and the quality of their judges.[88] For this reason, improvements in the selection procedures and practice are indispensable. Principles providing for the minimum conditions for the selection of international judges should be set out,[89] while the transparency and accountability of the nomination and election procedure should be safeguarded at the same time in order to banish from them 'extraneous political factors'.[90]

Against the background of the Independent Expert Review (IER), to be looked at more closely in a moment (below Section (4)(b)), it should be noted that the systematic problems of the Court identified by the IER (mistrust, bullying and harassment, lack of professionalism, qualification and a (political) attitude of infallibility)[91] may arguably be aggravated by insufficiently qualified judges.

[85] Thereto Heinze, in Bergsmo et al., *Power* (2020), pp. 155, 252–3. The terms for this epistemic community vary, with 'invisible college of international (criminal) lawyers' possibly the most popular, see the references in Heinze, ibid., p. 254 with n. 547.

[86] See <https://asp.icc-cpi.int/iccdocs/asp_docs/Publications/Compendium/Resolution-ElectionJudges-ENG.pdf>.

[87] The evaluation consists of four levels: highly qualified, well qualified, formally qualified, and not qualified, cf. ACN Report 2023, ICC-ASP/22/4, para. 11.

[88] See the foreword of Lord Woolf, in Mackenzie et al., *Selecting International Judges* (2010), p. viii: 'The legitimacy of the court will be damaged or even destroyed if it is perceived that the court's membership is largely the product of political bargaining between the states which are subject to the jurisdiction of the court'; Swart, *LJIL*, 24 (2011), 792 ('The importance of judicial selection cannot be overestimated. It could be said that the legitimacy of the entire system of international justice is at stake'); from a gender perspective, see Grossman, *ICLR*, 11 (2011), 643, who argues that the under-representation of women judges undercuts the legitimacy of the courts 'because men and women bring different perspectives to judging. Consequently, without both sexes, adjudication is inherently biased.'

[89] The 'Burgh House Principles on the Independence of the International Judiciary', reprinted in Mackenzie et al., *Selecting International Judges* (2010), p. 178: '2.1 In accordance with the governing instruments, judges shall be chosen from among persons of high moral character, integrity and conscientiousness, who possess the appropriate professional qualifications, competence and experience required for the court concerned. 2.2 While procedures for nomination, election and appointment should consider fair representation of different geographic regions and the principal legal systems, as appropriate, as well as of female and male judges, appropriate personal and professional qualifications must be overriding considerations in the nomination, election and appointment of judges. 2.3 Procedures for the nomination, election and appointment of judges should be transparent and provide appropriate safeguards against nominations, elections and appointments motivated by improper considerations. 2.4 Information regarding the nomination, election and appointment process and information about candidates for judicial office should be made public, in due time and in an effective manner, by the international organization or other body responsible for the nomination, election and appointment process.'

[90] Mackenzie et al., *Selecting International Judges* (2010), p. 179.

[91] Expert Group, *IER* (2020), p. 7.

## (4) Legal ethics

### *(a) The (original) Code of Judicial Ethics of 2005*

The Presidency of the Court drafted a Code of Judicial Ethics (CJE) adopted by the judges,[92] that is, a set of 'principles that characterize "right conduct" in the exercise of a profession'.[93] 'The principles embodied in this Code shall serve as guidelines' and 'are advisory in nature' setting out a code of conduct for the judges regarding 'ethical and professional issues'.[94]

Accordingly, a judge should be independent[95] and impartial.[96] The concepts can be defined by having recourse in particular to (European) human rights case law.[97] For the ECtHR both concepts are closely linked.[98] For independence 'regard must be had, inter alia, to the manner of appointment of the members and their term of office, the existence of guarantees against outside pressures and the question whether the body presents an appearance of independence'.[99] As to impartiality, the ECtHR distinguishes[100] between—subjectively—the freedom from personal bias of the relevant tribunal,[101] and—objectively—the existence

[92] cf. Reg. 126 RegC and CJE, ICC-BD/02-01-05; for a historic overview, see Seibert-Fohr, in Romano, Alter, and Shany, *International Adjudication* (2014), pp. 759–61; see also Rohan, in Rohan and Zyberi, *Defense Perspectives* (2017), pp. 68 ff. Generally, on the Presidency's important role with regard to the creation of administrative regulations, see Ambach and Rackwitz, *LCP*, 76 nos. 3 & 4 (2013), 123–4. The administrative regulations are contained in the Court's *Vademecum of Administrative Issuances*, <https://www.icc-cpi.int/sites/default/files/Vademecum/OT1513845_ICC%20INF%202012%20020.PDF>.

[93] Mégret, in Reydams, Wouters, and Ryngaert, *Prosecutors* (2012), p. 416. On violations of prosecutorial ethics in the Nuremberg Trials, see Sarvarian, *JICJ*, 10 (2012), 423.

[94] Art. 11 CJE. Stressing the non-binding, merely advisory nature of the CJE, Rohan, in Rohan and Zyberi, *Defense Perspectives* (2017), pp. 71–2.

[95] Art. 3 CJE. See also Seibert-Fohr, in Romano, Alter, and Shany, *International Adjudication* (2014), pp. 759–65. One should distinguish between independence in a personal (referring to the independence of judges as such) and an institutional sense (regarding the independence of the institution vis-à-vis political organs); cf. thereon Almqvist, *LJIL*, 28 (2015), 98 ff.

[96] Art. 4 CJE. See also Seibert-Fohr, in Romano, Alter, and Shany, *International Adjudication* (2014), pp. 765–71.

[97] Benzing, *MPYbUNL*, 7 (2003), 612; Razesberger, *Complementarity* (2006), p. 47; Stigen, *Relationship* (2008), pp. 300–5. Examining the jurisprudence in more detail, see van der Wilt and Lyngdorf, *ICLR*, 9 (2009), 51 ff.; Kleffner, *Complementarity* (2008), pp. 145–50; El Zeidy, *Complementarity* (2008), pp. 196–203; Stegmiller, *Pre-Investigation Stage* (2011), pp. 306–7. On the difference between impartiality and independence, cf. Seibert-Fohr, in Romano, Alter, and Shany, *International Adjudication* (2014), p. 765.

[98] ECtHR, *Findlay v. the UK*, Application No. 22107/93, Judgment (10 June 1996), para.73 ('First, the tribunal must be subjectively free of personal prejudice or bias. Secondly, it must also be impartial from an objective viewpoint, that is, it must offer sufficient guarantees to exclude any legitimate doubt in this respect'); recently *Guðmundur Andri Ástráðsson v. Iceland*, Application No. 26374/18, Judgment (1 December 2020), para. 218; for further (earlier) case law, see previous edition, p. 107 with n. 91; the same goes for the IACHR, cf. *Judicial Guarantees in States of Emergency* (Arts. 27 (2), 25, and 8) American Convention on Human Rights (ACHR)), Advisory Opinion OC-9/87 of 6/10/1987, IACHR (Series A) No. 9, para. 24.

[99] ECtHR, *Campbell and Fell v. UK*, Application No. 7819/77; 7878/77, Judgment (Merits and Just Satisfaction) (28 June 1984), para. 78; more recently *Thiam v. France*, Application No. 80018/12, Judgment (18 October 2018), para. 59; for further (earlier) case law, see previous edition, p. 107 with note 92; listing further indicators, ICC-OTP, *Policy Prelim. Examinations* (2013), para. 53.

[100] ECtHR, *Morice v. France*, Application No. 29369/10, Judgment (23 April 2015), paras. 73–8; *Volkov v. Ukraine*, Judgment, para. 104 ('impartiality denotes the absence of prejudice or bias. According to the Court's settled case-law, the existence of impartiality … must be determined according to: (i) a subjective test, where regard must be had to the personal conviction and behaviour of a particular judge—that is, whether the judge held any personal prejudice or bias in a given case; and (ii) an objective test, that is to say by ascertaining whether the tribunal itself and, among other aspects, its composition, offered sufficient guarantees to exclude any legitimate doubt in respect of its impartiality'). However, this distinction is not always possible, cf. *Micallef v. Malta*, Application No. 17056/06, Judgment (15 October 2009), para. 95 (there is no watertight division between subjective and objective impartiality since the conduct of a judge may not only prompt objectively held misgivings as to impartiality from the point of view of the external observer (objective test) but may also go to the issue of his or her personal conviction (subjective test)). For further (earlier) case law see previous edition, p. 108 with note 93.

[101] *Piersack v. Belgium*, Judgment (Merits), para. 30 ('personal conviction of a given judge in a given case'); *Demicoli v. Malta*, Application No. 13057/87, Judgment (Merits and Just Satisfaction) (27 August 1991), para.

of sufficient guarantees for impartiality.[102] Impartiality has been defined similarly by the ICTY in *Furundzija* stating that 'there is a general rule that a Judge should not only be subjectively free from bias, but also that there should be nothing in the surrounding circumstances which objectively gives rise to an appearance of bias'.[103] In sum, independence refers to external influence on the tribunals and proceedings,[104] whereas impartiality refers to the judge as a person and to the existence of any conflict of interest, which could lead to or could appear as bias.[105]

Furthermore, judges shall fulfil their duties conscientiously and faithfully.[106] Thus, judges shall conduct themselves with integrity, by not accepting 'any gift, advantage, privilege or reward that can reasonably be perceived as being intended to influence the performance of their judicial functions';[107] with confidentiality;[108] with diligence in the exercise of their duties;[109] with dignity towards themselves and the participants of the proceedings, equality, patience, and courtesy, avoiding racist, sexist, or otherwise degrading conduct or comments.[110] Finally, when judges express themselves in public, they shall do so 'in a manner that is compatible with their office and that does not affect or appear to affect judicial independence or impartiality'; in any case, they 'shall not comment on pending cases and shall avoid expressing views which may undermine the standing and integrity of the Court' and they shall not exercise any political function (Articles 9 and 10 CJE).[111]

### (b) *The Independent Expert Review of 30 September 2020*

In December 2019, the ASP established an 'Independent Expert Review' (IER) mechanism.[112] The Experts were mandated to 'identify ways to strengthen the ICC and the Rome Statute system in order to promote universal recognition of their central role in the global fight against impunity and enhance their overall functioning'.[113] Thus, the Experts

40 ('interest of a particular judge in a given case'); *De Cubber v. Belgium*, Application No. 9186/80, Judgment (26 October 1984), para. 25 ('had displayed any hostility or ill-will'); *Hauschildt v. Denmark*, Application No. 10486/83, Judgment (24 May 1989), para. 47 (the judge acted 'with personal bias'); *Kyprianou v. Cyprus*, Application No. 73797/01, Judgment (15 December 2005), para. 119 (the judge made special arrangements to be assigned with a case based on personal reasons).

[102] *Marin v. Romania*, Application No. 47448/13, Decision (2 September 2014), para. 22 (whether a judge 'offered guarantees sufficient to exclude any legitimate doubt in this respect'); *Warsicka v. Poland*, Application No. 2065/03, Judgment (16 January 2007), para. 37 ('quite apart from the personal conduct of any of the members of that body, there are ascertainable facts which may raise doubts as to its impartiality'); *Morel v. France*, Application No. 34130/96, Judgment (6 June 2000), para. 42 (the lack of impartiality 'can be held to be objectively justified'); *Ferarantelli and Santangelo v. Italy*, Application No. 19874/92, Judgment (7 August 1996), para. 58; *Fehr v. Austria*, Application No. 19247/02, Judgment (3 February 2005), para. 30; *Depiets v. France*, Application No. 53971/00, Judgment (10 February 2004), para. 35.

[103] *Prosecutor v. Furundžija*, No. IT-95-17/1, AC Judgment, 21 July 2000, para. 189. Listing further indicators, ICC-OTP, *Policy Prelim. Examinations* (2013), para. 54.

[104] Safferling, *Criminal Procedure* (2012), p. 133.

[105] cf. Razesberger, *Complementarity* (2006), p. 46; Safferling, *Criminal Procedure* (2012), p. 134, splitting impartiality into the personal link of a judge to a specific case (e.g. family link to the accused) and the professional link of the judge to this specific case (e.g. engaged in any proceedings at a prior stage); Jørgensen and Zahar, in Sluiter et al., *International Criminal Procedure* (2013), pp. 1181–2.

[106] Seibert-Fohr, in Romano, Alter, and Shany, *International Adjudication* (2014), pp. 771–3.

[107] Art. 5 CJE.

[108] Art. 6 CJE.

[109] Art. 7 CJE.

[110] Art. 8 CJE.

[111] Arts. 9 and 10 CJE.

[112] cf. Review of the ICC and the Rome Statute system, ICC-ASP/18/Res.7 (2019) and Expert Group, *IER* (2020), p. 7.

[113] Expert Group, *IER* (2020), p. 7

were tasked with making 'concrete, achievable and actionable recommendations aimed at enhancing the performance, efficiency and effectiveness of the Court and the Rome Statute system as a whole'.[114]

The final IER Report contains 348 pages. Several parts address both quality and ethics of judges at the ICC. The report reveals a shattering practice at the ICC, identified by Karnavas as an existential threat to international criminal justice. He concludes:

> [W]hat comes across page after page in the IER is that the ICC is a dysfunctional court at virtually every level. In fact, it would not be an exaggeration to say that were the ICC to continue to function as it currently does, it is doomed to suffer a prolonged, humiliating, unforgiving death by a thousand cuts.[115]

Two of perhaps the most central findings of the report are:

- 'The Court appears to suffer internally from distrust (inter-Organ, as well as between staff and senior/higher management) and a culture of fear.'[116]
- '[T]he working environment in Chambers has been affected by instances of harassment and bullying by some Judges, which have not been sufficiently tackled, partly due to the perceived unaccountability of Judges.'[117]

Clearly, such problems affect the productivity of a criminal justice system as well as its legitimacy. In a liberal and democratic system of justice the quality of lawyers and their ethics are interdependent. The IER Report contains numerous proposals to overcome the identified deficits, for example:

> There must be avenues where victims can safely report the behaviour and which will enable this to be investigated swiftly. Staff should be able to bring their concerns to managers and receive guidance and support as to the procedure to follow, should they wish to submit complaints. If the complaint is found to be valid, there must be consequences for the offender. The Experts conclude that such leadership in the Court has been lacking in the past. Too often the Experts heard that the Principals were reluctant to involve themselves in such staffing matters and left it to the Directors or other officials to deal with them—a particularly unsatisfactory response if the accused offender happens to be a close confidant or ally of the Director concerned.[118]

### *(c) The revised Code of Judicial Ethics of 19 January 2021*

As a consequence of the IER Report the judges amended the CJE. Article 5 of the revised CJE deals exclusively with the integrity of judges and stipulates, inter alia, the following:

2. Judges shall treat fellow Judges, Parties and participants, staff members and others with dignity and respect. Judges shall not engage in any form of discrimination, harassment, including sexual harassment, and abuse of authority.

[114] Ibid., p. 7.
[115] Karnavas, 'The ICC-ASP Independent Expert Review: Scrutinizing the Past/Proposing the Future, 2021-01-06', <http://michaelgkarnavas.net/blog/2021/01/06/independent-expert-review/>.
[116] Expert Group, *IER* (2020), para. 62.
[117] Ibid., para. 72.
[118] Ibid., para. 211.

3. Judges shall act at all times towards one another in a spirit of collegiality and professionalism.[119]

Furthermore, the revised Code provides explicitly for a duty of loyalty[120] and affirms the binding nature of the respective ethical obligations ('guidelines'), including for former judges as to the secrecy of deliberations and certain confidentiality issues.[121] However, the exact scope of the duties remains unclear.

*(d) The revised Code of Judicial Ethics of 18 September 2022*

Following a judges' retreat held in September 2022, it was agreed to further amend the CJE.[122] Building upon the pre-existing prohibition on judges from engaging in any form of discrimination, harassment, and abuse of authority, the judges have agreed to amend Article 5 (2) of the revised CJE with the following provision:

> '=The Court's Administrative Instruction on Investigations of Unsatisfactory Conduct and the Administrative Instruction on Addressing Discrimination, Harassment, Including Sexual Harassment, and Abuse of Authority, shall apply mutatis mutandis to the judges.[123]

With this amendment, the judges intended to enhance accountability and the application of consistent principles, procedures, and obligations to all persons working at the Court.[124] While this certainly is a laudable goal, the problem remains that there is no monitoring or compliance mechanism. Therefore, another review process—indeed, perhaps even a continuous one—will be necessary to ensure the implementation of and compliance with the (twice amended) Code.

## (5) Control and review (accountability)

While judges should be 'independent in the performance of their functions',[125] they are also to be held accountable if they do not behave 'in accordance with established standards of judicial conduct'.[126] After all, 'it is the duty [not only] of all governmental and other institutions to respect and observe the independence of the judiciary',[127] but also the judges themselves

[119] On the debate on collegiality, see Ambos, *Treatise ICL I* (2021), p. 38.

[120] Art. 8 revised CJE (2021).

[121] Art. 12 (1) revised CJE (2021).

[122] In accordance with Reg. 126 RegC.

[123] Art. 5 (2) revised CJE (2022).

[124] ICC, ICC Judges Amend Code of Judicial Ethics, Press Release (7 October 2022), <https://www.icc-cpi.int/news/icc-judges-amend-code-judicial-ethics-0>.

[125] Art. 40 (1) ICCS. See also Staker, Abtahi, and Young, 'Article 40', in Ambos, *Commentary* (2022), mn. 1 ('cardinal principle in the administration of Justice'); Ntoubandi, 'Article 40', in Fernandez et al., *Statut I* (2019), p. 1259 ('L'indépendance et l'impartialité ... principes fondamentaux'); Safferling, *Criminal Procedure* (2012), p. 133; McDermott, 'Article 40', in Klamberg et al., *Commentary ICC I* (2023), p. 969; Jørgensen and Zahar, in Sluiter et al., *International Criminal Procedure* (2013), pp. 1181–2; International Commission of Jurists, *Independence and Accountability* (2007), pp. 17–26.

[126] Basic Principles on the Independence of the Judiciary, GA Res. 40/32 (29 November 1985) and GA Res. 40/146 (13 December 1985), Art. 19; Seibert-Fohr, in Romano, Alter, and Shany, *International Adjudication* (2014), pp. 761 ff.; for the relation between independence and accountability, see International Commission of Jurists, *Independence and Accountability* (2007), pp. 55–9; cf. also Sifris, *ChiKentJIl&CompL*, 8 (2008), 96 ff.

[127] Basic Principles on the Independence of the Judiciary, Art. 1.

'shall not engage in any activity which is likely to interfere with their judicial functions or to affect confidence in their independence'.[128] Furthermore, 'a judge should not participate in any case in which his or her impartiality might reasonably be doubted on any ground'.[129] There are a series of such grounds:

- involvement 'in any capacity in that case before the Court or in a related criminal case at the national level involving the person being investigated or prosecuted';[130]
- 'personal interest in the case, including a spousal, parental or other close family, personal or professional relationship, or a subordinate relationship, with any of the parties';[131]
- 'performance of functions, prior to taking office, during which he or she could be expected to have formed an opinion on the case in question, on the parties or on their legal representatives that, objectively, could adversely affect the required impartiality of the person concerned';[132] or
- 'expression of opinions through ... the media, in writing or in public actions, that could affect [their] impartiality'.[133]

In such a case, the respective judge should request their excusal by the Presidency. Otherwise, a request for disqualification shall be made, either by the Prosecutor or the person being investigated.[134] In case of doubt about the independence or impartiality of a judge, the decision is, in both cases, to be taken by the absolute majority of the judges.

Apart from the excusal and the disqualification of a judge, which are actions taken with regard to a specific case, the ICCS and the RPE ICC provide for three general administrative proceedings holding judges accountable, that is, *removal from office*, *suspension from duty*, and *disciplinary measures*.[135] A judge can be removed from office if found to have committed serious misconduct—such as, inter alia, disclosure of confidential facts or information, concealment of information, abuse of judicial office, or serious breach of duty (such as being grossly negligent in the performance of their duty or failing to comply with the duty to request to be excused, knowing that there are grounds for it) or if a judge is unable to exercise

[128] Art. 40 (2) ICCS; cf. also McDermott, 'Article 40', in Klamberg et al., *Commentary ICC I* (2023), pp. 971–2.

[129] Art. 41 (2)(a) ICCS. On the notion of impartiality, cf. International Commission of Jurists, *Independence and Accountability* (2007), pp. 27–31; also Seibert-Fohr, in Romano, Alter, and Shany, *International Adjudication* (2014), pp. 765–71; Rohan, in Rohan and Zyberi, *Defense Perspectives* (2017), p. 71.

[130] Art. 41 (2)(a) ICCS. See also *Prosecutor v. Katanga and Ngudjolo*, Presidency Decision Replacing Judges in the Appeals Chamber, No. ICC-01/04-01/07-1266, 3 July 2009; *Prosecutor v. Lubanga*, Presidency Decision Replacing a Judge in the Appeals Chamber, No. ICC-01/04-01/06-2521, 20 July 2010.

[131] Rule 34 (1)(a) RPE ICC.

[132] Rule 34 (1)(c) RPE ICC.

[133] Rule 34 (1)(d) RPE ICC. See also Abtahi and Young, 'Article 41', in Ambos, *Commentary* (2022), mn. 6 ff.; McDermott, 'Article 41', in Klamberg et al., *Commentary ICC I* (2023), pp. 978–81; cf. also Ntoubandi, 'Article 41', in Fernandez et al., *Statut I* (2019), p. 1283, who distinguishes between grounds which lead automatically to the disqualification of the judge, and those where an evaluation is necessary. On the experience at the ICTY, see Rohan, in Rohan and Zyberi, *Defense Perspectives* (2017), pp. 72–4.

[134] Art. 41 (2)(b) ICCS and Rule 34 (2) RPE ICC. See also Schabas, *ICC Commentary* (2016), pp. 731–5; Markovic, *WashUGSLR*, 13 (2013), 25 ff. (nationality of judge as reason for excuse disqualification; thereon see also McDermott, 'Article 41', in Klamberg et al., *Commentary ICC I* (2023), p. 980); Bohlander, in Bohlander, *International Criminal Justice* (2007), pp. 368–82.

[135] Schabas, *Introduction* (2020), pp. 394–5, welcoming the provision for strengthening the judicial independence and impartiality; Schabas, *ICC Commentary* (2016), pp. 775–9 (removal), 615–18 (disciplinary measures); on removal from office, see, in detail, Karagiannakis, 'Article 46', in Ambos, *Commentary* (2022), mn. 6 ff.; Abline, 'Article 46', in Fernandez et al., *Statut I* (2019), pp. 1341 ff.; McDermott, 'Article 46', in Klamberg et al., *Commentary ICC I* (2023), p. 1018.

the functions required by the Statute.[136] If the misconduct is of a less serious nature, the judge is subject, with a decision taken by the Presidency, to the disciplinary measures of reprimand or pecuniary sanction.[137] The ASP decides on the removal from office.[138]

These disciplinary mechanisms are complemented by several oversight mechanisms. With regard to budgetary and financial concerns,[139] all organs of the ICC act under the supervision of the Office of the Internal Audit,[140] the External Auditor,[141] the Audit Committee, and the Committee on Budget and Finance.[142] Moreover, the Independent Oversight Mechanism (IOM), established by the ASP in 2009[143] and operational since November 2013,[144] has the mandate 'to conduct investigations on allegations of misconduct and to ensuring effective and meaningful oversight thereof'[145] including the authority to deal with possible unlawful acts by judges.[146] The IOM transmits the results of its investigation to the Presidency, Registrar, or Prosecutor of the Court, as appropriate, together with recommendations on possible disciplinary or jurisdictional action,[147] including referring the matter to national authorities for possible criminal investigation.[148] Thus, the IOM may serve, at least in theory, [149] as an important tool to assist the Prosecutor and the ASP in the exercise of their disciplinary powers and to enhance the effectiveness of the accountability measures described so far.[150] Yet the IOM itself has become the object of criticism and review by the ASP[151] and a 'facilitation' process has been initiated.[152] At its twentieth session, the ASP requested 'the Bureau to remain seized of the review' of the IOM, especially 'with

[136] Art. 46 ICCS and Rule 24 RPE ICC.

[137] Art. 47 ICCS and Rule 32 RPE ICC. See also Karagiannakis, 'Article 47', in Ambos, *Commentary* (2022), mn. 3 ff.; Abline, 'Article 47', in Fernandez et al., *Statut I* (2019), pp. 1351 ff.; McDermott, 'Article 47', in Klamberg et al., *Commentary ICC I* (2023), pp. 1023–5.

[138] Sifris, *ChiKentJIl&CompL*, 8 (2008), 108. On the relevant procedure, see Art. 46 (2)–(4) ICCS and Rules 26–9 and 31 RPE ICC; see also Schabas, *Introduction* (2020), p. 390; McDermott, 'Article 46', in Klamberg et al., *Commentary ICC I* (2023), pp. 1019–22.

[139] Generally, on budget and financial management, see Ambach and Rackwitz, *LCP*, 76 nos. 3 & 4 (2013), 147–55.

[140] Reg. 110.1 Financial Regulations and Rules. In areas falling under the authority of the Prosecutor (see Art. 42 (2) ICCS), the Internal Audit provides its comments and recommendations not only to the Registrar, but also to the Prosecutor.

[141] Reg. 12 Financial Regulations and Rules with explicit reference to the OTP in Reg. 12.8.

[142] In more detail, Olásolo et al., *Role of the IOM* (August 2011), pp. 39–42.

[143] cf. Art. 112 (4) ICCS, Rule 83 RPE ICC and Res. ICC-ASP/8/Res.1, Establishment of an Independent Oversight Mechanism, adopted at 7th plenary meeting on 26 November 2009.

[144] It adopted its operational mandate on 27 November 2013, ICC-ASP/12/Res. 6, Annex.

[145] Resolution ICC-ASP/8/Res.1, Annex, para. 7.

[146] ICC-ASP/12/Res. 6, Annex, para. 4, 28.

[147] Ibid., para. 40.

[148] Ibid., para. 41.

[149] Sceptically Heinze, *Disclosure* (2014), p. 469, criticizing the fact that the IOM has to take into consideration any objection by a head of an organ that its investigation would undermine the judicial or prosecutorial independence of that organ and, as the case may be, obtain permission to continue its investigation from a third party to be appointed by the Bureau; see ICC-ASP/9/Res. 5, IOM, adopted at the 5th plenary meeting on 10 December 2010, paras. 21–3. These restrictions on the operational independence of the IOM, however, are not included in the subsequent Resolution ICC-ASP/12/Res. 6, which merely states that the IOM 'will fully respect the judicial and prosecutorial independence' (para. 27). See, in a similar vein, the discussion by Alvarez, Cowdery, du Plessis/Gevers, Khan, and van der Wilt, <http://iccforum.com/oversight>. For a more detailed overview of the IOM's functions (namely 'inspection', 'evaluation', and 'investigation'), see Ambach, 'Article 112', in Ambos, *Commentary* (2022), mn. 61 ff.

[150] In particular on the potential role of the IOM in investigating serious financial mismanagement by the heads of organs, see Ambach and Rackwitz, *LCP*, 76 nos. 3 & 4 (2013), 156.

[151] First, the ASP decided to fully review the work and the operational mandate of the IOM. Then it decided to request the Bureau to continue the review and to complete it, including the consideration of amendments to the mandate to cover investigations of allegations against former officials, and to report thereon to the ASP (cf. ICC-ASP/15/Res.5; ICC-ASP/16/Res.6; ICC-ASP/17/Res.5, and ICCASP/18/Res.6).

[152] The facilitation shall review the Court's work on updating the regulatory framework to ensure consistency with the new operational mandate of the IOM adopted by the ASP's 19th session. On 21 February 2022, the

a view to considering also recommendations of the Independent Expert Review in this regard, and to report thereon to the Assembly at its twenty-first session'.[153] Recall what the IER Report had to say in this context:

> [T]he Experts have noted the inadequacy of the existing mechanisms in the Court to deal with complaints of bullying and harassment. Recommendations on new and more effective complaint investigation and dispute resolution mechanisms to address the phenomena have been made in that context. The Experts wish to note that the environment and practices that have allowed this behaviour to occur, often with impunity, also needs to change. [ … ] In the Court, this means that the issuance of an Administrative Instruction on bullying and harassment is going to be ineffective unless staff, both senior and junior, actually believe the Principals and senior managers care about the issue and will respond resolutely to breaches of the policy.[154]

At its twenty-first session, the ASP emphasized the importance of the IOM's mandate 'to investigate the alleged conduct of former elected officials and staff both while they were in office and when they separated from service'[155] and welcomed the complementary initiatives undertaken (inter alia) by the Bureau to ensure 'that the different organs of the Court have streamlined and updated [ … ] consistent ethics charters and codes of conduct'.[156]

## B. Prosecutor and Office of the Prosecution

### (1) Position: A separate and independent organ of the Court

In line with other international criminal tribunals,[157] the ICC's Office of the Prosecutor (OTP) is a separate and independent organ within the structure of the Court.[158] This institutional independence[159] means first and foremost that neither the ASP[160] nor any other

Bureau of the ASP appointed Mr Christian Nygård Nissen (Denmark) as facilitator to review the work and the operational mandate of the IOM.

153 ICC-ASP/20/Res.5.

154 IER Report (2020), paras. 210–11.

155 ICC-ASP/21/Res.2, para. 154.

156 ICC-ASP/21/Res.2, para. 150.

157 Arts. 16 (2) ICTYS, 15 (2) ICTRS, and 14 (2) IRMCTS; see also Arts. 15 (1) SCSLS, 14 (3) RSCSLS, 11 (2) STLS; in a similar vein, Rule 13 (1) IR ECCC ('independent office within the ECCC'). The Public Prosecution Service in East Timor, to the contrary, is a 'constituent organ of the civil administration of East Timor', Section 1.2 UNTAET Regulation No. 2000/16 on the Public Prosecution Service in East Timor. See also the comparative overview by Côté, in Reydams, Wouters, and Ryngaert, *Prosecutors* (2012), pp. 324–7. At the KSC the Specialist Prosecutor has an even stronger position, being fully autonomous and independent of the Court, see Art. 4 (1) and 24 (2) KSC Law and <https://www.scp-ks.org/en/specialist-prosecutors-office/role-spo>. For a detailed analysis of the KSC Specialist Prosecutor's Office, see Heinze, *JICJ* (2017), 988–90; Holvoet, *ICLR* (2020), 3–8.

158 Art. 42 (1) ICCS. See also Bergsmo, Harhoff, and Zhu, 'Article 42', in Ambos, *Commentary* (2022), mn. 3, 8; Moulier, 'Article 42', in Fernandez et al., *Statut I* (2019), p. 1272; McDermott, 'Article 42', in Klamberg et al., *Commentary ICC I* (2023), pp. 985, 992; Heinze, *Disclosure* (2014), p. 250; see also Ambach and Rackwitz, *LCP*, 76 nos. 3 & 4 (2013), 127; for a general overview of the managerial, strategic, and policy initiatives undertaken by the OTP, see Shoamanesh, *ICLR*, 18 (2018), 489–516.

159 Côté, in Reydams, Wouters, and Ryngaert, *Prosecutors* (2012), p. 324. See also the distinction between the independence of the Office itself and the independence of its members in Reg. 13 RegOTP.

160 See Goldston, *JICJ*, 8 (2010), 405, who rightly points out that it would be incompatible with Art. 42 (1) ICCS, if the ASP promulgated binding guidelines for the exercise of prosecutorial discretion. Generally, on the relationship between the ICC and the ASP, O'Donohue, in Stahn, *ICC* (2015), pp. 105 ff.

organ of the Court, that is, Presidency, Chambers, or Registry,[161] has the power to issue binding directions to the OTP in the exercise of its mandate.[162] Rather, the Office exercises its mandate in full autonomy.[163] For this reason, the functions of the OTP are clearly separated from those of the just mentioned other organs of the Court.[164] While these organs shall coordinate their administrative activities,[165] the OTP is administratively separated from the Presidency[166] and the Registry.[167] The Prosecutor also enjoys 'full authority over the management and administration of the Office, including the staff, facilities and other resources thereof'.[168] This kind of institutional independence of the OTP, supported by a strong administrative autonomy, is a novelty.[169] Its purpose is to prevent a factual dependency of the Office on the Registry as occurred in the early stages of the ICTR.[170] Nevertheless, the ASP provides management oversight to the Prosecutor and decides on the budget for the whole Court.[171] In doing so, the ASP allocates budgetary resources to the individual sections[172] and thus has the power to influence the funding of the Court's investigative and prosecutorial

161 On the structure and role of the Registry, see Ambach and Rackwitz, *LCP*, 76 nos. 3 & 4 (2013), 144 ff., distinguishing between its administrative and quasi-judicial functions.

162 Except as provided in the Statute, see e.g. Art. 53 (3)(b) ICCS. See generally Keen, *LJIL*, 17 (2004), 796; Ntanda Nsereko, *JICJ*, 3 (2005), 138; Wei, *Rolle des Anklägers* (2007), pp. 14–15; Bergsmo, Harhoff, and Zhu, 'Article 42', in Ambos, *Commentary* (2022), mn. 8; Bock, *Opfer* (2010), p. 214; Côté, in Reydams, Wouters, and Ryngaert, *Prosecutors* (2012), p. 328 Safferling, *Criminal Procedure* (2012), p. 150; Heinze, *Disclosure* (2014), p. 251. See *Prosecutor v. S. Milošević*, Reasons for Refusal of Leave to Appeal from Decision to Impose Time Limit, No. IT-02-54-AR73, 16 May 2002, para. 12: 'No government or other institution or person, including the judges of the Tribunal, can direct the Prosecutor as to whom he or she is to investigate or to charge.' Crit. with regard to the 'personal influence and authority' of some judges, Kuczyńska, *Accusation Model ICC* (2015), p. 40.

163 In the same vein, *Situation in the Islamic Republic of Afghanistan*, AC Judgment on the Appeal against the Decision on the Authorisation of an Investigation into the Situation in the Islamic Republic of Afghanistan, No. ICC-02/17-138, 5 March 2020, paras. 30–1.

164 Art. 42 (1) ICCS. See also Côté, in Reydams, Wouters, and Ryngaert, *Prosecutors* (2012), p. 327.

165 For this reason a 'Coordination Council' has been established, comprised of the President, the Prosecutor, and the Registrar; see Reg. 3 RegC and Ambach and Rackwitz, *LCP*, 76 nos. 3 & 4 (2013), 139–40.

166 Art. 38 (3)(a) ICCS. Art. 38 (4) ICCS, however, demands that the Prosecutor and the Presidency seek concurrence on all matters of mutual concern; on the practical implementation of this cooperation obligation, see Ambach and Rackwitz, *LCP*, 76 nos. 3 & 4 (2013), 138–9.

167 Art. 43 (1) ICCS. This general rule is reinforced by Rule 13 (1) RPE ICC with regard to the communication mandate of the Registry. See, however, on tensions between OTP and Registry regarding resources and because of the quasi-judicial functions of the latter (e.g. regarding witness protection), Ambach and Rackwitz, *LCP*, 76 nos. 3 & 4 (2013), 143–6. The AC stressed the particular need of cooperation between the OTP and the Registry with respect to witness protection where disagreement 'should not be resolved by the unilateral action of the Prosecutor ... but by an application to the relevant Chamber for a ruling on the matter'; in this area, see *Prosecutor v. Katanga and Ngudjolo*, Judgment on the Appeal of the Prosecutor Against the 'Decision on Evidentiary Scope of the Confirmation Hearing, Preventive Relocation and Disclosure under Article 67 (2) of the Statute and Rule 77 of the Rules' of Pre-Trial Chamber I, No. ICC-01/04-01/07-776, 26 November 2008, paras. 98–101.

168 Art. 42 (2) ICCS. See also Rwelamira, in Lee, *ICC* (1999), p. 168, who calls this 'operational independence'; Côté, in Reydams, Wouters, and Ryngaert, *Prosecutors* (2012), pp. 334–6, speaks of 'administrative or managerial independence'. This component of independence, however, does not preclude the Prosecutor from relying on the Registry's services, see Reg. 20 RegOTP.

169 See also Jones, in Cassese et al., *Rome Statute I* (2002), p. 273; Wouters, Verhoeven, and Demeyere, *ICLR*, 8 (2008), 277; Schabas, *Introduction* (2020), p. 394.

170 See UNGA, 'Report' (1997), UN Doc. A/51/789, Annex para. 8 ('The Registrar has declined to meet administrative requests from the judges or the Office of the Prosecutor where in his judgement they were insufficiently justified ... Because of this perception, almost no decision can be taken by the other organs of the Tribunal that does not receive his review and agreement or rejection'); in more detail, Côté, in Reydams, Wouters, and Ryngaert, *Prosecutors* (2012), pp. 335–6, see also Jones, in Cassese et al., *Rome Statute I* (2002), p. 273; Olásolo et al., *Role of the IOM* (August 2011), p. 54; Ambach and Rackwitz, *LCP*, 76 nos. 3 & 4 (2013), 142.

171 Art. 112 (2)(b) and (d) ICCS. In 2022 the programme budget amounted to approx. €154 Mio., cf. ICC-ASP/20/Res.l, p. 1. For 2023, the Court proposed an an increase of the budget of approx. 15.9 per cent, cf. ICC-ASP/21/10, para. 6. The ASP followed this proposal in large part and approved a total amount of approx. €173m for 2023, cf. ICC-ASP/21/Res.1, p. 1.

172 That is the judiciary, the OTP, the Registry, etc., see ICC-ASP/21/Res. 1, p. 1.

activities.[173] The risk of a budgetary dependency of the OTP, however, was mitigated by the establishment of a Contingency Fund that can meet 'costs associated with an unforeseen situation following a decision by the Prosecutor to open an investigation' as well as 'unavoidable expenses for developments in existing situations that could not be accurately estimated at the time of the adoption of the budget'.[174] This ensures that the Prosecutor enjoys the necessary financial flexibility to react promptly and freely from budgetary constraints to unexpected developments.[175] Also, the OTP received additional extrabudgetary funds which it may use for other investigations, for example in the context of the Ukraine investigation.[176] We will return to the general budget in the next section.

Institutional independence, however, does not mean that the OTP is not or must not be subject to (judicial) supervision.[177] Thus, it needs, for example, the authorization of the PTC to initiate *proprio motu* investigations[178] or issue arrest warrants and summons to appear.[179] Similarly, the PTC has the power to review the Prosecutor's decision to terminate investigations in case of State or Security Council referrals[180] and to decide on the confirmation of charges.[181] During trial, the Prosecutor's freedom of action is limited by the TC's power to manage the proceedings, especially by setting deadlines for submissions or other procedural activities.[182] Nevertheless, the Chambers must not interfere with the OTP's sole

[173] See also Stegmiller, *Pre-Investigation Stage* (2011), p. 54; Ambach and Rackwitz, *LCP*, 76 nos. 3 & 4 (2013), 153, 155; Bergsmo, Cissé, and Staker, in Arbour et al., *Prosecutor* (2000), p. 133; less crit. Wouters, Verhoeven, and Demeyere, *ICLR*, 8 (2008), 288.

[174] ICC-ASP/21/Res. 1, p. 3. See also Ambach and Rackwitz, *LCP*, 76 nos. 3 & 4 (2013), 150–2.

[175] Stegmiller, *Pre-Investigation Stage* (2011), pp. 54–5; see also Ambach and Rackwitz, *LCP*, 76 nos. 3 & 4 (2013), 155.

[176] ICC-OTP, *Statement Khan Ukraine* (May 2022) ('20 States have committed to provide financial contributions … multiplying the effectiveness of our activities in all situations addressed by my Office'); previously *Statement Khan* (March 2022) ('accelerate action across our investigations'). Generally, on the OTP's extrabudgetary resources, see ICC-ASP, *Budget 2024*, paras. 251 ff.; ICC-ASP, *Budget 2023*, paras. 169, 193–4, 211, 214.

[177] Bergsmo, Harhoff, and Zhu, 'Article 42', in Ambos, *Commentary* (2022), mn. 8–9; Côté, in Reydams, Wouters, and Ryngaert, *Prosecutors* (2012), p. 328; Heinze, *Disclosure* (2014), pp. 251–2; see also PTC I, *Situation in the DRC*, Prosecution's Reply on the Applications for Participation 01/04-1/dp to 01/04-6/dp, No. ICC-01/04-84, 15 August 2005, para. 32; *Prosecutor v. Ndindiliyimana*, TC II Decision on Urgent Oral Motion for a Stay of the Indictment, or in the Alternative a Reference to the Security Council, No. ICTR-2000-56-I, 26 March 2004, paras. 22–5; *Prosecutor v. Sesay et al.*, TC I Decision on Sesay Motion seeking Disclosure of the Relationship between Governmental Agencies of the United States of America and the Office of the Prosecutor, No. SCSL-04-15-T, 2 May 2005, para. 22; Ntanda Nsereko, *JICJ*, 3 (2005), 136, 138; Keen, *LJIL*, 17 (2004), 797; Friman, in Cryer et al., *ICL* (2019), pp. 410–11; Thalmann, in Kolb and Scalia, *DIP* (2012), p. 473; Tochilovsky, *Jurisprudence* (2014), p. 470; Kuczyńska, *Accusation Model ICC* (2015), pp. 40–2; from a comparative perspective, Ambos, in Livingstone, *Procedural Regime* (2002), pp. 16–21, 63.

[178] Art. 15 (3) ICCS; in more detail, see Chapter IV, A.(1)(a) and B.(3) in this volume.

[179] cf. Art. 58 ICCS; in detail, see Chapter IV, B.(6)(a) in this volume.

[180] Art. 53 (3) ICCS; see also Chapter IV, B.(3) in this volume.

[181] Art. 61 (7) ICCS. In more detail, see Chapter IV, A.(2)(b) in this volume.

[182] *Milošević*, No. IT-02-54-AR73, para. 13; see also *Prosecutor v. Furundžija*, TC's Formal Complaint to the Prosecutor Concerning the Conduct of the Prosecution, No. IT-95-17/1-PT, 5 June 1998, paras. 5–6; *Prosecutor v. Lubanga*, Redacted Decision on the Prosecution's Urgent Request for Variation of the Time-Limit to Disclose the Identity of Intermediary 143 or Alternatively to Stay Proceedings Pending Further Consultations with the VWU, No. ICC-01/04-01/06-2517, 8 July 2010, para. 27 ('No criminal court can operate on the basis that whenever it makes an order in a particular area, it is for the Prosecutor to elect whether or not to implement it, depending on his interpretation of his obligations'); *Prosecutor v. Lubanga*, Judgment on the Appeal of the Prosecutor against the Decision of Trial Chamber I of 8 July 2010 entitled 'Decision on the Prosecution's Urgent Request for Variation of the Time-Limit to Disclose the Identity of Intermediary 143 or Alternatively to Stay Proceedings Pending Further Consultations with the VWU', No. ICC-01/04-01/06-2582, 8 October 2010, para. 48. In more detail on the consequences of non-disclosure, see Chapter V, B.(5) in this volume. For an ethical duty of the OTP to comply with all Court orders, which, however, shall be subject to some exceptions, Markovic, *TexILJ*, 47 (2011–2012), 226. The Code of Conduct OTP falls short of this proposal by merely obliging OTP Members to 'act with due deference to the authority of Chambers' (Rule 71 (e)) without specifying under which circumstances an OTP Member shall be allowed to disobey an order.

responsibility to investigate and prosecute international crimes and its right to exercise its functions at its sole discretion.[183] For example, the Chambers may have the power to authorize *proprio motu* investigations, but it is the Prosecutor who decides on the course of the investigation, its focus (priorities) and the selection of cases.[184] In the same vein, the PTC does not interfere with the OTP's decision on opening or closing preliminary examinations under Article 15 of the ICC Statute.[185] There is, thus, a delicate balance between the OTP's autonomy and the supervisory powers of the Chambers[186] which requires the latter to exercise their oversight functions with great care and full respect for the OTP's independence.[187]

The Court's internal dimension of independence is complemented by the rule according to which no OTP member[188] shall 'seek or act on instructions from any *external* source'.[189] Similar provisions can be found in the law of the ad hoc and mixed international criminal tribunals.[190] They reaffirm that the OTP shall exercise its authority on its own behalf and unaffected by external influence or pressure from governments, international organizations, NGOs, or individuals.[191] As to the OTP's external independence, the Prosecutor and the Deputy Prosecutors must refrain from engaging in any activity which is likely to interfere with their prosecutorial functions or to affect confidence in their independence.[192] Moreover, they must not engage 'in any other occupation of a professional nature'.[193] The ICC's Staff Rules and Regulations and the OTP's Code of Conduct extend this limitation of outside activities to all OTP members[194] and complement it with a prohibition on accepting

[183] Crit. of the impact of the completion strategy of the ad hoc tribunals (thereon, see Ambos, *Treatise ICL I* (2021), p. 24); on the independence of the Prosecutor, Côté, in Reydams, Wouters, and Ryngaert, *Prosecutors* (2012), pp. 329–31; Heller, in Reydams, Wouters, and Ryngaert, *Prosecutors* (2012), pp. 906–9.

[184] Bergsmo, Harhoff, and Zhu, 'Article 42', in Ambos, *Commentary* (2022), mn. 9 with further examples; see also *Milošević*, No. IT-02-54-AR73, para. 12; *Prosecutor v. Jelisić*, AC Judgment, Partial Dissenting Opinion of Judge Wald, No. IT-95-10-A, 5 July 2001, paras. 4, 14; Mégret, in Reydams, Wouters, and Ryngaert, *Prosecutors* (2012), p. 429; de Meester et al., in Sluiter et al., *International Criminal Procedure* (2013), p. 185.

[185] See PTC I Decision on the 'Request for review of the Prosecutor's decision of 28 October 2021 to close the preliminary examination of the situation in Colombia' and Related Requests, No. ICC-RoC46(3)-01/22-6, 22 July 2022, paras. 6–11.

[186] See also *Prosecutor v. Bagosora et al.*, Decision on the Admissibility of the Prosecutor's Appeal from the Decision of a Confirming Judge Dismissing an Indictment against Théoneste Bagosora and 28 Others, No. ICTR-09-37-A, 8 June 1998, para. 31: '[T]he Prosecutor enjoys sole discretion in the execution of her mandate. Similarly, it is the sole prerogative of the Trial and Appeals Chambers, by applying the Statute and the Rules, to determine the limits of their own competence'; in a similar vein, *Sesay et al.*, No. SCSL-04-15-T, para. 22.

[187] In a similar vein, Mégret, in Reydams, Wouters, and Ryngaert, *Prosecutors* (2012), p. 460; see also ICC, *Chambers Practice Manual* (2016), p. 13 (limited and exceptional interference of PTC with regard to charges); in a decision issued on 12 April 2019, PTC II (ICC-02/17-33) refused for the first time to grant authorization to investigate in a situation initiated *proprio motu*; crit. Rossetti, *JICJ*, 17 (2019), 585–608.

[188] This provision applies to the Prosecutor, the Deputy Prosecutors, staff, and gratis personnel; see Schabas, *ICC Commentary* (2016), p. 741.

[189] Art. 42 (1) cl. 3 ICCS (emphasis added). cf. also McDermott, 'Article 42', in Klamberg et al., *Commentary ICC I* (2023), p. 992.

[190] Arts. 16 (2) ICTYS, 15 (2) ICTRS, 14 (2) IRMCTS, 15 (1) SCSL, 14 (2) RSCSLS 19 ECCC Law, 11 (2) STLS, and 35 (5) KSC Law.

[191] *Situation in the DRC*, No. ICC-01/04-84, para. 32; in a similar vein, Guariglia, in Stahn and Sluiter, *Practice* (2009), p. 212; Côté, in Reydams, Wouters, and Ryngaert, *Prosecutors* (2012), p. 337. See also Rule 101.3 (a) Staff Rules ('Staff members shall ensure their independence from any person, entity or authority outside the Court'); Wei, *Rolle des Anklägers* (2007), p. 13; Safferling, *Criminal Procedure* (2012), p. 151; deGuzman and Schabas, in Sluiter et al., *International Criminal Procedure* (2013), p. 167. Art. 42 (1)(3) ICCS does not, of course, forbid the prosecution to seek assistance from external sources, in particular from Member States, see *Sesay et al.*, No. SCSL-04-15-T, para. 44.

[192] Art. 42 (5) ICCS.

[193] See also Bock, *Opfer* (2010), p. 215; Schabas, *ICC Commentary* (2016), p. 741; Moulier, 'Article 42', in Fernandez et al., *Statut I* (2019), p. 1276.

[194] See in particular Rules 101.3 (a), (b), (g), 101.7 Staff Rules; Reg. 1.2 (n), (o) Staff Regulations; Rule 23 Code of Conduct OTP; in the same vein, Schabas, *ICC Commentary* (2016), p. 741.

gifts, remunerations, and favours from external sources.[195] Most notably, all these provisions conceive external independence as a subjective duty of the OTP members,[196] that is, a breach of the obligation to act independently may trigger accountability of OTP staff[197] and lead to disciplinary measures.[198] This holds true in particular for the Chief Prosecutor who—as the head of office—has to ensure that all Staff members maintain their full independence[199] and is thus vested with the overall responsibility for the OTP's compliance with Article 42 (1) ICCS.

The OTP's external independence is, however, also subject to some limitations which aim to reconcile the powers of the Prosecutor with the sovereign interests of States and the primary responsibility of the Security Council for maintaining international peace and security.[200] States have the power to render any ICC proceedings inadmissible by initiating genuine national investigations or prosecutions[201] and in doing so to force the OTP, by way of admissibility challenges,[202] to defer its (international) investigations.[203] The Security Council's power to defer any investigation and prosecution for a renewable period of twelve months[204] constitutes a further 'unquestionable limitation' of prosecutorial independence.[205] It is only acceptable if applied in a restrictive and transparent manner.[206]

Real independence can only be achieved if not only the OTP as an institution, but also its individual members are protected against undue interference and external pressure.[207] This means, first, that the OTP staff must enjoy economic security, that is, have an adequate and stable income, which guarantees freedom from economic pressure.[208] Salaries of all staff members are therefore determined in accordance with the UN Common System of Salaries,

[195] Rules 45–8 Code of Conduct OTP.

[196] Turone, 'Powers', in Cassese et al., *Rome Statute II* (2002), p. 1140; Guariglia, in Stahn and Sluiter, *Practice* (2009), p. 212; Bock, *Opfer* (2010), p. 214; see also PTC II, *Situation in Uganda*, Prosecution's Reply under Rule 89 (1) to the Applications for Participation of Applicants a/0010/06, a/0064/06 to a/0070/06, a/0081/06 to a/0104/06 and a/0111/06 to a/0127/06 in the Uganda Situation, No. ICC-02/04-85, 28 February 2007, para. 32; Wouters, Verhoeven, and Demeyere, *ICLR*, 8 (2008), 280; Safferling, *Criminal Procedure* (2012), p. 151; Mégret, in Reydams, Wouters, and Ryngaert, *Prosecutors* (2012), p. 434.

[197] Côté, in Reydams, Wouters, and Ryngaert, *Prosecutors* (2012), p. 338.

[198] Bergsmo, Harhoff, and Zhu, 'Article 42', in Ambos, *Commentary* (2022), mn. 22 with regard to breaches of the prohibition on outside activities; see also Moulier, 'Article 42', in Fernandez et al., *Statut I* (2019), p. 1276.

[199] Rule 22 Code of Conduct OTP.

[200] Turone, in Cassese et al., *Rome Statute II* (2002), p. 1140. On political interference in national criminal prosecutions, see the comparative analysis by Ambos, *EJCCLCJ*, 8 (2000), 109–12; the respective national reports are reproduced in Ambos, in Livingstone, *Procedural Regime* (2002), pp. 21–63.

[201] Art. 17 ICCS (principle of complementarity).

[202] Arts. 18 (2), 19 (2) ICCS.

[203] Turone, in Cassese et al., *Rome Statute II* (2002), p. 1140; see also Wouters, Verhoeven, and Demeyere, *ICLR*, 8 (2008), 283; Côté, in Reydams, Wouters, and Ryngaert, *Prosecutors* (2012), p. 354. In more detail on the complementarity principle, see Chapter III, B. in this volume.

[204] Art. 16 ICCS.

[205] Turone, in Cassese et al., *Rome Statute II* (2002), p. 1141 ('strong power of obstruction'); see also Wouters, Verhoeven, and Demeyere, *ICLR*, 8 (2008), 282; Côté, in Reydams, Wouters, and Ryngaert, *Prosecutors* (2012), p. 340; Kuczyńska, *Accusation Model ICC* (2015), p. 44; for a (further) restriction of the Prosecutor's discretion in case of a Security Council referral, see Ohlin, in Stahn and Sluiter, *Practice* (2009), pp. 189, 195, arguing that the ICC is a hybrid, security, and criminal Court and as to the former function bound by a SC referral (pp. 192 ff.).

[206] See also Cassese, *EJIL*, 10 (1999), 163.

[207] Côté, in Reydams, Wouters, and Ryngaert, *Prosecutors* (2012), p. 341; on the importance of personal independence, see also Wei, *Rolle des Anklägers* (2007), p. 17.

[208] Côté, in Reydams, Wouters, and Ryngaert, *Prosecutors* (2012), p. 348. See also No. 6 of the UN Guidelines on the Role of Prosecutors, adopted by the 8th United Nations Congress on the Prevention of Crime and the Treatment of Offenders (27 August to 7 September 1990): 'Reasonable conditions of service of prosecutors, adequate remuneration and, where applicable, tenure, pension and age of retirement shall be set out by law or published rules or regulations.' The correlation between independence and economic security is also stressed in ICC-ASP/4/11, para. 15.

Allowances, and Benefits.[209] Another important feature to safeguard personal independence is the protection of OTP members from 'unjustified exposure to civil, penal or other liability'.[210] For this reason the Prosecutor and the Deputy Prosecutors are vested with the same privileges and immunities as are accorded to heads of diplomatic missions, while all other OTP members (only) enjoy 'such privileges, immunities and facilities as are necessary for the independent performance of their functions'.[211] These general principles are further specified in the Agreement on the Privileges and Immunities of the ICC[212] which provides lists of the applicable immunities—among them immunity from personal arrest or detention, inviolability for all official papers and documents, and exemption from immigration restrictions or alien registration.[213] The personal independence of the Prosecutor and the Deputy Prosecutors is also affected by the rules on their qualifications, selection, tenure, and disqualification. We will return to these rules below.

## (2) Composition and structure

The ICC-OTP[214] is a hierarchical, pyramidal organization[215] headed by the Prosecutor with the assistance of 'one or more Deputy Prosecutors'.[216] At the beginning of 2024, the OTP counted approximately 380 staff members[217] and, apart from the above-mentioned contingency fund and additional funding, a budget of about €55m,[218] yet a (further) increase is under discussion.[219]

209 See in general <https://www.icc-cpi.int/jobs/conditions-of-employment-gs>; see in particular ICC-ASP/5/Res. 3, para. 29. The conditions of service and compensation of the Prosecutor and the Deputy-Prosecutors are the same as those of an Under-Secretary-General and an Assistant Secretary-General, respectively; see also ICC-ASP/21/10, para. 195 and p. 44.

210 No. 4 of the UN Guidelines on the Role of Prosecutors. See also Amnesty International, *Right Choices, Part II* (July 1997), p. 26; Beresford, *SanDiegoILJ*, 3 (2002), 85–6; Mochochoko, *FordhamILJ*, 25 (2001), 640; Nilsson, *LJIL*, 17 (2004), 560; Wei, *Rolle des Anklägers* (2007), p. 19; Karagiannakis, 'Article 48', in Ambos, *Commentary* (2022), mn. 3; Côté, in Reydams, Wouters, and Ryngaert, *Prosecutors* (2012), p. 348.

211 Art. 48 (2) ICCS. cf. McDermott, 'Article 48', in Klamberg et al., *Commentary ICC I* (2023), pp. 1029–33. See also the similar approaches in Arts. 30 ICTYS, 29 ICTRS/IRMCTS (applicability of the Convention on the Privileges and Immunities of the UN [13 February 1946]) and Arts. 12 SCSL Agreement, 10 RSCSL Agreement, 11 STL Agreement, 41 ECCC Law (applicability of the Vienna Convention on Diplomatic Relations [18 April 1961]).

212 Arts. 15, 16; ICC-ASP/1/3; for a detailed analysis, see Beresford, *SanDiegoILJ*, 3 (2002), 83; Mochochoko, *FordhamILJ*, 25 (2001), 638; Nilsson, *LJIL*, 17 (2004), 559.

213 In more detail, Beresford, *SanDiegoILJ*, 3 (2002), 110–20; Mochochoko, *FordhamILJ*, 25 (2001), 651–3.

214 As to the organization of the prosecution offices at other international tribunals, see the comparative analysis by Townsend, in Reydams, Wouters, and Ryngaert, *Prosecutors* (2012), pp. 171 ff.; Bergsmo, Cissé, and Staker, in Arbour et al., *Prosecutor* (2000), pp. 125–7. For an instructive analysis of the position and role of the ICC-OTP with a view to Damaška's hierarchical and coordinate ideal, see Heinze, *Disclosure* (2014), pp. 250 ff.; see further Birn, *LJIL*, 30 (2017), 987–1002 (presenting a '"best practices" model for interdisciplinary investigations adopted by a group of national and international prosecution units').

215 Heinze, *Disclosure* (2014), p. 250; Ambos, *Internationales Strafrecht* (2018), § 6 mn. 27; see also Kreß, in Grützner, Pötz, and Kreß, *Internationaler Rechtshilfeverkehr in Strafsachen* (2003), Part IV A 1 mn. 85; Turner, *NYUJIL&Pol'y*, 45 (2012), 245 and Rule 27 (c) Code of Conduct OTP; see alsoKuczyńska, *Accusation Model ICC* (2015), pp. 33, 39.

216 Art. 42 (2) ICCS.

217 See <https://www.icc-cpi.int/about/otp>.

218 cf. Res. ICC-ASP/21/Res.1, para. 1, <https://asp.icc-cpi.int/sites/asp/files/2022-12/ICC-ASP-21-Res1-AV-ENG.pdf>. The total budget of the Court is approx. €173m (ibid.). The budget for the OTP has increased over the years (as has the Court's total budget), cf. the programme budget for 2022 (which provides approx. €49m for the OTP), Res. ICC-ASP/20/Res.1, para. 1, <https://asp.icc-cpi.int/sites/asp/files/asp_docs/ASP20/ICC-ASP-20-Res1-AV-ENG.pdf>.

219 cf. ICC-ASP/21/INF.2, para. 22 ('The OTP does not presently benefit from sufficient resources in order to effectively discharge its mandate'), <https://asp.icc-cpi.int/sites/asp/files/2022-07/ICC-ASP-21-INF2-ENG.pdf>. On Budget Alignment, see ICC-OTP, *Strategic Plan* (2023), paras. 95–6, <https://www.icc-cpi.int/sites/default/files/2023-08/2023-strategic-plan-otp-v.3.pdf>. The discussion revolving around budgetary limitations vis-à-vis the OTP's (growing) size is not new, cf. ASP, *Report Basic Size OTP* (2015), where it is acknowledged that the

Originally, the first Prosecutor[220] chose to have two Deputies—Serge Brammertz from Belgium as 'Deputy Prosecutor (Investigation)'[221] and Fatou Bensouda from The Gambia as 'Deputy Prosecutor (Prosecution)'.[222] However, when Brammertz left the Court in 2005[223] and finally resigned in 2007, the position of the 'Deputy Prosecutor (Investigation)' remained vacant(Brammertz then became Prosecutor of the ICTY on 1 January 2008 and of the MICT on 29 February 2016, a position he holds until today)r. Between 2012 and 2021 the OTP was headed by Fatou Bensouda (The Gambia)[224] and Deputy Prosecutor James Stewart (Canada).[225] The current Prosecutor, Karim A.A. Khan (United Kingdom), took office on 16 June 2021.[226] His two Deputy Prosecutors are Mame Mandiaye Niang (Senegal)[227] and Nazhat Shameen Khan (Fiji).[228] In the first years since his inauguration, Prosecutor Khan has repeatedly stressed his intention to reform and restructure the OTP in order to improve the Office's internal processes and overall performance.[229]

In June 2023, the OTP published its first Strategic Plan during Khan's term. The Plan sets out a framework that is declared to reflect a 'renewed vision' for the mandate of the OTP and aims to make its work 'more dynamic, efficient and closer to those impacted by Rome Statute crimes',[230] also based on the recommendations of the IER.[231] Formerly, the Office was composed of three operational divisions and two support sections.[232] The *operational divisions* which reported directly to the Deputy Prosecutor[233] were the following, headed by three 'Directors of Division':

- the Jurisdiction, Complementarity and Cooperation Division (JCCD) headed by Phakiso Mochochoko (Lesotho);[234]
- the Investigation Division (ID) headed by Michel de Smedt (Belgium); and
- the Prosecution Division (PD) headed by Fabricio Guariglia (Argentina).

current size of the OTP is 'below the required level' (para. 4) and therefore an increase to a 'basic size' is demanded (staff increase from 405 to 540 persons, para. 11) in order to at least meet the expected demand 'without having to over-prioritise activities and constantly overstretch resources' (para. 8). See also ICC-OTP, *Strategic Plan* (2015), para. 4, subpara. (v) ('achieve a basic size which can respond to the demands').

[220] On the previous Prosecutors and their Deputy Prosecutors, see Ambos, *Treatise ICL I* (2021), pp. 39–43.

[221] Elected by the ASP on 9 September 2003 for a term of six years, see ASP, *Second Session* (2003), paras. 24, 26.

[222] Elected by the ASP on 8 September 2004 for a term of nine years, ASP, *Third Session* (2004), paras. 24–6.

[223] He went to Lebanon to work with the International Independent Investigation Commission investigating the assassination of Lebanese Prime Minister Rafic Hariri; cf. UNGA, 'Report ICC 2005-2006' (3 August 2006), UN Doc. A/61/217, paras. 61–2.

[224] Elected by the ASP on 12 December 2011 for a term of nine years. She was sworn in on 15 June 2012, <https://www.icc-cpi.int/news/ceremony-solemn-undertaking-icc-prosecutor-fatou-bensouda>.

[225] Elected by the ASP on 16 November 2012 for a term of nine years. He was sworn in on 8 March 2013, <https://www.icc-cpi.int/news/iccs-new-deputy-prosecutor-james-stewart-sworn>.

[226] Elected by the ASP on 12 February 2021 for a term of nine years, <https://www.icc-cpi.int/news/mr-karim-asad-ahmad-khan qc sworn-today-prosecutor-international-criminal-court>.

[227] Elected by the ASP on 10 December 2021 and sworn in on 7 March 2022, <https://www.icc-cpi.int/about/otp/who-s-who/nazhat-shameem-khan>.

[228] Elected by the ASP on 10 December 2021 and sworn in on 7 March 2022, <https://www.icc-cpi.int/news/iccs-new-deputy-prosecutor-james-stewart-sworn>.

[229] See e.g. ICC-OTP, *Statement Khan Darfur* (2023) ; see also Prosecutor of the ICC Karim A. A. Khan KC presents the Annual Report of the OTP, 5 December 2022, <https://www.icc-cpi.int/news/prosecutor-international-criminal-court-icc-karim-aa-khan-kc-presents-annual-report-office>.

[230] ICC-OTP, *Strategic Plan* (2023), para. 1.

[231] ICC-OTP, *Strategic Plan* (2023), paras. 7, 20.

[232] Reg. 5 RegOTP.

[233] cf. ASP, *Programme Budget 2014*, ICC-ASP/12/10 (19 July 2013), para. 135. Originally, the PD was headed by the Deputy Prosecutor. In order to enhance the strategic coordination of the OTP, however, his role was redefined and strengthened in 2013.

[234] About the (former) JCCD and its establishment as one of the operational divisions and 'diplomaticwing' of the OTP, Heinze, in Heinze and Dittrich, *ICC* (2021), pp. 83–4.

The *support sections* which belonged to the Immediate Office of the Prosecutor were the Legal Advisory Section and the Services Sections. The Office's main decision-making body, the *Executive Committee* (Excom), consisted of the Prosecutor and her Deputy, the (three) Divisional Directors and Divisional Coordinators,[235] the Heads of the Appeals Section, the Legal Advisory Section, and the Services Section.[236] It provided 'advice on major decisions, such as the initiation of investigations, ... promote[d] coordination of activities',[237] and was responsible for the development and adoption of the strategies, policies, and budget of the Office.[238] The basic structure was reproduced in the previous edition, at p. 119.

The three former Divisions (JCCD, ID, and PD)[239] were abolished under the reorganization of the OTP under Prosecutor Khan. Figure 1 displays the new structure with most recent amendments (contained in the 2025 Budget proposal to the ASP), i.e., at the second hierarchical level with an autonomous 'Division of Prosecutorial Administrative Services' (DPAS) and a reinforced tracking function under the 'Integrated Services Division' (ISD).[240] Under this new structure there is, as the first hierarchical level, the Prosecutor with several sections or units, especially the 'Immediate Office of the Prosecutor' (IOP), and, as the second hierarchical level, the two Deputy Prosecutors (Nazhat Khan and Mame Niang) as well as the ISD (headed by Michel de Smedt) and the most recently created DPAS.[241]

The *IOP* is non-operational in nature. It provides support and services to the Prosecutor in order to implement the Office's overall strategic vision.[242] As such, the IOP is put in place to ensure quality control and management of the Office, as well as communication, coordination and cooperation in the overall administration of the ICC, serving as an interface with other organs.[243] The OTP *HR Office* manages the human resources needs of the OTP.[244] It was first moved from the IOP following the reorganization of the OTP to report directly to the Prosecutor,[245] but has now included in the new DPAS (Fig. 1).

The *Legal Advisory Section* responds to requests for legal advice from the Prosecutor as well as the other sections of the Office, especially concerning institutional matters such as, for instance, contracts or other agreements.[246] As such, this section functions as an 'in-house counsel' and, at the same time, acts as the Office's legal representative in administrative and disciplinary proceedings—both internally and externally.[247]

[235] On the prosecution coordinator supervising the trial activities and reviewing all OTP submissions before filling, see Townsend, in Reydams, Wouters, and Ryngaert, *Prosecutors* (2012), p. 290.

[236] cf. Reg. 4 RegOTP (but only mentioning Prosecutor and Divisional Directors); see also ICC-OTP, *Strategic Plan* (2013), p. 11 with para. 14 and n. 2, p. 35 with para. 93 (expanding Excom to include the persons mentioned above in the text).

[237] UNGA, 'Report ICC 2004' (1 August 2005), UN Doc. A/60/177, para. 30; Stegmiller, *Pre-Investigation Stage* (2011), p. 50; Townsend, in Reydams, Wouters, and Ryngaert, *Prosecutors* (2012), p. 290.

[238] Reg. 4 RegOTP. See also ICC-ASP, *Programme Budget 2014*, ICC-ASP/12/10 (19 July 2013), para. 149; ASP, *Programme Budget 2015*, ICC-ASP/13/10 (18 September 2014), paras. 142–3.

[239] Their competences have been specified in Reg. 7-9 RegOTP as summarized in the previous edition at pp. 119–21.

[240] ICC-ASP, *Budget 2025*, pp. 40 ff.; for the previous (reorganized) structure see ICC-ASP, *Budget 2024*, p. 37 (without the autonomous DPAS and the reinforced tracking unit); see also previously on the reorganization ICC-ASP, *Budget 2023*, pp. 35 ff.; ICC-OTP, *Report 2023* (2023), p. 30. Unfortunately, at the time of writing (September 2024), the RegOTP have not been adjusted to the new structure.

[241] ICC-ASP, *Budget 2024*, pp. 37 ff.; ICC-ASP, *Budget 2023*, pp. 35, 192; most recently ICC-ASP, *Budget 2025*, para. 184 ff., 499 ff.

[242] ICC-ASP, *Budget 2024*, para. 284.

[243] ICC-ASP, *Budget 2024*, para. 285; ICC-ASP, *Budget 2025*, para. 255 ff.

[244] ICC-ASP, *Budget 2024*, para. 313; ICC-ASP, *Budget 2025*, para. 545 ff.

[245] ICC-ASP, *Budget 2024*, para. 318.

[246] ICC-ASP, *Budget 2024*, paras. 279–301; ICC-ASP, *Budget 2025*, para. 288 ff.

[247] ICC-ASP, *Budget 2024*, paras. 279, 300.

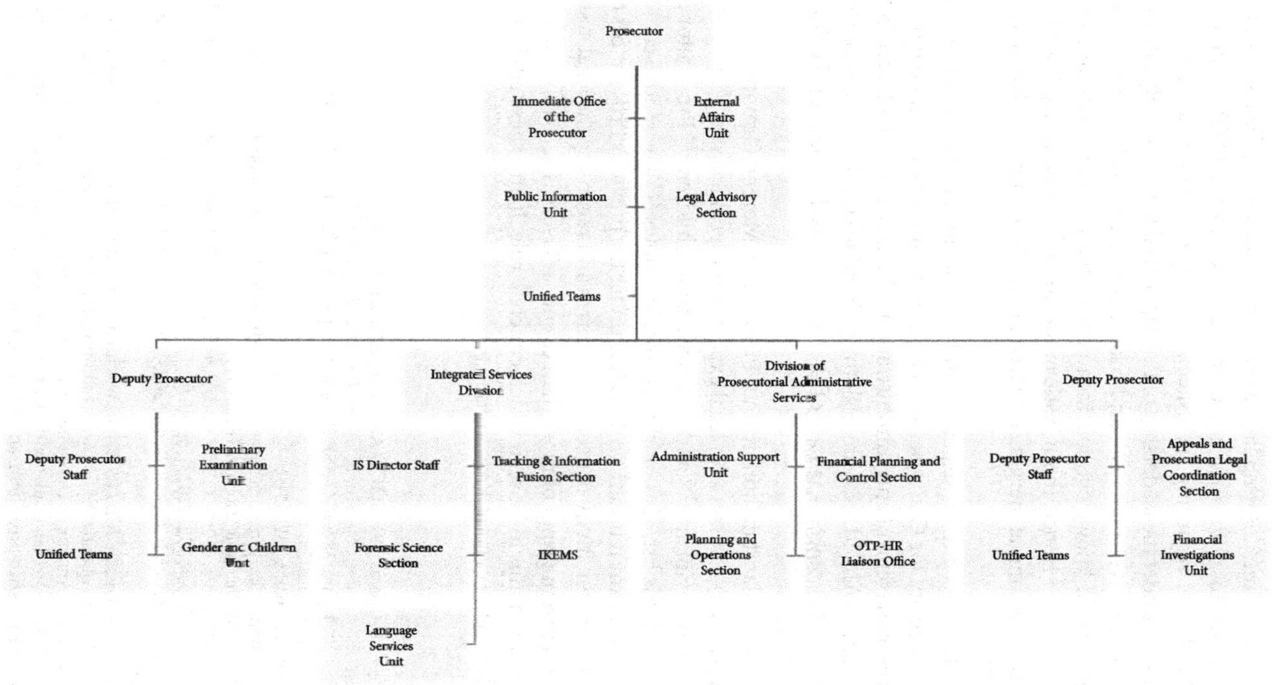


**Fig. 1.** New organizational structure ICC-OTP
*Source:* ICC-ASP, *Budget 2025*, p. 40

The External Affairs Section, now called 'Unit' (Fig. 1) is responsible for the guidance of diplomatic and external engagements of the OTP. This includes both external relations and judicial cooperation.[248]

The two prosecution pillars (formerly 'Pillar B1' and 'Pillar B2', now just 'Deputy Prosecutor', Fig. 1) are managed by the two Deputy Prosecutors under the delegated authority of Prosecutor Khan.[249] Both pillars are organized following the concept of '*Unified Teams*' which are constituted for each situation addressed by the OTP[250] but also exist at the first hierarchical level regarding the especially complex and demanding situations of Ukraine and Palestine under the leadership of Principal Trial Lawyers.[251] By integrating staff involved in the investigative, analytical, and trial stages of the OTP's work, these Unified Teams are meant to build knowledge specific to each situation and maintain continuity of resources and expertise.[252] Hence, this holistic model follows a multidisciplinary[253] and collaborative approach that aims at merging the strengths and skills represented in the different divisions of the OTP.

The *ISD* provides cross-cutting expertise and support to the OTP in areas such as logistics, safety and security for Court personnel, tracking and arrest, technology, forensics, language, as well as management and administration.[254] The recently reinforced 'Suspects at Large Tracking Team' (SALTT) – to diminish the (widening) gap between suspects wanted and actually in the ICC's power – is part of the 'Tracking & Information Fusion Section' which belongs to the ISD.[255]

In addition to the regular staff, both former Prosecutors Moreno Ocampo and Bensouda have appointed (external) *advisers* with legal expertise on specific issues,[256] in particular on sexual and gender-based violence[257] and violence against children.[258] Prosecutor Khan has considerably enlarged this list, also mostly for specific topics.[259] These advisers work on a pro bono basis if they do any relevant work. While under the previous Prosecutors the group of advisors lacked representativity in geographic terms and regarding the legal systems they represented,[260] the current group of more than twenty advisors is certainly more representative. At any rate, it remains to be seen which concrete role, if any, these advisors will play during the mandate of the current Prosecutor.

[248] ICC-ASP, *Budget 2024*, paras. 291–5; ICC-ASP, *Budget 2025*, para. 266 ff.

[249] ICC-ASP, *Budget 2024*, paras. 380, 418; ICC-ASP, *Budget 2025*, para. 331 ff.

[250] ICC-ASP, *Budget 2024*, para. 382; ICC-ASP, *Budget 2025*, para. 331-2, 341-5, 373-4, 384-6.

[251] ICC-ASP, *Budget 2025*, para. 299 ff.

[252] ICC-ASP, *Budget 2024*, paras. 382, 421.

[253] The Teams incorporate lawyers, investigators, analysts, international cooperation advisers, as well as country experts, cf. ICC-ASP, *Budget 2024*, para. 382.

[254] ICC-ASP, *Budget 2024*, para. 450; ICC-ASP, *Budget 2025*, para. 412 ff.; on the importance of technology for the OTP, see also ICC-OTP, *Report 2023* (2023), pp. 48 ff.

[255] In more detail on this section ICC-ASP, *Budget 2025*, para. 199, 21-4 (inability 'to effectively track individuals' as 'Risk 1'), 460 ff.

[256] See previously Ambos, *Treatise ICL I* (2021), p. 39 with n. 214 (listing, inter alia, Tim McCormack, advisor for IHL, who still serves). Subsequently the following (additional) advisors have been appointed: Patricia Sellers, Leila Sadat, and Diane Marie Amann in December 2012, <https://www.icc-cpi.int/news/icc-prosecutor-fatou-bensouda-appoints-patricia-sellers-leila-sadat-and-diane-marie-amann>; Mohammed Ayat in March 2013, <https://www.icc-cpi.int/news/icc-prosecutor-announces-appointment-mohammed-ayat-special-adviser-regional-cooperation-mena>.

[257] Special Advisor on Gender was Patricia V. Sellers, international criminal lawyer, see <https://www.icc-cpi.int/Pages/item.aspx?name=PR1352>.

[258] cf. Art. 42 (9) ICCS.

[259] At the time or writing (September 2024) there are 21 Special Advisors, see for details <https://www.icc-cpi.int/about/otp/special-advisers-to-the-prosecutor>.

[260] Crit. previous edition, Ambos, *Treatise ICL III* (2016), p. 121.

Moreover, on 27 June 2014 the OPT established a *Scientific Advisory Board* to provide recommendations on developments in new and emerging technologies and scientific methods and procedures which may assist the Office in its investigations.[261]

Last but not least, it should be mentioned that the Prosecutor often relies and depends on so-called *intermediaries* during his investigations.[262] Intermediaries are individuals or organizations familiar with the situation on the ground and therefore able to connect the Prosecutor—and other organs of the Court[263]—with the affected communities.[264] Concretely speaking, intermediaries help the Prosecutor to contact potential (victim) witnesses[265] and assist the Prosecutor otherwise in the investigation.[266] Of course, they must

[261] It should hold annual meetings, see for the 2020 (zoom) meeting, <https://www.icc-cpi.int/news/scientific-advisory-board-office-prosecutor-holds-7th-annual-meeting>. It is also mentioned in the ICC-ASP, *Budget 2023*, para. 405.

[262] The issue played a major role in the *Lubanga* proceedings; for a detailed treatment, see *Prosecutor v. Lubanga*, TC I Judgment pursuant to Article 74 of the Statute, No. ICC-01/04-01/06-2482, 14 March 2012, paras. 178 ff. and *passim*; see also the OTP submission as quoted in *Prosecutor v. Lubanga*, TC I Decision on Intermediaries, No. ICC-01/04-01/06-2434-Red2, 31 May 2010, para. 58, ('Prosecutor's mandate cannot succeed without the use of trusted and reliable intermediaries') and para. 88 ('undertake tasks in the field that staff members cannot fulfil without creating suspicion; they know members of the community, and they have access to information and places that are otherwise unavailable to the prosecution'). On their importance, see generally *Guidelines Intermediaries* (2014), p. 2 ('valuable support'); de Vos, *LJIL*, 26 (2013), 1024 ('[W]ithout them, the Court simply could not function'). On the elaboration of the Guidelines, esp. the role of NGOs and the ensuing professionalization of intermediaries, see Haslam and Edmunds, *CLF*, 24 (2013), 61 ff., 65 ff.; on the background, see also ICC-ASP, *Report Governance* (2014), paras. 34 ff.

[263] cf. *Guidelines Intermediaries* (2014), pp. 5–6 ('different organs or units of the Court and Counsel use different categories of intermediaries to perform different functions'); more detailed on their role, see Haslam and Edmunds, *CLF*, 24 (2013), 50–1, 54 ff. Each organ is responsible for the proper compliance with the Guidelines (*Guidelines Intermediaries* (2014), p. 18 with section 6 on monitoring the Guidelines; on a possible judicial supervision, see Haslam and Edmunds, *CLF*, 24 (2013), 77 ff.). As to the intermediaries' formal relationship with the Court the *Guidelines Intermediaries* (2014), p. 10, section 3 distinguish three types of intermediaries ((i) 'contracted intermediaries' to whom the entire Guidelines apply; (ii) others 'approved by the Court by way of affidavit to whom the Guidelines shall apply unless otherwise specified'; (iii) 'unapproved intermediaries' who are self-appointed or act on a one-off basis with the Guidelines only applying on a 'case-by-case basis'); in contrast, the OTP distinguishes between two types of intermediaries, i.e. contracted and voluntary ones (ICC-ASP, *Report Governance* (2014), para. 40); see thereon also Haslam and Edmunds, *CLF*, 24 (2013), 70–1; on concrete contracts, see *Lubanga*, No. ICC-01/04-01/06-2482, paras. 203 ff. In financial terms intermediaries either 'provide services on a voluntary basis and [do] not receive compensation' or 'they may receive compensation for the time required to perform the requested tasks'. (*Guidelines Intermediaries* (2014), p. 12 with detailed regulation in section 4; thereon also ASP, *Report Guidelines Intermediaries* (2013), para. 5); see thereon also the 'Model Contract for Intermediaries' also adopted in March 2014. On the concrete payment in *Lubanga*, see *Lubanga*, No. ICC-01/04-01/06-2482, paras. 198 ff.

[264] cf. *Guidelines Intermediaries* (2014), p. 5, section 1 ('[S]omeone who comes between one person and another; who facilitates contact or provides a link between one of the organs or unit of the Court or Counsel on the one hand, and victims, witnesses, beneficiaries of reparations and/or affected communities more broadly on the other'). For a perhaps too idealistic definition of intermediaries, see Dixon and Tenove, *IJTJ*, 7 (2013), 401–2 ('formal or informal civil society actors that help with ICC activities, including investigations, community outreach and liaising with victim participants'); equally broad and (erroneously) critical of the Court's reliance on this 'uncompensated labour', Kendall, *JICJ*, 13 (2015), 128 ('role ... wide ranging and diverse', 'widespread within the Court's informal economy').

[265] In the *Lubanga* investigation, twenty-three intermediaries (individuals or organizations) 'contacted or introduced potential incriminating witnesses or individuals' (*Lubanga*, No. ICC-01/04-01/06-2434-Red2, para. 3). Apart from contacting witnesses, they also assessed the security situation (*Lubanga*, No. ICC-01/04-01/06-2482, paras. 190, 193); more detailed, Haslam and Edmunds, *CLF*, 24 (2013), 58–61; also ICC-ASP, *Report Governance* (2014), para. 38.

[266] See also (former) head of the OTP's jurisdiction, complementarity, and cooperation Division, Béatrice Le Fraper du Hellen, 'Interview—ICC Prosecutors Will Refute Allegations That Intermediaries Manipulated Evidence in Lubanga Case', *International Justice Monitor* (15 March 2010), <www.lubangatrial.org/2010/03/15/interview-icc-prosecutors-will-refute-allegations-that-intermediaries-manipulated-evidence-in-lubanga-case> ('people in the field who put the OTP in contact with potential sources and witnesses, and describe to the OTP the situation on the ground ... do not investigate ... are not witnesses ... very committed persons, very supportive of international justice'). The interview, especially Le Fraper's remarks on intermediaries, produced a sharp reaction by the TC; cf. *Prosecutor v. Lubanga*, Decision on the Press Interview with Ms Le Fraper du Hellen, No. ICC-01/

neither perform core functions[267] of the prosecution, in particular take over their investigatory functions,[268] nor work in multiple, incompatible capacities.[269] Their use may also be questionable from an evidentiary and defence perspective, as we will see below.[270]

### (3) Qualifications, selection, and tenure

As regards the qualifications of Prosecutors, modern statutes of international criminal tribunals have a common baseline: International Prosecutors must be of high moral character,[271] exceptionally competent, and experienced.[272] The latter is particularly stressed by Article 42 (3) ICCS, which expects the Prosecutor to have '*extensive*[273] practical experience in the prosecution or trial of criminal cases'.[274] As prosecutorial or trial skills are mentioned in the alternative, all types of criminal law practitioners, including judges and defence attorneys, may be selected as Prosecutor.[275] Moreover, Article 42 ICCS does not demand previous *international* experience. Nevertheless, it is regarded as particularly valuable if Prosecutors have already worked on international cases, preferably at one of the ad hoc tribunals.[276] However, one must not overlook that the ICC Statute and its supplementary norms have created a unique procedural code which differs significantly from its predecessors.[277] Thus, staff switching from the ad hoc tribunals to the ICC must not stick to their familiar procedural routines, but should rather be able to reevaluate their former practice and align their approaches to the ICC's unique system. This additional challenge cannot be overestimated.

04-01/06-2433, 12 May 2010, paras. 34 ff., ('prejudicial to the ongoing proceedings' [41], 'seriously intruded on the role of the Chamber' [49], 'strongest disapproval' [53]).

267 Of course, the concept of core functions is ambiguous and varies according to the organ of the Court using intermediaries, cf. Haslam and Edmunds, *CLF*, 24 (2013), 75; *Guidelines Intermediaries* (2014), p. 2.

268 Crit. in this respect, *Lubanga*, No. ICC-01/04-01/06-2482, para. 482 ('prosecution should not have delegated its investigative responsibilities to the intermediaries'). See also *Guidelines Intermediaries* (2014), p. 3 (intermediaries 'are not a substitute'). The OTP has, as a consequence of the problems in the *Lubanga* proceedings, adopted various measures to better supervise the intermediaries; they are codified in the (confidential) OTP Operations Manual; cf. ICC-ASP, *Report Governance* (2014), para. 39. The OTP also reaffirmed that 'investigative activities are not outsourced to intermediaries.' (para. 41).

269 For a discussion, see Haslam and Edmunds, *CLF*, 24 (2013), 76–7.

270 See Chapter V, A.(3)(c) in this volume.

271 In more detail, Thompson, in Jalloh and Marong, *Promoting Accountability* (2015), p. 53, who concludes that the Prosecutor 'should be a highly principled individual'; Mudukti, *JICJ*, 19 (2021), 747.

272 See Arts. 16 (4) ICTYS, 15 (4) ICTRS, 14 (4) IRMCTS, 15 (3) SCSLS, 14 (2) RSCSLS, 11 (3) STLS, 19 ECCC Law, 42 (3) ICCS, 35 (7) KSC Law.

273 The ICCS does not specify the meaning of 'extensive'. The Preparatory Committee discussed introducing a minimum threshold of ten years of practical experience. This approach, however, was not agreeable to the majority; see Bergsmo, Harhoff, and Zhu, 'Article 42', in Ambos, *Commentary* (2022), mn. 15.

274 Emphasis added.

275 Wei, *Rolle des Anklägers* (2007), p. 23; FIDH et al., *Open Letter* (2011), p. 3; Moulier, 'Article 42', in Fernandez et al., *Statut I* (2019), p. 1279; Heinze, *Disclosure* (2014), p. 250; see also McDermott, 'Article 42', in Klamberg et al., *Commentary ICC I* (2023), p. 990; Bergsmo, Harhoff, and Zhu, 'Article 42', in Ambos, *Commentary* (2022), mn. 15, who, however, regard prosecutorial experience as 'decisive in the choice between two equally well-qualified candidates'.

276 Bergsmo, Harhoff, and Zhu, 'Article 42', in Ambos, *Commentary* (2022), mn. 15. See also Wei, *Rolle des Anklägers* (2007), pp. 24–5, according to whom the Prosecutor should possess experience and knowledge in international law, international humanitarian law, and human rights law.

277 cf. Nerlich, in Stahn and Sluiter, *Practice* (2009), p. 321; Ambos and Bock, in Reydams, Wouters, and Ryngaert, *Prosecutors* (2012), p. 531. The autonomy of the ICC with regard to its predecessors was also stressed by *Prosecutor v. Lubanga*, Decision Regarding the Practices Used to Prepare and Familiarise Witnesses for Giving Testimony at Trial, No. ICC-01/04-01/06-1049, 30 November 2007, para. 44: 'the Chamber does not consider the procedural rules and jurisprudence of the ad hoc Tribunals to be automatically applicable to the ICC without detailed analysis.' On witness proofing in that regard, see, in detail, Chapter V, A.(3)(d) in this volume.

The ICCS's emphasis on the practical skills of the Prosecutors has, however, been criticized by Schabas, according to whom this approach 'would arguably have eliminated such great international Prosecutors as Robert Jackson, Richard Goldstone, and Louise Arbour, all of whom had little or no "practical experience in the prosecution or trial of criminal cases"'.[278] This criticism is, ultimately, unconvincing. First, the requirement of criminal trial experience is by no means new but was already contained in both the ICTYS and ICTRS.[279] Secondly, while leadership ability, sure instinct, and strategic/conceptual skills are certainly important qualities of an international Prosecutor,[280] they cannot compensate for the technical-legal, procedural, and rhetoric skills necessary for the prosecution of international crimes.[281]

Apart from these personal and professional qualifications, excellent language skills regarding the working languages of the Court are required.[282] Further, the Prosecutor and the Deputy Prosecutors shall be of different nationalities, but—unlike the judges[283]—not necessarily from different legal systems.[284] Given the lack of a rule comparable to Article 36 (4)(b) ICCS—requiring the nationality of State Parties for the judges—it has been suggested that the Prosecutor or their Deputy need not have the nationality of a State Party, that is, even nationals of non-State Parties may become (Deputy) Prosecutor of the ICC.[285] However, the ASP has clarified the matter, applying the procedures for the nomination of judges *mutatis mutandis* to the nomination of the Prosecutor.[286]

The procedure for selecting and appointing international Prosecutors is closely linked to the way in which the respective tribunal was created.[287] The Prosecutors of the ICTY, ICTR, SCSL, and STL—tribunals which have been established by or with the involvement of the Security Council—have been appointed by the Security Council[288] or the UN Secretary-General.[289] Both Co-Prosecutors of the ECCC[290] have been appointed by the national Supreme Council of the Magistracy of Cambodia. As regards the International Co-Prosecutor, however, the Secretary-General has the right to nominate a candidate.[291] The

[278] Schabas, *ICC Commentary* (2016), pp. 742–3; see also Moulier, 'Article 42', in Fernandez, *Statut* (2019), pp. 1279–80.

[279] cf. Arts. 16 (4) ICTYS, 15 (4) ICTRS, and 14 (4) IRMCTS (requiring 'experience in the conduct of investigations and prosecutions of criminal cases').

[280] cf. Schabas, *ICC Commentary* (2016), p. 743; in a similar vein, FIDH et al., *Open Letter* (2011), p. 4.

[281] See also FIDH et al., *Open Letter* (2011), p. 3; even more restrictive, Côté, in Reydams, Wouters, and Ryngaert, *Prosecutors* (2012), p. 345 ('Professional qualifications should be, if not the sole criteria, at least the main criteria required to be an international prosecutor').

[282] cf. Art. 42 (3) ICCS.

[283] See Art. 36 (8)(i) ICCS.

[284] Art. 42 (2) ICCS; see also Bergsmo, Harhoff, and Zhu, 'Article 42', in Ambos, *Commentary* (2022), mn. 14; Moulier, 'Article 42', in Fernandez et al., *Statut I* (2019), p. 1280.

[285] Schabas, *ICC Commentary* (2016), pp. 742–3; Schabas, *Introduction* (2011), p. 377.

[286] cf. Resolution ICC-ASP/3/Res. 6, Procedure for the Nomination and Election of Judges, the Prosecutor and Deputy Prosecutors of the International Criminal Court—Consolidated Version, paras. 28 and 41, <https://asp.icc-cpi.int/iccdocs/asp_docs/Resolutions/ICC-ASP-3-Res.6-CONSOLIDATED-ENG.pdf>; see also Note Verbale of 7 February 2011, ICC-ASP/10/S/06, <https://asp.icc-cpi.int/iccdocs/asp_docs/Elections/EP2011/NV-Election-Prosecutor-2011-ENG.pdf>.

[287] In a similar vein, Côté, in Reydams, Wouters, and Ryngaert, *Prosecutors* (2012), pp. 342–5; see also the detailed overview on the various international and internationalized tribunals in Ambos, *Treatise ICL I* (2021), pp. 24–94.

[288] Arts. 16 (4) ICTYS, 15 (4) ICTRS, and 14 (4) IRMCTS.

[289] Arts. 15 (3) SCSLS, 14 (1) RSCSLS, 11 (3) STLS.

[290] The organizational structure of the ECCC Prosecution is unique. The office is headed by two Co-Prosecutors—one international and one Cambodian—who are equal in status and share the responsibility for the conduct of the prosecution; cf. thereto Ambos and Bock, in Reydams, Wouters, and Ryngaert, *Prosecutors* (2012), p. 521 with further references; also Townsend, in Reydams, Wouters, and Ryngaert, *Prosecutors* (2012), pp. 302–6.

[291] Art. 18 Law of the ECCC.

KSC Special Prosecutor has been appointed by the Head of the EU Common Security and Defence Policy Mission as 'Appointing Authority'.[292] In contrast, the ICC Prosecutors are elected by the ASP as the ICC's legislative treaty body.[293] The election is organized by the Bureau and the Secretariat of the ASP.[294] The details of the process are set out in the respective ASP resolution:[295] upon invitation by the ASP Secretariat, State Parties may nominate their candidates. Preferably, the aspirant should enjoy the support of multiple State Parties.[296] Each nomination should be accompanied by a statement on the qualification of the respective candidate.[297] In preparation of the 2011 elections, the Bureau of the ASP decided to set up a Search Committee which was mandated to 'receive expressions of interest from individuals, States, regional and international organizations, civil society, professional associations and other sources' and to 'actively identify and informally approach individuals who may satisfy the applicable criteria ... and who may subsequently express their interest to be considered'.[298] In doing so, the Bureau complemented the formal nomination process with a proactive search for suitable candidates—an innovative approach which might contribute to a desirable depoliticization of the selection process by putting a particular emphasis on the candidates' competencies and professional skills.[299] As to the actual election, the Statute allows for an absolute majority[300] of the ASP members, but the respective ASP Resolution urges them to come to a unanimous decision.[301] This can be seen as a measure to reinforce the OTP's independence.[302] The Deputy Prosecutors are elected in the same way, but from a list of three possible candidates provided by the Prosecutor.[303] This confirms the Chief Prosecutor's administrative independence.[304]

The last election procedure turned out to be more complicated. First, the Bureau of the ASP created the Terms of Reference of the Committee for the Election of the Prosecutor (Committee) on 3 April 2019. The Committee was assisted by a panel of five experts, who had 'extensive national or international criminal investigation, prosecution or judicial experience'.[305] At the end, the Committee produced an unranked short list of four candidates[306] which was, as we will see in a moment, however subsequently expanded. The entire election process was delayed and cumbersome and accompanied by a debate about prosecutorial

[292] Art. 35 (6) with 28 (3) KSC Law.

[293] Art. 42 (4) ICCS, Rule 86 RPE ASP.

[294] cf. Res. ICC-ASP/1/Res. 2, Nos. 27–31.

[295] Resolution ICC-ASP/1/Res. 2, Procedure for the Nomination and Election of Judges, the Prosecutor and the Deputy Prosecutor of the International Criminal Court, adopted at the 3rd Plenary Meeting, on 9 September 2002, amended by ICC-ASP/3/Res. 6.

[296] Res. ICC-ASP/1/Res. 2, No. 25.

[297] Ibid., No. 26.

[298] ICC-ASP/9/INF.2, No. 6, Search Committee for the Position of the Prosecutor of the International Criminal Court—Terms of Reference, adopted at the ninth session on 6 December 2010.

[299] See also Côté, in Reydams, Wouters, and Ryngaert, *Prosecutors* (2012), p. 345.

[300] Art. 42 (4) ICCS. An absolute majority requires the majority of all ASP members (including absent and abstaining members), and not merely the majority of all valid votes; see Bergsmo, Harhoff, and Zhu, 'Article 42', in Ambos, *Commentary* (2022), mn. 16.

[301] Res. ICC-ASP/1/Res. 2, No. 29.

[302] Côté, in Reydams, Wouters, and Ryngaert, *Prosecutors* (2012), p. 347; on the relationship between independence and appointment procedure, see also Kuczyńska, *Accusation Model ICC* (2015), pp. 37–8.

[303] Art. 42 (4) ICCS; Res. ICC-ASP/1/Res. 2, Nos. 32–7.

[304] Safferling, *Criminal Procedure* (2012), p. 149.

[305] ASP, *Bureau of the ASP: Election of the Prosecutor—Terms of Reference*, ICC-ASP/18/INF.2, 11 April 2019, para. 7, <https://asp.icc-cpi.int/sites/asp/files/asp_docs/ASP18/ICC-ASP-18-INF2-ENG-11Apr19-1600.pdf>. The five experts have been Marcin Czepelak (Poland), Lamin Faati (The Gambia), Andreas Mavroyiannis (Cyprus), Sabine Nölke (Canada), and Mario Oyarzábal (Argentina), cf. Kersten, *JiC* (2020).

[306] ICC-ASP, *Election Prosecutor* (2020), § 18. The four shortlisted candidates were M. A. Anyah (Nigeria), F. Gaynor (Ireland), S. Okalany (Uganda), and R. Roy (Canada).

ethics. The major shortcoming of the process has been seen in the failure to carry out vetting for high moral character,[307] i.e. to examine the candidates for soundness and integrity. This method was—especially in light of the IER Report 2020[308] and the IBA Report 2019[309]—supposed to be used to check candidates against their history of possible forms of workplace misconduct including fraud, corruption, bullying, and harassment;[310] this cannot be substituted by the candidates' signing of a declaration attesting to their high moral character.[311] Ultimately, the current Prosecutor, somewhat surprisingly, has been elected: initially, following the newly established system guiding the election,[312] he was not shortlisted by the Committee.[313] However, the dissatisfaction with the shortlist expressed by some State Parties led to an expansion of the list—including Karim Khan—and this list was ultimately voted on.[314]

As a rule,[315] the Prosecutor and the Deputy Prosecutors are appointed for a term of nine years without the possibility of re-election.[316] This relatively long tenure reflects the desire to ensure continuity in the work of the Office.[317] The prohibition of a second term, in turn, safeguards the personal independence of the heads of the OTP who have no need to stay on the good side of the State Parties just to ensure their reelection.[318] This constitutes a remarkable change vis-à-vis the ad hoc tribunals whose Prosecutor is appointed for a much shorter term of four years but with the prospect of a second mandate.[319]

### (4) Function and mandate

The ICC-OTP is 'responsible for receiving referrals and any substantiated information on crimes within the jurisdiction of the Court, for examining them and for conducting investigations and prosecutions before the Court'.[320] In carrying out its mandate, the prosecution is to 'extend the investigation to cover all facts and evidence relevant to an assessment of whether there is criminal responsibility under this Statute, and, in doing so, investigate incriminating

307 Mudukuti, *JICJ*, 19 (2021), 747.
308 See above note 113.
309 IBA, 'Us Too? Bullying and Sexual Harassment in the Legal Profession', 2019 <www.ibanet.org/bullying-and-sexual-harassment>.
310 Mudukuti, *JICJ*, 19 (2021), 750.
311 Mudukuti, *JICJ*, 19 (2021), 753.
312 See ICC ASP, *Election of Prosecutor* (2020), <https://asp.icc-cpi.int/elections/prosecutor/Prosecutor2020>.
313 ASP, *Report of the Committee on the Election of the Prosecutor*, ICC-ASP/19/INF.2, 30 June 2020, para. 3.
314 ASP, *Report of the Committee on the Election of the Prosecutor—Addendum—Appraisals of additional candidates*, ICC-ASP/19/INF.2/Add.3, 25 November 2020, para. 3. The Committee submitted its appraisal of five additional candidates, namely, C. Castresana Fernández (Spain), K. A. A. Khan (UK), F. Lo Voi (Italy), R. Petit (Canada), and B. Raynaud (France), see ibid., para. 7.
315 At the time of the election, the ASP may fix a shorter term. In this vein, the ASP elected Brammertz as a Deputy Prosecutor with a reduced tenure of six years, ASP, *Second Session* (2003), paras. 24, 26.
316 Art. 42 (4) ICCS.
317 Bergsmo, Harhoff, and Zhu, 'Article 42', in Ambos, *Commentary* (2022), mn. 18.
318 Jones, in Cassese et al., *Rome Statute I* (2002), p. 271; Wei, *Rolle des Anklägers* (2007), p. 17; Wouters, Verhoeven, and Demeyere, *ICLR*, 8 (2008), 276; Schabas, *Introduction* (2020), p. 391; Côté, in Reydams, Wouters, and Ryngaert, *Prosecutors* (2012), p. 348; see also Safferling, *Criminal Procedure* (2012), p. 80; Friman, in Cryer et al., *ICL* (2019), p. 417; Kuczyńska, *Accusation Model ICC* (2015), p. 38 and Bergsmo, Harhoff, and Zhu, 'Article 42', in Ambos, *Commentary* (2022), mn. 18, who, however, question if it was necessary to extend the bar of reelection to the Deputy Prosecutors.
319 Arts. 16 (4) ICTYS, 15 (4) ICTRS, and 14 (4) IRMCTS. On non-extensions of tenure, which might be interpreted as sanctions for undesired prosecutorial conduct, see Mégret, in Reydams, Wouters, and Ryngaert, *Prosecutors* (2012), p. 482.
320 Art. 42 (1) ICCS. See also McDermott, 'Article 42', in Klamberg et al., *Commentary ICC I* (2023), pp. 986–7.

and exonerating circumstances equally'.[321] Thus, the ICCS conceives the Prosecutor as an 'impartial organ of justice' bound by the principle of objectivity.[322] In this regard, it seems to depart from the approaches of the ad hoc tribunals whose procedural rules do not oblige the Prosecutor to *actively* investigate exculpatory evidence.[323] This turns the Prosecutor, in line with the adversarial model,[324] into a party to the proceedings,[325] focusing on the guilt of the suspect while leaving the identification of exculpatory circumstances to the defence.[326] It is important to note, though, that already the *Kupreškić* TC moved away from the purely adversarial understanding of the role of the Prosecutor holding that:

> the Prosecutor of the Tribunal is not, or not only, a Party to adversarial proceedings but is an organ of the Tribunal and an organ of international criminal justice whose object is not simply to secure a conviction but to present the case for the Prosecution, which includes

[321] Art. 54 (1) (a) ICCS and Reg. 24 RegOTP (demanding a 'consistent and objective method for the evaluation of sources, information and evidence' and the examination of 'multiple sources as a means of bias control'). The draft Regulations provided for 'truth-seeking standards' and the investigation of 'both incriminating and exonerating circumstances' (cf. de Meester et al., in Sluiter et al., *International Criminal Procedure* (2013), p. 190). This was expected to speed up the proceedings; cf. ICC-OTP, *Length of Proceedings* (2003), paras. 22 ff.; ICC-OTP, *Draft Policy Paper on Preliminary Examinations* (4 October 2010), p. 6. See also Safferling, *Criminal Procedure* (2012), p. 218; Gless, *Internationales Strafrecht* (2021), mn. 888; crit. Buisman, *LJIL*, 27 (2014), 211 ff. (non-compliance with duty to investigate exonerating circumstances). In the same vein, Rule 55 (5) IR ECCC on the Role of the Co-Investigating Judges before the ECCC. On the moral dimension of the Prosecutor's mandate, see Thompson, in Jalloh and Marong, *Promoting Accountability* (2015), p. 47.

[322] *Situation in Afghanistan*, No. ICC-02/17-138, para. 60 ('the Prosecutor ... is also subject to certain duties that affect the scope of her investigation. She is mandated ... to ... investigate incriminating and exonerating circumstances equally ... in order to obtain a full picture ... the Prosecutor must carry out an investigation into the situation as a whole'); *Situation in Uganda*, No. ICC-02/04-85, para. 32; *Situation in the DRC*, No. ICC-01/04-84, para. 32; see also *Prosecutor v. Lubanga*, Defence Response to the Appeals Chamber Order of 24 November 2006, No. ICC-01/04-01/06-734, 29 November 2006, para. 27 ('prosecutor as an impartial minister of justice'); Behrens, *HuV-I*, 11 (1998), 146; Cassese, *EJIL*, 10 (1999), 162; Turone, in Cassese et al., *Rome Statute II* (2002), p. 1165; Kreß, in Grützner, Pötz, and Kreß, *Internationaler Rechtshilfeverkehr in Strafsachen* (2003), Part IV A 1 mn. 103; Wouters, Verhoeven, and Demeyere, *ICLR*, 8 (2008), 307; Bock, *Opfer* (2010), p. 215; Schabas, *ICC Commentary* (2016), p. 849; Bensouda, *NCJIL&ComReg*, 36 (2011), 280; Ambos and Bock, in Reydams, Wouters, and Ryngaert, *Prosecutors* (2012), p. 537; Côté, in Reydams, Wouters, and Ryngaert, *Prosecutors* (2012), p. 359; Thalmann, in Kolb and Scalia, *DIP* (2012), p. 470; Klamberg, *Evidence* (2013), p. 208; Trüg, *ZStW*, 125 (2013), 48; de Meester et al., in Sluiter et al., *International Criminal Procedure* (2013), p. 189; Buisman, *LJIL*, 27 (2014), 205 ('neutral truth-finder'); Heinze, *Disclosure* (2014), p. 258; see also Zahar and Sluiter, *ICL* (2008), p. 374; Friman, in Cryer et al., *ICL* (2019), p. 412; Cassese et al., *ICL* (2013), p. 344; Kuczyńska, *Accusation Model ICC* (2015), p. 51; Thompson, in Jalloh and Marong, *Promoting Accountability* (2015), p. 51; on the principle of objectivity as part of the right to a fair trial, see Mégret, in Reydams, Wouters, and Ryngaert, *Prosecutors* (2012), p. 441; in a similar vein, Kuczyńska, *Accusation Model ICC* (2015), p. 52, yet arguing that this does not give the defendant the right to demand that the Prosecutor undertake specific actions to produce exculpatory evidence.

[323] Turone, in Cassese et al., *Rome Statute II* (2002), p. 1165; Zahar and Sluiter, *ICL* (2008), p. 55; Bock, *Opfer* (2010), p. 216; Bensouda, *NCJIL&ComReg*, 36 (2011), 281; Markovic, *TexILJ*, 47 (2011–2012), 211; Langer, *AJCompL*, 53 (2005), 861; Ambos and Bock, in Reydams, Wouters, and Ryngaert, *Prosecutors* (2012), p. 504; Thalmann, in Kolb and Scalia, *DIP* (2012), p. 467; de Meester et al., in Sluiter et al., *International Criminal Procedure* (2013), p. 177; Heinze, *Disclosure* (2014), p. 257; Tochilovsky, *Jurisprudence* (2014), p. 475; cf also Klamberg, *Evidence* (2013), pp. 208–9.

[324] See Chapter I, A.(1)(b) in this volume.

[325] cf. Rule 2 (A) RPE ICTY/ICTR/MICT and *Prosecutor v. Barayagwiza*, Prosecutor's Request for Review or Reconsideration, Separate Opinion of Judge Shahabuddeen, No. ICTR-97-19-AR72, 31 March 2000, para. 68; see also Behrens, *HuV-I*, 11 (1998), 146; Calvo-Goller, *Trial Proceedings* (2006), pp. 50–1; Kreß, 'Resolution 827 (1993)', in Grützner, Pötz, and Kreß, *Internationaler Rechtshilfeverkehr* (2002), Part III 27 mn. 37; Langer, *AJCompL*, 53 (2005), 860; Thalmann, in Kolb and Scalia, *DIP* (2012), p. 467.

[326] Calvo-Goller, *Trial Proceedings* (2006), p. 51; Ambos and Bock, in Reydams, Wouters, and Ryngaert, *Prosecutors* (2012), p. 504; Thalmann, in Kolb and Scalia, *DIP* (2012), p. 467; de Meester et al., in Sluiter et al., *International Criminal Procedure* (2013), p. 176; Buisman, *LJIL*, 27 (2014), 207; see also Safferling, *Criminal Procedure* (2012), p. 218; also *Prosecutor v. Blagojević et al.*, Joint Decision on Motions Related to Evidence, No. IT-02-60-PT, 12 December 2002, para. 26.

not only inculpatory, but also exculpatory evidence, in order to assist the Chamber to discover the truth in a judicial setting.[327]

Article 54 (1)(a) ICCS draws on this jurisprudence in making impartiality and objectivity statutory obligations.[328] In particular the Prosecutor's duty to search actively for exonerating information may be regarded as a measure to achieve factual equality of arms between prosecution and defence since the latter may lack the necessary resources and powers to conduct extensive investigations on its own.[329] Of course, it remains to be seen whether and how this prosecutorial duty can be implemented in practice.[330] In its Code of Conduct[331] and its first Strategic Plan,[332] the OTP puts a particular emphasis on its truth-finding mandate and explains that it will 'apply multiple case hypotheses—incriminating and exonerating—throughout the investigation'.[333] While the term 'truth' no longer appears in the second Strategic Plan, the Office confirms 'the need to consider multiple alternative case hypotheses and to consistently and objectively test case theories against the evidence—incriminating and exonerating'.[334] In the third Strategic Plan, performance, functioning, and success are primarily related to the aspects of speed, efficiency, and effectiveness.[335] The fourth Strategic Plan has a similar emphasis.[336] At any rate, some critics argued that the prosecution has so far 'largely ignored its obligation under Article 54 (1) (a)', 'failed to investigate any of its cases

[327] *Prosecutor v. Kupreškić et al.*, Decision on Communications between the Parties and their Witnesses, No. IT-95-16, 21 September 1998, ii; for further similar case law, see previous edition, p. 128 with notes 283–4; see also ICTY/ICTR, *Prosecutor's Regulation No. 2* (1999) establishing 'Standards of Professional Conduct for Prosecution Counsel' providing, inter alia, that prosecution counsel be 'objective and independent'. In the same vein, Zahar and Sluiter, *ICL* (2008), p. 55; Boas et al., *International Criminal Procedure* (2011), p. 106 ('sound investigative practice ... arguable something which all the international prosecutors engage in, legally duty-bound or not'); Safferling, *Criminal Procedure* (2012), p. 218; de Meester et al., in Sluiter et al., *International Criminal Procedure* (2013), pp. 177–9; dissenting Fairlie, *ICLR*, 4 (2004), 314–15; Wouters, Verhoeven, and Demeyere, in Doria, Gasser, and Bassiouni, *ICC* (2009), pp. 349 ff.; on the re-definition of the role of the prosecution in the case law of the ICTY, see Langer, *AJCompL*, 53 (2005), 890–3; on impartiality, see also Wouters, Verhoeven, and Demeyere, in Doria, Gasser, and Bassiouni, *ICC* (2009), pp. 351 ff. For a comparison of the Prosecutors of the IMT/IMTFE, ICTY, and ICC, see Eser, in *FS Nehm* (2006), pp. 113 ff.; Langer, *AJCompL*, 53 (2005), 839; Weigend, in Dressler, *Encyclopedia of Crime and Justice III* (2002), p. 1234.

[328] See also Bock, *Opfer* (2010), p. 216; Côté, in Reydams, Wouters, and Ryngaert, *Prosecutors* (2012), pp. 359–60; Heinze, *Disclosure* (2014), pp. 257–8.

[329] See also Buisman, *LJIL*, 27 (2014), 206; Thalmann, in Kolb and Scalia, *DIP* (2012), p. 467; Kuczyńska, *Accusation Model ICC* (2015), p. 52. This appears to resemble more a civil law ('inquisitorial') than a common law ('adversarial') type of Prosecutor. For, although the prosecution in the adversarial system is also obliged to follow the principles of truth and objectivity, the adversarial two-case approach entails that the submission of evidence by the prosecution is separated from the one by the defence, thereby forcing the Prosecutor more into a partisan party position; cf. Damaška, in Cassese, *Companion* (2009), p. 176, arguing that 'it becomes difficult' for the Prosecutor 'to refrain from using ... evidence selectively, focusing only on information favourable to their allegations'; see also Friman, in Lee, *ICC* (2001), p. 537; Tochilovsky, in Fischer, Kreß and Lüder, *Prosecution* (2001), p. 637; Safferling, *Criminal Procedure* (2012), pp. 79, 86; Ambos and Bock, in Reydams, Wouters, and Ryngaert, *International Prosecutors* (2012), p. 489; Heinze, *Disclosure* (2014), pp. 250, 253.

[330] Sceptical Boas et al., *International Criminal Procedure* (2011), p. 106 ('It remains unclear whether this prosecutorial duty to investigate exculpatory evidence has any practical substantive effect'); see also Zahar and Sluiter, *ICL* (2008), pp. 55, 374; Cassese et al., *ICL* (2013), p. 367.

[331] See in particular Rules 49–50 Code of Conduct OTP on objective truth-seeking. Several other Rules oblige the Prosecutor to be truthful and act in good faith, see e.g. Rule 51 (c) (no prosecution of innocent persons); Rule 63 (no presentation of false or forged evidence, no untrue statements of material facts to a judge, a Chamber, the Presidency, counsel, or Registry); Rule 68 (no influencing of witnesses or obstructing of testimonies); on the need to include such self-evident provisions in a Code of Conduct, see Mégret, in Reydams, Wouters, and Ryngaert, *Prosecutors* (2012), pp. 443–4.

[332] ICC-OTP, *Strategic Plan* (2013), paras. 9, 18, 54, 97.

[333] ICC-OTP, *Strategic Plan* (2013), para. 23.

[334] ICC-OTP, *Strategic Plan* (2015), para. 34.

[335] ICC-OTP, *Strategic Plan* (2019).

[336] ICC-OTP, *Strategic Plan* (2023).

with the thoroughness expected from a diligent prosecutor', and turned a blind eye to the weaknesses of its case.[337] The *Ngudjolo* TC, for example, criticized a lack of thoroughness and completeness in the investigations of the Office.[338] In the proceedings against Gbagbo, the PTC, quite straightforwardly, expressed doubts about whether the Prosecutor really had followed 'all relevant incriminating and exonerating lines of investigation in order to establish the truth'.[339] Even more alarming, the *Mbarushimana* PTC labelled the OTP's interrogation technique—inter alia, using frequently leading questions and manipulative feedback on witness testimony—as 'utterly inappropriate when viewed in light of the objective, set out in article 54 (1)(a) of the Statute, to establish the truth by "investigating incriminating and exonerating circumstances equally"'.[340] Given that the international and national public, including and in particular the victims and the organizations representing them, judge the ICC by its number of indictments and, even worse, convictions, it might be understandable that the OTP's main focus is on finding incriminating evidence.[341] This external pressure, however, does not release the prosecution from its statutory obligation to impartiality and objectivity. At any rate, to be fair to the OTP, one must acknowledge that this criticism gave rise to a strategic shift in 2013 in order to improve the OTP's investigative approach. Recently, in 2023, the Prosecutor withdrew all charges against one accused in the CAR situation after assessing that the case no longer offered a reasonable prospect of conviction.[342] We will look at this approach more closely in the next section.

The ICCS does not provide for a specific remedy for OTP violations of its obligations of impartiality and objectivity.[343] However, the above-mentioned restrictions on outside activities[344] operate as a safeguard for the Prosecutor's impartiality.[345] More importantly, the Prosecutor and the Deputy Prosecutor may be disqualified if their impartiality might reasonably be questioned.[346] These provisions will be discussed in more detail below in the context of accountability measures.

[337] Buisman, *LJIL*, 27 (2014), 223, 226. See also *Prosecutor v. Lubanga*, TC I Closing Submission of the Defence, No. ICC-01/04-01/06-2773, 15 July 2011, para. 13, arguing that the OTP has seriously failed to fulfil its obligation to investigate exculpatory circumstances. Similar complaints were made in *Prosecutor v. Muthaura et al.*, PTC II Public Redacted Version of Final Written Observations of the Defence Team of Ambassador Francis K. Muthaura on the Confirmation of Charges Hearing, No. ICC-01/09-02/11-374, 2 December 2011, paras. 71–2; *Prosecutor v. Abu Garda*, PTC I Decision on the Confirmation of Charges, No. ICC-02/05-02/09-243-Red, 8 February 2010, paras. 46–7; *Prosecutor v. Ruto et al.*, PTC II William Samoei Ruto Defence Brief following the Confirmation of the Charges Hearing, No. ICC-01/09-01/11-355, 24 October 2011, paras. 19–23; Cassese et al., *ICL* (2013), p. 344 ('the prosecutor is every bit as partisan as his counterparts at the ICTY and ICTR').

[338] *Prosecutor v. Ngudjolo*, TC II Judgment pursuant to Article 74 of the Statute, No. ICC-01/04-02/12-3, 18 December 2012, paras. 117–23. In a similar vein, *Prosecutor v. Gbagbo*, PTC I Decision Adjourning the Hearing on the Confirmation of Charges pursuant to Article 61 (7)(c)(i) of the Rome Statute, No. ICC-02/11-01/11-432, 3 June 2013, paras. 24–37.

[339] *Gbagbo*, No. ICC-02/11-01/11-432, para. 37.

[340] *Prosecutor v. Mbarushimana*, PTC I Decision on the Confirmation of Charges, No. ICC-01/04-01/10-465, 16 December 2011, para. 51.

[341] Ambos, *ICLR*, 12 (2012), 127. See also the reference to the 'degree of international and local pressure, once it was known that officials from the Court had arrived in the country' in *Prosecutor v. Lubanga*, TC I Judgment pursuant to Article 74 of the Statute, No. ICC-01/04-01/06-2842, 14 March 2012, para. 142; on the 'natural tendency of the prosecutors to sympathize with victims of crimes at the expense of ICC defendants', seeMarkovic, *TexILJ*, 47 (2011–2012), 209.

[342] See *Prosecutor v. Mokom*, PTC II Notice of Withdrawal of the Charges against Maxime Jeoffroy Eli Mokom Gawaka, No. ICC-01/14-01/22-275, 16 October 2023, paras. 1 ('Having considered the totality of the evidence ... the Prosecution does not consider that there is a reasonable prospect of conviction at trial even if the charges were confirmed'), 5, 10; see also ICC-OTP, *Report 2023* (2023), p. 17.

[343] Cassese et al., *ICL* (2013), p. 367; see also Wei, *Rolle des Anklägers* (2007), pp. 37–8.

[344] See Section B.(1) in this chapter.

[345] Côté, in Reydams, Wouters, and Ryngaert, *Prosecutors* (2012), p. 360.

[346] Art. 42 (7) and (8) ICCS.

### (5) Strategy and policy

Given the high number of international crimes committed in situations of crisis, it is practically impossible to prosecute all potential perpetrators at the international level. In fact, after more than twenty years of ICC experience we are slowly but surely becoming used to the fact that by far not all those most responsible will face international criminal justice, even if a situation (like most prominently Ukraine) is also the object of national investigations. In any case, the rational and transparent selection and prioritization of cases, accompanied by a coherent prosecution strategy, turns out to be of utmost importance for the success and legitimacy of any international criminal tribunal[347] and the international criminal justice system as a whole.[348] This holds particularly true for the ICC given that its Prosecutor (who is in charge of selection)[349] has not only the power to select individual defendants but also—for the first time in history—entire situations for investigations.[350] Accordingly, the complex process of selecting defendants and concrete charges[351] can be divided into two main steps: first, the primary selection of situations, and secondly, the subsequent extraction of cases from these situations.[352] This section focuses on the latter, which is a core issue for prosecutorial coherence. Questions of selecting situations will be discussed in more detail in connection with the referral (trigger) mechanisms.[353]

As a general rule, it follows from the principles of equality before the law and non-discrimination[354] that selection decisions must not be 'based on impermissible motives such as, inter alia, race, colour, religion, opinion, national or ethnic origin'.[355] The Prosecutor

[347] For an instructive comparative evaluation of the selection policies and practices of international criminal tribunals, see Vlaming, in Reydams, Wouters, and Ryngaert, *Prosecutors* (2012), pp. 547–70; deGuzman and Schabas, in Sluiter et al., *International Criminal Procedure* (2013), pp. 133–54; also Locke, in Reydams, Wouters, and Ryngaert, *Prosecutors* (2012), pp. 607–12; specifically on the ICTY, see Angermaier, in Bergsmo, *Criteria* (2010), pp. 27–43; on the ICTR, see Obote-Odora, in Bergsmo, *Criteria* (2010), pp. 45–67.

[348] See previously Ambos and Stegmiller, *Crime Law Soc Change*, 58 (2012), 392. See also HRW, *Selection* (2006), p. 7; HRW, *Business* (2011), pp. 4, 46; Bergsmo, in Bergsmo, *Criteria* (2010), pp. 8, 12, 14; Vlaming, in Reydams, Wouters, and Ryngaert, *Prosecutors* (2012), pp. 542–3; Locke, in Reydams, Wouters, and Ryngaert, *Prosecutors* (2012), p. 614; Côté, in Reydams, Wouters, and Ryngaert, *Prosecutors* (2012), pp. 354–5; deGuzman and Schabas, in Sluiter et al., *International Criminal Procedure* (2013), pp. 131–2; from a victims' perspective, see Dicker, in Bergsmo, *Criteria* (2010), pp. 267–8; Bock, *Opfer* (2010), p. 606; Thompson, in Jalloh and Marong, *Promoting Accountability* (2015), p. 54.

[349] See also *Prosecutor v. Bemba*, PTC II Decision on Request for Leave to Submit Amicus Curiae Observations Pursuant to Rule 103 of the Rules of Procedure and Evidence, No. ICC-01/05-01/08-453, 17 July 2009, para. 10, leaving the 'issue of selection of cases' to the Prosecutor.

[350] Ambos and Stegmiller, *Crime Law Soc Change*, 58 (2012), 392; see also Ambos and Bock, in Reydams, Wouters, and Ryngaert, *Prosecutors* (2012), pp. 532, 541; Smeulers, Weerdesteijn, and Hola, *ICLR*, 15 (2015), 2.

[351] In the case against Lubanga, the Prosecutor decided to concentrate on the recruitment and use of child soldiers and suspended investigations concerning other alleged crimes, in particular sex crimes; *Prosecutor v. Lubanga*, Prosecutor's Information on Further Investigations, No. ICC-01/04-01/06-170, 28 June 2006, para. 7. As expected the OTP did not bring additional charges in the course of the appeals proceedings. Thus, the first case concluded at the ICC has already shown that the selection of charges entails another discretionary decision that might enlarge the impunity gap; see Bock, *Opfer* (2010), pp. 322–3; Bock, *ZIS*, 8 (2013), 302; Ambos and Bock, in Reydams, Wouters, and Ryngaert, *Prosecutors* (2012), p. 538; also Seils, in Bergsmo, *Criteria* (2010), pp. 73–5; generally on the OTP's failure to charge Lubanga with sex crimes, see Ambos, *ICLR*, 12 (2012), 137–8 with n. 156; on its impact on the reparation decision, see Bock, *ZIS*, 8 (2013), 302–3.

[352] Regs. 34–5 RegOTP; see Smeulers, Weerdesteijn and Hola, *ICLR*, 15 (2015), 3.

[353] See Chapter III, A.4 (b) in this volume.

[354] Arts. 21 (3), 67 (1) ICCS.

[355] *Prosecutor v. Delalić et al.*, AC Judgment, No. IT-96-21-A, 20 February 2001, para. 605; see also *Prosecutor v. Bizimungu et al.*, TC II Decision on Defence Motions for Stay of Proceedings and for Adjournment of the Trial, including Reasons in Support of the Chamber's Oral Ruling delivered on Monday 20 September, No. ICTR-2000-56-T, 24 September 2004, para. 26; Côté, in Reydams, Wouters, and Ryngaert, *Prosecutors* (2012), pp. 364, 366–70; deGuzman and Schabas, in Sluiter et al., *International Criminal Procedure* (2013), pp. 146, 167; also Thompson, in Jalloh and Marong, *Promoting Accountability* (2015), p. 55.

is thus required to investigate, as a rule,[356] all sides of a conflict without favouring or discriminating against any person or groups.[357] In fact, this is a prerequisite to overcome the victor's justice stigma attached to international criminal justice since the Nuremberg and Tokyo precedents.[358] Apart from these human rights constraints, however, the prosecution is relatively free to develop its own prosecutorial policy. The need to integrate these broad discretionary powers into a transparent and coherent prosecutorial strategy is acknowledged by Reg. 14 RegOTP. It obliges the OTP to make public its strategy and make use of policy papers that reflect the key principles and criteria of this strategy.[359]

So far, the OTP has already issued several documents regarding policy and strategy.[360] First, the 2003 Policy Paper ('on some policy issues') attempts to define a general prosecutorial strategy, in particular by highlighting some priority tasks.[361] Its central point is the focus on those suspects who bear the greatest responsibility for the most serious crimes,[362] thus leaving the task of closing the ensuing impunity gap for middle- and low-ranking perpetrators to national justice systems.[363] Subsequent policy papers developed this further,[364] as we will see below. Secondly, the general guiding principle of 'focused investigations and prosecutions' is concretized, modified, and further developed by five strategy papers laying down some key strategic issues: (i) the Reports on Prosecutorial Strategy 2006,[365] and (ii) 2009–2012;[366] as well as (iii) the Strategic Plans 2012–2015,[367] (iv) 2016–2018,[368] (v) 2019–2021,[369] and (vi) 2023–2025.[370]

356 Exceptionally, though, the investigation is limited to the alleged perpetrators if jurisdiction is based on active personality pursuant to Art. 12 (2)(b) ICCS; see thereon Rastan, in Stahn, *ICC* (2015), p. 152 and generally Chapter III, A.(4)(a)(ii) in this volume.

357 Côté, in Reydams, Wouters, and Ryngaert, *Prosecutors* (2012), p. 370; deGuzman and Schabas, in Sluiter et al., *International Criminal Procedure* (2013), p. 167; see also Mégret, in Reydams, Wouters, and Ryngaert, *Prosecutors* (2012), p. 439; Takemura, in van den Herik and Stahn, *Diversification* (2012), p. 643. Against this background, the decision of the ICTY prosecution not to investigate alleged war crimes committed by NATO Forces during 'Operation Allied Forces' was heavily criticized; see Ambos and Bock, in Reydams, Wouters, and Ryngaert, *Prosecutors* (2012), p. 502 with further references. In general, on the difficulty and necessity of prosecuting peacekeepers on the international level, see O'Brien, *JICJ*, 10 (2012), 525.

358 Côté, in Reydams, Wouters, and Ryngaert, *Prosecutors* (2012), p. 370. In more detail on the limited competencies of the IMT and the IMTFE which had no jurisdiction over alleged war crimes of the Allies, see Ambos and Bock, in Reydams, Wouters, and Ryngaert, *Prosecutors* (2012), pp. 491–2, 497–8 with further references.

359 This corresponds to No. 17 of the UN Guidelines on the Role of Prosecutors ('In countries where prosecutors are vested with discretionary functions, the law or published rules or regulations shall provide guidelines to enhance fairness and consistency of approach in taking decisions in the prosecution process, including institution or waiver of prosecution'). A good example in this regard is ICC-OTP, *Policy Prelim. Examinations* (2013) setting out the principles and criteria of preliminary examinations (paras. 1 ff.) and aiming to promote transparency (para. 15). See also ICC-OTP, *Strategic Plan* (2015), especially para. 36, referring to the policy paper on preliminary examinations and to case identification and prioritization within a formal investigation.

360 For an overview, see <https://www.icc-cpi.int/about/otp/otp-policies>.

361 ICC-OTP, *Policy Paper* (2003), p. 1.

362 One, however, must not confuse the OTP's policy choice to limit prosecutions to certain high calibre cases with the admissibility threshold as a legal barrier to bring certain cases, in particular with the gravity threshold of Art. 17 (1)(d) ICCS; crit. as to the ('impossible to determine') notion of gravity, see Pues, *ICLR*, 17 (2017), 960; in more detail, see Chapter III, B.(2)(c) in this volume.

363 ICC-OTP, *Policy Paper* (2003), p. 7. As to the historical origin of the policy of targeting senior leaders/persons most responsible, see Locke, in Reydams, Wouters, and Ryngaert, *Prosecutors* (2012), p. 607.

364 For an overview, see <https://www.icc-cpi.int/about/otp/otp-policies>.

365 ICC-OTP, *Prosecutorial Strategy* (2006); on the relevant draft paper, see Seils, in Bergsmo, *Criteria* (2010), pp. 71–2.

366 ICC-OTP, *Prosecutorial Strategy* (2010); for a detailed analysis, see Ambos and Stegmiller, *Crime Law Soc Change*, 58 (2012), 394–407.

367 ICC-OTP, *Strategic Plan* (2013).

368 ICC-OTP, *Strategic Plan* (2015).

369 ICC-OTP, *Strategic Plan* (2019).

370 ICC-OTP, *Strategic Plan* (2023).

The Strategy Plan 2012–2015 marked a certain shift in that the OTP acknowledged the need to adjust its strategy in the light of past experience and judicial criticism, in particular by trying to achieve an earlier trial-readiness and a greater diversity in the evidence submitted[371] which in turn should be facilitated by a higher number of senior trial lawyers in charge of the investigations and prosecutions.[372] On a more abstract level, this plan formulated six strategic goals,[373] which have been turned by the 2016–2018 Plan, building on the former,[374] into six external challenges.[375] It pursues nine strategic goals organized around three major themes: the 'performance of the Office's mandate',[376] the 'conditions to fulfil the Office's mandate',[377] and the better coordination in investigation and prosecution.[378] The Strategic Plan 2019–2021 focused primarily on questions improving performance in relation to the Office's core activities (e.g. to achieve a high rate of success in court; to increase the speed, efficiency, and effectiveness of preliminary examinations, investigations, and prosecutions; and to develop strategies to increase the arrest rate of persons subject to outstanding ICC arrest warrants).[379] The last Strategic Plan 2023–2025 focuses on structural changes within the OTP, technological developments, and outreach within the framework of ten strategic goals.[380]

[371] ICC-OTP, *Strategic Plan* (2013), p. 5 (judges 'are expecting the OTP to be (more) trial-ready at an earlier stage in the proceedings and ... to submit more and different kinds of evidence') and pp. 12, 14; also ICC-OTP, *Strategic Plan* (2015), pp. 5 (with n. 1), 9, 15–16, 39, 41.

[372] ICC-OTP, *Strategic Plan* (2013), pp. 7, 16, 25, 26; ICC-OTP, *Strategic Plan* (2015), pp. 9, 11, 39, 45. On the shift from a horizontal to a vertical model of prosecution in this regard and recommending the latter, see Mettraux et al., *Expert Initiative Effectiveness ICC* (2014), pp. 63–5 (paras. 41–54).

[373] ICC-OTP, *Strategic Plan* (2013), p. 17: '1. Conduct impartial, independent, high-quality, efficient and secure preliminary examinations, investigations and prosecutions. 2. Further improve the quality and efficiency of the preliminary examinations, the investigations and the prosecutions. 3. Enhance the integration of a gender perspective in all areas of our work and continue to pay particular attention to sexual and gender based crimes and crimes against children. 4. Enhance complementarity and cooperation by strengthening the Rome System in support of the ICC and of national efforts in situations under preliminary examination or investigation. 5. Maintain a professional office with specific attention to gender and nationality balance, staff quality and motivation, and performance management and measurement; 6. Ensure good governance, accountability and transparency.'

[374] ICC-OTP, *Strategic Plan* (2015), paras. 1–2 (seeing a 'promising trend' in its shift of strategy brought about by the Plan 2012–2015).

[375] ICC-OTP, *Strategic Plan* (2015), para. 3 (referring to the (i) increasing complex security environment, (ii) necessity of cooperation, (iii) 'high pace of technological evolution' impacting on evidence gathering and presentation, (iv) time period between the crimes and their investigation with the ensuing problem of preservation of evidence, (v) insufficient resources, and (vi) lack of coordination of relevant actors).

[376] ICC-OTP, *Strategic Plan* (2015), para. 4: (i) 'conduct impartial, independent, high-quality, efficient and secure preliminary examinations, investigations and prosecutions'; (ii) 'continue to integrate a gender perspective in all areas of the work and to implement the policies in relation to sexual and gender based crimes and crimes against children'; (iii) 'further improve the quality and efficiency of the preliminary examinations, the investigations and the prosecutions'; (iv) 'further adapt the Office's investigative and prosecutorial capabilities and network to the complex and evolving scientific and technological environment'.

[377] ICC-OTP, *Strategic Plan* (2015), para. 4: (v) 'achieve a basic size which can respond to the demands' ; (vi) 'contribute to strengthening cooperation, and promoting general support towards the mandate and activities of the Office'; (vii) 'adapt the Office's protection strategies to the new security challenges'; (viii) 'ensure a professional, accountable, transparent and efficient management of the Office'.

[378] Ibid., para. 4: (ix) 'develop with partners a coordinated investigative and prosecutorial strategy to close the impunity gap'.

[379] ICC-OTP, *Strategic Plan* (2019).

[380] ICC-OTP, *Strategic Plan* (2023), proposing the following goals at pp. 12–22: 1. Increase the expeditiousness and efficiency of the Court's core activities (preliminary examinations, investigations, trials and reparations) while preserving the independence, fairness, and highest legal standards and quality of its proceedings, and protecting the safety and well-being of the persons involved, in particular victims and witnesses; 2. Further develop the Court's approach to victims in all phases of the judicial proceedings, including (in cooperation with the Trust Fund for Victims) reparations; 3. Further develop mainstreaming of a gender perspective in all aspects of the Court's work; 4. Further foster political support and develop modalities of cooperation and operational support for all parties as regards preliminary examinations, investigations, protection of witnesses, implementation of warrants of arrest and judicial proceedings; 5. Discuss and devise with States and other stakeholders new strategies

In 2022, the OTP joined, for the first time, a so-called Joint Investigation Team (JIT),[381] set up with regard to the Ukraine investigation by six countries (Lithuania, Poland, Ukraine, Estonia, Latvia, and Slovakia) and assisted by Eurojust.[382] It is noteworthy, however, that the OTP joined the JIT only as a 'participant', not as a formal 'member', as done subsequently with regard to a JIT dealing with alleged crimes against migrants in Libya.[383]

Thirdly, several policy papers of the OTP clarify other more concrete issues, such as the 'interests of justice',[384] victim's participation,[385] preliminary examinations,[386] the prosecution of sexual and gender-based crimes,[387] case selection and prioritization,[388] children,[389] cultural heritage,[390] situation completion,[391] the crime of gender persecution,[392] the recent updates both on gender-based crimes[393] and on children,[394] and the Policy on Complementarity and Cooperation.[395] We will come back to some of these papers in the following chapters if appropriate.

In sum, the OTP currently combines *strategy papers*, which clarify the Office's strategic objectives for a time period of three to four years, with *policy papers* addressing particular fundamental issues on which the Office wants to provide more clarity and transparency, not least for itself. The strategy papers are valid working agendas which—due to their temporal limitation—also give the OTP the opportunity to critically evaluate and, if necessary, adjust its strategy on a regular basis. A good example is the Office's decision to complement its sequential approach with a simultaneous approach. Originally, the OTP has, in line with its focus on persons most responsible, adopted a sequential approach, investigating

to increase the ability of the Rome Statute System to address the shared responsibility to close the impunity gap, including through encouraging domestic implementation of the Rome Statute and other measures of complementarity by States Parties (including providing support and assistance to victims); 6. Further strengthen professionalism, dedication and integrity in all of the Court's operations; 7. Ensure a safe and secure working environment in which staff wellbeing and continuous improvement are at the centre; 8. Achieve more equitable geopgraphical representation and gender balance, particularly at higher level posts; 9. Manage resources in an effective, coherent, transparent, responsible, and adaptable manner that reflects the culture of continuous improvement, and further develop the sustainability and resilience of the Court against identified risks; and 10. Building upon a strategy for the completion of situations under investigation.

[381] This innovative instrument of police/legal cooperation is provided for in Art. 20 AP II to the European Convention on Mutual Assistance in Legal Matters (1957) of 2001 (Council of Europe) and Art. 13 of the EU Mutual Assistance Convention of 2000. It is often employed in the investigation of cross-border criminality at the EU level in order to overcome the usual obstacles of traditional interstate cooperation. In the case at hand the JIT had to be based on the CoE AP II since Ukraine is not an EU Member State. See generally Ambos and Rackow, in Ambos and Rackow, *European Criminal Law* (2023), pp. 316–18.

[382] See ICC-OTP, *Statement Khan JIT Ukraine* (April 2022). See also ICC-OTP, *Report 2023* (2023), pp. 81–3; ICC-OTP, *Complementarity and Cooperation* (2024), paras. 102 ff.

[383] This JIT has been set up by Italy, the Netherlands, the UK, Ireland, and Spain and is supported by Europol. The OTP joined on 7 September 2022, see <https://www.icc-cpi.int/news/statement-icc-prosecutor-karim-aa-khan-qc-office-prosecutor-joins-national-authorities-joint-0>.

[384] ICC-OTP, *Interests of Justice* (2007).

[385] ICC-OTP, *Policy Victims' Participation* (2010).

[386] ICC-OTP, *Policy Prelim. Examinations* (2013); on the relevant draft paper, see Ambos and Stegmiller, *Crime Law Soc Change*, 58 (2012), 397–9; see also the OTP's annual reports on Preliminary Examination Activities from 2011, 2012, 2013, and 2014.

[387] ICC-OTP, *Policy Sexual Crimes* (2014); crit. Fowler, *JICL*, 2 (2021), 27–52.

[388] ICC-OTP, *Policy Case Selection* (2016); thereto Ambos, *ILM*, 57 (2018), 1131.

[389] ICC-OTP, *Policy Children* (2016).

[390] ICC-OTP, *Policy Cultural Heritage* (2021).

[391] ICC-OTP, *Situation Completion* (2021).

[392] ICC-OTP, *Policy Gender Persecution* (2022).

[393] ICC-OTP, *Policy Gender-Based Crimes* (2023); see also ICC-OTP, *Report 2023* (2023), p. 33.

[394] ICC-OTP, *Policy Children* (2023); see also ICC-OTP, *Report 2023* (2023), p. 34.

[395] ICC-OTP, *Complementarity and Cooperation* (2024); see also ICC-OTP, *Report 2023* (2023), p. 35.

cases within a situation one after another and selecting them according to their gravity.[396] Subsequently, the Office has been more flexible and, for example in the Kenya proceedings, moved to simultaneous investigations, bringing two cases for prosecution at the same time.[397] Accordingly, the Strategy 2009–2012—albeit adhering to the policy of focused investigations[398]—no longer explicitly contained the sequential approach.

Another shift in strategy was introduced by the Strategic Plan 2012–2015 and confirmed by the subsequent one of 2016–2019. As the evidentiary standards adopted by the (Pre-Trial) Chambers[399] were higher than expected by the OTP, the Office decided to replace the policy of focused investigations by 'the principle of in-depth, open-ended investigations while maintaining focus'.[400] In particular, in situations in which the OTP has limited investigative possibilities, this approach is meant to allow for 'a strategy of gradually building upwards', which means that the OTP will 'first investigate and prosecute a limited number of mid- and high-level perpetrators in order to ultimately have a reasonable chance to convict the most responsible'.[401] Depending on the evidence available, the OTP even considers limiting itself to the prosecution of low-level perpetrators, who have committed particular grave and notorious crimes, instead of initiating proceedings against persons most responsible with dubious prospects of success.[402] Last but not least, the paper on situation completion of 2021 deals with the highly relevant issue of how the Office will complete its work in a given 'situation' (as opposed to a 'case') once an investigation has been opened and how this completion is to be made public.[403] In a nutshell,[404] the paper proposes the following: while the completion of a case depends on its individual merits and 'the exhaustion of legal proceedings', 'there is no pre-determined legal threshold or procedure' with regard to the completion of a situation.[405] In that regard the OTP now introduces the concepts of 'Investigation' and 'Prosecution Phase', with the former determining 'the scope of the Office's caseload' in a given situation and the latter ensuring 'the necessary steps ... to complete the Office's responsibilities' with regard to the 'caseload' in that situation.[406] While there should be no 'artificial separation between investigative and prosecutorial activities' (the prosecution of a given case may start before the termination of the investigation of the overall situation), the 'transition from the Investigation Phase to the Prosecution Phase marks the point at which the Office's resources for a situation will be focused on completion of the defined

[396] ICC-OTP, *Policy Paper* (2003), p. 5; for critique, see HRW, *Selection* (2006), p. 5 ('negative implications for the perception of the prosecutor's impartiality'); Ambos, *Colombian Peace Process* (2010), p. 38.

[397] The case against Ruto, Kosgey, and Sang on the one hand, and the case against Muthaura, Kenyatta, and Hussein Ali on the other.

[398] ICC-OTP, *Prosecutorial Strategy* (2010).

[399] In more detail, see *in fine* Chapter IV, A.(2)(b) in this volume.

[400] ICC-OTP, *Strategic Plan* (2013), paras. 4, 23; also ICC-OTP, *Strategic Plan* (2015), para. 34; see also Mettraux et al., *Expert Initiative Effectiveness ICC* (2014), p. 8 (para. 11), p. 9 (para. 13) (investigations 'more efficient and focused', 'sufficient depth'), also ibid., pp. 51 ff. (paras. 4 ff.).

[401] ICC-OTP, *Strategic Plan* (2013), para. 22; also ICC-OTP, *Strategic Plan* (2015), para. 34.

[402] ICC-OTP, *Strategic Plan* (2013), para. 22 (stating that the required evidentiary standards together with limited investigative possibilities to prove the criminal responsibility of those most responsible 'might force the OTP to change its approach' leading in such cases to a 'strategy of gradually building upwards', including 'prosecuting lower level perpetrators where their conduct has been particularly grave and has acquired extensive notoriety'; adding that this strategy 'will in the end be more cost-effective than having no or failing prosecutions against the highest placed perpetrators').

[403] ICC-OTP, *Situation Completion* (2021), para. 2.

[404] I present a summary of the Executive Summary here, cf. ibid. paras. 5–12 (with an instructive figure 1); for more details see ibid. para. 20 ff. (situation strategy), 31 ff. (conclusion Investigation Phase), 55 ff. (conclusion Prosecution Phase), 99 ff. (conclusion situation activities).

[405] Ibid., para. 5 with n. 7.

[406] Ibid., para. 6.

caseload, as opposed to launching investigations into new cases'.[407] The Investigation Phase is concluded once warrants or summonses pursuant to Article 58 ICCS are granted with regard to those cases that are to be prosecuted, thus defining the 'Prosecutorial Programme' (in turn informed by the 'Situation Strategy').[408] The completion of the Investigation Phase will be publicly announced by the Office so that external stakeholders (especially victims) will better understand the state of play and can manage their expectations.[409] Once this 'Programme' is defined, the resources required for the actual prosecution of the selected cases may become predictable and resources may be transferred to other situations.[410] At any rate, in principle, the allocated resources will now be devoted to the Prosecution Phase which 'aims to conclude' all selected (prosecuted) cases. [411] A situation is (only) completed if both the Investigation and the Prosecution Phases are completed.[412]

While the different OTP documents show that a certain flexibility is useful and even necessary, in order to be able to react to legal or jurisprudential changes,[413] the OTP approach, as approved by the 2016–2018 Strategy,[414] suffers from the lack of a comprehensive, overall strategy.[415] The Strategic Plan 2012–2015, for example, emphasizes the prioritization ('pay particular attention') of sexual and gender-based crimes and crimes against children;[416] the current Strategic Plan 2023–2025 confirms this approach.[417] However, while there is no doubt that these crimes should be investigated thoroughly, neither the Strategic Plans nor the Policy Paper from 2003 nor the Policy Paper on Sexual and Gender-Based Crimes give any reason *why* these crimes should be prioritized instead of others. In other words, the Office fails to provide criteria of prioritization and explain the underlying rationale, if any, of its prioritization policy.[418]

Moreover, the practice of temporary strategies flies in the face of Reg. 14 RegOTP which requires a general and coherent prosecutorial strategy in one master document serving as the overall guidance. This does not mean that there can be no temporary, mid-term strategies which have to be adjusted after several years; yet, such mid-term plans do not make one main document with the overall general or specific goals of a prosecution strategy superfluous. For only such a permanent strategy indicates the general direction for the Office, both for the personnel of the Office and the interested public. It is also more practical to have the overall strategy in one document instead of in various documents which are produced

[407] Ibid., para. 7.
[408] Ibid., para. 8 and definition on p. 32.
[409] Ibid., para. 9.
[410] Ibid., para. 9.
[411] Ibid., para. 11.
[412] Ibid., para. 12.
[413] See also Goldston, *JICJ*, 8 (2010), 403.
[414] ICC-OTP, *Strategic Plan* (2015), paras. 1, 13 ff., arguing that the improved results, esp. in terms of confirmations of charges, demonstrate that the shift in strategy was appropriate and successful.
[415] Crit. alsoHRW, *Business* (2011) pp. 46–7.
[416] ICC-OTP, *Strategic Plan* (2013), paras. 58–63; also ICC-OTP, *Strategic Plan* (2015), para. 37 ('In prioritising investigations, the Office will continue to pay particular attention to prosecuting specific forms of crime. In line with the SGBC [Sexual and Gender Based Crimes] Policy, the Office has committed to focusing in particular on the investigation and prosecution of SGBC'); on the respective 'Gender and Children Unit' see ICC-ASP, *Budget 2025*, para. 351 ff.; also ICC-OTP, *Strategic Plan* (2019), p. 5 (the Office will 'continue to ensure a systematic application of its policies concerning traditionally underreported SGBC and those crimes against or affecting children over which the Rome Statute confers jurisdiction, and evaluate the implementation and effectiveness of these policies in practice').
[417] ICC-OTP, *Strategic Plan* (2023), paras. 58 ff. (Strategic Goal 6), esp. para. 59 ('The Office will prioritize the effective investigation and prosecution of SGBC and CAC crimes').
[418] See e.g. the philosophical justification of the prioritization of sex crimes by deGuzman, *ICLR*, 11 (2011), 515; deGuzman, in Bergsmo, *Thematic Prosecution* (2012), p. 11.

at different times and focus on different topics. Of course, there are also arguments against one master document or even the possibility to elaborate such a document in a meaningful way. The dynamics of international crimes, investigations, and jurisdictional triggers make it difficult if not impossible to formulate a general strategy in a comprehensive and reliable manner without taking recourse to generalities and platitudes. The Court is not the master of its investigations; new crime situations may come up virtually from day to day and may be referred to it by States or the Security Council. Given this volatility of the Court's situation and caseload it seems to be more prudent to elaborate general strategies only for limited time periods.

In any case, only a master document can set out a *leitmotif* from which focused strategies can be developed and on the basis of which periodic reflection can take place.[419] The 2003 Policy Paper (albeit unrestricted in terms of time) cannot fulfil this function: it is too general to serve as meaningful guidance and—more importantly—was at least partly overturned by the last three Strategic Plans.[420] It remains to be seen whether the 'renewed vision' of the current Strategic Plan, already mentioned above,[421] entails a more comprehensive and holistic approach. We will return to selection and prioritization and suggest possible criteria below.[422]

### (6) Professional ethics: The OTP's Code of Conduct

The above-mentioned statutory rules on independence, impartiality, objectivity, and equality are closely linked to questions of ethics, that is, they 'characterize "right conduct" in the exercise of a profession'.[423] In order to establish minimum standards of conduct applicable to all its members, the OTP introduced in 2013 a Code of Conduct[424] which identifies in Rule 8 the following six guiding principles for the work of the Office:

(a) independence of the Office;
(b) professional ethics and integrity;
(c) fair, impartial, effective, and expeditious[425] investigation and prosecution;
(d) respect for confidentiality of investigations and prosecutions;
(e) respect for human rights and fundamental freedoms recognized by international law in conformity with the Statute, and non-discrimination against any individual or groups of individuals; and
(f) a shared culture rooted in the principles and purposes of the Statute, without bias for the rules and methods of any national system.

[419] Ambos and Stegmiller, *Crime Law Soc Change*, 58 (2012), 394.

[420] See the change from the policy of 'focused investigations' to the 'principle of in-depth, open-ended investigations' as described above note 431 and accompanying text in this chapter.

[421] Above note 230 with main text.

[422] See Chapter IV, B.(1) in this volume.

[423] Mégret, in Reydams, Wouters, and Ryngaert, *Prosecutors* (2012), p. 416. On violations of prosecutorial ethics in the Nuremberg Trials, see Sarvarian, *JICJ*, 10 (2012), 423; Oriolo, *ICLR*, 16 (2016), 304.

[424] In detail on previous proposals or drafts for a Code of Conduct, see Heinze, *Disclosure* (2014), pp. 472–6; also Roosevelt, *GeoJLegalEthics*, 24 (2011), 844–8. On ethical standards for OTP lawyers according to ICC case law, see Oriolo, *ICLR*, 16 (2016), 10–15 (criticizing those standards because of their fragmentation and inconsistency [16]–[18] and calling for the judges 'as the "ultimate guardian of a fair and expeditious trial", ... to assess the conduct, good standing and professionalism of the OTP' [19]).

[425] Expeditiousness is particularly important if the accused is in custody; see *Furundžija*, No. IT-95-17/1-PT, para. 5; see also *Prosecutor v. Barayagwiza*, AC Decision, No. ICTR-97-19-AR72, 3 November 1999, para. 92.

These general principles are further specified in the Code's following chapters on standards of conduct, specific duties, working relations, and discipline. To some extent, the Code simply reiterates the general principles and rules enshrined in the ICCS[426] or stresses the OTP's obvious obligation to comply with the ICCS and its supplementary norms.[427] Although the additional benefit of the Code thus seems to be rather limited,[428] it contains at least some concretizations worth mentioning. Rules 45–8 provide useful guidance on the handling of gifts, remunerations, and favours from external sources which help the OTP's members to preserve their independence and to avoid any appearance of bias.[429] The OTP's obligation of impartiality is reinforced by restrictions on the staff's right to freedom of expression[430] and special rules on conflicts of interest which in particular empower the Prosecutor to relieve members of the Office from their duties if they have a personal or financial interest in a particular case.[431] Moreover, the Code deserves credit for emphasizing the OTP's confidentiality obligations[432] and its duties towards suspected and accused persons,[433] the defence,[434] victims, and witnesses.[435] The need for a Code of Conduct has, at any rate, been confirmed by the IER Report 2020 referring to 'distrust and a culture of fear' as well as 'bullying behaviour amounting to harassment … particularly in the OTP'.[436] The question of course is whether there exist internal compliance mechanisms which ensure that such a behaviour will be prevented and, if it nevertheless occurs, adequately sanctioned. This brings us to the issue of accountability.

## (7) Control and review (accountability)

The counterpart of professional ethics is accountability. Mechanisms of answerability and liability, which include the possibility of sanctioning misconduct, are indispensable for the effective enforcement of the numerous obligations of the prosecution, but they must be

426 See e.g. Rules 21, 23 Code of Conduct OTP (on independence), Rule 31 (on impartiality), Rule 49 (1) (on objective truth-seeking), or Rule 72 (on offences and misconduct that are likely to harm the administration of justice).

427 See e.g. generally Rule 7 Code of Conduct OTP as well as Rule 30 (on the presumption of innocence and disclosure) and Rule 34 (on confidentiality).

428 See also Heinze, *Disclosure* (2014), p. 471 ('basically a reference to the Staff Rules of the ICC'); Oriolo, *ICLR*, 16 (2016), 4 ('more comprehensive set of ethical standards' which, however, 'does not fully meet the current needs to balance the powers and faculties of the ICC Prosecutor in compliance with fair trial principles, the credibility of the Court and the sound administration of justice'). Less crit. Mégret, in Reydams, Wouters, and Ryngaert, *Prosecutors* (2012), p. 433, who regards the reiteration of the OTP's duty to respect rules as a useful affirmation.

429 In a similar vein, but less detailed, Reg. 1.2 (k)–(l) Staff Regulations; Rule 101.5 Staff Rules.

430 Rule 30 (b) Code of Conduct OTP. In light of these rules, the implicit comparison between Al Bashir and Hitler drawn by the former Prosecutor Moreno-Ocampo, and his implication that the PTC had already found Al Bashir guilty of the alleged crimes (see Moreno-Ocampo, *The Guardian* (15 July 2010)), constitutes a breach of professional ethics; also crit., Markovic, *TexILJ*, 47 (2011–2012), 230; Mégret, in Reydams, Wouters, and Ryngaert, *Prosecutors* (2012), p. 438; McDermott, 'Article 42', in Klamberg et al., *Commentary ICC I* (2023), p. 995. On possible infringements on the presumption of innocence through extra-judicial comments by OTP members, see also *Sesay*, No. SCSL-04-15-CCC32, para. 32; *Prosecutor v. Taylor*, TC II Decision on Motion for Disclosure of Evidence Underlying Prejudicial Statements Made by the Chief Prosecutor, Mr Stephen Rapp, No. SCSL-03-1-T, 6 February 2009, para. 30; *Lubanga*, No. ICC-01/04-01/06-2433, para. 51.

431 Rules 42–4 Code of Conduct OTP. In a similar vein, but less detailed, Rule 101.6 Staff Rules.

432 Rules 32–6 Code of Conduct OTP. See also Mégret, in Reydams, Wouters, and Ryngaert, *Prosecutors* (2012), pp. 446–7. In a similar vein, Regulation 1.2 (j) Staff Regulations; Rule 101.4 Staff Rules.

433 Rule 69 Code of Conduct OTP.

434 Rule 70 Code of Conduct OTP.

435 Rules 66–8 Code of Conduct OTP.

436 Expert Group, *IER* (2020), p. 45 para. 138; generally on workplace culture, see ICC-OTP, *Report 2023* (2023), pp. 99 ff.

carefully balanced against its autonomy and independence.[437] As a consequence, it is first and foremost the Prosecutor himself[438] who has to ensure that the OTP staff respects legal rules and principles of good professional practice.[439] In this vein, every staff member has to report to the supervisor or directly to the Prosecutor if they have reason to believe that a departure from these standards has occurred or is about to occur.[440] Based on this information, the Prosecutor may initiate disciplinary proceedings[441] and, if appropriate, sanction 'unsatisfactory conduct',[442] inter alia, with written censure, fine, demotion, or—in the case of serious misconduct—summary dismissal.[443] Notably, appeals against disciplinary decisions of the Prosecutor are dealt with by the Administrative Tribunal of the ILO,[444] which means that an external body participates in the OTP accountability procedure.[445]

Similar mechanisms apply in cases of possible bias. OTP staff members shall request to be excused from any matter in which their impartiality might reasonably be doubted, in particular because they have previously been involved in any capacity in that case before the Court or in a related criminal case at the national level involving the person being investigated or prosecuted.[446] In addition, they must disclose any personal or financial interest they may have in a given case to the Head of their Division or to the Prosecutor, who then decides how to proceed.[447] Failure to comply with these reporting obligations constitutes unsatisfactory conduct and thus may lead to disciplinary sanctions.

The Office internal disciplinary mechanisms are of no avail if the Prosecutor themselves, being the holder of the disciplinary powers, is suspected of misconduct. Although they may decide of their own volition to resign in face of the allegation (and thus to avert damage to the standing of the Office and the Court as a whole),[448] they cannot reasonably be expected to discipline themselves.[449] While the ad hoc tribunals could only treat prosecutorial

[437] On the tension between accountability and independence, see also Danner, *AJIL*, 97 (2003), 524; Mégret, in Reydams, Wouters, and Ryngaert, *Prosecutors* (2012), p. 418; Turner, in Stahn, *ICC* (2015), p. 382; see also the comparative analysis of various national control and accountability mechanisms by Ambos, *EJCCLCJ*, 8 (2000), 95–8, 101–13, 115, 116; on models of accountability, see also Stahn, in Stahn and Sluiter, *Practice* (2009), p. 259 ff., distinguishing between political accountability, process-based checks and balances, (self-) regulation, and judicial review.

[438] On external, civil society control (by NGOs), see Stahn, in Stahn and Sluiter, *Practice* (2009), p. 261; on informal sanctions/control mechanisms, see Turner, in Stahn, *ICC* (2015), pp. 402–4.

[439] Mégret, in Reydams, Wouters, and Ryngaert, *Prosecutors* (2012), p. 457; see also Markovic, *TexILJ*, 47 (2011–2012), 206; Turner, *NYUJIL&Pol'y*, 45 (2012), 256; Turner, in Stahn, *ICC* (2015), pp. 386–7; Olásolo et al., *Role of the IOM* (August 2011), p. 65. The Prosecutor, however, must delegate his or her disciplinary powers if s/he has a personal interest in the case, see *Mr C.P. v. ICC*, Judgment No. 2757 of the ILO Administrative Tribunal, 9 July 2008, para. 19.

[440] Rule 12 Code of Conduct OTP.

[441] Rule 75 Code of Conduct OTP, Chapter X Staff Rules.

[442] Rule 110.1 Staff Rules defines unsatisfactory conduct as '[f]ailure by a staff member to act in accordance with any official document of the Court governing rights and obligations of staff members, such as the Staff Regulations and Rules and the Financial Regulations and Rules, or any relevant resolutions and decisions of the Assembly of States Parties, or failure to observe the standards of conduct expected of an international civil servant'. Rule 74 Code of Conduct OTP clarifies that any conduct incompatible with the standards set forth in the Code is considered unsatisfactory.

[443] Rules 110.6, 110.7 Staff Rules.

[444] Rule 111.5 Staff Rules.

[445] Mégret, in Reydams, Wouters, and Ryngaert, *Prosecutors* (2012), p. 463. See e.g. on the unlawful dismissal of a media relations officer of the OTP who has accused the former Prosecutor Moreno-Ocampo of serious misconduct by committing sexual crimes, *Mr C.P. v. ICC*, Judgment No. 2757, 9 July 2008; on the removal of the senior trial lawyer from the *Lubanga Case*, see *Mr. E. W. v. ICC*, Judgment No. 3079, 8 February 2012.

[446] Art. 42 (7) ICCS; Rule 31 Code of Conduct OTP. Crit. thereof, Jones, 'Office', in Cassese et al., *Rome Statute I* (2002), p. 274 who deems Art. 42 (7) ICCS to be too strict.

[447] Rules 42–3 Code of Conduct OTP.

[448] See also Rule 37 RPE ICC; Mégret, in Reydams, Wouters, and Ryngaert, *Prosecutors* (2012), pp. 458–9

[449] Mégret, in Reydams, Wouters, and Ryngaert, *Prosecutors* (2012), p. 479; Heinze, *Disclosure* (2014), p. 469.

malpractice as misconduct of counsel[450] or contempt of the tribunal,[451] the ICCS fills this lacuna with a special disciplinary proceeding applicable to all high-ranking Court officials including the Prosecutor and the Deputy Prosecutors.[452] This accountability mechanism corresponds largely to that for disciplining judges,[453] the main difference being that the decision to sanction a Prosecutor's misconduct of a less serious nature[454] is taken by an absolute majority of the Bureau of the ASP.[455] In case of a Deputy Prosecutor, it is the Prosecutor who decides on whether to give a reprimand, while pecuniary sanctions are imposed by the Bureau of the ASP, but only upon recommendation of the Prosecutor.[456] This stresses the administrative authority of the Prosecutor and their primary responsibility for holding OTP members accountable.

In addition, the Prosecutor and the Deputy Prosecutor are subject to a similar disqualification system as the judges. They are obliged to disclose any ground that casts doubts on their impartiality[457] and ask, where appropriate, to be excused from their functions.[458] This duty is backed up by the right of the person being investigated or prosecuted to challenge the impartiality of the heads of the OTP and request their disqualification.[459] Such forced withdrawals must be ordered by the AC.[460] The equal treatment of judges, the Prosecutor, and Deputy Prosecutors in disqualification matters confirms the latter's role as impartial ministries of justice.[461] Given their mandate to investigate and prosecute international crimes, however, the impartiality requirements of the Prosecutors might be somewhat more flexible than those of the judges. In any case, Prosecutors, as well as judges,[462] benefit from a presumption that they exercise their functions correctly,[463] which includes a 'presumption of impartiality' which must be rebutted with clear evidence for malpractice.[464] Generally, it will be easier for defendants to challenge the Prosecutor's impartiality on objective grounds, for example, his or her family relationship with a party, rather than on breaches of professional ethics, including the duty to investigate both incriminating and exonerating circumstances.[465] Neither the Statute nor the Rules spell out the exact consequences of an excusal

[450] Rule 46 RPE ICTY/ICTR, 47 RPE MICT and Rule 63 RPE KSC. See e.g. *Prosecutor v. Niyitegeka*, TC I Decision on two Defence Motions Pursuant to, inter alia, Rule 5 of the Rules and the Prosecutor's Motion for Extension of Time to File the Modified Amended Indictment pursuant to the Trial Chamber II Order of 20 November 2000, No. ICTR-96-14-T, 27 February 2001, para. 37.

[451] Rule 77 RPE ICTY/ICTR and Rule 90 RPE MCT. At the KSC contempt is only addressed by way of a reference in Arts. 15 (2) and 16 (3) KSC Law to the Kosovo CC. See also Mégret, in Reydams, Wouters, and Ryngaert, *Prosecutors* (2012), p. 479. See also the conviction of Florence Hartman, a former spokesperson of the ICTY Prosecutor, for contempt of court by disclosing confidential information, AC *In the Case against Hartmann*, Judgment, No. IT-02-54-R55.5-A, 19 July 2011.

[452] cf. Art. 47 ICCS, Rules 23 ff. RPE ICC. See also Section A.(5) in this chapter.

[453] See Section A.(5) in this chapter.

[454] See Rule 25 RPE ICC.

[455] Rule 30 (2) RPE ICC.

[456] Rule 30 (3) RPE ICC. See, in more detail, Heinze, *Disclosure* (2014), pp. 465–6.

[457] See the non-exhaustive lists in Art. 42 (7) ICCS and Rule 34 (1) RPE ICC; cf. also McDermott, 'Article 42', in Klamberg et al., *Commentary ICC I* (2023), p. 995.

[458] Art. 42 (6) ICCS, Rule 35 RPE ICC.

[459] See also Bassiouni, *Introduction to ICL* (2013), p. 706.

[460] Art. 42 (8) ICCS. See also PTC II, *Situation in Kenya*, Decision on the Application for Leave to Participate under Arts. 58, 42 (5), (7)–(8)(a) of the Rome Statute and Rule 34 (1)(d) and (2) of the Rules of Procedure and Evidence, No. ICC-01/09-47, 18 February 2011, para. 8.

[461] Schabas, *ICC Commentary* (2016), p. 746.

[462] With regard to judges, see Section A.(5) in this chapter.

[463] *Delalić et al.*, No. IT-96-21-A, para. 611; Mégret, in Reydams, Wouters, and Ryngaert, *Prosecutors* (2012), p. 452.

[464] Côté, in Reydams, Wouters, and Ryngaert, *Prosecutors* (2012), p. 365; see also *Bizimungu et al.*, No. ICTR-2000-56-T, para. 26; Tochilovsky, *Jurisprudence* (2014), pp. 470–1.

[465] See also Côté, in Reydams, Wouters, and Ryngaert, *Prosecutors* (2012), p. 366.

or disqualification. This leaves crucial questions unanswered, since, unlike judges, the Prosecutor cannot fully withdraw from a case, as they still bear the overall responsibility for the prosecutorial strategy and thus are factually involved in any investigation and prosecution.[466] It is therefore, arguably, sufficient if the biased Prosecutor refrains from presenting the respective case in court and from giving detail instructions to the trial attorneys.

As the most radical disciplinary measure, Article 46 ICCS empowers the ASP to remove the Prosecutor or the Deputy Prosecutors from office if they have committed a serious misconduct (which requires more than mere 'unsatisfactory conduct')[467] or are unable to exercise the functions required by the ICCS.[468] Here again, judges, Prosecutor, and Deputy Prosecutors are put on an equal footing, although the removal of the latter merely requires an absolute majority of the State Parties and not—as in the case of judges—a two-thirds majority.[469] Nevertheless, Article 46 ICCS establishes a high threshold for removals from office which underlines the independence of the OTP leadership from the Member States and the ASP.[470]

Besides those disciplinary structures, the OTP operates under the supervision of the same oversight mechanisms as all other organs of the ICC.[471] Here it suffices to say that the Independent Oversight Mechanism (IOM) also has the authority to deal with possible unlawful acts of all OTP members, including the Prosecutor and the Deputy Prosecutors.[472]

Another form of ensuring accountability results from the already mentioned supervisory powers of the Chambers.[473] The decision whether or not to authorize *proprio motu* investigations,[474] to issue arrest warrants and summonses to appear,[475] to confirm a charge,[476] or a decision not to proceed[477] includes, to a certain degree, a control of prosecutorial discretion and good practices.[478] The Chambers may also resort to 'soft measures' and communicate their concerns on certain prosecutorial practices to the parties[479] or use interlocutory decisions to clarify the obligations of the OTP.[480] The most important judicial accountability instrument, however, is the granting of remedies to the defendant.[481] Possible reactions to

466 Jones, in Cassese et al., *Rome Statute I* (2002), p. 274; see also Schabas, *ICC Commentary* (2016), p. 747.

467 Thereto Rule 110.1 Staff Rules, Rule 74 Code of Conduct OTP, also Markovic, *TexILJ*, 47 (2011–2012), 207.

468 On the disciplinary proceedings against the former Prosecutor Moreno-Ocampo concerning alleged sexual offences, see *Mr C.P. v. ICC*, Judgment No. 2757, paras. 3–4. The complaint made by an OTP staff member, who was not the alleged victim of the crime, was dismissed as manifestly unfounded.

469 Crit. of these divergent standards, Kreß, in Grützner, Pötz, and Kreß, *Internationaler Rechtshilfeverkehr in Strafsachen* (2003), Part IV A 1 mn. 86.

470 cf. also Turner, in Stahn, *ICC* (2015), pp. 395–6.

471 The Office of the Internal Audit, the External Auditor, the Audit Committee, the Committee on Budget and Finance and the Independent Oversight Mechanism (IOM); on those oversight mechanisms, see the analysis in Section A.(5) of this chapter.

472 Res. ICC-ASP/12/Res. 6, Independent Oversight Mechanism, Annex, para. 28. On possible conflicts between the mandate of the IOM and the OTP's independence, see Olásolo et al., *Role of the IOM* (August 2011), pp. 70–6; Turner, *NYUJIL&Pol'y*, 45 (2012), 243–4; Turner, in Stahn, *ICC* (2015), pp. 397–400.

473 See above note 152 and accompanying text in this chapter. For a comparative perspective, see Ambos, *EJCCLCJ*, 8 (2000), 116.

474 Art. 15 ICCS.

475 Art. 58 ICCS.

476 Art. 61 (7) ICCS.

477 Art. 53 (3) ICCS.

478 Mégret, in Reydams, Wouters, and Ryngaert, *Prosecutors* (2012), pp. 429, 469–70; in a similar vein, Takemura, in van den Herik and Stahn, *Diversification* (2012), p. 653; on the dismissal of individual counts to cure indictment defects, see Turner, *NYUJIL&Pol'y*, 45 (2012), 225–8.

479 See e.g. *Lubanga*, No. ICC-01/04-01/06-2517-Red, para. 21; also *Furundžija*, No. IT-95-17/1-PT, para. 2. The *Furundžija* TC went a step further by issuing a formal complaint against the prosecution and in doing so arguably exceeded its competence; in more detail, Mégret, in Reydams, Wouters, and Ryngaert, *Prosecutors* (2012), p. 473; also Turner, *NYUJIL&Pol'y*, 45 (2012), 228–30; Turner, in Stahn, *ICC* (2015), p. 392.

480 See Mégret, in Reydams, Wouters, and Ryngaert, *Prosecutors* (2012), p. 471.

481 See generally Chapter VI, D.(1) in this volume.

prosecutorial misconduct are exclusion of evidence,[482] order of a stay of proceedings because of an abuse of process,[483] reduction of sentence,[484] order of retrial,[485] or imposition of sanctions for misconduct before the Court.[486] We will return to these forms of judicial review in Chapter IV.[487] At any rate, in this context too, the criticism and recommendation of the IER Report levelled at the IOM, mentioned above,[488] are to be taken seriously.

## C. Defence counsel

### (1) Right to counsel

#### *(a) Introduction*

The overarching right to defence, perhaps the most fundamental element of a fair trial, already discussed in Chapter I,[489] belongs to the defendant who needs to be assisted by counsel.[490] Indeed, the right to counsel is fundamental for the effective realization of the defence and thus the fair trial principle.[491] It is the starting point for an efficient defence since consultation with a specialist is indispensable to develop an efficient defence strategy. The right to counsel becomes even more important before international criminal tribunals where the accused is confronted with a unique procedural law in a wholly unfamiliar setting, often accompanied by linguistic and cultural obstacles.[492] In practical terms, the defence counsel will operate here as the adverse party to the Prosecutor, mainly because of the adversarial, party-driven collection and presentation of evidence.[493]

#### *(b) Legal framework and scope of protection*

The ICCS and the RPE ICC regulate the position of defence counsel only in a rudimentary fashion. They are supplemented by the more detailed Regulations of the Court,[494] the

[482] In more detail, Chapter V, A.(8) in this volume.
[483] See Ambos, *Treatise ICL I* (2021), pp. 559–62.
[484] See Ambos, *Treatise ICL II* (2021), p. 408; also Turner, *NYUJIL&Pol'y*, 45 (2012), 217–24.
[485] See Art. 84 ICCS. In more detail, Mégret, in Reydams, Wouters, and Ryngaert, *Prosecutors* (2012), p. 473 and Chapter VI, C. in this volume; see also Heinze, *Disclosure* (2014), pp. 452, 473–7; for an elaborate analysis of the relevant case law, see Turner, *NYUJIL&Pol'y*, 45 (2012), 185–204; Turner, in Stahn, *ICC* (2015), pp. 388–94, stressing, however, that 'case-determinative remedies inflict serious costs on other objectives of interational criminal justice, including the Court's primary goal of preventing impunity' (p. 386).
[486] Art. 71 ICCS. In more detail, Turner, *NYUJIL&Pol'y*, 45 (2012), 234–7; see also *Lubanga*, No. ICC-01/04-01/06-2582, para. 56; de Meester et al., in Sluiter et al., *International Criminal Procedure* (2013), pp. 378–9.
[487] See esp. Chapter IV, B.(3) in this volume.
[488] Above notes 151 ff. with accompanying text in this chapter.
[489] See Chapter I, D.(3)(d) and (e) in this volume.
[490] Arguably, defendant and counsel comprise together the 'defence'; cf. Safferling and Hartwig, *International Criminal Procedure* (2012), pp. 179–80; Zahar and Sluiter, *ICL* (2008), p. 64.
[491] Knoops, in Rohan and Zyberi, *Defense Perspectives* (2017), p. 40; Gallant and Kirsch, in Bohlander, Boed, and Wilson, *Defense in International Criminal Proceedings* (2006), p. 446 ('cornerstone of fair criminal justice'); Boas et al., *International Criminal Procedure* (2011), pp. 137–9; Tuinstra, *Defence Counsel* (2009), p. 13 ff.; Keita et al., 'Article 67', in Fernandez et al., *Statut II* (2019), pp. 1842–3. On the principle of equality of arms as an important tool to advance the interests of the defence, Fedorova, in Rohan and Zyberi, *Defense Perspectives* (2017), pp. 204 ff.
[492] On the efficiency of the legal representation in international criminal proceedings, and Buisman, Gumpert, and Hallers, *ICLR*, 5 (2005), 1 ff. On the challenges of defence counsel in international criminal trials, see Gibson, in Romano et al., *OxfHB IntAdjudication* (2014), pp. 693 ff., 705 ff.
[493] cf. Chapter V, A.(1) and (3)(a) in this volume. On the role of defence counsel at the trial stage, see Karnavas, in Rohan and Zyberi, *Defense Perspectives* (2017), pp. 277 ff.
[494] RegC, 26 May 2004, last amendment 12 November 2018 (ICC-BD/01-05-16).

Regulations of the Registry,[495] and the Code of Professional Conduct for Counsel.[496] From the relevant provisions derive three separate rights which, in fact, are based on the already analysed right to a full and effective defence,[497] that is, the right to counsel of accused's own choosing,[498] the right to free legal assistance, and the right to self-representation. This latter right will be analysed in connection with the position of the defendant.[499]

The accused is entitled 'to conduct the defence in person or through legal assistance of the accused's choosing' and, in the absence of legal assistance, 'to be informed ... of this right and to have legal assistance assigned by the Court in any case where the interests of justice so require, and without payment if the accused lacks sufficient means to pay for it'.[500] The right to counsel already applies at the investigation stage, that is, 'where there are grounds to believe that a person has committed a crime within the jurisdiction of the Court and that person is about to be questioned either by the Prosecutor, or by national authorities'.[501] Once a suspect is arrested they may request (from the PTC) the appointment of counsel[502] and are entitled to 'fully' communicate with him/her.[503] The defence acquires *all* procedural rights at latest from the moment of the first appearance.[504] A counsel may also be appointed by the PTC in relation to a unique investigative opportunity.[505]

It is unclear, however, at what exact *point in time* during the investigation the right to counsel applies.[506] According to the relevant provisions the right is granted to a person against whom 'there are grounds to believe' that she 'has committed a crime' or who is 'accused' of such a crime.[507] Yet, the ICCS does not determine when a person is considered to be 'accused'.[508] The systematic position of Article 67—in Part 6 of the ICCS covering the trial phase—seems to suggest that a suspect turns into an 'accused' only after the confirmation of the charges,[509] that is, at the end of the intermediate phase of the proceedings,

[495] RegR, 6 March 2006, last amendment 4 December 2013 (ICC-BD/03-03-13).

[496] On the Code of Professional Conduct for Counsel, Res. ICC-ASP/4/Res.1, 2 December 2005, see Section C.(2)(b) in this chapter.

[497] cf. Chapter I, D.(3)(e) in this volume.

[498] On the right to a defence counsel, either chosen by the accused or assigned by the Court, see Tochilovsky, *Jurisprudence* (2014), pp. 389 ff.; Tuinstra, *Defence Counsel* (2009), pp. 13 ff.; Keita et al., 'Article 67', in Fernandez et al., *Statut II* (2019), pp. 1831 ff.; Safferling and Hartwig, *International Criminal Procedure* (2012), pp. 179 ff.; Pérez-León-Acevedo and Elberling, 'Article 67', in Klamberg et al., *Commentary ICC II* (2023), pp. 277–81; before the ICTR, Niang, *CLF*, 13 (2002), 323 ff.; Meisenberg, in Decaux, Dieng, and Sow, *Human Rights* (2007), pp. 125 ff.

[499] Section D.(3) in this chapter.

[500] Art. 67 (1)(d) ICCS; cf. also Arts. 21 (4)(d) ICTYS, 20 (4)(d) ICTRS and 19 (4)(d) IRMCTS; Pérez-León-Acevedo and Elberling, 'Article 67', in Klamberg et al., *Commentary ICC II* (2023), pp. 277–81.

[501] Art. 55 (2)(c) ICCS; cf. thereon Hall and Jacobs, 'Article 55', in Ambos, *Commentary* (2022), mn. 13 ff.; Pérez-León-Acevedo and Elberling, 'Article 55', in Klamberg et al., *Commentary ICC II* (2023), pp. 62–5.

[502] Rule 117 (2) RPE ICC. There is no ICC case law but the ICTR has held that a failure to provide legal assistance during detention amounts to a serious human rights violation, cf. ICTR, *Prosecutor v. Rwamakuba*, Decision on Appropriate Remedy, No. ICTR-98-44C-T, 31 January 2007, para. 17.

[503] Reg. 97 (1) RegC.

[504] ICC, *Chambers Practice Manual* (2016), p. 8. On the first (or initial) appearance, see Chapter IV, A.(2)(a)(iv) and (2)(b)(ii) in this volume.

[505] Art. 56 (1)(b) and (2)(d) ICCS. See also *Situation in the DRC*, PTC I Decision on the Prosecutor's Request for Measures under Art. 56, No. ICC-01/04-21, 26 April 2005, p. 4; Safferling, *Criminal Procedure* (2012), pp. 255–7.

[506] On the different standards in domestic and international jurisdictions, see Skilbeck, *JICJ*, 8 (2010), 453–5.

[507] See Art. 55 (2) vs. Art. 67 ICCS.

[508] See also Gallant and Kirsch, in Bohlander, Boed, and Wilson, *Defense in International Criminal Proceedings* (2006), p. 449; on the terms 'suspect' and 'accused', see Friman, in Cryer et al., *ICL* (2019), p. 412; Safferling, *Criminal Procedure* (2012), p. 185; Hall, Ntanda Nsereko, and Ventura, 'Article 19', in Ambos, *Commentary* (2022), mn. 31 ff.; on 'suspect', see Tochilovsky, *Jurisprudence* (2014), pp. 715–16; Hall and Jacobs, 'Article 55', in Ambos, *Commentary* (2022), mn. 10.

[509] Art. 61 ICCS. In this vein, the *Lubanga* PTC, during the confirmation proceedings, ordered 'the Registrar to draft an explanatory note ... to inform the public that the status of Mr Thomas Lubanga Dyilo ... is a suspect, not

situated between the investigation and the trial.[510] This restrictive interpretation, however, is unconvincing for basically three reasons.

First, it cannot be reconciled with the situation under the human rights regime according to which the fair trial rights already apply during the pre-trial phase of the proceedings.[511] Secondly, the wording of Article 67 (1) ICCS—'in the determination of any charge', '*examen des charges*', '*determinación de cualquier cargo*'—speaks in favour of a broad interpretation.[512] The process of determining or examining the charges is not limited to the actual confirmation hearing but starts with the individualization of responsibility, that is, with the linking of certain persons to the crimes in question by the prosecution.[513] More concretely, the PTC must examine the charges when called to decide upon the issuance of an arrest warrant or summons to appear.[514] This is confirmed by Article 55 (2)(c) ICCS which triggers the right to counsel if 'there are grounds to believe' that a crime has been committed, that is, during the investigation.[515] Last but not least, a restrictive interpretation is inconsistent with Rule 121 (1) RPE ICC which already grants the Article 67 rights at the moment of the first appearance before the PTC.[516] Indeed, the PTC has to make sure that the person is aware of their rights.[517]

In any case, the application of the right to counsel should not depend on a formal definition, be it suspect or accused, but on the substantive question of whether and when individual rights are at stake. This is the case when effective investigative measures are carried out against a person since these measures affect individual rights and normally determine the outcome of the proceedings.[518]

Of course, the right to counsel also extends to the appeals stage of criminal proceedings and to the subsequent phase of enforcement of sentences, relocation, and release.[519]

an accused person' (*Prosecutor v. Lubanga*, PTC I Transcript, No. ICC-01/04-01/06-T-32-EN, 10 November 2006, p. 36, lines 15–22); conc. Friman, in Cryer et al., *ICL* (2019), p. 412; Hall, Ntanda Nsereko, and Ventura, 'Article 19', in Ambos, *Commentary* (2022), mn. 33 ('A suspect only becomes an accused upon the charges being confirmed'); in the same vein, Klamberg, 'Article 58', in Klamberg et al., *Commentary ICC II* (2023), p. 95; in favour of a broader reading, Hall and Ryngaert, 'Article 58', in Ambos, *Commentary* (2022), mn. 5 with n. 28, arguing that 'there are a number of earlier stages in the proceedings at which a person could become an accused'.

510 On the structure of the proceedings, see, in more detail, Chapter IV, A.(2) in this volume.

511 cf. Chapter I, D.(2)(d) in this volume. In a similar vein, Pérez-Leó-Acevedo and Elberling, 'Article 67', in Klamberg et al., *Commentary ICC II* (2023), p. 249 ('by virtue of article 21(3) ... applicable law shall be consistent with internationally recognised human rights and, thus, the broad concept of fair trial should embrace the judicial process in its entirety'), 250. On the role of defence counsel during pre-trial, inter alia, to ensure that a fair trial is granted already at this early stage, see Dieckmann and O'Leary, in Rohan and Zyberi, *Defense Perspectives* (2017), pp. 237 ff.

512 See also Schabas and McDermott, 'Article 67', in Ambos, *Commentary* (2022), mn. 8.

513 Schabas and McDermott, 'Article 67', in Ambos, *Commentary* (2022), mn. 8.

514 cf. Art. 58 (1)(a) ICCS and Gallant and Kirsch, in Bohlander, Boed, and Wilson, *Defense in International Criminal Proceedings* (2006), p. 450.

515 See also the explicit reference to the investigation in the title of Art. 55 ICCS; see Chapter I, D.(2)(d) in this volume.

516 Rule 121 (1) grants these rights to 'a person subject to a warrant of arrest or a summons to appear under article 58', i.e. to everyone appearing before the Court; see also Gallant and Kirsch, in Bohlander, Boed, and Wilson, *Defense in International Criminal Proceedings* (2006), p. 452; Pérez-León-Acevedo and Elberling, 'Article 67', in Klamberg et al., *Commentary ICC II* (2023), pp. 249–50.

517 Art. 60 (1) ICCS.

518 See Chapter I, D.(2)(d) in this volume.

519 For a detailed comparative analysis of the role of defence counsel on appeal at the ICTY, ICTR, and ICC, see Rohan and Ackerman, in Rohan and Zyberi, *Defense Perspectives* (2017), pp. 312 ff. For a defence perspective on post-conviction issues, esp. the relocation of released and acquitted, see Lecolle, *JICJ*, 21 (2023), 167 ff. On the role of defence in the context of the enforcement of sentences, see Petrov and Radisavljević, in Rohan and Zyberi, *Defense Perspectives* (2017), pp. 347 ff.

### *(c) Free choice of counsel*

The accused is entitled to freely choose legal assistance.[520] While this is an absolute right,[521] a counsel has, of course, to meet certain minimum qualifications[522] in order to ensure, at least theoretically, the high quality of legal representation before the Court.[523] Accordingly, the counsel shall have 'established competence in international or criminal law and procedure' pursuant to some practical experience in criminal proceedings[524] of 'at least ten years'.[525] Further, counsel must have language proficiency in one of the working languages of the Court (English or French)[526] and 'should not have been convicted of a serious criminal or disciplinary offence'.[527]

The counsel must be included in the list of counsel[528] maintained by the Registry.[529] The accused is, however, not limited to the list. They may also call another counsel 'who meets the required criteria and is willing to be included in the list'.[530] In this case, the counsel 'shall file a power of attorney with the Registrar'.[531] The right to free choice of counsel also applies to the person who is entitled to legal assistance (on that *infra* d)).[532]

Ultimately, if there is no other counsel available, the Registrar may appoint a *duty counsel*.[533] A 'duty counsel' is a lawyer who may be assigned to the accused to assist him in the

[520] Arts. 55 (2)(c), 67 (1)(d) ICCS. See also Arts. 21 (4)(c), 41 (4)(b) KSC Law.

[521] cf. Elberling, *Defendant in International Criminal Proceedings* (2012), pp. 82–3 ('absolute right'); *contra*, *Prosecutor v. Lubanga*, No. ICC-01/04-01/06-937, Presidency Decision on the 'Demande urgente en vertu de la Règle 21–3 du Règlement de procédure et de preuves' and on the 'Urgent Request for the Appointment of a Duty Counsel', 29 June 2007, para. 25, with further case law references in n. 2 ('this right is not absolute and is necessarily subject to certain limitations'); in the same vein, Keita et al., 'Article 67', in Fernandez et al., *Statut II* (2019), pp. 1840–42 ('ce droit n'est pas absolu et est nécessairement soumis à certaines limitations').

[522] On the qualifications in more detail, see Tuinstra, *Defence Counsel* (2009), pp. 40 ff.; see also Schabas and McDermott, 'Article 67', in Ambos, *Commentary* (2022), mn. 30, pointing out the difference between the criteria adopted by the ICC (focusing on substance) and the ad hoc tribunals (focusing on form); Gut, Kirsch, Mundis, and Taylor, in Sluiter et al., *International Criminal Procedure* (2013), pp. 1272 ff.; Dive, in Lee, *ICC* (2001), p. 284; Keita et al., 'Article 67', in Fernandez et al., *Statut II* (2019), p. 1866; Pérez-León-Acevedo and Elberling, 'Article 67', in Klamberg et al., *Commentary ICC II* (2023), pp. 277–81; Hall and Jacobs, 'Article 55', in Ambos, *Commentary* (2022), mn. 14 (arguing that the counsel's competence is 'an inherent requirement of the right to assigned counsel').

[523] cf. the ICC information sheet on the defence, stressing that '[a]ll members of the defence team have to meet certain qualifications to ensure that they can assist the defendant effectively and efficiently at the highest international standards'.

[524] cf. Rule 22 (1) RPE ICC.

[525] Reg. 67 (1) RegC: 'at least ten years for lead counsel and at least eight years for associate counsel'. See also KSC Directive on Counsel, sect. 5 (b): 'At least ten (10) years, and for purposes of acting as Co-Counsel at least seven (7) years, of proven relevant experience whether as a lawyer for defence or victims, as a prosecutor, a judge or in a comparable capacity in criminal proceedings.' For a comparative analysis of the requirements concerning defence counsels' practical experience as well as other qualifications in different international criminal courts and tribunals, esp. at the ICTY and ICTR, see Gibson, in Romano *et al.*, *OxfHB IntAdjudication* (2014), pp. 695 ff.

[526] cf. Rule 22 (1) RPE ICC ('excellent knowledge' and 'fluent'); see also Dive, in Lee, *ICC* (2001), p. 284 ('knowledge of languages . . . absolute condition'). See also KSC Directive on Counsel, sect. 5 (e): 'Written and oral proficiency in one of the official languages of the Specialist Chambers', i.e. Albanian, Serbian, or English.

[527] Reg. 67 (2) RegC. In the same vein, also KSC Directive on Counsel, sect. 5 (f).

[528] The current 'List of Counsel before the ICC' is available at <https://www.icc-cpi.int/sites/default/files/2023-06/list-of-counsel-eng.pdf>. On the criteria to be met to be included in the List and on the appointment, see Raimondo, *ICLR*, 16 (2016), 946 ff.

[529] Rule 21 (2) RPE ICC, Reg. 122 RegR and Reg. 69–72 RegC; Art. 34 (7) KSC Law and KSC Directive on Counsel, sects. 6, 7. Advocating a 'proactive attitude' of the Registry 'towards vetting the quality and effectiveness of counsel', Mettraux et al., *Expert Initiative Effectiveness ICC* (2014), p. 8 (para. 11), pp. 33–4, 35 (paras. 151–2, 158, 164), and pp. 207 ff.

[530] Rule 21 (2) RPE ICC.

[531] Rule 22 (2) RPE ICC.

[532] cf. Reg. 75 RegC. For a different view (before the adoption of the RegC), Schabas, *ICC Commentary* (2016), p. 1039 ('no right to choice of counsel when a defendant relies upon legal aid'). At the KSC, when a person does not have sufficient means to retain counsel, the Registrar takes into consideration the preferences expressed by the suspect or accused, cf. Reg. 20 (2) KSC Legal Aid Regulations.

[533] cf. Reg. 73 RegC. See also KSC Directive on Counsel, sect. 2 (2) and 17.

initial phase of the proceedings pending the appointment of counsel.[534] At the ICC, a duty counsel may also be appointed 'to represent the interests of the defence' in general.[535] Although appointed by the Registrar, the existence of a duty counsel corresponds with the concept of free choice of counsel, since the Registrar 'shall take into account the wishes of the person, the expertise of duty counsel, the geographical proximity of, and the languages spoken by, the counsel'.[536] In practice, the defendant is asked to 'provide the Registry with a prioritised list of persons by whom he would like to be represented',[537] but the Registrar takes the final decision.[538]

### *(d) Free legal assistance—legal aid*

While the remuneration of a counsel should be covered, as a rule, by the defendant, this is not the case if they 'lack[] sufficient means'.[539] Of course, the applicant has to provide all the necessary information to prove their indigence.[540] The Registrar shall determine whether 'full or partial payment' of legal fees is provided[541] inquiring into the 'means of all kinds in respect of which the applicant has direct or indirect enjoyment or power freely to dispose'.[542] If indigency is determined, 'all costs reasonably necessary ... for an effective and efficient defence' will be met by the Court.[543] Concretely speaking, this includes, on the basis of an

[534] Tuinstra, *Defence Counsel* (2009), p. 22; Jalloh, *PennStLR*, 117 (2012–2013), 712. Duty counsel has been appointed so far for the following reasons and purposes respectively: for the first appearance of the defendant (who has not chosen counsel yet) before the Chamber and the start of the disclosure process (*Prosecutor v. Katanga*, PTC I Decision Appointing Mr Jean Pierre Fofé as Duty Counsel for Mr Germain Katanga, No. ICC-01/04-01/07-52, 5 November 2007); for the purpose of responding to Court directions and the supplementation of certain documents (*Prosecutor v. Lubanga*, AC Corrigendum to the supplementation to the document entitled "Defence submissions on the scope of the right to appeal within the meaning of article 82(1)(b) of the Statute" of 7 February 2007, No. ICC-01/04-01/06-882-tEN, 4 May 2007); to provide submissions arising out of an ICC's (appeals) judgment (*Prosecutor v. Mokom*, PTC II Order to the Registry to Maintain the Mandate of Duty Counsel and to the Prosecution and Duty Counsel for Submissions, No. ICC-01/14-01/22-73, 22 July 2022); because of the failure to submit documents as a result of the non-appointment of counsel (*Prosecutor v. Lubanga*, AC Decision of the Appeals Chamber upon the Registrar's Requests of 5 April 2007, No. ICC-01/04-01/06-857, 3 April 2007); to advise the witness pursuant to Rule 74 RPE ICC (self-incrimination by a witness) (*Prosecutor v. Ngaïsona*, TC v. Decision on the Second Prosecution Request for Appointment of Duty Counsel for Purposes of Rule 74 of the Rules, No. ICC-01/14-01/18-1406, 13 May 2022 and *Prosecutor v. Ngaïsona*, TC v. Decision on the Third Prosecution Request for Appointment of Duty Counsel for Purposes of Rule 74 of the Rules, No. ICC-01/14-01/18-1491, 29 June 2022); and following the withdrawal of counsel (*Prosecutor v. Lubanga*, PTC I Appointment of Duty Council, No. ICC-01/04-01/06-870, 19 April 2007); see also Section C.(4), Figure 2 in this chapter.

[535] Reg. 73 (1) RegC; Tuinstra, *Defence Counsel* (2009), p. 22.

[536] Reg. 73 (2) RegC. See also *Lubanga*, No. ICC-01/04-01/06-937, para. 26.

[537] *Lubanga*, No. ICC-01/04-01/06-882-tEN, p. 2.

[538] *Lubanga*, No. ICC-01/04-01/06-937, para. 53; *Situation in Darfur*, PTC I Decision of the Registrar Appointing Mr Hadi Shalluf as ad hoc Counsel for the Defence, No. ICC-02/05-12, 25 August 2006 (appointing a counsel who 'is fluent in French and Arabic, and has a "good" command of the English language'); cf. also Schabas and McDermott, 'Article 67', in Ambos, *Commentary* (2022), mn. 30.

[539] Art. 67 (1)(d) ICCS. Generally, on the principles governing the legal aid system of the ICC, see Keita et al., 'Article 67', in Fernandez et al., *Statut II* (2019), p. 1843. Art. 67 ICCS is further developed by the ICC's Legal Aid Policy, cf. ICC, *Registry's Single Policy Document on the Court's Legal Aid System*, No. ICC-ASP/12/3, 4 June 2013. For a similar policy at the ICTY and KSC, see ICTY Trial Legal Aid Policy; ICTY Pre-Trial Legal Aid Policy; KSC Legal Aid Policy.

[540] Reg. 85 RegC and Reg. 132 RegR; Reg. 6 (1) KSC Legal Aid Regulation ('The burden to prove indigence or partial indigence lies with the suspect or the Accused'). See also Tuinstra, *Defence Counsel* (2009), p. 31. At the ICC, while victims do not have a right to legal aid, they may get financial assistance to cover the costs of their common legal representatives, which, however, is discretionary, cf. Rule 90 (5) RPE ICC; crit. Killean and Moffett, *JICJ*, 16 (2017), 728–30.

[541] Reg. 84 (1) RegC.

[542] Reg. 84 (2) RegC.

[543] Reg. 83 (1) RegC. Crit. however Buisman and Hooper, in Rohan and Zyberi, Defense Perspectives (2017), p. 522, arguing with respect to the 'limited' investigation budget that an 'effective investigation cannot be accomplished' with the means provided, also criticizing (at p. 533) that the Prosecutor regularly fails 'to conduct thorough investigations' despite its 'duty to investigate exonerating information'.

action plan established by the counsel,[544] 'the remuneration of counsel, his or her assistants and ... staff, expenditure in relation to the gathering of evidence, administrative costs, translation and interpretation costs, travel costs and daily subsistence allowances'.[545] In practice, most accused receive legal aid.[546] In any case, the Registrar shall reconsider the decision on payment of legal assistance 'if the financial situation of the person receiving such legal assistance is found to be different than indicated in the application, or if the financial situation of the person has changed since the application was submitted'.[547] The applicant may seek review of the decisions of the Registrar by the Presidency within fifteen days of notification of the relevant decision.[548] The decision of the Presidency is final.[549]

## (2) Defence attorney ethics

### *(a) Preliminary remarks*

Codes regulating the professional conduct of counsel are commonplace in national jurisdictions.[550] In international criminal proceedings, where diversity of legal traditions is a feature of both the proceedings in general and the practice of counsel in particular, such rules seem to be even more important; indeed, they are imperative.[551] At the ICC, the main legal basis for these rules is the Code of Professional Conduct for counsel which will be more closely examined in turn. It complements the statutory provisions on 'offences against the administration of justice' (Article 70) and 'misconduct before the Court' (Article 71).[552] These offences have been treated in more detail in the second volume of this Treatise.[553]

Other rather administrative rules can be found in the RegC, the RegR, and the RPE ICC.[554] Thus, for instance, there are rules on the elections of the members of the ICC Disciplinary Organs for Counsel (Disciplinary Board and the Disciplinary Appeals Board),[555] on the interdiction of counsel from exercising their functions before the Court for having refused to comply with Court directions,[556] and on the removal or suspension of counsel from the list of counsel as a result of disciplinary proceedings.[557]

544 Reg. 134 (1) RegR.

545 Reg. 83 (1) RegC. At the KSC, the concrete amount of legal aid depends on the stage of proceedings, the complexity of the case, the assumed team size, and the expected duration of the case, cf. KSC Legal Aid Regulations, Annex C.

546 Yet denying legal aid for an accused who elects to self-represent, cf. *Prosecutor v. Šešelj*, AC Public Redacted Version of 'Judgment' Issued on 30 May 2013, No. IT-03-67-R77.4-A, 30 May 2013. Crit. on the 'poorly conceived' provisions for legal aid for defence investigations at the ICC, Buisman and Hooper, in Rohan and Zyberi, *Defense Perspectives* (2017), p. 521.

547 Reg. 85 (2) RegC; see also Reg. 9 (4)(a) KSC Legal Aid Regulations.

548 Reg. 85 (3) RegC. At the KSC, the Registrar's decision on (partial) indigence can be appealed to the relevant Panel within seven days of notification of the relevant decision, cf. Reg. 18 (7) KSC Legal Aid Regulations.

549 Reg. 85 (3) RegC.

550 For a comparative law perspective, see Gut, *Counsel Misconduct* (2012), pp. 51–9.

551 cf. Tuinstra, *Defence Counsel* (2009), pp. 195–6.

552 cf. Piragoff, 'Article 70', in Ambos, *Commentary* (2022), mn. 6 ff.; Triffterer and Burchard, 'Article 71', in Ambos, *Commentary* (2022), mn. 3, 9, 10 ff.; Gut, *Counsel Misconduct* (2012), pp. 237–52, 256–65. On the provisional amendment of Rule 165 RPE ICC and the adoption of Reg. 66*bis* RegC, see above notes 32, 48, and 52 in this chapter.

553 Ambos, *Treatise ICL II* (2022), pp. 282 ff. (including analysis of the *Bemba et al.* case).

554 For an overview of ICC's framework for disciplining counsel, see Gut, *Counsel Misconduct* (2012), pp. 172–85.

555 Regs. 147–9 RegR.

556 Rules 171 and 172 RPE ICC.

557 Regulations 71 and 72 RegC.

### *(b) Code of Professional Conduct for counsel*

The code was adopted by the ASP in 2005.[558] It can be considered as an expression of general principles governing the practice and ethics of the legal profession.[559] It applies to all sorts of counsel, representing the accused, victims, or a State.[560] It prevails over any other (national) code of ethics or professional responsibility for practice before the ICC.[561] Its forty-six articles address terminological and technical issues,[562] the fundamental principles of the professional conduct for counsel and the duties towards the clients,[563] the rules for representation,[564] for the relations with the Court,[565] as well as the other participants,[566] and the disciplinary regime.[567]

Counsel shall exercise their duties with independence, integrity, and freedom, resisting any external pressure that could compromise them.[568] As far as their professional conduct is concerned, counsel shall be 'respectful and courteous' towards the other participants and persons involved in the proceedings,[569] comply with the ICCS, the RPE ICC, the RegC and all relevant rulings regarding conduct and procedure,[570] 'maintain a high level of competence',[571] and actively respect 'the professional secrecy and the confidentiality of

[558] Code of Professional Conduct for Counsel, Res. ICC-ASP/4/Res.1, 2 December 2005 adopted pursuant to Rule 8 RPE ICC. See for the ICTY: the 'Directive on Assignment of Defence Counsel', as amended on 11 July 2006 (IT/73/Rev. 11); the 'Code of Professional Conduct for Defence Counsel Appearing before the International Tribunal' as amended on 22 July 2009 (IT/125 Rev. 3); the 'Rules Governing the Detention of Persons Awaiting Trial or Appeals before the Tribunal or otherwise Detained on the Authority of the Tribunal', as amended on 21 July 2005 (IT/38/Rev. 9); the 'Regulations to Govern the Supervision of Visits to and Communications with Detainees', amended 4 August 2009 (IT/98/REV. 4); all available at <http://www.icty.org/en/documents>. On these legal instruments, see Ambos, *NStZ*, 18 (1998), 123 ff.; Martinez and Bohlander, in Bohlander, Boed, and Wilson, *Defense in International Criminal Proceedings* (2006), pp. 100 ff. (ICTY); Boed and Niang, in Bohlander, Boed, and Wilson, *Defense in International Criminal Proceedings* (2006), pp. 229 ff. (ICTR); Zahar and Sluiter, *ICL* (2008), pp. 319–20. The respective provisions for ICTR are available at <https://unictr.irmct.org/sites/unictr.org/files/legal-library/detention-rules_en_fr.pdf>, for the MICT at <https://www.irmct.org/sites/default/files/documents/181205-irmct-regulations-supervision-visits-communications-with-detainees-mict-23.pdf>, and for the (R)SCSL at <http://www.rscsl.org/Documents/Rules%20of%20Detention.pdf>. For the KSC see <https://www.scp-ks.org/en/documents/other-rules-and-regulations>. Generally, on the ad hoc tribunals' disciplinary regime regarding counsel misconduct, see Gut, *Counsel Misconduct* (2012), pp. 11–37 (ICTY), 37–45 (ICTR), 45–9 (SCSL); for a detailed presentation of international associations of defence counsel, see Bourgon, Ogetto, and Bendler, in Bohlander, Boed, and Wilson, *Defense in International Criminal Proceedings* (2006), pp. 483 ff.; St-Michel, Grandon, and Haage, *ICLR*, 18 (2018), 517 ff.

[559] See also Tuinstra, *Defence Counsel* (2009), p. 197; Gut, *Counsel Misconduct* (2012), p. 178; Rohan, in Rohan and Zyberi, *Defense Perspectives* (2017), p. 45; Gibson, in Romano et al., *OxfHB IntAdjudication* (2014), pp. 700–2.

[560] cf. Art. 1 Code counsel (2005). On the *personal jurisdiction* of the Code in more detail, see Gut, *Counsel Misconduct* (2012), pp. 185–90. TC V(B) even wants to apply the Code counsel to the OTP; cf. *Prosecutor v. Kenyatta*, TC V(B) Decision on the Defence Application Concerning Professional Ethics Applicable to Prosecution Lawyers and Concurring Separate Opinion of Judge Eboe-Osuji, No. ICC-01/09-02/11-747, 31 May 2013, para. 16; *Disciplinary Board*, Decision of the Disciplinary Board, SDO-2017-18-DB, 6 September 2017, pp. 6–8.

[561] Art. 4 Code counsel (2005). On the Code's primacy, see also Gut, *Counsel Misconduct* (2012), pp. 191–2; Rohan, in Rohan and Zyberi, *Defense Perspectives* (2017), p. 46.

[562] Arts. 1–5 Code counsel (2005).

[563] Arts. 6–10 Code counsel (2005).

[564] Arts. 11–22 Code counsel (2005).

[565] Arts. 23–5 Code counsel (2005).

[566] Arts. 26–9 Code counsel (2005).

[567] Arts. 30–44 Code counsel (2005).

[568] Art. 6 (2)(a) Code counsel (2005). On the related issue of defence counsel immunity and in favour, Zeegers, *ICLR*, 11 (2011), 869 ff. In favour of a 'principled approach' to both functional as well as personal immunity for defense counsel combined with a 'principled and consistent approach to waiver thereof', Sali and Zyberi, in Rohan and Zyberi, *Defense Perspectives* (2017), pp. 173 ff. (p. 202).

[569] Art. 7 (1) Code counsel (2005).

[570] Art. 7 (3) Code counsel (2005).

[571] Art. 7 (2) Code counsel (2005).

information'.[572] Counsel shall never act in a discriminatory manner, in particular in relation to their client.[573] They shall take into consideration 'the client's personal circumstances and specific needs',[574] ensure 'proper legal representation of the client', when the 'client's ability to make decisions . . . is impaired',[575] and not engage in 'any improper conduct', such as demanding sexual relations.[576]

The representation 'agreement is established when counsel accepts a request from a client'[577] and ends 'when the case has been finally determined',[578] or with the withdrawal of counsel,[579] or the discharge of counsel by the client.[580] Counsel shall withdraw from the agreement, when 'a conflict of interest arises',[581] when 'the client insists on pursuing an objective that counsel considers repugnant',[582] or when 'the client fails to fulfil an obligation to counsel regarding counsel's services'.[583] Moreover, counsel may be withdrawn by the Chamber, 'where counsel's physical or mental condition materially impairs his or her ability to represent the client'.[584] A conflict of interests can either be—depending on whether it arises before the establishment of the representation agreement or after—a reason for withdrawal of counsel or an impediment to representation and therefore reason for refusal of an agreement,[585] unless all potentially affected clients consent after consultation.[586] Representation may also be impeded if counsel participated in the proceedings, either representing another client[587] or being 'involved' or 'privy to confidential information as staff member of the Court' relating to the same case,[588] or if there is a 'substantial probability' that she will participate as a witness.[589] As to the second ground—'privy to confidential information as a staff member of the Court'—the *Muthaura and Kenyatta* AC held that 'prior association with the OTP does not, *per se*, disqualify a former OTP staff member from working for the defence'.[590] For an impediment to representation to arise, it is required that the 'counsel has to have had knowledge of confidential information relating to the case'[591] under consideration, that is,

572 Art. 8 (1) Code counsel (2005) (with exceptions). On ethical codes and free speech, esp. at the ICTY, Rohan, in Rohan and Zyberi, *Defense Perspectives* (2017), pp. 54 ff.

573 Art. 9 (1) Code counsel (2005) (providing for the classical discriminatory grounds).

574 Art. 9 (2) Code counsel (2005).

575 Art. 9 (3) Code counsel (2005).

576 Art. 9 (4) Code counsel (2005).

577 Art. 11 Code counsel (2005).

578 Art. 17 (1)(a) Code counsel (2005).

579 Art. 17 (1)(b) and (c) Code counsel (2005).

580 Art. 18 (3) Code counsel (2005).

581 Art. 16 (3)(a) Code counsel (2005).

582 Art. 18 (1)(a) Code counsel (2005).

583 Art. 18 (1)(b) Code counsel (2005). See also Reg. 78 RegC, which repeats that defence counsel should seek the leave of the Chamber before withdrawing.

584 Art. 18 (4) Code counsel (2005).

585 Arts. 12 (1)(a), 13 (2)(a), and 16 Code counsel (2005).

586 Art. 13 (1)(a) and (2) and Art. 16 (3)(b) Code counsel (2005).

587 Art. 12 (1)(a) Code counsel (2005); cf. also *Prosecutor v. Ntaganda*, PTC II Decision on the Request of the Defence of Mathieu Ngudjolo Chui in Relation to the Appointment of Andrea Valdivia as Member of the Defence Team of Bosco Ntaganda, No. ICC-01/04-02/06-112, 20 September 2013, para. 45; *Prosecutor v. Mokom*, No. ICC-01/14-01/22-26-Red, paras. 8, 10–13.

588 Art. 12 (1)(b) Code counsel (2005).

589 Art. 12 (3) Code counsel (2005).

590 *Prosecutor v. Muthaura and Kenyatta*, AC Judgment on the Appeal of the Prosecutor against the Decision of Pre-Trial Chamber II Dated 20 July 2011 Entitled 'Decision with Respect to the Question of Invalidating the Appointment of Counsel to the Defence', No. ICC-01/09-02/11-365, 10 November 2011, para. 58 (emphasis in the original); conc. *Prosecutor v. Muthaura and Kenyatta*, PTC II Second Decision with Respect to the Question of Invalidating the Appointment of Counsel to the Defence, No. ICC-01/09-02/11-405, 9 March 2012, para. 32.

591 *Muthaura and Kenyatta*, No. ICC-01/09-02/11-365, para. 64; *Prosecutor v. Nourain and Jerbo*, AC Judgment on the Appeal of the Prosecutor against the Decision of Trial Chamber IV of 30 June 2011 Entitled 'Decision on the Prosecution's Request to Invalidate the Appointment of Counsel to the Defence', No. ICC-02/05-03/09-252, 11 November 2011, para. 32.

'actual knowledge of confidential information', and not just 'potential knowledge' the person could have had.[592] Furthermore, the AC rejected the '*de minimis* standard' applied by the TC in *Bemba* and *Nourain and Jerbo* and by the PTC in *Muthaura and Kenyatta*,[593] holding that the meaning of 'privy to confidential information' 'need[s] not and should not be qualified in any way',[594] and that the '"*de minimis*" nature [of the information] is potentially only one factor that a Chamber may wish to consider'.[595]

Besides those impediments to representation, counsel has a duty to refuse an agreement, on personal grounds, when she is 'incapable of dealing with the matter diligently' or does not have 'the requisite expertise'.[596]

As long as the representation agreement exists, a mutual, candid, and trusted communication between the counsel and the client is expected to exist. Counsel shall 'consult the client on [how] the objectives of [defence] are to be pursued',[597] provide her 'with all explanations reasonably needed to make informed decisions',[598] and then comply with those decisions 'as long as they are not inconsistent with counsel's [legal] duties'.[599]

Correct and efficient professional conduct is predicated on transparent and clear *financial agreements* between counsel and client. Accordingly, the Code comprises detailed provisions on fees and remuneration of counsel. First of all, counsel is obliged to 'inform the client in writing of the rate of fees to be charged and the criteria for setting them'.[600] It is prohibited to accept remuneration from other sources without the consent of the client; to make the fees contingent on the outcome of the case; to mix the client's funds with those of the counsel, her employer's or associates'; or to borrow from the client.[601] When counsel is paid by the Court, the prohibitions to accept remuneration from other sources[602] and of fee-splitting are absolute.[603] A breach of either of them amounts 'to misconduct … subject to the disciplinary procedure pursuant to this Code'.[604]

Defence counsel has a twofold *role in the proceedings* before the Court. On the one hand, she has to represent her client; on the other hand, she is just (another) organ of the administration of justice. The latter obliges her to interact not only with her client but also with the other participants.[605] Counsel is 'personally responsible' for the client's

592 *Muthaura and Kenyatta*, No. ICC-01/09-02/11-405, para. 35.

593 *Prosecutor v. Bemba*, TC III Decision on the 'Prosecution's Request to Invalidate the Appointment of Legal Consultant to the Defence Team', No. ICC-01/05-01/08-769, 7 May 2010, para. 42 ('whilst working for the prosecution, became aware of more than *de minimis* confidential information relevant to the case, which a member of the defence team should not possess' [emphasis in the original]); conc. *Prosecutor v. Nourain and Jerbo*, TC IV Decision on the Prosecution's Request to Invalidate the Appointment of Counsel to the Defence, No. ICC-02/05-03/09-168, 30 June 2011, para. 16; *Prosecutor v. Muthaura and Kenyatta*, PTC II Decision with Respect to the Question of Invalidating the Appointment of Counsel to the Defence, No. ICC-01/09-02/11-185, 20 July 2011, para. 17, further holding that '[t]he information is deemed *de minimis* if it is "so insignificant that a court may overlook it in deciding an issue"' (emphasis in the original, fn. omitted).

594 *Muthaura and Kenyatta*, No. ICC-01/09-02/11-365, para. 65; *Nourain and Jerbo*, No. ICC-02/05-03/09-252, para. 34.

595 *Muthaura and Kenyatta*, No. ICC-01/09-02/11-365, para. 70 (emphasis in the original); *Nourain and Jerbo*, No. ICC-02/05-03/09-252, para. 34.

596 Art. 13 (2)(b) and (c) Code counsel (2005).

597 Art. 14 (2)(b) Code counsel (2005).

598 Art. 15 (1) Code counsel (2005).

599 i.e. under the ICCS, RPE ICC, and this Code, cf. Art. 14 (2)(a) Code counsel (2005).

600 Art. 20 Code counsel (2005).

601 Art. 21 Code counsel (2005).

602 Art. 22 (1) Code counsel (2005).

603 Art. 22 (2) Code counsel (2005). On fee-splitting, see also Tuinstra, *Defence Counsel* (2009), pp. 212–16.

604 Art. 22 (5) Code counsel (2005). On formal and informal means for addressing professional misconduct, see Zyberi, in Rohan and Zyberi, *Defense Perspectives* (2017), pp. 116–18.

605 cf. Zahar and Sluiter, *ICL* (2008), p. 65; Safferling, *Criminal Procedure* (2012), p. 186; Rohan, in Rohan and Zyberi, *Defense Perspectives* (2017), p. 46.

case;[606] she shall represent her in an expeditious manner;[607] her conduct must not be 'prejudicial to the ongoing proceedings' and 'not bring the Court into disrepute'.[608] The only way to 'make contact with a judge or Chamber relative to the merits of a particular case' is 'within the proper context of the proceedings'[609] and only 'through the Registry', when it comes to transmission of 'evidence, notes or documents'.[610] Counsel's duty to that extent is to always 'maintain the integrity of evidence ... submitted to the Court'[611] and to never introduce evidence knowingly incorrect.

While the counsel has primarily relations with her client, she may also enter into *relations with other persons*, who may be at the same time participants in the proceedings. The Code refers in this regard to 'unrepresented persons', 'other counsel', 'persons already represented by counsel', as well as victims and witnesses.[612] The gist of these provisions is that counsel shall always behave in line with the ethical standards already mentioned above. Thus, for example, she shall refrain immediately from engaging in any further contact or communication with an unrepresented person if there may be a potential conflict of interest.[613] Persons already represented by counsel may only be addressed 'through or with the permission of that counsel'.[614] Any exchange of information between counsel 'shall be presumed confidential and privileged'.[615] Any intimidation, harassment, or humiliation of witnesses and victims, or their subjection to disproportionate or unnecessary pressure is prohibited.[616]

The *disciplinary regime*, represented by three organs—the Disciplinary Commissioner, the Disciplinary Board (DB), the Disciplinary Appeals Board (DAB)—is complementary to national disciplinary regimes,[617] but the DB takes the final decision to close or continue the procedure due to the national decision.[618] The Commissioner is responsible for investigating complaints of misconduct[619] filed by the Chamber dealing with the case, the Prosecutor, the Registrar (*proprio motu*), or 'any person or group of persons whose rights or interests may have been affected by the alleged misconduct'.[620] Such misconduct may consist in an (attempted) violation (or knowing assistance or inducement of another person thereto, or through the acts of another person) of any provision of this Code or the other ICC rules in force, which impose 'substantial ethical or professional duty' on counsel; non-compliance with a prior disciplinary decision; ordering or approving a misconduct of

[606] Art. 24 (2) Code counsel (2005).
[607] Art. 24 (5) Code counsel (2005).
[608] Art. 24 (1) Code counsel (2005). In the same vein, 'Counsel shall not deceive or knowingly mislead the Court', actively correct any erroneous statement (Art. 24 (3)), 'shall not submit any request or document with the sole aim of harming one or more of the participants in the proceedings' (Art. 24 (4)).
[609] Art. 23 (a) Code counsel (2005).
[610] Art. 23 (b) Code counsel (2005).
[611] Art. 25 (1) Code counsel (2005).
[612] Arts. 26–9 Code counsel (2005).
[613] Art. 26 (3) Code counsel (2005).
[614] Art. 28 Code counsel (2005). Affirmative on the applicability of the Code counsel's ethical rules to the ICC's TFV, *Prosecutor v. Katanga*, TC II Decision on the Application by the Legal Representative for Victims regarding Compliance with Ethical Rules by the Parties and the Trust Fund for Victims in the Reparations Proceedings, No. ICC-01/04-01/07-3807-Red-tENG, 21 August 2018, paras. 20–4.
[615] Art. 27 (2) Code counsel (2005).
[616] Art. 29 (1) Code counsel (2005). On the examination of victim-witnesses, esp. concerning its confrontational character, see Zyberi, in Rohan and Zyberi, *Defense Perspectives* (2017), pp. 125–6.
[617] Art. 38 Code counsel (2005). For a crit. view on the complementarity in cases of misconduct, cf. Zahar and Sluiter, *ICL* (2008), p. 68; see also Gut, *Counsel Misconduct* (2012), pp. 291–300.
[618] Art. 38 (5) Code counsel (2005). For a comparative overview of the disciplinary regimes at the ICTY, ICTR, and SCSL, see Gut, *Counsel Misconduct* (2012), pp. 11–37 (ICTY), 37–45 (ICTR), 45–9 (SCSL); including the ICC, see Gibson, in Romano *et al.*, *OxfHB IntAdjudication* (2014), pp. 702–3.
[619] Art. 33 Code counsel (2005).
[620] Art. 34 Code counsel (2005).

counsel's assistants or staff; or failing to take any remedial action against such misconduct from those persons.[621]

The Commissioner can either dismiss a complaint or 'promptly investigate'; in the latter case she may either submit a report to the DB, bring the procedure to an end, or 'find an amicable settlement'.[622] The DB, after hearing the Commissioner and the counsel subject to the disciplinary procedure,[623] may either find a misconduct or not.[624] In the former case various sanctions—from admonishment to a permanent ban from the Court[625]—apply. The decision may be appealed before the DAB.[626] The counsel concerned has several rights, for example, the right to counsel, the right to remain silent, the right to 'full disclosure of the information and evidence gathered by the Commissioner', the right to adequate time for the preparation of the defence, and the right to question witnesses.[627]

### (3) Standby counsel

The notion of 'standby' counsel comes from common law and refers to a counsel who is assigned to an accused who wants to represent herself.[628] Standby counsel was appointed before the MICT, ICTY, ICTR, and SCSL[629] in cases where prominent defendants exercised their right to self-representation thereby 'substantially and persistently obstructing the proper and expeditious conduct' of their trial.[630] At the KSC, though representation by counsel is formulated as 'a right', in fact, self-representation is not allowed in the majority of situations.[631] In the proceedings before the ICC the appointment of standby counsel is envisaged 'where the interests of justice so require', leaving a wide discretion to Chambers.[632] Clearly, as can be seen from the practice of the ad hoc tribunals, the assignment of such a counsel serves the interests of justice in that obstruction of the trial is avoided or at least diminished.

621 Arts. 31 and 32 Code counsel (2005).

622 Art. 39 Code counsel (2005).

623 Art. 39 (7) Code counsel (2005). On the disciplinary hearings, see also Gut, *Counsel Misconduct* (2012), pp. 220–6.

624 Art. 41 (1) Code counsel (2005). Crit. as to the seemingly varying standards of proof at the ICTY and the ICC, Rohan, in Rohan and Zyberi, *Defense Perspectives* (2017), p. 52 ('The ICTY requires that misconduct be proved beyond a reasonable doubt. The ICC appears to require only clear and convincing evidence'), p. 53 ('international courts have not yet resolved questions as fundamental as whether misconduct requires proof of a culpable state of mind').

625 cf. Art. 42 Code counsel (2005). See also Gut, *Counsel Misconduct* (2012), pp. 227–30; Rohan, in Rohan and Zyberi, *Defense Perspectives* (2017), p. 53.

626 cf. Art. 43 Code counsel (2005). See also Gut, *Counsel Misconduct* (2012), pp. 230–4.

627 Art. 40 Code counsel (2005). See also Gut, *Counsel Misconduct* (2012), pp. 210–12.

628 cf. LaFave et al., *Criminal Procedure* (2017), §11.5 (f); Miller et al., *Criminal Procedures* (2019), p. 708; Boas et al., *International Criminal Procedure* (2011), pp. 163–4.

629 More recently on 'standby counsel', see *Prosecutor v. Šešelj*, AC Decision on Assignment of Standby Counsel for the Appeal Hearing, No. MICT-16-99-A, 11 October 2017; for earlier case law, see previous edition note 546; see also Tuinstra, *Defence Counsel* (2009), pp. 252–5; Jalloh, in Carter and Pocar, *International Criminal Procedure* (2013), pp. 127–8, 144 ff.; Harvey, in Rohan and Zyberi, *Defense Perspectives* (2017), pp. 86–105.

630 *Milošević*, No. IT-02-54-AR73.7, para. 17.

631 Art. 21 (5) KSC Law. It is unclear whether this provision, which goes back to the Kosovo civil law tradition, allows self-representation through standby counsel, see Karnavas, Kosovo Specialist Chambers—Part 3: Peculiar Features of the Statute (5 June 2023). In any case, when representation is mandatory, the competent Panel and the Registrar have the obligation to make sure that the accused is represented by Counsel, cf. e.g. Rules 26 (3), 92 (1), 96 KSC RPE; sects. 12 (1) and 14 (4) of the Directive on Counsel.

632 Reg. 76 (1) RegC ICC. See also Safferling, *Criminal Procedure* (2012), p. 192; *Šešelj*, No. IT-03-67-PT, para. 21 ('broad scope').

There seems to be an overlap of the standby and duty counsel's mandates. If the person concerned has not chosen counsel during the initial stages of proceedings (either because she is planning to represent herself or for other reasons), the interests of justice may require either the appointment of duty[633] or standby counsel.[634] It may be for this reason that *Jalloh* considers the duty counsel as a 'specific type of "standby counsel" '.[635] Yet, this understanding does not comply with the *ratio* of these different types of counsel: while duty counsel is appointed following a free choice of the defendant,[636] standby counsel is actually an alien element within the defendant's right to represent himself.[637] Despite the limitations regarding this right,[638] standby counsel's participation should not interfere with the accused's actual control over his defence.[639] Thus, despite the joint reference of both Reg. 73 (3) RegC and Reg. 76 (1) RegC to 'the interests of justice', the latter must be read in conjunction with Article 67 (1)(d) ICCS which suggests a rather strict interpretation with regard to standby counsel. Consequently, the last sentence of Reg. 76 (1) RegC ('This may include the appointment of standby counsel, if appropriate') attaches the appointment of standby counsel to further restricting conditions ('if appropriate'). This is also in line with the ICC case law so far: it applies Reg. 76 (1) RegC exclusively to the appointment of ad hoc counsel,[640] while the issue of standby counsel has not yet played a role before the ICC.[641]

The mandate of the standby counsel can 'vary considerably' from case to case as do 'the reasons for and specific parameters of each appointment'.[642] As the term 'standby' implies, the standby counsel shall 'attend the proceedings and remain available to step in at any time the Chamber determines it to be necessary'[643] and 'be prepared to take over representation' in exceptional circumstances.[644] Keeping in mind that any restrictions on the accused's right to self-representation 'must be limited to the minimum extent necessary to protect the tribunal's interest in assuring a reasonably expeditious trial',[645] a standby counsel may assist in the preparation of the accused's case throughout the proceedings, or even 'be engaged actively in the substantive preparation of the case', 'receive copies of all court documents, filings and disclosed materials that are received by or sent to the accused', 'address the Court', 'offer advice or make suggestions ... in particular on evidential and procedural issues', and

633 Reg. 73 (3) RegC.

634 Reg. 76 (1) RegC.

635 Jalloh, *PennStLR*, 117 (2012–2013), 712.

636 See Section C.(1)(c) in this chapter.

637 Art. 67 (1)(d) ICCS. See also Tuinstra, *Defence Counsel* (2009), p. 252.

638 See Section D.(3) in this chapter.

639 For US case law, see Tuinstra, *Defence Counsel* (2009), p. 252.

640 *Prosecutor v. Gaddafi and Al-Senussi*, PTC I Decision on the 'Defence request for an order of disclosure', No. ICC-01/11-01/11-392-Red-Corr, 1 August 2013, para. 31; *Prosecutor v. Gaddafi and Al-Senussi*, PTC I Decision on 'Request for Review of Registrar's Decision' by the Defence of Saif Al-Islam Gaddafi, No. ICC-01/11-01/11-390-Red, 30 July 2013, para. 35; *Situation in the DRC*, PTC I Decision Appointing Ad Hoc Counsel and Establishing a Deadline for the Prosecution and the Ad Hoc Counsel to Submit Observations on the Applications of Applicants a/0001/06 to a/0003/06, No. ICC-01/04-147, 18 May 2006, p. 4; *Situation in the DRC*, PTC I Decision on Protective Measures Requested by Applicants 01/04-1/dp to 01/04-6/dp, No. ICC-01/04-73, 21 July 2005, p. 4.

641 See only the reference in *Prosecutor v. Ongwen*, PTC II Decision Requesting Observations from the Defence on the Prosecutor's Application to Postpone the Confirmation Hearing and on the Choice of Counsel for Dominic Ongwen, No. ICC-02/04-01/15-197, 12 February 2015, para. 12.

642 *Karadžić*, No. IT-95-5/18-AR73.6, para. 35.

643 *Prosecutor v. Karadžić*, TC Decision on Appointment of Counsel and Order on Further Trial Proceedings, No. IT-95-5/18-T, 5 November 2009, para. 27; Jalloh, in Carter and Pocar, *International Criminal Procedure* (2013), p. 128.

644 *Prosecutor v. Norman et al.*, TC Consequential Order on Assignment and Role of Standby Counsel, No. SCSL-04-14-T, 14 June 2004; *Šešelj*, No. IT-03-67-PT, para. 30.

645 *Milošević*, No. IT-02-54-AR73.7, para. 17; crit. on the 'illusory' compromise between self-representation and standby counsel, Boas et al., *International Criminal Procedure* (2011), p. 164.

even 'put questions to witnesses, in particular sensitive or protected', 'in the event of abusive conduct by the accused'.[646]

A standby counsel can be taken from the list of counsel or, pursuant to Reg. 76 (2) RegC, be a member of the Office of Public Counsel for the defence (OPCD).[647] The OPCD has been established in order to 'constitute an institutional memory for the Defence and to establish a resource centre'.[648] It falls 'within the remit of the Registry solely for administrative purposes', but 'shall function in its substantive work as a wholly independent office'.[649] As a result of the *ReVision* Project of the Registry initiated in 2014,[650] the creation of a single Defence Office was envisaged, consolidating some of the support functions to defence teams currently provided by the Counsel Support Section (CSS), including the administration of legal aid, as well as the general assistance mandate of the OPCD, 'except for the representation function which OPCD may currently be called upon to exercise'.[651] However, these structural re-design proposals have not been implemented.[652] While the reasons for this were not communicated,[653] concerns related to the supposed increase in efficiency of the Defence Office appear to have played a key role in putting the planned transformation on hold.[654]

The work of the OPCD may include, apart from assignments as standby or duty counsel, representing and protecting the rights of the defence during the initial stages of the investigation;[655] providing general support and assistance to defence counsel and to the person entitled to legal assistance, including legal research and advice;[656] appearing, on the instruction or with the leave of the Chamber, in respect of specific issues;[657] and

[646] *Šešelj*, No. IT-03-67-PT, para. 30.

[647] Reg. 76 (2) RegC: 'When acting in accordance with sub-regulation 1 [appointment of defence counsel and standby counsel by a Chamber] ... The Chamber may, where the interests of justice so require, also appoint counsel from the Office of Public Counsel for the defence as defined in regulation 77, sub-regulation 3.' On the OPCD, see Safferling and Hartwig, *International Criminal Procedure* (2012), pp. 180–1; Tuinstra, *Defence Counsel* (2009), pp. 82–3; Boas et al., *International Criminal Procedure* (2011), p. 144.

[648] Reg. 77 (3) RegC, and Reg. 143-146 RegR; see also the ICC Website, *The Office of Public Counsel for the Defence*, <https://international.vlex.com/source/international-criminal-court-31167/c/office-of-public-counsel-for-defence>.

[649] Reg. 77 (2) RegC.

[650] The *ReVision* Project of the Registry was initiated by the ASP, which 'authorized the Registrar to reorganize and streamline the Registry's organizational structure', ASP, *Resolution ICC-ASP/12/Res.1*, 27 November 2013, sect H, para. 3. The Registrar thereupon established a project team to implement the so-called 'ReVision project', see ASP, *Report on the Review of the Organizational Structure of the Registry*, ICC-ASP/13/26, 28 October 2014, para. 2.

[651] See ASP, *Report of the Committee on Budget and Finance on the work of its Twenty-Third Session*, ICC-ASP/13/15, 18 November 2014, p. 17. About the proposals of the Registry in more detail, see Registry ReVision Project, Basic Outline of Proposals to Establish Defence and Victims Offices (Draft), pp. 6 ff., <https://michaelgkarnavas.net/files/Basic_Outline_Defence_and_Victims_Offices.pdf>. For a similar reform proposal (independent Defence Office with separate Legal Aid and Legal Advisory Units), see Mettraux et al., *Expert Initiative Effectiveness ICC* (2014), pp. 32–3, 36 (paras. 145–9, 167) and 204–7 (paras. 4–11). About the 'representation function' of the OPCD (as ad hoc counsel), see note 684 and main text in this chapter.

[652] ICC, *Report Registry* (2016), p. 12 ('The Registry has put these proposals [concerning, inter alia, the revision of the Office of Public Counsel for the Defence] on hold').

[653] cf. ibid., p. 110 (merely stating at n. 125 that the proposed changes would have required 'amendments to the Regulations of the Court'), 131–2.

[654] For a crit. analysis, see Clements, *JICJ*, 17 (2019), 281–3; Catallo, *MichJIL*, 41 (2020), 444 ff. In contrast, at the KSC a Defence Office has been put into practice. It has two main tasks: it administers both a list of defence counsel eligible to practice before the Specialist Chambers (on behalf of the Registrar) and a system of legal aid for the representation of (partially) indigent accused, cf. Art. 34 (7) of the KSC Law and Rule 23 (6) RPE KSC. The Defence Office does not get involved in the litigation or preparation of materials for defence teams.

[655] Reg. 77 (4)(a) RegC.

[656] Reg. 77 (4)(b) RegC.

[657] Reg. 77 (4)(c) RegC.

advancing submissions on behalf of the person entitled to legal assistance when defence counsel has not been secured or when the mandate of temporary counsel is limited to other issues.[658]

### (4) Ad hoc counsel

Compared to the other forms of legal representation before the ICC, the mandate of the ad hoc counsel is 'a *sui generis* appointment',[659] 'limited in time and scope',[660] 'strictly restricted' to the specific proceedings, and not applicable 'automatically to other proceedings at the pre-trial stage'.[661] Furthermore, the ad hoc counsel attends and represents the interests of the defence in general, not a concrete person[662] because such a person has not yet been arrested or even identified.[663] Consequently, there is no client-counsel relationship to which the provisions of the Code of Conduct regarding representation could apply.[664]

There are two legal bases governing the appointment of an ad hoc counsel. First, an ad hoc counsel may be appointed, pursuant to Article 56 (2)(d) ICCS, in cases where there is for the Prosecutor 'a unique opportunity to take testimony or a statement from a witness or to examine, collect or test evidence, which may not be available subsequently for the purposes of a trial'.[665] In that case, the PTC is entitled to take certain measures 'to ensure the efficiency and integrity of the proceedings and, in particular, to protect the rights of the defence'.[666] One of these measures may be to authorize 'counsel for a person who has been arrested, or appeared before the Court in response to a summons, to participate, or where there has not yet been such an arrest or appearance or counsel has not been designated, appointing another counsel to attend and represent the interests of the defence'.[667] Strictly speaking, only within the context of the latter alternative ('where there has not yet been such an arrest or appearance or counsel has not been designated') this counsel serves as an 'ad hoc counsel', representing 'the interests of the defence'. The second legal basis is Reg. 76 (1) RegC according to which '[a] Chamber, following consultation with the Registrar and, when appropriate, after hearing from the person entitled to legal assistance, may appoint counsel in the circumstances specified in the Statute, Rules and these Regulations or where the interests of justice so require'.

Although the application of both legal bases leads to the same result, that is, the appointment of an ad hoc counsel representing the interests of the defence, the apparent differences between them should not be overlooked: while Article 56 (2)(d) ICCS has a specific

[658] Reg. 77 (4)(d) RegC.

[659] *Prosecutor v. Kony et al.*, AC Judgment on the Appeal of the Defence against the 'Decision on the admissibility of the case under article 19 (1) of the Statute' of 10 March 2009, No. ICC-02/04-01/05-408, 16 September 2009, para. 56.

[660] IBAHRI, *Counsel Matters* (2012), p. 11.

[661] *Situation in Darfur, Sudan*, PTC I Decision on the Ad hoc Counsel for Defence Request of 18 December 2006, No. ICC-02/05-47, 2 February 2007.

[662] Safferling, *JICJ*, 9 (2011), 662 ff.

[663] See Dieckmann and Kerll, *ICLR*, 11 (2011), 106, 109 ff.

[664] *Kony et al.*, No. ICC-02/04-01/05-408, para. 56; see also Dieckmann and Kerll, *ICLR*, 11 (2011), 106, 127 ff., 135; Tuinstra, *Defence Counsel* (2009), pp. 239–41.

[665] Art. 56 (1)(a) ICCS. The respective provision of Rule 99 (3)(d) RPE KSC refers to a 'Specialist Counsel' and this is normally the counsel admitted to the List of (Specialist) Counsel (Rules 2, 26 (1) RPE KSC).

[666] Art. 56 (1)(b) ICCS; in the same vein, Rule 47 (2) RPE ICC. See also *Situation in the DRC*, PTC I Decision on the Prosecutor's Request for Measures under Article 56, No. ICC-01/04-21, 26 April 2005.

[667] Art. 56 (2)(d) ICCS.

material scope (unique opportunity to examine, collect, or test evidence, which may not be available subsequently for the purposes of the trial) and temporal scope (the person is neither arrested nor appeared voluntarily before the Court), Reg. 76 (1) RegC refers to the 'interests of justice' and appears—with its rather general notion—to be a kind of fall-back provision[668] for cases not covered by the more specific Article 56 (2)(d) ICCS.[669] This may be the reason why so far there have only been a few occasions where an ad hoc counsel was appointed on the basis of this provision.[670] Another perhaps more important reason may be the apparent overlap between the tasks of the PTC and the OPCD: while Article 56 (1)(b) ICCS entitles the PTC to take measures provided for in Article 56 (2)(d) ICCS, Reg. 77 (4) (a) RegC entrusts the OPCD with the protection of the rights of the defence for the application of Article 56 (2)(d) ICCS and Rule 47 (2) RPE ICC.[671] Thus, it is questionable whether

668 Based on the German '*Generalklausel*', Maxeiner calls this sort of provisions 'general clause', see Maxeiner, *VaparaisoULR*, 41 (2006–2007), 529 ('Effective methods of legislative drafting provide tools to enable legal systems to deal with uncertainty in law and society. These tools include general clauses that are deliberately vague to permit their development by those charged with applying them, exceptions to otherwise generally applicable rules, and authorizations to officials charged with rules exceptionally to depart from them. Effective methods of legislative drafting allow legal systems to grant discretion to officials and to provide for control of that discretion'). However, for a more principled approach to a definition of the term 'general clause' see Glendon et al., *Traditions* (1985), p. 205 ('The fact that the co-operation of jurists is called for in the formulation of the law, and not only in its application, is seen in the use of certain "super-eminent principles" (*Generalklauseln, principes généraux*). These are found sometimes in the enacted law . . . The recourse to these principles, and how they are used, are difficult for theorists of legislative positivism to explain; they bring to light the fact that in the Romano-Germanic family there is a subordination of law to the commands of justice, such as it is conceived at a given moment in a given period, and that this legal family is a *jurists' law*, not merely a system of legislative norms' [emphasis in the original]). The explanation is no longer contained in the new edition of 2016.

669 An illustrative example of this difference is provided by the conflict between the ad hoc counsel and PTC I in the *Darfur* Situation: in a decision filed on 24 July 2006, PTC I invoked Rule 103 RPE ICC and invited both the UN High Commissioner for Human Rights and the Chairperson of the International Commission of Inquiry on Darfur, Sudan, 'to submit in writing their observations on issues concerning the protection of victims and the preservation of evidence in Darfur, Sudan' (*Situation in Darfur, Sudan*, PTC I Decision Inviting Observations in Application of Rule103 of the Rules of Procedure and Evidence, No. ICC-02/05-10, 24 July 2006, p. 5). To that end, PTC I also ordered the Registrar to appoint 'an ad hoc counsel to represent and protect the general interests of the Defence in the Situation in Darfur, Sudan during the proceedings pursuant to rule 103 of the Rules' (p. 6), which the Registrar did on 25 August 2006 (*Situation in Darfur*, No. ICC-02/05-12). After the ad hoc counsel requested, inter alia, that the Chamber permit him to attend '*any* proceedings provided for in the Rome Statute, the Regulations of the Court and the Rules of Procedure and Evidence, related to the situation in Darfur' (*scil.* not only the Rule 103 proceedings, [emphasis added]), which the PTC denied (*Situation in Darfur*, No. ICC-02/05-47, pp. 4–6), he established that '[t]he appointment of counsel for the defence . . . is properly based on article 56 (2)(d) of the Statute' and argued that the Chamber violated this provision (*Situation in Darfur, Sudan*, PTC I Application Requesting Leave to Appeal from the Decision Rendered on 02/02/2007 on the Application Filed by the Defence Requesting 'The Presence and Participation of the Ad Hoc Counsel for the Defence during the Proceedings that the Office of the Prosecutor Will Undertake in Sudan', No. ICC-02/05-48-tEN, 8 February 2007, pp. 4–5). The PTC, however, clarified 'that the Ad hoc Counsel's mandate . . . is clearly not related to article 56 (2)(d) of the Statute [and] that, accordingly, no issues related to article 56 of the Statute were dealt with nor even impliedly considered by the Decision' (*Situation in Darfur, Sudan*, PTC I Decision on the Ad hoc Counsel for the Defence's Request for leave to Appeal the Decision of 2 February 2007, No. ICC-02/05-52, 21 February 2007, p. 6). In other words, because the Chamber did not base its initial decision to order the appointment of an ad hoc counsel on Art. 56 (2)(d) ICCS, it could circumvent the strict requirements of that provision. In fact, the Chamber's practice of not indicating any legal basis for the appointment of an ad hoc counsel might have facilitated the rejection of the ad hoc counsel's request mentioned above, but is questionable from the perspective of legality and fairness.

670 See *Situation in the DRC*, No. ICC-01/04-21; *Situation in the DRC*, PTC I Decision Establishing a Deadline for Final Submissions on the NFI's Additional Report, No. ICC-01/04-112, 8 February 2006, p. 2; see generally Dieckmann and Kerll, *ICLR*, 11 (2011), 106, 110.

671 Reg. 77 (4) RegC reads: 'When a conflict of interest does not arise, the tasks of the Office of Public Counsel for the defence shall include . . . Representing and protecting the rights of the defence during the initial stages of the investigation, in particular for the application of article 56, paragraph 2 (d), and rule 47, sub-rule 2. For this

there is a need to have, besides the OPCD, a (further) ad hoc counsel appointed, especially since OPCD staff acting as ad hoc counsel 'will not only be bound by the Staff Rules and Regulations of the Court, but also by the dictates of the Code of Professional Conduct for Counsel'.[672]

In every other instance, the Chambers based their decisions to appoint ad hoc counsel on Reg. 76 (1) RegC. Accordingly, the appointment of an ad hoc counsel will always be in order to address a specific issue, such as the collection of evidence,[673] the reply to applications for participation of the victims in the proceedings according to Rule 89 (1) RPE ICC,[674] or—as previously mentioned—the reply to *amicus curiae* briefs pursuant to Rule 103 (2) RPE ICC.[675] Unfortunately, the recourse to the fall-back provision of Reg. 76 (1) RegC produced some confusion with regard to the temporal scope of that provision, because it was not only applied to situations, that is, where a suspect has not yet been identified and where thus no attorney-client relationship exists, but also to cases.[676] At first sight, this seems to be contradictory, given that an ad hoc counsel, as already noted above, represents the interests of the defence in general and not a specific suspect. Notwithstanding, in *Kony et al.* an ad hoc counsel was appointed on several occasions although the suspects, being at large, had already been identified.[677] The AC clarified insofar that '[i]n circumstances, where the suspects are at large and counsel is appointed to represent their interests generally in proceedings, such counsel cannot speak on their behalf'.[678]

Figure 2, summarizing this section, displays the appointment of defence counsel with a view to the different stages of the proceedings.

purpose the Office of Public Counsel for the defence may, on the instruction or with the leave of the Chamber, make submissions concerning the needs of the defence in ongoing proceedings.' See also Dieckmann and Kerll, *ICLR*, 11 (2011), 106, 110; Khan and Dixon, *Archbold International* (2018), mn. 20–59.

672 Khan and Dixon, *Archbold International* (2018), mn. 20–59.

673 *Situation in the DRC*, No. ICC 01/04-21, p. 2 (forensic examination); Dieckmann and Kerll, *ICLR*, 11 (2011), 111–12.

674 *Situation in the DRC*, No. ICC-01/04-73, p. 4; Dieckmann and Kerll, *ICLR*, 11 (2011), 112–15.

675 *Situation in Darfur*, No. ICC-02/05-10, p. 5, although the Chamber did not indicate that it based its order to appoint an ad hoc counsel on that particular legal basis, see above note 702; Dieckmann and Kerll, *ICLR*, 11 (2011), 115.

676 On this distinction, see, in more detail, Chapter III, B.(2)(b) in this volume. For an illustration that the application to cases is indeed possible, see ICC, *List of Counsel*, p. 10 ('The mandates of ad hoc counsel are limited in time and scope and have a clear purpose in the context of a situation or case under the jurisdiction of the Court.')

677 The Chambers appointed ad hoc counsel for the following purposes: Response to victim's applications under ICC Rule 89: *Prosecutor v. Kony et al.*, PTC II Decision on Legal Representation, Appointment of Counsel for the Defence, Protective Measures and Time-Limit for Submission of Observations, No. ICC-02/04-01/05-134, 1 February 2007; *Prosecutor v. Kony et al.*, PTC II Decision on Legal Representation, Appointment of Counsel for the Defence, Criteria for Redactions of Applications for Participation, and Submission of Observations on Applications for Participation a/0014/07 to a/0020/07 and a/0076/07 to a/0125/07, No. ICC-02/04-01/05-312, 17 September 2008; *Prosecutor v. Kony et al.*, PTC II Decision on Victims' Applications for Participation, No. ICC-02/04-01/05-375, 10 March 2009; *Prosecutor v. Al Bashir*, PTC I Decision Ordering the Parties to Submit their Observations on the Applications for Victims' Participation in the Proceedings, No. ICC-02/05-01/09-38, 1 September 2009; *Prosecutor v. Al Bashir*, PTC I Decision Ordering the Parties to Submit their Observations on Applications a/0443/09 to a/0450/09 for Participation as Victims in the Proceedings, No. ICC-02/05-01/09-50, 6 November 2009; *Prosecutor v. Al Bashir*, PTC I Decision Setting a Time Limit for the Parties' Replies to 8 Applications for Victims' Participation in the Proceedings, No. ICC-02/05-01/09-85, 26 May 2010; submitting observations on the admissibility of a case: *Prosecutor v. Kony et al.*, PTC II Decision Initiating Proceedings under Article 19, Requesting Observations and Appointing Counsel for the Defence, No. ICC-02/04-01/05-320, 21 October 2008.

678 *Kony et al.*, No. ICC-02/04-01/05-408, para. 56.

| Trial stage | Context | General description | Provision |
|---|---|---|---|
| **Investigative stage general** | Case | Counsel available to certain persons for certain events/measures but no general right to counsel | Art. 55(2)(c) ICCS |
| **Before confirmation hearing (no arrest/appearance yet)** | Situation (ad hoc counsel) | Prosecution considers investigative measure to present unique opportunity to examine, collect or test evidence, which may not be available subsequently for trial | Art. 56(1)(a) ICCS<br>Art. 56(1)(b) ICCS<br>Art. 56(2)(d) ICCS<br>Rule 47(2) RPE ICC<br>[but see Reg 77(4)(a) RegC: OPCD is responsible for application of Art. 56(2)(d) und Rule 47(2)] |
| | Situation (ad hoc counsel) | RegC allow for the appointment of Counsel by Chamber following consultation with Registrar where specified in the Statute or Rules or where interests of justice so require = PTC appoints counsel before confirmation hearing in the interests of justice, whether or not there is a right to counsel under ICCS | Reg 76 (1) RegC |
| | Case (ad hoc counsel) | | Reg 76 (1) RegC |
| **'In the determination of any charge' (confirmation hearing and after)** | Case (duty counsel) | person is 'accused' at latest at the confirmation hearing<br>- 'accused' appears as the term for person charged in the ICCS's Part on trial | Art. 67(1)(d) ICCS<br>Art. 61 ICCS<br>Part 9 ICCS<br>Reg 73 RegC |
| **Entire proceedings** | Case (standby counsel) | Counsel appointed by the Court to assist an accused who is asserting the right to self-representation ("standby" = counsel steps in whenever the Court orders him to take over the defence case in exceptional circumstances)<br>[different from 'duty counsel', who provides initial legal advice and assistance to an accused pending the appointment of counsel] | Art. 64(2) ICCS<br>Reg 76(1) RegC |

**Fig. 2.** Appointment of defence counsel with a view to the stages of the proceedings
© Alexander Heinze

## (5) The International Criminal Bar (ICB) and International Criminal Court Bar Association (ICCBA)

There are two independent Defence Counsel Organisations (DCOs) for the ICC.[679] The ICB was established in Montreal in June 2002,[680] the ICCBA more than ten years later in

[679] On the other DCOs (for ICTY, ICTR, MICT, SCSL, STL, and ECCC), see Bourgon, Ogetto, and Bendler, in Bohlander, Boed, and Wilson, *Defense in International Criminal Proceedings* (2006), pp. 483 ff.; Kennedy and Düsterhöft, in Rohan and Zyberi, *Defense Perspectives* (2017), pp. 138 ff. (with organizations outside the tribunals/Registry only existing for ICTY, ICTR, and MICT); St-Michel, Grandon, and Haage, *ICLR*, 18 (2018), 517 ff. At the KSC, there exists also an independent body, the Independent Representative Body of Counsel Admitted to Practice before the KSC (IRB-KSC), referred to in Art. 19 (4) KSC Law and Rule 25 (4) RPE KSC; see also <https://www.scp-ks.org/en/specialist-counsel-establish-independent-representative-body>, and the Constitution of the IRB-KSC.

[680] See generally its website: <http://www.bpi-icb.com/en/>.

June 2016.[681] Yet, while the ICB was given observer status by the ASP in 2005,[682] it was never fully recognized in the RPE ICC or otherwise.[683] In contrast, the ICCBA was officially recognized at the eighteenth session of the ASP 'as an independent representative body of counsel which may be consulted by the Registrar' in accordance with Rule 20 (3) RPE ICC[684] and invited 'to report' to the ASP 'on its activities in advance of the nineteenth session'.[685]

The ICCBA is, according to its Constitution adopted by its General Assembly in June 2018,[686] an independent association of 'Counsel practising before the ICC and their Support Staff [ ... ] to uphold professional standards of conduct, reinforce the independence of the legal profession, and ensure the effective representation of their general and collective interests'.[687]

According to Art. 2 no. 1 ICCBA Constitution the primary objective of the ICCBA is 'to support the functions, efficiency and independence of Counsel practicing before the ICC'. To this effect, several organs have been established, inter alia, the already mentioned General Assembly, an Executive Council, and an Executive Director.[688]

## D. Defendants

### (1) Rights of the suspect/accused

The rights of the defendant (suspect/accused) are central in the procedural framework of the ICC.[689] The relevant provisions are Articles 55, 66, and 67 ICCS. While Article 66 guarantees the presumption of innocence,[690] Articles 55 and 67 provide for the specific fair trial rights resulting from the general fair trial principle. All these rights are based on the human rights law extensively discussed in Chapter I. It therefore suffices here to summarize the specific rights contained in Articles 55 and 67 from a predominantly procedural perspective.

The main difference between Articles 55 and 67 ICCS is their application *ratione temporis*. While Article 55 applies during the investigation stage—distinguishing between rights during investigation in general (para. 1) and vis-à-vis concrete investigative measures (para. 2)[691]—Article 67 applies to the trial stage. The latter provision ensures two categories of

681 See generally its website: <https://www.iccba-abcpi.org>.

682 According to Rule 93 RPE ASP the ICB may participate at the ASP as an NGO.

683 cf. Kennedy and Düsterhöft, in Rohan and Zyberi, *Defense Perspectives* (2017), pp. 142–3.

684 cf. ASP, Res. ICC-ASP/18/Res. 6, 6 December 2019, para. 80; see also <https://www.iccba-abcpi.org/about>.

685 ASP, Res. ICC-ASP/18/Res. 6, 6 December 2019, para. 81.

686 <https://www.iccba-abcpi.org/_files/ugd/ff5a5e_16c61a8eb72b4dd88477334b53d7f674.pdf>; see also St-Michel, Grandon, and Haage, *ICLR*, 18 (2018), 517 ff.

687 Preamble, ICCBA Constitution (2018).

688 cf. Arts. 4 ff. ICCBA Constitution (2018).

689 Schabas and McDermott, 'Article 67', in Ambos, *Commentary* (2022), mn. 1 ('the credibility of international justice depends on rigorous respect of the rights of the accused to a fair trial'); Zappalà, in Cassese et al., *Rome Statute II* (2002), p. 1320; Keita et al., 'Article 67', in Fernandez et al., *Statut II* (2019), p. 1822; Weissbrodt and Zinsmaster, in Brown, *Handbook ICL* (2011), pp. 265, 275 ff. (comparing them with those of the military commissions in Guantánamo).

690 See thereon Chapter I, D.(3)(b) in this volume.

691 cf. Schabas, *ICC Commentary* (2016), pp. 862–7; Hall and Jacobs, 'Article 55', in Ambos, *Commentary* (2022), mn. 1–4; Zappalà, in Cassese et al., *Rome Statute II* (2002), 1183; Mbaye and Shoamanesh, 'Article 55', in Fernandez et al., *Statut II* (2019), pp. 1548–49; Pérez-León-Acevedo and Elberling, 'Article 55', in Klamberg et al., *Commentary ICC II* (2023), pp. 59–61.

rights, namely, on the one hand, the general right to a fair, public hearing in full equality, and, on the other hand, the individual rights (or minimum guarantees) deriving from it.[692] This also correspondes to the structure of the relevant human rights provisions analysed in Chapter I.

As to the concrete rights, Articles 55 and 67 ICCS basically have the same scope of protection. Thus, to start with, the suspect/accused is entitled to be informed promptly and in detail about the case against her in a language which she fully understands and speaks.[693] Lacking the linguistic knowledge the accused is entitled to have, 'free of any cost', the assistance of a competent interpreter and the relevant documents translated as far as 'necessary to meet the requirements of fairness'.[694] These broad guarantees are to ensure that the accused will be capable, linguistically and intellectually, to comprehend the proceedings carried out against her[695] and thus be able to prepare an effective defence as early as possible.[696] In this regard, the explicit granting of these rights already during investigation is to be welcomed given the prejudicial character of this stage of the proceedings.[697] It is also to be welcomed that the respective 'record of questioning' shall contain the information that the suspect has been informed of her rights.[698] For the actual trial, this entails that the TC, when reading the charges to the accused at the commencement of the trial, 'shall satisfy itself that the accused

[692] Zappalà, in Cassese et al., *Rome Statute II* (2002), p. 1320; cf. also Pérez-León-Acevedo and Elberling, 'Article 67', in Klamberg et al., *Commentary ICC II* (2023), pp. 249–50.

[693] cf. Art. 55 (1)(c), (2)(a) ICCS with Art. 67 (1)(a) ICCS (referring to 'the nature, cause and content of the charge'); cf. also Arts. 21 (4)(a) ICTYS, 20 (4)(a) ICTRS, and 19 (4)(a) IRMCTS; for a comprehensive analysis, see Jordash and Coughlan, in Darcy and Powderly, *Judicial Creativity* (2010), pp. 286 ff.; Keita et al., 'Article 67', in Fernandez et al., *Statut II* (2019), pp. 1826–8; Safferling and Hartwig, *International Criminal Procedure* (2012), pp. 289–91; Pérez-León-Acevedo and Elberling, 'Article 55', in Klamberg et al., *Commentary ICC II* (2023), pp. 62–72; Pérez-León-Acevedo and Elberling, 'Article 67', in Klamberg et al., *Commentary ICC II* (2023), pp. 251–8.

[694] Arts. 55 (1)(c) and 67 (1)(f) ICCS; cf. also Arts. 21 (4)(f) ICTYS and 20 (4)(f) ICTRS, and 19 (4)(f) IRMCTS; Keita et al., 'Article 67', in Fernandez et al., *Statut II* (2019), p. 1850; Hall and Jacobs, 'Article 55', in Ambos, *Commentary* (2022), mn. 7; Schabas and McDermott, 'Article 67', in Ambos, *Commentary* (2022), mn. 41–3; Pérez-León-Acevedo and Elberling, 'Article 55', in Klamberg et al., *Commentary ICC II* (2023), pp. 62–5; Pérez-León-Acevedo and Elberling, 'Article 67', in Klamberg et al., *Commentary ICC II* (2023), pp. 288–92.

[695] cf. Schabas and McDermott, 'Article 67', in Ambos, *Commentary* (2022), mn. 42 ('an accused who does not understand is not "present" at trial'); in the same vein, Pérez-León-Acevedo and Elberling, 'Article 67', in Klamberg et al., *Commentary ICC II* (2023), p. 293 ('able to adequately follow the court proceedings and thus to be "present" in a meaningful sense').

[696] cf. *Prosecutor v. Tolimir*, AC Decision on Interlocutory Appeal against Oral Decision of the Pre-Trial Judge of 11 December 2007, No. IT -05-88/2-AR 73.1, 28 March 2008, para. 15 (but allowing for certain flexibility with regard to the language requirement: 'a language [the accused] can understand, ... does not translate into a right for an accused, ... to ... demand the production of documents in any language or script that he or she chooses', but only 'a language which the accused understands sufficiently in order to allow for the effective exercise of his right to conduct his defence'); conc. *Prosecutor v. Karadžić*, AC Decision on Interlocutory Appeal of the Trial Chamber's Decision on Prosecution Motion Seeking Determination that the Accused Understands English, No. IT-95-5/18-AR73.3, 4 June 2009, para. 11; *Prosecutor v. Bemba Gombo et al.*, PTC II Decision on the Defence Request for an Order Requiring the Translation of Evidence, No. ICC-01/05-01/13-177, 11 February 2014, para. 6 (only documents that are fundamental to ensuring that the accused fully understands the 'nature, cause and content of the charge and thus to adequately defend himself or herself' to be translated); *Prosecutor v. Gbagbo*, AC Decision on Mr Gbagbo's Request for Translation and an Extension of Time for the Filing of a Response to the Document in Support of the Appeal, No. ICC-02/11-01/11-489, 22 August 2013, para. 12; *Prosecutor v. Gbagbo*, TC I Decision on the Request for Suspension of the Limit to Respond to the Prosecutor's Trial Brief Submitted by the Defence for Mr Gbagbo, No. ICC-02/11-01/15-1141, 26 March 2018, para. 9 (translation of trial brief not necessary); *Prosecutor v. Gbagbo*, TC I Decision on Mr Gbagbo's Request for Revised and Corrected Translation of the Trial Brief and Related Orders, No. ICC-02/11-01/15-1177, 7 June 2018, para. 5 (clarifying at p. 7 that the lack of a revised French version of a Trial Brief 'does not adversely impact the rights of the Defence'); *Prosecutor v. Gbagbo*, AC Decision on Counsel for Mr Gbagbo's Request for Transmission of Draft English Translations of his Documents, No. ICC-02/11-01/15-1380, 22 September 2020, para. 3 (defendant's own documents not to be translated).

[697] cf. Chapter I, D.(2)(d) and (3)(e) in this volume.

[698] Rule 111 (2) RPE ICC.

understands the nature of the charges'.[699] Furthermore, the accused is entitled 'to have adequate time and facilities for the preparation of the defence' and to communicate freely and in confidence with counsel.[700] Yet, the right to counsel is already triggered at the investigation stage when investigative measures are directed against a person.[701] This communication is privileged and therefore only exceptionally subject to disclosure.[702]

In line with the *nemo tenetur* principle[703] the suspect/accused cannot be obliged to testify against herself and has a right to remain silent, without such silence being a consideration in the determination of guilt or innocence.[704] Article 55 distinguishes here—in line with its two-stage approach mentioned above—between the general prohibition of self-incrimination and the concrete right to remain silent in the face of being questioned.[705] Of course, the accused has the right to make a statement ('unsworn oral or written') in her defence,[706] but it is of dubious evidentiary value given that the accused, unlike the witness, is, as a consequence of the *nemo tenetur* principle, not obliged to tell the truth.[707] We will return to this issue below.[708]

Given the specific situation during the investigation, especially the sometimes vulnerable state of the suspect vis-à-vis the investigative authorities, Article 55 explicitly clarifies that the suspect 'shall not be subjected to any form of coercion, duress or threat, to torture or to any other form of cruel, inhuman or degrading treatment or punishment' nor 'be subjected to arbitrary arrest or detention'.[709]

The right to witness confrontation, already discussed previously,[710] is a clear consequence or expression of the adversarial structure of the proceedings. Yet, the accused has not only the right to obtain the attendance and examine, or have examined, the prosecution witnesses,

[699] Art. 64 (8)(a) ICCS. Of course, the possibility of an 'an admission of guilt', provided for by this same provision, is predicated on the full understanding of the charges, cf. Cotte and Saracco, 'Article 64', in Fernandez et al., *Statut II* (2019), pp. 1777–81; Klamberg, 'Article 64', in Klamberg et al., *Commentary ICC II* (2023), p. 213.

[700] Art. 67 (1)(b) ICCS; see also Arts. 21 (4)(b) ICTYS and 20 (4)(b) ICTRS, and 19 (4)(b) IRMCTS; Pérez-León-Acevedo and Elberling, 'Article 67', in Klamberg et al., *Commentary ICC II* (2023), pp. 259–63; on the right to counsel of the accused's choosing, see previously Section C (1)(c) in this chapter. Crit. with regard to the meaning of the notion 'adequate' in the context of defence, Karnavas, *ICLR*, (2019), 255–8. Crit. with regard to the broad victims' participation generating 'an increase in workload' and 'the processing of and responding to victim applications', thereby creating a tension with the defence rights, McGonigle Leyh, *ICLR*, 12 (2012), 397 ff.

[701] cf. Art. 55 (2)(c) (right to legal assistance) and (d) (right to presence of counsel during questioning unless waiver); see also Pérez-León-Acevedo and Elberling, 'Article 55', in Klamberg et al., *Commentary ICC II* (2023), pp. 66–70.

[702] cf. Rule 73 RPE ICC; generally on disclosure, see Chapter V, B. in this volume.

[703] *Nemo tenetur se ipsum accusare* ('nobody is bound to accuse himself'). For a detailed comparative analysis of the ensuing right to remain silent, see Damaška, *UPaLR*, 121 (1972–1973), 521 ff.

[704] Art. 67 (1)(g) ICCS; also Arts. 21 (4)(g) ICTYS, 20 (4)(g) ICTRS, and 19 (4)(g) IRMCTS. See also Safferling and Hartwig, *ZIS*, 4 (2009), 788 ff.; Keita et al., 'Article 67', in Fernandez et al., *Statut* (2019), pp. 1851–2; Schabas, *ICC Commentary* (2016), p. 864; Safferling and Hartwig, *International Criminal Procedure* (2012), p. 288; Pérez-León-Acevedo and Elberling, 'Article 67', in Klamberg et al., *Commentary ICC II* (2023), pp. 293–6.

[705] Art. 55 (1)(a) versus (2)(b); see also Safferling and Hartwig, *International Criminal Procedure* (2012), p. 288; Hall and Jacobs, 'Article 55', in Ambos, *Commentary* (2022), mn. 5 and 12; Pérez León Acevedo and Elberling, 'Article 55', in Klamberg et al., *Commentary ICC II* (2023), pp. 62–70.

[706] Art. 67 (1)(h) ICCS. See also Pérez-León-Acevedo and Elberling, 'Article 67', in Klamberg et al., *Commentary ICC II* (2023), pp. 297–9.

[707] *Abu Garda*, No. ICC-02/05-02/09-243-Red, para. 54; conc. *Prosecutor v. Bemba*, TC Decision on Unsworn Statement by the Accused pursuant to Article 67 (l)(h) of the Rome Statute, No. ICC-01/05-01/08-2860, 1 November 2013, para. 8.

[708] Chapter V, A.(3)(a) in this volume.

[709] Art. 55 (1)(b) and (d) ICCS; cf. thereon Hall and Jacobs, 'Article 55', in Ambos, *Commentary* (2022), mn. 6, 8–9; Pérez-León-Acevedo and Elberling, 'Article 55', in Klamberg et al., *Commentary ICC II* (2023), pp. 62–5; on the irregular apprehension of a suspect and the effects the ensuing violations may have on the fairness of the trial before the ICC, see McDermott, *JICJ*, 14 (2016), 147 ff.

[710] Chapter I, D.(3)(f) in this volume.

but also to raise defences and present other evidence.[711] This right suffers, however, some restrictions for the purpose of the protection of vulnerable witnesses, especially in cases of sexual violence.[712] We will return to the ensuing evidential issues regarding accused statements and the limitations on witness confrontation in Chapter V.[713]

Last but not least, the accused has the right to trial 'without undue delay'.[714] The term 'trial' refers to the whole proceedings, from the moment the accused is informed about a possible prosecution until the issuance of a final decision.[715] As explained previously, it cannot be determined in the abstract when a procedural delay turns out to be 'undue' but this depends on various factors relevant in the concrete case.[716] In the ICC context, the extensive victims' participation regime is certainly a factor which may increase the duration of proceedings but this is the price to be paid for the legitimate representation of victims' interests which, indeed, lie at the core of the Rome system and of international criminal justice in general. We will come back to this below.[717]

### (2) Presence at trial

We have already said above that the (fair trial) right to be present at the trial does not entail an absolute prohibition of *in absentia* trials.[718] In fact, such trials are common in several national jurisdictions[719] and the (now closed) Special Tribunal for Lebanon tried and convicted one defendant *in absentia*,[720] pursuant to its legal framework inspired by Lebanese law.[721]

Further, as a right, presence presupposes the fitness to stand trial.[722] The ICC Statute guarantees the right in Article 67 (1)(d) but the general presence requirement is contained in Article 63 (1) ICCS. This provision has come under fire in the Kenya proceedings with regard to President Uhuru Kenyatta and Deputy President William Samoei Ruto. The

[711] Art. 67 (1)(e) ICCS. See also Arts. 21 (4)(e) ICTYS, 20 (4)(e) ICTRS, and 19 (4)(e) IRMCTS.

[712] cf. Rules 68–73 RPE ICC; also Keita et al., 'Article 67', in Fernandez et al., *Statut II* (2019), p. 1849; Schabas and McDermott, 'Article 67', in Ambos, *Commentary* (2022), mn. 36–40; Pérez-León-Acevedo and Elberling, 'Article 67', in Klamberg et al., *Commentary ICC II* (2023), pp. 277–87.

[713] cf. Chapter V, A. in this volume, esp. (3)(a), and (b).

[714] Art. 67 (1)(c) ICCS; see also Arts. 21 (4)(c) ICTYS, 20 (4)(c) ICTRS, 19 (4)(c) IRMCTS and 21 (4)(d) KSC Law; see also Tochilovsky, *Jurisprudence* (2014), pp. 503–10; Pérez-León-Acevedo and Elberling, 'Article 67', in Klamberg et al., *Commentary ICC II* (2023), pp. 269–76; criticizing the length of the proceedings before the ICC, Kaul, *ZIS*, 2 (2007), 497; before the ad hoc tribunals, Hoven, *ZIS*, 6 (2011), 830 ff.; differentiating Whiting, *HarvILJ*, 50 (2009), 323 ff.; Damaška, *JICJ*, 10 (2012), 616; discussing the conflict between the right to adequate time for preparation and the right to trial without undue delay, Keita et al., 'Article 67', in Fernandez et al., *Statut II* (2019), p. 1831.

[715] Schabas and McDermott, 'Article 67', in Ambos, *Commentary* (2022), mn. 26.

[716] See Chapter I, D.3(h) in this volume.

[717] See below Section E., esp. (4).

[718] See Chapter I, D.3(a) in this volume.

[719] cf. Mertins, Proceedings *in absentia* (2022), pp. 282–407.

[720] *Prosecutor v. Ayyash et al.*, TC Summary of Judgment, No. STL-11-01/T/TC, 18 August 2020. Mr Ayyash was represented by defence counsel assigned by the Head of the Defence Office (*Prosecutor v. Ayyash et al.*, Pre-Trial Judge, Assignement of Counsel for the p-Proceedings Held *in absentia* Pursuant to Rule 106 of the Rules, No. STL-11-01/PT/PTJ, 2 February 2012) and was according to the TC aware of the charges and the possibility to participate in person (*Prosecutor v. Ayyash et al.*, TC Decision to Hold Trial *in absentia*, No. STL-11-01/I/TC, 1 February 2012, paras. 107–11.

[721] Art. 22 STLS, Part 5 sect. 6 STL RPE.

[722] See Schabas and Caruana, 'Article 63', in Ambos, *Commentary* (2022), mn. 48–60; Pérez-León-Acevedo and Elberling, 'Article 67', in Klamberg et al., *Commentary ICC II* (2023), pp. 277–81; for an overview of the case law of the ad hoc tribunals and the ICC thereon, see Freckelton and Karagiannakis, *JICJ*, 12 (2014), 707 ff.

implementation of the presence requirement becomes complicated if the accused is a sitting head of State or another highly important public official who certainly has other things to do than sit idly in a courtroom of the ICC. Of course, this was not an issue as long as the ICC did not prosecute such high officials or they just did not appear before the Court (e.g. Sudanese President Omar Al Bashir). With Kenyatta voluntarily appearing in The Hague the question then arose how his official duties as head of State can be reconciled with being present at his trial. The answer of the ASP was an amendment of the RPE at its twelfth session in November 2013 introducing Rules 134*bis*, *ter*, and *quater*.[723]

This amendment was preceded, apart from the usual political pressure and negotiations,[724] by some interesting case law attempting to solve the impasse via jurisprudential interpretation.[725] The AC considered that the TC had exceeded the limits of its discretionary power[726] and finally allowed the excusal of the accused under some conditions.[727] The *ratio decidendi* of the Appeals judgment has been basically incorporated into Rule 134*quater*.[728] This rule allows for an excusal from presence at trial due 'to extraordinary duties at the highest national level', on the condition that the person concerned is represented by counsel and waives[729] the right to be present.[730] The request must be directed to the TC, which grants it if 'it is in the interests of justice' and 'the rights of the accused are fully ensured'.[731] Of course, this rule leaves a broad discretion to the Chamber and it remains to be seen how its *ratione personae* scope (how low in the State hierarchy can be the 'highest national level')[732]

[723] Res. ICC-ASP/12/Res.7 Adopted on 27 November 2013; on the amended Rules regarding presence in light of Kenya proceedings, cf. also Ambos, 'Misguided Criticism', D&C, (2013), <http://www.dandc.eu/en/article/criticism-international-criminal-court-being-too-focussed-africa-misleading>; Knottnerus, *International Crimes Database Brief 5* (2014), 1 ff.

[724] On the 'intense' negotiations, see Schabas and Caruana, 'Article 63', in Ambos, *Commentary* (2022), mn. 17–18 with further references; Knottnerus, *LPICT*, 13 (2014), 270 ff.

[725] *Prosecutor v. Ruto and Sang*, TC Decision on Mr Ruto's Request for Excusal from Continuous Presence at Trial, No. ICC-01/09-01/11-777, 18 June 2013; *Prosecutor v. Kenyatta*, TC Decision on Defence Request for Conditional Excusal from Continuous Presence at Trial, No. ICC-01/09-02/11- 830, 18 October 2013; *Prosecutor v. Ruto and Sang*, AC Judgment on the Appeal of the Prosecutor against the Decision of Trial Chamber V(a) of 18 June 2013 entitled 'Decision on Mr Ruto's Request for Excusal from Continuous Presence at Trial', No. ICC-01/09-01/11-1066, 25 October 2013. On the procedural history leading to those two TC decisions and the AC Judgment, see Schabas and Caruana, 'Article 63', in Ambos, *Commentary* (2022), mn. 12 ff.; Knottnerus, *International Crimes Database Brief 5* (2014), 3 ff.; Knottnerus, *LPICT*, 13 (2014), 262 ff.; Le Floch, Lemey, and Paiola, *LPICT*, 14 (2015), 225 ff.

[726] *Ruto and Sang*, No. ICC-01/09-01/11-1066, paras. 61 ('the presence of the accused must remain the general rule ... article 63 (1) of the Statute clearly limits the Trial Chamber's discretion to excuse an accused person from presence during the trial') and 63 ('Trial Chamber in the present case interpreted the scope of its discretion too broadly and thereby exceeded the limits of its discretionary power').

[727] See *Ruto and Sang*, No. ICC-01/09-01/11-1066, para. 62 ('(i) the absence of the accused can only take place in exceptional circumstances and must not become the rule; (ii) the possibility of alternative measures must have been considered, including, but not limited to, changes to the trial schedule or a short adjournment of the trial; (iii) any absence must be limited to that which is strictly necessary; (iv) the accused must have explicitly waived his or her right to be present at trial; (v) the rights of the accused must be fully ensured in his or her absence, in particular through representation by counsel; and (vi) the decision ... must be taken on a case-by-case basis, with due regard to the subject matter of the specific hearings that the accused would not attend during the period for which excusal has been requested').

[728] cf. thereon, Schabas and Caruana, 'Article 63', in Ambos, *Commentary* (2022), mn. 79 ff.; Pérez-León-Acevedo and Elberling, 'Article 67', in Klamberg et al., *Commentary ICC II* (2023), pp. 277–87.

[729] On the quality of such a waiver, see *Prosecutor v. Nahimana et al.*, AC Judgment, No. ICTR-99-52-A, 28 November 2007, para. 109 ('free and unequivocal ... and done with full knowledge').

[730] Rule 134*quater* (1) RPE ICC.

[731] Rule 134*quater* (2) RPE ICC.

[732] Shortly after the new Rules came into force, Kenyan Deputy President Samoei Ruto submitted a request pursuant to Rule 134*quater*; cf. *Prosecutor v. Ruto and Sang*, Defence Request pursuant to Article 63 (1) of the Rome Statute and Rule 134*quater* of the Rules of Procedure and Evidence to Excuse Mr William Samoei Ruto from Attendance at Trial, No. ICC-01/09-01/11-1124, 16 December 2013. The TC V(A) 'decided to conditionally excuse Mr Ruto from presence at trial pursuant to Rule 134*quater*' requiring his presence in the courtroom for 'the

and the highly normative interests-of-justice clause[733] will be interpreted in the future case law of the Court.[734]

The new Rules provide for a three-stage system of exception from the presence requirement, allowing for a full absence only in the case of the highest officials mentioned above (third stage)[735] and for a partial absence of, in principle, any accused in case of 'exceptional circumstances' and the impossibility of 'alternative measures' (second stage);[736] virtual instead of physical presence by use of video technology is possible on a case-by-case basis (first stage).[737] Of course, also in this case, the person concerned must have good reasons for the physical absence although the Rule does not require that explicitly.[738]

In any case, it is unclear if Article 63 (1) ICCS allows for these exceptions in the first place and thus, whether, in light of Article 51 (5) ICCS giving prevalence to the Statute over conflicting Rules,[739] the new Rules can be applied at all. Article 63 (2) ICCS only allows for an exception from presence 'in exceptional circumstances' if the accused continuously disrupts the trial.[740] One may accept as a further exception the situation where an accused cannot be present for a prolonged period of time due to health reasons.[741] Apart from that, the absence

entirety of the closing statements of all parties and participants in the case', for 'when victims present their views and concerns in person', for 'the delivery of the judgment in the case', for 'the sentencing hearing', 'the sentencing', 'the victim impact hearings', 'the reparation hearings', 'for the first five days of hearing starting after a judicial recess as set out in regulation 19*bis* of the Regulations of the Court, ... and for any other attendance directed by the Chamber either *proprio motu* or other request of a party or participant as decided by the Chamber'; cf. *Prosecutor v. Ruto and Sang*, TC Reasons for the Decision on Excusal from Presence at Trial under Rule 134*quater*, No. ICC-01/09-01/11-1186, 18 February 2014, para. 79; crit. of that decision, Knottnerus, *International Crimes Database Brief 5* (2014), 4 ff.; Knottnerus, *LPICT*, 13 (2014), 281–2. On the cumulative requirements of 'extraordinary duties' and 'at the highest level', see also Schabas and Caruana, 'Article 63', in Ambos, *Commentary* (2022), mn. 81.

733 cf. *Ruto and Sang*, No. ICC-01/09-01/11-1186, paras. 72–4; Schabas and Caruana, 'Article 63', in Ambos, *Commentary* (2022), mn. 82. On this clause, see also Chapter IV, B.(4) in this volume.

734 Dismissing the criticism of Rule 134*quater* for inconsistency with other provisions of the ICCS, *Ruto and Sang*, No. ICC-01/09-01/11-1186, paras. 55, 59–61; conc. Schabas and Caruana, 'Article 63', in Ambos, *Commentary* (2022), mn. 85–7; Le Floch, Lemey, and Paiola, *LPICT*, 14 (2015), 227; *contra* Heller, *Opinio Juris* (2013); Knottnerus, *LPICT*, 13 (2014), 275–7, 283 ff.; Knottnerus, *International Crimes Database Brief 5* (2014), 7 ff.

735 Rule 134*quater* RPE ICC.

736 Rule 134*ter* RPE ICC; thereon Schabas and Caruana, 'Article 63', in Ambos, *Commentary* (2022), mn. 65–70; Pérez-León-Acevedo and Elberling, 'Article 67', in Klamberg et al., *Commentary ICC II* (2023), pp. 277–87.

737 134*bis* RPE ICC; thereon Schabas and Caruana, 'Article 63', in Ambos, *Commentary* (2022), mn. 30 ff.

738 For a discussion thereon, see Schabas and Caruana, 'Article 63', in Ambos, *Commentary* (2022), mn. 32 ff., 85, 88, arguing that 'the requirement, under article 63 (1) to be present at trial, can only be derogated from exceptionally' (mn. 88), but leaving to the Courts 'discretion in determining how narrowly or widely it interprets this requirement' and 'whether or not to grant the request' (mn. 39); arguing in favour of the exceptional character of virtual presence, Heller, *Opinio Juris* (2013) ('The drafters of Art. 63 (2) not only contemplated the use of videoconferencing, they very specifically considered it an exceptional mechanism'); see further Wheeler, *JICJ*, 17 (2019), 429, 430 (arguing that trials *in absentia* are not able to provide victims with a complete sense of justice and should therefore be avoided).

739 On the prevailing of the Statute over inconsistent or conflicting Rules, cf. Broomhall, 'Article 51', in Ambos, *Commentary* (2022), mn. 31–4; Malewa, 'Article 51', in Fernandez et al., *Statut I* (2019), pp. 1410–18.

740 Elberling, 'Article 63', in Klamberg et al., *Commentary ICC II* (2023), pp. 191–2.

741 cf. *Slobodan Milošević*, No. IT-02-54-AR73.7, paras. 14 ff., holding that the defendant can 'temporarily' be absent (para. 20), if his 'health, while good enough to engage in the ordinary and non-strenuous activities of everyday life, is not sufficiently robust to withstand all the rigors of trial work—the late nights, the stressful cross-examinations, the courtroom confrontations' (para. 14), and in any case, it shall be a weighing between 'self-representation [and the presupposed presence of the defendant at trial] and ... a reasonably expeditious resolution of the cases' (para. 19). On possible *in absentia* proceedings, incompatible with the ICCS, because of the accused's death, see Bachvarova, *JICJ*, 10 (2012), 547 ff.; Elberling, *Defendant in International Criminal Proceedings* (2012), pp. 14 ff., 18 ff.; for other possibilities of *in absentia* proceedings, see Elberling, 'Article 63', in Klamberg et al., *Commentary ICC II* (2023), pp. 193–4; crit. observing a recent change on how (*in absentia*) trials are conducted at the ICC, Wheeler, *ICLR*, 21 (2021), 97–125; on *in absentia* trials before the STL, see Jenks, *FordhamILJ*, 33 (2010), 57; Oehmichen, in Esser et al., *FS Kühne* (2013), pp. 613 ff.

of the accused is only explicitly allowed with regard to the confirmation hearing.[742] Thus, the gist of the issue is whether Article 63 (1) grants a right only (which then could be waived) or if it also entails a duty or at least relates to some public interest in the presence of the accused in ICC proceedings. The former view seems to be confirmed by the fact that the right to be present is also mentioned in the central rights provision of the Statute[743] and thus seems to constitute just another fair trial right.[744] However, Article 63 itself does not speak of a 'right' but the use of the term 'shall' (in para. 1) rather suggests a general presence requirement coming close to a duty.[745] On a more substantive note, the presence of the accused at trial does not only serve fair trial but also other interests, more akin to the purpose of a criminal trial, such as its truth-finding purpose or even the 'credibility of the criminal justice system' in general.[746] From this perspective, the presence requirement appears as a more general principle,[747] which at best, not amounting to a (fixed) rule,[748] allows for well-founded exceptions.[749] One may now argue that the State Parties, as the sovereign of the Rome Statute and its legislator, have made these exceptions with Rules 134*bis*, *ter*, and *quater*, although this argument leaves a bitter taste given the deeply divisive politicial struggle surrounding the

[742] Art. 61 (2) ICCS and Rule 124 (1) RPE ICC; cf. also Pérez-León-Acevedo and Elberling, 'Article 67', in Klamberg et al., *Commentary ICC II* (2023), pp. 277–87. On the special case of the *ex parte* hearing within the framework of the protection of national security information (Art. 72 (7) ICCS), see Rastan, 'Article 72', in Ambos, *Commentary* (2022), mn. 37 ff.

[743] cf. Art. 67 (1)(d) ICCS.

[744] In this vein, Safferling, *Towards an International Criminal Procedure* (2001), p. 241 (compare the title of the section [right] with the other sections [principles]); on *presence at trial* as the basic prerequisite for 'equality of arms', see Negri, in Bohlander, *International Criminal Justice* (2007), pp. 28 ff.

[745] In this vein, *Ruto and Sang*, No. ICC-01/09-01/11-777, paras. 38–44, 47–53, 104 (104: 'the presence of the accused during trial is not only a right (by virtue of article 67 (1)(d)), but also a duty on the accused (by virtue of 63 (1))'); conc. *Ruto and Sang*, No. ICC-01/09-01/11-1066-Anx, Joint Separate Opinion of Judge Erkki Kourula and Judge Anita Ušacka, para. 7; *Ruto and Sang*, No. ICC-01/09-01/11-777, Dissenting Opinion of Judge Herrera Carbuccia, para. 4; *Prosecutor v. Kenyatta*, TC Decision on Defence Request for Conditional Excusal from Continuous Presence at Trial, No. ICC-01/09-02/11-830, 18 October 2013, para. 124; *Prosecutor v. Kenyatta*, Partially Dissenting Opinion of Judge Ozaki, No. ICC-01/09-02/11-830- Anx2, 23 October 2013, para. 10, *Prosecutor v. Kenyatta*, No. ICC-01/09-02/11-863-Anx-Corr, Dissenting Opinion of Judge Eboe-Osuji, para. 35, ('the view that article 63(1) is about a right for the accused not a duty negate[s] the very notion of excusal from presence at trial'); Safferling, *International Criminal Procedure* (2012), pp. 399–400 ('a general principle of international criminal procedure'); Knottnerus, *LPICT*, 13 (2014), 263 ('statutory requirement', 'impose a duty on the accused to attend the complete trial'); Le Floch, Lemey, and Paiola, *LPICT*, 14 (2015), 227 ('It is now clear that … [Article 63(1)] provides for a duty on the accused'); Schabas and Caruana, 'Article 63', in Ambos, *Commentary* (2022), mn. 21–9 (mn. 24: 'the provision imposes a duty upon the accused'); Schabas and McDermott, 'Article 67', in Ambos, *Commentary* (2022), mn. 28 ('the presence of the accused is an obligation as well as a right').

[746] Friman, in Darcy and Powderly, *Judicial Creativity* (2010), p. 334; Safferling, *International Criminal Procedure* (2012), p. 397; for more arguments in favour of presence at trial, see Schabas and Caruana, 'Article 63', in Ambos, *Commentary* (2022), mn. 29.

[747] cf. *Ruto and Sang*, No. ICC-01/09-01/11-1066, para. 49 ('a general principle'); see also Schabas, *ICC Commentary* (2016), p. 862; Friman, in Darcy and Powderly, *Judicial Creativity* (2010), pp. 334–5; Preira, Mbaye, and Shoamanesh, 'Article 63', in Fernandez et al., *Statut* (2019), pp. 1720 ff.; Schabas and Caruana, 'Article 63', in Ambos, *Commentary* (2022), mn. 20 ff.

[748] As to the distinction between (rather flexible) principles and (fixed) rules, I follow Alexy, *Theorie der Grundrechte* (1986), pp. 71 ff. (English translation by Rivers, *A Theory of Constitutional Rights* (2002), pp. 44 ff.), according to whom principles and rules are two types of norm that both give reasons as to what should happen but that differ in a qualitative sense: principles demand that something must be realized to the greatest extent possible, they are 'optimization requirements' (*Optimierungsgebote*) that can only be satisfied to a certain extent, their actual fulfilment depends on the factual and legal possibilities; rules can either be fulfilled or not, they contain determinations (*Festsetzungen*, English translation, at p. 48: 'fixed points') within the factually and legally possible.

[749] Boas et al., *International Criminal Procedure* (2011), pp. 272; Safferling, *International Criminal Procedure* (2012), p. 400; *Nahimana et al.*, No. ICTR-99-52-A, para. 99; for further case law references of absence of the accused for short durations with a specific waiver of the right to be present, see Schabas and McDermott, 'Article 67', in Ambos, *Commentary* (2022), mn. 28.

adoption of these Rules. Be that as it may, it is now up to the Court to interpret these Rules restrictively in light of the importance of the presence requirement.[750]

### (3) Self-representation

While the accused is entitled to conduct the defence in person, the Court may assign legal assistance to this person 'in any case where the interests of justice so require'.[751] Thus, again, all depends on the interpretation of the highly ambiguous 'interests of justice' clause, the invocation of which could outplay the right to self-representation.

Unfortunately, the case law of the ad hoc tribunals[752] is inconclusive on the matter.[753] The approaches adopted vary from the recognition of an extensive right to self-representation, denying a compulsory imposition of a defence counsel,[754] to the imposition of a standby

[750] For a restrictive interpretation of Rule 134*bis* RPE ICC, see *Prosecutor v. Bemba*, TC VII Decision on 'Motion for Severance or, in the Alternative, Adjournment or Appearance Pursuant to Rule 134bis of the Rules', No. ICC-01/05-01/13-1269, 18 Sptember 2015, para. 21 (stressing the exceptionality of presence through video technology of the accused and demanding that 'compelling reasons must be advanced which will move the Chamber to conclude that derogation of this rule is warranted'). Equally restrictively applying Rules 134*bis* and 134*ter* RPE ICC, see *Prosecutor v. Gbagbo*, TC I, Public Redacted Version of the Decision on Mr Gbagbo's Detention, No. ICC-02/11-01/15-1038-Red, 25 September 2017, para. 72 ('Rules 134*bis* and 134*ter* of the Rules allow the exceptional absence of the accused person, but in no way establish a rule'). Departing from this rather cautious approach and permitting, in principle, to continue a trial outside of the physical or virtual presence of the accused on the basis of an implicit waiver derived from the accused's failure to appear, see *Prosecutor v. Gbagbo*, AC, Public Redacted Decision on Counsel for Mr Gbagbo's Request for Reconsideration of the 'Judgment on the Prosecutor's appeal against the oral decision of Trial Chamber I pursuant to article 81(3)(c)(i) of the Statute' and on the review of the conditions on the release of Mr Gbagbo and Mr Blé Goudé, No. ICC-02/11-01/15-1355-Red, 28 May 2020, paras. 68–71 (determining that in case of a wilful failure to reappear before the Court for any future proceedings, 'such proceedings could in principle continue without their physical presence' [at para. 68] and stating that '[t]he continuance of proceedings without the physical presence of the accused in cases of wilful absence is prohibited neither by the Statute properly understood, nor by general principles of law. As long as the right to a fair trial is scrupulously respected, particularly by ensuring proper representation of counsel, such proceedings are permissible' [at para. 70]). Crit. as to this possible change in the ICC's approach to the permissibility of *in absentia* trials, Wheeler, *EJIL: Talk!*, 3 July 2020.

[751] Art. 67 (1)(d) ICCS. If the accused chooses to defend herself in person, she shall so notify the Registrar in writing at the first opportunity (Rule 21 (4) RPE ICC). See also Art. 14 (3)(d) ICCPR and Arts. 21 (4)(d) ICTYS, 20 (4)(d) ICTRS, 19 (4)(d) IRMCTS, and 21 (4)(e) KSC Law.

[752] For a detailed jurisprudential analysis of self-representation, esp. at the ICTY, see Harvey, in Rohan and Zyberi, *Defense Perspectives* (2017), pp. 86 ff. There is not yet any KSC case law on the matter, but from Art. 21 (5) KSC Law it follows that a right to self-representation only exists in limited circumstances.

[753] cf. generally Kirsch, in Weigend, Walther, and Grunewald, *Strafverteidigung vor neuen Herausforderungen* (2008), pp. 85 ff.; Tochilovsky, *Jurisprudence* (2014), pp. 424 ff.; Petersdorf, *Eigenverteidigung* (2010), pp. 53 ff.; Jalloh, *PennStLR*, 117 (2012–2013), 717; Bonomy, in Boas, Schabas, and Scharf, *International Criminal Justice* (2012), pp. 53 ff.; Swoboda, *ZIS*, 5 (2010), 113; Bassiouni, *DukeJCompe&IL*, 3 (1993), 283–4; Tuinstra, *Defence Counsel* (2009), pp. 245 ff.; Scharf, in Brown, *Handbook ICL* (2011), pp. 284 ff.; Higgins, in Darcy and Powderly, *Judicial Creativity* (2010), pp. 252 ff.; in favour of a limited validity of the right to self-representation (with a comparative view of various legal systems) also Ambach, *ZIS*, 4 (2009), 289; *Damaška*, *JICJ*, 10 (2012), 617; Pérez-León-Acevedo and Elberling, 'Article 67', in Klamberg et al., *Commentary ICC II* (2023), p. 282 ('self-representation is not an absolute right and may be restricted when there is a continuous and substantial obstruction of trial').

[754] *Prosecutor v. Slobodan Milošević*, TC Reasons for Decision on the Prosecution Motion Concerning Assignment of Counsel, No. IT-02-54-T, 4 April 2003, paras. 18 ff. (admitting, however, that 'there may be circumstances ... where it is in the interest of justice to appoint counsel', para. 40); *Slobodan Milošević*, No. IT-02-54-AR73.7; imposing defence counsel in the *Milošević* case on the grounds of the health condition of the accused, cf. *Prosecutor v. Slobodan Milošević*, TC Reasons for Decision on Assignment of Defence Counsel, No. IT-02-54-T, 22 September 2004; crit. as to this 'excessiveness', cf. *Prosecutor v. Slobodan Milošević*, AC Decision on Interlocutory Appeal of the Trial Chamber's Decision on the Assignment of Defense Counsel, No. IT-02-54-AR73.7, 1 November 2004, para. 18 (calling at para. 19 for 'a careful course between allowing Milošević to exercise his fundamental right of self-representation and safeguarding the Tribunal's basic interest in a reasonably expeditious resolution of the case before it'); in favour of such a broad approach Schabas, *ICC Commentary* (2016), p. 1037; for a crit. view, see Damaška, *JICJ*, 3 (2005), 3 ff.; Sluiter, *JICJ*, 3 (2005), 9 ff.; Boas, 'The Right to Self-Representation', in Abtahi

counsel against the will of the accused.[755] The former position is based on the accused's position as a subject and not a mere object of criminal procedure.[756] In practice, however, counsel was assigned in every case where the accused invoked the right to self-representation,[757] regardless of the respective Chamber's theoretical approach.

Thus, in sum, while the right to self-representation is one of the minimum guarantees of the accused, it is lifted when a Chamber considers that the trial could effectively not be run without the assignment of defence counsel. In other words, the right to self-representation has to give in to the overarching interests of justice, that is, the interest of international criminal tribunals to conduct their trials as smoothly as possible. Beyond that, a Chamber also has the responsibility to guarantee a fair trial. To make a technical defence possible, this may entail assigning counsel even against the accused's will. From this perspective, the fair trial principle 'is not only a fundamental right of the accused, but also a fundamental interest of the tribunal related to its own legitimacy'.[758]

## E. Victims

### (1) A new concept in ICL: From victor's justice to justice for victims

In the historic war crimes trials victims played only a marginal role, if any. The Charters of the Nuremberg and Tokyo tribunals did not contain any provision on victim participation, treatment, or reparation; in fact, they made no reference to victims at all.[759] The emphasis

and Boas, *The Dynamics of International Criminal Justice* (2006), pp. 67 ff.; Bohlander, *CLF*, 16 (2005), 159 ff.; Bonomy, *JICJ*, 5 (2007), 355 ff.; Kreß and Wannek, 'Von den beiden internationalen Ad-Hoc-Tribunalen zum Internationalen Strafgerichtshof', in Kirsch, *Internationale Strafgerichtshöfe* (2005), p. 255; alsoChiavario, *JICJ*, 6 (2008), 77 ff.; on how the substitution of the presiding member of the three-judge panel potentially threatens the fair trial rights of the accused in the *Milošević* case Fairlie, *CLF*, 16 (2005), 107 ff.; *Prosecutor v. Krajišnik*, AC Judgement, No. IT-00-39-A, 17 March 2009, paras. 117–18 and ICTY, *Manual* (2009), pp. 90 ff.

[755] *Šešelj*, No. IT-03-67-PT, TC Decision with which the ICTY appointed a 'standby counsel' against the accused's will; crit., however, *Prosecutor v. Šešelj*, AC Decision on Appeal against the Trial Chamber's Decision (No. 2) on Assignment of Counsel, No. IT-03-67-AR73.4, 8 December 2006, paras. 18 ff., paras. 25–9 (finding at para. 27 that 'the Trial Chamber abused its discretion by immediately ordering the imposition of standby counsel, without first establishing additional obstructionist behaviour on the part of *Šešelj* warranting that imposition, with the clear possibility to take over the proceedings'). On the restriction of the right to self-representation at the pre-trial stage, *Prosecutor v. Šešelj*, AC Decision on Appeal against the Trial Chamber's Decision on Assignment of Counsel, No. IT-03-67-AR73.3, 20 October 2006, paras. 27–9. Assigning standby counsel for the appeal stage, *Prosecutor v. Šešelj*, AC Decision on Assignment of Standby Counsel for the Appeal Hearing, No. MICT-16-99-A, 11 October 2017. On the assignment of counsel *proprio motu*, cf. *Prosecutor v. Prlić*, AC Decision on Praljak's Request for Stay of Proceedings, No. IT-04-74-A, 27 June 2014, para. 16. Against self-representation Boas, *JICJ*, 9 (2011), 74 ff. On the right to self-representation in the *Šešelj* case (IT-03-67), cf. Badar and Karsten, *ICLR*, 7 (2007), 177 ff., Scharf, in Brown, *Handbook ICL* (2011), p. 299 (right to self-representation 'not ... an absolute right, but a qualified privilege'); crit. of the tribunal's handling of Šešelj's hunger strike, see Sluiter, *JICJ*, 5 (2007), 529 ff.; Zahar and Sluiter, *ICL* (2008), pp. vii–viii.

[756] In the same vein, Spaniol, in Burkhardt et al., *FG Eser* (2015), p. 432 (arguing that the right to self-representation derives from human dignity and the rule of law, according to which the defendant is not a mere object of the criminal procedure, but a subject with a right to take part and actively influence its course and outcome).

[757] The most prominent accused who represented themselves have been *Slobodan Milošević*, *Vojislav Šešelj*, *Zdravko Tolimir*, and *Radovan Karadžić*; *Momćilo Krajišnik* invoked this right in the appeals procedure.

[758] *Šešelj*, No. IT-03-67-PT, para. 18.

[759] Moffett, *ICLR*, 12 (2012), 252, 265; Garkawe, *ICLR*, 3 (2003), 347; see also Donat-Cattin, in Carlizzi et al., *Corte Penale Internazionale* (2003), p. 349 with n. 2; Stehle, *Strafverfahren* (2007), p. 209; Abo Youssef, *Stellung des Opfers* (2008), p. 7; Evans, *Right to Reparation* (2012), p. 88; de Brouwer and Heikkilä, in Sluiter et al., *International Criminal Procedure* (2013), p. 1300; Zegveld, *ICLR*, 19 (2019), 323–4. In preparation of the Nuremberg Trial, the idea of having a kind of *amicus curiae* representation of Jewish victims was discussed, but finally dismissed; see, in more detail, Marrus, *CardozoLR*, 27 (2006), 1653–6.

on the crime of aggression even indicates that not individuals but States were regarded as the primary victims of the Nazi atrocities.[760] Given the meticulous documentation of the crimes by the Nazis themselves,[761] victims were not even needed as witnesses. Indeed, the prosecution at the IMT only called fourteen victims to testify in court;[762] at the IMTFE twenty-seven victims testified.[763] In sum, it is fair to say that the tribunals' focus on the responsibility of the Nazi regime vis-à-vis the Allies did not leave much room nor need for a victim-oriented procedural approach.[764]

About fifty years later, probably under the influence of the international victims' rights movement,[765] the newly established *ad hoc tribunals* are obliged to ensure the protection of victims *and* witnesses[766]—a novel distinction, which implies that victims have a procedural status independent and distinct from that of a witness.[767] This general rule is further specified in Rules 69, 75, 79 (A) (ii) RPE ICTY/ICTR/SCSL[768] on specific protective measures such as non-disclosure of identity, closed session, or one-way circuit television, which may also be ordered at the request of the victim concerned.[769] Moreover, the ad hoc tribunals' procedural regime contains a (limited) recognition of the victims' right to reparation:[770] The TC may order a convicted person to return any property and proceeds acquired by the respective criminal conduct to the rightful owner.[771] Further, pursuant to Rules 106 RPE

[760] Moffett, *ICLR*, 12 (2012), 249–51, 256; see also Bass, *Stay the Hand* (2000), p. 148 ('the Allies saw themselves as the victims of German criminality'); Schabas, *Introduction* (2020), p. 355. See also Art. 28 IMTS, according to which stolen property has to be delivered to the Allied Control Council and not the rightful owner, i.e. the individual victim of the crime.

[761] At least 90 per cent of the evidence presented during the Nuremberg Trial consisted of the Nazis' own written records: Dodd, in Mettraux, *Perspectives* on the Nuremberg Trial (2008), p. 439; see also Ambos and Bock, in Reydams, Wouters, and Ryngaert, *Prosecutors* (2012), p. 493 with further references and Chapter I, B.(1)(a) in this volume.

[762] Moffett, *ICLR*, 12 (2012), 252; see also Garkawe, *ICLR*, 3 (2003), 347; Danieli, *CardozoLR*, 27 (2006), 1641; Chakravarti, *Constellations*, 15 (2008), 225; Schabas, *ICC Commentary* (2016), p. 1055; McGonigle Leyh, *Procedural Justice?* (2011), p. 136.

[763] Moffett, *ICLR*, 12 (2012), 266; see also Chapter I, B.(1)(b) in this volume.

[764] Moffett, *ICLR*, 12 (2012), 259, crit. on p. 258 ('Nuremberg neglected justice for many victims and survivors'); see also Chakravarti, *Constellations*, 15 (2008), 225; Bass, *Stay the Hand* (2000), p. 148; in a similar vein, Danieli, *CardozoLR*, 27 (2006), 1641 ('the Trials have not only missed a healing opportunity of welcoming demoralized survivors to a world with justice, but they added little meaning to the survivors and their re-emerging communities').

[765] In more detail and with further references, Bock, *Opfer* (2010), pp. 40–51; cf. also Garkawe, *ICLR*, 3 (2003), 347–8; Tolbert and Swinnen, in Abtahi and Boas, *Dynamics* (2006), pp. 194–5; Bassiouni, in Bassiouni, *Pursuit* (2010), pp. 578–83; Spiga, *JICJ*, 10 (2012), 1381–6.

[766] Arts. 22 ICTYS, 21 ICTRS, 20 IRMCTS and—broader—Art. 23 KSC Law. See also Art. 17 (2) SCSLS/RSCSLS, according to which the right of the accused to a fair and public hearing is subject 'to measures ordered by the Special Court [and/or the Residual Special Court, including] for the protection of victims and witnesses' (in a similar vein, Art. 21 (2) KSC Law).

[767] cf. also Tolbert and Swinnen, in Abtahi and Boas, *Dynamics* (2006), p. 196; Boas et al., *International Criminal Procedure* (2011), p. 309.

[768] See also Rules 75, 86, and 93 (A) RPE MICT as well as Rules 80, 81 RPE KSC.

[769] Rule 75 (A) RPE ICTY/ICTR/SCSL and Rule 86 (A) RPE MICT.

[770] cf. also Garkawe, *ICLR*, 3 (2003), 349; van Boven, in von Hebel, Lammers, and Schukking, *Reflections on the ICC* (1999), p. 81.

[771] Arts. 24 (3) ICTYS, 23 (3) ICTRS, 22 (4) IRMCTS and 44 (6) KSC Law; Rules 105 RPE ICTY/ICTR, 129 RPE MICT and 71 RPE KSC; see also Rule 104 (C) RPE SCSL, according to which the tribunal may order the return of forfeited property to the owner or its transfer to the State of Sierra Leone. In more detail, Abo Youssef, *Stellung des Opfers* (2008), pp. 91–6; Heikkilä, *International Criminal Tribunals* (2004), pp. 178–9; de Brouwer, *LJIL*, 20 (2007), 214–15; Chifflet, in Boas and Schabas, *ICL Developments* (2003), pp. 100–2; de Brouwer and Heikkilä, in Sluiter et al., *International Criminal Procedure* (2013), pp. 1355–8. The practical relevance of this provision, however, is limited, since a restitution order is only deemed possible if the accused is charged with the unlawful taking of property, *Prosecutor v. Musema*, Decision on Application by African Concern for Leave to Appear as Amicus Curiae, No. ICTR-96-13-T, 17 March 1999, para. 11; see also Boas et al., *International Criminal Procedure* (2011), p. 310.

ICTY/ICTR, 105 RPE SCSL, and 130 RPE MICT, victims may seek compensation for the injuries suffered in any other forum;[772] for the purposes of these compensation proceedings, the judgment of the tribunals shall be final and binding as to the criminal responsibility of the convicted person for such injury. However, the said Rules do not grant victims the right to claim reparation in the proceedings before the tribunals, nor do they oblige States to provide for compensation mechanism.[773] In essence, they merely contain a reference to existing domestic rules on reparation.[774]

From all this results that the ad hoc tribunals perceive victims primarily as a (passive) object of protection,[775] not yet as an (active) participant in the proceedings. Given the adversarial nature of the proceedings before the ad hoc tribunals,[776] the trial is dominated by defence and prosecution while the role of the victims is largely limited to that of a witness.[777] In fact, victims' testimonies have become the most important, in any case most spectacular,[778] source of international criminal proceedings.[779] Given their passive status before the ad hoc tribunals, victims may, however, only provide information about the respective crimes at the request of the parties, but not actively influence the course of the proceedings or ask for the presentation of additional evidence. In short, they are dependent on the Prosecutor to represent their interests.[780] Victims therefore have been described as the 'missing party' in international criminal proceedings.[781]

This situation changed radically with the adoption of the ICC Statute, which for the first time in the history of international criminal procedure—recognizes victims as persons and legal subjects in their own right[782] and grants them 'an independent voice and role in

[772] See also Rule 167 (2) RPE KSC; also Heikkilä, *International Criminal Tribunals* (2004), p. 175.

[773] Ibid.; see also Jorda and de Hemptinne, in Cassese et al., *Rome Statute II* (2002), p. 1393; Chifflet, in Boas and Schabas, *ICL Developments* (2003), pp. 99, 103; Donat-Cattin, in Carlizzi et al., *Corte Penale Internazionale* (2003), p. 357; de Brouwer, *LJIL*, 20 (2007), 215; Abo Youssef, *Stellung des Opfers* (2008), p. 93; Pérez-León-Acevedo, *Victims' Status* (2014), p. 581.

[774] Crit. Heikkilä, *International Criminal Tribunals* (2004), p. 176; Boas et al., *International Criminal Procedure* (2011), pp. 310–11; see also Donat-Cattin, in Carlizzi et al., *Corte Penale Internazionale* (2003), pp. 348, 357.

[775] Jorda and de Hemptinne, in Cassese et al., *Rome Statute II* (2002), p. 1389; cf. also Stehle, *Strafverfahren* (2007), p. 211.

[776] See Chapter I, B.(2)(a) and Chapter IV, A.(1) in this volume.

[777] Jorda and de Hemptinne, in Cassese et al., *Rome Statute II* (2002), p. 1390; Heikkilä, *International Criminal Tribunals* (2004), pp. 74, 154Abo Youssef, *Stellung des Opfers* (2008), p. 67; see also Donat-Cattin, in Lattanzi, *The ICC* (1998), p. 264; van Boven, in von Hebel, Lammers, and Schukking, *Reflections on the ICC* (1999), p. 80; Tolbert and Swinnen, in Abtahi and Boas, *Dynamics* (2006), p. 195; Boas et al., *International Criminal Procedure* (2011), p. 309; de Brouwer and Heikkilä, in Sluiter et al., *International Criminal Procedure* (2013), p. 1300; Kendall and Nouwen, *LCP*, 76 nos. 3 & 4 (2013), 238; Friman, in Cryer et al., *ICL* (2019), p. 445.

[778] Catani, *JICJ*, 10 (2012), 920 regards giving testimony as the 'arguably most meaningful form of participation'.

[779] In the proceedings before the ICTY, thousands of victims have been interviewed, and more than one hundred testified in court; see <http://www.icty.org/sid/324>, and <http://www.icty.org/en/in-focus/voice of the-victims>; see also Garkawe, *ICLR*, 3 (2003), 350; Chifflet, in Boas and Schabas, *ICL Developments* (2003), p. 98; Heikkilä, *International Criminal Tribunals* (2004), p. 74; Abo Youssef, *Stellung des Opfers* (2008), p. 67; Bock, *Opfer* (2010), p. 372; Kelly, in Bonacker and Safferling, *Victims* (2013), p. 48.

[780] cf. Jorda and de Hemptinne, in Cassese et al., *Rome Statute II* (2002), p. 1390; Chifflet, in Boas and Schabas, *ICL Developments* (2003), p. 109; Heikkilä, *International Criminal Tribunals* (2004), p. 155.

[781] Donat-Cattin, in Carlizzi et al., *Corte Penale Internazionale* (2003), p. 356; cf. also Chifflet, in Boas and Schabas, *ICL Developments* (2003), p. 98; Heikkilä, *International Criminal Tribunals* (2004), p. 164; Stahn, Olásolo, and Gibson, *JICJ*, 4 (2006), 220; Pena and Carayon, *IJTJ*, 7 (2013), 520–2; Perrin, *ICLR*, 15 (2015), 299; on the resulting dissatisfaction of victims, see Wemmers, *LJIL*, 23 (2010), 640; but see also, on Rule 61 Proceedings as the 'voice of victims', Safferling, *ZStW*, 115 (2003), 366; on the use of victim impact statements, McGonigle Leyh, *Procedural Justice?* (2011), pp. 143–5; on the impact of evidence introduced by the victims in the *Lubanga* and *Katanga* cases, see Wheeler, *ICLR*, 16 (2016), 536 ff. and 541 ff.

[782] Ambos, *ICLR*, 12 (2012), 115–16; Bock, in Klip and Freeland, *ALC*, XL (2013), p. 283; in a similar vein, Kendall and Nouwen, *LCP*, 76 nos. 3 & 4 (2013), 238–9; Hodgson, *CLF*, 34 (2023) 2.

the proceedings before the Court'.[783] Most notably, Article 68 ICCS does not only oblige the Court to 'take appropriate measures to protect the safety, physical and psychological well-being, dignity and privacy of victims and witnesses', but also empowers victims to present their views and concerns in the proceedings before the Court, if their personal interests are affected. In addition, the Court may order the convicted person to make reparations to victims.[784] All in all, the ICCS establishes a comprehensive victims' rights system consisting of four components, namely assistance, participation, protection, and reparation.[785] These components will be analysed in more detail below.[786] Similar provisions can only be found in the procedural law of subsequent (mixed) tribunals, namely the ECCC,[787] STL,[788] and in particular the KSC.[789]

The underlying idea of this *new victim-focus* in international criminal procedure is to bring the proceedings closer to the affected communities and, in doing so, strengthen their legitimacy.[790] The better integration of victims into the proceedings is also meant to prevent them from taking vengeance,[791] help them recover from their traumatic experiences,[792] and contribute to the reconciliation of the society.[793] This approach, however, is not without risks. The possible participation of thousands of victims[794] enhances the complexity of the proceedings, causes delays, and thus raises the principled question of whether

[783] PTC I, *Situation in the DRC*, Decision on the Applications for Participation in the Proceedings of VPRS 1, VPRS 2, VPRS 3, VPRS 4, VPRS 5, and VPRS 6, No. ICC-01/04-101, 17 January 2006, para. 51; *Prosecutor v. Kony et al.*, PTC II Decision on 'Prosecutor's Application to Attend 12 February Hearing', No. ICC-02/04-01/05-155, 9 February 2007, p. 4; see also *Prosecutor v. Katanga and Ngudjolo*, Single Judge, PTC I Decision on the Set of Procedural Rights Attached to Procedural Status of Victim at the Pre-Trial Stage of the Case, No. ICC-01/04-01/07-474, 13 May 2008, paras. 153–60; PTC I, *Situation in the Bolivarian Republic of Venezuela I*, Victims' Concerns arising from the Public Information regarding the Conclusion of the Prosecutor's Preliminary Examination concerning the Situation in the Bolivarian Republic of Venezuela I, No. ICC-02/18-11, 21 June 2021, para. 12.

[784] Art. 75 (2) ICCS.

[785] In a similar vein, Friman, in Cryer et al., *ICL* (2019), p. 445.

[786] cf. Section E.(3)–(6) in this chapter.

[787] Art. 33 ECCC Law, Rules 12*ter*, 23–23*quinquies* IR ECCC.

[788] Art. 12 (4), 17 STLS. The STL, however, cannot order compensation to victims. Just like Rule 106 RPE ICTY/ICTR, Art. 25 STLS refers reparation issues to the national level.

[789] Arts. 22–3 KSC Law, Rules 80, 81, 113, 114 RPE KSC.

[790] *Katanga and Ngudjolo*, No. ICC-01/04-01/07-474, para. 163; FIDH, *Victims' Rights* (November 2013), p. 7; in a similar vein, de Brouwer and Heikkilä, in Sluiter et al., *International Criminal Procedure* (2013), p. 1300; VRWG, *Victim Participation* (June 2014), p. 4; Moffet, *JICJ*, 13 (2015), 289; Moffet, *CLF*, 26 (2015), 260; Hodgson, *CLF*, 34 (2023), 16. See also ICC-OTP, *Complementarity and Cooperation* (2024), p. 13 (favouring 'close physical proximity and regular contact with affected communities'), p. 39 (para. 97) ('the Office will seek... to hold at least part of the proceedings ... as close as possible to the affected communities'); thereon Urueña, *Just Security* 26 August 2024.

[791] Garkawe, *ICLR*, 3 (2003), 349; Damaška, *ChicKentLR*, 83 (2008), 334.

[792] Donat-Cattin, in Carlizzi et al., *Corte Penale Internazionale* (2003), p. 362; Kaoutzanis, *UCDavisJIL&Pol'y*, 17 (2010), 127; Bock, *Opfer* (2010), p. 175; Tonellato, *EJCCLCJ*, 20 (2012), 324; Pena and Carayon, *IJTJ*, 7 (2013), 522; cf. also Garkawe, *ICLR*, 3 (2003), 350; de Hemptinne, *JICJ*, 8 (2010), 167–8; WCRO, *Victim Status* (December 2013), p. 6; also Pemberton et al., *ICLR*, 15 (2015), 360–3. More reluctant, Rauschenbach and Scalia, *IRRC*, 90 (2008), 445; Mohan, *ICLR*, 9 (2009), 740; Safferling, *ICLR*, 11 (2011), 215; Vasiliev, in Stahn, *ICC* (2015), p. 1195; in more detail on the (possible) therapeutic effect of international criminal trials, Doak, *ICLR*, 11 (2011), 263.

[793] Stahn, Olásolo, and Gibson, *JICJ*, 4 (2006), 221; Bock, *Opfer* (2010), p. 208; Ip, *ICLR*, 13 (2013), 868, 883; see also Horovitz, in Carter and Pocar, *International Criminal Procedure* (2013), p. 190; Suprun, *ICLR*, 16 (2016), 976–7.

[794] For instance, over 5,500 victims participated in the proceedings against Bemba: FIDH, *Victims' Rights* (November 2013), p. 18 and over 4,000 victims participated in the proceedings against Ongwen, see *Prosecutor v. Ongwen*, TC IX Trial Judgment, No. ICC-02/04-01/15-1762-Red, 4 February 2021, para. 25; for an overview on victim applications for participation per year and situation, see ICC-ASP, *Budget 2023*, p. 241 (para. 16), indicating, for example, a total of 6,900 in 2021 and of 7,800 in 2022. For 2024, a total of 10,500 victims are expected to apply for participation/ reparation, see ICC-ASP, *Budget 2024*, p. 200 (para. 18), indicating victims' numbers for the following situations: CAR II (1,500), Mali (1,000), DRC (1,500), UGA (1,500), Darfur (2,000), and UKR (3,000).

(international) criminal proceedings really are an appropriate forum for this empowerment exercise in the first place or if the (procedural) costs are rather too high.[795]

Apart from that, victims' participation in criminal proceedings always generates a conflict with the right of the accused to an expeditious[796] and fair[797] trial. In addition, the difficulties in implementing the victims' rights approach may even frustrate the goals it tries to pursue: some authors fear that the intervention of victims may undermine the strategy of the Prosecutor and thus hamper the prosecution and conviction of a defendant.[798] More importantly, the ICC's victim-friendly rules might create high expectations for victims and their constituencies[799] which—not least because of inherent procedural limitations—are impossible to fulfil and thus necessarily lead to disappointment and frustration.[800] These merely cursory considerations show that the development

[795] Trumbull IV, *MichJIL*, 29 (2008), 804–18; crit. van den Wyngaert, *CWRJIL*, 44 (2011), 489 ('criminal trial … not the appropriate forum for victims to express their feelings, as this would detract from the serenity of the trial and would not serve a useful purpose from the perspective of a criminal proceeding'); Safferling, *ICLR*, 11 (2011), 215 (referring to alternative TJ mechanisms); in a similar vein, Damaška, *ChicKentLR*, 83 (2008), 343; Damaška, *UCLA JIL & ForAff*, 14 (2009), 25–6, 28 ff. (calling for a restrictive interpretation of the victim participation rights, at 33–4); McGonigle Leyh, *ICLR*, 12 (2012), 407; Meloni, in Lupária, *Victims* (2015), p. 62; Ciorciari and Heindel, *VirgJIL*, 56 (2016), 301 ('The impulse of some victims in the courtroom to express rage, distress, or the desire for revenge, or to offer information extraneous to the charges, not only lengthens the proceedings, but also potentially jeopardizes the impartiality of the courtroom atmosphere'); cf. also Hoven, Feiler, and Scheibel, *Victims* (2013), p. 10; Stegmiller, *LJIL*, 27 (2014), 475 and the overview on the discussion by Hoyle and Ullrich, *JICJ*, 12 (2014), 688–92. In contrast, denying that the ICC's victim-centred approach is responsible for lengthy trials, Carayon and O'Donohue, *JICJ*, 15 (2017), 588 ('Judges involved in the first trials have also spoken publicly and positively of victim participation in those cases, opining that the rights of victims and the defence can be balanced without greatly extending the length of the cases').

[796] WCRO, *Victim Participation* (November 2007), pp. 26–7; Damaška, *ChicKentLR*, 83 (2008), 334; de Hemptinne, *JICJ*, 8 (2010), 168; Safferling, *ICLR*, 11 (2011), 213; Burnham, in van den Herik and Stahn, *Diversification* (2012), p. 675; see also Stahn, Olásolo, and Gibson, *JICJ*, 4 (2006), 223; Guhr, *ICLR*, 8 (2008), 120; de Hemptinne, *JICJ*, 8 (2010), 168; Trumbull IV, *MichJIL*, 29 (2008), 815–16; SáCouto and Cleary, *Transnat'lLCP*, 17 (2008), 83–4; Kaoutzanis, *UCDavisJIL&Pol'y*, 17 (2010), 128; Zappalà, *JICJ*, 8 (2010), 145–6; McGonigle Leyh, *ICLR*, 12 (2012), 399–400; and Hoven, Feiler, and Scheibel, *Victims* (2013), p. 79. See, however, also *Prosecutor v. Bemba*, Partly Dissenting Opinion of Judge Sylvia Steiner on the Decision on the Supplemented Applications by the Legal Representatives of Victims to Present Evidence and the Views and Concerns of Victims, No. ICC-01/05-01/08-2140, 23 February 2012, para. 8: 'Furthermore, it must be recalled that victims authorised to participate in the proceedings have been allowed, through their legal representatives, to question witness … and that at no point can their participation be seen as having had a negative impact on the expeditiousness of the trial'; for a different view, see van den Wyngaert, *CWRJIL*, 44 (2011), 493–4.

[797] Trumbull IV, *MichJIL*, 29 (2008), 823; Damaška, *ChicKentLR*, 83 (2008), 334; Damaška, *UCLA JIL & ForAff*, 14 (2009), 28–9; Safferling, *ICLR*, 11 (2011), 213; McGonigle Leyh, *Procedural Justice?* (2011), pp. 346–57; von Wistinghausen, in Bonacker and Safferling, *Victims* (2013), p. 166; cf. also de Brouwer and Heikkilä, in Sluiter et al., *International Criminal Procedure* (2013), pp. 1339–40; Spiga, *JICJ*, 10 (2012), 1391; see also Pemberton et al., *ICLR*, 15 (2015), 338–60 and the comments of legal practitioners of the ECCC as quoted in Hoven, *JICJ*, 12 (2014), 97–8, 103; Hoven, *ZIS*, 9 (2014), 691; but see also Vasiliev, in Stahn, *ICC* (2015), p. 1140, according to whom 'in the trials completed thus far, victim participation did not take the largest share of blame for endangering due process'. On the victim/offender dichotomy resulting in the demonization of the accused, see Kochhar and Hieramente, *LJIL*, 29 (2016), 229–30, 243; on the tension between the presumption of innocence and victim participation rights at the ICC, see Coleman, *ICLR*, 20 (2020), 379 ff.; on the conflict between the presumption of innocence and the presumption of victimhood, see Pues, *JICJ*, 13 (2015), 957–9.

[798] Trumbull IV, *MichJIL*, 29 (2008), 808–9; in a similar vein, Damaška, *ChicKentLR*, 83 (2008), 342; de Hemptinne, *JICJ*, 8 (2010), 168–9; van den Wyngaert, *CWRJIL*, 44 (2011), 466. See also the description of the role of civil parties in the proceedings before the EECC by a Prosecutor: 'Certainly not to approach the case in a way that would interfere with the Prosecution's strategy' (quoted in Hoven, Feiler, and Scheibel, *Victims* (2013), p. 46). On the (limited) impact of victim representations on Court decisions Perrin, *ICLR* 15 (2015), 337–8.

[799] On the motivations for victims to participate in the proceedings before the ECCC, see Hoven, Feiler, and Scheibel, *Victims* (2013), pp. 25–37; Hoven, *ZIS*, 9 (2014), 685–90; in general on the expectations of victims towards the (international) criminal justice system, see the comprehensive study of Kiza, Rathgeber, and Rohne, *Victims of War* (2006), pp. 95 ff.; with a particular focus on the ECCC, Killean, *ICLR*, 16 (2016), 1; Killean and Moffett, *JICJ*, 16 (2017), 720–1, 723 ff.

[800] WCRO, *Victim Participation* (November 2007), p. 44; FIDH, *Victims' Rights* (November 2013), p. 10; see also Scalia, in Strickler, *Place de la victime* (2009), p. 250; Rauschenbach and Scalia, *IRRC*, 90 (2008), 453;

and implementation of a meaningful victims' participation system, while at the same time safeguarding the rights of the accused, is an *enormous challenge* for all the actors in the respective proceedings.[801]

## (2) Definition of victims

According to Rule 85 (a) RPE ICC, '"Victims" means natural persons who have suffered harm as a result of the commission of any crime within the jurisdiction of the Court'.[802] Based on this provision, PTC I identified four requirements,[803] which individuals must meet in order to obtain victim status:

- They must be natural persons, that is, human beings,[804] which arguably includes deceased persons.[805]
- They must have suffered harm.[806]

SáCouto and Cleary, *Transnat'lLCP*, 17 (2008), 100; Stover, Balthazard, and Koenig, *IRRC*, 93 (2011), 545; van den Wyngaert, *CWRJIL*, 44 (2011), 489; Mohan, *ICLR*, 9 (2009), 738, 752–8 (referring to the experiences of the ECCC); Pemberton et al., *ICLR*, 15 (2015), 357–8; Moffet, *JICJ*, 13 (2015), 295; Killean and Moffett, *JICJ*, 16 (2017), 727–30; Vasiliev, in Stahn, *ICC* (2015), p. 1135 and Dixon and Tenove, *IJTJ*, 7 (2013), 410, 411, who conclude that victims have a high moral authority in ICL which may be used by other authorities who speak about (and not on behalf of) victims in order to pursue their own interests; in a similar vein, Kendall and Nouwen, *LCP*, 76 nos. 3 & 4 (2013), 253–8.

[801] See also Vasiliev, in Stahn, *ICC* (2015), pp. 1138–40; scrutinizing meaningful victim participation before the ICC, Sehmi, *JICJ*, 16 (2018), 579–87; Suprun, *ICLR*, 16 (2016), 982–94. See also Ullrich, who, beyond the more traditional approaches mentioned above, suggests to conceptualize victim participation as a form of labour which needs to be paid, Ullrich, *Victims and the Labour of Justice* (2024), p. 8 and passim; summarizing Ullrich, *EJIL: Talk!* 11 September 2024.

[802] Similarly Rule 2 (1) RPE KSC: 'suffered physical, material, or mental harm as a direct result of a crime alleged in an indictment confirmed by the Pre-Trial Judge'.

[803] Similarly KSC, *Prosecutor v. Thaci et al.*, AP Decision on Appeal Against "First Decision on Victims' Participation", No. KSC-BC-2020-06/IA005/F00008, 16 July 2021, para. 25.

[804] *Situation in the DRC*, No. ICC-01/04-101, para. 80; Dwertmann, *Reparation System* (2010), p. 78.

[805] *Prosecutor v. Bemba*, Fourth Decision on Victims' Participation, No. ICC-01/05-01/08-320, 12 December 2008, para. 40: 'a victim does not cease to be a victim because of his or her death'; in the same vein, *Prosecutor v. Ntaganda*, TC IV Fourth Decision on Victims' Participation in Trial Proceedings, No. ICC-01/04-02/06-805, 1 September 2015, para. 11; *Prosecutor v. Gbagbo and Blé Goudé*, TC Decision on the Resumption of Action Applications, No. ICC-02/11-01/15-1052, 11 October 2017, para. 14; for further (earlier) case law, see previous edition, p. 171 with note 700. For a different view, see *Prosecutor v. Muthaura, Kenyatta and Hussein Ali*, Decision on Victims' Participation at the Confirmation of Charges Hearing and in the Related Proceedings, No. ICC-01/09-02/11-267, 26 August 2011, para. 47; for further (earlier) case law, see previous edition, p. 172 with note 700; see also Bock, *Opfer* (2010), p. 476; cf. also the detailed analysis by Bachvarova, *ICLR*, 11 (2011), 672–82. The practical consequences of these diverging approaches are limited: either the applicants are allowed to participate on behalf of the deceased persons, or they may be recognized as (indirect) victims in their own right provided that they have suffered moral or mental harm resulting from the death of the direct victim, see e.g. *Katanga and Ngudjolo*, No. ICC-01/04-01/07-579, para. 63; *Prosecutor v. Katanga and Ngudjolo*, Grounds for the Decision on the 345 Applications for Participation in the Proceedings Submitted by Victims, No. ICC-01/04-01/07-1481, 12 September 2009, paras. 49–56, 86; *Muthaura, Kenyatta and Hussein Ali*, No. ICC-01/09-02/11-267, para. 47; cf. also Bock, *Opfer* (2010), p. 476. Without discussing the different views, the AC has accepted participation on behalf of deceased victims, *Prosecutor v. Lubanga*, Decision on 32 Applications to Participate in the Proceedings, No. ICC-01/04-01/06-3045, 27 August 2013, para. 168.

[806] Detailed on the distinction between 'personal' and 'direct' harm, *Prosecutor v. Lubanga*, AC Judgment on the Appeals of the Prosecutor and the Defence against Trial Chamber I's Decision on Victims' Participation of 18 January 2008, No. ICC-01/04-01/06-1432, 11 July 2008, paras. 17 ff.

- The alleged crimes must fall within the jurisdiction of the Court (see in particular Articles 5–8, 11, 12 ICCS).[807]
- There must be a causal link between these crimes and the harm suffered.[808]

The concept of harm is understood broadly and comprises any physical or mental injury, emotional suffering, or economic loss[809] with the sole limitation that the harm must be personal to the victim.[810] This definition is broad enough to cover indirect victims,[811] that is, persons who—like close relatives of the direct victim,[812] witnesses of particular

[807] *Prosecutor v. Lubanga*, TC I Decision on Victims' Participation, No. ICC-01/04-01/06-1119, 18 January 2008, para. 93; *Muthaura, Kenyatta and Hussein Ali*, No. ICC-01/09-02/11-267, para. 59; see also *Bemba*, No. ICC-01/05-01/08-320, para. 59; *Prosecutor v. Ntaganda*, PTC II Decision on Victims' Participation at the Confirmation of Charges Hearing and in the Related Proceedings, No. ICC-01/04-02/06-211, 15 January 2014, paras. 18, 24–7; *Prosecutor v. Ngaïssona*, PTC II Decision Establishing the Principles Applicable to Victims' Applications for Participation, No. ICC-01/14-01/18-14, 15 March 2019, para. 21; Baumgartner, *IRRC*, 90 (2008), 422; Kaoutzanis, *UCDavisJIL&Pol'y*, 17 (2010), 121; Bock, *Opfer* (2010), p. 212; Bachvarova, *ICLR*, 11 (2011), 702.

[808] *Situation in the DRC*, No. ICC-01/04-101, para. 79; confirmed, inter alia, in *Katanga and Ngudjolo*, No. ICC-01/04-01/07-579, para. 65; *Ntaganda*, No. ICC-01/04-02/06-211, paras. 18, 28–33; *Ngaïssona*, No. ICC-01/14-01/18-141, para. 21; *Prosecutor v. Abd-Al-Rahman*, PTC II Decision Establishing the Principles Applicable to Victims' Participation and Representation During the Confirmation Hearing, No. ICC-02/05-01/20-259, 18 January 2021, para. 17; see also *Prosecutor v. Ntaganda*, TC IV Decision on Victims' Participation in Trial Proceedings, No. ICC-01/04-02/06-449, 6 February 2015, para. 42; for further (earlier) case law, see previous edition, p. 172 with note 702.

[809] *Lubanga*, No. ICC-01/04-01/06-1119, para. 92; confirmed in *Prosecutor v. Lubanga*, AC Judgment on the Appeals of The Prosecutor and the Defence against Trial Chamber I's Decision on Victims' Participation of 18 January 2008, No. ICC-01/04-01/06-1432, 11 July 2008, paras. 1, 32; *Muthaura, Kenyatta and Hussein Ali*, No. ICC-01/09-02/11-267, para. 64 with illustrative examples of indirect economic consequences of international crimes in para. 38; *Ngaïssona*, No. ICC-01/14-01/18-141, para. 35; cf. also Pikis, *Rome Statute* (2010), mn. 709; Dwertmann, *Reparation System* (2010), pp. 79–84; Meloni, in Lupária, *Victims* (2015), p. 55. This broad interpretation is supported by international codifications, see Art. 2 (1)(a) of Directive 2012/29/EU of the European Parliament and of the Council of 25 October 2012 establishing minimum standards on the rights, support, and protection of victims of crime, and replacing Council Framework Decision 2001/220/JHA, OJ EU L 351/57 of 14 November 2012; Art. 8 of the UN Basic Principles and Guidelines on the Right to a Remedy and Reparation for Victims of Gross Violation of International Human Rights Law and Serious Violations of International Humanitarian Law, GA Res. 60/147 of 16 December 2005 (UN Basic Principles and Guidelines); No. 3.2 of the ECCC Practice Direction on Victim Participation; cf. also Bock, *Opfer* (2010), p. 210 and the detailed case law analysis by Bachvarova, *ICLR*, 11 (2011), 694–702.

[810] *Lubanga*, No. ICC-01/04-01/06-1432, para. 37. The requirement of personal harm is not incompatible with the collective dimension of victimization in ICL. As was rightly pointed out by the AC: 'there may clearly be harm that could be both personal and collective in nature. The fact that harm is collective does not mandate either its inclusion or exclusion of whether a person is a victim before the Court. The issue for determination is whether the harm is personal to the individual victim. The notion of harm suffered by a collective is not, as such, relevant or determinative' (para. 35). See also *Prosecutor v. Thaçi et al.*, AP Decision on Appeal Against 'First Decision on Victim's Participation', No. KSC-BC-2020-06/IA005/F00008, 16 July 2021, paras. 25, 27 (no consideration of 'collective suffering' as to determine personal, direct harm).

[811] *Lubanga*, No. ICC-01/04-01/06-1119, para. 91; *Lubanga*, No. ICC-01/04-01/06-1432, para. 38; *Muthaura, Kenyatta and Hussein Ali*, No. ICC-01/09-02/11-267, para. 68; *Ntaganda*, No. ICC-01/04-02/06-211, paras. 47–50. Common Rule 2 (A) RPE ICTY/ICTR/SCSL/MICT, to the contrary, defines victim as 'a person *against whom* a crime over which the Tribunal has jurisdiction has allegedly been committed' (emphasis added) and thus excludes indirect victims, Donat-Cattin, 'Article 68', in Ambos, *Commentary* (2022), mn. 35; Donat-Cattin, 'Role of Victims', in Lattanzi and Schabas, *Essays on the Rome Statute I* (2000), p. 261; Safferling, *ZStW*, 115 (2003), 365; Stehle, *Strafverfahren* (2007), p. 231.

[812] *Lubanga*, No. ICC-01/04-01/06-1432, para. 32 (parents as victims of the crime of enlisting and conscripting child soldiers); *Prosecutor v. Lubanga*, TC I Redacted Version of 'Decision on "Indirect Victims"', No. ICC-01/04-01/06-1813, 8 April 2009, paras. 49–50; *Abu Garda*, No. ICC-01/05-02/09-121, para. 13; Bock, *Opfer* (2010), p. 211 with further references; see also *Co-Prosecutors v. Kaing*, No. 001/18-07-2007/ECCC/TC, para. 643; *Prosecutor v. Ayyash et al.*, PTJ Decision on Victims' Participation in the Proceedings, No. STL-11-01/PT/PTJ, 8 May 2012, para. 46. Notably, the category of indirect victims is not limited to persons who have a personal relationship to the direct victim, *Situation in Uganda*, AC Decision on the Participation of Victims in the Appeal, No. ICC-02/04-164, 27 October 2008, para. 8.

violent and shocking crimes,[813] or persons who intervened to help the direct victim[814]—are not directly involved in the criminal act, but are nevertheless (indirectly) harmed by it.[815] Although the inclusion of such indirect victims significantly broadens the possible number of victims and, thus, participants in the proceedings, it is, as a matter of principle, the correct approach[816] given the huge collateral impact of international crimes on third persons and their sometimes immense emotional and psychological suffering.[817] In practice, the Chambers did not see the need to develop a comprehensive strategy with a view to limiting the number of indirect victim participants.[818] Rather, they have so far focused on effective trial management by grouping victims and assigning them to a common legal representative.[819]

Legal persons, such as organizations or institutions, may also qualify as victims,[820] but only if they 'have sustained direct harm to any of their property which is dedicated to religion, education, art or science or charitable purposes, and to their historic monuments, hospitals and other places and objects for humanitarian purposes'. Compared to Rule 85 (a) RPE ICC, the recognition of legal persons as victims is limited in three regards:[821] first, legal persons must be the *direct* victim of the relevant crime.[822] Secondly, the property harmed must fulfil a humanitarian purpose.[823] Thirdly, the Chambers enjoy full discretion whether or not to accord victim status to legal persons ('may include').[824]

813 *Situation in Uganda*, PTC II Decision on Victims' Applications for Participation . . . , No. ICC-02/04-101, 13 August 2007, para. 31; confirmed in *Situation in Uganda*, No. ICC-02/04-164, paras. 10, 12.

814 *Prosecutor v. Lubanga*, TC I Decision on the Applications by Victims to Participate in the Proceedings, No. ICC-01/04-01/06-1556, 15 December 2008, paras. 107–9; *Muthaura, Kenyatta and Hussein Ali*, No. ICC-01/09-02/11-267, para. 68.

815 Bock, in Klip and Freeland, *ALC*, XL (2013), p. 284. See also Schabas, *ICC Commentary* (2016), p. 1065 and the definition in *Situation in Uganda*, No. ICC-02/04-164, para. 8: 'victims who have suffered, inter alia, mental harm as a result of physical harm suffered by any person'. However, persons who suffered harm as a result of a later conduct of the direct victims do not qualify as indirect victims. This means, in particular, that victims of crimes committed by child soldiers are not victims of the crime of enlisting and conscripting child soldiers, cf. *Lubanga*, No. ICC-01/04-01/06-1813, para. 52; conc. Safferling, *International Criminal Procedure* (2012), p. 171; crit. Spiga, *JICJ*, 8 (2010), 183. On the different categories of victims, cf. Safferling and Petrossian, in Heinze and Dittrich, *International Criminal Court* (2021), pp. 465 ff.

816 cf. also Stehle, *Strafverfahren* (2007), pp. 235, 242; Donat-Cattin, 'Article 68', in Ambos, *Commentary* (2022), mn. 35–7; Bock, 'Commentary', in Klip and Freeland, *ALC*, XL (2013), p. 285; Pérez-León-Acevedo, *Victims' Status* (2014), pp. 302–3; crit. Trüg, *ZStW*, 125 (2013), 62.

817 In more detail on the possible impact of international crimes on third persons, see Bock, *Opfer* (2010), pp. 158–64 with further references.

818 See e.g. the approach proposed by Bock, *Opfer* (2010), pp. 446–7, who wants to take into account the personal relationship between the applicant and the direct victim as well as the extent of the (emotional or psychological) harm suffered by the indirect victim. According to Zappalà, *JICJ*, 8 (2010), 157, the participation of indirect victims should be limited to reparation proceedings. See also Spiga, *JICJ*, 8 (2010), 188–9; McGonigle Leyh, in Letschert et al., *Victimological Approaches* (2011), p. 501; de Hemptinne, *JICJ*, 8 (2010), 170; Ambos, *ICLR*, 12 (2012), 117; Bock, 'Commentary', in Klip and Freeland, *ALC*, XL (2013), p. 285.

819 See sub-section (4)(d) in this section.

820 In more detail on the recognition of legal persons as victims in ICL, Bachvarova, *ICLR*, 11 (2011), 683–91.

821 For a different approach, see No. 3.2 of the ECCC Practice Direction on Victim Participation (equal treatment of natural and legal persons with regard to victim status). The procedural law of the STL, to the contrary, only recognizes natural persons as victims, *Ayyash et al.*, No. STL-11-01/PT/PTJ, para. 30.

822 *Situation in Uganda*, OPCV's Observations on the Victims' Applications . . . to Participate in the Uganda Situation and in the Case The Prosecutor *v.* Joseph Kony, Vincent Otti, Okot Odhiambo, Raska Lukwiya, and Dominic Ongwen, No. ICC-02/04-89, 26 March 2007, para. 42; Dwertmann, *Reparation System* (2010), p. 89; Bock, in Klip and Freeland, *ALC*, XL (2013), p. 284; de Brouwer and Heikkilä, in Sluiter et al., *International Criminal Procedure* (2013), p. 1302; Friman, in Cryer et al., *ICL* (2019), p. 447–8.

823 cf. also Bachvarova, *ICLR*, 11 (2011), 701–2.

824 Bock, *Opfer* (2010), p. 213; cf. also Fernández de Gurmendi, in Lee, *ICC* (2001), p. 433; Safferling, *ZStW*, 115 (2003), 368; Safferling, *International Criminal Procedure* (2012), p. 169.

### (3) Assistance to victims by the Registry

The ICC's victim-oriented approach is reflected in its organizational structure. The Registry comprises three victim-support sections: the Victims and Witnesses Unit (VWU), the Victims Participation and Reparation Section (VPRS), and the Office of Public Counsel for Victims (OPCV).[825] The VWU provides protective measures and security arrangements, counselling, and other appropriate assistance for victims who appear before the Court.[826] The VPRS informs victims on the ICC in general and their rights relating to participation and reparation. It also assists them to submit applications to the Court and to obtain legal advice.[827] The OPCV, established by the Registry, provides general support and assistance to the legal representative of victims and to victims themselves, appears (if requested) before the Chamber in respect of specific victim-related issues, and, if need be, represents victims throughout the proceedings.[828] The OPCV—like the OPCD—falls within the remit of the Registry solely for administrative purposes but enjoys full independence regarding its substantial work.[829]

### (4) Victim participation

#### *(a) Article 68 (3) ICCS: The core provision on victim participation*

The central Article 68 (3) ICCS tries to square the circle by giving the victims the rights to present 'their views and concerns' if their 'personal interests' are 'affected', while, at the same time, pretending to avoid this being 'prejudicial to or inconsistent with the rights of the accused and a fair and impartial trial'. The provision, despite its location in Part 6 of the Statute, is not limited to the trial stage.[830] It rather vests victims with a general right to participate during the whole proceedings—the only limitation being that the Court deems the stage in which participation is sought to be 'appropriate'. This assessment must be done on a case-by-case basis taking into account, inter alia, 'such factors as the significance of any victims' participation to the proceedings, the constructiveness of the participation, the legal protected interests affected, judicial economy and whether not allowing an intervention at a particular time during the proceedings would affect the interests of the victims'.[831]

No stage of the trial is per se inappropriate for victim participation.[832] The ACs, however, understand the term 'proceeding' as referring to 'a judicial cause pending before a Chamber',

[825] On the OPCV, see Chapter I, C.(2)(c) in this volume. In order to avoid duplication of resources and expenses, Mettraux et al., *Expert Initiative Effectiveness ICC* (2014), pp. 29 (para. 128), 188–96 (paras. 43–71) suggest merging the VPRS and the OPCV into a unified 'Office for Victims', which should provide logistical and administrative support to enable victims to claim and establish their entitlement to participate and to victim's representatives in the exercise of their mandate.

[826] Art. 46 (6) ICCS, Rule 17 RPE ICC, Regs. 78–96 RegR.

[827] ICC, *Booklet* (undated), p. 13; Bock, *Opfer* (2010), p. 234.

[828] Reg. 81 RegC. In more detail on the role of the OPCV, Massidda and Pellet, in Stahn and Sluiter, *Practice* (2009), pp. 691–706.

[829] Reg. 81 (2) RegC.

[830] Donat-Cattin, in Lattanzi and Schabas, *Essays on the Rome Statute I* (2000), p. 269; Donat-Cattin, 'Article 68', in Ambos, *Commentary* (2022), mn. 9; Meloni, in Lupária, *Victims* (2015), p. 59.

[831] *Lubanga*, No. ICC-01/04-01/06-1119, para. 25; see also *Ntaganda*, No. ICC-01/04-02/06-211, para. 82; Horovitz, in Carter and Pocar, *International Criminal Procedure* (2013), p. 182.

[832] Boas et al., *International Criminal Procedure* (2011), p. 313; cf. also Friman, in Cryer et al., *ICL* (2019), pp. 458–9; Donat-Cattin, 'Article 68', in Ambos, *Commentary* (2022), mn. 9; Schabas, *ICC Commentary* (2016), p. 1062; Massidda and Walter, 'Article 68', in Fernandez et al., *Statut II* (2019), p. 1887; in detail, Bock, *Opfer* (2010), pp. 452–64. At the STL, to the contrary, victim participation is only possible after the confirmation of charges, Rule 86 (A) RPE STL.

not covering inquiries 'conducted by the Prosecutor into the commission of a crime'.[833] Thus, contrary to the (too) broad approach adopted initially by some PTCs,[834] victims cannot be granted a procedural status 'entitling them to participate in the investigation of a situation'.[835] Yet, the AC did not go so far as to categorically rule out victim participation at the investigation stage.[836] Instead it allows victims to present their views and concerns 'in any judicial proceeding, including proceedings affecting investigations',[837] that is, in judicial proceedings in relation to a unique investigative opportunity within the meaning of Article 56 ICCS.[838]

But when are the 'personal interests'[839] of victims affected? Originally, the AC demanded a clear-cut distinction between the personal interests of the victims and the role and mandate of the Prosecutor.[840] This seemed to indicate that victims have no personal interest in establishing the truth about their victimization or in proving the guilt or innocence of the

[833] *Situation in the DRC*, Judgment on the Victim Participation in the Investigation Stage of the Proceedings in the Appeal of the OPCD against the Decision of Pre-Trial Chamber I of 7 December 2007 and in the Appeals of the OPCD and the Prosecutor against the Decision of Pre-Trial Chamber I of 24 December 2007, No. ICC-01/04-556, 19 December 2008, para. 45; conc. *Situation in Darfur, Sudan*, AC Judgment on Victim Participation in the Investigation Stage of the Proceedings in the Appeal of the OPCD against the Decision of Pre-Trial Chamber I of 3 December 2007 and in the Appeals of the OPCD and the Prosecutor against the decision of Pre-Trial Chamber I of 6 December 2007, No. ICC-02/05-177, 2 February 2009, paras. 7–8.

[834] See in particular *Situation in the DRC*, No. ICC-01/04-101, para. 71: 'persons accorded the status of victims will be authorized, *notwithstanding any specific proceedings being conducted in the framework of such an investigation*, to be heard by the Chamber in order to present their views and concerns and to file documents pertaining to the current investigation of the situation in the DRC' (emphasis added); for a crit. view, see de Hemptinne and Rindi, *JICJ*, 4 (2006), 347–8; WCRO, *Victim Participation* (November 2007), pp. 44–8; Guhr, *ICLR*, 8 (2008), 117–29; SáCouto and Cleary, *Transnat'lLCP*, 17 (2008), 100–4; Guhr, *ZIS*, 3 (2008), 368; Baumgartner, *IRRC*, 90 (2008), 415–16; Vasiliev, 'Article 68 (3)', in Stahn and Sluiter, *Practice* (2009), pp. 646–8; Chung, *NWJIHR*, 6 (2008), 510–14; Pérez-León-Acevedo, *Victims' Status* (2014), pp. 376–7.

[835] *Situation in the DRC*, No. ICC-01/04-556, para. 59; *Situation in Darfur, Sudan*, No. ICC-02/05-177, paras. 7–8; crit. Bock, *Opfer* (2010), pp. 462–3; Bock, 'Commentary', in Klip and Freeland, *ALC*, XL (2013), pp. 290–2; Moffet, *CLF*, 26 (2015), 271–4; in favour of the original approach of the PTCs, also Tsereteli, in Stahn and van den Herik, *Perspectives* (2010), p. 639; see also Klamberg, *Evidence* (2013), pp. 91–2, who wants to apply the broad PTC approach at the situation stage of the proceedings.

[836] *Situation in Uganda*, No. ICC-02/04-191, para. 10; *Situation in Kenya*, Decision on Victims' Participation in Proceedings Related to the Situation in the Republic of Kenya, No. ICC-01/09-24, 3 November 2010, para. 9; *Situation in the DRC*, Decision on Victims' Participation in Proceedings Relating to the Situation in the Democratic Republic of the Congo, No. 01/04-593, 11 April 2011, para. 9; Tsereteli, in Stahn and van den Herik, *Perspectives* (2010), p. 657; Bock, *Opfer* (2010), p. 462; Bock, 'Commentary', in Klip and Freeland, *ALC*, XL (2013), pp. 292; FIDH, *Victims' Rights* (November 2013), p. 16; Friman, in Cryer et al., *ICL* (2019), p. 458; see also Schabas, *Introduction* (2020), p. 366; Boas et al., *International Criminal Procedure* (2011), p. 321; crit. Tonellato, *EJCCLCJ*, 20 (2012), 344.

[837] *Situation in the DRC*, No. ICC-01/04-556, para. 56; *Situation in Darfur, Sudan*, No. ICC-02/05-177, paras. 7–8.

[838] *Situation in Kenya*, No. ICC-01/09-24, para. 12; *Situation in the DRC*, No. 01/04-593, para. 10 with further examples; cf. also de Brouwer and Heikkilä, in Sluiter et al., *International Criminal Procedure* (2013), p. 1316.

[839] I note in passing that the limitation to 'personal' interests has led the AC and some authors to argue that victims are not parties to the proceedings, but merely participants; cf. *Prosecutor v. Lubanga*, TC I Decision on the Manner of Questioning Witnesses by the Legal Representatives of Victims, No. ICC-01/04-01/06-2127, 16 September 2009, para. 24; *Situation in the DRC*, No. ICC-01/04-556, para. 55; *Situation in Darfur, Sudan*, No. ICC-02/05-177, paras. 7–8; Chung, *NWJIHR*, 6 (2008), 465; Pikis, *Rome Statute* (2010), mn. 681; see also WCRO, *Victim Participation* (February 2009), p. 33. The distinction is more semantical than substantial given the effective participatory rights of victims, see Section E.(4)(d) in this chapter.

[840] *Prosecutor v. Lubanga*, AC Decision on the Appeals Chamber on the Joint Applications of Victims ... concerning the 'Directions and Decision of the Appeals Chamber' of 2 February 2007, No. ICC-01/04-01/06-925, 13 June 2007, para. 28: 'More generally, an assessment will need to be made in each case as to whether the interests asserted by victims do not, in fact, fall outside their personal interests and belong instead to the role assigned to the Prosecutor'; conc., *Prosecutor v. Lubanga*, Prosecution's Document in Support of Appeal against Trial Chamber I's 18 January 2008 Decision on Victim's Participation, No. ICC-01/04-01/06-1219, 10 March 2008, para. 21; ICC-OTP, *Policy Victims' Participation* (2010), p. 12; Trumbull IV, *MichJIL*, 29 (2008), 824; McGonigle Leyh, *ICLR*, 12 (2012), 407; Mettraux et al., *Expert Initiative Effectiveness ICC* (2014), pp. 26 (para. 113), 178 (para. 9), 181 (para. 18); in a similar vein, apparently, Burnham, in van den Herik and Stahn, *Diversification* (2012), p. 673.

accused because these questions fall into the (sole) responsibility of the Prosecutor.[841] Such a restrictive reading of Article 68 (3) ICCS would, however, ultimately limit the participatory rights of victims to reparation and protection issues[842] and therefore fly in the face of the *ratio* of Article 68 (3) ICCS, that is, to grant victims an independent voice. As convincingly argued by the PTCs, this independence must also be preserved vis-à-vis the Prosecutor.[843] This means, in turn, that the procedural role of victims cannot be defined in relation (and thus in dependence) to other parties or participants but autonomously on the basis of the victims' own standing.[844]

The victims' position is further informed by their right to truth and justice recognized in human rights law[845]—part of the ICC's legal sources[846]—and this right must be taken into account in interpreting the personal interest criterion.[847] Against this background, PTC I rightly concluded that victims also have—in addition to questions of reparation and protection—a personal interest in the outcome of a criminal trial; the establishment of the truth; and the identification, prosecution, and punishment of the perpetrator(s).[848] In a similar vein, the AC has meanwhile held that—pursuant to Article 68 (3) ICCS—victims may be allowed to tender or challenge evidence relating to the guilt or innocence of the accused,[849] thereby implicitly confirming that the enforcement of the right to truth and justice is an integral part of the victims' personal interests.[850]

[841] In this vein, *Lubanga*, No. ICC-01/04-01/06-925, paras. 21–2.

[842] cf. *Lubanga*, No. ICC-01/04-01/06-925, para. 28; Guhr, *ZIS*, 3 (2008), 369. See also Trüg, *ZStW*, 125 (2013), 83, who suggests limiting victim participation to the sentencing and reparation stage.

[843] *Kony et al.*, No. ICC-02/04-01/05-155, p. 4; *Situation in the DRC*, No. ICC-01/04-101, para. 51; cf. also *Prosecutor v. Abu Garda*, PTC I Decision on Victims' Modalities of Participation at the Pre-Trial Stage of the Case, No. ICC-02/05-02/09-136, 6 October 2009, para. 7; Tonellato, *EJCCLCJ*, 20 (2012), 326; Tochilovsky, *Jurisprudence* (2014), p. 746. The situation is different at the ECCC, where the victims may solely participate 'by supporting the prosecution' (Rule 23 (1) IR ECCC), cf. thereon McGonigle Leyh, *ICLR*, 12 (2012), 388; on the divergent interpretations of this clause by the civil parties and the Prosecutor, see Hoven, *JICJ*, 12 (2014), 90–2; Hoven, *ZIS*, 9 (2014), 692. On the 'complex relationship' between victims and the Prosecutor Perrin, *ICLR*, 15 (2015), 336.

[844] Bock, *Opfer* (2010), p. 450; Bock, in Klip and Freeland, *ALC*, XL (2013), p. 288; see also Tsereteli, in Stahn and van den Herik, *Perspectives* (2010), p. 642 arguing that establishing the truth and achieving justice is a personal matter for victims and not—as in the case of the Prosecutor—an objective duty. On the complex relationship between victims and the truth at the ICC, characterized by the antagonism between victims' right to truth and, at the same time, their obligation to assist the Court in establishing the truth, Stolk, *JICJ*, 13 (2015), 973.

[845] In detail, Ambos, in Ambos, Large, and Wierda, *Building a Future* (2009), pp. 34–6 with further references; cf. also Donat-Cattin, in Lattanzi, *The ICC* (1998), pp. 252–8; Letschert and van Boven, in Letschert et al., *Victimological Approaches* (2011), pp. 157–8; Bassiouni, in Bassiouni, *Pursuit* (2010), pp. 650–1. To give but one example: No. 24 of the UN Basic Principles and Guidelines grants victims and their representatives the right to seek and obtain information on the causes leading to their victimization and on the causes and conditions pertaining to gross violation of international human rights law and serious violations of international humanitarian law and to learn the truth in regard to these violations.

[846] Art. 21 (3) ICCS.

[847] See also the approach in *Katanga and Ngudjolo*, No. ICC-01/04-01/07-474, paras. 31–44; crit. ICC-OTP, *Policy Victims' Participation* (2010), p. 12.

[848] *Katanga and Ngudjolo*, No. ICC-01/04-01/07-474, paras. 34, 36, 39; in a similar vein, *Lubanga*, No. ICC-01/04-01/06-1119, para. 97; *Prosecutor v. Katanga and Ngudjolo*, Decision on the Modalities of Victim Participation at Trial, No. ICC-01/04-01/07-1788, 22 January 2010, paras. 59–60; *Abu Garda*, No. ICC-01/05-02/09-121, para. 3; cf. also Bock, *Opfer* (2010), pp. 449–50 with further references; de Brouwer and Heikkilä, in Sluiter et al., *International Criminal Procedure* (2013), p. 1319; Spiga, *JICJ*, 10 (2012), 1387; Pérez-León-Acevedo, *Victims' Status* (2014), pp. 324–5; for a crit. view, see Trumbull IV, *MichJIL*, 29 (2008), 798; Kelly, in Bonacker and Safferling, *Victims* (2013), p. 54.

[849] *Lubanga*, No. ICC-01/04-01/06-1432, para. 108; *Prosecutor v. Katanga and Ngudjolo*, AC Judgment on the Appeal of Mr Katanga against the Decision of Trial Chamber II of 22 January 2010 Entitled 'Decision on the Modalities of Victim Participation at Trial', No. ICC-01/04-01/07-2288, 16 July 2010, para. 1; see, in more detail, sub-section 3(d) in this section.

[850] cf. also *Lubanga*, No. ICC-01/04-01/06-925, Separate Opinion of Judge Sang-Hyun Song, paras. 10–11: 'the victims assert their interest in seeing the Appellant being prosecuted; in other words, the Victims want that justice is done'.

It follows from the personal interests criterion that only persons who have suffered harm as a result of the crimes charged may participate at the case stage of the proceedings; that is, there must be a *causal connection* between the alleged crimes and the harmful results;[851] the existence of the context element and its impact on alleged victims do not suffice.[852] However, the limitation of the personal scope of Article 68 (3) ICCS to the so-called 'victims of a case'[853] results in a considerable dependence of victims' rights on the prosecutorial strategy.[854] This is clear since the *Lubanga* proceedings where the Prosecutor's focus on the recruitment and use of child soldiers, in particular leaving out sexual crimes, resulted in the procedural exclusion of a great number of victims of those crimes by not having been included in the indictment.[855]

Last but not least, the challenge remains of preventing victim participation from being prejudicial to or inconsistent with the rights of the accused. In fact, this means that the Chambers must strike a balance between the rights of the accused and the interests of victims.[856] Given that Article 68 (3) ICCS grants victims the statutory *right*[857] to present their

[851] *Lubanga*, No. ICC-01/04-01/06-1432, paras. 62–5; cf. also *Nourain*, No. ICC-02/05-03/09-528, para. 21; *Prosecutor v. Ruto et al.*, First Decision on Victims' Participation in the Case, No. ICC-01/09-01/11-17, 30 March 2011, para. 6; *Prosecutor v. Blé Goudé*, Second Decision on Victims' Participation in the Pre-Trial Proceedings and Related Issues, No. ICC-02/11-02/11-111, 1 August 2014, para. 13; Calvo-Goller, *Trial Proceedings* (2006), p. 245; Greco, *ICLR*, 7 (2007), 540; Schabas, *ICC Commentary* (2016), p. 1065; Friman, in Cryer et al., *ICL* (2019), pp. 453–4; von Wistinghausen, in Bonacker and Safferling, *Victims* (2013), p. 167; Safferling, *International Criminal Procedure* (2012), p. 170. Originally, the *Lubanga* TC adopted a broader approach and approved applications for participation, if either there is 'a real evidential link between the victim and the evidence which the Court will be considering' or if the victim is 'affected by an issue arising during Mr. Thomas Lubanga Dyilo's trial because his or her personal interests are in a real sense engaged by it', *Lubanga*, No. ICC-01/04-01/06-1119, para. 134. This ruling was rightly overturned by the AC since 'the parameters set forth in the charges define the issues to be determined at trial and limit the Trial Chamber's authority to the determination of those issues', which means that the Chamber is not competent to decide on the procedural status of persons who were harmed by crimes not contained in charges, *Lubanga*, No. ICC-01/04-01/06-1432, para. 63; cf. also *Lubanga*, No. ICC-01/04-01/06-1119, Separate and Dissenting Opinion of Judge René Blattmann, para. 11; in the same vein, *Thaci et al.*, No. KSC-BC-2020-06/IA005/F00008, paras. 16 ff. ('crime(s) in relation to which an applicant claims to be a victim must fall under the material, geographical and temporal parameters of the charges, as specified in the Indictment' [para. 16]), with further references in para. 17 with nn. 40 ff.; see also Bock, *Opfer* (2010), pp. 451–2; Bock, in Klip and Freeland, *ALC*, XL (2013), p. 286; Chung, *NWJIHR*, 6 (2008), 516; Friman, *LJIL*, 22 (2009), 491; Tsereteli, in Stahn and van den Herik, *Perspectives* (2010), p. 645.

[852] *Thaci et al.*, No. KSC-BC-2020-06/IA005/F00008, para. 20.

[853] *Lubanga*, No. ICC-01/04-01/06-1119, Separate and Dissenting Opinion of Judge René Blattmann, paras. 9, 17; cf. also the general differentiation between victims of a situation (persons who seem to meet the definition of victims in relation to the situation in question) and victims of a case (persons who seem to meet the definition of victims in relation to the relevant case) introduced in *Situation in the DRC*, No. ICC-01/04-101, paras. 65–6.

[854] Bock, in Klip and Freeland, *ALC*, XL (2013), p. 286; see also McGonigle Leyh, *Procedural Justice?* (2011), p. 250; Moffet, *JICJ*, 13 (2015), 290; Kendall and Nouwen, *LCP*, 76 nos. 3 & 4 (2013), 241 ('juridified victimhood').

[855] cf. *Lubanga*, No. ICC-01/04-01/06-2842, para. 16; Ambos, *ICLR*, 12 (2012), 117; Bock, in Klip and Freeland, *ALC*, XL (2013), p. 286. For an in-depth discussion, see Grey, *Prosecuting Sexual and Gender-Based Crimes* (2019), pp. 128–42 and 235–41.

[856] *Prosecutor v. Mokom*, PTC II Decision on the Legal Representation of Victims, No. ICC-01/14-01/22-182, 27 March 2023, para. 27; *Abu Garda*, No. ICC-02/05-02/09-136, para. 8; *Ruto and Sang*, No. ICC-01/09-01/11-460, para. 16; *Prosecutor v. Gbagbo*, TC I Decision on Victims Participation, No. ICC-02/11-01/11-800, 6 March 2015, para. 26; Ambos, *ICLR*, 12 (2012), 116; see also Donat-Cattin, in Lattanzi, *The ICC* (1998), p. 266; Donat-Cattin, in Lattanzi and Schabas, *Essays on the Rome Statute I* (2000), p. 271; Moffet, *CLF*, 26 (2015), 262; for a crit. view, see McGonigle Leyh, *Procedural Justice?* (2011), pp. 360–2 (rejecting the 'balancing consciousness' and giving primacy to the rights of the accused). In a similar vein, Pues, *JICJ*, 13 (2015), 956 ff. (correctly arguing that only the accused has an individual right to a fair trial, while victims merely benefit from 'an overarching general component of fairness').

[857] cf. *Prosecutor v. Ruto and Sang*, TC V Decision on Victims' Representation and Participation, No. ICC-01/09-01/11-460, 3 October 2012, para. 9, noting that 'the Chambers of this Court *have an obligation* to permit victims whose personal interests are affected to have their views and concerns presented and considered' (emphasis added); see also *Mokom*, No. ICC-01/14-01/22-182, para. 27; *Situation in Uganda*, No. ICC-02/04-101, para. 8; ICC-OTP, *Policy Victims' Participation* (2010), p. 3; WCRO, *Victim Participation* (November 2007), p. 19; Vasiliev, 'Article 68 (3)', in Stahn and Sluiter, *Practice* (2009), p. 649.

views and concerns, the drafters of the Statute must have believed that victim participation and accused rights can be reconciled.[858] Thus, the gist of the issue is how this can be done in concrete proceedings with regard to specific forms of participation.

A good example of the balancing exercise required by Article 68 (3) ICCS is the treatment of anonymous victim participants. In recognition of their legitimate security concerns, several Chambers allowed victims to participate anonymously in the proceedings,[859] that is, without having their identity disclosed to the defence or the prosecution, but—in order to safeguard the right of the defendants to a fair trial and to protect them from anonymous accusers—only with limited participatory rights.[860] Take the example of PTC I which denied anonymous victim participants the right to have witnesses examined.[861] In a similar vein, the Chambers have accepted that victim participants testify as witnesses,[862] but this dual status may influence the scope of their participatory rights[863] and the evaluation of their testimony.[864]

### (b) *Specific participation and information rights*

Article 68 (3) ICCS is complemented by several specific rules on victim participation.[865] First of all, victims may submit information on alleged international crimes to the Prosecutor to trigger investigations.[866] Moreover, if the Prosecutor intends to request the authorization of *proprio motu* investigations from the PTC, she has to inform all victims

[858] Bock, *Opfer* (2010), pp. 464–5; Spiga, *JICJ*, 10 (2012), 1391; cf. also *Mokom*, No. ICC-01/14-01/22-182, para. 27; *Situation in the DRC*, No. ICC-01/04-101, para. 57; *Lubanga*, No. ICC-01/04-01/06-925, Separate Opinion of Judge Sang-Hyun Song, para. 27; Zappalà, *JICJ*, 8 (2010), 147; crit., however, *Prosecutor v. Lubanga*, Observation de la défense sur les demandes de participation à la procedure ..., No. ICC-01/04-01/06-561, 12 October 2006, para. 18; *Prosecutor v. Lubanga*, Response to the Application by Victims ... for Authorization to Participate in Appeal Proceedings Relating to the Decision on the Confirmation of Charges, No. ICC-01/04-01/06-901, 11 May 2006, para. 33; Calvo-Goller, *Trial Proceedings* (2006), p. 245; Trumbull IV, *MichJIL*, 29 (2008), 823; Guhr, *ICLR*, 8 (2008), 128; Burnham, in van den Herik and Stahn, *Diversification* (2012), p. 675.

[859] The participation of anonymous victim participants must not be confused with the testimony of anonymous witnesses, which will be discussed in more detail in Chapter V, A.(3)(c) in this volume.

[860] *Lubanga*, No. ICC-01/04-01/06-1119, para. 131; *Katanga and Ngudjolo*, No. ICC-01/04-01/07-474, paras 180–4; *Prosecutor v. Nourain*, Decision on the Participation of Victims in the Trial Proceedings, No. ICC-02/05-03/09-545, 20 March 2014, paras. 18–19; crit. Zappalà, *JICJ*, 8 (2010), 151. For a different approach, see *Bemba*, No. ICC-01/05-01/08-320, para. 99.

[861] *Abu Garda*, No. ICC-02/05-02/09-136, para. 22; cf. also *Katanga and Ngudjolo*, No. ICC-01/04-01/07-474, para. 182; crit. Bock, *Opfer* (2010), p. 532; in more detail, sub-section 4(d) in this section.

[862] *Lubanga*, No. ICC-01/04-01/06-1119, para. 134; *Prosecutor v. Katanga and Ngudjolo*, PTC I Decision on the Application for Participation of Witness 166, No. ICC-01/04-01/07-632, 23 June 2008, paras. 18–22; *Katanga and Ngudjolo*, No. ICC-01/04-01/07-1788, para. 110. At the ECCC, to the contrary, victim participants cannot be questioned as witnesses (Rule 23 (4) IR ECCC), see also McGonigle, in Ryngaert, *Effectiveness* (2009), p. 113; Pérez-León-Acevedo, *Victims' Status* (2014), pp. 159–62.

[863] *Lubanga*, No. ICC-01/04-01/06-1119, para. 134; see also *Nourain*, No. ICC-02/05-03/09-545, para. 22. PTC I, for example, limits the participatory rights of persons with dual status to those granted to anonymous victim participants, *Katanga and Ngudjolo*, No. ICC-01/04-01/07-632, para. 32; cf. also the guidelines set up in *Prosecutor v. Lubanga*, TC I Decision on Certain Practicalities Regarding Individuals who Have the Dual Status of Witness and Victim, No. ICC-01/04-01/06-1379, 5 June 2008, paras. 52 ff. On lifting redactions of certain information contained in the applications of dual status victim-witnesses, see *Ntaganda*, No. ICC-01/04-02/06-211, paras. 70–5.

[864] *Katanga and Ngudjolo*, No. ICC-01/04-01/07-1788, paras. 116–17; cf. also Bock, *Opfer* (2010), pp. 551–2; de Brouwer and Heikkilä, in Sluiter et al., *International Criminal Procedure* (2013), p. 1303; in more detail on the testimonies of victim-witnesses in the *Lubanga* case, Catani, *JICJ*, 10 (2012), 915–17.

[865] See also the overview on the victims' rights provisions of the ICCS and the RPE ICC by Funk, *Victims' Rights* (2010), pp. 81–5.

[866] Arts. 13 (c), 15 ICCS; see also *Situation in Uganda*, No. ICC-02/04-101, para. 92; *Situation in the DRC*, No. ICC-01/04-556, para. 53; *Situation in Darfur, Sudan*, No. ICC-02/05-177, para. 7; ICC-OTP, *Policy Victims' Participation* (2010), p. 6; Ambos, *International Peacekeeping*, 6 (2000), 70; Heikkilä, *International Criminal Tribunals* (2004), p. 144; Olásolo, *Triggering Procedure* (2005), p. 113; Stahn, Olásolo, and Gibson, *JICJ*, 4 (2006), 226; Trumbull IV, *MichJIL*, 29 (2008), 791; SáCouto and Cleary, *Transnat'lLCP*, 17 (2008), 91; Tsereteli, in Stahn

known to her to the VWU[867] in order to enable them to make representations in writing[868] to the PTC.[869] This right does not, in contrast to Article 68 (3) ICCS, depend on the relevant victim being personally affected, nor do the Chambers have the power to decide on the appropriateness of the participation.[870] In the following course of the proceedings, the Chamber may request additional information from any of the victims who have made representations.[871]

In proceedings concerning jurisdiction and admissibility issues, victims may also submit observations to the Court.[872] To give effect to this right, the Registry is obliged to inform all victims who have already communicated with the Court in relation to the respective case[873] on any challenge based on Article 19 (1)–(3) ICCS[874] and—subject to security restrictions—provide them with a summary of the grounds on which the jurisdiction of the Court or the admissibility of the case has been challenged.[875] Here again, victim participants need not to show that the challenge affects their personal interests.[876]

In addition, the RPE ICC vest victims 'that have communicated with the Court' with additional participation and information rights. The PTCs are obliged to seek their views

and van den Herik, *Perspectives* (2010), p. 631; in more detail, Bock, *Opfer* (2010), pp. 277–8; Carnero Rojo, 'Article 68', in Klamberg et al., *Commentary ICC II* (2023), pp. 315–17. Victims, however, cannot question the Prosecutor's selection of suspects and crimes for investigation and prosecution; for a crit. view, see Pena and Carayon, *IJTJ*, 7 (2013), 529–31.

867 Rule 50 (1) RPE ICC. In more detail on this information obligation, Stehle, *Strafverfahren* (2007), pp. 256–7.

868 *Situation in Kenya*, No. ICC-01/09-4, Order to the Victims Participation and Reparations Sections Concerning Victims' Representations Pursuant to Article 15 (3) of the Statute, 10 December 2009, para. 5; *Situation in Côte d'Ivoire*, No. ICC-02/11-6, Order to the Victims Participation and Reparations Section Concerning Victims' Representations Pursuant to Article 15 (3), 6 July 2011, para. 5; Stahn, Olásolo, and Gibson, *JICJ*, 4 (2006), 228.

869 Art. 15 (3) ICCS. See also *Situation in Palestine*, No. ICC-01/18, Decision on Information and Outreach for the Victims of the Situation, para. 10 (13 July 2018) ('right to provide information to, receive information from and communicate with the Court, regardless and independently from judicial proceedings'); Bock, *Opfer* (2010), p. 507; WCRO, *Victim Participation* (November 2007), pp. 23–4. On the application of Art. 15 (3) ICCS in praxis, see McGonigle Leyh, *Procedural Justice?* (2011), pp. 263–5 (situation in Kenya); Perrin, *ICLR* 15 (2015), 320–7 (situations in Kenya and Côte d'Ivoire).

870 Stahn, Olásolo, and Gibson, *JICJ*, 4 (2006), 225; Boas et al., *International Criminal Procedure* (2011), p. 314; see also Tsereteli, in Stahn and van den Herik, *Perspectives* (2010), p. 631. The Chambers, however, have to assess whether the participant qualifies as victim in terms of Rule 85 RPE ICC, *Situation in Kenya*, No. ICC-01/09-4, para. 8. In *Situation in Côte d'Ivoire*, No. ICC-02/11-6, para. 10, the Chamber delegated this task mainly to the VPRS. On the additional applicability of Art. 68 (3) ICCS in Art. 15 (3) proceedings, see Stehle, *Strafverfahren* (2007), pp. 303–4; Bock, *Opfer* (2010), pp. 507–8.

871 Rule 50 (4) RPE ICC.

872 Art. 19 (3) ICCS. See e.g. *Prosecutor v. Gaddafi and Al-Senussi*, Observations on Behalf of the Victims on the Application on Behalf of the Government of Libya relating to Abdullah Al-Senussi pursuant to Article 19 of the ICC Statute, No. ICC-01/11-01/11-353, 17 June 2013; in more detail, Perrin, *ICLR*, 15 (2015), 328–32.

873 'Victims having communicated with the Court' are victim participants (see *Prosecutor v. Lubanga*, PTC I Decision Inviting the Democratic Republic of the Congo and the Victims in the Case to Comment on the Proceedings Pursuant to Article 19 of the Statute, No. ICC-01/04-01/06-206, 24 July 2006, p. 4; *Prosecutor v. Kony et al.*, Decision Initiation Proceedings under Art. 19, Requesting Observations and Appointing Counsel for the Defence, No. ICC-01/04-01/05-320, 21 October 2008, p. 7), victim-applicants (i.e. persons whose application for participation are still pending, see *Situation in Uganda*, No. ICC-02/04-101, para. 93; *Kony et al.*, No. ICC-01/04-01/05-320, p. 7), and, arguably, victims who have actively contacted an organ of the Court in any other way: Stehle, *Strafverfahren* (2007), p. 258; Bock, *Opfer* (2010), p. 510. Crit. of this restriction ('victims who have already communicated with the Court' as compared to 'victims known to the Prosecutor or to the VWU'), see Stehle, *Strafverfahren* (2007), p. 258.

874 Rule 59 (1) RPE ICC. However, Art. 18 ICCS on preliminary rulings regarding admissibility does not contain a special rule on victim participation, which means that (only) the general Art. 68 (3) ICCS applies, Stahn, Olásolo, and Gibson, *JICJ*, 4 (2006), 231.

875 Rule 59 (2) RPE ICC.

876 Boas et al., *International Criminal Procedure* (2011), p. 315; cf. also Tsereteli, in Stahn and van den Herik, *Perspectives* (2010), p. 631.

in proceedings on conditional release.[877] As far as possible, they have to be informed of a decision of the Prosecutor not to initiate an investigation or not to prosecute pursuant to Article 53 ICCS,[878] and on upcoming hearings on confirmation of charges.[879] Based on this information, victims may apply for participation in the relevant proceedings.[880]

Another way of involving victims in the criminal process is offered by Rule 93 RPE ICC, which allows the Chambers to seek the views of victims independently of whether they participate or not in the proceedings.[881] In exercising this competence, however, the Chambers should ensure that victims are not forced into cooperation with the Court against their will.[882] Further, the Chambers are obliged to take into account the needs of victims when making any directions or order.[883] All this shows that sympathy and friendliness towards victims have become a guiding principle in international criminal procedural law.[884]

### (c) *The application process*

Except for the possibility to submit observations pursuant to Articles 15 (3), 19 (3) ICCS,[885] victims must be accepted as participants in order to be formally involved in the proceedings. The respective applications shall be made in writing to the Registrar, who transmits them together with a report thereon[886] to the relevant Chamber.[887] The prosecution and the defence receive copies of the applications and have the right to reply to them.[888] The applications may be redacted for security reasons.[889] Incomplete applications[890] are not

[877] Rule 119 (3) RPE ICC. In more detail, Boas et al., *International Criminal Procedure* (2011), pp. 315–16; Perrin, *ICLR*, 15 (2015), 327–8.

[878] Rule 92 (2) RPE ICC; in more detail, Perrin, *ICLR* 15 (2015), 316–19; see also *Situation on Registered Vessels of the Union of the Comoros, the Hellenic Republic and the Kingdom of Cambodia*, Decision on the Victims' Participation, No. ICC-01/13-18, 24 April 2015, para. 8.

[879] Rule 92 (3) RPE ICC.

[880] See also Bitti and Friman, in Lee, *ICC* (2001), p. 471.

[881] *Situation in the DRC*, No. ICC-01/04-556, para. 48; *Situation in Darfur, Sudan*, No. ICC-02/05-177, para. 7; Heikkilä, *International Criminal Tribunals* (2004), p. 149; Bitti and Friman, in Lee, *ICC* (2001), p. 473; cf. also Tsereteli, in Stahn and van den Herik, *Perspectives* (2010), p. 631.

[882] Bock, *Opfer* (2010), p. 506.

[883] Rule 86 RPE ICC.

[884] cf. also the overview on 'miscellaneous provisions related to victims' by Perrin, *ICLR*, 15 (2015), 314–16.

[885] Delagrange, *ICLR*, 18 (2018), 543–4; Bock, *Opfer* (2010), pp. 508, 510; Pérez-León-Acevedo, *Victims' Status* (2014), p. 304; see also *Situation in Uganda*, No. ICC-02/04-101, para. 94; Baumgartner, *IRRC*, 90 (2008), 413; Guhr, *ICLR*, 8 (2008), 111; Tsereteli, in Stahn and van den Herik, *Perspectives* (2010), p. 631; Guhr, *ICLR*, 8 (2008), 111.

[886] Reg. 86 (5) RegC. On the contents of the report, see *Situation in Uganda*, ICC-02/04-191, para. 26.

[887] Rule 89 RPE ICC. Establishing a detailed system for the transmission and admission of applications, *Ngaïssona*, No. ICC-01/14-01/18-141, para. 41. For a brief overview on the application procedure before the STL and the ECCC, see ASP, *Report*, ICC-ASP/11/22 (5 November 2012), paras. 76–84; in more detail on the law and practice of the ECCC, McGonigle Leyh, *Procedural Justice?* (2011), pp. 179–85.

[888] The applicants, however, have no right to respond to the observations of the parties, *Situation in the DRC*, Decision on the Request of the OPCV, No. ICC-01/04-418, 10 December 2007, para. 16. In more detail on the complex application process ASP, *Report*, ICC-ASP/11/22 (5 November 2012), paras. 7–11; Delagrange, *ICLR*, 18 (2018), 545 ff.; Bock, *Opfer* (2010), pp. 466–95; McGonigle Leyh, *Procedural Justice?* (2011), pp. 240–61; WCRO, *Victim Status* (December 2013), pp. 16–37; Vasiliev, in Stahn, *ICC* (2015), pp. 1147–63; Sehmi, *JICJ*, 16 (2018), 576–9.

[889] *Lubanga*, No. ICC-01/04-01/06-3045, paras. 20–3; *Prosecutor v. Gbagbo and Blé Goudé*, Decision on Victims' Participation Status, No. ICC-02/11-01/15-379, 7 January 2016, para. 38; see e.g. the redactions ordered in *Prosecutor v. Bemba*, TC III Decision on the Status of 54 Victims who Participated at the Pre-Trial Stage and Inviting the Parties' Observations on Applications for Participation by 86 Applicants, ICC-01/05-01/08-699, 22 February 2010, para. 33; *Prosecutor v. Nourain and Jerbo*, TC IV Decision on the Registry Report on Six Applications to Participate in the Proceedings, No. ICC-02/05-03/09-231, 17 October 2011, paras. 33–7; cf. in more detail, Bock, *Opfer* (2010), pp. 480–5 with further references.

[890] Applications shall contain the information listed in Reg. 86 (2) RegC; cf. also *Situation in the DRC*, Decision on the Requests of the Legal Representative of Applicants on Application Process for Victims' Participation and Legal Representation, No. ICC-01/04-374, 17 August 2007, para. 12. For a detailed discussion of the specific

considered.[891] The Chambers, however, may instruct the Registry to automatically request the missing information from the applicants before submitting their applications for decision.[892] Applicants who are denied victim status do not—unlike the Prosecutor and defence[893]—have a right to appeal the decision,[894] but may file a new application later in the proceedings.[895]

Applications may also be made by a person acting with the consent of the victim or persons acting on behalf of a victim, in the case of a victim who is a child or, when necessary, a victim who is disabled.[896] Closely connected individuals may also continue an action initiated by a participating victim who died during the proceedings.[897] However, the person acting on behalf of the victim need not to be a relative or legal guardian.[898] Even in the case of minors representation is not mandatory. Depending on their individual maturity, children may also apply in their own right for participation in the proceedings.[899] In *Al Hassan* the Single Judge (PTC I) allowed victim families to apply collectively and electronically (for participation or reparation or both).[900]

When deciding on the applications, the Chamber examines if the applicant is a victim pursuant to Rule 85 RPE ICC, and if the other criteria set forth in Article 68 (3) ICCS are

information required for the application to be considered complete, see *Ntaganda*, No. ICC-01/04-02/06-211, paras. 59–64. The standard application form comprises seven pages, see <https://www.icc-cpi.int/iccdocs/JUDSUMM/JSV_ICC_0104_374.pdf>. In order to facilitate the application process, PTC II has developed a simplified one-page application form, *Prosecutor v. Ntaganda*, Annex to the Decision Establishing Principles on the Victims' Application Process, No. ICC-01/04-02/06-67-Anx, 28 May 2013; but see also *Prosecutor v. Al Hassan*, Registry Observations on Aspects related to the Admission of Victims for Participation in the Proceedings, ICC-01/12-01/18-28, 9 May 2018, paras. 5–7, where the Registry requested a redesign of the application form from one to five pages because of the specific circumstances of the case.

891 See e.g. *Abu Garda*, No. ICC-02/05-02/09-147, para. 11; *Situation in Uganda*, ICC-02/04-191, para. 37; *Ruto et al.*, No. ICC-01/09-01/11-17, para. 12.

892 *Situation in the DRC*, No. ICC-01/04-374, paras. 8–11; see also *Prosecutor v. Ongwen*, PTC II Decision Concerning the Procedure for Admission of Victims to Participate in the Proceedings in the Present Case, No. ICC-02/04-01/15-299, 3 September 2015, para. 5. If possible, the VPRS staff in the field should ensure that only complete applications are transmitted to the Court, *Situation in Uganda*, Decision on Victim's Participation in Proceedings Related to the Situation in Uganda, ICC-02/04-191, 9 March 2012, para. 24; Delagrange, *ICLR*, 18 (2018), 550–2; Catani, *JICJ*, 10 (2012), 919; see also *Prosecutor v. Al Hassan*, PTC I Decision Establishing the Principles Applicable to Victims' Application for Participation, ICC-01/12-01/18-37-tENG, 24 May 2018, paras. 39-40 (reliable intermediaries shall assist victims during application period); see also Eckelmans, in Bonacker and Safferling, *Victims* (2013), p. 195. In more detail on the role of the VPRS in the application process, WCRO, *Representation of Victims* (December 2011), pp. 14–16.

893 They may file interlocutory appeals pursuant to Art. 82 (1)(d) ICCS.

894 *Situation in the DRC*, No. ICC-01/04-418, para. 16.

895 Rule 89 (2) RPE ICC.

896 Rule 89 (3) RPE ICC. Participation on behalf of disappeared persons is not possible since they are not available to provide consent. Their family members, however, may be recognized as indirect victims in their own right, PTC I, *Situation in Darfur, Sudan*, Corrigendum to Decision on the Applications for Participation in the Proceedings of Applicants a/0011/06 to a/0015/06, a/0021/07, a/0023/07 to a/0033/07 and a/0035/07 to a/0038/07, No. ICC-02-05-111-Corr, 14 December 2007, para. 35.

897 *Prosecutor v. Ongwen*, TC IX Decision on LRV Request Concerning the Deaths of Participating Victims, No. ICC-02/04-01/15-962, 30 August 2017, para. 3; *Prosecutor v. Ntaganda*, TC VI Tenth Decision on Victims' Participation in Trial Proceedings, No. ICC-01/04-02/06-2221, 12 February 2018, para. 3.

898 *Lubanga*, No. ICC-01/04-01/06-1556, para. 67.

899 Ibid., para. 94; concurring *Prosecutor v. Katanga and Ngudjolo*, Grounds for the Decision on the 345 Applications for Participation in the Proceedings Submitted by Victims, No. ICC-01/04-01/07-1491, 23 September 2009, para. 98; *Gbagbo and Blé Goudé*, No. ICC-02/11-01/15-379, para. 60; Bock, in Klip and Freeland, *ALC*, XL (2013), p. 287; for a different view, see *Situation in the DRC*, Decision on the Applications for Participation Filed in Connection with the Investigation in Democratic Republic of the Congo by Applicants, No. ICC-01/04-545, 4 November 2008, para. 33.

900 *Al Hassan*, ICC-01/12-01/18-37-tENG, paras. 35, 32, 24–9. On modern technology in the application process and in favour of greater reliance on it, Delagrange, *ICLR*, 18 (2018), 558–61.

fulfilled.[901] The burden of proof lies with the applicants,[902] who also have to establish their identity. Given the difficulties that victims may face in obtaining official documents, the Chambers accept a wide range of proof of identity, for example, voting cards, medical documents, church membership cards, or even statements signed by two credible witnesses attesting to the identity of the applicant.[903]

The standard of proof required increases during the course of the proceedings.[904] At the investigation stage, there must be 'grounds to believe' that all preconditions for participation are fulfilled.[905] The *Abu Garda* PTC assessed applications for participation in the confirmation proceedings on a *prima facie* basis;[906] other Chambers required a satisfactory level of proof[907] or established a 'substantial grounds to believe standard'.[908] At the trial stage, participation is granted if 'there are, *prima facie*, credible grounds for suggesting' that the applicant qualifies as victim in terms of Rule 85 RPE ICC.[909] These lower standards of proof—as compared to the one of 'beyond reasonable doubt'—are due to the fact that, when the Chambers decide on applications for participation, it is not yet clear whether the alleged crimes have actually been committed by the accused.[910] Nevertheless, more uniformity, in particular in the PTCs' case law, would be desirable.[911]

The case law also differs with regard to the scope and consequences of an admission for participation.[912] According to the so-called *systematic approach*, the analysis of whether the personal interests of a victim are affected is conducted with regard to the respective procedural stage as a whole. If this precondition is fulfilled, the applicants are granted the 'procedural status of victim', that is, they are generally accepted as participants at the pre-trial, trial,

[901] Rule 89 (2) RPE ICC.

[902] *Situation in the DRC*, No. ICC-01/04-101, para. 100; *Situation in Uganda*, No. ICC-02/04-101, para. 13; *Prosecutor v. Abu Garda*, PTC I Public Redacted Version of 'Decision on the 52 Applications for Participation at the Pre-Trial Stage of the Case', No. ICC-02/05-02/09-147, 9 October 2009, para. 18; *Bemba*, No. ICC-01/05-01/08-320, para. 31; Safferling, *ICLR*, 11 (2011), 205.

[903] See *Situation in the DRC*, No. ICC-01/04-374, para. 15; *Lubanga*, No. ICC-01/04-01/06-1119, paras. 87–8; *Bemba*, ICC-01/05-01/08-699, para. 699; *Nourain and Jerbo*, No. ICC-02/05-03/09-231, para. 22; *Ruto et al.*, No. ICC-01/09-01/11-17, paras. 7–8; *Ntaganda*, No. ICC-01/04-02/06-449, para. 45; cf. also *Lubanga*, No. ICC-01/04-01/06-3045, para. 17; more restrictive, however, *Situation in Uganda*, No. ICC-02/04-101, para. 16. Applicants who claim to have suffered harm as a result of the loss of a family member have to prove the identity of the direct victims and their relationship with the applicants, *Abu Garda*, No. ICC-02/05-02/09-147, para. 6.

[904] *Situation in the DRC*, No. ICC-01/04-101, paras. 97–8.

[905] Ibid., para. 99; in a similar vein, *Situation in Uganda*, No. ICC-02/04-101, para. 12 ('appears duly established').

[906] *Abu Garda*, No. ICC-02/05-02/09-147, para. 18; in the same vein, *Ayyash et al.*, No. STL-11-01/PT/PTJ, para. 61.

[907] *Bemba*, No. ICC-01/05-01/08-320, para. 31.

[908] *Situation in the DRC*, No. ICC-01/04-101, para. 98.

[909] *Lubanga*, No. ICC-01/04-01/06-1119, para. 99; cf. also *Bemba*, No. ICC-01/05-01/08-699, para. 35; *Nourain*, No. ICC-02/05-03/09-528, para. 22; *Ruto and Sang*, No. ICC-01/09-01/11-460, para. 37; *Ntaganda*, No. ICC-01/04-02/06-449, para. 44; *Prosecutor v. Ntaganda*, Second Decision on Victims' Participation in Trial Proceedings, No. ICC-01/04-02/06-650, 16 June 2015, para. 27; *Gbagbo and Blé Goudé*, ICC 02/11 01/15 379, para. 58; implicitly confirmed in *Lubanga*, No. ICC-01/04-01/06-3045, para. 16; on the similar approach of the ECCC, see Kroker, *Zivilparteien* (2012), pp. 145–6. However, as soon as the Chambers realize that their *prima facie* evaluation is incorrect, they may withdraw the applicants' right to participate in order to save the defence from unnecessary confrontations with 'false' victims, *Lubanga*, No. ICC-01/04-01/06-2842, paras. 484, 502; Ambos, *ICLR*, 12 (2012), 117–18; Pérez-León-Acevedo, *Victims' Status* (2014), p. 308. Catani, *JICJ*, 10 (2012), 920 argues for 'a greater involvement of VPRS staff in the field at the moment the applications are filled in' in order to avoid 'false victims' being admitted as participants.

[910] *Situation in the DRC*, No. ICC-01/04-101, para. 82; *Situation in Uganda*, No. ICC-02/04-101, paras. 13–14; Ambos, *ICLR*, 12 (2012), 117; in more detail, Bock, *Opfer* (2010), pp. 444–5; for a crit. view, see Trüg, *ZStW*, 125 (2013), 63.

[911] In the same vein, WCRO, *Victim Participation* (November 2007), pp. 51–2.

[912] cf. also the case law analysis by Olásolo, *NCLR*, 12 (2009), 520–7.

or appeals stage. In a second step, the Chambers decide on the rights attached to this procedural status and determine the concrete modalities of victim participation.[913] Chambers which follow the *casuistic approach* do not recognize a 'procedural status of victim', but rather decide on the rights of victims on a case-by-case basis, which in particular means that they assess the personal interest requirement with regard to every single procedural activity. In this vein, the *Lubanga* TC required victims 'in order to participate at any specific stage in the proceedings, e.g. during the examination of a particular witness or the discussion of a particular legal issue or type of evidence, . . . to show, in a discrete written application, the reasons why his or her interests are affected by the evidence or issue then arising in the case and the nature and extent of the participation they seek'.[914]

The AC seems to favour the casuistic approach,[915] but—to the best knowledge of the author—has not yet made a definitive ruling on this issue.[916] With a view to its procedural consequences, the systematic approach is preferable since it gives the victims and the parties more certainty on the procedural role of the former. In addition, it avoids multiple applications (including multiple reports, observations, and decisions on these applications) and thus enhances the efficient conduct of the proceedings.[917]

Generally, the application procedure is a very time-consuming and resource-intensive process for the victims, the parties, the Chambers, and the Registry.[918] It may seriously delay the proceedings and hamper efficient victim participation.[919] With regard to the right of the accused to an expeditious trial, but also in order to give effect to Article 68 (3) ICCS, all (legally admissible) attempts to streamline these proceedings are more than welcome.[920]

[913] cf. in particular PTC I, *Situation in Darfur, Sudan*, Decision on the Requests for Leave to Appeal the Decision on the Application for Participation of Victims in the Proceedings in the Situation, No. ICC-01/05-121, 6 February 2008, pp. 5–6; *Katanga and Ngudjolo*, No. ICC-01/04-01/07-474, para. 45; in a similar vein, *Situation in the DRC*, No. ICC-01/04-101, para. 63.

[914] *Lubanga*, No. ICC-01/04-01/06-1119, para. 96; see also the case-by-case approach adopted in *Ruto and Sang*, No. ICC-01/09-01/11-460, para. 13.

[915] cf. *Lubanga*, No. ICC-01/04-01/06-1432, para. 104; see also McGonigle Leyh, in Letschert et al., *Victimological Approaches* (2011), p. 513; Carnero Rojo, 'Article 68', in Klamberg et al., *Commentary ICC II* (2023), pp. 331–6.

[916] See also Olásolo, *NCLR*, 12 (2009), 526–7; Tsereteli, in Stahn and van den Herik, *Perspectives* (2010), p. 655; de Brouwer and Heikkilä, in Sluiter et al., *International Criminal Procedure* (2013), p. 1319. For an overview of the different applied approaches, see Ring, *JICJ*, 21 (2023), 36 ff.

[917] *Katanga and Ngudjolo*, No. ICC-01/04-01/07-474, paras. 47–8; *Situation in Darfur*, No. ICC-01/05-121, pp. 6–7; Tsereteli, in Stahn and van den Herik, *Perspectives* (2010), pp. 654–5; Bock, *Opfer* (2010), pp. 467–71, 542–3; see also *Lubanga*, No. ICC-01/04-01/06-1119, para. 22; Mohan, *ICLR*, 9 (2009), 747; McGonigle Leyh, in Letschert et al., *Victimological Approaches* (2011), p. 513; van den Wyngaert, *CWRJIL*, 44 (2011), 483. This is also acknowledged by Pérez-León-Acevedo, *Victims' Status* (2014), pp. 322–3, who, however, favours in the end the casuistic approach.

[918] WCRO, *Victim Participation* (November 2007), pp. 59–60; McGonigle, in Ryngaert, *Effectiveness* (2009), p. 103; McGonigle Leyh, *ICLR*, 12 (2012), 397–8; Bock, *Opfer* (2010), p. 495; Catani, *JICJ*, 10 (2012), 917; FIDH, *Victims' Rights* (November 2013), p. 14; WCRO, *Victim Status* (December 2013), p. 49; Smith-van Lin, in Schabas et al., *Research Companion ICL* (2013), p. 192; Vasiliev, in Stahn, *ICC* (2015), pp. 1141–2, 1150–2; Mettraux et al., *Expert Initiative Effectiveness ICC* (2014), p. 197 (para. 72); ICC-ASP, *Governance* (2015), pp. 24–5 (para. 41); Pues, *JICJ*, 13 (2015), 959; in particular on the capacity overload of the Registry ASP, *Report*, ICC-ASP/11/22 (5 November 2012), para. 12; see also Trüg, *ZStW*, 125 (2013), 63; with a view to the ECCC, see Sperfeldt, *JICJ*, 11 (2013), 1129.

[919] ASP, *Report*, ICC-ASP/11/22 (5 November 2012), para. 12. Several victims were excluded from participation in the *Lubanga* trial proceedings because their applications were not transmitted to the TC on time, see *Lubanga*, No. ICC-01/04-01/06-3045, para. 13; cf. also WCRO, *Victim Participation* (February 2009), pp. 12–13; WCRO, *Representation of Victims* (December 2011), pp. 17–18; Chung, *NWJIHR*, 6 (2008), 497, 508; Kaoutzanis, *UCDavisJIL&Pol'y*, 17 (2010), 128–30; Pena and Carayon, *IJTJ*, 7 (2013), 527–8; Haslam and Edmunds, *ICLR*, 12 (2012), 874; Kendall and Nouwen, *LCP*, 76 nos. 3 & 4 (2013), 246.

[920] In the same vein, Perrin, *ICLR* 15 (2015), 336. See also the comprehensive report and case law overview in ICC-ASP, *Governance* (2015), pp. 14 ff. (paras. 8 ff.), setting out the applicable legal framework (pp. 14–21 and paras. 8–28), the standard victim application system ('Standard System'), implemented during the Court's first

In particular, the Chambers tend to set deadlines for the submission of applications[921] and refrain in principle from re-assessing applications which have already been granted at a previous stage of the proceedings.[922] The *Ongwen* PTC even went a step further in holding that it will only examine the applications contested by a party while all other persons are automatically granted victim status.[923] Likewise, the *Ngaïssona* PTC held that in order to best accommodate both the interests of the victims and the accused, it will concentrate on a limited number of applications—namely 'those that pose assessment problems'.[924]

In the case against *Gbagbo*, the Registry developed, with the approval of the PTC, a group concept consisting of two elements: '(i) a group form, which allows for a number of individuals to describe elements common to them as a group ("Group Form"); and (ii) an individual declaration, which connects the individual application to the information provided in the Group Form and includes the information necessary under the statutory provisions ("Individual Declaration")'.[925] Despite the collective dimension of this approach, all applications are assessed individually and all applicants, who satisfy the requirements of Rule 89 RPE ICC, are admitted to participate as individuals.[926]

With regard to the high number of applications, TC V regarded the procedure set out in Rule 89 RPE ICC to be completely inappropriate. It therefore ruled that only victims who wish to exercise their participation rights in person have to submit applications. For victims who are represented by a common legal representative, the Chamber deemed it sufficient that they register with the Registry as victim participants without having to pass the regular application procedure.[927] Yet, regardless of whether such a purely collective approach is

decade of operation (pp. 21–4 and paras. 29–38), as well as a comparative analysis of the evolution of application systems used by Chambers (pp. 24–8 and paras. 39–60).

[921] See e.g. *Gbagbo*, Second Decision on Issues Relating to the Victims' Application Process, No. ICC-02/11-01/11-86, 5 April 2012, para. 37; *Ntaganda*, No. ICC-01/04-02/06-67, para. 40; *Ruto et al.*, No. ICC-01/09-01/11-17, para. 17; see also Bock, *Opfer* (2010), p. 477; Catani, *JICJ*, 10 (2012), 918; Eckelmans, in Bonacker and Safferling, *Victims* (2013), p. 195.

[922] See e.g. *Nourain and Jerbo*, No. ICC-02/05-03/09-231, paras. 15–16, where the Chamber took the view that victims authorized to participate in the proceedings at the pre-trial stage are automatically authorized to participate in the trial stage, unless (a) the alleged harm is linked to a charge which was not confirmed by the PTC or (b) new information has emerged; cf. also *Bemba*, No. ICC-01/05-01/08-699, paras. 18–19; crit., because this approach is time-consuming for the parties, see Pérez-León-Acevedo, *Victims' Status* (2014), p. 307. The AC also automatically granted all victims who participated in the *Lubanga* trial proceedings the right to participate in the appeals proceedings: *Prosecutor v. Lubanga*, AC Decision on the Participation of Victims in the Appeals against Trial Chamber I's Conviction and Sentencing Decisions, No. ICC-01/04-01/06-2951, 13 December 2012, para. 3. With regard to interlocutory appeals, however, the AC pursues a more restrictive approach and requires all victims (regardless of whether they have already been recognized as participants in the proceedings giving rise to the appeal) to file new applications, cf. e.g. *Situation in Darfur, Sudan*, PTC I Decision on Victim Participation in the Appeal of the Office of Public Counsel for the Defence against Pre-Trial Chamber I's Decision of 3 December and in the Appeals of the Prosecutor and the Office of Public Counsel for the Defence against Pre-Trial Chamber I's Decision of 6 December 2007, No. ICC-02/05-138, 18 June 2008, paras. 23–4; for a crit. view, see Bock, 'Commentary', in Klip and Freeland, *ALC*, XL (2013), pp. 293–4. The *Lubanga* TC, as well, found it necessary to review all applications granted by the PTC in *Lubanga*, No. ICC-01/04-01/06-1119, para. 112.

[923] *Ongwen*, No. ICC-02/04-01/15-299, para. 7; in a similar vein, Mettraux et al., *Expert Initiative Effectiveness ICC* (2014), pp. 30 (para. 136), 200 (para. 83).

[924] *Ngaïssona*, No. ICC-01/14-01/18-141, para. 44 (stressing that this system has the advantage of 'saving time and resources').

[925] *Gbagbo*, No. ICC-02/11-01/11-86, para. 17. This approach was also adopted in *Situation in Uganda*, No. ICC-02/04-191, para. 22 and (with slight modifications as regards the group application) in *Ntaganda*, No. ICC-01/04-02/06-67, para. 33; in more detail, WCRO, *Victim Status* (December 2013), pp. 24–30, 34–7; Vasiliev, in Stahn, *ICC* (2015), pp. 1153–5, 1158–9.

[926] *Gbagbo*, No. ICC-02/11-01/11-86, para. 35.

[927] *Ruto and Sang*, No. ICC-01/09-01/11-460, paras. 25, 48–55; *Prosecutor v. Muthaura and Kenyatta*, TC V Decision on Victims Representation and Participation, No. ICC-01/09-02/11-498, 3 October 2012, paras. 24, 47–54; in more detail, Vasiliev, in Stahn, *ICC* (2015), pp. 1155–8.

desirable in principle,[928] it violates Rule 89 RPE ICC which makes any victim participation dependent on a prior judicial evaluation of the eligibility criteria set out in Article 68 (3) ICCS.[929] Legitimate concerns for the rights of the accused and the interests of victims must not lead the Chambers to disregard binding procedural norms. If the current application procedure proves to be unworkable, it is for the State Parties to amend or adapt the Court's legal framework.[930]

### (d) *Modalities of victim participation*

The Statute is silent on the concrete modalities of victim participation and the RPE only provide for some general guidelines. Accordingly, victims have the right to choose a legal representative[931] but in order to safeguard the effectiveness of the proceedings[932] the Chambers insist on a common legal representation[933] of all or, at least, certain groups of victims.[934] If the victims are unable to agree on a common legal representative, the Chamber may ask the Registry to appoint one[935] or appoint counsel from the OPCV for

928 In favour of a fully collective approach as developed in the Kenya case, WCRO, *Victim Status* (December 2013), p. 50–60; see also van den Wyngaert, *CWRJIL*, 44 (2011), 483; Mettraux et al., *Expert Initiative Effectiveness ICC* (2014), pp. 30 (para. 133), 198 (para. 75) and Kaoutzanis, *UCDavisJIL&Pol'y*, 17 (2010), 134–49 (arguing for the adaption of the (civil) US class action device to the ICC's criminal proceedings); more reluctant, ASP, *Report*, ICC-ASP/11/22 (5 November 2012), paras. 44–7; Kendall and Nouwen, *LCP*, 76 nos. 3 & 4 (2013), 249; Dixon and Tenove, *IJTJ*, 7 (2013), 410; VRWG, *Victim Participation* (June 2014), p. 4; Moffet, *JICJ*, 13 (2015), 291; Killean and Moffett, *JICJ*, 16 (2017), 731–8; Zegveld, *ICLR*, 19 (2019), 334–6.

929 WCRO, *Victim Status* (December 2013), p. 60; Pérez-León-Acevedo, *Victims' Status* (2014), p. 310; Vasiliev, in Stahn, *ICC* (2015), pp. 1156–7; crit. also, Friman, in Cryer et al., *ICL* (2019), p. 457.

930 cf. Art. 51 (2) ICCS. See e.g. the proposals discussed in ASP, *Report*, No. ICC-ASP/11/22 (5 November 2012), paras. 39–49 (adoption of TC V's fully collective approach), 57–64 (decision-making on status of victims by judges, i.e. no observations on the applications by the defence and the prosecution), 65–71 (dealing with victims' applications only at the pre-trial stage). Despite reports and recommendations aiming at a review of the victim application process, the ASP has not yet adopted any reforms; crit. thereon Ring, *JICJ*, 21 (2023), 29 (arguing that the procedure stipulated in the legal framework of the ICC 'has proven inoperable'), 35 ('the ASP has acknowledged the limitations of the framework but issued no guidelines as to how the issue should be managed'); for earlier discussions, see also WCRO, *Victim Status* (December 2013), pp. 37–48; Vasiliev, in Stahn, *ICC* (2015), pp. 1159–63; Mettraux et al., *Expert Initiative Effectiveness ICC* (2014), pp. 30 (paras. 135–6), 199–201 (paras.79–89) (evaluation of the applications by the proposed 'Office for Victims').

931 Rule 90 (1) RPE ICC. Stressing the importance of this rule, *Ngaïssona*, No. ICC-01/14-01/18-141, para. 46 ('The Chamber places the utmost importance on the possibility for the victims to be represented, first and foremost, by a person they have chosen according to their interests and for their own reasons'). However, as the Court has repeatedly made clear, this right is not absolute, see e.g. *Prosecutor v. Al Mahdi*, Public redacted version of 'Decision on Victim Participation at Trial and on Common Legal Representation of Victims', No. ICC-01/12-01/15-97-Red, 8 June 2016, para. 36; see also Zegveld, *ICLR*, 19 (2019), 334 (stating that the freedom to choose a legal representative has in practice 'turned out to be an empty shell'), 335 (with further references in n. 47). Note that victims may also participate in the proceedings without the assistance of a legal representative: see *Kony et al.*, No. ICC-02/04-01/05-134, paras. 2–10; for a different view, see Calvo-Goller, *Trial Proceedings* (2006), p. 248. In contrast, at the ECCC the legal representation of participating victims is mandatory from the issuance of the Closing Order onwards (Rule 23*ter* (1) IR ECCC). In the proceedings before the STL, participation of unrepresented victims is possible only with the special leave of the PTC (Rule 86 (C)(ii) RPE STL). For an empirical analysis of victim legal representation both before the ICC and the ECCC, see Killean and Moffett, *JICJ*, 16 (2017), 713 ff.

932 Crit. discussing tensions between effectiveness and efficiency in relation to the participation process, Delagrange, *ICLR*, 18 (2018), 553–6.

933 In all proceedings before the ICC, victims are represented by common legal representatives; see van den Wyngaert, *CWRJIL*, 44 (2011), 480. Crit. Zegveld, *ICLR*, 19 (2019), 334–6.

934 Rule 90 (2) RPE ICC. See e.g. the 'geographical grouping' of victims in *Prosecutor v. Bemba*, No. ICC-01/05-01/08-1005, Decision on Common Legal Representative of Victims for the Purpose of Trial, 10 November 2010, para. 18 and the overview on the case law by Eckelmans, in Bonacker and Safferling, *Victims* (2013), p. 203; WCRO, *Representation of Victims* (December 2011), pp. 34–44; Haslam and Edmunds, *ICLR*, 12 (2012), 883–9; Smith-van Lin, in Schabas et al., *Research Companion ICL* (2013), pp. 198–203.

935 Rule 90 (3) RPE ICC, Reg. 79 RegC. Balancing the victim's interests and the efficiency of the proceedings while instructing the Registry to appoint counsel, *Mokom*, No. ICC-01/14-01/22-182, paras. 32–5. On the need to avoid conflicts of interest within the commonly represented group of victims, see *Bemba*, No. ICC-01/

that matter.[936] Although such a collective approach may be necessary in order to safeguard the right of the accused to an expeditious trial[937] and duly reflects the collective dimension of victimization in ICL,[938] it carries the inherent danger of a de-individualization of victims by reducing them to 'faceless numbers' and making it impossible to hear their individual views and concerns.[939] In any case, a common legal representation can at least ensure that the Court takes into consideration the *collective* interests of victims.[940] Of course, to satisfy the demands of the *individual* victims, the common legal representatives have to stay in close contact with their clients, ultimately with the help of field assistants.[941]

The legal representatives have special participatory rights (attending hearings, questioning witnesses etc.).[942] Thus, victims represented by counsel enjoy broader rights than unrepresented victims,[943] who would probably be confined to submitting written

05-01/08-1005, para. 13; *Prosecutor v. Ruto et al.*, PTC II Decision on Victims' Participation at the Confirmation of Charges Hearing and in the Related Proceedings, No. ICC-01/09-01/11-249, 5 August 2011, para. 65; Bock, *Opfer* (2010), p. 498; Ambos, *ICLR*, 12 (2012), 118; Donat-Cattin, in Carlizzi et al., *Corte Penale Internazionale* (2003), p. 361; Garkawe, *ICLR*, 3 (2003), 361; with a particular view of the legal representative's duty of loyalty to clients, Funk, *Victims' Rights* (2010), pp. 112–17; on the selection of suitable common representatives, see Haslam and Edmunds, *ICLR*, 12 (2012), 880–3. But note that the Chamber may also direct the Registry to terminate the appointment of counsel, see e.g. *Prosecutor v. Abd-Al-Rahman*, TC I Decision Terminating the Appointment of Counsel, No. ICC-01/09-01/11-249, 5 May 2022, para. 21.

[936] Reg. 80 (2) RegC; see e.g. *Lubanga*, No. ICC-01/04-01/06-2842, para. 20; *Situation in Uganda*, No. ICC-02/04-191, para. 30; *Ntaganda*, No. ICC-01/04-02/06-211, para. 79; *Prosecutor v. Ongwen*, PTC II Decision on Contested Victims' Applications for Participation, Legal Representation of Victims and their Procedural Rights, No. ICC-02/04-01/15-350, 27 November 2015, para. 19; in more detail, WCRO, *Representation of Victims* (December 2011), pp. 27–33, 44–7. It is, however, questionable whether it is wise to make use of this possibility. The main task of the OPCV is to provide support and assistance to the legal representatives of victims and to the victims themselves (Reg. 81 RegC), see e.g. *Prosecutor v. Abd-Al-Rahman*, TC I Decision on Victims' Participation and Legal Representation in Trial Proceedings, No. ICC-02/05-01/20-494, 19 October 2021, paras. 8, 10–11, in which the TC instructed the OPCV to support counsel with knowledge of Darfuri dialects and the victim communities. Given its very limited resources, the direct involvement of OPCV officials as participant to the proceedings might substantially reduce the Office's ability to exercise its support function in an adequate manner, see Bock, *Opfer* (2010), p. 503; Ambos, *ICLR*, 12 (2012), 118–19; crit. also FIDsH, *Victims' Rights* (November 2013), p. 22; WCRO, *Representation of Victims* (December 2011), pp. 49–52, 56–61; *de lege ferenda* in favour of the establishment of a permanent victims' office that assumes the tasks of coordinating outreach and victims' representation, Hoven, Feiler. and Scheibel, *Victims* (2013), p. 9; on the possible role and competences of such an '*Opferbeauftragten*', Hoven, *ZIS*, 9 (2014), 697–701. On financial assistance pursuant to Rule 90 (5) RPE ICC, see Killean and Moffett, *JICJ*, 16 (2017), 728–30.

[937] cf. *Lubanga*, No. ICC-01/04-01/06-1119, paras. 125–6; *Bemba*, No. ICC-01/05-01/08-1005, para. 9; *Ntaganda*, No. ICC-01/04-02/06-449, para. 53; see also Donat-Cattin, in Lattanzi and Schabas, *Essays I* (1999), p. 270; Timm, in Fischer, Kreß and Lüder, *Prosecution* (2001), p. 300; Greco, *ICLR*, 7 (2007), 544; de Brouwer and Heikkilä, in Sluiter et al., *International Criminal Procedure* (2013), p. 1347; Funk, *Victims' Rights* (2010), pp. 137–44 suggests that common legal representatives should compile a dossier summarizing their clients' experiences and submit it to the Chamber and the Prosecutor.

[938] Trüg, *ZStW*, 125 (2013), 66.

[939] cf. FIDH, *Victims' Rights* (November 2013), p. 23; also Dixon and Tenove, *IJTJ*, 7 (2013), 410; Pues, *JICJ*, 13 (2015), 962; Haslam and Edmunds, *JICJ*, 15 (2017), 931; Zegveld, *ICLR*, 19 (2019), 336. According to Catani, *JICJ*, 10 (2012), 919, participation through a legal representative, i.e. without victims personally attending the hearings, is merely symbolic; in a similar vein, WCRO, *Victim Participation* (February 2009), p. 50; Baumgartner, *IRRC*, 90 (2008), 429; Stover, Balthazard, and Koenig, *IRRC*, 93 (2011), 544; Haslam and Edmunds, *ICLR*, 12 (2012), 903. Victims seem to prefer to participate on an individual basis, see Mohan, *ICLR*, 9 (2009), 758; de Brouwer and Heikkilä, in Sluiter et al., *International Criminal Procedure* (2013), p. 1347.

[940] Bock, *Opfer* (2010), p. 498.

[941] FIDH, *Victims' Rights* (November 2013), p. 23; Wemmers, *LJIL*, 23 (2010), 642; Haslam and Edmunds, *ICLR*, 12 (2012), 891; Eckelmans, in Bonacker and Safferling, *Victims* (2013), pp. 203–4; Kaul, in Bonacker and Safferling, *Victims* (2013), p. 226; see also the proposed establishment of a 'support structure' for legal representatives by the Registry in *Bemba*, No. ICC-01/05-01/08-1005, paras. 25–6; *Ruto et al.*, No. ICC-01/09-01/11-249, para. 78.

[942] Rule 91 RPE ICC.

[943] *Kony et al.*, No. ICC-02/04-01/05-134, paras. 7, 10; Baumgartner, *IRRC*, 90 (2008), 430; Bock, *Opfer* (2010), p. 500; Friman, in Cryer et al., *ICL* (2019), pp. 458–9.

observations.[944] Victims have a right to be informed on the course of the proceedings by the Registry which has to notify them or their legal representatives, inter alia, on all relevant hearings, requests, submissions, motions, and decisions.[945]

Apart from these general rules, the procedural regime of the ICC leaves it to the discretion of the Chambers to decide on a case-by-case basis on the appropriate modalities of participation.[946] While this flexible approach allows the Chambers to respond to the particularities of the case at hand,[947] it leads to divergent decisions[948] and thus to an unequal treatment of victim participants.[949] It is to be hoped, though, that with the increasing practice some common guidelines of the ICC's victim participation system will be developed.[950]

At the *investigation stage*, victims' rights are rather limited. They have a right to be heard and to file documents and written observations.[951] In addition, they may ask the Chamber to initiate *proprio motu* proceedings, for example, to review a decision of the Prosecutor not to proceed pursuant to Article 53 (3) ICCS,[952] or request certain investigative steps from the

944 Friman, in Cryer et al., *ICL* (2019), p. 459. As yet, all victims participating in the ICC's proceedings have been represented by a legal representative, see WCRO, *Victim Status* (December 2013), p. 14.

945 Rule 92 RPE ICC.

946 See *Situation in Uganda*, No. ICC-02/04-101, para. 8; *Katanga and Ngudjolo*, No. ICC-01/04-01/07-1788, para. 46; *Bemba*, No. ICC-01/05-01/08-320, para. 85; Safferling, *ZStW*, 115 (2003), 375; Olásolo, *NCLR*, 12 (2009), 519–20; Coleman, *ICLR*, 20 (2020), 381.

947 Tonellato, *EJCCLCJ*, 20 (2012), 324; see also Vasiliev, in Stahn, *ICC* (2015), p. 1197.

948 *Katanga and Ngudjolo*, No. ICC-01/04-01/07-1788, para. 54; Vasiliev, 'Article 68 (3)', in Stahn and Sluiter, *Practice* (2009), p. 650; Vasiliev, in Stahn, *ICC* (2015), p. 1168; Meloni, in Lupária, *Victims* (2015), p. 56.

949 Bock, *Opfer* (2010), p. 443; Smith-van Lin, in Schabas et al., *Research Companion ICL* (2013), p. 187; see also WCRO, *Victim Participation* (November 2007), p. 57; Haslam, in McGoldrick, Rowe, and Donnelly, *Permanent ICC* (2004), p. 323; for a crit. view, see also Safferling, *International Criminal Procedure* (2012), p. 176 (no 'concise procedural structure'); Zappalà, *JICJ*, 8 (2010), 140 ('the ICC system lacks an appropriate level of clarity'); Coleman, *ICLR*, 20 (2020), 393 ('[t]he rights of victims should be the same in all Chambers'); McGonigle Leyh, *ICLR*, 12 (2012), 404; VRWG, *Victim Participation* (June 2014), p. 3; Moffet, *JICJ*, 13 (2015), 291–2; Mettraux et al., *Expert Initiative Effectiveness ICC* (2014), p. 177 (para. 7). See also Pues, *JICJ*, 13 (2015), 964 arguing that victims' participatory rights are not rights *stricto sensu*, but rather privileges.

950 On the procedural rights of victims in the proceedings before the ECCC, see Kroker, *Zivilparteien* (2012), pp. 220–318; Stover, Balthazard, and Koenig, *IRRC*, 93 (2011), 513–40 (regarding Case 001); McGonigle Leyh, *Procedural Justice?* (2011), pp. 185–223; McGonigle Leyh, *ICLR*, 12 (2012), 388–90; Pratlong, in Kolb and Scalia, *DIP* (2012), pp. 648–56; Studzinsky, in Bonacker and Safferling, *Victims* (2013), pp. 179–87; de Brouwer and Heikkilä, in Sluiter et al., *International Criminal Procedure* (2013), pp. 1313–14, 1318, 1322–3, 1326–7, 1329–30; 1331–2; Ip, *ICLR*, 13 (2013), 882–9; Sperfeldt, *JICJ*, 11 (2013), 1116–20; Stegmiller, *LJIL*, 27 (2014), 465 (stressing the increasing normative regulation and juridical restraint of victims' participatory rights); for a comparison between the ICC's and ECCC's approaches on victim participation, see McGonigle, in Ryngaert, *Effectiveness* (2009), p. 91; on victim participation before the STL, see de Hemptinne, *JICJ*, 8 (2010), 172–9; de Brouwer and Heikkilä, in Sluiter et al., *International Criminal Procedure* (2013), pp. 1314, 1318, 1323–4, 1327–8, 1330, 1332–3; for a comprehensive comparative analysis of the victim's status as participant/civil party before the ICTY, ICTR, ICC, ECCC, and STL, see Pérez-León-Acevedo, *Victims' Status* (2014), pp. 299–563; for the development of general principles on victim participation e.g. by an amendment of the RegC, see Mettraux et al., *Expert Initiative Effectiveness ICC* (2014), pp. 26 (para. 114), 180 (para. 14).

951 *Situation in the DRC*, No. ICC-01/04-101, para. 71. See, in more detail, Bock, *Opfer* (2010), pp. 510–35.

952 cf. *Situation in the DRC*, Decision on the Requests of the Legal Representative for Victims VPRS 1 to VPRS 6 regarding 'Prosecutor's Information on further Investigation', No. ICC-01/04-399, 26 September 2007, pp. 6–7. This right is arguably compatible with the AC's more restrictive approach towards victim participation in the investigation stage (see above note 871and main text), since it merely links Art. 68 (3) ICCS to a judicial proceeding. This seems not to preclude victims from intervening with a view to triggering judicial proceedings; see *Situation in Kenya*, Decision on the 'Victim's Request for Review of Prosecution's Decision to Cease Active Investigation', No. ICC-01/09-159, 5 November 2015, para. 7. Calling for an amendment of Art. 53 ICCS to enable victims to request judicial review of a decision not to open an investigation, Hodgson, *CLF*, (2023), 280. More reluctantly, see Friman, 'Victims', in Cryer et al., *ICL* (2019), pp. 458–9; de Brouwer and Heikkilä, 'Victim Issues', in Sluiter et al., *International Criminal Procedure* (2013), p. 1317; with a particular view to the right of victims to request the collection of evidence, Klamberg, *Evidence* (2013), pp. 218–22.

Prosecutor.[953] At this stage, the victims' rights must be carefully balanced against the need to safeguard the integrity of the proceedings. Victims are thus not allowed to participate in *confidential ex parte* proceedings relating to the issuance of an arrest warrant,[954] as this would increase the risk that the suspect becomes aware that s/he is under investigation,[955] unless the warrant is unsealed.[956]

In the *confirmation proceedings*, the victims representatives are, as a rule,[957] granted the right to make opening and closing statements;[958] to question witnesses;[959] to make submissions on all issues relating to the admissibility and probative value of the evidence and to examine such evidence;[960] to file written motions, responses, and replies;[961] to access all public and confidential filings contained in the record of the cases (but not *ex parte* documents);[962] and to attend all public and closed sessions related to the confirmation of charges.[963] However, in order to prevent the confirmation hearing from becoming 'a trial before the trial', victims are not allowed to present additional evidence.[964]

If the victims insist on anonymity, most Chambers limit the procedural rights of their representatives:[965] they are not entitled to question witnesses, may only attend public hearings

[953] *Katanga and Ngudjolo*, No. ICC-01/04-01/07-474, para. 83; see also *Situation in the DRC*, No. ICC-01/04-556, para. 54 ('Information that victims can provide to the Prosecutor about the scope of his investigations cannot but be welcome as it could provide nothing other than assistance'), *Situation in Darfur, Sudan*, No. ICC-02/05-177, para. 7.

[954] *Situation in Kenya*, Decision on the 'Application for Leave to Participate in the Proceedings before the Pre-Trial Chamber relating to the Prosecutor's Application under Article 58 (7)', No. ICC-01/09-42, 11 February 2011, paras. 9, 11, 13.

[955] Bock, *Opfer* (2010), p. 517; cf. also Pérez-León-Acevedo, *Victims' Status* (2014), p. 377.

[956] *Prosecutor v. Al Bashir*, Decision on the Second Application by Victims . . . to Participate in the Appeal against the 'Decision on the Prosecution's Application for a Warrant of Arrest against Omar Hassan Ahmad Al Bashir', No. ICC-02/05-01/09-70, 28 January 2010, para. 10.

[957] The Chambers may at any time limit the procedural rights of the victims' representative if 'necessary to safeguard another competing interest', *Katanga and Ngudjolo*, No. ICC-01/04-01/07-474, para. 147; *Abu Garda*, No. ICC-02/05-02/09-136, para. 9; Kelly, in Bonacker and Safferling, *Victims* (2013), p. 52.

[958] See also Rule 89 (1) RPE ICC; *Prosecutor v. Lubanga*, Decision on the Arrangements for Participation of Victims . . . at the Confirmation Hearing, No. ICC-01/04-01/06-462, 22 September 2006, p. 8; *Katanga and Ngudjolo*, No. ICC-01/04-01/07-474, para. 143; *Abu Garda*, No. ICC-02/05-02/09-136, para. 19; *Ruto et al.*, No. ICC-01/09-01/11-249, p. 48; *Prosecutor v. Mbarushimana*, Decision on the 138 Applications for Victims' Participation in the Proceedings, No. ICC-01/04-01/10-351, 11 August 2011, para. 42; *Blé Goudé*, No. ICC-02/11-02/11-111, para. 20; *Ntaganda*, No. ICC-01/04-02/06-211, para. 87. For suggestions on the contents and structure of an opening statement, see Funk, *Victims' Rights* (2010), pp. 186–9.

[959] *Katanga and Ngudjolo*, No. ICC-01/04-01/07-474, paras. 135–9; cf. also *Abu Garda*, No. ICC-02/05-02/09-136, paras. 22–3.

[960] *Katanga and Ngudjolo*, No. ICC-01/04-01/07-474, para. 134; *Ntaganda*, No. ICC-01/04-02/06-211, para. 86.

[961] *Katanga and Ngudjolo*, No. ICC-01/04-01/07-474, para. 142; *Abu Garda*, No. ICC-02/05-02/09-136, para. 25; *Ruto et al.*, No. ICC-01/09-01/11-249, para. 101; *Prosecutor v. Ongwen*, No. ICC-02/04-01/15-350, para. 33.

[962] *Katanga and Ngudjolo*, No. ICC-01/04-01/07-474, paras. 128–30. This includes the right to be notified of the relevant documents and to have access to the evidence contained in the case record, paras. 131–2; see also *Prosecutor v. Ongwen*, No. ICC-02/04-01/15-350, para. 29. In *Blé Goudé*, No. ICC-02/11-02/11-111, paras. 18–19, the legal representatives were only granted access to *public* filings and decisions. In the same vein, *Ntaganda*, No. ICC-01/04-02/06-211, paras. 89 ff., however reserving at para. 90 the option to decide on a case-by-case basis whether or not to grant access to filings and evidence that are classified 'confidential' (affirmatively at para. 95).

[963] *Katanga and Ngudjolo*, No. ICC-01/04-01/07-474, para. 140; see also *Prosecutor v. Ongwen*, No. ICC-02/04-01/15-350, para. 32. In *Blé Goudé*, No. ICC-02/11-02/11-111, paras. 18–19, the legal representatives were only granted the right to attend *public* sessions. If the Chamber holds closed or *ex parte* sessions, it will decide on a case-by-case basis whether or not the legal representatives may attend them. In the same vein, *Ntaganda*, No. ICC-01/04-02/06-211, para. 85.

[964] *Katanga and Ngudjolo*, No. ICC-01/04-01/07-474, paras. 101–13; see also ICC-OTP, *Policy Victims' Participation* (2010), p. 18; Bantekas, *ICL* (2010), p. 560; FIDH, *Victims' Rights* (November 2013), p. 16.

[965] See above notes 894, 895, and main text.

and access public documents, and cannot 'add any point of fact or any evidence';[966] their requests to intervene in Court sessions are decided by the Chambers on a case-by-case basis.[967] The *Bemba* PTC took, however, the opposing view that a 'differentiation in participatory rights should not be to the detriment of those requesting protective measures' and vested all legal representatives with the same (limited) rights, namely, to attend *public* hearings, to access *public* decisions and documents, to make oral submissions (if deemed appropriate), and to submit written submissions.[968]

At the *trial stage*, victims' representatives enjoy, as a rule, the same rights as in the confirmation proceedings.[969] The Chambers, however, tend to limit the right to access the case file to public documents and the right to attend hearings to public sessions.[970] Although this approach is understandable with regard to the protection of sensitive information, it gives too little credit to the fact that victims have a personal interest in the outcome of the proceedings: that is, that they (at least at the trial stage) must not be compared with the general (unconcerned) public.[971] This difference was acknowledged by the *Lubanga* TC itself encouraging the parties to determine the appropriate recipients of a confidential filing and to identify those filings which should be forwarded to the legal representatives.[972] The problem with this approach is that it leaves the decision of what concerns the victims to the parties, but they may not know. An alternative solution safeguarding the victim's own procedural standing would be to pick up on the distinction introduced by the PTCs and to grant the representatives general access to confidential filings and hearings (excluding *ex parte* ones)[973] or to provide them with a full, non-redacted version of the case record which would enable them to identify themselves the filings and hearings which are of concern to them.[974]

Most notably, the TCs strengthen the role of legal representatives in the hearing of evidence. They are not only granted the right to question witnesses, experts, and the

[966] *Lubanga*, No. ICC-01/04-01/06-462, p. 8; *Katanga and Ngudjolo*, No. ICC-01/04-01/07-474, para. 182; *Abu Garda*, No. ICC-02/05-02/09-136, paras. 13, 17, 22; cf. also *Mbarushimana*, No. ICC-01/04-01/10-351, para. 42; *Muthaura, Kenyatta and Hussein Ali*, No. ICC-01/09-02/11-267, paras. 103–18.

[967] *Lubanga*, No. ICC-01/04-01/06-462, p. 8; *Katanga and Ngudjolo*, No. ICC-01/04-01/07-474, para. 182; cf. also *Abu Garda*, No. ICC-02/05-02/09-136, para. 20 with regard to the attendance at closed sessions. See also *Ruto et al.*, No. ICC-01/09-01/11-249, paras. 100, 125 where the Chamber held that it will decide on requests of the common legal representatives (who also act on behalf of anonymous victims) for leave to question witnesses on a case-by-case basis. The same approach was adopted in *Muthaura, Kenyatta and Hussein Ali*, No. ICC-01/09-02/11-267, paras. 115–17.

[968] *Bemba*, No. ICC-01/05-01/08-320, paras. 101–10. Since no witness testified in the proceedings, the Chamber did not have to decide if the legal representative should be entitled to examine them, para. 109. In more detail on the equal or distinctive treatment of anonymous and non-anonymous victims, Bock, *Opfer* (2010), pp. 518, 523–4, 536; McGonigle Leyh, in Letschert et al., *Victimological Approaches* (2011), pp. 515–18.

[969] See *Lubanga*, No. ICC-01/04-01/06-1119, paras. 105–7 (access to the record, documents, and filings), 112–14 (participation in hearings/status conferences; filing of written submission), 117 (opening and closing statements), 118 (filing applications and requests); *Katanga and Ngudjolo*, No. ICC-01/04-01/07-1788, paras. 68 (opening and closing statements), 69–70 (attend and participate in hearings). In *Ruto and Sang*, No. ICC-01/09-01/11-460, para. 71, *Muthaura and Kenyatta*, No. ICC-01/09-02/11-498, para. 70, however, the Chambers granted only the OPCV but not the legal representative the right to attend public and confidential hearings. This approach is incompatible with Art. 68 (3) ICCS, 90 RPE ICC, since it factually denies the victims the right to act through their *chosen* representative; crit. also, FIDH, *Victims' Rights* (November 2013), p. 23.

[970] *Lubanga*, No. ICC-01/04-01/06-1119, paras. 105–6, 112–13; see also *Nourain*, No. ICC-02/05-03/09-545, paras. 34–6; *Ruto and Sang*, No. ICC-01/09-01/11-460, paras. 64–7.

[971] *Bock*, Opfer (2010), p. 525; Ambos, *ICLR*, 12 (2012), 119.

[972] *Lubanga*, No. ICC-01/04-01/06-1119, para. 107; see also *Nourain*, No. ICC-02/05-03/09-545, para. 36; *Ruto and Sang*, No. ICC-01/09-01/11-460, para. 67.

[973] In this vein, *Katanga and Ngudjolo*, No. ICC-01/04-01/07-1788, paras. 71, 121; with regard to participation in closed sessions, see *Nourain*, No. ICC-02/05-03/09-545, para. 41.

[974] *Bock*, Opfer (2010), pp. 512–13, 525–7, 536–7; Ambos, *ICLR*, 12 (2012), 119; Pérez-León-Acevedo, *Victims' Status* (2014), p. 430.

accused[975]—although with the manner of questioning to be determined by the TC[976]—but also to tender, examine, and challenge evidence,[977] which includes the right to ask the Chambers to call one or more of their clients as witnesses.[978] As was already pointed out above,[979] this approach acknowledges and implements the victim's right to truth and justice.[980] It is also compatible with the ICC's procedural regime, which imposes the responsibility for the presentation of evidence not exclusively on the parties.[981] Rather, Article 69 (3), (4) ICCS vest the Chamber with the power 'to request the submission of all evidence that it considers necessary for the determination of the truth' and to 'rule on the relevance and admissibility of evidence'. These powers may also be exercised at the request of the victims.[982] Thus, although victims do not have the direct right to present evidence, they may request the Chamber to order the production of evidence.[983]

975 *Katanga and Ngudjolo*, No. ICC-01/04-01/07-1788, paras. 72–8; see also *Lubanga*, No. ICC-01/04-01/06-1119, para. 108; *Nourain*, No. ICC-02/05-03/09-545, para. 31; in a similar vein, *Ruto and Sang*, No. ICC-01/09-01/11-460, para. 74, *Muthaura and Kenyatta*, No. ICC-01/09-02/11-498, para. 74, where the Chamber, however, again (see above note 971) grants this right to the OPCV, not to the legal representative. Notably, the Chambers have developed different views on the scope of the right to question witnesses, in particular on whether the legal representative may ask questions relating to the guilt of the accused: see McGonigle Leyh, *Procedural Justice?* (2011), pp. 298–300; Eckelmans, in Bonacker and Safferling, *Victims* (2013), pp. 212–13; Tochilovsky, *Jurisprudence* (2014), p. 751; Pérez-León-Acevedo, *Victims' Status* (2014), pp. 436–8; Vasiliev, in Stahn, *ICC* (2015), pp. 1176–80. Mettraux et al., *Expert Initiative Effectiveness ICC* (2014), pp. 26 (para. 113), 179–80 (para. 12) suggest that victims should not be permitted to question witnesses or to elicit evidence related to the responsibility of the accused.

976 *Lubanga*, No. ICC-01/04-01/06-2127, para. 21. See also Rule 91 (3) RPE ICC, according to which the Chamber may require the legal representative to submit the questions in writing prior to the relevant session for approval and decide to put the questions on behalf of the legal representative.

977 *Lubanga*, No. ICC-01/04-01/06-1119, paras. 108 9; confirmed in *Lubanga*, No. ICC-01/04-01/06-1432, para. 109; *Nourain*, No. ICC-02/05-03/09-545, paras. 24, 28, 30; *Katanga and Ngudjolo*, No. ICC-01/04-01/07-1788, paras. 81–5; *Prosecutor v. Bemba*, Decision on the Supplement Applications by the Legal Representatives of Victims to Present Evidence and the Views and Concerns of Victims, No. ICC-01/05-01/08-2138, 23 February 2012, para. 18; *Ruto and Sang*, No. ICC-01/09-01/11-460, para. 77; *Muthaura and Kenyatta*, No. ICC-01/09-02/11-498, para. 76; see also Donat-Cattin, 'Article 68', in Ambos, *Commentary* (2022), mn. 23 and the detailed analysis by Plevin, *CLF*, 25 (2014), 441 and Vasiliev, in Sluiter et al., *International Criminal Procedure* (2013), pp. 616–20; Vasiliev, in Stahn, *ICC* (2015), pp. 1166–76; crit. WCRO, *Victim Participation* (February 2009), p. 51–2; Burnham, in van den Herik and Stahn, *Diversification* (2012), p. 673; also Klamberg, *Evidence* (2013), pp. 360–2, 464–70, 513 (arguing that the role of victims should be downplayed in favour of a more adversarial approach towards the presentation of evidence).

978 *Katanga and Ngudjolo*, No. ICC-01/04-01/07-1788, paras. 86–93; confirmed in *Katanga and Ngudjolo*, No. ICC-01/04-01/07-2288, para. 3. On the differences between allowing a victim to give evidence as witness and allowing a victim to present his or her views and concerns in person, *Bemba*, No. ICC-01/05-01/08-2138, paras. 19–20.

979 See notes 849, 850 and accompanying text in this chapter.

980 For a different view, see Plevin, *CLF*, 25 (2014), 448 (victims' ability to introduce evidence as a 'truth finding mechanism that gives the Court powers to request the submission of additional evidence—far from any incarnation of an entitlement derived from human rights law').

981 In contrast, Art. 41 (2)(b) ICCS explicitly limits the right to request the disqualification of a judge to the Prosecutor and the person being investigated or prosecuted which seems to indicate that this right cannot be exercised by victims even if the participation of a biased judge affects their personal interests in terms of Art. 68 (3) ICCS, see *Prosecutor v. Katanga*, Annex to the Notification of the Decision on the Application of the Legal Representative for Victims for the Disqualification of a Judge in case ICC-01/04-01/07, No. ICC-01/04-01/07-3504-Anx, 22 July 2014, paras. 44–5.

982 Bock, in Klip and Freeland, *ALC*, XL (2013), pp. 289; cf. also *Katanga and Ngudjolo*, No. ICC-01/04-01/07-2288, para. 40; *Nourain*, No. ICC-02/05-03/09-545, para. 24; Plevin, *CLF*, 25 (2014), 444–5.

983 Tsereteli, in Stahn and van den Herik, *Perspectives* (2010), p. 650; Trüg, *ZStW*, 125 (2013), 65; Eckelmans, in Bonacker and Safferling, *Victims* (2013), p. 211; see also Friman, *LJIL*, 22 (2009), 494; crit. ICC-OTP, *Policy Victims' Participation* (2010), pp. 18–19; Guhr, *ZIS*, 3 (2008), 369; Chung, *NWJIHR*, 6 (2008), 517; Safferling, *International Criminal Procedure* (2012), p. 175; Tonellato, *EJCCLCJ*, 20 (2012), 354; Zappalà, *JICJ*, 8 (2010), 148 (arguing that the Chamber should use its competence to order the production of evidence only in favour of the accused); in a similar vein, McGonigle Leyh, *ICLR*, 12 (2012), 401.

Of course, the Chambers have to ensure that the victims' involvement does not prejudice the rights of the accused.[984] The unique role of victims and their legal representatives to assist the Chamber in the pursuit of the truth,[985] as participants rather than parties,[986] entails that the manner of questioning witnesses is to be determined by the Chamber and should take place in a rather neutral form.[987] This unique role does not mean, however, as argued by the *Lubanga* TC, that victims have to comply 'with their disclosure obligations'[988] for they simply do not have such obligations flowing directly from the Statute or the Rules.[989] Rather, if victims want to tender evidence, it is the Chamber's responsibility to adopt, on a case-by-case basis, all measures necessary to safeguard the rights of the accused,[990] including requesting victims to disclose evidence,[991] and in particular to ensure that the parties receive the relevant evidence sufficiently in advance to be able to prepare for trial.[992]

Victims are also allowed to participate in the *sentencing stage* by filing 'written submissions on the procedure to be adopted for sentencing ... and the principles to be applied by the Chamber when it considers the appropriate sentence to be imposed'.[993] Moreover, they have the right to appeal against an order for reparations,[994] but not against decisions of acquittal or convictions, sentence, or other decisions.[995] They, however, may present their views and concerns in (interlocutory) appeals, in particular by filing observations on the documents in support of the appeal[996] or (subject to leave by the AC) submissions on the substance of an appeal.[997]

[984] cf. Art. 69 (3) ICCS.

[985] *Lubanga*, No. ICC-01/04-01/06-2127, para. 27. On the importance of victim participation for the establishment of truth, see Wheeler, *ICLR*, 16 (2016), 528 (referring to the victims' representative closing statement in the *Lubanga* trial).

[986] See e.g. above note 920 and main text.

[987] *Lubanga*, No. ICC-01/04-01/06-2127, paras. 28–30; also Klamberg, *Evidence* (2013), p. 469 and Mettraux et al., *Expert Initiative Effectiveness ICC* (2014), pp. 26–8 (paras. 116–22), 182 (para. 21), 183–5 (paras. 28–32) (recommending that the questioning of witnesses or the presentation of evidence by legal representatives should be tightly guided and regulated by the Chambers; and to limit the active involvement of legal representatives to instances in which written submissions or the questioning of a witness by the Chamber are inadequate to outline the views and concerns of the victims).

[988] *Lubanga*, No. ICC-01/04-01/06-2842, para. 14 (vii).

[989] *Katanga and Ngudjolo*, No. ICC-01/04-01/07-1788, para. 105; Ibid., paras. 3, 81, 87; crit. van den Wyngaert, *CWRJIL*, 44 (2011), 488; Plevin, *CLF*, 25 (2014), 461–2.

[990] *Lubanga*, No. ICC-01/04-01/06-1432, para. 100; cf. also *Katanga and Ngudjolo*, No. ICC-01/04-01/07-2288, paras. 45, 52; Plevin, *CLF*, 25 (2014), 453, 459–60.

[991] *Katanga and Ngudjolo*, No. ICC-01/04-01/07-2288, para. 71; *Nourain*, No. ICC-02/05-03/09-545, para. 40; see also Klamberg, *Evidence* (2013), pp. 328–9.

[992] *Katanga and Ngudjolo*, No. ICC-01/04-01/07-1788, para. 107; Bock, *Opfer* (2010), pp. 540–1; Ambos, *ICLR*, 12 (2012), 120; cf. also Pikis, *Rome Statute* (2010), mn. 684.

[993] *Prosecutor v. Lubanga*, No. ICC-01/04-01/06-2844, Scheduling Order Concerning Timetable for Sentencing and Reparations, 14 March 2012, para. 3; in more detail, Pérez-León-Acevedo, *Victims' Status* (2014), pp. 509–17; Moffet, *CLF*, 26 (2015), 277–81; Pérez-León-Acevedo, *JICJ*, 17 (2019), 433–40; crit. de Hemptinne, *JICJ*, 8 (2010), 178–9. Funk, *Victims' Rights* (2010), pp. 226–7 suggests that legal representatives should prepare a memorandum which summarizes all facts relevant to sentencing.

[994] Art. 82 (4) ICCS and Chapter VI, B.(2)(b) in this volume; cf. also *Prosecutor v. Lubanga*, Decision on the Admissibility of the Appeals against Trial Chamber I's 'Decision Establishing the Principles and Procedures to be Applied in Reparations' and Directions on the Further Conduct of Proceedings, No. ICC-01/04-01/06-2953, 14 December 2012, para. 65; generally on the differentiated approach regarding victim participation in appeals under Arts. 81 and 82 ICCS, cf. Staker and Eckelmans, 'Article 83', in Ambos, *Commentary* (2022), mn. 60–65.

[995] See also Olásolo, *Triggering Procedure* (2005), p. 112; Horovitz, in Carter and Pocar, *International Criminal Procedure* (2013), p. 184.

[996] *Lubanga*, No. ICC-01/04-01/06-2951, para. 5; see also *Prosecutor v. Kenyatta*, , Decision on the Victims' Request to Participate in the Appeals Proceedings, No. ICC-01/09-02/11-1015, 14 April 2015, para. 12; in more detail, Pérez-León-Acevedo, *Victims' Status* (2014), pp. 530–4. More reluctant, Haslam, in McGoldrick, Rowe, and Donnelly, *Permanent ICC* (2004), p. 322, holding that victims 'are not entitled to argue against the accused on an appeal generally because they have no right to appeal themselves'; in a similar vein, Jorda and de Hemptinne, in Cassese et al., *Rome Statute II* (2002), p. 1406. In order to speed up proceedings, Mettraux et al., *Expert Initiative Effectiveness ICC* (2014), p. 23 (para. 100), suggest that victims should only be allowed to participate in interlocutory appeals, which 'could have a clear and important effect on their position in the proceedings'.

[997] *Al Bashir*, No. ICC-02/05-01/09-70, para. 12; *Prosecutor v. Ongwen*, AC Decision on the modalities of victim participation, No. ICC-02/04-01/15-1859, 11 June 2021, para. 8.

Victims are neither allowed to participate nor to present views and concerns in *compensation proceedings* following an acquittal (that was confirmed on appeal).[998] Such proceedings concern wrongful prosecutions but do not affect previous findings regarding victims' suffering and hence do not affect the personal interests of victims.[999]

## (5) Victim protection

Victims who come in touch with the international criminal justice system or even cooperate with international criminal tribunals may face threats, harassments, and retaliations. Many fear for their lives and that of their families if their liaison with the Court becomes public,[1000] especially in case of investigations into ongoing conflicts.[1001] Article 68 (1) ICCS acknowledges the particular vulnerable situation of victims and obliges the whole Court, that is, the Chambers, the Prosecutor, and the Registry,[1002] to protect their safety, physical and psychological well-being, dignity, and privacy.[1003] Possible protective measures are listed non-exhaustively in Rules 87, 88 RPE ICC. In making a protection order, the Chambers have, again, to ensure that the measures are not prejudicial to or inconsistent with the rights of the accused.[1004]

It is noteworthy that the ICC's procedural law provides for a common regulatory framework for the protection of both victims *and* witnesses. Apart from special questions linked to their participatory rights (redaction of applications,[1005] participation of anonymous victims[1006]), already discussed above, victims are thus protected in the same way as witnesses.[1007]

## (6) Reparations to victims

International law increasingly recognizes a State's duty to provide reparations for violations of international law, especially with regard to the non-compliance with human rights obligations.[1008] Accordingly, victims of gross violations of international human rights law and

[998] *Prosecutor v. Gbagbo and Blé Goudé*, Article 85 Chamber Decision on the OPCV Request for Victims to Participate in the Article 85 Proceedings, No. ICC 02/11 01/15-1420, 11 October 2021, paras. 3-7.

[999] *Gbagbo and Blé Goudé*, No. ICC-02/11-01/15-1420, para. 4. For a different view, see *Prosecutor v. Gbagbo and Blé Goudé*, Office of Public Counsel for Victims, Victims' Submissions on their Participation in Proceedings Held pursuant to Article 85 of the Statute, No. ICC-02/11-01/15-1419, 29 September 2021, paras. 17–22, arguing that the interests of the victims are affected in such proceedings and that their participation is not inappropriate.

[1000] See e.g. *Prosecutor v. Kony et al.*, Decision on Legal Representation, Appointment of Counsel for the Defence, Protective Measures and Time-Limit for Submission of Observations on Applications for Participation …, No. ICC-01/04-01/05-134, 1 February 2007, para. 18.

[1001] Whiting, *LCP*, 76 nos. 3 & 4 (2013), 179–82; Friman, in Cryer et al., *ICL* (2019), pp. 447–8.

[1002] Donat-Cattin, 'Article 68', in Ambos, *Commentary* (2022), mn. 12.

[1003] For an overview of protective measures, see Carayon and O'Donohue, *JICJ*, 15 (2017), 574–8.

[1004] Art. 68 (1) ICCS; for an instructive overview on the relevant case law, see Carnero Rojo, 'Article 68', in Klamberg et al., *Commentary ICC II* (2023), pp. 316 (with n. 3), 318; Perrin, *ICLR*, 15 (2015), 310–14.

[1005] See above note 924 and accompanying text.

[1006] See above note 1000 and accompanying text.

[1007] See thereon Chapter V, A.(4)(d) in this volume.

[1008] cf. Rombouts, Sardaro, and Vandeginste, in de Feyter et al., *Out of the Ashes* (2005), pp. 355–70; Dannenbaum, *WILJ*, 28 (2010), 237; WCRO, *Reparations Scheme* (June 2010), pp. 12–13; Letschert and van Boven, in Letschert et al., *Victimological Approaches* (2011), p. 158; Zegveld, *JICJ*, 8 (2010), 81–6; Bassiouni, in Bassiouni, *Pursuit* (2010), pp. 583–98; Evans, *Right to Reparation* (2012), pp. 31–43; with a particular view to the crimes committed in the former Yugoslavia during the 1990s, Palassis, *ICLR*, 14 (2014), 1. On the influence of human rights on reparations proceedings before the ICC, see Dijkstal, *ICLR*, 17 (2019), 391 ff. On the conceptual framework of reparations, see Owiso, *ICLR*, 19 (2019), 510–16.

serious violations of international humanitarian law should, as rule, be provided with full and effective reparation, including restitution, compensation, rehabilitation, satisfaction, and guarantees of non-repetition.[1009] For the IACtHR 'any violation of an international obligation that has caused harm entails the obligation to make adequate reparation' and this rule 'reflects a customary norm that constitutes one of the fundamental principles of contemporary international law on state responsibility'.[1010] Article 75 (2) ICCS combines this international right to reparation with the principle of individual responsibility by empowering the Court to 'make an order directly against a convicted person specifying appropriate reparations to, or in respect of, victims'.[1011] The rationale of integrating reparation proceedings into the (international) criminal justice system was summarized by the *Lubanga* TC as follows:

> Reparations fulfil two main purposes that are enshrined in the Statute: they oblige those responsible for serious crimes to repair the harm they caused to the victims and they enable the Chamber to ensure that offenders account for their acts. Furthermore, reparations can be directed at particular individuals, as well as contributing more broadly to the communities that were affected. Reparations in the present case must—to the extent achievable—relieve the suffering caused by these offences, afford justice to the victims by alleviating the consequences of the wrongful acts; deter future violations, and contribute to the effective reintegration of former child soldiers. Reparation can assist in promoting reconciliation between the convicted person, the victims of the crimes and the affected communities.[1012]

In sum, the Chamber closely links the Court's reparation mandate to the aims and functions of the international criminal justice system as a whole,[1013] that is, attributing individual responsibility, deterring crimes,[1014] and promoting reconciliation.[1015] Of course, awarding

[1009] Art. 18 of the UN Basic Principles and Guidelines.

[1010] cf. from the recent case law: IACHR, *Case of Osorio Rivera and Family Members v. Peru*, Judgment, Preliminary Objection, Merits, Reparations and Costs, para. 235 (26 November 2013); IACHR, *Case of J v. Peru*, Judgment, Preliminary Objection, Merits, Reparations and Costs, para. 383 (27 November 2013); IACHR, *Case of Liakat ali Alibux v. Surinam*, Judgment, Preliminary Objection, Merits, Reparations and Costs, para. 137 (10 January 2014); IACHR, *Case of Almeida v. Argentina*, Judgment, Merits, Reparations and Costs, para. 54 (17 November 2020); IACHR, *Case of Bissoon et al. v. Trinidad and Tobago*, Judgment, Merits and Reparations, para. 53 (14 November 2022); in more detail on the case law of the IACtHR, Ambos, in Ambos, Large, and Wierda, *Building a Future* (2009), pp. 38–9 (with further references).

[1011] Fischer, *EmoryILR*, 17 (2003), 200; Bock, *ZIS*, 8 (2013), 297–8; in more detail, McCarthy, 'Victim Redress', in Stahn, *ICC* (2015), pp. 1207–9. On the nature of the reparation order (civil claim, criminal sanction, or independent legal sanction), Timm, in Fischer, Kreß and Lüder, *Prosecution* (2001), pp. 306–8; see also McCarthy, *JICJ*, 10 (2012), 361–2; advocating a punitive nature Papachristopoulos, *LJIL*, 37 (2024), 737 ff.; crit. of the reparation regime, Damaška, *UCLA JIL & ForAff*, 14 (2009), 26–7, 30–2 (advocating a detachment of the reparation proceedings from criminal procedure, at 34); *Sperfeldt, ICLR*, 17 (2017), 351–77; Owiso, *ICLR*, 19 (2019), 506–7; Fisher, *ICLR*, 20 (2020), 329–31; Moffett and Sandoval, *LJIL*, 34 (2021), 749–69. For a comparative analysis covering the ICC, ICTR, ICTY, ECCC ,and STL, see Zegveld, *ICLR*, 19 (2019), 323–30.

[1012] *Prosecutor v. Lubanga*, TC I Decision Establishing the Principles and Procedures to be Applied to Reparations, No. ICC-01/04-01/06-2904, 7 August 2012, para. 179 [fn. omitted]; conc. *Prosecutor v. Lubanga*, AC Judgment on the Appeals against the 'Decision establishing the principles and procedures to be applied to reparations' of 7 August 2012 with Amended Order for Reparations (Annex A) and Public Annexes 1 and 2, No. ICC-01/04-01/06-3129, 3 March 2015, paras. 99, 202–3; see also *Prosecutor v. Lubanga*, Filing on Reparations and Draft Implementation Plan, No. ICC-01/04-01/06-3177-Red, 3 November 2015, paras. 176–80; *Prosecutor v. Al Mahdi*, TC VIII Reparations Order, No. ICC-01/12-01/15-236, 17 August 2017, paras. 2–8.

[1013] See Ambos, *Treatise ICL I* (2021), pp. 99–124.

[1014] Crit. of the possible deterrent effect of reparation orders, Dwertmann, *Reparation System* (2010), p. 41; Bock, *ZIS*, 8 (2013), 301.

[1015] On the 'expressivist function' of reparations, see McCarthy, *JICJ*, 10 (2012), 366–8; see also Sander, *ICLR*, 19 (2019), 1024–5; Fisher, *ICLR*, 20 (2020), 337–43.

victims of international crimes with 'appropriate, adequate and prompt reparations'[1016] is not an easy task. First, the physical, psychological, and emotional consequences of international crimes are typically irreparable;[1017] secondly, the high number of victims (in contrast to the limited recourses available for reparation purposes) makes it factually impossible to compensate all of them.[1018] At any rate, even imperfect reparations entail acknowledgement of the victims' suffering and thus may have an important symbolic value.[1019]

The ICCS and the RPE ICC give only little guidance on the content of a *reparation order*. According to the AC, it must contain the following five essential elements:

- It must be directed against the convicted person (personal liability).
- It must establish and inform the convicted person of his or her liability with respect to the reparations awarded in the order (amount of liability).
- It must specify, and provide reasons for, the type of reparations ordered, either collective, individual, or both (types and modalities of reparations).
- It must define the harm caused to direct and indirect victims as a result of the crimes for which the person was convicted, as well as identify the modalities of reparations that the TC considers appropriate (harm).
- It must identify the victims eligible to benefit from the awards for reparations or set out criteria of eligibility based on the link between the harm suffered by the victims and the crimes for which the person was convicted (victims).[1020]

First of all, Chambers can make reparation orders only against convicted persons, that is, individuals, but not against States.[1021] As regards the types of reparation, the ICCS explicitly

[1016] *Lubanga*, No. ICC-01/04-01/06-2904, para. 242; *Al Mahdi*, No. ICC-01/12-01/15-236, para. 33; *Ntaganda*, No. ICC-01/04-02/06-2659, para. 89. See also Ambos, in Stan and Nedelsky, *Encyclopedia I* (2023), p. 421.

[1017] cf. Correa, in Letschert et al., *Victimological Approaches* (2011), pp. 187–8; Hamber, in de Feyter et al., *Out of the Ashes* (2005), pp. 135–6; Bock, *Opfer* (2010), pp. 561–2; Ip, *ICLR*, 13 (2013), 891.

[1018] Shelton, *Reparations* (1999), p. 10; Wierda and de Greiff, *Reparations* (2004), p. 6; de Greiff and Wierda, in de Feyter et al., *Out of the Ashes* (2005), pp. 237–8; Rombouts, Sardaro, and Vandeginste, in de Feyter et al., *Out of the Ashes* (2005), pp. 468–9; Henzelin, Heiskanen, and Mettraux, *CLF*, 17 (2006), 339–40; Correa, in Letschertet et al., *Victimological Approaches* (2011), p. 188; see also Hoven, Feiler, and Scheibel, *Victims* (2013), p. 86.

[1019] Letschert and van Boven, in Letschert et al., *Victimological Approaches* (2011), pp. 160–1; Bock, *ZIS*, 8 (2013), 300; cf. also *Prosecutor v. Lubanga*, Public Redacted Version of ICC-01/04-01/06-2803-Conf-Exp-Trust Fund for Victims' First Report on Reparation, No. ICC-01/04-01/06-2803, 1 September 2011, para. 115; *Co-Prosecutors v. Kaing*, No. 001/18-07-2007/ECCC/TC, 26 July 2010, para. 661 with n. 1144; Hamber, in de Feyter et al., *Out of the Ashes* (2005), p. 135; Rombouts, Sardaro, and Vandeginste, in de Feyter et al., *Out of the Ashes* (2005), pp. 465–6; Peschke, in Bonacker and Safferling, *Victims* (2013), p. 321; Pemberton et al., *ICLR*, 15 (2015), 364–5; in detail, de Greiff, in de Greiff, *Handbook of Reparations* (2006), pp. 460–6.

[1020] *Lubanga*, No. ICC-01/04-01/06-3129, para. 32; confirmed by *Prosecutor v. Katanga*, TC II Order of Reparations pursuant to Article 75 of the Statute, No. ICC-01/04-01/07-3728-tENG, 24 March 2017, paras 29–30; conc. and expanding *Prosecutor v. Ntaganda*, No. ICC-01/04-02/06-2659, TC VI Reparations Order, 8 March 2021, paras. 30–103; see also *Prosecutor v. Ongwen*, No. ICC-02/04-01/15-1820, TC IX Order for Submissions on Reparations, 6 May 2021, p. 4; *Prosecutor v. Ongwen*, TC IX Reparations Order, No. ICC-02/04-01/15-2074, 28 February 2024, paras. 89 and 91 ff.; see further Capone, *JICJ*, 16 (2018), 645–61; crit. Stahn, *JICJ*, 13 (2015), 811–12 (arguing that the required individualization of harm is not always feasible and may create unreasonable expectations). In the event that a victim dies after having been awarded reparations, a family member may become the new holder of the right to reparations, cf. *Prosecutor v. Al Mahdi*, TC VIII Decision on the LRV Request for Resumption of Action for Deceased Victim a/20519/19, No. ICC-01/12-01/15-357, 21 April 2020, paras. 4, 5; *Prosecutor v. Katanga*, TC II Decision on the Application for Resumption of Action Brought by Family Members of Deceased Victim a/0195/08, No. ICC-01/04-01/07-3891, 9 November 2021, para. 5.

[1021] Art. 75 (2) ICCS. See also van Boven, in von Hebel, Lammers, and Schukking, *Reflections on the ICC* (1999), p. 88; Muttukumaru, in Lee, *The ICC* (1999), pp. 267–8; di Giovanni, *JILIR*, 2 (2005–2006), 44; Henzelin, Heiskanen, and Mettraux, *CLF*, 17 (2006), 330; Donat-Cattin, 'Article 75', in Ambos, *Commentary* (2022), mn. 23; crit. Evans, *Right to Reparation* (2012), p. 101. The same holds true for the ECCC, see Sperfeldt, *ICLR*, 12 (2012),

mentions restitution, compensation, and rehabilitation,[1022] but this list is not exhaustive.[1023] Reparation thus may be understood as any (material or immaterial) measure to alleviate and/or compensate the consequences of a crime,[1024] including 'issuing certificates that acknowledge the harm particular individuals experienced; setting up outreach and promotional programmes that inform victims as to the outcome of the trial; and educational campaigns that aim at reducing the stigmatization and marginalization of victims'.[1025]

The Court may award reparations on an individualized or a collective basis.[1026] In the latter case, the reparation is made to a group of individualized victims (e.g. the eight child soldiers recruited on a certain day in a certain village), to specific groups of victims (e.g. child soldiers in the DRC),[1027] or arguably even to the community affected by the crimes (community-based reparations).[1028] Collective reparations have the advantage that they may

480–2. Notably, however, pursuant to Art. 75 (6) ICCS the Court's reparation scheme does not prejudice the rights of victims under national or international law, i.e. victims may claim reparations from States in other forums.

1022 Art. 75 (2) ICCS. In detail on these forms of reparation, Abo Youssef, *Stellung des Opfers* (2008), pp. 165–71; Dwertmann, *Reparation System* (2010), p. 129–49; Bock, *Opfer* (2010), pp. 560–7; see also *Lubanga*, No. ICC-01/04-01/06-2904, paras. 223–36; *Lubanga*, No. ICC-01/04-01/06-3129-AnxA, paras. 35–43; *Al Mahdi*, No. ICC-01/12-01/15-236, paras. 45–9; *Ntaganda*, No. ICC-01/04-02/06-2659, paras. 82–7; *Ongwen*, No. ICC-02/04-01/15-2074, para. 88; de Greiff, 'Justice', in de Greiff, *Handbook of Reparations* (2006), p. 452; Henzelin, Heiskanen, and Mettraux, *CLF*, 17 (2006), 331–2; Letschert and van Boven, in Letschert et al., *Victimological Approaches* (2011), pp. 158–60; Ambach, in Ambach et al., *Protection of Non-Combatants* (2015), pp. 471–2; see also Friman, 'Article 75', in Klamberg et al., *Commentary ICC II* (2023), pp. 463–5; on their implementation in the *Lubanga* case, see *Lubanga*, No. ICC-01/04-01/06-3177, paras. 189–212.

1023 *Lubanga*, No. ICC-01/04-01/06-2904, para. 222; *Lubanga*, No. ICC-01/04-01/06-3129-AnxA, para. 34; *Al Mahdi*, No. ICC-01/12-01/15-236, para. 46; *Ntaganda*, No. ICC-01/04-02/06-2659, para. 82; *Ongwen*, No. ICC-02/04-01/15-2074, para. 612; Dwertmann, *Reparation System* (2010), p. 129; Henzelin, Heiskanen, and Mettraux, *CLF*, 17 (2006), 331; WCRO, *Reparations Scheme* (June 2010), p. 5; Bock, *ZIS*, 8 (2013), 299; for a different view, see Kelly, in Bonacker and Safferling, *Victims* (2013), p. 61, according to whom the Court is left with only monetary remedies.

1024 In this vein, *Lubanga*, No. ICC-01/04-01/06-2904, para. 179; see also *Al Mahdi*, No. ICC-01/12-01/15-236, para. 28; *Ongwen*, No. ICC-02/04-01/15-2074, para. 635; Bock, *ZIS*, 8 (2013), 299; see also Hamber, in de Feyter et al., *Out of the Ashes* (2005), p. 13; Ferstman, *LJIL*, 15 (2002), 668; di Giovanni, *JILIR*, 2 (2005–2006), 41, 42.

1025 *Lubanga*, No. ICC-01/04-01/06-2904, para. 239; see also *Ntaganda*, No. ICC-01/04-02/06-2659, para. 207; *Ongwen*, No. ICC-02/04-01/15-2074, para. 617. The ECCC can only award collective and moral reparations to civil parties, but no monetary payments (Rule 23*quinquies* IR ECCC). This limitation is—at least for some victims—hard to understand, see Mohan, *ICLR*, 9 (2009), 761; in more detail on the reparation scheme of the ECCC, Sperfeldt, *ICLR*, 12 (2012), 457; Pérez-León-Acevedo, *Victims' Status* (2014), pp. 620–41.

1026 Rule 91 (1) RPE ICC; *Lubanga*, No. ICC-01/04-01/06-2904, paras. 217–21; in more detail, *Lubanga*, No. ICC-01/04-01/06-3129, paras. 149–51; *Ntaganda*, No. ICC-01/04-02/06-2659, paras. 78–80. However, as the Court has repeatedly stressed, these categories are not mutually exclusive, hence individual and collective reparations can be awarded concurrently, see *Prosecutor v. Katanga*, AC Judgment on the appeals against the order of Trial Chamber II of 24 March 2017 entitled 'Order for Reparations pursuant to Article 75 of the Statute', No. ICC-01/04-01/07-3778-Red, 8 March 2018, para. 146; *Prosecutor v. Lubanga*, AC Judgment on the Appeals against Trial Chamber II's 'Decision Setting the Size of the Reparations Award for which Thomas Lubanga Dyilo is Liable', No. ICC-01/04-01/06-3466-Red, 18 July 2019, para. 40; *Al Mahdi*, No. ICC-01/12-01/15-236, paras. 45, 70 ff., 82–3; see also *Ntaganda*, No. ICC-01/04-02/06-2659, para. 9 ('collective reparations with individualized components'), conc. *Ongwen*, No. ICC-02/04-01/15-2074, para. 672. See also Chapter VIII, C. of this volume.

1027 See also the differentiation between 'collective reparations in their large sense' and 'collective reparations in their narrow sense', in *Prosecutor v. Lubanga*, Observations on Issues Concerning Reparations, No. ICC-01/04-01/06-2863, 18 April 2012, paras. 83–106.

1028 In this vein, *Prosecutor v. Lubanga*, Observations on Reparations in Response to the Scheduling Order of 14 March 2012, No. ICC-01/04-01/06-2872, 25 April 2012, para. 156; *Lubanga*, No. ICC-01/04-01/06-3177, paras. 170, 174; *Al Mahdi*, No. ICC-01/12-01/15-236, para. 83; *Ntaganda*, No. ICC-01/04-02/06-2659, paras. 80–1; *Ongwen*, No. ICC-02/04-01/15-2074, paras. 572, 574 ff.; see also Dwertmann, *Reparation System* (2010), p. 121; di Giovanni, *JILIR*, 2 (2005–2006), 46; Letschert and van Boven, in Letschert et al., *Victimological Approaches* (2011), p. 171; Correa, in Letschertet al., *Victimological Approaches* (2011), p. 208; Bock, *ZIS*, 8 (2013), 314; Sperfeldt, *ICLR*, 12 (2012), 471 and the reference to reparations with a 'transformative value' in *Lubanga*, No. ICC-01/04-01/06-2904, para. 222; *Ntaganda*, No. ICC-01/04-02/06-2659, para. 82; Zegveld, *ICLR*, 19 (2019), 337; in more detail on reparations and transformative justice, Hoyle and Ullrich, *JICJ*, 12 (2014), 692–9; Butti and McGonigle Leyh, *ICLR*, 19 (2019), 753. Note, however, that the AC clarified that only members of communities who have suffered harm as a result of the crimes the accused was convicted for are entitled to (collective)

reach a high number of victims and allow for an economic use of the limited recourses.[1029] If applied too broadly, however, they may lose the link to the crime and become more closely linked to development programmes or humanitarian aid.[1030] It may be for this reason that Rule 97 (1) RPE ICC establishes a primacy of individual reparations.[1031]

In procedural terms,[1032] reparation proceedings may be initiated by the Chamber upon request by a victim[1033] or on its own motion.[1034] These *proprio motu* powers aim to ensure that victims who—due to geographical remoteness, lack of information, or external pressure—are unable to file an application are not excluded from the reparation procedure.[1035] In any case, the Chambers enjoy full discretion on whether or not to make a reparation order.[1036] Article 75 ICCS thus grants victims merely a potential right to reparation.[1037] In the course of the reparation proceedings, the Chamber may appoint experts to assist it in determining the scope and extent of the harm suffered and in developing appropriate types and modalities of reparation.[1038] Victims, who naturally have a personal interest in the outcome of these proceedings, may present their views and concerns.[1039] If the Chamber issues a reparation order, all Member States are obliged to cooperate in its enforcement.[1040]

reparations, *Lubanga*, No. ICC-01/04-01/06-3129, para. 214; conc. Stahn, *JICJ*, 13 (2015), 807–8; see also above note 1099 and accompanying text.

[1029] Scalia, in Strickler, *Place de la victime* (2009), p. 243; Dwertmann, *Reparation System* (2010), pp. 121–2; Bock, *Opfer* (2010), pp. 571–4; Bock, *ZIS*, 8 (2013), 314; cf. also *Lubanga*, No. ICC-01/04-01/06-2904, para. 219; Rombouts, Sardaro, and Vandeginste, in de Feyter et al., *Out of the Ashes* (2005), pp. 460–1; de Brouwer, *LJIL*, 20 (2007), 233; Baumgartner, *IRRC*, 90 (2008), 438–9; Abo Youssef, *Stellung des Opfers* (2008), p. 177; Zegveld, *JICJ*, 8 (2010), 98; Sperfeldt, *JICJ*, 11 (2013), 1123.

[1030] Di Giovanni, *JILIR*, 2 (2005–2006), 25; Bock, *Opfer* (2010), p. 573; see also Letschert and van Boven, in Letschert et al., *Victimological Approaches* (2011), p. 177; Correa, in Letschert et al., *Victimological Approaches* (2011), pp. 209–10; Sperfeldt, *JICJ*, 11 (2013), 1134; Moffet, *CLF*, 26 (2015), 282–3;McCarthy, in Stahn, *ICC* (2015), p. 1220–1; see further Navarro, *ICLR*, 18 (2018), 67–96; Zegveld, *ICLR*, 19 (2019), 340.

[1031] Dwertmann, *Reparation System* (2010), p. 121; Bock, *Opfer* (2010), p. 571; crit. McCarthy, in Stahn, *ICC* (2015), p. 1218. Nevertheless, the AC did not challenge the approach of the *Lubanga* TC to award reparations on a collective basis only, *Lubanga*, No. ICC-01/04-01/06-3129, paras. 152–7. See also *Al Mahdi*, No. ICC-01/12-01/15-236, paras. 141–2. Identifying a tendency of the ICC to deal with reparation claims collectively rather than individually, Zegveld, *ICLR*, 19 (2019), 337 ff.

[1032] In detail on the reparation proceedings, Dwertmann, *Reparation System* (2010), pp. 195–283; Bock, *Opfer* (2010), pp. 589–99; Pérez-León-Acevedo, *Victims' Status* (2014), pp. 667–9.

[1033] Rule 94 RPE ICC; crit. of the 'emphasis on an applications-based approach to reparations', McCarthy, in Stahn, *ICC* (2015), p. 1217.

[1034] Rule 95 RPE ICC.

[1035] Muttukumaru, in Lee, *ICC* (1999), p. 269; Jorda and de Hemptinne, in Cassese et al., *Rome Statute II* (2002), p. 1407; Zegveld, *JICJ*, 8 (2010), 88; Bock, *Opfer* (2010), p. 558; Dwertmann, *Reparation System* (2010), p. 208; Evans, *Right to Reparation* (2012), p. 106.

[1036] Ingadottir, *Trust Fund* (1999), p. 16; Jorda and de Hemptinne, in Cassese et al., *Rome Statute II* (2002), p. 1407; Sarkin, in de Feyter et al., *Out of the Ashes* (2005), p. 180; de Brouwer, *LJIL*, 20 (2007), 220; Donat-Cattin, 'Article 75', in Ambos, *Commentary* (2022), mn. 22; Dwertmann, *Reparation System* (2010), pp. 45, 114; Pellet, 'Article 75', in Fernandez et al., *Statut* (2019), p. 1998; see also *Lubanga*, No. ICC-01/04-01/06-3129, para. 148 (b); McCarthy, in Stahn, *ICC* (2015), p. 1208; for a different view, see Ambach, in Ambach et al., *Protection of Non-Combatants* (2015), pp. 474–7, arguing that the Chamber's discretion concerns only 'the level of detail with which it intends to issue its decision' (476) and 'will normally reduce to … almost zero if and when victims have validly applied for reparations' (477).

[1037] Jorda and de Hemptinne, in Cassese et al., *Rome Statute II* (2002), p. 1407; Pérez-León-Acevedo, *Victims' Status* (2014), p. 607.

[1038] Rule 97 (2) RPE ICC.

[1039] cf. Art. 68 (3) ICCS; see also *Lubanga*, No. ICC-01/04-01/06-925, para. 28; *Lubanga*, No. ICC-01/04-01/06-3466-Red, paras. 89–90; Bock, *Opfer* (2010), p. 597; de Brouwer and Heikkilä, in Sluiter et al., *International Criminal Procedure* (2013), p. 1350; also Dwertmann, *Reparation System* (2010), pp. 217–22. Crit. as to the wide discretion of the Court,Zegveld, *ICLR*, 19 (2019), 332–3.

[1040] Art. 75 (5) ICCS, Rule 217 RPE ICC; see also *Lubanga*, No. ICC-01/04-01/06-2129-AnxA, para. 50; *Ntaganda*, No. ICC-01/04-02/06-2659, para. 102; *Ongwen*, No. ICC-02/04-01/15-2074, paras. 581, 816. On the enforcement in more detail, see Chapter VIII, C. in this volume.

This judicial reparation scheme is complemented by the Trust Fund for Victims (TFV) established by the ASP in 2002 pursuant to Article 79 (1) ICCS.[1041] The TFV is financed through voluntary contributions from, inter alia, States, international organizations, individuals, and corporations[1042] as well as money and other properties collected by the ICC through fines or forfeiture.[1043] The Fund has two mandates:[1044] first, it assists the Chambers in implementing their reparation orders[1045] and may complement insufficient funds of the convicted person with its own resources (reparation mandate).[1046] It is, however, controversial whether the Chambers may order the TFV to exercise its complementary function. The *Lubanga* TC answered this question in the affirmative holding that 'the Court is able to draw on the logistical and financial resources of the Trust Fund'.[1047] This view is not fully convincing and was rightly overturned by the AC.[1048] It does not sufficiently account for the institutional independence of the TFV nor for the wording of Article 75 (2) ICCS, that merely empowers the Court to order that reparations are made *through*—and not *by* or *out of*—the TFV.[1049] The TFV thus is free to decide whether or not to exercise its reparation mandate. If the Fund advances its resources in order to enable the implementation of a reparation order, it may claim the reimbursement from the convicted person.[1050]

Secondly, the TFV provides general support to victims of international crimes and their families in the form of physical and psychological rehabilitation and material support.[1051] Notably, the TFV can exercise this general assistance mandate in all situations the ICC is seized with. The beneficiaries must not necessarily be victims of a case, nor must the TFV wait for the completion of the trial.[1052] As a result, the compensation given by the TFV can reach a high

[1041] Resolution ICC-ASP/1/Res. 6, Establishment of a Fund for the Benefit of Victims of Crimes within the Jurisdiction of the Court, and of the Families of Such Victims, adopted at the 3rd plenary meeting on 9 September 2002.

[1042] Regs. 22–30 RegTFV.

[1043] Art. 75 (2) ICCS, Regs. 31–3 RegTFV; cf. also *Lubanga*, No. ICC-01/04-01/06-2803, paras. 116–21; Ingadottir, *Trust Fund* (1999), pp. 17–18; Garkawe, *ICLR*, 3 (2003), 364–6; Fischer, *EmoryILR*, 17 (2003), 215–21; Saabel, 'Article 79', in Fernandez et al., *Statut* (2019), pp. 2043–50; Ambach, in Ambach et al., *Protection of Non-Combatants* (2015), p. 493; crit. of the TFV's funding problems, Damaška, *UCLA JIL & ForAff*, 14 (2009), 31; Kendall, *JICJ*, 13 (2015), 124–5.

[1044] Peschke, in Bonacker and Safferling, *Victims* (2013), pp. 319–20; Song, 'Article 79', in Klamberg et al., *Commentary ICC II* (2023), pp. 545–6; Zegveld, *ICLR*, 19 (2019), 341 ('dual role').

[1045] Rule 98 (2), (3) RPE ICC, Regs. 59–72 RegTFV; see also Fischer, *EmoryILR*, 17 (2003), 204–5; Dwertmann, *Reparation System* (2010), pp. 267–72.

[1046] Reg. 56 RegTFV; see also *Lubanga*, No. ICC-01/04-01/06-2803, para. 122; *Lubanga*, No. ICC-01/04-01/06-3177, paras. 110, 127 (arguing that the term 'complement' has not only a financial connotation but comprises also various forms of administrative assistance like financial management or leveraging networks of partners in the implementation of reparations); Dwertmann, *Reparation System* (2010), pp. 272–7; Ferstman, *LJIL*, 15 (2002), 685; McCarthy, *JICJ*, 10 (2012), 360; de Brouwer and Heikkilä, in Sluiter et al., *International Criminal Procedure* (2013), p. 1361.

[1047] *Lubanga*, No. ICC-01/04-01/06-2872, para. 270.

[1048] *Lubanga*, No. ICC-01/04-01/06-3129, paras. 106–14.

[1049] Dannenbaum, *WILJ*, 28 (2010), 256–60; WCRO, *Reparations Scheme* (June 2010), p. 2; Bock, *ZIS*, 8 (2013), 316–17; for the same results, see van den Wyngaert, *CWRJIL*, 44 (2011), 491.

[1050] *Lubanga*, No. ICC-01/04-01/06-3129, para. 116; crit. *Lubanga*, No. ICC-01/04-01/06-3177, para. 123 (arguing that the convicted person owes the financial recources to the Court itself and not to the TFV).

[1051] Art. 75 (1) ICCS, Rule 98 (5) RPE ICC, Reg. 27 RegTFV; see also *Lubanga*, No. ICC-01/04-01/06-2803, para. 121; Peschke, in Bonacker and Safferling, *Victims* (2013), p. 320; de Baan and Saabel, 'Article 79', in Fernandez et al., *Statut* (2019), p. 2056; Song, 'Article 79', in Klamberg et al., *Commentary ICC II* (2023), pp. 545–6.

[1052] In more detail, *Bock*, Opfer (2010), pp. 579–82; Dannenbaum, *WILJ*, 28 (2010), 248–55; see also *Lubanga*, No. ICC-01/04-01/06-3129, para. 182; *Lubanga*, No. ICC-01/04-01/06-3177, para. 153; Wierda and de Greiff, *Reparations* (2004), p. 12; de Greiff and Wierda, in de Feyter et al., *Out of the Ashes* (2005), pp. 239–41; de Brouwer, *LJIL*, 20 (2007), 230; Zegveld, *JICJ*, 8 (2010), 89; Evans, *Right to Reparation* (2012), p. 106; McCarthy, *JICJ*, 10 (2012), 369; Peschke, in Bonacker and Safferling, *Victims* (2013), p. 320; Manirabona and Wemmers, *ICLR*, 13 (2013), 1004; Song, 'Article 79', in Klamberg et al., *Commentary ICC II* (2023), p. 549.

number of victims. For instance, in its first programme cycle between 2008 and 2017, the TFV has provided assistance for a total of 101,723 direct beneficiaries in the DRC and Uganda.[1053]

In order to complement the Statute's fragmentary rules on Court-ordered reparations, Article 75 (1) ICCS obliges the Court to establish principles[1054] which shall guide the Chambers in their reparation decisions.[1055] After attempts to develop general principles have failed,[1056] the responsibility to comply with Article 75 (1) ICCS shifted to the Chambers,[1057] that is, reparation principles are established on a case-by-case basis.[1058] The *Lubanga* TC delivered in 2012 an extensive decision in which it presented its approach towards reparations. Its core principles may be summarized as follows:[1059]

- All victims are to be treated fairly and equally as regards reparations. The right to reparation is not limited to victims who participated in the trial.[1060]
- Reparations may be granted to direct and indirect victims[1061] and to legal entities.[1062]
- The damage, loss, or injury, for which reparation is sought, must have resulted from the crimes the accused was convicted for,[1063] that is, there must exist a 'but/for' relationship between the crime and the harm, and, moreover, the crime must be the proximate cause of the respective harm.[1064]

[1053] See TFV, *Impact* (2024).

[1054] Donat-Cattin, 'Article 75', in Ambos, *Commentary* (2022), mn. 10; Dwertmann, *Reparation System* (2010), p. 45.

[1055] *Lubanga*, No. ICC-01/04-01/06-3129, para. 55: 'principles should be general concepts that, while formulated in light of the circumstances of a specific case, can nonetheless be applied, adapted, expanded upon, or added to by future Trial Chambers.'

[1056] Schabas, *ICC Commentary* (2016), p. 1139; Ambach, in Ambach et al., *Protection of Non Combatants* (2015), pp. 463–5.

[1057] Dwertmann, *Reparation System* (2010), p. 48; van den Wyngaert, *CWRJIL*, 44 (2011), 486; Bock, *ZIS*, 8 (2013), 305; Kaul, in Bonacker and Safferling, *Victims* (2013), p. 227; see also Pellet, 'Article 75', in Fernandez et al., *Statut* (2019), p. 1991 and *Lubanga*, No. ICC-01/04-01/06-3129, para. 55.

[1058] Crit., since this approach may give rise to legal uncertainty and an unequal treatment of victims, Bock, *ZIS*, 8 (2013), 305; cf. also Dwertmann, *Reparation System* (2010), p. 48; WCRO, *Reparations Scheme* (June 2010), pp 28–30; de Brouwer and Heikkilä, in Sluiter et al., *International Criminal Procedure* (2013), p. 1371.

[1059] -DonatCattin, 'Article 75', in Ambos, *Commentary* (2022), mn. 15–19; Chung, in Jeßberger et al., *Strafrecht und Systemunrecht* (2022), pp. 37–47. See also the detailed analysis by Bock, *ZIS*, 8 (2013), 305–17 and the overview on the decision in ASP, *Report* ICC-ASP/12/39 (8 October 2013), para. 12; Ambach, in Ambach et al., *Protection of Non-Combatants* (2015), pp. 467–9.

[1060] *Lubanga*, No. ICC-01/04-01/06-2904, para. 187 with a particular emphasis on the principle of non-discrimination in para. 191; confirmed in *Lubanga*, No. ICC-01/04-01/06-3129-AnxA, paras. 12, 16; see also de Brouwer, *LJIL*, 20 (2007), 222; SáCouto and Cleary, *Transnat'lLCP*, 17 (2008), 87; Dwertmann, *Reparation System* (2010), p. 77; McGonigle Leyh, in Letschert et al., *Victimological Approaches* (2011), p. 502; Evans, *Right to Reparation* (2012), p. 104; Tonellato, *EJCCLCJ*, 20 (2012), 322; Pérez-León-Acevedo, *Victims' Status* (2014), p. 605.

[1061] *Lubanga*, No. ICC-01/04-01/06-2904, para. 194; confirmed in *Lubanga*, No. ICC-01/04-01/06-3129-AnxA, para. 6; see also Henzelin, Heiskanen, and Mettraux, *CLF*, 17 (2006), 323.

[1062] *Lubanga*, No. ICC-01/04-01/06-2904, para. 197; confirmed in *Lubanga*, No. ICC-01/04-01/06-3129-AnxA, para. 8. According to the AC, however, the applicable standards and burden of proof are not 'principles', but elements of the reparation order, *Lubanga*, No. ICC-01/04-01/06-3129, para. 77.

[1063] *Lubanga*, No. ICC-01/04-01/06-2904, para. 247; confirmed in *Lubanga*, No. ICC-01/04-01/06-3129, para. 129, in particular with regard to collective and community-based reparations in paras. 213–14. The AC convincingly concluded that the sexual and gender-based violence committed against some of the child soldiers recruited by Lubanga cannot be defined as a harm resulting from the crimes for which Lubanga was convicted, para. 196. In favour of a broader approach, Mettraux et al., *Expert Initiative Effectiveness ICC* (2014), pp. 31 (para. 142), 187 (para. 40) (recommending to 'consider amending the Statute to remove the requirement that reparation for victims is conditioned upon the conviction of the accused so that victims could focus more effectively on establishing the harm done to them').

[1064] *Lubanga*, No. ICC-01/04-01/06-2904, para. 250; confirmed in *Lubanga*, No. ICC-01/04-01/06-3129-AnxA, para. 59; Gacka, *ICLR*, 22 (2022), 438–74, discussing if 'transgenerational harms' can be acknowledged, i.e. 'future victims' should receive reparations.

- The facts relevant for a reparation order must be proved on a balance of probabilities (and not beyond reasonable doubt).[1065]
- Reparations are entirely voluntary and the informed consent of the recipient is necessary prior to any award of reparation.[1066]
- When deciding on the scope of reparations, the Chamber may take into account any awards or benefits received by victims from other bodies.[1067]

Having established these general principles, the Chamber, somewhat surprisingly, declined to examine the individual applications for reparation and to issue any specific reparation orders.[1068] Instead of applying its reparation principles, it transmitted all applications for reparations to the TFV for further consideration. In particular, the Chamber left it to the TFV to decide on whether or not the applicants should be included in any of its reparation programmes.[1069] In doing so, the Chamber delegated its reparation mandate almost entirely to the TFV[1070] and reserved itself merely some monitoring and oversight functions.[1071] Although this decision might have disappointed the victims of the *Lubanga* case, it is the correct approach.[1072] As the TC rightly observed, it can only grant reparations to victims who were harmed by the crimes for which Lubanga was convicted.[1073] Court-ordered reparations therefore are necessarily very selective[1074] and necessarily entail an unequal treatment of victims by privileging those who were lucky enough that 'their crimes' were chosen by the Prosecutor.[1075] In contrast, the TFV, with its broad mandate, can avoid such injustice and ensure that its funds are spent in an economic, coherent, and truly non-discriminatory manner.[1076]

[1065] *Lubanga*, No. ICC-01/04-01/06-2904, paras. 251, 253; modified in *Lubanga*, No. ICC-01/04-01/06-3129-AnxA, para. 22: 'In determining the appropriate standard of proof in reparation proceedings, various factors specific to the case should be considered.' On the standard and burden of proof, see also Shelton, *Reparations* (1999), p. 11; Henzelin, Heiskanen, and Mettraux, *CLF*, 17 (2006), 329; WCRO, *Reparations Scheme* (June 2010), pp. 40–1; on the extensive discussions on the adequate standard of proof for reparations in the Preparatory Commission, see Lewis and Friman, in Lee, *ICC* (2001), pp. 484–6.

[1066] *Lubanga*, No. ICC-01/04-01/06-2904, para. 204; *Lubanga*, No. ICC-01/04-01/06-3129, para. 160 (even with regard to collective awards). This is an important clarification since some victims might not wish to accept 'blood money' from the perpetrator, see Lewis and Friman, in Lee, *ICC* (2001), p. 481.

[1067] *Lubanga*, No. ICC-01/04-01/06-2904, para. 201.

[1068] Ibid., para. 289.

[1069] Ibid., para. 284.

[1070] Bock, *ZIS*, 8 (2013), 320.

[1071] *Lubanga*, No. ICC-01/04-01/06-2904, para. 289; confirmed in *Lubanga*, No. ICC-01/04-01/06-3129, para. 237; *Lubanga*, No. ICC-01/04-01/06-3466-Red, paras. 139–40.

[1072] See also Bock, *ZIS*, 8 (2013), 320; Pérez-León-Acevedo, *Victims' Status* (2014), pp. 703–4; in favour of a strong role for the TFV, also McCarthy, in Stahn, *ICC* (2015), p. 1219; crit. Stahn, *JICJ*, 13 (2015), 804.

[1073] In more detail on this link requirement, Bock, *ZIS*, 8 (2013), 307–9; see also Abo Youssef, *Stellung des Opfers* (2008), p. 174; Dwertmann, *Reparation System* (2010), p. 93; WCRO, *Reparations Scheme* (June 2010), pp. 4–5; Evans, *Right to Reparation* (2012), p. 105; Pellet, 'Article 75', in Fernandez et al., *Statut* (2019), p. 1994; Chung, in Jeßberger et al., *Strafrecht und Systemunrecht* (2022), p. 43; for a broader approach (granting reparations also to 'other interested persons who suffered harm as a result of crimes other than those included in the charges'), ICC-OTP, *Policy Victims' Participation* (2010), p. 9.

[1074] Sarkin, in de Feyter et al., *Out of the Ashes* (2005), p. 180; de Greiff and Wierda, in de Feyter et al., *Out of the Ashes* (2005), p. 234; Dannenbaum, *WILJ*, 28 (2010), 275; cf. also WCRO, *Reparations Scheme* (June 2010), p. 2; di Giovanni, *JILIR*, 2 (2005–2006), 48, 58; McCarthy, *JICJ*, 10 (2012), 360, 363–4; Manirabona and Wemmers, *ICLR*, 13 (2013), 1003; Ambach, in Ambach et al., *Protection of Non-Combatants* (2015), pp. 504–6.

[1075] With a particular view to the *Lubanga* proceedings, Bock, *ZIS*, 8 (2013), 302–4; see also Dannenbaum, *WILJ*, 28 (2010), 278; less crit. Donat-Cattin, 'Article 75', in Ambos, *Commentary* (2022), mn. 19, according to whom 'it is not the role of the ICC to create equal opportunities on access to reparations for all victims in a given situation'.

[1076] In the same vein, Heikkilä, *International Criminal Tribunals* (2004), p. 182; Bock, *Opfer* (2010), pp. 599–600; Bock, *ZIS*, 8 (2013), 320; cf. also de Greiff and Wierda, in de Feyter et al., *Out of the Ashes* (2005), pp. 226, 234, 243; Wierda and de Greiff, *Reparations* (2004), pp. 2, 10; Kelly, in Bonacker and Safferling, *Victims* (2013), p. 63;

The AC[1077] largely confirmed the general principles set up by the TC,[1078] and added that a convicted person's liability for reparations must be proportionate to the harm caused and, inter alia, her participation in the commission of the crimes for which she was found guilty.[1079] As regards the application of these principles, the AC argued that the TC had ordered the TFV to make collective reparations to Lubanga's victims and, in doing so, ignored that 'an order for reparations has to be issued in all circumstances against the convicted person'.[1080] Moreover, it deemed the decision to be insufficiently detailed, since the TC delegated the task of defining the harms caused to victims as a result of Lubanga's crimes to the TFV.[1081] At the same time, the AC emphasized that Chambers are only obliged to *define* the harm, but may leave the task of *assessing* its extent for purposes of determining the size and nature of reparation awards to the TFV.[1082] In essence, the AC tries to strike a balance between preserving the TC's responsibility for the content of the reparation order and integrating the TFV's expertise in the judicial reparation scheme. It must, however, be kept in mind that the AC's decision is based on the—controversial—assumption that the TC has indeed issued a reparation order but addressed it to the wrong person. Arguably, future Chambers thus are still free to strengthen further the role of the TFV by refraining from exercising their reparation mandate.[1083]

The principles on reparation established in *Lubanga* were adapted and expanded by the *Ntaganda* TC in 2021, identifying six groups of principles:[1084] (i) principles related to victims,[1085] (ii) principles related to harm,[1086] (iii) principles related to the types and modalities of reparations,[1087] (iv) principles related to liability,[1088] (v) principles related to the rights of the defence,[1089] and (vi) other principles.[1090] As to the enforcement of reparations orders, the *Ongwen* TC took a rather restrictive approach in 2024. It highlighted that while previous Chambers have adopted different views as to their involvement regarding

Zegveld, *JICJ*, 8 (2010), 98; Dannenbaum, *WILJ*, 28 (2010), 297–8. On the need to complement the efforts of the TFV with national reparation programmes, Manirabona and Wemmers, *ICLR*, 13 (2013), 1007–10.

[1077] The decision of the TC was appealed by both the victims and the accused: *Prosecutor v. Lubanga*, Appeal against Trial Chamber I's Decision Establishing the Principles and Procedures to be Applied to Reparation of 7 August 2012, No. ICC-01/04-01/06-2914, 3 September 2012; *Prosecutor v. Lubanga*, Appeal against Trial Chamber I's Decision Establishing the Principles and Procedures to be Applied to Reparation of 7 August 2012, No. ICC-01/04-01/06-2909, 24 August 2012; *Prosecutor v. Lubanga*, Appeal of the Defence for Mr Thomas Lubanga against Trial Chamber I's Decision Establishing the Principles and Procedures to be Applied to Reparation rendered on 7 August 2012, No. ICC-01/04-01/06-2917, 6 September 2012. On the admissibility of the Appeals, see *Lubanga*, No. ICC-01/04-01/06-2953. See also the evaluation of the decisions by Friman, 'Article 75', in Klamberg et al., *Commentary ICC II* (2023), pp. 466–72. For a good overview, see Chung, in Jeßberger et al., *Strafrecht und Systemunrecht* (2022), pp. 43–7.

[1078] See above notes 1094 ff. and accompanying text.

[1079] *Lubanga*, No. ICC-01/04-01/06-3129, para. 118.

[1080] Ibid., para. 76. The indigence of the convicted person is deemed to be irrelevant, para. 102; conc. Stahn, *JICJ*, 13 (2015), 805–6.

[1081] *Lubanga*, No. ICC-01/04-01/06-3129, para. 184.

[1082] Ibid., para. 184.

[1083] The *Katanga* AC however confirmed the *Lubanga* AC's approach, see *Katanga*, No. ICC-01/04-01/07-3778-Red, para. 72 with nn. 158, 159.

[1084] *Ntaganda*, No. ICC-01/04-02/06-2659, paras. 30 ff.; conc. *Ongwen*, No. ICC-02/04-01/15-2074, paras. 57, 77, 87 (referring to the '*Ntaganda* principles').

[1085] *Ntaganda*, No. ICC-01/04-02/06-2659, paras. 31–67, amended in *Ongwen*, No. ICC-02/04-01/15-2074, paras. 79–86.

[1086] *Ntaganda*, No. ICC-01/04-02/06-2659, paras. 68–77.

[1087] *Ntaganda*, No. ICC-01/04-02/06-2659, paras. 78–95; amended in *Ongwen*, No. ICC-02/04-01/15-2074, para. 78.

[1088] *Ntaganda*, No. ICC-01/04-02/06-2659, paras. 96–100.

[1089] Ibid., para. 101.

[1090] Namely States and other stakeholders as well as the publicity of the proceedings, see *Ntaganda*, No. ICC-01/04-02/06-2659, paras. 102–3.

implementation processes in the past,[1091] it will merely 'retain limited oversight' on the TFV's Draft Implementation Plan and 'rule on exceptional matters only'.[1092] Interestingly, the TC did not base this position on a more principled argument but on the circumstances of the *Ongwen* case, namely the high number of victims elegible for reparations and the type of reparations awarded.[1093]

## F. *Amicus curiae*

*Amicus curiae*, 'friend of the court' (Latin),[1094] is a common law institution,[1095] which found its way into the international criminal justice institutions.[1096] *Amici curiae* are not a party in the proceedings,[1097] but mere independent participants[1098] providing experts' information on relevant issues[1099] where their 'specific expertise' is needed.[1100] If a Chamber 'considers it desirable for the proper determination of the case', it may 'invite or grant leave to a State, organization or person to submit, in writing or orally, any observation on any issue that the Chamber deems appropriate'.[1101]

*Amici curiae* can make their observations 'at any stage of the proceedings', either by appearing personally before the Court or by submitting a brief through the Registrar.[1102] The Prosecutor and the defence shall have the opportunity to respond to the respective observations,[1103] but only once 'the Chamber has decided to grant leave'.[1104] Given the broad

1091 *Ongwen*, No. ICC-02/04-01/15-2074, para. 40, giving a detailed overview in n. 109.

1092 In doing so, the *Ongwen* TC followed the restrictive approach already adopted in the *Ntaganda* Reparations Order, cf. *Ongwen*, No. ICC-02/04-01/15-2074, paras. 40 (with n. 109), 41.

1093 *Ongwen*, No. ICC-02/04-01/15-2074, para. 41.

1094 cf. the glossary of the STL, <https://www.stl-tsl.org/sites/default/files/documents/STL_Glossary.pdf>, according to which the *amicus curiae* is 'an independent party who appears in court or otherwise provides their legal opinion on matters or legal issues in order to assist the court in its deliberations'.

1095 cf. Garner, *Dictionary* (2019), p. 106: 'Someone who is not party to a lawsuit but who petitions the court or is requested by the court to file a brief in the action because that person has a strong interest in the subject matter.'

1096 For a brief account of the practice of *amici* in international proceedings other than those of the criminal tribunals, see Williams and Woolaver, *ICLR*, 6 (2006), 151–4; see more recently Kopylova, *JICJ*, 19 (2021), 1099–131; Imseis, *JICJ*, 18 (2020), 905–25; Williams and Woolaver, *JICJ*, 18 (2020), 891–904; Kent and Trinidad, *ICLR*, 17 (2017), 728–47; for *amici* participation in the ECtHR, see Dolidze, *EJIL*, 26 (2015), 861–80.

1097 Tuinstra, *Defence Counsel* (2009), p. 251; Tochilovsky, *Jurisprudence* (2014), p. 1343; cf. also *Prosecutor v. Krajišnik*, AC Decision on Momčilo Krajišnik's Request to Self-represent, No. IT-00-39-A, 11 May 2007, para. 20.

1098 *Krajišnik*, No. IT-00-39-A, para. 19.

1099 *Situation in the DRC*, No. ICC-01/04-373, para. 4; cf. also Schabas, *ICC Commentary* (2016), p. 988.

1100 *Prosecutor v. Ntaganda*, PTC II Decision on the Application by the Redress Trust to Submit Amicus Curiae Observations, No. ICC-01/04-02/06-259, 18 February 2014, para. 3.

1101 Rule 103 RPE ICC. For almost identical provisions, see Rules 74 RPE ICTY/ICTR/SCSL, 83 RPE MICT, 33 IR ECCC, 131 RPE STL, and 67 RPE KSC. See also Williams and Woolaver, *ICLR*, 6 (2006), 154–70 (ICTY), 170–4 (ICTR), 175–81 (SCSL), 181–2 and 184–9 (ICC); Boas et al., *International Criminal Procedure* (2011), pp. 166–8 (ICTY and ICTR), p. 168 (SCSL), pp. 168–9 (ICC); Tochilovsky, *Jurisprudence* (2014), pp. 1338–44.

1102 Rule 103 (3) RPE ICC.

1103 Rule 103 (2) RPE ICC.

1104 PTC II, *Situation in the Republic of Kenya*, Decision on Application to Appear as Amicus Curiae and Related Requests, No. ICC-01/09-14, 3 February 2010, para. 9 (holding that 'the *amicus curiae* procedure is governed by rule 103 of the Rules which is the *lex specialis*, and as such, none of the parties, participants or any other entity including the Applicants is entitled to file replies or responses until the Chamber has decided to grant leave' [emphasis in the original] and therefore rejecting all the requests); *Prosecutor v. Al Bashir*, AC Reasons for 'Decision on the Application of 20 July 2009 for Participation under Rule 103 of the Rules of Procedure and Evidence and on the Application of 24 August 2009 for Leave to Reply', No. ICC-02/05-01/09-51, 9 November 2009, para. 8 (where the AC, 'although the Prosecutor had not been granted leave', 'nevertheless decided to accept the Prosecutor's Response as it considered it to be in the interests of justice to do so'); *Prosecutor v. Ruto and Sang*, AC Decision on the Prosecutor's 'Request for Leave to Respond to the Government of the Republic of Kenya's Request to Participate as Amicus Curiae in the Appeal concerning the "Decision on Prosecution Request for Admission of

wording of Rule 103 RPE ICC, referring to 'State, organization or person', all kinds of organizations, and natural and legal persons may submit observations.[1105] It is, however, within the absolute discretion of the Chamber[1106] whether to grant leave or invite *amici* at all,[1107] which specific issues to have addressed,[1108] and at what length and within what time frame.[1109]

The admission decision shall be taken pursuant to three criteria. First, the intervention of *amici* shall be 'desirable for the proper determination of the case'.[1110] This can normally be excluded if the request refers to a legal issue since it is to be expected that international judges are in a position to resolve such issues on their own.[1111] Secondly, the observations made shall 'relate to an issue that the Chamber deems appropriate',[1112] and thirdly the intervention shall not be at the expense of 'the expeditiousness of the proceedings as one of the fundamental tenets of their fairness'.[1113] From this, together with the fact that the *amicus* is not a party to the proceedings, it follows that Chambers shall 'resort to amicus curiae observations only on an exceptional basis'.[1114] This may especially be the case in high-profile proceedings, such as those concerning Palestine/Israel and Afghanistan.[1115] For this reason, it came as a surprise that PTC I generously granted requests for leave to file *amicus curiae* observations in the (*ex parte*) arrest warrant proceedings in the Palestine situation.[1116]

Prior Recorded Testimony" (ICC-01/09-01/11-1972)', No. ICC-01/09-01/11-1975, 29 September 2015, paras. 4, 5; *Prosecutor v. Ruto and Sang*, AC Decision on Applications for Leave to Submit Amicus Curiae Observations Pursuant to Rule 103 of the Rules of Procedure and Evidence, No. ICC-01/09-01/11-1987, 12 October 2015, paras. 19, 20.

[1105] Boas et al., *International Criminal Procedure* (2011), p. 169 ('non-governmental organisations, mixed-membership organisations, and public intergovernmental organisations ... individuals and corporations or other legal person').

[1106] Generally on this discretion, see Tochilovsky, *Jurisprudence* (2014), pp. 1339–41; on the manifestation of this discretion in the practice of the Court to hardly provide reasons for rejecting an *amicus curiae* application, see Le Floch, Lemey, and Paiola, *LPICT*, 14 (2015), 223–4.

[1107] *Prosecutor v. Lubanga*, AC Decision on the application by Child Soldiers International for Leave to Submit Observations pursuant to Rule 103 of the Rules of Procedure and Evidence, No. ICC-01/04-01/06-3044, 16 August 2013, para. 11; *Prosecutor v. Lubanga*, AC Decision on 'Motion for Leave to File Proposed Amicus Curiae Submission of the International Criminal Bar Pursuant to Rule 103 of the Rules of Procedure and Evidence', No. ICC-01/04-01/06-1289, 22 April 2008, para. 8.

[1108] *Prosecutor v. Bemba*, PTC II Decision on Application for Leave to Submit Amicus Curiae Observations Pursuant to Rule 103 of the Rules of Procedure and Evidence, No. ICC-01/05-01/08-401, 9 April 2009, para. 12 (*Amicus curiae* 'must confine its submission to the legal aspects outlined in the Request and refrain from making any indication or link to the specific facts of the case'); *Prosecutor v. Lubanga*, TC I Decision Inviting Observations from the Special Representative of the Secretary General of the United Nations for Children and Armed Conflict, No. ICC-01/04-01/06-1175, 18 February 2008, para. 8.

[1109] *Prosecutor v. Bemba*, PTC II Decision on Request for Leave to Submit Amicus Curiae Observations pursuant to Rule 103 of the Rules of Procedure and Evidence, No. ICC-01/05-01/08-451, 17 July 2009, para. 14.

[1110] Rule 103 (1) RPE ICC; *Lubanga*, No. ICC-01/04-01/06-1289, para. 8.

[1111] *Bemba et al.*, TC VII Decision on Kilolo Defence Motion for Inadmissibility of Material, No. ICC-01/05-01/13-1257, 16 September 2015, para. 6.

[1112] Rule 103 (1) RPE ICC; PTC I, *Situation in the Democratic Republic of the Congo*, Decision on the Request Submitted pursuant to Rule 103 (1) of the Rules of Procedure and Evidence, No. ICC-01/04-373, 17 August 2007, para. 3; cf. also Williams and Woolaver, *ICLR*, 6 (2006), 187; Mundis, in Cassese, *Companion* (2009), p. 243; Boas et al., *International Criminal Procedure* (2011), pp. 168–9.

[1113] *Bemba*, No. ICC-01/05-01/08-451, para. 15.

[1114] *Ntaganda*, No. ICC-01/04-02/06-259, PTC II Decision on Amicus Curiae, para. 3.

[1115] *Situation in the State of Palestine*, PTC I Amicus Curiae Observations of the Republic of Austria, No. ICC-01/18-76, 15 March 2020; *Situation in Afghanistan*, paras. 73, 16 (with n. 23).

[1116] *Situation in the State of Palestine*, PTC I, Decision on requests for leave to file observations pursuant to rule 103 of the Rules of Procedure and Evidence, ICC-01/18-249, 22 July 2024; crit. Vasiliev, *EJIL:Talk!* 1 August 2024 and Ambos, *EJIL:Talk!* 19 August 2024.

Notwithstanding, in the ICTY's practice, *amici curiae* have been often called to play a more active role than just 'neutral friends' of the Court, especially when becoming de facto defence counsel in cases where an accused insisted on self-representation.[1117] Thus, perhaps most famously, the *Milošević* TC invited counsel to appear before it as *amici curiae*, 'not to represent the accused but to assist in the proper determination of the case' 'by way of preliminary or other pre-trial motion', or by 'making any submissions or objections to evidence ... and cross-examining witnesses as appropriate', or by 'drawing to the attention of the Trial Chamber any exculpatory or mitigating evidence', with the alleged objective 'to ensure that [the] trial is fair and that it is conducted with full respect for the rights of the accused'.[1118]

Subsequently, the *amicus*' role was extended even further, authorizing the *amici* 'to act in any way to protect and further the interests of his [accused's] Defence'.[1119] Of course, this approach, to assign an *amicus* to effectively overrule the defendant's decision to represent himself and perhaps to undermine a whole defence strategy given that the defendant does not control the *amicus*,[1120] is highly controversial. It can only be justified if one limits the right to self-representation in the sense explained above[1121] and if the *amicus* is seen as rendering an important service for the administration of justice with a view to ensure the right to an effective defence.[1122]

[1117] Crit. of the ICTY insofar, Williams and Woolaver, *ICLR*, 6 (2006), 188–9; Tuinstra, *Defence Counsel* (2009), pp. 249–52; Boas et al., *International Criminal Procedure* (2011), pp. 169–71; Mundis, in Cassese, *Companion* (2009), p. 243.

[1118] *Prosecutor v. Slobodan Milošević*, TC Order Inviting Designation of Amicus Curiae, No. IT-02-54-T, 30 September 2001; for a more restrictive approach, but still beyond the traditional role of *amicus curiae*, cf. *Krajišnik*, No. IT-00-39-A, AC Decision, paras. 19–21.

[1119] *Prosecutor v. Slobodan Milošević*, TC Order for Further Instruction to the *Amici Curiae*, No. IT-02-54-T, 6 October 2003.

[1120] cf. Art. 14 (2)(a) and (b) Code of Professional Conduct for Counsel, according to which counsel (but not *amicus*) shall 'abide by the client's decision concerning the objectives of his or her representation' and consult the client on the means by which these objectives 'are to be pursued'. For a crit. view, see Williams and Woolaver, *ICLR*, 6 (2006), 188–9; in a different vein, Tuinstra, *Defence Counsel* (2009), p. 252, who considers exactly that lack of representation agreement between *amicus* and defendant as the advantage of the institution.

[1121] Section D.(3) in this chapter.

[1122] See Boas et al., *International Criminal Procedure* (2011), pp. 170–1, pointing out that though 'extreme and unorthodox', the *Milošević* precedent may have perspectives 'in the delivery of fair and expeditious trials' in cases of self-represented defendants; similarly Jalloh, in Carter and Pocar, *International Criminal Procedure* (2013), p. 159; Tochilovsky, *Jurisprudence* (2014), pp. 1342–4.

# III
# Jurisdiction and Admissibility (Complementarity)

*The full chapter bibliography can be downloaded from

## A. Jurisdiction

### (1) Principles of national jurisdiction

#### *(a) The starting point: Principle of non-interference*

Jurisdiction is understood broadly here, that is, as a State's exercise of regulatory power with regard to persons and property[1] in the three areas normally accorded to its jurisdiction: legislation, adjudication, and enforcement.[2] While the German criminal law scholar Karl Binding still considered in 1885 that it lies in the sovereign domain of each State to determine the reach of its criminal jurisdiction[3] and this was indeed in line with the then dominant sovereignty-based reading of international law,[4] in the modern understanding sovereignty and thus jurisdiction are grounded in international law.[5] As a consequence, a State's jurisdiction is defined and limited by international law.[6]

[1] Mills, *BYbIL*, 84 (2014), 194; Bantekas, *ICL* (2010), p. 329; Noll, in Orford et al., *International Law* (2016), p. 601 (referring to 'a human being, a company, a territory, or a particular deed subjected to jurisdiction').

[2] See for the respective threefold distinction in jurisdiction to legislate (prescribe), adjudicate, and enforce, ALI, *Restatement* I (1987), pp. 230–1; ALI, *Restatement* (2018), pp. 139–41; Akehurst, *BYbIL*, 46 (1972/73), 145 ff.; Gilbert, *BYbIL*, 63 (1992), 416; O'Keefe, *JICJ*, 2 (2004), 736–7; Bantekas, *ICL* (2010), p. 329; Caeiro, *Fundamento* (2010), pp. 41 ff.; Oxman, in Wolfrum and Peters, *MPEPIL VI* (2007), p. 547; Mills, *BYbIL*, 84 (2014), 194–5; also Cryer, in Cryer et al., *ICL* (2019), pp. 49 ff.; O'Keefe, *ICL* (2015), pp. 4–6; Hernández, *IL* (2021), pp. 196–8; Ryngaert, *EJIL*, 32 (2021), 1455–6; Noll, in Orford et al., *International Law* (2016), p. 602; Liivoja, *Jurisdiction* (2017), pp. 46–7; crit. Currie and Rikhof, *I&TCL* (2020), p. 56 ('analytical and not watertight') prefering to distinguish '*prescriptive* jurisdiction from *enforcement* jurisdiction'. In the same vein, Ireland-Piper, *Accountability* (2017), p. 21; furthermore, see Mouland, *WashILJ*, 29 (2019), 176 ff. (concluding 'that reconsidering adjudicative jurisdiction as a possible manifestation of a state's enforcement jurisdiction is a worthy question for further exploration', 201).

[3] Binding, *Handbuch des Strafrechts I* (1885), p. 374.

[4] This approach has its origins in the so called positivist international law theory, as developed especially in the works of the nineteenth-century legal philosopher John Austin, who argued that legal obligations could only derive from the voluntary acts of sovereigns, i.e. States, and that this sovereignty is something a State possesses as an *a priori* consequence of statehood; cf. thereon Mills, *BYbIL*, 84 (2014), 191–3. As a consequence of this approach, jurisdiction too could be only derived, as an aspect of State sovereignty, from the voluntary acts of a State, leaving it in fact a practically unfettered discretion: 'States possessing independence and territorial as well as personal supremacy can naturally extend or restrict their jurisdiction as far as they like.' (Oppenheim, *International Law* (1905), § 143).

[5] Thus, sovereignty is not prior to, but a product of, international law; cf. Mills, *BYbIL*, 84 (2014), 193 (recalling the change in the 9th edition of *Oppenheim's International Law*).

[6] cf. Mills, *BYbIL*, 84 (2014), 193 ('The rules of international jurisdiction authorise an exercise of regulatory authority in limited and defined circumstances—an authorisation which can only be necessary because a regulatory act would be prohibited in its absence'); see also Bantekas, *ICL* (2010), pp. 329–30 (international law as 'acid test') and Noll, in Orford et al., *International Law* (2016), pp. 600–1; furthermore, see Rosen, *JICJ*, 19 (2021), 1072 ('perception of international law as having one of its main goals to regulate and restrict the scope of jurisdiction exercised by states').

This (modern) view may even be traced back to the seminal 1927 *Lotus* decision of the Permanent Court of International Justice (PCIJ)[7] although this decision, being somewhat ambiguous, may also be interpreted in line with the traditional view.[8] What is clear from the PCIJ's relevant considerations is that it limited jurisdiction to territoriality and thus recognized the principle of non-interference with regard to a State's jurisdiction to enforce:

> Now the first and foremost restriction imposed by international law upon a state is that—failing the existence of a permissive rule to the contrary—it may not *exercise* its power in any form in the territory of another state. *In this sense* jurisdiction is certainly territorial; it cannot be exercised by a state outside its territory, except by virtue of *permissive rule* derived from international custom or from a convention.[9]

At the same time, however, the PCIJ leaves States a wide discretion to determine their prescriptive and even adjudicative (criminal) jurisdiction:

> It does not, however, follow that international law prohibits a State from exercising jurisdiction in its own territory, in respect of any case which relates to acts which have taken place abroad, and in which it cannot rely on some permissive rule of international law … Far from laying down a general prohibition [international law] leaves [States] … a *wide measure of discretion* … every State remains free to adopt the principles which it regards as best and most suitable.
>
> In these circumstances, all that can be required of a state is that it should not overstep the limits which international law places upon its jurisdiction; within these limits, its title to exercise jurisdiction rests in its sovereignty.[10]

Of course, the PCIJ does not explicitly distinguish between the three forms of jurisdiction nowadays recognized. In fact, it even seems to use the term 'exercise' in a more general sense not limited to enforcement. Nevertheless, two conclusions may be drawn. On the one hand, there can be no enforcement without prescriptive jurisdiction, but there may be prescriptive jurisdiction which cannot be enforced: for example, the suspect is abroad and will not be extradited;[11] the limitation regarding the enforcement jurisdiction is accepted by *Lotus*.[12] On the other hand, the limits of international law, especially the principle of non-interference, must be observed; in this sense, the expansion of

[7] PCIJ, *The Case of the S.S. 'Lotus' (France v. Turkey)*, Judgment (7 September 1927).

[8] cf. Mills, *BYbIL*, 84 (2014) 190–1 characterizing it at 'best' as the 'high water mark' of the positivist approach explained above (note 4 in this chapter); in this vein also, ICJ, *Arrest Warrant of 11 April 2000 (Democratic Republic of the Congo v. Belgium)*, Judgment, ICJ Reports 2002 3, Joint Separate Opinion of Judges Higgins, Kooijmans, and Buergenthal, para. 51 (14 February 2002), arguing that the *Lotus* decision 'represents the high water mark of laissez-faire in international relations, and an era that has been significantly overtaken by other tendencies'; also Ryngaert, *Jurisdiction* (2015), pp. 37–8; Currie and Rikhof, *I&TCL* (2020), p. 60 ('approach to the entitlement of states to exercise prescriptive jurisdiction was extremely broad and permissive'); in a similar vein, Mouland, *WashILJ*, 29 (2019), 179; furthermore, see Beaulac, in Allen et al., *Jurisdiction*, (2019), pp. 47 ff.; Liivoja, *Jurisdiction* (2017), pp. 52–3; Payer, *Territorialität* (2021), pp. 13–15; Irarrázavel Zaldívar, *Grundlagen des Strafanwendungsrechts* (2024), pp. 34 ff.

[9] PCIJ, *Lotus*, Judgment (1927), pp. 18–19 (emphasis added); cf. also Garrod, *ICLR*, 12 (2012), 769–70 with further references.

[10] PCIJ, *Lotus*, Judgment (1927), p. 19 (emphasis added).

[11] See also Bowett, *BYbIL*, 53 (1982), 1; conc. Vagias, *Jurisdiction* (2014), p. 13.

[12] See also Hirst, *Jurisdiction* (2003), pp. 44–5 and Bantekas, *ICL* (2010), p. 330, both interpreting *Lotus* as formulating a 'permissive' rule, but limited to prescriptive and adjudicative jurisdiction.

territorial jurisdiction is limited by opposing counterclaims of other States, especially the territorial State.[13]

The principle of non-interference is now to be found in Article 2 (1) UN Charter establishing, in turn, the sovereign equality of States. The former applies not only to the vertical relationship between the States and the UN,[14] but also, albeit in a mitigated form,[15] horizontally in interstate relationships.[16] Consequently, the presumption of criminal jurisdiction with regard to extraterritorial matters may amount to interference in the internal affairs of the territorial State since it questions its exclusive jurisdiction and forces it to tolerate a *foreign* exercise of jurisdiction; in turn, the foreign State thereby executes its *own* penal power on *foreign* territory.[17] This may amount to an unlawful intervention if the foreign State's exercise of jurisdiction reaches a certain level of intensity or compulsion.

The ensuing clash of sovereign jurisdictions provides for a high conflict potential because what is a sovereign execution of penal power for one State, is interference in internal affairs for another.[18] Given that the prevention of such conflicts is one of the main goals of international law, the principle of non-interference must operate as the limitation of national criminal jurisdiction. This has also been recognized in several international agreements.[19] The idea of a *competence-competence (Kompetenz-Kompetenz)* of a nation State to determine its jurisdiction autonomously,[20] irrespective of the limits imposed by international law, is therefore no longer acceptable since it would subject international to national law. Such a view fails to recognize that interstate conflicts arising out of the sovereign equality of States can only be solved through supra- or transnational mechanisms, that is, through a *competence-competence* of international law.[21] Thus, one has to carry out a two-step analysis (as illustrated in Figure 3) to decide upon the compatibility of the extraterritorial exercise of jurisdiction—understood as a jurisdictional claim with 'no territorial nexus whatsoever with the regulating State'[22]—with the principle of non-interference.[23]

### (b) *Genuine links in international law*

As a first step one has to examine whether there is a close relation to or a sufficient link or connection with the State claiming jurisdiction in the respective case, that is, whether a genuine link exists.[24] Regarding the close relationship between a State and a person necessary to

[13] See also Bantekas, *ICL* (2010), p. 330 ('permissive rule' limited by State 'counter-opposing claims').

[14] cf. Art. 2 (7) UN Charter.

[15] Whereas the principle of non-interference between States only protects from interference by way of coercion (Heintschel von Heinegg, in Ipsen, *Völkerrecht* (2024), § 55 mn. 47), Art. 2 (7) UN Charter prohibits any interference by the UN in the *domaine réservé* of its Member States (ibid., § 55 mn. 43 ff.).

[16] For a nuanced view, Ziegenhain, *Exterritoriale Rechtsanwendung* (1992), pp. 33 ff.; see also Behrendt, *Verfolgung* (2005), p. 42; Cameron, *Protective Principle* (1994), pp. 343 ff.

[17] cf. also Merkel, in Jeßberger and Geneuss, *Zehn Jahre VStGB* (2013), p. 47.

[18] cf. Jennings and Watts, *Oppenheim's International Law* (1992), p. 457.

[19] cf. 'UN Convention against Transnational Organised Crime' (UNCTOC), 15 November 2000, UN Doc. A/55/383 (2225 *UNTS* 209) ('Palermo Convention'), which subjects the active and passive personality principles to the principle of non-interference (Art. 15 (2), (4)).

[20] See e.g. Walter, *JuS*, 10 (2006), 870–1; Satzger, *ICL* (2018), § 4 mn. 2; Satzger, 'Vorbemerkungen §§ 3–7', in Satzger et al., *StGB* (2024), mn. 4; Zöller, in Amelung, Günther, and Kühne, *FS Krey* (2010), p. 505, who, however, considers international law as an explicit limit to the competence-competence of States.

[21] cf. Jescheck, *IRuD*, 1 (1956), 83; Rosswog, *Vereinbarkeit* (1965), pp. 36 ff.; also Grant, in Kolb and Scalia, *DIP* (2012), p. 585; Böse, 'Vor §§ 3-7', in Kindhäuser et al., *NK I* (23), mn. 13.

[22] cf. Ryngaert, *Jurisdiction* (2015), p. 7.

[23] Gropp, in Sinn, *Jurisdiktionskonflikte* (2012), p. 44.

[24] Mann, *Recueil des Cours*, 111, 1 (1964), 46 ('the State which has a close, rather than the closest connection with the facts, a genuine link, a sufficiently strong interest'); also see ALI, *Restatement* (2018), p. 188: 'Customary international law permits exercises of prescriptive jurisdiction when a genuine connection exists between the state seeking to regulate and the persons, property, or conduct being regulated.'

| Stage 1: | Sufficient jurisdictional link? |
|---|---|
| **I. General rule** | |
| Territorial principle (including effects principle) | |
| **II. Exceptions** | |
| Extension of jurisdiction beyond the territorial principle:<br>1. Flag principle<br>2. Active personality principle<br>3. Protective principle<br>a. Protective principle *stricto sensu*<br>b. Principle of passive personality<br>4. Principle of universal jurisdiction<br>5. Principle of representation | |

| Stage 2: | Conflicting international prohibition? |
|---|---|
| I. General prohibition of arbitrariness and of abuse of right | |
| II. If several states claim jurisdiction on the basis of sufficient jurisdictional links (positive conflicts of jurisdiction):<br>1. Abstract hierarchy of the jurisdictional principles<br>2. Concrete balancing of the sovereign interests of the States concerned in the sense of the optimization principle | |

**Fig. 3.** Two-step analysis of criminal jurisdiction

grant diplomatic protection, the ICJ required a 'real link' or 'genuine connection'.[25] In the absence of such a link, the principle of non-interference is violated.

Some jurisdictional principles of international criminal law, such as the principles of territory, flag, active/passive personality, and protection, constitute legitimizing links since they embody territory, nationality, and real State interests.[26] Other principles, such as the principles of representation and of universal jurisdiction, renounce a legitimate link however. In the former case a State exercises criminal jurisdiction in representation of another State, that is, this other State's approval is required. If it exists, it excludes an unlawful interference in this State's affairs. In the latter case of universal jurisdiction, the protection of fundamental legal interests is at stake, that is, interests that do not belong to the exclusive domain of a single nation state, but to the international community as such. Therefore, the exercise of jurisdiction by third States cannot be considered as an undue interference in the affairs of the territorial State or State of nationality. We will analyse all these principles in more detail in the next section.

### *(c) Solving conflicts by balancing out the respective interests*

Only if a genuine link exists can one generally assume—as a first step—that the exercise of criminal jurisdiction is in line with international law. Only then, the second step of our analysis comes into play: that is, the question whether there is an explicit rule in international law, which prohibits the respective exercise of jurisdiction. While such an explicit prohibition will hardly exist, two general principles may veto the exercise of jurisdiction: the *prohibition of arbitrariness* and the *prohibition of the abuse of legal right*.[27]

[25] ICJ, *Nottebohm Case (Liechtenstein v. Guatemala)*, Judgment (6 April 1955), ICJ Reports 1955 4, p. 23; cf. ICJ, *Barcelona Traction, Light and Power Company, Limited (Belgium v. Spain)*, Judgment (5 February 1970), ICJ Reports 1970 3, para. 70 (relative test of 'genuine connection' also regarding legal persons); see also Arts. 5 and 91 (1) cl. 3 of the Convention on the High Seas (29 April 1958), 450 *UNTS* 11; cf. also Werle and Jessberger, *Principles ICL* (2020), mn. 256.

[26] See also Mills, *BYbIL*, 84 (2014), 196 (listing territoriality, nationality, and, though less strongly, essential interests and fundamental values).

[27] Mann, *Recueil des Cours*, 111, 1 (1964), 46–7. On the prohibition of arbitrariness, see Wendt, *Personalitätsprinzip* (1965), pp. 98–9; Martin, *Umweltbeeinträchtigung* (1989), p. 142; Heinrich, *Personalitätsprinzip* (1994), pp. 186 ff.; on the abuse of rights, see Dahm, *Völkerstrafrecht* (1956), pp. 38–9;

This second analytical step amounts, in essence, to the question whether the general link also legitimizes the concrete exercise of jurisdiction, that is, whether it appears to be reasonable[28] with a view to the concrete extension of the *ius puniendi*. The underlying 'rule of reason', as developed by Francis Mann,[29] and the ensuing requirement of *reasonableness* as an international law principle regarding criminal jurisdiction,[30] suffers, of course, from great uncertainty[31] and may even give room to a certain arbitrariness.[32] In addition, if reasonableness is made part of these links—for example, by requiring a reasonable link or 'relation'[33]—the call for reasonableness turns out to be circular since the conclusion (reasonableness of jurisdiction) is already included in the premise of the argument. In any case, reasonableness must not be invoked to justify any kind of criminal jurisdiction. Rather, it must be further developed in line with the recognized links of jurisdiction and other relevant principles of international law,[34] such as the principle of moderation and limitation of the exercise of extraterritorial criminal jurisdiction, developed by Judge Fitzmaurice in the *Barcelona-Traction* case.[35] Reasonableness so understood works both ways: as a justification of jurisdiction, but also as its limitation based on the argument that an unreasonable jurisdictional claim amounts to an unlawful intervention, an abuse of rights, or even a due process violation.[36]

Rosswog, *Vereinbarkeit* (1965), pp. 158 ff.; Cameron, *Protective Principle* (1994), pp. 337–8; Zieher, *Internationale Strafrecht* (1997), pp. 67–8; dissenting, Pappas, *Stellvertretende Strafrechtspflege* (1996), p. 89.

[28] cf. Oxman, in Wolfrum and Peters, *MPEPIL VI* (2007), p. 548.

[29] Mann, *Recueil des Cours*, 111, 1 (1964), 43 ('The problem, properly defined, involves the search for the State or States whose contact with the facts is such as to make the allocation of legislative competence just and reasonable').

[30] cf. Vagias, *Jurisdiction* (2014), pp. 33–5, 88, 106; on reasonableness (as part of US law), see also Mills, *BYbIL*, 84 (2014), 200; Struebing, *NCLR*, 21 (2018), 21–2; and esp. (with a view to the Restatement of the Law (Fourth)) Ryngaert, *EJIL*, 32 (2021), 1458–63 (agreeing 'with the drafters' doubts over the customary international law status of reasonableness'); also Bantekas, *ICL* (2010), p. 331.

[31] In the same vein, Vagias, *Jurisdiction* (2014), p. 33.

[32] In fact, reasonableness is used as a panacea in almost any legal dispute in common law jurisdictions, cf. Fletcher, *HarvLR*, 98 (1985), 949 ff. (953: 'reliance on reasonableness facilitates flat legal thinking. With syntactically mobile modifiers like "reasonable" and "substantial," each rule of the common law can contain placeholders for everything that one needs to know to resolve a particular problem'); Fletcher, *Grammar I* (2007), p. 138 (the way the word 'reasonable' is used facilitates a '[h]olistic legal thought', i.e. a legal thought based on the use of a single rule to resolve a complex legal problem); Fletcher and Sheppard, *American Law* (2005), p. 66; Fletcher, in Arnold et al., *Menschengerechtes Strafrecht* (2005), p. 744 ('reasonableness im common law ist wie eine Kanone ohne Zielrichtung').

[33] Mann, *Recueil des Cours*, 111 (1964-I), 46–7 (arguing that 'not every close contact will be legally accepted … to support international jurisdiction', but '[i]t must be possible to point to a reasonable relation, that is to say, to the absence of abuse of rights or of arbitrariness').

[34] For Vagias, *Jurisdiction* (2014), pp. 196, 202, it even encapsulates these principles, especially non-intervention and abuse of rights. Also see Ryngaert, *Jurisdiction* (2015), p. 182 ('there are a substantial number of principles of international law, such as non-intervention, proportionality, abuse of rights, equity, and genuine connection, that may be seen as buttressing an international rule of reason informed by interest-balancing … the rule of reason is, short of being a norm of customary international law, a general principle of international law'); Ryngaert, *EJIL*, 32 (2021), 1461.

[35] ICJ, *Barcelona Traction*, Judgment (1970), Separate Opinion of Judge Fitzmaurice, para. 70 ('It [international law] does however (*a*) postulate the *existence* of limits—though in any given case it may be for the tribunal to indicate what these are for the purposes of that case; and (*b*) involve for every State an obligation to exercise moderation and restraint as to the extent of the jurisdiction assumed by its courts in cases having a foreign element, and to avoid undue encroachment on a jurisdiction more properly appertaining to, or more appropriately exercisable by, another State'); see also Council of the EU, 'Expert Group on the Principle of Universal Jurisdiction Report (2009)', mn. 24; Bantekas, *ICL* (2010), p. 331 (no abusive or excessive jurisdiction).

[36] See, in this limiting sense, Vagias, *Jurisdiction* (2014), pp. 127–30 (on the use of the concept in human rights law), 196, 202, 207; Ryngaert, *EJIL*, 32 (2021), 1458–9 ('principle of reasonableness has the potential to limit the international havoc wrought by broadly construed permissive principles of jurisdiction—in particular the territoriality principle and its cousin the effects doctrine. It could provide a solution to international conflicts between

In concrete terms, this means that a balancing of the respective State and sovereignty interests is at stake; that is, the conflicting interests have to be reconciled, trying to do justice to both of them in the best form possible (optimization principle): while every State may extend its criminal jurisdiction as far as possible, in relation to other States it may do so only so far as necessary, so that those States' interests are not unduly affected.[37] This would be the case if their interests outweighed the interests of the State exercising jurisdiction; in this case, the exercise of criminal jurisdiction would amount to an illegitimate interference in the affected State's internal affairs. We will return to the possible reconciliation of the opposing States' interests by this balancing exercise below.

### (2) The legitimate genuine links in detail

#### *(a) Principle of territoriality*

*(i) General*

According to the territoriality principle, the State on whose territory—that is, its land, sea, and airspace[38]—a crime has occurred or has been committed possesses criminal jurisdiction over it, irrespective of the suspect's nationality.[39] At first sight, the principle seems to be straightforward, but the devil is in the detail, as we shall see below.

On the level of principle, it is clear that territoriality is an expression of State sovereignty and thus recognized under international treaty and customary law.[40] Also, the principle is sound for reasons of criminal policy since the territorial State is most proximate to the crime

states with concurring jurisdiction over a particular subject matter'); for a fundamental critique of the non-intervention principle's limited ability to effectively restrain a State's criminal jurisdiction, see recently Irarrázavel Zaldívar, *Grundlagen des Strafanwendungsrechts* (2024), pp. 26, 62–3, 141 ff., 457 ff.

[37] cf. in detail, Ziegenhain, *Exterritoriale Rechtsanwendung* (1992), pp. 36 ff.

[38] cf. for more details Ambos, *Internationales Strafrecht* (2018), § 3 mn. 14 ff.; also Bantekas, *ICL* (2010), pp. 336–7 (including occupied territory); Hernández, *IL* (2021), pp. 199–200; Oxman, in Wolfrum and Peters, *MPEPIL VI* (2007), p. 549; O'Keefe, *ICL* (2015), p. 10; on the implementation of the principle in various legal orders, see Satzger, *ICL* (2018), § 4 mn. 12–14.

[39] Werle and Jeßberger, 'Vorbemerkungen §§ 3 ff.', in Cirener et al., *Leipziger Kommentar StGB I* (2020), mn. 241; Eser and Weißer, 'Vorbemerkungen §§ 3-9', in Schönke and Schröder, *Strafgesetzbuch* (2019), mn. 17; Wolfrum, in Arnold et al., *Menschengerechtes Strafrecht* (2005), p. 977; Miller and Rackow, *ZStW*, 117 (2005), 379 (381); Satzger, *ICL* (2018), § 4 mn. 6; Satzger, *Internationales Strafrecht* (2022), § 4 mn. 6; Council of the EU, 'Expert Group on the Principle of Universal Jurisdiction Report (2009)', mn. 12; Jeßberger, *Geltungsbereich* (2011), p. 225; Eisele and Majer, *NStZ*, 31 (2011), 551; O'Keefe, *ICL* (2015), p. 10.

[40] cf. PCIJ, *Lotus*, Judgment (1927), pp. 18–20; see also Gilbert, *BYbIL*, 63 (1992), 416; Hirst, *Jurisdiction* (2003), p. 45; Mills, *BYbIL*, 84 (2014), 196–7; Vagias, *Jurisdiction* (2014), pp. 13–14; Ireland-Piper, *Accountability* (2017), p. 23 ('uncontroversial and universally recognized'); also Cryer, in Cryer et al., *ICL* (2019), pp. 52–3; Hernández, *IL* (2021), p. 199 ('easiest basis on which to claim jurisdiction'); Kindt, *Menschenrechte* (2009) p. 76; Wamser, *StraFo*, 7 (2010), 279; Ambos, 'Vorbemerkung § 3', in von Heintschel-Heinegg, *MüKo I* (2020), mn. 18, 133; Pocar and Maystre, in Bergsmo, *Complementarity* (2010), p. 251; Jeßberger, *Geltungsbereich* (2011), pp. 227 ff.; Cryer, in Cryer et al., *ICL* (2019), pp. 52–3; Le Nguyen, *JFinancCrime*, 27 (2020), 1365 ('most substantial basis for a state to claim criminal jurisdiction'); Hernández, *IL* (2021), p. 199 ('easiest basis on which to claim jurisdiction'); Irarrázavel Zaldívar, *Grundlagen des Strafanwendungsrechts* (2024), pp. 65–6; Ambos, 'Vorbemerkung § 3', in von Heintschel-Heinegg, *MüKo I* (2020), mn. 18, 133; from a comparative law perspective, Böse, Meyer, and Schneider, in Böse, Meyer, and Schneider, *Conflicts of Jurisdiction I* (2013), p. 412; on Switzerland , Gless, *Internationales Strafrecht* (2021), mn. 153–4; on the historical development, see Ryngaert, *Jurisdiction* (2015), pp. 51 ff.; The territorial principle is also recognized by Art. 12 (2)(a) ICCS as will be seen below in Section (4)(a). From a European perspective, Klip, *European Criminal Law* (2021), pp. 258 ff.; for a comparative law perspective, see Sinn, in Sinn, *Jurisdiktionskonflikte bei grenzüberschreitender Kriminalität* (2012), p. 543; from a human rights perspective, see Walther, in Arnold et al., *Menschengerechtes Strafrecht* (2005), pp. 938 ff., with alternatives pp. 943 ff.

and thus best suited to investigate and prosecute it.[41] From the perspective of international law, the main advantage of territoriality is that by limiting the penal power to the sovereign territory of a State, jurisdictional conflicts with other States are prevented.[42] Indeed, this has been the reason why common law States have traditionally only acknowledged territorial jurisdiction.[43] Of course, this advantage is getting lost, as we will see in a moment, with the broadening of territoriality and, even more so, with the extraterritorial expansion of criminal jurisdiction, occurring in practically all national criminal justice systems. As already acknowledged by the PCIJ in the *Lotus* case:

> Though it is true that in all systems of law the principle of the territorial character of criminal law is fundamental, it is equally true that all or nearly all these systems of law extend their action to offences committed outside the territory of the State which adopts them, and they do so in ways which vary from State to State. The territoriality of criminal law, therefore, is not an absolute principle of international law and by no means coincides with territorial sovereignty.[44]

In fact, different approaches exist to extend a State's criminal jurisdiction to extraterritorial events. Given that such a jurisdictional overreach entails interference in another State's territorial jurisdiction and thus in its internal affairs, it requires a justification under international law. It is provided by the generally recognized principles of (extraterritorial) jurisdiction, invoking the suspect's nationality (principle of active personality), the victim's nationality (principle of passive personality), essential State interests (protective principle), or even global legal interests (principle of representation, *aut dedere aut iudicare*, universal jurisdiction). Before we analyse these principles allowing for extraterritorial jurisdiction, we have to take a closer look at the already mentioned broadening of territoriality itself by the doctrines of ubiquity and effects, on the one hand, and the flag principle, on the other.[45]

*(ii) Objective territoriality/ubiquity vs. effects*

Objective territoriality captures territoriality 'objectively'[46] in that it requires for the jurisdictional claim of the territorial State that the crime was completed on its

[41] In this vein, also Bantekas, *ICL* (2010), p. 333.

[42] Ambos, 'Vorbemerkung § 3', in von Heintschel-Heinegg, *MüKo I* (2020), mn. 18; see also Böse, in Zöller et al., *Gesamte Strafrechtswissenschaft* (2013), p. 1327. Differently, probably from the perspective of the effects principle, Abelson, *UCDavisJIL&Pol'y*, 16 (2009), 16; also Werle and Jeßberger, 'Vorbemerkungen §§ 3 ff.', in Cirener et al., *Leipziger Kommentar StGB I* (2020), mn. 242; see also Wolswijk, in Böse, Meyer, and Schneider, *Conflicts of Jurisdiction I* (2013), p. 330.

[43] cf. Gilbert, *BYbIL*, 63 (1992), 416 (with a detailed analysis of the (traditional) English law [424 ff.], 'tied firmly to the territorial principle' [441] and 'out of step' with other States in terms of 'qualified territoriality' [442]).

[44] PCIJ, *Lotus*, Judgment (1927), p. 20; see also Jennings and Watts, *Oppenheim's International Law I* (1992), pp. 457, 468.

[45] In favour of a concept of 'qualified territoriality' to encompass all sub-forms and extensions of territoriality, Gilbert, *BYbIL*, 63 (1992), 417, 430.

[46] In contrast, subjective territoriality has been described as jurisdiction 'to prosecute and punish for crimes committed within the State but completed or consummated abroad' *Harvard Draft Convention* (1935), p. 484), more precisely, the conduct occurred in the State claiming jurisdiction (cf. Hirst, *Jurisdiction* (2003), p. 46; ALI, *Restatement* (2018), pp. 196–7 ('a state may exercise prescriptive jurisdiction over conduct that occurs or has begun within its territory, although the conduct has consequences in another state'); Bantekas, *ICL* (2010), pp. 333–4; furthermore, see Currie and Rikhof, *I&TCL* (2020), p. 66 ('jurisdiction over an offence that begins on its territory but is completed outside the territory'); in the same vein, Hernández, *IL* (2021), p. 200). In any case, this terminology is not undisputed (see e.g. Hirst, *Jurisdiction* (2003), p. 46: 'seldom … adopted in English cases'); subjective territoriality is sometimes difficult to delimit from objective territoriality and ubiquity (see e.g. Gilbert, *BYbIL*, 63 (1992), 430–1 equating ubiquity to subjective territoriality 'if an element of the offence takes place in the

territory[47] or, more precisely, as held in *Lotus*, that 'one of the constituent elements of the offence, and more especially its effects, have taken place there'.[48] While the doctrine is recognized under international law,[49] its precise scope is unclear since it has never been properly defined what the 'constituent elements' of an offence amount to.[50] In fact, the *Lotus* definition is only (more or less) precise in its first part referring to 'constituent elements', that is, elements of the *actus reus*, but it then loses all this precision by introducing a purely factual element with the concept of 'effects'. Thus, there is a tension between the legally understood objective territoriality and the factual effects principle entailing, as we will see below, an almost unlimited expansion of criminal jurisdiction.[51]

In addition, in *Lotus*, the principle was applied to a negligent perpetrator, but how can a negligent agent be aware of the impact of the respective act and thus held responsible without this knowledge? This is difficult to reconcile with the culpability principle, concretely with its requirement of foreseeability of the punishability. For this reason, the respective conduct must be punishable in both the State where it was performed and the one where the result occurred (requirement of double criminality).[52]

At any rate, there are some clear-cut cases of objective territoriality, especially in result crimes where the harmful result has occurred in a different place (territory) than the relevant conduct. Take the famous example of a shot that is fired from one side of the border killing someone on the other side. In this so-called distance crime, the State where the criminal act was performed differs from the State where the harmful result occurred but both States are entitled to claim jurisdiction on the basis of objective territoriality.[53] Of course, things are getting more complicated if several parties are involved in a crime, preparatory acts are at stake, or crimes are committed via or within the internet.[54]

prosecuting State'), and lost importance in light of the development of the latter concepts (cf. Vagias, *Jurisdiction* (2014), pp. 15–16).

[47] Akehurst, *BYbIL*, 46 (1972–73), 152–3; Hernández, *IL* (2021), p. 200 (with the example of 'the implantation of malware in State A that then temporarily shuts down the cyber infrastructure of State B. State A would claim to exercise *subjective* territorial jurisdiction. State B would claim to exercise *objective* territorial jurisdiction, as the consequences of implantation were suffered in its territory'); on the similar (English) 'terminatory theory of jurisdiction' Hirst, *Jurisdiction* (2003), pp. 115 ff.; furthermore, see Struebing, *NCLR*, 21 (2018), 21.

[48] PCIJ, *Lotus*, Judgment (1927), p. 23.

[49] Summarizing, Vagias, *Jurisdiction* (2014), p. 22; also Ryngaert, *Jurisdiction* (2015), pp. 77–9 ('necessary and sufficient that one constituent element of the act or situation has been consummated in the territory of the State that claims jurisdiction'); from a legal-historical perspective, see Liivoja, *Jurisdiction* (2017), pp. 20–1.

[50] See also Hirst, *Jurisdiction* (2003), p. 46; Vagias, *Jurisdiction* (2014), pp. 22–3; Vagias, *JCSL*, 21 (2016), 527 ('customary international law does not explain specifically how little of a crime must be committed on the territory of a state for that state to have jurisdiction in accordance with international law'); Ryngaert, *EJIL*, 32 (2021), 1457 ('does the use of US correspondent bank accounts to clear transactions denominated in US dollars qualify as a genuine territorial connection with the USA?'); on the issue of the applicability of US criminal law in the FIFA bribery scandal, cf. Struebing, *NCLR*, 21 (2018), 21 ff.; Krisch, *EJIL*, 33 (2022), 488–9.

[51] Crit. also Irarrázavel Zaldívar, *Grundlagen des Strafanwendungsrechts* (2024), pp. 70–1 ('universal jurisdiction through the backdoor' ['Einführung des Weltrechtsprinzips durch die Hintertür']).

[52] Gropp, in Sinn, *Jurisdiktionskonflikte* (2012), p. 46. In the same vein, Kunig and Uerpmann, *Jura*, 4 (1994), 193; see also Böse, 'Vor §§ 3-7', in Kindhäuser et al., *NK I* (23), mn. 16 (advocating a restriction to crimes of intent due to human rights and constitutional concerns); *contra*, focusing exclusively on the criminal result, PCIJ, *Lotus*, Judgment (1927), Dissenting Opinion of Judge Loder, p. 37 and Dissenting Opinion of Judge Moore, pp. 82–3; conc. Vagias, *Jurisdiction* (2014), p. 18.

[53] At the beginning of the twentieth century, jurisdiction in these cases has been based on the fiction of 'constructive presence', cf. PCIJ, *Lotus*, Judgment (1927, Dissenting Opinion of Judge Moore, p. 73; also Vagias, *Jurisdiction* (2014), p. 14 with references in n. 15; generally on the cross-border shooting case, also Bantekas, *ICL* (2010), p. 333; with regard to 'transnational bribery and money laundering offences' which 'can be conceived of as "conduct offences" and not as "result offences"', see Le Nguyen, *JFinancCrime*, 27 (2020), 1365.

[54] See, for more details, Vagias, *Jurisdiction* (2014), pp. 19–22; also Ambos, *Internationales Strafrecht* (2018), § 1 mn. 17–20.

The concept of *ubiquity* renders these definitional problems moot in that it does not require the existence of any constituent element of the offence, but turns to a wholly, effects-like factual definition merely requiring that 'a part of' the respective offence must have been committed in the territory of the State claiming jurisdiction.[55] Despite its considerable broadening of territorial jurisdiction,[56] the concept is widely applied in State practice[57] and recognized under international law.[58]

With its recourse to 'effects', the *Lotus* decision may well be related to the *effects doctrine*, but as a proper doctrine it came only into existence almost twenty years later with US courts addressing antitrust violations in transnational trade relations in the context of civil litigations.[59] According to this doctrine, a State can establish (territorial) jurisdiction over a crime committed abroad if it has an impact or effect within its territory.[60] Thus, even if the main part of the relevant conduct is performed abroad and therefore extraterritorial, the effects doctrine is part of the principle of territoriality focusing on the *intraterritorial* effects of the conduct.[61] This is in line with the above-mentioned understanding of 'extraterritoriality' as implying the absence of any link whatsoever to the territorial State.[62] In any case, given the broad understanding of 'effects' as 'economic repercussions or consequences' (in the context of antitrust law)[63] or even broader socio-political consequences (in the ICL context),[64] both of course outside the *actus reus* of the offence, certain limiting qualifiers are necessary to avoid jurisdictional overreach.[65] Insofar antitrust case law offers as common denominators that the effects should be of a certain magnitude ('substantial'), reasonably foreseeable, and causally connected to the offence ('direct').[66]

55 CoE, *Extraterritorial Criminal Jurisdiction* (1990), p. 8 ('offence as a whole may be considered to have been committed in the place where a part of it has been committed').

56 Crit. also CoE, *Extraterritorial Criminal Jurisdiction* (1990), p. 25.

57 See references in Cameron, *Protective Principle* (1994), p. 57; Vagias, *Jurisdiction* (2014), p. 24 with n. 71; on the German law (misquoted in Vagias, ibid.), see Ambos, *Internationales Strafrecht* (2018), § 1 mn. 17.

58 cf. Vagias, *Jurisdiction* (2014), p. 24.

59 The first US case dealt with antitrust violations in the aluminium market (cf. *US v. Aluminum Company of America et al.*, 148 F.2d 416 [No. 144, Circuit Court of Appeals, Second Circuit, 12 March 1945]) but only in 1997—after the respective criminalization of antitrust violations in the US—the doctrine was used in a criminal prosecution (*US v. Nippon Paper Industries Co.Ltd et al.*, 109 F.3d 1 [Court of Appeals, First Circuit, 17 March 1997]); for a detailed analysis and further (US) case law, see Vagias, *Jurisdiction* (2014), pp. 25 ff., 172 ff., 178 ff.; also Hirst, *Jurisdiction* (2003), pp. 47–8; Cameron, *Protective Principle* (1994), pp. 59 ff.; Currie and Rikhof, *I&TCL* (2020), p. 67; Hernández, *IL* (2021), p. 201.

60 Vagias, *Jurisdiction* (2014), p. 24.

61 cf. ibid., pp. 24, 183–5; also Podgor, *Stud. L. POL. & Soc'y*, 28 (2003), pp. 123 ff., considering it as a kind of defensive territoriality and limiting it to all cases where an effect on a governmental function is obvious; Ryngaert, *Antitrust Violations* (2008), pp. 15–16, regarding it, 'under classical criminal jurisdictional theory' as '"objective" territorial jurisdiction'; *contra* Doehring, *Völkerrecht* (2004), mn. 823 (variation of the protective principle); also Bantekas, *ICL* (2010), p. 342 (protection 'overlaps with the effects doctrine'); for a nuanced view, see Cameron, *Protective Principle* (1994), p. 64 ('either a principle of extraterritorial jurisdiction' or 'simply a means of localising crime', i.e., in the latter case, 'a form of the territoriality principle').

62 Note 22 in this chapter with main text.

63 cf. Ryngaert, *Antitrust Violations* (2008), p. 17; Wolswijk, *NILR*, 66 (1999), 366; crit. of the expansive US practice, Bantekas, *ICL* (2010), pp. 335–6.

64 cf. Vagias, *Jurisdiction* (2014), pp. 162–3 (referring to the mass exodus of civilian populations as a consequence of massacres).

65 Think of the example just given in the previous footnote in times of global refugee crises: should criminal jurisdiction really be conferred upon each State which receives these refugees? To ask this question means to answer it in the negative.

66 cf. Vagias, *Jurisdiction* (2014), pp. 190 ff. (195), 207; also Hirst, *Jurisdiction* (2003), pp. 46–7 ('significant adverse effect'); O'Keefe, *ICL* (2015), p. 16, rejecting the effects doctrine ('a highly dubious basis') beyond the bounds of 'direct and substantial harmful effect within the territory of the prescribing state'.

The effects principle is recognized under international law,[67] at least as a basis for civil jurisdiction pursuant to the widespread practice in antitrust law.[68] The Court of Justice of the European Union (ECJ) in fact, following the US precedents, decided in the case of *Ahlström v. Commission*,[69] that Article 85 EEC Treaty old version[70] (Article 101 TFEU[71]) is applicable due to the effects principle, given that a price-fixing agreement made outside the EC territory was to take effect inside and would thus affect it.[72] The Advocate General stated that the principle was laid down in Article 85 EEC Treaty itself,[73] and that the ECJ had approved of it.[74] He further argued that it is compatible with international law since it is derived from the principle of objective territoriality.[75] The principle was also used by the European Commission on several occasions,[76] referred to by the ICJ,[77] and can be found in ICL conventions.[78]

Thus, in sum, it can be concluded that the existence of the effects doctrine, also as a ground for criminal jurisdiction, has been widely accepted. The ongoing debate centres on an adequate interpretation of the admissible effects in the sense of the above-mentioned qualifiers and the possible extension of the doctrine to other areas of (criminal) law.[79] In any case, there is, as shown by Krisch,[80] a certain tendency in the context of (economic) globalization, to have recourse to territorial jurisdiction independently of the effects principle[81] and

[67] Akehurst, *BYbIL*, 46 (1972/73), 152; Ryngaert, *Antitrust Violations* (2008), pp. 15–16 ('Doubtless, public international law authorizes criminal jurisdiction by a State over an act of which the effects are felt in the territory of that State'); Mills, *BYbIL*, 84 (2014), 196; Vagias, *Jurisdiction* (2014), pp. 28–31; also Hernández, *IL* (2021), p. 218 ('Though the effects doctrine . . . has faced considerable international opposition, other jurisdictions have employed similar practices'); but seeing a lack of consistent State practice, Meng, *AVR*, 27 (1989), 183; crit. also Currie and Rikhof, *I&TCL* (2020), p. 67 ('no case can be made for its acceptance as a rule of customary international law').

[68] ECJ, *Air Transport Association of America and Others*, Case C–366/10, Opinion of Advocate General Kokott, para. 148 (6 October 2011); also see ALI, *Restatement* (2018), pp. 200–2. As to criminal jurisdiction, Vagias, *Jurisdiction* (2014), p. 182 rather cautiously concludes that 'there is [only] certain acceptance of the effects doctrine as an interpretation of territorial criminal jurisdiction' with regard to 'the most egregious violations of competition law'.

[69] ECJ, *Ahlström and Others v. Commission*, Case C–89/85, Judgment (27 September 1988); for further EU case law, see Vagias, *Jurisdiction* (2014), p. 29.

[70] Treaty establishing the European Economic Community, signed in Rome on 25 May 1957.

[71] Treaty on the Functioning of the European Union, 26 October 2012 (OJ 2012/C 326/01), <http://eur-lex.europa.eu/legal-content/EN/TXT/PDF/?uri=CELEX:12012E/TXT&from=EN>.

[72] ECJ, *Ahlström and Others v. Commission*, Judgment, para. 16: 'the decisive factor is . . . the place where it [the price-fixing agreement, K. Ambos] is implemented'.

[73] Art. 85 EEC Treaty concerns agreements, 'which have as their object or *effect* the prevention, restriction or distortion of competition within the common market' (emphasis added).

[74] ECJ, *Ahlström and Others v. Commission*, Case C–89/85, Opinion of Advocate General Darmon, para. 8 (25 May 1988).

[75] Ibid., paras. 15 ff.

[76] Meng, *AVR*, 27 (1989), 183; for international law references, see Oehler, in Börner et al., *Einigkeit und Recht und Freiheit I* (1984), pp. 436 ff.

[77] ICJ, *DRC v. Belgium*, Judgment (2002), Joint Separate Opinion of Judges Higgins, Koojimans, and Buergenthal, para. 47 (arguing that it is embraced by both the US and the EU).

[78] See e.g. Art. 15 (2)(c)(i) UNCTOC allowing for jurisdiction for an extraterritorial offence 'with a view to the commission of a serious crime within its territory'.

[79] cf. Vagias, *Jurisdiction* (2014), pp. 30–1 (referring, inter alia, to human rights violations, terrorism, and ordinary criminal law offences).

[80] Krisch, *EJIL*, 33 (2022), 481 ff. (arguing that the traditional concept of jurisdiction has been transformed to 'an "unbound" jurisdiction', especially with regard to global business activities, resulting in a 'jurisdictional assemblage' where 'a multiplicity of states have wide and overlapping jurisdictional claims' but in practice only 'a few powerful countries wield the capacity to set and implement the rules'; rebalancing this regime requires, according to Krisch, 'the introduction of new forms of accountability that respect self-government while providing effective tools to regulate multinational companies'); largely agreeing with this analysis but advocating the further use of the existing (treaty) law, O'Keefe, *EJIL*, 33 (2022), 515.

[81] Krisch, *EJIL*, 33 (2022), 485 (effects doctrine 'remains contested'), 496 ('not as prominent as one might have expected')

in a much more flexible ('unbound') way, based on thin and partial links and amounting to a 'jurisdictional assemblage' where a small group of powerful States defines and dominates jurisdictional claims.[82]

### *(iii) The flag principle*

According to the flag principle, ships, aircraft, and spacecraft stand under the authority of the flag State, that is, the State whose flag they carry or in which they are registered; from the perspective of public international law, they possess the nationality of that State. As a consequence, the flag State has jurisdiction over any crimes committed on that particular ship or aircraft, irrespective of its location at the time of the crime and of the offender's nationality. The flag principle is recognized since the *Lotus case*[83] where, in fact, the PCIJ even assimilated the Turkish vessel, as the *locus delicti*, to Turkish territory.[84] However, this doctrine of the '*territoires flottants*' has since been overcome[85] and the flag principle is no longer considered as expanding the flag State's sovereign territory, but only its jurisdiction.[86]

As a consequence, the flag principle is no more than a pragmatic extraterritorial expansion of sovereign and penal power, to close jurisdictional gaps on the high seas and in airspace with a view to upholding law and order.[87] This is also depicted by the fact that often, concurrent jurisdictions exist: the flag State of which the ship carries the flag may have exclusive jurisdiction on the high seas, but in the coastal areas its jurisdiction conflicts with the territorial one of the coastal State.[88] Furthermore, even on the high seas, the flag State's jurisdiction may collide with the jurisdiction of the suspect's State, as a result of the principle of active personality,[89] if the persons involved in the criminal event are not all nationals of the flag State.[90]

### *(b) The active personality principle*

The active personality principle links jurisdiction over the crime directly to the offender's nationality, irrespective of the place of the crime scene. Its rationale is, arguably, that a

[82] Ibid., 481, 495 ff.

[83] PCIJ, *Lotus*, Judgment (1927), p. 25 ('It is certainly true that ... vessels on the high seas are subject to no authority except that of the State whose flag they fly'). See also Art. 12 (2)(a) ICCS; thereon Schabas and Pecorella, 'Article 12', in Ambos, *Commentary* (2022), mn. 23; from a European perspective Klip, *European Criminal Law* (2021), p. 260; for a comperative law view cf. Böse, Meyer, and Schneider, in Böse, Meyer, and Schneider, *Conflicts of Jurisdiction I* (2013), p. 415.

[84] PCIJ, *Lotus*, Judgment (1927), p. 23 ('the offence produced its effects on the Turkish vessel and consequently in a place *assimilated* to Turkish territory in which the application of Turkish criminal law cannot be challenged, even in regard to offences committed there by foreigners'), p. 25 ('a ship on the high seas is *assimilated* to the territory of the State the flag of which it flies, for, *just as in its own territory*, that State exercises its authority, upon it, and no other State may do so') (emphasis added).

[85] Crit. previously, PCIJ, *Lotus*, Judgment (1927), Dissenting Opinion of Judge Finlay, p. 53 ('jurisdiction ... on a ship ... not of a territorial nature at all'); Liivoja, *Jurisdiction* (2017), p. 28 ('theory that ships are floating pieces of the territory of their flag State has been abandoned'); yet still defending the 'floating territory' approach, see Hernández, *IL* (2021), p. 200.

[86] cf. Gaeta, in Cassese, Chiavario, and De Francesco, *Problemi* (2005), pp. 522 ff.; in this sense, also Deumeland, *VR*, 50 (2004), 94; cf. also Ambos, 'Vorbemerkung § 3', in von Heintschel-Heinegg, *MüKo I* (2020), mn. 27; Kolbet et al., *ZaöRV*, 71 (2011), 217; Wolswijk, in Böse et al., *Conflicts of Jurisdiction I* (2013), p. 336.

[87] cf. German Federal Court [BGH], *NStZ*, 8 (2009), 464; Meyer, in Böse, Meyer, and Schneider, *Conflicts of Jurisdiction I* (2013), pp. 149–50. On the overlap of the flag principle with the protective principle, see Cameron, *Protective Principle* (1994), pp. 74–5. On the flag State's responsibility for persons rescued at the high seas by its ships, see Busco and Pizzuti, *EJIL: Talk!* 1 May 2024.

[88] cf. Art. 27 UNCLOS.

[89] cf. Art. 97 (1) UNCLOS deviating from the *Lotus* precedent.

[90] If one considers the active personality principle as the ruling principle (as in Germany from 1940 until 1975), it would even override the flag principle (cf. Rudolf, *NJW*, 6 (1954), 219).

State may extend its criminal law to extraterritorial events pursuant to that State's sovereignty over its own nationals or, more convincingly, pursuant to the allegiance owed to one's country of nationality.[91] This latter rationale manifests itself, probably most evidently, in the exclusive jurisdiction of the sending State for its soldiers stationed abroad in a receiving State.[92] The principle is recognized under international law (explicitly in Article 12 (2)(b) ICCS)[93] and widely used in many legal systems.[94] It is especially relevant in States that prohibit the extradition of their own citizens, particularly in Continental Europe (e.g. Germany[95]) and Latin America, which have similar legal systems.[96] Thus, if a German commits a crime outside the EU area,[97] they could avoid prosecution in the territorial State by returning to Germany and invoking Article 16 (2) clause 1 of the German Constitution (*Grundgesetz*).

*(i) Absolute active personality principle*

The principle of active personality in its absolute form subjects nationals committing crimes abroad to the domestic criminal law, irrespective of the punishability of the respective conduct in the foreign jurisdiction. This broad expansion of jurisdiction interferes with the sovereign jurisdiction of the territorial State since it disrespects this State's legal system by effectively setting aside its right to determine the punishability of conduct in its territory. Apart from that, it seems blatantly unfair to punish a person for conduct that is not punishable in the foreign jurisdiction in which they decided to reside and whose laws are alone relevant for them in accordance with the principle of territorial jurisdiction.

The absolute active personality principle can only be explained as an exaggeration of the linkage between the State and its citizens, that is, a kind of duty of absolute faithfulness of these citizens towards their home State.[98] This home State, in turn, appears to consider the enforcement of its own criminal law and the underlying values as more important than the international principle of non-interference. The reduction of the offenders to a sole object of their home State does not only defy the principle of non-interference, but portrays, in fact,

[91] For the latter, see Bantekas, *ICL* (2010), p. 338; demanding a closer, more substantive connection than mere nationality Irarrázavel Zaldívar, *Grundlagen des Strafanwendungsrechts* (2024), pp. 78, 88 ff.

[92] On the respective exclusion of territorial jurisdiction of the receiving State in the respective Statute of Forces agreements, see Bantekas, *ICL* (2010), pp. 350 ff.; Almqvist, *LJIL*, 28 (2015), 109–10.

[93] See Section A.(4)(a)(ii) in this chapter.

[94] cf. Gilbert, *BYbIL*, 63 (1992), 417; Cameron, *Protective Principle* (1994), pp. 67 ff.; Schmitz, *Das aktive Personalitätsprinzip* (2002), pp. 243 ff.; Bantekas, *ICL* (2010), pp. 338–9, 340; Cryer, in Cryer et al., *ICL* (2019), pp. 53–5; O'Keefe, *LJIL*, 26 (2013), 549; Jeßberger, *Geltungsbereich* (2011), pp. 240–1; Mills, *BYbIL*, 84 (2014), 198; O'Keefe, *ICL* (2015), p. 11; Le Nguyen, *JFinancCrime*, 27 (2020), 1366 ('application varies significantly'); Irarrázavel Zaldívar, *Grundlagen des Strafanwendungsrechts* (2024), pp. 76, 88; on its implementation in various national legal orders, see Satzger, *ICL* (2018), § 4 mn. 17–21; from the perspective of European criminal law, Klip, *European Criminal Law* (2021), pp. 261–3; crit. from a theoretical perspective, Pawlik, *ZIS*, 1 (2006), 274, 285–6.

[95] See e.g. Art. 16 (2) cl. 1 German Constitution (GG) stating that: 'No German may be extradited to a foreign country'. (Translation in Tomuschat and Currie, *Basic Law for the Federal Republic of Germany* (2020), p. 23.)

[96] cf. Cassese et al., *ICL* (2013), pp. 276, 307; Bantekas, *ICL* (2010), pp. 338 ff.; Currie and Rikhof, *I&TCL* (2020), pp. 69–70; Satzger, *ICL* (2018), § 4 mn. 15; Satzger, *Internationales Strafrecht* (2022), § 4 mn. 8; Jeßberger, *Geltungsbereich* (2011), pp. 243–4; see also Pocar and Maystre, in Bergsmo, *Complementarity* (2010), pp. 251–2; Švedas, in Böse, Meyer, and Schneider, *Conflicts of Jurisdiction I* (2013), p. 303.

[97] Extradition to EU Member States and to international courts to which Germany is a party are permitted, cf. Art. 16 (2) cl. 2 German Constitution (GG).

[98] Von Weber, *DStR*, (1940), 186; Doehring, *Völkerrecht* (2004), mn. 814; Schröder, *JZ*, 23 (1968), 241; crit. Jescheck, *IRuD*, 1 (1956), 83 ff.; Vogler, in Schroeder and Zipf, *FS Maurach* (1972), pp. 597 ff.; Oehler, *Internationales Strafrecht* (1983), mn. 139; Werle and Jeßberger, 'Vorbemerkungen §§ 3 ff.', in Cirener et al., *Leipziger Kommentar StGB I* (2020), mn. 253; Böse and Meyer, *ZIS*, 6 (2011), 342; Chatzinikolaou et al., in Böse, Meyer, and Schneider, *Conflicts of Jurisdiction I* (2013), p. 204; see also Pocar and Maystre, in Bergsmo, *Complementarity* (2010), p. 251.

the image of authoritarian State.[99] This all becomes even more unacceptable if the principle of active personality constitutes—as unfortunately happened during the Nazi regime[100]—the standard rule.[101]

*(ii) Limited active personality principle*

A limited or restricted version of the principle of active personality is in line with international law. For in this case the home State only prosecutes the extraterritorial conduct if it is also punishable in the respective foreign jurisdiction (double criminality requirement) and thus shows its respect for the legal system of the territorial State.[102] The active personality principle may also be combined with another principle of jurisdiction, such as the protective principle;[103] in this case, the actual limitation of jurisdiction is often brought about by the principle of active personality itself since the legal interests protected do not contain further limitations.

The limited active personality principle finds support, apart from the nationality allegiance to the offender's home State, in the idea of international solidarity, given that the prosecuting home State protects foreign legal interests against violation by its own nationals and thereby relieves the criminal justice system of the respective foreign territorial State.[104]

*(iii) Domicile or residence principle*

While in most cases the nationality of the offender serves as the jurisdictional link under the personality principle, in some cases the place of residence is also used. This turns the personality principle[105] into the so-called domicile principle.[106] There are two options: a State may

[99] Crit. also Council of Europe, *Extraterritorial Criminal Jurisdiction* (1990), pp. 27–8; Jescheck, *IRuD*, 1 (1956), 80 ff.; Caeiro, *KritV*, 4 (2010), 378; Böse, in Zöller et al., *Gesamte Strafrechtswissenschaft* (2013), pp. 1322–3 (stressing that within the EU the active personality principle can conflict with the right to free movement); for a different view, Jeßberger, *Geltungsbereich* (2011), p. 247 (arguing that the absolute active personality principle is permissible under international law); for a comparative overview of the different national provisions, cf. Sinn, in Sinn, *Jurisdiktionskonflikte* (2012), p. 547. In France, for instance, there is no double criminality requirement for some offences, see Lelieur, in Böse, Meyer, and Schneider, *Conflicts of Jurisdiction I* (2013), p. 118.

[100] Through the so-called '*NS-Geltungsbereichsverordnung*' of 6 May 1940 (RGBl. 1940 p. 754). On the §§ 3 ff. RStGB, see Mayer, *Ne-bis-in-idem-Wirkung europäischer Strafentscheidungen* (1992), pp. 24 ff.; Jeßberger, *Geltungsbereich* (2011), pp. 58 ff.; see also German Federal Court [BGH], *NJW*, 19 (1951), 769.

[101] Mayer, *JZ*, 7 (1952), 609 ff.; Rosswog, *Vereinbarkeit* (1965), pp. 173 ff. (175); Eser and Weißer, 'Vorbemerkungen §§ 3–9', in Schönke and Schröder, *Strafgesetzbuch* (2019), mn. 20; Böse, 'Vor §§ 3–7', in Kindhäuser et al., *NK I* (23), mn. 18.

[102] See also Gropp, in Sinn, *Jurisdiktionskonflikte* (2012), p. 47; Frände and Helenius, in Böse, Meyer, and Schneider, *Conflicts of Jurisdiction I* (2013), p. 74; Chatzinikolaou et al., in Böse, Meyer, and Schneider, *Conflicts of Jurisdiction I* (2013), p. 205. For a different view, see Hoyer, 'Vorbemerkungen §§3–7', in Wolter et al., *Systematischer Kommentar StGB I* (2017), 1 mn. 24, who does not pay enough respect to the international legal framework however. But see also ALI, *Restatement* (2018), p. 204: 'Some states condition active-personality jurisdiction on dual criminality, i.e., they require that the conduct was illegal in the state of nationality or residence and in the state in which the conduct took place. These limitations appear to be motivated by international comity rather that required under international law.'

[103] cf. Hoyer, 'Vorbemerkungen §§3–7', in Wolter et al., *Systematischer Kommentar StGB* (2017), mn. 22; similarly, Schmitz, *Das aktive Personalitätsprinzip* (2002), pp. 270 ff.

[104] Oehler, *Internationales Strafrecht* (1983), mn. 733 ff., 775 ff.; Vogler, in Oehler et al., *Aktuelle Probleme* (1970), p. 157; Werle and Jeßberger, 'Vorbemerkungen §§ 3 ff.', in Cirener, *Leipziger Kommentar StGB I* (2020), mn. 254; Satzger, *ICL* (2018), § 4 mn. 15; Satzger, *Internationales Strafrecht* (2022), § 4 mn. 8; crit. Irarrázavel Zaldívar, *Grundlagen des Strafanwendungsrechts* (2024), pp. 78 ff. For Böse and Meyer, *ZIS*, 6 (2011), 342 the active personality principle is not necessary in such a situation since nationals committing offences abroad could be prosecuted by their home State on the basis of the principle of representation.

[105] Werle and Jeßberger, 'Vorbemerkungen §§ 3 ff.', in Cirener, *Leipziger Kommentar StGB I* (2020), mn. 273; *contra* Oehler, *Internationales Strafrecht* (1983), mn. 137, who regards it as part of a principle of distribution of competence, which he rejects.

[106] cf. CoE, *Extraterritorial Criminal Jurisdiction* (1990), p. 11; Zieher, *Internationale Strafrecht* (1997), pp. 86 ff.; Jennings and Watts, *Oppenheim's International Law I* (1992), p. 469; Meng, *AVR*, 27 (1989), 185; crit. *Harvard Draft Convention* (1935), pp. 533 ff.; from a comparative perspective, Swart, in Cassese and Delmas-Marty,

use the offender's residence as an alternative jurisdictional link replacing the nationality requirement[107] or it may be used as an additional factor, that is, both nationality and residence are cumulatively required. While this approach is fully in line with international law since it operates as a further restriction of nationality,[108] the former approach represents an expansion of the principle of active personality (allowing for mere residence as a sufficient link) and thus generates a certain conflict with the principle of non-interference as explained above. In any case, the fact that mere residence serves as a jurisdictional link in several international instruments[109] speaks in favour of such a broader approach notwithstanding certain sovereignty concerns.

*(iv) Seat principle*

The seat principle connects to the legal place or seat of a legal person, for whose benefit or in whose name crimes are committed. Criminal jurisdiction is bestowed upon the seat State. This principle appears in some regional instruments.[110] Although the criminal responsibility of legal persons has not yet been recognized in all countries,[111] and thus legal persons are not subject to criminal prosecution on a universal scale pursuant to the active personality principle, the seat principle is, in essence, a form of the active personality principle, given that the 'active personality' of the legal person is the decisive factor determining the criminal jurisdiction.

*(c) The protective principle: Substantial State interests and passive personality*

According to the protective principle, the domestic criminal jurisdiction extends over crimes that harm or endanger national interests, regardless of where or by whom the respective crimes were committed. In practice, the principle mainly covers foreigners committing crimes abroad that affect domestic interests.[112] The principle allows for two forms of

*Juridictions nationales* (2002), pp. 573 ff.; from a European criminal law perspective, see Klip, *European Criminal Law* (2021), pp. 263–4.

[107] That is the case, for instance, in Lithuanian law, Švedas, in Böse, Meyer, and Schneider, *Conflicts of Jurisdiction I* (2013), p. 303; for an overview from a comparative view perspective, see Böse, Meyer, and Schneider, in Böse, Meyer, and Schneider, *Conflicts of Jurisdiction I* (2013), p. 416.

[108] See also Jeßberger, *Geltungsbereich* (2011), p. 251, arguing that a modern law for national prosecution of extraterritorial offences should apply the domicile principle.

[109] cf. UN GA, 'International Convention against the Taking of Hostages' (17 December 1979), Art. 5 (1)(b); UN GA, 'International Convention for the Suppression of Terrorist Bombings' (15 December 1997), Art. 6 (2)(c); UN GA, 'International Convention for the Suppression of Financing of Terrorism' (9 December 1999), Art. 7 (2)(d); UN GA, 'International Convention for the Suppression of Acts of Nuclear Terrorism' (13 April 2005), Art. 9 (2)(c); UN GA, 'Convention against Corruption' (31 October 2003), Art. 42 (2)(b); UN GA. 'Convention against Transnational Organized Crime (UNTOC)' (15 November 2000), Art. 15 (2)(b); UN GA, 'Optional Protocol to the Convention on the Rights of the Child on the Sale of Children, Child Prostitution and Child Pornography' (25 May 2000), *UNTS* 2171, 227, Art. 4 (2)(a). For regional instruments, see Council of Europe, 'Convention on Preventing and Combating Violence against Women and Domestic Violence' CETS No. 210 (Istanbul, 11 May 2011), Art. 44; Council Framework Decision on Combating Terrorism (13 June 2002) (2002/475/JHA), Art. 9 (1)(c); European Parliament and Council, Directive 2011/92/EU on Combating the Sexual Abuse and Sexual Exploitation of Children and Child Pornography (13 December 2011), Art. 17 (2)(c) (optional).

[110] See e.g. CFD on Combating Terrorism (2002/475/JHA), Art. 9 (1)(d); EU Council Framework Decision on the Fight against Organised Crime (24 October 2008) (2008/841/JHA), Art. 7 (1)(c). See also the last 2023 Draft of a 'Legally Binding Instrument to Regulate, in International Human Rights Law, the Activities of Transnational Corporations and other Business Enterprises', HRC, Open-ended Intergovernmental Working Group (OEIGWG), No Doc. No, July 2023, Art. 9 (1)(c)(i) and 9 (2) (referring to where a legal person is 'domiciled').

[111] Germany is a notable exception, dealing with this issue on the level of administrative sanctions (cf. s. 130a of the Act on Regulatory Offences [OWiG]).

[112] On the *raison d'être* and a historical overview of the principle, see Cameron, *Protective Principle* (1994), pp. 31 ff.

protection: the protection of the State (protective principle in the strict sense/*stricto sensu*), and the protection of individuals (passive personality principle).[113]

*(i) Protective principle* stricto sensu

The protective principle allowing for the protection of State interests is recognized under international law and widely used in domestic legal systems.[114] It is essentially based on the correct assumption that every State should have the right to act on attacks on its political or military integrity, especially since the State in which the crime was committed may not be able or willing to prosecute the respective crimes.[115] Indeed, it would lead to absurd consequences to require the approval of the territorial State.[116] Thus, on this assumption, West Germany, for instance, would have had to enter into an agreement with the (former) GDR allowing it to prosecute the GDR agents spying on West German territory.[117]

There is no double criminality requirement since the perpetrator herself creates a link to the affected State through her attack and this attack gives the State—similar to a 'self-defence' situation—the right to protect itself.[118] Nevertheless, this State should not be allowed, in light of the sovereignty of the territorial State, to abuse this 'right to self-defence' to extend its criminal jurisdiction extraterritorially in order to protect just any, even minor, domestic interest.[119] It may only protect itself against those attacks which clearly harm or endanger its existence or security, for instance, the commission of espionage and treason.[120] Following Jeßberger the scope of the protective principle should be determined in light of its purpose, taking into account three criteria: (i) the respective act must be directed against an important (own) interest of the protected State, which is normally not protected by other States; (ii) it must be immediately directed against this interest; and (iii) the harm of this interest should

[113] From a theoretical perspective, see Pawlik, *ZIS*, 1 (2006), 274, 287 ff. For Cameron, *Protective Principle* (1994), pp. 76 ff., passive personality and protective principles, albeit closely related, are distinct from each other.

[114] cf. Gilbert, *BYbIL*, 63 (1992), 419; Hirst, *Jurisdiction* (2003), p. 18; Kindt, *Menschenrechte* (2009), p. 78; Bantekas, *ICL* (2010), p. 342; Ambos, 'Vorbemerkung § 3', in von Heintschel-Heinegg, *MüKo I* (2020), mn. 36; Oxman, in Wolfrum and Peters, *MPEPIL VI* (2007), pp. 550–1; O'Keefe, *ICL* (2015), p. 12; Currie and Rikhof, *I&TCL* (2020), p. 73; Irarrázavel Zaldívar, *Grundlagen des Strafanwendungsrechts* (2024), p. 100; for a comparative law perspective, see Satzger, *ICL* (2018), § 4 mn. 23–5; Cameron, *Protective Principle* (1994), pp. 96 ff. (Sweden), 164 ff. (Denmark), 180 ff. (Norway), 210 ff. (US); from a European law perspective, see Klip, *European Criminal Law* (2021), pp. 264–5; on Belgium's legal system, see David, *Éléments* (2009), mn. 3.3.2. ff.; furthermore, see ALI, *Restatement* (2018), pp. 209–10.

[115] On the suppression of the protective principle within the EU, with a simultaneous horizontal extension of the assimilation principle (Member States' obligation to protect the legal interests of other Member States as their own), see Böse and Meyer, *ZIS*, 6 (2011), 343.

[116] For a more restrictive view, however, rejecting any such principle of protection, PCIJ, *Lotus*, Judgment (1927), Dissenting Opinion of Judge Finlay, pp. 55 ff.; crit. also Currie and Rikhof, *I&TCL* (2020), p. 73 ('problem with the protective principle is the potential for its abuse').

[117] cf. BVerfG 92, 277 (319), where it was stated that the State responsible for creating and supporting a secret service cannot prosecute its employees and agents for their work connected to this job.

[118] cf. again BVerfG 92, 277 (317 ff.) where it was stated that 'quite apart from the fact that in the time frame the alleged crimes were committed the Federal Republic of Germany was particularly subjected to operations of opposing secret services … it is, considering the transnational structures of modern secret services and their spying operations that circumvent all affairs of other States, generally *justified* to *protect* the *safety* of one's own State in a comprehensive form against *foreign operations* of alien secret services by means of criminal law' (author's translation; emphasis added); see also Jeßberger, *Geltungsbereich* (2011), pp. 253 ff.

[119] See e.g. Bantekas, *ICL* (2010), p. 344 ('significant national interests'); more broadly, however, Eser and Weißer, 'Vorbemerkungen §§ 3–9', in Schönke and Schröder, *Strafgesetzbuch* (2019), mn. 21.

[120] On these classical and other examples, see Gilbert, *BYbIL*, 63 (1992), 420–2; Bantekas, *ICL* (2010), pp. 342–4; Cameron, *Protective Principle* (1994), p. 46 (but giving less relevance to the idea of self-defence); crit. Irarrázavel Zaldívar, *Grundlagen des Strafanwendungsrechts* (2024), pp. 103 ff. (discussing 'vital' interests and pointing to abuses, esp. with regard to jurisdiction over drug offences).

be the 'primary effect' of the act.[121] Otherwise, the ensuing exception from the principles of non-interference and territorial jurisdiction cannot be justified.[122]

*(ii) Passive personality principle*

According to this principle, the home State's criminal jurisdiction is extended to crimes committed abroad by foreign nationals against its own nationals,[123] excluding thereby implicitly harm caused to other nationals in the same factual circumstances).[124] From a principled perspective, the extension of penal power in these cases is to be viewed critically, because the main goal here is not the protection of the State itself, as in the case of the protective principle *stricto sensu*, but 'only' of its nationals. In other words, here the State's interest in prosecution is weaker than in the case of existential threats against this same State. Further, the necessary link between the home country (claiming criminal jurisdiction) and the foreign territory is only established through the attack on one of that State's citizens. Thus, contrary to the situation of active personality, the necessary connection does not yet exist before the offence is committed. Instead, the victim's home State extends its penal power over foreign perpetrators who, in most cases, are not even aware of the fact that the victim of their attack is a foreigner and they could therefore be subjected to the criminal jurisdiction of that person's home State, that is, a State whose legal system is alien to them.

The ensuing conflict with the principle of culpability can only be resolved by requiring the double criminality of the respective conduct.[125] If this conduct is punishable in both jurisdictions, the offender cannot claim to have been subjected to a foreign penal power without their consent, for the conduct would have been prosecuted by the territorial State

[121] Jeßberger, *Geltungsbereich* (2011), p. 257; in a similar vein, Böse, 'Vor §§ 3-7', in Kindhäuser et al., *NKI* (23), mn. 19.

[122] Cameron, *Protective Principle* (1994), pp. 358 ff.

[123] Eser and Weißer, 'Vorbemerkungen §§ 3–9', in Schönke and Schröder, *Strafgesetzbuch* (2019), mn. 22; crit. Satzger, *ICL* (2018), § 4 mn. 26; Böse and Meyer, *ZIS*, 6 (2011), 341; Gropp, in Sinn, *Jurisdiktionskonflikte* (2012), p. 48; Meyer, in Böse, Meyer, and Schneider, *Conflicts of Jurisdiction I* (2013), p. 156; favouring a general international recognition of the principle, O'Keefe, *JICJ*, 2 (2004), 739; O'Keefe, *ICL* (2015), p. 13; Böse, 'Vorbemerkungen § 3', in Kindhäuser, Neumann, and Paeffgen, *NK I* (2023), mn. 20; Jeßberger, Kaleck, and Schueller, in Bergsmo, *Complementarity* (2010), p. 235; Jeßberger, *Geltungsbereich* (2011), p. 260; Pocar and Maystre, in Bergsmo, *Complementarity* (2010), p. 252; similarly Lee, in May and Hoskins, *ICL* (2010), p. 17; Mills, *BYbIL*, 84 (2014), 198–9; *contra* Marauhn and Simon, in Sinn, *Jurisdiktionskonflikte* (2012), p. 31; for a nuanced view, see Cryer, in Cryer et al., *ICL* (2019), pp. 55–6 (accepting its unlimited application in the cases of war crimes); in a similar vein, Bantekas, *ICL* (2010), pp. 340–1 (considering the principle only 'reasonable' if it operates as an 'auxiliary' form of criminal jurisdiction if the territorial State is unable or unwilling to prosecute); crit. also Irarrázavel Zaldívar, *Grundlagen des Strafanwendungsrechts* (2024), pp. 93 ff.; for the position at the beginning of the twentieth century rejecting criminal jurisdiction for the protection of nationals abroad out of hand, see PCIJ, *Lotus*, Judgment (1927), Dissenting Opinion of Judge Finlay, pp. 55 ff; from a comparative law perspective, Satzger, *ICL* (2018), § 4 mn. 27–9; Sinn, in Sinn, *Jurisdiktionskonflikte* (2012), pp. 534–5; Böse, Meyer, and Schneider, in Böse, Meyer, and Schneider, *Conflicts of Jurisdiction I* (2013), p. 418; on the traditionally limited recognition of the protective principle in the common law legal systems, see Hirst, in Böse, Meyer, and Schneider, *Conflicts of Jurisdiction I* (2013), p. 45.

[124] Convincing Yanev, *NILR*, 68 (2021), 169–70 criticizing, on the one hand, the prosecution's claim in the Dutch MH-17 trial to possess jurisdiction over the murder of non-Dutch passengers ('murder of all passengers', Opening Statement of 9 March 2020, <https://www.prosecutionservice.nl/topics/mh17-plane-crash/prosecution-and-trial/court-sessions-march-2020/opening-statement-9-march-2020>. On the other hand, Yanev argues that 'one can reasonably argue that the crime of "intentionally causing an aircraft to crash" is subject to Dutch passive personality jurisdiction because the conduct prescribed in this particular crime resulted in the victimization of Dutch citizens'.

[125] In this vein, Oehler, *Internationales Strafrecht* (1983), mn. 127 ff., mn. 666 ff.; Plutte, *Prüfung ausländischen Strafrechts* (1982), pp. 41 ff., 51; Satzger, *ICL* (2018), § 4 mn. 26; Gropp, in Sinn, *Jurisdiktionskonflikte* (2012), p. 48; cf. also Böse, 'Vor §§ 3-7' in Kindhäuser et al., *NK I* (2023), mn. 20; Böse and Meyer, *ZIS*, 6 (2011), 341; Chatzinikolaou et al., in Böse, Meyer, and Schneider, *Conflicts of Jurisdiction I* (2013), p. 212; diff. Werle and Jeßberger, 'Vorbemerkungen §§ 3 ff.', in Cirener, *Leipziger Kommentar StGB I* (2020), mn. 249.

(i.e. the offender's State) too. If the offender was mistaken about the victim's nationality and thus about the applicability of the foreign criminal law regime, this mistake would, in any case, be irrelevant since the respective conduct would also be punishable under the law of the territorial State (i.e. the offender's home State).[126]

While the double criminality requirement may satisfy the principle of culpability, and thus resolve the rights concerns, this requirement does not change the fact that the victim's home State interferes in the sovereign and exclusive exercise of criminal jurisdiction of the territorial State, by claiming to subject its nationals (i.e. the offenders) to alien criminal laws.[127] In fact, the passive personality principle does not only show distrust in the respective foreign criminal justice system,[128] but also generates jurisdictional conflicts instead of avoiding them. Of course, the ensuing interference in the criminal justice matters of the territorial State[129] is at least mitigated by the fact that its criminal law is accepted as a (primary) basis for prosecution and not simply ignored, as would be the case with an *absolute* passive personality principle setting aside the double criminality requirement. Clearly, from an international law perspective, the recognition of the criminal *lex loci* is necessary out of legal and political reasons; an absolute passive personality principle would contravene international law.[130]

The passive personality principle may—as the active personality principle—be linked to the domicile principle. Using both principles alternatively, the penal power would be extended; requiring them cumulatively, it would be limited.

State protection by way of the protective principle *stricto sensu* and protection of nationals by way of the passive personality principle are sometimes mixed up. Take the example of the home State's penal jurisdiction when crimes are committed against its diplomats. Jurisdiction in this case may be justified with both the protection of the State and protection of its nationals, for diplomats wear both hats, as representatives and as nationals of their State. Thus, one may speak of a double link to the diplomats' home State, displacing the principle of non-interference.

### *(d) Principle of universal jurisdiction*

#### *(1) Foundations*

The principle of universal jurisdiction (universality principle)[131] *allows*[132] for a global prosecution of extraterritorial crimes, irrespective of their place of commission or of the

[126] For an in-depth analysis, see Jeßberger, *Geltungsbereich* (2011), pp. 154 ff.

[127] Expressing concerns from an European law perspective, Böse, in Zöller et al., *Gesamte Strafrechtswissenschaft* (2013), p. 1322 (arguing that the application of this principle by an EU Member State violates the prohibition of discrimination given that the application of its criminal law depends upon the nationality of the victim); in a similar vein, Böse and Meyer, *ZIS*, 6 (2011), 342.

[128] Thereon, see also Pocar and Maystre, in Bergsmo, *Complementarity* (2010), p. 252; Irarrázavel Zaldívar, *Grundlagen des Strafanwendungsrechts* (2024), pp. 93 ff.

[129] Crit. Safferling, *Internationales Strafrecht* (2011), § 3 mn. 41.

[130] cf. Wendt, *Das passive Personalitätsprinzip* (1965), pp. 7 ff., 44 ff.; Rosswog, *Vereinbarkeit* (1965), pp. 179 ff. (181, 184), 190; Satzger, *ICL* (2018), § 4 mn. 26; very crit. Gilbert, *BYbIL*, 63 (1992), 418–19; for a different view, cf. Jeßberger, *Geltungsbereich* (2011), p. 263.

[131] For the historical and theoretical background, see Henzelin, *Le principe* (2000), pp. 33 ff.; Behrendt, *Verfolgung* (2005), pp. 54 ff.; Donnedieu de-Vabres, *JICJ*, 9 (2011), 906 ff.

[132] It is a right (entitlement), not a duty (obligation); cf. Cryer, *Prosecuting* (2005), pp. 87, 89, 101 ff. (109); Fleck, *JICJ*, 7 (2009), 851 ff.; Bantekas, *ICL* (2010), pp. 348–9. Mégret, in Stahn and El Zeidy, *Complementarity I* (2011), p. 370 ('option'); Oxman, in Wolfrum and Peters, *MPEPIL VI* (2007), p. 553; Einarsen, *Universal Crimes* (2012), p. 65. However, favouring a duty to prosecute in cases of genocide, Ben-Naftali and Sharon, *JICJ*, 5 (2007), 859, 864 ff.; *contra* ICJ, *Application of the Convention on the Prevention and Punishment of the Crime of Genocide (Bosnia and Herzegovina v. Serbia and Montenegro)*, Judgment (26 February 2007), ICJ Reports 2007 43, para. 442; for a nuanced view, see also Pocar and Maystre, in Bergsmo, *Complementarity* (2010), p. 262 ('principle of universal jurisdiction empowers—or requires in certain cases'); from a comparative law perspective, see Satzger,

offender's or victim's nationality.[133] The prosecuting State does not exercise universal jurisdiction in representation of the territorial State but executes its own distinct penal power representing the universal interests to be protected by universal jurisdiction. Thus, the principle, while 'still afflicted with the *haut gout* of interfering in foreign affairs',[134] is substantially different from traditional genuine links, given that the prosecuting State is not acting in its own interest, but as a representative of the international community as a whole.[135]

The universality principle can be justified either by pragmatic or by normative (value-based) considerations.[136] Under the former justification, a State prosecutes a crime pursuant to the universality principle in order to defend the common security interests of all States.[137] A typical example would be the prosecution of piracy, arguably the oldest crime of universal jurisdiction.[138] Here the prosecuting State helps to fill the jurisdictional gap which exists on

*ICL* (2018), § 4 mn. 33–9. On the duty to prosecute based on the grave breaches system of the GC, see Stewart, *JICJ*, 7 (2009), 870, 874 ff.; Henckaerts, *JICJ*, 7 (2009), 698–9; in a similar vein, based on *aut dedere aut iudicare*, but correctly stressing that there is 'no duty to establish universal jurisdiction', Zahar and Sluiter, *ICL* (2008), pp. 496, 498. On the different nature of *aut dedere aut iudicare*, see next sub-section (e) in this chapter.

[133] cf. O'Keefe, *JICJ*, 2 (2004), 745; O'Keefe, *ICL* (2015), p. 17; Currie and Rikhof, *I&TCL* (2020), pp. 74–5; Behrendt, *Verfolgung* (2005), p. 53; Bantekas, *ICL* (2010), p. 344; also Ambos, '§ 1 VStGB', in Safferling, *MüKo IX* (2022), mn. 5. For an overview of the discussions and the resolutions adopted at the 2009 ADIP's XVIII Congress of International Law in Istanbul, see Petrig, *ZStW*, 122 (2010), 468 ff., and AIDP, *ZStW*, 122 (2010), 488–91. From a European criminal law perspective, see Klip, *European Criminal Law* (2021), p. 265; for the universality principle in civil litigation based on the US-Alien Tort Claims Act, see Nolte, in Tomuschat and Thouvenin, *Fundamental Rules* (2006), pp. 373 ff.; crit. of the universality principle in the light of the theories of punishment, Pawlik, *ZIS*, 1 (2006), 274, 289 ff.

[134] Weigend, in Kohlmann et al., *Entwicklungen und Probleme des Strafrechts* (2004), p. 14 (own translation); also see Rosen, *JICJ*, 19 (2021), 1075–7. Crit. Langer, *AJIL*, 105 (2011), 1, arguing that the universality principle can be applied only against the so-called '*low-cost defendants*', against whom the criminal proceedings will not have any political cost (deterioration of diplomatic relations); in a similar vein, Ferstman and Schurr, in Letschert et al., *Victimological Approaches to International Crimes* (2011), pp. 456 ff.; Stephen, *ICLQ*, 61 (2012), 87; Zhou, in Bergsmo and Ling, *State Sovereignty* (2012), pp. 36–7; see also Kaleck, *APuZ*, 25/26 (2013), 40; *contra* van der Wilt, *JICJ*, 9 (2011), 1043; Chehtman, *Foundations* (2010), pp. 136 ff.; Weißer, *GA*, 152 (2012), 426; Weißer, in Jeßberger and Geneuss, *Zehn Jahre VStGB* (2013), p. 69 (correctly affirming that the cause of the problem is not the universality principle itself, but the selectivity of the national prosecution of international crimes in some otherwise well-functioning legal systems); in a similar vein, Pocar and Maystre, in Bergsmo, *Complementarity* (2010), p. 302.

[135] Jennings and Watts, *Oppenheim's International Law I* (1992), p. 468 n. 13; Scharf, *LCP*, 64 (2001), 76, 115; Joyner, *LCP*, 64 (2001), 165; Vogler, in Schroeder and Zipf, *FS Maurach* (1972), pp. 603 ff.; Doehring, *Völkerrecht* (2004), mn. 819. Weigend, in Kohlmann et al., *Entwicklungen und Probleme des Strafrechts* (2004), p. 14; García Arán, in García Arán and López Garrido, *Crímen internacional* (2000), pp. 66 ff.; Bassiouni, *VirgJIL*, 42 (2001), 82, (88, 96); Boister, *EJIL*, 14 (2003), 963; Rodrigues, in Faculdade de Direito da Universidade de Coimbra and Goethe-Institut Lisboa, *Direito penal internacional* (2003), p. 72; Burchards, *Verfolgung* (2005), pp. 24 ff.; Cryer, *Prosecuting* (2005), p. 84; Arbour, in Dolgopol and Gardam, *Challenge of Conflict* (2006), p. 313; Grant, in Kolb and Scalia, *DIP* (2012), pp. 593–4; Hernández, *IL* (2021), p. 208 ('irrespective of the nationality of the individuals, the nationality of the victims, or the place of the commission of the crime'); also AI, *Universal Jurisdiction* (2001), Introduction, pp. 28 ff. and ch. I, pp. 3 ff.

[136] For a similar twofold justification, see Bantekas, *ICL* (2010), p. 345 ('repugnant nature and scale of the conduct', e.g. crimes against humanity, and 'as a result of the inadequacy of domestic law and enforcement', e.g. in case of piracy); also Irarrázavel Zaldívar, *Grundlagen des Strafanwendungsrechts* (2024), p. 122. Hovell, *EJIL*, 29 (2018), 438 ff. identifies three main rationales for universal jurisdiction and ultimately argues that 'universal jurisdiction is best understood as being based in an individual's right of access to justice for victims of serious international crimes' (455). Yet, this does not go beyond the legal-interest-oriented approach advocated here (see below main text at note 140 ff.) for Hovell's approach entails the question of which 'serious international crimes' are qualifying for universal jurisdiction and which are not (see below main text at note 150 ff.).

[137] See also Garrod, *ICLR*, 12 (2012), 807–8 (advocating on this basis the prosecution of international crimes pursuant to the protective principle); Garrod, *HarvILJ*, 59 (2018), 132.

[138] For a detailed analysis of piracy, see Ambos, *Treatise ICL II* (2022), pp. 274 ff.; Ambos and Timmermann, in Safferling and Kirsch, *Völkerstrafrechtspolitik* (2014), pp. 30 ff.; also Kolb, Neumann, and Salomon, *ZaöRV*, 71 (2011), 211 ff.; O'Keefe, *ICL* (2015), pp. 17–21; Currie and Rikhof, *I&TCL* (2020), pp. 75–6; Hernández, *IL* (2021), p. 208 ('justification ... is not so much that piracy is inherently heinous, but due to the pragmatic fact that pirates operate on the open seas'); in the same vein, Bazuaye and Fenemigho, *Afr. J. Int. Comp. Law* 26 (2018),

the high seas and acts in the security interest of all States given that all States benefit from safe passage on the high seas for trade and other civilian purposes.[139]

From a normative perspective, a State prosecutes a certain crime because it harms *universally recognized legal interests* and thus interferes with the underlying values. Such a crime does not only concern the States in any way linked to it—by way of their territory, nationals, or substantial State interests—but the international community or even humanity as a whole since it constitutes an assault on their foundational moral values. This is especially recognized in the case of universally protected, fundamental human rights because these belong to all human beings and are entitlements *erga omnes*.[140] Thus, their violation affects, from a normative perspective, the interests of all States.[141] In other words, a so-understood normative concept of universal jurisdiction conceives the universal and transnational prosecution of international core crimes as the defence of universal values common to all mankind and part of *ius cogens*.[142] Such a normative foundation of universal jurisdiction may also be based on the (human) right of access to justice, which entails a right to universal jurisdiction as a form of individual sovereignty.[143] Last but not least, it also finds support in a normative theory of the supranational *ius puniendi* defended elsewhere.[144] In any case, irrespective of the justification of the universality principle applied, it is clear that the prosecuting State does not only act in its own interest, but on behalf of the entire international community and the world citizens represented by it.[145]

549; furthermore, see Hovell, *EJIL*, 29 (2018), 441–2; Irarrázavel Zaldívar, *Grundlagen des Strafanwendungsrechts* (2024), pp. 125–6. On the national practice, see Gardner, *JICJ*, 10 (2012), 797; from a German perspective, see Ladiges, *NZWehrr*, 52 (2012), 56; Brandt, in Safferling and Kirsch, *Völkerstrafrechtspolitik* (2014), pp. 279 ff.; Heinecke, in Strafverteidigervereinigungen, *Alternativen zur Freiheitsstrafe* (2013), pp. 151 ff.

[139] Kontorovich argues (*NotreDameLR*, 94 (2019), 1424 ff., 1431 ff.), from a factual perspective, that in the majority of universal jurisdiction cases the respective States had an own interest in criminal prosecution or could, in the historical and recent piracy procceedings, have claimed a genuine link other than universality, albeit difficult to be proven in some cases (1431 ff.).

[140] Duties *erga omnes*, especially if derived from *ius cogens* norms, do not only apply transnationally, but also to the international community itself; cf. ICJ, *Barcelona Traction*, Judgment (1970), para. 33; see also Ambos, '§ 1 VStGB', in Safferling, *MüKo IX* (2022), mn. 5 with n. 28.

[141] cf. Doehring, *Völkerrecht* (2004), mn. 94; Bungenberg, *AVR*, 39 (2001), 191; Broomhall, *NELR*, 35 (2001), 401 ff.; Joyner, *LCP*, 64 (2001), 969; García Arán, in García Arán and López Garrido, *Crímen internacional* (2000), pp. 69 ff.; Boister, *EJIL*, 14 (2003), 969; Zappalà, in Cassese, Chiavario, and De Francesco, *Problemi* (2005), pp. 555 ff.; Cosnard, in Tomuschat and Thouvenin, *Fundamental Rules* (2006), pp. 355 ff.; Zimmermann, in Tomuschat and Thouvenin, *Fundamental Rules* (2006), pp. 337 ff.; Cryer, *Prosecuting* (2005), pp. 86 ff.; Cryer, in Cryer et al., *ICL* (2019), p. 66; Currie and Rikhof, *I&TCL* (2020), p. 76; Bazuaye and Fenemigho, *Afr. J. Int. Comp. Law*, 26 (2018), 551–2 ('affront to all states'); from a human rights perspective, see Neubacher, *Grundlagen* (2005), pp. 100 ff., 111. On the legitimacy of universal jurisdiction also with regard to the accused, see also Merkel, in Jeßberger and Geneuss, *Zehn Jahre VStGB* (2013), pp. 55–6; crit. because the 'common interests of mankind' can be 'neither clearly defined' as to what they include, 'nor [is it] established who is qualified to represent all of mankind in exercising jurisdiction', Zhou, in Bergsmo and Ling, *State Sovereignty* (2012), p. 42. See also, for a legitimacy concept focusing on the 'principles of the participation of, and accountability to, the international community', Langer, *JICJ*, 11 (2013), 762 ff.; Langer, in Jeßberger and Geneuss, *Zehn Jahre VStGB* (2013), pp. 253 ff.

[142] cf. Bantekas, *ICL* (2010), p. 346.

[143] In a similar vein, Mills, *BYbIL*, 84 (2014), 219 ff. (arguing in favour of a right to universal civil jurisdiction in case of serious human rights violations as a consequence of the right to access to justice expressing a form of individual sovereignty); more recently Hovell, *EJIL*, 29 (2018), 438 ff. (455) as quoted above note 136.

[144] cf. Ambos, *OJLS*, 33 (2013), 293; summarizing Ambos, *Treatise ICL I* (2021), pp. 99 ff. For a justification of an (extraterritorial) ius puniendi pursuant to a close, substantive connection between the State (claiming jurisdiction) and the person (suspect), Irarrázavel Zaldívar, *Grundlagen des Strafanwendungsrechts* (2024), pp. 147 ff. (relying on the theory of a criminal law of the citizen, *Bürgerstrafrecht*).

[145] Cameron, *Protective Principle* (1994), pp. 81 ff.; Merkel, in Lüddersen, *Aufgeklärte Kriminalpolitik III* (1998), p. 252; Eser, in Eser et al., *Strafverfahrensrecht* (2001), p. 17; Benavides, *AMDI*, 1 (2001), 29; Kreß, *ZStW*, 114 (2002), 837; Rau, *HuV-I*, 16 (2003), 214; Hall, in Lattimer and Sands, *Justice for Crimes against Humanity* (2003), p. 56; Weigend, in Kohlmann et al., *Entwicklungen und Probleme des Strafrechts* (2004), p. 14; Randall, *AJIL*, 98 (2004), 627; Cryer, *Prosecuting* (2005), p. 85; Kreß, *ZIS*, 2 (2007), 517; Zahar and Sluiter, *ICL* (2008),

Against this background, it is clear that the universality principle does not violate the principle of non-interference: the protection of human rights does not belong to a State's internal affairs but is a matter of concern for all of mankind. Affairs concerning mankind as a whole cannot be subjected to the sovereignty claims of individual nation States. Therefore, these claims, illegitimate *ab initio*, cannot be violated when a State exercises universal jurisdiction.[146] If, however, the principle of non-interference is not even touched by the exercise of universal jurisdiction, an additional domestic genuine link to justify the exercise of this jurisdiction is wholly unnecessary,[147] for a legitimate sovereign claim does not exist in the first place. Thus, in sum, no territorial State that remains passive in the face of international crimes falling under the universality principle can claim that these crimes must not be prosecuted by a third State on behalf of the international community. As a further consequence, the traditional procedural obstacles to prosecution, in particular immunities, cannot set aside the exercise of universal jurisdiction.[148]

*(ii) Scope or subject matter*

This brings us to the gist of the issue, namely the scope or subject matter of the universality principle. While it is beyond dispute that the principle exists,[149] it is far less clear which legal

p. 497; Bock, *BelgianRIL*, 43 (2010), 50–1; Hall, in Bergsmo, *Complementarity* (2010), p. 203; Langer, *JICJ*, 13 (2015), 246 ff. (distinguishing between the 'active' 'global enforcer' universal jurisdiction—States have a role 'in preventing and punishing core international crimes committed anywhere in the world'—and the 'reactive' 'no safe haven' universal jurisdiction—States exercise it 'in order not to be a refuge for participants in core international crimes').

146 Convincingly Eser, in Eser et al., *Strafverfahrensrecht* (2001), p. 19 (arguing in the context of genocide that there can absolutely be no exclusive national sovereignty for the right to life of parts of mankind); Merkel, in Jeßberger and Geneuss, *Zehn Jahre VStGB* (2013), pp. 49 ff., 52 (arguing that in cases of grave core international crimes, the State loses its legitimacy and its sovereignty as international law subject); see also Rodrigues, in Faculdade de Direito da Universidade de Coimbra and Goethe-Institut Lisboa, *Direito penal internacional* (2003), p. 62; Neubacher, *Grundlagen* (2005), pp. 126 ff.; Werle, *Völkerstrafrecht* (2012), mn. 212; Werle and Jessberger, *Principles ICL* (2020), mn. 259; Kindt, *Menschenrechte* (2009) pp. 121 ff.; Gropp, in Sinn, *Jurisdiktionskonflikte* (2012), p. 48.

147 For the same view, see *Princeton Principles* (2001), 43; AI, *Universal Jurisdiction* (2001), ch. I, pp. 14 ff. ; Scharf, *LCP*, 64 (2001), 76; Broomhall, *NELR*, 35 (2001), 400; Joyner, *LCP*, 64 (2001) 169, 171; Blanco Cordero, *La Ley*, 5980 (2004), 5; Kreicker, in Eser, Sieber, and Kreicker, *Nationale Strafverfolgung VII* (2006), pp. 252 ff.; Höpfel, in Arnold et al., *Menschengerechtes Strafrecht* (2005), p. 773; Grant, in Kolb and Scalia, *DIP* (2012), pp. 584, 592; Munivrana Vajd, *ICLR*, 10 (2010), 336 ff.; Doumit, *GeoJIL*, 52 (2020), 273–4 in this respect (finding pure universality only in Germany, Norway, and Sweden, while in France, for example, the perpetrator must be a French national/citizen or a resident of France or be at least in France). For a different view, see Gierhake, *ZStW*, 120 (2008), 397 ff.

148 cf. Mills, *BYbIL*, 84 (2014), 211–12.

149 See e.g. ALI, *Restatement* (2018), p. 211 ('well established in criminal law'; 'well accepted in theory, prosecutions based on universal criminal jurisdiction are rare in practice and often attract controversy'); Rosen, *JICJ*, 19 (2021), 1073 ('universal jurisdiction to prescribe is recognized by customary international law'). For a recent radical critique, however, see Garrod, *ICLR*, 12 (2012), 782, 797, 807, 823, 826 (advocating the abandonment of universal jurisdiction since it has no basis in customary international law and its replacement by the protective principle, but without explaining his understanding of these two principles and several misleading assumptions, e.g. regarding lacking State practice at 812 ff.); furthermore, see Garrod, *HarvILJ*, 59 (2018), 169 (yet on a flawed methodological basis stating 'that none of the states in the sample provide for universal jurisdiction in their national laws'). Crit. of Garrod's methodological approach, Langer and Eason, *EJIL*, 30 (2019), 788 with n. 22 (arguing that Garrod bases his assessment on a 'survey ... by examining a range of sources, including: U.N. General Assembly and its Sixth Committee documents evaluating universal jurisdiction; LEXIS-NEXIS and Westlaw; specialized journals; websites such as Legislationonline and The Hague Justice Portal; NGO reports, such as Amnesty International, Human Rights Watch, Redress and Trial Watch; newspaper articles and other media documents; and the Google search engine' (169 with n. 282); on that basis Garrod identified six (!) international crimes prosecutions in Germany, for example, for the period from 1961 to 2016 (170). This alone makes clear that this method does not produce a comprehensive picture of the situation in countries like Germany (169 with n. 281). Instead, using a much more refined methodology, Langer and Eason, *EJIL*, 30 (2019), 780 with n. 2, 789 identify twelve completed jurisdiction trials for Germany for the same period, two of which are from 2017. On

interests and thus crimes are covered by it.[150] This question, which has been on the agenda of the GA's Sixth Committee for well over ten years so far,[151] can be answered, methodologically, by a twofold approach: first, by formally identifying universal legal interests recognized in the sources of international law as recognized by Article 38 (1) ICJ Statute, that is, international treaties, custom, and general principles of law; secondly, in line with the normative approach explained above, by focusing on the extraordinary wrongfulness of the respective acts.

Whether or not a certain act is covered by the universality principle is not decided by the States themselves, pursuant to their *competence-competence* (*Kompetenz-Kompetenz*),[152] but by looking at the objective indicators in the relevant sources of international law. In this regard, one can differentiate between a (real, absolute, or pure) universality principle in a narrow sense and a (conditional or limited) universality principle in a broad sense; that is, one can briefly differentiate between a narrow and a broad universality principle.[153] In the first case, international treaty or customary law explicitly or absolutely allows for universal prosecution. In the second case, sometimes also called universality jurisdiction *in absentia*, the actual jurisdiction to prosecute depends on other factors, such as the suspect's presence in the territory of the prosecuting State.[154] This is typically the case in international treaties, which provide for an '*aut dedere aut iudicare*' clause and therewith oblige the State Parties to either prosecute the respective crimes themselves or extradite the suspects to another forum.

the prosecution of war crimes committed in Syria by German courts on the basis of universal jurisdiction, cf. note 163-3 below.

[150] Garrod, *HarvILJ*, 59 (2018), 132 ('types of values that may be protected by universal jurisdiction are usually left insufficiently explained'); crit. also Irarrázavel Zaldívar, *Grundlagen des Strafanwendungsrechts* (2024), pp. 125–6, 127 ff. On the distinction between generally recognized crimes (manslaughter etc.) and crimes internationally prosecutable based on the universality principle, see Fletcher, *JICJ*, 3 (2005), 24 ff.

[151] cf. UN Doc. A/63/237, 23 July 2009, p. 2 ('While the African Union fully subscribes to and supports the principle of universal jurisdiction within the context of fighting impunity as well as the need to punish perpetrators of genocide, crimes against humanity and war crimes, it is, however, concerned about its ad hoc and arbitrary application, particularly towards African leaders'); UN GA, 'The Scope and Application of the Principle of Universal Jurisdiction' (UN Doc. A/RES/76/118, 17 December 2021), pp. 1–2 ('*Noting* the constructive dialogue in the Sixth Committee, including in the context of its working group, recognizing the diversity of views expressed by States, including concerns expressed in relation to the abuse or misuse of the principle of universal jurisdiction'; *Reiterating* its commitment to fighting impunity'; '*Decides* that the Sixth Committee shall continue its consideration of the scope and application of universal jurisdiction'). On this, also see Garrod, *HarvILJ*, 59 (2018), 132 ('unable to reach agreement').

[152] *Contra* Official collection German Supreme Court (BGH) vol. 27, at 30 (32); vol. 34, 334 (336).

[153] Wang, *Strafanspruch* (2005), p. 22; Bantekas, *ICL* (2010), p. 344; crit. of an unlimited universality principle, Lafontaine, *JICJ*, 10 (2012), 1277; Yee, *ChinJIL*, 10 (2011), 529–30, who recognizes it only for piracy; also crit. Fletcher, *JICJ*, 1 (2003), 580 ff.; against his position, Eser, *TulsaLR*, 39 (2004), 955 ff.; summing up Cryer, *Prosecuting* (2005), pp. 95 ff. For a different kind of distinction, namely the distinction between a unilateral, absolute, and relative universality principle, Henzelin, *Le principe* (2000), pp. 30, 117 ff.; thereto Ambos, 'Vorbemerkung § 3', in von Heintschel-Heinegg, *MüKo I* (2020), mn. 51. In favour of yet another distinction, Reydams, *Universal Jurisdiction* (2003), pp. 38 ff., 35 ff., 38 ff.; also Ambos, '§ 1 VStGB', in Safferling, *MüKo IX* (2022), mn. 19. D'Aspremont, *IsLR*, 43 (2010), 305 ff. distinguishes between a treaty-based, multilateral form of universal jurisdiction, committed to the '*aut dedere aut iudicare*' principle (305–8), and a unilateral one without a treaty basis (308–9), and considers that the absence of a conventional framework for the latter one, 'while not putting the legality of an exercise of universal jurisdiction into question' (315 ff.), 'jeopardizes the legitimacy of such domestic criminal proceedings because of the idea of consent inherent in the existence of a conventional framework' (325 ff.).

[154] See also Bantekas, *ICL* (2010), p. 344. Summarizing the multiple restrictions on the principle in thirty-three States, Kreicker, in Eser, Sieber, and Kreicker, *Nationale Strafverfolgung VII* (2006), pp. 191 ff.; regarding the factual subsidiarity in Belgium, Germany, France, Austria, and Spain, see Ryngaert, *CLF*, 19 (2008), 159 ff.; on the mandatory presence requirement in Europe, cf. HRW, *Universal Jurisdiction* (June 2006), p. 28; Cryer, *Prosecuting* (2005), pp. 90 ff.; on the role and ability of national courts to prosecute international crimes, see Ryngaert, *EJCCLCJ*, 14 (2006), 57 ff., 79.

Yet, as we will see in the next sub-section, universal jurisdiction must not be confused with *aut dedere aut iudicare*.[155] At any rate, the presence requirement is not a constitutive element of universal jurisdiction, but rather a factual date on which the enforcement of jurisdiction ('jurisdiction to enforce') depends.[156] 'Presence' as a factual requirement of jurisdiction to enforce must not be confused either with presence of the accused at trial as a legal requirement in many national systems.[157]

As to the second, normative method to determine the *scope of universal jurisdiction*, the decisive factor is the degree of wrongfulness embodied by the offences to be covered. Accordingly, the universality principle includes all crimes that protect collective or universally recognized legal interests, the perpetration of which would harm or endanger world peace and the security of mankind.[158] Concretely speaking, this includes, apart from the classical and already mentioned international crime of piracy,[159] the so-called core crimes of the ICC Statute, that is, genocide, crimes against humanity, and crimes of (international or non-international) armed conflicts.[160] This also finds growing support in international and national case law.[161]

155 Apparently overlooked by Bantekas, *ICL* (2010), pp. 347–8 (treating both equally).

156 cf. Weigend, in Arnold et al., *Menschengerechtes Strafrecht* (2005), p. 970; Weigend, in Triffterer, *GS Vogler* (2004), p. 207; agreeing Cryer, *Prosecuting* (2005), pp. 85 ff.; Cryer, in Cryer et al., *ICL* (2019), pp. 57–8; Grant, in Kolb and Scalia, *DIP* (2012), p. 593 ('different matter is the *exercise of this jurisdiction*'), 602 ff.; Lafontaine, *JICJ*, 10 (2012), 1302; for a different view, see Ryngaert, *EJCCLCJ*, 14 (2006), 52, 42; in more detail, Ambos, '§ 1 VStGB', in Safferling, *MüKo IX* (2022), mn. 8, 15; Lafontaine, *JICJ*, 10 (2012), 1280 ff.; Geneuss, *Völkerrechtsverbrechen und Verfolgungsermessen* (2013), pp. 126–7, 130 ff. For Langer, *JICJ*, 13 (2015), 250, 'formal requirements such as presence of the defendant or another link with the prosecuting state ... are epiphenomenal to the substantive discussion about the role that states should have in the extraterritorial enforcement'.

157 See Art. 63 ICCS and Chapter II, D.(2) in this volume.

158 Similarly ICJ, *DRC v. Belgium*, Judgment (2002), Joint Separate Opinion of Judges Higgins, Koojimans and Buergenthal, paras. 35, 37; Scharf, *LCP*, 64 (2001), 80; crit. Gierhake, *ZStW*, 120 (2008), 387 ff.

159 See also Ambos, *Treatise ICL II* (2022), pp. 274–7; O'Keefe, *ICL* (2015), pp. 17–21.

160 cf. Ambos, 'Vorbemerkung § 3', in von Heintschel-Heinegg, *MüKo I* (2020), mn. 53, with further references; Weißer, *GA*, 152 (2012), 418–19; Sánchez Legido, *Jurisdicción universal penal* (2004), pp, 118 ff. (247); Blanco Cordero, *La Ley*, 5980 (2004), 4 ff.; Weigend, in Arnold et al., *Menschengerechtes Strafrecht* (2005), pp. 967, 971 ff. (975); Beigbeder, *International Justice* (2005), pp. 48 ff.; Zimmermann, in Tomuschat and Thouvenin, *Fundamental Rules* (2006), pp. 335 ff.; Arbour, in Dolgopol and Gardam, *Challenge of Conflict* (2006), p. 307; Wang, *Strafanspruch* (2005), p. 165; Ryngaert, *EJCCLCJ*, 14 (2006), 59; Cryer, *Prosecuting* (2005), p. 93; Cryer, in Cryer et al., *ICL* (2019), p. 57; Bantekas, *ICL* (2010), pp. 346–7; Werle, *Völkerstrafrecht* (2012), mn. 212–13, 216; Werle and Jessberger, *Principles ICL* (2020), mn. 261; Borsari, *Diritto punitive* (2007), pp. 189 ff.; Grant, in Kolb and Scalia, *DIP* (2012), pp. 594 ff.; Gierhake, *ZStW*, 120 (2008), 393 ff.; Roht-Arriaza and Fernando, in Brown, *Handbook ICL* (2011), pp. 359 ff.; Jeßberger, Kaleck, and Schueller, in Bergsmo, *Complementarity* (2010), p. 236; Jeßberger, *Geltungsbereich* (2011), p. 278; Böse, Meyer, and Schneider, in Böse, Meyer, and Schneider, *Conflicts of Jurisdiction I* (2013), p. 423; Langer, *JICJ*, 13 (2015), 246; O'Keefe, *ICL* (2015), pp. 17–25, 371; Kindt, *Menschenrechte* (2009), pp. 80 ff., arguing that there is no constant and unanimous concept in applying the universality principle. Crit. of universal jurisdiction for war crimes in light of the trials after WWII, Garrod, *ICLR*, 12 (2012), 763 ff.; crit. also, Merkel, in Jeßberger and Geneuss, *Zehn Jahre VStGB* (2013), p. 54 (according to whom not all war crimes deploy the necessary norm destructive effect); for universal jurisdiction even for non-international conflict crimes, however, Weißer, *GA*, 152 (2012), 422; on GC violations, O'Keefe, *JICJ*, 7 (2009), 814; see also Ben-Naftali and Sharon, *JICJ*, 5 (2007), 859, 864 ff. (regarding genocide). For the French courts' jurisdiction to try Pascal Simbikangwa for his involvement in the Rwandan genocide, see Trouille, *JICJ*, 14 (2016), 209–13.

161 cf. *Prosecutor v. Kallon et al.*, No. SCSL-04-15-0059, AC Decision on Constitutionality and Lack of Jurisdiction, paras. 69 ff. (13 March 2004); cf. also ICJ, *DRC v. Belgium*, Judgment (2002), Separate Opinion of Judge Koroma, para. 9, Dissenting Opinion of Judge van den Wyngaert, paras. 59 ff., Joint Separate Opinion of Judges Higgins, Koojimans and Buergenthal, paras. 60 ff., Dissenting Opinion of Judge Al-Khasawneh, paras. 7, 8b; *contra* ICJ, *DRC v. Belgium*, Judgment (2002), Declaration of Judge Ranjeva, para. 7, Separate Opinion of President Guillaume, para. 17, Separate Opinion of Judge Rezek, para. 7; in more detail, Ambos, '§ 1 VStGB', in Safferling, *MüKo IX* (2022), mn. 18; summarizing, Hoffman, in Menzel, Pierlings, and Hoffmann, *Völkerrechtsprechung* (2005), pp. 439 ff.; Behrendt, *Verfolgung* (2005), pp. 92 ff.; Cryer, in Cryer et al., *ICL* (2019), pp. 58 ff. On State practice in this regard, Kreicker, in Eser, Sieber, and Kreicker, *Nationale Strafverfolgung VII* (2006), pp. 191 ff.; Rikhof, in Bergsmo, *Complementarity* (2010), pp. 45 ff.; on the European practice, see HRW, *Universal Jurisdiction*

While the principle has experienced a certain setback after the *Pinochet* effect at the turn of the century, bringing it closer to a cooperative or subsidiary, instead of a true absolute universality,[162] more recently universal jurisdiction has gained momentum due to a series of factors,[163] not least a focus on less prominent defendants.[164]

As to the crime of aggression, the relative lack of State practice even seems to point to rejection of the universality principle.[165] The discussion has gained some momentum in the context of the Ukraine war, with some States invoking universal jurisdiction to investigate and prosecute the Russian aggression.[166] As regards the so-called treaty-based crimes,[167] especially terrorism, drug trafficking, and torture (as an individual crime), we have already found in Volume II of this Treatise that the respective instruments do not provide for

(June 2006), pp. 37 ff.; concerning Belgium, Germany, France, Austria, and Spain, see Ryngaert, *CLF*, 19 (2008), 160 ff.; on France, see Sulzer, in Kaleck et al., *International Prosecution* (2007), pp. 125 ff.; Lelieur, in Böse, Meyer, and Schneider, *Conflicts of Jurisdiction I* (2013), pp. 128 ff.; on Belgium, see David, *Éléments* (2009), mn. 3.3.42 ff.; Pocar and Maystre, in Bergsmo, *Complementarity* (2010), pp. 282 ff.; on Switzerland, Kolb, in Kolb and Scalia, *DIP* (2012), pp. 254 ff.; Baumgartner, in Safferling and Kirsch, *Völkerstrafrechtspolitik* (2014), pp. 404 ff.; on Sweden, Cameron, *ICL from a Swedish Perspective* (2011), pp. 72 ff.; on Finland, Kimpimäki, *ICLR*, 11 (2011), 165 ff.; on Denmark, Laursen, *JICJ*, 10 (2012), 997; on Spain, Roht-Arriaza, in Kaleck et al., *International Prosecution* (2007), pp. 114 ff.; Carnero Rojo, *JICJ*, 9 (2011), 699 ff.; Pocar and Maystre, in Bergsmo, *Complementarity* (2010), pp. 275 ff.; with regard to the Spanish jurisprudence on the Argentinian military junta, see Tomuschat, *JICJ*, 3 (2005), 1074 ff.; Gil Gil, *JICJ*, 3 (2005), 1082 ff.; Pinzauti, *JICJ*, 3 (2005), 1092 ff.; Wilson, *ASIL Insight*, 12 (2008); Fernández-Pacheco, *JpD*, 61 (2008), 101 ff.; on the Netherland's appliance of the universality principle to war crimes, see Mettraux, *JICJ*, 4 (2006), 362 ff., as opposed by Ferdinandusse, *JICJ*, 4 (2006), 881 ff.; on Switzerland, see Gless, *Internationales Strafrecht* (2021), mn. 204. For relevant jurisprudence, see Weiss, in Kaleck et al., *International Prosecution* (2007), pp. 31 ff.; for an overview, see also Hall, in Bergsmo, *Complementarity* (2010), pp. 217 ff.; Zhu, in Bergsmo and Ling, *State Sovereignty* (2012), pp. 212 ff.; crit. of the implementation of universal jurisdiction in China (remaining behind its obligations under international law), Ma, in Bergsmo and Ling, *State Sovereignty* (2012), pp. 180 ff.

162 cf. Ambos, '§ 1 VStGB', in Safferling, *MüKo IX* (2022), mn. 16 ff.; Ambos, *CWRJIL*, 42 (2009), 405 ff.; Bock, *BelgianRIL*, 43 (2010), 60; Kourula, in Bergsmo and Ling, *State Sovereignty* (2012), pp. 138 ff.; van der Wilt, *JICJ*, 9 (2011), 1050, 1055 ff.; Lafontaine, *JICJ*, 10 (2012), 1286 ff.; Weißer, *GA*, 152 (2012), 430; Stigen, in Bergsmo, *Complementarity* (2010), pp. 136 ff.; Ryngaert, in Bergsmo, *Complementarity* (2010), pp. 181 ff.; on the recent setback in Spain, see Alija Fernández, *ZIS*, 9 (2014), 717 ff. For a nuanced approach regarding the history of universality in the last decades, Langer, *JICJ*, 13 (2015), 246 ff., arguing that what appears as the 'fall' of the principle in recent years is the 'on-going competition' between the role States should have 'in the universal jurisdiction regime', either that of the 'global enforcer' or that of the 'no safe haven', see note 145 in this chapter.

163 cf. Langer and Eason *EJIL*, 30 (2019), 791 ff. convincingly listing as factors for this trend: the introduction of ICC implementing legislation (791); the introduction of specialized investigative units (792–3); institutional learning/technological improvements (793–6), and last not least 'the high levels of conflict-based migration in the past decade' (796, 796–9); in a similar vein, Doumit, *GeoJIL*, 52 (2020), 279 ('Germany is home to more than 550,000 Syrian refugees, and these refugees may have evidence or first-hand accounts of some of the crimes that occurred'). See also the recent Resolution of the CoE's Parliamentary Assembly invoking universal jurisdiction with regard to Russia's aggressive war against Ukraine, cf. Res. 2482 (2023), para. 15.4.

164 Langer and Eason, *EJIL*, 30 (2019), 782 ('trials have focused on low-cost defendants and defendants who were already residing in the prosecuting country'), Doumit, *GeoJIL*, 52 (2020), 284 ('universal jurisdiction can play an important role here in holding lower-level officials accountable, while the ICC can hold higher-level officials accountable'). In detail on the prosecution of State sponsored torture in Syria by German courts, see Aboueldahab and Langmack, *Minn. J. Int. Law*, 31 (2022), 1.

165 Werle, *Völkerstrafrecht* (2012), mn. 212, 216; Werle and Jessberger, *Principles ICL* (2020), mn. 261; Zahar and Sluiter, *ICL* (2008), pp. 498 ff.; cf. also Oeter, in Jeßberger and Geneuss, *Zehn Jahre VStGB* (2013), p. 120. According to the UN GA, 'The Scope and Application of the Principle of Universal Jurisdiction' (UN Doc. A/65/181, 29 July 2010), p. 29, universal jurisdiction for aggression and 'crimes against peace' did exist only in four States (Azerbaijan, Belarus, Bulgaria, and Estonia) at the time. In the Czech Republic the preparation of war can be universally prosecuted. For a different view, see Hoven, in Safferling and Kirsch, *Völkerstrafrechtspolitik* (2014), pp. 363 ff., 366 (definition of aggression in ICCS as expression of no-impunity stance of international community).

166 See McDougall, *J. Confl. Secur. Law*, 28 (2023), 214–15 (referring to Lithuania); furthermore, see Sterio, *Case West. Reserve J. Int. Law*, 55 (2023), 488–9 ('uncertain whether the crime of aggression, particularly relevant in the Ukrainian context, is subject to universal jurisdiction').

167 On this concept, see Ambos, *Treatise ICL II* (2022), pp. 257–61.

universal jurisdiction, but for the *aut dedere aut iudicare* principle at best.[168] Thus, although all of these crimes protect important universal values, they are not universally prosecutable, save the just mentioned crime of piracy and, arguably, torture given its peremptory nature.[169]

### *(e) The principle of representation* (aut dedere aut iudicare)

The main purpose of the principle of representation (also called 'representational principle')[170] is to avoid prosecution gaps with regard to a suspect who flees the territorial State (being the State *locus delicti*). Concretely speaking, the principle concerns cases where prosecution may fail because of a legal or factual impossibility of extraditing the suspect to his home State (which is the territorial State where the crime was committed) so that they must be prosecuted by the custodial State, 'stepping into the shoes' of the home/territorial State.[171] This shows that the principle is based on *aut dedere aut iudicare*: if the suspect cannot be returned (extradited) to the home/territorial State (the *dedere* limb), they must be prosecuted[172] by the custodial State (the *iudicare* limb). The relationship between these two limbs—prevalence of one of the two or equal weight—depends on the 'context and applicable legal regime in particular situations' and is thus case-specific.[173] We will return to this below when taking a look at the relevant treaties.

Strictly speaking, the custodial State enforces the criminal law in representation or with the full consent of the home/territorial State; at least, if it does not act on the basis of its own obligation to prosecute, but pursuant to the non-extradition or surrender (in the sense of the distinction made above). This is the crucial difference with the universality principle: the prosecuting (arrest) State does not derive the legitimacy for exercising criminal jurisdiction from representing the interests of the international community, but simply from the home/territorial State, which delegates its jurisdiction.[174] The principle of representation may also be distinguished from cases of delegation of a territorial State's criminal jurisdiction to another State or a supranational tribunal.[175]

To be acceptable under international law, representation so understood requires more than the *factual* impossibility of extradition and the therewith associated factual subsidiarity

[168] cf. Ambos, *Treatise ICL II* (2022), pp. 269, 273–4, 281; also Ambos and Timmermann, in Safferling and Kirsch, *Völkerstrafrechtspolitik* (2014), pp. 309 ff., 333 ff.; on its application in various legal orders, see Satzger, *ICL* (2018), § 4 mn. 42.

[169] On torture (as an individual crime), see Ambos, *Treatise ICL II* (2022), pp. 278–82. Also including torture (and 'most serious forms of slavery'), Bantekas, *ICL* (2010), p. 347; Grant, in Kolb and Scalia, *DIP* (2012), pp. 599–600; including slavery and slave trade as a crime against humanity, O'Keefe, *ICL* (2015), pp. 21–2.

[170] Gilbert, *BYbIL*, 63 (1992), 423.

[171] Ibid., 423; crit. on the closing-prosecution-gaps rationale, Irarrázavel Zaldívar, *Grundlagen des Strafanwendungsrechts* (2024), pp. 136–7.

[172] Prosecuted but not necessarily convicted and punished; for this reason the second limb of the old version of the principle as formulated by Hugo Grotius (*aut dedere aut punire*) has been changed; cf. ILC, *Obligation to Extradite or Prosecute* (2014), para. 2. For a distinction between *aut dedere* and representation principle, see Irarrázavel Zaldívar, *Grundlagen des Strafanwendungsrechts* (2024), pp. 138 ff.

[173] cf. ILC, *Obligation to Extradite or Prosecute* (2014), paras. 4, 13.

[174] So understood, the custodial State exercises neither universal jurisdiction nor any other jurisdiction (in this sense however ILC, *Obligation to Extradite or Prosecute* (2014), para. 18) but the *aut dedere aut iudicare* principle constitutes a jurisdictional basis in its own right. Furthermore, see Garrod, *HarvILJ*, 59 (2018), p. 132 ('If the unique feature of universal jurisdiction is the absence of any link at all between the crime and the prescribing state, then jurisdiction arising out of treaty obligations to extradite or prosecute is its antithesis').

[175] cf. Yanev, *NILR* 68 (2021), 171–4 on the transfer of Ukrainian criminal jurisdiction to the Netherlands in the MH-17 case as the first example of the application of the CoE's Convention on the Transfer of Proceedings in Criminal Matters CETS No. 73 (15 May 1972). Also see Galand, *Security Council* (2019), pp. 16–17. On the possible delegation of Ukraine's jurisdiction to a Special Aggression Tribunal, cf. Ambos, *Verfassungsblog*, 6 January 2023.

of the home/territorial State.[176] For this State can refuse to prosecute a crime without consenting, at the same time, to the prosecution by the arrest State; it may prefer that a third State deals with the respective crime.[177]

A requirement of double criminality does not inform about the true will of the home/territorial State with regard to the prosecution of the relevant crime either. This can only be truly determined by an explicit declaration of the home/territorial State, in particular expressing its consent with the prosecution by the custodial State in its *representation*. In other words, the home/territorial State must explicitly transfer its criminal jurisdiction to the custodial State, thereby enabling that State to exercise criminal jurisdiction derivatively. Thus, we are faced with a 'derivative extension of criminal jurisdiction',[178] a 'subsidiary complementarity of foreign criminal jurisdiction',[179] or merely 'gap-filling'.[180]

This further means that the principle of representation does not provide—absent an explicit treaty basis to this effect (thereto in a moment)—for a link or justification for criminal prosecution in its own right but is rather based on a cooperation model in terms of legal assistance in criminal matters. Concretely speaking, it is based on the cooperation between the home/territorial and the custodial State with a view to ensuring criminal prosecution. Consequently, the custodial State has to respect any decision of the home State terminating criminal proceedings.[181] Last but not least, such an understanding also avoids any violation of the principle of non-interference: if the home/territorial State voluntarily delegates its original criminal jurisdiction to the custodial State (or another State), the consent implicit in this delegation excludes any sovereignty violation. Thus, the custodial State's jurisdiction is not based on a genuine link or principle of jurisdiction but on the consent of the home/territorial State.

The underlying *aut dedere aut iudicare* principle is included in a number of international treaties[182] some of which we have already discussed in the context of the treaty-based crimes in Volume II of this Treatise.[183] There are mainly two categories of treaties: on the one hand, those pursuant to which the prosecution obligation is triggered by the non-extradition (or surrender to an international tribunal[184]); on the other hand, those which impose the prosecution obligation on the custodial State *ipso facto* once the suspect enters national territory.[185] This latter approach has been adopted by many conventions adopted since 1970,

[176] See e.g. § 7 (2) no. 2 German StGB: 'is not extradited because a request for extradition within a reasonable period of time is not made, is rejected, or the extradition is not feasible'. (Translation by Bohlander, *German Criminal Code* (2008).)

[177] Correctly, Heinrich, *Personalitätsprinzip* (1994), p. 98; Pappas, *Stellvertretende Strafrechtspflege* (1996), pp. 95 ff.

[178] Pappas, *Stellvertretende Strafrechtspflege* (1996), p. 100 ('derivative Strafgewalterstreckung' [own translation]); similarly Zieher, *Internationale Strafrecht* (1997), p. 85.

[179] Herdegen, *ZaöRV*, 47 (1987), 235 ('subsidiäre Ergänzung fremder Strafgewalt' [translation K. Ambos]).

[180] Satzger, *ICL* (2018), § 4 mn. 40 ('purpose of filling regulatory gaps').

[181] cf. s. 7 (2) Alternative Draft of German PC (AE-StGB); Jescheck, *IRuD*, 1 (1956), 80, 91; Vogler, in Oehler et al., *Aktuelle Probleme* (1970), p. 157; Jescheck and Weigend, *Strafrecht—Allgemeiner Teil* (1996), p. 176. In regard to the impact of a general exemption from punishment, see Ambos, '§ 7', in von Heintschel-Heinegg, *MüKo I* (2020), mn. 12 ff.

[182] In contrast, the customary law nature of the principle is highly controversial; cf. ILC, *Obligation to Extradite or Prosecute* (2014), paras. 49–55; see also van Steenberghe, *JICJ*, 9 (2011), 1091 ff. (limited customary recognition regarding international core crimes).

[183] Ambos, *Treatise ICL II* (2022), pp. 257 ff.

[184] On this so-called—increasingly important—'third alternative', see ILC, *Obligation to Extradite or Prosecute* (2014), paras. 27, 35. It is stipulated, for example, in Art. 11 (1) of the 2006 International Convention for the Protection of All Persons from Enforced Disappearance.

[185] In this vein, see Separate Opinion of Judge Yusuf, *Questions relating to the Obligation to Prosecute or Extradite. Belgium v. Senegal*, Judgment (20 July 2012), ICJ Reports 2012 422, pp. 567–8, paras. 19–22; conc., ILC, *Obligation to Extradite or Prosecute* (2014), paras. 38–40. Distinguishing between four types of conventions pursuant to a 2010 survey by the Secretariat, ILC, *Obligation to Extradite or Prosecute* (2014), paras. 6 ff.

based on the so-called 'Hague formula'.[186] An important example in our context is the CAT, whose Article 7 (1) entails primacy of the prosecution over the extradition limb, the former creating an international obligation of the custodial State and the latter only an option.[187] If the custodial State does not comply with this obligation—be it the prosecution or the extradition/surrender limb—it incurs an international wrongful act.[188]

In fact, only in the latter case of the custodial State's primary duty to prosecute[189] one can speak of a transfer of criminal jurisdiction to this State, and of an ensuing derivative criminal jurisdiction of that State as explained above. And here again the conceptual difference with the universality principle becomes clear:[190] while both principles can be traced back to the *aut dedere aut iudicare* principle, the exercise of criminal jurisdiction pursuant to the representation principle must correctly be understood as a derivative and not an original exercise of jurisdiction (as in the case of the universality principle).[191] As a consequence, it is the universality principle which primarily aims at the prevention of impunity in territorial States, not the representation principle. Of course, this important consequence does not speak in favour of impunity, but in favour of a clear conceptual distinction of both principles although they may overlap in practical terms.[192] Whoever wants to prevent impunity must fill the gaps in the current '*aut dedere aut iudicare*' treaty regime[193] and strengthen the universality principle by including more international crimes in its subject-matter competence.

### (3) Conflicts of jurisdiction

According to the—above explained—two-step test to determine criminal jurisdiction in line with international law, one has first to identify a genuine link or jurisdictional principle which justifies the respective State's jurisdiction over the respective criminal event. The second step, searching for possible rules in international law prohibiting the jurisdictional claim, is irrelevant if only *one* State possesses the necessary jurisdictional link and its jurisdictional claim does not appear to be arbitrary.

The situation becomes more complicated if *several* States claim jurisdiction. This could lead to (positive) conflicts of jurisdiction, the resolution of which is not only difficult, but highly controversial (sub-section (b) in this section). A different situation arises where one State claims criminal jurisdiction on the basis of *several jurisdictional links*. Here a hierarchy of jurisdictional principles is unnecessary, but the State would want to invoke the broadest jurisdictional link to have the broadest jurisdiction possible.[194] Last but not least, the double jeopardy rule (*ne bis in idem*), that is, the prohibition on being prosecuted several times for

[186] ILC, *Obligation to Extradite or Prosecute* (2014), para. 13 (referring to the Secretariat survey).

[187] In this vein, with regard to Art. 7 (1) CAT ICJ, *Questions relating to the Obligation to Prosecute or Extradite. Belgium v. Senegal*, Judgment (20 July 2012), ICJ Reports 2012 422, paras. 94–5 (also referring to Art. 6 (2) CAT calling on the custodial State to 'immediately make a preliminary inquiry into the facts').

[188] ILC, *Obligation to Extradite or Prosecute* (2014), para. 26; ICJ, Judgment, ICJ Reports 2012 422, para. 95.

[189] On the implementation at the domestic level, in particular elements for national legislation and the scope of the investigation and prosecution obligations, see ILC, *Obligation to Extradite or Prosecute* (2014), paras. 15 ff.

[190] See also Hall, in Bergsmo, *Complementarity* (2010), pp. 204–5.

[191] For a different view, cf. Dahm, *Völkerstrafrecht* (1956), p. 33; Jescheck, *IRuD*, 1 (1956), 89; Oehler, *Internationales Strafrecht* (1983), mn. 147, 818.

[192] See also Gilbert, *BYbIL*, 63 (1992), 424.

[193] See, in this regard, ILC, *Obligation to Extradite or Prosecute* (2014), paras. 14, 31 ff. (with concrete proposals).

[194] Werle and Jeßberger, 'Vorbemerkungen §§ 3 ff.', in Cirener, *Leipziger Kommentar StGB I* (2020), mn. 281.

the same crime, comes into play if a person were to be subjected to criminal proceedings a second time or even more times. We will turn to this situation first.

### (a) *Conflict of jurisdiction in the broad sense and double jeopardy*

We can speak of a conflict of jurisdiction in a broad sense where the offender has already been tried for an offence in one country but is to be prosecuted again for the same offence in another.[195] While the double jeopardy rule prohibits such a practice in principle, the problem is that this rule is not fully recognized at the interstate level. The relevant human rights provisions explicitly refer to the acquittal or conviction according to the laws of the respective country,[196] that is, they do not rule out a prosecution and trial in *another* country.[197] Similarly, there is no general principle of international law, that is, a principle recognized by the major legal systems, embodying the double jeopardy rule. On the contrary, many States explicitly limit the rule to prosecutions and trials within their own criminal justice systems;[198] in the US federal system, where the States of the Federation are considered as sovereigns on their own, it is even limited at this interstate level by the 'dual sovereign exception.'[199] In addition, many States do not recognize the *lex mitior* principle[200] nor do they deduct the time already spent in detention for the same offence (rule of credit).[201]

From the perspective of international law the widespread non-recognition of a transnational *ne bis in idem* is mainly explained by the fact that a State cannot be deprived of its sovereign right to exercise criminal jurisdiction if it possesses a sufficient jurisdictional link and has a concrete interest to exercise its jurisdiction.[202] Of course, this view entails that a State's right to punish takes precedence over the individual right not to be prosecuted twice (or more times) for the same conduct. From a rights perspective this is a highly unsatisfactory solution, especially if one takes into account that a criminal investigation, prosecution, and trial as such have a highly intimidating and stigmatizing effect.[203] From this perspective,

[195] cf. Zöller, in Amelung, Günther, and Kühne, *FS Krey* (2010), p. 506.

[196] cf. Art. 14 (7) ICCPR (referring to the trial of 'each country') and Art. 4 AP VII ECHR.

[197] cf. in detail, with relevant jurisprudence, Henzelin, *ZStR*, 123 (2005), 354 ff.; see also Commission of the European Communities, 'Commission Staff Working Document—Annex to the Green Paper on Conflicts of Jurisdiction and the Principle of ne bis in idem in Criminal Proceedings' (23 December 2005), Annex pp. 44 ff., 67 ff.; Mangiaracina, *LP*, 2 (2006), 632–3. For a comparative analysis on the *ne bis in idem* principle, see Jegede, in Decaux, Dieng, and Sow, *From Human Rights to ICL* (2007), pp. 483 ff.; Mezei, in Badó, *Studies in the Fields of Comparative Law* (2012), pp. 109 ff.; Mezei, in Badó, *Fair Trial and Judicial Independence* (2014), pp. 197 ff.

[198] See e.g. the interpretation of Art. 103 (3) German Constitution (GG) by the German Constitutional Court, BVerfGE 6, 176 (177); or Art. 39 Constitution of Japan, <https://japan.kantei.go.jp/constitution_and_government_of_japan/constitution_e.html>, in conjunction with Art. 5 Japanese Penal Code, <http://www.japaneselawtranslation.go.jp/law/detail/?id=1960&vm=04&re=02>. For a different approach, however, see Art. 8 in relation with Art. 17 CP Colombia recognizing, as a rule, the *ne bis in idem* principle for foreign sentences; cf. implicitly, Corte Constitucional, Sentencia C-554/01, para. 3.9. (30 May 2001).

[199] That exception was reaffirmed in *Bartkus v. Illinois*, 359 U.S. 121 (1959) <http://www.law.cornell.edu/supremecourt/text/359/121>. While the context was a federal and state prosecution rather than prosecutions by two states, it is generally recognized that the principle operates in both contexts (cf. *Heath v. Alabama*, 474 U.S. 82 (1985), <http://www.law.cornell.edu/supremecourt/text/474/82>.

[200] Accordingly, the less severe applicable law (entailing a lower sentence) should be applied, cf. BGHSt 27, 30 (34) or s. 10 II Danish Criminal Code (*Bekendtgørelse af Straffeloven*).

[201] While this is recognized in some domestic systems (e.g. s. 51 (3) German Criminal Code (StGB): 'foreign sentence, to the extent it has been served, shall be credited towards the new sentence' or Art. 5 Japanese Penal Code: 'when the person has already served either the whole or part of the punishment abroad, execution of the punishment shall be mitigated or remitted'), it does not amount to a general principle of law given that it does not exist in many systems (German Federal Constitutional Court (BVerfG), *NJW*, 35 (1987), 2155 (2158)). See also Donnedieu de Vabres, *Annuaire de l'IDI*, 43, 2 (1950), 261; Schönke, in Englisch and Maurach, *FS Mezger* (1954), pp. 113 ff.; Satzger, *Europäisierung* (2001), p. 686. On the respective provisions in the international criminal tribunals, esp. Art. 78 (2) ICCS, see Ambos, *Treatise ICL II* (2022), pp. 323–4.

[202] Doehring, *Völkerrecht* (2004), mn. 815, 1152.

[203] cf. Feeley, *Process* (1992); European Criminal Policy Initiative, *ZIS*, 8 (2013), 430.

the correct approach is the one taken in Europe, that is, to codify the *ne bis in idem* principle at the EU level, on the one hand for the Schengen Member States (Article 54 CISA)[204] and on the other hand for the EU Member States (Article 50 EU Charter).[205] A similar approach is taken by the international criminal tribunals, which all recognize, in principle, the *ne bis in idem* rule in their (vertical) relationship with the domestic criminal justice systems.[206] In any case, States should, at least, give a person credit for the effective time already spent in custody.

### *(b) Settling conflicts of jurisdiction: A call for a hierarchy of the jurisdictional links*

A conflict of jurisdiction can emerge where several States claim to have an adequate jurisdictional link (so called positive[207] conflict of jurisdiction).[208] In fact, such conflicts are 'simply a part of the reality of international law'.[209] In this case, a concrete balancing of the sovereign interests of the States concerned must take place, in order to determine which State would be, in line with the above-mentioned optimization principle,[210] the most adequate to exercise jurisdiction.[211] While it has been questioned whether conflicts of jurisdiction can be properly described as a collision of sovereign interests and thus be resolved by balancing these interests,[212] the critical voices hardly provide convincing alternatives.[213] Thus, while, for example, one may conceive jurisdictional questions as part of the discourse on global governance,[214] the solution of conflicts of jurisdiction calls for sufficiently predictable and precise differentiations. As a consequence, for the time being, the best solution for jurisdictional conflicts of this kind still appears to be adopting international treaties with clear jurisdictional rules.[215] This helps to avoid or at least to reduce the costs such conflicts have

[204] Art. 54 CISA reads: 'A person whose trial has been finally disposed of in one Contracting Party may not be prosecuted in another Contracting Party for the same acts provided that, if a penalty has been imposed, it has been enforced, is actually in the process of being enforced or can no longer be enforced under the laws of the sentencing Contracting Party.'

[205] Art. 50 EU Charter ('Right not to be tried or punished twice in criminal proceedings for the same criminal offence') reads: 'No one shall be liable to be tried or punished again in criminal proceedings for an offence for which he or she has already been finally acquitted or convicted within the Union in accordance with the law.'

[206] cf. Arts. 10 ICTYS, 9 ICTRS, 7 IRMCTS, and 20 ICCS. See also Henzelin, *ZStR*, 123 (2005), 351 ff.; Hecker, *ZIS*, 6 (2011), 60.

[207] A *negative* conflict arises if no State with jurisdiction is interested in exercising it (take the case of the leader of the Kurdish PKK Öcalan, who was arrested in Italy, but finally not wanted by Germany as the State which issued the arrest warrant in the first place), cf. Vandermeersch, in Cassese and Delmas-Marty, *Juridictions nationales* (2002), pp. 608 ff.; Caeiro, *KritV*, 4 (2010), 369 ff.; Caeiro, in Correia, Machado, and Loureiro, *Estudos em Homenagem ao Canotilho III* (2012), pp. 196–7; Weißer, *GA*, 152 (2012), 432; Eisele, *ZStW*, 125 (2013), 2–3. The situation is different, however, if one person is prosecuted by several States because of several crimes.

[208] Linke, in Oehler et al., *Aktuelle Probleme* (1970), p. 85; Caeiro, *KritV*, 4 (2010), 373 ff.; Caeiro, in Correia, Machado, and Loureiro, *Estudos em Homenagem ao Canotilho III* (2012), p. 197. See, on the terminology, also Akehurst, *BYbIL*, 46 (1972/73), 167 ff. (even discussing cases of collision, where one legal system requires certain actions, which are forbidden under another legal system); see also the examples in Büchler and Kreuzer, in Sinn, *Jurisdiktionskonflikte* (2012), pp. 125 ff.

[209] Mills, *BYbIL*, 84 (2014), 199.

[210] Section A.(1)(a) in this chapter.

[211] For a similar approach, see Böse, in Zöller et al., *Gesamte Strafrechtswissenschaft* (2013), p. 1314 (arguing that in finding the best jurisdiction both the need for flexibility and the principle of legal certainty shall be taken into consideration); for an instructive overview of the (diverging) interests of States, suspects, and victims which should be taken into account in this case, see Eser, *Jurisdiktionskonflikte bei grenzüberschreitender Kriminalität* (2012), pp. 563 ff. With regard to the possible role of the ICC in solving conflicts of jurisdiction over international crimes, Zappalá, in Cassese, Chiavario, and De Francesco, *Problemi* (2005), pp. 556 ff.

[212] On Ryngaert's 'New Theory', see below note 249.

[213] Conceded by Krisch, *EJIL*, 33 (2022), 508.

[214] See Krisch, *EJIL*, 33 (2022), 503 ff.

[215] On the necessity to find common rules for the settling of jurisdiction conflicts within the EU, see Lelieur, in Brach-Thiel and Fourment, *Questions de droit pénal international* (2013), pp. 262 ff.

for the stability in international diplomatic relations.[216] Such treaties do not, however, exist in most cases.[217] Therefore, the only solution is to develop a *hierarchy or ranking order* of the internationally recognized jurisdictional principles.[218] At the European level, where conflicts of jurisdiction are occurring all the time, such a ranking was attempted by the 1965 'Draft European Convention on Conflicts of Jurisdiction in Criminal Matters'.[219] The EU Commission's Green Paper on 'Conflicts of Jurisdiction and the Principle of ne bis in idem in Criminal Proceedings' proposed an allocation based on a coordination and consultation model with the possible determination of a 'leading' jurisdiction at the moment of having an accusation or indictment prepared ('priority rule').[220] As to the relevant criteria to determine jurisdiction, the proposal opts for a 'flexible case-by-case approach' instead of an abstract ranking order, leaving the competent authorities a broad discretion.[221] The Council Framework Decision of 30 November 2009 'on prevention and settlement of conflicts of exercise of jurisdiction in criminal proceedings'[222] does not provide for concrete criteria amounting to a ranking,[223] but just establishes a system of consultation between competent,

[216] cf. Mills, *BYbIL*, 84 (2014), 238.

[217] cf. Abelson, *UCDavisJIL&Pol'y*, 16 (2009), 5; Council of the EU, 'Expert Group on the Principle of Universal Jurisdiction Report (2009)', mn. 14 ('no mandatory hierarchy of internationally permissible jurisdictions'); see also Böse and Meyer, *ZIS*, 6 (2011), 338; Marauhn and Simon, in Sinn, *Jurisdiktionskonflikte* (2012), p. 37. On the few existing treaties such as the ones mentioned in the main text, as well as CoE, 'European Convention on the Transfer of Proceedings in Criminal Matters' (15 May 1972) (CETS Nr. 073) and the UN GA, 'Model Treaty on Transfer of Proceedings in Criminal Matters' (14 December 1990) (UN Doc. A/RES/45/118), see Werle and Jeßberger, 'Vorbemerkungen §§ 3 ff.', in Cirener, *Leipziger Kommentar StGB I* (2020), mn. 49–50; on the suggestions of Art. 21 Palermo Convention (see above note 19), see Le Nguyen, *JFinancCrime*, 27 (2020), 1370–1.

[218] cf. Donnedieu de-Vabres, *Annuaire de l'IDI*, 43, 2 (1950), 260; also Herdegen, *ZaöRV*, 47 (1987), 235 ff.; Oxman, in Wolfrum and Peters, *MPEPIL VI* (2007), p. 55 5. Crit. of a hierarchical ranking, Walther, in Arnold et al., *Menschengerechtes Strafrecht* (2005), pp. 926 ff.; Werle and Jeßberger, 'Vorbemerkungen §§ 3 ff.', in Cirener, *Leipziger Kommentar StGB I* (2020), mn. 47; Jeßberger, Kaleck, and Schueller, in Bergsmo, *Complementarity* (2010), p. 237; Hecker, in Sinn, *Jurisdiktionskonflikte* (2012), pp. 97–8; Weißer, *GA*, 152 (2012), 430 ff.; Weißer, in Jeßberger and Geneuss, *Zehn Jahre VStGB* (2013), pp. 69 ff. (but arguing ultimately for a priority of the territoriality principle, from which one can deviate for pragmatic procedural reasons); crit. of the proposed approach, Wörner and Wörner, in Sinn, *Jurisdiktionskonflikte* (2012), p. 211–12; crit. from a practical legal perspective, Krisch, *EJIL*, 33 (2022), 502 ('state practice offers little indication of such rules to resolve conflicts, instead treating different grounds of jurisdiction on an equal footing').

[219] CoE, Parliamentary Assembly, 'Draft European Convention on Conflicts of Jurisdiction in Criminal Matters', 29 January 1965, Recommendation 420 (1965) on the Settlement of Conflicts of Jurisdiction in Criminal Matters; for a more detailed analysis, see Oehler, in Oehler et al., *Aktuelle Probleme* (1970), pp. 115 ff.; Vogler, in Schroeder and Zipf, *FS Maurach* (1972), pp. 609 ff.; Lagodny, *Gerichtskompetenz für Strafgewaltskonflikte* (March 2001), pp. 45–9; Lagodny, in Arnold et al., *Menschengerechtes Strafrecht* (2005), pp. 792 ff.; also Wörner and Wörner, in Sinn, *Jurisdiktionskonflikte* (2012), pp. 252 ff.

[220] Commission, *Green Paper on Jurisdiction* (2005), nos. 2.1. to 2.4. Crit. focusing on procedural rights, ECBA, 'Response to the Green Paper' (28 March 2006); Schomburg, Lagodny, Gleß, and Hackner, *Internationale Rechtshilfe* (2012), Einleitung mn. 73a, propose a more pragmatic, controlled procedure (located at Eurojust), by codifying transnational offences, which should help to avoid premature or multiple punishment. For a possible settlement of conflicts within the EU by means of assigning criminal procedures, cf. Hecker, *ZIS*, 6 (2011), 82; Hecker, in Sinn, *Jurisdiktionskonflikte* (2012), pp. 86 ff.; on respective approaches in Italy, see Foffani, Orlandi, and Ruggeri, in Sinn, *Jurisdiktionskonflikte* (2012), p. 324.

[221] Commission, *Green Paper on Jurisdiction* (2005), No. 2.5 (indicating as such criteria territoriality, active personality, victims and State interests, and 'other criteria related to efficiency and rapidity of the proceedings').

[222] Council Framework Decision 2009/948/JHA; cf. thereon Fikarova, 'Prospects of the Council Framework Decision 2009/948/JHA', in Sinn, *Jurisdiktionskonflikte* (2012), pp. 103 ff.; crit. of the FD, European Criminal Policy Initiative, *ZIS*, 8 (2013), 440.

[223] Crit. Böse and Meyer, *ZIS*, 6 (2011), 336; Fikarova, in Sinn, *Jurisdiktionskonflikte* (2012), p. 105; Sinn, *ZIS*, 8 (2013), 4; European Criminal Policy Initiative, *ZIS*, 8 (2013), 440; Lelieur, in Brach-Thiel and Fourment, *Questions de droit pénal international* (2013), p. 262. For Hecker, in Sinn, *Jurisdiktionskonflikte* (2012), p. 96, this does not constitute a problem, because a consensual solution can duly take account of the interests of the person concerned with a view to avoiding multiple prosecutions. This approach can already be found in Commission, *Green Paper on Jurisdiction* (2005), No. 2.1 ff., proposing a 'mechanism aiming to allocate cases to an appropriate jurisdiction', which relied however on early coordination and consultation between the interested States and (regarding the

central authorities.[224] Eurojust, in turn, proposes as a 'preliminary presumption' that 'a prosecution should take place in the jurisdiction in which the majority—or the most important part—of the criminality occurred or in which the majority—or the most important part—of the loss was sustained'.[225]

In any case, it is clear that any hierarchy that pretends to have a binding effect must be derived from international law; that is, the relevance and strength of a certain jurisdictional principle correlates to the degree of recognition of that principle under international law. The starting point is the above-mentioned principle of a moderate exercise of extraterritorial criminal jurisdiction.[226] As to the actual hierarchy, the *territorial principle* clearly comes first,[227] since it is the internationally most recognized principle and avoids, by limiting jurisdiction to the sovereign territory, any jurisdictional conflict.[228] As to extensions of the territoriality principle, both the effects and the flag principle prevail over the other extraterritorial principles although they do trigger, contrary to the strict territoriality principle, jurisdictional conflicts.

Thus, in the case of the effects principle, the effects (result or consequences) of the criminal conduct occur in a different place than the causal conduct.[229] In the case of the flag principle, there are cases where it conflicts with the territorial principle, for example, if a foreign ship moves into the coastal sea (i.e. the sovereign area of the respective territorial State). This conflict is solved by Article 27 UNCLOS granting the flag State precedence over the coastal State. The coastal State is only allowed to arrest a person of that foreign ship or investigate on the ship if a special connection to the coastal State exists[230] or the ship emerged from the coastal State's territorial waters.[231] Possible conflicts on the high seas are solved by Article 97 (1) UNCLOS, limiting jurisdiction to the flag State or the suspects'/perpetrators' State. These rules show in an exemplary fashion how international treaty provisions may solve conflicts of jurisdiction.

criteria for choosing jurisdiction, no. 2.5) on flexible criteria like reasonableness and due process, rather than on a ranking based on international law; crit. of that, with emphasis on the procedural rights of the person concerned, ECBA, 'Response to the Green Paper' (28 March 2006). See also the development of the criteria for determining the best jurisdiction in Art. 13 of the agreed jurisdiction model, Sinn, in Sinn, *Jurisdiktionskonflikte* (2012), pp. 581 ff.

[224] Hecker, in Sinn, *Jurisdiktionskonflikte* (2012), p. 95; see also Fikarova, in Sinn, *Jurisdiktionskonflikte* (2012), p. 104.

[225] Eurojust, *Guidelines for Deciding 'Which Jurisdiction should Prosecute?'*, p. 2.

[226] cf. sub-section (1)(a) in this section.

[227] Also Council of the EU, 'Expert Group on the Principle of Universal Jurisdiction Report (2009)', mn. 24, as well as Art. 3 (1), (3), Art. 4 (2), and Art. 5 Draft European Convention; Sánchez Legido, *Jurisdicción universal penal* (2004), pp. 320 ff.; Behrendt, *Verfolgung* (2005), p. 297; Sieber, in Ständige Deputation des Deutschen Juristentages, *Verhandlungen*, I/3 (2012), p. 141; taking a different view, Abelson, *UCDavisJIL&Pol'y*, 16 (2009), 26, who is not willing to accept a general priority of territorial principle over the passive personality principle. Crit. Wong, *Criminal Act* (2004), pp. 195 ff.; Eicker, *StV*, 25 (2005), 632 ff.; for a primacy, in principle, of the territoriality over the universality principle, see Jeßberger, Kaleck, and Schueller, in Bergsmo, *Complementarity* (2010), p. 238; similarly Lønseth, in Bergsmo, *Complementarity* (2010), p. 162; Böse and Meyer, *ZIS*, 6 (2011), 343. In favour of giving 'territoriality principle priority above other considerations', see 'the statutory determination model' in Sinn, in Sinn, *Jurisdiktionskonflikte* (2012), p. 609 ('If the accused acted within the territory of multiple Member States, jurisdiction lies with the State in which the criminal consequences also arose' or 'where the accused has his primary residence'); thereon, see Sinn, *ZIS*, 8 (2013), 6 ff.; in a similar vein, Eisele, *ZStW*, 125 (2013), 32.

[228] Misjudged by Scharf, *LCP*, 64 (2001), 111; regarding the general prevalence of the territorial principle, see *Harvard Draft Convention* (1935), p. 531; see also *Princeton Principles* (2001), p. 53.

[229] See also Art. 3 (3) Draft European Convention, according to which the place of the main conduct prevails over the place of assistance and the effects.

[230] Art. 27 (2) UNCLOS.

[231] Art. 27 (2) UNCLOS. cf. also Heintschel von Heinegg, in Ipsen, *Völkerrecht* (2024), § 41 mn. 24.

As to the remaining jurisdictional principles, a hierarchy is difficult to determine[232] since international law does not provide any 'hard and fast rules' for that matter.[233] In any case, a certain hierarchy may be derived from the *degree of international recognition* of the respective principles and their underlying rationales. As to the latter, one can inquire whether a State exercises its criminal jurisdiction to pursue its own, foreign, or truly international interests. The own interests' approach coincides, in essence, with the traditional idea of State self-preservation,[234] which is the basis of all principles that aim at protecting the territorial and institutional integrity of the State. Besides the territoriality principle (in the broad sense), this is the case of the *protective principle*.[235] This principle is comparable to the territoriality principle in that it aims to protect the State territory and the effective exercise of sovereign power. Given a territorial State's little or completely missing interest in protecting foreign States' real interests, these interests must be protected by the concerned State itself taking recourse to the protective principle. Therefore, this principle must possess the same rank as the territorial principle.[236]

At the same time, the protective principle overrides all those principles, which only indirectly pursue the protection of the self-preservation of the State and/or foreign interests. This applies to all principles which link jurisdiction to the nationality (of the perpetrator or the victim), that is, the active and passive *personality principles*. While the extraterritorial prosecution of a State's own nationals may contribute to the general preventive effect of the national criminal law,[237] and the prosecution of crimes committed against its own nationals may be demanded by a State's duty of diplomatic protection of its own nationals, the respective offences do not affect the foundations of the State concerned, that is, they do not affect its very safety and existence. The State invoking these principles does not act as a territorial State but as a victim or offender home State. From this perspective, this State is no longer pursuing primarily its own, but foreign interests, namely those of the territorial State. This State can, therefore, demand primary jurisdiction based on the territorial principle.[238] Against this background, the claim of extraterritorial jurisdiction by the victim or offender State on the basis of nationality only makes sense if, without this jurisdictional expansion, impunity would occur.[239]

As to the hierarchy of the jurisdictional principles, this means that the territorial principle and the protective principle prevail over the *nationality* (personality) *principle*. As to the latter, the active personality principle, entailing the protection of the victims of the national aggressor, overrides the passive personality principle, which is, anyway, controversial under international law. In fact, it is advisable to limit the latter principle to especially grave crimes against the own citizens.[240]

232 cf. Ziegenhain, *Exterritoriale Rechtsanwendung* (1992), pp. 50 ff.

233 See, in this vein, generally O'Keefe, *ICL* (2015), pp. 25–8 (concluding that no hierarchy is recognized under customary international law).

234 cf. Oehler, *Internationales Strafrecht* (1983), mn. 122 ff.; see also CoE, *Extraterritorial Criminal Jurisdiction* (1990), p. 26.

235 See also Oehler, *Internationales Strafrecht* (1983), mn. 126; Eser and Weißer, 'Vorbemerkungen §§ 3-9', in Schönke and Schröder, *Strafgesetzbuch* (2019), mn. 21.

236 cf. also Art. 7 Draft European Convention; likewise, Vogler, in Schroeder and Zipf, *FS Maurach* (1972), p. 603; Sieber, in Ständige Deputation des Deutschen Juristentages, *Verhandlungen*, I/3 (2012), p. 141; for an extensive interpretation, see Frimpong, in Eser and Lagodny, *Principles and Procedures* (1992), p. 31.

237 cf. Hoyer, 'Vorbemerkungen §§3-7', in Wolter et al., *Systematischer Kommentar StGB I* (2017), mn. 23.

238 Coming to a similar conclusion, Feller, *IsLR*, 16 (1981), 70.

239 Similarly, Vogler, in Schroeder and Zipf, *FS Maurach* (1972), pp. 604 ff.

240 cf. s. 5 Nr. 6 Alternative Draft of German PC (AE-StGB); conc. Vogler, in Oehler et al., *Aktuelle Probleme* (1970), p. 156.

The *representation principle* exclusively serves foreign interests. It could, at best, be explained with the, albeit somewhat ambiguous, concept of the solidarity of States,[241] which, of course, presupposes that the custodial State acts in fact 'in solidarity', that is, with the consent of the territorial State. In any case, the principle of representation is absolutely subsidiary to any other jurisdictional principle, including the personality principle.[242] In fact, the principle's subject matter has become increasingly irrelevant beside the universality principle. This is due to the fact that a foreign State may only be willing to assume criminal jurisdiction in representation of the territorial State if the offences concerned are of such seriousness that they also fall under the universality principle.

The *universality principle*, however, cannot be satisfactorily explained by the idea of solidarity of States, because, as we have just seen, this concept practically encompasses everything except acting in pure self-interest. In fact, the universality principle is not so much concerned with expressing solidarity with States, but rather with the victims of the crimes whose impunity it is supposed to prevent. At any rate, universality does not sit well with the traditional jurisdictional principles, for it is based upon the idea of an exercise of criminal jurisdiction on behalf of the international community enforcing its universal values[243] and, moreover, guided by a general mistrust in the territorial State's willingness and/or capacity to prosecute the respective crimes.[244]

Despite the existence of international criminal tribunals, universal jurisdiction is mostly invoked by national States to prosecute international crimes. Its decentralized application—in line with the indirect enforcement model[245]—leads to conflicts of jurisdiction, normally between the territorial State and the State invoking universal jurisdiction. It is questionable in such a case, for example that of General Pinochet, whether the territorial State (*in casu* Chile) should not have primary jurisdiction, even with regard to the universal jurisdiction State (*in casu* Spain).[246] This is certainly reasonable from a practical perspective since the territorial State's authorities are more familiar with the situation on the ground and normally have better access to evidence, suspects, and other materials relevant to the investigation. At the same time, however, this territorial State will often have no particular interest in carrying out an investigation and must therefore be substituted by a third State on the basis of the universality principle.

From a legal perspective, a subsidiary approach to universality gives rise to concerns since the truly international interests, to be pursued by the principle, cannot be conceptually subordinated to purely domestic interests, to be covered by the other jurisdictional principles. As a compromise, one could assume that the universality principle is *conditionally subsidiary* to the territorial principle. The condition would be that the territorial State is willing and able—in line with the rationale of the ICC's complementarity principle[247]—to investigate and prosecute the respective crime adequately. Under these same conditions, the universality principle should also be subsidiary to the personality principle, that is,

[241] cf. Oehler, *Internationales Strafrecht* (1983), mn. 133, 143 ff.; Council of the EU, 'Universal Jurisdiction (2009)', pp. 26 ff.

[242] Conc. Böse, 'Vor §§ 3-7', in Kindhäuser et al., *NK I* (23), mn. 33.

[243] This is being overlooked by Feller, *IsLR*, 16 (1981), 70.

[244] cf. AI, *Universal Jurisdiction* (2001), Introduction, p. 17 and *passim*.

[245] On this model, see Chapter VII, A. in this volume.

[246] cf. House of Lords per Lord Millett (24 March 1999), *WLR*, 1999, 825, 914.

[247] See Art. 17 ICCS; for an analysis, see Section B.(2) in this chapter.

one should generally give precedence to the territorial, victim, or offender States as long as these are willing and able to prosecute.[248] The subsidiarity approach would also enable a territorial State to prevent the abusive use of the universality principle by exercising primary jurisdiction.[249] If this State moreover claims that the crimes concerned do not fall under the universality principle but third States disagree, an independent international institution would have to decide the conflict. In this regard, the ICC could play an important role.[250]

A *combination* of several jurisdictional principles can influence the proposed hierarchy. First of all, one can say that any factor complementing the territorial principle strengthens its priority towards the other principles. Thus, for example, the combination of the territorial and active personality principles—if the territorial State prosecutes its own nationals—enjoys absolute priority over concurring claims of penal power, even if they are based on the protective principle that generally overrides the active personality principle.[251] On the other hand, in the case of a crime by a foreigner against a foreigner, a combination of the active and passive personality principles cannot override the territorial principle.

In sum, the following, fairly clear, hierarchy of jurisdictional principles may be suggested (see also Figure 4):

[248] cf. Kreicker, in Eser, Sieber, and Kreicker, *Nationale Strafverfolgung VII* (2006), pp. 268 ff. (speaking of a 'jurisdiction in stages'); Behrendt, *Verfolgung* (2005), pp. 293 ff., 298; Keller, *GA*, 146 (2006), 25, 34 ff.; Ryngaert, *CLF*, 19 (2008), 157 ff., 176, 178; Geneuss, *JICJ*, 7 (2009), 957; Munivrana Vajda, *ICLR*, 10 (2010), 342; Rosen, *JICJ*, 19 (2021), 1081–2; also Ambos, '§1 VStGB', in Safferling, *MüKo IX* (2022), mn. 23; ultimately in a similar vein, Weißer, *GA*, 152 (2012), 430. See also the three-stage jurisdictional system proposed by the German Federal Constitutional Court (BVerfG), *NStZ*, 31 (2011), 354 pursuant to § 153f StPO (precedence of the territorial, offender, or victim State, thereafter intervention of the ICC or other international tribunals, and only ultimately, at a third stage, any third States pursuant to the universality principle); in the same vein, Beck and Ritscher, *JICJ*, 13 (2015), 232. Crit., however, Roht-Arriaza and Fernando, in Brown, *Handbook ICL* (2011), p. 367; crit. the precedence given to the victim's State, Stigen, in Bergsmo, *Complementarity* (2010), p. 146.

[249] Tomuschat, in Cremer et al., *Tradition und Weltoffenheit des Rechts* (2002), pp. 339 ff. As far as universal jurisdiction is concerned, Ryngaert's 'New Theory' (Ryngaert, *Jurisdiction* (2015), pp. 189 ff.) does not, apparently, go substantially beyond the subsidiarity approach (cf. ibid., p. 229 where he calls to lift 'the nexus veil … if the State with the strongest nexus to the case is unable or unwilling to adequately deal with an internationally or transnationally relevant situation' and grant 'other States that are harmed' the right 'to *subsidiarily* exercise jurisdiction in the interest of the international community'). However, the more general an approach regarding jurisdictional conflicts (ibid., p. 231: 'another State … may step in, provided that its exercise of jurisdiction serves the global interest'), the greater is the tension with the requirements of criminal law in terms of precision and specifity, even, *in extremis*, possibly amounting to an abuse of (universal) jurisdiction (cf. in this respect the strong criticism from a TWAIL perspective by Chimni, *LJIL*, 35 (2022), 50: 'proposals of liberal jurisdictional internationalism are neoimperialist in their ambition and design'). These and other critical issues have not become decisively clearer in Ryngaert's follow-up work which is mainly due to the fact that the normative and the empirical are conflated in the research question (Ryngaert, *Intervention* (2020), p. 1: 'to identify the conditions enabling and constraining the exercise of unilateral jurisdiction in the common interest by states that have not necessarily the strongest connection to a situation') and methodology (p. 13 '"toolkit" methodology'). For a convincing critique, see Janis, *NILR* 68 (2021), 511 with regard to Ryngaert's summary (according to which 'third states' exercise of unilateral jurisdiction has its rightful place in the international legal order, as third state legal prescription and adjudication may well be the only means to safeguard common interests', Ryngaert, *Intervention* (2020), p. 220): 'Is this really enough for so detailed a study?' In yet another contribution (in Allen et al., *Jurisdiction* (2019)), Ryngaert, again conflating the normative and empirical levels, seems to suggest a kind of reconciliation of his 'New Theory' with more traditional perspectives when he speaks of 'the empowering real-life possibilities of a state exercising jurisdiction in the commen interest in ways that at the same time strengthen or reconstitute the territorially bounded political community which the state is supposed to serve, and to whose members … it owes fiduciary obligations given the relational character of state souvereigny' (pp. 226–7).

[250] On resolving jurisdictional conflicts between States and the ICC, cf. also Ambos, '§ 1 VStGB', in Safferling, *MüKo IX* (2022), mn. 22–4 with further references.

[251] cf. Herdegen, *ZaöRV*, 47 (1987), 236.

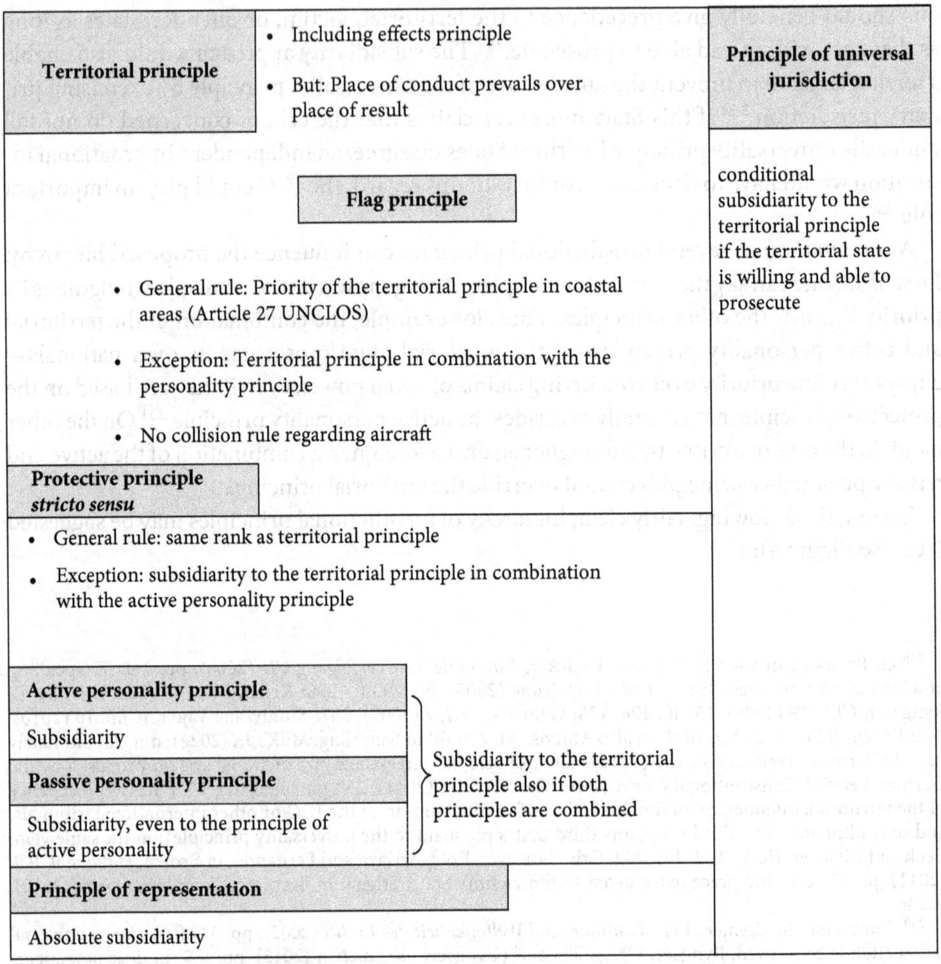


**Fig. 4.** Hierarchy of jurisdictional principles

1. territorial principle, including flag and effects principle, and protective principle
2. active and passive personality principle, and—at best complementary—3. principle of representation.

In parallel, the universality principle serves as a link between the national States and international criminal justice in order to enforce truly international interests. In concrete terms, this means that the international law standards of reasonableness and optimization, developed above,[252] allow for *flexible solutions*.[253] Other qualitative criteria may additionally be invoked. Flexibility may especially be achieved by procedural solutions giving discretion to the prosecutorial authorities.[254]

[252] See sub-section (1)(a) in this section.
[253] cf. Lagodny, in Donatsch et al., *Strafrecht, Strafprozessrecht und Menschenrechte* (2002), pp. 264 ff.; van der Beken, Vermeulen, and Lagodny, *NStZ*, 22 (2002), 625 ff.
[254] See e.g. regarding §153f StPO, Ambos, *CLF*, 18 (2007), 45 ff.; from the German Federal Prosecutor's perspective, see Beck and Ritscher, *JICJ*, 13 (2015), 229 ff.

## (4) Jurisdiction of the ICC vis-à-vis international criminal tribunals

### *(a) Jurisdiction of the ICC*

#### *(i) Preliminary remarks*

While ad hoc tribunals have by definition a very limited jurisdiction—limited to the place and time where the relevant criminal events have occurred[255]—the jurisdiction of a permanent international criminal court is, as a matter of principle, unlimited. As to the ICC,[256] distinguishing—in line with the AC—between four forms of jurisdiction (*ratione temporis, personae, materiae,* and *loci*),[257] we see the following: the ICC's temporal jurisdiction (jurisdiction *ratione temporis*) encompasses all *future* crimes within its subject matter jurisdiction,[258] that is, the crimes committed after the general entry into force of the Rome Statute,[259] or its entry into force for the respective State.[260] The ICC's *ratione personae*

[255] cf. Arts. 1, 8 ICTYS (limiting the ICTY's jurisdiction to the territory of the former Yugoslavia for crimes committed since 1991); Arts. 1, 7 ICTRS (limiting the ICTR's jurisdiction to 'the territory of Rwanda and Rwandan citizens responsible for such violations committed in the territory of neighbouring States between 1 January 1994 and 31 December 1994'), Art. 1 (1) IRMCTS (continuing 'the material, territorial, temporal and personal jurisdiction of the ICTY and the ICTR as set out in Arts. 1 to 8 of the ICTY Statute and Arts. 1 to 7 of the ICTR Statute') and Arts. 1 (1) SCSLS and 1 (2) RSCSLS (limiting the (R)SCSL's jurisdiction to crimes 'committed in the territory of Sierra Leone since 30 November 1996'); Art. 7, 8 KSC Law No. 05/L-053 (jurisdiction for crimes 'either commenced or committed in Kosovo' between 1 January 1998 and 31 December 2000); see also O'Keefe, *ICL* (2015), pp. 493–7 (ICTY/ICTR/MICT), 519–23 (SCSL). Crit. Cryer, *Prosecuting* (2005), pp. 223–4.

[256] cf. Bergsmo, *EJCCLCJ*, 6 (1998), 345 ff.; Kaul, *EJCCLCJ*, 6 (1998), 364 ff.; Olásolo, *CPI* (2003), pp. 160 ff.; Satzger, *ICL* (2018), § 12 mn. 6 ff.; Calvo-Goller, *Trial Proceedings* (2006), pp. 173 ff.; Calvo-Goller, *Procédure* (2012), pp. 107 ff.; in detail on the territorial jurisdiction (Art. 12 (2)(a) ICCS), see Vagias, *Jurisdiction* (2014); on the negotiations in detail (focusing on Art. 12 (2)(a)), Vagias, *Jurisdiction* (2014), pp. 41 ff., concluding that the 'account does not lend itself to uncontested legal conclusions' (p. 60); see also Schabas and Pecorella, 'Article 12', in Ambos, *Commentary* (2022), mn. 3 ff.; Rastan, in Stahn, *Practice* (2015), pp. 141–7.

[257] The case law requires explicitly *ratione materiae, temporis, and loci* jurisdiction; cf. e.g. ICC, *Prosecutor v. Bemba*, PTC III, Decision on the Prosecutor's Application for a Warrant of Arrest against Jean-Pierre Bemba Gombo, ICC-01/05-01/08-14-tENG, 10 June 2008, para. 12; *Prosecutor v. Gbagbo*, PTC III, Public Redacted Version of 'Decision on the Prosecutor's Application pursuant to Article 58 for a Warrant of Arrest against Laurent Koudou Gbagbo', ICC-02/11-01/11-9-Red, 30 November 2011, para. 9; *Prosecutor v. Ntaganda*, PTC II, Decision on the Prosecutor's Application under Article 58, ICC-01/04-02/06-36-Red, 13 July 2012, para. 8. Also including *ratione personae* jurisdiction, *Prosecutor v. Lubanga*, AC, Judgment on the Appeal of Mr Thomas Lubanga Dyilo against the Decision on the Defence Challenge to the Jurisdiction of the Court pursuant to article 19 (2) (a) of the Statute of 3 October 2006, ICC-01/04-01/06-772, 14 December 2006, para. 21; from more recent case law, cf. e.g. *Prosecutor v. Ongwen*, Public Redacted Trial Judgment, ICC-02/04-01/15-1762-Red 04-02-2021 975/1077 NM T, 4 February 2021, para. 2794 (*ratione materiae*); *Prosecutor v. Abd-Al-Rahman*, PTC II, Public Decision on the Defence 'Exception d'incompétence' (ICC-02/05-01/20-302), ICC-02/05-01/20-391, 17 May 2021, paras. 24, 36; *Prosecutor v. Ali Muhammad Ali Abd-Al-Rahman*, AC, Judgment on the Appeal of Mr Abd-Al-Rahman against the PTC II's 'Decision on the Defence "Exception d'incompétence" (ICC-02/05-01/20-302)', ICC-02/05-01/20-503, 1 November 2021, para. 42; ICC *Prosecutor v. Ongwen*, AC, Judgment on the Appeal of Mr Ongwen against the Decision of Trial Chamber IX of 4 February 2021 entitled 'Trial Judgment', ICC-02/04-01/15-2022-Red 15-12-2022 1/611 NM A, 15 December 2022, paras. 293, 1621; in the same vein, Nsereko and Ventura, 'Article 19', in Ambos, *Commentary* (2022), mn. 25; Rastan, in Stahn, *Practice* (2015), p. 146.

[258] i.e. genocide, crimes against humanity, war crimes, and the crime of aggression.

[259] Arts. 11 (1), 126 (1) ICCS. This was one of the reaons why French courts (instead of the ICC) tried Pascal Simbikangwa, who was found guilty on 14 March 2014 by the Paris Cour d'Assises for his involvement in the Rwandan genocide, see, in more detail, Trouille, *JICJ*, 14 (2016), 202–3.

[260] Arts. 11 (2), 126 (2) ICCS. On the prohibition of a retroactive application of the Statute (*nullum crimen sine lege praevia*), see Ambos, *Treatise ICL I* (2021), pp. 143 ff.; on the tricky issue of retroactivity regarding continuous crimes, see Ambos, *Treatise ICL II* (2022), pp. 129–30 (discussing the limitation with regard to enforced disappearance); in more detail, Rastan and Badar, 'Article 11', in Ambos, *Commentary* (2022), mn. 16–28. PTC III authorized the OTP to extend its investigation regarding continuous crimes even to those committed before the entry into force of the respective State (Bangladesh) 'in so far as the crimes continued after this date'; see *Situation in the People's Republic of Bangladesh/Republic of the Union of Myanmar*, PTC III, 'Decision Pursuant to Article 15 of the Rome Statute on the Authorisation of an Investigation into the Situation in the People's Republic of Bangladesh/Republic of the Union of Myanmar', ICC-01/19-27, 14 November 2019, para. 132. The continuous nature of certain crimes may also entail that they continue after the expiry of the force of the ICCS for a certain State and thus the OTP may continue its investigation after that date, see *Situation Burundi*, ICC-01/17-9-Red,

jurisdiction[261] extends to all natural persons aged over eighteen years.[262] The *ratione materiae* (subject matter) jurisdiction[263] covers the crimes included in Articles 5 to 8*bis* ICCS, all analysed in detail in Volume II of this Treatise. The *ratione loci* jurisdiction is, as we will see in a moment, basically governed by the territoriality principle. As to the crime of aggression, Articles 15*bis* and *ter* provide for specific jurisdictional rules;[264] the jurisdiction was activated by 17 July 2018.[265]

Of course, given that the Court has international legal personality[266] and that it is subject to international law, its jurisdiction is governed by the respective rules of international law discussed at the beginning of this chapter,[267] although it is not subject to the same limitations as that of a State.[268] Thus, the perhaps most important difference is that the Court has an inherent power—pursuant to the *compétence de la compétence* (*Kompetenz Kompetenz*) of international law mentioned earlier[269]—to determine its jurisdiction,[270] taking into account, of course, its jurisdictional framework and the relevant international principles discussed above.[271] This is especially true for the *ratione loci* jurisdiction to be analysed now.

*(ii)* Ratione loci *jurisdiction*

There have been two main opposing positions during the negotiations. States favourable to the Court, the so-called like-minded group, e.g. Canada, Germany, and Italy, argued on the basis of the universality principle, that—first—a State is bound by the automatic jurisdiction

para. 192. On how temporal jurisdiction could be used to limit the formal jurisdiction of the Court, see Scheffer, *JICJ*, 2 (2004), 26 ff.; specifically on the situation in Mali, see Stegmiller, *CLF*, 24 (2013), 489–90.

261 In detail, Kreß, in Grützner et al., *Internationaler Rechtshilfeverkehr* (2003), Part IV A 1, mn. 11 ff.; Schabas, *Introduction* (2020), pp. 64 ff.; Bassiouni, *Introduction ICL* (2013), pp. 59 ff., 660–1; Fakhouri Gómez, in Bacigalupo and Cancio M., *Derecho penal* (2005), pp. 100 ff.; Gless, *Internationales Strafrecht* (2021), mn. 980; on the problem of third party jurisdiction in particular, see Tsilonis, *Jurisdiction* (2019), pp. 33–5; Hoffmeister and Knoke, *ZaöRV*, 59 (1999), 795 ff.; Akande, *JICJ*, 1 (2003), 618 ff.; Danilenko, in Cassese et al., *Rome Statute II* (2002), pp. 1871 ff.; Paust, *VanderbiltJTL*, 11 (2000), 1 ff.; for a limited jurisdiction, Hafner, *JICJ*, 3 (2005), 329 ff.

262 Arts. 1, 25 (1), 26 ICCS; see also O'Keefe, *ICL* (2015), p. 542

263 cf. thereon, in detail, Rastan, in Stahn, *Practice* (2015), pp. 147–51; also O'Keefe, *ICL* (2015), pp. 538–9.

264 These have already been analysed in Ambos, *Treatise ICL II* (2022), pp. 226 ff., 247 ff.; see more recently Zimmermann and Freiburg-Braun, 'Article 15*bis*', in Ambos, *Commentary* (2022), mn. 1, 4 ff.; Aronsson-Storrier, 'Article 15*bis*', in Klamberg et al., *Commentary ICC I* (2023), pp. 565–82; Aronsson-Storrier, 'Article 15*ter*', in Klamberg et al., *Commentary ICC I* (2023), pp. 585–90.

265 In line with paras. 2 and 3 of Art. 15*bis* and 15*ter* ICCS, cf. Ambos, *Treatise ICL II* (2022), p. 250.

266 Art. 4 (1) ICCS.

267 In the same vein, Vagias, *Jurisdiction* (2014), p. 8; furthermore, see Tsilonis, *Jurisdiction* (2019), p. 34 arguing that the 'Achilles heel' of the ICC's jurisdictional system may be its exclusion of passive personality ('craftily excluded').

268 See also Bantekas, *ICL* (2010), p. 352.

269 See sub-section (1)(a) in this section.

270 cf. Art. 19 (1) ICCS (*proprio motu* power of Court regarding its jurisdiction) and ICC, *Situation in Uganda*, PTC II, Decision on the Prosecutor's Application that the Pre-Trial Chamber Disregard as Irrelevant the Submission Filed by the Registry on 5 December 2005, ICC-02/04-01/05-147, 9 March 2006, paras. 22–3; *Prosecutor v. Kony et al.*, PTC II, Decision on the Admissibility of the Case under Article 19 (1) of the Statute, ICC-02/04-01/05-377, 10 March 2009, para. 44; *Request under Regulation 46(3) of the Regulations of the Court*, PTC I, Decision on the 'Prosecution's Request for a Ruling on Jurisdiction under Article 19(3) of the Statute', ICC-RoC46(3)-01/18-37, 6 September 2018, paras. 30 ff. (32–3); PTC I, Decision on the 'Prosecution Request pursuant to Article 19(3) for a Ruling on the Court's Territorial Jurisdiction in Palestine'—Judge Péter Kovács' Partly Dissenting Opinion, ICC-01/18-143-Anx1 05-02-2021 1/163 EC PT, 5 February 2021, para. 49. See also Vagias, *Jurisdiction* (2014), pp. 10–11, 83–5, 86–8, 108, 111, 160, 206; Nsereko and Ventura, 'Article 19', in Ambos, *Commentary* (2022), mn. 4–5; Rastan, in Stahn, *Practice* (2015), pp. 162, 170; Abdou, 'Article 19', in Klamberg et al., *Commentary ICC I* (2023), pp. 645–6. This inherent power also entails that the Court's jurisdiction cannot be restricted by a State Party which, e.g., advocates a particularly restrictive interpretation of its territorial jurisdiction, cf. Rastan, *CLF*, 23 (2012), 20; Vagias, *Jurisdiction* (2014), pp. 109–11, 117, 160–1.

271 On another note, it has been stated that 'the rules of jurisdiction … do not preclude the Court from considering facts that in themselves occur outside its jurisdiction for the purpose of determining a matter within the jurisdiction.' (*Situation on the Registered Vessels of the Union of the Comoros, the Hellenic Republic and the Kingdom of Cambodia*, PTC I, Decision on the Request of the Union of the Comoros to Review the Prosecutor's Decision not to Initiate an Investigation, ICC-01/13-34, 16 July 2015, para. 17; conc. *Situation Bangladesh/ Myanmar*, ICC-01/19-27, para. 93.

of the Court as soon as that State becomes a party to the treaty, and—secondly—the Court must have universal jurisdiction.[272] At the other extreme, States sceptical towards the ICC, led by the US delegation, argued that one has to make a distinction between crimes of genocide on the one hand, and crimes against humanity and war crimes on the other. Automatic jurisdiction might be appropriate in the case of *genocide*, but for the other categories specific 'jurisdictional links' or additional prerequisites would be necessary to justify the ICC's jurisdiction.

A compromise proposal was made by the South Korean delegation. According to this so-called *South Korea proposal*, the Court would have jurisdiction if the territorial State (i.e. the State in which the crime has occurred) or the perpetrator's, victim's, or custodial State is either a State Party or has accepted the jurisdiction of the Court on an ad hoc basis. However, as to war crimes and crimes against humanity a so-called opt-in mechanism would have further been required, that is, a State Party would have to explicitly accept the ICC's jurisdiction by a declaration to that effect. As a sufficient jurisdictional link in these cases, the most restrictive view only accepted the perpetrator's (suspect's) State.[273] In any case, the Conference's Committee of the Whole (COW) rejected the distinction between genocide and the other crimes as confusing and arbitrary. A clear majority of States supported automatic jurisdiction and the South Korea proposal (as the compromise, which was closest to the German proposal of universal jurisdiction).[274]

In the end, the final proposal, adopted on the last day of the conference, provides for a three-stage model for jurisdiction, now contained in Article 12 ICCS and establishing 'preconditions for the exercise of jurisdiction':

- At the first stage, a State automatically accepts jurisdiction when it becomes a party to the treaty.[275] However, until recently a State Party could opt out[276] of the jurisdiction with respect to war crimes for a seven-year period after the Statute had come into force for that State;[277] this option was abolished by the 2015 ASP but the abolishment did not yet enter into force.[278]
- At the second stage, the territorial State or the suspect's State is recognized as alternative jurisdictional links.[279] The Court's jurisdiction is, therefore, established if the territorial

[272] For the same view, Rodrigues, in Faculdade de Direito da Universidade de Coimbra and Goethe-Institut Lisboa, *Direito penal internacional* (2003), pp. 70 ff.; considering it admissible, Cryer, *Prosecuting* (2005), p. 222. Ryngaert, *EJCCLCJ*, 14 (2006), 48, sees the universality principle as the basis of an ad hoc declaration under Art. 12 (3) ICCS and a Security Council referral. For a different view, see Abass, *ICLR*, 6 (2006), 349 ff.

[273] On these proposals, cf. also Arts. 7, 7*bis*, and 7*ter* of the Bureau's last two drafts of 6 July 1998 (A/Conf. 183/C.1/L.53) and 10 July 1998 (A/Conf. 183/C.1/L.59), cf. also *Zimmermann*, *ZaöRV*, 58 (1998), 84 5; *Kaul*, *EJCCLCJ*, 6 (1998), 364 ff.; Schabas and Pecorella, 'Article 12', in Ambos, *Commentary* (2022), mn. 5 ff.

[274] According to the 'Coalition for the ICC Monitor', the Conference Paper N. 2 (10 July 1998), 79 per cent of the States were in favour of the South Korea proposal.

[275] Art. 12 (1) ICCS. See, Schabas and Pecorella, 'Article 12', in Ambos, *Commentary* (2022), mn. 13; Zimmerman, revised by Guilfoyle, 'Article 12', in Klamberg et al., *Commentary ICC I* (2023), p. 489.

[276] In contrast, an opt in mechanism which was also discussed entails that a State is not (automatically) submitted to the Court's jurisdiction but must expressly declare its submission.

[277] Art. 124 ICCS. On history and rationale, see Nemane and Gunjal, *ICLR*, 15 (2015), 951 ff. This provision was crucial for France's acceptance of the Statute. Yet, only two States (France and Colombia) have made use of this possibility, but in both cases the opt-out is no longer valid (France withdrew its declaration on 13 August 2008 and the Colombian declaration expired on 1 November 2009). Recently, Ukraine has linked its envisaged ratification of the ICCS to invoke Art. 124, for a (critical) analysis see Heller, *Opinio Juris* 17 August 2024 and Zimmermann, *EJIL: Talk!* 20 August 2024. In any case, Art. 124 only applied to nationals of the State having made the declaration, not to protected aliens (e.g. refugees) on its territory (cf. Rastan, *CLF*, 23 (2012), 16–17, correctly rejecting the respective defence argument in *Mbarushimana*); problems could arise in case of concurrent jurisdiction between a State having made the declaration and another having not made it, cf. Nemane and Gunjal, *ICLR*, 15 (2015), 960 ff.

[278] At the (first) 2010 Kampala Review Conference (Art. 124 cl. 3 with Art. 123 (1) ICCS) Art. 124 was retained but made subject to further review 'during the fourteenth session of the Assembly of States Parties', i.e. the session of 2015, see Res. RC/Res. 4, <https://asp.icc-cpi.int/iccdocs/asp_docs/Resolutions/RC-Res.4-ENG.pdf>. The deletion only enters into force if seven-eights of the State Parties have ratified it (Art. 121 (4) ICCS). See, in more detail, Kravik, *EJIL: Talk!*, 12 April 2016. In favour of its deletion, Nemane and Gunjal, *ICLR*, 15 (2015), 949, 964 ff.

[279] Art. 12 (2)(b) refers to 'the person accused' ('*personne accusée*'), i.e., it embodies the active personality principle (cf. sub-section (2)(b) in this section, and thereon Schabas and Pecorella, 'Article 12', in Ambos, *Commentary*

State or the suspect's State is either a State Party (i.e. no special declaration of acceptance is necessary)[280] or has accepted the Court's jurisdiction with respect to one or more crimes 'of relevance' to a particular situation.[281] We will return to this form of ad hoc jurisdiction in a moment. Given the territorial focus of this part of the provision, it is fair to say that the Court's jurisdictional regime is basically one of territoriality, and thus rather conservative.[282] This territorial focus is also confirmed by Article 4 (2) ICCS according to which the 'Court may exercise its functions and powers' only on the territory of State Parties.

- At the third stage, a State[283] not party to the Statute,[284] but which is the territorial or suspect's State ('that State'), can accept the jurisdiction of the Court by an ad hoc

(2022), mn. 24; Zimmerman, revised by Guilfoyle, 'Article 12', in Klamberg et al., *Commentary ICC I* (2023), p. 495). However, the term suspect expresses more precisely the status of the person concerned at that point. On the notion of 'suspect' and 'accused', see Chapter I, D.(2)(d) and Chapter II, D.(1) in this volume.

[280] Art. 12 (2) ICCS. Thereto Fakhouri Gómez, in Bacigalupo and Cancio M., *Derecho penal* (2005), p. 112; Zimmerman, revised by Guilfoyle, 'Article 12', in Klamberg et al., *Commentary ICC I* (2023), pp. 490–5.

[281] Art. 12 (3) ICCS; Rule 44 (2) RPE ICC. For a summary, see Zimmerman, revised by Guilfoyle, 'Article 12', in Klamberg et al., *Commentary ICC I* (2023), pp. 496–9. On the nationality of the alleged offender as a basis for the assertion of criminal jurisdiction with an analysis of different scenarios, see Rastan, in Stahn, *Practice* (2015), pp. 151–63.

[282] See also Vagias, *Jurisdiction* (2014), p. 4, 282; Dicker, in Stahn, *ICC* (2015), p. 6 ('a limited jurisdictional regime'). On the territorial jurisdiction of the Court, with different scenarios of assertion or not of jurisdiction based on territoriality, see Rastan, in Stahn, *ICC* (2015), pp. 163–8.

[283] See thereon the discussion about Palestine's statehood pursuant to its Art. 12 (3) declaration in 2009 and 2014 in Ambos, *EJIL: Talk!* 6 May 2014; response by Azarov and Meloni, *EJIL: Talk!* 27 May 2014; Schabas and Pecorella, 'Article 12', in Ambos, *Commentary* (2022), mn. 33, all with further references; Cryer, in Stahn, *ICC* (2015), pp. 277–9; Stegmiller, 'Article 14', in Klamberg et al., *Commentary ICC I* (2023), pp. 533–7; crit. of the Prosecutor's position on the issue, Schabas, in Stahn, *ICC* (2015), p. 374; also crit. of 'the inconsistencies and legal errors in the former Prosecutor's approach', El Zeidy, in Stahn, *Practice* (2015), pp. 182–92. With GA Res. 67/19 of 4 December 2012 Palestine has become a 'Non-member State' of the UN and thus by now also meets the 'State' requirements in Art. 12 and other provisions of the ICCS (in the same vein calling for a functional approach, Dürr and von Maltitz, *ZStW*, 125 (2013) 922 ff.). An occupied territory, being a State, may also become a State Party since it retains, under general IHL, its sovereign power over this territory (cf. Vagias, *Jurisdiction* (2014), pp. 213–14, 241–2). The OTP did not only invoke Palestine's accession to the UN but also argued that Palestine was 'a State under relevant principles and rules of international law' (ICC OTP, *'Prosecution request pursuant to article 19(3) for a ruling on the Court's territorial jurisdiction in Palestine'*, OTP Request, ICC-01/18, 22 January 2020, paras. 7 and 9); also see the contributions of the symposium "Litigating Palestine Before the International Criminal Court', *JICJ*, 18 (2020), 881 ff. covering the further developments until 21 October 2020). In contrast, PTC I, by majority, explicitly considered any recourse to general international law as superfluous (*Situation in the State of Palestine*, PTC I, Decision on the 'Prosecution request pursuant to article 19(3) for a ruling on the Court's territorial jurisdiction in Palestine', ICC-01/18-143, 5 February 2021, paras. 88 and 89 ff.; summarizing Bayefsky, *ILM*, 60 (2021), 1038–9). This is hardly convincing, as it is apparent from Art. 12 (2)(a) ICCS ('if … States are Parties to this Statute') and Art. 12 (3) ICCS ('acceptance of a State which is not a Party to this Statute'), that the ICCS distinguishes between statehood in a jurisdictional sense and the status as an ICC State Party, see Situation in the State of Palestine, PTC I, Dissenting Opinion Judge Kovács, ICC-01/18-143-Anx1, 5 February 2021, para. 61. At any rate, Palestine's statehood can indeed be justified on the basis of the general international law due to collective recognition by the UN GA and the right of peoples to self-determination (see Ambos, *EJIL: Talk!* 2 March 2021; Tsilonis, *Jurisdiction* (2019), p. 53 ('recognized as a State by a large majority of UN member states'); also see Zimmermann, in Jeßberger et al., *Straftat und Systemunrecht* (2022), 455 arguing that it would be difficult to decisively apply the effective control criterion if the lack of effective control by the territorial State was based on the very war crimes in question.). Palestine was therefore within its rights when it made its Art. 12 (3) declaration of 31 December 2014 (ICC-CPI-20150105-PR1080) and acceded to the ICCS on 7 January 2015 (ICC-ASP-20150107-PR1082). On Israel's unwillingness to prosecute offences allegedly committed in the occupied territories, see Azarov and Weill, *ICLR*, 12 (2012), 913 ff.; for a detailed analysis, see Kearney and Reynolds, in Schabas et al., *Research Companion ICL* (2013), pp. 407 ff.; Dugard, *JICJ*, 11 (2013), 563 ff.; Zimmermann, *JICJ*, 11 (2013), 303 ff.; Ronen, *JICJ*, 12 (2014), 7 ff. The fact that Palestine has become a 'Non-member State' of the UN has not changed much in this regard, see Zimmermann, *JICJ*, 11 (2013), 306 ff.; thereon also Ronen, *JICJ*, 12 (2014), 10 ff.The issue has come up again – with regard to the Oslo Accords – in the arrest warrant proceedings in the Palestine Situation, cf. Prosecution's consolidated response" to the amicus curiae observations, ICC-01/18-346, 23 August 2024, para. 33 ff. <https://www.icc-cpi.int/sites/default/files/CourtRecords/0902ebd180949087.pdf>

[284] However, against this explicit wording, extending the provision to State Parties, Wills, *JICJ*, 12 (2014), 422 ff., advocating a broad, purpose-based reading and invoking Rule 44 (1) RPE ICC ('State … that has become a Party'), but these considerations cannot overrule the clear wording of the Statute which in any case prevails over conflicting Rules; cf. Art. 51 (5) ICCS and Zimmermann, *JICJ*, 11 (2013), 315.

declaration pursuant to Article 12 (3) ICCS. Such a declaration must be made by the legal representatives of the State[285] and deposited with the Court's Registry.[286]

Of course, this complex jurisdictional regime generates many questions, which cannot be dealt with here exhaustively.[287] As to the jurisdictional links included in Article 12 (2) ICCS—perhaps the core provision of the jurisdictional regime—the Court, while certainly within its right to determine its jurisdiction autonomously pursuant to its *compétence de la compétence* mentioned above,[288] must stick to the wording of the relevant provisions and take into account the principles and rules of international law analysed above. In particular, it will have to take issue with 'the conduct in question' as the decisive point of reference of its territorial jurisdiction.[289]

Given the thorough study on the subject by Michail Vagias[290] it suffices here to take note of some aspects in passing. While it is pretty clear that 'conduct' encompasses act and omission,[291] the very use of this term[292] makes it difficult to broaden the Court's jurisdiction *on this basis* to the mere (partial) commission of a crime on the respective territory,[293] including its preparatory acts or attempt, its consequences or effects, or any constituent element of this crime. Such a broad or expansive interpretation would only overcome the quite straightforward wording of Article 12 (2)(a) if a case could be made that a rather flexible territorial nexus requirement based on reasonableness,[294] and in line with the doctrines discussed

[285] That is, normally, the sitting government; see in this regard the failed attempt by representatives of former Egyptian President Morsi and his Freedom and Justice Party to lodge a declaration rejected by the OTP (for lack of standing, i.e. legal capacity to act on behalf of Egypt) and, pursuant to a 'request for review', as confirmed by PTC II twice; cf. ICC, Request under Regulation 46 (3) of the Regulations of the Court, PTC II, Decision on the 'Request for review of the Prosecutor's decision of 23 April 2014 not to open a Preliminary Examination concerning alleged crimes committed in the Arab Republic of Egypt, and the Registrar's Decision of 25 April 2014', ICC-RoC46(3)-01/14, 12 September 2014, rejecting the request *in limine* for lack of power to review the OTP's decision; see also ICC, Regulation 46 (3) of the Regulations of the Court, PTC II, Decision on a Request for Reconsideration or Leave to Appeal the 'Decision on the "Request for review of the Prosecutor's decision of 23 April 2014 not to open a Preliminary Examination concerning alleged crimes committed in the Arab Republic of Egypt, and the Registrar's Decision of 25 April 2014"', ICC-RoC46(3)-01/14-5, 22 September 2014, rejecting an application for reconsideration and leave to the appeal; on the former decision, see Schabas and Pecorella, 'Article 12', in Ambos, *Commentary* (2022), mn. 34; see generallyElDeeb, *ICLR*, 15 (2015), 733, 749 ff. (agreeing with the dismissal and criticizing the political use of Art. 12 (3) by the complainants). On whether the Palestinian Minister of Justice and the Attorney General of Gaza were entitled to lodge a declaration, see El Zeidy, in Stahn, *Practice* (2015), pp. 201–5 (arguing, on the basis of relevant ICJ case law, that such—minor—State authorities need to be vested explicitly with full powers which *in casu* were lacking).

[286] Art. 12 (3) cl. 1 ICCS; Rule 44 (2) RPE ICC.

[287] For (many) open questions not yet dealt with by the case law or literature, see Rastan, *CLF*, 23 (2012), 33–4; Rastan, in Stahn, *Practice* (2015), pp. 163–8.

[288] Note 270 and main text in this chapter.

[289] Art. 12 (2)(a) ICCS.

[290] Vagias, *Jurisdiction* (2014), pp. 79 ff., with an especially interesting part on internet crimes (pp. 130 ff.), especially online incitement to genocide (135, 153 ff.) where however 'no safe answers' regarding jurisdiction can be offered. Also, see Vagias, *JCSL*, 21 (2016), 527 ff. concluding regarding internet crimes that 'the construction of an offence' is relevant to the (territorial) jurisdiction (539: 'accessibility of the website might suffice to establish territorial jurisdiction over incitement to genocide') and finally suggesting that the ICC 'could follow its domestic counterparts'.

[291] Ambos, *Treatise ICL I* (2021), p. 369; see also Vagias, *Jurisdiction* (2014), pp. 91 ff., 100; Adell, 'Article 22', in Klamberg et al., *Commentary ICC I* (2023), pp. 716–19.

[292] Art. 30 ICCS in particular makes clear that 'conduct' must be distinguished from 'consequence' (or, for that matter, results or effects) and 'circumstance'. It is based on the general distinction between 'conduct' and 'consequence' in criminal law theory (see Ambos, *Treatise ICL I* (2021), pp. 139–40, 368–71). It is for this reason that national laws use the term 'commission' (of the crime) if they want to broaden the jurisdictional basis. Against this background, Vagias' recourse to Arts. 20 and 22 ICCS (pp. 99–100) does not change the matter.

[293] For this view, Vagias, *Jurisdiction* (2014), pp. 96 ff., 101 ('conduct in question' as 'crimes in question').

[294] In this vein, specifically advocating a (mere) 'reasonable nexus' between the crime and the territory of a State Party, Vagias, *Jurisdiction* (2014), pp. 88, 130, 160, 285.

above (objective territoriality, ubiquity, effects doctrine), is part of customary international law or amounts to a general principle within the meaning of the recognized sources of the Court.[295] This would be supported by a teleological reading of Article 12 (2)(a)[296] whereby the extensions of territoriality *stricto sensu*, especially the effects principle, could be seen as manifestations or subsets of territoriality and thus be covered by the territorial jurisdiction of the Court.[297] This has indeed been the view taken by PTC I in the case of the deportation of Rohingya people from Myanmar (non-State Party) to Bangladesh (State Party).[298] Such a broad reading of the Court's territorial jurisdiction also makes it easier to subject transnational non-State actors, such as IS, despite the usually lacking specific territorial link, to the Court's jurisdiction.[299]

With regard to the situation in Bangladesh/Myanmar,[300] PTC III found, on the basis of a textual and systematic interpretation, that the terms conduct and crime are used in an identical way in Article 12 (2)(a).[301] Accordingly, the term 'conduct' simply denotes 'the *actus reus* element underlying a crime subject to the jurisdiction ratione materiae of the Court'.[302] Yet, this understanding appears, at least terminologically, ambivalent for the very fact that the same PTC uses the term 'conduct' at a later point in order to link it with particular consequences.[303] Moreover, and more importantly, the concept of ubiquity or the 'effects doctrine' is likely to offer more appropriate or doctrinally sound solutions. Be that as it may, the PTC III then goes on to list extensive considerations as to 'whether article 12(2)(a) of the Statute requires that all the conduct takes place in the territory of one or more State

[295] cf. Art. 21 (1)(b) and (c) ICCS. In this vein, Vagias, *Jurisdiction* (2014), pp. 102–24, 159–60, 286, albeit admitting that the wording of Art. 12 (2)(a), by 'opting for the existing formulation', 'could be seen as a silent rejection' of such a broad interpretation and, generally (p. 285), that '[t]here are limits' to what the Court's territorial jurisdiction entails.

[296] cf. Vagias, *Jurisdiction* (2014), pp. 76–7, 163, 171, 205.

[297] cf. regarding the effects principle, Vagias, *Jurisdiction* (2014), pp. 171, 188, 206 (also advocating such a broad reading on some policy grounds which may be summarized as follows: closing of jurisdictional loopholes since ICL crimes causes a considerably greater harm than the antitrust violations for which the effects doctrine is recognized [pp. 163 ff., 205–6]; but also, being aware of the difficulties of his argument, proposing two limitations along the lines of the qualifiers recognized and the reasonableness of the jurisdictions claim [pp. 190–6, 207, cautious also at 286]); in favour of objective territoriality (including ubiquity), see also Rastan, *CLF*, 23 (2012), 17 ff.

[298] Decision Jurisdiction under Article 19 (3), ICC-RoC46(3)-01/18-37, paras. 50 ff. (regarding deportation pursuant to Art. 7 (1)(d) ICCS [para. 52 ff.]; 'support in the object and purpose of the Statute' [para. 69]; 'acts of deportation … fall within the parameters of article 12(2)(a)' [para. 73]), 74 ff. (affirmatively discussing this jurisdictional extension with regard to Art. 7 (1)(h) and 7 (1)(k)).

[299] For a first discussion regarding IS, see Stahn, *EJIL: Talk!*, 3 December 2014, arguing, inter alia, that the territorial nexus requirement makes it difficult to speak of a 'situation' with regard to an armed group only and thus to claim ICC jurisdiction; in a similar vein, Galand, *EJIL: Talk!*, 27 May 2015; affirming territorial jurisdiction over IS in connection with the Paris attacks on the basis of the effects principle Ambos, *EJIL: Talk!* 26 November 2015. Discussing the Court's jurisdiction pursuant to active personality (Art. 12 (1)(b) ICCS) Fry, *Contours* (2015), pp. 142–4 (correctly pointing to the fragmented investigation of the situation and the arbitrary selection of responsible because of the necessary jurisdictional focus on the nationals of State Parties).

[300] With regard to the jurisdictional questions arising from the situation, cf. also Schabas and Pecorella, 'Article 12', in Ambos, *Commentary* (2022), mn. 19.

[301] *Situation Bangladesh/Myanmar*, ICC-01/19-27, para. 48 ('At first glance, the term "conduct" appears to be distinct from the term "crime". However, the use of both "conduct" and "crime" in the language of article 12(2)(a) of the Statute indicates that the term conduct, short of crime, is a reference to criminal conduct absent legal characterization. The *travaux préparatoires* offer no explanation as to why the drafters selected to use a different word in relation to vessel/aircraft. There is no apparent reason why the threshold for territorial jurisdiction would be different based on whether the location of the conduct/crime is on land or vessel/aircraft').

[302] *Situation Bangladesh/Myanmar*, ICC-01/19-27, para. 49.

[303] Ibid., para. 51 ('particular consequence may be that the victim behaves, or is caused to behave, in a certain way as a result of conduct attributable to the alleged perpetrator').

Parties'.[304] In this regard, the Chamber concludes that jurisdiction *ratione loci* can be justified 'under the objective territoriality principle, the ubiquity principle, as well as the constitutive elements approach',[305] 'provided that at least part of the conduct' takes place 'in the territory of a State Party'.[306] In the situation of Bangladesh/Myanmar this was, according to PTC III, the case with regard to acts under Article 7 (1)(d) and (h) ICCS, given that the deported victims had crossed the border into Bangladesh.[307] Related to these questions is the problem that it is unclear whether the transboundary crime of deportation, when committed by sea, is completed when the deportees reach the high seas or only when they land in the first receiving State.[308]

As to the specific situation of occupation one must distinguish between the occupied and the occupying State: While the former may confer jurisdiction upon the ICC with accession to the Statute since it retains its sovereign power under general IHL,[309] it is unclear whether the occupying State, being a State Party, can extend the Court's jurisdiction to the occupied territory by way of its effective control.[310]

*(iii) Declaration under Article 12 (3) ICCS*

As to Article 12 (3) ICCS it is first worthwhile noting—complementing the considerations made above—that, so far, several States have deposited the required declarations,[311] including one State Party.[312] While this is not foreseen in Article 12 (3)—it only applies to 'a State which is not a Party'[313]—it is possible under Article 11 (2) *in fine* allowing a State Party

[304] Ibid., para. 54.
[305] Ibid., para. 62.
[306] Ibid., para. 61.
[307] Ibid., para. 62.
[308] On this in depth, Almasri, *EJIL: Talk!*, 25 September 2023.
[309] cf. Vagias, *Jurisdiction* (2014), pp. 213 ff., 241–2, 286.
[310] For an excellent discussion, see Vagias, *Jurisdiction* (2014), pp. 224 ff. concluding that, at the present state of the law, such an expansive application of Art. 12 (2)(a), on the basis of the human rights effective control test, would be 'doubtful' (p. 239) ultimately leaving the decision to the Court (pp. 241, 242, 286); furthermore, see Tsilonis, *Jurisdiction* (2019), p. 45, who opposes such a jurisdictional extension arguing that then State parties might find themselves tempted to occupy non-State Parties in order to establish ICC jurisdiction ('following the multiple terror attacks in the centre of Paris on the 13 November 2015, France could have invaded Palmyra in Syria for the ICC to establish jurisdiction without the interference of the Security Council').
[311] See the instructive overview in El Zeidy, in Peters, *MPEPIL* (2023), paras. 21 ff. On *Palestine*, see note 283 in this chapter; see also Shaw, *JICJ*, 9 (2011), 301 ff. On 18 April 2003, the government of President Gbagbo of *Ivory Coast* submitted such a declaration accepting the ICC's jurisdiction for acts committed since 19 September 2002. This declaration has—albeit legally not necessary—been 'confirmed' by his successor President Qattara on 14 December 2010 (*Situation Côte d'Ivoire*, ICC-02/11-14, paras. 10–11); see also thereon Stahn, *CLF*, 22 (2011), 183; *Gbagbo*, ICC-02/11-01/11-321, paras. 49, 55–6, 58–62. *Ukraine* lodged a declaration on 17 April 2014 accepting the Court's jurisdiction for crimes committed from 21 November 2013 to 22 February 2014 and another one on 8 September 2015 accepting jurisdiction for crimes committed since 20 February 2014 'for an indefinite duration'; on Ukraine's ad hoc jurisdictional acceptance, see Marchuk, *VanderbiltJTL*, 49 (2016), 323; El Zeidy, in Peters, *MPEPIL* (2023), paras. 58–60. On 15 November 2023, the Republic of *Armenia* accepted the ICC's jurisdiction retroactively from 10 May 2021. Discussing the deterrence effect of Art. 12 (3) declarations, see Shen, *Opinio Juris* 2 February 2024 (but it is unclear why this effect should be different under this jurisdictional basis).
[312] Uganda, despite being a State Party since 14 June 2002 (entry into force 1 September 2002 pursuant to Arts. 11 (2), 126 (2) ICCS), lodged such a declaration on 16 December 2003 (at the time of writing under seal) to give the Court full retroactive jurisdiction as of 1 July 2002, i.e. the general entry into force of the Statute. Thus, this is a case where an Art. 12 (3) declaration was used to fill a temporal (two months) jurisdictional gap; cf. Chaitidou, 'Article 14', in Ambos, *Commentary* (2022), mn. 13; Wills, *JICJ*, 12 (2014), 411–12.
[313] Note 284 in this chapter.

('that State') to make such a declaration.[314] While States having made such a declaration do not possess all the rights and obligations of a State Party, they are obliged to cooperate with the ICC, 'without any delay or exception', in accordance with Part 9 of the Statute.[315] Rule 44 (2) RPE ICC clarifies ('with respect to the crimes referred to in article 5 of relevance to the situation')—contrary to the insofar ambiguous wording of Article 12 (3) ('with respect to the crime in question')—that a State making an ad hoc declaration must not 'use the Court "opportunistically"', that is, only against certain parties to a conflict.[316] Instead, it must refer to the general conflict 'situation' and the resulting core 'crimes' or 'events' and all these crimes/events have to be investigated.[317]

There is a certain controversy as to the *temporal effect* of such a declaration, that is, if it is limited with regard to past and/or future events. While the wording of Article 12 (3), as just quoted, seems to limit the declaration to past crimes ('crime in question'), this interpretation is contradicted by Rule 44 (2) RPE ICC,[318] also just quoted. More importantly, it appears too formalistic in light of the purpose of Article 12 ICCS[319] as a provision establishing mere 'preconditions to the exercise of jurisdiction'.[320] The actual jurisdiction is only triggered by the referral mechanisms of Article 13, to be analysed in the next section, and it is perfectly possible that a referral of a 'situation' also includes future crimes developing out of this situation, sufficiently linked to it.[321] Thus, the mere wording of Article 12 (3) does not limit the scope of the declaration either way (with regard to past or future crimes) as correctly confirmed by the Appeals Chamber.[322] However, such a

[314] See also Rastan and Badar, 'Article 11', in Ambos, *Commentary* (2022), mn. 29. Yet, Art. 11 (2) *in fine* should be read narrowly, as extending only the *temporal* jurisdiction of the Court; see also note 323 in this chapter.

[315] cf. Art. 12 (3) ICCS and *Gbagbo*, ICC-02/11-01/11-321, para. 74; crit. on the limited enforcement, see Schabas and Pecorella, 'Article 12', in Ambos, *Commentary* (2022), mn. 30. On Part 9 ICCS, see Chapter VII in this volume.

[316] ICC, *Prosecutor v. Gbagbo*, PTC I, Decision on the 'Corrigendum of the challenge to the jurisdiction of the International Criminal Court on the basis of articles 12(3), 19(2), 21(3), 55 and 59 of the Rome Statute filed by the Defence for President Gbagbo (ICC-02/11-01/11-129)', ICC-02/11-01/11-212, 15 August 2012, para. 59. Crit. with regard to Ukraine's 2014 declaration (note 311 in this chapter) in that regard, Schabas and Pecorella, 'Article 12', in Ambos, *Commentary* (2022), mn. 34. On the drafting history, see Rastan, in Stahn and El Zeidy, *Complementarity I* (2011), p. 422 with n. 2 and p. 429 with n. 23 (also discussing Uganda's referral of the 'situation of LRA'). On Uganda's referral, see also Sainati, *VanderbiltJTL*, 49 (2016), 206–8; Vinjamuri, *LCP*, 79 (2016), 282.

[317] Rule 44 RPE ICC; ICC, *Prosecutor v. Gbagbo*, AC, Judgment on Appeal of Mr Laurent Koudou Gbagbo against the Decision of Pre-Trial Chamber I on Jurisdiction and Stay of Proceedings, ICC-02/11-01/11-321, 12 December 2012, para. 1. See also Gómez Colomer, in Gómez Colomer et al., *Corte Penal Internacional* (2003), p. 297 with n. 61; Olásolo, *CPI* (2003), pp. 180 ff.; Olásolo, *CLF*, 16 (2005), 295–6; Stahn, El Zeidy and Olásolo, *AJIL*, 99 (2005), 427 ff.; Klamberg, in van den Herik and Stahn, *Diversification and Fragmentation* (2012), p. 627; Zimmermann, *JICJ*, 11 (2013), 315–16; ElDeeb, *ICLR*, 15 (2015), 747–8; Schabas and Pecorella, 'Article 12', in Ambos, *Commentary* (2022), mn. 31; Zimmerman, revised by Guilfoyle, 'Article 12', in Klamberg et al., *Commentary ICC I* (2023), pp. 496–9.

[318] cf. *Gbagbo*, ICC-02/11-01/11-321, para. 80, clarifying that 'crime in question', as 'the words "crimes referred to in article 5" indicates … refers to the categories of crimes in article 5 of the Statute … and not to specific events in the past, in the course of which such crimes were committed'.

[319] For a teleological reading in this context, see also Wills, *JICJ*, 12 (2014), 409 ff.; Vagias, *Jurisdiction* (2014), p. 63.

[320] *Gbagbo*, ICC-02/11-01/11-321, para. 82. cf. also El Zeidy, in Stahn, *Practice* (2015), pp. 205–6.

[321] cf. ICC, *Situation in the Republic of Côte d'Ivoire*, PTC III, Decision pursuant to Article 15 of the Rome Statute on the Authorisation of an Investigation into the Situation in the Republic of Côte d'Ivoire, ICC-02/11-14, 3 October 2011, paras. 178–9 (holding that 'crimes that may be committed after the date of the Prosecutor's application will be covered by any authorisation' 'insofar as they are sufficiently linked to the situation of crisis referred to the Court as ongoing at the time of the referral'); thereon, see also Stegmiller, *CLF*, 24 (2013), 481 and notes 400 ff. in this chapter.

[322] *Gbagbo*, ICC-02/11-01/11-321, paras. 81, 83–4, stating that 'article 12(3) does not prevent a State from accepting the jurisdiction of the Court prospectively, with the consequence that the Court has jurisdiction in

limitation may be given to the declaration by the issuing State itself or it may follow from the Court's legal framework, especially with a view to the above mentioned 'opportunistic' declarations.

As to the latter, the question arises whether the Statute's substantive prohibition of retroactivity in the sense of the *nullum crimen sine lege praevia* principle,[323] confirmed by the Statute's jurisdictional non-retroactivity pursuant to Article 11, as already mentioned earlier, limits the temporal scope of such a declaration with regard to past crimes. As we have just seen, Article 12 (3) itself refers, on the face of it, to past crimes. However, can the ensuing retroactivity of an ad hoc declaration be reconciled with the Statute's general prohibition of retroactivity? The answer is given by the last part of Article 11 (2) which admits an exception in case of ad hoc declarations under Article 12 (3) ICCS.[324] Thus, it follows that a State may refer in such a declaration to crimes or events having occurred before the actual declaration is issued, that is, a State may give such a declaration a retroactive effect. However, this effect must not go beyond the date of general entry into force of the Statute, that is, not beyond 1 July 2002,[325] or beyond the coming into existence of that State.[326] In other words, a State may anticipate the *specific* entry into force[327]—or, more precisely, the jurisdictional effect of the declaration with regard to itself—but it must not include crimes in its declaration that occurred before the Statute's *general* entry into force. Insofar, the State's discretion pursuant to an Article 12 (3) declaration is limited by the Statute's general entry into force.[328] For otherwise, the substantive (human rights) dimension of the retroactivity prohibition, as embodied in Articles 22 (1) and 24 (1) ICCS, would be violated given that the 'conduct in question' referred to in this provision only turns into ('constitutes') a crime under the Statute with its general entry into force.[329]

A further limitation of the otherwise sovereign right of a State to give its Article 12 (3) declaration a (limited) retroactive effect has been suggested with regard to the rights of third

respect of any future events' (para. 83) and 'the phrase crime in question … neither limits the scope of a declaration to crimes that occurred in the past nor to crimes committed in a specific "situation"' (para. 84). In favour also, Ambos, *EJIL: Talk!* 6 May 2014; *contra* Zimmermann, *JICJ*, 11 (2013), 311 ff.; El Zeidy, in Stahn, *Practice* (2015), pp. 207–8; also, see Batros, in Guariglia et al., *AC ICC Commentary* (2018), 70.

[323] cf. Art. 22 (1) ICCS and Ambos, *Treatise ICL I* (2021), pp. 143 ff.

[324] cf. Art. 11 (2) *in fine*: 'unless … declaration under article 12, paragraph 3'; see Tsilonis, *Jurisdiction* (2019), pp. 60–1; for a different reading of this provision, cf. Kontorovich, *IsLR*, 47 (2014), 385–6, arguing that it only explains the effect of such a declaration vis-à-vis full membership, i.e. allows subsequent membership to refer back to the declaration, but does not give the declaration as such a retroactive effect.

[325] cf. Arts. 11 (1), 126 (1) ICCS. In the same vein, El Zeidy, in Stahn and Sluiter, *Practice* (2009), p. 70; O'Keefe, *ICL* (2015), pp. 542–3; Klamberg, 'Article 11' in Klamberg et al., *Commentary ICC I* (2023), pp. 482–3; Zimmerman, revised by Guilfoyle, 'Article 12', in Klamberg et al., *Commentary ICC I* (2023), pp. 496–9.

[326] This is relevant with regard to the Palestinian declaration discussed in note 283 in this chapter; against a retroactive effect of the Art. 12 (3) declaration beyond the date of the existence of the State, see Zimmermann, *JICJ*, 11 (2013), 318–20; Fry, *Contours* (2015), pp. 146–7; in favour, Wills, *JICJ*, 12 (2014), 428 ff.

[327] cf. Arts. 11 (2), 126 (2) ICCS; see also Rastan, *CLF*, 23 (2012), 30–1 (discussing PTC III's decision in the *Côte d'Ivoire* situation); also in favour of such a retroactive effect, ElDeeb, *ICLR*, 15 (2015), 748–9.

[328] Too broad, therefore, the view taken by the ICC-OTP when stating that the temporal jurisdiction depends on 'the date indicated' in the Art. 12 (3) declaration (ICC-OTP, *Prelim. Examinations* (2013), para. 37).

[329] For a too liberal reading in this regard, see Wills, *JICJ*, 12 (2014), 418–20, arguing in essence that Art. 12 (3) does not affect Art. 22 (1) since it only refers to the 'preconditions to the exercise of jurisdiction' and too lightly dismissing human rights concerns. If one understands 'jurisdiction' in Art. 22 (1) broadly, all jurisdictional provisions of the Statute are covered by this provision, including Art. 12; in the same vein, Broomhall, 'Article 22', in Ambos, *Commentary* (2022), mn. 34; cf. also Adell, 'Article 22', in Klamberg et al., *Commentary ICC I* (2023), pp. 716–19.

States, especially those States that are not Parties to the Statute. It has been argued—in line with the old US position as defended in Rome—that they cannot be bound by such a retroactive declaration, that is, it must only apply to the nationals of the declaring State.[330] This is not convincing. There is no difference between the strict territorial principle under Article 12 (2)(a) and its ad hoc backdating under Article 12 (3). In both cases the territorial State delegates its territorial jurisdiction to the Court and thus all persons falling under this territorial jurisdiction in the first place are covered.

Last but not least, in the context of the recent, above-mentioned invocation of Art. 124 by Ukraine a controversy about the relationship between former Art. 12(3) declarations and a subsequent ratification of the Statute arose. Can a State limit the Court's territorial jurisdiction excluding war crimes (by way of Art. 124) displacing previous Art. 12(3) declarations which did not contain such a (*ratione materiae*) limitation? Can such a limitation in itself be limited to the State's own nationals (Ukrainans) but exclude foreign nationals (Russians)?[331]

*(iv) Challenges to jurisdiction*

The existence of jurisdiction can either be examined by the Court *proprio motu* as part of its *compétence de la compétence*,[332] or pursuant to a challenge to be brought either by the accused/suspect[333] or by a State which has jurisdiction over the respective case and investigates/prosecutes it[334] or by a State whose consent, by way of an Article 12 (3) declaration, is required.[335] In addition, the Prosecutor may always seek a ruling on jurisdiction or

330 In the same vein, Scheffer, *JICJ*, 2 (2004), 32 ('would empower the Prosecutor to investigate the nationals of the non-Party State filing the Article 12(3) declaration, but not any other non-Party State's nationals absent state consent').

331 On this and other issues Heller, *Opinio Juris* 17 August 2024 and Zimmermann, *EJIL: Talk!* 20 August 2024.

332 cf. Art. 19 (1) ICCS, note 270 and main text in this chapter. The wording '*shall* satisfy', as opposed to 'may' regarding admissibility, may even be read as entailing an obligation of the Court to determine its jurisdiction; in this sense, Nouwen, *Complementarity* (2013), p. 81.

333 cf. Art. 19 (2)(a) ICCS. The reference to Art. 58 entails that, in line with this provision, a suspect is also covered; for more details, see Nsereko and Ventura, 'Article 19', in Ambos, *Commentary* (2022), mn. 30 ff. (discussing, inter alia, the terms 'suspect' and 'accused'). There have been several defence challenges to jurisdiction, starting with the *Lubanga* case (PTC I, Decision on the Defence Challenge to the Jurisdiction of the Court pursuant to Article 19 (2)(a) of the Statute, ICC-01/04-01/06-532, 3 October 2006; also *Lubanga*, ICC-01/04-01/06-772) and continuing with *Mbarushimana* (PTC I, Decision on the 'Defence Challenge to the Jurisdiction of the Court', ICC-01/04-01/10-451, 26 October 2011); *Ruto and Sang*, AP, Decision on the Appeals of Mr William Samoei Ruto and Mr Joshua Arap Sang against the Decision of Pre-Trial Chamber II of 23 January 2012 Entitled 'Decision on the Confirmation of Charges Pursuant to Article 61(7)(a) and (b) of the Rome Statute', ICC-01/09-01/11 OA3 OA4, 24 May 2012; *Gbagbo* (PTC I, Decision on the 'Corrigendum of the challenge to the jurisdiction of the International Criminal Court on the basis of articles 12(3), 19(2), 21(3), 55, and 59 of the Rome Statute filed by the Defence for President Gbagbo (ICC-02/11-01/11-129)', ICC-02/11-01/11-212, 15 August 2012; AC, Judgment on the Appeal of Mr Laurent Koudou Gbagbo against the Decision of PTC I on Jurisdiction and Stay of the Proceedings, ICC-02/11-01/11-321 (OA2), 12 December 2012); *Ntaganda* (TC VI, Decision on the Defence's Challenge to the Jurisdiction of the Court in respect of Counts 6 and 9, ICC-01/04-02/06-892, 9 October 2015; AC, Judgment on the Appeal of Mr Bosco Ntaganda against the 'Decision on the Defence's challenge to the jurisdiction of the Court in respect of Counts 6 and 9', ICC-01/04-02/06-1225, 22 March 2016); *Abd-Al-Rahman*, ICC-02/05-01/20-391.

334 cf. Art. 19 (2)(b) ICCS. An attempt to limit this possibility to State Parties failed, i.e. any State with jurisdiction can make a challenge (cf. Nsereko and Ventura, 'Article 19', in Ambos, *Commentary* (2022), mn. 36). On the same case/conduct test, which may be applicable here, see Section B.(2)(b) in this chapter. See also thereon Vagias, *Jurisdiction* (2014), p. 253; crit. of this part of the provision Nsereko and Ventura, 'Article 19', in Ambos, *Commentary* (2022), mn. 37.

335 cf. Art. 19 (2)(a)–(c) ICCS; for a crit. discussion, see Nsereko and Ventura, 'Article 19', in Ambos, *Commentary* (2022), mn. 43; for an overview of the early case law, Stahn, in Stahn, *Practice* (2015), pp. 229, 231 ff. (distinguishing between disputes regarding the 'merits of ICC engagement with domestic consent' and 'state

admissibility.[336] The procedural details are laid down in the Rules.[337] Here, it suffices to note some specific aspects.

First of all, it is important to mention that Article 19 refers to a 'case'[338] and concerns challenges to both the jurisdiction and the admissibility, the former having to be treated 'first'.[339] Issues of admissibility concern the complementarity principle and will therefore be dealt with in Section B. of this chapter,[340] but, as to Article 19, only insofar as they are different from jurisdictional challenges. The person and the State concerned can challenge the jurisdiction (and admissibility)—on the basis of the facts as they exist at the time of the challenge[341]—only once (with regard to the same person and conduct)[342] unless there are 'exceptional circumstances'[343] and the Court grants leave.[344] As to the exact timing of the submission of the challenge, Article 19 indicates different moments for the person concerned ('prior to or at the commencement of the trial')[345] and the State ('at the earliest opportunity'),[346] but

challenges to ICC intervention, grounded in transitional justice claims or more categorical objections to the exercise of ICC jurisdiction').

[336] cf. Art. 19 (3) ICCS. PTC I left the question open regarding the *Bangladesh/Myanmar* situation (Decision Jurisdiction under Article 19 (3), ICC-RoC46(3)-01/18-37, para. 28), with Judge Perrin de Brichambaut in a Partially Dissenting Opinion (paras. 5, 8–13) considering Art. 19 (3) not applicable at this early stage of the proceedings. Regarding the *Palestine* situation the same PTC considered a 'principal difference' in the more advanced procedural stage (with an investigation 'in principle … already initiated', *Situation in the State of Palestine*, ICC-01/18-143, para. 66) and thus Art. 19 (3) applicable (para. 67) advocating insofar a broad reading 'in accordance with the ordinary meaning' of Art. 19 (3) in its 'context and in light of the Statute's object and purpose' (paras. 68, 69 ff.). This time Judge Perrin de Brichambaut agreed (Partly Separate Opinion, paras. 5–6, 10–12, 15) and also Judge Kovács despite dissenting on the merits (Partly Dissenting Opinion, para. 1). Interestingly, PTC I made a kind of disclaimer limiting its decision explicitly to 'the territorial scope of its jurisdiction' without 'prejudging the question of any future borders' (para. 130). For a crit. discussion, see Nsereko and Ventura, 'Article 19', in Ambos, *Commentary* (2022), mn. 50 ff., linking para. 3 with para. 10 in order to apply the latter also in case of jurisdictional issues (mn. 105); see also Ambos, *EJIL: Talk!* 2 March 2021; in favour of invoking Art. 19 (3) regarding the Philippines situation, see Ventura, *Opinio Juris* (22 January 2024).

[337] Rules 58–62, 122 (2), 133 RPE ICC and also Reg. 38 (1)(c) RegC regarding page limit of challenge; on Reg. 46 (3) RegC in this context, see El Zeidy, in Stahn, *Practice* (2015), pp. 186, 198, see also Vaglas, *Jurisdiction* (2014), pp. 249 ff.; Nsereko and Ventura, 'Article 19', in Ambos, *Commentary* (2022), mn. 43 ff. On the Chamber's 'broad discretion' in the conduct of the proceedings, see *Gbagbo*, ICC-02/11-01/11-321, para. 39; on the importance of jurisdictional decisions highlighted by these provisions, see *Prosecutor v. Muthaura and Kenyatta*, AC, Decision on the Appeal of Mr Francis Kirimi Muthaura and Mr Uhuru Muigai Kenyatta against the Decision of Pre-Trial Chamber II of 23 January 2012 entitled 'Decision on the Confirmation of Charges Pursuant to Article 61(7)(a) and (b) of the Rome Statute', ICC-01/09-02/11-425, 24 May 2012, para. 28; see also Nsereko and Ventura, 'Article 19', in Ambos, *Commentary* (2022), mn. 46, with further references.

[338] cf. Art. 19 (1): 'in any case', 'admissibility of a case'. See also *Situation in DRC*, AC, Judgment on the Prosecutor's Appeal against the Decision of Pre-Trial Chamber I Entitled 'Decision on the Prosecutor's Application for Warrants of Arrest, Article 58', ICC-01/04-169, 13 July 2006, paras. 42, 47, 51–2. For a comparison with Art. 18 insofar, referring to a situation, see Section B.(2)(e) in this chapter.

[339] cf. Rule 58 (4) RPE ICC; also see Bachmann and Nwibo Eda, *Brook. J.Int'l. L.* 43 (2018), 485.

[340] See Section B.(2)(e) in this chapter, also on the relationship between Arts. 18 and 19.

[341] cf. *Prosecutor v. Gaddafi and Al-Senussi*, AC, Judgment on the Appeal of Libya Against the Decision of Pre-Trial Chamber I of 31 May 2013 entitled 'Decision on the Admissibility of the Case Against Saif Al-Islam Gaddafi', ICC-01/11-01/11-547-Red, 21 May 2014, para. 14, distinguishing this challenge insofar from an appeal; see also Stahn, in Stahn, *Practice* (2015), pp. 247–9; Nsereko and Ventura, 'Article 19', in Ambos, *Commentary* (2022), mn. 27.

[342] On the generous interpretation of the case law so far, see Nsereko and Ventura, 'Article 19', in Ambos, *Commentary* (2022), mn. 61.

[343] In favour of the application of the new evidence standard of Art. 84 (1)(a) insofar, Nsereko and Ventura, 'Article 19', in Ambos, *Commentary* (2022), mn. 64.

[344] cf. Art. 19 (4) ICCS.

[345] Art. 19 (4) ICCS; thereon, in passing, *Ntaganda*, ICC-01/04-02/06-892, para. 22 (advocating a narrow interpretation giving prevalence to exact deadlines set by a Chamber).

[346] Art. 19 (5) ICCS.

both standards are ambiguous and allow for different interpretations.[347] In fact, as to the commencement standard there are two conflicting PTC interpretations: one focusing on the constitution of a TC[348] and the other on the actual start of the trial with the calling of evidence and the presentations of the parties.[349] As to the 'earliest opportunity' standard, it can only safely be said that a State must bring its challenge as soon as possible—once it can 'actually assert a conflict of jurisdictions'[350] and 'substantiate that challenge'[351]—acting with due diligence.[352] At any rate, jurisdictional issues should be settled as early as possible in the proceedings.[353]

The burden of proof lies with the claimant, that is, the party who challenges the jurisdiction has to demonstrate the grounds for the challenge.[354] The grounds themselves, that is, the material scope of the challenge, have been defined rather narrowly, covering the existence of an (alleged) crime or a mode of liability, but not 'challenges relating to the contours or elements of crimes'.[355] The standard of proof is controversial[356] but the certainty standard advanced by the *Bemba* PTC[357] seems to be most convincing, since only if a Chamber is

347 cf. Vagias, *Jurisdiction* (2014), pp. 255–62, 281; Nsereko and Ventura, 'Article 19', in Ambos, *Commentary* (2022), mn. 62, 70–1; Abdou, 'Article 19', in Klamberg et al., *Commentary ICC I* (2023), pp. 651–3; crit. Stahn, in Stahn, *Practice* (2015), p. 247, arguing that a State may not yet have sufficiently developed its investigation at an early point in the ICC proceedings.

348 *Prosecutor v. Katanga and Chui*, ICC 01/04-01/07-1213-tENG, TC Reasons for the Oral Decision on the Motion Challenging the Admissibility of the Case (Article 19 of the Statute), paras. 49–50 (16 June 2009). The Chamber considered the challenge anyway, exercising its discretion; see *Katanga and Chui*, ICC 01/04-01/07-1213-tENG, paras. 56–8 and *Prosecutor v. Katanga and Chui*, AC, Judgment on the Appeal of Mr Germain Katanga against the Oral Decision of Trial Chamber II of 12 June 2009 on the Admissibility of the Case, ICC-01/04-01/07-1497, 25 September 2009, para. 38.

349 *Prosecutor v. Bemba*, TC, Decision on the Admissibility and Abuse of Process Challenges, ICC-01/05-01/08-802, 24 June 2010, para. 210. Favouring this approach, Vagias, *Jurisdiction* (2014), p. 262; leaving it open, Nsereko and Ventura, 'Article 19', in Ambos, *Commentary* (2022), mn. 62 ('uncertain').

350 *Prosecutor v. Ruto et al.*, AC, Judgment on the Appeal of the Republic of Kenya Against the Decision of Pre-Trial Chamber II of 30 May 2011 entitled 'Decision on the Application by the Government of Kenya Challenging the Admissibility of the Case Pursuant to Article 19(2)(b) of the Statute', ICC-01/09-01/11-307, 30 August 2011, paras. 46, 100; *Prosecutor v. Muthaura et al.*, AC, Judgment on the Appeal of the Republic of Kenya against the Decision of Pre-Trial Chamber II of 30 May 2011 entitled 'Decision on the Application by the Government of Kenya Challenging the Admissibility of the Case Pursuant to Article 19(2)(b) of the Statute', ICC-01/09-02/11-274, 30 August 2011, paras. 45, 98 (30 August 2011); conc. *Gaddafi*, ICC-01/11-01/11-547-Red, para. 84 ('present its challenge in such a way that it can show a conflict of jurisdictions'); *Prosecutor v. S. Gbagbo*, AC, Judgment on the Appeal of Côte d'Ivoire's Challenge to the Admissibility of the Case against Simone Gbagbo, ICC-02/11-01/12-75, 27 May 2015, para. 35.

351 *Gaddafi*, ICC-01/11-01/11-547-Red, para. 164 ('until it is in a position to substantiate that challenge'); *S. Gbagbo*, ICC-02/11-01/12-75, para. 35.

352 Nsereko and Ventura, 'Article 19', in Ambos, *Commentary* (2022), mn. 71. On possible tensions between this standard ('earliest opportunity') and the States' tactic 'to postpone the challenge until the latest possible moment, in order to enhance the scope of investigations or prosecutions and the quality of evidence' (as required by the ICC jurisprudence on Art. 17 (1)), thereby meeting the high threshold for a successful challenge, see Stahn, in Stahn, *Practice* (2015), pp. 246–7.

353 *Ntaganda*, ICC-01/04-02/06-1225, paras. 18, 41.

354 ICC, *Prosecutor v. Mbarushimana*, PTC I, Decision on the 'Defence Challenge to the Jurisdiction of the Court', ICC-01/04-01/10-451, 26 October 2011, para. 4; conc. Vagias, *Jurisdiction* (2014), p. 264; Vagias and Ferencz, *LJIL*, 28 (2015), 135–7, 149, 152; Nsereko and Ventura, 'Article 19', in Ambos, *Commentary* (2022), mn. 22.

355 cf. ICC, *Prosecutor v. Ruto et al.*, AC, Decision on the Appeals of Mr William Samoei Ruto and Mr Joshua Arap Sang against the Decision of Pre-Trial Chamber II of 23 January 2012 Entitled 'Decision on the Confirmation of Charges Pursuant to Article 61(7)(a) and (b) of the Rome Statute', ICC-01/09-01/11-414, 24 May 2012, para. 31 (referring to ICTY); conc. *Ntaganda*, ICC-01/04-02/06-892, para. 24.

356 For a detailed and crit. discussion of the conflicting case law offering three options (*prima facie* proof, certainty, and balance of probabilities), see Vagias and Ferencz, *LJIL*, 28 (2015), 138–43, 149, 152–3; also criticizing the case law, Nsereko and Ventura, 'Article 19', in Ambos, *Commentary* (2022), mn. 18, 23–4.

357 ICC, *Prosecutor v. Bemba*, PTC II, Decision pursuant to Article 6 1(7)(a) and (b) of the Rome Statute on the Charges of the Prosecutor Against Jean-Pierre Bemba Gombo, ICC-01/05-01/08-424, 15 June 2009, para. 24

certain of its jurisdiction, can one fairly say that it has 'satisfied itself' in that regard.[358] The challenges may be brought, depending on the procedural stage, to the PTC, TC, or AC,[359] but in practice the bulk goes to the Pre-Trial Division if only for the restrictive time frame allowing for such challenges.[360]

The suspension of the investigation upon a State challenge[361] does, arguably, not apply to a jurisdictional challenge for, basically, three reasons:[362] first, the last part of the provision ('until ... determination in accordance with article 17') makes clear that such a suspension is predicated upon an admissibility challenge. Secondly, the suspension only makes sense with regard to such a challenge since only an admissibility challenge entails that there are parallel national proceedings; this is not (necessarily) the case if the jurisdiction is challenged. Thirdly, Article 95, allowing for the postponement of the execution of cooperation requests, only applies to admissibility challenges.

In any case, the suspension only concerns the prosecutorial investigation: that is, neither a prosecution, nor judicial proceedings, nor investigative measures by a PTC under Article 56 (3) have to be suspended.[363] In addition, the Prosecutor may always seek authority from the Court to pursue certain necessary investigatory measures.[364] Previous prosecutorial acts or Court orders (especially arrest warrants) are not affected by the challenge.[365]

### *(b) Exercise of jurisdiction: Referral (trigger) mechanisms*

Once the 'preconditions' to the exercise of jurisdiction, including jurisdiction *ratione personae* and *temporis* are met, the Court can exercise its jurisdiction if it is triggered by one

('degree of certainty'); conc. *Prosecutor v. Muthaura et al.*, PTC II, Decision on the Confirmation of Charges pursuant to Article 61 (7)(a) and (b) of the Rome Statute, ICC-01/09-02-11-382-Red., 23 January 2012, para. 23. The standard goes back to the ICJ, *Military and Paramilitary Activities in and against Nicaragua (Nicaragua v. United States)*, Merits, Judgment (27 June 1986), ICJ Reports 1986 14, para. 29 (requiring 'certainty' supported by 'convincing evidence'). However, the *Kenya* AC left the question open considering that the issue of 'organizational policy' within the meaning of Art. 7 (2)(a) ICCS (thereon, see Ambos, *Treatise ICL II* (2022), pp. 76–9) referring to the subject matter jurisdiction of the Court has to be dealt with at the merits stage of the proceedings, cf. ICC *Prosecutor v. Muthaura et al.*, AC, Decision on the Appeal of Mr Francis Kirimi Muthaura and Mr Uhuru Muigai Kenyatta against the Decision of Pre-Trial Chamber II of 23 January 2012 Entitled 'Decision on the Confirmation of Charges Pursuant to Article 61(7)(a) and (b) of the Rome Statute', ICC-01/09-02/11-425, 24 May 2012, paras. 32 ff.; in the same vein, *Ruto et al.*, ICC-01/09-01/11-414, paras. 25 ff.; thereon see Vagias and Ferencz, *LJIL*, 28 (2015), 143–8, 153 (advocating a restrictive interpretation of this ruling limiting it to factual questions regarding the subject matter jurisdiction of the Court).

[358] cf. Art. 19 (1) ('satisfy itself that it has jurisdiction'); for a different view, cf. Nsereko and Ventura, 'Article 19', in Ambos, *Commentary* (2022), mn. 18, advocating a 'reasonable grounds to believe' test, at least when the decision is taken in the context of Art. 58 ICCS; discussing the options and calling the AC to rule on the matter, Vagias and Ferencz, *LJIL*, 28 (2015), 152–5.

[359] Art. 19 (6); see also Vagias, *Jurisdiction* (2014), pp. 270 ff. ('tiered system'); Nsereko and Ventura, 'Article 19', in Ambos, *Commentary* (2022), mn. 73 ff.; Abdou, 'Article 19', in Klamberg et al., *Commentary ICC I* (2023), pp. 654–5; on appeal pursuant to Art. 82 (1)(a), see Chapter VI, B.(2) in this volume.

[360] The case law on jurisdictional challenges has considerably increased since the first edition (where I referred to *Ntaganda*, ICC-01/04-01/06-892 and *Prosecutor v. Mbarushimana*, PTC I, Decision on the 'Defence Challenge to the Jurisdiction of the Court', ICC-01/04-01/10-451, 26 October 2011). See, for more recent case law, the various references above and below; for a summary of the case law, Nsereko and Ventura, 'Article 19', in Ambos, *Commentary* (2022), mn. 5 with n. 9, 10, mn. 6 with n. 12, mn. 25 with n. 75, 80 ff. and *passim*.

[361] Art. 19 (7); crit. Nsereko and Ventura, 'Article 19', in Ambos, *Commentary* (2022), mn. 84–5.

[362] For the same view, Vagias, *Jurisdiction* (2014), pp. 268–9; Nsereko and Ventura, 'Article 19', in Ambos, *Commentary* (2022), mn. 86; *contra* Schabas, *ICC Commentary* (2016), pp. 492–3; Safferling, *International Criminal Procedure* (2012), p. 213.

[363] cf. Nsereko and Ventura, 'Article 19', in Ambos, *Commentary* (2022), mn. 86 with case law references.

[364] cf. Art. 19 (8); see also Nsereko and Ventura, 'Article 19', in Ambos, *Commentary* (2022), mn. 87 ff., advocating an 'expansive interpretation' and a 'speedy determination' by Chambers (mn. 89).

[365] cf. Art. 19 (9); see also Nsereko and Ventura, 'Article 19', in Ambos, *Commentary* (2022), mn. 99.

of the three possibilities of referrals (trigger mechanisms)[366] provided for in Article 13:[367] a referral of a State Party, a referral of the UN Security Council, or a *proprio motu* investigation of the Prosecutor.[368] All these referrals have to be presented in written form.[369] Once a situation has been referred to the Prosecutor, or if she intends to proceed under Article 15, she must inform the Presidency of the Court,[370] which will then assign the respective situation to a PTC.[371] The Registry shall then open a 'situation record'.[372] Let us now take a closer look at the three referral mechanisms to better understand how they operate and distinguish themselves.

*(i) State referral, including self-referral*

Under the mechanism of a so-called State referral, a State Party—not just a State (not party) which has made an Article 12 (3) declaration[373]—can always request the Prosecutor to investigate a particular 'situation', that is, a course of events occurring in a given period of time and space (territory)[374] where crimes 'appear to have been committed'.[375] This involves a *prima facie* assessment of the respective State Party as to the possibility of crimes within the jurisdiction of the Court.[376] The request must 'specify the relevant circumstances' and 'be accompanied by' the available 'supporting documentation'.[377] The general requirements for jurisdiction and admissibility apply.[378] Whether they are met or not, in particular whether

[366] cf. thereon Hoffmeister and Knoke, *ZaöRV*, 59 (1999), 788 ff.; Kreß, in Grützner et al., *Internationaler Rechtshilfeverkehr* (2003), Part IV A 1, mn. 18 ff.; Quattrocolo, in Cassese, Chiavario, and De Francesco, *Problemi* (2005), pp. 298 ff.; Schabas, *HRLJ*, 27 (2006), 27 ff.; Werle, *Völkerstrafrecht* (2012), mn. 282; Werle and Jessberger, *Principles ICL* (2020), 337; Nsereko, *ZIS*, 2 (2007), 500–1; Kolb, in Kolb and Scalia, *DIP* (2012), pp. 277–8; Shraga, in Cassese, *Companion* (2009), pp. 168 ff.; Easterday, *ArizJICompL*, 26 (2009), 54; Gless, *Internationales Strafrecht* (2021), mn. 745; Satzger, *ICL* (2018), § 12 mn. 12 ff.; Stegmiller, *CLF*, 24 (2013), 477 ff.; Trüg, *ZStW*, 125 (2013), 51; Schabas, *Kein Frieden ohne Gerechtigkeit?* (2013), pp. 23 ff.; Ramsden and Hamilton, *ICLQ*, 66 (2017), 893.

[367] On the negotiations of this 'most complex and most sensitive' provision, (Kirsch and Holmes, *AJIL*, 93 (1999) 8) see Schabas and Pecorella, 'Article 13', in Ambos, *Commentary* (2022), mn. 1–13; on Art. 14, see Chaitidou, 'Article 14', in Ambos, *Commentary* (2022), mn. 1–8.

[368] For a summary of the situations over which the Court has exercised jurisdiction and the respective mechanism that triggered it, see Schabas, in Stahn, *Practice* (2015), pp. 366–7.

[369] Rule 45 RPE ICC. See also Chaitidou, 'Article 14', in Ambos, *Commentary* (2022), mn. 26 ('written declaration').

[370] Reg. 45 RegC.

[371] Reg. 46 (2) in relation with Reg. 45 RegC.

[372] Reg. 20 (1) RegR.

[373] See also Schabas and Pecorella, 'Article 13', in Ambos, *Commentary* (2022), mn. 15; Coco, 'Article 13', in Klamberg et al., *Commentary ICC I* (2023), pp. 511–14. It is for this reason that in the situation of Ivory Coast, which has made an Art. 12 (3) declaration (note 311 in this chapter), the Prosecutor, lacking a SC referral, had to investigate *proprio motu* and to request the authorization of an investigation (see note 448 and main text in this chapter).

[374] On the concept of situation, see also Section B.(2)(b) in this chapter; on how this concept has been defined by the case law in terms of 'territorial, temporal and possibly personal parameters', cf. ICC, *Prosecutor v. Lubanga*, PTC I, Decision on the Applications for Participation in the Proceedings of VPRS-1, VPRS-2, VPRS-3, VPRS-4, VPRS-5, VPRS-6, ICC-01/04-101-tEN-Corr, 17 January 2006, para. 65; more recently *Abd-Al-Rahman*, ICC-02/05-01/20-503, paras. 25–6 ('used loosely, specifically with a view to extending enough flexibility to the Prosecutor to investigate independently and impartially', 'situation of crisis or armed conflict from which the Prosecutor may select and investigate potential cases', 'greater or smaller than territory'); on the 'rather flexible' practice regarding the factual scope of the *situation*, see Chaitidou, 'Article 14', in Ambos, *Commentary* (2022), mn. 25, 29, 31, 34; on the discussion whether it is possible to refer a worldwide situation relating to a group to the Court (in this case IS), or whether the situation referred must be defined by reference to 'a particular geographical location or in a particular state', see Galand, *EJIL: Talk!* 27 May 2015; in favour, Fry, *Contours* (2015), pp. 141–2.

[375] Art. 13 (a) in conjunction with Art. 14 ICCS. For a more detailed account, see Olásolo, *CPI* (2003), pp. 510 ff.; Cassese, *JICJ*, 4 (2006), 436; El Zeidy, *LJIL*, 19 (2006), 749 ff.; Hoffmeister and Knoke, *ZaöRV*, 59 (1999), 788 ff.; Chaitidou, 'Article 14', in Ambos, *Commentary* (2022), mn. 29–31; crit. Cryer, *Prosecuting* (2005), pp. 224–5.

[376] Chaitidou, 'Article 14', in Ambos, *Commentary* (2022), mn. 30.

[377] Art. 14 (2) ICCS. See statement of the OTP on second self-referral by DRC, 15 June 2023.

[378] Arts. 11, 12, 17–19 ICCS.

the referral is compatible with the complementarity principle,[379] has to be determined, either by the Prosecutor or the Chambers,[380] according to the respective procedural stage.

It is worthwhile noting that referrals by third States, as arguably implicit in this provision,[381] have not been submitted in more than a decade of the Court's existence. This confirmed the experience from the human rights system where it is highly unlikely that States will make use of the possibility to file a complaint against another State given the diplomatic implications of such a move.[382] Instead, several African leaders[383] have used the State referral mechanism, quite unexpectedly, to submit so-called *self-referrals*.[384] The first ICC Prosecutor, Luis Moreno Ocampo, has even actively sought these self-referrals[385]—a questionable approach given the Prosecutor's rather passive role under Article 13 as a recipient of referrals.[386] In any case, it is fair to assume that the State, self-referring a situation to the Court, has effectively waived its right to invoke the complementarity objection, at least with regard to the situation in general[387] and if there is no fundamental change in the circumstances giving rise to the self-referral in the first place. Arguably, to invoke the complementarity objection under the same circumstances would have to be considered as *mala fide* conduct (*venire contra factum proprium*).[388] Only more recently the mechanism has

[379] cf. ICC, *Situation in the DRC*, PTC I, Decision on the Prosecutor's Application for Warrants of Arrest, Article 58, ICC-01/04-02/06-20-Anx2, 10 February 2006, paras. 35 ff.; Gioia, *LJIL*, 19 (2006), 1114; crit. the ICC's practice as 'rather laxly', Boas et al., *International Criminal Procedure* (2011), p. 93.

[380] cf. Chaitidou, 'Article 14', in Ambos, *Commentary* (2022), mn. 26, 29, 33, 40.

[381] The (historical, literal, and teleological) interpretation of Art. 14 (1) ICCS is, of course, controversial, see the excellent account by Robinson, *JICJ*, 9 (2011), 355, 361 ff. (arguing on the basis of the drafting history that, contrary to popular belief, the original focus was on the territorial State, i.e. self-referrals were implicitly envisaged).

[382] In a similar vein, Boas et al., *International Criminal Procedure* (2011), p. 93 ('rare in practice').

[383] Self-referrals have been made by Uganda (16 December 2003), DRC (3 March 2004), Central African Republic (18 December 2004 and 30 May 2014), Mali (13 July 2012), and the Union of Comoros (14 May 2013); see <https://www.icc-cpi.int/situations-under-investigations>; see also Chaitidou, 'Article 14', in Ambos, *Commentary* (2022), mn. 12 ff.; Stegmiller, 'Article 14', in Klamberg et al., *Commentary ICC I* (2023), pp. 533–7. The self-referral of the Union of Comoros has been the first under the flag principle, i.e. referring to alleged crimes committed on board of a vessel registered by the referring State; see also Chatidou, op. cit. (mn. 17).

[384] For a conceptual clarification, see Müller and Stegmiller, *JICJ*, 8 (2010), 1271 ff., discussing other terminology, such as 'auto-referral' and 'voluntary referral'; Bassiouni, *JICJ*, 4 (2006), 424 ff.; Kreß and Wannek in Kirsch, *Internationale Strafgerichtshöfe* (2005), p. 237. Crit. Arsanjani and Reisman, *AJIL*, 99 (2005), 387 ff.; Hoffmeister and Knoke, *ZaöRV*, 59 (1999), 788, 793; Kolb, in Kolb and Scalia, *DIP* (2012), pp. 277–9; Schabas, *CLF*, 19 (2008), 12 ff.; Stahn, *CLF*, 19 (2008), 110–12; for a nuanced view, see Wolfrum, in Arnold et al., *Menschengerechtes Strafrecht* (2005), p. 984; Kreß, in Neubacher and Klein, *Vom Recht der Macht zur Macht des Rechts?* (2006), pp. 108 ff.; Zahar and Sluiter, *ICL* (2008), pp. 455 ff.; Bock, *Opfer* (2010), pp. 271 ff.; Robinson, *JICJ*, 9 (2011), 357 ff. (discussing the criticism against 'self referrals' [357–77] and considering that the term 'is of very limited value, … ambiguous, … [and] legally useless, because … a territorial state referral is simply a subset of state party referral … [and] … all of the trigger mechanisms are legal' [378]); Robinson, in Cryer et al., *ICL* (2019), p. 151; focusing on Uganda and the DRC, Schabas, *HRLJ*, 27 (2006), 29 ff., 32 ff.; Akhavan, *CLF*, 21 (2010), 103 ff.

[385] In its first address to the ASP in 2003, albeit referring to his *proprio motu* power under Art. 15, he suggested 'a referral or active support from the DRC' and, in the next paragraph, 'from African and Western countries … as well as other States Parties', i.e. he invited both self-referrals and referrals from third States, cf. Second Assembly of States Parties to the Rome Statute of the ICC, Report of the Prosecutor of the ICC, Mr Luis Moreno-Ocampo, 8 September 2003, pp. 4–55, <http://www.icc-cpi.int/NR/rdonlyres/C073586C-7D46-4CBE-B901-0672908E8639/143656/LMO_20030908_En.pdf>. See also Section B.(3)(a) in this chapter.

[386] Crit. Kress, *JICJ*, 2 (2004), 947.

[387] On the situation–case distinction and the ensuing differentiation in the object of a complementarity objection, see Section B.(2)(b) in this chapter.

[388] cf. Benzing, *MPYbUN*, 7 (2003), 631; Kress, *JICJ*, 2 (2004), 946. On the legal issues connected to such a waiver, see El Zeidy, *ICLR*, 5 (2005), 99 ff., 118; Arsanjani and Reisman, *AJIL*, 99 (2005), 396–7; Bitti and El Zeidy, *LJIL*, 23 (2010), 321–2; Stahn, *LJIL*, 23 (2010), 314; Müller and Stegmiller, *JICJ*, 8 (2010), 1286 ff.; Jurdi, *ICC* (2011), pp. 135 ff.; on the distinction between a self-referral and a waiver, see Schabas, *CLF*, 19 (2008), 15–16; against a waiver, Nouwen, *Complementarity* (2013), p. 75. Of course, the compatibility of the referral with the complementarity principle will be determined by the Court, cf. *Situation in the DRC*, ICC-01/04-02/06-20-Anx2, paras. 35 ff.; Gioia, *LJIL*, 19 (2006), 1114; crit. Kress, *JICJ*, 2 (2004), 946.

been used by several State Parties to submit collective[389] referrals, so far with regard to Venezuela,[390] Ukraine,[391] and Palestine.[392]

Despite the initial criticism against the practice of self-referrals—with regard to the complementarity regime[393] and the risk of 'opportunistic' referrals attempting to use the Court as a political tool in a domestic conflict,[394] they have been accepted in the meantime as valid procedural triggers on the condition that an entire 'situation of crisis', not just certain crimes of certain parties to the conflict, is referred,[395] and the referring State is unable to undertake proper investigations.[396] In fact, the case law has accepted the practice so far without raising critical questions,[397] but the Appeals Chamber has also warned that the Court may at one point decide, 'depending on the circumstances of each case', 'not to act upon a State's relinquishment of jurisdiction in favour of the Court'.[398] This is a gentle reminder to State Parties that it is, in light of the complementarity principle, their primary duty to prosecute ICC

[389] A special case has been Palestine's '"complaint" against a third state' turning, with the opening of formal investigations by the OTP into the Palestine situation in spring of 2021, into the first third party referral, cf. <https://www.icc-cpi.int/palestine>; Stegmiller, 'Article 14', in Klamberg et al., *Commentary ICC I* (2023), pp. 533–7).

[390] The Venezuela I situation has been referred to the ICC on 27 September 2018 by six State Parties, cf. <https://www.icc-cpi.int/venezuela-i>. Before that Colombia's former president, Alvaro Uribe, had considered several times referring Venezuela's former president, Hugo Chávez, to the ICC, inter alia, for his alleged support of the FARC rebel group, see e.g. <http://www.eltiempo.com/archivo/documento/CMS-7851714>. Along the same lines, in September 2015, (then) Colombian Chief Prosecutor Eduardo Montealegre had threatened to refer Venezuela's current president, Nicolas Maduro, for expulsion amounting to forced displacements of Colombian citizens from Venezuela; see e.g. <https://www.eluniversal.com.co/colombia/bogota/montealegre-no-ha-presentado-la-denuncia-contra-maduro-ante-la-cpi-207659-GTEU309906>.

[391] The Ukraine situation has been referred to the ICC by forty-three State Parties in March/April 2022 after the Russian invasion, cf. <https://www.icc-cpi.int/ukraine>.

[392] This referral was submitted in the context of the Gaza/Israel war on 17 November 2023 by five State Parties (Bangladesh, Bolivia, Comores, Djibouti, and South Africa), cf. <https://www.icc-cpi.int/news/statement-prosecutor-international-criminal-court-karim-aa-khan-kc-situation-state-palestine>. On 18 January 2024 Chile and Mexico additionally submitted a referral, cf. <https://www.icc-cpi.int/sites/default/files/2024-01/2024-01-18-Referral_Chile__Mexico.pdf>

[393] See, in particular, Arsanjani and Reisman, *AJIL*, 99 (2005), 387 ff.; also El Zeidy, *Complementarity* (2008), pp. 218–19; Müller and Stegmiller, *JICJ*, 8 (2010), 1282 ff.; Nouwen, *Complementarity* (2013), pp. 350–1, 399, 407, arguing that this policy discouraged States from making use of their primary right and responsibility to exercise jurisdiction; for a summary of the discussion, see Stegmiller, 'Article 14', in Klamberg et al., *Commentary ICC I* (2023), pp. 533–7.

[394] Thus, as regards Uganda's self-referral 'concerning the LRA', the former Prosecutor Moreno Ocampo had to clarify that all acts of all parties involved in the conflict in Northern Uganda would be investigated (Letter of the 17 June 2004 to the President of the ICC); cf. Akhavan, *AJIL*, 99 (2005), 403 ff.; Chaitidou, 'Article 14', in Ambos, *Commentary* (2022), mn. 32; van der Wilt, in Stahn, *Practice* (2015), pp. 211–15; generally Boas et al., *International Criminal Procedure* (2011), p. 94; furthermore, see Zakerhossein, *Situation* (2017), p. 68.

[395] *Mbarushimana*, ICC-01/04-01/10-451, para. 27. In any case, the Court will always have to interpret a referral in this comprehensive sense; in this vein, see also Rastan, *CLF*, 23 (2012), 9–13 (but crit. of the notion 'situation of crisis'); Guariglia and Rogier, in Stahn, *Practice* (2015), pp. 352, 357; Chaitidou, 'Article 14', in Ambos, *Commentary* (2022), mn. 29; also see Zakerhossein, *Situation* (2017), p. 69.

[396] ICC, *Prosecutor v. Lubanga*, PTC I, Decision Concerning the PTC I's Decision of 10 February 2006 and the Incorporation of Documents into the Record of the Case against Mr Thomas Lubanga Dyilo, ICC-01/04-01/06-8-Corr, 24 February 2006; ICC, *Prosecutor v. Lubanga*, Annex I, PTC I, Decision on the Prosecutor's Application for Warrant of Arrest, Article 58, ICC-01/04-01/06-1-Corr-Red, 10 February 2006, para. 35, arguing that DRC's self-referral was valid in light of the complementarity regime since the judicial system was 'indeed unable to undertake the investigation and prosecution of the crimes'. For perhaps the earliest justification of this practice, see Kress, *JICJ*, 2 (2004), 945; also in favour, convincingly rejecting the counter-arguments, Robinson, *JICJ*, 9 (2011), 359 ff.; explicitly concurring with him, Buchan, *CLF*, 25 (2014), 472–3; also in favour, van der Wilt, in Stahn, *Practice* (2015), pp. 215 ff. (analysing the case law regarding inability or unwillingness of a self-referring State to carry out investigations or prosecutions, and advocating the use of self-referrals as a way for the Court to deal with non-State actors). On *inability* and *unwillingness*, see more in Section B.(2)(d)(iii)(2) and (3) in this chapter.

[397] cf. Chaitidou, 'Article 14', in Ambos, *Commentary* (2022), mn. 24 with references.

[398] *Katanga*, ICC-01/04-01/07-1497, para. 85; *Gbagbo*, ICC-02/11-01/11-436-Red, para. 29.

crimes committed on their territory[399] and that they must not lightly renounce their jurisdiction in favour of the Court.[400]

These considerations are also relevant with regard to the *temporal jurisdiction*. Here one must distinguish between events or crimes predating the referral and the ones succeeding it. As to the previous events, the cut-off date of any referral is the entry into force of the Statute for the respective State[401] or the date of an Article 12 (3) declaration, as discussed above; that is, the referral cannot cover events having occurred before the respective dates. Both previous and subsequent events (crimes) are only covered if they are 'sufficiently linked to the situation of crisis referred to the Court as on-going at the time of the referral';[402] otherwise, the (self-) referral would have an indefinite temporal effect and thereby undermine the—already mentioned—principle of complementarity.[403] This 'situational linkage' requirement may be further refined by objective criteria more precisely determining the necessary nexus between the respective crimes and the overall situation,[404] but it is, in any case, flexible enough to cope with the complex and sometimes ongoing crisis situations referred to the Court, and thus is more satisfactory and practical than a fixed cut-off date, based, for example, on the date of the referral or the prosecutorial request pursuant to Article 15 (3) ICCS.[405] The referral must be submitted—as a unilateral State act—by the

[399] cf. recital 6 of the Preamble of the ICCS ('duty of every State to exercise its criminal jurisdiction over those responsible for international crimes'); see recently also ICC-ASP, Res. ICC-ASP/21/Res. 2 (2022), para. 134 ('primary responsibility').

[400] In this vein, see also, with regard to the principle of complementarity, *Mbarushimana*, ICC-01/04-01/10-451, para. 21, stating that the 'Statute cannot be interpreted as permitting a State to permanently abdicate its responsibilities by referring wholesale present and future criminal activities comprising the whole of its territory, without any limitation whether in context or duration'; thereon also Rastan, *CLF*, 23 (2012), 6. See also van der Wilt, in Stahn, *Practice* (2015), pp. 223 ff. (in favour of self-referrals as a way for the Court to also prosecute non-State actors).

[401] cf. Arts. 11 and 126 ICCS.

[402] ICC, *Prosecutor v. Mbarushimana*, PTC I, Decision on the Prosecutor's Application for a Warrant of Arrest against Callixte Mbarushimana, ICC-01/04-01/10-1, 28 September 2010, para. 6; *Situation in Georgia*, PTC I, Decision on the Prosecutor's Request for Authorization of an Investigation, ICC-01/15-12, 27 January 2016, para. 64 (excluding events 'in and around South Ossetia' from the relevant situation 'unless they are sufficiently linked thereto'); *Situation Bangladesh/Myanmar*, ICC-01/19-27, para. 131, 133; *Prosecutor v. Mahmoud Mustafa Busayf Al-Werfalli*, PTC I, Warrant of Arrest, ICC-01/11-01/17-2, 15 August 2017, para. 23; *Situation in the Islamic Republic of Afghanistan*, AC, Judgment on the Appeal against the Decision on the Authorisation of an Investigation into the Situation in the Islamic Republic of Afghanistan, ICC-02/17-138 OA4, 5 March 2020, para. 79 ('other crimes ... sufficiently linked to the situation', overruling *Situation in the Islamic Republic of Afghanistan*, PTC II, Decision Pursuant to Article 15 of the Rome Statute on the Authorisation of an Investigation into the Situation in the Islamic Republic of Afghanistan, ICC-02/17-33, 12 April 2019, paras. 40–1). For a discussion with further references, Rastan, *CLF*, 23 (2012), 3 ff. (9); Stegmiller, *CLF*, 24 (2013), 481–2; Chaitidou, 'Article 14', in Ambos, *Commentary* (2022), mn. 37 and above note 321 with main text; crit. Vagias, *Jurisdiction* (2014), pp. 198 ff. (inter alia crit. that the PTC did not define the concept of 'situation of crisis' and did not explain its test in the light of international law). On the relevant case law regarding the situation-case linkage, see Section B.(2)(b) in this chapter.

[403] *Mbarushimana*, ICC-01/04-01/10-451, para. 16 ('This link is necessary ... to avoiding that referrals become instruments "permitting a State to abdicate its responsibility for exercising jurisdiction over atrocity crimes for eternity", which—as the defence correctly points out—"would be wholly antithetical to the concept of complementarity"'); see also Rastan, *CLF*, 23 (2012), 6; conc. Stegmiller, *CLF*, 24 (2013) 482.

[404] cf. ICC, *Situation in the Republic of Côte d'Ivoire*, PTC III, Corrigendum to 'Decision Pursuant to Article 15 of the Rome Statute on the Authorisation of an Investigation into the Situation in the Republic of Côte d'Ivoire', ICC-02/11-14-Corr, 15 November 2011, para. 179, referring to the same 'contextual elements' for all crimes, the 'same actors' and the same 'context' in terms of the attack and the conflict; for a discussion with further references, including the Prosecutor's splitting up of the second CAR situation, Marchesi and Chaitidou, 'Article 14', in Ambos, *Commentary* (2022), mn. 38–9; summarizing, Rastan, *CLF*, 23 (2012), 9, 32–3.

[405] cf. Rastan, *CLF*, 23 (2012), 20 ff. (crit. discussing the respective *Kenya* PTC Art. 15 decision, comparing it to the more flexible *Côte d'Ivoire* Art. 15 decision and concluding that the latter flexible approach was 'better suited to the many volatile situations that the Court will continue to confront', at 29).

competent organ of the respective State,[406] that is, its *ex officio* representatives (sitting[407] head of State or government, minister of foreign affairs)[408] or persons vested with the respective 'full powers',[409] for example, a senior cabinet member.[410] Last but not least, the self-referring State cannot simply change its mind and withdraw its referral, stripping the ICC of jurisdiction it originally conferred upon it,[411] since this would—notwithstanding the possibility of invoking the *proprio motu* powers of Article 15—set aside the Court's jurisdictional and admissibility regime and, in political terms, make a fool of the Court. Indeed, only the Security Council has the statutory power to roll back an original referral by way of Article 16 (to be looked at more closely in the next sub-section). The correct statutory approach for a State wishing to take a situation or case back to the domestic judicial system is an admissibility challenge under Articles 18 and 19 ICCS,[412] to be discussed in the second part of this chapter.[413]

*(ii) Security Council referral (and deferral)*

The second trigger is that of a Security Council referral.[414] The Council is thereby empowered to refer to the Court peace-threatening situations within the meaning of Chapter VII of the UN Charter, in which ICCS crimes have allegedly been committed.[415] The threshold is rather high since only the commission of crimes accompanied by the respective context element[416] can amount to a threat to or breach of the peace within the meaning of Article 39 UN Charter.[417] At any rate, the Statute's Preamble itself assumes such a peace-threatening impact of 'such grave crimes'[418] which may explain the rather lax Council practice in trying to justify such an impact. As the Council's competence flows directly from the UN Charter, it can also refer situations of UN Member States, not being State Parties of the

[406] See Principle No. 4 of ILC, 'Guiding Principles Applicable to Unilateral Declarations of States capable of Creating Legal Obligations (2006)', UN-YB ILC II, 366, 372, ('A unilateral declaration binds the State internationally only if it is made by an authority vested with the power to do so. By virtue of their functions, heads of State, heads of Government and ministers for foreign affairs are competent to formulate such declarations. Other persons representing the State in specified areas may be authorized to bind it, through their declarations, in areas falling within their competence.')

[407] On the lack of standing of a former government or governing party, see note 285 in this chapter with regard to Egypt.

[408] cf. Art. 7 (2) VCLT.

[409] Ibid.

[410] Thus, the self-referral of Mali was signed by the Minister of Justice; see Stegmiller, *CLF*, 24 (2013) 479. See also Chaitidou, 'Article 14', in Ambos, *Commentary* (2022), mn. 11.

[411] For the same view, see El Zeidy, in Stahn and Sluiter, *Practice* (2009), pp. 55 ff.; Chaitidou, 'Article 14', in Ambos, *Commentary* (2022), mn. 27 with further references; Stegmiller, 'Article 14', in Klamberg et al., *Commentary ICC I* (2023), pp. 533–7; for the opposing view, see Maged, *ICLR*, 6 (2006) 422 ff. (basically arguing with State sovereignty).

[412] cf. Stegmiller, *CLF*, 24 (2013), 485; Stegmiller, 'Article 14', in Klamberg et al., *Commentary ICC* I (2023), pp. 533–7.

[413] See Section B.(2)(e) in this chapter.

[414] Art. 13 (b) ICCS.

[415] cf. Kurth, *IStGH* (2006), pp. 61 ff.; Hoffmeister and Knoke, *ZaöRV*, 59 (1999), 789–90; Olásolo, *CPI* (2003), pp. 134 ff., 481 ff.; Wolfrum, in Arnold et al., *Menschengerechtes Strafrecht* (2005), pp. 984–5; Fixson, in Kirsch, *Internationale Strafgerichtshöfe* (2005), pp. 216–17; crit. Cryer, *Prosecuting* (2005), p. 225; Ohlin, in Stahn and Sluiter, *Practice* (2009), pp. 189–90; Yigzaw, *ICLR*, 23 (2023), 642 (even advocating the removal of the SC powers).

[416] Attack on a protected group or, arguably, organized and systematic commission (genocide), systematic or widespread attack (crimes against humanity), armed conflict (war crimes), cf. Ambos, *Treatise ICL II* (2022), pp. 16–18, 50 ff., 142 ff.

[417] In a similar vein, see Trahan, *CLF*, 24 (2013), 420–3, 468–9.

[418] cf. Preamble, recital 3 ('[R]ecognizing that such grave crimes threaten the peace'); thereto Triffterer/Bergsmo/Ambos, 'Preamble', in Ambos, *Commentary* (2022), mn. 9–11.

Rome Statute;[419] this in fact happened regarding the situations in Darfur (Sudan)[420] and Libya.[421]

Sadly, the drafting of these resolutions leaves much to be desired.[422] On the one hand, the nationals of non-State Parties are excluded from the referral[423] and the ensuing financial burden must be exclusively borne by the ICC.[424] On the other hand, cooperation obligations are only imposed on the State Parties and the situation States (Sudan and Libya), explicitly excluding non-State Parties,[425] and no follow-up mechanism (as for example in the Council's sanctions regime) has been established.[426]

[419] See also O'Keefe, *ICL* (2015), p. 541; Zakerhossein, *Situation* (2017), p. 74; Galand, *Security Council* (2019), pp. 47 ff.; rather melodramatic Tsilonis, *Jurisdiction* (2019), p. 37 ('titanium legal spear that penetrates the principle of state sovereignty'); Coco, 'Article 13', in Klamberg et al., *Commentary ICC I* (2023), pp. 515–22 (arguing that in such a situation the SC does not just trigger but 'create[s] jurisdiction'). A SC referral may also overrule an Art. 124 declaration, cf. Nemane and Gunjal, *ICLR*, 15 (2015), 960.

[420] cf. UNSC Res. 1593, 31 March 2005 (Darfur); crit. Condorelli and Ciampi, *JICJ*, 3 (2005), 594 ff.; Schabas, *HRLJ*, 27 (2006), 37; Zimmermann, in Dupuy et al., *FS Tomuschat* (2006), pp. 689 ff.; Kurth, *IStGH* (2006) pp. 73–4; Cryer, *LJIL*, 19 (2006), 195 ff.; Jurdi, *ICC* (2011), pp. 199 ff., 210 ff.; more positive Kreß, in Kempf, Jansen, and Müller, *FS Richter II* (2006), p. 326 and Cassese, *JICJ*, 4 (2006), 436 ff.; on the alleged invalidity of para. 7 of this Resolution (referring to the expenses incurred in the Darfur situation) and the impact on jurisdiction *Abd-Al-Rahman*, ICC-02/05-01/20-503, paras. 43 ff. ('would not strike at the heart of the resolution', para. 45).

[421] cf. UNSC Res. 1970, 26 February 2011 (Libya); for an in-depth analysis thereon, see Frau, *AVR*, 49 (2011), 276; Frau, *ZIS*, 6 (2011), 784 ff.; Brunner and Frau, *HuV-I*, 2011, 192 ff.; Domestici-Met, *GoJIL*, 3 (2011), 861 ff., 872 ff.; Fink, in Meng, Ress and Stein, *Europäische Integration und Globalisierung* (2011), pp. 137 ff.; Janssen-Holldiek, *DGAPanalyse*, 4 (October 2011); Stahn, *JICJ*, 10 (2012), 325 ff.; on both SC referrals, also see Zakerhossein, *Situation* (2017), pp. 82–5; on the punitive character of this Resolution, see Hehir and Lang, *CLF*, 26 (2015), 170 ff., referring, however, erroneously to Res. 1973.

[422] Crit. of the Security Council's involvement in the field of international criminal justice with regard to exclusion of certain cases from prosecution and judicial independence, see also Almqvist, *LJIL*, 28 (2015), 91 ff.; also crit. of the SC's 'flawed' practice regarding '(i) selectivity, (ii) substantive shortcomings in the referral resolutions, and (iii) the lack of meaningful follow-up', Dicker, in Stahn, *Practice* (2015), pp. 3 ff.; Ruiz Verduzco, in Stahn, *Practice* (2015), pp. 36 ff.

[423] cf. UNSC Res. 1593/2005, para. 6 and UNSC Res. 1970/2011, para. 6, assigning the 'exclusive jurisdiction' for 'nationals, current or former officials or personnel' from a non-State Party to that State. Crit. also Trahan, *CLF*, 24 (2013), 454–62, 472, doubting the validity of such an exclusion in light of the wording of Art. 13 (b) providing for a referral of the comprehensive situation; Schabas and Pecorella, 'Article 13', in Ambos, *Commentary* (2022), mn. 20–2, arguing that the resolutions are therefore incompatible with the ICCS; in a similar vein, Dicker, in Stahn, *Practice* (2015), p. 7 ('This exemption codifies a double standard in applying justice'); Ruiz Verduzco, in Stahn, *Practice* (2015), pp. 36–8 (criticizing the exemption clause of the Resolutions as one going 'against the Rome Statute' and highlighting 'the application of double standards', arguing, however, that these 'exemptions did not play a meaningful role in practice' [p. 38]); Rastan, in Stahn, *Practice* (2015), pp. 158 ff.; Birdsall, *CLF*, 26 (2015), 66 ff.; cf. also Mégret, *CLF*, 26 (2015), 128 ff. (arguing that this exemptions actually 'echoed a certain pattern of the UN's own actions' often seeking to 'de-emphasize the legal obligations of peace operations' [129]).

[424] Both Resolutions disallow the UN (GA) from allocating the respective funding, cf. UNSC Res. 1593/2005, para. 7 and UNSC Res. 1970/2011, para. 8 ('none of the expenses incurred in connection with the referral, including expenses related to investigations or prosecutions in connection with that referral, shall be borne by the United Nations'). Crit. also Fletcher and Ohlin, *JICJ*, 4 (2006), 428 ff.; Nsereko, *ZIS*, 2 (2007), 501; Trahan, *CLF*, 24 (2013), 450–4, 470–1 (arguing that the question of funding should be left to the GA in line with Art. 17 (1) of the Charter); Mettraux et al., *Expert Initiative Effectiveness ICC* (2014), p. 76 (paras. 95–6) (recommending a funding by the UNSC); Kendall, *JICJ*, 13 (2015), 126–7; Schabas and Pecorella, 'Article 13', in Ambos, *Commentary* (2022), mn. 23; Dicker, in Stahn, *Practice* (2015), p. 7. For an analysis of the financial needs of the ICC, see Ford, in Stahn, *Practice* (2015), pp. 84 ff.; Ruiz Verduzco, in Stahn, *Practice* (2015), pp. 39–42.

[425] cf. UNSC Res. 1593/2005, para. 2 and UNSC Res. 1970/2011, para. 5. Crit. also Trahan, *CLF*, 24 (2013), 462–4, 472, calling upon the Security Council to impose cooperation obligations on all UN Member States; also crit. Dicker, in Stahn, *Practice* (2015), p. 7; Ruiz Verduzco, in Stahn, *Practice* (2015), pp. 42–4 ('The failure of the Council to create obligations on cooperation runs against the very *raison d'être* of the system of referrals').

[426] Crit. also Trahan, *CLF*, 24 (2013), 465–7, 472–3 (suggesting a 'Security Council working group for ICC referrals' similar to the working group on tribunals); Dicker, in Stahn, *Practice* (2015), p. 7 ('The sense of political instrumentalization of the Court has been exacerbated by Council inaction after referral'); Stahn, *CLF*, 26 (2015), 41; see also Mettraux et al., *Expert Initiative Effectiveness ICC* (2014), pp. 42–3 (paras. 188, 194) (Prosecutor should suspend investigation if UNSC fails to provide support; UNSC should include in referral resolution possible sanctions).

The Security Council is not obliged to refer a situation to the Court.[427] This follows from the wording of Articles 39 ff. UN Charter[428] and from the fact that an ICC referral is but one option to react to a breach of or threat to the peace; it may be neither a necessary nor a sufficient one.[429] However, if the Council opts for a referral, it should follow up on it and support the Court, especially the Prosecutor, to implement its mandate. Unfortunately, the Council's practice so far has been to the contrary.[430]

In legal terms, a Security Council referral cannot bind the Court since the latter is an autonomous organ of international law whose obligations only follow from the Rome Statute. This states that the Court '*may* exercise its jurisdiction' pursuant to a referral[431] and thus makes clear that it is ultimately the Court's decision if it exercises jurisdiction.[432] Thus, it is always upon the Court alone to determine its jurisdiction *ratione materiae* and *temporis*,[433] even if the respective resolution broadens it;[434] equally, it is for the Court to decide on the admissibility of a situation or a case along the lines of the gravity threshold and the complementarity principle.[435] As to the *ratione temporis* jurisdiction it is worthwhile noting that the

427 Generally on the relationship between the ICC and the SC, see Ruiz Verduzco, in Stahn, *Practice* (2015), pp. 31–5 (distinguishing between three models describing the practice so far: 'Council-related functionality, institutional autonomy, and Rome Statute-centred functionality').

428 cf. Art. 39 ('shall') and Arts. 40–2 ('may') UN Charter; on the SC's legal constraints in that regard Almqvist, *LJIL*, 28 (2015), 108–9.

429 In the same vein, Birdsall, *CLF*, 26 (2015), 51 ff. (criticizing the instrumental use of ICC in the Libya and Syria situations [71] and suggesting that a SC 'referral is not the best way forward', but rather its association with R2P [72]). See also Trahan, *CLF*, 24 (2013), 424–8, 432, 469 (arguing, however, that 'an increasingly solidifying legal obligation to act in the face of large scale atrocity crimes' may arise from the 'responsibility to protect' doctrine and referring insofar, understandably, to the conflict in Syria [430–1]); generally on the R2P, see Ralph, *CLF*, 26 (2015), 1 ff.; on the R2P with regard to international criminal justice, see Stahn, *CLF*, 26 (2015), 13 ff. (analysing the ensuing problems for the ICC [35 ff.] as well as the role of the SC [40 ff.] and rejecting the use of R2P in a punitive sense [43 ff.]); on R2P and the ICC, see also Mills, *CLF*, 26 (2015), 73 ff. (suggesting that both can 'be part of a strategy to deal with potential or ongoing atrocities' [87 ff., 95 ff.]); on the relationship of the R2P and the ICC with regard to peace operations, see Mégret, *CLF*, 26 (2015), 102 ff., 116 ff. (discussing the idea of accountability for a peace operation's failure to protect [137 ff.]); on R2P, the Security Council and the ICC, see also Hehir and Lang, *CLF*, 26 (2015), 153 ff., 175 ff. (criticizing that the SC operates as an impediment to ICC intervention and that the existing system of post-R2P and ICC 'remains fundamentally corrupted by the constitutional competencies of the UNSC, specifically the P5' [177]).

430 This unfortunate situation has been explicitly addressed by Prosecutor Bensouda in her December 2014 Report to the SC, UN Doc. S/PV.7337, 12 December 2014, p. 2 (complaining of a lack of 'strategic recommendation', 'lack of foresight' of the Council forcing her to suspend investigations in Darfur, <http://www.securitycouncilreport.org/atf/cf/%7B65BFCF9B-6D27-4E9C-8CD3-CF6E4FF96FF9%7D/s_pv_7337.pdf>; more recently criticizing the (still) lacking cooperation of the Sudanese government Prosecutor Khan, Statement of 26 January 2023, <https://www.icc-cpi.int/news/statement-icc-prosecutor-karim-khan-kc-united-nations-security-council-situation-darfur>; crit. also Stahn, *EJIL: Talk!*, 3 December 2014 ('use of the ICC as a "dropbox" for unresolved accountability problems') and the references quoted in note 424 in this chapter.

431 Art. 13 ICCS (emphasis added).

432 cf. deGuzman and Schabas, in Sluiter et al., *International Criminal Procedure* (2013), p. 144; Trahan, *CLF*, 24 (2013) 420, 423–4; Schabas and Pecorella, 'Article 13', in Ambos, *Commentary* (2022), mn. 17; for a different, *de lege ferenda* view, Ohlin, in Stahn and Sluiter, *Practice* (2009), pp. 189, 195, arguing, at 192 ff., that the ICC is a hybrid, both security and criminal Court and, as to the former function, bound by a SC referral since only the SC is entitled to decide on question of international peace and security.

433 Arts. 5, 11 ICCS.

434 cf. Sadat, in Schabas and Bernaz, *Handbook ICL* (2011), pp. 197 ff.; Jessberger, in Cassese, *Companion* (2009), p. 209.

435 The Court held so in several decisions—despite Art. 18 ICCS giving standing only to a State concerned and the Prosecutor—and examined the admissibility of cases arising out of Darfur, Sudan, and Libya; see esp. ICC, *Prosecutor v. Gaddafi and Al-Senussi*, PTC I, Decision Requesting Libya to Provide Observations Concerning the Court's Request for Arrest and Surrender of Abdullah Al-Senussi, ICC-01/11-01/11-254, 18 January 2013, para. 10 ('The legal framework of the Statute applies equally to situations referred by the Security Council, including with respect to the complementarity and cooperation regimes, as this is in line, inter alia, with articles 1, 13 and 21 of the Statute which mandate the applicability of the Statute regardless of how the exercise of jurisdiction is triggered in the particular situation'); ICC, *Prosecutor v. Gaddafi and Al-Senussi*, PTC I, Decision on Libya's Postponement of the Execution of the Request for Arrest and Surrender of Abdullah Al-Senussi pursuant to Article 95 of the

Security Council may well backdate the Court's jurisdiction—as a State under Articles 12 (3) and 13 (a) ICCS[436]—but it cannot do so going before the entry into force of the Statute.[437]

Chapter VII of the Charter is also the basis of the Security Council's *deferral power* pursuant to Article 16 ICCS, that is, to request the Court not to begin an investigation or a prosecution or to suspend it for a (renewable) period of up to twelve months.[438] While this power of the Council applies to all referral mechanisms, including a referral by the Council itself,[439] it is to be interpreted narrowly, since such a deferral restricts the Court's autonomy considerably.[440] First, it requires an actual threat to or breach of the peace, or an act of aggression within the meaning of Article 39 UN Charter. Secondly, it applies only to a concrete investigation and prosecution; in particular, prosecutorial measures during the preliminary examinations phase cannot be prevented[441] and the Prosecutor may take the necessary measures to preserve evidence pursuant to Article 54 (3)(f) ICCS.[442] Thirdly, such a deferral may be incompatible with conflicting obligations under the ICC Statute, especially the non-immunity provision of Article 27 considering that even a limited suspension of an investigation or prosecution of a person covered by this provision may amount to a prohibited immunity.[443] The only use of Article 16 so far—in 2002 and 2003 by the US Bush Junior administration in order to prevent the ICC from investigating peacekeepers from the US and other non-Party States[444]—did not meet all of these

Rome Statute and Related Defence Request to Refer Libya to the UN Security Council, ICC-01/11-01/11-354, 14 June 2013, para. 20; *Gaddafi*, ICC-01/11-01/11-547-Red, paras. 73–4, 78; *Prosecutor v. Al Bashir*, AC, Judgment in the Jordan Referral re Al-Bashir Appeal, ICC-02/05-01/09-397-Corr, 6 May 2019, para. 135 ('Court bound by the provisions of the Statute'); *Abd-Al-Rahman*, ICC-02/05-01/20-503, para. 80; see also Nouwen, *Complementarity* (2013), pp. 75–6, 105, 333–4 (here arguing that the SC should consider complementarity for policy reasons in order to 'imbue' its 'discretionary decision with legal principle'); also, see Schabas and Pecorella, 'Article 13', in Ambos, *Commentary* (2022), mn. 18; Bo, *CLF*, 25 (2014), 508 ff.; *contra* Ohlin, in Stahn and Sluiter, *Practice* (2009), pp. 193, 195 (ICC as a security Court 'not subject to the usual constraints of complementarity').

436 Note 324 and main text in this chapter.

437 See e.g. ICC, *Prosecutor v. Abu Garda*, PTC I, Decision on the Prosecutor's Application under Article 58, ICC-02/05-02/09-1, 7 May 2009, para. 2; *Prosecutor v. Ntaganda*, PTC II, Decision on the Prosecutor's Application under Article 58, ICC-01/04-02/06-36-Red, 13 July 2012, paras. 8, 10; conc. Fry, *Contours* (2015), p. 139; too broad again (as previously mentioned, note 329 in this chapter, regarding an Art. 12 (3) declaration) ICC-OTP, *Prelim. Examinations* (2013), para. 37, stating that the temporal jurisdiction depends on 'the date specified in a Security Council referral'. In detail, Galand, *Security Council* (2019), pp. 120 ff.

438 In detail, Olásolo, *CPI* (2003), pp. 232 ff.; Kurth, *IStGH* (2006), pp. 75 ff.; also Hoffmeister and Knoke, *ZaöRV*, 59 (1999), 803 ff., arguing that such a resolution cannot bind the—independent (Art. 42)—Prosecutor (pp. 804–5.); also Fixson, in Kirsch, *Internationale Strafgerichtshöfe* (2005), pp. 218–19; Ambos, in Ambos et al., *Building a Future* (2009), p. 82 (para. 50); Quesada-Alcalá, in Fernández-Sánchez, *New Challenges* (2005), pp. 298 ff.; Gallavin, *CLF*, 17 (2006), 50 ff.; Nsereko, *ZIS*, 2 (2007), 502–3; Robinson, in Cryer et al., *ICL* (2019), pp. 153–4; crit. Cryer, *Prosecuting* (2005), pp. 226–7; Kolb, in Kolb and Scalia, *DIP* (2012), pp. 284 ff.; Ruiz Verduzco, in Stahn, *Practice* (2015), pp. 52 ff.; O'Keefe, *ICL* (2015), pp. 549–51; Brunger, 'Article 16', in Klamberg et al., *Commentary ICC I* (2023), pp. 591–600; Zakerhossein, *Situation* (2017), p. 77; regarding the proceedings against Al Bashir, see Hoven, *ZIS*, 6 (2011), 230 ff. On the negotiations, see Bergsmo and Zhu, 'Article 16', in Ambos, *Commentary* (2022), mn. 1–9.

439 cf. Bergsmo and Zhu, 'Article 16', in Ambos, *Commentary* (2022), mn. 25.

440 cf. Trahan, *CLF*, 24 (2013), 433–49, 470–1; Ruiz Verduzco, in Stahn, *Practice* (2015), p. 53 (arguing that it is 'the most powerful tool for the Council to directly influence investigations and prosecution of the ICC', and expressing some concerns on the impact deferrals can have on the interests of the accused, of the victims or other State Parties [p. 60]).

441 In the same vein, Bergsmo and Zhu, 'Article 16', in Ambos, *Commentary* (2022), mn. 16; Brunger, 'Article 16', in Klamberg et al., *Commentary ICC I* (2023), p. 591. On the different procedural phases (preliminary examinations, investigation, prosecution), see Chapter IV, A. in this volume.

442 cf. Bergsmo and Zhu, 'Article 16', in Ambos, *Commentary* (2022), mn. 20–1.

443 In this sense, apparently, Trahan, *CLF*, 24 (2013), 442–6, 449, 470, also discussing an incompatibility with Art. 12 (2) ICCS and prohibiting for reasons of 'good policy' a kind of self-serving deferral benefiting a person or a State who created the peace threatening situation in the first place.

444 cf. UNSC Res. 1422, 12 July 2002, renewed by UNSC Res. 1487, 12 June 2003; see Boas et al., *International Criminal Procedure* (2011), pp. 95–6; Bergsmo and Zhu, 'Article 16', in Ambos, *Commentary* (2022), mn. 11; crit.

requirements.[445] Of course, both a Security Council referral and deferral face the problem of a possible veto by a permanent member of the Council and require a majority decision of the fifteen Council members.[446]

*(iii) Proprio* motu *investigation by the Prosecutor*

Last but not least, the Prosecutor themselves can operate as a trigger by initiating investigations *ex officio* on the basis of information from any reliable source, including intergovernmental organizations and non-governmental organizations.[447] If they are of the opinion that a reasonable basis for an investigation exists, they must apply to the PTC for an authorization to proceed with the investigation.[448] This has happened so far in seven situations, namely Kenya,[449] Ivory Coast,[450] Georgia,[451], Burundi,[452] Bangladesh/Myanmar,[453] Afghanistan,[454] and, most recently, the Philippines.[455]

El Zeidy, *VanderbiltJTL*, 35 (2002), 1503 ff.; Mokhtar, *ICLR*, 3 (2003), 295 ff.; Zakerhossein, *Situation* (2017), pp. 77–8; also crit. and rejecting the more recent deferral requests by Sudan and Kenya for lack of an actual threat to peace, Trahan, *CLF*, 24 (2013), 433–49, 470–1; for an overview of deferral requests, see Ruiz Verduzco, in Stahn, *Practice* (2015), pp. 53 ff. See also Triggs, in Dolgopol and Gardam, *Challenge of Conflict* (2005), p. 325; Ambos, *RDP*, 15 (2005), 108 ff.; Kurth, *IStGH* (2006), pp. 123 ff.; Stahn, *EJIL*, 14 (2003), 103–4; Cryer, *Prosecuting* (2005), pp. 227–8; Robinson, in Cryer et al., *ICL* (2019), pp. 165–7.

[445] On how these requirements are interpreted differently for different situations, see Ruiz Verduzco, in Stahn, *Practice* (2015), pp. 57–60; also see Tladi, in Jeßberger et al., *Systemunrecht* (2022), p. 326 pointing out that '[i]t was not lost on African States that when Article 16 was to the benefit of one of the permanent members, it was granted without much fanfare.'

[446] Art. 27 (3) UN Charter. Similarly Bock, *Opfer* (2010), pp. 335–6; furthermore, see Brunger, 'Article 16', in Klamberg et al., *Commentary ICC I* (2023), pp. 591–600. Even if one takes into account the potential of the GA and the HRC to influence the relevant SC decisions, 'the extent of UNGA/HRC influence is inevitably limited in the "hard case" where the interest of a UNSC permanent member is implicated' (see Ramsden and Hamilton, *ICLQ*, 66 (2017), 895 ff., 899). See Zakerhossein, *Situation* (2017), p. 70 ('selective justice arising from the Council is maybe better than nothing').

[447] Art. 13 (c), in conjunction with Art. 15 ICCS. For more details, see Olásolo, *CPI* (2003), pp. 403 ff.; Hoffmeister and Knoke, *ZaöRV*, 59 (1999) 790 ff.; Radosavljevic, *ICLR*, 13 (2013), 1021; De Vos, *LJIL*, 26 (2013), 1012 ff.; Stegmiller, 'Article 15', in Klamberg et al., *Commentary ICC I* (2023), pp. 549–51.

[448] Art. 15 (3) ICCS.

[449] The OTP's 'request for authorization of an investigation' of (*Situation in the Republic of Kenya*, PTC II, Request for Authorisation of an Investigation pursuant to Article 15, ICC-01/09-3, 26 November 2009) was accepted by PTC II on 31 March 2010 (*Situation in the Republic of Kenya*, PTC II, Decision Pursuant to Article 15 of the Rome Statute on the Authorization of an Investigation into the Situation in the Republic of Kenya, ICC-01/09-19, 31 March 2010); thereon, see Ambos, in Bruinsma and Weisburd, *Encyclopedia of Criminology and Criminal Justice* (2013), p. 1038.

[450] The OTP's 'request for authorization of an investigation' (*Situation in the Republic of Cote d'Ivoire*, PTC III, Request for Authorisation of an Investigation pursuant to Article 15, ICC-02/11-3, 23 June 2011) was accepted by PTC III on 3 October 2011 (*Situation in the Republic of Cote d'Ivoire*, ICC-02/11-14).

[451] The OTP's 'request for authorization of an investigation' (*Situation in Georgia*, PTC I, Request for Authorisation of an Investigation pursuant to Article 15, ICC-01/15-4, 13 October 2015) was accepted by PTC I on 27 January 2016 (*Situation in Georgia*, ICC-01/15).

[452] The OTP's 'request for authorization of an investigation' (*Situation in the Republic of Burundi*, PTC III, Request for Authorisation of an Investigation pursuant to Article 15, ICC-01/17-X-5-US-Exp., 5 September 2017) was accepted by PTC III on 25 October 2017 (*Situation in the Republic of Burundi*, ICC-01/17-X).

[453] The OTP's 'request for authorization of an investigation' (*Situation in the People's Republic of Bangladesh/Republic of the Union of Myanmar*, PTC III, Request for Authorisation of an Investigation pursuant to Article 15, ICC-01/19-7, 4 July 2019) was accepted by PTC III on 14 November 2019 (*Situation in the People's Republic of Bangladesh/Republic of the Union of Myanmar*, ICC-01/19-27).

[454] The OTP's 'request for authorization of an investigation' (*Situation in the Islamic Republic of Afghanistan*, AC, ICC- 02/17-7-Conf-Exp, 20 November 2017) was finally accepted by the AC on 5 March 2020 (*Situation in the Islamic Republic of Afghanistan*, ICC-02/17 OA4). PTC II initially had rejected the Prosecutor's request, see below note 718.

[455] The OTP's 'request for authorization of an investigation' (*Situation in the Republic of the Philippines*, PTC I, ICC-01/21-7-SECRET-Exp, 24 May 2021) was accepted by PTC I on 15 September 2021 (*Situation in the Republic of the Philippines*, ICC-01/21-12).

The relatively early control of the Prosecutor's *proprio motu* activity[456] has been the price to afford them this possibility in the first place.[457] Only if the PTC is satisfied that there is a sufficient basis for an investigation can the Prosecutor actually commence the proper investigation.[458] In case of a negative decision, the Prosecutor may present, at a later stage, another request on the basis of other facts or fresh evidence.[459] If the Prosecutor, before applying to the PTC, realizes that the information is insufficient, they must inform the parties concerned; this, too, does not preclude further investigations on the basis of fresh facts or evidence.[460]

In sum, it is fair to say that the jurisdictional control is most intense in a case of *proprio motu* initiation by the Prosecutor and less intense in a case of Security Council referral. Yet, it is worth noting that in the former situation the threshold is relatively low, and even in the latter situation the Court is not a blind executor of the Council's will but has to carry out a proper examination of its jurisdictional requirements. Indeed, the OTP clarified that the preliminary examinations 'will be conducted in the same manner irrespective' of the trigger mechanism.[461]

## B. Admissibility, in particular the complementarity test

### (1) Primacy vs. subsidiarity (complementarity)

Once an international criminal tribunal has jurisdiction, the question arises whether there is a national criminal justice system that may also claim jurisdiction and effectively does so. If this is the case, the further question arises how the factual *concurrence* between the international and the national jurisdiction will be resolved. Of course, such a concurrence does not arise in the rather exceptional situations that an *exclusive* jurisdiction of an international tribunal[462] exists, or that there is no national jurisdiction over the respective crime since it has been committed in a place that does not belong to the territory of a State and no other jurisdictional link exists either.[463] Yet, in the normal situation of an effective concurrence between the international and the national jurisdiction, that is, a jurisdictional claim by both jurisdictions, *rules of priority* have to be established along the following basic lines: either the international tribunal enjoys primacy, or it is subsidiary (complementary) to the respective national jurisdiction. Of course, primacy and subsidiarity rarely exist in a pure, absolute form; rather, they are arranged, in the concrete law and practice of international criminal tribunals, in a more flexible and relative fashion.[464] In practice, there may even be

[456] Normally a control of prosecutorial activity—coercive measures aside—will take place once investigations have actually been completed, for instance, by the French *Chambre d'Accusation*, the US *Grand Jury*, or the pre-trial judge in the German *Zwischenverfahren* (interlocutory proceedings); cf. Ambos, *The Review* (*International Commission of Jurists*), 58/59 (1997), 50 ff., with references.

[457] See also Coco, 'Article 13', in Klamberg et al., *Commentary ICC I* (2023), pp. 523–4 ('avoiding abuse of the *proprio motu* power for politicized or frivolous investigations'); Zakerhossein, *Situation* (2017), pp. 90–1.

[458] Art. 15 (4) ICCS. On the distinction between the preliminary investigation (examinations) and the formal investigation, see Chapter IV, A.(1) in this volume.

[459] Art. 15 (5) ICCS; see also Stegmiller, 'Article 15', in Klamberg et al., *Commentary ICC I* (2023), p. 562.

[460] Art. 15 (6) ICCS.

[461] ICC-OTP, *Prelim. Examinations* (2013), para. 12. Indeed, the factors to be taken into account are identical, cf. Rule 48 RPE ICC referring to Art. 53 (1)(a) to (c) ICCS; thereon also Chapter IV, A.(1)(a) in this volume.

[462] So far, the jurisdiction of international criminal tribunals has been 'concurrent', see Nouwen and Lewis, in Sluiter et al., *International Criminal Procedure* (2013), pp. 117 ff., 126 (analysing all tribunals since Nuremberg).

[463] On the possible jurisdictional links, see Section A.(2) in this chapter.

[464] See also Nouwen and Lewis, in Sluiter et al., *International Criminal Procedure* (2013), p. 117 ('somewhere in between, rendering the tribunal's jurisdiction more or less primary and more or less complementary').

an approximation between these two concepts as we shall see with regard to Rule 11*bis* primacy at the ad hoc tribunals and complementarity at the ICC.

### *(a) Primacy*

The primacy approach has been employed in the case of the ad hoc tribunals,[465] that is, they supersede the national jurisdiction and adjudicate the cases they consider important enough. To be fair, it must be said that Rule 9 RPE ICTY provides for three (alternative) grounds for a prosecutorial request for deferral,[466] but the Rule is broad enough to justify any deferral.[467] In practice, TCs have generously granted the respective requests,[468] relying normally on the third ground of the close relationship of the respective issue with the case before the tribunal.[469] To effectively implement primacy, the Prosecutor may request a State to forward all relevant information regarding an investigation[470] and the tribunal may, at any stage of the proceedings, 'formally request national courts to defer' to its competence.[471] This is possible even if the national authorities have already started with an investigation and indicted a specific person. Thus, in the very first case of the ICTY, that of Duško Tadić, the suspect was already detained and indicted by the prosecutorial authorities of the German state (Land) of Bavaria, but the tribunal asked the German authorities to surrender Tadić to the tribunal.[472]

Of course, the advantage of the primacy approach—apart from expressing a hierarchical superiority vis-à-vis national jurisdictions[473]—is that it avoids lengthy jurisdictional disputes between the concurrent jurisdictions. The rule is clear: there is nothing the domestic jurisdiction can do against the international tribunal's interference with

465 cf. Arts. 9 (2) ICTYS, 5 (2) IRMCTS, 8 (2) ICTRS/SCSLS/RSCSLS and Art. 10 (1), 54 KSC Law (note the slight difference regarding the object of reference of the primacy rule: 'national courts', 'national courts of all states', 'national courts of Sierra Leone', 'all other courts in Kosovo'). In practice, the ICTY case law also extended the primacy to all UN Member States; see *Prosecutor v. Tadić*, No. IT-94-1, Decision on the Defence Motion for Interlocutory Appeal on Jurisdiction, paras. 56–60 (esp. 58) (2 October 1995). cf. also Wolfrum, in Arnold et al., *Menschengerechtes Strafrecht* (2005), pp. 980 ff.; Cryer, *Prosecuting* (2005), pp. 127 ff.; Zahar and Sluiter, *ICL* (2008), pp. 450 ff.; O'Keefe, *ICL* (2015), pp. 499–500 (ICTY/ICTR), 526 (SCSL); Greenawalt, in deGuzman and Oosterveld, *Elgar Companion ICC* (2020), pp. 62 and 65; furthermore, see Bachmann and Nwibo Eda, *Brook. J.Int'l. L*, 43 (2018), 475–7 and Zhao, *China* (2017), pp. 13–16.

466 cf. Rule 9 RPE ICTY allowing for a request if either the relevant conduct may be characterized as an 'ordinary crime', there is a 'lack of impartiality or independence', or 'what is in issue is closely related to, or otherwise involves, significant factual or legal questions which may have implications for investigations or prosecutions before the Tribunal'. In contrast, Rules 9 (ii) RPE ICTR/SCSL and Rule 11 (B) RPE MICT refer to the 'seriousness of the offence', the 'status of the accused', and the 'general importance of the legal questions involved in the case'. Nouwen and Lewis, in Sluiter et al., *International Criminal Procedure* (2013), pp. 119, 127 speak therefore of 'conditional' primacy that is, however, 'most unconditional', in the case of the STL (ibid., p. 121). At the KSC a transfer of proceedings may only be ordered 'to the Specialist Chambers and the Specialist Prosecutor', Art. 54 (2) KSC Law.

467 Crit. also Cryer, *Prosecuting* (2005), p. 130 ('demand transfer ... whenever [they] want').

468 cf. Boas et al., *International Criminal Procedure* (2011), pp. 55–6, referring, in n. 40, to one 'rare partial denial' of a request with regard to the Former Yugoslav Republic of Macedonia and indicating that the requests either refer to a 'particular case' or a 'general group of incidents'; in the same vein, Nouwen and Lewis, in Sluiter et al., *International Criminal Procedure* (2013), p. 121 ('never declined a prosecutor's request').

469 cf. Nouwen and Lewis, in Sluiter et al., *International Criminal Procedure* (2013), p. 120.

470 Rules 8 RPE ICTY/ICTR/SCSL and 9 RPE MICT.

471 cf. Arts. 9 (2) ICTYS, 5 (2) IRMCTS, and 8 (2) ICTRS/SCSLS/RSCSLS.

472 cf. Boas et al., *International Criminal Procedure* (2011), p. 56.

473 Newton, *MilLR*, 167 (2001), 42 ('jurisdictional hierarchy'); Bachmann and Nwibo Eda, *Brook. J.Int'l. L*, 43 (2018), 473 ('primacy regime essentially creates a hierarchy of jurisdiction'); see also Boas et al., *International Criminal Procedure* (2011), p. 48; Trahan, *CornILJ*, 45 (2013), 574. This also has consequences with regard to the rather vertical than mixed cooperation regime of the ad hoc tribunals, as we will see in Chapter VII in this volume.

its investigation. Indeed, the international tribunal alone has the authority to decide if it wants to take care itself of a certain case/suspect or leave it to the national system. Against this background the formal recognition of 'concurrent jurisdiction'[474] appears as mere lip service.[475]

Equally, the primacy rule gives an international tribunal the authority to 'outsource' investigations to the national authorities of the territorial State, as indeed has been done by ICTY/ICTR—as a consequence of their completion strategies[476]—with their Rule 11*bis* procedures.[477] According to this lengthy and complex Rule, a 'Referral Bench' (composed of three Permanent Judges from the TCs), at the request of the Prosecutor or *proprio motu*,[478] shall determine, after confirmation of the indictment and before the commencement of the trial, whether a given case shall be referred to the authorities of the territorial, arrest, or any other State which has jurisdiction and is 'willing and adequately prepared to accept such a case'.[479] However, the referral is predicated on the assumption that the respective State offers a fair trial and does not impose the death penalty.[480] Further, at the ICTY, the gravity of the alleged conduct and the 'level of responsibility of the accused' must be taken into account.[481] Interestingly, admissibility as a procedural concept has only become relevant at the ad hoc tribunals with the completion strategy and the ensuing deferral of cases,[482] although it must be said that only the ICTY judges introduced a kind of admissibility rule in their law by filtering out indictments which do not concentrate 'on one or more of the most senior leaders suspected of being most responsible'.[483] Ultimately, the Rule 11*bis* procedure as applied in judicial practice has become strikingly similar to the complementary regime of the ICC[484] to be looked at more closely now.

[474] cf. Arts. 9 (1) ICTYS, 8 (1) ICTRS/SCSLS, and 5 (1) IRMCTS. See also Nouwen and Lewis, in Sluiter et al., *International Criminal Procedure* (2013), pp. 118–19.

[475] It is surprising therefore that Boas et al., *International Criminal Procedure* (2011), p. 47 put the ad hoc tribunals on an equal footing with the ICC.

[476] cf. Boas et al., *International Criminal Procedure* (2011), p. 57, pointing to the decrease in deferral requests since the early 2000s, 58 ('product of the completion strategy'); Nouwen and Lewis, in Sluiter et al., *International Criminal Procedure* (2013), p. 122 ('part of their "completion strategy"'). On the completion strategy, see previously Ambos, *Treatise ICL I* (2021), p. 25; crit. on how the 'completion strategy' influences the selection of cases at ICC, Bergsmo, in Bergsmo, *Criteria for Prioritizing* (2010), p. 12; on the relationship between 'completion strategy' and 'positive complementarity', see note 1063 in this chapter.

[477] cf. Boas et al., *International Criminal Procedure* (2011), pp. 58 ff.; O'Keefe, *ICL* (2015), pp. 500–1; see also El Zeidy, *ICLQ*, 57 (2008), 406 ff.; Pinto Soares, *IsLR*, 46 (2013), 331–2, Shany, *IsLR*, 46 (2013), 438–9; Kindt, *Menschenrechte* (2009), pp. 134–5; Lindemann, *Referral of Cases* (2013), pp. 70 ff.; see also Angermaier, in Bergsmo, *Criteria for Prioritizing* (2010), pp. 40 ff.; Donlon, in Darcy and Powderly, *Judicial Creativity* (2010), pp. 353 ff.; Bekou, *FordhamILJ*, 33 (2010), 723; Carter, *FordhamILJ*, 32 (2009), 1614.

[478] Rule 11*bis* (B) RPE ICTY/ICTR and Article 6 (4) IRMCTS; according to Rule 11*bis* (B) RPE SCSL only at the request of the Prosecutor.

[479] Rule 11*bis* (A) RPE ICTY/ICTR and Art. 6 (2)(iii) IRMCTS; according to Rule 11*bis* (A) RPE SCSL a referral is possible only to 'a State having jurisdiction'. In practice, the ICTY Referral Bench has normally chosen the State with the strongest nexus to the alleged criminal conduct (Blumenstock and Pittman, *HuV*-I, 21 (2008), 111–12).

[480] Rules 11*bis* (B) RPE ICTY/SCLS, 11*bis* (C) RPE ICTR, Art. 6 (4) IRMCTS.

[481] Rule 11*bis* (C) RPE ICTY; cf. also Art. 6 (3) IRMCTS. On further principles derived from the primacy rule, see Boas et al., *International Criminal Procedure* (2011), pp. 61–3.

[482] Boas et al., *International Criminal Procedure* (2011), pp. 57–8.

[483] cf. Rule 28 (A) RPE ICTY; in the same vein, Art. 1 (2) IRMCTS. The ICTR judges did not adopt such a rule, arguing that it would infringe the Prosecutor's independence, cf. Sautenet, *ChinJIL*, 4 (2005), 562 with n. 248.

[484] cf. El Zeidy, *ICLQ*, 57 (2008), 405 ff. (arguing that the move away from absolute primacy to complementarity started with the amendment on 10 June 2004 [410] and the underlying idea is burden-sharing between international and national courts [411], thereby creating 'a third model of complementarity comparable in *principle* to the Rome Statute complementarity model' [413, emphasis in the original]).

*(b) Subsidiarity (complementarity)*

The ICC regime opts for a subsidiarity approach, that is, it grants, as a matter of principle, primacy to the respective national jurisdiction.[485] More precisely, *any* State, that is, not necessarily a State Party,[486] 'which has jurisdiction over' a case,[487] that is, which can ground its jurisdiction on one of the recognized jurisdictional titles under international law,[488] may claim primacy towards the ICC, that is, it can 'trump' its jurisdiction.[489] This form of subsidiarity appears only insofar as it is 'complementary to national criminal jurisdictions'[490] in that both—the international and the national—jurisdictions strive to close the impunity gap for international core crimes and thus 'complement' each other, forming part of the international criminal justice system already alluded to in Volume I of this Treatise.[491]

On the face of it, a State's jurisdiction may also rest on less traditional jurisdictional principles, like *aut dedere aut iudicare* (principle of representation) and universal jurisdiction.[492] The case law has not yet dealt with the issue, but policy reasons support a restrictive interpretation. While it is fair to assume that the drafter did not want to leave it to the Court to decide about the (prescriptive) jurisdiction of the States, the rationale of the establishment of the ICC calls for a restrictive interpretation. For one of the main reasons for its establishment was to avoid far-fetched third State jurisdiction for extraterritorial events ('Pinochet situation'),[493] not least to avoid diplomatic tensions between the States concerned. In practical terms, such jurisdiction entails many problems regarding access to evidence, investigations on the ground, etc. Of course, the Court has to struggle with the same problems, but one would assume that, as an international institution embedded in the international system, it can better cope with the respective problems and, in any case, its intervention does not generate the kind of tensions known from interstate jurisdictional conflicts. Thus, while it is reasonable to give States with a close jurisdictional link (territoriality, nationality) jurisdictional primacy over the Court, this makes less sense with regard to a jurisdictional title which renounces such a link.[494] Importantly, this is not so much a normative claim—as the normative basis for universal jurisdiction is the same for the national or supranational level—but a decision based on practical and policy considerations.

In any case, a State is free to limit its universal jurisdiction to cases which are not investigated by the ICC, thereby giving primacy to the Court in universal jurisdiction cases.[495]

485 Stressing the function of complementarity 'as primary right' to investigation, prosecution, and adjudication of States, Nouwen, *Complementarity* (2013), pp. 338–9; in a similar vein, in favour of the adoption of an Optional Protocol to the Rome Statute enshrining in the admissibility system an express and enforceable obligation to exercise national jurisdiction, Akhavan, *JICJ*, 8 (2010), 1247, 1262 ff.; Akhavan, *JICJ*, 14 (2016), 1045; furthermore, see Rastan, *JICJ*, 15 (2017), 3 (rightly emphasizing that the final decision is taken by the ICC); Bachmann and Nwibo Eda, *Brook. J.Int'l. L*, 43 (2018), 479–80 ('passive model'); Minow, *HarvILJ*, 60 (2019), 5 ('basic idea is that the ICC is to "complement" domestic justice systems, not replace them'). See also note 1133 in this chapter in connection with positive complementarity, Section (3)(b).

486 Art. 17 (1)(a) and (b) ICCS refer to 'a State', not a State Party; see also Nouwen, *Complementarity* (2013), p. 71; O'Keefe, *ICL* (2015), p. 555.

487 cf. Art. 17 (1)(a) and (b) ICCS.

488 cf. Section A.(2) in this chapter.

489 O'Keefe, *ICL* (2015), p. 554.

490 cf. Preamble, recital 10; thereto Triffterer, Bergsmo, and Ambos, 'Preamble', in Ambos, *Commentary* (2022), mn. 22; Bachmann and Nwibo Eda, *Brook. J.Int'l. L*, 43 (2018), 485 (rightly pointing out that 'the question of admissibility and jurisdiction, in terms of exercising competences over specific cases, is distinguishable').

491 Thereon see Ambos, *Treatise ICL I* (2021), pp. 97–9.

492 See also the same formulation in Arts. 18 (1), (2), and 19 (2)(b). See also recital 6 of the Preamble of the Statute referring to 'criminal jurisdiction' in a general sense.

493 ICC-OTP, *Prosecutorial Strategy* (2010), para. 16; thereon Ambos and Stegmiller, *Crime Law Soc Change*, 58 (2012), 417 ff.

494 cf. Benvenuti, in Lattanzi and Schabas, *Essays on the Rome Statute I* (2000), pp. 48–9; Kreß, *NStZ*, 20 (2000), 625; Höpfel, in Arnold et al., *Menschengerechtes Strafrecht* (2005), p. 773.

495 See e.g. the German solution in s. 153f (1) cl. 2 German CPC (StPO) (refraining from criminal prosecution of a German (!) suspect if the offence is being prosecuted, inter alia, by an international court) and 153f (2) no. 4 (no

Further, the Court shall only complement the domestic criminal justice systems,[496] that is, only take care of cases within its jurisdiction if the competent national jurisdiction is—in line with the complementarity *stricto sensu* test[497]—either (totally) inactive or unwilling/unable to do so. Thus, while such a system upholds State sovereignty—probably the most important rationale of the complementarity principle[498]—by creating a general presumption in favour of the competent domestic jurisdiction, this presumption only holds—going beyond the just mentioned 'slogan version' focusing on unwillingness/inability[499]—if the respective domestic jurisdiction actually investigates and/or prosecutes the (same) 'case' within the meaning of Article 17 (1)(a) ICCS.[500] The respective provisions of the ICC Statute (Articles 17–19) provide for rules on the (in)admissibility[501] of situations and cases[502] before the ICC. In fact, all provisions carry the term 'admissibility' already in their headings. They apply irrespective of the referral mechanisms, including a Security Council referral.[503]

Of course, a system of subsidiarity or—to use the ICC term—'complementarity'[504] generates a series of difficult questions of legal interpretation and policy[505] and therefore needs

German prosecution of extraterritorial crime by and against foreigner if, inter alia, an international court takes care of it); see also Werle and Jessberger, *Principles ICL* (2020), mn. 347 with n. 784. In a similar vein, Constitutional Court of South Africa, *National Commissioner of the South African Police Service v. Southern African Human Rights Litigation Centre and Another*, Case CCT 02/14, (30 October 2014), para. 61 ('However, the universal jurisdiction to investigate international crimes is not absolute. It is subject to at least two limitations ... we may not investigate or prosecute international crimes in breach of considerations of complementarity and subsidiarity').

[496] Werle and Jessberger, *Principles ICL* (2020), mn. 314. For a reversed (mis)understanding in Uganda, considering the domestic justice system as 'complementary' to the ICC, see Nouwen, *Complementarity* (2013), pp. 239–40.

[497] See sub-section (2)(d) in this section.

[498] cf. Bergsmo, Bekou, and Jones, *GoJIL*, 2 (2010), 794–5 ('balance between ... State sovereignty and judicial independence'); Nouwen, *Complementarity* (2013), p. 16 with further references in n. 16 (criticizing the—alleged—de facto limitation of sovereignty by the Court's subordination of States' under its 'anti-impunity struggle' at p. 409); Werle and Jessberger, *Principles ICL* (2020), mn. 315; Heller, *JICJ*, 14 (2016), 639; Jackson, *JICJ*, 14 (2016), 1068; Bachmann and Nwibo Eda, *Brook. J.Int'l. L*, 43 (2018), 475 ('overarching rationale'); see also for this and further purposes of complementarity, Trahan, *CornILJ*, 45 (2013), 578–80; Zhao, *China* (2017), p. 12 (arguing that 'complementarity plays at least two roles under the Rome Statute: the judicial disputes settlement mechanism and the burden-sharing system'), for a nuanced approach with regard to a post-conflict/transitional situation Stahn, in Stahn, *Practice* (2015), pp. 227–8 (arguing that in this situation 'the very essence of sovereignty and the state itself is in flux'); on the conflict between sovereignty interests and prosecution by the ICC, see Brighton, *ICLR*, 12 (2012), 631 ff.

[499] Crit. of this 'slogan version', Robinson, in Stahn and El Zeidy, *Complementarity I* (2011), pp. 462, 463 ff.

[500] *Muthaura et al.*, ICC-01/09-02/11-274, para. 43; *Ruto et al.*, ICC-01/09-01/11-307, para. 44, arguing that Art. 17 (1) ICC favours the domestic jurisdictions 'only to the extent that there actually are, or have been, investigations and/or prosecutions at the national level'; conc. *Gaddafi*, ICC-01/11-01/11-547-Red, para. 78; *S. Gbagbo*, ICC-02/11-01/12-75, paras. 2, 59.

[501] On the negative drafting of Art. 17 using 'inadmissible', instead of 'admissible', see Schabas and El Zeidy, 'Article 17', in Ambos, *Commentary* (2022), mn. 23.

[502] El Zeidy, *CLF*, 19 (2008), 35, 39; Ambos, *Colombian Peace Process* (2010), p. 44; crit. Schabas, *ICC Commentary* (2016), pp. 451–2; WCRO, *Situation* (2009), pp. 28 ff.

[503] See Section A.(4)(b)(ii) in this chapter. See also Satzger, *ICL* (2018), § 12 mn. 24; Tillier, *ICLR*, 13 (2013), 515–16. However, it is debatable whether the UN Security Council can instruct the States not to exercise their jurisdiction, cf. ICC-OTP, *Complementarity* (2003), paras. 67 ff.; see also Hoffmeister and Knoke, *ZaöRV*, 59 (1999), 798; Nsereko, *LJIL*, 26 (2013), 430 ff.

[504] cf. Ambos, *Colombian Peace Process* (2010), pp. 37 ff.; Stahn, *LJIL*, 23 (2010), 315 ff.; Eberechi, *AfrJICompL*, 20 (2012), 24 ff.; Krings, *GoJIL*, 4 (2012), 746 ff.; Rastan, in Bergsmo, *Complementarity* (2010), pp. 83 ff.; Ellis, in Muller and Zouridis, *Law and Justice* (2012), pp. 178 ff.; Lafleur, *Komplementarität* (2011), *passim*; generally on the notion of complementarity, see Tharakan, *Konkretisierung* (2009), pp. 5 ff.; Sadat, in Schabas and Bernaz, *Handbook ICL* (2011), pp. 197 ff.; El Zeidy, in Schabas and Bernaz, *Handbook ICL* (2011), pp. 211 ff.; Jessberger, in Cassese, *Companion* (2009), pp. 208, 212; Nouwen, in Brown, *Handbook ICL* (2011), p. 206; Mendes, *Peace* (2010), pp. 27 ff..; Gordon, *OregonLR*, 88 (2009), 627 ff.; Benoit-Landale, in Ziegler et al., *Kriegsverbrecherprozesse* (2009), pp. 247 ff.; Jurdi, *ICC* (2011), pp. 9 ff.; Pinto Soares, *CLF*, 23 (2012), 186–7; on shaping the principle of complementarity taking into account the practice of the national jurisdictions when applying subsidiarity on the basis of universality, see Ryngaert, *CLF*, 19 (2008), 177 ff.; on the relation to 'responsibility to protect', see Benzing, in König et al., *International Law Today* (2008), pp. 25 ff.; on a 'gender approach to complementarity', see Chappell, Grey, and Waller, *ICTJ*, 7 (2013), 455 ff.

[505] For a crit. approach, see e.g. Vinjamuri, in Stahn, *Practice* (2015), pp. 23–4 (expressing concerns as to complementarity leading to 'a bifurcated system of global justice, with weak states subject to international authority

a closer analysis, to be carried out in the following section. To be sure, this analysis will be primarily a legal one, that is, it will be limited to complementarity as an admissibility requirement for situations and cases brought before the ICC. Any broader political or even philosophical meaning of the concept is not encompassed by this inquiry,[506] apart from some considerations on 'positive complementarity'—rather belonging to complementarity's political limb[507]—at the end of this chapter.

### (2) Admissibility (Article 17 ICCS): Gravity and complementarity *stricto sensu*

#### *(a) Introductory remarks*

The complementarity test[508] is an *ongoing process* and may be revisited several times before the commencement of the trial.[509] The *Kony* PTC made the continuing nature of the test clear, stressing the possibility of 'multiple determinations' of, and 'multiple challenges'[510] to admissibility in a given case.[511] It concluded:

and stronger democratic states answerable only to themselves', and suggesting as a necessary solution a possible abandonment of the 'goal of the decentralized justice' and of complementarity).

[506] For the 'double life' of complementarity, as a technical-legal concept and a 'big idea', see Nouwen, *Complementarity* (2013), pp. 11, 15–16, listing in total nine complementarity 'developments and paradoxes' (11–14); on the two dimensions of complementarity, law and policy, see Pinto Soares, *IsLR*, 46 (2013), 319 ff.

[507] cf. Nouwen, *Complementarity* (2013), pp. 20–1 (discussing it as a 'big idea'); furthermore, see Bachmann and Nwibo Eda, *Brook. J.Int'l. L*, 43 (2018), 490 (arguing that 'contrasting interpretations of the complementarity principle ... in terms of the actual purpose that the principle is designed to achieve in practice ... contribute to the ICC's sociopolitical amalgamation and involvement in national jurisdictions, which in itself is a direct result of the failure to resolve the many challenges associated with the theory and practice of complementarity').

[508] I draw here on my previous study with regard to Colombia , Ambos et al., *Procedimiento de la Ley de Justicia y Paz* (2010) and Ambos, *Colombian Peace Process* (2010). On the historical development of the concept, see Stahn, in Stahn and El Zeidy, *Complementarity I* (2011), pp. 5–6; see also Holmes, in Lee, *ICC* (1999), pp. 41–78; El Zeidy, in Stahn and El Zeidy, *Complementarity I* (2011), pp. 71–141; Politi, in Stahn and El Zeidy, *Complementarity i I* (2011), pp. 142–9; regarding the ICC negotiations, see Schabas and El Zeidy, 'Article 17', in Ambos, *Commentary* (2022), mn. 5 ff.; defining complementarity as the distinction between the *ratione materiae* jurisdiction of the ICC and its exercise, Satzger, *ICL* (2018), § 12 mn. 17; Satzger, *Internationales Strafrecht* (2022), § 14 mn. 17. On the purpose of complementarity, see Batros, in Stahn and El Zeidy, *Complementarity I* (2011), pp. 589–96; Schabas, *ICC Commentary* (2016), pp. 447–51; Stegmiller, *Pre-Investigation Stage* (2011), pp. 281–3. On a prospective assessment of complementarity, see Carter, *SouthwesternJIL*, 18 (2011), 201–5.

[509] See also Stigen, *Relationship* (2008), p. 245; Stigen, in Stahn and El Zeidy, *Complementarity I* (2011), pp. 504–6; Nouwen, in Brown, *Handbook ICL* (2011), pp. 227–8; Nouwen, *Complementarity* (2013), pp. 79–83; Satzger, *ICL* (2018), § 12 mn. 17; O'Keefe, *ICL* (2015), pp. 555–6; also ICC-OTP, *Complementarity and Cooperation* (2024), paras. 146, 167. On the double effect of this dynamic character of complementarity (vis-à-vis States but also vis-à-vis the ICC), see Olásolo, in Almqvist and Espósito, *Justitia Transicional* (2009), p. 279.

[510] I draw here on my previous study with regard to Colombia, Ambos et al., *Procedimiento de la Ley de Justicia y Paz* (2010) and Ambos, *Colombian Peace Process* (2010). On potential scenarios of admissibility challenges, see Stigen, in Stahn and El Zeidy, *Complementarity I* (2011), pp. 532–56; see also Batros, in Stahn and El Zeidy, *Complementarity I* (2011), pp. 583–8. On preliminary rulings regarding admissibility according to Art. 18 ICCS, see e.g. Schabas, *ICC Commentary* (2016), pp. 474–82; on admissibility challenges pursuant to Art. 19 ICCS, see e.g. Schabas, *ICC Commentary* (2016), pp. 483–501. See also in depth, Safferling, *International Criminal Procedure* (2012), pp. 197–215; Boas et al., *International Criminal Procedure* (2011), pp. 85–92; Nouwen, in Brown, *Handbook ICL* (2011), pp. 222–7, arguing that once an investigation has been opened, it becomes difficult for the State in question to get the case back (222–4); Safferling and Farthofer, *International Criminal Procedure* (2012), pp. 100–2; Nouwen and Lewis, in Sluiter et al., *International Criminal Procedure* (2013), p. 126.

[511] *Kony et al.*, ICC-02/04-01/05-377, paras. 25–6; on this decision, see Batros, in Stahn and El Zeidy, *Complementarity I* (2011), pp. 562–4. For a 'dynamic' complementarity assessment, see Nouwen, *Complementarity* (2013), pp. 79–83.

> Considered as a whole, the corpus of these provisions delineates a system whereby the determination of admissibility is meant to be an ongoing process throughout the pre-trial phase, the outcome of which is subject to review depending on the evolution of the relevant factual scenario. Otherwise stated, the Statute as a whole enshrines the idea that a change in circumstances allows (or even, in some scenarios, compels) the Court to determine admissibility anew.[512]

The Afghanistan PTC stressed the preliminary nature of its authorization for the OTP to resume the investigation, given that the circumstances could change with regard to jurisdiction and admissibility and thus a new challenge could arise.[513]

It follows that complementarity is to be examined at a very *early stage* during pre-trial proceedings, or, more exactly, during the *preliminary examinations* or pre-investigation stage of the proceedings.[514] In fact, once the OTP has affirmed the ICC's jurisdiction in all its aspects (*ratione temporis, personae, and materiae*), it has to analyse the complementarity issue. Only if the (potential) cases of a situation are considered admissible is the Prosecutor in a position to analyse more closely whether a formal investigation in these cases pursuant to Article 53 (1) ICCS may be opened.[515] In fact, Article 53 (1)(a) and (b) themselves require a positive decision with regard to jurisdiction and admissibility before coming to the more policy-based and discretional criteria of subparagraph (c). The Article 53 decision is at least as complex as the decision under Article 17 and the criteria to be applied, especially the 'interests of justice' test,[516] may even be considered more relevant with regard to the specific challenges posed by transitional justice processes.[517] This could be seen, for example, in the Colombian situation where—before the Prosecutor decided to close the preliminary examination on 28 October 2021[518]—it was possible that certain cases of a certain situation may have been considered admissible, but, still, an investigation has not (formally) been opened for the reasons spelt out in Article 53 (1) ICCS.[519]

[512] *Kony et al.*, ICC-02/04-01/05-377, paras. 25 ff. (28), 52.

[513] ICC, *Situation in the Islamic Republic of Afghanistan*, PTC II, Decision pursuant to Article 18(2) of the Statute Authorizing the Prosecution to Resume Investigation, ICC-02/17-196, 31 October 2022, para. 60 ('present ruling is *preliminary* ... based on the current circumstances' and thus 'without prejudice to any future challenge' to jurisdiction or admissibility [emphasis in original]); see also *Situation in the Bolivarian Republic of Venezuela I*, PTC I, Decision Authorising the Resumption of the Investigation pursuant to Article 18 (2) of the Statute, ICC-02/18-45, 27 June 2023, para. 134; *Situation in the Republic of the Philippines*, PTC I, Public Redacted Version of 'Authorisation pursuant to article 18(2) of the Statute to resume the investigation', ICC-01/21-56-Red, 26 January 2023, para 99.

[514] cf. Art. 53 (1)(b) and Art. 18 (2) ICCS in conjunction with Rule 55 (2) RPE ICC; thereto, see *Situation in Kenya*, ICC-01/09-19, paras. 43–8 (explaining that 'case' in Art. 53 (1)(b) 'actually refers to the admissibility of one or more potential cases *within the context of a situation*' [para. 48, emphasis added]). On admissibility during preliminary examinations, see Stigen, in Stahn and El Zeidy, *Complementarity I* (2011), pp. 506–11; also Nouwen, *Complementarity* (2013), pp. 71–2.

[515] On the structure of the pre-trial phase, see Chapter IV, A.(1) and (2) in this volume.

[516] Art. 53 (1)(c), (2)(c) ICCS.

[517] See, for an analysis of the interests of justice clause, Chapter IV, B.(4) in this volume.

[518] cf. https://www.icc-cpi.int/news/icc-prosecutor-mr-karim-khan-qc-concludes-preliminary-examination-situation-colombia; see Ambos, *EJIL: Talk!* 3 November 2021.

[519] For an in-depth assessment of the situation in Colombia and complementarity, see Ambos et al., *Procedimiento de la Ley de Justicia y Paz* (2010) and Ambos, *Colombian Peace Process* (2010). On complementarity decisions at the ICC regarding Colombia, see also Pinto Soares, *IsLR*, 46 (2013), 326–9; Valiñas, in Stahn and van den Herik, *Perspectives* (2010), pp. 278 ff.; Burke-White, in Stahn and El Zeidy, *Complementarity I* (2011), pp. 347–8; Tillier, *ICLR*, 13 (2013), 530–1. On prevention and complementarity in Colombia, see Méndez, in Stahn and El Zeidy, *Complementarity I* (2011), pp. 47–8. See also Seils, in Stahn and El Zeidy, *Complementarity II* (2011), pp. 1003–11. Considering, albeit with further analysis, that the Colombian justice system is 'unable' to conduct genuine prosecutions, Safferling and Farthofer, *International Criminal Procedure* (2012), pp. 104–5. On gender justice and complementarity in Colombia, see Chappell, Grey, and Waller, *ICTJ*, 7 (2013), 455–75.

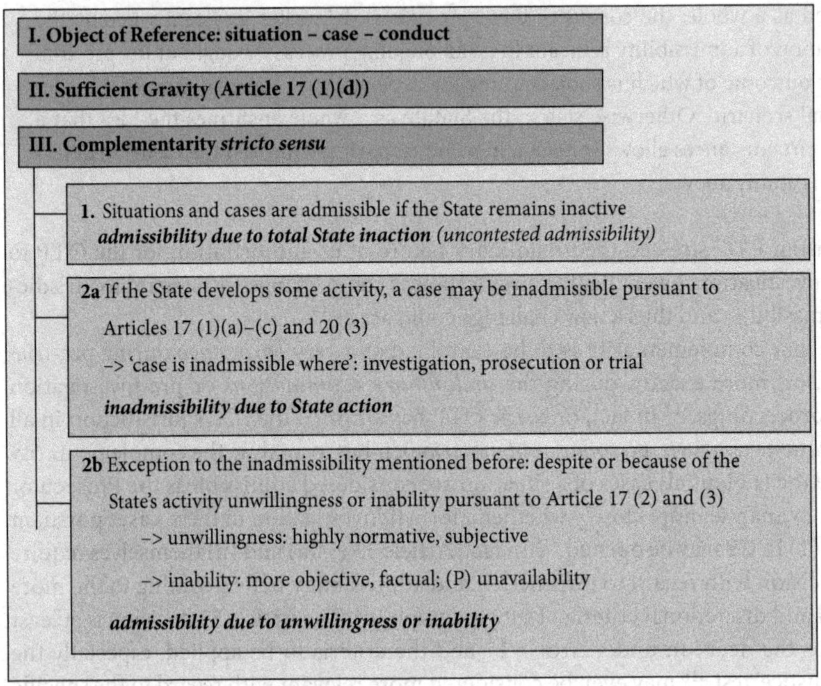


**Fig. 5.** The admissibility test (Article 17 ICCS)

In the following, we will first discuss the concepts of situation and case as the objects of reference of the admissibility test (sub-section (b)). Then, the actual admissibility test will be analysed distinguishing between the gravity threshold of Article 17 (1)(d) ICCS[520] (sub-section (c)) and complementarity *stricto sensu* pursuant to Article 17 (1)(a)–(c), (2) and (3) ICCS (sub-section (d)); see also Figure 5. This distinction follows from the considerations of the *Lubanga* PTC according to which the gravity concept constitutes an additional threshold, different from complementarity *stricto sensu*.[521] This implies, in turn, that

[520] *Situation in the DRC*, ICC-01/04-02/06-20-Anx2, paras. 42 ff.; Ambos, *Colombian Peace Process* (2010), pp. 43 ff.; in detail, Murphy, *CLF*, 17 (2006), 281 ff.; see also Ambos, in Ambos et al., *Building a Future* (2009), pp. 73–4; Cárdenas, *Zulässigkeitsprüfung* (2005), pp. 88 ff.; Robinson, in Cryer et al., *ICL* (2019), pp. 161–2; Rohrer, *Legalitäts- oder Opportunitätsprinzip* (2010), pp. 198 ff.; Jurdi, *ICC* (2011), pp. 55 ff.; crit. Arzt, in Arnold et al., *Menschengerechtes Strafrecht* (2005), pp. 700–1; deGuzman, *ColJTransnat'lL*, 51 (2012/13), 18 ff.; Takemura, in van den Herik and Stahn, *Diversification and Fragmentation* (2012), p. 634.

[521] *Situation in the DRC*, ICC-01/04-02/06-20-Anx2, para. 29 ('The Chamber considers that the admissibility test of a case arising from the investigation of a situation has two parts. The first part of the test relates to national investigations, prosecutions and trials concerning the case at hand insofar as such a case would be admissible only if those States with jurisdiction over it have remained inactive in relation to that case or are unwilling or unable, within the meaning of Art. 17 (1)(a) to (c), 2 and 3 of the Statute. The second part of the test refers to the gravity threshold which any case must meet to be admissible before the Court. Accordingly, the Chamber will treat them separately' [fn. omitted]). In the same vein, *Lubanga*, ICC-01/04-01/06-1-Corr-Red, para. 41 ('this gravity threshold is in addition to … the crimes included in Articles 6 to 8 of the Statute'); *Situation in Côte d'Ivoire*, ICC-02/11-14, para. 201; *Prosecutor v. Al Hassan Ag Abdoul Aziz Ag Mohamed Ag Mahmoud*, AC, Judgment on the Appeal of Mr Al Hassan against the Decision of Pre-Trial Chamber I Entitled 'Décision relative à l'exception d'irrecevabilité pour insuffisance de gravité de l'affaire soulevée par la défense', ICC-01/12-01/18-601-Red OA, 19 February 2020, para. 53 ff. See also ICC-OTP, *Report on Activities* (2006), para. 2: 'Although any crime falling within the jurisdiction of the Court is a serious matter, the Rome Statute … clearly foresees and

complementarity *strictu sensu* only becomes relevant if the respective case is of sufficient gravity in the first place. It therefore seems logical to examine gravity first, and only then if the gravity standard is satisfied, the complementarity *stricto sensu*.[522] In actual practice, however, the case law tends to look at complementarity (*stricto sensu*) first, unless there is a particular gravity challenge.[523] In other words, the practice will usually not follow any logical order but treat the more relevant and, perhaps, controversial issue first.

### *(b) Situation and case—The objects of reference of the admissibility test*

While Article 17 and 53 ICCS explicitly only refer to (individual) '*cases*'[524]—that is, 'specific incidents during which one or more crimes ... seems to have been committed by one or more identified suspects'[525]—it is clear that not cases, but (general) '*situations*'—'generally defined in terms of temporal, territorial, and in some cases personal parameters'[526]—are referred to the Prosecutor[527] under the triggering procedure.[528] This also follows from PTC I's *situation-case demarcation* focusing on the issuance of a warrant of arrest or a summons to

requires an additional consideration of "gravity"'. See also Guariglia, in Stahn and Sluiter, *Practice* (2009), p. 213 ('overarching consideration ... analyzed before any decision to investigate'); Boas et al., *International Criminal Procedure* (2011), p. 72 ('two-pronged inquiry', i.e. questions relating to state action and gravity); van der Merwe, *ICLR*, 15 (2015), 43–4; Schabas, in Stahn, *Practice* (2015), pp. 379–80 ('gravity' not necessarily synonymous with complementarity); Schabas and El Zeidy, 'Article 17', in Ambos, *Commentary* (2022), mn. 23 (gravity as 'second limb' of admissibility); Abdou, 'Article 17', in Klamberg et al., *Commentary ICC I* (2023), pp. 614–15. See also Ambos, *Colombian Peace Process* (2010), pp. 43 ff.; for a case law overview, see Pinto Soares, *IsLR*, 46 (2013), 322 ff.

[522] This has also been the approach taken by the ICC-OTP. Thus, in the Iraq situation the Prosecutor reached a negative conclusion on 'gravity', and therefore found it unnecessary to elaborate on complementarity (ICC-OTP, *Update on Communications* (2006), Annex—Iraq Response, p. 9); on this, see deGuzman and Schabas, 'Initiation and Selection', in Sluiter et al., *International Criminal Procedure* (2013), p. 144; Boas et al., *International Criminal Procedure* (2011), p. 85. For a similar solution, see Meißner, *Zusammenarbeit* (2003), p. 79; see also Werle and Jessberger, *Principles ICL* (2020), mn. 344–5 (arguing that the gravity threshold as a procedural limitation 'arises from considerations of judicial economy'). However, according to ICC-OTP, *Prelim. Examinations* (2013), para. 42, the ICCS does not 'stipulate any mandatory sequence in the consideration of complementarity and gravity'.

[523] Schabas and El Zeidy, 'Article 17', in Ambos, *Commentary* (2022), mn. 24 with further references; similarly, assessing gravity after complementarity *stricto sensu* and therefore only speaking of a 'presumptive' admissibility when affirming the former, Boas et al., *International Criminal Procedure* (2011), pp. 72–3.

[524] See also Benzing, *MPYbUNL*, 7 (2003), 603; Zakerhossein, *Situation* (2017), p. 28.

[525] *Situation in the DRC*, ICC-01/04-101-tEN-Corr, para. 65; *Lubanga*, ICC-01/04-01/06-1-Corr-Red, para. 31; *Prosecutor v. Harun and Abd-Al-Rahman*, PTC I, Decision on the Prosecution Application under Article 58 (7) of the Statute, ICC 02/05-01/07-1-Corr, 27 April 2007, para. 14; *Prosecutor v. Gbagbo*, PTC III, Decision on the Prosecutor's 'Application pursuant to Article 58 for a Warrant of Arrest against Laurent Koudou Gbagbo', ICC-02/11-01/11-9-US-Exp, 30 November 2011, para. 10. See also *Gaddafi*, ICC-01/11-01/11-547-Red, para. 1, defining 'case' with regard to investigated suspect and alleged conduct; crit. *Gaddafi*, ICC-01/11-01/11-547-Anx2, Dissenting Opinion of Judge Anita Ušacka, paras. 24 ff. On this definition, adopted in the subsequent case law, also Olásolo, *Triggering Procedure* (2005), pp. 40 ff.; Stegmiller, *Pre-Investigation Stage* (2011), pp. 115–19.

[526] *Situation in the DRC*, ICC-01/04-101-tEN-Corr, para. 65 and above note 374; for a detailed analysis, see Rastan, in Stahn and El Zeidy, *Complementarity I* (2011), pp. 422–36; see also Olásolo, *ICLR*, 3 (2003), 99–100; Kleffner, *Complementarity* (2008), p. 199; WCRO, *Situation* (2009), pp. 21–2; Stegmiller, *Pre-Investigation Stage* (2011), pp. 100–14; Schabas, in Stahn, *Practice* (2015), pp. 366–8; cf. in detail on this, Zakerhossein, *Situation* (2017), pp. 37–51; on the drafting history of the terms 'situation' and 'case', in the ICCS, see Stegmiller, *Pre-Investigation Stage* (2011), pp. 95–100; furthermore, see Bådagård and Klamberg, *GeoJIL* 48 (2017), 659–60.

[527] Chaitidou, 'Article 14', in Ambos, *Commentary* (2022), mn. 34, 36; also see Zakerhossein, *Situation* (2017), p. 32 stressing the relevance of the 'situation-oriented approach' for the impartiality of the investigation (of a situation): 'A situation-oriented approach provides the Prosecutor with an opportunity to adopt a holistic and far-reaching approach to conflict and to conduct a thorough investigation into crimes allegedly committed by each party involved.'

[528] Art. 13 ICCS. For a discussion, see Section A.(4)(b) in this chapter.

appear, that is, considering that a case only starts with Article 58 proceedings.[529] Accordingly, the *procedural development* from a situation to a case is as follows:[530]

(1) the Office of the Prosecutor
   (a) obtains *notitia criminis*;
   (b) starts pre-investigating;
   (c) identifies a situation;
   (d) checks the criteria enshrined in Articles 53 (1), 15 (3) ICCS, Rule 48 with regard to the situation as a whole;
   (e) starts a formal investigation (in the case of a referral), or asks for authorization of a formal investigation (in the case of information under Article 15 ICCS);
   (f) investigates and, ideally, identifies individual suspects; and
   (g) ultimately, applies for a warrant of arrest, or summons to appear if the reasonable grounds standard of Article 58 (1) and (7) ICCS are met; and
(2) the Pre-Trial Chamber issues a warrant of arrest or summons to appear.

Only with this last step does a formal or legal case exist.[531] At any rate, the procedural stages mentioned above are blurry in practice since the OTP will most likely focus on individuals before a legal case in the sense of Article 58 arises. In fact, a case could begin at three potential stages:

(1) during pre-investigation and investigation stages;
(2) at the moment the Prosecutor makes an application for an arrest warrant or summons to appear; or
(3) when the PTC issues a decision to issue a warrant of arrest or summons to appear.[532]

Therefore, one may distinguish between cases in a *broad* and *narrow sense*. While the latter refer to the (strict) legal cases that only come into being once a warrant of arrest or summons to appear is issued, cases in a broad sense may evolve factually very early during investigations and even at the preliminary examination stage. As soon as the OTP bundles allegations against one or more specific individuals, and possibly even generates a 'case file' with their names, a case in the broader sense arises. Such a broad case constitutes, in fact, a '*case hypothesis*', that is, a likely set of cases or potential cases that may arise from the investigation of a situation.[533] The design of a solid case hypothesis is fundamental for the subsequent process, and it must cover:

[529] *Situation in the DRC*, ICC-01/04-101-tEN-Corr, para. 65; see also *Situation in DRC*, PTC I, Decision Following the Consultation Held on 11 October 2005 and the Prosecution's Submission on Jurisdiction and Admissibility Filed on 31 October 2005, ICC-01/04-93, 9 November 2005, p. 4; *Abd-Al-Rahman*, ICC-02/05-01/20-391, paras. 25–7; later confirmed by the AC, *Abd-Al-Rahman*, ICC-02/05-01/20-503, paras. 25–9. See also Olásolo, *LJIL*, 20 (2007), 194; Rastan, *CLF*, 19 (2008), 442–3; Boas et al., *International Criminal Procedure* (2011), pp. 68–9. For an overview on situations and cases at the ICC, see on the ICC website, 'Situations and Cases'.

[530] cf. Stegmiller, *Pre-Investigation Stage* (2011), pp. 119, 215–23 (modified). On the detailed structure of the preliminary examinations according to the recent OTP policy paper, see Chapter IV, A.(1)(a) in this volume.

[531] cf. *Harun and Abd-Al-Rahman*, ICC-02/05-01/07-1-Corr, para. 18; conc. *Situation in Kenya*, ICC-01/09-19, para. 44; *Situation in the State of Palestine*, ICC-01/18-143, para. 67.

[532] Rastan, *CLF*, 19 (2008), 440.

[533] Originally, Rastan, *CLF*, 19 (2008), 441; now Reg. 34 RegOTP; see also, albeit without explicitly using the term 'case hypothesis', ICC-OTP, *Prelim. Examinations* (2013), paras. 43 and 46. See also Burke-White and

(1) the status of authority or role of the suspect;
(2) the structure of the organization instrumental to the crime and subordinated or associated to the suspect;
(3) the pattern and *modus operandi* of the criminal events; and
(4) a conclusion on the mode of responsibility.[534]

At any rate, it is clear that cases—understood broadly or narrowly—may only result from a long and thorough investigation[535] and they cannot exceed the parameters of the respective situation.[536]

Within a situation, the OTP originally applied a *sequential or 'sequenced' approach*,[537] that is, it investigated specific cases within a situation one after another rather than all at once, whereby cases inside the situation are selected according to gravity.[538] Later, the Office has become more flexible also carrying out simultaneous investigations[539] and replacing the term 'sequenced' by the more flexible concept of 'focused investigations'.[540] This concept has since been replaced by the 'principle of in-depth, open-ended investigations' and the Office works with 'multiple case hypotheses'.[541] Upon completion of each case the Office examines whether other cases in the situation warrant investigation—bearing in mind the gravity threshold and the complementarity test—or whether to select a new situation.[542] The latest Strategic Plan reiterates this approach of 'open-ended, in-depth investigations with a stronger evidence base and with the aim to be trial-ready as early as possible and in any event no later than the confirmation of charges hearing', while 'respecting all the rights of victims, witnesses, suspects and accused persons'.[543] In any case, with the abolishment of the rather formal sequenced approach and the simultaneous pursuit of multiple case hypotheses each investigation is governed by the facts on the ground and the concrete progress of the sub-investigations.

Kaplan, in Stahn and Sluiter, *Practice* (2009), p. 88 ('investigative hypothesis'); Burke-White and Kaplan, *JICJ*, 7 (2009), 260.

534 Agirre Aranburu, in Bergsmo, *Criteria for Prioritizing* (2010), pp. 148–9.

535 See also Stigen, *Relationship* (2008), p. 91; Kleffner, *Complementarity* (2008), pp. 195–203; Razesberger, *Complementarity* (2006), pp. 32–3; Stahn, in Stahn and Sluiter, *Practice* (2009), p. 268.

536 cf. Chaitidou, 'Article 14', in Ambos, *Commentary* (2022), mn. 35–8, discussing the relevant case law regarding the *Mbarushimana* case.

537 ICC-OTP, *Report on Activities* (2006), p. 8; ICC-OTP, *Prosecutorial Strategy* (2006), para. 2b. On a previous draft paper on criteria for the selection of situations and cases, see also Seils, in Bergsmo, *Criteria for Prioritizing* (2010), pp. 56–7; ICC-OTP, *Update on Communications* (2006), pp. 1, 5; ICC-OTP, *Report on Activities* (2006), p. 8; see also Swaak-Goldman, in ICC-OTP, *Second Public Hearing* (2006), Session 1: Interested States; Guariglia, in Stahn and Sluiter, *Practice* (2009), p. 215; Guariglia and Rogier, in Stahn, *Practice* (2015), p. 362. Sceptical, Mattioli, in ICC-OTP, *Second Public Hearing* (2006), Session 2: NGOs and Other Experts, who fears 'delays in the investigations and consequences for the preservation of evidence or serious problems of perception for the Office;' similarly, Bernard, 'International Federation for Human Rights (FIDH)', in ICC-OTP, *Second Public Hearing* (2006), Session 2: NGOs and Other Experts; Dicker, in ICC-OTP, *Second Public Hearing* (2006), Session 4: NGOs and Other Experts ('selective justice'); Schiff, *Building the ICC* (2008), pp. 118–19;

538 Regarding gravity, see ICC-OTP, *Prosecutorial Strategy* (2010), para. 20; ICC-OTP, *Prelim. Examinations* (2013), para. 66; insofar in favour, Mattioli, in ICC-OTP, *Second Public Hearing* (2006), Session 2: NGOs and Other Experts.

539 See e.g. regarding the *Kenya* situation, Ambos and Stegmiller, *Crime Law Soc Change*, 58 (2012), 395.

540 ICC-OTP, *Prosecutorial Strategy* (2010), paras. 2, 3, 15, 18 ff.

541 ICC-OTP, *Strategic Plan* (2013), paras. 4a, 23; cf. also Guariglia and Rogier, in Stahn, *Practice* (2015), pp. 361–2; Bådagård and Klamberg, *GeoJIL* 48 (2017), 689–91.

542 ICC-OTP, *Update on Communications* (2006), pp. 1, 5. On a possible application of the concept of 'completion' (as understood within the framework of the completion strategy of the ad hoc tribunals) to ICC situations, see Evenson and Smith, in Stahn, *Practice* (2015), pp. 1263 ff.

543 ICC-OTP, *Strategic Plan* (2019), para. 14.a.

From all this it follows that the Prosecutor examines the admissibility, at the pre-investigation stage, with regard to a given *situation*,[544] but focuses on the said potential cases being part of this situation.[545] Thus, at this stage, the Prosecutor checks admissibility only in a 'generalized manner'[546] and in a preliminary way,[547] albeit taking into account its general selection criteria, in particular the importance of the suspect and their role in the crimes.[548] Only if the Prosecutor has identified concrete cases, potential criminal conduct, and/or suspects, within the course of the Article 53 decision,[549] does the admissibility test shift to the *case*[550] and become *case-specific*.[551]

As a further consequence, the process of substantiating a situation into a case requires a *sufficiently close relationship* or linkage between the two. Thus, PTC I held that:

> for the *case* at hand not to exceed the parameters defining the DRC situation under investigation, the crimes referred to in the Prosecutor's Application must have occurred in the *context of the ongoing situation of crisis* that triggered the jurisdiction of the Court... [I]t is only within the *boundaries of the situation of crisis* for which the jurisdiction of the Court was activated that subsequent prosecutions can be initiated. Such a situation can include not only crimes that had already been or were being committed at the time of the referral, but also crimes committed after that time, in so far as they are *sufficiently linked* to the situation of crisis referred to the Court as ongoing at the time of the referral.[552]

In other words: each situation triggering the Court's jurisdiction is characterized by an underlying crisis ('situation of crisis') which continues (or ceases) to exist independent of

[544] See also Kleffner, *Complementarity* (2008), pp. 195–203. On the admissibility of a situation, see Stegmiller, *Pre-Investigation Stage* (2011), pp. 285–9; Olásolo and Carnero-Rojo, in Stahn and El Zeidy, *Complementarity I* (2011), pp. 393–420.

[545] cf. *Situation in Kenya*, ICC-01/09-19, para. 50: 'Accordingly, admissibility at the situation phase should be assessed against certain criteria defining a "potential case" such as: (i) the groups of persons involved that are likely to be the focus of an investigation for the purpose of shaping the future case(s); and (ii) the crimes within the jurisdiction of the Court allegedly committed during the incidents that are likely to be the focus of an investigation for the purpose of shaping the future case(s). The Prosecutor's selection of the incidents or groups of persons that are likely to shape his future case(s) is preliminary in nature and is not binding for future admissibility assessments.' Confirmed in subsequent case law, e.g. *Situation in Côte d'Ivoire*, ICC-02/11-14-Corr, para. 190; *Situation Georgia*, ICC-01/15-12, paras. 36–7, 39. See also ICC-OTP, *Complementarity and Cooperation* (2024), para. 151 ('potential cases' during preliminary examination).

[546] Stahn, in Stahn and Sluiter, *Practice* (2009), pp. 268–9; on the relevant criteria, see Olásolo, *Triggering Procedure* (2005), pp. 164 ff. See also *Situation in Côte d'Ivoire*, ICC-02/11-14, para. 190 ('consideration of one or more potential cases within the broader context of the "situation"').

[547] cf. *Situation Georgia*, ICC-01/15-12, para. 37 ('selection ... likely to shape the Prosecutor's future case(s) at this stage is preliminary, and ... may change'); see also *Situation in Afghanistan*, ICC-02/17-138 OA4, para. 39.

[548] For this *ratione personae* limitation, see also Olásolo, in Almqvist and Espósito, *Justitia Transicional* (2009), pp. 267–8. For a critique in the context of the gravity test, see note 667 in this chapter with main text.

[549] See para. 1 (b): 'case is or would be admissible'; para. 2 (b): 'case is admissible.'

[550] On this shift from a situation to a case, see Rastan, in Stahn and El Zeidy, *Complementarity I* (2011), pp. 454–8; Schabas, in Stahn, *Practice* (2015), pp. 375 ff.

[551] See also Nouwen, *Complementarity* (2013), pp. 72–3; also ICC-OTP, *Complementarity and Cooperation* (2024), para. 150.

[552] *Mbarushimana*, ICC-01/04-01/10-1, para. 6 (emphasis added); similarly ('situation in crisis') *Mbarushimana*, ICC-01/04-01/10-451, para. 16; *Prosecutor v. Mudacumura*, PTC II, Decision on the Prosecutor's Application under Article 58, ICC-01/04-01/12-1-Red, 13 July 2012, para. 16 ('linked to the situation'); see also *Situation in Bangladesh/Myanmar*, ICC-01/19-27, para. 129. See also Stegmiller, *CLF*, 24 (2013), 480–3; Marchesi and Chaitidou, 'Article 14', in Ambos, *Commentary* (2022), mn. 37; Guariglia and Rogier, in Stahn, *Practice* (2015), p. 352 ('situation' to be understood as 'situation of crisis' selected); crit. Rastan, *CLF*, 23 (2012), 9 ff. (concept of 'crisis' as an ambiguous 'shorthand' to establish the territorial and temporal link between case and situation, at 13); Vagias, *Jurisdiction* (2014), pp. 198 ff. (inter alia crit. the PTC because it did not define the concept of 'situation of crisis' and does not explain its test in light of international law).

the Court's jurisdiction over the cases/crimes occurring within the context of this crisis. As already explained above,[553] the Court's jurisdiction extends to all cases that are sufficiently linked to the respective situation (of crisis) which, in turn, may constitute a 'single situation … involving a prolonged political dispute and power-struggle' culminating in events triggering the Court's jurisdiction and object of its investigation.[554] Of course, the tight relationship between situation and case should not, normatively speaking, displace the strict separation between jurisdiction and admissibility under the Rome Statute.[555] At any rate, the situational linkage requirement also aims at reminding States of their primary jurisdiction as a consequence of the complementarity principle, thereby deterring them from abdicating their 'responsibility for exercising jurisdiction over atrocity crimes for eternity'.[556]

The procedural development—from the investigation of a general situation to a more concrete case—makes clear that the *object of reference* of the national proceedings vis-à-vis the ICC proceedings, that is, the 'case' within the meaning of Article 17 (1)(a) ICCS,[557] can only have more concrete contours if the investigation is sufficiently advanced, that is, has reached the concrete case stage.[558] Only then does the question arise whether the 'case' being investigated by the domestic authorities 'sufficiently mirrors the one that the Prosecutor [of the ICC] is investigating'.[559] In fact, only then does a State have a realistic chance to challenge the investigation on the basis of complementarity since before, at the (preliminary) situation stage, there will normally be so many (potential) cases that it is practically impossible for a State to claim that it is investigating the same case as the ICC Prosecutor.[560] In addition, at this stage there is no legal possibility of forcing the Prosecutor to take a decision, either ending the preliminary examination or opening a formal investigation.[561]

[553] See Section A.(4)(b)(i) in this chapter in connection with a discussion of the temporal jurisdiction.

[554] ICC, *Situation in the Republic of Côte d'Ivoire*, PTC II, Decision on the Prosecution's Provision of further Information Regarding Potentially Relevant Crimes Committed between 2002 and 2010, ICC-02/11-36, 22 February 2012, para. 36, referring to the 'violent events in Côte d'Ivoire in the period between 19 September 2002 and 28 November 2010 … reaching varying levels of intensity at different locations and at different times'; see also Vagias, *Jurisdiction* (2014), pp. 202–4 ('case needs to fall within the parameters of a situation').

[555] Crit. of the *Mbarushimana* PTC thereon, Vagias, *Jurisdiction* (2014), pp. 198–9 ('seems to infuse admissibility concerns in jurisdiction'); for a discussion with regard to Art. 12 (3) declaration, see Section A.(4)(b) in this chapter.

[556] *Mbarushimana*, ICC-01/04-01/10-451, para. 16; see Section A.(4)(a)(i) in this chapter with note 398.

[557] cf. *Ruto et al.*, ICC-01/09-01/11-307, para. 37, holding that 'under article 17 (1)(a), first alternative, the question is not merely a question of "investigation" in the abstract, but is whether the same case is being investigated by both the Court and a national jurisdiction'; cf. also *Muthaura et al.*, ICC-01/09-02/11-274, para. 36; in the same vein, *Prosecutor v. Alfred Yekatom and Patrice-Edouard Ngaïssona*, TC V, Decision on the Yekatom Defence's Admissibility Challenge, ICC-01/14-01/18-493, 28 April 2020, para. 20.

[558] cf. *Ruto et al.*, ICC-01/09-01/11-307, para. 39, correctly holding that the 'meaning of the words "case being investigated", in article 17 (1)(a) of the Statute must … be understood in the context to which it is applied'.

[559] *Gaddafi*, ICC-01/11-01/11-547-Red, paras. 2, 73; cf. also Stahn, in Stahn, *Practice* (2015), pp. 230 ff.; O'Keefe, *ICL* (2015), pp. 557–9.

[560] Crit. thereon Nouwen, *Complementarity* (2013), pp. 73–4, 409, therefore advocating a change of the ICCS allowing for a 'situation-based assessment of complementarity' but arguably such a general assessment already takes place and all depends on the flexibility of the Prosecutor's approach. See also Heller, *JICJ*, 14 (2016), 645 ('state will … be able to forestall a formal OTP investigation only by accurately predicting which conduct ("incidents") the OTP will target if it decides to open an investigation') and Newton, *IsLR*, 54 (2021), 158 ('domestic enforcement efforts cannot be evaluated against hypothetical charges in some indeterminate future "case"'); also, see below at note 611. The *Kenya* PTC has asked for a certain precision of the Prosecutor with regard to the cases to be investigated so that a complementarity challenge pursuant to Art. 18 (2) does not become completely futile: see *Situation in Kenya*, ICC-01/09-19, paras. 49–51 (para. 51: 'The Chamber emphasizes that defining the scope of potential case(s) at this stage may well serve an effective application of article 18 of the Statute').

[561] Crit. Nouwen, *Complementarity* (2013), p. 78, 106, regarding the end of an investigation. We will return to this issue of the (limited) judicial supervision of the OTP at this stage in Chapter IV, B.(3) in this volume.

As to the same case requirement, the prevailing jurisprudence tends towards an identity requiring that the national proceedings must refer to the OTP's case encompassing 'both the *person* and the *conduct* which is the subject of the case before the Court'.[562] While the reference to the same person, that is, the suspect, is hardly controversial,[563] the determination of the same conduct gives rise to several problems. What quality of the conduct and degree of identity ('sameness')[564] between the conduct under domestic and ICC investigation is required? While the case law itself prepared the ground for a more flexible approach with the *Kenya* AC's addition of the qualifier 'substantially' to the 'same conduct',[565] the significance

562 *Situation in the DRC*, ICC-01/04-02/06-20-Anx2, para. 31 (emphasis added); *Prosecutor v. Harun and Abd-Al-Rahman*, PTC I, Decision on the Prosecution Application under Article 58 (7) of the Statute, ICC-02/05-01/07-1, 27 April 2007, para. 24; *Prosecutor v. Ngudjolo*, PTC I, Decision on the Evidence and Information provided by the Prosecution for the Issuance of a Warrant of Arrest for Mathieu Ngudjolo Chui, ICC-01/04-02/07-3, 6 July 2007, para. 21; *Prosecutor v. Katanga*, PTC I, Decision on the Evidence and Information Provided by the Prosecution for the Issuance of a Warrant of Arrest for Germain Katanga, ICC-01/04-01/07-4, 6 July 2007, para. 20; *Prosecutor v. Bemba*, PTC III, Decision on the Prosecutor's Application for a Warrant of Arrest against Jean-Pierre Bemba Gombo, ICC-01/05-01/08-14-tENG, 10 June 2008, para. 16; *Prosecutor v. Al Bashir*, PTC I, Decision on the Prosecution's Application for a Warrant of Arrest against Omar Hassan Ahmad Al Bashir, ICC-02/05-01/09-2-Conf, 4 March 2009, para. 50; *Prosecutor v. Abu Garda*, PTC I, Decision on the Prosecutor's Application under Article 58, ICC-02/05-02/09-1-Conf, 7 May 2009, para. 4; *Kony et al.*, ICC-02/04-01/05-377, paras. 17–18; *Prosecutor v. Ruto et al.*, PTC II, Decision on the Application by the Government of Kenya Challenging the Admissibility of the Case pursuant to Article 19 (2)(b) of the Statute, ICC-01/09-01/11-101, 30 May 2011, para. 54; *Muthaura* et al., ICC-01/09-02/11-96, para. 48; *Muthaura et al.*, ICC-01/09-02/11-274, paras. 38–40; *Ruto et al.*, ICC-01/09-01/11-307, paras. 39–41; *Prosecutor v. Gaddafi and Al-Senussi*, PTC I, Decision on the Admissibility of the Case against Saif Al-Islam Gaddafi, ICC-01/11-01/11-344-Red, 31 May 2013, para. 61, ('settled jurisprudence', with further references in n. 125); *Prosecutor v. Gaddafi and Al-Senussi*, PTC I, Decision on the Admissibility of the Case against Abdullah Al-Senussi, ICC-01/11-01/11-466-Red, 11 October 2013, para. 66(i); *Gaddafi*, ICC-01/11-01/11-547-Red, paras. 1 (referring to 'conduct' defining the 'case' as 'both that of the suspect and that described in the incidents under investigation'), 61, 70; *Situation Afghanistan*, ICC-02/17-196, para. 46; *Situation Philippines*, ICC-01/21-56-Red, para.13; *Situation in the Bolivarian Republic of Venezuela I*, PTC I, Decision Authorizing the Resumption of the Investigation pursuant to Article 19 (2) of the Statute, ICC-02/18-45, 27 June 2023, para. 65; for a good overview of the case law, see *Gaddafi*, ICC-01/11-01/11-547-Anx2, Dissenting Opinion Judge Ušacka, paras. 27 ff., 85; see also ICC-OTP, *Prelim. Examinations* (2013), para. 47. For the scholarly debate, see El Zeidy, *Complementarity* (2008), p. 161; Rastan, *CLF*, 19 (2008), 436–7; Stigen, *Relationship* (2008), p. 261; Hansen, *MelbJIL*, 13 (2012), 223–5; Abdou, 'Article 17', in Klamberg et al., *Commentary ICC I* (2023), pp. 612–13; Bo, *CLF*, 25 (2014), 517 ff., crit. discussing the *Gaddafi* PTC's approach to the conduct requirement; Heller, Complementarity, *Opinio Juris* (24 May 2024). For a different view of Ruto's Defence, see *Prosecutor v. Ruto et al.*, PTC II, Application on Behalf of the Government of the Republic of Kenya pursuant to Article 19 of the ICC Statute, ICC-01/09-01/11-19, 31 March 2011, para. 32 ('persons at the same level in the hierarchy being investigated by the ICC'); *contra* also *Gaddafi*, ICC-01/11-01/11-547-Anx2, Dissenting Opinion Judge Ušacka, paras. 47 ff., arguing that the same person/conduct test undermines the principle of complementarity and that 'conduct' is but one possible element of a case; what is required is 'a complementarity scheme that contains multiple criteria that are assessed by reference to the concrete circumstances of each specific case' (para. 58) and a broader understanding of 'conduct' basically only requiring 'a nexus between the conduct being investigated and prosecuted domestically and that before the Court' (para. 58); in addition, one should focus on the 'genuine will' of a State to investigate (para. 59); in a similar vein, *Gaddafi*, ICC-01/11-01/11-547-Anx1, Separate Opinion Judge Sang-Hyun Song, paras. 3 ff., arguing that an overlap between incidents 'is not a relevant factor' with regard to the same conduct test since 'incidents are interchangeable and the non-investigation of one particular incident by the domestic authorities does not mean that they are investigating different conduct', i.e. to require the investigation of the 'same incidents' or the 'same acts of murder and persecution would make the national investigators' task impossible' and, ultimately, the complementarity principle 'redundant' (para. 6). In the same vein, Nouwen, *Complementarity* (2013), pp. 51–9, 106–7, warning that a too strict test leaves complementarity with 'little role to play' (51) and makes it 'impossible for a state to win an admissibility challenge' (51, 107); in a similar vein, Wierda, *Impact* (2023), pp. 59, 66–7, 81 ('distortions' re the *Saif Al Islam Gaddafi* case and generally 'distorting effect' by focusing 'on a few individual cases'); from a gender perspective, Chappell, Grey, and Waller, *ICTJ*, 7 (2013), 463–4.

563 The scenario outlined by Greenawalt ultimately concerns the appropriateness of the OTP's decisions to prosecute certain individuals as 'most responsible' rather than less responsible ones, cf. Greenawalt, in deGuzman and Oosterveld, *Elgar Companion ICC* (2020), p. 71 ('Suppose that a state attempts a fairly comprehensive investigation into international crimes but fails, for one reason or another, to target the particular person whom the ICC Prosecutor wishes to pursue').

564 *Gaddafi*, ICC-01/11-01/11-547-Red, para. 59.

565 *Muthaura et al.*, ICC-01/09-02/11-274, para. 39; *Ruto et al.*, ICC-01/09-01/11-307, para. 40 ('national investigation must cover ... *substantially the same conduct* as alleged in the proceedings before the Court' [emphasis

of the specific 'conduct' follows, apparently, from the interplay of Articles 17 (1)(c) and 20 (3) ICCS,[566] the former referring to conduct 'subject of the complaint' and the latter to the 'same conduct'.[567] Thus, 'conduct', in this sense, that is, in the sense of the 'idem' (the same) of the *ne bis in idem* principle enshrined in Article 20 ICCS,[568] is to be understood as the specific factual or procedural conduct of the respective case[569] and as *incident-specific*.[570] The respective incidents, underlying the case, refer to the 'historical event[s], defined in time and place, in the course of which crimes within the jurisdiction of the Court were allegedly committed by one or more direct perpetrators.'[571]

Such a factual, incident-based approach does not entail a full legal identity with regard to the offences charged or even the mode of liability.[572] As to the former, it suffices if the

added]); conc. *Gaddafi*, ICC-01/11-01/11-547-Red, paras. 63 ff.; *S. Gbagbo*, ICC-02/11-01/12-75, para. 98; more recently see *Prosecutor v. Saif Al-Islam Gaddafi*, PTC I, Decision on the 'Admissibility Challenge by Dr. Saif Al-Islam Gadafi pursuant to Articles 17(1), 19 and 20(3) of the Rome Statute', ICC-01/11-01/11-662 05-04-2019 1/29 RH PT, 5 April 2019, para. 5; *Prosecutor v. Saif Al-Islam Gaddafi*, AC, Judgment on the Appeal of Mr Saif Al-Islam Gaddafi against the decision of Pre-Trial Chamber I entitled 'Decision on the "Admissibility Challenge by Dr. Saif Al-Islam Gaddafi pursuant to Articles 17(1)(c), 19 and 20(3) of the Rome Statute"' of 5 April 2019, ICC-01/11-01/11-695 09-03-2020 1/43 EO PT OA8, 9 March 2020, para. 12; crit., *Gaddafi*, ICC-01/11-01/11-547-Anx2, Dissenting Opinion Judge Ušacka, para. 37 (missing an explanation of this term); crit. also Stahn, in Stahn, *Practice* (2015), p. 242 ('mysteriously added'); Schabas and El Zeidy, 'Article 17', in Ambos, *Commentary* (2022), mn. 35–7 (missing a legal basis); in the same vein, Heller, *JICJ*, 14 (2016), 646–7; for a discussion, see also Abdou, 'Article 17', in Klamberg et al., *Commentary ICC I* (2023), pp. 612–13.

[566] Rastan, *CLF*, 19 (2008), 437; conc. Sedman, in Stahn and van den Herik, *Perspectives* (2010), pp. 262 ff.; ICC, *Prosecutor v. Gaddafi and Al-Senussi*, Prosecution's Response to 'Libyan Government's further submissions on issues related to the admissibility of the case against *Saif Al-Islam Gaddafi*', ICC-01/11-01/1 l-276-Red2, 12 February 2013, para. 27 with n. 55, arguing, referring to the *Kenya* AC and to Arts. 17 (1)(c), 20 (3), and 90 ICCS that '[t]he same person/same conduct test is deeply rooted in the Statute itself'. Furthermore, see Rastan, *JICJ*, 15 (2017), 5–6 stressing that Arts. 20 (3) and 17 (1)(c) ICCS share the same definition ('Article 20(3) explains how a case should be defined for Article 17(1)(c)'); in addition, Art. 90 (1) ICSS would also suggest a same person/conduct oriented approach (ibid., 6–7).

[567] See also Art. 90 (1) ICCS; thereon Nouwen, *Complementarity* (2013), pp. 53–4. In addition, Art. 17 (1)(a) and (b) refer to the more specific 'case', instead of 'situation'. See also Arts. 89 (4), 94 ICCS referring to a 'different' crime or case with regard to domestic prosecutions.

[568] On the relation between complementarity and *ne bis in idem*, see Conway, *CLF*, 14 (2003), 351 ff. with further references; Conway, 'Article 20', in Klamberg, in Klamberg et al., *Commentary ICC I* (2023), pp. 663–71; distinguishing between the two, deGuzman and Schabas, in Sluiter et al., *International Criminal Procedure* (2013), p. 144; Boas et al., *International Criminal Procedure* (2011), pp. 81–2; Safferling and Farthofer, *International Criminal Procedure* (2012), pp. 106–7; on the relation between complementarity and *ne bis in idem* in case of a prior ICC judgment, see Labuda, *Opinio Juris* (13 April 2016); see also Chapter VIII, B.(1)(b) *in fine* in this volume.

[569] This corresponds to the general understanding of the *ne bis in idem* principle, as particularly discussed with regard to the 'European' *ne bis in idem* Rule of Art. 54 Schengen Agreement and Art. 50 EU Charter of Fundamental Rights, cf. Ambos, *EurCrL* (2018), pp. 146 ff.

[570] cf. Rastan, *CLF*, 19 (2008), 438 ff.; see also Stigen, *Relationship* (2008), p. 199 ('case specific'); Pichon, *ICLR*, 8 (2008), 225–6 with regard to Ali Abd-Al-Rahman (Sudan); Schabas and El Zeidy, 'Article 17', in Ambos, *Commentary* (2022), mn. 36. On the related *'specificity' test*, see Rastan, *CLF*, 19 (2008), 436; Stegmiller, *Pre-Investigation Stage* (2011), pp. 297–8. Crit. Nouwen, *Complementarity* (2013), pp. 54–5, but interpreting 'incident' too narrowly. For a discussion, see also Abdou, 'Article 17', in Klamberg et al., *Commentary ICC I* (2023), pp. 612–13. See also *Situation Afghanistan*, ICC-02/17-196, para. 46 and *Situation Philippines*, ICC-01/21-56-Red, para. 12 (both stressing, regarding Arts. 18 and 19, the 'specific context' to which 'case' in Art. 17 (1)(a) ICCS refers).

[571] *Gaddafi*, ICC-01/11-01/11-547-Red, para. 62; see also *Al Hassan*, ICC-01/12-01/18-601-Red OA, para. 65.

[572] The AC's reference to conduct 'imputed to the suspect' (*Gaddafi*, ICC-01/11-01/11-547-Red, paras. 62, 72, 85) should therefore not be interpreted in this narrow sense (unconvincing in this regard, see Schabas and El Zeidy, 'Article 17', in Ambos, *Commentary* (2022), mn. 35–6). Indeed, the AC itself sticks to the 'substantially the same conduct' test, see *Gaddafi*, ICC-01/11-01/11-547-Red, paras. 63 ff.; see also O'Keefe, *ICL* (2015), p. 560 (no identity re 'legal characterization'). In the same vein against the same mode of liability, Nouwen, *Complementarity* (2013), pp. 54–5 with n. 69, 242; ICC-OTP, *Complementarity and Cooperation* (2024), para. 156 (not 'the same legal label'). But see also Greenawalt, in deGuzman and Oosterveld, *Elgar Companion ICC* (2020), p. 73, who emphasizes that it is not always possible to make a clear distinction between 'conduct as opposed to legal characterization' ('the two concepts are not always so easily separated') and suggests that 'domestic charges' must 'capture the core harm manifested by the conduct', which, in his view, would be doubtful if, for example, rape were prosecuted

domestic authorities investigate/prosecute the respective incidents as ordinary crimes, in particular if the ICC crimes have not been implemented at the national level;[573] at any rate, any investigation, be it merely administrative/disciplinary or already criminal, must be carried out with a view to a criminal prosecution.[574] Of course, whether the 'degree of overlap'[575] between the conduct under investigation at the domestic and the ICC level amounts to 'substantially the same conduct' cannot be determined in the abstract but only on a case-by-case basis,[576] taking as a standard of comparison the suspect's conduct and the underlying incidents under investigation.[577] For the purpose of this comparison, 'the contours' or 'defining parameters' of the national investigation must be clear.[578]

Thus, in *Lubanga* and *Ntaganda* the PTC held, albeit finding a total inactivity of the Congolese authorities with regard to the relevant cases,[579] that the DRC's arrest warrants issued against the suspects did not encompass the same (factual) conduct of the Prosecutor's application,[580] namely the specific incidents relating to the 'alleged UPC/FPLC's policy/practice of enlisting into the FPLC, conscripting into the FPLC and using to participate actively in hostilities children under the age of fifteen between July 2002 and December

'under the label of "disturbing the peace", or "insulting the honor" of the victim's family'. Furthermore, see Batros, in Guariglia et al., *AC ICC Commentary* (2018), pp. 77–8 pointing out (with reference to the AC Judgment on *Al-Senussi's* Appeal on the Admissibility of the Case, see below note 603) that 'the legal characterization may well matter as it does shed light on the true nature of the domestic case'.

573 Thus, the reference to Arts. 6-8 ICCS in Art. 20 (3) has to be interpreted as a generic reference ('also proscribed') not implying a requirement of normative identity. In the same vein, Nouwen, *Complementarity* (2013), pp. 49–50; Bo, *CLF*, 25 (2014), 526 ff.; Samir Hassanein, *ICLR*, 15 (2015), 113 ff. (arguing that the existence and prosecution of ordinary crimes is, in principle, sufficient if the respective offences are broad enough and adequate sentences are meted out); similarly, Zhao, *China* (2017), pp. 37–8 using the example of the 'improper use of a flag of truce', making it clear that there must at least be a sufficiently '"corresponding"' ordinary crime; Abdou, 'Article 17', in Klamberg et al., *Commentary ICC I* (2023), pp. 612–13; *contra* El Zeidy, *Complementarity* (2008), pp. 286–92; Mégret, in Stahn and El Zeidy, *Complementarity I* (2011), pp. 383–4, arguing that judging for ordinary crimes 'will be the equivalent of denying a crucial contextual and systemic aspect of their acts'. The flexible interpretation is also supported by the lack of an explicit obligation implementation in the Statute (see also Mégret, in Stahn and El Zeidy, *Complementarity I* (2011), p. 367; Nouwen, *Complementarity* (2013), pp. 40–1, 104).

574 cf. ICC, *Situation in the Republic of Burundi*, PTC III, Public Redacted Version of 'Decision Pursuant to Article 15 of the Rome Statute on the Authorization of an Investigation into the Situation in the Republic of Burundi', ICC-01/17-X-9-US-Exp, 25 October 2017, ICC-01/17-9-Red, 9 November 2017, paras. 152, 165 (considering that mere evidence gathering does not lead to inadmissibility since 'an investigation must be carried out with a view to conducting criminal prosecutions'); more recently *Situation Afghanistan*, ICC-02/17-196, para. 45; *Situation Philippines*, ICC-01/21-56-Red, para. 14; crit. Newton, *IsLR* 54 (2021), 167–8 (claiming that administrative investigations can be or 'are designed to fold into subsequent prosecutorial processes').

575 *Gaddafi*, ICC-01/11-01/11-547-Red, para. 72, arguing that between the two extreme ends—an identical domestic investigation or no domestic investigation of any of the incidents investigated by the ICC—the 'real issue' is 'the degree of overlap' with regard to the 'substantially the same' conduct test; there will be no overlap '[i]f it has only been established that "discrete aspects" of the case before the Court are being investigated domestically' (para. 77); the degree of overlap should be judicially assessed taking into consideration 'the interests of victims and the impact on them of any decision that a case is inadmissible at the Court despite not all of the incidents being investigated domestically' (para. 74).

576 *Gaddafi*, ICC-01/11-01/11-344-Red, para. 77; *Al-Senussi*, ICC-01/11-01/11-466-Red, para. 66 (iii); *Gaddafi*, ICC-01/11-01/11-547-Red, paras. 62, 71 ('depend upon the facts of the specific case ... not possible to set down a hard and fast rule'); conc. in this regard, see *Gaddafi*, ICC-01/11-01/11-547-Anx2, Dissenting Opinion Judge Ušacka, para. 40 and *Gaddafi*, ICC-01/11-01/11-547-Anx1, Separate Opinion Judge Song, para. 4.

577 *Gaddafi*, ICC-01/11-01/11-547-Red, para. 73; see also paras. 2, 62, 73, 85.

578 Ibid., paras. 2 ('necessary for a Chamber to know the contours or parameters of the investigation being carried out both by the Prosecutor and by the State'), 83, 85; *S. Gbagbo*, ICC-02/11-01/12-75, para. 88; crit. of the 'contours', *Gaddafi*, ICC-01/11-01/11-547-Anx2, Dissenting Opinion Judge Anita Ušacka, para. 44.

579 *Situation in the DRC*, ICC-01/04-02/06-20-Anx2, para. 41 ('no State with jurisdiction over the cases against Mr Thomas Lubanga Dyilo and Mr Bosco Ntaganda is acting, or has acted, in relation to those cases').

580 *Situation in the DRC*, ICC-01/04-02/06-20-Anx2, para. 38. On how complementarity was articulated in DRC, see Pinto Soares, *IsLR*, 46 (2013), 322–4; Tillier, *ICLR*, 13 (2013), 524–6; Maunganidze and du Plessis, in Stahn, *Practice* (2015), pp. 72–3.

2003'.[581] In *Katanga* and *Ngudjolo Chui* the admissibility assessment did not even reach this level of specificity because the Chamber focused on the lack of any relevant domestic investigative activity in the first place. Thus, the total inactivity of the Congolese authorities rendered the *Katanga* case admissible without further ado; the Chamber did not need to decide on the 'same conduct test'.[582]

In the Libyan situation[583] matters have become more complicated. While in the case against *Saif Al-Islam Gaddafi* both PTC I[584] and the AC,[585] Judge Ušacka dissenting, found the case admissible, in *Al-Senussi* the same PTC I granted Libya's admissibility challenge and declared the case inadmissible.[586] In *Gaddafi*, PTC I, while not requiring the Libyan investigations to cover 'exactly the same acts of murder and persecution mentioned in the Article 58 Decision', assessed 'whether the alleged domestic investigation addresses the same conduct ... namely that: Mr Gaddafi used his control over relevant parts of the Libyan State apparatus and Security Forces to deter and quell, by any means, including by the use of lethal force, the demonstrations of civilians'.[587] Concretely, the Chamber found that, albeit the national authorities investigated the case to some extent,[588] Libya failed to prove that the domestic prosecution covered the same conduct as the ICC case.[589] The majority of the AC dismissed Libya's appeal since it could not find, in line with its standard of review,[590] any revelant errors or unreasonability in the PTC's findings.[591] Judge Ušacka, on the basis of a more flexible interpretation of the same case requirement,[592] would have reversed the PTC's decision since she considered that the Chamber asked for too much and its findings showed 'lack of reasoning' and 'uncertainty'.[593] Judge Song, while agreeing with the majority in the result (with regard to Libya's inability to obtain the accused pursuant to Article 17 (3) ICCS), disagreed with the majority's interpretation of the term 'case'[594] and considered, assessing the evidence as a whole, that Libya 'is investigating the same case'.[595] After having

[581] *Situation in the DRC*, ICC-01/04-02/06-20-Anx2, paras. 39, 40.

[582] *Prosecutor v. Katanga and Chui*, ICC-01/04-01/07-1213-tEng, Reasons for the Oral Decision on the Motion Challenging the Admissiblity of the Case (Article 19 of the Statute), para. 95 (16 June 2009).

[583] See, for a general analysis, Tillier, *ICLR*, 13 (2013), 518–20.

[584] *Gaddafi*, ICC-01/11-01/11-344-Red.

[585] *Gaddafi*, ICC-01/11-01/11-547-Red.

[586] *Al-Senussi*, ICC-01/11-01/11-466-Red; cf. Greenawalt, in deGuzman and Oosterveld, *Elgar Companion ICC* (2020), p. 73 ('the domestic labels provided an adequate substitute for the international labels').

[587] *Gaddafi*, ICC-01/11-01/11-344-Red, paras. 82, 133.

[588] Ibid., para. 134.

[589] Ibid., para. 135.

[590] On this standard, see Chapter VI, B.(1)(b) in this volume. As to the object of the appeal in *temporal terms*, the AC clarified that it refers to the admissibility proceedings before the PTC; see on that *Gaddafi*, ICC-01/11-01/11-547-Red, paras. 41–4, adopting *Prosecutor v. Ruto et al.*, AC, Decision on the 'Filing of Updated Investigation Report by the Government of Kenya in the Appeal against the Pre-Trial Chamber's Decision on Admissibility', ICC-01/09-01/11-234, 28 July 2011, paras. 10–11; *Prosecutor v. Muthaura et al.*, AC, Decision on the 'Filing of Updated Investigation Report by the Government of Kenya in the Appeal against the Pre-Trial Chamber's Decision on Admissibility', ICC-01/09-02/11-202, 28 July 2011, para. 9 (*time of the proceedings* is 'the time of the proceedings on the admissibility challenge before the Pre-Trial Chamber and not to the subsequent proceedings on appeal'. Consequently, 'events which fall outside the scope of the relevant pre-trial or trial proceedings fall outside the scope of the appeal concerning those proceedings and should be rejected in limine'); conc. *S. Gbagbo*, ICC-02/11-01/12-75, paras. 32–3, 43–5.

[591] *Gaddafi*, ICC-01/11-01/11-547-Red, paras. 104–8, 111, 116, 119, 120, 125, 126, 132, 135, 139, 144–5, 163 ff., 177, 179, 194, 203, 210, 211.

[592] See note 562 in this chapter.

[593] *Gaddafi*, ICC-01/11-01/11-547-Anx2, Dissenting Opinion Judge Ušacka, para. 46; on this, cf. in more detail, Greenawalt, in deGuzman and Oosterveld, *Elgar Companion ICC* (2020), p. 74, who, however, recognizes as an advantage of the more rigid 'same person/same conduct' standard that 'it allows the Court to avoid the more negative assessments of state action that would be required to sustain admissibility under a broader-ranging evaluation of the state's efforts'.

[594] See note 562 in this chapter.

[595] *Gaddafi*, ICC-01/11-01/11-547-Anx1, Separate Opinion Judge Song, paras. 1, 37–8.

been sentenced to death by the Tripoli Court of Assize,[596] on 5 June 2018 Gaddafi filed a second admissibility challenge contending that 'on 28 July 2015, he was convicted by the Tripoli Criminal Court for substantially the same conduct as alleged in the proceedings before this Court',[597] which was again dismissed by PTC I on 5 April 2019.[598] This decision was (unanimously) confirmed by the Appeals Chamber on 9 March 2020,[599] convincingly arguing on the basis of the complementarity principle:

[B]efore the Court is called to determine the admissibility of a case on the basis that a person has been tried, a State's judicial system should be given the opportunity to remedy deficiencies in proceedings if, and to the extent that, such means to do so are available. This is ensured by an interpretation of articles 17(1)(c) and 20(3) of the Statute that requires finality of the domestic trial.

In *Al-Senussi*, PTC I declared the case inadmissible since it considered that Libya has presented sufficient evidence regarding its domestic proceedings dealing with the same case within the meaning of Article 17 (1)(a) ICCS;[600] further, the Chamber did not find an inability 'to obtain the accused and the necessary evidence'[601] given that Al Senussi was being detained in Tripoli and thus under the control of the central authorities.[602] On 24 July 2014, the AC unanimously confirmed the PTC I's decision.[603]

In sum, for a case to be declared inadmissible, national proceedings, if there are any, must refer to the *same suspects and substantially the same conduct* as are the objects of the ICC proceedings.[604] While a determination of admissibility does not constitute 'a judgement or reflection on the national justice system as a whole', but always refers to concrete proceedings,[605] a too strict and specific admissibility test may nevertheless overly restrict a State's legitimate prosecutorial choices[606] and thus ultimately undermine the complementarity's main rationale, that is, to protect State sovereignty.[607] Indeed, if the complementarity

596 On the verdict, see UNSMIL & OHCHR, Report on Case 630/2012, 21 February 2017 <https://unsmil.unmissions.org/sites/default/files/regime-trial-report-english.pdf>, pp. 47–50. Gaddafi has appealed against the death sentence to the Libyan Supreme Court. The Tripoli Court of Assize's proceedings leading to the death sentence allegedly violated the defendant's fair trial rights (UNSMIL & OHCHR, Report on Case 630/2012, 21 February 2017, p. 54); see also IntComJur, Libyan Proceedings, 2020, pp. 9–10; on the fair trial shortcomings in this case other Libyan proceedings see Wierda, *Impact* (2023), pp. 73 ff.

597 ICC, *Prosecutor v. Saif Al-Islam Gaddafi*, PTC I, Admissibility Challenge by Dr. Saif Al-Islam Gadafi pursuant to Articles 17 (1)(c), 19 and 20 (3) of the Rome Statute, ICC-01/11-01/11-640 08-06-2018 1/57 RH PT, 5 June 2018, para. 2.

598 *Gaddafi*, ICC-01/11-01/11-662 05-04-2019 3/29 RH PT. The PTC argues with the wording of Article 17 (1)(c) (para. 36 'formulation "a trial by the Court is not permitted" suggests that the person has been the subject of a completed trial') and relevant case law (paras 37 ff.).

599 *Gaddafi*, ICC-01/11-01/11-695 09-03-2020 1/43 EO PT OA8, para. 59. Also, see below main text at note 866.

600 *Al-Senussi*, ICC-01/11-01/11-466-Red., paras. 167–8, 311.

601 Art. 17 (3) ICCS.

602 *Al-Senussi*, ICC-01/11-01/11-466-Red, paras. 309–10, 311.

603 *Prosecutor v. Gaddafi and Al-Senussi*, AC, Judgment on the Appeal of Mr Abdullah Al-Senussi against the Decision of PTC I of 11 October 2013 Entitled 'Decision on the admissibility of the case against Abdullah Al-Senussi', ICC-01/11-01/11-565, 24 July 2014, paras. 66 ff.

604 For a thorough discussion, see Rastan, *JICJ*, 15 (2017), 7 ff.

605 ICC-OTP, *Prelim. Examinations* (2013), para. 46; in a similar vein, Nouwen, *Complementarity* (2013), pp. 74–5.

606 In the same vein, Nouwen, *Complementarity* (2013), pp. 51–9, 106, advocating a more liberal reading allowing for national prosecutorial discretion (52–3) and 'some deference to prosecutorial choices of the domestic justice system' (57); otherwise 'inequality in discretion' (53), with regard to the OTP's full-fledged discretion, would ensue. Crit. of the same conduct test in this regard, see also Stahn, in Stahn, *Practice* (2015), pp. 229–30, 239 ff., 258 (arguing that it reflects a 'tension between ICC-centricity and contextualization', giving primacy to the former and thereby undermining domestic justice efforts). Crit. also Heller, *JICJ*, 14 (2016), 648 ff. (arguing that the substantiality requirement (still) makes it too difficult for States to ensure inadmissibility through their own actions and thus ultimately undermines the complementarity principle). See also the dissenting views of Judges Ušacka and Song, as quoted in note 562 in this chapter.

607 Note 498 in this chapter and main text.

regime aims—in line with the so-called positive complementarity concept, to be discussed below[608]—to encourage domestic proceedings,[609] States should have a certain margin of appreciation as to their prosecutorial policies.[610] Thus, the identity of the domestic and ICC proceedings must be construed dynamically and flexibly, taking into account the different context of domestic and international proceedings[611] and allowing for a comprehensive comparison with regard to the overall scope of both proceedings.[612] Arguably, the 'sufficiently mirror' test developed with regard to Article 18 litigation, i.e. to require that domestic proceedings sufficiently mirror the content of an Article 18 (1) notification,[613] offers a more flexible approach. Ultimately, a 'qualified deference' to domestic jurisdictions is necessary in order to counterbalance a too strict reading of the same conduct test.[614]

### *(c) Sufficient gravity (Article 17 (1)(d) ICCS)*

#### *(i) The standard in practice*

The situation/case distinction discussed above also plays out with regard to the determination of the gravity threshold in that one must distinguish between situation- and case-related gravity, that is, with a view to the initiation of the investigation of a *situation* and of the *case*(*s*) arising from this situation.[615]

[608] Section B.(3) in this chapter.

[609] For a thorough discussion, see Kleffner, *Complementarity* (2008), pp. 309–39; Stahn, in Stahn, *Practice* (2015), pp. 232–40; see also El Zeidy, *Complementarity* (2008), pp. 298–305, discussing positive vs. traditional complementarity.

[610] See, convincingly, Kleffner, *Complementarity* (2008), p. 201; Nouwen, *Complementarity* (2013), pp. 52–3, 57; in a similar vein, ICC, *Prosecutor v. Muthaura et al.*, AC, Judgment on the Appeal of the Republic of Kenya against the Decision of Pre-Trial Chamber II of 30 May 2011 entitled 'Decision on the Application by the Government of Kenya Challenging the Admissibility of the Case Pursuant to Article 19 (2)(b) of the Statute', Dissenting Opinion of Judge Anita Ušacka, ICC-01/09-02/11-342, 20 September 2011, para. 19 and *Gaddafi*, ICC-01/11-01/11-547-Anx2, Dissenting Opinion Judge Ušacka, paras. 19, 57, 62 (understanding complementarity as a form of 'cooperation and communication' leaving some discretion to the State, especially if undergoing a transitional justice process). But crit. re sovereignity protection as (main) rationale for complementarity, Rastan, *JICJ*, 15 (2017), 18–19 ('unclear what role a margin of appreciation would play if the central issue under the first limb of admissibility is a determination of whether there is an actual conflict of jurisdiction'; 'better rationale is the peril to which a suspect may be exposed if tried twice for the same conduct').

[611] cf. Nouwen, *Complementarity* (2013), p. 55. Going much further, Heller, *JICJ*, 14 (2016), 664 (advocating a '"radical complementarity"', according to which inadmissibility should already be assumed if the State in question is 'making a genuine effort to bring a suspect to justice'). In Heller's view 'the "same person requirement"' should be relaxed by the judges 'to permit pyramidal (and similar) investigative strategies', whereas the (substantially) same conduct requirement should be eliminated by (if necessary) amending the ICCS. Conc. Jackson, *JICJ*, 14 (2016), 1071.

[612] See note 575 ff. in this chapter and main text, as well as Nouwen, *Complementarity* (2013), p. 59 (referring to the defence position in *Katanga*); see also Kleffner, *Complementarity* (2008), pp. 202–3; in favour of a flexible approach, also Bo, *CLF*, 25 (2014), 526.

[613] *Situation Philippines*, ICC-01/21-56-Red, para. 98 ('totality of the national investigations and proceedings ... do not sufficiently, or at all, mirror[,] the Court's investigation'); *Situation Venezuela I*, ICC-02/18-45, para. 131 ('domestic investigations appear to not sufficiently mirror the forms of criminality the Prosecution intends to investigate'); confirmed by *Situation in the Bolivarian Republic of Venezuela I*, AC, Judgment on the appeal of the Bolivarian Republic of Venezuela against Pre-Trial Chamber I's "Decision authorising the resumption of the investigation pursuant to article 18(2) of the Statute", ICC-02/18-89, 1 March 2024, paras. 247–9.

[614] The concept of 'qualified deference' goes back to Drumbl, *Atrocity* (2007), pp. 193–4 and Drumbl, in Stahn and El Zeidy, *Complementarity I* (2011), pp. 222–32; subsequently, Stahn, in Stahn, *Practice* (2015), pp. 230, 253 ff., 258 (criticizing the 'binary "either/or" choice' of admissibility challenges as artificial and advocating 'qualified deference' in order to connect 'ICC practice more closely to longer-term visions of complementarity' and balance 'the strict application of the "same conduct" test, and the more generous granting of deference under Article 17(2) and (3)'); conc. (apparently) Wierda, *Impact* (2023), p. 60 (but tracing the concept back to Stahn).

[615] *Situation in the DRC*, ICC-01/04-02/06-20-Anx2, para. 44. See also WCRO, *Gravity* (2008), pp. 21–5, 25–8; El Zeidy, *CLF*, 19 (2008), 39; Kontorovich, *IsLR*, 47 (2014), 381; De Meester, *Investigation Phase* (2015), pp. 250 ff.; Stahn, *JICJ*, 15 (2017), 427 ('unresolved tension between the use of gravity as an argument of situational analysis, and its connection to hypothetical cases'); in a similar vein, Heller, *Opinio Juris* 1 December 2017 criticizing the notion that the OTP 'must investigate any situation in which at least one case is grave enough to be admissible';

*(1) **Office of the Prosecutor*** Indeed, the OTP has so far[616] applied gravity in this twofold way regarding situations and cases.[617] Originally, the OTP had not systematically elaborated the gravity criteria or even proposed a more sophisticated gravity theory. Later, the Office developed its approach further giving it a more precise shape, by taking into account quantitative and qualitative considerations[618] and referring to 'various factors, including their scale, nature, manner of commission, and impact'[619] and 'bearing in mind the potential cases that would likely arise from an investigation of the situation'.[620] This more nuanced approach is a result of an ongoing process of external and internal consultation that has seen many changes. As to the specific factors mentioned—equally applicable to situations and cases[621]—the Office has offered definitions in declarations, papers, and submissions.

As to the '*scale*' the Office referred, as in the Iraq case mentioned above,[622] to the number of victims[623] and also took the geographic and temporal scope of the crimes into account.[624] This approach has been criticized because of the difficulty of establishing exact victim

furthermore, see Zakerhossein, *Situation* (2017), pp. 217–18; crit. regarding situational gravity, WCRO, *Situation* (2009), pp. 28–36; Nouwen, *Complementarity* (2013), pp. 90–1; Smeulers, Weerdesteijn, and Hola, *ICLR*, 15 (2015), 5 ff.; for a crit. account from the perspective of human rights law, see Deprez, *ICLR*, 12 (2012), 733–7.

616 Between mid-2003 and 2005 gravity played no role, see Schabas, in Stahn and Sluiter, *Practice* (2009), pp. 229–31. Interestingly, it did not attract much attention either in the negotiation history of the ICCS; cf. thereon Stahn, in Stahn and Sluiter, *Practice* (2009), p. 267; Stegmiller, *Pre-Investigation Stage* (2011), pp. 317–18.

617 ICC-OTP, *Case Selection* (2016), para. 36 ('Gravity of crime(s) as a case selection criterion is assessed similarly to gravity as a factor for admissibility under article 17(1)(d). However, given that many cases might potentially be admissible under article 17, the Office may apply a stricter test when assessing gravity for the purposes of case selection than that which is legally required for the admissibility test under article 17'); ICC-OTP, *Report on Activities* (2006), p. 8. See also Ambos, in Ambos et al., *Building a Future* (2009), pp. 73–4, para. 38; El Zeidy, *CLF*, 19 (2008), 39; WCRO, *Gravity* (2008), pp. 25–8; Stegmiller, *ICLR*, 9 (2009), 557; Stegmiller, *Pre-Investigation Stage* (2011), pp. 318–22; Abdou, 'Article 17', in Klamberg et al., *Commentary ICC I* (2023), pp. 614–15; for an empirical assessment of the OTP's selection of situations with a view to their gravity, see Smeulers, Weerdesteijn, and Hola, *ICLR*, 15 (2015), 1 ff., concluding, on the basis of an analysis of secondary data on violence and human rights violations, that 'the Prosecutor is generally focusing on the gravest situations where international crimes are supposedly committed' (1, 35–6, 38), but at the same time admitting intrinsic limitations of their approach, especially their focus on broad country situations different from the OTP's approach on narrower situations/potential cases (36–8); also the focus on broad country situations does not account for the—procedurally more important—selection of cases *within* a given situation.

618 ICC-OTP, *Prelim. Examinations* (2013), para. 61; *Prelim. Examinations* (2020), para. 69, 260, 284; see also ICC-OTP, *Mali—Article 53 Report* (2013), para. 143.

619 Regulation 29 (2) RegOTP; ICC-OTP, *Prelim. Examinations* (2013), paras. 9, 59 ff.; ICC-OTP, *Prelim. Examinations* (2014), para. 7; *Prelim. Examinations* (2019), para. 7; *Prelim. Examinations* (2020), para. 7. See previously ICC-OTP, *Prosecutorial Strategy* (2010), para. 20; ICC-OTP, *Report on Activities* (2006), p. 6 and ICC-OTP, *Prosecutorial Strategy* (2006), para. 2b. See also Seils, in Bergsmo, *Criteria for Prioritizing* (2010), p. 57; Guariglia and Rogier, in Stahn, *Practice* (2015), pp. 359–60; for a crit. discussion, see Kontorovich, *IsLR*, 47 (2014), 387 ff.; crit. also Schabas, in Stahn, *Practice* (2015), p. 380arguing that '[g]ravity provides the prosecutor with a seemingly objective but ultimately an extraordinarily subjective standard'. On the ensuing discretion of the OTP, see Rohrer, *Legalitäts- oder Opportunitätsprinzip* (2010), pp. 234 ff.

620 ICC-OTP, *Prelim. Examinations* (2019), para. 7; *Prelim. Examinations* (2020), para. 7.

621 El Zeidy, *CLF*, 19 (2008), 43.

622 ICC-OTP, *Update on Communications* (2006), Annex—Iraq Response, p. 8; more recently *Prelim. Examinations* (2020), paras. 7, 240, 260, 284.

623 ICC-OTP, *Statement by Luis Moreno-Ocampo* (2005), p. 6; Waugaman, *IAR*, 15 (2006), 2; ICC-OTP, *Case Selection* (2016), para. 38 ('number of direct and indirect victims'); *Prelim. Examinations* (2019), para. 299 ('in view of the scale of the alleged crimes and the number of approximately 600,000 to one million Rohingya victims allegedly forcibly displaced from Myanmar to Bangladesh, the case clearly reached the gravity threshold'); *Prelim. Examinations* (2020), para. 224.

624 ICC-OTP, *Case Selection* (2016), para. 38 ('geographical or temporal spread (high intensity of the crimes over a brief period or low intensity of crimes over an extended period'); DeGuzman, *FordhamILJ*, 32 (2008), 1451; Guariglia, in Stahn and Sluiter, *Practice* (2009), p. 214.

numbers,[625] the lack of qualitative criteria,[626] and a proper methodology as to what to compare.[627] Meanwhile, the Office acknowledges, as part of the damage caused by crimes, the 'bodily or psychological harm caused to the victims and their families' as a particular factor to assess the scale.[628] As to the 'geographical and temporal spread' it puts on an equal footing the 'high intensity of the crimes over a brief period or low intensity of crimes over an extended period'.[629]

With respect to the *nature* of the crimes, the OTP considers that while all ICC crimes 'are crimes of concern to the international community and, as such, grave in themselves',[630] their nature is manifest in 'the specific elements of each offence'.[631] On the assumption that there is an inherent hierarchy of crimes,[632] killing, rape, sexual and gender violence, crimes against children, persecution, or the imposition of destructive conditions on a group are considered crimes of particular concern.[633] One may also refer in this context to the Preamble which speaks of 'grave crimes', in referring back to 'unimaginable atrocities that deeply shock the conscience of mankind';[634] this implies a very high gravity threshold.[635] Further, as to war crimes, Article 8 distinguishes between the grave breaches and the other (armed conflict) crimes not amounting to such grave breaches.[636]

Regarding the *manner of the commission*, the OTP refers, as objective criteria, to 'the means employed'; the 'degree of participation'; the system, organization, or official involvement in the crimes ('policy');[637] and 'elements of particular cruelty', including the attack on especially vulnerable victims and the use of sexual violence. As subjective criteria, the

[625] See, on this issue, Brunborg, 'Session 3: Transcript', in ICC-OTP, *First Public Hearing* (2003), p. 2.

[626] See for the prioritization of qualitative criteria, i.e. the systematicity of the crimes, the social alarm caused, and State involvement, Heller, in Stahn and van den Herik, *Perspectives* (2010), pp. 229–53, arguing, essentially, that his qualitative approach would lend greater legitimacy to the Court and produce a greater impact in terms of deterrence and general prevention ('greater expressive value', p. 236). Yet, Heller's approach, albeit certainly thought-provoking and allegedly principled, is from a theoretical perspective, and apart from its practical implications, full of consequentalist assumptions and thus 'more like a prudent concession to practical *realpolitik*, ... than a strong, independent argument for what the ICC is really about, what it is truly for'. (Osiel, in Stahn and van den Herik, *Perspectives* (2010), p. 258).

[627] Schabas, *JICJ*, 6 (2008), 741, 747–8; Schabas, in Stahn and Sluiter, *Practice* (2009), pp. 245–6; Zakerhossein, *Situation* (2017), p. 223; see also Ambos, in Bohlander, *International Criminal Justice* (2007), p. 439.

[628] ICC-OTP, *Prelim. Examinations* (2013), para. 62.

[629] Ibid.

[630] ICC-OTP, *Criteria for Selection* (2006), para. 16.

[631] ICC-OTP, *Prelim. Examinations* (2013), para. 63.

[632] cf. Seils, in Bergsmo, *Criteria for Prioritizing* (2010), p. 57; Heller, in Stahn and van den Herik, *Perspectives* (2010), pp. 230 ff.; Kontorovich, *IsLR*, 47 (2014), 383, 389; see also Ambos, *Treatise ICL II* (2022), pp. 296 ff.

[633] ICC-OTP, *Prelim. Examinations* (2013), para. 63; similarly, ICC-OTP, *Case Selection* (2016), para. 39 ('The nature of the crimes refers to the specific factual elements of each offence such as killings, rapes, other sexual or gender-based crimes, crimes committed against or affecting children, persecution, or the imposition of conditions of life on a group calculated to bring about its destruction'); previously Guariglia, in Stahn and Sluiter, *Practice* (2009), p. 214; deGuzman, *FordhamILJ*, 32 (2008), 1452 (referring to crimes resulting in death and rape). See also *Prosecutor v. Sesay, Kallon and Gbao*, No. SCSL-04-15-T, TC I, Sentencing Judgment, paras. 188 and 204 (8 April 2009) qualifying crimes against UN personnel and child soldiers as 'inherently grave'.

[634] cf. Preamble ICCS, recital 3 referring back ('such') to recital 2.

[635] See also Kontorovich, *IsLR*, 47 (2014), 392, therefore excluding, in principle, the crime of transfer of population of the Occupying Power pursuant to Art. 8 (2)(b)(viii) ICCS.

[636] cf. Art. 8 (2)(a) ['grave breaches'] as compared to (b) ['other serious violations']; less clear, Art. 8 (2) (c) ['serious violations'] as compared to (e) ['other serious violations']; see also Kontorovich, *IsLR*, 47 (2014), 392; furthermore, see ICC-OTP, *Prelim. Examinations* (2019), para. 278 ('information available at this stage suggests in particular that members of armed anti-government entities have generally committed detention-related alleged crimes of a more severe nature and on a significantly larger scale than members of Ukrainian Government Forces').

[637] ICC-OTP, *Case Selection* (2016), para. 40; see also Nouwen, *Complementarity* (2013), p. 91 (state involvement as 'independent and sufficient indication of gravity, because of the high risk of impunity').

(presumed) intent of the perpetrator and possible discriminatory motives are taken into account.[638]

Ultimately, the—long controversial[639]—*impact* criterion has finally been adopted. The Office now wants to assess impact in light of 'the sufferings endured by the victims and their increased vulnerability', 'the terror subsequently instilled' or the 'social, economic and environmental damage inflicted on the affected communities'.[640] This very much reminds one of the 'social alarm' criterion employed by the case law and, in any case, appears more as a policy[641] than a strictly legal criterion. We will return to this issue in a moment. Last but not least, the OTP also stresses in the gravity context its focus on the *most responsible* as an additional factor.[642]

In practical terms, the Office often has affirmed gravity without further reasoning, for example in the situations of the DRC, Uganda, Sudan, Mali, Ivory Coast, and the Central African Republic (II),[643] as well as more recently with regard to the situations in Nigeria and Ukraine.[644] In contrast, the OTP has dealt rather extensively with the gravity threshold in relation to the situation in Afghanistan[645] and

[638] ICC-OTP, *Case Selection* (2016), para. 40; *Prelim. Examinations* (2013), para. 64; previously (slightly different) ICC-OTP, *Criteria for Selection* (2006), para. 17. See also deGuzman, *FordhamILJ*, 32 (2008), 1453; Guariglia, in Stahn and Sluiter, *Practice* (2009), p. 214.

[639] The first Prosecutor Moreno Ocampo mentioned impact on various occasions; cf. thereon ICC-OTP, *Statement by Luis Moreno-Ocampo* (2005), p. 6; ICC-OTP, *Third Report UNSC* (2006), p. 2; his Office also referred to the 'nature, manner and impact' regarding the Haskanita attack in the Darfur situation, ICC-OTP, *Eighth Report UNSC* (2008), para. 56. In contrast, senior (former) staff members seem to have been critical of this criterion, cf. Guariglia, in Stahn and Sluiter, *Practice* (2009) pp. 212–18; Seils, in Bergsmo, *Criteria for Prioritizing* (2010), p. 59. Guariglia has been the OTP's Appeals' coordinator and Seils the Head of the Situation Analysis Section (August 2004 to October 2008) and mainly responsible, inter alia, for a 2006 OTP paper (ICC-OTP, *Criteria for Selection* (2006), para. 12) which did not include this criterion.

[640] ICC-OTP, *Case Selection* (2016), para. 40; *Prelim. Examinations* (2013), para. 65. See previously Schabas, *JICJ*, 6 (2008), 742, quoting a June 2006 OTP draft document referring to 'the broader impact of crimes on the community and on regional peace and security, including longer term social, economic and environmental damage'; see also Hall, *Suggestions* (2003), p. 21; Stegmiller, *ICLR*, 9 (2009), 560–1; Meißner, *Zusammenarbeit* (2003), p. 79; deGuzman, *FordhamILJ*, 32 (2008), 1453; Osiel, *The Hague Justice Portal* (2009), p. 2.

[641] cf. Art. 53 (1)(c) and (2)(c) ICCS.

[642] cf. ICC-OTP, *Case Selection* (2016), paras. 42–44; *Prelim. Examinations*, para. 66; cf. also Guariglia and Rogier, in Stahn, *Practice* (2015), pp. 360–1, for whom the gravity of the case 'includes both the *gravity of the crimes* and the *extent of responsibility of the perpetrator*'.

[643] ICC-OTP, *Report on Activities* (2006), para. 11: 'The Office selected the DRC and Northern Uganda as the first situations because they were the gravest admissible situations under the Statute's jurisdiction, and, after the referral, the Office confirmed that the Darfur situation clearly met the gravity standard. The Office will continue to adhere to the rigorous standard of gravity established in the Statute.' On Mali, see ICC-OTP, *Mali—Article 53 Report* (2013), paras. 142–70; on Ivory Coast, see ICC, *Situation in the Republic of Côte D'Ivoire*, PTC III, Prosecution's Request for Authorisation of an Investigation pursuant to Article 15, ICC-02/11-3, 23 June 2011, paras. 54 ff.; on the CAR II, see ICC-OTP, *Situation CAR II* (2014), paras. 252–64; crit. Stegmiller, *CLF*, 24 (2013), 497–8 (498: 'cursory analysis'); for a profound analysis of the Uganda and Sudan situations, see Nouwen, *Complementarity* (2013), pp. 111 ff., 244 ff., identifying catalysing complementarity effects in both situations (141 ff., 234, 266 ff., 328), but no increase in domestic prosecutions (228 ff., 234, 306 ff., 328).

[644] ICC-OTP, *Prelim. Examinations* (2020), paras. 260, 284 (merely affirming 'sufficient gravity').

[645] See ICC-OTP, *Prelim. Examinations* (2017), para. 263 (regarding the Taliban, 'crimes were committed in a manner calculated to inflict maximum harm and injury on the largest number of victims, such as through suicide bombings'; 'widespread use of perfidious tactics has also placed the civilian population at increased risk of attack from governmental and international forces'; 'alleged crimes have had a particularly broad and severe impact on women and girls'), paras. 265–6 (regarding the Afghan National Security Forces: 'alleged crimes have been committed on a large scale'; 'torture has been practised institutionally in certain facilities'; 'manner in which these crimes are alleged to have been committed also appears to have been particularly cruel, prolonged and severe, calculated to inflict maximum pain and has included acts of sexual violence'; 'alleged crimes had severe short-term and long-term impacts on detainees') and paras. 272–4 (regarding the US Armed Forces and the CIA 'groups of persons likely to be the focus of future investigations include persons who devised, authorised or bore oversight responsibility for the implementation'; 'acts allegedly committed were serious both in their number and in their effect, and although implemented pursuant to authorised interrogation policies adopted locally rather than at

Burundi.[646] With regard to the situation in Bangladesh/Myanmar, the OTP considered the nature of the crimes or the manner in which they were committed, as well as the underlying discriminatory intent.[647]

Gravity was rejected regarding possible crimes of UK forces in the *Iraq* situation[648] and the flotilla incident.[649] In the *UK/Iraq* situation gravity was rejected comparing the relatively low number of victims (four to twelve) of alleged crimes by British troops with the large-scale violence in the situations of DRC, Uganda, and Sudan. While this has been criticized as 'comparing apples and oranges',[650] there was not much choice for the OTP given that it only had jurisdiction over British troops by way of the active personality (nationality) principle.[651] The preliminary examination was re-opened on 13 May 2014 based on new information but it was then terminated, despite the affirmation of gravity,[652] on 9 December 2020, invoking complementarity.[653] The OTP could have avoided criticism by taking a more systematic and consistent approach to gravity in the first place, especially by clarifying the concrete factors it has considered.[654] In the flotilla incident the Prosecutor basically argued that the killing of ten passengers out of five hundred and the injury of fifty to

headquarters level, implicated personal responsibility within the command structure'; 'treatment of CIA detainees appears to have been particularly grave on a qualitative assessment. The alleged crimes appear to have been committed with particular cruelty, involving the infliction of serious physical and psychological injury, over prolonged periods, and including acts committed in a manner calculated to offend cultural and religious values, and leaving victims deeply traumatised').

[646] ICC-OTP, *Prelim. Examinations* (2017), paras. 305–6.

[647] *Prelim. Examinations* (2019), para. 260 ('alleged coercive acts of killings, arbitrary arrests, infliction of pain and injuries, sexual violence, and destruction of houses and buildings. The victims' representations also reflected the immense gravity of the alleged crimes and their alleged commission with discriminatory intent').

[648] ICC-OTP, *Update on Communications* (2006), Annex—Iraq Response, pp. 8–9; Stegmiller, *ICLR*, 9 (2009), 558–9; Schüller, *HuV-I*, 21 (2008), 77; Murphy, *CLF*, 17 (2006), 309 ff.; see also Ambos, in Bohlander, *International Criminal Justice* (2007), pp. 438–9; Greenawalt, in deGuzman and Oosterveld, *Elgar Companion ICC* (2020), pp. 86–7.

[649] ICC-OTP, *Comoros, Greece and Cambodia* (2014), paras. 119–51. On the background and facts of the case, see Buchan, *CLF*, 25 (2014), 466–9 (who affirms gravity because of accompanying 'aggravating factors' as set out in the referral letter of the flag State Comoros (495–8)), and Knoops and Zwart, *ICLR*, 15 (2015), 1070–3 (rejecting the 'social alarm' criterion and thus gravity for this case (1082 ff.)). Rejecting gravity with regard to Israeli settlement policy in the Palestinian territories, arguably a war crime under Art. 8 (2)(b)(viii) ICCS, Kontorovich, *IsLR*, 47 (2014), 379 ff., basically arguing that this crime is not a 'grave breach', but only a malum *prohibitum* (390) and thus may only reach the gravity threshold if it 'fundamentally change[s] the demographic composition of the occupied territory' or is committed 'alongside other grave crimes' (399); in favour of gravity, Buchan, *CLF*, 25 (2014), 465. For further procedural developments regarding the flotilla incident, see below notes 655 ff. and main text.

[650] Schabas, *JICJ*, 6 (2008), 741; Schabas, in Stahn and Sluiter, *Practice* (2009), p. 240. Schabas further criticizes that the Prosecutor did not compare the total number of deaths in Iraq with the total in the DRC or Uganda, nor did he compare the total number of deaths resulting from the crimes attributed to specific perpetrators with those blamed on the British troops in Iraq (Schabas, *JICJ*, 6 (2008), 747 and Schabas, in Stahn and Sluiter, *Practice* (2009), p. 240). Crit. also El Zeidy, *CLF*, 19 (2008), 40–1; Heller, in Stahn and van den Herik, *Perspectives* (2010), p. 234 and *passim*; Stahn, *JICJ*, 15 (2017), 427; Bådagård and Klamberg, *GeoJIL* 48 (2017), 714–15. Against any comparison, but for an absolute assessment of gravity, deGuzman and Schabas, in Sluiter et al., *International Criminal Procedure* (2013), p. 145.

[651] Art. 12 (2)(b) ICCS.

[652] *Prelim. Examinations* (2020), para. 240 (seeing an aggravating factor in the fact that 'the underlying conduct arose, in part, from institutional factors related to unclear doctrine, training programmes that encouraged maintaining or prolonging the "shock of capture" without sufficient regard for humane treatment, and from command and supervisory failings across the Ministry of Defence and the British army, particularly in the early phases of Operation Telic, to prevent the occurrence of such crimes').

[653] cf. ICC-OTP, *Iraq/UK Final Report* (2020); *Prelim. Examinations* (2017), para. 174; *Prelim. Examinations* (2020), paras. 241–7.

[654] See previously Ambos, in Bohlander, *International Criminal Justice* (2007), p. 439; in a similar vein, also crit., Schüller, *HuV-I*, 21 (2008), 78; deGuzman, *FordhamILJ*, 32 (2008), 1432–3, 1435; Stegmiller, *ICLR*, 9 (2009), 562; Stegmiller, in Stahn and El Zeidy, *Complementarity I* (2011), pp. 606–21.

fifty-five passengers was not sufficient to meet the gravity threshold.[655] Thus, the 'potential case(s) that could be pursued as a result of an investigation into this situation [was] limited to an event encompassing a limited number of victims ... with limited countervailing qualitative considerations'.[656] Despite two PTC decisions that provided guidelines for the OTP with regard to, inter alia, gravity withing the meaning of Article 17 (1)(d) ICCS, including the instruction to reconsider its decision,[657] confirmed by the AC,[658] the OTP adapted the respective reasoning but ultimately closed the case in 2019, arguing, inter alia, that only relatively few people had been subjected to 'direct violence'.[659] As we will see below,[660] neither PTC I nor the Appeals Chamber agreed with the OTP's position and the litigation has grown into a kind of clash between the OTP and Chambers as to the judicial control of the OTP's discretion.[661]

***(2) Chambers*** As to *judicial pronouncements* on gravity, the issue remains largely unsettled at the ICC level. While the *Lubanga* PTC[662] proposed at least some abstract criteria regarding a case—the nature and social impact ('social alarm') of the crimes (systematic or large-scale?), the manner of commission (e.g. particular brutality or cruelty), and the status and role of the suspected perpetrators (are they the most responsible?)—this decision has not only received widespread criticism,[663] but also, more importantly, has been reversed

[655] ICC-OTP, *Comoros, Greece and Cambodia* (2014), para. 138; for more details and crit., see Longobardo, *JICJ*, 14 (2016), 1019 and 1024 ff. (arguing that the OTP should have had considered 'the lower threshold required to establish admissibility—including sufficient gravity—at the preliminary examination stage' (1025) and the specific case law for operations on board a vessel (1028)).

[656] ICC-OTP, *Comoros, Greece and Cambodia* (2014), para. 144.

[657] First review decision: ICC, *Situation on Registered Vessels of the Union of the Comoros, the Hellenic Republic and the Kingdom of Cambodia*, PTC I, Decision on the Request of the Union of the Comoros to Review the Prosecutor's Decision not to Initiate an Investigation, ICC-01/13-34, 16 July 2015. After the OTP stood by its decision (ICC-OTP, 'Statement of ICC Prosecutor, Fatou Bensouda, on the Situation on registered vessels of the Union of the Comoros et al.', 30 November 2017), the PTC issued a second review decision and decided that the OTP failed to comply with the initial guidelines, PTC I, Decision on the 'Application for Judicial Review by the Government of the Union of the Comoros', ICC-01/13-68, 15 November 2018.

[658] The AC rejected the Prosecutor's appeal and instructed her to 'reconsider her decision not to open an investigation in accordance with the 16 July 2015 Decision and the present judgment and to notify the Pre-Trial Chamber and those participating in the proceedings of her final decision by 2 December 2019', ICC, *Situation on Registered Vessels of the Union of the Comoros, the Hellenic Republic and the Kingdom of Cambodia*, AC, Judgment on the Appeal of the Prosecutor against Pre-Trial Chamber I's 'Decision on the "Application for Judicial Review by the Government of the Union of the Comoros"', ICC-01/13-98, 2 September 2019, para. 1.

[659] ICC-OTP, Final Decision of the Prosecutor concerning the 'Article 53(1) Report' (ICC-01/13-6-AnxA), dated 6 November 2014, ICC-01/13-99-Anx1 02-12-2019 1/44 NM PT, 2 December 2019, para. 38; for more details, see Chaitidou, *ZIS*, 15 (2020), 559–60. There was, so to speak, a third review decision where, again, the PTC criticized the erroneous application of its guidelines by the OTP but did not issue a further instruction to reconsider, due to its reading of the AC decision (above note 658), see ICC, *Situation on Registered Vessels of the Union of the Comoros, the Hellenic Republic and the Kingdom of Cambodia*, PTC I, Decision on the 'Application for Judicial Review by the Government of the Comoros', ICC-01/13-111, 16 September 2020. On 22 September 2020, the Government of Comoros sought leave to appeal this decision, TC I, Application on Behalf of the Government of the Union of the Comoros for Leave to Appeal the 'Decision on the "Application for Judicial Review by the Government of the Comoros"' of 16 September 2020, ICC-01/13-112, 22 September 2020, which was eventually rejected, cf. AC, Decision on the Request for Leave to Appeal the 'Decision on the "Application for Judicial Review by the Government of the Comoros"', ICC-01/13-115, 21 December 2020.

[660] Below note 680 ff. and main text.

[661] cf. Heinze, in Heinze and Dittrich, *ICC* (2021), pp. 56–7; Sadat, in Heinze and Dittrich, *ICC* (2021), pp. 138–9; Chaitidou, *ZIS*, 15 (2020), 558; Greenawalt, in deGuzman and Oosterveld, *Elgar Companion ICC* (2020), pp. 92–4and Billis, *BergenJCLCJ*, 10 (2022), 3–7 (concluding that 'it could be a step forward to set clear normative limits to decision-making processes involving the aspect of "gravity", even if that means further restricting prosecutorial discretion'); see also Chapter IV, B.(3).

[662] *Situation in the DRC*, ICC-01/04-02/06-20-Anx2, paras. 29, 42, 46, 50–4, 63; crit. Boas et al., *International Criminal Procedure* (2011), p. 84.

[663] See Schüller, *HuV-I*, 21 (2008), 80; Schabas, *JICJ*, 6 (2008), 743; WCRO, *Gravity* (2008), pp. 36–51, recommending a 'sufficiently flexible' analysis (p. 42) and taking into account exceptional circumstances as 'the impact

by the Appeals Chamber.[664] It held that the PTC's gravity test is flawed and thus constitutes an error of law.[665] In particular, as to the social alarm criterion, the Chamber opined that it has no basis in the Statute and would politicize the gravity determination by relying on 'subjective and contingent reactions to crimes rather than upon their objective gravity'.[666] Further, as to the status and role of the suspect—a criterion used by the OTP only as an additional factor with regard to its focus on the 'most responsible'[667]—the Chamber correctly pointed out that the 'predictable exclusion of many perpetrators' on these grounds 'could severely hamper the preventive, or deterrent role of the Court'.[668] However, the AC did not propose an alternative test;[669] only Judge Pikis, in his separate and partly dissenting opinion, tried to determine gravity,[670] without, however, proposing a concrete test.

In the subsequent case law, the *Kenya* PTC II treated the gravity issue more profoundly.[671] In its Article 15 decision, PTC II did not only rely on the number of victims,[672] that is, a quantitative factor, but 'rather (on) the existence of some aggravating or qualitative factors

of victims, the manner in which the crimes were carried out, and the vulnerability of the victim population'; crit. in particular on the 'social alarm' criterion, Schüller, *HuV-I*, 21 (2008), 80–1; deGuzman, *FordhamILJ*, 32 (2008), 1461–2; Osiel, *The Hague Justice Portal* (2009), p. 6; WCRO, *Gravity* (2008), pp. 5, 39; El Zeidy, *CLF*, 19 (2008), 45 ('weird novelty'), who additionally points out (p. 44) that these factors are illustrative and not exclusive; Murphy, *CLF*, 17 (2006), 288 ff. (esp. 289); Smith, *ICLR*, 8 (2008), 340 ff.; Stegmiller, *ICLR*, 9 (2009), 551–2; Kontorovich, *IsLR*, 47 (2014), 398–9; Knoops and Zwart, *ICLR*, 15 (2015), 1093–7; Stahn, *JICJ*, 15 (2017), 426 ('well-intended, but partly misguided'); crit. also ICC, *Situation in IRC*, AC, Judgment on the Prosecutor's Appeal against the Decision of Pre-Trial Chamber I Entitled 'Decision on the Prosecutor's Application for Warrants of Arrest, Article 58', Separate and Partly Dissenting Opinion of Judge Georghios M. Pikis, ICC-01/04-169, 13 July 2006, paras. 34, 38–41; *contra* Heller, in Stahn and van den Herik, *Perspectives* (2010), pp. 233 ff., invoking this criterion as part of his qualitative approach (pp. 229–53); against this position, Osiel, in Stahn and van den Herik, *Perspectives* (2010), p. 257. Crit. as to the quantitative approach, Schabas, *CLF*, 19 (2008), 28–32; Schabas and El Zeidy, 'Article 17', in Ambos, *Commentary* (2022), mn. 62–4; crit. from a human rights perspective, Deprez, *ICLR*, 12 (2012), 733–4; also crit. Heller, in Stahn and van den Herik, *Perspectives* (2010), pp. 227 ff. See also El Zeidy, *MichJIL*, 23 (2002), 905; Cárdenas, *Zulässigkeitsprüfung* (2005), pp. 93–100 focusing on the international concern ('internationaler Belang', pp. 98, 100) of the matter; and see Stegmiller, *Pre-Investigation Stage* (2011), pp. 324–5. Crit. on the gravity standard, also Ohlin, in Stahn and Sluiter, *Practice* (2009), pp. 185, 200 ('unclear what kind of legal threshold is established'). On the difficult relations between OTP and Chambers in this matter, see El Zeidy, *CLF*, 19 (2008), 51 ff.

[664] *Situation in DRC*, ICC-01/04-169, paras. 54–82 (esp. 68–82); conc. *Prosecutor v. Al Bashir*, PTC I, Decision on the Prosecutor's Application for a Warrant of Arrest against Omar Hassan Ahmad Al Bashir, ICC 02/05 01/09-3, 4 March 2009, para. 48 with n. 51; for an analysis, see Stegmiller, *Pre-Investigation Stage* (2011), pp. 322 ff., 335–6; furthermore, see Schabas, *Introduction* (2020), pp. 198–9.

[665] On the respective standard pursuant to Art. 81 (1)(i)-(iii) ICCS, see Chapter VI, B. (1)(b)(ii) in this volume.

[666] *Situation in DRC*, ICC-01/04-169, para. 72.

[667] See above note 642 and main text; see also, previously, Guariglia, in Stahn and Sluiter, *Practice* (2009), pp. 214–15; Schabas, in Stahn and Sluiter, *Practice* (2009), p. 243; calling for flexibility if using this criterion at all, WCRO, *Gravity* (2008), pp. 43–51 (esp. 50–1); in a similar vein, Seils, in Bergsmo, *Criteria for Prioritizing* (2010), p. 56.

[668] *Lubanga*, ICC-01/04-169, para. 75. See also Seils, in Bergsmo, *Criteria for Prioritizing* (2109), p. 56.

[669] Crit. of the AC thereon and generally of its too strict approach, Schabas and El Zeidy, 'Article 17', in Ambos, *Commentary* (2022), mn. 64.

[670] *Situation in DRC*, ICC-01/04-169, Separate and Partly Dissenting Opinion of Judge Pikis, paras. 38–41. He focused on the ordinary meaning of the term and understands it as 'weightiness' (para. 39) excluding cases 'unworthy of consideration' by the Court, i.e. cases that are 'insignificant in themselves; where the criminality on the part of the culprit is wholly marginal; borderline cases' (para. 40) and holds a crime to be insignificant if 'the acts constituting the crime are wholly peripheral to the objects of the law in criminalising the conduct'.

[671] In *Bemba*, TC III affirmed gravity without further ado, cf. *Bemba*, ICC-01/05-01/08-802, para. 249. Regarding the situation in the Ivory Coast, PTC III basically followed *Kenya* PTC II (see above main text), focusing on the gravity of the alleged crimes ('scale and nature, the manner in which they were carried out, their impact on the victims, and any aggravating circumstances'), see *Situation in Côte d'Ivoire*, ICC-02/11-14, para. 204. In *Abu Garda*, PTC II took at least 'the qualitative dimension of the crime' into consideration; cf. *Prosecutor v. Abu Garda*, PTC I, Decision on the Confirmation of Charges, ICC-02/05-02/09-243-Red, 8 February 2010, para. 31.

[672] *Situation in Kenya*, ICC-01/09-19, paras. 190–1 (referring, inter alia, to 1,113 to 1,220 killings).

attached to the commission of crimes, which made it grave'.[673] The gravity must be assessed 'against the backdrop of a potential case within the context of a situation', thereby examining whether the suspects 'bear the greatest responsibility' (sic!) and the gravity of the respective crimes, 'guided by factors such as the scale, nature, manner of commission, impact of crimes committed on victims and the existence of aggravating circumstances'.[674] In its confirmation decision, PTC II explicitly rejects the *Lubanga* PTC test[675] and the defence argument that sufficient gravity only exists in case of active conduct or direct perpetration.[676] As to the positive factors to be taken into account for the determination of sufficient gravity the Chamber refers to the (sentencing) Rule 145 (1)(c) RPE ICC and quotes, by way of example, 'scale, nature and manner of commission of the alleged crimes, their impact on victims, and the existence of any aggravating circumstances'.[677]

With this the Chamber correctly affirms that gravity as a primary consideration ('litmus test') in the context of sentencing, treated in more detail in Volume II of this Treatise,[678] cannot, from a conceptual perspective, be understood differently from gravity as an admissibility criterion. In other words, there is but *one uniform concept of gravity*, equally valid at the pre-investigation (admissibility) and sentencing stage of the proceedings. This, in turn, means that the rich jurisprudence of the ICTY, ICTR, and SCSL on gravity in sentencing,[679] albeit not formally binding for the ICC, may provide important elements of a general gravity concept.

This combined quantitative-qualitative approach taking into account various factors has been confirmed by PTC I in its review decision regarding the flotilla incident.[680] The Chamber, drawing on the Court's previous case law, considers the 'gravity determination' as 'a generic assessment (general in nature and compatible with the fact that an investigation is yet to be opened)' focusing on persons 'who may bear the greatest responsibility for the alleged crimes' and adopting 'both a "quantitative" and "qualitative" viewpoint' taking into account 'factors such as nature, scale and manner of commission of the alleged crimes, as well as their impact on victims'.[681] As to the application of these factors to the circumstances

673 *Situation in Kenya*, ICC-01/09-19, para. 62; it further referred to the sentencing factors of the RPE, see Ambos, *Treatise ICL II* (2022), p. 336. On gravity in *Kenya*, see also Sriram and Brown, *ICLR*, 12 (2012), 219–44, 234–7; see also de Guzman and Schabas, in Sluiter et al., *International Criminal Procedure* (2013), p. 145.

674 *Situation in Kenya*, ICC-01/09-19, para. 188; affirming the gravity in paras. 198–200.

675 ICC, *Prosecutor v. Muthaura, Kenyatta and Ali*, PTC II, Decision on the Confirmation of Charges pursuant to Article 61 (7)(a) and (b) of the Rome Statute, ICC-01/09-02/11-382-Red, 23 January 2012, para. 44.

676 *Muthaura et al.*, ICC-01/09-02/11-382-Red, paras. 46, 47.

677 Ibid., para. 50.

678 See Ambos, *Treatise ICL II* (2022), pp. 335 ff.

679 See ibid., p. 336 on the case law; on the ad hoc tribunals' jurisprudence in detail, see also Stegmiller, *Pre-Investigation Stage* (2011), pp. 341–9.

680 ICC, *Situation on the Registered Vessels of the Union of the Comoros, the Hellenic Republic and the Kingdom of Cambodia*, PTC I, Decision on the Request of the Union of the Comoros to Review the Prosecutor's Decision not to Initiate an Investigation, ICC-01/13-34, 16 July 2015, paras. 20 ff.; *contra*, *Situation on the Vessels of Comoros*, ICC-01/13-34-Anx-Corr, Partly Dissenting Opinion of Judge Kovács, paras. 14 ff. (16 July 2015) (discussing at paras. 31 ff. the existence of war crimes depending on the legality of the Israeli blockade and its ensuing right to stop the vessels). For an analysis, see Knoops and Zwart, *ICLR*, 15 (2015), 1070 ff., 1082 ff., criticizing the PTC's intrusion 'on the prosecutorial discretion without the existence of exceptional circumstances' and the majority's 'undue emphasis [placed] on the political and international attention that the Mavi Marmara incident had been given'. Crit. also Greenawalt, in deGuzman and Oosterveld, *Elgar Companion ICC* (2020), pp. 93–4, identifying as the core statement of the decision that 'the gravity threshold is less onerous than' made by the Prosecutor and missing considerations on the 'question of relative gravity': 'How should the Prosecutor proceed, for example, when it lacks the capacity and resources to pursue every case within the Court's jurisdiction that meets some minimum threshold of admissibility?'

681 *Situation on the Vessels of Comoros*, ICC-01/13-34, para. 21; essentially conc. *Situation on the Vessels of Comoros*, AC, Judgment on the Appeal of the Prosecutor against Pre-Trial Chamber I's 'Decision on the "Application for Judicial Review by the Government of the Union of the Comoros"', ICC-01/13-98 02-09-2019 30/36 SL PT OA2, 2 September 2019, para. 81 ('the assessment of gravity involves, as in the case at hand, the

of the concrete incident, the PTC's majority considered first that the Prosecutor failed to consider whether a possible investigation would include the *most responsible*.[682] Regarding the *scale of the crimes*, the majority opined that the fact that the number of the victims of the situation at issue was 'exceeding the number of casualties in actual cases that were previously not only investigated but even prosecuted by the Prosecutor' was 'a compelling indicator of sufficient ... gravity'.[683] Importantly, Dissenting Judge Kovács rejected the majority's view by introducing, for the first time in the jurisprudence of the Court, a kind of comparative gravity, that is, he compared the flotilla situation with the one of Kenya arguing that there the scale of the violence was much broader.[684] At any rate, he further argued that in a situation like the one *sub judice* the scale cannot be determined solely by the number of victims, but should be 'accompanied by another qualitative factor(s) or aggravating circumstances surrounding the situation or case'.[685]

Applying the *nature of the crimes* criterion, PTC I discussed the war crimes of torture or inhuman treatment and of outrages upon personal dignity,[686] criticizing the Prosecutor's lack of proper analysis and premature exclusion of the former—more serious—war crime instead of taking it—pursuant to the 'reasonable basis' standard of Article 53 (1) ICCS—into account for the gravity assessment.[687] Further, as to the *manner of commission*, the Prosecutor's flawed or missing consideration of the use of live fire, the 'cruel and abusive treatment of detained passengers in Israel', and the '[u]nnecessarily' cruel treatment of passengers and attempts to conceal the crimes' amounted to her 'unsustainable' conclusion that a systematic and thus sufficiently grave commission was lacking.[688] Last but not least, as to the *impact of the crimes*, the majority found that 'physical, psychological or emotional harm suffered by the direct and indirect victims of the identified crimes', but also—'going beyond the suffering of the direct and indirect victims'—'the attention and concern that these events attracted from the parties involved, also leading to several fact-finding efforts on behalf of States and the United Nations in order to shed light on the events' sufficiently indicate a

evaluation of numerous factors and information relating thereto'); furthermore, see *Situation on the registered Vessels of the Union of the Comoros, the Hellenic Republic and the Kingdom of Cambodia*, PTC I, Decision on the 'Application for Judicial Review by the Government of the Comoros', ICC-01/13-111 16-09-2020 1/51 EC PT, 16 September 2020, para. 18 ('at the situation stage, gravity ... is assessed against the "potential cases" arising from the situation, which are defined by two parameters: (i) the groups of persons likely to be the object of the investigation; and (ii) the crimes within the jurisdiction of the Court allegedly committed during the incidents that are likely to be the focus of the investigation') and para. 20 ('Prosecutor must consider both quantitative and qualitative criteria, which relate to four main factors established in the jurisprudence of the Court'); in the same vein, *Situation Georgia*, ICC-01/15-12, paras. 51–2 ('generic assessment', 'quantitative and qualitative viewpoint'); on these factors, see Knoops and Zwart, *ICLR*, 15 (2015), 1092–6.

682 *Situation on the Vessels of Comoros*, ICC-01/13-34, paras. 23, 49; *contra*, *Situation on the Vessels of Comoros*, ICC-01/13-34-Anx-Corr, Partly Dissenting Opinion of Judge Kovács, paras. 27–9 (despite prosecutorial omission no relevant material error); furthermore, see *Situation on Vessels if Comoros*, ICC-01/13-111 16-09-2020 1/51 EC PT, paras. 38–45, esp. para. 40 ('Prosecutor erred by prematurely confining the scope of the potential cases and excluding from the scope of the investigation certain categories of persons'); on the criterion of the hierarchical position of the individuals most responsible, see Lafontaine and Magnoux, in Heinze and Dittrich, *ICC* (2021), pp. 267–9; furthermore Chaitidou, *ZIS*, 15 (2020), 561.

683 *Situation on the Vessels of Comoros*, ICC-01/13-34, paras. 26, 49.

684 *Situation on the Vessels of Comoros*, ICC-01/13-34-Anx-Corr, Partly Dissenting Opinion of Judge Kovács, para. 19.

685 Ibid., para. 20.

686 cf. Arts. 8 (2)(a)(ii) and 8 (2)(b)(xxi) ICCS.

687 *Situation on the Vessels of Comoros*, ICC-01/13-34, paras. 29–30, 49; also see *Situation on the Vessels if Comoros*, ICC-01/13-111 16-09-2020 1/51 EC PT, paras. 51–71 further clarifying, inter alia, that the Prosecutor failed by not taking into account the relevant legal characterization of alleged acts (paras. 65–6).

688 *Situation on the Vessels of Comoros*, ICC-01/13-34, paras. 33–45 (summary at para. 44 and conclusion at para. 45), 49.

relevant impact.[689] Here again, Judge Kovács made a noteworthy counter-argument, namely that the assessment of gravity *in casu* must be distinguished from the 'overall humanitarian crisis suffered by the Palestinian civilian population' as a result of the ongoing Palestinian-Israeli conflict.[690] In the result, Judge Kovács, agreeing with the Prosecutor, denies gravity given that the actual situation 'is narrow in scope with much less qualitative impact' than other situations.[691]

More recently, PTC I, with reference to the *Abu Garda* and *Kenya* decisions,[692] reiterated that the gravity criterion is not to be examined exclusively from a quantitative perspective but rather with a focus on qualitative considerations.[693] In the same vein and more explicitly, the Appeals Chamber rejected a mere reference to quantitative criteria alone as the deciding factor and concluded:

> In sum, the Appeals Chamber considers that the gravity assessment under article 17(1)(d) of the Statute must be made on a case-by-case basis. It involves a holistic evaluation of all relevant quantitative and qualitative criteria, including some of the factors relevant to the determination of the sentence of a convicted person. Quantitative criteria alone, including the number of victims, are not determinative of the gravity of a given case.[694]

With regard to the numbers of victims the AC stated that, '[i]n determining the number of victims, the number of participating victims may provide some indication of the scope of victimhood within the context of a case', even if 'quantitative criteria are not per se determinative of the gravity of a given case'.[695]

Summarizing this case law on the basis of our previous considerations in Volume II of this Treatise with regard to sentencing gravity,[696] it is fair to say that the ad hoc tribunals have taken a *case-specific approach* and considered both *quantitative* and *qualitative* factors, referring, on the one hand, to the gravity of the crime (taking into account factors such as scale, systematic character, continuing nature, genocide and rape, discriminatory nature, vulnerability of victims, manner of commission, and effects on victims), and, on the other, to the individual circumstances of the accused (taking into account, inter alia, planning, form of participation, motive, position, and role).[697] Thus, as concerns gravity, this jurisprudence has recourse to the same factors as the ones contained in Rule 145 (1)(c) RPE ICC and adopted by the ICC case law so far. While each decision ultimately depends on the concrete circumstances of the respective situation/case it is clear that the above-mentioned

[689] Ibid., paras. 46–48, 49, 51; furthermore, see *Vessels if Comoros*, ICC-01/13-111, para. 79 (stressing that '[s]cale and impact are two separate factors in the gravity assessment, which should not be confused or collapsed into one another').

[690] *Situation on the Vessels of Comoros*, ICC-01/13-34-Anx-Corr, Partly Dissenting Opinion of Judge Kovács, para. 21; in a similar vein, Knoops and Zwart, *ICLR*, 15 (2015), 1093–7, arguing that the '"social alarm" should therefore not have had any bearing on the assessment of the gravity of a case or situation'.

[691] *Situation on the Vessels of Comoros*, ICC-01/13-34-Anx-Corr, Partly Dissenting Opinion of Judge Kovács, paras. 22–3.

[692] See above note 671 ff. with main text.

[693] ICC, *Prosecutor v. Al Hassan Ag Abdoul Aziz Ag Mohamed Ag Mahmoud*, PTC I, Decision on the Admissibility Challenge raised by the Defence for Insufficient Gravity of the Case, ICC-01/12-01/18-459-tENG, 27 September 2019, para. 47 with further references ('"rather the qualitative dimension"'; '"rather the existence of some aggravating or qualitative factors"').

[694] *Al Hassan*, ICC-01/12-01/18-601-Red OA, para. 94.

[695] *Al Hassan*, ICC-01/12-01/18-601-Red 1 OA, para. 97.

[696] See above notes 678 and 679 with main text.

[697] Ambos, *Treatise ICL II* (2022), p. 336. On the distinction between gravity of the case and of the crime, see Kuczyńska, *Accusation Model ICC* (2015), pp. 88–92.

qualitative considerations, e.g. looking at the nature of the underlying conflict and the status of the suspects, may outweigh a quantitative assessment which would otherwise entail a rejection of sufficient gravity.[698] Last but not least, it is worth mentioning that the ICC's *Independent Expert Review* suggested a generally higher gravity threshold to ensure that the Court only has to 'investigate and prosecute "the most serious crimes of concern to the international community as a whole," '.[699] Yet, the Court's response was, to put it mildly, sceptical, inter alia, implying that an even higher threshold would exclude too many situations.[700]

*(ii) The own approach*

In order to understand gravity in its full meaning and to develop a consistent gravity concept, one has to start from a distinction between the two forms of gravity referred to in Article 53, that is, *legal* (non-discretionary) gravity pursuant to Articles 53 (1)(b), 17 (1)(d) ICCS and *relative* (discretionary) gravity pursuant to Article 53 (1)(c) ICCS.[701] Gravity applies, in principle, to all situations equally, independent of the trigger mechanism (Article 13 ICCS) bringing the situation before the Court.[702] Taking an even broader perspective and considering the proceedings as a whole, there is, in line with the considerations made above, only one uniform concept of gravity encompassing both pre-investigation (admissibility) and sentencing gravity.

However, legal and relative gravity, as pre-investigation thresholds, differ in that the former—as a mere admissibility criterion—conditions the Court's exercise of jurisdiction and for that reason is to be understood strictly in a legal sense while the latter constitutes—like 'interests of victims' (Article 53 (1)(c) ICCS)—a sub-criterion of the interests of justice clause thereby leaving the Prosecutor a broad discretion.[703] The gravity factors referring to

[698] On this basis, affirming gravity in the UK/Iraq situation, Schabas and El Zeidy, 'Article 17', in Ambos, *Commentary* (2022), mn. 68. Such (broader) qualitative considerations may also influence the gravity assessment of crimes committed in the occupied Palestinean territories, including the (possible) crime of transfer under Art. 8 (2)(b)(viii) ICCS; they are understated by Kontorovich, *IsLR*, 47 (2014), 388–90, 391–2 and note 649 ff. in this chapter, focusing on rather narrow considerations like the nature of the crime; in favour of a broad reading of gravity Satzger, *ICL* (2010), § 12 mn. 21 (criterion only 'exceptionally not met').

[699] Expert Group, *IER* (2020), pp. 210–11.

[700] ICC, *IER Reponse* (2021), p. 93 (formulating the 'practical question whether, if the gravity threshold were to be pitched even higher than it is now, would any of the current situations fail to meet that threshold?').

[701] This part is based on a proposal developed by my former doctoral student Ignaz Stegmiller, cf. Stegmiller, *Pre-Investigation Stage* (2011), pp. 332–5; Stegmiller, *ICLR*, 9 (2009), 561 ff. For a dual use of gravity, see also deGuzman, *FordhamILJ*, 32 (2008), 1405–6; deGuzman, *ColJTransnat'lL*, 51 (2012/13), 61–8, arguing against both a too narrow and a too broad interpretation, and calling instead for a balance of the interests *pro* and *contra* international prosecution: 'Instead, they should explain why the interests of the international community in adjudicating the case of situation are sufficiently strong to overcome whatever interests mitigate against such adjudication' (p. 68); WCRO, *Gravity* (2008), pp. 7–8, 51–7. For an autonomous gravity concept in the sense of Art. 17 (1)(d), see *Situation in DRC*, ICC-01/04-169, Separate and Partly Dissenting Opinion of Judge Pikis, para. 29. On proportionality with regard to gravity in Art. 53 (1)(c), (2)(c) and Art. 17 (1)(d), see Rohrer, *Legalitäts- oder Opportunitätsprinzip* (2010), pp. 206–7.

[702] For a different view apparently, deGuzman, *FordhamILJ*, 32 (2008), 1410–11, arguing that in case of a (Security Council or State) referral the Prosecutor '*must* initiate an investigation' of any admissible case and 'does not appear to have discretion to reject a referred situation at this preliminary stage based on a relative gravity determination' while in case of acting *proprio motu* 'upon receiving information, the Prosecutor can evaluate its seriousness and decide not to reach a decision regarding the existence of a reasonable basis when the potential cases presented are relatively less serious than other actual or potential cases available to the Court'. Yet, this would mean that even less grave cases would have to be considered admissible for the mere fact that they have been referred by a State or the Security Council. Art. 17 (1)(d) does not make this distinction. Apart from that, there is a general consensus that complementarity applies to all trigger mechanisms, including a Security Council referral; cf. thereon Stigen, *Relationship* (2008), pp. 238–45; Kleffner, *Complementarity* (2008), pp. 165–6, 213–23; Pichon, *ICLR*, 8 (2008), 188 ff.; Bothe, *Friedens-Warte*, 83 (2008), 67; Nouwen, *Complementarity* (2013), pp. 75–6; see also Hobbs, *Eyes on the ICC*, 9 (2012/13), 19, 51.

[703] On prosecutorial discretion in more detail, see Chapter IV, B.(3) in this volume.

the crimes, that is, scale, nature, and manner of commission (on impact see in a moment), constitute elements of legal gravity; in contrast, individual circumstances referring to the concrete perpetrator and his role in the crime ('most responsible'), involve subjective considerations to be taken into account when analysing the relative gravity of a concrete case.[704]

The legal–relative gravity dichotomy also determines the application of *quantitative and qualitative factors* in assessing gravity.[705] As the value and weight of qualitative factors, being vague and highly normative, are per se controversial,[706] they should primarily be applied to relative gravity and only exceptionally to legal gravity; in contrast, quantitative factors can be applied to both legal and relative gravity. The exceptional application of qualitative factors to legal gravity may be reasonable in cases where the quantitative factors alone would not overcome the admissibility threshold despite the qualitative importance of the crime, for example, in the case of a quantitatively small but qualitatively highly relevant commission of genocide as an inherently grave crime.[707] Last but not least, the *impact* criterion, albeit usually connected to crimes,[708] also belongs to relative gravity in that it refers—like impact on victims—to the 'interests of victims'[709] and even more broadly—like impact on the community and on regional peace—to policy (interest of justice) considerations.

As to the general interpretation of legal vs. relative gravity it follows that the former should be interpreted—to be understood strictly legally—narrowly with regard to the admissibility threshold, that is, the threshold should be low. It must be recalled that legal gravity was originally introduced with a broader subject matter jurisdiction of the Court (including e.g. treaty crimes) in mind.[710] Now, given the Court's limited jurisdiction over international core crimes, it may be reasonably argued that the 'definitional' gravity of the ICC crimes entails a presumption in favour of legal gravity[711] and that the additional gravity threshold is practically only relevant with regard to war crimes.[712] This would also explain and, indeed, justify the rather superficial affirmation of gravity at the pre-investigative admissibility stage by the case law discussed in the previous section. Be that as it may, a low legal gravity threshold would also reduce the risk that a lack of situational gravity hinders the investigation and prosecution of really grave cases and the ensuing crimes.[713] In contrast, relative

[704] cf. Art. 53 (2)(c) ICCS explicitly referring to the 'alleged perpetrator'.

[705] For a both quantitative and qualitative interpretation of the term complementarity, see Stigen, *Relationship* (2008), p. 188; for three visions of admissibility (complementarity), stressing correctly the respect for State sovereignty Burke-White and Kaplan, in Stahn and Sluiter, *Practice* (2009), pp. 91–101; Burke-White and Kaplan, *JICJ*, 7 (2009), 262–8.

[706] See also Osiel, *The Hague Justice Portal,* (2009), 4–5. This is the main criticism against Heller's approach (Heller, in Stahn and van den Herik, *Perspectives* (2010), pp. 229–36); on this criticism, see Osiel, in Stahn and van den Herik, *Perspectives* (2010), pp. 256 ff. pointing, in addition, to the risk of political manipulation inherent in this approach.

[707] In this sense, Heller's approach is helpful since it elaborates the argument of quantitatively small, but qualitatively important (= grave) situations; cf. Heller, in Stahn and van den Herik, *Perspectives* (2010), pp. 229–53 (esp. 234–5, 243, 249).

[708] cf. Reg. 29 (2) RegOTP referring to 'gravity of the crimes'.

[709] Art. 53 (1)(c), 53 (2)(c) ICCS.

[710] See the discussion previously in the UN-YB ILC 1994 I, 25 (para. 41) and 27 (para. 59); Draft Code 1994, UN-YB ILC 1994 II, 1, 32, 35–6. See also WCRO, *Gravity* (2008), pp. 12–17; deGuzman, *FordhamILJ*, 32 (2008), 1420–1.

[711] For a general affirmation of gravity, see Cárdenas, in Kleffner and Kor, *Complementary Views* (2006), p. 120; regarding genocide Cárdenas, *Zulässigkeitsprüfung* (2005), p. 99; Cárdenas, in Werle, *Justice in Transition* (2006), p. 244; Cárdenas, in Hankel, *Macht und Recht* (2008), p. 138. For higher gravity of genocide and crimes against humanity vis-à-vis war crimes, see Schabas, *CLF*, 19 (2008), 25–32.

[712] DeGuzman, *FordhamILJ*, 32 (2008), 1457–8.

[713] Out of this concern, WCRO, *Situation* (2009), pp. 28–36 (esp. 31, 35–6) wants to limit the application of the gravity threshold to cases (35: 'ICC should not forgo prosecuting the relevant cases solely on the ground that the situation does not involve a wider range of cases that could be prosecuted by the Court'). The same concern has been expressed by the AC, see above note 666. These concerns, however, can also be adequately addressed by a low

gravity gives the Prosecutor a broad discretion expressed by the 'interests of justice' clause and thus enables her to take out comparably less grave cases. This means that the relative gravity threshold is rather high, in any case higher than the legal gravity threshold.

Taking into account the double twofold approach explained above—on the one hand with regard to the case/situation dichotomy and, on the other hand, with regard to the one of legal and relative gravity—the following four scenarios must be distinguished:[714]

- *legal* gravity with regard to *situations* pursuant to Articles 53 (1)(b), 17 (1)(d) ICCS;
- *relative* gravity with regard to *situations* under the 'interests of justice' concept pursuant to Article 53 (1)(c) ICCS;
- *legal* gravity with regard to *cases* pursuant to Articles 53 (2)(b), 17 (1)(d) ICCS;
- *relative* gravity with regard to *cases* under the 'interests of justice' concept pursuant to Article 53 (2)(c) ICCS.

Both situation- and case-related *legal* gravity have a generally low threshold while situation- and case-related *relative* gravity call for a high, or at least higher threshold.[715] The difference between situations and cases consists only of the scope of the factual information available to the Prosecutor when assessing gravity: in the former case it refers in a still quite abstract way to all possible crimes committed in a situation, while cases refer to more specific and individualized crimes. Examining relative gravity the Prosecutor may invoke non-legal policy arguments for their decision not to initiate an investigation based on considerations of comparable gravity of situations or cases. At this stage, it is evident that a stricter selection must take place in light of the limited resources of the OTP and the Court as a whole. In any case, the Prosecutor must—finally setting aside their earlier practice of conflating legal and relative gravity—make clear when their decision is based on legal gravity as an admissibility threshold and when on relative gravity on the basis of the discretional prioritizing of situations or cases for policy ('interest of justice') reasons. In terms of the available criteria the difference is that in the latter case the Prosecutor may also have recourse to the already mentioned qualitative factors and, as to cases, individual circumstances[716] and the impact criterion. This allows them to make a comparable gravity analysis of all situations and cases before the Court. Thus, while the legal gravity test is limited to crime-related quantitative factors, the relative gravity analysis also embraces qualitative and subjective factors and thus enables the Prosecutor to concentrate the Court's resources on the most serious situations and, generally, on the most serious cases within each situation.[717] With regard to the further question of whether the PTC in *proprio motu* proceedings is to make a positive finding on the 'interest of justice' requirement (Article 53 (1)(c) ICCS),[718] the AC has found that 'the pre-trial chamber need only consider whether there is a reasonable factual basis to proceed with an investigation':[719] In particular, Article 15 ICCS 'does not refer to the interests of

threshold and/or the recourse to qualitative criteria in the sense of Heller's approach (Heller, in Stahn and van den Herik, *Perspectives* (2010), pp. 229–53).

[714] I follow here Stegmiller, *Pre-Investigation Stage* (2011), pp. 353–6, 462.
[715] See also deGuzman, *FordhamILJ*, 32 (2008), 1456, 1458, 1459–60.
[716] See Art. 53 (2)(b) ICCS.
[717] See also deGuzman, *FordhamILJ*, 32 (2008), 1459–61.
[718] cf. *Situation Afghanistan*, ICC-02/17-33, para. 35 ('scrutiny mandated to the Pre-Trial Chamber in the proceedings under article 15 is not limited to determining whether there is a reasonable basis to believe that crimes under the Court's jurisdiction have been committed, but must include a positive determination to the effect that investigations would be in the interests of justice').
[719] *Situation in Afghanistan*, ICC-02/17-138 OA4, para. 34.

justice or article 53 of the Statute';[720] moreover, Article 53 (1)(b) ICCS shows that not all the requirements of Article 53 ICCS can be meaningfully applied in the context of an Article 15 procedure;[721] furthermore, as stressed by the AC, Regulation 49 of the RegC only provides for the Prosecutor to submit information 'of a limited and very general nature' to the PTC and does not require 'to provide her reasoning (if any) or justify her conclusion regarding the interests of justice';[722] finally, the drafting history of Article 15 ICCS also runs counter to an understanding that the PTC addresses admissibility issues in the context of Article 15 (4) ICCS.[723] As a consequence of the AC's (convincing) decision the prosecution has been considerably strengthened in the context of *proprio motu* proceedings.[724]

#### (d) *Complementarity stricto sensu (Article 17 (1)(a)–(c), (2), and (3) ICCS)*

In the case of complementarity *stricto sensu*, it follows from the wording of Article 17 (1) ICCS[725] that admissibility is *presumed*[726] and that this presumption may be refuted—apart from insufficient gravity[727]—by some action (activity) on the part of the relevant State with regard to its investigation and prosecution of cases falling within the Court's jurisdiction.[728] If such action is lacking at all, that is, in the case of (total) inaction, admissibility may be presumed without extensive further reasoning.[729] If the respective State action complies with the requirements established in Article 17 (1)(a)–(c) ICCS the situation or case is inadmissible. If, however, the relevant State action indicates or entails unwillingness or inability in the sense of Article 17 (2) and (3) ICCS the situation or case must be declared admissible.

After some confusion at the beginning of the ICC's practice this test has been accepted as a *twofold test*: action (activity) first, unwillingness/inability second.[730] Of course, these two

720 *Situation in Afghanistan*, ICC-02/17-138 OA4, para. 34. For a different view insofar, Separate Opinion of Judge del Carmen Ibáñez Carranza, ICC-02/17-138-Anx-Corr OA4, 6 March 2020, para. 7 ('From the plain reading of article 53(1), there is nothing in its last sentence that restricts the application of article 53(1) to only referrals'); in the same vein, Chigowe, *LJIL*, 35 (2022), 704 adding that the drafting history of Arts. 15 and 53 (1) ICCS 'indicates that the two provisions are connected'.

721 *Situation in Afghanistan*, ICC-02/17-138 OA4, para. 40.

722 Ibid., para. 39.

723 Ibid., para. 41.

724 Crit. Chigowe, *LJIL*, 35 (2022), 718: 'Given the already existing tensions between some ICC states parties and the ICC regarding the way the *proprio motu* powers have been exercised, it is imprudent to weaken the PTC's oversight role over the Prosecutor.'

725 '[T]he Court shall determine that a case is inadmissible where ...'.

726 cf. Cárdenas, *Zulässigkeitsprüfung* (2005), p. 116; see also Meißner, *Zusammenarbeit* (2003), pp. 70–1; Kleffner, *Complementarity* (2008), pp. 104–5; Stegmiller, *Pre-Investigation Stage* (2011), pp. 289; Safferling and Farthofer, *International Criminal Procedure* (2012), pp. 99–100; Kelly, *GeoJIL*, 48 (2017), 812. *Contra*, apparently, Gómez Pardo, *Revista Debate Interamericano* [2009], 141 without however analysing Art. 17 properly.

727 Art. 17 (1)(d).

728 Art. 17 (1)(a)–(c) ICCS.

729 For references, see below note 741.

730 cf. *Gaddafi*, ICC-01/11-01/11-344-Red, para. 58: 'Article 17 (1)(a) of the Statute contemplates a two-step test, according to which the Chamber, in considering an admissibility challenge, shall address in turn two questions: (i) whether, at the time of the proceedings in respect of an admissibility challenge, there is an ongoing investigation or prosecution of the case at the national level; and, in case the answer to the first question is in the affirmative, (ii) whether the State is unwilling or unable genuinely to carry out such investigation or prosecution' (but later examining inability although inactivity had been found, paras. 134–5, 137–8). See also *Katanga*, ICC-01/04-01/07-1497, paras. 1, 75–9 (25 September 2009) (para. 78: 'To do otherwise would be to put the cart before the horse'); *Muthaura et al.*, ICC-01/09-02/11-274, para. 40; *Ruto et al.*, ICC-01/09-01/11-307, para. 41; *S. Gbagbo*, ICC-02/11-01/12-75, para. 27; *Gaddafi*, ICC-01/11-01/11-547-Red, para. 213; *Yekatom*, ICC-01/14-01/18-493, para. 17; *Situation Philippines*, ICC-01/21-56-Red, para. 11. Summarizing the case law, Schabas and El Zeidy, 'Article 17', in Ambos, *Commentary* (2022), mn. 24–32; Batros, in Guariglia et al., *AC ICC Commentary* (2018), pp. 72–4; ICC-OTP, *Complementarity and Cooperation* (2024), para. 147 ff. As to the scholarly debate, see El Zeidy, *Complementarity* (2008), p. 161; Robinson, *CLF*, 21 (2010), 102; Robinson, in Stahn and El Zeidy, *Complementarity I* (2011), pp. 463 ff.; Hansen, *MelbJIL*, 13 (2012), 219–23; Jurdi, *SAYbIL*, 34 (2009), 29–30;

limbs of the admissibility test are 'intimately and inextricably linked', especially as concerns the evidence presented by a State to demonstrate sufficient investigatory activity.[731] In any case, starting from this twofold test, the full complementarity *stricto sensu* test may be structured in a threefold way, distinguishing at the level of activity between a priori inaction and a posteriori action (see Figure 5):[732]

- First, situations and cases are admissible if the State remains inactive (*admissibility due to total State inaction*, sub-section (i) in this section);
- Secondly, if the State develops some activity, a case may be inadmissible pursuant to Articles 17 (1)(a)–(c) and 20 (3) ICCS (*inadmissibility due to State action*, subsection (ii) in this section);
- Thirdly, as an exception to the inadmissibility mentioned before, despite or because of the State activity, unwillingness or inability on the part of the State is established pursuant to Article 17 (2) and (3) ICCS (*admissibility due to unwillingness or inability*, subsection (iii) in this section).

### (i) *Admissibility due to total State inaction*

International treaty and customary law provides for a general duty of States to investigate, prosecute, and punish international core crimes.[733] While this duty, mainly derived from human rights law,[734] preceded the existence of the ICC regime, it has been reinforced with

Burke-White and Kaplan, in Stahn and Sluiter, *Practice* (2009), pp. 86–7; Burke-White and Kaplan, *JICJ*, 7 (2009), 260; Marong, *GeorgiaJI&CompL*, 40 (2011/12), 76; Nouwen, in Brown, *Handbook ICL* (2011), pp. 209–12; Nouwen, *Complementarity* (2013), pp. 43–5; Abdou, 'Article 17', in Klamberg et al., *Commentary ICC I* (2023), pp. 601–2; Brighton, *ICLR*, 12 (2012), 635–40, distinguishing two tiers (activity and unwillingness/inability) with three elements (activity, unwillingness, and inability), i.e. subdistinguishing the second tier; Nouwen and Lewis, in Sluiter et al., *International Criminal Procedure* (2013), p. 123; Bo, *CLF*, 25 (2014), 507; Heller, *Opinio Juris* 24 May 2024. Interestingly, the current Spanish Law on Universal Jurisdiction (which, in fact, abolished universal jurisdiction) copied the wording of Art. 17 (2) and (3) ICCS (Ley Orgánica 1/2014, de 13 de marzo, de modificación de la Ley Orgánica 6/1985, de 1 de Julio, del Poder Judicial, relativa a la justicia universal, *Boletín Oficial del Estado*, no. 63, 14 March 2014, section I, p. 23026, Art. 1 para. 5); for the development, see Cancio M., in Topuridze, *Issues* (2021), 226 ff.

[731] cf. *Al-Senussi*, ICC-01/11-01/11-466-Red, para. 210, arguing that evidence demonstrating the 'genuineness' of national investigations may be 'relevant for both limbs'; similarly *Prosecutor v. Simone Gbagbo*, PTC I, Decision on Côte d'Ivoire's Challenge to the Admissibility of the Case against Simone Gbagbo, ICC-02/11-01/12-47-Red, 11 December 2014, para. 30.

[732] cf. Stegmiller, *Pre Investigation Stage* (2011), pp. 289–302, 461; Stegmiller, *CLF*, 20 (2010), 159–74; Stegmiller, *CLF*, 24 (2013), 484 and 495.

[733] See Ambos, in Ambos et al., *Building a Future* (2009), pp. 29–31, para. 8; Ambos, in Haldemann and Unger, *Impunity* (2018), pp. 205 ff.; see also Rastan, in Stahn and El Zeidy, *Complementarity I* (2011), p. 449.

[734] It has been, most prominently, developed by the IACtHR since the seminal case of *Velásquez-Rodríguez v. Honduras*, Serie C No. 4, Judgment (29 July 1988), paras. 162 ff., 166, 174, and since then several times confirmed; see more recently Gómez Virula y Otros v. Guatemala, Serie C No. 393, Judgment (21 November 2019), paras, 56, 64, 65; Maidanik y Otros *v.* Uruguay, Serie C No. 444, Judgment (15 November 2021), paras. 136, 137, 138, 139, 151, 211; Digna Ochoa y Familiares *v.* México, Serie C No. 447, Judgment (25 November 2021), paras. 98, 99, 221; *Pavez Pavez v. Chile*, Serie C No. 449, Judgment (4 February 2022), paras. 104–6; *Sales Pimenta v. Brasil*, Serie C No. 454, Judgment (30 June 2022), paras. 82 ff.; *Flores Bedregal y otras v. Bolivia*, Serie C No. 467, Judgment (17 October 2022), para. 100; *Baraona Bray v. Chile*, Serie C No. 481, Judgment (24 November 2022), para. 33; *Aguinaga Aillón v. Ecuador*, Serie C No. 483, Judgment (30 January 2023) para. 67; *Núñez Naranjo y otros v. Ecuador*, Serie C No. 492, (23 May 2023), paras. 106, 131; *Comunidad Garífuna de San Juan y sus miembros v. Honduras*, Serie C No. 496. Judgment (29 August 2023) paras. 120, 154, 176; *Baptiste y otros v. Haití*, Serie C No. 503. Judgment (1 September 2023), para. 75; *Córdoba v. Paraguay*, Serie C No. 505, Judgment (4 September 2023), para. 16; for earlier case law, see previous edition p. 297 with note 662. The ECtHR has adopted the same view: see *Marguš v. Croatia*, Application No. 4455/10, Judgment (27 May 2014), paras. 125, 127 (with references to previous case law); Olewnik-Cieplińska *v.* Poland, Application No. 20147/15, Judgment (5 December 2019),

regard to the Statute crimes and the State Parties.[735] Consequently, if a State Party remains inactive in the face of genocide, crimes against humanity, war crimes, or the crime of aggression[736] within the meaning of Articles 5 to 8*bis* ICCS, it fails to comply with its duty flowing both from the Statute and from general international law. This inaction alone must then make, as already said above,[737] the case admissible under Article 17 ICCS.[738] This also follows, as correctly held by the *Lubanga* PTC,[739] from an *a contrario* interpretation of Article 17 (1)(a)–(c), for, as this provision requires at least some action (initial investigative steps)[740] for a case to be declared inadmissible, no action whatsoever makes the case admissible without further ado.[741]

paras. 135, 136; Makuchyan and Minasyan v. Azerbaijan and Hungary, Application No. *17247/13, Judgment (12 October 2020), paras. 48, 154–7;* Ribcheva and Others *v.* Bulgaria, Applications Nos. 37801/16 and 2 others, Judgment (30 June 2021), para. 125 ('effective official investigation'). See also HRCt, General Comment No. 31 (UN Doc. CCPR/C/21/Rev.1/Add.13 (2004)), paras. 10, 15, 18 (deriving this duty from the positive obligation to protect human rights, esp. the rights to life and physical integrity; responsible to be 'brought to justice'); General Comment No. 36 (UN Doc. CCPR/C/GC/36 (2019)), paras. 21–3, 27, 63; General Comment No. 37 (UN Doc. CCPR/C/GC/37 (2020)), para. 90 ('obligation to investigate effectively, impartially and in a timely manner any allegation or reasonable suspicion of unlawful use of force or other violations by law enforcement officials).

[735] Ambos, in Ambos et al., *Building a Future* (2009), p. 31, para. 8. This position has been reaffirmed by the ICC Kampala Review Conference; see the document on Review Conference, 'Complementarity' (8 June 2010) (RC/Res. 1), Preamble recital 3 (stating that '[international crimes] must not go unpunished and . . . their effective prosecution must be ensured by taking measures at the national level'), and para. 1 ('[Recognizing] the primary responsibility of States to investigate and prosecute the most serious crimes of international concern'), <https://asp.icc-cpi.int/sites/asp/files/asp_docs/Resolutions/RC-Res.1-ENG.pdf>; similarly the sixth preambular recital of the ICCS ('duty of every State to exercise its criminal jurisdiction'); on the review conference in this regard, see Bergsmo, Bekou, and Jones, *GoJIL*, 2 (2010), 797–803. On the duty to prosecute and complementarity, see also Politi, in Stahn and El Zeidy, *Complementarity I* (2011), pp. 144–5; Krings, *GoJIL*, 4 (2012), 749; on the (in)compatibility of the duty to prosecute with the 'inactivity' criterion, see Schabas, in Stahn and El Zeidy, *Complementarity I* (2011), pp. 158–64; crit. of any relevance of such a duty with regard to the national proceedings requirement, Robinson, in Stahn and El Zeidy, *Complementarity I* (2011), pp. 495–8; generally crit. of such a duty, based on the ICCS, Nouwen, *Complementarity* (2011), pp. 18–19, 36–40, arguing that complementarity could only have 'a catalysing effect on normative grounds', in that regard; Nouwen, in Brown, *Handbook ICL* (2011), pp. 214–16.

[736] On complementarity with regard to the crime of aggression, see Clark, in Stahn and El Zeidy, *Complementarity II* (2011), pp. 721–44; Trahan, *CornILJ*, 45 (2013), 569–601, concerned about states being 'all too willing' to prosecute (583–5, 594–601); van Schaak, *JICJ*, 10 (2012), 133–64, advocating primacy of the ICC in case of aggression.

[737] Above note 729 and main text.

[738] cf. Benzing, *MPYbUNL*, 7 (2003), 105, 115; Boas et al., *International Criminal Procedure* (2011), pp. 73–8 (reviewing jurisprudence).

[739] *Lubanga*, ICC-01/04-01/06-1-Corr-Red, para. 29 with n. 19.

[740] Kleffner, *Complementarity* (2008), p. 105; Robinson, in Stahn and El Zeidy, *Complementarity I* (2011), pp. 463 ff., arguing that Art. 17 expressly requires national proceedings.

[741] *Lubanga*, ICC-01/04-01/06-1-Corr-Red, para. 29 with n. 19; *Situation in the DRC*, ICC-01/04-02/06-20-Anx2, para. 41; *Kony et al.*, ICC-02/04-01/05-377, para. 44; *Katanga*, ICC-01/04-01/07-1497, para. 78; *S. Gbagbo*, ICC-02/11-01/12-75, para. 30; *Yekatom*, ICC-01/14-01/18-493, para. 17; see previously ICC-OTP, *Complementarity* (2003), paras. 17–18 ('First, the most straightforward scenario is where no State has initiated any investigation (the inaction scenario). In such a scenario, none of the alternatives of Articles 17 (1)(a)–(c) are satisfied and there is no impediment to admissibility. Thus, there is no need to examine the factors of unwillingness or inability; the case is simply admissible under the clear terms of Article 17'); similarly ICC-OTP, *Prelim. Examinations* (2013), para. 47. See also Stigen, *Relationship* (2008), p. 201; Kleffner, *Complementarity* (2008), pp. 104–5, 342; El Zeidy, *Complementarity* (2008), pp. 106, 161, 230, 318; Schabas, *CLF*, 19 (2008), 7–8; Schabas and El Zeidy, 'Article 17', in Ambos, *Commentary* (2022), mn. 28; O'Keefe, *ICL* (2015), pp. 556 ('*ipso facto* admissible', [emphasis in the original]); Stahn, *CLF*, 19 (2008), 105–6; Carnero Rojo, *LJIL*, 18 (2005), 833; Ambos, in Ambos et al., *Building a Future* (2009), p. 72, para. 37; Robinson, in Stahn and El Zeidy, *Complementarity I* (2011), pp. 463 ff., stressing the national proceedings requirement; Schabas, in Stahn and El Zeidy, *Complementarity I* (2011), pp. 158–64 (p. 161: 'unwritten third criterion'); Buchan, *CLF*, 25 (2014), 491–2; crit. Reisman and Arsanjani, *AJIL*, 99 (2005), 385–403; Schabas, *JICJ*, 6 (2008), 757; anticritique (esp. *contra* Reisman and Arsanjani), Robinson, in Stahn and El Zeidy, *Complementarity I* (2011), pp. 478–83, 487–8.

In practice, the inaction scenario has been confirmed. The OTP relies heavily on the dichotomy of inaction–some action[742] and alleges an '*uncontested admissibility*' in the former case.[743] Given the strict same case/person/conduct test[744] inaction also ensues if there are investigations or prosecutions for a different conduct and/or against different persons.[745] PTC I held in *Lubanga* that 'in the absence of any acting State, the Chamber need not make any analysis of unwillingness or inability'.[746] PTC II confirmed the admissibility of the case against Kony et al., invoking the Court's *proprio motu* powers under Article 19 (1) ICCS, because the scenario of 'total inaction' has not substantially changed, given that the February 2008 Agreement and its Annex providing for the establishment of a special division of the Ugandan High Court had, at the time of the decision, still not been implemented.[747] Thus, it is settled that if no State[748] is acting in relation to the specific case under investigation at the ICC, a further analysis of unwillingness or inability is not warranted.[749] In *Katanga*, the AC acknowledged this kind of automatic admissibility on the basis of inaction without

[742] cf. Seils and Wierda, 'ICC and Conflict Mediation' (2005), p. 6; Burke-White, *HarvILJ*, 49 (2008), 78; regarding the Darfur investigation, see Pichon, *ICLR*, 8 (2008), 219–20; generally crit. of the operation of complementarity insofar, Fouladvand, *ICLR*, 14 (2014), 1028, 1050 ff.

[743] See e.g. ICC-OTP, *Eighth Report UNSC* (2008), para. 13 (Prosecution cases admissible for lack of 'proceedings in the Sudan against Ahmad Harun and Ali Abd-Al-Rahman, against Omar Al Bashir, or against the three rebel commanders of the Haskanita attack'); more recently ICC-OTP, *Prelim. Examinations* (2013), para. 47 ('absence of national proceedings, i.e. domestic inactivity, … sufficient to make the case admissible'). See also Sheng, *ILSAJICL*, 13 (2006/2007), 419; Schabas, in Stahn and Sluiter, *Practice* (2009), pp. 236–7; Schabas and El Zeidy, 'Article 17', in Ambos, *Commentary* (2022), mn. 285–32; crit. of the potential abuse by State Parties, by remaining inactive and self-referring situations to the ICC in the expectation that it will only prosecute their enemies, Schabas, in Stahn and El Zeidy, *Complementarity I* (2011), p. 163 ('*ad hominem* prosecution'); in favour of the *inaction* approach also in self-referral cases, Stegmiller, *Pre-Investigation Stage* (2011), pp. 136–7; Bock, *Opfer* (2010), p. 296; Greenawalt, in deGuzman and Oosterveld, *Elgar Companion ICC* (2020), pp. 68–70.

[744] See Section B.(2)(b) in this chapter.

[745] Boas et al., *International Criminal Procedure* (2011), p. 75; see also Nouwen and Lewis, in Sluiter et al., *International Criminal Procedure* (2013), pp. 123–4.

[746] *Situation in the DRC*, ICC-01/04-02/06-20-Anx2, para. 41. On this case, see Smith, *ICLR*, 8 (2008), 335–6; El Zeidy, *Complementarity* (2008), pp. 228–32.

[747] *Kony et al.*, ICC-02/04-01/05-377, para. 52. Meanwhile an 'International Crimes Division' has been established at the High Court of Uganda; cf. thereon, 'The High Court [International Crimes Division] Practice Directions, 2011', Legal Notice 10/2011, *Uganda Gazette* No. 38 Vol CIV (31 May 2011) and Uganda implemented the ICCS into national law (International Criminal Court Act, Act 11/2010, *Uganda Gazette* No. 39 Vol CIII [25 June 2010]). Still, the Amnesty Act 2000 (Laws of Uganda, vol. XII, ch. 294, [21 January 2000]) impedes any prosecution of conflict-related crimes by this or any other Ugandan judicial entity. In fact, this amnesty law grants full immunity from prosecution to any LRA rebel who 'renounces and abandons involvement in the war or armed rebellion' (s. 4 (1)), being the withdrawal from fighting an inherent condition of any amnesty. According to *Avocats sans Frontières* et al. (2022), para. 62, there is a complete lack of prosecutions/convictions due to the amnesty. For a discussion of the Ugandan situation, see Burke-White and Kaplan, in Stahn and Sluiter, *Practice* (2009), pp. 79–84, 103–8; Burke-White and Kaplan, *JICJ*, 7 (2009), 257–9, 270–4; Peschke, in Brown, *Handbook ICL* (2011), pp. 178–205; Seils, in Stahn and El Zeidy, *Complementarity II* (2011), pp. 1000–3; Marong, *GeorgiaJI&CompL*, 40 (2011/12), 67–103; Wierda and Otim, in Stahn and El Zeidy, *Complementarity II* (2011), 1155–79; Nouwen, in Stahn and El Zeidy, *Complementarity II* (2011), 1120–54; Nouwen, *Complementarity* (2013), pp. 111–243, identifying seven catalysing effects of complementarity (141 ff., 243), but no increase in domestic prosecutions (33, 228 ff., 234); Pinto Soares, *IsLR*, 46 (2013), 324–6; Tillier, *ICLR*, 13 (2013), 522–6; Roach, *ICLR*, 13 (2013), 249–68; Maunganidze and du Plessis, in Stahn, *Practice* (2015), pp. 77–9; Wierda, *Impact* (2023), pp. 92 ff., 129 ff., 141–2, 150 ff., 201 ff., 218 ff.; on amnesties in the African context, see Eberechi, *AfrJICompL*, 20 (2012), 25–9.

[748] On the relevance of quasi-criminal proceedings carried out by non-State actors, see Kleffner, in Stahn and El Zeidy, *Complementarity II* (2011), pp. 707–20, distinguishing between Arts. 17 (1)(a), (b) and 17 (1)(c), 20 (3) ICCS and arguing that only the latter recognize non-State prosecutions, while the wording of the former ('by a State', pp. 716–18) excludes this possibility; in any case, on a policy level, the OTP should take into account all non-State investigations within its discretion (pp. 718–20). De facto authorities established or supported by another State 'are not capable of meeting' the complementarity requirements, cf. *Situation Georgia*, ICC-01/15-12, para. 41 (regard the authorities of South Ossetia in Georgia).

[749] See ICC-OTP, *Prelim. Examinations* (2013), para. 47; Abdou, 'Article 17', in Klamberg et al., *Commentary ICC I* (2023), pp. 610–11; previously, Ambos, in Bohlander, *International Criminal Justice* (2007), p. 448; El Zeidy, *Complementarity* (2008), p. 161.

analysing in-depth unwillingness or inability;[750] further, it was argued that this does not affect an additional determination of *ne bis in idem* and gravity in accordance with Article 17 (1)–(c) and (d) ICCS.[751] This was confirmed by subsequent case law.[752]

As to the *burden of proof*, it is clear that it falls on the State that advocates sufficient investigatory activity,[753] or on the individual challenging admissibility.[754] The *standard of proof* was discussed, for the first time, in the *Kenya* situation: PTC II demanded 'concrete evidence' of investigatory and prosecutorial activities and considered unsubstantiated claims of ongoing national investigations as insufficient.[755] This was confirmed and further developed by the Appeals Chamber holding that 'the State must provide the Court with evidence of a sufficient degree of specificity and probative value that demonstrates that it is indeed investigating the case. It is not sufficient merely to assert that investigations are ongoing.'[756] In the cases of *Gaddafi* and *Al-Senussi* the AC confirmed this standard.[757]

[750] *Katanga*, ICC-01/04-01/07-1497, para. 78 ('To do otherwise would be to put the cart before the horse').

[751] *Katanga and Chui*, ICC-01/04-01/07-1213-tEng, paras. 21, 81; *Katanga*, ICC-01/04-01/07-1497, paras. 73, 96–7, 111–13.

[752] *Prosecutor v. Bemba*, ICC-01/05-01/08-962-Corr, AC Judgment on the Appeal of Mr Jean-Pierre Bemba Gombo against the Decision of Trial Chamber III of 24 June 2010 Entitled 'Decision on the Admissibility and Abuse of Process Challenges', paras. 74, 107–9 (19 October 2010); also *Gaddafi*, ICC-01/11-01/11-547-Red, para. 213; *Al-Senussi*, ICC-01/11-01/11-565, para. 68; *S. Gbagbo*, ICC-02/11-01/12-75, para. 30; *Situation Georgia*, ICC-01/15-12, para. 41 (no 'further progress of relevant national proceedings' by Georgian authorities and thus 'situation of inactivity'); *Yekatom*, ICC-01/14-01/18-493, para. 17 ('in the case of inactivity, the question of unwillingness and inability does not arise').

[753] cf. *Muthaura et al.*, ICC-01/09-02/11-274, para. 2, 61; *Ruto et al.*, ICC-01/09-01/11-307, para. 62; confirmed in *Gaddafi*, ICC-01/11-01/11-344-Red, para. 52; see also *Al-Senussi*, ICC-01/11-01/11-466-Red, para. 66 (v), (vi); *S. Gbagbo*, ICC-02/11-01/12-75, paras. 29, 128; for further references, see Schabas and El Zeidy, 'Article 17', in Ambos, *Commentary* (2022), mn. 38–9. See also El Zeidy, *Complementarity* (2008), p. 163; Abdou, 'Article 17', in Klamberg et al., *Commentary ICC I* (2023), pp. 603–9, 612–3; ICC-OTP, *Complementarity* (2003), paras. 54 and 56 (indicating examples of a shifting of the burden).

[754] *Gaddafi*, ICC-01/11-01/11-662, para. 32.

[755] ICC, *Prosecutor v. Muthaura et al.*, PTC II, Decision on the Application by the Government of Kenya Challenging the Admissibility of the Case pursuant to Article 19 (2)(b) of the Statute, ICC-01/09-02/11-96, 30 May 2011, para. 60 ('concrete evidence' of 'current initiatives' of 'investigative activities' necessary, mere reliance on 'judicial reform actions', insufficient); *Prosecutor v. Ruto et al.*, PTC II, Decision on the Application by the Government of Kenya Challenging the Admissibility of the Case pursuant to Article 19 (2)(b) of the Statute, ICC-01/09-02/11-101, 30 May 2011, para. 64. On this, see also Hansen, *MelbJIL*, 13 (2012), 225–7.

[756] *Muthaura et al.*, ICC-01/09-02/11-274, paras. 2, 61–2; *Ruto et al.*, ICC-01/09-01/11-307, paras. 2, 62–3, providing 'tangible proof', 'sufficient degree of specificity and probative value'. See also *Muthaura et al.*, ICC-01/09-02/11-342, Dissenting Opinion of Judge Ušacka, paras. 21, 24, 28, arguing that PTC II should have requested additional information from Kenya instead of dismissing the admissibility challenge without further ado. Crit. of the Kenyan decisions, Brighton, *ICLR*, 12 (2012), 663–4, arguing that 'the interpretation and application of the law ... appears to have been influenced by political considerations and concerns' and was 'incorrect and inappropriate' (p. 664). See also Sriram and Brown, *ICLR*, 12 (2012), 232–4, seeing a 'missed opportunity', in the failure to take into account the Kenyan Truth, Justice and Reconciliation Commission with regard to admissibility (p. 234); furthermore, see Bachmann and Nwibo Eda, *Brook. J.Int'l. L*, 43 (2018), 486.

[757] *Gaddafi*, ICC-01/11-01/11-547-Red, para. 116 (State 'must support its statement with tangible proof to demonstrate that it is actually carrying out relevant investigations'), following *Muthaura et al.*, ICC-01/09-02/11-96, para. 60 and *Ruto et al.*, ICC-01/09-02/11-101, para. 64; see also para. 178 (burden of proof on Libya), 205 (discussing and following the PTC's considerations); see also *Al-Senussi*, ICC-01/11-01/11-565, para. 166 (holding that 'a State challenging admissibility needs to prove ... that it is conducting a genuine investigation or prosecution—which requires proof of both limbs of the provision'); see also *Gaddafi*, ICC-01/11-01/11-344-Red, paras. 54, 66 (vii); *Gaddafi*, ICC-01/11-01/11-662, para. 32; *Situation in Afghanistan*, ICC-02/17-33, para. 72; *contra*, *Gaddafi*, ICC-01/11-01/11-547-Anx2, Dissenting Opinion Judge Ušacka, paras. 60–1, arguing that it is unfair to impose the burden of proof only on the State and not the other participants as well; but this begs the question how other participants can get hold of information about domestic proceedings; see also *S. Gbagbo*, ICC-02/11-01/12-75, paras. 28, 122, 128. On the potential evidentiary submissions, see *Al-Senussi*, ICC-01/11-01/11-466-Red, para. 66 (viii), referring to *Prosecutor v. Gaddafi and Al-Senussi*, PTC I, Decision Requesting Further Submissions on Issues Related to the Admissibility of the Case against Saif Al-Islam Gaddafi, ICC-01/11-01/11-239, 7 December 2012, paras. 10–11. Crit. Newton, *IsLR* 54 (2021), 153 (arguing that '*Gaddafi* and *al-Senussi* holdings effectively amended Article 17' given that it follows from this provision 'that a case is inadmissible unless the decisions of the domestic state are non-compliant with the statutory test').

While inaction is primarily an empirical, not a normative, concept,[758] it is not limited to factual scenarios of inaction, but also extends to *'normative' inaction* in the narrow sense, that is, situations where inactivity is due to normative (procedural) obstacles,[759] in particular a blanket amnesty, as the Ugandan Amnesty Act 2000 already mentioned above.[760] While such obstacles impeding the investigation and prosecution of international core crimes are under international law generally inadmissible,[761] with regard to complementarity two situations may arise: first, a (substantive) investigation is *a limine* precluded since the investigative organs are only authorized to apply the respective procedural obstacle to the case at hand and terminate the proceedings if it is applicable; this case can be considered as one of (a priori) inaction.[762] Secondly, some investigative steps are undertaken and it is then decided not to prosecute the case (a posteriori inaction).[763] This case falls under Article 17 (1)(b) ICCS[764] and its admissibility depends on the unwillingness or inability test to be analysed in the following section.[765]

*(ii) Inadmissibility due to State action (Article 17 (1)(a)–(c) and Article 20 (3) ICCS)*

By distinguishing between investigation,[766] prosecution,[767] and trial[768] the provision aims to cover *all procedural stages* from investigation to the actual court trial. The criteria are considered to be exhaustive.[769] The distinction in the various procedural stages corresponds to the different moments of application of possible exemptions from prosecution or punishment. An amnesty, for example, normally impedes, as just discussed, a prosecution[770] or even an investigation,[771] while a pardon is a typical post-conviction exemption only

[758] Ambos, in Ambos, Large, and Wierda, *Building a Future* (2009), p. 72, para. 37.

[759] See also ICC-OTP, *Policy Paper Preliminary Examinations* (2013), para. 48.

[760] See note 747 in this chapter. See also Ambos, *Colombian Peace Process* (2010), pp. 55 ff.; Stegmiller, *Pre-Investigation Stage* (2011), pp. 289 ff., 409 ff.; Schabas, in Brown, *Handbook ICL* (2011), pp. 374 ff., 381 ff.; King, *GeoWashILR*, 41 (2010), 577; Jurdi, *ICC* (2011), p. 37; Batros, *LJIL*, 23 (2010), 353 ff.; Robinson, *CLF*, 21 (2010), 67 ff.; differentiating SáCouto and Cleary, *LJIL*, 23 (2010), 364, 368 ff.; cf. also Stahn, *LJIL*, 23 (2010), 315 ff.; crit., Reisman and Arsanjani, *AJIL*, 99 (2005), 390–1; on the African context, see Eberechi, *AfrJICompL*, 20 (2012), 25 ff.

[761] For a discussion with regard to amnesties, see Ambos, *Treatise ICL I* (2021), pp. 516 ff. with further references, distinguishing between blanket—inadmissible—and conditional—potentially admissible—amnesties. The ICCS is silent on the matter; see also Nouwen, *Complementarity* (2013), p. 18 (at best discouraging effect by complementarity). As regards the case law, see *Gaddafi*, ICC-01/11-01/11-695, para. 96 ('international law is still in the developmental stage on the question of acceptability of amnesties'); *Gaddafi*, ICC-01/11-01/11-662, para. 61 ('strong, growing, universal tendency that grave and systematic human rights violations—which may amount to crimes against humanity by their very nature—are not subject to amnesties or pardons under international law').

[762] Ambos, in Ambos et al., *Building a Future* (2009), pp. 75–6, para. 40; see also Stigen, *Relationship* (2008), p. 322; Kleffner, *Complementarity* (2008), p. 264; Razesberger, *Complementarity* (2006), p. 160; Burke-White and Kaplan, in Stahn and Sluiter, *Practice* (2009), p. 104 (regarding Uganda); Burke-White and Kaplan, *JICJ*, 7 (2009), 271; Olásolo, in Almqvist and Espósito, *Iustitia Transicional* (2009), p. 270.

[763] For the *a priori–a posteriori* distinction, see Olásolo, *Triggering Procedure* (2005), pp. 149–50, 166; Olásolo, in Almqvist and Espósito, *Justitia Transicional* (2009), pp. 260–1; furthermore, see Zakerhossein, *Situation* (2017), pp. 291–3 on instances of *a posteriori* inaction.

[764] See also Benzing, *MPYbUNL*, 7 (2003), 601 with n. 50; Kleffner, *Complementarity* (2008), p. 264; Werle, 'Transitional Justice', in Müller et al., *FS Eisenberg* (2009), p. 804; Olásolo, in Almqvist and Espósito, *Justitia Transicional* (2009), pp. 271 ff.

[765] Similarly ICC-OTP, *Policy Prelim. Examinations* (2013), para. 49.

[766] Art. 17 (1)(a) ICCS; cf. thereon Abdou, 'Article 17', in Klamberg et al., *Commentary ICC I* (2023), pp. 603–9.

[767] Art. 17 (1)(b) ICCS; cf. also Abdou, 'Article 17', in Klamberg et al., *Commentary ICC I* (2023), pp. 610–11.

[768] Art. 17 (1)(c) referring to Art. 20 (3) ICCS.

[769] At first sight, the text seems to leave this question open. However, no open wording—like 'including'—was used that would have indicated a non-exhaustive nature of the criteria, and, moreover, the word 'considers' has been interpreted as deliberately limiting the criteria to the mentioned factors; cf. Benzing, *MPYbUNL*, 7 (2003), 606; Meißner, *Zusammenarbeit* (2003), pp. 72–3; Gropengießer and Meißner, *ICLR*, 5 (2005), 282; Kleffner, *Complementarity* (2008), p. 104; Nouwen, *Complementarity* (2013), p. 69; Schabas and El Zeidy, 'Article 17', in Ambos, *Commentary* (2022), mn. 73.

[770] Art. 17 (1)(b).

[771] Art. 17 (1)(a).

applicable after a trial;[772] such a post-conviction measure can hardly constitute a ground for admissibility since it will be difficult to demonstrate that it was taken to shield the person concerned from criminal responsibility.[773]

The implicit *temporal distinction* as to the procedural stage of the investigation[774] is of secondary importance since ultimately the admissibility depends on the unwillingness and the inability test referred to in both subparagraphs (a) and (b) and also in subparagraph (c) of Article 17 by way of the reference to the 'upwards' *ne bis in idem*[775] in Article 20 (3) ICCS.[776] The Court will always have to assess the State's unwillingness/inability at the moment of its decision, that is, it is possible that subsequent/new State activity, after the Prosecutor's start of an investigation, retroactively revokes the basis of a previous admissibility decision.[777] While this is challenging for the Prosecutor, it gives States in transition processes a certain flexibility to catch up and comply with the demands of the ICC Statute.[778]

At any rate, the provision presupposes, as already explained above, some *State action*,[779] more concretely that the case is 'being investigated or prosecuted'[780] and, if there is enough evidence, ultimately tried.[781] The investigation and prosecution requirements must be read together[782] since, in any case, once an investigation is finished a decision to prosecute or not to prosecute must be taken. In other words, while an investigation in the sense of subparagraph (a) may block the intervention of the ICC for a certain period of time (namely, as long as the case is 'being investigated'), afterwards a decision in favour of or against prosecution must be taken and in this precise moment Article 17 (1)(b) ICCS becomes applicable.[783] In the case of a decision in favour of prosecution the decision-making authority shifts to the trial judge[784] and Article 17 (1)(c) ICCS becomes applicable. A decision not to

[772] Art. 17 (1) (c); see also Ambos, in Ambos et al., *Building a Future* (2009), p. 74, para. 39; see also Stigen, *Relationship* (2008), pp. 429–30, discussing amnesty.

[773] Art. 17 (1)(c) in connection with Art. 20 (3)(a) ICCS. See also Stigen, *Relationship* (2008), pp. 334–5; Kleffner, *Complementarity* (2008), pp. 266–7, criticizing the respective lacuna of Art. 17 in case of clemency measures without retroactive effect as to the validity of the conviction.

[774] See Ambos, in Ambos et al., *Building a Future* (2009), p. 73, para. 38.

[775] El Zeidy, *MichJIL*, 23 (2002), 931; Kleffner, *Complementarity* (2008), pp. 118–19; Meyer, *ICLR*, 6 (2006), 554; van den Wyngaert and Ongena, in Cassese et al., *Rome Statute I* (2002), pp. 724 ff. See also Boas et al., *International Criminal Procedure* (2011), pp. 81–2; Nouwen and Lewis, in Sluiter et al., *International Criminal Procedure* (2013), p. 125.

[776] I made this point less forcefully earlier in Ambos, in Ambos et al., *Building a Future* (2009), p. 74, para. 39. For this reason it is, for example, of secondary importance if the investigation must be completed (see Kleffner, *Complementarity* (2008), p. 117) or, with regard to Art. 17 (1)(c), the local remedies be exhausted (Kleffner, *Complementarity* (2008), pp. 124–5).

[777] cf. Pichon, *ICLR*, 8 (2008), 199–200.

[778] cf. Akhavan, *JICJ*, 14 (2016), 1044 ff. ('complementarity is a complex compromise between the unyielding exigencies of expeditious and fair trials on the one hand, and the humbling realities of messy transitions on the other'), therefore advocating sufficient time for domestic jurisdictions (1047: 'the ICC should avoid to rush to a judgment'); conc. Bachmann and Nwibo Eda, *Brook. J.Int'L.* 43 (2018), 487–8 ('Justice therefore demands that post-conflict societies be given more time and resources to satisfy these admissibility conditions in terms of institutional capacity building, as part of a wider post-conflict transformation process').

[779] Benzing, *MPYbUNL*, 7 (2003), 600–1 with n. 48; Kleffner, 'Complementarity as Catalyst', in Kleffner and Kor, *Complementary Views* (2006), pp. 79, 82.

[780] Art. 17 (1)(a) ICCS.

[781] HRW, 'Benchmarks' (May 2007), 4–10 requires, apart from credible, impartial, and independent investigation and prosecution and penalties that reflect the gravity of the crimes, also the rigorous adherence to international fair trial standards. The trial conditions are however irrelevant for the question of admissibility, cf. *Katanga and Chui*, ICC-01/04-01/07-1213-tEng, para. 84.

[782] See Ambos, in Ambos et al., *Building a Future* (2009), p. 74, para. 39; in a similar vein, Nouwen, *Complementarity* (2013), p. 60 ('followed by prosecution').

[783] This temporal aspect has apparently been overlooked by Cárdenas, *Zulässigkeitsprüfung* (2005), pp. 159–65, who distinguishes too artificially between investigation and prosecution and therefore applies Art. 17 (1)(a) too schematically to an amnesty.

[784] Meißner, *Zusammenarbeit* (2003), p. 77.

prosecute renders the case inadmissible, that is, the Statute also accepts, in principle, negative prosecutorial decisions,[785] unless they result from unwillingness or inability.[786] A decision to stop national proceedings in order to refer the case to the ICC does not, however, amount to a non-prosecution decision within the meaning of Article 17 (1)(b); otherwise, the absurd result would ensue that the case could be prosecuted neither at the domestic nor at the international level.[787]

While the trial requirement of subparagraph (c) poses little problem[788] (apart from the upwards *ne bis in idem* test of Article 20 (3) ICCS which refers, partly, back to the unwillingness standard of Article 17 (2)(a) and (c) ICCS to be dealt with below), it is controversial and crucial how (strictly) the terms 'investigations' and 'prosecutions', in subparagraphs (a) and (b) are to be interpreted. As to the *investigation requirement*, it is debatable whether a criminal investigation by the respective criminal justice organs is necessary or alternative, even non-judicial forms of investigation,[789] in particular a (effective) Truth and Reconciliation Commission ('TRC'),[790] would suffice.[791] A literal interpretation does not clarify the issue since, on the one hand, the term 'investigation' only implies a systematic and careful inquiry[792] and, on the other hand, the ICCS neither states that a 'criminal' investigation is necessary[793] nor does it deal with alternative forms of accountability.[794] It seems clear, though, that the 'investigation' must be carried out by State organs, that is, non-judicial organs like a TRC must at least be set up and supported by the State,[795] since the duty to investigate and prosecute rests upon the State.[796] Accordingly, investigations or prosecutions by non-State actors can not be taken into account either, unless they can be attributed to a State.[797]

785 In the same vein, Mégret, in Stahn and El Zeidy, *Complementarity I* (2011), p. 382.

786 cf. Art. 17 (1)(b) *in fine*.

787 cf. *Katanga*, ICC-01/04-01/07-1497, para. 82; *Bemba*, ICC-01/05-01/08-962-Corr, paras. 68, 74. In the same vein, Schabas and El Zeidy, 'Article 17', in Ambos, *Commentary* (2022), mn. 29; cf. also Abdou, 'Article 17', in Klamberg et al., *Commentary ICC I* (2023), pp. 610–11.

788 With regard to the Gaddafi admissibility challenge, cf. above note 596 with main text.

789 See thereon Ambos, in Ambos et al., *Building a Future* (2009), pp. 40–9, paras. 12–18. In this line, calling upon the ICC to take a broader approach of complementarity and to recognize restorative options, Gordon, in Stahn and El Zeidy, *Complementarity II* (2011), pp. 745–802; for a recognition of (African) restorative justice forms while assessing complementarity, see also Eberechi, *AfrJICompL*, 20 (2012), 40–1, pointing to damaging effects by the disregard of the alternative justice mechanisms (pp. 39–40). For a hypothetical study on alternative complementarity justice mechanisms in the USA regarding crimes committed by US nationals in Afghanistan, see Vaid, *NYUJILe&Pol'y*, 44 (2011/12), 573–628 (esp. 625–7), rejecting a pure criminal law approach.

790 On the criteria such an effective TRC must fulfil, see Ambos, in Ambos et al., *Building a Future* (2009), pp. 40–9 (esp. 46), paras. 13–19 (esp. 16).

791 The question is left open by Robinson, *EJIL*, 14 (2003), 499–500, but his general flexible approach indicates that he prefers a 'slightly broader approach'; undecided also Benzing, *MPYbUNL*, 7 (2003), 602 and El Zeidy, *Complementarity* (2008), p. 315; for Stigen, *Relationship* (2008), p. 211 punishment must be 'an option'; in a similar vein, Nouwen, *Complementarity* (2013), pp. 60, 105 ('not alternative mechanisms'); on the definition of 'investigated' and 'prosecuted' in the *Uganda* Situation, see Greenawalt, *VirgJIL*, 50 (2009), 125 ff.

792 For a definition, see Stigen, *Relationship* (2008), p. 203.

793 Stahn, *JICJ*, 3 (2005), 697; Scharf, *CornILJ*, 32 (1999), 525; Bartelt, *AVR*, 43 (2005), 206; Majzub, *MelbJIL*, 3 (2002), 267; Razesberger, *Complementarity* (2006), p. 180; Valiñas, in Stahn and van den Herik, *Perspectives* (2010), pp. 273–4.

794 Meyer, *ICLR*, 6 (2006), 565; Minow, *HarvILJ*, 60 (2019), 5 ('Statute is silent about what happens to ICC jurisdiction when the state proceeds with a response other than adversarial criminal litigation').

795 See also Cárdenas, *Zulässigkeitsprüfung* (2005), pp. 177, 183; for a judicial investigation, see also El Zeidy, *Complementarity* (2008), p. 315.

796 Note 733 in this chapter.

797 In this sense, also *Situation Georgia*, ICC-01/15-12, para. 40 ('the de facto authorities of South Ossetia are not capable of meeting the requirements of article 17 of the Statute, due to South Ossetia not being a recognized State') and subsequently leaving the question open in *Prosecutor v. Al-Werfalli*, PTC I, Second Warrant of Arrest, ICC-01/11-01/17-13, 4 July 2018, para. 27 ('The Chamber finds that irrespective of whether the entity exercising authority in the territory controlled by the LNA can be considered a State for the purposes of article 17 of the Statute, there remains a situation of inactivity'). On the case law, see Nuridzhanian, *LAPE*, 18 (2019), 220–2 (advocating the inclusion of non-governmental courts where their proceedings can be attributed to a State

Apart from that, a systematic and teleological interpretation of Article 17 suggests that the *objective* of any 'investigation' is criminal prosecution or adjudication, namely to avoid that the suspect be shielded 'from criminal responsibility'[798] and 'to bring the person concerned to justice'.[799] While this does not exclude a *preliminary* investigation by a TRC with respective powers (i.e. to recommend criminal proceedings),[800] and indeed the wording of Article 17 (1)(a) ICCS ('being investigated') leaves room for such alternative investigations,[801] their ultimate objective must always be a criminal prosecution *stricto sensu*[802] where the legal and factual prerequisites of such a prosecution are fulfilled.[803] In turn, this means that investigations of a general nature about past events which do not individualize responsibility and therefore cannot serve as basis for a criminal prosecution or adjudication do not satisfy the investigation requirement of Article 17 ICCS.

In sum, as a minimum, a *systematic inquiry* into the facts and circumstances of the case[804]—the already mentioned initial or *minimal investigative steps*[805]—with a view to a

according to customary international law, 227 ff.); furthermore, see Amoroso, *JICJ*, 16 (2018), 1063 ff. (considering investigations by non-State actors to be relevant since the wording of Art. 17 (1)(c) does not exclude it [1084–6] and the command responsibility within such actors as well as especially the *ne bis in idem* principle speak in favour of their inclusion [1087–8, 1088–9]); also, see below note 855.

798 Art. 17 (2)(a) ICCS.

799 Art. 17 (2)(b) and (c) ICCS. In this sense, see also Gavron, *ICLQ*, 51 (2002), 111, arguing that 'to bring someone to justice' is to be interpreted in the legal, not wider moral sense. Even stricter, Holmes, in Lee, *ICC* (1999), p. 77 ('Statute's provisions on complementarity are intended to refer to criminal investigations.'). In the same vein, Kleffner, *Complementarity* (2008), pp. 268–70 and Zhao, *China* (2017), p. 32.

800 A good example is a Commission of Inquiry like the Israeli Kahan Commission established to investigate the responsibility of Israeli government and military officials, including the then Minster of Defense Ariel Sharon, for the atrocities committed in the Sabra and Shatila refugee camps in Lebanon in September 1982 since it had, pursuant to the Israeli Commissions of Inquiry Law of 1968 (reprinted in English in Ministry of Justice of Israel, *ILM*, 22 (1983), 658 ff.), the authority to recommend criminal prosecution. In the same vein, Zhao, *China* (2017), p. 32 ('there must be a possibility to subsequently refer the case to a prosecuting body').

801 See also Seibert-Fohr, *MPYbUNL*, 7 (2003), 569 and Stahn, *JICJ*, 3 (2005), 697, 711 arguing against the requirement of a criminal investigation since it is not expressly contained in Art. 17. In a similar vein, Cárdenas, *Zulässigkeitsprüfung* (2005), pp. 58–9, 101; Cárdenas, 'Admissibility Test', in Kleffner and Kor, *Complementary Views* (2006), p. 129; Razesberger, *Complementarity* (2006), pp. 180–1. Too restrictive, Meißner, *Zusammenarbeit* (2003), p. 76 requiring investigations within the framework of criminal proceedings; see also Schomburg and Nemitz, 'Internationale Strafgerichtsbarkeit', in Schomburg et al., *Internationale Rechtshilfe* (2006), p. 1730, arguing against an upward *ne bis in idem* effect (towards international courts) [in subsequent editions omitted].

802 In this sense also Seibert-Fohr, *MPYbUNL*, 7 (2003), 569 linking the investigation to the prosecution requirement; see also Stigen, *Relationship* (2008), p. 203; Kleffner, *Complementarity* (2008), p. 269; Gropengießer and Meißner, *ICLR*, 5 (2005), 287, arguing that 'proceedings which do not have the *quality of a criminal proceeding* cannot rule out prosecution by the Court' (emphasis added) and Stegmiller, *Pre-Investigation Stage* (2011), pp. 290–1; similarly, Cárdenas, *Zulässigkeitsprüfung* (2005), p. 137 stressing the need of criminal prosecutions after the TRC's work has been finished; conc., modifying his earlier position, Robinson, *EJIL*, 14 (2003), 144–5 (possibility of a criminal prosecution after investigation); in the same vein, Minow, *HarvILJ*, 60 (2019), 15–16 with further references ('truth commission could be sufficient, especially if it does not preclude prosecution at the national level'); see also Nouwen and Werner, *JICJ*, 13 (2015), 174 (complementarity in legal sense creates only alternative *criminal* justice space, at national level, but not space for an alternative conception of justice).

803 See also Stahn, *JICJ*, 3 (2005), 711–12.

804 Cárdenas, *Zulässigkeitsprüfung* (2005), p. 58; Cárdenas, in Kleffner and Kor, *Complementary Views* (2006), p. 117, 119; Murphy, *Eyes on the ICC*, 3 (2006), 44. See also Stahn, *JICJ*, 3 (2005), 710; Seibert-Fohr, *MPYbUNL*, 7 (2003), 588; Stigen, *Relationship* (2008), p. 203.

805 cf. also *Ruto et al.*, ICC-01/09-01/11-307, para. 41, holding that the expression 'the case is being investigated' must be understood as requiring the taking of 'concrete and progressive investigative steps' to ascertain whether the person is responsible for the alleged conduct. Those steps undertaken by the domestic authorities may include 'interviewing witnesses or suspects, collecting documentary evidence, or carrying out forensic analyses'; *Muthaura et al.*, ICC-01/09-02/11-274, para. 41 (investigative 'steps directed at ascertaining whether ... suspects are responsible'; mere 'preparedness to take such steps' insufficient); also, see *Al-Werfalli*, ICC-01/11-01/17-13, para. 28 ('tangible, concrete and progressive investigative steps'); *Situation Burundi*, ICC-01/17-9-Red, para. 148, both with further references; crit. with regard to a progressive steps requirement Heller, *JICJ*, 14 (2016), 641–2 (arguing that Art. 17 ICCS 'suggests that *any* investigative steps involving the same suspect will satisfy the

criminal prosecution is required. This does not mean that the 'messy realities'[806] of post-conflict societies and certain post-colonial sensibilities with regard to 'Western-style prosecutions'[807] are overlooked or underestimated. At the same time, however, alternative justice processes must comply with certain minimum requirements to have, legitimately, an effect on ICC prosecutions.[808] For the ICC derives its legitimacy essentially from its 'core function as a neutral adjudicator of agreed-upon rules of international law'.[809] As a consequence, it seems to be more adequate to evaluate alternative justice mechanisms within the framework of the interest of justice clause of Article 53 (1)(c) and (2)(c) ICCS.[810]

This interpretation is confirmed by the second requirement, the *decision to prosecute*.[811] Such a decision can only be taken if a substantial investigation of *concrete* acts and *individual* suspects has been carried out in the first place. In other words, a decision to prosecute presupposes a criminal or at least individualized investigation, which precedes and prepares it.[812] Clearly, prosecution refers to criminal prosecution,[813] but only the 'decision' to prosecute is required, not the prosecution itself. This presupposes that the organ that takes this decision must at least have two options, namely either to prosecute or not to prosecute.[814]

### *(iii) Admissibility due to unwillingness or inability (Article 17 (2) and (3) ICCS)*

*(1)* ***Preliminary remarks*** If one understands, as suggested here, complementarity *stricto sensu* in a threefold way, all State action mentioned in Article 17 (1)(a)–(c) ICCS only creates a presumption of inadmissibility[815] which may be refuted by the establishment of unwillingness or inability pursuant to Article 17 (2) and (3) ICCS. This also holds true for subparagraph (1)(c) since it introduces the criteria of subparagraphs (2)(a)–(c) by having recourse to Article 20 (3) ICCS.[816] Thus, to declare a situation or case admissible ultimately requires the establishment of unwillingness[817] or inability[818] on the part of the respective national justice system.

investigation requirement', especially since otherwise the difference between inactivity and unwillingness would be blurred). See also previously Kleffner, *Complementarity* (2008), p. 105; conc. also Stahn, in Stahn, *Practice* (2015), p. 236.

806 Akhavan, *JICJ*, 14 (2016), 1059.

807 Minow, *HarvILJ*, 60 (2019), 17 (arguing that this would entail the criticism 'that the Rome Statute elevates the Global North's adversarial legal traditions over others').

808 See with a view to an 'effective TRC' already above note 790 with main text. See also Minow, *HarvILJ*, 60 (2019), 42 (arguing that 'alternative justice' processes can only be treated 'as preclusive of international criminal process' if they identify the responsible and produce sanctions or 'a public report or transparent outcome, and is itself a mechanism for restoring communal trust or building the rule of law domestically').

809 Greenawalt, in deGuzman and Oosterveld, *Elgar Companion ICC* (2020), p. 79.

810 In a similar vein apparently, O'Keefe, *ICL* (2015), p. 562 with n. 156.

811 See previously Ambos, in Ambos et al., *Building a Future* (2009), p. 76, para. 41.

812 See also Stahn, *JICJ*, 3 (2005), 712; El Zeidy, *Complementarity* (2008), p. 315 (noting that '[w]hen [article 17] paragraph [1] (a) refers to a "prosecution", which is always a judicial activity, carried out by a purely judicial body, one gets the sense that Art. 17(1) is concerned with "judicial proceedings" as opposed to alternative mechanisms of justice').

813 cf. Cárdenas, *Zulässigkeitsprüfung* (2005), pp. 58, 101; Stigen, *Relationship* (2008), p. 205; Kleffner, *Complementarity* (2008), pp. 268–9; broader Schabas and El Zeidy, 'Article 17', in Ambos, *Commentary* (2022), mn. 51 ('judicial activity').

814 Robinson, *EJIL*, 14 (2003), 500; see also Stahn, *LJIL*, 18 (2005), 463.

815 See also Schabas, *ICC Commentary* (2016), p. 459.

816 Deeming Art. 17 (1)(c) superfluous, Schabas, *ICC Commentary* (2016), p. 461.

817 Art. 17 (1)(a)–(c) in connection with para. (2).

818 Art. 17 (1)(a), (b) in connection with para. (3).

The *burden of proof* rests, as a rule, on the Prosecutor, that is, they must prove the unwillingness or inability.[819] Yet, the Court depends on the respective State's cooperation in providing the information regarding the action taken by its national justice system;[820] in fact, in light of the inaction scenario[821] and the ensuing admissibility, it is in the best interests of the State concerned to provide compelling evidence demonstrating that it is acting accordingly,[822] imposing on it a kind of burden of production.[823] The unwillingness/inability test comes only into play if the State has convincingly shown that an investigation or prosecution has taken place.[824] Recently, the Prosecutor considered this to be the case regarding Colombia and terminated its investigation.[825]

The interpretation of the criteria contained in paras. (2) and (3) of Article 17 is controversial and unsettled, not least because they are highly normative and open to value judgement.[826] An alternative approach merging unwillingness and inability into one requirement has been proposed,[827] but it does not help to overcome the definitional issues with regard to the relevant criteria, that is, if they are to be understood objectively, subjectively, or both.[828] It seems to be clear that the term '*genuinely*'[829]—'the least objectionable word'—was inserted to give the unwillingness/inability test a more concrete and objective meaning.[830] Yet, the term is highly normative, calling for good faith and seriousness[831] on the part of the respective State with regard to investigation and prosecution.[832] From human rights jurisprudence it

[819] See El Zeidy, *Complementarity* (2008), p. 163; see also ICC-OTP, *Complementarity* (2003), paras. 55, 56, which however, as the rule, propose to impose the burden on the party raising a specific issue (para. 54); similarly Fairlie and Powderly, inStahn and El Zeidy, *Complementarity I* (2011), 648–82.

[820] Rules 51, 55 (2) RPE ICC.

[821] See Section B.(2)(d)(i) in this chapter.

[822] Razesberger, *Complementarity* (2006), pp. 53–4, but later, arguing for the deletion of Rule 51 (pp. 55–6); Burke-White and Kaplan, in Stahn and Sluiter, *Practice* (2009), p. 110; Burke-White and Kaplan, *JICJ*, 7 (2009), 276; O'Keefe, *ICL* (2015), p. 557.

[823] Following the well-known distinction between burden of proof (persuasion) and burden of production (evidential burden), esp. relevant with regard to defences, cf. Roberts, *Evidence* (2022), pp. 243–5.

[824] *Katanga*, ICC-01/04-01/07-1497, paras. 78, 97; *Bemba*, ICC-01/05-01/08-962-Corr, paras. 107–8; *Al-Senussi*, ICC-01/11-01/11-565, paras. 68–9, 176.

[825] cf. ICC-OTP, *Report on Colombia* (2023), paras. 21 ff.

[826] See previously Ambos, in Ambos et al., *Building a Future* (2009), p. 76, para. 42 with further references; in the same vein, El Zeidy, *Complementarity* (2008), p. 236; Bothe, *Friedens-Warte*, 83 (2008), 65.

[827] See Kleffner, *Complementarity* (2008), pp. 161, 342, suggesting the 'effectiveness of the national proceedings' as an overall criterion.

[828] On the drafting process of the OTP policy paper, see Dicker, in ICC-OTP, *First Public Hearing* (2003). On the subjective-objective approach, see also Wei, *Rolle des Anklägers* (2007), p. 73. On some States' opposition to subjective elements, Holmes, in Lee, *ICC* (1999), p. 49; El Zeidy, *MichJIL*, 23 (2002), 899. Crit. on the term's substance, Kleffner, *Complementarity* (2008), pp. 115–16.

[829] Art. 17 (1)(a), (b) ICCS.

[830] cf. Holmes, in *Lee, ICC* (1999), p. 50; Holmes, in Cassese et al., *Rome Statute I* (2002), p. 674; see also El Zeidy, *Complementarity* (2008), pp. 163–70 (esp. 166); El Zeidy, *MichJIL*, 23 (2002), 900; Cárdenas, *Zulässigkeitsprüfung* (2005), p. 110; Kelly, *GeoJIL*, 48 (2017), 812.

[831] Holmes, in Cassese et al., *Rome Statute I* (2002), p. 674; Benzing, *MPYbUNL*, 7 (2003), 605; Cárdenas, *Zulässigkeitsprüfung* (2005), pp. 110–11; cf. Ambos, *Colombian Peace Process* (2010), pp. 59 ff.; Stegmiller, *Pre-Investigation Stage* (2011), pp. 289 ff.; Kelly, *GeoJIL*, 48 (2017), 812–13 (pointing out that the debates regarding the word 'genuine' 'reflect the tension' between the ICC as a 'court of last resort' and its role in the fight against impunity); on an autonomous meaning of the term 'genuinely', see Jensen, in Kleffner and Kor, *Complementary Views* (2006), pp. 147 ff.; Cárdenas, in Kleffner and Kor, *Complementary Views* (2006), pp. 168–9; El Zeidy, *Complementarity* (2008), pp. 164–5; Razesberger, *Complementarity* (2006), p. 52; Nouwen, *Complementarity* (2013), p. 62; Nouwen and Lewis, , in Sluiter et al., *International Criminal Procedure* (2013), p. 124 ('normative requirement'); Bishop, *MinnesotaJIL*, 22 (2013), 396. Using 'good faith' and 'genuinely', interchangeably ECJ, *Commission v. Spain*, Case C-499/99, Judgment (2 July 2002), para. 24; ECJ, *Commission v. Germany*, Case C-105/02, Judgment (5 October 2006), paras. 93–4; ECJ, *Commission v. Belgium*, Case C-275/04, Judgment (5 October 2006), paras. 82–3. The ICC has been so far silent on the matter. On possible standards, see also Stigen, *Relationship* (2008), pp. 218–29.

[832] It does not refer to the preceding terms 'unwilling or unable', but to the last part of subparas. (a) and (b) referring to investigation and prosecution, cf. El Zeidy, *Complementarity* (2008), p. 165; Stigen, *Relationship* (2008),

follows that the State has 'the obligation to use all the legal means at its disposal' to conduct serious and effective investigations and prosecutions leading to the identification and punishment of the responsible;[833] only then can one speak of a 'genuine' investigation or prosecution.[834] On the other hand, alternative good faith efforts, for example, the establishment of an effective TRC with the ultimate goal of peace in mind, cannot be considered, *a limine*, as showing 'genuine' unwillingness.[835] The same applies to lenient sentences instead of amnesties or pardons.[836] In any case, the term implies a double objective-subjective test[837] and is indirectly defined by paragraphs (2) and (3) of Article 17.[838]

In addition, one may identify a *structural distinction* between unwillingness and inability in the following sense: while in the former case an, in principle, functioning judicial system is politically manipulated to generate impunity for powerful and influential perpetrators, in the latter case such a system does not, in the worst case, physically even exist or is substantially collapsed or unavailable.[839] Of course, these crucial concepts have to be explored further in the following two sections, but the Court should generally pursue a flexible case-by-case approach in line with the above-mentioned 'qualified deference' to domestic jurisdictions.[840]

### *(2) Unwillingness*

*1.* General Unwillingness is not defined in the Statute. Article 17 (2) ICCS only spells out the criteria that have to be considered: (1) the purpose of shielding, (2) unjustified delay, and (3) the lack of independence and impartiality.[841] The threshold of paragraph (2) is

p. 216 with n. 701; Schabas and El Zeidy, 'Article 17', in Ambos, *Commentary* (2022), mn. 46. The French version of the Statute expresses this more unequivocally ('*véritablement à bien*'), see Morel, *Complémentarité* (2005), pp. 99–100; Kleffner, *Complementarity* (2008), p. 115. The Spanish version ('*realmente*') sounds a little emphatic. Apparently for a different view, Nouwen, *Complementarity* (2013), p. 62 (not 'independent of unwillingness and inability').

833 See e.g. IACtHR, *Paniagua Morales et al v. Guatemala*, Serie C No. 37, Judgment (8 March 1998), para. 173; see also *Zambrano Vélez v. Ecuador*, Serie C No. 166, Judgment (4 July 2007), para. 123; *Escué Zapata v. Colombia*, Serie C No. 165, Judgment (4 July 2007), para. 106; for more recent case law, see note 734 in this chapter. Extensively on applicable human rights standards in this context, see Stigen, *Relationship* (2008), pp. 219–29; El Zeidy, *Complementarity* (2008), pp. 175–80. In this context, one may understand 'genuinely' as 'effectively' and combine it with 'inability', cf. Nouwen, *Complementarity* (2013), pp. 62–3.

834 In a similar vein, van der Wilt and Lyngdorf, *ICLR*, 9 (2009), 39 ff., arguing that the ECHR's case law on the duty to properly investigate flagrant human rights violations and its concrete assessment of State practice serves as a useful guideline as to these or other States' unwillingness or inability; see also van der Wilt, in Stahn and El Zeidy, *Complementarity II* (2011), pp. 686–705. See also El Zeidy, *Complementarity* (2008), p. 167, implying, incorrectly however, that the said human rights jurisprudence explicitly defines the term 'genuine'.

835 Seibert Fohr, *MPYbUNL*, 7 (2003), 570; Kelly, *GeoJIL*, 48 (2017), 815, 832 (referring to 'alternative sanctions' in the context of the Colombian TJ process not addressed by Art. 17 ICCS, also see below main text at note 876 ff.). Yet, also see Schabas, *ICC Commentary* (2016), p. 455 ('unlikely interpretation').

836 For a detailed analysis, see Mayans-Hermida and Holá, *JICJ*, 18 (2020), 1110 f.f, also see below note 977; on alternative sanctions in Colombia, South Africa, and Rwanda, see Kelly, *GeoJIL*, 48 (2017), 821 ff.

837 Stigen, *Relationship* (2008), p. 216.

838 cf. ibid., p. 218.

839 For a general analysis, see Benzing, *MPYbUNL*, 7 (2003), 613–17; for a similar distinction, see Seils and Wierda, 'ICC and Conflict Mediation' (2005), p. 6; see also Cárdenas, *Zulässigkeitsprüfung* (2005), pp. 138–40; for a concrete proposal and analysis of inability criteria with regard to the DRC, see Burke-White, *LJIL*, 18 (2005), 576 ff., who suggests (p. 576) four criteria 'to judge the effectiveness of judicial systems in states recovering from a total or substantial judicial collapse', namely availability of experienced and unbiased judicial personnel, a viable legal infrastructure, adequate operative law, and a sufficient police capability. For Arsanjani and Reisman, in Sadat and Scharf, *Theory and Practice of ICL* (2008), p. 329, inability exists if 'the system ... is unable to obtain the accused or the necessary evidence and testimony or (is) otherwise unable to carry out its proceedings'.

840 Note 614 in this chapter and main text.

841 cf. Ambos, *Colombian Peace Process* (2010), pp. 59 ff.; Stegmiller, *Pre-Investigation Stage* (2011), pp. 302 ff.; Tharakan, *Konkretisierung* (2009), pp. 105 ff.; Kindt, *Menschenrechte* (2009), pp. 150 ff.; Jurdi, *ICC* (2011), pp. 37 ff.; Azarov and Weill, *ICLR*, 12 (2012), 910 ff.; Abdou, 'Article 17', in Klamberg et al., *Commentary ICC I* (2023),

generally considered as high.[842] The list in subparagraphs (a)–(c) is exhaustive[843] and is to be applied—as clearly indicated by the wording ('one or more of the following')—in the alternative.[844]

While subparagraph (a) of Article 17 (2) ICCS calls for a rather subjective interpretation, subparagraphs (b) and (c) are to be interpreted more objectively.[845] Although the notion of 'intent', present in both subparagraphs, normally carries a subjective meaning, it must be read in context, and this context, referring to such objective criteria as 'unjustified delay', independence and impartiality, and the 'circumstances', implies an overall objective reading, albeit always indicating bad faith.[846]

The *Katanga and Ngudjolo Chui* TC has, albeit not explicitly provided for in Article 17 ICCS, identified a 'second form of "unwillingness"' (in relation to subparagraph 2 (a)), where a State 'aims to see the person brought to justice, but not before national courts'.[847] The Chamber argues 'that a State which chooses not to investigate or prosecute a person before its own courts, but has nevertheless every intention of seeing that justice is done, must be considered as lacking the will referred to in Article 17'.[848] This interpretation is difficult to bring into line with the overall goal of Article 17—to avoid impunity—since impunity would effectively be avoided if a third State assumes the jurisdiction to enforce. In addition, this interpretation is neither covered by the wording of Article 17 (2) nor can it create—*ex nihilo*—a further cause of unwillingness expanding the—exhaustive—list of paragraph 2.[849] In fact, if a State foregoes the exercise of its jurisdiction, it does not fulfil its duty to investigate the ICC crimes and thus falls under the inaction scenario discussed above.[850] In any case, the existence of one of the unwillingness criteria of Article 17 (2) does not automatically entail a finding of unwillingness since the Court 'shall consider' these criteria to determine unwillingness,[851] that is, they are necessary but not sufficient factors to determine unwillingness.[852] Also, (un)willingness may vary according to the State and/or institution concerned.[853]

pp. 618–20; on the extent to which the ICC can influence domestic due process rights, see Fry, *CLF*, 23 (2012), 40 ff.; on the admissibility of amnesties or other similar measures in this context, see Ambos, in Ambos et al., *Building a Future* (2009), pp. 78–9; see also Benoit-Landale, in Ziegler et al., *Kriegsverbrecherprozesse in der Schweiz* (2009), pp. 250–1; Jurdi, *ICC* (2011), pp. 73 ff.

[842] El Zeidy, *Complementarity* (2008), p. 170.

[843] See Stigen, *Relationship* (2008), pp. 257–8, 314; Kleffner, *Complementarity* (2008), p. 104; El Zeidy, *Complementarity* (2008), p. 168; Pichon, *ICLR*, 8 (2008), 191; Stegmiller, *Pre-Investigation Stage* (2011), p. 303; Boas et al., *International Criminal Procedure* (2011), p. 80; Bishop, *MinnesotaJIL*, 22 (2013), 397; in the same vein, but confusing, Razesberger, *Complementarity* (2006), pp. 42–3, 57; *contra* Morel, *Complémentarité* (2005), p. 117 ('critères énoncés … sont qu'illustratifs … ne saurait être qualifiée d'exhaustive', relying on the wording); Chappell, Grey, and Waller, *ICTJ*, 7 (2013), 460 (conc. with the *Katanga and Chui* TC discussed in the text).

[844] Morel, *Complémentarité* (2005), p. 116; Kleffner, *Complementarity* (2008), p. 134; for a discussion thereon, see Valiñas, in Stahn and van den Herik, *Perspectives* (2010), pp. 274–6.

[845] Benzing, *MPYbUNL*, 7 (2003), 610; see also El Zeidy, *Complementarity* (2008), pp. 168, 316; El Zeidy, *MichJIL*, 23 (2002), 901; Nouwen, *Complementarity* (2013), pp. 6–13; Schabas and El Zeidy, 'Article 17', in Ambos, *Commentary* (2022), mn. 74.

[846] Stigen, *Relationship* (2008), p. 290.

[847] See *Katanga and Chui*, ICC-01/04-01/07-1213-tEng, para. 77.

[848] Ibid., para. 77.

[849] In the same vein, Boas et al., *International Criminal Procedure* (2011), p. 80; crit. also Nouwen, *Complementarity* (2013), p. 64.

[850] See Section B.(2)(d)(i) in this chapter; in the same vein, *Katanga*, ICC-01/04-01/07-1497, para. 97; Boas et al., *International Criminal Procedure* (2011), p. 80.

[851] Art. 17 (2) ICCS.

[852] Stigen, *Relationship* (2008), pp. 258, 290 (as to 'unjustified delay').

[853] cf. ICC-OTP, *Complementarity and Cooperation* (2024), para. 160 ('different national institutions may demonstrate varying and inconsistent degrees of willingness/unwillingness').

On another note, it is important to stress that the obligation to investigate rests on the State. Thus, as already noted above,[854] it cannot be substituted by non-State actors and/or international entities unless their exercise of jurisdiction can be attributed to a State.[855] Thus, any efforts to delegate the national criminal jurisdiction to a regional court, for example, the African Court of Justice and Human Rights,[856] would not make a situation/case inadmissible before the ICC. Also, the unwillingness must be attributed to the State,[857] it must reflect—contrary to inability[858]—its policy.[859] Yet, as most States are not monolithic but pluralist and complex entities composed of different organs with sometimes opposing objectives and interests, there may not exist a uniform policy of promoting or blocking criminal investigations and prosecutions.[860] It may well be possible that one State organ (e.g. the national government) intends to block an investigation while another organ (e.g. the Attorney General) is willing to carry out the very same investigation. In this scenario, the situation or case must still be considered admissible if, on the basis of an overall assessment, the unwillingness of only one organ frustrates the whole investigation. In other words, a State cannot hide behind the positive actions of one organ if other organs boycott the investigation.[861]

*2.* Specific criteria As to the first element—'*purpose of shielding the person concerned from criminal responsibility*'[862]—the term 'purpose' suggests a *subjective* interpretation in the sense of the State's specific intention, objective, or desire to protect the individual responsible from (criminal) justice.[863] This must not be the only or ultimate intention.[864] It constitutes, at the same time, an expression of *bad faith* of the respective State with regard to the intention to bring the person(s) responsible to justice,[865] encompassing the entire (first and second instance) proceedings.[866]

[854] Note 797 with main text.

[855] See Kleffner, *Complementarity* (2008), pp. 109–10 and concretely on criminal proceedings by non-State actors Kleffner, in Stahn and El Zeidy, *Complementarity II* (2011), pp. 707–20. With regard to regional tribunals Jackson, *JICJ*, 14 (2016), 1066 ff. argues that they may exercise State-delegated jurisdiction (1066) and thus meet the requirements of Art. 17 (1)(a) ICCS, provided the tribunal genuinely exercises jurisdiction and 'there is no impunity gap' (1069).

[856] On the respective African efforts, see Murungu, *JICJ*, 9 (2011), 1067–88; Rau, *MinnesotaLR*, 97 (2012), 669–708; on the recently created Court, see du Plessis, *EJIL: Talk!*, 27 August 2012; Abass, *NILR*, 60 (2013), 27 ff.; Nmehielle, *AfrJLS*, 7 (2014), 7 ff.; Maunganidze and du Plessis, in Stahn, *Practice* (2015), pp. 79–82.

[857] For a discussion, see Stigen, *Relationship* (2008), pp. 253–6.

[858] See Section B.(2)(d)(iii)(3) in this chapter.

[859] Stigen, *Relationship* (2008), p. 275.

[860] See Kleffner, *Complementarity* (2008), pp. 106–7. On this broader understanding of complementarity emerging in Africa, cf. Maunganidze and du Plessis, in Stahn, *Practice* (2015), pp. 71 ff., referring to the examples of DRC (72–3), South Africa (74–7), and Uganda (77–9).

[861] Kleffner, *Complementarity* (2008), p. 107. On possible 'unwillingness' of Israel, see Azarov and Weill, *ICLR*, 12 (2012), 913–35.

[862] Art. 17 (2)(a). On shielding from a (legal) historical perspective, see Adigun, *Nigeria* (2017), pp. 35–7.

[863] Arbour and Bergsmo, in von Hebel et al., *Reflections on the ICC* (1999), p. 131 ('devious intent'); Cárdenas, *Zulässigkeitsprüfung* (2005), pp. 115–16; El Zeidy, *Complementarity* (2008), p. 316; Razesberger, *Complementarity* (2006), p. 43. For Kleffner, *Complementarity* (2008), p. 135, the purpose-requirement resembles *dolus directus* and he refers to State intention in the sense of Art. 16 of the ILC Draft on State Responsibility (135–6).

[864] Kleffner, *Complementarity* (2008), pp. 137–8. See also El Zeidy, *Complementarity* (2008), p. 170, pointing out that the drafters introduced 'shielding' as an objective criterion.

[865] El Zeidy, *Complementarity* (2008), p. 175.

[866] *Gaddafi*, ICC-01/11-01/11-695, para. 59 ('This is because it is conceivable that a domestic trial is carried out genuinely at the first-instance level, but that the appellate phase is used to shield the person concerned from criminal responsibility... Conversely, it is also conceivable that any shortcomings of a domestic first-instance trial will be corrected on appeal'). Also, see above, main text at note 599.

Clearly, such a high subjective threshold raises the difficult question of the correct standard of proof[867] and necessarily requires recourse to *indicia* (circumstantial evidence) from which the 'bad faith purpose' may be inferred.[868] Such indicia may constitute, for example,[869] the bypassing of the normal legal procedure by appointing a special investigator who is politically close to the accused, the transfer of a case to secret or special (military) tribunals,[870] the inadequate allocation of resources, or the lack of support and cooperation with the investigators. Some of these indicia may also serve as an expression of unavailability in the sense of paragraph (3), for example, the limited access to the justice system,[871] the decision to grant blanket amnesties and immunities,[872] or a considerable mitigation of punishment.[873]

While the former examples entail a total shielding, the latter implies a partial shielding.[874] In this sense, the Colombian Constitutional Court, while accepting amnesties that comply with the standards of IHL, excludes those that 'are the product of decisions which do not offer effective access to justice.'[875] Yet, while an amnesty may demonstrate bad faith under certain circumstances, this is not always and necessarily the case.[876] Imagine a situation where a State pursues the higher objective of peace and it grants, in good faith, an amnesty as a necessary means to achieve this higher end; then a 'bad faith purpose' can hardly be assumed.[877] Similarly, if one recognizes the right to a peaceful transition, it would be inconsistent to argue that the granting of exemptions in order to assure this transition can be considered as shielding a person and thus as demonstrating unwillingness in the sense of

867 Kleffner, *Complementarity* (2008), p. 135; Benzing, *MPYbUNL*, 7 (2003), 609–10; Stigen, *Relationship* (2008), pp. 261–2; Bekou, in Ulrich, *Challenges and Prospects* (2005), pp. 73–4; Meißner, *Zusammenarbeit* (2003), p. 84; Evans, *HRLC*, 1 (2005), 2–3; Gavron, *ICLQ*, 51 (2002), 111; Morel, *Complémentarité* (2005), p. 120 ('une des tâche les plus ardues du Procureur'); Bothe, *Friedens-Warte*, 83 (2008), 65.

868 Stigen, *Relationship* (2008), pp. 252, 259, 262; Kleffner, *Complementarity* (2008), pp. 136–7; see also Stegmiller, *Pre-Investigation Stage* (2011), p. 304.

869 For further indicators, see ICC-OTP, *Policy Prelim. Examinations* (2013), para. 51; for a thorough discussion, see Stigen, *Relationship* (2008), pp. 262–88.

870 Holmes, in Cassese et al., *Rome Statute I* (2002), p. 675.

871 For a discussion, see Section B.(2)(d)(iii)(3) in this chapter with notes 964 ff. (969). In this context, see also Stigen, *Relationship* (2008), pp. 266–7.

872 Kleffner, *Complementarity* (2008), p. 136; Pichon, *ICLR*, 8 (2008), 194–5 (considering, however, that amnesties are rather a case of unavailability in the sense of Art. 17 (3), see note 972 in this chapter); Adigun, *Nigeria* (2017), pp. 101–8 (also considering the recourse to Art. 17 (3) ICCS [105 with n. 147]), pp. 84–100 (on immunities) and pp. 108–17 (on pardons). Against blanket amnesties in this context, also El Zeidy, *Complementarity* (2008), p. 175 ('clear-cut example' of shielding); Stahn, *JICJ*, 3 (2005), 714; Gropengießer and Meißner, *ICLR*, 5 (2005), 285.

873 Kleffner, *Complementarity* (2008), p. 137 ('sentence ... manifestly insufficient in light of the gravity of the crime(s) in question and the form of participation of the accused'), yet also pointing to the 'large margin of appreciation' with regard to sentencing. See also with regard to Uganda's regime of alternative sentences, Burke-White and Kaplan, in Stahn and Sluiter, *Practice* (2009), pp. 106, 111; Burke-White and Kaplan, *JICJ*, 7 (2009), 273, 277.

874 On this distinction, see Stigen, *Relationship* (2008), p. 260 mentioning explicitly an inferior penalty as a form of partial shielding.

875 Constitutional Court of Colombia [30 July 2002] Judgment C–578, MP Cepeda Espinosa, s. 4.1.2.1.7: '*que son producto de decisiones que no ofrezcan acceso efectivo a la justicia*' ('which are product of decisions which do not offer an effective access to justice'; translation K. Ambos).

876 For a flexible approach, see also Stigen, *Relationship* (2008), pp. 424–67 (esp. 426, 463–7); too strict, Cárdenas, *Zulässigkeitsprüfung* (2005), pp. 117, 164, 183–4; Cárdenas, in Kleffner and Kor, *Complementary Views* (2006), p. 130.

877 Seibert-Fohr, *MPYbUNL*, 7 (2003), 570; Adigun, *Nigeria* (2017), p. 107 (proposes five requirements for an admissible amnesty: (1) inevitable to peace and reconciliation, (2) combined with other accountability measures like truth commissions, (3) product of negotiated peace with assistance of entities like the UN or of peace negotiated between an outgoing government and an incoming one, (4) only apply to those that are least culpable and (5) would only cover the ring leaders in the most stringent circumstances'); on this transitional justice dilemma, see also Stigen, *Relationship* (2008), pp. 420–2, 429–31, 462–7; on the same question from the perspective of broad or narrow prosecutorial discretion, see Rodman, *LJIL*, 22 (2009), 101 ff.

Article 17 (2)(a) ICCS.[878] Consequently, the fact that impunity will be a certain side effect of an exemption measure is not per se sufficient to qualify this measure as pursuing a bad faith purpose.[879] In any event, the Court should seek to understand the objectives and motives of the relevant national actors in dialogue with them and take them into account consistently.[880] Apart from that, the decision or procedure entailing impunity must be undertaken 'for the purpose of shielding'[881] or, in other words, the non-prosecution must have 'resulted from'[882] this decision or procedure. Thus, there must be some causal link between the State's action (purpose) and the consequence (shielding).[883]

An *'unjustified' delay* requires less from the State than an 'undue' delay in that it gives the State the possibility to justify the delay and thereby avoid the unwillingness verdict for this reason; in fact, the drafters wanted to give State Parties this possibility and therefore preferred 'unjustified' over 'undue'.[884] As the Statute does not define the concept, recourse must be taken to the relevant provisions of human rights instruments, taking into account, as already set out in Chapter I in this volume,[885] several criteria, especially the complexity of the case and the conduct of the parties.[886] A further factor to be considered is the (comparative) length of ordinary criminal proceedings in the respective State.[887] The OTP assesses unjustified delay with factors such as 'the pace of investigative steps and proceedings', the objective circumstances of the proceedings, and in view of the 'evidence of a lack of intent to bring the person(s) concerned to justice'.[888]

A delay may be 'unjustified', in particular, if it could have been avoided by employing the adequate care;[889] economic or administrative restraints are no justification. In any event, the decision on whether there was (i) a delay and (ii) it was 'unjustified, cannot be taken *in abstracto* but only on a case-by-case basis taking due account of the circumstances of the respective case.[890] An unjustified delay in this sense only entails unwillingness, however, if it runs counter to the very purpose of Article 17 ICCS, that is, to bring the suspect to justice.[891] This is, in fact, the third requirement of the three—cumulative—requirements of subparagraph (b).

[878] See, however, Gavron, *ICLQ*, 51 (2002), 111–12.

[879] Stricter, Cárdenas, in Kleffner and Kor, *Complementary Views* (2006), p. 131 arguing that impunity as certain 'collateral damage' must be considered as part of the purpose.

[880] Kelly, *GeoJIL*, 48 (2017), 835 demanding (convincingly) 'that these policies do not change drastically with each new Prosecutor'.

[881] Art. 17 (2)(a).

[882] Art. 17 (1)(b).

[883] See also Stigen, *Relationship* (2008), p. 260.

[884] Benzing, *MPYbUNL*, 7 (2003), 610–11; Stigen, *Relationship* (2008), p. 289; see also Holmes, in Lee, *ICC* (1999), p. 54; El Zeidy, *Complementarity* (2008), p. 181; El Zeidy, *MichJIL*, 23 (2002), 900; Razesberger, *Complementarity* (2006), p. 45; Morel, *Complémentarité* (2005), p. 121; Stegmiller, *Pre-Investigation Stage* (2011), pp. 305–6; Abdou, 'Article 17', in Klamberg et al., *Commentary ICC I* (2023), p. 619.

[885] See Chapter I, D.(3)(h).

[886] See generally Benzing, *MPYbUNL*, 7 (2003), 610–11; Morel, *Complémentarité* (2005), p. 122; Bekou, 'Complementarity and the ICC', in Ulrich, *Challenges and Prospects* (2005), p. 74; Kleffner, *Complementarity* (2008), pp. 140–1; El Zeidy, *Complementarity* (2008), pp. 183 ff.; for a recent detailed analysis, see Schabas and El Zeidy, 'Article 17', in Ambos, *Commentary* (2022), mn. 79 ff.

[887] El Zeidy, *Complementarity* (2008), p. 194; Pichon, *ICLR*, 8 (2008), 195; Razesberger, *Complementarity* (2006), p. 45. See, in this regard, also Rule 51 RPE according to which the Court may consider information provided by the respective State as to the practice of its courts with regard to 'internationally recognized norms and standards'.

[888] ICC-OTP, *Policy Prelim. Examinations* (2013), para. 52.

[889] cf. Cárdenas, *Zulässigkeitsprüfung* (2005), pp. 119–20.

[890] See Kleffner, *Complementarity* (2008), p. 140; El Zeidy, *Complementarity* (2008), pp. 182, 184; Bekou, in Ulrich, *Challenges and Prospects* (2005), p. 75; van der Wilt and Lyngdorf, *ICLR*, 9 (2009), 60.

[891] El Zeidy, *Complementarity* (2008), pp. 183, 317.

Subparagraph 2 (c) of Article 17—requiring *independent and impartial proceedings*—is based on Articles 10 (2) ICTYS, 9 (2) ICTRS, which use the terms in the context of *ne bis in idem*.[892] The case would be admissible because of unwillingness if national proceedings, including the respective investigations,[893] were *either* not independent *or* not impartial. These concepts have already been explained in Chapter II in this volume.[894] In short, independence refers to external influence on the tribunals and proceedings, whereas impartiality is concerned with possible bias of the judicial personnel itself. An 'effective' TRC, that is, an above all independent and impartial TRC,[895] may refute a lack of independence and impartiality.[896] The ICC made pronouncements on this subparagraph in the *Situation of Venezuela I*, stating that the prosecution's submissions were too general for the Chamber to reach any conclusive determination on the matter.[897] Rather, in the *Al-Senussi* proceedings, the PTC's inadmissibility decision was based on the—somewhat arbitrary—assessment of factual information provided by the Libyan government which, in the Chamber's view, did not indicate 'a systemic lack of independence and impartiality of the judiciary' within the meaning of Article 17 (2)(c).[898] More concretely, the Chamber did not consider, for example, sufficient in that regard statements by public officials undermining the accused's right to be presumed innocent.[899] Thus, regrettably, the Chamber conducted a factual analysis in a vacuum, without taking issue with the legal meaning of the relevant concepts.

Both subparagraphs (b) and (c) require that the unjustified delay and lack of independence or impartiality are 'inconsistent with an intent to *bring the person concerned to justice*'.[900] This requirement operates in addition to the former ones[901] and adds an element of subjectivity to them.[902] It refers back to subparagraph (a), in that it confirms that the person concerned must not be shielded from but brought to justice, that is, criminally investigated and prosecuted.[903] If one defends a broad concept of justice, as I have done elsewhere,[904] a quasi-judicial procedure, conducted, for example, by an effective TRC, would, in principle, suffice in this regard as long as a possibility of a subsequent criminal process and sanction exists.[905]

It is controversial, however, whether the corresponding domestic judicial procedure must satisfy *due process* standards.[906] While the wording of Article 17 ICCS, especially the

892 See also Art. 7 (2) IRMCTS and Art. 20 (3)(b) ICCS.

893 cf. Stigen, *Relationship* (2008), pp. 300, 308–9.

894 See Chapter II, A.(4) with further references.

895 On the criteria of 'effectiveness', see the reference in note 790 in this chapter.

896 See Ambos, in Ambos et al., *Building a Future* (2009), p. 78, para. 43; also Razesberger, *Complementarity* (2006), p. 181.

897 ICC, *Situation Venezuela I*, ICC-02/18-45, paras. 127–9.

898 *Al-Senussi*, ICC-01/11-01/11-466-Red, paras. 241–58.

899 Ibid., para. 241.

900 Emphasis added.

901 cf. Kleffner, *Complementarity* (2008), pp. 143, 149–50.

902 Carnero Rojo, *LJIL*, 18 (2005), 835.

903 See note 798 in this chapter and main text.

904 Ambos, in Ambos et al., *Building a Future* (2009), pp. 22–3, para. 2 with further references. See also Stigen, *Relationship* (2008), pp. 433–40, 446–51.

905 See Ambos, in Ambos et al., *Building a Future* (2009), p. 78, para. 43 with further references.

906 See, for a fundamental critique of this 'due process thesis', Heller, *CLF*, 17 (2006), 260 ff.; see, in the same vein, Carnero Rojo, *LJIL*, 18 (2005), 836 ff. (852 ff.); Pichon, *ICLR*, 8 (2008), 192 ff.; Stegmiller, *Pre-Investigation Stage* (2011), pp. 306–8; Mégret, in Stahn and El Zeidy, *Complementarity I* (2011), p. 372; Safferling and Farthofer, *International Criminal Procedure* (2012), pp. 102–3; Nouwen, *Complementarity* (2013), pp. 67–70; Bishop, *MinnesotaJIL*, 22 (2013), 410 ff.; Trahan, *CornILJ*, 45 (2013), 584–6, 596–7; Stahn, in Stahn, *Practice* (2015), pp. 244–6 (crit. with regard to the stricter deferral standard of Rule 11*bis* RPE ICTY); Bo, *CLF*, 25 (2014), 532 ff. (considering due process violations only as relevant 'if intented to shield the accused from criminal liability' [537]), Wierda, *Impact* (2023), pp. 70 ff. ('blindness' re due process, basically following Heller). See also Abdou, in Klamberg et al., *Commentary ICC I* (2023), pp. 620–1. For a more nuanced approach, see Mégret and Giles

reference to 'principles of due process recognized by international law',[907] and also the references to unjustified delay[908] and independence/impartiality[909] as more concrete due process standards, seem to suggest just that this is the case,[910] the drafting history and the *rationale* of Article 17 speak against any due process requirement.[911] Proposals to include procedural fairness were rejected during the negotiations.[912] A broader, due process reading of Article 17 (2)(b) and (c) ICCS would only be plausible if the due process criteria and the intent-to-bring-the person-to-justice requirement were to be phrased disjunctive ('or') instead of conjunctive ('and').[913] Instead, this requirement demonstrates the mainly anti-impunity function of Article 17 ICCS, that is, to put pressure on States to prosecute and punish international core crimes and, in the negative, to refer these cases to the ICC, but not guarantee, in any case not primarily, due process.[914] In short, Article 17 is about admissibility, not due process. The ICC is a criminal, not a human rights court, and thus should not 'be involved in supervising domestic trial standards per se'.[915]

The case law has so far not really addressed the problem. Only PTC I stated in *Al Senussi* that 'alleged violations of the accused's procedural rights are not per se grounds for a finding of unwillingness or inability under article 17 of the Statute'.[916] While the Chamber acknowledges that certain rights violations 'may be relevant to the assessment of the independence and impartiality of the national proceedings', it stresses that these criteria have to be

Samson, *JICJ*, 11 (2013), 574–6, 577 ff., developing, on the one hand, a ten-step argument in favour of tolerance with regard to flawed domestic proceedings (577–83), but, on the other, acknowledging that minimum due process must always be fulfilled; van der Merwe, *ICLR*, 15 (2015), 40, 57 ff., rejecting the due process thesis, but advocating a limited version focusing on the risk of losing/the genuine chance of an acquittal; for a moderate approach also Fry, *Contours* (2015), pp. 115–16, 120–35; we will return to these more nuanced approaches below. Following Heller with regard to gender justice, and arguing that the complementarity regime does not take into account the gender perspective, and thus identifying a 'gender justice shadow of complementarity', Chappell, Grey, and Waller, *ICTJ*, 7 (2013), 455 ff. For indicators of due process in this regard, see ICC-OTP, *Policy Prelim. Examinations* (2013), para. 55 (Art. 67 and international law); for a good summary of the debate, van der Merwe, *ICLR*, 15 (2015), 46 ff.

[907] Art. 17 (2) ICCS.

[908] Art. 17 (2)(b) ICCS.

[909] Art. 17 (2)(c) ICCS.

[910] Heller, *CLF*, 17 (2006), 258–9; see also Kleffner, *Complementarity* (2008), pp. 127–52; El Zeidy, *Complementarity* (2008), p. 169; *contra* Carnero Rojo, *LJIL*, 18 (2005), 837–8, 852 considering a literal interpretation as 'not decisive' and stressing the ambivalent meaning of 'justice' as 'trial' (process) or 'accountability' (resulting).

[911] For a more detailed interpretation and discussion, see Carnero Rojo, *LJIL*, 18 (2005), 838 ff., 840 ff., concluding that the drafting history clearly shows that the drafters favoured the intervention of the ICC only when the unfair domestic proceedings were intended to shield the person from justice (p. 852). See also Heller, *CLF*, 17 (2006), 262–3, 270 ff., Pichon, *ICLR*, 8 (2008), 193; Trahan, *CornILJ*, 45 (2013), 583–6, 596–7; Batros, in Guariglia et al., *AC ICC Commentary* (2018), p. 79; also Benzing, *MPYbUNL*, 7 (2003), 597 (arguing that Art. 17 begs the question).

[912] Holmes, in Lee, *ICC* (1999), p. 49; Heller, *CLF*, 17 (2006), 272–3; Carnero Rojo, *LJIL*, 18 (2005), 849; Pichon, *ICLR*, 8 (2008), 193.

[913] See Heller, *CLF*, 17 (2006), 279–80 with a further reform proposal for Art. 14; conc. Fry, *Contours* (2015), p. 120; Jurdi, *LIJL*, 30 (2017), 204; Greenawalt, in deGuzman and Oosterveld, *Elgar Companion ICC* (2020), p. 75. Interpreting the due process clause in a broader sense, as referring to principles and standards with regard to duly investigate, prosecute, and punish international crimes, Kleffner, *Complementarity* (2008), pp. 131–4.

[914] See also Stigen, *Relationship* (2008), p. 221; Pichon, *ICLR*, 8 (2008), 193; Kleffner, *Complementarity* (2008), p. 152 ('blind spot vis-à-vis unfair proceedings'); Bishop, *MinnesotaJIL*, 22 (2013), 411–12; Jurdi, *LIJL*, 30 (2017), 205–6.

[915] cf. Mégret and Giles Samson, *JICJ*, 11 (2013), 581; in the same vein, Nouwen, *Complementarity* (2013), pp. 67–8; O'Keefe, *ICL* (2015), p. 561; Jurdi, *LIJL*, 30 (2017), 206; van der Merwe, *ICLR*, 15 (2015), 56, but acknowledging (60–3) the interdependence of human rights and ILC; see also Libya's submission in *Gaddafi*, ICC-01/11-01/11-344-Red, para. 195.

[916] *Al-Senussi*, ICC-01/11-01/11-466-Red, para. 235.

read together with the intent to bring the person to justice.[917] In contrast, in *Saif Al-Islam Gaddafi* PTC I took note only of certain rights violations within the framework of 'unavailability' in the sense of Article 17 (3) ICCS, concluding that the 'national system cannot yet be applied in full in areas or aspects relevant to the case, being thus "unavailable"', including 'existing difficulties in securing a lawyer for the suspect'.[918] The alleged fair trial violations have not been (further) discussed with regard to Libya's (un)willingness to carry out genuinely an investigation or a prosecution since the Chamber had already determined Libya's inability.[919] The AC endorsed the *Al-Senussi* PTC's view in principle, arguing that the ICC is not a human rights court[920] and that (therefore) the due process part of Article 17 (2)[921] 'should generally be understood as referring to proceedings which will lead to a suspect evading justice, in the sense of not appropriately being tried genuinely'.[922] However, at the same time, the Chamber acknowledges that the genuineness of the proceedings may be frustrated by 'egregious' rights violations 'so that they should be deemed, in those circumstances, to be "inconsistent with an intent to bring the person to justice"'.[923] Thus, while the Chamber confirms that, from the perspective of the complementarity principle, due process rights have to take a back seat vis-à-vis criminal investigation and prosecution, it also leaves the door for human rights considerations open. As I will argue now, such a nuanced approach is the best one can achieve under the ambiguous wording of Article 17 (2) ICCS.[924]

A strict, outcome-oriented reading of Article 17 may produce results which are difficult to accept for those who defend a principled approach to ICL, modelled after the criminal law of a liberal *Rechtsstaat.* Such an approach raises difficulties to accepting a special regime with regard to Article 17, a regime which in fact advocates the production of criminal accountability at any cost, with the end (accountability) serving the means (any, even an unfair process), equating the concept of justice referred to in the provision[925] with 'conviction'.[926] The Libya admissibility proceedings are indeed a case in point. Can one really, in the admissibility context, accept any domestic criminal trial, no matter how seriously due process rights are violated, as long as it results in a criminal conviction of the defendant? Even if domestic proceedings fall so drastically below due process standards that one cannot talk of proper proceedings any more?[927] The answer must be in the negative and a more nuanced approach—in line with the AC's approach just quoted above—is called for. Kevin Heller's attempt to modify his anti-due process thesis in light of the *Saif Al-Islam Gaddafi* is a step in the right direction. Heller now proposes a 'modified due process thesis' which takes

[917] Ibid.

[918] *Gaddafi*, ICC-01/11-01/11-344-Red, paras. 205, 215.

[919] *Gaddafi*, ICC-01/11-01/11-344-Red, para. 216.

[920] *Al-Senussi*, ICC-01/11-01/11-565, para. 219.

[921] The AC refers in particular to Art. 17 (2)(c): 'being conducted in a manner which, in the circumstances, is inconsistent with an intent to bring the person concerned to justice'.

[922] *Al-Senussi*, ICC-01/11-01/11-565, paras. 2–3, 230.

[923] Ibid.; conc. Greenawalt, in deGuzman and Oosterveld, *Elgar Companion ICC* (2020), p. 76 (considering that the AC's approach 'strikes a sensible and textually justifiable balance').

[924] Conc. Schabas and El Zeidy, 'Article 17', in Ambos, *Commentary* (2022), mn. 76; crit. Jurdi, *LJIL*, 30 (2017), 209–13.

[925] cf. Art. 17 (2)(b) and (c).

[926] For a correct broader understanding insofar, van der Merwe, *ICLR*, 15 (2015), 60–2, 65, arguing that justice in this context also includes due process.

[927] See, on the blatant due process violation in the Libyan proceedings against Al-Saif Gaddafi, *Prosecutor v. Gaddafi and Al-Senussi*, ICC-01/11-01/11-190-Corr-Red, Public Redacted Version of the Corrigendum to the 'Defence Response to the "Application on behalf of the Govemment of Libya pursuant to Article 19 of the ICC Statute"' (31 July 2012). In the same vein, Bishop, *MinnesotaJIL*, 22 (2013), 408–10, 417–18; see also Werle and Jessberger, *Principles ICL* (2020), mn. 351.

serious domestic rights violations then into account if they make it 'increasingly unlikely' that the domestic prosecution can be brought to a successful end.[928] To be sure, in Heller's view the outcome, criminal accountability-oriented interpretation of Article 17, still prevails over any due process considerations. These considerations are only relevant insofar as domestic rights violations may jeopardize a successful prosecution and trial since fair trial minded and independent judges may exclude unlawfully obtained evidence (e.g. a confession) or even impose a stay of proceedings and *thereby* impede the successful conclusion of the proceedings. Of course, this modified due process thesis is predicated on the assumption that serious domestic rights violations entail the said serious procedural consequences (as most probably will be the case in the US Federal system which Heller takes as an example); but what if the defendant is convicted anyway since judges are neither fair nor independent in the respective domestic system? What if the prosecution is politically motivated, as part of the new regime's coping with the past regime, and the Prosecutors and judges act on behalf of the new regime organizing a show trial? What if the judicial system in a post-conflict situation is not able to effectively act independently and impartially since Prosecutors and judges receive death threats and defence lawyers will be killed if they assume the defence of former regime members?[929] Heller does not ask these questions but only states, somewhat naïvely, that 'Libya has an independent judiciary'.[930] This begs the question whether flagrant domestic rights violations should make a case admissible before the ICC irrespective of the domestic consequences of these violations.

I think the answer must be in the affirmative. The effect of domestic rights violations on admissibility cannot depend on the effective independence, impartiality, and fairness of the domestic justice system since that would mean in most cases of prosecution of macrocriminality that the cases would be inadmissible, for the defendants would be convicted anyway. This would further mean that the ICC would, in a way, approve of these domestic rights violations since it would accept them as making ICC proceedings inadmissible. For the principled theory of ICL[931] defended here this is not acceptable. The hard question is when the due process violations are so serious that they cannot be accepted in terms of admissibility, even if they result in the conviction of the defendants and thus, apparently, comply with Article 17's primarily anti-impunity function. Mégret and Giles Samson rightly argue that 'there may be a point where' such violations 'nullify an ability or intent to prosecute'[932] and list a series of factors, for example the lack of any access to due process rights, where this entails 'to deprive a trial of its character as a trial'.[933] Fry's moderate approach fixes the 'limit to what the Court can ignore' in 'core fair trial' rights.[934] In a similar vein, van der Merwe advocates a 'limited due process thesis' whereby admissibility ensues as a result of 'specific due process violations creating either not risk of losing (leading to inability) or virtually no risk of losing (resulting in unwillingness on the part of the national prosecution authority)'.[935] While such a nuanced due process approach certainly needs further

[928] cf. Heller, *Opinio Juris* (2 August 2012); in the same vein, Bishop, *MinnesotaJIL*, 22 (2013), 389, 415 ff.; for an amendment of Art. 17 to cover 'overzealous' national prosecutions by 'all too willing' States resulting in fair trial violations, see Trahan, *CornILJ*, 45 (2013), 572, 598–9. Previously, Frank Meyer, *ICLR*, 6 (2006), 567, already advocated 'minimal standards' since 'impunity could also result de facto from conduct under the color of law'.

[929] Crit. also Mégret and Giles Samson, *JICJ*, 11 (2013), 582–3; Jurdi, *LIJL*, 30 (2017), 206–7.

[930] Heller, *Opinio Juris* 2 August 2012.

[931] Such a theory counts 'fairness' as one of its guiding principles, see Ambos, *Treatise ICL I* (2021), pp. 152–4.

[932] In this vein, Mégret and Giles Samson, *JICJ*, 11 (2013), 583.

[933] In this vein, ibid., 586–7.

[934] Fry, *Contours* (2015), p. 135.

[935] van der Merwe, *ICLR*, 15 (2015), 74–5; in detail, see pp. 66 ff., distinguishing, between extreme show trials 'flawed beyond all recognition' and without any risk to lose ('no risk trials') amounting to inability (p. 68); and

refinement it should be beyond controversy that there is a point where a State's failure to provide for proper proceedings amounts to either unwillingness or inability;[936] most probably, it would render the proceedings 'inconsistent with an intent to bring the person concerned to justice'.[937]

Comparing subparagraphs (a), (b), and (c) of Article 17 (2) it may be concluded that *bad faith* lies at the core of the unwillingness test.[938] The crucial point is whether the proceedings are not 'genuine', in the sense explained above, that is, whether the deviation from a genuine proceeding is such that it must be considered as an expression of the State's bad faith and thus unwillingness.[939] Consequently, the 'unwillingness' test is about the quality of the proceedings, their seriousness, and good faith with a view to bringing the person to justice; it is not about passing moral judgements about the national justice system concerned.[940] There may be legitimate reasons not to investigate, prosecute, or convict; for example, a lack of evidence, no public interest, or policy considerations.[941] In addition, the threshold of subparagraph (a) is considerably higher than the ones of subparagraphs (b) and (c). Thus, it seems as if subparagraph (a) encompasses subparagraphs (b) and (c)[942] so that it may be advisable for the Prosecutor to first examine these criteria and only if they are satisfied, to then examine subparagraph (a).[943]

*(3)* ***Inability*** While the inability concept is more objective and factual than its counterpart of unwillingness,[944] its correct interpretation is still controversial.[945] Inability is determined by three disabling events: (1) a 'total' collapse, (2) a 'substantial' collapse, or (3) the 'unavailability' of the national judicial system.[946] The said events must entail the State's inability[947] 'to obtain the accused or the necessary evidence and testimony or otherwise ... to carry out

other show trials 'which may have the effect of significantly and unfairly increasing the probability of the accused's conviction' and thus may result in unwillingness.

936 As discussed above in the main text, a due process reference can be found in both unwillingness and inability. In practice and scholarly writings, a clear preference is usually missing. See e.g. leaving it open, *Al-Senussi*, ICC-01/11-01/11-466-Red, para. 235, as quoted in note 916 of this chapter and in main text; in favour of inability, apparently, ICC-OTP, *Policy Prelim. Examinations* (2013), para. 57 ('violations of fundamental rights of the accused' as factor of inability); with a slight preference for unwillingness (albeit mostly referring to both standards), Mégret and Giles Samson, *JICJ*, 11 (2013), 571, 584, 588; with the same tendency, Bishop, *MinnesotaJIL*, 22 (2013), 397–8, 415–16.

937 cf. Art. 17 (2)(c), as correctly invoked by *Al-Senussi*, ICC-01/11-01/11-565, paras. 2–3, 230, quoted earlier.

938 Cárdenas, *Zulässigkeitsprüfung* (2005), p. 113; Stigen, *Relationship* (2008), p. 290; El Zeidy, *Complementarity* (2008), pp. 168, 236.

939 Stigen, *Relationship* (2008), p. 252; ICC-OTP, *Policy Prelim. Examinations* (2013), para. 58 ('impact on the proceedings to such extent as to vitiate their genuineness').

940 cf. Stigen, *Relationship* (2008), p. 252; with a similar result, Jurdi, *LIJL*, 30 (2017), 209 (requiring the domestic system to *bona fide* investigate and prosecute the respective conduct).

941 For a discussion of these reasons, see Stigen, *Relationship* (2008), pp. 309–12.

942 See also El Zeidy, *Complementarity* (2008), p. 170.

943 Pichon, *ICLR*, 8 (2008), 195–6.

944 Holmes, in Cassese et al., *Rome Statute I* (2002), p. 677; Wei, *Rolle des Anklägers* (2007), p. 74; Evans, *HRLC*, 1 (2005), 4; Morel, *Complémentarité* (2005), p. 129; Kleffner, *Complementarity* (2008), pp. 152–3; El Zeidy, *Complementarity* (2008), p. 222; Boas et al., *International Criminal Procedure* (2011), p. 80; Satzger, *ICL* (2018), § 12 mn. 19; Schabas and El Zeidy, 'Article 17', in Ambos, *Commentary* (2022), mn. 88.

945 See El Zeidy, *Complementarity* (2008), p. 227 with references for both positions.

946 Arsanjani and Reisman, in Sadat and Scharf, *Theory and Practice of ICL* (2008), p. 329; van der Wilt, in Stahn, *Practice* (2015), pp. 215 ff.; ICC-OTP, *Complementarity* (2003), para. 49; El Zeidy, *MichJIL*, 23 (2002), 903; Philips, *CLF*, 10 (1999), 79; ICC-OTP, *Policy Prelim. Examinations* (2013), para. 56. For the practically less relevant question of whether the qualifier 'total or substantial' also refers to unavailability, see Kleffner, *Complementarity* (2008), p. 153; considering this generally a 'low threshold', Wierda, *Impact* (2023), p. 72.

947 'Judicial system' must be understood broadly, see Kleffner, *Complementarity* (2008), p. 154.

its proceedings'.[948] The point of reference of the inability assessment is the legal system of the State in question. As correctly held by PTC I in the Libyan *Gaddafi* case, (in)ability:

> must be assessed in the context of the relevant national system and procedures. In other words, the Chamber must assess whether the Libyan authorities are capable of investigating or prosecuting Mr. Gaddafi in accordance with the substantive and procedural law applicable in Libya.[949]

A *total collapse* presupposes that the judicial system as a whole does not function for a considerable period of time.[950] In this sense, a total collapse may be equated with inaction as discussed above.[951] This is for example the case if the State authorities have lost control over their territory to an extent that the administration of justice has broken down completely, or where the authorities, while still exercising (some) effective (military or police) control over the territory, do not perform such administration of justice.[952] Thus, the total collapse may be defined as 'a complete breakdown of the national administration of justice, either due to the State's loss of control over the territory or due to the national decision to efface the national administration of justice'.[953] Of course, the effect of such a collapse of the national justice system may go well beyond the specific case and extend to the situation as a whole.[954]

As to a *substantial collapse*, it is controversial whether the provision embraces a quantitative and/or qualitative assessment.[955] Given that the original term 'partial' was replaced by 'substantial', in order to increase the admissibility threshold and reinforce the primacy of national jurisdictions,[956] and given that there must remain a scope of application for the unavailability criterion, a strict interpretation is called for. The collapse is 'substantial' if it has a great or significant impact on the functioning of the national justice system.[957] This system must be damaged to an extent that it is generally no longer capable of ensuring the

[948] Art. 17 (3) ICCS. For a discussion, see Stigen, *Relationship* (2008), pp. 326–8; distinguishing between causes (collapse etc.) and consequences (inability to carry out proceedings), Nouwen, *Complementarity* (2013), pp. 64; in a similar vein, Abdou, 'Article 17', in Klamberg et al., *Commentary ICC I* (2023), pp. 622–4; listing concrete factors, also *Gaddafi*, ICC-01/11-01/11-344-Red, paras. 199–215; *Al-Senussi*, ICC-01/11-01/11-466-Red, para. 235; ICC-OTP, *Policy Prelim. Examinations* (2013), para. 57; ICC-OTP, *Complementarity* (2003), paras. 44 ff. (with an extensive list of indicia for both criteria at pp. 28 ff.); Tharakan, *Konkretisierung* (2009), pp. 123 ff.; Kindt, *Menschenrechte* (2009), p. 156; Benoit-Landale, in Ziegler et al., *Kriegsverbrecherprozesse in der Schweiz* (2009), pp. 251–2; Jurdi, *ICC* (2011), pp. 48 ff.; also Ambos, *Colombian Peace Process* (2010), pp. 80 ff.; on the DRC in this regard, see Burke-White, *LJIL*, 18 (2005), 574 ff. (586); on both criteria, see Easterday, *ArizJICompL*, 26 (2009), 57 ff.; van der Wilt and Lyngdorf, *ICLR*, 9 (2009), 9 ff.; from a gender perspective, Chappell, Grey, and Waller, *ICTJ*, 7 (2013), 463–4.

[949] *Gaddafi*, ICC-01/11-01/11-344-Red, para. 200; also *Al Senussi*, ICC-01/11-01/11-466-Red, para. 203. On the whole discussion regarding a possible inability in those cases, see Fry, *CLF*, 23 (2012), 35 ff. (updated in Fry, *Contours* (2015), pp. 113 ff.); Stahn, *JICJ*, 10 (2012), 332 ff.; Mégret and Giles Samson, *JICJ*, 11 (2013), 581 ff.

[950] Cárdenas, in Kleffner and Kor, *Complementary Views* (2006), p. 125; Cárdenas, *Zulässigkeitsprüfung* (2005), p. 126; Stigen, *Relationship* (2008), pp. 314–15 ('could arguably be temporary, albeit not too brief'); van der Wilt, in Stahn, *Practice* (2015), p. 215 (no incidental failure).

[951] Section B.(2)(d)(i) in this chapter; cf. Kleffner, *Complementarity* (2008), pp. 154, 160.

[952] Benzing, *MPYbUNL*, 7 (2003), 614; Meißner, *Zusammenarbeit* (2003), p. 86; Greppi, in Politi and Goia, *National Jurisdictions* (2008), p. 64; Samir Hassanein, *ICLR*, 15 (2015), 104.

[953] Pichon, *ICLR*, 8 (2008), 196; see also Razesberger, *Complementarity* (2006), p. 48; Ellis, *FloridaJIL*, 15 (2002), 215, 238 ff.

[954] cf. Bergsmo, *EJCCLCJ*, 6 (1998), 345; Cárdenas, *Zulässigkeitsprüfung* (2005), pp. 130–1.

[955] For 'relevant facts and evidence', see ICC-OTP, *Complementarity* (2003), para. 50.

[956] Arsanjani and Reisman, in Sadat and Scharf, *Theory and Practice of ICL* (2008), pp. 330–1; Hoffmeister and Knoke, *ZaöRV*, 59 (1999), 798; Philips, *CLF*, 10 (1999), 79; Morel, *Complémentarité* (2005), p. 132; El Zeidy, *Complementarity* (2008), pp. 224–8; Razesberger, *Complementarity* (2006), pp. 48–9; Boas et al., *International Criminal Procedure* (2011), p. 81.

[957] Stigen, *Relationship* (2008), p. 316; El Zeidy, *Complementarity* (2008), p. 226.

investigation of the case and the prosecution of the individuals.[958] A geographically limited collapse may suffice, that is, if the State's effective control does not extend to the whole territory but fails in some parts;[959] a good example is the situation in the Ituri region of the Democratic Republic of the Congo.[960] If, however, such a partial (substantial) collapse can be compensated by shifting the resources and proceedings to another venue, the threshold is not reached.[961] A revival of a once substantially collapsed (local) justice system may also be possible.[962]

The determination of *unavailability* is more difficult,[963] not least because it partly overlaps with the substantial or total collapse requirement.[964] A broad literal interpretation may reveal three potential facets: the non-existence of something, the non-accessibility of something, and the non-usefulness of a remedy, irrespective of its existence and accessibility.[965] This literal reading[966] is confirmed by systematic and teleological arguments. As to the former, Article 88 ICCS, referring to 'availability of procedures under national law', uses the term 'availability', in a broader sense than existence of legislation only. As to the latter, 'unavailability' must be construed broad enough to reduce the number of situations the ICC must refer to national proceedings despite the State's actual inability to carry out proceedings.[967] Such a broad reading would also allow for including situations under unavailability where a legal system is generally in place but *in concreto* does not provide for effective judicial remedy or access to the courts, be it for political, legal, or factual reasons (capacity overload), or is not able to produce the desired result (bring the responsible to justice).[968] If this is accepted, human rights case law as to an effective judicial remedy against serious human rights violations can provide important guidelines for the complementarity test.[969]

958 Benzing, *MPYbUNL*, 7 (2003), 614; Stigen, *Relationship* (2008), p. 316; Samir Hassanein, *ICLR*, 15 (2015), 104.

959 Hall, *Suggestions* (2003), p. 17; El Zeidy, *MichJIL*, 23 (2002), 903–4; Kleffner, *Complementarity* (2008), pp. 32–3; Razesberger, *Complementarity* (2006), pp. 48–9; differentiated, Stigen, *Relationship* (2008), pp. 315–16.

960 Wouters and Verhoeven, 'Cases Identified', in Ankumah and Kwakwa, *African Perspectives* (2005), p. 138.

961 cf. Kleffner, *Complementarity* (2008), p. 155; El Zeidy, *Complementarity* (2008), p. 225; cf. also van der Wilt, in Stahn, *Practice* (2015), p. 215, arguing that 'the replacement of the initial adjective "partial" with "substantial" [collapse] made the criteria more rigid'.

962 In this vein, *Situation in the DRC*, ICC-01/04-02/06-20-Anx2, para. 37, arguing that the DRC's justice system inability 'does not wholly correspond to the reality any longer'.

963 Crit. the lack of clarity, Morel, *Complémentarité* (2005), p. 133.

964 cf. Kleffner, *Complementarity* (2008), pp. 155, 160 (regarding substantial collapse); Jurdi, *LJIL*, 30 (2017), 202 (considering it 'very difficult' to distinguish unavailability from total collapse: 'Probably, the only scenario where these criteria can be different from each other is when a newly political system has been established with no judicial system in place yet').

965 Stigen, *Relationship* (2008), pp. 316–17; for possible factors entailing an unavailability, see Boas et al., *International Criminal Procedure* (2011), p. 81.

966 In contrast, Cárdenas, in Kleffner and Kor, *Complementary Views* (2006), p. 124; Cárdenas, *Zulässigkeitsprüfung* (2005), p. 128 argues—based on the authentic Spanish version of Art. 17 (3) ('*al hecho de que carece*')—that a system is *only* unavailable when it is non-existent. See also Burke-White, *CLF*, 19 (2008), 74 ('lack of judicial infrastructure'); *contra* Hall, *Suggestions* (2003), p. 17; El Zeidy, *Complementarity* (2008), pp. 226–7.

967 See ICC-OTP, *Complementarity* (2003), para. 49 with n. 15: 'It is suggested that the term "unavailability" should be given a broad interpretation, so as to cover the various "inability" scenarios in the latter part of Article 17 (3) and to cover typical cases of inability'. See also Stigen, *Relationship* (2008), pp. 317–18; Kleffner, *Complementarity* (2008), p. 153 ('any unavailability') and Meißner, *Zusammenarbeit* (2003), p. 87, functioning judiciary exists, but it cannot deal with the particular case for normative or factual reasons.

968 For a detailed discussion, see Stigen, *Relationship* (2008), pp. 319–24; see also Benzing, *MPYbUNL*, 7 (2003), 614 ('capacity overload'); El Zeidy, *Complementarity* (2008), pp. 227–8; Razesberger, *Complementarity* (2006), p. 49; Nouwen, *Complementarity* (2013), p. 65; van der Wilt, in Stahn, *Practice* (2015), p. 220.

969 This argument has been further developed by van der Wilt and Lyngdorf, *ICLR*, 9 (2009), 39 ff., arguing that the ECHR's case law on the duty to properly investigate flagrant human rights violations and its concrete assessment of State practice serves as a useful guideline as to these or other States' unwillingness or inability. See also Stigen, *Relationship* (2008), p. 318.

In this sense, *exemption provisions* conceded in processes of transition may not only be considered as a problem of unwillingness,[970] but also as one of inability in the sense of '*human rights unavailability*', that is, a lack of an effective judicial remedy or access to the courts.[971] Also, the absence or inadequacies of national legislation regarding international criminal law, especially regarding the ICC core crimes, could render a national system unavailable.[972] As a consequence, the ICC would qualify a State's legal system as 'unavailable', in the sense of Article 17 (3) ICCS. The opposite, narrower, view rejects such quality judgements about a national justice system.[973] It argues that the drafters did not consider the scenario of an overburdened justice system since, inter alia, this is an assessment which is ultimately up to the State concerned.[974] Thus, one cannot demand more than 'some existent national infrastructure' and the fulfilment of some minimum international standards with a view to ensure the security for victims, witnesses, judges, and defendants.[975] As to the existence of international crimes in the national legislation, it is sufficient, pursuant to this correct, more liberal, view, that the concrete acts can be appropriately punished, be it on the basis of international or national crimes.[976]

[970] cf. Gropengießer and Meißner, *ICLR*, 5 (2005), 282 ff.; Kreicker, in Eser, Sieber, and Kreicker, *Nationale Strafverfolgung VII* (2006), p. 305.

[971] In this sense, O'Shea, *Amnesty* (2002), p. 126, arguing that a failure to prosecute based on amnesty would amount to an inability to prosecute owing to the unavailability of the State's national judicial system; for inability due to a blanket amnesty, see also Burke-White, *LJIL*, (2005), 582; Stigen, *Relationship* (2008), p. 322 (law not 'at disposal'); Razesberger, *Complementarity* (2006), pp. 160–1. See also Pichon, *ICLR*, 8 (2008), 195 arguing that 'amnesties have to be subsumed in general under the notion of unavailability, since it would contradict the whole purpose of an amnesty if it could easily be lifted in a concrete case' and concluding with regard to Sudan (p. 223) that immunity 'leads to unavailability'. See also Kleffner, *Complementarity* (2008), p. 106 (regarding amnesty) and pp. 157–8 ('statutory limitations', 'bar to carrying out the proceedings'); El Zeidy, *Complementarity* (2008), p. 227; Nouwen, *Complementarity* (2013), p. 65; Samir Hassanein, *ICLR*, 15 (2015), 122.

[972] Kleffner, *JICJ*, 1 (2003), 89; Kleffner, *Complementarity* (2008), pp. 156–7; El Zeidy, *Complementarity* (2008), p. 227; Razesberger, *Complementarity* (2006), pp. 49–51; Bekou, in Ulrich, *Challenges and Prospects* (2005), p. 78; Terracino, *JICJ*, 5 (2007), 435; Mégret, in Stahn and El Zeidy, *Complementarity I* (2011), pp. 380–1; Samir Hassanein, *ICLR*, 15 (2015), 113 ff. ('substantive legal inability'); from a victim's perspective, see Moffett, *JICJ*, 13 (2015), 297 ff.; McCarthy, in Stahn, *Practice* (2015), pp. 1211 ff. (in favour of taking into consideration 'as part of an assessment of whether cases are admissible before the Court', 'the existence or otherwise of reparations schemes at the national level'). Crit. Nouwen, *Complementarity* (2013), p. 50 with n. 57. An example provides the ICTR decision in the case of *Prosecutor v. Bagaragaza*: though not in the context of the ICCS, the ICTR had to decide on a comparable issue when Norway requested a referral of the just mentioned case to its authorities based on Rule 11*bis* ICTR RPE. Since Norway had not implemented the crime of genocide into its national criminal law, the ICTR's Trial Chamber came to the conclusion that Norway lacked jurisdiction *ratione materiae* over the crimes as charged in the indictment, and consequently 'Bagaragaza's alleged criminal acts cannot be given their full legal qualification under Norwegian criminal law, and the request for the referral to the Kingdom of Norway falls to be dismissed' (*Prosecutor v. Bagaragaza*, No. ICTR 2005-86-R11, Decision on the Prosecution's Motion for Referral to the Kingdom of Norway, para. 16 (19 May 2006)).

[973] Arsanjani and Reisman, in Sadat and Scharf, *Theory and Practice of ICL* (2008), pp. 329 ff.; Philips, *CLF*, 10 (1999), 79; Holmes, in Lee, *ICC* (1999), p. 48.

[974] Arsanjani and Reisman, in Sadat and Scharf, *Theory and Practice of ICL* (2008), pp. 331 ff.

[975] Burke-White, *LJIL*, (2005), 579. Advocating a gender-sensitive witness protection, Chappell, Grey, and Waller, *ICTJ*, 7 (2013), 464; crit. of a narrow interpretation of admissibility, as the criteria of same conduct and genuine proceedings do not include due process concerns with regard to victims, Moffett, *JICJ*, 13 (2015), 298–9.

[976] See note 573 in this chapter with main text; in the same vein, Pichon, *ICLR*, 8 (2008), 197; Stigen, *Relationship* (2008), pp. 321, 336; Razesberger, *Complementarity* (2006), pp. 51, 153–4; Nouwen, *Complementarity* (2013), pp. 49–50; Jurdi, *LJIL*, 30 (2017), 203 assumes unavailability when a domestic judicial system's 'failure to act has led to the materialization of impunity'. For the same result, also Kleffner, *Complementarity* (2008), pp. 119–25 (esp. 123); Rastan, in Stahn and El Zeidy, *Complementarity I* (2011), p. 450, focusing on the legal qualification instead of the crimes' label. Similarly Heller, *HarvILJ*, 53 (2012), 85–133, advocating a 'sentence-based theory' of complementarity, only comparing the possible domestic sentence with the one of the ICC; crit. on this, Robinson, *HarvILJOnline*, 53 (2012), 165 ff.; Robinson, in Schabas et al., *Research Companion ICL* (2013), pp. 369 ff.; also crit. Satzger, *ICL* (2018), § 12 mn. 19, arguing that '[i]n spite of a potentially adequate punishment, an appropriate legal qualification is … missing'; Stahn, *HarvILJ*, 53 (2012), 183 ff.; crit. on the (non-)application of Art. 17 by the OTP regarding the *Colombia* Situation, see Pinto Soares, *IsLR*, 46 (2013), 326 ff.; Chappell, Grey, and Waller, *ICTJ*, 7 (2013), 464 ff. For a different interpretation, stressing the difference between ordinary and international

A convincing and sensible interpretation should find a middle ground between the broad and narrow interpretations. A too narrow interpretation would make the 'total or substantial collapse' criteria superfluous and is therefore not convincing. On the other hand, a too broad interpretation would ignore that by using the term 'substantial', instead of 'partial' (collapse), the mere inefficient functioning of a judicial system, its internal deficiencies, should not fall under the unavailability concept.[977] Thus, in the result, the existence of substantial legal or factual obstacles[978] entailing a lack of effective remedies may only constitute unavailability if this qualification can be made by an external observer without entering into value (quality) judgements regarding the *internal* functioning of the national justice system concerned. The qualification must be based on objective (quantitative) factors which are easily verifiable from outside of the system, for example empirical information indicating that that there is no effective remedy for human rights violations. Under these circumstances it is possible that a capacity overload might render the judicial system unavailable, either due to the sheer magnitude of the crimes committed or due to a lack of personal or other resources.[979]

As a consequence of the collapse or unavailability of the judicial system, the State may be 'unable to obtain the accused or the necessary evidence and testimony' or is—catch-all clause[980]—'otherwise unable to carry out the proceedings'.[981] The case law, albeit cautious so far,[982] has produced some examples in this regard. In *Bemba*, TC III, in an *obiter dictum*, took the national justice system's lack of capacity 'to handle these proceedings' as an 'otherwise' unavailability.[983] As to *Saif Al-Islam Gaddafi*, PTC I, without discussing the conditions of unavailability further, considered the Libyan judicial system as unavailable given 'substantial difficulties in exercising its judicial powers fully across the entire territory'.[984] The Chamber emphasized in particular the challenges with regard to 'the effectiveness and accountability of the police service, the security for the courts and participants in the proceedings, to reform the detention centers and to bring practices of torture to an end'.[985] Interestingly, the same PTC I came to a different result in the *Al Senussi* case. Comparing the (detention) situation of Gaddafi and Al-Senussi the Chamber concluded that the same security challenges, in particular with regard to the protection of witnesses, do not prejudice the proceedings against Al-Senussi given that 'a considerable amount of evidence' has already been collected and continues to be collected and that these proceedings 'are currently progressing and have recently reached the accusation stage'.[986]

crimes, El Zeidy, *Complementarity* (2008), pp. 290–8; similarly, albeit too superficial, Sedman, in Stahn and van den Herik, *Perspectives* (2010), pp. 265–6; relying on ICTR jurisprudence with regard to international crimes, Marong, *GeorgiaJI&CompL*, 40 (2011/12), 93–4. See also *Gaddafi*, ICC-01/11-01/11-344-Red, paras. 85–8, 108–13; *Al-Senussi*, ICC-01/11-01/11-466-Red, para. 66 (iv) ('whether domestic investigations are carried out with a view to prosecuting "international crimes"' or 'ordinary crimes' 'is not determinative ... to the extent that the case covers the same conduct'); upheld by the AC in *Al-Senussi*, ICC-01/11-01/11-565, para. 119.

[977] Stigen, *Relationship* (2008), p. 323, limiting factual obstacles to external ones.

[978] Discussing substantive and procedural legal obstacles under 'legal inability', Samir Hassanein, *ICLR*, 15 (2015), 112 ff.

[979] cf. Stigen, *Relationship* (2008), pp. 329–30. See also Stegmiller, *Pre-Investigation Stage* (2011), pp. 311–13.

[980] El Zeidy, *Complementarity* (2008), pp. 223–4.

[981] Art. 17 (3) ICCS.

[982] For a discussion, see Schabas and El Zeidy, 'Article 17', in Ambos, *Commentary* (2022), mn. 88; Abdou, 'Article 17', in Klamberg et al., *Commentary ICC I* (2023), pp. 622–4.

[983] *Bemba*, ICC-01/05-01/08-802, paras. 245–6; see also Safferling and Farthofer, *International Criminal Procedure* (2012), p. 105; van der Wilt, in Stahn, *Practice* (2015), pp. 215 ff.

[984] *Gaddafi*, ICC-01/11-01/11-344-Red, para. 205.

[985] Ibid., paras. 204 and 206 ff. (with a detailed analysis of these aspects).

[986] *Al-Senussi*, ICC-01/11-01/11-466-Red, paras. 294 ff. (298–9).

An inability 'to obtain the accused' within the meaning of Article 17 (3) has been discussed, again, with regard to Saif Al-Islam Gaddafi since, albeit being in custody on Libyan territory, it was not possible to transfer him from the detention centre of the Zintan militia in the north of the country to proper State custody in Tripoli. Thus, PTC I, seeing no concrete progress that this will happen in future, determined a lack of ability on the part of the Libyan State.[987] In the same decision an inability to obtain testimony has been determined since the national authorities lacked full control over the detention facilities and failed to provide adequate witness protection.[988] Last but not least, the 'otherwise' inability to carry out proceedings has also been discussed in both Libya admissibility proceedings. In *Gaddafi*, PTC I affirmed such an inability because of the Libyan authorities' inability to provide the suspect with a defence counsel.[989] In contrast, however, the same PTC I was not disturbed by the same situation with regard to Al-Senussi since he was in custody of the central authorities in Tripoli and 'many local lawyers from Mr Al-Senussi's tribe have indicated their willingness to represent Mr. Al-Senussi'.[990]

### *(e) Challenges to admissibility (Articles 18, 19)*

The shift from situation to case is also reflected in Articles 18 and 19 ICCS which regulate the procedural challenges against jurisdiction and admissibility (and thus display the adversarial nature of complementarity litigation):[991] while Article 18 refers to 'a situation' referred[992] and 'criminal acts which may constitute crimes',[993] Article 19 provides for challenges as to the admissibility (and jurisdiction) of 'a case'.[994] Thus, it has correctly been argued that the specificity increases from a comparatively general standard[995]—via Article 18 ICCS—to selecting individual cases,[996] until it reaches the highest level of concrete cases in the narrow sense (Article 19 ICCS).[997] As a consequence, admissibility must be assessed, as already explained above,[998] both at the situation and case levels, that is, with regard to preliminary admissibility rulings (focusing on potential cases) pursuant to Article 18 ICCS and (proper, case-related) admissibility rulings pursuant to Article 19 ICCS.[999]

987 *Gaddafi*, ICC-01/11-01/11-344-Red, paras. 206–8.

988 Ibid., paras. 209–11 (pointing to torture of detainees in detention centres and insufficient witness protection programmes).

989 Ibid., paras. 212–14; see also Abdou, 'Article 17', in Klamberg et al., *Commentary ICC I* (2023), pp. 622–4.

990 *Al-Senussi*, ICC-01/11-01/11-466-Red, para. 308.

991 See also Wierda, *Impact* (2023), pp. 60 ff. (rather adversarial than 'amicable').

992 Art. 18 (1).

993 Art. 18 (2).

994 See previously note 338 in this chapter.

995 Art. 53 (1).

996 Art. 53 (2); cf. e.g. Rastan, in Stahn and El Zeidy, *Complementarity I* (2011), pp. 456–7.

997 *Muthaura et al.*, ICC-01/09-02/11-274, paras. 38–9, 44, pointing to the relative vagueness of situations within the meaning of Art. 18 ICCS as compared to the higher specificity of cases within the meaning of Art. 19 ICCS; in the same vein, *Ruto et al.*, ICC-01/09-01/11-307, paras. 39–40, 45; see also *Gaddafi*, ICC-01/11-01/11-547-Red, para. 60. See also Kleffner, *Complementarity* (2008), pp. 197–8 (see also his preceding analysis of Arts. 18, 19 at pp. 168–91); for a detailed analysis, see also El Zeidy, *Complementarity* (2008), pp. 239–82; Razesberger, *Complementarity* (2006), pp. 32–3, 72–84, 123–38; Taylor, 'Article 18', in Klamberg et al., *Commentary ICC I* (2023), pp. 625–41; Abdou, 'Article 19', in Klamberg et al., *Commentary ICC I* (2023), pp. 643–59.

998 Section B.(2)(b) in this chapter.

999 *Muthaura et al.*, ICC-01/09-02/11-274, para. 37; *Ruto et al.*, ICC-01/09-01/11-307, para. 38. See also Rule 55 (2) RPE ICC ordering the PTC to consider Art. 17 when making a preliminary admissibility ruling. For a literature overview, see Stahn, *CLF*, 19 (2008), 106; Olásolo, in Almqvist and Espósito, *Justicia Transicional* (2009), pp. 266–7.

*Article 18*[1000] basically ensures that interested State Parties,[1001] that is, especially those that 'would normally exercise jurisdiction',[1002] are properly informed[1003] so that they can challenge admissibility by informing the Court[1004] that they already conduct proceedings regarding the respective criminal acts.[1005] With this, Article 18 confirms the States' primary jurisdiction and entails an early[1006] control of the Prosecutor by the respective State or the PTC.[1007] This purpose also speaks in favour of a broad interpretation of the provision with regard to a State's initiation of national proceedings once it receives a notification.[1008] However, the provision does not apply to Security Council referrals.[1009] Upon the 'request' of the State, the Prosecutor may 'defer' to its investigation,[1010] assuming that the State acts in good faith;[1011] otherwise, if no State reacts, the Prosecutor may go on with the investigation.[1012] Alternatively, the Prosecutor may themselves request the PTC to authorize the investigation,[1013] thereby overriding the State's primary jurisdiction.[1014] PTCs have recently granted such requests with regard to the situations of Afghanistan,[1015] the Philippines,[1016] and Venezuela.[1017] At any rate, given that Article 18 applies at the

[1000] For the procedural details, see Rules 52–7 RPE ICC and Reg. 38 (1)(b) RegC. On the drafting history, see Nsereko and Ventura, 'Article 18', in Ambos, *Commentary* (2022), mn. 1–9.

[1001] While the wording of Art. 18 (1) is ambiguous (referring unspecifically to 'those States'), it follows from Art. 18 (5) (referring to 'States Parties') and the *travaux* that the provision only applies to State Parties; cf. Nsereko and Ventura, 'Article 18', in Ambos, *Commentary* (2022), mn. 34-6; more broadly apparently, ICC-OTP, *Policy Paper* (2003), p. 5 only referring to 'States'; in favour of an application with regard to non-State Parties, Taylor, 'Article 18', in Klamberg et al., *Commentary ICC I* (2023), pp. 625–8.

[1002] Art. 18 (1).

[1003] On the method and contents of the notification, see Nsereko and Ventura, 'Article 18', in Ambos, *Commentary* (2022), mn. 37–8 with further references; Taylor, 'Article 18', in Klamberg, in Klamberg et al., *Commentary ICC I* (2023), pp. 629–31. The Prosecutor may notify 'on a confidential basis', e.g. to prevent destruction of evidence; cf. Art. 18 (1) last sentence; Nsereko and Ventura, 'Article 18', in Ambos, *Commentary* (2022), mn. 39-40; Taylor, 'Article 18' in Klamberg et al., *Commentary ICC I* (2023), pp. 629–31.

[1004] The 'Court', in both Arts. 18 and 19 refers to the Chambers as the adjudicatory organs, i.e. not to the 'Court', in a broad sense as defined in Art. 34 ICCS. This follows from the separate reference to the 'Prosecutor', in Art. 18 (1) and to the Chambers in Art. 19 (6); on the latter, see also Nouwen, *Complementarity* (2013), p. 81 with n. 184.

[1005] Art. 18 (2), Rule 53 RPE ICC. See also ICC-OTP, *Policy Paper* (2003), p. 5, stating that the notification under Art. 18 'will alert States with jurisdiction to the possibility of taking action themselves'; Nsereko and Ventura, 'Article 18', in Ambos, *Commentary* (2022), mn. 33; Razesberger, *Complementarity* (2006), 67 ff.; crit. Damaška, *UCLA JIL & ForAff*, 14 (2009), 23–4; Nouwen, in Brown, *Handbook ICL* (2011), pp. 222–3; Rohrer, *Legalitäts- oder Opportunitätsprinzip* (2010), pp. 143–4.

[1006] cf. Nsereko and Ventura, 'Article 18', in Ambos, *Commentary* (2022), mn. 15.

[1007] cf. *Situation in Kenya*, ICC-01/09-19, para. 43 ('review . . . does not otherwise arise before the stage of article 18'). On the purposes of the provision, see Nsereko and Ventura, 'Article 18', in Ambos, *Commentary* (2022), mn. 10.

[1008] In the same vein, ICC-OTP, *Policy Paper* (2003), p. 5 ('possibility of taking action'); Nsereko and Ventura, 'Article 18', in Ambos, *Commentary* (2022), mn. 42 ('State that has not yet started investigations but is otherwise able and willing to do so must be given a chance to do so').

[1009] Art. 18 (1) only refers to Art. 13 (a) and (c), but not to 13 (b) ICCS; see also Nouwen, *Complementarity* (2013), p. 77; Nsereko and Ventura, 'Article 18', in Ambos, *Commentary* (2022), mn. 11; Taylor, 'Article 18', in Klamberg et al., *Commentary ICC I* (2023), pp. 629–31.

[1010] Art. 18 (2), last sentence first part.

[1011] Nsereko and Ventura, 'Article 18', in Ambos, *Commentary* (2022), mn. 44.

[1012] Ibid.

[1013] Art. 18 (2), last sentence ('on the application of the Prosecutor, decides to authorize').

[1014] Nsereko and Ventura, 'Article 18', in Ambos, *Commentary* (2022), mn. 47.

[1015] *Situation Afghanistan*, ICC-02/17-196, concluding 'Afghanistan is not presently carrying out genuine investigations and . . . has not acted in a manner that shows an interest in pursuing the Deferral Request' (para. 58).

[1016] *Situation Philippines*, ICC-01/21-56-Red, concluding that the domestic activities 'do not amount to tangible, concrete and progressive investigative steps being carried out with a view to conducting criminal proceedings, in a way that would sufficiently mirror the Court's investigation as authorised in the Article 15 Decision' (para. 96); and that despite limited investigations regarding low-level perpetrators 'the totality of the national investigations and proceedings . . . do not sufficiently, or at all, mirror[,] the Court's investigation', so that 'relevant investigations' or 'a real or genuine effort to carry out such investigations' has not been shown (para. 98).

[1017] *Situation Venezuela I*, ICC-02/18-45, concluding that '[w]hile Venezuela is taking some investigative steps, its domestic criminal proceedings do not sufficiently mirror the scope of the Prosecution's intended

situation stage, and a situation normally contains a series of potential cases all linked to a given (broad) situation (situation linkage),[1018] new events may not easily produce a new situation[1019] and the comparison with domestic investigations/prosecutions may be difficult given that these may already focus on specific cases and/or individuals.[1020] Also, a Prosecutor's deferral of a certain (concrete) investigation will not impede the continuation of other (concrete) investigations and thus be 'of little help to a state that wishes to prevent the ICC from investigating the situation as a whole'.[1021] In fact, the ICC regime does not provide for a legal framework for deferrals comparable to that of the ad hoc tribunals.[1022]

In the case of deference to the national proceedings, the Prosecutor may review the State's activity after six months or 'at any time when there has been a significant change of circumstances based on the State's unwillingness or inability genuinely to carry out the investigation'.[1023] It may request the State to be periodically informed, 'without undue delay', of the state of the proceedings.[1024] Pending a PTC ruling, the Prosecutor may seek authority from the PTC 'to pursue necessary investigative steps', in case of a 'unique opportunity' to preserve and obtain important evidence.[1025] Given that this is an exceptional possibility[1026] the Prosecutor has to show, with cogent evidence, the urgent need for it.[1027] If authorized, the investigative steps are to be carried out notwithstanding any postponement of execution of

investigation. [ ... ] Venezuela is not investigating (and does not express any intention to investigate) the factual allegations underlying the contextual elements of crimes against humanity ([ ... ] the focus of the domestic investigations appear to generally be on direct/low level perpetrators. (para. 130) and that 'Venezuela appears to have taken limited investigative steps ... periods of unexplained investigative inactivity ... the domestic investigations appear to not sufficiently mirror the forms of criminality the Prosecution intends to investigate ... discriminatory intent underlying the alleged crimes and the insufficient investigation of crimes of a sexual nature' (para. 131).

[1018] See Section B.(2)(b).

[1019] The issue came recently up with regard to the post-7 October 2023 Gaza war investigation and the Prosecutor's application of arrest warrants with regard to Israel's Prime Minister Netanyahu and Defence Minister Gallant, see Heller, *Opinio Juris* 24 May 2024 (arguing that the Art. 18 stage has been passed and thus Israel/the suspects can only invoke Art. 19); in the same vein Ambos, EJIL:Talk! 19 August 2024; *contra* Cohen and Shany, *Just Security* 25 May 2024 ('Israel ... deprived ... of invoking complementarity under article 18 ...').

[1020] See also *Situation Afghanistan*, ICC-02/17-196, para. 46; *Situation Philippines*, ICC-01/21-56-Red, para. 13: 'comparison of two very different sets of information that cannot easily be compared'; *Situation Venezuela I*, ICC-02/18-45, para. 65; for a clear distinction that yet allows to draw conclusions from one to the other, see *Situation Venezuela I*, ICC-02/18-89, para. 248 (supporting the PTC's approach to enquire whether domestic investigations had identified particular perpetrators in order to assess whether any relevant investigations or prosecutions have been conducted).

[1021] Nouwen, *Complementarity* (2013), p. 78; Taylor, 'Article 18', in Klamberg, in Klamberg et al., *Commentary ICC I* (2023), pp. 632–5; see previously note 560 in this chapter and main text. On the ICC framework on deferral of cases and the post-admissibility monitoring, see Stahn, in Stahn, *Practice* (2015), pp. 250–3.

[1022] See note 476 in this chapter and main text. Crit. of the lack of a proper deferral and post-(in)admissibility monitoring system, also Stahn, in Stahn, *Practice* (2015), pp. 250–3.

[1023] Art. 18 (3).

[1024] Art. 18 (5). Stressing the State's obligation to inform swiftly, Nsereko and Ventura, 'Article 18', in Ambos, *Commentary* (2022), mn. 61; crit. Stahn, in Stahn, *Practice* (2015), p. 240 ('dead letter'). Non-State Parties have no such obligation to inform, rendering 'it particularly difficult for the Prosecution to assess the progress of the case, as the Prosecution also has no right to conduct investigations in non-State parties', cf. thereon Taylor, 'Article 18', in Klamberg et al., *Commentary ICC I* (2023), pp. 638–9.

[1025] Art. 18 (6). On the PTC's authority in this regard, see Art. 56 ICCS; see also Taylor, 'Article 18', in Klamberg et al., *Commentary ICC I* (2023), p. 640.

[1026] cf. Art. 18 (6): 'on an exceptional basis'. This limitation is not contained in Art. 19 (8) ICCS.

[1027] cf. Nsereko and Ventura, 'Article 18', in Ambos, *Commentary* (2022), mn. 62; Cryer, *Prosecuting* (2005), pp. 164 ff. (esp. on Art. 18 (3) and (5)); Friman, 'Procedures', in Cryer et al., *ICL* (2014), pp. 443–4 (omitted in the 2019 edition authored by Vasiliev).

a cooperation request under Article 95 ICCS.[1028] The respective PTC decisions may be appealed by the State concerned or the Prosecutor.[1029]

As to *Article 19*, the considerations made regarding jurisdiction[1030] apply, *mutatis mutandis*, to admissibility challenges under this provision. If a State has, however, already challenged a PTC admissibility ruling under Article 18, it can only do so again under Article 19—with regard to the respective 'case'—'on the grounds of additional significant facts or significant change of circumstances'.[1031] Apart from that there are some further differences as compared to jurisdictional challenges. First of all, as to the standard of proof, the wording of Article 19 (1) makes a distinction between jurisdiction and admissibility requiring for the latter a lower standard than for the former.[1032] Thus, the certainty standard applicable to jurisdiction[1033] seems to be too strict for admissibility, where therefore something less, e.g. a balance of probabilities or reasonable conviction, should suffice.[1034] Secondly, a challenge to a case only brought at the commencent of the trial or even later (with the leave of the Court)[1035] can only be based on a violation of the *ne bis in idem* principle;[1036] otherwise, as to all other admissibility challenges, the previous admissibility decision by the Court is to be considered *res judicata*.[1037] Thirdly, as already explained above,[1038] the suspension of the investigation upon a State challenge[1039] only applies to an admissibility challenge.[1040]

Fourthly, the Prosecutor may request a review of an inadmissibility decision—to the Chamber that made the latest ruling[1041]—if 'new facts have arisen which negate the basis on which the case had previously been found inadmissible'.[1042] A comparison with the French and Spanish versions[1043] makes clear that these facts must have only become known after the

[1028] cf. Art. 95 *in fine* ('unless the Court has specifically ordered'); see also Chapter VII, B.(2)(a)(ii)(1) in this volume and Nsereko, 'Article 18', in Ambos, *Commentary* (2022), mn. 62–3.

[1029] Art. 18 (4). For more details, see Nsereko and Ventura, 'Article 18', in Ambos, *Commentary* (2022), mn. 56–60; Taylor, 'Article 18', in Klamberg et al., *Commentary ICC I* (2023), p. 637.

[1030] See Section A.(4)(a)(iv) in this chapter. For more details, see Rules 58–62, 122 (2), 133 RPE ICC, and Reg. 38 (1)(c) RegC.

[1031] Art. 18 (7). For examples of such grounds, see Nsereko and Ventura, 'Article 18', in Ambos, *Commentary* (2022), mn. 68, e.g. end of war, regime change etc., but, of course, always with implications for willingness to genuinely prosecute. Absent such grounds, the State is estopped from filing a further challenge, cf. Nouwen, *Complementarity* (2013), p. 83 with n. 193 (analogical application).

[1032] Compare Art. 19 (1), cl. 1 regarding jurisdiction ('satisfy itself') with sentence 2 regarding admissibility (merely 'determine'). The further difference as to the verbs 'shall' and 'may' (obligation versus discretion), however, yields no further consequences since Art. 19 (1) cl. 2 refers to the admissibility test of Art. 17 which also uses the stricter 'shall'; in the same vein, Nouwen, *Complementarity* (2013), pp. 81–2.

[1033] See Section A.(4)(a)(iv) in this chapter and below.

[1034] See e.g. *Bemba*, ICC-01/05-01/08-802, para. 204 (the AC has not pronounced itself on the standard) and for further (inconsistent) case law, Nsereko and Ventura, 'Article 19', in Ambos, *Commentary* (2022), mn. 17-8, 23-4, 29; see also ICC-OTP, *Complementarity* (2003), para. 52; Vagias and Ferencz, *LJIL*, 28 (2015), 149–52 (against an analogical application of the admissibility standard to jurisdiction since the two concepts are too different).

[1035] While a State may always adjudicate a case, even after the Court has issued an arrest warrant (Nouwen, *Complementarity* (2013), pp. 78–9), the admissibility may only be challenged once and, as a rule, 'prior to or at the commencement of the trial' (Arts. 19 (4) cll. 1 and 2).

[1036] cf. Art. 19 (4) last sentence referring to Art. 17 (1)(c) which in turn refers to Art. 20 (3) ICCS; see also Abdou, 'Article 19', in Klamberg at al., *Commentary ICC I* (2023), pp. 651–2.

[1037] cf. Nouwen, *Complementarity* (2013), p. 81.

[1038] See Section A.(4)(a)(iv) in this chapter.

[1039] Art. 19 (7).

[1040] For a detailed analysis, see Nsereko and Ventura, 'Article 19', in Ambos, *Commentary* (2022), mn. 84–6.

[1041] Rule 62 (1) RPE ICC. This would normally be a PTC or TC, see Nsereko and Ventura, 'Article 19', in Ambos, *Commentary* (2022), mn. 101–2.

[1042] Art. 19 (10). The provision only refers to admissibility, not jurisdiction; for a restrictive interpretation, also Nouwen, *Complementarity* (2013), p. 85; crit. Nsereko and Ventura, 'Article 19', in Ambos, *Commentary* (2022), mn. 105 ('oversight').

[1043] 'des faits nouvellement apparus' and 'han aparecido nuevos hechos'.

last decision, and they must have not also occurred since that decision.[1044] In any case, this review possibility confirms that the factual situation on the basis of which admissibility (or jurisdictional) decisions are taken is not 'static, but ambulatory',[1045] that is, that the complementarity test is an ongoing process[1046] taking into account the facts as they exist at the time of the (pre)trial (not appeals) proceedings.[1047] As to the new facts, the Prosecutor must also be certain in the sense of the certainty standard mentioned above,[1048] going beyond a mere balance of probabilities.[1049]

Last but not least, the Prosecutor, having deferred an investigation of a case for the reasons spelt out in Article 17, may request 'information on the proceedings' from the relevant State.[1050] This mirrors the identical information obligation of States under Article 18 (5) regarding situations, except that this provision demands State Parties to respond 'without undue delay'. However, under Article 19 (11) a State Party has the same duty to promptly comply with the said information obligation. It follows, implicitly, from its general, good faith cooperation obligation as a State Party under Article 86 ICCS.[1051] It is less clear whether Article 19 (11) only addresses a voluntary deferral by the Prosecutor or also a suspension of an investigation pursuant to Article 19 (7). While the latter, broader view would make sense with regard to the Prosecutor's supervisory function under the complementarity regime since they can only comply with this function on the basis of State information on relevant domestic proceedings, the delicate balance between Court and State interests under this regime makes it difficult to impose an obligation on States where it is not explicitly provided for in the Statute. Thus, it seems to better conform to the rationale of the complementarity regime to limit the obligation information to the situation under Article 19 (11) where it is explicitly provided for.[1052]

At any rate, a State which challenges admissibility under Article 18 (2) or under Article 19 (2)(b) and (c) bears the *burden* of showing that investigations or prosecutions have taken place or are taking place;[1053] this burden rests, *mutatis mutandis*, on the accused under

[1044] In the same vein, Nsereko and Ventura, 'Article 19', in Ambos, *Commentary* (2022), mn. 104.

[1045] *Katanga*, ICC-01/04-01/07-1497, para. 56, further noting that the admissibility of a case must be determined on the basis of the facts as they exist at the 'time of proceedings' concerning the admissibility challenge and that '[t]hese activities may change over time' and 'a case that was originally admissible may be rendered inadmissible by a change of circumstances in the concerned States and vice versa'. See also *Kony et al.*, ICC-02/04-01/05-377, paras. 27–9. For further case law, Nsereko and Ventura, 'Article 19', in Ambos, *Commentary* (2022), mn. 21, 27. See also Nouwen, *Complementarity* (2013), pp. 83, 105 (facts dynamic); Stahn, in Stahn, *ICC* (2015), p. 230.

[1046] See Section B.(2)(a) in this chapter with note 509 and main text.

[1047] *Katanga*, ICC-01/04-01/07-1497, para. 56 (admissibility must be determined on the basis of the facts as they exist at the 'time of proceedings' concerning the admissibility challenge and that '[t]hese activities may change over time' and 'a case that was originally admissible may be rendered inadmissible by a change of circumstances in the concerned States and vice versa'); *Ruto et al.*, ICC 01/09-01/11-234, para. 10 ('time of the proceedings' refers to the 'time of the proceedings on the admissibility challenge before the Pre-Trial Chamber and not to the subsequent proceedings on appeal'); *Muthaura et al.*, ICC-01/09-02/11-202, para. 9; *Situation Afghanistan*, ICC-02/17-196, para. 47 ('time ... of the request for deferral'); *Situation Philippines*, ICC-01/21-56-Red., para. 17 ('time ... of the Prosecution's request to resume its investigation'); see also note 590 in this chapter referring to *Gaddafi*, ICC-01/11-01/11-547-Red, paras. 41–4 (distinguishing an appeal insofar from the Art. 19 (4) challenge).

[1048] Above note 1034 with main text.

[1049] Similarly Nsereko and Ventura, 'Article 19', in Ambos, *Commentary* (2022), mn. 104 ('fully satisfied', 'higher than that for admissibility determinations under Article 19(1)').

[1050] Art. 19 (11) ICCS.

[1051] In the same vein, Nsereko and Ventura, 'Article 19', in Ambos, *Commentary* (2022), mn. 107–8.

[1052] For a restrictive view, also Nouwen, *Complementarity* (2013), p. 86; for a broader interpretation, see Nsereko and Ventura, 'Article 19', in Ambos, *Commentary* (2022), mn. 109–10, invoking, inter alia, the intention of the drafters, but the mere intention cannot compensate for the lack of an explicit information obligation under Art. 19 (7).

[1053] cf. (regarding Art. 18) *Situation Afghanistan*, ICC-02/17-196, para. 45; *Situation Philippines*, ICC-01/21-56-Red., para. 14; *Situation Venezuela I*, ICC-02/18-45, para. 63; *Situation Venezuela I*, ICC-02/18-89, para. 77;

Article 19 (2)(a). For the State/accused have all means and information at their disposal with regard to domestic investigations, prosecutions, or trials. The respective State/accused must 'provide the Court with evidence with a sufficient degree of specificity and probative value that demonstrates that it is indeed investigating' the situation or case.[1054] It must be shown that 'tangible, concrete and progressive' as well as 'proactive investigative steps' are undertaken;[1055] 'sparse and disparate' activities are as insufficient[1056] as mere assertions of ongoing investigations.[1057] Relevant materials to comply with this burden of production may include, but are not limited to, 'police reports, charges or other official allegations, copies of evidence, referrals to prosecutors or other bodies, as well as relevant court fillings and court records'.[1058] Having the burden the State must also ensure that these materials are provided in one of the working languages of the Court so that a Chamber is able to analyse them.[1059]

### (3) Positive complementarity

#### *(a) Origin and concept*

As already mentioned above,[1060] positive complementarity may be understood, notwithstanding certain controversies,[1061] as a concept aimed at encouraging domestic and other (international, regional) criminal justice systems to conduct their own criminal proceedings.[1062] The concept originated in an OTP policy paper from 2003 where the Office

(regarding Art. 19) *Muthaura et al.*, ICC-01/09-02/11-274, para. 61 (holding that 'a State that challenges the admissibility of a case bears the burden of proof to show that the case is inadmissible'); *Ruto et al.*, ICC-01/09-01/11-307, para. 62; *S. Gbagbo*, ICC-02/11-01/12-75, para. 128. In the same vein, Ellis, *Sovereignty and Justice* (2014), pp. 180–1 (explaining the 'less demanding burden' in *Bemba* with the fact that the applicant was the defendant whereas in *Kenya* the applicant was the State); Nsereko and Ventura, 'Article 19', in Ambos, *Commentary* (2022), mn. 22, 29 with further references to case law in notes 65, 66, 87.

1054 *Muthaura et al.*, ICC-01/09-02/11-274, paras. 2, 61, 68; *Gaddafi and Al-Senussi*, ICC-01/11-01/11-344-Red, para. 54; *Situation Afghanistan*, ICC-02/17-196, para. 45; *Situation Philippines*, ICC-01/21-56-Red., para. 14; *Situation Venezuela I*, ICC-02/18-45, para. 66; *Situation Venezuela I*, ICC-02/18-89, para. 181.

1055 *Gbagbo*, ICC-02/11-01/12-47-Red, paras. 30, 65; *Al-Werfalli*, ICC-01/11-01/17-13, para. 28; more recently with further references *Situation Afghanistan*, ICC-02/17-196, para. 45; *Situation Philippines*, ICC-01/21-56-Red., para. 14.

1056 *Gbagbo*, ICC-02/11-01/12-47-Red, para. 65; *Situation Philippines*, ICC-01/21-56-Red., para. 14.

1057 *Muthaura et al.*, ICC-01/09-02/11-274, paras. 2, 61; *Situation Afghanistan*, ICC-02/17-196, para. 45

1058 *Situation Philippines*, ICC-01/21-56-Red., para. 15.

1059 *Situation Afghanistan*, ICC-02/17-196, para. 50 (if, however, the prosecution provides a translation due to the inactivity of the respective State 'it must be assumed that the State accepts the translation, as well as the selection made by the Prosecution as being reflective of the materials submitted').

1060 Section B.(2)(b) in this chapter with note 608.

1061 cf. ICC-ASP, *Complementarity* (2021), p. 3 (Ch. Nissen, advisor at the Danish embassy, stating that there is 'no universally agreed definition'); see also ILA, *Positive Complementarity* (2022), pp. 17 ff. with further references. Much of the controversy is due to the use of different terminology, see ILA, *Positive Complementarity* (2022), p. 48 (recommending uniform terminology) and the following note.

1062 For a recent comprehensive definition ILA, *Positive Complementarity* (2022), p. 19: 'any cooperation with a criminal jurisdiction aimed at enhancing the capacity and willingness of that jurisdiction to investigate and prosecute crimes within the ICC's subject-matter jurisdiction' (distinguishing between the concept as an admissibility rule or a policy and not limiting it to the OTP); for a similar distinction, see Expert Group, *IER* (2020), para. 720 (distinguishing between complementarity 'for the assessment of jurisdiction' and 'positive complementarity activities'); see also ICC-ASP, *Report Complementarity* (2022), para. 58 (enabling domestic jurisdictions in the fight against impunity by way of cooperation). See previously Burke-White, *CLF*, 19 (2008), 62 (defining positive complementarity as the OTP 'actively encourag[ing] investigation and prosecution of international crimes within the Court's jurisdiction by States where there is reason to believe that such States may be able or willing to undertake genuine investigations and prosecutions and where the active encouragement of national proceedings offers a resource-effective means of ending impunity'); crit. of this and other 'complementarity obligations' Nouwen, *Complementarity* (2013), pp. 18–19; see also Burke-White, *HarvILJ*, 49 (2008), 54 with n. 4 (prefering the term

stressed—within the framework of 'a two-tiered approach to combat impunity'—the responsibility of domestic systems to prosecute international crimes and expressed its intent to 'encourage' and 'facilitate' them to do so.[1063] This may include assistance in 'strengthening and rebuilding national justice systems, by providing international assistance to those systems or by some other means'.[1064]

Thus, the OTP suggests a division of labour between the ICC and the national criminal justice systems whereby the former goes after the most responsible and the latter prosecute the other, more low-level perpetrators,[1065] although this does not exclude that 'in other instances', international and national efforts may be combined to 'ensure that perpetrators of serious international crimes are brought to justice'.[1066] In any case, in the OTP's view, the national systems 'are often best placed to carry out some of the tasks assigned to the Office'.[1067]

In the 2003 Expert Paper on Complementarity a whole section is dedicated to '[P]artnership and dialogue with States'.[1068] Apart from repeating the States' 'first

'proactive complementarity' as one better reflecting the nature of the policy and better highlighting its distinction from passive complementarity); in the same vein, Pampalk and Knust, *ZIS*, 5 (2010), 672 with n. 30; Arbia and Bassy, in Stahn and El Zeidy, *Complementarity I* (2011), p. 55; Ryngaert, in Bergsmo, *Complementarity* (2010), pp. 172 ff.; Bekou, in Stahn, *Practice* (2015), pp. 1252 ff.; on positive complementarity as a second pillar of complementarity, see Ambach, in Stahn, *Practice* (2015), pp. 1281–2; also El Zeidy, *Complementarity* (2008), pp. 298 ff.; Ambos and Stegmiller, *Crime Law Soc Change*, 58 (2012), 426 ff.; furthermore, see Bachmann and Nwibo Eda, *Brook. J.Int'l. L*, 43 (2018), 478–82 (differentiating between 'Passive Complementarity', i.e. the 'ICC's role in prosecuting international crimes' (479), 'Positive Complementarity' and 'Proactive Complementarity, i.e. 'a policy of formal requests by States for assistance from the ICC, and a corresponding agreement by the ICC to support national justice systems' (482)); ICC-ASP, *Report complementarity* (2022), para. 58 (equating 'complementary activities' with positive complementarity); distinguishing 'positive complementarity' from a 'positive approach to complementarity' (as echoed by the OTP after Kampala) ILA, *Positive Complementarity* (2022), pp. 10 ff., 48 (understanding the latter as a policy factor used in the assessment of a State's willingness and ability to prosecute and thus render situations/cases inadmissible).

[1063] ICC-OTP, *Policy Paper* (2003), pp. 3, 5; see also ICC-OTP, *Annex Policy Paper* (2003), pp. 4 ('encourage genuine national proceedings'), 6 ('encourage and assist national proceedings where possible'), L. Moreno Ocampo, 'Ceremony for the Solemn Undertaking of the Chief Prosecutor of the International Criminal Court' (The Hague, 16 June 2003) <http://www.icc-cpi.int/NR/rdonlyres/D7572226-264A-4B6B-85E3-2673648B4896/143585/030616_moreno_ocampo_english.pdf> (States' 'primary responsibility to prevent, control and prosecute atrocities'); Moreno-Ocampo, in Stahn and El Zeidy, *Complementarity I* (2011), pp. 24–5. On the early implementation of positive complementarity by the OTP, see Hall, in Stahn and Sluiter, *Practice* (2009), pp. 219–28; on the earlier origins of the concept, see El Zeidy, *Complementarity* (2008), pp. 299–300; on the development, see also ILA, *Positive Complementarity* (2022), p. 5.

[1064] ICC-OTP, *Policy Paper* (2003), pp. 3, 7; Moreno-Ocampo, in Stahn and El Zeidy, *Complementarity I* (2011), pp. 26–8; ICC-OTP, *Prosecutorial Strategy* (2010), para. 17; thereon Pinto Soares, *IsLR*, 46 (2013), 320, see also Pampalk and Knust, *ZIS*, 5 (2010), 673–4. On the ICC Legal Tools Project and its role in positive complementarity, see Tillier, *ICLR*, 13 (2013), 566 ff.; Bergsmo, Bekou, and Jones, *GoJIL*, 2 (2010), 804 ff.; Bergsmo, Bekou, and Jones, *HRLR*, 10 (2010), 715 ff.; Bergsmo, Bekou, and Jones, in Bergsmo, *Active Complementarity* (2011), pp. 25–42; Bergsmo, Bekou, and Jones, in Bergsmo, *Active Complementarity* (2011), pp. 15 ff.; cf. also the 'Legal Tools Database' website, <https://www.legal tools.org/>. A service of Legal Tools is the Case Matrix, see <https://www.casematrixnetwork.org/icc-legal-tools-database/>; see also Bergsmo, Bekou, and Jones, in Bergsmo, *Active Complementarity* (2011), pp. 43 ff. On effective positive complementarity comparing it to the completion strategy of the ad hoc tribunals, see Pinto Soares, *IsLR*, 46 (2013), 329 ff. On positive complementarity in the service of a possible completion strategy of the Court, see Evenson and Smith, in Stahn, *Practice* (2015), pp. 1269 ff. For further means in this regard, see also Lafleur, *Komplementarität* (2011), pp. 345 ff.; Kuhli, *GA*, 152 (2012), 765; Orentlicher, *JICJ*, 11 (2013), 524 ff.

[1065] ICC-OTP, *Policy Paper* (2003), p. 7 ('If the ICC has successfully prosecuted the leaders of a State or organisation, the situation in the country concerned might then be such as to inspire confidence in the national jurisdiction. The reinvigorated national authorities might now be able to deal with the other cases.')

[1066] Ibid.

[1067] Ibid., pp. 8–9. The OTP even suggest that 'States Parties take ownership of the Court in a number of ways' (p. 6).

[1068] ICC-OTP, *Complementarity* (2003), pp. 5 ff. (sect. II.); thereon, see also Schabas and El Zeidy, 'Article 17', in Ambos, *Commentary* (2022), mn. 26.

responsibility and right to prosecute' and their 'best access to evidence and witnesses and the resource to carry out the proceedings',[1069] the paper stresses the cooperative relationship between States and the ICC in the fight against impunity which may sometimes entail 'a consensual division of labour'.[1070] States are to be reminded of their responsibility to enact relevant legislation and to be encouraged to investigate and prosecute international crimes.[1071] The OTP shall provide 'direct assistance and advice' consisting of technical advice, training, and other forms of assistance.[1072] Assistance to concrete national investigations and prosecutions[1073] should be used 'as an incentive to encourage co-operation on the part of the State concerned'.[1074] Yet, the potential tension between these two contradictory roles—the partnership/dialogue role and the supervisory/monitoring role—is acknowledged and it is rightly pointed out that this gives rise to the 'potential danger that if the OTP gets too closely involved in providing training, advice and assistance to a national proceeding, it may be difficult to extricate the OTP to credibly criticize and question the process if it subsequently proves to be a non-genuine proceeding'.[1075]

In 2006, in its report on its first three years of activities, the OTP referred to the concept of complementarity 'meaning that it encourages genuine national proceedings ... relies on national and international networks; and participates in a system of international co-operation'.[1076] It further defined complementarity as a kind of universal international criminal justice system[1077] whose effectiveness must therefore not be measured by the number of cases reaching the Court, but taking into account national proceedings: 'In this circumstance, Office inactivity with regard to investigation and prosecution should be measured as a success'.[1078] In 2010, setting out its Strategy 2009 to 2012, the Office defined the concept as 'a proactive policy of cooperation aimed at promoting national proceedings'.[1079] More concretely, it advocated the encouragement of national proceedings, 'relying on its

[1069] ICC-OTP, *Complementarity* (2003), p. 3.

[1070] Ibid., pp. 3–4. On the terms required for a successful division of labour, see Burke-White, *HarvILJ*, 49 (2008), 101–5; Burke-White, *CLF*, 19 (2008), 81–4.

[1071] ICC-OTP, *Complementarity* (2003), p. 5.

[1072] Ibid., pp. 5–6.

[1073] cf. Art. 93 (10) ICCS and Chapter VII, B.(3)(a)(i) in this volume with further references on this 'reverse' cooperation.

[1074] ICC-OTP, *Complementarity* (2003), p. 6.

[1075] Ibid., p. 7.

[1076] ICC-OTP, *Report on Activities* (2006), para. 58.

[1077] Ibid. ('much of the work done toward achieving the goals of the Statute may take place in national systems around the world'); similarly Moreno-Ocampo, in Stahn and El Zeidy, *Complementarity I* (2011), pp. 21–3. The idea of a global criminal justice system in this context was probably first advocated by Burke-White, *LJIL*, 18 (2005), 558 ff. (advocating a 'multi-level global governance model of interaction between the Court and national governments created by the complementarity regime', rather than a 'simple substitution model of complementarity' where 'the ICC will merely step in when domestic courts are unable or unwilling to act'); see also Burke-White, *CLF*, 19 (2008), 60–1 ('the Rome System of Justice'); Burke-White, *HarvILJ*, 49 (2008), 56 ff. ('the Rome Statute creates a tiered system of prosecutorial authority that could be characterized the "Rome System of Justice"'. Within this system, both the domestic and international levels of governance have interrelated international legal duties to provide accountability for international crimes' (fn. omitted)); Burke-White, in Stahn and El Zeidy, *Complementarity I* (2011), p. 353 comparing it with the US federal criminal justice system (pp. 353 ff.). Crit. Nouwen, *Complementarity* (2013), pp. 19–20 and Tsilonis, *Jurisdiction* (2019), pp. 215 ff. (worrying about '"reverse" interpretation and practical application' (215) or even a politicization of the complementarity principle (221)).

[1078] ICC-OTP, *Report on Activities* (2006), para. 58.

[1079] ICC-OTP, *Prosecutorial Strategy 2009–2012* (2010), para. 16. Crit. Burke-White, *HarvILJ*, 49 (2008), 55–6 (arguing that the former Prosecutor moved away from such a policy ever since, focusing on the direct prosecution of international crimes); Burke-White, in Stahn and El Zeidy, *Complementarity I* (2011), p. 346; similarly Pinto Soares, *IsLR*, 46 (2013), 320–1 (holding that 'the declared commitment of the OTP to positive complementarity has barely materialised in practice').

various networks of cooperation', without, however, 'involving the Office directly in capacity building or financial or technical assistance'.[1080] This approach includes four aspects, namely, (i) providing information on request within the framework of national investigations pursuant to Article 93 (10); (ii) involving 'officials, experts and lawyers from situation countries to participate in OTP investigative and prosecutorial activities' and 'sharing with them expertise and trainings'; (iii) 'providing information about the judicial work of the Office' to national or international mediators; and (iv) 'acting as a catalyst with development organizations and donors' conferences to promote support for relevant accountability efforts'.[1081]

The 'Policy Paper Preliminary Examinations' confirmed the cooperative approach[1082] and restated the idea, first expressed in the 2006 Activities Report,[1083] of the creation of 'an interdependent, mutually reinforcing international system of justice'.[1084] The Office also reiterates the risk, as previously stated in the Expert Paper,[1085] of a too close cooperation with the national authorities with regard to (future) admissibility proceedings.[1086] It wants to minimize this risk by *a limine* excluding that such cooperation can be 'construed as a validation of the national proceedings'.[1087]

In its strategic plan 2012–2015, the Office proclaims, as a fourth strategic goal, to 'enhance complementarity and cooperation by strengthening the Rome System in support of the ICC and of national efforts in situations under preliminary examination or investigation'.[1088] Thus, cooperation is seen as the essential tool to support (positive) complementarity[1089] which, in turn, means national investigations and prosecutions[1090] in order to obviate 'the need for the Court's intervention'.[1091] In fact, the Office makes a virtue of necessity and invokes its limited resources as a reason 'to reinforce the complementarity idea',[1092] that is, to leave the investigation and prosecution to domestic jurisdictions. This iunctim between cooperation and complementarity shall also be applied to other situations and cases not under preliminary investigation by the Court.[1093] Insofar the OTP seeks 'to develop stronger relationships with national authorities' and, together with Interpol, 'create a common platform for improved interaction between the relevant members of the law enforcement community'.[1094] The 2016–2018 Strategy basically confirmed this approach[1095] and the 2019–2021

[1080] ICC-OTP, *Prosecutorial Strategy 2009–2012* (2010), para. 17.

[1081] Ibid.

[1082] ICC-OTP, *Policy Prelim. Examinations* (2013), para. 100 ('requires national judicial authorities and the ICC to function together').

[1083] Note 1080 in this chapter and main text.

[1084] ICC-OTP, *Policy Prelim. Examinations* (2013), para. 100.

[1085] Note 1078 in this chapter and main text.

[1086] ICC-OTP, *Policy Prelim. Examinations* (2013), para. 102 ('engage with national jurisdictions provided that it does not risk tainting any possible future admissibility proceedings').

[1087] Ibid., para. 102.

[1088] ICC-OTP, *Strategic Plan* (2013), para. 5 no. 4, para. 32 no. 4, and para. 21 (positive complementarity as strategic principle).

[1089] See also ibid., paras. 66, 69.

[1090] See also ibid., paras. 66 ('enable a State to genuinely investigate and prosecute'), 69 ('encouraging genuine national proceedings').

[1091] See also ibid., para. 66; see also para. 9 (limiting the Court's intervention through complementarity).

[1092] Ibid., para. 15.

[1093] In a similar vein, Evenson and Smith, in Stahn, *Practice* (2015), pp. 1269 ff. arguing in favour of applying positive complementarity at the stage of (and for the preparation of) the completion of a situation or case.

[1094] ICC-OTP, *Strategic Plan* (2013), para. 67.

[1095] ICC-OTP, *Strategic Plan* (2015), para. 23 (goal 4 to 'enhance complementarity and cooperation by strengthening the Rome Statute System ... and of national efforts in situations under preliminary examination or investigation'), para. 29 (achieving 'a higher level of coordination and complementarity').

Strategy stressed once more the role of positive complementarity with a view to closing the impunity gap and contributing to the completion of ongoing investigations.[1096]

Under the leadership of current Prosecutor Khan the OTP is meant to become 'a hub for accountability efforts'[1097] with (positive) complementarity playing a central role to strengthen the cooperative relationship between the ICC and States ('two-way street of co-operation').[1098] The recently launched 'Policy on Complementarity and Cooperation' develops this further, conceiving the OTP not as 'the apex of the international criminal justice movement' but rather, as just said, as 'a hub at the centre of our collective accountability efforts'.[1099] The original concept of positive complementarity is now complemented, if not substituted, by 'dynamic' complementarity, striving to bring 'justice closer to communities'[1100] and putting more emphasis on the already mentioned cooperative relationship between the ICC (OTP) and States ('two track approach'),[1101] considering that this close relationship is firmly entrenched in the Court's legal framework.[1102] It is questionable though if, apart from the new terminology, this implies a substantive change in policy. If positive complementarity means, as explained at the beginning of this subsection, encouraging domestic systems to genuinely investigate and prosecute the Rome Statute crimes, a closer cooperation with States appears as a logical and necessary consequence and entails an increased deference to national investigations terminating or at least suspending ICC preliminary examinations.[1103] With this dynamic, complementarity turns out to be a form of positive complementarity under a different name. At any rate, the OTP recognizes 'four key pillars on which the Office's efforts to deepen its engagement with national authorities will be based', namely the creation of a 'Community of Practice' through, among other things, (i) new forms of information exchange ('establishing new forums, platforms and modalities'); (ii) the improvement of its technical infrastructure; (iii) an increased presence in the field 'to strengthen its investigative activities and deepen its engagement with national

[1096] ICC-OTP, *Strategic Plan* (2019), para. 49 ('can help to progress the goal of closing the impunity gap as well promote a faster implementation of the completion strategy'); see also Expert Group, *IER* (2020), para. 736 with R265 (to be 'considered in the design of completion strategies'). On the role of the Court and the ASP with regard to positive complementarity in the context of a completion strategy, see previously Evenson and Smith, in Stahn, *ICC* (2015), pp. 1273–5.

[1097] ICC-OTP, *Strategic Plan* (2023), paras. 32 ff.

[1098] ICC-OTP, *Report 2022* (2022), p. 32–3; also para. 54 ('vision of the complementary role of the ICC and its relationship with national criminal jurisdictions').

[1099] ICC-OTP, *Complementarity and Cooperation* (2024), Preface, p. 1; also paras. 34 and 51. On this new policy see Urueña, *Just Security* 26 August 2024 (and further blogs at the respective symposium).

[1100] ICC-OTP, *Complementarity and Cooperation* (2024), Preface, pp. 1–2 ('bring our work closer to communities'); also paras. 27, 72 ff. Crit. from a victim's perspective Chinwenmeri Uche, *EJIL: Talk!*,25 April 2024; from an African perspective Lugano, *Just Security* 8 July 2024.

[1101] ICC-OTP, *Complementarity and Cooperation* (2024), Preface, p. 3; also paras. 1 ff., 91, 118.

[1102] cf. ICC-OTP, *Complementarity and Cooperation* (2024), para. 13 ('The provisions of the Court's regulatory framework that address complementarity and cooperation straddle multiple provisions of the Statute and Rules and their full utilization gives better expression to the relationship of complementarity and cooperation … Many of the areas treated in this policy have traditionally been subsumed under the overall umbrella of complementarity or the phrase 'positive complementarity'.)

[1103] See, regarding *Colombia* above, note 518 with main text and Ambos, *EJIL: Talk!* 3 November 2021 (discussing, inter alia, the respective MoU); on Colombia as a (new) positive complementarity model, see also ICC-OTP, *Report on Colombia* (2023), paras. 48–54, 66. While the *Venezuela I* preliminary examination concluded with an opening of an investigation, the respective MoU also refers to positive complementarity (focusing on cooperation and contributing to the Venezuelan 'efforts … to carry out genuine national proceedings'); see also Prosecutor Khan's remarks at the respective press conference ('committed to working collaboratively … with full regard to the principle of positive complementarity'). On these situations as well as CAR and Guinea, see also ICC-OTP, *Report 2022* (2022), pp. 37 ff. (stating at p. 54 that the 'implementation of completion strategies … offers tangible expression to the core principles of cooperation and complementarity'); ICC-OTP, *Complementarity and Cooperation* (2024), paras. 125 ff., 134 ff.

stakeholder and local CSOs'; and, last but not least, (iv) the utilization of cooperation mechanisms.[1104] Given that positive complementarity is a policy question within the OTP's domain and not a question of the interpretation of Article 17 proper, it is understandable that, within the Court, primarily the Prosecutor speaks to this practice.[1105] Apart from that, only the Registry has stressed its role in positive complementarity,[1106] while there is only relevant judicial pronouncement in the *Kenya* proceedings. There the PTC dealt with the reverse cooperation under Article 93 (10) ICCS, mentioned earlier as one element of positive complementarity,[1107] and held that this concerns exclusively the cooperation regime under Part IX of the Statute and 'has no linkage with the issue of admissibility'.[1108] Interestingly, in these same proceedings the OTP dismissed its out-of-court stance with regard to positive complementarity, described in detail above, arguing that the domestic proceedings in Kenya 'should be in principle carried out without the assistance of the Court'.[1109]

### (b) *Assessment: A realistic role for positive (or cooperative) complementarity*

Generally, positive complementarity is to be welcomed in that it shows respect for the national criminal justice systems and thus better accommodates local cultural sensitivities.[1110] Ideally, it empowers national criminal justice systems and assists them in overcoming accountability obstacles.[1111] It thus contributes to a more positive relationship between the ICC/OTP[1112] and States and, ultimately, may make ICC intervention wholly

[1104] ICC-OTP, *Complementarity and Cooperation* (2024), paras. 27 ff.

[1105] On the alignment of a proactive complementarity policy with the OTP, see also Burke-White, *HarvILJ*, 49 (2008), 82–5 (suggesting concrete strategies and tactics the OTP could utilize to implement it at 85 ff.). For Seils, in Stahn, *Practice* (2015), pp. 305 ff., 'there is a limited amount the ICC and the OTP in particular can do in promoting national prosecutions' (making some suggestions for steps to be taken by the OTP at pp. 326–7) in order 'to contribute not only to occasional prosecutions but to restored justice systems capable of protecting human rights and worth trusting' (p. 327).

[1106] cf. Arbia and Bassy, in Stahn and El Zeidy, *Complementarity I* (2011) , pp. 55 ff. Accordingly, this non-judicial role of the Registry includes every aspect of a broad understanding of national proceedings, from the implementation of legislation (ibid., 65–6), to ensuring adequate legal representation (ibid., 57–9), witness protection (ibid., 59–60) and effective court management and detention conditions (ibid., 60–2), to the outreach of the Court (ibid., 62–4) and the positive impression the Court leaves behind after leaving the situation country (ibid., 64–5).

[1107] Note 1076 in this chapter and main text.

[1108] *Muthaura et al.*, ICC-01/09-02/11-96, paras. 30–1. See also Judge Ušacka's dissent in the *Gaddafi* Appeals Decision acknowledging that the Statute's goal 'to combat impunity can also be achieved ... through means of active cooperation with the domestic authorities'; *Gaddafi*, ICC-01/11-01/11-547-Anx2, Dissenting Opinion Judge Ušacka, para. 65, further stating that in this regard the Court is 'in an ideal position to actively assist domestic authorities in conducting such proceedings, be it by the sharing of materials and information collected or of knowledge and expertise'. Crit. of the strict separation also, Stahn, in Stahn, *Practice* (2015), pp. 236–7 (arguing that it leaves 'limited space to take into account domestic justice efforts'); see also ILA, *Positive Complementarity* (2022), pp. 6–7 (stressing the breadth of the provision covering 'serious crime[s] under international law' [Art. 93 (1)(a)] and/or crimes not investigated by the ICC).

[1109] ICC, *Situation in the Republic of Kenya*, PTC II, Prosecution's Response to 'Request for Assistance on behalf of the Government of the Republic of Kenya pursuant to Article 93 (10), Article 96 and Rule 194', ICC-01/09-80, 6 October 2011, paras. 6, 24. See also Tillier, *ICLR*, 13 (2013), 528–30; crit. thereon Nouwen, *Complementarity* (2013), p. 109.

[1110] On these, regarding the *Darfur* investigation, Fouladvand, *ICLR*, 14 (2014), 1028, 1050 ff.

[1111] See, for a list of accountability barriers and countermeasures on the basis of positive complementarity ILA, *Positive Complementarity* (2022), pp. 19 ff. The Report lists quite common (legal) obstacles (e.g. lack of codification of core crimes, *nullum crimen sine lege*, immunities) but also discusses rather uncommon (more factual) ones mentioned in some country reports (e.g. a jurisdictional custody or presence requirement, governments seeing accountability efforts against their interests, political instability, patronage).

[1112] ICC, *IER Response* (2021), para. 503 ('supporting the work of national jurisdictions ... can be one of the most effective ways to build positive connections between the Court and national authorities, enhancing the Court's perception and credibility among key stakeholders'); see also ICC-OTP, *Report 2022* (2022), pp. 32–3, 54 where this cooperative relationship is stressed.

unnecessary.[1113] Of course, as rightly acknowledged by the OTP, a too close cooperation with the investigative authorities of the territorial State entails the risk that the Office loses the neutrality and distance necessary to assess the national activities in light of Article 17 ICCS.[1114] It is therefore right that the Office takes steps to exclude at the outset that such a close cooperation could amount to a 'validation of the national proceedings'.[1115] At the same time, positive complementary is not limited to the preliminary examination phase but may well continue to be relevant during investigation[1116] and as part of a completion strategy.[1117]

At any rate, one should be aware that positive complementarity has intrinsic *limitations* and entails some *risks*.[1118] First of all, the Court/OTP, albeit able to support domestic proceedings in various ways,[1119] is not a development agency[1120] and the OTP certainly lacks the resources[1121] to act as a meaningful facilitator of international assistance.[1122] To proclaim otherwise, as in some of the (early) statements quoted above, is counterproductive since it creates unrealistic expectations whose non-fulfilment only leads to generalized frustration about the Court's performance.[1123] The ASP therefore rightly limited the OTP's role to concrete assistance in national proceedings without getting involved 'in capacity building, financial support and technical assistance'.[1124] These activities should

[1113] Regarding empowerment as a success criterion of international criminal justice, see Akhavan, *JICJ*, 11 (2013), 532; on how the national capacity can be strengthened, see Bekou, in Stahn, *Practice* (2015), pp.1254 ff.; on the contribution of proactive complementarity regarding some of the ICC's goals, see Burke-White, *HarvILJ*, 49 (2008), 73–6. On some examples of positive complementarity in the first years of the Court (Colombia, Uganda, Kenya), see Burke-White, in Stahn and El Zeidy, *Complementarity I* (2011), pp. 347–52; on a more recent example (Colombia), Ambos, *EJIL: Talk!* 3 November 2021.

[1114] Crit. also Nouwen, *Complementarity* (2013), pp. 100–1 (risk of losing impartiality); crit. previously, Stahn, *CLF*, 19 (2008), 100 ff., esp. on the risks with regard to the independence of the OTP (103, 107–8); on the differences with the ICTR and ICTY, see Hall, in Stahn and Sluiter, *Practice* (2009), pp. 220 ff.

[1115] Note 1090 in this chapter and main text.

[1116] cf. ICC, *IER Response* (2021), para. 498 ('may remain a live issue'), responding to Expert Group, *IER* (2020), para. 734 ('exclusive to the PE stage'). On the controversial debate with regard to the role of positive complementarity at the preliminary examination phase, see ILA, *Positive Complementarity* (2022), pp. 13 ff., 47–8 (arguing that there are 'strong reasons to give complementarity a serious chance' during that phase).

[1117] Above note 1099.

[1118] For a fundamental, but too far-reaching critique, see Nouwen, *Complementarity* (2013), pp. 378 ff., criticizing, inter alia, the inconsistency, in particular between out-of-court statements and in-court practice, and stressing the risk of the OTP's approach to the primary jurisdiction of States (see also the following references); crit. of the too far-reaching and overambitious implementation demands linked to complementarity, Mégret, in Stahn and El Zeidy, *Complementarity I* (2011), pp. 365 ff., arguing that some activist scholars and NGOs use complementarity as a 'Trojan horse' to achieve the implementation of full-fledged legal and judicial reforms (361, 367 ff.), understanding it as an orthodox 'universalizing mechanism', instead of 'a device to accommodated diversity' (361, 398–90).

[1119] cf. ILA, *Positive Complementarity* (2022), p. 49.

[1120] As itself acknowledged by the OTP, cf. ICC-OTP, *Strategic Plan* (2015), para. 57 ('not act as a development agency').

[1121] Crit. also Nouwen, *Complementarity* (2013), pp. 101, 401 ('illusion' created by complementarity in that regard); Tillier, *ICLR*, 13 (2013), 551–2; Wierda, *Impact* (2023), pp. 64–6 (complementarity cannot fix systemic problems in domestic systems), 69–70, 81 (Court cannot remedy situations of absolute inability, inherits same obstacles as exist in domestic systems, insofar complementarity creates 'illusion'); on the Court's limited resources in this regard, see Burke-White, *HarvILJ*, 49 (2008), 66–7.

[1122] All the relevant information on the complementarity resources and on the actors working in the field of complementarity can be found at the website of the ASP under 'Complementarity', <https://asp.icc-cpi.int/en_menus/asp/complementarity/Pages/COMP_default.aspx>.

[1123] See generally Damaška, *ChicKentLR*, 83 (2008), 329, 331 ff., warning of the 'overabundance' of the Court leading to exaggerated expectations and calling for more 'modesty in setting objectives' to avoid '[d]isillusionment stemming from unfulfilled expectations and inconsistencies' (364–5).

[1124] ICC-ASP, Res. ICC-ASP/8/Res. 9 (2010), Annex 4 para. 16; see also paras. 42, 52; see also ICC-ASP, Res. ICC-ASP/11/Res. 6 (2012), paras. 3 and 10; Res. ICC-ASP/12/Res. 4 (2013), paras. 3 and 8; Res. ICC-ASP/21/Res. 2 (2022), para. 143 ('recalling the Court's limited role in strengthening national jurisdictions').

be left to the technical cooperation agencies of donor countries and international organizations,[1125] with the ASP itself serving as a kind of 'matchmaker'.[1126] For this very reason the OTP's new aspiration as a 'hub' for global accountability efforts, as expressed in the recent policy paper already mentioned above,[1127] gives rise to certain concerns if this entails activities, for example the creation of 'a new global Complementarity and Cooperation Forum through which a community of practitioners can be formed',[1128] which are not proper of an entity whose primary function is to investigate international crimes and prosecute the (most) responsible.

Secondly, the so-called policy of positive (or dynamic) complementarity is indeed a mere prosecutorial policy, largely operating without an explicit or implicit legal basis in the Statute.[1129] The only provision explicitly providing for such a basis, the already mentioned Article 93 (10) ICCS,[1130] is limited to judicial assistance in the context of concrete proceedings[1131] and, in addition, rather belongs to the cooperation regime.[1132] Of course, if States explicitly ask for assistance or even greater involvement in their national criminal justice processes,[1133] the Court/OTP may enter into agreements with the respective State.[1134] Indeed, it is not legally impeded from responding to such requests, but the factual problems—potential loss of neutrality and limited resources—remain. In any case, positive complementarity must not be understood or operate in such a way that it discourages States from complying with their primary responsibility to exercise jurisdiction.[1135]

[1125] ICC-ASP, Res. ICC-ASP/8/Res. 9 (2010), Annex 4, para. 16; Res. ICC-ASP/21/Res. 2 (2022), para. 136 ff. See, for concrete examples of assistance in that regard, ILA, *Positive Complementarity* (2022), pp. 50–2.

[1126] ILA, *Positive Complementarity* (2022), p. 12 (but crit. of its performance at p. 13); see also Expert Group, *IER* (2020), para. 736 ('division of labour between the OTP and the ASP', the latter 'facilitating partnerships' between OTP and States/organizations'); conc. ICC, *IER Response* (2021), para. 498; see also ICC-ASP, *Report Complementarity* (2022), para. 19 ff. (summary of first meeting on 'division of labour between Court and ASP'); ICC-ASP, Res. ICC-ASP/21/Res. 2 (2022), para. 140 ('Bureau to remain seized of... capacity-building activities'), 141 ('mandate to facilitate the exchange of information'). On the role of the ASP in promoting complementarity, see also O'Donohue, in Stahn, *ICC* (2015), pp. 136 ff. Crit. of the ASP's focus, Nouwen, *Complementarity* (2013), pp. 385, 406–7, arguing that it is based 'on incorrect assumptions about the obstacles to domestic proceedings'.

[1127] Above notes 1102 ff. and main text.

[1128] ICC-OTP, *Complementarity and Cooperation* (2024), paras. 38 ('Sharing ideas, good practices and expert knowledge is essential in building future bridges for cooperation which will enhance the Rome Statute system and assist the Court in the delivery of its mandate'), 38 ff.; see also Chinwenmeri Uche, *EJIL: Talk!*, 25 April 2024 ('a platform for sharing expertise and discussing and developing common standards').

[1129] cf. Nouwen, *Complementarity* (2013), p. 98. For a different view apparently ICC-OTP, *Complementarity and Cooperation* (2024), para. 13 (already quoted above note 1105).

[1130] On positive complementarity within this framework, see Tillier, *ICLR*, 13 (2013), 553–4. One may also see a basis in the sixth recital of the Preamble (stressing the States's duty to exercise jurisdiction over the ICC crimes), but the Preamble lacks the binding force of the actual treaty text, see Triffterer, Bergsmo, and Ambos, 'Preamble', in Ambos, *Commentary* (2022), mn. 4 (legal importance of the Preamble), 16–17 (sixth recital). See also Burke-White, *HarvILJ*, 49 (2008), 76–82; Burke-White, *CLF*, 19 (2008), 63–70 (inferring implicit and explicit legal support for proactive complementarity from the ICCS, its Preamble and the provisions on admissibility and the OTP); a basis in paras. 4 to 6 of the Preamble, El Zeidy, *Complementarity* (2008), pp. 301–4 (but crit. of Burke-White's reference to the ICCS).

[1131] Nouwen, *Complementarity* (2013), p. 99.

[1132] Note 1111 in this chapter and main text.

[1133] A recourse to the ASP (acquiescing in positive complementarity measures), as suggested by Nouwen, *Complementarity* (2013), p. 100, is therefore not necessary.

[1134] cf. Art. 54 (3)(d); on such agreements with regard to the positive complementarity, see Tillier, *ICLR*, 13 (2013), 581 ff.

[1135] Crit. in this regard of a 'literal' understanding of the term and the above-mentioned 'division of labour' Nouwen, *Complementarity* (2013), pp. 340–4, 397–8, 407–8, arguing that this approach, further fostered by a 'pro-ICC ideology' (352 ff., 398, 407), undermines the States' primary obligation to exercise jurisdiction and thus entails 'the normative paradox of complementarity' (345–51), i.e. displacing the States' jurisdiction instead of encouraging it. This goes too far however. A thorough reading of the OTP's understanding of positive complementarity, as presented above in the main text, clearly shows that any division of labour between States and the Court

On a more modest and realistic note, positive complementarity may surely help a willing State to overcome *inability*[1136]—if its national justice system is not totally collapsed in the sense defined in the previous section—but it will never be able to do this alone, that is, without efforts by the State itself and assistance by international donors. Also, positive complementarity can hardly contribute to overcome *unwillingness*[1137] since, as explained earlier,[1138] this concept implies a political manipulation of the criminal justice system by the ruling elite. Such political manipulation can only be overcome by structural reforms which must come from within the system. Thus, in sum, positive complementarity may help willing States to overcome a selective or limited inability.

does not change the formers' primary responsibility. See also Burke-White, *HarvILJ*, 49 (2008), 62–4 (arguing that proactive complementarity would restore the burden of prosecuting international crimes on those States which want to shift it to the ICC); similarly Satzger, *ICL* (2018), § 12 mn. 26 (arguing that complementarity is 'exerting (political) pressure on the Member States to prosecute international crimes primarily on a national level'). On the importance of a positive victim-orientated complementarity to end impunity, see Moffett, *JICJ*, 13 (2015), 300 ff., suggesting 'three areas where complementarity might be made more victim-orientated and therefore more effective in tackling impunity: legislation, procedural rules and substantive outcomes' (302 ff.), and stressing the role of the ASP (as oversight) (305 ff.) and regional organizations to facilitate that change (307 ff.).

1136 See also Gioia, in Stahn and El Zeidy, *Complementarity II* (2011), pp. 807–29 (arguing that such cooperation 'might prove attractive to a state wishing to overcome its "unavailability" and to prevent the ... ICC from stepping in', at 807); in a similar vein, Nouwen, *Complementarity* (2013), pp. 395, 401; Burke-White, *HarvILJ*, 49 (2008), 68, 92 ff.; Burke-White, *CLF*, 19 (2008), 74–81; Bekou, in Stahn, *Practice* (2015), pp. 1254.

1137 See also Nouwen, *Complementarity* (2013), p. 401; Burke-White, *HarvILJ*, 49 (2008), 87–91; Burke-White, *CLF*, 19 (2008), 70–4; Bekou, in Stahn, *Practice* (2015), pp. 1254.

1138 See Section B.(2)(d)(iii)(1) in this chapter.

# IV
# Proceedings before the ICC and the Ad Hoc Tribunals—Overview of and Special Issues

*The full chapter bibliography can be downloaded from

## A. Overview

International criminal proceedings may be divided, up to the first instance verdict, into *three separate phases*: the investigation phase, the intermediate proceedings, and the trial. The *investigation* phase consists of all 'activities undertaken by the Prosecutor ... for the collection of information and evidence'.[1] It may be further subdivided into a pre-investigation and a formal (actual) investigation phase, but the former is only of relevance at the ICC in the form of the so-called preliminary examination. As we have already seen in the previous chapter, the investigation develops from a situation to a case, and the precise definition and delimitation of these concepts are already relevant at the level of jurisdiction and, in particular, of admissibility (complementarity).[2] The *intermediate proceedings* basically serve to review the indictment or charges as the actual result of the prosecutorial investigation. These proceedings have, again, special importance at the ICC with the so-called confirmation proceedings. Once charges are confirmed, the case is transferred to a trial chamber or trial division.[3] The *trial phase* may be further subdivided into three phases: the (normally quite extensive) trial preparation phase, the actual trial with the verdict ('decision')[4] upon the guilt or innocence of the accused, and the phase meting out the sentence ('sentencing').[5]

In this chapter, we will first give an overview of the three phases of international criminal procedure, subdividing the investigation phase into 'preliminary examination' and 'formal investigation'. For readers more interested in the complex details of international criminal procedure we will then examine more closely some special issues in the second section (Section B.) of this chapter. Both the law of evidence and the law on appeal, revision, and other remedies will be treated separately in Chapters V and VI. The course of the whole procedure before the ICC, including the post-trial phase, is illustrated in Figure 6.

[1] Rule 2 (A) MICT; see also Rule 2 (A) RPE ICTY/ICTR and SCSL. See also the definition of 'investigation' in the KSC RPE, Rule 2 (1): 'All activities undertaken by the Specialist Prosecutor's Office under the Law and the Rules, or the SITF pursuant to Kosovo criminal law and procedure for the collection of information and evidence'. See also Zeegers, *International Criminal Tribunals* (2016), p. 142.

[2] See, in detail, Chapter III, B.(2)(d) in this volume. See also von Maltitz and Körner, in Heinze and Dittrich, *ICC* (2021), pp. 649 ff.

[3] See Expert Group, *IER* (2020), p. 165. About the IER in general, Sadat, in Heinze and Dittrich, *ICC* (2021), pp. 121, 147–8; Hale, in Heinze and Dittrich, *ICC* (2021), pp. 159, 168 ff.

[4] cf. Art. 74 ICCS.

[5] cf. Art. 76 ICCS.

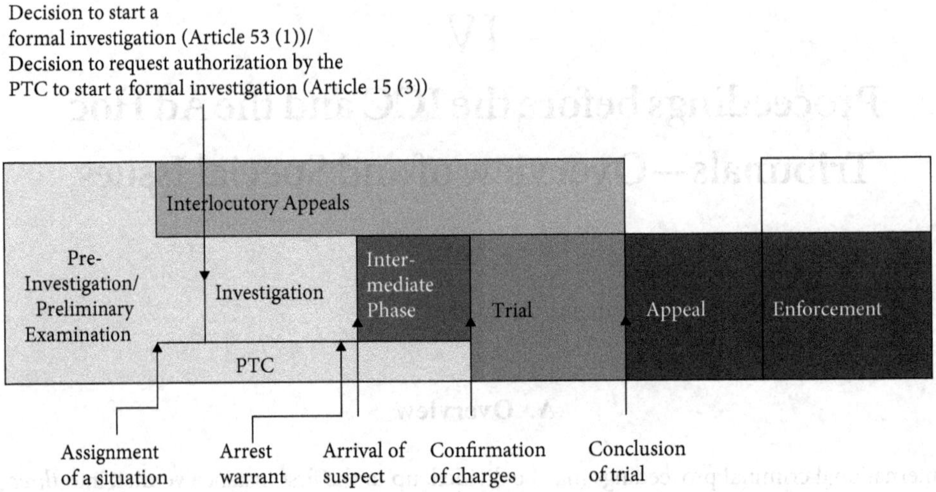


**Fig. 6.** Overview of the ICC Procedure

*Source:* This figure is based partly on the Report on the Court Capacity Model, ICC-ASP, 5th session, 21.08.2006, ICC-ASP/5/10, p. 5 and on Stegmiller, *Pre-Investigation Stage* (2011), p. 66.

It is important to note that the ICC's procedural framework is much more elaborated than that of the ad hoc tribunals.[6] Thus, while only eleven of thirty-four articles of the ICTYS refer to procedural issues *stricto sensu*,[7] the ICCS comprises much more and more detailed procedural provisions.[8] These are further specified, interpreted, and implemented[9] by the other sources mentioned in Article 21 ICC Statute, such as the RPE,[10] which shall be consistent with the Statute,[11] and to a lesser extent by Regulations of the different organs of the Court.[12] In accordance with Article 21 (2) ICC Statute, another important source is previous decisions taken by the ICC, but without providing for a binding effect in terms of the *stare decisis* doctrine known in most common law jurisdictions.[13] The term 'previous decisions' arguably includes best practices such as the Chambers *Practice Manual*.[14] Yet, it is not formally binding and it has indeed been criticized that judges are giving it improper weight in determining how to assess evidence.[15]

[6] Boas et al., *Procedure* (2011), p. 38.

[7] Arts. 18–23, 25–9 ICTYS.

[8] Guariglia, in Cassese et al., *Rome Statute II* (2002), pp. 1113–14 ('full procedural scheme'); Olásolo, *ICLR*, 5 (2005), 122 distinguishes three types of procedures (triggering, criminal, and civil) carried out through seven different types of proceedings.

[9] Guariglia, in Cassese et al., *Rome Statute II* (2002), p. 1124.

[10] See Chapter I, B.(2)(b) of this volume.

[11] Art. 51 (4); see also Broomhall, 'Article 51', in Ambos, *Commentary* (2022), mn. 31–2; Malewa, 'Article 51', in Fernandez et al., *Commentaire CPI I* (2019), pp. 1399 ff.

[12] cf. Chapter I, B.(2)(b) in this volume, and in more detail in Chapter II in connection with the respective organs.

[13] On the doctrine of *stare decisis* ('to stand by things decided') within the ICL framework, see Ambos, *Treatise ICL I* (2021), p. 133 with n. 317.

[14] ICC, *Practice Manual* (2023).

[15] ICC, *Prosecutor v. Al Mahdi*, PTC I, Separate Opinion of Judge Péter Kovács, ICC-0-1/12-01/15-84-Anx, 9 May 2016, paras. 13–15; see also McDermott, *JICJ*, 15 (2017), 873, 904.

## (1) Investigation

### *(a) Preliminary examination*

#### *(i) Overview, function, structure*

Other than the procedural law of the ad hoc tribunals (ICTY and ICTR), which only set out a pre-investigation phase limited to the initial assessment of the 'information' received by the Prosecutor,[16] the ICC proceedings provide for a so-called 'preliminary examination' as an autonomous procedural stage, that is, a form of a pre-investigation that precedes the actual 'formal' investigation of a situation[17] and subsequently a case.[18] Thus, one has to distinguish between the preliminary examination and the actual formal investigation,[19] with the former requiring a mere initial suspicion regarding the possible commission of ICC crimes, that is, less than 'a reasonable basis to proceed'—'a sensible or reasonable justification for a belief' that crimes have been committed[20]—within the meaning of Articles 15 (3), 53 (1) ICCS.[21] The information need not 'point towards only one conclusion'.[22] In fact, the preliminary

[16] cf. Art. 18 (1) ICTYS, Art. 17 (1) ICTR. The comparable Art. 38 (1) KSC Law only authorizes the Prosecutor 'to conduct investigations'. See also Liu, in Bergsmo and Stahn, *Fact-Finding* (2020), pp. 152–3; Namakula, *ICLR*, 17 (2017), 941–2; Cayley, in Bergsmo and Stahn, *Preliminary Examination I* (2018), pp. 35, 36 ff.; previously van Heeck, *Weiterentwicklung* (2006), pp. 164 ff.; Safferling, *Criminal Procedure* (2012), p. 231; De Meester, *Investigation Phase* (2015), pp. 143–4.

[17] On the respective 'situation record' opened by the Registry (Reg. 20 (1) RegR), see Chapter III, A.(4)(b) in this volume at the beginning; on the procedural development from a situation to a case, see Chapter III, B.(2)(b) in this volume.

[18] cf. Art. 15 (6) ICCS as referring to Art. 15 (1), (2) and Reg. 25–31 RegOTP. Similarly, Olásolo, *CPI* (2003), pp. 118–19 distinguishing between the pre investigative phase (solely led by the prosecution) and the actual investigation that begins with the individualization pursuant to Art. 58 and ends with the confirmation hearing as described in Art. 61 ICCS. See generally Adekunle, in Heinze and Dittrich, *ICC* (2021), pp. 409, 413 ff.; see also Bosco, *AJIL*, 111 (2017), 395; Wharton and Grey, *CanYbIL*, 56 (2018), 1–57.

[19] See also van Heeck, *Weiterentwicklung* (2006), p. 145; Lorenz, in Kühne et al., *Völkerstrafrecht* (2007), pp. 328–9; Schabas, *Introduction* (2020), pp. 252 ff.; Safferling, *JICJ*, 9 (2011), 652, who uses the term 'pre-investigative phase'; Kuczyńska, *Accusation Model ICC* (2015), pp. 73–4, 77; De Meester, 'Article 53', in Klamberg et al., *Commentary ICC II* (2023), pp. 1–4; Rodríguez Pineda, in Bergsmo and Stahn, *Preliminary Examination II* (2018), pp. 321, 330 ff.; Jacobs and Naouri, in Bergsmo and Stahn, *Preliminary Examination II* (2018), pp. 469, 476. For further information on the procedure, see Wouters, Verhoeven, and Demeyere, *ICLR*, 8 (2008), 294 ff. (= Wouters, Verhoeven, and Demeyere, in Doria, Gasser, and Bassiouni, *Legal Regime* (2009), pp. 365 ff.); Stegmiller, *Pre-Investigation Stage* (2011), p. 57; Stegmiller, *CLF*, 24 (2013), 485 ff.; on preliminary examinations, see also Wei, *Rolle* (2007), pp. 67 ff.; Lounici, in Kolb, *DIP* (2008), pp. 273 ff. (the contribution has not been updated in the second edition); on the practice, see Guariglia and Rogier, in Stahn, *Practice* (2015), pp. 353 ff. (giving a short summary of the completed and ongoing examinations to the date of writing); vague in this respect, Gless, *Internationales Strafrecht* (2021), mn. 984 ff.

[20] ICC, *Situation in the Republic of Kenya*, PTC II, Decision pursuant to Article 15 of the Rome Statute on the Authorization of an Investigation into the Situation in the Republic of Kenya, ICC-01/09-19, 31 March 2010, para. 35; *Situation in Georgia*, PTC I, Decision on the Prosecutor's Request for Authorization of an Investigation, ICC-01/15-12, 27 January 2016, para. 25; *Situation in the Republic of Burundi*, PTC III, Public Redacted Version of 'Decision pursuant to Article 15 of the Rome Statute on the Authorization of an Investigation into the Situation in the Republic of Burundi', ICC-01/17-X-9 US Exp, 25 October 2017, ICC-01/17-9-Red, 9 November 2017, para. 30; *Situation in the Islamic Republic of Afghanistan*, PTC II, Decision pursuant to Article 15 of the Rome Statute on the Authorisation of an Investigation into the Situation in the Islamic Republic of Afghanistan, ICC-02/17-33, 12 April 2019, para. 31. In more detail, Schabas, *ICC Commentary* (2016), p. 833; Rodríguez Pineda, in Bergsmo and Stahn, *Preliminary Examination I* (2018), pp. 321, 333 ff. Crit. of this standard, Jacobs, in Sluiter et al., *International Criminal Procedure* (2013), p. 1135.

[21] See also ICC-OTP, *Case Selection* (2016), para. 17 ('[T]he Office will select cases only if the information available or accessible to the Prosecution can *reasonably justify* the selection of a case for investigation and prosecution' [emphasis added]). On the different degrees of suspicion, see Ambos and Miller, *ICLR*, 7 (2007), 339–40.

[22] *Situation in the Republic of Kenya*, ICC-01/09-19, para. 38. See also *Situation in the Republic of Burundi*, ICC-01/17-9-Red, para. 30; *Request under Regulation 46(3) of the Regulations of the Court*, PTC I, Decision on the 'Prosecution's Request for a Ruling on Jurisdiction under Article 19(3) of the Statute', ICC-RoC46(3)-01/18, 6 September 2018, para. 85 ('the preliminary examination as such "does not necessitate any complex or detailed

examination has the sole purpose of ascertaining whether there are sufficient grounds ('reasonable basis') to commence a formal investigation;[23] it thus serves as a kind of procedural filter for the OTP.[24] In the words of PTC I, the preliminary examination serves as a 'pre-investigative assessment through which the Prosecutor analyses the seriousness of the information "received" or "made available" to her against the factors set out in Article 53(1) (a)–(c) of the Statute'.[25] In an earlier decision, the same Chamber held that the Prosecutor's assessment of the criteria listed in Article 53 (1) 'does not necessitate any complex or detailed process of analysis'.[26] However, this seems to be a bit of an understatement, as will be seen below, especially due to the expressivist, policy-related impact of a preliminary examination[27] and the larger goal of prevention.[28]

As we have already seen in the first volume of this Treatise,[29] the bulk of the situations referred to the ICC are in the preliminary examination phase, and given the time the OTP needs in order to take decisions in some of these situations, it seems somewhat euphemistic to call this phase 'preliminary'. In fact, the length of preliminary examinations has always been a major point of critique[30] and the IER thus suggests that it should 'last no longer than two years'.[31] Yet, such a strict deadline does not sufficiently account for the dynamics of this

process of analysis", and the information available is not expected to be "comprehensive" or "conclusive", particularly taking into account the limited investigative powers at the Prosecutor's disposal, compared to those provided for in Article 54 of the Statute at the investigation Stage' [fn. omitted]); *Situation in the Islamic Republic of Afghanistan*, ICC-02/17-33, para. 31. Thereto Bergsmo and Bekou, 'Article 53', in Ambos, *Commentary* (2022), mn. 12.

[23] van Heeck, *Weiterentwicklung* (2006), pp. 181–2; deGuzman and Schabas, in Sluiter et al., *International Criminal Procedure* (2013), p. 144, stressing the reasonable basis requirement; Kuczyńska, *Accusation Model ICC* (2015), p. 74; Cross, in Bergsmo and Stahn, *Preliminary Examination I* (2018), pp. 213, 218 ff.

[24] Stegmiller, *CLF*, 24 (2013), 486 ('procedural filtering tool'). See also Expert Group, *IER* (2020), p. 154 ('The pre-trial proceedings were intended to constitute a filter, allowing only those charges that meet the test of confirmation to proceed to trial'); Recommendation 191 ('Throughout the conduct of confirmation proceedings, Judges should have regard to the purpose of the confirmation process as a filter for inadequately supported charges and to ensure the fair trial rights of the accused, including by conducting efficient and expeditious proceedings leading to a clear and unambiguous confirmation of charges decision.')

[25] *Request under Regulation 46(3) of the Regulations of the Court*, ICC-RoC46(3)-01/18-37, para. 82. Thereto Adekunle, in Heinze and Dittrich, *ICC*, (2021), pp. 409, 414.

[26] ICC, *Situation on the Registered Vessels of the Union of the Comoros, the Hellenic Republic and the Kingdom of Cambodia*, PTC I, Decision on the Request of the Union of the Comoros to Review the Prosecutor's Decision not to Initiate an Investigation, ICC-01/13-34, 16 July 2015, para. 13. Conc. Cross, in Bergsmo and Stahn, *Preliminary Examination II* (2018), pp. 213, 223 ('would seem to support a more formalistic approach, focusing on the characteristics of an individual referral, communication, or piece of information, and not on an overall assessment of whether the inference to be drawn—for example, an element of a crime—is reasonable').

[27] Stahn, Bergsmo, and Chan, in Bergsmo and Stahn, *Preliminary Examination I* (2018), pp. 4 ff. ('States do not necessarily fear preliminary examinations because of their coercive consequences, but rather due to their stigma and reputational damage that come with public "naming and shaming" of situation countries' [13]); Stahn, *JICJ*, 15 (2017), 418 ('gateway approach'), 419 ('"consequentialist approach" … admits that preliminary examinations may serve a number of rationales other than facilitating ICC investigations and prosecutions'), 422 ('ICC thus faces a conundrum'). Generally Adekunle, in Heinze and Dittrich, *ICC* (2021), pp. 409, 414–15 ('The preliminary examination, therefore, presents an opportunity (i) to condemn criminality and gross violations of human rights; (ii) to incentivize domestic investigations or prosecutions; (iii) to demonstrate that the ICC remains vigilant despite domestic action; (iv) to address State inaction in relation to atrocities that fall within ICC jurisdiction and (v) to generally send strong signals about the seriousness of alleged crimes.')

[28] Stahn, Bergsmo, and Chan, in Bergsmo, Morten, and Stahn, *Preliminary Examination I* (2018), p. 11.

[29] cf. Ambos, *Treatise ICL I* (2021), pp. 49 ff.

[30] Crit. on the different speed with respect to different situations, Stegmiller, *CLF*, 24 (2013), 488; crit. also Adekunle, in Heinze and Dittrich, *ICC* (2021), pp. 409, 433 ff.; Gumpert and Nuzban, in Heinze and Dittrich, *ICC* (2021), pp. 553, 559 ff.

[31] Expert Group, *IER* (2020), p. 232. See generally Heinze, in Heinze and Dittrich, *ICC* (2021), p. 70; Jones, *JICJ*, 8 (2021), 825–50. On timelines for preliminary examinations, Pues, *JICJ*, 15 (2017), 436.

kind of investigation. In practice, any fixed deadline will only work as a principle with exceptions leaving sufficient flexibility.[32]

While the OTP has set up a special section on preliminary examinations on the Court's website,[33] there is still little transparency during this phase and for an 'outsider' it is impossible to assess the fate of the thousands of communications sent to the OTP.[34] This lack of transparency stands, apparently, in contrast to the importance and impact of preliminary examinations, unless it is seen as part of their 'mystery' which makes them appear more important than they actually are. [35] At any rate, given the large number of situations, conducting preliminary examinations is one of the core tasks of the OTP, alongside formal investigations and prosecutions.[36]

Although the term 'preliminary examination' is explicitly mentioned only in Article 15 (6) ICCS and Regs. 25–31 RegOTP, this examination takes place in all proceedings, regardless of the mechanism used to trigger the ICC's operation (whether through a referral by a State Party, or the UN Security Council, or by a *proprio motu* initiation of the Prosecutor).[37] Of course, in case of a *proprio motu* investigation of the Prosecutor, the preliminary investigation will usually be more thorough and take more time. More importantly, it is contingent on a PTC authorization (as we will see more closely in sub-section (ii)).[38] Furthermore, Rules 48 and 104 RPE ICC partly conflate the requirements of Articles 15 and 53: Rule 48 makes the criteria of Article 53 (1)(a)–(c) applicable to the determination of a reasonable basis within the meaning of Article 15 (3) and Rule 104 transfers the essential contents of Article 15 (2) to the Article 53 (1) evaluation.[39]

[32] In a similar vein, ICC, *IER Response* (2021), p. 103 ('It does, by suggesting a simple formula—a two-year rule for PEs, with an extension in only exceptional and justified circumstances—appear to ignore certain dynamics of the PE process, which have proven highly beneficial to the Rome Statute system … , advantages it would be a shame to sacrifice without a careful cost/benefit assessment'); Stahn, Bergsmo, and Chan, in Bergsmo and Stahn, *Preliminary Examination I* (2018), p. 8 ('In some contexts, it is better to keep preliminary examinations short and to pass on to formal investigation, since investigation entails greater pressure for compliance. In other contexts, it is precisely the unpredictability and surprise element of preliminary examinations that makes them a powerful instrument.')

[33] Available at <https://www.icc-cpi.int/>, under the heading 'Situation and Cases'.

[34] See also the analysis in Expert Group, *IER* (2020), pp. 237 ff.; Stahn, Bergsmo, and Chan, in Bergsmo and Stahn, *Preliminary Examination I* (2018), p. 8 ('Preliminary examinations are convenient for the OTP because they are less legalized than investigations, pre-trial or trial proceedings'); but see (in the same volume!) on the 'legalistic nature' of a preliminary examination, Gawronski, in Bergsmo and Stahn, *Preliminary Examination I* (2018), pp. 181 ff.

[35] The scholarly treatment is ambiguous, to say the least; see esp. Stahn, Bergsmo, and Chan, in Bergsmo and Stahn, *Preliminary Examination I* (2018), p. 4 (described as 'marked paradoxes and curiosities') and p. 13 ('In practice, preliminary examinations are clouded by mystery. Their shadow is often bigger than their actual core. Their impact may be more powerful than actual cases. They make the ICC relevant as object of reference in accountability discussions, even before any concrete investigations'); previously Stahn, *JICJ*, 15 (2017), 413–34.

[36] In a similar vein, Expert Group, *IER* (2020), p. 225.

[37] ICC-OTP, *Referrals and Communications* (2003), p. 7; Wouters, Verhoeven, and Demeyere, *ICLR*, 8 (2008), 294 (= Wouters, Verhoeven, and Demeyere, in Doria, Gasser, and Bassiouni, *Legal Regime* (2009), p. 365); de Meester, Pitcher, Rastan, and Sluiter, in Sluiter et al., *International Criminal Procedure* (2013), p. 182; Ambos and Stegmiller, *Crime Law Soc Change*, 59 (2013), 420 ff.; Rodríguez Pineda, in Bergsmo and Stahn, *Preliminary Examination II* (2018), pp. 321, 329–30; on the three trigger mechanisms, see Chapter III, A.(4)(b) in this volume.

[38] cf. Art. 15 (3) ICCS. See thereon Ambach and Rackwitz, *LCP*, 76 nos. 3 & 4 (2013), 141 ('safeguard against politically motivated investigations'); crit. Wouters, Verhoeven, and Demeyere, *ICLR*, 8 (2008), 282 (= Wouters, Verhoeven, and Demeyere, in Doria, Gasser, and Bassiouni, *Legal Regime* (2009), p. 353: wrongly considering this as a sign of lacking independence); cf. also Kuczyńska, *Accusation Model ICC* (2015), p. 77 (considering this authorization as the borderline between preliminary examination and the investigation proper).

[39] For the relationship between Arts. 15 and 53, see also Friman, in Lee, *ICC* (2001), pp. 494 ff.; Olásolo, *CPI* (2003), pp. 71–2; Schabas, *ICC Commentary* (2016), p. 394; Stegmiller, *Pre-investigative Stage* (2011), p. 213; deGuzman and Schabas, in Sluiter et al., *International Criminal Procedure* (2013), p. 143; Bergsmo, Kruger, and Bekou, 'Article 53', in Ambos, *ICC Commentary* (2022), mn. 8; Kuczyńska, *Accusation Model ICC* (2015), pp. 74–6; De Meester, *Investigation Phase* (2015), pp. 144–5. See also ICC, *Situation in Côte d'Ivoire*, PTC III, Judge Fernandez de Gurmendi's Separate and Partially Dissenting Opinion to the Decision pursuant to Article 15 of the

Structurally, preliminary examinations are the task of the OTP's Preliminary Examinations Section (PES) that is now located under the new Pillar A headed by Deputy Prosecutor Nazhat Khan.[40] The PES is responsible for 'processing and analysing all incoming Article 15 communications, assessing jurisdiction and admissibility of the situations, as well as the interests of justice' and 'reports its findings directly to the Prosecutor'.[41] The Prosecutor always had two main options with regard to the preliminary examination: either continuing with a formal investigation or closing the preliminary examination. A third (informal) option has only been formalized recently: leaving the preliminary examination open but freezing or hibernating it.[42]

The OTP's Policy Paper on Preliminary Examinations[43] structured the preliminary examination in four phases as illustrated in Figure 7 in the previous edition (p. 338). Later the OTP emphasized, while maintaining the phases in principle, that the assessment is holistic, not mechanical.[44] The holistic approach has also been noted as a response to the IER's critique of the phased approach.[45] Under the current Prosecutor, the Office has sought to implement the IER's recommendation on the phases. The 2023 ASP Report on implementation of the IER sees a positive, ongoing implementation.[46] Graphically, the current approach may be displayed as follows (Figure 7):

*Phase one*, now referred to as a filtering stage,[47] is concerned with the evaluation of the 'communications', that is, the information submitted on alleged crimes received in accordance with Article 15 (1) ('information on alleged crimes').[48] The internal timeline set by the OTP for this evaluation is one year.[49] The incoming information must be duly registered[50] and itseception formally acknowledged.[51] The seriousness of the information is analysed with a view to filtering out the alleged crimes which appear to be (manifestly) outside the jurisdiction of the Court, or which are already under preliminary examination or investigation.[52] The 'appear to be' standard is lower than 'reasonable basis': 'the information available

Rome Statute on the Authorisation of an Investigation into the Situation in the Republic of Côte d'Ivoire, ICC-02/11-15, 3 October 2011, paras. 21 ff.; dissenting, esp. with regard to Security Council referrals, Ohlin, in Stahn and Sluiter, *Practice* (2009), pp. 185 ff., 207.

[40] On the OTP's new structure, see Chapter II, B.(2) in this volume.

[41] Expert Group, *IER* (2020), p. 231 (R254: 'consider carrying out the PE activities more holistically'); *contra* ICC, *IER Response* (2021), p. 102 (paras. 468–9).

[42] See Kersten, in Bergsmo and Stahn, *Preliminary Examination II* (2018), pp. 655, 661; Adekunle, in Heinze and Dittrich, *ICC* (2021), pp. 409, 414.

[43] ICC-OTP, *Policy Prelim. Examinations* (2013), paras. 77–84; see also Regs. 25–31 RegOTP; see also Stegmiller, *CLF*, 24 (2013), 487; Lubin, in Bergsmo and Stahn, *Preliminary Examination II* (2018), pp. 77, 87 ff. On the OTP's previous practical approach, see Ambos, in Kaleck et al., *International Prosecution of Human Rights Crimes* (2006), pp. 56 ff.; Ambos, in Bohlander, *International Criminal Justice* (2007), pp. 435 ff.; Ambos, *APuZ*, 42 (2006), 14–15; Stegmiller, *CLF*, 24 (2013), 486–7.

[44] ICC-OTP, *Report Prelim. Examinations* (2020), paras. 1–16.

[45] Expert Group, *IER* (2020), p. 228 (Table 1).

[46] ICC-ASP, *Review* (2023), pp. 9–10 ('OTP is considering options and suggestions on how a reasonable duration of PE could be part of the general plan at the opening of each PE ... The Preliminary Examinations Section has been considering options and suggestions on how a reasonable duration could be part of the general plan at the opening of each preliminary examination.')

[47] ICC-OTP, *Report 2022* (2022), pp. 76–7 ('filtering activities').

[48] ICC-ASP, *Report Basic Size OTP* (2015), p. 39. See, in detail, Gawronski, in Bergsmo and Stahn, *Preliminary Examination II* (2018), pp. 186–7, 201 ff.; Khojasteh, in Bergsmo and Stahn, *Preliminary Examination I* (2018), pp. 223 ff.

[49] Expert Group, *IER* (2020), p. 228 (Table 1).

[50] cf. Reg. 26 RegOTP.

[51] cf. Reg. 28 (1) RegOTP.

[52] ICC-OTP, *Policy Prelim. Examinations* (2013), para. 75; ICC-OTP, *Report Prelim. Examinations* (2020), para. 29; Khojasteh, in Bergsmo and Stahn, *Preliminary Examination I* (2018), p. 228.

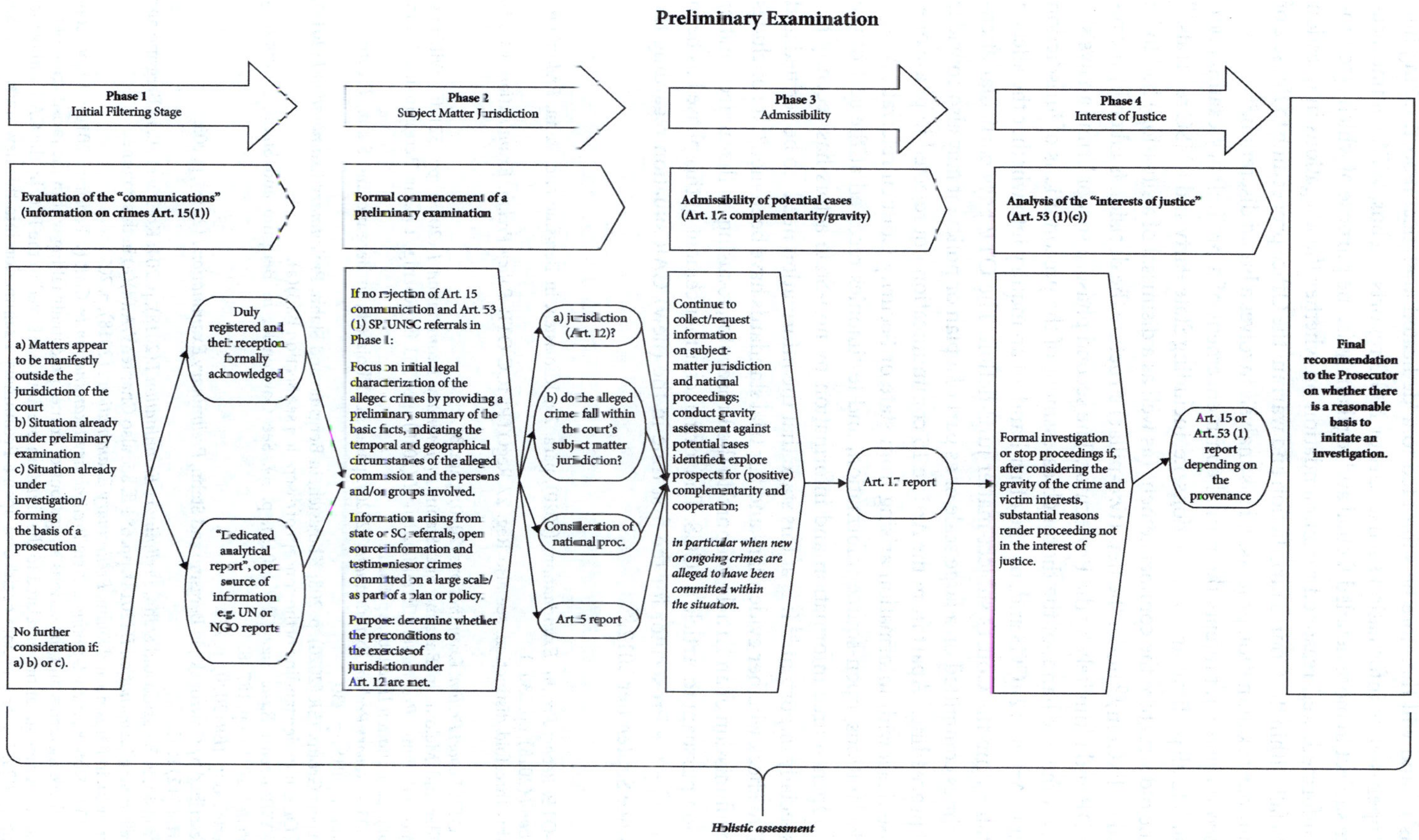


**Fig. 7.** Structure of Preliminary Examination
*Source:* own elaboration on the basis of different OTP documents

must *tend to suggest* that the alleged acts *could* amount to crimes within the jurisdiction of the Court'.[53] All other communications warrant further analysis[54] (so-called 'WFA communications')[55] and will therefore be submitted to a 'dedicated analytical report', taking into account open-source information such as UN or NGO reports.[56] Thus, WFA communications 'are subject to more detailed factual and legal analysis, the purpose of which is to provide an informed, well-reasoned recommendation on whether the allegations in question appear to fall within the Court's jurisdiction and warrant the Office proceeding to Phase 2 of the preliminary examination process'.[57] This analysis involves a broad discretion.[58]

The *second phase* represents the formal commencement of a preliminary examination and applies to all preliminary examinations, i.e. including State Party and UNSC referrals.[59] Under the old structure the commencement (as well as a dismissal of a situation) had to be approved by ExCom;[60] under the new (two-pillar) structure the decision is taken by the respective DP and ultimately by the Prosecutor. The second phase, a sort of 'crime analysis',[61] consists, on the one hand, of the thorough assessment of the preconditions of jurisdiction pursuant to Article 12 ICCS and, on the other hand, of an inquiry into whether the alleged crimes fall within the Court's subject-matter jurisdiction. The OTP pays particular attention to crimes committed on a large scale or as part of a plan or policy; it may also consider national proceedings. Apart from the Article 15 communication not rejected in phase one, this phase deals with information arising from state or Security Council referrals, Article 12 (3) declarations, open-source information, and testimonies received at the seat of the Court.[62] Open-source information and information by non-State actors has recently become especially important.[63] It is at this stage that the information needs to be verified and the OTP to check whether evidentiary and fair trial standards have been met.[64] It concludes with the submission of an 'Article 5 report' to the Prosecutor, focusing on the subject-matter jurisdiction pursuant to Article 5 ICCS. The formal commencement of this phase has been announced by the Prosecutor for the first time in the (new) CAR situation regarding the events since September 2012.[65]

[53] ICC-OTP, *Report Prelim. Examinations* (2020), para. 29; Khojasteh, in Bergsmo and Stahn, *Preliminary Examination I* (2018), pp. 230–1.

[54] On this threefold distinction, see also Reg. 27 RegOTP; ICC-OTP, *Policy Prelim. Examinations* (2013), para. 78.

[55] ICC-OTP, *Report Prelim. Examinations* (2020), para. 31.

[56] Schüller and Meloni, in Bergsmo and Stahn, *Preliminary Examination I* (2018), pp. 521 ff.; Williams, in Bergsmo and Stahn, *Preliminary Examination II* (2018), pp. 553 ff.; Koenig et al., in Bergsmo and Stahn, *Preliminary Examination II* (2018), pp. 681 ff.

[57] ICC-OTP, *Report Prelim. Examinations* (2020), para. 31; Khojasteh, in Bergsmo and Stahn, *Preliminary Examination I* (2018), p. 230.

[58] cf. Expert Group, *IER* (2020), p. 208; Khojasteh, in Bergsmo and Stahn, *Preliminary Examination I* (2018), pp. 238 ff. On our understanding of the concept of discretion see Section B.(3)(a).

[59] ICC-ASP, *Report Basic Size OTP* (2015), p. 39. See Gawronski, in Bergsmo and Stahn, *Preliminary Examination I* (2018), pp. 187–8.

[60] Expert Group, *IER* (2020), p. 228.

[61] As described by Gawronski, in Bergsmo and Stahn, *Preliminary Examination I* (2018), p. 203.

[62] cf. Art. 15 (2) ICCS.

[63] Gawronski, in Bergsmo and Stahn, *Preliminary Examination I* (2018), p. 204; Koenig et al., in Bergsmo and Stahn, *Preliminary Examination II* (2018), pp. 681 ff. See also Chapter V, A.(4)(e) in this volume.

[64] Gawronski, in Bergsmo and Stahn, *Preliminary Examination I* (2018), p. 207.

[65] ICC-OTP, *Statement on Opening a New Preliminary Examination in CAR* (7 February 2014): 'I have concluded that these incidents and the serious allegations of crimes potentially falling within the jurisdiction of the ICC constitute a new situation, unrelated to the situation previously referred to the ICC by the CAR authorities in December 2004. I have therefore decided to open a Preliminary Examination into this new situation' ). See more recently ICC-OTP, *Statement on Opening Preliminary Examinations into the Situations in the Philippines and in Venezuela* (8 February 2018) and *Statement on Opening a Preliminary Examination concerning the Alleged Deportation of the Rohingya People from Myanmar to Bangladesh* (18 September 2018).

The *third phase* is concerned with the admissibility of 'potential' cases—defined cases do not exist yet[66]—in terms of complementarity and gravity according to Article 17 ICCS.[67] The Office continues to collect information on the subject-matter jurisdiction and prepares an 'Article 17 report' to the Prosecutor. The focus of information shifts from crime information to information 'about any existing, planned or pending investigative and prosecutorial proceedings and about the judicial systems carrying them out'.[68] In addition, the OTP might also act in a more forward-looking way and pursue a 'positive complementarity agenda'.[69] This phase appears as the most time consuming for the OTP.[70] Take for example the Nigeria situation: after the publication of the Article 5 report on 5 August 2013 (presenting the preliminary findings on jurisdictional issues),[71] it lasted seven years (until 11 December 2020)[72] before that the situation was concluded. In the meantime, the OTP published updates on the subject-matter assessment on 12 November 2015[73] and 5 December 2019.[74]

The *fourth phase* analyses the 'interests of justice' pursuant to Article 53 (1)(c),[75] and results in the corresponding 'Articles 15/53 (1) report'.[76] This report contains an 'initial legal characterization of the alleged crimes' and a preliminary summary of the basic facts, indicating the temporal and geographical circumstances of the alleged commission, and the persons and/or groups involved. It serves as a basis to determine whether to commence a formal investigation in accordance with Article 53 (1), or whether to stop proceedings in the just mentioned 'interests of justice'.[77]

In sum, the preliminary examination phase deals—contrary to the more limited wording of Article 53 (1)[78]—with all formal and substantive requirements of jurisdiction: that is, jurisdiction *ratione temporis*,[79] *ratione personae*,[80] *ratione materiae*,[81] and the preconditions of jurisdiction,[82] as well as with the admissibility requirement of complementarity.[83] Thus, it is a complex preliminary investigation, certainly more complex than envisaged by PTC I as

[66] ICC, *Situation in the Republic of Kenya*, PTC II, Request for Authorisation of an Investigation pursuant to Article 15, ICC-01/09-3, 26 November 2009, paras. 51, 107 and *Situation in the Republic of Kenya*, ICC-01/09-19, paras. 50, 182, 188 (assessment of admissibility 'against certain criteria defining a "potential case"').

[67] ICC-ASP, *Report Basic Size OTP* (2015), p. 39. See Gawronski, in Bergsmo and Stahn, *Preliminary Examination I* (2018), pp. 188 ff.; Armenian, *ICLR*, 16 (2016), 642 ff.; Ezennia, *ICLR*, 16 (2016), 448 ff.

[68] Gawronski, in Bergsmo and Stahn, *Preliminary Examination I* (2018), p. 209. The Expert Group, *IER* (2020), p. 210 (para. 648) recommended assessing gravity already in the first phase before the decision to open a preliminary examination is taken.

[69] Ibid., p. 211. On positive (cooperative) complementarity see already Ch. III B. (3).

[70] Adekunle, in Heinze and Dittrich, *ICC* (2021), pp. 409, 425, Badagard and Klamberg, *GeoJIL*, 48 (2017), 667.

[71] ICC-OTP, *Situation in Nigeria* (2013).

[72] ICC-OTP, *Statement of the Prosecutor, Fatou Bensouda, on the Conclusion of the Preliminary Examination of the Situation in Nigeria* (11 December 2020).

[73] ICC-OTP, *Report Prelim. Examinations* (2015), paras. 195–216.

[74] ICC-OTP, *Report Prelim. Examinations* (2019), paras. 182–7. For an overview, see ICC-OTP, *Report Prelim. Examinations* (2020), paras. 248 ff. See also Adekunle, in Heinze and Dittrich, *ICC* (2021), pp. 409, 431 ff.

[75] CC-ASP, Report Basic Size OTP (2015), p. 40. See Gawronski, in Bergsmo and Stahn, *Preliminary Examination I* (2018), pp. 192 ff.

[76] cf. Reg. 29 (1) RegOTP also referring to Art. 15 (3) ICCS. See Gawronski, in Bergsmo and Stahn, *Preliminary Examination I* (2018), pp. 194–5.

[77] cf. Regs. 29 and 31 RegOTP.

[78] Art. 53 (1)(a) only refers to 'a crime within the jurisdiction', i.e. apparently, the *ratione materiae* jurisdiction; see also Safferling, *Criminal Procedure* (2012), p. 233.

[79] cf. Arts. 11, 126 ICCS.

[80] cf. Arts. 1, 25 (1), 26 ICCS.

[81] cf. Art. 5 ICCS.

[82] cf. Art. 12 ICCS. See, in this sense, the reference to 'jurisdiction' in Art. 15 (4), Reg. 49 (1)(b) RegC and Reg. 27, 29 (1) RegOTP. On these requirements, see Chapter III, A.(4)(a)(ii) in this volume.

[83] cf. Art. 17 ICCS, analysed in Chapter III, B.(2)(d) in this volume; cf. also Kuczyńska, *Accusation Model ICC* (2015), pp. 81–6.

quoted above.[84] While the complexity seems to be reduced by the four-phased structure and the ensuing sequenced approach, this approach may prove to be too strict and static in the face of the concrete circumstances of a situation and the time and depth of the examination during each phase.[85]

*(ii)* Proprio motu *investigation*

In the case of a *proprio motu* investigation,[86] the Prosecutor, if finding a 'reasonable basis to proceed', must seek permission from the PTC to continue with the investigation.[87] This request is obligatory;[88] the Presidency of the Court is to be informed so that the situation can be assigned to a PTC.[89] Under national procedural laws, the decision to initiate an investigation generally rests with the prosecution.[90] At any rate, such an early judicial control of the investigation can be better explained from an inquisitorial than from an adversarial perspective,[91] since the inquisitorial system generally bestows a greater importance on the judge—in the sense of a more active and intervening role—than the adversarial system. Against this background, it is not surprising that most concerns, expressed during the ICC negotiations, regarding the judicial control of an independent prosecutor came from Anglo-American delegates.[92] They had also to admit, however, that the alternative of a political control through the UN Security Council, as proposed by States rather hostile towards the ICC project, would be much more detrimental to this project. In that case, the Prosecutor would be forced to submit to a highly politicized body—with three (China, the Russian Federation, and the USA) of its five permanent members outside the ICC regime—who could, at best, be expected to be neutral towards the ICC. The judicial control model was therefore ultimately

[84] Note 26 and main text in this chapter.

[85] cf. Stahn, Bergsmo, and Chan, in Bergsmo and Stahn, *Preliminary Examination I* (2018), p. 16 ('Like the sorcerer's apprentice, the OTP might have locked itself in too much through its phased-based model. There is a certain tension between a sequenced and a parallel consideration of selection criteria. The idea to break preliminary examination down into phases seems to suggest that the analysis is sequenced. It implies that one phase comes after the next. According to this approach, analysis may get stuck by comprehensive scrutiny at one phase, like jurisdiction, for years, without considering information relating to other phases. Such a strict sequencing is not directly required by the Statute. It might be preferable to adopt a more flexible approach in order to avoid that the OTP get stuck in its own methodology.') See also Lubin, in Bergsmo and Stahn, *Preliminary Examination II* (2018), pp. 87 ff.; Khojasteh, in Bergsmo and Stahn, *Preliminary Examination I* (2018), pp. 241 ff.

[86] Art. 15 (1) ICCS.

[87] cf. Art. 15 (3) ICCS. See von Maltitz and Körner, in Heinze and Dittrich, *ICC* (2021), pp. 652–3.

[88] cf. the wording of Art. 15 (3) ('shall'). For a crit. view, see Schabas, *ICC Commentary* (2016), pp. 404–5, arguing that while 'shall' suggests an obligation to get the PTC involved, this makes little practical sense, since the Statute does not provide for any enforcement mechanism or remedies, if such an authorization is not sought by the Prosecutor; going beyond the request of the Prosecutor, ICC, *Situation in the Republic of Côte d'Ivoire*, PTC III, Corrigendum to 'Decision pursuant to Article 15 of the Rome Statute on the Authorisation of an Investigation into the Situation in the Republic of Côte d'Ivoire' ICC-02/11-14-Corr, 15 November 2011; for further information thereon, see Rastan, *CLF*, 23 (2012), 23 ff.

[89] Reg. 45, 46 (2) RegC.

[90] From a comparative perspective, cf. Bergsmo, Cissé, and Staker, in Arbour et al., *Prosecutor* (2000), pp. 121 ff.; Ambos, *EJCCLCJ*, 8 (2000), 89 ff.; Fairlie, *ICLR*, 4 (2004), 248–9; Fyfe and Heinze, in Ambos et al., *Core Concepts I* (2020), pp. 367 ff.; Fyfe and Heinze, in Ambos et al., *Core Concepts II* (2022), pp. 169, 191 ff.; Ruggeri, in Wright, Levine, and Gold, *OxfHB Prosecutors* (2021), pp. 3, 5 ff.

[91] cf. also Friman, in Lee, *ICC* (2001), p. 537; and similarly Friman, in Fischer, Kreß and Lüder, *Prosecution* (2001), p. 192; Fernández de Gurmendi, in Lee, *ICC* (1999), p. 223 ('civil law proposals'); Guariglia, in Lee, *ICC* (1999), p. 228; Sadat and Carden, *GeoLJ*, 88 (2000), 399; Kreß, in Grützner, Pötz ,and Kreß, *Internationaler Rechtshilfeverkehr in Strafsachen* (2003), Part IV A 1, mn. 108; Swoboda, *Verfahrens- und Beweisstrategien* (2013), p. 208; Heinze and Fyfe, in Bergsmo und Stahn, *Preliminary Examination II* (2018), pp. 61 ff.; more conciliatory, Friman, in Stahn, *Practice* (2015), p. 910 (PTC as a bridge between civil and common law traditions).

[92] cf. Guariglia, in Lee, *ICC* (1999), p. 228.

accepted, even by the sceptics among the ICC-friendly (common law) States, as 'the lesser of two evils'.[93]

In any case, in determining the 'reasonable basis' within the meaning of Article 15 (3) ICCS the Prosecutor shall, as already stated above, consider the factors set out in Article 53 (1)(a)–(c).[94] These factors will be discussed in the next section. The authorization request to the PTC must be in writing and contain the crimes allegedly committed, a statement of the facts, and a declaration of the Prosecutor that the Court has jurisdiction.[95] The OTP may only commence the formal investigation if the PTC is satisfied, in light of the requirements of Article 53 (1),[96] that there is a reasonable basis to conduct such an investigation.[97] The PTC may also authorize only a part of the requested investigation by the OTP.[98] At any rate, its decision will not affect any later decisions on jurisdiction and admissibility. If the PTC finds that there is no reasonable basis to proceed with an investigation, the OTP may submit a new request based on new facts or evidence.[99] However, the OTP may also conclude, prior to seeking the PTC's authorization, that there is insufficient information to justify the continuation of the investigation. In this case, the PTC will not be involved,[100] but the information providers have to be informed.[101] This does not exclude the possibility of resuming the investigation at a later stage on the basis of new evidence.[102] Overall, with Article 15, rooted in an Argentinean-German initiative and supported by the group of ICC like-minded States, the project of an *independent Prosecutor* won the day.[103] Instead of political control by the UN Security Council, as suggested by the United States, with the PTC authorization a judicial control mechanism was implemented, which however intervenes at an earlier stage than similar controls at the national level.[104]

[93] For a more distinct affiliation to the continental-European (inquisitorial) model, see Damaška, in Cassese, *Companion* (2009), p. 182; for an enhanced role of the judges, see Zappalà, in Cassese, *Companion* (2009), p. 223; generally on the role of the PTC, Jorda and Saracco, in Decaux, Dieng, and Sow, *Human Rights* (2007), pp. 419 ff.; Schabas, *ICC Commentary* (2010), p. 881; Pitcher, *Judicial Responses* (2018), pp. 261 ff.; but see also for (possible) forms of political review of the prosecution in the ICC regime, Kuczyńska, *Accusation Model ICC* (2015), pp. 155–60.

[94] cf. Rule 48 RPE ICC; also de Meester, Pitcher, Rastan, and Sluiter, in Sluiter et al., *International Criminal Procedure* (2013), p. 182; Cross, in Bergsmo and Stahn, *Preliminary Examination II* (2018), pp. 213 ff., 217 ff.

[95] Rule 50 (2) RPE and Reg. 49 (1) RegC. The statement of facts shall indicate, as a minimum, the place of commission (as precisely as possible), the time of commission, and the persons or groups involved (Reg. 49 (2) RegC). See also de Meester, Pitcher, Rastan, and Sluiter, in Sluiter et al., *International Criminal Procedure* (2013), pp. 182–3.

[96] Although there is no Rule 48 RPE ICC for the PTC, the standard of Art. 53 (1) must also apply to the PTC examination, for reasons of logic and consistency; see also *Situation in the Republic of Kenya*, ICC-01/09-19, para. 21; conc. Bergsmo, Pejić, and Zhu, 'Article 15', in Ambos, *ICC Commentary* (2022), mn. 21; Safferling, *Criminal Procedure* (2012), pp. 236–7; contra, Hoffmeister and Knoke, *ZaöRV*, 59 (1999), 792 (only examination of facts and evidence presented required under Art. 53 (1) ICCS).

[97] Art. 15 (4) ICCS.

[98] Rule 50 (5) RPE ICC.

[99] Art. 15 (5) ICCS.

[100] Most notably, Art. 53 (3) will not be applicable; cf. Rule 105 (2) RPE ICC, and Gropengießer and Meißner, *ICLR*, 5 (2005), 298 with further references.

[101] Art. 15 (6) cl. 1 ICCS.

[102] Art. 15 (6) cl. 2 ICCS.

[103] cf. 'Freiburg Declaration', in Arbour et al., *Prosecutor* (2000), pp. 667 ff. (in German, English, French, and Spanish); see also Planchadell Gargallo, in Gómez Colomer et al., *CPI* (2003), pp. 185 ff.; Cryer, *Prosecuting International Crimes* (2005), pp. 162–3. For a different view, see Gómez Colomer, in Gómez Colomer et al., *CPI* (2003), pp. 301–2; see also Goldston, *JICJ*, 8 (2010), 383 ff.

[104] Usually, prosecution activity is—with the exception of coercive measures—not judicially controlled until the termination of the investigation; see e.g. the French *chambre d'accusation*, the American Grand Jury, or the German *Zwischenverfahren*; cf. Ambos, *The Review (IntComJur)*, 58/59 (1997), 50 ff., with further references; Fyfe and Heinze, in Ambos et al., *Core Concepts I* (2020), pp. 367 ff.; Fyfe and Heinze, in Ambos et al., *Core Concepts II* (2022), pp. 169, 191 ff.; Ruggeri, in Wright, Levine, and Gold, *OxfHB Prosecutors* (2021), pp. 3, 5 ff. Crit. on the early control mechanism, Bergsmo, Cissé, and Staker, in Arbour et al., (2000), p. 142; Safferling,

*(iii) Powers*

While a preliminary examination may have a expressivist, policy-related impact, as already mentioned above,[105] the (legal) powers of the Prosecutor are very limited during the preliminary examination, perhaps at best comparable to an international commission of inquiry.[106] The Prosecutor may seek information from States, UN organs, intergovernmental or non-governmental organizations, and other reliable sources,[107] but she does not possess the powers of investigation of Article 54 at this stage; in particular, she does not possess any coercive powers (as will be discussed below),[108] but may only 'receive' witness statements at the seat of the Court, that is, these witnesses have to come forward voluntarily[109] (although the attendance of witnesses can be required through a *subpoena* as explained below[110]). Part 9 of the Rome Statute, on cooperation, does not apply to preliminary examinations.[111]

This lack of coercive powers also explains preference of the OTP for State referrals.[112] In contrast, as previously mentioned in Chapter I in this volume,[113] the suspect[114] already possesses a broad spectrum of rights in the pre-trial phase.[115] Finally, yet importantly, it is worth mentioning that *victims* already have a say at this stage of the proceedings, that is, they are entitled to make representations.[116] The victims concerned must also be informed, if the

*Criminal Procedure* (2012), pp. 81, 177; Planchadell Gargallo, in Gómez Colomer et al., *CPI* (2003), pp. 187–8; Gómez Colomer, in Gómez Colomer et al., *CPI* (2003), pp. 279–80, 293–4, 301; Kreß and Wannek, in Kirsch, *Internationale Strafgerichtshöfe* (2005), pp. 248–9; Ntanda Nsereko, *JICJ*, 3 (2005), 138 ff.; Byrne, *LJIL*, 26 (2013), 999; Kuczyńska, *Accusation Model ICC* (2015), p. 78 (considering judicial control necessary due to the Prosecutor's power in the selection of cases). On the PTC's review pursuant to Art. 53 (3), see Section B.(3)(b) in this chapter.

105 Above note 27 with main text.

106 cf. de Meester, Pitcher, Rastan, and Sluiter, in Sluiter et al., *International Criminal Procedure* (2013), p. 181. See also, regarding 'function and mandate', Chapter II, B.(4) in this volume.

107 Art. 15 (2) ICCS.

108 Section B.(5) in this chapter. See also van Heeck, *Weiterentwicklung* (2006), p. 153; Safferling, *Criminal Procedure* (2012), p. 262; Damaška, *JICJ*, 10 (2012), 613.

109 cf. Art. 15 (2) ICCS, Rule 47 RPE ICC. According to Rule 47 (1), such testimony must be taken in accordance with the rules governing the 'record of questioning' set out in Rules 111, 112 RPE ICC, i.e. the persons questioned, especially the suspect, have to be informed of their rights and the interview has to be recorded (see Chapter I, D.(3)(c) in this volume). Similarly, at the ad hoc tribunals questioning of suspects has to be recorded (Rule 43 RPE ICTY/ICTR/SCSL, Rule 41 RPE MICT, Rule 44 RPE KSC). In favour of a principle regarding recording of both suspect/accused and witness interviews, de Meester, Pitcher, Rastan, and Sluiter, in Sluiter et al., *International Criminal Procedure* (2013), pp. 254, 281; on the problem of undue pressure during the break in the recording, see ibid., pp. 232, 236, welcoming the more detailed ICC Rules according to which interruptions in the course of recording shall also be recorded (Rule 112 (1)(c)); Razesberger, *Complementarity* (2006), pp. 64–5; cf. also Vasiliev, in Cryer et al., *ICL* (2019), pp. 422–4; on the practice of the ad hoc tribunals and the ICC, see Jackson and M'Boge, *LJIL*, 26 (2013), 956 ff.

110 In more detail, Chapter V, A.(3)(a) and Chapter VII, B.(3)(a)(ii).

111 See also Stahn, Bergsmo, and Chan, in Bergsmo and Stahn, *Preliminary Examination I* (2018), p. 6.

112 Bosco, *AJIL*, 111 (2017), 395–407; Adekunle, in Heinze and Dittrich, *ICC* (2021), pp. 409, 420. For a crit. view, see Schabas, *CLF*, 19 (2008), 5 ff.

113 Chapter I, D.(3) in this volume.

114 The ICC Statute deliberately avoids the term 'suspect'. According to *Marchesiello*, the person concerned may be considered as 'suspect' prior to the formal investigation, as 'investigated' after the formal investigation has been authorized, and as 'indicted' or 'accused' during the pre-trial and trial phases, see Marchesiello, in Cassese et al., *Rome Statute II* (2002), pp. 1231, 1234 ff. Crit. Ambos and Miller, *ICLR*, 7 (2007), 339, 340; about the definition of suspect in more detail, De Meester, *Investigation Phase* (2015), pp. 332 ff. See, in relation to the *ratione temporis* application of the ECtHR, Chapter I, D.(2)(d) in this volume. In recent years, an alternative term has increasingly been used, namely 'person of interest', see ICC-OTP, *Annual Report* (2022), p. 75; see generally Heinze, *NCLR*, 24 (2021), 212, 214.

115 See, on the one hand, Art. 55 ICCS (thereon Gordon, *ColJTransnat'lL*, 45 (2007), 663) and, on the other, Arts. 17 ICTRS, 18 ICTYS, Rules 42 and 55 (A) RPE ICTY/ICTR (thereon Safferling and Hartwig, *ZIS*, 4 (2009), 789), Rules 40, 57 RPE MICT as well as Art. 38 (3) KSC Law and Rules 42 and 43 RPE KSC.

116 cf. Art. 15 (3) ICCS and Rule 50 (3) RPE ICC. See also Hoffmeister and Knoke, *ZaöRV*, 59 (1999), 792; Bock, *Opfer* (2010), pp. 507–8 with further references and Chapter II, E.(4) in this volume.

Prosecutor seeks an authorization pursuant to Article 15 (3)[117] and concludes that there is no sufficient basis for an investigation pursuant to Article 15 (6).

### *(b) Formal investigation*

In all international criminal tribunals, the formal investigations are initiated and directed by the Prosecutor.[118] The Prosecutor is responsible 'for conducting investigations and prosecutions'[119] and shall decide whether the available information constitutes a 'sufficient' or 'reasonable' basis[120] to proceed with the investigation.[121] In this regard she exercises a broad discretion;[122] in the ICC system this is especially manifest in the concept of 'interests of justice',[123] to be looked at in more detail below.[124]

If the (ICC) Prosecutor decides to commence an investigation, she has to notify the State Parties and those States exercising jurisdiction.[125] As already explained above,[126] the ICC

[117] Rule 50 (1) RPE ICC.

[118] cf. de Meester, Pitcher, Rastan, and Sluiter, in Sluiter et al., *International Criminal Procedure* (2013), pp. 172 ff., 184 ff.; see also Safferling, *Criminal Procedure* (2012), p. 262; Jackson, *JICJ*, 7 (2009), 17, 24 ff.; Tuinstra, *Defence Counsel in ICL* (2009), p. 131; Bensouda, *NCJIL&ComReg*, 36 (2010–2011), 279; De Meester, *Investigation Phase* (2015), pp. 162 ff.; on the investigative practices, see De Vos, *LJIL*, 26 (2013), 1014 ff.

[119] Arts. 42 (1), 54 ICCS. See also ICC, *Situation in Darfur, Sudan*, PTC I, Decision on Application under Rule 103, ICC-02/05-185, 4 February 2009, para. 12, referring to Art. 54 ICCS and stating that the Prosecutor is 'the organ of the Court primarily entrusted with the investigation ... in the relevant situation'. See also ICC, *Situation in the Islamic Republic of Afghanistan*, AC, Judgment on the Appeal against the Decision on the Authorisation of an Investigation into the Situation in the Islamic Republic of Afghanistan, ICC-02/17-138, 5 March 2020, para. 63 ('[A]rticle 42(1) recognises the independence of the Prosecutor and her responsibility for the conduct of investigations.')

[120] Arts. 18 (1) ICTYS, 17 (1) ICTRS, 15 (3), and 53 (1) ICCS. At the KSC only Art 38 (4) requires a 'well-grounded suspicion' but regarding an indictment.

[121] Generally on Art. 53 see Razesberger, *Complementarity* (2006), pp. 99 ff.; Hoffmeister and Knoke, *ZaöRV*, 59 (1999), 793 ff.; Reisert, *StV*, 25 (2005), 637–8, Delmas-Marty, *RSC*, 3 (2005), 478 ff.; Wouters, Verhoeven, and Demeyere, *ICLR*, 8 (2008), 312 ff. (= Wouters, Verhoeven, and Demeyere, in Doria, Gasser, and Bassiouni, *Legal Regime* (2009), pp. 382 ff.); Rohrer, *Legalitäts- oder Opportunitätsprinzip* (2010), pp. 164 ff.

[122] In detail, see ICC-OTP, *Interests of Justice* (2007), pp. 3 ff.; Rohrer, *Legalitäts- oder Opportunitätsprinzip* (2010), pp. 160 ff., 234 ff. (regarding gravity); see also Quattrocolo, in Cassese, Chiavario, and De Francesco, *Problemi* (2005), pp. 314 ff.; Gropengießer and Meißner, *ICLR*, 5 (2005), 294 ff.; Ambos, in Ambos, Large, and Wierda, *Building a Future* (2009), pp. 82–6; Meyer, *ICLR*, 6 (2006), 579–80; Stahn, in Stahn and Sluiter, *Practice* (2009), pp. 249, 252 ff., 267 (discretion privileged over accountability), 270; Nouwen, *Complementarity* (2013), pp. 92 ff., distinguishing between the 'relatively narrow discretion' regarding the investigation decision pursuant to Art. 53 (1) and the 'broad leeway as to whom to charge and with which crimes' regarding the prosecution decision pursuant to Art. 53 (2) (p. 94); for a restrictive interpretation (re interests of justice), see Friman, in Cryer et al., *ICL* (2010), pp. 445–6; less focusing on discretion now Vasiliev, in Cryer et al., *ICL* (2019), p. 422; De Meester, *Investigation Phase* (2015), pp. 214 ff.; crit. of a (too) broad discretion and thus of Art. 53, Ohlin, in Stahn and Sluiter, *Practice* (2009), pp. 201–9, arguing, on the basis of a dualist individualist-retributive and collective security theory of ICL, that the ICC and its Prosecutor must only act pursuant to individualist-retributive considerations, leaving collective security and policy considerations to the UN Security Council (207, 209). On the DRC in this context, see Arsanjani and Reisman, *AJIL*, 99 (2005), 398 ff.; on Uganda, see El Zeidy, *ICLR*, 5 (2005), 111 ff. On the wide discretion of the prosecutor in the US system, see Safferling, *Criminal Procedure* (2012), p. 175; Cummings, *CardozoLR*, 31 (2009–2010), 2146. On the discretion of the Crown Prosecution Service in England & Wales, see Marsh, *Criminal Justice* (2004), pp. 166–7; Davies, *Criminal Justice* (2015), pp. 249 ff.; Spencer, in Delmas-Marty and Spencer, *European Criminal Procedures* (2002), p. 161. From a comparative perspective, Fyfe and Heinze, in Ambos et al., *Core Concepts II* (2022), pp. 169, 187 ff.; Fyfe and Heinze, *Core Concepts I* (2020), pp. 368 ff. On the concept of discretion generally, see Section B.(3)(a).

[123] Art. 53 (1)(c), (2)(c) ICCS.

[124] Section B.(4) in this chapter.

[125] Art. 18 (1) ICCS. In case of a Security Council referral, the Security Council is notified through the UN Secretary General (Reg. 30 RegOTP).

[126] Chapter II, B.(4) in this volume.

system has departed from the ad hoc tribunals in that it has purposed the Prosecutor rather as 'an officer of justice … than a partisan advocate'.[127]

In the ICC system there is the already mentioned[128] partial overlap between Article 15 (3) and Article 53 (1) ICCS, since in both cases—the Prosecutor acting *proprio motu*,[129] or upon a State or Security Council referral[130]—will consider the factors set out in Article 53 (1). Based on the assessment of the available information, the ICC-OTP will determine whether the available information suffices to assume that a crime has been committed, and whether an investigation would be in accordance with the principle of complementarity and the 'interests of justice';[131] for the latter assessment the Prosecutor shall take into account the gravity of the crime[132] and the interests of victims—concepts already analysed in previous chapters.[133]

Once the requirements of Article 53 (1) ICCS are met, it is presumed that a formal investigation will be initiated ('shall').[134] PTC I has interpreted the word 'shall' as expressing a 'presumption … that the Prosecutor investigates in order to be able to properly assess the relevant facts', that is, 'to provide clarity' by investigating unclear information.[135] This is not entirely convincing, though, given the four phases of the preliminary examination and the clarifying effect they may have—before the formal investigation under Article 53 (1) is opened.

At any rate, at this stage, normally, one or various cases will have evolved from the situation—'case' in Article 53 (1)(b) refers to potential cases[136]—and the respective case records opened.[137] The OTP shall identify 'the most serious crimes committed within a situation' and take into account the factors of Article 53 (1) when selecting cases within a situation.[138] A 'provisional *case hypothesis*', indicating the most serious and representative crimes, the 'most responsible' suspects, and the 'main types of victimisation' shall be elaborated;[139] according to Reg. 34 (3) RegOTP it must (still) be approved by ExCom but this unit has

[127] Kreß, *JICJ*, 1 (2003), 608; conc. de Meester, Pitcher, Rastan, and Sluiter, in Sluiter et al., *International Criminal Procedure* (2013), p. 190; similarly Swart, *JICJ*, 6 (2008), 109, for whom, however, ultimately decisive is how the Prosecutor executes her role.

[128] Sub-section (1) of this section with note 39.

[129] Arts. 13 (c), 15 ICCS.

[130] Arts. 13 (a), (b), 14, 53 ICCS.

[131] Kuczyńska, *Accusation Model ICC* (2015), pp. 86–8.

[132] Crit. thereon, Stahn, in Stahn and Sluiter, *Practice* (2009), p. 268, arguing that the assessment of gravity is 'mission impossible' without having concrete cases. About practical difficulties applying the gravity test, see Mégret, *LJIL*, 29 (2016), 203.

[133] On the 'gravity of the crime', see Chapter III, B.(2)(c)(i) in this volume; on the interests of victims pursuant to Art. 68 (3) ICCS, see Chapter II, E.(4)(a) in this volume.

[134] ICC-OTP, *Interests of Justice* (2007), pp. 1, 3; see also Safferling, *Criminal Procedure* (2012), p. 220 ('obliged'); Bergsmo and Bekou, 'Article 53', in Ambos, *Commentary* (2022), mn. 6 ('obliged').

[135] *Situation on the Vessels of Comoros*, ICC-01/13-34, para. 13; see also ICC, PTC I, Request under Regulation 46(3) of the Regulations of the Court, Decision on the 'Prosecution's Request for a Ruling on Jurisdiction under Article 19(3) of the Statute, ICC-RoC46(3)-01/18-37, 6 September 2018, para 84. Conc. Chaitidou, *ZIS* (2016), 840; Bergsmo and Bekou, 'Article 53', in Ambos, *Commentary* (2022), mn. 6 with n. 15. Generally Sadat, in Heinze and Dittrich, *ICC* (2021), pp. 121, 137–8.

[136] In the same vein, Bergsmo and Bekou, 'Article 53', in Ambos, *Commentary* (2022), mn. 20; Kuczyńska, *Accusation Model ICC* (2015), pp. 80–1.

[137] cf. Reg. 20 (2) RegR.

[138] Reg. 33 RegOTP. The OTP also develops a Case Selection Plan, 'which identifies in broad terms the potential cases within the situation' and 'will be based on the conclusions from the preliminary examination stage', see ICC-OTP, *Case Selection* (2016), para. 7.

[139] Reg. 34 (3) RegOTP. The provisional case hypotheses will be identified in the Case Selection Plan, ICC-OTP, *Case Selection* (2016), para. 7. See also Expert Group, *IER* (2020), pp. 47 ff. and 215 ('The Experts agree with the Prosecutor that "the most responsible" does not refer only to those occupying the highest positions, whether armed forces or political.')

disappeared with the new organization of the OTP.[140] At the time of writing (September 2024) the RegOTP have, unfortunately, not been adjusted in line with this new organization. Further, the investigative activities must be planned, inter alia, by developing an 'evidence collection plan' and a 'cooperation plan', and continuously reviewed and adjusted in light of new evidence.[141] Also, a joint team was to be formed, composed of members of the three divisions of the OTP (JCCD, ID, and PD),[142] in order to ensure a coordinated approach throughout the investigation.[143] Each joint team had to report to ExCom in order to receive strategic guidance.[144]

At the end of the formal investigation ('upon investigation'),[145] the Prosecutor must decide if there is a 'sufficient basis' for a 'prosecution', that is, to file charges against a concrete person or persons.[146] We will look more closely at the charging in the following sub-section and return to the delimitation between paragraphs (1) and (2) of Article 53 later.[147] It should be noted, however, that by no means all investigations lead directly to an arrest, surrender, or voluntary appearance. In the event the Court does not get hold of a suspect, the investigation turns into a 'hibernated' one, that is, it is basically frozen.[148] Otherwise, if the suspect is surrendered or comes voluntarily to the Court, he shall appear 'promptly' before the competent PTC,[149] that is, 'normally within 48 to 96 hours after arrival at the seat of the Court upon surrender, or on the date specified in the summons to appear'.[150]

## (2) Charges and judicial review: Confirmation proceedings

### *(a) Indictment (ad hoc tribunals) and Document Containing the Charges (ICC)*

#### *(i) General remarks*

Although neither the procedural law of the ad hoc tribunals nor that of the ICC provides for a formal distinction between the investigation and (intermediate) pre-trial phase, it is safe to say that the investigation phase ends with the presentation of the indictment (ICTY/ICTR/KSC) or the charges (ICC).[151] The indictment presupposes a *prima facie*

[140] See Chapter II, B.(2) in this volume.

[141] Reg. 35 RegOTP. The case hypothesis and these plans are internal documents and therefore not subject to the disclosure obligations of OTP (Reg. 35 (5) RegOTP); see also Chapter V, B.(2)(a) in this volume.

[142] On the (new) structure of the ICC-OTP, see Chapter II, B.(2) in this volume. See also the recommendations in Expert Group, *IER* (2020), p. 40.

[143] Reg. 32 (1), (2) RegOTP.

[144] Reg. 32 (4) RegOTP.

[145] Art. 53 (2) ICCS.

[146] cf. Safferling, *Criminal Procedure* (2012), pp. 242–3; Kuczynska, *Accusation Model ICC* (2015), pp. 92–3; for a more specific definition of prosecution with a view to the procedural stage (arrest warrant [Art. 58] or confirmation of charges [Art. 61]), see Bergsmo, Pejić, and Zhu, 'Article 16', in Ambos, *Commentary* (2022), mn. 15 ('actions taken once charges against an individual have been confirmed ... totality of actions undertaken by the Prosecutor to secure the conviction of a person against whom charges have been confirmed').

[147] Section B.(2) in this chapter.

[148] See ICC-ASP, *Report Basic Size OTP* (2015), pp. 33–4, 37, 44, 57–8.

[149] Rule 121 (1) RPE ICC.

[150] ICC, *Practice Manual* (2022), para. 7.

[151] ICTY, *Manual Practices* (2009), pp. 35 ff.; however, 'it must be possible for the Prosecutor to continue his investigation in respect of crimes that are not covered by the document containing the charges'; ICC, *Prosecutor v. Lubanga*, AC, Judgment on the Prosecutor's Appeal against the Decision of Pre-Trial Chamber I Entitled 'Decision Establishing General Principles Governing Applications to Restrict Disclosure pursuant to Rule 81 (2) and (4) of the Rules of Procedure and Evidence', ICC-01/04-01/06-568, 13 October 2006, paras. 49, 51; Heinze, *Disclosure* (2014), pp. 524 ff. See also Chapter V, B.(2)(a) in this volume.

case,[152] that is, 'a credible case, which (if not contradicted by the defence) would be a sufficient basis on which to convict the accused on the charge'.[153] Interestingly, the KSC Law requires, instead of a 'prima facie case', a 'well-grounded suspicion' of a commission of an offence within the KSC's jurisdiction.[154] This has been defined as requiring a conviction ... beyond mere theory or suspicion, that: (i) the contextual elements of the crime (if any) are present; (ii) the underlying acts or crimes have indeed occurred; and (iii) the suspect committed or participated in the commission of the crime ....[155]

The indictment contains the 'charges',[156] it is the 'accusatory instrument',[157] to be formulated by the Prosecutor.[158] While the term 'charges' is sometimes limited to crimes, that is,

[152] Arts. 18 (4) ICTYS, 17 (4) ICTRS. At the SCSL the Prosecutor need only be 'satisfied in the course of the investigation that a suspect has committed a crime' (Rule 47 (B) RPE SCSL) or 'that the allegations ... amount to a crime' (Rule 47 (E) RPE SCSL); see thereon Jacobs, in Sluiter et al., *International Criminal Procedure* (2013), p. 1133. For a crit. view of the additional preliminary test provided for by Rule 28 (A) RPE ICTY, Jacobs, ibid., p. 1131.

[153] ICTY, *Prosecutor v. Kordić and Čerkez*, TC, Decision on the Review of the Indictment, IT-95-14/2-T, 10 November 1995, p. 3, adopting the ILC's definition given in its Report on the ICC Draft Statute (Report of the International Law Commission on the Work of its 46th Sess., UN GAOR, 49th Sess., at 95, UN Doc. A/49/10 (1994)); conc. ICTY, *Prosecutor v. S. Milošević*, TC, Decision on Review of Indictment, IT-01-51-I, 22 November 2001, para. 14; ICTY, *Prosecutor v. Mladić*, Confirming Judge's Order Granting Leave to File an Amended Indictment and Confirming the Amended Indictment, IT-95-5/18-1, 8 November 2002, para. 26; ICTY, *Prosecutor v. Pavković et al.*, TC, Order on Confirmation of Indictment, IT-03-70-I, 2 October 2003; ICTY, *Prosecutor v. Mladić*, Single Judge Decision on Amendment of Indictment, T-09-92-I, 27 May 2011, para. 14. Thereto Vasconcelos, in Bergsmo, Rackwitz, and Song, *Historical Origins V* (2017), p. 866 with n. 80. The standard has been put in more concrete terms by Rule 47 (B), previously 47 (A), RPE ICTY/ICTR and Rule 48 (B) RPE MICT ('sufficient evidence to provide reasonable grounds for believing that a suspect has committed a crime within the jurisdiction of the Tribunal'), although this appears, arguably, to be a higher standard (in this vein, Safferling, *Criminal Procedure* (2012), p. 317). See more recently MICT, *Prosecutor v. Turinabo*, Decision on the Prosecution Motion to Amend the Indictment, 17 October 2019, para 29 (explaining that the supporting material must provide a credible case which would, if not contradicted by the defence, be a sufficient basis to convict the accused on the charge); STL, *Prosecutor v. Ayyash et al.*, AC, Interlocutory Decision on the Applicable Law: Criminal Association and Review of the Indictment, STL-17-07/I/AC/R176bis/F0021/20171018/R000800-R000844/EN/dm, 18 October 2017, para. 110 ('[T]he Pre-Trial Judge's task under Article 18 of the Statute and Rule 68 (F) requires him to assess whether the supporting materials provided by the Prosecutor demonstrate a credible case which could, if not contradicted, be a sufficient basis to convict the suspect on the charge(s) in the indictment.') See also Hunt, in May et al., *Essays on ICTY Procedure and Evidence* (2001), pp. 137 ff.; Vohrah, in McDonald and Swaak-Goldman, *Substantive and Procedural Aspects* (2000), pp. 491–2; Turone, in Cassese et al., *Rome Statute II* (2002), p. 1173; Vasiliev, in Cryer et al., *ICL* (2019), pp. 427–8; Boas et al., *Procedure* (2011), pp. 181–2; crit. Jacobs, in Sluiter et al., *International Criminal Procedure* (2013), pp. 1132–3.

[154] Art. 38 (4) KSC Law; Rule 86 (1) RPE KSC.

[155] *Prosecutor v. Mustafa*, PTJ, Public Redacted Version of Decision on the Confirmation of the Indictment Against Salih Mustafa, KSC-BC-2020-05, F00008/RED, 5 October 2020, para. 37 (further explaining that this conviction is to be based 'on concrete and tangible supporting material, demonstrating a clear line of reasoning underpinning the charges in the indictment' and the relevant material has to be examined 'holistically, without scrutinising each item of evidentiary material in isolation'); subsequently conc. *Prosecutor v. Thaçi et al.*, PTJ, Public Redacted Version of Decision on the Confirmation of the Indictment against Hashim Thaçi, Kadri Veseli, Rexhep Selimi, Jakup Krasniqi, KSC-BC-2020-06, F00026/RED, 30 November 2020, paras. 45–9; *Prosecutor v. Shala*, PTJ, Public Redacted Version of the Decision on the Confirmation of the Indictment against Pjetër Shala, KSC-BC-2020-04, F00007/RED, 6 May 2021, paras. 34–8.

[156] cf. e.g. Rules 47 (C), 50 (B), 73*bis* (D), 85 (A)(vi), 87 (B) RPE ICTY; Rules 48 (C), 50 (B), 81 (D), 102 (A) (vi), 104 (B) RPE MICT; Art. 38 (4) KSC Law and Rule 86 (2) RPE KSC. See also Boas et al., *Procedure* (2011), pp. 178–9.

[157] Friman, Brady, Costi, Guariglia, and Stuckenberg, in Sluiter et al., *International Criminal Procedure* (2013), pp. 383, 385, 447.

[158] See also ICC, *Practice Manual* (2022), para. 38 ('fully within the responsibility of the Prosecutor'); also ICC-ASP, *Report Study Group on Governance* (2015), p. 32 (para. 17); Pues, *Prosecutorial Discretion* (2020), p. 113.

the legal allegation[159] ('nature ... of the charges'[160]), or to facts or evidence, that is, the factual allegation[161] ('cause of the charges'[162]), it also comprises both the factual and legal allegation, that is, it is 'the minimum combination of factual and legal allegations sufficient to justify the imposition of criminal liability'.[163]

The combined understanding of charges is also common under the ICC regime,[164] where the Prosecutor must provide the person charged, 'no later than 30 days' before the confirmation hearing,[165] with a 'Document Containing the Charges' (DCC):[166] that is, 'an assertion ... that he intends to bring a person to trial for the specific crimes set out in the document'.[167] The DCC contains, apart from personal information regarding the suspect,[168] a 'statement of the facts' and their 'legal characterisation'.[169] The 'facts' in this sense must be distinguished from the evidence to be adduced by the Prosecutor to support these facts.[170] Further, the 'statement of the facts' is, arguably, broader than 'the facts and circumstances' which form the basis of a verdict of a TC pursuant to Article 74 (2) ICCS.[171] There is also

[159] See e.g. Rules 11*bis* (C), 47 (C), 73*bis* (D) RPE ICTY, 48 (C), 81 (D), RPE MICT; also Art. 38 (3) KSC Law and Rule 86 (3) RPE KSC ('crimes' or 'crime charged').

[160] ICTY, *Prosecutor v. Kupreškić et al.*, AC, Judgment, IT-95-16-A, 23 October 2001, para. 88; conc. ICTR, *Prosecutor v. Ntagerura et al.*, TC, Judgment and Sentence, ICTR-99-46-T, 25 February 2004, para. 29; distinguishing between 'counts or charges', and 'material facts' ICTY, *Prosecutor v. Đorđević*, AC, Judgment, IT-05-87/1-A, 27 January 2014, para. 574, with further references in n. 1897; ICTY, *Prosecutor v. Prlić et al.*, AC, Judgment, Vol. I, IT- 04-74-A, 29 November 2017, para. 27 *in fine* ('In order to provide proper notice to the accused, the Prosecution is required to plead in an indictment all of the charges and the underpinning material facts with sufficient precision, but is not required to set out the evidence by which the material facts are to be proven'); KSC, *Prosecutor v. Gucati and Haradinaj*, CoAP, Decision on the Defence Appeals against Decision on Preliminary Motions, KSC-BC-2020-07/IA004/F00007, 23 June 2021, para. 35.

[161] See e.g. Art. 65 (1)(c) ('facts contained in ... charges'), Art. 74 (2) ('fact and circumstances described in the charges') ICCS and Rule 69 RPE ICC (as facts within the framework of evidentiary agreements); see also Art. 38 (4) KSC Law ('statement of the facts ... with which the person is charged').

[162] *Kupreškić et al.*, IT-95-16-A, para. 88.

[163] Boas et al., *Procedure* (2011), p. 198; conc. Safferling, *Criminal Procedure* (2012), p. 249 (factual commission at specific time and place by a person amounting to a crime or crimes); see also Fry, *Contours* (2015), pp. 84–5.

[164] ICC, *Prosecutor v. Ongwen*, AC, Judgment on the Appeal of Mr Ongwen against the Decision of Trial Chamber IX of 4 February 2021 Entitled 'Trial Judgment', ICC-02/04-01/15-2022-Red, 15 December 2022, para. 236; *Prosecutor v. Al Hassan*, Judgment on the Appeal of Mr Al Hassan against the Decision of Trial Chamber X Entitled 'Decision on application for notice of possibility of variation of legal characterisation pursuant to Regulation 55(2) of the Regulations of the Court', ICC-01/12-01/18-1562-Red, 1 July 2021, para. 39; *Prosecutor v. Al Hassan*, PTC I, Decision on the Defence Request concerning the Time Limit for the Prosecutor to File the Document Containing a Detailed Description of the Charges, ICC-01/12-01/18-143-tENG, 5 October 2018, para. 30. For previous case law, see first edition p. 346 with note 119. See also Schabas, Chaitidou, and El Zeidy, 'Article 61', in Ambos, *Commentary* (2022), mn. 15 ('facts and their legal characterization together form the "charge"' [emphasis omitted]).

[165] Rule 121 (3) RPE ICC. For a stricter time limit, see WCRO, *Confirmation* (2015), pp. 4, 94 (within thirty days since first appearance).

[166] Art. 61 (3)(a) ICCS. For a broad use of the term, see also Art. 64 (8)(a) ('charges ... confirmed') and Art. 67 (1)(a) ('nature, cause and content of the charge'). For a detailed analysis of the DCC, see Schabas, Chaitidou, and El Zeidy, 'Article 61', in Ambos, *Commentary* (2022), mn. 30 ff.

[167] *Lubanga*, ICC-01/04-01/06-568, para. 51.

[168] The suspect must be notified 'by way of personal service' (Reg. 31 (3)(c) RegC).

[169] cf. Reg. 52 RegC.

[170] cf. Art. 61 (5) ICCS ('support each charge with sufficient evidence') and ICC, *Prosecutor v. Lubanga*, AC, Judgment on the Appeals of Mr Lubanga Dyilo and the Prosecutor against the Decision of Trial Chamber I of 14 July 2009 Entitled 'Decision giving notice to the parties and participants that the legal characterisation of the facts may be subject to change in accordance with Regulation 55 (2) of the Regulations of the Court', ICC-01/04-01/06-2205, 8 December 2009, para. 90 with n. 163, stating: 'the term "facts" refers to the factual allegations which support each of the legal elements of the crime charged. These *factual allegations* must be distinguished from the *evidence* put forward by the Prosecutor at the confirmation hearing to support a charge' (emphasis added). In the same vein, Triffterer and Kiss, 'Article 74', in Ambos, *Commentary* (2022), mn. 46, 47.

[171] See the quoted passage in preceding note 170 from *Lubanga*, ICC-01/04-01/06-2205, para. 90 with n. 163, which continues that the *factual allegations* must be distinguished 'as well ... from *background or other information* that, although contained in the document containing the charges or the confirmation decision, does not

the (controversial) distinction between 'material' and 'subsidiary' facts[172]— to be presented separately[173]— to which we will return below.[174] There is no explicit evidentiary standard for the DCC, but it follows from Article 61 (5) and (7) ICCS that the 'substantial grounds to believe' standard of the confirmation hearing applies.[175] We will return to this standard at the end of this section.

*(ii) Form and content of the charging document*

The combined factual-legal understanding of the charges also determines the requirements as to the form and content of the charging document.[176] The relevant provisions require, generally, a concise, detailed, and self-contained statement of both the alleged facts and the respective crimes to be attributed to the person(s) charged.[177] More concretely, it must be specified 'the name and particulars of the suspect',[178] the 'full name' and 'any other relevant identifying information',[179] 'the time and place of the alleged crimes',[180] as well as a 'legal characterization of the fact', including the 'precise form of participation'.[181]

A rich, albeit not always consistent, case law has developed around these requirements.[182] The evidence presented must be linked to the factual allegations and these to the specific

support the legal elements of the crime charged' (emphasis added). Referring to Art. 74 (2), however, ICC, *Practice Manual* (2022), para. 36.

[172] The distinction, introduced in 2011 (cf. Bitti, in Agirre et al., *Quality Control* (2020), pp. 905, 929 ff.), was generally supported by the PTCs. Accordingly, 'material facts' are those which support a specific charge, while 'subsidiary facts' refer to background information or other information (in the sense of *Lubanga*, ICC-01/04-01/06-2205) from which the existence of 'material facts' may be inferred; cf. ICC, *Prosecutor v. Banda and Jerbo*, PTC I, Corrigendum of the 'Decision on the Confirmation of Charges', ICC-02/05-03/09-121-Corr-Red, 7 March 2011, paras. 36–7; *Prosecutor v. Ruto et al.*, PTC II, Decision on the Confirmation of Charges, ICC-01/09-01/11-373, 23 January 2012, paras. 47–8; *Muthaura et al.*, PTC II, Decision on the Confirmation of Charges pursuant to Article 61 (7)(a) and (b) of the Rome Statute, ICC-01/09-02/11-382-Red, 23 January 2012, paras. 59–60; *Prosecutor v. Gbagbo*, PTC I, Decision on the Date of the Confirmation of Charges Hearing and Proceedings Leading thereto, ICC-02/11-01/11-325, 14 December 2012, para. 27; *Prosecutor v. Ongwen*, PTC II, Transcript of Hearing, ICC-02/04-01/15-T-6-ENG, 19 May 2015, p. 21; implicitly, *Prosecutor v. Ongwen*, PTC, Decision on the Confirmation of Charges against Dominic Ongwen, ICC-02/04-01/15-422-Red, 23 March 2016, Disposition pp. 71 ff. In contrast, the distinction has sometimes been rejected by the ACs, see below the references in note 1221.

[173] cf. ICC, *Practice Manual* (2022), paras. 31 ff. (either separate filings, or, if subsidiary/supporting facts included in the DCC, separate sections). According to the *Practice Manual* 'material facts' are 'the facts and circumstances that must be described in the charges [ . . . ] and which are the only facts subject to judicial determination to the applicable standard of proof at confirmation and trial stages, respectively and their legal characterisation'; in contrast, 'subsidiary facts' are 'those facts that are relied upon by the Prosecutor as part of his/her argumentation in support of the charges and, as such, are functionally "evidence"' (ibid., paras. 35–6).

[174] Section B.(7)(b)(iii) in this chapter with notes 1221 ff.

[175] cf. Friman, Brady, Costi, Guariglia, and Stuckenberg, in Sluiter et al., *International Criminal Procedure* (2013), pp. 389–90.

[176] Generally on the form and content of the indictment and the DCC, see Tochilovsky, *Jurisprudence* (2014), pp. 4 ff.; Kuczyńska, *Accusation Model ICC* (2015), pp. 126–30. On law and practice at the IMT, IMTFE, SPSC, ECCC, and STL, see Friman, Brady, Costi, Guariglia, and Stuckenberg, in Sluiter et al., *International Criminal Procedure* (2013), pp. 383–4, 394–7.

[177] cf. Arts. 18 (4) ICTYS, 17 (4) ICTRS, Rule 47 (C) RPE ICTY/ICTR/SCSL, Rule 48 (C) RPE MICT, Art. 38 (4) KSC Law and Rule 86 (3) RPE KSC. Reg. 52 RegC and Reg. 58 RegOTP. Rule 121 (3) RPE ICC only refers to the 'detailed description of the charges' without defining them more precisely, but see ICC, *Practice Manual* (2022), paras. 35 ('clear, exhaustive and self-contained') and 36 (consequently, no footnotes with cross-references or reference to evidence allowed). See also Mettraux et al., *Effectiveness ICC* (2014), pp. 14, 18 (paras. 51, 78c): 'clear, tight and precise DCC', but possibly 'footnoted'.

[178] Rule 47 (C) RPE ICTY/ICTR/SCSL, Rule 48 (C) RPE MICT.

[179] Reg. 52 (a) RegC.

[180] Reg. 52 (b) RegC.

[181] Reg. 52 (c) RegC; as to the form of participation, see also Reg. 58 (2) RegOTP (referring to 'mode or modes of liability').

[182] See the references in note 164. See also ICC, *Prosecutor v. Ntaganda*, Public Redacted Version of Judgment on the Appeals of Mr Bosco Ntaganda and the Prosecutor against the Decision of Trial Chamber VI of 8 July

elements of the crimes or modes of liability.[183] The Prosecutor must plead all 'material facts'—as opposed to subsidiary or background facts[184]—but materiality is an ambiguous concept that cannot be determined in the abstract, but rather depends on the particularities of the Prosecution's case, especially the nature of the relevant conduct.[185] At any rate, the charges must be pleaded with a view to the relevant criminal acts and the respective conduct of the accused.[186]

The Prosecutor is not allowed to frame the factual allegations (too) openly,[187] but specific incidents should be dated as precisely as possible (although the list of all incidents need not be complete).[188] Of course, it is difficult to determine precisely which formulations are still acceptable[189] and which are too broad and ambiguous.[190] Simply listing categories of crimes 'or stating, in broad general terms, the temporal and geographical parameters of the charge' is insufficient.[191] Specificity is also necessary with regard to the identity of the victims and the

2019 entitled 'Judgment', ICC-01/04-02/06-2666-Red, 30 March 2021, para. 322; ICC, *Prosecutor v. Yekatom and Ngaïssona*, Judgment on the Appeal of Mr Alfred Yekatom against the Decision of Trial Chamber V of 29 October 2020 Entitled 'Decision on motions on the Scope of the Charges and the Scope of Evidence at Trial', ICC-01/14-01/18-874, 5 February 2021, para. 53; *Gucati and Haradinaj*, KSC-BC-2020-07/IA004/F00007, para. 35. For previous case law, see first edition p. 347 with note 137. See also Gallmetzer, in Guariglia et al., *AC ICC Commentary* (2018), p. 179; Smith, in Rohan and Zyberi, *Defense Perspectives* (2017), pp. 385, 402 ff.; Tochilovsky, *Jurisprudence* (2014), pp. 1 ff. (18 ff.); Klann, in Decaux, Dieng, and Sow, *Human Rights* (2007), pp. 109 ff.; Boas et al., *Procedure* (2011), pp. 192–4; Friman, Brady, Costi, Guariglia, and Stuckenberg, in Sluiter et al., *International Criminal Procedure* (2013), pp. 385–8, 391–2, 403, 483 (formulating a 'principle'); Vasiliev, in Cryer et al., *ICL* (2019), pp. 427–8; esp. on the ICC DCC, see Schabas, Chaitidou, and El Zeidy, 'Article 61', in Ambos, *Commentary* (2022), mn. 30 ff.; Triffterer and Kiss, 'Article 74', in Ambos, *Commentary* (2022), mn. 46–7. Crit. on the practical application, Tochilovsky, *CLF*, 15 (2004), 340–1; Möller, in Kirsch, *Internationale Strafgerichtshöfe* (2005), p. 52; Zahar and Sluiter, *ICL* (2008), pp. 336 ff.

[183] See the case law on the in-depth analysis chart below in Chapter V, B.(2)(c)(iii). See also ICC, *Prosecutor v. Lubanga*, PTC I, Decision on the Final System of Disclosure and the Establishment of a Timetable, ICC-01/04-01/06-102, 15 May 2006, paras. 59–60 ('(i) each item of evidence is linked to the factual statement it intends to prove, and (ii) each factual statement is linked to the specific element of the crime or mode of liability, or both'); *Prosecutor v. Abu Garda*, PTC I, Second Decision on Issues Relating to Disclosure, ICC-02/05-02/09-35, 15 July 2009, p. 17; *Prosecutor v. Mbarushimana*, PTC I, Decision on Issues Relating to Disclosure, ICC-01/04-01/10-87, 30 March 2011, para. 13; *Prosecutor v. Ruto et al.*, PTC II, Decision Setting the Regime for Evidence Disclosure and Other Related Matters, ICC-01/09-01/11-44, 6 April 2011, paras. 21–2; ICC, *Prosecutor v. Muthaura et al.*, PTC II, Decision Setting the Regime for Evidence Disclosure and Other Related Matters, ICC-01/09-02/11-48, 6 April 2011, paras. 22–3.

[184] See note 172 in this chapter.

[185] cf. ICTY, *Prosecutor v. Blaškić*, AC, Judgment, IT-95-14-A, 29 July 2004, paras. 209–10; *Prosecutor v. Stanković*, TC, Decision on the Defence Preliminary Motion on the Form of the Indictment, IT-96-23/2-PT, 15 November 2002, para. 8; *Ntagerura et al.*, ICTR-99-46-T, para. 31; *Prlić et al.*, IT-04-74-A, para. 28.See also Boas et al., *Procedure* (2011), p. 193.

[186] See also Triffterer and Kiss, 'Article 74', in Ambos, *Commentary* (2022), mn. 44 ('charges may be pleaded by reference to parameters or at the level of individual criminal acts').

[187] Summarizing the case law, Schabas, Chaitidou, and El Zeidy, 'Article 61', in Ambos, *Commentary* (2022), mn. 38–9.

[188] ICC, *Prosecutor v. Bemba*, PTC II, Decision pursuant to Article 61 (7)(a) and (b) of the Rome Statute on the Charges of the Prosecutor Against Jean-Pierre Bemba Gombo, ICC-01/05-01/08-424, 15 June 2009, paras. 65–8.

[189] The geographic reference to 'Busurungi and surrounding villages' (ICC, *Prosecutor v. Mbarushimana*, PTC I, Decision on the Confirmation of Charges, ICC-01/04-01/10-465-Red, 16 December 2011, para. 84) and the temporal one of 'on or about' a particular date (*Bemba*, ICC-01/05-01/08-424, paras. 67–8) have been accepted as sufficiently precise.

[190] The formulation 'including but not limited to' has been considered too broad: *Mbarushimana*, ICC-01/04-01/10-465-Red, paras. 82–3; *Ruto et al.*, ICC-01/09-01/11-373, paras. 99, 101, 103; *Muthaura et al.*, ICC-01/09-02/11-382-Red, para. 106. See generally Schabas, Chaitidou, and El Zeidy, 'Article 61', in Ambos, *Commentary* (2022), mn. 38.

[191] ICC, *Prosecutor v. Bemba*, AC, Judgment on the Appeal of Mr Jean-Pierre Bemba Gombo against Trial Chamber III's 'Judgment pursuant to Article 74 of the Statute', ICC-01/05-01/08-3636-Red, 8 June 2018, para. 4.

means of commission,[192] but ICC PTCs do not consider it necessary to set out the identity of all victims.[193] Modes of liability require a particular high degree of specificity,[194] allowing, however, for 'different levels of specificity' with regard to the suspect's role and contribution, depending on the circumstances of the particular case.[195] Summarizing the requirements the *Al Hassan* PTC held:

> [T]he degree of specificity expected from the Prosecutor in her description of the facts depends on the nature of the crimes in question and the circumstances of the case brought by the Prosecutor ... Where crimes such as torture or rape are concerned, the Prosecutor must describe the criminal acts in issue, stating the date and place of the acts, along with the number of victims, or at the very least a clear estimate of that number, and their identities as far as at all possible. However, where by their nature the crimes are directed against a group or collectivity of people, as in the case of the crime of persecution, a like degree of specificity cannot be expected of the Prosecutor's description of the facts; nonetheless, the Prosecutor must endeavor to pinpoint as much as possible places, times and approximate numbers of victims and to provide the necessary particulars to make out the elements of the crimes.[196]

Thus, an indictment has been considered defective by an ICTY AC 'when the material facts are pleaded without sufficient specificity, such as, unless there are special circumstances, when the times refer to broad date ranges, the places are only generally indicated, and the victims are only generally identified'.[197] Consequently, at the ad hoc tribunals, Chambers have allowed the prosecution to cure defective indictments 'by timely, clear and consistent information ... detailing the factual basis underpinning the charges'.[198] In apparent contrast, at the ICC, defence submissions with respect to a lack of precision of a DCC have been regularly rejected by PTCs.[199]

192 *Blaškić*, IT-95-14-A, para. 213; ICTR, *Prosecutor v. Niyitegeka*, AC, Judgment, ICTR-96-14-A, 9 July 2004, para. 193; ICTY, *Prosecutor v. Gotovina et al.*, AC, Decision on Joint Defence Interlocutory Appeal against Trial Chamber's Decision on Joint Defence Motion to Strike the Prosecution's Further Clarification of Identity of Victims, IT-06-90-AR73.3, 26 January 2009, para. 19.

193 ICC, *Prosecutor v. Katanga and Ngudjolo*, PTC I, Decision on the Three Defences' Requests Regarding the Prosecution's Amended Charging Document, ICC-01/04-01/07-648, 25 June 2008, para. 28; *Bemba*, ICC-01/05-01/08-424, para. 134.

194 See e.g. ICTY, *Prosecutor v. Brđanin and Talić*, TC, Decision on Objections by Momir Talić to the Form of the Amended Indictment, IT-99-36 and IT-99-36/1, 20 February 2001, para. 20; *Ntagerura et al.*, ICTR-99-46-T, para. 33; SCSL, *Prosecutor v. Brima et al.*, AC, Judgment, SCSL-04-16-A-675, 22 February 2008, para. 38.

195 cf. ICC, *Prosecutor v. Lubanga*, AC, Judgment on the Appeal of Mr Thomas Lubanga Dyilo against his Conviction, ICC-01/04-01/06-3121-Red, paras. 122–3 ('greatest degree of specificity possible in the circumstances'), quoting the ICTY *Blaškić*, IT-95-14-A; thereto Triffterer and Kiss, 'Article 74', in Ambos, *Commentary* (2022), mn. 43; Nerlich, in Fernandez et al., *Commentaire CPI II* (2019), p. 1976; similarly ICC, *Practice Manual* (2022), paras. 40–3; on the ICTY approach, also Boas et al., *Procedure* (2011), p. 193.

196 *Al Hassan*, ICC-01/12-01/18-143-tENG, para. 30; conc. ICC, *Prosecutor v. Yekatom and Ngaïssona*, Decision on the 'Prosecution's Request to Postpone the Confirmation Hearing and all Related Disclosure Deadlines', ICC-01/14-01/18-199, 15 May 2019, para. 41. Thereto Schabas, Chaitidou, and El Zeidy, 'Article 61', in Ambos, *Commentary* (2022), mn. 37.

197 *Prlić et al.*, IT-04-74-A, para. 29.

198 cf. Friman, Brady, Costi, Guariglia, and Stuckenberg, in Sluiter et al., *International Criminal Procedure* (2013), pp. 421–2 (with case law references), 450.

199 cf. Schabas, Chaitidou, and El Zeidy, 'Article 61', in Ambos, *Commentary* (2022), mn. 41.

The evidence is to be presented separately[200] and in an orderly fashion.[201] The DCC need not 'strictly follow the factual and legal foundations' of an arrest warrant or summons to appear,[202] given that the Prosecution can continue its investigation[203] and thus amend the charges.[204] It should be noted, though, that the OTP aims at being trial-ready 'as early as possible in the judicial proceedings and in any event no later than the confirmation of charges hearing'.[205] Furthermore, the AC recognized that, 'ideally, it would be desirable for the investigation to be complete by the time of the confirmation hearing' although this is 'not a requirement of the Statute'.[206] Thus, apparently, the formerly rather relaxed approach to the OTP's trial readiness has been tightened due to expediency concerns.[207]

The rather strict requirements in framing the charges are in line with and, arguably, even demanded by the (human) right to be adequately informed of the charges.[208] Against this background, it is misleading to argue that the person concerned is only—'formally' or 'actually'—charged after the confirmation of the charges.[209] Apart from the terminological confusion created by such an argument, in substantive terms, it sets aside the structural and functional separation between prosecutorial and judicial functions, that is, the shift of authority from the OTP—as investigative and charging authority—to the PTC—as adjudicatory authority assessing the charges by way of an intermediate (review or confirmation) procedure.[210] The fact that charges are reviewed or to be confirmed by judges does

[200] For the ICC this already follows from Art. 61 (3)(b) ICCS and Rule 121 (3) RPE ICC, which refer separately to the evidence to be presented (in Rule 121 (3) even more explicitly to the 'list of evidence' to be presented with the charges); see also note 173 in this chapter and main text and, in more detail, Chapter V, B.(2)(c)(i) and (e) in this volume. For the ICTY/ICTR it has been clarified by the case law, e.g. *Blaškić*, IT-95-14-A, para. 209; *Niyitegeka*, ICTR-96-14-A, para. 193; ICTR, *Prosecutor v. Nyiramasuhuko et al. (Butare)*, AC, Judgment I, ICTR-98-42-2183/01, 14 December 2015, para. 492. See also Friman, Brady, Costi, Guariglia, and Stuckenberg, in Sluiter et al., *International Criminal Procedure* (2013), pp. 386, 392.

[201] cf. ICC, *Practice Manual* (2022), para. 40 ('consecutively in any clear order'; no 'chart linking the factual allegations … and the evidence submitted thereof'); in favour of such 'in-depth-analysis charts', however, Trendafilova, in *FS Werle* (2022), pp. 331 ff.; Mettraux et al., *Effectiveness ICC* (2014), pp. 13–14 (paras. 48, 49, 52). On the IDAC, in more detail, Chapter V, B.(2)(c)(iii).

[202] cf. Art. 58 ICCS and, in detail, Section B.(6) in this chapter.

[203] cf. Art. 61 (4) ICCS.

[204] *Mbarushimana*, ICC-01/04-01/10-465-Red, para. 88; see also ICC, *Prosecutor v. Bemba et al.*, PTC II, Decision on 'Narcisse Arido's Request for an Order Rejecting the Prosecution's Document Containing the Charges (ICC-01/05-01/13-526-AnxB1) and for an Order to the Prosecution to File an Amended and Corrected Document Containing the Charges', ICC-01/05-01/13-567, 15 July 2014, pp. 4–5. With regard to the factual expansion of the charges, see ICC, *Practice Manual* (2022), paras. 31 ff.

[205] ICC-OTP, *Strategic Plan* (2019), p. 13.

[206] *Lubanga*, ICC-01/04-01/06-102, para. 54; reiterated by ICC, *Practice Manual* (2023), para. 14

[207] Expert Group, *IER* (2020), p. 158 ('Several Judges and counsel emphasised the need for the investigation being completed before the initiation of proceedings. A suggestion put forward by Judges consisted of a requirement upon the Prosecutor, at the commencement of the proceedings, to specify clearly the stage reached in the investigation. Trial non-readiness by the OTP was mentioned as one of the main reasons for the lengthy pre-trial phase.')

[208] On this right, see Chapter I, D.(3)(c) in this volume; ICC, *Prosecutor v. Bemba*, TC III, Judgment pursuant to Article 74 of the Statute, ICC-01/05-01/08-3343, 21 March 2016, para. 33 with further references; for the same assessment with regard to ICTY/ICTR and ICC, but considering that the SCSL practice falls short of this standard, see Friman, Brady, Costi, Guariglia, and Stuckenberg, in Sluiter et al., *International Criminal Procedure* (2013), pp. 456, 480; regarding the ICC DCC, see Schabas, Chaitidou, and El Zeidy, 'Article 61', in Ambos, *Commentary* (2022), mn. 33–4.

[209] In this sense, Safferling, *Criminal Procedure* (2012), pp. 317, 325, 337.

[210] On this shift of authority, see also ICC, *Prosecutor v. Bemba et al.*, TC VII, Decision on the Submission of Auxiliary Documents, ICC-01/05-01/13-992, 10 June 2015, para. 12; also Schabas, Chaitidou, and El Zeidy, 'Article 61', in Ambos, *Commentary* (2022), mn. 132; Bitti, in Agirre et al., *Quality Control* (2020), 905, 932.

not turn them into something preliminary, provisional, or 'informal' from the perspective of the investigative authority;[211] on the contrary, the filing of charges brings an investigation, at least with regard to the respective facts and/or crimes charged, to an end. Of course, from the perspective of the whole proceedings, the charges are always preliminary or provisional since they need to be accepted by the judges or jurors; but this does not deprive them of their character as 'charges'. In any case, the charges fulfil a double function; that is, they inform the accused about the case against him and determine the factual framework of the proceedings.[212]

### (iii) *Adding or subtracting charges*

The above-mentioned shift of authority from the investigation (OTP) to the confirmation proceedings (PTC) also makes clear that the charges, once confirmed by the PTC, cannot be 'updated' or in any other way *amended* by the OTP.[213] It simply lacks the authority to do so. Indeed, the PTC 'commit[s] the person to a Trial Chamber for trial *on the charges as confirmed*';[214] its 'confirmation decision constitutes the final, authoritative document setting out the charges'.[215] There is no further (intermediate) instrument between the confirmation and the trial proceedings. From this perspective, an updated DCC is incompatible with the procedural regime of the ICC since it 'is an updated version of a document given a specific purpose in the statutory scheme [i.e. to confirm or decline the charges]—and this purpose has been served when the confirmation decision is rendered'.[216] In addition, an updated DCC is unnecessary since the charges are (partially) confirmed or rejected by the PTC and its decision should set out clearly enough the factual allegations and their legal characterization for the trial proceedings.[217]

The final decision of a Trial Chamber must not 'exceed the facts and circumstances described in the charges and any amendments to the charges'.[218] This provision, although referring to the trial phase to be dealt with below, became a matter of controversy in both the *Bemba* and *Ntaganda* cases with regard to the charges confirmed and the above-mentioned

[211] In this vein, however, Kirsch, in Ahlbrecht et al., *Internationales Strafrecht* (2017), mn. 1415.

[212] cf. Friman, Brady, Costi, Guariglia, and Stuckenberg, in Sluiter et al., *International Criminal Procedure* (2013), p. 383.

[213] Convincingly *Bemba et al.*, ICC-01/05-01/13-992, paras. 8–20; *contra* ICC, *Prosecutor v. Bemba et al.*, TC VII, Decision on the Submission of Auxiliary Documents, Partly Dissenting Opinion of Judge Eboe-Osuji, ICC-01/05-01/13-992-Anx-Corr, 16 June. 2015, who, however after long and in part unnecessarily theoretical considerations, admits that an updated DDC 'is not required by the Statute or Rules', but 'is a matter entirely for the discretion of the TC' (para. 136); ICC, *Prosecutor v. Bemba et al.*, AC, Judgment on the Appeals of Mr Jean-Pierre Bemba Gombo, Mr Aimé Kilolo Musamba, Mr Jean-Jacques Mangenda Kabongo, Mr Fidèle Babala Wandu and Mr Narcisse Arido against the Decision of Trial Chamber VII Entitled 'Judgment pursuant to Article 74 of the Statute', ICC-01/05-01/13-2275-Red, 8 March 2018, para. 197; ICC, *Prosecutor v. Al Hassan*, TC X, Decision Setting the Commencement Date of the Trial, ICC-01/12-01/18-548, 6 January 2020, para. 18. See also Bitti, 'Article 64', in Ambos, *ICC Commentary* (2022), mn. 14. Apparently overlooked by Friman, Brady, Costi, Guariglia, and Stuckenberg, in Sluiter et al., *International Criminal Procedure* (2013), p. 392.

[214] Art. 61 (7)(a) ICCS; emphasis added. For further provisions referring to the charges as confirmed by the PTC, see *Bemba et al.*, ICC-01/05-01/13-992, para. 15.

[215] ICC, *Practice Manual* (2022), para. 57.

[216] *Bemba et al.*, ICC-01/05-01/13-992, para. 16.

[217] Previously against an updated DCC, see e.g. ICC, *Prosecutor v. Gbagbo and Blé Goudé*, TC I, Order Setting the Commencement Date for Trial, ICC-02/11-01/15-58, 7 May 2015, para. 17; *Bemba et al.*, ICC-01/05-01/13-992, para. 19.

[218] Art. 74 (2) ICCS.

specificity requirements. *Bemba* was convicted partly for individual acts of murder, rape, and pillaging committed against particular victims at specific times and places that had not been confirmed in the confirmation decision.[219] The Prosecutor listed a number of alleged criminal acts of murder, rape, and pillaging in the amended DCC, but, through the use of expressions such as 'include' or 'include but are not limited to', suggested that this list was not complete or exhaustive.[220] The PTC confirmed *in broad terms* charges of murder and rape as war crimes and crimes against humanity, and pillaging as a war crime.[221] Following the confirmation of charges, the TC requested the Prosecutor to provide a second amended document containing the charges,[222] which was eventually submitted.[223] *Bemba* thought that this document added new allegations that were not confirmed.[224] TC III argued that the PTC's confirmation decision was broad enough so that new allegations could be included without a new confirmation decision.[225] The question therefore was: how concretely have the charges to be formulated and how much evidence must the Prosecutor provide in their support? Is it acceptable to formulate them in such a broad way that the Prosecutor can add criminal acts whenever she wishes to do so, with leave of the TC after the trial has begun? The majority of the AC, in line with the strict requirements in charging mentioned above, rejected this broad approach, finding: 'Simply listing the categories of crimes with which a person is to be charged or stating, in broad general terms, the temporal and geographical parameters of the charge is not sufficient'.[226] In line with this view, the IER recommends 'that the OTP might concentrate on narrower charges and more focused cases'.[227] In contrast, the *Ntaganda* AC took a more flexible approach: while emphasizing that the DCC 'may also list or make reference to specific criminal acts', it pointed out that 'the scope of the case is not necessarily limited to them—"other criminal acts not mentioned in the document containing the charges may still fall within the—broadly described—facts and circumstances of the charges'".[228]

[219] ICC, *Prosecutor v. Bemba*, TC III, Judgment pursuant to Article 74 of the Statute, ICC-01/05-01/08, 21 March 2016, paras. 752–3. Thereto Heinze, *Opinio Juris* (18 June 2018). Crit. Fyfe, in Heinze and Dittrich, *ICC* (2021), pp. 679, 699.

[220] ICC, *Prosecutor v. Bemba*, PTC II, Annex 3 to 'Prosecution's Submission of Amended Document Containing the Charges, Amended List of Evidence and Amended In-Depth Analysis Chart of Incriminatory Evidence', ICC-01/05-01/08-395-Anx3, 30 March 2009, paras. 33–7.

[221] *Bemba*, ICC-01/05-01/08-424, para. 140.

[222] *Prosecutor v. Bemba*, PTC III, Transcript, ICC-01/05-01/08-T-14-ENG, 7 October 2009, p. 13, ll. 5–10.

[223] Regarding the second amended Document Containing the Charges, see ICC, *Prosecutor v. Bemba*, TC III, Redacted Annex to 'Prosecution's Submission of the Document Containing the Charges as Confirmed by the Pre-Trial Chamber filed in accordance with the Chamber's Order of 7 October 2009', ICC-01/05-01/08-593-Anx-Red, 4 November 2009.

[224] Regarding reference to crimes not previously confirmed by the TC, see ICC, *Prosecutor v. Bemba*, TC III, Requête aux fins d'obtenir une Décision ordonnant la correction et le dépôt du Second Document Amendé Contenant les Charges, ICC-01/05-01/08-694, 12 February 2010, para. 36.

[225] *Bemba*, ICC-01/05-01/08, paras. 42 ff.

[226] ICC, *Prosecutor v. Bemba*, AC, Judgment on the appeal of Mr Jean-Pierre Bemba Gombo against Trial Chamber III's 'Judgment pursuant to Article 74 of the Statute, ICC-01/05-01/08-3636-Red', 8 June 2018, para. 110. The majority was formed by Judges van den Wyngaert, Morrison, and Eboe-Osuji, the latter concurring in the result, cf. Concurring Separate Opinion of Judge Eboe-Osuji, ICC-01/05-01/08-3636-Anx3, 14 June 2018, paras. 118–34 (disagreeing that a TC is in principle precluded from amending the indictment after the commencement of trial, employing a teleological and contextual interpretation of Art. 74 (2) in conjunction with Art. 69 (9) ICCS). *Contra* Dissenting Opinion of Judge Sanji Mmasenono Monageng and Judge Piotr Hofmański, paras. 20 ff.

[227] Expert Group, *IER* (2020), p. 217.

[228] *Ntaganda*, ICC-01/04-02/06-2666-Red, para. 326.

Of course, if PTCs do not comply with their task to define the charges sufficiently precise an updated DCC may still be warranted in order to dispel the ensuing doubts and make it crystal clear to the parties what the trial is about, thereby enabling in particular the defence to adequately prepare its case.[229] However, even in such a situation the preparation of an updated DCC bears the risk of having the opposite effect, that is, to create further confusion as to the charges thereby engaging the parties in further discussion which unnecessarily prolongs the proceedings.[230] In any case, even such an exceptional updated DCC must never exceed the scope of the charges as confirmed by the PTC as the sole adjudicatory authority at this stage of the proceedings.[231] Of course, the PTCs must determine 'the facts and circumstances'[232] of the case as precisely as possible,[233] giving proper notice especially to the defence.[234] One must not overlook, however, that in ICL prosecutions involving macrocriminal conduct, it is a Herculean task for both the prosecution and the PTC to identify and cover all factual details underlying the charges.[235] Perhaps it is for this reason that the *Ntaganda* AC considered that the accused was sufficiently informed—notwithstanding that the prosecution updated the DCC (as authorized by the TC), that the defence argued that new facts had not been considered by the PTC and that not only individual acts formed the basis of the DCC.[236]

*(iv) Individualization, review, and (pre-)trial management*

The charging presupposes the *individualization of the initial suspicion* and the issuance of a warrant of arrest or a summons to appear.[237] The DCC 'shall be based' on the Article 58 request,[238] that is, it is produced afterwards. In fact, unlike the review procedure at the ad hoc tribunals, the confirmation proceedings take place after the issuance of an arrest warrant and, in principle, in the presence of the suspect who is supposed to be at the seat of the Court.[239] The relevant requirements and the procedure will be analysed below.[240] Here it

[229] This clarification and thus fairness purpose of the updated DCC is, for example, stressed by ICC, *Prosecutor v. Ruto and Sang*, TC V, Order for the Prosecution to File an Updated Document Containing the Charges, ICC-01/09-01/11-439, 5 July 2012, para. 6; *Prosecutor v. Ntaganda*, TC VI, Decision on the Updated Document Containing the Charges, ICC-01/04-02/06-450, 6 February 2015, paras. 16–20, both stressing the accused's right to be informed in detail of the charges; also *Bemba et al.*, ICC-01/05-01/13-992-Anx-Corr, para. 136 and *passim*; *Prosecutor v. Said*, Decision on the Defence Request for Leave to Appeal the 'Decision on the "Prosecution's application to amend the charges"', ICC-01/14-01/21-456, 19 August 2022, para. 12. In a similar vein, Triffterer and Kiss, 'Article 74', in Ambos, *Commentary* (2022), mn. 41, 52.

[230] *Bemba et al.*, ICC-01/05-01/13-992, para. 17 (with previous case law in n. 22).

[231] See also *Ntaganda*, ICC-01/04-02/06-450, para. 19; *Bemba et al.*, ICC-01/05-01/13-992-Anx-Corr, para. 136; in ICC, *Prosecutor v. Bemba*, TC III, Decision on the Defence Application for Corrections to the Document Containing the Charges and for the Prosecution to File a Second Amended Document Containing the Charges, ICC-01/05-01/08-836, 20 July 2010, para. 80, TC III found that the 'introduction ... of the "systematic" element in the Second Amended DCC exceeds the scope of the charges'; see also *Bemba*, ICC-01/05-01/08-3343, para. 65.

[232] Art. 74 (2) ICCS. See generally Nerlich, in *FS Werle* (2022), pp. 235 ff.

[233] For attempts in this respect, see Schabas, Chaitidou, and El Zeidy, 'Article 61', in Ambos, *Commentary* (2022), mn. 132–3; Triffterer and Kiss, 'Article 74', in Ambos, *Commentary* (2022), mn. 55; see also Mettraux et al., *Effectiveness ICC* (2014), pp. 12, 16–17 (paras. 39, 74–5) (recommending clear and consistent confirmation of material facts, 'short, precise and detailed description', 'specificity and detailed particularisation of charges').

[234] ICC, *Practice Manual* (2023), paras. 35–6, 42; Triffterer and Kiss, 'Article 74', in Ambos, *Commentary* (2022), mn. 55.

[235] In a similar vein, *Chaitidou*, ZfIStW 1 (2022), 662, 667.

[236] *Ntaganda*, ICC-01/04-02/06-2666-Red, para. 332. See also Chaitidou, *ZfIStW*, 1 (2022), 662, 667.

[237] Art. 58 ICCS; see Schabas, *ICC Commentary* (2016), pp. 886 ff.; on the 'initial appearance' at the ICTY, see Möller, in Kirsch, *Internationale Strafgerichtshöfe* (2005), pp. 19 ff.

[238] Reg. 58 (1) RegOTP.

[239] See also Friman, Brady, Costi, Guariglia, and Stuckenberg, in Sluiter et al., *International Criminal Procedure* (2013), p. 399.

[240] Section B.(6)(b) in this chapter.

suffices to say that the request for an arrest warrant triggers an *ex parte* exchange[241] between the Prosecutor and the PTC with a view to relevant information '[a]t any time after the initiation of an investigation'.[242] Furthermore, *defence counsel* must have been appointed, at latest, at this stage. This already follows, generally, from the application of the right to defence at the pre-trial stage.[243]

Once the charges have been issued and the indictment (ICTY/ICTR/SCSL) or DCC (ICC) has been prepared, the question of the *nature of the judicial review* arises.[244] So far, significant discrepancies between the ICTY/ICTR/SCSL and the ICC exist,[245] with the KSC partly merging the two approaches. The regime of the ad hoc tribunals only provides for a (normally quite superficial[246]) review of the indictment by just one judge,[247] that is, the judge has to establish whether a *prima facie* case, as defined above,[248] exists. Other, potentially more effective, review mechanisms have been introduced later, in particular the possibility—along the lines of the common law 'no case to answer' procedure—for a TC to enter a 'judgment of acquittal' with regard to charges not supported by any evidence 'capable of supporting a conviction'.[249] Further, it is noteworthy in this context, that Pre-Trial and Pre-Defence Conferences, fulfilling a similar function to the (previous) Status Conferences,[250]

[241] cf. ICC, *Practice Manual* (2022), para. 3.

[242] cf. Art. 58 (1) ICCS; Boas et al., *Procedure* (2011), p. 180.

[243] cf. Art. 55 (2)(c) ICCS ('during an investigation'), Art. 56 (1)(b) (PTC's role in protecting 'rights of the defence' with regard to unique investigative opportunity) and (2)(d) ICCS (appointment of counsel); see also Safferling, *Criminal Procedure* (2012), pp. 255–7 (regarding the ICC's pre-investigative stage); De Meester, *Investigation Phase* (2015), pp. 338–43; and, generally, Chapter I, D.(2)(d) and (3)(d), (e) as well as Chapter II, C.(1) in this volume.

[244] See generally Kreß, in Grützner, Pötz, and Kreß, *Internationaler Rechtshilfeverkehr in Strafsachen* (2003), Part IV A 1, mn. 126 ff.; Ambos, in Bohlander, *International Criminal Justice* (2007), pp. 454 ff.; Satzger, *Internationales Strafrecht* (2022), § 14 mn. 32; Satzger, *ICL* (2018), § 12 mn. 32; Calvo-Goller, *Trial Proceedings* (2006), pp. 169 ff.

[245] On IMT, IMTFE, SPSC, ECCC, and STL, see Friman, Brady, Costi, Guariglia, and Stuckenberg, in Sluiter et al., *International Criminal Procedure* (2013), pp. 397, 411–15; on the IMT, also see Safferling, *Criminal Procedure* (2012), pp. 316–17; pointing out the differences between the ad hoc tribunals and the ICC, Zahar and Sluiter, *ICL* (2008), p. 55; cf. also, on the other hand, Thalmann, in Kolb and Scalia, *DIP* (2012), pp. 466 ff., pointing out the extended possibilities for judicial intervention in the pre-investigation phase.

[246] Boas et al., *Procedure* (2011), p. 185 ('remarkable little analysis'), also Safferling, *Criminal Procedure* (2012), p. 317 ('mere' review); Friman, Brady, Costi, Guariglia, and Stuckenberg, in Sluiter et al., *International Criminal Procedure* (2013), pp. 398 ('low threshold'), 448 ('quick and uncontested').

[247] Arts. 19 ICTYS, 18 ICTRS, Rule 47 (E) RPE ICTY/ICTR/SCSL, Rule 48 (E) RPE MICT (the SCSLS does not contain a provision); see thereon Zahar and Sluiter, *ICL* (2008), pp. 47 ff.; Langer, *AJCompL*, 53 (2005), 863; Ambos and Bock, in Reydams, Wouters, and Ryngaert, *International Prosecutors* (2012), p. 505. This judge is delegated as a duty judge by the president; cf. Rule 28 (A) RPE ICTY, Rule 28 (1) RPE ICTR, Rule 28 RPE MICT, ICTY, *Manual* (2009), pp. 39 ff. At the KSC, the Pre-Trial Judge exercises this function, see below note 258 with main text.

[248] Note 153 in this chapter.

[249] cf. Rule 98*bis* RPE ICTY/ICTR/SCSL, Rule 121 RPE MICT; see also the equivalent Rule 130 RPE KSC ('Dismissal of Charges'). The Chamber may act *proprio motu* or pursuant to a defence motion. The case law has made clear that this procedure shall only 'bring to an end ... proceedings in respect of a charge for which there is no evidence', i.e. 'merely weak' evidence may suffice (ICTY, *Prosecutor v. Strugar*, Decision on Defence Motion Requesting Judgment of Acquittal pursuant to Rule 98*bis*, IT-01-42-T, 21 June 2004, para. 20); for further references, see Friman, Brady, Costi, Guariglia, and Stuckenberg, in Sluiter et al., *International Criminal Procedure* (2013), pp. 425–7; Klamberg, *Evidence* (2013), pp. 145–7. At the KSC, there have been two such motions but both have been rejected by the respective Trial Panels, cf. KSC, *Prosecutor v. Gucati and Haradinaj*, TP, Decision on Motions to Dismiss Charges, KSC-BC-2020-07/F00450, 26 November 2021, and *Prosecutor v. Mustafa*, TP, Decision on the Defense Rule 130 (1) Motion to Dismiss any or all Charges of the Indictment, 23 February 2022, KSC-BC-2020-05/F00326/RED. See, in more detail, Section A.(4)(b).

[250] Rule 65*bis* RPE ICTY/ICTR, Rule 69 RPE MICT. See also Vohrah, in McDonald and Swaak-Goldman, *Substantive and Procedural Aspects* (2000), pp. 541 ff.; Möller, in Kirsch, *Internationale Strafgerichtshöfe* (2005), pp. 48, 50–1; Harmon, *JICJ*, 5 (2007), 387–8; crit. Fairlie, *ICLR*, 4 (2004), 300 ff.

have been introduced,[251] and a Pre-Trial Judge, albeit with limited powers, has been created (at the ICTY).[252] At the KSC, a Pre-Trial Judge existed from the outset[253] and has broad, managerial powers[254] to expedite proceedings,[255] going well beyond the mere review/confirmation of the indictment.[256]

The latter development shows the tendency towards a greater judicial management already at the pre-trial stage of proceedings, confirming the general 'rise of managerial judging'[257] and the shift to 'managed adversarialism'[258] in international criminal procedure.[259] Indeed, such managerial tendencies exist at all stages of the proceedings,[260] and effective pre-trial and trial management by Chambers is necessary to streamline and speed up proceedings.[261] This presupposes that dates and deadlines given by Chambers are

[251] Rules 73*bis* and 73*ter* RPE ICTY/ICTR, Rules 81, 82 RPE MICT; see thereon Kwon, *JICJ*, 5 (2007), 372 ff.; dissenting, Zahar and Sluiter, *ICL* (2008), p. 50.

[252] cf. Rules 65*ter* RPE ICTY, 70 RPE MICT (power of coordination rather than investigation during the pre-trial phase); see also Orie, in Cassese et al., *Rome Statute II* (2002), p. 1465; Möller, in Kirsch, *Internationale Strafgerichtshöfe* (2005), pp. 47 ff.; Sluiter, *ICLR*, 6 (2006), 615; Bonomy, *JICJ*, 5 (2007), 352 ff.; Boas et al., *Procedure* (2011), pp. 243–4; Kuczyńska, *Accusation Model ICC* (2015), pp. 329–32; Carlson, *Model(ing) Justice* (2018), p. 86; for the prosecution perspective, see Harmon, *JICJ*, 5 (2007), 377, 384 ff. (389: 'pre-trial Judge must be pro-active'); and for the defence perspective, see Higgins, *JICJ*, 5 (2007), 398–9.

[253] cf. esp. Art. 25 (1)(a), 33 (1)(a), 39 KSC Law and Rules 85, 95 RPE KSC.

[254] cf., inter alia, Rule 85 (3), cl. 1 RPE KSC ('Pre-Trial Judge and the Specialist Prosecutor may hold meetings during the investigation and prior to the confirmation of the indictment') and Rule 96 RPE KSC ('Status Conferences').

[255] cf., inter alia, Rule 85 (2) RPE KSC ('rule expeditiously on requests by the Specialist Prosecutor related to the conduct of the investigation') and Rule 95 (2) KSC RPE ('ensure that the proceedings are not unduly delayed and shall take all necessary measures for the expeditious preparation of the case for trial').

[256] cf. Art. 39 (1), (2) KSC Law and Rule 86 (4), (5) RPE KSC.

[257] cf. Langer, *AJCompL*, 53 (2005), 835 ff., demonstrating how the ICTY's predominantly adversarial procedure changed to a 'managerial judging model' (853–905), and identifying the features of such a model largely modelled after US civil procedure (874–85); cf. also McDermott, *Fairness* (2016), pp. 11–12; Ambos, in Jackson and Summers, *Fairness* (2018), pp. 179, 182–3; Langer and Doherty, *YaleJIL*, 36 (2011), 245–51, summarizing the managerial judging reforms at the ICTY; Jones, *ICLR*, 19 (2019), 445, 450 ff.; for the inconsistent approach of different TCs at the ICTR, see Byrne, *LJIL*, 26 (2013), 1004–6. See also below note 671 with main text.

[258] Stahn, in Stahn and Sluiter, *Practice* (2009), p. 264, referring to Carmichael Keen, *LJIL*, 17 (2004), 767 ff. and his theory of 'tempered adversariality'; in the same vein, Kuczyńska, *Accusation Model ICC* (2015), pp. 336–7. For a comparative (inquisitorial vs. adversarial) view of managerial judging, Luzon, *CardozoJConfRes*, 20 (2019), 597 ff.

[259] Generally Turner, in Heller et al., *Oxford HB ICL* (2020), pp. 39, 41. On pre-trial case management at the ICTY, ICTR, and SCSL, see Boas et al., *Procedure* (2011), pp. 243–7; Kuczyńska, *Accusation Model ICC* (2015), p. 333; for more 'proactive management' with regard to evidence admission and production, Mettraux et al., *Effectiveness ICC* (2014), p. 18 (paras. 78, 79).

[260] See e.g. the particularly controversial power of ICTY TCs (not granted to the ICTR and SCSL) to reduce the scope of the indictment regarding 'number of counts' and 'crimes sites or incidents' pursuant to Rule 73*bis* (D) RPE ICTY; see thereon Boas et al., *Procedure* (2011), p. 246; Friman, Brady, Costi, Guariglia, and Stuckenberg, in Sluiter et al., *International Criminal Procedure* (2013), pp. 419–20, 487 (recommending the abolition of this Rule since it entails an interference with prosecutorial discretion); Kuczyńska, *Accusation Model ICC* (2015), pp. 330–1, 333–5 (in favour). Regarding the PTC's management responsibility within the framework of Art. 60 (4) ICCS, see also Section B.(6)(b) in this chapter, note 1035 and main text. For the KSC see Rules 116–19 KSC RPE (providing for the 'management of proceedings' by way of 'trial management orders', 'Status Conferences', 'Trial Preparation Conferences', a 'Specialist Prosecutor's Preparation Conference', and a 'Defence Preparation Conference'). See also Heinze, *JICJ*, 15 (2017), 1001–3.

[261] In favour of a balanced approach, Boas et al., *Procedure* (2011), pp. 247, 374 (attempt 'to strike an appropriate balance between the demands of trial management and the goal of producing reasoned, persuasive, and well-founded judgements', albeit 'not always successful'); but see also Langer and Doherty, *YaleJIL*, 36 (2011), 252–89 (showing that the ICTY reforms did not produce the desired overall results in terms of pre-trial and trial duration and explaining that with the judges' limited or deficient use of their management powers and the parties' resistance) and 289–97 (explaining and referring to two empirical studies on US civil procedure, the structural obstacles and implementation challenges of such a reform, and concluding that 'it seems unrealistic to expect that most managerial judging techniques will bring substantial time gains, and that we should be wary when specific techniques bring substantial time gains, because they may also compromise accuracy, fairness, and the

binding and can only be postponed or prolonged in exceptional circumstances.[262] While the ICC's procedural framework seems to be flexible enough to allow for such management practices and efficiency has been at the core of relevant reform efforts,[263] immediate results can be more easily and quickly achieved by judicial practice (laid down in practice manuals like the Chambers *Practice Manual*) than by proper normative reforms (via amendments of the RPE or even the Statute). Of course, management is not only a concern of the judicial proceedings but also, perhaps even more so, of the—two-tiered—investigation stage in the hands of the Prosecutor.[264]

Under the ICC regime, while a 'no case to answer' procedure is not explicitly provided for[265] and a status conference at this stage can only be convened with regard to disclosure,[266] the case arising out of a situation is managed by the PTC,[267] which reviews the charges in a complex confirmation procedure, the centre of which is an *inter partes*, oral, and adversarial '*confirmation hearing*'.[268] This procedure needs to be looked at more closely now.

### (b) *Confirmation proceedings, hearing, and decision*

#### (i) *Purpose and aims*

The purpose of the confirmation procedure is first of all—similar to any judicial review procedure at the domestic level[269]—to prevent prosecutorial overreach by checking the charges

other goals of the legal process' [297]); crit. also, Byrne, *LJIL*, 26 (2013), 998. On managerial practices at the ICC, but regarding the relevant organs and their relationship, see Ambach and Rackwitz, *LCP*, 76 nos. 3 & 4 (2013), 120 ff., 127 ff.; on the need for efficient management of judicial proceedings at the ICC, see Ambach, in Stahn, *Practice* (2015), pp. 1283–4; on the ICC as 'a model of public administration', see ICC, 'Guidelines Governing the Relations between the Court and Intermediaries—For the Organs and Units of the Court and Counsel Working with Intermediaries', (March 2014), p. 2, <https://www.icc-cpi.int/iccdocs/lt/GRCI-Eng.pdf>; for recommendations regarding 'institution building and administration', see Mettraux et al., *Effectiveness ICC* (2014), pp. 36–42 (paras. 168–85) and pp. 216 ff. (more detailed analysis); thereon, Lindenmann, *ZIS*, 10 (2015), 529–31, crit. the State Parties' tendency for micromanagement instead of strategic oversight of the Court and stressing the need to assume a more active role (531); calling for 'changes of practice' (and only subsidiary for normative changes), ICC-ASP, *Report Study Group on Governance* (2015), p. 3 (para. 14).

262 For a good example in this regard, see ICC, *Prosecutor v. Bemba et al.*, TC VII, Decision on Defence Request to Postpone the Commencement of the Trial, ICC-01/05-01/13-1254, 15 September 2015, paras. 15 ff. (16: commencement date for trial binding and postponement 'exceptional measure'; *in casu* rejecting the defence postponement request); also *Prosecutor v. Said*, TC VI, Decision on Defence Request for Suspension of Deadline for Response to the Trial Brief and Postponement of Commencement of Trial pending Translation of Trial Brief, ICC-01/14-01/21-408, 14 July 2022, paras. 13 ff. (19: rejecting the defence postponement request since 'good cause has not been shown to delay the filling of a response to the Trial Brief'). See also Chapter V, B.(2)(a) in this volume.

263 Ambos, in Jackson and Summers, *Fairness* (2018), pp. 179, 182–3 with further references.

264 In more detail, below note 671 with main text.

265 Arguably, such a procedure may be applied within the general authority of a TC under Art. 64 (3)(a) ICCS (see e.g. ICC, *Prosecutor v. Ruto and Sang*, TC V, Decision on the Conduct of Trial Proceedings (General Directions), ICC-01/09-01/11-847-Corr, 9 August 2013, para. 32), but it is difficult to reconcile with the ICC's case-by-case system of presentation of evidence (cf. Rule 140 (1) RPE ICC, and Chapter V, A.(3)(a) in this volume) and the potential role of victims in the production of evidence. Furthermore, such a procedure does not seem to be necessary, given the thorough review by the confirmation procedure; see also Friman, Brady, Costi, Guariglia, and Stuckenberg, in Sluiter et al., *International Criminal Procedure* (2013), pp. 430–1, 450, 486; in favour, however, see Mettraux et al., *Effectiveness ICC* (2014), p. 21 (paras. 85, 91) and p. 158 (para. 49). See, in more detail, Section A.(4)(b).

266 cf. Rule 121 (2)(b) RPE ICC; advocating a greater use of status conferences, ICC, *Practice Manual* (2022), para. 19 ('increasing efficiency and eliminating the need for cumbersome written decisions'); see further notes 446 and 723 ff. in this chapter with main text.

267 As a permanent chamber with a fixed composition, cf. Reg. 46 (1) RegC.

268 cf. Art. 61 ICCS.

269 See also Friman, Brady, Costi, Guariglia, and Stuckenberg, in Sluiter et al., *International Criminal Procedure* (2013), pp. 463–4 ('common in domestic criminal systems'); from a comparative law perspective, Kuczyńska, *Accusation Model ICC* (2015), pp. 140–8.

and filtering out the weaker and, perhaps, less important ones.[270] This, in turn, means, that it serves, on the one hand, to protect the suspect against (wholly) unfounded charges[271] by dismissing those that do not comply with the evidentiary standard of 'substantial grounds' (to be discussed below);[272] on the other hand, the remaining (confirmed) charges should be clearly set out.[273] Further, this procedure aims to reduce time-consuming disputes over questions of evidence during the trial phase,[274] that is, it shall serve the efficiency and expediency of the (main) proceedings[275] and thus has a preparatory function with a view to the trial.[276]

[270] cf. ICC, *Prosecutor v. Abd-Al-Rahman*, Decision on the Confirmation of Charges against Ali Muhammad Ali Abd-Al-Rahman ('Ali Kushayb'), ICC-02/05-01/20-433, 9 July 2021, paras. 33 ff.; *Prosecutor v. Said*, Decision on the Confirmation of Charges against Mahamat Said Abdel Kani, ICC-01/14-01/21-218-Red, 9 December 2021, paras. 34 ff.; *Prosecutor v. Yekatom and Ngaïssona*, Public Redacted Version of the Decision on the Confirmation of Charges against Yekatom and Ngaïssona, ICC-01/14-01/18-403-Red, 20 December 2019, paras. 13 ff. For previous case law, see first edition p. 354 with note 198. See also Friman, in Lee, *ICC* (2001), p. 537; Marchesiello, in Cassese et al., *Rome Statute II* (2002), p. 1238; Ambos and Miller, *ICLR*, 7 (2007), 341 ('check and balance the Prosecutor'); Boas et al., *Procedure* (2011), p. 248 ('process of winnowing'); Safferling, *Criminal Procedure* (2012), pp. 341 with n. 124, 342 ('avoid the prosecutor from becoming a kind of superpower'); Friman, Brady, Costi, Guariglia, and Stuckenberg, in Sluiter et al., *International Criminal Procedure* (2013), pp. 399 ('pre-trial filter'), 411, 448; Vasiliev, in Cryer et al., *ICL* (2019), pp. 429–30; Stahn, *JICJ*, 12 (2014), 832; Stegmiller, in Stahn, *Practice ICC* (2015), p. 897 (protect suspect 'against wrongful prosecution', 'judicial economy', 'monitors the prosecutor's activities'); Schabas, Chaitidou, and El Zeidy, 'Article 61', in Ambos, *Commentary* (2022), mn. 6; crit. Lewis, in Fischer, Kreß, and Lüder, *Prosecution* (2001), pp. 223 ff. From a defence perspective, Turner, in Heller et al., *Oxford HB ICL* (2020), pp. 39, 64; Stahn, *Introduction ICL* (2019), p. 367; Chaitidou, *ZfIStW* 1 (2022), 662, 667. For further literature, see first edition p. 354 with note 198.

[271] See also ICC, *Prosecutor v. Al Hassan*, PTC I, Rectificatif à la Décision relative à la confirmation des charges portées contre Al Hassan Ag Abdoul Aziz Ag Mohamed Ag Mahmoud, ICC-01/12-01/18-461-Corr-Red, 13 November 2019—original decision registered on 30 September 2019, para. 42; *Yekatom and Ngaïssona*, ICC-01/14-01/18-403-Red, para. 14; ICC, *Prosecutor v. Al Mahdi*, PTC I, Decision on the Confirmation of Charges against Ahmad Al Faqi Al Mahdi, ICC-01/12-01/15-84-Red, 24 March 2016, para. 15; *Ongwen*, ICC-02/04-01/15-422-Red, para. 14; Boas et al., *Procedure* (2011), p. 183; Safferling, *Criminal Procedure* (2012), p. 342; Friman, Brady, Costi, Guariglia, and Stuckenberg, in Sluiter et al., *International Criminal Procedure* (2013), p. 448; Nerlich, *JICJ*, 10 (2012), 1354; Schabas, Chaitidou, and El Zeidy, 'Article 61', in Ambos, *Commentary* (2022), mn. 6–7; Mariniello, *JICJ*, 13 (2015), 583–4; crit. WCRO, *Confirmation* (2015), pp. 81 ff.

[272] cf. Art. 61 (7) ICCS; also Schabas, Chaitidou, and El Zeidy, 'Article 61', in Ambos, *Commentary* (2022), mn. 7, 133. Facts not explicitly mentioned in the confirmation decision do not form part of the charges as confirmed (mn. 132). On this linkage between the 'substantial grounds' standard and the purposes of the confirmation proceedings, see also Stegmiller, in Stahn, *Practice* (2015), p. 897; in a similar vein, Mariniello, *JICJ*, 13 (2015), 583 ff., 593 ff., 595 ff. (but crit. the 'largely completed investigation' requirement as setting the evidentiary threshold too high for the confirmation hearing, transforming it to 'a miniature judgment', to a '*pre-judgment* of the accused's guilt'); also crit. Kuczyńska, *Accusation Model ICC* (2015), pp. 152–5 (arguing that 'the [judicial] control over the Prosecutor's actions has become a goal in itself').

[273] Expert Group, *IER* (2020), p. 154 ('precise description of charges', 'set out clearly the charges'; but crit., inter alia, that decisions often fail 'to clearly delineate the charges separately from the legal analysis').

[274] cf. Bitti, in Fischer, Kreß, and Lüder, *Prosecution* (2001), p. 276; Fourmy, in Cassese et al., *Rome Statute II* (2002), p. 1225; on the character of the confirmation hearing from a comparative point of view, see Heinze, *Disclosure* (2014), pp. 408 ff.; crit. Gómez Colomer, in Gómez Colomer et al., *La Corte Penal Internacional* (2003), p. 320; Kreß and Wannek, in Kirsch, *Internationale Strafgerichtshöfe* (2005), pp. 250–1; Kreß, *JICJ*, 1 (2003), 610; Nerlich, *JICJ*, 10 (2012), 1354–5 (crit. the limited contribution of the confirmation proceedings to the disclosure of evidence); Mariniello, *JICJ*, 13 (2015), 599. In detail on the *Lubanga* case, see Lounici, in Kolb and Scalia, *DIP* (2012), pp. 298 ff.

[275] ICC, *Prosecutor v. Ongwen*, AC, Judgment on the Appeal of Mr Dominic Ongwen against Trial Chamber IX's 'Decision on Defence Motions Alleging Defects in the Confirmation Decision', ICC-02/04-01/15-1562, 17 July 2019, paras. 130, 147; Safferling, *Criminal Procedure* (2012), p. 342; Friman, Brady, Costi, Guariglia, and Stuckenberg, in Sluiter et al., *International Criminal Procedure* (2013), p. 448. For Turner and Weigend, in Sluiter et al., *International Criminal Procedure* (2013), p. 1408, efficiency 'is not an independent goal of international criminal justice', but it is demanded by practical considerations; Schabas, Chaitidou, and El Zeidy, 'Article 61', in Ambos, *Commentary* (2022), mn. 8; Mariniello, *JICJ*, 13 (2015), 583; crit. WCRO, *Confirmation* (2015), pp. 85–6.

[276] cf. Nerlich, *JICJ*, 10 (2012), 1348–54 (preparation of several aspects of the trial, such as the definition of its subject matter [1348–50], the determination of the applicable law [1350–1], the compilation and disclosure of evidence [1351–3], and the organization of victims' participation [1353–4]); Friman, in Stahn, *Practice* (2015), p. 914; Schabas, Chaitidou, and El Zeidy, 'Article 61', in Ambos, *Commentary* (2022), mn. 8, 10; Mariniello, *JICJ*, 13 (2015), 599.

These aims have been confirmed by the case law.[277] Thus, in the first confirmation decision, the *Lubanga* PTC stressed the hearing's purpose to commit for trial 'only those persons against whom sufficiently compelling charges going beyond mere theory or suspicion have been brought', thereby protecting the suspect 'against wrongful and wholly unfounded charges'.[278] Other PTCs confirmed this view.[279] The *Katanga and Ngudjolo* PTC held that the confirmation hearing must be seen as a 'means to distinguish those cases that should go to trial from those that should not go to trial'.[280] It shall 'ensure that no case proceeds to trial without sufficient evidence', thereby protecting 'the rights of the Defence against wrongful and wholly unfounded charges';[281] it shall also ensure judicial economy.[282]

At any rate, the confirmation hearing should not amount to 'a mini-trial or a trial before the trial'.[283] Of course, if one takes this call seriously, a confirmation decision need not and should not deal with all substantive and evidentiary questions in detail,[284] but limit itself

[277] Summing up the different views regarding the purposes of the confirmation proceedings, Stegmiller, in Stahn, *Practice* (2015), pp. 892–3, 897 (arguing, however, that the main, prevailing purpose is the determination 'whether a case should be sent to trial and to filter the prosecution's allegations' [p. 908]). For a detailed overview of the confirmation proceedings held up to October 2015 and a critical analysis, see WCRO, *Confirmation* (2015), pp. 16 ff.; for an updated statistic, Schabas, Chaitidou, and El Zeidy, 'Article 61', in Ambos, *Commentary* (2022), mn. 9; for previous overviews, see Nerlich, *JICJ*, 10 (2012), 1345–7;Safferling, *Criminal Procedure* (2012), pp. 326 ff.; Friman, Brady, Costi, Guariglia, and Stuckenberg, in Sluiter et al., *International Criminal Procedure* (2013), pp. 405 ff. In the same vein, Expert Group, *IER* (2020), p. 154.

[278] ICC, *Prosecutor v. Lubanga*, PTC I, Decision on the Confirmation of Charges, ICC-01/04-01/06-803-tEN, 29 January 2007, para. 37.

[279] ICC, *Prosecutor v. Said*, Decision on the 'Prosecution's application to amend the charges', ICC-01/14-01/21-396, 14 July 2022, para. 13; ICC, *Prosecutor v. Abd-Al-Rahman*, Decision on the 'Prosecution's application to amend the charges', ICC-02/05-01/20-626, 14 March 2022, para. 15; ICC, *Prosecutor v. Abd-Al-Rahman*, Corrected Version of 'Decision on the confirmation of charges against Ali Muhammad Ali Abd-Al-Rahman ('Ali Kushayb')', ICC-02/05-01/20-433-Corr, 9 July 2021, para. 37.

[280] ICC, *Prosecutor v. Katanga and Ngudjolo*, PTC I, Corrigendum to the Decision on Evidentiary Scope of the Confirmation Hearing, ICC-01/04-01/07-428-Corr, 25 April 2008, para. 6.

[281] ICC, *Prosecutor v. Katanga and Ngudjolo*, PTC I, Decision on the Confirmation of Charges, ICC-01/04-01/07-717, 30 September 2008, para. 63. Conc. *Said*, ICC-01/14-01/21-396, para. 14.

[282] ICC, *Prosecutor v. Bemba*, PTC II, Decision on the Evidence Disclosure System and Setting a Timetable for Disclosure between the Parties, ICC-01/05-01/08-55, 31 July 2008, paras. 15, 19 ('avoiding superfluous proceedings', 'filtering function').

[283] *Katanga and Ngudjolo*, ICC-01/04-01/07-717, para. 64; *Said*, ICC-01/14-01/21-396, para. 14; See also ICC, *IER Response* (2021), p. 85: 'confirmation process must not turn into a mini-trial.... the objectives of the confirmation process must be appreciated not only by the judges, but also by the parties and participants to the proceedings, in particular the Office of the Prosecutor'). Crit. in this regard De Beco, *ICLR*, 7 (2007), 481 (concerned that there may be a pre-emption of the main trial); see also Stahn, *JICJ*, 12 (2014), 833 (calling for better Court management and 'self restraint in scholarly discussion'); Nerlich, *JICJ*, 10 (2012), 1347–8; Mettraux et al., *Effectiveness ICC* (2014), pp. 11–13 (paras. 38, 40, 42, 44), pp. 94–5, 97–9 (paras. 25–7, 35–40) (more active judicial control, 'police' and limit the scope, 'streamline' trial process, avoiding *obiter* and scholarly discussion, 'management efforts'); Gallmetzer, in Guariglia et al., *AC ICC Commentary* (2018), p. 185.; Stahn, *Introduction ICL* (2019), p. 368; Fernández de Gurmendi, *JICJ*, 16 (2018), 341, 359; see also Schabas, Chaitidou, and El Zeidy, 'Article 61', in Ambos, *Commentary* (2022), mn. 10 ('Proper case management and expeditious decision-making are key to the success of the confirmation process'); Mariniello, *JICJ*, 13 (2015), 595–7, 598–9; calling for a reform (if above recommendations unsuccessful), Mettraux et al., *Effectiveness ICC* (2014), p. 14 (para. 56) (*ex parte* hearing similar to ad hoc tribunals or 'court-driven' confirmation process, i.e. giving a greater role to the PTC); also Friman, in Stahn, *Practice* (2015), pp. 915–6, 929–30 (crit. a truth-finding function of the PTC and stressing the need for a 'further developed and standardized' 'relationship between the confirmation of charges and the trial processes'); WCRO, *Confirmation* (2015), pp. 3–6, 90–103, 104 (advocating a 'scaling back' of the confirmation procedure to an essentially written procedure to be completed within ninety days from the first appearance, where the defence responds in a written form to the DCC, the hearing is limited to a 'non-evidentiary, non-testimonial hearing', strict time limits are imposed, and disclosure is limited to the evidence relevant for confirmation); see also Ambach, in Stahn, *Practice* (2015), pp. 1287–8; Kuczyńska, *Accusation Model ICC* (2015), pp. 153–4.

[284] In the same vein, Mariniello, *JICJ*, 13 (2015), 591 ff., 599 (crit. the 'largely completed investigation' requirement). In more concrete terms, the PTC I in *Al Mahdi*, ICC-01/12-01/15-84-Red, para. 19 remarked that its determinations at that stage will be 'presumptive' and that it was 'not in a position to conclusively determine issues of probative value of evidence, including with respect to credibility of witnesses'; see also *Ongwen*, ICC-02/04-01/15-422-Red, para. 18.

to affirming or rejecting the 'substantial grounds' required by Article 61 (7) ICCS. The first confirmation decisions may have exceeded these limits and thus slowed down the proceedings as a whole, thereby contravening the goal of expediency.[285] In contrast, since mid-2014 there has been a tendency towards 'slimmer' confirmation decisions, relying on the increasingly consolidated case law and basically focusing on the charges' compliance with the required substantial grounds standard.[286]

The confirmation procedure has so far operated as a quite effective screening mechanism[287]—far more effective than the review mechanisms at the ad hoc tribunals—as is demonstrated by the fact that by no means all charges are confirmed.[288] In the future, a reasonable balance between these two competing interests—fair trial for the suspect by proper screening of the charges, and expediency of the proceedings—must be found,[289] keeping the 'trial readiness'[290] in mind.[291] Surely, the concerns expressed in the IER should also be taken seriously:

> that the pre-trial stage is lengthy and cumbersome at times.... practices followed by different Chambers can be inconsistent and contradictory; that the roles of the Pre-Trial and Trial Chambers are duplicated; that some decisions rendered are unnecessarily voluminous.[292]

The report points to an average length of 362 days for pre-trial proceedings at the ICC.[293] As a result, the recent version of the Chambers *Practice Manual* addresses the Court's efficiency

[285] Crit. in this vein, Safferling, *Criminal Procedure* (2012), pp. 343–4; Friman, Brady, Costi, Guariglia, and Stuckenberg, in Sluiter et al., *International Criminal Procedure* (2013), pp. 448–9, 470, 481 ('time-consuming'), 471 ('too protracted'); Stegmiller, in Stahn, *Practice* (2015), pp. 892, 905–6.

[286] cf. ICC, *Prosecutor v. Ntaganda*, PTC II, Decision on the Confirmation of Charges, ICC-01/04-02/06-309, 9 June 2014, paras. 99–100, considering alternative charges as mainly evidentiary question with final qualification left to TC; ICC, *Prosecutor v. Gbagbo*, PTC I, Decision on the Confirmation of Charges, ICC-02/11-01/11-656-Red, 12 June 2014, paras. 22, 203, 227, stressing the 'limited scope as purpose of the confirmation of charges' (para. 22) and confirming alternative charges upon existence of 'substantial grounds' and leave final decision to TC (paras. 203, 227); cf. thereon Mariniello, *JICJ*, 13 (2015), 589 ff.; similarly short (ninety pages), ICC, *Prosecutor v. Blé Goudé*, PTC I, Decision on the Confirmation of Charges against Charles Blé Goudé, ICC-02/11-02/11-186, 11 December 2014; also short, fifty-five pages, ICC, *Prosecutor v. Bemba et al.*, PTC II, Decision pursuant to Article 61 (7)(a) and (b) of the Rome Statute, ICC-01/05-01/13-749, 11 November 2014. In favour of 'more precise and more narrowly focused' decisions also Mettraux et al., *Effectiveness ICC* (2014), p. 83 (para. 9 b). For a model of a 'typical' or ideal structure of a confirmation decision, see ICC, *Practice Manual* (2023), para. 66.

[287] Friman, Brady, Costi, Guariglia, and Stuckenberg, in Sluiter et al., *International Criminal Procedure* (2013), pp. 448 ('proper screening mechanism'), 470, 481 ('by far the most exhaustive and fairest' review procedure).

[288] More recently charges were only partially confirmed in *Said*, ICC-01/14-01/21-218-Red; *Yekatom and Ngaïssona*, ICC-01/14-01/18-403-Red. For previous case law, see first edition p. 357 with note 214. Acknowledging the success of the confirmation process in 'weeding out "weaker" cases', Mettraux et al., *Effectiveness ICC* (2014), p. 85 (para. 10). On the possible reasons responsible for non-confirmation of charges in the recent ICC case law, see SáCouto and Cleary Thompson, in Stahn, *Practice* (2015), pp. 341–5; considering that the lengthy confirmation procedure was unnecessary in these cases since charges 'have been so weak' that they 'could have been easily disposed of' by a smoother procedure, WCRO, *Confirmation* (2015), pp. 2, 77.

[289] See also Friman, Brady, Costi, Guariglia, and Stuckenberg, in Sluiter et al., *International Criminal Procedure* (2013), pp. 470, 486.

[290] There are two schools of thought regarding 'trial readiness': according to one view the case should be ready for trial almost immediately upon confirmation (including with all disclosure essentially done pre-confirmation), see Bitti, in Fischer et al., *Prosecution* (2001), pp. 276–7. Another view is that post-confirmation disclosure and other preparations are necessary, appropriate, and better in line with the legal regime, see Brady, in Fischer et al., *Prosecution* (2001), pp. 264–5.

[291] cf. Stahn, *JICJ*, 12 (2014), 833, advocating the following: (i) effective anticipation of disclosure issues, (ii) preparation of redactions and protective measures, (iii) settlement of victim participation in relation to the 'case', and (iv) the arrangement of a proper transfer of the pre-trial record to trial.

[292] Expert Group, *IER* (2020), pp. 151–2.

[293] Ibid., p. 157.

at length.[294] I note in passing that, at the KSC, the Pre-Trial Judge is obliged to 'set a target date' for his confirmation decision 'which, subject to the specificities of the case, shall be no later than six (6) months from the filing of the indictment and all supporting material'.[295] So far, the KSC (trial and appeals) proceedings have also turned out to be highly expedient.[296]

An effective, yet underestimated tool for efficient pre-trial proceedings is Rule 121 RPE ICC, especially subparagraph 2, which gives the PTCs several (managerial) powers that have not been fully used so far.[297] Rule 121 (9) allows for the PTC to require written submissions by both the Prosecutor and the 'person' (suspect). A more managerial (albeit arguably excessive) use of Rule 121 can be seen in the *Al-Rahman* (formerly '*Ali Kushayb*') case: upon realizing that the prosecution was unable to discharge various obligations prior to the confirmation hearing, eventually delaying proceedings, Single Judge Aitala ordered the Prosecutor 'to submit, every other week starting on Monday, 24 August 2020, a detailed report to keep the Chamber abreast of any progress made with regard to the evidence review, translation and disclosure process'.[298]

*(ii) Procedure*

The confirmation hearing has to be prepared by the respective PTC—being the sole adjudicatory authority at this stage—in cooperation with the parties. The PTC sets the date for the hearing 'within a reasonable time after the person's surrender or voluntary appearance before the Court'.[299] The *Practice Manual* suggests four to six months as a target date after the first appearance but acknowledges that there should be flexibility with regard to 'the circumstances of each particular case'.[300] The PTC has also to supervise the disclosure process,[301] to be analysed in more detail in Chapter V.[302] The Prosecutor must provide to the PTC the already mentioned DCC accompanied by the relevant evidence no later than thirty days before the hearing;[303] in case of a factual expansion of the charges, the PTC may order the Prosecutor to inform the defence 'in advance' of this expansion by way of a 'formal

294 ICC, *Practice Manual* (2023), paras. 2, 94–8.

295 cf. Art. 39 (2) KSC Law and Rule 85 (5) RPE KSC. See also Heinze, in Heinze and Dittrich, *ICC* (2021), p. 69.

296 In the first case on administration of justice offences (*Gucati and Haradinaj*) the pre-trial and trial phase lasted 19 months and 24 days—the accused were transferred to the KSC on 25 and 26 September 2020 and the TJ was pronounced on 18 May 2022—and the AJ was delivered in less than one year on 2 February 2023. In the second case on war crimes (*Mustafa*) the pre-trial and trial phase lasted 26 months and 22 days—the accused was transferred to the KSC on 24 September 2020 and the TJ was pronounced on 16 December 2022—the AJ was delivered in less than one year on 14 December 2023. In the third case on war crimes (*Shala*) the pre-trial and trial phase lasted 39 months—the accused was arrested on 16 March 2021, transferred to the KSC on 15 April 2021 and the TJ was pronounced on 16 July 2024—the AJ is expected to be delivered in 2025.

297 In the same vein, Expert Group, *IER* (2020), p. 159. Especially when it comes to disclosure obligations, the Chamber can save time using Rule 121 RPE and hence a good case management, see Chapter V, A.(7) and B.(1)(c) in this volume. Conc. regarding the use of Rule 121, see ICC, *IER Response* (2021), p. 84.

298 ICC, *Prosecutor v. Abd Al Rahman*, PTC II, Order on Disclosure and Related Matters, ICC-02/05-01/20-116, 17 August 2020, para. 17. While this decision does not explicitly refer to Rule 121 (2) RPE ICC, the Rule is mentioned in a previous decision, cf. *Prosecutor v. Abd-Al-Rahman*, PTC II, Order Seeking Observations on Disclosure and Related Matters, ICC-02/05-01/20-14, 2 July 2020, paras. 6, 7.

299 Art. 61 (1) ICCS; Rule 121 (1) RPE ICC; see above sub-section (1)(b) *in fine*. See also Schabas, Chaitidou, and El Zeidy, 'Article 61', in Ambos, *Commentary* (2022), mn. 13–17; on the importance of the right timing for the confirmation hearing with a view to its objective(s), see Nerlich, *JICJ*, 10 (2012), 1355–6; in a similar vein, Stegmiller, in Stahn, *Practice* (2015), pp. 906–7.

300 ICC, *Practice Manual* (2023), paras. 12–13.

301 Art. 61 (3) *in fine* ICCS; Rule 121 (2) RPE ICC.

302 Chapter V, B.(1)(c) and (2)(c) in this volume.

303 cf. Rule 121 (3) RPE ICC; cf. also Schabas, Chaitidou, and El Zeidy, 'Article 61', in Ambos, *Commentary* (2022), mn. 50.

notification in the record of the case'.[304] The suspect must provide his evidence, if any, to the PTC no later than fifteen days before the hearing.[305] Charges and evidence 'presented after the time limit' will not be taken into consideration.[306] However, submissions 'on points of fact and law', in particular grounds excluding responsibility, are possible until three days before the hearing.[307]

At the hearing, before discussing the merits, the presiding judge shall ask the Prosecutor and the defence whether they intend to raise objections concerning the proper conduct of the proceedings prior to the hearing,[308] including the form and contents (not the merits) of the charges.[309] Of course, the actual conduct of the hearing very much depends on the background and culture of the respective judges. The Chambers *Practice Manual* strives therefore for a certain uniformity by providing guidelines on the conduct of the hearing.[310] At any rate, the Prosecutor may seek a postponement of the confirmation hearing, if she needs more time to complete her case.[311] The Registry shall create and maintain 'a full and accurate record of all proceedings' before the PTC.[312] The withdrawal or amendment of charges or evidence will be analysed in more detail below.[313] The pre-trial brief, introduced by one of the various amendments of the RPE ICTY/ICTR,[314] is comparable to the ICC list of evidence/information,[315] except that it is subsequently amendable by the parties.[316] Indeed, before the ICC, the filing of a pre-trial brief, explaining the case theory and listing the respective evidence, is now standard practice.[317]

The actual confirmation hearing must be held *publicly* unless a private hearing is ordered for reasons of witness protection.[318] It must also be held in the *presence* of the accused, unless

[304] cf. ICC, *Practice Manual* (2023), para. 32 (how much 'in advance' before the confirmation hearing this 'notification' needs to be provided depends on the particular circumstances of the case).

[305] cf. Rule 121 (6) RPE ICC; cf. also Ambos and Miller, *ICLR*, 7 (2007), 344; Heinze, *Disclosure* (2014), pp. 411 ff.; *Lubanga*, ICC-01/04-01/06-803-tEN, para. 143; Ambos, in Kotsalis, Courakis, and Mylonopoulos, *FS Karras* (2010), p. 986.

[306] cf. Rule 121 (8) RPE ICC.

[307] cf. Rule 121 (9) RPE ICC.

[308] Rule 122 (3) RPE ICC.

[309] cf. ICC, *Practice Manual* (2023), paras. 39 ff. (at paras. 45 ff. further explaining the scope of Rule 122 (3) referring to formal challenges and Rule 122 (4) precluding such challenges subsequently).

[310] ICC, *Practice Manual* (2023), paras. 49–54.

[311] cf. Rule 121 (7) RPE ICC; cf. also Schabas, Chaitidou, and El Zeidy, 'Article 61', in Ambos, *Commentary* (2022), mn. 16; SáCouto and Cleary Thompson, in Stahn, *Practice* (2015), pp. 345–8 (suggesting ways for the OTP to strengthen its case before going to the confirmation hearing).

[312] cf. Rule 121 (10) RPE ICC.

[313] Section B.(7)(a) in this chapter.

[314] cf. Rule 65*ter* (E) RPE ICTY, Rule 73*bis* RPE ICTR, Rule 70 RPE MICT and Rule 86, esp. paras. 3, 4, and 5 RPE KSC.

[315] Despite the explicit usage of the term 'evidence' in Rule 121 (3) RPE ICC, to be understood narrowly (see Chapter V, A.(1)(a) in this volume), one may add the term 'information' given that the disclosure obligation of the Prosecutor refers more broadly to 'material to the preparation of the defence' (Rule 77 RPE ICC), i.e. to *all* objects that are relevant for the preparation of the defence (in contrast to those that the Prosecutor intends to rely on at the confirmation hearing), see, in more detail, Chapter V, B.(2)(e) in this volume.

[316] On the ICTY, see Wasef, *CLF*, 20 (2009), 452; Jones and Powles, *International Criminal Practice* (2003), p. 646; ICTY, *Manual* (2009), pp. 57–8; see also ICTY, *Prosecutor v. Tolimir*, TC II, Decision on Accused's Preliminary Motion pursuant to Rule 72 (A) (ii), IT-05-88/2-PT, 10 February 2010, para. 17.

[317] ICC, *Practice Manual* (2023), para. 76. For earlier case law, see first edition p. 358 with note 235.

[318] ICC, *Prosecutor v. Lubanga*, PTC I, Order Authorising the Taking of Photographs at the Hearing on 9 November 2006, ICC-01/04-01/06-671-tEN, 6 November 2006; ICC, *Prosecutor v. Bemba*, PTC III, Decision Authorising Photographs at the Confirmation of the Charges Hearing on 12 January 2009, ICC-01/05-01/08-351, 8 January 2009; Schabas, *Introduction* (2020), p. 289; cf. also Schabas, Chaitidou, and El Zeidy, 'Article 61', in Ambos, *Commentary* (2022), mn. 17. In *Ongwen*, ICC-02/04-01/15-422-Red, paras. 24–8, PTC II accepted that certain charges were made in closed session for reasons of witness protection, but eventually made them public in light of Art. 61 (7) and the accused's right to a public trial.

he has waived his right to be present or cannot be brought before the Court.[319] A combined reading of Article 61 (2) and the relevant Rules 123–6 RPE ICC, taking into account the importance of the presence of a suspect in an adversarial confirmation hearing, makes clear that the possibility of an *in absentia* hearing should only be used in highly exceptional circumstances.[320] In fact, so far it has been of little practical importance.[321] The law provides for two exceptional scenarios where it may take place. Under both exceptions counsel should—contrary to the ambiguous wording of the last sentence of Article 61 (2)[322] be assigned 'in the interests of justice'[323] and represent the suspect to the best possible extent.[324] The first exception allowing for a waiver presupposes that the suspect 'is available to the Court' and understands the consequences of a waiver; further, he may observe the hearing and make written observations.[325] While a waiver is possible during the hearing,[326] the suspect must not waive his presence for parts of the hearing to 'pick and choose the days he wishes to attend';[327] yet, it has been considered possible for a suspect to attend the hearing and to waive his or her right 'for the remaining of the confirmation hearing'.[328]

The second exception presupposes the absolute and definitive unavailability of the suspect,[329] that is, that he or she cannot be brought before the Court despite 'all reasonable steps' that have been undertaken to secure their appearance.[330] This exception has been invoked by the OTP—for the first time in the history of the Court—requesting PTC II to

[319] Art. 61 (2) ICCS; also ICC, *Prosecutor v. Lubanga*, AC, Judgment on the Appeal of Lubanga Dyilo against the Decision of Pre-Trial Chamber I Entitled 'Décision sur la demande de mise en liberté provisoire de Thomas Lubanga Dyilo', Separate Opinion of Judge Pikis, ICC-01/04-01/06-824, 13 February 2007, para. 2 ('held in the absence of the person ... must ... be ... exceptional'); Trendafilova, in Stahn and Sluiter, *Practice* (2009), pp. 452–7; Billis, *Die Rolle des Richters* (2015), p. 420; largely descriptive Zakerhossein and de Brouwer, *CLF*, 26 (2015), 192–4.

[320] For a detailed analysis, see Schabas, Chaitidou, and El Zeidy, 'Article 61', in Ambos, *Commentary* (2022), mn. 20–5. For a historical overview of 'total' and 'partial' in *absentia* proceedings in international criminal justice, see Zakerhossein and de Brouwer, *CLF*, 26 (2015), 184 ff., 209 ff., pointing to the IMT, IMTFE, and STL as the only tribunals allowing for total *in absentia* trials, which the authors reject (223). See also Carnero Rojo, 'Article 61', in Klamberg, *Commentary ICC II* (2023), p. 141.

[321] cf. Schabas, Chaitidou, and El Zeidy, 'Article 61', in Ambos, *Commentary* (2022), mn. 23.

[322] The reference to 'that case' seems to imply that the right to counsel applies only under subpara. (b), but given the importance of this right it has to apply to both situations.

[323] Art. 61 (2)(b) *in fine* ICCS.

[324] See the references to counsel in Rules 123 (2), 124 (1), 125 (1), and 126 (2) RPE ICC.

[325] cf. Rule 124 RPE ICC. In the trial against *Katanga*, the PTC was informed by Katanga's defence lawyer that his client would not be present throughout the trial (ICC, *Prosecutor v. Katanga and Ngudjolo*, PTC I, Transcript of Confirmation of Charges Hearing, ICC-01/04-01/07-T-45-ENG, 9 July 2008, p. 1) and submitted a waiver of his right to be present at the confirmation hearing (ICC, *Prosecutor v. Katanga and Ngudjolo*, Mr Katanga's Waiver of his Right to be Present at the Confirmation Hearing pursuant to Rule 124 of the Rules of Procedure and Evidence, ICC-01/04-01/07-670-AnxA, 9 July 2008). The PTC accepted the waiver, *Katanga and Ngudjolo*, ICC-01/04-01/07-T-46-ENG, pp. 23–4. In the Sudan/Darfur case of *Abakaer Nourain* and *Jerbo Jamus* the confirmation hearing also took place in absence of the accused; cf. ICC, *Prosecutor v. Banda and Jerbo*, PTC I, Decision on Issues Related to the Hearing on the Confirmation of Charges, ICC-02/05-03/09-103, 17 November 2010, paras. 1–4; *Banda and Jerbo*, ICC-02/05-03/09-121-Corr-Red, para. 19.

[326] ICC, *Prosecutor v. Katanga and Ngudjolo*,PTC I, Transcript of Confirmation of Charges Hearing, ICC-01/04-01/07-T-46-ENG, 11 July 2008, p. 24 .

[327] ICC, *Prosecutor v. Ruto et al.*, PTC II, Decision on the 'Defence Request pursuant to Rule 124 (1) for Mr William Ruto to Waive his Right to be Present for Part of the Confirmation of Charges Hearing', ICC-01/09-01/11-302, 29 August 2011, para. 12.See also Bourguiba, in Fernandez et al., *Commentaire CPI II* (2019), p. 1682.

[328] *Katanga and Ngudjolo*, ICC-01/04-01/07-T-46-ENG, p. 24. See also Schabas, *ICC Commentary* (2016), p. 931.

[329] For a different view, see Safferling, *Criminal Procedure* (2012), p. 323, arguing that an *in absentia* hearing is only possible if the suspect 'has at some stage been in the custody of the Court'. This clearly goes against the wording of Art. 61 (2)(b) and overlooks the difference between subparas. (a) and (b), as explained in the text.

[330] cf. Art. 61 ((2)(b) ICCS and Rule 123 RPE ICC.

hold a confirmation hearing against *Joseph Kony* in his absence.[331] The request is a consequence of prior developments:[332] The *Kony* case was originally joined with the *Ongwen* case and, following the latter's initial appearance, PTC II requested the Prosecutor to 'provide observations on whether or not confirmation of charges proceedings *in absentia* against the other co-suspects in this case', amongst them *Kony*.[333] In its decision severing the case against *Ongwen* from that against *Kony et al.*, PTC II decided against holding a confirmation hearing *in absentia* against the latter, stating that '(i) currently, the Court lacks the necessary resources to proceed against the other co-suspects *in absentia*; and that (ii) this course of action would have significant but unjustified budgetary implications, considering the circumstances of the case'.[334] The Prosecutor's request shortly before the AC's judgment against *Ongwen*[335] suggests a connection between the request and the final conviction of *Ongwen*. Another (more strategic) reason could be to test confirmation hearings *in absentia* with regard to the Ukraine investigations.[336] Be that as it may, PTC II decided on 23 November 2023 that, despite the exceptional nature of *in absentia* proceedings even at the confirmation stage,[337] there is sufficient cause to hold a confirmation hearing against Kony in his absence and that he 'qualifies as a person who cannot be found' within the meaning of Article 61 (2)(b).[338] Yet, as the actual taking place of a confirmation hearing (in presence or absence) presupposes that the accused is properly informed of the charges, the Chamber ordered the prosecution to first present charges and use all reasonable (alternative) means to inform Kony of these charges.[339] In its second decision of 4 March 2024 the Chamber then set the date for the commencement of this hearing.[340]

Rule 122 RPE ICC provides for some technical rules for the proceedings in the presence of the person charged. Most importantly, it is up to the presiding judge 'to determine how the hearing is to be conducted' and the evidence presented.[341] The parties shall be allocated a certain amount of time to make their respective presentations on the merits.[342] The actual confirmation of charges requires 'sufficient evidence to establish substantial grounds to

[331] ICC, *Prosecutor v. Kony and Otti*, Public Redacted Version of the 'Prosecution's Request to Hold a Hearing on the Confirmation of Charges against Joseph Kony in his Absence', ICC-02/04-01/05-446-Red, 24 November 2022.

[332] For an overview, see Schabas, Chaitidou, and El Zeidy, 'Article 61', in Ambos, *Commentary* (2022), mn. 23.

[333] ICC, *Prosecutor v. Kony et al.*, PTC II (Single Judge Trendafilova), Transcript of Hearing, ICC-02/04-01/05-T-11-Conf-Exp-ENG, 28 January 2015, p. 25, ll. 16–17.

[334] ICC, *Prosecutor v. Kony et al.*, PTC II, Decision Severing the Case Against Dominic Ongwen, ICC-02/04-01/05-424, 6 February 2015, para. 7.

[335] Issued on 15 December 2022, *Ongwen*, ICC-02/04-01/15-2022-Red.

[336] Thereto Fesefeldt, *DriZ*, 100 (2022), 410 ff.

[337] ICC, *Prosecutor v. Kony*, PTC II, Decision on the Prosecution's Request to hold a Confirmation of Charges Hearing in the Kony Case in the Suspect's Absence, ICC-02/04-01/05-466, 23 November 2023, para. 37 ('extraordinary procedural step', 'narrowly construed'). Notwithstanding, the PTC declared, *obiter*, that 'a trial in absentia' should have been foreseen and 'it would be valuable to States Parties to reconsider' the issue (ibid., para. 70).

[338] *Kony*, ICC-02/04-01/05-466, para. 31 ff. and disposition. Crit. Andrian, *EJIL: Talk!*, 5 December 2023 ('ill-reasoned' negligence of 'Defense's rights'). The PTC equates 'cannot be found' (Art. 61 (2)(b)) with 'was never available'; crit. Andrian, just quoted (who, however, agrees that a first appearance before the Court is not necessary).

[339] *Kony*, ICC-02/04-01/05-466, para. 45 ff. (51); conc. Andrian, *EJIL: Talk!*, 5 December 2023. The OTP submitted the requested charges (by way of a DCC) on 19 January 2024, <https://www.icc-cpi.int/sites/default/files/CourtRecords/CR2024_00006.PDF>. On 26 January 2024, the PTC II issued an order regarding notification efforts and outreach activities, *Prosecutor v. Kony*, PTC II, Order to Initiate Notification Efforts and Related Outreach Activities, ICC-02/04-01/05-475, 26 January 2024.

[340] ICC, *Prosecutor v. Kony*, PTC II, Second Decision on the Prosecution's Request to Hold a Confirmation of Charges Hearing in the Kony Case in the Suspect's Absence, ICC-02/04-01/05-481, 4 March 2024 (commencement on 15 October 2024).

[341] Rule 122 (1) RPE ICC.

[342] cf. ICC, *Practice Manual* (2023), para. 51.

believe that the person committed each one of the crimes charged'.[343] In order to meet this standard the Prosecutor must 'support each charge with sufficient evidence'[344] but the implementation of this requirement, as to the quantity and quality of evidence, has not been uniform.[345] At any rate, Chambers have different opinions as to their own powers. Both evidentiary standard on the one hand and judicial powers on the other are often confused. For instance, with regard to the overall assessment of the PTC (i.e. all decisions taken by it), Judge Kovács opined that the role of the PTC was 'not to conduct a "marginal assessment"'. Rather, its role is, inter alia, to 'provide a clear and well-reasoned decision, which presents a full account of the relevant facts and law in order to reveal transparency of the judicial process and guarantee a considerable degree of persuasiveness'.[346] It is important to note that Judge Kovács does not address the evidentiary standard in this context but what he calls 'the seriousness of a Chamber's examination'.[347] This distinction—between evidentiary standard and depth of the inquiry—might not be self-explanatory from the common law perspective with the judge as a more passive umpire; it is convincing, though, from the perspective of judicially-led confirmation proceedings. Judge Kovács is therefore correct in stating that:

> the pre-trial phase does not justify a light assessment of facts or disregarding the proper presentation of evidence submitted. It simply means that the assessment should be carried out against the evidentiary standard required for the particular stage of the judicial process, be it low or high.[348]

Of course, this does not affect the guideline that PTCs should limit their reasoning to what is strictly necessary.[349] Yet, this is still not fully implemented and, at any rate, the practice is rather inconsistent, as recent confirmation decisions show: slim confirmation decisions were issued in the cases against *Abd-Al-Rahman* (*'Ali Kushayb'*)[350] and *Said*,[351] extensive ones in *Al Hassan*[352] and *Yekatom and Ngaïssona*.[353]

The Prosecutor may predominantly or exclusively rely on documentary or summary evidence.[354] In fact, given the need for expediency, PTCs seem to prefer rather fewer than more live witnesses at the confirmation hearing, including 'core witnesses',[355] and thus tend very much to limit the number of witnesses.[356] The identity of witnesses does not need to be fully

[343] Art. 61 (7) ICCS.
[344] Art. 61 (5) ICCS.
[345] cf. Expert Group, *IER* (2020), p. 155 (para. 486: 'non consistent application').
[346] *Prosecutor v. Al Mahdi*, PTC I, Separate Opinion of Judge Péter Kovács, ICC-01/12-01/15-84-Anx, 9 May 2016, para. 6 (fn. omitted).
[347] *Al Mahdi*, ICC-01/12-01/15-84-Anx, para. 7.
[348] Ibid., para. 7.
[349] cf. ICC, *Practice Manual* (2023), para. 63.
[350] Abd-Al-Rahman, ICC-02/05-01/20-433 (71 pp.).
[351] *Said*, ICC-01/14-01/21-218-Red. (62 p.).
[352] *Al Hassan*, ICC-01/12-01/18-461-Corr-Red. (467 p.).
[353] *Yekatom and Ngaïssona*, ICC-01/14-01/18-403-Red. (108 pp.).
[354] Art. 61 (5) ICCS.
[355] cf. ICC, *Prosecutor v. Katanga and Ngudjolo*, PTC I, Decision on the Admissibility for the Confirmation Hearing of the Transcripts of Interview of Deceased Witness 12, ICC-01/04-01/07-412, 18 April 2008, p. 4; ordering a reduction of live witnesses to a maximum of two for each suspect, *Prosecutor v. Ruto et al.*, PTC II, Order to the Defence to Reduce the Number of Witnesses to Be Called to Testify, ICC-01/09-01/11-221, 25 July 2011, paras. 9, 11–14, 15, 19, 23 ; *Prosecutor v. Muthaura et al.*, PTC II, Order to the Defence to Reduce the Number of Witnesses to Be Called to Testify, ICC-01/09-02/11-226, 10 August 2011, para. 24 ; *Prosecutor v. Muthaura et al.*, PTC II, Decision on the 'Defence Application for Allocation of Time to Present Viva Voce Witnesses at the Confirmation Hearing', ICC-01/09-02/11-240, 15 August 2011, para. 4; see also Schabas, Chaitidou, and El Zeidy, 'Article 61', in Ambos, *Commentary* (2022), mn. 94–9.
[356] Schabas, Chaitidou, and El Zeidy, 'Article 61', in Ambos, *Commentary* (2022), mn. 97, 107 ff.

disclosed.[357] In the past, PTCs have asked the Prosecutor to make modifications to the evidentiary summaries 'where this proves to be necessary ... so as to ensure better protection of the witness's identity or, conversely, make more information available to the Defence'.[358]

The person charged may object to the charges, challenge the evidence, or present his own evidence.[359] Both parties may make final 'observations' at the end of the hearing,[360] without, however, using the observations to raise new arguments.[361]

*(iii) Evidentiary threshold and possible decisions*

The requisite standard of proof—the existence of *substantial* grounds—is higher than the reasonable grounds required for the issuance of an arrest warrant[362] and, *a fortiori*, the 'grounds to believe' standard,[363] but lower than the burden required for a conviction, that is proof beyond reasonable doubt.[364] The substantial grounds standard is also higher than the *prima facie* standard of ICTY/ICTR,[365] even if one interpreted this standard as requiring 'reasonable grounds for believing that a suspect has committed a crime'.[366] Arguably, it is also higher or at least more precise than the 'well-grounded suspicion' threshold applicable at the KSC for

357 ICC, *Prosecutor v. Lubanga*, AC, Judgment on the Appeal of Mr Thomas Lubanga Dyilo against the Decision of Pre-Trial Chamber I Entitled 'Second Decision on the Prosecution Requests and Amended Requests for Redactions under Rule 81', ICC-01/04-01/06-774, 14 December 2006, paras. 40, 47 (redaction pursuant to Rule 81 (2) RPE ICC is permissible, since 'the threshold for the confirmation of the charges is lower than for a conviction', this threshold can be reached 'even if the reliability of the witnesses and other evidence was not fully tested'). In order to meet the 'sufficient evidence' standard, the prosecution may even use inclusive language 'such as the phrase "include, but ... not limited to" certain acts', see *Bemba*, ICC-01/05-01/08-3343, para. 41.

358 ICC, *Prosecutor v. Al Hassan*, PTC I, Decision on the Prosecution Requests for Authorization to Withhold the Identities of Witnesses P-0100, P-0111, P-0130, P-0576, P-0581, P-0583, P-0589, P-0592, P- 0593 and P-0594, ICC-01/12-01/18-174-Red2, 28 January 2019 (original decision registered on 6 November 2018), paras. 29, 67; see also *Prosecutor v. Yekatom and Ngaïssona*, PTC II, Decision on the 'Joint Defence Motion for Disclosure of Anonymous Summaries for [REDACTED] and [REDACTED]', ICC-01/14-01/18-256-Red, 3 February 2020 (original decision registered on 26 July 2019), para. 20; *Prosecutor v. Yekatom and Ngaïssona*, PTC II, Decision on the Prosecutor's Request to Use Anonymised Summaries of Witness Statements, ICC-01/14-01/18-261-Red2, 3 February 2020 (original decision registered on 31 July 2019), paras. 26, 29.

359 Art. 61 (6) ICCS; see also Schabas, Chaitidou, and El Zeidy, 'Article 61', in Ambos, *Commentary* (2022), mn. 102 ff.

360 Rule 122 (8) RPE ICC.

361 See also ICC, *Practice Manual* (2023), para. 52 *in fine* (only responding to each other's submissions, no new arguments).

362 Art. 58 (1)(a) ICCS. See the following sub-section (6).

363 Art. 55 (2) ICCS.

364 *Ruto et al.*, ICC-01/09-01/11-373, para. 40; Rules 87 (A) RPE ICTY/ICTR/SCSL, 104 (A) RPE MICT; Art. 66 (3) ICCS. See previously Ambos and Miller, *ICLR*, 7 (2007), 345–6; Ambos, in Bohlander, *International Criminal Justice* (2007), pp. 455–6; see also Cross, in Bergsmo and Stahn, *Preliminary Examination II* (2018), pp. 213 ff.; De Beco, *ICLR*, 7 (2007), 476; Safferling, *Criminal Procedure* (2012), p. 339; Friman, Brady, Costi, Guariglia, and Stuckenberg, in Sluiter et al., *International Criminal Procedure* (2013), p. 407 (p. 457 stressing the compatibility with the ECtHR case law); on the importance of the burden with regard to the equality of arms, see Jackson, *JICJ*, 7 (2009), 17, 28; on the 'progressively higher evidentiary thresholds applicable in the course of the proceedings', see Schabas, Chaitidou, and El Zeidy, 'Article 61', in Ambos, *Commentary* (2022), mn. 91–2; Friman, in Stahn, *Practice* (2015), p. 914 ('evidentiary threshold ... increasingly onerous for the prosecution to meet'); Mariniello, *JICJ*, 13 (2015), 598; see also Stegmiller, in Stahn, *Practice* (2015), pp. 896–7. All these standards are taken from Anglo-American law; see e.g. the 'probable cause to believe' standard, necessary in the US to issue a warrant of arrest (Rule 4 FedRCrimProc; *Ortega v. Superior Court*, 135 CalApp 3d 244 (1982)); or 'sufficient evidence' for the commencement of the main trial (Rule 5:30 FedRCrimProc; *Somers v. Superior Court*, 31 CalApp 3d 961 (1973)); or 'beyond reasonable doubt' to prove guilt in the main trial (e.g. *In Re Winship*, 397 US 358 (1970)).

365 Arts. 19 (1) ICTYS, 18 (1) ICTRS; Rules 47 (E) RPE ICTY/ICTR, 48 (E) RPE MICT. For the same view, see Miraglia, *JICJ*, 6 (2008), 498, arguing that 'the evaluation of the ICC PTC is not based on a "prima facie" standard', since it 'must consider all of the evidentiary materials proposed by the Prosecutor in light of the materials, allegations and evidence tendered by the Defence, and even any defence which may be raised by the suspect'; Safferling, *Criminal Procedure* (2012), p. 341; Mariniello, *JICJ*, 13 (2015), 598; for a different view, see Ntanda Nsereko, *JICJ*, 3 (2005), 140 ('equivalent of the prima facie standard used by the ad hoc Tribunal').

366 Rule 47 (B) RPE ICTY/ICTR, quoted in note 153 in this chapter; Rule 48 (B) RPE MICT.

the review of the indictment[367] for the latter only requires that the evidence 'would satisfy an objective observer that a criminal offence has occurred and the defendant has committed the offence'.[368]

The term 'substantial' grounds has been put on an equal footing with 'strong', 'significant', or 'solid' grounds.[369] The case law rightly requires 'concrete and tangible proof demonstrating a clear line of reasoning underpinning its specific allegations' and assesses the presented evidence comprehensively.[370] A case will only be ready for trial when 'a limited and careful selection of the best evidence' available gives rise to the requisite level of suspicion.[371] Of course, the requisite level of suspicion is satisfied with the 'substantial grounds' standard of Article 61 (7) ICCS, that is, there is no need to evaluate whether there is sufficient evidence with a view to a future conviction.[372]

The Chamber may take one of the *three decisions* provided for in Article 61 (7)(a)–(c) ICCS with regard to 'each of the crimes charged':[373] confirm or decline charges right away, or adjourn the hearing requesting further activity from the Prosecutor.[374] Thus, it must take a separate decision on each charge,[375] that is, it may also combine the options provided for in Article 61 (7). The *Practice Manual* introduced guidelines as to how to formulate the confirmation decision.[376] The PTC may make adaptions to the charges to conform to its findings, but must not expand their factual scope.[377] When declining charges the Chamber may have to provide a more detailed analysis than when confirming, since the non-confirmation entails that proceedings are, at least with regard to the respective charges, terminated.[378] In any case, the Prosecutor 'shall not be precluded from subsequently requesting' their confirmation on the basis of 'additional evidence';[379] also, the Prosecutor may seek an amendment of

[367] Art. 39 (2) KSC Law, Rule 86 (1), (4) RPE KSC.

[368] Art. 19 no. 1.12. Kosovo CPC 2012.

[369] See, on the one hand, *Lubanga*, ICC-01/04-01/06-803-tEN, para. 38 ('strong') and, on the other hand, *Bemba*, ICC-01/05-01/08-424, para. 29 ('significant', 'solid', 'material', 'well built', 'real'). See also *Ruto et al.*, ICC-01/09-01/11-373, para. 40.

[370] *Al Hassan*, ICC-01/12-01/18-461-Corr-Red, para. 44; *Said*, ICC-01/14-01/21-218-Red, para. 38; *Yekatom and Ngaïssona*, ICC-01/14-01/18-403-Red, para. 17. For earlier case law, see previous edition p. 361 with note 263. See also Schabas, Chaitidou, and El Zeidy, 'Article 61', in Ambos, *Commentary* (2022), mn. 93 ff.; Expert Group, *IER* (2020), p. 156; Mariniello, *ICLR*, 19 (2019); 979, 990; crit. De Beco, *ICLR*, 7 (2007), 481.

[371] *Katanga and Ngudjolo*, ICC-01/04-01/07-428-Corr, para. 81; *Banda and Jerbo*, ICC-02/05-03/09-121-Corr-Red, para. 40; *Ruto et al.*, ICC-01/09-01/11-373, para. 48.

[372] *Abu Garda*, ICC-02/05-02/09-243-Red, para. 40 ('The Chamber, therefore, shall not evaluate whether the evidence is sufficient to sustain a future conviction. Such a high standard is not compatible with the standard under article 61 (7) of the Statute'); in the same vein, ICC, *Practice Manual* (2023), para. 63 ('keep the reasoning strictly limited to what is necessary'); WCRO, *Confirmation* (2015), pp. 2–3; Mariniello, *JICJ*, 13 (2015), 595–8, 599. For a stricter view, see ICC, *Prosecutor v. Gbagbo*, Dissenting Opinion of Judge Christine Van den Wyngaert, ICC-02/11-01/11-656-Anx, 12 June 2014, para. 4: '[C]harges should only be confirmed if the evidence has a realistic chance of supporting a conviction beyond reasonable doubt . . . [T]here must be at least enough of an evidentiary basis to sustain a possible conviction on the assumption that these questions are resolved in favour of the Prosecutor at trial.'

[373] Art. 61 (7) ICCS.

[374] On these three options, see also Stegmiller, in Stahn, *Practice* (2015), pp. 898–901; cf. also Kuczyńska, *Accusation Model ICC* (2015), p. 151 (suggesting a 'fourth option: rather than adjourning the hearing . . . [the PTC] may modify the legal characterisation of facts'—but this is not a separate, but an implicit option, see also Section B.(7) in this chapter).

[375] Safferling, *Criminal Procedure* (2012), p. 324.

[376] ICC, *Practice Manual* (2023), paras. 65–6; conc. Expert Group, *IER* (2020), p. 157. For a crit. view regarding the admission of evidence and disclosure, see Chapter V, A.(1)(b), (4) and B. in this volume.

[377] ICC, *Practice Manual* (2023), para. 64.

[378] cf. Ibid.

[379] Art. 61 (8) ICCS. See also ICC, *Prosecutor v. Al Hassan*, PTC I, Decision on the Applicable Procedure following the Prosecutor's Filing of Her Request for Corrections and Amendments of the Decision to Confirm the Charges, ICC-01/12-01/18-608-Red-tENG, 21 February 2020, para. 44.

the already confirmed charges, especially adding new charges or substituting more serious ones, 'with the permission of the Pre-Trial Chamber' which will normally hold a hearing.[380]

Otherwise, once charges are confirmed, the case should move to the TC as swiftly as possible, but there are, apart from unclear charges,[381] two procedural scenarios causing delays. In the first scenario, the Chamber confirms some charges, but adjourns the hearing on other charges. The person's committal to trial may then be deferred 'pending the continuation of the hearing' with regard to the adjourned charges.[382] An alternative approach would be to refer the case regarding the confirmed charges to the TC and continue to work on the remaining (adjourned) charges. This would avoid a general delay regarding the whole case. In the second scenario, (unresolved) requests for leave to appeal a PTC decision delay the transfer of the case to the TC, since it is the respective PTC that has first to decide on the leave request.[383] To avoid this delay, allowing the case to be transferred to the TC should be considered even though not all pending issues are resolved.

The written decision must be delivered within sixty days after the end of the hearing.[384] A deviation from this time limit is exceptionally possible for 'good cause'.[385] The parties must be notified[386] and the record of proceedings sent to the Presidency. The Presidency will constitute a TC[387] and transmit the confirmation decision and the record of proceedings to it.[388] The OTP sets up an 'interdivisional trial team'.[389]

As to the record of proceedings it is noteworthy that PTC II has made clear that, pursuant to Rule 129 RPE ICC, the record has to be transmitted 'in its entirety' to the TC and that there is no 'discretion ... vested in the Chamber for the purposes of reducing, amending or otherwise intervening on the content of the record'.[390] This full transmission of the record

380 Art. 61 (9) ICCS. See also ICC, *Lubanga*, ICC-01/04-01/06-2205, para. 73 ff., 94; *Al Hassan*, ICC-01/12-01/18-608-Red-tENG, para. 44. On the relationship of Art. 61 (9) ICCS with Reg. 55 RegC, see Section B.(7)(b)(ii) in this chapter.

381 cf. Expert Group, *IER* (2020), p. 154 ('Not having clearly defined charges has also been attributed as a factor for delay in the start of trials.').

382 cf. Rule 127 RPE ICC.

383 Rule 155 RPE ICC.

384 Reg. 53 RegC; see also ICC, *Practice Manual* (2023), para. 55; Expert Group, *IER* (2020), p. 156; Safferling, *Criminal Procedure* (2012), p. 325. The hearing ends with the last final observation pursuant to Rule 122 (8) RPE ICC. Taking into account the above suggested four to six months from the first appearance to the hearing (note 302 and main text in this chapter) the confirmation decision would then be issued in about eight months since the initial appearance (the actual hearing lasting only a few days). However, in practice, in the first twelve confirmation decisions up to October 2015, it took from seven months to more than two and a half years to reach a decision (WCRO, *Confirmation* (2015), pp. 1, 16 ff., with instructive figures at pp. 105 ff.; therefore advocating a 'scaling back' to complete the confirmation proceedings within ninety days [sic!] (see further note 285 in this chapter), including a PTC decision within thirty days after defence submission; ibid., pp. 5–6, 99); on the length, see also Mettraux et al., *Effectiveness ICC* (2014), pp. 82, 93 (paras. 7–8, 22).

385 cf. Reg 35 (2) RegCourt ('The Chamber may extend or reduce a time limit if good cause is shown and, where appropriate, after having given the participants an opportunity to be heard. After the lapse of a time limit, an extension of time may only be granted if the participant seeking the extension can demonstrate that he or she was unable to file the application within the time limit for reasons outside his or her control.') This provision was invoked by Single Judge Trendafilova in *ICC, Prosecutor v. Ruto et al.*, PTC II, Decision on the Issuance of the Decision pursuant to Article 61 (7) of the Rome Statute, ICC-01/09-01/11-357, 26 October 2011, para. 14. In *Al Hassan* PTC I issued its confirmation decision seventy-four days after the end of the confirmation hearing, cf. *Prosecutor v. Al Hassan*, PTC I, Rectificatif à la Décision relative à la confirmation des charges portées contre Al Hassan Ag Abdoul Aziz Ag Mohamed Ag Mahmoud, ICC-01/12-01/18-461, 30 September 2019; crit. Expert Group, *IER* (2020), pp. 162–3.

386 Rule 129 RPE ICC.

387 This has so far taken up to three months (WCRO, *Confirmation* (2015), p. 1).

388 Rule 130 RPE ICC; see thereon also ICC, *Practice Manual* (2023), paras. 70–1.

389 Reg. 32 (5) RegOTP.

390 ICC, *Prosecutor v. Yekatom and Ngaïssona*, PTC II, Decision on the Prosecutor's Request for Reconsideration or, in the Alternative, Leave to Appeal the 'Decision on the Confirmation of Charges against Alfred Yekatom and

entails that the material contained in it is treated—very much like in the civil law case file system—as evidence by mere submission (as opposed to its admission).[391]

## (3) Trial

### *(a) General overview*

As in domestic systems, extensive *pre-trial preparations* are necessary before the actual trial starts.[392] At the ICC,[393] once the TC has been constituted,[394] it will hold a status conference to set the date for the trial and hold further status conferences, discussing with the parties relevant issues to ensure a proper conduct of the proceedings.[395] As to the timing, 'Trial Chamber should generally issue the scheduling order for the first status conference within a week of its composition. The first status conference pursuant to Rule 132 (1) of the Rules should generally be held within a month of this scheduling order.'[396]

A judge may be designated to take care of the preparation of the trial.[397] She may refer specific issues to the TC for its decision,[398] hold (further) status conferences, render orders and decisions, as well as establish a 'work plan' containing the obligations of the parties and respective deadlines.[399] Preparatory issues to be dealt with by this judge include the proper disclosure between the parties, the ordering of protective measures if necessary, deciding on victims' applications for participation, dealing with the conditions of detention.[400] The full Chamber may rule on 'any issue concerning the conduct of the proceedings',[401] including the determination of the language,[402] motions challenging admissibility or jurisdiction,[403] and disclosure.[404] Any objections by the parties must be raised at the commencement of the trial.[405] To streamline these elements in the trial's preparation, it has, in line with the *Practice*

Patrice-Edouard Ngaïssona', ICC-01/14-01/18-447, 11 March 2020, para. 38; further, ICC, *Prosecutor v. Yekatom and Ngaissona*, The Presidency, Decision Constituting Trial Chamber V and Referring to it the Case of The Prosecutor v. Alfred Yekatom and Patrice-Edouard Ngaïssona, Presidency, ICC-01/14-01/18-451, 16 March 2020, p. 5; in detail, Heinze, *Opinio Juris* (25 June 2020).

[391] See also Heinze, 'Disclosure: International Criminal Courts and Tribunals', *MPEiPro* (2020) (arguing that this is an indication, amongst others, that the ICC relies on a case file system). On this and the submission vs. admission of evidence, see, in more detail, Chapter V, B.(1)(c).

[392] See generally Schabas, *Introduction* (2020), pp. 297 ff.; Safferling, *Criminal Procedure* (2012), pp. 419 ff.; Vasiliev, in Cryer et al., *ICL* (2019), pp. 436–8; Tochilovsky, *Jurisprudence* (2014), pp. 117–18, 252.

[393] For the ad hoc tribunals, see Rules 51, 72–73*ter* RPE ICTY/ICTR; Rules 55, 70, 79–80 RPE MICT; Rules 54, 73–73*ter* RPE SCSL.

[394] Art. 61 (11) ICCS, Rule 130 RPE ICC.

[395] Art. 64 (3)(a) ICCS, Rule 132 RPE ICC, Reg. 54 RegC; see thereon Bitti, 'Article 64', in Ambos, *Commentary* (2022), mn. 21 ff.

[396] ICC, *Practice Manual* (2023), para. 72. See also Bitti, 'Article 64', in Ambos, *Commentary* (2022), mn. 22.

[397] Art. 64 (3)(a) ICCS in connection with Rule 132*bis* (1) RPE ICC; see thereon Bitti, 'Article 64', in Ambos, *Commentary* (2022), mn. 22; Bitti, in Stahn, *Practice* (2015), p. 416.

[398] Rule 132*bis* (3) RPE ICC.

[399] Rule 132*bis* (4) RPE ICC.

[400] Rule 132*bis* (5) RPE ICC. In more detail, ICC, *Practice Manual* (2023), para. 73; see also Bitti, 'Article 64', in Ambos, *Commentary* (2022), mn. 22.

[401] Rule 134 (1) RPE ICC.

[402] Art. 64 (3)(b) ICCS; see thereon Bitti, 'Article 64', in Ambos, *Commentary* (2022), mn. 28.

[403] Rule 133 in connection with Rule 58 RPE ICC. On such challenges, see Chapter III, A.(4)(a)(iv) and B.(2)(e) in this volume.

[404] Art. 64 (3)(c) ICCS; see thereon, in detail, Chapter V, B. in this volume.

[405] Rule 134 (2) RPE ICC.

*Manual*,[406] become best practice for PTCs to issue protocols. Given all these issues and rules it is little surprising that the period from confirmation until the actual trial starts may last months or even years.[407]

The actual trial[408] stage has, notwithstanding the structurally adversarial nature of international criminal procedure, various inquisitorial features.[409] Before the *ad hoc tribunals* the trial commences with a 'case presentation',[410] the requirements of which appear to follow the adversarial system: opening statements by the Prosecutor and the defence;[411] presentation of evidence[412] by both parties including rebuttal[413] and rejoinder,[414] examination-in-chief, cross-examination and re-examination,[415] closing stage,[416] and presentation of sentencing evidence.[417] Upon closer analysis, it becomes clear, however, that the TC may deviate from

[406] ICC, *Practice Manual* (2023), paras. 78 ff.

[407] The trials against Lubanga, Gbagbo, and Blé Goudé started almost two years after the confirmation of charges. The preparation of other trials took more than a year (*Katanga* and *Ngudjolo*: one year and two months; *Ntaganda*: one year and three months; *Bemba*: more than one year and five months; *Ruto* and *Sang*: more than one year and seven months; *Yekatom* and *Ngaïssona*: more than one year and one month). See on the length of the pre-trial proceedings (preliminary examination, investigation, confirmation proceedings) notes 30, 294 ff. with main text in this chapter.

[408] The 'trial' also comprises the phases of judgment, deliberation, and sentencing; cf. ICC, *Prosecutor v. Bemba*, AC, Public Redacted Version of Judgment on the Appeal of Mr Jean-Pierre Bemba Gombo against the decision of Trial Chamber III of 23 December 2014 Entitled 'Decision on "Defence Urgent Motion for Provisional Release"', ICC-01/05-01/08-3249-Red, 20 May 2015, para. 38 (thereto Heinze, in Bergsmo et al., *Power* (2020), p. 215); *Prosecutor v. Bemba et al.*, TC VII, Decision on Mr Bemba's Application for Release, ICC-01/05-01/13-2291, 12 June 2018, para. 11. For a conceptual analysis, see Heinze, in Wright, Levine and Gold, *OxfHB Prosecutors* (2021), pp. 117, 118–19.

[409] On the legal nature of the international criminal proceedings, see Carmichael Keen, *LJIL*, 17 (2004), 767 ff., who speaks of 'tempered adversariality' (see esp. 811 ff.); see also Byrne, *LJIL*, 26 (2013), 995; Heinze, in Bergsmo et al., *Power* (2020), pp. 155 ff.; Fairlie, *GeorgiaJI&CompL*, 47 (2019), 619, 620 ff.; Sorvatzioti, *ICLR*, 22 (2022), 895, 911. On the adversarial structure of the main trial of the ad hoc tribunals, see Rohan, in Aksenova et al., *Mass Atrocities* (2019), pp. 95, 108 ff.; Findlay and Ying, *International Criminal Justice* (2019), pp. 12 ff.; Nemitz, in Kirsch, *Internationale Strafgerichtshöfe* (2005), pp. 53 ff.; Zahar and Sluiter, *ICL* (2008), pp. 38–9, 43–2; Swart, *JICJ*, 6 (2008), 109–10; Doherty, *LJIL*, 26 (2013), 943 ff. See also Chapter V, A.(1)(c), (3)(a), and (4)(c) in this volume.

[410] Rules 82–7 (section 2) RPE ICTY/ICTR/SCSL, 100–4 RPE MICT, and 124–36 RPE KSC; see thereon Boas et al., *Procedure* (2011), pp. 278 ff.; in great detail, Vasiliev, in Sluiter et al., *International Criminal Procedure* (2013), pp. 569–600.

[411] Rules 84 RPE ICTY/ICTR, 100 RPE MICT, and 126 RPE KSC; cf. also Vasiliev, in Sluiter et al., *International Criminal Procedure* (2013), pp. 545–6; Heinze, in Wright, Levine, and Gold, *OxfHB Prosecutors* (2021), pp. 117, 122 ff.

[412] From a comparative perspective, Heinze, in Wright, Levine, and Gold, *OxfHB Prosecutors* (2021), pp. 117, 125 ff.

[413] Rules 85 (A) RPE ICTY/ICTR/SCSL, 102 (A) RPE MICT, and 127 (2)(d) RPE KSC; cf. also Combs, in Sluiter et al., *International Criminal Procedure* (2013), pp. 736 ff.

[414] Rules 85 (A) RPE ICTY/ICTR, 102 (A) RPE MICT, and 127 (2)(e) RPE KSC. The RPE SCSL do not provide for defence rejoinder.

[415] Rules 85 (B) RPE ICTY/ICTR/SCSL, 102 (B) RPE MICT, and 127 (3) RPE KSC. See also Combs, in Schabas and Bernaz, *Routledge Handbook ICL* (2011), pp. 323, 325 ff.; Schuon, *International Criminal Procedure* (2010), pp. 180 ff.; Vasiliev, in Sluiter et al., *International Criminal Procedure* (2013), pp. 586 ff.

[416] Arguably, the closing stage is more than the mere closing arguments/presentation, see Heinze, in Wright, Levine, and Gold, *OxfHB Prosecutors* (2021), pp. 117, 130 ff. At the ad hoc tribunals, for instance, where there was no order/decision on the conduct of the proceedings, the closing stage often started with a scheduling order by the TC; see e.g. *Prosecutor v. Prlic et al.*, TC, Dissenting Opinion of the Presiding Judge of the Chamber, Jean-Claude Antonetti, Concerning the Decision on the Prosecution's Motion to Re-open its Case, IT-04-74, 6 October 2010, p. 27. This shows the importance of the closing stage: in the *Ntaganda* trial, for instance, the Prosecutor's closing brief was 361 pages long and subject to a judicial dispute, see ICC, *Prosecutor v. Ntaganda*, TC VI, Decision on the Defence Request for an Extension of Time to File its Closing Brief, ICC-01/04-02/06-2291, 29 May 2018, and Gumpert and Nuzban, in Heinze and Dittrich, *ICC* (2021), pp. 553, 570.

[417] See note 471 and main text in this chapter. For the different stages of a trial from a comparative perspective, see Heinze, in Wright, Levine, and Gold, *OxfHB Prosecutors* (2021), pp. 117, 119–20.

the said order if necessary 'in the interest of justice';[418] also, it may order the production of additional evidence if deemed necessary.[419] As to the accused, it deserves to be mentioned that he is allowed to 'make a statement under the control of the Trial Chamber',[420] turning him, at least conceptually, from a mere object of the proceedings into an active participant as known from modern (reformed) inquisitorial systems.[421] The accused may also appear as a witness in his own defence,[422] which resembles the status of the accused in adversarial systems.[423] As opposed to the opening statement of the accused, his testimony as a witness will be of greater evidential value, as it is made under oath and subjected to cross-examination. We will return to this issue in the next chapter.[424] In 1998, the ICTY ascertained that a witness called upon by either party will become a so-called 'witness of truth' once sworn in, rather than a witness for that particular party.[425] Against this background, it is fair to say that the influence of the inquisitorial system has significantly increased, thereby abandoning the originally purely adversarial procedure of the ad hoc tribunals.[426]

The trial before the *ICC* starts by reading out to the accused the charges from the DCC, previously confirmed by the PTC; these charges, not the PTC's reasoning, are binding on the TC.[427] The reading of the charges may be determined by Directions on the Conduct of the Proceedings,[428] for example allowing for summarizing the charges if the accused waived the right to have them read out.[429] The Chamber shall then satisfy itself that the accused understands the nature of the charges and give him the opportunity to make an admission of guilt,[430] or to plead not guilty.[431] The prosecution or the defence may make an opening

[418] Rules 85 (A) RPE ICTY/ICTR/SCSL, 102 (A) RPE MICT. Rule 127 (2) RPE KSC allows for a different order if 'directed by the Panel'. On the meaning of 'the interest of justice' clause in Rule 115 (A) RPE ICTY, see *Kupreškić et al.*, IT-95-16-A, paras. 52 ff., 61 ff.

[419] Rules 85 (A)(v) and 98 RPE ICTY/ICTR, 85 (A)(iv) RPE SCSL, and 102 (A)(v), 120 RPE MICT and 132 RPE KSC. This is only a power, not a duty. See e.g. Kirsch, in Weigend, Walther, and Grunewald, *Strafverteidigung* (2008), p. 87; in a similar vein, Swart, *JICJ*, 6 (2008), 110, stressing the central importance of the presiding judge; see also Ambos and Bock, in Reydams, Wouters, and Ryngaert, *International Prosecutors* (2012), pp. 539, 541; Boas et al., *Procedure* (2011), pp. 278 ff.

[420] Rules 84*bis* RPE ICTY, 101 (A) RPE MICT, and 142 (1) RPE KSC.

[421] Orie, in Cassese et al., *Rome Statute II* (2002), p. 1468.

[422] cf. Rules 85 (C) RPE ICTY/ICTR/SCSL, 102 (C) RPE MICT, and 142 (4) RPE KSC; see also May and Wierda, *ColJTransnat'lL*, 37 (1999), 742; Terrier, in Cassese et al., *Rome Statute II* (2002), pp. 1307–8; Tochilovsky, *CLF*, 15 (2004), 336–7.

[423] cf. Kreß, in Fischer, Kreß, and Lüder, *Prosecution* (2001), pp. 321–2; Terrier, in Cassese et al., *Rome Statute II* (2002), p. 1308; Orie, in Cassese et al., *Rome Statute II* (2002), p. 1468. About the normative framework of the trial stage in more detail, see Heinze, in Wright, Levine, and Gold, *OxfHB Prosecutors* (2021), pp. 117, 119.

[424] Chapter V, A.(3)(a) in this volume.

[425] ICTY, *Prosecutor v. Kupreškić et al.*, TC, Decision on Communications between the Parties and Their Witnesses, IT-95-16, 21 September 1998, p. 3, consideration 3 (iii): 'a witness, either for the Prosecution or Defence, once he or she has taken the Solemn Declaration pursuant to Rule 90 (B) of the Rules of Procedure and Evidence, is a witness of truth before the Tribunal and, inasmuch as he or she is required to contribute to the establishment of the truth, not strictly a witness for either party.' See also Stahn, *Introduction ICL* (2019), pp. 318–19.

[426] cf. Bassiouni and Manikas, *Law of the ICTY* (1996), p. 955; Terrier, in Cassese et al., *Rome Statute II* (2002), pp. 1295–6; Orie, in Cassese et al., *Rome Statute II* (2002), p. 1492; similarly Bonomy, *JICJ*, 5 (2007), 348, 350–1, who points out several rules that allow for a 'judicial control'; also Kwon, *JICJ*, 5 (2007), 360 ff. ('internationalization'); stressing the mixed and pragmatic approach Friman, in Cryer et al., *ICL* (2019), pp. 427–8 ('mixed' but 'primarily adversarial in nature') and now Vasiliev, in Cryer et al., *ICL* (2019), p. 407 ('combine ... the best of two worlds'; '"procedural narcissism" gave way to a more pragmatic approach whereby the advantages of different systems could be recruited in the construction of a fair und effective international procedure by fusing their elements into a hybrid framework').

[427] ICC, *Practice Manual* (2023), para. 62 (the operative part of the decision); cf. also ICC-ASP, *Report Governance* (2015), p. 31 (para. 16).

[428] *Ongwen*, ICC-02/04-01/15-2022-Red, para. 182.

[429] Ibid., para. 183.

[430] cf. Art. 65 ICCS; on this procedure, see Section B.(9)(b)(ii) in this chapter.

[431] cf. Art. 64 (8)(a) ICCS; also Safferling, *Criminal Procedure* (2012), p. 443.

statement, although this is not explicitly provided for in the ICCS or the RPE ICC.[432] Then the presentation of evidence starts,[433] to be looked at in more detail in the next chapter.[434]

The TC takes up a predominant role in the ICC's procedural system.[435] The Chamber's functions include: carrying out the proceedings,[436] ordering the production of evidence,[437] adopting various protocols,[438] and deciding on 'any other relevant matters',[439] including issuing a series of different orders at a status conference.[440] The trial is generally directed by the presiding judge;[441] only if he refuses to give any directions, the prosecution and defence may strike an agreement about the modalities of submitting evidence.[442] This flexible approach of the law makes clear that those modalities may vary from Chamber to Chamber, and from case to case.[443]

The dominant position of the Chamber and the presiding judge led to significant frictions between civil law and common law lawyers whilst negotiating the procedural rules in Rome and thereafter.[444] Observers described it as a 'clash of cultures',[445] with civil law negotiators arguing in favour of a powerful judge to lead the proceedings and their common

[432] Vasiliev, in Sluiter et al., *International Criminal Procedure* (2013), p. 550; cf. also ICC, *Prosecutor v. Lubanga*, TC I, Decision on Opening and Closing Statement, ICC-01/04-01/06-1346, 22 May 2008, paras. 14–16.

[433] Vasiliev, in Sluiter et al., *International Criminal Procedure* (2013), p. 563; Boas et al., *Procedure* (2011), pp. 278 ff.; Safferling, *Criminal Procedure* (2012), pp. 448 ff. On the law of evidence, see Chapter V, A. in this volume.

[434] Chapter V, A.(1)(c) and (3)(a) in this volume.

[435] cf. also Ambos, *ZIS*, 7 (2012), 317; Trüg, *ZStW*, 125 (2013), 48; Friman, in Stahn, *Practice* (2015), pp. 926–30; for further information on the role of the Prosecutor at trials before international and hybrid tribunals, see Vasiliev, in Reydams, Wouters, and Ryngaert, *International Prosecutors* (2012), pp. 700 ff.; Heinze and Fyfe, in Bergsmo and Stahn, *Preliminary Examination II* (2018), pp. 27 ff.; Pues, *Prosecutorial Discretion* (2020), pp. 30 ff.

[436] Arts. 64 (6)(a) and 61 (11) ICCS.

[437] Art. 64 (6)(b) and (d) ICCS. As to Art. 64 (6)(b), see ICC, *Prosecutor v. Ruto and Sang*, AC, Judgment on the Appeals of William Samoei Ruto and Mr Joshua Arap Sang against the Decision of Trial Chamber V (A) of 17 April 2014 Entitled 'Decision on Prosecutor's Application for Witness Summonses and resulting Request for State Party Cooperation', ICC-01/09-01/11-1598, 9 October 2014, paras. 1, 106–8, holding that the TC has 'the power to compel witnesses to appear before it, thereby creating a legal obligation for the individuals concerned' (para. 1), thereby confirming the TC's view (paras. 36–8).

[438] ICC, *Practice Manual* (2023), paras. 78 ff.

[439] Art. 64 (6)(f) ICCS; crit. Byrne, *LJIL*, 26 (2013), 996 ff.

[440] cf. Rule 132 RPE ICC and Reg. 54 RegC. See generally Report of the International Criminal Court, 1 August 2005 (UN GA, A/60/177), para. 25; Safferling, *Criminal Procedure* (2012), p. 255; Kuczyńska, *Accusation Model ICC* (2015), pp. 332–3; Bitti, 'Article 64', in Ambos, *Commentary* (2022), mn. 21 ff., 42 ff.

[441] Art. 64 (8)(b) ICCS. Generally, on the role of the judges in the ICC procedures, see Wharton, in deGuzman and Oosterveld, *Elgar Companion ICC* (2020), pp. 204 ff.; Powderly, *Judges* (2020), pp. 277 ff.; Christensen, *JICJ*, 17 (2019), 537 ff.; De Smet, in Stahn and Sluiter, *Practice* (2009), pp. 418 ff.; Bock, *Opfer* (2010), pp. 346 ff.; Mégret, *UCLA JIL & ForAff*, 14 (2009), 69.

[442] Rule 140 (1) RPE ICC. For a detailed analysis of first ICC practice, see Vasiliev, in Sluiter et al., *International Criminal Procedure* (2013), pp. 601–7; see also Safferling, *Criminal Procedure* (2012), p. 443; Jackson and M'Boge, *LJIL*, 26 (2013), 955–6.

[443] ICC, *Prosecutor v. Katanga and Ngudjolo* TC II, Corrigendum Directions for the Conduct of the Proceedings and Testimony in Accordance with Rule 140, Annex, ICC-01/04-01/07-1665-Corr, 1 December 2009; *Ruto and Sang*, ICC-01/09-01/11-847-Corr; Friman, in Stahn, *Practice* (2015), pp. 929–30 (stressing the uncertainty and delays such a practice causes and calling for further standardized trial proceedings); on the 'discernible difference in the roles of the judges and lawyers' at the ICTR, see Byrne, *LJIL*, 26 (2013), 996–7, 1001 ff.

[444] The TC of the ECCC proves to be even more dominant. It is in charge of conducting the hearing (Internal Rule 90 (1)), including the hearing of evidence which becomes especially pertinent in the (inquisitorial) way the interrogation is conducted; cf. ECCC, *Prosecutor v. Kaing Guek Eav*, TC, Direction on the Scheduling of the Trial, 001/18-07-2007-ECCC/TC, 20 March 2009; see also Gibson and Rudy, *JICJ*, 7 (2009), 1010; on the '"inquisitorial" by nature' scheme of presentation of evidence before the ECCC, see also Vasiliev, in Sluiter et al., *International Criminal Procedure* (2013), pp. 624–9, 631 ff., 647–9.

[445] cf. Gallmetzer, in Guariglia et al., *AC ICC Commentary* (2018), p. 309; Lewis, in Lee, *ICC* (2001), pp. 547 ff.; Fernández de Gurmendi, in Lee, *ICC* (2001), p. 252; Kreß, in Fischer, Kreß and Lüder, *Prosecution* (2001), p. 352; Kuczyńska, *Accusation Model ICC* (2015), p. 349. On the ICTY, see Tochilovsky, *CLF*, 15 (2004), 332 ff.; Eser, in Müller-Dietz et al., *FS Jung* (2007), pp. 167 ff.

law counterparts preferring a neutral judge, who would leave the general procedural questions to the parties and not interfere with their cross-examination of the witnesses.[446] The compromise that was finally reached can be found in Rule 140 (2) RPE ICC, which states that the Prosecutor and the defence may question a witness without any interference by the Chamber, which, in turn, may only interrogate the witness itself either prior to or after the interrogation by the parties.[447] The possibility of cross-examination is thus explicitly recognized, but whether and how this possibility is used is ultimately left to the judges. Once the evidentiary phase is closed,[448] the presiding judge shall invite the Prosecutor and the defence to make their closing statements.[449] Witnesses at the ICC are called 'witnesses of the Court',[450] yet, this does not turn the adversarial structure of the ICC process into an inquisitorial one, as rightly observed by Judge Schmitt in *Yekatom and Ngaïssona*:

> [I]f we look at the structure of the proceedings at the ICC, we have a party-driven process: Prosecution, Defence, Victims present their evidence. They call witnesses. They are not their witnesses, they are witnesses of the Court indeed, but they are called the witnesses. So we follow in principle sort of a common law procedure in that regard.[451]

The defence always has the opportunity to speak last,[452] but the parties may seek 'a right to reply and rejoinder, subject to the Trial Chamber's discretion'.[453] Victims may deliver closing statements through their legal representatives pursuant to Rule 89 (1) RPE ICC and when so authorized by the Chamber,[454] but after the prosecution and before the

[446] Bohlander, *LJIL*, *24* (2011), 395. Of course, the rather active or passive role of the judge also varies among common law jurisdictions; while English judges are usually more active, their US colleagues are more passive, see thereon Heinze, in Bergsmo et al., *Power* (2020), pp. 155, 167, 202 ff.; Stahn, *Introduction ICL* (2019), pp. 295 ff.; van Kessel, *NotreDameLR*, 67 (1991–1992), 429, 433, 434, 481; Spencer, in Delmas-Marty and Spencer, *European Criminal Procedures* (2002), p. 26.

[447] On this Rule in more detail, Chapter V, A.(3)(c) in this volume. In favour of a more active role of the TC, Stahn, *Introduction ICL* (2019), p. 297; Gallmetzer, in Stahn and Sluiter, *Practice* (2009), pp. 506–7; Bock, *Opfer* (2010), pp. 348–9; Heinze, *Disclosure* (2014), pp. 499 ff.; Friman, in Stahn, *Practice* (2015), pp. 928–9. About 'judge-led trials' at the ICC, Fairlie, *JICJ*, 16 (2018), 295 ff. About managerialism as a narrative, Clements, *LJIL*, 32 (2019), 149 ff.

[448] Rule 141 (1) RPE ICC.

[449] Rule 142 (2) RPE ICC. At the ad hoc tribunals it is called 'closing arguments', cf. Rules 86 RPE ICTY/ICTR/SCSL, 103 RPE MICT; see thereon Vasiliev, in Sluiter et al., *International Criminal Procedure* (2013), pp. 658–60.

[450] cf. ICC, *Prosecutor v. Lubanga*, PTC I, Decision on the Practices of Witness Familiarisation and Witness Proofing, ICC-01/04-01/06-679, 8 November 2006, para. 26 and *Prosecutor v. Lubanga*, TC I, Decision Regarding the Practices Used to Prepare and Familiarise Witnesses for Giving Testimony at Trial Decision, ICC-01/04-01/06-1049, 30 November 2007, paras. 33–4; see also *Katanga and Ngudjolo*, ICC-01/04-01/07-428-Corr, para. 30; *Prosecutor v. Muthaura et al.*, PTC II, Decision on Variation of Summons Conditions, ICC-01/09-02/11-38, 4 April 2011, para. 10; *Prosecutor v. Ruto et al.*, Corrigendum of the 'Decision Establishing Modalities to be Observed When Complying with Summons Conditions', ICC-01/09-01/11-38-Corr, 6 April 2011, para. 9. See also Farthofer, in Heinze and Dittrich, *ICC* (2021), pp. 525, 536. On adversarial elements at the ICC, cf. also Vasiliev, in Cryer et al., *ICL* (2019), pp. 410 ff. On witnesses of the prosecution and the defence, see Tochilovsky, *CLF*, 15 (2004), 329 ff. With regard to disclosure obligations, see Chapter V, B.(2)(a) *in fine*.

[451] ICC, *Prosecutor v. Yekatom and Ngaïssona*, Hearing Transcript, ICC-01/14-01/18-T-014-ENG, 16 February 2021, pp. 20–1.

[452] Rule 141 (2) 2nd sentence RPE ICC. See also ICC, *Prosecutor v. Katanga and Ngudjolo* TC II, Ordonnance relative aux modalités de présentation des conclusions orales, ICC-01/04-01/07-3274, 20 April 2012, para. 10 (oral declaration under Art. 67 (1)(h) as 'last word').

[453] ICC, *Prosecutor v. Katanga and Ngudjolo,* TC II, Order on the Arrangement for the Filing of the Written and Oral Closing Statements (Regulation 54 of the Regulations of the Court), ICC-01/04-01/07-3218-tENG, 15 December 2011, para. 14; *Katanga and Ngudjolo*, ICC-01/04-01/07-3274, para. 9.

[454] See Chapter II, E.(4)(d) in this volume; also Vasiliev, in Sluiter et al., *International Criminal Procedure* (2013), pp. 661–2.

defence/accused.[455] TCs have streamlined the closing stage by ordering final trial briefs and issuing directions regarding length and content of the briefs and the oral statements.[456]

After the closing statements[457] the TC shall retire to deliberate.[458] If the accused is found guilty, it shall determine the appropriate sentence at the same hearing.[459] However, Article 76 (2) ICCS provides that, except from cases of admission of guilt,[460] the TC *may* hold—on its own motion—or *shall* hold—at the request of the Prosecutor or the accused—a separate sentencing hearing, to hear any additional evidence or submissions relevant to the sentence. The Statute provides for both procedures leaving the choice to the Chambers and the participants:[461] the bifurcated procedure followed by the SCSL,[462] and the unified one followed by the ad hoc tribunals[463] and the KSC,[464] whose judgments contain both the decision on guilt or innocence and the sentence.[465] Although a separate sentencing hearing entails a prolongation of the proceedings,[466] it has been the preferred option at the ICC.[467] Yet, the right to a separate sentencing hearing is eliminated, pursuant to (provisional) Rule 165 (2) cl. 1 RPE ICC,[468] for Article 70 proceedings.[469]

455 *Katanga and Ngudjolo*, ICC-01/04-01/07-1665-Corr, para. 2; ICC, *Prosecutor v. Katanga and Ngudjolo*, TC II, Decision on the Modalities of Victim Participation at Trial, ICC-01/04-01/07-1788-tENG, 22 January 2010, para. 68; ICC, *Prosecutor v. Lubanga*, TC I, Order on the Timetable for Closing Submissions, ICC-01/04-01/06-2722, 12 April 2011, para. 7. The order is thus prosecution, victims, and defence/accused. See also Vasiliev, in Sluiter et al., *International Criminal Procedure* (2013), pp. 680–2 (suggesting respective principles and rules).

456 cf. Reg. 54 (a) RegC; in more detail, see Vasiliev, in Sluiter et al., *International Criminal Procedure* (2013), pp. 662–4, 680–1 (suggesting respective principles and rules).

457 On the (exceptional) re-opening of the trial hearing after the closing statements, see ICC, *Prosecutor v. Katanga*, AC, Judgment on the Appeal of Mr Germain Katanga against the Decision of Trial Chamber II of 21 November 2012 Entitled 'Decision on the implementation of regulation 55 of the Regulations of the Court and severing the charges against the accused persons', Dissenting Opinion of Judge Cuno Tarfusser, ICC-01/04-01/07-3363, 27 March 2013, para. 17.

458 More on that below in Section A.(4)(i).

459 Art. 76 (1) ICCS.

460 Art. 65 ICCS.

461 In the cases so far that resulted in a conviction, separate sentencing hearings were held, cf. ICC, *Prosecutor v. Lubanga*, TC I, Decision on Sentence pursuant to Art. 76 of the Statute, ICC-01/04-01/06-2901, 20 July 2012; *Prosecutor v. Katanga*, TC II, Decision on Sentence pursuant to Art. 76 of the Statute, ICC-01/04-01/07-484, 23 May 2014; *Prosecutor v. Bemba*, Transcript, ICC-01/05-01/08-T-368-ENG ET WT 16-05-2016 1/116 SZ T, 16 May 2016; *Prosecutor v. Bemba et al.*, Hearing Transcript, ICC-01/05-01/13-T-59-ENG, 4 July 2018; *Prosecutor v. Ntaganda*, Hearing Transcript, ICC-01/04-02/06-T-269-ENG, 7 November 2019; *Prosecutor v. Ongwen*, Order Providing Further Details on the Schedule of the Hearing on Sentence, ICC-02/04-01/15-1802, 23 March 2021; *Prosecutor v. Ongwen*, Hearing Transcript, ICC-02/04-01/15-T-260-ENG, 14 April 2021. No separate sentencing hearing in ICC, *Prosecutor v. Al Mahdi*, Judgment and Sentence ICC-01/12-01/15-171, 27 September 2016.

462 Rule 100 RPE SCSL. See also STL, *Prosecutor v. Ayyash et al.*, Order Scheduling Hearing on Sentencing, Tuesday 10 November 2020, STL-11-01/S/TC, F3851, 30 October 2020.

463 Rules 87 (C) RPE ICTY/ICTR, 104 (C) RPE MICT; on the distinction between bifurcated and single trials, cf. also Acquaviva, in Sluiter et al., *International Criminal Procedure* (2013), p. 534.

464 Rule 162 (1), (4) RPE KSC. In the first three Trial Judgments (*Gucati & Haradinaj*, *Mustafa* and *Shala*) the respective TP did not opt ('Unless otherwise decided') for a separate sentencing hearing; cf. <https://www.scp-ks.org/en/cases/hysni-gucati-nasim-haradinaj/en>, <https://www.scp-ks.org/en/cases/salih-mustafa/en> and <https://www.scp-ks.org/en/cases/pjeter-shala>.

465 In favour of a separate sentencing hearing due to reasons of coherency and protection of the right against self-incrimination, Boas et al., *Procedure* (2011), pp. 290–1; in the same vein, Safferling, *Criminal Procedure* (2012), p. 462; similarly, esp. emphasizing the importance of the sentence for the broader public, Harmon and Gaynor, *JICJ*, 5 (2007), 707 ff.; cf. also Acquaviva, in Sluiter et al., *International Criminal Procedure* (2013), pp. 535 ff.

466 Gumpert and Nuzban, in Heinze and Dittrich, *ICC* (2021), pp. 553, 581.

467 cf. Schabas, *ICC Commentary* (2016), p. 1147 ('Holding a distinct sentencing hearing is presented as an option, but given that it is mandatory upon the request of either the Prosecutor or the convicted person, it seems likely that there will be a separate sentencing hearing in virtually all cases'); Marchuk and Wanigasuriya, 'Article 76', in Klamberg, *Commentary ICC II* (2023), pp. 500–4.

468 'Articles 39(2)(b), 53, 57(2), 59, 76(2) and 82(1)(d), and any rules thereunder, shall not apply.'

469 ICC, *Prosecutor v. Gicheru*, Judgment on the Appeal of the Office of Public Counsel for the Defence against the Decision of Pre-Trial Chamber A of 10 December 2020 Entitled 'Decision on the Applicability of Provisional

### (b) *Presence of the accused and joinder/severance*

The above-mentioned opening procedure before an ICC TC, especially the accused's possibility of admitting his guilt, presupposes his *presence*.[470] However, the case law has flexibilized the presence requirement during the Kenya proceedings in light of the conflicting, extraordinary obligations of two of the accused, namely President Kenyatta and Deputy President Ruto.[471] The ASP has reacted to this situation by introducing the new Rules 134*bis*, *ter*, and *quarter* RPE ICC.[472] This move has been criticized as political interference.[473] The new Rules provide for exceptions from the presence requirement in three different constellations with increasing absence and decreasing requirements at the accused's request: presence through the use of video technology on a case-by-case basis,[474] excusal from presence under exceptional, strict circumstances and with limited absence,[475] and excusal from presence due to extraordinary public duties 'at the highest national level' (*lex Kenyatta*').[476] Trial Chambers have subsequently reaffirmed the presence requirement,[477] but Judge Tarfusser criticized the narrow reading of Article 63, 'virtually transforming it into a sort of "arrest" for any accused not detained or not having his permanent residence in The Hague'; a broader interpretation 'would have made' Rules 134*ter* and 134*quarter* RPE ICC

Rule 165 of the Rules of Procedure and Evidence', ICC-01/09-01/20-107, 8 March 2021, para. 102. On Rule 165 ICC RPE and its history, see already Ambos, *Treatise ICL II* (2022), pp. 281–2.

470 See also Art. 63 (1) ICCS.

471 cf. ICC, *Prosecutor v. Ruto and Sang*, TC V(a), Decision on Mr Ruto's Request for Excusal from Continuous Presence at Trial, ICC-01/09-01/11-777, 18 June 2013, p. 52, and ICC, *Prosecutor v. Kenyatta*, TC V(b), Decision on Defence Request for Conditional Excusal from Continuous Presence at Trial, ICC-01/09-02/11-830, 18 October 2013, p. 54, by which the excusal requests were granted with the exception of the sessions listed in the decisions, and under the condition that the absence of the accused must always 'be seen to be directed towards performance of [the accused's] duties of state'. The excusal of the accused from presence during trial was further limited by the AC, setting out concrete criteria; cf. ICC, *Prosecutor v. Ruto and Sang*, AC, Judgment on the Appeal of the Prosecutor against the Decision of Trial Chamber V(a) of 18 June 2013, ICC-01/09-01/11-1066, 25 October 2013, para. 62; referring to this judgment and applying its criteria, ICC, *Prosecutor v. Kenyatta*, TC V(b), Decision on the Prosecution's Motion for Reconsideration of the Decision Excusing Mr Kenyatta from Continuous Presence at Trial, ICC-01/09-02/11-863, 26 November 2013, para. 16. See generally Schabas and Caruana, 'Article 63', in Ambos, *Commentary* (2022), mn. 12 ff.; Heinze, 'Commentary', in Klip and Freeland, *ALC LXI* (2020), pp. 426–7.

472 Res. ICC-ASP/12/Res. 7, 12th plenary meeting, 27 November 2013. See, in more detail, Wheeler, *JICJ*, 17 (2019), 413, 418.

473 See McDermott, *JICJ*, 15 (2017), 873, 881 ('politicization of Rule amendments); FIDH, 'Justice at Risk—States Parties to the ICC Statute Concede to Political Pressure', 28 November 2013, <http://www.fidh.org/en/international-justice/international-criminal-court-icc/14308 justice at-risk-states-parties-to-the-icc-statute-concede-to-political>; crit. also Heller, *Opinio Juris* (28 November 2013); in favour, Karnavas, *ICL Blog* (12 December 2013); also Zakerhossein and de Brouwer, *CLF*, 26 (2015), 213–22.

474 Rule 134*bis* RPE ICC.

475 Rule 134*ter* RPE ICC.

476 Rule 134*quater*. This Rule has been modelled after *Ruto and Sang*, ICC-01/09-01/11-1066, para. 62. Immediately after the adoption of the new Rules, Ruto and Kenyatta invoked Rule 134*quater*: ICC, *Prosecutor v. Ruto and Sang*, TC V(a), Defence Request pursuant to Article 63 (1) of the Rome Statute and Rule 134quater of the Rules of Procedure and Evidence to Excuse Mr William Samoei Ruto from Attendance at Trial, ICC-01/09-01/11-1124, 16 December 2013; ICC, *Prosecutor v. Kenyatta*, TC V(b), Defence Request pursuant to Article 63 (1) of the Statute and Rule 134quater of the Rules of Procedure and Evidence to Excuse Uhuru Muigai Kenyatta from Continuous Attendance at Trial, ICC-01/09-02/11-882, 15 January 2014. However, shortly afterwards Kenyatta withdrew his request; ICC, *Prosecutor v. Kenyatta*, TC V(b), Defence Withdrawal of its Request, ICC-01/09-02/11-888, 27 January 2014.

477 ICC, *Prosecutor v. Gbagbo and Blé Goudé*, TC I, Decision on Mr Gbagbo's Detention, ICC-02/11-01/15-846, 10 March 2017, para. 22; *Prosecutor v. Gbagbo and Blé Goudé*, TC I, Public Redacted Version of the Decision on Mr Gbagbo's Detention, ICC-02/11-01/15-1038-Red, 25 September 2017, para. 72; see also *Prosecutor v. Ntaganda*, TC VI, Transcript, ICC-01/04-02/06-T-126-ENG, 8 September 2016, p. 10, ll. 10–11.

'superfluous'.[478] Also, in 2020, the Appeals Chamber considered that the Court may proceed *in absentia* against defendants who have been released from custody and subsequently fail to show up for the trial.[479] Yet, this view has not been confirmed by subsequent case law. At any rate, these Rules have been a necessary response to a practical problem. The issue of the accused's presence during delivery of the judgment has not been addressed yet.

If there are *several accused*,[480] the TC may order that charges be joined and thus a single trial will take place.[481] A combined reading of Article 64 (5) ICCS and Rule 136 (1) RPE ICCS[482] makes clear that the ICC system starts from a presumption of a joined trial.[483] Indeed, this has been the interpretation of PTC I in perhaps the most prominent case so far (*Katanga and Ngudjolo*),[484] where the charges have first been joined at the pre-trial stage[485] but later, at the trial stage, been severed (again).[486] Apart from the radical u-turn of the Court in one and the same case, what matter here are the reasons given for the different decisions. While Article 64 (5) ICCS as the only statutory provision grants the TC—in line with ad hoc tribunals' practice[487]—a broad discretion[488] (it 'may, as appropriate') but does not express any preference as to joinder or severance, Rule 136 as the only relevant Rule does so, establishing the said presumption. In the PTC's view, relying on the ICTY and ICTR case law, joint proceedings are in line with the 'object and purpose of the Statute and the Rules', since they enhance 'the fairness as well as the judicial economy of the proceedings' (avoiding witnesses having to testify more than once and thus reducing expenses, avoiding duplication of evidence, avoiding inconsistency in the presentation of the evidence, and therefore affording equal treatment to the persons prosecuted) and minimize 'the potential impact on witnesses' and 'better facilitate the protection of the witnesses' physical and mental well-being'.[489] The AC confirmed the PTC's interpretation[490]

[478] ICC, *Prosecutor v. Gbagbo and Blé Goudé*, Dissenting Opinion of Judge Cuno Tarfusser, ICC-02/11-01/15-846-Anx, 10 March 2017, para. 23. See also Schabas and Caruana, 'Article 63', in Ambos, *Commentary* (2022), mn. 25.

[479] ICC, *Prosecutor v. Gbagbo and Blé Goudé*, AC, Decision on Counsel for Mr Gbagbo's Request for Reconsideration of the 'Judgment on the Prosecutor's appeal against the oral decision of Trial Chamber I pursuant to article 81(3)(c)(i) of the Statute' and on the Review of the Conditions on the Release of Mr Gbagbo and Blé Goudé, 28 May 2020, ICC-02/11-01/15-1355-Red, para. 68 ff. For a crit. discussion, see Wheeler, *EJIL: Talk!*, 3 July 2020 (position 'lacks sufficient legal support').

[480] Of course, against one accused charges should and will usually be joined unless this would entail a too complex and long procedure (the proceedings against former Serb president Milošević, are the prime example; see thereon recently Uertz-Retzlaff, *ZIS*, 10 (2015), 533–4).

[481] Art. 64 (5) alternative 1 ICCS.

[482] 'Persons accused jointly shall be tried together.'

[483] In the same vein, Linton, in Sluiter et al., *International Criminal Procedure* (2013), p. 519; Bitti, 'Article 64', in Ambos, *Commentary* (2022), mn. 39.

[484] Conc. ICC, *Prosecutor v. Yekatom and Ngaïssona*, PTC II, Decision on the Joinder of the Cases against Alfred Yekatom and Patrice-Edouard Ngaïssona and Other Related Matters, ICC-01/14-01/18-121, 20 February 2019, para. 9.

[485] ICC, *Prosecutor v. Katanga and Ngudjolo*, PTC I, Decision on the Joinder of the Cases against Germain Katanga and Mathieu Ngudjolo Chui, ICC-01/04-01/07-257, 10 March 2008, pp. 7, 9.

[486] ICC, *Prosecutor v. Katanga and Ngudjolo*,TC II, Decision on the Implementation of Regulation 55 of the Regulation of the Court and Severing the Charges against the Accused Persons, ICC-01/04-01/07-3319-tENG/FRA, 21 November 2012.

[487] See generally Rules 2, 48, 49, 82 RPE ICTY/SCSL, Rules 2, 48, 48*bis*, 49, 82 RPE ICTR, and 49, 97 RPE MICT; in detail, see Boas et al., *Procedure* (2011), pp. 197–8, 200–7; Linton, in Sluiter et al., *International Criminal Procedure* (2013), pp. 493–518. Interestingly, the IMT and IMTFE did not have any rules in this regard (cf. Linton, in Sluiter et al., *International Criminal Procedure* (2013), pp. 492–3), although they have conducted the paradigmatic trials against multiple accused for system crimes.

[488] In the same vein, Linton, in Sluiter et al., *International Criminal Procedure* (2013), pp. 495, 515, 518, 522, 533, finding that this discretion has not led to arbitrary decision but that there is consistency in the case law. On our understanding of the concept of discretion, see Section B.(3)(a).

[489] *Katanga and Ngudjolo*, ICC-01/04-01/07-257, p. 8.

[490] ICC, *Prosecutor v. Katanga and Ngudjolo*, AC, Judgment on the Appeal against the Decision on the Joinder Rendered on 10 March 2008 by the Pre-Trial Chamber in the Germain Katanga and Mathieu Ngudjolo Chui Cases, ICC-01/04-01/07-573, 9 June 2008, para. 7 ('joinder of more than one person ... is the norm').

and explained that joinder 'tallies with the object of the Statute being, in this regard, the assurance of the efficacy of the criminal process, and promotes its purpose that proceedings should be held expeditiously'.[491] In contrast, the TC, ordering the severance of the proceedings, invoked one of the three exceptions[492] to the said presumption, namely the 'serious prejudice to the accused' that a joint trial—here its continuation—would entail.[493] In the same vein, PTC II accords 'broad discretion' to a Chamber 'to join or sever charges against more than one person'.[494]

Taking together these considerations it follows that the decision for or against joinder depends on the impact that this decision has on the expediency and fairness of the proceedings.[495] These general considerations are also captured by the second exception mentioned in Rule 136 (1) RPE ICC, that is, the 'interests of justice', a highly normative concept already known from a different context[496] and also relevant in the previous ICTY/ICTR/SCSL practice on joinder and severance.[497] Fairness considerations are, on the other hand, explicitly repeated in Rule 136 (2) RPE ICC, providing, again in line with the previous practice of the ad hoc tribunals,[498] that the accused 'shall be accorded the same rights' either tried jointly or separately. The previous practice also provides the substantive criterion for any joinder, namely the 'same transaction' test according to which the crimes object of the joinder must have been committed 'in the course of the same transaction',[499] meaning 'a number of acts or omissions whether occurring as one event or a number of events, at the same or different locations and being part of a common scheme, strategy or plan'.[500] In sum, a joinder is 'appropriate' within the meaning of Article 64 (5) ICCS, leaving a broad discretion to Chambers, if it serves the judicial economy and fairness and the respective conduct is based on the same transaction. Along these lines, PTC II decided to join the cases against *Yekatom* and *Ngaïssona* after noting 'that the contextual elements of the alleged crimes against humanity and war crimes in both cases are virtually indistinguishable in that they constitute the same widespread and systematic attack against the civilian population [ ... ] and the same armed conflict not of an international character [ ... ]'.[501] As a result, the PTC created a joint case record.[502]

491 *Katanga and Ngudjolo*, ICC-01/04-01/07-573, para. 8.

492 cf. Rule 136 (1) RPE ICC: 'unless the Trial Chamber ... orders that separate trials are necessary in order to avoid serious prejudice to the accused, to protect the interests of justice or because a person jointly accused has made an admission of guilt'.

493 *Katanga and Ngudjolo*, ICC-01/04-01/07-3319-tENG/FRA, para. 61, arguing that the application of Reg. 55 RegC, to be discussed in detail below (Section B.(7)(b) in this chapter), would prolong the proceedings and thus be prejudicial to Ngudjolo Chui.

494 *Yekatom and Ngaïssona*, ICC-01/14-01/18-121, para. 10 (referring to Art. 64 (5) ICCS and Rule 136 RPE ICC).

495 cf. Art. 64 (2) ICCS and the respective reference to 'the dual requirement of fairness and expeditiousness established by article 64 of the Statute', in *Katanga and Ngudjolo*, ICC-01/04-01/07-3319-tENG/FRA, para. 62.

496 cf. Art. 53 (1)(c) and (2)(c) ICCS, see, in detail, Section B.(4) in this chapter.

497 cf. Linton, in Sluiter et al., *International Criminal Procedure* (2013), pp. 502–4, 505–6, 511, 513–15.

498 cf. Rule 82 (A) RPE ICTY/ICTR/SCSL, Rule 96 (A) RPE MICT.

499 cf. Rules 48, 49 RPE ICTY/ICTR/SCSL, Rule 48*bis* RPE ICTR, Rule 49 RPE MICT.

500 cf. Rule 2 RPE ICTY/ICTR/SCSL and Rule 49 (C) RPE MICT; for analysis of the case law, see Linton, in Sluiter et al., *International Criminal Procedure* (2013), pp. 495–8, 508–10, 516–17. The same transaction test can already be found in *Katanga and Ngudjolo*, ICC-01/04-01/07-257, pp. 3–4 when the PTC refers to the suspects' 'joint participation in the same attack'.

501 *Yekatom and Ngaïssona*, ICC-01/14-01/18-121, para. 11.

502 Ibid., para. 19.

## (4) Judgment

### *(a) General remarks*

For the (final) judgment[503] to be valid, all judges of the respective Chamber have to be physically and mentally *present*[504] throughout all stages of the trial,[505] that is, from the moment the evidentiary hearings begin[506] until the deliberations.[507] Otherwise, a Chamber would not be able to base its decision 'on its evaluation of the evidence'.[508] Indeed, it is a consequence of the principles of *orality, immediacy, and publicity*[509] that a TC shall base its decision on a free evaluation of the evidence, discussed before it in an oral and immediate form during the trial.[510] It is therefore reason for concern that a trial before the ad hoc tribunals may continue for up to five working days even in the absence of a judge, when it is in the interests of justice;[511] a similar ICC rule was proposed by the judges in 2014 but has never been considered by the ASP.[512] The IER brought the issue back to the agenda supporting a temporary, exceptional excusal of a judge to be authorized by the respective Chamber pursuant to Article 64 (3)(a) ICCS[513] and making a relevant recommendation.[514] At any event,

[503] cf. Arts. 23 ICTYS, 22 ICTRS, 18 SCSLS, and 74 ICCS. Generally, on judgment, see Tochilovsky, *Jurisprudence* (2014), pp. 1017 ff.; Kreß, in Grützner, Pötz, and Kreß, *Internationaler Rechtshilfeverkehr in Strafsachen* (2003), Part IV A 1, mn. 168 ff.; Bernaz, in Schabas and Bernaz, *Routledge Handbook ICL* (2011), pp. 289 ff.; Öberg, *CLF*, 24 (2013), 113 ff.; Triffterer and Kiss, 'Article 74', in Ambos, *Commentary* (2022), mn. 1 ff. (historical overview) and 9 ff. (general remarks).

[504] On presence through video technology, see Triffterer and Kiss, 'Article 74', in Ambos, *Commentary* (2022), mn. 17.

[505] Art. 74 (1) ICCS; cf. also Boas et al., *Procedure* (2011), pp. 259–62; Jørgensen and Zahar, in Sluiter et al., *International Criminal Procedure* (2013), p. 1170.

[506] Triffterer and Kiss, 'Article 74', in Ambos, *Commentary* (2022), mn. 13.

[507] The deliberations are, despite the apparent distinction in Art. 74 (1) ICCS, part of the trial, cf. *Bemba*, ICC-01/05-01/08-3249-Red, paras. 25–6, 37–8, 41.

[508] Art. 74 (2) cl. 1 ICCS.

[509] See also Safferling, *Criminal Procedure* (2012), p. 522.

[510] Olásolo, *CPI* (2003), p. 124. Generally, on the 'free proof principle', see Damaška, *Evidence Law* (1997), pp. 20 ff.; Damaška, *AJCompL*, 43 (1995), 343 ff.; Heinze, in Caeiro et al., *Elgar Encyclopedia* (2023); Schauer, in Dahlman et al., *Evidence Law* (2021), p. 69; on the highly demanding task of evaluation of evidence at international criminal trials, due to their complexity, see Öberg, *CLF*, 24 (2013), 115 ff.; Sorvatzioti, *ICLR*, 22 (2022), 895 ff.

[511] cf. Rule 15*bis* (A) RPE ICTY/ICTR; Rule 16 (A) RPE SCSL and Rule 19 (A) RPE MICT; crit. Fairlie, *VanderbiltJTL*, 48 (2015), 92 ff.; see also Jørgensen and Zahar, in Sluiter et al., *International Criminal Procedure* (2013), p. 1163. On how the ICC TCs dealt with physically absent judges, see Triffterer and Kiss, 'Article 74', in Ambos, *Commentary* (2022), mn. 14–16. The KSC legal framework does not allow for such a temporary absence, cf. Rule 19 RPE KSC, esp. paras. 1, 5.

[512] The ICC's Working Group on Amendments discussed this proposal of a new Rule 140*bis* on the temporary absence of a judge at its meeting on 5 November 2014. According to the proposed Rule 'where a Trial Chamber judge is absent for illness or other unforeseen and urgent personal reasons, the remaining judges of the Chamber may continue hearing the case to complete a specific matter, provided that such continuation is in the interests of justice and the parties consent', see ICC-ASP, *Report of the Working Group on Amendments*, ICC-ASP/13/31 (7 December 2014), para. 19. However, the Working Group stopped short of making a recommendation to the ASP, because 'some delegations had still some concerns and/or needed further clarification' (para. 17). See also Schabas, *ICC Commentary* (2016), p. 1132; crit. Fernández de Gurmendi, *JICJ*, 16 (2018), 341, 349; McDermott, *JICJ*, 15 (2017), 873, 883.

[513] Expert Group, *IER* (2020), pp. 182–3.

[514] Ibid., p. 189 with R206: 'The ASP and/or the Judges should make provision … for proceedings to continue in the absence of one Judge for illness or other urgent personal reasons for such period as they consider appropriate on the basis that the remaining Judges are satisfied that to do so will have no adverse impact on the fairness of the trial.'

to avoid any delays or other undesired procedural consequence, the Presidency could use the possibility to appoint alternate[515] or reserve[516] judges—as regularly done at the KSC[517] and surely the better solution than to continue a hearing without the full bench.[518]

The Chamber is bound by the 'facts and circumstances described in the charges and any amendments to the charges'.[519] The interpretation of this part of the provision is controversial with a view to a legal recharacterization of the charges. We will return to this issue below.[520] The Chamber may take into account the 'entire proceedings' to get a more complete picture,[521] but its decision has to be based 'only on evidence submitted and discussed before it at the trial',[522] that is, the evidence as part of the trial record.[523] This is a manifestation of the *immediacy principle*.[524] However, it is not necessary that each piece of evidence is 'discussed' in detail before the Chamber; rather, it suffices that the parties had the opportunity to make submissions on each piece of evidence.[525] We will analyse the evidentiary rules, including the submission vs. admission approach, in detail in Chapter V.

As to the determination of the guilt or innocence of the accused, the standard of proof '*beyond reasonable doubt*'[526] applies.[527] Concretely speaking, it applies to the facts constituting the elements of the relevant crime and the mode of responsibility as well as to the facts that are indispensable for the conviction.[528] Thus, as emphasized by the AC, 'not each and every fact in the Conviction Decision must be proved beyond reasonable doubt'[529] but

[515] Art. 74 (1) ICCS; Rule 16*bis* RPE SCSL. Regarding alternate judges at the ICC, see also Triffterer and Kiss, 'Article 74', in Ambos, *Commentary* (2022), mn. 20–5; Expert Group, *IER* (2020), pp. 192–3.

[516] Rule 15*ter* RPE ICTY and Rule 20 RPE MICT. The RPE ICTR do not provide for such an alternative.

[517] So far in all KSC trial proceedings a (fourth) reserve judge has, in line with Rule 18 RPE KSC, been assigned to the competent TP.

[518] See the quite sophisticated KSC legal framework generally providing for a reserve judge (Rule 18 RPE KSC), an adjournment of proceedings in case of absence (Rule 19 (4)), and the assignment of another judge in case of an absence 'longer than of short duration' with the possibility of a rehearing of the missed parts with the full bench (Rule 19 (5)).

[519] cf. Art. 74 (2) cl. 2 ICCS; see also *Muthaura et al.*, ICC-01/09-02/11-382-Red, paras. 56–7; *Ruto et al.*, ICC-01/09-01/11-373, para. 45; Fyfe, in Heinze and Dittrich, *ICC* (2021), pp. 679, 697–8.

[520] Section B (7)(b) in this chapter.

[521] Art. 74 (2) cl. 1 ICCS. This is to be understood restrictively, namely as referring to diverse information from other procedural stages (e.g. the conduct of the parties in terms of strategies, submissions etc.) which may 'help forge a comprehensive view of the evidence'; cf. Triffterer and Kiss, 'Article 74', in Ambos, *Commentary* (2022), mn. 39; more broadly apparently Triffterer and Kiss, 'Article 74', in Ambos, *Commentary* (2016), mn. 37 (arguing that '[a]n overall view of the "entire proceedings" may be more enlightening than the mere addition of single aspects').

[522] Art. 74 (2) cl. 3 ICCS.

[523] ICC, *Prosecutor v. Lubanga*, TC I, Judgment pursuant to Article 74 of the Statute, ICC-01/04-01/06-2842, 14 March 2012, para. 98; ICC, *Prosecutor v. Katanga*, TC II, Judgment rendu en application de l'article 74 du Statut, ICC-01/04-01/07-3436, 7 March 2014, para. 78. On the trial record ('record of proceedings') in more detail, see Chapter V, A.(7) and B.(1)(c) in this volume.

[524] Triffterer and Kiss, 'Article 74', in Ambos, *Commentary* (2022), mn. 56.

[525] *Katanga*, ICC-01/04-01/07-3436, para. 78; also Triffterer and Kiss, 'Article 74', in Ambos, *Commentary* (2022), mn. 59.

[526] Rule 87 (A) RPE ICTY/ICTR/SCSL, Rule 104 (A) RPE MICT, Art. 66 (3) ICCS.

[527] cf. *Ongwen*, ICC-02/04-01/15-2022-Red, para. 319; ICTY, *Prosecutor v. Aleksovski*, AC, Judgment, IT-95-14/1-A, 24 March 2000, para. 64; ICTY, *Prosecutor v. Mucić et al.*, AC, Judgment, IT-96-21-A, 20 February 2001, para. 458; ICTY, *Prosecutor v. Halilović*, AC, Judgment, IT-01-48-A, 16 October 2007, paras. 118 ff.; ICTY, *Prosecutor v. Haradinaj et al.*, AC, Judgment, IT-04-84-A, 19 July 2010, para. 221; also Triffterer and Kiss, 'Article 74', in Ambos, *Commentary* (2022), mn. 38. See also Ambos, in Jackson and Summers, *Fairness* (2018), p. 179, 180 with further references in n. 6.

[528] cf. *Ongwen*, ICC-02/04-01/15-2022-Red, para. 319; ICC, *Prosecutor v. Ngudjolo*, TC II, Judgment pursuant to Article 74 of the Statute, ICC-01/04-02/12-3-tENG, 18 December 2012, para. 35. See also STL, *Prosecutor v. Merhi and Oneissi*, AJ, STL-11-01/A-2/AC/F0051/20220310/R007727-R007979/EN/af, 10 March 2022, para. 84; *Halilović*, IT-01-48-A, para. 125; ICTY, *Prosecutor v. Blagojević and Jokić*, AC, Judgment, IT-02-60-A, 9 May 2007, para. 226; ICTR, *Prosecutor v. Ntagerura et al.*, AC, Judgment, ICTR-99-46-A, 7 July 2006, para. 174; *Kupreškić et al.*, IT-95-16-A, para. 226.

[529] *Ongwen*, ICC-02/04-01/15-2022-Red, para. 321.

a 'clear distinction must be made between facts constituting the elements of the crime and mode of liability... and any other set of facts introduced by the different types of evidence'.[530] The KSC AP adopted this view.[531] Of course, the evidentiary standard is difficult to define in the abstract, as we will see in the chapter on evidence.[532]

Ultimately, all conviction standards leave a considerable discretion to the judges[533] and can only be delimited in relation to other (lower) standards as has been done above.[534] As a minimum, a conviction must always be based on reasons and, indeed, must be reasoned.[535] This follows from legitimacy and fair trial considerations.[536] In more practical terms, any reasonable review presupposes that the fact finder has given reasons for her decision and observed the rules of logic, consistency, and common sense;[537] purely subjective, intuition-based decision-making cannot be reasonably tested in a review procedure.[538]

To be sure, defendants may also be acquitted (as for example former President Laurent Gbabgo).[539] This is merely a consequence of a fair trial with a sufficiently high conviction threshold, notwithstanding the quality of the prosecutorial investigation and the evidence.[540]

[530] *Bemba et al.*, ICC-01/05-01/13-2275-Red, para. 868; conc. *Ongwen*, ICC-02/04-01/15-2022-Red, para. 321.

[531] KSC, *Prosecutor v. Gucati and Haradinaj*, AP, AJ, KSC-CA-2022-01/F00114, 2 February 2023, paras. 327 ff.

[532] Chapter V, A.(2)(a) and (b) in this volume.

[533] In the same vein, see also De Smet, in Stahn, *Practice* (2015), pp. 866–7 (putting on an equal footing the subjective and beyond reasonable doubt standards in this context).

[534] Above note 369 and main surrounding text in this chapter. Similarly De Smet, in Stahn, *Practice* (2015), p. 888 (no overlapping with other standards). Demanding a more precise conviction standard, Jacobs, in Sluiter et al., *International Criminal Procedure* (2013), p. 1149.

[535] On the importance of (legal) reasoning and a respective recommendation, see also Jacobs, in Sluiter et al., *International Criminal Procedure* (2013), p. 1149; Frisch, in A. Bruns et al., *FS Stürner* (2013), pp. 868–9, 871; Klamberg, *Evidence* (2013), pp. 159–60; Roberts, *JICJ*, 13 (2015), 489–92 (pointing, inter alia, to 'adjudication' as a 'rational process'); summarizing four formal models aspiring to a formal, more rational standard of proof, De Smet, in Stahn, *Practice* (2015), pp. 872–82, 889.

[536] On the fair trial requirement to give adequate reasons for a decision, see ECtHR, *Hadjianastassiou v. Greece*, Application No. 12945/87, Judgment (16 December 1992), paras. 33 ('The national courts must, however, indicate with sufficient clarity the grounds on which they based their decision. It is this, inter alia, which makes it possible for the accused to exercise usefully the rights of appeal available to him'), 37 ('the applicant did not have the benefit of a fair trial'); see also ECtHR, *Boldea v. Romania*, Application No. 19997/02, Judgment (15 February 2007), paras. 28–34 (para. 29: 'article 6 § 1 oblige les tribunaux à motiver leurs décisions', para. 33: 'il aurait fallu une décision motivée de manière détaillée et complete ... pour pouvoir qualifier d'équitable la procédure'); ECtHR, *Grădinar v. Moldova*, Application No. 7170/02, Judgment (8 April 2008), para. 107; ECtHR, *Taxquet v. Belgium*, Application No. 926/05, Judgment (16 November 2010), para. 91.

[537] cf. ICTR, *Prosecutor v. Rutaganda*, AC, Judgment, ICTR-96-3-A, 26 May 2003, para. 488 (reasonable doubt standard to 'be based on logic and common sense, and have a rational link to the evidence'); conc. ICC, *Prosecutor v. Ngudjolo*. AC, Judgment on the Prosecutor's Appeal against the Decision of Trial Chamber II Entitled 'Judgment Pursuant to Article 74 of the Statute', ICC-01/04-02/12-271-Corr, 7 April 2015, para. 109.

[538] This is indeed one of the major problems of the subjective (*intime conviction*) approach, cf. De Smet, in Stahn, *Practice* (2015), pp. 871, 889 (rational discussion impossible); for a more principled treatment see Ambos, *Quaestio Facti*, 4 (2023) 167 ff.

[539] TC I issued its decision first orally, acquitting *Gbagbo* and co-defendant *Charles Blé Goudé* from all charges of crimes against humanity allegedly committed in Côte d'Ivoire in 2010 and 2011 (*Prosecutor v. Gbagbo and Blé Goudé*, TC I, Transcript, ICC-02/11-01/15-T-234-ENG, 16 January 2019; Judge Carbuccia dissenting, Dissenting Opinion to the Chamber's Oral Decision of 15 January 2019, ICC-02/11-01/15-1234, 15 January 2019); only six months later the detailed written reasons were given (*Prosecutor v. Gbagbo and Blé Goudé*, TC I, Reasons for Oral Decision of 15 January 2019 on the Requête de la Défense de Laurent Gbagbo afin qu'un jugement d'acquittement portant sur toutes les charges soit prononcé en faveur de Laurent Gbagbo et que sa mise en liberté immédiate soit ordonée; on Blé Goudé's no case to answer motion, see ICC-02/11-01/15-1263, 16 July 2019). The AC confirmed the acquittal (*Prosecutor v. Gbagbo and Blé Goudé*, AC, Judgment in the Appeal of the Prosecutor against TC I's Decision on the No Case to Answer Motions, ICC-02/11-01/15-1400, 31 March 2021. Separate Concurring Opinions by Judge Eboe-Osuji [*Gbagbo and Blé Goudé*, ICC-02/11-01/15-1400-Anx1-Red]; Judge Morrison [*Gbagbo and Blé Goudé*, ICC-02/11-01/15-1400-Anx2]; and Judge Hofmański [*Gbagbo and Blé Goudé*, ICC-02/11-01/15-1400-Anx3]), Judges Judge Ibáñez and Bossa dissenting (ICC-02/11-01/15-1400-Anx4-Red and ICC-02/11-01/15-1400-Anx5).

[540] In more detail, Heinze, in Heinze and Dittrich, *ICC* (2021), p. 48 (correctly arguing that an acquittal does not necessarily indicate a bad investigation or even a failure of the ICL system). In contrast, Labuda, *Völkerrechtsblog*, 18 January 2019 sees an 'evidence problem' of the ICC after the Gbabgo acquittal.

A criminal trial is not a game in which the Prosecutor is a contestant who wins with a conviction and loses with an acquittal.[541] Instead, acquittals contribute to the legitimacy of any criminal justice system, including an international one.[542] In more practical terms an acquittal triggers cooperation with a State: the Court must find one which is willing to let the person enter its territory.[543] We will return to this aspect below.[544]

The judges shall *deliberate* in private.[545] Insofar the IER's sharp critique of the ICC's deliberation culture gives rise to concern. [546] The judges shall try to achieve *unanimity* in their decision.[547] If a unanimous decision is not possible, a majority decision could, exceptionally, be adopted.[548] In this case, the opinions of the majority and the minority shall be clearly set out.[549] The decision shall be in writing and fully reasoned, so that the parties can effectively appeal it and the interested public can critically analyse it.[550] Of course, the requirement of a reasoned decision must not be overstretched. Indeed, 'a Trial Chamber is not obliged to give a detailed answer for every argument raised during a trial.'[551] At any rate, it is not a recommende practice to give the full written reasoning only six months after the issuing of the judgment[552] and, to make matters worse, in the form of separate opinions of the judges.[553]

[541] See Heinze, *Disclosure* (2014), pp. 226, 257 ff., with further references. The game analogy has received both applause and criticism. For a nuanced account, see King, *ACLR*, 58 (2021), pp. 47 ff., esp. 54 ff.

[542] Irving, *Human Rights Protection* (2020), pp. 93 ff.

[543] See Irving, *Human Rights Protection* (2020), p. 39.

[544] cf. Chapter VIII, B.(1)(b).

[545] Rule 142 (1) RPE ICC ('in camera'). See also Jørgensen and Zahar, in Sluiter et al., *International Criminal Procedure* (2013), pp. 1159–60 (ICTY, ICTR, and SCSL); Triffterer and Kiss, 'Article 74', in Ambos, *Commentary* (2022), mn. 19, 65–8.

[546] Expert Group, *IER* (2020), p. 198 ('Lack of communication between the Judges and problematic relationships among the members of some benches were such as to evoke the description of the Chamber as dysfunctional. In one instance, a Judge deliberately chose not to circulate the Judge's opinion before the point of delivery.')

[547] Art. 74 (3) ICCS. See also Maučec and Dothan, *LJIL*, 35 (2022), 945, 947.

[548] cf. Arts. 23 (2) ICTYS, 22 (2) ICTRS, 18 SCSLS, and 74 (3) and (4) ICCS; Jørgensen and Zahar, in Sluiter et al., *International Criminal Procedure* (2013), pp. 1161–3 (ICTY, ICTR, and SCSL), 1196; Triffterer and Kiss, 'Article 74', in Ambos, *Commentary* (2022), mn. 61–4.

[549] Rules 88 (C) RPE ICTR/SCSL, 98*ter* (C) RPE ICTY, and 122 (C) RPE MICT; cf. also Jørgensen and Zahar, in Sluiter et al., *International Criminal Procedure* (2013), p. 1161; SCSL, *Prosecutor v. Brima et al.*, AC, Decision on Brima-Kamara Defence Appeal Motion against Trial Chamber II Majority Decision on Extremely Urgent Confidential Joint Motion for the Re-Appointment of Kevin Metzger and Wilbert Harris as Lead Counsel for Alex Tamba Brima and Brima Bazzy Kamara, SCSL-04-16-AR73, 8 December 2005, para. 21 ('concurring/dissenting opinions shall be filed together with the majority decision, in order to put the parties in a position to decide whether or not to apply for leave to appeal'); see also Öberg, *CLF*, 24 (2013), 120–1; Safferling, *Criminal Procedure* (2012), pp. 525–7; Boas et al., *Procedure* (2011), pp. 383–4; Triffterer and Kiss, 'Article 74', in Ambos, *Commentary* (2022), mn. 63–4. For an empirical analysis of dissenting opinions at the ICC, see Maučec and Dothan, *LJIL*, 35 (2022), 945 ff.; see also Jain, *EJIL*, 28 (2017), 1163 ff.

[550] cf. Arts. 23 (2) 2 ICTYS, 22 (2) ICTRS, and 18 SCSLS, Rule 98*ter* (A) and (C) RPE ICTY, Rule 88 (A) and (C) RPE ICTR/SCSL, Rule 122 (A) and (C) RPE MICT, Art. 74 (5) ICCS; see further Rules 142–4 RPE ICC; Safferling, *Criminal Procedure* (2012), pp. 523–4; Boas et al., *Procedure* (2011), pp. 377–83; Jørgensen and Zahar, in Sluiter et al., *International Criminal Procedure* (2013), pp. 1163–8 (ICTY, ICTR, and SCSL), 1170–1 (ICC), 1197; *Ntagerura et al.*, ICTR-99-46-A, para. 169; Triffterer and Kiss, 'Article 74', in Ambos, *Commentary* (2022), mn. 69–73.

[551] ICTR, *Prosecutor v. Bagilishema*, AC, Judgment, ICTR-95-1A, 3 July 2002, para. 44 in the same vein, *Mucić et al.*, IT-96-21-A, para. 481 ('A Trial Chamber is not required to articulate in its judgement every step of its reasoning in reaching particular findings'); ICTY, also *Prosecutor v. Furundžija*, AC, Judgment, IT-95-17/1-A, 21 July 2000, para. 69 (extent of duty to give a 'reasoned opinion ... may vary according to the nature of the decision and can only be determined in the light of the circumstances of the case' [citing ECtHR case law]); cf. also Triffterer and Kiss, 'Article 74', in Ambos, *Commentary* (2022), mn. 71.

[552] As just mentioned (above note 545 with references) in *Gbagbo and Blé Goudé* the TC pronounced its majority decision and reasons first (on 15 January 2019) only *orally* supported by a decision of merely eight pages.

[553] *Gbagbo and Blé Goudé*, ICC-02/11-01/15-1263; ibid., ICC-02/11-01/15-1263-AnxA; ibid., ICC-02/11-01/15-1263-AnxB-Red; ibid., ICC-02/11-01/15-1263-AnxC-Red.

The verdict shall be pronounced in open court[554] and in the presence of the accused;[555] in case of a separate sentencing hearing, the same applies to the sentence.[556]

Pursuant to Article 75 (1) ICCS and the principles relating to *reparations* to victims, the Court[557] is called upon to determine, either upon request or on its own motion in exceptional circumstances, the scope and extent of any damage, loss, and injury to victims.[558] In this regard, the Court may make reparation orders against a convicted person, or in respect of victims.[559] It may give effect to them in accordance with the provisions for cooperation[560] and enforcement of fines and forfeiture measures.[561] Where appropriate, the Court may order that the award for reparations be made through the Trust Fund provided for in Article 79.[562]

### (b) *No case to answer?*

In the *Ruto and Sang* case the question arose of what would be the right judgment when the evidence fails to meet the required threshold due to witness tampering and political interference which eventually forces the prosecution to close its case. In a decision of 3 June 2014, the TC defined the test for a 'no case to answer motion' as 'whether there is evidence on which a reasonable Trial Chamber *could* convict'.[563] In the same decision the Chamber explained that the consequence of a successful no case to answer motion—that is, lack of sufficient prosecution evidence to convict—is an acquittal.[564] The much anticipated decision of

554 Safferling, *Criminal Procedure* (2012), p. 524; Jørgensen and Zahar, in Sluiter et al., *International Criminal Procedure* (2013), pp. 1160–1 (ICTY, ICTR, and SCSL), 1169–70 (ICC); Triffterer and Kiss, 'Article 74', in Ambos, *Commentary* (2022), mn. 75–8.

555 Rule 100 (B) RPE ICTY/ICTR, Rule 124 (B) RPE MICT, Art. 76 (4) ICCS.

556 See note 465 and main text in this chapter.

557 In reality, the Court has shifted this responsibility onto the Chambers, see Bock, *ZIS*, 8 (2013), 304–5. In this context, regarding the ad hoc tribunals, see also Rules 106 (B) RPE ICTY/ICTR and 130 (B) RPE MICT, according to which 'a victim or persons claiming through him may bring an action in a national court or other competent body to obtain compensation'. Pursuant to Rule 106 (C) RPE ICTY/ICTR and 130 (C) RPE MICT, 'the judgement ... shall be final and binding as to the criminal responsibility of the convicted person for such injury'.

558 The first decision of that kind was ICC, *Prosecutor v. Lubanga*, TC I, Decision Establishing the Principles and Procedures to be Applied to Reparations, ICC-01/04-01/06-2904, 7 August 2012; see thereon Bock, *ZIS*, 8 (2013), 305 ff.; see also Donat-Cattin, 'Article 75', in Ambos, *Commentary* (2022), mn. 20–1. See afterwards ICC, *Prosecutor v. Katanga*, TC II, Ordonnance de réparation en vertu de l'article 75 du Statut, ICC-01/04-01/07-3728, 24 March 2017; *Prosecutor v. Al Mahdi*, TC VIII, Reparations Order, ICC-01/12-01/15-236, 17 August 2017; *Prosecutor v. Al Mahdi*, AC, Public Redacted Judgment on the Appeal of the Victims against the 'Reparations Order', ICC-01/12-01/15-259-Red2, 8 March 2018; *Prosecutor v. Ntaganda*, Reparations Order, ICC-01/04-02/06-2659, 8 March 2021; *Prosecutor v. Ntaganda*, AC, Judgment on the Appeals against the Decision of Trial Chamber VI of 8 March 2021 Entitled 'Reparations Order', ICC-01/04-02/06-2782, 12 September 2022. See generally Cohen, *Reparative Justice* (2020), pp. 75 ff.

559 Art. 75 (2) ICCS.

560 Art. 93 (1) ICCS.

561 Art. 109 ICCS.

562 Art. 75 (2); also *Lubanga*, ICC-01/04-01/06-2904, paras. 281 ff.; concurring, Bock, *ZIS*, 8 (2013), 317 ff.; cf. also Bock, *Opfer* (2010), pp. 578 ff.; Burnham, in van den Herik and Stahn, *Diversification and Fragmentation* (2012), pp. 676 ff.; McCarthy, *JICJ*, 10 (2012), 359 ff., 369–70; Mouthaan, *ICLR*, 11 (2011), 790; Manirabona and Wemmers, *ICLR*, 13 (2013), 1001, 1004; see, on the Trust Fund, Chapter II, E.(6) in this volume.

563 ICC, *Prosecutor v. Ruto and Sang*, TC V(a), Decision No. 5 on the Conduct of Trial Proceedings (Principles and Procedure on 'no case to answer' Motions), ICC-01/09-01/11-1334, 3 June 2014, para. 32 (emphasis in the original). See also ICTY, *Prosecutor v. Kordić and Čerkez*, Decision on Defence Motions for Judgment of Acquittal, IT-95-14/2-T, 6 April 2000, para. 26; ICTY, *Prosecutor v. Sikirica et al.*, Judgment on Defence Motions to Acquit, IT-95-8-T, 3 September 2001, paras. 4, 8; ICTR, *Prosecutor v. Imanishimwe et al.*, Separate and Concurring Decision of Judge Williams on Imanishimwe's Defence Motion for Judgment of Acquittal on Count of Conspiracy to Commit Genocide Pursuant to Rule 98*bis*, ICTR-99-46-T, 13 March 2002, para. 3. See generally Boas et al., *Procedure* (2011), pp. 287–90; Calvo-Goller, *Trial Proceedings* (2006), pp. 98–101.

564 *Ruto and Sang*, ICC-01/09-01/11-1334, para. 23; in the same vein, ICC, *Prosecutor v. Ruto and Sang*, TC V(a), Decision on Defence Applications for Judgments of Acquittal, Reasons of Judge Fremr, ICC-01/09-01/11-2027-Red, 5 April 2016, para. 1.

5 April 2016 demonstrates the exceptionalism of the case, because four possible outcomes found resonance amongst the judges: first, Judge Fremr argued, on the basis of a full evaluation of the evidence, that there was no case to answer for the accused.[565] Secondly, Judge Eboe-Osuji, albeit fully concurring with Judge Fremr's evidentiary evaluation,[566] declared a mistrial, because of the 'serious tainting of the trial process by way of witness interference and political intimidation of witnesses'.[567] Thirdly, notwithstanding this, for the majority, a judgment of acquittal was not the right outcome given that the flawed evidentiary situation was due to witness tampering to be attributed to the Kenyan government and benefiting the accused. Thus, the majority 'vacated' the charges against the accused and 'discharged' them 'without prejudice to their prosecution afresh in future'.[568] Fourthly, this result was rejected by dissenting Judge Herrera Carbuccia, arguing that it departed from the legal standard established in the above quoted TC's decision of 3 June 2014.[569] Instead, she considered that the prosecution case had not 'broken down' and that there was sufficient evidence upon which, if accepted, a reasonable TC could convict the accused.[570]

In essence, the decision stages a conflict on a micro level that has been probing the ICC ever since on the macro level, namely the interference of important political players in its proceedings. In a way, the legal issue at this stage of the proceedings—whether the accused have a case to answer—was displaced by the 'special circumstances of the case', that is, the tampering of prosecution witnesses effectively benefiting the accused.[571] Against this background any anticipated termination of the trial—either an acquittal due to a 'no case to answer' scenario or a (permanent) stay of proceedings because of a mistrial[572]—would seem to be somewhat counter-intuitive. Indeed, if witness tampering of this sort entails the effective discharging of an accused it appears to be a recipe for other States or governments to follow the Kenyan model to ensure the frustration of the trial.[573] Judge Eboe-Osuji takes

[565] *Ruto and Sang*, ICC-01/09-01/11-2027-Red, Reasons of Judge Fremr, para. 1.

[566] Ibid., Reasons of Judge Eboe-Osuji, para. 2.

[567] Ibid., ('[W]as the Prosecution's case weak because there really was no better evidence left to be obtained and tendered without the factor of witness interference and political intimidation? Or was it weak because the prosecution did the best they could with the only evidence they could eke out amidst difficult circumstances of witness interference and political intimidation? Because of the tainted process, I am unable to say. It is for that reason that I prefer declaration of a mistrial as the right result.') For a strong, perhaps overstated critique, Heller, *Opinio Juris* (28 April 2016) ('disregard for Ruto and Sang's right to a fair trial'); crit. also Schabas, *PhD Studies in Human Rights* (8 April 2016).

[568] *Ruto and Sang*, ICC-01/09-01/11-2027-Red, p. 1.

[569] ICC, *Prosecutor v. Ruto and Sang*, TC V(a), Decision on Defence Applications for Judgments of Acquittal, Dissenting Opinion of Judge Herrera Carbuccia, ICC-01/09-01/11-2027-AnxI, 5 April 2016, para. 1.

[570] Ibid., para. 2.

[571] *Ruto and Sang*, ICC-01/09-01/11-2027-Red, Reasons of Judge Fremr, para. 148 ('they did profit from the interference, inter alia, by the falling away of several key witnesses that this Chamber found to have been interfered with').

[572] On this as a remedy in case of procedural violations, see Chapter VI, D.(1)(b) in this volume.

[573] cf. *Ruto and Sang*, ICC-01/09-01/11-2027-Red, Reasons of Judge Eboe-Osuji, para. 156 ('A verdict of acquittal is particularly unjustifiable in the circumstances, not only because it will vindicate the illicit objectives of the unseen hands that had engaged in witness interference, the obvious aim of which is to frustrate the trial of the accused; but it may also encourage future unseen hands to interfere with a criminal trial. What was done against this trial ... must not become a case study for others inclined to emulate such tactics in future cases of this Court. It may not be too much to speak of such tactics in terms of efforts whose aim is to hold justice hostage, with acquittals of accused persons as the envisaged ransom. Hence, for purposes of a mistrial—resulting from obstruction of justice intended to benefit the accused—it does not matter at all that there is no evidence showing the accused as a culprit of the interference. It is enough that the aim of a mistrial is to hold out some hope that justice may be seen to be done sooner or later. And those seeking to obstruct the course of justice, for the benefit of the accused, are made to realise that their efforts will come to nought. On the contrary, it may in the end only inconveniently prolong the process for the accused, as it does for the prosecution and the victims. No one is the winner. But declaration of mistrial and allowing the case to start afresh in the future is better than rewarding the interference and political meddling with a verdict of acquittal.')

this unintended consequence as the main reason to opt for a mistrial instead of an outright acquittal,[574] but both solutions appear equally unconvincing if one assumes that the accused themselves did not interfere with witnesses so as to 'render the trial null and void',[575] and that the witness tampering was done on purpose and with the knowledge of the accused to spare them from conviction.[576] Against this background a vacation of charges with the possibility of a new prosecution (that is without any preclusionary effect within the meaning of Article 20 ICCS)[577] is a defensible compromise.[578] At any rate, the case shows that judges are not well equipped to counter political interference by a territorial State whose government does everything possible to frustrate the prosecution and trial of its leaders.[579]

There has been subsequent practice on no case to answer.[580] The *Ntaganda* TC emphasized the case-by-case notion of the concept, refuting the generalization of the *Ruto and Sang* approach.[581] The AC confirmed this case-by-case approach leaving the procedure to the discretion of the Chamber.[582] Of course, a consequence of this casuistic approach is an inconsistent case law and thus a lack of clear guidance on the matter. Thus, for example, the *Gbagbo/Blé Goudé* TC,[583] deciding on a 'no case to answer' motion by the defence of *Blé Goudé*,[584] seems to have departed from the (evidentiary) standard in *Ruto*.[585]

[574] *Ruto and Sang*, ICC-01/09-01/11-2027-Red, Reasons of Judge Eboe-Osuji, para. 8 (acquittal right outcome 'had there been no incidence of interference or political meddling').

[575] Ibid., Reasons of Judge Fremr, para. 147 ('Although these circumstances had an effect on the proceedings and appear to have influenced the Prosecution's ability to produce more (credible) testimonies, I do not consider the impact to have been of such a level so as to render the trial null and void.') For a definition of a mistrial in general, see Chapter VI, D.(1)(b).

[576] While it 'has not been shown, or argued, that the accused were involved in the interference of witnesses', *Ruto and Sang*, ICC-01/09-01/11-2027-Red, Reasons of Judge Fremr, para. 148; Reasons of Judge Eboe-Osuji, para. 153 ('[I]t must be made clear that there was no evidence to the effect that Mr Ruto or Mr Sang had instructed or encouraged anyone to engage in witness interference. The Prosecution acknowledged that gap in the evidence'), it would be naive to believe that they were not aware of it and it was not done with the purpose to 'save them', see e.g. the statement of Njonjo Mue, Chairperson of the International Commission of Jurists Kenya: '[I]t is also common knowledge that the Kenyan cases at the ICC have systematically collapsed under the weight of contamination of evidence through victim interference and an orchestrated political and diplomatic campaign to intimidate and discredit the Court by the Kenyan government under Uhuru Kenyatta and William Ruto.' <https://ciccglobaljustice.wordpress.com/2016/04/07/rutosang-icc-case-thrown-out-explanation-and-reaction/>).

[577] The *ne bis in idem* principle would not impede a second prosecution if it were limited to (final) judgments, see Chapter I, D.(3)(j) in this volume. A revision is only possible in case of a conviction, see Art. 84 (1) ICCS; thereon Chapter VI, C.(1) in this volume.

[578] Crit. however Heller, *Opinio Juris* (28 April 2016); Schabas, *PhD Studies in Human Rights* (8 April 2016). In essence, both authors consider it unfair that the accused may be reprosecuted, but this is a merely theoretical, far-fetched possibility and, more importantly, this focus understates their—albeit not proven, but very probable—involvement in the witness tampering (see note 582 and main text in this chapter).

[579] cf. Kersten, 7 April 2016, <https://justiceinconflict.org/2016/04/07/a-missed-trial-or-a-mistrial-the-end-of-the-icc-cases-against-ruto-and-sang/> ('story about a state and government against an international court and institution').

[580] A list of AC decisions with regard to 'no case to answer' motions (and the ensuing decisions) can be found in Guariglia et al., *Appeals Chamber* (2018), pp. 343–5.

[581] ICC, *Prosecutor v. Ntaganda*, TC VI, Decision on Defence Request for Leave to File a 'no case to answer' Motion, ICC-01/04-02/06-1931, 1 June 2017, para. 28.

[582] ICC, *Prosecutor v. Ntaganda*, AC, Judgment on the Appeal of Mr Bosco Ntaganda against the 'Decision on Defence Request for leave to file a "no case to answer" motion', ICC-01/04-02/06-2026, 5 September 2017, para. 44 ('A decision on whether or not to conduct a 'no case to answer' procedure is thus discretionary in nature and must be exercised on a case-by-case basis in a manner that ensures that the trial proceedings are fair and expeditious pursuant to article 64 (2) and 64 (3) (a) of the Statute').

[583] On the two to one acquittal, see already above note 545 with main text.

[584] ICC, *Prosecutor v. Gbagbo and Blé Goudé*, Defence, Public Redacted Version of 'Corrigendum to the "Blé Goudé Defence No Case to Answer Motion" (ICC-02/11-01/15-1198-Conf), 23 July 2018,' 3 August 2018, ICC-02/11-01/15-1198-Conf-Corr, ICC-02/11-01/15-1198-Corr-Red, 28 September 2018.

[585] ICC, *Prosecutor v. Gbagbo and Blé Goudé*, TC I, Transcript, ICC-02/11-01/15-T-232-ENG, 15 January 2019. In more detail and crit., Bradfield, *Opinio Juris* 20 January 2019; see also Robinson, *EJIL: Talk!* 5 November 2019.

Notwithstanding this inconsistency and the lack of an explicit legal basis,[586] the IER approves of the 'no case to answer' procedure with a view to judicial economy.[587] At least, it rightly recommends the inclusion of the procedure in the statutory regime of the ICC.[588]

## B. Special Issues

### (1) Selection and prioritization as key elements of a prosecutorial strategy

The flip side of impunity gaps at the level of the national criminal justice systems is an (increasingly) high number of international crimes that may be referred to the ICC. Thus, the ICC turns, in fact, into the lone enforcer of ICL, at least the most visible one, but it cannot cope with the investigative and prosecutorial burden this implies. This has further implications for the kind of justice that is delivered by the Court. In an ideal system of (criminal) justice, each suspect receives the quantum of retributive justice deserved in line with the wrongfulness of the respective conduct and the ensuing blame (*culpa*) to be accorded to her. In the real world, though, matters are more complicated. In practically all domestic criminal justice systems justice is distributed selectively according to certain, often policy-based criteria.[589] Of course, one would expect the criminal justice systems of developed liberal democracies (*Rechtsstaaten*) to be disposed towards fairer selection mechanisms than less democratic, rather authoritarian systems are, but ultimately these are only distinctions of degree.

Be that as it may, international criminal justice, as represented by the ICC, is also a real system but with additional difficulties and certain peculiarities, mainly its subject-matter focus on macrocriminality. Although this subject matter is currently limited to three major crimes (with a limited jurisdiction on aggression as the fourth crime),[590] it in fact entails an expansion of jurisdiction beyond the classical limits of territoriality and the contours of traditional, individualistic criminal law. More concretely speaking, the ICC faces massive and complex situations of criminality in distant territories but does not expend sufficient human and other resources to deal with this challenge nearly adequately. The Court thus suffers, as famously expressed by Damaška, from an 'endogenous powerlessness'[591] and this more so than the ad hoc or hybrid tribunals, because these not only have a more limited mandate, but also have always received the specific support of certain interested States or groups of

[586] Crit. insofar Tarfusser and Chiarini, *Opinio Juris* 13 April 2021 ('It is my very firm belief that no judge is allowed to "create" procedural rules, by borrowing them from other national or international legal frameworks Even less is it allowed to create them based on the phantomatic—also unwritten and unregulated—"inherent powers". Judges have to stick to the law!').

[587] Expert Group, *IER* (2020), p. 170: '[T]he principal question is how to ensure its consistent application in a way that will not unduly lengthen the trial proceedings.'

[588] Ibid., p. 172.

[589] See Jehle and Wade, *Prosecutorial Power* (2006), pp. 24, 60–1; Kotecha, *JICJ*, 18 (2020), 107 ff.; Heinze and Fyfe, in Ambos et al., *Core Concepts I* (2020), 343, 348 ff.; Lorca, *LJIL*, 35 (2022), 421, 427 ('All systems of criminal justice act selectively because they all have legal, political, economic and even technological constraints that prevent them from investigating and judging all crimes under their jurisdiction'); see also Damaška, *ChicKentLR*, 83 (2008), 362–3, referring to the discrimination from a historical perspective; from a comparative perspective, with a view to mandatory prosecution or prosecutorial discretion (principle of opportunity), see Kuczyńska, *Accusation Model ICC* (2015), pp. 94–106. From a critical theory perspective, Vasiliev, in Heller et al., *Oxford HB ICL* (2020), pp. 627 ff.

[590] cf. Ambos, *Treatise ICL II* (2022), pp. 226 ff.

[591] Damaška, *UCLA JIL & ForAff*, 14 (2009), 21.

States.[592] Thus, the idealistic aspirations of the Court are severely restrained by the harsh realities of the prosecution of international core crimes in the real word.[593]

At any event, given its situation and case overload, the ICC cannot deliver classical retributive, but only a kind of distributive criminal justice, where the main challenge is not so much the fair or just delivery of sanctions to individual defendants, but the *fair distribution of justice* to a selected number of suspects/perpetrators.[594] In making this selection, it is an enormous challenge for the Court to avoid the impression that it only prosecutes individuals of weak States and thus reproduces the structural (post-colonial) inequalities between States existing at the international level.[595] If this were the case, the Court would discriminate on the basis of nationality and rightly face the charge of using disturbing double standards. Matters are further complicated by the fact that suspects are not selected as bare individuals—as is normally the case in domestic proceedings—but as representatives of certain perpetrator groups (the Serbs, the Croats, the Hutus, the Tutsies ...) and thus the selection entails the distribution of blame to their respective States or groups. As convincingly argued by Mégret, 'the choice of indictees is always seen as also reflecting some distributive allocation of blame between different national or sub-national groups'; selection 'is likely to be interpreted as a veritable verdict on the relative responsibilities of various communities'.[596] This, in fact, explains why States often make it their national cause to get their nationals acquitted, at least if they belong to the high echelons of civilian or military power.

Against this background it is evident, as already argued above,[597] that the rational, fair, and transparent selection and prioritization of cases, accompanied by a coherent prosecution strategy, turns out to be of utmost importance for the success and legitimacy of any international criminal tribunal, especially the ICC.[598] After the OTP has drafted a series of

592 See also Robinson, *LJIL*, 28 (2015), 333 with n. 35 (pointing to the worse situation of the ICC as compared to the ad hoc tribunals in terms of resources).

593 On the ideal (normative, aloof, transcendental) and real (grounded, engaged, effective) tension in the Court's assignment, see also Robinson, *LJIL, 28* (2015), 331; see also De Meester, *Investigation Phase* (2015), pp. 270–1.

594 cf. also Mégret, *JICJ*, 13 (2015), 81 ('justice between rather than justice to'), 83–4 (fair distribution), 89, 95; see also Robinson, *LJIL*, 28 (2015), 332, referring to the 'problem of *choice*' as consequence of the overload (emphasis in the original). Generally on selection, Schabas, in Stahn, *Practice* (2015), p. 365 ('extreme selectivity' of the international system of criminal prosecution); Kuczyńska, *Accusation Model ICC* (2015), pp. 111–15, (115: 'selection of defendants stands at the basis of [ICC's] effective and correct functioning' and 'the "impunity gap" is an indispensable—and therefore necessary—element of the selection strategy'); De Meester, *Investigation Phase* (2015), pp. 261 ff.

595 cf. Damaška, *ChicKentLR*, 83 (2008), 360 ff.; Sainati, *VanderbiltJTL*, 49 (2016), 210–14. On the structural inequality also regarding the 'ICL we', see Tallgren, *JICJ*, 13 (2015), 155.

596 Mégret, *JICJ*, 13 (2015), 90, also 84 ('distributing blame'), 94 ('distribution of cases, ultimately, interacts with forms of justice that are better understood as inter-community or, quite simply, international'). A similar point was previously made by Damaška, *JICJ*, 10 (2012), 1239 ff. with regard to unindicted persons or States.

597 Chapter II, B.(5) in this volume.

598 cf. Schabas, *JMarshallLR*, 43 (2010), 544 and 547–8 (selection necessary but to be explained with a view to the general public); Guariglia and Rogier, in Stahn, *Practice* (2015), p. 352 (arguing that selectivity is a reality and calling for 'the formulation of transparent criteria and the scrutiny of the manner in which those criteria are applied in practice'); Levi, Hagan, and Dezalay, *LCP*, 79 (2016), 313; about the selection of cases at the ICTR in more detail, see Schabas, in Jalloh and Marong, *Promoting Accountability* (2015), pp. 58 ff. See also ICC-OTP, *Policy Case Selection* (2016), para. 5. For a comparison between the ICTY and the ICC with regard to prosecutorial policies, Brammertz, in Stahn et al., *Legacies of the ICTY* (2020), pp. 31 ff.; Heinze, in Heinze and Dittrich, *ICC* (2021), pp. 64–5. See also the insightful account of Goldstone, in Bergsmo and Dittrich, *Integrity* (2020), pp. 1065 ff.

strategy and policy papers already discussed above,[599] and following a related Draft paper of 2006,[600] it recently published a *Policy on Situation Completion* as part of a 'trilogy'[601] complementing the previous Policy Papers on Preliminary Examinations[602] and on Case Selection and Prioritisation.[603] It follows from the previous considerations on 'strategy and policy',[604] gravity,[605] and the investigatory activity of the Prosecutor at the preliminary examination and formal investigation stages[606] as well as from the just mentionedtrilogy[607] that the Prosecutor is only bound by the general principles of equality before the law and non-discrimination, that is, she must act independently, impartially,[608] and objectively investigating all parties to a conflict without favouring or discriminating against any one of them.[609]

In fact, the OTP has broad discretion with regard to case selection and prioritization,[610] and this discretion operates in a threefold way: as discretion to select a situation and make a preliminary case selection; once a situation is selected, it has discretion to deprioritize situations, select cases, and deprioritize cases; once cases are selected, it has discretion about which suspects to charge.[611] This discretion is guided by certain *policy criteria*,[612] namely:

599 Chapter II, B.(5) in this volume.

600 ICC-OTP, *Criteria for Selection* (2006).

601 ICC-OTP, *Situation Completion* (2021), para. 2 ('trilogy of policy papers describing the life cycle of the Office's operations in a situation').

602 ICC-OTP, *Policy Prelim. Examinations* (2013). Thereto Kersten, in deGuzman and Oosterveld, *Elgar Companion* (2020), pp. 183 ff.

603 ICC-OTP, *Policy Case Selection* (2016). For a detailed analysis see Bernaz, *JICJ*, 15 (2017), 527–42.

604 Chapter II, B.(5) in this volume.

605 Chapter III B.(2)(c) in this volume.

606 Section A.(1) and (2) in this chapter, esp. referring to Art. 53 ICCS.

607 The *Policy Paper on Case Selection and Prioritisation* explicitly 'draws from many of the same principles and criteria that are applied at the preliminary examination stage', ICC-OTP, *Policy Case Selection* (2016), para. 4. However, the paper also clarifies that 'by its nature, case selection requires the application of a more focused test than the one conducted at the situation stage. For each case selected for investigation and prosecution, jurisdiction, admissibility and the interests of justice will be considered in relation to identified incidents, persons and conduct' (para. 25). About the legal criteria governing case selection in more detail, see paras. 20–32.

608 'Impartiality' can be understood, however, in either procedural or political terms. See Rosenberg, *JICJ*, 15 (2017), 471–90; Heinze and Fyfe, in Bergsmo und Stahn, *Preliminary Examination II* (2018), pp. 1, 47 ff.

609 ICC-OTP, *Policy Case Selection* (2016), paras. 16–23. On the principle of objectivity in more detail, De Meester, *Investigation Phase* (2015), pp. 295 ff.

610 The OTP spoke of 'broad discretion' itself in the Draft Paper on Selection (2006), paras. 4, 12 ('Nonetheless, the Office has broad discretion in selecting individual cases for investigation and prosecution'), quoted according to Heinze and Fyfe, in Bergsmo und Stahn, *Preliminary Examination II* (2018), pp. 1, 47–8. Interestingly, the same language was not used in the final version, cf. ICC-OTP, *Policy Case Selection* (2016), para. 4. On our understanding of the concept of discretion see Section B.(3)(a); see also Governa, *Discretion* (2023), pp. 211–17.

611 cf. Expert Group, *IER* (2020), p. 207. See also Kersten, in deGuzman, and Oosterveld, *Elgar Companion ICC* (2020), p. 183; Heinze, in Heinze and Dittrich, *ICC* (2021), pp. 64 ff.; with regard to the (alleged) Africa-focus of the ICC see Kiyani, in deGuzman and Oosterveld, *Elgar Companion ICC* (2020), pp. 309 ff.

612 ICC-OTP, *Policy Case Selection* (2016), paras. 37 ff. On the governing principles of the selection process by the OTP, see also Guariglia and Rogier, in Stahn, *Practice* (2015), pp. 358–9; Kuczyńska, *Accusation Model ICC* (2015), pp. 112–15; Heinze and Fyfe, in Bergsmo und Stahn, *Preliminary Examination II* (2018), pp. 1–75, 47. In favour of the 'aggressor status' as a further criterion for case selection, Combs, *Pace Int'l L.Rev.*, 36 (2024), 102, 115 ff. (arguing that this would serve as 'a limited form of retribution and deterrence on aggressors by enhancing the likelihood of prosecution' [116] but considering this status 'only when there is clear and convincing evidence that one party acted in a manifestly wrongful way when initiating the conflict' [117]; further arguing, with reference to some African situations, that this aggressor status has already been used as a selection factor, although 'sub silentio' [117 ff.]).

- *Ratione personae*: focus on the 'most responsible',[613] with this concept having been interpreted more flexibly in recent years,[614] including also mid- and low-level perpetrators;[615]
- *Ratione materiae*: focus on specific crimes because of a special international/public interest/expressivist function (e.g. sexual and gender-based crimes and crimes against children),[616] 'scale, nature, manner of commission, and impact' (gravity requirements);[617]
- Focus on specific situations/cases because of certain qualitative considerations (quality and importance of the respective conflict, involvement of certain actors);
- Focus on incidents that are 'most representative of the scale and impact of the crimes' and on 'crimes that have been traditionally under-prosecuted';[618]
- Interests of justice within the meaning of Article 53;[619]
- Practical considerations (e.g. access to crime sites, available evidence, feasibility of arrest).[620]

[613] cf. e.g. *Situation in the Republic of Kenya*, ICC-01/09-19, para. 188; *Prosecutor v. Al Hassan*, PTC I, Decision on the Admissibility Challenge Raised by the Defence for Insufficient Gravity of the Case, ICC-01/12-01/18-459, 27 September 2019, paras. 50–2; see also Reg. 34 (1) RegOTP. See also, regarding other tribunals, Rule 28 (A) RPE ICTY (additional screening of indictment, introduced as part of completion strategy in 2004, to ensure that it 'concentrates on one or more of the most senior leaders suspected of being most responsible'; see thereon Friman, Brady, Costi, Guariglia, and Stuckenberg, in Sluiter et al., *International Criminal Procedure* (2013), p. 385) and Art. 1 (1) SCSLS (limiting the mandate to 'persons who bear the greatest responsibility'); Guariglia and Rogier, in Stahn, *Practice* (2015), pp. 351–2 (regarding ICTY), 360–1; Lafontaine and Magnoux, in Heinze and Dittrich, *ICC* (2021), pp. 241 ff.; with regard to the ECCC, esp. in the context of expressivism ('aesthetics'), DeFalco, *Invisible Atrocities* (2022), pp. 166 ff.

[614] See also Lafontaine and Magnoux, in Heinze and Dittrich, *ICC* (2021), pp. 241, 245.

[615] ICC-OTP, *Policy Case Selection* (2016), para. 42; ICC-OTP, *Strategic Plan* (2019), para. 5 (1) ('focusing on the most responsible perpetrators, if needed through a building upwards strategy'), also p. 19, para. 24 ('it might also imply a strategy of building upwards by focusing on mid-level or notorious perpetrators first, with the aim of reaching the level of the most responsible persons at a later stage'); ICC-OTP, *Report Prelim. Examinations* (2020), p. 4 with n. 3.

[616] cf. ICC-OTP, *Strategic Plan* (2013), paras. 58–63, *Strategic Plan* (2019), pp. 5 and 9 regarding the results of the 'Strategic Plan 2016–2018'; *Strategic Plan* (2023), pp. 17 and 19. About the 'Strategic Plan 2012–2015' see also Bensouda, in Jalloh and Marong, *Promoting Accountability* (2015), pp. 329 ff. Crit. on 'thematic prosecution of sex crimes', i.e. the primary selection and prioritization of these crimes over others, Ambos, in Bergsmo, *Thematic Prosecution of International Sex Crimes* (2018), pp. 303 ff.; crit. of the ICC practice so far, but optimistic because of the new course under Prosecutor Bensouda as evidenced by the OTP Policy Paper, Hayes, in Stahn, *Practice* (2015), pp. 801 ff. About institutional interests in case and situation selection, Kersten, in deGuzman and Oosterveld, *Elgar Companion ICC* (2020), pp. 185 ff.; see also Sander, *Justice to History* (2021), pp. 10 and 61 ff. (examining practices that have 'influenced the selection of prosecutorial targets in different institutional settings and the implications that have followed for the scope and content of the historical narratives constructed by international criminal courts in their judgments') and van Sliedregt, *LJIL*, 34 (2021), 283–90.

[617] cf. Reg. 29 (2) RegOTP and ICC-OTP, *Draft Policy Case Selection* (2016), para. 32; ICC-OTP, *Prelim. Examinations* (2013), paras. 9, 59 ff.; ICC-OTP, *Prelim. Examinations* (2020), para. 7; Guariglia and Rogier, in Stahn, *Practice* (2015), pp. 359–60; *Situation in the Republic of Kenya*, ICC-01/09-19, para. 188; *Muthaura et al.*, ICC-01/09-02/11-382-Red, para. 50, referring to sentencing Rule 145 (1)(c) RPE. For a discussion, see Chapter III, B.(2)(c) in this volume. The OTP points out that it 'may apply a stricter test when assessing gravity for the purposes of case selection than that which is legally required for the admissibility test under article 17': see ICC-OTP, *Policy Case Selection* (2016), para. 36, thereto Bernaz, *JICJ*, 15 (2017), 527, 528. About the preliminary examination of a situation and gravity, see Greenawalt, in deGuzman and Oosterveld, *Elgar Companion ICC* (2020), pp. 87 ff. See, on the gravity threshold already, Chapter III, B.(2)(c).

[618] Regulation 34 (2) RegOTP; ICC-OTP, *Policy Case Selection* (2016), paras. 45–6.

[619] See sub-section B.(4) in this chapter.

[620] cf. e.g. ICC-OTP, *Referrals and Communications* (2003), p. 1 ('feasibility of conducting an effective investigation in a particular territory'); ICC-OTP, *Policy Issues* (2003), p. 2 (availability of the necessary cooperation); ICC-OTP, *Policy Case Selection* (2016), para. 51 ('conduct an effective and successful investigation leading to a prosecution with a reasonable prospect of conviction'). See also Expert Group, *IER* (2020), pp. 206, 212, 218 (feasibility considerations with regard to the delay of execution of arrests warrants, e.g. in the case of 'Ali Kushayb' arrested thirteen years after the issuance of the first warrant of arrest).

Of course, the concrete application of these criteria is situation- and case-specific, that is, the ultimate selection or prioritization decision cannot be precisely determined by abstract criteria but remains in the hands of the Prosecutor whose discretion is only subject to a limited judicial review.[621] In particular the OTP's broad discretion has been acknowledged with regard to the selection of cases (acts, incidents, persons) within an authorized investigation of a certain situation.[622] At any event, the development of abstract criteria and the broadest possible transparency in the selection process will not make this process immune from criticism[623]—in fact, it is easy to criticize any prosecutorial choice as 'political' or biased for other reasons[624]—but only help to better explain the respective decisions. To counter the mentioned criticism, the OTP, in its 2016 Policy Paper on Case Selection and Prioritisation, dedicated an entire sub-section to the so-called 'Case Selection Document' which is meant to identify 'in broad terms the potential cases across all situations',[625] but remains confidential.[626] At any rate, the Expert Report still queried that 'there is no comprehensive mapping of all potential cases within each situation'.[627]

In contrast, the above-mentioned OTP *Policy on Situation Completion* is a (first) response to the IER's criticism that '[n]o policy for hibernation or closure of investigations has been adopted'.[628] Here, again, an internal document comparable to the 'Case Selection Document', the so-called 'Situation Strategy', seems to be the strategic centrepiece.[629] This (confidential) document is supposed to 'set out the lines of inquiry to be pursued before the investigation may be considered to be complete'.[630] It 'is framed around broad lines of inquiry—rather than pre-determined objectives (such as targeting particular individuals or groups, or bringing a certain number of prosecutions)—to ensure consistency with the core mandate of the Office: the open-ended investigation of cases, with a view to potential

[621] Only pursuant to legal regulation, esp. Art. 53 (3) ICCS. It is however questionable to interpret Art. 53 (1) (a) and (b) as providing for 'exacting legal requirements' (*Situation on the Vessels of Comoros*, ICC-01/13-34, para. 14); on the criticism regarding the trigger and scope of the judicial review, see Guariglia and Rogier, in Stahn, *Practice* (2015), pp. 362–3.

[622] cf. ICC, *Situation in Georgia*, Corrected Version of 'Request for authorisation of an investigation pursuant to article 15', 16 October 2015, ICC-01/15-4-Corr, ICC-01/15-4-Corr2, 17 November 2015, para. 51, holding that 'the Prosecution should be permitted to expand or modify its investigation with respect to these or other alleged acts, incidents, groups or persons and/or adopt different legal qualifications, so long as the cases brought forward for prosecution are sufficiently linked to the authorised situation'. See also ICC, *Situation in the Islamic Republic of Afghanistan*, Public Redacted Version of 'Request for authorisation of an investigation pursuant to article 15', ICC-02/17-7-Red, 20 November 2017, para. 38, *Situation in the People's Republic of Bangladesh/Republic of the Union of Myanmar*, PTC III, Decision pursuant to Article 15 of the Rome Statute on the Authorisation of an Investigation into the Situation in the People's Republic of Bangladesh/Republic of the Union of Myanmar, ICC-01/19-27, 14 November 2019, para. 126.

[623] Crit. of the prosecutorial practice regarding the selection of situations ('a primarily objective determination') and cases (discretion), e.g. Schabas, in Stahn, *Practice* (2015), pp. 380–1; crit. regarding case selection Expert Group, *IER* (2020), p. 213 (stressing 'the issues regarding unequal investigations into all sides of the conflict (e.g. DRC, Uganda), the time lag between investigating different parties to the conflict (e.g. Cote d'Ivoire (CIV)); the choice of charges which insufficiently represent the underlying crime patterns (e.g. Lubanga), suspects of low hierarchical position (e.g. Al Werfalli), or situations/cases with low feasibility').

[624] cf. Robinson, *LJIL*, 28 (2015), 334–6, 343, discussing selection as one of five inescapable dyads of the ICC, esp. referring to the factual criterion of feasibility of arrest (336); Guariglia and Rogier, in Stahn, *Practice* (2015), pp. 363–4 (arguing that such criticism is inherent in the international prosecution of crimes); Adekunle, in Heinze and Dittrich, *ICC* (2021), pp. 409, 419.

[625] ICC-OTP, *Policy Case Selection* (2016), para. 10.

[626] Ibid., para. 15.

[627] Expert Group, *IER* (2020), p. 220.

[628] Ibid., p. 222.

[629] ICC-OTP, *Situation Completion* (2021), paras. 20 ff.

[630] Ibid., para. 23.

prosecution if justified on the basis of the evidence.'[631] The Situation Strategy identifies lines of inquiry that, in turn, refer to the following (non-exhaustive) list of factors:

- Representing the gravity of the alleged criminality in the situation (quantitatively and qualitatively), taking into account the likely charges and the likelihood that they will meet the Office's standard for prosecution, and the interest in bringing at least some cases to trial at the Court within a reasonable time;
- The interests of victims and affected communities;
- The types of evidence available in the situation (witnesses, documents, open-source material, electronic data, imagery, financial data, scientific and other expert evidence, etc.), its volume and accessibility, and any anticipated threats to its preservation;
- The prospects and requirements for cooperation with the Office, including from State Parties, other relevant States, international organizations, and non-governmental organizations ('NGOs');
- The prospects for relevant genuine proceedings in other jurisdictions, and especially possible accountability partnerships with relevant States;
- The operational conditions affecting the Office's ability to conduct successful investigations and prosecutions, and to execute arrest strategies, while discharging its protection duties under the Statute; and
- The resources anticipated to be required to investigate and, if necessary, prosecute relevant cases.

Of most practical relevance is the question of how to deal with a situation where it turns out that possible cases arising out of it might never be prosecuted. Eventually, this question does not only affect the fate of the possible cases but of the entire situation. Here the OTP's new '*depriorisation*' policy with regard to cases becomes relevant. It means that the Prosecutor may suspend the investigation of a case 'pending a material change in external circumstances.'[632] The OTP does not hide the fact that deprioritization is also, perhaps even mainly, resource-driven.[633] In addition, it is also due to an increase in the number of situations.[634] This illustrates the interrelation between situations and cases and their completion. The OTP emphasizes that deprioritized cases have an impact on the situation, 'since they prevent the Office from fully pursuing all lines of inquiry in the Situation Strategy and thereby proceeding to conclude the Investigation Phase.'[635] An example of such a deprioritization is the ICC Prosecutor's decision on 27 September 2021 to deprioritize certain aspects of the Afghanistan investigation, for example alleged crimes by CIA members and US armed forces.[636] This deprioritization illustrates the conflict of feasibility aspects on the one hand (prospect of a conviction) and gravity on the other. In this regard, the Afghanistan situation

[631] Ibid., para. 24.
[632] Ibid., paras. 36, 43.
[633] Ibid., para. 44.
[634] Ibid., para. 45: 'Rapid expansion of the Office's docket of situations may mean that cases (or even, consequently, a situation as a whole) will be deprioritised or suspended more frequently and that certain cases may be deprioritised for much longer, as new cases are selected and prioritised instead.'
[635] Ibid., para. 46.
[636] ICC-OTP, *Statement Khan* (27 September 2021). At the same time the Prosecutor sought authorization to resume the OTP investigation in the Afghanistan situation focusing 'on crimes allegedly committed by the Taliban and the Islamic State—Khorasan Province ("IS-K")', cf. ICC, *Situation in the Islamic Republic of Afghanistan*, PTC II, Request to Authorize Resumption of Investigation under Article 18 (2) of the Statute, ICC-02/17-161, 27 September 2021

may well decide the future course of preliminary examinations.[637] Thus, arguably, the *Policy on Situation Completion* revolves around resources and feasibility at the dispense of gravity and thus seems to contradict the Policy on case selection and prioritization.[638]

### (2) The fine distinction between Article 53 (1) and (2) ICC Statute

As we have already said above, the decision to investigate under Article 53 (1) marks the end of the preliminary examination (pre-investigation) phase, while the decision to prosecute under Article 53 (2)—'upon investigation'—terminates the investigation phase.[639] Apart from the procedural stage when the respective decisions are taken, their difference is twofold: on the one hand, the Article 53 (2) decision requires a slightly higher threshold than the one under Article 53 (1), that is, a 'sufficient' instead of a mere 'reasonable' basis.[640] On the other hand, the listed factors to be taken into account are—apart from admissibility (complementarity) and interests of justice[641]—distinct in that the question of jurisdiction is settled under Article 53 (1)(a), while Article 53 (2)(a) presupposes a sufficiently advanced individualization to seek a warrant or summons under Article 58.[642] This corresponds to the previously mentioned development from a situation (preliminary examination) to a case (formal investigation, prosecution); that is, it merely stresses the increasing individualization in line with the advancement of the procedure notwithstanding the further requirement to actually issue such a warrant or summons (to be examined more closely below).[643] In any case, as Article 53 (2) presupposes a negative decision (not to prosecute), the Prosecutor need not take any formal decision with regard to a warrant or summons, if she wants to discontinue the proceedings. In contrast, if she sees a sufficient basis to prosecute, she will regularly request—Article 53 (2)(a) *e contrario*—an arrest warrant or summons to appear.[644]

The advanced individualization also explains the further difference between Article 53 (1) and (2) with regard to the listed factors to be taken into account to assess the countervailing consideration of the 'interests of justice' under subparagraph (c):[645] apart from 'gravity of the crime' and 'interests of victims', Article 53 (2) refers to 'the age or infirmity of the alleged perpetrator, and his or her role in the alleged crime', given that at this stage of the investigation there is a concrete suspect ('alleged perpetrator'). Thus, the interests of justice may speak against a prosecution, if a suspect may not survive the proceedings because of his advanced age or his state of health ('infirmity'), or if he had only a minor, secondary role in the alleged crime(s).[646] Also, the list in subparagraph 2 (c) is not exhaustive ('all the circumstances, including').[647] Given these differences between Article 53 (1) and (2), it is not

[637] See also Stahn, Bergsmo, and Chan, in Bergsmo and Stahn, *Preliminary Examination I* (2018), p. 6 ("'Nicaragua moment" for the ICC that can make it or break it').

[638] EP, *ICC* (2021); AI, 'Afghanistan' (2021); Trahan, *Opinio Juris* (1 October 2021).

[639] See also Safferling, *Criminal Procedure* (2012), p. 229.

[640] See also ibid., p. 240 ('slightly different threshold'); Bergsmo, Kruger and Bekou, 'Article 53', in Ambos, *Commentary* (2022), mn. 11.

[641] cf. subparas. (b) and (c) of Art. 53 (1) and (2).

[642] cf. Art. 53 (2)(a) providing negatively—as a reason for the lack of a *sufficient basis to prosecute—that there 'is not a sufficient legal or factual basis to seek a warrant* or summons'. For a crit. view, see Safferling, *Criminal Procedure* (2012), pp. 240–1, arguing that 'there is no logical reason for the application of the arrest warrant test' since there are, apart from the level of suspicion, other factors to be taken into account.

[643] Section B.(6)(a) in this chapter.

[644] See also Safferling, *Criminal Procedure* (2012), p. 242.

[645] cf. subparas. (c) of Art. 53 (1) and (2).

[646] See also Safferling, *Criminal Procedure* (2012), pp. 226–7.

[647] See also Bergsmo, Kruger and Bekou, 'Article 53', in Ambos, *Commentary* (2022), mn. 41.

entirely convincing that Reg. 29 RegOTP shall equally (*mutatis mutandis*) apply to both paragraphs.[648] This only makes sense in mere administrative terms, that is, as to the preparation of the respective Article 53 (1) and (2) reports[649] and to the ongoing nature of the evaluation.[650]

### (3) Prosecutorial discretion vs. judicial supervision during preliminary examination and investigation

#### (a) *General remarks, especially the concept of discretion*

The term 'discretion' has already been used at various times in this chapter and previously. It is now time to take a closer look at this concept. In its broad meaning, which is the one employed here, 'discretion' includes both the drawing of a legal conclusion/consequence from a given set of facts (in German *Rechtsfolgeermessen*) and the decision on whether the prerequisites for the exercise of legal power have been fulfilled (*Beurteilungsspielraum*/margin of appreciation/scope for judgment/interpretive judgment).[651] Authorities use this interpretive judgment when there are indeterminate/vague legal concepts (*unbestimmte Rechtsbegriffe*) such as 'public interest', 'reasonable suspicion', 'public safety', etc., and they are tasked with applying these concepts to the facts at hand.[652]

While in international criminal procedure 'discretion' is usually employed for both the interpretive judgment and the conclusion from a given set of facts, it is worth noting that the distinction plays a role in two regards: first, with regard to judicial review and secondly, because many discretionary decisions taken by the Prosecutor are in fact forms of interpretive judgment. This can be illustrated with the 'reasonable basis to proceed' clause in Article 53 (1)(c) ICCS:[653] '[t]he Prosecutor *shall* [ ...] iniiate an investigation unless he or she determines that there is no *reasonable basis* to proceed under this Statute' (emphasis added). The legal conclusion is the initiation of an investigation, and the word 'shall' indicates that the Prosecutor is *obliged* to investigate once the requirements of the provision are met.[654] Thus, the Prosecutor has *no discretion* with regard to the legal conclusion. Yet, the situation is different with regard to the element 'reasonable basis to proceed', where, arguably, the Prosecutor enjoys *full discretion*.[655] Legal systems such as Germany would not use the term 'discretion' in the latter case: in their understanding, discretion can only exist with regard to the legal conclusion of a provision, otherwise—with regard to the legal requirements of a provision, especially if they are vaguely formulated (like 'reasonable basis')—the Prosecutor (or any deciding authority) rather has an interpretive judgment or a margin of appreciation with regard to *the facts*. As a further consequence, in these systems courts do not only have full review powers but are 'even entitled to exercise a *de novo* review—that is, they define the undefined/vague concepts themselves and do not ask whether the agency's application was

[648] Reg. 29 (5) RegOTP.
[649] Reg. 29 (1) RegOTP.
[650] Reg. 29 (4) RegOTP.
[651] In detail, Fyfe and Heinze, in Ambos et al., *Core Concepts II* (2022), pp. 169, 174–7.
[652] Fyfe and Heinze, in Ambos et al., *Core Concepts II* (2022), pp. 169, 174. Following this understanding, Cross in Bergsmo and Stahn, *Preliminary Examination II* (2018), pp. 213, 238 uses a narrow interpretation of 'discretion' if he states: 'To be clear, the application of the standard of proof in Articles 53(1)(a) and (b) allows no discretion in the legal sense at all. Rather, the only discretion lies in Article 53(1)(c)'.
[653] Fyfe and Heinze, in Ambos et al., *Core Concepts II* (2022), pp. 169, 175.
[654] Bergsmo and Bekou, 'Article 53', in Ambos, *Commentary* (2022), mn. 6.
[655] Ibid., mn. 6.

correct'.[656] Discretionary decisions *stricto sensu* (referring to the legal conclusion), by contrast, may be reviewed, albeit with some limitations.[657] As we will see later, the ICC regime, too, makes an implicit distinction between interpretive judgment and discretion *stricto sensu*, especially in the context of standards of proof and the 'interests of justice' (to be dealt with in more detail in the next section). The preliminary examination phase is especially full of discretionary decisions.[658]

If we now turn to the distribution of responsibilities between the prosecutorial and judicial authorities during the investigative phase of the proceedings, it is the rule that the Prosecutor of an international criminal tribunal fully controls this phase and it is her responsibility alone to formulate the charges.[659] As already mentioned in Chapter II, with regard to the ICC, Chambers have 'to exercise their oversight functions with great care and full respect for the OTP's independence'.[660] At the ad hoc tribunals and the KSC this already follows from the adversarial structure of the proceedings and the full prosecutorial autonomy in carrying out the investigation;[661] under the ICC regime it results from Article 42 (1) and Article 54 (1)(b) ICCS already quoted above.[662] However, a closer look reveals that there are some important differences between the ad hoc tribunals/KSC and the ICC, and between the preliminary examination and the investigation phase of the proceedings. As to the former, it is plain that the OTP of the ad hoc tribunals/KSC has much more autonomy and a higher degree of discretion than that of the ICC.[663] The former can independently decide when to submit an indictment and when to withdraw it and this decision can only be subjected to a (subsequent) judicial review by way of a review procedure.[664] The latter faces greater judicial control, especially in case of a *proprio motu* investigation (as we will see in a moment). This can be explained by the OTP's broad range of unregulated and informal activities especially during a preliminary examination. This has led one to speak of a 'prosecutorial managerialism', by analogy with the already mentioned 'judicial managerialism'.[665] Arguably, in a way, the ICCS balances one form of managerialism against the other.

### *(b) Review of the Prosecutor's* proprio motu *investigation*

The ICC Prosecutor's *proprio motu* investigation is subject, as already mentioned above,[666] to an early judicial control through the PTC.[667] In fact, once a situation is triggered, it is

[656] Fyfe and Heinze, in Ambos et al., *Core Concepts II* (2022), pp. 169, 180 with further references.

[657] Ibid., pp. 169, 183–4.

[658] Stahn, Bergsmo, and Chan, in Bergsmo and Stahn, *Preliminary Examination I* (2018), p. 14: '[P]rosecutorial discretion plays an important role in preliminary examinations. It underpins fundamental aspects of preliminary examination.'

[659] See above note 158 with main text.

[660] Chapter II, B.(1) in this volume.

[661] cf. Art. 18 ICTYS/Art. 17 ICTRS (esp. para. 1) and Art. 35 KSC Law (esp. paras. 1, 5); see also Boas et al., *Procedure* (2011), p. 104; see also Friman, in Cryer et al., *ICL* (2014), p. 438, linking the adversarial procedure to prosecutorial independence: ('Prosecutor's institutional independence and large functional autonomy' as 'adversarial features', but 'impartiality … more inquisitorial' pointing to a 'role as "an officer of justice" rather than a partisan party'); apparently giving up this view now Vasiliev, in Cryer et al., *ICL* (2019), pp. 416–17. See also Cayley, in Bergsmo and Stahn, *Preliminary Examination I* (2018), pp. 35, 36 ff.

[662] Note 119 and main text in this chapter.

[663] See the provisions mentioned above note 667 and also Zahar and Sluiter, *ICL* (2008), p. 55.

[664] cf. Art. 19 ICTYS, Arts. 17 (4), 18 ICTRS, and Rules 47 RPE ICTY/ICTR, 48 RPE MICT; Art. 39 (1), (2) KSC Law and Rule 86 (4) RPE KSC; see also Zahar and Sluiter, *ICL* (2008), pp. 47 ff.; Langer, *AJCompL*, 53 (2005), 863; Stahn, in Stahn and Sluiter, *Practice* (2009), p. 266.

[665] Stahn, Bergsmo, and Chan, in Bergsmo and Stahn, *Preliminary Examination I* (2018), p. 10.

[666] See Section A.(1)(a)(i) in this chapter; on other (non-judicial) forms of control, see Chapter II, B.(7) in this volume.

[667] For the role of the Pre-Trial Division regarding the crime of aggression, see Art. 15*bis* (8) ICCS. Crit. with regard to judicial control during a preliminary examination and its impact on the length of proceedings, Gumpert and Nuzban, in Heinze and Dittrich, *ICC* (2021), pp. 553, 564–5; see also Governa, *Discretion* (2023), pp. 271–3.

assigned to a PTC by the Presidency and this PTC 'shall be responsible for any matter, request or information arising out of the situation assigned to it'.[668] As explained above, the extent of judicial review does not only depend on the drawing of a legal conclusion from a given set of facts (*Rechtsfolgeermessen*) but also on the fulfilment of the prerequisites for the exercise of legal power (*Beurteilungsspielraum*). The latter encompasses the interpretation of the concept of 'situation'.[669] PTCs have traditionally used their review power broadly to correct the temporal scope of a situation as determined by the OTP.[670] In the Afghanistan situation, for instance, PTC II did not approve of the Prosecutor's request 'to be permitted to expand or modify its investigation ... so long as the cases brought forward for prosecution [were] *sufficiently* linked to the authorized situation',[671] but instead required a '*close* link [...] with one or more of the incidents specifically authorised'.[672]

Yet, judicial control has its limits, even in *proprio motu* investigations. The Afghanistan situation illustrates this well. In two regards, the AC limited the PTC's judicial review power and emphasized the OTP's broad discretion.[673] First, it supported the latter's flexible approach of expanding or modifying its investigation as long as it is *sufficiently* linked to the authorized situation.[674] Secondly, the AC considered that the PTC interpreted its judicial review powers too broadly in deciding on the OTP's request under Article 15 (3) ICCS.[675] The OTP decided that all requirements of Article 53 (1) ICC Statute had been met, including the absence of the negative interests of justice criterion.[676] Put differently, the OTP did not consider that the investigations would *not* serve the interests of justice and therefore did not even mention this requirement. However, the PTC decided not to authorize the opening

[668] Reg. 46 (2) in relation with Reg. 45 RegC. See also ICC, *Situation in the CAR*, PTC III, Decision Requesting Information on the Status of the Preliminary Examination of the Situation in the Central African Republic, ICC-01/05-6, 30 November 2006, p. 3.

[669] von Maltitz and Körner, in Heinze and Dittrich, *ICC* (2021), pp. 649, 660 ff.

[670] ICC, *Situation in the Republic of Kenya*, PTC II, Corrigendum of the Decision Pursuant to Article 15 of the Rome Statute on the Authorization of an Investigation into the Situation in the Republic of Kenya, ICC-01/09-19-Corr, 1 April 2010, para. 203 ('In the Chamber's opinion, the reference to the phrases "including" but not limited to" and "in relation to the post election violence of 2007–2008", is too broad, and as such, it is the responsibility of the Chamber to define the temporal scope of the authorization for investigation with respect to the situation under consideration'); *Situation in the Republic of Côte d'Ivoire*, PTC III, Decision on the 'Prosecution's provision of further information regarding potentially relevant crimes committed between 2002 and 2010', ICC-02/11-36, 22 February 2012, para. 36 ('[T]he Chamber is of the view that the violent events in Côte d'Ivoire in the period between 19 September 2002 and 28 November 2010, although reaching varying levels of intensity at different locations and at different times, *are to be treated as a single situation*, in which an ongoing crisis involving a prolonged political dispute and power-struggle culminated in the events in relation to which the Chamber earlier authorised an investigation', emphasis added), para. 37 ('Accordingly, the Chamber expands its authorisation for the investigation in Côte d'Ivoire to include crimes within the jurisdiction of the Court allegedly committed between 19 September 2002 and 28 November 2010').

[671] ICC, *Situation in the Islamic Republic of Afghanistan*, PTC III, Public Redacted Version of 'Request for authorisation of an investigation pursuant to article 15', 20 November 2017, ICC-02/17-7-Conf-Exp, ICC-02/17-7-Red, 20 November 2017, para. 38 (emphasis added).

[672] *Situation in the Islamic Republic of Afghanistan*, ICC-02/17-33, para. 41 (emphasis added).

[673] Chigowe, *LJIL*, 35 (2022), 699 ff.

[674] *Situation in the Islamic Republic of Afghanistan*, ICC-02/17-138, para. 64: '[T]he Appeals Chamber finds that the Pre-Trial Chamber erred in finding that the scope of any authorisation granted would be limited to the incidents mentioned in the Request and those closely linked thereto.'

[675] cf. ICC, *Situation in the Islamic Republic of Afghanistan*, AC, Written Submissions in the Proceedings Relating to the Appeals Filed Against the 'Decision Pursuant to Article 15 of the Rome Statute on the Authorisation of an Investigation into the Situation in the Islamic Republic of Afghanistan' Issued on 12 April 2019 (ICC-02/17-33) and pursuant to 'Decision on the participation of amici curiae, the Office of Public Counsel for the Defence and the cross-border victims' Issued on 14 October 2019 (ICC-02/17–97), ICC-02/17-108, 14 November 2019 and *Annex*, ibid. ICC-02/17-108-Anx.

[676] Thereto, in more detail, Section B.(4).

of an investigation for allegedly not serving the interests of justice.[677] Even though the AC overturned this decision authorizing, by majority, the investigation,[678] the PTC's decision struck a nerve in the ICC's judicial control system. Of course, it is the Chamber which carries the burden of proof/persuasion that the investigation would *not* serve the interests of justice. If the Chamber, in reviewing[679] the decision of the Prosecutor (under Article 15 (4) ICC Statute), does not see any reasons why the investigation would not be in the interests of justice, it does not have to spend a single word on that issue. This was already decided in the *Kenya* Authorisation Decision:

> Unlike sub-paragraphs (a) and (b) [of Art. 53 (1) ICCS], which require an affirmative finding, sub-paragraph (c) does not require the Prosecutor to establish that an investigation is actually in the interests of justice. Indeed, the Prosecutor does not have to present reasons or supporting material in this respect. Thus, the Chamber considers that a review of this requirement is *unwarranted* in the present decision, taking into consideration that the Prosecutor has not determined that an investigation 'would not serve the interests of justice', which would prevent him from proceeding with a request for authorization of an investigation. [ ... ] It is only when the Prosecutor decides that an investigation would not be in the interests of justice that he or she is under the obligation to notify the Chamber of the reasons for such a decision, thereby triggering the review power of the Chamber.[680]

The Chamber's formulation 'that a review of this requirement is unwarranted', in combination with the referral to Article 53 (3)(b) ICCS, which triggers its 'review power', suggests that it understands 'unwarranted' as 'unlawful' or not based on any authority. A similar wording can be found in the *Côte d'Ivoire* Authorisation Decision[681] and the position has, in fact, been confirmed in the *Afghanistan* authorization decision.[682] This seems to go beyond the mere issue of burden of proof in Article 53 (1)(c) ICCS,[683] which might lead to the argument that due to the different standard of proof in subparagraph (1)(c) ('substantial reasons to believe') prosecutorial discretion is broader than in subparagraphs (1)(a) and (b) and hence less limited by way of a review. The aforementioned decisions, however, seem even to go beyond that, suggesting that a review of the negative interests of justice clause is prohibited by law.

This is, arguably, too narrow a reading. For to deny a PTC the possibility to conduct a review of the negative interests of justice criterion within Article 53 (1)(c) ICCS, even if the prosecution makes no determination to that end, would openly disregard the drafting history of Article 53.

[677] *Situation in the Islamic Republic of Afghanistan*, ICC-02/17-33, paras. 89 ff. (12 April 2019). On the Afghanistan situation in more detail, Adekunle, in Heinze and Dittrich, *ICC* (2021), pp. 409, 427 ff.; on this decision in more detail, see Section B.(4)(c).

[678] *Situation in the Islamic Republic of Afghanistan*, ICC-02/17-138, Disposition.

[679] The use of 'reviewing' here is not supposed to preclude the debate about whether this is—in fact—a review. The AC rejected this reading: '[T]he process under paragraphs 3–5 of article 15 *is not a review* of the Prosecutor's determination. Rather the Prosecutor seeks the pre-trial chamber's authorisation to proceed and that authorisation should be based on the application by the pre-trial chamber of the separate factors specified in paragraph 4, to the Prosecutor's application. Thus the pre-trial chamber is required to reach its own determination under article 15(4) of the Statute as to whether there is a reasonable basis to proceed with an investigation. It is not called to review the Prosecutor's analysis of the factors under article 53(1)(a) to (c) of the Statute'; *Situation in the Islamic Republic of Afghanistan*, ICC-02/17-138, para. 45 (emphasis added). Crit. Chigowe, *LJIL*, 35 (2022), 699, 701 ff.

[680] *Situation in Republic of Kenya*, ICC-01/09-19-Corr, para. 63 (emphasis added).

[681] *Situation in the Republic of Côte d'Ivoire*, ICC-02/11-14-Corr, para. 207 *in fine*.

[682] *Situation in the Islamic Republic of Afghanistan*, ICC-02/17-138, para. 37.

[683] Cross, in Bergsmo and Stahn, *Preliminary Examination II* (2018), pp. 213, 218 ff.

Delegates would not have agreed upon the inclusion of the interests of justice clause in Article 53 (1) ICCS if it had been formulated positively and connected with a low standard of proof; nor would they have agreed upon the inclusion without the specific review mechanism provided for in Article 53 (3)(b) ICCS.[684] Admittedly, the procedural constellation is different where the Prosecutor requests the authorization to open an investigation pursuant to Article 15; yet, the *telos* of the procedural control remains the same in both procedural constellations: a judicial review is supposed to make sure that the negative interests of justice criterion will not be used as a gateway for political pressure.[685] The rationale of refraining from judicial review when the Prosecutor decides *not* to investigate is that a Chamber is 'not empowered to substitute a negative decision with its own prosecution';[686] by contrast, a decision *to* investigate can indeed be reviewed—including all conditions of the relevant provision, whether positive or negative. Thus, unlike the *Kenya* and *Côte d'Ivoire* PTCs, PTC I in the *Georgia* Authorisation Decision did not conclude that it had no authority to speak to the interests of justice clause (if not explicitly dealt with by the prosecution) but formulated cautiously: 'the Chamber *considers* that there are indeed no substantial reasons to believe that an investigation would not serve the interests of justice.'[687] The use of the word 'considers' shows that the Chamber *decided* not to review the negative interests of justice element—instead of assuming a (formal) *prohibition* to review it. The same wording appears in the *Burundi* Authorisation Decision.[688] This is the more convincing approach.

#### *(c) Review in case of State or Security Council referrals*

Preliminary examinations in case of State or Security Council referrals[689] are usually less formalized and more comprehensive than the ones following a *proprio motu* initiation. The OTP may decide 'to initiate an investigation',[690] when it considers its preliminary examination concluded—there is no time limit in the Statute or Rules[691]—and only from that moment on can the PTC formally review the respective OTP decision. The PTC, in particular, is entitled to review OTP non-investigation or non-prosecution decisions under Article 53 (1) and (2) pursuant to Article 53 (3) ICCS. Insofar as the OTP has, first of all, certain information obligations: it 'shall' inform the PTC of a non-investigation decision based solely on the 'interests of justice',[692] and generally of a non-prosecution decision;[693] it shall also inform a State or the Security Council, if they have referred the respective situation.[694]

[684] Bitti, *EJIL: Talk!*, 14 August 2019; see, in more detail, Section B.(4).

[685] The Afghanistan situation is a paradigmatic example for such pressure and its possible effect on judges, see already Ambos, *Treatise ICL I* (2021), p. 62. In a similar vein, Cullen, Kastner, and Richmond, in ibid, *Politics* (2021), pp. 5–6: 'appears to have had a direct impact on the work of the Court. For example, the decision of Pre-Trial Chamber II in April 2019 that stopped the Prosecutor from opening a formal investigation into crimes allegedly committed by Taliban, American and Afghan forces in Afghanistan based in part on the assumption that little co-operation with the Court could be expected from the US.'

[686] Friman et al., in Sluiter et al., *International Criminal Procedure* (2013), pp. 381, 390.

[687] *Situation in Georgia*, ICC-01/15-12, para. 58 *in fine* (emphasis added).

[688] *Situation in the Republic of Burundi*, ICC-01/17-9-Red, para. 190 *in fine* ('Chamber considers that there are indeed no substantial reasons to believe that an investigation would not serve the interests of justice.')

[689] cf. Art. 13 (a) and (b) ICCS.

[690] Art. 53 (1) ICCS.

[691] cf. Nouwen, *Complementarity* (2013), p. 94.

[692] Art. 53 (1) *in fine*, Rule 105 (4) RPE ICC.

[693] Art. 53 (2) *in fine*, Rule 106 (1) RPE ICC.

[694] Art. 53 (2) *in fine*, Rules 105 (1), 106 (1) RPE ICC.

The PTC 'may'[695] then review the non-investigation or non-prosecution decision,[696] either upon the request of the respective State or the Security Council[697] or upon its own initiative, if the decision rests only on the interests of justice clause.[698] If the Chamber reviews upon request, the review is triggered by the disagreement between the Prosecutor and the referring entity and indeed 'limited by the parameters of this disagreement'.[699] In the latter case, the OTP's decision must be confirmed by the PTC to become 'effective'.[700]

In all these cases, the PTC exercises legitimate judicial oversight without unduly encroaching upon the Prosecutor's independence.[701] Last but not least, the Prosecutor depends on measures and orders of the PTC in relation to a unique investigative opportunity[702] and possible other pre-trial orders.[703]

### (d) *Limits of judicial review, especially with regard to prosecutorial inaction*

However, there are serious restraints on the judicial review of prosecutorial decisions or rather non-decisions. In fact, the architects of the Statute neglected the problem of *prosecutorial inaction*.[704] Generally, there is—either legally or factually—no possibility of judicial review in case of prosecutorial inaction. Thus, a decision not to initiate an investigation under Article 15 cannot be reviewed.[705] PTC I has decided that there is nothing to review where no decision has been taken by the OTP.[706] Also, there is no judicial review with regard to investigative measures

[695] It is not legally obliged to do so, but enjoys discretion; cf. ICC, *Situation on the Vessels of Comoros*, PTC I, Partly Dissenting Opinion of Judge Kovács, ICC-01/13-34-Anx-Corr, 16 July 2015, paras. 2–5.

[696] See generally ICC, *Situation in the DRC*, PTC I, Decision on the Requests of the Legal Representative for Victims VPRS1 to VPRS 6 regarding 'Prosecutor's information on further investigation', ICC-01/04-399, 26 September 2007, pp. 5, 6; ICC, *Situation in the DRC*, PTC I, Decision on the Request Submitted pursuant to Rule 103 (1) of the Rules of Procedure and Evidence, ICC-01/04-373, 17 August 2007, para. 5; *Situation in the Islamic Republic of Afghanistan*, ICC-02/17-138, 5 March 2020, paras. 28–9; see also Schabas, *ICC Commentary* (2016), pp. 841 ff.; Guariglia, in Stahn and Sluiter, *Practice* (2009), p. 216; Safferling, *Criminal Procedure* (2012), pp. 238–9.

[697] Art. 53 (3)(a); on formal requirements and decision, see Rules 107, 108 RPE ICC.

[698] Art. 53 (3)(b); on formal requirements and decision, see Rules 109, 110 RPE ICC.

[699] *Situation on the Vessels of Comoros*, ICC-01/13-34, paras. 9 (distinguishing this review from the one under Art. 15) and 10 ('limited to the issues that are raised in the request for review and have a bearing on the Prosecutor's conclusion not to investigate'). The PTC applies the standard of review adopted by the AC with regard to interlocutory appeals (ibid., para. 12; on this standard, see Chapter VI, B.(2) in this volume); crit. in this regard, *Situation on the Vessels of Comoros*, ICC-01/13-34-Anx-Corr, paras. 6–8 (in favour of a more deferential approach regarding the Prosecutor's discretion).

[700] Art. 53 (3)(b) second cl.

[701] cf. *Situation on the Vessels of Comoros*, ICC-01/13-34, para. 15; *Situation on the Vessels of Comoros*, AP, Judgment on the Appeal of the Prosecutor against Pre-Trial Chamber I's 'Decision on the "Application for Judicial Review by the Government of the Union of the Comoros"', ICC-01/13-98, 2 September 2019, paras. 93–4; ICC, *Situation in the Bolivarian Republic of Venezuela I*, PTC I, Public Redacted Version of 'Decision on the "Request for judicial control submitted to the Pre-Trial Chamber I of the International Criminal Court by the Bolivarian Republic of Venezuela pursuant to Articles 15 and 21.3 of the Statute and Rule 46.2 of the Rules of the regulations of the Court"', ICC-02/18-9-Red, 14 June 2021, paras. 16–18. See also Chaitidou, *ZfIStW*, 1 (2022), 662, 671–2.

[702] Art. 56 ICCS.

[703] Art. 57; also Rules 115, 116 RPE ICC; generally on pre-trial orders, see Boas et al., *Procedure* (2011), pp. 210–13.

[704] cf. Stahn, in Stahn and Sluiter, *Practice* (2009), p. 267.

[705] cf. ibid., p. 255.

[706] cf. *Situation in the DRC*, PTC I, Decision on the Request of the Legal Representative of Victims VPRS 3 and VPRS 6 to Review an Alleged Decision of the Prosecutor not to Proceed, ICC-01/04-582, 25 October 2010, pp. 4–5 (arguing that in absence of an OTP decision under Art. 53 on 'interest of justice' grounds 'there is no decision for the Chamber to review and there is, accordingly, no basis for it to exercise its powers under article 53 (3)(b) of the Statute'); crit. Stahn, in Stahn and Sluiter, *Practice* (2009), pp. 277–8; in the same vein recently, ICC, *Situation in the Republic of Kenya*, PTC II, Decision on the 'Victims' request for review of Prosecution's decision to cease active investigation', ICC-01/09-159, 5 November 2015, paras. 19 ff. (no judicial review where no non-investigation

under Article 54 ICCS.[707] The PTC's review authority is conclusively regulated by Article 53 (3) ICCS.[708]

In practical terms, it is unclear how specific the information obligations of the OTP with respect to non-investigation or prosecution decisions are: does it suffice to report only a non-investigation/prosecution decision in a given situation generally, or does the Office need to report any single case it decides not to investigate or prosecute?[709] This lack of clarity directly derives from the ambiguous wording of Article 53 (1) and (2), which fails to precisely define the object of the investigation or prosecution *ratione personae* or *materiae* beyond the above-mentioned situation/case divide.[710] The case law has not yet (explicitly) ruled on the matter,[711] but it seems clear that a too strict interpretation would go against the logic of the trigger mechanisms (situations instead of cases) and the structure of the preliminary examination phase, which gives the Prosecutor a broad discretion, especially, as we have seen above, regarding selection and prioritization of situations and cases.[712] In addition, a kind of micro-level control of prosecutorial decisions (why commander A and not B, why village C and not D) is hardly practical given that only the concrete investigator working on the respective case has sufficient information to take these decisions and it is generally difficult for an outside organ to get involved so deeply in a prosecutorial investigation.[713] After all, the decision to investigate or prosecute belongs to the realm of the Prosecutor, being the *dominis litis* over this part of the proceedings, and thus cannot be substituted by a judicial organ.[714]

If it is correct, as we said before, that the PTC can only intervene—by formally undertaking a judicial review—once the OTP has taken the Article 53 (1) decision, the Prosecutor

or prosecution decision under Art. 53 has been taken. Generally, on judicial control of a refusal to prosecute, see Kuczyńska, *Accusation Model ICC* (2015), pp. 160–5.

707 *Situation in the Republic of Kenya*, ICC-01/09-159, para. 13 with further references in n. 9. See also Cross, in Bergsmo and Stahn, *Preliminary Examination II* (2018), pp. 213, 246.

708 *Situation in the Republic of Kenya*, ICC-01/09-159, para. 18 (arguing that therefore there is no lacuna which allows to invoke general principles of law pursuant to Art. 21 (1) ICCS).

709 The answer to this question also determines the scope of the PTC's review pursuant to Art. 53 (3) ICCS; leaving it open, deGuzman and Schabas, in Sluiter et al., *International Criminal Procedure* (2013), p. 147.

710 Regarding the non-prosecution decision under Art. 53 (2), see Stahn, in Stahn and Sluiter, *Practice* (2009), pp. 270–1, giving four possible interpretations (regarding a specific person, a group of persons, certain crimes, or no prosecution at all); see also Ohlin, in Stahn and Sluiter, *Practice* (2009), pp. 190–2, 207 (distinguishing between the particular discretion of a Prosecutor regarding the individual culpability of particular defendants and the general prosecutorial discretion regarding the collective dimensions of international crimes, the latter amounting to an intrusion of the Security Council's discretion); Governa, *Discretion* (2023), pp. 311–13.

711 The two decisions quoted by Nouwen, *Complementarity* (2013), p. 95 with nn. 243–4 do not speak to our problem. The decision *Situation in Uganda*, PTC II, Decision to Convene a Status Conference on the Investigation in the Situation in Uganda in Relation to the Application of Article 53, ICC-02/04-01/05-68, 2 December 2005, para. 17, convening a status conference, concerns the control of an investigation at the preliminary examination stage. The decision *Situation in the DRC*, ICC-01/04-373, albeit referring to a decision 'not to prosecute a particular person or … a person for particular crimes' (para. 5), rejects the respective *amicus curiae* request pursuant to Rule 103 RPE ICC and thus does not deal with the substance of the matter; crit. of this decision, Stahn, in Stahn and Sluiter, *Practice* (2009), pp. 276–7, arguing that the PTC 'postponed its consideration of Article 53 review'.

712 In a similar vein, ICC-OTP, *Policy Situation Completion* (2021), paras. 52–4 ('this requirement to mean that it must notify the Pre-Trial Chamber and the referring entity if it proposes to complete the Investigation Phase of a referred situation without initiating at least one prosecution by making an application under article 58' [53]; to inform about 'each decision not to prosecute a given case … inconsistent with discretionary nature of the Prosecutor's powers [54]).

713 See also Stahn, in Stahn and Sluiter, *Practice* (2009), p. 257; Nouwen, *Complementarity* (2013), pp. 95–6.

714 In a similar vein, Stahn, in Stahn and Sluiter, *Practice* (2009), p. 255; Friman, Brady, Costi, Guariglia, and Stuckenberg, in Sluiter et al., *International Criminal Procedure* (2013), p. 390 (Chamber 'not empowered to substitute a negative decision with its own prosecution').

can exercise her broad discretion[715] basically unaffected by judicial interference.[716] In particular, there is no judicial interference in the preliminary examination phase. Earlier attempts by more pro-active judges to put some pressure on the OTP by convening *status conferences*[717]—invoking the protection of victims and witnesses and preservation of evidence[718] and the general power of any Chamber pursuant to Regulation 30 RegC[719]—or even asking the Prosecutor to produce a status report regarding a preliminary examination, 'including an estimate of when the preliminary examination ... will be concluded and when a decision pursuant to article 53 (1) of the Statute will be taken',[720] have not changed the balance of power between OTP and Chambers.[721] As to status conferences, it must be recalled that they are not provided for in Article 57 (3)(c) but only in two situations, that is, before the confirmation hearing to ensure adequate disclosure and before the trial to ensure the 'fair and expeditious conduct of the proceedings'.[722] Of course, Regulation 30 RegC does not limit them to a certain procedural phase but this alone does not constitute a legal or policy argument to use status conferences as a means to control or even achieve prosecutorial expediency. In any case, irrespective of the appropriate instrument—status conference, *ex parte* hearing, or progress report—the substantive issue is whether such an early control of the prosecutorial activity is legally demanded at all. While one may advocate information rights of the parties to the proceedings during preliminary examinations,[723] especially of the victims, given their privileged status in the ICC system,[724] it is another question whether the right to a trial without undue delay[725] entails, as argued by PTC III, that the preliminary examination of a situation 'must be completed within a reasonable time', even 'regardless of its complexity'[726] and that therefore the OTP will have to provide an 'estimate' regarding the conclusion of the examination and the Article 53 (1) decision.[727]

This goes too far for various reasons. First, the right to a trial without undue delay presupposes a certain concretization of the object of the proceedings, especially the individualization with regard to the suspect(s), since only then can this right be violated with regard to concrete persons. Of course, victims may already be identified at the preliminary examination/situation stage but they are not protected by this right (being a right of the accused).[728] Secondly, this right prohibits an 'undue' delay, that is, positively speaking, it grants a right to

[715] On this discretion, see note 122 in this chapter.

[716] Boas et al., *Procedure* (2011), pp. 103 ('facilitating without controlling'), 105, 133.

[717] See notes 268 and 446 in this chapter with main text.

[718] Art. 57 (3)(c) ICCS. See generally De Meester, *Investigation Phase* (2015), pp. 177–9.

[719] ICC, *Situation in the DRC*, PTC I, Decision to Convene a Status Conference, ICC-01/04-9, 17 February 2005, p. 3, invoking Art. 57 (3)(c) and Reg. 30 RegC; *Situation in Uganda*, ICC-02/04-01/05-68, para. 17, invoking Art. 53 (3)(b) and Regs. 30, 48 RegC; also ICC, *Situation in Uganda*, PTC II, Decision to Postpone the Status Conference on the Investigation in the Situation in Uganda in Relation to the Application of Article 53, ICC-02/04-01/05-72, 9 December 2005.

[720] *Situation in the CAR*, ICC-01/05-6, p. 5; conc. Mettraux et al., *Effectiveness ICC* (2014), p. 8 (para. 9) (require Prosecution 'to provide periodic *ex parte* reports' with a view to the 'prompt completion' of investigation); Kuczyńska, *Accusation Model ICC* (2015), p. 78 (arguing that the PTC's role 'is very similar to that of official supervision in hierarchically structured prosecution offices, especially in the light of seizing even more controlling powers than provided expressly by the Statute').

[721] Crit. Stahn, in Stahn and Sluiter, *Practice* (2009), p. 276 ('problems of Article 53 ... unresolved').

[722] cf. Rules 121 (2)(b) and 132 RPE ICC and Reg. 54 RegC.

[723] Regarding the State that referred the situation, see *Situation in the CAR*, ICC-01/05-6, p. 3; see also PTC I, Decision on the 'Prosecution's Request for a Ruling on Jurisdiction under Article 19(3) of the Statute', ICC-RoC46(3)-01/18-37, 6 September 2018, para. 84.

[724] cf. Chapter II, E.(4)(b) in this volume; see also the reference in Art. 57 (3)(c) ICCS.

[725] Art. 67 (1)(c) ICCS and Chapter I, D.(3)(h) in this volume.

[726] *Situation in the CAR*, ICC-01/05-6, p. 4.

[727] Ibid., p. 5.

[728] See title of Art. 67.

a reasonably speedy trial. Such highly normative criteria ('undue', 'reasonably', 'complexity') do not allow for a fixed time frame—indeed, it is not provided for in the Statute or Rules—but only call for the determination of the reasonableness of the length of the proceedings on a case-by-case basis, taking into account various factors, especially—contrary to the affirmation by PTC III—the complexity of the proceedings.[729] Thirdly, to demand a fixed time frame and an 'estimate' regarding the conclusion of a certain investigatory phase is impractical and normally impossible, since an investigation is dynamic and dependent on the circumstances of the concrete situation or case.[730] Fourthly, too early an intervention into the prosecutorial investigation, that is, even before the Article 53 (1) decision, would shift the procedural balance between the Prosecutor and Chambers too much in the direction of a *juge d'instruction* system[731] clearly rejected by the drafters.[732]

All in all, this means that, given the tension between the Prosecutor's institutional independence and accountability as an agent of justice,[733] one has to strike a proper balance between 'activist interventionism' and 'prudent oversight',[734] with a view to victims' rights and a reasonably speedy investigation. In more concrete terms, this means that, albeit there are no fixed time limits and, as a matter of principle, there is no judicial review during preliminary examinations, the Prosecutor always has to comply with the standard of due diligence, that is, to investigate with proper care, present evidence as soon as possible, and take into account the rights of suspect/accused and victims.[735] Yet, this does not fully address the problem of prosecutorial inaction already mentioned above. Prosecutorial inaction may, de facto, amount to a decision not to prosecute, if it lasts forever, that is, if the Prosecutor just does not take any decision (not even to terminate a preliminary examination).[736] If in such a scenario judicial scrutiny was *a limine* precluded, it would be too easy for the Prosecutor to prevent just that. In practical terms, here the PTC is faced with a problem of a lack of information: if it does not receive any information from the Prosecutor on the state of the investigation, it lacks any factual basis to intervene.[737] But what can the PTC do about that? At best, the PTC may activate Regulation 48 RegC to obtain information regarding the status

[729] In the same vein, ICC, *Situation in the CAR*, PTC III, Prosecution's Report Pursuant to PTC III's 30 November 2006 Decision Requesting Information on the Status of the Preliminary Examination of the Situation in the Central African Republic, ICC-01/05-7, 15 December 2006, p. 5, ('the OTP, while committed to reaching decisions under Article 53 (1) as expeditiously as possible, submits that no provision in the Statute or the Rules establishes a definitive time period for the purposes of the completion of the preliminary examination. The OTP submits that this was a deliberate legislative decision that provides the required flexibility to adjust the parameters of the assessment or analysis phase to the specific features of each particular situation. That choice, and the discretion that it provides, should remain undisturbed.')

[730] See also *Situation in the CAR*, ICC-01/05-7, pp. 2, 5, 8 (concrete estimate 'not possible at this time').

[731] In this vein, see De Hemptinne and Rindi, *JICJ*, 4 (2006), 349–50 and De Hemptinne, *JICJ*, 5 (2007), 414 ff.; *contra* Scheffer, *LJIL*, 21 (2008), 152–3, 157–8, 161–2.

[732] cf. Guariglia and Hochmayr, 'Article 56', in Ambos, *Commentary* (2022), mn. 2–3; see also Miraglia, *JICJ*, 4 (2006), 192–3, arguing that a (too) early setting of a status conference shifts 'the equilibrium between the legal traditions reached in Rome' bringing the system closer to an investigating judge; in a similar vein, Scheffer, *LJIL*, 21 (2008), 151, 158, warning of an intervention into the Prosecutor's discretionary power; also crit. of a too early intervention, El Zeidy, *CLF*, 19 (2008), 51 ff., who however acknowledges the risk of too long and unchecked preliminary examinations (54–5); Kuczyńska, *Accusation Model ICC* (2015), pp. 154–5; in favour or more rigorous judicial scrutiny, Stahn, in Stahn and Sluiter, *Practice* (2009), pp. 278–9.

[733] cf. Stahn, in Stahn and Sluiter, *Practice* (2009), p. 258.

[734] Scheffer, *LJiL*, 21 (2008), 158, 162.

[735] cf. de Meester, Pitcher, Rastan, and Sluiter, in Sluiter et al., *International Criminal Procedure* (2013), pp. 179–81, 191, 211 (as principle indirectly derived from Art. 84 (1)(a) ICCS and Reg. 17 RegOTP).

[736] cf. Friman, Brady, Costi, Guariglia, and Stuckenberg, in Sluiter et al., *International Criminal Procedure* (2013), p. 390.

[737] See also Stahn, in Stahn and Sluiter, *Practice* (2009), pp. 267, 271–2, criticizing the PTC's total dependence on the Prosecutor information policy and thus 'virtually no power of control and no information on the activities of the Prosecutor'.

of proceedings but even this weak remedy is limited to three specific procedural situations, that is, the ones envisaged in Articles 53 (3)(b), 56 (3)(a), and 57 (3)(c) ICCS.[738] In general, it seems that the PTCs are still trying to find the right balance between their judicial review powers and both the independence and discretion of the Prosecutor.[739]

## (4) The interests of justice clause

*(a) Conceptual remarks*

The concept of 'interests of justice'[740] within the meaning of Article 53 (1)(c) and (2)(c) is nowhere defined in the ICC's legal framework. The OTP understands the concept as 'a potential *countervailing* consideration that might produce a reason *not* to proceed' even where jurisdiction and admissibility are satisfied.[741] Thus, 'interests of justice' is a negative requirement[742] that may exclude an investigation (or prosecution), even if the positive requirements of Article 53 (1) and (2) are met. It will only be applied 'in exceptional circumstances' as a kind of last resort.[743]

The notion of '*justice*' in the interests of justice clause is to be understood broadly,[744] mirroring the peace vs. justice debate.[745] In both adversarial and inquisitorial procedural systems[746] the Prosecutor is, regardless of other specific duties, expected to seek justice.[747] While the particular features of what constitutes justice vary between, and sometimes within, legal systems, the concept is usually tied to the principle of fairness.[748] Thus, 'justice' in this sense does not focus only on the situation or case itself[749] and is not limited to typical criminal justice considerations,[750] but encompasses alternative forms of justice and entails

[738] See, in more detail, De Meester, *Investigation Phase* (2015), pp. 265–7.

[739] In a similar vein, Stahn, Bergsmo and CHAN, in Bergsmo and Stahn, *Preliminary Examination I* (2018), p. 16 ('One missing part in the architecture of preliminary examinations is the limited ability of the Prosecutor to seek guidance from the Pre-Trial Chamber on status issues.')

[740] I draw here on my previous analysis in Ambos, 'Legal Framework TJ', in Ambos et al., *Peace and Justice* (2009), pp. 19, 82–6. On the public interest criterion in English and Welsh law in general, see Duff, in Langer and Sklansky, *Prosecutors* (2017), pp. 9, 24–32.

[741] ICC-OTP, *Interests of Justice* (2007), pp. 2–3 (emphasis in the original).

[742] *Situation in the Islamic Republic of Afghanistan*, ICC-02/17-138, paras. 21, 49; Lafontaine and Magnoux, in Heinze and Dittrich, *ICC* (2021), p. 241, 272. On the consequences for judicial review see above Section (3)(b).

[743] ICC-OTP, *Interests of Justice* (2007), p. 3. See also Rohrer, *Legalitäts- oder Opportunitätsprinzip* (2010), pp. 253–4, 313.

[744] In a similar vein, deGuzman, *Gravity* (2020), pp. 130 and 134 ff.; reviewed by Lingenfelter, *ICLR*, 21 (2021), 398 ff.; see also Heinze, in Heinze and Dittrich, *ICC* (2021), pp. 65–6. Summarizing the broad and narrow views, Stegmiller, *Pre-Investigation Stage* (2011), pp. 357 ff.; De Meester, *Investigation Phase* (2015), pp. 256 ff.; Buchan, *CLF*, 25 (2014), 498–503 (in favour of a narrow view). See also Rohrer, *Legalitäts- oder Opportunitätsprinzip* (2010), pp. 243 ff. (applying the usual methods of interpretation in order to define the notion of interest of justice).

[745] Lafontaine and Magnoux, in Heinze and Dittrich, *ICC* (2021), pp. 241, 272; see also Tachou-Sipowo and Lafontaine, in Bernard and Scalia, *Les Dossiers de la RDPC*, Vol. 21 (2014), pp. 219–35.

[746] About the meaning, Heinze, *Disclosure* (2014), pp. 117 ff.; Ambos and Heinze, in Bergsmo, *Abbreviated Criminal Procedures* (2017), pp. 28 ff.

[747] Boyne, *German Prosecution Service* (2014), p. 5. The fact that the search for truth in inquisitorial systems is a constitutive feature (Heinze, *Disclosure* (2014), p. 107) does not render the ensuing ethical obligation less relevant, see Peters, *Strafprozeß* (1985), p. 82. In the same vein, Kubicek, *America's Court System* (2006), p. 37 with further references; Ingraham, *Criminal Procedure* (1987), p. 13.

[748] See, e.g., ICC, *Prosecutor v. Lubanga*, AC, Judgment on the Appeal of Mr Thomas Lubanga Dyilo against the Decision on the Defence Challenge to the Jurisdiction of the Court pursuant to Article 19 (2) (a) of the Statute of 3 October 2006, ICC-01/04-01/06-772, 14 December 2006, para. 37; see also Namakula, *ICLR*, 17 (2017), 935–6. See generally Heinze and Fyfe, in Bergsmo and Stahn, *Preliminary Examination II* (2018), p. 51.

[749] Gavron, *ICLQ*, 51 (2002), 110.

[750] Namely, considerations which concern the proper administration of justice, e.g. the admission of additional evidence on the basis of 'interests of justice', cf. *Kupreškić et al.*, IT-95-16-A, paras. 52–4, 61–9 (on former Rule 115 (B)

an overall assessment of the situation taking into account peace and reconciliation as the ultimate goals of every process of transition.[751] This does not put 'interests of justice' on an equal footing with 'interests of peace',[752] but only acknowledges, in line with the OTP's comprehensive approach,[753] that interests of justice also play a role in transitional justice processes where peace may be the final overarching goal.[754]

*(b) The notion of 'justice'*

With regard to the decision-making process of a Prosecutor, fairness is to be understood threefold, as substantive, procedural, and distributive fairness.[755] Thus, the Prosecutor's specific obligations in preliminary examinations involve both deontological and consequentialist considerations.[756]

Ultimately, it is for the Prosecutor to strike the right balance and decide, on a case-by-case basis, whether the formal initiation of an investigation or prosecution[757] would jeopardize higher justice interests in the broad sense.[758] Yet, it must not be overlooked that taking into account the possible (negative) consequences of criminal prosecutions implies speculating about hypothetical future events and is therefore fraught with insecurity. In addition, the possibility of adverse State reactions to the investigation or prosecution of its officials must not subject the Prosecutor or the Court as a whole to blackmail by powerful States. Otherwise, the Court would rightly face criticism that it only prosecutes weak States and thus undermine its legitimacy. While the Court is certainly dependent on State cooperation, it still needs a critical distance from States, especially from those where its criminal situations take place; it cannot make (political) concessions to States with regard to the investigation and prosecution of their officials, since this would clearly delegitimize the Court. Also, the

RPE ICTY); for more examples, see Stegmiller, *Pre-Investigation Stage* (2011), p. 367; also ICC-OTP, *Interests of Justice* (2007), p. 8 (to be understood more broadly 'than criminal justice in a narrow sense').

[751] See also Goldstone and Fritz, *LJIL*, 13 (2000), 662; Robinson, *EJIL*, 14 (2003), 488; Meyer, *ICLR*, 6 (2006), 579; Rodman, *LJIL*, 22 (2009), 101 ff., 108 ff.; Stegmiller, *Pre-Investigation Stage* (2011), pp. 358, 367–8, 378–9; Rohrer, *Legalitäts- oder Opportunitätsprinzip* (2010), pp. 314 ff. On judicial intervention in ongoing atrocities and the assumption that justice can be pursued neutrally during conflicts, see Vinjamuri, in Stahn, *Practice* (2015), pp. 20–5; on the interests of justice in conjunction with the principle of positive complementarity, see Tillier, *ICLR*, 13 (2013), 542–5.

[752] ICC-OTP, *Interests of Justice* (2007), pp. 1 (interests of peace to be dealt with by other institutions), 4 (distinguishing it from 'interests of peace' with regard to *Uganda* situation), 8–9 ('not be conceived of so broadly as to embrace all issues related to peace and security', 'within the mandate of other institutions'); conc. Bergsmo and Bekou, 'Article 53', in Ambos, *Commentary* (2022), mn. 26; crit. Stegmiller, *Pre-Investigation Stage* (2011), p. 364; Davis, *ICLR*, 15 (2015), 179–80.

[753] ICC-OTP, *Interests of Justice* (2007), p. 8 'fully' endorsing 'the complementary role that can be played by domestic prosecutions, truth seeking, reparations programs, institutional reform, and traditional justice mechanisms in the pursuit of a broader justice' and ensuring 'that all efforts are as complementary as possible in developing a Comprehensive approach'.

[754] cf. Vinjamuri, in Stahn, *Practice* (2015), pp. 15–8 (advocating a double role for justice in post-conflict and transitional States, namely by deterring future perpetrators and by strengthening the rule of law); Lafontaine and Magnoux, in Heinze and Dittrich, *ICC* (2021), pp. 241, 272.

[755] On their meaning, Heinze and Fyfe, in Bergsmo and Stahn, *Preliminary Examination II* (2018), pp. 7 ff.

[756] Ibid, p. 8. See also ICC, *Situation in the Islamic Republic of Afghanistan*, PTC II, Concurring and Separate Opinion of Judge Antoine Kesia-Mbe Mindua, ICC-02/17-33-Anx-Corr, 31 May 2019, para. 39 (referring to legal and 'non-legal' factors).

[757] Arts. 53 (1) and (2) ICCS.

[758] See e.g. Stahn, *JICJ*, 3 (2005), 698, arguing that abstinence from (immediate) prosecution may be allowed if otherwise reconciliation would be seriously put a risk; or Gropengießer and Meißner, *ICLR*, 5 (2005), 296, arguing that it is 'possible to suspend the punishment even of serious offences in favour of higher-priority-interests' (similarly, van der Voort and Zwanenburg, *ICLR*, 1 (2001), 329–30) or, at 297, that the Prosecutor makes 'his *own* decision on prognosis and balance' (emphasis in the original). For considerations governing the timing of indictments, see ICTJ, *UN Guidelines Meeting* (2005), 3 ff.

broad reading of the notion of justice has its natural limits in the core meaning of justice, that is, it does not allow for the total absence of justice, for example, by deference to a national exemption measure without mechanisms of compensation. In other words, the interests of justice clause can only be invoked if the reason(s) that cause the Prosecutor to abstain from investigation and prosecution can really be traced back or are linked to justice interests, that is, if the abstention really serves these (broad) justice interests.[759]

The views on the notion of justice are reflected by broader and narrower views in the literature. Various authors consider 'interests of justice' as the most explicit gateway of the ICC Statute for the recognition of alternative processes of national reconciliation, including the granting of an amnesty or other exemption measures for the sake of achieving peace.[760] Such a broad reading, giving the Prosecutor an interpretative discretion,[761] is considered to be in line with the ICC's primary expressivist goal.[762] A more radical view even advances a 'strategic interpretation' of the concept, using it against the opening of an investigation—despite the existence of a reasonable basis within the meaning of Article 53 (1)(a)—if such an investigation were detrimental to the Court's 'viability'.[763] This, however, allows for abuse, since it is unclear what exactly is detrimental to the Court's viability. Also, this approach goes too far for the reasons explained above, because it may entail—pursuant to an ambivalent concept of 'soft power'[764]—giving in to powerful States claiming that the Court allegedly needs to fulfil its anti-impunity mission. In contrast, as a representative of a more restrictive view, Seibert-Fohr doubts that Article 53 is the appropriate legal basis for a broad, alternative reading and argues that the interests of justice clause does not provide for additional criteria that would go beyond Article 17.[765] Consequently, in her view, 'it can hardly be argued that the prosecution is not in the interests of justice', if the case is admissible under Article 17.[766] Another, even more restrictive view argues that the object and purpose of the ICC Statute (the fight against impunity) and the use of 'interests of justice' in other provisions of the ICC and other Statutes[767] indicate that the non-investigation/prosecution cannot be based on transitional justice considerations.[768]

759 Contrary to HRW, *Interests of Justice* (2005), pp. 19–20 the victims' justice interests cannot be limited to the interests of a criminal prosecution excluding *a limine* their possible interests in peace, traditional reconciliation, etc. It is equally unconvincing to adduce as an additional factor in favour of criminal prosecution the victims' interest in the memory since this can normally be better preserved by a TRC.

760 Dugard, *LJIL*, 12 (1999), 1014; Dugard, in Cassese et al., *Rome Statute I* (2002), p. 702; Goldstone and Fritz, *LJIL*, 13 (2000), 656, 662; Robinson, *EJIL*, 14 (2003), 486; Olásolo, *ICLR*, 3 (2003), 111 (referring to a TRC); Brubacher, *JICJ*, 2 (2004), 81–2 (referring to post-conflict reconciliation processes); Seils and Wierda, *ICC* (2005), p. 12 ('most direct significance to mediators'); Meyer, *ICLR*, 6 (2006), 579; Rodman, *LJIL*, 22 (2009), 101 ff., 108 ff. (considering the goal of peace at the core of his broad, consequentialist approach); Valiñas, in Stahn and van den Herik, *Perspectives* (2010), pp. 277–8; Stegmiller, *Pre-Investigation Stage* (2011), pp. 358, 367–8, 378–9; less emphatic, Scharf, *CornILJ*, 32 (1999), 524.

761 Pues, *Prosecutorial Discretion* (2020), pp. 15 ff.; summarizing Pues, *ICLR*, 17 (2017) 960–84; see also Greenawalt, in deGuzman and Oosterveld, *Elgar Companion ICC* (2020), pp. 81 ff.; Heinze, in Heinze and Dittrich, *ICC* (2021), pp. 65–6.

762 deGuzman, *Gravity* (2020), pp. 130 and 131 ff. (broad discretion instead of applying a rather legalistic approach given the expressivist function of the ICC, cf. ibid., pp. 13, 27 ff., 140 ff.).

763 Davis, *ICLR*, 15 (2015), 172, 174, 188–9.

764 Ibid., 184–5, 189, arguing that the ICC must make State comply, i.e. to convince them to comply, even granting them concessions, since only they can bring about the Court's anti-impunity goals.

765 Seibert-Fohr, *MPYbUNL*, 7 (2003), 578 ff.

766 Ibid., 580.

767 See HRW, *Interests of Justice* (2005), p. I, referring to Arts. 55 (2)(c), 61, 65, 67 ICCS and (in n. 17) to Statutes of earlier international criminal tribunals where the notion was always understood in the sense of a fair administration of justice.

768 See HRW, *Interests of Justice* (2005), pp. 4 ff. stating that 'the prosecutor may not fail to initiate an investigation or decide not to proceed with the investigation because of national efforts, such as truth commissions, national amnesties, or traditional reconciliation methods, or because of concerns regarding an ongoing peace process' (at 4–5).

While these narrower views deserve credit for trying to overcome the broad prosecutorial discretion built into the interests of justice clause and a possible political interference by limiting the legal analysis to the more precise criteria of Article 17, they are difficult to reconcile with the wording of Article 53 and the sheer existence of the interests of justice clause—clearly a normative, potentially broad concept.[769] One may, with the benefit of hindsight, regret this but the drafters of the ICC Statute wanted to give the Prosecutor—albeit without having a clear or even unanimous understanding of the concept[770]—an additional instrument to exercise her discretion going beyond the rather 'technical' requirements of Article 17.[771] Indeed, there could be situations, which would be considered admissible under Article 17 and therefore could only be taken away from the ICC, if at all, by invoking the interests of justice clause. Take, for example, the scenario that a TRC undertakes an investigation which can, however, never lead to a prosecution, since the relevant conduct is covered by an amnesty. Such a TRC investigation would not satisfy the investigation requirement of Article 17 (1) (b), because there is no true prosecution option,[772] that is, the case would be admissible and the only way to avoid an interference with the TRC's ongoing work would be—apart from an intervention of the Security Council[773]—a recourse to the interests of justice clause.[774]

### *(c) Political considerations*

Clearly, there is no other clause in the ICC Statute allowing so explicitly for policy considerations[775]—in particular Article 15 only provides for an evidentiary test ('reasonable basis to proceed') but does not entail a value judgement as to the appropriateness of any exemption measure[776]—and thus granting such a broad discretion to the Prosecutor.[777]

The policy element of the interests of justice clause has of course the—perhaps unintended—consequence that the OTP and the Court as a whole may be put under (external) pressure or at least appear as having taken certain decisions under such pressure. This has become manifest in the PTC's non-authorization of the opening of the *Afghanistan* investigation (inter alia targeting US forces)[778] given the Trump administration's full-blown attack on the ICC in this context.[779] In concrete terms, the PTC based its decision on a

[769] See also deGuzman and Schabas, in Sluiter et al., *International Criminal Procedure* (2013), p. 145.

[770] cf. HRW, *Interests of Justice* (2005), pp. 3–4 with further references.

[771] Olásolo, *ICLR*, 3 (2003), 135 ff. even argues that the drafters of the ICC Statute have with the interests of justice clause granted unlimited political discretion to the Prosecutor 'through the back-door', unmaking the core policy choices against impunity of the Preamble (p. 149). In favour of an, albeit narrow, discretion of the Prosecutor on the basis of this clause, see Rohrer, *Legalitäts- oder Opportunitätsprinzip* (2010), pp. 341–2.

[772] See Chapter III, B.(2)(d)(ii) in this volume.

[773] Art. 16 ICCS, see Chapter III, A.(4)(b)(ii) in this volume.

[774] See also Robinson, in Kleffner and Kor, *Complementarity* (2006), p. 145; Valiñas, in Stahn and van den Herik, *Perspectives* (2010), p. 277.

[775] cf. Arsanjani, in ASIL, *Proceedings* (1999), p. 67 ('broad range of possibilities'); Goldstone and Fritz, *LJIL*, 13 (2000), 662–3; Brubacher, *JICJ*, 2 (2004), 80 ff. (81: 'broader interests of the international community'); Seils and Wierda, *ICC* (2005), p. 12; Meyer, *ICLR*, 6 (2006), 580. Gallavin, *KCLJ*, 14 (2003), 195, 197, draws a comparison to the 'public interest' criterion in English and Welsh law arguing that while the Prosecutor must be independent she must at the same time be aware of the political realities; on this parallel, see also Brubacher, *JICJ*, 2 (2004), 80.

[776] cf. Seibert-Fohr, *MPYbUNL*, 7 (2003), 581–2, convincingly against Dugard, *LJIL*, 12 (1999), 1014 who argues that the Prosecutor can decline to proceed under Art. 15 because of the existence of a national amnesty. At best, the reconsideration under Art. 15 (5) (see also Art. 53 (4)) implicitly confers upon the Prosecutor political discretion (cf. Olásolo, *ICLR*, 3 (2003), 128 ff.).

[777] Stressing the discretion, also Stegmiller, *Pre-Investigation Stage* (2011), p. 379; deGuzman and Schabas, in Sluiter et al., *International Criminal Procedure* (2013), p. 146; Nouwen, *Complementarity* (2013), p. 92; Davis, *ICLR*, 15 (2015), 179.

[778] *Situation in the Islamic Republic of Afghanistan*, ICC-02/17-33.

[779] Ambos, *Treatise ICL I* (2021), pp. 61–2.

broad interpretation of the clause, stressing the (envisaged) lack of cooperation of the States concerned (USA and Afghanistan) and thus the low probability of success of the investigation.[780] While a detailed analysis of the decision would go beyond the scope of this chapter, it is worthwhile to recall at least two main flaws of the decision: first, the Chamber converted the 'justice', whose 'interests' are at stake, into a utilitarian efficiency clause, which is thus no longer a value in itself, but to be measured by the mere prospect of success. Secondly, the PTC's approach is categorically wrong and hardly compatible with the wording of Article 53 (1)(c) ICCS.[781]

The first issue touches upon the controversial question of whether the interests of justice clause may be invoked to stop potentially futile investigations, be it for a lack of State cooperation or for other reasons. It is certainly appropriate for a prosecutor and may even be obligatory in some instances to consider the potential consequences of the prosecutorial decisions and priorities.[782] In every legal system, concerns about the substantive outcomes of criminal trials, the overall performance or record of a prosecutor, or social and political impacts play a role in prosecutorial decision-making.[783] Thus, an inquiry into whether an investigation would not be in the 'interests of justice' may involve consequentialist political considerations and these considerations should take place before the start of the trial. However, prosecutorial conduct should also be limited by deontological constraints[784] and it would go too far to construe the interests of justice clause as granting an 'unlimited political discretion',[785] be it with regard to a possible amnesty exception[786] or the prevention of (whatever) detrimental effects to the Court's viability.[787] Otherwise, there is a risk that the Prosecutor be 'mired in making political judgements that would ultimately undermine' his work, authority, and indeed legitimacy, subjecting him to 'political pressures' and potential manipulations by governments, rebel groups, and other actors.[788] Thus, the Prosecutor must always 'judicialize the politics' without being a political actor herself.[789] This view is also supported by a historical interpretation of Article 53: As Gilbert Bitti—a member of the French delegation—wrote on the basis of his personal recollection of the debates in Rome, the developments in the negotiations regarding the interests of justice criterion were spurred

[780] *Situation in the Islamic Republic of Afghanistan*, ICC-02/17-33, paras. 89 ff., thereon crit. Jacobs, *Spreading the Jam* (12 April 2019); Menon, in Ruiz Fabri et al., *Legitimacy* (2020), pp. 71, 81; Romm, *ICLR*, 20 (2020), 862, 865 ff. See also the analysis by Chaitidou, *ZIS*, 12 (2020), 563 ff.; Lafontaine and Magnoux, in Heinze and Dittrich, *ICC* (2021), pp. 241, 274 ff.

[781] cf. Ambos, *EJIL: Talk!*, 11 June 2019. See also Rona, *Opinio Juris* (15 April 2019); Jacobs, *Spreading the Jam* (12 April 2019); Heller, *Opinio Juris* (13 April 2019).

[782] Adekunle, in Heinze and Dittrich, *ICC* (2021), p. 409, 419.

[783] Markovits, *Adversary Advocacy* (2008), p. 8; Jehle and Wade, *Prosecutorial Power* (2006), pp. 24, 60–1. A Prosecutor with an impeccable record of respect for defendants' rights, faced with the prospect of removal due to her failure to convict several of these defendants, may even consider whether she should treat a few defendants as a means to maintain her job, cf. Heinze and Fyfe, in Bergsmo and Stahn, *Preliminary Examination II* (2018), p. 11.

[784] Danner, *AJIL*, 97 (2003), 536–7. This is acknowledged by the OTP itself in several policy papers, see e.g. ICC-OTP, *Policy Children* (2023), para. 37 ff.; see also Heinze and Fyfe, in Bergsmo and Stahn, *Preliminary Examination II* (2018), pp. 35 ff.

[785] See Olásolo, *ICLR*, 3 (2003), 110–1, 135 ff., esp. 141 distinguishing (at 110–11) between a limited discretion regarding the goals to be achieved with the prosecutorial decision and an unlimited discretion regarding the convenience of a prosecution with a view to these goals; Olásolo critically concludes that the combination gives 'the broadest possible scope of political discretion'.

[786] In the same vein, Stahn, *JICJ*, 3 (2005), 717–18.

[787] In this vein, Davis, *ICLR*, 15 (2015), 172, 174, 188–9.

[788] HRW, *Interests of Justice* (2005), p. 14.

[789] Stegmiller, *Pre-Investigation* (2011), p. 379; in a similar vein, Brubacher, *JICJ*, 2 (2004), 95, arguing that prosecutorial 'discretion must exclude partisan politics, but not the more statesmanlike politics of persuading state compliance'.

on by a fear of unequal treatment of States before the Court.[790] The drafters expressed concerns that (powerful) States may push the Prosecutor, by for example threatening non-cooperation, and thus use the interests of justice criterion to preclude an investigation or a prosecution with a view to protecting their own nationals.[791]

As a consequence of the above, the interests of justice clause may only be invoked in terms of consequentialist (political) considerations in limited circumstances, namely when either an investigation might endanger the very existence and functioning of the ICC or when it can *never and under no circumstances* lead to a prosecution. Feasibility in itself cannot be one of those considerations.[792] Indeed, by recurring to feasibility arguments, the *Afghanistan* PTC[793] turned the interests of justice clause on its head, ultimately undermining the legitimacy of the Court. The PTC's decision, in fact, on the one hand, vindicated the neo-colonial or even racist criticism of the ICC by African States;[794]on the other hand, it received highly dubious applause by the former US administration,[795] i.e. the very administration which launched an unprecedented attack on the Court.

### (d) Gravity and the interests of victims

One may distinguish subparagraph 1 (c) from subparagraph 2 (c) of Article 53 in that the former construes 'interests of justice' as an autonomous factor to be distinguished from the other factors listed in these subparagraphs, that is, as a factor which may 'nonetheless'[796]—as a countervailing consideration—entail a non-investigation decision, and subparagraph 2 (c) construes the concept as an element of the 'circumstances of the case'.[797] Yet, this distinction does not convert the interests of justice clause in a fully free-standing factor but it must still be read with reference to the other factors mentioned and already analysed in this and other chapters of this volume.[798] These factors, in turn, make clear that the Prosecutor has to take a legally substantiated decision on a case-by-case basis and cannot, as already explained above, merely invoke general policy considerations in their own right

Against this background it is clear that the *Afghanistan* PTC should have balanced the factors speaking against the opening of the investigation against gravity and the interests of victims, but this balancing exercise did not take place. While the PTC rightly points out at the beginning of its analysis that 'the gravity of the crime and the interests of victims' have to be taken into account,[799] the 'gravity' has in fact not been considered in the following[800] and the interests of victims are only addressed in one paragraph:

> It is worth recalling that only victims of specific cases brought before the Court could ever have the opportunity of playing a meaningful role [in] as participants in the relevant proceedings; in the absence of any such cases, this meaningful role will never materialise in spite of the

790 Bitti, 'Article 53', in Fernandez et al., *Commentaire CPI II* (2019), pp. 1447 ff.

791 Bitti, *EJIL: Talk!*, 13 August 2019; cf. Bitti, 'Article 53', in Fernandez et al., *Commentaire CPI II* (2019), pp. 1447 ff.

792 ICC-OTP, *Policy Prelim. Examinations* (2013), para. 70.

793 *Situation in the Islamic Republic of Afghanistan*, ICC-02/17-33, paras. 90 ff.

794 Ambos and Heinze, *Criminology and Criminal Justice* (20 November 2018).

795 See Pompeo, *U.S. Department of State* (12 April 2019).

796 Art. 53 (1)(c).

797 cf. Gallavin, *KCLJ*, 14 (2003), 185 ff., distinguishing between an external/extrinsic and internal/intrinsic interpretation with regard to subparas. 1 (c) and 2 (c) of Art. 53 and giving subpara. 1 (c) precedence over subpara. 2 (c) (187). For HRW, *Interests of Justice* (2005), p. 19, subpara. 2 (c) gives a broader discretion than para. 1 (c).

798 cf. ICC-OTP, *Interests of Justice* (2007), pp. 4 ff., analysing 'interests of justice' with regard to these factors; see also HRW, *Interests of Justice* (2005), pp. 16 ff., 23–4.

799 *Situation in the Islamic Republic of Afghanistan*, ICC-02/17-33, paras. 87 ff.

800 In the same vein, Rossetti, *JICJ*, 17 (2019), 597–8.

investigation having been authorised; victims' expectations will not go beyond little more than aspirations. This, far from honouring the victims' wishes and aspiration that justice be done, would result in creating frustration and possibly hostility vis-a-vis the Court and therefore negatively impact its very ability to pursue credibly the objectives it was created to serve.[801]

This paragraph does not show that victims' interests have effectively been taken into account, but it is rather overly paternalistic.[802] Moreover, that 'victims' expectations will not go beyond little more than aspirations' is speculative. Last but not least, even though the reference to possible hostilities against the Court may be considered a legitimate consequentialist motive,[803] it is unsubstantiated. Similarly, it is unsubstantiated to see, as Judge Mindua does in his concurring and separate opinion, the existence of the Court in danger if it cannot 'proceed smoothly'.[804]

Apart from that, the Prosecutor has to take into account the legal situation and debate on the admissibility of amnesties or other exempting measures in the course of peace processes for she is bound by the international *lex lata* by way of Article 21 ICCS.[805] Last but not least, the possibility[806] of a *proprio motu* judicial review by the PTC of a non-prosecution decision based on a lack of interests of justice[807] clearly shows that the Prosecutor has no *unfettered* discretion; indeed, while the PTC must not replace the prosecutorial discretion by its own, it is entrusted with the review of the legality of the Prosecutor's decision.[808]

*(e) 'substantial reasons ... that an investigation would not serve the interests of justice'*

As to this part of the interest of justice clause three issues will be briefly addressed.

First, Article 53 (1)(c) is formulated in a negative manner ('... not serve ...'). Thus, there is a presumption that the investigation serves the interests of justice. Such negative formulations have normally not just the effect that the party invoking them must make their meaning public or explicit,[809] but they also reverse the burden of proof/persuasion. We have already seen above that the case law regarding Article 53 (1)(c) does not take issue with the Prosecutor if he is silent on the interests of justice, i.e. assumes tacitly that a lack of interests of justice does not hinder the opening of the investigation.[810] Given that the drafters decided to formulate the interests of justice as an exception, it would go beyond the common rules of interpretation to treat the exception as a leading condition.[811] The drafting history of Article 53 is very telling in this regard: from the ILC Draft Statute to the Rome Conference, drafts

801 *Situation in the Islamic Republic of Afghanistan*, ICC-02/17-33, para. 96.

802 Ibid.

803 See Section B.(4)(c).

804 *Situation in the Islamic Republic of Afghanistan*, ICC-02/17-33-Anx-Corr, para. 44 ('[H]ow can the ICC proceed smoothly if the Prosecutor cannot collect or preserve evidence, because of security problems?').

805 See also Gropengießer and Meißner, *ICLR*, 5 (2005), 297; ICC-OTP, *Interests of Justice* (2007), pp. 8 ff.

806 The PTC is not obliged, but 'may' review the prosecutorial decision (Art. 53 (3)(b), see also Rule 109 RPE ICC granting the PTC a period of 180 days to decide on the review).

807 Art. 53 (3)(b) ICCS. See also Robinson, *EJIL*, 14 (2003), 487–8, advocating a 'necessity exception' in these cases (495–6); Brubacher, *JICJ*, 2 (2004), 86–7; Seils and Wierda, *ICC* (2005), p. 5; HRW, *Interests of Justice* (2005), p. 4; Gropengießer and Meißner, *ICLR*, 5 (2005), 297–8; very critical on the judicial review mechanisms, Olásolo, *ICLR*, 3 (2003), 142; unclear insofar Davis, *ICLR*, 15 (2015), 186–7, arguing that the PTC should not be influenced by political considerations, but how is this possible if the OTP's decision, to be reviewed by this very Chamber, is based, according to this author, on political considerations?

808 cf. Gropengießer and Meißner, *ICLR*, 5 (2005), 299; ICC-OTP, *Interests of Justice* (2007), p. 3.

809 In this vein, Akande and de Souza Dias, *EJIL: Talk!*, 18 April 2019.

810 Above note 694 with main text.

811 Assuming that many rules are constructed in a threefold way: leading condition + legal rule + exception, cf. Salambier, *Legislative Drafting* (2009), p. 52.

of Article 53 either included a positive or negative formulation of the 'interests of justice' clause.[812] At no point was there a premise that both formulations carried the same meaning. On the contrary, a comparison of the Draft Statute of 18 June 1998 with the text of Article 53 adopted at Rome shows that a negative formulation of the clause was expressly preferred over a positive one.[813]

Secondly, as to the relationship between Article 15 (4) and 53 (1) ICCS, both provisions stipulate a 'reasonable basis to proceed' standard. Subparagraph (1)(c) of Article 53, however, provides for a 'substantial reasons to believe' standard[814] which is a consequence of the negative formulation of this subparagraph establishing an exception. If the drafters had wanted subparagraph 1(c) to be another leading condition, they would have employed the same 'reasonable basis to proceed' standard for it as in subparagraphs (1)(a) and (b). The inclusion of the higher 'substantial reasons' standard fulfils two purposes: first, it was supposed to compensate for the fact that the 'interests of justice' clause is formulated rather vaguely; secondly, it worked as a compromise to motivate delegations to eventually agree on the inclusion of the clause.[815] In other words, both the negative formulation of the clause and the high evidentiary standard had been adopted deliberately and had a great significance in drafting the provision.

Thirdly, as previously explained, the term 'substantial' reasons/grounds corresponds to 'strong', 'significant', or 'solid' grounds.[816] The PTC *Afghanistan* Decision may again serve as an example of an erroneous application of this standard, since it rests largely on assumptions, conjecture, and speculation.[817] The Chamber notes for instance that,

> even by international criminal justice standards, the preliminary examination in the situation in Afghanistan was particularly long. As many as about eleven years (which were marked by heightened political instability, in Afghanistan and elsewhere) elapsed between the start of the preliminary examination and the filing of the Request.[818]

With this and other considerations the following questions, relevant for the applicable evidentiary standard, remain unanswered: first, what exactly are 'the international criminal justice standards' referred to by the PTC? Secondly, what is *tertium comparationis* if the PTC criticizes the length of the *Afghanistan* investigation? Intuitively, reference should be made to a preliminary examination that involves a major power like the USA but such a comparison (or any other) is not drawn. Instead, the PTC remarks:

> *[S]ubsequent changes within the relevant political landscape* both in Afghanistan and in key States (both parties and non-parties to the Statute), coupled with the complexity and volatility of the political climate still surrounding the Afghan scenario, make it extremely difficult to gauge the prospects of securing meaningful cooperation from relevant authorities for the future.[819]

812 Bitti, *EJIL: Talk!*, 13 August 2019.
813 Ibid.
814 In detail, Section B.(2).
815 Bitti, *EJIL: Talk!*, 14 August 2019.
816 Above note 375 with main text.
817 In the same vein, Vasiliev, *EJIL: Talk!*, 19 April 2019.
818 *Situation in the Islamic Republic of Afghanistan*, ICC-02/17-33, para. 92.
819 Ibid., para. 94 (emphasis added).

Why are changes within the relevant political landscape so peculiar in this situation? To quote former KSC Judge Keith Raynor: 'What then is the current political landscape and the surrounding political reality? Well, the landscape has changed in the past 20-odd years and it continues to change by the month, week and day.'[820] In fact, the evidentiary standard would have required the PTC to provide concrete information. Instead, it continues to speculate that 'it seems *reasonable* to assume that these difficulties will prove even trickier in the context of an investigation proper'.[821] This kind of formulation—'seems reasonable to assume'—certainly does not meet the required evidentiary standard.

### (5) Investigatory powers of the Prosecutor (simple and qualified investigative measures)

#### *(a) Overview*

As to the investigatory powers of the Prosecutor, one must make a twofold distinction. On the one hand, one must distinguish with regard to the *nature* of the investigative measure between those that do not interfere with human or fundamental rights (mere or simple investigative measures) and those that have a coercive or compulsory nature interfering with individual rights (qualified investigative measures).[822] On the other hand, a distinction as to the *procedural phase* is necessary, that is, one must distinguish between measures performed within the context of a preliminary examination or a formal investigation.

Apart from this distinction a specific feature of the investigation by an international Prosecutor—who lacks her own police force and a territory—is the fact that she practically always faces the limits of territorial sovereignty, that is, she depends on State cooperation. It is for this reason that Article 54 ICCS—as the key provision of the ICC system with regard to investigative duties and powers of the Prosecutor—refers the Prosecutor to the cooperation regime of Part IX of the Statute[823] or, for that purpose, to the PTC;[824] further, it authorizes her to seek the cooperation of States on an ad hoc basis or by way of an agreement.[825] The particularities of this cooperation regime will be examined in more detail in Chapter VII. Here it suffices to say that a lack of consent of the territorial State as to investigative measures on its territory can only be overruled by an authorization of the PTC pursuant to Article 54 (2)(b) in conjunction with Article 57 (3)(d) ICCS. However, such an authorization, to be requested by the Prosecutor,[826] presupposes that the relevant State is party to the Rome Statute and is 'clearly unable'[827] to comply with the cooperation request, that is, that it can be equated to a failed State.[828] Even if this were to be the case, it is by no means clear if the security situation in this State allows international investigators to carry out investigative measures. Equally, it is not clear whether the relevant State will comply with a PTC order

[820] Raynor, *The Guernica Group* (24 May 2019).
[821] *Situation in the Islamic Republic of Afghanistan*, ICC-02/17-33, para. 94, emphasis added.
[822] This terminology is taken from Safferling, *Criminal Procedure* (2012), pp. 257–8. The distinction also applies to measures within the framework of the cooperation regime pursuant to Art. 54 (2)(a) in relation with Art. 93 (1), (ibid.) pp. 271–3.
[823] In more detail, see Chapter VII in this volume.
[824] Art. 54 (2); see, in this context, also Safferling, *Criminal Procedure* (2012), pp. 270 ff.
[825] Art. 54 (3) (c), (d); see also Safferling, *Criminal Procedure* (2012), pp. 263 ff.
[826] cf. Rule 115 RPE ICC.
[827] cf. Art. 57 (3)(d) ICCS.
[828] cf. Rastan, *LJIL*, 21 (2008), 438; de Meester, Pitcher, Rastan, and Sluiter, in Sluiter et al., *International Criminal Procedure* (2013), p. 292.

pursuant to Article 57 (3)(d) and allow the Prosecutor to carry out the necessary investigative measures on its territory. If it refuses to do so, that is, in the case of non-compliance with a Court order, the Court could only make the appropriate finding and refer the matter to the ASP.[829] The same applies when the State is just unwilling to cooperate.[830]

### (b) *Preliminary examination, especially* 'unique investigative opportunity', *and formal investigation*

During the preliminary examination *phase* the Prosecutor can only, as already mentioned above, seek information from States, UN organs, and so forth, and receive voluntary testimony at the Court.[831] Additionally, in cases where a '*unique investigative opportunity*' arises,[832] the OTP[833] may ask the PTC to authorize the necessary investigative measures to obtain the relevant evidence.[834] The relevant provision (Article 56 ICCS), albeit situated after Article 53 ICCS, also applies to the preliminary examination phase. This follows from Rule 47 (2) RPE ICC, which basically repeats the substance of Article 56 ICCS with regard to the Article 15 preliminary examination.[835] A unique investigative opportunity exists where there is a witness or other evidence that may not be available 'subsequently for the purposes of a trial',[836] for instance, because of the death of a witness, and must therefore already be preserved during the investigation.[837] The provision must be interpreted strictly though, since the mere transfer of such preserved evidence to the trial entails a limitation of defendant's rights: this evidence cannot be thoroughly examined at trial, a witness cannot be questioned by the defence. Thus, a mere risk for a witness ('vulnerable witness') is to be dealt with by the general provisions for victims/witnesses protection;[838] Article 56 is inapplicable in so far.[839] Concrete measures to be taken by the PTC, 'to ensure the efficiency and integrity of the proceedings and, in particular, to protect the rights of the defence',[840] are listed in Article 56 (2), including the appointment of defence counsel.[841] The list is not exhaustive

829 cf. Art. 87 (7) ICCS.

830 Rastan, *LJIL*, 21 (2008), 438.

831 Art. 15 (2) ICCS.

832 Art. 56 ICCS. The Statutes of the ad hoc tribunals contained similar provisions: Rule 71 ICYS and ICTRS, later Rule 71*bis* ICTRS; now Rules 77 and 78 MICTS; Rule 71 SCSLS and Rule 123 STLS. Thereto Bradfield, *ICLR*, 19 (2019), 373, 379–80.

833 Note that a suspect may also request measures under Art. 56 pursuant to Art. 57 (3)(b); see Safferling, *Criminal Procedure* (2012), p. 252.

834 cf. ICC, *Situation in the DRC*, PTC I, Decision to Hold Consultation under Rule 114, ICC-01/04-19, 21 April 2005; ICC, *Situation in the DRC*, PTC I, Decision on the Prosecutor's Request for Measures under Article 56, ICC-01/04-21, 26 April 2005. See also Coalition for the ICC, *Insight ICC*, 5 (2005), 10. Furthermore Kreß, *JICJ*, 1 (2003), 607–8; Karnavas, in Bohlander, *International Criminal Justice* (2007), pp. 85 ff.; dissenting, De Smet, in Stahn and Sluiter, *Practice* (2009), pp. 421, 426 ff., who believes that a broad interpretation of Art. 56 could bear the danger of 'freezing' evidence for the main trial.

835 For the same result, Safferling, *Criminal Procedure* (2012), p. 251. This is also confirmed by Art. 18 (6) which enables the Prosecutor to seek authority from the PTC to carry out investigative measures 'for the purpose of preserving evidence where there is a unique opportunity to obtain important evidence'.

836 Art. 56 (1)(a) ICCS. The wording 'for the purpose' was used since it is as yet unclear at the early preliminary examination stage whether a trial will take place at all (Fourmy, in Cassese et al., *Rome Statute II* (2002), p. 1218). On the introduction of previously recorded testimony outside Art. 56, see Rule 68 RPE ICC.

837 cf. *Ongwen*, ICC-02/04-01/15-2022-Red, para. 136. See also Fourmy, in Cassese et al., *Rome Statute II* (2002), p. 1218; Guariglia and Hochmayr, 'Article 56', in Ambos, *Commentary* (2022), mn. 7; Bradfield, *ICLR*, 19 (2019), 373, 378.

838 Art. 68 ICCS; see, in this regard, the discussion in Chapter II, E.(4)(a) in this volume.

839 See also Safferling, *Criminal Procedure* (2012), pp. 253–4. The question was left open during the negotiations, cf. Guariglia and Hochmayr, 'Article 56', in Ambos, *Commentary* (2022), mn. 7.

840 Art. 56 (1)(b) ICCS.

841 Art. 56 (2)(d); accordingly, counsel represents 'the interests of the defence' if a suspect has not yet been determined, i.e. during the preliminary examination; see also Safferling, *Criminal Procedure* (2012), pp. 256–7, pointing to four issues which concern these defence interests.

('include') and subparagraph (f) authorizes the PTC, by way of a catch-all provision, to take 'such other action ... necessary to collect or preserve evidence'.[842] The PTC may take these measures also on its own initiative after having consulted with the Prosecutor,[843] but this *proprio motu* power should be interpreted restrictively, given the division of labour between the Prosecutor (in charge of the investigation) and the PTC (in charge of judicial review, not being a *juge d'instruction*);[844] this power could be invoked, though, when the preservation of evidence is 'essential for the defence'.[845]

Article 56 has become the subject of extensive debate in the *Ongwen* case.[846] In its appeal, the defence took issue with (i) the propriety of a judge's 'concurrent' (parallel) involvement in the taking of testimony under Article 56 and the conduct of confirmation proceedings; (ii) alleged procedural irregularities of the Article 56 proceedings; and (iii) the manner in which the TC dealt with the defence's objections to the submission of the evidence obtained under Article 56 and its subsequent reliance on that evidence in the conviction decision.[847] The AC found no harm in the 'dual role' of the Single Judge in taking the testimony of witnesses under Article 56 and concurrently conducting the confirmation of charges proceedings.[848] Further, the alleged 'procedural irregularities' seem to be based on the premise that Article 56 proceedings require notice of *all* charges against the suspect but this is not the case since under Article 56: 'evidence may be preserved ... even before the surrender or voluntary appearance of the person concerned'.[849]

During the (formal) *investigation* the above-mentioned dichotomy between simple and qualified investigative measures applies. These measures include onsite investigations, the summoning and interrogation of the accused, victims and witnesses, as well as the collection and examination of other evidence.[850] 'Other evidence' means all non-testimonial, material evidence, including documents, data, and movable and immovable objects.[851] 'Collection' means to obtain physical power over this evidence, 'examination' its forensic analysis.[852]

As a general rule, only *simple investigative measures*, that is, the ones not interfering with individual rights, can be carried out by the Prosecutor of his own accord. The ICTY/ICTR/SCSL/KSC Prosecutors may even request from a State certain 'provisional measures'

[842] See also Guariglia and Hochmayr, 'Article 56', in Ambos, *Commentary* (2022), mn. 16, 21. For a concrete application of the provision, see *Situation in the DRC*, ICC-01/04-21.

[843] cf. Art. 56 (3)(a) ICCS. The decision is to be taken by the full Chamber (Rule 114 (2) RPE ICC), which may request additional information from the Prosecutor (Reg. 48 RegC); for a restrictive interpretation, see Guariglia and Hochmayr, 'Article 56', in Ambos, *Commentary* (2022), mn. 27.

[844] In a similar vein, Guariglia and Hochmayr, 'Article 56', in Ambos, *Commentary* (2022), mn. 24.

[845] cf. Art. 56 (3)(a) ICCS with an explicit reference to the defence in cl. 1; ICC, *Situation of Uganda*, PTC II, Decision on Prosecutor's Applications for Leave to Appeal Dated the 15th Day of March 2006 and to Suspend or Stay Consideration of Leave to Appeal Dated the 11th Day of May 2006, ICC-02/04-01/05-90-US-Exp, 10 July 2006, para. 35 also invoking Art. 57 (3)(c); *contra* Guariglia and Hochmayr, 'Article 56', in Ambos, *Commentary* (2022), mn. 25, who are in favour, though, of consultations with the defence (mn. 28).

[846] About the application of Art. 56 in the *Ongwen* case at the (pre-)trial stage, generally Bradfield, *ICLR*, 19 (2019), 373, 382 ff.

[847] *Ongwen*, ICC-02/04-01/15-2022-Red, para. 114 ff.

[848] Ibid., para. 138 ('There is nothing in the applicable law to suggest that a judge of the pre-trial chamber who has participated in a unique investigative opportunity should be excluded from subsequent proceedings during the pre-trial phase. On the contrary, all these procedural steps are part of the same pre-trial phase, of which the same pre-trial chamber is in charge.')

[849] Ibid., para. 148.

[850] cf. Arts. 18 (2) ICTYS, 17 (2) ICTRS, Rule 39 (i), (ii) ICTY/ICTR RPE, Art. 54 (3)(a) and (b) ICCS. See also Boas et al., *Procedure* (2011), p. 105; de Meester, Pitcher, Rastan, and Sluiter, in Sluiter et al., *International Criminal Procedure* (2013), pp. 176–7, 234.

[851] Safferling, *Criminal Procedure* (2012), pp. 266–7.

[852] Ibid., p. 267.

with a certain compulsory effect, such as a provisional arrest.[853] However, most investigative measures, such as the arrest of the accused[854] (to be examined more closely in the next sub-section) and non-custodial measures (such as search and seizure,[855] surveillance, genetic/electronic identification, interception of communications, or corporal/mental examinations[856]) are *qualified* in that they affect individual rights and therefore require judicial authorization in order to be legitimate.[857] Notwithstanding, the Prosecutors of the ad hoc tribunals seek a judicial warrant only exceptionally, namely only when the respective national authorities refuse to directly cooperate with them and such a warrant is therefore necessary to increase the pressure on the relevant State to cooperate.[858] In this vein, TCs have required 'reasonable efforts' to directly obtain cooperation before issuing the respective court request.[859]

### *(c) Non-custodial measures, especially proportionality*

The above-mentioned non-custodial measures, while not explicitly provided for in the legal instruments of the ad hoc tribunals or the ICC (with the exception of the urgent seizure of

[853] Rule 40 (i) RPE ICTY, Rule 40 (A)(i) RPE ICTR/SCSL, Rule 37 (A)(i) RPE MICT, Arts. 35 (2), 38 (2) KSC Law, and Rule 52 RPE KSC; see also Zahar and Sluiter, *ICL* (2008), p. 56, dissenting on the function of judicial control, pp. 367–8.

[854] According to Art. 19 (2) ICTYS and 18 (2) ICTRS a judicial arrest warrant may only be issued upon confirmation of the indictment. On the interplay between Rule 39 (ii) and 54 RPE ICTY/ICTR, see Safferling, *Criminal Procedure* (2012), p. 261.

[855] For the need of an inventory of all items and documents seized, see Rules 41 (B) RPE ICTR/SCSL and 39 (B) RPE MICT; in favour also de Meester, Pitcher, Rastan, and Sluiter, in Sluiter et al., *International Criminal Procedure* (2013), pp. 288, 311–12.

[856] Of course, in this regard the human rights prohibition of torture and inhuman treatment (Arts. 7 ICCPR, 3 ECHR, 5 ACHR, 5 ACHPR) must be observed. This is not a merely academic exercise, as has been shown in ECtHR, *Jalloh v. Germany*, Application No. 54810/00, ECtHR Grand Chamber Judgment (11 July 2006), finding a violation of Art. 3 ECHR by Germany by submitting the applicant to an inhuman and degrading treatment by forcibly administering him emetics to obtain evidence, i.e. the drugs in his body; cf. Ambos, *IsrLR*, 42 (2009), 383–4. It must be noted, however, that a forcible medical procedure in order to obtain evidence from a suspect is not prohibited *as such* by Arts. 3 and 8 ECHR (*Jalloh v. Germany*, para. 70). Under 'a strict scrutiny of all the surrounding circumstances', taking into consideration 'the seriousness of the offence', the existence or lack of 'alternative methods of recovering the evidence', and that 'the procedure must not entail any risk of lasting detriment to a suspect's health' (*Jalloh v. Germany*, para. 71) a forcible medical intervention may not violate Art. 3; in this vein, also ECtHR, *Bogumil v. Portugal*, Application No. 35228/03, Judgment (7 October 2008), paras. 70, 77–81.

[857] cf. Art. 57 (3)(a) ICC, Rules 39 (iv), 54 RPE ICTY/ICTR/SCSL and Rules 36 (B)(iv) and 55 RPE MICT. For a human rights analysis of the relevant measures, see Safferling, *Criminal Procedure* (2012), pp. 276 ff.; de Meester, Pitcher, Rastan, and Sluiter, in Sluiter et al., *International Criminal Procedure* (2013), pp. 303 ff.

[858] cf. de Meester, Pitcher, Rastan, and Sluiter, in Sluiter et al., *International Criminal Procedure* (2013), pp. 284–5.

[859] ICTR, *Prosecutor v. Bagosora et al.*, TC, Decision on the Defence for Bagosora's Request to Obtain the Cooperation of the Republic of Ghana, ICTR-98-41-T, 25 May 2004, para. 6 ('The party seeking the request by the Trial Chamber must … show that efforts to obtain the assistance have been unsuccessful'); ICTR, *Prosecutor v. Bizimungu et al.*, TC, Decision on Nzuwonemeye's Motion Requesting Cooperation from the Government of Belgium pursuant to Article 28 of the Statute, ICTR-00-56-T, 7 June 2006, paras. 6–7 with further case law references in n. 11 ('the party seeking an order under Article 28 … must also demonstrate that efforts have been made to obtain such assistance, and that these efforts have been unsuccessful' … 'the Defence has made reasonable efforts to obtain the assistance of the Government of Belgium'); ICTR, *Prosecutor v. C. Bizimungu et al.*, TC, Decision on Prosper Mugiraneza's Motion Regarding Cooperation with the Republic of Burundi, ICTR-99-50-T, 30 October 2008, para. 14 (a party shall not 'exhaust *all* possible mechanisms before seeking intervention by the Chamber. Rather, the party must merely demonstrate that prior reasonable efforts to obtain cooperation were unsuccessful'); ICTR, *Prosecutor v. Setako*, TC, Decision on Extremely Urgent and *Ex Parte* Defence Motion for Cooperation of the Kingdom of Belgium, ICTR-04-81-T, 31 March 2009, paras. 2, 4. With regard to Rule 68 RPE ICC, see ICC, *Prosecutor v. Ntaganda*, Decision on certain requests related to the admission of the prior recorded testimony of Witness D-0080, ICC-01/04-02/06-2242-Red, 22 February 2018, para. 32.

evidence[860]), are inherent to the general investigatory powers of the Prosecutor.[861] Similarly, at the ad hoc tribunals and at the KSC, the freezing of assets has been based on the general competence of the judge to issue orders 'as may be required for the conduct of the trial'.[862] In contrast, according to Article 57 (3)(e) ICCS, a PTC may seek State cooperation pursuant to Article 93 (1)(k) ICCS[863] 'for the purpose of forfeiture, in particular for the ultimate benefit of victims', but only when an arrest warrant or a summons to appear has been issued[864] and 'having due regard to the strength of the evidence and the rights of the parties concerned'. Thus, this provision, on the one hand, introduces a specific and high threshold linking the forfeiture to the issuing of an arrest warrant, and, on the other, seeks to ensure an early seizure or freezing of assets to prevent countermeasures of the suspect/accused.[865] The respective request may relate to any proceeds, property, or assets owned or controlled by the suspect, that is, it is not limited—as suggested by Article 77 (2)(b) ICCS ('derived directly or indirectly from that crime')—to those derived from the crime(s) under investigation.[866]

As to Article 57 (3)(a) ICCS, it has been argued that it does not explicitly require a judicial authorization for specific measures—as Article 58 does—and therefore the decision whether or not such an authorization is necessary 'is left to the discretion of the Court'.[867] This is a flawed proposition, which, in fact, turns the requirement of a legal basis for qualified

[860] Rules 40 (ii) RPE ICTY, 40 (A)(ii) RPE ICTR/SCSL, Rule 37 (A)(i) RPE MICT. An ICTR TC held that search and seizure incidental to an arrest may be considered as an urgent measure in light of the possible destruction of evidence (ICTR, *Prosecutor v. Nyiramasuhuko*, TC (Single Judge), Decision on the Defence Motion for Exclusion of Evidence and Restitution of Property Seized, ICTR-97-21-T, 12 October 2000, para. 24). See also, regarding physical/mental examinations, Rule 113 RPE ICC; on the *travaux*, see Friman, in Lee, *ICC* (2001), pp. 504–6.

[861] As embodied in Arts. 18 (2) ICTYS, 17 (2) ICTRS, 15 (2) SCSLS, and 54 (3)(a) ICCS; see also Rule 39 (i) and (ii) RPE ICTY/ICTR/SCSL, Rule 36 (B)(i) and (ii) RPE MICT, Art. 35 (2), 38 (2) KSC Law; see also de Meester, Pitcher, Rastan, and Sluiter, in Sluiter et al., *International Criminal Procedure* (2013), pp. 287, 291, 294, 297, 302, 311, considering the inherent power as a principle.

[862] cf. Arts. 19 (2) ICTY, 18 (2) ICTRS; see also Rules 47 (H)(i) RPE ICTY/ICTR, 48 (H)(i) RPE MICT, 48 (2) KSC RPE; see also ICTY, *Prosecutor v. S. Milošević et al.*, TC (Single Judge Hunt), Decision on Review of Indictment and Application for Consequential Orders, IT-99-37-I, 24 May 1999, paras. 27–8, rejecting any limitation by Rule 61 (D) RPE ICTY at the stage of the confirmation of the indictment; crit. de Meester, Pitcher, Rastan, and Sluiter, in Sluiter et al., *International Criminal Procedure* (2013), p. 289 with n. 938. At the ICTR, the Prosecutor requested the French authorities to freeze the assets of one accused and they complied; see ICTR, *Prosecutor v. Kabuga*, AC, Decision, Appeal of the Family of Felicien Kabuga against Decisions of the Prosecutor and President of the Tribunal, ICTR-98-44, 22 November 2002. However, Single Judge Thompson of the SCSL rejected a similar order for the lack of an explicit legal basis in a pre-conviction setting (as an additional penalty it is provided for by Art. 19 (3) SCSLS) and stressed that such a freezing would, in any case, only be admissible if the respective property has, as demonstrated by 'clear and convincing evidence', either been 'acquired unlawfully or as a result of criminal conduct'; cf. SCSL, *Prosecutor v. Norman et al.*, TC, Decision on Inter Partes Motion by Prosecution to Freeze the Account of the Accused Sam Hinga Norman at Union Trust Bank (SL) Limited or at any other Bank in Sierra Leone, SCSL-04-14-PT-59, 19 April 2004, paras. 10–11, 13, citing Art. 19 (3) SCSLS, Rules 88 (b), 104 (C) RPE SCSL.

[863] It provides for the 'identification, tracing and freezing or seizure of proceeds, property and assets and instrumentalities of crimes for the purpose of eventual forfeiture'.

[864] cf. Art. 58 ICCS.

[865] cf. ICC, *Prosecutor v. Lubanga*, PTC I, Decision Concerning PTC I's Decision of 10 February 2006 and the Incorporation of Documents into the Record of the Case against Mr Thomas Lubanga Dyilo, ICC-01/04-01/06-8-US-Corr, 24 February 2006, para. 137 . The PTC also criticized the Prosecutor for not having made an early application for forfeiture (para. 141). This possibility is now set out in Reg. 54 RegOTP, suggesting that the Prosecutor should consider requesting the respective measures at the moment of preparing a request under Art. 58 ICCS.

[866] cf. de Meester, Pitcher, Rastan, and Sluiter, in Sluiter et al., *International Criminal Procedure* (2013), p. 297, referring to the *Bemba* PTC's request to Portugal, ICC, *Prosecutor v. Bemba*, Decision et demande en vue d'obtenir l'identification, la localisation, le gel et la saisie des biens et avoirs adressées a la republique portugaise, ICC-01/05-01/08-8-US-Exp, 27 May 2008, para. 3.

[867] Guariglia and Hochmayr, 'Article 57', in Ambos, *Commentary* (2022), mn. 14; similarly, de Meester, Pitcher, Rastan, and Sluiter, in Sluiter et al., *International Criminal Procedure* (2013), p. 293.

investigative measures on its head. To be sure, an explicit provision for the judicial control of these measures is not required—a general provision along the lines of Article 57 (3)(a) ICCS suffices in this respect—but explicit provisions are required to authorize such measures in the first place. In other words, the critical issue is whether the general investigatory powers of the Prosecutor lend sufficient legitimacy to these measures or whether, instead, these measures need to be based on an explicit authorization provision as in the case of custodial measures. That such provisions are perfectly feasible demonstrates the various proposals during the ICC negotiations and the detailed rules of the ECCC, SPSC, and KSC.[868] This issue cannot be solved by the recourse to the applicable national law of the State that executes the requested measure. While this State's domestic law certainly governs the execution of requests by international criminal tribunals (*lex loci* principle),[869] this does not dispense the international tribunals from ensuring the human rights of the persons investigated by setting out specific authorizing provisions[870] and granting the judges the exclusive competence to apply them.[871] As a consequence, contrary to what has been held by the ICTR,[872] the national law of the requested State does not suffice as a legal basis for the respective measure for the simple reason that it may not, as required by Article 21 (3) ICCS, be (completely) compatible with human rights.[873]

In any case, irrespective of the competent organ to order investigative measures affecting individual rights, these orders cannot be issued without further ado but must comply with some *substantive requirements*. This follows from the applicable human rights framework set out in Chapter I of this volume. Of course, if the Prosecutor is obliged to 'fully respect the rights' of suspects[874] and these rights are to be fully respected during the proceedings as a whole, there must be some material criteria to allow a rights-infringing investigative measure. The first criterion refers to the *threshold of suspicion* necessary to authorize such a measure. While comparative law normally provides for an increased threshold, for example, 'probable cause'[875] or an enhanced degree of suspicion,[876] the law of the ad hoc tribunals

[868] cf. Rules 55–70 ECCC Internal Rules, Section 9.4 of Transitional Rules of Criminal Procedure (UNTAET/REG/2000/30 (25 September 2000) as amended by 2001/25 (14 September 2001)), Rules 34-41 KSC RPE; see also de Meester, Pitcher, Rastan, and Sluiter, in Sluiter et al., *International Criminal Procedure* (2013), pp. 298 ff., 302.

[869] See explicitly Art. 99 (1) ICCS: 'in accordance with the relevant procedure under the law of the requested State.'

[870] During the ICC negotiations, a proposal was made for an explicit provision on privacy rights regarding search and seizure: Art. 60 [41] para. 3: 'The right to all persons to be secure in their homes and to secure their papers and effects against entries, searches and seizures shall not be impaired by the Court except upon warrant issued by the [Court] [PTC], on the request of the Prosecutor, in accordance with Part 9[7] or the Rules of the Court, for adequate cause and particularly describing the place to be searched and things to be seized, or except on such grounds and in accordance with such procedures as are established by the Rules of the Court.' (Zutphen Draft Statute for the International Criminal Court, Report of the Inter-Sessional Meeting from 19 to 30 January 1998 in Zutphen, the Netherlands, UN Doc. A/AC.249/1998/l.13 (4 February 1998)).

[871] Also in favour of a judicial authorization from a human rights perspective, de Meester, Pitcher, Rastan, and Sluiter, in Sluiter et al., *International Criminal Procedure* (2013), pp. 303–4, 310–11 (strongly recommending such a rule), 341–2, 348 (judicial warrant as principle), but not considering it—disagreeing with Ambos, *EJCCLCJ*, 8 (2000), 107 ff.—a general principle of law (Sluiter et al., ibid., pp. 306–7, 310, 345–6) and even arguing that the respective requirement in the ICC law is 'far too strict' (Sluiter et al., ibid., p. 346). This goes, however, too far. How can a rule based on human rights law be too strict? Stressing the human rights affected (by search and seizure), also *Nyiramasuhuko*, ICTR-97-21-T, para. 23.

[872] ICTR, *Prosecutor v. Muvunyi*, TC, Decision on the Prosecutor's Motion pursuant to TC's Directives of 7 December 2005 for the Verification of the Authenticity of Evidence Obtained out of Court Pursuant to Rules 89 (C) & (D), ICTR-2000-55A-T, 26 April 2006, paras. 24–5, referring to the English Police and Criminal Evidence Act, 1984, ss. 17 (1) and 18.

[873] In addition, the international judge may be in a better position to authorize the measure, see de Meester, Pitcher, Rastan, and Sluiter, in Sluiter et al., *International Criminal Procedure* (2013), p. 309.

[874] Art. 54 (1)(c) ICCS.

[875] cf. Fourth Amendment US Constitution.

[876] See Fyfe and Heinze, in Ambos et al., *Core Concepts II* (2022), p. 169, 189 (US: 'reasonable suspicion' for so-called Terry stop-and-frisks); Nan and Verrest, in Bachmaier Winter, Thaman, and Lynn, *Right to Counsel* (2020),

only knows the general 'sufficient basis to proceed'[877] and the ICC the 'reasonable basis to believe that a crime' has been committed.[878] This is too unspecific and low a threshold. It should be replaced, as a rule, by the 'probable cause' threshold[879] or the KSC's 'grounded suspicion'.[880]

A second criterion refers to the measure itself, requiring that it be *reasonable or proportional*. Both standards are well known in various areas of substantive (international) criminal law and have been dealt with in the previous volumes of this Treatise.[881] As to the proportionality standard, the ICTY AC has correctly held that, with regard to restrictions of fundamental rights, 'many jurisdictions are guided by some variant of a basic proportionality principle', requiring 'a sufficiently important objective' and impairing the respective right 'no more than ... necessary to accomplish the objective.'[882] The ICTY itself has been guided by a 'general principle of proportionality' with regard to restrictions on the right to liberty and the respective provisional release requests. Accordingly, 'a measure in public international law is proportional only when (1) it is suitable, (2) it is necessary, and (3) its degree and scope remain in a reasonable relationship to the envisaged target'.[883] Further, it was held that 'procedural measures should never be capricious or excessive' and that 'a more lenient measure ... must be applied', if it is sufficient.[884] This latter test corresponds to the necessary criterion mentioned in the general definition of proportionality; it entails the subsidiarity of the measure concerned as compared to equally effective but more lenient

p. 205, 228 (Netherlands: 'reasonable suspicion' for search and seizure); Roberts, *Evidence* (2022), p. 625 ('reasonable suspicion for police surveillance); Hodgson, *Criminal Justice* (2020), p. 102; Lippke, in Brown, Turner, and Weißer, *OxfHb Criminal Process* (2019), p. 27 ('"reasonable suspicion" of criminal activity on the part of those they stop'). For older literature, see previous edition p. 397 with note 616.

[877] Arts. 18 (1) ICTYS, 17 (1) ICTRS. See also de Meester, Pitcher, Rastan, and Sluiter, in Sluiter et al., *International Criminal Procedure* (2013), pp. 286–7; De Meester, *Investigation Phase* (2015), p. 138.

[878] Arts. 15 (3), 53 (1)(a) ICCS. See also de Meester, Pitcher, Rastan, and Sluiter, in Sluiter et al., *International Criminal Procedure* (2013), p. 294, 302.

[879] In the same vein, de Meester, Pitcher, Rastan, and Sluiter, in Sluiter et al., *International Criminal Procedure* (2013), p. 311, but arguing (p. 342) that the threshold applied is higher than the standard of reasonable suspicion and therefore in line with human rights law, concluding in the same vein (p. 347).

[880] Rule 34 (1) KSC RPE.

[881] On the ambiguous catch all concept of reasonableness, see in particular Ambos, *Treatise ICL I* (2021), pp. 306, 313, 454, 474, 486–7; Ambos, *Treatise ICL II* (2022), pp. 83 (with n. 304), 107 (with n. 515), 332; on proportionality, see Ambos, *Treatise ICL I* (2021), pp. 110 (with n. 133), 445–6, 454, 513, 544; Ambos, *Treatise ICL II* (2022), pp. 174, 206, 209, 327–9. For a philosophical account, see Gardiner, *P&PA*, 47 (2019), 288 ff.; for a Bayesian approach to 'reasonable suspicion' see Ball, *ACLR*, 55 (2018), 511 ff.

[882] ICTY, *Prosecutor v. S. Milošević*, AC, Decision on the Interlocutory Appeal of the TC's Decision on the Assignment of Defence Counsel, IT-02-54-AR73.7, 1 November 2004, para. 17, quoting English, US, Canadian, and ECtHR case law.

[883] ICTY, *Prosecutor v. E. Hadžihasanović et al.*, TC II, Decision Granting Provisional Release to E. Hadžihasanović, IT-01-47-PT, 19 December 2001, para. 8 (identically the provisional release decisions of the same date regarding M. Alagić and A. Kubura); conc. ICTY, *Prosecutor v. Mrđa*, TC, Decision on Darko Mrđa on Request for Provisional Release, IT-02-59-PT, 15 April 2002, para. 31; ICTY, *Prosecutor v. Stakić*, TC II, Order to the Registry of the Tribunal to Provide Documents, IT-97-24-T, 5 July 2002; ICTY, *Prosecutor v. Blagojević et al.*, Decision on Vidoje Blagojević's Application for Provisional Release, IT-02-60-PT, 22 July 2002, para. 29; confirmed by ICTY, *Prosecutor v. Limaj et al.*, AC Decision on F. Limaj's Request for Provisional Release, IT-03-66-AR65, 31 October 2003, para. 13 (identically the provisional release decisions of the same date regarding H. Bala and I. Musliu); conc., *S. Milošević*, IT-02-54-AR73.7, para. 17 (regarding a restriction on the fundamental right to liberty); ICTY, *Prosecutor v. Krajišnik*, AC, Decision on M. Krajišnik's Request to Self-Represent, on Counsel's Motions in Relation to Appointment of Amicus Curiae, and on the Prosecution Motion of 16 February 2007, Fundamentally Dissenting Opinion of Judge Schomburg on Right to Self-Representation, IT-00-39-A, 11 May 2007, para. 69.

[884] *Hadžihasanović et al.*, IT-01-47-PT, para. 8; conc. *Mrđa*, IT-02-59-PT; *Stakić*, IT-97-24-T; confirmed by *Limaj et al.*, IT-03-66-AR65, para. 13. Crit. on the German (constitutional law) origins of this test, de Meester, Pitcher, Rastan, and Sluiter, in Sluiter et al., *International Criminal Procedure* (2013), p. 286 (but referring to it themselves at pp. 308–9, together with French and Dutch law).

measures.[885] The KSC Appeals Panel has similarly stressed the importance of the proportionality principle in the context of pre-trial detention, especially invoking the ECHR and the ECtHR's case law.[886]

The ICC invoked the proportionality principle, also relying on ECtHR case law,[887] in *Lubanga* with regard to a search on his private premises in the DRC.[888] More specifically, it has been held that requests to seek cooperation under Article 57 (3)(b) ICCS have to meet the conditions of '(i) specificity (ii) relevance and (iii) necessity'.[889] 'Specificity' means that the concrete (cooperation) measure has to be precisely indicated and sufficient information be provided.[890] 'Relevance' implies that the measure 'may be material to the proper determination of the issues being adjudicated'.[891] 'Necessity' requires that all other possibilities to obtain the desired information or evidence have been exhausted.[892] The same conditions apply to requests for general orders and warrants within the meaning of Article 57 (3)(a) ICCS, since these orders have to be 'required for the purposes of an investigation', that is, they must be necessary,[893] and, in order to avoid 'fishing expeditions', specific and relevant.[894]

885 Similarly de Meester, Pitcher, Rastan, and Sluiter, in Sluiter et al., *International Criminal Procedure* (2013), p. 286.

886 cf. KSC, *Prosecutor v. Hysni Gucati and Nasin Haradinaj*, AP, Decision on Hysni Gucati's Appeal on Matters Related to Arrest and Detention, KSC-BC-2020-07, IA001-F00005, 9 December 2020, paras. 72–3 ('considering whether an applicant's detention on remand was strictly necessary to ensure his presence at the trial or whether other, less stringent, measures could have been sufficient for that purpose'). See also KSC, *Prosecutor v. Hashim Thaçi et al.*, Decision on Kadri Veseli's Appeal against Decision on Interim Release, AP, KSC-BC-2020-06, IA001/F00005, 30 April 2021, para. 56; Public Redacted Version of Decision on Jakup Krasniqi's Appeal Against Decision on Interim Release, AP, KSC-BC-2020-06, IA002/F00005/RED, 30 April 2021, para. 69; Public Redacted Version of Decision on Rexhep Selimi's Appeal Against Decision on Interim Release, AP, KSC-BC-2020-06, IA003/F00005/RED, 30 April 2021, para. 79; Public Redacted Version of Decision on Jakup Krasniqi's Appeal against Decision on Review of Detention, AP, KSC-BC-2020-06, IA006/F00005/RED, 1 October 2021, para. 41; Public Redacted Version of Decision on Hashim Thaçi's Appeal Against Decision on Review of Detention, AP, KSC-BC-2020-06, IA010/F00008/RED, 27 October 2021, para. 49; Public Redacted Version of Decision on Kadri Veseli's Appeal against Decision on Remanded Detention Review and Periodic Review of Detention, AP, KSC-BC-2020-06, IA014/F00008/RED, 31 March 2022, para. 61; Decision on Rexhep Selimi's Appeal against Decision on Remanded Detention Review and Periodic Review of Detention, AP, KSC-BC-2020-06, IA015/F00005, 25 March 2022, para. 56; Public Redacted Version of Decision on Hashim Thaçi's Appeal against Decision on Review of Detention, AP, KSC-BC-2020-06, IA017/F00011/RED, 5 April 2022, para. 64.

887 For a summary, see de Meester, Pitcher, Rastan, and Sluiter, in Sluiter et al., *International Criminal Procedure* (2013), pp. 304–5. See also Pitcher, *Pre-Trial Procedural Violations* (2018), pp. 21 ff.

888 *Lubanga*, ICC-01/04-01/06-803-tEN, paras. 79–82 (82: violation of principle of proportionality 'as a violation of internationally recognised human rights'); ICC, *Prosecutor v. Lubanga*, TC, Decision on the Admission of Material from the 'bar table', ICC-01/04-01/06-1981, 24 June 2009, para. 38 ('disproportionate to the objective of the national authorities, as hundreds of documents were indiscriminately seized that were unrelated to the purpose of the search'). See also Pitcher, *Pre-Trial Procedural Violations* (2018), pp. 328 ff.

889 ICC, *Prosecutor v. Banda and Jerbo*, TC, Decision on 'Defence Application pursuant to articles 57 (3)(b) & 64 (6)(a) of the Statute for an order for the preparation and transmission of a cooperation request to the Government of the Republic of the Sudan', ICC-02/05-03/09-169, 1 July 2011, para. 17; less precisely, previously, ICC, *Prosecutor v. Katanga and Ngudjolo*, Decision on the 'Defence Application pursuant to Article 57 (3)(b) of the Statute to Seek the Cooperation of the Democratic Republic of Congo (DRC)', ICC-01/04-01/07-444, 25 April 2008, p. 5; generally, De Meester, *Investigation Phase* (2015), pp. 173–4; Klamberg, 'Article 57' in Klamberg, *Commentary ICC II* (2023), pp. 87–9.

890 *Banda and Jerbo*, ICC-02/05-03/09-169, paras. 18–24; Rule 116 (1)(b) RPE ICC.

891 Rule 116 (1)(c) RPE ICC.

892 *Banda and Jerbo*, ICC-02/05-03/09-169, paras. 25–31. The necessity requirement follows directly from Art. 57 (3)(b): 'may be necessary to assist'.

893 Kreß, *JICJ*, 1 (2003), 615; Guariglia and Hochmayr, 'Article 57', in Ambos, *Commentary* (2022), mn. 17.

894 In the same vein, de Meester, Pitcher, Rastan, and Sluiter, in Sluiter et al., *International Criminal Procedure* (2013), pp. 293–4, 302, 311 (rule); Guariglia and Hochmayr, 'Article 57', in Ambos, *Commentary* (2022), mn. 17.

In sum, a proportionality test entails that qualified, rights-interfering investigatory measures have to be as specific as possible, relevant, and necessary.[895] Ultimately, proportionality implies a balancing of the interests at stake in the sense of the proportionality *stricto sensu*.[896] In a criminal process this comes down to a balance between the rights affected and the interest to thoroughly investigate the alleged crimes and prosecute those responsible.

### (6) Individualization: Arrest and pre-trial detention, summons to appear and release

#### (a) *Issuance of an arrest warrant*

As we have already seen above,[897] once the Prosecutor decides to initiate a formal investigation pursuant to Article 53 (1) ICCS, she must have a provisional case hypothesis, including possible suspects. Thus, she may also be in a position to apply for an arrest warrant pursuant to Article 58.[898] Indeed, para. 1 of this provision authorizes the PTC to issue an arrest warrant '[a]t any time after the initiation of an investigation', that is, after the Article 53 (1) decision. This presupposes, of course, that the Court has jurisdiction and the corresponding investigation is admissible pursuant to the complementarity principle.[899]

The PTC acts at the request of the Prosecutor, whose application shall contain precise information with regard to the person sought and the alleged crimes committed.[900] The Prosecutor must also explain why the arrest of the person is necessary;[901] she carries the burden of proof.[902] On this basis, the PTC must determine whether the two requirements for an arrest warrant—'reasonable grounds to believe' that the respective person has committed a crime, and the necessity of the arrest[903]—are fulfilled. If this is the case, the warrant 'typically sets forth ... the conclusion of the judge or chamber that the allegations against the suspect or accused have satisfied the relevant legal standards'.[904] The warrant may be sealed,

[895] Requiring specificity with regard to persons and places involved, de Meester, Pitcher, Rastan, and Sluiter, in Sluiter et al., *International Criminal Procedure* (2013), p. 312.

[896] See Ambos, *Treatise ICL I* (2021), p. 544.

[897] Section A.(1)(b) in this chapter.

[898] On the *ex parte* procedure, see Section A.(2)(a)(iv) in this chapter with note 243.

[899] ICC, *Prosecutor v. Said*, PTC II, Public Redacted Version of 'Warrant of Arrest for Mahamat Said Abdel Kani', 7 January 2019, ICC-01/14-01/21-2-US-Exp, ICC 01/14 01/21-2-Red2, 17 February 2021, paras. 4–5; *Prosecutor v. Al Hassan*, Decision on the Prosecutor's Application for the Issuance of a Warrant of Arrest for Al Hassan Ag Abdoul Aziz Ag Mohamed Ag Mahmoud, ICC-01/12-01/18-35-Red2-tENG, 22 May 2018, paras. 10 ff.; *Prosecutor v. Al-Werfalli*, PTC I, Warrant of Arrest, ICC-01/11-01/17-2, 15 August 2017, paras. 23 ff.; ICC, *Prosecutor v. Lubanga*, Decision on the Prosecutor's Application for a Warrant of Arrest, Article 58, CC-01/04-01/06-1 Corr Red, 10 February 2006, para. 18 (originally Annex I to *Lubanga*, ICC-01/04-01/06-8-US-Corr, and under seal, reclassified as public by Decision ICC-01/04-01/06-37, later separated from its main document). For earlier case law, see previous edition p. 399 with note 637. See also ICC, *Practice Manual* (2023), para. 4; Ryngaert, 'Article 58', in Ambos, *Commentary* (2022), mn. 3–4 with further case law references; see also El Zeidy, *LJIL*, 19 (2006), 746.

[900] Art. 58 (2)(a)–(d) ICCS; for more details, see Ryngaert, 'Article 58', in Ambos, *Commentary* (2022), mn. 22–7.

[901] Art. 58 (2)(e) ICCS.

[902] ICC, *Prosecutor v. Katanga and Ngudjolo*, PTC I (Single Judge Kuenyehia), Decision on the Powers of the PTC to Review *Proprio Motu* the Pre-Trial Detention of Germain Katanga, ICC-01/04-01/07-330, 18 March 2008, p. 6.

[903] Art. 58 (1) ICCS. See also Art. 58 (6), (7) (a summons may be issued if 'there are reasonable grounds to believe that the person committed the crime alleged'). On this standard, Cross, in Bergsmo and Stahn, *Preliminary Examination II* (2018), pp. 213, 227 ff.

[904] Boas et al., *Procedure* (2011), p. 208.

if this increases the chance to get the respective person(s) arrested.[905] Notwithstanding, Chambers usually authorize the Prosecutor and the Registry to communicate a warrant of arrest (even if sealed) 'to any State or international organisation, or, as the case may be, to reveal its existence, for the purposes of its execution'.[906] The arrest warrant can be reclassified as public by the PTC upon the request of the Prosecutor as long as the PTC is competent to issue the warrant, that is, until the end of the investigation phase;[907] in substantive terms this may be done if, for example, 'reclassifying the warrant of arrest as public may facilitate [the suspect's] arrest and surrender as all states will then be aware of its existence' and 'could foster support and cooperation for an arrest operation from the international community'.[908]

The 'reasonable grounds' standard of Article 58[909] lies between the lower 'grounds to believe' of Article 55 (2),[910] the arguably lower 'reasonable basis',[911] and the—already examined[912]—higher 'substantial grounds to believe' of Article 61 (7) ICCS.[913] The OTP combines the standards of Article 53 (1) ('reasonable basis') and Article 58 requiring for the latter 'a reasonable prospect of conviction at the end of trial'.[914] The AC equates this standard to the 'reasonable suspicion' in Article 5 (1)(c) ECHR[915] and adopts the interpretation of the ECtHR, according to which there must be 'facts or information which would satisfy an

[905] cf. Ryngaert, 'Article 58', in Ambos, *Commentary* (2022), mn. 10.

[906] ICC, *Prosecutor v. Yekatom*, PTC II, Public Redacted Version of 'Warrant of Arrest for Alfred Yekatom', ICC-01/14-01/18-1-US-Exp, 11 November 2018, ICC-01/14-01/18-1-Red, 17 November 2018, para. 23.

[907] cf. Art. 58 (6) ICCS; Ryngaert, 'Article 58', in Ambos, *Commentary* (2022), mn. 34.

[908] ICC, *Prosecutor v. Al-Werfalli*, PTC I, Warrant of Arrest, ICC-01/11-01/17-2, 15 August 2017, paras. 2–4.

[909] On the drafting history, see Ramsden and Chung, *JICJ*, 13 (2015), 558–9.

[910] Irving, *Human Rights Protection* (2020), pp. 42 ff. On the applicability and scope of Art. 55 during the Preliminary Examination phase, Jacobs and Naouri, in Bergsmo and Stahn, *Preliminary Examination II* (2018), pp. 469, 506 ff.

[911] *Situation in the Republic of Kenya*, ICC-01/09-19, para. 34 ('Mindful of this interpretation and bearing in mind that the "reasonable basis" standard under article 15 of the Statute is even lower than that provided under article 58 of the Statute (the subject-matter of the said Appeals judgment), the Chamber considers that in the context of the present request, all the information provided by the Prosecutor certainly need not point towards only one conclusion'); ICC-OTP, *Report Prelim. Examinations* (2017), para. 11 with n. 6 ('In this respect, it is further noted that even the higher "reasonable grounds" standard for arrest warrant applications under article 58 does not require that the conclusion reached on the facts be the only possible or reasonable one. Nor does it require that the Prosecutor disprove any other reasonable conclusions. Rather, it is sufficient to prove that there is a reasonable conclusion alongside others (not necessarily supporting the same finding), which can be supported on the basis of the evidence and information available'). Crit. Cross, in Bergsmo and Stahn, *Preliminary Examination II* (2018), pp. 213, 229 ff. (rejecting a differentiation between 'grounds' and 'basis' with semantic and teleological arguments).

[912] Section A.(2)(b)(ii) in this chapter.

[913] See also Safferling, *Criminal Procedure* (2012), p. 293; Dumbryte, in Stahn, *Practice* (2015), pp. 1068–70; Ryngaert, 'Article 58', in Ambos, *Commentary* (2022), mn. 11; crit. Jacobs, in Sluiter et al., *International Criminal Procedure* (2013), p. 1136; also crit. Ramsden and Chung, *JICJ*, 13 (2015), 568–70 (comparing the 'reasonable grounds' standard with four other standards and arguing that its 'association' with the purposefully low 'reasonable basis to proceed' pursuant to Art. 15 (3), 53 (1) ICCS entails its lowering).

[914] ICC-OTP, *Situation Completion* (2021), para. 35; see also Karnavas, *ICL Blog* 25 May 2021.

[915] ICC, *Prosecutor v. Al Bashir*, AC, Judgment on the Appeal of the Prosecutor against the 'Decision on the Prosecution's Application for a Warrant of Arrest against Omar Hassan Ahmad Al Bashir', ICC-02/05-01/09-73, 3 February 2010, para. 31; thereon, Carnero Rojo, *Merkourios UJIEL*, 27 (2010), 61–4; see also ICC, *Prosecutor v. Gbagbo*, PTC III, Decision on the Prosecutor's Application Pursuant to Article 58 for a Warrant of Arrest against Laurent Koudou Gbagbo, ICC-02/11-01/11-9-Red, 30 November 2011, para. 27 ('the Chamber has borne in mind the "reasonable suspicion" standard under Article 5 (1)(c) of the European Convention for the Protection of Human Rights and Fundamental Freedoms' and 'has also been guided by the jurisprudence of the Inter-American Court of Human Rights ("IACHR") as regards the fundamental right to liberty which is enshrined in Article 7 of the American Convention on Human Rights'); ICC, *Prosecutor v. Ntaganda*, PTC II, Decision on the Prosecutor's Application Pursuant to Article 58, ICC-01/04-02/06-36-Red, 13 July 2012, para. 16; crit. of this equation, Ramsden and Chung, *JICJ*, 13 (2015), 563–5, arguing that the two provisions serve different purposes and therefore it is not appropriate to borrow the 'reasonable suspicion' threshold since it provides a lower evidentiary standard compared to 'reasonable grounds to believe'.

objective observer that the person concerned may have committed the offence',[916] that is, neither is certainty required[917] nor must a certain finding be the 'only reasonable conclusion'.[918] In any case, the PTC's practice so far entails a thorough examination of the factual and legal sufficiency of the Prosecution's allegations[919] on the basis of all available evidence,[920] looking first at the context elements of the alleged crimes and then at the individual acts.[921]

While there is no comparable provision for the ICTY/ICTR and the KSC,[922] an arrest warrant there presupposes the confirmation of the indictment,[923] that in turn presupposes the existence of a *prima facie* case already defined above.[924] This seems to be a higher standard than the 'reasonable grounds' standard of the ICC.[925]

As to the second requirement—the necessity of the arrest—Article 58 (1)(b) ICCS gives three *alternative*[926] grounds: (i) to ensure the person's appearance at trial; (ii) to prevent any obstruction or endangering of the investigation or court proceedings; (iii) and to prevent the

[916] ECtHR, *Fox et al. v. UK*, Application Nos. 122444/86, 12245/86, 12383/86, Judgment (30 August 1990), para. 32; conc. ECtHR, *Labita v. Italy*, Application No. 26772/95, Judgment (6 April 2000), para. 155; ECtHR, *Berktay v. Turkey*, Application No. 22493/93, Judgment (1 March 2001), para. 199; ECtHR, *O'Hara v. UK*, Application No. 37555/97, Judgment (16 October 2001), para. 34; ECtHR, *Bulduş v. Turkey*, Application No. 64741/01, Partial Decision (1 June 2004), para. 2; ECtHR, *Baş v. Turkey*, Application No. 66448/17, Judgment (3 March 2020), para. 171; ICC, *Prosecutor v. Gbagbo and Blé Goudé*, Dissenting Opinion of Judge Cuno Tarfusser, ICC-02/11-01/15-1156-Anx, 20 April 2018, para. 6.

[917] *Al Bashir*, ICC-02/05-01/09-73, para. 31.

[918] Ibid., paras. 32–3, rejecting ICC, *Prosecutor v. Al Bashir*, PTC I, Decision on the Prosecution's Application for a Warrant of Arrest against Omar Hassan Ahmad Al Bashir, ICC-02/05-01/09-3, 4 March 2009, paras. 158–9 (Judge Ušacka dissenting); this standard was confirmed by the PTC in ICC, *Prosecutor v. Al Bashir*, PTC I, Second Decision on the Prosecution's Application for a Warrant of Arrest, ICC-02/05-01/09-94, 12 July 2010, para. 1; conc. ICC, *Prosecutor v. Mudacumura*, PTC II, Decision on the Prosecutor's Application Pprsuant to Article 58, ICC-01/04-01/12-1-Red, 13 July 2012, para. 19. See also Carnero Rojo, *Merkourios UJIEL*, 27 (2010), 63–4; crit. Ramsden and Chung, *JICJ*, 13 (2015), 559 ff. (esp. 561–3), arguing that if 'it suffices for evidence to point to one reasonable conclusion' then 'the standard is too low'; Cross, in Bergsmo and Stahn, *Preliminary Examination II* (2018), pp. 213, 228, referring to the Separate Opinion of Judge Pikis in *Lubanga*, ICC-01/04-01/06-824, para. 5, according to whom Art. 58 requires '"grounds" *founded on evidential material* giving rise to a reasonable belief that a crime has been committed' (emphasis in original).

[919] *Lubanga*, ICC-01/04-01/06-8-Corr, Annex 1, paras. 79–96, examining three questions, namely whether (i) there are reasonable grounds to believe that a crime has been committed, (ii) Lubanga is responsible for it under Art. 25 ICCS, and (iii) his arrest appears to be necessary; in the same vein, *Prosecutor v. Harun and Abd-Al-Rahman*, PTC I, Decision on Application for a Warrant of Arrest, ICC-02/05-01/07-1-Corr, paras. 29–134 (27 April 2007). Less strict, however, *Prosecutor v. Bemba et al.*, PTC II (Single Judge Tarfusser),Warrant of Arrest for Jean-Pierre Bemba Gombo, Aimé Kilolo Musamba, Jean-Jacques Mangenda Kabongo, Fidèle Babala Wandu, and Narcisse Arido, ICC-01/05-01/13-1-Red2, 20 November 2013, para. 11, while pointing to the 'lack of concision' of the application with regard to the 'temporal and geographic circumstances' of the alleged commission of the crimes pursuant to Art. 70 ICCS [!] nevertheless 'able to navigate the body of evidence' and in the result granting the application.

[920] *Prosecutor v. Ngudjolo*, PTC I, Decision on the Evidence and Information Provided by the Prosecution for the Issuance of a Warrant of Arrest for Mathieu Ngudjolo Chui, ICC-01/04-02/07-3, 6 July 2007, para. 26 ('on the basis of the overall evidence and information contained in the Prosecution Application, the Prosecution Supporting Materials and the Prosecution Response'); *Mudacumura*, ICC-01/04-01/12-1-Red, paras. 28–9, taking into account the expanded evidentiary record; crit., however, Ramsden and Chung, *JICJ*, 13 (2015), 566 ff., 576 (arguing that ICC judges have no express powers 'to assess relevance, reliability and probative value' of provided evidence, being therefore unable to assess its reasonableness and thereby forced to accept it 'at face value').

[921] See *Yekatom*, ICC-01/14-01/18-1-Red, paras. 6 ff.; cf. Ryngaert, 'Article 58', in Ambos, *Commentary* (2022), mn. 13 with case law references.

[922] cf. de Meester, Pitcher, Rastan, and Sluiter, in Sluiter et al., *International Criminal Procedure* (2013), p. 313 (crit. of the lack of detailed rules in the RPE).

[923] Arts. 19 (2) ICTYS, 18 (2) ICTR, 17 (2) MICTS, 39 (1) (2) (3) KSC Law.

[924] Section A.(2)(a)(i) in this chapter with note 153. In the same vein, Jacobs, in Sluiter et al., *International Criminal Procedure* (2013), p. 1133.

[925] For the same view, Safferling, *Criminal Procedure* (2012), p. 294; for a different view, Mariniello, *JICJ*, 13 (2015), 585–6 ('the confirmation of indictment before the ICTY and ICTR presents similarities with the "reasonable grounds to believe" standard within the meaning of Art. 58(1)(a) of the ICC Statute').

[926] *Prosecutor v. Abd-Al-Rahman*, PTC II, Decision on the Defence Request for Interim Release, ICC-02/05-01/20-115, 14 August 2020, para. 25.

person from continuing to commit 'that' or a 'related' crime arising 'out of the same circumstances'.[927] Given that it suffices that the arrest 'appears necessary',[928] the occurrence of one of these three grounds need not be inevitable but only possible.[929] As a consequence, 'the evidence presented in relation to the necessity of continued detention ... does not have to be of the same nature and strength as the evidence required to establish reasonable grounds to believe that the person has committed one or more crimes'.[930] As held by the AC, '[i]t is the responsibility of the relevant chamber, on the basis of the available evidence, to weigh such evidence and, on that basis, to make a prediction as to the likelihood of future events'.[931]

The *first ground* is, perhaps, the most important one, since the ICC does not, in principle,[932] allow for *in absentia* trials.[933] While assessing the flight risk 'necessarily involves an element of prediction',[934] case law has taken into account the international contacts, the position, and the financial and professional background of the suspect[935] as well as the suspect and/or host/territorial State's unwillingness to cooperate.[936] In *Lubanga*, the AC has more generally argued that the gravity of the crimes 'may make the person more likely to abscond'.[937] However, this proposition is certainly too unspecific to justify detention.[938] Thus, the AC's more cautious formulation in *Said* ('may have greater incentive') is to be welcomed.[939] If it is to be expected that the suspect will appear voluntarily, a summons to

[927] In more detail, Dumbryte, in Stahn, *Practice* (2015), pp. 1070–8; Ryngaert, 'Article 58', in Ambos, *Commentary* (2022), mn. 18.

[928] cf. Art. 58 (1)(b) ICCS.

[929] *Prosecutor v. Said*, AC, Judgment on the Appeal of Mr Mahamat Said Abdel Kani against the Decision of Trial Chamber VI Entitled 'Decision on the Defence Application for Interim Release of Mahamat Said Abdel Kani and Contact Restrictions', ICC-01/14-01/21-318, 19 May 2022, paras. 1, 33; *Situation in the CAR II*, PTC II, Public Redacted Version of 'Warrant of Arrest for Mahamat Nouradine Adam', 7 January 2019, ICC-01/14-41-US-Exp, ICC-01/14-41-Red, 28 July 2022, para. 25; *Situation in Georgia*, PTC I, Public Redacted Version of 'Arrest warrant for David Georgiyevich Sanakoev', ICC-01/15-42-Red, 30 June 2022, paras. 33 ff.; *Prosecutor v. Abd-Al-Rahman*, AC, Judgment on the Appeal of Mr Ali Muhammad Ali Abd-Al-Rahman against the Decision of Pre-Trial Chamber II of 14 August 2020 entitled 'Decision on the Defence Request for Interim Release', ICC-02/05-01/20-177, 8 October 2020, para. 33 ('[T]he Appeals Chamber recalls that, when determining whether detention appears necessary under article 58(1)(b) of the Statute, "[t]he question evolves around the possibility, not the inevitability, of a future occurrence"' [fn. omitted]). For earlier case law, see previous edition p. 402 with note 661.

[930] *Prosecutor v. Ntaganda*, PTC II, Decision on the Defence's Application for Interim Release, ICC-01/04-02/06-147, 18 November 2013, para. 47; conc. *Abd-Al-Rahman*, ICC-02/05-01/20-115, para. 28; *Abd-Al-Rahman*, ICC-02/05-01/20-177, para. 31.

[931] *Said*, ICC-01/14-01/21-318, paras. 1, 33.

[932] On the exceptions due to the *Kenya* proceedings, see Section A.(3)(b) in this chapter.

[933] Ryngaert, 'Article 58', in Ambos, *Commentary* (2022), mn. 18.

[934] *Said*, ICC-01/14-01/21-318, para. 34.

[935] Ibid., para. 34; *Prosecutor v. Khaled*, PTC I, Warrant of Arrest for Al-Tuhamy Mohamed Khaled with under seal and ex parte Annex, ICC-01/11-01-13-1, 18 April 2013, para. 13 ('including his alleged possession of at least 10 different passports, some issued under other identities'). For earlier case law, see previous edition p. 402 with note 663.

[936] *Al Bashir*, ICC-02/05-01/09-3, paras. 228–31; ICC, *Situation in the Libyan Arab Jamahiriya*, PTC I, Decision on the Prosecutor's Application pursuant to Article 58 as to Muammar Mohammed Abu Minyar Gaddafi, Saif Al Islam Gaddafi and Abdullah Al Senussi, ICC-01/11-12, 27 June 2011, para. 93; ICC, *Prosecutor v. Blé Goudé*, PTC III, Decision on the Prosecutor's Application Pursuant to Article 58 for a Warrant of Arrest against Charles Blé Goudé, ICC-02/11-02/11-3, 6 January 2012, para. 41; ICC, *Prosecutor v. Hussein*, PTC I, Decision on the Prosecutor's Application Under Article 58 Relating to Abdel Raheem Mohammad Hussein, ICC-02/05-01/12-1-Red, 1 March 2012, para. 44; *Ngudjolo*, ICC-01/04-02/07-3, para. 63. See also Dumbryte, in Stahn, *Practice* (2015), pp. 1074–6. A list of further reasons with references to case law can be found in Ryngaert, 'Article 58', in Ambos, *Commentary* (2022), mn. 18 *in fine*.

[937] *Lubanga*, ICC-01/04-01/06-824, para. 136.

[938] Crit. also, Khan, 'Article 60', in Ambos, *Commentary* (2022), mn. 8 with n. 29; Dumbryte, in Stahn, *Practice* (2015), pp. 1072–3 ('showing that it is easy or possible for the detainee to abscond is insufficient').

[939] *Said*, ICC-01/14-01/21-318, para. 44 ('A Chamber may find that, given the gravity of the charges, an accused may have greater incentive to abscond. However, detention pending trial is a temporary measure subject to periodic review.')

appear, as a less intrusive measure, is sufficient;[940] in this case, conditions 'provided for by national law' can be imposed.[941] If the suspect fails to comply with the summons, the PTC may review its decision and issue an arrest warrant;[942] if the suspect complies with the summons and appears before the Court, her detention would require an arrest warrant.[943]

The *second ground* has been interpreted broadly so as to include any behaviour—from destruction of evidence to the intimidation of witnesses—which may jeopardize the investigation or proceedings.[944] Previous behaviour in this regard may serve as an indicator for further interference.[945] In determining the risk of witness intimidation, Chambers may have to rely on public sources, especially newspaper articles and other media reports in general. While the ensuing element of prediction entails a certain flexibility in the standard the AC rejected the defence observation in *Said* that 'it will always be possible to justify detention by claiming—absent evidence—that there might be someone who might want to interfere with the proceedings or that the Accused himself—again, absent any concrete evidence—might want to'.[946] The reliance on media reports has been confirmed by the AC,[947] including their

[940] cf. Art. 58 (7) ICCS. The ICC has issued summonses in the situations of Sudan/Darfur (for Abu Garda, Abakaer Nouran, and Jerbo Jamus) and Kenya (Arap Sang, Hussein Ali, Muthaura, Kenyatta, Kosgey, and Ruto). It was refused in the Darfur situation with regard to Al Harun and Abd-Al-Rahman because the PTC was not satisfied that it would ensure their appearance for trial (*Harun and Abd-Al-Rahman*, ICC 02/05-01/07-1-Corr, para. 133). For more details, see Ryngaert, 'Article 58', in Ambos, *Commentary* (2022), mn. 40 ff. (at mn. 44 listing grounds where a summons is not an option).

[941] See Art. 57 (7) and Rule 119 (5) RPE ICC; crit. for the ad hoc tribunals, see Rules 65 (C) RPE ICTY/ICTR, 68 (C) RPE MICT; see also Safferling, *Criminal Procedure* (2012), pp. 334–5; Ryngaert, 'Article 58', in Ambos, *Commentary* (2022), mn. 46.

[942] *Abu Garda*, ICC-02/05-02/09-1, para. 32 ('The Chamber reserves its right to review this finding either proprio motu or at the request of the Prosecutor, however, particularly if the suspect fails to appear on the date specified in the summons or fails to comply with the orders contained in the summons to appear issued by the Chamber'); *Prosecutor v. Banda and Jerbo*, PTC I, Second Decision on the Prosecutor's Application Under Article 58, ICC-02/05-03/09-1-US, 27 August 2009, para. 35; *Prosecutor v. Ruto et al.*, PTC II, Decision on the Prosecutor's Application for Summons to Appear for William Samoei Ruto, Henry Kiprono Kosgey and Joshua Arap Sang, ICC-01/09-01/11-01, 8 March 2011, para. 56 ('the Chamber reserves the right to replace the summonses to appear with warrants of arrest under article 58 of the Statute and rule 119(4) of the Rules of Procedure and Evidence (the "Rules")'); *Prosecutor v. Muthaura et al.*, PTC II, Decision on the Prosecutor's Application for Summonses to Appear for Francis Kirimi Muthaura, Uhuru Muigai Kenyatta and Mohammed Hussein Ali, ICC-01/09-02/11-01, 8 March 2011, para. 55.

[943] This situation is not regulated in the applicable law. In particular, Art. 60 (3) ICCS (which will be analysed further down the main text) does not cover this situation since it refers to Art. 60 (2) which presupposes the existence of an arrest warrant and fails to mention a mere summons to appear; thus, if the person appearing under a summons should be detained the Prosecutor would have to apply for an arrest warrant under Art. 58; cf. Khan, 'Article 60', in Ambos, *Commentary* (2022), mn. 16.

[944] *Al Bashir*, ICC-02/05-01/09-3, para. 233; *Harun and Abd-Al-Rahman*, ICC-02/05-01/07-1-Corr, paras. 129–31; *Ngudjolo*, ICC-01/04-02/07-3, para. 63; *Prosecutor v. Bemba*, PTC III, Decision on the Prosecutor's Application for Warrant of Arrest against Jean Pierre Bemba Gombo, ICC-01/05-01/08-14, 10 June 2008, para. 89; *Prosecutor v. Mbarushimana*, Decision on the Prosecutor's Application for Warrant of Arrest against Callixte Mbarushimana, ICC-01/04-01/10-1, 28 September 2010, para. 48; *Hussein*, ICC-02/05-01/12-1-Red, para. 47; *Situation in the Libyan Arab Jamahiriya*, ICC-01/11-12, paras. 97, 101; *Gbagbo*, ICC-02/11-01/11-9-Red, para. 84; *Blé Goudé*, ICC-02/11-02/11-3, para. 42; *Prosecutor v. S. Gbagbo*, Decision on the Prosecutor's Application pursuant to Article 58 for a Warrant of Arrest against Simone Gbagbo, ICC-02/11-01/12-2-Red, 2 March 2012, paras. 42, 44; *Mudacumura*, ICC-01/04-01/12-1-Red, para. 73. For a case law analysis of the second ground, see also Dumbryte, in Stahn, *Practice* (2015), pp. 1076–7 (calling upon the Court to 'accord greater weight to the accused's actual ability and willingness to obstruct proceedings').

[945] *Harun and Abd-Al-Rahman*, ICC-02/05-01/07-1-Corr, paras. 129–31; *S. Gbagbo*, ICC-02/11-01/12-2-Red, para. 44; *Situation in the Libyan Arab Jamahiriya*, ICC-01/11-12, para. 93.

[946] *Said*, ICC-01/14-01/21-318, para. 36.

[947] ICC, *Prosecutor v. Gbagbo*, AC, Judgment on the Appeal of Mr Laurent Koudou Gbagbo against the decision of Pre-Trial Chamber I of 13 July 2012 entitled 'Decision on the "Requête de la Défense demandant la mise en liberté provisoire du président Gbagbo"', ICC-02/11-01/11-278-Red, 26 October 2012, para. 91; *Abd-Al-Rahman*, ICC-02/05-01/20-177, para. 34 (conc. with the AC decision in *Gbagbo*, while clarifying that the decision was still relevant, even though it involved a single NGO report: 'The fact that in that case the pre-trial chamber relied on a number of newspaper articles rather than a single NGO report does not affect the relevance of the Pre-Trial

probative value,[948] but Chambers will have to justify why they give preference to certain media reports. We will return to this issue in Chapter V.[949] Both *Gbagbo* and *Said* felt that the fact that the prosecution disclosed evidence to the defence was used to their disadvantage, namely as indicating an increase of the risk of witness intimidation with the increase of the defendant's knowledge. Thus, the *Said* defence argued that this was 'putting the accused in the impossible position of having to choose between two fundamental rights: the right to be informed of the charges and the right to the enjoyment of liberty pending trial'.[950] Yet, while the AC acknowledged that '[i]n making an assessment pursuant to article 58(1)(b)(ii) of the Statute, disclosure may be a factor for consideration' in assessing the obstruction ground 'as disclosure enhances a detained person's knowledge of the Prosecution's investigation',[951] this is just one factor amongst others.[952]

As to the *third ground*, Chambers have taken the maintaining of a position of power or retaining control over armed forces as sufficient to justify the issuing of an arrest warrant.[953] At any rate, this ground is difficult to reconcile with the rationale of pre-trial detention, that is, to ensure that the trial take place in presence of the accused and with all the relevant evidence in an untainted form.[954] Indeed, it is not the purpose of pre-trial detention to prevent the suspect from committing further crimes, but only to make sure that he can be put to trial for the ones he allegedly committed. In addition, this ground conflicts with the presumption of innocence, since it is predicated on the assumption that the identified suspect has already committed a crime ('that crime'), but this needs to be proven in the first place.[955] Notwithstanding, the AC does not see a problem with the presumption of innocence, if pre-trial detention is based on *any* of the grounds of Article 58 (1).[956]

Chamber's reference to that decision when determining the case at hand'). See also *Prosecutor v. Gbagbo*, PTC I, Decision on the 'Requête de la Défense demandant la mise en liberté provisoire du président Gbagbo', ICC-02/11-01/11-180-Red, 13 July 2012, para. 54 (rejecting the defence objection to rely on such material: 'there does not exist in the applicable law any impediment to the use of such material, or any requirement that it be corroborated. Rather, the Single Judge must analyse all the material placed before it, in order to determine what weight must be given to it for the purpose of the determination as to whether continued detention "appears necessary"').

[948] *Abd-Al-Rahman*, ICC-02/05-01/20-177, para. 34 *in fine* ('Likewise, the Appeals Chamber finds that Mr Abd-Al-Rahman failed to articulate why the Pre-Trial Chamber's approach would be contrary to the application of article 69 to various stages of the proceedings'); *contra* the defence submission, cf. *Prosecutor v. Abd-Al-Rahman*, AC, Corrected Version of the 'Mémoire d'appel de la décision ICC-02/05-01/20-115 en vertu de l'Article 82-1-b du Statut de Rome', ICC-02/05-01/20-120-Corr-tENG, 19 August 2020, paras. 22–3.

[949] Chapter V, A.(3)(c) and (4)(b).

[950] ICC, *Prosecutor v. Said*, Defence, Public Redacted Version of the 'Defence Appeal Brief against the "Decision on the Defence Application for Interim Release of Mahamat Said Abdel Kani and Contact Restrictions" (ICC-01/14-01/21-247-Conf) of Trial Chamber VI Deciding to Continue Mr Said's Detention and Maintain the Restrictions on His Communications' Filed on 21 March 2022, ICC-01/14-01/21-265-Red-tENG, 22 March 2022, para. 62; *Said*, ICC-01/14-01/21-318, para. 69.

[951] *Said*, ICC-01/14-01/21-318, para. 74; *Gbagbo*, ICC-02/11-01/11-278-Red, para. 65.

[952] Ibid.

[953] *Al Bashir*, ICC-02/05-01/09-3, paras. 235–6; *Mbarushimana*, ICC-01/04-01/10-1, para. 49; *Situation in the Libyan Arab Jamahiriya*, ICC-01/11-12, paras. 93–4, 97–8, 101; *Mudacumura*, ICC-01/04-01/12-1-Red, para. 74.

[954] cf. Llobet Rodríguez, *Unschuldsvermutung* (1995), pp. 97 ff.; Llobet Rodríguez, *Prisión preventiva* (2010), pp. 179 ff. In the same vein, identifying as the relevant factors for a restriction of liberty the risk of flight and obstruction of justice (as a general rule), de Meester, Pitcher, Rastan, and Sluiter, in Sluiter et al., *International Criminal Procedure* (2013), p. 348, but adopting all grounds listed in Art. 58 (1)(b) ICCS (p. 349); similarly restrictive, Khan, 'Article 60', in Ambos, *Commentary* (2022), mn. 10; generally crit. also, Orlandi, *ZStW*, 127 (2015), 462–5.

[955] Crit. also, Ryngaert, 'Article 58', in Ambos, *Commentary* (2022), mn. 20; Dumbryte, in Stahn, *Practice* (2015), pp. 1077–8 (criticizing the Chambers for considering 'contrary to domestic and human rights courts ... primarily external factors rather than individual intentions'); for a principled critique, see Llobet Rodríguez, *Unschuldsvermutung* (1995), pp. 134 ff.; Llobet Rodríguez, *Prisión preventiva* (2010), pp. 203 ff.

[956] *Said*, ICC-01/14-01/21-318, para. 39; *Prosecutor v. Abd-Al-Rahman*, AC, Public Redacted Version of Judgment on the Appeal of Ali Muhammad Ali Abd-Al-Rahman against Trial Chamber I's 'Decision on the

The arrest warrant must be precise and concrete: that is, indicate the name of the person sought and other identifying information, the alleged crimes, and the relevant factual basis.[957]

While too broad arrest grounds are, from a human rights perspective, not completely satisfactory, the PTCs try, arguably, to make sure that detention is the exception and not the rule,[958] especially by issuing a summons to appear instead of an arrest warrant, if possible.[959] In any case, the situation at the ad hoc tribunals has been worse. Their law does not even require any specific ground for an arrest and makes it 'a purpose in and of itself', thereby turning detention into the rule instead of the exception[960] and strikingly interfering with the human right to personal liberty.[961] An alternative, less intrusive, measure to an arrest, such as a summons to appear, is not provided for.[962] Also, both the ICTY and ICTR have set a high threshold with regard to objections against the legality of the detention or the period of detention.[963] At the KSC, pre-trial detention also has turned out to be the rule; recently the first interlocutory appeal has been granted.[964]

review of detention', ICC-02/05-01/20-542-Red, 17 December 2021, para. 41; ICC, *Prosecutor v. Bemba et al.*, AC, Judgment on the Appeal of Mr Aimé Kilolo Musamba against the Decision of Pre-Trial Chamber II of 14 March 2014 Entitled Decision on the 'Demande de mise en liberté provisoire de Maître Aimé Kilolo Musamba', ICC-01/05-01/13-558, 11 July 2014, paras. 67–8 ('pre-trial detention, whilst to be ordered exceptionally, does not breach internationally recognised human rights or criminal law principles such as the presumption of innocence where it is justified under articles 58 (1) and 60 (2) of the Statute'); see also ICC, *Prosecutor v. Bemba et al.*, AC, Judgment on the Appeal of Mr Fidele Babala Wandu against the Decision of Pre-Trial Chamber II of 14 March 2014 Entitled 'Decision on the "Requête urgente de la Défense sollicitant la mise en libert provisoire de monsieur Fidele Babala Wandu"', ICC-01/05-01/13-559, 11 July 2014, para. 66.

[957] Art. 58 (3) ICCS. This subparagraph refers back to Art. 58 (2) where the information required in the application of the Prosecutor is listed, see note 908 and main text in this chapter. See also ICC, *Practice Manual* (2023), para. 4.

[958] ICC, *Prosecutor v. Bemba*, PTC II, Decision on the Interim Release of Jean-Pierre Bemba Gombo and Convening Hearings with the Kingdom of Belgium, the Republic of Portugal, the Republic of France, the Federal Republic of Germany, the Italian Republic, and the Republic of South Africa, ICC-01/05-01/08-475, 14 August 2009, para. 36; Abd-Al-Rahman, ICC-02/05-01/20-542-Red, para. 39; thereto Irving, *Human Rights Protection* (2020), pp. 31–2; for earlier case law, see previous edition p. 404 with note 678; in the same vein, de Meester, Pitcher, Rastan, and Sluiter, in Sluiter et al., *International Criminal Procedure* (2013), p. 317; Dumbryte, in Stahn, *Practice* (2015), p. 1064; generally crit. of the ICC's practice, Ramsden and Chung, *JICJ*, 13 (2015), 558 ff., 571 ff. (arguing that the applied threshold is too low, undermining the role of the Prosecutor, the credibility of the ICC, and the defendant's right to liberty).

[959] Note 948 in this chapter.

[960] cf. de Meester, Pitcher, Rastan, and Sluiter, in Sluiter et al., *International Criminal Procedure* (2013), pp. 315, 339; Dumbryte, in Stahn, *Practice* (2015), pp. 1064–5.

[961] cf. Arts. 9 (1) ICCPR, 5 (1) ECHR, 7 (1) ACHR; see de Meester, Pitcher, Rastan, and Sluiter, in Sluiter et al., *International Criminal Procedure* (2013), pp. 340–1, seeing a violation of this right in the 'presumption in favour of detention' esp. at the ad hoc tribunals.

[962] Crit. de Meester, Pitcher, Rastan, and Sluiter, in Sluiter et al., *International Criminal Procedure* (2013), p. 315.

[963] De Meester, Pitcher, Rastan, and Sluiter, in Sluiter et al., *International Criminal Procedure* (2013), pp. 315–16. See also ICTR, *Prosecutor v. Barayagwiza*, AC, Decision, ICTR-97-19-AR72, 3 November 1999, para. 74 , applying the *abuse of process doctrine* only in cases of 'serious and egregious violations of the accused's rights'; ICTR, *Prosecutor v. Barayagwiza*, AC, Decision, Prosecutor's Request for Review or Reconsideration, ICTR-97-19-AR72, 31 March 2000, para. 71; ICTY, *Prosecutor v. Dragan Nikolić*, TC, Decision on Defence Motion Challenging the Exercise of Jurisdiction by the Tribunal, IT-94-2-PT, 9 October 2002, para. 111 ('in order to prompt a Chamber to use this doctrine [*abuse of process*], it needs to be clear that the rights of the Accused have been egregiously violated').

[964] KSC, *Prosecutor v. Isni Kilaj*, Public Redacted Version of Decision on the Specialist Prosecutor's Office's Appeal against Decision on Isni Kilaj's Review of Detention, AP, KSC-BC-2018-01/IA007/F00007/RED, 13 May 2024. Previous appeals have been dismissed: KSC, *Prosecutor v. Hashim Thaçi et al.*, Decision on Selimi Appeal against 'Decision on Periodic Review of Detention of Rexhep Selimi', AP, KSC-BC-2020-06, IA021/F00005/RED, 2 August 2022; Decision on Jakup Krasniqi's Appeal against Decision on Periodic Review of Detention, 2 August 2022; AP, KSC-BC-2020-06, IA020/F00005/RED, 2 August 2022; and Decision on Hashim Thaçi's Appeal against Decision on Periodic Review of Detention, AP, KSC-BC-2020-06, IA022/F00005/RED, 22 August 2022. On

### (b) Arrest, review, and (interim) release

For the execution of their international arrest warrants, international criminal tribunals depend on the cooperation of States or international organizations.[965] Thus, the judge or Chamber 'directs the competent authorities to arrest, detain, and transfer the individual to the custody of the Court'; its decision 'includes a direction to the administrative arm of the Court to prepare a "request" to the custodial state for arrest and surrender of the suspect'.[966] While the ICC's cooperation regime will be examined in detail in Chapter VII, some remarks are apposite here. The ICC's 'inability to secure arrests of fugitives'[967] has led the OTP to set up a Suspects-At-Large Tracking Team (SALTT) in 2018,[968] composed of a small team of staff members working on regular cases.[969] In addition, the OTP has had specific arrest guidelines since 2010[970] and may conclude agreements with States to facilitate the surrender of suspects. Take for example the MoU of 17 August 2021 with Sudan[971]—not an ICC State Party—which was preceded by the surrender of former militia leader *Abd-Al-Rahman* ('Ali Kushayb') which finally led to his transfer to the ICC on 9 June 2020.[972]

my concerns, with a special reference to the 'Third State option' see Separate Concurring Opinion of Judge Kai Ambos, in Decision on Hashim Thaçi's Appeal against Decision on Interim Release, KSC-BC-2020-06/IA004/F00005/RED, 30 April 2021.

965 While the cooperation of non-State entities in arrest operations is not regulated in the ICCS or the ICC RPE, there are some specific agreements between the ICC and such organizations to that effect; see e.g. the MoU between the UN and the ICC Concerning Cooperation between the UNO Mission in the DRC (MONUC [now MONUSCO]) and the ICC, 8 November 2005, <https://treaties.un.org/doc/publication/unts/volume%202363/ii-1292.pdf> and UNSC Res. 2098, 28 March 2013, para. 12; further agreements of this kind are, for instance, the MoU with the MINUSCA in the CAR (UNSC Res. 2149, 10 April 2014, para. 29(f)), with the UNOCI in Côte d'Ivoire (MoU, 12 June 2013, and UNSC Res. 2162, 25 June 2014, para. 12), with the UPEACE (<https://www.icc-cpi.int/news/icc-and-un-university-peace-sign-memorandum-understanding>, 15 June 2022), with La Francophonie (<https://www.icc-cpi.int/news/icc-signs-memorandum-understanding-international-organisation-la-francophonie>, 28 September 2012), with the European Committee (<https://rm.coe.int/pdf/1680765d7a>, 2 November 2017) and the EU (<https://www.consilium.europa.eu/uedocs/cms_data/docs/pressdata/en/er/Memo.eng.htm>, 21 September 1999); see also ICC-ASP, *Ongoing Cooperation* (2013), paras. 24, 51 ff.

966 Boas et al., *Procedure* (2011), p. 208, referring to *Al Bashir*, ICC-02/05-01/09-3, p. 93.

967 Expert Group, *IER* (2020), p. 247. Crit. also Hale, in Heinze and Dittrich, *ICC* (2021), pp. 159, 178 ff. (demanding that the OTP prioritize the arrest of fugitives over other actions. Hale's comparison with the arguably more effective arrest regime at the ICTY downplays, however, the fundamental differences in the cooperation regime).

968 Expert Group, *IER* (2020), p. 247. Generally, on this kind of 'tracking units', see Hale, in Heinze and Dittrich, *ICC* (2021), pp. 159, 180 ff. About the efforts of the (former) Prosecutor to arrest fugitives, see Shoamanesh, *ICLR*, 18 (2018), pp. 489–516.

969 It is part of the OTP budget, see ASP, Proposed Budget 2022, ICC-ASP/20/10, 16 August 2021, p. 199, where it is mentioned in Annex IV (e) referring to the OTP. Crit. of the lack of sufficient resources, Expert Group, *IER* (2020), p. 248; Hale, in Heinze and Dittrich, *ICC* (2021), p. 183.

970 ICC-OTP, *Prosecutorial Strategy* (2010), para. 48: a) eliminate non-essential contacts with individuals subject to an arrest warrant issued by the Court. When contacts are necessary, attempt first to interact with individuals not subject to an arrest warrant;

b) in bilateral and multilateral meetings, proactively express support for the enforcement of the Court's decisions, request cooperation with the Court, and demand that crimes, if ongoing, cease immediately;

c) contribute to the marginalization of fugitives and take steps to prevent that aid and funds meant for humanitarian purposes or peace talks are diverted for the benefit of persons subject to an arrest warrant; and

d) make collaborative efforts to plan and execute arrests of individuals subject to an arrest warrant issued by the Court, including by providing operational or financial support to countries willing to conduct such operations but lacking the capacity to do so.'

971 cf. <https://www.icc-cpi.int/news/prosecutor-international-criminal-court-mr-karim-khan-qc-concludes-his-first-visit-sudan>.

972 *Situation in Darfur (Sudan): Ali Kushayb is in ICC custody*, 'Press Release', 9 June 2020, ICC-CPI-20200609-PR1525, <https://www.icc-cpi.int/news/situation-darfur-sudan-ali-kushayb-icc-custody>. Previously, a second arrest warrant was issued, cf. ICC, *Prosecutor v. Harun and Abd-Al-Rahman*, PTC II, Public Redacted Version of 'Second warrant of arrest for Ali Muhammad Ali Abd-Al-Rahman ('Ali Kushayb')', 16 January 2018, ICC-02/05-01/07-74-Secret-Exp, ICC-02/05-01/07-74-Red, 11 June 2020.

The Court may—'on the basis of the warrant of arrest'[973]—either request the surrender or arrest of the respective person[974] or, in urgent cases, request his *provisional* arrest.[975] The request must contain all necessary information so that the requested State is able to comply with it.[976] The provisional arrest must not exceed sixty days, since this is the time the Court has to present the request for surrender to the relevant State.[977] In implementing the request for (provisional) arrest, the competent judicial authority of the custodial State shall determine whether the warrant applies to the person arrested, whether it has been properly executed and the rights of the person have been respected.[978] It is important to note that the arrest always requires the respective warrant by a PTC,[979] which may then have to act quickly.[980] It goes without saying that the rights of the person have to be respected when the arrest is being executed.[981]

In contrast, at the ad hoc tribunals and at the KSC, in case of urgency, it is the Prosecutor who may, without judicial involvement, request the respective State to provisionally arrest the suspect with a view to his subsequent surrender to the tribunal.[982] The prosecutorial request for a provisional arrest does not require—like the 'normal' arrest[983] already described earlier—the confirmation of the indictment and thus no *prima facie* case. There is no explicit time limit for this provisional detention at the national level; the analogous application of Rule 40*bis* RPE ICTY/ICTR—actually applicable to the detention at the tribunals—to this situation by the *Barayagwiza* AC[984] has never been incorporated into the Rules.[985] This means that a suspect could remain detained in the custodial State until transferred to the tribunal—in line with the arrest-for-surrender logic mentioned above—unless the custodial

[973] Art. 58 (5) ICCS. Given this wording, the request must be based on the original arrest warrant although details must be developed by the case law; cf. Ryngaert, 'Article 58', in Ambos, *Commentary* (2022), mn. 31–3.

[974] Arts. 58 (5), 89 ICCS. See Irving, *Human Rights Protection* (2020), pp. 3, 49 ff.

[975] Arts. 58 (5), 92 (1) ICCS. While it has been the usual practice that the PTC made such requests (ICC, *Prosecutor v. Bemba,* Demande d'arrestation provisoire de M. Jean-Pierre Bemba Gombo adressée au Royaume de Belgique, ICC-01/05-01/08-3, 23 May 2008, p. 4), today it is the Registrar's task to prepare and transmit a request for cooperation, *Mudacumura*, ICC 01/04-01/12-1-Red, pp. 29–30; *Mbarushimana*, ICC-01/04-01/10-1, p. 28; ICC, *Prosecutor v. Al Bashir*, Decision Regarding Omar Al Bashir's Travel to the United Arab Emirates and his Potential Travel to the Kingdom of Saudi Arabia, the State of Kuwait and the Kingdom of Bahrain, ICC-02/05-01/09-224, 24 February 2015, p. 6; ICC, *Prosecutor v. Blé Goudé,* Warrant of Arrest for Charles Blé Goudé, ICC-02/11-02/11-1, 21 December 2011, p. 9; ICC, *Prosecutor v. Gaddafi,* Decision on the 'Prosecutor's Application Pursuant to Article 58 as to Muammar Mohammed Abu Minyar Gaddafi, Saif Al-Islam Gaddafi and Abdullah Al-Senussi', ICC-01/11-01/11-1, 27 June 2011, p. 42.

[976] Art. 91 ICCS. See also de Meester, Pitcher, Rastan, and Sluiter, in Sluiter et al., *International Criminal Procedure* (2013), p. 318, stressing that the 'warrant itself should ... anticipate the obligations under Article 91'.

[977] Art. 92 (3) with Rule 188 RPE ICC.

[978] Art. 59 (2) ICCS. This includes the right to be promptly informed about the reasons of the arrest (Arts. 9 (2) ICCPR, 5 (2) ECHR, 7 (4) ACHR), cf. de Meester, Pitcher, Rastan, and Sluiter, in Sluiter et al., *International Criminal Procedure* (2013), p. 343; Ryngaert, 'Article 59', in Ambos, *Commentary* (2022), mn. 14.

[979] cf. de Meester, Pitcher, Rastan, and Sluiter, in Sluiter et al., *International Criminal Procedure* (2013), pp. 318, 321, stating that this is also the rule with regard to the other tribunals.

[980] See e.g. *Bemba*, ICC-01/05-01/08-14, paras. 4–10, limiting the warrant to only a few of the offences charged notwithstanding the issuance of a new warrant at a later stage.

[981] Arts. 55 and 59 (2) ICCS; see also Irving, *Human Rights Protection* (2020), p. 55.

[982] Rules 40 (i) RPE ICTY, 37 (A)(i) RPE MICT, 40 (A)(i) RPE ICTR, Arts. 35 (2) (h), 38 (2) KSC Law, and Rule 52 RPE KSC. The ICTR Rule regulates detention at the national level in more detail, in particular the release by the custodial state (Rule 40 (B) RPE ICTR); see also de Meester, Pitcher, Rastan, and Sluiter, in Sluiter et al., *International Criminal Procedure* (2013), pp. 316, 349–50, recommending this as a model for the ICC Prosecutor. About the practice at the ICTR in more detail, see Mochochoko, in Jalloh and Marong, *Promoting Accountability* (2015), pp. 83 ff.

[983] cf. Arts. 19 (2) ICTYS, 18 (2) ICTRS.

[984] *Barayagwiza*, ICTR-97-19-AR72, para. 46 (3 November 1999), referring to the time limits contained in Rule 40*bis*.

[985] Crit., de Meester, Pitcher, Rastan, and Sluiter, in Sluiter et al., *International Criminal Procedure* (2013), p. 316.

State would consider, in its own right, that such a detention would be too long or not justified for other reasons.[986] To avoid such a situation the KSC Law limits this arrest to forty-eight hours,[987] to be prolonged only by a judicial decision.[988]

As to a possible interim release at the ICC, one must distinguish between the situation before surrender (with the person still in the custody of the relevant State) and after surrender (with the person in the custody of the Court). In the former situation, the custodial State decides on the interim release upon a request by the arrested person.[989] This authority shows, among other features, that the ICC cooperation regime is rather of a horizontal or mixed than vertical nature.[990] While the custodial State must not examine the grounds given by the Court for the warrant (this is the exclusive competence of the PTC),[991] it has, taking into account the recommendations of the competent PTC,[992] to take a substantive decision as to 'whether, given the gravity of the alleged crimes, there are urgent and exceptional circumstances to justify interim release and whether necessary safeguards exist to ensure that the custodial State can fulfil its duty to surrender the person to the Court'.[993] It has been argued that the custodial State's duty to surrender entails that it 'cannot terminate the detention permanently';[994] in any case, it must prevent the escape of the persons sought by the Court.[995] Arguably, the custodial State may be able to ensure surrender without detention, for example, by monitoring the person sought with electronic means. On the other hand, the reference to 'urgent and exceptional circumstances'[996] makes clear that the threshold for a provisional release is high and, at any rate, subject to the fulfilment of the surrender obligation.[997]

If interim release is granted, the PTC can request periodic reports on the status of the release from the competent national authority.[998] While one may consider Article 59 ICCS an 'ambitious provision'[999] in that it tries to reconcile the custodial State's duty to surrender the person sought with the protection of the rights of this person by this very State, it is open to debate whether and to what extent the ICC has the power to control or even review the domestic

[986] cf. de Meester, Pitcher, Rastan, and Sluiter, in Sluiter et al., *International Criminal Procedure* (2013), pp. 322–3, referring to provisional release decisions by French and Texan Courts with regard to ICTR cases.

[987] Art. 35 (2)(h), 38 (2) KSC Law.

[988] Rule 52 (2) RPE KSC.

[989] Art. 59 (3) ICCS.

[990] Ryngaert, 'Article 59', in Ambos, *Commentary* (2022), mn. 16 considers the national authority's responsibility regarding provisional release as 'a dramatic shift'.

[991] cf. Art. 59 (4) cl. 2 with Rule 117 (3) RPE ICC ('not be open to the competent authority of the custodial State to consider whether the warrant of arrest was properly issued'). See also Ryngaert, 'Article 59', in Ambos, *Commentary* (2022), mn. 17, 22. However, Rule 117 RPE ICC is only applicable when the person is detained in the custodial State, see ICC, *Prosecutor v. Osapiri Barasa*, Decision on the 'Defence challenge to the warrant for the arrest of Walter Osapiri Barasa', ICC-01/09-01/13-35, 10 September 2015, para. 2; Irving, *Human Rights Protection* (2020), p. 57.

[992] Art. 59 (5) ICCS, Rule 117 (4) RPE ICC. See also Ryngaert, 'Article 59', in Ambos, *Commentary* (2022), mn. 23–4.

[993] Art. 59 (4) ICCS. See also Ryngaert, 'Article 59', in Ambos, *Commentary* (2022), mn. 19, considering as that kind of an exceptional circumstance, for example, the advanced stages of a terminal illness.

[994] De Meester, Pitcher, Rastan, and Sluiter, in Sluiter et al., *International Criminal Procedure* (2013), p. 329.

[995] Art. 59 (5) *in fine* ICCS. See also Ryngaert, 'Article 59', in Ambos, *Commentary* (2022), mn. 26.

[996] Art. 59 (4) ICCS. On the similar requirement of 'exceptional circumstances' in old Rule 65 (B) RPE ICTY/ICTR, see later in this section. At the KSC, it is up to the Pre-Trial Judge ('Panel') to decide on the continuation of the detention, cf. Rule 52 (2) RPE KSC.

[997] For a discussion, see also de Meester, Pitcher, Rastan, and Sluiter, in Sluiter et al., *International Criminal Procedure* (2013), p. 330.

[998] Art. 59 (6) ICCS, Rule 117 (5) RPE ICC. On the almost obligatory nature of these reports pursuant to Rule 117 (5), see Ryngaert, 'Article 59', in Ambos, *Commentary* (2022), mn. 27.

[999] De Meester, Pitcher, Rastan, and Sluiter, in Sluiter et al., *International Criminal Procedure* (2013), p. 318 (but notwithstanding recommending it at p. 350).

arrest proceedings.[1000] In any case, again the situation is worse under the regime of the ad hoc tribunals, since there is no provision granting national authorities a comparable release power. Indeed, the relevant Rules[1001] leave no discretion to the national authorities but treat them as pure executors of the tribunals' orders.[1002] At the KSC, arrests in Kosovo are anyway done by the SPO's own police force or by the Kosovo police under the former's instruction.[1003]

Once the person is surrendered to the ICC, he shall 'promptly' appear before the PTC,[1004] which has to ensure that he is informed of the alleged crimes and his rights.[1005] He may directly apply—in writing[1006]—for interim release to the PTC.[1007] While Article 60 (2) ICCS seems to limit this application to the pre-trial phase ('pending trial'), Trial Chambers have often conducted interim release reviews after the commencement of the trial and the AC has reviewed such rulings routinely.[1008] Article 60 (2) ICCS 'aims to provide the detainee with an early opportunity to contest his or her arrest and sequential detention'[1009] and thus provides for the human right to challenge the lawfulness of the detention.[1010] It presupposes that the applicant must rebut the facts that justified the original arrest warrant,[1011] that is, the onus of rebuttal is imposed on him.[1012] This can only be compatible with the non-reversal guarantee of Article 67 (1)(i) ICCS if one limits the scope of this provision to the charges; this indeed seems to follow from the chapeau of the provision, which refers to the 'determination of any charge'.[1013] In any case, the *Bemba* AC has clarified that while 'the Prosecutor

1000 In fact, the ICC has left so far a broad discretion to the national authorities; cf. *Lubanga*, ICC-01/04-01/06-772, para. 41, thereto Irving, *Human Rights Protection* (2020), p. 58. For the same restrictive view, see Rastan, *LJIL*, 21 (2008), 449–53; crit. Sluiter, in Stahn and Sluiter, *Practice* (2009), pp. 468–75; leaving the question open, de Meester, Pitcher, Rastan, and Sluiter, in Sluiter et al., *International Criminal Procedure* (2013), p. 331.

1001 Rules 55–8 RPE ICTY/ICTR, 57–60 RPE MICT.

1002 In the same vein, Safferling, *Criminal Procedure* (2012), p. 298.

1003 cf. Art. 35 (3) KSC Law.

1004 cf. Art. 60 (1) ICCS, Rule 121 (1) RPE ICC; see Section A.(1)(b)(iii) in this chapter.

1005 Art. 60 (1) ICCS; also Khan, 'Article 60', in Ambos, *Commentary* (2022), mn. 4.

1006 Rule 118 (3) RPE ICC.

1007 Art. 60 (2) ICCS, Rule 118 (1) RPE ICC.

1008 See ICC, *Prosecutor v. Bemba*, AC, Judgment on the Appeal of Mr Jean-Pierre Bemba Gombo against the Decision of Trial Chamber III of 27 June 2011 Entitled 'Decision on Applications for Provisional Release', ICC-01/05-01/08-1626-Red, 19 August 2011; ICC, *Prosecutor v. Bemba*, AC, Public Redacted Version—Judgment on the Appeal of Mr Jean-Pierre Bemba Gombo against the Decision of Trial Chamber III of 6 January 2012 Entitled 'Decision on the defence's 28 December 2011 "Requête de mise en liberté provisoire de M. Jean-Pierre Bemba Gombo"', ICC-01/05-01/08-2151-Red, 5 March 2012; ICC, *Prosecutor v. Gbagbo and Blé Goudé*, AC, Judgment on the Appeal of Mr Laurent Gbagbo against the Decision of Trial Chamber I of 10 March 2017 Entitled 'Decision on Mr Gbagbo's Detention', ICC-02/11-01/15-992-Red, 19 July 2017; *Bemba et al.*, ICC-01/05-01/13-2291, para. 11.

1009 *Katanga and Ngudjolo*, ICC-01/04-01/07-572, para. 12.

1010 cf. Arts. 9 (4) ICCPR, 5 (4) ECHR, and 7 (6) ACHR. This right has been recognized by ICC, *Prosecutor v. Bemba*, AC, Judgment on the Appeal of Mr Jean-Pierre Bemba Gombo against the Decision of Pre-Trial Chamber III Entitled 'Decision on application for interim release', ICC-01/05-01/08 323, 16 December 2008, para. 32; in the same vein, de Meester, Pitcher, Rastan, and Sluiter, in Sluiter et al., *International Criminal Procedure* (2013), pp. 344, 350, recommending a judicial review; Irving, *Human Rights Protection* (2020), pp. 66 ff. See also Chapter I, D.(3)(c) in this volume.

1011 cf. ICC, *Prosecutor v. Bemba*, PTC III, Decision on Application for Interim Release, ICC-01/05-01/08-80-Anx, 20 August 2008, para. 52 , noting 'that the defence has not put forward any material fact or argument to rebut these grounds [of detention, K.A.] and considers that they still stand'; ICC, *Prosecutor v. Bemba*, Decision on Application for Interim Release, ICC-01/05-01/08-321, 16 December 2008, para. 34 .

1012 Safferling, *Criminal Procedure* (2012), p. 305, even sees a reversal of the burden of proof; in a similar vein, Dumbryte, in Stahn, *Practice* (2015), pp. 1065–7 (justifying such a shifting of the burden of proof in the ICC case law regarding interim release on the basis of the seriousness of the charges and the influential positions the suspects have).

1013 In the same vein, apparently, Schabas and McDermott, 'Article 67', in Ambos, *Commentary* (2022), mn. 8 ('rights ... do not apply necessarily ... in other proceedings before the Court'); for a broader interpretation, apparently, however, Keïta et al., 'Article 67', in Fernandez et al., *Commentaire CPI II* (2019), pp. 1821 ff., calling for protection of the rights of the accused in all procedural phases ('Le droits de l'accusé doivent être protégés lors de *toutes les phases* de la procédure devant la CPI.'). In a similar vein, Art. 66 (2) ICCS imposes the onus on the Prosecutor regarding 'the guilt of the accused'.

does not have to re-establish circumstances that have already been established, he [she] must show that there has been no change in those circumstances'. Thus, she must inform the PTC 'as to whether there has been any change in the circumstances that previously justified detention' and 'bring to the attention of the Chamber any other relevant information'.[1014] This means that the PTC is not restricted to arguments brought forward by the defence.[1015] In addition, the AC found that the 'necessity of continued detention' may be established 'on the basis of an analysis of all relevant factors taken together' and not just 'on the basis of one factor taken in isolation'.[1016] If the PTC determines—'without delay'[1017]—that the requirements of Article 58 (1) are still met[1018] the arrest continues; otherwise, it 'shall release' the person with or without conditions.[1019]

The PTC shall review 'its ruling' at least every 120 days and at any time upon request of the person or Prosecutor.[1020] The 'ruling' in this sense refers to the Article 60 (2) decision ordering the continuation of the detention; consequently, the time limits for the periodic review run from the first release application under Article 60 (2).[1021] Without the Article 60 (2) ruling, the periodic review under Article 60 (3) is not triggered, that is, the mere existence of an arrest warrant does not trigger this periodic review.[1022] This does not only follow from a systematic interpretation—both Article 60 (3) ICCS and Rule 118 (2) RPE ICC appear directly after Article 60 (2)[1023]—but above all from the fact that Article 60 (4) imposes upon the PTC the duty to ensure that a person is not detained for an 'unreasonable period prior to trial due to inexcusable delay by the Prosecutor'.[1024] This is a self-standing review

[1014] cf. ICC, *Prosecutor v. Bemba*, AC, Judgment on the Appeal of Mr Jean-Pierre Bemba Gombo against the Decision of Trial Chamber III of 28 July 2010 Entitled 'Decision on the review of the detention of Mr Jean-Pierre Bemba Gombo pursuant to Rule 118 (2) of the Rules of Procedure and Evidence', ICC-01/05-01/08-1019, 19 November 2010, para. 51. This clarification was apparently caused by the Dissenting Opinion of Judge Pikis in *Bemba*, ICC-01/05-01/08-323, Dissenting Opinion of Judge Georghios M. Pikis; see de Meester, Pitcher, Rastan, and Sluiter, in Sluiter et al., *International Criminal Procedure* (2013), p. 333; Zeegers, *International Criminal Tribunals* (2016), p. 276.

[1015] ICC, *Prosecutor v. Bemba et al.*, PTC II, Decision on the First Review of Fidèle Babala Wandu's Detention pursuant to Article 60 (3) of the Statute, ICC-01/05-01/13-538, 4 July 2014, para. 2; ICC, *Prosecutor v. Gbagbo*, Sixth Decision on the Review of Laurent Gbagbo's Detention pursuant to Article 60 (3) of the Rome Statute, ICC-02/11-01/11-668, 11 July 2014, para. 18; ICC, *Prosecutor v. Bemba et al.*, Decision on the First Review of Aimé Kilolo Musamba's Detention pursuant to Article 60 (3) of the Statute, ICC-01/05-01/13-611, 5 August 2014, para. 2. See Zeegers, *International Criminal Tribunals* (2016), pp. 276–7.

[1016] *Bemba*, ICC-01/05-01/08-323, para. 55; conc. *Abd-Al-Rahman*, ICC-02/05-01/20-177, para. 35. In this case, the AC further noted 'that the fact that a suspect surrendered himself voluntarily to the Court can be understood as an indication of his willingness to cooperate with the Court in its proceedings'; *Abd-Al-Rahman*, ICC-02/05-01/20-542-Red, para. 27.

[1017] Rule 118 (1) RPE ICC.

[1018] In this regard confusing, Safferling, *Criminal Procedure* (2012), p. 300 (arguing that 'at least with regard to a decision in accordance with Art. 60 (2) ... the requirements of Art. 58 (1) must be assessed and affirmed'). See also *Bemba et al.*, ICC-01/05-01/13-2291, para. 14.

[1019] Art. 60 (2) ICCS. The onerous requirements of Art. 59 (4) do not apply; cf. Khan and Ellis, 'Article 60', in Ambos, *Commentary* (2022), mn. 7. See also Khan at al., *International Criminal Courts* (2018), mn. 7–137 and 7–154. Rule 119 RPE ICC provides for a non-exhaustive list of conditions of release which may be imposed by the Chamber; crit. Khan and Ellis, 'Article 60', in Ambos, *Commentary* (2022), mn. 9.

[1020] Art. 60 (3) ICCS, Rule 118 (2) RPE ICC.

[1021] See also Khan and Ellis, 'Article 60', in Ambos, *Commentary* (2022), mn. 15.

[1022] *Lubanga*, ICC-01/04-01/06-824, paras. 3, 94–100; conc. *Bemba*, ICC-01/05-01/08-1019, para. 45; *Gbagbo*, ICC-02/11-01/11-278-Red, paras. 23–4.

[1023] *Lubanga*, ICC-01/04-01/06-824, para. 94.

[1024] In ICC, *Prosecutor v. Bemba et al.*, Decision Ordering the Release of Aimé Kilolo Musamba, Jean-Jacques Mangenda Kabongo, Fidèle Babala Wandu and Narcisse Arido', ICC-01/05-01/13-703, 21 October 2014, p. 5, the PTC II considered that even if the duration of the detention of the suspect was not due to the Prosecutor's 'inexcusable delay', it still had a 'distinct and independent obligation ... to ensure that a person is not detained for an unreasonable period prior to trial under article 60(4) of the Statute'. The AC, however, rejected this interpretation of Art. 60 (4) ICCS, finding that Art. 60 (4) was 'unequivocal' and only 'addresses situations in which detention prior to trial has been for an unreasonable period of time "due to inexcusable delay by the Prosecutor"', see ICC, *Prosecutor*

obligation of the PTC[1025] that aims to bring the ICC regime in line with the general human rights obligations already discussed in Chapter I in this volume.[1026] It entails a management responsibility of the PTC in the sense that it must do everything possible and necessary to speed up proceedings, for example by setting fixed dates for submissions of the parties and limit these submissions.[1027]

While the reasonableness and 'inexcusable' standards cannot be determined in the abstract, but depend—taking into account the human rights case law on the trial without undue delay[1028]—on the circumstances of the concrete case,[1029] once the unreasonableness of the detention is determined the person should be released. Given the the flexible wording ('shall consider') of Article 60 (4) the release is not automatic though.[1030] In any case, the best way to prevent an unreasonably long detention is to speed up proceedings making use of the just mentioned pre-trial and trial management possibilities.

Contrary to the wording ('delay by the Prosecutor'), one has to take into account delays caused by any organ of the Court.[1031] After all, the prolonged pre-trial detention at

*v. Bemba et al.*, AC, Judgment on the Appeals against Pre-Trial Chamber II's Decisions Regarding Interim Release in Relation to Aimé Kilolo Musamba, Jean-Jacques Mangenda, Fidèle Babala Wandu, and Narcisse Arido and Order for Reclassification, ICC-01/05-01/13-969, 29 May 2015, para. 42. See also ICC, *Prosecutor v. Abd-Al-Rahman*, PTC II, Decision on the Review of Detention, ICC-02/05-01/20-338, 12 April 2021, para. 22. For the same interpretation for Rule 56 (2) KSC RPE, see the KSC AP in *Prosecutor v. Thaçi et al.*, Decision on Jakup Krasniqi's Appeal against Decision on Remanded Detention Review and Periodic Review of Detention, KSC-BC-2020-06/IA016/F00005/RED, 25 March 2022, para. 47. On the 'unreasonableness' standard, see Dumbryte, in Stahn, *Practice* (2015), pp. 1078–9; Irving, *Human Rights Protection* (2020), pp. 68 ff.

1025 *Lubanga*, ICC-01/04-01/06-824, paras. 98, 120 (98: 'distinct and independent obligation ... to ensure that a person is not detained for an unreasonable period prior to trial', 120: 'Article 60 (4) is independent of article 60 (2) in the sense that even if a detainee is appropriately detained ... the Pre-Trial Chamber shall consider releasing the detainee ... if ...detained for an unreasonable period prior to trial'); see also Boas et al., *Procedure* (2011), p. 120.

1026 See Arts. 9 (3) ICCPR ('trial within a reasonable time or to release'), 5 (3) ECHR, and 7 (5) ACHR, in part adopted by Art. 67 (1)(c) ICCS; see also Chapter I, D.(1) and (3)(h) in this volume. See also de Meester, Pitcher, Rastan, and Sluiter, in Sluiter et al., *International Criminal Procedure* (2013), pp. 342–3, 350, recommending this rule.

1027 In a similar vein, Khan and Ellis, 'Article 60', in Ambos, *Commentary* (2022), mn. 22.

1028 See Chapter I, D.(3)(h) in this volume.

1029 *Lubanga*, ICC-01/04-01/06-824, para. 122 ('cannot be determined in the abstract, but has to be determined on the basis of the circumstances of each case'); ICC, *Prosecutor v. Katanga and Ngudjolo*, Second Review of the Decision on the Application for Interim Release of Mathieu Ngudjolo (Rule 118 (2) of the Rules of Procedure and Evidence), ICC-01/04-01/07-750-tENG, 19 November 2008, para. 19, referring to ICC, *Prosecutor v. Lubanga*, PTC I, Second Review of the 'Decision on the Application for Interim Release of Thomas Lubanga Dyilo', ICC-01/04-01/06-924, 11 June 2007, and stressing the public interest which may outweigh the right to liberty when assessing the reasonableness ('to assess the reasonableness of detention, it must determine whether the requirement of public interest shall outweigh the rule of respect for individual liberty'); *Bemba*, ICC 01/05-01/08-321, para. 47; ICC, *Prosecutor v. Katanga and Ngudjolo*, Third Review of the Decision on the Application for Interim Release of Mathieu Ngudjolo (Rule 118 (2) of the Rules of Procedure and Evidence), ICC-01/04-01/07-965-tENG, 17 March 2009, para. 11; conc. Boas et al., *Procedure* (2011), p. 120; Dumbryte, in Stahn, *Practice* (2015), p. 1080; crit. Khan and Ellis, 'Article 60', in Ambos, *Commentary* (2022), mn. 18 (discussing the delay issue in mn. 17–21); discussing fixed terms of pre-trial detention in this context, but leaving it open, de Meester, Pitcher, Rastan, and Sluiter, in Sluiter et al., *International Criminal Procedure* (2013), p. 350.

1030 I deviate here from the previous edition, p. 410 with note 736. In the same vein, Khan and Ellis, 'Article 60', in Ambos, *Commentary* (2022), mn. 17, arguing that the Chamber 'is not obliged to release that person'; for obligatory release de Meester, Pitcher, Rastan, and Sluiter, in Sluiter et al., *International Criminal Procedure* (2013), p. 343.

1031 ICC, *Prosecutor v. Lubanga*, PTC I, Decision on the Application for the Interim Release of Thomas Lubanga Dyilo, ICC-01/04-01/06-586-tEN, 18 October 2006, p. 7 ('the organs of the Court have acted swiftly and that at no moment were proceedings dormant'); *Bemba et al.*, ICC-01/05-01/13-703, p. 5; see also de Meester, Pitcher, Rastan, and Sluiter, in Sluiter et al., *International Criminal Procedure* (2013), pp. 335, 343; Khan and Ellis, 'Article 60', in Ambos, *Commentary* (2022), mn. 19; cf. also Dumbryte, in Stahn, *Practice* (2015), pp. 1079, 1082, arguing that 'Article 60 (4) should extend the application of the due diligence standard to all the organs of the Court' (p. 1082) since their delays today 'will not permit granting interim release' (p. 1078).

international criminal tribunals—normally considerably longer than in domestic proceedings of a liberal *Rechtsstaat*[1032]—gives rise to concern, although the conditions of detention, subject to a series of detailed rules,[1033] do not only comply with the minimum detention standards but go well beyond them.[1034] In any case, while the PTC is—as a consequence of the above interpretation—not *obliged* to take a decision under Article 60 (3) ICCS without a 'ruling' under Article 60 (2), it is nevertheless *entitled* to carry out such a review 'as the ultimate guarantor of the rights of the Defence' during the investigation stage of the proceedings.[1035] Such an interpretation takes due account of the importance given by human rights law to the judicial supervision of deprivation of liberty in the course of criminal proceedings.[1036]

If the periodical review mechanism under Article 60 (3) ICCS applies, a *hearing* must be held at least once a year.[1037] The PTC 'may' modify its ruling if 'changed circumstances so require'.[1038] According to the AC, 'changed circumstances' exist either with 'a change in some or all of the facts underlying a previous decision' or with 'a new fact' bringing about the change (for example a change in the defendant's health).[1039] The term 'may' seems to imply that the Chamber has discretion but this discretion must, at least, be considerably reduced if the conditions of Article 58 (1) are—due to the 'changed circumstances'—no longer met.[1040] The wording 'so require' in Article 60 (3) also suggests that the Chamber should

[1032] See also—somewhat overstating—Boas et al., *Procedure* (2011), pp. 104 ('shockingly long in comparison to national criminal prosecutions'), 119–20 (too general referring to all domestic proceedings), 134.

[1033] For the ICC, see 'Chapter 6—Detention Matters' of the RegC (Regs. 89–106 RegC) and 'Chapter 5—Detention Matters' of the RegR (Regs. 150–223 RegR); cf. also ICTY, 'Rules Governing the Detention of Persons Awaiting Trial or Appeal before the Tribunal or otherwise Detained on the Authority of the Tribunal', adopted 5 May 1994, as amended on 15 November 2016 (IT38/Rev. 10), <https://www.icty.org/x/file/Legal%20Library/Detention/161115-it38-rev10-rules-of-detention.pdf>; ICTR, 'Rules Covering the Detention of Persons Awaiting Trial or Appeal before the Tribunal or otherwise Detained on the Authority of the Tribunal', adopted 5 June 1998, <http://www.unictr.org/sites/unictr.org/files/legal-library/detention-rules_en_fr.pdf>; SCSL, 'Rules Governing the Detention of Persons Awaiting Trial or Appeal before the Special Court for Sierra Leone or otherwise Detained under the Authority of the Special Court for Sierra Leone', adopted on 7 March 2003, as amended on 14 May 2005, <http://www.rscsl.org/Documents/rulesofdetention.pdf>,.

[1034] The best example is the Scheveningen detention centre in The Hague which is part of Scheveningin prison and hosts detainees from the ICC, KSC and MICT (official visit on 17 May 2023); see also Boas et al., *Procedure* (2011), pp. 118–19.

[1035] cf. ICC, *Prosecutor v. Katanga and Ngudjolo*, PTC I (Single Judge Steiner), Decision Concerning the Pre-Trial Detention of Germain Katanga, ICC-01/04-01/07-222, 21 February 2008, p. 6; conc. *Katanga and Ngudjolo*, ICC-01/04-01/07-330, pp. 7–10, explicitly referring to the *Lubanga* AC decision quoted previously. Conc. also Safferling, *Criminal Procedure* (2012), p. 307; Zeegers, *International Criminal Tribunals* (2016), p. 250.

[1036] See the references to the IACtHR case law in *Lubanga*, ICC-01/04-01/06-8-Corr, Annex 1, para. 12 with n. 6; *Harun and Abd-Al-Rahman*, ICC-02/05-01/07-1-Corr, para. 28 with n. 22; for European case law in this respect, see e.g. ECtHR, *Nikolova v. Bulgaria*, Application No. 31195/95, Grand Chamber Judgment (25 March 1999), ECtHR, *H. B. v. Switzerland*, Application No. 26899/95, Judgment (5 April 2001), regarding the meaning of a 'judge' before whom a person detained should appear; regarding the notion of *promptness* of the appearance before an officer authorized by law to exercise judicial power, see ECtHR, *Brogan et al. v. UK*, Application Nos. 11209/84, 11234/84, 11266/84, and 11386/84, Judgment (29 November 1988); ECtHR, *Harkmann v. Estonia*, Application No. 2192/03, Judgment (11 July 2006); ECtHR, *Kandzhov v. Bulgaria*, Application No. 68294/01, Judgment (6 November 2004); ECtHR, *Mamedova v. Russia*, Application No. 7064/05, Judgment (1 June 2006); on the duty to account for custody, see ECtHR, *Kurt v. Turkey*, Application No. 24276/94, Judgment (25 May 1998). See also OHCHR, *Human Rights in the Administration of Justice* (2003), pp. 185 ff.

[1037] Rule 118 (3) RPE ICC.

[1038] Art. 60 (3) ICCS.

[1039] ICC, *Prosecutor v. Bemba*, AC, Judgment on the Appeal of the Prosecutor against Pre-Trial Chamber II's 'Decision on the Interim Release of Jean-Pierre Bemba Gombo and Convening Hearings with the Kingdom of Belgium, the Republic of Portugal, the Republic of France, the Federal Republic of Germany, the Italian Republic, and the Republic of South Africa', ICC-01/05-01/08-631-Red, 2 December 2009, para. 60. See also *Bemba*, ICC-01/05-01/08-1019, para. 51.

[1040] See also Safferling, *Criminal Procedure* (2012), pp. 306–7, pointing further to Rule 65 (B) RPE ICTY/ICTR, which, using the term 'may', seems to give discretion to the judges, thereby violating the human right to liberty and the presumption of innocence.

order the release.[1041] The confirmation of charges may amount to a changed circumstance increasing the risk that the defendant escapes.[1042] This does not reverse the standard principle that liberty is the rule and detention the exception[1043] given that a decision on interim release has to be made on a case-by-case basis, taking into account various factors, including a confirmation of charges.[1044]

If the PTC considers that the period of detention is unreasonable within the meaning of the already mentioned Article 60 (4) ICCS, the person should be released 'with or without conditions';[1045] a list of possible conditions and the procedure are contained in Rule 119 RPE ICC.[1046] The Rule was invoked in the *Gicheru* (Article 70) case by Single Judge Alapini-Gansou to 'adequately' mitigate the ongoing risk under Article 58 (1)(b) ICCS and grant the request for the defendant's interim release.[1047]

The PTC may re-issue a warrant of arrest 'to secure the presence' of the person released,[1048] that is, not against a person otherwise at liberty.[1049] The re-issuance may particularly become necessary if the person concerned has failed to comply with conditions imposed,[1050] but is not limited to this situation, given that a person may also be released without any condition, and/or her presence may also be put at risk for other reasons than the non-compliance with conditions imposed.

The Chamber must indicate a State willing to receive the suspect,[1051] that is, the release depends on the voluntary cooperation of a State.[1052] States may sign an agreement on (interim) release with the ICC.[1053] Regulation 51 RegCourt, requires the PTC, for the purpose

[1041] cf. *Lubanga*, ICC-01/04-01/06-824, para. 134 ('not of a discretionary nature'); *Bemba*, ICC-01/05-01/08-631-Red, para. 59; conc. Boas et al., *Procedure* (2011), p. 130; de Meester, Pitcher, Rastan, and Sluiter, in Sluiter et al., *International Criminal Procedure* (2013), p. 332.

[1042] *Prosecutor v. Abd-Al-Rahman*, TC I, Decision on the Review of Detention, ICC-02/05-01/20-502, 1 November 2021, paras. 22 ff.

[1043] As argued by the defence, cf. ICC, *Prosecutor v. Abd-Al-Rahman*, Defence, Appeal Brief against Decision ICC-02/05-01/20-502, ICC-02/05-01/20-518-tENG, 16 November 2021, para. 7.

[1044] ICC, *Prosecutor v. Abd-Al-Rahman*, AC, Public Redacted Version of Judgment on the Appeal of Ali Muhammad Ali Abd-Al-Rahman against Trial Chamber I's 'Decision on the review of detention', ICC-02/05-01/20-542-Red, 17 December 2021, paras. 37–8, 41.

[1045] Art. 60 (4) cl. 2 ICCS.

[1046] See also de Meester, Pitcher, Rastan, and Sluiter, in Sluiter et al., *International Criminal Procedure* (2013), pp. 334–5.

[1047] ICC, *Prosecutor v. Gicheru*, PTC A (Article 70), Public Redacted Version of 'Decision on Mr Gicheru's Request for Interim Release', ICC-01/09-01/20-90-Red2, 29 January 2021, para. 45 ff. (imposing a series of conditions at para. 47, including the payment of a financial security of one million Kenyan shillings, compliance with orders of the Chamber, obligations to report and to abstain from contacting witnesses).

[1048] Art. 60 (5) ICCS.

[1049] In this sense, the broader Rules 65 (H) RPE ICTY/ICTR, 68 (H) RPE MICT; cf. Khan and Ellis, 'Article 60', in Ambos, *Commentary* (2022), mn. 23.

[1050] cf. Rule 119 (4) RPE ICC. Insofar the PTC must be 'convinced', i.e. be sure beyond reasonable doubt; cf. Khan and Ellis, 'Article 60', in Ambos, *Commentary* (2022), mn. 23.

[1051] cf. *Bemba*, ICC-01/05-01/08-475, para. 79 ('pending a decision by the Chamber on ... the State to which he is to be released'); see also *Bemba*, ICC-01/05-01/08-631-Red, para. 106 ('in order to grant conditional release the identification of a State willing to accept the person concerned ... is necessary'). According to the AC, once a Chamber has concluded that 'there is no condition short of detention at the seat of the Court that would be sufficient to mitigate the accused's flight risk', it is not obliged 'to convene a status conference with State representatives "to discuss the implementation of appropriate conditions and logistical arrangements for an eventual period of provisional release"', see *Bemba*, ICC-01/05-01/08-3249-Red, para. 90. Thus, it follows, *e contrario*, that once the requirements for conditional release are met, the Chamber may indeed have an obligation to seek observations from States that have an agreement with the ICC relating to interim release but have not yet made an offer to accept the accused.

[1052] Crit. de Meester, Pitcher, Rastan, and Sluiter, in Sluiter et al., *International Criminal Procedure* (2013), pp. 334, 341 ('*de facto* presumption of detention').

[1053] ICC, *Cooperation Agreements* (2023), pp. 12 ff with a model agreement on pp. 33 ff. At the time of writing (Septemberl 2024), Belgium and Argentina are the only two States to have done so, cf. <https://www.icc-cpi.int/news/argentina-and-icc-sign-agreements-interim-release-and-release-persons-reinforcing-argentinas>.

of the release decision, to 'seek observations from the host State and from the State to which the person seeks to be released'. Yet, this obligation only ensues, as convincingly held by the AC, by majority,[1054] if the respective PTC 'intends to grant interim release or envisages the possibility thereof', i.e. not before it has made up its mind on the granting of the release.[1055] In the same vein, the KSC Appeals Panel requires consultations with a third State only once the Pre-Trial Judge has decided to release the suspect.[1056]

Both parties can appeal, without leave,[1057] a decision on interim release,[1058] but the grounds must already be set out in the notice of appeal,[1059] to expedite appeal proceedings.[1060] While Article 60 and the respective RPE also apply at trial,[1061] during the appeal proceedings a convicted person shall, as a rule, remain in custody,[1062] unless the time in custody exceeds the expected imprisonment[1063] or the person is acquitted.[1064] Compensation as a possible remedy in case of an unlawful detention will be analysed below.[1065]

[1054] Judge Ibáñez Carranza dissenting, see her Separate Concurring Opinion, ICC-02/05-01/20-177-Anx, 8 October 2020. She sees an obligation by the Chamber to 'seek observations from the relevant State or States regardless of whether or not it is minded to grant an application for interim release'. This is not convincing. Not only is her reading of the word 'shall' (para. 20)—a term of art for a certain form of discretion—based on a dictionary definition questionable, but, more importantly, her view is counterintuitive and against judicial economy asking a Chamber to do something (to seek State observations) which is only relevant if it has taken, previously, a certain decision (namely to grant release).

[1055] ICC, *Prosecutor v. Abd-Al-Rahman*, Judgment on the Appeal of Mr Ali Muhammad Ali Abd-Al-Rahman against the Decision of Pre-Trial Chamber II of 14 August 2020 Entitled 'Decision on the Defence Request for Interim Release', ICC-02/05-01/20-177, 8 October 2020, para. 52 ff. (55). In a similar vein, Irving, *Human Rights Protection* (2020), p. 71.

[1056] KSC, *Prosecutor v. Thaçi*, AP, Decision on Hashim Thaçi's Appeal against Decision on Review of Detention, KSC-BC-2020-06, IA010/F00008/RED, 27 October 2021, para. 64 ('At the outset, the Panel agrees with the assessment of the Pre-Trial Judge according to which consultations with a Third State to which a detained person seeks to be released ... is compulsory only when the panel intends to grant interim release or envisages the possibility thereof. This finding results from the plain meaning of the relevant provisions. Notably, Article 41 (11) of the Law stipulates that "*[i]f released*, any person detained in the Specialist Chambers' detention facilities in the Host State [...]" and according to Rule 56(4) of the Rules, a "detained person *shall not be released* in the Third State without the consent of that State". It is also supported by the ICC jurisprudence on which the Pre-Trial Judge relied' [fn. omitted, emphasis in the original]); KSC, *Prosecutor v. Thaçi*, AP, Decision on Hashim Thaçi's Appeal against Decision on Review of Detention, KSC-BC-2020-06, IA017/F00011/RED, 5 April 2022, para. 59 ('The Panel further recalls that consultations, including at an oral hearing, with a Third State to which a detained person seeks to be released are compulsory only when the panel intends to grant interim release or envisages the possibility thereof' [fn. omitted]).

[1057] Rule 154 (1) ICC RPE.

[1058] Art. 82 (1)(b) ICCS.

[1059] Reg. 64 (5) RegC (amendment entered into force on 20 July 2017). The AC, by majority, dismissed Gbagbo's appeal on the basis of this amended version *in limine*, cf. ICC, *Prosecutor v. Gbagbo and Blé Goudé*, AC, Decision on Mr Laurent Gbagbo's Notice of Appeal, ICC-02/11-01/15-1047, 5 October 2017, para. 5 ('[I]t appears that Counsel for Mr Gbagbo relied on an outdated version of the Regulations of the Court, which is no longer in force'), para. 7: ('In light of the strict timelines prescribed by regulation 64 of the Regulations of the Court for the efficient conduct of proceedings on interim release, the Appeals Chamber considers that to allow Mr Gbagbo to re-file his Notice of Appeal at this stage of the proceedings would unduly infringe on these timelines. The Notice of Appeal is therefore dismissed *in limine*'). Considering the importance of the accused's right to liberty and the mere formal nature of regulations, the majority should have dealt with the appeal invoking the interests of justice clause of Reg. 29 RegC (which deals with violations of the Regulations); in this vein, ICC, *Prosecutor v. Gbagbo and Blé Goudé*, Dissenting Opinion of Judge Howard Morrison, ICC-02/11-01/15-1047-Anx, 5 October 2017, para. 2 ('[I]n my view the broader interests of justice could have been better served by condoning the non-compliance with a strong caution to Mr Gbagbo and his Counsel to be more attentive in the future to amendments to the applicable law before the Court.')

[1060] *Gbagbo and Blé Goudé*, ICC-02/11-01/15-1047, para. 6.

[1061] Unconvincing, therefore, Boas et al., *Procedure* (2011), p. 132 ('nothing ... requires a trial chamber to review *proprio motu* whether an accused should be granted interim release').

[1062] Art. 81 (3)(a) ICCS.

[1063] Art. 81 (3)(b) ICCS.

[1064] Art. 81 (3)(c) ICCS.

[1065] Chapter VI, D.(1) in this volume.

While the procedure before the ICC is quite complex, at the ICTY, ICTR, SCSL, and KSC the 'provisional release' is regulated in just one provision.[1066] It is, however, not identical for all tribunals and has undergone an important change with the removal of the requirement of 'exceptional circumstances' for granting a provisional release.[1067] In practical terms, however, this change only had an impact in the ICTY case law, leading to a significant increase in the number of provisional releases;[1068] in contrast, at the ICTR, the restrictive jurisprudence remained in place and no provisional release was ever granted—despite some corrections made by the AC.[1069] Equally, at the SCSL, no provisional release was granted,[1070] despite the absence of the exceptional circumstances requirement and the incorporation of the more liberal Anglo-American concept of bail.[1071] Also, the burden of proof continued to rest with the accused.[1072] Recently, however, at the KSC Isni Kilaj has been released provisionally under 'strict conditions'.[1073] The Single Judge weighed the risk of obstructing witnesses against Kilaj's fundamental right to liberty and found that the latter prevailed,[1074] which—in the view of the CoAP—was not a discernable error in exercising his discretion.[1075]

In sum, at all tribunals the existing Rule 65 gives the judges a broad discretion, which they used, at best, to take some release decisions on a case-by-case basis focusing in particular on official assurances that the accused will appear at trial and on compelling humanitarian grounds.[1076] The release decision, be it positive or negative, can be appealed.[1077] In addition,

[1066] cf. Rules 65 RPE ICTY/ICTR/SCSL, 68 RPE MICT, and 57 RPE KSC. On Rule 64 RPE ICTY/ICTR regulating the detention facility and allowing the President of the Tribunal to request the modification of the conditions of detention, see de Meester, Pitcher, Rastan, and Sluiter, in Sluiter et al., *International Criminal Procedure* (2013), p. 323; cf. also Rule 67 RPE MICT. At the SCSL, the accused shall be detained at the detention facility of the tribunal (Rule 64 RPE SCSL).

[1067] cf. Rule 65 (B) RPE ICTY (1999) and ICTR (2003); Rule 65 RPE SCSL never contained such a requirement, nor does Rule 68 RPE MICT.

[1068] De Meester, Pitcher, Rastan, and Sluiter, in Sluiter et al., *International Criminal Procedure* (2013), p. 325. The TC may impose conditions pursuant to Rules 65 (C) RPE ICTY/ICTR, 68 (C) RPE MICT; see on that Safferling, *Criminal Procedure* (2012), pp. 309–10.

[1069] De Meester, Pitcher, Rastan, and Sluiter, in Sluiter et al., *International Criminal Procedure* (2013), pp. 327–8, arguing that the AC's reversals 'proved to be essentially symbolic' and providing various case law examples.

[1070] De Meester, Pitcher, Rastan, and Sluiter, in Sluiter et al., *International Criminal Procedure* (2013), p. 328.

[1071] Nowadays the possibility of bail also exists in civil law systems; see de Meester, Pitcher, Rastan, and Sluiter, in Sluiter et al., *International Criminal Procedure* (2013), p. 346.

[1072] This did not change with the amendment of the Rules in 1999; see ICTY, *Prosecutor v. Miodrag Jokić*, TC Order on Miodrag Jokić's Motion for Provisional Release, IT-01-42-PT, 20 February 2002, para. 18; ICTY, *Prosecutor v. Ljubičić*, TC Decision on Second Application for Provisional Release, IT-00-41-PT, 26 July 2005, para. 17. See also Boas et al., *Procedure* (2011), p. 124, crit. Safferling, *Criminal Procedure* (2012), pp. 305–6; de Meester, Pitcher, Rastan, and Sluiter, in Sluiter et al., *International Criminal Procedure* (2013), pp. 323, 325.

[1073] KSC, *Prosecutor v. Isni Kilaj*, Public Redacted Version of Corrected Version of Decision on Review of Detention of Isni Kilaj, TP (Single Judge), KSC-BC-2018-01/F00658/COR/RED, 3 May 2014, upheld on appeal: KSC, *Prosecutor v. Isni Kilaj*, Public Redacted Version of Decision on the Specialist Prosecutor's Office's Appeal against Decision on Isni Kilaj's Review of Detention, AP, KSC-BC-2018-01/IA007/F00007/RED, 13 May 2024. For references about rejected requests for release, see above note 972 with main text.

[1074] KSC, *Prosecutor v. Isni Kilaj*, Public Redacted Version of Corrected Version of Decision on Review of Detention of Isni Kilaj, TP (Single Judge), KSC-BC-2018-01/F00658/COR/RED, 3 May 2014, para. 62. Concretely, the Single Judge was mindful that '(i) Mr Kilaj has been detained for nearly six months, since his arrest on 6 November 2023; (ii) the offences for which Mr Kilaj is considered a suspect carry a possible penalty between one (1) and five (5) years; and (iii) while an Indictment has been filed against him, followed by a revised indictment on 11 March 2024, the SPO has now requested the suspension of the Pre-Trial Judge's consideration of the Revised Indictment, in light of its intent to file an amended indictment [ … ], substantially delaying the timeline of the proceedings'.

[1075] KSC, *Prosecutor v. Isni Kilaj*, Public Redacted Version of Decision on the Specialist Prosecutor's Office's Appeal against Decision on Isni Kilaj's Review of Detention, AP, KSC-BC-2018-01/IA007/F00007/RED, 13 May 2024, paras. 40 ff. (re the balancing right to liberty and risk of obstruction, see para. 50).

[1076] See, for an analysis of the case law, esp. of the ICTY, de Meester, Pitcher, Rastan, and Sluiter, in Sluiter et al., *International Criminal Procedure* (2013), pp. 324–9.

[1077] cf. Rule 65 (D) RPE ICTY/ICTR, Rule 68 (D) RPE MICT, and Rule 65 (E) RPE SCSL.

although no explicit right to review comparable to Article 60 (2) ICCS is provided for in the law of the ad hoc tribunals, it is by now accepted—since the *Barayagwiza* AC's recognition of a *habeas corpus* right[1078]—that a right to review follows from the rules on 'other motions'.[1079] At the KSC, a regular, highly demanding two-month review by the Pre-Trial Judge and the respective interlocutory appeal is explicitly provided for.[1080]

Notwithstanding the ICC's more flexible legal regime, so far the Court's case law has taken a similar restrictive approach with regard to continued detention, dismissing any request for interim release,[1081] except in the Article 70 proceedings against Gicheru as already mentioned above.[1082] Thus, in *Bemba* the continued detention of the defendant pursuant to Article 58 (1)(a) ICCS has been justified with the increased flight risk at a later procedural stage.[1083] To establish such a risk, it suffices that the possibility of a flight 'remains visible' and that it does not appear as 'imaginary'.[1084] In *Katanga and Ngudjolo* the mere possibility to influence witnesses has been considered sufficient for an obstruction of justice within the meaning of Article 58 (1)(b)(ii).[1085] In the same vein, the *Abd-Al-Rahman* AC took 'the

[1078] cf. *Barayagwiza*, ICTR-97-19-AR72, paras. 88–9 (3 November 1999); Irving, *Human Rights Protection* (2020), p. 61.

[1079] Rules 73 RPE ICTY, 72 (A) RPE ICTR, 80 RPE MICT; see also Boas et al., *Procedure* (2011), pp. 121–2, 123–9, 134; Safferling, *Criminal Procedure* (2012), p. 308; crit. on the lack of effective remedies, de Meester, Pitcher, Rastan, and Sluiter, in Sluiter et al., *International Criminal Procedure* (2013), pp. 315–16.

[1080] cf. Art. 41 (10) KSC Law and Rule 57 (1), (2) RPE KSC.

[1081] Thomas Lubanga was almost released, but this was not due to an unreasonable delay but to the Prosecutor's mishandling of her disclosure obligations in relation to Art. 54 (3)(e) ICCS, cf. Ambos, *NCLR*, 12 (2009), 543 ff. The *Bemba* PTC granted its fourth application for interim release (*Bemba*, ICC-01/05-01/08-475), but this decision was overturned on appeal by the Prosecutor (*Bemba*, ICC-01/05-01/08-631-Red). The same occurred with the *Bemba et al.* PTC ordering the release of Musamba, Kabongo, Wandu, and Arido (*Bemba et al.*, ICC-01/05-01/13-703), with its decision being also overturned by the AC (*Bemba et al.*, ICC-01/05-01/13-969,). See also Boas et al., *Procedure* (2011), pp. 130–1.

[1082] Above note 1055 with main text; *Gicheru*, ICC-01/09-01/20-90-Red2. Thereto Marchesi and Fusari, *EJIL: Talk!*, 8 March 2021 (arguing that while Art. 70 suspects may be released, Art. 5 ones will not).

[1083] *Bemba*, ICC-01/05-01/08-631-Red, paras. 70 ('the finding ... that there were substantial grounds to believe that Mr Bemba committed the crimes charged, increased the likelihood that he might abscond. In addition, the length of sentence ... likely to serve if convicted ... is a further incentive for him to abscond'), 74 ('the financial status of Mr Bemba to be a relevant factor in determining whether he would have the means to abscond'). See also *Ntaganda*, ICC-01/04-02/06-147, para. 55; *Prosecutor v. Bemba et al.*, PTC II, Decision on the 'Requête urgente de la Défense sollicitant la mise en liberté provisoire de monsieur Fidèle Babala Wandu', ICC-01/05-01/13-258, 14 March 2014, para. 22; *Prosecutor v. Bemba et al.*, PTC II, Decision on the 'Demande de mise en liberté provisoire de Maître Aimé Kilolo Musamba', ICC-01/05-01/13-259, 14 March 2014, paras. 20 ff.; *Prosecutor v. Bemba et al.*, PTC II, Decision on the 'Requête de mise en liberté' submitted by the Defence for Jean Jacques Mangenda, ICC-01/05-01/13-261, 14 March 2014, para. 31; *Prosecutor v. Ntaganda*, PTC II, Second Decision on Bosco Ntaganda's Interim Release, ICC-01/04-02/06-284, 17 March 2014, para. 36; *Bemba et al.*, ICC-01/05-01/13-558, para. 113; *Prosecutor v. Ntaganda*, PTC II, Third Decision on Bosco Ntaganda's Interim Release, ICC-01/04-02/06-335, 17 July 2014, para. 35.

[1084] *Katanga and Ngudjolo*, ICC-01/04-01/07-572, para. 24; crit. de Meester, Pitcher, Rastan, and Sluiter, in Sluiter et al., *International Criminal Procedure* (2013), p. 333, arguing that this leaves a too broad discretion and puts the onus regarding the lack of an imaginary flight possibility on the defence, p. 341, demanding 'more efforts and better reasoning to establish certain risks'.

[1085] *Prosecutor v. Katanga and Ngudjolo*, TC, Second Review of the Decision on the Conditions of Detention of Germain Katanga, ICC-01/04-01/07-794, 12 December 2008, para. 13 ('to determine whether the release of Germain Katanga would not be *likely* to obstruct or endanger the proceedings' [emphasis added]); *Katanga and Ngudjolo*, ICC-01/04-01/07-572, para. 26 ('the possibility of the appellant obstructing or endangering the investigations or the court proceedings'); see also *Ntaganda*, ICC-01/04-02/06-147, para. 59 ('the possibility of him influencing, threatening or intimidating witnesses and victims'); *Ntaganda*, ICC-01/04-02/06-284, para. 38; *Bemba et al.*, ICC-01/05-01/13-558, para. 113; *Ntaganda*, ICC-01/04-02/06-335, para. 37. Although the AC found that the evaluation of the possibility to influence witnesses cannot be made by merely referring to a decision of 'another Single Judge in other proceedings' (see *Katanga and Ngudjolo*, ICC-01/04-01/07-572, para. 26, quoted above, where the Single Judge simply adopted the findings of another Single Judge, who 'found that from the facts laid before her, it appeared that the appellant had the capacity to interfere with ongoing or further investigations, or Prosecution witnesses, victims, or members of their families'), it later clarified that this only applies where the

safety of witnesses' into account 'regardless of whether they are currently reachable by the Prosecutor'.[1086] The Single Judge in *Bemba* held, however, that the obstruction risk must be linked to a 'specific act or conduct' of the detainee.[1087] This more restrictive interpretation of the non-interference with witnesses or victims, as an expression of an obstruction of justice, is in line with the post-1999 ICTY case law, according to which the existence of such a risk has to be established objectively and concretely.[1088] Also, regarding Article 58 (1)(b) (iii) ICCS, it has been held that specific information must be available to assume that the defendant might commit the same or a related crime.[1089]

From a human rights perspective, that is, the right to liberty and the presumption of innocence, the current practice is not fully satisfactory. Chambers should therefore strive for a more liberal approach, distinguishing between the stage of the issuance of an arrest warrant[1090] and the stage of interim release.[1091] At the former stage, only a summons to appear constitutes an alternative, less intrusive measure,[1092] but it may often be insufficient to secure the presence of the suspect. In contrast, at the interim release stage a greater flexibility is feasible, given the broad range of conditions that can be imposed upon a release to secure the presence of the suspect. In this regard, Chambers should be more courageous in making use of these conditions.[1093] Of course, the better approach is to avoid unreasonable long pre-trial detention[1094] in the first place by streamlining the pre-trial and trial phase of the proceedings. This presupposes strict judicial oversight by experienced trial judges who are able to manage the respective schedules and guide the parties with a view to procedural efficiency.[1095]

findings that are relied upon are made 'in an entirely different context', see *Bemba*, ICC-01/05-01/08-3249-Red, para. 726.

[1086] *Abd-Al-Rahman*, ICC-02/05-01/20-177, para. 27.

[1087] *Bemba*, ICC-01/05-01/08-475, para. 72 ('the arguments … reflect a general concern rather than an apprehension linked to any specific act or conduct … the submissions … ought to be based on more concrete information').

[1088] ICTY, *Prosecutor v. Mićo Stanišić*, AC, Decision on Prosecution's Interlocutory Appeal of Mićo Stanišić's Provisional Release, IT-04-79-AR65.1, 17 October 2005, para. 27 (it must be demonstrated that 'the Accused would represent a concrete risk of harm to victims and witnesses upon release' and 'that he has influenced or threatened them in the past or intends to do so in the future'); ICTY, *Prosecutor v. Haradinaj et al.*, AC, Decision on Ramush Haradinaj's Modified Provisional Release, IT-04-84-AR65.1, 10 March 2006, paras. 43, 46 (43: 'constitute harm or a concrete threat to witnesses or victims', 46: '[s]ubjective witness fear and concern is not *per se* a reason to refuse a provisional release … The Accused['s] … conduct, past and future, is at issue, not other people's perceptions of that conduct'); *Prosecutor v. Prlić et al.*, AC, Decision on Motions for Re-Consideration, Clarification, Request for Release and Applications for Leave to Appeal, IT-04-74-AR65.1, IT-04-74-AR65.2, IT-04-74-AR65.3, 8 September 2004, para. 27 ('identify *in concreto* any indication that the accused would try to abscond or interfere with the administration of justice'). See also de Meester, Pitcher, Rastan, and Sluiter, in Sluiter et al., *International Criminal Procedure* (2013), p. 325.

[1089] *Bemba*, ICC-01/05-01/08-475, para. 76 ('no information is available … indicating that Mr Jean-Pierre Bemba would interfere or act in the CAR and commit the same or related crimes').

[1090] Art. 58 ICCS.

[1091] Arts. 59, 60 ICCS.

[1092] Recommending it as a rule to be considered *proprio motu* in each case, de Meester, Pitcher, Rastan, and Sluiter, in Sluiter et al., *International Criminal Procedure* (2013), p. 349.

[1093] In a similar vein, Khan and Ellis, 'Article 60', in Ambos, *Commentary* (2022), mn. 9.

[1094] cf. Art. 60 (4) ICCS and the discussion above in the main text.

[1095] In a similar vein, Khan and Ellis, 'Article 60', in Ambos, *Commentary* (2022), mn. 22; see notes 263 and 264 in this chapter with further references.

## (7) Charging: amendment/withdrawal of charges, cumulative/alternative charging, and recharacterization of facts

### *(a) Amendment/withdrawal of charges and presentation of new evidence*

The emergence of new facts or information may entail the amendment or withdrawal of charges,[1096] including with regard to a confession,[1097] and/or the presentation of new evidence. As to the *amendment of charges*, in temporal terms one must distinguish between the situation before and after their confirmation. While in the former situation the amendment is generally possible, with reasonable notice to the Chamber and, particularly, to the accused fifteen days before the hearing,[1098] any amendment after confirmation requires judicial authorization.[1099] Thus, at the ad hoc tribunals and at the KSC, the Prosecutor may seek leave from the (confirming) judge to amend charges after confirmation;[1100] in case of new charges, additional safeguards are provided for.[1101] Similarly, at the ICC, the Prosecutor may only amend the charges, 'before the trial has begun', with the permission of the PTC and after notice to the accused.[1102]

Two points deserve special attention here: First, the explicit temporal reference in both Article 69 (1) clause 1 ICCS and Rule 128 (1) RPE ICC—'*before* the trial has begun'[1103]—leaves no doubt that, contrary to the ad hoc tribunals' practice,[1104] amendments *after* the commencement of the trial are not possible.[1105] However, as the actual trial only begins with the reading out of the charges and possible opening statements of the parties,[1106] the Prosecutor may still request amendments in the preceding preparatory phase, that is, the

[1096] For a comparative overview regarding amendment and withdrawal, see Friman, Brady, Costi, Guariglia, and Stuckenberg, in Sluiter et al., *International Criminal Procedure* (2013), pp. 464–6; see also Stegmiller, in Stahn, *Practice* (2015), pp. 900–5.

[1097] cf. ICC-OTP, *Guidelines Admission of Guilt* (2020), para. 20: '[T]here may be instances in which amendment or withdrawal of charges in accordance with article 61(9) is appropriate, such as for example where discussions between the Prosecution and Defence elicit facts that cause the Prosecution to revise its view of the accused's criminal responsibility or its ability to prove particular charges at trial.'

[1098] cf. Rule 50 (A)(i)(a) RPE ICTY/ICTR; Rule 50 (A) alt. 1 RPE SCSL; Art. 61 (4) ICCS and Rule 121 (4) RPE ICC; see also Boas et al., *Procedure* (2011), p. 186; Friman, Brady, Costi, Guariglia, and Stuckenberg, in Sluiter et al., *International Criminal Procedure* (2013), pp. 415, 422, 449, 484; Vasiliev, in Cryer et al., *ICL* (2019), pp. 427–9; Zahar and Sluiter, *ICL* (2008), p. 57. On the other deadlines, see Section A.(2)(b) in this chapter.

[1099] There is a situation, however, where the PTC should intervene even prior to confirmation, namely when the Prosecutor amends the charges without notice sufficiently in advance, see Schabas, Chaitidou and El Zeidy, 'Article 61', in Ambos, *Commentary* (2022), mn. 149 ('failure on the part of the Prosecutor to provide such notice sufficiently in advance or her failure to do so at all … relevant PTC should either intervene *proprio motu* or in response to an application lodged by the suspect in order to preserve the fairness of the proceedings, including the rights of the defence').

[1100] cf. Rule 50 (A)(i) RPE ICTY/ICTR/MICT as well as Rule 50 (A) alt. 2 RPE SCSL and 90 (1) RPE KSC; thereon, Boas et al., *Procedure* (2011), pp. 186–90; Friman, Brady, Costi, Guariglia, and Stuckenberg, in Sluiter et al., *International Criminal Procedure* (2013), pp. 387 with n. 50 and 415–18, 449, 484 (both on the conditions developed by the case law, esp. the fair trial requirements); also Vasiliev, in Cryer et al., *ICL* (2019), p. 427.

[1101] cf. Rule 50 (B) and (C) RPE ICTY/ICTR/MICT, Rule 50 (b) RPE SCSL (additional hearing and period of thirty days); see thereon Friman, Brady, Costi, Guariglia, and Stuckenberg, in Sluiter et al., *International Criminal Procedure* (2013), pp. 422 (discussing the distinction between 'new charges' from other amendments), 484.

[1102] Art. 61 (9) cl. 1 ICCS and Rule 128 (1), (2) RPE ICC.

[1103] Emphasis added.

[1104] cf. e.g. Rules 50 (A)(i)(c) RPE ICTY and 90 (1)(c) RPE KSC; see also Friman, Brady, Costi, Guariglia, and Stuckenberg, in Sluiter et al., *International Criminal Procedure* (2013), pp. 415–16, 449.

[1105] cf. ICC, *Prosecutor v. Lubanga*, TC I, Minority Opinion (Judge Fulford) on the 'Decision giving notice to the parties and participants that the legal characterisation of facts may be subject to change in accordance with Regulation 55(2) of the Regulations of the Court', ICC-01/04-01/06-2054, 17 July 2009, para. 15; Friman, Brady, Costi, Guariglia, and Stuckenberg, in Sluiter et al., *International Criminal Procedure* (2013), p. 422; Safferling, *Criminal Procedure* (2012), p. 326.

[1106] See Section A.(3)(a) in this chapter.

phase between the constitution of a TC after confirmation[1107] and the actual opening of the trial. Secondly, the reference to the accused makes clear that the key challenge of any amendment is the preservation of his/her fair trial rights.[1108] If the Prosecutor intends to add charges or substitute charges by more serious ones, a new hearing before the PTC must be held.[1109] Once authorized, the implementation of the amendment rests with the prosecution.[1110]

In contrast, a *withdrawal of charges* is, in principle, even possible after commencement of the trial.[1111] A combined reading of Article 61 (4) and (9) ICCS suggests a threefold distinction:[1112] Prior to confirmation the Prosecutor must only give reasons;[1113] after confirmation she needs the permission of the PTC, and after commencement of the trial the permission of the TC.[1114] In the *Kenyatta* proceedings, the Prosecutor withdrew the charges after confirmation and the TC terminated the proceedings accordingly without further ado.[1115] While in this case the reason was the lack of compelling evidence, charges may also be withdrawn because of the death of the accused or for reasons of prosecutorial strategy.[1116] Recently the charges against *Mokom* have been withdrawn before the confirmation hearing because the Prosecutor did not see 'a reasonable prospect of conviction at trial', even with (the) charges confirmed;[1117] as a result, PTC II terminated the proceedings.[1118]

As to the presentation of *new evidence*, one must also distinguish between the situation before or after confirmation. Before the confirmation hearing, new evidence may be presented to support an amendment of the charges[1119] or for other reasons.[1120] In both cases, the Prosecutor must respect the fifteen days' deadline before the confirmation hearing.[1121] For the situation after confirmation, no explicit rule exists, but if the Chamber authorizes the amendment of the charges, it follows that the introduction of new evidence must also be permitted. In fact, the amendment will normally be triggered by the emergence of new

1107 Art. 61 (11) ICCS, Rule 130 RPE ICC.

1108 Esp. his right to be informed promptly and in detail pursuant to Art. 67 (1)(a) ICCS; see also notes 1236 ff. in this chapter with respect to Reg. 55 RegC, and Safferling, *Criminal Procedure* (2012), p. 325; Friman, Brady, Costi, Guariglia, and Stuckenberg, in Sluiter et al., *International Criminal Procedure* (2013), pp. 422, 449, 481; Vasiliev, in Cryer et al., *ICL* (2019), p. 427.

1109 Art. 61 (9) cl. 2 ICCS and Rule 128 (3) RPE ICC.

1110 For the ICTY, cf. Vohrah, in McDonald and Swaak-Goldman, *Substantive and Procedural Aspects* (2000), p. 493; Schabas, *Criminal Tribunals* (2006), pp. 371 ff.

1111 cf. Rule 51 (A)(iii) RPE ICTY/ICTR/MICT and Rule 51 (C) RPE SCSL; Art. 61 (9) cl. 3 ICCS; see also Stegmiller, in Stahn, *Practice* (2015), p. 902; Schabas, Chaitidou, and El Zeidy, 'Article 61', in Ambos, *Commentary* (2022), mn. 85–90 (before the confirmation hearing), 146–56.

1112 Similarly Rule 51 (A) RPE ICTY/ICTR/MICT and Rule 51 (C) RPE SCSL; thereon, Boas et al., *Procedure* (2011), p. 195.

1113 Art. 61 (4) cl. 3 ICCS.

1114 Art. 61 (9) cl. 3 ICCS, explicitly referring to the situation after commencement of the trial.

1115 ICC, *Prosecutor v. Kenyatta*, TC V(B), Decision on the Withdrawal of Charges against Mr Kenyatta, ICC-01/09-02/11-1005, 13 March 2015. About the *Kenya* situation in more detail, Adekunle, in Heinze and Dittrich, *ICC* (2021), pp. 409, 429 ff.

1116 On the practice of the ad hoc tribunals insofar, see Boas et al., *Procedure* (2011), pp. 195–7.

1117 ICC, *Prosecutor v. Mokom*, OTP, Notice of Withdrawal of the Charges against Maxime Jeoffroy Eli Mokom Gawaka, ICC-01/14-01/22-275, 16 October 2023, para. 1.

1118 ICC, *Prosecutor v. Mokom*, PTC II, Order in Relation to the Prosecution's 'Notice of Withdrawal of the Charges against Maxime Jeoffroy Eli Mokom Gawaka', ICC-01/14-01/22-276, 17 October 2023.

1119 cf. Art. 61 (4) ICCS and Rule 121 (4) RPE ICC.

1120 cf. Rule 121 (5) RPE ICC; thereon, Schabas, Chaitidou and El Zeidy, 'Article 61', in Ambos, *Commentary* (2022), mn. 84. This is also independent of the Prosecutor's obligation to disclose exculpatory evidence under Art. 67 (2) ICCS and Rule 77 RPE ICC; see thereon Chapter V, B.(2)(d) in this volume.

1121 It operates either as a notification period or a presentation period (cf. Rule 121 (4) with Rule 121 (5) RPE ICC) and must be distinguished from the general thirty days' deadline as to the presentation of charges (Rule 121 (3) RPE ICC).

evidence[1122] and this evidence will then have to be presented. Of course, the Prosecutor may also present (new) evidence, previously not disclosed and independent of any amendment, to better support the confirmed charges.[1123] In sum, the presentation of new evidence is, in principle, possible at every stage of the proceedings and linked to or independent of the amendment of charges.

### (b) *Cumulative/alternative charging and recharacterization of facts (Regulation 55)*

The above considerations make clear that the charges as set out in the DCC are, as a rule, binding. The existence of an updated DCC, notwithstanding the controversy surrounding it, does not change this situation, since it will always have to be in line with the confirmation decision.[1124] It is unclear however, how far this binding effect of the DCC goes, that is, whether it is limited to the factual contents of the charges, or whether it also encompasses—in the sense of the above explained combined factual-legal concept of charges[1125]—the legal characterization of these facts in the charges. The answer to this question does not only depend on the concept of charges, but also on the distribution of authority between prosecution and judges in criminal proceedings.[1126] From a civil law perspective, with the termination of the investigation and the respective instrument of accusation, the authority shifts from the prosecutor to the judge(s). They have the power to amend the charges in their legal dimension in line with the principle *iura novit curia* ('the court knows the law').[1127] From a common law (especially US) perspective, any judicial amendment of the charges—in both their factual and legal contents—appears unacceptable, since their determination belongs to the exclusive domain of the prosecution and thus can only be amended by this

1122 cf. Schabas, Chaitidou, and El Zeidy, 'Article 61', in Ambos, *Commentary* (2022), mn. 42 ('in light of new evidence'), 89 ('necessary in light of new evidence').

1123 Ibid., mn. 132.

1124 See Section A.(2)(a)(iii) in this chapter.

1125 Section A.(2)(a)(i).

1126 On this structural aspect, see also ICC, *Prosecutor v. Katanga and Ngudjolo,* Décision relative à la mise en œuvre de la norme 55 du Règlement de la Cour et prononçant la disjonction des charges portées contre les accusés, Dissenting Opinion of Judge van den Wyngaert, ICC-01/04-01/07-3319, 21 November 2012, paras. 54–7, focusing on the—adversarial or inquisitorial—conduct of the concrete trial; in the same vein, ICC, *Prosecutor v. Katanga*, TC II, Judgment pursuant to Article 74 of the Statute, Minority Opinion of Judge van den Wyngaert, ICC-01/04-01/07-3436-AnxI, 7 March 2014, paras. 93–6; focusing on the truth-seeking function pursuant to Art. 69 (3) ICCS, Klinkner, *ICLR*, 15 (2015), 408–10, without however offering concrete solutions regarding Reg. 55 RegC.

1127 cf. Friman, in Fischer et al., *Prosecution* (2001), pp. 208–9; Vasiliev, in Cryer et al., *ICL* (2019), pp. 429–30; also Stahn, *CLF*, 16 (2005), 5–6, 21–3; from a comparative and human rights perspective, see Friman, Brady, Costi, Guariglia, and Stuckenberg, in Sluiter et al., *International Criminal Procedure* (2013), pp. 427–8, 458–60, 464–6; on the controversy regarding the principle during the ICC negotiations, see Friman et al., ibid., pp. 431–2; Kreß, in Grützner, Pötz, and Kreß, *Internationaler Rechtshilfeverkehr in Strafsachen* (2003), Part IV A 1, mn. 170; generally crit. also, Gómez Colomer, in Gómez Colomer et al., *CPI* (2003), pp. 308–9; from a comparative law perspective, see Kuczyńska, *Accusation Model ICC* (2015), pp. 165–73. At the ad hoc tribunals this principle was first rejected (ICTY, *Prosecutor v. Kupreškić et al.*, TC, Judgment, IT-95-16-T, 14 January 2000, para. 740, with a comparative overview in paras. 733–7), but later recognized regarding the close of the proceedings (ICTR, *Prosecutor v. Karemera et al.*, TC III, Decision on the Prosecutor's Motion for Leave to Amend the Indictment—Rule 50 of the Rules of Procedure and Evidence, ICTR-98-44-T, 13 February 2004, para. 47 ['At the close of the proceedings the Chamber will decide, on the basis of its own knowledge of the law (according to the principle *iura novit curia*)'], thereto Stahn, *Introduction ICL* (2019), p. 372 with n. 642; *Ntagerura et al.*, ICTR-99-46-T, para. 38 ['defects in legal qualification may not be fatal because the Chamber can apply the correct material law to the factual findings regardless of the qualification indicated by the Prosecution']); crit. Stahn, *CLF*, 16 (2005), 8–10. See also ICC, *Situation in Afghanistan*, PTC II, Decision Regarding Applications Related to the Prosecution's 'Notification on status of the Islamic Republic of Afghanistan's article 18(2) deferral request', ICC-02/17-156, para. 19 ('[T]he Chamber considers in accordance with the principle '*Iura novit curia*' that it does not require any support to interpret the law applicable to the issue *sub judice*.'); KSC, *Prosecutor v. Gucati and Haradinaj*, TP II, Trial Judgment, Separate Opinion of Judge Barthe, KSC-BC-2020-07/F00611/RED, 18 May 2022, para. 11.

institution itself.[1128] Exceptionally, the trial court may convict (only!) for a less serious—'lesser included'[1129]—offence.[1130]

*(i) Cumulative vs. alternative charging and defence rights*

As a consequence, to avoid a factually incomplete or legally inaccurate indictment, common law systems (especially the U.S.) normally allow for a broad *cumulative or alternative charging*, that is, either an overcharging—charging of the same conduct cumulatively with different offences—or a charging of the same conduct with—at least—two alternative offences, for example, murder or extermination as a crime against humanity,[1131] or with different modes of responsibility.[1132] It is then left to the judges to choose the charge/offence they consider appropriate. We have previously rejected the practice of *cumulative charging* at the ad hoc tribunals,[1133] since it overbroadens the prosecution case and thus makes it more difficult, if not impossible, for the defence to adequately and precisely react.[1134] This has also been the view of the *Bemba* PTC.[1135] However, cumulative charging can be justified—in line with the different elements (speciality) test ('Blockburger') developed by the ad hoc tribunals in connection with cumulative (multiple) convictions[1136]—if the respective offences differ in at least one material (objective or subjective) element,[1137] for, in this case, it is necessary to charge the same conduct with these different offences to capture the whole wrongfulness of the perpetrator's conduct.[1138] Whether these cumulative charges can (all) be confirmed or even lead to a conviction, depends, of course, on the evidence available to the respective PTC and TC.[1139] Following a similar line of argument, the *Ongwen* PTC deemed cumulative charging permissible, since 'questions of concurrence of offences are

[1128] cf. Friman, Brady, Costi, Guariglia, and Stuckenberg, in Sluiter et al., *International Criminal Procedure* (2013), p. 465, esp. stressing the 'firm and prohibitive' view of US Federal Law based on the Fifth Amendment grand jury requirement; see also Stahn, *CLF*, 16 (2005), 4–5; Vasiliev, in Cryer et al., *ICL* (2019), p. 429; Majola, in Jalloh and Marong, *Promoting Accountability* (2015), pp. 203 ff.

[1129] On the concept of the lesser included offence, see Ambos, *Treatise ICL II* (2022), pp. 291–2.

[1130] For England/Wales and the USA, see *Kupreškić et al.*, IT-95-16-T, paras. 729–32.

[1131] Art. 7 (1)(a) vs. 7 (1)(b) ICCS.

[1132] cf. *Ntaganda*, ICC-01/04-02/06-309, paras. 99–100, regarding Art. 25 (3)(a), (b), (d)(i), or (ii), (f), and/or Art. 28 (a) ICCS; also *Ruto et al.*, ICC-01/09-01/11-373, paras. 284–5. On the ad hoc tribunals' practice, see Boas et al., *Procedure* (2011), pp. 198–200; Kuczyńska, *Accusation Model ICC* (2015), pp. 131–4.

[1133] See e.g. ICTR, *Prosecutor v. Ndindiliyimana et al.*, AC Judgment, ICTR-00-56-A, 11 February 2014, para. 149; ICTR, *Prosecutor v. Nyiramasuhuko et al.*, AC Judgment, ICTR-98-42-A, 14 December 2015, para. 530; ICTY, *Prosecutor v. Seselj*, TC, Judgment, IT-03-67-T, 31 March 2016, para. 18; MICT, *Prosecutor v. Karadzic*, AC Judgment, MICT-13-55-A, 20 March 2019, para. 56.

[1134] cf. Ambos, *Treatise ICL II* (2022), pp. 298–9; crit. also *Ongwen*, ICC-02/04-01/15-422-Red, paras. 30–1; Kuczyńska, *Accusation Model ICC* (2015), pp. 334, 335–6.

[1135] *Bemba*, ICC-01/05-01/08-424, para. 202; on that and on the subsequent case law, see Kuczyńska, *Accusation Model ICC* (2015), pp. 134–6.

[1136] cf. Ambos, *Treatise ICL II* (2022), pp. 296–300.

[1137] See also *Ruto et al.*, ICC-01/09-01/11-373, paras. 279–81, comparing persecution with murder and deportation/forcible transfer as crimes against humanity; less explicitly *Al Bashir*, ICC-02/05-01/09-3, paras. 95–6, comparing murder and extermination as crimes against humanity; for 'a more flexible approach to charging', see also WCRO, *Regulation 55* (2013), pp. 2, 55.

[1138] In a similar vein, *Ongwen*, ICC-02/04-01/15-422-Red, para. 32 ('[C]ertain crimes under the Statute may, although based on the same set of facts, be not alternative to each other, but concurrently lead to a conviction. Notably, this is the case when each of these crimes requires proof of a distinct legal element or offends a different protected interest'). On a different but not less interesting note, the recourse to the concept of 'protected interest' implies the usefulness of the *Rechtsgut* concept for ICL; see, in more detail, Ambos, *Treatise ICL I* (2021), pp. 106 ff.

[1139] See also ICC, *Practice Manual* (2023), para. 68. (PTC will confirm if sufficient evidence and defer to TC as to ensuing questions of concurrence of offences).

better left to the determination of the Trial Chamber'.[1140] It further infers the permissibility of cumulative charging from a plain reading of Article 61 (7).[1141]

From this perspective, *alternative charging* is more problematic, since it entails a situation where the defence does not know which charge it should reasonably try to rebut. Take, for example, the *Ntaganda* case, where the accused was charged, in the alternative, with effectively eight (!) forms of individual responsibility.[1142] Notwithstanding, so far ICC PTCs have admitted this practice 'as long as each charge is supported by sufficient evidence', turning the issue into 'mainly an evidentiary question'.[1143] In their view, this 'more flexible approach' is 'desirable' with a view 'to reduce further delays at trial' and provide 'early notice to the Defence of the different legal characterisations' to 'be considered by the trial judges'.[1144] It is, however, questionable whether alternative charging will bring the desired effects and really help the defence. In general, given that all charges must be disposed of at one point in time, at the latest at the trial stage, it is certainly true that a higher number of charges entail, on the whole, a prolongation of the proceedings. In addition, to allow for alternative charging without any substantive limitation leads to a de facto unlimited overcharging, where the prosecution charges any offence or mode of liability that somewhat fits to the respective conduct. The *Ntaganda* confirmation decision with its eight highly distinct modes of responsibility is a case in point. In such a case it is also difficult to see to what extent the defence should be in a better position than in cases of only one or—to be more flexible—two charges, that is, those that correspond best with the conduct in question.[1145] In fact, to defend an accused against eight or a similar high number of charges is a bit like shadow-boxing: you think you have struck out one charge, but it was most probably not the right one. At any rate, if the judges are free, as under the *iura novit curia* principle, to change the legal characterization of the (factual) conduct, a wrong legal characterization by the prosecution does not entail the risk of impunity; thus, this judicial authority makes cumulative or alternative charging unnecessary.[1146]

[1140] *Ongwen*, ICC-02/04-01/15-422-Red, para. 30. Unsurprisingly, the issue returned in the form of 'cumulative convictions', see *Prosecutor v. Ongwen*, TC IX, Trial Judgment, ICC-02/04-01/15-1762-Red, 4 February 2021, paras. 2792 ff; *Prosecutor v. Ongwen*, AC, Judgment on the Appeal of Mr Ongwen against the Decision of Trial Chamber IX of 4 February 2021 Entitled 'Trial Judgment', ICC-02/04-01/15-2022-Red, 15 December 2022, paras. 1630 ff. See also Chaitidou, *ZfIStW*, 1 (2022), 662, 665.

[1141] In the PTC's view, a plain reading of Article 61 (7) ICCS enables the Chamber 'to decline to confirm charges only when the evidence does not provide substantial grounds to believe that the person committed the charged crime and not when one possible legal characterisation of the relevant facts is to be preferred over another, equally viable': *Ongwen*, ICC-02/04-01/15-422-Red, para. 30.

[1142] *Ntaganda*, ICC-01/04-02/06-309, para. 99, referring to the above-mentioned (note 1140) provisions distinguishing—regarding Art. 25 (3)(a)—between direct perpetration, direct and indirect co-perpetration, and—regarding Art. 25 (3)(b)—between ordering and inducing.

[1143] *Ntaganda*, ICC-01/04-02/06-309, para. 100; see also *Prosecutor v. Yekatom and Ngaïssona*, PTC II, Corrected Version of 'Decision on the confirmation of charges against Alfred Yekatom and Patrice-Edouard Ngaïssona', ICC-01/14-01/18-403-Corr-Red, 28 June 2021, para. 121 (accepting alternative and cumulative charges); *Abd-Al-Rahman*, ICC-02/05-01/20-433-Corr, 9 July 2021, paras. 26–9 (accepting cumulative charges and alternative modes of liability); but see, on the application of the 'materially distinct elements' test regarding concurrence of crimes/multiple/cumulative convictions, *Ongwen*, ICC-02/04-01/15-1762-Red, para. 2792; *Bemba et al.*, ICC-01/05-01/13-1989-Red, para. 951; *Bemba*, ICC-01/05-01/08-3343, paras. 747-749. In the same vein, ICC, *Practice Manual* (2023), paras. 67–8.

[1144] *Gbagbo*, ICC-02/11-01/11-656-Red, para. 228, confirming charges (paras. 203, 227), with an 'alternative qualification' or 'alternative legal characterisations' and leaving the 'final determination' to the TC; in this regard, conc. *Gbagbo*, ICC-02/11-01/11-656-Anx, para. 3 ('alternate modes of liability ... should be applied as early as possible' to avoid the application of Regulation 55); conc. also *Blé Goudé*, ICC-02/11-02/11-186, para. 133; in the same vein, ICC, *Practice Manual* (2023), paras. 67–8.

[1145] Sceptical regarding the defence position, see also Stahn, *JICJ*, 12 (2014), 831 ('may ... compromise the prospects of the Defence to mount a targeted strategy').

[1146] See also Stuckenberg, in Stahn, *Practice* (2015), p. 853; Kuczyńska, *Accusation Model ICC* (2015), pp. 136–7.

*(ii) The ICC regime, especially Regulation 55*

The ICC's legal regime pursues, as often, a line of compromise implementing the *iura novit curia* principle[1147] at the trial stage: on the one hand, while the PTC may confirm or reject 'those charges',[1148] that is, the charges as presented by the Prosecutor in the DCC, any amendment of the charges is left to the Prosecutor.[1149] Consequently, the PTC must not—contrary to the *Lubanga* confirmation decision[1150]—amend the charges itself, but may only request the OTP to do so.[1151] In addition, any subsequent amendment of charges and their withdrawal, albeit to be authorized by the PTC (amendment) or TC (withdrawal), has to be requested by the Prosecutor.[1152] This confirms—in line with the *travaux* of the ICC Statute[1153]—the prosecutorial prerogative as to the *factual* component of the charges and thus the separation of powers between the Prosecutor and the Chambers.[1154]

On the other hand, the TC (not the PTC!) has, pursuant to Regulation 55 RegC,[1155] the competence of amending the *legal* nature of the charges—in one singular procedure[1156]—as

[1147] In a similar vein, Stahn, *CLF*, 16 (2005), 29–30 ('fair balance' with 'preference over civil law methodology').

[1148] Art. 61 (7)(a) and (b) ICCS.

[1149] Art. 61 (7)(c)(ii) ICCS.

[1150] *Lubanga*, ICC 01/04-01/06-803-tEN, paras. 202–4; cf. also thereon Stegmiller, in Stahn, *Practice* (2015), p. 901.

[1151] ICC, *Prosecutor v. Bemba*, Request for Clarification on Document Containing the Charges, ICC-01/05-01/08-20, 4 November 2008, paras. 1 and 7 ; ICC, *Prosecutor v. Ruto and Sang*, PTC II, Decision on the 'Request by the Victims' Representative for authorization by the Chamber to make written submissions on specific issues of law and/or fact', ICC-01/09-01/11-274, 19 August 2011, paras. 7–8 , and ICC, *Prosecutor v. Ruto and Sang*, TC V, Decision on the Content of the Updated Document Containing the Charges, ICC-01/09-01/11-522, 28 December 2012, paras. 13–19. In the same vein, Jacobs, in Schabas et al., *Research Companion ICL* (2013), p. 209; Friman, Brady, Costi, Guariglia, and Stuckenberg, in Sluiter et al., *International Criminal Procedure* (2013), pp. 486–7; Friman, in Cryer et al., *ICL* (2019), p. 430, for discussion of relevant case law, see Friman, Brady, Costi, Guariglia, and Stuckenberg, in Sluiter et al., *International Criminal Procedure* (2013), pp. 408–11, 449.

[1152] cf. Art. 61 (9) ICCS and Art. 61 (11) ICCS, the latter paragraph applying para. 9 to the TC ('subject to paragraph 9'); thereon also *Lubanga*, ICC-01/04-01/06-2054, paras. 12–17, 53, ii; Stahn, *CLF*, 16 (2005), 15; Jacobs, in Schabas et al., *Research Companion ICL* (2013), p. 213; Heller, in Stahn, *Practice* (2015), pp. 984–9, but interpreting Art. 61 (9) too broadly as the prohibition of *any* amendment, including legal ones, thereby blurring the distinction between factual and legal amendments.

[1153] cf. Guariglia and Hochmayr, 'Article 56', in Ambos, *Commentary* (2022), mn. 2–3, explaining the drafters' intent to avoid 'excessive judicial interference' at the pre-trial stage and thus with regard to the factual framing of the charges; specifically on Reg. 55 RegC, see Stahn, *CLF*, 16 (2005), 10–11.

[1154] See also *Lubanga*, ICC-01/04-01/06-2205, paras. 77, 94; in a similar vein, Jacobs, in Schabas et al., *Research Companion ICL* (2013), pp. 209 ('shifting balance'), 213; Schabas, Chaitidou, and El Zeidy, 'Article 61', in Ambos, *Commentary* (2022), mn. 40 ('PTC ... not entitled to go beyond the factual scope of ... DCC ... not an investigative chamber'), 43 ('statement of the facts' cannot change), 132 (facts 'frozen'). This separation of powers and the ensuing shift of authority from the Prosecutor (note 212 in this chapter and main text) to Chambers (PTC and TC) is overlooked by Heller, in Stahn, *Practice* (2015), pp. 994–6, adopting a too adversarial reading of the ICC procedure (e.g. at 994: 'adversarial nature' and referring to the—US dominated—Nuremberg proceedings as 'accepted part of international criminal practice').

[1155] For a radical critique, see Heller, in Stahn, *Practice* (2015), pp. 981–1006, concluding that it 'represents the most indefensible form of judicial law-making', but his view is predicated on a too unilateral, adversarial reading of the ICC Statute (note 1162 in this chapter) and blurs the distinction between the factual and legal components of the charges (we will return to his position more specifically in the following text); crit. also Jacobs, in Schabas et al., *Research Companion ICL* (2013), pp. 215–8, 221 ('difficult' to 'be reconciled with the Statute', additional amendment procedure cannot be read into the Statute, judicial lawmaking; but also defending a too adversarial reading of the Statute [p. 219]); Boas et al., *Procedure* (2011), pp. 190–1 (regarding the *Lubanga* case). For my previous views, see Ambos, in Bohlander, *International Criminal Justice* (2007), pp. 462–3 and Ambos and Miller, *ICLR*, 7 (2007), 358–60.

[1156] *Lubanga*, ICC-01/04-01/06-2205, paras. 88 ff., convincingly reversing the TC's 'split' interpretation of Reg. 55 where the TC distinguished between para. 1 and paras. 2 and 3 providing for two distinct procedures, the latter of which allows for a change of the legal characterization of charges which have not been in the original DCC as long as there is a procedural unity; cf. ICC, *Prosecutor v. Lubanga*, TC, Decision Giving Notice to the Parties and Participants that the Legal Characterisation of the Facts May Be Subject to Change in Accordance with Regulation 55 (2) of the Regulations of the Court, ICC-01/04-01/06-2049, 14 July 2009, paras. 27–8 ; *Prosecutor v. Lubanga*, Clarification and Further Guidance to Parties and Participants in Relation to the 'Decision giving notice to the

long as this does not unduly restrict defence rights.[1157] The TC is the master of the Regulation 55 proceedings.[1158] The parties may bring a possible modification to the attention of the Chamber,[1159] but it is the Chamber that takes the respective decision. It also decides when it initiates the procedure by giving notice to the participants and allows them, afterwards, to make submissions.[1160] While Regulation 55, as explained above, surely must not be applied at the pre-trial stage,[1161] it is unclear whether it could be invoked by the AC.[1162] If at all, this could only be done by way of an analogy ('Chamber' in Regulation 55 means the TC) and under the same strict conditions to be discussed in the following, in particular without exceeding 'the facts and circumstances described in the charges'.[1163] The ensuing additional fact-finding by the AC—*de novo*—has found support in the *Bemba* AC judgment:

> [I]f the original trial chamber is no longer available, the Appeals Chamber may also decide to determine de novo the factual question at hand, analysing the relevant evidence that was before the trial chamber. If the Appeals Chamber's assessment of this evidence leads it to adopt the same factual finding as that adopted by the trial chamber, the Appeals Chamber will confirm the impugned decision in relation to the factual finding despite the insufficient or lacking reasoning. If, however, the Appeals Chamber, based on its own assessment of the evidence, adopts a factual finding that is different from the one adopted by the trial chamber, the Appeals Chamber will then need to consider the impact, if any, of this new factual finding on the finding as to the guilt or innocence of the accused person.[1164]

While Regulation 55 is compatible with the statutory framework in general, in particular with the judges' mandate under Article 52 (1) ICCS,[1165] it has to be interpreted in strict conformity with Articles 61 (9) and 74 (2) ICCS. In particular, the relationship between

parties and participants that the legal characterisation of the facts may be subject to change in accordance with Regulation 55(2) of the Regulations of the Court', ICC-01/04-01/06-2093, 27 August 2009, para. 8 ; in favour of 'an indivisible or singular process' created by Reg. 55, also *Lubanga*, ICC-01/04-01/06-2054, paras. 4, 21–33, 53.

[1157] On the different theoretical options ('freezing theory', 'amendment theory', compromise of Reg. 55), see Stahn, *CLF*, 16 (2005), 13–6. Crit. from a defence perspective, Jacobs and Naouri, in Bergsmo and Stahn, *Preliminary Examination II* (2018), pp. 469, 487 ('pervasive use of Regulation 55 in most cases at the ICC thus far').

[1158] cf. Stahn, *CLF*, 16 (2005), 26–7. The respective power of the TC may also be inferred from its general competence under Art. 64 (6)(f) ICCS and its implied powers; cf. Stahn, *CLF*, 16 (2005), 17–18.

[1159] e.g. in a status conference pursuant to Rule 132 (2) RPE ICC.

[1160] Reg. 55 (2) RegC; see also *Prosecutor v. Bemba et al.*, TC VII, Decision on Prosecution Application to Provide Notice pursuant to Regulation 55, ICC-01/05-01/13-1250, 15 September 2015, para. 8 (distinguishing these stages and considering the actual recharacterization decision as a third stage).

[1161] In the same vein, Friman, Brady, Costi, Guariglia, and Stuckenberg, in Sluiter et al., *International Criminal Procedure* (2013), pp. 486–7, 487–8; Stegmiller, in Stahn, *Practice* (2015), p. 905; on the case law regarding Reg. 55, see Friman, in Stahn, *Practice* (2015), pp. 916 ff.—I hereby deviate from my earlier position in Ambos, in Bohlander, *International Criminal Justice* (2007), pp. 462–3 and Ambos and Miller, *ICLR*, 7 (2007), 360.

[1162] See Eckelmans, 'Article 83', in Ambos, *Commentary* (2022), mn. 20.

[1163] Art. 74 (2) cl. 2 ICCS.

[1164] *Bemba*, ICC-01/05-01/08-3636-Red, para. 56.

[1165] *Lubanga*, ICC-01/04-01/06-2205, paras. 66 ff., basically arguing, at paras. 68–72, as to the 'routine functioning' as the limiting element of the judges' competence in Art. 52 (1) ICCS, that the fact that the drafters did not reach an agreement on the issue meant that it had to be solved by the judges who did so by introducing Reg. 55; in the same vein, Stahn, *CLF*, 16 (2005), 12, arguing that 'Article 52 is broad enough to allow for the adoption of regulations which clarify elements of the trial procedure or provide the capacity to function effectively as a Court'; *contra* Heller, in Stahn, *Practice* (2015), pp. 982–4; crit. also, Jacobs, in Schabas et al., *Research Companion ICL* (2013), p. 217; Staker and Jacobs, 'Article 52', in Ambos, *Commentary* (2022), mn. 8, 14, 15.

Article 61 (9) ICCS, regulating the amendment of already confirmed charges as mentioned above,[1166] and Regulation 55 is controversial.[1167] The *Lubanga* AC pointed out that:

> Article 61(9) addresses primarily the powers of the Prosecutor to seek an amendment, addition or substitution of the charges, at his or her own initiative and prior to the commencement of the trial; the terms of the provision do not exclude the possibility that a Trial Chamber modifies the legal characterization of the facts on its own motion ... Thus, ... Article 61(9) of the Statute and Regulation 55 address different powers of different entities at different stages of the procedure, and the two provisions are therefore not inherently incompatible.[1168]

A recent example where the Prosecutor invoked Article 61 (9) ICCS to seek an amendment of the already confirmed charges is the *Al Hassan* case.[1169] The Prosecutor asked the Chamber

> to make three types of corrections or amendments to the Confirmation Decision, *viz.*: (i) 'correct/amend' some charges confirmed in the Confirmation Decision because of errors made by the Prosecutor ('Part I' of the Request); (ii) 'reconsider and correct/amend' some existing charges on the basis of information already provided in the DCC ('Part II' of the Request); and (iii) 'to amend' some charges to incorporate new facts on the basis, in part, of new evidence ('Part III' of the Request).[1170]

PTC I rejected Parts I and II of the request, finding that they 'do not concern an amendment of the factual scope of the charges already confirmed within the meaning of article 61(9) of the Statute'.[1171] It considered that Article 61 (9) does not give a Chamber 'the task of revisiting the facts as found or the assessment of evidence previously presented and included in its Confirmation Decision and of making "corrections" thereto'.[1172] This could (only) be done at trial, though.[1173] Especially additional modes of responsibility 'could also be canvassed *before the Trial Chamber* pursuant to *regulation 55* of the Regulations of the Court'.[1174] PTC I returns to the term 'amendment' and seems to insinuate that the OTP tried in fact to reach a 'reconsideration'[1175] through the term 'amendment'.[1176] Ultimately, PTC I granted Part III

[1166] Above in this chapter Section A.(2)(b).

[1167] For a detailed analysis see Schabas, Chaitidou and El Zeidy, 'Article 61', in Ambos, *Commentary* (2022), mn. 146 ff.

[1168] *Lubanga*, ICC-01/04-01/06-2205, para. 77. Thereto Schabas, Chaitidou, and El Zeidy, 'Article 61', in Ambos, *Commentary* (2022), mn. 147.

[1169] *Al Hassan*, ICC-01/12-01/18-461-Corr-Red. PTC I found that there were substantial grounds to believe that *Al Hassan* was responsible for directly committing crimes against humanity and war crimes, for assisting in the commission of those crimes, and/or for contributing in any other way to the crimes (different modes of liability in Art. 25 of the ICC Statute applied). See, in more detail, Chaitidou, *ZIS*, 16 (2021), 46 ff.

[1170] *Al Hassan*, ICC-01/12-01/18-608-Red-tENG, para. 25.

[1171] *Al Hassan*, ICC-01/12-01/18-608-Red-tENG, para. 44. See, for an analysis, Schabas, Chaitidou and El Zeidy, 'Article 61', in Ambos, *Commentary* (2022), mn. 156.

[1172] *Al Hassan*, ICC-01/12-01/18-608-Red-tENG, para. 44.

[1173] Ibid., para. 45.

[1174] Ibid., para. 47 (emphasis added).

[1175] As will be shown in Chapter V, the ICCS does not know the concept of reconsideration or an equivalent, see also Chapter VI C.(3).

[1176] *Al Hassan*, ICC-01/12-01/18-608-Red-tENG, para. 48 ('[T]he Prosecutor, in addition to requesting an amendment of the charges, uses a specific lexicon to seek the "correction" of what she sees as errors in the Confirmation Decision: she requests the Chamber to "reconsider" its decision. Specifically, she submits that the Chamber committed certain errors of fact, which she views as "apparent errors", and that "exceptional circumstances" justify such reconsideration by the Chamber of its decision').

of the Prosecutor's request to amend the charges,[1177] thus modifying a part of them[1178] and making clear that Article 61 (9) may go beyond Regulation 55 RegC whenever the facts and their legal characterization cannot be clearly distinguished.

As to Article 52 ICCS, we have just explained above that it refers to the pre-trial stage and basically regulates the relationship between Prosecutor and PTC at this stage, while Regulation 55 addresses the trial stage and the TC. Accordingly, one could again conclude with the *Lubanga* AC (albeit it referred to Article 61 (9)), that these 'two provisions are not inherently incompatible.'[1179]

Article 74 (2) ICCS provides that the TC's decision 'shall not exceed the *facts and circumstances* described in the charges and any amendments to the charges.'[1180] As a consequence, *e contrario*, it is not prohibited, as stated by Regulation 55, to 'modify the legal characterization of facts.'[1181] From this perspective Regulation 55 crystallizes and refines Article 74 (2).[1182] In other words, this provision contains, as correctly held by the *Lubanga* AC, a double message: on the one hand, it 'confines the scope of Regulation 55 to the facts and circumstances described in the charges and any amendment thereto'; on the other, it 'does not make reference to the legal characterisation of these facts and circumstances.'[1183] As a result, '[i]t follows *a contrario* [sic][1184] that article 74 (2) of the Statute does not rule out' such a legal modification.[1185] It further follows that Regulation 55, in principle, is not limited as to possible legal modifications,[1186] in particular not to lesser included offences (in the sense of the above-mentioned common law approach) or to modes of liability.[1187] Indeed, on the face of it, Regulation 55 even applies to changes of (objective or subjective) elements within one offence or form of responsibility.[1188] If it were otherwise, Regulation 55 could not fulfil one of its major purposes, namely, to prevent the risk of acquittals by allowing the TC to correct an incorrect legal characterization of an alleged conduct.[1189] If the TC were to be bound by

[1177] ICC, *Prosecutor v. Al Hassan*, PTC I, Public Redacted Version of 'Prosecution Request for corrections and amendments concerning the Confirmation Decision', 30 January 2020, ICC-01/12-01/18-568-Conf, ICC-01/12-01/18-568-Red, 17 February 2020.

[1178] ICC, *Prosecutor v. Al Hassan*, PTC I, Version publique expurgée du Rectificatif de la Décision portant modification des charges confirmées le 30 septembre 2019 à l'encontre d'Al Hassan Ag Abdoul Aziz Ag Mohamed Ag Mahmoud, 23 avril 2020, ICC-01/12-01/18-767-Conf, ICC-01/12-01/18-767-Corr-Red, 8 May 2020.

[1179] *Lubanga*, ICC-01/04-01/06-2205, para. 77, 78.

[1180] Emphasis added.

[1181] *Bemba*, ICC-01/05-01/08-424, para. 203 ('under regulation 55 of the Regulations, the Trial Chamber may re-characterise a crime to give it the most appropriate legal characterisation'); in the same vein, Stahn, *CLF*, 16 (2005), 16–17.

[1182] Stahn, *CLF*, 16 (2005), 31.

[1183] *Lubanga*, ICC-01/04-01/06-2205, para. 93.

[1184] The correct Latin term is '*e contrario*' (Kramer, *Methodenlehre* (2019), p. 212 with n. 658; Hager, *Rechtsmethoden* (2009), pp. 52–3; Linderfalk, *Interpretation of Treaties* (2007), pp. 279, 299–303) but '*a contrario*' is indeed used often in common law sources, see e.g. Garner, *Dictionary* (2019), p. 133.

[1185] *Lubanga*, ICC-01/04-01/06-2205, para. 93.

[1186] Ibid., para. 100, arguing that Reg. 55 'does not stipulate … what changes in the legal characterisation may be permissible'; in the same vein, Stahn, *CLF*, 16 (2005), 24–5 (wide scope of application); Schabas, Chaitidou, and El Zeidy, 'Article 61', in Triffterer and Ambos, *Commentary* (2016), mn. 7 ('unrestricted powers'); recently apparently more cautiously id., 'Article 61' in Ambos, *Commentary* (2022), mn. 7 (omitting 'unrestricting').

[1187] This limitation has been suggested by Judge Fulford in his Minority Opinion, *Lubanga*, ICC-01/04-01/06-2054, para. 20; for a restrictive interpretation, see also *Katanga*, ICC-01/04-01/07-3363, paras. 5 ff.

[1188] See, in this vein, ICC, *Prosecutor v. Bemba*, TC III, Decision Giving Notice to the Parties and Participants that the Legal Characterisation of the Facts May be Subject to Change in Accordance with Regulation 55 (2) of the Regulation of the Court, ICC-01/05-01/08-2324, 21 September 2012, regarding a possible change of the mental element of Art. 28 (a)(i) ICCS from 'knowledge' to 'should have known'; see also *Bemba*, ICC-01/05-01/08-3343, paras. 51–7, 62.

[1189] See also *Lubanga*, ICC-01/04-01/06-2205, para. 77 (pointing to the risk of acquittals and considering as 'a principal purpose' of Reg. 55 'to close accountability gaps'); conc. *Katanga*, ICC-01/04-01/07-3363, para. 22; also *Katanga and Ngudjolo*, ICC-01/04-01/07-3319, para. 7 and *Katanga*, ICC-01/04-01/07-3436-AnxI, para. 10 (note

the original legal characterization of the Prosecutor and/or the PTC, it would have to acquit the accused in such a situation, since it could not convict her on the basis of a legal characterization it considers to be incorrect.[1190] The only way to avoid this result would be to allow for broad alternative charging, which, however, is not necessarily a better approach in terms of the defence rights of the accused. Of course, the possibility of a legal modification of the charges should not produce the same result, that is, an overbroad factual charging to enable the TC to pick and choose the appropriate crime and mode of responsibility.[1191]

Last but not least, Regulation 55 is not limited, per se, in temporal terms; on the contrary, a legal modification may occur 'at any time during the trial',[1192] that is, until its closure pursuant to a decision under Article 74 ICCS.[1193] Of course, this does not mean that the Chamber can exhaust this period, if the possibility of a legal change 'appears'[1194] to it; rather, it must give notice to the accused as soon as it becomes aware of this possibility,[1195] i.e. even prior to the hearing of opening statements.[1196] Also, it is clear that the later the notice is given, the stricter become the fair trial requirements to be observed by the Chamber. We will discuss these requirements in a moment but can already anticipate here that the late notice given in the *Katanga* proceedings has become the gist of the fair trial issue in this case.[1197]

*(iii) The gist of the issue: Distinguishing law and facts and ensuring a fair trial*

While the wording of Regulation 55 (1) is clear enough in distinguishing between law ('legal characterisation') and 'facts', it entails the question whether this fine line can always

however the caveat that this should not infringe upon the rights of the accused, para. 50); Stahn, *CLF*, 16 (2005), 25; Friman, Brady, Costi, Guariglia, and Stuckenberg, in Sluiter et al., *International Criminal Procedure* (2013), p. 451; Stegmiller, in Stahn, *Practice* (2015), pp. 904–5 ('important new procedural tool'); *contra* Heller, in Stahn, *Practice* (2015), pp. 1003–5; crit., see also Jacobs, in Schabas et al., *Research Companion ICL* (2013), p. 217; Staker and Jacobs, 'Article 52', in Ambos, *Commentary* (2022), mn. 8.

[1190] Stahn, *CLF*, 16 (2005), 3; in a similar vein, crit. of a binding effect of the confirmation decision on the TC, Friman, in Stahn, *Practice* (2015), pp. 918–21. This issue is not addressed by the dissenting judges. Esp. Judge Tarfusser does not discuss the consequences of his quite radical view (*Katanga*, ICC-01/04-01/07-3363, Dissenting Opinion of Judge Cuno Tarfusser, paras. 5 ff.): Would the inapplicability of Reg. 55 bind the TC to the original charges, thereby provoking an acquittal, or could it modify the charges without further ado? The latter approach would make things worse for the accused and therefore does not seem to be compatible with Judge Tarfusser's view.

[1191] Cautioning in this regard, see Jacobs, in Schabas et al., *Research Companion ICL* (2013), p. 218; Heller, in Stahn, *Practice* (2015), p. 1002.

[1192] Reg. 55 (2) RegCourt.

[1193] cf. *Katanga*, ICC-01/04-01/07-3363, paras. 14–24; conc. insofar *Katanga*, ICC-01/04-01/07-3363, Dissenting Opinion of Judge Tarfusser, para. 2. *In casu*, the notice was given at the deliberation stage more than one year after the close of the evidentiary phase, i.e. after the hearing within the meaning of Reg. 55 (2) cl. 2 alternative 1; but the Chamber (para. 23) correctly points to the possibility to order a separate hearing in this situation pursuant to Reg. 55 (2) cl. 2 alternative 2 ('or, if necessary'). *Contra* Heller, in Stahn, *Practice* (2015), p. 993, arguing that the deliberations phase must be distinguished from the actual trial phase but this misreads the Statute; Part 6 clearly refers to the trial phase including the deliberations (Art. 74 (4) ICCS) and its closure with the delivery of the verdict in open court (Art. 74 (5) ICCS); similarly in favour of a temporal limit, WCRO, *Regulation 55* (2013), pp. 2, 52 (until presentation of defence case before TC).

[1194] Reg. 55 (2) RegC.

[1195] In this vein, also *Katanga*, ICC-01/04-01/07-3363, para. 24 (notice 'should always be given as early as possible'); more flexible, *Bemba et al.*, ICC-01/05-01/13-1250, paras. 9–12 (early prosecution request rejected for lack of 'exceptional circumstances').

[1196] ICC, *Prosecutor v. Gbagbo and Blé Goudé*, Judgment on the Appeal of Mr Laurent Gbagbo against the Decision of Trial Chamber I Entitled 'Decision giving notice pursuant to Regulation 55(2) of the Regulations of the Court', ICC-02/11-01/15-369, 18 December 2015, paras. 47–55.

[1197] cf. *Katanga and Ngudjolo*, ICC-01/04-01/07-3319, Dissenting Opinion of Judge van den Wyngaert, paras. 25 ff., stressing several times the (too) late notice to the accused and 'the particular circumstances of this case' (para. 50) and concluding that 'in the current stage of the proceedings ... the 25 (3)(d) Notice Decision cannot be implemented fairly' (para. 53).

be convincingly drawn in each case before a TC. Judge Fulford questioned, albeit without elaborating further, whether it is possible at all to modify the legal characterization of the facts 'without *ipso facto* amending' the respective charges.[1198] In other words, 'can a charge remain "unamended" if one of the necessary ingredients, the legal characterisation, has changed?'[1199] Ultimately, this is, in his view, 'a question of fact and degree, to be assessed on a case-by-case basis'.[1200] In a similar vein, Judge van den Wyngaert argued in *Katanga*, albeit acknowledging the 'merit' of Regulation 55 'as a tool ... to adjust the legal characterisation to better accord with the facts and circumstances described in the charges',[1201] that a change in the mode of liability—from co-perpetration to contribution in a collective crime[1202]—cannot be done without affecting the factual basis of the charges and therefore exceeding the facts and circumstances as described in the charges.[1203] Van den Wyngaert agrees with Judge Fulford that the question of a violation of Article 74 is one 'of fact and degree'.[1204] However, she interprets the *Lubanga* AC's prohibition of a change 'in the statement of the facts'[1205] as a prohibition to 'change the narrative of the facts ... so fundamentally that it exceeds the facts and circumstances described in the charges'.[1206] She sees such a fundamental and thus inadmissible change in the majority's 'factual acrobatics' to find factual support for the change regarding Katanga's mode of responsibility in the confirmation decision.[1207] In her view, the ensuing transformation of the mode of responsibility entails a 'drastic change' in the factual narrative of the case, which is no longer covered by Article 74 (2) ICCS and Regulation 55 (1).[1208] In general terms, whether such a drastic change exists, can be evaluated, in her view, by questioning 'whether a reasonably diligent accused would have conducted substantially the same line of defence against both the old and new charge'.[1209] Van den Wyngaert further argues that there is a distinction between 'material' and 'subsidiary facts' and only the former ones—actually underlying the charges—are open to a recharacterization, while the latter ones cannot be relied upon to that effect.[1210]

The latter argument—which can be traced back to the distinction by the *Lubanga* Appeals Chamber and the ensuing PTC case law[1211]—finds no basis in either Article 74 (2) ICCS or

[1198] *Prosecutor v. Lubanga*, ICC-01/04-01/06-2054, TC I (Judge Fulford) Minority Opinion on the 'Decision giving notice to the parties and participants that the legal characterisation of facts may be subject to change in accordance with Regulation 55(2) of the Regulations of the Court', 17 July 2009, para. 18.

[1199] *Lubanga*, ICC-01/04-01/06-2054, (Judge Fulford) para. 18.

[1200] Ibid., para. 53, iii.

[1201] *Katanga and Ngudjolo*, ICC-01/04-01/07-3319, para. 5.

[1202] Art. 25 (3)(a) vs. 25 (3)(d) ICCS. *Katanga and Ngudjolo*, ICC-01/04-01/07-3319, paras. 42–4, is right if she rejects the lesser included offence argument of the majority since these two modes of responsibility have different objects of reference ('plan' *versus* 'crime'); also *Katanga*, ICC-01/04-01/07-3436-AnxI, para. 38.

[1203] *Katanga and Ngudjolo*, ICC-01/04-01/07-3319;*Katanga*, ICC-01/04-01/07-3436-AnxI, paras. 9 ff. (regarding TJ).

[1204] *Katanga*, ICC-01/04-01/07-3436-AnxI, para. 29.

[1205] *Lubanga*, ICC-01/04-01/06-2205, para. 97.

[1206] *Katanga and Ngudjolo*, ICC-01/04-01/07-3319, para. 13; *Katanga*, ICC-01/04-01/07-3436-AnxI, paras. 17, 29.

[1207] *Katanga and Ngudjolo*, ICC-01/04-01/07-3319, paras. 20–1; *Katanga*, ICC-01/04-01/07-3436-AnxI, paras. 19–26, arguing that the majority introduced new facts to justify the conviction.

[1208] *Katanga and Ngudjolo*, ICC-01/04-01/07-3319, para. 22; also *Katanga*, ICC-01/04-01/07-3436-AnxI, paras. 12, 27–49, 129 ('textbook example' of 'drastic change', para. 49); replying, ICC, *Prosecutor v. Katanga*, TC II, Judgment pursuant to Article 74 of the Statute, Concurring Opinion of Judges Diarra and Cotte, ICC-01/04-01/07-3436-AnxII-tENG, 7 March 2014, para. 2, stressing the identical 'factual allegations' of the TJ; basically conc. with Judge van den Wyngaert, WCRO, *Regulation 55* (2013), pp. 2, 50–2.

[1209] *Katanga*, ICC-01/04-01/07-3436-AnxI, para. 35.

[1210] For the distinction as made in the case law and *Chambers Practice Manual*, see above notes 172, 173. See also *Katanga and Ngudjolo*, ICC-01/04-01/07-3319, paras. 14–15.

[1211] Notes 171, 172, and main text in this chapter.

Regulation 55[1212] and has thus been rejected by the AC.[1213] More importantly, the proposed distinction would lead to unsurmountable problems of delimitation.[1214] In contrast, van den Wyngaert's first argument deserves serious consideration. Judge Tarfusser's Dissent in the Katanga AC Judgment, albeit advocating a restrictive interpretation of Regulation 55, does not directly address the difficult issue of the impact of a legal recharacterization on the facts underlying the charges.[1215]

The starting point to addressing this complex issue is, again, the factual-legal concept of charges as already defined above.[1216] Such a dualist concept, explicitly adopted by Regulation 52 with regard to the DCC,[1217] presupposes that the distinction between the factual and legal contents of the charges is possible and that, in principle, charges may be amended as to their legal component (i.e. kind of crime and mode of responsibility) without thereby changing their factual component (the statement of facts).[1218] Of course, such a legal modification affects the charges[1219] but this is beside the point, since Regulation 55 explicitly allows it as long as the facts remain the same.[1220] In this regard the dispute between the *Katanga* majority and Judge van den Wyngaert touches upon the *gist of the issue*: did the TC only stress the relevant facts or did it make them 'salient' ('mise en relief'),[1221] or did it actually alter the facts as alleged by van den Wyngaert.[1222] This, of course, cannot be decided without having been actively involved in the proceedings but it clearly shows that the fine distinction between an admissible, purely legal recharacterization of the facts and their inadmissible modification as a result of the recharacterization depends on the concrete circumstances of each case. It is, as rightly said by Judge Fulford, Judge van den Wyngaert concurring, 'a question of fact and degree, to be assessed on a case-by-case basis'.[1223] At any rate, one lesson

[1212] cf. *Katanga*, ICC-01/04-01/07-3363, para. 50 (against the *Katanga* defence which adopted van den Wyngaert's position, but admitting that 'facts and circumstances' may be 'narrowly or broadly understood'). Interestingly, van den Wyngaert in *Katanga*, ICC-01/04-01/07-3436-AnxI, no longer pursues this distinction.

[1213] *Katanga*, ICC-01/04-01/07-3363, para. 50; *Prosecutor v. Gbagbo*, AC, Judgment on the Appeal of the Prosecutor against the Decision of Pre-Trial Chamber I of 3 June 2013 Entitled 'Decision adjourning the hearing on the confirmation of charges pursuant to Article 61(7)(c)(i) of the Rome Statute', ICC-02/11-01/11-572, 16 December 2013, paras. 37–47; *Bemba*, ICC-01/05-01/08-3636-Red. For more references, see Schabas, Chaitidou, and El Zeidy, 'Article 61', in Ambos, *Commentary* (2022), mn. 34.

[1214] Crit. regarding the clarity of the distinction, also Schabas, Chaitidou, and El Zeidy, 'Article 61', in Triffterer and Ambos, *Commentary* (2016), mn. 32 with n. 59 and mn. 129) but now with a rather descriptive account of the ensuing AC case law, ibid., 'Article 61', in Ambos, *Commentary* (2022), mn. 34; crit. also Bourguiba, in Fernandez et al., *Commentaire II* (2019), p. 1691.

[1215] *Katanga*, ICC-01/04-01/07-3363, Dissenting Opinion of Judge Tarfusser, paras. 5–20, arguing that Reg. 55 should only encompass 'those modifications which, being significant, are suitable to have a meaningful impact on the "nature, cause and content" of the charges' (para. 8) and, as to the forms of responsibility, limiting its application to changes from Art. 25 to Art. 28 and *vice versa* but not within Art. 25, these being of minor significance (paras. 10–20).

[1216] Section A.(2)(a)(i) in this chapter.

[1217] cf. Reg. 52 (b) and (c) RegC; in this vein, also *Lubanga*, ICC-01/04-01/06-2205, paras. 96–7 ('distinction between facts and their legal characterisation should be respected for the interpretation of Regulation 55 as well').

[1218] In the same vein, Stahn, *CLF*, 16 (2005), 17, correctly distinguishing between the factual and legal components of the charges.

[1219] Correct in this regard, see Jacobs, in Schabas et al., *Research Companion ICL* (2013), p. 215 and Heller, in Stahn, *Practice* (2015), pp. 987–9, but understating the dualist nature of charges.

[1220] For this reason, the analogy, proposed by WCRO (WCRO, *Regulation 55* (2013), pp. 2, 44 ff.), to the ad hoc tribunals' practice of 'curing' defective indictments (note 210 and main text in this chapter) is problematic since it is structurally different from Reg. 55 in that it entails the addition of new facts (as correctly acknowledged WCRO, *Regulation 55* (2013), pp. 46, 50; distinguishing between the ad hoc tribunals and the ICC in this regard, also Friman, Brady, Costi, Guariglia, and Stuckenberg, in Sluiter et al., *International Criminal Procedure* (2013), pp. 421–2, 423, and 450).

[1221] ICC, *Prosecutor v. Katanga*, TC II, Judgment pursuant to Article 74 of the Statute, ICC-01/04-01/07-3436-tENG, 7 March 2014, paras. 1476, 1479 ('certain aspects of the case are made salient' [French original: 'mise en relief de certains aspects du dossier']).

[1222] Note 1211 and main text in this chapter.

[1223] Note 1218 and main text in this chapter.

learnt from the *Katanga* proceedings is that the precise 'facts and circumstances' should be made clearer at the outset, that is, in the confirmation decision, making an updated DCC[1224] or any other subsequent clarification unnecessary.[1225]

This brings us—notwithstanding the different approaches of common and civil law jurisdictions to the problem of a legal recharacterization in the course of the proceedings—to the key prerequisite of any recharacterization of the facts, that is, the safeguarding of the *fair trial rights* of the accused,[1226] especially[1227] his right to 'be informed promptly and in details of the nature, cause and content of the charge',[1228] to 'have adequate time and facilities for the preparation of the defence',[1229] and to 'be tried without undue delay'.[1230] The first of these rights protects the accused from being taken by surprise and therefore demands that he is *as soon as possible*—that is, by the investigation stage—*informed* about the charges.[1231] Yet, this right does not prohibit a subsequent change in the legal characterization of the facts at the trial stage,[1232] especially since the TC is under an obligation to 'give notice' of such a change.[1233] Also, a correction or adjustment of the legal characterization that better fits the

[1224] See Section A.(2)(a) in this chapter.

[1225] In the same vein, Stahn, *JICJ*, 12 (2014), 833.

[1226] For Judge van den Wyngaert (*Katanga and Ngudjolo*, ICC-01/04-01/07-3319, para. 10) this is the 'second step' of a two-step-test analysis embodied in Reg. 55 RegC (the first step being the recharacterization without exceeding the facts and circumstances); similarly, without explicitly mentioning the two-step test, *Katanga*, ICC-01/04-01/07-3436-AnxI, paras. 16 ff. and 50 ff. (sub-sect. A and B. of sect. II of the Opinion). See also Rohan, in Aksenova, van Sliedregt, and Parmentier, *Mass Atrocities* (2019), p. 107.

[1227] The alleged violation of the *right to an impartial trial* (see thereon Chapter I, D.(2)(a) in this volume), brought forward by the *Katanga* defence, is too far-fetched. Given that the Chamber is explicitly authorized to act on the basis of Reg. 55, it does not perform 'a prosecutorial function', but 'a neutral judicial act' which does not impinge upon its impartiality (*Katanga*, ICC-01/04-01/07-3363, para. 104); *Katanga*, ICC-01/04-01/07-3436-AnxII-tENG, para. 2, stressing that they have 'no intention of encroaching' on the Prosecution's authority; following the defence position, however, see Jacobs, in Schabas et al., *Research Companion ICL* (2013), pp. 220–1; Heller, in Stahn, *Practice* (2015), p. 1005 (arguing that judges act 'as advocates, not as neutral umpires'); Rohan, in Aksenova, van Sliedregt, and Parmentier, *Mass Atrocities* (2019), pp. 95, 107–8 ('[I]t appears that the *Katanga* Majority, unlike the *Ntaganda* Chambers, was *not* willing to rely on the assumed neutrality or the assumed thoroughness of pre-trial procedures, such as the confirmation of charges hearing, and the evidence produced at that time as a basis for in-trial legal rulings. That inconsistency appears to rest on the legally impermissible basis of the application, between ICC chambers, of random, subjective legal standards rather than the objective standards required by the rule of law', emphasis in the original). It is also unconvincing to invoke the *right to remain silent* (*Katanga and Ngudjolo*, ICC-01/04-01/07-3319, para. 45; *Katanga*, ICC-01/04-01/07-3436-AnxI, paras. 51–9, 130; conc. Heller, in Stahn, *Practice* (2015), pp. 1000–1) if the accused has voluntarily waived this right and testified to the facts underlying the charges; it is then a question of the concrete case if the facts have been changed to the accused's detriment. For further general fair trial violations in *Katanga*, see *Katanga*, ICC-01/04-01/07-3436-AnxI, paras. 109–17, alleging 'that the Majority has systematically turned a blind eye towards the Defence's repeated requests to terminate the regulation 55 proceedings'. Crit. also WCRO, *Regulation 55* (2013), pp. 1–2, 44, 50–2; Stahn, *JICJ*, 12 (2014), 830, 833 ('critical dilemmas of late notice and self-incrimination', 'findings compromise the idea of protection of defence interests ... inherent in the regulation', 'in contrast to ... fairness'); Schabas and McDermott, 'Article 67', in Ambos, *Commentary* (2022), mn. 20. Van den Wyngaert's outspoken opinion has provoked a reaction by the majority expressing 'astonishment' and stressing that it took an 'approach' 'informed' by 'the principle of legality as well as that of fair and impartial proceedings'; see *Katanga*, ICC-01/04-01/07-3436-AnxII-tENG, para. 3.

[1228] cf. Art. 67 (1)(a) ICCS. See also Ambos, in Jackson and Summers, *Fairness* (2018), p. 179, 180 with further references in n. 8.

[1229] cf. Art. 67 (1)(b) ICCS.

[1230] cf. Art. 67 (1)(c) ICCS.

[1231] See, in detail, Chapter I, D.(3)(c) in this volume.

[1232] For the same result, *Lubanga*, ICC-01/04-01/06-2205, para. 84; *Katanga*, ICC-01/04-01/07-3363, para. 93 (both with references to human rights case law which allows for a change to the legal characterization of the facts 'at late stages of the proceedings'); see also the discussion by Friman, Brady, Costi, Guariglia, and Stuckenberg, in Sluiter et al., *International Criminal Procedure* (2013), pp. 458–60.

[1233] Reg. 55 (2) RegC. For such a decision, see *Bemba*, ICC-01/05-01/08-2324.

facts corresponds to the principle of 'fair labelling'[1234] and thus is plainly in the interests of the accused.[1235] Of course, the Chamber may need to indicate the 'specific facts' upon which it intends to rely.[1236] In any case, it is up to the TC to determine the level of detail needed; if it considers 'that further information is required', it should be provided to the accused 'as soon as possible'.[1237]

The right to '*have adequate time and facilities*' seeks to ensure that the defence always has sufficient time to react to changes of the prosecution case during the proceedings.[1238] This is exactly accounted for by the just mentioned 'give notice' obligation regarding a possible change in the legal characterization and the further obligation to 'give the participants the opportunity to make oral or written submissions', including ordering a suspension of the proceedings[1239] and a separate hearing to discuss the proposed change(s). In fact, Regulation 55 (3) specifically refers to this right and, in addition, to the right to examine a witness and present new evidence pursuant to Article 67 (1)(e) ICCS.[1240] Thus, Regulation 55 itself sets out 'several stringent safeguards for the protection of the rights of the accused', whose concrete application depends, of course, on the circumstances of the concrete case.[1241] It is for this reason that the *Katanga* ACs omitted a final determination with regard to possible fair trial violations by the application of Regulation 55 in that case. In the Chamber's view, this will depend 'to a large extent upon how the TC conducts the further proceedings and, in particular, on the measures it will take to protect Mr Katanga's rights'.[1242] Its considerations have therefore been preliminary and 'without prejudice' to any future ruling.[1243] As to the subsequent proceedings, the majority of the TC saw no violation of Articles 67 (1)(b) and (e) ICCS.[1244]

[1234] On this principle, see generally Ashworth and Horder, *Principles* (2013), pp. 77–9; Zawati, *Fair Labelling* (2014), pp. 25 ff.; regarding the codification and prosecution of gender-based crimes at the international criminal tribunals, Zawati, ibid., pp. 87 ff.

[1235] See also *Katanga and Ngudjolo*, ICC-01/04-01/07-3319, para. 5, acknowledging 'that there is merit' in this principle; following her (para. 32) one may also identify fair labelling concerns in the majority decision stating that it is the Chambers' task to find 'the most suitable [normative] response to the charges'; cf. *Katanga and Ngudjolo*, ICC-01/04-01/07-3319-tENG/FRA, para. 8.

[1236] *Katanga*, ICC-01/04-01/07-3363, para. 101.

[1237] Ibid., para. 102; contra, *Katanga*, ICC-01/04-01/07-3363, Dissenting Opinion of Judge Tarfusser, paras. 22–7, requiring more detailed—'specific and precise'—information (para. 26) and '*at the same time*' when the Chamber gives notice (para. 27, emphasis in original); for a stricter standard, see also *Katanga*, ICC-01/04-01/07-3436-AnxI, paras. 60–85, considering that the right has been violated in *Katanga*.

[1238] See, in detail, Chapter I, D.(3)(d) in this volume. See also Ambos, in Jackson and Summers, *Fairness* (2018), p. 179, 181.

[1239] See e.g. ICC, *Prosecutor v. Bemba*, TC III, Decision on the Temporary Suspension of the Proceedings pursuant to Regulation 55 (2) of the Regulation of the Court and Related Procedural Deadlines, ICC-01/05-01/08-2480, 13 December 2012.

[1240] See Reg. 55 (3)(a) and (b) RegC, as applied e.g. in *Bemba*, ICC-01/05-01/08-2480, paras. 13 ff.

[1241] *Lubanga*, ICC-01/04-01/06-2205, para. 85; conc. *Katanga*, ICC-01/04-01/07-3363, para. 88; in a similar vein, Stahn, *CLF*, 16 (2005), 18–24, stressing that the safeguards go beyond domestic systems; Friman, Brady, Costi, Guariglia, and Stuckenberg, in Sluiter et al., *International Criminal Procedure* (2013), p. 460, stressing the safeguards of Reg. 55 and of the *Lubanga* AC.

[1242] *Katanga*, ICC-01/04-01/07-3363, para. 91.

[1243] Ibid., paras. 91 and 95 ('premature' to rule on Katanga's argument regarding his right to adequately prepare the defence), 98 (arguments regarding trial without delay 'premature'), 102 (conclusive determination as to right to be informed 'only at the end of the trial').

[1244] *Katanga*, ICC-01/04-01/07-3436-tENG, paras. 1538 (arguing that 'further investigations or searches for new evidence are not the only possible means of mounting a defence'), 1568 ff. (insufficient diligence of defence, in particular it did not seize alternative avenues of investigation offered by the TC); *contra Katanga*, ICC-01/04-01/07-3436-AnxI, paras. 86–108, 130, inter alia calling for 'a meaningful and realistic opportunity' for the defence 'to investigate' relevant factual issues (para. 90).

As to the right to a *trial without undue delay* one cannot assume without further ado that the application of Regulation 55 will entail such a delay 'automatically'.[1245] While, arguably, the practical application of Regulation 55 has caused several delays,[1246] including in the *Katanga* case contrary to the AC's cautious ruling,[1247] this effect depends on the application of the provision in each concrete case. In other words, its cautious application, as advocated here, can avoid intolerable delays. Apart from that, it is difficult to determine a relevant delay and the concrete causes for it.[1248] In fact, as already discussed earlier,[1249] the filing of additional charges and broad overcharging may also cause relevant delays.

Summing up these considerations, one should not, throwing out the baby with the bathwater, abolish or totally disregard Regulation 55, but apply it in a cautious and responsible way.[1250] It should be recalled, notwithstanding the obvious shortcomings in the practical application of Regulation 55, that its clear purpose was to make broad overcharging superfluous and instead to encourage precise charging from the beginning of the proceedings[1251] and thus 'to allow for shorter, more focused, trials'.[1252] This is, not least in light of the experience of the ad hoc tribunals, to be welcomed. Regulation 55 and the underlying *iura novit curiae* principle do not per se violate basic fair trial guarantees.[1253] Unacceptable fair trial violations in proceedings can be avoided by its cautious and exceptional application to situations where a TC considers the legal qualification of the facts, as confirmed by the PTC, as clearly flawed and thus has no alternative to a recharacterization in order to avoid an acquittal on such technical grounds. Of course, such a recharacterization should—for fair trial reasons and despite the open wording of Regulation 55[1254]—be announced as early as possible and, in principle, be avoided after the presentation of the defence case.[1255] If notice is only given at this late stage of the trial proceedings, an additional hearing—pursuant to Regulation 55 (2) clause 2 alternative 2 ('or, if necessary')—should be held where the defence, with enough time for preparation, can set out its case in light of the recharacterization.

[1245] *Lubanga*, ICC-01/04-01/06-2205, para. 86; conc. *Katanga*, ICC-01/04-01/07-3363, para. 97; *contra* Jacobs, in Schabas et al., *Research Companion ICL* (2013), p. 220 (possible slowing down of proceedings); Heller, in Stahn, *Practice* (2015), p. 1002, arguing that Reg. 55 is 'likely to frustrate efficient trial management' and especially makes the use of Rule 69 RPE ICC highly improbable.

[1246] cf. WCRO, *Regulation 55* (2013), pp. 1, 43, 54–5; Stahn, *JICJ*, 12 (2014), 829.

[1247] *Katanga*, ICC-01/04-01/07-3363, paras. 98–9 (arguments insofar 'premature', 'at the present time … not clear' but TC 'will need to be particularly vigilant'); seeing already at that stage 'an unfair delay', *Katanga and Ngudjolo*, ICC-01/04-01/07-3319, paras. 48–52, arguing that the radical change in the mode of responsibility 'may have the effect of triggering an entirely new trial' and force the defence 'to present an entirely new case' (para. 49); confirmed at trial stage in *Katanga*, ICC-01/04-01/07-3436-AnxI, paras. 118–28, 131, inter alia arguing that 'the length of the post-notice proceedings (21 November 2012–7 March 2014) has shown the Majority to be wrong' (para. 119) and generally criticizing the overall length of the proceedings. Interestingly, the TC in *Katanga and Ngudjolo*, ICC-01/04-01/07-3319-tENG/FRA, para. 61, has justified the severance of the trial against Ngudjolo Chui with the application of Reg. 55 with regard to Katanga, which 'clearly has the potential consequence of prolonging the proceedings against him'.

[1248] See generally Chapter I, D.(3)(h) in this volume.

[1249] Notes 1270, 1152 and main text in this chapter.

[1250] In a similar vein, Stahn, *JICJ*, 12 (2014), 831 ('Regulation 55 may have been stretched beyond its limits in Katanga. But this does not mean that it is feasible to "throw out the baby with the bathwater".'); for a similar (preliminary) nuanced assessment, see Friman, Brady, Costi, Guariglia, and Stuckenberg, in Sluiter et al., *International Criminal Procedure* (2013), p. 450–1, advocating its 'cautious' application in light of the *Lubanga* AJ.

[1251] Stahn, *CLF*, 16 (2005), 30.

[1252] *Katanga*, ICC-01/04-01/07-3436-AnxI, para. 90 (purpose of Reg. 55); similarly Stahn, *CLF*, 16 (2005), 26 ('safeguards against an overflow of request for re-classification'), 28 ('[P]reservation of judicial economy').

[1253] In the same vein, Friman, Brady, Costi, Guariglia, and Stuckenberg, in Sluiter et al., *International Criminal Procedure* (2013), pp. 458–60, analysing relevant human rights law.

[1254] Note 1200 and main text in this chapter.

[1255] In this sense, the WCRO proposal (WCRO, *Regulation 55* (2013), pp. 2, 52) of a temporal limit (until presentation of defence case before TC) is to be welcomed although I would allow, in exceptional circumstances, for later notice under the conditions set out in the main text above.

### (8) Continuous investigation versus premature termination

The prosecutorial investigation does not stop with the filling of the charges or their confirmation.[1256] Given that the Prosecutor is to search for the truth and investigate both incriminating and exculpatory circumstances,[1257] there can be no fixed, formal endpoint of the investigation. In any case, such an endpoint would be plainly unreasonable, for it may entail that important information or evidence cannot be taken into account at the trial stage and thus not inform the final verdict. In this sense, the *Lubanga* ICC AC correctly held that the Prosecutor's investigation need not 'be brought to an end before the confirmation hearing' and that she is in particular entitled to investigate 'other crimes' not yet covered by the charges presented at the confirmation hearing.[1258] The applicable law is silent on the matter; it only contains rules with regard to the amendment of charges—to be looked at in a moment—but not on the termination of the investigation in general.[1259]

Of course, from a defence perspective and also in terms of expediency of the proceedings, it is desirable that the prosecution investigate its case as thoroughly and rapidly as possible up to the confirmation hearing,[1260] but this is merely an aspirational goal and not, as just said, a specific legal obligation of the Prosecutor. Indeed, 'ideally', as nicely put by the *Lubanga* AC, 'it would be desirable for the investigation to be complete by the time of the confirmation hearing',[1261] but, as acknowledged by the Chamber in the same paragraph, 'this is not a requirement of the Statute'.[1262] Unfortunately, the post-*Lubanga* case law converted the aspirational goal of an early termination of the investigation into a legal principle without, however, indicating any explicit legal basis for this interpretation.[1263] Most importantly, the *Mbarushimana* AC formulated, explicitly relying on *Lubanga*,[1264] but with a more compulsory undertone, that 'the investigation should largely be completed at the stage of the confirmation of charges hearing'.[1265] Thus, the *Lubanga* 'ideal' was converted into something obligatory ('should'), misreading *Lubanga*[1266] and, in addition, discussing

[1256] cf. de Meester, Pitcher, Rastan, and Sluiter, in Sluiter et al., *International Criminal Procedure* (2013), pp. 174–6 (discussing the continuing investigation of the ICTY/ICTR Prosecutor up to the trial and further amendments regarding crime sites or incidents, exhibits, and witness lists pursuant to Rules 73*bis* (F) RPE ICTY and 73*bis* (E) RPE ICTR), 191–2 (discussing the continuous investigation under the ICC regime) and 212 (establishing as a rule that the 'prosecutor may continue his investigation after the confirmation of charges').

[1257] cf. Art. 54 (1)(a) ICCS; see Chapter II, B.(4) in this volume.

[1258] *Lubanga*, ICC-01/04-01/06-568, paras. 49, 51. See also Heinze, *Disclosure* (2014), pp. 524 ff.

[1259] See also *Lubanga*, ICC-01/04-01/06-568, para. 54 ('not a requirement of the Statute') and the Dissenting Opinions of Judges Eboe-Osujii and Fernández de Gurmendi, quoted in note 1276 in this chapter; also Whiting, *LCP*, 76 nos. 3 & 4 (2013), 164, 166–7.

[1260] In this sense, see ICC, *Prosecutor v. Gbagbo*, PTC I, Decision Adjourning the Hearing on the Confirmation of Charges pursuant to Article 61 (7)(c)(i) of the Rome Statute, ICC-02/11-01/11-432, 3 June 2013, para. 25; see also Schabas, Chaitidou, and El Zeidy, 'Article 61', in Ambos, *Commentary* (2022), mn. 46.

[1261] *Lubanga*, ICC-01/04-01/06-568, para. 54.

[1262] Ibid.

[1263] For a useful analysis, see Whiting, *LCP*, 76 no. 3 & 4 (2013), 168–73; also WCRO, *Confirmation* (2015), pp. 16 ff. (crit. analysing twelve cases up to the confirmation decision); crit. of this case law, Mariniello, *JICJ*, 13 (2015), 580 ff.

[1264] ICC, *Prosecutor v. Mbarushimana*, AC, Judgment on the Appeal of the Prosecutor against the Decision of Pre-Trial Chamber I of 16 December 2011 Entitled 'Decision on the confirmation of charges', ICC-01/04-01/10-514, 30 May 2012, para. 44 with n. 89 ('[A]s previously indicated by the Appeals Chamber').

[1265] *Mbarushimana*, ICC-01/04-01/10-514, para. 44.

[1266] The *Lubanga* AC did clearly *not*, as suggested by the *Mbarushimana* AC (*Mbarushimana*, ICC-01/04-01/10-514), '*indicate*' that 'the investigation should largely be completed at the stage of the confirmation of charges hearing'.

the issue in the different context of the evaluation of the (mostly written) evidence at the confirmation hearing.[1267] Nevertheless, subsequent PTC case law, basically relying on the *Mbarushimana* interpretation, essentially presumed that the prosecutorial investigation should be completed by the time of the confirmation hearing, absent some exceptional circumstances to be adduced by the prosecution.[1268] Only the majority of the *Kenyatta* TC took a more nuanced approach,[1269] with Judge Eboe-Osujii even advocating a more flexible position.[1270]

The future case law should, in line with the convincing *Lubanga* AC precedent, advocate the termination of the prosecutorial investigation by the time of the confirmation hearing as an aspirational goal but not a legal obligation. For this does not only reflect the law, but also duly takes account of the enormous difficulties faced by prosecutorial investigations into macrocriminal events and the dynamic nature of such investigations that makes any rigid termination date simply unreasonable.[1271] Of course, the right to continue the investigation

[1267] *Mbarushimana*, ICC-01/04-01/10-514, paras. 16 ff.

[1268] *Prosecutor v. Muthaura and Kenyatta*, PTC II (Single Judge Trendafilova), Decision Requesting Observations on the 'Prosecution's Request to Amend the Final Updated Document Containing the Charges Pursuant to Article 61 (9) of the Statute', ICC-01/09-02/11-614, 29 January 2013, para. 9 ('principled approach is that the Prosecutor should be ready with the investigation during said phase and any delay in doing so is exceptional and should be justified'); *Prosecutor v. Kenyatta*, PTC II (Single Judge Trendafilova), Corrigendum to 'Decision on the "Prosecution's Request to Amend the Final Updated Document Containing the Charges Pursuant to Article 61 (9) of the Statute"', ICC-01/09-02/11-700-Corr, 21 March 2013, para. 35 (while acknowledging that 'the Prosecutor is not barred from continuing her investigations post confirmation of charges hearing when there is a genuine need to pursue certain investigative activities crucial for her case and for the principal goal of determining the truth', in the same paragraph confirming that 'continuing investigations after the charges have been confirmed cannot be the rule, but rather the exception, and should be justified on a case-by-case basis'); *Gbagbo*, ICC-02/11-01/11-432, para. 25 ('Chamber must assume that the Prosecutor has presented her strongest possible case based on a *largely completed investigation*' [emphasis added]); *Prosecutor v. Gbagbo*, PTC I, Decision Adjourning the Hearing on the Confirmation of Charges, Dissenting Opinion of Judge Silvia Fernández de Gurmendi, ICC-02/11-01/11-432-Anx, 3 June 2013; *Prosecutor v. Al Hassan*, ICC-01/12-01/18-608-Red-tENG, paras. 53-4; in the same vein, Mettraux et al., *Effectiveness ICC* (2014), p. 9 (para. 13) and p. 66 (paras. 56–8) ('largely conclude primary investigations'); crit. of the requirement of the 'strongest possible case based on a largely completed investigation', Mariniello, *JICJ*, 13 (2015), 587–9, 591 ff.

[1269] *Prosecutor v. Kenyatta*, TC V, Decision on Defence Application pursuant to Article 64 (4) and Related Requests, ICC-01/09-02/11-728, 26 April 2013, paras. 119–21 (on the one hand acknowledging that there are 'no formal preconditions' (119) and 'the Prosecution is [not] prohibited from conducting further investigations after the confirmation stage' (120), indicating reasons for post-confirmation investigation; on the other hand arguing that 'under the procedural framework of the Statute, the Prosecution is expected to have largely completed its investigation prior to the confirmation hearing' (119) and 'that the Prosecution should not continue investigating post-confirmation for the purpose of collecting evidence which it could reasonably have been expected to have collected prior to confirmation' (121)).

[1270] *Prosecutor v. Kenyatta*, TC V, Decision on Defence Application pursuant to Article 64 (4) and Related Requests, Corrigendum of Concurring Separate Opinion of Judge Eboe-Osuji, ICC-01/09-02/11-728-Anx3-Corr2-Red, 2 May 2013, paras. 87 ff., expressing concern that majority position 'will presently undermine the Prosecutor's confidence in conducting post-confirmation investigations when she sees the need'; considering 'such a development is unjustifiable as a matter of law and inhospitable to substantive justice. Additionally, its sustainability is highly questionable as a matter of policy and practical implementation.' (87), demonstrating that the majority misreads AC precedents and correctly concluding that 'the AC's *ratio decidendi* in *Lubanga* remains the controlling law' (88–92), discussing the practicality of a limitation of post-confirmation investigation, especially with regard to the defence (93–100), and concluding that there is 'little justification in limiting the prosecutorial right to post-confirmation investigations as a matter of general principle that would permit such investigations only in "exceptional circumstances"' (100). In a similar vein, *Gbagbo*, ICC-02/11-01/11-432-Anx, paras. 12 ff., criticizing the majority's interpretation of the *Mbarushimana* AJ and keeping with the *Lubanga* AC Judgment, therefore considering it 'problematic that a policy objective [desirability of early completion of investigation] has been turned by the Majority into a legal requirement, something that cannot be done without amendments to the legal framework' (15).

[1271] For a detailed account of the 'realities of OTP investigations' at the ICC, see Whiting, *LCP*, 76 nos. 3 & 4 (2013), 173 ff. (discussing budget constraints, witness security, cooperation dependence, and the dynamic nature

post confirmation does not dispense the prosecution from its due diligence duty to exhaustively investigate any matter in line with the applicable standard of proof.[1272] The possibility of a continuous investigation does not exist to correct deficient or otherwise poor investigations.[1273] It is equally clear that it must not restrict essential defence rights.[1274]

### (9) Guilty plea versus 'admission of guilt'

'Negotiated justice' has long been an exclusive domain of common law jurisdictions,[1275] but for decades it has been creeping into the procedural systems of civil law countries.[1276] In international criminal procedure the move from the guilty plea (ad hoc tribunals) to an 'admission of guilt' (Article 65 ICCS) demonstrates, at first sight, once more the willingness to attempting a compromise between—from the perspective of ideal types—the settlement-friendly adversarial and the truth-focused inquisitorial approaches in criminal procedure.[1277]

of investigation, and therefore concluding that a too 'rigid and formalistic' insistence on completion up to the confirmation hearing 'presumes an unrealistic investigative practice' (165) and is 'unwise' (189)).

[1272] On the dependence of the prosecution case and the respective evidence on the standard of proof, see Whiting, *LCP*, 76 nos. 3 & 4 (2013), 165–6.

[1273] In a similar vein, de Meester, Pitcher, Rastan, and Sluiter, in Sluiter et al., *International Criminal Procedure* (2013), p. 212, referring to the parties' general duty of due diligence.

[1274] See also Whiting, *LCP*, 76 nos. 3 & 4 (2013), 164 (maintain 'essential procedural protections for the defense' and making it 'aware of the allegations against it sufficiently before trial to allow it to investigate and prepare'), 167 (provide defence 'with the results of the OTP's investigation with sufficient time to prepare'), 189 ('rights of the defense require that it know the case that it must answer').

[1275] Recall in particular the famous paper by John Langbein on Germany as the 'land without plea bargaining' in *MichLR*, 78 (1979), 204 ff. This was, of course, not even true in actual court practice at that time as famously denounced by an anonymous author (Detlef Deal) in the German journal *StV*, 2 (1982), 545. At any rate, plea bargaining is much more widespread in the USA, where more than 90 per cent of all criminal cases are decided by plea offers: see *Lafler v. Cooper*, 132 S. Ct. 1376, 1388 (2012) ('Ninety-seven percent of federal convictions and ninety-four percent of state convictions are the result of guilty pleas'); for more detail on the use of plea bargaining in the USA, see the recent critique by Schehr, *Tex. A&M L. R.*, 2 (2015), 385 ff.

[1276] See generally Tulkens, in Delmas-Marty and Spencer, *European Criminal Procedures* (2002), pp. 546 ff.; Turner and Weigend, in Sluiter et al., *International Criminal Procedure* (2013), pp. 1376, 1400 ff.; Turner and Weigend, in Ambos et al., *Core Concepts I* (2019), pp. 389 ff.; Heinze and Fyfe, in Ambos et al., *Core Concepts I* (2019), pp. 368–9; Vasiliev, in Cryer et al., *ICL* (2019), p. 435; Guariglia and Hochmayr, 'Article 65', in Ambos, *Commentary* (2022), mn. 4. Concretely on individual civil law jurisdictions, see regarding France, Ambroise-Casterot and Bonfils, *Procédure pénale* (2022), mn. 142–5; Bouloc, *Procédure pénale* (2022), mn. 777, 1079–80; Pradel, *Procédure Pénale* (2019), mn. 613–15, 879–80. Regarding Italy, see Maffei, *JICJ*, 2 (2004), 1067. On Germany, see s. 257c German StPO and Weigend and Turner, *GermanLJ*, 15 (2014), 81 ff., analysing this provision and the respective Constitutional Court decision; from a comparative law perspective (Germany–USA), see Trüg, *ZStW*, 120 (2008), 331 ff.; Kuczyńska, *Accusation Model ICC* (2015), pp. 244–61. On the shortened procedure in Swiss procedural law, see Gless, *Internationales Strafrecht* (2021), mn. 992. On the USA, see Schuon, *International Criminal Procedure* (2010), pp. 76 ff.

[1277] In this sense, interpreting Art. 65 ICCS as a compromise between common and civil law, see Combs, in Sluiter et al., *International Criminal Procedure* (2013), p. 688 ('mediate between ... common ... and civil law'); Turner and Weigend, in Sluiter et al., *International Criminal Procedure* (2013), p. 1389; Guariglia and Hochmayr, 'Article 65', in Ambos, *Commentary* (2022), mn. 10 ('third avenue'), 14 ('hybrid'); see also Fernández de Gurmendi, in Lee, *ICC* (1999), p. 223; Beltrán Montoliu, in Gómez Colomer et al., *CPI* (2003), p. 357.

### *(a) Ad hoc tribunals*

At the ad hoc tribunals,[1278] the guilty plea procedure was modelled after the common law approach,[1279] giving the accused in her initial appearance the possibility to enter a plea of guilty or not guilty with regard to each count.[1280] Interestingly though, plea-bargaining[1281] has only been introduced later.[1282] In case of a valid guilty plea, the proceedings would automatically be brought to a separate sentencing stage,[1283] whose only purpose is to determine the actual sentence of the defendant[1284] (now to be considered guilty). If the Chamber considers the plea invalid, it must reject it and allow the accused to re-plead.[1285] While there have been a series of guilty pleas at the ICTY and—less often—at the ICTR, nobody ever pleaded guilty at the SCSL.[1286]

The system came under attack in the (in)famous *Erdemović* case, where the accused formally pleaded guilty but at the same time claimed to have acted under duress.[1287] The TC initially accepted *Erdemović*'s guilty plea,[1288] but the AC overturned this decision setting out three preconditions for a valid guilty plea, that is, that it be voluntary, informed, and

1278 On the IMT and IMTFE, where a guilty plea was possible (Arts. 24 (b) IMTS, 15 (b) IMTFES), but never became practical (let alone any plea bargaining), see Combs, in Sluiter et al., *International Criminal Procedure* (2013), p. 683; Turner and Weigend, in Sluiter et al., *International Criminal Procedure* (2013), p. 1377. On the new mixed tribunals which either followed the ICTY/ICTR (STL) or the ICC (SPSC) or rejected a guilty plea altogether (ECCC), see Combs, in Sluiter et al., *International Criminal Procedure* (2013), p. 685; Turner and Weigend, in Sluiter et al., *International Criminal Procedure* (2013), pp. 1392–5. For the KSC following the ICC, see below note 1329 and main text.

1279 Schuon, *International Criminal Procedure* (2010), p. 196; Safferling, *Criminal Procedure* (2012), p. 438; Turner and Weigend, in Sluiter et al., *International Criminal Procedure* (2013), p. 1377; Vasiliev, in Cryer et al., *ICL* (2019), pp. 435-6. Generally on guilty plea before the ad hoc tribunals, see Kuczyńska, *Accusation Model ICC* (2015), pp. 266–76.

1280 cf. Art. 20 (3) ICTYS and Rule 62 (A)(iii)–(vi) RPE ICTY; Art. 19 (3) ICTRS, and Rule 62 (A)(iii)–(v) RPE ICTR; Rule 64 (A)(iii)–(iv), (B) and (C) MICT; Rule 61 (iii)–(v) RPE SCSL (no reference in the SCSL Statute).

1281 For a concise definition, see Carlson, in Christensen and Levi, *Criminal Justice* (2018), p. 131: 'Plea bargaining is the practice of encouraging defendants to plead guilty to a crime, thus invalidating the need to prove the defendant's guilt through a criminal trial.'

1282 See Rules 62*ter* (A) RPE ICTY; 62*bis* (A) RPE ICTR (adopted in 2001 and 2003 respectively); see also Rauxloh, *ICLR*, 10 (2010), 746; Burens, *ZIS*, 8 (2013), 327; Turner and Weigend, in Sluiter et al., *International Criminal Procedure* (2013), pp. 1377–8, all pointing, inter alia, to US Federal Judge McDonald's important role as President of the ICTY in introducing this practice.

1283 cf. Rules 62 (A)(vi) with 62*bis in fine* RPE ICTY; 62 (A)(v) with 62 (B) *in fine* RPE ICTR; 61 (v) with 62 (B) RPE SCSL; 64 (B) and (C) *in fine* RPE MICT; on the ICTY, see also Vohrah, in McDonald and Swaak-Goldman, *Substantive and Procedural Aspects* (2000), pp. 511 ff.; Scharf, *JICJ*, 2 (2004), 1072 ff.; Combs, in Sluiter et al., *International Criminal Procedure* (2013), p. 684.

1284 cf. Rules 100 RPE ICTY/ICTR/SCSL and 124 RPE MICT.

1285 Combs, in Sluiter et al., *International Criminal Procedure* (2013), p. 684.

1286 For an empirical analysis, see Meernik, *ICLR*, 14 (2014), 206–7 with table 1, showing that as of January 2013, 20 per cent or approx. 17 per cent of the ICTY accused and 9 per cent or approx. 13 per cent of the ICTR accused have pleaded guilty. See also Schuon, *International Criminal Procedure* (2010), pp. 200 ff.; Boas et al., *Procedure* (2011), p. 214; see also Zahar and Sluiter, *ICL* (2008), p. 42; Safferling, *Criminal Procedure* (2012), pp. 440–1 (both regarding ICTY); Rauxloh, *ICLR*, 10 (2010), 746–9, distinguishing three phases at the ICTY; Turner and Weigend, in Sluiter et al., *International Criminal Procedure* (2013), pp. 1377–8, 1383, referring in n. 7 to the only guilty plea at the SCSL, but in contempt proceedings; Guariglia and Hochmayr, 'Article 65', in Ambos, *Commentary* (2022), mn. 12–13 (ICTY/ICTR).

1287 Langer, *AJCompL*, *53* (2005), 864–5; Harmon, in Doria, Gasser, and Bassiouni, *Legal Regime* (2009), pp. 163 ff.; Turner and Weigend, in Sluiter et al., *International Criminal Procedure* (2013), pp. 1378–9; Carlson, *Model(ing) Justice* (2018), pp. 93 ff. (arguing that 'the appearance of Drazen *Erdemović*, in the person of a contrite, cooperative witness, and in the situation of participant in genocide ... was ... a fantastic stroke of luck for the fledgling institution. Yet when *Erdemović* cooperated with the ICTY, there was no procedure under the ICTY's rules that permitted a judicially meaningful admission of guilt'); Carlson, in Christensen and Levi, *Criminal Justice* (2018), pp. 132 ff. From a defence perspective, Dieckmann and O'Leary, in Rohan and Zyberi, *Defense Perspectives* (2017), pp. 272 ff.

1288 ICTY, *Prosecutor v. Erdemović*, Sentencing Judgment, IT-96-22-T, 29 November 1996, para. 10.

unequivocal.[1289] While the Chamber found that the plea was voluntary,[1290] and—despite Erdemović's invocation of duress—also unequivocal,[1291] it did not consider it informed, since Erdemović was apparently not fully aware of the consequences of the plea.[1292] The AC's requirements for a valid guilty plea have been subsequently adopted by the Rules of the ad hoc tribunals, adding as a fourth condition that there must be a 'sufficient factual basis for the crime and the accused's participation in it'.[1293] Conceptually, these requirements determine the 'formal' validity of a plea; its 'substantive' validity speaks to its role in the overall defence strategy.[1294] In actual practice, the different Chambers of the tribunals have adopted 'widely varying approaches' in satisfying themselves that the said requirements have been met.[1295]

In procedural terms, the parties may conclude a plea agreement—normally at the pre-trial stage[1296]—which enables the Prosecutor 'to amend the indictment accordingly' and apply for 'a specific sentence or sentencing range', and obliges her to 'not oppose' a respective request of the accused.[1297] With the introduction of this quite precise framework, the judges considerably restricted the parties' negotiating powers, especially as compared to the broad charge and sentence bargaining practices known from common law systems.[1298] The ensuing plea agreements may be quite detailed;[1299] normally, they entail the exchange of the guilty plea for the withdrawal of charges and sentencing recommendations of the Prosecutor.[1300] As a rule, the agreements shall be disclosed in open session, exceptionally in closed session.[1301] In any case, the TC is not bound by such an—inter-party—agreement,[1302] since 'its fundamental obligation is [in line with the fourth condition of a valid plea mentioned above] to

[1289] ICTY, *Prosecutor v. Erdemović*, AC Judgment, IT-96-22-A, 7 October 1997, paras. 18–20. See the analysis of Carlson, *Model(ing) Justice* (2018), pp. 96–7.

[1290] *Erdemović*, IT-96-22-A, para. 18 (unanimous decision by all five judges).

[1291] Ibid., para. 19 and Disposition, (4). This part of the decision was taken by three votes (Judges McDonald, Li, and Vohrah) to two (Judges Cassese and Stephen), the majority arguing that duress does not constitute a complete defence in the case of the killing of innocent persons and that therefore the plea was unequivocal. For a discussion of this highly contentious finding, see Ambos, *Treatise ICL I* (2021), pp. 466–9.

[1292] *Erdemović*, IT-96-22-A, para. 20. This part of the decision was taken by four votes to one (Judge Li), see Ibid., Disposition, (3).

[1293] cf. Rules 62*bis* ICTY RPE, 62 (B) ICTR RPE, 62 (A) SCSL RPE. This requirement has been first mentioned in *Erdemović*, IT-96-22-A, Separate and Dissenting Opinion of Judge Cassese, para. 10.

[1294] For this distinction, see *Erdemović*, IT-96-22-T, paras. 11, 13; conc. Boas et al., *Procedure* (2011), p. 215.

[1295] cf. Rauxloh, *ICLR*, 10 (2010), 754–61, criticizing that 'judges are not very diligent in investigation the validity of a guilty plea' and pursue a 'hodgepodge' (Cook) approach; Boas et al., *Procedure* (2011), p. 221 (from brief 'one- or two-word responses to broad inquiries' and 'detailed questions' to the accused); Turner and Weigend, in Sluiter et al., *International Criminal Procedure* (2013), pp. 1379–83 (esp. 1381); Carlson, *Model(ing) Justice* (2018), pp. 159 ff.; Vriend, *Criminal Trial* (2016), pp. 143 ff.

[1296] But parties are not precluded from concluding them during trial; cf. Turner and Weigend, in Sluiter et al., *International Criminal Procedure* (2013), p. 1384.

[1297] Rules 62*ter* (A) RPE ICTY; 62*bis* (A) RPE ICTR; 65 (A) RPE MICT.

[1298] cf. Boas et al., *Procedure* (2011), pp. 221–2; Turner and Weigend, in Sluiter et al., *International Criminal Procedure* (2013), p. 1385 (esp. pointing to the limitation of 'fact bargaining').

[1299] See e.g. the agreement reached in ICTY, *Prosecutor v. Sikirica et al.*, TC, Sentencing Judgment, IT-95-8-S, 13 November 2001, paras. 17 ff. ; ICTY, *Prosecutor v. M. Jokić*, AC, Judgment on Sentencing Appeal, IT-01-42/1-A, 30 August 2005, paras. 9 ff. ; see also Gallagher, *LJIL*, 18 (2005), 526–7; on the ICTY practice, see Tieger and Shin, *JICJ*, 3 (2005), 666 ff.; on the ICTR and East Timor Special Panels, see Othman, *Accountability for International Humanitarian Law Violations* (2005), pp. 299 ff.; on both ICTY and ICTR, see Boas et al., *Procedure* (2011), pp. 222–3, giving various examples and stating that the convicts have sometimes not fulfilled 'their end of the bargain'.

[1300] For more details on the contents, see Turner and Weigend, in Sluiter et al., *International Criminal Procedure* (2013), pp. 1384–6.

[1301] Rules 62*ter* (C) RPE ICTY; 62*bis* (C) RPE ICTR; 65 (C) RPE MICT. See also Turner and Weigend, in Sluiter et al., *International Criminal Procedure* (2013), p. 1384.

[1302] Rules 62*ter* (B) RPE ICTY; 62*bis* (B) RPE ICTR; 65 (B) RPE MICT. See also Turner and Weigend, in Sluiter et al., *International Criminal Procedure* (2013), pp. 1384 ('unlimited discretion'), 1387–8, 1397–8; calling for binding plea agreements, Pittmann, *HuV-I*, 20 (2007), 157.

ensure that there is a sufficient factual basis for the crime and the accused's participation in it'.[1303] It is for this reason that the prosecution normally submits an additional document setting out the factual basis of the plea agreement.[1304] Only if it enters a finding of guilt the Chamber must consider the agreement and draw on it when determining the sentence to be imposed.[1305]

In fact, however, both ICTY and ICTR Chambers have in some cases, albeit not the majority,[1306] imposed higher sentences than expected (and agreed) by the accused,[1307] and it was found, in an empirical study, that 'there is a reasonable, if not significant, doubt that plea bargains lead to lighter sentences'.[1308] At any rate, given the crucial importance of the certainty of sentencing discounts within the framework of negotiated justice,[1309] it is not surprising that the countervailing sentencing practice of some (civil law) judges considerably reduced the attractiveness of guilty pleas. A case in point is the *Kambanda* case before the ICTR, where the defendant ended with a life sentence despite a guilty plea.[1310] Unsurprisingly, this led to a much lower number of guilty pleas at the ICTR[1311] (ten in total)[1312] as compared to the ICTY (twenty).[1313]

[1303] *Sikirica et al.*, IT-95-8-S, para. 48.

[1304] cf. Turner and Weigend, in Sluiter et al., *International Criminal Procedure* (2013), p. 1382.

[1305] ICTY, *Prosecutor v. Jelisić*, AC, Judgment, IT-95-10-A, 5 July 2001, para. 87; *Sikirica et al.*, IT-95-8-S, para. 49.

[1306] cf. Meernik, *ICLR*, 14 (2014), 203 (defendants 'usually' sentenced within expected range); Turner and Weigend, in Sluiter et al., *International Criminal Procedure* (2013), p. 1388–9, 1398 (on average one-third reduction); Guariglia and Hochmayr, 'Article 65', in Ambos, *Commentary* (2022), mn. 12 (at ICTY majority of sentences within agreed framework).

[1307] cf. Boas et al., *Procedure* (2011), p. 224 with further references; Turner and Weigend, in Sluiter et al., *International Criminal Procedure* (2013), p. 1378; crit. of this practice of the tribunals, Kuczyńska, *Accusation Model ICC* (2015), pp. 282–3.

[1308] Meernik, *ICLR, 14* (2014), 216 (drawing on a nuanced statistical analysis taking into account several variables); Turner, *McGeorge L.Rev.*, 48 (2017), 238–9 (smaller discounts than in national systems). On the guilty plea as a mitigating factor within the framework of sentencing, see also Ambos, *Treatise ICL II* (2022), pp. 339–43 with further references.

[1309] cf. Combs, *VanderbiltLR*, 59 (2006), 75 ('to induce such a defendant to plead guilty, a prosecutor must be able to offer the defendant a fairly certain sentence reduction in exchange for his guilty plea'), 92–100 (100: 'Now that the recommendations no longer provide that certainty, ICTY defendants apparently prefer to take their chances on a trial'); Combs, *Guilty Pleas in International Criminal Law* (2007), pp. 89–90 ('it is only through the chambers' adherence to the prosecution's recommendations that the promise of a particular recommendation will persuade defendants to plead guilty'); see also Turner and Weigend, in Sluiter et al., *International Criminal Procedure* (2013), p. 1378; Vasiliev, in Cryer et al., *ICL* (2019), pp. 435–6.

[1310] *Prosecutor v. Kambanda*, TC, Judgment and Sentence, ICTR 97-23-S, 4 September 1998, paras. 3–7. Kambanda tried then to withdraw his guilty plea but his appeal was unanimously rejected, cf. ICTR, *Prosecutor v. Kambanda*, AC, Judgment, ICTR-97-23-A, 19 October 2000, paras. 49–95; thereto Zyberi, in Rohan and Zyberi, *Defense Perspectives* (2017), p. 128.

[1311] Explaining this with the *Kambanda* precedent Rauxloh, *ICLR*, 10 (2010), 762–3; Boas et al., *Procedure* (2011), p. 224; Burens, *ZIS*, 8 (2013), 328; Meernik, *ICLR*, 14 (2014), 208; see also Turner and Weigend, in Sluiter et al., *International Criminal Procedure* (2013), p. 1378 (indicating, albeit erroneously, that since 2007 no further guilty pleas have been entered at either tribunal); Guariglia and Hochmayr, 'Article 65', in Ambos, *Commentary* (2022), mn. 12. Note however that there may be multiple (other) reasons why a defendant enters a guilty plea and therefore a clear causality is difficult to establish; cf. see thereon Meernik, *ICLR*, 14 (2014), 201.

[1312] Apart from *Kambanda* just quoted, see ICTR, *Prosecutor v. Bagaragaza*, TC III, Sentencing Judgment, ICTR-05-86-S, 17 November 2009, paras. 8, 10–11, 14–16; *Bisengimana*, TC II, ICTR-00-60-T, 13 April 2006, paras. 12, 19–25; *Nzabirinda*, TC II, Sentencing Judgment, ICTR-2001-77-T, 23 February 2007, paras. 7–14; *Rugambarara*, TC II, Sentencing Judgment, ICTR-00-59-T, 16 November 2007, paras. 4–9; *Ruggiu*, TC I, Judgment and Sentence, ICTR-97-32-I, 11 April 2000, paras. 7, 10; *Rutaganira*, TC III, Judgment and Sentence, ICTR-95-1C-T, 14 March 2005, paras. 27–30; *Serugendo*, TC I, Judgment and Sentence, ICTR-2005-84-1, 12 June 2006, paras. 2–11; *Serushago*, TC I, Sentence, ICTR-98-39-S, 5 February 1999, paras. 4–9; *GAA*, TC III, Judgment and Sentence, ICTR-07-90-R77-I, 4 December 2007, paras. 2–4. See also ICC-OTP, *Guidelines Admission of Guilt* (2020), para. 2.

[1313] UN, International Criminal Tribunal for the former Yugoslavia, *Guilty Pleas*, <https://www.icty.org/en/cases/guilty-pleas>. See also Hodge, *Balkans* (2019), p. 257 (listing the respective defendants); Carlson, in

### (b) *International Criminal Court*

#### (i) *Preliminary remarks*

The ICC law, albeit partly based on the *Erdemović*-precedent[1314] and the Rules mentioned, is fundamentally different from the law of the ad hoc tribunals in that it does not recognize a 'guilty plea' as such,[1315] but only an 'admission of guilt' which—despite the terminological similarity[1316]—rather resembles a (non-binding) 'confession'[1317] as known from civil law jurisdictions[1318] (and recently followed by the KSC[1319]). For, in procedural terms, an accused at the ICC is not asked to plead guilty or not guilty, but only afforded 'the opportunity to make an admission of guilt'[1320] at the commencement of the trial,[1321] that is, once the charges are confirmed.[1322] Note, however, that the accused is not prevented from making an admission of guilt at a later stage in the proceedings,[1323] which enables the TC to trigger abbreviated proceedings under Article 65 (2) or (4)(a) ICCS.[1324]

Article 65 ICCS basically leaves the decision on the acceptance of the accused's admission to the TC and thus opts for a cautious judge-led or at least judge-controlled approach.[1325]

Christensen and Levi, *Criminal Justice* (2018), pp. 138 ff.; Zyberi, in Rohan and Zyberi, *Defense Perspectives* (2017), p. 116. At the SCSL guilty pleas have only been made in contempt proceedings, cf. SCSL, *Independent Counsel v. Brima et al.*, TC I, Sentencing Judgment in Contempt Proceedings, SCSL 05-02-119-132, 21 September 2005, the four accused in the case pleaded guilty, and SCSL, *Independent Counsel v. Bangura et al.*, TC II, Sentencing Judgment in Contempt Proceedings, SCSL 11-02-T-071, 11 October 2012, the accused Kargbo pleaded guilty.

1314 cf. Behrens, in Lee, *ICC* (1999), pp. 241–2.

1315 See also Boas et al., *Procedure* (2011), p. 225; Safferling, *Criminal Procedure* (2012), p. 439; Bitti, 'Article 64', in Ambos, *Commentary* (2022), mn. 56; Kuczyńska, *Accusation Model ICC* (2015), pp. 283–8; for a more nuanced view, see Friman, in Cryer et al., *ICL* (2014), p. 471 ('provision does not prevent plea bargaining as such'), and Vasiliev, in Cryer et al., *ICL* (2019), p. 436 ('leaves scope for agreements between parties'). See also ICC-OTP, *Guidelines Admission of Guilt* (2020), para. 1: 'Article 65 uses the term "admission of guilt" (rather than "guilty plea") and prescribes an abbreviated trial procedure by which the Trial Chamber may accept, or reject, the admission of guilt.'

1316 See the definition of 'guilty plea' as a 'formal admission in court of having committed the charged offense', in Garner, *Dictionary* (2019), p. 1393.

1317 On the distinction, see Turner and Weigend, in Sluiter et al., *International Criminal Procedure* (2013), p. 1376 (confession as statement of fact part of the evidence, guilty plea as 'procedural declaration without factual content'), similarly p. 1392.

1318 cf. Safferling, *Criminal Procedure* (2012), p. 440 (but see also p. 445: 'not a confession in the Continental European sense'); Burens, *ZIS*, 8 (2013), 332; Vasiliev, in Cryer et al., *ICL* (2019), p. 436 ('leans more towards the civil-law view that a confession is merely one piece of evidence'); see also Orie, in Cassese et al., *Rome Statute II* (2002), p. 1481; Swart, *JICJ*, 6 (2008), 107. But see also Guariglia and Hochmayr, 'Article 65', in Ambos, *Commentary* (2022), mn. 10 ('between the classic "common law" and "civil law" approaches').

1319 cf. Rule 93 RPE KSC. See also previously s. 29A of Transitional Rules of Criminal Procedure (UNTAET/REG/2000/30 (25 September 2000) as amended by 2001/25 (14 September 2001)); thereon Sluiter, in Stahn and van den Herik, *Perspectives* (2010), p. 594.

1320 The admission has to be made personally; cf. Guariglia and Hochmayr, 'Article 65', in Ambos, *Commentary* (2022), mn. 17. This, however, still leaves room for written agreements, see *Al Mahdi*, ICC 01/12-01/15-171, para. 30; Bishop-Burney, *AJIL*, 111 (2017), 126, 130.

1321 Art. 64 (8)(a) ICCS.

1322 Given the fact that the admission has as its object of reference the charges it would not make sense to admit any charges, which have not yet been confirmed; also, the PTC is not competent to receive an admission of guilt since it is not mentioned in Arts. 64 (8)(a), 65 (but only the TC); on the other hand, it is perfectly possible that the accused admits charges after the commencement of the trial; cf. Safferling, *Criminal Procedure* (2012), pp. 443–4; Guariglia and Hochmayr, 'Article 65', in Ambos, *Commentary* (2022), mn. 16, 18. On the controversy whether the opportunity to make the admission should already be given at the first status conference before the TC, see Bitti, 'Article 64', in Ambos, *Commentary* (2022), mn. 56.

1323 Conc. Schabas, *ICC Commentary* (2016), pp. 997–8.

1324 Guariglia and Hochmayr, 'Article 65', in Ambos, *Commentary* (2022), mn. 16.

1325 See also Turner and Weigend, in Sluiter et al., *International Criminal Procedure* (2013), p. 1396 ('greater role for judges'); in favour, Safferling, *Criminal Procedure* (2012), p. 442 ('luckily a rather cautious approach'); Combs, in Sluiter et al., *International Criminal Procedure* (2013), p. 688 (recommending this approach); Dieckmann and O'Leary, in Rohan and Zyberi, *Defense Perspectives* (2017), p. 273.

In fact, it is explicitly stated that the 'Court' is not in any way bound by '[a]ny discussions' between the parties 'regarding modification of the charges, the admission of guilt or the penalty to be imposed'.[1326] Of course, the very reference to such 'discussions' presupposes that negotiations between the Prosecutor and the defence are not ruled out[1327] and the OTP emphasizes the 'significant advantages' of the resulting agreements.[1328]

Interestingly, in the first and so far only Article 65 case of *Ahmad Al Faqi Al Mahdi*[1329] TC VIII emphasized the implications of an admission of guilt for the goals of the Court, invoking most ambitious policy aspirations: Al Mahdi's admission of guilt 'may also further peace and reconciliation in Northern Mali by alleviating the victims' moral suffering through acknowledgement of the significance of the destruction' and 'may have a deterrent effect on others tempted to commit similar acts in Mali and elsewhere'.[1330] Moreover, from the perspective of special prevention,[1331] his admission demonstrated 'that he is likely to successfully reintegrate into society'.[1332] Arguably, the Chamber's approach does not only underline the Janus-faced nature of the admission of guilt procedure between expediency and truth-seeking, or—more broadly—between *Realpolitik* and *Idealpolitik*, it also gives a taste of what the Court is determined to do to convince its critics that it can operate expediently and fairly at the same time. This may motivate other accused to admit guilt to avoid a lengthy trial and a high sentence in return[1333] although so far no further Article 65 proceedings have taken place. One reason may be that the necessary unequivocal evidence (to the detriment of the accused) is the exception rather than the rule.[1334] At any rate, the *Al Mahdi* case should not be underestimated in its communicative effect[1335] on all those who are willing to reintegrate into society after having been involved in an armed conflict and the accompanying atrocities.[1336]

*(ii) Article 65 ICCS*

According to the core part of the provision the Chamber:

[1326] Art. 65 (5) ICCS and ICC-OTP, *Guidelines Admission of Guilt* (2020), paras. 7, 13. This corresponds to the situation in comparative law; see Turner and Weigend, in Sluiter et al., *International Criminal Procedure* (2013), pp. 1404–5. The non-binding nature has considerable impact on defence tactics, see for an analysis (with concrete guidelines for defence counsel) by Dieckmann and O'Leary, in Rohan and Zyberi, *Defense Perspectives* (2017), pp. 274–5.

[1327] Guariglia and Hochmayr, 'Article 65', in Ambos, *Commentary* (2022), mn. 40; conc. Safferling, *Criminal Procedure* (2012), p. 442; Turner and Weigend, in Sluiter et al., *International Criminal Procedure* (2013), p. 1390.

[1328] ICC-OTP, *Guidelines Admission of Guilt* (2020), para. 8 ('Such agreements, which have preceded most of the guilty pleas at the *ad hoc* tribunals, have a number of significant advantages').

[1329] The case dealt with the destruction of ten sites of historical, religious, and cultural significance in Timbuktu, Mali, charged under Art. 8 (2)(e)(iv) ICCS (on that, in more detail, Ambos, *Treatise ICL II* (2022), pp. 182–3; Kersten, in deGuzman and Oosterveld, *Elgar Companion ICC* (2020), pp. 185 ff.). *Al Mahdi* declared in a closed confirmation hearing on 1 March 2016 his intent to enter a guilty plea and then entered this plea before the TC on 22 August 2016 (about the plea itself in more detail, see Casaly, *JICJ*, 14 (2016), 1217–18). As a result, the shortest trial in the history of the ICC (Cole, *TempleICLJ*, 31 (2017), 446; Guariglia and Hochmayr, 'Article 65', in Ambos, *Commentary* (2022), mn. 21; Gumpert and Nuzban, in Heinze and Dittrich, *ICC* (2021), p. 559) produced a judgment of merely forty-nine pages.

[1330] *Al Mahdi*, ICC-01/12-01/15-171, para. 100. See also Guariglia and Hochmayr, 'Article 65', in Ambos, *Commentary* (2022), mn. 8.

[1331] About special prevention as a goal of international criminal justice, see Ambos, *Treatise ICL I* (2021), p. 120.

[1332] *Al Mahdi*, ICC-01/12-01/15-171, para. 97.

[1333] See Karnavas, *International Criminal Law Blog* 30 August 2016.

[1334] Suhr, *Völkerrechtsblog* 3 October 2016.

[1335] In more detail, see Ambos, *Treatise ICL I* (2021), pp. 122–3.

[1336] Ambos and Heinze, in Bergsmo, *Abbreviated Criminal Procedures* (2017), pp. 98–100.

1. ... shall determine whether:
   (a) The accused understands the nature and consequences of the admission of guilt;
   (b) The admission is voluntarily made by the accused after sufficient consultation with defence counsel; and
   (c) The admission of guilt is supported by the facts of the case that are contained in:
      (i) The charges brought by the Prosecutor and admitted by the accused;
      (ii) Any materials presented by the Prosecutor which supplement the charges and which the accused accepts; and
      (iii) Any other evidence, such as the testimony of witnesses, presented by the Prosecutor or the accused.

*Subparagraph (a)* is most clearly based on the *Erdemović* precedent with the AC's holding, regarding the informed requirement, that the accused must understand the nature of the charges and the consequences of a guilty plea, including the nature and distinction between alternative charges.[1337] Thus, the accused must understand, on the one hand, the nature of the charges, that is, the interplay between factual and legal elements, the distinction between alternative charges, and the possible penalties arising from these charges.[1338] On the other hand, the accused must understand the procedural 'consequences', that is, she must be aware of the ensuing waiver of procedural rights, especially regarding the *nemo-tenetur* right.[1339] While it is upon the TC to 'determine' that the accused understands all this, the defence has an important role to play here in sufficiently informing the accused.[1340] At any rate, a waiver should not be read as precluding the accused from making submissions at the sentencing stage,[1341] nor does the accused forgo his right to appeal.[1342] The ICC law is silent on this matter but this right is too important to be lost without further ado, that is, an explicit provision to that effect or, at least, an explicit waiver of this right[1343] as part of a comprehensive

[1337] *Erdemović*, IT-96-22-A, para. 18 in relation with *Erdemović*, IT-96-22-A, Joint Separate Opinion of Judges McDonald and Vohrah, para. 14 ('an informed plea would require that the Appellant understand (a) the nature of the charges against him and the consequences of pleading guilty generally; and (b) the nature and distinction between the alternative charges and the consequences of pleading guilty to one rather than the other'); *Kambanda*, ICTR-97-23-A, para. 75, explicitly referring to 'the standard ... articulated by Judges McDonald and Vohrah in Erdemović'; *Al Mahdi*, ICC-01/12-01/15-171, para. 42.

[1338] cf. Guariglia and Hochmayr, 'Article 65', in Ambos, *Commentary* (2022), mn. 23–5; Turner, 'Article 65' in Klamberg, *Commentary ICC II* (2023), pp. 224–5; also Turner and Weigend, in Sluiter et al., *International Criminal Procedure* (2013), pp. 1380–1, pointing, at 1380, to the *Kunarac* TC's rejection of a plea since the accused did not understand the nature of rape as a crime against humanity. See also ICC-OTP, *Guidelines Admission of Guilt* (2020), para. 4.

[1339] Safferling, *Criminal Procedure* (2012), p. 445; Turner and Weigend, in Sluiter et al., *International Criminal Procedure* (2013), pp. 1380–1, criticizing that the ad hoc tribunals have not always established whether the accused understands these waivers; Guariglia and Hochmayr, 'Article 65', in Ambos, *Commentary* (2022), mn. 22, 25. On *nemo tenetur*, see Chapter I, D.(2)(a) and (b) in this volume.

[1340] cf. ICC, *Prosecutor v. Al Mahdi*, TC VIII, ICC-01/12-01/15-T-3-Red-ENG WT 24-05-2016 1-26 SZ T, ICC-01/12-01/15-T-3-Red-ENG, 24 May 2016, p. 22 ll. 20–5 (TC VIII asking the defence in a status conference to confirm that they discussed with the accused: 'The rights that the accused is waiving by making an admission of guilt, that's the first; any possible defences that he may have; the maximum sentence that could be imposed by the Chamber; the possibility of having an order issued against him for reparations; and the fact that the Chamber is not required to accept the admission of guilt or the recommended sentencing range, that covers the range—the nature and consequences of the admission').

[1341] In the same vein, Guariglia and Hochmayr, 'Article 65', in Ambos, *Commentary* (2022), mn. 25.

[1342] Apparently undecided, Guariglia and Hochmayr, 'Article 65', in Ambos, *Commentary* (2022), mn. 26 (requiring at any case full information of the accused).

[1343] Germain Katanga discontinued his appeal against the TJ of 7 March 2014 and waived his right to appeal against the Sentencing Judgment of 23 May 2014; see ICC, *Prosecutor v. Katanga*, Defence Notice of Discontinuance of Appeal, ICC-01/04-01/07-3497, 25 June 2014; ICC, *Prosecutor v. Katanga*, Notice of Discontinuance of the Prosecution's Appeal against the Article 74 Judgment of Conviction of Trial Chamber II dated 7 March 2014 in

plea agreement would be necessary.[1344] To be sure, human rights law does not prohibit the respective waiver if it has been informed, voluntary, and unequivocal.[1345] According to the OTP Guidelines regarding Admission of Guilt a waiver of appeal 'should generally be subject to an exception preserving the parties' ability to appeal sentences outside a range specified in the agreement, and shall preserve the parties' rights to appeal any error that manifestly undermines the fairness of the proceedings.'[1346] Al Mahdi waived his right to 'appeal a conviction or sentence, provided the sentence is not in excess of the recommended sentencing range',[1347] which the TC admitted.[1348]

As to *subparagraph (b)*, the ICTY/ICTR AC has established two elements with regard to the 'voluntary' requirement, namely that the accused must be mentally sufficiently fit to understand the consequences of the plea and that it must not have resulted from any undue pressure.[1349] While the former element is already covered by subparagraph (a)—a mentally unfit accused[1350] cannot understand the 'nature and consequences' of his admission—the latter represents the core of the voluntary requirement and, at the same time, the 'weak spot of any system of bargaining'.[1351] Thus, the accused must be free from any form of coercion or improper promise when making the admission of guilt.[1352] While the unfulfilled expectation of a lower sentence does not qualify as an improper promise,[1353] any undue pressure or promise of the investigative authorities does;[1354] such pressure can also be exerted by

relation to Germain Katanga, ICC-01/04-01/07-3498, 25 June 2014. In his personal notification attached as Annex A ('notification du retrait') to the defence notice Katanga confirms the notice and assures that he is 'pleinemeint informé par son conseil des conséquences juridiques de cette decision', especially of the fact that 'il est censé avoir volontairement abandonné son droit d'interjeter appel'.

[1344] On the ad hoc tribunals insofar, see Turner and Weigend, in Sluiter et al., *International Criminal Procedure* (2013), p. 1385, where such waivers have never been challenged but are also more limited as comparable waivers at national level.

[1345] cf. Turner and Weigend, in Sluiter et al., *International Criminal Procedure* (2013), p. 1400; also Combs, in Sluiter et al., *International Criminal Procedure* (2013), p. 688. National law may explicitly prohibit such a waiver (cf. e.g. s. 302 (1) cl. 2 German CPC [StPO]), but this does not seem to be the majority position (Turner and Weigend, in Sluiter et al., *International Criminal Procedure* (2013), pp. 1403, 1408–9).

[1346] ICC-OTP, *Guidelines Admission of Guilt* (2020), para. 12.

[1347] TC VIII treated *Al Mahdi's* admission of guilt—in the tradition of the civil law system—as a mitigating factor, citing ICTY case law, and imposed with nine years the lowest sentence imposed thus far; *Al Mahdi*, ICC-01/12-01/15-171, para. 100.

[1348] *Al Mahdi*, ICC-01/12-01/15-171, para. 30; thereto Guariglia and Hochmayr, 'Article 65', in Ambos, *Commentary* (2022), mn. 26.

[1349] cf. *Erdemović*, IT-96-22-A, para. 18 in relation with *Erdemović*, IT-96-22-A, Joint Separate Opinion of Judges McDonald and Vohrah, para. 10 ('Voluntariness involves two elements. Firstly, an accused person must have been mentally competent to understand the consequences of his actions when pleading guilty ... Secondly, the plea must not have been the result of any threat or inducement other than the expectation of receiving credit for a guilty plea by way of some reduction of sentence'); *Kambanda*, ICTR-97-23-A, para. 61, holding that '[n]o pressure must have been brought to bear upon [on the accused] to sign the plea agreement'. Summarizing, Boas et al., *Procedure* (2011), pp. 217–18; Turner and Weigend, in Sluiter et al., *International Criminal Procedure* (2013), pp. 1379–80.

[1350] This corresponds, as a rule, to the required fitness to stand trial although not completely, cf. Turner and Weigend, in Sluiter et al., *International Criminal Procedure* (2013), p. 1379, discussing contradicting expert opinions as to the fitness to stand trial.

[1351] Turner and Weigend, in Sluiter et al., *International Criminal Procedure* (2013), pp. 1403 (from a comparative perspective), 1409 ('critical issue' from a human rights perspective).

[1352] Safferling, *Criminal Procedure* (2012), p. 445; Guariglia and Hochmayr, 'Article 65', in Ambos, *Commentary* (2022), mn. 28.

[1353] *Kambanda*, ICTR-97-23-A, para. 63 ('If the Appellant pleaded guilty instead of going to trial in the hope of receiving a lighter sentence, he cannot claim that the plea was involuntary merely because he received a life-term after pleading guilty to several counts of genocide and crimes against humanity.')

[1354] cf. ECtHR, *Deweer v. Belgium*, Judgment, 6903/75, 27 February 1980, paras. 50–4 (threat by Prosecutor with a heavy fine and closure of company) ('the applicant waived the guarantees of Article 6 par. 1 (art. 6-1) only

excessive charge and sentencing differences.[1355] The further requirement of sufficient consultation with counsel—one of the two differences to the Rules of the ad hoc tribunals[1356]—is meant to reinforce the voluntariness in that the accused is made fully aware[1357] of the consequences by counsel and also protected against undue pressure.[1358] It depends on the circumstances of each case if the accused was sufficiently advised by counsel.[1359]

*Subparagraph (c)* refers to three different situations regarding the factual basis of the admission. It obliges the Chamber to embark upon a 'trial-factual basis-procedure',[1360] carefully inquiring into the facts supporting the admission, that is, the facts as contained in the charges (lit. (i)), the 'materials presented by the Prosecutor' (lit. (ii)), and 'any other evidence' (lit. (iii)).[1361] All *literae* refer to the facts 'supporting' the charges within the meaning of Article 61 (3)(b) ICCS, not merely 'supplementing' them as wrongly suggested in lit. (ii).[1362] This already follows from the chapeau of subparagraph (c), referring to the 'admission … supported by the facts'. As can be inferred from the practice of the ad hoc tribunals,[1363] it may often not be easy to properly establish the factual basis of the admission. It is upon the prosecution to produce the relevant evidence and facts—perhaps in a separate document, different from the actual plea agreement[1364]—so that the Chamber can take an informed decision. While Rule 63 (4) RPE ICC generally rejects any kind of corroboration requirement,[1365] the 'materials' to be 'presented by the Prosecutor which supplement the charges' (within the meaning of subparagraph (c)(ii)) serve to corroborate the charges and the accused's admission (within the meaning of subparagraph (c)(i)).[1366] Thus, the *Al Mahdi* TC, while acknowledging that 'there is no corroboration requirement when assessing evidence', focused on 'whether evidence could establish the facts independently of the Accused's admissions',[1367] i.e. it relied on the accused's admission as confirmed by the supplementary material of the Prosecutor and witness testimony.[1368] Despite the differences to the Rules of the ad hoc tribunals, the requirements set out in Article 65 (1) ICCS are

"under the threat of [the] serious prejudice" that the closure of his shop would have caused him'); Guariglia and Hochmayr, 'Article 65', in Ambos, *Commentary* (2022), mn. 44 (promise of Prosecutor she is not able to fulfil).

[1355] For this reason the ICC should establish a framework of permissible charge and sentence reductions, cf. Turner and Weigend, in Sluiter et al., *International Criminal Procedure* (2013), p. 1412. See also Guariglia and Hochmayr, 'Article 65', in Ambos, *Commentary* (2022), mn. 28 (referring to the previous volume of this Treatise in note 89).

[1356] The other one is the omission of the requirement of an 'unequivocal' admission. This was relevant in the above discussed *Erdemović* case, but the situation of the invocation of a defence may also be covered by the subparas. (a) and (b) of Art. 65 (1); see also Boas et al., *Procedure* (2011), pp. 219, 226; Guariglia and Hochmayr, 'Article 65', in Ambos, *Commentary* (2022), mn. 27 (covered by subpara. (a)); considering this requirement as a 'generally accepted principle', Turner and Weigend, in Sluiter et al., *International Criminal Procedure* (2013), p. 1403.

[1357] On the importance of advice by counsel to obtain the necessary knowledge, see Turner and Weigend, in Sluiter et al., *International Criminal Procedure* (2013), p. 1402.

[1358] cf. Safferling, *Criminal Procedure* (2012), p. 445; Turner and Weigend, in Sluiter et al., *International Criminal Procedure* (2013), p. 1399.

[1359] cf. Safferling, *Criminal Procedure* (2012), p. 445.

[1360] Guariglia and Hochmayr, 'Article 65', in Ambos, *Commentary* (2022), mn. 30.

[1361] Stressing the difference between the groups of evidence referred to in lit. (ii) and (iii), see Guariglia and Hochmayr, 'Article 65', in Ambos, *Commentary* (2022), mn. 31.

[1362] Guariglia and Hochmayr, 'Article 65', in Ambos, *Commentary* (2022), mn. 31 with n. 96.

[1363] cf. Turner and Weigend, in Sluiter et al., *International Criminal Procedure* (2013), pp. 1382–3.

[1364] See note 1312 and main text in this chapter.

[1365] On the definition of corroboration evidence see Chapter V, A.(3)(b).

[1366] See also Guariglia and Hochmayr, 'Article 65', in Ambos, *Commentary* (2022), mn. 31 with n. 96 (inter alia referring to this volume).

[1367] *Al Mahdi*, ICC-01/12-01/15-171, para. 29 *in fine*.

[1368] cf. *Al Mahdi*, ICC-01/12-01/15-171, para. 29: 'For each of the established facts, the Chamber has relied upon: (i) the admissions of the Accused; (ii) the supplementary material presented by the Prosecution

essentially identical.[1369] It is also to be expected that admissions of guilt will be laid down in (written)[1370] plea agreements,[1371] as indeed was done in *Al-Mahdi*.[1372] Such agreements should contain more than a plain admission—a mere affirmation of the charges—that is, a detailed admission whereby the accused gives a full account of the crimes and his role in them.[1373] Only general agreements as to evidence[1374] before the ICC were so far reached in *Ongwen*, *Yekatom and Ngaïssona*, and *Ntaganda* as well as Banda *and Jerbo*.[1375]

The TC has *three options* to decide, always accompanied by the respective reasoning.[1376] First, it convicts the accused for the crimes he admitted to, provided that it is satisfied that the above requirements are met and thus the respective crimes are proved;[1377] given that this entails a conviction which brings the trial directly to the sentencing stage,[1378] the admission of guilt and any underlying (written) agreement[1379] should be examined in an open hearing;[1380] this does not preclude a previous written agreement[1381] but it should always be presented and examined in an (open) hearing.[1382]

and accepted by the Accused; and (iii) the testimony of the witnesses who appeared before this Chamber' (fn. Omitted). See also Guariglia and Hochmayr, 'Article 65', in Ambos, *Commentary* (2022), mn. 31.

[1369] In a similar vein, Boas et al., *Procedure* (2011), p. 226 ('accused before the ICC does not seem to be in an appreciably different position').

[1370] cf. ICC-OTP, *Guidelines Admission of Guilt* (2020), para. 16 ('[A]ll terms of an agreement regarding admission of guilt shall be in writing. All agreements shall be signed by the Prosecutor, the accused, and the accused's counsel before becoming final.')

[1371] cf. Guariglia and Hochmayr, 'Article 65', in Ambos, *Commentary* (2022), mn. 18; see also ICC-OTP, *Guidelines Admission of Guilt* (2020), para. 12, 14.

[1372] *Al Mahdi*, ICC-01/12-01/15-171, para. 3 and *Al Mahdi*, Annex 1 to the Version publique expurgée du 'Dépôt de l'Accord sur l'aveu de culpabilité de M. Ahmad Al Faqi Al Mahdi', 25 février 2016, ICC-01/12-01/15-78-Conf-Exp, ICC-01/12-01/15-78-Anx1-tENG-Red, 9 September 2016.

[1373] For this distinction, see Turner and Weigend, in Sluiter et al., *International Criminal Procedure* (2013), pp. 1392, 1411–12 (calling for a detailed admission); in a similar vein, for a detailed document to be added to the plea agreement, Burens, *ZIS*, *8* (2013), 332.

[1374] cf. Rule 69 RPE ICC.

[1375] ICC, *Prosecutor v. Ongwen*, TC IX, Trial Judgment, ICC-02/04-01/15-1762-Red, 4 February 2021, para. 850 ('As provided in Rule 69 of the Rules, the Prosecution and Defence submitted 23 agreed facts related to Dominic Ongwen's background, the parentage of certain children, geographical facts, the meaning of certain acronyms and the occurrence of an attack on Pajule. These agreed facts are proven for the purposes of the judgment' [notes omitted]); ICC, *Prosecutor v. Yekatom and Ngaïssona*, Decision on the Joint Submission of Agreed Facts, ICC-01/14-01/18-835, 19 January 2021, para. 2; ICC, *Prosecutor v. Ntaganda*, TC VI, Trial Judgment, ICC-01/04-02/06-2359, 8 July 2019, para. 46 ('The Chamber may consider alleged facts as being proven if the parties agree that these facts are not contested. The parties in this case agreed only on a limited number of facts. The Chamber considered it to be in the interests of justice, in accordance with Rule 69 of the Rules, to find such agreed facts to be proven' [notes omitted]); Banda and *Jerbo* agreed to contest only specific issues which they explicitly listed and to submit additional evidence as to the agreed issues which have been detailed in a confidential Annex, ICC, *Prosecutor v. Banda and Jerbo*, TC IV, Joint Submission by the OTP and the Defence regarding Contested Issues at the Trial of Accused Persons, ICC-02/05-03/09-148, 16 May 2011. As to the previous evidentiary agreement regarding the confirmation of charges, see *Banda and Jerbo*, ICC-02/05-03/09-121-Corr-Red, paras. 44–7, with the PTC taking a 'cautious approach' and not bound by the agreement.

[1376] See also ICC-OTP, *Guidelines Admission of Guilt* (2020), para. 5. While Rule 139 (1) RPE ICC refers to the Art. 65 (4) decision, Rule 139 (2) has to be interpreted as requiring 'reasons' for all admission of guilt decisions; for the same result, see Guariglia and Hochmayr, 'Article 65', in Ambos, *Commentary* (2022), mn. 19. On a possible appeal against such a decision pursuant to Art. 82 (1)(d) ICCS, see Chapter VI, B.(2) in this volume.

[1377] Art. 65 (2) ICCS.

[1378] Art. 76 ICCS; Section A.(4)(a) in this chapter. See also Schabas, *ICC Commentary* (2016), p. 1147; Guariglia and Hochmayr, 'Article 65', in Ambos, *Commentary* (2022), mn. 36.

[1379] Above notes 1338, 1381 and main text.

[1380] Guariglia and Hochmayr, 'Article 65', in Ambos, *Commentary* (2022), mn. 17

[1381] As done in *Al Mahdi* the admission of guilt was presented in closed session after the plea agreement has been signed, cf. *Al Mahdi*, ICC-01/12-01/15-T-3-Red-ENG, p. 3 ll. 14–19 and above note 1382; see also Guariglia and Hochmayr, 'Article 65', in Ambos, *Commentary* (2022), mn. 17.

[1382] See also Rule 62*ter*(c) RPE ICTY: 'If a plea agreement has been reached by the parties, the Trial Chamber shall require the disclosure of the agreement in *open session* or, on a showing of good cause, in *closed session*, at the

Secondly, the TC orders the continuance of the trial ignoring the admission, since it is not satisfied that the requirements are met.[1383] Thirdly, it considers that a 'more complete presentation of the facts of the case' is necessary 'in the interests of justice, in particular the interests of the victims',[1384] either requesting additional evidence from the Prosecutor[1385] or ordering the continuation of the trial in the sense mentioned above.[1386]

This latter option—which contains the just mentioned two sub-options[1387]—goes beyond the first two options embodied in Article 65 (2) and (3) ICCS in that it enables the Chamber to strive for 'a more complete presentation of the facts' notwithstanding the validity of the admission of guilt.[1388] This follows from the lack of any reference to the admission of guilt in the chapeau of paragraph (4) of Article 65, contrary to paras. (2) and (3). Indeed, the focus of this paragraph does not lie so much on the admission as the basis of the accused's guilt, but rather on the broader picture, that is, the 'more complete presentation of the facts of the case' as required by the 'interests of justice, in particular the interests of victims'. In other words, what really matters here is not so much the concrete guilt of the respective accused with regard to the respective charges, but the broader 'truth' of the case.[1389] This has clearly an inquisitorial undertone[1390] and entails the risk of an unnecessary prolongation of the trial for the sake of the search for an abstract truth—detached from the parameters of the concrete case as reflected in the DCC and the admission of guilt—to the detriment of the accused.[1391] Thus, a restrictive interpretation is called for, limiting the TC's authority to order additional evidence or the continuation of the ordinary trial to absolutely exceptional situations, where the interests of the victims—being the only relevant 'justice' interests in this context—compellingly demand the presentation and examination of further evidence.[1392] This requires more than a general call for the judicial establishment of a historical record,[1393] since this, albeit arguably a goal of international criminal justice,[1394] goes beyond

time the accused pleads guilty in accordance with Rule 62 (vi), or requests to change his or her plea to guilty' (emphases added).

[1383] Art. 65 (3) ICCS.

[1384] Art. 65 (4) ICCS, chapeau. In this context it 'may invite the views of the Prosecutor and the defence' (Rule 139 (1) RPE ICC).

[1385] Art. 65 (4)(a) ICCS.

[1386] Art. 65 (4)(b) ICCS.

[1387] Subparas. (a) and (b) of Art. 65 (4) as summarized in the two previous notes with main text. For this reason Safferling, *Criminal Procedure* (2012), p. 444, counts in total four (instead of three) options.

[1388] For the same result (although without explicit explanation), see Safferling, *Criminal Procedure* (2012), pp. 446–7.

[1389] In favour, Turner and Weigend, in Sluiter et al., *International Criminal Procedure* (2013), p. 1390. In the same vein, ICC-OTP, *Guidelines Admission of Guilt* (2020), para. 19 ('[T]he Prosecutor shall not enter into any agreement in which the accused disputes the essential facts establishing his or her guilt, namely, the facts underlying the elements of the charged crimes and the applicable modes of liability. The Prosecutor should insist, as a condition of every agreement regarding admission of guilt, that the accused person provide the Prosecutor with a full and truthful account of his or her own conduct relevant to the charged crimes.')

[1390] Thus, rather than a 'compromise between legal systems that do not allow a summary end to the trial or an automatic conviction in case of an admission of guilt and the common law approach on guilty pleas' (Guariglia and Hochmayr, 'Article 65', in Ambos, *Commentary* (2022), mn. 39), Art. 65 (4) espouses a clear inquisitorial tendency which is incompatible with an adversarial guilty plea. *Contra* also Safferling, *Criminal Procedure* (2012), p. 446. For a more nuanced definition of truth, related to the concept of fairness, see Heinze and Fyfe, in Ambos, Duff, Roberts and Weigend, *Core Concepts I* (2019), pp. 346–7 (see esp. n. 16).

[1391] Crit. also Safferling, *Criminal Procedure* (2012), pp. 446–7, seeing, with regard to subpara. (a), the 'danger that the accused is made an object of the proceedings, having to suffer a prolonged procedure for some higher goal' and, with regard to subpara. (b), a trial amounting to 'a judge-led truth commission'.

[1392] In the same vein, Safferling, *Criminal Procedure* (2012), pp. 446–7.

[1393] In favour of such a (overambitious) goal, Rauxloh, *ICLR*, 10 (2010), 739–44; Burens, *ZIS*, 8 (2013), 322, 324–6 (with criminal trials complementing TRCs).

[1394] See Chapter I, C.(2)(a) in this volume.

the mandate and capacity of a criminal court[1395] and should be left to interdisciplinary Truth Commissions.[1396]

If the trial is to be continued, it shall—contrary to the more liberal wording ('may')[1397]—be remitted to another TC, since only a new Chamber will be sufficiently impartial and able to ignore the—actually existing—admission of guilt.[1398] This applies to both Article 65 (3) and (4)(b) ICCS, although in the latter case the remission to a new TC is even more compelling, since the trial is only continued 'in the interests of justice' despite the existence of a—possibly valid—admission of guilt.[1399] In any case, to consider 'the admission of guilt as not having been made'[1400] amounts to an exclusionary or at least inadmissibility rule as to the admission as a piece of evidence and the ensuing consequences (waivers of procedural rights).[1401] This should also extend, for reasons of fairness, to any statement of the defendant or information given in the course of the plea negotiations.[1402] Similar considerations of fairness apply to the situation—also not regulated by the ICC law—where a plea agreement is breached by one of the parties.[1403] The respective Chamber should then—in line with Article 65 (3) and (4)(b) ICCS—consider the admission of guilt as not having been made and remit the case to another TC.[1404] The Court should also have the authority to impose appropriate remedies.[1405]

1395 In the same vein, Damaška, *ChicKentLR*, 83 (2008), 332, 335–6, 340–2, 364, arguing that international criminal tribunals lack the institutional competence to write history and should therefore take a more modest role with a view to 'making a historical record of events'; Turner and Weigend, in Sluiter et al., *International Criminal Procedure* (2013), p. 1406 (while acknowledging—case-related—truth-finding as a goal of international criminal justice correctly admitting that 'a criminal court does not have the means, the methodology, or the time available to historians and thus cannot "write history"'); Heinze, in Cullen et al., *Politics* (2021), 27, 48 (goal of creating a historical record as a mere ambition, not necessarily achievable, juxtaposed to a purpose); from an evidentiary perspective in favour of 'truth in its narrow sense', Klamberg, *Evidence* (2013), p. 513; crit. of the common law guilty plea as impairing the truth-seeking function, Combs, in Sluiter et al., *International Criminal Procedure* (2013), p. 687.

1396 See the discussion in Chapter I, C.(3) in this volume. On (effective) TRCs, see Chapter III., B.(2)(d)(ii) in this volume.

1397 cf. Art. 65 (3) *in fine* and (4)(b) *in fine* ICCS.

1398 For the same result, Turner and Weigend, in Sluiter et al., *International Criminal Procedure* (2013), pp. 1400, 1405; see also Guariglia and Hochmayr, 'Article 65', in Ambos, *Commentary* (2022), mn. 41 ('Subpara. (b) allows the TC to retain jurisdiction over the case after deciding that the trial should continue under normal trial procedures, instead of requiring the case to be remitted to another TC'). On the related right to an impartial tribunal, see Chapter II, D.(2)(a) in this volume.

1399 See also Safferling, *Criminal Procedure* (2012), pp. 446 and 447, in the former case in favour of the remission to a new TC for the lack of impartiality, in the latter case for a mandatory remission; regarding para. (4)(b), see also Guariglia and Hochmayr, 'Article 65', in Ambos, *Commentary* (2022), mn. 40, calling on the TC to 'prudently exercise' these powers.

1400 Art. 65 (3) ICCS.

1401 See also Guariglia and Hochmayr, 'Article 65', in Ambos, *Commentary* (2022), mn. 37 (admission or waiver 'cannot result in any prejudice whatsoever to the accused. It is null and void, and can only be stricken from the record, with no implications adverse to the accused being drawn from it'); conc. Turner and Weigend, in Sluiter et al., *International Criminal Procedure* (2013), pp. 1392, 1405, 1409 (inadmissibility as general principle of law and from a human rights perspective); Turner, 'Article 65', in Klamberg et al., *Commentary ICC II* (2023), pp. 231–2; Schabas, *ICC Commentary* (2016), 999–1000.

1402 On the parallel problem at the ad hoc tribunals, see ICTY, *Manual* (2009), para. 72 (stating that such 'discussions remain confidential' when plea negotiations fail); Turner and Weigend, in Sluiter et al., *International Criminal Procedure* (2013), pp. 1386–7.

1403 For a discussion regarding the ad hoc tribunals, where the law does not solve the issue either, see Turner and Weigend, in Sluiter et al., *International Criminal Procedure* (2013), pp. 1388–7.

1404 In the same vein ibid., p. 1392.

1405 cf. ibid., p. 1413.

There are, of course, variations to the admission of guilt scenario. An accused may admit his guilt only to some charges. The Chamber may then use the abbreviated procedure of Article 65 (2) ICCS—if the admission of guilt is valid—for the charges covered by the admission and continue with the ordinary procedure for the remaining charges. Alternatively, the Chamber may proceed with the ordinary trial with regard to all charges—invoking Article 65 (4)(b) in its broad interpretation mentioned above—and consider the admission of guilt together with the other evidence during trial.[1406] In fact, in this scenario the broader interpretation of Article 65 (4)(b) is convincing, since it would avoid the splitting of the trial against the same accused.[1407] There may be several accused but only some of them admit guilt; here again—to complicate things further—there may be a split admission covering some, but not all charges. For the basic situation Rule 136 (1) RPE ICC provides for the possibility of separate trials, explicitly referring to the situation of an admission of guilt; one of the advantages of a separation is that the accused, having made the admission, can be called as a witness in the trial against the other accused.[1408] In the more complicated situation—partial admission by one of the accused—the above solution of an ordinary trial applies to this accused but it may be sensible for practical reasons to separate this trial from the others pursuant to Rule 136 (1) RPE ICC.

In sum, the ICC regime presents a truly mixed picture: on the one hand, the accused may admit guilt and the parties may have 'discussions' regarding charges and sentence,[1409] on the other hand victims are encouraged to debate the 'historical truth' of events in public proceedings.[1410] In fact, the privileged role of victims before the ICC, confirmed by the above discussed reference to the 'interests of the victims' in Article 65 (4) ICCS,[1411] turns them into unpredictable third parties that may well become a spoiler in any adversarial bargaining process,[1412] unless they too prefer a negotiated settlement, since it saves them from being called onto the witness stand, running the risk of being re-traumatized or threatened.[1413]

[1406] cf. Guariglia and Hochmayr, 'Article 65', in Ambos, *Commentary* (2022), mn. 34; Schabas, *ICC Commentary* (2016), p. 999.

[1407] For the same result, see Safferling, *Criminal Procedure* (2012), p. 448.

[1408] cf. Guariglia and Hochmayr, 'Article 65', in Ambos, *Commentary* (2022), mn. 35; also Safferling, *Criminal Procedure* (2012), p. 448.

[1409] Art. 65 (5) ICCS and ICC OTP, *Guidelines Admission of Guilt* (2020), para. 11.

[1410] cf. Behrens, in Lee, *ICC* (1999), p. 242; Wei, *Rolle* (2007), pp. 260–1; Bock, *Opfer* (2010), pp. 353–4; on the therewith achieved inquisitorial effect, see Swart, *JICJ*, 6 (2008), 106–7; on the historical truth, see also Diggelmann, *AVR*, 45 (2007), 394–5. On the limited role of victims at the ad hoc tribunals, see Turner and Weigend, in Sluiter et al., *International Criminal Procedure* (2013), p. 1388.

[1411] See also Rule 93 RPE ICC allowing the Chamber to seek the views of victims with regard to Rule 139, i.e. an admission of guilt; see Chapter II, E.(4)(b) in this volume *in fine*. In favour, Turner and Weigend, in Sluiter et al., *International Criminal Procedure* (2013), pp. 1406–7; Guariglia and Hochmayr, 'Article 65', in Ambos, *Commentary* (2022), mn. 20.

[1412] See also Ambos and Heinze, in Bergsmo, *Abbreviated Criminal Procedures* (2017), p. 96. In a similar vein, Safferling, *Criminal Procedure* (2012), pp. 442–3; Heinze, in Heinze and Dittrich, *ICC* (2021), pp. 79–80; on the impact of victims' participation in this regard see already Chapter II, E.(1) with note 767.

[1413] On this side of the coin, see ICC-OTP, *Guidelines Admission of Guilt* (2020), para. 15 ('An admission of guilt will ordinarily eliminate or reduce the need for victims and witnesses to testify at trial, which can be a traumatic experience. Witnesses who might require intrusive security measures or even relocation as a result of their testimony can also be spared this significant disruption to their lives.') See also Schuon, *International Criminal Procedure* (2010), pp. 220–1, 240–1 (regarding ICTY practice); Turner and Weigend, in Sluiter et al., *International Criminal Procedure* (2013), pp. 1406, 1408; Guariglia and Hochmayr, 'Article 65', in Ambos, *Commentary* (2022), mn. 7.

In any case, while victims may be heard in the bargaining process, they should not have a veto right.[1414]

The compromise reached demonstrates the civil law influence, where the search for the truth—the cornerstone of the inquisitorial mode—is a key feature of criminal procedure and any negotiation of the truth is considered to undermine the truth-seeking mission of the court.[1415] While this view ignores that an admission of guilt may also contribute to the truth, at least regarding the charges it refers to,[1416] it leaves little, if any, room for charge bargaining—despite the acknowledgment of the respective 'discussions' in Article 65 (5)[1417]—since the ensuing omission of complete charges regarding international core crimes effectively distorts the historical case record.[1418] In addition, the Prosecutor is only free to amend or withdraw charges until the confirmation hearing.[1419] In any case, Article 65 ICCS modifies a crucial structural feature of the adversarial system to an extent that one could speak, from the perspective of procedural expediency, of an 'overregulation' of the guilty plea in a manner that undermines its function as a procedural shortcut.[1420] Clearly, it has been accepted by the ICC drafters that procedural speed is not an end in itself and, in any case, should not completely displace the truth-seeking function of procedure.[1421] Of course, how this legal regime will, beyond the quite unique *Al-Mahdi* case, play out in practice before the Court is an open question. Given the fact that the ICC pursues those most

[1414] In the same vein, Turner and Weigend, in Sluiter et al., *International Criminal Procedure* (2013), p. 1412. This corresponds to comparative law in that plea bargains do normally not depend on the victims' consent but they are at least consulted, including in common law jurisdictions (cf. Turner and Weigend, in Sluiter et al., *International Criminal Procedure* (2013), p. 1404 with further references). It is also consistent with international law in that there is no subjective right of victims for a specific punishment of the concrete defendant; in the same vein, Turner and Weigend, in Sluiter et al., *International Criminal Procedure* (2013), pp. 1407–8.

[1415] See also Burens, *ZIS*, 8 (2013), 321, 326, 331; Turner and Weigend, in Sluiter et al., *International Criminal Procedure* (2013), p. 1376; Guariglia and Hochmayr, 'Article 65', in Ambos, *Commentary* (2022), mn. 5 (plea bargaining as 'erosion of fact-finding mission of the criminal procedure'); regarding ICTY, see Schuon, *International Criminal Procedure* (2010), p. 268; generally in favour of truth-seeking, *Katanga and Ngudjolo*, ICC-01/04-01/07-3319-tENG/FRA, para. 8; crit. of 'an unqualified truth seeking mission' of TCs, *Katanga and Ngudjolo*, ICC-01/04-01/07-3319, paras. 34–5.

[1416] cf. Tieger and Shin, *JICJ*, 3 (2005), 671; Rauxloh, *ICLR*, 10 (2010), 767, 769–70 (arguing that plea bargaining, fulfilling certain conditions, can be used 'as a mechanism to build the historical record'); Schuon, *International Criminal Procedure* (2010), pp. 208–20, 224–5, 232–40, 242–3 (crit. discussion of ICTY practice); Burens, *ZIS*, 8 (2013), 328–9 ('[t]o a certain extent'), 333 (partial truth); Meernik, *ICLR*, 14 (2014), 201, 204 (but also, at 204–5, pointing to the risk of 'insincere confessions' and the harm to the historical record by dropping charges).

[1417] As already said earlier (note 1337 with main text) the provision assumes that 'discussions' 'regarding modification of charges' take place; see also Guariglia and Hochmayr, 'Article 65', in Ambos, *Commentary* (2022), mn. 43 ('charge bargaining is admissible').

[1418] In a similar vein, Rauxloh, *ICLR*, 10 (2010), 752 (charge bargaining as main problem regarding historical record); Burens, *ZIS*, 8 (2013), 328 (exclusion of sex violence at ICTR), 329–30, 332 (considering it inadmissible); Turner and Weigend, in Sluiter et al., *International Criminal Procedure* (2013), pp. 1406, 1407; with a view to the discussion at the ICTY, see Schuon, *International Criminal Procedure* (2010), pp. 206–8, 249–54, 269–70.

[1419] cf. Section B.(7)(a) in this chapter. See also Guariglia and Hochmayr, 'Article 65', in Ambos, *Commentary* (2022), mn. 43; Turner and Weigend, in Sluiter et al., *International Criminal Procedure* (2013), pp. 1390–1.

[1420] cf. Creta, *HoustonJIL*, 20 (1998), 407; dissenting, Arzt, in Arnold et al., *Menschengerechtes Strafrecht* (2005), p. 701 ('faktische Bindungswirkung').

[1421] In a similar vein, Safferling, *Criminal Procedure* (2012), pp. 441–2.

responsible, that is, civilian or military leaders, it is difficult to imagine that these kinds of people, mostly rejecting the Court as a matter of political principle, will 'admit their guilt'.[1422] Rather, one would expect that only low- or mid-level defendants would use this instrument to get off the hook of the Court or at least in order to obtain a lighter sentence. Their information may then be used, as in classical organized crime investigations, to get to the top of the organization.[1423]

[1422] In a similar vein, Combs, *VanderbiltLR*, 59 (2006), 119 (regarding ICTR); conc. Rauxloh, *ICLR*, 10 (2010), 766; in a similar vein, Meernik, *ICLR*, 14 (2014), 216.

[1423] In a similar vein, Meernik, *ICLR*, 14 (2014), 217.

# V
# Evidence and Disclosure

*The full chapter bibliography can be downloaded from

This chapter is divided into two main sections. Section A will examine the law of evidence in general and specific terms. After some general remarks (Section A.(1)) and the discussion of the relevant principles and concepts (Section A.(2)), the main areas of evidence before international criminal tribunals, that is, witness and documentary evidence, will be analysed (Section A.(3) and (4)). Then, some specific rules and issues have to be explored (Section A.(5) to (7)) before we conclude this section with the important problem of the inadmissibility (exclusion) of evidence due to rights violations (Section A.(8)). Section B will analyse the highly relevant disclosure regime, distinguishing, after a brief introduction (Section B.(1)), between prosecution and defence disclosure (Section B.(2) and (3)) and discussing disclosure restrictions (Section B.(4)).

While, as in previous chapters, we take into account both the ad hoc tribunals and the ICC, the focus will be on the ICC although its case law on the matter is largely informed by the case law of the ad hoc tribunals.

## A. Evidence

### (1) General remarks

Before taking a closer look at the principles governing the taking and admission of evidence in international criminal procedure, some conceptual clarifications are appropriate, especially with regard to the types of evidence (below (a)). Afterwards we will consider free assessment and admissibility ((b)) and the submission of evidence ((c)).

#### *(a) Conceptual clarifications*

First, the term '*evidence*' must be distinguished from the more general terms '*material*' or '*information*'. While 'evidence' refers more narrowly to the forms of evidence legally prescribed and permitted, that is, 'any species of proof legally presented at the trial of an issue, by the act of the parties and through the medium of witnesses, records, documents, concrete objects, and the like',[1] in particular witness and documentary evidence explicitly mentioned in Article 69 (1) and (2) ICCS;[2] 'material' encompasses any information and does

[1] Garner, *Dictionary* (2019), pp. 697–703. See also Ingram, *Criminal Evidence* (10th edn, 2009), p. 24 ('Legal evidence is that which is used or is intended to be used at the trial or at inquiries before courts, judges, commissioners, referees, etc.'); Jämsä, *Rules of Evidence* (2023), p. 22; Fishman and McKenna, *Jones on Evidence I* (2020), para. 1.2: '"Evidence" is what a litigant submits to the factfinder in the hopes of "proving" a fact'. Evidence according to this definition is also called 'judicial evidence', see Brandl, *Criminal Investigations* (2021), p. 39 ('Judicial evidence is evidence that is admissible in court and meets the rules of evidence'). Pursuant to a broader definition, evidence is 'something (including testimony, documents, and tangible objects) that tends to prove or disprove the existence of an alleged fact', see Garner, *Dictionary* (2019), p. 697.

[2] Paras. (1) and (2) of Art. 69 refer to witness testimony, para. (2) to 'documents or written transcripts'. See also Safferling, *International Criminal Procedure* (2012), p. 463.

not in itself have to be admissible in evidence.[3] In addition, the body of evidence law has several connotations and no uniform understanding across the legal systems. Most notably, while the procedural rules on evidence may form a separate body of 'Evidence Law', e.g. in England and Wales, they may also merely be a part of criminal, civil, or administrative procedure, as in civil law jurisdictions like Germany.[4]

Secondly, there are numerous ways to structure or categorize evidence and this may serve several purposes.[5] In this chapter, the purpose is to systematize the fragmented body of international criminal evidence. Categorization of evidence is relevant, as will be seen in the second part of the chapter, with regard to the access to evidence by way of disclosure and inspection; disclosure rules vary, depending on the category of the respective evidence.[6]

The categorization into *direct* and *circumstantial* evidence follows the criterion of 'proximity to the facts in issue'.[7] The same applies to the distinction between 'direct' and 'collateral' evidence, with the former going directly to the facts in issue and the latter not.[8] The categorization into *primary* and *secondary* evidence speaks to both proximity and value, with primary evidence meaning 'the best and highest kind' and secondary 'inferior or substitutionary evidence'.[9] The categories *testimonial*, *real*, *demonstrative*, or *documentary* evidence follow the criterion of the nature or form of the evidence.[10] The same applies to the categories of testimony, documentary evidence, and tangible objects or exhibits;[11] or testimony, real evidence, and demonstrative evidence.[12] A categorization along the lines of the purposes of establishing proof would include the following types of evidence: *corpus delicti* evidence, corroborative evidence, cumulative evidence, associative evidence, identification evidence, or behavioural evidence.[13]

Evidence can be *incriminatory* (incriminating) or *exculpatory*. Generally speaking, evidence is incriminatory if it tends 'to establish guilt or from which a fact-trier can infer guilt';[14] this follows, *e contrario*, from the definition of exculpatory evidence in Article 67 (2) ICCS according to which such evidence 'shows or tends to show the innocence of the accused, or to mitigate the guilt of the accused', or may, in addition, 'affect the credibility of prosecution evidence'.[15]

Finally, the admissibility of evidence is the criterion behind the categorization into *judicial* and *extrajudicial* evidence: While the former is admissible in court, hence complying with the evidentiary rules, the latter is not: 'it is any information on which an investigative decision can be based but that is not allowed in court proceedings.'[16]

[3] This follows, *e contrario*, from the ICTY case law on the term 'evidence' as used in Rule 68 RPE ICTY, where evidence in light of the term's narrow meaning has been explicitly defined broadly as 'not restricted to material in a form that would be admissible in evidence', see, in more detail, Section B.(2)(d)(ii).

[4] Heinze, in Caeiro, Gless, and Mitsilegas, *Elgar Encyclopedia* (2022).

[5] The following part is taken from Heinze, in Caeiro, Gless, and Mitsilegas, *Elgar Encyclopedia* (2022). See also Trendafilova, *CLF*, 34 (2023), 449, 450.

[6] Heinze, *Disclosure* (2014), p. 309; Heinze, in Ruiz Fabri, *MPEIPro* (2020), mn. 2.

[7] De Smet, in Bergsmo and Stahn, *Fact-Finding* (2020), p. 119; Roberts, *Evidence* (2022), p. 119.

[8] Roberts, *Evidence* (202 2), p. 122.

[9] Malek, in Malek, *Phipson on Evidence* (2022), para. 1.15.

[10] Doak, McGourlay, and Thomas, *Evidence* (2018), pp. 11 ff.; De Smet, in Bergsmo and Stahn, *Fact-Finding* (2020), p. 119.

[11] Fishman and McKenna, *Jones on Evidence I* (2020), para. 1.3; Melillo, in Ruiz Fabri, *MPEIPro* (2020), mn. 5.

[12] Bergman, Hollander, and Duncan, *Wharton's Criminal Evidence I* (2021), para. 1.6.

[13] Brandl, *Criminal Investigation* (2021), p. 124.

[14] Garner, *Dictionary* (2019), p. 700.

[15] See, in more detail, in the context of (prosecution) disclosure, Section B.(2)(d) in this chapter, esp. subsection (ii).

[16] Brandl, *Criminal Investigation* (2021), p. 99.

### *(b) Free assessment and admissibility*

Generally speaking, the evidence law of international criminal tribunals is governed by the principle of the free assessment of all evidence,[17] leaving 'maximum flexibility'[18] and 'broad discretion' to TCs when deciding on the admissibility and probative value of evidence;[19] judges are not bound by any strict technical rules of evidence as known in the old inquisitorial procedure of continental Europe.[20] However, free assessment of evidence should not be confused with arbitrary or unfettered discretion. As we will see below[21] there are rules to follow and, in any case, what is to be assessed freely is not so much the admission of a certain piece of evidence but its probative value (weight). Apart from that, the evidentiary system of international criminal tribunals is premised on the expertise of professional judges who are expected, 'by virtue of their training and experience', to properly and fairly assess the relevant evidence and 'accord it appropriate weight'.[22] Of course, there is reason to doubt that this premise is fully matched by reality. It is no secret that States do not always send their best judges to international (criminal) tribunals[23] and there has indeed been criticism that a number of international judges have either no (proper) legal training at all or lack sufficient

[17] cf. Rule 63 (2) RPE ICC ('assess freely all evidence'); also ICC, *Prosecutor v. Lubanga*, TC I, Decision on the Admissibility of Four Documents, ICC-01/04-01/06-1399, 13 June 2008, paras. 24, 32; previously Art. 19 IMT Charter. See also Bantekas, *ICL* (2010), pp. 545–6; Klamberg, *Evidence* (2013), p. 418 (general principle).

[18] Boas et al., *Procedure* (2011), p. 336.

[19] For the ICTY, see ICTY, *Prosecutor v. Aleksovski*, AC, Decision on Prosecutor's Appeal on Admissibility of Evidence, IT-95-14/1-AR73, 16 February 1999, para. 15; ICTY, *Prosecutor v. Kordić* and *Čerkez*, AC, Decision on Appeal Regarding Statement of a Deceased Witness, IT-95-14/2-AR73.5, 21 July 2000, para. 20; ICTY, *Prosecutor v. Aleksovski*, AC, Judgment, IT-95-14/1-A, 24 March 2000, para. 63; ICTY, *Prosecutor v. Šešelj*, TC III, Judgment, IT-03-67-T, 31 March 2016, para. 27; for the ICTR, see ICTR, *Prosecutor v. Musema*, AC, Judgment, ICTR-96-13-A, 16 November 2001, paras. 37–8; for the SCSL, see SCSL, *Prosecutor v. Norman et al.*, Appeal against Decision Refusing Bail, SCSL-04-14-AR65, 11 March 2005, para. 26 (purpose of Rule 89 I 'to avoid sterile legal debate over admissibility'); for the ICC, see *Lubanga*, ICC-01/04-01/06-1399, para. 23 ('wide discretion'); ICC, *Prosecutor v. Bemba*, TC III, Judgment pursuant to Article 74 of the Statute, ICC-01/05-01/08-3343, 21 March 2016, para. 222 ('In deciding on the admission of the various items ... the Chamber is afforded a measure of discretion.'); STL, *Prosecutor v. Ayyash et al.*, TC, Judgment, STL-11-01/T/TC/F3839/20200818/R331945-R334626/EN/dm, 18 August 2020, para. 293; on the IMT, see Chapter I, B.(1)(a) in this volume. See also Bantekas, *ICL* (2010), pp. 477–8; Schuon, *International Criminal Procedure* (2010), pp. 136–7, 165 ff. (discussing reasons for this flexibility); Boas et al., *Procedure* (2011), pp. 338, 373; Klamberg, *Evidence* (2013), pp. 335 ff.; Klamberg, in Sluiter et al., *International Criminal Procedure* (2013), pp. 1017, 1018–20, 1036, 1043 (general rule); Friman, in Cryer et al., *ICL* (2019), p. 433; crit. Zahar and Sluiter, *ICL* (2008), p. 394 ('insufficient guidance', 'uncertain, obscure, and unworkable body of law'); Caianiello, 'Indeterminatezza' in Delmas-Marty, Fronza, and Lambert-Abdelgawad, *Droit international pénal* (2004), pp. 343 ff.; Gallmetzer, in Stahn and Sluiter, *ICC* (2009), pp. 507–8; Combs, in Schabas and Bernaz, *Handbook ICL* (2011), pp. 326 ff.; in contrast, in favour of an (even) greater margin of discretion and the option of permitting a lower standard of proof in exceptional cases, Henham, *ICLR*, 9 (2009), 817 ff. For the ECtHR's 'flexible' approach on the matter, see Chapter I, D.(4) in this volume.

[20] cf. Frisch, in Bruns et al., *FS Stürner* (2013), pp. 851–2.

[21] Notes 182 ff. in this chapter and main text.

[22] ICTY, *Prosecutor v. Tadić*, TC, Decision on Defence Motion on Hearsay, IT-94-1-T, 15 August 1996, para. 17; ICTY, *Prosecutor v. Prlic et al.*, AC, Judgment Vol. I Part 1, IT-04-74-A, 29 November 2017, para. 195 ('The Appeals Chamber recalls in this regard the broad discretion of the Trial Chamber in considering relevant factors on a case-by-case basis and assessing the appropriate weight and credibility to be accorded to the testimony of a witness since it is best placed to assess these issues, and that the Appeals Chamber's review is limited to establishing whether the challenging party has demonstrated that the trial chamber has committed an error'); ICC, *Prosecutor v. Ongwen*, AC, Judgment on the Appeal of Mr Ongwen against the Decision of Trial Chamber IX of 4 February 2021 entitled 'Trial Judgment', ICC-02/04-01/15-2022-Red, 16 December 2022, para. 814; *Ayyash et al.*, STL-11-01/T/TC/F3839/20200818/R331945-R334626/EN/dm, para. 293 ('Under the general principles of international criminal law, a trial chamber has a broad discretion in assessing the credibility of witness testimony and deciding the appropriate weight to give it. The Trial Chamber as the trier of fact that has heard the evidence is best placed to make this assessment').

[23] On the discussion of the selection of international judges and the need for quality control in this regard, see Chapter II, A.(3) in this volume; cf. also Ambos, *CLF*, 23 (2012), 223–8 with further references.

(criminal) trial experience.[24] In addition, as will be seen in the context of the 'submission' vs. 'admission approach', the background of the judges has a crucial impact.

The '*admissibility*' of a given piece of evidence[25] depends on its 'relevance'[26] and 'probative value'[27] and the absence of any serious rights violation.[28] As to the latter, 'reliability' as a third criterion comes in,[29] although, as we will see below,[30] it is applied as an inherent element of probative value by case law. ICC TCs have translated these criteria in a *three-step test* distinguishing explicitly between (i) relevance and (ii) probative value, and then (iii) weighing the probative value of the evidence against its prejudicial effect.[31] While up to 2016 the three-step test mainly applied to evidence 'other than direct oral testimony',[32] it is now fair to say that it is applied to all types of evidence mentioned above, with the minor exception of the weight component.[33] However, the first two steps cannot, in practice, be so neatly separated and are often taken together to draw a conclusion regarding—much, little, or no—probative value.[34] Thus, it is more plausible to structure the operation in a *two-step test*: evidence must first pass the admissibility test (relevance and probative value, including reliability)[35] and then a fairness or rights test which may bar the consideration of otherwise admissible evidence. This last fairness test will be analysed in more detail at the end of this section.[36]

In any case, admissibility *stricto sensu* (entailing the exclusion of evidence due to serious unfairness) should not be overstated to the detriment of the actual evaluation of the

[24] See, in detail, Ambos, *Treatise ICL I* (2021), pp. 37 ff. See also Boas et al., *Procedure* (2011), p. 337, quoting former ICTY Judge David Hunt; Byrne, *LJIL*, 26 (2013), 995; Bohlander, 'Article 36', in Ambos, *Commentary* (2022), mn. 3 ff.

[25] cf. Rule 89 (C) RPE ICTY/ICTR/SCSL and Rule 105 (C) RPE MICT ('may admit'); Arts. 64 (9)(a) and 69 (4) ICCS (authorizing the TC to 'rule' on the 'admissibility' of evidence), Rule 63 (2) RPE ICC ('determine ... admissibility').

[26] cf. Rule 89 (C) RPE ICTY/ICTR/SCSL and Rule 105 (C) RPE MICT (referring to 'relevant' evidence); Arts. 64 (9)(a) and 69 (4) ICCS (authorizing the TC to 'rule' on the 'relevance' of evidence), Rule 63 (2) RPE ICC (determine 'relevance').

[27] cf. Rule 89 (C) RPE ICTY/ICTR and Rule 105 (C) RPE MICT ('probative value' as criterion, besides 'relevance', for admission), Art. 69 (4) ICCS ('probative value' as criterion to decide on admissibility and relevance), Rule 72 (2) RPE ICC ('sufficient degree of probative value' as a factor be taken into account with regard to evidence related to sexual violence). The omission of 'probative value' in Rule 89 (C) RPE SCSL led the SCSL to focus exclusively on relevance; cf. SCSL, *Prosecutor v. Taylor*, AC, Decision on 'Prosecution Notice of Appeal and Submissions Concerning the Decision Regarding the Tender of Documents', SCSL-03-01-T-721, 6 February 2009, para. 37; also Boas et al., *Procedure* (2011), p. 340 with further references in n 18.

[28] cf. esp. Rules 89 (D) RPE ICTY and 105 (D) RPE MICT ('need to ensure a fair trial' as balancing factor with regard to exclusion of evidence); Art. 69 (4) ICCS (possible 'prejudice' to 'fair trial or 'fair evaluation of the testimony of a witness' as criterion to decide on admissibility and relevance), Rule 72 (2) RPE ICC (possible 'prejudice' within meaning of Art. 69 (4) ICCS as factor be taken into account with regard to evidence related to sexual violence). See generally Jämsä, *Rules of Evidence* (2023), p. 25.

[29] cf. Rules 95 RPE ICTY/ICTR and 117 RPE MICT; Art. 69 (7)(a) ICCS.

[30] Section A.(2) in this chapter.

[31] See originally *Lubanga*, ICC-01/04-01/06-1399, paras. 27–31; the subsequent case law followed this approach, see e.g. ICC, *Prosecutor v. Katanga*, TC II, Decision on the Prosecutor's Bar Table Motions, ICC-01/04-01/07-2635, 17 December 2010, para. 14: *Bemba*, ICC-01/05-01/08-3343, para. 223. See also De Arcos Tejerizo, *LJIL*, 36 (2023), 749, 762; Bitti, 'Article 64', in Ambos, *Commentary* (2022), mn. 65; Piragoff and Clarke, 'Article 69', in Ambos, *Commentary* (2022), mn. 58; Freeman, *FordhamILJ*, 41 (2018) 283, 294.

[32] See previous edition at p. 448; see also *Lubanga*, ICC-01/04-01/06-1399, para. 26; *Bemba*, ICC-01/05-01/08-3343, para. 236.

[33] Freeman, *FordhamILJ*, 41 (2018) 283, 295 ff. ('more nuanced').

[34] In the same vein, Boas et al., *Procedure* (2011), pp. 339–40 (collapsing the two first steps, conclusion regarding some probative value).

[35] Similarly, Khan et al., *International Criminal Courts* (2018), § 9 mn. 57. This comes close to the separate admissibility stage in common law proceedings; cf. Schuon, *LJIL*, 25 (2012), 516.

[36] Section A.(8) in this chapter.

evidence.[37] The ultimate decision on the probative value of a piece of evidence—in terms of its weight[38]—is to be taken, 'in the context of all other evidence'[39] and on the basis of an individual assessment at the end of the trial.[40]

Against this background, it does not appear to be sensible to take an—in any case, preliminary (*prima facie*)—admissibility decision (including relevance and probative value) when a piece of evidence is submitted—the so-called 'admission approach'.[41] In the previous edition of this volume we reported that most Chambers followed this approach,[42] but preferred the alternative ('submission') approach allowed by the *Bemba* AC and later *Ongwen* TC, i.e., deferring this decision 'until the end of the proceedings'.[43] The submission approach was then adopted by TC X in the *Al Hassan* case[44] and by TC V in the *Yekatom and Ngaïssona* case.[45] The submission approach has arguably become common (if not best) practice at Trial Chamber level, even though the *Practice Manual* has been silent on the matter so far.[46]

[37] On John Wigmore's critique in that regard (focus on 'admissibility' instead of 'proof'), see Roberts, *JICJ*, 13 (2015), 493 with further references.

[38] On the synonymous use of the terms 'probative value' and 'weight', see Section A.(2).

[39] ICTR, *Prosecutor v. Musema*, TC, Judgment and Sentence, ICTR-96-13-T, 27 January 2000, para. 41; ICTY, *Prosecutor v. Boškoski and Tarčulovski*, AC, Judgment, IT-04-82-A, 19 May 2010, para. 198. On the respective totality approach see also note 83 in this chapter.

[40] cf. ICTR, *Prosecutor v. Nyiramasuhuko*, AC, Decision on Pauline Nyiramasuhuko's Appeal on Admissibility of Evidence, ICTR-98-42-AR73.2, 4 October 2004, para. 6 (assessment as to probative value 'made by the Trial Chamber at the end of the case'); ICC, *Prosecutor v. Bemba*, AC, Judgment on the Appeals of Mr Jean-Pierre Bemba Gombo and the Prosecutor against the Decision of TC III entitled 'Decision on the admission into evidence of materials contained in the prosecution's list of evidence', ICC-01/05-01/08-1386, 3 May 2011, para. 37; also *Katanga*, ICC-01/04-01/07-2635, paras. 13, 15; ICC, *Prosecutor v. Ruto and Sang*, TC V(a), Decision on the Prosecution's Request for Admission of Documentary Evidence, ICC-01/09-01/11-1353, 10 June 2014, para. 18; ICC, *Prosecutor v. Ruto and Sang*, TC V(a), Decision on the Prosecution's Request for Admission of Documentary Evidence, Separate Further Opinion of Judge Eboe-Osuji, ICC-01/09-01/11-1353-Anx, 10 June 2014, para. 10. See also Boas et al., *Procedure* (2011), pp. 340, 341–2, 343–4 (decisions on admissibility as 'preliminary conclusions' on probative value before 'final assessment' on actual probative value); in a similar vein, Klamberg, in Sluiter et al., *International Criminal Procedure* (2013), p. 1026.

[41] cf. *Bemba*, ICC-01/05-01/08-1386, para. 37, arguing that the word 'may' in Art. 69 (4) allows a TC to take this approach; *Bemba*, ICC-01/05-01/08-3343, para. 222; explicitly Schmitt, *JICJ*, 19 (2021), 485, 497 ('Indeed, if the nonoral evidence is assessed in light of the standard criteria against the low *prima facie* standard, then any howsoever relevant piece of evidence with some potential probative value will always meet this standard. For the judges, however, the gain from this exercise will be marginal. The time the judges spend to filter, by way of *prima facie* decisions, a rather negligible amount of irrelevant and/or inadmissible evidence is a rather expensive investment, especially when bearing in mind that the assessment of the evidence will have to be undertaken again at the stage of the Article 74 judgment. Resulting litigation and judicial decision-making will divert the attention of the judges from substantial issues of the case').

[42] *Treatise ICL III* (2016), 449. See e.g. *Katanga*, ICC-01/04-01/07-2635, para. 15 and further examples below in the course of the main text. For a similar approach at the ICTY, see Schuon, *International Criminal Procedure* (2010), pp. 137–8 (shift from admissibility to weight/reliability).

[43] *Bemba*, ICC-01/05-01/08-1386, para. 37; in the same vein, ICC, *Prosecutor v. Bemba et al.*, TC VII, Decision on Prosecution Requests for Admission of Documentary Evidence (ICC-01/05-01/13-1013-Red, ICC-01/05-01/13-1113-Red, ICC-01/05-01/13-1170-Conf), ICC-01/05-01/13-1285, 24 September 2015, para. 9. The defence's request for leave to appeal was rejected, mainly for being 'premature' by TC VII; see ICC, *Prosecutor v. Bemba et al.*, TC VII, Decision on Babala and Arido Defence Request for Leave to Appeal the Trial Chamber's 'Decision on Prosecution Requests for Admission of Documentary Evidence' (ICC-01/05-01/13-1285), ICC-01/05-01/13-1361, 12 October 2015. See also ICC, *Prosecutor v. Ongwen*, TC IX, Initial Directions on the Conduct of the Proceeding, ICC-02/04-01/15-497, 13 July 2016, paras. 24 ff.; ICC, *Prosecutor v. Ongwen*, TC IX, Decision on Request to Admit Evidence Preserved Under Article 56 of the Statute, ICC-02/04-01/15-520, 11 August 2016, para. 7. See generally Schmitt, *JICJ*, *19* (2021), 485, 493 ff.

[44] ICC, *Prosecutor v. Al Hassan*, TC X, Annex A to the Decision on the Conduct of Proceedings, ICC-01/12-01/18-789-AnxA, 6 May 2020, paras. 29 ff.

[45] ICC, *Prosecutor v. Yekatom and Ngaïssona*, TC V, Initial Directions on the Conduct of the Proceedings, ICC-01/14-01/18-631, 26 August 2020, paras. 52–9.

[46] *Practice Manual* (2023); crit. McDermott Rees, *Völkerrechtsblog* 14 July 2022 ('Abandon the "submission" model for evidence').

A definitive (in)admissibility decision at the moment of submission is only warranted if an item of evidence is irrelevant on its face[47] or its admission would seriously prejudice the proceedings.[48] Such a flexible approach does not only make it easier to assess admissibility with a view to probative value—'in the context of all other evidence'[49]—but will also increase the overall expediency of the proceedings since time-consuming preliminary admissibility decisions can be avoided or at least be reduced.[50]

The shift from an admission to a submission approach has once again disclosed the cultural differences at the ICC with regard to procedural law.[51] The most telling example is, arguably, the *Gbagbo and Blé Goudé* case, where TC I opted for the submission approach by majority[52] but Judge Henderson (who is from common-law-dominated Trinidad and Tobago) forcefully dissented, painting a bleak and outdated picture of the so-called inquisitorial system.[53] Judge Henderson's dissent is paradigmatic for common law jurists' unease with anything that they consider an inquisitorial feature and explains the continuing resistance to the submission approach, often leading to time-consuming disputes within Chambers. Take for example the *Gbagbo and Blé Goudé* case: after the Chamber majority had introduced the approach, it was only a question of time when an issue would arise challenging its application. The issue then came up with regard to the authenticity of documents where the defence requested an admissibility decision excluding the respective documents.[54] The issue was then used, with Judge Henderson's support, to challenge the submission approach generally. What unfolded was a procedural tug-of-war that was decided by the AC in support of the TC's majority preference for the submission approach.[55] Judge Henderson, in his dissent to the (impugned) TC I decision, essentially repeated his critique of the submission approach (as he did again in his reasons for an acquittal of the accused).[56] This was also noted years later by Judge Ibáñez Carranza in her dissenting opinion to the AC decision on the appeal by the Prosecutor against the acquittal of the accused.[57] Judge Ibáñez addressed

[47] Similarly, for a preliminary admissibility exam limited to relevance, Klamberg, *Evidence* (2013), pp. 357, 513; Klamberg, *JICJ*, 13 (2015), 552. An early exclusion of obviously irrelevant evidence accounts for the criticism of a too generous admission of evidence which entails the risk that judges are getting lost in the sheer amount of evidence; cf. Murphy, *IJEP*, 12 (2008), 1 ff.; conc. and in favour of exclusion of 'more evidence' (regarding the ad hoc tribunals), Bantekas, *ICL* (2010), pp. 507–8, 546.

[48] cf. *Bemba et al.*, ICC 01/05 01/13-1285, para. 12.

[49] Note 39 in this chapter.

[50] See also *Bemba et al.*, ICC-01/05-01/13-1285, paras. 10–11.

[51] Guariglia, *JICL*, 16 (2018), 315. On the common law-civil law dimension of the dispute, see Carlson, *Model(ing) Justice* (2018), p. 76; Fairlie, *GeorgiaJI&CompL*, 47 (2019), 619–28.

[52] ICC, *Prosecutor v. Gbagbo and Blé Goudé*, TC I, Decision on the Submission and Admission of Evidence, ICC-02/11-01/15 405, 29 January 2016, paras. 12 ff., with Dissenting Opinion of Judge Henderson: Annex to Decision on the Submission and Admission of Evidence, ICC-02/11-01/15-405-Anx, 29 January 2016, paras. 13, 16 ff.

[53] *Gbagbo and Blé Goudé*, ICC-02/11-01/15-405, paras. 7, 12 ff. In more detail, Heinze, in Klip and Freeland, *ALC LXXII* (2024), pp. 87-8.

[54] ICC, *Prosecutor v. Gbagbo and Blé Goudé,* TC I, Decision Concerning the Prosecutor's Submission of Documentary Evidence on 13 June, 14 July, 7 September, and 19 September 2016, ICC-02/11-01/15-773, 9 December 2012, para. 39.

[55] ICC, *Prosecutor v. Gbagbo and Blé Goudé,* AC, Judgment on the Appeals of Mr Laurent Gbagbo and Mr Charles Blé Goudé against Trial Chamber I's Decision on the Submission of Documentary Evidence, ICC-02/11-01/15 OA 11 OA 12, 24 July 2017.

[56] ICC, *Prosecutor v. Gbagbo and Blé Goudé,* TC I, Reasons for Oral Decision of 15 January 2019 on the Requête de la Défense de Laurent Gbagbo afin qu'un jugement d'acquittement portant sur toutes les charges soit prononcé en faveur de Laurent Gbagbo et que sa mise en liberté immédiate soit ordonnée, Reasons of Judge Geoffrey Henderson, ICC-02/11-01/15-1263-AnxB-Red, 16 July 2019, paras. 21–3.

[57] ICC, *Prosecutor v. Gbagbo and Blé Goudé,* AC, Judgment in the Appeal of the Prosecutor against Trial Chamber I's Decision on the No Case to Answer Motions, Annex 4: Dissenting Opinion of Judge Luz del Carmen Ibáñez Carranza to the Judgment on the Appeal of the Prosecutor against the Oral Verdict of Trial Chamber 1 of

explicitly the disagreement between Judges Henderson and Tarfusser on the 'system of admissibility of evidence'.[58] Her words are the last reckoning with the division within TC I:

> These issues [the system for the admissibility of evidence, inter alia, K.A.] remained unresolved after Judges Henderson and Tarfusser entered the acquittals, and even when they tried to put their findings on the evidence and their conclusions in writing. Besides affecting the rights of the victims, the trial and the acquittals as entered violated the principles of legality and pacta sunt servanda, as shown above, and they also affected the due process of law and the fairness of the proceedings.[59]

The episode points to the meaning of a ruling on admissibility. The *Gbagbo and Blé Goudé* TC clarified that the 'authenticity of the documents [was] disputed' and continued: 'Without going into further detail, the Chamber observes that further evidence may be necessary to determine the authenticity of some of the documents submitted.'[60] The descriptive reference to *documents* and their authenticity is not an analysis of the probative value or relevance of *evidence*.[61] The AC, too, separated the authenticity issue from an admissibility ruling:

> To the extent that Mr Gbagbo argues that, as a matter of logic, the authenticity of a document must be determined by reference only to the document concerned and that there is therefore no reason to defer a ruling in this regard, the Appeals Chamber disagrees.

While the Statutes of the ad hoc tribunals[62] do not contain a provision on evidence (apart from the general Rule 89 RPE),[63] the KSC RPE established in Rule 138 (1) standard admissibility criteria that the Panel shall apply when making a discretionary[64] assessment as to the admissibility of an evidentiary item (relevance, authenticity, probative value, and prejudicial effect).[65] The ICC Statute contains a detailed provision with Article 69.[66] There are, however, some more substantive differences between the ad hoc tribunals and the ICC. First of all, looking more closely at the relevant provisions,[67] it is striking that the concept

15 January 2019, with written reasons issued on 16 July 2019, ICC-02/11-01/15-1400-Anx4-Red, 31 March 2021, para. 9 with n. 6 ('Judge Henderson continued to hold a different position until the end of the case').

[58] *Gbagbo and Blé Goudé*, ICC-02/11-01/15-1400-Anx4-Red, para. 15 *in fine*.
[59] Ibid., para. 128.
[60] *Gbagbo and Blé Goudé*, ICC-02/11-01/15-773, para. 39.
[61] In more detail, Heinze, in Klip and Freeland, *ALC LXXII* (2024), p. 92.
[62] On the IMT, IMTFE, and the new hybrid tribunals also focusing on probative value and following the free assessment rule, see Klamberg, in Sluiter et al., *International Criminal Procedure* (2013), pp. 1017–18, 1021–2, 1024.
[63] On this generally, Rule 89 ICTY/ICTR and the seminal decision in ICTY, *Prosecutor v. Brđanin and Talić*, TC, Order on the Standards Governing the Admission of Evidence, IT-99-36-T, 15 February 2002, paras. 15 ff.; cf. Nemitz, in Kirsch, *Internationale Strafgerichtshöfe* (2005), p. 56; Bantekas, *ICL* (2010), pp. 290 ff.; White, *LJIL*, 37 (2024), 231; Karnavas, in Stahn et al., *Legacies of the ICTY* (2020), pp. 252, 269; Jordash and Kulinowski, in Rohan and Zyberi, *Defense Perspectives* (2017), pp. 416, 426 ff.; highly crit. of ICTY practice regarding Rule 89 (C) from a common law perspective, Murphy, *JICJ*, 8 (2010), 567 ff.; on the ICTR, see Alexis, in Decaux, Dieng, and Sow, *Human Rights* (2007), pp. 467 ff.
[64] KSC, *Prosecutor v. Shala*, CoAP, Decision on Shala's Appeal Against Decision Concerning Prior Statements, KSC-BC-2020-04/IA006/F00007, 5 May 2023, para. 8 ('The Panel stresses that decisions related to the admission of evidence are generally treated as discretionary, and that appellate intervention in that respect is warranted only in very limited circumstances').
[65] See also KSC, *Prosecutor v. Mustafa*, TP I, Decision on the Submission and the Admissibility of Evidence, KSC-BC-2020-05/F00169, 25 August 2021, para. 13.
[66] On the *travaux*, see Behrens, in Lee, *ICC* (1999), pp. 242 ff.; Piragoff and Clarke, 'Article 69', in Ambos, *Commentary* (2022), mn. 1 ff. For Schabas, *ICC Commentary* (2016), p. 1078, the provision is too detailed to be in the Statute.
[67] Notes 17 and -28 in this chapter.

of 'admissibility' of evidence is used differently: at the ad hoc tribunals it is understood as a kind of umbrella term, at the ICC it is put on an equal footing with 'relevance' of evidence.[68] Further, at the ICC, the clear-cut separation between pre-trial (confirmation) and trial stages entails different standards with regard to the admissible evidence[69] and the probative threshold[70] as well as different organizational responsibilities.[71] Last but not least, while the law of the ad hoc tribunals provides explicitly for exclusionary rules in case of serious fair trial violations, the ICC regime only takes such considerations into account with regard to admissibility and relevance of the respective evidence[72] or generally as an admissibility criterion.[73] We will return to this conceptual issue below.[74]

The above-mentioned highly flexible and discretionary evidentiary regime is most explicit in Rules 89 (B) RPE ICTY/ICTR/SCSL and 105 (B) RPE MICT, according to which 'a Chamber shall apply rules of evidence which will best favour a fair determination of the matter before it and are consonant with the spirit of the Statute and the general principles of law'.[75] This so-called 'best evidence rule'[76] refers to the 'best evidence available in the circumstances of the case'[77] and more specifically to the respective piece of evidence under

[68] cf. provisions quoted in notes 26 and 27 in this chapter.

[69] cf. Art. 61 (5), second sentence versus Art. 69 (2), first sentence ICCS (the former expressing a preference for 'documentary or summary evidence' without the need to 'call the witnesses expected to testify at the trial'); see also *Bemba*, ICC-01/05-01/08-1386, para. 80 ('rules regarding orality in the pre-trial phase ... more relaxed'); ICC, *Prosecutor v. Ruto and Sang*, PTC II, Decision on the Confirmation of Charges pursuant to Article 61 (7)(a) and (b) of the Rome Statute, ICC-01/09-01/11-373, 23 January 2012, para. 65 (admission of summaries of statements of non-ICC witnesses at the confirmation hearing since the 'use of such documentary evidence' is not precluded 'nor is there any indication that this evidence is otherwise inadmissible'); thereto also Klamberg, *Evidence* (2013), pp. 393–5; Klamberg, *JICJ, 13* (2015), 550–1; Schabas, Chaitidou, and El Zeidy, 'Article 61', in Ambos, *Commentary* (2022), mn. 94 ff.

[70] cf. 'substantial grounds to believe' (Art. 61 (7) ICCS) and 'beyond reasonable doubt' (Art. 66 (3) ICCS); cf. Chapter IV, A.(2)(b)(i) and (iii); also Schabas, Chaitidou and El Zeidy, 'Article 61', in Ambos, *Commentary* (2022), mn. 91 ff.; Khan et al., *International Criminal Courts* (2018), § 9 mn. 55; regarding the ad hoc tribunals, see also Klamberg, in Sluiter et al., *International Criminal Procedure* (2013), pp. 1026–7, distinguishing between the admission stage and final determination of evidence.

[71] PTC and TC; cf. ICC, *Prosecutor v. Katanga*, PTC I (Single Judge Steiner), Decision on the Defences' Applications for Leave to Appeal the 'Decision on the admissibility for the confirmation hearing of the transcripts of interview of deceased witness 12', ICC-01/04-01/07-496, 22 May 2008, p. 7, (distinguishing between admissibility of evidence at confirmation hearing and trial stage); ICC, *Prosecutor v. Katanga*, PTC I, Decision on the Confirmation of Charges, ICC-01/04-01/07-717, 30 September 2008, para. 189; ICC, *Prosecutor v. Abd-Al-Rahman*, PTC II, Decision on Defence Requests and Procedural Challenges, ICC-02/05-01/20-402, 21 May 2021, para. 43 ('The Chamber therefore firmly rejects the suggestion that it would be necessary to declare entire categories of evidence inadmissible in bulk on the basis of speculations about possible risks of interference. This would be especially inapposite in the context of the confirmation process, which is based largely on written statements that are obviously not subject to interference on account of the absence of confidentiality markings.')

[72] cf. provisions quoted in note 28 in this chapter.

[73] cf. Art. 69 (7) ICCS ('shall not be admissible').

[74] Section A.(8)(a) in this chapter.

[75] See also ICTY, *Prosecutor v. Karadžić*, TC, Public Redacted Version of Judgment Issued on 24 March 2016, IT-95-5/18-T, 24 March 2016, para. 8, highlighting the *in dubio pro reo* principle. See also MICT, *Prosecutor v. Stanišić and Simatović*, AC, Judgment, MICT-15-96-A, 31 May 2023, para. 591, emphasizing the 'bounds of discretion' as set forth in that rule.

[76] In US criminal procedure, this rule is also referred to as the 'original documents rule'. Accordingly, as a rule, the original documents are required. However, there are circumstances when a copy or other evidence of its contents may be admissible instead (see Rule 1004 of the Federal Rules of Evidence, allowing for 'other evidence of the content of a writing, recording, or photograph' under certain circumstances). On the common law origin, see Bantekas, *ICL* (2010), p. 487; Klamberg, in Sluiter et al., *International Criminal Procedure* (2013), pp. 1038–9; Wong, in Ruiz Fabri, *MPEiPro* (2023), mn. 1; crit., Gaynor, in Sluiter et al., *International Criminal Procedure* (2013), p. 1072. It should be noted, though, that in most common law jurisdictions, statutes have, more or less, abolished the 'best evidence rule', see Heinze, in Caeiro, Gless, and Mitsilegas, *Elgar Encyclopedia* (2022); Pattenden, in Malek, *Phipson on Evidence* (2022), para. 41.03–04.

[77] cf. ICTY, *Prosecutor v. Delalić et al.*, TC, Decision on the Tendering of Prosecution Exhibits 104–108, IT-96-21-T, 9 February 1998, para. 15 (referring to 'the old English case of *Omychund v. Barker* (1745) 1 Atk. 21 at p. 49, where Lord Hardwicke is quoted as saying, that 'the judges and sages of the law have laid it down that there is but

consideration.[78] If it is understood as expressing a preference of first-hand, original, direct evidence over second-hand, derivative, indirect evidence, it comes close to the immediacy principle known in civil law jurisdictions.[79] Rule 89 (B) was held to be an expression of 'common sense' and a 'reasonable' path,[80] creating a 'golden opportunity to craft a workable and just procedural and evidentiary regime that will foster the interests of international justice'.[81]

The relevant ICC law leaves it to the Court to rule on the admissibility of evidence on the basis of relevance, probative value, and fair trial considerations.[82] Chambers are free to take a 'holistic' and overall assessment approach with regard to the specific facts to be proven.[83] The *Bemba* PTCs and TCs had established a kind of presumption of admissibility (*prima*

one general rule of evidence, the best that the nature of the case will allow'. In the circumstances of this case, the Trial Chamber will guide its consideration of the evidence relying on this aphorism. The principle of a fair trial is dominant in our consideration. The Trial Chamber will rely on the best evidence available in the circumstances of the case.'); ICTY, *Prosecutor v. Gotovina et al.*, TC I, Reasons for the Decision, IT-06-90-T, 27 May 2008, para. 11 ('Trial Chambers at the Tribunal have interpreted the best evidence rule to mean that they will rely on the best available evidence'); ICTY, *Prosecutor v. Perišić*, TC I, Order for Guidelines on the Admission and Presentation of Evidence and Conduct of Counsel in Court, Annex, IT-04-81-T, 29 October 2008, para. 36; see also Schuon, *International Criminal Procedure* (2010), p. 161; Klamberg, *Evidence* (2013), pp. 342–3; Wong, in Ruiz Fabri, *MPEiPro* (2023), mn. 13. On IMT, IMTFE, and the hybrid tribunals, see Klamberg, in Sluiter et al., *International Criminal Procedure* (2013), p. 1019 (limiting it to the weight of the evidence); Wong, in Ruiz Fabri, *MPEiPro* (2023), mn. 12.

[78] cf. *Brđanin and Talić*, IT-99-36-T, Standards Order, para. 22 ('best evidence will depend on the particular circumstances attached to each document and to the complexity of this case and the investigations that preceded it'); ICTY, *Prosecutor v. Šešelj*, TC, Order Setting Out the Guidelines for the Presentation of Evidence and the Conduct of the Parties During the Trial, IT-03-67-T, 15 November 2007, para. 12 (determining 'best evidence available to each party with a mind to the burden of proof incumbent on that party and the particular circumstances of each piece of evidence, to the complexity of the case and to the investigations which preceded its production').

[79] cf. Klamberg, in Sluiter et al., *International Criminal Procedure* (2013), p. 1039; Vriend, *Criminal Trial* (2016), pp. 42 ff. For a comparative study on the immediacy principle, see the papers published in *ZStW*, 126 (2014), 173 ff. (for Switzerland, Riklin at 173; for France, Leblois-Happe at 185; for Spain, Bachmaier Winter at 194; for Italy, Negri at 2014; for England, Vogler at 239; for the Netherlands, Groenhuijsen and Selçuk at 248).

[80] cf. Dixon, *Transnat'lLCP*, 7 (1997), 100.

[81] Ntanda Nsereko, *CLF*, 5 (1994), 554.

[82] cf. Arts. 64 (9)(a), 69 (4) ICCS; also Rule 63 (2) RPE ICC. The reference to other factors ('inter alia') in Art. 69 (4) is also an expression of this discretion; see also Piragoff and Clarke, 'Article 69', in Ambos, *Commentary* (2022), mn. 69.

[83] ICC, *Prosecutor v. Yekatom and Ngaïssona*, TC, First Decision on the Prosecution Requests for Formal Submission of Prior Recorded Testimonies pursuant to Rule 68 (2)(b) of the Rules, ICC-01/14-01/18-1833-Corr-Red, 17 April 2023, para. 42 ('Chamber's holistic assessment when deliberating its judgment pursuant to Article 74(2) of the Statute'); ICC, *Prosecutor v. Ongwen*, TC IX, Judgment, ICC-02/04-01/15-1762-Red, 4 February 2021, para. 227; ICC, *Prosecutor v. Ntaganda*, TC VI, Judgment, ICC-01/04-02/06-2359, 8 July 2019 (with public annexes A, B, C), para. 45; ICC, *Prosecutor v. Lubanga*, AC, Judgment on the Appeal of Mr Thomas Lubanga Dyilo against his Conviction, ICC-01/04-01/06-3121-Red, 1 December 2014, para. 22 ('holistic evaluation and weighing of *all the evidence taken together* in relation to the fact at issue', referring to the ICTY and ICTR totality of the evidence approach); *Bemba*, ICC-01/05-01/08-3343, para. 218, pointing out, however, that the Chamber is free to ignore certain pieces of evidence ('[the Chamber] is under no obligation "to refer to the testimony of every witness or every piece of evidence on the trial record"' (para. 227)); *Karadžić*, IT-95-5/18-T, Judgment, para. 9 ('[T]he Chamber adopted an approach that favoured the admissibility of evidence, provided it was relevant and had probative value, and assessed the weight to be ascribed to each piece of evidence in its overall consideration of the entire trial record' (notes omitted)); previously also *Lubanga*, ICC-01/04-01/06-1399, para. 29 ('consider the position overall'). See also Bantekas, *ICL* (2010), pp. 531–2; Kiss, 'Article 74', in Ambos, *Commentary* (2022), mn. 38 with further references. Klamberg, *Evidence* (2013), pp. 151, 167 ff., 506 and Klamberg, *JICJ*, 13 (2015), 546–9 combines the totality of the evidence with the evaluation of a single piece ('combined' approach) and further advocates a 'comprehensive evaluation' consisting of three steps (identifying relevant facts, structuring the evidence, and determing probative value and weight). Crit. on the respective totality approach before ICTY/ICTR, McDermott, *LJIL*, 26 (2013), 985–8, 989, questioning the complex admissibility procedure with a view to consideration of the 'totality of the evidence' and the feasibility of this approach given the sheer amount of available evidence; in the same vein, McDermott, *JICJ*, 13 (2015), 520 ('immensely challenging').

*facie* admissibility)[84] stating that 'any evidence may be admitted ... unless it is expressly ruled inadmissible ... upon a challenge by any of the participants'.[85] The timing of this *prima facie* admissibility depends on the choice between the above-mentioned submission and admission approach:[86] where the evidence is merely being submitted and the admission decision is made at the end of the proceedings, *prima facie* admissibility consequently only plays a role within the holistic analysis of the evidence.[87] Upon closer analysis, however, the suggested '*prima facie* admissibility' turns out to be a red herring: the *Bemba* TC III seems to simply advocate for a submission approach, albeit using the slightly misleading term '*prima facie* admissibility'.[88] In addition, the *Lubanga* PTC, relied on by the *Bemba* TC III,[89] is not a valid authority since the PTC decided within a pre-trial context, where admissibility considerations are relaxed anyway. In any case, the admissibility decision, usually taken at the end of the proceedings, does not relieve TCs from a cautious item-by-item examination of the evidence, especially the one incriminating the accused.[90] Apart from that, a *prima facie* admissibility entails a too complicated three-tiered admissibility process where the actual admissibility of an item of evidence may remain unclear until the end of the trial phase thereby creating considerable uncertainty for the parties who do not know whether they can rely or not on it.[91]

With regard to the timing of admissibility rulings, ICC case law suggests discretion in so far as the TC 'will have to *consider* the relevance, probative value and the potential prejudice of each item of evidence at some point in the proceedings'.[92] This provides little guidance and 'leaves a lot of uncertainty'.[93]

[84] Crit. on this approach, esp. the consequences with a view to *prima facie* exclusion of evidence, *Ruto and Sang*, ICC-01/09-01/11-1353-Anx, para. 13.

[85] ICC, *Prosecutor v. Lubanga*, PTC I, Decision on the Schedule and Conduct of the Confirmation Hearing, ICC-01/04-01/06-678, 7 November 2006, p. 9; conc. ICC, *Prosecutor v. Bemba*, TC III, Decision on the Admission into Evidence of Materials Contained in the Prosecution's List of Evidence, ICC-01/05-01/08-1022, 19 November 2010, para. 10; *contra* ICC, *Prosecutor v. Bemba*, TC III, Dissenting Opinion of Judge Ozaki on the Decision on the Admission into Evidence of Materials Contained in the Prosecution's List of Evidence, ICC-01/05-01/08-1028, 23 November 2010, paras. 4–5, arguing that such a *prima facie* admissibility has no basis in the Court's legal framework.

[86] Notes 41 ff. in this chapter and main text.

[87] See ICC, *Prosecutor v. Ongwen*, TC IX, Decision on Prosecution Request to Submit Interception Related Evidence, ICC-02/04-01/15-615, 1 December 2016, para. 7: 'The Chamber emphasises that its general approach does not involve making any relevance, probative value or potential prejudice assessments at the point of submission—not even on a *prima facie* basis [ ... ] Article 74(2) of the Statute stipulates that the Chamber's final judgment can be based only on evidence "submitted and discussed" before it at the trial. Nowhere does this provision—or any other in the Court's applicable law—mandate that the evidence to be considered for the final judgment must have also been previously declared "admitted" or that a formal procedural step of "admission" of each item of evidence is otherwise required' [fn. omitted]). See also Schuon, *LJIL*, 25 (2012), 518 (correctly distinguishing the *Bemba* PTC's approach from the *Lubanga* TC's approach).

[88] See esp. *Bemba*, ICC-01/05-01/08-1022, para. 9.

[89] See above note 85 and main text.

[90] cf. *Bemba*, ICC-01/05-01/08-1386, paras. 78, 81. On the evaluation of each piece of evidence 'on its own merits', see also McDermott, *JICJ*, 13 (2015), 529–31 (discussing *Katanga* TJ and *Ngudjolo* AJ, Dissenting Opinion).

[91] For a convincing critique on the *Bemba* TC's approach, see Schuon, *LJIL*, 25 (2012), 516–19 (also correctly distinguishing it, at 518, from the *Lubanga* TC's approach which only referred to a *prima facie* [preliminary] admission as opposed to the ultimate assessment of probative value).

[92] ICC, *Prosecutor v. Bemba et al.*, AC, Judgment on the appeals of Mr Jean-Pierre Bemba Gombo, Mr Aimé Kilolo Musamba, Mr Jean-Jacques Mangenda Kabongo, Mr Fidèle Babala and Mr Narcisse Arido against the Decision of Trial Chamber VII entitled 'Judgment pursuant to Article 74 of the Statute', ICC-01/05-01/13-2275-Red, 8 March 2018, para. 594; *Ongwen*, ICC-02/04-01/15-2022-Red.

[93] Piragoff and Clarke, 'Article 69', in Ambos, *Commentary* (2022), mn. 47.

### *(c) Submission of evidence*

Notwithstanding the adversarial tendency of international criminal procedure,[94] leaving the submission of evidence to the parties[95] (or even the identification of the specifically relevant evidence),[96] the TC (presiding judge)[97] is fully entitled to direct the respective proceedings[98] as well as to request[99] (additional) evidence[100] and evaluate all evidence in the record,[101] guided by the ultimate procedural goal of the *'ascertainment' or 'determination' of*

[94] See, in more detail, Chapter I A.(2) in this volume. Crit. about the suitability of the adversarial-inquisitorial dichotomy, Heinze, in Bergsmo et al., *Power* (2020), pp. 155 ff.

[95] cf. Rules 85 (A) RPE ICTY/ICTR/SCSL and 102 (A) RPE MICT; Art. 69 (3) cl. 1 ICCS ('parties may submit evidence'); thereon, Kirsch, *ICLR*, 6 (2006), 288 ff.; also Rule 140 (1) RPE ICC *e contrario* (parties 'shall agree on the order and manner' if no judicial directions), thereto Schmitt, *JICJ*, 19 (2021), 485, 490–1 with further references; see also ICC, *Prosecutor v. Katanga and Ngudjoloi*, TC II, Corrigendum—Decision on the Disclosure of Evidentiary Material Relation to the Prosecutor's Site Visit to Bogoro on 28, 29, and 31 March 2009, ICC-01/04-01/07-1515-Corr, 9 October 2009, para. 68 ('adversarial principle' regarding expert evidence); generally see Bantekas, *ICL* (2010), p. 477 ('largely adversarial'); Schuon, *International Criminal Procedure* (2010), p. 170 ('remained adversarial'); Boas et al., *Procedure* (2011), p. 356 ('still predominantly adversarial'); Klamberg, *Evidence* (2013), pp. 203 ff. (distinguishing between Prosecutor, defence, and victims); Friman, in Cryer et al., *ICL* (2019), p. 433; Kuczyńska, *Accusation Model ICC* (2015), pp. 312, 314 ('strictly adversarial' regarding ad hoc tribunals); in detail on the order of presentation of evidence (from the IMT to the hybrid tribunals), see Klamberg, *Evidence* (2013), pp. 426 ff.; Vasiliev, in Sluiter et al., *International Criminal Procedure* (2013), pp. 565–635 (demonstrating the 'predominantly adversarial' structure [570] and the use of 'common law terminology' [585], e.g. evidence in rebuttal and rejoinder, in Rule 85 (A) RPE ICTY/ICTR/SCSL [569 ff.]); see Chapter IV, A.(3) in this volume. From a comparative perspective, Kuczyńska, *Accusation Model ICC* (2015), pp. 312–14.

[96] ICC, *Prosecutor v. Lubanga*, TC I, Judgment pursuant to Article 74 of the Statute, ICC-01/04-01/06-2842, 14 March 2012, para. 95. 'Parties', understood broadly as participants, includes victims, see Chapter II, E.(1) and (4)(d) in this volume *in fine*.

[97] On the dominant role of the TC and the presiding judge, see Chapter IV, A. (3)(a) in this volume.

[98] cf. Rules 90 (F) RPE ICTY/ICTR/SCSL and 106 (F) RPE MICT ('exercise control over the mode and order of interrogating witnesses and presenting evidence'); Art. 64 (8)(b) ICCS ('presiding judge may give directions', 'parties may submit evidence' only 'subject' to these directions); in the same vein, Rule 140 (1) RPE ICC ('[I]f the Presiding Judge does not give directions'); also Reg. 43 RegC ('determine the mode and order of interrogating witnesses and presenting evidence'). See also Combs, in Sluiter et al., *International Criminal Procedure* (2013), p. 733 (principle); Klamberg, *Evidence* (2013), pp. 222 ff. (on judicial intervention); Kuczyńska, *Accusation Model ICC* (2015), pp. 317–19, 324–6(on ICC law and practice); crit. on the *Lubanga* TC's direction to the parties to highlight the relevant evidence as 'burden-shifting' to the defence, see Roberts, *JICJ*, 10 (2012), 931–4, 943. Note that Art. 64 ICCS, esp. its para. 3, is generally applicable by way of the general *renvoi* in Art. 69 (3); thereto Piragoff and Clarke, 'Article 69', in Ambos, *Commentary* (2022), mn. 42. Generally, on the role of the judges in the ICC procedure, see De Smet, in Stahn and Sluiter, *ICC* (2009), pp. 418 ff.; Bock, *Opfer* (2010), pp. 346 ff.; Mégret, *UCLA JIL & ForAff*, 14 (2009), 69; from a comparative perspective, Kuczyńska, *Accusation Model ICC* (2015), pp. 337–46.

[99] A German proposal introducing a 'duty' to call evidence has however been rejected; cf. Piragoff and Clarke, 'Article 69', in Ambos, *Commentary* (2022), mn. 2; also Klamberg, *Evidence* (2013), pp. 150–1.

[100] Rules 98 RPE ICTY/ICTR and 120 RPE MICT and Art. 69 (3) 2nd cl. ICCS ('authority to request'); see also the general power by way of Rules 54 RPE ICTY/ICTR/SCSL and 55 RPE MICT and more specifically Rules 85 (B) RPE ICTY/ICTR and 102 (B) RPE MICT (judge 'may at any stage put any question to the witness') and Art. 64 (6)(b) ('require the attendance and testimony'), Art. 64 (6)(d) ICCS ('order the production of evidence'). See also *Lubanga*, ICC-01/04-01/06-1399, para. 20; *Lubanga*, ICC-01/04-01/06-2842, para. 97 (reviewing 'other items of evidence as appropriate'); *Bemba et al.*, ICC-01/05-01/13-1285, para. 5; ICC, *Prosecutor v. Ruto and Sang*, TC V(a), Separate, Partly Concurring Opinion of *Judge Eboe-Osuji* on the 'Decision of Prosecution Request for Admission of Prior Recorded Testimony', ICC-01/09-01/11-1938-Anx-Red, 19 August 2015, paras. 27–9 (para. 28: 'expression of the plenitude of a Trial Chamber's incidental jurisdiction to do justice'). On the ad hoc tribunals' practice, see Vasiliev, in Sluiter et al., *International Criminal Procedure* (2013), p. 570: evidence to 'be called at the proper time' (refering to Delalić et al. in n. 511), pp. 578–9 (Rule 98 discretionary, *extrema ratio* but not 'dead letter'), 585 (normally first examination of witness by Chamber), 594–8 (sophisticated analysis of Rule 85 (B) and the ensuing tensions depending on the judge's style); see also Combs, in Sluiter et al., *International Criminal Procedure* (2013), pp. 691–3, 699 (principle); Terrier, 'Powers of the Trial Chamber', in Cassese et al., *Rome Statute II* (2002), p. 1273; Bonomy, *JICJ*, 5 (2007), 355; Heinze, *Disclosure* (2014), pp. 243–4. On the ICC, see Kuczyńska, *Accusation Model ICC* (2015), pp. 350–1; too restrictive and somewhat inconsistent, Piragoff and Clarke, 'Article 69', in Ambos, *Commentary* (2022), mn. 44 (no 'own authority' but 'for the Court alone to decide whether ... sufficient evidence'); see also Ambos, *ICLR*, 12 (2012), 121–3; Sato, *Structures ICL* (2021), p. 98. On similar powers at the IMT, IMTFE, SPSC, ECCC, and STL, see Combs, in Sluiter et al., *International Criminal Procedure* (2013), pp. 691, 694, 721, 728–9.

[101] ICC, *Prosecutor v. Katanga*, TC II, Judgment pursuant to Article 74 of the Statute, ICC-01/04-01/07-3436-tENG, 7 March 2014, para. 81. On the 'record of proceedings', see Sections A.(7) and B.(1)(c) in this chapter.

*the truth*.[102] This has an inquisitorial undertone[103] but it must be stressed that the order of the presentation of evidence is not structurally different at the tribunals, including the ICC.

At the ICC, in a nutshell, the great bulk of the evidence is presented and submitted respectively[104] by the prosecution and defence and each of these two evidentiary blocks is presented in one separate phase.[105] To be sure, the ICC's legal regime allows for an alternative—either more adversarial or inquisitorial—organization of the trial proceedings,[106] albeit overcoming the two parties dichotomy of the pure adversarial system[107] by bringing the victims in as a further participant.[108] At the same time, this mixed approach causes, arguably, disorder in the formerly ordered world of autopoietic procedural systems,[109] leaving the final trial organization to the judges who may consult with the parties.[110] Indeed, given the widespread fragmentation among international criminal tribunals, the only common denominator appears to be the TCs' authority to determine the order and mode of the presentation of evidence,[111] including their right to put questions to the witness at any time.[112]

The ICC's *Chambers' Practice Manual* tries to streamline the conduct of the proceedings through a 'a model for the decision on "Directions for the Conduct of Proceedings" which is appended to the present manual by way of a confidential annex'.[113] The regular sequence

[102] References to the 'truth' can be found in Rules 90 (F)(i) RPE ICTY/ICTR/SCSL, 106 (F)(i) RPE MICT, Art. 69 (3) *in fine* ICCS, and Rule 143 (4)(a) KSC RPE ('effective for the ascertainment of the truth'). See also *Gbagbo and Blé Goudé*, ICC-02/11-01/15-405, para. 12; Pitcher, *Judicial Responses* (2018), p. 281.

[103] See also Hofstetter, *Verfahrensrecht* (2005), pp. 109–10; Heinze, in Bergsmo et al., *Power* (2020), pp. 155, 166 ff. From a national perspective, see e.g. s. 244 (2) German CPC (*StPO*) setting out the establishment of the truth as the main goal of German criminal procedure and thus the guiding principle of the courts' performance in the evidentiary process; thereto Bohlander, *German Criminal Procedure* (2021), pp. 163–5. On the other hand, common law judges will rarely use their authority to call witnesses in order to avoid any appearance of unfairness or a lack of impartiality; for the same reasons great caution is displayed when questioning witnesses, especially in jury trials; cf. Combs, in Sluiter et al., *International Criminal Procedure* (2013), pp. 697–8, 704–5. From a comparative perspectiveCH, Heinze and Fyfe, in Ambos et al., *Core Concepts I* (2020), p. 343, 347.

[104] There is a separate procedure for the submission of (documentary) evidence, see e.g. ICC, *Prosecutor v. Said*, TC VI, Directions on the Conduct of the Proceedings, ICC-01/14-01/21-251, 9 March 2022, paras. 22 ff.

[105] cf. Vasiliev, in Sluiter et al., *International Criminal Procedure* (2013), pp. 570–1 (regarding ad hoc tribunals) and pp. 601–7 (analysing the directions pursuant to Rule 140 (1) RPE ICC in the first four ICC cases and concluding that the difference to the ad hoc tribunals lies mainly in the intervention by victims and the flexibility regarding Chamber witnesses). This is clearly a common law feature, cf. op. cit., p. 639 with references in n. 1092. For the same result from a comparative perspective, see Kuczyńska, *Accusation Model ICC* (2015), p. 320, discussing the civil law 'thematic organisation model' but concluding that the ICC so far has followed the presentation in block in line with the ad hoc tribunals. Crit. of the ensuing binary structure of case presentation and the bifurcation of the trial with regard to the goals of international criminal justice, e.g. determination of the truth, satisfaction of victims' interests, and national reconciliation, Damaška, *ChicKentLR*, 83 (2008), 337–8, 342–3, 357–8; Damaška, *Companion* (2009), pp. 176–7, 180–1; Eser, 'The "Adversarial" Procedure', in Kruessmann, *ICTY* (2008), pp. 218–20, 224–5, 226 (trial used by the parties as a stage); also Vasiliev, in Sluiter et al., *International Criminal Procedure* (2013), pp. 642–5, 651; Heinze, in Wright, Levine, and Gold, *OxfIIB Prosecutors* (2021), pp. 117–51, 125 ff.

[106] Generally on the structure of the trial, see Chapter IV, A.(3)(a) in this volume. See also Kreß, *JICJ*, 1 (2003), 605; Vasiliev, in Sluiter et al., *International Criminal Procedure* (2013), pp. 600–1.

[107] In a similar vein, ibid., p. 601, in this regard, speaking of a mixed or *sui generis* model, Klamberg, *Evidence* (2013), pp. 504–5.

[108] Chapter II, E.(4) in this volume.

[109] Vasiliev, in Sluiter et al., *International Criminal Procedure* (2013), p. 631 ('"postmodernist" suspense and uncertainty embodied in the ICC Statute').

[110] See Chapter IV, A.(4)(a) in this volume and, in addition to the above-mentioned Art. 64 (8)(b) ICCS and Rule 140 (1) RPE ICC, Art. 64 (3)(a) ICCS (pre-trial consultations with a view to organise trial) and Art. 64 (6)(b) ICCS ('require the attendance and testimony of witnesses and production of documents and other evidence'); see also the powers of the Chamber under Reg. 54 RegC.

[111] cf. Vasiliev, in Sluiter et al., *International Criminal Procedure* (2013), pp. 631–2. This is also the (only) common principle in comparative law, cf. pp. 641–2, 652 (proposing it as a general principle).

[112] cf. ibid., p. 654 (recommending TC's control over 'mode and order of interrogating witnesses and presenting evidence' as a general rule).

[113] ICC, *Practice Manual* (2023), para. 84. See also Schmitt, *JICJ*, *19* (2021), 485, 490. McDermott Rees, *Völkerrechtsblog* 14 July 2022, supports the model direction but criticizes that it is 'procedural law-making through the back door'.

of the presentation of evidence is, in line with Articles 64 (6)(b) and 69 (3) ICCS: 'i) presentation of evidence by the Prosecution; ii) any presentation of evidence by the LRV, should leave to do so be granted; and iii) any presentation of evidence by the Defence'.[114] Rejoinder and rebuttal are an option only after leave is sought.[115] A modified (discretionary)[116] model is followed by the KSC, where evidence at trial is usually presented in the following sequence: (i) evidence called by the SPO; (ii) evidence called by victims' counsel, as ordered by the Panel, if any; (iii) evidence called by the defence; (iv) evidence called by the Panel pursuant to Rule 132 of the Rules, if any; (v) SPO evidence in rebuttal, with leave of the Panel; and (vi) defence evidence in rejoinder, with leave of the Panel.[117] According to Rule 127 RPE KSC, '[a] Judge may at any stage put any question to the witness', which corresponds to Rule 85 (B) RPE ICTY/ICTR[118] and Rule 140 (2)(c) RPE ICC.[119] The KSC CoAP clarified that trial panels have a wide discretion in questioning witnesses and questions do not have to be related to questions posed by one of the parties.[120]

In any case, it should not be overlooked that truth-seeking is by no means alien to adversarial procedure;[121] rather, there it takes a more discursive and dialectic route[122] than in an inquisitorial system, resulting in the juxtaposition of (inquisitorial) *substantive* versus (adversarial) *procedural truth*.[123] As Heinze and Fyfe note, the distinction between procedural and substantive truth largely corresponds to the common law distinction between procedural and substantive fairness.[124] From this perspective, the above-mentioned best evidence rule, to be observed by the parties when submitting evidence,[125] is informed by

[114] See *Said*, ICC-01/14-01/21-251, para. 10.

[115] Ibid.

[116] KSC, *Prosecutor v. Thaçi et al.*, CoAP, Public Redacted Version of Decision on Thaçi, Selimi and Krasniqi Appeal against Oral Order on Trial Panel Questioning, KSC-BC-2020-06/IA028/F00011/RED, 4 July 2023, para. 10 ('The Panel stresses that decisions concerning trial management issues and the conduct of proceedings are generally treated as discretionary').

[117] KSC, *Prosecutor v. Shala*, TP I, Public Redacted Version of Decision on the Conduct of the Proceedings, KSC-BC-2020-04/F00434/RED, 24 February 2023, para. 9.

[118] Both providing that 'a Judge may at any stage put any question to the witness'.

[119] Providing that '[t]he Trial Chamber has the right to question a witness before or after a witness is questioned by a participant'; thereto Schmitt, *JICJ*, 19 (2021), 485, 500, who cautions, however: '[T]he mere fact that something is permissible under the ICC's instruments does not necessarily mean that it has to be done in this way.'

[120] KSC, *Prosecutor v. Thaçi, Veseli, Selimi and Krasniqi*, CoAP, Public Redacted Version of Decision on Thaçi, Selimi and Krasniqi Appeal against Oral Order on Trial Panel Questioning, KSC-BC-2020-06/IA028/F00011/RED, 4 July 2023, paras. 10 and 32.

[121] See Safferling, *International Criminal Procedure* (2003), pp. 18–19; Piragoff and Clarke, 'Article 69', in Ambos, *Commentary* (2022), mn. 5 (active role of judges in adversarial systems too); Gleß, *Beweisrechtsgrundsätze* (2006), pp. 89 ff.; Weigend, in Bernsmann and Fischer, *FS Rissing-van Saan* (2011), pp. 749 ff.; Lippke, in Brown, Turner, and Weißer, *OxfHb Criminal Process* (2019), p. 31.

[122] Some consider this discursive and dialectic path even better suited to ascertaining the truth, see e.g. Luban, *The Good Lawyer* (1983), pp. 83, 99; Goodpaster, *JCL&Crim*, 78 (1987–1988), 124; see also the examples in Jackson and M'Boge, *LJIL*, *26* (2013), 949 ff., esp. 954. On the issue as a whole, Heinze, *Disclosure* (2014), pp. 112, 122, 218 ff.

[123] cf. Volk, *Wahrheit und materielles Recht im Strafprozeß* (1980), pp. 15 ff.; for further references, see Ambos, *ZStW*, 115 (2003), 617–18. On 'substantive truth' in Germany and France on the one hand and 'procedural truth' in England and Wales on the other hand, see Gleß, *Beweisrechtsgrundsätze* (2006), pp. 81 ff. On the USA, see Langer, *AJCompL*, 53 (2005), 862; Trüg, *ZStW*, 120 (2008), 346 ff.; Murphy, *JICJ*, 8 (2010), 547 ff. The German Federal Court of Justice (*Bundesgerichtshof*) has explicitly underlined the role of procedural truth in criminal procedure: '[a]cceptance and legitimacy of criminal judgments are not based on the trust in a "correctness", understood as a material truth that is discovered in the course of a criminal trial. Instead, trust in the "procedural truth" is both necessary and sufficient. The "procedural truth" is created through a trial that complies with both the substantial and procedural law and is therefore fair.' See BGH, Judgment from 10 June 2015 – 2 StR 97/14, in *NStZ* 2016, 52, 58 (translation K.A.); thereto Heinze, in Bergsmo and Dittrich, *Integrity*, (2020), 615, 696–7.

[124] Heinze and Fyfe, in Ambos et al., *Core Concepts I* (2020), 343, 347 with n. 19.

[125] cf. *Gotovina et al.*, IT-06-90-T, Reasons for the Decision, para. 11; also ICTY, *Prosecutor v. Haradinaj et al.*, TC I, Decision on Admission into Evidence of Documents Tendered during Testimony of Achilleas Pappas,

the probative value of the respective evidence with a view to the establishment of the truth. In other words, the evidence must contribute to the determination of the truth, that is, it must be new and relevant.[126] The fact that the parties present evidence does not make the search for truth any less relevant. This is demonstrated by Statutes on international criminal tribunals that endorse judicial questioning on matters beyond clarification of a witness's testimony.[127] The right to challenge a piece of evidence[128] is triggered by the moment of submission of this evidence[129] unless the relevant issue only becomes known later.[130] The burden to rebut this challenge rests with the party who seeks to introduce the respective evidence.[131]

The 'submission' of evidence within the meaning of Article 74 (2) last clause ICCS and Rule 64 (1) RPE ICC, must, however, be distinguished from the mere filing of a 'list of evidence' with the respective material.[132] As clarified by the *Bemba* AC, 'evidence is "submitted" if it is presented to the Trial Chamber by the parties on their own initiative or pursuant to a request by the Trial Chamber for the purpose of proving or disproving the facts in issue before the Chamber' and this submission conforms 'to the directions of the Presiding Judge or the manner agreed upon by the parties'.[133] The submission may also take place outside the trial hearing if the respective procedure has been clearly determined.[134]

## (2) Relevance, probative value (reliability), and fundamental procedural principles

### *(a) Relevance, probative value, and reliability*

The above mentioned key concepts—'relevance' and 'probative value'—require, of course, a more precise determination. Evidence is *relevant* if it tends to prove or disapprove a material

IT-04-84-T, 17 September 2007, para. 6 ('Prosecution's task to sift through its collection of documents and carefully select the best evidence to present to the Chamber in the most comprehensible and efficient manner').

[126] In a similar vein, ICTY, *Prosecutor v. Kordić and Čerkez*, TC, Decision on Prosecutor's Submissions Concerning 'Zagreb Exhibits' and Presidential Transcripts, IT-95-14/2-T, 1 December 2000, para. 36 (not formerly available evidence, not cumulative/repetitious and of 'significant relevance'); on the ad hoc tribunals' 'good cause' test to recall a witness in rebuttal or rejoinder, see Vasiliev, in Sluiter et al., *International Criminal Procedure* (2013), pp. 576–7; Combs, in Sluiter et al., *International Criminal Procedure* (2013), pp. 736, 737–8, 740, 742 (general rule); on the extraordinary reopening of the (prosecution or defence) case and the submission of 'fresh evidence', see Vasiliev, in Sluiter et al., *International Criminal Procedure* (2013), pp. 581–4; Combs, in Sluiter et al., *International Criminal Procedure* (2013), p. 736–7, 738, 740, on rebuttal, rejoinder, and general re-examination before the ICC, see Vasiliev, in Sluiter et al., *International Criminal Procedure* (2013), pp. 602, 604, 615–16; for a general rule regarding presentation of new evidence after close of the case if such evidence 'is newly obtained and could not have been obtained before', Vasiliev, ibid., p. 652; more restrictively Combs, in Sluiter et al., *International Criminal Procedure* (2013), pp. 742–3.

[127] *Thaçi, Veseli, Selimi, and Krasniqi*, KSC-BC-2020-06/IA028/F0001/RED, para. 34 with n. 83; Bitti, 'Article 64', in Ambos, *Commentary* (2022), mn. 45.

[128] See generally Klamberg, in Sluiter et al., *International Criminal Procedure* (2013), pp. 1030–2.

[129] Rule 64 (1) cl. 1 RPE ICC ('must be raised at the time when the evidence is submitted').

[130] Rule 64 (1) cl. 2 RPE ICC ('may be raised immediately after the issue has become known').

[131] *Lubanga*, ICC-01/04-01/06-1399, para. 25 (invoking the ICTY case law).

[132] On the list of evidence at the ad hoc tribunals (Rule 65*ter* (E)(ii) and (G)(i) RPE ICTY, Rule 70 (E)(ii) and (M)(i) RPE MICT, and Rules 73*bis* (B)(iv) and (E) and 73*ter* (B)(iii) and (E) RPE ICTR/SCSL) and the Chamber's discretion to vary them, see Vasiliev, in Sluiter et al., *International Criminal Procedure* (2013), pp. 572–3; Klamberg, *Evidence* (2013), pp. 458–60.

[133] *Bemba*, ICC-01/05-01/08-1386, para. 43, rejecting the TC's admission as evidence of the Prosecutor's list of evidence (paras. 44–6).

[134] *Bemba*, ICC-01/05-01/08-1386, para. 43.

issue[135] or if it 'makes the existence of a fact at issue more or less probable'.[136] Contrary to the ambiguous wording of Article 69 (4) ICCS, relevance is distinct from admissibility in that the latter is the umbrella concept and the former one factor to determine admissibility.[137]

Relevance is a relational concept in that it relates to a specific item of evidence and the fact it seeks to prove or disprove;[138] it defines the purpose of this item in the proceedings.[139] Relevance speaks to the 'rational probativeness of the evidence' with regard to the respective fact, that is, 'the question is whether the item of evidence is rationally probative to a fact in issue'.[140] 'Probativeness' comes close to 'probative value', demonstrating the nexus between 'relevance' and 'probative value' to be revisited in a moment. The relational character of the relevance criterion also finds its expression in its relation to the specific case, that is, the respective piece of evidence must be 'relevant'[141] or 'material'[142] to the case, to one issue or accused.[143] This gives Chambers a broad discretion to exclude certain pieces of evidence on certain subject matters—perhaps the most important purpose of the relevance test[144]—as

[135] May and Wierda, *International Criminal Evidence* (2002), p. 102.

[136] *Katanga*, ICC-01/04-01/07-2635, para. 16; *Ruto* and *Sang*, ICC-01/09-01/11-1353, para. 15. ICC, *Prosecutor v. Ruto and Sang*, TC V(a), Public Redacted Version of Decision on the Ruto Defence's Request for Admission of Documentary Evidence, ICC-01/09-01/11-1943-Red, 28 August 2015, date of public redacted version: 11 December 2017, para. 9 ('The Chamber recalls, in particular, when making general admissibility assessments, the document sought for admission must be *prima facie* relevant. It must relate to a material issue or fact that is to be properly considered by the Chamber in the sense of making it more or less probable, that is, tending to prove or disprove the material issue or fact in question'). See also KSC, *Prosecutor v. Mustafa*, AC, Public Redacted Version of Appeal Judgment, KSC-CA-2023-02/F00038/RED, 14 December 2023, para. 37 ('For the purposes of deciding on the admissibility of evidence, relevance is assessed on the basis of whether the proposed evidence relates to elements of the offence(s) or mode(s) of liability pleaded in the indictment, or to other facts or circumstances material to the parties' case').

[137] In a similar vein, *Katanga*, ICC-01/04-01/07-2635, para. 16 (relevance as 'legal precondition to admissibility'); ICC, *Prosecutor v. Abd-Al-Rahman*, AC, Judgment on the Appeal of Mr Ali Muhammad Ali Abd-Al-Rahman against the Decision of Trial Chamber I of 17 February 2023 Entitled 'Decision on the admissibility of video (DAR-OTP-0216-0119) and records of telephone calls (DAR-OTP-0216-0127, DAR-OTP-0216-0128)', ICC-02/05-01/20-982, 28 June 2023, para. 79 ('relevance and/or admissibility'); also ICTY, *Prosecutor v. Delalić et al.*, TC, Decision on the Prosecution's Oral Requests for the Admission of Exhibit 155 into Evidence and for an Order to Compel the Accused, Zdravko Mucic, to Provide a Handwriting Sample, IT-96-21-T, 19 January 1998, para. 29; ICTY, *Prosecutor v. Delalić et al.*, TC, Decision on the Motion of the Prosecution for the Admissibility of Evidence, IT-96-21, 19 January 1998, para. 17; *Mustafa*, KSC-CA-2023-02/F00038/RED, para. 37 ('The Panel recalls that a decision on whether to admit or exclude evidence pursuant to Rule 138(1) of the Rules is one that lies within a trial panel's discretion in its assessment of the relevance, authenticity and probative value of the submitted evidence. A trial panel may refuse to admit evidence where no reasonable showing of relevance has been made' [notes omitted]). See also Piragoff and Clarke, 'Article 69', in Ambos, *Commentary* (2022), mn. 52 ('related but distinct concepts'); Safferling, *International Criminal Procedure* (2012), p. 490 (relevance as 'part of admissibility').

[138] On the nexus between relevance and the subject matter, see *Tadić*, IT-94-1-T, Hearsay Decision, para.18; ICTY, *Prosecutor v. Kupreškić et al.*, TC, Decision on Evidence of the Good Character of the Accused and the Defence of Tu Quoque, IT-95-16-T, 17 February 1999; *Musema*, ICTR-96-13-A, para. 39; also *Lubanga*, ICC-01/04-01/06-1399, para. 27 (evidence 'relevant' if 'it relates to the matters that are properly to be considered' with regard to the charges). See also Klamberg, *Evidence* (2013), p. 345 ('logical fit'); Piragoff and Clarke, 'Article 69', in Ambos, *Commentary* (2022), mn. 52; Gaynor, *BCLR*, 63 (2022), 37, 42.

[139] See also *Katanga*, ICC-01/04-01/07-2635, para. 17 (considering this as one of the purposes of the relevance criterion). Generally Schmitt, *JICJ*, *19* (2021), 485, 492.

[140] Piragoff and Clarke, 'Article 69', in Ambos, *Commentary* (2022), mn. 52; Schabas, *ICC Commentary* (2016), p. 1088; cf. also *Delalić et al.*, IT-96-21-T, Exhibit 155 Decision, para. 29; *Delalić et al.*, IT-96-21, Admissibility of Evidence Decision, para. 17; *Ruto and Sang*, ICC-01/09-01/11-1943-Red, para. 9 (as quoted above note 1369). See also James, *CalLR*, 29 (1941), 689 ff.

[141] cf. Art. 69 (3) cl. 1 ICCS; thereon also Piragoff and Clarke, 'Article 69', in Ambos, *Commentary* (2022), mn. 42 (stressing that it may be relevant 'to other issues in the case').

[142] cf. Broun, *McCormick on Evidence* (2014), pp. 395–6 ('Materiality concerns the fit between the evidence and the case'). Thus, 'materiality' is, besides probative value, the second component of relevance; cf. Klamberg, *Evidence* (2013), p. 344; Klamberg, in Sluiter et al., *International Criminal Procedure* (2013), pp. 1039, 1042; Ho, *Philosophy* (2008), p. 10.

[143] cf. *Katanga*, ICC-01/04-01/07-2635, para. 18 (relevance to only one accused 'not a ground for objection' by the other accused). See also *Taylor*, SCSL-03-01-T-721, para. 38 (relation of document to witness).

[144] *Katanga*, ICC-01/04-01/07-2635, para. 17 (purpose of relevance criterion).

being irrelevant for the case at hand.[145] Thus, for example, evidence on the 'historical, political or military background' of the alleged crimes has been excluded as irrelevant.[146] The case law has taken a restrictive approach so far,[147] that is, evidence is generally considered to be relevant using a rather low threshold.[148]

Depending on the procedural stage (and the standard of proof required), a Chamber may only make 'a prima facie assessment of the relevance of any material, on the basis that it appears to be *a priori* relevant to the case'.[149] For evidence submitted by victims,[150] their special right under Article 68 (3) ICCS must be taken into account.[151] In any case, irrelevant evidence should be excluded at the outset for reasons of expediency and the right to a speedy trial.[152] Indeed, it is one of the few outstanding and uncontroversial principles of the international (criminal) law of evidence that 'needless consumption of time' is to be avoided[153] and thus 'the parties and/or participants shall refrain from long, compound, or repetitive questions'.[154] At the ICC, the application of evidence and disclosure law has been identified as one of the reasons for lengthy trials, especially the debate revolving around the submission vs. admission approaches[155] and witness preparation/proofing.[156] Here a TC's managerial capacity with regard to evidence presentation[157] takes centre stage.[158] At the KSC, for instance, status conferences are used to discuss the conduct of proceedings, especially with

[145] See also Piragoff and Clarke, 'Article 69', in Ambos, *Commentary* (2022), mn. 54.

[146] ICTY, *Prosecutor v. Kunarac et al.*, TC II, Decision on Prosecution's Motion for Exclusion of Evidence and Limitation of Testimony, IT-96-23 & 23/1-T, 3 July 2000; see also Rules 92*bis* (A)(i)(b) RPE ICTY/ICTR and 100 (A)(i)(b) RPE MICT (requiring 'relevant' evidence on 'background'). There is no comparable ICC rule.

[147] *Kupreškić et al.*, IT-95-16-T, Decision on Evidence, p. 5 (evidence irrelevant that is supposed to show that the 'other side' may have committed crimes or may have started the conflict); similarly *Kunarac et al.*, IT-96-23 & 23/1-T, Prosecution's Motion Decision, para. 6, excluding parts of a report by a defence expert witness, which contained analysis of historical reasons for the conflict, information on the responsible, and crimes committed by the other side.

[148] Safferling, *International Criminal Procedure* (2012), p. 493.

[149] *Bemba*, ICC-01/05-01/08-1022, para. 10. For a similar approach, see *Lubanga*, ICC-01/04-01/06-1399, paras. 26–7 ('Chamber must ensure that the evidence is prima facie relevant to the trial'); *Ongwen*, ICC-02/04-01/15-1762-Red, para. 247.

[150] Pursuant to Art. 69 (3) ICCS, note 95 in this chapter.

[151] cf. ICC, *Prosecutor v. Nourain*, TC IV, Decision on the Participation of Victims in the Trial Proceedings, ICC-02/05-03/09-545, 20 March 2014, para. 29 ('combined effect' of Art. 68 (3) and Arts. 64 (9) and 69 (4) ICCS), Piragoff and Clarke, 'Article 69', in Ambos, *Commentary* (2022), mn. 40 with further references to case law.

[152] ICTY, *Prosecutor v. Orić*, TC II, Order Concerning Guidelines on Evidence and the Conduct of Parties During Trial Proceedings, IT-03-68-T, 21 October 2004, para. 10, generally referring to fairness ('irrelevant evidence must be, and will be, excluded in the most unequivocal way in the interest of a fair and expeditious trial').

[153] cf. Rules 90 (F)(ii) RPE ICTY/ICTR and 106 (F)(ii) RPE MICT; also Rule 90 (F)(ii) RPE SCSL ('Avoid the wasting of time') and Reg. 43 (b) RegC ('Avoid delays and ensure the effective use of time').

[154] Vasiliev, in Sluiter et al., *International Criminal Procedure* (2013), p. 635 (with further references in n. 1065). See also note 126 in this chapter regarding the presentation of new evidence.

[155] Expert Group, *IER* (2020), pp. 177–8, paras. 546 ff. ('Should this continue to be a problem … , which is thought to be unlikely, the matter could be resolved by adopting a presidential directive or incorporating appropriate provisions into the Regulations of the Court, introducing the solution agreed among the Judges').

[156] Ibid., pp. 178–9, para. 551. For an overview, see also Gumpert and Nuzban, in Heinze and Dittrich, *ICC* (2021), pp. 553 ff.

[157] See above notes 98 ff. in this chapter and main text. See also Expert Group, *IER* (2020), p. 180, para. 556 ('Proactive judicial case management is as important to the fairness and expeditiousness of trial proceedings as it is to pre-trial proceedings').

[158] On the importance of the respective managerial powers of judges, see ibid., p. 166, para. 513; see also Kuczyńska, *Accusation Model ICC* (2015), pp. 327, 354–5; Gumpert and Nuzban, in Heinze and Dittrich, *ICC* (2021), p. 582 ('Within trial proceedings, more hands-on management by presiding judges could significantly shorten the giving of evidence. Judges could query the relevance of certain lines of questioning at an early stage and rule out those which are not relevant to central issues in the case. Trial Chambers could refuse to hear witnesses unlikely to cast light on the allegations made by the Prosecution, or at least require that their statements be submitted in writing under Rule 68 of the Rules of Procedure and Evidence').

a view to reducing evidence (witness) presentation to the absolutely necessary;[159] also, the presiding judge of a Trial Panel may issue 'trial management orders'.[160] This list of possible orders is not exhaustive, it ranges from disclosure orders to 'other preparatory orders'.[161] At the ICC, both the updated versions of the *Practice Manual* and amended Regulations of the Court have tried to address the issue of lengthy proceedings.[162]

Given the sheer amount of evidence in international criminal trials,[163] case charts may be useful to order, systematize, and link evidence to the relevant facts and elements of crime;[164] Protocols should be standardized, including the one on the Electronic Document Management System ('E-Court'),[165] and prior recorded testimony and live testimony should be used by means of audio- or video-link technology;[166] Artificial Intelligence can be used to save time and costs for translations and transcriptions.[167] In *Ongwen*, the Single Judge of TC IX directed the parties and participants to make requests and motions by email.[168]

*Probative value* has, in the context of the law of evidence, a twofold meaning.[169] On the one hand, it refers to the degree of relevance of certain evidence with regard to a certain fact. This is most explicit in Article 69 (4) ICCS according to which 'relevance' is assessed, inter alia, by taking into account the 'probative value' of the evidence.[170] The relationship is more neutral under the law of the ad hoc tribunals: relevant evidence must have probative value[171] or, in other words, probative value relates to whether certain evidence 'tends to prove an issue' which is relevant to the proceedings.[172]

159 The number of witnesses and the ensuing length of proceedings have been a particular concern in the trial against the (former) UCKA leadership (*Hashim Thaçi et al.*, see <https://www.scp-ks.org/en/cases/hashim-thaci-et-al>). The trial started on 3 April 2023 and its length, especially with a view to the number of witnesses to be heard, has been discussed in a status conference of 20 March 2023 (before the start of the trial) and subsequently in a status conference of 21 February 2024. The target date for the closing of the prosecution (SPO) case has been set by the Panel as 1 April 2025.

160 Rule 116 (4) RPE KSC; in more detail, see Heinze, *JICJ*, 15 (2017), 985, 1001–5; Heinze, in Heinze and Dittrich, *ICC* (2021), p. 68.

161 Rule 116 (4) cl. 3 RPE KSC.

162 See e.g. Regs. 20 (2), 24 (5), 33 (1)(d), 34, 36, 38 and 44 (1) RegC concerning page limits, time limits, and other procedural matters. See, in more detail, Gumpert and Nuzban, in Heinze and Dittrich, *ICC* (2021), p. 579.

163 See e.g. McDermott, *JICJ*, 13 (2015), 507–8 (inter alia referring to the *Katanga* trial).

164 Advocating neo-Wigmorian charting in this regard, Roberts, *JICJ*, 13 (2015), 492 ff. (explaining how it can assist evidential analysis in ICL); McDermott, *JICJ*, 13 (2015), 514 ff. (arguing that it facilitates trial preparation for the parties and judicial reasoning and defending it against criticisms); about the uses and limitations of 'Modified Wigmorean Analysis' and its particular application to witness credibility at the ICTR, see Anderson and Twining, *CLF*, 26 (2015), 374 ff.; advocating also other methods and guiding the structuring of evidence with five questions, Klamberg, *Evidence* (2013), pp. 170–1; Klamberg, *JICJ*, 13 (2015), 547–8.

165 Expert Group, *IER* (2020), p. 166, para. 513.

166 Ibid., pp. 179-80, para. 552 ff.; ICC, *IER Response* (2021), para. 378 ('The Chambers of the Court already make use of the possibility to introduce prior recorded testimony into the proceedings and to allow presentation of evidence through electronic and other means. It is both the obligation and the prerogative of each Chamber in each case to ensure that the evidence is presented in the most appropriate way, ensuring that proceedings are conducted fairly, expeditiously and efficiently. Further regulation in this regard does not appear to be required or indeed desirable. That said, the Judiciary has taken good note of the recommendation, which will be given due attention going forward').

167 Gumpert and Nuzban, in Heinze and Dittrich, *ICC* (2021), pp. 570–1.

168 ICC, *Prosecutor v. Ongwen,* TC IX, Decision on Publicity of Case Record, ICC-02/04-01/15-700, 7 February 2017, para. 5.

169 cf. Dennis, *Evidence* (2010), p. 110.

170 So understood, 'relevance' encompasses 'probative value'; cf. *Ruto and Sang,* ICC-01/09-01/11-1353-Anx, paras. 4–7.

171 Rules 89 (C) RPE ICTY/ICTR and 105 (C) RPE MICT; also Rule 138 (1) RPE KSC. See also Schuon, *International Criminal Procedure* (2010), pp. 138–9; Piragoff and Clarke, 'Article 69', in Ambos, *Commentary* (2022), mn. 55–6.

172 *Delalić et al.*, IT-96-21-T, Exhibit 155 Decision, para. 29; Ibid., Admissibility of Evidence Decision, para. 17.

On the other hand, probative value is also used as a synonym for the '*weight*' of the evidence with regard to a fact in issue.[173] Weight in this sense speaks to 'the degree to which the evidence does affect the probability of a fact in issue, on the assumption that the factfinder has found the evidence to have a degree of credibility and reliability.'[174] In other words, evidentiary weight 'is the relative importance that is attached to an item of evidence in deciding whether a certain issue has been proven or not'.[175] Alternatively, the concepts of 'robustness', 'resilience', or 'comprehensiveness' of the evidence are employed.[176] As already stated above,[177] the final decision on the weight of the evidence will be taken at the end of the trial, 'when items of evidence are weighted against each other'.[178]

The *assessment* of the probative value of evidence, albeit free, must not be arbitrary but must observe the rules of logic, consistency, and common sense.[179] In the words of the *Delalić et al.* TC, it must be based on 'human experience as well as logic, and will depend upon the particular circumstances of the case and the nature of the evidence'.[180] Here the scientific methods of evidentiary analysis and evaluation come into play,[181] to be distinguished, at the risk of oversimplification, by either a mathematical, statistical (Pascalian),[182] or rather psychological, cognitive (Baconian) approach.[183] While the former methods are particularly useful in assessing the value of hard scientific evidence, for example, drawing inferences from DNA evidence,[184] they do not produce sufficiently reliable results where the 'human factor' comes into play, such as in practically all cases of witness evidence.[185] Thus, it is not surprising that the case law prefers (if any) Baconian

[173] See e.g. *Bemba*, ICC-01/05-01/08-1022, para. 9 ('By probative value, the Majority refers, inter alia, to the reliability and weight to be attached to the evidence concerned.'; a few lines before, however, putting 'probative value and appropriate weight' on an equal footing); but see also ICC, *Prosecutor v. Bemba*, PTC II, Decision pursuant to Article 61 (7)(a) and (b) of the Rome Statute on the Charges of the Prosecutor against Mr Jean-Pierre Bemba Gombo, ICC-01/05-01/08-424, 15 June 2009, para. 59 (referring to 'weight' in relation to 'probative value' and 'relevance'); *Ongwen*, ICC-02/04-01/15-2022-Red, para. 1550.

[174] Dennis, *Evidence* (2010), pp. 109–10, further distinguishing 'weight' from 'relevance' in that the latter refers to the 'potential weight' of the evidence, not its actual weight which is predicated on its relevance. As to weight, see also May and Wierda, *International Criminal Evidence* (2002), p. 109–11. See also Klamberg, *Evidence* (2013), p. 345 (probative value indicating 'actual strength' of evidence 'in terms of reliability and/or credibility').

[175] *Katanga*, ICC-01/04-01/07-2635, para. 13.

[176] cf. Klamberg, *JICJ*, 13 (2015), 545 (with further references and himself opting for 'robustness', 544 ff.); on 'robustness' in more detail, see Klamberg, *Evidence* (2013), pp. 153–6, 183, 511, arguing that robust evidence presupposes an 'adequate investigation' and its probative value cannot be changed by additional evidence.

[177] Note 40 in this chapter and main text.

[178] Klamberg, in Sluiter et al., *International Criminal Procedure* (2013), p. 1026 (referring to Anderson et al.).

[179] See also Frisch, in Bruns et al., *FS Stürner* (2013), pp. 857, 862–3 (not only limited but guided by 'reason and experience' and rules of logic); Klamberg, *Evidence* (2013), pp. 157–8; Klamberg, *JICJ*, 13 (2015), 536 (referring to the general theory of knowledge, that is, epistemology); McGregor Richmond, *ICLR*, 22 (2022), 847, 859 ff.

[180] *Delalić et al.*, IT-96-21-T, Admissibility of Evidence Decision, para. 17; also ICTR, *Prosecutor v. Simba*, AC, Judgment, ICTR-01-76-A, 27 November 2007, para. 132; ICTR, *Prosecutor v. Bizimungu*, AC, Judgment, ICTR-00-56B-A, 30 June 2014, para. 210; ICTY, *Prosecutor v. Popović et al.*, AC, Judgment, IT-05-88-A, 30 January 2015, para. 90.

[181] In this regard, advocating 'Wigmorean analysis', i.e. using the above-mentioned (see note 164 in this chapter) neo-Wigmorian charting method for the construction and evaluation of inferential arguments, see Roberts, *JICJ*, 13 (2015), 480, 481–2, 492 ff.; McDermott, *JICJ*, 13 (2015), 507, 509 ff.; McGregor Richmond, *ICLR*, 22 (2022), 847 ff.

[182] Roberts, in du Bois-Pedain and Eldar, *Beccaria* (2022), p. 192 with n. 166.

[183] For a more detailed analysis with further references, see Klamberg, *Evidence* (2013), pp. 158 ff.; Klamberg, *JICJ, 13* (2015), 537 ff; for a similar distinction, McDermott, *JICJ*, 13 (2015), 510 with n. 16.

[184] cf. Klamberg, *JICJ*, 13 (2015), 540.

[185] See also ibid., 541, referring to alibi counter-evidence where probative value of the primary evidence cannot be determined by simply subtracting the probative value of the former, but difficult considerations regarding its credibility come into play; thereon, ICTR, *Prosecutor v. Zigiranyirazo*, AC, Judgment, ICTR-01-73-A, 16 November 2009, para. 18; ICTY, *Prosecutor v. Delalić et al.*, AC, Judgment, IT-96-21-A, 20 February 2001, para. 581. See also, with regard to the ICC's *Ongwen* trial, Nistor, *ICLR*, 24 (2024), 3, 13.

methods focusing on the totality of the evidence[186] and eliminating unreasonable alternative hypotheses.[187]

As to the criterion of *reliability* we have already said above that it is explicitly mentioned only in the context of the second step of the admissibility test, that is, with regard to rights violations and their possible impact on reliability.[188] Notwithstanding,[189] the case law has applied reliability already in the context of the first step, that is, the actual admissibility test,[190] either considering it as an inherent or implicit element to be analysed together with relevance and probative value,[191] or as a separate element to be considered after admissibility *stricto sensu* (but before the second step of the test).[192] The dispute shows that different Chambers start from a different understanding of admissibility, some limiting it to the relevance of the evidence,[193] others including probative value.[194] ICC Chambers followed the inclusive approach, considering reliability 'as a component of the evidence[195] when determining its weight'.[196] Thus, reliability is an inherent element of probative value,[197] which is determined, as stated before, by taking into account, inter alia, the weight of the evidence. *Prima facie* proof of reliability on the basis of sufficient indicia is enough at the admissibility stage, that is, there is no particularly high threshold.[198] This is also in line with the above-mentioned alternative approach[199] to take the substantive admissibility decision (especially regarding the probative value of the respective evidence) at the end of the

186 See note 83 in this chapter.

187 On the 'alternative hypothesis approach' (and other approaches) with references to the case law, see Klamberg, *JICJ*, 13 (2015), 542–4; previously, Klamberg, *Evidence* (2013), pp. 3, 124, 134, 139, 143, 161, 164–8, 183–96, 200–1, 506–8, 511 ('exclusion of every reasonable hypothesis of innocence method'); in the same vein, Frisch, in Bruns et al., *FS Stürner* (2013), pp. 858 ff. (exclusion of competing hypothesis on the basis of evidence).

188 cf. Rules 95 RPE ICTY/ICTR and 117 RPE MICT; Art. 69 (7)(a) ICCS; Rule 138 RPE KSC.

189 Some Chambers have acknowledged the lack of any legal basis of 'reliability' within admissibility *stricto sensu*; cf. e.g. *Delalić et al.*, IT-96-21, Exhibit 155 Decision, para. 32 ('neither necessary nor desirable to add to the provisions Sub-rule 89 (C) a condition of admissibility which is not expressly prescribed by that provision').

190 For a different interpretation, see Boas et al., *Procedure* (2011), p. 341.

191 *Tadić*, IT-94-1-T, Hearsay Decision, paras. 7, 15–6, 19; *Delalić et al.*, IT-96-21, Exhibit 155 Decision, para. 32 ('inherent and implicit component of each element of admissibility'); *Delalić et al.*, IT-96-21, Admissibility of Evidence Decision, paras. 17, 20 ('implicit requirement ... when assessing the relevance and probative value'); *Delalić et al.*, IT-96-21, Exhibit 155 Decision, para. 32 ('implicit requirement ... invisible golden thread which runs through all components of admissibility'); *Musema*, ICTR-96-13-A, paras. 38–9; *Brđanin and Talić*, Standards Order, IT-99-36-T, para. 24 (not 'separate condition of admissibility'); for the ICC, see *Katanga*, ICC-01/04-01/07-717, para. 78; *Lubanga*, ICC-01/04-01/06-1399, paras. 28, 30; ICC, *Prosecutor v. Ruto and Sang*, TC V(A), Decision of Prosecution Request for Admission of Prior Recorded Testimony, ICC-01/09-01/11-1938-Corr-Red2, 19 August 2015, para. 151 (reliability as 'component' of 'weight' or 'probative value').

192 *Norman et al.*, SCSL-04-14-AR65, para. 24 ('Evidence is admissible once it is shown to be relevant: the question of its reliability is determined thereafter, and is not a condition for its admission.')

193 Ibid., as just quoted.

194 See the references quoted in note 191 in this chapter, but see also *Kordić* and *Čerkez*, IT-95-14/2-AR73.5, para. 24 (while including reliability in admissibility, excluding weight (!): 'the reliability of a statement is relevant to its admissibility, and not just to its weight').

195 See also Bantekas, *ICL* (2010), p. 481 ('prerequisite to ... probative value').

196 *Katanga*, ICC-01/04-01/07-717, para. 78 (calling this, confusingly, an 'alternative approach' only because the defence has advanced two 'alternative' interpretations, para. 68); *Bemba*, ICC-01/05-01/08-3343, paras. 225–7; further references in note 191 in this chapter.

197 Piragoff and Clarke, 'Article 69', in Ambos, *Commentary* (2022), mn. 41 ('In determining probative value, the Chamber should consider the reliability of the item of evidence, taking into account its authenticity, nature and origin, characteristics, precision of the information contained within, understandability of the document, purpose for the creation of the document, etc.')

198 ICTY, *Prosecutor v. Popović et al.*, AC, Decision on Joint Defence Interlocutory Appeal Concerning the Status of Richard Butler as an Expert Witness, IT-05-88-AR73.2, 30 January 2008, para. 22; ICTR, *Prosecutor v. Nahimana et al.*, AC, Judgment, ICTR-99-52-A, 28 November 2007, para. 199. See also Boas et al., *Procedure* (2011), pp. 341–2 with further references.

199 Note 43 in this chapter and main text.

proceedings. The relationship between reliability and credibility will be examined below in the context of witness testimony.[200]

### *(b) Fundamental principles, in particular the 'beyond reasonable doubt' standard*

The taking and evaluation of evidence is governed by some fundamental principles of modern criminal procedure.[201] Most importantly, the principles of *orality and immediacy* apply. These principles are generally expressed in the context of the 'requirements for the decision' within the meaning of Article 74 ICCS already mentioned above:[202] on the one hand, by way of the permanent presence of the judges throughout the trial and the deliberations;[203] on the other hand, by the rule that their decision has to be based 'only on evidence submitted and discussed before it at the trial.'[204] In addition, the principle of *orality* finds an important manifestation in evidence law in the primacy of oral testimony as affirmed by the written law[205] and the case law,[206] notwithstanding the shift to written testimony at the ICTY at the beginning of the twenty-first century.[207]

These principles are prerequisites of a fair trial but they must be distinguished from the fair trial principles *stricto sensu*, which have been analysed in detail in Chapter I in this volume.[208] In the evidentiary context, these principles play an important role as admissibility limitations, at the second stage of the admissibility test, as we will see more closely below.[209] However, they also inform, at the first stage of the admissibility test, the actual taking and evaluation of evidence. Insofar the most important principles are the proof 'beyond reasonable doubt' standard as the basis for any conviction,[210] the presumption of innocence,[211]

[200] Note 314 in this chapter and main text.
[201] See also Kiss, 'Article 74', in Ambos, *Commentary* (2022), mn. 28.
[202] See Chapter IV, A.(4)(a) in this volume.
[203] Art. 74 (1) cl. 1 ICCS.
[204] Art. 74 (2) cl. 3 ICCS; *Bemba*, ICC-01/05-01/08-3343, para. 224.
[205] cf. Rule 90 (A) RPE ICTR/SCSL and Art. 69 (2), 1st cl. ICCS; Rule 141 (1) RPE KSC ('testimony ... given in person')
[206] cf. ICTR, *Prosecutor v. Akayesu*, AC, Judgment, ICTR-96-4, 1 June 2001, para. 134 ('The general principle is that Trial Chambers of the Tribunal shall hear live, direct testimony ... and ... prior statements of witnesses who appear in court are as a rule relevant only insofar as they are necessary to a Trial Chamber in its assessment of the credibility of a witness. It is not the case ... that they should or could generally in and of themselves constitute evidence that the content thereof is truthful. For this reason, live testimony is primarily accepted as being the most persuasive evidence before a court' [footnotes omitted]); *Simba*, ICTR-01-76-A, para. 103 ('general, though not absolute, preference for live testimony'); ICTR, *Prosecutor v. Nyiramasuhuko et al.*, AC, Decision in the Matter of Proceedings under Rule 15*bis* (D), ICTR 98-42-A15*bis*, 24 September 2003, para. 25 ('preference for live testimony to be heard by each and every judge'); *Bemba*, ICC-01/05-01/08-1386, para. 76 (Art. 69 (2) 1st cl. as expression of 'in court personal testimony [as] the rule, giving effect to the principle of orality'); less emphatic, *Bemba*, ICC-01/05-01/08-1022, para. 14 ('presumption in favour of oral testimony, but no prevalence of *orality* ... as a whole' [emphasis in the original]); thereon also Schuon, *LJIL*, 25 (2012), 519–20; Roberts, *JICJ*, 10 (2012), 935–6; Sorvatzioti, *ICLR*, 22 (2022), 895, 904; Farthofer, in Heinze and Dittrich, *ICC* (2021), 525, 527. See also KSC, *Prosecutor v. Shala*, TP I, Decision on the Submission and Admissibility of Non-Oral Evidence, KSC-BC-2020-04/F00161, 17 March 2023, para. 30. See generally Klamberg, *Evidence* (2013), pp. 362 ff., 417 (general principle); Rigney, *Fairness* (2022), p. 136.
[207] Rigney, *Fairness* (2022), p. 136; Schmitt, *JICJ*, 19 (2021), 485, 492–3. See also Section A.(4)(c) in this chapter.
[208] Chapter I, D. in this volume.
[209] Section A.(8)(b) in this chapter.
[210] cf. Rules 87 (A) RPE ICTY/ICTR/SCSL and 104 (A) RPE MICT, Art. 66 (3) ICCS, and Chapters I, D.(1) and IV, A.(4) in this volume. In this context, see also Jacobs, in Sluiter et al., *International Criminal Procedure* (2013), pp. 1139–43, 1148; Klamberg, *Evidence* (2013), p. 197 (both considering it as a general principle); McDermott, *CLF*, 26 (2015), 354 ff.
[211] cf. Art. 66 (1) ICCS and Chapter I, D.(1) and (3)(b) in this volume. See also Roberts, *JICJ*, 10 (2012), 925–7; Jacobs, in Sluiter et al., *International Criminal Procedure* (2013), pp. 1139–42, 1148; Klamberg, *Evidence* (2013), pp. 118 ff., 197, 488 (both considering it a general principle).

and—as a consequence of the former—the prosecutorial onus to prove the guilt[212] as well as the non-reversal of the burden of proof or onus of rebuttal.[213] It further follows that any (reasonable) doubt must benefit the accused (*in dubio pro reo*).[214]

The *burden* as to the relevance and probative value of a concrete piece of evidence rests with the party who wants to introduce this evidence.[215] The ICTY has however applied a different standard of proof to prosecution and defence: while the former must prove admissibility 'beyond reasonable doubt', for the latter a 'balance of probabilities' suffices.[216] More direct defence rights, derived from the principles of fair trial and equality of arms,[217] may also influence the taking and evaluation of evidence. Take for example the right to confrontation, which operates as a kind of checks and balances of witness evidence.[218] We will take a closer look at this kind of evidence in the next section.

As already discussed in the previous chapter,[219] the 'beyond reasonable doubt' standard is difficult to define in the abstract.[220] It appears more objective and thus rational than the classical, more subjective French standard of *intime conviction*,[221] more familiar to civil law jurisdictions;[222] yet, it does not necessarily entail more certainty, as demonstrated by the definitional attempts of the Nuremberg case law alluding to 'moral certainty'[223] and the highly diverse definitional attempts in common law jurisdictions.[224] In fact, a 'conviction' can only be based on (inter-subjective) reason in the Kantian sense[225] and this common

[212] cf. Art. 66 (2) ICCS and Chapter I, D.(1) and (3)(b) in this volume. See also Bantekas, *ICL* (2010), pp. 532–3; Roberts, *JICJ*, 10 (2012), 927–8; Jacobs, in Sluiter et al., *International Criminal Procedure* (2013), pp. 1139–43, 1148 (principle).

[213] cf. Art. 67 (1)(i) ICCS and Chapter I, D.(1) in this volume. On the reversal of the burden of proof in case of mental health defences and psychiatric expert evidence, see Radosavljevic, *ICLR*, 13 (2013), 1017–18.

[214] Chapters I, D.(3)(b) and IV, A.(4)(a) in this volume. See also Bantekas, *ICL* (2010), p. 533; Jacobs, in Sluiter et al., *International Criminal Procedure* (2013), pp. 1140, 1142, 1148; Klamberg, *Evidence* (2013), pp. 123, 197, both considering it a general principle.

[215] ICTY, *Prosecutor v. Delalić et al.*, AC, Decision on Application of Defendant Zejnil Delalic for Leave to Appeal against the Decision of the Trial Chamber of 19 January 1998 for the Admissibility of Evidence, IT-96-21-A, 4 March 1998, para. 17; ICTR, *Prosecutor v. Bagosora et al.*, TC, Decision on Request to Admit United Nations Documents into Evidence under Rule 89 (C), ICTR-98-41-T, 25 May 2006, para. 2 (*prima facie* showing that evidence is relevant and has probative value).

[216] ICTY, *Prosecutor v. Delalić et al.*, TC, Judgment, IT-96-21-T, 16 November 1998, para. 603; *Orić*, IT-03-68-T, p. 5 (Guideline (ii) *in fine*). See also Bantekas, *ICL* (2010), pp. 506–7; Klamberg, *Evidence* (2013), p. 130; Kuczyńska, *Accusation Model ICC* (2015), pp. 310–11.

[217] cf. Chapter I, D.(2) in this volume.

[218] See Chapter I, D.(3)(f) in this volume.

[219] Chapter IV, A.(4) in this volume.

[220] For a comparative and theoretical treatment, see Ambos and Lee, in Ambos et al., *Core Concepts III* (2025) (forthcoming).

[221] See Chapter I, D.(1) in this volume.

[222] See Arts. 304, 353, and 427 French CCP and also, albeit to be understood more objectively, s. 261 German *StPO* (decision pursuant to 'free conviction based on the entirety of the trial' ['*nach seiner freien, aus dem Inbegriff der Verhandlung geschöpften Überzeugung*']). Thereto, see also Jacobs, in Sluiter et al., *International Criminal Procedure* (2013), pp. 1145–6; De Smet, in Stahn, *Practice* (2015), pp. 865–6; on the origins in the French jury trial, see Frisch, in Bruns et al., *FS Stürner* (2013), pp. 854–5.

[223] See e.g. *US v. Pohl et al.*, in US-GPO, *TWC*, v (1948), p. 965 ('It is such a doubt as, after full consideration of all the evidence, would leave an unbiased, reflective person charged with the responsibility of decision, in such a state of mind that he could not say that he felt an abiding conviction amounting to a moral certainty of the truth of the charge'). For further references, see Schabas and McDermott, 'Article 66', in Ambos, *Commentary* (2022), mn. 24; Schabas, *Introduction ICC* (2020), p. 327.

[224] cf. Combs, *Fact-Finding* (2010), p. 344 with n. 1415 (demonstrating the controversy surrounding the precise meaning); De Smet, in Stahn, *Practice* (2015), pp. 867–70, demonstrating that the definitions of this standard are largely elusive and thus it also leaves a broad discretion to the adjudicator, be it a professional judge or a jury. For (other) jurisdictions applying this standard, see the references in Combs, *Fact-Finding* (2010), p. 346 with n. 1424.

[225] cf. Frisch, in Bruns et al., *FS Stürner* (2013), p. 868.

basis in reason approximates 'intime conviction' to 'reasonable doubt'.[226] Indeed, it is all about reason and rational reconstruction of past events.[227] Thus, on the face of it, 'beyond reasonable doubt' does not require that there is not 'any' doubt at all but not 'a doubt that is founded in reason'.[228] While such a doubt must benefit the accused (*in dubio pro reo*),[229] this does not help much to clearly draw the line between 'simple' and 'reasonable' doubts[230] and surely does not answer the question whether 'all hypothetically possible contrary inferences' have to be rejected to come to a conviction.[231]

The case law does not offer an unambiguous definition either. The *Tadić* AC, following the TC, held that 'not every hypothesis or possibility of innocence' but only a 'fair or rational hypothesis' excluding the guilt must be taken into account.[232] The ICTR AC referred to 'logic and common sense' and to the relationship between the standard and the evidence in that it must 'have a rational link to the evidence, lack of evidence or inconsistencies in the evidence'.[233] At the ICC, the majority of the *Katanga* TC convicted the accused invoking the 'beyond reasonable doubt' standard,[234] explicitly excluding 'certainty',[235] but Judge van den Wyngaert found 'another reasonable reading of the evidence' possible and thus would have acquitted Katanga.[236] In *Bemba et al.*, the TC follows an 'exclusion of every other reasonable hypothesis' approach, finding that 'when the Chamber concludes that, based on the evidence, there is only one reasonable conclusion to be drawn from the facts *sub judice*, the conclusion is that they have been established 'beyond reasonable doubt'.[237]

To be sure, the *Katanga* dispute[238] points to the broader, underlying issue of whether the nature and complexity of international criminal proceedings does not call for a more

[226] For a similar, more objective (rational) understanding of 'intime conviction', see also Klamberg, *Evidence* (2013), pp. 129, 131, putting it on an equal footing with 'beyond reasonable doubt'.

[227] Recall the requirement of a reasoned opinion; cf. Chapter IV, A.(4)(a) in this volume.

[228] Schabas and McDermott, 'Article 66', in Ambos, *Commentary* (2022), mn. 26; Schabas, *Introduction ICC* (2020), p. 327.

[229] See Chapter I, D.(3)(b) in this volume.

[230] For a discussion of the fine distinctions ('any doubt', 'shadow of a doubt', 'substantive doubt', 'absolute certainty', or 'moral certainty'), see Schabas and McDermott, 'Article 66', in Ambos, *Commentary* (2022), mn. 26; see also De Smet, in Stahn, *Practice* (2015), pp. 869–70, giving an overview of available definitions excluding 'absolute certainty' and minor doubts.

[231] *Contra*, ICC, *Prosecutor v. Ngudjolo*, OTP, Prosecution's Document in Support of Appeal against the 'Jugement rendu en application de l'article 74 du Statut', ICC-01/04-02/12-39-Red2, 3 April 2013, para. 2. However, the AC found no error in the TC's assessment of the facts leading to the acquittal of the accused; cf. ICC, *Prosecutor v. Ngudjolo*, AC, Judgment on the Prosecutor's Appeal against the Decision of Trial Chamber II entitled 'Judgment pursuant to Article 74 of the Statute', ICC-01/04-02/12-271-Corr, 7 April 2015; but see also ICC, *Prosecutor v. Ngudjolo*, AC, Joint Dissenting Opinion of Judge Ekaterina Trendafilova and Judge Cuno Tarfusser, ICC-01/04-02/12-271-AnxA, 27 February 2015. On the 'alternative hypothesis approach' see above note 187 with main text; its proponent examines alternative hypothesis as a third factor—after weighing the evidence and checking its robustness—when determing the reasonable doubt standard (Klamberg, *JICJ*, 13 (2015), 549).

[232] ICTY, *Prosecutor v. Tadić*, AC, Judgment, IT-94-1-A, 15 July 1999, para. 174 (referring to the TC).

[233] ICTR, *Prosecutor v. Rutaganda*, AC, Judgment, ICTR-96-3-A, 26 May 2003, para. 488. Crit. of the ICTR's (and esp. the SCSL's) 'cavalier treatment' of testimonial deficiencies, effectively downplaying the 'beyond reasonable doubt' standard, Combs, *Fact-Finding* (2010), pp. 7–8, 189 ff., 224, 254, 271, 343, arguing that these tribunals omit to mention these 'testimonial deficiencies' and overlook 'severe inconsistencies' in witness testimonies.

[234] *Katanga*, ICC-01/04-01/07-3436-tENG, paras. 68–70.

[235] ICC, *Prosecutor v. Katanga*, TC II, Judgment pursuant to Article 74 of the Statute, Concurring Opinion of Judges Diarra and Cotte, ICC-01/04-01/07-3436-AnxII-tENG, 13 March 2004, para. 4.

[236] ICC, *Prosecutor v. Katanga*, TC II, Judgment pursuant to Article 74 of the Statute, Minority Opinion of Judge van den Wyngaert, ICC-01/04-01/07-3436-AnxI, 7 March 2014, paras. 133 ff.

[237] ICC, *Prosecutor v. Bemba et al.*, TC VII, Public Redacted Version of Judgment pursuant to Article 74 of the Statute, ICC-01/05-01/13-1989-Red, 19 October 2016, para. 188. See also Schabas and McDermott, 'Article 66', in Ambos, *Commentary* (2022), mn.

[238] Thereon also Stahn, *JICJ*, 12 (2014), 827 ff.

flexible conviction standard than applied in ordinary domestic proceedings. Indeed, the majority defends its position with the argument that, given the complexity of international criminal proceedings, one has to find a middle ground between 'necessary rigour' and 'excessive rigidity'.[239] Yet, while it is clear that the conviction standard must remain manageable in ICC proceedings and absolute certainty is surely not required,[240] the majority's position should not be read as a call for a lowering the usual 'beyond reasonable doubt' standard.[241] This would be incompatible with the Statute and the relevant human rights law which do not allow for any different standards to the detriment of the accused.

The 'beyond reasonable doubt' standard 'applies to those facts which are indispensable for entering a conviction, namely those constituting the elements of the crime(s) charged, including the causal nexus, and the alleged modes of liability'.[242] As to negative facts which may amount to a ground excluding responsibility, there is normally a burden of production with the defence while the prosecution then carries the burden to disprove the respective ground.[243] Yet, the *Ongwen* TC held that 'the Prosecutor does not bear the burden per se to "disprove each element" of a ground excluding an accused's criminal responsibility'.[244]

### (3) Witness testimony, including expert witnesses

#### *(a) General: Order and manner of interrogation*

As already stated above,[245] the taking of evidence, including that of witnesses,[246] may be directed by the Chamber (the presiding judge), but otherwise witness interrogation follows the

[239] *Katanga*, ICC-01/04-01/07-3436-AnxII-tENG, Concurring Opinion of Judges Diarra and Cotte para. 5 (finding the 'excessive rigidity' 'incompatible with the functions of the judge in general and cases of the kind brought before the Court in particular').

[240] See, in this regard, *Ngudjolo*, ICC-01/04-02/12-271-Corr, paras. 42–63, rejecting the Prosecutor's submission that the TC applied a standard of 'absolute certainty'.

[241] In the same vein, Stahn, *JICJ*, 12 (2014), 828. For a different view, however, Combs, *Fact-Finding* (2010), pp. 10, 345 ff., arguing essentially, relying on utilitarian considerations regarding the societal function of a standard of proof and recent approaches in favour of a variable, case-related standard, that the nature and seriousness of international crimes 'put the defendant's innocence in a different light' than that of a domestic defendant (353) and thus justifies convicting international defendants without having 'near certainty' (353), making wrongful convictions less costly than for ordinary crimes at the domestic level (353–7) but wrongful acquittals more costly (358–9); rightly *contra* De Smet, in Stahn, *Practice* (2015), pp. 885–6. On a principled level, Combs's view invites the classical deontological reaction that it makes the individual defendant the object of considerations of utility and thus disrespects his unique dignity (cf. Ambos, *Treatise ICL I* (2021), p. 115 with further references). She indeed takes issue with this criticism, offering the rebuttal that a variable standard does not mean a lower standard of proof, but that it only accounts for the necessary variations 'over space and time' inherent to criminal cases (Combs, *Fact-Finding* (2010), pp. 363–4).

[242] *Mustafa*, KSC-CA-2023-02/F00038/RED, para. 368; see also ICC, *Prosecutor v. Ongwen*, AC, Judgment, ICC-02/04-01/15-2023, 15 December 2022, para. 338; *Ntaganda*, ICC-01/04-02/06-2359, para. 44.

[243] On the classic disctinction between burden of proof (persuasive burden) and burden of production (evidential burden) see Roberts, *Evidence* (2022), pp. 243–5; also KSC, *Prosecutor v. Gucati and Haradinaj*, CoAP, Judgment, KSC-CA-2022-01/F00114, 2 February 2023, para. 330.

[244] *Ongwen*, ICC-02/04-01/15-2023, para. 338.

[245] Notes 95 ff. in this chapter and main text.

[246] Neither the Rules of the ad hoc tribunals nor those of the ICC define what constitutes a witness statement. According to the AC in *Blaškić*, '[t]he usual meaning of a witness statement in trial proceedings is an account of a person's knowledge of a crime, which is recorded through due procedure in the course of an investigation into the crime', see ICTY, *Prosecutor v. Blaškić*, AC, Decision on the Appellant's Motions for the Production of Material, Suspension or Extension of the Briefing Schedule, and Additional Filings, IT-95-14-A, 26 September 2000, para. 15.

adversarial mode at the ICC[247] (despite the use of neutral terminology):[248] questioning by the party that presented the witness, then by prosecution and defence, then—or first, that is before any participant[249]—by the Chamber and lastly (again) by the defence.[250]

This order entails the judicial right to question the witness 'at any stage'[251] and the parties' right to examine her regarding all 'relevant matters',[252] at least in the sense of the just mentioned right to confrontation, although not necessarily amounting to an adversarial-style *cross-examination*.[253] Indeed, this special interrogation method is explicitly mentioned, inter alia, in the law of the ad hoc tribunals;[254] one may also read it into Rule 140 (2)(b)

[247] At the ad hoc tribunals, the adversarial mode follows from the general Rules 85 (A), (B) RPE ICTY/ICTR/SCSL, 102 (A), (B) RPE MICT, and the specific Rules 90 (F) RPE ICTY/ICTR/SCSL, 106 (F) RPE MICT ('order of interrogating witnesses'); for a detailed analysis, see Vasiliev, in Sluiter et al., *International Criminal Procedure* (2013), pp. 584 ff.; also Combs, in Sluiter et al., *International Criminal Procedure* (2013), p. 698 (summoning of witnesses mainly by parties) and ibid., pp. 735 ff. (demonstrating that Trial Chambers may alter this order, pp. 735, 740); Kuczyńska, *Accusation Model ICC* (2015), pp. 323–4. On the classical common law approach distinguishing between 'examination-in-chief, cross-examination and re-examination', as used in the just mentioned Rule 85 (B), see Vasiliev, op. cit., pp. 639–40 (taking England and Wales as an example) and Combs, op. cit., p. 741; from a comparative perspective, Kuczyńska, *Accusation Model ICC* (2015), pp. 320–3. On IMT, IMTFE, SPSC, ECCC, and STL, see Combs, op. cit., pp. 734–5, 739–40.

[248] Specific common law terminology, as referred to in the previous footnote, was, as in other parts of the ICC legal regime, deliberately avoided in order not to to prejudge the procedural approach to be taken; cf. Lewis, in Lee, *ICC* (2001), pp. 549–50; Kreß, *JICJ*, 1 (2003), 605; Vasiliev, in Sluiter et al., *International Criminal Procedure* (2013), pp. 608, 609–10, 633 (crit. of the inconsistent terminology by Chambers). Still, the common law expressions may be used 'as terms of convenience' by the parties (cf. ICC, *Prosecutor v. Lubanga*, TC I, Decision on the Manner of Questioning Witnesses by the Legal Representatives of Victims, ICC-01/04-01/06-2127, 16 September 2009, para. 22).

[249] Rule 140 (2) RPE ICC ('before or after a witness is questioned by a participant'). The Rule is to ensure that questioning by a participant is not interrupted by the Chamber, cf. Lewis, in Lee, *ICC* (2001), p. 550; Vasiliev, in Sluiter et al., *International Criminal Procedure* (2013), pp. 608, 620–2.

[250] Rule 140 (2)(a)–(d) RPE ICC; in more detail, see Vasiliev, in Sluiter et al., *International Criminal Procedure* (2013), pp. 607–22, discussing the 'sequence of questioning' in the prosecution and defence phase, by each party pursuant to the order given by Rule 140 (2) and, in addition, by the victims' representative), 633–5 (summarizing), 652 (general rule); see also Combs, in Sluiter et al., *International Criminal Procedure* (2013), pp. 738–9, correctly affirming that the ICC is more flexible than the ad hoc tribunals. See also Chapter IV, A.(3)(a) in this volume.

[251] Rules 85 (B) RPE ICTY/ICTR/SCSL and 102 (B) RPE MICT *in fine*. In the same vein, proposing a general rule for judicial questioning 'at any time', Vasiliev, in Sluiter et al., *International Criminal Procedure* (2013), p. 654, and even arguing that this rule should be formulated as a positive obligation for the sake of the determination of the truth; in the same vein, Combs, in Sluiter et al., *International Criminal Procedure* (2013), p. 706; also Kuczyńska, *Accusation Model ICC* (2015), p. 326 (proposing a 'free witness narration' directed by the judges at the start of witness interrogation). Such judicial dominance seems to go beyond Rule 140 (2)(c) RPE ICC insofar as judicial questioning is limited 'before or after a witness is questioned by a participant' (above note 249), but this rule has been interpreted in a more flexible way as allowing questioning at any time (cf. Vasiliev, in Sluiter et al., *International Criminal Procedure* (2013), p. 621). On the ad hoc tribunals' practice, see also Combs, op. cit., pp. 700–2; on IMT, IMTFE, SPSC, ECCC, and STL, see Combs, op. cit., pp. 700, 702–3. On common law judges' restraint in that regard, see above note 103.

[252] cf. Rule 140 (2)(b) RPE ICC (referring also to 'other relevant matters') and ICC, *Prosecutor v. Lubanga*, TC I, Decision on Various Issues Related to Witnesses' Testimony during Trial, ICC-01/04-01/06-1140, 29 January 2008, para. 32 (referring to trial, sentencing, and reparation issues). See also Rules 85 (B) and 90 (H) RPE ICTY/90 (G) RPE ICTR and 102 (B), 106 (H) RPE MICT; Rules 67 (1), 68 (2)(a) RPE ICC. On the ad hoc tribunals' case law, giving a broad discretion to Chambers to direct and limit questioning, Combs, in Sluiter et al., *International Criminal Procedure* (2013), pp. 721–6; crit. of these too broad cross-examination rules and in favour of tighter judicial control, Gaynor, in Sluiter et al., *International Criminal Procedure* (2013), pp. 1078, 1082. On the ICC, see Kuczyńska, *Accusation Model ICC* (2015), p. 351. On specific problems in multiple-defendant cases, see Vasiliev, in Sluiter et al., *International Criminal Procedure* (2013), pp. 598–600.

[253] On cross-examination in general, Zahar and Sluiter, *ICL* (2008), pp. 377–8; Safferling, *International Criminal Procedure* (2012), p. 452 (rightly distinguishing it from the mere right to confrontation); Vasiliev, in Sluiter et al., *International Criminal Procedure* (2013), p. 640; Klamberg, *Evidence* (2013), pp. 425–6 (purpose and techniques); on its negative impact with regard to the failure to elicit the relevant evidence, see Combs, *Fact-Finding* (2010), pp. 308–9.

[254] cf. generally Rules 85 (B) RPE ICTY/ICTR and 102 (B) RPE MICT and Rules 90 (H) RPE ICTY/90 (G) RPE ICTR/106 (H) RPE MICT, as well as several other, more specific witness provisions, e.g. Rule 92*ter* (ii), 94*bis* (B) (ii) RPE SCSL; see also Rule 143 (3) RPE KSC. See also *Prlic et al.*, IT-04-74-A, AC Judgment, para. 39. For a detailed analysis, see Vasiliev, in Sluiter et al., *International Criminal Procedure* (2013), pp. 587–93; Combs, in

RPE ICC.[255] In any case, the right to cross-examination is not absolute, that is, key witness evidence may be admitted even if not subjected to cross-examination;[256] of course, such evidence would require corroboration if it is meant to support a conviction.[257] Any *additional* cross-examination of a witness by one party would violate the principle of equality of arms, at least if understood in a strict, formal sense.[258]

On a more general level, further reflection and research is needed as to whether cross-examination of victim-witnesses in international criminal proceedings contributes at all to the determination of the truth—in line with the classic common law view of cross-examination as 'the greatest legal engine ever invented for the discovery of the truth'[259]—or, instead, given its aggressive and hostile performance,[260] rather disturbs and alienates the witness who will then not only suffer a re-victimization,[261] but may also be unwilling and/or unable to speak to the truth.[262] Indeed, from this perspective the more informal and conversational witness interrogation by a judge, as practised in modern civil law systems, may be more appropriate since it will put the witness at ease and thus create an atmosphere where she can tell her story, which, in turn, is more conducive to fact- and truth-finding.[263] At any

Sluiter et al., *International Criminal Procedure* (2013), pp. 721–3 (on possible restrictions); see also Jackson, *JICJ*, 7 (2009), 30–1; O'Sullivan and Montgomery, *JICJ*, 8 (2010), 512; Safferling, *International Criminal Procedure* (2012), pp. 454–5; Doherty, *LJIL*, 26 (2013), 944–5; from a practical point of view, Jackson and M'Boge, *LJIL*, 26 (2013), 961 ff.; crit. Schuon, *International Criminal Procedure* (2010), pp. 170–1. On the use of cross-examination before IMT and IMTFE, see Vasiliev, in Sluiter et al., *International Criminal Procedure* (2013), pp. 568–9; on the IMT, see Safferling, op. cit., pp. 452–3.

[255] Given that this sub-rule provides for the right of the prosecution and defence 'to question' the witness 'about relevant matters' related to her testimony, it comes close to cross-examination although it does not use the term. In this vein, ICC, *Prosecutor v. Katanga and Ngudjolo*, TC II (Single Judge), Directions for the Conduct of the Proceedings and Testimony in Accordance with Rule 140, Annex, ICC-01/04-01/07-1665-Corr, 1 December 1999, para. 68 (right to 'cross-examine' witness); also Safferling, *International Criminal Procedure* (2012), p. 456; Vasiliev, in Sluiter et al., *International Criminal Procedure* (2013), pp. 612–14 (discussing the sub-rule under 'cross-examination); but see also ICC, *Prosecutor v. Bemba*, TC III, Decision on Directions for the Conduct of the Proceedings, ICC-01/05-01/08-1023, 19 November 2010, paras. 7 ff. (omitting the term 'cross-examination').

[256] cf. ICTY, *Prosecutor v. Blagojević and Jokić*, TC I, Section A, First Decision on Prosecution's Motion for Admission of Witness Statements and Prior Testimony pursuant to Rule 92*bis*, IT-02-60-PT, 12 June 2003, para. 14 ('the right to cross-examine witnesses is not an absolute right'); ICTY, *Prosecutor v. Kordić and Čerkez*, TC III, Decision on the Prosecution Application to Admit the Tulica Report and Dossier into Evidence, IT-95-14/2-T, 29 July 1999, paras. 25, 27, 28; ICTY, *Prosecutor v. Martić*, TC, Decision on Defence Motion to Exclude the Testimony of Milan Babic, Together with Associated Exhibits, from Evidence, IT-95-11-T, 9 June 2006, para. 56; ICTY, *Prosecutor v. Martić*, AC, Decision on Appeal against the Trial Chamber Decision on the Evidence of Witness Milan Babic, IT-95-11-AR73.2, 14 September 2006, para. 12 ('it is settled law before the International Tribunal that the right of an accused to cross-examine a witness is not absolute').

[257] *Martić*, IT-95-11-AR73.2, para. 20 ('evidence which has not been cross-examined ... will require corroboration if used to establish a conviction'). See also Schuon, *International Criminal Procedure* (2010), pp. 147, 169; Bantekas, *ICL* (2010), p. 485.

[258] cf. ICTY, *Prosecutor v. Delalić et al.*, TC, Decision on the Motion on Presentation of Evidence by the Accused, Esad Landzo, IT-96-21-T, 1 May 1997, paras. 28, 29; May and Wierda, *ColJTransnat'lL*, 37 (1999), 739–40.

[259] Wigmore, *Treatise on Evidence I* (1940), § 1367, comparing cross-examination in this regard to torture as employed in the mediaeval system of the Continent.

[260] But note trial judges' authority to limit (abusive) cross-examination, cf. Combs, in Sluiter et al., *International Criminal Procedure* (2013), pp. 731–3.

[261] In this vein, Bock, *Opfer* (2010), pp. 424 ff.; Tonellato, *EJCrim*, 20 (2012), 321, 328.

[262] In a similar vein, *Lubanga*, ICC-01/04-01/06-2127, paras. 27–9 (advocating 'a presumption in favour of a neutral approach' in questioning instead of 'combative' cross-examination by victims' legal representative since his purpose is to assist the Chamber in the pursuit of the truth); crit. also Damaška, *ChicKentLR*, 83 (2008), 342 (difficult to reconcile with vindicating victims' rights); Vasiliev, in Sluiter et al., *International Criminal Procedure* (2013), pp. 644–5, questioning cross-examination in the context of international criminal justice with regard to search for truth and victims' rights; Rigney, *Fairness* (2022), p. 135 ('Adversarial cross-examination may result in the counsel or witness selecting passages from documents and thereby distorting the overall effect of the document, which can be "counter-productive" and "not the best way of getting at the truth"').

[263] In a similar vein, Combs, *Fact-Finding* (2010), pp. 303 ff., arguing, inter alia, that 'judges are more apt than lawyers to elicit accurate and complete testimony' (307) and adversarial style cross-examination reduces

rate, cross-examination should not interfere with the protection and/or respectful treatment of a witness.[264]

As a rule, witnesses have to *appear* for their interrogation *in person* (principle of live testimony).[265] Their attendance can be required by the Court,[266] including by—like the ad hoc tribunals[267]—issuing a *subpoena*.[268] The authority to compel the attendance of a witness must be distinguished from the State's role in interrogating witnesses for the Court or bringing them before it.[269] Also, it must be distinguished from the Court's authority to compel a witness to provide testimony.[270] At most international criminal tribunals, a witness 'shall' give an undertaking as to the truthfulness of her testimony[271] unless she does not understand the nature of this undertaking.[272] It is unclear if the witness can be forced to give

the quantity of relevant evidence and thus the 'opportunity costs of adversarial questioning' are high (308–9); yet, she further distinguishes between an unable and an unwilling witness and only considers the nonadversarial questioning to be more adequate in the former case while the adversarial approach is preferable in the latter, especially to uncover perjury (303, 312 ff.). Crit. of cross-examination also Schuon, *International Criminal Procedure* (2010), pp. 170–1 (arguing that an inquisitorial inquest is more efficient since it does not entail a dispute about complex admissibility rules (171) and in favour of 'a strong judge' (266)); for a rather inquisitorial, truth-oriented procedure, see also Kuczynska, *Accusation Model ICC* (2015), pp. 346–9, 353 (ICC judge 'coordinate officialdom' (in more detail, Heinze, *Disclosure* (2014), p. 502): 'play umpire of a contest' but searching for the truth). On the narrative evidence theory as the basis of a civil law, judge-led interrogation, see Klamberg, *Evidence* (2013), pp. 166–7.

264 cf. ICC, *Prosecutor v. Katanga and Ngudjolo*, TC II [Judge Cotte], Directions for the Conduct of the Proceedings and Testimony in Accordance with Rule 140, ICC-01/04-01/07-1665, 20 November 2009, paras. 74–6 ('cross-examination must at all times remain civil and respectful to the witness. The Chamber will not allow parties to assault the dignity or exploit the vulnerability of witnesses during cross-examination' [para. 75]). Thereto CH Pérez-León-Acevedo, in Heinze and Dittrich, *ICC* (2021), p. 515.

265 cf. ICTY, *Prosecutor v. Tadić*, Decision on the Defence Motions to Summon and Protect Defence Witnesses and on the Giving Evidence by Video-Link, IT-94-1-T, 25 June 1996, para. 19, ('It cannot be stressed too strongly that the general rule is that a witness must physically be present at the seat of the International Tribunal'); *Lubanga*, ICC-01/04-01/06-1140, para. 41; ICC, *Prosecutor v. Lubanga*, TC I, Decision on the Prosecution's Application for Admission of Four Documents from the Bar Table pursuant to Article 64 (9), ICC-01/04-01/06-2662-Cont, 16 December 2010, para. 13 (presumption of oral testimony), *Bemba*, ICC-01/05-01/08-1386, para. 76; ICC, *Prosecutor v. Katanga and Ngudjolo*, TC II, Decision on Defence Request to Admit into Evidence Entirety of Document DRC-OTP-1017-0572, ICC-01/04-01/07-2954, 25 May 2011, para. 4. See also Rule 90 (A) RPE ICTR/SCSL, Rule 141 (1), first sentence, RPE KSC and Art. 69 (2) ICCS. The original Rule 90 (A) RPE ICTY, still valid at the time of the quoted *Tadić* decision, was deleted by the 19th amendment of the RPE ICTY in December 2000 in the course of the reforms consequent on the Expert Report, see Section A.(4). On IMT, IMTFE, SPSC, ECCC, and STL, see McDermott, in Sluiter et al., *International Criminal Procedure* (2013), pp. 860–1, 870–2.

266 cf. Art. 64 (6)(b) ICCS ('[r]equire the attendance and testimony of witnesses'), thereto Schmitt, *JICJ*, 19 (2021), 485, 490; implicitly also Art. 64 (6)(d) ICCS; see also Piragoff and Clarke, 'Article 69', in Ambos, *Commentary* (2022), mn. 25 *in fine*; also Safferling, *International Criminal Procedure* (2012), p. 468 (but without legal basis). Mixing up accused and witnesses, McDermott, in Sluiter et al., *International Criminal Procedure* (2013), p. 868.

267 cf. Rules 54 RPE ICTY/ICTR/SCSL and 55 RPE MICT. See, in detail, Combs, in Sluiter et al., *International Criminal Procedure* (2013), pp. 707–12 (ICTY/ICTR/SCSL), 706–7, 713 (IMT, IMTFE, SPSC, ECCC, and STL).

268 This has been confirmed by the AC in ICC, *Prosecutor v. Ruto and Sang*, AC, Judgment on the Appeals of William Samoei Ruto and Mr Joshua Arap Sang against the Decision of Trial Chamber V (A) of 17 April 2014 Entitled 'Decision on Prosecutor's Application for Witness Summonses and resulting Request for State Party Cooperation', ICC-01/09-01/11-1598, 9 October 2014, para. 1. For a more detailed treatment, see Chapter VII, A.(2) and B.(3)(a)(i) in this volume, with an analysis of TC V's decision in ICC, *Prosecutor v. Ruto and Sang*, TC V(a), Decision on Prosecutor's Application for Witness Summonses and Resulting Request for State Party Cooperation, ICC-01/09-01/11-1274-Corr2, 17 April 2014, para. 83. On the common law origin of the *subpoena* power, see Combs, in Sluiter et al., *International Criminal Procedure* (2013), p. 715–16, recognizing it as a principle of international criminal procedure (717).

269 On this issue, belonging to the realm of cooperation, see Chapter VII, B.(3)(a)(ii) in this volume.

270 Rule 65 RPE ICC.

271 Rule 90 (A) RPE ICTY, Rule 90 (B) RPE ICTR/SCSL, Rule 106 (A) RPE MICT; Art. 69 (1) ICCS, Rule 66 RPE ICC. See also McDermott, in Sluiter et al., *International Criminal Procedure* (2013), p. 877 (principle).

272 Rule 66 (2) RPE ICC; also Rule 90 (B) RPE ICTY, Rule 90 (C) RPE ICTR/SCSL, Rule 106 (B) RPE MICT.

the undertaking. If the presiding judge issues a direction to that effect, its non-compliance may give rise to sanctions;[273] yet, a sanction would certainly be disproportionate if the witness had good reason to refuse to give the undertaking.

An *unsworn statement* has two important consequences: on the one hand, false (unsworn) testimony is not punishable according to Article 70 (1)(a) ICCS;[274] on the other hand, an unsworn statement has a lower probative value.[275] The latter consequence marks an important difference between an unsworn statement of a witness and of an accused:[276] Since the latter can neither be obliged to tell the truth nor be questioned by the parties[277]—for they cannot be obliged to testify in the first place due to the *nemo tenetur* principle[278]—the unsworn statement does not constitute evidence within the meaning of Article 74 (2) ICCS.[279] Thus, it can only be taken into account as part of the defence submission—of the 'proceedings' within the meaning of Article 74 (2) first sentence[280]—and should therefore also be made during the closing statement.[281] The accused's statement can only be considered as evidence if it is made in the form of a witness testimony[282] with the above-mentioned undertaking;[283] the TC can then freely assess it, considering it in part credible and in other parts not.[284] The accused is not obliged to give a sworn statement and testify under solemn undertaking, but has, in line with Article 67 ICCS, the right to do so.[285]

[273] cf. Rule 171 (1) RPE ICC; it may even amount to 'misconduct' within the meaning of Art. 71 (1) ICCS; cf. Piragoff and Clarke, 'Article 69', in Ambos, *Commentary* (2022), mn. 23.

[274] The offence requires ('obligation pursuant') the undertaking pursuant to Art. 69 (1) ICCS; see also Piragoff and Clarke, 'Article 69', in Ambos, *Commentary* (2022), mn. 23–4.

[275] Piragoff and Clarke, 'Article 69', in Ambos, *Commentary* (2022), mn. 23.

[276] cf. Art. 67 (1)(h) ICCS. See also Chapter IV, A.(3)(a) in this volume.

[277] ICC, *Prosecutor v. Abu Garda*, PTC I, Decision on the Confirmation of Charges, ICC-02/05-02/09-243-Red, 8 February 2010, para. 54; see also ICC, *Prosecutor v. Bemba*, TC III, Decision on Unsworn Statement by the Accused pursuant to Article 67 (1)(h) of the Rome Statute, ICC-01/05-01/08-2860, 1 November 2013, para. 8 (no right to questioning by prosecution).

[278] Art. 67 (1)(g) ICCS.

[279] cf. *Abu Garda*, ICC-02/05-02/09-243-Red, paras. 54–5 ('the suspect, unlike witnesses, who are obliged to tell the truth, is under no such obligation and may therefore provide unreliable information to a Chamber ... an unsworn statement cannot be used as evidence' [Note omitted]); *Bemba*, ICC-01/05-01/08-2860, para. 8; ICC, *Prosecutor v. Ngudjolo*, TC II, Judgment pursuant to Article 74 of the Statute, ICC-01/04-02/12-3-tENG, 18 December 2012, para. 67; ICC, *Prosecutor v. Ntaganda*, AC, Public Redacted Version of Judgment on the Appeals of Mr Bosco Ntaganda and the Prosecutor against the Decision of Trial Chamber VI of 8 July 2019 Entitled 'Judgment', Annex 5: Partly Concurring Opinion of Judge Chile Eboe-Osuji, ICC-01/04-02/06-2666-Anx5-Corr, 30 March 2021, para. 6; in the same vein, against the evidentiary value of an unsworn statement, Schabas and McDermott, 'Article 67', in Ambos, *Commentary* (2022), mn. 48, arguing that '[t]he word "may"' in the latter decision indicates 'that there is no obligation on the Trial Chamber to take the unsworn statement into account when reaching its final judgment'; in the same vein, Keita et al., 'Article 67', in Fernandez et al., *Statut* (2019), p. 1852; Kiss, 'Article 74', in Ambos, *Commentary* (2022), mn. 34, arguing that 'Statements of the accused not provided under oath are not "evidence" for the purposes of the Judgment'; less strict, however, *Prosecutor v. Ngudjolo*, AC, Decision on the Prosecutor's Request to Establish Parameters for Mr Ngudjolo's Personal Address at the Appeal Hearing, ICC-01/04-02/12-217, 17 October 2014, para. 9, holding that 'an unsworn oral or written statement' by the accused 'may attract evidentiary weight'. See Chapter II, D.(1) in this volume.

[280] See also Kiss, 'Article 74', in Ambos, *Commentary* (2016), mn. 34.

[281] *Abu Garda*, ICC-02/05-02/09-243-Red, para. 55; *Bemba*, ICC-01/05-01/08-2860, para. 7.

[282] But note that it is difficult to conceive the accused as a witness due to the above mentioned *nemo tenetur* principle (see also Safferling, *International Criminal Procedure* (2012), p. 451 but limited to the German system).

[283] See *Bemba*, ICC-01/05-01/08-2860, para. 8 (distinguishing explicitly between a statement with undertaking and an unsworn statement).

[284] *Katanga*, ICC-01/04-01/07-3436-tENG, paras. 101, 105. See also Rule 142 (3) RPE KSC: 'The Accused shall not be compelled to make a solemn declaration before making statements or answering questions. The Judges shall assess the probative value, if any, of the Accused's statements or answers to questions.'

[285] ICC, *Prosecutor v. Ntaganda*, AC, Public Redacted Version of Judgment on the Appeals of Mr Bosco Ntaganda and the Prosecutor against the Decision of Trial Chamber VI of 8 July 2019 Entitled 'Judgment', ICC-01/04-02/06-2666-Red, 30 March 2021, para. 580.

The strict distinction between a sworn, 'witness-like' statement and an unsworn statement of the accused has clearly a common law origin[286] and is not entirely convincing in light of the free assessment principle. If the Chamber is free to assess the evidence, it should not be limited by such a formal distinction, but the evidentiary value of the statement should depend on its relevance and reliability. This can also be tested by other means than the questioning of the witness, for example, by corroborating the statement by means of other evidence.[287] Implicitly, that is what the *Ntaganda* TC and AC decided: a decision of the accused to testify under oath does have an impact on the evaluation of evidence insofar as they waive their right to remain silent and 'if [they] decline[] to respond to a permissible question, the Chamber may draw adverse inferences, as appropriate'.[288] The solution via the evaluation of evidence may be considered a compromise between an absolute (civil law) understanding of the *nemo tenetur* principle (with the consequence of prohibiting any inferences from testifying under oath, even if the accused declines to respond)[289] and a more flexible (common law) one (allowing these inferences).[290]

Also, the possibility to forego the undertaking, exceptionally allowed for in the rules,[291] makes clear that witness statements can have evidential value without the solemn undertaking too.

Each testimony should be taken separately[292] to avoid witnesses mutually influencing each other.[293] Witnesses may perceive the same facts completely differently and therefore cannot legitimately comment on each other's testimonies.[294] Witness testimony is based on personal perception and thus is highly subjective. It is—if it goes to the conduct of the accused and links it to the criminal events[295]—one of the major sources of false convictions.[296] Indeed, in her groundbreaking study on witness testimony at the ICTR, SCSL, and SPSC,

[286] Usually, in common law jurisdictions the accused can only give evidence appearing as a witness, while in civil law jurisdictions s/he is considered a party and may give an unsworn statement; cf. Vasiliev, in Sluiter et al., *International Criminal Procedure* (2013), p. 571; also Safferling, *International Criminal Procedure* (2012), p. 469. See also *Ntaganda*, ICC-01/04-02/06-2666-Red, para. 583 ('The Appeals Chamber notes that common law and civil law systems have different approaches to the issue of whether an accused person may testify under oath in their own defence and the scope of the related right to remain silent and privilege against self-crimination.')

[287] Similarly Safferling, *International Criminal Procedure* (2012), p. 457; crit. also Safferling, ibid., p. 469.

[288] ICC, *Prosecutor v. Ntaganda*, TC VI, Decision on further matters related to the testimony of Mr Ntaganda, ICC-01/04-02/06-1945, 8 June 2017, para. 24; *Ntaganda*, ICC-01/04-02/06-2666-Red, para. 581.

[289] *Ntaganda*, ICC-01/04-02/06-2666-Red, para. 583 with n. 1146 (view of Judge Ibáñez Carranza).

[290] Ibid., para. 583 with n. 1147 (view of Judge Eboe-Osuji).

[291] Note 272 in this chapter and main text.

[292] Rule 90 I RPE ICTY, Rule 106 I RPE MICT, Rule 90 (D) RPE ICTR/SCSL, Rule 140 (3) RPE ICC; Rule 141 (4) RPE KSC.

[293] For the same reason witnesses have, in the course of their 'familiarisation', to be accommodated separately, see below note 376 with main text.

[294] Stricter even ICTY, *Prosecutor v. Kupreškić et al.*, TC, Transcript, IT-95-16-T, 25 August 1998, p. 54 (prohibiting the asking of one witness to comment on the evidence of another witness since he can only speculate in this regard).

[295] On the ensuing distinction between 'linkage' and 'crime base' (witness) evidence, the former linking the accused to the crimes charged, and the latter testifying with regard to the circumstances of the crime scene, see Boas et al., *Procedure* (2011), p. 352 with nn. 84 and 85; Klamberg, *Evidence* (2013), pp. 117–18. On linkage, crime-base, and context-related evidence, see Jacobs, in Alston and Knuckey, *HR Fact-Finding* (2016), 268 ff.; Wiley, in Bergsmo and Stahn, *Fact-Finding* (2020), 547 ff.; Brown and Wiley, in Bergsmo and Dittrich, *Integrity* (2020), 529 ff. See also Mettraux et al., *Effectiveness ICC* (2014), p. 9 (para. 19) and p. 69 (paras. 68–9) (recommending that '[i]nvestigations should place a greater emphasis on the acts and conducts of the accused, i.e. on linkage rather than crime base evidence'); for background of this Expert Initiative and a summary of the recommendations, see Lindenmann, *ZIS*, 10 (2015), 529 ff. On the importance of crime-base investigations, Retzlaff, *ZIS*, 10 (2015), 533.

[296] According to the US Innocence Project, 63 per cent of wrongful convictions, as detected by subsequent DNA analysis, are caused by eyewitness misidentification; cf. <http://www.innocenceproject.org/causes-wrongful-conviction>. For Germany, see Velten, *GA*, 162 (2015), 392; generally Combs, *Fact-Finding* (2010), pp. 14–20; Roberts, *JICJ*, 10 (2012), 936–8 (discussing four main concerns).

Nancy Combs reveals that 'eyewitness testimony . . . is of highly questionable reliability' and therefore the factual determinations of these tribunals, mainly relying on such testimony,[297] are of limited accuracy.[298] More concretely, Combs finds, examining all SCSL cases and 'a handful' of ICTR cases, 'that more than 50 percent of the prosecution witnesses appearing in these trials testified in a way that was seriously inconsistent with their pretrial statements' as regards, for example, date, time, or place of the crime, and also its nature and the accused's involvement in it.[299] Further, Combs suggests that the incidence of perjury is higher at these tribunals than in domestic proceedings given the specific cultural and ethnic context and background of international crimes where victims regularly belong to one of the groups involved.[300] Of course, these findings are preliminary[301] and limited to the ICTR, SCSL, and SPSC. Yet, they are not completely surprising given domestic experiences with witness testimony.[302] In any case, the findings, albeit not challenging the foundations of international criminal justice at its core,[303] are important enough to call for an even more cautious use of witness evidence, especially in assessing its probative value (reliability). As a consequence, one should try to improve the quality of this testimony and complement it, to the greatest extent possible, by other testimony.

While *live testimony* is certainly a consequence of the principles of orality and immediacy, as explained above, there are several *exceptions* due to reasons of witness protection[304] or unavailability. Live testimony may then be replaced by audio- or video-link technology[305] or by the introduction of prior recorded witness statements at trial.[306] While the former, especially, testimony via (live) video-link, still respects the principle of orality, the latter entails the replacement of oral by written testimony. It will therefore be more closely analysed in the next section on documentary evidence.

297 Combs, *Fact-Finding* (2010), pp. 6, 12 ff.

298 Ibid., pp. 4, 167 ('virtually every ICTR and SCSL case features some false testimony'); for a detailed analysis of the factual deficiencies, see pp. 21 ff.; for an update of these findings, see Combs, *CLF*, 26 (2015), 394 ff.; for the causes (lack of education and life experiences, cultural background, linguistic difficulties, etc.), see Combs, *Fact-Finding* (2010), pp. 63 ff.; on the inconsistent approaches towards testimonial evidence at the ICTR, see also Byrne, *LJIL*, 26 (2013), 1002–4; McDermott, *CLF*, 26 (2015), 352.

299 Combs, *Fact-Finding* (2010), p. 5; for a detailed analysis (including the causes of inconsistencies), see pp. 106 ff.

300 Ibid., pp. 5–6, 130 ff. (arguing, at p. 6, that 'my review of ICTR cases shows that more than 90 per cent of them featured an alibi or another example of diametrically opposing testimony from defense and prosecution witnesses').

301 Ibid., p. 366.

302 See the references in note 296 of this chapter.

303 Indeed, Combs herself, while questioning the fact-finding competence of 'Western-style' international criminal tribunals (Combs, *Fact-Finding* (2010), p. 7), advocates two reformist paths to overcome the evidentiary problems (9): improving the quality of fact-finding, especially witness testimony (by improving the quality of investigators interviewing witnesses, conducting more on-site visits, punishing perjury, and procedural reforms, [273 ff.]) or adjusting the charges to the evidence (321 ff.). In addition, she proposes a more nuanced understanding of the beyond-reasonable-doubt standard, see previously note 241 in this chapter.

304 cf. Art. 68 ICCS (as referred to in Art. 69 (2) 1st cl.). On the protection measures, see note 573 in this chapter.

305 Rule 67 RPE ICC; also Rules 81*bis* RPE ICTY, 106 RPE MICT, and 85 (D) RPE SCSL; ICC, *Practice Manual* (2023), para. 38 ('If the calling party or participant is unable to travel to the particular location where the interview is to be conducted, the parties and participants shall endeavour to reach an agreement concerning alternative arrangements for the participation of a representative of the calling party, such as participation by video link or holding the interview with the witness at another location'). There is no explicit ICTR rule but Rule 54 RPE ICTR serves as a general basis (Bantekas, *ICL* (2010), p. 490). On the exceptional testimony 'par liaison vidéo', see *Katanga*, ICC-01/04-01/07-3436-tENG, para. 74.

306 Rule 68 RPE ICC. Crit. of this Rule, Zahar and Sluiter, *ICL* (2008), pp. 390–1; Caianiello, *JICJ*, 9 (2011), 393 ff.

Testimony via video- or audio-link can be authorized 'whenever necessary',[307] that is, if the testimony is important and the witness cannot appear for important enough reasons.[308] This may especially happen in cases concerning sexual violence.[309] The testimony should be taken in an appropriate venue where the safety of the witness is ensured.[310] The virtual approach is, in principle, compatible with the right to confrontation, since the witness can be questioned.[311] Of course, given the physical distance of the witness, such virtual testimony has a lower probative value (weight) although its value is still higher than pure written testimony.[312] In any case, the use of the—nowadays well-advanced—video-link technology may help to get access to otherwise unavailable witnesses and be preferable in economic and logistical terms to the transfer of the witness to the seat of the tribunal.[313]

*(b) Probative value, reliability, credibility, and corroboration*

The probative value of a witness statement depends on its reliability and credibility. We have already seen above,[314] that these concepts speak to the probative value or weight of the evidence and that reliability in particular is an inherent element of probative value. As to witness evidence both concepts can be found in the written law[315] and have been recognized by the case law.[316] However, one must distinguish reliability from credibility in that the latter refers to the truthfulness of the witness's testimony, while the former speaks to the fact to which the testimony is directed, that is, whether it can prove this fact.[317] In this sense, reliability

[307] *Lubanga*, ICC-01/04-01/06-1140, para. 41; ICC, *Prosecutor v. Bemba*, TC III, Redacted Decision on the 'Request for the conduct of the testimony CAR-OTP-WWWW-0108 by video-link', ICC-01/05-01/08-947-Red, 12 October 2010, para. 10.

[308] cf. *Tadić*, IT-94-1-T, Video Link Decision, para. 19 ('allow video-link testimony if certain criteria are met, namely that the testimony of a witness is shown to be sufficiently important to make it unfair to proceed without it and that the witness is unable or unwilling to come to the International Tribunal'); ICTR, *Prosecutor v. Zigiranyirazo*, TC III, Decision on Defence Motion for a Hearing by Video-Link for Witness BNZ60, ICTR-2001-73-T, 14 March 2007, para. 2 ('The Chamber may authorize testimony by video-link where it is in the interests of justice, based on a consideration of (i) the importance of the testimony; (ii) the inability or unwillingness of the witness to attend; and (iii) a good reason adduced for the witness' inability or unwillingness to attend the trial proceeding. Where the witness is unwilling to attend, the refusal must be genuine and well-founded, giving the Chamber reason to believe that the testimony will not be heard unless the video-link is authorised'); see also Bantekas, *ICL* (2010), pp. 490–1; Schuon, *International Criminal Procedure* (2010), p. 162; McDermott, in Sluiter et al., *International Criminal Procedure* (2013), p. 877 (general rule).

[309] Farthofer, in Heinze and Dittrich, *ICC* (2021), pp. 539 ff.

[310] *Tadić*, IT-94-1-T, Video-Link Decision, para. 22; also Rule 67 (3) RPE ICC and *Lubanga*, ICC-01/04-01/06-1140, para. 41; also McDermott, in Sluiter et al., *International Criminal Procedure* (2013), pp. 877–8 (general rule).

[311] In the same vein, *Bemba*, ICC-01/05-01/08-947-Red, paras. 11–12; also McDermott, in Sluiter et al., *International Criminal Procedure* (2013), pp. 865 (ad hoc tribunals), 869.

[312] cf. McDermott, in Sluiter et al., *International Criminal Procedure* (2013), p. 865with case law references.

[313] See also ibid., p. 876 (on the latter point). See also AIDP, 'Resolutions of the Nineteenth International Congress of Penal Law', reprinted in *ZStW*, 127 (2015), 470 ff., advocating at 495 an increased use of digital technology in the courtroom ('Virtual Court Room').

[314] Section A.(2)(a) in this chapter.

[315] See e.g. Rules 68 (i), 90 (H)(i) RPE ICTY and 73 (A), 106 (H)(i) RPE MICT (credibility), and Rules 92*quinquies* (B)(ii)(a) RPE ICTY and 113 (B)(ii)(a) RPE MICT (reliability); Rule 140 (2)(b) RPE ICC (both reliability and credibility); in the same vein, Rule 139 (4) RPE KSC.

[316] See e.g. ICTY, *Prosecutor v. Kunarac et al.*, TC II, Decision on Motion for Acquittal, IT-96-23 & 23/1-T, 3 July 2000, para. 7; *Lubanga*, ICC-01/04-01/06-3121-Red, paras. 57 and 239 (but stating incorrectly that the RPR do 'not specifically refer to these concepts' considering them therefore (implicitly) contained in Art. 74 (2) ICCS); *Mustafa*, KSC-CA-2023-02/F00038/RED, para. 38: 'assess the credibility of a witness and the reliability of the evidence presented', para. 153 (in both paras. referring to the credibility of a witness and the reliability of the evidence/testimony); *Ongwen*, ICC-02/04-01/15-2022-Red, para. 320. See also Boas et al., *Procedure* (2011), pp. 344–6; Klamberg, *Evidence* (2013), pp. 172–4 both with further references.

[317] cf. *Kunarac et al.*, IT-96-23 & 23/1-T, Motion for Acquittal Decision, para. 7 ('Credibility depends upon whether the witness should be believed. Reliability assumes that the witness is speaking the truth, but depends

constitutes, arguably, an umbrella term encompassing credibility.[318] In any case, reliability can be 'divided', that is, the testimony may be reliable with regard to some issues but not with regard to others.[319]

The probative value (reliability) and credibility of a testimony must be evaluated on a case-by-case basis,[320] considering 'inconsistencies' in light of the 'evaluation of the overall credibility of each particular witness'.[321] To assess credibility various factors have to be taken into account, for example, the witness's demeanour in Court, her role in the relevant events, and the plausibility and clarity of the testimony.[322] A witness must be protected against self-incrimination by either informing her about the right not to testify or assuring that the statement will not be used against her.[323] Yet, if such an assurance is given, the witness may be compelled to testify under certain circumstances.[324] A witness has also the (dispensable) right to refuse to testify if his testimony would incriminate family members.[325] In both cases only incriminating answers are covered by the privilege.[326]

Low credibility of a witness statement or other factors affecting its probative value, especially the lack of confrontation or cross-examination,[327] may make *corroboration* necessary. However, corroboration does not operate as an explicit legal requirement;[328] on the contrary, the free assessment principle entails that—contrary to the old inquisitorial *unus testis, nullus testis* rule (one witness, no witness)[329]—even one piece of evidence may prove

upon whether the evidence, if accepted, proves the fact to which it is directed'); also *Lubanga*, ICC-01/04-01/06-3121-Red, para. 239 (noting 'that there is a strong link between the two concepts' but only defining credibility 'as referring to whether a witness is testifying truthfully'); *Bemba*, ICC-01/05-01/08-3343, paras. 228–30. On the factors to assess reliability, see below note 654 with main text.

[318] cf. ICTR, *Prosecutor v. Karemera et al.*, AC, Decision on Joseph Nzirorera's Appeal of Decision on Admission of Evidence Rebutting Adjudicated Facts, ICTR-98-44-AR73.17, 29 May 2009, para. 15 with n. 38 ('Given the large meaning of the term "reliability", the Appeals Chamber considers that the requirement of *prima facie* reliability indisputably encompasses the requirement of *prima facie* credibility'); Klamberg, *Evidence* (2013), p. 174; Klamberg, in Sluiter et al., *International Criminal Procedure* (2013), p. 1025 ('wider concept').

[319] *Lubanga*, ICC-01/04-01/06-2842, para. 104; *Katanga*, ICC-01/04-01/07-3436-tENG, para. 84. See also Boas et al., *Procedure* (2011), p. 346 (with references to ICTY/ICTR/SCSL case law in n. 47).

[320] cf. Bantekas, *ICL* (2010), p. 531.

[321] *Akayesu*, ICTR-96-4, para. 136; *Ongwen*, ICC-02/04-01/15-2022-Red, para. 320. See also Bantekas *ICL* (2010), pp. 541–2.

[322] *Nahimana et al.*, ICTR-99-52-A, para. 194; confirmed e.g. by ICTR, *Prosecutor v. Bikindi*, AC, Judgment, ICTR-01-72-A, 18 March 2010, para. 114; ICTR, *Prosecutor v. Nchamihigo*, AC, Judgment, ICTR-2001-63-A, 18 March 2010, para. 47; ICTR, *Prosecutor v. Nzabonimana*, AC, Judgment, ICTR-98-44D-A, 29 September 2014, para. 45; *Popović et al.*, IT-05-88-A, para. 132.

[323] cf. Rules 90 I RPE ICTY/ICTR/SCSL and 106 I RPE MICT; Rule 151 RPE KSC; more detailed Rule 74 RPE ICC; thereto McDermott, in Sluiter et al., *International Criminal Procedure* (2013), pp. 862, 868.

[324] cf. *Mustafa*, KSC-CA-2023-02/F00038/RED, para. 141 (referring to Rule 151 (2) RPE KSC).

[325] cf. Rule 75 RPE ICC.

[326] Piragoff and Clarke, 'Article 69', in Ambos, *Commentary* (2022), mn. 77 *in fine*.

[327] cf. *Aleksovski*, IT-95-14/1-AR73, para. 15.

[328] cf. Rule 63 (4) RPE ICC (explicitly stating that it is no legal requirement); see also *Lubanga*, ICC-01/04-01/06-3121-Red, para. 218 (no corroboration regarding video excerpts); *Stanišić and Simatović*, MICT-15-96-A, para. 294 (corroboration 'not a requirement for admission of evidence'); *Mustafa*, KSC-CA-2023-02/F00038/RED, para. 38 ('corroboration is neither a condition nor a guarantee of reliability of a single piece of evidence. A trial panel has the discretion to decide, in the circumstances of each case, whether corroboration of evidence is necessary, and to rely on uncorroborated, but otherwise credible, witness testimony'); see previously ICTY, *Prosecutor v. Tadić*, TC, Opinion and Judgment, IT-94-1-T, 7 May 1997, para. 537 ('it is not correct to say that in present day civil law systems corroboration remains a general requirement'); *Delalić et al.*, IT-96-21, TC Judgment, para. 594 ('corroboration of evidence is not a customary rule of international law, and as such should not be ordinarily required by the International Tribunal'); ICTY, *Prosecutor v. Limaj et al.*, AC, Judgment, IT-03-66-A, 27 September 2007, para. 203; on the ad hoc tribunals, see also Bantekas, *ICL* (2010), pp. 533–4; Schuon, *International Criminal Procedure* (2010), p. 161; Klamberg, *Evidence* (2013), pp. 179 ff.

[329] See in this regard *Tadić*, IT-94-1-T, TC Judgment, paras. 536–8 (stressing the free evaluation of the evidence); ICTR, *Prosecutor v. Akayesu*, TC, Judgment, ICTR-96-4-T, 2 September 1998, para. 135 ('the Chamber

the respective fact.[330] Of course, corroboration may increase the probative value (reliability, weight) of certain evidence.[331] It may even amount to so-called 'concurrent (corroborative) evidence', if the same fact is proven by two or more pieces of evidence, for example, two witnesses testifying to the same fact.[332] Yet, corroboration does not automatically entail the credibility and thus probative value of the witness statement but is only one factor to be taken into account by a reasonable trier of fact in assessing it.[333]

Indeed, the credibility of a witness may be impugned to such an extent that the reliability of her statement cannot be achieved by corroboration of any sort.[334] In such a situation the quantitative approach underlying the concurrent evidence thesis does not help either.[335] Another factor to be taken into account could be a prior (out-of-court) statement of the same witness which may—if admitted into evidence pursuant to the rules to be discussed in the next section—either confirm or rebut his in-court-statement.[336] The ICTR Appeals Chamber stated with regard to the mutual corroboration of two testimonies:

> [T]wo testimonies corroborate one another when one *prima facie* credible testimony is compatible with the other *prima facie* credible testimony regarding the same fact or a sequence of linked facts. It is not necessary that both testimonies be identical in all aspects or describe the same fact in the same way. Every witness presents what he has seen from his own point of view at the time of the events, or according to how he understood the events recounted by others. It follows that corroboration may exist even when some details differ

can rule on the basis of a single testimony'); *Limaj et al.*, IT-03-66-A, para. 203 ('Corroboration is neither a condition nor a guarantee of reliability of a single piece of evidence'). About the rule generally, Roberts, in du Bois-Pedain and Eldar, *Beccaria* (2022), pp. 187–8.

[330] *Lubanga*, ICC-01/04-01/06-2842, para. 110; *Katanga*, ICC-01/04-01/07-3436-tENG, para. 110: *Bemba*, ICC-01/05-01/08-3343, paras. 245–6 (all adopting a case-by-case approach); *Ntaganda*, ICC-01/04-02/06-2666-Red, para. 690; *Mustafa*, KSC-CA-2023-02/F00038/RED, para. 30. See also *Karadžić*, IT-95-5/18-T, Judgment, para. 12; Bantekas, *ICL* (2010), p. 534 with further references in n. 360, Agirre, in Agirre et al., *Quality Control* (2020), pp. 224 ff.

[331] cf. *Lubanga*, ICC-01/04-01/06-803-tEN, para. 121 ('Chamber ... will attach a higher probative value to those parts of the children's ... evidence which have been corroborated'); conc. *Katanga*, ICC-01/04-01/07-717, para. 150, also paras. 159–60, stressing probative value with regard to Rule 63 (4) and impact of corroboration. With regard to the ad hoc tribunals, see *Stanišić and Simatović*, MICT-15-96-A, para. 294 ('[C]orroboration ... goes to the reliability of the evidence and whether, once admitted, it will be relied upon to support a conviction. If such evidence is to support a conviction, it must be corroborated'); see also Bantekas, *ICL* (2010), pp. 534–6; Agirre, in Agirre et al., *Quality Control* (2020), pp. 224 ff.

[332] cf. Klamberg, *Evidence* (2013), pp. 178–9, 180; Klamberg, *JICJ*, 13 (2015), 541; see also Combs, *Fact-Finding* (2010), pp. 169–70 (referring to Matthew Hale and Robert Boyle already making this point in the seventeenth and eighteenth centuries, respectively).

[333] *Limaj et al.*, IT-03-66-A, para. 203; *Prosecutor v. D. Milošević*, AC, Judgment, IT-98-29/1-A, 12 November 2009, para. 248.

[334] *Ngudjolo*, ICC-01/04-02/12-271-Corr, paras. 1–2, 168–71, 192, holding that a TC in such a situation may also 'reject potentially corroborative evidence when making its credibility assessments'.

[335] For a crit. discussion, see Combs, *Fact-Finding* (2010), pp. 170–4.

[336] See e.g. ICTY, *Prosecutor v. D. Tadić*, AC, Judgment on Allegations of Contempt against Prior Counsel, Milan Vujin, IT-94-1-A-R77, 31 January 2000, para. 93 (holding that a prior out-of-court statement, which is inconsistent with the in-court testimony, 'is admissible so as to prove the truth of what was said, acknowledging nevertheless that the weight to be afforded to that material will usually be less than that given to the testimony of a witness who has given it under a form of oath and who has been cross-examined, although even this will depend upon the infinitely variable circumstances which surround hearsay material'); see also ICTY, *Prosecutor v. Naletilić and Martinović*, TC, Decision on the Admission of Witness Statements into Evidence, IT-98-34-T, 14 November 2001 (use of prior statement to test credibility of witness); *Lubanga*, ICC-01/04-01/06-2842, para. 102 (assessing possible contradiction with prior statements admitted into evidence). See also Safferling, *International Criminal Procedure* (2012), pp. 480–1(discussing this issue under 'impeachment documents' challenging evidence of the opposing party); McDermott, in Sluiter et al., *International Criminal Procedure* (2013), p. 861.

between testimonies, provided that no credible testimony describes the facts in question in a way which is not compatible with the description given in another credible testimony.[337]

### *(c) Hearsay evidence, including intermediaries*

Hearsay evidence is a form of testimonial evidence and belongs to the category of indirect evidence.[338] It can be defined as '[e]vidence from any witness which consists of what another person stated (whether verbally, in writing, or by any other method of assertion)'.[339] It is admissible in principle.[340] This has been settled case law since the *Tadić* hearsay decision,[341] confirmed by the AC.[342] Still, this is striking in light of the classic common law rule[343] and of

[337] *Nahimana et al.*, ICTR-99-52-A, para. 428. See also ICTR, *Prosecutor v. Karera*, AC, Judgment, ICTR-01-74-A, 2 February 2009, para. 173.

[338] Heinze, in Caeiro, Gless, and Mitsilegas, *Elgar Encyclopedia* (2022).

[339] Glover, *Evidence* (2017), 10.1.1, p. 293, reproducing the definition given by Murphy in earlier editions. According to Rule 801 I of the US Federal Rules of Evidence, hearsay is 'a statement, other than one made by the declarant while testifying at the trial or hearing, offered in evidence to prove the truth of the matter asserted'; see also Binder, *Hearsay Handbook* (2021), para. 1.1. Under common law, hearsay evidence is 'any statement, other than one made by a witness in the course of giving his evidence in the proceedings in question, by any person, whether it was made on oath or unsworn and whether it was made orally, in writing, or by signs and gestures, which is offered as evidence of the truth of its contents' (Keane and McKeown, *The Modern Law of Evidence* (2022), p. 11; for more definitions see Pattenden, in Malek, *Phipson on Evidence* (2022) paras. 28.03, 30.04); from a comparative perspective, Choo, in Assy and Higgins, *Principles, Procedure, and Justice* (2020), p. 25; for England and Wales, see s. 114 of the Criminal Justice Act 2003; for Ireland, Charleton et al., *Charleton and McDermott's Criminal Law and Evidence* (2020), para. 3.02; for a similar definition, invoking US and UK law, see *Karadžić*, IT-95-5/18-T, Judgment, para. 13 ('Hearsay evidence is any statement other than one made by a witness while giving evidence in the proceedings and which is offered to prove the truth of the matter asserted in the statement'). A rather ponderously formulated definition can be found in *Aleksovski*, IT-95-14/1-AR73, para. 14: hearsay is 'the statement of a person made otherwise than in the proceedings in which it is being tendered, but nevertheless being tendered in those proceedings in order to establish the truth of what that person says'.

[340] See also Bantekas, *ICL* (2010), pp. 508–11; Schuon, *International Criminal Procedure* (2010), pp. 143–7 (stressing the practical usefulness of this kind of evidence at 146–7), 163; Combs, in Schabas and Bernaz, *Handbook ICL* (2011), pp. 326–7; Klamberg, *Evidence* (2013), pp. 368 ff.; crit. Boas et al., *Procedure* (2011), pp. 347–9; Gillet, *Prosecuting Environmental Harm* (2022), pp. 164–5; Gillett, *MichJIL*, 44 (2023), 320; Sorvatzioti, *ICLR*, 22 (2022) 904 ff. On the use in Nuremberg and Tokyo, see Chapter I, B.(1) and (2) in this volume.

[341] *Tadić*, IT-94-1-T, Hearsay Decision, paras. 7, 13 ff. (with Dissenting Opinion by Judge Stephen); thereto also Murphy, *JICJ*, 8 (2010), 563; *Tadić*, IT-94-1-T, TC, Judgment, para. 555 ('The mere fact that particular testimony was in the nature of hearsay did not operate to exclude it from the category of admissible evidence'); see also ICTY, *Prosecutor v. Blaškić*, TC I, Decision on the Standing Objection of the Defence to the Admission of Hearsay with no Inquiry as to its Reliability, IT-95-14-T, 21 January 1998, para. 10 (arguing that 'professional judges ... possess the necessary ability to begin by hearing hearsay evidence and then to evaluate it so they can make a ruling as to its relevance and probative value'); ICTY, *Prosecutor v. Blaškić*, TC, Decision on the Defence Motion to Compel the Disclosure of Rule 66 and 68 Material Relating to Statements Made by a Person Known as 'X', IT-95-14-T, 15 July 1998, paras. 10–12. For the ICTR, see *Musema*, ICTR-96-13-A, para. 51 ('hearsay evidence is not inadmissible per se, even when it cannot be examined at its source or when it is not corroborated by direct evidence'). For the ICC, see *Katanga*, ICC-01/04-01/07-2635, para. 27 lit. e. ('no prohibition'); also Art. 69 (4) ICCS ('*any* evidence', emphasis added); thereto Safferling, *International Criminal Procedure* (2012), p. 498. See also *Bemba et al.*, ICC-01/05-01/13-2275-Red, para. 874. For the KSC, see next note; for the ECCC see McDermott, *JICJ*, 18 (2020), 747–64 with further references. On this as a whole, May and Wierda, *International Criminal Evidence* (2002), pp. 114–19; Ambos, in Bohlander, *International Criminal Justice* (2007), pp. 483–4.

[342] *Aleksovski*, IT-95-14/1-AR73, para. 15, thereto Karnavas, in Stahn et al., *Legacies of the ICTY* (2020), pp. 251, 265; also ICTY, *Prosecutor v. Kordić* and *Čerkez*, AC, Judgment, IT-95-14/2-A, 17 December 2004, paras. 281–4; *Mustafa*, KSC-CA-2023-02/F00038/RED, para. 125 with n. 296 ('The Panel recalls that hearsay evidence is generally admissible, but the weight and probative value, if any, to be afforded to the evidence must be assessed on a case-by-case basis, including a consideration of the Defence's opportunity to test and challenge the evidence'); Schuon, *International Criminal Procedure* (2010), pp. 143 ff.

[343] Hearsay evidence is only permissible in exceptional cases under common law; see *Tadić*, IT-94-1-T, Hearsay Decision, paras. 8 ff.; similarly *Tadić*, IT-94-1-T, Hearsay Decision, Dissenting Opinion of Judge Stephen. Yet, there are quite a few exceptions, cf. Laudan, *Truth* (2006), p. 121, reporting twenty-nine exceptions and further exceptions to these; Heinze, in Caeiro, Gless, and Mitsilegas, *Elgar Encyclopedia* (2022). In the US, hearsay evidence is for example admissible within the context of so-called *grand jury proceedings*; thereon McCord and McCord, *Criminal Law and Procedure* (2006), p. 440; Boas et al., *Procedure* (2011), p. 347; Heinze, *Disclosure* (2014), p. 394.

the best evidence rule explained above. In fact, hearsay is far from the best evidence; rather it is secondary evidence and thus, in terms of probative value and reliability, worse than primary evidence, that is, direct witness testimony.[344] Also, given the absence of the primary witness, a confrontation or cross-examination is not possible.[345] As a consequence, hearsay as secondary evidence should only be admitted if no primary evidence is available, provided that it meets the general requirements, that is, it is relevant and has (still) probative value.[346]

Indeed, the gist of the issue is the probative value (reliability) of hearsay.[347] It depends on 'the context and character of the evidence in question'[348] and is to be assessed at the end of the trial 'on a case by case basis taking into account factors such as the consistency of the information itself and its consistency with the evidence as a whole, the reliability of the source and the possibility for the defence to challenge the source'.[349] Of course, as already said above, hearsay has a lower probative value than direct witness evidence,[350] and

On the fundamental incompatibility with an adversarial trial, Damaška, *Faces of Justice* (1986), pp. 15, 64, 80, 130; Swart, *JICJ*, 6 (2008), 98; on the English 'rule against hearsay', see Gleß, *Beweisrechtsgrundsätze* (2006), pp. 259–60, 324–6. cf. also May and Wierda, *ColJTransnat'lL*, 37 (1999), 745, where reference is made to the Dissenting Opinion of Judge Pal in the *Tokyo* Judgment and the *Nuremberg* Judgment; also Safferling, *International Criminal Procedure* (2003), pp. 292, 306; see also Murphy, *JICJ*, 8 (2010), 563, who suggests rules for hearsay evidence; crit. also Radosavljevic, *ICLR*, 13 (2013), 1029–32 (but misstating the common law approach). For the perspective of civil law, see e.g. the decision of the German Constitutional Court BverfG, 21.08.1996-2 BvR 1304/96, reprinted in *StV*, 17 (1997), 2–3 ('Der Beweiswert der auf diese Weise eingeführten Angaben zum Tatgeschehen ist besonders kritisch zu überprüfen, wenn sie auf Bekundungen eines nicht näher bekannten Gewährsmannes zurückgehen. Die Angaben des Gewährsmannes reichen grundsätzlich nicht, wenn sie nicht durch andere, nach der Überzeugung des Fachgerichts wichtige Gesichtspunkte gestützt werden.')

344 In a similar vein, Miebach, *NStZ*, 41 (2021), 403, 408; less crit. Heinze, in Caeiro, Gless, and Mitsilegas, *Elgar Encyclopedia* (2022).

345 *Aleksovski*, IT-95-14/1-AR73, para. 27; Karnavas, in Stahn et al., *Legacies of the ICTY* (2020), 251, 265; Brandl, *Criminal Investigation* (2021), p. 116 ('(1) the person who made the original statement was not under oath and therefore was not obligated to tell the truth and (2) the person who originally made the statement cannot be cross examined to test his or her perception, memory, veracity, and ability to be articulate'). Of course, the lacking oath is only a convincing argument for those jurisdictions where a witness statement is regularly taken under oath.

346 See also *Orić*, IT-03-68-T, para. 3, where the TC 'views primary evidence as the best evidence. However, where only secondary evidence is available of a relevant document, it may be admitted without prejudice, provided that the reliability is not at issue.' See also Sorvatzioti, *ICLR*, 22 (2022), 895, 905; Pittman and Öberg, in Stahn et al., *Legacies of the ICTY* (2020), pp. 282, 299.

347 cf. *Akayesu*, ICTR-96-4, para. 286 ('so lacking in terms of the indicia of reliability that it is not "probative"'; citing *Kordić* and *Čerkez*, IT-95-14/2-AR73.5, para. 24). See *Nahimana et al.*, ICTR-99-52-A, para. 509 ('settled jurisprudence that hearsay evidence is admissible as long as it is of probative value'); ICTY, *Prosecutor v. Naletilić and Martinović*, AC, Judgment, IT-98-34-A, 3 May 2006, para. 217; *Lubanga*, ICC 01/04 01/06-803-tEN, para. 103 ('objections pertaining to the use of anonymous hearsay evidence do not go to the admissibility of the evidence, but only to its probative value'); also *Katanga*, ICC 01/04-01/07-717, para. 137; *Bemba*, ICC-01/05-01/08-3343, para. 238 ('The Chamber took a cautious approach in assessing evidence originating from hearsay. It did not rule out such evidence *ab initio*, instead assessing the weight to be accorded to it') [emphasis in the original]. See also Sorvatzioti, *ICLR*, 22 (2022), 895, 905.

348 *Aleksovski*, IT-95-14/1-AR73, para. 15 ('reliable for that purpose, in the sense of being voluntary, truthful and trustworthy as appropriate; and for this purpose [a Chamber] may consider both the content of the hearsay statement and the circumstances under which the evidence arose'); also *Nahimana et al.*, ICTR-99-52-A, para. 831 (focusing on the 'source and precise character' of the information); conc. *Lubanga*, ICC-01/04-01/06-1399, para. 28 (following *Aleksovski*); for specific criteria of reliability, see *Kordić* and *Čerkez*, IT-95-14/2-AR73.5, paras. 23 ff.

349 *Katanga*, ICC-01/04-01/07-717, para. 141; also *Akayesu*, ICTR-96-4, para. 292 ('at the end of trial when weighing and evaluating the evidence as a whole, in light of the context and of the nature of the evidence itself, including the credibility and reliability of the relevant witness') and *Karadžić*, IT-95-5/18-T, Judgment, para. 13. Sceptical, Boas et al., *Procedure* (2011), p. 349 ('unlikely that most Chambers actually expend a great deal of time assessing the reliability of each item of hearsay at the end of a lengthy trial'), also generally at 374.

350 *Aleksovski*, IT-95-14/1-AR73, para. 15 ('weight or probative value to be afforded to that evidence will usually be less than that given to the testimony of a witness who has given it under a form of oath and who has been cross-examined'); also ICTY, *Prosecutor v. Rajić*, TC, Review of the Indictment pursuant to Rule 61 of the Rules of Procedure and Evidence, Separate Opinion of Judge Sidhwa, IT-95-12-T, 13 September 1996, para. 28 ('not a

the more persons take part in the chain of transmission of the original statement ('multiple hearsay'[351] or 'hearsay upon hearsay'[352]) the lower the probative value becomes. Similarly, anonymous hearsay—having no or insufficient information about the primary source—has an even lower probative value and may at best be used to corroborate other evidence.[353] In any case, a TC shall be particularly 'cautious in considering such evidence'[354] and should strive to corroborate it by additional evidence.[355]

The so-called *intermediaries*, already discussed in Chapter II,[356] produce, at best, hearsay evidence which will often have no probative value and/or be unreliable.[357] Their use is

witness to the occurrence' and therefore 'cannot be permitted to give evidence as to what the eye-witness of the case told him because his evidence would be against the best evidence rule'); ICC, *Prosecutor v. Gbagbo*, PTC I, Decision Adjourning the Hearing on the Confirmation of Charges pursuant to Art. 61 (7)I(i) of the Rome Statute, ICC-02/11-01/11-432, 3 June 2013, para. 28 ('less probative value'). See also Schuon, *International Criminal Procedure* (2010), p. 145; O'Sullivan and Montgomery, *JICJ*, 8 (2010), 513; Klamberg, *JICJ*, *13* (2015), 540 (comparing it in this regard to successive chain evidence).

[351] The terminology of the case law is not consistent; see on the one hand *Kordić and Čerkez*, IT-95-14/2-AR73.5, para. 27 ('first hand hearsay') and on the other *Nahimana et al.*, ICTR-99-52-A, paras. 508, 509 ('second degree' and 'third degree hearsay'). See also Bantekas, *ICL* (2010), p. 539 ('[d]ouble hearsay'); Schuon, *International Criminal Procedure* (2010), p. 144.

[352] Spencer, *Hearsay Evidence* (2014), p. 213.

[353] This has even been held with regard to the pre-trial stage: *Lubanga*, ICC-01/04-01/06-803-tEN, para. 106; *Katanga*, ICC-01/04-01/07-717, paras. 119, 140; ICC, *Prosecutor v. Mbarushimana*, PTC I, Decision on the Confirmation of Charges, ICC-01/04-01/10-465-Red, 16 December 2011, para. 78 ('low probative value in view of the inherent difficulties in ascertaining the truthfulness and authenticity of such information ... used only for the purpose of corroborating other evidence'); more detailed, *Gbagbo*, ICC-02/11-01/11-432, paras. 29–32 (one the one hand concerned with regard to defence rights and the corroboration by anonymous hearsay, on the other distinguishing between hearsay presented by the Prosecutor and based on third sources, e.g. NGO reports). On press and NGO reports to corroborate other pieces of evidence, see also *Bemba*, ICC-01/05-01/08-3343, paras. 269–71. Due to the failure to meet the reliability and probative value requirements, the TC in *Karadžić*, IT-95-5/18-T, Judgment, para. 21 also rejected the admissibility of media reports as such; they were only admitted 'when a witness testified to the accuracy of the information contained therein and attested that they had not been manipulated in any way'. Against the use of anonymous hearsay, also Mettraux et al., *Effectiveness ICC* (2014), p. 19 (para. 16: 'The Prosecution should cease in principle to rely on evidential use of anonymous hearsay. Investigators must find the source of the hearsay and conduct their own independent interview and assessment of the witness'); also pp. 67–8 (paras. 62–4); in particular, crit. of the use of NGO reports, pp. 9 (paras. 15, 21), 67, 69 (paras. 61, 70) (recommending its limited use).

[354] ICTY, *Prosecutor v. Ndindabahizi*, AC, Judgment, ICTR-01-71-A, 16 January 2007, para. 115; *Katanga*, ICC-01/04-01/07-717, para. 70 ('when the Chamber determines that the probative value of an item of evidence or portions thereof is affected, for example because the evidence contains only anonymous hearsay statements or inconsistencies, the Chamber will exercise caution in using such evidence in order to affirm or reject any assertion made by the Prosecution'); also *Katanga*, ICC-01/04-01/07-2635, para. 27 lit. e. ('Chamber is conscious of the inherent risks in this type of evidence. It may therefore take such risks into consideration when attributing the appropriate probative value to items of evidence consisting mainly or exclusively of hearsay').

[355] *Nahimana et al.*, ICTR-99-52-A, para. 473; *Katanga*, ICC-01/04-01/07-717, para. 70 ('as with any evidence presented, the Chamber will try, whenever possible, to cite additional evidence in the record which also supports the Chamber's conclusions'). See also ICC, *Prosecutor v. Bemba*, AC, Judgment on the Appeal of Mr Jean-Pierre Bemba Combo against Trial Chamber III 'Judgment pursuant to Article 74 of the Statute', Separate Opinion of Judge Christine Van den Wyngaert and Judge Howard Morrison, ICC-01/05-01/08-3636-Anx2, 8 June 2018, and Concurring Separate Opinion of Judge Eboe-Osuji, ICC-01/05-01/08-3636-Anx3, 14 June 2018, para. 8 ('Whereas hearsay is not per se inadmissible before the Court, this does not mean that it is permissible to make findings beyond a reasonable doubt on this basis, especially when the Trial Chamber does not seem to have tried to establish the reliability of the source of the information. Although the Trial Chamber accepted the need to be cautious when relying on hearsay evidence, it appears that in practice it often threw its own caution to the wind'); thereto Sorvatzioti, *ICLR*, 22 (2022), 895, 906. See also Bantekas, *ICL* (2010), pp. 538–9.

[356] Chapter II, B.(2) in this volume *in fine*. On intermediators as mere 'translators' as used in the domestic context, see Combs, *Fact-Finding* (2010), pp. 300–2.

[357] ICC, *Prosecutor v. Lubanga*, TC I, Judgment pursuant to Article 74 of the Statute, ICC-01/04-01/06-2482, 14 March 2012, para. 374; see also de Vos, *LJIL*, 26 (2013), 1022. The *Lubanga* TC also withdrew the status of victims because of their interactions with the controversial intermediaries, cf. *Lubanga*, ICC-01/04-01/06-2482, para. 484. The AC approved the steps taken by the TC with regard to the controversial intermediaries, cf. *Lubanga*, ICC-01/04-01/06-3121-Red, paras. 163, 206, 352, 521.

troubling if they are neither properly selected[358] nor supervized[359] and manipulate witnesses pursuing interests alien to the purpose of criminal proceedings.[360] In this case they may have to be called to appear in court since their testimony may, inter alia, contribute to resolve possible 'conflicts in the evidence'.[361] The disclosure of the intermediary's identity may then be 'material to the preparation of the defence'[362] since otherwise, keeping their identity secret, the defence will not be able to find out whether a possibly untrue testimony 'was influenced by untoward behaviour' of an intermediary.[363] We will return to this issue in the context of disclosure.[364]

### (d) *Preparation of witnesses ('proofing') versus mere 'familiarization'*

Another controversial issue at the ICC is the preparation of witnesses, understood, with regard to the concrete witness testimony, as 'proofing' or 'coaching'.[365] This practice is well known in common law systems, especially the USA,[366] and has thus—not surprisingly—been widely practised at the ad hoc tribunals.[367] In essence, *witness proofing* focuses on the concrete witness testimony and is used by the calling party to make sure that the witness testifies to its full satisfaction. A less straightforward definition used early by the OTP at the ICC refers to a 'practice whereby a meeting is held between a party to the proceedings and a witness, before the witness is due to testify in Court, the purpose of which is to re-examine the witness's evidence to enable more accurate, complete and efficient testimony'.[368]

[358] *Lubanga*, ICC-01/04-01/06-2482, para. 195 ('no formal recruitment procedure ... matter of circumstance'). For selection criteria, see ICC, 'Guidelines Intermediaries' (2014), pp. 7–10, sect. 2; Haslam and Edmunds, *CLF*, 24 (2013), 72 ff. In this regard, see also the ICC, *Guidelines Intermediaries* (2014) which establishes the relevant rules of conduct and possible sanctions.

[359] Crit. on the lack of proper supervision, ICC, *Prosecutor v. Lubanga*, TC I, Redacted Decision on Intermediaries, ICC-01/04-01/06-2434-Red2, 31 May 2010, para. 146; *Lubanga*, ICC-01/04-01/06-2482, para. 482 ('unsupervised actions'); see also de Vos, *LJIL*, 26 (2013), 1012, 1022.

[360] *Lubanga*, ICC-01/04-01/06-2434-Red2, para. 140 (referring to two intermediaries who 'may have misused their positions in varying ways', in particular it is alleged 'that they have persuaded or invited witnesses to give false testimony to the Court'); *Lubanga*, ICC-01/04-01/06-2482, paras. 482 (witnesses 'vulnerable to manipulation'), 483 (possible crimes under Art. 70 ICCS). See also Mettraux et al., *Effectiveness ICC* (2014), p. 9 (para. 16: while acknowledging the importance of intermediaries at the same time cautioning against their use in the selection of witnesses), also pp. 59, 68 (paras. 24–6, 65–6); on the possible manipulation of victims, see Haslam and Edmunds, *CLF*, 24 (2013), 56–7.

[361] *Lubanga*, ICC-01/04-01/06-2434-Red2, paras. 141, 150 (iii) (therefore requesting the appearance of the two intermediaries mentioned in the previous footnote pursuant to an abuse of process application by the defence, para. 54).

[362] cf. Rule 77 RPE ICC.

[363] *Lubanga*, ICC-01/04-01/06-2434-Red2, para. 143.

[364] Section B.(2)(e) in this chapter *in fine* and (5) with note 1161.

[365] cf. KSC, *Prosecutor v. Shala*, TP I, Decision on Witness Familarisation, KSC-BC-2020-04/F00435, 24 February 23, para. 9 with n. 12 (understanding witness preparation 'broadly, covering a number of expressions, including, inter alia, "witness proofing", "witness training", and "witness coaching", used in different jurisdictions in connection with practices aimed at preparing a witness to give oral testimony'). See generally Skilbeck, *JICJ*, 8 (2010), 457 ff.; Swoboda, *Verfahrens- und Beweisstrategien* (2013), pp. 665 ff.; Heinze, *Disclosure* (2014), pp. 387 ff.; Heinze, in Klip und Freeland, *ALC LXI* (2020), 307, 431 ff.

[366] See Ambos, in Stahn and Sluiter, *ICC* (2009), pp. 605–11. The practice in adversarial systems is, of course, not uniform; it is especially more restrictive in England and Wales; see pp. 606–9, and Jackson and Brunger, *JICJ*, 13 (2015), 606.

[367] ICTY, *Prosecutor v. Limaj et al.*, TC II, Decision on the Defence Motion on Prosecution Practice of 'Proofing Witnesses', IT-03-66-T, 10 December 2004, p. 2; for further references, see Ambos, in Stahn and Sluiter, *ICC* (2009), pp. 603–5; crit. of the tribunals' lack of an uniform approach, Jordash, *LJIL*, 22 (2009), 504. Recently, the STL has also approved of the practice; cf. STL, *Prosecutor v. Ayyash et al.*, TC, STL-11-01/TC, 16 January 2014, pp. 2 ff. (guidelines on the conduct of proceedings) and para. 18 with n. 4 (citing, inter alia, the ICC *Kenya* decisions to be discussed below).

[368] ICC, *Prosecutor v. Lubanga*, TC I, Prosecution Submissions Regarding the Subjects that Require Early Determination: Procedures to be Adopted for Instructing Expert Witnesses, Witness Familiarization and Witness

A similar definition has been given more recently by TC V with regard to 'witness preparation' as 'a meeting between a witness and the party calling that witness, taking place shortly before the witness's testimony, for the purpose of discussing matters relating to the witness's testimony'.[369] Thus, 'proofing' and 'preparation' mean basically the same, but it is preferable to use the latter term—to be distinguished from pre-trial preparation at the witness's location of origin[370]—being the less controversial one.[371]

In contrast, '*witness familiarisation*', in essence, means that the VWU[372] helps the witness to accommodate in The Hague and become familiar with the Court's infrastructure and procedures to be generally able to testify in the first place,[373] that is, it is a more general measure without a focus on the concrete testimony. In fact, while witnesses may be allowed to 'refresh their memory' reviewing their prior statements or other relevant documents before their actual in-court testimony and may have a 'courtesy meeting' with relevant counsel, all this takes place under the supervision of the VWU and the evidence to be given by the witness shall not be touched upon.[374]

While 'familiarisation' has never been controversial[375]—it only had to be developed and improved on the basis of practical experiences to be translated into the respective 'Familiarisation Protocol'[376]—and is indeed both necessary,[377] and encouraged,[378] witness

Proofing, ICC-01/04-01/06-952, 12 September 2007, para. 15 (following ICTY, *Prosecutor v. Haradinaj et al.*, TC I, Decision on Defence Requests for Audio-Recording of Prosecution Witness Proofing Sessions, IT-04-84-T, 23 May 2007, para. 8, which, however, encompasses both preparation and familiarization of the witness).

369 ICC, *Prosecutor v. Ruto and Sang*, TC V, Decision on Witness Preparation, ICC-01/09-01/11-524, 2 January 2013, para. 4.

370 The so-called 'preparation phase' starts with the introduction of the witness by the calling party to the VWU 'prior to the scheduled travel ... to the location of testimony', i.e. in her location of origin; cf. ICC, *Prosecutor v. Bemba et al.*, TC VII, Unified Protocol on the Practices Used to Prepare and Familiarise Witnesses for Giving Testimony before the Court, ICC-01/05-01/13-1252-Anx, 15 September 2015, paras. 5 ff.

371 On the unclear origin of the term 'witness proofing', not commonly used in adversarial systems, see Jackson and Brunger, *JICJ*, 13 (2015), 603.

372 On this organ, see Chapter II, E.(3) in this volume.

373 Ambos, in Stahn and Sluiter, *ICC* (2009), pp. 599–600.

374 cf. ICC, *Prosecutor v. Bemba et al.*, TC VII, Decision on Witness Preparation and Familiarisation, ICC-01/05-01/13-1252, 15 September 2015, paras. 26–7 and the annexed Protocol *Bemba et al.*, ICC-01/05-01/13-1252-Anx, paras. 25 ff.

375 Ambos, in Stahn and Sluiter, *ICC* (2009), p. 600; Ciorciari and Heindel, *VirgJIL*, 56 (2017), 306.

376 See more recently *Ruto and Sang*, ICC-01/09-01/11-524, para. 4, referring to the Registry's 'Unified Protocol on the Practices Used to Prepare and Familiarize Witnesses for Giving Testimony', i.e. the 'Familiarisation Protocol'; also ICC, *Prosecutor v. Ntaganda*, TC VI, Decision on the Protocol on Witness Familiarisation, ICC-01/04-02/06-656, 17 June 2015 (where 'participants and VWU agree on all aspects of the proposed' Protocol 'with the exception of two paragraphs relating to travel and accommodation arrangements for witnesses' [para. 5] and the Chamber grants the VWU 'a certain level of discretion' [para. 12] but orders, regarding accommodation, 'the separation of witnesses once they have commenced their testimony' [para. 14]) and the respective (amended) Protocol published as Annex A of the Decision (ICC, *Prosecutor v. Ntaganda*, TC VI, Protocol on the Practices to be Used to Familiarise Witnesses for Giving Testimony at Trial, ICC-01/04-02/06-656-AnxA, 17 June 2015); most recently *Bemba et al.*, ICC-01/05-01/13-1252, paras. 26 ff. and the (newly amended) Protocol *Bemba et al.*, ICC-01/05-01/13-1252-Anx, paras. 25 ff. (interestingly, the issue of accommodation is again dealt with slightly differently, providing, as a rule, for joint accommodation reminding the witnesses not to 'discuss their impending evidence with each other' and for separation only 'once a witness commences giving evidence' if 'there is a risk of evidence being tainted by contact', paras. 32–4); ICC, *Prosecutor v. Al Hassan*, TC X, Decision on Witness Preparation and Familarisation, Annex, ICC-01/12-01/18-666-Anx, 17 March 2020. The equivalent at the KSC are the 'WPSO Guidelines on Services to Witnesses Appearing Before the Specialist Chambers', KSC-BD-42/Rev2, Registry Instruction. WPSO Guidelines on Services to Witnesses Appearing Before the Specialist Chambers, 7 October 2022, annexed as Annex 1 to WPSO Submissions, pp. 24–34. See also *Shala*, KSC-BC-2020-04/F00435, paras. 11 ff.

377 Ambos, in Stahn and Sluiter, *ICC* (2009), p. 600 with references in n. 7.

378 ICC, *Practice Manual* (2023), para. 79 ('The Trial Chamber should consider adopting a familarisation protocol governing the period of time shortly before a witness commences his/her testimony').

preparation has become quite early the object of a controversy between OTP and Chambers which has been turned into a judicial controversy by more recent case law. Initially, the *Lubanga* PTC and TC (I) rejected the practice in light of the special role of witnesses—as witnesses of the Court and thus the truth, not of one of the parties[379]—and the spontaneity of the examination situation calling for an untainted, fresh witness.[380] The *Bemba* TC (III) adopted the same view by majority.[381] The *Katanga* TC (II) did not explicitly pronounce on the issue but no witness preparation took place during the proceedings.[382]

However, the *Kenya* TCs (V) have taken a more flexible view permitting the preparation of witnesses[383] as long as this takes place in accordance with the so-called 'Witness Preparation Protocol'.[384] The same view has been adopted by the *Ntaganda* TC (VI)[385] and, more recently, by TC X in *Al Hassan*[386] and TC VI in *Said*.[387] In a nutshell, these Chambers argue that Article 64 ICCS, leaving a broad discretion to the judges to manage the trial in a 'fair and expeditious' manner,[388] provides a sufficient legal basis for witness preparation if a party wants to make use of this practice.[389] The practice 'could, in principle, advance the fairness and expeditiousness of [the] trial and at the same time help protect the well-being of witnesses'.[390] It helps to obtain 'relevant, accurate and complete witness testimony'

[379] Ambos, in Stahn and Sluiter, *ICC* (2009), pp. 602–3.

[380] ICC, *Prosecutor v. Lubanga*, PTC I, Decision on the Practices of Witness Familiarisation and Witness Proofing, ICC-01/04-01/06-679, 8 November 2006, paras. 18 ff., 28 ff. (while it is admissible 'to assist the witness … so as to prevent the witness from finding himself or herself in a disadvantageous position, or from being taken by surprise as a result of his or her ignorance' [para. 20], no general legal principle exists that permits 'witness proofing', rather there is a 'duty of the Prosecution to refrain from undertaking' this practice [para. 42]); conc. ICC, *Prosecutor v. Lubanga*, TC I, Decision Regarding the Practices Used to Prepare and Familiarise Witnesses for Giving Testimony at Trial, ICC-01/04-01/06-1049, 30 November 2007, paras. 28 ff., 45, 53 ff., 57. On the *Lubanga* Chamber, see also Badar and Karsten, *ICLR*, 7 (2007), 183 ff.; Friman, in Schabas and Bernaz, *Handbook ICL* (2011), p. 274; Skilbeck, *JICJ*, 8 (2010), 457 ff.; Jackson and M'Boge, *LJIL*, 26 (2013), 961–2 (with views of court staff, 963–4); Nerlich, *LJIL*, 26 (2013), 778; Bock, 'Commentary (Witnesses)', in Klip and Sluiter, *ALC XXXIII* (2013), pp. 89 ff.; in favour of 'proofing', Karemaker, Taylor, and Pittman, *LJIL*, 21 (2008), 683; for a counter-argument, see Ambos, *LJIL*, 21 (2008), 911; for a rebuttal, Karemaker, Taylor, and Pittman, *LJIL*, 21 (2008), 917 ff.; on this debate Thorne, *Witness* (2023), p. 22; crit. of proofing, see also Jordash, *LJIL*, 22 (2009), 501 ff., Vasiliev, *CLF*, 20 (2009), 193 ff.; Bock, *Opfer* (2010), p. 390 ff.; differentiating, Sluiter, 'Trends in the Development of a Unified Law', in Stahn and van den Herik, *Future Perspectives* (2010), p. 586 ff.; crit. as to the procedural differentiation between the procedural systems of the ad hoc tribunals on the one hand and the ICC on the other, Sluiter, ibid., pp. 590 ff.

[381] ICC, *Prosecutor v. Bemba*, TC III, Decision on the Unified Protocol on the Practices Used to Prepare and Familiarize Witnesses for Giving Testimony at Trial, ICC-01/05-01/08-1016, 18 November 2010; with ICC, *Prosecutor v. Bemba*, TC III, Partly Dissenting Opinion of Judge Kuniko Ozaki on the Decision on the Unified Protocol on the Practices Used to Prepare and Familiarize Witnesses for Giving Testimony at Trial, ICC-01/05-01/08-1039, 24 November 2010.

[382] cf. ICC, *Prosecutor v. Ntaganda*, TC VI, Decision on Witness Preparation, ICC-01/04-02/06-652, 16 June 2015, para. 15 with n. 25.

[383] *Ruto and Sang*, ICC-01/09-01/11-524 and ICC, *Prosecutor v. Muthaura and Kenyatta*, TC V, Decision on Witness Preparation, ICC-01/09-02/11-588, 2 January 2013.

[384] As annexed to the respective decision, cf. e.g. ICC, *Prosecutor v. Ruto and Sang*, TC V, Witness Preparation Protocol, ICC-01/09-01/11-524-Anx, 7 February 2013. Generally Schmitt, *JICJ*, 19 (2021), 485, 504.

[385] *Ntaganda*, ICC-01/04-02/06-652.

[386] *Al Hassan*, ICC-01/12-01/18-666, para. 9 ('In the exercise of its discretion pursuant to Article 64(2) of the Statute, the Chamber finds it appropriate, for the reasons set out below, to adopt a witness preparation protocol for the Al Hassan trial proceedings').

[387] *Prosecutor v. Said*, TC VI, Directions on the Conduct of Proceedings, Annex: Witness preparation protocol, ICC-01/14-01/21-251-AnxA, 9 March 2022.

[388] Art. 64 (2) ICCS.

[389] *Ruto and Sang*, ICC-01/09-01/11-524, para. 27; *Muthaura and Kenyatta*, ICC-01/09-02/11-588, para. 31; *Ntaganda*, ICC-01/04-02/06-652, paras. 13–16. For the same result, see Jackson and Brunger, *JICJ*, 13 (2015), 606–8, arguing that it is not structurally incompatible with the ICC procedure and that the alleged underlying 'systemic divide' is 'overdrawn'.

[390] *Ruto and Sang*, ICC-01/09-01/11-524, para. 31; *Ntaganda*, ICC-01/04-02/06-652, para. 17; in a similar vein, ICC, *Prosecutor v. Al Hassan*, TC X, Decision on Witness Preparation and Familarisation, ICC-01/12-01/18-666, 17 March 2020, para. 18.

which in turn contributes to 'a fair, effective and expeditious trial'.[391] It further facilitates the introduction of prior recorded testimony[392] 'insofar as the witnesses have a further opportunity to confirm the truth of their written statement for the purposes of its admission into evidence'.[393] Against this background 'it is neither practical nor reasonable to prohibit pre-testimony meetings between parties and the witnesses they will call to testify at trial'.[394]

However, in yet another move, the *Bemba et al.*, TC (VII) and the majority of the *Gbagbo and Blé Goudé* TC (I), while accepting the 'broad discretion' of trial Chambers in that matter,[395] returned to the original position of the *Lubanga* Chambers: they reaffirmed that witness preparation cannot be considered a general principle of law;[396] in addition, it affects the 'spontaneity and reliability' of witness testimonies, risks which *in casu* 'are not outweighed by the benefits' of the practice.[397] Instead, the Chambers stress the 'particular importance' of the 'spontaneity' of witness testimony[398] and of the principles of orality and immediacy with regard to the testing of any eventual inconsistent or additional evidence to be tested in the courtroom.[399]

It remains to be seen how the case law further develops but, in any case, decisions are always case-specific[400] and, clearly, the more permissive position of TCs V and VI must be interpreted in light of the increasing formalization of witness preparation by way of the already mentioned '*Witness preparation protocol*'. The last version, as adopted by the *Said* TC V,[401] consists of eight sections[402] with thirty-two Rules, two of which had been previously added by the *Ntaganda* Chamber.[403] In essence, the Protocol opts for a reasonable

[391] *Ntaganda*, ICC-01/04-02/06-652, para. 18; in a similar vein, *Al Hassan*, ICC-01/12-01/18-666, para. 16.

[392] Thereon, in more detail, in the next section.

[393] *Ntaganda*, ICC-01/04-02/06-652, para. 18; in a similar vein, *Al Hassan*, ICC-01/12-01/18-666, para. 16.

[394] *Ruto and Sang*, ICC-01/09-01/11-524, para. 50 and *Muthaura and Kenyatta*, ICC-01/09-02/11-588, para. 52; also approvingly referred to by *Ntaganda*, ICC-01/04-02/06-652, para. 15.

[395] *Bemba et al.*, ICC-01/05-01/13-1252, para. 20; ICC, *Prosecutor v. Gbagbo and Blé Goudé*, TC I, Decision on Witness Preparation and Familiarization, ICC-02/11-01/15-355, 2 December 2015, para. 15 (referring to Art. 64 (2) ICCS); leave to appeal rejected by ICC, *Prosecutor v. Gbagbo and Blé Goudé*, TC I, Decision on the Request for Leave to Appeal the 'Decision on witness preparation and familiarization', ICC-02/11-01/15-388, 13 January 2016, Judge Henderson dissenting.

[396] *Bemba et al.*, ICC-01/05-01/13-1252, para. 20; *Gbagbo and Blé Goudé*, ICC-02/11-01/15-355, para. 15.

[397] *Bemba et al.*, ICC-01/05-01/13-1252, para. 22, therefore considering it, at para. 21, 'unnecessary and inappropriate' in the case at hand which concerns alleged offences of Art. 70 ICCS of Bemba and his defence team. In the same vein, the majority in *Gbagbo and Blé Goudé*, ICC-02/11-01/15-355, para. 17, Judge Henderson dissenting (Partially Dissenting Opinion of Judge Henderson, ICC-02/11-01/15-355-Anx1, paras. 7 ff.).

[398] *Bemba et al.*, ICC-01/05-01/13-1252, para. 23; *Gbagbo and Blé Goudé*, ICC-02/11-01/15-355, para. 17.

[399] *Bemba et al.*, ICC-01/05-01/13-1252, para. 25. OTP leave to appeal requests have been rejected by way of an oral decision; cf. ICC, *Prosecutor v. Bemba et al.*, PTC, Transcript of Hearing, ICC-01/05-01/13-T-10-Red-FRA, 29 September 2015, p. 10 (lines 6–22). Previously in favour of more oral (instead of written) decisions, Klamberg, *Evidence* (2013), p. 514.

[400] This is a consequence of the TCs' discretion and is stressed in *Bemba et al.*, ICC-01/05-01/13-1252, paras. 21–4 ('in this case', 'in the particular circumstances of this case', 'in these circumstances', 'in the present case').

[401] *Said*, ICC-01/14-01/21-251-AnxA. Previously, inter alia, ICC, *Prosecutor v. Ntaganda*, TC VI, Witness Preparation Protocol, ICC-01/04-02/06-652-Anx, 16 June 2015, annexed to *Ntaganda*, ICC-01/04-02/06-652. As a matter of fact, in the most recent approach to witness preparation, TC I annexed its decision a 'Unified Protocol on the Practices Used to Prepare and Familiarize Witnesses for Giving Testimony at Trial' (ICC, *Prosecutor v. Gbagbo and Blé Goudé*, TC I, Unified Protocol on the Practices Used to Prepare and Familiarize Witnesses for Giving Testimony at Trial, ICC-02/11-01/15-355-Anx, 2 December 2015). However, due to its rejection of witness preparation per se (see above notes 396 and 397 with main text), the Chamber, by majority, 'reject[ed] the request by the parties and the LRV to adopt a Witness Preparation Protocol' (*Gbagbo and Blé Goudé*, ICC-02/11-01/15-355, p. 12). Thus, despite the (misleading) title of the protocol ('practices used to *prepare* and familiarize witnesses', emphasis added), it cannot be qualified at a witness preparation protocol.

[402] General principles (I), responsibility for conducting witness preparation (II), location (III), timing (IV), record keeping (V), required and permissible conduct (VI), prohibited conduct (VII), disclosure (VIII).

[403] Rules 13 (requirements for access to video recording by non-calling party) and 32 (provision of materials shown to witness by calling to non-calling party) have been added to the version as adopted by the TC V; see

compromise between witness familiarization as a mere general preparatory measure and full-fledged witness proofing as known from US practice amounting to coaching, training, or rehearsing.[404] The former is too little since it does not prepare the witness with a view to her concrete testimony,[405] the latter too much since it entails the risk of a manipulation of the witness.[406] As a consequence, the Protocol determines two main 'purposes' of witness preparation, namely, with regard to the witness, 'to help ensure' that she 'gives relevant, accurate and structured testimony' and her 'well-being' and, with regard to the calling party, 'to assess and clarify the witness' evidence in order to facilitate the focused, efficient and effective questioning of the witness during the proceedings'.[407] To guarantee a good faith and ethically sound preparation the Protocol contains, on the one hand, several information and instruction duties of the calling party's lawyer[408] with regard to the witness;[409] on the other hand, it explicitly prohibits 'seeking new evidence or continuing the calling party's investigations',[410] influencing 'a witness to testify to factual events' she 'did not observe or perceive', including '[C]oaching, training or practising',[411] seeking 'to influence the substance of the witness' answers'[412] and 'inform the witness of the evidence of other witnesses'.[413] Further, the duty to video record the preparation session[414] is a further guarantee that the calling party does not manipulate or otherwise illicitly influence the witness.[415] Last but not least, the explicit reference to disclosure obligations of the calling party confirms that the general disclosure regime applies.[416]

The Protocol is a first step to formalize witness preparation in line with a 'principled pragmatism'[417] but will, probably, have to be further refined by future practice. Its perhaps most

*Ruto and Sang*, ICC-01/09-01/11-524 Anx; for a discussion, see *Ntaganda*, ICC-01/04-02/06-652, paras. 28–32 and 33–8.

[404] cf. Ambos, in Stahn and Sluiter, *ICC* (2009), pp. 609–11.

[405] See also Jackson and Brunger, *JICJ*, *13* (2015), 614, arguing that familiarization may not even guarantee a sufficient general preparation of the witnesses.

[406] *Contra* also Safferling, *International Criminal Procedure* (2012), pp. 458–60.

[407] *Said*, ICC-01/14-01/21-251-AnxA, Rule 1; *Ntaganda*, ICC-01/04-02/06-652-Anx, Rule 1; *Al Hassan*, ICC-01/12-01/18-666-Anx, para. 1.

[408] The calling party, i.e. her lawyer, is responsible for conducting the witness preparation (*Said*, ICC-01/14-01/21-251-AnxA, Rules 5, 6; *Ntaganda*, ICC-01/04-02/06-652-Anx, Rules 5, 6) but shall coordinate with the VWU (Rule 5). Crit. on the unclear delimitation of the functions of VWU and calling party in this regard, Jackson and Brunger, *JICJ*, 13 (2015), 619.

[409] *Said*, ICC-01/14-01/21-251-AnxA, Rules 16–27; *Ntaganda*, ICC-01/04-02/06-652-Anx, Rules 16–27 (reiterate the witness's obligation to tell the truth, explain purpose of session, review and possibly confirm prior statements, explain relevant topics of examination in trial, explain situation in court, role of participants, etc.).

[410] *Ntaganda*, ICC-01/04-02/06-652-Anx, Rule 2.

[411] Ibid., Rule 3; in the same vein, Rule 29 prohibiting 'to train the witness or practice the questions and answers expected during the witness's in-court testimony so that the witness memorises those questions and answers'

[412] Ibid., Rule 28.

[413] Ibid., Rule 30.

[414] Ibid., Rule 12. To get access to the recording the non-calling party must indicate reasons why this is 'necessary' and 'warranted' (Rule 13); in favour of an unrestricted access for the parties, Jackson and Brunger, *JICJ*, 13 (2015), 623.

[415] See also *Ntaganda*, ICC-01/04-02/06-652, para. 24 ('important safeguard to prevent and disclose potential abuse by the calling party ... efficient tool to identify alleged acts of misconduct, as well as to resolve misunderstandings').

[416] *Ntaganda*, ICC-01/04-02/06-652-Anx, Rules 31, 32 (with Rule 31 applying the same terminology ['as soon as practicable'] as Art. 67 (2) ICCS with regard to the general disclosure obligation of the Prosecutor); see also *Ntaganda*, ICC-01/04-02/06-652, paras. 32, 37. Crit. of the lack of a more concrete timetable, esp. with regard to the possibility of a preparation session up to twenty-four hours before the in-court witness testimony (Rule 11), Jackson and Brunger, *JICJ*, 13 (2015), 620–1.

[417] Jackson and Brunger, *JICJ*, 13 (2015), 601, 602, 613 ff., arguing that this 'principled pragmatism' rests on two 'guiding principles', i.e. the well-being of the witnesses and the integrity of the evidence, and stressing the

important gap is the lack of a sanction regime in case of non-compliance[418] which would go beyond the existing Codes of Conduct.[419]

### (e) *Expert witnesses*

In addition to ordinary witnesses, international tribunals may also rely on the oral and written testimony of expert witnesses. In fact, in all completed trials at the ICC so far, parties or Chambers have relied on experts.[420] In evidentiary terms experts are witnesses and thus treated equally in various aspects,[421] especially regarding the possible order of protective measures.[422] Neither the ICCS nor the RPE ICC define 'expert' or 'expert witness' but the ICC's case law, following the ad hoc tribunals,[423] defines them as witnesses with a 'specialized knowledge regarding a technical, scientific, or otherwise discrete set of ideas or concepts that is expected to lie outside the lay person's ken'[424] or, more recently, 'a person who, by virtue of some specialised knowledge, skill or training can assist the Chamber in understanding or determining an issue of a technical nature that is in dispute'.[425] It is for this reason that experts, in contrast to ordinary (lay or 'fact')[426] witnesses, can always be present, including during witness interrogations,[427] and provide assistance to the Chamber and the parties.[428]

connection between the two in that protecting 'witness well-being ... can assist the truth-finding function of the ICC'. This corresponds to Rule 1 (see note 407 in this chapter with main text).

418 See also ibid., 623.

419 These Codes provide (only) for administrative sanctions by the respective court organ; see Chapter II, B.(6) and C.(2)(b) in this volume.

420 Nuzban, *JICJ*, 21 (2023), 931–57.

421 They are therefore treated together with ordinary witnesses in various provisions, e.g. Arts. 48 (4), 93 (2), 100 (1)(a) ICCS. See also *Bemba et al.*, ICC-01/05-01/13-1989-Red, para. 20 ('The term "witness" also extends to an "expert" witness who provides specialised knowledge on a particular question of fact or law and by doing so may give his or her opinion which need not be based on first-hand knowledge or experience'). See generally and from a comparative perspective, Pérez Marín, in Caeiro, Gless, and Mitsilegas, *Elgar Encyclopedia* (2022); also Nuzban, *JICJ*, 21 (2023) 933.

422 ICC, *Prosecutor v. Yekatom and Ngaïssona*, Yekatom Defence, Public Redacted Version of 'Yekatom Defence Response to the Prosecution's Request for in court protective measures, 15 January 2021, ICC-01/14-01/18-828-Conf', ICC-01/14-01/18-828-Red, 25 January 2021, para. 54; *Prosecutor v. Yekatom and Ngaïssona*, Transript, ICC-01/14-01/18-T-031-Red-ENG, 11 May 2021, p. 5. See also Nuzban, *JICJ*, 21 (2023), 954.

423 cf. Nuzban, *JICJ*, 21 (2023), 933 with further references.

424 ICTR, *Prosecutor v. Semanza*, AC, Judgment, ICTR-97-20-A, 20 May 2005, para. 303; also ICTY, *Prosecutor v. Delalić et al.*, TC, Decision on the Motion by the Prosecution to Allow the Investigators to Follow the Trial during Testimonies of the Witnesses, IT-96-21-T, 20 March 1997, para. 10, ('specially skilled in the field of knowledge about which he is required to testify' but 'only necessary and required where the expert can furnish the Trial Chamber with scientific, technical or such information that is ordinarily outside the experience and knowledge of the judges of facts'). On the rather controversial application of the standard at the ICTR, see Linton, in Sluiter et al., *International Criminal Procedure* (2013), p. 893. The areas of expertise recognized by the case law include history, linguistics, forensics, and military analysis; cf. Boas et al., *Procedure* (2011), pp. 357–8 with further references. In favour of an expansion of (psychiatric) expert testimony with regard to substantive defences, e.g. duress or diminished responsibility, Radosavljevic, *ICLR*, 13 (2013), 1019–20 (discussing concrete examples at 1020 ff.).

425 ICC, *Prosecutor v. Abd-Al-Rahman*, TC I, Decision on the Defence Request to Admit Dr Philippe Gout as an Expert Witness, ICC-02/05-01/20-1044, 30 November 2023, para. 9.

426 Lately, the ICC OTP seems to have been using the categories 'expert witness' and 'fact witness', see ICC, *Prosecutor v. Yekatom and Ngaïssona*, OTP, Public Redacted Version of 'Prosecution's Response to the "Request of Mr. Yekatom to exclude the proposed Prosecution background expert P-2926 and his report" (ICC-01/14-01/18-780-Conf), 24 December 220, ICC-01/14-01/18-797-Conf', ICC-01/14-01/18-797-Red, 14 January 2021, para. 24.

427 Rule 90 I RPE ICTY, Rule 106 I RPE MICT, Rule 90 (D) RPE ICTR/SCSL, Rule 140 (3) RPE ICC ('other than an expert'). See also Boas et al., *Procedure* (2011), p. 358; Safferling, *International Criminal Procedure* (2012), p. 475. For this reason, they 'may also be jointly accommodated' (*Bemba et al.*, ICC-01/05-01/13-1252-Anx, para. 35).

428 See e.g. ICTY, *Prosecutor v. Karadžić*, TC, Decision on Accused's Request for Assistance of Defence Experts in the Courtroom During Testimony of Expert Witness Theunens, IT-95-5/18-T, 14 June 2011, para. 4.

This being said, the line between lay and expert testimony is sometimes difficult to draw,[429] especially with regard to digital open-source information.[430] The distinction has no impact on possible criminal responsibility for false testimony in line with Article 70 (1) (a) ICCS.[431] In the more adversarial procedure of the ad hoc tribunals experts are usually called by a party[432]—notwithstanding the general power of Chambers regarding additional evidence[433]—and the ensuing lack of impartiality has led to complex disputes regarding the admission of their evidence,[434] often focusing on the 'ultimate issue rule'.[435]

At the ICC, there is a shift to civil law procedure[436] with a more active (Pre-Trial or Trial) Chamber[437] which may (discretion[438]) designate and instruct its own experts.[439] Thus, even though expert witnesses are still appearing as witnesses of a certain party, their duty is to the Court.[440] Details about the handling of expert witnesses are usually determined by the respective TC in its decision on the conduct of proceedings.[441] The ICC Registry maintains a list of experts[442] but '[t]he Chamber has discretion to allow the introduction of expert evidence from persons who are not on the list of experts'.[443] Regulation 44 (2) gives the Chamber discretion to 'direct the joint instruction of an expert by the participants'; this may be discussed at a status conference (Regulation 54 (m) RegC). The *Lubanga* TC has favoured a joint expert and a joint instruction, since the interest of justice 'would be significantly assisted if a single, impartial and suitably qualified expert is afforded the best possible opportunity to investigate areas of dispute, having been provided with the detail of the rival contentions'.[444] However, the 'Chamber may separately instruct an expert witness

[429] In more detail and from a comparative perspective, Heinze, in Caeiro, Gless, and Mitsilegas, *Elgar Encyclopedia* (2022).

[430] cf. Gillett and Fan, *JICJ*, 21 (2023), 661 ff. (proposing a six-factor test to identify sufficiently qualified experts in this area and to maintain 'rigorous fact-finding standards').

[431] *Bemba et al.*, ICC-01/05-01/13-1989-Red, para. 20 ('does not impact the scope of Article 70(1)(a) of the Statute').

[432] Rules 94*bis* (A) RPE ICTY/ICTR/SCSL and 116 (A) RPE MICT ('called by a party'). On the IMT and IMTFE, SPSC, ECCC, and STL, see Linton, in Sluiter et al., *International Criminal Procedure* (2013), pp. 879–80, 909–15.

[433] Rules 98 RPE ICTY/ICTR and 120 RPE MICT, n. 67.

[434] cf. Bantekas, *ICL* (2010), pp. 514–21.

[435] According to this Rule, the ultimate decision on the guilt of the accused is to be taken by the judge(s), cf. ibid., p. 514.

[436] In the same vein, Linton, in Sluiter et al., *International Criminal Procedure* (2013), p. 924.

[437] cf. Reg. 44 (5) RegC (broad authority of Chamber regarding subject of expert report, number of experts, mode of instruction, manner of presentation, and time limits); see also *Said*, ICC-01/14-01/21-251, para. 43.

[438] ICC, *Prosecutor v. Al Hassan*, TC X, Public Redacted Version of the Decision on Prosecution's Proposed Expert Witnesses, ICC-01/12-01/18-989-Red, 21 October 2020, para. 16.

[439] cf. Art. 56 (2)I ICCS (appointment by PTC) and Reg. 44 RegC, esp. para. 4 (*proprio motu* instruction by Chamber).

[440] Nuzban, *JICJ*, 21 (2023), 955.

[441] See e.g. *Said*, ICC-01/14-01/21-251, paras. 10 ff.

[442] Reg. 44 (1) RegC., Reg. 56 RegR provide further details regarding the application and review process, leaving the ultimate decision to the Presidency; see e.g. ICC, *Presidency*, Decision on the Application to Review the Decision of the Registrar Denying the Admission of X to the List of Experts, ICC-RoR56-02/09-3-Red, 5 November 2009); see also Piragoff and Clarke, 'Article 69', in Ambos, *Commentary* (2022), mn. 58.

[443] The practice of the Court had been translated into Reg. 44 (1) RegC on 9 December 2016, see <https://www.icc-cpi.int/news/icc-judges-amend-regulations-court>. Previous case law: ICC, *Prosecutor v. Lubanga*, TC I, Decision on the Procedures to be Adopted for Instructing Expert Witnesses, ICC-01/04-01/06-1069, 10 December 2007, para. 25 (in para. 24 criticizing the list is too limited and must be expanded). On this decision, as an important forerunner of the elaboration of guidelines for expert witnesses before the ICC, similar to the ones existing in national jurisdictions, see Linton, in Sluiter et al., *International Criminal Procedure* (2013), pp. 926–7, 935 (referring to common law jurisdictions).

[444] *Lubanga*, ICC-01/04-01/06-1069, paras. 14–16; conc. ICC, *Prosecutor v. Bemba*, TC III, Decision on the Procedures to be Adopted for Instructing Expert Witnesses, ICC-01/05-01/08-695, 2 October 2010, paras. 11–12; similarily also *Katanga and Ngudjolo*, ICC-01/04-01/07-1515-Corr, paras. 70–1. Summarizing, Linton, in Sluiter et al., *International Criminal Procedure* (2013), pp. 908–9.

if it believes there are relevant issues that are not under consideration by the parties'.[445] The matter remained theoretical until 2021, when TC I in the *Abd-Al-Rahman* case instructed the parties 'to seek joint agreement on various issues, including the selection of an expert witness' and the parties eventually 'sent a signed letter containing joint instructions'.[446] In any case, the role of an expert is that of 'a neutral and important' source of information for a TC.[447]

It has become regular practice at the ICC to call expert witnesses on contextual issues such as history, anthropology, sociology, and political science. Such experts ('overview experts' or 'background experts') were called in the cases against *Abd-Al-Rahman*, *Al Hassan*, *Lubanga*, *Ntaganda*, *Ongwen*, *Ruto and Sang*, and *Yekatom and Ngaïssona*.[448] The *Al Hassan* TC X has emphasized that 'expert evidence has to be technical in order to qualify as such' and considered that there 'may be areas of expertise that are not technical in nature, particularly as regards social sciences and specific areas such as culture'.[449] It is difficult to distinguish, in substance, between a background expert and an *amicus curiae*, if only for the procedural modality that the latter is to be invited by the TC pursuant to Rule 103 RPE ICC.[450]

If the parties do not agree on a joint expert and therefore want to call separate experts, they have to indicate their reasons.[451] The party calling the expert must, in any case, demonstrate that the expert possesses the necessary knowledge.[452] The other party may challenge the expertise[453] and present her own expert.[454] In any case, an entirely unilateral appointment and use of experts does not sit well with the above-mentioned concept of a neutral and impartial expert to be jointly instructed by the parties and the predominantly adversarial manner of evidence gathering.[455] As a consequence, the other party (defence) should, 'to

[445] *Lubanga*, ICC-01/04-01/06-1069, para. 22 referring to Reg. 44. The *Lubanga* TC has issued several decisions regarding the instructions of Court's experts; see e.g. ICC, *Prosecutor v. Lubanga*, TC I, Instructions to the Court's Expert on Child Soldiers and Trauma, ICC-01/04-01/06-1558, 17 December 2008; ICC, *Prosecutor v. Lubanga*, TC I, Instructions to the Court's Expert on Background and Context, ICC-01/04-01/06-1671, 6 February 2009; ICC, *Prosecutor v. Lubanga*, TC I, Instructions to the Court's Expert on Names and Other Social Conventions in the DRC, ICC-01/04-01/06-1934, 5 June 2009; see also ICC, *Prosecutor v. Katanga and Ngudjolo*, TC II, Order Instructing Experts pursuant to Regulation 44 of the Regulations of the Court, ICC-01/04-01/07-1300, 14 July 2009, para. 3, ordering two experts to ascertain whether Katanga understands French sufficiently so that an interpretation into his native language Lingala is no longer necessary; ICC, *Prosecutor v. Said*, TC VI, Decision Setting the Commencement Date of the Trial and Related Deadlines, ICC-01/14-01/21-243, 21 February 2021, para. 35. Generally Knoops, *CLF*, 30 (2019), 48.

[446] ICC, *Prosecutor v. Abd-Al-Rahman*, TC I, Transcript, ICC-02/05-01/20-T-013-ENG, 8 September 2021, p. 23, ll. 20–5 and p. 24, ll. 1–8; ICC, *Prosecutor v. Abd-Al-Rahman*, TC I, Joint Prosecution and Defence Submission of the Expert Report, ICC-02/05-01/20-582, 5 February 2022, para. 2.

[447] *Katanga and Ngudjolo*, ICC-01/04-01/07-1515-Corr, para. 68; *Ongwen*, ICC-02/04-01/15-1762-Red, 4, para. 2531: 'It is not in the role of a forensic expert to sustain a relationship of trust and confidence with the person to be examined for the court, and the expert must in fact take care to remain as objective and detached as possible'; *Al Hassan*, ICC-01/12-01/18-989-Red, para. 17 ('utmost neutrality and objectivity').

[448] cf. Nuzban, *JICJ*, 21 (2023), 932, 936 with an instructive overview in table 1. See e.g. ICC, *Prosecutor v. Abd-Al-Rahman*, TC I, Transcript, ICC-02/05-01/20-T-020-Red-ENG, 4 June 2022, p. 74.

[449] *Al Hassan*, ICC-01/12-01/18-989-Red, para. 25. See also Nuzban, *JICJ*, 21 (2023), 935.

[450] See also Nuzban, *JICJ*, 21 (2023), 942.

[451] *Lubanga*, ICC-01/04-01/06-1069, para. 17.

[452] ICTY, *Prosecutor v. Galić*, TC, Decision Concerning the Expert Witnesses Ewa Tabeau and Richard Philipps, IT-98-29-T, 3 July 2002, p. 3.

[453] Rule 94*bis* (B)(iii) RPE ICTY/ICTR/SCSL.

[454] ICTY, *Prosecutor v. S. Milošević*, TC, Decision on the Admissibility of Expert Report of Kosta Cavoski, IT-02-54-T, 1 March 2006, p. 2; ICTY, *Prosecutor v. Stanišić and Župljanin*, TC II, Decision pursuant to Rule 94*bis* Accepting Ewan Brown and Affirming Ewa Tabeau as Prosecution Expert Witnesses, and Written Reasons for the Oral Ruling Accepting Andreas Riedlmayer as an Expert Witness, IT-08-91-T, 29 September 2010, paras. 10, 12.

[455] See, in this regard, the criticism of the OTP in *Katanga and Ngudjolo*, ICC-01/04-01/07-1515-Corr, paras. 65 ff. (OTP expert mission to Bogoro, DRC, in March 2009 without having informed TC or defence in advance but only 'a few months before the … hearings on the merits' [para. 68], 'unfortunate situation' [para. 74]).

the extent possible, be invited to participate in the expertise from an early stage onwards', 'to be allowed to comment upon the selection', 'the precise nature and scope of the instructions' and 'the working method ... in particular with regard to the selection of sources, and to make suggestions for additional investigative measures'.[456] Otherwise, in case of an entirely unilateral approach by one party, the other party will not be able to effectively comment on the expert evidence and will have to appoint its own expert if it wants to challenge it; this, in turn, will further prolong the proceedings.[457]

As to the admissibility of the (oral or written) expert report[458] or testimony the same general criteria—relevance and probative value (reliability)—apply,[459] including regarding the preference for the admission or submission approach.[460] In addition, the Chamber has discretion as to the admissibility decision, albeit a more limited one.[461] In general terms, the criteria of expertise, added value, and relevance apply:[462] first of all, the testimony must fall within the expert's area of 'specialised knowledge' in the sense of the above-mentioned definition;[463] secondly, it must 'be of assistance to the Chamber'; and thirdly, 'the content of the report and/or the anticipated testimony does not usurp the functions of the Chamber as the ultimate arbiter of fact and law'.[464] As to the reliability of the expert testimony,[465] the *Katanga* TC considered 'scientific evidence to be objective', even if the expert was called by one party.[466]

[456] *Katanga and Ngudjolo*, ICC-01/04-01/07-1515-Corr, para. 68.

[457] cf. *Katanga and Ngudjolo*, ICC-01/04-01/07-1515-Corr, paras. 68, 72, stressing the time-saving effect of 'the early resolution of any possible disputes surrounding the expertise'.

[458] Experts prepare a report prior to their testimony. The report is submitted into evidence under Rule 68 (3) RPE ICC. See, in more detail, Nuzban, *JICJ*, 21 (2023), 940–1.

[459] cf. *Lubanga*, ICC-01/04-01/06-2842, para. 112 (referring, inter alia, to 'general reliability'); conc. *Ngudjolo*, ICC-01/04-02/12-3-tENG, para. 60; *Katanga*, ICC-01/04-01/07-3436-tENG, para. 94. See also Knoops, *CLF*, 30 (2019), 33, 36.

[460] ICC, *Prosecutor v. Yekatom and Ngaïssona*, TC V, Decision on the Yekatom Defence Request to Exclude Expert Witness P-2926, ICC-01/14-01/18-881, 11 February 2021, para. 8.

[461] cf. ICTY, *Prosecutor v. Stakić*, AC, Judgment, IT-97-24-A, 22 March 2006, paras. 150, 158; ICTR, *Prosecutor v. Bizimungu et al.*, TC II, Decision on Casimir Bizimungu's Urgent Motion for the Exclusion of the Report and Testimony of Déo Sebahire Mbonyinkebe (Rule 89 I), ICTR-99-50-T, 2 September 2005, para. 10. See also Radosavljevic, *ICLR*, 13 (2013), 1016 with further references in note 21.

[462] See also Nuzban, *JICJ*, 21 (2023), 945 ff.

[463] See e.g. *Abd-Al-Rahman*, ICC-02/05-01/20-1044, para. 10; ICC, *Prosecutor v. Al Hassan*, TC X, Decision on Defence's Proposed Expert Witnesses and Related Applications Seeking to Introduce Their Prior Recorded Testimony under Rule 68 (3) of the Rules, ICC-01/12-01/18-2206, 28 April 2022, para. 9; *Al Hassan*, ICC-01/12-01/18-989-Red, paras. 14, 16; ICC, *Prosecutor v. Bemba et al.*, TC VII, Decision on Prosecution Request to Exclude Defence Witness D22-0001, ICC-01/05-01/13-1653, 24 February 2016, para. 11. See also ICTY, *Prosecutor v. D. Milošević*, TC III, Decision on Admission of Expert Report of Robert Donia, IT-98-29/1-T, 15 February 2007, para. 6 (with four requirements in total); ICTY, *Prosecutor v. Tolimir*, TC II, Decision on Admission of Expert Report of Ratko Škrbić with Separate Opinion of Judge Mindua and Dissenting Opinion of Judge Nyambe, IT-05-88/2-T, 22 March 2012, paras. 13, 17; ICTY, *Prosecutor v. Karadžić*, TC, Decision on Prosecution's Motion to Exclude the Expert Report of Kosta Čavoški, IT-95-5/18-T, 5 April 2013, para. 13; ICTR, *Prosecutor v. Karemera et al.*, TC, Decision on Edouard Karemera's Motion for the Admission of an Expert Witness, ICTR-98-44-T, 22 May 2009, paras. 5, 6, (with five requirements in total); ICTR, *Prosecutor v. Renzaho*, AC, Judgment, ICTR-97-31-A, 1 April 2011, para. 287; ICTR, *Prosecutor v. Nyiramasuhuko et al.*, TC II, Judgment and Sentence, ICTR-98-42-T, 24 June 2011, para. 198; SCSL, *Prosecutor v. Brima et al.*, TC II, Decision on Prosecution Requrest for Leave to Call an Additional Witness (Zainab Hawa Bangura) pursuant to Rule 73*bis* I and on Joint Defence Notice to Inform the Trial Chamber of It, SCSL-04-16-T-365, 5 August 2005, para. 31; *Lubanga*, ICC-01/04-01/06-2842, para. 112 ('established competence'); conc. *Katanga*, ICC-01/04-01/07-3436-tENG, para. 94. See also Bantekas, *ICL* (2010), p. 544; for a narrower approach apparently, Mettraux et al., *Effectiveness ICC* (2014), p. 20 (para. 82) ('much narrower view of (i) what may be said to constitute "expertise" for the purpose of the evidential process and (ii) what issues could/should be subject to expert evidence').

[464] *Abd-Al-Rahman*, ICC-02/05-01/20-1044, para. 10; *Al Hassan*, ICC-01/12-01/18-2206, para. 9; *Al Hassan*, ICC-01/12-01/18-989-Red, para. 16; *Bemba et al.*, ICC-01/05-01/13-1653, para. 11.

[465] Thereto also *D. Milošević*, IT-98-29/1-T, Expert Report Decision, para. 6.

[466] *Ngudjolo*, ICC-01/04-02/12-3-tENG, para. 60; *Katanga*, ICC-01/04-01/07-3436-tENG, para. 94 ('considered scientific evidence to be objective').

This is in line with the case law of the ad hoc tribunals.[467] As to the probative value, the ICTY has more specifically required a minimum degree of 'transparency in the sources and methods used'.[468] The *Lubanga* TC also referred to 'the methodologies used' and 'the extent to which the findings made were consistent with other evidence in the case'.[469]

A certain degree of specificity regarding the sources and methods is necessary to allow the opposing counsel to effectively examine the witness.[470] This is, again, a consequence of the fair trial right to confrontation,[471] but the testimony may also be accepted without further ado.[472] Effective (cross-)examination also presupposes the timely disclosure of the (written) testimony[473] pursuant to the disclosure rules analysed in the second section of this chapter. A Chamber is, of course,[474] not bound by an expert opinion;[475] it may only admit parts of it[476] and determine its probative value (weight) at the end of the trial in the context of all available evidence.[477]

## (4) Documentary evidence

### *(a) Concept and forms: Testimonial and other written evidence*

The term 'documentary evidence' is not defined in the written law but it is to be understood broadly, basically encompassing 'anything in which information of any description is recorded', that is, not only written documents but also 'maps, sketches, plans, calendars, graphs, drawings, computerized records, mechanical records, electro-magnetic records, digital records, databases, sound tracks, audio-tapes, video-tapes, photographs, slides and negatives'.[478]

'Digital evidence', already alluded to in the previous quote by 'digital records', has become increasingly relevant more recently. It is documentary evidence produced by electronic devices,[479] often taken from satellite images (via YouTube, Google Earth, and other internet sources).[480] Digital evidence is often combined with testimonial evidence by an expert.[481]

[467] cf. Linton, in Sluiter et al., *International Criminal Procedure* (2013), pp. 883–4, 895, 900. Note that in common law systems too there are strict rules on the quality of expert testimony entailing objectivity, cf. ibid., pp. 926–7.

[468] See e.g. ICTY, *Prosecutor v. Popović et al.*, TC, Decision on Defence Rule 94*bis* Notice Regarding Prosecution Expert Witness Richard Butler, IT-05-88-T, 19 September 2007, para. 30; see generally *Karadžić*, IT-95-5/18-T, Judgment, para. 19. See also Bantekas, *ICL* (2010), p. 544–5.

[469] *Lubanga*, ICC-01/04-01/06-2842, para. 112; conc. *Ngudjolo*, ICC-01/04-02/12-3-tENG, para. 60; *Katanga*, ICC-01/04-01/07-3436-tENG, para. 94.

[470] ICTY, *Prosecutor v. Galić*, TC, Decision on the Expert Witness Statements Submitted by the Defence, IT-98-29-T, 27 January 2003, p. 5; see also Safferling, *International Criminal Procedure* (2012), p. 482 (report must include sources); Piragoff and Clarke, 'Article 69', in Ambos, *Commentary* (2022), mn. 56.

[471] See also Rules 94*bis* (B)(ii) RPE ICTY/ICTR/SCSL and 116 (B)(iii) RPE MICT.

[472] cf. Rules 94*bis* (B)(i) RPE ICTY/ICTR/SCSL and 116 (B)(i) RPE MICT.

[473] See also Rules 94*bis* (A) RPE ICTY/ICTR/SCSL and 116 (A) RPE MICT.

[474] As usually in national procedure, cf. Linton, in Sluiter et al., *International Criminal Procedure* (2013), p. 925.

[475] ICTY, *Prosecutor v. Gotovina et al.*, TC I, Decision on Admission of Expert Report of Geoffrey Corn, IT-06-90-T, 22 September 2009, para. 6; ICTY, *Prosecutor v. Brđanin and Talić*, TC, Decision on Prosecution's Submission of Statement of Expert Witness Ewan Brown, IT-99-36-T, 3 June 2003.

[476] cf. ICTR, *Prosecutor v. Bizimungu et al.*, TC, Decision on the Admissibility of the Expert Testimony of Dr Binaifer Nowrojee, ICTR-99-50-T, 8 July 2005, paras. 10–12.

[477] *Brđanin and Talić*, Statement of Expert Decision.

[478] *Musema*, ICTR-96-13-A, para. 53.

[479] Brandl, *Criminal Investigation* (2021), p. 120; Laux, *AVR*, 56 (2019) 324, 341; Freeman, *FordhamILJ*, 41 (2018), 283 ff.; Piragoff and Clarke, 'Article 69', in Ambos, *Commentary* (2022), mn. 35; Heinze, in Caeiro, Gless, and Mitsilegas, *Elgar Encyclopedia* (2022).

[480] Heinze, in Caeiro, Gless, and Mitsilegas, *Elgar Encyclopedia* (2022).

[481] On expert evidence see Section A.(3)(e).

The reliability of blockchain evidence, for instance, is usually demonstrated by an expert witness.[482] Digital evidence has gained momentum on the international level by becoming not only a relevant source of information[483] but also impacting the type of information.[484] As a result, projects and guidelines have been dedicated to the analysis of and recommendation of how to search, use, and store digital material, such as the Harvard Signal Code Programme,[485] the Berkeley Protocol on Digital Open Source Investigations,[486] or the Leiden Guidelines on Digitally Derived Evidence.[487] However, as will become apparent throughout this chapter, the use of digital evidence creates a plethora of evidentiary and procedural problems. These problems involve, inter alia, its authenticity, its storage, and its use.[488]

Taking a more systematic approach one may distinguish five groups of documentary evidence, the last four of which belong to the other documentary evidence: (i) written statements or transcripts, (ii) impeachment documents, (iii) court documents, (iv) reports, books, and similar documents, and (v) forensic evidence and other expert reports.[489] As to the character and/or source one may distinguish between public, judicial, and private documentary evidence.[490]

Thus, written evidence is everything that is not oral evidence but with the further—for civil lawyers unusual—distinction between written *testimonial* evidence (i.e. witness statements in a written form) and all *other* documentary evidence,[491] which can further be divided into such evidence introduced through a witness or directly as so-called bar table evidence (to be dealt with below). Yet, there is no distinction, as known from some national jurisdictions, between documentary evidence *stricto sensu* and evidence by inspection.[492]

Out-of-court statements, normally taken by a court official, like depositions[493] and affidavits,[494] belong to the first group of testimonial written evidence.[495] Investigators'

482 Polydor, *SJBLP*, 3 (2020), 96, 97.

483 Heinsch, *ZfIStW*, 3 (2024), 1, 2. On information documented through apps, see Aboueldahab and Freixo, *JICJ*, 21 (2021), 505 ff.

484 D'Alessandra, *JICJ*, 21 (2023), 551, 567.

485 Greenwood et al., *Signal Code* (2017).

486 OCHR and Human Rights Center, *Berkeley Protocol on Digital Open Source Investigations* (2022). Thereto Koenig and Freeman, *HastLJ*, 73 (2022), 1233, 1239–40.

487 Leiden Guidelines (2022); thereto in detail, Heinsch, *ZfIStW*, 3 (2024), 1 ff. See also De Arcos Tejerizo, *LJIL*, 36 (2023), 749 ff.; Solomon, *GeorgiaJI&CompL*, 51 (2023), 373, 375; Lahmann, *AJIL*, 116 (2022), 810, 814 ff.

488 Solomon, *GeorgiaJI&CompL*, 51 (2023), 373, 376.

489 Safferling, *International Criminal Procedure* (2012), pp. 477 ff.

490 Pattenden, in Malek, *Phipson on Evidence* (2022), para. 41.51. See also Heinze, in Caeiro, Gless, and Mitsilegas, *Elgar Encyclopedia* (2022).

491 For this distinction, see Klamberg, *Evidence* (2013), pp. 373–4; Gaynor, in Sluiter et al., *International Criminal Procedure* (2013), pp. 1045–6, listing under the first category written witness statements, depositions, and affidavits and under the second category documents, reports, records, intercepts, cellphone date, photographs, and video footage (see also his list at p. 1081).

492 See e.g. the distinction between 'Urkunds- und Augenscheinsbeweis' in Germany; cf. Volk and Engländer, *Grundkurs StPO* (2021), pp. 219–21 and 221–2; for Spain, see Armenta Deu, *Lecciones* (2018), p. 162; for France, see Art. 456 CCP providing for inspection of the site of the crime ('Le tribunal ... peut ordonner tous transports utiles en vue de la manifestation de la verité') but generally a distinction is made between documentary evidence (preuve littérale) and the documents themselves as objects of evidence to be admitted otherwise (either 'constatations directes' or 'indices'), cf. Merle and Vitu, *Traité de droit criminel*, ii (2001), pp. 212–13.

493 cf. Rules 71 (A) RPE ICTY/ICTR/SCSL and 77 (A) RPE MICT (giving of sworn evidence out of court to an official appointed by the Court 'in the interests of justice'). Thereto Bantekas, *ICL* (2010), p. 489; Gaynor, in Sluiter et al., *International Criminal Procedure* (2013), p. 1053; Klamberg, *Evidence* (2013), pp. 380–2.

494 cf. former Rule 94*ter* RPE ICTY; thereto Defrancia, *VirginiaLRev*, 87 (2001), 1496 ff.; on affidavits in the case law since Nuremberg, see Klamberg, *Evidence* (2013), pp. 383 ff.; on affidavits at the IMT, IMTFE, see Chapter I, B.(1)(a) and (b) in this volume.

495 cf. Gaynor, in Sluiter et al., *International Criminal Procedure* (2013), p. 1045.

reports[496] belong to other documentary evidence;[497] if they summarize witness evidence, the rules on hearsay discussed above apply. In temporal terms, a document may have been produced before or at the occurrence of the relevant event (contemporaneous document), for example, a military order, or afterwards (*ex post facto* document), for example, a written report.[498]

Clearly, the importance of (other) documentary evidence in macrocriminality trials cannot be overstated,[499] although most modern criminals do not document their crimes as meticulously as the Nazis and Japanese did.[500]

### (b) *Admissibility: General principles*

As to the admissibility of documentary evidence the same general principles apply, that is, it depends on its relevance and probative value (reliability).[501] Thus, it is within the discretion of the respective TC to make an admissibility decision at the end of the trial.[502] The Chamber has discretion to either:

> (i) recognise the submission of such item of evidence by a party without a prior ruling on its relevance and/or admissibility and consider its relevance and probative value as part of the holistic assessment of all evidence submitted when deciding on the guilt or innocence of the accused; or (ii) rule on the relevance and/or admissibility of such item of evidence as a pre-condition for recognising it as 'submitted' within the meaning of Article 74(2) of the Statute, and assess its weight at the end of the proceedings as part of its holistic assessment of all evidence submitted.[503]

The two paths relate to the assessment of the general relevance and probative value of the respective documentary evidence but not to its possible exclusion or inadmissibility which would require a separate evidentiary decision.[504] As mentioned above, the submission

496 See e.g. Bantekas, *ICL* (2010), pp. 512–14.
497 *Ongwen*, ICC-02/04-01/15-1762-Red, 4, para. 847.
498 Safferling, *International Criminal Procedure* (2012), pp. 476–7.
499 cf. Gaynor, in Sluiter et al., *International Criminal Procedure* (2013), pp. 1045–6. But see also Combs, *Fact-Finding* (2010), pp. 6, 12–14, finding that ICTR, SCSL, and SPSC basically relied on witness testimony with only the latter also receiving significant forensic evidence.
500 See Combs, *Fact-Finding* (2010), p. 11; Gaynor, in Sluiter et al., *International Criminal Procedure* (2013), p. 1048 (referring to the contemporaneous diary of the accused Kido, principal advisor to the Japanese Emperor, which contained almost six thousand entries and has been described as the single most important document admitted at the IMTFE). On how the IMT and IMTFE dealt with the great amount of documents admitted into evidence, see Chapter I, B.(1)(a) and (b) in this volume.
501 See also *Brđanin and Talić*, IT-99-36-T, Standards Order, para. 18; *Musema*, ICTR-96-13-A, para. 56; *Katanga*, ICC-01/04-01/07-2635, paras. 13 ff.; *Ruto and Sang*, ICC-01/09-01/11-1353, paras. 13 ff., 37 (referring to general principles re bar table evidence and applying a case-by-case assessment). See also Bantekas, *ICL* (2010), pp. 503–5 (on ICTY); crit. of a too generous admission, pp. 507–8.
502 See Section A.(1)(a).
503 *Ongwen*, ICC-02/04-01/15-1762-Red, 4, para. 234; *Bemba et al.*, ICC-01/05-01/13-2275-Red, paras. 8, 598.
504 *Ongwen*, ICC-02/04-01/15-1762-Red, 4, para. 238 (refer 'to the relevance and probative value of the items of documentary evidence submitted in the course of the trial, and not issues related to the potential operation of specific exclusionary rules which would render a certain item of evidence inadmissible before the Court and which a trial chamber is mandated to consider separately for the purpose of a distinct evidentiary ruling'). See also *Bemba et al.*, ICC-01/05-01/13-2275-Red, para. 580 ('[i]n the context of the potential operation of any such exclusionary rule, a distinct determination on the admissibility of certain items of evidence must be conducted—whether in the course of the trial or at the end of the proceedings—separately from the assessment of the evidence for the purpose of establishing the guilt or innocence of the accused').

approach for documentary evidence now seems to be preferred by most Chambers.[505] It has also been approved by the AC.[506]

As to *written testimonial evidence*, the case law of the ad hoc tribunals basically took two factors into account with regard to admissibility *stricto sensu*, namely whether the witness was alive and could be cross-examined and whether his evidence concerned the conduct of the accused.[507] In the latter case, the evidence can only be admitted if the witness is actually cross-examined unless she is unable to testify.[508] Thus, the testing of evidence through cross-examination takes on a particular significance here.[509]

As to probative value, much depends of the nature of the prior statement and the conditions under which it was provided.[510] In case of a *deposition*, defined above, the person making the testimony is normally not available to the Court. For this reason depositions subvert the principle of immediacy in regard to the questioning of the direct witnesses[511] unless the other party can (cross-)examine the witness during the deposition;[512] only then may they be admissible under the ICC regime, which contains no explicit provision.[513] In any case, depositions are rarely used and only to corroborate other witnesses' testimony or to prove background issues.[514] At any rate, the ICTY AC held that a conviction cannot be based solely, or in a decisive manner, on the written statement of one single witness which could not be examined.[515] This, in fact, reintroduces the *unus testis, nullus testis* rule, difficult to reconcile with the free assessment principle.[516]

As to the admission of (*other*) *documentary evidence* through a witness this witness must either be the author of the respecive piece of evidence or be able to speak to its origin or contents; there must be a nexus between this witness and the evidence.[517] With respect to the reliability of a document the case law of the ad hoc tribunals has adduced some factors to be taken into account, namely: (i) the place where the document was seized, (ii) the chain of

[505] *Ongwen*, ICC-02/04-01/15-1762-Red, 4, para. 241; See ICC, *Prosecutor v. Bemba et al.*, TC VII, Decision on Prosecution Requests for Admission of Documentary Evidence (ICC-01/05-01/13-1013-Red, ICC-01/0501/13-1113-Red, ICC-01/05-01/13-1170-Conf), ICC-01/05-01/13-1285, 24 September 2015; ICC, *Prosecutor v. Gbagbo and Blé Goudé*, TC I, Decision on the Submission and Admission of Evidence, ICC-02/11-01/15-405, 29 January 2016; *Al Hassan*, ICC-01/12-01/18-789-AnxA, paras. 27–34; *Yekatom and Ngaïssona*, ICC-01/14-01/18-631, paras. 52–65.

[506] *Bemba et al.*, ICC-01/05-01/13-2275-Red, paras. 572–601. See also Expert Group, *IER* (2020), para. 547 ('Which approach to follow in relation to the bulk of documentary productions has been recognised by the Appeals Chamber as a decision that falls within the discretion of the Trial Chamber Judges').

[507] For a detailed analysis, see Gaynor, in Sluiter et al., *International Criminal Procedure* (2013), pp. 1049–53.

[508] Ibid., p. 1052.

[509] cf. *Kordić* and *Čerkez*, IT-95-14/2-T, Tulica Report Decision, para. 23; *Kordić and Čerkez*, IT-95-14/2-T, 'Zagreb Exhibits' Decision, para. 40. From a historical perspective, cf. May and Wierda, *ColJTransnat'lL*, 37 (1999), 749 ff.; see also Ambos, *ICLR*, 3 (2003), 25.

[510] cf. Bantekas, *ICL* (2010), p. 543 with further references.

[511] cf. May and Wierda, *ColJTransnat'lL*, 37 (1999), 759–60; Nemitz, in Kirsch, *Internationale Strafgerichtshöfe* (2005), pp. 67–8; Harmon, *JICJ*, 5 (2007), 382–3.

[512] Rules 71 I RPE ICTY/ICTR/SCSL and 77 I RPE MICT.

[513] Klamberg, *Evidence* (2013), pp. 382, 462 (only Rule 68 RPE ICC).

[514] cf. Schuon, *International Criminal Procedure* (2010), pp. 162–3; see also Bantekas, *ICL* (2010), p. 489 ('last recourse').

[515] ICTY, *Prosecutor v. Haraqija and Morina*, AC, Judgment, IT-04-84-R77.4-A, 23 July 2009, para. 61 ('when a conviction is based solely, or in a decisive manner, on the depositions of a witness whom the accused has had no opportunity to examine or to have examined either during the investigation or at trial ... without sufficient corroboration'); ICTY, *Prosecutor v. Prlić et al.*, AC, Decision on Appeals against Decision Admitting Transcript of Jadranko Prlić's Questioning into Evidence, IT-04-74-AR73.6, 23 November 2007, paras. 53, 59. See also Schuon, *International Criminal Procedure* (2010), p. 148 (written evidence insufficient as sole basis for conviction).

[516] See note 329 in this chapter and main text.

[517] cf. Gaynor, in Sluiter et al., *International Criminal Procedure* (2013), pp. 1054 (with case law references) and 1081 (principle).

custody after seizure of the document, (iii) corroboration of the contents of the document with other evidence, and (iv) the nature of the document itself such as signature, stamps, handwriting.[518] None of these requirements is absolute[519] and they may differ according to the type of document.

Given that, from the five groups of documentary evidence mentioned above, usually only written statements or transcripts speak to the guilt or innocence of the accused while the other documents normally provide mere background information,[520] the admissibility threshold should be higher in the case of the former.[521] Contemporaneous documents carry, as a rule, a higher degree of reliability and probative value than *ex post facto* documents.[522] The authorship of a document is not a question of admissibility but of its weight (probative value).[523] When introducing documentary evidence, the tendering party must explain how the content of the document relates to a material issue.[524]

### (c) *Ad hoc tribunals: The move to written evidence*

In more general terms the perhaps most noteworthy development at the ad hoc tribunals, especially the ICTY, has been the gradual displacement of the principle of live testimony[525] by rules on *written evidence*.[526] Thus, Rule 90 (A) RPE ICTY[527] was deleted[528] and Rule 89 (F) RPE ICTY[529] inserted in December 2000, thereby authorizing the TC to 'receive the evidence of a witness orally or, where the interests of justice allow, in written form'.[530] The determination of the 'interest of justice' must be made on a case-by-case basis, in relation to each individual witness, in light of not only the surrounding circumstances, but also the evidence to be given by the witness.[531]

[518] ICTR, *Prosecutor v. Bagosora et al.*, TC I, Decision on Admission of Tab 19 of Binder Produced in Connection with Appearance of Witness Maxwell Nkole, ICTR-98-41-T, 13 September 2004, para. 8; see also *Delalić et al.*, IT-96-21-A, Leave to Appeal Decision, para. 18 and *Kordić and Čerkez*, IT-95-14/2-T, 'Zagreb Exhibits' Decision, paras. 43–4.

[519] Bantekas, *ICL* (2010), p. 506.

[520] See, in more detail, Safferling, *International Criminal Procedure* (2012), pp. 477 ff.

[521] In detail on the admission of other documentary evidence (media reports, intercepts, forensic evidence, letters, and books), see Gaynor, in Sluiter et al., *International Criminal Procedure* (2013), pp. 1057–60.

[522] In a similar vein, Safferling, *International Criminal Procedure* (2012), pp. 476–7.

[523] *Brđanin and Talić*, IT-99-36-T, Standards Order, paras. 18, 19; ICTY, *Prosecutor v. Martić*, TC, Decision Adopting Guidelines on the Standards Governing the Admission of Evidence, Annex A 5, IT-95-11-T, 19 January 2006.

[524] ICTY, *Prosecutor v. Prlić et al.*, AC, Decision on Jadranko Prlić's Interlocutory Appeal against the Decision on Prlić Defence Motion for Reconsideration of the Decision on Admission of Documentary Evidence, IT-04-74-A, 3 November 2009, para. 13.

[525] Note 265 in this chapter. See also *Shala*, KSC-BC-2020-04/F00461, para. 30.

[526] On this development, see also Boas et al., *Procedure* (2011), pp. 353–5; Gaynor, in Sluiter et al., *International Criminal Procedure* (2013), p. 1049; Khan et al., *International Criminal Courts* (2018), § 9 mn. 58; previously also Ambos, in Bohlander, *International Criminal Justice* (2007), pp. 485–6 (first reform in December 2000); Prosperi and Zammit Borda, in Stahn et al., *Legacies of the ICTY* (2020) pp. 174, 184.

[527] It read: 'Witnesses shall, in principle, be heard directly by the Chambers unless a Chamber has ordered that the witness be heard by means of a deposition as provided for in Rule 71 or where, in exceptional circumstances and in the interests of justice, a Chamber has authorized the receipt of testimony via video-conference link.'

[528] Also Rule 94*ter* RPE ICTY on affidavits has been deleted.

[529] Thereon Langer, in Baigún et al., *Homenaje al Maier* (2005), pp. 694–5; Langer and Doherty, *YaleJIL*, 36 (2011), 249 ff.; Sluiter, *ICLR*, 6 (2006), 614–15; Kwon, *JICJ*, 5 (2007), 363 ff.; Zahar and Sluiter, *ICL* (2008), p. 387; Jackson, *JICJ*, 7 (2009), 19; Sato, *Structures ICL* (2021), p. 109; crit. De Smet, in Stahn and Sluiter, *ICC* (2009), pp. 420 ff.

[530] See also Rule 105 (F) RPE MICT and Rule 141 (1) 2nd sentence RPE KSC (introduction of written witness evidence 'in a way not prejudicial to or inconsistent with the rights of the Accused').

[531] ICTY, *Prosecutor v. S. Milošević*, AC, Decision on Interlocutory Appeal on the Admissibility of Evidence-in-Chief in the Form of Written Statements, IT-02-54-AR73.4, 30 September 2003, para. 21 and disposition (written witness statement admissible under Rule 89 (F) when the witness: (i) is present in court; (ii) is available for cross-examination and any questioning by the judges; and (iii) attests that the statement accurately reflects his or her declaration and what he or she would say if examined).

Rule 89 (F) is supplemented by Rule 92*bis* (A) RPE ICTY/ICTR,[532] according to which 'a written statement' or 'transcript of evidence'[533] may be admitted 'in lieu of oral testimony' if it 'goes to proof of a matter other than the acts and conduct of the accused as charged in the indictment'.[534] The Rule contains a non-exhaustive list of 'factors' that aims to regulate the admissibility of written evidence and is based largely on the ICTY case law.[535] The Rule leaves broad discretion to the Chamber ('may dispense');[536] it may even call the witness for cross-examination.[537] This is surprising given that evidence submitted under this Rule must not go to proof of acts or conduct of the accused relevant for his guilt or innocence. In fact, this limitation arises out of concerns regarding the right of confrontation and the ensuing impossibility to assess the credibility of a witness who is not available.[538]

Rule 92*ter* RPE ICTY, introduced in the second reform move in September 2006, goes still further permitting 'other admission of written statements and transcripts' even if it goes to proof of conduct of the accused;[539] yet the witness must be present in court, available for cross-examination, and attest the accuracy of the transcript.[540] Rule 92*quater* RPE ICTY,[541] in turn, allows for the admission of statements or transcripts of witnesses who are no longer available for personal testimony if the Chamber is satisfied of the unavailability and the reliability of the statement.[542] The evidence so given may also go to proof of conduct of the accused but 'this may be a factor against' its admission.[543] Last

[532] According to the TC in *Karadžić*, IT-95-5/18-T, Judgment, para. 21, Rules 92*bis*, *ter*, *quater*, and *quinquies* constitute *leges speciales* to Rule 89. Rule 105 (F) RPE MICT is accordingly supplemented by Rule 110 (A) RPE MICT. Similar but much shorter, Rule 92*bis* RPE SCSL.

[533] The latter change regarding transcripts was made in September 2006. On transcripts from related trials, see Klamberg, *Evidence* (2013), pp. 387–9.

[534] cf. Kwon, *JICJ*, 5 (2007), 363 ff.; Harmon, *JICJ*, 5 (2007), 379–81; Bantekas, *ICL* (2010), pp. 491–4; Schuon, *International Criminal Procedure* (2010), pp. 151–5, 164–5; McDermott, *CLF*, 26 (2015), 360; differentiating, Zahar and Sluiter, *ICL* (2008), pp. 341 ff., 376, 387 ff.; O'Sullivan and Montgomery, *JICJ*, 8 (2010), 516; Prosperi and Zammit Borda, in Stahn et al., *Legacies of the ICTY* (2020) pp. 184–5; Sato, *Structures ICL* (2021), p. 110; on ICTY, *Prosecutor v. Gotovina et al.*, TC I, Decision Guidance on the Admissibility into Evidence of Unattested Parts of Rule 92*ter* Statements as Previous Inconsistent Statements, IT-06-90-T, 30 March 2010, paras. 7 ff. For the KSC see Rule 153 RPE KSC and *Shala*, KSC-BC-2020-04/F00461, para. 32.

[535] cf. e.g. Rule 92*bis* (A) RPE ICTY/ICTR and Rule 110 (A) RPE MICT, distinguishing between factors in favour of and against admission.

[536] In performing this discretion, the Chambers have to consider the following factors: (i) whether the statement or transcript sought to be admitted satisfies Rule 89 I, in that it is relevant and has probative value; (ii) whether it goes to proof of a matter other than the acts and conduct of the accused as charged in the indictment; (iii) whether the formal requirements of Rule 92*bis* (B) have been met; (iv) whether to admit the statement in the exercise of the Trial Chamber's discretion; see ICTR, *Prosecutor v. Bagosora et al.*, TC, Decision on Prosecutor's Motion for the Admission of Written Witness Statements under Rule 92*bis*, ICTR-98-41-T, 9 March 2004, para. 16; see also ICTY, *Prosecutor v. S. Milošević*, AC, Decision on Admissibility of Prosecution Investigator's Evidence, IT-02-54-AR73.2, 30 September 2002, para. 18.

[537] cf. Rule 92*bis* I RPE ICTY, Rule 92*bis* I RPE ICTR, and Rule 110 I RPE MICT.

[538] cf. Boas et al., *Procedure* (2011), pp. 355–6.

[539] Rule 92*ter* (B) RPE ICTY; thereon Bantekas, *ICL* (2010), p. 495; Schuon, *International Criminal Procedure* (2010), pp. 156, 165; Gaynor, in Sluiter et al., *International Criminal Procedure* (2013), p. 1057; Sato, *Structures ICL* (2021), p. 110. On the equal treatment of *viva voce* and written evidence pursuant to Rule 92*ter* RPE ICTY, see *Karadžić*, IT-95-5/18-T, Judgment, para. 11; however in *Šešelj*, IT-03-67-T, para. 26, it was held that there is a 'préférence généralement donnée à un témoignage *viva voce*' (emphasis in the original), and the judges should always give reasons if they decide to reverse it in favour of a prior recorded testimony. See also Rule 111 (B) RPE MICT.

[540] cf. Rule 92*ter* (A)(i)–(iii) RPE ICTY; also Rule 111 (A)(i)–(iii) RPE MICT.

[541] See also Rule 112 RPE MICT, Rule 92*bis* I RPE ICTR, Rule 92*quater* RPE SCSL, and Rule 155 (1) RPE KSC. Thereon, Bantekas, *ICL* (2010), pp. 495–6; Schuon, *International Criminal Procedure* (2010), pp. 156–9; Gaynor, in Sluiter et al., *International Criminal Procedure* (2013), p. 1051; McDermott, *LJIL*, 26 (2013), 980–1; Sato, *Structures ICL* (2021), p. 110.

[542] Rule 92*quater* (A) RPE ICTY/SCSL, Rule 92*bis* (C) RPE ICTR, and Rule 112 (A) RPE MICT. About the advantages of Rules 92*bis* and *quater* from a Prosecutor's perspective, see Uertz-Retzlaff, *ZIS*, 10 (2015), 534–5.

[543] Rules 92*quater* (B) RPE ICTY/SCSL and 112 (B) RPE MICT; also Rule 92*bis* (D) RPE ICTR (without this limitation).

but not least, Rule 92*quinquies*, introduced in December 2009, permits the admission of statements and transcripts of persons who failed to attend as witnesses or have not given full evidence due to improper interference.[544] This normative change has also been reflected in the case law, which has put the preference for live testimony in more relative terms.[545]

The move to written evidence has received strong criticism, basically out of fairness considerations, in particular with regard to the equality of arms and the accuracy of factual findings.[546] As worthy of consideration as this criticism seems in principle, one must not overlook that already the general Rule 89 (C)[547] has given Chambers a broad enough discretion to admit written evidence[548] and it always remains applicable as a fallback provision to the newly introduced Rules operating as *leges speciales*.[549] More specifically, the central Rule 92*bis* (A)[550] clearly prohibits that written statements may be used as proof of the accused person's individual responsibility for the concrete matter with which she is charged. Accordingly, live testimony remains indispensable for proving the *personal guilt* of the accused.[551] This view was confirmed by the ICTY.[552] Incidentally, live testimony seems to have maintained a more important role at the ICTR,[553] a rule similar to Rule 89 (F) RPE ICTY has not been introduced and attempts to apply the ICTY Rule by analogy have not been successful.[554] Both tribunals have developed strict fair trial standards, especially with regard to

[544] On Rule 92*quinquies*, see Bantekas, *ICL* (2010), p. 496; Gaynor, in Sluiter et al., *International Criminal Procedure* (2013), pp. 1051–2, 1080, 1082 (in favour); McDermott, *LJIL*, 26 (2013), 981 (not used); Cryer, *LJIL*, 27 (2014), 198; Sato, *Structures ICL* (2021), p. 110; on the origins of this rule in recent legislative developments in common law jurisdictions, see Gaynor, op. cit., p. 1073. For the KSC, see Rule 155 (2), (3) RPE KSC and *Shala*, KSC-BC-2020-04/F00461, para. 32. We will return to the problem of witness interference ('tampering') below, note 573 and main text in this chapter.

[545] See e.g. *Nyiramasuhuko et al.*, ICTR-98-42-A15bis, para. 25 ('preference for live testimony ... does not represent an unbending requirement ... exceptions can be made. The exceptions may relate even to evidence involving an assessment of demeanour, various ways being available to assist a new judge to overcome any disadvantages'); ICTR, *Prosecutor v. Karemera et al.*, AC, Decision on Appeals pursuant to Rule 15*bis* (D), ICTR- 98-44-AR15bis.3, 20 April 2007, para. 42; ICTY, *Prosecutor v. Krajišnik*, TC I, Decision pursuant to Rule 15*bis* (D), IT-00-39-T, 16 December 2004, para. 11: ICTY, *Prosecutor v. Šešelj*, AC, Decision on Appeal against Decision on Continuation of Proceedings, IT-03-67-Arl5bis, 6 June 2014, para. 37.

[546] cf. Boas et al., *Procedure* (2011), p. 357 ('[E]xcessive reliance on written evidence ... poses significant concerns for equality of arms ... and accuracy of factual findings, and thus ultimately the overall fairness of the trial'); also Wald, *HarvILJ*, 42 (2001), 548 (also 545: 'emerging dominance of written testimony'); Defrancia, *VirginiaLRev*, 87 (2001), 1424 ff.; Stein, *Foundations* (2005), pp. 190–1; Jackson, *JICJ*, 7 (2009), 17, 31; Bantekas, *ICL* (2010), p. 496 (quoting Judge Hunt). Arguing in favour of written evidence from a prosecutorial perspective, Nice and Vallières-Roland, *JICJ*, 3 (2005), 365 ff.; Nice and Vallières-Roland, in Abtahi and Boas, *Dynamics of ICJ* (2006), pp. 154–5; on the dependence of the admission of written evidence on the composition of the respective chamber, see McDermott, *LJIL*, 26 (2013), 976–81, esp. 977–8 (with an analysis ICTY/ICTR case law from January 2011 to June 2012).

[547] See also subsequently Rule 105 I RPE MICT.

[548] See e.g. on the admission of suspect interviews against a co-accused, Bantekas, *ICL* (2010), pp. 500–3.

[549] cf. Schuon, *International Criminal Procedure* (2010), p. 150. On the broad Rule 89 I, see abovr note 19 and main text.

[550] See also Rule 110 (A) RPE MICT.

[551] cf. Guariglia, in Fischer et al., *Prosecution* (2001), p. 678; Robinson, in Abtahi and Boas, *Dynamics of ICJ* (2006), p. 181; Jackson, *JICJ*, 7 (2009), 29; also Schuon, *International Criminal Procedure* (2010), pp. 141 (still 'general preference for live evidence'), 169.

[552] See ICTY, *Prosecutor v. Naletilić and Martinović*, TC, Decision on the Prosecutor's Request for Public Version of Trial Chamber's 'Decision on the Motion to Admit Statement of Deceased Witnesses' of 22 January 2002, IT-98-34-T, 27. February 2002; concurring with this narrow interpretation, Safferling, *YbIHL*, 5 (2002), 237–8.

[553] See *Simba*, ICTR-01-76-A, para. 132 ('AC recalls that it has already dismissed the argument that as a matter of law documentary evidence should be preferred to oral testimony'); *Nyiramasuhuko et al.*, ICTR-98-42-T, paras. 177 ff.; ICTR, *Prosecutor v. Ndahimana*, TC, Judgment and Sentence, ICTR-01-68-T, 30 December 2011, paras. 45 ff.; on the 'continued value of oral testimony' in the ICTY/ICTR case law, see McDermott, *LJIL*, 26 (2013), 982–5; McDermott, *CLF*, 26 (2015), 357.

[554] See ICTR, *Prosecutor v. Bagosora et al.*, TC, Case Minute, 2.a., ICTR-98-41-T, 20 November 2003.

the reliability of evidence.[555] The admission of written testimony is, apart from the general conditions mentioned above (relevance and probative value), subject to strict conditions: (i) the testimony must be sufficiently important, (ii) the witness must be unwilling or unable to participate in the trial, and (iii) the defendant's right to confrontation must be observed.[556] Of course, the right to confrontation can only be observed if the witness is available and in court.

On a more general level, it is important to recall that the move to written evidence at the ad hoc tribunals was a reaction to the general criticism with regard to the excessive length of proceedings,[557] mainly caused by the extensive taking of oral witness evidence,[558] with the questioning of a witness lasting one day on average. Also, the completion strategies exerted pressure on the ad hoc tribunals to bring their trials (more quickly) to a close.[559] Against this background, it is unsurprising that the UN expert group recommended using other forms of evidence, in particular written 'prepared statements'.[560] Furthermore, the report cited the views of judges according to whom the excessively long trials were due to the lack of judicial

[555] cf. ICTY, *Naletilić and Martinović*, TC, Prosecutor's Request for Public Version Decision, IT-98-34-T, Considerations 11 and 14; see also, on the inadmissibility of a record of interrogation of a witness later turned into an accused for reasons of fair trial and the right to remain silent, cf. ICTY, *Prosecutor v. Halilović*, AC, Judgment, IT-01-48-A, 16 October 2007, paras. 28–41. On the Chamber's discretion when applying Rule 92*bis*, see *Ndidabahizi*, ICTR-01-71-A, para. 94; Schuon, *International Criminal Procedure* (2010), pp. 151 ff.

[556] See *Tadić*, IT-94-1-T, Video-Link Decision, para. 19; on the third condition, see ICTY, *Prosecutor v. Delalić et al.*, TC, Decision on the Motion to Allow K, L, and M to Give Their Testimony by Means of Video-Link Conference, IT-96-21-T, 28 May 1997, para. 15, and Rules 92*ter* (A)(ii) RPE ICTY and 111 (A)(ii). RPE MICt. cf. also Vohrah, in McDonald and Swaak-Goldman, *ICL I* (2000), pp. 534–5; Nice and Vallières-Roland, in Abtahi and Boas, *Dynamics of ICJ* (2006), pp. 161–2.

[557] See Tochilovsky, in Fischer et al., *Prosecution* (2001), p. 632; Guariglia, in Fischer et al., *Prosecution* (2001), p. 677; May and Wierda, in May et al., *Essays on ICTY* (2001), pp. 259, 261 (defending written witness evidence for the sake of expediency); also Rodrigues and Tournaye, in May et al., *Essays on ICTY* (2001), p. 302; Nemitz, in Kirsch, *Internationale Strafgerichtshöfe* (2005), p. 66; Gaynor, in Sluiter et al., *International Criminal Procedure* (2013), pp. 1075–6; Kuczyńska, *Accusation Model ICC* (2015), p. 329; on the reasons for this excessive length, see Eser, in Müller-Dietz et al., *FS Jung* (2007), pp. 172 ff.; Fernández and Friman, in Doria, Gasser, and Bassiouni, *Legal Regime* (2009), pp. 809 ff.; differentiating, Whiting, *HarvILJ*, 50 (2009), 323 ff.; Heinsch, in Stahn and Sluiter, *ICC* (2009), pp. 479 ff.; on the problems of 'judicial evaluation of evidence' caused by excessively long proceedings, see Öberg, *CLF*, 24 (2013), 118 ff. On further ways of speeding up proceedings, Robinson, in Abtahi and Boas, *Dynamics of ICJ* (2006), pp. 175 ff.; crit. Fairlie, *ICLR*, 4 (2004), 295 ff., 317 ff.

[558] Usually between 100 and 200 witnesses. In the *Milošević* Trial, it was reckoned there would be between 380 and 600 witnesses; cf. ICTY, *Prosecutor v. S. Milošević*, TC, Decision on Prosecution's Motion for Joinder, IT-99-37-PT, IT-01-50-PT & IT-01-51-PT, 13 December 2001, para. 47. In this respect, see also the so-called 'Witness List for the Prosecution Case—Kosovo Phase' (12 February 2002) and the 'Witness List for the Prosecution Case—Croatia and Bosnia Phase' (26 September 2002), which included 298 witnesses in total, <http://www.icty.org/x/cases/slobodan_milosevic/pros/en/Kosovophase020212.htm> and <http://www.icty.org/x/cases/slobodan_milosevic/pros/en/CroatiaBosniaphase020926.htm>. On the significance of witness evidence (and intelligence) in international criminal law trials in general, see Moranchek, *YaleJIL*, 31 (2006), 478–9; specifically on the context of the *Eichmann* Trial, see Bilsky, *JICJ*, 12 (2014), 39 ff.; arguing against this with an emphasis on documentary evidence, ICC, *Prosecutor v. Katanga and Ngudjolo*, PTC I, Corrigendum to the Decision on Evidentiary Scope of the Confirmation Hearing, Preventive Relocation and Disclosure under Article 67 (2) of the Statute and Rule 77 of the Rules, ICC-01/04-01/07-428-Corr, 25 April 2008, paras. 75–6; similarly Gaynor, in Sluiter et al., *International Criminal Procedure* (2013), pp. 1076–7 (oral method 'not necessarily appropriate for a modern war crimes trial'); for 'alternative forms of evidence' given the increased lapses in witnesses' memory, also ICC-OTP, 'Strategic Plan' (2013), para. 44.

[559] cf. Boas et al., *Procedure* (2011), p. 353; Levi, Hagan, and Dezalay, *LCP*, 79 (2016), 306.

[560] UN GA, 'Report of the Expert Group to Conduct a Review of the Effective Operation and Functioning of the International Tribunal for the Former Yugoslavia and the International Criminal Tribunal for Rwanda', A/54/634, 22 November 2009, paras. 85 ff., 88 incl. Recommendation 12; in a similar vein, Gaynor, in Sluiter et al., *International Criminal Procedure* (2013), pp. 1077–9, 1082 (proposing to 'generally dispense with oral direct examination' with three caveats and rather rely on 'well-organized, comprehensive written witness statements' which would form the basis of a 'tightly controlled' cross-examination), 1082–3 (recommending the combination of statements and 'rigorous training' to ensure quality of statements).

direction and organization in the (main) trial.[561] Thus, the length of proceedings was cited as a reason in favour of a greater judicial direction of the trial displacing the completely free interaction between parties. Incidentally, other innovations, especially the introduction of the Electronic Document Management System ('E-Court'),[562] also aim to reduce the length of proceedings. Of course, as we have already seen in the previous chapter,[563] such managerial tendencies in international criminal procedure do not guarantee more efficient and expeditious proceedings.[564]

### *(d) ICC: Admission of written evidence, especially Rule 68 RPE ICC*

At the ICC, documentary evidence is not only permitted—in a more generous way—at the pre-trial stage,[565] but also at the trial stage.[566] While the first sentence of Article 69 (2) ICCS provides for the principle of oral testimony,[567] this same sentence contains exceptions for reasons of witness protection under Article 68 and in accordance with the RPE.[568] The protection clause and thus the exception from oral and immediate testimony applies to all persons who are 'at risk on account of the activities of the Court', including the above mentioned intermediaries.[569] Accordingly, Article 68 (2) allows the Court to 'conduct any part of the proceedings in camera or allow the presentation of evidence by electronic or other special means', especially in cases of sexual violence.[570] Rule 87 RPE ICC, implementing the protective regime of Article 68, provides for 'protective measures', for example, non-identification of the witness and *in camera* hearing;[571] Rule 88 RPE ICC goes further and

[561] UN GA, 'Expert Group ICTY/ICTR Report' (2002), para. 77. Thereto, see also Hofstetter, *Verfahrensrecht* (2005), pp. 108–9; Öberg, *CLF*, 24 (2013), 118 ff.; in favour of stronger judicial direction, Bonomy, *JICJ*, 5 (2007), 349 ff.; in regard to the educational impact (through general deterrence) of international criminal trials, see Damaška, *ChicKentLR*, 83 (2008), 357 ff.

[562] This is to give trial participants electronic access to all documents, evidence, and information of relevance to the trial, cf. ICTY, *Manual* (2009), pp. 95–6, 117 <http://www.icty.org/x/file/About/Reports%20and%20Publications/manual_developed_practices/icty_manual_on_developed_practices.pdf>. See generally Re, in Agirre et al., *Quality Control* (2020), pp. 772 ff.

[563] See Chapter IV, A.(2)(a)(iv) in this volume.

[564] cf. Langer and Doherty, *YaleJIL*, 36 (2011), 252–89, showing that the ICTY reforms did not produce the desired overall results in terms of pre-trial and trial duration and explaining that by the judges' limited or deficient use of their management powers and the parties' resistance.

[565] Note 69 in this chapter.

[566] In the view of the majority of the *Bemba* TC, the admission of written evidence is in line with the Chamber's role to direct the proceedings (*Bemba*, ICC-01/05-01/08-1022, paras. 11, 12); *Ongwen*, ICC-02/04-01/15-1762-Red, 4, para. 238; *Bemba et al.*, ICC-01/05-01/13-1989-Red, para. 206.

[567] See also *Bemba*, ICC-01/05-01/08-1386, para. 76, as quoted above note 206; Klamberg, 'Article 69–Evidence', in Klamberg et al., *Commentary ICC II* (2023), p. 361; Piragoff and Clarke, 'Article 69', in Ambos, *Commentary* (2022), mn. 25 ff.

[568] See also *Lubanga*, ICC-01/04-01/06-1399, para. 22 ('clear recognition that a variety of other means of introducing evidence may be appropriate'); conc. *Lubanga*, ICC-01/04-01/06-2842, para. 107; also *Bemba*, ICC-01/05-01/08-1386, para. 77; *Bemba*, ICC-01/05-01/08-1022, para. 14; thereto also Piragoff and Clarke, 'Article 69', in Ambos, *Commentary* (2022), mn. 26–9. See also ICC, *Prosecutor v. Yekatom and Ngaïssona*, TC V, Decision Setting the Commencement Date of the Trial, ICC-01/14-01/18-589, 16 July 2020, para. 24, thereto Pérez-León-Acevedo, in Heinze and Dittrich, *ICC* (2021), pp. 487, 492; Marchesi, *ICLR*, 22 (2022), 920, 922. See also Rules 100 (1), 153–5 RPE KSC.

[569] cf. ICC, *Prosecutor v. Katanga*, AC, Judgment on the Appeal of the Prosecutor against the Decision of PTC I entitled 'First Decision on the Prosecution Request for Authorisation to Redact Witness Statements', ICC-01/04-01/07-475, 13 May 2008, paras. 1, 36–54, referring to the relevant provisions of the Statute and the RPE, esp. Rule 81 (4) RPE ICC, and concluding that these indicate that persons 'at risk on account of the activities of the Court' should not be 'unjustifiably exposed to risk through the activities of the Court'; see also ICC, 'Guidelines Intermediaries' (2014), pp. 4, 14–17 (sect. 5 providing security and protection); see also Rule 87 (3) RPE ICC ('at risk on account of testimony'). See also Combs, in Holá, Nyseth Nzitatira, and Weerdesteijn, *OxfHB Atrocity Crimes* (2022), 617, 634.

[570] See Section A.(5)(c) in this chapter.

[571] Rule 87 (3) RPE ICC. See also Pérez-León-Acevedo, in Heinze and Dittrich, *ICC* (2021), pp. 492–3.

allows 'special measures' for vulnerable witnesses entailing a full anonymity[572] of the witness.[573] While these protective measures may often be necessary[574]—although hardly efficient outside the courtroom[575]—they conflict with the rights of the accused, especially his confrontation right,[576] and should therefore be exceptional. We will return to this issue in the context of disclosure.[577]

In addition, the second sentence of Article 69 (2) ICCS permits a Chamber to admit 'viva voce (oral) or recorded testimony of a witness by means of video or audio technology, as well as the introduction of documents or written transcripts'. This authority is different from the one under the first sentence of Article 69 (2), that is, it refers to cases where not protection but the general unavailability of the witness is an issue.[578] This includes especially testimony taken by the PTC under Article 56 (1) ICCS,[579] for example, an audio-video-recorded testimony of a deceased witness.[580]

[572] On the distinction between anonymous victim participants and witnesses, and the possibility of the former to testify, see Chapter II, E.(4)(a) in this volume *in fine*.

[573] For a more detailed treatment of the available protective measures (redactions, pseudonyms, non-disclosure, technical means, and *in camera* hearings), see Acquaviva and Heikkilä, in Sluiter et al., *International Criminal Procedure* (2013), pp. 818 ff. (from IMT to hybrid tribunals); Safferling, *International Criminal Procedure* (2012), pp. 516–21; Klamberg, *Evidence* (2013), pp. 442–51; see also de Brouwer, *ICLR*, 15 (2015), 704–6; Donat-Cattin, 'Article 68', in Ambos, *Commentary* (2022), mn. 19 ff.; Piragoff and Clarke, 'Article 69', in Ambos, *Commentary* (2022), mn. 26, 39 (esp. discussing the controversy around Rule 88 RPE ICC and arguing that the right to know the accusing witness would take precedence pursuant to the case law of the ad hoc tribunals); generally on victims' protection, see Chapter II, E.(5) in this volume. Rules 87, 88 RPE ICC are the equivalent of Rules 75, 79 RPE ICTY, ICTR and SCSL, Rule 133 RPE STL, and Rule 29 Internal Rules ECCC; thereto Pérez-León-Acevedo, in Heinze and Dittrich, *ICC* (2021), p. 492; for the KSC, see Rules 80, 81 (protective measures).

[574] For a discussion of case law regarding witness tampering, i.e. the threatening or otherwise unduly influencing of witnesses, see Cryer, *LJIL*, 27 (2014), 193 ff.; for concrete numbers regarding ICTY, ICTR, and ICC as well as concrete risks, see de Brouwer, *ICLR*, 15 (2015), 703–4 (e.g. protective measures for over 650 witnesses until the beginning of 2015), 708 ff. (risks resulting from disclosure of identities and witness interference); also for 'alternative forms of evidence' with a view to better witness protection, see ICC-OTP, 'Strategic Plan' (2013), para. 44. Such a one-size-fits-all approach fails to recognise, however, that victim witnesses may benefit psychologically from making their own statements.

[575] cf. ICTY, *Prosecutor v. Haradinaj et al.*, TC, Judgment, IT-04-84-T, 3 April 2008, para. 49 (quoting a witness who renounced protective measures since they 'do not exist in reality' but only 'within the boundaries of this courtroom') and the discussion by Cryer, *LJIL*, 27 (2014), 199 ff. (seeing the limited possibilities of protection as a problem of the lacking enforcement apparatus of international criminal tribunals); more detailed on the conditions in the country of origin influencing the willingness to testify, de Brouwer, *ICLR*, 15 (2015), 716 ff.; on breaches of protective measures by the media, see de Brouwer, *ICLR*, 15 (2015), 721 ff.; recommending 'an ICC-wide witness protection scheme' to counter these problems, Mettraux et al., *Effectiveness ICC* (2014), p. 43 (paras. 191–3).

[576] Art. 68 ICCS cautions various times that the measures 'shall not be prejudicial to or inconsistent with the rights of the accused' (para. 1 and others).

[577] Section B.(2)(f) in this chapter.

[578] cf. Piragoff and Clarke, 'Article 69', in Ambos, *Commentary* (2022), mn. 30.

[579] cf. Ibid.; also Guariglia and Hochmayr, 'Article 56', in Ambos, *Commentary* (2022), mn. 30 ('delegations decided not to specify the relative weight to be attached to evidence taken under article 56, but rather to leave the determination of its probative value, as well as its admissibility, to the Trial Chamber under the principles established in article 69 … Accordingly, the Trial Chamber is free to rule on the admissibility and relevance of evidence obtained pursuant to article 56, subject to the criteria set forth in article 69 para 4 and in the Rules of Procedure and Evidence, and even to decide its exclusion in the scenario envisaged by article 69 para 7'). On the procedure, see Rule 114 RPE ICC.

[580] See OTP, in ICC, *Prosecutor v. Katanga and Ngudjolo*, TC II, Prosecution's Consolidated Response to 'Defence Objections to Admissibility in Principal and in Substance' (ICC-01/04-01/07-1558) and 'Requête de la Défense en vue d'obtenir une décision d'irrecevabilité des documents liés aux témoins décédés référencés sous les numéros T-167 et T-258' (ICC-01/04-01/07-1556), ICC-01/04-01/07-1645, 16 November 2009, paras. 19 ff. On written testimony of a deceased witness as a principle, see Gaynor, in Sluiter et al., *International Criminal Procedure* (2013), pp. 1081–2; Klamberg, 'Article 69—Evidence', in Klamberg et al., *Commentary ICC II* (2023), p. 360.

As to the RPE, Rule 68 is of special importance[581] and, indeed, may be considered as *lex specialis* with regard to the admission of prior recorded testimony.[582] Such testimony broadly[583] refers to 'previously recorded audio or video testimony of a witness, or the transcript or other documented evidence of such testimony',[584] including written witness statements taken under Rules 111 and 112.[585] The Chamber has, as always, broad discretion to admit such testimony[586] (upon the request of a party);[587] it must basically be 'satisfied'[588] of its 'sufficient specificity and probative value'[589] and of its sufficient 'indicia of reliability'.[590] The person giving a statement must understand 'that he or she is providing information which may be relied upon in the context of legal proceedings'.[591] Prior testimony may also be used to refresh the memory of the present witness[592] or confront her oral in-court-testimony and clarify possible contradictions.[593] Yet, the (full) prior recorded testimony should not be admitted for the mere corroboration of the oral testimony given by a witness who is present in court.[594] In general, according to TC III, Rule 68 should only be applied 'in cases

[581] See also *Bemba*, ICC-01/05-01/08-1386, para. 77. For *Judge Eboe-Osuji* the purpose of the Rule is to 'make trials simpler and shorter' (*Ruto and Sang*, ICC-01/09-01/11-1938-Anx-Red, para. 18).

[582] In this vein, *Ruto and Sang*, ICC-01/09-01/11-1938-Corr-Red2, para. 149 (rejecting therefore the prosecution's invocation of the general rule of Art. 69 (2) ICCS since its application 'would amount to a circumvention of the applicable law', i.e. Rule 68); in a similar vein, also against a circumvention, Piragoff and Clarke, 'Article 69', in Ambos, *Commentary* (2022), mn. 32.

[583] ICC, *Prosecutor v. Gicheru*, TC III, Decision on the Prosecution's Second Request to Introduce Evidence Other than Through a Witness, ICC-01/09-01/20-299, 15 March 2022, para. 11.

[584] Rule 68 (1) RPE ICC. See also the broad definition of the 'Working Group on Lessons Learnt': 'video or audio recorded records, transcripts and written witness statements' (in ICC-ASP, *Report Study Group on Governance* (2013), p. 22, para. 13).

[585] Rules 111, 112 RPE ICC set out the formalities for the recording of witness statements (normally taken by the prosecution), including suspects for whom special rules under Rule 112 (esp. audio- or video-recording of statements) apply. These Rules also apply to witness testimony under Art. 15 (2) ICCS (cf. Rule 47 (1) RPE ICC). *Ruto and Sang*, ICC-01/09-01/11-1938-Corr-Red2, paras. 32–3 held that Rule 68 applies to Rule 111 or 112 statements, notwithstanding the formal requirements under Rule 68 (2)(b)(ii) and (iii), including '[E]xhibits associated with these recordings ... so long as the witness uses or explains them in the prior recorded testimony, and particularly when these are necessary to read and understand the prior recorded testimony being introduced'. *Contra Judge Eboe-Osuji* in *Ruto and Sang*, ICC-01/09-01/11-1938-Anx-Red, paras. 2, 19–26, arguing that Rule 68, given the ordinary meaning of the term 'testimony' as opposed to 'statement', only applies to the former requiring as 'essential element ... an oath or solemn affirmation', i.e. it is not applicable to the statements *in casu*; Rule 68 (2)(b)(ii) does not contradict this interpretation but only 'highlight confusion or ambiguity in the drafting'.

[586] In *Ongwen*, for instance, the Chamber allowed the introduction, pursuant to Rule 68 (2)(b) or (c) RPE ICC, of the prior recorded testimony of a total of further forty-nine witnesses, see *Ongwen*, ICC-02/04-01/15-1762-Red, 4, para. 254.

[587] ICC, *Prosecutor v. Yekatom and Ngaïssona*, TC V, Decision on the Prosecution Extension Request and Initial Guidance on Rule 68 of the Rules, ICC-01/14-01/18-685, 16 October 2020, para. 23 ('decision whether to use Rule 68 of the Rules is—in principle—up to the calling party'); see also ICC, *Prosecutor v. Ongwen* TC IX, Public Redacted Version of Decision on Prosecution Request to Introduce Evidence of Defence Witnesses via Rule 68 (2)(b), ICC-02/04-01/15-1322-Red, 16 August 2018, para. 12.

[588] cf. Rule 68 (2)I(i) and (d)(i) RPE ICC.

[589] *Ruto and Sang*, ICC-01/09-01/11-1938-Corr-Red2, para. 37 (rejecting, in para. 36, a higher standard, esp 'beyond reasonable doubt').

[590] cf. Rule 68 (2)(b)(i), (c)(i) and (d)(i); also *Ruto and Sang*, ICC-01/09-01/11-1938-Corr-Red2, para. 65, holding that the reliability assessment is 'preliminary' at this stage, taking into account 'the circumstances in which the testimony arose', e.g. if it was given under oath, accompanied by a declaration as to its truthfulness, tested by cross-examination, translated by an interpreter; yet, possible indicia are neither 'exhaustive' nor 'definitive'. In a similar vein, *Judge Eboe-Osuji* in *Ruto and Sang*, ICC-01/09-01/11-1938-Anx-Red, para. 46 lit d. (admission does not entail 'Irrebuttable presumption of credibility', rather it 'will be assessed in the usual manner, taking into account the foregoing and other factors').

[591] *Gicheru*, ICC-01/09-01/20-299, para. 11.

[592] *Ongwen*, ICC-02/04-01/15-1762-Red, 4, para. 256. See also McDermott, in Sluiter et al., *International Criminal Procedure* (2013), p. 861; also Bantekas, *ICL* (2010), pp. 498–500.

[593] *Ongwen*, ICC-02/04-01/15-1762-Red, 4, para. 256. See note 336 in this chapter.

[594] *Katanga and Ngudjolo*, ICC-01/04-01/07-2954, paras. 5–7 (admitting the relevant extracts of the prior testimony into evidence since they have not been read aloud but rejecting the admission of the whole recorded in line with TC II's 'moderated approach').

where the tendering party wishes to adduce the prior recorded testimony for the truth of its contents'.[595]

Of course, it is explicitly stated—again[596]—that all these exceptions to the principle of oral testimony 'shall not be prejudicial to or inconsistent with the rights of the accused'.[597] This calls for a 'cautious assessment' of each piece of written evidence, taking into account, inter alia, '(i) whether the evidence relates to issues that are not materially in dispute; (ii) whether that evidence is not central to core issues in the case, but only provides relevant background information; and (iii) whether the evidence is corroborative of other evidence'.[598] The decision in favour of prior recorded testimony instead of the oral examination of the witness will often—unless the witness is unavailable—entail a balancing exercise taking into account the importance (probative value) of the statement of the respective witness and the consequences for the rights of the accused.[599]

The situation of the *present* witness is, in this regard, less of a problem since his presence makes an examination possible and this possibility accounts for the right to confrontation. His testimony is, strictly speaking, not exclusively 'written', since it does not replace the oral testimony but complements it.[600] Thus, in this situation, pursuant to Rule 68 (3) RPE ICC,[601] the introduction of the prior testimony is possible if the witness does not object and can be examined by Prosecutor, defence, and Chamber.[602] Similarly, the video interrogation of a witness can be reconciled with the right to confrontation since the witness is, in fact, virtually present and can thus be examined.[603]

595 *Gicheru*, ICC-01/09-01/20-299, para. 11 *in fine*.

596 See regarding Art. 68 ICCS, note 576 in this chapter.

597 Art. 69 (2) last sentence ICCS; also Rule 68 (1) RPE ICC *in fine*; exact same wording in Rule 141 (1) 2nd sentence RPE KSC. See also *Ruto and Sang*, ICC-01/09-01/11-1938-Corr-Red2, para. 150, balancing authenticity, relevance, and probative value vis-à-vis the prejudice caused to the accused and concluding, preliminarily, that the 'prima facie probative value [of the prior recorded testimonies] outweighs any prejudicial effect caused to the accused'; similarly, *Yekatom and Ngaïssona*, ICC-01/14-01/18-685, paras. 20, 25 ff.; *Ntaganda*, ICC-01/04-02/06-2666-Red, para. 629.

598 *Bemba*, ICC-01/05-01/08-1386, para. 78; also para. 81 ('cautious item-by-item analysis'); *Ntaganda*, ICC-01/04-02/06-2666-Red, para. 630. In the view of the AC the TC (*Bemba*, ICC-01/05-01/08-1022) has not applied this strict analysis and therefore violated Art. 69 (2) ICCS (ICC-01/05-01/08-1386, paras. 79–81). Explicitly following the AC's instruction regarding an 'item-by-item analysis', see e.g. *Ruto and Sang*, ICC-01/09-01/11-1353, para. 37; previously ICC, *Prosecutor v. Lubanga*, TC I, Decision on the Admission of Material from the 'Bar Table', ICC-01/04-01/06-1981, 24 June 2009, para. 49 ('document-by-document approach'). Consequently, cautioning against an extensive use of 'written proceedings', Mettraux et al., *Effectiveness ICC* (2014), p. 24 (para. 105).

599 See, in this vein, ICC, *Prosecutor v. Katanga and Ngudjolo*, TC II, Decision on Prosecutor's Request to Allow the Introduction into Evidence of the Prior Recorded Testimony of P-166 and P-219, ICC-01/04-01/07-2362, 3 September 2010, para. 19 ('Chamber will assess the relative importance of the statement and determine whether it is more appropriate to hear the testimony directly from the witness. Factors to be taken into consideration, in this regard, are whether direct oral testimony is likely to provide any additional information and, in particular, whether the Chamber deems it necessary to observe the giving of evidence by the witness in full. In certain cases there may also be prejudice to the Defence if the witness does not make his or her allegations against the accused in open court.') Similarly *Judge Eboe-Osuji*, in *Ruto and Sang*, ICC-01/09-01/11-1938-Anx-Red, para. 45 ('balancing act').

600 *Yekatom and Ngaïssona*, ICC-01/14-01/18-685, para. 30.

601 Note that Rule 68 always provided for the possibility to examine the witness; cf. Piragoff and Clarke, 'Article 69', in Ambos, *Commentary* (2022), mn. 3 *in fine*. See also Rule 154 RPE KSC; thereto *Shala*, KSC-BC-2020-04/F00461, para. 32.

602 Rule 68 (3) RPE ICC is identical with the earlier version of Rule 68 (b); thereto Guariglia, in Fischer et al., *Prosecution* (2001), pp. 673–4; Kreß and Wannek, in Kirsch, *Internationale Strafgerichtshöfe* (2005), p. 253. On the Rule change, see the Report of the ASP Working Group and the ASP President, ASP, Twelfth Session, 20–28 November 2013, Official Records Vol. I, Annex II, p. 71, Annex IX, p. 85. Advocating a principle, Gaynor, in Sluiter et al., *International Criminal Procedure* (2013), p. 1081.

603 In a similar vein, *Delalić et al.*, IT-96-21-T, Video-Link Conference Decision, para. 15, holding that 'video-conferencing is, in actual fact, merely an extension of the Trial Chamber to the location of the witness' and 'the accused is therefore neither denied his right to confront the witness, nor does he lose materially from the fact of the physical absence of the witness' but admitting that it has a lower probative value than the personal witness interrogation; see also *Tadić*, IT-94-1-T, Video-Link Decision, para. 22; *Bemba et al.*, ICC-01/05-01/13-1989-Red, para. 205.

In contrast, in case of a *non-present* witness the ensuing restriction of the right to confrontation entails stricter and more precision conditions to allow for the introduction of the written testimony. As a consequence, Rule 68 (2) RPE ICC, as amended by the ASP on 27 November 2013,[604] allows for the introduction of the prior recorded testimony in four instances which are modelled after Rules 92*bis* to 92*quinquies* RPE ICTY[605] set out above: (i) Prosecutor and defence had the opportunity to examine the witness during the recording, (ii) the prior testimony 'goes to proof of a matter other than the acts and conduct of the accused', (iii) 'comes from a person who has subsequently died, must be presumed dead, or is, due to obstacles that cannot be overcome with reasonable diligence, unavailable to testify orally' or, (iv) 'comes from a person who has been subjected to interference.'[606] The *Ruto and Sang* TC has admitted in total five testimonies into evidence—four pursuant to Rule 68 (2)(d) and one pursuant to Rule 68 (2)(c)—and rejected the admission of one testimony.[607]

Interestingly enough, the argument of a violation of the non-retroactivity principle by Rule 68, already rejected by the Chamber,[608] was revitalized by Kenya and some other African States at the 2015 ASP Meeting: in a request for a supplementary agenda item at the 14th session, Kenya addressed the 'legislative intent' of Rule 68 RPE ICC.[609] In more concrete terms, Kenya asked the ASP, for obvious reasons, to find that the rule cannot be

[604] ICC-ASP/12/Res.7. The amendment, in essence, introduced sub-rules (2)I and (d) of Rule 68 as additional possibilities to introduce prior recorded testimony; cf. *Ruto and Sang*, ICC-01/09-01/11-1938-Corr-Red2, para. 12; *Yekatom and Ngaïssona*, ICC-01/14-01/18-685, para. 29. See also Vasiliev, in Bergsmo et al., *Power* (2020), p. 524.

[605] Contrary to Piragoff and Clarke, 'Article 69', in Ambos, *Commentary* (2022), mn. 30 in this regard, there is no 'clear departure' from the Rules of the ad hoc tribunals.

[606] cf. Rule 68 (2)(a)–(d) RPE ICC setting out more specific sub-requirements as to the above-mentioned options (ii)–(iv) in subparas. (b)–(d) of Rule 68 (2), largely introduced by the amendment mentioned in the previous note.

[607] *Ruto and Sang*, ICC-01/09-01/11-1938-Corr-Red2, pp. 54–5. In the case of the four testimonies *admitted* pursuant to Rule 68 (2)(d) the Chamber applied the second alternative of the provision according to which a witness who attended the hearing 'has failed to give evidence with respect to a material aspect' included in the prior testimony. The gist of the issue was 'whether a witness who appears, but whose testimony deviates from his/her prior recorded testimony, falls within the scope of the rule' (ibid., para. 40). In the Chamber's view, this is the case since the sub-rule applies, in principle, to persons who 'do not testify at all or recant fundamental aspects of their prior recorded testimony' (ibid., paras. 41–2). The Chamber further held that the alleged interference need not be attributable to the accused (ibid., paras. 43–4). Concretely, the Chamber examined, in line with the sub-rule, the nature of the testimony, whether reasonable efforts have been made to secure all material facts known to the witness, whether the failure to give evidence has been materially influenced by improper interference, whether the admission would serve the interests of justice, and whether the prior testimony has sufficient indicia of reliability (ibid., paras. 45 ff.). As to the 'interests of justice' the Chamber basically focuses on the importance of the evidence (in line with Art. 69 (3) ICCS: 'necessary') and the 'systematicity of the interference … which gives rise to the impression of an attempt to methodically target witnesses … in order to hamper the proceedings' (similarly *Judge Eboe-Osuji*, in *Ruto and Sang*, ICC-01/09-01/11-1938-Anx-Red, para. 44: 'interests of justice … perturbed'); an 'unproven link between the improper interference and the accused' is, in line with the above statement, irrelevant in this regard (ibid., para. 60). In the case of the *not admitted* testimony it was not satisfied that a sufficient interference existed (ibid., paras. 96–7). In the case of the testimony admitted pursuant to Rule 68 (2)I (ibid., paras. 134 ff.) the Chamber was satisfied that the witness is 'unavailable' since he could neither be contacted by the prosecution nor appeared for testimony on the scheduled date (para. 138). For essentially the same result, but with a different reasoning in line with its dismissal of Rule 68 (n 474) Judge Eboe-Osuji, in *Ruto and Sang*, ICC-01/09-01/11-1938-Anx-Red, paras. 2, 27–48, admitting all prior witness statements 'due to the 'exceptional circumstances of this case' pursuant to Art. 69 (3) ICCS but those already admitted in the record only partially, namely limited to the questions asked by prosecution and defence and the answers to these questions.

[608] The Chamber did not see a violation of the prohibition of retroactivity within the meaning of Art. 51 (4) ICCS since Rule 68 'is a rule of neutral application', i.e. it 'is not inherently detrimental to the accused'. (*Ruto and Sang*, ICC-01/09-01/11-1938-Corr-Red2, paras. 23–6 [25] with reference to ICTY case law); conc. in this regard, Judge Eboe-Osuji, in *Ruto and Sang*, ICC-01/09-01/11-1938-Anx-Red, para. 18 with n. 2, arguing that the ASP did not provide for the prohibition of retroactivity when amending the Rule.

[609] ASP, Fourteenth session, *List of supplementary items requested for inclusion in the agenda of the fourteenth session of the Assembly*, Addendum, ICC-ASP/14/35/Add.2, 6 November 2015, p. 1: 'Kenya requests that the

applied retroactively to ICC investigations commenced prior before its entry into force (27 November 2013), thereby excluding its application in the ongoing proceedings against members of the Kenyan government. Kenya proposed that an ASP Resolution should contain a text that basically formulated Kenya's view of the 'legislative intent' of Rule 68.[610] The proposal quite frankly constituted a direct attack on the independence of the Court given that the issue is a judicial one which was, at that time, still under review before the Appeals Chamber pursuant to a defence challenge.[611] Notwithstanding, Kenya's proposed text was not rejected outright by the (other) State Parties but only banished into a report—instead of a proper ASP resolution—that addressed the matter in a rather ponderous language by referring to the Statute in general and to the already mentioned Resolution ICC-ASP/12/Res.7.[612] This at least gives some hope that the State Parties did not—again—give in to Kenya's pressure (which feeds on the hostility of some African States towards the ICC) and concede more than has already been conceded by the 2013 amendment with regard to the presence of the accused.[613] In the end, the AC reversed the TC Decision:[614] it invoked Article 51 (4) ICCS according to which any amendment to the RPE ICC 'shall not be applied retroactively to the detriment' of the accused, interpreting 'detriment' as 'disadvantage, loss, damage or harm to the accused including, but not limited to, the rights of that person'.[615] While this is a plausible approach the second argument of the Chamber, namely that the relevant assessment does not only entail 'an analysis of the amended law, but also how that law was applied in a particular case',[616] is less convincing. If this were correct new procedural rules might be applied retroactively or not depending on the circumstances of the concrete case. A better test would be to ask whether the respective rule *generally* operates to the detriment of the accused. This is certainly not the case for Rule 68 since prior recorded evidence may also operate in favour of the accused; think, for example, of a (written) testimony which confirms an alibi.

A side benefit of the admission of written witness testimony is that the risk of intimidating witnesses before trial is reduced, since an interested party would know that the prior

legislative intent of rule 68 be placed before the Assembly for discussion.' See also Vasiliev, in Bergsmo et al., *Power* (2020), pp. 551 ff.

610 ASP, ICC-ASP/14/35/Add.2, 6 November 2015, A. 1.: '*Recalling* further that in amending rule 68, the Assembly of States Parties was mindful of article 51(4) of the Rome Statute according to which amendments to the Rules of Procedure and Evidence shall not be applied retroactively to the detriment of the person who is being investigated or prosecuted, with the understanding that the rule as amended is without prejudice to article 67 of the Rome Statute related to the rights of the accused' (underlining in the original).

611 See ICC, *Prosecutor v. Ruto and Sang*, AC, Public Redacted Version of Sang Defence Appeal against the decision of Trial Chamber V (A) of 19 August 2015 entitled 'Decision on Prosecution Request for Admission of Prior Recorded Testimony', ICC-01/09-01/11-1982-Red, 13 October 2015, para. 13, submitting 'that the Trial Chamber erred in its finding that amended Rule 68 of the Rules can be applied ... without offending Arts. 24(2) and 51(14) of the Statute' and criticizing the 'erroneous finding that the application of the amended Rule 68 ... would not be retroactive in the context of Article 51(4)'. See also Vasiliev, in Bergsmo et al., *Power* (2020), pp. 552–3.

612 This Resolution, while introducing the amendment of Rule 68 RPE ICC, merely emphasized 'article 51, paragraph 4, of the Rome Statute according to which amendments to the Rules of Procedure and Evidence shall not be applied retroactively to the detriment of the person who is being investigated or prosecuted', Res. ICC-ASP/12/Res.7, para. 2.

613 See Chapter IV, A.(3)(b) in this volume.

614 ICC, *Prosecutor v. Ruto and Sang*, AC, Judgment on the Appeals of Mr William Samoei Ruto and Mr Joshua Arap Sang against the Decision of Trial Chamber V(A) of 19 August 2015 Entitled 'Decision on Prosecution Request for Admission of Prior Recorded Testimony', ICC-01/09-01/11-2024, 12 February 2016, paras. 78 ff. Thereto and crit. in detail, Vasiliev, in Bergsmo et al., *Power* (2020), pp. 556–7.

615 *Ruto and Sang*, ICC-01/09-01/11-2024, para. 78.

616 Ibid., para. 88.

testimony may be admitted anyway, and this diminishes the incentive to intimidate the witness.[617] This brings us right back to perhaps the most important justification of the use of written in lieu of oral evidence in international criminal proceedings, already mentioned above: that is, the need to protect certain witnesses.

*(e) Bar table evidence and authenticity of documents*

Documentary evidence may be introduced through a witness,[618] but the already mentioned bar table evidence, that is, the 'submission of documentary evidence other than through a witness' directly from the 'bar table' to the judges,[619] has become increasingly important at the ICC too.[620] At the ad hoc tribunals, the practice has been approved by the *Blaškić* TC,[621] acknowledging that it may be smoother to directly submit documentary evidence to the judges without involving a witness.[622] Yet, it has been limited to certain documents and purposes, for example, it has not been allowed to challenge the credibility of a witness with a bar table motion.[623] Furthermore, when bar table evidence is introduced complementing a witness testimony, the distinction between a bar table motion and the introduction of prior recorded testimony of a present witness (Rule 68 (3) RPE ICC) becomes blurred. Thus, TC X has rejected the use of Rule 68 (3) to circumvent seeking the submission of evidence via the bar table.[624]

The Single Judge in *Katanga/Ngudjolo* listed several factors to consider when deciding on the admission of such documentary evidence, inter alia, the nature and origin of the document, the case-relevance of its contents, and its authenticity.[625] The tendering party shall prepare a table with all documents, explaining their relevance; the opposing party has the right to make observations.[626] The full *Katanga* TC, while taking a liberal approach regarding the admission of documentary exhibits[627] and limiting its exam to the items whose admission was contested between the parties,[628] stressed that the lack of witness authentication in the case of bar table evidence is an important factor in the assessment of its admissibility (probative value).[629]

[617] cf. also Ambos, *ICLR*, 12 (2012), 126; in a similar vein, Bibas and Burke-White, *DukeLJ*, 59 (2010), 697 (pointing to the risk that, in an adversarial system, 'full discovery creates far too much temptation to kill or silence the complaining witnesses').

[618] cf. *Katanga and Ngudjolo*, ICC-01/04-01/07-1665-Corr, para. 97 (tendering party shall introduce document through witness if there is 'inherent correlation' between the two).

[619] *Bemba*, ICC-01/05-01/08-1386, para. 44; previously *Lubanga*, ICC-01/04-01/06-1981, para. 1 (but limiting the submission to 'counsel', instead of 'party'); see also Gaynor, in Sluiter et al., *International Criminal Procedure* (2013), p. 1054; Piragoff and Clarke, 'Article 69', in Ambos, *Commentary* (2022), mn. 41.

[620] See e.g. *Ruto and Sang*, ICC-01/09-01/11-1353, para. 13 ('practice established in the jurisprudence', with further references); *Bemba et al.*, ICC-01/05-01/13-1285, para. 1 (OTP request of admission of 1028 documents!); *Bemba et al.*, ICC-01/05-01/13-1989-Red, para. 190. See also Boas et al., *Procedure* (2011), p. 360 (regarding contemporaneous documents); Gaynor, in Sluiter et al., *International Criminal Procedure* (2013), pp. 1064–7 (crit. of too strict ICC requirements), 1079, 1082 (advocating a rule regulating bar table evidence in order to encourage its use). On the practice before the IMT and IMTFE, see Gaynor, in Sluiter et al., *International Criminal Procedure* (2013), p. 1048.

[621] ICTY, *Prosecutor v. Blaškić*, TC, Judgment, IT-95-14-T, 3 March 2000, para. 35.

[622] cf. Gaynor, in Sluiter et al., *International Criminal Procedure* (2013), pp. 1054–5; also Schuon, *International Criminal Procedure* (2010), pp. 160, 165.

[623] For a detailed analysis, see Gaynor, in Sluiter et al., *International Criminal Procedure* (2013), pp. 1055–7 with case law references; Piragoff and Clarke, 'Article 69', in Ambos, *Commentary* (2022), mn. 41.

[624] *Al Hassan*, ICC-01/12-01/18-989-Red, para. 119: '[T]he Chamber agrees with the Defence that Rule 68 (3) of the Rules is not a substitute or alternative to seeking the submission of evidence via the bar table.'

[625] cf. *Katanga and Ngudjolo*, ICC-01/04-01/07-1665-Corr, para. 100.

[626] Ibid., paras. 101–2.

[627] *Katanga*, ICC-01/04-01/07-2635, para. 8 (only rejecting admission 'if there are compelling reasons').

[628] Ibid., para. 10.

[629] Ibid., para.12. In a similar vein, *Ayyash et al.*, STL-11-01/T/TC/F3839/20200818/R331945-R334626/EN/dm, para. 354 ('The Trial Chamber may give less weight to such evidence, if, for instance, the creator of a

Indeed, the probative value of any particular item of documentary evidence depends on its *reliability* and the *impact* it has on the determination of the issue it refers to.[630] The latter is determined by the significance of the respective evidence with regard to the relevant issues before a Chamber, either significantly helping it to reach a conclusion about the existence or non-existence of a material fact or to assess the reliability of other evidence.[631] In other words, the tendered bar table evidence must fit into the case.[632] Reliability, in turn, depends foremost on the authenticity of the document[633] and some other criteria.

*Authenticity* is 'whether a document is what it professes to be in origin and authorship'[634] and thus a form of reliability in that the latter is predicated on the former.[635] Authenticity is disjunctive and cannot—like reliability—be fulfilled gradually.[636] In other words, a document can only be reliable if it is authentic since 'the fact that the document is what it purports to be enhances the likely truth of the contents thereof'.[637] Thus, authenticity speaks to the probative value of a document, be it in the form of the just mentioned reliability or of its evidentiary weight.[638] Authenticity will be weighed at the end of the proceedings when the Chamber has to decide on the final probative value of each piece of evidence.[639] Whether this precludes the Chamber from making any authenticity remarks in the course of the trial became an issue in the case against *Gbagbo and Blé Goudé*. The AC asked

> whether the Trial Chamber in this instance correctly *balanced its discretion*, when it decided not to rule on the admissibility of the documents in question despite finding potential deficiencies in the authenticity of same with its obligations under article 64 (2) of the Statute.[640]

document could not be cross-examined. However, depending on the circumstances, considerable weight could be given to a document admitted from the bar table.')

[630] *Katanga*, ICC-01/04-01/07-2635, para. 20.

[631] Ibid., para. 34 (distinguishing, at para. 35, between 'degrees of significance', from 'little to none' and 'some to considerable').

[632] Gaynor, in Sluiter et al., *International Criminal Procedure* (2013), p. 1081 (principle).

[633] *Katanga*, ICC-01/04-01/07-2635, para. 22; *Bemba*, ICC-01/05-01/08-3343, para. 237; see also Boas et al., *Procedure* (2011), p. 346.

[634] *Ayyash et al.*, STL-11-01/T/TC/F3839/20200818/R331945-R334626/EN/dm, para. 356. See also Braga da Silva, *ICLR*, 22 (2022), 941, 945.

[635] *Ayyash et al.*, STL-11-01/T/TC/F3839/20200818/R331945-R334626/EN/dm, para. 356 ('may be relevant in assessing whether a document is *prima facie* reliable').

[636] Braga da Silva, *ICLR*, 22 (2022), 941, 946.

[637] *Bagosora et al.*, ICTR-98-41-T, Admission of Tab 19 Decision, para. 8 (considering authenticity and reliability as 'overlapping concepts'). See also the reference to reliability in the context of authenticity in ICC, *Prosecutor v. Bemba*, TC III, Public Redacted Version of Decision on the Prosecution's Application for Admission of Materials into Evidence pursuant to Article 64 (9) of the Rome Statute of 6 September 2012, ICC-01/05-01/08-2299-Red, 8 October 2012, para. 9, (document can 'shown to be *authentic and reliable* by the tendering party through provision of sufficient information to enable the Chamber to verify that the documents are what they purport to be' [emphasis added]).

[638] ICTY, *Prosecutor v. Blaškić*, TC, Decision on the Defence Motion for Reconsideration of the Ruling to Exclude from Evidence Authentic and Exculpatory Documentary Evidence, Disposition, IT-95-14-T, 30 January 1998 ('the weight to be ascribed to it will depend on the additional elements which will have, if necessary, been provided and which permit attesting to its authenticity'). See also Boas et al., *Procedure* (2011), p. 341 (discussing it in relation to reliability).

[639] cf. *Orić*, IT-03-68-T, pp. 5–6; *Brđanin and Talić*, IT-99-36-T, Standards Order, paras. 18–20; *Mustafa*, KSC-CA-2023-02/F00038/RED, para. 99: '[A]bsolute proof of authenticity is not required for admissibility. Rather, it is a consideration in the Trial Panel's determination of the weight to be given to the Evidence.'

[640] *Gbagbo and Blé Goudé*, ICC-02/11-01/15 OA 11 OA 12, 24 July 2017, para. 46.

In the impugned Decision, the TC had admitted that the authenticity of the relevant documents was 'disputed'. It then observed, without further elaboration, 'that further evidence may be necessary to determine the authenticity of some of the documents submitted'.[641] Arguably, the descriptive reference to *documents* and their authenticity is not an analysis of the probative value or relevance of *evidence*. In this vein, the AC then distinguished the authenticity remark from an admissibility ruling and rejected the defence's request to make a a ruling in this regard.[642]

Trial Chambers are afforded discretion to assess a document's authenticity.[643] The case law has developed specific standards, with the ICC (so far) being stricter than the ad hoc tribunals.[644] According to the *Blaškić* TC any document 'produced by a party and identified or recognized by a witness' is to be admitted into evidence; its authenticity is, at best, a question of weight if it is challenged.[645] The *Katanga* PTC, quite generously, observed, in line with previous ICTY case law, 'that the fact that a document is not signed or dated does not automatically make it inauthentic'.[646] Yet, the *Katanga* TC unequivocally held that 'unauthenticated documentary evidence' has 'no probative value' and to admit such evidence 'would unjustifiably burden the record of the trial with non-probative material and serve no purpose in the determination of the truth'.[647] The authenticity must be proven by the party tendering the evidence using the reasonable grounds standard.[648] The Chamber then sets out specific requirements for different kinds of documents that generally call for authentication unless the document concerns open-source information or the authenticity is uncontested.[649] Ultimately, if the tendering party cannot prove authenticity, 'the Chamber may exercise its discretion to allow the unauthenticated document if there are other indicia of reliability'.[650] In a more flexible vein, the *Bemba* TC held that 'there is no strict requirement that every document be authenticated officially or by a witness in court', rather documents can be (i) 'self-authenticating' (being official documents), (ii) 'agreed upon by the parties as authentic', (iii) '*prima facie* reliable',[651] (iv) 'shown to be authentic and reliable by the tendering party through provision of sufficient information'.[652]

[641] *Gbagbo and Blé Goudé*, ICC-02/11-01/15-773, para. 39.

[642] ICC, *Prosecutor v. Gbagbo and Blé Goudé*, AC, Judgment on the appeals of Mr Laurent Gbagbo and Mr Charles Blé Goudé against Trial Chamber I's decision on the submission of documentary evidence, ICC-02/11-01/15-995, 24 July 2017, para. 52 ('To the extent that Mr Gbagbo argues that, as a matter of logic, the authenticity of a document must be determined by reference only to the document concerned and that there is therefore no reason to defer a ruling in this regard, the Appeals Chamber disagrees').

[643] *Mustafa*, KSC-CA-2023-02/F00038/RED, para. 99.

[644] See, in this regard, Rules 89 I RPE ICTY, 105 I RPE MICT and 89 (D) RPE ICTR ('verification of the authenticity of evidence'). On the ad hoc tribunals, see also Bantekas, *ICL* (2010), p. 537; Schuon, *International Criminal Procedure* (2010), pp. 159–60, 168.

[645] *Blaškić*, IT-95-14-T, Documentary Evidence Decision, para. 10 and disposition (stricter only with regard to documents 'forming part of exculpatory evidence' where the Prosecutor must transmit to the defence 'any material relevant to the authenticity'); but see also regarding intercepts, Gaynor, in Sluiter et al., *International Criminal Procedure* (2013), p. 1058–9 (referencing the ad hoc tribunals' case law according to which intercepts 'bear no *prima facie* indicia of authenticity or reliability').

[646] *Katanga*, ICC-01/04-01/07-717, para. 112 (referring to ITCY case law in n. 150).

[647] *Katanga*, ICC-01/04-01/07-2635, para. 22.

[648] Ibid., para. 23.

[649] cf. Ibid., para. 24 (discussing open-source information, official documents, private documents, videos, films, photographs, and audio recordings).

[650] Ibid., para. 25.

[651] *Bemba*, ICC-01/05-01/08-2299-Red, para. 9 (bearing 'sufficient indicia of reliability such as a logo, letter head, signature, date or stamp, and appear to have been produced in the ordinary course of the activities of the persons or organisations who created them'). In a similar vein, *Ayyash et al.*, STL-11-01/T/TC/F3839/20200818/R331945-R334626/EN/dm, para. 356. See also Braga da Silva, *ICLR*, 22 (2022), 941, 947–8.

[652] *Bemba*, ICC-01/05-01/08-2299-Red, para. 9, as quoted in note 637 in this chapter. See also Braga da Silva, *ICLR*, 22 (2022), 941, 947–8.

As to the *other criteria*, apart from authenticity, there is 'no finite list' or an automatic exclusion,[653] but the *Katanga* TC identified five 'key factors' to be taken into account.[654] Further, the 'chain of custody', that is, the document's production process from its creation to the submission to a Chamber, is to be considered.[655] While it is not possible 'to lay down strict criteria', the *Katanga* TC opined 'that by their very nature, certain types of documentary evidence are generally more likely to have sufficient probative value to be admitted, whereas other types of evidence will generally lack such probative value'.[656]

### (5) Special rules due to subject matter or other reasons

As we have seen previously, expediency and judicial economy are important goals of evidentiary rules. Judicial notice and non-contestation of facts are important instruments to foster these goals but, as always, they must not operate to the detriment of the rights of the accused, especially his right to confrontation. It is for this reason that the so-admitted facts must not relate to the guilt or innocence of the accused.[657] In contrast, there are other rules, especially regarding evidence on sexual violence, which put the accused in a less advantageous position.

#### *(a) Judicial notice*

A Chamber 'shall not', pursuant to Article 69 (6) ICCS, 'require proof of facts of common knowledge but may[658] take judicial notice of them'.[659] Facts of *common knowledge* are 'facts which are so notorious that they do not require formal proof'[660] or, at least, are

[653] *Katanga*, ICC-01/04-01/07-2635, para. 27.

[654] cf. Ibid., para. 27 (source of the information, nature and characteristics of the item of evidence, contemporaneousness, purpose, adequate means of evaluation); see previously *Lubanga*, ICC-01/04-01/06-1399, para. 29 (referring to origin, provenance, and character of the document); see also *Musema*, ICTR-96-13-A, para. 42; *Tadić*, IT-94-1-T, Hearsay Decision, para. 19 (referring to four factors, i.e. the circumstances under which the evidence arose, its content, a possible corroboration, as well as its truthfulness, voluntariness, and trustworthiness).

[655] *Lubanga*, ICC-01/04-01/06-2842, para. 109; *Katanga*, ICC-01/04-01/07-3436-tENG, para. 91.

[656] *Katanga*, ICC-01/04-01/07-2635, para. 28 (discussing thereafter, at paras. 29–33, reports by the UN, NGOs, States, the press and letters, manifestos, political statements, and other documents).

[657] See e.g. ICTY, *Prosecutor v. Popović et al.*, TC II, Decision on Prosecution Motion for Judicial Notice of Adjudicated Facts, IT-05-88-T, 26 September 2006, paras. 12–13 (adjudicated facts must not be related to the acts, mental state, or conduct of the accused). This is also stressed by Boas et al., *Procedure* (2011), pp. 363, 365. With regard to written statements, see also Rule 92*bis* (A) RPE ICTY, referred to in notes 550, 551 and in main text in this chapter.

[658] In favour of a discretionary rule ('may'), also Gaynor, in Sluiter et al., *International Criminal Procedure* (2013), p. 1128.

[659] See—apart from Art. 69 (6) ICCS—Rule 94 (A) RPE ICTY/ICTR/SCSL, Rule 105 (A) RPE MICT; Rule 160 (A) RPE STL and Rule 157 (1) RPE KSC; ; thereon *Bemba*, ICC-01/05-01/08-3343, paras. 219–20; see also UN GA, 'Expert Group ICTY/ICTR Report' (2002), para. 85 including Recommendation 11; Nice and Vallières-Roland, *JICJ*, 3 (2005), 375; Nemitz, in Kirsch, *Internationale Strafgerichtshöfe* (2005), pp. 68–9; Bonomy, *JICJ*, 5 (2007), 359; Kwon, *JICJ*, 5 (2007), 368 ff.; Harmon, *JICJ*, 5 (2007), 381–2; Zahar and Sluiter, *ICL* (2008), pp. 356 ff.; Safferling, *International Criminal Procedure* (2012), pp. 485–7; Gaynor, in Sluiter et al., *International Criminal Procedure* (2013), pp. 1109 ff. (1127, 1128: general principle); Klamberg, *Evidence* (2013), pp. 472–4. The rule already existed in Art. 21 IMT Charter; thereto Gaynor, in Sluiter et al., *International Criminal Procedure* (2013), p. 1109; Klamberg, *Evidence* (2013), pp. 476–7 (but considering it as a separate rule for documentary evidence). On the mixed tribunals, Gaynor, in Sluiter et al., *International Criminal Procedure* (2013), pp. 1121–3. At the ECCC there is no equivalent provision, cf. ECCC, *Co-Prosecutors v. Nuon Chea et al.*, TC, Decision on Ieng Sary's Motions Regarding Judicial Notice of Adjudicated Facts from Case 001 and Facts of Common Knowledge Being Applied in Case 002, E69/1, 4 April 2011, p. 3.

[660] Piragoff and Clarke, 'Article 69', in Ambos, *Commentary* (2022), mn. 78.

not reasonably subject to dispute,[661] for example, geographical information or historical data[662] or a 'consistent pattern of conduct relevant to serious violations of IHL'[663] but not legal concepts or findings.[664] Facts of common knowledge 'include facts which are capable of ready determination by resort to sources whose accuracy cannot reasonably be questioned'.[665] Article 69 (6) ICCS, as quoted above, is somewhat inconsistent in that it is mandatory ('shall') in the first, but discretionary ('may') in the second part.[666] This is arguably the result of the fact that one of the ICC's goals is to establish a historical record and, thus, judicial efficiency has sometimes to be balanced against the search for truth.[667] In procedural terms, TC I reads into Article 69 (6) ICCS that 'the Chamber may raise *proprio motu* or a party may request that the Chamber take judicial notice of facts of common knowledge'.[668]

The distinguishing line between facts and law may sometimes be difficult to draw.[669] Thus, the *Karemera et al.* AC recognized the Rwandan genocide as a fact of common knowledge being beyond reasonable dispute,[670] but distinguished from that the (legal) question of the individual responsibility of the accused which needs to be determined in an adversarial procedure.[671] In fact, the ICTR AC did not so much focus on the facts–law distinction, but on the level of controversy surrounding the respective question. As long as this question is not reasonably disputed, a Chamber can take judicial notice of it.[672] At any rate, the

[661] ICTY, *Prosecutor v. Simić et al.*, TC, Decision on Pre-trial Motion by the Prosecution Requesting the Trial Chamber to Take Judicial Notice of the International Character of the Conflict in Bosnia-Herzegovina, IT-95-09-PT, 25 March 1999; ICTR, *Prosecutor v. Karemera et al.*, TC III, Decision on Appeals Chamber Remand of Judicial Notice, ICTR-98-44-T, 11 December 2006, para. 10. A voluntary admission of the accused does not necessarily make a fact indisputable; cf. ICTR, *Prosecutor v. Semanza*, TC III, Decision on the Prosecutor's Motion for Judicial Notice and Presumptions of Facts pursuant to Rules 94 and 54, ICTR-97-20-I, 3 November 2000, para. 34. For the broader US position during the negotiations, see Safferling, *International Criminal Procedure* (2012), p. 486.

[662] Piragoff and Clarke, 'Article 69', in Ambos, *Commentary* (2022), mn. 78. In favour of including information regarding the existence or nature of an armed conflict ICC-OTP, 'Informal Expert Paper, Length of Proceedings' (2003), para. 114.

[663] Rules 93 RPE ICTY/ICTR/SCSL and 114 RPE MICT. See also *Šešelj*, IT-03-67-T, TC III Judgment, para. 29 ('le pouvoir discrétionnaire donné aux Juges d'user ou non d'éléments de preuve relatifs à une ligne de conduite délibérée doit être exercé avec prudence').

[664] SCSL, *Prosecutor v. Norman et al.*, AC Fofana, Decision on Appeal Against 'Decision on Prosecution's Motion for Judicial Notice and Admission of Evidence', SCSL-2004-14-AR73, 16 May 2005, para. 32 ('legal conclusions as well as facts which constitute legal findings cannot be judicially noticed'); ICTY, *Prosecutor v. Perišić*, TC I, Decision on Motion for Judicial Notice of ICTY Convictions, IT-04-81-PT, 25 September 2008, para. 17, (convictions by other Chambers not facts 'of common knowledge').

[665] ICC, *Prosecutor v. Bemba et al.*, TC VII, Decision on Prosecution Motion for Clarification of Rule 68 (3) Direction in Conduct of Proceedings Decision", ICC-01/05-01/13-1249, 15 September 2015, para. 5, referring to, inter alia, ICTR, *Prosecutor v. Bagosora et al.*, TC, Decision on the Prosecutor's Motion for Judicial Notice pursuant to Rules 73, 89 and 94, ICTR-98-41-T, 11 April 2003, para. 44.

[666] ICC, *Prosecutor v. Bemba et al.*, TC VII, Decision on Prosecution Request for Judicial Notice, ICC-01/05-01/13-1473, 9 November 2015, para. 4. Crit. Gaynor, in Sluiter et al., *International Criminal Procedure* (2013), p. 1121; see also Vriend, *Criminal Trial* (2016), pp. 159, 171.

[667] See also Piragoff and Clarke, 'Article 69', in Ambos, *Commentary* (2022), mn. 11 *in fine* ('[s]uch a balancing process may prompt a Chamber to take judicial notice in one context and decline to do so in another, even when the same facts are at issue').

[668] See ICC, *Prosecutor v. Gbagbo and Blè Goudé*, TC I, Directions on the Conduct of the Proceedings, ICC-02/11-01/15-205, 3 September 2015, para. 61. See also Vriend, *Criminal Trial* (2016), pp. 159–60.

[669] See also McDermott Rees, *Völkerrechtsblog* 14 July 2022. Describing a clear separation between law and facts regarding evidence: Jämsä, *Rules of Evidence* (2023), p. 23.

[670] ICTR, *Prosecutor v. Karemera et al.*, AC, Decision on Prosecutor's Interlocutory Appeal of Decision on Judicial Notice, ICTR-98-44-AR73I, 16 June 2006, para. 35; crit. Boas et al., *Procedure* (2011), p. 362; Safferling, *International Criminal Procedure* (2012), p. 487.

[671] *Karemera et al.*, ICTR-98-44-AR73(C), paras. 36–7.

[672] Ibid., para. 29 and n. 44; *Semanza*, ICTR-97-20-A, para. 197. See also Gaynor, in Sluiter et al., *International Criminal Procedure* (2013), pp. 1111–12.

respective facts are not evidence,[673] but can be admitted into the evidentiary record without being proven again although a party is free to challenge them.[674] On a different note, the ICTR AC has warned that 'the practice of judicial notice must not be allowed to circumvent the presumption of innocence and the defendant's right to a fair trial, including his right to confront his accusers'; in particular, criminal responsibility cannot be based on judicially noticed facts.[675]

At the ad hoc tribunals, a Chamber may, in addition, take judicial notice, at the request of a party or *proprio motu*, of '*adjudicated facts* and or of the authenticity of documentary evidence from other proceedings';[676] at the STL and the KSC the judicial notice is limited to the adjudicated facts.[677] Yet, this form of judicial notice is limited at various levels. First of all, for such facts to be admitted they must be explicitly accepted in a final judgment ('adjudicated');[678] they must be distinct, concrete, and identifiable and the relevant parts of the respective judgment must be clearly identified.[679] In addition to this admissibility test, it is always in the Chamber's discretion[680] to refuse the notification if it is contrary to the interests of justice.[681] As with 'facts of common knowledge', the distinction between facts and law generates difficult questions of delimitation.[682] As to '*documentary*

[673] ICTY, *Prosecutor v. Prlić et al.*, TC II, Decision on 'Prosecution Motion for Judicial Notice of Facts of Common Knowledge and Admission of Documentary Evidence pursuant to Rules 94 (A) and 89 (C)', IT-04-74-PT, 3 February 2006 ('a fact of common knowledge, since it requires no proof, cannot be considered "evidence"').

[674] cf. ICTY, *Prosecutor v. S. Milošević*, AC, Decision on the Prosecution's Interlocutory Appeal against the Trial Chamber's 10 April 2003 Decision on Prosecution Motion for Judicial Notice of Adjudicated Facts, IT-02-54-AR73.5, 28 October 2003 ('by taking judicial notice of an adjudicated fact, a Chamber establishes a well-founded presumption for the accuracy of this fact, which therefore does not have to be proven again at trial, but which, subject to that presumption, may be challenged at that trial', fn. omitted); ICTY, *Prosecutor v. Ljubicić*, TC I, Decision on Prosecution's Motion for Judicial Notice of Adjudicated Facts, IT-00-41-PT, 23 January 2003, p. 6; for a different view, see *Norman et al.*, SCSL-2004-14-AR73, Separate Opinion of Judge Robertson, para. 5 ('facts that are judicially noticed are thenceforth taken for granted and cannot be the subject of further evidence or dispute in the trial'). In the same vein, Gaynor, in Sluiter et al., *International Criminal Procedure* (2013), p. 1117 ('established conclusively').

[675] ICTR, *Prosecutor v. Karemera et al.*, AC, Decision on Prosecutor's Interlocutory Appeal of Decision on Judicial Notice, ICTR-98-44-AR73(C), 16 June 2006, para. 47 ('it would plainly be improper for facts judicially noticed to be the "basis for proving the Appellant's criminal responsibility" (in the sense of being sufficient to establish that responsibility)'). See also *Semanza*, ICTR-97-20-A, para. 192.

[676] Rule 94 (B) RPE ICTY/ICTR/SCSL; Rule 105 (B) RPE MICT (emphasis added). Thereon, Klamberg, *Evidence* (2013), pp. 474–6; Prosperi and Zammit Borda, in Stahn et al., *Legacies of the ICTY* (2020) p. 174, 185; Rigney, *Fairness* (2022), pp. 132, 134 ff.; for detailed principles governing judicial notice of adjudicated facts, see *Karadžić*, IT-95-5/18-T, Judgment, paras. 25–31, see also *Šešelj*, IT-03-67-T, TC III Judgment, para. 30.

[677] Rule 160 (B) RPE STL and Rule 157 (2) RPE KSC.

[678] ICTY, *Prosecutor v. Sikirica et al.*, TC, Decision on Prosecution Motion for Judicial Notice of Adjudicated Facts, IT-95-8-T, 27 September 2000 ('not in the proper sense adjudicated as they are the subject of ongoing appellate proceedings [and hence not yet final]'); ICTY, *Prosecutor v. Kupreskić et al.*, AC, Decision on the Motions of Drago Josipović, Zoran Kupreskić and Vlatko Kupreskić to Admit Additional Evidence pursuant to Rule 115 and for Judicial Notice to be taken pursuant to Rule 94 (B), IT-95-16-A, 8 May 2011, para. 6 ('Only facts in a judgement, from which there has been no appeal, or as to which any appellate proceedings have concluded, can truly be deemed "adjudicated facts" within the meaning of Rule 94(B)').

[679] cf. ICTY, *Prosecutor v. Stanišić and Simatović*, TC I, Decision on Prosecution's Motion for Judicial Notice of Adjudicated Facts, IT-03-69-T, 25 November 2009, paras. 27, 32; *Popović et al.*, IT-05-88-T, Adjudicated Facts Decision, paras. 6 (distinct, concrete, and identifiable), 7 (not substantially different from the original judgment), 9 (fact identified with adequate precision). See also Gaynor, in Sluiter et al., *International Criminal Procedure* (2013), pp. 1113, 1115, 1116, with further references.

[680] cf. Rules 94 (B) RPE ICTY/ICTR/SCSL and 115 (B) RPE MICT ('may') with Rules 94 (A) RPE ICTY/ICTR/SCSL and 115 (A) RPE MICT ('shall').

[681] cf. *Popović et al.*, IT-05-88-T, Adjudicated Facts Decision, para. 4; *Karemera et al.*, ICTR-98-44-T, Judicial Notice Decision, paras. 23, 51. On this two-stage test, see also Boas et al., *Procedure* (2011), p. 363.

[682] For a discussion with case law references, see Gaynor, in Sluiter et al., *International Criminal Procedure* (2013), pp. 1114, 1116 (regarding facts which go directly to the responsibility of the accused), 1117 (exclusion of convictions) with case law references.

*evidence*', the judicial notice only goes to the authenticity of the documents, not to their contents and probative value.[683] The judicial notice of such an (adjudicated) fact will only raise the prosecution's initial burden of production (and not affect the burden of persuasion of guilt)[684] and may—being of a merely presumptive nature—be challenged by 'reliable and credible evidence to the contrary'.[685] The main driving force behind allowing judicial notice of adjudicated facts and documentary evidence was to foster 'consistency and uniformity of decisions on factual issues where diversity in factual findings would be unfair'.[686]

At the ICC, there is no specific rule for judicial notice of adjudicated facts and documentary evidence.[687] Instead there are other (general) rules, in particular the above discussed Rule 68 RPE ICC, which suggest that judicial notice may be used more restrictively than at the ad hoc tribunals.[688] While there, as mentioned above, judicial notice of adjudicated facts is mainly driven by consistency considerations, at the ICC—having a different institutional architecture and a broader jurisdiction—such consistency is strived for by other means. In *Katanga and Ngudjolo*, Katanga requested in his closing brief that the findings in the *Lubanga* judgment regarding the use of intermediaries be admitted as evidence, or alternatively that the Trial Chamber have regard to *Lubanga* findings as 'the findings of another Chamber on a question of fact relevant to [the *Katanga and Ngudjolo*] case'.[689] Since Article 69 (6) ICCS, as mentioned, does not provide a basis for such a request, the defence suggested that it 'may fall under the general power of the Trial Chamber to ensure that the trial is fair under article 64(2) of the Statute'.[690] Yet, the TC found, rejecting the request, that 'there is no express legal basis for taking judicial notice of facts tried in other cases brought before the Court which are related to matters at issue in the current proceedings'.[691]

683 For the discussion in the case law, see Gaynor, in Sluiter et al., *International Criminal Procedure* (2013), pp. 1117–19; Prosperi and Zammit Borda, in Stahn et al., *Legacies of the ICTY* (2020) p. 174, 185.

684 ICTY, *Prosecutor v. D. Milošević*, TC III, Decision on Prosecution's Motion for Judicial Notice of Adjudicated Facts and Prosecution's Catalogue of Agreed Facts with Dissenting Opinion of Judge Harhoff, IT-98-29/1-T, 10 April 2007, para. 29; *Popović et al.*, IT-05-88-T, Adjudicated Facts Decision, para. 21; See also Boas et al., *Procedure* (2011), p. 362; Gaynor, in Sluiter et al., *International Criminal Procedure* (2013), p. 1113.

685 cf. *Karemera et al.*, ICTR-98-44-AR73(C), para. 42; *S. Milošević*, IT-02-54-AR73.5 ('subject to that presumption, [for the accuracy] may be challenged at that trial'); ICTY, *Prosecutor v. D. Milošević*, AC, Decision on Interlocutory Appeals Against Trial Chamber's Decision on Prosecution Motion for Judicial Notice of Adjudicated Facts and Prosecution's Catalogue of Agreed Facts, IT-98-29/1-AR73.1, 26 June 2007, para. 16; ICTY, *Prosecutor v. Šešelj*, TC III, Decision on Prosecution Motion for Judicial Notice of Facts Adjudicated by *Krajišnik* Case, IT-03-67-T, 23 July 2010, para. 6; ICTY, *Prosecutor v. Karadžić*, TC, Decision on Prosecution's Motion to Admit Evidence in Rebuttal, IT-95-5/18-T, 21 March 2014, para. 11. See also Boas et al., *Procedure* (2011), pp. 362, 365 (crit. of the shift of the burden of persuasion to the accused); Gaynor, in Sluiter et al., *International Criminal Procedure* (2013), pp. 1113, 1115, 1117 with further references.

686 ICTR, *Prosecutor v. Semanza*, TC, Decision on the Prosecutor's Motion for Judicial Notice and Presumptions of Facts pursuant to Rules 94 and 54, ICTR-97-20-T, 3 November 2000, para. 20. See also Vriend, *Criminal Trial* (2016), p. 173.

687 In favour of such rules, Gaynor, in Sluiter et al., *International Criminal Procedure* (2013), p. 1128.

688 See also Piragoff and Clarke, 'Article 69', in Ambos, *Commentary* (2022), mn. 79; Klamberg, *Evidence* (2013), p. 476.

689 ICC, *Prosecutor v. Katanga and Ngudjolo*, Defence, Urgent Defence Request for Leave to Reply, ICC-01/04-01/07-3278, 26 April 2012, para. 1. See also ICC, *Prosecutor v. Katanga and Ngudjolo*, Defence, Public Redacted Version—Second Corrigendum to the Defence Closing Brief, ICC-01/04-01/07-3266-Corr2-Red, 29 June 2012, paras. 465–75.

690 *Katanga and Ngudjolo*, ICC-01/04-01/07-3266-Corr2-Red, para. 469.

691 ICC, *Prosecutor v. Katanga and Ngudjolo*, TC II, Decision on the Request by the Defence for Germain Katanga Seeking to Admit Excerpts from the Judgment Rendered in *Lubanga*, ICC-01/04-01/07-3279-tEng, 26 April 2012, para. 12.

With regard to the relevance of adjudicated facts, the ICC's approach differs from that of the ad hoc tribunals: while the ICTY/ICTR AC has emphasized 'that the adjudicated facts sought to be judicially noticed must be relevant to the matters at issue',[692] the ICC TC VII held that 'the Chamber may take judicial notice of facts of common knowledge without first assessing the relevance of these facts to the case at hand'.[693] However, the TC qualifies this approach in that a TC 'always has the discretion to decline to take judicial notice of clearly irrelevant facts'.[694]

While, in case of judicial notice, a Chamber relies on written evidence, if it conducts a *judicial site visit* it draws conclusions based on its own perceptions, for example, regarding the context and topography of locations involved in the alleged crimes.[695] Such site visits, which can be based on the Chambers' general power to obtain evidence 'necessary for the determination of the truth'[696] or in the interest of justice,[697] have been made by the ad hoc tribunals[698] and the *Katanga* TC.[699]

### *(b) Agreed ('not contested') facts*

Rule 69 RPE ICC provides for a *consensual approach* to evidence: Prosecutor and defence may agree that a relevant fact is 'not contested' and a Chamber 'may' accordingly consider such a fact 'as being proven' unless it deems a 'more complete presentation' necessary.[700] The word 'may' makes clear that it lies in the Chamber's discretion whether it considers the uncontested facts as proven or not.[701] It may also issue any necessary order at a status conference with regard to 'the evidence to be introduced under rule 69 as regards agreed facts'.[702] The wording underlines the difference between fact and evidence: agreed facts are not (yet) evidence but may become evidence. The Chamber shall be guided by 'the interests of justice', especially 'the interests of victims'[703] and, of course, the general procedural and

[692] See also *D. Milošević*, IT-98-29/1-AR73.1, para. 13; *Semanza*, ICTR-97-20-A, para. 189.

[693] *Bemba et al.*, ICC-01/05-01/13-1170, para. 6.

[694] Ibid., para. 6 with n. 11.

[695] cf. Kiss, 'Article 74', in Ambos, *Commentary* (2022), mn. 36; also *Katanga*, ICC-01/04-01/07-3436-tENG, para. 108.

[696] cf. Art. 69 (3); also Art. 64 (6)(d) ICCS. Combs, in Sluiter et al., *International Criminal Procedure* (2013), p. 718, finds the basis in Art. 62 ICCS, but this provision does not refer to the collection of evidence. In contrast, Rule 4 RPE ICTY/ICTR/SCSL more specifically allows a Chamber to 'exercise its functions at a place other than the seat of the Tribunal' and therefore encompasses on-site visits; also ibid., pp. 717–18. The truth-seeking function of such an on-site visit also explains that the practice is common in civil law jurisdictions, esp. in macrocriminality trials; cf. ibid., pp. 719–20.

[697] Rule 4 RPE ICTY/ICTR/SCSL/MICT *in fine*; see also Combs, in Sluiter et al., *International Criminal Procedure* (2013), pp. 720 (principle) and 721 (advocating its greater use).

[698] cf. Combs, in Sluiter et al., *International Criminal Procedure* (2013), p. 721 (referring to three ICTS on-site visits).

[699] *Katanga*, ICC-01/04-01/07-3436-tENG, paras. 106–7 with further references.

[700] See specifically ICC, *Prosecutor v. Nourain and Jerbo*, TC IV, Decision on the Joint Submission Regarding the Contested Issues and the Agreed Facts, ICC-02/05-03/09-227, 28 September 2011, para. 20; leaving only three issues uncontested, ibid., paras. 24, 46; also *Katanga*, ICC-01/04-01/07-3436-tENG, para. 73 (for agreed facts considered 'established'); *Lubanga*, ICC-01/04-01/06-2842, para. 245 (for agreed written statements considered not credible); thereon also Klamberg, *Evidence* (2013), pp. 479–80. The ad hoc tribunals have in part different rules, see e.g. Rule 65*ter* (H) RPE ICTY according to which '[t]he pre-trial Judge shall record the points of agreement and disagreement on matters of law and fact'; see also Rules 73*bis* (B)(ii) and (F), 73*ter* (B)(i), and 108*bis* (C) RPE ICTR; Rule 70 (N) RPE MICT; Rule 122 RPE STL; Rules 73*bis* (B)(ii) and (F), 73*ter* (B)(i), and 109 (C) RPE SCSL as well as Rules 80 (3)(e) and 87 (6) RPE ECCC; On these Rules, see also Gaynor, in Sluiter et al., *International Criminal Procedure* (2013), pp. 1119–21, concluding (at 1128), that this is a general principle; Klamberg, *Evidence* (2013), pp. 478–9. In contrast, Rule 156 RPE KSC follows Rule 69 RPE ICC.

[701] See also *Nourain and Jerbo*, ICC-02/05-03/09-227, para. 23 ('not mandatory').

[702] Reg. 54 (n) RegC.

[703] Rule 69 RPE ICC *in fine*.

evidentiary principles ('fair and expeditious conduct of the proceedings',[704] 'determination of the truth'[705]).[706]

Any decision is always preliminary insofar as it is taken at a specific procedural stage and the Chamber may always request additional evidence and/or submission on the respective facts in the interests of justice.[707] Victims can challenge any such an agreement,[708] in particular they may request to question a witness or have her questioned by the Chamber if a certain fact results from this witness's statement.[709]

### (c) Others

As regards *character* evidence—which may be submitted in written form[710]—the *Kupreškić et al.* TC has generally considered it inadmissible with a view to the accused's propensity to act in conformity with his (alleged) character. This is in line with the common law approach according to which such evidence is excluded since it tends to be irrelevant with regard to the concrete charges but, instead, seriously prejudges the accused.[711] Thus, the Chamber argued:

> (i) generally speaking, evidence of the accused's character prior to the events for which he is indicted before the International Tribunal is not a relevant issue inasmuch as (a) by their nature as crimes committed in the context of widespread violence and during a national or international emergency, war crimes and crimes against humanity may be committed by persons with no prior convictions or history of violence, and that consequently evidence of prior good, or bad, conduct on the part of the accused before the armed conflict began is rarely of any probative value before the International Tribunal, and (b) as a general principle of criminal law, evidence as to the character of an accused is generally inadmissible to show the accused's propensity to act in conformity therewith.[712]

[704] Art. 64 (3)(a) ICCS; also Art. 64 (2) ICCS.

[705] Art. 69 (3) ICCS.

[706] In the so far only Rule 69 case, TC IV further referred to the general powers of the Chamber to conduct proceedings pursuant to Art. 64 ICCS, Rules 134 (1), 140 (1) RPE ICC, and Reg. 54 (h) RegC; cf. *Nourain and Jerbo*, ICC-02/05-03/09-227, para. 20.

[707] See also *Nourain and Jerbo*, ICC-02/05-03/09-227, paras. 24, 37, 45–6 (decision 'at this stage' of proceedings, Chamber not limited by agreement).

[708] cf. Art. 68 (3) ICCS and Rule 69 RPE ICC *in fine* (explicitly referring to the interests of victims); see also the considerations in *Nourain and Jerbo*, ICC-02/05-03/09-227, paras. 26 ff.

[709] cf. Rule 91 (3) RPE ICC; also Piragoff and Clarke, 'Article 69', in Ambos, *Commentary* (2022), mn. 29.

[710] Rules 92*bis* (A)(i)(e) RPE ICTY/ICTR and 110 (A)(i)(e) RPE MICT. See also ICTY, *Prosecutor v. Prlić et al.*, TC, Decision on Prlić Defence Motion for Admission of Written Statements pursuant to Rule 92*bis*, IT-04-74-T, 25 November 2008, para. 12; *Prlić et al.*, IT-04-74-A, AC Judgment, para. 146.

[711] cf. Bantekas, *ICL* (2010), p. 522; Heinze, in Caeiro, Gless, and Mitsilegas, *Elgar Encyclopedia* (2022). For a profound treatment, Spencer, *Character* (2016), p. ix, who is in favour of admitting the defendant's previous misconduct (arguing that this is 'neither dangerous nor unjust, provided there is other solid evidence that links him to the offence. The danger arises where such evidence is allowed to be used as a substitute for more convincing evidence where the case against him is otherwise weak'). From an ethical perspective: Smith and Gardiner, *PI*, 31 (2021), 334–54. It should be noted, though, that the common law distinguishes between defendant and non-defendant (witness) bad character evidence. UK law especially has been considerably changed recently in this regard, see ss. 98–113 of the Criminal Justice Act (CJA) 2003 and Thomason, *IJEP*, 27 (2023), 26–50; Mirfield, *CambLJ*, 82 (2023), 395 ff.

[712] *Kupreškić et al.*, IT-95-16-T, TC Decision on Evidence, p. 1. However, in the amended indictment against *Hadžihasanović et al.*, the Prosecutor referred to a criminal matter when he described the military position of Amir Kubura (ICTY, *Prosecutor v. Hadžihasanović et al.*, Prosecution, Amended Indictment, IT-01-47-PT, 11 January 2002, para. 58). This may be interpreted as a reference to the character; see Jones and Powles, *International Criminal Practice* (2003), p. 733.

Such evidence may only be admitted if it points to a 'consistent pattern of conduct' within the meaning of Rules 93 RPE ICTY/ICTR/SCSL and 114 RPE MICT.[713] At the ICC, there is no comparable rule, but such evidence may be admitted—in line with the general rules—if it is relevant to the charges and does not cause unfair prejudice to the accused.

The importance and particularities of *sexual violence* in armed conflicts which is mainly directed against women and thus is a manifestation of general discriminatory practices[714] has led to a number of special rules which can be summarized as follows (the ICC law has essentially adopted the SCSL approach):[715]

- Corroboration of the victim's testimony is not required (to avoid re-traumatization);[716]
- Consent shall not be allowed as a defence if there are circumstances of generalized violence and fear which did not allow the victim to act with full autonomy;[717] if the accused wants to adduce consent he must satisfy the Chamber that his evidence is 'relevant and credible';[718]
- Prior sexual conduct of the victim shall not be admitted in evidence.[719]

Given the specific defence challenges in *Bemba* as to 'evidence identifying individuals, in particular, alleged perpetrators', TC III developed useful general principles on how to assess such evidence. Accordingly, a Chamber may consider, inter alia,

> the circumstances in which a witness observed the perpetrator, the length of the observation, distance between the perpetrator and the witness, obstruction of the observation, interactions between the witness and the perpetrators or their group, and the manner in which the witness describes the perpetrators, for example, whether there are inconsistencies, misidentification followed by later identification, or delayed assertion of memory

[713] cf. Bantekas, *ICL* (2010), pp. 522–3.

[714] cf. Boas et al., *Procedure* (2011), p. 350 with further references.

[715] On the evidentiary issues, see previously Ambos, in Bergsmo, *Thematic Prosecution of International Sex Crimes* (2012), pp. 296–301 (amounting to the 'satisfactory evidence' or 'strong case' problem); generally Klamberg, *Evidence* (2013), pp. 406–8; on the *travaux* regarding Rules 70–2 RPE ICC, see Piragoff and Clarke, 'Article 69', in Ambos, *Commentary* (2022), mn. 9.

[716] Rule 96 (i) RPE ICTY/ICTR; Rule 118 (i) RPE MICT; Rule 63 (4) RPE ICC (no corroboration requirement 'in particular' in case of 'crimes of sexual violence'). See also ICTY, *Prosecutor v. Kunarac et al.*, AC, Judgment, IT-96-23-A and IT-96-23/1-A, 12 June 2002, para. 281 (TC was 'entitled not to require corroboration').

[717] Rule 96 (ii) RPE ICTY/ICTR; Rule 118 (ii) RPE MICT; Rule 96 (i), (ii) RPE SCSL, Rule 148 (1)(a) RPE KSC and Rule 70 (a), (b) RPE ICC (both referring to a 'coercive environment' and situation where victim is 'incapable of giving genuine consent'); also Rule 96 (iii) RPE SCSL, Rule 148 (1)(c) RPE KSC, and Rule 70 (c) RPE ICC (no inference of consent from 'silence of, or lack of resistance' of victim) as well as Rule 148 (1)(b) RPE KSC (no inference of consent 'by reason of any words or conduct' where genuine consent impossible). On the respective (case) law on consent as a defence in rape cases, see previously Ambos, *Treatise ICL I* (2021), p. 506.

[718] Rule 96 (iii) RPE ICTY/ICTR; Rule 118 (iii) RPE MICT.

[719] Rule 96 (iv) RPE ICTY/ICTR; Rule 118 (iv) RPE MICT; Rule 148 (1)(d) and (2) RPE KSC; Rule 71 RPE ICC; also, albeit less explicitly, Rule 96 (iv) RPE SCSL and Rule 70 (d) RPE ICC. In *Delalić et al.*, a witness gave evidence of her rape and torture. During cross-examination and in a public court session, she stated that she had an abortion. The TC took the view that the information on abortion constituted evidence of prior sexual conduct: 'Sub-rule 96 (iv) seeks to prevent situations where the admission of certain evidence may lead to a confusion of the issues, therefore offending the fairness of the proceedings. Furthermore, when adopting Sub-rule 96 (iv), due regard was given to the fact that in rape or other sexual assault cases, evidence of prior sexual conduct of the victims mainly serves to call the reputation of the victim into question. Moreover, it was considered that the value, if any, of information about the prior sexual conduct of a witness in the context of trials of this nature was nullified by the potential danger of further causing distress and emotional damage to the witnesses.' (ICTY, *Prosecutor v. Delalić et al.*, TC, Decision on the Prosecution's Motion for the Redaction of the Public Record, IT-96-21-T, 5 June 1997, para. 48). See also *Halilović*, IT-01-48-A, paras. 10–11.

coupled with the clear possibility that the witness had been influenced by the suggestion of others.[720]

It goes without saying that the criteria enumerated by the Chamber are not supposed to restrict the Chambers in their approach to identification evidence. In fact, the Chambers might deem it necessary to consider 'various criteria in identifying accused persons and their subordinates'.[721] Arguably, these specific rules, although limiting the Chambers' discretion,[722] can be traced back to the general principles of relevance and probative value and thus are not more prejudicial to the rights of the accused than any other evidentiary determination.[723] Take for example the non-admission of the prior sexual conduct of the victim which can be explained with the general consideration that it will normally lack the 'rational probativeness' with respect to the concrete fact in issue[724]—the concrete sexual assault—and must therefore not be admitted.[725]

### (6) Direct versus indirect (circumstantial) evidence

Direct evidence directly proves a matter, for example, a credible witness testifies to the accused's presence at the crime scene. In contrast, indirect or circumstantial evidence provides only an 'indirect' proof, for example, the accused's business card found with the victim indicates that they had contact or the accused's weapon found at the crime scene indicates that he committed the crime or at least was involved in it.[726] The distinction between direct and indirect (circumstantial) evidence follows the criterion of 'proximity to the facts in issue'.[727] Here the above-mentioned alternative hypothesis approach[728] is particularly relevant since circumstantial evidence leaves room for more alternative hypotheses which need to be eliminated in the first place to arrive at one convincing hypothesis.[729]

720 *Bemba*, ICC-01/05-01/08-3343, para. 242.

721 Ibid., para. 243 ('including the position and role of the accused at the time of the charges, the presence in and control of an area by the perpetrators and commanders, the direction from which a perpetrator came, composition of the troops, a perpetrator's uniform—including insignia, footwear, headwear, arms, and clothing, his or her language, and the perpetrator's specific behaviour' (footnotes omitted)).

722 cf. Boas et al., *Procedure* (2011), p. 350.

723 cf. Piragoff and Clarke, 'Article 69', in Ambos, *Commentary* (2022), mn. 59 *in fine*.

724 Section A.(2)(a) in this chapter.

725 See also Piragoff and Clarke, 'Article 69', in Ambos, *Commentary* (2022), mn. 67 ('not rationally related to the conduct or issue in question').

726 For this distinction, see also Klamberg, *Evidence* (2013), pp. 116 (although quoting Greenstein who, inter alia, rejects this traditional distinction), 407–8, 417, 489 (admission of circumstantial evidence as general principle). A more general definition is provided by *Karadžić*, IT-95-5/18-T, Judgment, para. 14 ('Circumstantial evidence is evidence of a number of different circumstances surrounding an event from which a fact at issue may be reasonably inferred'). On the definition in the practice of the ad hoc tribunals, see Windridge, *CLF*, 26 (2015), 404 ff.

727 De Smet, in Bergsmo and Stahn, *Fact-Finding* (2020), p. 119; Roberts, *Evidence* (2022), p. 119. See also Heinze, in Caeiro, Gless, and Mitsilegas, *Elgar Encyclopedia* (2022). But see also the principled critique of the distinction by Greenstein, *Hous L Rev*, 45 (2009), 1801, 1804 (rejecting the logic behind the distinction arguing that: '[t]here simply is no category of evidence that brings us into direct contact with crucial facts because no such contact is possible. All facts are a function of interpretation, and this unavoidability of interpretation makes all facts a matter of inference and all evidence, whether called "direct" or "circumstantial," nothing more or less than a contribution to that inferential process').

728 See note 186 in this chapter.

729 cf. Frisch, in Bruns et al., *FS Stürner* (2013), pp. 860–2; Klamberg, *Evidence* (2013), pp. 194–5.

Circumstantial evidence generally involves the drawing of inferences 'in addition to the testimonial inferences'[730] and may also qualify as otherwise categorized evidence.[731] Examples of circumstantial evidence are an alibi,[732] the person's physical ability to commit a crime, the method by which the crime was committed, the existence of an identifiable motive,[733] and prior behaviour/statements by the suspect and character witnesses,[734] who may testify that 'the offence was completely out of character and that they are convinced nothing like it will ever happen again'.[735]

In international case law, circumstantial evidence is regularly used to prove intent, especially 'specific intent'.[736] Thus, the ICTY AC held that in the absence of pertinent direct evidence the genocidal intent to destroy can be proved through a variety of (external) factors and circumstances, for example through the overall context in which the acts were perpetrated, through the perpetration of other crimes against the same (national, ethnic, racial, or religious) group, the severity of hostilities, the systematicity of the conduct against the victims based on their belonging to the respective group, or through the repetition of destructive and discriminating acts.[737] In *Kvočka et al.*, the accused persons' knowledge of the atrocities committed in a concentration camp was deduced from the fact that they either worked regularly in the camp or were present there in any event.[738] Circumstantial evidence indicating knowledge of the respective joint criminal enterprise with regard to the camp[739] may include: (1) the position that the respective accused held in the camp; (2) the time he spent there; (3) the functions performed by the accused; (4) the possibility of moving freely throughout the camp; and (5) contact with prisoners, other members of camp staff, or visitors to the camp.[740]

It is also necessary to resort to circumstantial evidence to prove superior or command responsibility,[741] for example if the superior denies knowledge of crimes committed by her subordinates. In this respect, the superior's knowledge cannot be presumed.[742] Depending on whether the superior's position is legal or factual or military or non-military in nature, the quality of the circumstantial evidence is subject to very different requirements. Thus, a military commander's knowledge of his subordinates' crimes will be easier to prove than that of a civilian superior because of the comprehensive reporting and supervisory duties that usually exist in a military context.

730 Fishman and McKenna, *Jones on Evidence I* (2020) para. 1.5.

731 Heinze, in Caeiro, Gless, and Mitsilegas, *Elgar Encyclopedia* (2022).

732 cf. Rule 79 (1)(a) RPE ICC: 'the notification shall specify the place or places at which the accused claims to have been present at the time of the alleged crime and the names of witnesses and any other evidence upon which the accused intends to rely to establish the alibi.'

733 Munday, *Cross and Tapper on Evidence* (2018), p. 33 ('reason why the crime was commited'); Brandl, *Criminal Investigation* (2021), p. 112.

734 Munday, *Evidence* (2019), p. 232.

735 Sprack and Engelhardt-Sprack, *A Practical Approach to Criminal Procedure* (2019), para. 22.54; Imwinkelried, in Mosteller, *McCormick on Evidence* (2020), pp. 135–6. For the list see also Heinze, in Caeiro, Gless, and Mitsilegas, *Elgar Encyclopedia* (2022). This is different to bad character evidence, see above note 711.

736 See also Schuon, *International Criminal Procedure* (2010), pp. 140, 168; Klamberg, *Evidence* (2013), pp. 192–3. See also *Bemba*, ICC-01/05-01/08-3343, para. 239, wher the Chamber remarked, that the existence of the mental elements of crimes 'can be inferred from relevant facts and circumstances', citing para. 3 of the General Introduction to the Elements of Crimes.

737 ICTY, *Prosecutor v. Jelisić*, AC, Judgment, IT-95-10-A, 5 July 2001, para. 47.

738 *Prosecutor v. Kvočka et al.*, TC, Judgment, IT-98-30/1-T, 2 November 2001, para. 324.

739 On this so-called JCE II, see Ambos, *Treatise ICL I* (2021), pp. 186–92 (186, 189).

740 *Kvočka et al.*, IT-98-30/1-T, para. 324.

741 On this form of responsibility, see Ambos, *Treatise ICL I* (2021), pp. 257 ff.

742 *Delalić et al.*, IT-96-21-T, TC Judgment, para. 386.

Of course, the relevant circumstantial evidence itself must be established beyond any reasonable doubt, that is, be indisputable or proven, before any conclusion can be drawn from it to the detriment of the accused. For a conviction cannot be based on anything less than the usual standard of proof.[743] If, on the other hand, there is only one reasonable conclusion to be drawn from particular facts so proven, a Chamber may properly conclude that it has been established 'beyond reasonable doubt'.[744] The matter of both standard of proof and standard of inference with regard to circumstantial evidence received major attention in the *Karadžić* case, where both genocide charges were based on circumstantial evidence.[745] The TC inferred from the available evidence that Karadžić 'shared with Mladić, Beara, and Popović the intent that every able-bodied Bosnian Muslim male from Srebrenica be killed, which, in the Chamber's view, amounts to the intent to destroy the Bosnian Muslims in Srebrenica'.[746] Apart from the fact that it seems questionable whether this is the 'only reasonable inference',[747] genocidal intent can only be proven 'watertight' by direct evidence; if such evidence is not available, as in this case, the 'only reasonable inference' test, if interpreted at face value, is, arguably, too high a threshold.[748] The only reasonable inference test qualifies the inferential process of making deductions and narrows the 'beyond reasonable doubt' standard in focusing on the '*only* reasonable' inference. It thus entails a higher threshold than the ordinary 'beyond reasonable doubt' standard, since under this standard it suffices that the trial judge is convinced that the requisite specific intent follows from the totality of evidence, including any relevant and reasonable inference.[749] That the 'only reasonable inference' test (as the process of deduction) is aligned with the 'beyond reasonable doubt' standard as a standard of proof has already been demonstrated by the ICTR AC in *Zigiranyirazo* with regard to an inference by an accused. Here the Chamber stated, however, that an accused's inference based on circumstantial evidence 'need not be the only reasonable one' because 'an accused does not bear a burden of proof, by contrast with the burden of the prosecution in establishing a conviction'.[750]

[743] This is also recognized in national criminal procedure, cf. *in lieu* of many, Volk and Engländer, *Grundkurs StPO* (2021), § 23 mn. 4; also McDermott, *JICJ*, 13 (2015), 532 (no inference from dubious facts).

[744] ICC, *Prosecutor v. Al Bashir*, AC, Judgment on the Appeal of the Prosecutor against the 'Decision on the Prosecution's Application for a Warrant of Arrest against Omar Hassan Ahmad Al Bashir', ICC-02/05-01/09-73, 3 February 2010, para. 33; *Lubanga*, ICC-01/04-01/06-2842, para. 111; *Katanga*, ICC-01/04-01/07-3436-tENG, para. 109.

[745] The following considerations draw on my discussion in *EJIL: Talk!*, see Ambos, *EJIL: Talk!*, 1 April 2016.

[746] *Karadžić*, IT-95-5/18-T, Judgment, para. 5830.

[747] The evidence presented by the Chamber, especially Karadzic's certain knowledge of the events at Srebrenica, allows for many (reasonable) inferences. In particular, that he had the intention to remove the Bosnian Muslims from Srebrenica—in fact, there are many references to that effect (e.g. takeover of Srebrenica 'devised with the intent to permanently remove the Bosnian Muslim population living there', *Karadžić*, IT-95-5/18-T, Judgment, para. 5801)—as a strategic step in his plan to create an ethnically pure Bosnia and Herzegovina.

[748] In fact, an 'inference' is the process of making deductions and reaching conclusions, whereby the 'only reasonable' wording serves as a qualification of that process. Proof (or non-proof) 'is the result—the conclusion to be reached after the inferences have been evaluated' (Anderson, Schum, and Twining, *Analysis of Evidence* (2005), p. 94).

[749] Admittedly, it seems that the TC had that in mind when it stated: 'Where that inference was not the only reasonable inference, it [the Chamber] found that the Prosecution had not proved its case. The Chamber further notes that while it has not always reiterated the phrase "beyond reasonable doubt" in all of its findings, this standard of proof was applied throughout the Judgement': *Karadžić*, IT-95-5/18-T, Judgment, para. 10. But why use the high 'only reasonable inference' threshold for reaching the conclusion that there is a logical relationship between two propositions, i.e. that the evidence mentioned above (proposition one) supports Karadzic's intent to destroy (proposition two) the Bosnian Muslims in Srebrenica, if the ultimate standard of proof applicable is 'beyond reasonable doubt'?

[750] *Zigiranyirazo*, ICTR-01-73-A, para. 49 with n. 136.

In *Bemba et al.*, the AC emphasized the importance of the 'only reasonable conclusion approach':

> If there is another conclusion reasonably open from the evidence, and which is consistent with the innocence of the accused, he or she must be acquitted. For alleged errors of fact in relation to factual findings that were based on inferences drawn from circumstantial evidence, the Appeals Chamber will therefore, in keeping with the standard of review for factual errors, consider whether no reasonable trier of fact could have concluded that the inference drawn was the only reasonable conclusion that could be drawn from the evidence.[751]

At any rate, more recent practice has confirmed the 'only reasonable inference' test[752] although a large quantity of circumstantial evidence in connection with its 'holistic assessment'[753] may flexibilize the test.[754] After all, there is still judicial discretion as to which of the possible reasonable inferences is the 'only reasonable one'.

Also, indirect evidence may prove a fact (directly) in accumulated or combined form (successive or cumulative indicia).[755]

However, a certain organizational responsibility or status alone does not suffice to infer from it concrete criminal responsibility of the respective superior or commander. Otherwise the—at least normatively—overcome doctrine of organizational or membership responsibility[756] would be reintroduced and evidence gathering substituted by official status or position.[757] An 'overall evaluation' of all circumstantial evidence for and against the defendant is necessary before a guilty verdict can be pronounced.[758]

751 *Bemba et al.*, ICC-01/05-01/13-2275-Red, para. 868.

752 See, in particular, Rule 140 (3) RPE KSC explicitly providing that the 'beyond reasonable doubt' standard re circumstantial evidence 'is only satisfied if the inference from that evidence is the only reasonable one that could be drawn from the evidence presented'; cited in KSC, *Prosecutor v. Gucati and Haradinaj*, TP II, Judgment, KSC-BC-2020-07/F00611/RED, 18 May 2022, para. 37 and KSC, *Prosecutor v. Mustafa*, TP I, Judgment, KSC-BC-2020-05/F00494/RED2/COR, 16 December 2022, para. 29; on both cases, Meisenberg, *ZfIStW*, 3 (2024), 11, 12–13. From (other) case law, see *Bemba et al.*, ICC-01/05-01/13-2275-Red, para. 868 (stressing that 'merely *a* reasonable conclusion' [emphasis added] does not suffice); *Bemba*, ICC-01/05-01/08-3343, para. 192 (regarding 'proof of an accused's state of mind'); conc. ICC, *Prosecutor v. Bemba*, AC, Dissenting Opinions Mmasenono and Hofmanski, ICC-01/05-01/08-3636-Anx1-Red, 8 June 2016, para. 268-9; STL, *Prosecutor v. Merhi and Oneissi*, AC, Judgment, STL-11-01/A-2/AC, 10 March 2022, paras. 48, 55, 95 (only reasonable inference or conclusion from all evidence); see also implicitly *Ntaganda*, ICC 01/04-02/06-2666-Red, para. 939 (concluding co-perpetration from certain findings by inference 'reasonable' since defence did 'not set out any alternative conclusion'); see also HRC, *Myanmar Report* (2018), paras. 1434 ff. (excluding other reasonable inferences). But note that the only reasonable inference test is not applicable if the accused makes an inference based on circumstantial evidence since s/he does not bear the burden of proof, cf. *Zigiranyirazo*, ICTR-01-73-A, para. 49.

753 See e.g. *Lubanga*, ICC-01/04-01/06-3121-Red, para. 22 ('holistic evaluation and weighing of *all the evidence taken together* in relation to the fact at issue', emphasis in original). See also Section A.(1)(a) in this chapter with further references in note 83.

754 cf. implicitly Renno, in Ruiz Fabri, *MPEiPro* (2020), mn. 40.

755 May and Wierda, in May et al., *Essays on ICTY* (2001), p. 256.

756 cf. Ambos, *Treatise ICL I* (2021), pp. 170, 248.

757 Crit. with regard to ICTS, SCSL, and SPSC, Combs, *Fact-Finding* (2010), pp. 8–9, 239–54, arguing that guilt was often not determined on the basis of facts but inferred from the official position or affiliation of the defendant, in fact adopting the membership liability approach of IMT and IMTFE; however, Combs herself later advocates the use of the same or structurally equal doctrines of collective criminality (like JCE), in light of suboptimal evidence, 'to create a better fit between the evidence … received and the convictions … entered' (321 ff.) and concludes that 'in many cases inferences drawn from official position create such a compelling picture of criminal liability as to easily satisfy the beyond-a-reasonable-doubt standard' (334 and 335–9).

758 cf. Kahn et al., *International Criminal Courts* (2003), § 9 mn. 17 b (no longer contained in new edition); Zahar and Sluiter, *ICL* (2008), pp. 417 ff. See also ICTY, *Prosecutor v. Kordić and Čerkez*, TC, Judgment, IT-95-14/2-T, 26 February 2001, paras. 828–31.

### (7) Documentation ('record of proceedings')

The Registry[759] is to maintain 'a full and accurate record of all proceedings before the Pre-Trial Chamber'.[760] This record should not only contain all evidence communicated to the PTC, but also written submissions of parties and participants, orders and decisions of the Presidency and Chambers, and other important documents and information.[761] It is controversial whether all evidence must be taken into the record[762] or only the one the parties want to rely on in the confirmation hearing (i.e. as far as the Prosecutor is concerned, the incriminating evidence).[763] The former view is supported by Rule 121 (2)(c) RPE ICC according to which 'all evidence disclosed ... shall be communicated to the Pre-Trial Chamber'.[764] The latter view finds support in Reg. 52 (2) RegR, according to which participants shall submit to the Registry 'the evidence they intend to use at the hearing'.[765] Yet, the RegR provide only an internal regulatory framework for the Registry without an explicit statutory basis[766] and are overruled by the RPE that are applicable law *qua* Article 51 ICCS. For a while both approaches existed at the Court[767] and all evidence included in the record had remained there until the end of the trial;[768] the former approach as proposed by the *Bemba* PTC seems to have become the established practice now.[769] This is also reflected in the current version of the *Practice Manual*.[770] Also, evidence that forms the basis of the Chamber's decision must have been 'submitted and discussed before it at the trial',[771] that is, it must have become part of the trial record.[772]

[759] On the Registry's role in trials before the ICC, see Lachowska, in Doria, Gasser, and Bassiouni, *Legal Regime* (2009), pp. 396 ff.; Dubuisson, Bertrand, and Schauder, in Stahn and Sluiter, *ICC* (2009), pp. 566 ff.; Tuinstra, *Defence Counsel in ICL* (2009), p. 130 incl. further references.

[760] cf. Rules 121 (10), 131 (1) RPE ICC. See also Nerlich, *JICJ, 10* (2012), 1352; Safferling, *International Criminal Procedure* (2012), p. 375; Bitti, 'Article 64', in Ambos, *Commentary* (2022), mn. 20. On the question of whether the record of proceedings can take on the role of a case file, see Heinze, *Disclosure* (2014), pp. 265 ff., 510 ff. and Section B.(1)(c) in this chapter.

[761] cf. Rule 15 (1) RPE ICC ('particulars of each case'); Reg. 21 RegR (referring in addition, inter alia, to a list of witnesses and victims and official translations).

[762] ICC, *Prosecutor v. Bemba*, Decision on the Evidence Disclosure System and Setting a Timetable for Disclosure between the Parties, ICC-01/05-01/08-55, 31 July 2008, para. 55.

[763] ICC, *Prosecutor v. Lubanga*, PTC I, Decision on the Final System of Disclosure and the Establishment of a Timetable, ICC-01/04-01/06-102, 15 May 2006, paras. 41, 50 ff.

[764] In more detail, Orie, in Cassese et al., *Rome Statute II* (2002), p. 1484; Ambos, in Bohlander, *ICJ* (2007), p. 473; Heinze, *Disclosure* (2014), p. 528; Kuczyńska, *Accusation Model* (2015), pp. 236–7; Bitti, 'Article 64', in Ambos, *Commentary* (2022), mn. 20.

[765] Also in favour of this approach, Re, in Agirre et al., *Quality Control* (2020), pp. 782 ff. ('most rational interpretation'; 'far more consistent with Article 67(2)').

[766] The RegR are based on Rule 14 RPE ICC and shall deal with the 'organization and management of the Registry'; in contrast, Art. 52 ICCS refers to the RegC which therefore have a higher rank than the RegR.

[767] For a detailed presentation of the two positions in the case law with relevant references, see Schabas, Chaitidou, and El Zeidy, 'Article 61', in Ambos, *Commentary* (2022), mn. 77-84; see also Heinze, *Disclosure* (2014), pp. 34 ff. For a contextual interpretation of Rule 121 (2)(c) and its drafting history, see *Bemba*, ICC-01/05-01/08-55, paras. 43–4. See also Bourguiba, 'Article 61', in Fernandez et al., *Commentaire CP II* (2019) p. 1689.

[768] Once a piece of evidence is introduced in the case record, it is not removed again. This follows from Rule 15 RPE ICC and the whole idea of a case record.

[769] Schabas, Chaitidou, and El Zeidy, 'Article 61', in Ambos, *Commentary* (2022), mn. 81.

[770] ICC, *Practice Manual* (2023), para. 26 ('According to Rule 121(2)(c) of the Rules, all evidence disclosed between the parties "for the purposes of the confirmation hearing" is communicated to the Pre-Trial Chamber. This should be understood as encompassing all evidence disclosed between the parties during the pre trial proceedings, i.e. between the person's initial appearance (or, in particular circumstances, even before) and the issuance of the confirmation decision'). Crit. Re, in Agirre et al., *Quality Control* (2020), pp. 783–4.

[771] Art. 74 (2) last sentence ICCS.

[772] *Lubanga*, ICC-01/04-01/06-2842, para. 98 ('through the assignment of an evidence number'); *Katanga*, ICC-01/04-01/07-3436-tENG, para. 78.

From a common law perspective, the mere existence of such a record (even though it will probably not be as extensive as the French *dossier*,[773] the Spanish *expediente*, or the German *Akte*)[774] is seen as alarming,[775] as it entails the risk that the TC will base its verdict (only) upon this record, instead of reaching a decision—pursuant to Article 74 (2) ICCS—based upon the evidence presented immediately and orally before the Chamber.[776] On the other hand, the experience with such a record in modern (reformed) inquisitorial systems shows that judges will have to discuss, anyway, any piece of evidence they want to rely on in open court and with the parties. In other words, judges need to have access to all evidence and cannot depend on the submission by the parties in that regard.[777] Consequently, recourse to the record does not undermine the principles of immediacy and orality if it is only used as a reference tool or for background information and anything with evidentiary relevance is discussed in open court.[778] Also, the practical use of such a record, in particular in systematizing the background information on a particular case, cannot be overstated.[779] Last but not least, access to the record also makes it easier for the defence to prepare 'its case'.[780]

The record is sent—with the confirmation decision—by the PTC to the Presidency,[781] which then passes it on to the TC once it is constituted.[782] Arguably, recent developments turn the record of the proceedings from a conceptual perspective into a case file:[783] in the *Yekatom* case, PTC II rejected a request by the defence to 'not include any ex parte evidentiary

[773] This term was deliberately avoided by the drafters; cf. Kreß, *JICJ*, 1 (2003), 605. Heinsch even considers the term 'record of the proceedings' to be problematic (Heinsch, in Stahn and Sluiter, *ICC* (2009), p. 490).

[774] cf. Orie, in Cassese et al., *Rome Statute II* (2002), p. 1485 (on the ICTY records at pp. 1470–1); on the *dossier* in a procedural context, see De Smet, in Stahn and Sluiter, *ICC* (2009), pp. 412 ff.; on its functions, see De Smet, ibid., pp. 421, 434 ff.; Damaška, *Faces of Justice* (1986), p. 50; Langer, *AJCompL*, 53 (2005), 847; Heinze, *Disclosure* (2014), pp. 264 ff., 513 ff. (identifying three constituent components of the *dossier*: knowledge, structure, and probative value); Kuczyńska, *Accusation Model* (2015), pp. 186 ff.; in favour of a dossier, Schuon, *International Criminal Procedure* (2010), p. 266; considering the (electronic) case record as 'functionally equivalent', Kuczyńska, *Accusation Model ICC* (2015), p. 327.

[775] On the debate during the negotations on the ICC, see Brady, in Fischer et al., *Prosecution* (2001), p. 270; see also Whiting, in Stahn, *Practice* (2015), pp. 1017–18.

[776] Keen, *LJIL*, 17 (2004), 807. On the differences between civil law and common law concerning this question, see Brady, in Lee, *ICC* (2001), pp. 424 ff.; Lewis, in Lee, *ICC* (2001), p. 540; Tochilovsky, in Fischer et al., *Prosecution* (2001), p. 634; Fairlie, *ICLR*, 4 (2004), 278–9; representatively on the concerns from a common law perspective, Freedman, *ChapmanLR*, 1 (1998), 77; see also Trendafilova, in Stahn and Sluiter, *ICC* (2009), p. 442 (acknowledging the advantages of such a case file approach but at the same time pointing out that 'the dossier approach to disclosure in ICC proceedings is absent any basis in the statutory documents').

[777] In the same vein, Heinze, *Disclosure* (2014), pp. 512 ff.; Kuczyńska, *Accusation Model* (2015), pp. 236–7.

[778] See also Heinze, *Disclosure* (2014), pp. 520 ff.; for a nuanced view, see also Kreß and Wannek, in Kirsch, *Internationale Strafgerichtshöfe* (2005), pp. 252–3.

[779] From the OTP perspective, cf. Nice and Vallières-Roland, *JICJ*, 3 (2005), 358 ff.; Nice and Vallières-Roland, in Abtahi and Boas, *Dynamics of ICJ* (2006), pp. 147 ff.; from a practical perspective, Jackson and M'Boge, *LJIL*, 26 (2013), 966–7; Jackson, in Jackson, Langer, and Tillers, *Crime, Procedure and Evidence* (2008), p. 241, arguing that it increases the effectiveness of witness questioning by the judge. Even in the US, there are calls to render pretrial proceedings more effective by obliging the prosecution to disclose its complete investigation file, see Brown, *CalLR*, 93 (2005) 1636–8 ('a full account of the investigation').

[780] cf. Kirsch, *StV*, 23 (2003), 640; see, regarding the disclosure of the prosecutorial investigation file to the judges in the US, Capra, *FordhamLR*, 53 (1984–1985), 427–8 (arguing that the 'access to exculpatory evidence ... can actually be useful in presenting a meaningful defense' 'because the defendant will receive evidence determined to be favorable by an unbiased, independent adjudicator.'); Brown, *CalLR*, 93 (2005) 1637.

[781] Rule 129 cl. 2 RPE ICC.

[782] cf. Rule 130 cl. 1 RPE ICC; also Heinze, *Disclosure* (2014), pp. 245, 265–6. On the 'case file' within the context of the trial before the ECCC, see Internal Rules 69, 86, 87 (3), and Gibson and Rudy, *JICJ*, 7 (2009), 1010–11; see also ICC, *Practice Manual* (2023), paras. 69–71; on the (similar) practice of the ad hoc tribunals, see e.g. ICTR, *Prosecutor v. Akayesu*, TC, Decision by the Tribunal on its Request to the Prosecutor to Submit the Written Witness Statements, ICTR-96-4-T, 28 January 1997.

[783] In fact, the defence in *Ongwen* expressly called it 'case file', see ICC, *Prosecutor v. Ongwen*, Defence, Public Redacted Version of 'Corrected Version of "Defence Closing Brief", filed on 24 February 2020', ICC-02/04-01/15-1722-Corr-Red, 13 March 2020, para. 98.

material in the record of the proceedings when it transmits that record to the Presidency'.[784] The Chamber noted inter alia that Rule 129 ICC RPE 'unequivocally points to the transmission of the record *in its entirety* and rules out that any discretion may be vested in the Chamber for the purposes of reducing, amending or otherwise intervening on the content of the record'.[785] This, combined with the submission approach mentioned above,[786] means that the record of the proceedings largely contains material that is treated as evidence by the mere means of submission (as opposed to admission) which fulfils the weight component of a case file and has a considerable impact on the disclosure regime.[787] The *Ongwen* TC confirmed that the record of the proceedings contains material with the ensuing informations 'as to their relevance to the facts of the case and their probative value'.[788]

The TC has full access to the record but its concrete use ultimately depends on each judge and her approach to the proceedings: if she really wants to direct the conduct of the proceedings—as permitted by Article 64 (8) (b) ICCS—then she will have to make herself thoroughly familiar with all the (relevant) information contained in the record;[789] if, in contrast, she prefers to leave, following the adversial mode, the unfolding of the trial largely in the hands of the parties, a detailed knowledge of all the information contained in the record is dispensable.

### (8) Inadmissibility (exclusion) of evidence due to rights violations

As already pointed out at the beginning of this chapter, the fairness or rights test is the second step to be passed to finally admit otherwise admissible evidence. In the words of the *Bagosora et al.* AC the question in this regard is whether the 'prejudicial effect' of 'otherwise relevant and probative evidence' 'will adversely affect the fairness or expeditiousness of the proceedings'.[790] The *Lubanga* TC similarly stressed that it must 'ensure that it is not unfair to admit' evidentiary material.[791] More specifically, Article 69 (7) ICCS—being *lex specialis*[792]—focuses on the impact of the violation on the reliability of the evidence and

[784] *Prosecutor v. Yekatom and Ngaïssona*, TC V, Decision on Yekatom Defence Request not to Include Ex Parte Evidentiary Material in the Record of the Proceedings, ICC-01/14-01/18-463, 24 March 2020, para. 1.

[785] ICC, *Prosecutor v. Yekatom and Ngaïssona*, PTC II, Decision on the Prosecutor's Request for Reconsideration or, in the Alternative, Leave to Appeal the 'Decision on the Confirmation of Charges against Alfred Yekatom and Patrice-Edouard Ngaïssona', ICC-01/14-01/18-447, 11 March 2020, para. 38 (emphasis added); further, ICC, *Prosecutor v. Yekatom and Ngaïssona*, Presidency, Decision Constituting Trial Chamber V and referring to it the Case of The Prosecutor v. Alfred Yekatom and Patrice-Edouard Ngaïssona, ICC-01/14-01/18-451, 16 March 2020, para. 5; in detail, Heinze, *Opinio Juris* (25 June 2020).

[786] See Section A.(1)(a).

[787] See also Heinze, in Ruiz Fabri, *MPEIPro* (2020), mn. 8 *in fine*.

[788] *Ongwen*, ICC-02/04-01/15-1762-Red, 4, para. 245.

[789] cf. ICTY, *Prosecutor v. Dokmanović*, TC, Order, IT-95-13a-PT, 28 November 1997 and ICTY, *Prosecutor v. Dokmanović*, TC, Corrigendum to Order Dated 28 November 1997, IT-95-13a-PT, 15 January 1998; Heinsch, in Stahn and Sluiter, *ICC* (2009), p 488; Damaška, *AJCL*, 45 (1997), 851.

[790] ICTR, *Prosecutor v. Bagosora et al.*, AC, Decision on Prosecutor's Interlocutory Appeals Regarding Exclusion of Evidence, ICTR-98-41-AR93 & ICTR-98-41-AR93.2, 19 December 2003, para. 16 ('Trial Chamber may . . . exclude otherwise relevant and probative evidence where its prejudicial effect will adversely affect the fairness or expeditiousness of the proceedings').

[791] *Lubanga*, ICC-01/04-01/06-1399, para. 31.

[792] See previously Ambos, *IsLR*, 42 (2009), 375; also *Lubanga*, ICC-01/04-01/06-1981, para. 34 (quoting the German version of my article in n. 66); *Katanga*, ICC-01/04-01/07-2635, para. 39 (*lex specialis* as compared to Art. 69 (4) ICCS); ICC, *Prosecutor v. Al Hassan*, TC X, Public Redacted Version of 'Decision on requests related to the submission into evidence of Mr Al Hassan's statements', ICC-01/12-01/18-1475-Red, 20 May 2021, para. 30 ('Article 69(7) of the Statute is *lex specialis* when compared with the general admissibility provisions set out

the general integrity of the proceedings. We will return to this provision in the second subsection below. First, some conceptual groundwork is needed.

### (a) *Conceptual foundations: Exclusionary rules versus prohibitions of use*

We already referred at the beginning of this chapter to the apparent difference between exclusionary rules and the mere inadmissibility of tainted evidence. This difference is another divide between adversarial and inquisitorial systems with the former, generally speaking, applying exclusionary rules, that is, prohibiting the introduction of the tainted evidence in the first place,[793] and the latter[794] merely prohibiting its use.[795] In other words, while exclusionary rules prevent any contact between the adjudicatory authority (in particular a jury[796]) and the tainted evidence,[797] mere prohibitions of use allow for this contact but it is assumed or expected that the adjudicatory authority will not be influenced by the respective evidence anyway. It must not be overlooked, however, that this difference in the methodological approach to deal with unlawful evidence does not predetermine the substantive outcome as to the admission or non-admission of this evidence. On the contrary, the comparative picture is somewhat mixed, showing rather liberal or rather strict admission regimes in both common and civil law jurisdictions.[798]

At first sight, the exclusionary approach is taken by the ad hoc tribunals,[799] where a Chamber 'may *exclude* evidence if its probative value is substantially outweighed by the need to ensure a fair trial'[800] or 'if obtained by methods which cast substantial doubt on its

elsewhere in the Statute'). See also Heinze, in Bergsmo and Dittrich, *Integrity* (2020), pp. 615, 704; Pitcher, *Judicial Responses* (2018), p. 324.

[793] See the classic definition in Burkoff, in Kadish, *Encyclopedia of Crime and Justice II* (1983), p. 715: 'a rule that generally operates to exclude from admission at a criminal trial evidence obtained as a result of unlawful activity'.

[794] In international criminal justice the perhaps most 'inquisitorial' approach has been adopted by the ECCC where, pursuant to (Internal) Rule 87 (1) and (2) RPE ECCC, all evidence is first admitted and subsequently (only) its use 'rejected' in case of serious fairness violations.

[795] On the distinction, see Ambos, *Beweisverwertungsverbote* (2010), pp. 19 with n. 16, 129 ff.; from an international perspective, see May and Wierda, *ColJTransnat'lL*, 37 (1999), 745; Robinson, *EJIL*, 11 (2000), 579; Piragoff, in Lee, *ICC* (2001), pp. 351–4; Defrancia, *VirginiaLRev*, 87 (2001), 1397–8, 1402; Rodrigues and Tournaye, in May et al., *Essays on ICTY* (2001), pp. 295 ff.; Fidalgo Gallardo, *Las 'pruebas ilegales'* (2003), pp. 49 ff.; Caianiello, in Delmas-Marty, Fronza, and Lambert-Abdelgawad, *Droit international pénal* (2004), pp. 347–8; Hofstetter, *Verfahrensrecht* (2005), pp. 104 ff., 109 ff.; Zahar and Sluiter, *ICL* (2008), pp. 379–80; Gibson and Rudy, *JICJ*, 7 (2009), 1010; Sluiter, in Stahn and van den Herik, *Future Perspectives* (2010), p. 595; Heinze, in Bergsmo and Dittrich, *Integrity* (2020), pp. 615–738, 618. About the semantic difference between those two in more detail, albeit misleadingly described as 'linguistics', Giannoulopoulos, *Improperly Obtained Evidence* (2019), pp. 6–7.

[796] While historically, the existence of the jury may have had an impact on the development of exclusionary rules (Wang, *IJEP*, 24 (2020), 329, 331 ff. with further references) conceptually the two are independent, see Schauer, in Dahlman, Stein, and Tuzet, *Evidence Law* (2021), pp. 75 ff.; Heinze, in Caeiro, Gless, and Mitsilegas, *Elgar Encyclopedia* (2022) with further references.

[797] Deciding on admissibility in a 'trial within a trial' (*voir dire* procedure) without the participation of the jury, cf. Klamberg, in Sluiter et al., *International Criminal Procedure* (2013), p. 1030.

[798] Take e.g. Italy, with the prohibition on use of any illegally obtained evidence (Art. 191 CPP [*Prove illegittimamente acquisite*]), Germany with the flexible balancing doctrine (*Abwägungslehre*) and England with the focus on the relevance of the evidence, cf. Ambos, *Beweisverwertungsverbote* (2010), pp. 22, 43 with further references; Klamberg, in Sluiter et al., *International Criminal Procedure* (2013), p. 1040.

[799] *Contra* Safferling, *International Criminal Procedure* (2012), p. 495 (but without further analysis). No exclusionary rules existed at the IMT and IMTFE, cf. Klamberg, in Sluiter et al., *International Criminal Procedure* (2013), p. 1032; Piragoff and Clarke, 'Article 69', in Ambos, *Commentary* (2022), mn. 12–13. On the hybrid tribunals (SPSC, ECCC, STL), see Klamberg, in Sluiter et al., *International Criminal Procedure* (2013), p. 1036; Fallah, in Ruiz Fabri, *MPEIPro* (2020), mn. 11 ff.

[800] Rules 89 (D) RPE ICTY and 105 (D) RPE MICT (emphasis added); but there is no such provision in RPE ICTY and SCSL. See also *Stanišić and Simatović*, MICT-15-96-A, para. 590; Heinze, in Bergsmo and Dittrich, *Integrity* (2020), 615–738, 698.

reliability or if its admission is antithetical to, and would seriously damage, the integrity of the proceedings.'[801] Interestingly, the term 'exclusion' is used in the second provision only in its title,[802] but in the actual text the Rule speaks of 'admissible' or 'admission'. This, in turn, is the term used by the ICCS (evidence obtained by rights violations shall, as a rule, not be 'admissible'[803]) and the RPE KSC (Rule 138 (2): 'shall be inadmissible').

It is unclear whether these terms—exclusion and (in)admissibility—really have a different meaning. The French versions of the relevant sources speak of 'irrecevabilité'[804] and 'admissibilité',[805] with Rule 95 RPE ICTR putting 'irrecevabilité' and admissibility on an equal footing since the term 'recevable' is used for the English 'admissible'.[806] In addition, Rule 64 (3) RPE ICC provides that 'irrelevant or inadmissible' evidence 'shall not be *considered* by the Chamber'.[807] In other words, inadmissibility entails non-consideration of the respective evidence, that is, its exclusion from the trial record. Finally, given that Article 69 (7) ICCS is a copy of Rule 95 RPE ICTY/ICTR it makes little sense to assume that these identical provisions should produce different results.

Thus, in sum, it can safely be concluded that both at the tribunals and at the Court inadmissibility of evidence means that this evidence cannot be taken into account ('considered') although the Judges may come into contact with it.[808] In light of this result it is more important whether the Chamber is obliged to 'exclude' ('not consider') the evidence ('shall')[809] or whether this is within its discretion ('may').[810] Yet, even in the former case, exclusion is not automatic[811] but depends on specific requirements to be analysed more closely below.

### *(b) The substantive (two-step) test: Nature of violation and impact*

Apart from this conceptual issue, the substantive reasons not to consider evidence are basically the same: fair trial considerations,[812] use of illicit methods which negatively affect the reliability of the evidence[813] or which are of such gravity to be 'antithetical to, and would seriously damage, the integrity of the proceedings'.[814] The burden to show that these criteria

[801] Rules 95 RPE ICTY/ICTR and 117 RPE MICT; also Rule 95 RPE SCSL (exclusion if 'admission would bring the administration of justice into serious disrepute'). See also *Bagosora et al.*, ICTR-98-41-AR93 & ICTR-98-41-AR93.2, as quoted in note 790 in this chapter; *Stanišić and Simatović*, MICT-15-96-A, para. 590; Heinze, in Bergsmo and Dittrich, *Integrity* (2020), p. 698; Fallah, in Ruiz Fabri, *MPEIPro* (2020), mn. 12.

[802] Rules 95 RPE ICTY/ICTR/SCSL and 117 RPE MICT all refer in their titles to 'exclusion of [certain] evidence'.

[803] Art. 69 (7) ICCS. Also, Art. 69 (4) ICCS speaks of 'admissibility' in relation to possible fair trial violations.

[804] cf. Rule 95 RPE ICTR French version.

[805] Art. 69 (4) ICCS, French version; also Art. 69 (7) ICCS: 'admissibles', 'admission'.

[806] cf. English and French versions of Rule 95 RPE ICTR.

[807] Emphasis added.

[808] In favour of strict adherence to 'exclusionary' Rule 95, Safferling, *YbIHL*, 5 (2002), 242–3; see also Nemitz, in Kirsch, *Internationale Strafgerichtshöfe* (2005), p. 70; crit. Fairlie, *ICLR*, 4 (2004), 283 ff.; O'Sullivan and Montgomery, *JICJ*, 8 (2010), 514; on a corresponding defence, see Zahar and Sluiter, *ICL* (2008), pp. 407 ff.; treating all rules equally as exclusionary rules, Friman, in Cryer et al., *ICL* (2019), p. 434.

[809] cf. e.g. Rules 95 RPE ICTY, 117 RPE MICT, 138 (2) RPE KSC and Art. 69 (7) ICCS.

[810] cf. e.g. Rules 89 (D) RPE ICTY and 105 (D) RPE MICT, and Art. 69 (4) ICCS. In favour of 'mandatory exclusion', Zahar and Sluiter, *ICL* (2008), pp. 380–2.

[811] See, in this regard, e.g. *Ruto and Sang*, ICC-01/09-01/11-1353, paras. 24, 37 (no automatic exclusion of documentary evidence but according to general principles and case by case).

[812] Rules 89 (D) RPE ICTY and 105 (D) RPE MICT; Art. 69 (4) ICCS.

[813] Rules 95 alternative 1 RPE ICTY/ICTR and 117 alternative 1 RPE MICT; Rule 138 (2)(a) RPE KSC; Art. 69 (7)(a) ICCS.

[814] Rules 95 alternative 2 RPE ICTY/ICTR and 117 alternative 2 RPE MICT; Rule 138 (2)(b) RPE KSC; Art. 69 (7)(b) ICCS; also Rule 95 RPE SCSL (exclusion if 'admission would bring the administration of justice into serious disrepute'). See also ICC, *Prosecutor v. Al Hassan*, TC X, Public redacted version of 'Decision on requests related to the submission into evidence of Mr Al Hassan's statements', ICC-01/12-01/18-1475-Red, 20 May 2021, para. 32, highlighting the rationales 'to avoid reliance on unreliable evidence; and to preserve the integrity of the

have been met rests with the party bringing the motion under Article 69 (7) ICCS.[815] The fair trial considerations, usually stressed by the case law,[816] operate here as an interpretative guideline to help to reasonably apply the more concrete exclusionary rules.[817]

The focus lies on the *means* used to obtain the evidence, the *nature* of a possible rights violation, and its *impact* (effect) on the proceedings.[818] This represents the individual and collective dimension of exclusionary rules, the former referring to the *violation* of the individual's fair trial and/or human rights, the latter focusing on the *impact* of the rights violation on the integrity of the proceedings and the administration of justice.[819] These dimensions, being expressions of procedural justice,[820] have to be counterbalanced against considerations of material justice, that is, the realization of the *ius puniendi* by the investigation, prosecution, and adjudication of international crimes and their perpetrators.[821] There is a tension between these two forms of justice since the more evidence is excluded, the more difficult it is to bring the proceedings to a successful end and achieve some form of truth (assuming, of course, that the evidence excluded is not always irrelevant or unreliable evidence). Thus, contrary to the *Lubanga* TC,[822] the probative value of a piece of evidence (which may have been obtained illegally) in this regard indeed informs the decision on its admissibility,[823] unless the rights violation is so serious that there is no room for any balancing.

Also, while the application of exclusionary rules does not and cannot, as a matter of principle, depend on the alleged crime(s) committed by the accused,[824] the nature of this

Court's proceedings' and of 'disciplining or deterring irregular or unlawful conduct by law enforcement officials'. For a general overview of the rationale of exclusionary rules, see Heinze, in Bergsmo and Dittrich, *Integrity* (2020), pp. 615, 648 ff. ('Various rationales have been advanced with respect to the question of how to address procedural violations committed in the pre-trial phase of criminal proceedings: the "reliability" rationale, the "disciplinary" rationale, the "protective" (or "remedial") rationale, and the "integrity" rationale(s)'); with regard to the exclusion of illegal material collected by private entities and individuals, see also Heinze, *NCLR*, 24 (2021), 212, 230 ff.

[815] ICC, *Prosecutor v. Al Hassan*, TC X, Public Redacted Version of 'Decision on requests related to the submission into evidence of Mr Al Hassan's statements', ICC-01/12-01/18-1475-Red, 20 May 2021, para. 37.

[816] See the references at the beginning of this section.

[817] This also determines the (unclear) relationship between Art. 69 (4) and (7) ICCS with the former (referring to fairness) being a mere statement of principle in the context of exclusionary rules; leaving the decision to the Court, Piragoff and Clarke, 'Article 69', in Ambos, *Commentary* (2022), mn. 65.

[818] On the *travaux* in this regard, see also Piragoff and Clarke, 'Article 69', in Ambos, *Commentary* (2022), mn. 16–17. Similarly *Katanga*, ICC-01/04-01/07-2635, para. 38 (cause and effect of prejudice).

[819] See previously Ambos, *IsLR*, 42 (2009), 365–6 with further references; Heinze, in Bergsmo and Dittrich, *Integrity* (2020), pp. 649 ff.; Heinze, *NCLR*, 24 (2021) 230 ff.). As rightly argued by *Lubanga*, ICC 01/04-01/06-1981, paras. 45–6, the purpose to discipline or deter non-law-abiding investigatory authorities by means of exclusionary rules, well known from the debate in national law (cf. Ambos, *Beweisverwertungsverbote* (2010), pp. 19–20; Heinze, in Bergsmo and Dittrich, *Integrity* (2020), pp. 649–51), cannot be relevant at an international criminal tribunal lacking, being a 'head without hands' (Chapter VII, A.(1) in this volume), any authority over these national agents in the first place.

[820] Heinze, in Bergsmo and Dittrich, *Integrity* (2020), p. 654.

[821] On these conflicting interests, see also ICTY, *Prosecutor v. M. Nikolić*, AC, Decision on Interlocutory Appeal Concerning Legality of Arrest, IT-94-2-AR73, 5 June 2003, para. 30 (balance between 'rights of the accused' and 'interests of the international community in the prosecution'). In the same vein, Bantekas, *ICL* (2010), p. 527; similarly Klamberg, *Evidence* (2013), pp. 396, 399, 406; Heinze, in Bergsmo and Dittrich, *Integrity* (2020), pp. 651–3.

[822] *Lubanga*, ICC-01/04-01/06-1981, paras. 43, 49 (arguing that probative value cannot inform admissibility and 'arguments directed at' probative value 'are irrelevant' since Art. 69 (7) ICCS, being *lex specialis*, does not provide for that); conc. *Katanga*, ICC-01/04-01/07-2635, para. 64. The argument overlooks that Art. 69 (7) refers to 'reliability' and thus makes probative value part of the equation; it also has been contradicted by the *Lubanga* TC in a later decision, see the following note.

[823] In a similar vein, see *Lubanga*, ICC-01/04-01/06-2662-Conf, para. 16 ('probative value outweighs any prejudicial effect'); see also *Ruto and Sang*, ICC-01/09-01/11-1353, para. 16 (exclusion of prejudicial evidence on a case-by-case basis and 'comparing any identified prejudice against the probative value, including reliability').

[824] *Lubanga*, ICC-01/04-01/06-1981, para. 44; conc. ICC, *Prosecutor v. Bemba et al.*, TC VII, Decision on Kilolo Defence Motion for Inadmissibility of Material, ICC-01/05-01/13-1257, 16 September 2015, para. 8 (application regarding Art. 70 ICCS).

or these crimes indeed informs the above-mentioned interest in the realization of the *ius puniendi*: this interest increases with the gravity of the alleged crimes. By way of example: the commission of a crime of genocide entails a higher interest in the effective realization of the *ius puniendi*—and thus the use of all available evidence to have the broadest possible evidentiary basis for the final verdict—than an offence against the administration of justice.[825] It would have a similar detrimental effect if the decision of excluding crucial evidence was the result of a relatively minor violation of legal procedure. The ICTY AC in *Karadžić* highlighted this imbalance by recalling

> that the Appellant is charged with genocide, crimes against humanity and war crimes. The public interest in the prosecution of an individual accused of such offences, universally condemned, is unquestionably strong. Against the legitimate interest of the international community in the prosecution of the Appellant for Universally Condemned Offences stands the alleged violation of the Appellant's expectation that he would not be prosecuted by the Tribunal, pursuant to the alleged Agreement.[826]

All in all, the decision in favour of or against exclusion of evidence often entails a difficult balancing exercise[827] and there is no 'simple, algorithmic, all-purpose rule'[828] that helps us to take this decision lightly. At any rate, an exclusionary rule only speaks to the non-use of evidence in court, it leaves open the question whether this (unlawfully obtained) evidence may be used for other (investigatory) purposes. Take the example of a statement obtained by torture, relevant in the case against *Ieng Thirith* before the ECCC. The defence requested the co-investigating judges not only to hold this statement inadmissible, but also to decide against its use as 'lead evidence'. With regard to the latter request, of interest in our context, the Judges decided:

> [T]here is nothing objectionable in using the information contained in confessions as investigative leads to other sources of information, even if the information within the confession is ultimately deemed unreliable. A great deal of 'lead evidence' used in investigations is inherently unreliable and as such, would not be relied on in the Closing Order. However, during the course of the investigation, the Co-Investigating Judges need not rule out any hypothesis and it is not necessary for them to believe the assertions in the confessions to be true in order to use them to develop new avenues for searching out the truth, without this affecting the integrity of the proceedings.[829]

[825] Although Art. 69 (7) also applies, of course, to this offence, as just stated in the previous note.

[826] ICTY, *Prosecutor v. Karadžić*, AC, Decision on Karadžić's Appeal of Trial Chamber's Decision on Alleged Holbrooke Agreement, IT-95-5/18-AR73.4, 12 October 2009, para. 49. In a similar vein, KSC, *Prosecutor v. Shala*, CoAP, Decision on Shala's Appeal Against Decision Concerning Prior Statements, KSC-BC-2020-04/IA006/F00007, 5 May 2023, paras. 77 ff., esp. 79 ('That being said, although a violation of the standards of human rights law has been established and therefore the first prong of the test under Rule 138(2) of the Rules has been met, the violation is limited'). See also Pitcher, *Judicial Responses* (2018), p. 277.

[827] This approach is confirmed by the ECtHR case law which is 'flexible' with regard to the admissibility of unlawfully obtained evidence using an 'overall assessment' approach; see Chapter I, D.(4) in this volume. See also Heinze, in Bergsmo and Dittrich, *Integrity* (2020), pp. 615, 655; Heinze, *NCLR*, 24 (2021), 221; Campbell, Ashworth, and Redmayne, *The Criminal Process* (2019), pp. 42 ff.

[828] Roberts, *Evidence* (2022), p. 207.

[829] ECCC, *Prosecutor v. Ieng Thirith*, Office of the Co-Investigating Judges, Order on Use of Statements Which Were or may Have Been Obtained by Torture, C002/19-09-2007-ECCC-OCIJ, 28 July 2009, para. 26.

The concrete decision involves a *two-step test*.[830] First, the evidence must have been obtained by a rights violation—'of this Statute or internationally recognized human rights'[831] (but not necessarily affecting the accused)[832]—which, secondly, must be serious enough[833] to either 'cast substantial doubt' on its reliability or its admission would be 'antithetical to' and 'seriously damage the integrity of the proceedings'.[834] In other words, there must be a rights violation in the first place,[835] but only a serious one can ever have the said effect or impact.[836] In short, there must be a serious violation with the corresponding impact. For this reason the source of the violated right—the Statute[837] or recognized human rights—is of secondary importance; in any case, any violation of a recognized human right within the meaning of Article 21 (3) ICCS[838] triggers the possible exclusionary consequence.

Equally, a violation of national evidence rules by national authorities may be relevant[839] if serious enough. The fact that the Court 'shall not rule on the application of the State's national law'[840] only means that it must not legally assess national law[841] but it does not mean that it can admit without further ado evidence obtained by national authorities by way of serious rights violations.[842] It is not the source of the evidence—national or international authority—which decides its admissibility, but the nature and quality of the violation. A flagrant non-compliance by national authorities with their own law speaks to the seriousness

[830] Similarily Piragoff and Clarke, 'Article 69', in Ambos, *Commentary* (2022), mn. 92 ('dual test' regarding Art. 69 (7)(b) ICCS); *Bemba et al.*, ICC-01/05-01/13-1257, para. 9.

[831] Art. 69 (7) ICCS.

[832] cf. *Lubanga*, ICC-01/04-01/06-1981, para. 37 (correctly arguing that Art. 69 (7) does not contain a limitation to violations of the rights of the accused); in the same vein, Klamberg, *Evidence* (2013), p. 403.

[833] On the ICC drafters' intent to avoid a too broad prohibition, see Piragoff and Clarke, 'Article 69', in Ambos, *Commentary* (2022), mn. 14 ff.; Heinze, in Bergsmo and Dittrich, *Integrity* (2020), pp. 709–10. *Contra Lubanga*, ICC-01/04-01/06-1981, para. 35 (arguing that 'even a non-serious violation' may suffice since only the second limb of Art. 69 (7) ICCS refers to 'seriousness'; but this overlooks the interplay between the chapeau and the two subparas. of para. 7 and the—just mentioned—intent of the drafters).

[834] Rules 95 RPE ICTY/ICTR and 117 RPE MICT; 138 (2)(b) RPE KSC; Art. 69 (7)(a) and (b) ICCS.

[835] See, for a concrete example, *Bemba et al.*, ICC-01/05-01/13-1257, paras. 10–21 (given the crime/fraud exception to the lawyer-client privilege the respective communication may be intercepted lawfully and the obtained material duly separated into privileged and non-privileged ones so that there is no rights violation in the sense of Art. 69 (7) in the first place and the second step of the test need not even be examined). See also KSC, *Prosecutor v. Shala*, CoAP, Decision on Shala's Appeal Against Decision Concerning Prior Statements, KSC-BC-2020-04/IA006/F00007, 5 May 2023, paras. 77 ff., esp. para. 79.

[836] In this vein, see also *Lubanga*, ICC-01/04-01/06-803-tEN, para. 86 ('only a serious human rights violation can lead to the exclusion of evidence').

[837] On the discussion whether violations of the RPE would also be covered, see Piragoff and Clarke, 'Article 69', in Ambos, *Commentary* (2022), mn. 84–5; *contra*, but without discussion, Safferling, *International Criminal Procedure* (2012), p. 500. The issue is of little importance though since, as argued in the main text, all depends on the seriousness of the rights violation.

[838] See also Piragoff and Clarke, 'Article 69', in Ambos, *Commentary* (2022), mn. 87; Klamberg, 'Article 69—Evidence', in Klamberg et al., *Commentary ICC II* (2023), p. 373; Heinze, in Bergsmo and Dittrich, *Integrity* (2020), p. 693. This may include the *right to privacy* as held by *Bemba et al.*, ICC-01/05-01/13-2275-Red, para. 20 ('the internationally recognised right to privacy is not absolute, but may be subject to legitimate interference in accordance with the law, and as necessary for the protection of important public interests. The possibility of legitimate interference with the right to privacy raises the question of the scope of the inquiry the Court should undertake concerning compliance with national laws for the purposes of a determination under Article 69 para. (7) of the Statute.')

[839] In the same vein, Piragoff and Clarke, 'Article 69', in Ambos, *Commentary* (2022), mn. 81 (on the controversial discussion during the negotiations, mn. 19–21); *contra Lubanga*, ICC-01/04-01/06-1981, para. 36, but see note 846 in this chapter and main text.

[840] cf. Art. 69 (8) ICCS, Rule 63 (5) RPE ICC.

[841] cf. Piragoff and Clarke, 'Article 69', in Ambos, *Commentary* (2022), mn. 96–7.

[842] With regard to the relationship between subparas. 7 and 8 in Art. 69, see *Bemba et al.*, ICC-01/05-01/13-2275-Red, para. 340 ff. and Separate Opinion of Judge Geoffrey Henderson, ICC-01/05-01/13-2275-Anx, 8 March 2018, para. 30 ff.

of the violation.[843] The *Lubanga* PTC's and TC's decisions that a house search illegal under Congolese law does not make the collected evidence automatically inadmissible[844]—or similar decisions by the ad hoc tribunals[845]—does not contradict this view for it can be explained by the insufficient seriousness of the violation[846] and the already mentioned balancing test which led in this case to the admission of the evidence.

It is, of course, difficult to determine in the abstract when evidence-gathering methods are so grossly unlawful or unfair as to negatively affect the reliability of the so obtained evidence or to be 'antithetical to' and 'seriously damage the integrity of the proceedings'. There are only a few clear-cut cases, in particular the use of torture to obtain a confession or witness statements,[847] which will have a clear impact on both reliability and integrity and thus automatically entail the exclusion of the respective evidence. In contrast, violations of classic fair trial rights, such as the right to silence[848] or to counsel,[849] do not (necessarily) impact on reliability but may cause inacceptable damage to the integrity of the proceedings.[850] At any rate, it goes too far to see in any violation of the tribunal's or Court's Statute and Rules a sufficiently prejudicial impact on the integrity of the proceedings.[851] In assessing the integrity

[843] In a similar vein, Piragoff and Clarke, 'Article 69', in Ambos, *Commentary* (2022), mn. 97 (non-compliance as 'factual matter ... relevant to the admissibility').

[844] cf. *Lubanga*, ICC-01/04-01/06-803-tEN, paras. 62, 69 and *Lubanga*, ICC-01/04-01/06-1981, paras. 48–50. See thereon Ambos, in Kotsalis, Courakis, and Mylonopoulos, *FS Karras* (2010), p. 985; Schabas, *ICC Commentary* (2016), pp. 1234 ff.; Safferling, *International Criminal Procedure* (2012), pp. 501–2;Klamberg, in Sluiter et al., *International Criminal Procedure* (2013), pp. 1034–5. See also ICC, *Prosecutor v. Katanga and Ngudjolo*, TC II, Decision on the Prosecutor's Bar Table Motions, ICC-01/04-01/07-2635, 17 December 2010, para. 55 ('[T]he violation has to impact on international, as opposed to national, standards on human rights. [...] Therefore, evidence obtained in breach of national procedural laws, even though those rules may implement national standards protecting human rights, does not automatically trigger the application of Article 69(7) of the Statute' [fn. omitted]). Thereto and on the *Lubanga* decision, Heinze, in Bergsmo and Dittrich, *Integrity* (2020), pp. 667, 709.

[845] cf. Boas et al., *Procedure* (2011), pp. 342–3; Safferling, *International Criminal Procedure* (2012), pp. 500–1; Klamberg, in Sluiter et al., *International Criminal Procedure* (2013), pp. 1032–3. For a decision in favour of exclusion despite being a national measure, see also ICTY, *Prosecutor v. Delalić et al.*, TC, Decision on Zdravko Mucic's Motion for the Exclusion of Evidence, IT-96-21-T, 2 September 1997, paras. 43, 52 (Austrian interrogation without counsel); for further references, see Bantekas, *ICL* (2010), p. 526 with n. 318.

[846] In the same vein, ICTY, *Prosecutor v. Brđanin and Talić*, TC II, Decision on the Defence 'Objection to Intercept Evidence', IT-99-36-T, 3 October 2003, paras. 63–7, admitting transcripts of telephone conversations intercepted by national authorities since considering that the violations have been 'minor' ('it would constitute a dangerous obstacle to the administration of justice if evidence which is relevant and of probative value could not be admitted merely because of a minor breach of procedural rules which the Trial Chamber is not bound to apply'); also *Lubanga*, ICC-01/04-01/06-1981, paras. 47–8 (ultimately focusing—in line with Art. 69 (7) ICCS—on the impact of the integrity of the proceedings and the reliability of the respective evidence).

[847] cf. Ambos, *IsLR*, 42 (2009), 369–77, arguing that the use of torture casts serious doubts on the reliabiliy of the evidence and is so grossly inhuman that it seriously damages the integrity of the proceedings, also if the respective evidence is so obtained by third parties. For the same result, see Safferling, *International Criminal Procedure* (2012), p. 500; Klamberg, in Sluiter et al., *International Criminal Procedure* (2013), p. 1034 (duress in interrogation affecting reliability); Klamberg, *Evidence* (2013), p. 402 (following my view); Piragoff and Clarke, 'Article 69', in Ambos, *Commentary* (2022), mn. 93; in a similar vein, Ernst, *Torture Evidence* (2015), pp. 91–7 (unreliability of torture evidence), 97–101 (unfairness of proceedings), 113–19 (also when obtained by third parties) 188, but differentiating at pp. 107–13, 188 with regard to exculpatory torture evidence. From a philosophical perspective: Ho, *MLR*, 84 (2021), 30 ff.

[848] See in this regard *Katanga*, ICC-01/04-01/07-2635, paras. 63, 65 (statement obtained violating right to silence and privilege against self-incrimination cannot be admitted into evidence).

[849] See e.g. *Delalić et al.*, IT-96-21-T, Exclusion of Evidence Decision, para. 43; ICTR, *Prosecutor v. Karemera et al.*, TC III, Decision on the Prosecution Motion for Admission into Evidence of Post-Arrest Interviews with Joseph Nzirorera and Mathieu Ngirumpatse, ICTR-98-44-T, 2 November 2007, paras. 23–32 (both regarding exclusion for violation of right to counsel).

[850] For the same view regarding the right to counsel, see Safferling, *International Criminal Procedure* (2012), p. 503. For the impact of fair trial violations as 'specific forms of prejudice', see *Katanga*, ICC-01/04-01/07-2635, paras. 40 ff.

[851] Sluiter, *International Criminal Adjudication* (2002), p. 225.

of the proceedings threshold, Chambers at the ICC have considered the following elements: '(i) the nature and gravity of the violation; (ii) whether the rights violated related to the accused; and (iii) the Prosecution's degree of control over the evidence gathering process or power to prevent the improper or illegal activity.'[852] This also means that the violation of the rights of a third party, for instance through the use of artificial intelligence tools that violate the right to privacy of another person, does not meet the criteria of Article 69 (7) ICCS.[853]

Whether exclusionary rules apply to private individuals or entities (e.g. investigatory commissions) is controversial given that, in principle, private individuals/entities are not addressed by criminal procedure rules.[854] At any rate, given the importance of the evidence collected by these actors, e.g. the Syria CIJA, their material should be admitted if their work meets international standards.[855] Thus, exclusionary rules should be applied to privately acquired evidence on the basis of a holistic approach according to which this evidence forms part and is an integral element of the (official) proceedings as a whole.[856] On that basis it can be argued that exclusionary rules (withing the meaning of Article 69 (7) ICCS) do also address private investigators and thus must be respected by them.[857] This is also supported by the rationale of exclusionary rules,[858] namely the safeguarding of the integrity of (international) criminal proceedings as such; this rationale would be undermined if private investigators were not bound by these rules.[859]

It is particularly difficult to determine when the use of certain evidence is so prejudicial to the accused that it amounts to a sufficiently serious fair trial violation triggering the exclusion of the evidence. The *Lubanga* PTC observed that 'evidence of slight or minimal probative value has the capacity to prejudice the Chamber's fair assessment of the issues in the case' and thus should not be admitted in the first place.[860] The *Bemba* TC reserved itself the right to determine at the end of the trial 'whether the probative value of the evidence is outweighed by its prejudicial effect.'[861] This statement shows that the prejudicial effect also

[852] ICC, *Prosecutor v. Al Hassan*, TC X, Public Redacted Version of 'Decision on requests related to the submission into evidence of Mr Al Hassan's statements', ICC-01/12-01/18-1475-Red, 20 May 2021, para. 34. See also *Prosecutor v. Bemba et al.*, TC VII, Decision on Requests to Exclude Western Union Documents and Other Evidence pursuant to Article 69 (7), ICC-01/05-01/13-1854, 29 April 2016, paras. 65, 68-9; *Prosecutor v. Bemba et al.*, TC VII, Decision on Request in Response to Two Austrian Decisions, ICC-01/05-01/13-1948, 14 July 2016, paras. 33, 36–7, 39.

[853] In favour of including third party rights: McIntyre and Vialle, *Opinio Juris* 11 October 2023.

[854] For an application to private individuals or entities focusing on the 'investigatory context', Heinze, in Bergsmo and Dittrich, *Integrity* (2020), p. 663 ff.; Heinze, *NCLR*, 24 (2021), 214 ff. (basically arguing that the application of exclusionary rules to an 'extra-investigatory context' is required by the principle of integrity and, more broadly, the rule of law, partially relying on Ambos, *IsLR*, 42 (2009), 366).

[855] Rankin, *Global Resp. Protect*, 9 (2017), 403; Heinze, in Bergsmo and Dittrich, *Integrity* (2020), p. 733.

[856] Heinze, *NCLR*, 24 (2021), 222–30, see also Heinze, in Bergsmo and Dittrich, *Integrity* (2020), p. 640 (rightly pointing out that '[t]he question is thus how evidence that was obtained by private individuals who, in whatever form acted illegally or unethically, is and should be treated').

[857] Heinze, *NCLR*, 24 (2021), 230; Heinze, in Bergsmo and Dittrich, *Integrity* (2020), p. 678 ('Understood this way, the addressees of exclusionary rules are not so much either public officials or private citizens, or both, but are all those who factually conduct an investigation') and p. 686 ('The remark that "authorities have done nothing wrong" in cases when private individuals illegally obtained evidence somehow insiniuates that exclusionary rules are exclusively addressed to those authorities').

[858] See also ICC, *Prosecutor v. Al Hassan*, TC X, Public Redacted Version of 'Decision on requests related to the submission into evidence of Mr Al Hassan's statements', ICC-01/12-01/18-1475-Red, 20 May 2021, para. 32 ('In its assessment, the Chamber may be guided by the text of Article 69(7) which provides an indication of some of the rationales for this exclusionary rule: to avoid reliance on unreliable evidence; and to preserve the integrity of the Court's proceedings').

[859] Heinze, *NCLR*, 24 (2021), 234 ff.; Heinze, in Bergsmo and Dittrich, *Integrity* (2020), pp. 693 ff.

[860] *Lubanga*, ICC-01/04-01/06-1399, para. 31.

[861] *Bemba*, ICC-01/05-01/08-1022, para. 9. See also *Bagosora et al.*, ICTR-98-41-AR93 & ICTR-98-41-AR93.2, para. 16 (exclusion of relevant and probative evidence where 'prejudicial effect will adversely affect the

influences the probative value of the evidence. The question then is, again, when the prejudicial effect is such as to completely displace the probative value ('disproportionate prejudicial effect').[862]

In sum, one may at best formulate a rule of thumb according to which the likelihood that the admission would be 'antithetical' and would 'seriously damage' the proceedings so as to produce an unacceptable prejudice increases with the intensifying gravity of the rights violation. Yet, ultimately the decision must be taken on a case-by-case basis, taking into account the characteristics of the relevant item of evidence and the countervailing interests.[863] Of course, Chambers have a fair amount of discretion in line with the general discretion in evidentiary matters.[864]

## B. Disclosure

### (1) Introduction

#### *(a) Conceptual clarification*

Disclosure[865] describes 'the mandatory divulging of information to a litigation opponent according to procedural rules.'[866] It is one of the key elements of adversarial criminal procedure,[867] goes to the heart of every trial,[868] and is now recognized in many legal systems.[869] Most commonly, the terms 'disclosure' and 'discovery' are used interchangeably. While in England and Wales, disclosure describes 'the provision of relevant information by one party to the other',[870] discovery in the USA is understood as 'the process by which each party to a

fairness ... of the proceedings'); ICTR, *Prosecutor v. Ngeze and Nahimana*, AC, Decision on the Interlocutory Appeals, Separate Opinion of Judge Shahabuddeen, ICTR-97-27-AR72, 5 September 2000, para. 19 ('[I]t being recognized that all relevant prosecution evidence is prejudicial to the accused and the more probative the more prejudicial, still it is possible in some cases to say that the probative value of the particular evidence is outweighed by its prejudicial effects; in such a case the evidence is to be excluded'). See also Rules 89 (D) RPE ICTY and 105 (D) RPE MICT as quoted in note 800 in this chapter.

[862] cf. Piragoff and Clarke, 'Article 69', in Ambos, *Commentary* (2022), mn. 59; also Bantekas, *ICL* (2010), p. 485 (prejudice may outweigh probative value).

[863] In a similar vein, *Katanga*, ICC-01/04-01/07-2635, para. 40; Piragoff and Clarke, 'Article 69', in Ambos, *Commentary* (2022), mn. 91.

[864] Note 19 in this chapter and main text.

[865] In more detail, Heinze, *Disclosure* (2014), pp. 309 ff.; Tochilovsky, *Law and Jurisprudence* (2014), pp. 95 ff.; Tochilovsky, in Doria, Gasser, and Bassiouni, *Legal Regime* (2009), pp. 843 ff.; De Smet, in Stahn and Sluiter, *ICC* (2009), pp. 421, 426 ff; Trendafilova, in ibid., pp. 441, 442 ff.; Scheffer, in ibid., pp. 585 ff; also Ambos and Miller, *ICLR*, 7 (2007), 341 ff.; Gómez Colomer, and Beltrán, in Gómez Colomer et al., *CPI* (2002), pp. 337 ff.; Ambos, in Bohlander, *ICJ* (2007), pp. 464 ff.; De Beco, *ICLR*, 7 (2007), 472–3; Zahar and Sluiter, *ICL* (2008), pp. 373 ff.; Lounici, in Kolb, *Droit International Pénal* (2008), 286 ff.; von Braun, *HuV- I*, 18 (2005), pp. 96–7; Morrissey, in Boas, Schabas, and Scharf, *ICJ* (2012), pp. 68 ff.; Klamberg, *Evidence* (2013), pp. 223 ff.; on the ICTY, Pruitt, in May et al., *Essays on ICTY* (2001), pp. 305 ff.; May and Wierda, *ColJTL*, 37 (1999), 756 ff.; Safferling, *YIHL*, 5 (2002), 239 ff.; Tochilovsky, *CLF, 15* (2004), 341 ff.; Möller, in Kirsch, *Internationale Strafgerichtshöfe* (2005), pp. 35 ff.; from the point of view of the defence, Robinson, in Kirsch, *Internationale Strafgerichtshöfe* (2005), pp. 120–1; on the ICTR, Nahamya and Diarra, *CLF*, 13 (2002), 339 ff.; see also Kreß, in Grützner et al., *Rechtshilfeverkehr* (2003), Part IV A 1 mn. 127.

[866] Lexical definition by Garner, *Dictionary* (2019), p. 583. About the term, see also Kuczyńska, *Accusation Model* (2015), p. 192.

[867] Ambos and Miller, *ICLR*, 7 (2007), 341; Rigney, *Fairness* (2022), pp. 101–2.

[868] Brady, in Lee, *ICC* (2001), p. 403; see also Swoboda, *Beweisstrategien* (2013), p. 659; Heinze, in Ruiz Fabri, *MPEIPro* (2020), mn. 4; Guariglia et al., *AC ICC Commentary* (2018), p. 205.

[869] Schabas, *UN Tribunals* (2006), p. 398.

[870] Gibson and Cavadino, *The Criminal Justice System* (2008), p. 112; a similar definition is provided by Pitcher, *Judicial Responses* (2018), p. 397.

case learns of the evidence that the opposition will present'.[871] Thus, it seems that 'discovery by the defense corresponds to disclosure by the prosecution, discovery by the prosecution to disclosure by the defense',[872] that is, that disclosure and discovery are virtually two sides of the same coin. Yet, this downplays the existing differences between disclosure and discovery. After all, discovery could also be seen as 'merely one species of disclosure'.[873]

At the ICC, the Statute and the Rules distinguish between disclosure *stricto sensu* and communication: while disclosure refers to 'the exchange of materials between the parties and/or participants to the proceedings', communication describes the provision of the (*inter partes*) disclosed material to the Chamber.[874]

### (b) *The Human Rights Law dimension of disclosure*

We have already stressed in Chapter I in this volume the importance of disclosure with a view to the principle of equality of arms[875] and the defence rights of the accused.[876] It suffices to recall here that the ECtHR found 'that it is a requirement of fairness ... that the prosecution authorities disclose to the defence all material evidence for or against the accused'.[877] The lack of such disclosure would lead to the accused being severely handicapped in the preparation of his defence, resulting in an infringement of his rights under Article 6 ECHR,[878] although disclosure is not an absolute right.[879] As to equality of arms the late European Commission of Human Rights held in *Jespers v. Belgium* that this principle imposes on prosecuting and investigating authorities an obligation to disclose any material in their possession, or to which they could gain access, which may assist the accused in exonerating themselves or in obtaining a reduction in sentence.[880] The ECtHR,[881] the ICTY,[882]

[871] Worrall, *Criminal Procedure* (2018), p. 169.

[872] Ambos, *NCLR*, 12 (2009), 561.

[873] Abrahamson, Dwyer, and Fitzpatrick, *Discovery and Disclosure* (2019), pp. 3–4.

[874] cf. Rule 121 (2)I RPE ICC; Rastan, 'Article 72', in Ambos, *Commentary* (2022), mn. 3, who, however, suggests 'that the term "disclosure" within the meaning of article 72 should be construed broadly to govern the divulging of material to any third party, including the judges. In particular, it might be argued that the intended scope of the provision is to insulate a State against the consequences that may flow from a Chamber decision with respect to the onward handling of its information or documents. However, this would arguably disrupt the ordinary usage of the term throughout the Statute, including those provisions cross-referenced within paragraph 1.'

[875] cf. Chapter I, D.(2)(b) in this volume. The principle referred to in Arts. 64 (3)(c) and 67 (2) ICCS.

[876] cf. Chapter I, D.(1), (3)(c) and (d) in this volume *in fine*.

[877] ECtHR, *Edwards v. United Kingdom*, Judgment 13071/87, 16 December 1992; *M v. The Netherlands*, Judgment 2156/10, 25 July 2017, para. 66; Schabas and McDermott, 'Article 67', in Ambos, *Commentary* (2022), mn. 24; Re, in Agirre et al., *Quality Control* (2020), pp. 742 ff.

[878] cf. Emson, *Evidence* (2010), p. 513; Bitti, 'Article 64', in Ambos, *Commentary* (2022), mn. 32; Jämsä, *Rules of Evidence* (2023), p. 46. On these rights in detail, see Chapter I, D.(3) in this volume.

[879] cf. *Prosecutor v. Gucati and Haradinaj*, CoAP, Public Redacted Version of Decision on the Appeals Against Disclosure Decision, KSC-BC-2020-07/IA005/F00008/RED, 29 July 2021, para. 35 (while stressing the disclosure's impact on fairness, arguing that 'disclosure of relevant evidence is not an absolute right', clarifying that 'in some cases, it may be necessary to withhold certain evidence from the Defence in order to preserve the fundamental rights of another individual or to safeguard an important public interest').

[880] *Jespers v. Belgium*, no. 8403/78, Commission's report of 14 December 1981, DR 27, para. 58, thereto Jämsä, *Rules of Evidence* (2023), p. 48.

[881] cf. ECtHR, *Lietzow v. Germany*, Judgment, 13 February 2001, para. 44; ECtHR, *Schops v. Germany*, Judgment, 13 February 2001, para. 44 and ECtHR, *Garcia Alva v. Germany*, Judgment, 13 February 2001, para. 39; ECtHR, *Murray v. United Kingdom*, App. no. 18731/91, Reports 1996–1, 70. See also Calvo-Goller, *Trial Proceedings* (2006), pp. 45, 46; Safferling, *International Criminal Procedure* (2012), p. 412; generally Fedorova, *Equality of Arms* (2012), pp. 115 ff. with further references.

[882] See e.g. ICTY, *Prosecutor v. Brdjanin and Talić*, TC II, Public Version of the Confidential Decision on the Alleged Illegality of Rule 70 of 6 May 2002, IT-99-36-PT, 23 May 2002, para. 22 ('It is also equally important and inherent in the concept of equality of arms that each party be afforded a reasonable opportunity to present his or her case under conditions that do not place him at an appreciable disadvantage vis-à-vis his opponent'), citing

and the ICC[883] decided in a similar vein. A subcategory of the equality of arms—of no less importance for disclosure—is the right to have adequate time and facilities to prepare the defence.[884]

### (c) *The role of the Chamber and the Registry*

While the ICC Statute only provides for some basic norms on disclosure,[885] the RPE contain more detailed rules, applicable to both Prosecutor and defence.[886] When in doubt, the Trial Chamber—much like an arbitrator[887]—determines the extent of disclosure and when it has to take place.[888] Therefore, evidence must also be communicated to the respective Chamber but the scope of this communication requirement[889] is disputed, with the *Bemba* PTC advocating broad communication[890] and the *Lubanga* PTC a more restrictive approach.[891]

*Bulut v. Austria* (1996) 24 EHRR 84, paras. 47–50; see also ICTY, *Prosecutor v. Krajisnik and Plavšić*, TC, Decision on Prosecution Motion for Clarification in Respect of Application of Rules 65*ter*, 66 (B) and 67 (C), IT-00-39 and 40-PT, 1 August 2001, para. 7 ('The Prosecution, by not disclosing the documents prior to trial, places the Defence in a position in which it will not be able to prepare properly; and it is this fact that is likely to lead to a violation of the principle of equality of arms'); see also Negri, *ICLR*, 5 (2005), 513, 560 ff.; McIntyre, *LJIL*, 16 (2003), 269, 272 ff.; May and Wierda, *ColJTransnat'lL*, 37 (1999), 725, 757; Safferling, *International Criminal Procedure* (2012), p. 413.

[883] See e.g. ICC, *Prosecutor v. Lubanga*, TC I, Decision on the Consequences of Non-Disclosure of Exculpatory Materials Covered by Article 54 (3)(e) Agreements and the Application to Stay the Prosecution of the Accused, Together with Certain Other Issues Raised at the Status Conference on 10 June 2008, ICC-01/04-01/06-1401, 13 June 2008, para. 79. See also Art. 67 (2) ICC Statute; ICC, *Prosecutor v. Katanga and Ngudjolo*, Judgment on the Appeal of Mr Germain Katanga against the Decision of Pre-Trial Chamber I Entitled 'First Decision on the Prosecution Request for Authorisation to Redact Witness Statements', ICC-01/04-01/07-476, 13 May 2008, para. 63 ('More generally, if non-disclosure would result in the hearing to confirm the charges, viewed as a whole, to be unfair to the suspect, the requested redactions should not be authorised. In addition, adequate procedural safeguards should be in place to ensure that the interests of the Defence are protected so as to comply, as far as possible, with the requirements of adversarial proceedings and equality of arms.')

[884] Art. 67 (1)(b) ICCS; *Bemba*, ICC-01/05-01/08-55, paras. 20, 23, 65; ECtHR, *Murtazaliyeva v. Russia*, Judgment, 18 September 2019, para. 91; *Kordic and Cerkez*, IT-95-14/2-A, AC Judgment, para. 175 ('The principle of equality of arms falls within the guarantee of a fair trial provided by the Statute, and has been described as obligating a judicial body to ensure that neither party is put at a disadvantage when presenting its case. The Appeals Chamber, in considering the scope for application of the principle, has held that at a minimum "a fair trial must entitle the accused to adequate time and facilities for his defence" under conditions which do not place him at a substantial disadvantage as regards his opponent' [fn omitted]). See also UNICRI, *ICTY Manual on Developed Practices* (2009), p. 182, para. 22, regarding access to IT for the accused in order to prepare his/her defence: 'The UNDU must maintain security when considering whether to allow detainees to information technology. At the same time, the principle of "equality of arms" requires that detainees be able to access materials to conduct their defence, including the ability to review vast quantities of disclosure materials released by the Prosecution in searchable digital format.' See also Calvo-Goller, *Trial Proceedings* (2006), pp. 227, 228; May and Wierda, *International Criminal Evidence* (2002), p. 272, noting, however, that '[t]his does not mean that the time allotted to the defense to prepare must be exactly equal to that of the prosecut'on's investigations. However, it must, at a minimum, be "adequate". What time is adequate depends on the circumstances of the case.' Previously, Chapter I, D.(3)(d) in this volume.

[885] cf. Arts. 54 (3)(e), 61 (3) and (6), 67 (2), 68 (5), and 72 ICCS.

[886] Ambos, *NCLR*, 12 (2009), 543, 546. Schabas and McDermott even refer to 'the *Statute's* extensive disclosure obligations', see Schabas and McDermott, 'Article 67', in Ambos, *Commentary* (2022), mn. 24 (emphasis in the original); see also Piragoff and Clarke, 'Article 69', in Ambos, *Commentary* (2022), mn. 43.

[887] cf. Rules 76–84, 121 RPE ICC; cf. May and Wierda, *ColJTransnat'lL*, 37 (1999), 758.

[888] cf. Art. 61 (3) ICCS, Rule 66 (C) ICTY/ICTR, Rule 66 (A)(ii) RPE SCSL, Rules 71 (A)(ii), (C), 72 RPE MICT. See also Brady, in Lee, *ICC* (2001), pp. 403 ff.; Lewis, in Fischer et al., *Prosecution* (2001), pp. 226–7.

[889] About the definition of the term 'communication', see Section B.(1)(a) with note 874 in this chapter.

[890] *Bemba*, ICC-01/05-01/08-55, para. 28.

[891] ICC, *Prosecutor v. Lubanga*, PTC I, Decision on the Final System of Disclosure and the Establishment of a Timetable, ICC-01/04-01/06-102, 15 May 2006, paras. 41, 50 ff. See, in more detail, Schabas, Chaitidou, and El Zeidy, 'Article 61', in Ambos, *Commentary* (2022), mn. 51; Heinze, *Disclosure* (2014), pp. 34 ff., 508 ff.

As demonstrated above,[892] the *Bemba* approach has now become the dominant one at the ICC.[893] It has also been adopted at the KSC.[894]

The 'record of all proceedings' to be maintained by the Registry, already mentioned above,[895] contains all evidence communicated to the Pre-Trial Chamber, 'irrespective of whether it is eventually included in the parties' lists of evidence under rules 121(3) and (6) of the Rules'.[896] The practical use of such a record for disclosure purposes and thus an adequate defence cannot be overstated.[897] The controversial question of whether the disclosure process should be merely *inter partes* or also facilitated through the Registry[898] has been resolved in favour of the latter.[899] The same applies to disclosure at the KSC.[900]

Both the ICC's record of proceedings and the disclosure practice itself have deviated, in structural terms, from its original scope: disclosure at the ICC regularly takes place by giving the defence access to the prosecution's evidence database, i.e. it goes beyond the original meaning of disclosure as explained at the beginning of this section.[901] Everything is uploaded to the record management database of the Registry and accessible to everybody working on the respective situation or case.[902] In some instances, disclosure of the databases takes place through the E-Court (which led to (alleged) disclosure violations in *Ongwen*),[903] and in accordance with the E-Court Protocol, established through Regulation 26 (1) RegC. This electronic system 'is designed to ensure that all the necessary information is available electronically during the proceedings to the Court'.[904] The ICC's E-court system is the result

892 See above note 769 and main text.

893 See e.g. ICC, *Prosecutor v. Yekatom*, PTC II, Public Redacted Version of 'Decision on Disclosure and Related Matters', ICC-01/14-01/18-64-Red, 23 January 2019, para. 17.

894 KSC, *Prosecutor v. Shala*, PTJ, Framework Decision on Disclosure of Evidence and Related Matters, KSC-BC-2023-11/F00023, 19 December 2023, para. 42 ('In order to fulfil this duty, all evidence exchanged between the Parties, regardless of whether it will be relied upon at trial, shall be communicated to the Pre-Trial Judge. Such communication will also assist the Pre-Trial Judge to ensure that the disclosure of evidence takes place under satisfactory conditions.')

895 Section A.(7) in this chapter.

896 ICC, *Practice Manual* (2023), para. 27.

897 See notes 780 and 781 with main text in this chapter.

898 See e.g. *Lubanga*, ICC-01/04-01/06-102, para. 61.

899 See ICC, *Prosecutor v. Al Hassan*, PTC I, Decision on the Evidence Disclosure Protocol and Other Related Matters, ICC-01/12-01/18-31-tENG, 16 May 2018, para. 36; ICC, *Prosecutor v. Ongwen*, PTC II, Decision Setting the Regime for Evidence Disclosure and Other Related Matters, ICC-02/04-01/15-203, 27 February 2015, para. 10; ICC, *Practice Manual* (2023), para. 10 ('Disclosure of evidence between the parties takes place through the Registry in accordance with the E-court protocol developed for this purpose'). The *Practice Manual* was first published as *Pre-Trial Practice Manual* by Judges Cuno Tarfusser, President of the Pre-Trial Division, Marc Perrin de Brichambaut, Antoine Kesia-Mbe Mindua, Péter Kovács, and Chang-ho Chung, 'recording what has been identified as best practice to be followed in pre-trial proceedings and stating the expectations that pre-trial Judges have from the Prosecutor and Defence counsel', see the press release from 4 September 2015, <https://www.icc-cpi.int/Pages/item.aspx?name=ptd_stat_150904>, and then became the *Practice Manual*. See also ICC, *Prosecutor v. Blé Goudé*, PTC I, Decision establishing a system for disclosure of evidence, ICC-02/11-02/11-57, 14 April 2014, para. 4 ('As is standard practice before the Court, disclosure of evidence between the parties shall take place through the Registry. For this purpose, the Registry shall file in the record of the case the latest version of the e-court protocol').

900 At the KSC *inter partes* disclosure is also 'organised and facilitated by the Registry, acting as a communication channel between the Parties and the Panel' (*Shala*, KSC-BC-2023-11/F00023, para. 40).

901 See also Heinze, in Ruiz Fabri, *MPEIPro* (2020), mn. 9.

902 See also Chung, in Werle and Zimmermann, *ICC* (2019) p. 9, 15 ('All case records or submissions produced by all bodies including judges' decisions are filed into the record management database of the registry, and then distributed to the people at court entitled to be notified of such case record').

903 ICC, *Prosecutor v. Ongwen*, TC IX, Decision on Defence Request for Remedies in Light of Disclosure Violations, ICC-02/04-01/15-1734, 22 April 2020, para. 30.

904 ICC, *Prosecutor v. Yekatom*, PTC II, Annex to the Decision on Disclosure and Related Matters, E-Court Protocol, ICC-01/14-01/18-64-Anx, 23 January 2019, para. 1; ICC, *Prosecutor v. Abd-Al-Rahman*, PTC II (Single

of a trend to digital evidence and the ensuing disclosure and/or discovery,[905] something that has its origins in civil procedure.[906] At the ICTY, the electronic character of disclosure is made clear by the so-called 'Electronic Disclosure Suite' (EDS).[907] At the KSC, too, disclosure takes place electronically with the parties obliged to upload all evidence and other material into the E-Court management system ('Legal Workflow').[908]

### (2) Prosecution disclosure

In all international criminal tribunals, the Prosecutor is obliged to disclose most (incriminating) evidence and information on witnesses and certain other material either *ex officio* or at the request of the defence at all stages of the trial (Figure 8).[909] Disclosure is an ethical obligation of the Prosecutor,[910] who is expected to act in good faith.[911]

#### (a) General remarks

While it is 'desirable for the investigation to be complete by the time of the confirmation hearing',[912] the prosecution is required to discharge the disclosure obligation 'on an ongoing basis', that is, going beyond the trial stage and extending into the appeals stage.[913] Even if the

Judge), Annex 1 to the Order on Disclosure and Related Matters, ICC-02/05-01/20-116-Anx1, 17 August 2020, para. 2.

905 In more detail, Freeman, *FordhamILJ*, 41 (2018), 283, 283 ff.

906 In more detail, Turner, *JCL&Crim*, 109 (2019), 237, 237 ff.

907 In more detail, Rigney, *Fairness* (2022), pp. 107 ff.

908 *Shala*, KSC-BC-2023-11/F00023, para. 40 ('through the electronic software provided to this effect, as stipulated in Rules 98(1)(b) and 109(a) of the Rules. The Parties shall abide by the Registry Instruction on Uploading Records to Legal Workflow when disclosing evidence electronically.')

909 See e.g. Rule 66 RPE ICTY/ICTR; Art. 61 (3) ICCS, Rules 76, 77, 112, 121 (2) RPE ICC. See also ICTY, *Prosecutor v. Furundžija*, TC, Decision, IT-95-17/1-T, 16 July 1998, para. 19. cf. also Pruitt, in May et al., *Essays on ICTY* (2001), pp. 309 ff.; Wu Wei, *Prosecutor of the ICC* (2007), pp. 202 ff.; Tuinstra, *JICJ*, 8 (2010), 463, 479; Schuon, *International Criminal Procedure* (2010), pp. 111 ff., 275 ff.; Heinze, *Disclosure* (2014), pp. 355 ff., 376 ff. On the definition of 'exculpatory material', Harmon and Karagiannakis, in May et al., *Essays on ICTY* (2001), pp. 315 ff.; about disclosure in the confirmation hearing in general terms, Caianiello, *ICLR*, 10 (2010), 26–7; in detail with a comparative account, Heinze, *Disclosure* (2014), pp. 391 ff.

910 Heinze and Fyfe, in Bergsmo and Stahn, *Preliminary Examination II* (2018) 1, 32 ff.; Shah, *GeoJLegalEthics*, 32 (2019), 213, 218 ff.

911 ICC, *Prosecutor v. Yekatom and Ngaïssona*, PTC II, Decision on the Yekatom Defence Second Motion for Disclosure of Rule 76 Material, ICC-01/14-01/18-341-Conf, ICC-01/14-01/18-341-Red, 13 September 2019, para. 25; *Prosecutor v. Gucati and Haradinaj*, CoAP, Public Redacted Version of Decision on Defence Motions for Alternate Relief Relating to Rule 103 Disclosure Violations, KSC-CA-2022-01/F00083/RED, 31 January 2023, para. 23 ('presumption of good faith on the Prosecution's part when discharging its disclosure obligations'); Oriolo, in Ruiz Fabri, *MPEIPro* (2022), mn. 27 ff.

912 ICC, *Prosecutor v. Lubanga*, AC, Judgment on the Prosecutor's Appeal against the Decision of Pre-Trial Chamber I Entitled 'Decision Establishing General Principles Governing Applications to Restrict Disclosure pursuant to Rule 81 (2) and (4) of the Rules of Procedure and Evidence', ICC-01/04-01/06-568, 13 October 2006, para. 54; reiterated by ICC, *Practice Manual* (2023), para. 14; also *Al Hassan*, ICC-01/12-01/18-666, para. 15. See already Chapter IV, B.(7)(a) in this volume.

913 Rule 84 RPE ICC, Reg. No. 55 (2) RegOTP, Rule 67 (D) RPE ICTR; see also *Blaškić*, IT-95-14-A, paras. 29 ff. (42); ICTY, *Prosecutor v. Kordić and Čerkez*, AC, Decision on Appellant's Notice and Supplemental Notice of Prosecution's Non-Compliance with its Disclosure Obligation under Rule 68 of the Rules, IT-95-14/2-A, 11 February 2004, para. 17; ICTR, *Prosecutor v. Rutaganda*, Decision on the Urgent Defence Motion for Disclosure and Admission of Additional Evidence and Scheduling Order, ICTR-96-3-A, 12 December 2002; also ICTR, *Prosecutor v. Karemera, Ngirumpatse and Nzirorera*, AC, Decision on Joseph Nzirorera's Appeal From Decision on Alleged Rule 66 Violation, ICTR-98-44-AR73.18, 17 May 2010, para. 24, where the AC clarified that Rule 67 (D) RPE ICTR (obligation to notify the other party in the event of a discovery of additional material which should have been produced earlier) 'also applies to materials subject to an inspection request pursuant to Rule 66(B) of

<table>
<tr><th>Prior Confirmation Hearing</th><th>After Confirmation Hearing/Prior Trial</th><th>Trial</th></tr>
<tr><td>Art. 61 (3)<br>- disclosure of the charging document<br>- disclosure of evidence the prosecution intends to rely<br>- within reasonable time before the hearing</td><td>Art. 64 (3)(c)<br>- documents or information not previously disclosed</td><td>Art. 69<br>- general evidence provision</td></tr>
<tr><td>Rule 121 (Art. 61 (3))<br>- list of evidence and information<br>- only evidence sufficient to establish substantial grounds</td><td>Art. 64 (6)(d)<br>Trial Chamber may order the production of evidence</td><td>No rule…<br>… saying that evidence disclosed inter partes should be given to the Trial Chamber</td></tr>
<tr><td>Rule76, ICTY/ICTR/SCSL-Rules 69 (C) [identity], 66 [statements]<br>- disclosure of names and of statements all witnesses = contrary to Rule 121 (3) (list), but consistent with Art. 61 (3)</td><td>No rule…<br>… saying that the record of the proceedings can be inspected and updated by the Trial Chamber</td><td>Rule 130<br>- Trial Chamber receives the record of the proceedings</td></tr>
<tr><td colspan="3">Rule 77<br>- Inspection of books, docs, photographs, other tangible objects that assist the defence in the preparation of its case/intended by the Prosecution to be relied upon in the confirmation hearing or at trial<br>1.) material to the preparation of the defence<br>2.) intended for use by the prosecutor as evidence for the purposes of the confirmation hearing or at trial<br>3.) obtained from or belonged to the person<br>[applicability at the confirmation hearing controversial]</td></tr>
<tr><td>Rule 112 (iunctio Art. 93 (1)(c), 99 (1))<br>- disclosure of a copy of his or her transcribed interview to the accused<br>- disclosure of statements towards national authority (iunctio Art. 93 (1)(c), 99 (1))</td><td></td><td></td></tr>
<tr><td colspan="3">Art. 67 (2), ICTY/ICTR/SCSL-Rule 68<br>- disclosure of (potentially) exculpatory evidence<br>- as soon as practicable</td></tr>
<tr><td colspan="3">Rule 83 (Art. 67 (2))<br>- Request for ex parte hearing</td></tr>
<tr><td colspan="3">Rule 84<br>Disclosure is an ongoing process</td></tr>
<tr><td colspan="2">Bulk or 'all' material?<br>Lubanga PTC vs. Bemba PTC</td><td></td></tr>
</table>

**Fig. 8.** Prosecution Disclosure ICC
*Source:* Heinze, *Disclosure* (2014), p. 420

trial has already started, the Prosecutor could apply for an 'extension of a time limit' to add newly discovered incriminating evidence to its list, if she 'can demonstrate that he or she

the Rules … Accordingly, where such materials come into the Prosecution's possession subsequent to an inspection request from the Defence, the Prosecution is under a *continuous obligation to promptly notify the Defence* of their existence' (emphasis added). cf. also Brady, in Lee, *ICC* (2001), p. 422; Safferling, *YIHL*, 5 (2002), 241; Möller, in Kirsch, *Internationale Strafgerichtshöfe* (2005), p. 37; Khan and Buisman, in Stahn, *Practice* (2015), 1038.

was unable to file the application within the time limit for reasons outside his or her control'.[914] Take the following practical example: in *Katanga* the charges were confirmed on 26 September 2008.[915] The trial started on 24 November 2009. On 28–31 March 2009, i.e. six months after the confirmation of charges and seven months prior to the start of the trial, the prosecution sent a forensic expert mission to the Institut de Bogoro in the Democratic Republic of Congo's Ituri region. It produced additional material that the prosecution sought to disclose under Rule 77, which the TC II granted (while rejecting an application to extend the 'List of Incriminating Witnesses').[916]

According to the ICTY Trial Chamber in *Blagojević*, the expression 'continuing obligation' should be understood to mean that the prosecution must, on a continuous basis, search 'all material known to the Prosecutor', including all its files, in whatever form, and in relation to all accused, 'for the existence of material which in any way tends to suggest the innocence or mitigate the guilt of the accused or may affect the credibility of prosecution evidence, and disclose the existence of such material completely to the Defence'.[917] The ICTY Trial Chamber clarified that a representative of the prosecution must certify that a full search of all relevant material has been conducted.[918] In any case, as we will see in the following sub-sections, the extent of disclosure obligations depends on the stage of the proceedings and the kind of material which is due to be disclosed. It will also become clear that the ICC's disclosure regime is filled with vague terms that require interpretation. In fact, disclosure is one of the major procedural issues at the ICC. It is useful to be aware of the disclosure context at the ICC. The Prosecutor has broad disclosure obligations extending to witness statements,[919] objects material to the preparation of the defence,[920] objects intended for use

[914] Reg. 35 (2) RegC. According to the ICC's AC, the Prosecution could only invoke Reg. 35 (2) if it demonstrated 'the existence of "exceptional circumstances", such as incapacitating illness, to demonstrate that there is a "reason outside his/her control"'; see ICC, *Prosecutor v. Katanga*, TC II, Decision on the 'Prosecution's Urgent Application to Be Permitted to Present as Incriminating Evidence Transcripts and Translations of Videos and Video DRCOTP- 1042-0006 pursuant to Regulation 35 and Request for Redactions (ICC-01/04-01/07-1260)', ICC-01/04-01/07-1336, 27 July 2009, para. 7, with reference to ICC, *Prosecutor v. Lubanga*, AC, Reasons for the 'Decision of the Appeals Chamber on the Request of Counsel to Mr Thomas Lubanga Dyilo for Modification of the Time Limit pursuant to Regulation 35 of the Regulations of the Court of 7 February 2007' issued on 16 February 2007, ICC-01/04-01/06-834, 21 February 2007, paras. 9–10. In addition to the requirements of Reg. 35 (2), the TC imposed two further conditions to submit new incriminating material: the Chamber may only use its powers under Arts. 64 (6)(d) and 69 (3) ICCS and allow this submission 'if it can be shown that (i) the new material is either significantly more compelling than other items of evidence already disclosed to the Defence, or brings to light a previously unknown fact which has a significant bearing upon the case, and (ii) the late addition will not cause undue prejudice to the Defence in relation to the latter's right to have adequate time and facilities to prepare in accordance with article 67(l)(b) of the Statute'; see ICC, *Prosecutor v. Katanga*, TC II, Decision on Prosecution Requests ICC-01/04-01/07-1386 and ICC-01/04-01/07-1407 Made pursuant to Regulation 35 of the Regulations, ICC-01/04-01/07-1552, 23 October 2009, para. 14. See generally Khan and Buisman, in Stahn, *Practice* (2015), pp. 1039–40.

[915] ICC, *Prosecutor v. Katanga and Ngudjolo*, PTC I, Decision on the Confirmation of the Charges, ICC-01/04-01/07-716-Conf, 26 September 2008.

[916] ICC, *Prosecutor v. Katanga and Ngudjolo*, TC II, Decision on the Disclosure of Evidentiary Material Relating to the Prosecutor's Site Visit to Bogoro, 28, 29, and 31 March 2009, ICC-01/04-01/07-1305,1345,1360,1401,1412 and 1456), ICC-01/04-01/07-1515, 7 October 2009, para. 1 and disposition; see also Freeman, *FordhamILJ*, 41 (2018), 283, 304.

[917] ICTY, *Prosecutor v. Blagojević and Jokić*, TC II, Joint Decision on Motions Related to Production of Evidence, IT-02-60-PT, 12 December 2002, para. 29; ICTY, *Prosecutor v. Blaškić*, TC I, Decision on the Defence Motion for Sanctions for the Prosecutor's Failure to Comply with Sub-rule 66 (a) of the Rules and the Decision of 27 January 1997 Compelling the Production of all Statements of the Accused, IT-95-14, 15 July 1998, p. 3.

[918] ICTY, *Proseculor v. Krnojelac*, TC, Decision on Motion by Prosecution to Modify Order for Compliance with Rule 68, IT-97-25-PT, 1 November 1999, para. 11.

[919] Rule 76 RPE ICC: 'The names of witnesses whom the Prosecutor intends to call to testify and copies of any prior statements made by those witnesses.'

[920] Rule 77 RPE ICC: 'Any books, documents, photographs and other tangible objects in the possession or control of the Prosecutor, which are material to the preparation of the defence.'

as evidence[921] and exculpatory material.[922] These obligations mirror the ones at most international criminal tribunals and do not change in a constellation where the Chamber (in lieu of the parties or participants) calls the witness—as is the case at the MICT,[923] the STL,[924] or the KSC.[925]

### *(b) Disclosure relating to an arrest warrant*

The ICC Statute fails to define the moment when the disclosure process is triggered.[926] According to the ICC's Pre-Trial Chamber interpretation of Rule 121 (2) RPE ICC, the disclosure process starts at the initial appearance of the suspect.[927] Central disclosure obligations by the prosecution usually evolve around the confirmation hearing. Yet, disclosure may take place earlier. In the *Mbarushimana* case, for instance, prior to *Mbarushimana's* surrender to the ICC, the defence filed a disclosure request for material related to the arrest of *Mbarushimana*, in particular 'information forming the basis for the Prosecutor's application pursuant to Article 58 of the Rome Statute', 'material sought in three requests for disclosure made by the Defence to the Prosecutor', and 'exculpatory and/or materially relevant information necessary for the pursuit of challenges under Article 19(2)(a) of the Rome Statute and Rule 117(3)'.[928] The Chamber noted that the right to disclosure of documents for the three purposes identified by the defence was 'not expressly set forth in the Statute or the Rules'.[929]

However, the right to such disclosure for the purpose of an application for interim release was confirmed by the Appeals Chamber in *Bemba*.[930] Partially granting the request of the defence, the Pre-Trial Chamber affirmed the defence right to have access to documents which are essential for the purpose of applying for interim release and challenging the validity of the arrest warrant, but limited the scope of disclosure because of the sensitive nature

921 Rule 77 RPE ICC: 'Any books, documents, photographs and other tangible objects in the possession or control of the Prosecutor, which [ ... ] are intended for use by the Prosecutor as evidence [ ... ] at trial.'

922 Article 67 (2) ICCS: 'Evidence in the Prosecutor's possession or control which [ ... ] she believes shows or tends to.' See also ICC, *Prosecutor v. Ntaganda*, AC, Judgment on the Appeal of Mr Bosco Ntaganda against the 'Decision on Defence Request Seeking Disclosure Orders and a Declaration of Prosecution Obligations to Record Contacts with Witnesses', ICC-01/04-02/06-1330, 20 May 2016, para. 23.

923 Rule 120 RPE MICT: 'A Trial Chamber may order either Party to produce additional evidence. It may proprio motu summon witnesses and order their attendance.'

924 Rule 165 RPE STL: 'After hearing the Parties, the Trial Chamber may, *proprio motu* or at the request of a Party, order either Party or a victim participating in the proceedings to produce additional evidence. It may, after hearing the Parties, *proprio motu* summon witnesses and order their attendance.' See also STL, *Prosecutor v. Ayyush et al.*, TC, Reasons for the Trial Chamber's Decision Dismissing the Sabra Defence Application to Order Prosecution Disclosure of Documents Related to Mr Michael Taylor, STL-11-01/T/TC/F3710/20180713/R311213-R311231/EN/dm, 13 July 2018, para. 15; Re, in Agirre et al., *Quality Control* (2020), pp. 758–9.

925 Rule 132 RPE KSC: 'After hearing the Parties and, where applicable, Victims' Counsel, the Panel may invite the submission of or *proprio motu* call additional evidence not produced by the Parties, including expert evidence, where it considers it necessary for the determination of the truth.'

926 Schabas, Chaitidou, and El *Zeidy*, 'Article 61', in Ambos, *Commentary* (2022), mn. 54.

927 ICC, *Prosecutor v. Gaddafi and Al-Senussi*, PTC I, Decision on the 'Request for an order for the commencement of the pre-confirmation phase' by the Defence of Saif Al-Islam Gaddafi, ICC-01/11-01/11-440, 10 September 2013, para. 27 ('No provision of the Statute or the Rules would therefore compel the Chamber rganizeise the disclosure of materials related to the merits of the case when the suspect has not yet appeared before the Court and no date for the commencement of the confirmation of charges hearing has been set.'); Schabas, Chaitidou, and El Zeidy, 'Article 61', in Ambos, *Commentary* (2022), mn. 54.

928 ICC, *Prosecutor v. Mbarushimana*, PTC I, Decision on the Defence Request for Disclosure, ICC-01/04-01/10-47, 27 January 2011, paras. 1–3.

929 Ibid., para. 10.

930 ICC, *Prosecutor v. Bemba*, AC, Judgment on the Appeal of Mr Jean-Pierre Bemba Gombo against the Decision of Pre-Trial Chamber III Entitled 'Decision on application for interim release', ICC-01/05-01/08-323, 16 December 2008, para. 28.

of the material.[931] At any rate, the prosecution does not have to provide a so-called in-depth analysis chart, as required within the context of the confirmation hearing,[932] for purposes of the issuing of a warrant of arrest or summons to appear.[933]

### (c) *Disclosure prior and at the confirmation hearing*

#### (i) *The legal regime*

The suspect[934] must receive, 'a reasonable time' before the confirmation hearing, a copy of the Document Containing the Charges (DCC)—already explained above[935]—and a list of the evidence on which the Prosecutor intends to rely.[936] Rule 121 RPE ICC, complementing Art. 61 (3) ICCS, provides for a 'a detailed regime governing disclosure of evidence prior to the confirmation hearing',[937] including the record to be maintained by the Registry.[938] According to that provision, the Pre-Trial Chamber must receive—no later than thirty days before the date of the confirmation hearing[939] (i.e. later submission would be 'unreasonable' within the meaning of Article 61 (3) ICCS)—all evidence disclosed between the Prosecutor and the suspect, making necessary orders for disclosure, and organizing status conferences to ensure that disclosure occurs under satisfactory conditions.[940]

#### (ii) *Extent of disclosure*

How much material actually has to be disclosed *inter partes* prior to the confirmation hearing is controversial and largely depends on what function is attributed to the confirmation hearing:[941] while the *Bemba* PTC required the prosecution 'to disclose the evidence which is of true relevance to the case, whether that evidence be incriminating or exculpatory',[942]

[931] *Mbarushimana*, ICC-01/04-01/10-47, paras. 15 ff.

[932] See Section B.(2)(c)(iii) in this chapter.

[933] Van der Vyver, *CrimLBull*, 48 no. 4 (2012), 10.

[934] On the person becoming a suspect, see Chapter I, D.(2)(d) in this volume; generally on the term in the ICCS Chapter IV, A.(1)(a)(iii) in this volume.

[935] See Chapter IV, A.(2)(a) in this volume.

[936] cf. Art. 61 (3) ICCS; see for more details Rule 121 (3) RPE ICC; Reg. 51 RegC. See generally Khan and Buisman, in Stahn, *Practice* (2015), pp. 1032 ff.

[937] Brady, in Lee, *ICC* (2001), p. 407.

[938] See Sections A.(7) and B.(1)(c) in this chapter.

[939] Rule 121 (3) RPE ICC. See also ICC, *Practice Manual* (2023), para. 22; Schabas, Chaitidou, and El Zeidy, 'Article 61', in Ambos, *Commentary* (2022), mn. 50. See, in addition, Rule 121 (4) RPE ICC ('Where the Prosecutor intends to amend the charges pursuant to article 61, paragraph 4, he or she shall notify the Pre-Trial Chamber and the person *no later than 15 days* before the date of the hearing of the amended charges together with a list of evidence that the Prosecutor intends to bring in support of those charges at the hearing' (emphasis added)) and Rule 121 (5) RPE ICC ('Where the Prosecutor intends to present new evidence at the hearing, he or she shall provide the Pre-Trial Chamber and the person with a list of that evidence *no later than 15 days* before the date of the hearing' (emphasis added)). Compared to the ad hoc tribunals, these deadlines are regarded as rather short, see Khan and Buisman, in Stahn, *Practice* (2015), pp. 1032 ff.

[940] Brady, in Lee, *ICC* (2001), p. 407; Re, in Agirre et al., *Quality Control* (2020), p. 782.

[941] See Chapter IV, A.(2)(b)(i) in this volume. See also Heinze, *Disclosure* (2014), p. 417; Schabas, Chaitidou, and El Zeidy, 'Article 61', in Ambos, *Commentary* (2022), mn. 5 ff.

[942] *Bemba*, ICC-01/05-01/08-55, para. 67. The majority of the *Gbagbo* PTC addressed the question what evidence the Prosecutor may hold back before the confirmation hearing in surprisingly clear language: '[T]he Prosecutor in this case may not have deemed it necessary to present all her evidence or largely complete her investigation, following all relevant incriminating and exonerating lines of investigation in order to establish the truth. The Chamber does not exclude that the Prosecutor might be able to present or collect further evidence and is therefore, out of fairness, prepared to give her a limited amount of additional time to do so. As the Appeals Chamber noted when discussing summary evidence, when the evidence is insufficient the "Pre-Trial Chamber need not reject the charges but may adjourn the hearing and request the Prosecutor to provide further evidence".' (*Gbagbo*, ICC-02/11-01/11-432, para. 37); see also Friman, in Stahn, *Practice* (2015), p. 923. In the negotiation process of the ICC's RPE, France was particularly in favour of extensive disclosure prior to the confirmation of charges, see Broomhall, 'Article 51', in Ambos, *Commentary* (2022), mn. 48 with n. 94. The ICC's *Practice Manual*,

the *Lubanga* PTC considered it sufficient to disclose the 'bulk' of exculpatory evidence prior to the confirmation hearing and all exculpatory evidence thereafter.[943] This bulk rule certainly entails a more flexible approach in that it limits the Prosecutor's disclosure obligations to the bulk of the evidence, instead of requiring every piece of exculpatory evidence to be disclosed.[944] Nevertheless, as correctly noted by Judge Trendafilova, acting as Single Judge of Pre-Trial Chamber II, 'the "bulk rule" as a term and concept is nowhere enshrined in the Court's statutory documents' and there was no obligation whatsoever to follow this rule just because other Pre-Trial Chambers did—in fact rather inconsistently[945]—in previous cases.[946] At any rate, it seems to have become common practice for the OTP to disclose the 'bulk' of incriminating evidence by the confirmation hearing or within the deadline(s) set by the Chamber.[947]

Apart from the bulk rule, Judge Steiner in the *Katanga and Ngudjolo* case also discussed 'alternative measures in lieu of actual disclosure', as suggested by the OTP.[948] These include the transmission of summaries containing the exculpatory information identified in documents within the meaning of Article 54 (3)(e) ICCS and the 'principle of analogous

however, rejects any kind of obligation for the prosecution to also disclose all incriminating evidence prior to the confirmation hearing, see ICC, *Practice Manual* (2023), para. 22: 'As far as the incriminating evidence is concerned, it is the Prosecutor's own choice to disclose to the Defence as much as he/she considers warranted.'

[943] *Lubanga*, ICC-01/04-01/06-102, paras. 119 ff., 124. See also ICC, *Prosecutor v. Katanga and Ngudjolo*, PTC I, Decision on Article 54 (3)(e) Documents Identified as Potentially Exculpatory or Otherwise Material to the Defence's Preparation for the Confirmation Hearing, ICC-01/04-01/07-621, 20 June 2008, paras. 8, 45, 124; ICC, *Prosecutor v. Abu Garda*, PTC I, Second Decision on issues relating to Disclosure, ICC-02/05-02/09-35, 16 July 2009, para. 11 ('[A]ll materials subject to disclosure on which the parties do not intend to rely upon at the confirmation hearing do not need to be filed in the record of the case'); ICC, *Prosecutor v. Mbarushimana*, PTC I, Decision on issues relating to disclosure, ICC-01/04-01/10-87, 30 March 2011, p. 14. In support of this approach Friman, in Stahn, *Practice* (2015), p. 922; WCRO, *Confirmation of Charges* (2015), pp. 4–5, 94–9; crit. Khan and Buisman, in Stahn, *Practice* (2015), pp. 1036–7. See generally Ambos, *NCLR*, 12 (2009), 548–9; Heinze, *Disclosure* (2014), pp. 34 ff., 412 ff.; Kuczyńska, *Accusation Model* (2015), pp. 227–8; Schabas, *ICC Commentary* (2016), pp. 1050 ff.

[944] Ambos, *NCLR*, 12 (2009), 548.

[945] The Single Judge observed that 'the "bulk rule" is a notion appearing only in *some* pre-trial proceedings. Even if, for the sake of argument, one was to accept the existence of a "bulk rule" ... this jurisprudence is seemingly *not applied consistently* in the pre-trial proceedings, including the proceedings before Pre-Trial Chambers II and III. In fact, Pre-Trial Chambers II/(III) apply consistently the disclosure regime following the principles established in the Disclosure Decision, which lack any reference to the "bulk rule"'. cf. ICC, *Prosecutor v. Ruto and Sang*, PTC II, Decision on the 'Prosecution's Application for leave to Appeal the "Decision Setting the Regime for Evidence Disclosure and Other Related Matters" (ICC-01/09-01/11-44)', ICC-01/09-01/11-74, 2 May 2011, para. 26 (notes omitted, emphases added). As a result, the Single Judge was 'not persuaded why and how full disclosure of exculpatory evidence in the Prosecutor's possession or control would "unfairly hamper" his ability to prepare himself for the upcoming confirmation of charges hearing' (ibid., para. 27). In the same vein, Heinze, *Disclosure* (2014), pp. 34 ff.; more generally also Heinze, in Bock et al., *Strafrecht* (2015), pp. 196–7. Demanding a 'more consistent or uniform disclosure management' also Mettraux et al., *Effectiveness ICC* (2014), p. 15 (para. 58), who recommend that the 'Chambers should adopt a uniform Redaction Protocol to be applied to all cases for both pre trial and trial' (see, in more detail, ibid., pp. 109 ff. (paras. 19 ff.)).

[946] *Ruto and Sang*, ICC-01/09-01/11-74, para. 25. See generally Khan and Buisman, in Stahn, *Practice* (2015), p. 1041.

[947] See e.g. ICC, *Prosecutor v. Said*, PTC II, Decision on the Defence's Request for Postponement of the Confirmation Hearing, ICC-01/14-01/21-196, 5 October 2021, para. 23 ('The packages were disclosed on a rolling basis beginning in early March 2021 and the bulk of the incriminating evidence was disclosed in packages 29–35 on 7 July 2021. Although two packages were disclosed after the deadline set in the Disclosure Order, the Prosecution expressly indicated that it would not rely on that material for the purpose of the confirmation of charges hearing.' [fn. omitted]). For the same approach at the KSC see *Prosecutor v. Thaçi, Veseli, Selimi and Krasniqi*, PTJ, Decision on Prosecution Request for Extension of Time Limit to Provide its Rule 102 (3) Notice, KSC-BC-2020-06/F00370, 24 June 2021, para. 14.

[948] ICC, *Prosecutor v. Katanga and Ngudjolo*, OTP, Prosecution's Fifth Report on the Status of the Procedures Initiated under Articles 54 (3)(e), 73 and 93 in Relation to Those Items Identified as of a Potentially Exculpatory Nature under Article 67 (2) of the Statute or as Material to the Defence under Rule 77 of the Rules, ICC-01/04-01/07-502, 23 May 2008, paras. 3, 5.

information',[949] according to which disclosure may be limited to material 'containing information analogous to that identified in Article 54 (3)(e)'.[950] Both of these 'alternative measures' may satisfy the OTP's disclosure obligations at the pre-confirmation stage given the less demanding evidentiary standard at the confirmation hearing.[951]

Yet, any flexibilization of the Prosecutor's disclosure obligations should not go to the detriment of the defence. Thus, Pre-Trial Chamber I rejected the prosecution's contention that the major part of exculpatory material need only be disclosed after the confirmation hearing.[952] Instead, it found that this can be done only in exceptional circumstances, in order to guarantee the accused's right to adequately prepare his or her defence and the confirmation hearing.[953]

*(iii) The obligation to provide an analysis chart*

Pursuant to the *Bemba* PTC 'the evidence exchanged between the parties and communicated to the Chamber[954] must be the subject of a sufficiently detailed *legal analysis* relating the alleged facts with the constituent elements corresponding to each crime charged'.[955] The nature and extent of this demanding 'legal analysis'[956] gave birth to the so-called In-Depth Analysis Chart ('IDAC'),[957] also named 'element-based chart'.[958] Its legal basis is found[959] in the PTC's power 'to issue orders regarding the disclosure of information'[960] and 'take the necessary decisions regarding disclosure'.[961] Its purpose was to 'streamline the disclosure of evidence, to ensure that the defence [sic] be prepared under satisfactory conditions, to

[949] *Katanga and Ngudjolo*, ICC-01/04-01/07-621, paras. 65, 77–82. In favour of summaries for the purpose of the confirmation hearing, also Mettraux et al., *Effectiveness ICC* (2014), p. 15 (para. 59).

[950] *Katanga and Ngudjolo*, ICC-01/04-01/07-621, paras. 77, 85.

[951] Ibid., paras. 1–7, 66–7, 78–86.

[952] *Lubanga*, ICC-01/04-01/06-102, p. 8 and paras. 119, 124–31.

[953] Pursuant to Art. 61 (3) and 67 (1)(b) and (2) ICCS.

[954] See Section B.(1)(c) in this chapter.

[955] *Bemba*, ICC-01/05-01/08-55, para. 66 (emphasis added); also Kuczyńska, *Accusation Model* (2015), p. 212; Re, in Agirre et al., *Quality Control* (2020), p. 765.

[956] *Bemba*, ICC-01/05-01/08-55, para. 69: 'Each piece of evidence must be analysed—page by page or, where required, paragraph by paragraph—by relating each piece of information contained in that page or paragraph with one or more of the constituent elements of one or more of the crimes with which the person is charged, including the contextual elements of those crimes, as well as the constituent elements of the mode of participation in the offence with which [a] person is charged.' The PTC continued to specify that the in-depth analysis chart 'should be presented in the form of a summary table which shows the relevance of the evidence presented in relation to the constituent elements of the crimes with which the person is charged' (para. 70). See also ICC, *Prosecutor v. Katanga*, TC II, Order Concerning the Presentation of Incriminating Evidence and the E-Court Protocol, ICC-01/04-01/07-956, 13 March 2009, which reminded the Prosecutor 'to submit a proposal for "an ordered and systematic presentation of [its] evidence"' (para. 1) and 'directed the Prosecution to submit a proposal for a table linking the charges confirmed by Pre-Trial Chamber I and the modes of responsibility with the alleged facts as well as the evidence on which it intends to rely at trial' (para.1).

[957] See, in more detail, Schabas, Chaitidou, and El Zeidy, 'Article 61', in Ambos, *Commentary* (2022), mn. 73 ff.; Re, in Agirre et al., *Quality Control* (2020), pp. 764 ff. Generally about case charts that systematize and link evidence to the relevant facts and elements of crime, see Section A.(2)(a) in this chapter.

[958] ICC, *Prosecutor v. Gbagbo*, PTC III, Decision Establishing a Disclosure System and a Calendar for Disclosure, ICC-02/11-01/11-30, 24 January 2012, para. 40.

[959] cf. ICC, *Prosecutor v. Ongwen*, AC, Judgment on the Appeal of the Prosecutor against the Decision of Pre-Trial Chamber II entitled 'Decision Setting the Regime for Evidence Disclosure and Other Related Matters', ICC-02/04-01/15-25, 17 June 2015, paras. 1, 33. See also van der Vyver, *CrimLBull*, 48 No. 4 (2012), 17; Bekou and Bergsmo, in Bergsmo, *Active Complementarity* (2011), pp. 324, 327–9. In contrast, the Prosecutor opined that these provisions 'by their express terms relate to the Pre-Trial Chamber's "general discretionary power to regulate the disclosure process" and do not empower the Single Judge to order in-depth analysis charts', ICC, *Prosecutor v. Ongwen*, OTP, Prosecution's Appeal against the 'Decision Setting the Regime for Evidence Disclosure and Other Related Material', ICC-02/04-01/15-225, 28 April 2015, paras. 11–12.

[960] Art. 61 (3) ICCS.

[961] Rule 121 (2) RPE ICC.

expedite proceedings and to prepare properly for the confirmation hearing'.[962] The case law has become progressively more specific as to extent and format of the chart.[963] Another move was the so-called 'law-driven' approach whereby the parties were required to present 'each piece of evidence according to its relevance in relation to the constituent elements of the crimes presented by the Prosecutor in [her] application under article 58 of the Statute and taken into account by the Chamber in its [decision on the said application]'.[964] In *Gbagbo*, the TC 'invited' the Prosecutor to submit within thirty days 'a trial brief illustrating her case and detailing the evidence in support of the charges'.[965]

On a more general level, the introduction of the analysis chart forms part of a broader strategy to counter the increasing uncertainty and inconsistency of the disclosure process[966] by determining the form, timing, and extent of disclosure to the greatest extent possible.[967] Indeed, the fact that a (former) President of the Court in his address to the 9th ASP-Session in December 2010 mentioned the IDAC[968] demonstrates that is not just a mere technicality of disclosure, but regarded as an important step towards more efficient and expeditious trials. In fact, the Court has identified a disclosure reform as one of the steps that must be taken to improve its functioning, as suggested by the so-called 'Lessons Learnt' initiative.[969]

[962] *Bemba*, ICC-01/05-01/08-55, para. 72. In more detail, van der Vyver, *CrimLBull*, 48 no. 4 (2012), 12 ff.; Bekou and Bergsmo, in Bergsmo, *Active Complementarity* (2011), pp. 321 ff.

[963] In *Katanga*, ICC-01/04-01/07-956, the Chamber was of the view 'that the proposed template does not meet the needs of the Chamber and the Defence. The information provided by the proposed table would be largely outdated and would not enable the parties or the Chamber to have an ordered, systematic and sufficiently detailed overview of the incriminating evidence' (para. 9). As a result, the TC imposed specific conditions as to the content and format of the template (paras. 9 ff.). In a more flexible vein, the *Bemba* PTC requested the Prosecutor 'to submit an updated, consolidated version of the in-depth analysis chart of incriminating evidence following the structure of the model chart annexed to the present decision' (ICC, *Prosecutor v. Bemba*, PTC III, Decision on the Submission of an Updated, Consolidated Version of the In-depth Analysis Chart of Incriminatory Evidence, ICC-01/05-01/08-232, 10 November 2008, para. 8); see also *Mbarushimana*, ICC-01/04-01/10-87, pp. 15–16; ICC, *Prosecutor v. Ruto and Sang*, PTC II, Decision Setting the Regime for Evidence Disclosure and Other Related Matters, ICC-01/09-01/11-44, 6 April 2011, para. 22; ICC, *Prosecutor v. Kenyatta*, PTC II, Decision Setting the Regime for Evidence Disclosure and Other Related Matters, ICC-01/09-02/11-48, 6 April 2011, para. 23.

[964] cf. *Ongwen*, ICC-02/04-01/15-203, para. 37, basically drawing on *Bemba*, ICC-01/05-01/08-55, paras. 66–70; *Ruto and Sang*, ICC-01/09-01/11-44, para. 21; *Kenyatta*, ICC-01/09-02/11-48, para. 22. See generally Schabas, Chaitidou, and El Zeidy, 'Article 61', in Ambos, *Commentary* (2022), mn. 75 ff.

[965] ICC, *Prosecutor v. Gbagbo and Blé Goudé*, TC I, Order on the Further Conduct of the Proceedings, ICC-02/11-01/15-1124, 9 February 2018, p. 9. Thereto Re, in Agirre et al., *Quality Control* (2020), p. 767.

[966] The case-by-case-approach to issues of disclosure, in connection with the lack of precedent, leads to legal inconsistency, encouraging the parties to file as many motions as possible. In more detail, Heinze, *Disclosure* (2014), p. 28; Heinze, in Bock et al., *Strafrecht* (2015), pp. 196–7, 203, 210–11; Whiting, in Stahn, *Practice* (2015), pp. 1007–8. with a list of case law at the ad hoc tribunals in n. 1.

[967] Bekou and Bergsmo, in Bergsmo, *Active Complementarity* (2011), p. 315.

[968] Statement by Judge Sang-Hyun Song, President of the ICC, 'Remarks to the Assembly of States Parties 9th Session', p. 3 (6 December 2010), <https://asp.icc-cpi.int/iccdocs/asp_docs/ASP9/Statements/ICC-ASP9-statements-SangHyunSong-ENG.pdf> ('In 2008, the Pre-Trial Chamber introduced an innovative legal tool called the in-depth analysis chart. It directs the Prosecutor to link every piece of evidence with a specific element of the crimes and mode of liability as contained in the charges, making the review of evidence more efficient and enabling the judges to organise the presentation of evidence in an expeditious manner.').

[969] The 'Working Group on Lessons Learnt' was, together with a 'Roadmap on Reviewing the Criminal Procedures of the International Criminal Court', established by the ASP in November 2011 to consider recommendations on proposals to amend the ICC's RPE. In its first report, the Working Group came to the conclusion that '[a] discussion [was] needed regarding the system of disclosure, including the possibility of establishing a standard system of disclosure, a unified e-Court protocol and a simplified system for applying and lifting redactions'. (ICC-ASP, *Report Study Group on Governance* (2012), Annex, p. 4). Thus, the latest Report of the Study Group contains more detailed recommendations for disclosure amendments, see ICC-ASP, *Report Study Group on Governance* (2015), paras. 17, 31 ff., which explicitly bases its findings on the ICC, *Pre-Trial Practice Manual* (September 2015), also taken into account in this chapter (recently updated as: ICC, *Practice Manual* (2023)). About the Lessons Learnt initiative, see generally Ambach, in Stahn, *Practice* (2015), pp. 1277, 1284 ff.

While the IDAC certainly has the potential to make international criminal trials more efficient and expeditious,[970] and may even 'be of significant benefit to domestic jurisdictions both in terms of disclosure policy and as a framework for the investigation and prosecution of alleged crimes',[971] it bears two main risks also identified by the prosecution: first, to produce such a chart, albeit not affecting the OTP's independence,[972] requires additional resources which the prosecution is lacking.[973] Secondly, and more importantly, the creation of such a chart entails certain determinations that should actually be addressed at the confirmation hearing. Concretely speaking, the Prosecutor is now obliged not only to disclose information, but also to draw inferences from that information[974] and that would have otherwise been presented at the confirmation hearing. In this context the prosecution reminded the Chamber of Rule 81 (1) RPE ICC protecting '[r]eports, memoranda or other internal documents' as work product and excluding them from disclosure.[975] Against this background it comes as no surprise that the production of an IDAC may be considered 'disproportionate' in terms of the resources required and the procedural delay implied.[976]

A related, albeit more profound, concern is that the in-depth analysis provided by the chart converts the Pre-Trial Chamber into an investigative judge who will be in a position to pre-judge the case based on the parties' analysis before it is actually discussed at the confirmation hearing.[977] Thus, such a chart may make the Chamber lose its 'virgin mind'.[978] Be that as it may, it is clear that the chart does not enjoy popularity amongst all judges, as demonstrated by the recently published *Pre-Trial Practice Manual* and its successor, the *Practice Manual*,[979] stating unequivocally: 'No submission of any "in-depth analysis chart", or *similia*, of the evidence disclosed can be imposed on either party.'[980] Thus, there is an awkward split between the case law (at times imposing an obligation or at least an equivalent) and the *Practice Manual* (denying such an obligation).

970 Bekou and Bergsmo, in Bergsmo, *Active Complementarity* (2011), p. 343. In favour, also Mettraux et al., *Effectiveness ICC* (2014), pp. 13–14 (paras. 48, 52), who recommend that the Chart 'should include reference to relevant documentary evidence as well as witness evidence' (p. 18, para. 78 b)).

971 Bekou and Bergsmo, in Bergsmo, *Active Complementarity* (2011), p. 346.

972 As guaranteed by Art. 41 (1) ICCS and suggested by OTP, cf. *Ongwen*, ICC-02/04-01/15-225, paras. 18, 33.

973 On the contrary, the OTP is trying to increase its budget and staff; see Chapter II, B.(2) in this volume; see also *Ongwen*, ICC-02/04-01/15-225, para. 18 ('[T]he Decision imposes a significant extra-statutory duty on the Prosecution before the confirmation hearing by compelling it to direct resources towards the burdensome preparation of an IDAC, and away from other tasks that it believes are necessary to investigate and prosecute this and other cases.')

974 *Ongwen*, ICC-02/04-01/15-225, para. 12.

975 ICC, *Prosecutor v. Bemba*, OTP, Prosecution's Submissions on the Trial Chamber's 8 December 2009 Oral Order Requesting Updating of the In-Depth-Analysis Chart, ICC-01/05-01/08-656, 15 December 2009, para. 9; ICC, *Prosecutor v. Katanga and Ngudjolo*, TC II, Decision on the 'Prosecut'on's Application for Leave to Appeal the "Order concerning the Presentation of Incriminating Evidence and the E-Court Protocol"' and the 'Prosecution's Second Application for Extension of Time Limit Pursuant to Regulation 35', ICC-01/04-01/07-1088, 2 May 2009, para. 13.

976 See e.g. ICC, *Prosecutor v. Al Hassan*, PTC I, Decision on the In-depth Analysis Chart of Disclosed Evidence, ICC-01/12-01/18-61-tENG, 29 June 2018, para. 22 (weighing the advantages of the IDAC against the disadvantages, the Single Judge decided that ordering an IDAC would be 'disproportionate'); *Prosecutor v. Yekatom and Ngaïssona*, PTC II, Second Decision on Disclosure and Related Matters, ICC-01/14-01/18-163, 4 April 2019, paras. 23–4 (no ordering of IDAC because of possible postponement of confirmation hearing). Thereto Heinze, in Ruiz Fabri, *MPEIPro* (2020), mn. 26.

977 *Ongwen*, ICC-02/04-01/15-225, para. 21.

978 Damaška, *Faces of Justice* (1986), p. 137; Heinze, *Disclosure* (2014), pp. 242 ff., 495, 503.

979 See thereon note 899 in this chapter.

980 ICC, *Practice Manual* (2023), para. 24, see also Re, in Agirre et al., *Quality Control* (2020), p. 766. It remains a matter of speculation whether it is coincidence that the Manual, including its clear rejection of the IDAC, had not been published until the retirement of the Court's former President Song (who was a promoter of that chart, see above note 968). Similar reservations against the in-depth-analysis chart are expressed in ICC-ASP, *Report Study Group on Governance* (2015), para. 29.

At any rate, an IDAC or a similar procedural instruction may also serve as a management tool to improve the efficiency of proceedings. This can be seen by the KSC's approach where the SPO is required to submit the indictment with a 'detailed outline demonstrating the relevance of each item of evidentiary material to each allegation, with particular reference to the conduct of the suspect with respect to the alleged crime(s)'.[981] This requirement is supposed to improve the efficiency of the proceedings.[982] At the same time, with the effectiveness of international criminal trials, especially at the ICC, coming under increased scrutiny, the balancing exercise between the rights of the accused and streamlined proceedings seems to go increasingly in favour of the latter.[983]

### (d) *Exculpatory evidence*

#### (i) *The importance of an obligation to disclose exculpatory evidence*

The obligation to disclose exculpatory evidence[984] is independent from the trial stage and goes to the heart of an accused's right to a fair trial.[985] It is the most important,[986] if not the only, instrument for the defence to counterbalance the greater resources of the prosecution[987] and achieve some kind of 'equality of arms'.[988] It 'is not a secondary' obligation, 'to be complied with after everything else is done' but 'it is as important as the obligation to prosecute'.[989]

Yet, while at ICTY and ICTR the respective Rule 68 RPE has not, given the adversarial nature of the proceedings, been interpreted as forcing the prosecution 'to replace the Defence in conducting investigations or gathering material that may assist the Defence',[990] at the ICC this obligation is derived from the general duty to investigate incriminating and exonerating circumstances equally in order to find the truth.[991]

[981] Rule 86 (3)(b) KSC RPE. See also Heinze, in Ruiz Fabri, *MPEIPro* (2020), mn. 27.

[982] cf. Heinze, *JICJ*, 15 (2017), 994–5; Heinze, *CLF*, 30 (2019), 118–19.

[983] See esp. Heinze, *CLF*, 30 (2019), 119–20.

[984] On the distinction between 'material' and 'evidence', see Section A.(1) in this chapter. As the ICC disclosure regime uses the word (exculpatory) 'evidence', I use the same term throughout this section, mindful of the fact that the term is—as an exception in the context of disclosure—interpreted broadly, see (next) Section B.(2)(d)(ii) in this chapter *in fine*.

[985] cf. *Lubanga*, ICC 01/04-01/06-1401, paras. 77 ff., 92. According to the ICTY AC the disclosure of exculpatory material is fundamental to the fairness of proceedings before the tribunal, see ICTY, *Prosecutor v. Krstić*, AC, Judgment, IT-98-33-A, 19 April 2004, para. 180. See also Brady, in Lee, *ICC* (2001), p. 403; Kuczyńska, *Accusation Model* (2015), p. 186.

[986] cf. *Blagojević and Jokić*, IT-02-60-PT, para. 24; ICTY, *Prosecutor v. Brđanin*, TC, Decision on 'Motion for Relief from Rule 68 Violations by the Prosecutor and for Sanctions to be imposed Pursuant to Rule 68bis and Motion for Adjournment While Matters Affecting Justice and a Fair Trial can be Resolved', IT-99-36-T, 30 October 2002, para. 23 (disclosure of evidence that in any way tends to suggest the innocence or mitigate the guilt of the accused is one of the most onerous responsibilities of the prosecution).

[987] Mosteller, in Dressler, *Encyclopedia* (2002), p. 534; Brady, in Lee, *ICC* (2001), p. 403.

[988] Dennis, *Evidence* (2020), mn. 9-006 *in fine*; Swoboda, *CLF*, 19 (2008), 472.

[989] ICTY, *Prosecutor v. Kordić and Čerkez*, TC, Decision on Motions to Extend for Filing Appellant's Briefs, IT-95-14/2, 11 May 2001, para. 14. See also Khan and Buisman, in Stahn, *Practice* (2015), p. 1040 with further references.

[990] *Blagojević and Jokić*, IT-02-60-PT, para. 26; in a similar vein, ICTR, *Prosecutor v. Bizimungu et al.*, TC, Decision on Jerome-Clement Bicamumpaka's motion for judicial notice of a Rwandan judgement of 8 December 2000 and in the alternative for an order to disclose exculpatory evidence, ICTR-99-50-T, 15 December 2004, para. 26 ('Rule 68 (A) does not impose an obligation on the Prosecution to hunt for and disclose materials which are not in its possession or control').

[991] Art. 54 (1)(a) ICCS. See also Tochilovsky, in Doria, Gasser, and Bassiouni, *Essays in Honour of Blishchenko* (2009), p. 846 (arguing the the ad hoc tribunals' approach would not be applicable before the ICC). According to Mettraux et al., *Effectiveness ICC* (2014), p. 17 (para. 76), 'the Pre-Trial Chamber should verify the Prosecution's compliance with its obligations under Article 54(1) ICC Statute'; Turner, in Heller et al., *Oxford HB ICL* (2020) pp. 39, 54.

*(ii) Definition of 'exculpatory evidence'*

Exculpatory evidence is evidence that 'shows or tends to show the innocence of the accused, or to mitigate the guilt of the accused, or which may affect the credibility of prosecution evidence'.[992] The fact that a statement contains incriminatory elements 'is no reason to disregard any potentially exculpatory factor(s) contained therein'.[993]

According to the latest version of the similar Rule 68 RPE ICTY[994] the exculpatory character of the evidence has to be 'in the actual knowledge' of the Prosecutor. This 'narrows the obligation to disclose'[995] since it only applies to material which is not only already in the *possession* of the Prosecutor (i.e. no obligation to search for such material)[996] but of whose exculpatory character the Prosecutor also has 'actual knowledge'.[997] The SCSL and its residuary mechanism refer to 'evidence known to the Prosecutor'.[998] At the ICC and the KSC (actual) knowledge is not (exclusively) required. At the ICC it suffices that the Prosecutor, with regard to evidence in its 'possession or control' (including material publicly available),[999] 'believes' it to have an exculpatory tendency.[1000] At the KSC it suffices that information, in the SPO's 'custody, control *or* actual knowledge', 'reasonably suggest[s]' an exculpatory tendency.[1001]

While Article 67 (2) ICCS refers to 'evidence', the new Rule 68 RPE ICTY replaced this term[1002] by 'material' in 2001.[1003] This change was due to a rather broad interpretation of

[992] Art. 67 (2) ICCS. See e.g. *Lubanga*, ICC-01/04-01/06-1401, para. 59. See also Rule 103 RPE KSC.

[993] ICC, *Prosecutor v. Yekatom and Ngaïssona*, TC V, Decision on the Yekatom Defence Request Concerning Disclosure Violation and Disclosure of Exculpatory Material, ICC-01/14-01/18-595, 22 July 2020, para. 21.

[994] Rule 68 (1) RPE ICTY. The original version of the Rule from 4 October 1994 provided: 'The Prosecutor shall, as soon as practicable, disclose to the defence the existence of evidence known to the Prosecutor which in any way tends to suggest the innocence or mitigate the guilt of the accused of a crime charged in the indictment.' This rule caused a heavy workload for prosecution teams and produced lengthy debates with the defence, delaying proceedings, or the prosecution simply claimed that it did not possess the evidence sought by the defence, see Zappalà, *JICJ*, 2 (2004), 623. Thus, the new version quoted above was introduced in 2003 and 2004. It 'was intended to further the interests of justice, providing safeguards for ongoing or future investigations, increasing the expediency of proceedings, and protecting the confidentiality interests of states or other sensitive sources which could be prejudiced by disclosure', Zappalà, *JICJ*, 2 (2004), 624. For more details, see Heinze, *Disclosure* (2014), pp. 345 ff.; Re, in Agirre et al., *Quality Control* (2020), pp. 747–8.

[995] Fedorova, *Equality of Arms* (2012), pp. 252 ff.; on the reference to Rule 70 RPE ICTY taking into account the conflict between confidentiality and the disclosure obligations of the Prosecutor, pp. 254 ff.

[996] ICTY, *Prosecutor v. Bralo*, AC, Decision on Motions for Access to *Ex Parte* Portions of the Records on Appeal and for Disclosure of Mitigating Material, IT-95-17-A, 30 August 2006, para. 30; ICTY, *Prosecutor v. Hadzihasanovic et al.*, AC, Decision on Appeal from Refusal to Grant Access to Confidential Material in another Case, IT-01-47-AR73, 23 April 2002, p. 3. See generally Tochilovsky, *Law and Jurisprudence* (2014), pp. 161–2.

[997] On the restrictive impact of the 'actual knowledge'-requirement see Re in Agirre et al., *Quality Control* (2020), p. 749: 'No matter how well motivated prosecution officials are, the possibility always exists of undisclosed exculpatory information remaining in the prosecution's possession. This possibility is amplified by assigning the searching of holdings for disclosable information to junior staff. And it is further magnified by the challenges of finding this information in collections of evidence in languages not spoken or read by the reviewing officials, including in videos, evidence on CDs or other electronic forms. It may also be delegated—with instructions of what to look for—to language assistants. Inevitably things may be overlooked.'

[998] Rule 68 (B) RPE SCSL and Rule 68 (B) RPE RSCSL; thereto Re, in Agirre et al., *Quality Control* (2020), p. 747.

[999] ICC, *Prosecutor v. Banda and Jerbo*, AC, Judgment on the Appeal of Mr Abdallah Banda Abakaer Nourain and Mr Saleh Mohammed Jerbo Jamus against the Decision of Trial Chamber IV of 23 January 2013 Entitled 'Decision on the Defence's request for disclosure of documents in the possession of the Office of the Prosecutor', ICC-02/05-03/09-501, 28 August 2013, para. 34; Guariglia et al., *AC ICC Commentary* (2018), p. 205.

[1000] cf. Art. 67 (2) ICCS.

[1001] Rule 103 RPE KSC.

[1002] cf. Rule 68 RPE ICTY of 10 July 1998, IT/32/Rev. 13: 'The Prosecutor shall, as soon as practicable, disclose to the defence the existence of *evidence* known to the Prosecutor which in any way tends to suggest the innocence or mitigate the guilt of the accused or may affect the credibility of prosecution evidence' (emphasis added); Tochilovsky, in Doria, Gasser, and Bassiouni, *Essays in Honour of Blishchenko* (2009), p. 848. See Zappalà, *JICJ*, 2 (2004), 623, 627.

[1003] Rule 68 (i) RPE ICTY of 8 July 2015, IT/32/Rev.50: 'Subject to the provisions of Rule 70, the Prosecutor shall, as soon as practicable, disclose to the Defence any *material* which in the actual knowledge of the Prosecutor

the term 'evidence' by the case law,[1004] holding that the term 'evidence' was 'not restricted to material in a form that would be admissible in evidence' but included 'all information in any form which falls within the quoted description'.[1005] According to *Tochilovsky*, 'evidence' so understood includes 'any information which may affect the credibility of prosecution evidence'.[1006] As a consequence, the term 'evidence' in Article 67 (2) ICCS has to be interpreted rather broadly.[1007]

*(iii) Discretionary decision by the prosecution*

The classification of evidence as incriminating or exculpatory is at the discretion of the Prosecutor.[1008] Although there is no *prima facie* requirement—absent an order of the Trial Chamber[1009]—as a matter of practice and with a view to a fair and expeditious trial, the prosecution should normally indicate which material it is disclosing as exculpatory.[1010] The same applies under Article 67 (2) ICCS.[1011] In contrast, at the KSC the classification of the material as incriminating or exculpatory is not in the Prosecutor's discretion but to be decided on the basis of a reasonableness test.[1012]

When there is doubt about the application of this disclosure obligation, the ICC Prosecutor may request the Chamber to rule on the (exculpatory) nature of the evidence.[1013] This may also be the case when the prosecution is bound by conflicting duties, such as having to keep material confidential on the basis of national security interests,[1014] or when it has obtained material on the condition that it be kept confidential and used to generate new evidence only.[1015] The defence may also request the PTC or the TC to order the disclosure of

may suggest the innocence or mitigate the guilt of the accused or affect the credibility of Prosecution evidence' (emphasis added). See also Zappalà, *JICJ*, 2 (2004), 623, 627; Kuczyńska, *Accusation Model* (2015), p. 207.

[1004] cf. ICTY, *Prosecutor v. Brđanin and Talić*, TC II, Decision on Motion by Momir Talić for Disclosure of Evidence, IT-99-36-PT, 27 June 2000, para. 8; also Tochilovsky, in Doria, Gasser, and Bassiouni, *Essays in Honour of Blishchenko* (2009), p. 848.

[1005] *Kordić and Čerkez*, IT-95-14/2, para. 9; *Brđanin and Talić*, IT-99-36-PT, para. 8; *Krnojelac*, IT-97-25-PT, paras. 2, 11 ('The expression "evidence" is intended to include any material which may put the accused on notice that material exists which may assist him in his defence, and it is not limited to material which is itself admissible in evidence.')

[1006] Tochilovsky, in Doria, Gasser, and Bassiouni, *Essays in Honour of Blishchenko* (2009), p. 848.

[1007] *Lubanga*, ICC-01/04–01/06-1401, paras. 88–9. See also Ambos, *NCLR*, 12 (2009), 550 ff.; Whiting, in Stahn, *Practice*, p. 1011.

[1008] cf. Art. 67 (2) ICCS ('which [the Prosecutor] believes shows or tends to show'); see also *Prosecutor v. Gucati and Haradinaj*, CoAP, Appeal Judgment, KSC-CA-2022-01/F00114, 2 February 2023, para. 34; *Prosecutor v. Gucati and Haradinaj*, CoAP, Public Redacted Version of Decision on the Appeals Against Disclosure Decision, KSC-BC-2020-07/IA005/F00008/RED, 29 July 2021, para. 38; Tochilovsky, in Doria, Gasser, and Bassiouni, *Essays in Honour of Blishchenko* (2009), p. 846; Jackson, *JICJ*, 7 (2009), 27. About the difficulties the prosecution is facing with regard to the decision whether material is in fact exculpatory, see Whiting, in Stahn, *Practice* (2015), pp. 1022 ff.; Re, in Agirre et al., *Quality Control* (2020), pp. 750 ff.

[1009] *Krstić*, IT-98-33-A, para. 190 (order under Rule 68 RPE ICTY requiring prosecution to identify the material being disclosed to the defence as exculpatory).

[1010] ICTY, *Prosecutor v. Krajišnik*, TC III, Decision on Motion from Momcilo Krajisnik to Compel Disclosure of Exculpatory Evidence pursuant to Rule 68, IT-00-39 & 40-PT, 19 July 2001, p. 2.

[1011] Tochilovsky, in Doria, Gasser, and Bassiouni, *Essays in Honour of Blishchenko* (2009), p. 847.

[1012] cf. Rule 103 RPE KSC: 'Specialist Prosecutor shall immediately disclose ... any information ... which may *reasonably* suggest the innocence or mitigate the guilt of the Accused' (emphasis added). See also Heinze, *JICJ*, 15 (2017), 1008.

[1013] cf. Art. 67 (2) 2nd sentence ICCS and Rule 83 RPE ICC; see also Schuon, *International Criminal Procedure* (2010), p. 277.

[1014] Pursuant to Art. 72 ICCS.

[1015] Pursuant to Art. 54 (3)(e) ICCS.

exculpatory evidence by the prosecution with a view to the confirmation hearing[1016] or the trial.[1017]

*(iv) Timing and form*

Exculpatory evidence must be disclosed 'as soon as practicable',[1018] that is, when the accused is transferred to the court prior to the confirmation hearing[1019] or 'immediately after having identified any such evidence'.[1020] This is in line with the (stricter) Rule 103 RPE KSC.[1021]

At any rate, to avoid any kind of surprise caused by new evidence and a resulting late disclosure, the investigation and the corresponding disclosure are to be completed by the time of the confirmation hearing.[1022] Clearly, while there may be room for some flexibility before the confirmation hearing, afterwards every piece of exculpatory evidence must be disclosed.[1023]

The exculpatory evidence needs to be disclosed in its original form and not just in summary form.[1024] However, the prosecution may hand over the material with redactions where appropriate,[1025] 'without need for a prior authorisation of the Chamber',[1026] bearing in mind however that any redacted versions or extracted forms of exculpatory evidence must be 'sufficiently cohesive, understandable and usable' and not taken out of context.[1027] The *Practice Manual* emphasizes that 'the Prosecutor retains the burden of proof to justify the challenged redaction'.[1028] The prosecution must explain its case 'by reference to the witnesses' and all

[1016] Art. 61 (3) ICCS.

[1017] Art. 64 (3)(c) ICCS. See generally Schuon, *International Criminal Procedure* (2010), p. 277; Brady, in Lee, *ICC* (2001), pp. 403, 412.

[1018] Art. 67 (2) ICCS, Rules 83, 84 RPE ICC; see also Rule 68 (i) RPE ICTY/ICTR, Rule 73 (A) RPE MICT. See e.g. *Krajisnik and Plavsic*, IT-00-39 & 40 PT, para. 10. cf. also Schabas, Chaitidou, and El Zeidy, 'Article 61', in Ambos, *Commentary* (2022), mn. 55; Vohrah, in McDonald and Swaak-Goldman, *ICL I* (2000), pp. 519–20; Wu Wei, *Prosecutor of the ICC* (2007), p. 211; Billis, *Rolle des Richters* (2015), p. 427; with regard to the ICC's defence system and the *Lubanga* case, Katzman, *NWUJIHR*, 8 (2009), 88. On the question of whether the defence must submit a prior request before the ICTR according to Rule 66 (B), see ICTR, *Prosecutor v. Kalimanzira*, TC, Judgment, ICTR-05-88-T, 22 June 2009, para. 44. The inspection of such evidence that is 'material' for the case preparation must be permitted, whereby this evidence must be 'relevant'; see, for more detail, ICTY, *Prosecutor v. Karadžić*, TC, Decision on the Accused's Motion for Postponement of Trial, IT-95-5/18-T, 26 February 2010, para. 36.

[1019] *Lubanga*, ICC-01/04-01/06-102, paras. 86, 121; see in general Schuon, *International Criminal Procedure* (2010), p. 277; Heinze, *Disclosure* (2014), pp. 347–8. For an instructive statistic summarizing 'the amount of time between each suspect's initial appearance and the first disclosure of exonerating evidence, based on the publicly available court records', see WCRO, *Confirmation of Charges* (2015), pp. 97–8 with figure four.

[1020] '[S]hall disclose such evidence immediately after having identified any such evidence', see e.g. *Ongwen*, ICC-02/04-01/15-203, para. 18. See also *Al Hassan*, ICC-01/12-01/18-31-tENG, para. 24; ICC, *Prosecutor v. Al Hassan*, PTC I, Ordonnance fixant une date butoir pour le dépôt des requêtes en vue du dépôt du document contenant les charges, ICC-01/12-01/18-255, 25 February 2019, para. 18; *Yekatom*, ICC-01/14-01/18-64-Red, para. 16.

[1021] 'shall immediately disclose'; see also Heinze, *JICJ*, 15 (2017), 985, 1008.

[1022] See previously Ambos, *NCLR*, 12 (2009), 547; also ICC, *Prosecutor v. Lubanga*, AC, Judgment on the Prosecutor's Appeal Against the Decision of Pre-Trial Chamber I Entitled Decision Establishing General Principles Governing Applications to Restrict Disclosure Pursuant to Rule 81 (2) and (4) of the Rules of Procedure and Evidence, ICC-01/04-1/06-568, 13 October 2006, para. 54; ICC, *Prosecutor v. Lubanga*, TC I, Hearing Transcript, ICC-01/04-1/06-T-75, 13 February 2008, paras. 5–7; in more detail, Heinze, *Disclosure* (2014), pp. 524 ff.

[1023] Ambos, *NCLR*, 12 (2009), 549. See also Brady, in Lee, *ICC* (2001), p. 407; Swoboda, *CLF*, 19 (2008), 454.

[1024] *Blagojević and Jokić*, IT-02-60-PT, para. 24; *Brđanin*, Decision, IT-99-36-T, para. 26; Tochilovsky, in Doria, Gasser, and Bassiouni, *Essays in Honour of Blishchenko* (2009), p. 843, 846.

[1025] *Brđanin*, Decision, IT-99-36-T, para. 26; Tochilovsky, in Doria, Gasser, and Bassiouni, *Essays in Honour of Blishchenko* (2009), p. 847. See, in more detail, with a description of ICC case law, Friman, in Stahn, *Practice* (2015), pp. 924–5.

[1026] ICC, *Practice Manual* (2023), para. 99.

[1027] *Blagojević and Jokić*, IT-02-60-PT, para. 24; *Brđanin*, Decision, IT-99-36-T, para. 26.

[1028] ICC, *Practice Manual* (2023), para. 99.

the other evidence it intends to rely upon at trial. It must also explain how the evidence disclosed relates to the charges.[1029]

A redaction of the identity of a witness (i.e. anonymity) at the pre-trial stage[1030] must be specifically authorized 'upon motivated request by the Prosecutor'.[1031] The case law is inconsistent and perhaps too deferential to the prosecution.[1032] Thus, the guidelines of the *Practice Manual* are particularly detailed with regard to disclosure and redactions, even suggesting a template for the first decision regulating disclosure following the initial appearance.[1033]

At the STL, as a general rule, '[a] Party may choose to fulfil some or all of its disclosure obligations in electronic form, together with appropriate computer software to allow for searching of the material'.[1034] This provision mirrors Rule 68 (ii) ICTY RPE and Rule 68 (B) ICTR RPE.[1035] Consequently, referring to the case law of the ad hoc tribunals, the STL AC clarified that Rule 121 (A) 'does not create new disclosure obligations and is merely a way for the Prosecutor to discharge existing obligations efficiently'.[1036] At the ICC, disclosure regularly takes place by giving the defence access to the prosecution's evidence database.[1037]

### *(e) Documents and tangible objects*

According to Rule 77 RPE ICC—identical to Rule 66 (B) RPE ICTY/ICTR and Rule 110 (B) RPE STL—the prosecution shall 'permit the defence to inspect any books, documents, photographs and other tangible objects in the possession or control of the Prosecutor, which are material to the preparation of the defence or are intended for use by the Prosecutor as evidence for the purposes of the confirmation hearing or at trial'. This formulation makes clear that it is the Prosecutor who determines in what category the disclosure material falls: as the Prosecutor decides what qualifies as exculpatory, he decides whether objects are material to the preparation of the defence or whether he (merely) intends to use them.[1038] The KSC CoAP has acknowledged the fact that this means that questions about the materiality will often have to be decided by a Chamber without the defence having had prior access

[1029] ICC, *Prosecutor v. Lubanga*, TC I, Decision Regarding the Timing and Manner of Disclosure and the Date of Trial, ICC-01/04-01/06-1019, 9 November 2007, para. 26; ICC, *Prosecutor v. Lubanga*, TC I, Hearing Transcript, ICC-01/04-01/06-T-52, 1 October 2007, para. 40; ICC, *Prosecutor v. Lubanga*, TC I, Decision on Victim's Participation, ICC-01/04-01/06-1119, 18 January 2008, paras. 110, 138 (b).

[1030] Rule 81 (4) RPE ICC RPE. See, in more detail, Guariglia et al., *AC ICC Commentary* (2018), pp. 209 ff.

[1031] ICC, *Practice Manual* (2023), para. 100.

[1032] cf. Turner, in Heller et al., *Oxford HB ICL* (2020) 39, 55 (quoting defence attorneys who believed that judges were 'overly deferential to the prosecution in authorizing redactions').

[1033] ICC, *Practice Manual* (2023), para. 101. In more detail, Heinze, in Ruiz Fabri, *MPEIPro* (2020), mn. 39.

[1034] Rule 121 (A) RPE STL.

[1035] Heinze, in Ruiz Fabri, *MPEIPro* (2020), mn. 40.

[1036] STL, Prosecutor v. *Ayyash et al.*, AC, Public Redacted Version of 19 September 2013 Decision on Appeal by Counsel for Mr Oneissi Against Pre-Trial Judge's 'Decision on Issues Related to the Inspection Room and Call Data Records', STL-11-01/PT/AC/AR126.4, 2 October 2013, para. 33 (where the AC decided unanimously that Rule 121 (A) extends to the provision of certain software and that the PTJ erred in finding that the provision of that software did not entail an obligation by the prosecution because it was new work product); see also ICTR, *Prosecutor v. Karemera et al.*, AC, Decision on Interlocutory Appeal Regarding the Role of the Prosecutor's Electronic Disclosure Suite in Discharging Disclosure Obligations, ICTR-98-44-AR73.7, 30 June 2006, para. 13.

[1037] On the ensuing broader understanding of disclosure, see Section B.(1)(a).

[1038] See also *Ntaganda*, ICC-01/04-02/06-1330, para. 23 *in fine* ('The Appeals Chamber notes that the main difference between disclosure in item 1) above (witness statements) and disclosure in items 3) and 4) above (rule 77 of the Rules and article 67 (2) of the Statute), is the nature of the Prosecutor's assessment of material subject to disclosure. Article 67 (2) of the Statute requires disclosure of evidence which the Prosecutor *believes* meets the criteria set out therein. Similarly, rule 77 of the Rules leaves to the Prosecutor the assessment of whether objects are "material to the preparation of the defence" and their inspection should thus be permitted' [emphasis in the original]).

to the material and hence without 'informed submissions' by the defence.[1039] As a result, the Chamber must exercise 'particular caution' when evaluating 'materiality' to the defence under Rule 102 (3) RPE KSC.[1040]

As to the key part of this rule—'material to the preparation of the defence'—no explicit definition exists,[1041] but the case law provides some insights. The ICTY TC resorted to the interpretation of Rule 16 (a)(1)(E) of the US Federal Rules of Criminal Procedure,[1042] which was used as a model for Rule 66(B) RPE ICTY.[1043] The ICC AC confirmed this approach[1044] and suggested a broad understanding 'referring to all objects that are relevant for the preparation of the defence'.[1045] Both the STL AC and the KSC CoAP also advocate a broad approach,[1046] with the latter clarifying that 'the test for relevance is wider than the test of

[1039] *Prosecutor v. Gucati and Haradinaj*, CoAP, Public Redacted Version of Decision on the Specialist Prosecutor's Office's Request Regarding Item 206, KSC-CA-2022-01/F00075/RED, 31 January 2023, para. 21.

[1040] *Prosecutor v. Gucati and Haradinaj*, CoAP, Public Redacted Version of Decision on the Specialist Prosecutor's Office's Request Regarding Item 206, KSC-CA-2022-01/F00075/RED, 31 January 2023, para. 21.

[1041] See also *Ayyash et al.*, STL-11-01/PT/AC/AR126.4, 19 September 2013 Decision, para. 21 ('[n]either Rule 110 (B) nor any other Rule offers guidance as to the interpretation of "materiality" in this context'); *Prosecutor v. Gucati and Haradinaj*, CoAP, Public Redacted Version of Decision on the Appeals Against Disclosure Decision, KSC-BC-2020-07/IA005/F00008/RED, 29 July 2021, para. 38 ('[N]either the Rules nor the Law offer guidance as to the interpretation of the concepts of "relevance to the case" and "material to the Defence preparation"').

[1042] ICTY, *Prosecutor v. Delalić*, TC II, Decision on the Motion by the Accused Zejnil Delalić for the Disclosure of Evidence, IT-96-21-PT, 26 September 1996, para. 7: 'The significant jurisprudence in the United States federal courts on the scope of "materiality" demonstrates that it is generally accepted that to be material, the requested information must have "more than … [an] abstract logical relationship to the issues."' See e.g. *United States v. Ross*, 511 F.2d 757, 762 (U.S. Ct. App· 5th Cir.), cert. denied 423 U.S. 836 (U.S. Supreme Court 1975). The requested evidence must be 'significantly helpful to an understanding of important inculpatory or exculpatory evidence'; it is material if there 'is a strong indication that … [the evidence] will "play an important role in uncovering admissible evidence, aiding witness preparation, corroborating testimony, or assisting impeachment or rebuttal."' *United States v. Jackson*, 850 F. Supp. 1481, 1503 (U.S. Dist. Ct. D. Kan. 1994), quoting *United States v. Lloyd*, 992 F.2d 348, 351 (U.S. Ct. App. D.C. Cir. 1993)'.

[1043] *Delalić*, IT-96-21-PT, para. 6. About Rule 66 (B) RPE ICTY, see also Kuczyńska, *Accusation Model* (2015), pp. 207 ff. About the references to English and US Law by the ICC and the ICTY, see Heinze, *Disclosure* (2014), pp. 355 ff.; Whiting, in Stahn, *Practice* (2015), p. 1011.

[1044] ICC, *Prosecutor v. Lubanga*, AC, Judgment on the Appeal of Mr Lubanga Dyilo against the Oral Decision of Trial Chamber I of 18 January 2008, ICC-01/04-01/06-1433, 11 July 2008, para. 78 (Judge Pikis and Judge Song dissenting).

[1045] *Lubanga*, ICC-01/04-01/06-1433, paras. 76, 77, overruling the TC: '[A]ccording to the Trial Chamber's view, only material that relate to issues which would either directly undermine the "Prosecution case" or support a line of argument of the defence are material to the preparation of the defence … The Appeals Chamber finds that the Trial Chamber interpreted rule 77 of the Rules of Procedure and Evidence too narrowly because it excluded objects which, while not directly linked to exonerating or incriminating evidence, may otherwise be material to the preparation of the defence. The wording of rule 77 of the Rules of Procedure and Evidence does not suggest that the term "material to the preparation of the defence" should be construed as narrowly as the Trial Chamber did. Rather, the term should be understood as referring to all objects that are relevant for the preparation of the defence.' See also Kuczyńska, *Accusation Model* (2015), pp. 211 ff. Crit., however, Brady, in Lee, *ICC* (2001), pp. 403, 411, arguing that a broad interpretation of 'material to the preparation' basically makes Rule 121 (3) RPE ICC (which is applicable to the confirmation hearing) meaningless. In the same vein, Schuon (*International Criminal Procedure* (2010), p. 278) doubts that the drafters intended to require only a 'list of evidence' favouring a broad interpretation of 'material to the defence' at the same time. See also Heinze, *Disclosure* (2014), pp. 355 ff.

[1046] STL, *Prosecutor v. Ayyash et al.*, AC, Public Redacted Version of 'The Defence for Hussein Hassan Oneissi Appeal to The Pre-Trial Judge's "Decision on Issues Related to the Inspection Room and Call Data Records" Dated 18 June 2013', STL-11-01/PT/AC/AR126.4, 16 October 2013, paras. 22–3 (referring to ICTY, ICTR, and ICC, which 'have recognised that "preparation is a broad concept"' and rejecting the Pre-Trial Judge's interpretation of Rule 110 (B) RPE STL, being too restrictive and going 'against its clear wording and the jurisprudence of other international tribunals'); KSC, *Shala*, KSC-BC-2023-11/F00023, para. 63 ('The formulation *material to the Defence preparation* shall be construed broadly and refers to all documents and objects of relevance to the preparation of the Defence case, in the exercise of the Accused's rights under the Law and the Rules. What is *material* in this context should not necessarily be limited by the temporal scope of the Confirmed Indictment or confined to issues which would either directly undermine the SPO's case or support a line of argument of the defence' [fn. omitted, emphasis in original]); *Prosecutor v. Gucati and Haradinaj*, CoAP, Public Redacted Version of Decision

materiality to the preparation of the Defence'.[1047] Thus, the broad understanding of 'material to the defence' seems widely accepted today.[1048] It encompasses material such as requests for assistance submitted by the Prosecutor, even though those requests are not expressly covered by the ICC's disclosure regime,[1049] as well as 'individual protection assessments', 'biographical security questionnaires', and 'psycho-social assessment[s]'.[1050] Note, however, that Rule 102 (3) RPE KSC goes further than Rules 77 RPE ICC and 66 (B) RPE ICTY: the defence can 'request' the Prosecutor to disclose material and inspect objects in its 'custody or control' which the defence deems 'to be material to its preparation'.

Rule 66 (B) RPE ICTY—and thus the basically identical Rule 77 RPE ICC—'requires a *prima facie* showing of materiality to the preparation of the Defence of the evidence requested'.[1051] The defence has to specifically identify evidence, material to the preparation of the defence, which is being withheld by the Prosecutor.[1052] This corresponds to Rule 102 (3) RPE KSC, i.e. the defence must specifically identify the material it requests and cannot just generally ask for it.[1053] In contrast, Rule 77 RPE ICC does not—as Rule 66(B) RPE ICTY—ask the defence to file a request to trigger the inspection right. The relevant proposal[1054] was ultimately rejected since it was considered inappropriate to make this important defence right dependant upon such a request.[1055] The AC, explicitly resorting to the jurisprudence of the ad hoc tribunals, placed a low burden on the defence by finding that '[i]t may be that information that is material to the preparation of the defence is ultimately not used as evidence at the trial or may not turn out to be relevant to it. Yet, the defence is still entitled to this information on the basis of a *prima facie* assessment'.[1056] The defence fails to meet this 'low' threshold where it merely indicates that a 'database "may potentially" include

on the Appeals Against Disclosure Decision, KSC-BC-2020-07/IA005/F00008/RED, 29 July 2021, para. 41 ('It transpires from well-established jurisprudence from international criminal tribunals that the concept of 'material to the preparation of the defence' is to be interpreted broadly [ . . . ]').

[1047] *Prosecutor v. Gucati and Haradinaj*, CoAP, Public Redacted Version of Decision on the Appeals against Disclosure Decision, KSC-BC-2020-07/IA005/F00008/RED, 29 July 2021, para. 42.

[1048] See also Heinze, in Ruiz Fabri, *MPEIPro* (2020), mn. 42.

[1049] ICC, *Prosecutor v. Yekatom and Ngaïssona*, PTC II, Decision on the Defence Motion for an Extension of Time to File List of Evidence and Related Motions, ICC-01/14-01/18-315-Red, 3 February 2020, paras. 66 ff.

[1050] *Ongwen*, ICC-02/04-01/15-1734, para. 22.

[1051] ICTY, *Prosecutor v. Naletilić and Martinović*, TC, Decision on Joint Motions for Order Allowing Defence Counsel to Inspect Documents in the Possession of the Prosecution, IT-98-34-T, 16 September 2002, p. 3. For STL jurisprudence, see e.g. *Ayyash et al.*, STL-11-01/PT/AC/AR126.4, para. 21 ('[t]he defence must demonstrate *prima facie* that what is requested is "material to the preparation of the defence"' [emphasis in the original]).

[1052] *Delalić*, IT-96-21-PT, para. 11.

[1053] See also Heinze, *JICJ*, 15 (2017), 985, 1007.

[1054] PrepCom, *Proceedings of the Preparatory Commission at its first session* (16–26 February 1999), PCNICC/1999/L.3/Rev.1, 2 March 1999, Rule 5.16 (a): 'The Prosecutor shall *on request* permit the defence to inspect any books, documents, photographs, and tangible objects in his or her possession or control which are material to the preparation of the defence or are intended for use by the Prosecutor as evidence for the purposes of the confirmation hearing or at trial or were obtained from or belonged to the person' (emphasis added).

[1055] PrepCom, *Revised discussion paper proposed by the Coordinator: Part 5 of the Statute: Rules 5.1 to 5.4 Decision of the Prosecutor on the initiation of an investigation*, PCNICC/1999/WGRPE/RT.6, 5 August 1999, Rule 5.29; Brady, in Lee, *ICC* (2001), pp. 410, 411.

[1056] *Banda and Jerbo*, ICC-02/05-03/09-501. The reference to the case law of the ICTY and ICTR can be found in n. 103: 'The Appeals Chamber also notes that this standard is used at the ICTY and ICTR in relation to rule 66 (B) of their Rules of Procedure and Evidence. See, by way of example, ICTR, *Prosecutor v. Karemera et al.*, AC, Decision on the Prosecution's Interlocutory Appeal Conceming Disclosure Obligations, ICTR-98-44-AR73.11, 23 January 2008, para. 12. Given the similarity of rule 66 (B) to rule 77, the Appeals Chamber has previously considered that the jurisprudence of those tribunals in this respect is useful when interpreting rule 77. See *Lubanga* OA 11 judgment [i.e. *Lubanga*, ICC-01/04-01/06-1433, para. 78, K.A.]'. In support of this broad reading of Rule 77 RPE ICC, Khan and Buisman, in Stahn, *Practice* (2015), pp. 1042–3.

information on alleged human rights violations'.[1057] Contrary to Rule 76, Rule 77 RPE ICC does not include an obligation for the OTP to translate all the documents made available for inspection under that rule.[1058]

The request requirement in Rule 102 (3) RPE KSC is slightly softened by clause 1 of the Rule, according to which the Specialist Prosecutor shall 'provide detailed notice to the Defence of any material and evidence in his or her possession'. This requirement is unparalleled in other disclosure regimes of International(ized) Criminal Tribunals and basically obliges the SPO 'to first provide a list of any material and evidence in its possession, ahead of any request from the Defence for inspection or disclosure of information material to the Defence's preparation'.[1059] Disclosure according to Rule 102 (3) KSC RPE thus is a three-stage-process, starting with the SPO's 'detailed notice to the Defence of any material and evidence', followed by 'requests by the Defence for the disclosure or inspection of material in the custody or control of the SPO, which is deemed by the Defence to be material for its preparation, or was obtained from or belonged to the Accused', finishing with possible disputes regarding the materiality.[1060] The clause might render the defence request less of a fishing expedition, yet it does not change the general critique against the request requirement.[1061] At any rate, to receive the necessary information is not just a procedural matter but a (constitutional[1062]) right, as repeatedly stressed in human rights case law.[1063] This right exists 'whether or not a specific request for disclosure of details of scientific evidence is made by the defence'.[1064]

At the STL, the question arose—in connection with Rule 110 (B)—whether the prosecution was obliged to disclose material in a certain format, if the material in its possession was not in such a format.[1065] The STL Pre-Trial Judge pointed out that the prosecution was 'not obliged to perform analyses or to create work products which are not in its custody or control, possession or actually known to it' and that the prosecution 'cannot disclose or allow the inspection of materials that it does not have'.[1066] The Appeals Chamber confirmed this view.[1067] Another reason for the rejection of an obligation 'to perform analyses or to create work products' might be Rule 55 (C) RPE STL, for it provides that the Prosecutor should

1057 See e.g. *Ongwen*, ICC-02/04-01/15-1734, para. 22.

1058 ICC, *Prosecutor v. Al Hassan*, PTC I, Public Redacted Version of the 'Decision on the "Defence Request for Remedy for Disclosure Violation"', ICC-01/12-01/18-290-Red2-tENG, 3 June 2020, para. 27.

1059 *Prosecutor v. Gucati and Haradinaj*, CoAP, Public Redacted Version of Decision on the Appeals against Disclosure Decision, KSC-BC-2020-07/IA005/F00008/RED, 29 July 2021, para. 40.

1060 *Prosecutor v. Gucati and Haradinaj*, CoAP, Public Redacted Version of Decision on Prosecution Notifications, KSC-CA-2022-01/F00044/RED, 31 January 2023, para. 21; *Prosecutor v. Gucati and Haradinaj*, CoAP, Public Redacted Version of Decision on the Specialist Prosecutor's Office's Request Regarding Item 206, KSC-CA-2022-01/F00075/RED, 31 January 2023, para. 17; *Prosecutor v. Gucati and Haradinaj*, CoAP, Public Redacted Version of Decision on the Appeals against Disclosure Decision, KSC-BC-2020-07/IA005/F00008/RED, 29 July 2021, para. 38.

1061 In more detail, Heinze, in Ruiz Fabri, *MPEIPro* (2020), mn. 46.

1062 Dennis, *Evidence* (2020), mn. 9-001; instructive also Brown, in Brown, Turner, and Weißer, *OxfHB Criminal Process* (2019) pp. 544, 547.

1063 See Section B.(1)(b).

1064 Court of Appeal, *R. v. Ward*, 1993, (1993) 96 Cr App Rep 1, 52; see also Epp, *Disclosure* (2001), p. 104.

1065 *Ayyash et al.*, STL-11-01/PT/AC/AR126.4, 19 December 2013 Decision, para. 25; Heinze, in Klip and Freeland, *ALC XLIX* (2017) pp. 670, 670 ff.

1066 STL, *Prosecutor v. Ayyash et al.*, PTJ, Public Redacted Version 'Decision on Issues Related to the Inspection Room and Call Data Records' Dated 18 June 2013, STL-11-01/PT/PTJ, 19 September 2013, para. 52; *Ayyash et al.*, STL-11-01/PT/AC/AR126.4, 19 December 2013 Decision, para. 27.

1067 *Ayyash et al.*, STL-11-01/PT/AC/AR126.4, 19 December 2013 Decision, paras. 27 ff. (affirming that '[t]his certainly holds true for Rule 110(B)' and by referring to the established case law of both the ad hoc tribunals and national jurisdictions).

'assist the judges in establishing the truth' but is not obliged to investigate both incriminating and exculpatory evidence equally, as is the case at the ICC.[1068]

Rule 77 RPE ICC may even be invoked when it comes to the disclosure of certain information regarding the above-mentioned intermediaries,[1069] such as 'the general purpose, or purposes, for which such contact [with the intermediary] was made',[1070] the 'dates of contact' with an intermediary,[1071] etc.[1072] However, the *identity* of an intermediary must only be disclosed when '*prima facie* grounds have been identified for suspecting that the intermediary in question had been in contact with one or more witnesses whose incriminating evidence has been materially called into question'.[1073]

*(f) Witness disclosure and limitations*

Rule 76 (1) RPE ICC obliges the prosecution to disclose to the defence names of witnesses whom the Prosecutor intends to call to testify and copies of any *prior statements* made by those witnesses.[1074] Rule 76 (1) RPE ICC does not, unlike Rule 77, contain a 'materiality' test. The term 'prior statements' is understood rather broadly and 'requires the Prosecutor to disclose any prior statements, irrespective of the form in which they are recorded'.[1075] Yet, not all witness statements fall under Rule 76: according to the *Ntaganda* TC,[1076] confirmed by the AC,[1077] information relating to 'security concerns or purely logistical matters', i.e. information not related to the 'knowledge of the case in the course of its investigation', falls under Rule 77 RPE ICC.[1078] Unsurprisingly, the defence rejected this interpretation,[1079] since under Rule 77 the disclosure obligation only arises if the respective information is

[1068] In more detail, Heinze, in Klip and Freeland, *ALC XLIX* (2017), p. 673.

[1069] Chapter II, B.(2) in this volume *in fine* and in this chapter, Section A.(3)(c) *in fine*.

[1070] ICC, *Prosecutor v. Ruto and Sang*, TC V(a), Decision on Disclosure of Information Related to Prosecution Intermediaries, ICC-01/09-01/11-904-Red, 4 September 2013, para. 50.

[1071] Ibid., para. 52.

[1072] A summary of the information regarding intermediaries that has to be disclosed can be found in Khan and Buisman, in Stahn, *Practice* (2015), p. 1045. For examples where Chambers issued a stay of proceedings due to the failed compliance of the prosecution with court orders to disclose information regarding intermediaries see Section B.(5) with note 1161 in this chapter. See also Buisman and Hooper, in Rohan and Zyberi, *Defense Perspectives* (2017), p. 525.

[1073] *Lubanga*, ICC-01/04-01/06-2434-Red2, para. 139. The AC thereby rejected the three-stage approach suggested by the prosecution, providing '[f]irst, that an "appropriate" representative of the prosecution gives evidence about the use of intermediaries. Second, if, following that evidence, the Chamber determines that it remains necessary for one or more of the intermediaries to be called, this should be during an in camera hearing at which neither party is present. Third, only as a final measure should the Chamber consider revealing the role of intermediaries' (para. 91 (fn. omitted)).

[1074] See generally Tochilovsky, in Doria, Gasser, and Bassiouni, *Essays in Honour of Blishchenko* (2009), p. 843, 852; Khan and Buisman, in Stahn, *Practice* (2015), pp. 1037 ff.; Re, in Agirre et al., *Quality Control* (2020), pp. 755 ff.

[1075] ICC, *Prosecutor v. Banda*, AC, Judgment on the Appeal of the Prosecutor against the Decision of Trial Chamber IV of 12 September 2011 Entitled 'Reasons for the Order on translation of witness statements (ICC-02/05-03/09-199) and additional instructions on translation', ICC-02/05-03/09-295, 17 February 2012, para. 23. See also Re, in Agirre et al., *Quality Control* (2020), p. 755 with a more detailed definition ('Witness statements evolve and may comprise formally recorded question and answer style interviews, whether audio or video recorded or written, statements written in a prescribed or habitual form, notes of the utterances of witnesses recorded in note or other form, drafts of formal statements, or any combination of these').

[1076] ICC, *Prosecutor v. Ntaganda*, TC VI, Decision on Defence Requests Seeking Disclosure Orders and a Declaration of Prosecution Obligation to Record Contacts with Witnesses, ICC-01/04-02/06-904, 16 October 2015, para. 28 ff.

[1077] *Ntaganda*, ICC-01/04-02/06-1330, para. 16.

[1078] See also Re, in Agirre et al., *Quality Control* (2020), p. 756.

[1079] ICC, *Prosecutor v. Ntaganda*, Defence, Document in Support of the Appeal on Behalf of Mr Ntaganda against Trial Chamber VI's 'Decision on Defence requests seeking disclosure orders and a declaration of Prosecution obligation to record contacts with witnesses', ICC- 01/04-02/06-904, 9 December 2015, paras. 14 ff.

'material to the preparation of the defence' unless the Prosecutor intends to use it at trial as evidence. Rule 102 RPE KSC integrates both Rules 76 and 77 RPE ICC.

While Rule 76 (1) refers to 'names' of witnesses, Rule 69 (C) RPE ICTY uses the term identity, which requires more than the mere provision of a name but 'further particulars',[1080] excluding the present addresses of the witnesses.[1081] Rule 102 (1)(b)(i) RPE KSC requires, in contrast to Rule 76 (1) RPE ICC and Rule 69 (C) RPE ICTY, the disclosure of witness statements but not their identity.[1082] In fact, at the time of the confirmation of the indictment, the Pre-Trial Judge (PTJ) usually authorizes the temporary non-disclosure of the identity of witnesses, victims, or other persons at risk from the accused, pursuant to Rule 105 (1) KSC RPE, until 'appropriate protective measures have been ordered'.[1083] In the confirmation decision the PTJ then sets, with a view to meeting the thirty-day time limit under Rule 102 (1)(a) KSC RPE, a deadline for the SPO to submit a proper request for protective measures.

Rule 66 RPE ICTY/ICTR/SCSL and Rule 71 RPE MICT require the disclosure of all witness statements in the possession of the prosecution, regardless of their form or source.[1084] 'Pre-interview assessments',[1085] which are conducted prior to taking a formal statement from a witness in order to decide whether or not they should testify,[1086] are not proper witness statements, but may be disclosed as exculpatory evidence pursuant to Article 67 (2) ICCS and Rule 77 RPE ICC.[1087] TC V emphasized that while screening notes (i.e. 'notes prepared by the prosecution on the basis of an initial contact or interview with a person in connection

1080 ICTY, *Prosecutor v. Delalić et al.*, TC, Decision on the Defence Motion to Compel the Discovery of Identity and Location of Witnesses, IT-96-21-T, 18 March 1997, para. 17 ('[t]o identify the witnesses, therefore, it is necessary for the Defence to know further particulars about them, this in turn to satisfy the right of the accused to an adequate preparation of his defence').

1081 Ibid., para. 20. The disclosure of witness reports is governed by Rule 94*bis* RPE ICTY/ICTR; see, in more detail, Linton, in Sluiter et al., *International Criminal Procedure* (2013), pp. 880, 892.

1082 Heinze, *JICJ*, 15 (2017), 985, 1007.

1083 See also Heinze, in Ruiz Fabri, *MPEIPro* (2020), mn. 49.

1084 See also SCSL, *Prosecutor v. Brima et al.*, TC, Decision on Joint Defence Motion on Disclosure of All Original Witness Statements, Interview Notes and Investigators' Notes pursuant to Rules 66 and/or 68, SCSL-04-16-T, 4 May 2005, para. 16, deciding that '[a]ny statement or declaration made by a witness in relation to an event he or she witnessed and recorded in any form by an official in the course of an investigation, falls within the meaning of a "witness statement" under Rule 66(A)(i). Accordingly, facts contained in an investigator's interview notes which constitute statements made by the witness in the course of an investigation come within the meaning of "witness statements" under Rule 66(A)(i).' The Chamber continues that 'Rule 66 requires disclosure of all witness statements in the possession of the Prosecution, regardless of their form or source, save for any material covered by Rule 70(A)'. (see generally Swoboda, *Beweisstrategien* (2013), pp. 315 ff.). This definition is, in line with the case law on exculpatory evidence, broader than the definition of witness statements given in n. 184 (according to the AC in *Blaškić*: '[t]he usual meaning of a witness statement in trial proceedings is an account of a person's knowledge of a crime, which is recorded *through due procedure* in the course of an investigation into the crime' [emphasis added]). While for the purpose of Rule 66 (A)(i), any statement 'recorded in any form' qualifies as a witness statement, the definition of the *Blaškić* AC only includes material recorded 'through due procedure', thereby narrowing the definition.

1085 According to Heinze, in Heinze and Dittrich, *ICC* (2021), p. 74 with n. 167 the correct terminology is 'pre-interview assessment', even though TC III changes it to 'pre-assessment interview' in para. 31 (adopted by Safferling, *International Criminal Procedure* (2012), p. 355). Yet, since TC III uses 'pre-interview assessment' throughout the decision, the change of terminology seems to be a mistake.

1086 ICC, *Prosecutor v. Bemba*, TC III, Public Redacted Version of 'Decision on the Defence Request for Disclosure of Pre-Interview Assessments and the Consequences of Non-Disclosure', ICC-01/05-01/08-750-Red, 9 April 2010, para. 31; Safferling, *International Criminal Procedure* (2012), p. 355.

1087 *Bemba*, ICC-01/05-01/08-750-Red, para. 33: '[P]ut generally, it [the Prosecution, K.A.] must disclose exculpatory evidence and documents etc, that are material to the preparation of the defence case. This will involve fact-specific decisions for each pre-interview assessment, and critically the prosecution must ensure that if there has been a later formal statement, all the exculpatory material in the screening notes has been disclosed within the statement, along with any information that is material to defence preparation. If this has not occurred, the prosecution must disclose the screening notes, or the relevant information.'

with an investigation'),[1088] interview notes, or investigators' notes may constitute a statement (screening notes only fall under Rule 76 if 'witnesses are questioned about their knowledge of the case in the course of an investigation and they accept or adopt the screening notes as their own'),[1089] 'not all items containing information obtained from a witness will necessarily constitute a "statement" within the meaning of [Rule 76]'.[1090]

According to Rule 76 (3) ICC RPE, '[t]he statements of prosecution witnesses shall be made available in original *and* in a language which the accused fully understands and speaks'.[1091] In the *Yekatom and Ngaïssona* case, the prosecution conducted interviews where the answers were translated immediately by the investigator from Sango into French, and subsequently only these French translations disclosed. Single Judge Schmitt found—albeit *obiter* since the prosecution had not made a final determination of whom it would call to testify—that 'the questions originally posed in Sango and the answers provided in response by the witness in Sango fall under the definition of "original" pursuant to Rule 76(3)'.[1092]

There is a potential conflict with Rule 121 (3) RPE ICC: While Rule 76 RPE ICC refers to 'names of witnesses ... *and* copies of any prior statements made by those witnesses',[1093] Rule 121 (3) RPE ICC, which applies to the confirmation hearing, requires the disclosure of '*a list* of the evidence which [the prosecution] intends to present at the hearing'.[1094] There are two ways to solve this inconsistency: one may either deny the application of Rule 76 RPE ICC to the confirmation hearing or oblige the prosecution to disclose not only a 'list' of statements but both the (copied)[1095] statements *and* the names of the witnesses.[1096] The latter solution was preferred by the *Lubanga* PTC, which came to the conclusion

> that, as a general rule, statements must be disclosed to the Defence in full. Any restriction on disclosure to the Defence of the names or portions, or both, of the statements of the witnesses on which the Prosecution intends to rely at the confirmation hearing must be authorised by the single judge under the procedure provided for in rule 81 of the Rules.[1097]

As already stated above,[1098] witnesses in international criminal proceedings face considerable risks which entail certain *protection measures*. This, in turn, may cause the curtailment of defence rights, for example by not disclosing the identity of (prosecution) witnesses.[1099] However, a refusal to disclose (witness) evidence is to be based upon a careful examination

[1088] ICC, *Prosecutor v. Yekatom and Ngaïssona*, TC V, Decision on the Yekatom Defence Motion for Disclosure of Screening Notes, ICC-01/14-01/18-618, 10 August 2020, para. 10.

[1089] *Yekatom and Ngaïssona*, ICC-01/14-01/18-618, para. 12.

[1090] *Yekatom and Ngaïssona*, ICC-01/14-01/18-315-Red, para. 39.

[1091] Emphasis added.

[1092] ICC, *Prosecutor v. Yekatom and Ngaïssona*, TC V, Decision on the Yekatom Defence Request for Disclosure of Witness Statements in their Original Language, ICC-01/14-01/18-535, 29 May 2020, para. 11.

[1093] Emphasis added.

[1094] Emphasis added.

[1095] *Lubanga*, ICC-01/04-01/06-102, para. 103: 'Under rule 76, the Prosecution has the obligation only to provide the Defence with "copies" of the relevant statements and not the originals. However, as previously mentioned, the originals must be filed by the Prosecution in the record of the case as soon as practicable after copies have been provided to the Defence as part of the process for communicating to the Pre-Trial Chamber the evidence which the Prosecution intends to use at the confirmation hearing.'

[1096] In the same vein, Brady, in Lee, *ICC* (2001), p. 410.

[1097] *Lubanga*, ICC-01/04-01/06-568, para. 101. For more details, see Heinze, *Disclosure* (2014), pp. 377 ff.

[1098] Section A.(4)(d) in this chapter.

[1099] ICC, *Prosecutor v. Yekatom and Ngaïssona*, PTC II, Decision on the 'Joint Defence motion for disclosure of anonymous summaries for [Redacted] and [Redacted]', ICC-01/14-01/18-256-Red, 26 July 2019, para. 20.

of the individual case in question[1100] and to be justified as transparently and concretely as possible since adequate defence requires more than 'a blind confrontation in the courtroom'.[1101] Given the importance of the rights of the accused 'to know the identity of his accusers and challenge their testimony', these rights will often 'take precedence over the interests of victims and witnesses to not have their identities disclosed'.[1102]

Concerns about witness safety have also led the the ad hoc tribunals, SCSL, and ICC to permit the so-called '*rolling disclosure*' of the witness's identity, that is, instead of disclosing the identities of all witnesses prior to trial, disclosure takes place witness by witness in line with the respective witness's interrogation.[1103] In the *Katanga* case, for instance, due to 'real risks' faced by some witnesses,[1104] the TC II granted the Prosecutor's request to have the identity of one of the two key posecution witnesses disclosed to the accused only forty-five days before being summoned to testify.[1105] At the same time, the Chamber stressed that rolling disclosure could only be granted exceptionally, namely where it proved to be 'strictly necessary' and when the defence had temporary access, 'to either summaries of statements or redacted versions of the transcripts of ... witnesses'.[1106] However, Single Judge Prost, preparing the *Al Hassan* trial, considered that it was generally 'desirable for the disclosure of material to be made on a rolling basis'.[1107] Before the ICTR, the prosecution was permitted rolling disclosure by providing witness' statements 'no later than thirty-five days before the date of testimony of a particular witness, or when the witness comes under the protection of the Tribunal, whichever is earlier'.[1108]

Apart from serious concerns for witness safety, other circumstances involved Covid-19.[1109] In *Al Hassan*, the prosecution demonstrated serious obstacles to their investigation due to the temporary closure of the ICC premises and various measures by the Netherlands

1100 *Lubanga*, ICC-01/04–01/06-1401, para. 89 ('a thorough assessment will need to be made by the Pre-Trial Chamber of the potential relevance of the information to the Defence on a case by case basis'). See also Kuschnik, *ICLR*, 9 (2009), 165. It is certainly controversial whether the rather nebulous reference of the *Lubanga* TC to 'the present circumstances', under which 'no further disclosure is possible' (ICC, *Prosecutor v. Lubanga*, TC I, Judgment pursuant to Article 74 of the Statute, ICC-01/04-01/06-2842, 14 March 2012, para. 117) meets these requirements, see Ambos, *ICLR*, 12 (2012), 126; Ambos, *ZIS*, 7 (2012), 320; Trüg, *ZStW*, 125 (2013), 65.

1101 *Delalić et al.*, IT-96-21, paras. 17, 19, 20; in the same vein, also ICC, *Katanga and Ngudjolo*, PTC I, Decision on Evidentiary Scope of the Confirmation Hearing, Preventive Relocation and Disclosure under Art. 67 (2) of the Statute and Rule 77 of the Rules, ICC-01/04–01/07–428-Corr, 18 April 2008, para. 18 and *passim*; from a comparative perspective, Heinze, *Disclosure* (2014), pp. 359 ff.

1102 cf. Piragoff and Clarke, 'Article 69', in Ambos, *Commentary* (2022), mn. 39 (referring to the case law of the ad hoc tribunals).

1103 Combs, in Schabas and Bernaz, *Handbook ICL* (2011), p. 324. On 'rolling disclosure' based on Rule 69 (A) RPE ICTY/ICTR also Zahar and Sluiter, *ICL* (2008), p. 374; Swoboda, *Beweisstrategien* (2013), pp. 710–11; Heinze, *Disclosure* (2014), pp. 385–6; Croquet, *Melbourne JIL*, 11 (2010), 50; Rigney, *Fairness* (2022), pp. 112 ff.

1104 ICC, *Prosecutor v. Katanga and Ngudjolo*, TC II, Public Redacted Version of the Decision on the Protection of Prosecution Witnesses 267 and 353 of 20 May 2009 (ICC-01/04-01/07-1156-Conf-Exp), ICC-01/04-01/07-1179-tENG, 29 May 2009, para. 31.

1105 Ibid., paras. 46 ff.; Croquet, *Melbourne JIL*, 11 (2010), 55.

1106 *Katanga and Ngudjolo*, ICC-01/04-01/07-1179-tENG, para. 34 (as cited in note 1104 with main text).

1107 ICC, *Prosecutor v. Al Hassan*, TC X, Decision on the Evidence Disclosure Protocol and Other Related Matters, ICC-01/12-01/18-546, 30 December 2019, para. 8.

1108 ICTR, *Prosecutor v. Bagosora et al.*, TC, Decision and Scheduling Order on the Prosecution Motion for Harmonisation and Modification of Protective Measures for Witnesses, ICTR-98-41-I, 5 December 2001, para. 24 and *passim*.

1109 As Covid-19 and the restrictions imposed on travelling, contacts, etc., had a considerable impact on the daily routine of domestic courts around the world (see e.g. Ritscher, *JICJ*, 18 (2020), 1077–80), it goes without saying that this also applies to the ICC (see generally Abtahi, *JICJ*, 18 (2020), 1069–76). And since the daily routine involves, to a large extent, decisions about disclosure, the disclosure process at the ICC is subject to restraints. For instance, in the case against *Abd-Al-Rahman*, instead of holding a status conference, Single Judge Aitala sought detailed observations from the parties in writing, see ICC, *Prosecutor v. Abd-Al-Rahman*, PTC II, Order Seeking Observations on Disclosure and Related Matters, ICC-02/05-01/20-14, 3 July 2020, para. 8.

'that inevitably have an effect on the overall functioning of the Court'.[1110] To minimize a detrimental effect on the rights of the accused, TC X reconsidered the disclosure deadlines and permitted rolling disclosure instead.[1111]

The disclosure of witness statements is especially relevant with regard to the practice of witness preparation.[1112] As previously mentioned,[1113] the defence has been highlighting the danger of late disclosure as a by-product of permitting the preparation of witnesses. While in the *Ruto and Sang* case the Chamber merely reiterated the disclosure rules that already apply,[1114] two years later, TC VI added a new paragraph 32 to the Witness Preparation Protocol with regard to late disclosure. It reads:

> The calling party shall provide the non-calling party with a list of all materials that have been shown to the witness, and, if applicable, all of the information that is subject to the calling party's disclosure obligations, including:
> a) any clarifications, changes or corrections made by the witness to his or her previous statements and the reasons advanced by the witness, if any, to justify the change or correction; and
> b) any new information obtained from the witness.[1115]

## (3) Defence and victim disclosure

The disclosure obligations of the defence are much more limited than those of the Prosecutor.[1116] They only exist, as set out in Figure 9, with regard to certain defences, for example, with regard to the existence of an alibi.[1117] Yet, at the ICC the obligation to provide an in-depth analysis chart also applies to the defence.[1118] The defence must present its evidence

[1110] ICC, *Prosecutor v. Al Hassan*, TC X, Decision on the Prosecution Request for Extension of Deadlines Relating to the Disclosure of Evidence and a Postponement of the Starting Date for Trial, ICC-01/12-01/18-677, 20 March 2020, para. 6.

[1111] *Al Hassan*, ICC-01/12-01/18-677, para. 10.

[1112] Heinze, in Ruiz Fabri, *MPEIPro* (2020), mn. 57.

[1113] See Section A.(3)(d) in this chapter.

[1114] *Ruto and Sang*, ICC-01/09-01/11-524-Anx, para. 30.

[1115] *Ntaganda*, ICC-01/04-02/06-652-Anx; see also *Al Hassan*, ICC-01/12-01/18-666-Anx, para. 32. See also Heinze, in Klip and Freeland, *ALC LXI* (2020), pp. 307 ff.; for the ICTY practice, see the instructive account by McHenry and Ursini, in Bergsmo and Dittrich, *Integrity* (2020), pp. 909–10.

[1116] Abrahamson, Dwyer, and Fitzpatrick, *Discovery and Disclosure* (2019), p. 412; Ambos, *NCLR*, 12 (2009), 546; Kuschnik, *ICLR*, 9 (2009), 161.

[1117] cf. Rule 67 RPE ICTY/ICTR; Rules 78, 79 RPE ICC; Rule 104 RPE KSC. See also Schabas, Chaitidou, and El Zeidy, 'Article 61', in Ambos, *Commentary* (2022), mn. 100 ff.; Nerlich, *JICJ*, 10 (2012), 1352; Vohrah, in McDonald and Swaak-Goldman, *ICL I* (2000), pp. 517–18; Möller, in Kirsch, *Internationale Strafgerichtshöfe* (2005), pp. 36, 44–5; Zahar and Sluiter, *ICL* (2008), p. 423 ff.; Tochilovsky, *Law and Jurisprudence* (2014), pp. 163 ff.; Schuon, *International Criminal Procedure* (2010), pp. 279 ff.; Kuczyńska, *Accusation Model* (2015), p. 215; Re, in Agirre et al., *Quality Control* (2020), p. 770. Also ICTY, *Prosecutor v. Gotovina et al.*, TC I, Decision on Requests for Permanent Restraining Orders Directed to the Republic of Croatia, IT-06-90-T, 12 March 2010, para. 34; ICTR, *Prosecutor v. Rukundo*, TC II, Judgment, ICTR-2001-70-T, 27 February 2009, para. 539; specifically on the extent of defence disclosure in connection with the notification of an alibi, ICTR, *Prosecutor v. Ngirabatware*, TC II, Decision on Prosecution Motion for an Order to Compel the Accused to Disclose Particulars of his Alibi, ICTR-99-54-T, 16 February 2010, paras. 29 ff.

[1118] In a Decision by the *Bemba* PTC the Chamber criticized the defence because it 'did not include a chart analysing each piece of evidence in accordance with the Decision on Disclosure and the Model Chart', and noted 'that although the Defence may organize its strategy as it deems appropriate, it is still obliged to do so within the parameters of the law and the decisions of the Chamber', see ICC, *Prosecutor v. Bemba*, PTC III, Decision on the Disclosure of Evidence by the Defence, ICC-01/05-01/08-311, 5 December 2008, para. 9. See also *Ruto and Sang*, ICC-01/09-01/11-44, para. 22; ICC, *Prosecutor v. Ntaganda*, PTC II, Decision Setting the Regime for Evidence

<table>
<tr><th>Prior to/at Confirmation Hearing</th><th>After Confirmation Hearing/Prior Trial</th><th>Trial</th></tr>
<tr><td>Art. 61 (6)(c)<br>- person may present evidence</td><td></td><td>Rule 80 (Art. 31 (3))<br>- defence shall give notice to the Trial Chamber and prosecution if it intends to raise a ground for excluding criminal responsibility (Art. 31 (3))</td></tr>
<tr><td colspan="3">Rule 78<br>- inspection of books, docs, photos, other tangible objects<br>- intended for use by def. as evidence</td></tr>
<tr><td colspan="3">Rule 79<br>In case the defence intends to raise the existence of an alibi or a ground for excluding criminal responsibility, it shall (a) notify the prosecutor (b) specify names of witnesses and any other evidence<br>contrary to Art. 67 (1)(g) (privilege against self-incrimination)<br>disputed, whether it applies prior to the confirmation hearing</td></tr>
<tr><td>Rule 121<br>- proceedings before the confirmation hearing</td><td></td><td></td></tr>
<tr><td colspan="3">Rule 84<br>Disclosure is an ongoing process</td></tr>
</table>

**Fig. 9.** Defence Disclosure at the ICC
© Alexander Heinze

no later than fifteen days before the date of the confirmation hearing,[1119] that is, the same time limit applies to the respective disclosure obligations.

The defence cannot be required to disclose incriminating evidence as this would violate the *nemo tenetur* principle[1120] and the principle of equality of arms taking into account the structural superiority of the prosecution.[1121] Notwithstanding, the concept of a pre-defence conference, as envisaged by Rule 73*ter* RPE ICTY/ICTR/SCSL and Rule 82 RPE MICT, implies that the identity of defence witnesses (only their identity, not their statement!) must be disclosed in order to avoid lengthy interrogations during trial.[1122]

As far as *victims* are concerned they have no general *obligation* to disclose to the parties evidence in their possession.[1123] Nevertheless, since the Chambers 'set the modalities' for

Disclosure and Other Related Matters, ICC-01/04-02/06-47, 12 April 2013, para. 30; Schabas, Chaitidou, and El Zeidy, 'Article 61', in Ambos, *Commentary* (2022), mn. 101.

[1119] cf. Rule 121 (6) RPE ICC.

[1120] Art. 67 (1)(g) ICCS; see also Brady, in Lee, *ICC* (2001), p. 414; Kuczyńska, *Accusation Model* (2015), p. 215; see previously Ambos, *LJIL*, 15 (2002), 155 ff. (finding that Rule 74 RPE ICC has its origin in the *nemo tenetur* principle as it is embodied in common law jurisdictions, 166 and *passim*); generally Chapter I, D.(2)(a) and (3)(b) in this volume.

[1121] May and Wierda, *ColJTL*, 37 (1999), 760–1; Safferling, *International Criminal Procedure* (2003), pp. 194, 202, 374; on the superiority of the prosecution, also Zahar and Sluiter, *ICL* (2008), pp. 364 ff.; on equality of arms, esp. on the 'inequality of resources', see Jalloh and DiBella, in Schabas et al., *Research Companion ICL* (2013), pp. 251 ff.; on the link between equality of arms and disclosure in general, Heinze, *Disclosure* (2014), pp. 311 ff.; generally on equality of arms, see Chapter I, D.(2)(b) in this volume.

[1122] May and Wierda, *ColJTL*, 37 (1999), 761; also see Vohrah, in McDonald and Swaak-Goldman, *ICL I* (2000), p. 542.

[1123] See also Rigney, *Fairness* (2022), p. 123.

the exchange of information, it is within their discretion to order the victim(s) to disclose or present evidence to ensure a fair trial.[1124]

## (4) Disclosure restrictions

Disclosure restrictions and privileges are known at all international criminal tribunals. They are the exception to the principle or rule of full disclosure.[1125] At the same time, international criminal trials could not take place without disclosure restrictions, with the ICC probably having the most elaborate and specific ones.[1126] They apply both to the defence and, under some circumstances, to the public.[1127] Chambers take a two-step approach with a first step finding that certain information is in fact disclosable but—second step—protected by rules governing disclosure restrictions and matters of privilege.[1128] This second step and the ensuing non-disclosure is 'a measure of last resort'.[1129]

Disclosure restrictions apply to reports, memoranda, and other internal documents[1130] with regard to certain confidential information,[1131] and when disclosure may prejudice

[1124] ICC, *Prosecutor v. Katanga and Ngudjolo*, TC II, Decision on the Modalities of Victim Participation at Trial, ICC-01/04-01/07-1788-tENG, 22 January 2010, paras. 105–7; ICC, *Prosecutor v. Katanga and Ngudjolo*, AC, Judgment on the Appeal of Mr Katanga against the Decision of Trial Chamber II of 22 January 2010 Entitled 'Decision on the Modalities of Victim Participation at Trial', ICC-01/04-01/07-2288, 16 July 2010, paras. 43–8; Braga da Silva, *JICJ*, 18 (2020), 59, 76; crit. Bilsky, in Heller et al., *Oxford HB ICL* (2020) pp. 473, 489–90.

[1125] In that vein, *Shala*, KSC-BC-2023-11/F00023, para. 90 ('full disclosure of all material and relevant evidence is the principle, while withholding information is the exception').

[1126] Boas et al., *Procedure* (2011), pp. 366 ff.; Schabas, Chaitidou, and El Zeidy, 'Article 61', in Ambos, *Commentary* (2022), mn. 65; Kuczyńska, *Accusation Model* (2015), pp. 229 ff. About the attorney-client privilege in particular, Safferling, *International Criminal Procedure* (2012), pp. 506 ff.; Piragoff and Clarke, 'Article 69', in Ambos, *Commentary* (2022), mn. 62 ff. For domestic disclosure restrictions, see Abrahamson, Dwyer, and Fitzpatrick, *Discovery and Disclosure* (2019), pp. 521 ff.

[1127] About non-disclosure to the public, see, in more detail, Khan and Buisman, in Stahn, *Practice* (2015), pp. 1054 ff.

[1128] A classic example of this two-step approach can be found in *Ruto and Sang*, ICC-01/09-01/11-904-Red, para. 47.

[1129] In ICC, *Prosecutor v. Katanga*, PTC I, First Decision on the Prosecution Request for Authorisation to Redact Witness Statements, ICC-01/04-01/07-224-Anx, 23 February 2008, para. 60, for instance, Single Judge Sylvia Steiner considered 'less intrusive measures' than non-disclosure. The phrase 'a measure of last resort' is actually used by Judge Pikis in his Dissenting Opinion to the AC's judgment in *Katanga*, ICC-01/04-01/07-475, para. 4, and—albeit unsurprisingly given the defence lawyer's perspective—by Khan and Buisman, in Stahn, *Practice* (2015), p. 1047.

[1130] Rule 70 RPE ICTY; Rule 81 RPE ICC. Although neither the ICTY Statute nor the RPE contain any specific provisions on journalists, Rule 70 (D) RPE ICTY may be applicable in that regard, providing that '[i]f the Prosecutor calls a witness to introduce in evidence any information provided under this Rule, the Trial Chamber may not compel that witness to answer any question relating to the information or its origin, if the witness declines to answer on grounds of confidentiality'; see, in more detail, Linton, in Sluiter et al., *International Criminal Procedure* (2013), p. 881, with a detailed description of the ICTY case law on pp. 887 ff. Crit. on the prosecution's right to withhold statements, especially the specialist knowledge and identity of expert witnesses, even though their influence upon the outcome of the trial has hitherto been underestimated, Rothe and Overthon, *ICLR*, 10 (2010), 345 ff. On ICTY Rule 70, see UNICRI, *ICTY Manual on Developed Practices* (2009), pp. 20–1, 27, 88; Klip, *JICJ*, 10 (2012), 652 ff. The STL AC has clarified that, despite its character as internal, the document can still be exculpatory and hence subject to disclosure, see STL, *Prosecutor v. El Sayed*, AC, Decision on Partial Appeal by Mr El Sayed of Pre-Trial Judge's Decision of 12 May 2011, CH/AC/2011/01, 19 July 2011, para. 97; STL, *Prosecutor v. Ayyash et al.*, TC, Decision Denying the Sabra Defence Application for Disclosure of a UNIIIC Internal Memorandum on Mr Wissam Al-Hassan (Witness PRH680) Under Rules 110 (B) and 113, STL-11-01/T/TC/F3562/20180207/R306883-R306898/EN/dm, 7 February 2018, para. 12; *Ayyash et al.*, STL-11-01/T/TC/F3710/20180713/R311213-R311231/EN/dm, para. 32. Generally Re, in Agirre et al., *Quality Control* (2020), pp. 748, 768 ff.

[1131] Art. 54 ICCS, Rules 81 (4) and 82 RPE ICC, No. 55 (3) RegOTP. About confidentiality within the context of State cooperation with the ICC, see Kreß and Prost, 'Article 93', in Ambos, *Commentary* (2022), mn. 70. About the ICRC's privilege of non-disclosure for confidentiality reasons, see ICRC, *IRRC*, 97 (2015), 436–40.

investigations[1132] or certain persons require protection.[1133] When considering whether to authorize the non-disclosure of the identity of a witness pursuant to Rule 81 (4) RPE ICC, taking into account the danger and proportionality of disclosure,[1134] Chambers are asked to weigh the following factors:

(i) the witness' personal circumstances;
(ii) whether there are currently protection or security measures in place for the witness;
(iii) the relevant security situation in the area where the witness or their family currently resides;
(iv) whether the witness or their family members have received any threats on account of his/her (perceived) involvement with the Court;
(v) whether the witness him-/herself has undertaken any activity to endanger his/her personal safety; and
(vi) whether the witness consented that their identity be disclosed to the defence (without prejudice to the Chamber's *proprio motu* assessment whether to disclose such identity).[1135]

At the KSC, a Panel may order, *proprio motu* or upon request, appropriate measures for the protection, safety, physical and psychological well-being, dignity, and privacy of witnesses, victims participating in the proceedings, as well as other persons at risk on account of testimony given by witnesses.[1136] Such measures may include the redaction of names and other identifying information in order to prevent disclosure to the accused and/or the public, where necessary, of the identity and/or whereabouts of a witness, a victim participating in the proceedings, or a person related to or associated with them.[1137]

Privileges, especially the lawyer-client privilege, are also to be observed.[1138] The main restrictions at the ICC have been summarized in Figure 10.

[1132] Rule 81 (2) RPE ICC.

[1133] Art. 68 ICCS, Rule 81 (4) RPE ICC; Art. 21 (6) KSC Law with Rules 80 (1) and 108 (1) RPE KSC. For more detail, see Kuschnik, *ICLR*, 9 (2009), 166 ff.; Whiting, in Stahn, *Practice* (2015), pp. 1013 ff.; Schuon, *International Criminal Procedure* (2010), pp. 281 ff.; Rigney, *Fairness* (2022), pp. 127 ff. In this context, the use of *intermediaries* (see Section A.(3)(c) in this chapter *in fine*) appears problematic. As the option of anonymized witness testimonies has not yet been clarified (see Sections A.(4)(d) and B.(2)(e) in this chapter), in individual cases the TC requires disclosure pursuant to Rule 77 RPE ICC if (i) the intermediary was in contact with witnesses whose credibility is doubted (particularly if the intermediary may have incited them to make a false statement), and (ii) the intermediaries are guaranteed protection by the VWU (see *Lubanga*, ICC-01/04-01/06-2434-Red2, paras. 139 ff.). About the national security privilege (Arts. 72, 93 (4) ICCS), see Rastan, 'Article 72', in Ambos, *Commentary* (2022), mn. 1 ff.; Zemach, *IsLR*, 47 (2014), 331 ff.; about the ICTY's approach to the national security privilege, see ICTY, *Prosecutor v. Blaškic*, AC, Judgment on the Request of the Republic of Croatia for Review of the Decision of Trial Chamber II of 18 July 1997, IT-95-14-AR, 29 October 1997, paras. 64–5.

[1134] *Katanga and Ngudjolo*, ICC-01/04-01/07-224-Anx, para. 67 and paras. 69–73; ICC, *Prosecutor v. Yekatom and Ngaïssona*, PTC II, Decision on the Prosecutor's Request to Use Anonymised Summaries of Witness Statements, ICC-01/14-01/18-261-Red2, 3 February 2020, para. 21.

[1135] ICC, *Prosecutor v. Ntaganda*, PTC II, Redacted First Decision on the Prosecutor's Requests for Redactions and Other Related Requests, ICC-01/04-02/06-117-Red3, 1 October 2013, para. 34; ICC, *Prosecutor v. Yekatom and Ngaïssona*, PTC II, Decision on the 'Prosecution's Urgent Request for the Non-Disclosure of Witness Identities', ICC-01/14-01/18-273-Red2, 3 February 2020, para. 27. See also Heinze, in Ruiz Fabri, *MPEIPro* (2020), mn. 63.

[1136] Art. 23 (1) KSC Law, and Rules 80 (1), 108 (1)(b) RPE KSC.

[1137] Rule 80 (4)(a)(i)–(iii), (d), and (e) RPE KSC.

[1138] Rules 73 RPE ICC, 97 RPE ICTY. On counsel/defendant generally in this regard, see Chapter II, C.(2)(b) and D.(1) in this volume. About privilege for journalists under that provision, see ICTY, *Prosecutor v. Brđanin and Talić*, AC, Decision on Interlocutory Appeal, IT-99-36-AR73.8, 11 December 2002, paras. 35 ff.; Piragoff and Clarke, 'Article 69', in Ambos, *Commentary* (2022), mn. 72.

| | Restriction | Provision (RPEICC/ICCS) |
|---|---|---|
| 1. | *'Internal Documents'* such as a report that is connected with the investigation or preparation of the case, and is prepared by the Leading Council for the defence or the OTP, or its assistants or representatives | Rule 81 (1) |
| 2. | Disclosure of concerned material 'may *prejudice further or ongoing investigations'* of the OTP | Rule 81 (2) |
| 3. | Disclosure hinders the *generating of new evidence*<br><br>--> limited to situations where the obtainment of such evidence is based on a guarantee of the OTP to the provider of the information that the *received information is treated confidentially* | Rule 82 *iunctio* Art. 54 (3)(e) |
| 4. | The non-disclosure ensures the confidentiality of information | Rule 81 (4) *iunctio* Arts. 54, 72 and 93 |
| 5. | The non-disclosure is aimed to 'protect the *safety of witnesses and victims* and members of their families' | Rule 81 (4) *iunctio* Art. 68 |
| | --> submitting mere *summaries* of the information to the defence | Rule 81 (5), (6) *iunctio* Art. 68 (5) |

**Fig. 10.** Disclosure Restrictions at the ICC
© Alexander Heinze

In the *Lubanga* case, the Chamber had the difficult task of striking a proper balance between the rights of the defence and those of witnesses and victims with regard to (inter alia) protective measures for witnesses due to security concerns.[1139] Indeed, most confidentiality issues have so far come up because of security risks for witnesses or in the context of Article 54 (3)(e) ICCS with information providers invoking the respective assurances.[1140] In these circumstances the ICC case law provides for three general principles in case of non-disclosure: (1) protective measures should only be granted after exhausting the possibility of employing less extreme measures (principle of necessity); (2) they must be strictly limited to the exigencies of the situation (principle of proportionality); and (3) they must not infringe the right of the defendant to a fair and impartial trial.[1141] Thus, in line with the Court's 'last

[1139] *Lubanga*, ICC-01/04-01/06-2842, para. 115.

[1140] Ambos, *ICLR*, 12 (2012), 125. See generally Bergsmo and Bekou, 'Article 54', in Ambos, *Commentary* (2022), mn. 35 ff.; Schabas, Chaitidou, and El Zeidy, 'Article 61', in Ambos, *Commentary* (2022), mn. 69; Bitti, 'Article 64', in Ambos, *Commentary* (2022), mn. 29; Caianiello, *ICLR*, 10 (2010), 31 ff. About confidentiality in the context of Art. 54 (3)(e) and (f) vis-à-vis Art. 72 (3) ICCS (protection of national security information), see Rastan, 'Article 72', in Ambos, *Commentary* (2022), mn. 19 ff.

[1141] ICC, *Prosecutor v. Lubanga*, AC, Judgment on the Appeal of Mr Thomas Lubanga Dyilo against the Decision of Pre-Trial Chamber I Entitled 'First Decision on the Prosecution Requests and Amended Requests for Redactions under Rule 81', ICC-01/04-01/06-773, 14 December 2006, paras. 21, 33–4; *Katanga*, ICC-01/

resort' approach, a decision in favour of confidentiality should not be made lightly, for example because of an alleged general (unspecific) risk of (prosecution) witnesses testifying against the accused.[1142]

Another problem of non-disclosure decisions based on confidentiality is the assumption that the accused will intimidate witnesses (or attempt to do so) once their identity is disclosed, thereby converting the presumption of innocence into one of guilt.[1143] As a consequence, Chambers adopted, as already explained above,[1144] a careful case-by-case approach to non-disclosure.[1145]

To specify matters of confidentiality, the *Practice Manual* has annexed a 'Protocol on the Handling of Confidential Information During Investigations and Contact Between a Party or Participant and Witnesses of the Opposing Party or of a Participant', which '[t]he Chamber, acting under articles 57(3)(c) and 68(1) of the Statute, should order the parties and participants to comply with'.[1146] Article 54 (3)(e) in particular becomes relevant upon the provision of material by investigative mechanisms, private investigators, and private investigative entities.[1147] The disclosure of confidentially obtained information is particularly controversial with regard to the information exchange between ICTs and other entities such as truth and reconciliation commissions.[1148]

### (5) Consequences of non-disclosure

The written law is scarce with regard to *concrete* sanctions,[1149] Rule 110 RPE KSC being the only concrete provision on 'non-compliance with disclosure obligations'.[1150] Otherwise judicial sanctions for violations of disclosure obligations may be inherent to the general judicial

04-01/07-475, para. 64; Ambos, *ICLR*, 12 (2012), 125. cf. Schabas, Chaitidou, and El Zeidy, 'Article 61', in Ambos, *Commentary* (2022), mn. 66; Kuschnik, *ICLR*, 9 (2009), 164.

[1142] Ambos, *ICLR*, 12 (2012), 125. To specify matters of confidentiality, the ICC *Practice Manual* has annexed a 'Protocol on the Handling of Confidential Information During Investigations and Contact Between a Party or Participant and Witnesses of the Opposing Party or of a Participant', which '[t]he Chamber, acting under articles 57(3)(c) and 68(1) of the Statute, should order the parties and participants to comply with'; see ICC, *Practice Manual* (2023), p. 30 and annex.

[1143] One could even go further and argue, from a national law enforcement perspective, that the protection of witnesses is a preventive measure and, thus, within the competence of the police or another law enforcement agency, see Schenke, *Polizei- und Ordnungsrecht* (2023), § 1 mn. 10 ff. By contrast, the main function of an international criminal tribunal is to prosecute and punish past crimes, i.e. it acts in a repressive, backward-looking fashion (see Kingreen and Poscher, *Polizei- und Ordnungsrecht* (2022), § 2 mn. 5). As a consequence, it might be argued that preventive protective measures of witness protection, e.g. by non-disclosure, are none of its business.

[1144] cf. Section B.(2)(f) in this chapter.

[1145] *Lubanga*, ICC-01/04–01/06-1401, para. 89. See also Kuschnik, *ICLR*, 9 (2009), 165.

[1146] ICC, *Practice Manual* (2023), paras. 101–3 and annex.

[1147] Heinze, *ZIS*, *14* (2019), 169, 178–80.

[1148] See e.g. Jalloh, *Legacy of the SCSL* (2020), pp. 321 ff.

[1149] This also corresponds to the law in England, where the Criminal Procedure and Investigations Act 1996 (CPIA) sets out sanctions against the defence, but not against the prosecution; see Sharpe, *JCL*, 63 (1999), 80. However, certain sanctions can be based on s. 78 of the Police and Criminal Evidence Act 1984; in more detail, Campbell, Ashworth, and Redmayne, *The Criminal Process* (2019), pp. 275 ff. The opposite model exists in the US State of California, where s. 1054.5 (b) Califnia Penal Code lists seven kinds of sanction; see, in more detail, Pipes and Gagen, *California Criminal Discovery* (2008), pp. 677 ff.; in general on the legal situation in England and the USA, Ambos, *NCLR*, 12 (2009), 556 ff.; Schuon, *International Criminal Procedure* (2010), pp. 13 ff.

[1150] Rule 110 reads: 'The Panel may decide, upon request by a Party or proprio motu, on measures to be taken as a result of the non-compliance with disclosure obligations pursuant to the Rules, including a stay of proceedings and the exclusion of evidence, except for exculpatory evidence.' The Rule partly resembles Rule 114 RPE STL but is modelled after domestic rules such as s. 1054.5 (b) California Penal Code mentioned in the previous note.

authority and function.[1151] A glance at the case law teaches us that the choice of sanction depends on the individual case and is subject to judicial discretion.[1152] Thus, for example, a delayed disclosure does not automatically render the proceedings unfair but only if, first, the accused suffered material prejudice as a result of it[1153] and, secondly, it is not cured by the later full disclosure or by allowing additional evidence on appeal.[1154] This reminds us of the ECtHR's overall assessment approach in order to determine an ultimate fair trial violation.[1155]

One possible response to non-disclosure could be a *stay of proceedings*—albeit regarded as a 'drastic' and 'exceptional' remedy[1156]—if such non-disclosure amounts to an abuse of process.[1157] As we will see in Chapter VI,[1158] the ICC AC has taken a more critical approach to this doctrine. At any rate, the gist of the issue is the seriousness of the violation. As to disclosure violations the *Lubanga* TC once referred to the rupture of the trial process 'to such a degree that it is now impossible to piece together the constituent elements of a fair trial'.[1159] In case of disclosure violations by the prosecution a stay has been imposed in connection with Article 54 (3)(e) ICCS[1160] and the identity of certain intermediaries.[1161]

[1151] cf. Rule 68*bis* RPE ICTY; thereon Jones and Powles, *International Criminal Practice* (2003), pp. 667–8. At the ICC, a sanction may be constructed via Rule 121 (8) RPE: 'The Pre-Trial Chamber shall not take into consideration charges and evidence presented after the time limit, or any extension thereof, has expired.' In detail, Heinze, *Disclosure* (2014), pp. 452 ff., with a comparative law account at pp. 421 ff.; Rohan, in Schabas et al., *Research Companion ICL* (2013), pp. 292 ff.; Kuczyńska, *Accusation Model* (2015), pp. 221–2. Consequently, Mettraux et al., *Effectiveness ICC* (2014), p. 16 (para. 71) recommend that 'Chambers should develop a regime of credible sanctions to be applicable to disclosure violations regardless of whether or not the belatedly disclosed evidence is admitted at trial.'

[1152] ICTR, *Prosecutor v. Nteziryayo*, TC, Decision on Alphonse Nteziryayo's motion for exclusion of evidence, ICTR-97-29-T—Joint Case ICTR-98-42-T, 25 February 2009, paras. 26–7; ICTR, *Prosecutor v. Karemera et al.*, TC III, Oral Decision Relating to the Late Disclosure Regarding Witness T, ICTR-98-44-T, 24 May 2006; see Caianiello, *ICLR*, 10 (2010), 36–7 with further references.

[1153] ICTY, *Prosecutor v. Blaškić*, AC, Judgment, IT-95-14-A, 29 July 2004, para. 285; *Krstić*, IT-98-33-A, para. 153; conc. *Stakić*, IT-97-24-A, para. 188. See also Ambos, in Bohlander, *ICJ* (2007), p. 465.

[1154] cf. Rule 115 RPE ICTY; *Krstić*, IT-98-33-A, para. 187; conc. *Stakić*, IT-97-24-A, paras. 191 ff. Crit. Bohlander, *ERA Forum*, 4 (2005), 549; Calvo-Goller, *Trial Proceedings* (2006), pp. 263–4; *Yekatom and Ngaïssona*, ICC-01/14-01/18-595, para. 19; see also Pitcher, *Judicial Responses* (2018), p. 411; Turner, in Heller et al., *Oxford HB ICL* (2020) p. 55.

[1155] See Chapter I, D (4) in this volume.

[1156] See ICC, *Prosecutor v. Lubanga*, AC, Judgment on the Appeal of the Prosecutor against the Decision of Trial Chamber I of 8 July 2010 Entitled 'Decision on the Prosecution's Urgent Request for Variation of the Time-Limit to Disclose the Identity of Intermediary 143 or Alternatively to Stay Proceedings Pending Further Consultations with the VWU', ICC-01/04-01/06 2582, 8 October 2010, para. 55; Kuczyńska, *Accusation Model* (2015), p. 222. See generally Turner, *NYUJILP*, 45 (2012), 198 ff. On the consequences of a stay of proceedings as a reaction to an abuse of process, see ICTR, *Prosecutor v. Barayagwiza*, AC, Decision, ICTR-97-19, 3 November 1999, paras. 73 ff.; ICTY, *Prosecutor v. Nikolić*, TC II, Decision on Defence Motion Challenging the Exercise of Jurisdiction by the Tribunal, IT-94-2-PT, 9 October 2002, paras. 106 ff.; see also ECCC, *Prosecutor v. Guek Eav*, Order of Provisional Detention, 002/14-08-2006, 31 July 2007, paras. 21 ff.

[1157] Thereon Ryngaert, *LJIL*, 21 (2008), 719, 729 ff.; Ambos, *Treatise I* (2021), pp. 559 ff. with further references; Kochhar and Hieramente, *LJIL*, 29 (2016), 236.

[1158] Chapter VI, D.(1)(b) in this volume.

[1159] *Lubanga*, ICC-01/04–01/06-1401, para. 93.

[1160] See previously note 949 in this chapter. A conflict arose between the Prosecutor's right to obtain confidential 'lead' evidence pursuant to Art. 54 (3)(e) ICCS, and its responsibility to disclose potentially exculpatory evidence under Art. 67 (2) ICCS, cf. Whiting, *UCLA JIL & ForAff*, 14 (2009), 209, who points out that this conflict 'is built right into the Statute of the ICC'; Ambos, *ICLR*, 12 (2012), 124; Kuczyńska, *Accusation Model* (2015), pp. 224 ff. For a discussion esp. of Art. 54 (3)(e) ICCS, see Ambos, *NCLR*, 12 (2009), 543–68; Schabas, Chaitidou, and El Zeidy, 'Article 61', in Ambos, *Commentary* (2022), mn. 69; Bitti, 'Article 64', in Ambos, *Commentary* (2022), mn. 29; Schabas and McDermott, 'Article 67', in Ambos, *Commentary* (2022), mn. 54; Rigney, *Fairness* (2022), pp. 128 ff. For instances where the Chambers issued a stay of the proceedings following non-disclosure by the prosecution, see Heinze, *Disclosure* (2014), pp. 454 ff. Given this inherent conflict, Mettraux et al., *Effectiveness ICC* (2014), p. 10 (para. 25) correctly recommend that 'the OTP must continue to be extremely careful when entering into confidentiality agreements under Article 54(3)(e) ICC Statute. The Prosecutor should negotiate Article 54(3)(d) and (e) agreements in a way that protects the interests of the provider or state while ensuring that the Prosecutor can meet her other obligations under the Statute' (see also para. 64).

[1161] About the function and definition of intermediaries, see Section A.(3)(c) in this chapter *in fine*. During the proceedings against *Lubanga* the suspicion arose that certain intermediaries had bribed various persons to

Another possible sanction for disclosure violations is *disciplinary measures*.[1162] Under this approach such violations are considered as serious misconduct and serious breaches of duty,[1163] which may entail a reprimand or even a pecuniary sanction as a disciplinary measure.[1164] Then the oversight mechanisms[1165] as well as the Staff Rules[1166] and Codes of Conduct,[1167] setting out disciplinary measures for misconduct of members of the Court, come into play.

## (6) Conclusion

Disclosure obligations are arguably an expression of the adversarial model,[1168] for its *two cases approach*—already referred to above[1169]—is predicated on reciprocal disclosure giving the parties full access to all relevant information and enabling them to deal with each other 'on an equal footing'.[1170] Given the structural superiority of the prosecution, its higher disclosure obligations operate as compensation in order to achieve a fair balance between the parties and to come close to the ideal of an equality of arms.

By contrast, such reciprocal disclosure is unnecessary in the traditional inquisitorial system where—in line with a *one case approach*[1171]—the investigation lies in the hands of the prosecuting authority, which is obliged to investigate both incriminating and exculpatory evidence equally. Notwithstanding this obligation the suspect is entitled to get information

prepare false evidence for alleged former child soldiers, ICC, *Prosecutor v. Lubanga*, TC I, Transcript of hearing on 13 March 2009, ICC-01/04-01/06-T-147-ENG WT 13-03-2009 1-1 NB T, p. 3, l. 11–8, cited in *Lubanga*, ICC-01/04-01/06-2434-Red2, para. 16. This turned the formerly incriminating evidence into evidence that was material for the preparation of the defence case. The TC ordered the prosecution to disclose confidentially to the defence the identity ('names and other identifying information' plus the 'professional background') of certain intermediaries, *Lubanga*, ICC-01/04-01/06-2434-Red2, para. 150. After the prosecution did not comply with that order and another order of additional disclosure, the defence applied for a permanent stay of proceedings which was however denied by the TC; ICC, *Prosecutor v. Lubanga*, TC I, Redacted Decision on the 'Defence Application Seeking a Permanent Stay of the Proceedings', ICC-01/04-01/06-2690-Red, 2 March 2011, para. 224. See also Schabas and McDermott, 'Article 67', in Ambos, *Commentary* (2022), mn. 54; Burchard, 'Article 71', in Ambos, *Commentary* (2022), mn. 23; Re, in Agirre et al., *Quality Control* (2020), pp. 762 ff.

[1162] In detail, Heinze, *Disclosure* (2014), pp. 465 ff.; Kuczyńska, *Accusation Model* (2015), p. 223.

[1163] Art. 47 ICCS, Rules 25–7, 30 RPE ICC, Reg. 120 RegC. In practice, Art. 47 ICCS is directed primarily at the prosecution; cf. Mégret, in Reydams et al., *International Prosecutors* (2012), p. 479; Heinze, *Disclosure* (2014), pp. 465–6.

[1164] Rule 32 RPE ICC.

[1165] See Chapter II, A.(5), B.(7) in this volume.

[1166] See Chapter II, B.(1), C.(4) in this volume.

[1167] See Chapter II, B.(6), C.(2)(b) in this volume.

[1168] Ambos and Miller, *ICLR*, 7 (2007), 341; Ambos, *ICLR*, 3 (2003), 15 with further references ('From a conceptual perspective, such disclosure rules are a clear expression of the adversarial model since its "two cases approach" makes (mutual) disclosure necessary to ensure that both parties have the same level of information'); Schuon, *International Criminal Procedure* (2010), pp. 15, 16; Ward and Akhtar, *Walker and Walker's English Legal System* (10th edn, 2008), p. 606 ('The effective working of the adversarial system depends, in part, upon proper disclosure', citing *R v. McIlkenny* [1992] 2 All ER 417).

[1169] Chapter I, A.(1)(b) in this volume.

[1170] cf. Safferling, *International Criminal Procedure* (2003), p. 198; Möller, in Kirsch, *Internationale Strafgerichtshöfe* (2005), pp. 35–6, 54. Strictly speaking, the legal institution of disclosure is foreign to purely adversarial, conflict-solving criminal procedure, as this procedure is characterized precisely by the fact that both parties investigate and present their case independently of one another. However, it can be explained by the principle of the equality of arms. See Damaška, *Faces of Justice* (1986), p. 131; Swoboda, *Beweisstrategien* (2013), p. 179 ff.; Heinze, *Disclosure* (2014), pp. 317 ff.

[1171] Chapter I, A.(1)(a) in this volume.

of the case against him by requesting access to the case file (*dossier*)[1172] at some point before the beginning of the trial.[1173]

Given the importance of disclosure for the largely adversial trial[1174] before the ICC it comes as no surprise that it was one of the main issues during the negotiations of the RPE demonstrating the different approaches of common and civil law systems.[1175] This said it must not be overlooked that there is actually a connection between the dossier and the disclosure rules insofar as the object of the disclosure obligation must be contained in the dossier. Indeed, for this very reason Rule 121 (2)(c) RPE ICC requires that all disclosed evidence be communicated to the Pre-Trial Chamber.[1176] For the purpose of the confirmation hearing, this 'dossier' would even, in line with the *Bemba* approach,[1177] contain all relevant information and not only the bulk of it. Last but not least, the fact that both the confirmation decision and the record of the proceedings are to be transmitted to the Trial Chamber[1178] reaffirms the view that the ICC regime leaves room for a dossier.[1179]

Of course, it should not be overlooked that, in practice, civil law Prosecutors may also investigate *their* case and may succumb to the temptation to increase the chances of conviction by withholding exculpatory evidence.[1180] Likewise, even a proactive, fair-trial minded civil law judge may find it difficult to balance out the advantages of the prosecution that arise from the investigation. For this reason, independently of the respective procedural model, only comprehensive disclosure obligations are able to guarantee an effective right to adequate defence. In this sense, the 'all cards on the table' approach of the RPE ICC (particularly Rules 77, 78) is to be welcomed.[1181] And this also explains the existence of disclosure at the KSC which does not follow a purely adversarial procedural model.

1172 See Section A.(7) with note 774 in this chapter.

1173 See Friman, in Lee, *ICC* (2001), p. 213; Langer, *AmJCompL*, 53 (2005), 847.

1174 cf. Section A.(1)(c) in this chapter.

1175 Broomhall, 'Article 51', in Ambos, *Commentary* (2022), mn. 47; Schabas and McDermott, 'Article 67', in Ambos, *Commentary* (2022), mn. 6; WCRO, *Confirmation of Charges* (2015), pp. 12–13.

1176 See Sections A.(7) and B.(1)(c) in this chapter.

1177 About the disclosure regime established in *Bemba*, see Section B.(2)(c)(ii) in this chapter. In the same vein, Friman, in Stahn, *Practice* (2015), p. 923. In more detail, see Heinze, *Disclosure* (2014), pp. 509 ff.

1178 Rule 130 RPE ICC.

1179 See, in detail, Heinze, *Disclosure* (2014), pp. 245, 265, 503. As argued above (Section B.(1)(c) in this chapter), it seems that the record of the proceedings and its transmission from PTC to Presidency to TC comes close to the concept of a dossier. This view is also confirmed by the *Practice Manual* that seems to imply that the contents of Rule 130 might be viewed as another step further in the direction of a dossier: 'Considering that the Trial Chamber will ultimately conduct its own assessment as to the admissibility of evidence, its inclusion in the record of proceedings before professional judges is not problematic. The transmission of the complete record with all its contents is also preferred because of its simplicity' (ICC, *Practice Manual* (2023), para. 71; crit. Re, in Agirre et al., *Quality Control* (2020), pp. 786: 'It is not easy to comprehend the policy rationale for this. International criminal proceedings, in accordance with international human rights law, are adversarial. The ICC has neither an investigating judge nor chamber nor a dossier'.) The phrasing of that paragraph certainly carries a justificatory overtone, anticipating reservations to be expected by common law lawyers, similar to the ones made during the RPE negotiations (see notes 942 and 1175 in this chapter with accompanying text). Of course, the Manual's pro-dossier stance is rather unsurprising giving the civil law background of the judges that promoted the Manual: Cuno Tarfusser—Italy; Marc Perrin de Brichambaut—France; Antoine Kesia-Mbe Mindua—DRC (based on Belgian law); Péter Kovács—Hungary; Chang-ho Chung—Republic of Korea. Recommending a '(quasi-)"dossier" approach', Mettraux et al., *Effectiveness ICC* (2014), p. 18 (para. 78 a)): 'Trial Chambers could demand of the prosecution that it should provide prior to trial copies of witness statements, expert reports and exhibits that it proposes to use at trial. Chambers could also consider inviting the Defence to share its views on the nature of the evidence provided by the Prosecution at this early stage.'

1180 See Damaška, in Cassese, *Companion* (2009), pp. 176–7.

1181 In the same vein, Guariglia, in Cassese et al., *Rome Statute II* (2002), p. 1127; in favour of an 'independent investigative commission' to create fairness and transparency, Higgins, *JICJ*, 5 (2007), 396 ff.

# VI
# Appeal, Revision, and Other Remedies

*The full chapter bibliography can be downloaded from

## A. Preliminary remarks

The legal remedies available in the modern[1] international criminal tribunals are appeal and revision. *Appeal* in its original meaning (Latin '*appellare*') refers to an 'appeal to a higher court' as well as 'calling upon a magistrate' to intercede.[2] In international criminal procedure the appeal is the ordinary remedy against a first instance (trial) judgment of acquittal or conviction with a view to correcting possible errors of fact and law ('final appeal');[3] it can also be lodged against other decisions at the pre-trial or trial stage ('interlocutory appeal').[4] Notwithstanding this distinction as to the procedural stage of the appeal, the legal principles governing these appeals, especially with regard to the grounds of appeal, are largely the same.[5] The ICC Appeals Chamber consists of five judges—instead of three sitting in a Trial Chamber—and constitutes a 'higher court' only in a functional sense given that its judges have the same qualification as the trial judges and come from the same pool of judges elected to the tribunal or Court.[6]

[1] Neither the Statute of the IMT nor that of the IMTFE or CCL 10 allowed for an appeal by a higher tribunal (cf. Art. 26 IMTS and Art. 17 IMTFES; Calvo-Goller, *Trial Proceedings* (2006), pp. 115, 126, 304; Boas, Jackson, Roche, and Taylor III, in Sluiter et al., *International Criminal Procedure* (2013), p. 943). However, under the IMTFE regime and the CCL 10 there was at least an executive review system. Under the former, the Supreme Commander for the Allied Powers (General Douglas MacArthur) could reduce or alter the sentence (Art. 17 IMTFES); under the latter, the convicts could seek mercy from the Clemency Board of the High Commission for Occupied Germany. In 1952 US President Truman established a 'Clemency and Parole Board for War Criminals'; see Re, in Reydams, Wouters, and Ryngaert, *International Prosecutors* (2012), pp. 797–8; on the clemency boards, cf. also Heller, *Nuremberg Military Tribunals* (2011), pp. 362–7; Eckelmans, 'Article 81', in Ambos, *Commentary* (2022), mn. 2.

[2] cf. Hofstetter, *Verfahrensrecht* (2005), p. 135 with n. 549; Eckelmans, 'Article 81', in Ambos, *Commentary* (2022), mn. 4–5.

[3] At the KSC, mirroring the Kosovo domestic system, there is a third instance appeal to a Supreme Court Panel under certain limited circumstances, see Art. 47 KSC Law, Rule 186 RPE KSC. In addition, there is the possibility of a petition to a Constitutional Court Chamber for alleged constitutional violations, see Art. 49 KSC Law and the specific Rules of Procedure for this Chamber (as Part II of the RPE KSC).

[4] See generally Tracol, *CLF*, 12 (2001), 141 ff.; Lundqvist, *LJIL*, *15* (2002), 641 ff.; Hofstetter, *Verfahrensrecht* (2005), pp. 176 ff.; Wirth, in Kirsch, *Internationale Strafgerichtshöfe* (2005), pp. 75 ff.; Calvo-Goller, *Trial Proceedings* (2006), pp. 115 ff.; Meernik, *ICLR*, 7 (2007), 117 ff.; Cryer et al., *ICL* (2019), pp. 438 ff.; Tochilovsky, *Jurisprudence* (2014), pp. 1118 ff.; Friman, in Schabas and Bernaz, *Routledge Handbook ICL* (2011), pp. 278 ff.; *ICTY Manual*, pp. 129 ff.; on the 'right to appeal', see Zahar and Sluiter, *ICL* (2008), pp. 315 ff.; on the appeal before the ECCC, see O'Neill and Sluiter, *MelbJIL*, 10 (2009), 596; Shahabuddeen, *ChinJIL*, 10 (2011), 488 ff.; Mosna, in Allegrezza, *Appeal Proceedings* (2023), p. 76.

[5] With regard to Arts. 81 and 82 ICCS cf. *Prosecutor v. Lubanga*, AC, Judgment on the Appeal of Mr Thomas Lubanga Dyilo against his Conviction, ICC-01/04-01/06-3121-Red, 1 December 2014, para. 17; *Prosecutor v. Ngudjolo Chui*, AC, Judgment on the Prosecutor's Appeal against the Decision of Trial Chamber II Entitled 'Judgment Pursuant to Article 74 of the Statute', ICC-01/04-02/12-271-Corr, 7 April 2015, para. 19.

[6] cf. Nerlich, in Stahn, *ICC* (2015), pp. 964–6, arguing that the only difference of the AC compared to the (P) TC is functional ('power to review . . . the Decisions of the other Chambers of the Court') and not hierarchical ('no hierarchy in status', 'coming from the same pool', 'This transferability of judges from first-instance Chambers to the

The appeal before international criminal tribunals does not allow for a full-fledged review by a higher court, as is common in civil law jurisdictions,[7] but it is rather modelled after the Anglo-American appeal, providing for a selective, mixed factual-legal review, a kind of '*extended cassation*'.[8] Thus, in short, the appeal does not allow for a trial *de novo*, but only for a selective, corrective review pursuant to the grounds of appeal submitted by the parties.[9] However, the Appeals jurisprudence has also recognized that there are situations where an AC is not bound by the parties' submissions, namely either when considering legal arguments not raised by an appellant in relation to an alleged error of law,[10] regarding issues of general significance (even

Appeals Chamber further underlines the equal status of each judge of the Court, irrespective of the Chamber to which he or she is assigned'); see also on the one hand Safferling and Farthofer, *International Criminal Procedure* (2012), p. 147 ('highest judicial authority of the Court') and Safferling and Hartwig, *International Criminal Procedure* (2012), p. 534 (arguing in favour of the 'higher nature' of the AC, but 'only in the hierarchical sense' and not 'structurally'); for a more nuanced view on the other hand, see CHBoas, in Sluiter and Vasiliev, *International Criminal Procedure* (2009), p. 451 ('the appellate body simply reflects a larger number of judges, who are not selected ... on the basis of any seniority or particular experience'); also Zappalá, in Cassese, *Companion* (2009), p. 246.

[7] See e.g. for *France* ('*réexamen de l'affaire*') Arts. 380–1 (2), 380–14 (3) CPP and Cour de Cassation, Chambre Criminelle 2 February 2005, *Bull. Crim.*, No. 39, (2005), p. 115 ('*cour d'assises d'appel, ... réexamine l'affaire en son entier*'); for *Germany*, see ('*Berufung*') s. 312 ff. German CCP (StPO); for *Italy* ('*appello*') Art. 593 ff. CPP (but not necessarily devolutive effect); but see also for Spain, which has a more limited appeal ('*impugnación*'), Art. 790 ff. LEC and Bachmaier Winter and del Moral García, 'Spain', in Verbruggen and Franssen, *IEL Criminal Law* (2012), pp. 314–15; Allegrezza, in Allegrezza, *Appeal Proceedings* (2023), pp. 437–44.

[8] Kirsch, *StV*, 23 (2003), 637; cf. also Lundqvist, *LJIL*, 15 (2002), 655 ff.; Wirth, in Kirsch, *Internationale Strafgerichtshöfe* (2005), pp. 75–7; Ambos, in Bohlander, *International Criminal Justice* (2007), p. 495; for a historical and comparative legal analysis, see Hofstetter, *Verfahrensrecht* (2005), pp. 135 ff. (176 ff.); Re, in Reydams, Wouters, and Ryngaert, *International Prosecutors* (2012), pp. 797 ff.; Klamberg, *Evidence* (2013), pp. 411–12; Kuczyńska, *Accusation Model ICC* (2015), pp. 361–2, 372, 380, 390–1.

[9] See fundamentally *Prosecutor v. Tadić*, AC, Decision on Appellant's Motion for the Extension of the Time-Limit and Admission of Additional Evidence, IT-94-1-A, 15 October 1998, paras. 41–2 (denying a trial *de novo* and focusing on the corrective nature); *Prosecutor v. Ntaganda*, AC, Judgment on the Appeal of Mr Bosco Ntaganda against the 'Decision on the Defence's Challenge to the Jurisdiction of the Court in respect of Counts 6 and 9', ICC-01/04-02/06-1225, 22 March 2016, para. 23 with further references in note 39; *Prosecutor v. Al Hassan et al.*, AC, Judgment on the Appeal of Mr Al Hassan against the Decision of Pre-Trial Chamber I Entitled 'Décision relative à l'exception d'irrecevabilité pour insuffisance de gravité de l'affaire soulevée par la défense', ICC-01/12-01/18 OA, 19 February 2020, para. 39; *Prosecutor v. Ntaganda*, AC, Judgment on the Appeals of Mr Bosco Ntaganda and the Prosecutor against the Decision of Trial Chamber VI of 8 July 2019 Entitled 'Judgment', ICC-01/04-02/06 A A2, 30 March 2021, para. 45. See also Kreß, in Grützner, Pötz, and Kreß, *Internationaler Rechtshilfeverkehr in Strafsachen* (2003), IV A1 mn. 174; Zappalá, in Cassese, *Companion* (2009), p. 247; Eckelmans, 'Article 81', in Ambos, *Commentary* (2022), mn. 53, 113 ('corrective nature'); Re, in Reydams, Wouters, and Ryngaert, *International Prosecutors* (2012), p. 804; Safferling and Hartwig, *International Criminal Procedure* (2012), p. 532; Boas, Jackson, Roche, and Taylor III, in Sluiter et al., *International Criminal Procedure* (2013), p. 1003 (but apparently overlooking the civil law *cassation*); Tochilovsky, *Jurisprudence* (2014), pp. 1083–4; Trigeaud, 'Article 83', in Fernandez et al., *Statut II* (2019), p. 2112; leaving it open, Klamberg, 'Article 81', in Klamberg, *Commentary ICC* (2017), n. 651; in contrast Roth and Henzelin, in Cassese *et al.*, *Rome Statute II* (2002), p. 1539 (stressing the 'extreme flexibility' of the ICC appeals procedure); Allegrezza, in Allegrezza, *Appeal Proceedings* (2023), p. 427. For the KSC, see Art. 46 (2) KSC Law.

[10] *Prosecutor v. Erdemović*, AC, Judgment, IT-96-22-A, 7 October 1997, para. 16; *Tadić*, IT-94-1-A, 15 July 1999, para. 247. *Prosecutor v. Đorđević*, AC, Judgment, IT-05-87/1-A, 27 January 2014, para. 13 with further references in note 51; *Prosecutor v. Prlić et al.*, AC, Judgment, IT-04-74-A, 29 November 2017, para. 19; IRMCT, *Prosecutor v. Karadžić*, AC, Judgment, MICT-13-55-A, 20 March 2019, para. 15; for further (earlier) case law, see previous edition, p. 549 with note 9; for the ICTR, *Kambanda v. Prosecutor*, ICTR-97-23-A, 19 October 2000, para. 98; for the SCSL, cf. *Prosecutor v. Sesay et al.*, AC, Judgment, SCSL-04-15-A-1321-1, 26 October 2009, para. 31; *Prosecutor v. Fofana and Kondewa*, AC, Judgment, SCSL-04-14-A-829, 28 May 2008, para. 32; *Prosecutor v. Taylor*, AC, Judgment, SCSL-03-01-A, 26 September 2013, para. 25; for the STL, *Prosecutor v. Ayyash et al.*, AC, Decision on the Defence Appeals against the Trial Chamber's 'Decision on the Defence Challenges to the Jurisdiction and Legality of the Tribunal', STL-11-01/PT/AC/AR90.1, 24 October 2012, para. 10; in the same vein, also KSC, *Prosecutor v. Gucati and Haradinaj*, Decision on Hysni Gucati's Appeal on Matters Related to Arrest and Detention, KSC-BC-2020-07/IA001/F00005, 9 December 2020, para. 12 (holding that, '[e]ven if the party's arguments are insufficient to support the contention of an error, the Panel may find for other reasons that there is an error of law'); *Prosecutor v. Gucati and Haradinaj*, Appeal Judgment, KSC-CA-2022-01/F00114/2, 2 February

if they would not invalidate the judgment),[11] or even when, albeit more exceptionally, *proprio motu* raising errors of law where 'the interests of justice so require' (in particular with respect to sentencing).[12] In a similar vein, under the ICC regime, the Appeals Chamber has 'all the powers' of the Trial Chamber[13] and may itself also call evidence to determine an issue.[14]

In contrast to the appeal, the *revision* is an extraordinary remedy against a final judgment of conviction or sentence. In addition, there are *other remedies* with regard to prosecutorial investigation or prosecution decisions, procedural rights' violations, and administrative decisions. While the first group of reviews has already been analysed in Chapter IV,[15] the two last groups will be considered in the last section of this chapter.

## B. Appeal

### (1) Appeal against final (trial) decision or sentence

#### (a) Procedure

The appeal—be it an ordinary or an interlocutory one—is primarily a written procedure.[16] Yet, at least one substantive appeal hearing, apart from rather formal status conferences, will usually take place,[17] depending on the circumstances of the case and the utility of such a hearing with a view to clarifying and resolving the relevant issues.[18] The scope of the appeal

2023, para. 22 ('find an error of law based on other reasons'); *Prosecutor v. Mustafa*, Appeal Judgment, KSC-CA-2023-02/F00038/RED, 14 December 2023, para. 18.

[11] See ICTY, *Erdemović*, IT-96-22-A, para. 16; *Prosecutor v. Krnojelac*, AJ, IT-97-25-A, 17 September 2003, para. 6; *Prosecutor v. Galić*, AJ, IT-98-29-A, 30 November 2006, para. 6; ICTY, *Prosecutor v. Boškoski and Tarčulovski*, AJ, IT-04-82-A, 19 May 2010, para. 9; *Prosecutor v. Haradinaj et al.*, AJ, IT-04-84-A, 19 July 2010, para. 9; ICTR, *Nahimana et al. v. Prosecutor*, AJ, ICTR-99-52-A, 28 November 2007, para. 12; STL, *Prosecutor v. Merhi and Oneissi*, AJ, STL-11/01/A-2/AC, 10 March 2022, para. 30; *In the Case Against Al Jadeed [Co.] S.A.L./New T.V. S.A.L. (N.T.V.) and Al Khayat*, Public Redacted Version of Judgment on Appeal, STL-14-05/A/AP, 8 March 2016, para. 12.

[12] See ICTY, *Prosecutor v. Kordic and Cerkez*, AJ, IT-95-14/2-A, 17 December 2004, para. 1031; *Krnojelac*, IT-97-25-A, para. 6; ICTR, *Ndindabahizi v. Prosecutor*, AJ, ICTR-01-71-A, 16 January 2007, para. 13; regarding sentencing, see ICTY, *Prosecutor v. Jokic*, AC, Judgment on Sentencing Appeal, IT-01-42/1-A, 30 August 2005, para. 26 ('in the case of an error of law, the Appeals Chamber has the discretionary power to correct this error *proprio motu* if the interests of justice so require'); *Kordic and Cerkez*, IT-95-14/2-A, para. 1031 (considering *proprio motu* the issue of cumulative convictions not raised by the respective accused); *Ndindabahizi*, ICTR-01-71-A, para. 13 (raising *proprio motu* the issue of alternative convictions not raised by the parties); see also ECCC, AJ, Case 002/19-09-2007, 23 December 2022, paras. 25, 32_3; AJ (F36), Case 002/01, 23 November 2016, paras. 1138–42; AJ (F28), Case 001, 3 February 2012, para. 15.

[13] Art. 83 (1) ICCS; cf. *Lubanga*, ICC-01/04-01/06-3121-Red, para. 54; Eckelmans, 'Article 81', in Ambos, *Commentary* (2022), mn. 20; Eckelmans, 'Article 83', in Ambos, *Commentary* (2022), mn. 4; Trigeaud, 'Article 83', in Fernandez et al., *Statut II* (2019), p. 2110; Schabas, *ICC Commentary* (2016), pp. 1243–4.

[14] Art. 83 (2) 2nd cl. ICCS. See Schabas, *ICC Commentary* (2016), p. 1244; Trigeaud, 'Article 83', in Fernández et al., *Statut II* (2019), p. 2111–12.

[15] See Chapter IV, B.(3) in this volume.

[16] See, in particular, Rules 111–13 RPE ICTY/ICTR; Rules 138–40 RPE MICT; Rules 72 (3) (re offences against the administration of justice), 162 (4), 180 RPE KSC; Rules 150, 151, 156 (3) RPE ICC, Regs. 57–61 RegC.

[17] cf. Rules 114 RPE ICTY/ICTR/SCSL and 141 RPE MICT; Rules 178, 180 RPE KSC; cf. also Boas, Jackson, Roche, and Taylor III, in Sluiter et al., *International Criminal Procedure* (2013), pp. 957–8; Eckelmans, 'Article 83', in Ambos, *Commentary* (2022), mn. 5, 66. Generally on the development of the ICC appeals procedure, see Doria, in Doria, Gasser, and Bassiouni, *Legal Regime* (2009), pp. 947–8; Beltrán, in Gómez Colomer et al., *La Corte Penal Internacional* (2003), pp. 368 ff.; Kreß, *JICJ*, 1 (2003), 608; Calvo-Goller, *Trial Proceedings* (2006), pp. 306 ff.

[18] *Prosecutor v. Mathieu Ngudjolo Chui*, AC, Scheduling Order for a Hearing before the Appeals Chamber, ICC-01/04-01/12-199, 18 September 2014, paras. 12, 13 ('should be based primarily on the potential utility of an oral hearing, namely whether it would assist the Appeals Chamber in clarifying and resolving the issues raised in the appeal'); *Prosecutor v. Dominic Ongwen*, AC, Order Scheduling a Hearing before the Appeals Chamber, ICC-02/04-01/15-1909, 17 November 2021, para. 6 ('appropriate' to schedule a hearing).

is mainly determined by the submissions of the parties although the Appeals Chamber possesses the above-mentioned *proprio motu* authority. The procedure is governed by some formalities regarding deadlines for filing, length of the submissions, and the like.[19] Thus, for example, before the ad hoc tribunals the 'notice of appeal', setting out the grounds to be elaborated in more detail later,[20] shall be filed 'not more than thirty days' from the pronouncement of the judgment.[21]

Before the ICC, the 'notice of appeal'[22] against a conviction, an acquittal, a sentence, or a reparation order should be filed with the Registrar in writing within thirty days[23] of the appealing party being notified of the decision[24] and the document in support of the appeal (the actual appellate brief) shall not exceed 100 pages.[25] Upon the filing of the appeal, the trial record is transmitted to the AC.[26] The full appeal of one party may consist, as at the ad hoc tribunals, of three or even four documents: the already mentioned notice of appeal, the actual appellate brief, the response, and, if leave is granted, the reply.[27] The ICC law does not explicitly provide for a *pre-appeal (single) judge* as known from the ad hoc tribunals,[28] but it may be assigned pursuant to an (analogous) application of Rule 132*bis* (via Rule 149) RPE ICC.[29]

The parties have to submit the grounds of appeal (to be analysed below), present arguments in support of these grounds, and explain how the alleged errors affect the appealed decision.[30] The grounds raised must, in principle, have been indicated already in the

[19] See Boas, Jackson, Roche, and Taylor III, in Sluiter et al., *International Criminal Procedure* (2013), pp. 947–9 (ICTY, ICTR, SCSL), 956–7 (ICC), 960 (SPSC), 961 (ECCC), 962 (STL); on those formalities, see also Eckelmans, 'Article 83', in Ambos, *Commentary* (2022), mn. 48 ff.

[20] On the purpose of this requirement, see *Prosecutor v. Nahimana et al.*, AC, Decision on Appellant Jean-Bosco Barayagwiza's Motions for Leave to Submit Additional Grounds of Appeal, to Amend the Notice of Appeal and to Correct his Appellant's Brief, ICTR-99-52-A, 27 August 2006, para. 50 (arguing that it serves to better understand the arguments of the appellant and 'focus the mind of the Respondent').

[21] Rule 108 RPE ICTY/ICTR; cf. also the slightly different wording of Rule 133 RPE MICT, setting the deadline for filing a notice of appeal to 'thirty days from the date on which the written judgement was *filed*' (emphasis added); see also Rule 176 (1) RPE KSC. Before the SCSL, this deadline is set to '14 days from the *receipt* of the full judgment and sentence' (Rule 108 RPE SCSL, emphasis added).

[22] Reg. 57 RegC. On the *travaux* in this respect, see Boas, Jackson, Roche, and Taylor III, 'Appeals, Reviews, and Reconsideration', in Sluiter et al., *International Criminal Procedure* (2013), p. 956; also Eckelmans, 'Article 83', in Ambos, *Commentary* (2022), mn. 49.

[23] According to Rule 150 (2) RPE ICC, the Appeals Chamber may extend, upon application and under exceptional circumstances, the time limit for an appeal, as long as the applicant demonstrates that it is for a 'good cause'. Good cause is also a reason to vary time limits regarding the submission of documents (Reg. 35 (2) in conjunction with Reg. 34 RegC; on the calculation of time limits, see Reg. 33 RegC). In this context 'good cause' has been defined by the *Lubanga* AC as follows: 'valid reasons for non-compliance with the procedural obligations of a party to the litigation associated with a party's duties and obligations in the judicial process. A cause is good, if founded upon reasons associated with a person's capacity to conform to the applicable procedural rule or regulation or the directions of the Court.' (*Prosecutor v. Lubanga*, AC, Reasons for the 'Decision of the Appeals Chamber on the request of counsel to Mr Thomas Lubanga Dyilo for modification of the time limit pursuant to regulation 35 of the Regulations of the Court of 7 February 2007' issued on 16 February 2007, ICC-01/04-01/06 834, 7 February 2007, para. 7).

[24] Rule 150 (1) and (3) RPE ICC.

[25] Reg. 58 (5) RegC.

[26] Rule 151 (1) RPE ICC. For the trial record before the ad hoc tribunals, see Rules 109 RPE ICTY/ICTR, 110 RPE SCSL, and 136 RPE MICT.

[27] Regs. 57–60 RegC. On the formalities regarding those documents, see Eckelmans, 'Article 83', in Ambos, *Commentary* (2022), mn. 57–59.

[28] cf. Rule 108*bis* RPE ICTR, 109 RPE SCSL ('pre-hearing judge'), 135 RPE MICT and implicitly Rule 127 (B) RPE ICTY; see also Boas, Jackson, Roche, and Taylor III, in Sluiter et al., *International Criminal Procedure* (2013), pp. 949, 957, 1012.

[29] cf. Eckelmans, 'Article 83', in Ambos, *Commentary* (2022), mn. 69.

[30] *Prosecutor v. Krajišnik*, AC, Judgment, IT-00-39-A, 17 March 2009, para. 12; *Prosecutor v. D. Milošević*, AC, Judgment, IT-98-29/1-A, 12 November 2009, para. 13; for the SCSL, cf. e.g. *Prosecutor v. Taylor*, AC, Judgment, SCSL-03-01-A-1389, 26 September 2013, paras. 25, 27; for further case law, see previous edition p. 551 note 27; for the ICC, cf. *Prosecutor v. Lubanga*, AC, Judgment, ICC-01/04-01/06 A 5, 1 December 2014, para. 30 ; *Prosecutor*

(previous) notice of appeal, i.e. one could speak of a kind of congruence requirement and an AC may decline to consider grounds not contained in the notice of appeal.[31] Still, a variation of the grounds is possible under certain, more or less strict circumstances but it must, at any rate, be authorized by the AC.[32] The parties must not merely repeat on appeal arguments that did not succeed at trial unless they can demonstrate that the TC's rejection of those arguments constituted an error warranting the intervention of the AC.[33] Arguments that do not have the potential to cause the impugned decision to be reversed need not be considered on the merits, and may be immediately dismissed.[34] If an issue that could have been raised before the TC but was not due to a failure of the respective party it cannot be raised for the first time before the AC since the right to object may be considered to have been waived ('waiver principle'); while the ICTY has taken this view, the ICC has not yet addressed the matter but takes, in considering procedural errors, into account the conduct of the respective party at the trial stage.[35]

The ICTY/ICTR Appeals Chamber has identified a series of deficient submissions, which are to be summarily dismissed,[36] for example:

- Arguments that fail to identify the challenged factual findings, misrepresent the factual findings or the evidence, or ignore other relevant factual findings;
- Arguments that are clearly irrelevant, or that lend support to or are not inconsistent with the challenged finding;
- Arguments that challenge a TC's reliance or failure to rely on one piece of evidence, without explaining why the conviction should not stand on the basis of the remaining evidence;

*v. Bemba*, AC, Judgment, ICC-01/05-01/08-3636-Red, 8 June 2018 paras. 63–6. On how the grounds of appeal form the basis for the appeal, see Eckelmans, 'Article 81', in Ambos, *Commentary* (2022), mn. 38.

[31] See ICTY, *Marijačić and Rebić*, AJ, IT-95-14R77.2-A, 27 September 2006, para. 18; KSC, *Gucati and Haradinaj*, KSC-CA-2022-01/F00114/2, para. 30; *Mustafa*, KSC-CA-2023-02/F00038/RED, para. 31.

[32] cf. Rules 108 RPE ICTY/ICTR, 133 RPE MICT and Rule 176 (3) RPE KSC; for the ICC, see Reg. 61 RegC. Rules of ICTY, ICTR, MICT and KSC require good cause but the AC of ICTY/ICTR has authorized a variation even in the absence of good cause if otherwise a miscarriage of justice ensued; cf. Boas, Jackson, Roche, and Taylor III, 'Appeals, Reviews, and Reconsideration', in Sluiter et al., *International Criminal Procedure* (2013), pp. 949–50 with case law references in note 70. Reg. 61 RegC is mainly of a formal nature, esp. requiring that the application shall be filed 'as soon as the reasons warranting it become known' (para. 2); see also op. cit., p. 958.

[33] *Prosecutor v. Simić*, AC, Judgment, IT-95-9-A, 28 November 2006, para. 12; for further case law, see previous edition p. 352 note 29; for the ICC, see *Lubanga*, ICC-01/04-01/06-3121-Red, para. 31; *Prosecutor v. Bemba*, AC, Judgment, ICC-01/05-01/08 A, 8 June 2018, para. 64 ('Accordingly, the appellant has to substantiate that the Trial Chamber's interpretation of the law was incorrect; [...] this may be done including by raising arguments that were previously put before the Pre-Trial and/or Trial Chamber. In addition, the appellant must substantiate that the decision under review would have been substantially different, had it not been for the error').

[34] *Prosecutor v. Mrkšić and Šljivančanin*, AC, Judgment, IT-95-13/1-A, 5 May 2009, para. 16; for further case law, see previous edition p. 352 note 30; more recently *Prosecutor v. Šešelj*, Judgment, MICT-16-99-A, 11 April 2018, para. 49; for the ICC, see *Lubanga*, ICC-01/04-01/06-3121-Red, paras. 20, 30; *Prosecutor v. Bemba et al.*, AC, Judgment on the Appeals of the Prosecutor, Mr Jean-Pierre Bemba Gombo, Mr Fidèle Babala Wandu, and Mr Narcisse Arido against the Decision of Trial Chamber VII Entitled 'Decision on Sentence pursuant to Article 76 of the Statute', ICC-01/05-01/13-2276-Red, 8 March 2018, paras. 9-56; *Bemba*, ICC-01/05-01/08-3636-Red, paras. 47, 59, 64.

[35] cf. Eckelmans, 'Article 81', in Ambos, *Commentary* (2022), mn. 53–5 with references to ICTY/IRMCT case law. On gross negligence of counsel and whether it can be attributed to the defendant, see Section B.(1)(c) in this chapter.

[36] For relevant case law, see previous edition p. 552 note 33; more recently *Niyitegeka v. Prosecutor*, Decision Dismissing a Request, MICT-12-16-R, 13 April 2018. See also Boas, Jackson, Roche, and Taylor III, in Sluiter et al., *International Criminal Procedure* (2013), pp. 948–9; Tochilovsky, *Jurisprudence* (2014), pp. 1092–3; Eckelmans, 'Article 81', in Ambos, *Commentary* (2022), mn. 39 (on the difference between *rejection* and *dismissal* of a ground of appeal), 49–50 (on summary dismissal).

- Arguments contrary to common sense;
- Challenges to factual findings where the relevance of the factual finding is unclear and hasn't been explained by the appealing party;
- Mere repetition of arguments that were unsuccessful at trial without any demonstration that their rejection by the TC constituted an error warranting the intervention of the AC;
- Allegations based on material not on record;
- Mere assertions unsupported by any evidence, undeveloped assertions, or failure to articulate the error;
- Mere assertions that the TC failed to consider relevant evidence or to give sufficient weight to evidence, without showing that no reasonable trier of fact, based on the evidence, could have reached the same conclusion as the TC did.

The Prosecutor or the convict may appeal against the *decision itself* or against the *sentence* imposed where it is deemed to be disproportionate.[37] The Prosecutor's right to appeal even against an acquittal[38]—also allowed under the law of the ad hoc tribunals[39]—is difficult to reconcile with the common law's understanding of the double jeopardy rule (*ne bis in idem*), which prohibits subjecting the accused to a criminal trial for a second time.[40] However, it may be justified by the Prosecutor's impartial (non-partisan) position,[41] which carries the obligation to investigate both incriminating and exonerating circumstances.[42]

If the appeal has only been lodged by the convict or the Prosecutor on his behalf,[43] the principle *reformatio in peius* applies: the decision or sentence cannot be amended to the detriment of the convict.[44] If, during an appeals process concerning the sentence imposed, the AC has any doubts as to the underlying decision itself, it may ask the Prosecutor and the convict to extend the appeal to cover this matter, that is, to submit the respective grounds.[45] The same procedure applies in the reverse scenario, that is, if the AC considers that an appeal against the conviction should be extended only to the sentence.[46] As long as the Trial Chamber does not order otherwise, the convict must remain in custody for the duration of the appellate proceedings.[47]

The parties may discontinue their appeal. The right to appeal can be waived[48] (before the appeal is filed) or the appeal can be discontinued (after it has been filed). In both cases, the competent Chamber must make sure that the respective decision of the defendant has been informed, voluntary, and unequivocal. Thus, for example, Germain Katanga discontinued

[37] Art. 81 (1)(a), (b), and (2)(a) ICCS.

[38] From a comparative law perspective, see Kuczyńska, *Accusation Model ICC* (2015), pp. 366–71.

[39] Arts. 25 (1) ICTYS, 24 (1) ICTRS, 23 (1) IRMCTS, 20 (1) SCSLS, 21 (1) RSCSLS.

[40] Thomas III, *Double Jeopardy* (1998), pp. 216–19, 229–31; Stuckenberg, *Double Jeopardy* (2001), pp. 13 ff.; Brady and Jennings, in Lee, *ICC* (1999), p. 297; previously Ambos, in Bohlander, *International Criminal Justice* (2007), pp. 494–5. On *ne bis in idem* considerations upon revision, see below note 260 and main text.

[41] See Chapter II, B.(4) in this volume.

[42] Art. 54 (1)(a) ICCS. In a similar vein, Boas, Jackson, Roche, and Taylor III, in Sluiter et al., *International Criminal Procedure* (2013), p. 1004; Kuczyńska, *Accusation Model ICC* (2015), pp. 365–6.

[43] See Wei, *Ankläger* (2007), pp. 273 ff. (appeal by the Prosecutor on behalf of the convict), 288 ff. (against the sentence).

[44] Art. 83 (2) ICCS *in fine*. For further details, see Doria, in Doria, Gasser, and Bassiouni, *Legal Regime* (2009), pp. 950 ff.; Eckelmans, 'Article 83', in Ambos, *Commentary* (2022), mn. 31–2; Kuczyńska, *Accusation Model ICC* (2015), pp. 382–3; Allegrezza, in Allegrezza, *Appeal Proceedings* (2023), pp. 435–7.

[45] Art. 81 (2)(b) ICCS.

[46] Art. 81 (2)(c) ICCS. On appeals against sentence, see Eckelmans, 'Article 81', in Ambos, *Commentary* (2022), mn. 106–16.

[47] Art. 81 (3)(a) ICCS. On the suspension of the execution of the sentence during appeal, see Eckelmans, 'Article 81', in Ambos, *Commentary* (2022), mn. 116–41.

[48] On such a waiver in the context of a guilty plea, see Chapter IV, B.(9) in this volume.

his appeal against the Trial Judgment of 7 March 2014 and waived his right to appeal against the Sentencing Judgment of 23 May 2014.[49] In his personal notification attached as Annex A (‘*notification du retrait*’) to the defence notice, Katanga confirmed the notice and that he was fully aware of its consequences.[50]

### (b) *Standard of review and grounds of appeal*

The standard of review has been developed over the years by the case law. One has to distinguish between different grounds of appeal based on different errors, namely, errors of fact and errors of law[51] or both types of errors in the context of discretionary decisions. The more or less clear-cut fact/law dichotomy has been—not always for convincing reasons—complicated by further grounds of appeal, that is, procedural errors,[52] the unwritten ground of issues of general significance to the tribunals’ jurisprudence, and—to the benefit of the convict only—‘any other ground that affects the fairness or reliability of the proceedings or decision’.[53] These grounds will be analysed in turn.

#### (i) *Errors of fact*

The threshold for a review of errors of fact, by their very nature, must be high. For, if the AC, as already said above, does not conduct a full-fledged second trial *de novo*, that is, does not take, in principle, the evidence anew, but relies on the trial record and the submissions of the parties, it cannot lightly interfere with the factual findings of a TC.[54] Indeed, it is the TC that is best placed to assess the evidence.[55] The point was compellingly made by the *Kupreškić et al.* AC:

> Pursuant to the jurisprudence of the Tribunal, the task of hearing, assessing and weighing the evidence presented at trial is left primarily to the Trial Chamber. Thus, the Appeals

[49] cf. *Prosecutor v. Katanga*, AC, Defence Notice of Discontinuance of Appeal against the ‘Jugement rendu en application de l’Article 74 du Statut’ rendered by Trial Chamber II on 7 April 2014, ICC-01/04-01/07-3497, 25 June 2014; *Prosecutor v. Katanga*, AC, Notice of Discontinuance of the Prosecution’s Appeal, ICC-01/04-01/07-3498, 25 June 2014; for a waiver in the context of an admission of guilt, see *Prosecutor v. Al Mahdi*, TC VIII, Judgment and Sentence, ICC-01/12-01/15-171, 27 September 2016, para. 30.

[50] Annex A to the Defence Notice previously quoted where it is stated: ‘Il a été pleinement informé par son conseil des conséquences juridiques de cette Décision’, especially of the fact that ‘il est censé avoir volontairement abandonné son droit d’interjeter appel’.

[51] Arts. 25 (1) ICTYS, 24 (1) ICTRS, 23 (1) IRMCTS, 20 (1) SCSLS, 21 (1) RSCSLS; Art. 46 (1) KSC Law; Art. 81 (1) ICCS. It is for the AC to determine the kind of (possible) error, depending on what and how it is challenged; e.g. a challenge to the factual finding which forms the basis of the law is considered an error of fact; cf. thereon *Prosecutor v. Simone Gbagbo*, Judgment on the Appeal of Côte d’Ivoire against the Decision of Pre-Trial Chamber I of 11 December 2014 Entitled ‘Decision on Côte d’Ivoire’s challenge to the admissibility of the case against Simone Gbagbo’, ICC-02/11-01/12-75-Red, 27 May 2015, paras. 1, 46, 62.

[52] Art. 20 (1) SCSLS, 21 (1) RSCSLS; Art. 81 (1) ICCS.

[53] Art. 81 (1)(b)(iv) ICCS.

[54] *D. Milošević*, IT-98-29/1-A, para. 15; for further case law, see previous edition p. 555 note 52; more recently *Šešelj*, MICT-16-99-A, para. 103; *Karadzic*, MICT-13-55-A, para. 17; for the SCSL, cf. *Fofana and Kondewa*, SCSL-04-14-A-829, para. 33; *Sesay et al.*, SCSL-04-15-A-1321-1, para. 32; *Taylor*, SCSL-03-01-A-1389, para. 26; for the ICC, *Lubanga*, ICC-01/04-01/06-3121-Red, paras. 21, 26-7; conc. *Ngudjolo*, ICC-01/04-02/12-271-Corr, para. 22; *Bemba*, ICC-01/05-01/08-3636-Red, para. 65; for the KSC, see the first AJ in *Gucati and Haradinaj*, KSC-CA-2022-01/F00114/2, para. 20 ff. (at para. 26 affirming that a TJ will only be overturned in case of a ‘miscarriage of justice’ and that, at any rate, the AP ‘will not lightly overturn the Trial Panel’s factual findings’); conc. *Mustafa*, KSC-CA-2023-02/F00038/RED, para. 24. See also Eckelmans, ‘Article 81’, in Ambos, *Commentary* (2022), mn. 88; Boas et al., *International Criminal Procedure* (2011), p. 445 with references to previous case law in note 142; identical, Boas, Jackson, Roche, and Taylor III, ‘Appeals, Reviews, and Reconsideration’, in Sluiter et al., *International Criminal Procedure* (2013), p. 945 with references to previous case law in note 25.

[55] *Fofana and Kondewa*, SCSL-04-14-A-829, para. 33; *Sesay et al.*, SCSL-04-15-A-1321-1, para. 32; *Taylor*, SCSL-03-01-A-1389, para. 26; *Lubanga*, ICC-01/04-01/06-3121-Red, paras. 24, 57.

Chamber must give a margin of deference to a finding of fact reached by the Trial Chamber. Only where the evidence relied on by the Trial Chamber couldn't have been accepted by *any reasonable tribunal* of fact or where the evaluation of the evidence is '*wholly erroneous*' may the Appeals Chamber substitute its own finding for that of the Trial Chamber.[56]

The written law confirms this restrictive and highly deferential approach when requiring that an error of fact must occasion a miscarriage of justice.[57] 'Miscarriage of justice' refers in this context to any factual error relevant for the guilt or innocence of the accused.[58] Thus, a relevant error of fact only exists if—the reasonableness standard—no reasonable trier of fact could have reached the original decision and if—additional consequence—this error amounted to a miscarriage of justice.[59]

In a similar vein, the ICC AC initially took a similarly deferential approach refraining from interfering with factual findings of a first instance Chamber unless that Chamber committed 'a clear error, namely, misappreciated the facts, took into account irrelevant facts, or failed to take into account relevant facts'.[60] As to the misappreciation of facts, the AC made clear that it will only interfere where the TC's appreciation of the facts was wholly unreasonable, that is, where it 'cannot discern how the Chamber's conclusion could have reasonably been reached from the evidence before it'.[61] This reasonableness standard, relying, apparently, on the more than seventy-year-old English 'Wednesbury unreasonableness',[62] is of

[56] *Kupreškić et al.*, IT-95-16-A, para. 30 (emphasis added); for further case law, see previous edition p. 555 note 54; more recently *Šešelj*, MICT-16-99-A, para. 103; *Karadzic*, MICT-13-55-A, para. 17; for the SCSL, cf. *Fofana and Kondewa*, SCSL-04-14-A-829, paras. 33–4; *Sesay et al.*, SCSL-04-15-A-1321-1, para. 32; *Taylor*, SCSL-03-01-A-1389, para. 26; for the KSC, see *Gucati and Haradinaj*, KSC-CA-2022-01/F00114/2, paras. 25–6 (only in case of 'miscarriage of justice'); *Mustafa*, KSC-CA-2023-02/F00038/RED, para. 24.

[57] Arts. 25 (1)(b) ICTYS, 24 (1)(b) ICTRS, 23 (1)(b) IRMCTS, 20 (1)(c) SCSLS, 21 (1)(c) RSCSLS, 46 (1)(b) KSC Law.

[58] *Prosecutor v. Furundžija*, AC, Judgment, IT-95-17/1-A, 21 July 2000, para. 37 quoting *Prosecutor v. Serushago*, Reasons for Judgment, ICTR-98-39-A, 6 April 2000, para. 22; cf. also Garner, *Dictionary* (2019), p. 1195; *Kupreškić et al.*, IT-95-16-A, para. 29; *Sesay et al.*, SCSL-04-15-A-1321-1, para. 32; *Taylor*, SCSL-03-01-A-1389, para. 27. cf. also Tochilovsky, *Jurisprudence* (2014), pp. 1087–8; Schabas, *ICC Commentary* (2016), p. 1243; , 'Article 81', in Ambos, *Commentary* (2022), mn. 87 (any errors relevant for establishing the elements of the crime and individual criminal responsibility).

[59] *Krajišnik*, IT-00-39-A, para. 14, first referring to the reasonableness standard and then to a miscarriage of justice as a basis of a reversal of the first instance decision; for further case law, see previous edition p. 556 note 57; more recently *Prosecutor v. Šešelj*, Decision on Request to be Allowed to Exercise the Right to Appeal and Have a Deadline Set for the Notice of Appeal, MICT-16-99, 27 November 2018, paras. 7–9; *Karadzic*, MICT-13-55-A, para. 14; for the SCSL, cf. *Sesay et al.*, SCSL-04-15-A-1321-1, para. 32; *Taylor*, SCSL-03-01-A-1389, para. 26; for the KSC, *Gucati and Haradinaj*, KSC-CA-2022-01/F00114/2, para. 26; *Mustafa*, KSC-CA-2023-02/F00038/RED, para. 24; for the ICC conc. with the ICTY, *Lubanga*, ICC-01/04-01/06-3121-Red, para. 24; conc., *Ngudjolo*, ICC-01/04-02/12-271-Corr, para. 24. See also, on the ad hoc Tribunals' case law, Eckelmans, 'Article 81', in Ambos, *Commentary* (2022), mn. 85 ff.

[60] *Lubanga*, ICC-01/04-01/06-3121-Red, para. 21; *Ngudjolo*, ICC-01/04-02/12-271-Corr, para. 22; *Prosecutor v. Ntaganda*, Public Redacted Judgment on Mr Bosco Ntaganda's Appeal against the Decision Reviewing Restrictions on Contacts of 7 September 2016, ICC-01/04-02/06 OA 4, 8 March 2017, para. 24.

[61] *Lubanga*, ICC-01/04-01/06-3121-Red, para. 21; *Ngudjolo*, ICC-01/04-02/12-271-Corr, para. 22; see in the same vein, several interlocutory appeal decisions (in part referred to by the *Lubanga* AC): *Prosecutor v. Gaddafi*, AC, Judgment on the Appeal of Libya against the Decision of Pre-Trial Chamber I of 31 May 2013 Entitled 'Decision on the admissibility of the case against Saif Al-Islam Gaddafi', ICC-01/11-01/11-547-Red, 21 May 2014, para. 93, referring, inter alia, to *Prosecutor v. Ruto et al.*, AC, Judgment on the Appeal of the Republic of Kenya against the Decision of Pre-Trial Chamber II of 30 May 2011 Entitled 'Decision on the Application by the Government of Kenya Challenging the Admissibility of the Case Pursuant to Article 19 (2)(b) of the Statute', ICC-01/09-01/11-307, 30 August 2011, para. 56; *Prosecutor v. Gaddafi and Al-Senussi*, AC, Judgment on the Appeal of Mr Abdullah Al-Senussi against the Decision of Pre-Trial Chamber I of 11 October 2013, ICC-01/11-01/11-565, 24 July 2014, para. 241; *Lubanga*, ICC-01/04-01/06-3121-Red, para. 21; *Simone Gbagbo*, ICC-02/11-01/12-75-Red, paras. 38–9.

[62] Court of Appeal of England and Wales, *Associated Provincial Picture House Ltd v. Wednesbury Corporation*, Judgment of 10 November 1947, [1947] EWCA Civ 1 ('If a decision on a competent matter is so unreasonable that no reasonable authority could ever have come to it, then the courts can interfere'). See also Southey and Fulford,

course far from precise, perhaps not even reasonable itself. At any rate, lack of reasonableness can, arguably, be equated in this respect with an error of rationality or logic amounting to a ground of appeal in the sense of the continental European *cassation* or *Revision*.[63] Apart from that, the error of fact must have 'materially affected' the appealed decision.[64]

The *Bemba* Appeals Chamber took issue with the deferential approach of the previous case law regarding factual errors, stating:

> The Appeals Chamber is of the opinion that it may interfere with the factual findings of the first-instance chamber whenever the failure to interfere may occasion a miscarriage of justice, and not 'only in the case where [the Appeals Chamber] cannot discern how the Chamber's conclusion could have reasonably been reached from the evidence before it'. The Appeals Chamber must be careful not to constrain the exercise of its appellate discretion in such a way that it ties its own hands against the interest of justice, particularly in circumstances where the Rome Statute does not provide for the notion of appellate deference or require the Appeals Chamber to apply that particular notion.[65]

Thus, the AC, by majority, clearly takes a stricter approach with the trial judge. While her factual findings cannot be overturned pursuant to 'mere preferences or personal impressions of the appellate judges', 'serious doubts about the accuracy of a given finding' articulated by 'a reasonable and objective person' strongly indicate 'that the trial chamber may not have respected the standard of proof and, accordingly, that an error of fact may have been made'.[66] The dissenting minority of the *Bemba* AC saw in the majority's approach a deviation from the 'conventional standard of review' and stressed that the AC's review is merely 'corrective and only serves the purpose of assessing the reasonableness of the impugned findings'.[67] While the majority approach has received quite some criticism,[68] it is questionable whether the *Bemba* majority really wanted to deviate from the established standard of review for it relied otherwise on the established AC jurisprudence.[69] At any rate, the subsequent case law confirmed the standard as follows:

> When assessing the reasonableness of a factual finding, the Appeals Chamber will have regard not only to the evidence relied upon, but also to the trial chamber's reasoning in analysing it. In particular if the supporting evidence is, on its face, weak, or if there is significant contradictory evidence, deficiencies in the trial chamber's reasoning as to why it

*Judicial Review* (2004), p. 31, quoting Lord Diplock as applying this doctrine 'to a Decision which is so outrageous in its defiance of logic ... that no sensible person who had applied his mind to the question to be decided could have arrived at it'.

[63] For *France*, see Desportes and Lazerges-Cousquer, *Traité de procédure pénale* (2013), pp. 2184–5; Pradel, *Procédure pénale* (2019), pp. 1022 ff.; for *Germany*, Nagel, '§ 337', in Radtke and Hohmann, *StPO Kommentar* (2011), mn. 3 with further references.

[64] Art. 83 (2) ICCS. The *materially affected* standard seems to require less than a *miscarriage of justice*, cf. Eckelmans, 'Article 81', in Ambos, *Commentary* (2022), mn. 94. On the AC's 'stringent approach' regarding the 'material effect' requirement under Art. 83 (2) of the Statute, see Nerlich, in Stahn, *ICC* (2015), pp. 978–9.

[65] *Bemba*, ICC-01/05-01/08-3636-Red, para. 40.

[66] Ibid., para. 45.

[67] *Bemba*, ICC-01/05-01/08-3636-Anx1-Red, paras. 14 ff.

[68] cf. Sadat, *EJIL: Talk!* 12 June 2018; Sadat, *ICC Forum*, 27 May 2019; AI, 10 October 2018; AI, 8 October 2018; Fornel Poutou, *ICC Forum*, 27 May 2019; Amann, *ICC Forum*, 27 May 2019; defending the judgment, Heinze, *Opinio Juris* (18 June 2018); Newton, *ICC Forum*, 27 May 2019; for a nuanced approach, Jackson, *ICC Forum*, 27 May 2019. See also Bradley and de Beer, ICLR, 20, (2020), 163–213.

[69] Eckelmans, 'Article 81', in Ambos, *Commentary* (2022), mn. 91 (with references in n. 7), 92.

> found that evidence persuasive may lead the Appeals Chamber to conclude that the finding in question was such that no reasonable trier of fact could have reached. Nevertheless, the emphasis of the Appeals Chamber's assessment is on the substance: whether the evidence was such as to allow a reasonable trial chamber to reach the finding it did beyond reasonable doubt. [70]

While the said standard applies, in principle, equally to an appeal against an acquittal (by the Prosecutor) and against a conviction (by the defendant), the perspective of the respective appeal is different: in the former case the Prosecutor must show that the evidence presented before the TC does not leave any (reasonable) doubt as to the guilt of the accused; in the latter case, the defendant must argue that the alleged factual error(s) create (reasonable) doubts as to his guilt.[71] Thus, the ICC AC, confirming the *Ngudjolo* acquittal and invoking the reasonableness standard of the ad hoc tribunals,[72] held that '[it] will reverse only if it finds that no reasonable trier of fact could have failed to make the particular finding of fact beyond reasonable doubt and the acquittal relied on the absence of this finding'.[73]

*(ii) Errors of law*

Errors of law refer to the correct interpretation of the law,[74] be it of a substantive or procedural nature.[75] They arise when an incorrect legal standard is applied[76] or in the absence of a reasoned opinion.[77] From this strictly legal approach it follows that, unlike in the case of factual errors, the AC does not treat the TC's legal conclusions deferentially,[78] but decides on the correct interpretation of the law and applies the TC's factual findings to its legal interpretation.[79] This also follows from the—above-

[70] *Prosecutor v. Ntaganda*, AC, Judgment, ICC-01/04-02/06-2666-Red, 30 March 2021, para. 42; *Prosecutor v. Gbagbo and Blé Goudé*, AC, Judgment, ICC-02/11-01-15-1400, 31 March 2021, paras. 66–72.

[71] *Mrkšić and Šljivančanin*, IT-95-13/1-A, para. 15; *Boškoski and Tarčulovski*, IT-04-82-A, para. 15; *Šainović et al.*, IT-05-87-A, para. 24; *Đorđević*, IT-05-87/1-A, para. 18; for the SCSL, see *Sesay et al.*, SCSL-04-15-A-1321-1 para. 33; *Taylor*, SCSL-03-01-A-1389, para. 26 with n. 40; for the ICTR, see *Karemera and Ngirumpatse*, ICTR-98-44-A, para. 16; *Nzabonimana*, ICTR-98-44D-A, para. 10; *Nizeyimana*, ICTR-00-55C-A, para. 10. See also Eckelmans, 'Article 81', in Ambos, *Commentary* (2022), mn. 85–92.

[72] *Ngudjolo*, ICC-01/04-02/12-271-Corr, paras. 23–6 with references.

[73] Ibid., para. 26 (quoting the ICTY *Blagojević and Jokić* and *Brđanin* ACs in n. 18).

[74] cf. also Trigeaud, 'Article 81', in Fernandez et al., *Statut II* (2019), pp. 2079–81, according to whom 'error of law' includes basically three areas: errors in the identification of the applicable law, errors in its interpretation, and errors in its application.

[75] In the same vein, Kuczyńska, *Accusation Model ICC* (2015), pp. 375–6; Klamberg, 'Article 81', in Klamberg, *Commentary ICC* (2017), n. 652.

[76] *Krajišnik*, IT-00-39-A, para. 13; for further case law, see previous edition, p. 558 note 74; *Karadzic*, MICT-13-55-A, para. 72; for the ICC, see *Lubanga*, ICC-01/04-01/06-3121-Red, para. 19; *Prosecutor v. Bemba et al.*, AC, Judgment on the appeals of Mr Jean-Pierre Bemba Gombo, Mr Aimé Kilolo Musamba, Mr Jean-Jacques Mangenda Kabongo, Mr Fidèle Babala Wandu and Mr Narcisse Arido against the decision of TC VII entitled 'Judgment pursuant to Article 74 of the Statute', ICC-01/05-01/13-2275-Red, 8 March 2018, para. 90; *Bemba*, ICC-01/05-01/08-3636-Red, para. 37; *Al Hassan et al.*, ICC-01/12-01/18 OA, para. 38.

[77] *Prosecutor v. Brđanin*, AJ, IT-99-36-A, 3 April 2007, para. 9; for further case law, see previous edition, p. 558 note 75; *Prosecutor v. Mladic*, Judgment, MICT-13-56-A, 8 June 2021, para. 437; *Karadzic*, MICT-13-55-A, para. 700; for the SCSL, *Sesay et al.*, SCSL-04-15-A-1321-1, paras. 345, 694; *Taylor*, SCSL-03-01-A-1389, para. 25; for the ICC, *Bemba et al.*, ICC-01/05-01/13-2275-Red, para. 90; *Bemba*, ICC-01/105-01/08-3636-Red, paras. 49–55; see also Eckelmans, 'Article 81', in Ambos, *Commentary* (2022), mn. 77-81.

[78] Eckelmans, 'Article 81', in Ambos, *Commentary* (2022), mn. 60–1; Boas et al., *International Criminal Procedure* (2011), p. 443; identical, Boas, Jackson, Roche, and Taylor III, 'Appeals, Reviews, and Reconsideration', in Sluiter et al., *International Criminal Procedure* (2013), p. 944; in the same vein, Safferling and Hartwig, *International Criminal Procedure* (2012), p. 537; Tochilovsky, *Jurisprudence* (2014), p. 1091.

[79] *Prosecutor v. Blaškić*, AJ, IT-95-14-A, 29 July 2004, para. 24 (b); for further case law, see previous edition, p. 558 note 77; more recently *Šešelj*, MICT-16-99-A, para. 20; for the KSC, see *Gucati and Haradinaj*, KSC-CA-2022-01/F00114/2, para. 22 ('review the Trial Panel's findings of law to determine whether they are correct'); conc. *Mustafa*, KSC-CA-2023-02/F00038/RED, para. 18; for the ICC, *Lubanga*, ICC-01/04-01/06-3121-Red, para. 18

mentioned[80]—AC's power to discuss errors of law independent of the parties' submissions. At any rate, difficult issues of delimitation between errors of fact and law, often amounting to mixed factual-legal errors, may arise.[81] Also, the AC's own interpretation of the law to the facts raises the question of whether it can substitute immediately the TC's decision with its own decision or if it must return the case to the first instance Chamber.[82]

Independent of the nature of the decision (binding or discretionary), any error of law must have had an *impact* on the decision. The law of the ad hoc tribunals requires that the error invalidate the appealed decision.[83] Under the ICC regime the error must have 'materially affected' the impugned decision,[84] that is, the TC would have rendered a different decision, had it not made the error[85] or had it not improperly exercised its discretion.[86] In other words, the AC will uphold the appealed decision if the error had no effect on its outcome.[87]

*(iii) Erroneous exercise of discretion*

The distinction between errors of fact and law becomes more blurred if the error consists of an (erroneous) exercise of discretion by a TC. Discretionary decisions, for example on disclosure or the admissibility of evidence, are largely fact based and thus an AC will have to accord deference to a TC decision and may only intervene under limited circumstances.[88] The test established by the case law of the ad hoc tribunals runs along the lines of

(referring to *Banda and Jerbo*); *Ngudjolo*, ICC-01/04-02/12-271-Corr, para. 20; also *Simone Gbagbo*, ICC-02/11-01/12-75-Red, para. 40; *Ntaganda*, ICC-01/04-02/06-1225, para. 33; *Bemba et al.*, ICC-01/05-01/13-2275-Red, para. 90; *Bemba*, ICC-01/05-01/08-3636-Red, para. 37; *Al Hassan et al.*, ICC-01/12-01/18 OA, para. 38; *Ntaganda*, ICC-01/04-02/06 A A2, para. 36.

[80] See above Section A.

[81] cf. Eckelmans, 'Article 81', in Ambos, *Commentary* (2022), mn. 66–7; Mosna, in Allegrezza, *Appeal Proceedings* (2023), p. 73.

[82] Eckelmans, 'Article 81', in Ambos, *Commentary* (2022), mn. 61–5.

[83] Arts. 25 (1)(a) ICTYS, 24 (1)(a) ICTRS, 23 (1)(a) IRMCTS, 20 (1)(b) SCSLS, 21 (1)(b) RSCSLS; in the same vein, Art. 46 (1)(a) KSC Law.

[84] Art. 83 (2) ICCS.

[85] See *Bemba*, ICC-01/05-01/08-3636-Red, para. 36; *Bemba et al.*, ICC-01/05-01/13-2275-Red, para. 90; *Al Hassan et al.*, ICC-01/12-01/18 OA, para. 39; for earlier case law, see previous edition, p. 560 note 93; cf. also Schabas, *ICC Commentary* (2016), pp. 1213–14, pointing out that the ad hoc tribunals' standard is 'more demanding' than that of the ICC.

[86] *Prosecutor v. Kenyatta*, AC, Judgment on the Prosecutor's Appeal against TC V(B)'s 'Decision on Prosecution's application for a finding of non-compliance under Art. 87(7) of the Statute', ICC-01/09-02/11-1032, 19 August 2015, para. 22; for earlier case law, see previous edition, p. 561 note 94; more recently *Bemba et al.*, ICC-01/05-01/13-2276-Red, para. 90; *Ntaganda*, ICC-01/04-02/06 A A2, paras. 45–6; *Al Hassan et al.*, ICC-01/12-01/18 OA, para. 39.

[87] *D. Milošević*, IT-98-29/1-A, para. 13; for further case law, see previous edition, p. 561 note 95; more recently *Jojic & Radeta*, Decision on Republic of Serbia's Appeal against the Decision Re-examining Referral of the Case, MICT-17-111-R90-AR14.1, 24 February 2020, para. 12; *Karadzic*, MICT-13-55-A, para. 85; *Niyitegeka*, Decision on Appeals of Decision Rendered by a Single Judge, MICT-12-16-R, 9 August 2017, para. 14; for the SCSL, *Fofana and Kondewa*, SCSL-04-14-A-829, para. 32; *Sesay et al.*, SCSL-04-15-A-1321-1, para. 32; *Taylor*, SCSL-03-01-A-1389, para. 25; for the ICC, see *Lubanga*, ICC-01/04-01/06-3121-Red, paras. 18, 56; *Ntaganda*, ICC-01/04-02/06 A A2, para. 45; *Al Hassan et al.*, ICC-01/12-01/18 OA, para. 39; for KSC, *Gucati and Haradinaj*, KSC-CA-2022-01/F00114/2, para. 22 ('no prospect of changing the outcome of the decision'); conc. *Mustafa*, KSC-CA-2023-02/F00038/RED, para. 18.

[88] ICTR, *Prosecutor v. Bagosora et al.*, Decision on Prosecutor's Interlocutory Appeals Regarding Exclusion of Evidence, ICTR-98-41-AR93 and ICTR-98-41-AR93.2, 19 December 2003, para. 11; *Prosecutor v. Simba*, Judgment, ICTR-01-76-A, 27 November 2007, para. 19; ICTY, *Prosecutor v. Halilović*, Judgment, IT-01-48-A, 16 October 2007, para. 39; KSC, *Prosecutor v. Gucati and Haradinaj*, Decision on Nasim Haradinaj's Appeal Against Decision on Prosecution Requests in Relation to Proposed Defence Witnesses, KSC-BC-2020-07, IA006/F00006, 7 January 2022, para. 14; *Gucati and Haradinaj*, KSC-CA-2022-01/F00114/2, para. 34–5, 93; *Mustafa*, KSC-CA-2023-02/F00038/RED, para. 36, 39 ('discernible error').

an impermissible abuse or excess of discretion and its (still) reasonable exercise.[89] The AC held that the TC's exercise of discretion has been erroneous if it

> has misdirected itself either as to the principle to be applied, or as to the law which is relevant to the exercise of the discretion, or that it has given weight to extraneous or irrelevant considerations, or that it has failed to give weight or sufficient weight to relevant considerations, or that it has made an error as to the facts upon which it has exercised its discretion.[90]

Further, the AC has inferred the TC's erroneous exercise of discretion from its decision as being highly unreasonable and plainly unjust.[91]

The ICC AC has so far addressed discretionary decisions by its Chambers in the context of interlocutory appeals but, given that the relevant principles are largely the same,[92] we can take a look at them here. Generally speaking, the AC has taken a restrictive approach focusing its review on the proper exercise of the discretion by the first instance Chamber, that is, whether it has not been 'vitiated by an error of law, an error of fact, or a procedural error'.[93] The case law of the ICC AC summarized the standard, with regard to a non-compliance finding under Article 87 (7) ICCS, as follows: the AC will not interfere with a Chamber's discretion for the mere fact that its decision could have been different but only where one of the above-mentioned errors has been shown, namely where this decision is either (i) based

[89] See the examples given by Eckelmans, 'Article 81', in Ambos, *Commentary* (2022), mn. 72 (as possible errors of law under the ICTY/ICTR legal regime).

[90] *Prosecutor v. S. Milošević*, AC, Reasons for Decision on Prosecution Interlocutory Appeal from Refusal to Order Joinder, IT-99-37-AR73, 18 April 2002, para. 5; for further case law, see previous edition, p. 559 note 81; *Jojic & Radeta*, MICT-17-111-R90-AR14.1, para. 12; for the SCSL, *Fofana and Kondewa*, SCSL-04-14-A-829, para. 467; *Sesay et al.*, SCSL-04-15-A-1321-1, paras. 35, 1203; *Taylor*, SCSL-03-01-A-1389, para. 29; for KSC, see *Gucati and Haradinaj*, KSC-BC-2020-07/IA001/F00005, para. 14; *Prosecutor v. Gucati and Haradinaj*, Decision on the Defence Appeals Against Decision on Preliminary Motions, KSC-BC-2020-07/IA004/F00007, 23 June 2021, para. 11 ('discernible error in that the decision is: (i) based on an incorrect interpretation of governing law; (ii) based on a patently incorrect conclusion of fact; or (iii) so unfair or unreasonable as to constitute an abuse of the lower level panel's discretion'); conc., *Mustafa*, KSC-CA-2023-02/F00038/RED, para. 36.

[91] *Prosecutor v. Mejakić et al.*, AC, Decision on Joint Defence Appeal against Decision on Referral under Rule 11*bis*, IT-02-65-AR11*bis*.1, 7 April 2006, para. 10 ('its Decision was so unreasonable and plainly unjust that the Appeals Chamber is able to infer that the Referral Bench must have failed to exercise its discretion properly'); for further case law, see previous edition, p. 559 note 81; more recently *Prosecutor v. Kamuhanda*, Decision on Kamuhanda's Appeal of Decision on Motion for Appointment of Amicus Curiae Prosecutor to Investigate Prosecution Witness GEK, MICT-13-33-AR90/018.1, 8 December 2015, para. 16; *Prosecutor v. Stanisic & Simatovic*, Decision on Motion for Partial Reconsideration of Decision on Stanisic's Request for Stay of Proceedings, MICT-15-96-PT, 7 April 2017, para. 7; *Prosecutor v. Mladic*, MICT-13-56-A, 26 June 2018, p. 2; for the SCSL, *Fofana and Kondewa*, SCSL-04-14-A-829, para. 467; *Sesay et al.*, SCSL-04-15-A-1321-1, para. 1203; for the ICC, *Bemba* et al., ICC-01/05-01/13-2276-Red, para. 90; *Ntaganda*, ICC-01/04-02/06 A A2, paras. 45–6; *Al Hassan et al.*, ICC-01/12-01/18 OA, para. 39.

[92] See above note 5 with main text.

[93] *Kony et al.*, ICC-02/04-01/05-408, para. 80 (regarding a determination under Art. 19 ICCS); for further (earlier) ICC case law, see previous edition, p. 559 note 82; *Prosecutor v. Bemba et al.*, AC, Judgment on the Appeal of Mr Aimé Kilolo Musamba against the Decision of Pre-Trial Chamber II of 14 March 2014 Entitled 'Decision on the "Demande de mise en liberté provisoire de Maître Kilolo Musamba"', ICC-01/05-01/13-558, 11 July 2014, para. 47 (regarding whether to hold a hearing); *Prosecutor v. Bemba et al.*, AC, Judgment on the Appeal of Mr Fidele Babala Wandu against the Decision of Pre-Trial Chamber II of 14 March 2014, ICC-01/05-01/13-559, 11 July 2014, para. 18 (regarding interim release); *Gaddafi and Al-Senussi*, ICC-01/11-01/11-565, para. 151 (regarding the participatory rights of Al-Senussi); *Prosecutor v. Lubanga*, AC, Judgment on the Appeal of Mr Thomas Lubanga Dyilo against the 'Decision on Sentence pursuant to Article 76 of the Statute', ICC-01/04-01/06-3122, 1 December 2014, paras. 34, 40–4 (regarding sentencing); *Prosecutor v. Al Hassan*, AC, Judgment on the Appeal of Mr Al Hassan against the Decision of Pre-Trial Chamber I Entitled 'Décision relative à l'exception d'irrecevabilité pour insuffisance de gravité de l'affaire soulevée par la défense', ICC-01/12-01/18-601-Red, 19 February 2020, para. 39; *Ntaganda*, ICC-01/04-02/06 A A2, para. 45.

upon an 'erroneous interpretation of the law' or (ii) upon 'a patently incorrect conclusion of fact' or (iii) 'amounts to an abuse of discretion'.[94] As to an 'erroneous interpretation of the law' the AC will 'arrive at its own conclusions' applying 'the appropriate law' to the relevant facts.[95] As to an 'incorrect conclusion of fact' the AC applies a reasonableness standard, already discussed in the previous sub-section with regard to errors of fact, thereby granting 'a margin of deference' to the first instance Chamber.[96] Finally, an 'abuse of discretion' occurs 'when the decision is so unfair or unreasonable' as to show a lack of judicious exercise of discretion, for example, by taking into account irrelevant consideration and overlooking relevant ones.[97] The degree of the Chamber's discretion may depend on 'the nature of the decision in question'.[98]

*(iv) Procedural and other errors*

With the recognition of procedural errors[99] and two further grounds of appeal regarding issues of general significance and the fairness or reliability of the proceedings[100] difficult problems of delimitation arise.

The SCSL AC has defined procedural errors as those that 'vitiate the proceedings' and amount to a fair trial violation.[101] With this definition a procedural error cannot reasonably be distinguished from the fairness ground of appeal of Article 81 (1)(b)(iv) ICCS. Of course, one may employ a broader, generic reading and include in the concept of procedural errors all those that entail a wrongful interpretation and/or application of the procedural law, in particular as regards the rights of the accused within the meaning of Article 67 ICCS and the exercise of discretion.[102] So understood, procedural errors would form a subgroup of errors of law, that is, errors of procedural law, but this would make them equally redundant.[103]

The ICC AC offered a marked procedural definition—errors occurring 'in the proceedings leading up to the impugned decision',[104] that is, including errors prior to the impugned decision as long as they are 'germane to the legal correctness or procedural fairness of the Chamber's decision'[105]—but it is merely formalistic and bare of any substantive criterion. In fact, any error—be it procedural, factual, or legal—occurs in the (pre-trial or trial) proceedings and concerns 'the impugned decision itself'.[106] Last but not least, for a procedural error

[94] *Kenyatta*, ICC-01/09-02/11-1032, paras. 22–5, esp. para. 22; conc. *Bemba*, ICC-01/05-01/08 A, para. 48; *Bemba et al.*, ICC-01/05-01/13 A6 A7 A8 A9, para. 22; *Ntaganda*, ICC-01/04-02/06 A A2, para. 45; *Al Hassan et al.*, ICC-01/12-01/18 OA, para. 39.

[95] *Kenyatta*, ICC-01/09-02/11-1032, para. 23; *Al Hassan et al.*, ICC-01/12-01/18 OA, para. 38; *Ntaganda*, ICC-01/04-02/06 A A2, para. 36.

[96] *Kenyatta*, ICC-01/09-02/11-1032, para. 24; *Bemba*, ICC-01/05-01/08 A, para. 38.

[97] *Kenyatta*, ICC-01/09-02/11-1032, para. 25; *Bemba et al.*, ICC-01/05-01/13 A6 A7 A8 A9, para. 22; *Ntaganda*, ICC-01/04-02/06 A A2, para. 46.

[98] *Kenyatta*, ICC-01/09-02/11-1032, para. 25; *Bemba et al.*, ICC-01/05-01/13 A6 A7 A8 A9, para. 22; *Ntaganda*, ICC-01/04-02/06 A A2, para. 46.

[99] Art. 20 (1)(a) SCSLS; Art. 21 (1)(a) RSCSLS; Art. 81 (1)(a)(i) and (b)(i) ICCS.

[100] Art. 81 (1)(b)(iv) ICCS.

[101] *Sesay et al.*, SCSL-04-15-A-1321-1, para. 34; *Taylor*, SCSL-03-01-A-1389, para. 28 ('errors which occasioned a miscarriage of justice vitiating the proceedings and affecting the fairness of the trial').

[102] cf. Eckelmans, 'Article 81', in Ambos, *Commentary* (2022), mn. 57; similarly Roth and Henzelin, in Cassese et al., *Rome Statute II* (2002), p. 1544 ('any formal violations'); Trigeaud, 'Article 81', in Fernandez et al., *Statut II* (2019), pp. 2083–85; Kuczyńska, *Accusation Model ICC* (2015), p. 375; Klamberg, 'Article 81', in Klamberg, *Commentary ICC* (2017), n. 652.

[103] Safferling and Hartwig, *International Criminal Procedure* (2012), p. 537; similarly Eckelmans, 'Article 81', in Ambos, *Commentary* (2022), mn. 56.

[104] *Lubanga*, ICC-01/04-01/06-3121-Red, para. 20 (referring to *Kony et al.*, ICC-02/04-01/05-408, paras. 46–7).

[105] *Ngudjolo*, ICC-01/04-02/12-271-Corr, paras. 3, 21.

[106] In this vein, Eckelmans, 'Article 81', in Ambos, *Commentary* (2022), mn. 56, following the AC and distinguishing between procedural and legal error (concerns 'impugned Decision itself').

to be relevant it must, like any error of law, materially affect the impugned decision.[107] Thus, as a result, procedural errors will often amount to errors of law, i.e. if they refer to the correct interpretation of the law[108] and not merely to its (correct) application.[109]

As to the 'catch-all provision'[110] of Article 81 (1)(b)(iv) ICCS it can be argued that the *grounds affecting the fairness or reliability of the proceedings* will usually amount to procedural errors since they will affect the rights of the accused within the meaning of Article 67 ICCS.[111] In addition, it is questionable whether the reliability limb of this provision has an autonomous meaning, given that, pursuant to Article 83 (2) ('unfair ... affected the reliability'), unreliability appears as a consequence of unfairness.

In contrast, allowing an appeal in which *a legal issue of general significance to the jurisprudence* is raised[112] goes in a structurally different direction: this ground does not speak to the validity of the first instance decision—indeed, it may leave this decision intact, but its rationale is to further develop the case law of the ad hoc tribunals, and thus contribute to the consolidation and consistency of this law.[113] In any case, the issue under consideration must have a nexus with the case and it is always in the AC's discretion whether it applies this ground of appeal.

*(v) Appeal against sentence*

As has been demonstrated in Volume II of this Treatise, a TC has a broad discretion in matters of sentencing.[114] As a consequence the rules regarding appeals against discretionary decisions discussed above[115] apply, in principle, also to appeals against the sentence.[116] The

[107] Art. 83 (2) ICCS. cf. *Lubanga*, ICC-01/04-01/06-3121-Red, paras. 16, 20, 32, 56; *Ngudjolo*, ICC-01/04-02/12-271-Corr, para. 21 ('appellant needs to demonstrate that, in the absence of the procedural error, the Decision would have substantially differed from the one rendered'); *Bemba*, ICC-01/05-01/08 A, para. 66 ('the lack of adequate reasoning renders the finding unreviewable, thereby constituting a serious procedural error'); for interlocutory appeals, see *Prosecutor v. Gbagbo*, AC, Judgment on the Appeal of Mr Laurent Koudou Gbagbo against the Decision of Pre-Trial Chamber I on Jurisdiction and Stay of the Proceedings, ICC-02/11-01/11-321, 12 December 2012, para. 44; *Gaddafi*, ICC-01/11-01/11-547-Red, para. 146.

[108] See the definition above in sub sect. (ii).

[109] Stressing 'the higher substantiation requirements for procedural errors', Eckelmans, 'Article 81', in Ambos, *Commentary* (2022), mn. 58.

[110] Klamberg, 'Article 81', in Klamberg, *Commentary ICC* (2017), n. 652; similarly, Eckelmans, 'Article 81', in Ambos, *Commentary* (2022), mn. 104, who only sees a possibility of applying this ground where the unfairness was not caused by the (P)TC, but by other parties.

[111] In a similar vein, Eckelmans, 'Article 81', in Ambos, *Commentary* (2022), mn. 100; apparently also Kuczyńska, *Accusation Model ICC* (2015), pp. 376–7, giving, however, examples of 'circumstances that put the accused in an unfavourable position, although not by reason of the Court's erroneous application of law or its proceedings'; for an, albeit artificial, distinction between this ground and procedural errors (the latter being rather formal, the former more 'substantive'), Roth and Henzelin, in Cassese et al., *Rome Statute II* (2002), p. 1544.

[112] cf. *D. Milošević*, IT-98-29/1-A, para. 12 (with references to previous case law in n. 35); more recently see *Ngirabatware v. Prosecutor*, AJ, MICT-12-29-A, 18 December 2014, paras. 6–12; for the SCSL, *Sesay et al.*, SCSL-04-15-A-1321-1, para. 31. See also above note 11 and for earlier case law, see previous edition, p. 562 note 108 and Eckelmans, 'Article 81', in Ambos, *Commentary* (2022), mn. 146–7; see also Re, in Reydams, Wouters, and Ryngaert, *International Prosecutors* (2012), pp. 812–13; Maystre, in Carter and Pocar, *International Criminal Procedure* (2013), pp. 202–3

[113] *Prosecutor v. Akayesu*, AC, Judgment, ICTR-96-4-A, 1 June 2001, para. 21 ('ensure the development of the Tribunal's jurisprudence ... Appeals Chamber's role in unifying the applicable law ... provide guidance to the Trial Chambers in interpreting the law ... role of "the final arbiter of the law of the Tribunal"'); for further case law, see previous edition, pp. 562–3 note 109. *Gbagbo and Blé Goudé*, ICC-02/11-01-15-1400, para. 65. On the ICC AC's 'approach of judicial restraint' and its 'reluctance to give "advisory opinions"' on the one hand, and its 'ability to ensure coherence and consistency of the law' on the other, cf. Nerlichin Stahn, *ICC* (2015), pp. 979–80; in the same vein, cf. Eckelmans, in Ambos, *Commentary* (2022), mn. 145 ('Exceptionally, the ICC AC addresses issues that are not immediately relevant to the resolution of the appeal').

[114] Thereto previously Ambos, *Treatise ICL II* (2022), pp. 311 ff.

[115] Sub-section (iii).

[116] *Lubanga*, ICC-01/04-01/06-3122, para. 1; *Gucati and Haradinaj*, KSC-CA-2022-01/F00114/2, para. 414 and *Mustafa*, KSC-CA-2023-02/F00038/RED, para. 453 (applying the same test as for discretionary decisions in

appellant[117] must demonstrate that the TC has committed an error in exercising its discretion; that it operated outside its (broad) discretionary framework in imposing the sentence,[118] and that the imposed sentence was 'disproportionate' to the crime,[119] and therefore materially affected by the error.[120]

### (c) *Presentation of additional evidence*

The AC, in line with its *proprio motu* powers,[121] may itself call new ('additional') evidence or receive it under certain conditions.[122] The respective written law of the ad hoc tribunals[123] is more explicit and elaborate than that of the ICC.[124] In fact, the ICC has no comparable

general, see above note 90 *in fine*). See also Eckelmans, 'Article 81', in Ambos, *Commentary* (2022), mn. 112–13; Mosna, in Allegrezza, *Appeal Proceedings* (2023), pp. 69–73.

[117] On the Prosecutor's right to appeal the sentence, see Kuczyńska, *Accusation Model ICC* (2015), pp. 377–8; Klamberg, 'Article 81', in Klamberg, *Commentary ICC* (2017), n. 653.

[118] *Kupreškić et al.*, IT-95-16-A, para. 408; for further case law, see previous edition, p. 557 note 69; more recently *Prosecutor v. Karadzic*, Decision on Radovan Karadzic's Notice of Sentencing Appeal and the Related Motion for Assignment of Counsel and Extension of Time, MICT-13-55-A, 2 April 2019, p. 2; for the SCSL, see *Fofana and Kondewa*, SCSL-04-14-A-829, paras. 466–7; *Sesay et al.*, SCSL-04-15-A-1321-1, paras. 1202–3; *Taylor*, SCSL-03-01-A-1389, para. 30; for KSC, see *Gucati and Haradinaj*, KSC-CA-2022-01/F00114/2, para. 414; *Mustafa*, KSC-CA-2023-02/F00038/RED, para. 453 ('discernible error'). A 'discernible error' has been recognized for example in *Prosecutor v. M. Nikolić*, AC, Judgment on Sentencing Appeal, IT-02-60/1-A, 8 March 2006, paras. 6–8, 61–2, 103, 106–7, 111, 113; *Sesay et al.*, SCSL-04-15-A-1321-1, paras. 1236–7, 1250, 1273, 1282, 1307, 1320; for the ICC, see *Lubanga*, ICC-01/04-01/06-3122, paras. 1–3, 40; *Prosecutor v. Ntaganda*, AC, Judgment on the Appeals of Mr Bosco Ntaganda and the Prosecutor against the Decision of Trial Chamber VI of 8 July 2019 entitled 'Judgment', ICC-01/04-02/06, 30 March 2021, para. 22; for the KSC see *Mustafa*, KSC-CA-2023-02/F00038/RED, para. 479 (disproportionate sentence as compared to similar cases as 'discernible error') and *Mustafa*, Decision on New Determinaton of Salih Mustafa's Sentence, KSC-CA-2023-02/F00045, 10 September 2024 (further sentencing reduction due to a Supreme Court Panel decision on a request for Protection of Legality, KSC-SC-2024-02/F00018, 29 July 2024). See also Eckelmans, 'Article 81', in Ambos, *Commentary* (2022), mn. 108–13; crit. On the limited success of prosecutorial sentencing appeals, Re, in Reydams, Wouters, and Ryngaert, *International Prosecutors* (2012), pp. 811–12; Mosna, in Allegrezza, *Appeal Proceedings* (2023), p. 71.

[119] *Lubanga*, ICC-01/04-01/06-3122, paras. 1–3, 39–46; *Bemba et al.*, ICC-01/05-01/13-2276-Red, para. 21; *Prosecutor v. Bemba et al.*, AC, Judgment on the Appeal of Mr Jean-Pierre Bemba Gombo against the Decision of Trial Chamber VII of 17 September 2018 Entitled 'Decision Re-sentencing Mr Jean Pierre Bemba Gombo, Mr Aimé Kilolo Musamba and Mr Jean-Jacques Mangenda Kabongo', ICC-01/05-01/13-2351, 27 November 2019, para. 29; *Mustafa*, KSC-CA-2023-02/F00038/RED (as quoted in previous note). For a distinction between the ICTY standard of a discernible error of the TC in exercising its discretion and the ICC standard of 'disproportion between the crime and the sentence', the former being narrower than the latter, Kuczyńska, *Accusation Model ICC* (2015), pp. 374, 377–8.

[120] *Lubanga*, ICC-01/04-01/06-3122, paras. 4, 45; *Ntaganda*, ICC-01/04-02/06, para. 32.

[121] See above note 10 with main text; for the ICC, see explicitly Art. 83 (1) ICCS ('powers of the Trial Chamber') and Art. 83 (2) 2nd cl. ICCS ('call evidence'); thereto *Lubanga*, ICC-01/04-01/06-3121-Red, para. 54 (referring to Art. 83 and stressing the power under para. 1). In a similar vein, Klamberg, *Evidence* (2013), pp. 415–16; Kuczyńska, *Accusation Model ICC* (2015), p. 389.

[122] On the admission of additional evidence on appeal, see Klamberg, *Evidence* (2013), pp. 411–16, arguing that 'the answer [on allowing or prohibiting additional evidence on appeal] should be sought in the powers of the Appeals Chamber and the purpose of the appeal proceedings' (p. 415) and 'balance the interest of expediting the proceedings against the concern of avoiding miscarriages of justice' (p. 416); cf. also Eckelmans, 'Article 83', in Ambos, *Commentary* (2022), mn. 70 ff. For a comparative law perspective, see Kuczyńska, *Accusation Model ICC* (2015), pp. 383–7. On the possibility of an oral hearing, see Rules 115 (C) RPE ICTY/ICTR/SCSL and 142 (D) RPE MICT; see also Boas, Jackson, Roche, and Taylor III, in Sluiter et al., *International Criminal Procedure* (2013), p. 951; *Lubanga*, ICC-01/04-01/06-3121-Red, paras. 26, 54, 57–8 ('the admission of additional evidence on appeal, without further restriction, entails a real risk of litigation strategies').

[123] Rules 115, 117 (A) RPE ICTY; 115, 118 (A) RPE ICTR/SCSL; 142, 144 (A) RPE MICT; 181 RPE KSC. The SCSL AC held in *Prosecutor v. Sesay et al.*, AC, Decision on Gbao Motion to Admit Additional Evidence Pursuant to Rule 115, SCSL-04-15-A-1311, 5 August 2009, para. 8, that Rule 115 RPE SCSL is 'materially similar' to Rule 115 of RPE ICTY/ICTR and that their interpretation could therefore be followed; conc., *Prosecutor v. Taylor*, AC, Decision on Defence Motion to Present Additional Evidence Pursuant to Rule 115, SCSL-03-01-A, 18 January 2013, para. 7. On the SPSC, ECCC, STL, see Boas, Jackson, Roche, and Taylor III, in Sluiter et al., *International Criminal Procedure* (2013), pp. 960, 961, 962; on the historical tribunals, see Klamberg, *Evidence* (2013), p. 412.

[124] Art. 83 (2) 2nd cl. ICCS; Reg. 62 RegC.

provision in its Statute or the Rules but only in the Regulations (Reg. 62). While Article 83 (2), 2nd clause ICCS, allowing the AC to 'itself call evidence', may well be interpreted as encompassing the AC's power to receive additional evidence submitted by the parties,[125] it does not establish any concrete rules. In contrast, Article 84 (1)(a) ICCS indeed indicates two criteria for new evidence but this provision applies to revision proceedings to be looked at below.[126] Finally, Reg. 62 RegC, given its inferior legal source, cannot establish any substantive standard and is, in fact, a purely procedural provision.[127]

Against this background it is not surprising that the *Lubanga* AC took recourse to the case law of the ad hoc tribunals, acknowledging that it 'may be of assistance'[128] and that it is 'in many respects similar' to the criteria developed by the Chamber from the ICC law.[129] Thus, the AC may 'seek guidance' from this case law,[130] although the Chamber hastened to stress that it has its 'legal texts provide for the criteria that are applicable with regard to the admissibility of evidence of appeal'.[131]

It is also noteworthy in this regard that the Chamber considers the previous case law on the admission of additional evidence within the context of interlocutory appeals[132] as 'specific to those appeals', that is, the AC jurisprudence seeks to develop, for the first time, a proper standard with regard to additional evidence within the context of a final appeal.[133] This differentiated approach with regard to additional evidence—which, of course, does not affect the otherwise largely identical standard for appeals under Articles 81 and 82 mentioned above—seems to be confirmed by Article 83 (2) ICCS allowing the consideration of new evidence only for 'these purposes', that is, only in case of a reversal/amendment of an appealed TC decision or a re-trial before a new TC but not in case of an interlocutory

[125] See above note 122 and—somewhat unenthusiastically—*Lubanga*, ICC-01/04-01/06-3121-Red, para. 54 ('does not restrict it from hearing evidence on appeal').

[126] Section C. in this chapter.

[127] See also *Lubanga*, ICC-01/04-01/06-3121-Red, para. 64 ('silent as to any standard for its admission' [of additional evidence]); also *Bemba et al.*, ICC-01/05-01/13 A6 A7 A8 A9, paras. 112, 159.

[128] *Lubanga*, ICC-01/04-01/06-3121-Red, para. 53.

[129] Ibid., para. 63; see also *Bemba et al.*, ICC-01/05-01/13 A6 A7 A8 A9, paras. 112, 159.

[130] *Lubanga*, ICC-01/04-01/06-3121-Red, para. 63; *Bemba et al.*, ICC-01/05-01/13 A6 A7 A8 A9, paras. 112, 159. See also Eckelmans, 'Article 81', in Ambos, *Commentary* (2022), mn. 97–9 *in fine* (arguing that Reg. 62 (2) RegC is consistent with the ICTY/ICTR approach); Trigeaud, 'Article 83', in Fernandez et al., *Statut II* (2019), p. 2112; Kuczyńska, *Accusation Model ICC* (2015), pp. 390–1.

[131] *Lubanga*, ICC-01/04-01/06-3121-Red, para. 53.

[132] *Prosecutor v. Bemba*, AC, Judgment on the Appeal of Mr Bemba against the Decision of Trial Chamber III of 24 June 2010 entitled 'Decision on the Admissibility and Abuse of Process Challenges', ICC-01/05-01/08-962, 19 October 2010, para. 32; *Prosecutor v. Muthaura et al.*, AC, Decision on the 'Filing of Updated Investigation Report by the Government of Kenya in the Appeal against the Pre-Trial Chamber's Decision on Admissibility', ICC-01/09-02/11-202, 28 July 2011, paras. 10 ff., esp. paras. 12–13 (additional evidence in appeal admissibility challenges under Art. 19 only admissible if it pre-dates the impugned decision; subsequent evidence, postdating this decision, is to be brought by way of a second challenge); in the same vein, *Gaddafi and Al-Senussi*, ICC-01/11-01/11-565, paras. 57–8: more recently *Prosecutor v. Bemba et al.*, AC, On the Appeal of Mr Jean-Pierre Bemba Gombo against the Decision of Trial Chamber VII of 17 September 2018 entitled 'Decision Re-sentencing Mr JeanPierre Bemba Gombo, Mr Aimé Kilolo Musamba and Mr Jean-Jacques Mangenda Kabongo', ICC-01/05-01/13 A10, 27 November 2019, para. 23; *Prosecutor v. Ntaganda*, AC, Decision on Request for the Admission of Additional Evidence on Appeal of 22 October 2020 (ICC-01/04-02/06-2617-Conf), ICC-01/04-02/06-2617-Red, 13 November 2020, paras. 15, 20.

[133] *Lubanga*, ICC-01/04-01/06-3121-Red, para. 41; also *Prosecutor v. Lubanga*, AC, Decision on the Prosecutor's Application for Leave to Reply to 'Conclusions de la défense en réponse au mémoire d'appel du Procureur', ICC-01/04-01/06-424, 12 September 2006, paras. 5–6; *Bemba*, ICC-01/05-01/08-962, para. 32 (leaving the application of Reg. 62 RegC to Art. 82 open, but referring in n. 39 to the just quoted *Lubanga* AC Decision). See also Schabas, *ICC Commentary* (2016), p. 1240; Safferling and Hartwig, *International Criminal Procedure* (2012), p. 554; Trigeaud, 'Article 83', in Fernandez et al., *Statut II* (2019), pp. 2109–10, arguing that the powers described in Art. 83 (1) ICCS are reserved for the appeals provided for in the Article, while the appeals of Art. 82 follow an autonomous procedure; in a similar vein, Eckelmans, 'Article 83', in Ambos, *Commentary* (2022), mn. 29, 84; Klamberg, 'Article 83', in Klamberg, *Commentary ICC* (2017), n. 664.

appeal. Also, the applicable Rules for interlocutory appeals under Article 82 ICCS (Rules 153 (1) and 158 (1))[134] do not speak to additional evidence.

At any rate, it follows from the corrective nature of the appeal mentioned at the beginning of this chapter that the presentation of new evidence cannot be unfettered but is subject to strict requirements.[135] Following the case law of the ad hoc tribunals these requirements have been summarized by the *Lubanga* AC in three points:[136] (i) the evidence must be 'additional', that is, it must not yet have been 'available' at trial[137] or not already 'adduced' before the TC;[138] (ii) it must be *prima facie* credible and relevant;[139] and (iii) it must have an impact on the verdict, that is, this evidence—going beyond its mere link to a ground of appeal[140]—could have led the TC to enter a different verdict.[141]

The party presenting the new evidence must convincingly explain why it was not presented at trial and that it undertook all necessary efforts to obtain it.[142] In particular it must show that counsel exercised due diligence in seeking to obtain all relevant evidence[143] although the AC has recognized that evidence is to be considered not to have been 'available' if counsel acted with 'gross negligence'.[144] The reason for this exception is that the counsel's (gross) negligence cannot go to the detriment of the defendant, in particular if the exclusion of the new evidence would lead to a miscarriage of justice[145] in the sense defined above.[146]

134 Rule 153 (1) RPE ICC applies to Art. 82 (4) ICCS and Rule 158 (1) to Art. 82 (1) and (2).

135 In the same vein, Eckelmans, 'Article 81', in Ambos, *Commentary* (2022), mn. 97, 114; Eckelmans, 'Article 83', in Ambos, *Commentary* (2022), mn. 74; Nerlich, in Stahn, *ICC* (2015), p. 975; dissenting, Trigeaud, 'Article 83', in Fernandez et al., *Statut II* (2019), p. 2112.

136 *Lubanga*, ICC-01/04-01/06-3121-Red, para. 50.

137 Rules 115 (B) RPE ICTY/ICTR/SCSL, 142 (C) RPE MICT and 181 (3) RPE KSC.

138 Reg. 62 (1)(b) RegC (indicate reasons why it 'was not adduced'). See also *Lubanga*, ICC-01/04-01/06-3121-Red, paras. 50–1, 58; regarding interlocutory appeals, see *Bemba*, ICC-01/05-01/08-962, para. 32; more recently *Ntaganda*, ICC-01/04-02/06-2617-Red, para. 20.

139 *Lubanga*, ICC-01/04-01/06-3121-Red, paras. 50–1; see also *Bemba et al.*, ICC-01/05-01/13 A10, para. 22.

140 Rules 115 (A) RPE ICTY/ICTR/SCSL, 142 (A) RPE MICT and 181 (1) RPE KSC ('identifying with precision the specific factual finding of the Trial Chamber to which the additional evidence is directed'); also Reg. 62 (1)(b) RegC (requiring to show the relevance of the evidence to a ground of appeal).

141 *Lubanga*, ICC-01/04-01/06-3121-Red, paras. 1, 59 (going insofar beyond Reg. 62 (1)(b) RegC); *Bemba et al.*, ICC-01/05-01/13 A10, para. 16; *Ntaganda*, ICC-01/04-02/06-2617-Red, paras. 15, 20; Eckelmans, 'Article 83', in Ambos, *Commentary* (2022), mn. 77.

142 *Tadić*, IT-94-1-A, paras. 52–3; for further case law, see previous edition, p. 565 note 131; more recently *Prosecutor v. Uwinkindi*, Decision on Requests for Admission of Additional Evidence on Appeal, MICT-12-25-AR14.1, 22 September 2016, para. 5; *Prosecutor v. Karadzic*, Decision on a Motion to Admit Additional Evidence on Appeal, MICT-13-55-A, 2 March 2018, para. 7; *Prosecutor v. Mladic*, Decision on Motions for Admission of Additional Evidence on Appeal, MICT-13-56-A, 11 March 2020, para. 6; *Prosecutor v. Stanisic & Simatovic*, Decision on Jovica Stanisic's Motion for Admission of Additional Evidence, MICT-15-96-A, 21 December 2022, para. 6; for the ICC, *Lubanga*, ICC-01/04-01/06-3121-Red, para. 1; *Ntaganda*, ICC-01/04-02/06-2617-Red, paras. 15, 20.

143 cf. Eckelmans, 'Article 83', in Ambos, *Commentary* (2022), mn. 75; Boas, Jackson, Roche, and Taylor III, Sluiter et al., *International Criminal Procedure* (2013), p. 951, both with references.

144 *Tadić*, IT-94-1-A, paras. 48–50, 65, 66; for further case law, see previous edition, p. 565 note 133; cf. also Tochilovsky, *Jurisprudence* (2014), pp. 1117–18; Eckelmans, 'Article 83', in Ambos, *Commentary* (2022), mn. 75.

145 *Prosecutor v. Jelisić*, AC, Decision on Request to Admit Additional Evidence, IT-95-10-A, 15 November 2000; for further case law, see previous edition, p. 566 note 134; more recently *Uwinkindi*, MICT-12-25-AR14.1, para. 6; *Prosecutor v. Karadzic*, Decision on a Motion to Admit Additional Evidence on Appeal, MICT-13-55-A, 2 March 2018, para. 7; *Prosecutor v. Mladic*, Decision on Motions for Admission of Additional Evidence on Appeal, MICT-13-56-A, 11 March 2020, para. 6; *Stanisic & Simatovic*, MICT-15-96-A, para. 6, ('Where evidence was available, it can be admitted if it can be shown that it would have been a decisive factor in the Impugned Decision and that a miscarriage of justice would occur if the evidence was excluded'). In the same vein, Boas, Jackson, Roche, and Taylor III, in Sluiter et al., *International Criminal Procedure* (2013), pp. 951–2, who at 1012 criticize the too high threshold. See, in this context, also the two-stage test (impact and veracity of evidence) of the previous case law as discussed by Eckelmans, 'Article 81', in Ambos, *Commentary* (2022), mn. 97–9.

146 See above note 58 with main text.

If a party is, ultimately, allowed to present new evidence, the AC must determine if it is 'relevant and credible' and 'a decisive factor in reaching the decision at trial'.[147] In fact, the same criteria applicable at the trial stage and already discussed above[148] also apply, *mutatis mutandis*, at the appeals stage.[149] To be *relevant* the evidence must have probative value, that is, make the existence of a fact more or less probable;[150] to be *credible* it must be '*prima facie* credible'.[151] In the result, evidence will only be inadmissible where it does not appear to be 'reasonably capable of belief or reliance'.[152] As to the decisiveness of the evidence, the party must clearly specify the possible impact of the evidence upon the appealed decision.[153] New evidence may also be admissible if it refers to the fairness of the proceedings.[154] The *Lubanga* AC invoked the revision standard of Article 84 ICCS[155] in this context, arguing that new evidence admissible in revision proceedings must be admissible, *a fortiori*, in appeals proceedings, since otherwise a person's conviction could first be 'confirmed on appeal because the evidence could not be considered, only then to be overturned in revision proceedings'.[156]

Of course, the evaluation of the respective evidence must not take place in isolation but take into account the context in which this evidence would have been presented at trial.[157] The AC may also take into account further evidence presented by the other party in rebuttal since this evidence may directly affect the substance of the additional evidence admitted.[158]

The usual deferential approach of the AC towards the factual findings of the TC can reasonably only be upheld with regard to the (old) evidence already presented at trial. Thus, the

[147] Rule 115 (B) RPE ICTY/ICTR/SCSL, 142 (C) RPE MICT and 181 (3) RPE KSC; cf. also Klamberg, *Evidence* (2013), pp. 414, 416.

[148] Chapter V, A.(2)(a) and (3)(b) in this volume.

[149] *Lubanga*, ICC-01/04-01/06-3121-Red, para. 54.

[150] *Prosecutor v. Nahimana et al.*, AC, Decision on Appellant Jean-Bosco Barayagwiza's Motions for Leave to Present Additional Evidence Pursuant to Rule 115 of the Rules of Procedure and Evidence, ICTR-99-52-A, 8 December 2006, para. 5 ('With regards to relevance ... [when] the proposed evidence ... relates to a material issue'); for further case law, see previous edition, p. 566 note 139; more recently *Prosecutor v. Mladic*, Decision on Motions for Admission of Additional Evidence on Appeal, MICT-13-56-A, 11 March 2020, para. 6.

[151] *Nahimana et al.*, Rule 115 Decision, ICTR-99-52-A, paras. 28, 40; *Karadzic*, MICT-13-55-A, para. 128; *Prosecutor v. Mladic*, MICT-13-56-A, para. 6; *Lubanga*, ICC-01/04-01/06-3121-Red, paras. 50, 54.

[152] *Prosecutor v. Kupreškić et al.*, AC, Decision on the Motions of Appellants to Admit Additional Evidence, IT-95-16-A, 26 February 2001, para. 28; for further case law, see previous edition, p. 566 note 141; more recently *Prosecutor v. Mladic*, Decision on Motions for Admission of Additional Evidence on Appeal, MICT-13-56-A, 11 March 2020, para. 9; cf. also Boas, Jackson, Roche, and Taylor III, in Sluiter et al., *International Criminal Procedure* (2013), p. 952.

[153] *Prosecutor v. Krstić*, AC, Decision on Applications for Admission of Additional Evidence on Appeal, IT-98-33-A, 5 August 2003, p. 3; for further case law, see previous edition, p. 566 note 142; more recently *Prosecutor v. Mladic*, Decision on Motions for Admission of Additional Evidence on Appeal, MICT-13-56-A, 11 March 2020, para. 6; *Stanisic & Simatovic*, MICT-15-96-A, para. 6; for the ICC, *Lubanga*, ICC-01/04-01/06-3121-Red, paras. 50, 59; *Ntaganda*, ICC-01/04-02/06 A A2, para. 15; Eckelmans, 'Article 83', in Ambos, *Commentary* (2022), mn. 77–8.

[154] *Lubanga*, ICC-01/04-01/06-3121-Red, paras. 60–1; also Eckelmans, 'Article 83', in Ambos, *Commentary* (2022), mn. 79; Nerlich, in Stahn, *ICC* (2015), p. 976.

[155] See below Section C. in this chapter.

[156] *Lubanga*, ICC-01/04-01/06-3121-Red, para. 61 (also invoking 'interests of justice and the proper and expeditious administration of judicial proceedings').

[157] *Krstić*, IT-98-33-A, p. 3; for further case law, see previous edition, p. 567 note 146.

[158] *Prosecutor v. Kvočka et al.*, AC, Decision on Prosecution's Motion to Adduce Rebuttal Material, IT-98-30/1-A, 12 March 2004; *Prosecutor v. Nahimana et al.*, AC, Decision on Motions Relating to the Appellant Hassan Ngeze's and the Prosecution's Requests for Leave to Present Additional Evidence of Witnesses ABC1 and EB, ICTR-99-52-A, 27 November 2006, para. 42 (rebuttal evidence admitted 'if it directly affects the substance of the additional evidence admitted'); for further case law, see previous edition, p. 567 note 147; more recently *Prosecutor v. Mladic*, Judgment, MICT-13-56-A, 8 June 2021, paras. 55–6; *Karadzic*, MICT-13-55-A, para. 131; *Lubanga*, ICC-01/04-01/06-3121-Red, paras. 49, 52; *Prosecutor v. Ongwen*, AC, Judgment on the Appeal of Mr Dominic Ongwen against the Decision of Trial Chamber IX of 6 May 2021 entitled 'Sentence', ICC-02/04-01/15-2023, 15 December 2022, para. 364; see also Eckelmans, 'Article 83', in Ambos, *Commentary* (2022), mn. 83; Boas, Jackson, Roche, and Taylor III, in Sluiter et al., *International Criminal Procedure* (2013), pp. 952, 953.

previous case law requiring the traditional reasonableness test with regard to the trial evidence together with the additional evidence[159] only made sense if the old trial evidence had an overwhelming impact, practically unaffected by the new evidence. In any case, given that the AC becomes a trier of fact with regard to the new evidence and this evidence must be, by definition, decisive, the new approach according to which the AC must be itself convinced beyond reasonable doubt as to the guilt[160] is the correct one.

In sum, it is fair to say that the ICC's law on the matter draws, on the one hand, largely on the case law of the ad hoc tribunals but, on the other, is still developing and takes a more liberal approach than that of the ad hoc tribunals. In fact, the original approach by the *Lubanga* AC, confirmed by subsequent case law, goes beyond the above-mentioned criteria by granting Chambers 'discretion to admit additional evidence, which should be done on a case-by-case basis and in light of the specific circumstances of each case', even 'despite a negative finding on one or more of the above mentioned criteria, if there are compelling reasons for doing so.'[161]

### (d) *Appeals judgment*

At the end of the—ordinary[162]—appeals proceedings the AC delivers a verdict which either upholds ('affirms', 'may confirm') the appealed *decision* or overturns it.[163] In the latter case, the AC may reverse the decision, amend it directly,[164] or order a re-trial before a different TC.[165] The determination of issues of fact, albeit provided for in Article 83 (2) 2nd clause ICCS ('may itself... determine the issue'), should, as a rule, remain in the hands of the TC, that is, the AC should rather remand the issue back to the TC instead of taking an own decision. This restrictive interpretation follows from the—already mentioned—corrective nature of the appeal and the general division of labour between the TC and AC.[166] At any rate, one must not overlook that, in an international criminal justice system, given its specific time and budgetary constraints an AC may be more inclined to decide the case itself and

[159] *Kupreškić et al.*, IT-95-16-A, para. 76.

[160] *Blaškić*, AC, Judgment, IT-95-14-A, paras. 22–3, 24 (c); for further case law, see previous edition, p. 567 note 150; more recently *Šešelj*, MICT-16-99-A, para. 118; *Prosecutor v. Stanisic & Simatovic*, Judgment, MICT-15-96-T, 30 June 2021, para. 595 (if there is another conclusion, which is also reasonably open from the evidence, and which is consistent with the non-existence of the fact, the conclusion of guilt beyond reasonable doubt cannot be drawn). See also Boas, Jackson, Roche, and Taylor III, in Sluiter et al., *International Criminal Procedure* (2013), pp. 953–4, 1013; Maystre, 'Right to Appeal', in Carter and Pocar, *International Criminal Procedure* (2013), pp. 234–6; Eckelmans, 'Article 81', in Ambos, *Commentary* (2022), mn. 98.

[161] *Lubanga*, ICC-01/04-01/06-3121-Red, paras. 1, 62; conc. *Ntaganda*, ICC-01/04-02/06-2617-Red, para. 15.

[162] Art. 83 ICCS does not apply to Art. 82; generally see Nerlich, 'Article 82', in Ambos, *Commentary* (2022), mn. 4; Eckelmans, 'Article 83', in Ambos, *Commentary* (2022), mn. 4; see also Nerlich, in Stahn, *ICC* (2015), p. 966 ('final' in contrast to 'interlocutory appeals').

[163] Arts. 25 (2) ICTYS, 24 (2) ICTRS, 23 (2) IRMCTS, 20 (2) SCSLS, 21 (2) RSCSLS; Art. 46 (3) KSC Law and Rule 182 (3) RPE KSC; Art. 83 (2) ICCS; Rules 153 (1), 158 (1) RPE ICC. See Eckelmans, 'Article 83', in Ambos, *Commentary* (2022), mn. 18–25.

[164] See, for an example, *Šešelj*, MICT-16-99-A, paras. 3–5, 175 ff., where the IRMCT AC on appeal fully reversed the acquittal of Mr Šešelj and entered a conviction and a ten-year sentence of imprisonment. See also the double sentencing reduction (the second one pursuant to a protection of legality remedy) at the KSC in *Mustafa*, as quote above note 118.

[165] Arts. 25 (2) ICTYS, 24 (2) ICTRS, 23 (2) IRMCTS, 20 (2) SCSLS, 21 (2) RSCSLS; Art. 46 (4)–(6) KSC Law; Rules 117 (C) RPE ICTY, 118 (C) RPE ICTR/SCSL, 144 (C) RPE MICT; Rule 183 (5) RPE KSC; Art. 83 (2) ICCS. On the AC's powers when 'one or several errors meet the relevant standard of review', see Eckelmans, 'Article 83', in Ambos, *Commentary* (2022), mn. 18–24; on the 're-trial', see Lundqvist, *LJIL*, 15 (2002), 661 ff.; crit. Re, in Reydams, Wouters, and Ryngaert, *International Prosecutors* (2012), p. 810; see also Trigeaud, 'Article 83', in Fernandez et al., *Statut II* (2019), p. 2118, according to whom the AC will itself determine the issue in cases of acquittal.

[166] In a similar vein, Eckelmans, 'Article 83', in Ambos, *Commentary* (2022), mn. 24; Eckelmans, 'Article 81', in Ambos, *Commentary* (2022), mn. 114.

thus terminate proceedings instead of returning the case to a TC.[167] The more recent Kosovo Specialist Chambers are a good case in point: the same Trial Panel whose judgment was appealed is already busy with a new trial so that returning the case to it would only delay the course of the new trial and thus is not a reasonable option. In fact, Article 46 (3) KSC Law anticipates this problem by providing that a return of the case to the TP should only be considered if this TP 'is available' in the first place.

An appeal against a *sentence* allows the AC to 'vary' the sentence if it finds it to be disproportionate.[168] If the AC reverses or amends the decision (appealed pursuant to Article 81 (1) ICCS) and this affects—by way of a lower (overall) gravity of the crimes and/or the number of remaining counts—the sentence, it may equally be amended. This follows, at least implicitly, from Article 83 (2)(a) where the amendment of the sentence is allowed in case of reversal or amendment of the decision.[169] Article 83 (2)(a) also allows for the direct amendment of a joint sentence pursuant to Article 78 (3) ICCS.[170]

The judgment of the Appeals Chamber must be delivered in open court,[171] state the reasons,[172] and be adopted by a majority;[173] judge(s) in minority may deliver a separate or dissenting opinion,[174] under the ICC regime limited to 'a question of law'.[175] The judgment may be delivered in absence of the respective defendant;[176] in contrast, before the TC the accused shall be present 'wherever possible' (Article 76 (4)), that is, a temporal impediment of the accused may entail an adjournment of the respective hearing.[177]

## (2) (Interlocutory) appeal against other decisions

### (a) *General, including legal standing*

The interlocutory appeal is usually, as already stated above,[178] a written procedure.[179] Notwithstanding, it may take months until the appeal is resolved.[180] It allows for an appeal

[167] See also Boas, Jackson, Roche, and Taylor III, in Sluiter et al., *International Criminal Procedure* (2013), p. 1013.

[168] Art. 83 (3) ICCS.

[169] In the same vein, Eckelmans, 'Article 81', in Ambos, *Commentary* (2022), mn. 108–9; Eckelmans, 'Article 83', in Ambos, *Commentary* (2022), mn. 26. See also Rules 117 (D) RPE ICTY, 118 (D) RPE ICTR/SCSL, 144 (D) RPE MICT, and 184 RPE KSC (referring to Rules 162–4).

[170] For the same result, see Eckelmans, 'Article 83', in Ambos, *Commentary* (2022), mn. 26.

[171] Art. 83 (4) 1st cl. ICCS; Rules 117 (D) RPE ICTY, 118 (D) RPE ICTR, 118 (E) SCSL, 144 (D) RPE MICT and 183 (2) RPE KSC.

[172] Art. 83 (4) 2nd cl. ICCS; Rules 117 (B) RPE ICTY, 118 (B) RPE ICTR/SCSL, 144 (B) RPE MICT and 183 (3) RPE KSC. On the scope of the reasoning, see Eckelmans, 'Article 83', in Ambos, *Commentary* (2022), mn. 39.

[173] Art. 83 (4) 1st cl. ICCS; Rules 117 (B) RPE ICTY, 118 (B) RPE ICTR/SCSL, and 144 (B) RPE MICT; Art. 46 (7) 1st cl. KSC Law.

[174] Rules 117 (B) RPE ICTY, 118 (B) RPE ICTR/SCSL, and 144 (B) RPE MICT; Art. 46 (7) 2nd cl. KSC Law.

[175] Art. 83 (4) 3rd cl. ICCS. On the *travaux*, see Eckelmans, 'Article 83', in Ambos, *Commentary* (2022), mn. 35. On the applicability of this provision to appeals under Art. 82, see ibid. mn.15; see also Klamberg, 'Article 83', in Klamberg, *Commentary ICC* (2017), n. 667 (concerns 'in relation to a procedural error or error of fact should be expressed within the judgement').

[176] Art. 83 (5) ICCS; cf. Eckelmans, 'Article 83', in Ambos, *Commentary* (2022), pp. 41–2 (the AC 'needs to primarily weigh [the accused's] right to be present against the need to conclude the proceedings expeditiously', at 20).

[177] On the loosening of the general presence requirement in trial proceedings, see Chapter IV, A.(3)(b).

[178] See above note 16 with main text.

[179] See only Rule 156 (3) RPE ICC leaving it to the AC to convene, exceptionally, a hearing; generally in favour of a hearing, Mettraux et al., *Expert Initiative Effectiveness ICC* (2014), p. 22 (para. 94), p. 164 (para. 12).

[180] See, for the ICC (as long as seven months), crit. Mettraux et al., *Expert Initiative Effectiveness ICC* (2014), pp. 160–1, 165, 166 (paras. 2–5, 14, 15, 17) (therefore advocating, inter alia, strict deadlines, focused and, if possible, oral decisions).

against a series of decisions (other than a final sentence). At the ICC, this includes decisions on jurisdiction, admissibility, detention, a unique investigative opportunity, or even against reparation orders.[181] This list has been considered to be exhaustive by the Appeals Chamber.[182] At the ad hoc tribunals, the Rules allow for interlocutory appeals (not provided for in the respective Statutes[183]) only in limited circumstances.[184] This is in line with the applicable human rights regime which does not provide for a general right to an interlocutory appeal (but only for a general appeal pursuant to Article 14 (5) ICCPR).[185]

The different possibilities of interlocutory appeal under the ICC regime may be distinguished with a view to the legal standing to file the appeal and the (more or less specific) grounds or reasons of appeal. In addition, in some cases, namely under Article 82 (1)(d) and (2),[186] leave to appeal ('certification') is required to be granted[187] by the *iudex a quo* (the original judge or Chamber).[188] Given that thereby this Chamber must decide in its own cause and thus may not be fully impartial, it would be better and fairer, if a leave needs to be maintained at all, to entrust a different Chamber.[189]

As to the structure of Article 82, it is useful, in respect of the reasons of appeal (to be dealt with in the next sub-section), to distinguish the more specific paragraphs (1)(a)–(c), (2), and

[181] Arts. 81 (3)(c)(ii) and 82 (1), (2), (4) ICCS; Rules 153, 154–8 RPE ICC. In further detail, Lounici, in Kolb, *Droit international pénal* (2008), pp. 303 ff.; Cryer et al., *ICL* (2019), pp. 440–1; Eckelmans, in Stahn/Sluiter, *Practice* (2009), pp. 538 ff.; Friman, in Stahn and Sluiter, *Practice* (2009), pp. 553 ff.; de Hoyos, in Ambos and Hoyos, *Cuestiones esenciales* (2008), pp. 23 ff.; Nerlich, in Stahn, *ICC* (2015), pp. 966 ff.; on the terminology, see Nerlich, 'Article 82', in Ambos, *Commentary* (2022), mn. 1; Schabas, *ICC Commentary* (2016), pp. 1222–3; Mosna, in Allegrezza, *Appeal Proceedings* (2023), pp. 76–7. On the appeal against reparation orders which is, in fact, final, see below note 217 with main text.

[182] *Situation in the DRC*, AC, Judgment on the Prosecutor's Application for Extraordinary Review of Pre-Trial Chamber I's 31 March 2006 Decision Denying Leave to Appeal, ICC-01/04-168, 13 July 2006, para. 39; *Prosecutor v. Lubanga*, Decision on the 'Urgent Request for Directions' of the Kingdom of the Netherlands of 17 August 2011, ICC-01/04-01/06-2799, 26 August 2011, p. 4; *Prosecutor v. Katanga*, AC, Decision on the Admissibility of the Appeal against the 'Decision on the Application for the Interim Release of Detained Witness', ICC-01/04-01/07-3424, 20 January 2014, para. 28; *Prosecutor v. Bemba et al.*, PTC II, Decision on the 'Demande en reconsidération de la décision ICC-01/05-01/13-460 05-06-2014' submitted by the Defence for Mr Mangenda on 12 June 2014, ICC-01/05-01/13-498, 17 June 2014, p. 3; *Prosecutor v. Bemba*, Decision on the Request for Leave to Appeal the 'Decision on Mr Bemba's claim for compensation and damages', No. ICC-01/05-01/08, 1 October 2020, para. 6; cf. also El Abdallah, 'Article 82', in Fernandez et al., *Statut II* (2019), p. 2093; *contra* Nerlich, in Stahn, *ICC* (2015), pp. 966–7 ('this list is not complete').

[183] But see Art. 45 KSC Law, complemented by Rules 58, 77, 169–71 RPE KSC.

[184] See Rules 72, 73 RPE ICTY/ICTR/SCSL, and 79, 80 RPE MICT; see also Boas, Jackson, Roche, and Taylor III, in Sluiter et al., *International Criminal Procedure* (2013), pp. 963–4; previously Boas et al., *International Criminal Procedure* (2011), pp. 435 ff.

[185] See e.g. *Situation in the DRC*, ICC-01/04-168, para. 38 (contrasting interlocutory to a general appeal against final decisions); see also *Prosecutor v. Norman et al.*, AC, Decision on the Application for a Stay of Proceedings and Denial of Right to Appeal, SCSL-03-08-PT-108, 4 November 2003, para. 20; *Katanga*, ICC-01/04-01/07-3424, para. 28; *Prosecutor v. Ntaganda*, AC, Decision on Request to Suspend the Trial Proceedings, ICC-01/04-02/06 OA6, 28 June 2017, para. 8 ('is a remedy unknown to the Statute and wholly separate from the one envisaged by article 82 (3) of the Statute'); cf. also Tochilovsky, *Jurisprudence* (2014), p. 1120. Crit. of the (early) restrictive practice of the PTC, WCRO, *Interlocutory Appellate Review* (2008), pp. 2, 3–7, 19 ff.

[186] See also Rule 155 RPE ICC and Reg. 65 RegC.

[187] See Rules 72 (B)(ii) RPE ICTY/ICTR, 79 (B)(ii) RPE MICT and Art. 45 (2) KSC Law; see also *Situation in the DRC*, ICC-01/04-168, para. 20; *Prosecutor v. Ruto and Sang*, AC, Decision on Prosecution's Application for Leave to Appeal the 'Decision on Mr Ruto's Request for Excusal from Continuous Presence at Trial', ICC-01/09-01/11-817, 18 July 2013, para. 16; *Prosecutor v. Ruto and Sang*, AC, Decision on Defence Applications for Leave to Appeal the 'Decision on Prosecutor's Application for Witness Summonses', ICC-01/09-01/11-1313, 23 May 2014, para. 33. See also Mosna, in Allegrezza, *Appeal Proceedings* (2023), pp. 79–86.

[188] cf. Rule 155 (1) RPE ICC ('Chamber that gave the decision'). On its broad discretion, see Boas et al., *International Criminal Procedure* (2011), pp. 436 ff.

[189] In this vein, see Mettraux et al., *Expert Initiative Effectiveness ICC* (2014), pp. 22–3 (paras. 92, 95, 96, 101) and pp. 162–3, 164–5 (paras. 6, 9, 11, 13) (separate TC responsible for the leave and a 'strict time frame' with regard to the leave decision).

(4) from the rather general paragraph (1)(d). Yet, this distinction does not correspond to the distinction between appeals as *of right* and *on leave* just mentioned.

As to the *legal standing*, appeals under Article 82 (1) can be filed by '[e]ither party'. While the term 'party' is not explicitly defined in the ICC law, it generally[190] refers to the Prosecutor and the defence.[191] Thus, legal standing under Article 82 (1) is accorded to these two parties.[192] This also explains why legal standing is explicitly extended to other participants in Article 82 (2) and (4): namely, to the State concerned (apart from the Prosecutor) and to legal representatives of victims, the convict, or a *bona fide* owner of property if they are affected by a reparations order under Article 75.[193]

However, there seems to be an inconsistency between Article 82 (1) and some specific provisions it refers to, namely Articles 18 (4) and 19 (2) and (6) via Article 82 (1)(a) (by reference to decision on jurisdiction or admissibility).[194] Both Articles 18 (4) and 19 (2)(b) extend the *locus standi* to a relevant State. While in the latter case this extension only refers to the primary challenge to jurisdiction or admissibility, and regarding the appeal a reference to Article 82 is made,[195] Article 18 (4), albeit also referring to Article 82, apparently contradicts this provision by giving standing to the 'State concerned'.[196] It remains to be seen how this inconsistency will be dealt with by the jurisprudence, but it seems most plausible to read Article 18 (4) as a *lex specialis* extension of standing to States concerned.[197] As a consequence, under Article 19 the State concerned would not have a right to appeal unless one applies Article 18 (4) or Article 82 (2)—referred to by Article 19 (6) but limited to decisions under Article 57 (3)(d)—by way of analogy to a State appeal against an Article 19 decision. Interestingly, Rule 108*bis* (A) RPE ICTY has granted broader standing to a 'State directly

[190] See Chapter II, B.(4), C.(1)(a), and E.(4)(a)(d) in this volume (prosecution and defence as parties, victims as participants).

[191] See e.g. Rule 2 (A) RPE ICTY/ICTR/SCSL/MICT/KSC. In the same vein, *Prosecutor v. Lubanga*, TC, Decision on Two Requests to Appeal, ICC-01/04-01/06-2779, 4 August 2011, para. 11; *Prosecutor v. Gaddafi and Al-Senussi*, AC, Decision on the Admissibility of the 'Appeal Against Decision on Application Under Rule 103' of Ms Mishana Hosseinioun of 7 February 2012, ICC-01/11-01/11-74, 10 March 2012, para. 9; excluding victims as parties (in the context of Art. 15 ICCS), *Situation in Afghanistan*, Reasons for the Appeals Chamber's oral decision dismissing as inadmissible the victims' appeals against the decision rejecting the authorisation of an investigation into the situation in Afghanistan, ICC-02/17-137, 4 March 2020, para. 21; cf. also Schabas, *ICC Commentary* (2016), p. 1222; Nerlich, 'Article 82', in Ambos, *Commentary* (2022), mn. 9; Hall, Ntanda Nsereko, and Ventura, 'Article 19', in Ambos, *Commentary* (2022), mn. 75–7 with references in nn. 185–6; also Calvo-Goller, *Cour Pénale Internationale* (2012), p. 293 (arguing that the concept of party at the ICC is broader than the one at the ICTY covering the accused and the Prosecutor); leaving it open, Friman, 'Article 82', in Klamberg, *Commentary* ICC (2017), n. 657 (arguing that 'no one else than a party may appeal or be granted leave to appeal', without however defining 'party').

[192] In the same vein, Nerlich, 'Article 82', in Ambos, *Commentary* (2022), mn. 9; regarding appeals under Art. 81 (1) and (2), see Eckelmans, 'Article 83', in Ambos, *Commentary* (2022), mn. 45; for a different view, Abdou, 'Article 19', in Klamberg, *Commentary ICC* (2017), n. 239 (arguing that the State concerned is a party to the proceedings having an automatic right to appeal but then Art. 82 (2) ICCS would be redundant; see also the discussion below in this section of the chapter).

[193] See in addition Arts. 18 (4), 19 (6) ICCS; see also Friman, 'Article 82', in Klamberg, *Commentary ICC* (2017), n. 662.

[194] For a discussion, see also Boas, Jackson, Roche, and Taylor III, in Sluiter et al., *International Criminal Procedure* (2013), p. 967.

[195] cf. Art. 19 (6) ICCS.

[196] The impugned decision need not exclusively concern admissibility or jurisdictional matters but may also refer to other matters if these affect the jurisdiction or admissibility; cf. Hall, Ntanda Nsereko, and Ventura, 'Article 19', in Ambos, *Commentary* (2022), mn. 75–7 (referring to an appeal against an arrest warrant decision).

[197] In the same vein, El Abdallah, 'Article 82', in Fernandez et al., *Statut II* (2019), p. 2096 (arguing in favour of extension of standing to States concerned since a State is not a *stricto sensu* party); similarly, Schabas, *ICC Commentary* (2016), p. 1225 ('special provision'); for a different view, Nerlich, 'Article 82', in Ambos, *Commentary* (2022), mn. 14 ('The specific reference to States in that provision [Art. 18 (4)] suggests that potential suspects of an investigation by the Prosecutor do not have a right to appeal against preliminary admissibility rulings').

affected by an interlocutory decision of a Trial Chamber'[198] going beyond the usual limitation of this right to a 'party'[199] in the traditional sense, that is, Prosecutor and defence.[200]

Last but not least, it is worthwhile mentioning that Article 56 (3)(b) ICCS limits the right to appeal to the Prosecutor, excluding, contrary to Article 82 (1), the defence.[201] While this, at first sight, seems to be incompatible with the equality of arms principle, it can be explained with the kind of investigative measures covered by Article 56 (3)(b) ICCS, that is, measures 'to preserve evidence ... essential for the defence'. Thus, given that such measures are favourable to the defence, it does not need a right to appeal against them.

### *(b) Reasons of appeal and formalities*

As to the reasons of appeal, it should be noted, first of all, that Article 82 ICCS does not explicitly provide for any 'grounds' within the meaning of Article 81. In the view of the AC this entitles the parties to raise 'any relevant ground of appeal', including the ones specified in Article 81 (1),[202] 'that may be germane to the legal correctness or procedural fairness'.[203]

Following the structural distinction made above we will first look at the more specific paragraphs (1)(a)–(c), (2), and (4) of Article 82. Jurisdictional and admissibility decisions within the meaning of *paragraph 1(a)*[204] concern the ones taken under Part 2 of the Statute,[205] in particular Articles 18 (4) and 19 (6) ICCS. The right to appeal is strictly limited to the said decisions,[206] but it includes an appeal against a TC's *proprio motu* decision on jurisdiction[207] and against a TC's decision rejecting a challenge under Article 19 on the ground that the challenge does not concern a jurisdictional question.[208] Under certain circumstances, 'the question of whether the facts alleged correspond to the crime charged may

198 See also Boas, Jackson, Roche, and Taylor III, in Sluiter et al., *International Criminal Procedure* (2013), pp. 962–3 (referring to the *Blaškić* subpoena decision which triggered this extension).

199 e.g. Rules 72 (C), 73 (A) RPE ICTY; see also Rule 134 (A) RPE MICT, identical to Rule 108*bis* (A) RPE ICTY, as opposed to the limitations of this right to a 'party' e.g. by Rules 79 (C) and 80 (A) RPE MICT.

200 See above note 191 with main text.

201 Conc. Brady, in Lee, *ICC* (2001), pp. 579–80.

202 *Situation in the DRC*, AC, Judgment on the Prosecutor's Appeal against the Decision of Pre-Trial Chamber I Entitled 'Decision on the Prosecutor's Application or Warrants of Arrest, Article 58', ICC-01/04-168, 13 July 2006, paras. 32, 33; *Prosecutor v. Kony et al.*, AC, Judgment on the Appeal of the Defence against the 'Decision on the admissibility of the case under Article 19 (1) of the Statute' of 10 March 2009, ICC-02/04-01/05-408, 16 September 2009, para. 47; *Simone Gbagbo*, ICC-02/11-01/12-75-Red, para. 37. In this vein, Friman, 'Article 82', in Klamberg, *Commentary ICC* (2017), no. 656.

203 *Kony et al.*, ICC-02/04-01/05-408, para. 46; *Ruto et al.*, ICC-01/09-01/11-307, para. 87; more recently *Prosecutor v. Abd-Alrahman*, AC, Judgment on the Appeal of Mr Abd-Al-Rahman against Pre-Trial Chamber II's 'Decision on the review of detention' of 5 July 2021, ICC-02/05-01/20 OA9, 27 August 2021, para. 23; *Prosecutor v. Ntaganda*, AC, Judgment on the Appeals against the Decision of Trial Chamber VI of 8 March 2021 Entitled 'Reparations Order', ICC-01/04-02/06-2782, 12 September 2022, para. 738.

204 In more detail, Nerlich, in Stahn, *ICC* (2015), pp. 967–9; Friman, 'Article 82', in Klamberg, *Commentary* ICC (2017), n. 658.

205 Arts. 5–21.

206 *Situation in the Republic of Kenya*, AC, Decision on the Admissibility of the 'Appeal of the Government of Kenya', ICC-01/09-78, 10 August 2011, paras. 15–17; *Gaddafi and Al-Senussi*, ICC-01/11-01/11-74, paras. 10–11; *Prosecutor v. Ruto et al.*, AC, Decision on the Appeals of Mr William Samoei Ruto and Mr Joshua Arap Sang against the Decision of Pre-Trial Chamber II of 23 January 2012, ICC-01/09-01/11-414, 24 May 2012, paras. 23, 29; *Katanga*, ICC-01/04-01/07-3424, para. 33; *Prosecutor v. Ntaganda*, AC, Judgment on the Appeal of Mr Bosco Ntaganda against the 'Decision on the Defence's challenge to the jurisdiction of the Court in respect of Counts 6 and 9', ICC-01/04-02/06 OA 2, 22 March 2016, para. 15; see also Nerlich, 'Article 82', in Ambos, *Commentary* (2022), mn. 12–13; Vagias, *Territorial Jurisdiction* (2014), pp. 274 ff.; Mosna, in Allegrezza, *Appeal Proceedings* (2023), pp. 63–4.

207 Art. 19 (1) ICCS; cf. Vagias, *Territorial Jurisdiction* (2014), p. 276.

208 Such a first instance decision is considered a 'decision with respect to jurisdiction' within the meaning of Art. 82 (1)(a); cf. *Ntaganda*, ICC-01/04-02/06-1225, para. 20.

also acquire a jurisdictional dimension', namely if a certain restrictive interpretation of the relevant crime excluded the charges from its subject-matter jurisdiction.[209]

Decisions granting or denying the release of suspects ('person being investigated or prosecuted') within the meaning of *paragraph 1(b)*[210] refer primarily to those under Article 60 ICCS.[211] Sentence reduction decisions under Article 110 are not covered since they do not concern suspects and, more importantly, are taken by an AC panel[212] whose decisions, by definition, are not appealable; indeed, such decisions are necessarily discretionary and already afford an additional, continuous[213] right to the convict so that there is no need for an appeal.[214] *Paragraph 1(c)* allows for an appeal against the PTC's decision regarding a unique investigative opportunity under Article 56 (3) ICCS.[215]

*Paragraph 2* of Article 82 permits, 'on an expedited basis',[216] an appeal against a PTC decision authorizing investigative measures of the Prosecutor on the territory of a State Party pursuant to Article 57 (3)(d) ICCS. Last but not least, *paragraph 4* allows for a specific appeal against reparation orders pursuant to Article 75; this is not an interlocutory but a final appeal.[217] It has been argued that a legal representative of victims may also appeal against a refusal to make such an order.[218]

In contrast, *paragraph 1(d)*,[219] modelled after Rule 73 (B) RPE ICTY,[220] provides for a more general ground of appeal, namely with regard to an issue 'that would significantly affect the fair and expeditious conduct of the proceedings or the outcome of the trial, *and* for which ... an immediate resolution by the Appeals Chamber may materially advance the proceedings'.[221] While the first requirement is modelled after Article 81 (1)(b)(iv), the second

[209] *Ntaganda*, ICC-01/04-02/06-1225, paras. 39–40 (regarding the question of whether child soldiers can also be victims of the war crimes of rape and sexual slavery committed by the same armed group pursuant to Art. 8 (2)(e)(vi) ICCS).

[210] In more detail, Nerlich, in Stahn, *ICC* (2015), pp. 969–70; Friman, 'Article 82', in Klamberg, *Commentary ICC* (2017), n. 659.

[211] See Chapter IV, B.(6)(b) in this volume.

[212] cf. Rule 224 (1) RPE ICC (three judges of AC).

[213] According to Art. 110 (5) ICCS, Rule 224 (4) RPE ICC the review period is, as a rule, three years.

[214] cf. Nerlich, 'Article 82', in Ambos, *Commentary* (2022), mn. 16; also Schabas, *ICC Commentary* (2016), pp. 1417–18. Para. (1)(b) decisions do not cover either appeals against a confirmation D-decision; cf. *Prosecutor v. Lubanga*, AC, Decision on the Admissibility of the Appeal of Mr Thomas Lubanga Dyilo against the Decision of Pre-Trial Chamber I Entitled 'Décision sur la confirmation des charges' of 29 January 2007, ICC-01/04-01/06-926, 13 June 2007, paras. 14–15; *Situation in the Republic of Kenya*, AC, Decision on the Admissibility of the 'Appeal of the Government of Kenya against the Request for Assistance', ICC-01/09-78, 10 August 2011, para. 17; *Prosecutor v. Mbarushimana*, AC, Reasons for 'Decision on the appeal of the Prosecutor of 19 December 2011' of 20 December 2011, ICC-01/04-01/10-483, 24 January 2012, paras. 22–3; see also El Abdallah, 'Article 82', in Fernandez et al., *Statut II* (2019), pp. 2097–8.

[215] In more detail, Nerlich, in Stahn, *ICC* (2015), pp. 970–1.

[216] See also Rule 156 (4) RPE ICC.

[217] cf. *Prosecutor v. Lubanga*, AC, Decision on the Admissibility of the Appeals against Trial Chamber I's 'Decision establishing the principles and procedures to be applied to reparations' and Directions on the Further Conduct of Proceedings, ICC-01/04-01/06-2953, 14 December 2012, paras. 51 ff (esp. paras. 63–4) ('final judicial Decision in respect of reparations'); conc. *Prosecutor v. Lubanga*, AC, Judgment on the Appeals against the 'Decision establishing the principles and procedures to be applied to reparations' of 7 August 2012 with Amended Order for Reparations (Annex A) and Public Annexes 1 and 2, ICC-01/04-01/06-3129, 3 March 2015, para. 30; cf. also Nerlich, in Stahn, *ICC* (2015), pp. 966, 974, 976.

[218] cf. Nerlich, 'Article 82', in Ambos, *Commentary* (2022), mn. 33, who differentiates between the right to appeal which 'lies with the victims themselves', and the exercise of this right which 'may only be brought with the assistance of a legal representative'; for a summary of the case law regarding appeals against reparation orders, see Nerlich, in Stahn, *ICC* (2015), p. 976.

[219] In more detail, Nerlich, in Stahn, *ICC* (2015), pp. 971–4; Friman, 'Article 82', in Klamberg, *Commentary ICC* (2017), n. 660.

[220] cf. also Rules 73 (B) RPE ICTR, 80 (B) RPE MICT and the slightly different wording of Rule 73 (B) RPE SCSL ('in exceptional circumstances and to avoid irreparable prejudice to a party').

[221] Emphasis added.

requirement entails a restrictive application of this ground[222] since, apart from obtaining leave of appeal,[223] the appellant must concretely demonstrate that the appeal 'materially' advances the proceedings. Already the *DRC* PTC stressed the 'restrictive character of the remedy' and, in addition, 'the irrelevance or non-necessity at this stage … to address arguments relating to the merit or substance of the appeal'.[224] The AC took the same restrictive approach by stressing the specific nature of the 'issue' that must be involved in this appeal, namely,

> an identifiable subject or topic requiring a decision for its resolution, not merely a question over which there is a disagreement or conflicting opinion … a subject the resolution of which is essential for the determination of matters arising in the judicial cause under examination …[225] [and which is] apt to 'significantly affect', that is, in a material way, either a) 'the fair and expeditious conduct of the proceedings' or b) 'the outcome of the trial'.[226] … [I]ts immediate resolution … will settle the matter …, ridding thereby the judicial process of possible mistakes that might taint either the fairness of the proceedings or mar the outcome of the trial.[227]

It is unclear whether the decisions of a Trial Chamber with regard to an *admission of guilt*[228]—notwithstanding the question of leave to be granted[229]—can be appealed. A judgment based on an admission of guilt can, of course, be appealed under Article 81 but what about the decisions taken in the context of the Article 65 procedure? While these decisions are clearly 'other decisions' within the meaning of Article 82 ICCS, they do not fall easily under Article 82 (1)(d) ICCS—as the only possible appeals ground—given its restrictive interpretation just set out. From the defendant's perspective, any of these decisions—either sending the trial directly to the sentencing stage or ordering the continuance of the ordinary

222 In the same vein, Nerlich, 'Article 82', in Ambos, *Commentary* (2022), mn. 20.

223 '[I]n the opinion of the Pre-Trial or Trial Chamber' (Art. 82 (1)(d) ICCS).

224 *Situation in the DRC*, PTC, Decision on the Prosecution's Application for Leave to Appeal the Chamber's Decision of 17 January 2006 on the Applications for Participation in the Proceedings of VPRS 1, VPRS 2, VPRS 3, VPRS 4, VPRS 5 and VPRS 6, ICC-01/04-135-tEN, 31 March 2006, paras. 19, 25, 29–31; *Situation in Uganda*, PTC, Decision on Prosecutor's Application for Leave to Appeal in Part Pre-Trial Chamber II's Decision on the Prosecutor's Applications for Warrants of Arrest under Article 58, ICC-02/04-01/05-20-US-Exp, 19 August 2005, paras. 15, 22–3; *Situation in the Republic of Kenya*, AC, Decision on the Government of Kenya's Application for Leave to Appeal Pursuant to Article 82 (l)(d) of the Rome Statute, ICC-01/09-86, 29 May 2012, para. 9; *Prosecutor v. Ntaganda*, PTC II, Decision on the Defence Request for Leave to Appeal, ICC-01/04-02/06-207, 13 January 2014, para. 8. See previously Ambos, in Bohlander, *International Criminal Justice* (2007), pp. 496–8; for a broader interpretation of 'fairness' and a 'more generous approach' with regard to the effect on the trial, see WCRO, *Interlocutory Appellate Review* (2008), pp. 9–10, 62 ff.

225 *Situation in the DRC*, ICC-01/04-168, para. 9; *Ntaganda*, ICC-01/04-02/06-207, para. 11; *Prosecutor v. Bemba*, AC, Decision on 'Defence Request for Leave to Appeal "Decision on Defence Motion on Privileged Communications"', ICC-01/05-01/08-3114, 14 August 2014, para. 15; more recently *Prosecutor v. Gbagbo and Blé Goudé*, TC, Decision on Request for Leave to Appeal the Decision concerning the Prosecutor's Submission of Documentary Evidence on 13 June, 14 July, 7 September, and 19 September 2016, ICC-02/11-01/15-901, 4 May 2017, para. 11; *Prosecutor v. Al Hassan*, TC, Decision on Defence Request for Reconsideration, ICC-01/12-01/18-734, 9 April 2020, para. 13; *Prosecutor v. Said*, AC, Decision on the Admissibility of the Appeal, ICC-01/14-01/21-514, 25 October 2022, para. 14.

226 *Situation in the DRC*, ICC-01/04-168, para. 10; *Situation in the Republic of Kenya*, ICC-01/09-86, para. 10; *Ntaganda*, ICC-01/04-02/06-207, para. 10; *Al Hassan*, ICC-01/12-01/18-734, para. 12.

227 *Situation in the DRC*, ICC-01/04-168, paras. 14, 19 ('to pre-empt the repercussions of erroneous Decisions on the fairness of the proceedings or the outcome of the trial'); *Situation in the Republic of Kenya*, ICC-01/09-86, para. 9; *Ntaganda*, ICC-01/04-02/06-207, para. 10; *Bemba*, ICC-01/05-01/08-3114, para. 16; *Said*, ICC-01/14-01/21-514, para. 15.

228 cf. Art. 65 (2)–(4) ICCS; see also Chapter IV, B.(9) in this volume.

229 See above notes 187 and 223 with main text.

trial—affects 'the fair and expeditious conduct of the proceedings', but it is questionable if an AC decision would 'materially advance the proceedings'. This may be possible if the decision to be impugned concerns the impact of the admission on the truth to be produced by the respective proceedings and a decision of the AC could contribute to the clarification of the matter. Of course, the application of Article 82 (1)(d) ICCS depends on the circumstances of the concrete case.

As in the appeals against final decisions, there exist also a number of *formal rules* regarding timing, length of submissions, and so forth.[230] At the ICTY an expedited appeals procedure has been introduced in 2005 with Rule 116*bis* RPE ICTY;[231] at the KSC, expediency is generally required at the appeals stage.[232] At the ICC, the appeal must be filed within a period of maximum two to five days after notification.[233] The interlocutory appeal has no suspensive effect unless so ordered by the AC upon request.[234] The AC has often invoked Reg. 29 RegC to speed up interlocutory appeals.[235] All these rules try to compensate for the overall procedural delay caused by any interlocutory appeal. It is not easy to strike a proper balance between the general aim of expediency of proceedings and the early solution of legal issues by way of interlocutory appeal.[236] In any case, relevant procedural errors which 'materially' affect[237] a TC's decision pursuant to Article 74 ICCS may also be raised as part of the final appeal,[238] that is, an interlocutory appeal could then be dispensed with.

### (c) *Standard of review*

As to the standard of review, both the AC of the ad hoc tribunals and of the ICC took the same restrictive approach as in the case of appeals against final decisions, distinguishing between the kind of error, and its possible impact on the appealed decision.[239] As to the latter, the ICC AC held that the error must 'materially affect' the impugned decision.[240]

[230] cf. Eckelmans, in Stahn and Sluiter, *Practice* (2009), pp. 544 ff.; Boas, Jackson, Roche, and Taylor III, in Sluiter et al., *International Criminal Procedure* (2013), pp. 974–7 (ICC), 965–6 (ad hoc tribunals); Vagias, *Territorial Jurisdiction* (2014), pp. 278–80.

[231] See also Rule 143 RPE MICT.

[232] cf. Rule 77 (3) RPE KSC. For the formal requirements of an (interlocutory) appeal, see *Gucati and Haradinaj*, KSC-BC-2020-07/IA004/F00007, paras. 14–17.

[233] Rules 154 (1), (2), and 155 (1) RPE ICC.

[234] Art. 82 (3) ICCS and 156 (5) RPE ICC. See also Friman, 'Article 82', in Klamberg, *Commentary ICC* (2017), n. 661; with regard to the appeal under Art. 82 (1)(a), Vagias, *Territorial Jurisdiction* (2014), p. 278.

[235] *Prosecutor v. Lubanga*, AC, Decision on the 'Observations de la Défense relatives à l'irrecevabilité du "Prosecution's Document in Support of Appeal against Trial Chamber I's Decision of 8 July to stay the proceedings for abuse of process" daté du 26 juillet 2010', ICC-01/0-01/06-2543, 30 July 2010, paras. 12–14; *Prosecutor v. Bemba et al.*, AC, Judgment on the Appeals against Pre Trial Chamber II's Decisions Regarding Interim Release in Relation to Aimé Kilolo Musamba, Jean-Jacques Mangenda, Fidèle Babala Wandu, and Narcisse Arido and Order for Reclassification, ICC 01/05-01/13 OA 5, OA 6, OA 7, OA 8, OA 9, 29 May 2015, para. 17.

[236] For a discussion, see Boas, Jackson, Roche, and Taylor III, in Sluiter et al., *International Criminal Procedure* (2013), pp. 1005–7, 1012.

[237] cf. Art. 83 (2) ICCS.

[238] *Kony et al.*, ICC-02/04-01/05-408, paras. 46–7; conc. *Ngudjolo*, ICC-01/04-02/12-271-Corr, paras. 3, 247.

[239] For an excellent summary (up to 2011), see Boas, Jackson, Roche, and Taylor III, 'Appeals, Reviews, and Reconsideration', in Sluiter et al., *International Criminal Procedure* (2013), pp. 964–5, 971–4. For the KSC, see *Gucati and Haradinaj*, KSC-BC-2020-07/IA001/F00005, paras. 4–14; *Gucati and Haradinaj*, KSC-BC-2020-07/IA004/F00007, paras. 8–11 (applying the standard for appeals against judgments *mutatis mutandis*).

[240] cf. *Prosecutor v. Lubanga*, AC, Judgment on the Prosecutor's Appeal against the Decision of Pre-Trial Chamber I Entitled 'Decision Establishing General Principles Governing Applications to Restrict Disclosure pursuant to Rule 81 (2) and (4) of the Rules of Procedure and Evidence', ICC-01/04-01/06-568, 13 October 2006, para. 15; *Prosecutor v. Bemba*, Judgment on the Appeal of Mr Jean-Pierre Bemba Gombo against the Decision of Trial Chamber III of 26 September 2011, ICC-01/05-01/08-1937-Red2, 15 December 2011, para. 68; *Nourain and Jerbo Jamus*, ICC-02/05-03/09-295, para. 20; *Prosecutor v. Mbarushimana*, AC, Judgment on the Appeal of the Prosecutor against the Decision of Pre-Trial Chamber I of 16 December 2011 entitled 'Decision on the Confirmation of charges', ICC-01/04-01/10-514, 30 May 2012, para. 15; *Gbagbo*, ICC-02/11-01/11-321, para. 76; *Ntaganda*, ICC-01/04-02/06-271-Red, para. 32; *Gaddafi*, ICC-01/11-01/11-547-Red, paras. 49, 146;

An error of law must render the AC's decision 'substantially different'.[241] As to an error of fact, the AC, first of all, emphasized that its review is 'corrective and not *de novo*'.[242] Thus, it will defer to the (Pre-)Trial Chamber's factual findings unless it has committed a 'clear error', that is, 'it misappreciates facts, disregards relevant facts or takes into account facts extraneous to the *sub judice* issues'.[243] If the appeal concerns a *discretionary decision* of a PTC, the AC's scope of review is even more limited as we have already seen above.[244]

## C. Revision, including reconsideration

### (1) General, including standing and standard

In a nutshell, revision is an extraordinary remedy against a final judgment on the grounds that newly discovered facts indicate that this judgment amounted to a miscarriage of justice.[245] It is provided for in the law of the ad hoc tribunals[246] and of the ICC,[247] but there are considerable differences. Both regimes have in common that the application can only be directed, in line with the general nature of revision just mentioned, against *final* judgments,[248] that is, any decision terminating the original proceedings.[249]

As to the *standing*, before the ICC, the claim can only be made by the convict (or, after death, relatives or a person instructed) or the Prosecutor on his behalf,[250] whereas, before

*Simone Gbagbo*, ICC-02/11-01/12-75-Red, para. 40; *Bemba et al.*, ICC-01/05-01/13-2275-Red, para. 90. See also Eckelmans, in Stahn and Sluiter, *Practice* (2009), pp. 543–4; Eckelmans, 'Article 81', in Ambos, *Commentary* (2022), mn. 40.

241 *Simone Gbagbo*, ICC-02/11-01/12-75-Red, para. 41; *Bemba et al.*, ICC-01/05-01/13-2275-Red, para. 90; see also *Gucati and Haradinaj*, KSC-BC-2020-07/IA001/F00005, para. 12 ('changing the outcome of a decision').

242 *Ruto et al.*, ICC-01/09-01/11-307, para. 56; *Nourain and Jerbo Jamus*, ICC-02/05-03/09-295, para. 20; *Mbarushimana*, ICC-01/04-01/10-514, para. 15; *Gbagbo*, ICC-02/11-01/11-321, para. 76; *Ntaganda*, ICC-01/04-02/06-271-Red, para. 29; *Bemba et al.*, ICC-01/05-01/13-559, para. 18; *Gaddafi and Al-Senussi*, ICC-01/11-01/11-565, para. 57; *Bemba et al.*, ICC-01/05-01/13-2275-Red, para. 96; similarly *Gucati and Haradinaj*, KSC-BC-2020-07/IA001/F00005, para. 13 (requiring 'miscarriage of justice'). See also Eckelmans, 'Article 81', in Ambos, *Commentary* (2022), mn. 88.

243 *Bemba*, ICC-01/05-01/08-1626-Red, paras. 44–5; see also *Ruto et al.*, ICC-01/09-01/11-307, paras. 56–7; *Ntaganda*, ICC-01/04-02/06-271-Red, paras. 29–30; *Bemba et al.*, ICC-01/05-01/13-559, paras. 18–19; *Simone Gbagbo*, ICC-02/11-01/12-75-Red, para. 38; summarizing *Bemba et al.*, ICC-01/05-01/13-2275-Red, paras. 91 ff.; see also *Gucati and Haradinaj*, KSC-BC-2020-07/IA001/F00005, para. 14 ('discernible error', above note 90).

244 Section B.(1)(b)(iii) in this chapter.

245 cf. Art. 14 (6) ICCPR; see also Darbyshire, in Vogler and Huber, *Criminal Procedure in Europe* (2008), pp. 120 ff.; Vogler, ibid., p. 223; Huber, ibid., p. 322; Šugman Stubbs, ibid., pp. 512–13; Gascón Inchausti and Villamarín López, ibid., pp. 597–8; Terrill, *World Criminal Justice Systems* (2007), p. 175 (Canada), p. 636 (China); Nerlich, 'Article 84', in Ambos, *Commentary* (20122), mn. 4; Klamberg, 'Article 84', in Klamberg, *Commentary ICC* (2017), n. 669.

246 Arts. 26 ICTYS, 25 ICTRS, 24 IRMCTS, 21 SCSLS, 22 RSCSLS; Rules 119–22 RPE ICTY, 120–3 RPE ICTR, 120–2 RPE SCSL and 146–8 RPE MICT. The KSC legal framework speaks of 're-opening of criminal proceedings', cf. Art. 48 (1)–(4) KSC Law and Rules 187–90 RPE KSC.

247 Art. 84 ICCS, Rules 159–61 RPE ICC, Reg. 66 RegC. See generally Cryer et al., *ICL* (2019), pp. 440–1; Doria, in Doria, Gasser, and Bassiouni, *Legal Regime* (2009), pp. 967 ff.; Friman, in Schabas and Bernaz, *Routledge Handbook ICL* (2011), pp. 281 ff.; Maia, 'Article 84', in Fernandez et al., *Statut II* (2019), pp. 2122 ff.; Nerlich, in Stahn, *ICC* (2015), pp. 976–7.

248 Art. 84 (1) ICCS; Rules 119 (A) RPE ICTY, 120 (A) RPE ICTR/SCSL, and 146 (A) RPE MICT; see also Art. 48 (2) KSC Law and Rule 187 (1) RPE KSC ("terminated by a final judgment").

249 *Prosecutor v. Barayagwiza*, AC, Decision (Prosecutor's Request for Review or Reconsideration), ICTR-97-19-AR72, 31 March 2000, para. 49; *Prosecutor v. Blaškić*, AC, Decision on Prosecutor's Request for Review or Reconsideration, IT 94-14-R, 23 November 2006, paras. 22–3. See also Nerlich, 'Article 84', in Ambos, *Commentary* (2022), mn. 10–12; Boas, Jackson, Roche, and Taylor III, in Sluiter et al., *International Criminal Procedure* (2013), p. 981; Calvo-Goller, *Cour Pénale Internationale* (2012), pp. 300–1, 302; Maia, 'Article 84', in Fernandez et al., *Statut II* (2019), pp. 2130–1.

250 Art. 84 (1) ICCS.

the ad hoc tribunals, the Prosecutor may also apply for it to the detriment of the person concerned, albeit only up to one year after the pronouncement of the final judgment;[251] at the KSC, any party may request the reopening[252] but only in limited circumstances to the detriment of the 'accused'.[253] Thus, the convict is clearly in a more favourable position before the ICC (and, to a limited extent, also before the KSC) where the purpose of the revision, basically, consists of the correction of miscarriages of justice to the detriment of the convict, that is, it operates to her benefit. As a further consequence, the *reformatio in peius* principle, enshrined in Article 83 (2) last clause ICCS, should be applied by analogy.[254]

As to the *standard* of review, the ICC (and the KSC) regime is also more beneficial to the convict in that it allows for more grounds of revision. While at the ad hoc tribunals a revision is predicated on the discovery of a new fact unknown to the respective party at the time of the proceedings,[255] the ICC (and KSC) law refers, apart from 'new evidence', to false decisive (old) evidence and serious misconduct of the respective judges as potential grounds of a revision.[256] Let us have a closer look at these grounds.

### (2) Grounds of revision

As to the first, typical ground of revision (discovery of new evidence), contained in subparagraph (a) of Article 84 (1) ICCS, one must first note the difference between '*new evidence*' and '*new fact*'[257] although not all authentic versions of the ICCS speak of new evidence.[258] The difference is of course relevant since the requirement of new facts—which is in line with Article 14 (6) ICCPR—creates a higher threshold.[259] The applicant may be able to present new evidence regarding the same facts—similar to the additional evidence in appeals proceedings discussed above[260]—but not necessarily wholly new facts not yet dealt with at the original proceedings. Indeed, the 'mere subsequent discovery of evidence of a fact ... is not in itself a new fact'[261] since it is linked to the fact(s) already known during the

[251] Rules 119 (A) RPE ICTY, 120 (A) RPE ICTR/SCSL, and 146 (A) RPE MICT. Nerlich, 'Article 84', in Ambos, *Commentary* (2022), mn. 7 rightly stresses the *ne bis in idem* problem which led the ILC not to allow a revision to the detriment of the convict. In the same vein, Zappalà, in Cassese, *Companion* (2009), p. 246; Calvo-Goller, *Cour Pénale Internationale* (2012), p. 302; Maia, 'Article 84', in Fernandez et al., *Statut II* (2019), p. 2131.

[252] Art. 48 (1) KSC Law and Rule 187 (1) RPE KSC ('[A] party').

[253] It follows from Art. 48 (3) KSC Law that in case of the grounds of revision stipulated in subpara. (a) and (b) of Art. 48 (2) criminal proceedings may be reopened to the detriment of the accused only in exceptional circumstances; yet, regarding the grounds mentioned in subpara. (c) and (d) this limitation does not apply.

[254] cf. Nerlich, 'Article 84', in Ambos, *Commentary* (2022), mn. 7.

[255] Arts. 26 ICTYS, 25 ICTRS, 24 IRMCTS, 21 SCSLS, 22 (1) RSCSLS; Rules 119 (A) RPE ICTY, 120 (A) RPE ICTR/SCSL, 146 (A) RPE MICT.

[256] Art. 84 (1) ICCS and similarly Art. 48 (2) KSC Law.

[257] Compare Art. 84 (1)(a) ICCS (and Art. 48 (2)(c) KSC Law) with Arts. 26 ICTYS, 25 ICTRS, 24 IRMCTS, 21 (1) SCSLS, 22 (1) RSCSLS. For a discussion, see Nerlich, 'Article 84', in Ambos, *Commentary* (2022), mn. 16; Boas, Jackson, Roche, and Taylor III, in Sluiter et al., *International Criminal Procedure* (2013), pp. 982–3; Maia, 'Article 84', in Fernandez et al., *Statut II* (2019), pp. 2126–30; Calvo-Goller, *Cour Pénale Internationale* (2012), pp. 303–5; Tochilovsky, *Jurisprudence* (2014), pp. 1160–1.

[258] The Spanish ('*nuevas pruebas*'), Arab 'ادل ةديدج', Chinese (新证据), and Russian ('обнаружились новые доказательства, которые') versions all do, Rule 190 RPE STL also speaks of 'new evidence', but not the French version ('*fait nouveau*'). Art. 48 (2)(c) KSC Law refers to both 'new facts' and 'new evidence'.

[259] Crit. of the restrictive approach of the ICTY/ICTR with alternative interpretations, Galbraith, *LJIL*, 21 (2008), 133 ff., 147 ff.; on the restrictive review practice at the ICTY/ICTR, Re, in Reydams, Wouters, and Ryngaert, *International Prosecutors* (2012), pp. 864–5; Tochilovsky, *Jurisprudence* (2014), p. 1161.

[260] Section B.(1)(c) in this chapter; cf. also Nerlich, 'Article 84', in Ambos, *Commentary* (2022), mn. 16; *Lubanga*, ICC-01/04-01/06-3121-Red, para. 61.

[261] *Tadić*, IT-94-1-A, para. 32; *Barayagwiza*, ICTR-97-19-AR72, para. 41.

original proceedings. In contrast, a new fact refers to 'new information of an evidentiary nature of a fact that was not in issue during the trial or appeal proceedings'.[262] While the discovery of new evidence is easier than that of new facts, both terms have in common that only factual changes or discoveries, not merely legal ones (e.g. change in law), can give rise to a revision.[263]

Also, neither the new facts nor the evidence must have been known[264] or available at the trial[265] and this lack of knowledge/availability must not have been caused by a lack of 'due diligence' of the respective party or that party's counsel,[266] that is, it must not be 'attributable to the party making the application'.[267] This requirement may, however, be outweighed by 'wholly exceptional circumstances', that is, when the new fact is so crucial that it 'is of such strength that it *would* affect the verdict'[268] and its non-consideration would entail a miscarriage of justice.[269] In any case, the importance of the new fact or evidence with a view to the trial outcome is a further factor to be taken into account, with both legal regimes again using a substantively similar language: while the new fact 'could have been a decisive factor in reaching a decision',[270] the new evidence must be 'sufficiently important' so that it 'would have been likely to have resulted in a different verdict'.[271] While it is clear that this requires less than the just mentioned miscarriage of justice, it is unclear whether these two standards can be precisely distinguished.[272]

The two further grounds of Article 84 (1)(b) and (c) ICCS do not exist in the law of the ad hoc tribunals.[273] *Subparagraph (b)* requires that 'it has been newly discovered that decisive evidence ... upon which the conviction depends, was false, forged or falsified'. This seems

[262] *Prosecutor v. Blaškić*, AC, Decision on Prosecutor's Request for Review or Reconsideration, IT-95-14-R, 23 November 2006, para. 14. Thus, for example, new information that sheds doubts on the credibility of a previous witness is not a 'new fact'; ; *Prosecutor v. Lukic*, Decision on Milan Lukic's Application for Review, MICT-13-52-R.1, 7 July 2015, para. 6; *Prosecutor v. Lukic*, Decision on Sreten Lukic's Application for Review, MICT-14-67-R.1, 8 July 2015, para. 6; *Niyitegeka v. Prosecutor*, Decision on Niyitegeka's Request for Review and Assignment of Counsel, MICT-12-16-R, 13 July 2015, para. 7; *Semanza v. Prosecutor*, Decision on a Request for Access and Review, MICT-13-36-R, 9 April 2018, para. 13; *Prosecutor v. Lukic*, Decision on Milan Lukic's Request for Review and for Assignment of Counsel, MICT-13-52-R1, 15 December 2020, para. 10; for further (earlier) case law, see previous edition p. 578 mn. 248.

[263] See also Nerlich, 'Article 84', in Ambos, *Commentary* (2022), mn. 17; Boas, Jackson, Roche, and Taylor III, in Sluiter et al., *International Criminal Procedure* (2013), p. 983.

[264] Rules 119 (A) RPE ICTY, 120 (A) RPE ICTR/SCSL, 146 (A) RPE MICT; Art. 48 (2)(c) KSC Law.

[265] Art. 84 (1)(a)(i) ICCS.

[266] Rules 119 (A) RPE ICTY, 120 (A) RPE ICTR/SCSL, 146 (A) RPE MICT; no reference to lack of due diligence in Art. 48 (2)(c) KSC Law.

[267] Art. 84 (1)(a)(i) ICCS. On the structural similarity of these criteria, see also Nerlich, 'Article 84', in Ambos, *Commentary* (2022), mn. 18; Calvo-Goller, *Cour Pénale Internationale* (2012), p. 303; Tochilovsky, *Jurisprudence* (2014), pp. 1160–1.

[268] *Šljivančanin*, Decision, IT-95-13/1-R.1, pp. 2, 3 with further references (emphasis added); also *Prosecutor v. Šljivančanin*, AC, Review Judgment, IT-95-13/1-R.1, 8 December 2010, para. 23; *Prosecutor v. Nahimana*, Decision on Nahimana's Request for Review, MICT-13-37-R.1, 16 November 2015, paras. 17–19 .

[269] *Barayagwiza*, ICTR-97-19-AR72, para. 65; *Prosecutor v. Šljivančanin*, AC, Decision with Respect to Veselin Šljivančanin's Application for Review, IT-95-13/1-R.1, 14 July 2010, pp. 2–3; *Nahimana*, MICT-13-37-R.1, paras. 8, 17–19; *Lukic*, MICT-13-52-R.1, para. 7; *Lukic*, MICT-14-67-R.1, para. 7; *Prosecutor v. Coric*, Decision on a Request for Review, MICT-17-112-R.1, 16 March 2018, para. 6; *Semanza*, MICT-13-36-R, para. 14. See also Nerlich, 'Article 84', in Ambos, *Commentary* (2022), mn. 21; Boas, Jackson, Roche, and Taylor III, in Sluiter et al., *International Criminal Procedure* (2013), p. 983; Knoops, *Redressing Miscarriages of Justice* (2013), pp. 93–6; Tochilovsky, *Jurisprudence* (2014), pp. 1159–60.

[270] Rules 120 RPE ICTY, 121 RPE ICTR, 120 (A) RPE SCSL, 146 (A), 147 RPE MICT; Art. 48 (2)(c) KSC Law.

[271] Art. 84 (1)(a)(ii) ICCS. Although, strictly speaking, the 'verdict', referring to the decision within the meaning of Art. 74 ICCS, must be distinguished from the 'sentence' within the meaning of Art. 76 ICCS (see Chapter IV, A. at the beginning, in this volume), new evidence may also affect the sentence and thus trigger its revision; cf. Nerlich, 'Article 84', in Ambos, *Commentary* (2022), mn. 24.

[272] cf. Nerlich, 'Article 84', in Ambos, *Commentary* (2022), mn. 23.

[273] But see Art. 48 (2)(a) and (b) KSC Law.

to be a higher threshold than the 'likely' standard of subparagraph (a).[274] *Subparagraph (c)* provides for a wholly different ground speaking to the 'serious misconduct' or 'serious breach of duty' of the judges involved in the original proceedings. As to the latter the reference to the removal procedure of Article 46 involving the ASP points to an interesting—and certainly uneasy—division of labour between the AC and the ASP: while the AC has to determine whether the sufficient level of gravity has been attained that would justify a removal, the ASP has to actually execute it with a two-thirds majority upon a recommendation of two-thirds of all ICC judges (i.e. twelve, not just the five of the AC);[275] yet, even if the removal procedure has not been initiated by the ASP, the AC can still consider that a sufficiently serious breach has been committed.[276] Subparagraph (c) requires 'a breach of duty of sufficient gravity to *justify* the removal';[277] it is not required—and would be difficult to prove given the secrecy of the deliberations[278]—that the misconduct/breach affected the outcome of the proceedings.[279]

As to the *procedure*, apart from some formal rules regarding timing and so forth,[280] it consists of two stages:[281] First, the competent (Trial or Appeals) Chamber[282] must take a preliminary decision on the merit of the application; only if this decision is in the affirmative can the second stage, that is, a more substantive analysis taking into account the new fact(s), follow. At the first stage, a kind of 'filter mechanism',[283] the Chamber must come to the conclusion that the new fact could have been a 'decisive factor in reaching a decision'[284] or, less demanding, that the application is 'meritorious'.[285] At the second stage, the ICC AC may reconvene the original TC, constitute a new TC, or exercise jurisdiction over the matter itself, to take the actual decision on the revision.[286] For this purpose, a full hearing shall be convened[287] and the relevant Chamber shall take the decision on the revision by majority pursuant to the rules on appeal.[288] In fact, the revision proceedings would have to encompass the new trial since there is no provision authorizing the ordering of a retrial.[289]

274 Conc. Calvo-Goller, *Cour Pénale Internationale* (2012), p. 1535 ('un critère plus exigeant'). Explaining it with the different perspective of subparagraphs (a) and (b) (prediction vs. actual importance), Nerlich, 'Article 84', in Ambos, *Commentary* (2022), mn. 26.

275 Art. 46 (2) ICCS.

276 Nerlich, 'Article 84', in Ambos, *Commentary* (2022), mn. 28.

277 Emphasis added. See also Nerlich, 'Article 84', in Ambos, *Commentary* (2022), mn. 28.

278 Art. 74 (4) ICCS.

279 In the same vein, Nerlich, 'Article 84', in Ambos, *Commentary* (2022), mn. 29; Calvo-Goller, *Cour Pénale Internationale* (2012), p. 305.

280 cf. Rules 119 RPE ICTY, 120 RPE ICTR/SCSL, 146 RPE MICT and Rules 159, 160 RPE ICC, Reg. 66 RegC. See also Boas, Jackson, Roche, and Taylor III, in Sluiter et al., *International Criminal Procedure* (2013), pp. 983–4, 985–6.

281 In the same vein, Nerlich, 'Article 84', in Ambos, *Commentary* (2022), mn. 30–1; Schabas, *ICC Commentary* (2016), pp. 1252–3; Calvo-Goller, *Cour Pénale Internationale* (2012), p. 306; Maia, 'Article 84', in Fernandez et al., *Statut II* (2019), pp. 2131–4; Klamberg, 'Article 84', in Klamberg, *Commentary ICC* (2017), n. 671.

282 Before the ICC the application goes to the AC (Art. 84 ICCS).

283 Nerlich, 'Article 84', in Ambos, *Commentary* (2022), mn. 30; Maia, 'Article 84', in Fernandez et al., *Statut II* (2019), pp. 2131–2.

284 Rules 120 RPE ICTY, 121 RPE ICTR, and 147 RPE MICT; Art. 48 (2)(c) KSC Law.

285 Art. 84 (2) ICCS and Rule 159 (2) RPE ICC; Rule 121 RPE SCSL.

286 Art. 84 (2) ICCS. Similarly, Art. 21 (2) SCSLS, and Rule 121 RPE SCSL (reconvene TC or retain jurisdiction) as well as Art. 48 (4)(b) KSC Law (reconvene or 'determine the matter itself'); cf. also Art. 22 (2) RSCSLS according to which the President and not the AC determines whether to reconvene the original TC or constitute a new one.

287 Rule 161 (1), (2) RPE ICC.

288 Rule 161 (3) RPE ICC in connection with Art. 83 (4) ICCS.

289 cf. Nerlich, 'Article 84', in Ambos, *Commentary* (2022), mn. 32; on the possibility of an appeal against the revised judgment, see ibid., mn. 34.

### (3) Reconsideration

The revision must be distinguished from a reconsideration of previous decisions. While both remedies are of an exceptional nature, they are different in that the reconsideration has no explicit legal basis in the law of the ad hoc tribunals[290] and it is not directed against final judgments but, quite to the contrary, previous decisions which have not yet been finalized. Notwithstanding the absence of a legal basis, the ad hoc tribunals have recognized an inherent right to reconsider their own decisions up until the judgment if either new circumstances have arisen, or the decision was erroneous and thus caused prejudice to the moving party.[291] Of course, this leaves a wide discretion to any chamber receiving an application for reconsideration.[292] The KSC's approach is more restrictive, in line with Rule 79 (1) RPE KSC which only allows for a reconsideration in 'exceptional circumstances', either because of 'a clear error of reasoning' or 'to avoid injustice'.[293]

At the ICC, PTCs have first taken a restrictive approach, basically limiting the remedies to the ones explicitly recognized by its law, especially an appeal against interlocutory decisions under Article 82.[294] Thus, PTC II has rejected a prosecutorial application for reconsideration with regard to certain redactions pointing to the insofar only available remedy of Article 82 (1)(d) ICCS and the ensuing time limits which the Prosecutor attempted to bypass by this type of application.[295] The position has changed with the decision of the *Lubanga* TC finding that it had the power to reconsider not only 'administrative' decisions of a case-management nature, but also more substantive decisions,

[290] But see Rule 79 RPE KSC.

[291] cf. Boas, Jackson, Roche, and Taylor III, in Sluiter et al., *International Criminal Procedure* (2013), pp. 997, 1001 with case law references in n. 489; see also Boas et al., *International Criminal Procedure* (2011), pp. 292–4; Nerlich, 'Article 82', in Ambos, *Commentary* (2022), mn. 8; Nerlich, 'Article 84', in Ambos, *Commentary* (2022), mn. 5.

[292] On the discretionary nature, see also *Prosecutor v. Tolimir*, Decision on Zdravko Tolimir's Request for Reconsideration of Appeals Chamber's Decision of 28 March 2008, IT-05-88/2-AR73.1, 18 June 2008, para. 8; *Prosecutor v. Norman et al.*, TC I, Decision on Urgent Motion for Reconsideration of the Orders for Compliance with the Order Concerning the Preparation and Presentation of the Defence Case, SCSL-04-14-T-0507, 7 December 2005, para. 12; more recently *Kamuhanda*, MICT-13-33-AR90/018.1, para. 16; *Stanisic & Simatovic*, MICT-15-96-PT, para. 7; *Prosecutor v. Mladic*, Decision on a Motion for Reconsideration and Certification to Appeal Decision on a Motion to Vacate the Trial Judgment and Stay the Proceedings, MICT-13-56-A, 26 June 2018, p. 2; for further (earlier) case law, see previous edition p. 580 with n. 275.

[293] See also KSC, AP, Public Redacted Version of Decision on Defence Applications for Reconsideration of 'Decision on Defence Requests to Amend the Notices of Appeal Pursuant to Rule 176(3) of the Rules', KSC-CA-2022-01, 3 November 2022, para. 13 (where the CoAP recalls, invoking Rule 79 (1) RPE KSC, the exceptional character of reconsideration).

[294] See, for an albeit not conclusive, summary Boas, Jackson, Roche, and Taylor III, in Sluiter et al., *International Criminal Procedure* (2013), pp. 998–9; also Nerlich, 'Article 82', in Ambos, *Commentary* (2022), mn. 8.

[295] *Situation in Uganda*, PTC II, Decision on the Prosecutor's Position on the Decision of Pre-Trial Chamber II to Redact Factual Descriptions of Crimes from the Warrants of Arrest, Motion for Reconsideration, and Motion for Clarification, ICC-02/04-01/05-60, 28 October 2005, paras. 18, 20, 22, 25 ('Outside such specific instances, the only remedy of a general nature is the interlocutory appeal against Decisions other than final Decisions', 'To allow such a possibility of review would indeed "render the stipulated time-limit ineffective" and create "procedural uncertainty ... contrary to the objective of ensuring fair and expeditious proceedings"'). See also *Prosecutor v. Lubanga*, PTC I, Decision Requesting Observations of the Prosecution and the Duty Counsel for the Defence on the System of Disclosure and Establishing an Interim System of Disclosure, ICC-01/04-01/06-54, 23 March 2006, pp. 3–4, arguing that 'the statutory framework' does not provide for this remedy; *Prosecutor v. Bemba*, TC, Decision on the 'Requête de la Défense aux fins d'obtenir de la Chambre de Première Instance III des décisions appropriées avant l'ouverture du Procès prévue pour le 22 Novembre 2010', ICC-01/05-01/08-1010, 16 November 2010, paras. 9–10 (recalling the previous jurisprudence, in particular arguing that 'the instruments governing the Court's procedure make no provision for such a broad remedy as an unqualified "motion for reconsideration" ... [and by doing so] [t]he defence seems to intend to obtain from the Chamber a remedy not provided for in the Court's legal framework'); *Bemba et al.*, ICC-01/05-01/13-498, p. 3.

which 'can be varied if they are manifestly unsound and their consequences are manifestly unsatisfactory'.[296]

## D. Other remedies

### (1) Remedies in case of rights violations

*(a) General*

The respect for procedural rights and rules must be guaranteed by sanctions in case of their violation. This is the understanding of 'remedies' in this section: the consequences of rights or rules violations by the investigatory authorities or other organs of the tribunals, that is, adequate sanctions or other compensatory measures for these violations. Such sanctions or measures may specifically attach to the rule violation or affect the procedure as a whole. In the former case, the person concerned may be compensated for the violation either by receiving a financial or symbolic compensation or a sentence reduction. More specifically, with regard to the law of evidence as already discussed above,[297] illegally obtained evidence may be excluded from the trial. As to the procedure as a whole, a permanent or temporary stay of proceedings may be imposed. The purpose of the said remedies is threefold: 'to provide a remedy for the violation of the accused's rights; to deter future misconduct; and to enhance the integrity of the judicial process'.[298]

Sometimes—more often under the ICC regime than under one of the ad hoc tribunals—such remedies are explicitly provided for in the applicable law; sometimes they may be inferred from the inherent powers of the tribunals or the human rights norms binding upon them. The most relevant example for the latter is Article 21 (3) ICCS according to which the ICC exercises jurisdiction 'in accordance with internationally recognized human rights norms'.[299] More specifically, common Rule 5 RPE ICTY/ICTR/SCSL/MICT authorizes a Trial Chamber to 'grant relief' in case of 'non-compliance with the Rules or Regulations' if it considers 'that the alleged non-compliance is proved and that it has caused material prejudice to that party';[300] according to Rule 6 RPE KSC, in case of non-compliance 'causing

[296] *Prosecutor v. Lubanga*, Decision on the Defence Request to Reconsider the 'Order on numbering of evidence' of 12 May 2010, ICC-01/04-01/06-2705, 30 March 2011, paras. 15–18 (esp. para. 18); relying thereon *Prosecutor v. Kenyatta*, TC V(b), Decision on the Prosecution's Motion for Reconsideration of the Decision Excusing Mr Kenyatta from Continuous Presence at Trial, ICC-01/09-02/11-863, 26 November 2013, para. 11; *Prosecutor v. Ntaganda*, TC VI, Decision on the Defence Request for Reconsideration and Clarification, ICC-01/04-02/06-483, 27 February 2015, para. 13 with n. 19; *Prosecutor v. Ntaganda*, TC VI, Decision on the Defence Request for Reconsideration, ICC-01/04-02/06-611, 27 May 2015, para. 12 with n. 17; *Prosecutor v. Bemba et al.*, Decision on Defence Request for Reconsideration of or Leave to Appeal 'Decision on "Defence Request for Disclosure and Judicial Assistance"', ICC-01/05-01/13-1282, 22 September 2015, para. 8; more recently *Prosecutor v. Ntaganda*, TC VI, Decision on Defence Request seeking Partial Reconsideration of the 'Decision on Defence request for admission of evidence from the bar table', ICC-01/04-02/06-2241, 22 February 2018, para. 4; *Prosecutor v. Ongwen*, TC IX, Decision on Defence Request for Reconsideration of or Leave to Appeal the Directions on Closing Briefs and Closing Statements, ICC-02/04-01/15-1259, 11 May 2018, para. 12; see also Nerlich, 'Article 82', in Ambos, *Commentary* (2022), mn. 8.

[297] Chapter V, A.(8) in this volume.

[298] *Prosecutor v. Barayagwiza*, AC, Decision, ICTR-97-19, 3 November 1999, para. 76; see also *Prosecutor v. Uwinkindi*, Decision on Uwinkindi's Request for Revocation, MICT-12-25-R14.1, 22 October 2015, para. 9 ('A determination concerning the conditions for a fair trial must necessarily take due consideration of the possibility and availability of remedies for any procedural irregularities at the trial and appeal stage of the national proceedings'); *Karadzic*, MICT-13-55-A, para. 41 ('Any violation of the right to a fair trial of an accused requires a remedy').

[299] cf. de Meester, Pitcher, Rastan, and Sluiter, in Sluiter et al., *International Criminal Procedure* (2013), p. 375.

[300] Rule 5 RPE SCSL slightly differs in wording (Chamber or judge 'may grant relief if the non-compliance has caused material prejudice to the objecting party').

material prejudice', a Panel may 'take any measure deemed appropriate to ensure the fairness and integrity of the proceedings'. In the law of evidence, as just mentioned, evidence may be excluded for reasons of fairness, reliability of the evidence, or integrity of the proceedings,[301] and sanctions may be imposed for the violation of disclosure obligations.[302]

### (b) *Stay of proceedings*

The most far-reaching sanction for a procedural violation is a stay of proceedings. A permanent stay entails that the case against the defendant will be definitively dismissed, and the defendant released since a fair trial is no longer considered possible. A non-permanent stay implies a temporary hold on the proceedings until the fair trial issue, for example, the lack of an adequate defence,[303] is solved.[304] The imposition of a stay is not explicitly provided for in the written law of the tribunals (the KSC, as often, being the exception)[305] but may be inferred from the *abuse of process doctrine*, which has been declared applicable by the ICTY/ICTR AC 'as a matter of discretion'.[306] According to this doctrine, as interpreted by the AC on the basis of the English common law,[307] the exercise of jurisdiction may be declined 'in cases where to exercise that jurisdiction in light of serious and egregious violations of the accused's rights would prove detrimental to the court's integrity'.[308] Thus, the doctrine may be invoked in two situations:

(1) where delay has made a fair trial for the accused impossible; and
(2) where in the circumstances of a particular case, proceeding with the trial of the accused would contravene the Court's sense of justice, due to pre-trial impropriety or misconduct.[309]

Although the first *Barayagwiza* AC decision at the ICTR ordering a permanent stay of proceedings[310] has later been overturned by another bench of the AC,[311] the standard focusing on the 'serious and egregious' nature of the violations seriously impairing the integrity of the proceedings has, in principle, been endorsed by subsequent jurisprudence.[312] Arguably, the

[301] Rules 89 (D) and 70 (G) RPE ICTY; Rules 89 (C) and 70 (F) RPE ICTR; Rule 70 (F) RPE SCSL; Rules 105 (D) and 76 (G) RPE MICT; Rules 95 RPE ICTY/ICTR/SCSL and 117 RPE MICT; Rule 138 (2), (3) RPE KSC; Art. 69 (4), (7) ICCS. See Chapter V, A.(8) in this volume.

[302] Rule 68*bis* RPE ICTY, 74 RPE MICT, and 110 RPE KSC. See Chapter V, B.(5) in this volume.

[303] See e.g. *Prosecutor v. Nahimana et al.*, Pre-Appeal Judge, Decision on Ngeze's Motion for a Stay of Proceedings, ICTR-99-52-A, 4 August 2004 (stay of proceedings until new lead counsel assigned).

[304] On the distinction in more detail, see de Meester, Pitcher, Rastan, and Sluiter, in Sluiter et al., *International Criminal Procedure* (2013), pp. 355–6.

[305] cf. Rule 110 RPE KSC (stay of proceedings as possible consequence of violation of disclosure obligation).

[306] *Barayagwiza*, ICTR-97-19, Decision, para. 74. See also *Prosecutor v. Mladic*, Decision on a Motion to Reconsider the Decision for Reconsideration and Certification to Appeal the Decision on a Request for Provisional Release, MICT-13-56, 16 July 2018, p. 2 ('Repeating requests for relief that the Appeals Chamber determined is not available ... does not serve the interests of justice and may amount to an abuse of process'). On the abuse of process doctrine in general and before international courts and tribunals in particular, see McDermott, *JICJ*, 14 (2016), 148–50, 159 ff., 167 (examining it with regard to irregular apprehensions and the effect the ensuing violations can have on the trial of the suspects).

[307] See Spencer, *CambLJ*, 73 (2014), 14, describing the 'common law power to stay a prosecution as an abuse of process' as 'surely ... one of the most astonishing developments in the history of English criminal justice'.

[308] *Barayagwiza*, ICTR-97-19, Decision, para. 74.

[309] Ibid., para. 77.

[310] Ibid., paras. 74–5, 113.

[311] *Barayagwiza*, ICTR-97-19-AR72, paras. 74–5 (arguing that the violations were less extensive than previously thought and therefore a permanent stay not justified).

[312] *Prosecutor v. Dragan Nikolić*, TC, Decision on Defence Motion Challenging the Exercise of Jurisdiction by the Tribunal, IT-94-2-PT, 9 October 2002, para. 111, and *Prosecutor v. Dragan Nikolić*, AC, Decision on Interlocutory Appeal Concerning Legality of Arrest, IT-94-2-AR73, 5 June 2003, paras. 29–33; also *Prosecutor*

ICTY *Dragan Nikolić* AC took a more prosecution-oriented stance when it held that a permanent stay will, in the light of the nature of the violations, 'usually be disproportionate' and the 'essential interests of the international community in the prosecution' outweighed the rights of the accused.[313] In any case, the gist of the issue remains whether the rights violation is so serious as to make a fair trial at the outset impossible and thus to irretrievably impair the integrity of the proceedings.

At the ICC, Chambers have taken a more critical approach to the abuse of process doctrine.[314] On the one hand, the *Lubanga* AC held that the 'power to stay proceedings for abuse of process' is neither provided for in the Statute nor 'generally recognised as an indispensable power of a court of law'.[315] On the other hand, the same Chamber acknowledged its responsibility to protect the fair trial rights, as recognized in the Statute,[316] which may entail a stay of proceedings.[317] Of course, not every breach of fair trial rights is tantamount to an abuse of process entailing the need to stay the proceedings.[318] Rather, the violation must reach a certain level of seriousness,[319] amount to a 'gross violation'[320] since 'it would be a contradiction in terms to put the person on trial' where a fair trial, focusing on the 'judicial process in its entirety', and a proper defence become impossible,[321] and where the violation cannot be

*v. Kajelijeli*, AC, Judgment, ICTR-98-44A-A, 23 May 2005, para. 206; *Prosecutor v. Karadžić*, AC, Decision on Karadžić's Appeal of Trial Chamber's Decision on Alleged Holbrooke Agreement, IT-95-5/18-AR73.4, 12 October 2009, para. 51 (holding that proceedings would have to 'contravene to the Tribunal's sense of justice or ... be detrimental to the Tribunal's integrity, due to pre-trial impropriety or misconduct amounting to serious and egregious violations of the Appellant's rights'); *Prosecutor v. Stanisic & Simatovic*, Decision on Stanisic's Request for Stay of Proceedings, MICT-15-96-T, 2 February 2017, para. 22.

313 *Dragan Nikolić*, IT-94-2-AR73, para. 30; conc. *Kajelijeli*, ICTR-98-44A-A, para. 206.

314 cf. *Prosecutor v. Mbarushimana*, Decision on the 'Defence request for a permanent stay of proceedings', ICC-01/04-01/10-264, 1 July 2011, p. 4 with further references; *Prosecutor v. Nourain and Jerbo*, Decision on the Defence Request for a Temporary Stay of Proceedings (and concurring Separate Opinion of Judge Eboe-Osuji), ICC-02/05-03/09-410, 26 October 2012, para. 80; more recently *Prosecutor v. Al Hassan*, TC, Decision on the Defence Request to Terminate the Proceedings and Related Requests, ICC-01/12-01/18-1009-Red, 29 October 2020, para. 57.

315 *Prosecutor v. Lubanga Dyilo*, Judgment on the Appeal of Mr Thomas Lubanga Dyilo against the Decision on the Defence Challenge to the Jurisdiction of the Court pursuant to Article 19 (2) (a) of the Statute of 3 October 2006, ICC-01/04-01/06-772, 14 December 2006, para. 35.

316 Arts. 55, 67 ICCS and Art. 21 (3) ICCS (fair trial as part of human rights); thereto generally De Guzman, 'Article 21', in Ambos, *Commentary* (2022), mn. 58 ff.; Heinze, 'Article 10', in Ambos, *Commentary* (2022), mn. 28.

317 *Lubanga*, ICC-01/04-01/06-772, paras. 36–7 (acknowledging the 'human rights dimension in that the causes for which the power of the Court to stay or discontinue proceedings were largely associated with breaches of the rights of the litigant, the accused in the criminal process, such as delay, illegal or deceitful conduct on the part of the prosecution and violations of the rights of the accused in the process of bringing him/her to justice'); in the same vein, *Mbarushimana*, ICC-01/04-01/10-264, p. 4; see also *Al Hassan*, ICC-01/12-01/18 1009 Red; para. 61 ('In exceptional cases, the abuse of process doctrine may be invoked in cases where serious violations of the right of the accused cannot be directly attributed to an organ of the Court'). For a discussion, see de Meester, Pitcher, Rastan, and Sluiter, in Sluiter et al., *International Criminal Procedure* (2013), pp. 363–4. Stressing the fair trial limb of the staying power also Spencer, *CambLJ*, 73 (2014), 14 ('virtually open-ended power ... to force a halt to any criminal proceedings which they feel to be fundamentally unfair').

318 *Mbarushimana*, ICC-01/04-01/10-264, p. 4.

319 See e.g. the violations concerning evidence gathering discussed in Chapter V, A.(8)(b) of this volume.

320 *Lubanga*, ICC-01/04-01/06-772, para. 24; conc. *Prosecutor v. Mbarushimana*, ICC-01/04-01/10-264, pp. 4–5; in a similar vein, McDermott, *JICJ*, 14 (2016), 164 ff., for whom stay of proceedings should be an exceptional remedy even in cases of irregular apprehensions (168); in favour of a general rule in this regard, de Meester, Pitcher, Rastan, and Sluiter, in Sluiter et al., *International Criminal Procedure* (2013), p. 378.

321 *Lubanga*, ICC-01/04-01/06-772, paras. 37, 39 (where breaches make defence impossible 'no fair trial can take place and the proceedings can be stayed'); *Mbarushimana*, ICC-01/04-01/10-264, pp. 4–5 ('only gross violations of those rights, such as to make it impossible for the accused "to make his/her defence within the framework of his rights" justify that the course of justice be halted').

rectified or corrected in the subsequent course of the proceedings.[322] Ultimately, as already suggested by the ICTY *Dragan Nikolić* AC, a balancing exercise needs to be undertaken, that is, 'the interest of the world community to put persons accused of the most heinous crimes ... on trial' must be weighed against the 'need to sustain the efficacy of the judicial process as the potent agent of justice.'[323]

The declaration of a *mistrial*, as discussed in the context of the termination of the *Ruto and Sang* proceedings,[324] also may be characterized as a permanent stay of proceedings but with the possibility to prosecute the respective accused anew if new evidence arises. In adversarial proceedings the concept is used to declare a trial invalid before it is completed, in situations where grave errors occur such as 'the introduction of inflammatory evidence and prejudicial remarks by the judge or the prosecution.'[325] Although this implies that it is usually the defence that files a motion for a mistrial, several jurisdictions allow for a mistrial in exactly those situations the *Ruto and Sang* TC dealt with, that is, 'where there has been a mistrial leading to an acquittal, due to ... an interference with witnesses or evidence.'[326]

Admittedly, the ICC Statute and the RPE do not explicitly provide for a mistrial, but it may be declared for reasons of fairness on the basis of the judges' inherent authority and broad discretion pursuant to Article 64 (2) ICCS.[327]

### (c) *Other remedies*

Other, lesser remedies include financial compensation, sentence reduction, declaratory relief, and administrative sanctions.

*Financial compensation* is only explicitly provided for by Article 85 ICCS;[328] at the ad hoc tribunals this right has been inferred from their inherent powers regarding unlawful pre-trial detention,[329] but stopping short of Article 85 (3) ICCS.[330] Article 85 ICCS foresees compensation 'to an arrested or convicted person' in three scenarios: the person was unlawfully arrested or detained (para. 1); the conviction has been reversed on the basis of new facts

[322] *Mbarushimana*, ICC-01/04-01/10-264, p. 5 ('[B]ehaviours which may trigger a stay of proceedings are those that entail unfairness of such a nature that it cannot be resolved, rectified or corrected in the subsequent course of the proceedings').

[323] *Lubanga*, ICC-01/04-01/06-772, para. 39.

[324] See Chapter IV, A.(4)(b) in this volume.

[325] Del Carmen, *Criminal Procedure* (2016), p. 59.

[326] Butler, in Carter and Palmer, *Roles and Perspectives in the Law* (2002), p. 117 with n. 14. In England and Wales, for instance, the Criminal Procedure and Investigations Act 1996 (CPIA 1996) explicitly provides for a so-called 'Tainted acquittal procedure', see ss. 54–7 CPIA 1996. The procedure applies to an acquitted person, who 'has been convicted of an administration of justice offence involving interference with or intimidation of a juror or a witness (or potential witness) in any proceedings which led to the acquittal' (s. 54 (1)(b)) or where 'there is a real possibility that, but for the interference or intimidation, the acquitted person would not have been acquitted' (s. 54 (2)(a)).

[327] On the judge's broad discretion to conduct proceedings under Art. 64, see Chapter V, A.(1)(b) and (3)(d) in this volume; regarding a mistrial, see *Prosecutor v. Ruto and Sang*, Decision on Defence Applications for Judgments of Acquittal, Reasons of Judge Eboe-Osuji, ICC-01/09-01/11-2027-Red, 5 April 2016, paras. 190–1; *contra*, Schabas, 'The Mistrial, an Innovation in International Criminal Law', *PhD Studies In Human Rights* (8 April 2016) (inference from Art. 64 (2) unconvincing); Heller, *Opinio Juris* (28 April 2016).

[328] In favour, Friman, 'Procedures', in Cryer et al., *Introduction ICL* (2014), p. 453 (no longer in new edition); generally Michels, *JICJ*, 8 (2010), 407 ff.

[329] cf. *Prosecutor v. Rwamakuba*, TC, Decision on Appropriate Remedy, ICTR-98-44C-T, 31 January 2007, para. 58; *Prosecutor v. Rwamakuba*, AC, Decision on Appeal against Decision on Appropriate Remedy, ICTR-98-44C-A, 13 September 2007, para. 19. This has been the only case where such compensation (USD 2000) has been ordered for a violation of the right to legal assistance during pre-trial detention; generally see Nerlich, 'Article 85', in Ambos, *Commentary* (2022), mn. 2–3; Zahar and Sluiter, *ICL* (2008), pp. 316 ff.; de Meester, Pitcher, Rastan, and Sluiter, in Sluiter et al., *International Criminal Procedure* (2013), pp. 359–61, 375.

[330] *Rwamakuba*, ICTR-98-44C-A, paras. 6, 10 (rejecting the analogy to Art. 85 (3) ICCS since such a right does not exist in customary international law).

which show that there has been a miscarriage of justice and the non-disclosure of these facts cannot be (partially) attributed to the person concerned (para. 2);[331] and in 'exceptional circumstances' in case of a 'grave and manifest' miscarriage of justice, where a person has been acquitted or proceedings terminated, within the discretion of the Court (para. 3).[332]

Paragraph 3 of Article 85 clearly stipulates a higher threshold than paragraph 2.[333] The restrictive wording is meant to prevent compensation being granted in cases where proceedings are terminated for factual reasons, especially due to a work-overload of the Court,[334] or where, as a result, the convict's guilt has never been ascertained. Of course, this should not be taken as an easy way out of the obligation for compensation if the Court keeps a suspect in pre-trial detention for an excessive time. After all, if the prolonged detention can be attributed to the Court it should be held accountable for it. Apart from that, it is unclear whether the right only arises if the unlawful arrest or detention is attributable to the Court or if State involvement also suffices.[335]

A request for compensation is to be filed in writing within a period of six months of notification of the decision and will be decided upon by a Chamber of three judges.[336] When setting the amount of compensation, the consequences of the unlawful detention or conviction for the affected person's personal situation should be taken into account.[337]

*Sentence reduction* is not explicitly provided for in any of the relevant legal instruments. However, a broad interpretation of the term 'compensation' in Article 85 ICCS—which has not been limited to financial compensation[338]—may encompass other non-financial compensation, including sentence reduction.[339] In practice, sentence reduction has been used by the ICTR, relying on its inherent powers, as an alternative to the more radical stay of proceedings[340] or a release of the accused.[341] It should be noted, however, that sentence reduction on the ground of rights violations conflicts with the general principles of sentencing law, in particular the culpability of the accused as the main (subjective) factor to determine the just sentence;[342] indeed, the rights violation does not affect in any way the culpability of the defendant and thus must not be taken into account in sentencing determination in a culpability-based sentencing system.

331 While Art. 85 (1) is modelled after Art. 9 (5) ICCPR, Art. 85 (2) corresponds in substance to Art. 14 (6) ICCPR; cf. also Klamberg, 'Article 85', in Klamberg, *Commentary ICC* (2017), nn. 673–4.

332 See also de Meester, Pitcher, Rastan, and Sluiter, in Sluiter et al., *International Criminal Procedure* (2013), pp. 366–7, 376 (stressing that in particular para. 3 of Art. 85 constitutes an improvement compared to Art. 9 (5) ICCPR); Dreyssé, 'Article 85', in Fernandez et al., *Statut II* (2019), pp. 2142–3; Klamberg, 'Article 85', in Klamberg, *Commentary ICC* (2017), n. 675.

333 cf. Nerlich, 'Article 85', in Ambos, *Commentary* (2022), mn. 22.

334 cf. for instance, the ICTY's termination of fourteen cases (ICTY-Bulletin 21, 27 July 1998, 4).

335 Crit. Nerlich, 'Article 85', in Ambos, *Commentary* (2022), mn. 10.

336 Rule 173 RPE ICC.

337 Rule 175 RPE ICC.

338 Ibid., speaking of 'amount of compensation', refers only to Art. 85 (3) ICCS where sentence reduction would not be an adequate remedy anyway.

339 See also de Meester, Pitcher, Rastan, and Sluiter, 'Investigation, Coercive Measures, Arrest, and Surrender', in Sluiter et al., *International Criminal Procedure* (2013), p. 367.

340 *Barayagwiza*, No. ICTR-97-19-AR72, paras. 74–5 (sentence reduction or financial compensation); more recently *Karadzic*, MICT-13-55-A, para. 753; *Prosecutor v. Mladic*, Judgment, MICT-13-56-A, 8 June 2021, para. 553; for further (earlier) case law, see previous edition, p. 587 note 323.

341 *Semanza*, Decision, ICTR-97-20-A, para. 129 and Disposition (either financial compensation or sentence reduction); *Prosecutor v. Semanza*, TC, Judgment and Sentence, No. ICTR-97-20-T, 15 May 2003, paras. 579–80 (reduction by six months); upheld by *Prosecutor v. Semanza*, AC, Judgment, ICTR-97-20-A, 20 May 2005, paras. 323–9: *Prosecutor v. Turinabo et al.*, Decision on Prosecution Appeal Against Decision Granting Marie Rose Fatuma Provisional Release, MICT-18-116-AR68.1, 6 June 2019, para. 5.

342 cf. Ambos, *Treatise ICL II* (2022), pp. 329 ff.

*Declaratory relief* has been granted by the ad hoc tribunals on the assumption that 'any violation, even if it entails a relative degree of prejudice, requires a proportionate remedy'.[343] This relief consists in the finding of a violation irrespective of the degree of prejudice suffered by the accused.[344]

*Administrative sanctions* can be imposed by a Chamber pursuant to Article 71 ICCS if the parties do not comply with its orders. The *Lubanga* AC invoked this provision with regard to the Prosecutor's non-compliance with its disclosure orders, as a less 'drastic' remedy than a stay of proceedings, to maintain control of the proceedings and bring about compliance.[345] On that basis a Chamber may also remove the respective person from the courtroom or impose a fine.[346]

Usually, the remedies mentioned presuppose that the respective rights violations can be *attributed* to the tribunal or Court, that is, they would have to be caused by one of its organs, or these must have at least been involved in one way or another in the respective violation. It was therefore correct when the *Lubanga* AC required a 'concerted action of any substance' between the Prosecutor and the Congolese authorities with regard to alleged violations during Mr Lubanga's pre-trial detention in the DRC. It further held that '[m]ere knowledge on the part of the Prosecutor of the investigations carried out by the Congolese authorities' is not sufficient as it does not prove its substantial 'involvement' in these investigations.[347] This attributory nexus is required independently of the gravity of the violations. Contrary to the *Barayagwiza* AC's finding[348] the nexus requirement cannot be displaced by the nature of the violation; nor it is 'irrelevant' to determine the entity responsible for the violation, at least if it may be attributed to an entity not belonging to the Court or to a third party.[349] This has also been held in ICTY case law.[350] It is also worthwhile noting in this regard that in the only case where financial compensation was granted, the violation was attributed to the ICTR Registry.[351] The MICT has declared itself incompetent to provide compensation for violations at the ICTR (and thus ICTY for that matter).[352]

343 *Semanza*, Decision, ICTR-97-20-A, para. 125; conc. *Rwamakuba*, ICTR-98-44C-A, para. 24; *Prosecutor v. Bagosora et al.*, TC, Judgment and Sentence, ICTR-98-41-T, 18 December 2008, paras. 96–7 ('minimal, if any, prejudice'); see also *Prosecutor v. Karadžić*, TC, Decision on Accused's Sixtieth, Sixty-First, Sixty-Third, and Sixty-Fourth Disclosure Violation Motions, IT-95-5/18-T, 22 November 2011, para. 37 (instead of exclusion of undisclosed evidence ordering disclosure of relevant evidence); *Karadzic*, MICT-13-55-A, para. 41; *Prosecutor v. Turinabo et al.*, Decision on Order to Show Cause, MICT-18-116-PT, 1 October 2019, para. 12. Recommending this practice, de Meester, Pitcher, Rastan, and Sluiter, in Sluiter et al., *International Criminal Procedure* (2013), p. 379.

344 Crit. thereof, *Prosecutor v. Karadžić*, TC, Decision on Accused's Thirty-Seventh to Forty-Second Disclosure Violation Motions, Partial Dissenting Opinion of Judge Kwon, IT-95-5/18-T, 29 March 2011, paras. 4–6 (arguing that is 'unnecessary, moot or even frivolous' to find a violation if the accused has not suffered any prejudice); *Turinabo et al.*, MICT-18-116-PT, para. 12.

345 *Lubanga*, ICC-01/04-01/06-2582, paras. 59–61 (arguing that a fair trial could still become possible, i.e. a stay is not yet necessary).

346 See Art. 71 (1) ICCS and Rules 170, 171 RPE ICC. On Art. 71 Ambos, *Treatise ICL II* (2022), pp. 289–91.

347 *Lubanga*, ICC-01/04-01/06-772, para. 42.

348 *Barayagwiza*, Decision, ICTR-97-19, para. 73; see also Paulussen, *Male captus* (2010), pp. 518, 546.

349 Leaving the question open, de Meester, Pitcher, Rastan, and Sluiter, in Sluiter et al., *International Criminal Procedure* (2013), pp. 357, 365, 371.

350 *Prosecutor v. Karadžić*, TC, Decision on the Accused's Motion for Remedy for Violation of Rights in Connection with Arrest, IT-95-5/18-PT, 31 August 2009, para. 6, (arguing that the violation must be attributed to one of the organs of the tribunal); *Rwamakuba*, ICTR-98-44C-A, para. 28 (considering the violations 'attributable to the Tribunal').

351 *Rwamakuba*, ICTR-98-44C-T, paras. 67 ff. and *Rwamakuba*, ICTR-98-44C-A, paras. 16 ff.

352 cf. *Prosecutor v. Nzuwonemeye*, Decision on Motion for Compensation and Damages for Violations of the Fundamental Rights of F.X. Nzuwonemeye, MICT-13-43, 4 August 2015, para. 17 ('IRMCT has no jurisdiction to provide compensation for a violation of rights at the ICTR').

### (2) Review of administrative decisions

At both the ad hoc tribunals and the ICC, the Registries are responsible for a series of decisions, which concern the rights of the accused, such as the right to counsel and the conditions of detention.[353] These decisions are, in principle, reviewable by the President[354] or Presidency[355]—generally responsible for the 'proper administration of the Court', excluding OTP[356]—or, rather exceptionally, by the Chambers.[357] However, the case law of the ad hoc tribunals has clearly recognized an inherent jurisdiction of the (Trial and Appeals) Chambers to review administrative decisions if fair trial rights are concerned,[358] including a right to appeal against a TC decision.[359]

Two questions, at least, arise in this context. First, it is unclear whether the Chambers' right to review may even set aside or override the authority of other organs entrusted with the review, especially the ICC Presidency. While, as just mentioned, the Chambers' authority to intervene in fair trial issues is essentially recognized, the case law is not clear on the relationship between the Chambers and other organs involved in the review process, especially the Presidency.[360] While the ICC *Bemba* TC has affirmatively stressed its 'overarching statutory

[353] For the ICC, see Regs. 70 (2) and 71 (1), (2) RegC (inclusion/removal/suspension list of counsel), Regs. 125–6 RegR (list of assistants to counsel, removal), Reg. 73 (2) RegC, and Reg. 129 RegR (appointment of duty counsel), Reg. 83 RegC (determination of scope/payment of legal assistance, indigence of applicant; see also Regs. 130–5 RegR), Reg. 90 (1) RegC (overall responsibility of detention centre; see also Regs. 186–204 RegR), Regs. 151–85 RegR (rights and detention conditions), Regs. 212, 215 RegR (isolation of detained person upon order of Chief Custody Officer; right to address registry); Regs. 217–20 RegR (complaints procedure regarding detention conditions/measures from Chief Custody Officer to Registrar); see also Chapter II, C.(1)(c) and (4) (regarding counsel), E.(3) and (4)(b) (regarding victims) in this volume. For the ad hoc tribunals, see Boas, Jackson, Roche, and Taylor III, in Sluiter et al., *International Criminal Procedure* (2013), pp. 987–8. For the KSC, see Art. 34 (7), (12) KSC Law ('Defence Office', list of defence counsel and detention function) and Rules 25, 26 RPE KSC.

[354] While the ad hoc tribunals have a 'President' (Arts. 14 ICTYS, 13 ICTRS, 11 IRMCTS, 12 (3) SCSLS, 12 RSCSLS, Arts. 30 (4), 32 KSC Law), the ICC has a 'Presidency' (Art. 38 ICCS); on this departure from the ICTY/ICTR practice, see also Abtahi and Young, 'Article 38', in Ambos, *Commentary* (2022), mn. 10.

[355] See e.g. Rule 21 (3) RPE ICC (review refusal request for assignment of counsel), Regs. 44 (1) RegC and 56 (4) RegR (review of negative decision regarding list of experts), Regs. 72 (1) RegC and 125 (4), 126 (3) RegR (review of decision regarding inclusion/removal/suspension list of counsel), Regs. 137 (5) and 138 (3) RegR (review of selection/removal list of professional investigators), Reg. 85 (3) RegC (review of decision regarding payment legal assistance), Regs. 95 (2) RegC and 216 RegR (right to address Presidency in case of disciplinary procedure during detention), Regs. 213 (2) and 216 RegR (right to address Presidency in case of isolation and release from isolation cell upon order from Presidency), Reg. 221 RegR (right to address Presidency as final instance in complaints procedure regarding detention conditions). For the ad hoc tribunals, see Boas, Jackson, Roche, and Taylor III, in Sluiter et al., *International Criminal Procedure* (2013), pp. 988–9.

[356] Art. 38 ICCS. In 'exceptional circumstances' the respective decision may be taken by the members of the Presidency 'immediately available' (Reg. 11 (3) RegC). See for a detailed analysis Ambach and Rackwitz, *LCP*, 76 nos. 3 & 4 (2013), 127 ff.; on the role of the Presidency, see Chapter II, A.(2) in this volume *in fine*.

[357] See e.g. Reg. 83 (4) RegC (review of Decision regarding scope of legal assistance), Reg. 135 (2) RegR (review of Decision concerning payment of counsel fees). For the ad hoc tribunals, see Boas, Jackson, Roche, and Taylor III, 'Appeals, Reviews, and Reconsideration', in Sluiter et al., *International Criminal Procedure* (2013), pp. 989–90. At the KSC, there is no administrative oversight of Registry decisions by the President but by the competent panel of judges, see e.g. Art. 9 PD on Detainees (Complaints), KSC-BD-11-Rev1.

[358] *Prosecutor v. Delalić et al.*, AC, Order on Esad Landzo's Motion for Expedited Consideration IT-96-21-A, 15 September 1999; for further case law, see previous edition, p. 589 note 340; more recently *Turinabo et al.*, Decision on Joint Defence Motion Seeking an Order Addressed to the Registrar concerning a Search and Seizure Operation Conducted on 1 May 2019 at the United Nations Detention Facility, MICT-18-116-PT, 13 June 2019, p. 2; *Prosecutor v. Mladic*, Order on Defence Submissions on 25 and 27 March 2020, MICT-13-56-A, 31 March 2020, p. 3.

[359] *Prosecutor v. Karadžić*, AC, Decision on Interlocutory Appeal of the Trial Chamber's Decision on Adequate Facilities, IT-95-5/18-AR73.2, 7 May 2009, paras. 9, 11; *Mladic*, MICT-13-56-A, p. 3.

[360] For the ad hoc tribunals, see Boas, Jackson, Roche, and Taylor III, in Sluiter et al., *International Criminal Procedure* (2013), pp. 989–90 with multiple, albeit contradictory, references (esp. referring to *Prosecutor v. Blagojević & Jokić*, AC, Public and Redacted Reasons for Decision on Appeal, IT-02-60-AR73.4, 7 November 2003, para. 7); see also *Prosecutor v. Nahimana et al.*, Decision on Appellant Jean-Bosco Barayagwiza's Motion Contesting the Decision of the President Refusing to Review and Reverse the Decision of the Registrar Relating

responsibility under Article 64 (2) ICCS' to ensure a fair trial[361] and a duty to 'rectify' fair trial violations pursuant to Article 67 ICCS,[362] and this apparently implies a final say on fair trial issues, the *Lubanga* AC took a much more cautious approach in the absence of specific authoritative provisions on the matter.[363] In short, while it seems clear that administrative decisions must always be reviewable by Chambers if fair trial issues are at stake it is unclear if this also holds if the legal review of a matter is conferred on the Presidency and the decisions of the latter are considered (as some are) to be 'final'.[364]

The second question concerns the standard of review. In this respect, the ICTY *Kvočka* AC et al. held that the review concerns the 'propriety of the procedure' employed by the Registrar, and that the impugned administrative decision will be repealed under four alternative conditions: (i) the Registry has failed to comply with the requirements of the relevant legal authorities, (ii) legal provisions, fundamental rules of justice or of procedural fairness have not been observed, (iii) irrelevant information has been taken into account and/or relevant information ignored, or (iv) a conclusion has been drawn that no reasonable person could have reached.[365] In a practically identical fashion, the ICC Presidency has repeatedly referred to the 'propriety of the procedure', and as a general standard considers whether the Registrar has 'acted without jurisdiction, committed an error of law, failed to act with procedural fairness, acted in a disproportionate manner, [has] taken into account irrelevant factors, failed to take into account relevant factors or reached a conclusion which no sensible person who has properly applied his or her mind to the issue could have reached'.[366]

to the Withdrawal of Co-Counsel, ICTR-99-52-A, 23 November 2006, para. 9; for further case law, see previous edition, p. 589 note 342; more recently *Prosecutor v. Ngirabatware*, Decision on Motion to Quash Decision of Suspension and to Re-instate Defence Team Legal Assistant, MICT-12-29-A, 19 March 2013, para. 8; *Prosecutor v. Karadzic*, Decision on Motion for Review of Decision on Assignment of Counsel on Appeal, MICT-13-55, 4 February 2016, para. 16; *Prosecutor v. Karadzic*, Decision on Motion for Disqualification and Motion Challenging Jurisdiction, MICT-13-55, 28 October 2019, para. 11; *Prosecutor v. Turinabo et al.*, Decision on Request for Review of Registrar's Decision, MICT-18-116-PT, 25 January 2019, para. 20; *Prosecutor v. Mladic*, Decision on Detention Complaint, MICT-13-56-A, 16 June 2020, para. 10.

361 *Prosecutor v. Bemba*, TC, Redacted Version of 'Decision on legal assistance for the accused', ICC-01/05-01/08-567-Red, 26 November 2009, para. 106; *Prosecutor v. Lubanga*, TC, Redacted Decision on the Prosecution's Urgent Request for Variation of the Time-Limit to Disclose the Identity of Intermediary 143, ICC-01/04-01/06-2517-Red, 8 July 2010, para. 24.

362 *Bemba*, ICC-01/05-01/08-567-Red, para. 107; *Prosecutor v. Ngudjolo Chui*, AC, Decision on the Defence Request to Reply to the Registrar's Observations Pursuant to Regulation 24*bis* of the Regulations of the Court (ICC-01/04-02/12-25 A), ICC-01/04-02/12-43, 20 March 2013, paras. 11, 12, allowing submissions by the defendant on the Registrar's Observations 'bearing in mind the principle of equality of arms and the need for expeditious proceedings' and 'considering the interests of fairness', although the submissions of the Registrar 'are *sui generis* in nature and outside the ambit of regulation 24 of the Regulations of the Court'.

363 *Prosecutor v. Lubanga*, Decision of the Appeals Chamber upon the Registrar's Requests of 5 April 2007, ICC-01/04-01/06-873, 27 April 2007, paras. 6–7 ('not invested with original jurisdiction') and *Prosecutor v. Lubanga*, AC, Decision on the 'Registrar's Submissions under Regulation 24*bis* of the Regulations of the Court in Relation to Trial Chamber I's Decision ICC-01/04-01/06-2800' of 5 October 2011, ICC-01/04-01/06-2823, 21 November 2011, paras. 15, 17, (impermissible 'to circumvent the limits on its jurisdiction').

364 cf. Rule 21 (3) RPE ICC; Regs. 72 (4), 85 (3) RegC; Regs. 56 (4) and (11), 125 (6) and 126 (5), 137 (7) and 138 (5), 147 (n) RegR. With regard to Reg. 85 (3) RegC, see in particular *Bemba*, No. ICC-01/05-01/08-567-Red, para. 106.

365 *Prosecutor v. Kvočka et al.*, Decision on Review of Registrar's Decision to Withdraw Legal Aid from Zoran Žigić, IT-98-30/1-A, 7 February 2003, para. 13; more recently *Prosecutor v. Karadzic*, Decision on a Motion to Review the Registrar's Decision on Indigence, MICT-13-55-A, 24 June 2016, pp. 5–6; for further (earlier) case law, see previous edition, p. 590 note 347.

366 Presidency, Decision on the Application to Review the Decision of the Registrar Denying the Admission of X to the List of Experts, ICC-RoR56-02/09-3-Red, 5 November 2009, para. 14 with references to previous decisions; reiterated most recently in Presidency, ICC-RoR125-01/15-5-Red, Public Redacted Version of 'Decision on the "Request for Review of Decision to Deny the Applicant admission to the List of Assistant to Counsel Pursuant to Regulation 125(4) of the Regulations of the Registry", 4 September 2015, ICC-RoR125-01/15-5-Conf-Exp', 1 October 2015, para. 27; Decision on the Request to Review the Decision of the Registrar denying the Inclusion of Ms. Ana Christina Rodríguez Pineda in the List of Counsel, ICC-RoC72-01/18-6, 20 April 2018, para. 17. See also Boas, Jackson, Roche, and Taylor III, in Sluiter et al., *International Criminal Procedure* (2013), pp. 993–4 with references in mn. 466–8.

# VII
# The Cooperation Regime

*The full chapter bibliography can be downloaded from

## A. Introductory remarks

### (1) Importance, nature, and forms of cooperation

International Law can be enforced by national courts *directly* (direct enforcement model) or *indirectly* (indirect enforcement model).[1] However, a truly direct enforcement of international law only exists if the relevant international court possesses *supranational* competences to validate its own decisions and judgments by, for instance, arresting suspects or conducting investigations on the territory of sovereign States. This could conceivably only be the case with tribunals set up by occupying powers such as the Nuremberg International Military Tribunal, the Tokyo International Military Tribunal for the Far East, and the Iraqi Special Tribunal (before it was turned into a national tribunal), having, of course, a jurisdiction limited to the occupied territories but the capacity to enforce their decisions and orders within this jurisdiction.[2] Thus, 'ordinary', international criminal tribunals[3] depend, as a general rule, on the cooperation of the relevant territorial State(s)[4] not only with regard to the investigation and prosecution of the crimes committed on the State territory, but also for the enforcement of the respective sentences (to be dealt with in the next chapter).[5]

Apart from that, the tribunals could also seek the cooperation of international or regional organizations or even local actors independent of the territorial State. Thus, the ICC[6] has signed, pursuant to Article 87 (6) 2nd clause ICCS, cooperation agreements with various organizations, in particular the UNO and its sub-organizations,[7] but also with regional

[1] Werle and Jessberger, *Principles* (2020), mn. 303 ff.; Bassiouni, *Introduction ICL* (2013), pp. 22 ff., 487 ff..; Burchards, *Die Verfolgung* (2005), pp. 21 ff.; Vest, *Humanitätsverbrechen* (2006), pp. 31 ff., 140; Gless, *Internationales Strafrecht* (2021), mn. 728 ff.

[2] cf. Ciampi, in Cassese et al., *Rome Statute II* (2002), pp. 1711–12.

[3] Generally on the ICC's approach to cooperation, see Rastan, in Stahn and Sluiter, *ICC* (2009), pp. 171 ff.; Calvo-Goller, *Cour Pénale Internationale* (2012), pp. 133; cf. also ICC-ASP, *Report Cooperation* (2014) and ICC-ASP, *Cooperation* (2014), paras. 51–4; for a more recent account, see ICC-ASP, *Report Cooperation* (2021), pp. 6–7; ICC-ASP, *Report Cooperation* (2022), para. 43; ICC-ASP, *Report Cooperation* (2023), p. 9; ICC-OTP, *Report 2023* (2023), pp. 35–6; on the practice of the other tribunals, see Paulussen, *Male captus* (2010), pp. 347 ff., 582 ff.

[4] On the cooperation of Latin American States with the ICC, see Ambos, Malarino, and Elsner, *Cooperación* (2007); Herencia Carrasco, *implementación del Estatuto de Roma* (2009), pp. 109 ff.; on the cooperation of African States, see Du Plessis, in Du Plessis, *African Guide* (2008), p. 127.

[5] See generally Kreß and Prost, 'Part 9—Preliminary Remarks', in Ambos, *Commentary* (2022), mn. 1; Ciampi, in Cassese et al., *Rome Statute II* (2002), pp. 1607–8; Swart, in Cassese et al., *Rome Statute II* (2002), pp. 1589–90; Schomburg, in Kirsch, *Internationale Strafgerichtshöfe* (2005), p. 129; Kreß and Wannek, in Kirsch, *Internationale Strafgerichtshöfe* (2005), p. 255; Moranchek, *YaleJIL*, 31 (2006), 485; Abels, *Prisoners* (2012), p. 446.

[6] Both the Presidency (Reg. 107 RegC) and the Prosecutor (Art. 54 (3)(d) ICCS) may sign such agreements.

[7] For the UNO as such, see the UN GA, *Relationship Agreement* (2004) and the related UN GA, *Best Practices Manual* (2016); see also UN GA, 65th Session, Report of the International Criminal Court, UN Doc. A/65/313 (19 August 2010), paras. 86 ff.; thereon, Fixson, in Kirsch, *Internationale Strafgerichtshöfe* (2005), pp. 221–2; Knoops, *International Criminal Tribunals* (2014), pp. 305–8; Buitelaar and Hirschmann, *EJIL*, 27 (2021), 548. See also the partnership agreement between the UNDP and the ICC on 27 October 2022, <https://www.undp.org/

organizations.[8] Of course, the activity of these organizations on State territory also depends on the authorization of the respective State, that is, States are and remain the key actor in the cooperation in criminal matters.[9]

Against this background, it is fair to say that international tribunals are, to quote a famous dictum of the German procedural law scholar Eduard Kern, similar to a national prosecution service dependent upon the police, like a 'head without hands',[10] or, in the words of the first President of the ICTY, 'a giant without arms and legs'.[11] Thus, a truly direct enforcement of international criminal law does not exist; rather, international criminal tribunals have to rely on the mechanisms provided for by the indirect enforcement model.[12]

news/undp-and-international-criminal-court-sign-new-partnership-agreement>. For the cooperation between the ICC and the MONUC (now MONUSCO) in the DRC, cf. the Memorandum of Understanding between the United Nations and the International Criminal Court Concerning Cooperation between the United Nations Organization Mission in the Democratic Republic of the Congo (MONUC) and the International Criminal Court, 8 November 2005 (<https://www.icc-cpi.int/sites/default/files/RelatedRecords/CR2008_01795.PDF>) and UNSC Res. 2098, 28 March 2013, para. 12; thereon, Melillo, *JICJ*, 11 (2013), 766 ff., esp. 780 ff.; Hamann, *ZStW*, 118 (2006), 814 ff. Further agreements between the ICC and UN sub-organizations at this level are, for instance, the one with the MINUSCA in the CAR (UNSC Res. 2149, 10 April 2014, para. 28) and the UNOCI in Côte d'Ivoire (Memorandum of Understanding, 12 June 2013, and UNSC Res. 2162, 25 June 2014, para. 12); thereon cf. also ASP, Report of the Court on the Status of Ongoing Cooperation between the International Criminal Court and the United Nations, Including in the Field, twelfth session, ICC-ASP/12/42, 14 October 2013, paras. 12 ff.; Unger and Wierda, in Ambos, Large, and Wierda, *Building a Future* (2009), pp. 282–3.

8 On the cooperation with the *EU* (Agreement between the International Criminal Court and the European Union on Cooperation and Assistance, 10 April 2006, ICC-PRES/01-01-06, <http://www.legal-tools.org/doc/4e8e0a/>); thereon, see Antoniadis and Bekou, *ICLR*, 7 (2007), 625 ff.; Moschetta, in Politi and Gioia, *The ICC and National Jurisdictions* (2008), pp. 123 ff.; furthermore, see Behrmann, in Bekou and Birkett, *Cooperation* (2016), pp. 297 ff. On the cooperation with the *Council of Europe*, see Res. 1644 (2009) of its Parliamentary Assembly, 'Co-operation with the International Criminal Court (ICC) and its Universality' (27 January 2009) <https://assembly.coe.int/nw/xml/XRef/Xref-XML2HTML-en.asp?fileid=17701&lang=en.pdf>; regarding the *OAS*, see the Resolution AG/RES. 2728 (XLII-O/12), 'Promotion of the International Criminal Court' (4 June 2012), <http://www.oas.org/en/sla/dil/docs/AG-RES_2728_XLII-O-12_eng.pdf>, and the 'Exchange of Letters between the ICC and OAS for the establishment of a Framework Cooperation Arrangement', <http://www.legal-tools.org/doc/51dcab>; see also the more recent cooperation agreement between the ICC and ILANUD (11 January 2024), <https://www.icc-cpi.int/news/icc-president-concludes-cooperation-agreement-ilanud>; regarding the *Commonwealth*, see Memorandum of Understanding between the International Criminal Court and the Commonwealth on Cooperation, 13 July 2011, ICC-PRES/10-04-11 <http://www.legal-tools.org/en/doc/dc14ab/>; with the *AALCO*, cf. the Memorandum of Understanding between the International Criminal Court and the Asian-African Legal Consultative Organization, ICC-PRES/05-01-08, 5 February 2012, <http://www.legal-tools.org/doc/121e2a/>; with the *IACtHR*, cf. the Memorandum of Understanding between the International Criminal Court and the Inter-American Court of Human Rights, 15 February 2016, <https://www.icc-cpi.int/iccdocs/oj/MoU_CR_En.pdf>. On the cooperation with *other tribunals*, see UN GA, 62nd Session, Report of the International Criminal Court, UN Doc. A/62/314 (31 August 2007), paras. 56 ff.; UN GA, 65th Session, Report of the International Criminal Court, UN Doc. A/65/313 (19 August 2010), paras. 103 ff.; more recently UN GA, 77th Session, Report of the International Criminal Court, UN Doc. A/77/305 (19 August 2022), paras. 62 ff.; UN GA, 78th Session, Report of the International Criminal Court, UN Doc. A/78/322 (21 August 2023), paras. 61 ff.; Vasiliev, in Cryer et al., *Introduction ICL* (2019), pp. 489 ff.; furthermore, see Turlan, in Bekou and Birkett, *Cooperation* (2016), p. 71.

9 See also Robinson, *LJIL*, 28 (2015), 339. But recall the Prosecutor's general competence under Art. 54 (3)(d) ICCS, already mentioned, which allows it to enter into cooperation agreements with, inter alia, any 'person'.

10 Kern, *Gerichtsverfassungsrecht* (1965), p. 227 ('Kopf ohne Hände').

11 Cassese, *EJIL*, 9 (1998), 13; concurring Vasiliev, in Cryer et al., *Introduction ICL* (2019), p. 503; Damaška, *UCLA JIL & ForAff*, 14 (2009), 22, speaking in this context, at 21, of an 'endegenous powerlessness' of international criminal courts; on the dependence of cooperation, see also Damaška, *ChicKentLR*, 83 (2008), 329–30; Robinson, *LJIL*, 28 (2015), 338–41; Mochochoko, in Jalloh and Alhagi, *Promoting Accountability* (2015), pp. 71–3; for an overview of the literature thereon, see Ali, *ChicJIL*, 14 (2014), 415 ff.; furthermore, see Bassiouni and Schabas, *History II* (2016), pp. 759–60; Kerr, *MichJIL*, 42 (2021), 210 emphasizing the importance of Art. 98 (1) precisely against this background. With regard to the KSC, the situation is, however, different (see note 329 below).

12 cf. Bassiouni, *Introduction ICL* (2013), pp. 22 ff., 536 ff.; regarding the ICC, see *Prosecutor v. Al Bashir*, PTC II, Decision on the Cooperation of the Democratic Republic of the Congo Regarding Omar Al Bashir's Arrest and Surrender to the Court, ICC-02/05-01/09-195, 9 April 2014, para. 33 (stressing the lack of direct enforcement mechanisms); thereon Boschiero, *JICJ*, 13 (2015), 626 ff.; also Robinson, *LJIL*, 28 (2015), 338–41 (arguing

This goes to show that certain forms and rules of cooperation are necessary to regulate the relationship between international criminal tribunals and States. As regards the *forms* of cooperation, the same forms (extradition/surrender of persons, other forms of legal assistance, enforcement assistance) traditionally used in interstate cooperation in criminal matters generally apply. However, there are significant distinctions in the cooperation terminology, conditions, and procedure. As to the *rules* of cooperation, it must first be noted that the cooperation between a supranational organization and a State is characterized by its *vertical* nature[13] as opposed to the horizontal cooperation between equally sovereign States.[14] In the latter case no general obligation to cooperate exists, but cooperation is rather dependent on the sovereign decisions of the States involved.[15] This is why interstate cooperation has several requirements, such as the principle of reciprocity and the observance of certain obstacles, which usually limit their efficiency.[16] Indeed, the very goal of an efficient (regional) system of horizontal interstate cooperation, such as the one between the Member States of the Council of Europe and the European Union,[17] is to overcome these obstacles.

In a regime of vertical cooperation, cooperation will not depend, as a matter of principle, on the sovereign decision of the State, but it is based on the legal obligation to cooperate. The paradigmatic examples of such a regime are the ICTY and ICTR as ad hoc tribunals established by the UN Security Council. They may direct binding requests and orders at/to UN Member States. In this case, the States' obligation to cooperate can be derived from the binding effect of the respective Security Council resolutions[18] and from the respective provisions of the tribunals' Statutes[19] that are based on these resolutions.[20] Bilateral cooperation agreements between States and the tribunals are not necessary;[21] States have only to

that the ICC's cooperation regime is predicated upon the Court's two limbs—international/criminal—the former demanding respect of territoriality and therefore State cooperation, while the latter calls for 'detachment, distance and avoidance of inappropriate contact' with regard to State agents).

[13] ICTY, *Prosecutor v. Blaškić*, AC, Judgment on the Request of the Republic of Croatia for Review of the Decision of Trial Chamber II of 18 July 1997, IT-95-14, 29 October 1997, paras. 47 and 54. Further on the vertical character of the cooperation, Sluiter, *Evidence* (2002), pp. 82 ff.; Sluiter, in Fischer et al., *Prosecution* (2001), pp. 688–9; Sluiter, in Cassese, *Companion* (2009), pp. 190–1; Swart, in Cassese et al., *Rome Statute II* (2002), pp. 1592 ff.; Meißner, *Zusammenarbeit* (2003), pp. 10 ff.; Cryer, *Prosecuting* (2005), pp. 132 ff.; Zahar and Sluiter, *ICL* (2008), pp. 459 ff.; Currie, *CLF*, 18 (2007), 376–7.

[14] cf. Swart, in Cassese et al., *Rome Statute II* (2002), pp. 1590 ff.; Sluiter, *Evidence* (2002), pp. 81 ff.; Ambos, *FYbIL*, 9 (1998), 413 ff.; Schomburg et al., *Internationale Rechtshilfe* (2020), p. 3; Vervaele and Klip, *European Cooperation* (2002), pp. 35–6; Kreß, in Grützner et al., *Rechtshilfeverkehr* (2003), IV A 1 mn. 205; Kreß and Prost, 'Part 9—Preliminary Remarks', in Ambos, *Commentary* (2022), mn. 5; Wilkitzki, *ICLR*, 2 (2002), 198; Meißner, *Zusammenarbeit* (2003), pp. 10 ff., 275 ff.

[15] Nagel, *Beweisaufnahme im Ausland* (1988), p. 72; Grützner, in Bassiouni and Nanda, *Treatise on ICL II* (1973), pp. 234–5; Swart, in Cassese et al., *Rome Statute II* (2002), pp. 1590–1; Ciavola, in Cassese et al., *Problemi attuali* (2005), pp. 432–3; Sluiter, in Cassese, *Companion* (2009), p. 189.

[16] cf. Swart, in Cassese et al., *Rome Statute II* (2002), pp. 1590 ff.; Bassiouni, *Introduction ICL* (2013), pp. 487 ff.; Sluiter, *Evidence* (2002), pp. 81 ff.; Meißner, *Zusammenarbeit* (2003), pp. 12 ff.; McDermott, *ICLR*, 15 (2015), 283 ff.

[17] cf. Ambos, *EuCrL* (2018), pp. 411 ff. (setting out the different regimes within the CoE and the EU, the latter quickly advancing towards a system of mutual recognition); specifically on extradition, see Caeiro and João Costa, in Ambos and Rackow, *European Criminal Law* (2023), pp. 254–82; on other legal assistance, Bachmaier Winter, in ibid., pp. 283–305; and on police cooperation, ibid., pp. 306–26; see also Stahn, *Introduction ICL* (2019), p. 233.

[18] cf. Art. 25 UN Charter.

[19] e.g. Arts. 29 ICTYS, 28 ICTRS, and 28 IRMCTS.

[20] cf. Chaumette, *ICLR*, 4 (2004), 357 ff.; Schomburg, in Kirsch, *Internationale Strafgerichtshöfe* (2005), pp. 129 ff.; Zahar and Sluiter, *ICL* (2008), pp. 462 ff.; Sluiter, in Cassese, *Companion* (2009), p. 192; Boas et al., *International Criminal Procedure* (2011), pp. 48–9 with various case law references; Bisset, *ICLR*, 20 (2020), 556; Klamberg, *Evidence* (2013), pp. 232–4. On the cooperation with the STL, see Swart, *JICJ*, 5 (2007), 1153 ff.; Korecki, *JICJ*, 7 (2009), 928 ff.

[21] cf. Sluiter, *Evidence* (2002), pp. 63 ff. (referring to the ones between the USA and the ICTY/ICTR); Godinho, *JICJ*, 1 (2003), 502 ff.; in favour, however, Kushen, *JICJ*, 1 (2003), 517 ff.

ensure that domestic cooperation legislation exists. The Statutes themselves do usually not provide for any reason or ground for noncompliance and even conflicting national laws or international treaty obligations cannot be used to justify a refusal to cooperate.[22] A failure to comply with a cooperation request can lead, at least in theory, to the imposition of sanctions by the UN Security Council against the State in question.[23]

In contrast, for the ICC, being treaty-based, most States did not envisage such a cooperation regime of strict verticality.[24] Thus, during the negotiations, the less ICC-friendly States advocated a regime of cooperation modelled after the traditional horizontal regime of interstate assistance, whereas the like-minded States proposed a *sui generis* type of cooperation regime that would reflect the ICC's special status.[25] In the end, the delegates opted for a *mixed regime of cooperation*, which is, on the one hand, less vertical than that of the ad hoc tribunals but, on the other, extends beyond a mere horizontal interstate cooperation regime.[26] It has been called a 'two pillar system', consisting of a judicial pillar (ICC) and an enforcement pillar (State Parties).[27] This compromise solution can be explained with the fact that the ICC Statute is the result of a controversially negotiated international treaty rather than a resolution imposed by the Security Council.

[22] cf. *Blaškić*, IT-95-14, paras. 26, 47, 54, and 63, as well as Arts. 25, 103 Charter of the UN. See also Kreß, in Grützner et al., *Rechtshilfeverkehr* (2003), IV A 2 mn. 57; Swart, in Cassese et al., *Rome Statute II* (2002), pp. 1592 ff.; Ciampi, in Cassese et al., *Rome Statute II* (2002), pp. 1610–11; Cassese, *ICL* (2013), pp. 347–8; Sluiter, *Evidence* (2002), pp. 47 ff., 139 ff.; Zahar and Sluiter, *ICL* (2008), pp. 326–7.

[23] *Blaškić*, IT-95-14, paras. 33 ff. and Rules 7*bis*, 11, 59 (B), and 61 (E) RPE ICTY/ICTR and Rules 8, 13, 61 (B), and 63 (E) RPE MICT; referring to *Blaškić*, ICC, *Prosecutor v. Harun and Kushayb*, PTC, Decision Informing the United Nations Security Council about the Lack of Cooperation by the Republic of the Sudan, ICC-02/05-01/07-57, 25 May 2010, p. 6; *Al Bashir*, ICC-02/05-01/09-195, para. 34 and p. 17. See also ICTR, *Prosecutor v. Nzabonimana*, TC, Decision on Nzabonimana's Motion Asking the Chamber to Request the President to Report the Matter of France's Refusal to Cooperate to the Security Council, ICTR-98-44D-T, 19 October 2009, para. 18, arguing that the imposition of sanctions is only an option where a breach of the duty to cooperate was 'deliberate, in bad faith, or ... intended to impede the fair and expeditious conduct of the proceedings'; furthermore, the calling of the SC should be a last resort. cf. also Schomburg, in Kirsch, *Internationale Strafgerichtshöfe* (2005), p. 132; Scharf, *DePaulLR*, 49 (2000), 938 ff.; Zahar and Sluiter, *ICL* (2008), pp. 472 ff.; Boas et al., *International Criminal Procedure* (2011), pp. 65–6 (correctly pointing to the rare exercise of the sanctioning powers by the Security Council); furthermore, see Stahn, *Introduction ICL* (2019), p. 234 and Vasiliev, in Cryer et al., *Introduction ICL* (2019), p. 502 (more sceptical than Friman in the previous edition).

[24] But see the language in ICC, *Prosecutor v. Gaddafi and Al-Senussi*, Defence (OPCD), Public Redacted Version of the 'Response to the Request to Postpone the Surrender of Mr Saif Al Islam Gaddafi Pursuant to Article 95 of the Statute', ICC-01/11-01/11-141-Red, 11 May 2012, para. 37 (vertical cooperation regime with regard to Art. 13 (b) referrals as compared to 'horizontal' Art. 13 (a) and (c) referrals). See also ICC, *Prosecutor v. Al-Bashir*, AC, Judgment in the Jordan Referral re Al-Bashir Appeal, ICC-02/05-01/09-397, 6 May 2019, paras. 121–32 (on the vertical dimension of the cooperation regime concerning arrest and surrender) and paras. 135–43 (on the scope of Art. 13 referrals).

[25] In detail on the negotiations, Mochochoko, in Lee, *ICC* (1999), pp. 305 ff.; Kreß, *EJCCLCJ*, 6 (1998), 449–50; Kreß and Prost, 'Part 9—Preliminary Remarks', in Ambos, *Commentary* (2022), mn. 5; Schabas, *ICC Commentary* (2016), pp. 1265 ff.; cf. also Raspail, 'Article 88', in Fernandez et al., *Commentaire CPI II* (2019), pp. 2201 ff.; Kreß and Prost, 'Article 88', in Ambos, *Commentary* (2022), mn. 1–3; Hiéramente, 'Article 88', in Klamberg et al., *Commentary ICC II* (2023), pp. 657–8; Prost, *JICJ*, 16 (2018), 364 ('Part 9 ... had not received much attention from those focused on the highly sensitive political issues in New York and Rome') and Sluiter, *JICJ*, 16 (2018), 384 ('drafters did not focus to any significant degree on a situation of conflict between States Parties and the Court').

[26] For examples of horizontal and vertical elements, see Kreß, in Grützner et al., *Rechtshilfeverkehr* (2003), IV A 1 mn. 206; Swart, in Cassese et al., *Rome Statute II* (2002), pp. 1594 ff.; Kreß and Prost, 'Part 9—Preliminary Remarks', in Ambos, *Commentary* (2022), mn. 5; Ambos, *FYbIL*, 9 (1998), 413 ff.; Sluiter, *Evidence* (2002), pp. 82 ff.; Meißner, *Zusammenarbeit* (2003), pp. 275 ff.; Caeiro, in Caeiro and Moreira, *TPI* (2004), p. 69; Schomburg, in Kirsch, *Internationale Strafgerichtshöfe* (2005), pp. 133 ff.; Kreß and Wannek, in Kirsch, *Internationale Strafgerichtshöfe* (2005), p. 256; Cryer, *Prosecuting* (2005), pp. 149 ff.; Palma, in Malaguti, *Cooperation* (2007), pp. 203 ff.; Rastan, *LJIL*, 21 (2008), 432 ff.; Klamberg, *Evidence* (2013), pp. 235, 236, 241, 259; crit. Damaška, *UCLA JIL & ForAff*, 14 (2009), 24; furthermore, see Stahn, *Introduction ICL* (2019), pp. 235 ff.; Bekou, *ICLR*, 19 (2019), 913.

[27] Rastan, in Stahn and Sluiter, *ICC* (2009), pp. 164–5.

At any rate, the vertical–horizontal dichotomy should not be overstated. In practical terms, the Security Council has not in fact ever asserted its supranational authority to enforce ICTY/ICTR findings of non-compliance or to assist the ad hoc tribunals otherwise. In fact, as concerns the ICTY, enforcement has largely been carried out by other actors such as the EU, NATO, and the World Bank—a quite unique situation as compared to other ad hoc tribunals and the ICC.[28] Also, the fact that the ICC can refer non-compliance to the UNSC in case of UNSC referrals, as will be seen in the following sub-section, creates the mirror image of ICTY/ICTR, at least in terms of normative hierarchy. Hence, from a practical perspective, verticalism in the context of the ad hoc tribunals may bear very little distinction with the ICC 'mixed' model.[29]

### (2) Cooperation obligations and non-compliance

The general obligation to cooperate pursuant to Article 86 ICCS,[30] to be looked at more closely below,[31] only applies to State Parties. A State not Party to the Statute[32] may be invited to cooperate on the basis of an ad hoc arrangement or agreement or 'any other appropriate basis'[33] pursuant to Article 87 (5) ICCS.[34] Otherwise, a non-State Party can only be obliged to cooperate either where it voluntarily lodges an Article 12 (3) declaration accepting the exercise of jurisdiction by the Court,[35] or where the Security Council refers a situation to the Court,[36] thereby imposing, inter alia,[37] cooperation obligations on the respective UN Member State pursuant to the binding effect of Security Council resolutions under Chapter VII of the UN

[28] See also Mettraux et al., *Expert Initiative Effectiveness ICC* (2014), p. 242 (para. 5); in the same vein, Stahn, *Introduction ICL* (2019), pp. 234–5; Carter et al., *Global Justice* (2018), pp. 117 ff.

[29] cf. Rastan, in Stahn and Sluiter, *ICC* (2009), pp. 166–9.

[30] See in this regard, on abstract (primary) and concrete (secondary) cooperation obligations (the latter referring to concrete requests), Kreß and Prost, 'Article 87', in Ambos, *Commentary* (2022), mn. 48.

[31] Section B.(1) in this chapter.

[32] For a detailed analysis of the relationship between the ICC and non-State Parties, see Cryer, in Stahn and Sluiter, *ICC* (2009), pp. 115 ff.; Cryer, in Stahn, *Practice* (2015), pp. 262 ff; Klamberg, *Evidence* (2013), pp. 235–7.

[33] According to Rastan, *LJIL*, 21 (2008), 442 with note 46 this applies to UNSC referrals where the regime is no ad hoc arrangement or agreement.

[34] In more detail, Kreß and Prost, 'Article 87', in Ambos, *Commentary* (2022), mn. 31–42; also Kowalski, 'Article 86', in Klamberg et al., *Commentary ICC II* (2023), pp. 613–23; Kowalski, 'Article 87', in Klamberg et al., *Commentary ICC II* (2023), pp. 637–43; previously Sluiter, *Evidence* (2002), pp. 68 ff.; Ciampi, in Cassese et al., *Rome Statute II* (2002), pp. 1615 ff.; Palmisano, in Lattanzi and Schabas, *Rome Statute I* (2000), pp. 402 ff.; Zahar and Sluiter, *ICL* (2008), pp. 465 ff.; furthermore, see Bekou, *ICLR*, 19 (2019), 915.

[35] See Chapter III, A.(4)(a)(iii) in this volume. Rule 44 provides that such a declaration entails the consequence that 'the provisions of Part 9, and any rules thereunder concerning State Parties, shall apply'. Thereon Rastan, 'Article 72', in Ambos, *Commentary* (2022), mn. 42.

[36] Art. 13 (b) ICCS.

[37] See, for a broader language (application of 'entire legal framework of the Statute' in case of UNSC referrals) ICC, *Prosecutor v. Banda and Jerbo*, TC IV, Decision on 'Defence Application pursuant to Articles 57 (3) (b) & 64 (6)(a) of the Statute for an order for the preparation and transmission of a cooperation request to the Government of Sudan', ICC-02/05-03/09-169, 1 July 2011, para. 15; *Prosecutor v. Gaddafi and Al Senussi*, PTC I, Decision on the Postponement of the Execution of the Request for Surrender of Saif Al-Islam Gaddafi pursuant to Article 95 of the Rome Statute, ICC-01/11-01/11-163, 1 June 2012, paras. 28–30 and PTC I, Decision on the 'Urgent Application on behalf of Abdullah Al-Senussi for Pre-Trial Chamber to order the Libyan Authorities to comply with their obligations and the orders of the ICC', ICC-01/11-01/11-269, 6 February 2013, para. 21; ICC, *Prosecutor v. Gaddafi*, PTC I, Decision on the Non-compliance by Libya with Requests for Cooperation by the Court and Referring the Matter to the United Nations Security Council, ICC-01/11-01/11-577, 10 December 2014, para. 21; *Prosecutor v. Al Bashir*, PTC II, Decision on the Prosecutor's Request for a Finding of Non-compliance against the Republic of the Sudan, ICC-02/05-01/09-227, 9 March 2015, paras. 15, 19; ICC-OTP, *Policy Case Selection* (2016), para. 28.

Charter.[38] Thus, one must distinguish between three scenarios:[39] (i) a general cooperation obligation, which only applies to State Parties[40] and, with regard to non-State Parties, (ii) a voluntary obligation on the basis of an Article 12 (3) declaration or an ad hoc arrangement, and so forth pursuant to Article 87 (5), or (iii) an obligation pursuant to a Security Council Resolution.

In temporal terms, the cooperation obligation is activated after the (preliminary) examination phase, that is, when the ICC-OTP commences a (formal) investigation,[41] be it upon the PTC authorization[42] or with the Prosecutor's own decision to do so.[43] At the preliminary examination stage itself there is no cooperation obligation since Article 86 ICCS refers to 'investigation and prosecution'. It may be in the interests of States to cooperate with the OTP,[44] especially with regard to a possible complementarity objection, but they are not obliged to do so. As we will see below,[45] States may also have some national security concerns and may want to communicate to the OTP as early as possible.

As regards the *non-compliance* with a cooperation obligation, the same threefold distinction applies:[46] where a State Party fails to fulfil its cooperation obligation, thereby incurring

[38] Art. 25 UN Charter. See also ICC, *Prosecutor v. Al Bashir*, PTC I, Decision on the Prosecution's Application for a Warrant of Arrest against Omar Hassan Ahmad Al Bashir, ICC-02/05-01/09-3, 4 March 2009, paras. 242–9; *Banda and Jerbo*, ICC-02/05-03/09-169, para. 14; ICC, *Prosecutor v. Gaddafi and Al-Senussi*, PTC I, Decision on Libya's Submissions Regarding the Arrest of Saif Al-Islam Gaddafi, ICC-01/11-01/11-72-Conf, 7 Mar. 2012, paras. 12–13; ICC, *Prosecutor v. Al Bashir*, PTC II, Decision on the Prosecutor's Request for a Finding of Non-Compliance against the Republic of the Sudan, ICC-02/05-01/09-227, 9 March 2015, paras. 13–15; *Prosecutor v. Al Bashir*, AC, Judgment in the Jordan Referral re Al-Bashir Appeal, ICC-02/05-01/09 OA2, 6 May 2019, paras. 140–1; cf. also Kreß and Prost, 'Article 86', in Ambos, *Commentary* (2022), mn. 3.

[39] On these three scenarios, see ICC, *Prosecutor v. Gaddafi and Al-Senussi*, PTC I, Decision on the Request of the Defence of Abdullah Al-Senussi to Make a Finding of Non-cooperation by the Islamic Republic of Mauritania and Refer the Matter to the Security Council, ICC-01/11-01/11-420, 28 August 2013, para. 12; cf. also Kowalski, 'Article 86', in Klamberg et al., *Commentary ICC II* (2023), pp. 613–23.

[40] Art. 86 ICCS; ICC, *Prosecutor v. Al Bashir*, PTC I, Corrigendum to the Decision Pursuant to Article 87 (7) of the Rome Statute on the Failure by the Republic of Malawi to Comply with the Cooperation Requests Issued by the Court with Respect to the Arrest and Surrender of Omar Hassan Ahmad Al Bashir, ICC-02/05-01/09-139-Corr, 12 December 2011, p. 21; *Prosecutor v. Al Bashir*, PTC I, Decision pursuant to Article 87 (7) of the Rome Statute on the Refusal of the Republic of Chad to Comply with the Cooperation Requests Issued by the Court with Respect to the Arrest and Surrender of Omar Hassan Ahmad Al Bashir, ICC-02/05-01/09-140-tENG, 13 Dec. 2011, para. 9 and p. 8; *Prosecutor v. Al Bashir*, PTC II, Decision Regarding Omar Al-Bashir's Visit to the Federal Republic of Nigeria, ICC-02/05-01/09-157, 15 July 2013, para. 7; *Prosecutor v. Kenyatta*, TC V(B), Decision on Prosecution's Application for a Finding of Non-compliance under Article 87 (7) of the Statute, ICC-01/09-02/11-982, 3 December 2014, para. 37; *Prosecutor v. Al Bashir*, PTC II, Decision under Article 87 (7) of the Rome Statute on the Non-compliance by South Africa with the Request by the Court for the Arrest and Surrender of Omar Al-Bashir, ICC-02/05-01/09-302, 6 July 2017, para. 61; cf. also Klamberg, *Evidence* (2013), p. 264.

[41] On the distinction between the preliminary examination and the formal investigation, see Chapter IV, A.(1) in this volume.

[42] Art. 15 (4) ICCS.

[43] Art. 53 (1) ICCS; see also ICC-OTP, *Complementarity* (2003), p. 10; ICC-OTP, *Fact-finding* (2003), p. 7; ICC-OTP, *Complementarity and Cooperation* (2024), para. 146; Kreß and Prost, 'Article 86', in Ambos, *Commentary* (2022), mn. 11–14.

[44] Originally, within the OTP, the 'Jurisdiction, Cooperation and Complementarity Division' (JCCD) dealt with matters of cooperation. Subsequently, however, the OTP introduced a 'revised cooperation model', according to which the JCCD is responsible for taking care of the strategic contacts of the cooperation network, whereas the operative contacts are in the hands of the 'Investigation Division' (ICC-OTP, *Strategic Plan* (2013), para. 64); under the current Prosecutor the JCCD has been abolished (Chapter II, B.(2)). In any case, it is to be noted that the OTP has only limited means to carry out the necessary investigations (ibid., para. 19); cf. also Bergsmo and Bekou, 'Article 54', in Ambos, *Commentary* (2022), mn. 34 with further references on such agreements in note 35. On the reality of the OTP cooperation with other actors when investigating cases, where the 'cooperation is largely outside the control of the office' and therefore 'the investigative practice of the office must adjust to different circumstances', see Whiting, *LCP*, 76, nos. 3 & 4 (2013), 182–5, arguing that '[t]he difficulty ... is not with the specified forms of cooperation, but rather with the enforcement'.

[45] cf. Section B.(2)(a)(ii) in this chapter.

[46] See generally Ciampi, in Cassese et al., *Rome Statute II* (2002), pp. 1608 ff.; Sluiter, *Evidence* (2002), pp. 67 ff.; Schomburg, in Kirsch, *Internationale Strafgerichtshöfe* (2005), p. 137; Zahar and Sluiter, *ICL* (2008), pp. 474 ff.;

an international wrongful act,[47] the ICC 'may make a finding to that effect'[48] and refer the case to the ASP or, where the Security Council referred the matter to the Court, to the Council;[49] or it may 'otherwise address the lack of cooperation by the requested State'.[50] On determining whether a referral to the ASP or the Security Council would be appropriate or not, it should be kept in mind that 'non-compliance proceedings and proceedings against an accused before the Court are distinct proceedings' and 'the interests and rights at stake are not interchangeable between these two'.[51] Thus, the 'future cooperation by the requested State is indeed a factor to be taken into account when deciding on the appropriateness of a referral', regardless of the status of the proceedings against the accused.[52] At any rate, the discussion about the recipient of the referral of a non-cooperation finding seems somewhat moot given that so far neither the ASP nor the Security Council has taken any action in that regard.[53] To be sure, both have this authority—the UNSC pursuant to Chapter VII of the UN Charter[54] and the ASP pursuant to the (customary) law on State responsibility given that the non-compliance amounts, as just said, to an international wrongful act permitting countermeasures[55]—but they should also use it by imposing sanctions on non-compliant State Parties.[56]

Sluiter, in Cassese, *Companion* (2009), p. 199; Schabas, *ICC Commentary* (2016), pp. 1278–9, 1439–40; Ciampi, 'Article 87', in Fernandez et al., *Commentaire CPI II* (2019), pp. 2192 ff.; Klamberg, *Evidence* (2013), pp. 258–61; Kreß and Prost, 'Article 87', in Ambos, *Commentary* (2022), mn. 48–68.

[47] cf. Bekou, *ICLR*, 19 (2019), 926; Kreß and Prost, 'Article 87', in Ambos, *Commentary* (2022), mn. 49 discussing the respective ILC Articles. Also see Turlan, in Bekou and Birkett, *Cooperation* (2016), p. 61 stressing that Art. 86 ICCS 'does not provide for a remedy in case of failure to execute this obligation [to cooperate]'.

[48] For Boschiero, *JICJ*, 13 (2015), 636, '[t]he competence of the Court to make a judicial finding on non-cooperation strengthens the vertical structure of the ICC cooperation regime'; yet, it is questionable whether there exists such a 'vertical structure' in the first place or rather a mixed regime, as argued in note 26 in this chapter. Sceptical , Sluiter and Talontsi, in Bekou and Birkett, *Cooperation* (2016), p. 91 ('the judicial finding on States' co-operation is a form of dispute settlement that does not fit into the realms of criminal procedure').

[49] Arts. 87 (7) and 112 (2)(f) ICCS. Crit. Sluiter, *JICJ*, 16 (2018), 307–8 ('the relevant Chamber does not bear the final responsibility'; 'when the Article 87(7) proceedings are of insufficient quality, this will inevitably affect the follow-up phase at the ASP or UNSC'); furthermore, see Ochs, *MichJIL*, 42 (2021), 588 (criticizing the fact that 'the Rome Statute lacks any defined repercussions that may complement this type of referral').

[50] cf. *Prosecutor v. Kenyatta*, AC, Judgment on the Prosecutor's Appeal against Trial Chamber V(B)'s 'Decision on Prosecution's Application for a Finding of Non-compliance under Article 87 (7) of the Statute', ICC-01/09-02/11-1032, 19 August 2015, paras. 1, 41 ff., 55, holding that the discretionary power of the Chambers comprises both whether to make or not make a finding of non-compliance and 'whether it is appropriate to refer the matter to the ASP or the UNSC in order to seek external assistance to obtain cooperation with the request at issue or to otherwise address the lack of cooperation by the requested State'. See also *Al Bashir*, ICC-02/05-01/09-139, para. 47; *Al Bashir*, ICC-02/05-01/09-140 tENG, para. 14, *Al Bashir*, ICC-02/05-01/09-195, para. 34. Crit. on the broad discretionary approach of the *Kenyatta* TC Kreß and Prost, 'Article 87', in Ambos, *Commentary* (2022), mn. 60 ff. (62). We have, of course, argued already that the ICC regime is rather a mixed one, see above note 26 and main text.

[51] *Kenyatta*, ICC-01/09-02/11-1032, para. 73.

[52] Ibid., para. 77.

[53] Crit. also Kreß and Prost, 'Article 87', in Ambos, *Commentary* (2022), mn. 67; Fulford, *AJIL*, 112 (2018), 169 ('Assembly of States Parties seems to have little appetite for reprimanding states'); also Bekou, *ICLR*, 19 (2019), 915–16 (defending the combination of a Chamber finding on non-cooperation with referral to the ASP as 'entirely appropriate': 'This two-pronged approach … aims to tackle non-cooperation by utilising both legal and political tools'). Crit. of the lack of support of the UNSC re the Libya and Sudan situations Sluiter, *JICJ* 16 (2018), 388 and Carter et al., *Global Justice* (2018), p. 134.

[54] See also Kreß and Prost, 'Article 87', in Ambos, *Commentary* (2022), mn. 39. According to Mettraux et al., *Effectiveness ICC* (2014), p. 43 (para. 194) and p. 244 (para. 9) the UNSC should include possible sanctions in the referral resolution.

[55] Kreß and Prost, 'Article 87', in Ambos, *Commentary* (2022), mn. 66.

[56] In this vein, see Mettraux et al., *Effectiveness ICC* (2014), p. 43 (para. 190) and pp. 243–4 (para. 8) (alternatively advocating the suspension of the voting rights of non-compliant State Parties).

With regard to a non-State Party bound by an ad hoc arrangement or agreement,[57] the ICC may also—albeit without making the above mentioned judicial finding—refer the matter to the ASP or—in case of a UNSC referral—to the Security Council.[58] In the latter case, the non-compliance can be communicated to the Council.[59] If the cooperation obligation is only derived from the respective UNSC referral resolution, that is, the non-State Party has not entered into an ad hoc agreement, it has been argued in some case law that the Court is vested with 'inherent powers' to inform the Security Council about an instance of non-compliance.[60] Recourse to the 'inherent powers' was deemed necessary as the Statute does not contain any sanction mechanism for this scenario (in particular Article 87 (7) does not help since it explicitly refers to a 'State Party').[61] Other Chambers have applied Article 87 (7), despite its clear wording, to non-State Parties, arguing that they are to be treated like State Parties by way of the UNSC referral.[62]

Neither of these solutions is convincing. On the one hand, given the determination of the cooperation obligation by the Security Council in this situation—indeed, the scenario is comparable to the above mentioned vertical cooperation regime common to Security Council established ad hoc tribunals with the ensuing enforcement authority of the Council[63]—the ICCS can, in principle, neither impose any rights or obligations on a *non*-State Party nor establish the

[57] In favour of a limited duty for non-State Parties to cooperate, in absence of an ad hoc agreement, on the basis of the 'responsibility to protect', see Benzing, in König et al., *International Law Today* (2008), p. 32.

[58] Art. 87 (5)(b) ICCS. In the same vein, Klamberg, *Evidence* (2013), p. 260. On the discussion of the formality of such an agreement, see on the one hand Heller, *Opinio Juris* 9 March 2016, arguing that Art. 87 (5) 'applies only when a non-party State makes a formal commitment to cooperate with the Court and then breaks that commitment… [not] any time a non-party State voluntarily provides the Court with information and then decides to stop providing it'; on the other hand, Kwast, *Opinio Juris* 16 March 2016, rejecting such 'a formality-condition into the text of 87(5)(b)'.

[59] cf. Kreß and Prost, 'Article 87', in Ambos, *Commentary* (2022), mn. 39 ('can be informed'); Bekou, *ICLR*, 19 (2019), 916 ('may be referred'). PTC II also 'informed the ASP', cf. *Al Bashir*, ICC-02/05-01/09-227, para. 19 and notification sheet. On the special role of the SC, cf. Palmisano, in Lattanzi and Schabas, *Rome Statute I* (2000), pp. 416 ff.; Gargiulo, in Lattanzi and Schabas, *Rome Statute I* (2000), pp. 100 ff.; Frau, *Verhältnis* (2010), pp. 238–9; crit. of the limited possibilities of enforcement, Wartanian, *GeoJIL*, 36 (2005), 1297–8; Cryer, *Prosecuting* (2005), pp. 159–60; crit. of the SC's unwillingness to follow up referrals of non-compliance, Cryer, in Stahn, *Practice* (2015), pp. 271–3 (Sudan), 273–5 (Libya); Ciampi, 'Article 87', in Fernandez et al., *Commentaire CPI II* (2019), pp. 2197–8; Kaye, *The Council and the Court* (2013), pp. 4 ff.; thereon also ICC Prosecutor, 'Statement to the United Nations Security Council on the Situation in Darfur, pursuant to UNSCR 1593 (2005)' (29 June 2015), <http://www.icc-cpi.int/en_menus/icc/press%20and%20media/press%20releases/Pages/29-06-15-otp-report-unsc.aspx>, paras. 28 ff., urging the SC, in the light of 'the number of such non-compliance communications to the Council [amounting] to ten' (para. 28) 'to ensure Sudan's compliance with UN Security Council Resolution 1593, and equally call on States Parties to the Rome Statute to promote cooperation and effect the arrest of individuals wanted by the ICC in the Darfur situation' (para. 32).

[60] *Harun and Kushayb*, ICC-02/05-01/07-57, p. 6; crit. thereon Kreß and Prost, 'Article 87', in Ambos, *Commentary* (2022), mn. 39–40. See also ICC, *Prosecutor v. Gaddafi and Al-Senussi*, Renewed Application on behalf of Mr Abdullah Al-Senussi to Refer Libya and Mauritania to the UN Security Council with Public Annex 1 and Confidential and Ex Parte (Registry only) Annexes 2 and 3, ICC-01/11-01/11-304, 19 March 2013, paras. 11 ff. In this case the Court invokes, inter alia, a decision of the ICTY AC (*Blaškić*, IT-95-14, para. 33) but this is misleading since the Court is not—unlike the ICTY—a Security Council organ established under Chapter VII of the UN Charter; crit. also Klamberg, *Evidence* (2013), pp. 260–1. On the differences between the ad hoc tribunals and the ICC in that regard, see also Wenqui, *IRRC*, 88 (2006), 94 ff., 108. Generally on the recognition of the 'doctrine of implied powers' in Art. 4 (1) ICCS, *Prosecutor v. Ruto and Sang*, Decision on Prosecutor's Application for Witness Summonses and Resulting Request for State Party Cooperation, ICC-01/09-01/11-1274-Corr2, 17 April 2014, para. 83.

[61] cf. Sluiter, *JICJ*, 6 (2008), 884 ('[I]f the ICC Statute is to apply in substance to states non-parties, it should explicitly say so').

[62] cf. *Al Bashir*, ICC-02/05-01/09-3, para. 248; *Prosecutor v. Gaddafi*, PTC I, Decision on the Non-compliance by Libya with Requests for Cooperation by the Court and Referring the Matter to the United Nations Security Council, ICC-01/11-01/11-577, 10 December 2014, paras. 20–2 (finding Libya in non-compliance under Art. 87 (7)).

[63] See above note 23 and main text.

procedure to be followed in case of a failure to cooperate.[64] On the other hand, in the absence of an alternative (Security Council) cooperation procedure, Part 9 of the Statute remains applicable.[65] Yet, the clear wording of Article 87 (7) excludes an application of this provision to non-State Parties. Treating these like State Parties by way of a UNSC referral undermines this provision and the will of the drafters. Still, it is not necessary to invoke the concept of inherent powers to allow the Court to refer the non-compliance of a non-State Party to the Council. Instead one could apply Article 87 (5)(b) ICCS by way of analogy considering that the Security Council referral replaces the lacking ad hoc agreement.[66] In fact, the UNSC referral could be considered the 'other appropriate basis' mentioned in Article 85 (5)(a); the omission of this part in the following subparagraph (b) seems to be a mere drafting error.[67]

Before making a non-compliance finding, a Chamber should first hear the requested State[68] unless that would be futile since the respective State 'has constantly refused to engage in any sort of dialogue with the responsible organs of the Court'.[69] In making the finding the Chamber 'should take into account all relevant factors, including the evidence that was required in the cooperation request and the conduct of the parties to the proceedings', 'whether ... judicial measures to obtain the cooperation had been exhausted and consultations had reached a deadlock'.[70]

## B. The cooperation regime in more detail

### (1) General aspects

The cooperation rules between international criminal tribunals and the national jurisdictions are normally laid down in *specific procedural laws*.[71] This model follows, for example, Germany, where the Law on Cooperation with the ICC ('ICC Cooperation Act') has been adopted;[72] similarly, in Australia, the rules can be found in the ICC Act of 2002;[73] in Canada,

[64] See, in detail, Ntoubandi, *ZaöRV*, 69 (2009), 142 ff.; also Akande, *JICJ*, 10 (2012), 308.

[65] cf. *Banda and Jerbo*, ICC-02/05-03/09-169, para. 15 (holding that in case of non-State Parties the SC Resolution obliging them to cooperate 'does not provide for an autonomous legal regime for cooperation that would replace the ICC regime or represent an alternative to it' and therefore 'the cooperation regime of the Statute under Part 9' is applicable); conc. Kreß and Prost, 'Article 86', in Ambos, *Commentary* (2022), mn. 3; Kreß and Prost, 'Article 95', in Ambos, *Commentary* (2022), mn. 5; *contra Gaddafi and Al-Senussi*, ICC-01/11-01/11-141-Red (OPCD), para. 33 ('patently inadequate').

[66] In this vein, Kreß and Prost, 'Article 87', in Ambos, *Commentary* (2022), mn. 39 (to avoid the otherwise 'absurd result'), 40 (instead of inherent powers).

[67] In a similar vein, Rastan, 'Article 72', in Ambos, *Commentary* (2022), mn. 42 with note 163.

[68] Reg. 109 (3) RegC.

[69] *Al Bashir*, ICC-02/05-01/09-227, para. 19.

[70] *Kenyatta*, ICC-01/09-02/11-1032, para. 95; confirmed in *Prosecutor v. Kenyatta*, TC V(b), Second Decision on Prosecution's Application for a Finding of Non-compliance under Article 87 (7) of the Statute, ICC-01/09-02/11-1037, 19 September 2016, para. 17.

[71] See e.g. the Belgian Cooperation Law, *Loi concernant la coopération avec la Cour pénale internationale et les tribunaux pénaux internationaux*, 29 March 2004 (last amended on 6 December 2022 by *Loi visant à rendre la justice plus humaine, plus rapide et plus ferme IIbis*), <https://www.ejustice.just.fgov.be/cgi_loi/change_lg.pl?language=fr&la=F&cn=2004032930&table_name=loi>.

[72] *Gesetz über die Zusammenarbeit mit dem Internationalen Strafgerichtshof*, BGBl 2002 I, 2144, last amended by Art. 6 of the Act of 10 December 2019: BGBl 2019 I, 2128; <https://www.gesetze-im-internet.de/istghg/IStGHG.pdf>; English translation available at <https://www.gesetze-im-internet.de/englisch_istghg/englisch_istghg.pdf>. For *Austria*, see the 'Bundesgesetz über die Zusammenarbeit mit dem Internationalen Strafgerichtshof' (BGBl 2002 I, Nr. 135; last amended by BGBl 2020 I, Nr. 20); original version <https://www.ris.bka.gv.at/GeltendeFassung/Bundesnormen/20002154/IStGH-ZG%2c%20Fassung%20vom%2023.05.2023.pdf>. For *Switzerland*, see the 'Bundesgesetz über die Zusammenarbeit mit dem Internationalen Strafgerichtshof' (AS 2002 1493; last amended by AS 2019 625); original version in German, French, and Italian at: <https://www.fedlex.admin.ch/eli/cc/2002/237/de>.

[73] <https://www.legislation.gov.au/Details/C2021C00313>.

the Extradition Act[74] and the Mutual Legal Assistance in Criminal Matters Act[75] have been amended to ensure an efficient cooperation with the ICC; the Netherlands adopted the ICC (Implementation) Act in 2002;[76] France adjusted its *Code de Procédure Pénale* in 2002.[77] Departing from this model, however, the UK adopted the ICC Act of 2001, where besides the rules on cooperation with the ICC also rules of substantive and procedural law are to be found.[78]

Very much like the interstate regime of horizontal cooperation (mutual assistance), the cooperation with international criminal tribunals encompasses *three areas*: arrest and surrender of persons, other legal assistance, and execution of sentences and other decisions.[79] The first two areas are regulated together,[80] but separately from the enforcement regime,[81] to be analysed more closely in the following chapter. Despite this formal separation, there is a factual connection insofar as both arrest/surrender/other legal assistance and execution of sentences/other decisions concern the cooperation between States and the tribunals.[82] The tribunals require the cooperation of States both in the investigation and adjudication phase as well as in the enforcement phase. Due to this factual connection, Parts 9 and 10 of the ICC Statute were initially discussed together under the heading of 'international cooperation and judicial assistance'.[83] As to the structure of cooperation, however, the cooperation in the area of enforcement seems less 'vertical' than the surrender of persons and the other legal assistance.[84]

### *(a) ICC*

Part 9 ICCS contains general and specific provisions on cooperation establishing a kind of minimum standard which States are free to improve (enhanced cooperation).[85] The

[74] <https://www.laws-lois.justice.gc.ca/PDF/E-23.01.pdf>.

[75] <https://laws-lois.justice.gc.ca/PDF/M-13.6.pdf>.

[76] English version available at <https://cjad.nottingham.ac.uk/en/legislation/54/keyword/512/>.

[77] cf. Loi No. 2002-268 du 26 février 2002 relative à la coopération avec la Cour Pénale Internationale, <https://www.legifrance.gouv.fr/loda/id/JORFTEXT000000776756>, to include matters of cooperation with the ICC.

[78] <https://www.legislation.gov.uk/ukpga/2001/17/contents>.

[79] Sluiter, *Evidence* (2002), p. 7; Calvo-Goller, *Trial Proceedings* (2006), p. 204. cf. also ICC-ASP, *Report Cooperation* (2014) (on recommendations for the improvement of cooperation between the ICC and State Parties, international organizations, and NGOs); generally, Ambos and Gronke, in Ambos et al., *Rechtshilferecht* (2020), pp. 69–70.

[80] cf. Art. 29 ICTYS, Art. 28 ICTRS/IRMCTS, Art. 53 (1) KSC Law; Part 9 ICCS.

[81] cf. Art. 27 ICTYS, Art. 26 ICTRS, Art. 25 IRMCTS, Art. 50 KSC Law; Part 10 ICCS.

[82] cf. Kreß and Sluiter, in Cassese et al., *Rome Statute II* (2002), p. 1752; Kreß, in Grützner et al., *Rechtshilfeverkehr* (2003), IV A 1 mn. 203.

[83] cf. Kreß and Sluiter, in Cassese et al., *Rome Statute II* (2002), p. 1752.

[84] See also Chapter VIII, A., and B.(1)(a) with note 64 ff. and C. with notes 139 ff. and main text in this volume.

[85] cf. ICC, *Prosecutor v. Ruto and Sang*, AC, Judgment on the appeals of William Samoei Ruto and Mr Joshua Arap Sang against the decision of Trial Chamber V (A) of 17 April 2014 entitled 'Decision on Prosecutor's Application for Witness Summonses and Resulting Request for State Party Cooperation', ICC-01/09-01/11-1598, 9 October 2014, para. 112 ('Part 9 of the Statute generally and article 93 (1) of the Statute in particular, establish primarily *minimum* obligations of cooperation that States Parties have *vis-à-vis* the Court. However, States Parties are at liberty to cooperate more extensively with the Court, if they so wish (so-called "enhanced cooperation")' [emphasis in the original]; *Prosecutor v. Bemba et al.*, AC, Judgment on the Appeals of Mr Jean-Pierre Bemba Gombo, Mr Aimé Kilolo Musamba, Mr Jean-Jacques Mangenda Kabongo, Mr Fidèle Babala Wandu, and Mr Narcisse Arido against the Decision of Trial Chamber VII Entitled 'Judgment pursuant to Article 74 of the Statute', ICC-01/05-01/13-2275-Red, 8 March 2018, para. 319 ('while Part 9 of the Statute safeguards the competences of States, the Court may request, and the requested States may provide, forms or modalities of cooperation in addition to those foreseen in Part 9 of the Statute provided that they are not contrary to the Statute, including internationally recognised human rights, in accordance with article 21 (3) of the Statute'). See also the note by then ICC President, Silvia Fernández de Gurmendi, calling on the UN General Assembly for enhanced cooperation with the Court, 'ICC President addresses United Nations General Assembly, calls for enhanced cooperation and support', ICC-CPI-20171030-PR1341, 30 October 2017.

general provisions pertain mostly to common procedural rules that are just as applicable to the special provisions on surrender of persons[86] as to the other measures of legal assistance.[87] Furthermore, cooperation related provisions are not limited to Part 9 of the Statute—indeed, Article 86 itself refers to 'provisions of this Statute'[88]—but can be found throughout its text.[89] On the other hand, Part 5, primarily dealing with the investigation phase, contains with Article 54 (3)(c) a provision that authorizes the OTP to seek cooperation from States or intergovernmental organizations.[90] Finally, Rules 176–97 RPE ICC complement the provisions of Part 9.[91]

Article 86 ICCS provides for a *general cooperation obligation* of State Parties regarding the 'investigation and prosecution of crimes within the jurisdiction of the Court'.[92] It has been said that the provision 'amounts to an overarching *interpretative guideline*' giving answers to the 'somewhat indeterminate compromise formulas' of Part 9.[93] To meet this cooperation obligation, State Parties have not only to adjust their procedural laws accordingly but, more concretely, provide for concrete 'procedures ... for all of the forms of cooperation' specified in Part 9 of the Statute.[94] A State Party cannot decline a cooperation request arguing that its national law does not provide for one of the forms of cooperation provided for in Part 9 ICCS.[95]

With regard to the already mentioned general cooperation provisions, it is to be noted that the *transmission* of a cooperation request for surrender or other legal assistance should first be made via diplomatic or other appropriate means, as designated by the State Party concerned; the request may also be transmitted via *Interpol* or via any other appropriate regional organization.[96] Most State Parties have made declarations to that

[86] Arts. 89–92, 101–2 ICCS.

[87] Arts. 93–6, 99 ICCS.

[88] See also the references in Arts. 89 (2), 90 (2)(a), 95 ICCS.

[89] See e.g. Art. 57 (3)(b) (seeking of cooperation by PTC to assist suspect in defence), Art. 64 (6)(b) (attendance and testimony of witnesses required by TC), Art. 70 (2) in conjunction with Rule 167 RPE ICC (cooperation with regard to offences against administration of justice according to domestic law) and Art. 109 (cooperation of States regarding enforcement of fines and forfeiture measures). See also Kreß and Prost, 'Article 87', in Ambos, *Commentary* (2022), mn. 15 (State's obligation to cooperate 'is created through a combination of provisions', 'which must be read together', 'rather than a single general statement').

[90] On this interaction, cf. in detail Kreß and Prost, 'Part 9—Preliminary Remarks', in Ambos, *Commentary* (2022), mn. 3; Kreß, in Grützner et al., *Rechtshilfeverkehr* (2003), IV A 1 mn. 207; Bergsmo and Bekou, 'Article 54', in Ambos, *Commentary* (2022), mn. 30–4.

[91] Extensively on these provisons, Harhoff and Mochochoko, in Lee, *ICC* (2001), pp. 637 ff.; Gartner, in Fischer et al., *Prosecution* (2001), pp. 423 ff.

[92] In detail, Kreß and Prost, 'Article 86', in Ambos, *Commentary* (2022), mn. 1–16; previously Ciampi, in Cassese et al., *Rome Statute II* (2002), pp. 1612 ff.; Kreß, in Grützner et al., *Rechtshilfeverkehr* (2003), IV A 1 mn. 211 ff.; Meißner, *Zusammenarbeit* (2003), p. 39; Giannone, in Kühne et al., *Völkerstrafrecht* (2007), pp. 314–15; Mbaye, 'Article 86', in Fernandez et al., *Commentaire CPI II* (2019), p. 2147; furthermore, see Turlan, in Bekou and Birkett, *Cooperation* (2016), p. 61.

[93] Kreß and Prost, 'Article 86', in Ambos, *Commentary* (2022), mn. 10.

[94] Art. 88 ICCS; recommending concrete measures to manage cooperation requests 'efficiently and expediently', Mettraux et al., *Effectiveness ICC* (2014), pp. 42–3 (para. 189) and p. 243 (para. 7) (e.g. designating a contact person/office).

[95] cf. ICC, *Prosecutor v. Kenyatta*, TC, Decision on Prosecution's Applications for a Finding of Non-compliance pursuant to Article 87 (7) and for an Adjournment of the Provisional Trial Date, ICC-01/09-02/11-908, 31 March 2014, para. 47; cf. also Kreß and Prost, 'Article 88', in Ambos, *Commentary* (2022), mn. 4; Ciampi, in Cassese et al., *Rome Statute II* (2002), pp. 1621 ff.; Malaguti, in Malaguti, *Cooperation* (2007), pp. 103 ff.; Schabas, *ICC Commentary* (2016), pp. 1281 ff.; Raspail, 'Article 88', in Fernandez et al., *Commentaire CPI II* (2019), pp. 2201 ff.; Hiéramente, 'Article 88', in Klamberg et al., *Commentary ICC II* (2023), pp. 657–66.

[96] Art. 87 (1) ICCS. For the procedure, see Art. 87 (3) ICCS and Rules 176–7, 180 RPE ICC. In ICC, *Prosecutor v. Gaddafi*, PTC I, Decision on 'Decision on the Prosecutor's "Request for an order directing the Registrar to transmit the request for arrest and surrender to Mr al-'Ajami Al-'Atiri, Commander of the Abu-Bakr Al Siddiq Battalion in Zintan, Libya"', ICC-01/11-01/11-634-Red, 21 November 2016, paras. 13–16. PTC I highlighted that 'matters of transmission of cooperation requests are regulated comprehensively in article 87 of the Statute and rule 176 of the Rules'. Therefore, the Court had to communicate via the competent national authorities of

effect.[97] Thus, *Germany* stated that requests may be transmitted directly to the Ministry of Justice. Requests addressed to the ICC may also be made by the Ministry of Justice directly or by any other competent authority (with permission of the Ministry of Justice). Requests and other documents must however be translated into the German language.[98] In *France*, requests, always in French language, may be transmitted in cases of urgency by any means to the *Procureur de la République antiterroriste*, who shall then pass them through the diplomatic channel.[99] In the *UK*, requests are to be directed to the Secretary of State only[100] and only they may transmit information or requests to the ICC.[101] In *Canada*, requests are to be directed to the Minister of Justice.[102] Requests for provisional arrest only may also be made through Interpol.[103] The *Australian* law explicitly allows the ICC to transmit requests via the Attorney General or anyone they have delegated such power to, or 'through the International Criminal Police Organisation or any other appropriate regional organisation'.[104] For the *Netherlands*, Antilles, and Aruba, the ICC's requests are to be directed to the respective Minister of Justice or any 'authorities designated by him for this purpose'.[105] If they are however directed to another authority, this authority should forward them to the Minister.[106] Only the Minister of Justice is capable of requesting cooperation from the ICC, upon request of any Dutch authorities.[107]

If a State Party, whilst processing a request, notes problems that could prevent or impede its execution, the Court should be consulted immediately.[108] This, of course, does not mean that the said problems constitute, *ipso facto*, legitimate grounds of refusal or that the obligation to give effect to the request is suspended; rather, this is a different question to be decided by the Court.[109] The 'ordinary costs of execution', meaning the costs that emerge on its territory due to necessary measures for the execution, are to be borne by the requested State; all

Libya. Crit. Kreß and Prost, 'Article 87', in Ambos, *Commentary* (2022), mn. 17 ('The resulting problem with this strict approach ... is that the Court may face significant issues given the *de facto* authorities operating in several situations').

[97] The declarations are available at <https://treaties.un.org/pages/ViewDetails.aspx?src=IND&mtdsg_no=XVIII-10&chapter=18&clang=_en#EndDec>.

[98] The German declaration reads: 'The Federal Republic of Germany declares, pursuant to article 87 (1) of the Rome Statute, that requests from the Court can also be transmitted directly to the Federal Ministry of Justice or an agency designated by the Federal Ministry of Justice in an individual case. Requests to the Court can be transmitted directly from the Federal Ministry of Justice or, with the Ministry's agreement, from another competent agency to the Court. The Federal Republic of Germany further declares, pursuant to article 87 (2) of the Rome Statute, that requests for cooperation to Germany and any documents supporting the request must be accompanied by a translation into German' (<https://treaties.un.org/pages/ViewDetails.aspx?src=IND&mtdsg_no=XVIII-10&chapter=18&clang=_en#EndDec>). cf. also § 68 IStGHG.

[99] Art. 627-1 of the French *Code de Procédure Pénale.*

[100] Sections 1 (1) and 27 (1) UK ICC Act 2001, note 79 in this chapter.

[101] Sections 5 and 41 UK ICC Act 2001.

[102] Sections 11 (1) Extradition Act 1999 and 9.1 (1) Mutual Legal Assistance Act 1985, in this chapter, notes 75 and 76 respectively.

[103] Section 11 (2) Extradition Act 1999.

[104] Section 8 sub-sections (1)(a), (2), and (1)(b) of ICC Act 2002, note 74 in this chapter.

[105] Section 2 (1), (2) and 3 (1), (5) ICC (Implementation) Act 2002, note 77 in this chapter.

[106] Section 3 (2) ICC (Implementation) Act 2002.

[107] Section 5 (1) ICC (Implementation) Act 2002.

[108] Art. 97 ICCS. In more detail, Meißner, *Zusammenarbeit* (2003), pp. 45 ff.; Rinoldi and Parisi, in Lattanzi and Schabas, *Rome Statute I* (2000), pp. 382 ff.; Zhang, 'Article 97', in Klamberg et al., *Commentary ICC II* (2023), pp. 823–8; stressing the importance of this consultation mechanism, Boschiero, *JICJ*, 13 (2015), 633–4. On the drafting history, see Sluiter, *JICJ*, 16 (2018), 385, who criticizes Art. 97 ('very unhelpful in terms of an effective cooperation regime', 'ambiguous language', the wording 'resolve the matter' may 'amount to changing, even withdrawing the request, in the face of a persistent, non-cooperative state').

[109] cf. Boschiero, *JICJ*, 13 (2015), 635.

other costs, associated for instance with travel or translation, are to be covered by the ICC.[110] The Court may only direct its requests at *States*,[111] or *intergovernmental organizations*[112] but not—as the ICTY, ICTR, and KSC (to be looked at in a moment)—at their organs or private persons.[113] The ICC law would have to enshrine this authority explicitly but there is no rule to that effect;[114] on the contrary, relevant provisions refer to the (territorial) State as the facilitator of investigatory measures with regard to witnesses,[115] although the AC has recently held that the requested State has to assist the Court in compelling the appearance of witnesses before the Court.[116] The cooperation request must be specific, relevant, and necessary.[117] If all conditions are met, it is the responsibility of the requested State to have the domestic procedures in place[118] to obtain the required result, for example, to serve an arrest warrant on a legal entity or a person.[119] The Court may have to take special measures for the protection of victims and witnesses.[120]

### (b) *Ad hoc tribunals and KSC*

As to the ICTY and ICTR, all UN Member States have a general cooperation obligation pursuant to Articles 29 (1) ICTYS, 28 (1) ICTRS, and 28 (1) IRMCTS respectively in connection with Article 25 UN Charter.[121] At the KSC, the cooperation obligation extends to 'all entities and persons in Kosovo'.[122] Thus, concrete types of cooperation include the identification of persons, the production of evidence, service of documents, and arrest and surrender of persons.[123] Apart from that, the Prosecutor is allowed to operate directly on the State territory,

[110] Art. 100 ICCS. In detail thereon, cf. Zhang, 'Article 100', in Klamberg et al., *Commentary ICC II* (2023), pp. 851–8.

[111] cf. Art. 87 (1)(a) and (5)(a) ICCS.

[112] Art. 87 (6) ICCS; cf. Klamberg, *Evidence* (2013), pp. 248–9; Kowalski, 'Article 87', in Klamberg et al., *Commentary ICC II* (2023), pp. 644–7; Kreß and Prost, 'Article 87', in Ambos, *Commentary* (2022), mn. 43–7.

[113] cf. previously Ambos, *LJIL*, 15 (2002), 169 ff.; also Kreß, in Grützner et al., *Rechtshilfeverkehr* (2003), IV A 1 mn. 214 ff.; Sluiter, *Evidence* (2002), pp. 79–80; Frau, *Verhältnis* (2010), p. 233; Mbaye, 'Article 86', in Fernandez et al., *Commentaire CPI II* (2019), p. 2160; Kreß and Prost, 'Article 86', in Ambos, *Commentary* (2022), mn. 6–7.

[114] The reference to 'person' in Art. 54 (3)(d) ICCS is only relevant with regard to OTP arrangements or agreements which, in any case, presuppose a voluntary contractual obligation of the respective State.

[115] See e.g. Arts. 64 (6)(b), and 93 (1)(e) ICCS.

[116] *Ruto and Sang*, ICC-01/09-01/11-1598, paras. 117 ff.; thereon in more detail, Section B.(3)(a)(i) with note 378 in this chapter.

[117] cf. *Banda and Jerbo*, ICC-02/05-03/09-169, para. 17 ('the Chamber may seek cooperation under Part 9 when the requirements of (i) specificity (ii) relevance and (iii) necessity are met'); ICC, *Prosecutor v. Banda and Jerbo*, TC IV, Decision on 'Defence application pursuant to Articles 57(3)(b) & 64(6)(a) of the Statute for an order for the preparation and transmission of a cooperation request to the African Union', ICC-02/05-03/09-170, 1 July 2011, para. 14; *Prosecutor v. Blé Goudé*, PTC I, Decision on the Defence Request for State Party Cooperation, ICC-02/11-02/11-63, 17 April 2014, para. 5; *Kenyatta*, ICC-01/09-02/11-937, para. 32; *Ruto and Sang*, ICC-01/09-01/11-1274-Corr2, paras. 181 ff.; *Prosecutor v. Bemba et al.*, TC VII, Decision on the 'Prosecution's Requests under Articles 64(6)(b) and 93 of the Rome Statute to Summon Witnesses', ICC-01/05-01/13-1343-Red, 3 December 2015, para. 18; see also *Prosecutor v. Yekatom and Ngaïssona*, TC V, Public Redacted Version of the 'Defence Response to the "Confidential redacted version of 'Prosecution's Request under Articles 64(6)(b) and 93 of the Rome Statute for Further Measures to Compel the Attendance of a Witness' (ICC-01/14- 01/18-1519-Conf-Red)' ICC-01/14-01/18-1534-Conf, 1 August 2022, ICC-01/14-01/18-1534-Red, 31 January 2023, para. 11; see also Kreß and Prost, 'Article 87', in Ambos, *Commentary* (2022), mn. 44.

[118] cf. Art. 88 ICCS; note 95 in this chapter.

[119] See e.g. ICC, *Prosecutor v. Kenyatta*, TC V(B), Decision on the Prosecution's Revised Cooperation Request, ICC-01/09-02/11-937, 29 July 2014, para. 47 ('additional steps' to be 'undertaken in parallel and in a timely manner').

[120] Art. 87 (4) ICCS. For more details, see Kreß and Prost, 'Article 87', in Ambos, *Commentary* (2022), mn. 26–30. On witness protection, see previously Chapter V, A.(4)(d) in this volume.

[121] See Sluiter, in Fischer et al., *Prosecution* (2001), pp. 691 ff.; de los Reyes, in Decaux, Dieng, and Sow, *Human Rights* (2007), pp. 55 ff.; Giannone, in Kühne et al., *Völkerstrafrecht* (2007), p. 295 (ICTY) and p. 309 (ICTR); Vasiliev, in Cryer et al., *Introduction ICL* (2019), pp. 485–6.

[122] Art. 53 (1) KSC Law; Rule 200 RPE KSC.

[123] Arts. 29 (2) ICTYS and 28 (2) ICTRS/IRMCTS; Art. 53 (1) KSC Law.

without the need for letters rogatory or any other traditional interstate request for assistance;[124] yet, one must not overlook that the ICTY and ICTR also had to request judicial assistance from the domestic authorities and the real difference to a treaty-based system like the ICC consists in the existence (or lack) of an enforcement pillar in the form of an UN run transitional administration with—similar to an occupation force—executive powers and the respective international support;[125] the KSC is put on an equal footing with national judicial authorities.[126] The former enumeration is not conclusive ('not limited to'); the general cooperation obligation can be and has been further developed by the case law.[127] In addition, the RPE ICTY/ICTR/KSC are to be taken into account, especially Rules 39–40*bis*, 54–61, 90*bis* RPE ICTY/ICTR, and Rules 198–211 RPE KSC.[128]

From a conceptual perspective, the cooperation obligation under the regime of the ad hoc tribunals is stronger than the one provided for by Article 86 ICCS, at least if cooperation obligations under the ICC regime are not equally—in case of a UNSC referral—based on a Security Council mandate. Consequently, Rules 58 RPE ICTY/ICTR and 60 RPE MICT establish the primacy of the cooperation obligation[129] over any legal obstacles existing in national law or extradition agreements. Thus, the traditional grounds of refusal, to be looked at more closely below,[130] do not apply.[131] In addition, the *Blaškić* TC held that the ad hoc tribunals may direct *binding orders* or requests for assistance *at States* (but not to individual civil servants in their official function).[132] Under certain conditions the tribunals may even direct

[124] Arts. 18 (2) ICTYS, 17 (2) ICTRS, 16 (2) IRMCTS, 15 (2) SCSLS, and 14 (4) RSCSLS. See also Rules 39–40 RPE ICTY/ICTR, 36–7 RPE MICT; Boas et al., *International Criminal Procedure* (2011), p. 64.

[125] See, with regard to the authority of occupying powers and the specific support for the ICTY, Section A.(1) in this chapter.

[126] Art. 53 (2) KSC Law: 'An order by the Specialist Chambers shall have the same force and effect as an order issued by any other Kosovo court or judge.' See also Rule 200 RPE KSC.

[127] In detail on the content of the general cooperation obligation, Sluiter, *Evidence* (2002), pp. 145 ff.; Sluiter, in Fischer et al., *Prosecution* (2001), pp. 681 ff..; Sluiter, in Cassese, *Companion* (2009), pp. 194 ff..; Maikowski, *Kooperationspflichten* (2002), pp. 54 ff.. and 147 ff.; Cassese, *ICL* (2013), pp. 357–8; Swart, in Cassese et al., *Rome Statute II* (2002), pp. 1592 ff.; Ciampi, in Cassese et al., *Rome Statute II* (2002), pp. 1712 ff.; Kreß, in Grützner et al., *Rechtshilfeverkehr* (2003), IV A 2 mn. 56 ff.; Knoops, *International Criminal Tribunals* (2014), pp. 300 ff.

[128] See now Rules 36–8, 55–63, and 107 RPE MICT; for the SCSL, cf. Rules 39–40*bis*, 54–9 RPE SCSL.

[129] But see Klamberg, *Evidence* (2013), p. 263, arguing that despite the vertical relationship between the tribunals and the States—'which involves far-reaching obligations of the States towards the tribunals and the mechanism with a lack of reciprocity and the final say in disputes attributed to the requesting side'—'the powers of the *ad hoc* tribunals and the mechanism are limited'.

[130] Section B.(2)(a)(ii)(1) and (3)(a)(ii) in this chapter.

[131] On the rejection of the 'political offence' exception as such a traditional ground, cf. for instance ICTY, *Prosecutor v. Furundžija*, TC, Judgment, IT-95-17/1-T, 10 December 1998, para. 157; ICTY, *Prosecutor v. Tadić*, AC, Decision on the Defence Motion for Interlocutory Appeal on Jurisdiction, IT-94-1, 2 October 1995, para. 57; Sluiter, in Cassese, *Companion* (2009), pp. 194–5.

[132] *Blaškić*, IT-95-14, paras. 26 ff., 38 ff. (para. 26: 'The exceptional legal basis of Article 29 accounts for the novel and indeed unique power granted to the International Tribunal to issue orders to sovereign States', and para. 38: 'The Appeals Chamber dismisses the possibility of the International Tribunal addressing subpoenas to State officials acting in their official capacity. Such officials are mere instruments of a State and their official action can only be attributed to the State. They cannot be the subject of sanctions or penalties for conduct that is not private but undertaken on behalf of a State'). In more detail on *Blaškić* and the respective Rule 54*bis* RPE ICTY, see Giannone, in Kühne et al., *Völkerstrafrecht* (2007), pp. 301–2; Vasiliev, in Cryer et al., *Introduction ICL* (2019), pp. 487–8; Swoboda, *Verfahrens- und Beweisstrategien* (2013), pp. 588 ff.; Klamberg, *Evidence* (2013), pp. 238–41. According to ICTR, *Prosecutor v. Ngirabatware*, TC, Decision on Defence Motion Requesting an Order Directed at the World Bank pursuant to Article 28, ICTR-99-54-T, 27 April 2010, requests can also be directed to international organizations, although it is debatable, whether these would be binding. The fact that Art. 28 ICTRS is explicitly only directed at States, and SC Res. 955 (establishing the ICTR) merely calls upon international organizations 'to contribute funds, equipment and services to the International Tribunal, including the offer of expert personnel' speaks against this view. However, in favour of a binding effect, see ICTY, *Prosecutor v. Milutinović et al.*, AC, Decision on Request of the North Atlantic Treaty Organization for Review, IT-05-87-AR108bis.l, 15 May 2006, para. 8; ICTY, *Prosecutor v. Simić et al.*, TC, Decision on Motion for Judicial Assistance to be Provided by SFOR and Others, IT-95-9-PT, 18 October 2010, para. 46, concluding at para. 58 that the Chamber 'is competent to issue a binding order … to SFOR'.

binding orders at *private individuals*, for instance, to summon them as witnesses or to demand the surrender of objects;[133] at the KSC this is explicitly provided for in the Law.[134] This still goes, at least from a conceptual perspective, beyond the finding of the ICC AC in *Ruto and Sang*[135] since the latter would always have to act through the respective State authorities, using them as facilitators.

## (2) Surrender and provisional arrest of persons

### *(a) The ICC regime and national implementation*

#### *(i) Basic principles and rules*

The provisions on the surrender and provisional arrest of persons in the ICC Statute are amongst the most important regulations in the Statute.[136] The term '*surrender*'[137] is to be distinguished from the term '*extradition*':[138] the former describes the handover/transfer of a person through a State to the ICC,[139] whereas the latter refers to the transfer of a person from one State to another.[140] While this sophisticated terminological distinction pretends to clarify that the interstate law on extradition cannot be applied to the ICC surrender regime,[141] and therefore constitutional prohibitions of the extradition of nationals—quite common in civil law jurisdictions[142]—do not hinder the surrender of nationals to the ICC, it

[133] *Blaškić*, IT-95-14, paras. 46 ff.; see also the general Rule 54 RPE ICTY/ICTR/SCSL and Rule 55 RPE MICT; cf. Chaumette, *ICLR*, 4 (2004), 363 ff.; Swoboda, *Verfahrens- und Beweisstrategien* (2013), pp. 584 ff., crit. pp. 595 ff., 780 ff.; Klamberg, *Evidence* (2013), pp. 243–4.

[134] Art. 53 (1) KSC Law ('persons'), (2) ('Every natural person'); see also Rule 200 RPE KSC ('any ... person').

[135] Note 117 in this chapter.

[136] Arts. 89–92, 101–2 ICCS. Kaul, *ZIS*, 2 (2007), 498 deems the issue of arrest and surrender to be *the* most essential unresolved problem. On the challenges the ICC faces with regard to the execution of arrest warrants, see Mochochoko, in Jalloh and Alhagi, *Accountability* (2015), pp. 79–84, arguing that approaches 'tailored to fit the particular circumstances of each situation' are necessary with regard to the cooperation of the ICC with the States on arrest issues (pp. 84 ff.).

[137] On surrender, understood as the suspect's personal and political act of voluntarily surrendering to the Court (as opposed to being arrested), see Meernik, *ICLR*, 15 (2015), 926 ff. (analysing, from the perspective of political theory, why and how surrender could be encouraged by the international tribunals in order to secure the presence of a suspect before them). On possible violations of individual rights through surrender, see Schrotz, *Individualrechtsverletzungen* (2006), pp. 85 ff. (146).

[138] For a historical overview of extradition and an analysis of the difficulties generated by the classical model of extradition regarding the international cooperation on transferring suspects, cf. McDermott, *ICLR*, 15 (2015), 257 ff., 283 ff.

[139] At the ad hoc tribunals the terms 'surrender' or 'transfer' are used interchangeably to describe the handing-over of a person to the tribunals (Arts. 19 (2), 29 (2)(e) ICTYS, 18 (2), 28 (2)(e) ICTRS, and 17 (2), 28 (2)(e) IRMCTS); in more detail, see Swart, in Cassese et al., *Rome Statute II* (2002), p. 1666; Caeiro, in Caeiro and Moreira, *TPI* (2004), pp. 72 ff.; Plachta, in AIDP, *ICL: Quo Vadis?* (2004), pp. 465 ff.; Ciavola, in Cassese et al., *Problemi attuali* (2005), pp. 435 ff.; Deen-Racsmány, *LJIL*, 20 (2007), 167 ff.).

[140] Art. 102 ICCS. On the negotiations, see Kreß and Prost, 'Article 102', in Ambos, *Commentary* (2022), mn. 1–3. Explicitly on the distinction, see ECtHR, *Naletilic v. Croatia*, Application No. 51891/99 (4 May 2000).

[141] cf. Swart, in Cassese et al., *Rome Statute II* (2002), pp. 1678 ff.; Kreß, *EJCCLCJ*, 6 (1998), 452–3; Schabas, *Introduction* (2020), pp. 277–9; Rinoldi and Parisi, in Lattanzi and Schabas, *Rome Statute I* (2000), pp. 345 ff.; Caeiro, in Caeiro and Moreira, *TPI* (2004), p. 74; Vasiliev, in Cryer et al., *Introduction ICL* (2019), p. 493; Quirico, 'Article 102', in Fernandez et al., *Commentaire CPI II* (2019), pp. 2355, 2357; Påle-Bartes, 'Article 102', in Klamberg et al., *Commentary ICC II* (2023), p. 865; Kreß and Prost, 'Article 102', in Ambos, *Commentary* (2022), mn. 2–3.

[142] cf. Art. 16 (2) cl. 1 German Constitution (*Grundgesetz*): 'No German may be extradited to a foreign country' (Translation in Tomuschat et al., *Basic Law* (2022), p. 4). For similar provisions, see Art. 5, LI [para. 51] *Brazilian* Constitution. In *Spain* the extradition of nationals is prohibited by the Act of Passive Extradition (*Ley de Extradición Pasiva*) of 1985 (Art. 3) unless based on an international treaty (Art. 1); then it is admissible on the basis of reciprocity (Art. 13.3. Spanish Constitution). But see also e.g. France and Argentina where the Constitution is silent on the matter. In *France*, the *Conseil d'État* held in its opinion (*avis*) No. 356–641 of 24

does not change the rationale of the extradition prohibition, that is, the lack of confidence in any foreign or alien jurisdiction, be it the one of another State or an international tribunal.[143] It is therefore more convincing to explicitly establish an exception from the extradition prohibition with regard to international criminal tribunals[144] than to rely on the Statute's terminological twist.

The *national implementation* of the surrender obligation only varies in the details, but not in its core substance. In *Germany*, the ICC has been recognized as an interstate organization within the meaning of Article 24 (1) *Grundgesetz* and thus its decisions and orders are, in principle, directly applicable.[145] The surrender of persons, including German nationals (in line with the above-mentioned constitutional amendment), is regulated in §§ 2–33 of the German Act on Cooperation with the International Criminal Court (ICC Act, IStGHG).[146] According to § 2 (1) IStGHG there is a mandatory obligation to surrender. The surrender procedure—modelled after the extradition procedure[147]—is generally divided into a judicial admissibility and an executive approval procedure.[148] The Higher Regional Court (*Oberlandesgericht*) is the competent authority to decide on the admissibility of the surrender, based on the file prepared by the General Prosecutor's Office which, in turn, is in charge of the execution of the surrender.[149] Exceptionally, a simplified procedure of surrender—forgoing the judicial procedure—may be applied, if the person sought consents to the simplified procedure after being cautioned by a judge.[150]

In *France*, arrest and surrender of persons are regulated in Article 627-4 of the *Code de Procédure Pénale* (CPP).[151] The execution of an ICC request is not explicitly mandatory and surrender may be refused if an evident error exists.[152] The competent authority to decide on

November 1994 that the principle of non-extradition of French nationals neither has a basis in an individual right of the *Déclaration des droits de l'homme de 1789* or the Préambule de la Constitution of 1946 nor as a 'principe fondamental reconnu par les lois de la République' which has constitutional rank according to the Préambule de la Constitution of 1946). In *Argentina*, nationals may be extradited pursuant to Law 24.767, (<http://infoleg.mecon.gov.ar/infolegInternet/anexos/40000-44999/41442/norma.htm>). In other countries, such as *Italy*, extradition of nationals is allowed pursuant to international treaties (Art. 26 Italian Constitution).

[143] cf. Kreß, in Grützner et al., *Rechtshilfeverkehr* (2003), IV A 1 mn. 372, with further references (criticizing the equal treatment of 'surrender' and 'extradition' under the German *Grundgesetz* and calling for a qualitative and not just terminological difference between them); in a similar vein, Kreß and Prost, 'Article 102', in Ambos, *Commentary* (2022), mn. 7, for whom 'the legal significance of article 102 is very limited', since 'it constitutes a matter of interpretation of the respective national constitution' whether the use of the term *extradition* serves only to terminologically distinguish it from *surrender* or whether it has a qualitative value as well (excluding the prohibition of extradition of nationals to surrender).

[144] See e.g. Art. 16 (2) 2nd cl. German *Grundgesetz* (GG): 'The law may provide otherwise for extraditions to a member state of the European Union or to an *international court*, provided that the rule of law is observed.' (Translation in Tomuschat et al., *Basic Law* (2022), p. 4 [emphasis added]).

[145] cf. Keller, in Ambos et al., *Rechtshilferecht* (2020), p. 1486; but see also pp. 1482 ff. (analysing the constitutional limitations of the ensuing verticality, esp. regarding the individual rights and the constitutive structures of the *Grundgesetz*).

[146] *Gesetz über die Zusammenarbeit mit dem Internationalen Strafgerichtshof (IStGH-Gesetz—IStGHG)*. This Act is contained, as Art. 1, in the Act on the Implementation of the ICCS (*IStGH-Ausführungsgesetz*, BGBl. I 2002 p. 2144).

[147] Thereon, see Rackow, in Ambos et al., *Rechtshilferecht* (2020), pp. 105–08.

[148] § 6 IStGHG.

[149] §§ 7–8 IStGHG.

[150] § 32 IStGHG. In detail on the judicial duty to caution and crit. of §§ 13, 14 IStGHG, Reisert, *StV*, 11 (2005), 638 ff.

[151] Amended by Art. 10 Law No 2020-1672, 24 December 2020, <https://www.legifrance.gouv.fr/codes/section_lc/LEGITEXT000006071154/LEGISCTA000006167496/#LEGISCTA000024966849>. For other examples, see Arts. 11–15 Belgian Cooperation Law, 29 March 2004 and Arts. 30–9 Argentinian Law on the Implementation of the Rome Statute, *Ley 26.200*, 13 December 2006, <https://www.argentina.gob.ar/normativa/nacional/ley-26200-123921/texto>.

[152] Art. 627-8 CPP.

surrender and arrest is the Investigation Chamber of the Paris Appeal Court (*Chambre de l'Instruction de la Cour d'Appel de Paris*), which basically has to check the suspect's identity, that is, to verify whether it is the person requested; if there is no evident error, the Chamber shall order the surrender or arrest of the person, leaving all other issues to be decided by the ICC.[153] A simplified procedure is possible if the person sought is under provisional arrest and consents to be surrendered to the ICC.[154]

Like in Germany, the law of the *Netherlands*, specifically Section 11 of the ICC (Implementation) Act, makes the execution of an ICC request for the surrender of persons mandatory ('shall be surrendered'). The Act also provides for a two-phased surrender procedure, that is, a judicial admissibility procedure[155] and an executive approval mechanism.[156] The Hague District Court has the exclusive competence to deal with matters of assistance to the ICC,[157] and is therewith also, upon application by the Public Prosecutor,[158] the competent court to conduct the public hearing[159] of the person sought with a view to determining their identity, the admissibility of the request, and the scope for granting the request.[160] The District Court may only refuse the surrender where it is of the opinion that the person brought before it is not the person requested.[161] There is no legal remedy against the ruling.[162] After the District Court's ruling, the executive decision on the surrender is to be made by the Minister of Justice.[163] An expedited procedure is also provided for:[164] if the person sought, after being cautioned by a judge, consents, the Public Prosecutor is competent to decide on the surrender.[165]

In the *UK*, arrest and surrender are regulated in Part 2 of the ICC Act 2001. Section 2 implies that there are no alternatives to the execution of an ICC request, thus making it mandatory. Before being surrendered, the person is to be brought in front of a 'competent court',[166] which must make a delivery order for the surrender to go ahead, in accordance with the requirements of Section 5. Where the competent court in England and Wales refuses to make a delivery order as outlined in Section 8, the Secretary of State may appeal against this decision to the High Court.[167] If this fails, the Secretary of State may further appeal to the Supreme Court of England and Wales (previously to the House of Lords).[168] The Procedure in Scotland is similar, but an appeal cannot go further up than to the High Court of Justiciary.[169] Where the person sought or their representative consents to the surrender in accordance with Section 7, the competent court is obliged to make a delivery order and the suspect loses their right to apply for review.[170]

153 Art. 627-7, 8 CPP; see also Bitti, in Kreß et al., *Domestic Legal Orders* (2005), pp. 99–100.
154 Art. 627-14 CPP; thereon Bitti, in Kreß et al., *Domestic Legal Orders* (2005), p. 101.
155 Sections 21–9 ICC (Implementation) Act.
156 Sections 30–5 ICC (Implementation) Act.
157 Section 4 ICC (Implementation) Act.
158 Section 21 (1) ICC (Implementation) Act.
159 Section 23 (1) ICC (Implementation) Act.
160 Section 24 (1) ICC (Implementation) Act.
161 Section 27 (2) in connection with Sections 25 (1) and 27 (3) ICC (Implementation) Act.
162 Section 27 (4) ICC (Implementation) Act.
163 Section 30 ICC (Implementation) Act.
164 Sections 36–40 ICC (Implementation) Act.
165 Section 37 (1) ICC (Implementation) Act.
166 Section 5 (1) ICC Act.
167 Section 9 (1) ICC Act.
168 Section 9 (3) ICC Act.
169 Section 10 UK ICC Act.
170 Section 7 (4) ICC Act.

Part 3 of the *Australian* ICC Act 2002 deals with requests by the ICC for arrest and surrender. The surrender is not explicitly mandatory and may be refused on the basis of Section 31 of the Act. According to Section 28, the surrender is merely dependent on the Attorney-General of Australia issuing a surrender warrant in the form specified in Section 43.

In *Canada*, the transfer of persons to the ICC is regulated in Part 2 of the Extradition Act 1999. The surrender may only occur once a detailed surrender order, containing the conditions set out in Section 58, has been issued by the Minister of Justice. This firstly requires the Minister of Justice (who is to receive the request according to Section 11 of the Extradition Act) to issue an authority to proceed (which can subsequently be amended or withdrawn at any time in accordance with Section 23), allowing the Attorney General to apply for the surrender order on behalf of the ICC at the competent court (defined in Section 2 of the Act) in the province he believes the requested person to be in.[171] A transfer to a competent court in a different province will always be possible on the basis of Section 22. The court will then hold an extradition hearing[172] to decide whether to issue an order of committal in accordance with Section 29 to keep the person in custody to await surrender. If the order of committal is issued, the Minister of Justice may order the surrender of the requested person, as stated in Section 40 (1). The requested person may lodge an appeal against the order of committal to the Court of Appeal,[173] or apply for judicial review of the Minister's order of surrender.[174] Alternatively to this lengthy procedure, the requested person may consent in writing, before a judge, to committal or surrender, which would oblige the judge to order committal and allow the Minister to proceed with his order for surrender.[175]

The ICC can direct a *request for surrender* to any State where the person sought allegedly resides.[176] If this State is a State Party to the ICC—or has cooperation obligations as a non-State Party under the above-mentioned requirements[177]—it is obliged to comply with the request in accordance with the rules of Part 9 and its relevant procedural law.[178] This entails taking all necessary measures, especially the arrest of the person.[179] Analogous to these provisions, the German §§ 9 ff. IStGHG, Section 2 UK ICC Act, the Canadian Section 16 Extradition Act, the Australian Sections 20 ff. ICC Act, and the Dutch Sections 13 ff. ICC (Implementation) Act include provisions for the prosecution and arrest of the accused. The committing judge of the requested State must confirm the identity of the arrested person, the compliance with the proper process, and the observance of the individual rights.[180] The

171 Sections 15 (1) and 16 (1) Extradition Act.
172 Section 24 Extradition Act.
173 Sections 49–56 Extradition Act.
174 Section 57 Extradition Act.
175 Sections 70 and 71 Extradition Act.
176 On the efficiency of the procedure, cf. Roper and Barria, *LJIL*, 21 (2008), 460, 463 ff.; Burke-White, *LJIL*, 21 (2008), 477 ff. Crit. on the PTCs' early practice to direct requests for surrender routinely at *all* State Parties, Kreß and Prost, 'Article 89', in Ambos, *Commentary* (2022), mn. 15–23, arguing that this practice is 'contrary to the clear intent of Article 89' (mn. 16) and 'undermines the strength of the cooperation obligation' (mn. 18), therefore favouring a more limited approach following the *Nourain* TC, ICC, *Prosecutor v. Nourain*, Warrant of Arrest for Abdallah Banda Abkaer Nourain, ICC-02/05-03/09-606, 11 September 2014, para. 26 (iv) and (v). ICC, *Practice Manual* (2023), para. 6 proposes that both State and non-State Parties should be informed via a *note verbale* by the Registrar if a person sought by the Court travels through their territory; non-State Parties should be reminded of Art. 87 (5)(a) ICCS.
177 Above Section A.(2) at the beginning.
178 Art. 89 (1) ICCS.
179 Art. 59 (1) ICCS.
180 Art. 59 (2) ICCS; also e.g. § 14 (2) and (3) IStGHG. Crit. of Art. 59 (2) ICCS, El Zeidy, *JICJ*, 4 (2006), 448 ff., 465. This provision first became relevant in the *Bemba* case, where, however, a violation was not established; cf. ICC, *Prosecutor v. Bemba*, PTC, Decision on Application for Interim Release, ICC-01/05-01/08-73-Conf, 20 August 2008, para. 49. On the related question of the effect of an unlawful arrest or abduction, see Currie, *CLF*, 18 (2007), 360 ff. (374 ff.).

legality of the ICC's warrant of arrest pursuant to Article 58 (1) ICCS may however not be questioned;[181] it can only be challenged before the competent PTC.[182] The arrested person may apply for interim release to the competent national authority.[183] The ICC will review the legitimacy of the arrest *ex officio* or upon application once the person has been transferred to the Court.[184] State Parties also have an obligation to authorize the *transportation* of a person being surrendered through its territory.[185]

The *competent national authority* within the meaning of Article 59 (3) ICCS is normally a judge or chamber. In *Germany* the decision lies, as in extradition proceedings according to § 23 German Act on International Cooperation in Criminal Matters (*IRG*),[186] with the Higher Regional Court ('Oberlandesgericht', § 14 (5) IStGHG). In *France*, an interim release can be requested, according to Article 627-9 CPP, at any time before the *Chambre de l'Instruction de la Cour d'Appel de Paris* which proceeds in accordance with Article 59 ICCS and the procedure of Article 148-1 to 148-8 CPP.[187] In the *Netherlands,* it would be a judge at the Hague District Court.[188] In *Canada*, such applications are to be directed to the competent court of the province the person was arrested.[189] When deciding on the application, the Court, at the request of the Attorney General, must adjourn to await recommendations on the interim release by the ICC's PTC;[190] these have to be considered in its decision.[191] The decision may be appealed against at the Court of Appeal.[192] In the *UK*, any court normally competent to deal with applications for bail may deal with the application;[193] it must, however notify the Secretary of State (England and Wales) or the competent Scottish Ministers, who must in turn notify the ICC, whose recommendations are to be considered in the decision.[194] In *Australia*, the Attorney-General must inform the ICC of such applications and the magistrate considering the application must consider the ICCs recommendations when deciding on them.[195]

[181] Art. 59 (4), 2nd sentence ICCS. Furthermore, see Rules 117, 184 RPE ICC and Meißner, *Zusammenarbeit* (2003), pp. 161 ff.; Swart, in Cassese et al., *Rome Statute II* (2002), pp. 1247 ff.; Kreß, in Grützner et al., *Rechtshilfeverkehr* (2003), IV A 1 mn. 116 ff.

[182] Rule 117 (3) RPE ICC; thereon ICC, *Prosecutor v. Barasa*, PTC II, Decision on the 'Defence challenge to the warrant for the arrest of Walter Osapiri Barasa', ICC-01/09-01/13-35, 10 September 2015, para. 2.

[183] Art. 59 (3) ICCS.

[184] Art. 60 ICCS. See in more detail on the review procedure, Chapter IV, B.(6)(b) in this volume.

[185] Art. 89 (3) ICCS, Rule 182 RPE ICC. In detail, Kreß and Prost, 'Article 89', in Ambos, *Commentary* (2022), mn. 38–51; Kreß, in Grützner et al., *Rechtshilfeverkehr* (2003), IV A 1 mn. 257 ff.; Schabas, *ICC Commentary* (2016), pp. 1294–5; seeing an improvement of the arrest and surrender procedures, cf. ICC-ASP, *Report Cooperation* (2013), paras. 19 ff.; ICC-ASP, *Report Cooperation* (2014), paras. 8 ff.; more recently ICC-ASP, *Report Cooperation* (2022), Annex I, paras. 2–6; ICC-ASP, *Report Cooperation* (2023), paras. 34–5. On the surrender procedure in Switzerland, see Gless, *Internationales Strafrecht* (2021), mn. 1017–18; Benoit-Landale, in Ziegler et al., *Kriegsverbrecherprozesse* (2009), pp. 256 ff.

[186] *Gesetz über die internationale Rechtshilfe in Strafsachen (IRG).*

[187] According to this procedure, the *Chambre de l'Instruction* shall issue a decision on an application for release within twenty days, after hearing the person requesting the release and the Public Prosecutor, whose submissions must be written and reasoned (Art. 148-2, and 148-4 CPP). Apart from the release, Art. 148-5 CPP provides for the possibility of an—exceptional—escorted release at any stage of the proceedings, that is, even before the *Chambre de l'Instruction* decides on the release, and in any case, for instance, even if the request is denied. In order to ensure that the duty to surrender the person to the Court can be fulfilled, the person is obliged, before the release, to indicate an address and to notify of any change (Art. 148-3 CPP); cf. also Bitti, in Kreß et al., *Domestic Legal Orders* (2005), p. 98.

[188] Sections 18 (2), 20, and 4 ICC (Implementation) Act.

[189] Section 2 Extradition Act.

[190] Section 18 (1.1) Extradition Act.

[191] Section 18 (1.2) Extradition Act.

[192] Section 18 (2) Extradition Act.

[193] Section 16 ICC Act.

[194] Section 18 ICC Act.

[195] Section 24 ICC Act.

The *ICC request* for arrest or surrender must be in writing and contain information on the requested person, their probable location, a copy of the arrest warrant, and other documents that are required in accordance with the requested State's laws.[196] In cases where the person has already been convicted the request should contain a copy of the arrest warrant and of the judgment, and information allowing the identification of the person.[197] The explicit reference to the '*surrender process in the requested State*'[198] can be explained by the concerns of common law States with regard to an autonomous standard of proof, instead demanding the consideration of national standards. These national standards should, however, not be misunderstood as a ground for refusal or lead to an undue delay of the surrender. This is why Article 91 (2)(c) ICCS explicitly calls for a 'not ... more burdensome' procedure than in interstate extradition proceedings.[199] It is questionable whether 'probable cause' as a requirement for surrender, contained in the legal assistance treaties between the USA and the ICTY/ICTR, meets this demand, since it constitutes a substantive condition which may entail the denial of surrender in not a few cases and thus the non-compliance with the SC Resolutions establishing the tribunals.[200]

In urgent cases, the ICC may request a State to make a *provisional arrest* until the submission of the surrender request.[201] This request must contain—besides information on the person sought—the alleged crimes and relevant facts as well as a statement of the existence of the arrest warrant and the convicting judgment.[202] The requested State may release the person sought if the surrender request is not provided within sixty days.[203] Before this period expires, the detainee may also agree to a simplified surrender procedure, making a request for surrender unnecessary.[204] The release from arrest does not however exclude the possibility of a later surrender of the same person.[205]

The surrendered person may only be prosecuted for the (alleged) 'conduct' or 'course of conduct'[206] referred to in the surrender request.[207] This corresponds to the *rule of speciality* as known from traditional extradition law[208] although the reference to 'course of

[196] Art. 91 (1), (2) ICCS.

[197] Art. 91 (3) ICCS. More generally on the wording of a request, cf. Art. 87 (2) ICCS, Rules 178 ff., 187 RPE ICC; cf. also Kowalski, 'Article 87', in Klamberg et al., *Commentary ICC II* (2023), pp. 631–2.

[198] Art. 91 (2)(c) ICCS.

[199] cf. Swart, in Cassese et al., *Rome Statute II* (2002), pp. 1672–3 and 1689 ff.; Kreß, in Grützner et al., *Rechtshilfeverkehr* (2003), IV A 1 mn. 229; Schabas, *ICC Commentary* (2016), p. 1307; Kreß, *EJCCLCJ*, 6 (1998), 453–4; Meißner, *Zusammenarbeit* (2003), pp. 116 ff.; Rinoldi and Parisi, in Lattanzi and Schabas, *Rome Statute I* (2000), pp. 379 ff.; Kreß and Prost, 'Article 91', in Ambos, *Commentary* (2022), mn. 13–14; summarizing the relevant discussion, Cazala, 'Article 91' in Fernandez et al., *Commentaire CPI II* (2019), pp. 2245–6.

[200] Crit. Godinho, *JICJ*, 1 (2003), 511 ff.; Mochochoko, in Jalloh and Alhagi, *Accountability* (2015), p. 76; in favour Kushen, *JICJ*, 1 (2003), 518.

[201] Art. 92 (1) ICCS. See Chapter IV, B.(6)(b) in this volume.

[202] Art. 92 (2) ICCS.

[203] Art. 92 (3) ICCS in conjunction with Rule 188 RPE ICC.

[204] Art. 92 (3) ICCS, Rule 189 RPE ICC.

[205] Art. 92 (4) ICCS. In detail, Swart, in Cassese et al., *Rome Statute II* (2002), pp. 1692–3; Rinoldi and Parisi, in Lattanzi and Schabas, *Rome Statute I* (2000), pp. 351 ff.; Meißner, *Zusammenarbeit* (2003), pp. 176 ff.; Cazala, 'Article 92', in Fernandez et al., *Commentaire CPI II* (2019), pp. 2251 ff.; Kreß and Prost, 'Article 92', in Ambos, *Commentary* (2022), mn. 15.

[206] Art. 101 (1) ICCS.

[207] In more detail, Wilkitzki et al., 'Article 101', in Ambos, *Commentary* (2022), mn. 1 ff.; Meißner, *Zusammenarbeit* (2003), pp. 168 ff.; Swart, in Cassese et al., *Rome Statute II* (2002), pp. 1698 ff.; Rinoldi and Parisi, in Lattanzi and Schabas, *Rome Statute I* (2000), pp. 373 ff.; Kreß, in Grützner et al., *Rechtshilfeverkehr* (2003), IV A 1 mn. 251; Veneziano, in Cassese et al., *Problemi attuali* (2005), pp. 464 ff.; Quirico, 'Article 101', in Fernandez et al., *Commentaire CPI II* (2019), pp. 2345 ff.; Klamberg, 'Article 101', in Klamberg et al., *Commentary ICC II* (2023), pp. 859–60; crit. Swart, in Cassese et al., *Rome Statute II* (2002), pp. 1700 ff.; Schabas, *ICC Commentary* (2016), pp. 1364–5; Gless, *Internationales Strafrecht* (2021), mn. 1013.

[208] cf. Wilkitzki et al., 'Article 101', in Ambos, *Commentary* (2022), mn. 1 ('conduct'); Ambos and Gronke, in Ambos et al., *Rechtshilferecht* (2020), p. 85 with mn 58 (normally factual basis, sometimes also offence).

conduct' appears, at first sight, somewhat broader, accounting for the systematic nature of ICC crimes.[209] This does not exclude a different *legal* assessment of the *same* facts.[210] Also, the rule of speciality does not apply in case of a voluntary appearance before the Court.[211] Finally, the requested State may waive the speciality requirement if the ICC so requests[212] and is indeed encouraged to do so.[213] To be sure, the broad interpretation of the rule and its non-application in case of voluntary appearance and a waiver reflect the controversy about its inclusion in the Statute in the first place.[214]

### *(ii) Limitations*

*(1)* ***General*** Similarly to the ad hoc tribunals, the traditional interstate *grounds of refusal* cannot be applied to the ICC.[215] Notwithstanding, national interests can be taken into account otherwise. For one, the admissibility of the surrender may be challenged with respect to the *ne bis in idem* principle as recognized in Article 20 ICCS,[216] that is, the person sought may claim to have been investigated or prosecuted already for the same conduct by the requested or a third State.[217] In such a situation a consultation between the Court and the State concerned must take place.[218] The surrender may be postponed if the ICC's admissibility ruling[219] is still pending,[220] that is, the Court has not yet decided upon the respective

[209] cf. ICC, *Prosecutor v. Blé Goudé*, PTC I (Single Judge), Decision on the 'Defence request to amend the document containing the charges for violation of the rule of speciality', ICC-02/11-02/11-151, 11 September 2014, para. 10 (but Art. 101 (1) is not 'much broader' than the classical rule and the reference to the UN Model Treaty on Extradition is misleading given that it focuses too narrowly on an offence). On the limited scope and purpose of the rule of speciality (also concerning ancillary matters such as protective measures), see ICC, *Prosecutor v. Al Hassan*, TC X, Public Redacted Version of 'Decision on the Defence request to terminate the proceedings and related requests', ICC-01/12-01/18-1009-Red, 29 October 2020, paras. 29, 37.

[210] See similarly ICC, *Prosecutor v. Bemba et al.*, PTC II (Single Judge), Decision on 'Narcisse Aiido's Request for an Order Rejecting the Prosecution's Document Containing the Charges (ICC-01/05-01/13-526-AnxBl) and for an Order to the Prosecution to File an Amended and Corrected Document Containing the Charges', ICC-01/05-01/13-567, 15 July 2014, p. 5 ('linked to the underlying facts rather than the legal qualification'); also Kreß *EJCCLCJ*, 6 (1998), 155.

[211] cf. ICC, *Prosecutor v. Muthaura et al.*, PTC II, Decision on the 'Preliminary Motion Alleging Defects in the Documents Containing the Charges (DCC) and List of Evidence (LoE) and Request that the OTP be ordered to re-file an Amended DCC & LoE' and the 'Defence Request for a Status Conference Concerning the Prosecution's Disclosure of 19 August 2011 and the Document Containing the Charges and Article 101 of the Rome Statute', ICC-01/09-02/11-315, 12 September 2011, para. 16; left open by ICC, *Prosecutor v. Ongwen*, PTC II, Decision Postponing the Date of the Confirmation of Charges Hearing, ICC-02/04-01/15-206, 6 March 2015, para. 32 with note 64; see also ICC, *Prosecutor v. Ongwen*, PTC II (Single Judge), Decision on the Applicability of Art. 101 of the Rome Statute in the Proceedings against Dominic Ongwen, ICC-02/04-01/15-260, 7 July 2015, paras. 12–13 (consent to surrender 'irrelevant', in fact no voluntary appearance since no freedom of movement after arrest/surrender by authorities of CAR); cf. also Klamberg, 'Article 101', in Klamberg et al., *Commentary ICC II* (2023), pp. 859–62.

[212] Art. 101 (2) ICCS, Rules 185, 196, 197 RPE ICC.

[213] See e.g. ICC, *Prosecutor v. Ongwen*, PTC II (Single Judge), Order to the Registrar to Transmit a Request for Cooperation under Article 101 of the Rome Statute to the Central African Republic, ICC-02/04-01/15-319-Red, 15 October 2015, paras. 4–6 and orders at pp. 5–8 (ordering the Registrar to inform the CAR about the charges and 'request' it 'to provide a waiver'). In a similar vein, ICC, *Practice Manual* (2023), para. 34.

[214] cf. Wilkitzki et al., 'Article 101', in Ambos, *Commentary* (2022), mn. 10.

[215] In the same vein, Kreß and Prost, 'Article 89', in Ambos, *Commentary* (2022), mn. 10 (no '*stricto sensu*' grounds for refusal, but means to take State concerns into account without putting the obligation to surrender as such in question). In more detail, Swart, in Cassese et al., *Rome Statute II* (2002), pp. 1681 ff.; Vasiliev, in Cryer et al., *Introduction ICL* (2019), pp. 492–3; on the discussion in the Ad Hoc Committee, see Bassiouni and Schabas, *History II* (2016), p. 790.

[216] On the *ne bis in idem* principle which also is an individual right, see Chapter I, D.(3)(j) in this volume.

[217] Art. 89 (2) cl. 1 ICCS; see e.g. § 3 IStGHG; also Nemitz et al., in Schomburg et al., *Internationale Rechtshilfe* (2020), p. 2547.

[218] Art. 89 (2) cl. 1 ICCS; Rule 181 RPE ICC (competent Chamber to obtain from State relevant information).

[219] cf. Arts. 17 (1)(c), 20 (3) ICCS.

[220] Art. 89 (2) cl. 3 ICCS.

admissibility challenge pursuant to Articles 18 or 19 ICCS;[221] if the admissibility has been affirmed, the request shall be carried out,[222] unless the affirmative decision is appealed and the AC gives the appeal a suspensive effect.[223] At any rate, an underlying arrest warrant remains valid until otherwise ordered.[224]

A different situation arises if the person sought is prosecuted or serves a sentence for *another crime* than that forming the basis of the surrender request. In this situation, the requested State shall grant the request first, then consult with the ICC and finally temporarily surrender the person.[225] The interplay of Article 89 (4) ICCS and Rule 183 RPE ICC is somewhat confusing[226] since the former explicitly obliges the State to grant the request first ('after making its decision to grant the request'), while the latter apparently gives the State discretion regarding the actual surrender ('may') and allows for a 'temporary surrender'. At any rate, the Statute takes precedence over the Rules.[227] Also, Article 94 (1) ICCS makes clear that the interference with national proceedings at best allows for a temporary postponement of the execution of an ICC request ('for a period of time agreed upon with the Court') and 'no longer than ... necessary to complete the relevant investigation or prosecution'.[228] While this provision, to which we will return below,[229] applies to other forms of cooperation under Article 93, Article 89 (4) being *lex specialis* for surrender,[230] the general idea underlying it confirms the ultimate prevalence of ICC requests vis-à-vis States which are under an obligation to cooperate. As to the substantive criteria to be considered by the requested State one can take recourse to Article 90 (7) ICCS which, albeit for the situation of competing requests, refers in particular to 'the relative nature and gravity of the conduct in question'.[231] Given the lacuna left by Article 89 (4) as to the issue of priority these provisions can be applied by way of analogy to the situation of surrender.

[221] On Arts. 18, 19 ICCS, see Chapter III, A.(4)(a)(iv) and B.(2)(e) in this volume. Art. 95 ICCS refers to these provisions and to a 'request under this Part', that is surrender and other requests; conc. *Gaddafi and Al-Senussi*, ICC-01/11-01/11-163, para. 37. For a discussion, see Kreß and Prost, 'Article 95', in Ambos, *Commentary* (2022), mn. 4–17 (esp. on the difficult delimitation between non-compliance and postponement); also Meißner, *Zusammenarbeit* (2003), pp. 157 ff.; Kreß, in Grützner et al., *Rechtshilfeverkehr* (2003), IV A 1 mn. 233; Hiéramente, 'Article 95', in Klamberg et al., *Commentary ICC II* (2023), pp. 795–812.

[222] Art. 89 (2) cl. 2 ICCS. cf. Meißner, *Zusammenarbeit* (2003), pp. 134 ff.; Swart, in Cassese et al., *Rome Statute II* (2002), pp. 1694; Rinoldi and Parisi, in Lattanzi and Schabas, *Rome Statute I* (2000), pp. 349–50; Schabas, *Commentary* (2016), pp. 1293–4.

[223] cf. Art. 82 (3); cf. Kreß and Prost, 'Article 89', in Ambos, *Commentary* (2022), mn. 33; Cazala, 'Article 89', in Fernandez et al., *Commentaire CPI II* (2019), p. 2222. The AC has not granted suspensive effect in ICC, *Prosecutor v. Gaddafi*, AC, Decision on the Request for Suspensive Effect and Related Issues, ICC-01/11-01/11-387, 18 July 2013, para. 27; ICC, *Prosecutor v. Ntaganda*, AC, Decision on Suspensive Effect, ICC-01/04-02/06-1968, 19 June 2017, para. 10; ICC, *Prosecutor v. Abd-Al-Rahman*, AC, Decision on the Request for Suspensive Effect, ICC-02/05-01/20-134, 25 August 2020, paras. 7–9; and ICC, *Prosecutor v. Al Hassan*, AC, Decision on suspensive effect, CC-01/12-01/18-1417, 19 April 2021, para. 8.

[224] Art. 58 (4) ICCS; see also Ntanda Nsereko and Ventura, 'Article 19', in Ambos, *Commentary* (2022), mn. 99–100 with case law references.

[225] cf. Art. 89 (4) ICCS and Rule 183 RPE ICC. cf. Meißner, *Zusammenarbeit* (2003), pp. 137 ff.; Kreß and Prost, 'Article 89', in Ambos, *Commentary* (2022), mn. 52–62; Kreß, in Grützner et al., *Rechtshilfeverkehr* (2003), IV A 1 mn. 234; Schabas, *ICC Commentary* (2016), pp. 1295–6.

[226] Crit. also Kreß and Prost, 'Article 89', in Ambos, *Commentary* (2022), mn. 59 ('ambiguous', 'confusing').

[227] Art. 51 (5) ICCS.

[228] See also Kreß and Prost, 'Article 89', in Ambos, *Commentary* (2022), mn. 62 ('marks the outer limit of the requested State's right to postpone').

[229] Section B.(3)(a) in this chapter.

[230] ICC, *Prosecutor v. Gaddafi and Al-Senussi*, PTC I, Decision on Libya's Submissions Regarding the Arrest of Saif Al-Islam Gaddafi, ICC-01/11-01/11-72, 7 March 2012, para. 15; conc. ICC, *Prosecutor v. Blé Goudé*, PTC I, Decision on Public Côte d'lvoire's Request to Postpone the Surrender of Charles Blé Goudé to the Court, ICC-02/11-02/11-41, 3 March 2014, paras. 7–8.

[231] See also Kreß and Prost, 'Article 89', in Ambos, *Commentary* (2022), mn. 62.

The national implementation legislation examined here largely supports the statutory approach. The *UK* ICC Act 2001 basically follows it in Schedule 2. Section 2 (3) states that the Secretary of State should, upon making the delivery order, consult with the ICC before ordering the execution and may instruct the discontinuation of the national proceedings. Where a custodial sentence is already being served in the UK, the time spent in custody of the ICC or a third State enforcing the sentence of the ICC after surrender 'shall be counted towards the completion' of the sentence imposed in the UK.[232] The *Argentinian* Implementation Law is more flexible in that the government 'shall consult' with the ICC regarding the conditions to which the temporary surrender shall be subject—without, however, specifying said conditions.[233] In contrast, the *German* law provides that the temporary surrender of a person to the ICC—where in Germany a process takes place or a sentence is to be enforced against this person[234]—is possible as long as the return of the person is guaranteed.[235] Germany may however waive this right to return.[236] Any deprivation of liberty up to the point of return or the waiver of such right may however also be credited to the sentence imposed in Germany.[237] The *Canadian* law takes a similar approach through the figure of 'temporary surrender' outlined in Section 66 of the Extradition Act 1999. Section 64 (1) explicitly states that, generally, persons accused of an offence or serving a sentence in Canada should not be surrendered until they have been discharged 'by acquittal, by expiry of the sentence or otherwise', subject to the discretion of the Minister of Justice. According to Section 66, the Minister may however also order the temporary surrender of a person serving a sentence of imprisonment in Canada for a trial or an appeal, which includes a guarantee that the person will be returned after they have been tried.[238] Time spent in custody abroad will also be credited to a sentence to be served in Canada.[239] Also, Sections 24 and 25 of the Mutual Legal Assistance Act 1985 allow for the surrender of detained persons, as long as they are returned after a specified period and the transfer has been approved by a judge of the province in which the person is detained, in the form of a transfer order.[240] In *Australia*, Section 46 (1) of the ICC Act also credits the time spent in ICC custody to the time still to be spent imprisoned in Australia. If the term of imprisonment expires whilst the person is in ICC custody, the Attorney-General must inform the ICC of the matter.[241] Where there are ongoing criminal proceedings against the person sought by the ICC for different conduct,[242] Sections 32–5 of the ICC Act 2002 apply. According to Section 32 (1)(b) the execution of a request to surrender may be postponed where there is an ongoing investigation or prosecution for different conduct in Australia, which it might interfere with. Section 34 is more specific and proscribes that the Attorney-General must consult with the ICC before making his decision, and then either execute the request or postpone its execution.[243] According to *Dutch* law, specifically section 35 of the ICC (Implementation) Act 2002, the person requested may still be surrendered to the ICC for the purpose of the trial[244] but must

[232] Section 5 (1) of Schedule 2 of the ICC Act.
[233] Art. 39 Ley 26.200, 13 December 2006.
[234] Art. 89 (4) ICCS, Rule 183 RPE ICC.
[235] § 27 (1) IStGHG.
[236] § 27 (2) IStGHG.
[237] § 27 (3), (4) IStGHG.
[238] Section 66 (1), (3), and (4) Extradition Act.
[239] Section 68 Extradition Act.
[240] Section 25 Mutual Legal Assistance Act.
[241] Section 47 ICC Act.
[242] Art. 89 (4) ICCS, Rule 183 RPE ICC.
[243] Section 34 (2) ICC Act.
[244] Section 35 (2) ICC (Implementation) Act.

be returned thereafter, although the period of ICC detention will be deducted from his sentence in the Netherlands.[245] In *France*, the provisional surrender to the ICC and the ensuing procedures will suspend any national prosecution of the person concerned or the execution of a sentence.[246] However, this suspension is only provisional and will end after the person has been judged by the ICC.[247]

In cases of *conflicting or competing requests*,[248] that is, where there is an ICC surrender request and an extradition request by a State for the same person and conduct, the requested State being a *State Party* 'shall give priority' to the ICC request, provided that the proceedings before the ICC would be admissible pursuant to Articles 17–19 ICCS.[249] While most national laws follow this approach,[250] in Canada the Minister of Justice is free to decide in which order competing requests are to be authorized.[251] Under the Statute, if an admissibility ruling has not yet been made by the Court, the requested State shall postpone the extradition until such a ruling has been made.[252] If the requesting State is a *non-State Party*, the ICC request should still be treated as having precedence if the requested State does not have any primary international obligations towards the requesting State and if the surrender would be admissible.[253] If a decision on the admissibility has not yet been made, the requested State may base its decision on its own discretion.[254] If, upon admission of proceedings by the ICC, a prior international obligation towards the requesting non-State Party exists, the requested State must make a discretionary decision, taking into account, inter alia, matters such as the interest of the requesting State in the extradition of the person sought based on certain factors (crime committed on its territory, offender or victim being a national of that State).[255] If the ICC deems the matter inadmissible, but an extradition to the requesting State is refused too, the requested State should notify the ICC of that matter.[256] If there are conflicting requests concerning the same person but with regard to *different conduct*,[257] the decisive factor will once more be whether the requested State has a prior international obligation towards the requesting State or not. If this is not the case, the surrender to the ICC will prevail;[258] if such an obligation does exist however, the requested State has to make a discretionary decision based on factors such as the nature and gravity of the crime.[259]

[245] Section 35 (3) ICC (Implementation) Act.

[246] Art. 627-11 CPP.

[247] Bitti, 'France', in Kreß et al., *Domestic Legal Orders* (2005), p. 100.

[248] Art. 90 ICCS. In detail, Meißner, *Zusammenarbeit* (2003), pp. 142 ff.; Swart, in Cassese et al., *Rome Statute II* (2002), pp. 1695 ff.; Rinoldi and Parisi, in Lattanzi and Schabas, *Rome Statute I* (2000), pp. 353 ff.; Keitner, *UCLA JIL & ForAff*, 6 (2001), 228 ff.; Kreß, in Grützner et al., *Rechtshilfeverkehr* (2003), IV A 1 mn. 235 ff.; Caeiro, in Caeiro and Moreira, *TPI* (2004), pp. 89 ff., Fixson, in Kirsch, *Internationale Strafgerichtshöfe* (2005), pp. 227–8; Schabas, *ICC Commentary* (2016), pp. 1300 ff.; Kreß and Prost, 'Article 90', in Ambos, *Commentary* (2022), mn. 1–29; Hiéramente, 'Article 90', in Klamberg et al., *Commentary ICC II* (2023), pp. 705–28; Carter et al., *Global Justice* (2018), pp. 84–5.

[249] Art. 90 (2) ICCS.

[250] cf. § 4 (3) IStGHG; s. 31 Dutch ICC Implementation Act; s. 37–8 Australian ICC Act 2002.

[251] Section 15 (2) Extradition Act 1999.

[252] Art. 90 (3) ICCS. In the same vein, § 4 (3) IStGHG; s. 8 (1) Dutch ICC Implementation Act; s. 5 (4) UK ICC Act 2001; s. 40 (5)(a) Canadian Extradition Act 1999; s. 32 (1)(a) Australian ICC Act 2002.

[253] Art. 90 (4) ICCS. On how the provision balances the priority to requests from the Court with the complementarity regime established by the ICCS, cf. Kreß and Prost, 'Article 90', in Ambos, *Commentary* (2022), mn. 16–18.

[254] Art. 90 (5) ICCS.

[255] cf. Art. 90 (6) ICCS; cf. also Kreß and Prost, 'Article 90', in Ambos, *Commentary* (2022), mn. 24.

[256] Art. 90 (8) ICCS; Rule 186 RPE ICC.

[257] Art. 90 (7) ICCS.

[258] Art. 90 (7)(a).

[259] Art. 90 (7)(b). Crit. on the broad discretion given to the State Parties by Art. 90 (7), Cazala, 'Article 90', in Fernandez et al., *Commentaire CPI II* (2019), pp. 2237–8; Swart, in Cassese et al., *Rome Statute II* (2002), p. 1702.

*(2) **Immunity and other conflicting obligations (Article 98 ICCS)***

Article 98 ICCS is intended to appropriately deal with *issues of conflicting international obligations* of the requested State and thereby intends to accommodate the sovereign interests of States.[260] It should be noted that the provision relates to 'surrender' and (other) 'assistance', but not to any preceding act, especially the arrest of the person sought. Hence, Article 98 does not prevent a State from arresting a person, but only from proceeding with her surrender, pending a determination by the Court. In other words, the person can be held pending a resolution to the Article 98 objection. Similarly, there is no suspensive effect per Article 98 to the arrest obligation. Further, it should be noted that Article 98 does not deprive the Court of jurisdiction per se—it continues to exist on the basis of Articles 12 and 27—but only of the power to require a particular requested State to surrender a person. That fugitive will still be sought by the ICC and can be arrested if he travels to another State not subject to similar conflicting obligations.

*1.* Article 98 (1) Paragraph 1 deals with the *immunity* of persons or property of a 'third State'[261] towards the 'requested State', which can be an obstacle to an ICC assistance request;[262] the term 'requested State' only refers to State Parties, while 'third State' also encompasses non-State Parties.[263] Thus, here, the interstate ('horizontal') immunity between the requested State and the affected third State is concerned, not the 'vertical' immunity of a third State towards the ICC; in this case, Article 27 (2) ICCS would exclude any immunity if the third State is a State Party[264] or is otherwise, as explained above,[265] under a cooperation obligation. Of course, these other obligations stem from different legal bases and they may need to be treated differently. Yet, the fact that the case law has recognized the application of the 'entire legal framework of the Statute' in case of UNSC referrals,[266] that is, State Parties and otherwise obliged non-State Parties are basically treated alike, at least for the purpose of

[260] cf. Rosenfeld, *WashUGISLR*, 2 (2003), 278–9 ('legal and psychological confidence building measure'); on the legislative history, see Senn, *Immunitäten* (2010), pp. 228 ff.

[261] According to Tladi, *ZIS*, 10 (2015), 498 the passage 'State or diplomatic immunity of a person' should not apply to Al Bashir, being 'neither a diplomat nor a state'; also Tladi, *JICJ*, 13 (2015), 1043. This is unconvincing, though, since it is clear from the context that Art. 98 (1) refers to the (State or diplomatic) 'immunity of a person' and thus clearly covers *ratione personae* immunity derived from State immunity, i.e. in particular heads of State; see also Kreß, 'Article 98', in Ambos, *Commentary* (2022), mn. 15.

[262] On the different types of immunities, see previously Ambos, *Treatise I* (2021), pp. 529–32 with further references.

[263] cf. Senn, *Immunitäten* (2010), pp. 241 ff., 265–6, 267 ff., 324; see also *Al Bashir*, ICC-02/05-01/09-139, para. 18 (discussing it with regard to State and non-State Parties); Kreß, 'Article 98', in Ambos, *Commentary* (2022), mn. 11 ('"third State" in this paragraph thus means "a State other than the requested State"'); Adell, 'Article 98', in Klamberg et al., *Commentary ICC II* (2023), pp. 831–4; see also Zenginkuzucu, *JICJ*, 2 (2021), 11–12; van der Wilt, in Ruys et al., *HB Immunities* (2019), pp. 603–4; for a crit. discussion, see Ubéda-Saillar, 'Article 98', in Fernandez et al., *Commentaire CPI II* (2019), pp. 2313–15 (but no longer containing the quote from the previous edition: Ralph, 'Article 98', in Fernandez and Pacreau, *Commentaire CPI II* (2012), p. 1914: 'un État autre que l'état requis, qu'il soit partie ou non au Statut').

[264] cf. Du Plessis, in Ambos and Maunganidze, *Power and Prosecution* (2013), p. 38; Kreicker, *Völkerrechtliche Exemtionen I* (2007), pp. 287 ff.; Akande, *AJIL Unbound*, 112 (2018), 173; Kerr, *MichJIL*, 42 (2021), 209 with note 101 (Art. 27 'only applies to States that *are* party to the Statute'); dissenting, Jacobs, in Stahn, *Practice* (2015), pp. 291–2, arguing that a literal interpretation of Art. 27 (2) dictates its unitarian application to all cases regardless of whether the person concerned is a national of a State Party or a non-State Party. On Arts. 98 and 27 ICCS, see also Gevers, in Ambos and Maunganidze, *Power and Prosecution* (2013), pp. 94 ff.; de Wet, *JICJ*, 13 (2015), 1054–7; on the drafting history of Arts. 27 and 98, see Sadat, in deGuzman and Oosterveld, *Elgar Companion ICC* (2020), pp. 101–4, 117 ('Article 98 did not receive much attention in Rome').

[265] See the beginning of Section A.(2) in this chapter (referring to such an obligation pursuant to an Art. 12 (3) declaration, or an ad hoc arrangement, agreement, or any other appropriate basis pursuant to Art. 87 (5) ICCS, esp. a UNSC referral).

[266] Above note 37 with main text.

the cooperation regime, speaks in favour of the same interpretation with regard to the other grounds for a cooperation obligation. After all, a non-State Party which voluntarily accepts the jurisdiction of the Court (pursuant to Article 12 (3)) or enters into an agreement with it (pursuant to Article 87 (5)) has consented to the ensuing (cooperation) obligations and thus can no longer be considered a 'third State' vis-à-vis the Statute within the meaning of Article 34 VCLT.[267]

From this follows equally, however, that an immunity cannot pose an obstacle to an ICC prosecution in the horizontal relation between State Parties[268] since their non-cooperation would otherwise undermine their general obligation to cooperate[269] and imply a disregard for the non-immunity rule of Article 27 (2) ICCS, to which they voluntarily agreed when becoming State Parties.[270] Indeed, a State's accession to the ICC Statute is to be interpreted as an automatic waiver to any form of immunity, therefore making an explicit waiver of immunity in the sense of Article 98 (1) ICCS redundant.[271] The Appeals Chamber has explicitly endorsed this view in the *Jordan* case:

> States Parties to the Rome Statute, have, by virtue of ratifying the Statute, accepted that Head of State immunity cannot prevent the Court from exercising jurisdiction—which is in line with customary law. There is no reason why article 27(2) should be interpreted in a way that would allow a State Party to invoke Head of State immunity in the horizontal relationship if the Court were to ask for the arrest and surrender of the Head of State by making a request to that effect to another State Party.[272]

Conversely, as regards non-State Parties, which are not subject to any (voluntary) cooperation obligation as mentioned above, Articles 98 and 27 ICCS entail that interstate immunities, as a rule, have to be taken into account, as long as these immunities also take effect in relation to the requested State, that is, have an *erga omnes* effect;[273] further, that the affected State has not waived the immunity,[274] and it is not superseded by international criminal or

[267] The consenting State is no longer a third State 'without ... consent' but rather falls under Art. 35 VCLT applicable to third States accepting certain obligations of a treaty. See also Bekou, *ICLR*, 19 (2019), 917–18, who even wants to apply Art. 87 (7) to such States.

[268] *Al Bashir*, ICC-02/05-01/09-195, para. 29; ICC, *Prosecutor v. Al Bashir*, PTC II, Decision Following the Prosecutor's Request for an Order Further Clarifying that the Republic of South Africa is under the Obligation to Immediately Arrest and Surrender Omar Al Bashir, ICC-02/05-01/09-242, 13 June 2015, para. 7.

[269] cf. Art. 86 ICCS.

[270] In a similar vein, Meißner, *Zusammenarbeit* (2003), pp. 123–4; Kreß, in Grützner et al., *Rechtshilfeverkehr* (2003), IV A 1 mn. 244; Caeiro, in Caeiro and Moreira, *TPI* (2004), pp. 100 ff. In any case, a State Party shall never be prevented 'from discharging its obligations as a State Party to the Statute' regarding a problem related to Art. 98 (1), since, pursuant to Art. 97, the State Parties have an obligation to consult or notify the Court, cf. *Al Bashir*, ICC-02/05-01/09-195, paras. 15–16; such consultations 'do not trigger any suspension or stay of this standing obligation' to enforce a court request for arrest and surrender, cf. *Al Bashir*, ICC-02/05-01/09-242, para. 8.

[271] Conc., *Al Bashir*, ICC-02/05-01/09-139, para. 18; ICC, *Prosecutor v. Al Bashir*, PTC II, Decision under Article 87 (7) of the Rome Statute on the Non-compliance by South Africa with the Request by the Court for the Arrest and Surrender of Omar Al-Bashir, ICC-02/05-01/09-302, 6 July 2017, para. 93 ('no immunity needs to be waived'). In the same vein, Blommestijn and Ryngaert, *ZIS*, 5 (2010), 439; Kreicker, *ZIS*, 4 (2009), 350; more detailed Senn, *Immunitäten* (2010), pp. 253 ff. (266–7, 273 ff.), 324–5; Cryer, in Stahn, *Practice* (2015), p. 264; Jacobs, in Stahn, *Practice* (2015), p. 282; Kreß, 'Article 98', in Ambos, *Commentary* (2022), mn. 16–18; Carter et al., *Global Justice* (2018), p. 91 ('States Parties explicitly waive any applicable immunities'); Galand, *Security Council* (2019), 161; crit. Tladi, *ZIS*, 10 (2015), 498 ('notion of an implicit waiver of immunity ... a fiction'); also Tladi, *JICJ*, 13 (2015), 1043.

[272] *Al Bashir*, ICC-02/05-01/09-397, paras. 4 and 127.

[273] This is the case for State immunity, but not for diplomatic immunities (cf. Senn, *Immunitäten* (2010), pp. 282 ff., 325); cf. also Pedretti, *Immunity* (2015), pp. 408–9.

[274] Art. 98 (1) ICCS *in fine*. See also Senn, *Immunitäten* (2010), pp. 285 ff., 325; Kreß, 'Article 98', in Ambos, *Commentary* (2022), mn. 156–7.

human rights law[275] or by a Security Council referral[276] pursuant to Article 13 (b) ICCS.[277] The possible conflict of obligations, described here, should already be considered by the Court before making the request and, where appropriate, should be resolved through negotiations with the affected third State.[278]

If one applies these principles to the possible (horizontal) immunity of the incumbent President of Sudan, Al-Bashir, it seems, at first sight, to follow that he enjoys immunity, since Sudan is not an ICC State Party, his is a personal '*erga omnes*' (state-)immunity, and Sudan has never waived its immunity right. However, the UN Security Council did refer the situation in Darfur to the ICC by way of Resolution 1593/2005 and explicitly committed the Sudan to cooperate.[279] This means that the 'obligations under international law' within the meaning of Article 98 (1) ICCS that result from Al-Bashir's immunity are overruled,

[275] Kreicker, *ZIS*, 4 (2009), 355–6, with further references; Kreicker, *Völkerrechtliche Exemtionen I* (2007), pp. 290 ff.; Kreicker, in Grützner et al., *Rechtshilfeverkehr* (2010), III E mn. 14 ff., 33; Senn, *Immunitäten* (2010), p. 325 (on functional immunities: pp. 76 ff., 87 ff., 97–8); Mettraux et al., *ICLR*, 18 (2018), 593 ff., at 595 (arguing, focusing on the 'nature of the offence', in favour of a CIL exclusion of immunities which applies to international *and* domestic international criminal law proceedings); in the same vein, Eboe-Osuji, *JICJ*, 21 (2023), 484 ('no doubt that customary international law no longer accepts immunity for anyone, including heads of state, suspected or accused of gross human rights violation in the order of international crimes, especially when the suspect is being prosecuted before an international criminal tribunal'); more restrictive with regard to domestic proceedings McDougall, *JCSL* 28 (2023), 216 ('customary law exception to functional immunity for serious international crimes regardless whether they are committed in an official capacity'; 'foreign domestic courts will be unable to exercise jurisdiction over persons who enjoy personal immunity (including President Putin) during their term in office'). For a profound analysis of the scholarly opinions, see Kreß, 'Article 98', in Ambos, *Commentary* (2022), mn. 93 ff. (concluding, at mn. 115–16, 121, that 'a strong argument can be made ... that the CIL rule of personal immunity has never been applicable before an international criminal court with a credible universal orientation' [mn. 115] or at least that 'an exception to that rule has developed' through State practice [mn. 116, 121]); arguing in favour of a CIL exclusion of immunities before an international court with regard to international crimes, albeit accepting limitations of this exception, for otherwise Arts. 27 and 98 would be redundant, Talmon, 'Immunität von Staatsbediensteten', in Paulus et al., *Immunität* (2014), pp. 359 ff; Pedretti, *Immunity* (2015), pp. 274 ff., 304 ff.; yet, also see Sadat, in deGuzman and Oosterveld, *Elgar Companion ICC* (2020), p. 117 ('Article 98's adoption was not meant to undermine the principle that "irrelevance of official position" effectively removed immunities *ratione materiae* as well as "temporal immunity" from prosecution', see also above at note 265); dissenting, Ralph, 'Article 98', in Fernandez and Pacreau, *Commentaire II* (2012), p. 1915; contra a CIL exception at least with regard to the horizontal level, Akande, *AJIL Unbound*, 112 (2018), 175; previously against a human rights exception, Wuerth, *AJIL*, 106 (2012), 768. Recently for an immunity exclusion with regard to Israeli Prime Minister Netanyahu (calling for a same treatment as President Putin) Ambos, Bock, Geneuss, Jeßberger, Kreß, Paulus, Talmon, Oeter and Zimmermann, *Verfassungsblog* 14 June 2024.

[276] The applicable resolution would then supersede conflicting 'obligations under international law' in the sense of Art. 98 (1) ICCS, cf. Senn, *Immunitäten* (2010), pp. 288 ff., 325–6; Tladi, *JICJ*, 11 (2013), 208 ff.; Kreß, 'Article 98', in Ambos, *Commentary* (2022), mn. 141–8 (discussing the relevant case law); de Wet, *JICJ*, 13 (2015), 1057–63. This view has been taken with regard to the Darfur referral Resolution (1593/2005) by PTC II in *Al Bashir*, ICC-02/05-01/09-195, paras. 29–30; in the same vein, *Al Bashir*, ICC-02/05-01/09-302, para. 83 ('obligations defined in the Statute may become incumbent upon a State not as a result of its acceptance of the Statute, but as a result of, and under, the Charter of the United Nations'). Thereon, see van der Wilt, in Ruys et al., *HB Immunities* (2019), pp. 600–1.

[277] cf. also Kreß, in Grützner et al., *Rechtshilfeverkehr* (2003), IV A 1 mn. 243 ff.; Meißner, *Zusammenarbeit* (2003), p. 125; Scheffer, *JICJ*, 3 (2005), 336–7; Fixson, in Kirsch, *Internationale Strafgerichtshöfe* (2005), pp. 225–6; dissenting van Alebeek, *Immunity of States* (2009), pp. 281 ff.; Akande, *AJIL*, 98 (2004), 418 ff.

[278] cf. Meißner, *Zusammenarbeit* (2003), pp. 120–1; Kreß, in Grützner et al., *Rechtshilfeverkehr* (2003), IV A 1 mn. 242; Sluiter, *Evidence* (2002), p. 171; Jacobs, in Stahn, *Practice* (2015), p. 284; Kreß and Prost, 'Article 98', in Ambos, *Commentary* (2022), mn. 156; Akande, *EJIL: Talk!*, 31 March 2016; cf. also Rule 195 (1) RPE ICC. On the role of the ICC as addressee of the provisions, see Friman, 'State Cooperation', in Cryer et al., *Introduction ICL* (2014), pp. 520–1 (no longer explicitly maintained by Vasiliev in the 2019 edition). On the proceedings before the Pre-Trial Chamber, see Senn, *Immunitäten* (2010), pp. 290 ff.

[279] The operative part of the Resolution (para. 2) places Sudan and 'all other parties to the conflict in Darfur' under an obligation to cooperate; (other) non-Party States are however not obliged to cooperate and the jurisdiction should not be extended to include the personnel of these States (para. 6). See also Lindemann, in Ziegler et al., *Kriegsverbrecherprozesse* (2009), pp. 236–7.

as mentioned above, by the SC Resolution in relation to Sudan as a 'third State'.[280] ICC PTCs have reached the same result but took different routes,[281] either advocating a lifting of Al-Bashir's immunity by way of SC Resolution 1593 (2005)[282] or by a general customary international law exception to Article 98 (1).[283] The Appeals Chamber[284] ultimately combined both approaches[285] and stressed that Article 98 (1) is merely a procedural norm.[286]

[280] This is the prevailing view; cf. Kreicker, *HuV-I*, 21 (2008), 162–3 ('der Sicherheitsrat völkerrechtliche Immunitäten … auch insoweit implizit für unbeachtlich erklärt hat'); Frau, *Verhältnis* (2010), pp. 359–60; Akande, *JICJ*, 7 (2009), 340 ff. ('puts Sudan in an analogous position to a party to the Statute. The only difference is that Sudan's obligations to accept the provisions of the Statute are derived not from the Statute directly, but from a UN Security Council resolution and the Charter'); Akande, *EJIL: Talk!* 29 March 2016; Papillon, *ICLR*, 10 (2010), 284 ff.; Kreß, in Bergsmo and Ling, *State Sovereignty and ICL* (2012), pp. 241–2; also Senn, *Immunitäten* (2010), pp. 288 ff. (leaving it open however in n. 1205); Pedretti, *Immunity* (2015), pp. 288–90; Ohlin, *Opinio Juris* 17 June 2015; de Wet, *JICJ*, 13 (2015), 1058–63; Ventura, *JICJ*, 13 (2015), 1017–22; for the same result, albeit with a different reasoning, Kreß, 'Article 98', in Ambos, *Commentary* (2022), mn. 141 ('In view of the fact that the CIL rule of personal immunity does not apply in proceedings for crimes under CIL before the ICC including the horizontal limb of the triangular legal relationship between the ICC, a requested State Party and a third State, the question of whether the SC could, through a legally binding resolution, displace any applicable CIL personal immunity is essentially a theoretical one'); furthermore, see with regard to the *Jordan* decision mn. 148 with n. 457('the non-State Party concerned is accordingly placed, by virtue of a binding Security Council decision, in a legal position analogous to that of a State Party') ; Boschiero, *JICJ*, 13 (2015), 636 ff. (650: 'since Sudan is de facto in a position analogous to that of states parties, a waiver of immunity under Article 98(1) would not be necessary'); Burghardt and Geneuss, *ZIS*, 4 (2009), 140–1 (differentiating between State Parties for which the request is binding and non-State Parties, for which no obligation can be derived from the Statute or indirectly from the SC Resolution, but only a right); Cryer, in Stahn, *Practice* (2015), pp. 268–71 (favouring the absence of immunity in the *Al Bashir* case, on the basis of the 'duty not to evade treaty obligations' and invoking the principles *ex injuria jus non oritur* and *ex delicto non oritur actio*). For a dissenting view, see Gaeta, *JICJ*, 7 (2009), 327 ff. (arguing that 'the request to states parties [let alone non-Party States] to surrender him [Al Bashir] is not in accordance with the terms of the ICC Statute and therefore not binding upon them'); see also Blommestijn and Ryngaert, *ZIS*, 5 (2010), 440 (arguing that Sudan has not become a State Party by virtue of the SC referral); Tladi, *JICJ*, 11 (2013), 211–13.

[281] For a summary and crit. discussion, Kreß, in Bergsmo and Ling, *State Sovereignty and ICL* (2012), pp. 227 ff. (distinguishing between the 'Security Council' and the 'customary law avenue' and in favour of the former); see also Schabas, *ICC Commentary* (2016), pp. 1348–9; Cryer, in Stahn, *Practice* (2015), p. 271; Jacobs, in Stahn, *Practice* (2015), pp. 289–91; Galand, *Security Council* (2019), 162 ff.; Sadat, in deGuzman and Oosterveld, *Elgar Companion ICC* (2020), p. 116 ('Pre-Trial Chambers … have not been consistent in their reasoning'); summarizing, Horsthemke, *Immunitäten* (2019), pp. 172 ff.

[282] *Al Bashir*, ICC-02/05-01/09-3, paras. 41 ff. (45: SC 'has also accepted that the investigation into the said situation … will take place.'); *Al Bashir*, ICC-02/05-01/09-195, para. 31; *Al Bashir*, ICC-02/05-01/09-242, para. 6. PTC II varied the general overruling thesis by way of a Chapter VII resolution by adding the waiver argument, *Al Bashir*, ICC-02/05-01/09-195, paras. 29–30 and above note 275 with main text; *contra*, e.g. Blommestijn and Ryngaert, *ZIS*, 5 (2010), 440 ('*until* the Government of Sudan has actually officially waived the immunity of Al-Bashir, this restriction on the Court *remains fully in place*. As long as Sudan refuses to act on its obligation to waive Al-Bashir's immunity, the Court is not given the authority to simply ignore the immunity from prosecution that Al-Bashir continues to hold' [emphasis in the original]); Tladi, *ZIS*, 10 (2015), 497 ff. (498); Tladi, *JICJ*, 13 (2015), 1042 ff. (1043).

[283] *Al Bashir*, ICC-02/05-01/09-139-Corr, paras. 18, 43 (no immunity for heads of State of non-State Parties in respect of proceedings before the ICC); conc. *Al Bashir*, ICC-02/05-01/09-140-tENG, para. 13. In the same vein, e.g. Kreicker, *ZIS*, 4 (2009), 356 (CIL exception to immunity); against such an exception with regard to sitting heads of State, Supreme Court of Appeal of South Africa, *The Minister of Justice and Constitutional Development v. The Southern African Litigation Centre*, No. 867/15, Judgment, para. 84, 15 March 2016 (with regard to Al Bashir's presence at the AU summit in South Africa and the non-execution of the ICC arrest warrant by the South African authorities; thereon Akande, *EJIL: Talk!* 29 March 2016); cautious also van der Wilt, in Ruys et al., *HB Immunities* (2019), pp. 600, 605 ('evidence advanced for the existence of customary international law is rather thin'; 'no strong evidence').

[284] Advocating an advisory opinion of the ICJ (being a more neutral Court) Akande, *EJIL: Talk* 31 March 2016 ('key to making progress on this contentious issue').

[285] For a methodological critique in this respect, Nouwen, *CambLJ*, 78 (2019), 605 ('judgement and accompanying texts leave ambiguous whether the international-criminal-court-exception route is an independent avenue to deny the relevance of immunity, or whether the Security-Council-analogous-to-state-party route was still necessary in order to address the horizontal relationship').

[286] *Al Bashir*, ICC-02/05-01/09-397, para. 5 ('procedural rule that determines how the Court is to proceed where any immunity exists such that it could stand in the way of a request for cooperation'); on this aspect, see Mudukuti, *AJIL*, 114 (2020), 105.

A decisive factor then was that Sudan, as a UN Member State, was obligated to cooperate fully under SC Resolution 1593 and that, as a result, Article 27 (2) (also) applied horizontally at the interstate level.[287] On a more general level, the Chamber held that immunity *ratione personae* before an international court has no support in customary international law.[288] As a consequence, ICC arrest warrants against heads of State, as the more recent one against President Putin[289] and a possible one against Prime Minister Netanyahu,[290] have to be executed, i.e. the ICC's immunity exclusion also concerns the horizontal, interstate relationship.[291] While from the Court's perspective the *Jordan* AC decision has then settled the matter,[292] the controversy is still going on in State capitals and scholarly circles.[293] Thus, it remains to be seen whether a renewed litigation of the matter before the ICC will produce the same results.

As a result of the above considerations one should distinguish between three groups of States: State Parties, non-State Parties with (other) cooperation obligations, and those without any such obligations (third States within the meaning of Article 34 VCLT). As to the second group of States one can further distinguish between States which have voluntarily contracted into the ICC regime (by way of an Article 12 (3) declaration or an Article 87 (5) agreement) and those that have been subjected to it by way of a UNSC referral (so far Sudan and Libya). As to the first two groups of States (State Parties and non-State Parties with obligations), any immunity will, in principle, be suspended also with regard to third States, that is, Article 27 ICCS prevails over Article 98 (1) ICCS, since those States (including the ones referred to the Court by a UNSC resolution)[294] are under a primary obligation to

[287] *Al Bashir*, ICC-02/05-01/09-397, paras. 7, 135–45. On this, see Sadat, in deGuzman and Oosterveld, *Elgar Companion ICC* (2020), pp. 122–3 ('combined effect of Articles 27, 13(b) and Security Council Resolution 1593'; 'Appeals Chamber relied upon customary law as well'); crit. Ubéda-Saillard, 'Article 98', in Fernandez et al., *Commentaire CPI II* (2019), p. 2321 ('se retranche derrière la résolution 1593 (2005)').

[288] *Al Bashir*, ICC-02/05-01/09-397, para. 113 ('there is neither State practice nor opinio juris that would support the existence of Head of State immunity under customary international law *vis-à-vis* an international court'); furthermore, see the Joint Concurring Opinion of Judges Eboe-Osuji, Morrison, Hofmański, and Bossaparas, *Al Bashir*, ICC-02/05-01/09-397-Anx1, paras. 239 ff., 252 ('customary international law harbours no rule that contradicts Nuremberg Principle III relative to the jurisdiction of an international court'). See also above notes 273 and 276 and main text.

[289] <https://www.icc-cpi.int/news/situation-ukraine-icc-judges-issue-arrest-warrants-against-vladimir-vladimirovich-putin-and>.

[290] On the application of 20 May 2024 see <https://www.icc-cpi.int/news/statement-icc-prosecutor-karim-aa-khan-kc-applications-arrest-warrants-situation-state>.

[291] *Al Bashir*, ICC-02/05-01/09-397, para. 114 ('The absence of a rule of customary international law recognising Head of State immunity vis-à-vis international courts is relevant not only to the question of whether an international court may issue a warrant for the arrest of a Head of State and conduct proceedings against him or her, but also for the horizontal relationship between States when a State is requested by an international court to arrest and surrender the Head of State of another State').

[292] cf. Jackson, *EJIL: Talk!* 21 March 2023.

[293] The gist of the issue is of course if the AC's position is supported by State practice; crit. Vasiliev, in Cryer et al., *Introduction ICL* (2019), p. 530; Nouwen, *CambLJ*, 78 (2019), 608; Akande, *EJIL: Talk!*, 6 May 2023 ('reasoning appears to assert that parties to the Rome Statute, have, by creating the Court, taken away the rights of non-party states under international law'); Liu, *EJIL: Talk!*, 14 April 2023 ('debatable'; 'seems to render Article 98(1) meaningless'); on State practice before the AC decision, cf. Horsthemke, *Immunitäten* (2019), pp. 172 ff. (ultimately leaving the question open, at 297); for a methodological critique see Kjeldgaard-Pedersen, *JICJ*, 19 (2021), 951 ('Appeals Chamber ... turns the burden of proof of the existence of a customary rule on its head. Instead of arguing that an exception to personal immunity of Heads of State has developed, the Appeals Chamber claims that there is, as a starting point, no immunity before "an international court", and that there is no state practice and *opinio juris* to support such a rule'); for views in favour of an immunity exclusion, see above note 276. The ILC has in its Draft on *Immunity of State officials from foreign criminal jurisdiction*, as adopted on first reading in its 73rd session in 2022 (A/CN.4/L.969, 31 May 2022), proposed to exclude (functional) immunity *ratione materiae* for certain 'crimes under international law' (genocide, CaH, war crimes, apartheid, torture, enforced disappearance). Yet, it remains to be seen whether this Draft Art. 7 will finally be adopted on second reading.

[294] Thus, Sudan is explicitly placed under an obligation through SC Res. 1593, see note 288 in this chapter. See also Akande, *JICJ*, 10 (2012), 299.

enforce an ICC (surrender) request.[295] Thus, the conflicting 'obligations under international law' referred to in Article 98 (1) ICCS only become relevant in respect to (full) third States.

To be sure, a non-State Party which, like Sudan or Libya, has been subjected to the ICC regime by a UNSC referral, is under a general cooperation obligation pursuant to the respective UNSC resolution, thereby triggering the rule of precedence of the UN Charter[296] by way of the binding nature of SC resolutions.[297] Yet, third States can only be bound in this respect by the same resolutions. If these—as the here relevant Resolutions 1593/2005 (Sudan) and 1979/2011 (Libya)—do *not* contain such an explicit cooperation obligation for third States (but only for the State referred to the Court by the resolution), one can at best assume a permission (a right) for them to cooperate (but not an obligation!) with regard to the arrest and surrender of fugitives of the State(s) referred to the Court.[298] This result does not change with the extension of the arrest warrant to include the crime of genocide,[299] for the Genocide Convention by itself does not give rise to an obligation to cooperate.[300]

*2.* Article 98 (2) Under Article 98 (2) the Court may not proceed with a surrender request in respect of a *national of a sending State* if this would force the requested State to act against an international agreement which allows for such surrender only with the permission of that State.[301] Once again, the bilateral relationship between the requested State[302] (host or receiving State) and the sending State is of relevance here, more specifically the possible treaty obligation of the requested towards the sending State that prohibits the former to surrender

[295] cf. Akande, *JICJ*, 7 (2009), 337 ff. Therefore, *Al Bashir*, ICC-02/05-01/09-242, paras. 9–10, held that 'the Republic of South Africa [for instance] is already aware of its obligation under the Rome Statute to immediately arrest Omar Al-Bashir and surrender him to the Court, as it is aware of the Court's explicit position ... that the immunities granted to Omar Al Bashir under international law and attached to his position as a Head of State have been implicitly waived by the Security Council'.

[296] Art. 103 UN Charter.

[297] cf. Art. 25 UN Charter. In the same vein, Tladi, *ZIS*, 10 (2015), 499, 500, arguing that such conflicts (could have been and) can be avoided if the SC (had placed and) places 'an obligation on all states to cooperate with the Court'; also Tladi, *JICJ*, 13 (2015), 1045, 1047.

[298] Convincingly Akande, *JICJ*, 7 (2009), 340 ff.; see also references in note 281 and Kowalski, 'Article 86', in Klamberg et al., *Commentary ICC II* (2023), pp. 613–23; Tladi, *JICJ*, 11 (2013), 208 ff. (however excluding 'Head of State Immunity' from Art. 98, note 262 in this chapter); for a different view, see Jacobs, in Stahn, *Practice* (2015), pp. 295–6, arguing that Sudan's duty to cooperate in conformity with the Rome Statute also includes Art. 27, and therefore 'immunities would not any more be an issue under Article 98 (1) in the context of a request for cooperation than if the third state was indeed a State Party to the Rome Statute, which is generally accepted'; see also Boschiero, *JICJ*, 13 (2015), 649–52 (arguing that 'No impediments exist in respect to the triangular relationship between Sudan, the ICC and the DRC'); Blommestijn and Ryngaert, *ZIS*, 5 (2010), 441–3 (differentiating between Sudan (being subject 'to a strict legal obligation to "cooperate fully with and provide any necessary assistance to the Court and the Prosecutor", thereby expanding the international duty to cooperate beyond the States Parties alone' [fn. omitted]) and other non-State Parties, which are 'under no international obligation to act upon any Court request for Al-Bashir's arrest' but 'have strict obligations under customary international law to abide by the rules of immunity' and therefore are not '*permitted* under international law to arrest Al-Bashir' [emphasis in the original]); with respect to the US, see Slye, in Gore, *Beyond Kampala* (2010), pp. 21–2. In any case, the ICC directed its request for assistance at both State Parties and non-State Parties (*Al Bashir*, ICC-02/05-01/09-3, p. 93).

[299] ICC, *Prosecutor v. Al Bashir*, PTC I, Second Warrant of Arrest for Omar Hassan Ahmad Al Bashir, ICC-02/05-01/09-95, 12 July 2010.

[300] cf. Akande, *JICJ*, 7 (2009), 348 ff.; Jacobs, in Stahn, *Practice* (2015), pp. 296–9; for a different view, Sluiter, *JICJ*, 8 (2010), 368 ff., 378–82 (arguing that applying 'the more effective regime set out in the Genocide Convention, which contains no explicit grounds for refusal' 'as an additional basis for support for and cooperation with the Court', 'increases both the quantity and quality of the duty to cooperate'); Ohlin, *Opinio Juris* 17 June 2015 ('the duty to prosecute or extradite any individual accused of genocide ... is a jus cogens obligation that prevails over any supposed legal obligation under the law of diplomatic relations').

[301] In detail, Senn, *Immunitäten* (2010), pp. 343 ff.; Kreß, 'Article 98', in Ambos, *Commentary* (2022), mn. 158–76; Prost, *JICJ*, 16 (2018), 365 ('discussion among the cooperation experts at the time focused solely on pre-existing obligations of a general nature').

[302] cf. Senn, *Immunitäten* (2010), pp. 346–7, 414.

nationals of the latter to the ICC without the latter's permission.[303] Thus, in fact, Article 98 (2) ICCS is not about obligations of or towards the ICC, but interstate obligations.[304]

The term '*sending State*' seems to imply that the provision mainly pertains to so-called 'Status of Forces Agreements' (SOFAs).[305] For the 'sending' of a person presumes that the presence of that person on the territory of the requested State is a direct result of an official act by the sending State.[306] In any case, the collision outlined in Article 98 (2) ICCS only arises if the sending State is not a State Party to the ICC.[307] For, if it were a State Party, it would be obliged to surrender the person to the ICC itself[308] and could not therefore make a surrender through the requested (host) State dependent on its consent.[309] If the sending State is not a State Party however, one must differentiate as follows: for 'agreements' concluded between the requested and the sending State *before* the signing of the ICC Statute, Article 98 (2) ICCS will be applicable, but for those concluded there*after* it will not.[310] While this interpretation does not directly follow from the wording of Article 98 (2) ICCS (as it is not limited, as Article 97 (c) ICCS is, to 'pre-existing' agreements),[311] it can be inferred from its legislative history, and especially from the following teleological argument:[312] from the moment of signing up to the ICCS the respective State is prohibited from acting in a manner that runs contrary to the 'object and purpose' of the treaty,[313] that is, in the case of

303 On the permission requirement in detail, see Senn, *Immunitäten* (2010), pp. 351 ff.

304 cf. Keitner, *UCLA JIL & ForAff*, 6 (2001), 254–5; Kreß, in Grützner et al., *Rechtshilfeverkehr* (2003), IV A 1 mn. 247; Meißner, *Zusammenarbeit* (2003), p. 126; Ambos, *NJW*, 54 (2001), 409. On the controversies surrounding Rule 195 (2) RPE ICC in this sense, see Harhoff and Mochochoko, in Lee, *ICC* (2001), pp. 664 ff.; Gartner, in Fischer et al., *Prosecution* (2001), pp. 430 ff.; Keitner, *UCLA JIL & ForAff*, 6 (2001), 248 ff. (260 ff.); Schabas, *ICC Commentary* (2016), p. 1349; Kreß, 'Article 98', in Ambos, *Commentary* (2022), mn. 158.

305 Kreß, 'Article 98', in Ambos, *Commentary* (2022), mn. 162–3; Meißner, *Zusammenarbeit* (2003), pp. 128 ff.; Keitner, *UCLA JIL & ForAff*, 6 (2001), 233 ff.; Kreß, in Grützner et al., *Rechtshilfeverkehr* (2003), IV A 1 mn. 248; Scheffer, *JICJ*, 3 (2005), 338 ff.; Schomburg, in Kirsch, *Internationale Strafgerichtshöfe* (2005), p. 136; Cryer, *Prosecuting International Crimes* (2005), p. 154; Quesada-Alcalá, in Fernández-Sánchez, *Challenges of Humanitarian Law* (2005), pp. 303–4; Robinson, in Cryer et al., *Introduction ICL* (2019), p. 167; Adell, 'Article 98', in Klamberg et al., *Commentary ICC II* (2023), pp. 835–6. According to Fleck, *JICJ*, 1 (2003), 651 ff., 'Standard-SOFAs', such as the NATO Status of Forces Agreement, do not fall under Art. 98 (2) ICCS, but only under (1). These agreements generally establish a *concurring* jurisdiction between the sending State and the territorial (host) State, where usually the former will be granted primary jurisdiction to deal with crimes committed during or in connection with the service, and the latter for crimes in all other cases (generally see Rosenfeld, *WashUGlSLR*, 2 (2003), 280 ff.). According to Stein, in Bröhmer et al., *Menschenrechte* (2005), pp. 301–2, van der Wilt, *LJIL*, 18 (2005), 100–1, and Senn, *Immunitäten* (2010), pp. 384 ff. (387–8), 414, Art. 98 (2) ICCS can generally be applied to all immunity agreements. On the transfer of a person subjected to extradition to a third State, cf. Meißner, *Zusammenarbeit* (2003), p. 128.

306 Sendel, *ZIS*, 2 (2007), 122; Crawford et al., *ICCS and Bilateral Agreements* (2003), para. 43.

307 Dissenting, Jia, in Cassese, *Companion* (2009), pp. 165–6, for whom the collision can also exist when the sending State is a non-State Party.

308 Art. 89 (1), (2) ICCS.

309 Agreements within the meaning of Art. 98 (2) ICCS concluded *before* accession to the treaty will be overtaken by the *lex posterior* rule of Art. 30 (3) VCLT, but *later* agreements cannot require a consent for surrenders to the ICC (cf. Senn, *Immunitäten* (2010), pp. 367 ff., 415; also Kreß, in Grützner et al., *Rechtshilfeverkehr* (2003), IV A 1 mn. 249; Meißner, *Zusammenarbeit* (2003), pp. 131–2; Fixson, in Kirsch, *Internationale Strafgerichtshöfe* (2005), p. 226).

310 Similarly, but in more detail, Kreß, in Grützner et al., *Rechtshilfeverkehr* (2003), IV A 1 mn. 250; Kreß, 'Article 98', in Ambos, *Commentary* (2022), mn. 167–74; see also Keitner, *UCLA JIL & ForAff*, 6 (2001), 238, 250; Meißner, *Zusammenarbeit* (2003), pp. 126–7, 132 ff.; van der Wilt, *LJIL*, 18 (2005), 105; previously Ambos, *NJW*, 54 (2001), 409; essentially in the same vein, Stein, in Bröhmer et al., *Menschenrechte* (2005), pp. 302 ff. (306); Ralph, 'Article 98', in Fernandez and Pacreau, *Commentaire CPI II* (2012), pp. 1919 ff.; unconvinced, Zappalà, *JICJ*, 1 (2003), 122 ff.; dissenting, Scheffer, *JICJ*, 3 (2005), 340–1; Sendel, *ZIS*, 2 (2007), 123.

311 In the same vein, Wilmshurst, in Cryer et al., *Introduction ICL* (2010), p. 176; Prost, *JICJ*, 16 (2018), 366 ('with the benefit of hindsight, the language of Article 98 could have been more clearly articulated').

312 cf. also Kreß, in Grützner et al., *Rechtshilfeverkehr* (2003), IV A 1 mn. 250; Meißner, *Zusammenarbeit* (2003), pp. 126–7, 133–4.

313 cf. Art. 18 VCLT.

the ICCS, putting an end to impunity (cf. paragraph 5 of its preamble).[314] The fulfilment of the ICC's purpose is—where the territorial/sending State does not prosecute the crime[315]—predicated on the surrender of the suspect, given that a trial *in absentia* is not provided for in the Statute.[316] Finally, from the moment of accession to the ICCS, the requested State is obliged to surrender the suspect.[317] It could only avert this obligation by committing itself to prosecute and punish the crime or by obtaining a guarantee from the sending State, as home State of the suspect, that it will prosecute and punish the crime accordingly.[318]

For the above-mentioned reasons the *bilateral non-surrender agreements*[319] concluded by the US invoking Article 98 (2) ICCS are inadmissible and therefore void if they were reached with a Signatory State or even a State Party and/or if they extend *ratione personae* beyond the nationals sent by the US.[320] This is why the 'Guiding Principles' agreed upon by the EU Foreign Ministers[321] recommend that such bilateral agreements should only be concluded where pre-existing international agreements with the US, especially SOFAs and agreements on the legal assistance in criminal matters, do not suffice to accommodate US concerns. Additionally, the following *guidelines* apply to any new agreements concluded:

- It must be ensured that any person not surrendered to the ICC will be appropriately prosecuted in their national jurisdiction (*guarantee of prosecution*).
- Such agreements may not contain any exemptions for nationals of a State Party.
- Only persons that reside on the territory of the requested State because they were sent there by their home State may be exempted from surrender to the ICC.

The standard US Agreements cannot be reconciled with these guidelines in at least two aspects: they make national prosecution dependant on an inclusion of 'appropriate operative provisions' and they extend the scope *ratione personae* to all nationals and all other persons contracted by the US ('contracted personnel').[322]

[314] Stein, in Bröhmer et al., *Menschenrechte* (2005), p. 302 wants to draw on the underlying motive for concluding the immunity agreement; in relation to the US agreements, however, the sole motive is to exempt a particular group of persons from the ICC's jurisdiction.

[315] This possibility is emphasized by Keitner, *UCLA JIL & ForAff*, 6 (2001), 237; Zappalà, *JICJ*, 1 (2003), 122 ff.;Stein, in Bröhmer et al., *Menschenrechte* (2005), p. 303; and Souza, in Ambos and Japiassú, *Tribunal Penal Internacional* (2005), pp. 116–17. The US agreements only provide for these in a limited manner, as will be seen in the following main text.

[316] See Arts. 62, 67 (1)(d) ICCS; but see, for the Kenyatta exceptions, Chapter IV, A.(3)(b) in this volume. For a more detailed analysis, see Beltrán, in Gómez Colomer et al., *CPI* (2003), pp. 361–2; Hofstetter, *Verfahrensrecht* (2005), pp. 86 ff.; on the alternative Rule 61 RPE ICTY procedure, see Hofstetter, ibid., pp. 81 ff.

[317] Art. 89 (1) cl. 2 ICCS.

[318] Similarly Sendel, *ZIS*, 2 (2007), 123 ff.; Senn, *Immunitäten* (2010), pp. 403 ff., 416.

[319] For a list of non-surrender agreements, see <https://guides.ll.georgetown.edu/c.php?g=363527&p=2456099>; for a similar agreement envisaged by Egypt with a view to the non-surrender of Sudan's president Al-Bashir, see Fouladvand, *ICLR*, 14 (2014), 1048–9.

[320] On these (generally) additional agreements in detail, Steinberger-Fraunhofer, *Internationaler Strafgerichtshof* (2008), pp. 260 ff.; Senn, *Immunitäten* (2010), pp. 334 ff.; cf. also Ambos, *RDP*, 15 (2005), 110 ff.; Sendel, *ZIS*, 2 (2007), 124; also crit., Cryer, *Prosecuting* (2005), pp. 155–6; Kolb, in Kolb and Scalia, *Droit international pénal* (2012), pp. 286–7; on the discussion surrounding these agreements, see Kreß, 'Article 98', in Ambos, *Commentary* (2022), mn. 4–8. The reference in the preamble of SC Res. 1593 (2005) cannot lend legitimacy to these agreements; accurately, Wilmshurst, in Cryer et al., *Introduction ICL* (2007), p. 145.

[321] Guiding Principles concerning Arrangements between a State Party to the Rome Statute of the ICC and the United States regarding the Conditions to Surrender of Persons to the Court, reproduced in Benzing, *Max Planck UNYB*, 8 (2004) 193–5 (the former pdf available online disappeared); Zappalà, *JICJ*, 2003, 126 ff.; Triggs, in Dolgopol and Gardam, *Challenges*(2006), pp. 323–4; crit. by Kreß, in Grützner et al., *Rechtshilfeverkehr* (2003), IV A 1 mn. 250.

[322] cf. Stein, in Bröhmer et al., *Menschenrechte* (2005), pp. 303–4; van der Wilt, *LJIL*, 18 (2005), 104 ff.; Schomburg, in Kirsch, *Internationale Strafgerichtshöfe* (2005), p. 136; cf. also Scheffer, *JICJ*, 3 (2005), 339 ff., who points out that the US delegation in Rome did not—in contrast to the Bush government—want to extend the agreements to include US citizens that serve in a private, non-official manner (under the 'overall direction' of the

### (b) ICTY, ICTR, and KSC

The UN Member States have a general obligation to make provisional arrests and surrender persons if so requested by the ICTY/ICTR.[323] The applicable procedure is regulated in the RPE.[324] Interstate grounds for refusal are irrelevant. A requested State should however be allowed to consult the tribunals if there are doubts as to the arrested person's identity or if the request refers to a crime that is not within the jurisdiction of the tribunal.[325] As opposed to the ICC rules, the release from detention of persons to be surrendered to the ICTY/ICTR may only be decided upon by the tribunals themselves.[326] The rule of speciality does not apply.[327]

The situation at the KSC differs significantly from that of the other international criminal tribunals in that its Special Prosecutor's Office (SPO) has a proper police force which has the same authority as the Kosovo Police and thus may exercise powers on the territory of Kosovo;[328] an arrest warrant issued by the KSC has the same effect as a national one.[329] Of course, cooperation beyond Kosovo with third States or other entities depends on the respective agreements between this third State and the KSC,[330] unless it may be based on a (multilateral) mutual legal assistance agreement[331] or a third State cooperates on a voluntary basis (in principle, only to be expected from the KSC supporting States[332]).[333] A KSC Panel may issue an international arrest warrant, upon request by

US government) abroad. This restrictive interpretation also finds support in the respective provisions of the ASPA and the respective SC Resolutions (see Scheffer, *JICJ*, 3 (2005), 350 ff.).

[323] Arts. 29 (2)(d), (e) ICTYS and 28 (2)(d), (e) ICTRS/IRMCTS. For Rwanda, see Mochochoko, in Jalloh and Alhagi, *Accountability* (2015), pp. 74–8.

[324] cf. Rules 40, 40*bis*, 54–61, 64–5 RPE ICTY/ICTR, and 37, 38, 55–63, 67–8 RPE MICT; cf. also Rules 40, 40*bis*, 54–9 and 64–5 RPE SCSL. Extensively on the tribunals' system of surrender, Swart, in Cassese et al., *Rome Statute II* (2002), pp. 1249 ff. and Swart, in Cassese et al., *Rome Statute II* (2002), pp. 1664 ff.; Sluiter, *Evidence* (2002), pp. 177 ff.; Kirsch, in Beulke and Müller, *FS Bundesrechtsanwaltskammer* (2006), pp. 271 ff.

[325] In this sense, Swart, in Cassese et al., *Rome Statute II* (2002), p. 1249, and Swart, in Cassese et al., *Rome Statute II* (2002), pp. 1672–3.

[326] Rules 65 RPE ICTY/ICTR/SCSL and 68 RPE MICT. Crit. on the ICTY's provisions on detention, Swoboda, *GA*, 153 (2006), 642; Zahar and Sluiter, *ICL* (2008), pp. 286 ff., 322; Sluiter, in Darcy and Powderly, *Judicial Creativity* (2010), pp. 328 ff.

[327] See e.g. ICTY, *Prosecutor v. Zoran Žigić*, AC, Decision Stating Reasons for Appeals Chamber's Order of 29 May 1998, IT-97-24-AR73, 2 July 1998, para. 37. In the same vein, MICT, *Prosecutor v. Milan Kovačević*, Decision on Zoran Žigić's request to withhold consent for the execution of the Republic of Austria's Extradition Decision, MICT-14-81-ES.1, 12 December 2014, para. 13.

[328] cf. Art. 35 (3) KSC Law ('The police within the Specialist Prosecutor's Office shall have the authority and responsibility to exercise powers given to Kosovo Police under Kosovo law in accordance with the modalities established by this law'); also see Heinze, *JICJ*, 15 (2017), 990.

[329] cf. Art. 53 (3) KSC Law.

[330] cf. Art. 55 (1) KSC Law; see also Rule 208 (1)(a) RPE KSC. There are only a few such agreements and they are confidential; the SPO has one with Albania; for the agreement with EUROPOL, see <https://www.europol.europa.eu/cms/sites/default/files/documents/working_arrangement_establishing_cooperative_relations_between_the_kosovo_specialist_chambers_and_specialist_prosecutors_office_and_europol.pdf>.

[331] cf. Art. 55 (2) KSC Law; see also Rule 208 (1)(b) RPE KSC. A MLAA has been invoked in the *Goxhaj* case, concerning Kosovo and Albania, see <https://www.scp-ks.org/en/dritan-goxhaj-arrested-albania-pursuant-arrest-warrant-kosovo-specialist-chambers>.

[332] Supporting States are the EU Member States as well as Canada, Norway, Switzerland, Turkey, and the United States of America, cf. <https://www.scp-ks.org/en/background>.

[333] For a concrete example, see the Belgian Cooperation Law, 29 March 2004, which explicitly includes the cooperation with the KSC in the new Section VI*ter*, <https://etaamb.openjustice.be/fr/loi-du-29-mars-2004_n2004009246.html>. Another approach is the analogous application of the rules on inter-State cooperation to 'international courts or other inter- or supranational bodies with criminal justice function', cf. Art. 1 (3*bis* and 3*ter*) Swiss Federal Act on International Mutual Assistance in Criminal Matters, <https://www.fedlex.admin.ch/eli/cc/1982/846_846_846/en>

the SPO or *proprio motu*, 'to be transmitted to all States through any relevant international body'.[334] Third States may then execute such an arrest warrant under the abovementioned circumstances.[335]

### (3) Other mutual legal assistance

*(a) ICC regime*

*(i) General rules and national implementation*

Article 93 (1)(a)–(k) ICCS enumerates the following '*other forms of cooperation*' to be requested by the 'Court'[336] from State Parties: the localization of persons or items; taking evidence; questioning persons being investigated or prosecuted; servicing documents; facilitating the appearance of witnesses and experts before the ICC, the temporary transfer of detainees; the examination of places or sites, searches, and seizures; the provision of records and documents; the protection of witnesses and victims; and the preservation of evidence.[337] Furthermore, the ICC may request State Parties, by way of the 'residual provision' of subparagraph (l),[338] to provide '[a]ny other type of assistance' not prohibited by their national law.[339] This may include such measures as the surveillance of telecommunication systems.[340] Thus, in the Article 70 proceedings against *Bemba et al.*, Single Judge Tarfusser authorized the Prosecutor 'to seize the relevant authorities in Belgium and the Netherlands' to collect logs and recordings of telephone calls placed or received by two accused without, however, discussing the legal basis of these measures.[341] In any case, before prematurely

[334] Rule 54 RPE KSC. On the role of the Registry in transmitting such arrest warrants, see Rule 198 (1) RPE KSC.

[335] Rule 55, esp. para. 2 RPE KSC.

[336] The term 'Court' should be interpreted widely for the purposes of Art. 93 (1), including the prosecution, cf. *Kenyatta*, ICC-01/09-02/11-908, para. 27; Kreß, 'Article 93', in Ambos, *Commentary* (2022), mn. 12.

[337] cf. extensively on these measures, Kreß, in Grützner et al., *Rechtshilfeverkehr* (2003), IV A 1 mn. 263 ff.; Kreß, 'Article 93', in Ambos, *Commentary* (2022), mn. 18–39; Påle-Bartes, 'Article 93', in Klamberg et al., *Commentary ICC II* (2023), pp. 757–81; also Ciampi, in Cassese et al., *Rome Statute II* (2002), pp. 1728 ff.; Meißner, *Zusammenarbeit* (2003), pp. 190 ff.; De Cesari, in Malaguti, *Cooperation* (2007), pp. 58 ff.; on collection of evidence and State cooperation, see Klamberg, *Evidence* (2013), pp. 231 ff. For recommendations with respect to these measures, cf. ASP, Report on the Bureau on Cooperation, sixth session, ICC-ASP/6/21, 19 October 2007, paras. 29 ff.

[338] *Ruto and Sang*, ICC-01/09-01/11-1598, para. 128, holding that Art. 93 (1)(l) ICCS 'serves as a residual provision, covering forms of cooperation not otherwise covered by article 93 (1)(a) to (k) of the Statute'; see previously *Banda and Jerbo*, ICC-02/05-03/09-169, para.19 ('"catch all" provision'); *Ruto and Sang*, ICC-01/09-01/11-1274-Corr2, paras. 147–56.

[339] See, in detail, Kreß, 'Article 93', in Ambos, *Commentary* (2022), mn. 40–1; also Påle-Bartes, 'Article 93', in Klamberg et al., *Commentary ICC II* (2023), p. 757 (favouring a broad interpretation of 'assistance' not limiting it to a legal one).

[340] Kreß, in Grützner et al., *Rechtshilfeverkehr* (2003), IV A 1 mn. 279; apart from that it may cover the surveillance by technical means of private premises or the interception and recording of communications by technical means outside private premises, cf. Keller, in Ambos et al., *Rechtshilferecht* (2020), pp. 1519–21; for more examples of such assistance, cf. Kreß, 'Article 93', in Ambos, *Commentary* (2022), mn. 40, endorsing (mn. 20) the *Ruto and Sang* AC's view that a video-based witness interview shall be covered rather by a broader reading of Art. 93 (1)(b) than by a special interpretation of lit. l (*Ruto and Sang*, ICC-01/09-01/11-1598, para. 130); see previously, in favour of a teleological reduction with respect to video-based hearings, Kreß, in Grützner et al., *Rechtshilfeverkehr* (2003), IV A 1 mn. 266.

[341] ICC, *Prosecutor v. Bemba et al.*, PTC II (Single Judge), Decision on the Prosecutor's 'Request for judicial order to obtain evidence for investigation under Article 70', ICC-01/05-52-Red2, 29 July 2013, 3 February 2014 [public redacted version], paras. 3 ff. Only in a follow-up decision is reference made to Art. 93 but only in general without any analysis, cf. ICC, *Prosecutor v. Bemba et al.*, PTC II, Decision on the 'Prosecution's notice of receipt of communication from Dutch authorities concerning seized material' and related filings, ICC-01/05-01/13-135, 28 January 2014, p. 4.

assuming that the measure would be prohibited, the requested State should verify that there are no alternative means of carrying out the request in compliance with its national law,[342] or if it could not be subjected to certain conditions, or provided at a later date.[343]

The *national implementing legislation* follows by and large the statutory rules, albeit with a different degree as to their mandatory character. In *Germany*, § 47 (1) IStGHG provides for a mandatory duty to provide legal assistance—defined broadly by § 47 (2) IStGHG[344]—where the requirements of the ICC Statute are met. Such assistance could consist of searches, seizures, and the confiscation of assets[345] as well as the surveillance of telecommunication systems and measures of observation.[346] Furthermore, the law allows the ICC to hold hearings in Germany and to carry out other autonomous non-coercive measures on German territory.[347] In the *UK*, Part 3 of the ICC Act 2001 provides a detailed outline of any 'other forms of legal assistance' and sets these out in detail in Sections 28–38. These include questioning, taking and production of evidence, transfer of prisoners, entry, search and seizure, taking fingerprints and non-intimate samples, and investigations of proceeds and freezing orders. The *Argentinian* Implementation Law equally provides for a—broadly framed—section concerning 'other forms of legal assistance'. ICC requests for assistance 'shall' be executed as long as they are within the scope of the ICC Statute and do not affect national security.[348] According to *Canada*'s Mutual Legal Assistance Act 1985, the provision of legal assistance is not mandatory (Section 8 (2): 'may'). The Act provides for legal assistance in the form of searches and seizures,[349] transfer of detained persons,[350] lending exhibits,[351] and anything else specified in an agreement for mutual legal assistance such as the ICC Statute.[352] Sections 17–23.1 allow the ICC to carry out certain specified autonomous investigatory measures, upon application to the competent court, via the Minister of Justice. In *Australia*, Part 4 of the ICC Act 2002 deals with legal assistance apart from arrest and surrender. These measures, however, are by no means mandatory, and Division 3[353] contains a long list of restrictions on the provision of assistance. Where these do not apply, assistance may include identifying or locating persons or things,[354] taking evidence and producing documents,[355] questioning of persons,[356] temporary transfer of prisoners,[357] and searches and seizures and the examination of places or sites.[358] Part 5 of the Act allows the ICC to conduct investigations or sittings in Australia in accordance with the ICC Statute. In the *Netherlands*, the other forms of cooperation are dealt with in Chapter 3 of the ICC (Implementation) Act.

[342] In the same vein, Caeiro and Lemos, 'Commentary', in Klip and Freeland, *Annotated Leading Cases* (2013), p. 614, arguing further that *other forms of cooperation* do not include a request to the competent judicial authorities of the State Party to initiate an investigation.

[343] Art. 93 (5) ICCS.

[344] § 47 (2) IStGHG speaks of 'all support given to the Court in its activities based upon the Rome Statute, independent of whether the mutual assistance is carried out by a court or by a government office.' (translation by the German Federal Foreign Office (*Auswärtiges Amt*), <https://www.gesetze-im-internet.de/englisch_istghg/index.html>. See also MacLean, *ZRP*, 35 (2002), 260, 263–4.

[345] § 52 IStGHG.

[346] § 59 IStGHG.

[347] §§ 61–2 IStGHG.

[348] Arts. 40–44 Ley 26.200, 13 December 2006.

[349] Sections 10–16 Mutual Legal Assistance Act.

[350] Sections 24–9 Mutual Legal Assistance Act.

[351] Sections 30–4 Mutual Legal Assistance Act.

[352] Section 8 (1) Mutual Legal Assistance Act.

[353] Sections 51–62 ICC Act.

[354] Section 63 ICC Act.

[355] Sections 64–9 ICC Act.

[356] Section 70 ICC Act.

[357] Sections 74–5 ICC Act.

[358] Sections 76–8 ICC Act.

According to Section 45 (1), requests by the ICC for such forms of cooperation 'shall, to the extent possible, be executed in the desired manner'. They include placing (voluntary) prisoners at the disposal of the ICC as witnesses or for other measures of cooperation,[359] the seizure of evidence,[360] telecommunication tapping, systematic surveillance, infiltration, undercover entry, etc.[361]

In turn, the ICC may also provide legal *assistance to State Parties* or non-State Parties in relation to crimes that fall within its jurisdiction or other serious crimes.[362] In this case of a so-called 'reverse' cooperation,[363] already discussed in relation to the so-called positive complementarity concept,[364] the ICC could, for instance, provide relevant evidence—possibly with the consent of the affected State and taking into account relevant provisions on witnesses and victims' protection—or interrogate persons that are in its custody. However, the ICC does not have a duty to provide assistance, it only 'may' do so if it considers it appropriate;[365] the relationship of cooperation between the ICC and a State is not based on reciprocity.[366]

A request for other legal assistance should be made in writing and should specify,[367] amongst others, its purpose and legal basis, information on the whereabouts of the suspect, and regarding identification, the essential facts the request is based upon and any information required in accordance with the laws of the requested State.[368] The requested State may inform the ICC as to the requirements under its national laws.[369] The ICC should safeguard

[359] Section 48 ICC (Implementation) Act.

[360] Section 50 (1)(d) ICC (Implementation) Act.

[361] Section 52 ICC (Implementation) Act.

[362] Art. 93 (10) ICCS.

[363] For more details, see Kreß, 'Article 93', in Ambos, *Commentary* (2022), mn. 76–87 with case law references; also Stahn, *CLF*, 19 (2008), 107, 112; also Cryer, *Prosecuting* (2005), p. 156; Gioia, in Malaguti, *Cooperation* (2007), pp. 75 ff.; Gioia, *LJIL*, 19 (2006), 1117–19; Gioia, in Stahn and El Zeidy, *Complementarity II* (2011), pp. 807 ff.; Tillier, *ICLR*, 13 (2013), 554 ff.; Påle-Bartes, 'Article 93', in Klamberg et al., *Commentary ICC II* (2023), pp. 779–80. On the question of requests and measures directed at the ICTY or ICTR by States, see Sluiter, *Evidence* (2002), pp. 85–6.

[364] See Chapter III, B.(3) in this volume. Note, however, that complementarity and (reverse) cooperation are separate issues, cf. ICC, *Prosecutor v. Muthaura et al.*, PTC II, Decision on the Application by the Government of Kenya Challenging the Admissibility of the Case pursuant to Article 19 (2)(b) of the Statute, ICC-01/09-02/11-96, 30 May 2011, paras. 30–31, also referred to in Chapter III in this volume. On positive complementarity, see *Situation in Venezuela I*, PTC I Public Redacted Version of 'Decision on the "Request for judicial control submitted to the Pre-Trial Chamber I of the International Criminal Court by the Bolivarian Republic of Venezuela pursuant to Articles 15 and 21.3 of the Statute and Rule 46.2 of the Rules of the regulations of the Court"', ICC-02/18-9-Red, 2 March 2022, para. 19. See also ICC-OTP, *Complementarity and Cooperation* (2024), para. 13, and the discussion by Burke-White, *ICC Forum* (2023).

[365] cf. ICC, *Situation in the Republic of Kenya*, PTC II, Decision on the Request for Assistance Submitted on Behalf of the Government of the Republic of Kenya pursuant to Article 93 (10) of the Statute and Rule 194 of the Rules of Procedure and Evidence, ICC-01/09-63, 19 June 2011, para. 29; conc., ICC, *Situation in the Republic of Kenya*, Decision on the Second Request for Assistance Submitted on Behalf of the Government of the Republic of Kenya pursuant to Article 93 (10) of the Statute and Rule 194 of the Rules of Procedure and Evidence, ICC-01/09-97, 12 July 2012, para. 17; see also ICC, *Prosecutor v. Ruto et al.*, PTC II, Decision on the Application by the Government of Kenya Challenging the Admissibility of the Case pursuant to Article 19 (2)(b) of the Statute, ICC-01/09-01/11-101, 30 May 2011, para. 35. On the OTP's new system for receiving requests for assistance, which incorporates new technologies to enhance efficiency, see ICC-OTP, *Report 2023* (2023), pp. 83–4.

[366] In detail, Sluiter, *Evidence* (2002), pp. 84–6; Ciampi, in Cassese et al., *Rome Statute II* (2002), pp. 1742–4; Palmisano, in Lattanzi and Schabas, *Rome Statute I* (2000), pp. 411–12; Gioia, in Malaguti, *Cooperation* (2007), pp. 75 ff., esp. 78, 87–9; Détais and de Sena, 'Article 93', in Fernandez et al., *Commentaire CPI II* (2019), pp. 2270–1.

[367] On the required *specificity* of the cooperation requests, cf. *Banda and Jerbo*, ICC-02/05-03/09-169, paras. 20 ff.; Kreß and Prost, 'Article 96', in Ambos, *Commentary* (2022), mn. 8–9; Détais and de Sena, 'Article 96', in Fernandez et al., *Commentaire CPI II* (2019), pp. 2299–300.

[368] Art. 96 (1), (2) ICCS; for further procedural details with regard to the different forms of cooperation in Art. 93, see Rules 190–3 RPE ICC; for procedural details regarding the reverse cooperation under Art. 93 (10) ICCS, see Rule 194 RPE ICC.

[369] Art. 96 (3) ICCS; see also the parallel provision of Art. 91 (4) regarding surrender. Both provisions aim to avoid a too burdensome procedure for the Court; cf. Kreß and Prost, 'Article 96', in Ambos, *Commentary* (2022),

the confidentiality of documents and certain information.[370] Evidence transmitted on a confidential basis may be disclosed at a later point.[371]

Article 93 (1)(e) ICCS ('voluntary appearance') implies that *witnesses* and experts have to appear voluntarily before the Court leaving some discretion to State Parties ('[f]acilitating').[372] Similarly, the temporary transfer of detained persons for the purpose of identification or interrogation requires the (free and informed) consent of the person concerned and of the requested State.[373] Consequently, it has long been argued that State Parties are not obliged to compel witnesses to appear before the ICC and it has been controversial whether State Parties may include such a duty for witnesses in their national implementation laws.[374] The underlying 'principle' of the voluntary appearance of witnesses, albeit typical for the traditional horizontal interstate legal assistance,[375] is however difficult to reconcile with an, at least partially, vertical cooperation regime of an international criminal court. In fact, in the relationship between State Parties and the Court, such a principle can only refer to the State Parties' duty to facilitate the voluntary appearance of witnesses at the seat of the Court,[376] but it cannot exempt them from their cooperation obligation, which also includes assistance in the taking of witness evidence. This also follows from Article 93 (1)(b) ICCS, which compels State Parties to take evidence, including testimony, on behalf of the Court;[377] to comply with this obligation, the States may employ the coercive measures to ensure witness attendance provided for in their national laws. However, going beyond the taking of evidence by the State itself, from this provision also follows, as now recognized by the Appeals Chamber, a State Party's obligation to produce the testimony of witnesses before the Court, by requiring their attendance on the territory of the requested State Party for such testimony to be provided to the Court sitting *in situ* or transmitted to it via video conference.[378] With

mn. 14–15; Kreß and Prost, 'Article 91', in Ambos, *Commentary* (2022), mn. 24; Zhang, 'Article 96', in Klamberg et al., *Commentary ICC II* (2023), p. 821. On the language to be used, see Arts. 87 (2), 99 (3) ICCS and Rules 178–80 RPE ICC.

[370] Art. 93 (8)(a) ICCS.

[371] Art. 93 (8)(b), (c) ICCS. Further thereon, Kreß and Prost, 'Article 93', in Ambos, *Commentary* (2022), mn. 72; Kreß and Prost, 'Article 87', in Ambos, *Commentary* (2022), mn. 24–5; Détais and de Sena, 'Article 93', in Fernandez et al., *Commentaire CPI II* (2019), p. 2267.

[372] Crit. also Kreß, in Grützner et al., *Rechtshilfeverkehr* (2003), IV A 1 mn. 270; Kreß, in Fischer et al., *Prosecution* (2001), pp. 324–5; Kreß and Prost, 'Article 93', in Ambos, *Commentary* (2022), mn. 27 ('serious weakness'); Påle-Bartes, 'Article 93', in Klamberg et al., *Commentary ICC II* (2023), p. 762; also Sluiter, *Evidence* (2002), pp. 253 ff., 346 ff.; Meißner, *Zusammenarbeit* (2003), p. 194; Kreß and Wannek, in Kirsch, *Internationale Strafgerichtshofe* (2005), p. 257; Zahar and Sluiter, *ICL* (2008), pp. 368 ff.; Klamberg, *Evidence* (2013), pp. 244–6. On the interaction with Art. 64 (6)(b) ICCS and Rule 65 RPE ICC, Vasiliev, in Cryer et al., *Introduction ICL* (2019), p. 488. On the question of the right to silence of witnesses, once they appear before the Court/tribunals, cf. Ambos, *LJIL*, 15 (2002), 155 ff.

[373] Art. 93 (1)(f), (7) ICCS, Rule 192 RPE ICC. However, this does not apply to persons already sentenced by the Court (Rule 193 RPE ICC). Both the consent of the person concerned and that of the requested State shall be in writing; cf. Kreß and Prost, 'Article 93', in Ambos, *Commentary* (2022), mn. 58–9, with case law references. For a case law overview on asylum claims being brought by transferred witnesses, see Kreß and Prost, 'Article 93', in Ambos, *Commentary* (2022), mn. 63–9.

[374] *Contra*, Sluiter, *Evidence* (2002), pp. 253–4; Sluiter, *CLF*, 14 (2003), 452–3; Ciampi, in Cassese et al., *Rome Statute II* (2002), pp. 1728–9; in favour, Kreß, in Grützner et al., *Rechtshilfeverkehr* (2003), IV A 1 mn. 271; Kreß, *JICJ*, 1 (2003), 616; Kreß, in Fischer et al., *Prosecution* (2001), p. 325.

[375] See e.g. Arts. 8 and 11 of the 1959 European Convention on Mutual Assistance in Criminal Matters of the Council of Europe.

[376] In this vein, see now *Ruto and Sang*, ICC-01/09-01/11-1598, paras. 123 ff. (denying the existence of 'a general "principle of voluntary appearance"', limiting it only 'to the facilitation of the voluntary appearance of witnesses at the seat of the Court, involving international travel').

[377] Conc., Kreß and Prost, 'Article 93', in Ambos, *Commentary* (2022), mn. 21–2.

[378] *Ruto and Sang*, ICC-01/09-01/11-1598, paras. 2, 117 ff., following thereby Kreß, as quoted in note 375 in this chapter; see also Kreß and Prost, 'Article 93', in Ambos, *Commentary* (2022), mn. 22, 28. For a much more profound analysis, see *Ruto and Sang*, ICC-01/09-01/11-1274-Corr2: TC V found several legal bases for a TC to

this, the Appeals Chamber has put, in a way, the taking of witness evidence by a State on an equal footing with that by the Court. This is convincing if one understands that the Court and State Parties pursue one and the same interest in terms of evidence, that is, to ensure that the necessary evidence is gathered.

*(ii) Limitations*

The traditional *grounds of refusal* of the interstate legal assistance are, as in the case of surrender, largely not applicable to the other forms of cooperation. All in all, however, these forms of cooperation are subjected to stronger limitations than the surrender of suspects.[379] In several cases, a State is entitled, due to certain State interests or the rights of third parties, to delay or reject a request. As a first step, Article 93 (3) ICCS provides for a mechanism of consultation between the requested State and the ICC, for cases where the execution of a 'particular measure of assistance' contravenes a 'fundamental legal principle of general application' of the requested State. This is a high threshold though,[380] relating to the execution required, not to the form of co-operation itself.[381] Mere 'practical or administrative difficulties' in the execution of the request 'do not constitute fundamental legal principles' which can prevent its execution.[382] If the requested measure cannot be realized in a different manner or under certain conditions, the ICC must alter its request accordingly.[383]

Further, a State may reject a request for reasons of the protection of *national security interests* in the sense of Article 72 ICCS.[384] The procedure referred to in Article 72 ICCS is based

compel the appearance of witnesses, i.e. the implied powers doctrine (paras. 84–7, 94: basis of a TC's 'incidental competence ... to compel the appearance of witnesses' [para. 87]), 'customary international criminal procedural law' (para. 88–92: relying on the ad hoc tribunals and arguing that 'it would require very clear language indeed for the States Parties to the Rome Statute to be taken to have intended that the ICC ... should be the only known criminal court in the world ... that has no power to subpoena witnesses to appear for testimony' [para. 92]) and the Statute itself, esp. Art. 64 (6)(b) (paras. 93, 94–100). It further found that a State Party is obliged 'to employ compulsory measures against the witness' to enforce a respective TC request (paras. 102–56: relying, again, on implied powers and the relevant provisions of the Statute, esp. Art. 93 (1)(l), and rejecting the defence argument that the adjective 'voluntary' in Art. 93 (1)(e) precludes any compulsory effect [114–18, 141–56, esp. 149–54]; further relying on the rule of good faith [120–9], the *Blaškić* precedent [130–3]), and considerations of complementarity [134–40]). Finally, it found no provision in the law of Kenya, esp. its ICC Act, that would prohibit the requested assistance (paras. 157–79) and that, *in casu*, the prosecution request to issue summonses to compel the appearance of eight witnesses was justified (paras. 180–92). On the requirement for State Parties to amend their national laws to provide a legal basis for compelling witnesses to testify in accordance with Art. 88 ICCS to comply with Art. 93 (1)(b) ICCS requests, see *Prosecutor v. Ruto and Sang*, TC V(A), Decision on Prosecution Request for Issuance of a Summons for Witness 727 of 17 February 2015, ICC-01/09-01/11-1817-Red, 17 February 2015, paras. 29–30.

379 Kreß, in Grützner et al., *Rechtshilfeverkehr* (2003), IV A 1 mn. 261 and 282; Klamberg, *Evidence* (2013), p. 242.

380 cf. Kreß and Prost, 'Article 93', in Ambos, *Commentary* (2022), mn. 46.

381 In this regard, the residual provision of Art. 93 (1)(l) (see note 339 in this chapter) allows for types of assistance 'not prohibited by the law of the requested State'.

382 cf. *Kenyatta*, ICC-01/09-02/11-937, para. 34; thereon, Kreß and Prost, 'Article 87', in Ambos, *Commentary* (2022), mn. 7; Kreß and Prost, 'Article 93', in Ambos, *Commentary* (2022), mn. 47.

383 In detail, Kreß and Prost, 'Article 93', in Ambos, *Commentary* (2022), mn. 43–51; Schabas, *ICC Commentary* (2016), p. 1322; crit. on this limitation of the obligation to cooperate, Kreß, in Grützner et al., *Rechtshilfeverkehr* (2003), IV A 1 mn. 284–5; Sluiter, *Evidence* (2002), pp. 161 ff.

384 Art. 93 (4) ICCS. Comprehensively on the scope of Art. 72 ICCS, Rastan, 'Article 72', in Ambos, *Commentary* (2022), mn. 3 ff.; in this context, see Kreß and Prost, 'Article 93', in Ambos, *Commentary* (2016), mn. 52–4; Détais and de Sena, 'Article 93', in Fernandez et al., *Commentaire CPI II* (2019), p. 2270; Vasiliev, in Cryer et al., *Introduction ICL* (2019), pp. 495–7; previously Kreß, in Grützner et al., *Rechtshilfeverkehr* (2003), IV A 1 mn. 291 ff.; Ambos, *ZStW*, 111 (1999), 200–1; Rinoldi and Parisi, in Lattanzi and Schabas, *Rome Statute I* (2000), pp. 368–9; Sluiter, *Evidence* (2002), pp. 163 ff.; Meißner, *Zusammenarbeit* (2003), pp. 218 ff.; Schomburg, in Kirsch, *Internationale Strafgerichtshöfe* (2005), pp. 135–6; Moranchek, *YaleJIL*, 31 (2006), 480 ff.; Schabas, *ICC Commentary* (2016), pp. 1119 ff.; crit. Damaška, *UCLA JIL & ForAff*, 14 (2009), 24.

on the ICTY's *Blaškić* decision,[385] although the ICCS clearly places greater weight on national security interests;[386] in case of third-party information the Court should direct its request to this third party as the 'originator' of the information.[387] At any rate, the Court is the ultimate arbiter on whether the respective material should be provided and can (where held in the hands of third parties) order disclosure over the objection of the State, or otherwise hold the State in non-compliance. It may also draw an inference as to a material fact at issue.[388] Finally, a further obstacle to legal assistance may follow from the *rights of immunity* of Article 98 (1), already discussed above.[389]

If a request for assistance concerns *ongoing investigations or proceedings* of another case(s) in the requested State, its execution may be postponed—'for a period of time agreed upon with the Court' and as a maximum up to the completion of the respective investigation or prosecution.[390] Also, the State has to consider alternatives to immediately granting the assistance, for instance, subjecting it to 'certain conditions'.[391] Otherwise it has to demonstrate that the assistance would prejudice its ongoing investigation or prosecution.[392] In case of a postponement, measures to secure evidence in accordance with Article 93 (1)(j) ICCS may be sought by the Prosecutor.[393] The execution of an assistance request may also be postponed[394] if there is an *admissibility challenge*[395] pending, unless the Court has authorized the Prosecutor to undertake the respective investigatory measures.[396]

Where the requested State Party receives *competing assistance requests* from the ICC and another State (pursuant to an international obligation), the requested State should meet, where possible, its obligations towards both parties, possibly through postponement or by attaching certain conditions to the execution.[397] Should this be impossible, the rules on competing requests for the surrender of persons apply.[398] If the request is based on information provided by third States or international organizations, the ICC must consult these directly.[399] The request will be executed by national authorities in accordance with their laws,

[385] *Blaškić*, IT-95-14, paras. 61 ff.; Klamberg, *Evidence* (2013), pp. 255–8; cf. also Rule 54*bis* RPE ICTY and Rule 56 RPE MICT.

[386] In more detail, Ciampi, in Cassese et al., *Rome Statute II* (2002), pp. 1720–1; Meißner, *Zusammenarbeit* (2003), pp. 220 ff.; Cassese, *ICL* (2013), pp. 359–60; crit. Kreß, in Grützner et al., *Rechtshilfeverkehr* (2003), IV A 1 mn. 291; Moranchek, *YaleJIL*, 31 (2006), 499–500.

[387] Art. 73 ICCS; thereon, Rastan, 'Article 73', in Ambos, *Commentary* (2022), mn. 1 ff.

[388] cf. Art. 72 (7) and Rastan, 'Article 72', in Ambos, *Commentary* (2022), mn. 1, 37 ff.

[389] Thereon, Kreß, in Grützner et al., *Rechtshilfeverkehr* (2003), IV A 1 mn. 295; Sluiter, *Evidence* (2002), pp. 169 ff.; Meißner, *Zusammenarbeit* (2003), pp. 210 ff.; Ciampi, in Cassese et al., *Rome Statut II* (2002), p. 1736; Palmisano, in Lattanzi and Schabas, *Rome Statute II* (2000), pp. 409–10.

[390] Art. 94 (1) ICCS; on the relation of Art. 94 with Arts. 89 (2), (4) and 95, see Hiéramente, 'Article 94', in Klamberg et al., *Commentary ICC II* (2023), p. 783 and Hiéramente, 'Article 95', in Klamberg et al., *Commentary ICC II* (2023), pp. 795–812.

[391] Art. 94 (1) last cl.

[392] Art. 94 (1) 1st cl. requires an 'inference' with the national investigation or prosecution; see also Kreß and Prost, 'Article 94', in Ambos, *Commentary* (2022), mn. 4.

[393] Art. 94 (2) ICCS. Extensively, Meißner, *Zusammenarbeit* (2003), pp. 236 ff.

[394] Art. 95 ICCS; thereon, note 221 in this chapter.

[395] cf. Arts. 18 and 19 ICCS; see note 221 in this chapter. Generally, on how this challenge shall be 'properly made' in order to justify a postponement pursuant to Art. 95, cf. ICC, *Prosecutor v. Gaddafi and Al-Senussi*, PTC I, Decision on Libya's Postponement of the Execution of the Request for Arrest and Surrender of Abdullah Al-Senussi pursuant to Article 95 of the Rome Statute and Related Defence Request to Refer Libya to the UN Security Council, ICC-01/11-01/11-354, 14 June 2013, paras. 29 ff.; crit. Kreß and Prost, 'Article 95', in Ambos, *Commentary* (2022), mn. 12–17 ('dangerous precedent').

[396] cf. Arts. 18 (6), 19 (8) ICCS; in more detail, Meißner, *Zusammenarbeit* (2003), pp. 155 ff., 236; Sluiter, *Evidence* (2002), pp. 173–4.

[397] Art. 93 (9)(a)(i) ICCS.

[398] Art. 93 (9)(a)(ii) ICCS.

[399] Art. 93 (9)(b) ICCS; see also Art. 73 ICCS. In depth, Meißner, *Zusammenarbeit* (2003), pp. 230 ff.; Ciampi, in Cassese et al., *Rome Statute II* (2002), pp. 1734 ff.; Schabas, *ICC Commentary* (2016), p. 1325; Kreß, in Grützner

although the modalities of the execution are to be determined—in the absence of contravening national laws—by the request itself, such as following a particular procedure outlined in the request or to allow persons specified by the ICC to be present at and assist in the execution process.[400]

The primacy of the national execution applies absolutely to requests involving coercive measures such as house searches and seizures,[401] except in the limited 'failed State' scenario regulated by Article 57 (3)(d) where the PTC may authorize the Prosecutor to execute such measures directly.[402] The general national primacy follows, as an *argumentum e contrario*, from Article 99 (4) ICCS, according to which the Prosecutor can execute requests not involving coercive measures, such as taking (voluntary) evidence from persons or the examination of public sites, autonomously.[403] The rights of the Prosecutor under Article 99 (4) are part of the most controversial provisions of Part 9 ICCS.[404] Here one must distinguish as follows: the direct execution of the measure is not predicated upon a formal permission (but a 'consultation') of the requested State if the crime was committed on its territory and the proceedings are admissible in accordance with Articles 18 and 19 ICCS.[405] In all other cases, the requested State may establish 'reasonable conditions'.[406] In either case, Article 72 ICCS may be invoked with regard to the protection of national security interests.[407] The rules concerning '*on-site-investigations*' are based on the common practice of the ICTY/ICTR and the SCSL.[408]

### (b) *ICTY, ICTR, and KSC*

Examples of other mutual legal assistance referred to in Articles 29 (2)(a)–(c) ICTYS and 28 (2)(a)–(c) ICTRS/IRMCTS include the identification and location of persons, the production of evidence, and the service of documents. These measures are further defined in the RPE.[409] The measures resemble those of the ICC. In contrast to the ICC, however, the ICTY and ICTR have the competence to compel the appearance of witnesses.[410]

et al., *Rechtshilfeverkehr* (2003), IV A 1 mn. 293–4; Kreß and Prost, 'Article 93', in Ambos, *Commentary* (2016), mn. 73–5.

[400] Art. 99 (1) ICCS; cf. also Zhang, 'Article 99', in Klamberg et al., *Commentary ICC II* (2023), pp. 838–9. Crit. of the 'limited' attention paid to the terms of reference of the request, Kreß, in Grützner et al., *Rechtshilfeverkehr* (2003), IV A 1 mn. 298–9; Sluiter, *Evidence* (2002), pp. 208 ff.

[401] Sluiter, *Evidence* (2002), p. 301; Kreß, in Grützner et al., *Rechtshilfeverkehr* (2003), IV A 1 mn. 301; Kreß, *JICJ*, 1 (2003), 615; Ambos, *ZStW*, 111 (1999), 207; Kreß and Prost, 'Article 99', in Ambos, *Commentary* (2022), mn. 19. On the (disputed) question whether a (*ex ante*) warrant of the Court or at least a (*ex post*) review is necessary Vasiliev, in Cryer et al., *Introduction ICL* (2019), pp. 498–9.

[402] cf. de Meester, 'Article 54', in Klamberg et al., *Commentary ICC II* (2023), pp. 43–4.

[403] *Banda and Jerbo*, ICC-02/05-03/09-169, para. 23 ('the direct execution of measures is *lex specialis* to be applied within the terms and conditions of Article 99 (4).'); cf. also Kreß and Prost, 'Article 99', in Ambos, *Commentary* (2022), mn. 28; Zhang, 'Article 99', in Klamberg et al., *Commentary ICC II* (2023), pp. 844–5.

[404] In detail, see Kreß and Prost, 'Article 99', in Ambos, *Commentary* (2022), mn. 1–4.

[405] Art. 99 (4)(a) ICCS; cf. also Zhang, 'Article 99', in Klamberg et al., *Commentary ICC II* (2023), pp. 846–7.

[406] Art. 99 (4)(b) ICCS. cf. Meißner, *Zusammenarbeit* (2003), pp. 243 ff.; Sluiter, *Evidence* (2002), pp. 293 ff.; Ciampi, in Cassese et al., *Rome Statute II* (2002), pp. 1736 ff.; Kreß, in Grützner et al., *Rechtshilfeverkehr* (2003), IV A 1 mn. 300 ff.; Kreß and Prost, 'Article 99', in Ambos, *Commentary* (2022), mn. 31–4; Schabas, *ICC Commentary* (2016), pp. 1357–8; Vasiliev, in Cryer et al., *Introduction ICL* (2019), pp. 497–8; Zhang, 'Article 99', in Klamberg et al., *Commentary ICC II* (2023), p. 848.

[407] Art. 99 (5) ICCS; cf. thereon, Zhang, 'Article 99', in Klamberg et al., *Commentary ICC II* (2023), p. 848.

[408] Arts. 18 (2), 29 ICTYS; 17 (2), 28 ICTRS, 16 (2), 28 IRMCTS; Rules 4, 39 (i), 54 RPE ICTY/ICTR; 4, 36 (B) (i), 55 RPE MICT; Arts. 15 (2) SCSLS and 14 (4) RSCSLS and Rules 4, 39 (i), 54 RPE SCSL. See, in detail, Sluiter, *Evidence* (2002), pp. 305 ff.; Klamberg, *Evidence* (2013), pp. 249–55.

[409] See e.g. Rules 39–40, 54, 54*bis* [only in relation to the ICTY], 56, 59, and 90*bis* RPE ICTY/ICTR; see also Rules 36–7, 55, 56, 58, 61, and 107 RPE MICT.

[410] Art. 29 (2)(b) read with 19 (2) ICTYS; Art. 28 (2)(b) read with 18 (2) ICTRS; Art. 28 (2)(b) read with 17 (2) IRMCTS; Rules 54, 56, and 90*bis* RPE ICTY/ICTR and 55, 58, and 107 RPE MICT. cf. also *Blaškić*, IT-95-14,

Furthermore, assistance aimed at the collection of evidence is primarily based on the request itself, the Statutes, and the RPE. Thus, the ICTY considered evidence collected at the national level as inadmissible since the rules of ICTYS and the RPE ICTY have not been taken into account.[411]

As to the KSC, it has already been explained above that, as far as Kosovo territory is concerned, the KSC act like the Kosovo courts and thus their cooperation orders must be executed by all Kosovo national authorities, especially the police.[412] As to the cooperation with third States or other entities, either specific bilateral agreements or (applicable) mutual legal assistance treaties must exist,[413] unless such States/entities cooperate on a voluntary basis.

paras. 57 ff. In depth, Sluiter, *Evidence* (2002), pp. 255 ff.; Ciampi, in Cassese et al., *Rome Statute II* (2002), pp. 1717 ff.; Swoboda, *Verfahrens- und Beweisstrategien* (2013), pp. 590 ff., emphasizing that this option is used with caution (pp. 592 ff., 977–8).

[411] cf. ICTY, *Prosecutor v. Delalić et al.*, TC, Decision on Zdravko Mucic's Motion for the Exclusion of Evidence, IT-96-21, 2 September 1997. On this subject, Kreß, in Grützner et al., *Rechtshilfeverkehr* (2003), IV A 2 mn. 58; Sluiter, *Evidence* (2002), p. 208; Gómez Colomer and Beltrán, in Gómez Colomer et al., *CPI* (2003), pp. 334–5; Zahar and Sluiter, *ICL* (2008), pp. 282–3. On confidential information and the right to silence, cf. Rules 70 RPE ICTY/ICTR/SCSL and 76 RPE MICT; on the former, see also Swoboda, *Verfahrens- und Beweisstrategien* (2013), p. 590.

[412] cf. Art. 53 (2) KSC Law, above notes 126 and 329 with main text.

[413] cf. Art. 55 KSC Law and Rule 208 (1) RPE KSC; above Section B.(2)(b). Also see Heinze, *JICJ*, 15 (2017), 993.

# VIII
# Enforcement of Sentences and Other Penalties

* The full chapter bibliography can be downloaded from

## A. Introductory remarks

It has been said by two prominent authors that the enforcement regime of international criminal tribunals constitutes 'the backbone of the system of international criminal justice' and its practical application 'must form part of a complete judgment about the legitimacy of this system'.[1] Against this background, it is surprising that the subject has so far received relatively little attention in academic writing, especially as far as the ICC[2] and empirical studies[3] are concerned.[4]

The starting point of any enforcement regime is the rule on the applicable penalties to be enforced. As to the ICC, Article 77 ICCS provides for imprisonment as the main penalty and fines and forfeiture of proceeds, property, and assets as additional ('in addition') penalties. This sentencing regime has been extensively analysed in the second volume of this Treatise.[5] Its division between deprivation of liberty and other, financial measures will also inform our analysis of the enforcement regime. Thus, in this chapter we will analyse the enforcement of sentences of imprisonment as opposed to the enforcement of fines and other financial measures. The relevant Part 10 of the ICC Statute (Articles 103–11)[6] is complemented by

[1] Kreß and Sluiter, in Cassese et al., *Rome Statute II* (2002), p. 1753; similarly stressing the legitimacy aspect, Mulgrew, *International Penal System* (2013), pp. 336 ff. and *passim*.

[2] For two more recent monographs and an edited volume covering, inter alia, the ICC's enforcement regime more in depth, see Mulgrew and Abels, *RH Penal System* (2016); Mulgrew, *International Penal System* (2013); and Rochner, *Strafvollstreckung* (2014). Earlier works essentially deal with the ad hoc tribunals, esp. the ICTY: cf. Klip, *EJCCLCJ*, 5 (1997), 144; Tolbert, *LJIL*, 11 (1998), 655; van Zyl Smit, *ICLQ*, 54 (2005), 357; Hoffmann, *ZIS*, 6 (2011), 838; further references in Holá and van Wijk, *JICJ*, 12 (2014), 110 with n. 2.

[3] See Holá and van Wijk, *JICJ*, 12 (2014), 109 ff. (dealing with the post-conviction phase focusing on early release and crit. concluding [at 131] that the enforcement regime 'is not transparent, conceptually underdeveloped and leads to inequalities in the treatment of international prisoners'; in a similar vein, Kelder, Holá, and van Wijk, *ICLR* 14 (2014), 1177 ff. (focusing on rehabilitation and calling for a more critical assessment of the respective information and a more systematic reporting by the enforcing States, at 1202); Holá and van Wijk, in Mulgrew and Abels, *RH Penal System* (2016), pp. 274 ff.; Holá, Kelder, and van Wijk, in Hayashi and Bailliert, *Legitimacy* (2017), pp. 351 ff. (crit. assessing how international criminal tribunals may achieve rehabilitation, a 'crucial, yet understudied aspect of international criminal justice', at 353).

[4] Crit. also Sluiter, in Mulgrew and Abels, *RH Penal System* (2016), p. 248 ('still a matter that could receive more attention'); Fernández-Pacheco Estrada, *ICLR*, 22 (2022), 566 ('a typically neglected area'); Stiel and Stuckenberg, 'Article 103', in Klamberg et al., *Commentary ICC II* (2023), p. 867 ('the least advanced part of international criminal justice').

[5] Ambos, *Treatise ICL II* (2022), pp. 311 ff.

[6] See generally Calvo-Goller, *Trial Proceedings* (2006), pp. 327 ff.; Vasiliev, in Cryer et al., *ICL* (2019), pp. 477–8; Piva, *ZIS*, 3 (2008), 141, 152; Gless, *Internationales Strafrecht* (2015), mn. 863–71; on the negotiations, cf. Chimimba, in Lee, *The ICC* (1999), pp. 345 ff.; Prost, in Lee, *The ICC* (2001), pp. 673 ff.; Marchesi, in Lattanzi and Schabas, *Rome Statute I* (1999), pp. 427 ff.; Rochner, *Strafvollstreckung* (2014), pp. 272 ff.; Harmsen and Strijards, 'Articles 103–104', in Ambos, *Commentary* (2022), pp. 2701–24; Clark and Hohler, 'Articles 105–107', in Ambos, *Commentary* (2022), pp. 2725–38; Schabas, 'Articles 108–109', in Ambos, *Commentary* (2022), pp. 2739–52; Harmsen and Strijards, 'Articles 110–111', in Ambos, *Commentary* (2022), pp. 2753–66; Stiel and Stuckenberg,

Rules 198–225 RPE ICC and Regulations 113–18 RegC.[7] The ad hoc tribunals' enforcement regime is basically regulated in Article 27 ICTYS, Article 26 ICTRS, and Article 25 MICTS, the KSC's in Article 50 KSC Law. A detailed analysis will follow in the next section (Section B.(1) and (2)).

The ICC enforcement regime does not only constitute a sequel to the Court's sentencing regime, but has also, as already seen in the previous chapter,[8] a material connection to the cooperation regime of Part 9 of the Statute. In fact, the enforcement of sentences and other judicial decisions is—together with extradition and other legal assistance (especially regarding evidence gathering)—a fundamental part of interstate cooperation in criminal matters.[9] As such, it operates, in essence, in a decentralized fashion through enforcement by (willing and able) States, although one may consider the international tribunals' detention facilities (IDFs)[10] as the nucleus of a centralized international enforcement or even an international penal system.[11]

In any case, given that enforcement is part of the broader cooperation regime, it is reasonable to argue that the State Parties' general obligation to cooperate,[12] discussed in the previous chapter,[13] includes the obligation to enforce the sentences of the Court. However, Part 10 of the Statute does not follow this logic.[14] On the one hand, it does not only refer to State Parties, but to States in general,[15] that is, the enforcing State need not necessarily be a State Party. On the other hand and more importantly, Part 10 makes the enforcement

'Articles 103–106', in Klamberg et al., *Commentary ICC II* (2023), pp. 867–912; Stiel, 'Article 107', in Klamberg et al., *Commentary ICC II* (2023), pp. 915–24; Stiel and Stuckenberg, 'Articles 108–109', in Klamberg et al., *Commentary ICC II* (2023), pp. 925–47; Oehmichen, 'Article 110', in Klamberg et al., *Commentary ICC II* (2023), pp. 951–70; Stiel and Stuckenberg, 'Article 111', in Klamberg et al., *Commentary ICC II* (2023), pp. 991–6; on the ad hoc tribunals, see Zahar and Sluiter, *ICL* (2008), pp. 320–1.

[7] Extensively on the rules, see Prost, in Lee, *The ICC* (2001), pp. 674 ff..; Gartner, in Fischer et al., *Prosecution* (2001), pp. 434 ff.

[8] Chapter VII, B.(1) in this volume.

[9] cf. Ambos and Gronke, in Ambos et al., *Rechtshilferecht* (2020), pp. 69–70.

[10] On these (IDFs) existing in The Hague (ICTY, ICC), Arusha (ICTR), and Freetown (SCSL), see, in detail, Mulgrew, *International Penal System* (2013), pp. 103 ff., 176, discussing, inter alia, the de facto equal treatment of indictees and convicts (106–7), the concrete conditions regarding visits, external contacts, medical care (107 ff.), the harmonious co-existence between former enemies (121–2), the oversight mechanisms (131 ff.), the generally high standards (143 ff.) and the lack of a special release procedure (151 ff.); see also Stiel and Stuckenberg, 'Article 103', in Klamberg et al., *Commentary ICC II* (2023), p. 867.

[11] For such a system, Mulgrew, *International Penal System* (2013), pp. 273 ff., seeing it as 'the logical institutional evolution of the international criminal justice system' (277) and proposing a joint venture between the UN and the ICC (282) drawing on nearly fifty years of UN experience (counting since the Spandau prison on the Control Council in post-WW II Germany, 281) and with several units in different locations, a kind of network of international prisons under international authority (278–9, 283 ff.); in sum, an international prison system based on resocialization, restoration, and accountability (341). While such a system would have several benefits, especially with a view to the logical connection between imposition and enforcement of sentences (in the same vein, Mulgrew, ibid., p. 194), its implementation ultimately depends on the will of the ICC State Parties, especially the host State and the other States where detention units should be located. In any case, as Mulgrew herself admits (280, 294), the historical precedent of Spandau does not provide a convincing blueprint for such an international system. See also Penrose, in Mulgrew and Abels, *RH International Penal System* (2016), pp. 423 ff. (arguing that with the creation of a permanent international criminal court '[t]he time has come for a permanent prison solution', at 444).

[12] Art. 86 ICCS.

[13] Chapter VII, A.(2) and B.(1) in this volume.

[14] See generally also Harmsen and Strijards, 'Article 103', in Ambos, *Commentary* (2022), mn. 1; Clark and Hohler, 'Article 105', in Ambos, *Commentary* (2022), mn. 1–3; Stiel and Stuckenberg, 'Article 103', in Klamberg et al., *Commentary ICC II* (2023), pp. 872–4.

[15] cf. Art. 103 ICCS.

completely dependent on the 'willingness' of the States concerned[16] and gives them the possibility to attach 'conditions' to their acceptance.[17]

Thus, the Court is put—quite similarly to the essentially 'vertical' arrangement of the ad hoc tribunals and the KSC[18]—in a 'penitentiary predicament',[19] and its enforcement regime is treated as an autonomous, separate form of cooperation.[20] Pursuant to this logic the drafters of the Statute, at least the majority of them, considered the ICC as a foreign jurisdiction with foreign sentences which need to be transformed at the national level by some sort of *exequatur* procedure.[21] An ILC proposal providing for an explicit recognition of the Court's judgments by the State Parties was rejected.[22] Thus, in sum, the Court, despite much more supportive cooperation legislation adopted by most State Parties,[23] depends on the goodwill of States, falls short of a full *auctoritas rei iudicatae*,[24] and its sentences enjoy only a relative recognition.[25] Still, there is no viable alternative to decentralized enforcement,[26] at least as long as an autonomous international penal system set up under the authority of the ICC or another suitable international authority is lacking.[27] As things stand now, one can only try to make the existing (decentralized) enforcement system as efficient and smooth as possible.

## B. Enforcement of sentences of imprisonment

### (1) The ICC regime and the role of States

#### *(a) General willingness of States, concrete designation, and acceptance of convicts*

States are crucial in the enforcement of prison sentences. In fact, they enforce the ICC's prison sentences in their national prison facilities. The ICC regime provides for a two-step procedure. First, a State must declare its general willingness to accept sentenced persons and it will then be put on a respective State's list, established, and maintained by the Registry.[28]

[16] cf. Art. 103 (1)(a) ICCS; cf. also Stiel and Stuckenberg, 'Article 103', in Klamberg et al., *Commentary ICC II* (2023), pp. 867–71.

[17] Art. 103 (1)(b) ICCS; cf. also Stiel and Stuckenberg, 'Article 103', in Klamberg et al., *Commentary ICC II* (2023), pp. 867, 875.

[18] On the ICTY in this regard, see Tolbert, *LJIL*, 11 (2008), 657–8, criticizing the lack of a specific enforcement obligation in Art. 27 ICTYS as compared to the cooperation obligation in Art. 29 ICTYS.

[19] Harmsen and Strijards, 'Article 103', in Ambos, *Commentary* (2022), mn. 18.

[20] In the same vein, Harmsen and Strijards, 'Article 103', in Ambos, *Commentary* (2022), mn. 5; similarly Mulgrew, *International Penal System* (2013), pp. 33–4 (pointing out that there is no obligation to enforce but only the general duty to cooperate).

[21] *Exequatur* (Latin: 'let him perform/execute') means, in international law, the admission of a consul through his official recognition by the receiving State (Verdross and Simma, *Universelles Völkerrecht* (1984), §§ 920, 924). In the civil procedure of many States, the term is used to describe the order of a national court to enforce foreign judgments within the domestic legal order (see e.g. §§ 722, 723 German Civil Procedure Act—*Zivilprozessordnung*). In the area of legal assistance in criminal matters, it concerns the enforcement of foreign prison sentences.

[22] Art. 58 of the 1994 ILC Draft Statute; for a good overview of the discussion, see Harmsen and Strijards, 'Article 103', in Ambos, *Commentary* (2022), mn. 1–4; see also Rochner, *Strafvollstreckung* (2014), p. 280.

[23] See Section D. in this chapter, and Rochner, *Strafvollstreckung* (2014), pp. 286–7 (with further references) and 325–6 (against an *exequatur* procedure).

[24] This is the authority, validity, or legal power to issue final judgments and decisions as recognized in Roman law. '*Res iudicata* creates a new legal situation between the parties to the trial thus finished and "is considered as truth"', cf. Berger, *Encyclopedic Dictionary of Roman Law* (2004), p. 678; also Puza, *Res Iudicata* (1973), p. 113.

[25] Harmsen and Strijards, 'Article 103', in Ambos, *Commentary* (2022), mn. 2, 3, 17; for criticism, see Stiel and Stuckenberg, 'Article 103', in Klamberg et al., *Commentary ICC II* (2023), pp. 867–71.

[26] In the same vein, Rochner, *Strafvollstreckung* (2014), pp. 318 ff.

[27] Calling for such a system, however, Mulgrew, *International Penal System* (2013), above note 11, and Penrose, in Mulgrew and Abels, *RH Penal System* (2016), pp. 423 ff.

[28] Art. 103 (1)(a) ICCS, Rule 200 (1) RPE ICC. Comprehensively Kreß and Sluiter, in Cassese et al., *Rome Statute II* (2002), pp. 1784 ff.; Kreß, in Grützner, Pötz, Kreß, and Gazeas, *Internationaler Rechtshilfeverkehr in Strafsachen*

A State's acceptance is not only voluntary,[29] but it may also, as already said above, attach certain conditions to its acceptance,[30] for example, with regard to the length of the sentence, modalities of early release, or the nature of the penitentiary administration.[31] These conditions must not, however, deviate from the general statutory scheme and have to be accepted by the Presidency of the Court.[32]

Here, the prominent role of the Presidency in the enforcement area in general,[33] and in drawing up the States' list in particular, becomes clear. It may decide not to include a given State because of unacceptable conditions demanded by the latter; any amendments or additions to conditions also have to be confirmed by the Presidency.[34] Also, a State may want to impose conditions which are unacceptable for the Court in order to avoid any designation.[35] In any case, a State may withdraw at any time from the list; this may not affect, however, the enforcement with regard to persons already accepted.[36] Currently, the list is made up of the States with which the Court, represented by the Presidency,[37] has concluded bilateral enforcement agreements pursuant to Rule 200 (5) RPE ICC.[38]

The second step consists of the *concrete designation* of a State of enforcement by the Presidency.[39] In doing so, the Presidency shall strive, on the one hand, for a fair

(2003), IV A 1, mn. 321 ff.; Marchesi, in Lattanzi and Schabas, *Rome Statute I* (1999), pp. 430 ff.; Beltrán Montoliu, in Gómez Colomer et al., *Corte Penal Internacional* (2003), pp. 376 ff.; Schabas, *ICC Commentary* (2016), pp. 1377–80; Ntoubandi, 'Article 103', in Fernandez and Pacreau, *Commentaire CPI II* (2019), pp. 2363 ff.; Harmsen and Strijards, 'Article 103', in Ambos, *Commentary* (2022), mn. 4–5, 18, 24–6; Stiel and Stuckenberg, 'Article 103', in Klamberg et al., *Commentary ICC II* (2023), pp. 872–4.

29 Crit. Kreß and Sluiter, in Cassese et al., *Rome Statute II* (2002), pp. 1818–19; Kreß, in Grützner et al., *Rechtshilfeverkehr* (2022), IV A 1, mn. 323. On the enforcement of sentences through non-Party States, cf. Palmisano, in Lattanzi and Schabas, *Rome Statute I* (1999), pp. 412 ff.

30 Art. 103 (1)(b) ICCS.

31 cf. Harmsen and Strijards, 'Article 103', in Ambos, *Commentary* (2022), mn. 24; Clark and Hohler, 'Article 105', in Ambos, *Commentary* (2022), mn. 4; Kreß and Sluiter, in Cassese et al., *Rome Statute II* (2002), pp. 1787–8; Schabas, *ICC Commentary* (2016), pp. 1380–1; Stiel and Stuckenberg, 'Article 103', in Klamberg et al., *Commentary ICC II* (2023), pp. 875–6.

32 cf. Art. 103 (1)(b) ICCS in connection with Rule 200 (2), (5) RPE ICC; cf. Fall, 'Article 105', in Fernandez and Pacreau, *Commentaire CPI II* (2019), p. 2376; Stiel and Stuckenberg, 'Article 103', in Klamberg et al., *Commentary ICC II* (2023), pp. 875–6; welcoming this in contrast to the ad hoc tribunals' regime, Mulgrew, *International Penal System* (2013), pp. 77–8, 83, 185, but also pointing to the ICC's enforcement agreement with Denmark (78–9) which provides, inter alia, for the possibility of pardon not foreseen in the ICCS.

33 cf. also Regs. 113–18 RegC, especially Reg. 113, establishing an 'enforcement unit' within the Presidency; see also Harmsen and Strijards, 'Article 103', in Ambos, *Commentary* (2022), mn. 26.

34 Rule 200 (3) RPE ICC.

35 Crit. thereon, Harmsen and Strijards, 'Article 103', in Ambos, *Commentary* (2022), mn. 24 ('overall escape-clause').

36 Rule 200 (4) RPE ICC. In the same vein, Art. 22 of the ICC-Austria Agreement establishes that the termination of the agreement will not 'affect sentences in force at the time of the termination': quoted in Harmsen and Strijards, 'Article 103', in Ambos, *Commentary* (2022), mn. 8.

37 cf. Reg. 114 RegC.

38 The Court has, at the time of writing (September 2024), concluded agreements with fourteen State Parties (Argentina, Austria, Belgium, Colombia, Denmark, Finland, France, Georgia, Mali, Norway, Serbia, Slovenia, Sweden, and the United Kingdom) and some international organisations, cf. ICC Official Journal at <https://www.icc-cpi.int/resource-library/official-journal>. See also ICC, *Cooperation Agreements* (2023), pp. 16 ff., with a model agreement on pp. 53 ff.

39 cf. ICC, *Prosecutor v. Katanga*, Presidency, Decision Designating a State of Enforcement, ICC-01/04-01/07-3626, 8 December 2015, pp. 5–6; ICC, *Prosecutor v. Lubanga*, Presidency, Decision Designating a State of Enforcement, ICC-01/04-01/06-3185, 8 December 2015, p. 5; ICC, *Prosecutor v. Ntaganda*, Presidency, Decision Designating a State of Enforcement and on the 'Additional submissions regarding Mr Ntaganda's transfer to a State of enforcement', dated 26 September 2022 (ICC-01/04-02/06-2784-Conf-Exp), ICC-01/04-02/06-2787, 27 October 2022, paras. 10 ff.; ICC, *Prosecutor v. Ongwen*, Presidency, Decision Designating a State of Enforcement, ICC-02/04-01/15-2065-Conf-Exp, 9 November 2023, paras. 6 ff. In detail on the designation procedure, see Mulgrew, *International Penal System* (2013), pp. 39 ff.

burden-sharing between the enforcing States on the basis of principles of equitable distribution;[40] on the other hand, it shall take into account normative factors, namely the international treaty standards regarding the treatment of prisoners, the views of the sentenced person, as well as their nationality and, even more broadly, '[s]uch other factors regarding the circumstances of the crime or the person sentenced, or the effective enforcement of the sentence, as may be appropriate in designating the State of enforcement'.[41] The consideration of the views of the sentenced person[42] and their right to be heard and assisted in expressing their views[43] is noteworthy and also foreseen at the KSC[44] but not at the ad hoc tribunals. It also exists in case of a potential change of the enforcement State, although it is in the discretion of the Presidency to consider presentations of the sentenced person in that case.[45] If the Presidency refuses to change the enforcement State it shall inform, inter alia, the sentenced person.[46]

Especially the requirement of minimum prison standards excludes de facto many States from the ICC enforcement regime.[47] Indeed, if one understands this requirement as referring to the UN minimum rules,[48] going—contrary to the wording of Article 103 (3)(b) and Article 106 (1), (2) ICCS ('treaty')—beyond primary treaty law,[49] and, in addition, if one

[40] cf. Art. 103 (3) ICCS and Rule 201 RPE ICC. The Rule refers in this respect, apart from 'any other relevant factors', more concretely to the principle of equitable geographical distribution, the need to afford each State on the list an opportunity to receive sentenced persons, and the number of sentenced persons already sent to enforcing States (penitentiary capacity). On the original (almost exclusive) focus on geographical factors, see Harmsen and Strijards, 'Article 103', in Ambos, *Commentary* (2022), mn. 20.

[41] Art. 103 (3)(e) ICCS; cf. also Stiel and Stuckenberg, 'Article 103', in Klamberg et al., *Commentary ICC II* (2023), pp. 880–3.

[42] Art. 103 (3)(c) ICCS. However, the sentenced person does not have a right to have the sentence enforced in their home State.

[43] Rule 203 RPE ICC.

[44] cf. Rule 166 (1) RPE KSC ('having heard the Accused').

[45] Rule 210 (1)(b) RPE ICC.

[46] Rule 210 (3) RPE ICC.

[47] In the same vein, Stiel and Stuckenberg, 'Article 106', in Klamberg et al., *Commentary ICC II* (2023), pp. 907–9.

[48] See, generally, Compendium of United Nations Standards and Norms in Crime Prevention and Criminal Justice, UN Sales. No.: E.92.IV.1 (1992); more specifically, see 'Standard Minimum Rules for the Treatment of Prisoners', adopted by the First United Nations Congress on the Prevention of Crime and the Treatment of Offenders on 30 August 1955 at Geneva, approved by the Economic and Social Council in resolutions 663 (XXIV) on 31 July 1957 and 2076 (LXII) of 13 May 1977; UN 'Body of Principles for the Protection of All Persons under Any Form of Detention or Imprisonment', GA Res. 43/173 (1988); UN Basic Principles for the Treatment of Prisoners, GA Res. 45/111 (1990); ICTY, Rules Governing the Detention of Persons Awaiting Trial or Appeal before the Tribunal or otherwise Detained on the Authority of the Tribunal, 24 November 2016 <https://www.icty.org/x/file/Legal%20Library/Detention/161115-it38-rev10-rules-of-detention.pdf>); on a regional level, see also 'Kampala Declaration on Prison Conditions in Africa', Economic and Social Council Resolution 1997/36, annex; 'Arusha Declaration on Good Prison Practice', Economic and Social Council Resolution 1999/27, annex; cf. also the European Prison Rules (Recommendation Rec (2006) 2 of the CoE Committee of Ministers, <https://wcd.coe.int/ViewDoc.jsp?id=955747>), which replaced the old European Prison Rules (Recommendation Rec (1987) 3 of CoE); 'Principles and Best Practices on the Protection of Persons Deprived of Liberty in the Americas', approved by the Inter-American Commission on Human Rights during its 131st regular period of sessions, held from 3–14 March 2008 <http://www.oas.org/en/iachr/mandate/Basics/principlesdeprived.asp>; 'Inter-American Convention to Prevent and Punish Torture', adopted on 9 December 1985, at the 15th regular session of the General Assembly <http://www.oas.org/en/iachr/mandate/Basics/5.CONVENTION%20TORTURE.pdf>; see also Ntoubandi, 'Article 103', in Fernandez and Pacreau, *Commentaire CPI II* (2019), pp. 2368–9; Stiel and Stuckenberg, 'Article 106', in Klamberg et al., *Commentary ICC II* (2023), pp. 907–9.

[49] In this vein, Clark and Hohler, 'Article 106', in Ambos, *Commentary* (2022), mn. 2 (referring to the *travaux*), 5 (referring to the ICC-Austria enforcement agreement including, inter alia, the rules mentioned in the previous footnote); Mulgrew, *International Penal System* (2013), p. 46 (minimum rules as interpretative guidance and referred to in enforcement agreements). But see also the tendency to limit the standards to the ones provided for by treaties in order to lower the threshold during the 1997 PrepCom, as discussed in Harmsen and Strijards, 'Article 103', in Ambos, *Commentary* (2022), mn. 27; on this discussion, see also Rochner, *Strafvollstreckung* (2014), pp. 283–4, 291 ff. (including the ICCPR and the UNCAT as 'treaties', in this sense) and 331–2, 332 (crit. of the treaty reference and in favour of including the UN minimum standards); in a similar vein, Stiel and Stuckenberg, 'Article 106', in Klamberg et al., *Commentary ICC II* (2023), p. 908 ('this choice of words [widely accepted international

excludes the territorial State as a potential enforcing State,[50] it is pretty obvious that sentences will basically be served in European and a few non-European countries with acceptable prison conditions.[51] Indeed, this is one of the lessons learnt from the practice of the ad hoc tribunals as will be seen below.[52] Thus, the existence of minimum prison standards should already play a decisive role in drawing up the general list of potential enforcement States since it does not make much sense to, first, list States with insufficient prison standards in order to, then, exclude these very States in the designation phase.

If no (other) State is designated in a given case, the sentence will be served in the *Netherlands* as the ICC *host State*.[53] While the Court 'shall endeavour to designate a State of enforcement', and this obligation is a continuous one,[54] the Netherlands is equally obliged to accept the convict if the Court's efforts fail. In other words, Article 103 (4) ICCS, as the only enforcement provision, imposes an obligation upon the host State being a 'last resort'.[55] The 'prison facility' referred to in Article 103 (4) ICCS is considered an extension of the ICC premises,[56] but the host State enforces the sentences, as any other State, pursuant to its national law.[57]

While the enforcement costs (only) in this case shall be borne by the Court, they normally fall on the enforcing State;[58] costs for transport of the sentenced person and certain costs generated by the Court are to be borne by it.[59] Against this background, the State's economic and financial capacity is another factor to be taken into account in the process of designation,[60] and it may limit the group of possible enforcing States even further. The only remedy

treaty standards] was intended to exclude the applicability of soft law like recommendatory minimum rules which the ad hoc Tribunals used to refer to').

[50] cf. Harmsen and Strijards, 'Article 103', in Ambos, *Commentary* (2022), mn. 23.

[51] In the same vein, Harmsen and Strijards, 'Article 103', in Ambos, *Commentary* (2022), mn. 19, 23. Exceptions, like the enforcement of the sentences of Lubanga and Katanga in the DRC (press release of 19 December 2015, ICC-CPI-20151219-PR1181) confirm the rule; see thereon Vojta, *F3*, 14 (2018), 29 ff. Note, however, that there are some developing countries on the list of States willing to take ICC convicts; see above note 38. On the relationship between international courts, enforcing States, and the Committee for the Prevention of Torture as monitoring body, see Snacken and Kiefer, in Mulgrew and Abels, *RII Penal System* (2016), pp. 322 ff.; generally on international prison standards and transnational criminal justice, see van Zyl Smit, *JITCL*, 4 (2019), 97; crit. pointing out the varying prison conditions amongst European States, Vojta, *EJIL: Talk!*, 2024.

[52] Below notes 168 ff. and main text.

[53] Art. 103 (4) ICCS. For details, see Art. 49 (2) of the Headquarters Agreement between the ICC and the Host State, ICC-BD/04-01-08, 1 March 2008, pursuant to Art. 3 (2) ICCS, <http://www.legal-tools.org/doc/45e340/>.

[54] Arts. 49 (1) and (3) Headquarters Agreement; see also Mulgrew, *International Penal System* (2013), p. 154; Harmsen and Strijards, 'Article 3', in Ambos, *Commentary* (2022), mn. 51; Harmsen and Strijards, 'Article 103', in Ambos, *Commentary* (2022), mn. 30.

[55] cf. Sections 66 (b), 68 (1) Dutch ICC (Implementation) Act confirming the mandatory enforcement by Netherlands as host State; see also Ntoubandi, 'Article 103', in Fernandez and Pacreau, *Commentaire CPI II* (2019), pp. 2369–70; Mulgrew, *International Penal System* (2013), pp. 153–4; Rochner, *Strafvollstreckung* (2014), p. 285; Stiel and Stuckenberg, 'Article 103', in Klamberg et al., *Commentary ICC II* (2023), pp. 884–5; also Abels, *Prisoners* (2012), pp. 458 ff., pointing out that the Dutch government sees this residual provision as a last resort only, favouring the principle of equitable distribution; cf. also Schabas, *ICC Commentary* (2016), pp. 1383–4.

[56] Harmsen and Strijards, 'Article 103', in Ambos, *Commentary* (2022), mn. 29. But note that pursuant to Art. 1 (x) of the Headquarters Agreement 'premises of the Court' are only buildings and so forth with regard to '*detention* of a person' (emphasis added), but not enforcement of the sentence. Consequently, 'the ICC Detention Centre ... is not a facility made for the purposes of managing a regime of convicted prisoners', cf. <https://www.icc-cpi.int/sites/default/files/iccdocs/PIDS/publications/DetentionCentreEng.pdf>. Notwithstanding, the first two ICC convicts (Lubanga and Katanga) have been detained in the detention centre waiting for their transfer to the DRC as enforcement State (above note 51).

[57] cf. Art. 49 (4) s. 2 Headquarters Agreement ('The conditions of imprisonment shall be governed by the law of the host State, as provided in article 106, paragraph 2, of the Statute'). For a discussion, see Rochner, *Strafvollstreckung* (2014), pp. 285–6.

[58] Compare Art. 103 (4) 2nd cl. ICCS with Rule 208 (1) RPE ICC.

[59] cf. Rule 208 (1) RPE ICC and Art. 100 (1)(c), (d), and (e) ICCS.

[60] cf. Harmsen and Strijards, 'Article 103', in Ambos, *Commentary* (2022), mn. 21.

against this effect would be to exempt financially weaker States from the enforcement costs, either by imposing them on the Court, drawing on the host State rule,[61] or on economically more potent States on the basis of trilateral enforcement agreements.[62]

Once a State is designated, the Presidency notifies it and transmits the relevant information.[63] Yet, this State is not subject to a full cooperation obligation since Rule 198 RPE ICC only declares applicable Article 87 ICCS and the corresponding Rules 176–80 RPE ICC, that is, it only authorizes the Court to direct requests to this State. In fact, the State is, at best, obliged to cooperate under the enforcement part (Part 10) of the Statute.[64] Apart from that, the State, here again, may object in different ways. For one, it may reject the concrete designation out of hand—invoking, for example, the already mentioned principle of fair burden-sharing[65]—and thereby force the Presidency to designate another State from the list.[66] Alternatively, the State may invoke 'circumstances' which could 'materially affect the terms or extent of the imprisonment', including one of the conditions mentioned above;[67] this shows that these conditions may constitute a serious obstacle to enforcement.[68] If such circumstances are not acceptable for the Court—which must have been given forty-five days' notice[69]—it may change the designation of the State of enforcement.[70] In any event, the Presidency can always change the State of enforcement, either on its own motion or at the request of the sentenced person or the Prosecutor;[71] in addition, it will have to do so if the designated State rejects the designation.[72]

The bilateral agreements between the Court and potential enforcing States mentioned above[73] may contribute to a greater certainty of the enforcement system. To this effect, the Presidency of the Court has prepared a model enforcement agreement, which incorporates the dispositions of the Statute and the RPE.[74] The Presidency provides States with this model and requests their listing. Once a State signals preliminary interest in joining, a negotiation process ensues, in which the State may invoke the above-mentioned conditions.[75]

[61] Art. 103 (4) ICCS. In this vein, see Rochner, *Strafvollstreckung* (2014), pp. 330–1. Arguably, such an arrangement requires a Statute amendment given that State Parties will not accept picking up the enforcement bill through assessed contributions by way of an analogy to Art. 103 (4) ICCS.

[62] Such agreements would be concluded between the Court, the (poorer) enforcement and the (richer) funding State; see on this and the respective amendment of Art. 103 (1)(a) ICCS proposed by Norway during the Kampala Review conference, Mulgrew, *International Penal System* (2013), pp. 192–3.

[63] Rule 204 RPE ICC. The Presidency shall transmit 'name, nationality, date and place of birth of the sentenced person', copy of judgment and sentence imposed, length of sentence still to be served, and possible information on the health of the person (Rule 204 RPE ICC). On the transfer and possible delays, see Mulgrew, *International Penal System* (2013), pp. 42 ff.

[64] cf. Kreß and Sluiter, in Cassese et al., *Rome Statute II* (2002), p. 1790 (arguing that with the designation, either an enforcement agreement is concluded or a unilateral binding promise of the State to enforce arises).

[65] According to Mulgrew, *International Penal System* (2013), p. 43 this is one 'of the most frequent reasons for refusing to enforce a particular sentence'.

[66] Art. 103 (1)(c) ICCS, Rule 205 RPE ICC.

[67] Art. 103 (2)(a) ICCS.

[68] cf. Mulgrew, *International Penal System* (2013), pp. 37–8.

[69] Art. 103 (2)(a) ICCS.

[70] Arts. 103 (2)(b), 104 ICCS.

[71] Art. 104 ICCS, Rule 209 RPE ICC. For the procedure, see Rule 210 RPE ICC. For details, see the existing bilateral enforcement agreements; on the ICC-Austria agreement, see Harmsen and Strijards, 'Article 104', in Ambos, *Commentary* (2022), mn. 3; see also Mulgrew, *International Penal System* (2013), p. 39 with n. 55; Ntoubandi, 'Article 104', in Fernandez and Pacreau, *Commentaire CPI II* (2019), pp. 2371–3; cf. also Stiel and Stuckenberg, 'Article 103', in Klamberg et al., *Commentary ICC II* (2023), pp. 880–3; Stiel and Stuckenberg, 'Article 104', in Klamberg et al., *Commentary ICC II* (2023), pp. 889–93.

[72] Rule 205 RPE ICC.

[73] Above note 38.

[74] It has been supplemented by provisions of previous models of the UN ad hoc tribunals as well as a UN Model Agreement drafted by the UN Office of Legal Affairs. See also Mulgrew, *International Penal System* (2013), p. 36.

[75] Abtahi, *MPEiPro* (2019), mn. 10.

From the States considered more closely in this chapter, so far the *UK* and *Sweden*, have concluded such an agreement with the ICC, formally declaring their willingness to enforce ICC sentences and detailing the conditions in accordance with Article 103 ICCS.[76] In contrast, *Germany* has refrained from concluding such an agreement and instead opted for ad hoc agreements on a case-by-case basis, given that, due to its federal nature, the enforcement of sentences lies in the competence of its Federal States (*Bundesländer*).[77] In any case, the direct and unreserved enforcement of ICC sentences pursuant to § 41 (2) of the German ICC Act (*IStGHG*)[78] entails that Germany will not attach any conditions within the meaning of Articles 103 (2)(b) and 105 (1) ICCS.[79] In *Australia*, the conditions for the enforcement of prison sentences are laid out in Part 12 of the ICC Act.[80] Section 160 allows the Attorney-General to declare Australia's willingness to enforce such sentences based on the conditions there defined. Once Australia is designated by the ICC, the Attorney-General must consider the designation in accordance with Section 162, and before accepting, ask—due to Australia's federal nature—for the consent of the State Minister of the State in which the ICC prisoner should serve the sentence.[81]

### (b) *The actual enforcement*

Once the designated State of enforcement accepts the designation, the sentenced person shall be 'delivered' to it.[82] To that effect, the Registrar of the Court coordinates with the authorities of this State and the host State.[83] The enforcement as such, that is, the conditions of imprisonment, is governed by the law of the enforcing State but it must comply with the above-mentioned international prison standards;[84] yet, ICC prisoners must not be treated less or more favourably than national prisoners convicted of similar offences.[85] If one were to understand this non-discrimination clause strictly, it would create an insoluble dilemma for the Court: on the one hand, it cannot transfer its prisoners to States which do not meet

[76] Agreement between the Government of the United Kingdom of Great Britain and Northern Ireland and the International Criminal Court on the enforcement of sentences imposed by the International Criminal Court of December 8th, 2007, ICC-PRES/04-01-07, <http://www.icc-cpi.int/NR/rdonlyres/C540B3EF-F3FF-4AD0-93F5-DA85E96B1522/0/ICCPres040107ENG.pdf>; Agreement between the International Criminal Court and the Government of Sweden on the enforcement of sentences of the International Criminal Court of April 24th, 2017, ICC-PRES/20-02-17, <https://www.icc-cpi.int/sites/default/files/itemsDocuments/170424-oj-sa-Sweden.pdf>.

[77] Nemitz, in Schomburg et al., *Internationale Rechtshilfe* (2020), p. 2545; Hess, Knust and Schuon, *FYbIL*, 16 (2005), 133, 160; Elberling, *GYbIL*, 54 (2011), 665, 670; Mulgrew, *International Penal System* (2013), p. 36.

[78] German Law on Cooperation with the International Criminal Court (ICC Act) (*Gesetz über die Zusammenarbeit mit dem Internationalen Strafgerichtshof (IStGH-Gesetz—IStGHG)*, <http://www.gesetze-im-internet.de/bundesrecht/istghg/gesamt.pdf>.

[79] cf. Keller, in Ambos et al., *Rechtshilferecht* (2020), p. 1510.

[80] ICC Act 2002 <http://www.comlaw.gov.au/Details/C2004A00992>.

[81] Sections 163 and 164 (1)(c) Australian ICC Act.

[82] Rule 206 (2) RPE ICC. According to Mulgrew, *International Penal System* (2013), p. 83, the use of the term 'delivery', instead of 'transfer' (as in the case of the ad hoc tribunals) is more appropriate since it makes clear that the international tribunals 'do not completely transfer responsibility' to enforcing States but merely 'delegate the practical aspects of implementation of sentences'. On the other hand, this author criticizes the existing system of decentralized enforcement because it entails 'the forced exile of prisoners to a foreign land' and 'bears the hallmarks of penal transportation' (p. 275). Yet, this is an overstatement given that the extradition or surrender of persons is the common, unavoidable feature of any system of mutual assistance in criminal matters.

[83] Rule 206 (3) RPE ICC.

[84] Art. 106 (2) ICCS. cf. Kreß and Sluiter, in Cassese et al., *Rome Statute II* (2002), pp. 1797 ff.; Kreß, in Grützner et al., *Rechtshilfeverkehr* (2022), IV A 1 mn. 345 and 347 ff.; Schabas, *ICC Commentary* (2016), pp. 1391 ff.; Clark and Hohler, *MPEiPro* (2022), mn. 25 ff.; Marchesi, in Lattanzi and Schabas, *Rome Statute I* (1999), pp. 437 ff.

[85] Art. 106 (2) *in fine* ICCS; cf. also Stiel and Stuckenberg, 'Article 106', in Klamberg et al., *Commentary ICC II* (2023), pp. 907–11. Contrary to Clark and Hohler, 'Article 106', in Ambos, *Commentary* (2022), mn. 10, this does not refer to the nature of the sentence (capital punishment).

the minimum prison standards; on the other hand, it must not request an enforcing State to upgrade these standards since this would violate the non-discrimination clause, creating double standards between international and national prisoners. Against the background of the ad hoc tribunals' enforcement practice, to be treated later in this chapter, the principle of equitable distribution and the Court's claim of universality leave it no other option than to encourage States to upgrade their prison conditions, with the potential positive side effect that this would also benefit the national prisoners. This has been, indeed, the approach with regard to the African prison facilities for the ICTR and SCSL.[86]

The enforcing States' adherence to international standards is ensured by the supervision of the ICC,[87] which in turn is predicated upon the 'unimpeded and confidential' communication between the sentenced person and the Court to be guaranteed, constituting a positive obligation,[88] by the enforcing State.[89] Apart from the ICC, the ICRC should also have access to the prison facilities of the enforcing State pursuant to a clause in the bilateral enforcement agreements to be included at the request of the ICC.[90] Apart from that, given that the prison conditions are governed by the national law of the enforcing State, the ICC prisoner may also use the available domestic remedies to challenge these conditions, especially if they violate the prisoner's individual—constitutionally protected—rights.[91]

The ICC's supervisory function is, of course, not only to the benefit of the sentenced person, but also gives the Court full control over any measure entailing the *reduction* or suspension of the *sentence* and, to a lesser extent, the flexibilization of the prison regime.[92] In sum, it is fair to say that the drafters opted for a model which seeks an adequate balance between the enforcing States and the Court: while the sentences are served in the prison facilities of the enforcing States according to their laws, the sentence imposed by the Court is binding and its enforcement supervised by the Court.[93]

Accordingly, the enforcing State has no influence upon the length of the prison sentence; any sentence reduction has to be decided by the Court alone.[94] The only exception to this binding effect of the Court's sentence may be agreed in advance as a condition attached by the State to its general acceptance to receive sentenced persons pursuant to Article 103 (1)

[86] See below note 178 with main text.

[87] Art. 106 (1) ICCS. On this supervision regarding the concrete prison conditions ('welfare of the international prisoner'), see Mulgrew, *International Penal System* (2013), pp. 45 ff.; on the possible external inspection bodies (esp. ICRC and CPT), see Mulgrew, op. cit., pp. 51 ff.; thereon, see also Stiel and Stuckenberg, 'Article 106', in Klamberg et al., *Commentary ICC II* (2023), pp. 904–6; crit. of the lack of uniformity regarding the oversight bodies and the lack of systemic overview, see Mulgrew, op. cit, pp. 185 ff.

[88] In the same vein, Clark and Hohler, 'Article 106', in Ambos, *Commentary* (2022), mn. 11; Ntoubandi, 'Article 106', in Fernandez and Pacreau, *Commentaire CPI II* (2019), pp. 2384–5; Stiel and Stuckenberg, 'Article 106', in Klamberg et al., *Commentary ICC II* (2023), p. 912.

[89] Art. 106 (3) ICCS. For details, see Rule 211 RPE ICC that, inter alia, authorizes the Court to send a judge or staff member to visit the sentenced person in order to hear their views *in situ*.

[90] The ICC has taken up this obligation in Art. 14 of its agreement with the ICRC; see Agreement between the ICC and the ICRC on Visits to Persons deprived of Liberty Pursuant to the Jurisdiction of the International Criminal Court, ICC-PRES/02-01-06, dates of signature: 29 March and 13 April 2006, entry into force: 13 April 2006, available in the ICC Official Journal <http://www.icc-cpi.int/NR/rdonlyres/A542057C-FB5F-4729-8DD4-8C0699DDE0A3/140159/ICCPRES020106_English.pdf>.

[91] With regard to Germany, see Keller, in Ambos et al., *Rechtshilferecht* (2020), p. 1511; in the same vein, Rochner, *Strafvollstreckung* (2014), pp. 209 ff., 314–15, 326–7 (crit. the lack of effective remedies in all tribunals and calling for a national review regarding fundamental rights), 329–30 (calling for a remedy against the Presidents' decisions).

[92] See, in detail, Mulgrew, *International Penal System* (2013), pp. 56 ff.

[93] Abtahi, in *MPEiPro* (2019), mn. 6. See also Holá, Kelder, and van Wijk, in Hayashi and Bailliert, *Legitimacy* (2017), crit. at 358 the limited scope of the supervisory role, esp. the lack of a proactive approach towards rehabilitation (not only concerning the ICC).

[94] Art. 110 (1), (2) ICCS. On sentence review, see also below notes 104 ff. and main text.

(b) ICCS.[95] However, any such condition must be compatible with the applicable provisions of the Statute and Rules.[96] Any application for appeal or revision is to be decided by the Court,[97] that is, no litigation in this regard, binding on the ICC, is possible in the courts of the enforcing State;[98] yet, this State must not impede such an application, that is, it must make it possible (positive obligation).[99]

Any *flexibilization*, for example, out-of-prison activity or temporal leave as part of domestic resocialization programmes, shall be communicated to the Presidency so that it can exercise its supervisory function.[100] While the Presidency may object to such a measure, it cannot prevent it as long as it does not entail an effective reduction of the sentence, that is, an interruption of enforcement. This follows from the interplay of the Court's clear authority regarding any sentence reduction,[101] including its right to be informed,[102] and the mere supervision of the concrete enforcement which remains in the hands of the enforcement State.[103] Ultimately, if the Court considers that the flexibilization goes too far, it can terminate the enforcement in the respective State and designate another enforcing State.

As to a possible sentence *reduction*,[104] the Court—concretely, a panel of three judges of the Appeals Chamber (AC) appointed for that reason[105]—shall make a first review after a period of two-thirds of the sentence (in case of a limited sentence) or after twenty-five years (in case of life imprisonment).[106] This review is 'an automatic and mandatory' one

[95] cf. Art. 105 (1) ICCS. See Kreß and Sluiter, in Cassese et al., *Rome Statute II* (2002), pp. 1791 ff.; Kreß, in Grützner et al., *Rechtshilfeverkehr* (2022), IV A 1 mn. 342 ff.; Stiel and Stuckenberg, 'Article 105', in Klamberg et al., *Commentary ICC II* (2023), pp. 895–8.

[96] For example, a provision on a possible sentence reduction before two-thirds have been served would, arguably, violate Art. 110 (3) ICCS explicitly establishing this minimum time of execution of the sentence.

[97] Art. 105 (2) cl. 1 ICCS.

[98] Clark and Hohler, 'Article 105', in Ambos, *Commentary* (2022), mn. 7; Fall, 'Article 105', in Fernandez and Pacreau, *Commentaire CPI II* (2019), p. 2378; Stiel and Stuckenberg, 'Article 105', in Klamberg et al., *Commentary ICC II* (2023), pp. 899–900.

[99] Art. 105 (2) cl. 2 ICCS. See Clark and Hohler, 'Article 105', in Ambos, *Commentary* (2022), mn. 8; Fall, 'Article 105', in Fernandez and Pacreau, *Commentaire CPI II* (2019), p. 2378 ('l'Etat d'administration ... a une obligation de faciliter').

[100] Rule 211 (2) RPE ICC. See, as an example of a national rule, § 41 (4)(2) IStGHG according to which a decision of the ICC has to be requested if the German law provides for a (temporary) delay or suspension of enforcement, the crediting of time already spent in detention, or a flexible enforcement regime mechanism. On these rules in detail, see Rochner, *Strafvollstreckung* (2014), pp. 299 ff.

[101] Art. 110 ICCS.

[102] Rule 211 (2) RPE ICC. In a similar vein, Mulgrew, *International Penal System* (2013), p. 56 (referring to enforcement agreements); Rochner, *Strafvollstreckung* (2014), pp. 297 ff.

[103] Art. 106 ICCS.

[104] The ICC regime, unlike the ICTY/ICTR/SCSL (below note 181), does not provide for a pardon, cf. Rochner, *Strafvollstreckung* (2014), p. 306. For a detailed comparative analysis of the respective Tribunals' early release systems, see Fernández-Pacheco Estrada, *ICLR*, 22 (2022), 452 ff.

[105] cf. Rules 223, 224 RPE ICC.

[106] Art. 110 (3) ICCS. Welcoming this rule as introducing 'transparency, predictability and consistency', Mulgrew, *International Penal System* (2013), p. 60; in a similar vein, Oehmichen, 'Article 110', in Klamberg et al., *Commentary ICC II* (2023), pp. 962–3 ('clearer guidance, which may contribute to their rehabilitation. Moreover, disparities that were observed at the ICTY and ICTR practice, due to diverging and conflicting domestic provisions on early release can thus be reduced'); welcoming it as being autonomous and not dependent upon national law, Rochner, *Strafvollstreckung* (2014), pp. 328–9. See also Fernández-Pacheco Estrada, *ICLR*, 22 (2022), 565, who welcomes this rule ('valuable step forward, as it ensures foreseeability and equality among those convicted') while at the same time calling for additional amendments in light of international human rights (esp. related to exceptional circumstances, such as grave illness). For the first ICC decisions, see ICC, *Prosecutor v. Lubanga*, AC, Decision on the Review Concerning Reduction of Sentence of Mr Thomas Lubanga Dyilo, ICC-01/04-01/06-3173, 22 September 2015 and *Prosecutor v. Lubanga*, AC, Second Decision on the Review Concerning Reduction of Sentence, ICC-01/04-01/06-3375, 3 November 2017; ICC, *Prosecutor v. Katanga*, AC, Decision on the Review Concerning Reduction of Sentence of Mr Germain Katanga, ICC-01/04-01/07-3615, 13 November 2015; ICC, *Prosecutor v. Ahmad Al Faqi Al Mahdi*, AC, Decision on the Review Concerning Reduction of Sentence, ICC-01/12-01/15-434-Red3, 25 November 2021.

and no application by the sentenced person is required.[107] However, the 'ultimate decision of whether to reduce the sentence is discretionary in nature'.[108] In making this decision, the AC has to consider various factors, namely: the sentenced person's willingness to cooperate with the Court's investigations, prosecutions, and enforcement measures regarding the applicable penalties;[109] the person's conduct in detention[110] (as an indication of 'a clear and significant change of circumstances' justifying a sentence reduction[111]); the prospect of resocialization and reintegration;[112] the social effects of an early release (prevention of 'significant social instability');[113] any beneficial action regarding the victims and their families, in particular the expression of regret;[114] as well as the

[107] *Lubanga*, ICC-01/04-01/06-3173, paras. 20, 32 ('the initial review of sentence . . . is not triggered by an application of a sentenced person, but rather is an automatic and mandatory review once the threshold of having served two thirds of a sentence has been met'); *Katanga*, ICC-01/04-01/07-3615, para. 113; *Al Mahdi*, ICC-01/12-01/15-434-Red3, para. 17 ('a mandatory *proprio motu* review').

[108] *Lubanga*, ICC-01/04-01/06-3173, para. 21; *Katanga*, ICC-01/04-01/07-3615, para. 20; *Al Mahdi*, ICC-01/12-01/15-434-Red3, para. 15.

[109] Art. 110 (4)(a), (b) ICCS; cf. also *Lubanga*, ICC-01/04-01/06-3173, para. 36, emphasizing that cooperation or willingness to cooperate have to be continuous 'beyond the conviction and imposition of sentence' or that they have to have an 'additional post-sentence impact on the Court's investigations or prosecution'; *Katanga*, ICC-01/04-01/07-3615, para. 34, holding that '"cooperation" within the meaning of article 110 (4) (a) ICCS must contribute to the efficient administration of justice at the Court' and the accused's withdrawal of his appeal 'as a result of acknowledging that he or she is guilty of the crimes committed and publicly apologising therefore' is an example of such post-sentence cooperation. In its second reduction of sentence decision concerning Lubanga, the panel held that an active participation in the context of the reparation process 'cannot constitute an indication of cooperation' within the meaning of Article 110 (4) (a) ICCS when it is limited to merely exercising procedural rights, cf. *Lubanga*, ICC-01/04-01/06-3375, para. 43; *Al Mahdi*, ICC-01/12-01/15-434-Red3, paras. 24–5 (stressing that conduct prior to the imposition of sentence may, depending on the individual case, qualify as an indicator of "early" cooperation—which it confirmed in the present case, given Mr Al Mahdi's 'continued adherence to his admission of guilt, his continued compliance with the Agreement and his cooperation . . . post-sentence' [at para. 31]).

[110] On the meaning of the accused person's conduct while in detention, cf. *Lubanga*, ICC-01/04-01/06-3173, paras. 45–7, holding that a 'good conduct while in detention generally or vis-à-vis other detainees and the Detention Centre staff is [not] sufficient on its own to establish the necessary connection between this conduct and a dissociation' from the accused person's crimes within the meaning of Rule 223 (a) RPE ICC, and requiring that the accused person shall accept responsibility and express remorse for having committed those criminal acts; *Lubanga*, ICC-01/04-01/06-3375, para. 57; *Katanga*, ICC-01/04-01/07-3615, paras. 47–9; *Al Mahdi*, ICC-01/12-01/15-434-Red3, para. 41 (requiring a 'clear and significant change of circumstances' from the time the sentence was imposed that shows that the dissociation from the crime is of a 'genuine' character. Accordingly, even a person who has shown remorse and sympathy toward the victims at the time of sentencing is not exempt from this standard and therefore must demonstrate a level of commitment beyond their prior conduct—which the panel, surprisingly, did not confirm in the present case, despite the fact that Mr Al Mahdi continued to express remorse post-conviction, read a statement addressed to the victims, and asked for their forgiveness [paras. 43–5]). Crit. on the lack of a clear and consistent conceptualization of remorse, also in the context of early release, Kapoor, *JICJ*, 4 (2023), 877 ff.

[111] Art. 110 (4)(c) ICCS; cf. also *Lubanga*, ICC-01/04-01/06-3173, para. 30, holding that 'a person's cooperation or assistance which was taken into account in the original sentence and has not continued post-conviction' may be taken into account on a case-by-case basis, if 'the original sentence imposed' does 'not fully capture the extent of the assistance provided, the benefit it provides to the victims, nor the degree to which it furthered the Court's investigations and prosecutions'.

[112] cf. also *Lubanga*, ICC-01/04-01/06-3173, paras. 52–3. *Katanga*, ICC-01/04-01/07-3615, paras. 57–8; *Lubanga*, ICC-01/04-01/06-3375, para. 61; *Al Mahdi*, ICC-01/12-01/15-434-Red3, paras. 52–3.

[113] cf. also *Lubanga*, ICC-01/04-01/06-3173, paras. 63–4; *Katanga*, ICC-01/04-01/07-3615, paras. 74–6, emphasizing that 'some degree of social instability' is not enough and the instability shall be 'significant' (para. 76); *Lubanga*, ICC-01/04-01/06-3375, paras. 72–4, stressing once again the threshold of significance (para. 74); *Al Mahdi*, ICC-01/12-01/15-434-Red3, paras. 58–9 (arguing that significant (temporary) social instability also exists when an early release has the potential to jeopardize the implementation of individual and collective reparations [para. 59]).

[114] *Katanga*, ICC-01/04-01/07-3615, paras. 50, 87, 90, 91, 93–4, 96–105. See also relevant ad hoc tribunal jurisprudence on the relevance of the convict's expression of acceptance of guilt, regret, and/or remorse: ICTY, *Prosecutor v. Stakić*, Decision of the President on Early Release, IT-97-24-ES, 15 July 2011, paras. 24 ff. Crit. as to the lack of special strategies in order 'to guide prison staff on how to encourage future ICC convicts to genuinely

individual circumstances of the sentenced person, especially in terms of their health and age.[115]

Of course, taking the prisoner's future lawful conduct in society (resocialization, reintegration) as a decisive factor for early release is predicated on the assumption that relevant programmes and services are offered in prison. If, however, the imprisonment of international prisoners operates as pure confinement without any kind of treatment,[116] as sadly demonstrated in some (early) enforcement cases of the ad hoc tribunals,[117] such requirements can hardly be met by the respective prisoners.[118]

In procedural terms, the decision shall be prepared by a hearing with the presence of the sentenced person, their counsel, the Prosecutor, the enforcing State, and the victims (or their representatives), all of which shall make written and/or oral observations.[119] Where the AC decides not to reduce the sentence, it must repeat the review procedure at least every three years.[120] In this case, written submissions are the rule.[121] Where the AC decides in favour of early release it may, arguably, impose certain conditions drawing on an analogy to Rule 119 RPE ICC. Of course, these conditions restrict the liberty, but if they are the price to regain liberty in the first place, they may be worth it. The Chamber must ensure compliance with and supervision of these conditions.[122] At the time of writing (September 2024),

dissociate from past crimes or take actions to the benefit of victims', difficulties arising from the fact that the prisons are usually located far away from the country where the crimes were committed and where the victims reside, as well as to the limited role of rehabilitation in the early release decisions of the ad hoc tribunals, see Holá, Kelder, and van Wijk, in Hayashi and Bailliert, *Legitimacy* (2017), p. 375; crit. as to the granting of unconditional early release at the ICTY, see Yarnell *JHR*, 5 (2023), 589 ff.

[115] Rule 223 RPE ICC. On these criteria and the procedure in detail, see Mulgrew, *International Penal System* (2013), pp. 70 ff.; Oehmichen, 'Article 110', in Klamberg et al., *Commentary ICC II* (2023), pp. 971–85.

[116] cf. Mulgrew, *International Penal System* (2013), pp. 188–9 ('"cheap and convenient" custody system in which national prisons act "as babysitters" for international prisoners', 'basic and regressive system').

[117] See below notes 196 ff. and main text.

[118] Crit. also Holá, Kelder, and van Wijk, in Hayashi and Bailliert, *Legitimacy* (2017), calling for a high level of specialization and expertise to promote rehabilitation, p. 375; Mulgrew, *International Penal System* (2013), p. 99. For a critical, theoretical approach to early release in international criminal law, see Choi, *YaleLJ*, 123 (2014), 1808 ff.

[119] Rule 224 (1) RPE ICC. On the importance of such hearings—esp. vis-à-vis the written procedure ad hoc tribunals, see Fernández-Pacheco Estrada, *ICLR*, 22 (2022), 547–8.

[120] Art. 110 (5) ICCS; Rule 224 (3) RPE ICC; cf. Kreß, in Grützner et al., *Rechtshilfeverkehr* (2022), IV A 1 mn. 338 ff.; Kreß and Sluiter, in Cassese et al., *Rome Statute II* (2002), pp. 1793–4; Pulvirenti, in Cassese, Chiavario, and De Francesco, *Problemi* (2005), pp. 481 ff.; Nemitz, in Haveman and Olusanya, *Sentencing and Sanctioning* (2006), p. 143; Oehmichen, 'Article 110', in Klamberg et al., *Commentary ICC II* (2023), pp. 986–7. However, in *Lubanga*, with a remaining sentence of less than four-and-a-half years the review panel reduced the three-year interval to two years after the first review (*Lubanga*, ICC-01/04-01/06-3173, para. 79); alternatively, it could have stuck to the existing rule and abstained from a further review. In its second (and final) review in 2017, the review panel denied reduction of Lubanga's remaining sentence of three years since it did not see a 'significant change in circumstances since the date of the First Sentence Review Decision that would merit a reduction', see *Lubanga*, ICC-01/04-01/06-3375, para. 94.

[121] Rule 224 (4) RPE ICC.

[122] In this line, regarding conditional release from pre-trial detention (Rule 119 RPE ICC), see ICC, *Prosecutor v. Bemba*, AC, Judgment on the Appeal of the Prosecutor against Pre-Trial Chamber II's 'Decision on the Interim Release of Jean-Pierre Bemba Gombo and Convening Hearings with the Kingdom of Belgium, the Republic of Portugal, the Republic of France, the Federal Republic of Germany, the Italian Republic, and the Republic of South Africa', ICC-01/05-01/08-631-Red, 2 December 2009, paras. 104 ff., esp. para. 105 regarding the specification of conditions ('decision that grants conditional release … is only possible if specific conditions are imposed.'), and paras. 106–7, regarding the supervision of the enforcement of those conditions (106: 'identification of a State willing to accept the person concerned as well as enforce related conditions is necessary' and 107: 'State cooperation in … accepting a person who has been conditionally released as well as ensuring that the conditions imposed by the Court are enforced.'). On the denial of interim release due to the 'absence of a State willing to accept a person and enforce related conditions', see ICC, *Prosecutor v. Mokom Gawaka*, PTC II, Public Redacted Version of 'Decision on interim release', ICC-01/14-01/22-173-Red, 8 March 2023, paras. 48 ff., esp. para. 59. Generally crit. as to the effective implementation of such conditions' supervision, Fernández-Pacheco Estrada, *ICLR*, 22 (2022),

the first request of the first ICC convict on the reduction of sentence, Mr Lubanga, has been denied twice,[123] but a similar request by the second ICC convict, Mr Katanga,[124] and also the more recent request by Mr Al Mahdi[125] were granted. The AC's decision on early release cannot be appealed.[126]

The Court's 'penitentiary primacy'[127] with regard to the length and possible reduction of the sentence may give rise to conflicts with the (constitutional) law of State Parties.[128] If, for example, the national law demands an earlier revision of the Court's prison sentence than after twenty-five years (life imprisonment) or two-thirds (limited imprisonment),[129] the respective State Party would have to violate its national law in order to comply with its enforcement obligation towards the ICC. From a legal perspective, the State concerned has only two options in such a situation: either it attaches, from the outset, the respective conditions to its declaration of acceptance[130] or it tries to bring its national law in line with the international enforcement regime.[131] If this is not done, the sentenced person may have to be returned to the ICC to avoid a violation of national (constitutional) law.[132]

If the sentenced person *escapes* from custody, the enforcing State 'may', after consulting with the ICC, request their surrender from the State they are located in (horizontal approach);[133] alternatively, the enforcing State 'may' ask the ICC to make such a request pursuant to the cooperation rules, in particular Article 91 ICCS (vertical approach).[134] The Presidency may also designate another enforcing State.[135]

565–6; in the same vein, Riegler, *ICLR*, 20 (2020), 710 (crit. that '[n]o mechanism is in place at the Tribunals nor at the ICC to supervise or even monitor prisoners once they have been released').

[123] *Lubanga*, ICC-01/04-01/06-3173, para. 77; *Lubanga*, ICC-01/04-01/06-3375, para. 94.

[124] *Katanga*, ICC-01/04-01/07-3615, para. 116; the original sentence of Mr Katanga was reduced by a third (three years and eight months).

[125] *Al Mahdi*, ICC-01/12-01/15-434-Red3, para. 77; the AC reduced the original sentence (of nine years' imprisonment) by two years.

[126] Crit. Fernández-Pacheco Estrada, *ICLR*, 22 (2022), 567 (identifying this as 'the greatest flaw' [esp. when compared to the possibility of appeal concerning many minor decisions adopted at previous stages of the trial—such as, for example, decisions concerning pre-trial conditional release] and calling for a respective amendment as an 'urgent and crucial matter' in order to avoid 'a certain sense of arbitrariness or even impunity, which could heavily undermine the Court's authority'). – There is only one State Party (Argentina) which has signed a release of persons agreement with the Court, cf. ICC, *Cooperation Agreements* (2023), p. 15; for a model agreement ibid., pp. 44 ff.

[127] Harmsen and Strijards, 'Article 110', in Ambos, *Commentary* (2022), mn. 1; in the same vein regarding the ICTY, Tolbert, *LJIL*, 11 (2008), 659; here, see below note 183.

[128] With regard to the (constitutional) prohibition of life imprisonment in Latin America and the respective early release mechanisms in countries like Germany, see Rochner, *Strafvollstreckung* (2014), pp. 288–90; with a view to Latin America, see Ambos et al., *Dificultades* (2007) with country reports; regarding ICTY practice, see Hoffmann, *ZIS*, 6 (2011), 838; Rochner, *Strafvollstreckung* (2014), pp. 212 ff., 232 ff. (with a view to Germany and Italy).

[129] Art. 110 (3) ICCS. For such an earlier review see e.g. § 57a of the German Penal Code (*Strafgesetzbuch*—StGB) which, pursuant to a decision of the German Constitutional Court (Case no. BvR 1041/88, Decision of 3 June 1992), calls for a revision of life imprisonment after fifteen years.

[130] Art. 103 (1)(b) ICCS.

[131] On a possible interpretation in conformity with the international rules, see Rochner, *Strafvollstreckung* (2014), p. 241.

[132] This has been the case for ICTY convicts who had been delivered to France to purge their sentences, and were eligible for early release/remission of sentence after less than two-thirds under applicable French law (see Arts. 721 ff. of the French CPP). See e.g. *Stakić*, IT-97-24-ES, paras. 22 ff., 38; ICTY, *Prosecutor v. Bala*, Decision on Application of Harandin Bala for Sentence Remission, IT-03-66-ES, 10 October 2010, paras. 13 ff.

[133] Art. 111 ICCS.

[134] For the practically literal implementation in enforcement agreements, see Harmsen and Strijards, 'Article 111', in Ambos, *Commentary* (2022), mn. 2–9, taking as an example the one between the ICC and Austria; on States' discretion to opt either for the 'horizontal' or the 'vertical' approach, see Stiel and Stuckenberg, 'Article 111', in Klamberg et al., *Commentary ICC II* (2023), pp. 991–6. Generally, on the differences and commonalities between horizontal and vertical cooperation, see van der Wilt, in Mulgrew and Abels, *RH Penal System* (2016), pp. 193 ff.

[135] Art. 111 ICCS. For more details, see Rule 225 RPE ICC.

Upon completion of the sentence, the convict is to be transferred to the State which 'is obliged' to receive them, that is, their home State,[136] or another State willing to take them, unless the enforcing State permits them to remain.[137] While the wishes of the person concerned are to be taken into account, they are not obligatory for the Court,[138] and Article 107 (1) ICCS distinguishes between the home and another State. As to the former, there seems to exist a certain priority since it 'is obliged to receive' the convict; as to the latter, its consent is needed in the first place ('agrees to receive') and, apparently, only with regard to that State the wishes of the person concerned are to be taken into account ('taking into account ... to that State').[139] Of course, if a transfer to the home State entails the risk of being persecuted in violation of fundamental human rights,[140] the person concerned must not be transferred, even if the recognition of refugee status would have to be excluded due to Article 1 F (a) of the Geneva Refugee Convention.[141] A transfer would in such a case result in the attribution of possible human rights violations committed by the home State to the Netherlands as the transferring State; this, in turn, would trigger the Netherlands' responsibility under the ECHR.[142]

With respect to a potential *further prosecution* by the enforcing State or the extradition by this State to a third State,[143] the *rule of specialty* applies,[144] that is, a further prosecution for crimes committed *before* the delivery to the enforcing State is generally not permitted. However, the Court may—as well as the State which surrenders a person to the Court[145] and after having heard the person concerned[146]—waive the specialty requirements at the request

[136] cf. the wording of Art. 107 (1) and Clark and Hohler, 'Article 107', in Ambos, *Commentary* (2022), mn. 6; cf. also Dosen and Ntoubandi, 'Article 107', in Fernandez and Pacreau, *Commentaire CPI II* (2019), pp. 2387–97; Stiel, 'Article 107', in Klamberg et al., *Commentary ICC II* (2023), pp. 918–21.

[137] Art. 107 (1) ICCS. See Kreß and Sluiter, in Cassese et al., *Rome Statute II* (2002), pp. 1813 ff.; Kreß, in Grützner et al., *Rechtshilfeverkehr* (2022), IV A 1 mn. 353; Marchesi, in Lattanzi and Schabas, *Rome Statute I* (1999), pp. 439–40; Schabas, *ICC Commentary* (2016), pp. 1397 ff.

[138] See also Clark and Hohler, 'Article 107', in Ambos, *Commentary* (2022), mn. 8 ('strongest attention').

[139] *Contra* this literal interpretation in favour of taking into account the wishes 'in all cases', Clark and Hohler, 'Article 107', in Ambos, *Commentary* (2022), mn. 8.

[140] cf. the case of Mathieu Ngudjolo Chui who applied for asylum in the Netherlands after his acquittal by the Court, see Holvoet and Yabasun, *EJIL: Talk!*, 2013; thereon also Savadogo, *ICLR*, 15 (2015), 803 ff.

[141] Art. 1 F of the Geneva Refugee Convention reads: 'The provisions of this Convention shall not apply to any person with respect to whom there are serious reasons for considering that: (a) He has committed a crime against peace, a war crime, or a crime against humanity, as defined in the international instruments drawn up to make provision in respect of such crimes.' On the legal issues arising from the relocation of persons acquitted, esp. by the ICTR and ICC, in their home countries, see Savadogo, *ICLR*, 15 (2015), 790 ff., 807 ff., following the *Katanga and Ngudjolo Chui* TC's view (ICC, *Prosecutor v. Katanga and Ngudjolo*, TC II, Decision on an Amicus Curiae Application and on the 'Requête tendant àobtenir présentations des témoins DRC-D02-P-0350, DRC-D02-P-0236, DRC-D02-P-0228 aux autorités néerlandaises aux fins d'asile' (Arts. 68 and 93 (7) of the Statute), (ICC-01/04-01/07), ICC-01/04-01/07-3003-tENG, 9 June 2011, para. 64), where the TC found that while it 'cannot disregard the customary rule of non-refoulement ... it is unable to implement the principle within its ordinary meaning' and 'only a State which possesses territory is actually able to comply with the non-refoulement principle' (811–14), proposing instead the use of diplomatic assurances for safely returning an acquitted person to their home country (814–18). On the protection of ICC witnesses through non-refoulement claims in the Netherlands and the limitations of such an alternative source of protection, see Irving, *JICJ*, 12 (2014), 1151 ff.; generally on the ICC's obligations pursuant to the principle of non-refoulement, see Pulvirenti, *LJIL*, 35 (2022), 433 ff.

[142] On the ECHR's obstacles to extradition/surrender/transfer in this regard, see Ambos, *Internationales Strafrecht* (2018), § 12 mn. 34 ff.

[143] Art. 107 (3) ICCS.

[144] Art. 108 (1) ICCS. See Kreß and Sluiter, in Cassese et al., *Rome Statute II* (2002), pp. 1809 ff.; Kreß, in Grützner et al., *Rechtshilfeverkehr* (2022), IV A 1 mn. 351–2; Schabas, *ICC Commentary* (2016), pp. 1402 ff.; Ntoubandi, 'Article 108', in Fernandez and Pacreau, *Commentaire CPI II* (2019), pp. 2399–403; Schabas, 'Article 108', in Ambos, *Commentary* (2022), mn. 1 ff.; Stiel and Stuckenberg, 'Article 108', in Klamberg et al., *Commentary ICC II* (2023), pp. 925 ff.

[145] Art. 101 ICCS.

[146] Art. 108 (2) ICCS.

of the enforcing State.[147] In its first application of Article 108 (1) ICCS, at the request of the DRC, the Presidency interpreted the specialty principle rather as an exception than the rule, holding that 'the Court's approval should only be denied when the [domestic] prosecution, punishment or extradition of sentenced persons may undermine certain fundamental principles or procedures of the Rome Statute or otherwise affect the integrity of the Court',[148] for example if 'there is a potential undermining of the key relevant principle of *ne bis in idem*'.[149] The specialty restriction also ceases to apply if the sentenced person remains voluntarily, after completion of the sentence, for more than thirty days in the territory of the enforcing State or returns to this State after having left it first.[150] Under these circumstances, the enforcing State may prosecute or surrender the convict to a third State.[151]

## (2) ICTY, ICTR, SCSL, and KSC

### (a) *General willingness of States, concrete designation, and acceptance of convicts*

The enforcement regime of the ad hoc tribunals resembles that of the ICC in that a *double consent* is required:[152] first, States have to indicate their *general willingness* to receive sentenced persons to the UN Security Council; on this basis the tribunals draw up a *list* of possible enforcing States[153] and may conclude bilateral enforcement agreements (which may contain certain conditions);[154] secondly, these States have to agree to accept *specific* convicts on an ad hoc basis.[155] While, regarding the ICTY, the States of the Former Yugoslavia had

[147] Art. 108 (1) ICCS. For procedural details, see Rules 214–16 RPE ICC distinguishing between a prosecution by the enforcing State or by a third State after extradition by the enforcing State. See also Reg. 115 RegC calling on the Presidency, with regard to the procedure sub Rule 214 (4) RPE ICC, to 'have due regard to the principles of international law on re-extradition'.

[148] ICC, *Prosecutor v. Katanga*, Presidency, Decision pursuant to Article 108 (1) of the Rome Statute, ICC-01/04-01/07-3679, 7 April 2016, para. 20. Crit. thereon, Labuda, *Opinio Juris* (13 April 2016).

[149] *Katanga*, ICC-01/04-01/07-3679, para. 21; further factors which can be taken into consideration as having the potential to undermine other fundamental principles or procedures or otherwise affect the integrity of the Court are, for example, whether 'the procedure for the designation of a State of enforcement having been used inappropriately as a guise to obtain custody over a sentenced person' (para. 27), whether the crimes are 'punishable by death' in the enforcing State (para. 28), or whether the person will be prosecuted for offences of a political character (para. 29).

[150] Art. 108 (3) ICCS.

[151] Arts. 107 (3), 108 (1) ICCS.

[152] In further detail, Kreß and Sluiter, in Cassese et al., *Rome Statute II* (2002), pp. 1771 ff.; Kreß and Gut, in Grützner et al., *Rechtshilfeverkehr* (2019), IV A 2 mn. 68 ff.; Nemitz, in Haveman and Olusanya, *Sentencing and Sanctioning* (2006), pp. 125 ff.; Holá and van Wijk, *JICJ*, 12 (2014), 115–16; Stiel and Stuckenberg, 'Article 108', in Klamberg et al., *Commentary ICC II* (2023), pp. 925–37.

[153] Arts. 27 ICTYS, 26 ICTRS, 25 IRMCTS, 22 (1) SCSLS, 23 (1) RSCSLS, and 50 (1) SC Law.

[154] At the time of writing (September 2024), such agreements existed between the *ICTY* and Albania, Belgium, Austria, Poland, the United Kingdom, Norway, Slovakia, Denmark, Finland, Estonia, Spain, Italy, Portugal, France, Ukraine, and Sweden; in addition to five ad hoc agreements with Germany regarding *Đorđević, Tarčulovski, Galić, Kunarac*, and *Tadić* (all available at <http://www.icty.org/sid/137#sentences>). The *ICTR* concluded such agreements with Senegal, Rwanda, Sweden, Italy, France, Mali, Benin, and Swaziland, and an Agreement Concerning the Headquarters of the ICTR with Tanzania (all available at <http://unictr.unmict.org/en/documents/bilateral-agreements>). See generally Klip, *EJCCLCJ*, 5 (1997), 146 ff. (detailed analysis of implementing legislation); Kreß and Sluiter, in Cassese et al., *Rome Statute II* (2002), pp. 1773 ff.; Harmsen and Strijards, 'Article 103', in Ambos, *Commentary* (2022), mn. 19; Nemitz, in Haveman and Olusanya, *Sentencing and Sanctioning* (2006), pp. 126–7; on the ICTY model agreement, see Yb ICTY (1996), 227; Tolbert, *LJIL*, 11 (2008), 664. At the KSC such agreements do not—at the time of writing (September 2024)—yet exist.

[155] For details, see the respective Practice Directions on the Procedure for the Designation of the Enforcing State: ICTY, 'Practice Direction on the Procedure for the International Tribunal's Designation of the State in which a Convicted Person is to Serve His/Her Sentence of Imprisonment', IT/137/Rev., 1 September 2009, <http://www.icty.org/x/file/Legal%20Library/Practice_Directions/it_137_rev1_en.pdf>; ICTR, 'Practice

been originally excluded as enforcing States,[156] as to the ICTR Rwanda is explicitly mentioned as a potential enforcing State.[157] At the SCSL explicit priority is given to Sierra Leone, and only '[i]f circumstances so require' may a sentence be served in another State, that is, one on the ICTY/ICTR lists or indeed a State with which a specific enforcement agreement has been concluded.[158] Regarding the KSC Kosovo has been excluded as an enforcing State by way of Article 162 (8) of the (amended) Constitution.[159] While the Netherlands serve as a fallback host State in the case of the ICC,[160] this is excluded for other tribunals sitting in the Hague.[161] At the time of writing (September 2024) there are no enforcement agreements with third States.

The *designation* is decided by the President of the respective tribunal,[162] who has a broad discretion in that regard.[163] Originally, the *Erdemović* Sentencing Judgment indicated some criteria,[164] which have then been taken up and complemented by the respective ICTY Practice Direction pointing, inter alia, to the equitable distribution of convicted persons;[165] the views of the person concerned can be disregarded.[166] In practice, however, the criteria

Direction on the Procedure for Designation of the State in which a Convicted Person is to Serve His/Her Sentence of Imprisonment', 23 September 2008, <https://unictr.irmct.org/sites/unictr.org/files/legal-library/pd-designation_state%20%281%29.pdf>; SCSL, 'Practice Direction for Designation of State for Enforcement of Sentence', 10 July 2009, <http://www.rscsl.org/Documents/PRACTICE_DIRECTION_Designation_State_Enforcement Sentence.pdf>; MICT, 'Practice Direction on the Procedure for Designation of the State in Which a Convicted Person is to Serve his or her Sentence of Imprisonment', MICT 2/Rev.1, 24 April 2014, <http://www.unmict.org/sites/default/files/documents/pd_mict2_rev1_en.pdf>; KSC, 'Practice Direction on the Designation of State of Enforcement', KSC-BD-45, 19 May 2022, <https://www.scp-ks.org/sites/default/files/public/content/documents/20220519_ksc-bd-45_pddesignationofstateofenforcement-public.pdf>.

[156] Report of the Secretary General pursuant to paragraph 2 of SC Resolution 808 (1993), UN Doc. S/25704, 3 May 1993, para. 121. This was, of course, inconsistent with the Rule 11*bis* transfer practice and the domestic prosecution of international crimes in these countries since all this entails local (localized) enforcement; see also below note 171 and main text.

[157] Art. 26 ICTRS. Against such a reading regarding this Article, Rochner, *Strafvollstreckung* (2014), p. 253, arguing that this provision only implies that Rwanda is not excluded as an enforcing State.

[158] Arts. 22 (1) SCSLS and 23 (1) RSCSLS. There are Special Enforcement Agreements with Finland, Rwanda, Sweden, and the UK (all available at the <https://rscsl.org/the-scsl/documents/>).

[159] According to Art. 162 (8) of the Constitution introduced by the 2015 amendment, a sentence is to be served 'in a third country, outside the territory of Kosovo'. See also the treaty-like 2014 Exchange of Letters between the EU and Kosovo (ratified by Kosovo Law No. 04/L-274), letter of President of Kosovo to EU High Representative C. Ashton, 14 April 2014, p. 3 ('service abroad of sentences of imprisonment if the trial results in convictions'), <https://www.scp-ks.org/sites/default/files/public/04-l-274_a.pdf>.

[160] See above note 53.

[161] See e.g. Agreement between the Kingdom of the Netherlands and the Republic of Kosovo concerning the Hosting of the Kosovo Relocated Specialist Judicial Institution in the Netherlands, Art. 44 (2): 'A sentence of imprisonment shall not be served in the Host State.', <https://www.scp-ks.org/sites/default/files/public/bwbv0006581-geldend_van_15-02-2016_tm_heden_zichtdatum_30-11-2016.pdf>.

[162] cf. Rules 103 (A) RPE ICTY/ICTR, 127 (A) RPE MICT; 103 (B) RPE SCSL and Art. 50 (1) KSC Law and Rule 166 (1) RPE KSC; see previously Tolbert, *LJIL*, 11 (2008), 668.

[163] Holá and van Wijk, *JICJ*, 12 (2014), 116.

[164] ICTY, *Prosecutor v. Erdemović*, TC, Sentencing Judgment, IT-96-22-T, 29 November 1996, para. 70 (due process, proper administration of justice, equal treatment for convicts, possible measures for reduction of disparities resulting from the execution of sentences); thereto Klip, *EJCCLCJ*, 5 (1997), 156–7.

[165] ICTY Practice Direction, para. 3 (b) (see above note 155 in this chapter); further criteria may be 'the national law of the relevant State in relation to pardon and commutation of sentence, the maximum sentence enforceable by the State, and any other relevant consideration related to the ability of States to enforce a particular sentence' (para. 3 (a)), and 'the proximity to the convicted person's relations.' (para. 5); see also ICTY, *Manual* (2009), <http://www.icty.org/x/file/About/Reports%20and%20Publications/manual_developed_practices/icty_manual_on_developed_practices.pdf>, p. 152 (indicating the geographical distance between the enforcing State and the Former Yugoslavia as a further factor to be taken into account).

[166] ICTY, *Prosecutor v. Kvočka et al.*, President's Decision on Request of Zoran Žigić, IT-98-30/1-ES, 31 May 2006, para. 2 ('not ... necessary to do so in the exercise of my discretion, ... there is no right conferred on a convicted person to be heard on this issue'); crit. Hoffmann, *ZIS*, 6 (2011), 841; Mulgrew, *International Penal System* (2013), p. 41.

have not been consistently applied and practical/political considerations prevail.[167] ICTY convicts are distributed around fifteen European countries ('dispersion model'), while ICTR and SCSL convicts are concentrated in three African countries ('concentrated model');[168] at the KSC the first sentence to be enforced was one for administration of justice offences,[169] the second one for war crimes.[170] Interestingly, despite the normative preference in the Statutes mentioned above, none of the ICTR or SCSL convicts serve their sentences in either Rwanda or Sierra Leone as territorial States of their crimes ('localised enforcement').[171]

### *(b) The actual enforcement*

The enforcement takes place in line with the law of the enforcing State, but is subject to the *supervision* by the tribunals.[172] This supervision refers generally to the conditions of imprisonment in the enforcing State. While the enforcing State is entrusted with the management of the day-to-day imprisonment,[173] the prison conditions must correspond to the international minimum standards already mentioned[174] and the international prisoner must have the possibility to turn to the tribunal to that effect.[175] Of course, in practice, prison conditions

[167] cf. Hoffmann, *ZIS*, 6 (2011), 841 ('something like a lottery'); Holá and van Wijk, *JICJ*, 12 (2014), 116–17, 131.

[168] Holá and van Wijk, *JICJ*, 12 (2014), 116–18 with Table 2; see also Mulgrew, *International Penal System* (2013), p. 84 ('dispersal' and 'consolidation' model). At the time of writing (September 2024), ICTY sentences of imprisonment are being enforced in Austria, Belgium, Estonia, Finland, France, Germany, Norway, Poland, Sweden and the UK (<https://www.irmct.org/sites/default/files/2024-09/2024-09-IRMCT-Enforcement%20of%20sentences%20ENGLISH.pdf>); ICTR sentences in Benin and Senegal (< https://www.irmct.org/sites/default/files/2024-09/2024-09-IRMCT-Enforcement%20of%20sentences%20ENGLISH.pdf>); SCSL sentences are only enforced in Rwanda with the exception of Charles Taylor's serving his sentence in the UK, cf. Holá and van Wijk, *JICJ*, 12 (2014), 114 with n. 22. For the respective enforcement agreements, see above notes 154 and 159.

[169] KSC, *Prosecutor v. Gucati and Haradinaj*, AC, Judgment, KSC-CA-2022-01/F00114, 2 February 2023. This is a final enforceable judgment notwithstanding the extraordinary remedy of a protection of legality request to the Supreme Court Panel pursuant to Art. 48 (6) to (8) KSC Law and Rule 193 RPE KSC. While the sentence of Hysni Gucati has been commuted by the KSC President pursuant to Art. 51 (2) KSC Law and Rules 195-197 RPE KSC and he has been released (cf. Decision on Commutation, Modification or Alteration of Sentence with Confidential and Ex Parte Annexes, KSC-SC-2023-01/CS001, 12 October 2023), the respective decision regarding Nasim Haradinaj was first in the negative (cf. Public Redacted Version of the Decision on Commutation, Modification or Alteration of Sentence, KSC-SC-2023-01/CS002, 12 October 2023) but he was then released on 12 December 2023 (Decision on Modification of Sentence, KSC-SC-2023-01/CS002/F00005, 12 December 2023).

[170] KSC, *Prosecutor v. Mustafa*, AC, Judgment, KSC-CA-2023-02/F00038/RED, 14 December 2023.

[171] cf. Mulgrew, *International Penal System* (2013), pp. 156 ff., discussing also the Rule 11*bis* transfers to the territory of the Former Yugoslavia and Rwanda (160 ff.); Holá and van Wijk, *JICJ*, 12 (2014), 114, indicating that Rwanda's prison facility Mpanga only hosts SCSL convicts and persons transferred to Rwanda for domestic prosecution; welcoming this regarding Rwanda, Rochner, *Strafvollstreckung* (2014), p. 270.

[172] Arts. 27 ICTYS, 26 ICTRS, 25 IRMCTS, 22 (2) SCSLS, 23 (2) RSCSLS, and 50 (2) SC Law; cf. also Rules 104 RPE ICTY/ICTR/SCSL, 128 RPE MICT and for more details the respective Practice Directions, above note 155 in this chapter; see also Abels, *Prisoners* (2012), pp. 450–1; Holá, Kelder, and van Wijk, in Hayashi and Bailliert, *Legitimacy* (2017), p. 358.

[173] In this sense, the supervision operates as a cooperative relationship between the enforcing State and the tribunal; cf. Tolbert, *LJIL*, 11 (2008), 661; see also Mulgrew, *International Penal System* (2013), p. 83.

[174] See above note 48 in this chapter. See also *Erdemović*, IT-96-22-T, paras. 68 ff., esp. 74 ff., calling for the respect of these minimum standards; in a similar vein, respecting 'domestic laws as well as European and international standards governing prison conditions ... that protect prisoners both *before* and *after* conviction' (emphasis added), ICTY, *Prosecutor v. Stanković*, AC, Decision on Rule 11*bis* Referral, IT-96-23/2-AR11bis.1, 1 September 2005, para. 37; more recently see ICTR, *Prosecutor v. Uwinkindi*, AC, Decision on Uwinkindi's Appeal against the Referral of his to Rwanda and Related Motions, ICTR-01-75-AR11*bis*, 16 December 2011, para. 22; for earlier case law, see previous edition n. 165. These standards are also referred to in the enforcement agreements, cf. Rochner, *Strafvollstreckung* (2014), pp. 257–8, 268. However, according to the ICTR and SCSL Designation Practice Directions (above note 155), paras. 3 (vi) and 4 (viii) respectively, in the process of designation the prison conditions shall only be taken into account 'if possible'. On the potential of strengthening the domestic rule of law by ensuring the implementation of these minimum standards, see Brodersen, *GoJIL*, 9 (2018), 231.

[175] cf. Klip, *EJCCLCJ*, 5 (1997), 159–60, recognizing this right of the convicted person along with, alternatively, the use of 'local remedies or even international supervisory mechanisms'; see also Tolbert, *LJIL*, 11 (1998), 659–61, who in the discussion of the supervision responsibilities of the tribunal argues that the tribunal can intervene only 'when some fundamental aspect of the sentence is affected'; Mulgrew, *International Penal System* (2013), pp. 83–4.

do not only differ substantially across the major regions of the world, but also within those regions, for example, among the European countries.[176] The non-compliance with the said minimum standards may make the setting up of a wholly different prison system for international prisoners necessary[177] which, in turn, would encompass privileged treatment of these prisoners with regard to ordinary national prisoners ('double standards').[178]

The supervision entails the tribunals' ultimate authority with regard to the length of the sentence, that is, the enforcing State is bound by it;[179] a pardon or commutation[180] of the sentence depends ultimately on the tribunals' consent.[181] However, the prisoner is 'eligible' for such a measure 'pursuant to the applicable law' of the enforcing State[182] and conditions included in bilateral enforcement agreements and State practice have tended to undermine the tribunals' authority with regard to the ultimate determination of the length of the sentence.[183] The respective early release procedure can be initiated by the enforcing State or the prisoner.[184] The tribunals have to be notified by that State, and the President, in consultation

[176] cf. Holá and van Wijk, *JICJ*, 12 (2014), 118–22 (apart from the general conditions focusing on visits, leave, and rehabilitation), 131 ('inequalities in the treatment', 'largely differing prison conditions'); in the same vein, Kelder, Holá, and van Wijk, *ICLR*, 14 (2014), 1181; on prison conditions in Africa, see Mulgrew, *International Penal System* (2013), pp. 47 ff. See also Fernández-Pacheco Estrada, *ICLR*, 22 (2022), 566 (arguing that 'the disparity among enforcement states is the greatest challenge of the enforcement system as adopted by the international tribunals').

[177] See, with regard to the upgrading of the respective prisons in the ICTR enforcing States Benin and Mali and the SCSL enforcing State Rwanda (Mpanga prison), Mulgrew, *International Penal System* (2013), pp. 47 ff.; Rochner, *Strafvollstreckung* (2014), pp. 268, 316 ('enforcement *sui generis*').

[178] cf. Mulgrew, *International Penal System* (2013), p. 50 (hoping that this will be a catalyst for national prison reform); generally on these double standards between national and international prisoners but also between international prisoners in different countries, Mulgrew, ibid., pp. 85 ff., 182 ff.

[179] cf. explicitly Art. 22 (2) 2nd cl. SCSLS and 23 (2) 2nd cl. RSCSLS as well as Art. 50 (1) KSC Law ('duration of the sentence imposed') and Art. 50 (2) cl. 2 KSC Law ('Only the Specialist Chambers can alter the duration'). Accordingly, the ICTY model agreement does not provide for an *exequatur* procedure, see Tolbert, *LJIL*, 11 (2008), 665.

[180] Crit. on the equal treatment of pardon with the other forms of early release given the former's nature as an executive measure with a political connotation, Rochner, *Strafvollstreckung* (2014), pp. 242–3; similarly crit. referring to different State practice and the doubtful role of pardon in international criminal justice, Mulgrew, *International Penal System* (2013), pp. 61–2; previously Klip, *EJCCLCJ*, 5 (1997), 161 (doubting if there will be impassioned calls for pardons in this context).

[181] Arts. 28 ICTYS, 27 ICTRS, 26 IRMCTS, 23 SCSLS, 24 RSCSLS, and 51 (2) KSC Law. See also *Erdemović*, IT-96-22-T, paras. 71 ff. (74: 'President of the International Tribunal who ... is entitled to review pardons or commutations of penalties before such measures are granted or enforced'); crit. in this regard Klip, *EJCCLCJ*, 5 (1997), 157–8 (referring to the IMTFE), 163; see also Tolbert, *LJIL*, 11 (2008), 661, 665. In this sense, one may read 'supervision' as 'primacy', in line with Art. 9 ICTYS (Tolbert, *LJIL*, 11 (2008), 659) although this view is difficult to reconcile with the ICC regime where supervision exists (Art. 106 ICCS) without primacy.

[182] See, again, Arts. 28 ICTYS, 27 ICTRS, 26 IRMCTS, 23 SCSLS, 24 RSCSLS, and 51 (2) KSC Law. Crit. on the unclear relationship between the ICTY/ICTR's authority and the applicable national law/the national authorities' involvement, Klip, *EJCCLCJ*, 5 (1997), 158–9, 164 (in favour of unconditional application of national enforcement rules); Mulgrew, *International Penal System* (2013), p. 62; Rochner, *Strafvollstreckung* (2014), pp. 201 ff.; on conflicts with the enforcement regimes in France, Spain, Italy, Austria, and Germany, see Rochner, *Strafvollstreckung* (2014), pp. 222 ff.; on the problem with regard to life imprisonment, see above note 129 and main text.

[183] cf. Klip, *EJCCLCJ*, 5 (1997), 158, distinguishing between continued enforcement and conversion on the basis of the enforcement agreements; Mulgrew, *International Penal System* (2013), pp. 72 ff., 185.

[184] See MICT, 'Practice Direction on the Procedure for the Determination of Applications for Pardon, Commutation of Sentence, or Early Release of Persons Convicted by the ICTR, the ICTY or the Mechanism', (MICT/3/Rev.3), 15 May 2020, paras. 3–5, <https://www.irmct.org/sites/default/files/documents/200515-mict3-rev3_en.pdf>; ICTY, 'Practice Direction on the Procedure for the Determination of Applications for Pardon, Commutation of Sentence, and Early Release of Persons Convicted by the International Tribunal', IT/146/Rev.3, 16 September 2010, paras. 1, 2, <http://www.icty.org/x/file/Legal%20Library/Practice_Directions/IT146Rev3en.pdf>; see also ICTR, 'Practice Direction on the Procedure for the Determination of Applications for Pardon, Commutation of Sentence, and Early Release of Persons Convicted by the International Criminal Tribunal for Rwanda', 10 May 2000 (not available online, on file with the author); SCSL, Practice Direction on the Conditional Early Release of Persons Convicted by the Special Court for Sierra Leone, 1 October 2013, para. 3 (A), <http://www.rscsl.org/Documents/PRACTICE_DIRECTION_Conditional_Early_Release.pdf>. On the original recognition of the prisoner's right to apply in the ICTY case law and for more details, see Rochner, *Strafvollstreckung* (2014), pp. 206, 242; also Mulgrew, *International Penal System* (2013), p. 57.

with the judges and after giving the prisoner the opportunity to be heard,[185] shall decide the matter 'on the basis of the interests of justice and the general principles of law'.[186] This power of the President turns the early release decision—which, in addition, cannot be challenged[187]—into one of a merely administrative nature, unlike the ICC, where the AC has to decide this matter.[188] One should note, however, that the relevant factors for the early release decision, that is, the 'gravity of the crime', the 'treatment of similarly-situated prisoners', the 'prisoner's demonstration of rehabilitation', and his 'substantial cooperation' with the Prosecutor,[189] partly correspond to the sentencing factors[190] and are similar to those contained in Article 110 (4) ICCS. If the President's decision is not acceptable to the State concerned and/or it may infringe upon fundamental principles of its national law, the convict must be transferred back to the tribunal.[191]

In practice, the vast majority of convicts do not serve their full sentence but are released after having served two-thirds[192] of their respective imprisonment terms.[193] Thus, on average, the actual enforcement has been reduced by three years (ICTY) or two years (ICTR) as compared to the sentence imposed.[194] Of course, this does not exclude that some convicts receive life or long prison sentences.[195] While both at the ICTY and ICTR there

[185] See e.g. ICTY Determination Practice Direction (see previous note), para. 5.

[186] Arts. 28 ICTYS, 27 ICTRS, 26 IRMCTS, 23 SCSLS, 24 RSCSLS, and 51 (2) KSC Law. See also Rules 123–5 RPE ICTY, 124–6 RPE ICTR, 149–51 RPE MICT, and 123–4 RPE SCSL; for a detailed treatment, see Abels, *Prisoners* (2012), pp. 451 ff.; Mulgrew, *International Penal System* (2013), pp. 63 ff.; Rochner, *Strafvollstreckung* (2014), pp. 198 ff., 259 ff.

[187] Crit. Klip, *EJCCLCJ*, 5 (1997), 162 (referring to human rights mechanisms); Rochner, *Strafvollstreckung* (2014), pp. 209 ff. (with a view to the effective remedy guarantees of Art. 13 ECHR and Art. 19 (4) GG).

[188] Above note 105 and main text. Crit. also Hoffmann, *ZIS*, 6 (2011), 840.

[189] Rules 125 RPE ICTY, 126 RPE ICTR, 151 RPE MICT, and 196 RPE KSC. On the practical application of these factors, see Mulgrew, *International Penal System* (2013), pp. 63 ff.; Holá and van Wijk, *JICJ*, 12 (2014), 123–9; Holá, Kelder and van Wijk, in Hayashi and Bailliert, *Legitimacy* (2017), pp. 360, 367 ff. (calling for a clearer conceptualization of rehabilitation and better assessment as well as crit. of the lack of a crit. evaluation of sources that are thought to demonstrate prisoners' rehabilitation); in the same vein, Riegler, *ICLR*, 20 (2020), 707 ('precise definition … is lacking'), 726 ('there is considerable incoherence in the conceptualisation of rehabilitation, both within the ICTY as well as between the ICTY and the ICC'); crit. on rehabilitation in terms of its practical operationalization and success rate, see Mulgrew, *International Penal System* (2013), pp. 65 ff., 85, 96 ff.; Kelder, Holá, and van Wijk, *ICLR*, 14 (2014), 1185–92; crit. of rehabilitation as an early release factor in this context, also Hoffmann, *ZIS*, 6 (2011), 841; on the risk of possible double standards in the context of rehabilitation of war criminals, Holá and Munivrana, *JICJ*, 21 (2023), 89–112; on the importance of the gravity of the crime as an early release factor, Fernández-Pacheco, *LJIL*, 37 (2024) (stressing the distinction between ICTY / ICTR and ICC, the latter giving less weight to gravity).

[190] cf. Ambos, *Treatise ICL II* (2022), pp. 321 ff.; crit. regarding the risk of double-counting, van Zyl Smit, *ICLQ*, 54 (2005), 373.

[191] See e.g. § 8 (2) of the Ad Hoc-Agreement in the case of *Tarčulovski*, <http://www.icty.org/x/file/Legal%20Library/Member_States_Cooperation/enforcement_agreement_germany_tarculovski_en.pdf>; for the same clause in the *Galić* enforcement agreement between Germany and the ICTY, see Hoffmann, *ZIS*, 6 (2011), 841 with n. 28.

[192] This is explicitly provided for as a minimum in Rule 124 RPE SCSL; in favour, with regard to State practice previously Tolbert, *LJIL*, 11 (2008), 666.

[193] cf. Holá and van Wijk, *JICJ*, 12 (2014), 112–13 (demonstrating that, as of 16 July 2013, forty-six of a total fifty-five ICTY convicts already released have been granted early release), 124–5; also Kelder, Holá, and van Wijk, *ICLR*, 14 (2014), 1183; Mulgrew, *International Penal System* (2013), pp. 57 ff.; Rochner, *Strafvollstreckung* (2014), pp. 202, 221–2, 225, 229–31 (explaining deviations before the ICTY in three cases), 246, 259 ff. (discussing how the original 3/4 rule of the ICTR was superseded by the 2/3 rule with the entry into force of the UNMICT, at 262–3 and 317); Hoffmann, *ZIS*, 6 (2011), 840.

[194] cf. Holá and van Wijk, *JICJ*, 12 (2014), 127–8 with Table 4.

[195] See e.g. Milomir Stakić (life imprisonment at first instance, later reduced by the AC to forty years' imprisonment, ICTY, *Prosecutor v. Stakić*, AC, Judgment, Disposition, IT-97-24-A, 22 March 2006, p. 141); Stanislav Galić (sentenced by the ICTY AC to life imprisonment; early release denied by the MICT President, MICT-14-83-ES, 23 June 2015); Charles Taylor (fifty-year prison sentence by TC, SCSL-03-01-T, 30 May 2002, upheld by the AC); and Pauline Nyiramashuko et al. (AC reducing the convicts' long sentences—except for Mr Kanyabashi's—only marginally, Judgment, Disposition, ICTR-98-42-A, 14 December 2015, p. 1208); Radovan Karadžić (forty years' imprisonment at first instance, later extended by the AC to life imprisonment, AC, MICT-13-55-A, 20 March 2019).

is no institutional preparation of convicts for release,[196] and once released they are completely on their own since there is no institutional or any other oversight or follow-up,[197] the SCSL was the first international tribunal to design a conditional early release programme.[198] In order to qualify for such early release, prisoners must agree to the conditions set out in a 'Conditional Early Release Agreement', which stipulates, inter alia, that the released will be subjected to intensive monitoring.[199] As a consequence, a monitoring authority has to submit annual reports to the SCSL's Registrar regarding the ex-prisoners' compliance with the conditions established in the abovementioned Agreement.[200] Non-compliance is investigated by the SCSL Prosecutor and may lead to a special hearing before a judge and even to re-incarceration and deprivation of liberty. The monitoring terminates with the expiry date of the respective sentence.[201] The SCSL procedure is quite detailed and focuses on the prisoners' reintegration prospects as well as their post-release plans.[202]

The ICTYS, ICTRS, SCSLS and KSC Law do not—unlike the ICCS—provide for a specialty rule.

## C. Enforcement of fines and other financial measures, including reparation orders

While the ad hoc tribunals' legal framework does not contain any provisions dealing with the enforcement of fines and forfeitures,[203] the ICCS contains such a provision in Article 109. The lack of previous practice and the sparse regulation in the ICCS reflects the limited use of this form of an economic penalty in the history of international criminal law.[204] This, in turn, can partly be explained by the fact that any economic sanction in the form of a criminal penalty—such as fine and forfeiture according to Article 77 (2)(a) and (b) ICCS—requires a

[196] cf. Mulgrew, *International Penal System* (2013), pp. 100 ff.

[197] cf. Holá and van Wijk, *JICJ*, 12 (2014), 129–31; see also Kelder, Holá, and van Wijk, *ICLR*, 14 (2014), 1198; on release, deportation, and relocation, Mulgrew, *International Penal System* (2013), pp. 79 ff.

[198] Doherty and Fisher, in Mulgrew and Abels, *RH Penal System* (2016), pp. 370 ff.; Fernández-Pacheco Estrada, *ICLR*, 22 (2022), 544, 562–3.

[199] SCSL, Practice Direction on the Conditional Early Release of Persons (above note 184), Art. 2 (D). For a detailed analysis of monitoring at the SCSL vis-à-vis the ICTY and ICTR, see Holá, Kelder, and van Wijk, in Hayashi and Bailliert, *Legitimacy* (2017), pp. 370 ff.

[200] SCSL, Practice Direction on the Conditional Early Release of Persons (above note 184), Art. 11 (A). See also Fernández-Pacheco Estrada, *ICLR*, 22 (2022), 566 (suggesting to take the SCSL supervision model as an example to be followed by the ICC: 'as done in SCSL, it should be made possible to impose conditions upon those released early, and that they should be subject to some supervision').

[201] SCSL, Practice Direction on the Conditional Early Release of Persons (above note 184), Art. 13. In addition to the annual reports, the monitoring authority may also impose certain conditions, for example, not to contact certain persons, see ibid., Annex C., No. 5 (p). See also Doherty and Fisher, in Mulgrew and Abels, *RH Penal System* (2016), p. 373; Holá, Kelder, and van Wijk, in Hayashi and Bailliert, *Legitimacy* (2017), pp. 370 ff.

[202] For instance, the former prisoners have to provide information regarding their address of residence and their financial situation, cf. SCSL, Practice Direction on the Conditional Early Release of Persons (above note 184), Art. 5 (B). The SCSL President shall not grant an early release if this information is not provided, or if the community in the proposed area of residence is unwilling to accept the prisoner, cf. ibid., Art. 8 (C)(ii)(b). Crit. as to the effective implementation of this monitoring system, see Holá, Kelder, and van Wijk, in Hayashi and Bailliert, *Legitimacy* (2017), p. 373.

[203] But see Rules 88 (B), 104 RPE SCSL and Art. 44 (6) KSC Law respectively, providing for forfeiture of property. At the ICTY/ICTR the payment of a fine is only provided for with regard to contempt of court or false testimony (e.g. Rule 77*bis* RPE ICTY with Rules 77 and 91 RPE ICTY/ICTR/SCSL and Rule 91 RPE MICT with Rules 90 and 108 RPE MICT); in addition, property resulting from the crime may be restituted (Rules 105 RPE ICTY/ICTR with 98*ter* (B) RPE ICTY and 88 (B) RPE ICTR; Rule 129 RPE MICT with Rule 122 (B) RPE MICT).

[204] With regard to forfeiture, cf. Galvis Martínez, *JICJ*, 12 (2014), 193 ff. pointing to the rare practice in the *Nuremberg Krupp* case and lamenting the 'constant failure by international courts to impose forfeitures' (194).

causal link to the crime committed, and thus to the person convicted.[205] Thus, forfeiture as a criminal penalty has always an *in personam* and not an *in rem* character.[206]

Another factor to consider is that the imposition of economic sanctions adds a reparative and reconciliatory element to sentencing which makes more sense if there is a natural person, that is, a victim as a potential recipient of the ensuing compensation, on the receiving end. Thus, economic sanctions are much more promising in a victim-centred Court like the ICC (or the KSC)[207] than in the previous ad hoc tribunals where the victims have not been considered as recipients of reparations[208] and were only present in the courtroom as witnesses or in the public gallery as passive observers.[209]

Unlike the situation with prison sentences, State Parties are obliged to enforce fines and forfeitures, without prejudice to the rights of *bona fide* third parties and in accordance with their procedures under national law.[210] Also, the ICC Presidency is authorized to ('shall') request cooperation ('seek cooperation and measures for enforcement') from relevant States.[211] It shall contact these States—the State of nationality, domicile, or residence of the sentenced person, or where their assets and property appear to be located, or the victim's State—and inform them of possible third-party claims.[212] Apart from such third-party rights, a State Party cannot claim any reason to refuse the enforcement of the fine and/or forfeiture order. Similarly, the State must not modify the fine imposed.[213]

Where a State Party is unable to enforce a *forfeiture order*, it shall, pursuant to Article 109 (2) ICCS, take measures to recover the respective value of the proceeds, property, or assets ordered by the Court to be forfeited.[214] However, this important possibility of a value-based

[205] Correctly in this regard, Galvis Martínez, *JICJ*, 12 (2014), 206–7.

[206] For the distinction, see Martínez, ibid, 215, who however does not draw the right conclusion from this distinction with regard to the relevant ICC provisions. Contrary to his view, these provisions cannot have a completely *in rem* character since they constitute criminal penalties. Only measures which focus on the crime proceeds or objects as such, notwithstanding their causal link to the criminal act and agent, can have a purely *in rem* character. See e.g. the distinction between '*Verfall*' (confiscation, § 73 StGB) and '*Einziehung*' (deprivation, § 74 StGB) in German law, the former focusing on the proceeds of crime and thereby being an autonomous tort-like sanction with an *in rem* character, the latter focusing on the objects used in or produced by crime being a criminal-like sanction with both an *in rem* and *in personam* character (cf. Eser and Schuster, in Schönke and Schröder, *StGB* (2019), pp. 1248–50; Hochmayr, *ZStW*, 124 (2012), 64 ff. [on German and Austrian law]); see also the distinction between *civil* (*in rem*) and *criminal* (*in personam*) forfeiture in the US American Law, where for the former 'the property is treated as the offender' and 'the guilt or innocence of the property owner is irrelevant', while for the latter 'confiscation is possible only upon the conviction of the owner of the property' (cf. Doyle, *Crime and Forfeiture* (2015), pp. 5–6; see also Garner, *Dictionary* (2019), p. 792; Garretson, *SCaliforniaRL&SocJ*, 18 (2008–2009), 45 ff.; Saltzburg and Capra, *American Criminal Procedure* (2010), pp. 1426–30); for England and Wales, and the distinction between confiscation of the proceeds of the crime, forfeiture of the objects and instrumentalities of the crime, and the civil recovery (confiscation without conviction), see Alldridge, *Money Laundering Law* (2003), pp. 46 ff., 110 ff. (forfeiture), 123 ff. (confiscation), 223 ff., 229 (civil recovery).

[207] At the KSC victims have a similar *partie civile* status as at the ICC, see Chapter II E. (4)(a) of this volume; as to payment of compensation or forfeiture to the benefit of victims, see Art. 44 (6) KSC Law.

[208] Unless these victims could claim to be 'rightful owners' of 'any property and proceeds acquired by criminal conduct', in which case the tribunals could order the return of such property, see Arts. 24 (3) ICTYS, 23 (3) ICTRS, and 19 (3) SCSLS.

[209] In the same vein, Gallant, *ICLR*, 19 (2019), 300, yet pointing to the limitations of the ICC reparations regime at 306–7.

[210] Art. 109 (1) ICCS. In more detail, Kreß, in Grützner et al., *Rechtshilfeverkehr* (2022), IV A 1 mn. 355 ff.; Kreß and Sluiter, in Cassese et al., *Rome Statute II* (2002), pp. 1823 ff.; Beltrán Montoliu, in Gómez Colomer et al., *Corte Penal Internacional* (2003), pp. 381–2; Schabas, *ICC Commentary* (2016), pp. 1408 ff.; Fall, 'Article 109', in Fernandez and Pacreau, *Commentaire CPI II* (2019), pp. 2405–10; Schabas, 'Article 109', in Ambos, *Commentary* (2022), mn. 1 ff.; Stiel and Stuckenberg, 'Article 109', in Klamberg et al., *Commentary ICC II* (2023), pp. 939–46.

[211] cf. Rule 217 cl. 1 RPE ICC.

[212] cf. Rule 217 cl.2 RPE ICC. On the contents of an order of forfeiture, see Rule 218 (1), (2) RPE ICC.

[213] Rule 220 RPE ICC.

[214] Art. 109 (2) ICCS; cf. also Stiel and Stuckenberg, 'Article 109', in Klamberg et al., *Commentary ICC II* (2023), p. 947.

forfeiture is not provided for by Articles 77 (2)(b) and 93 (1)(k) ICCS, being the primary provisions of the execution provision of Article 109 (2) ICCS. This seems to imply, on the one hand, that such a value-based forfeiture is, as per Article 93 (1)(k) ICCS, not possible during the investigation or prosecution phase of the proceedings.[215] On the other hand, the forfeiture of instrumentalities is possible during these phases,[216] but it is not covered by the sentencing and enforcement provisions of Articles 77 (2)(b) and 109 (2) ICCS.[217]

Property and the proceeds from its sale must be transferred to the Court.[218] The decision regarding the allocation of property or assets realized through an enforcement order is taken by the Presidency.[219] In practical terms, it must be taken into account that there may be assets which are not realizable by way of forfeiture (for example if they are blocked by a UN Security Council Resolution) or the costs created by the forfeiture of these assets exceed their net value.[220]

State Parties are also obliged to enforce *reparation orders*.[221] As in the case of fines and forfeiture orders, the Presidency contacts the affected State.[222] Reparation orders are equally binding, especially with regard to the scope and extent of the damage, loss, or injury determined by the Court and the principles stated in the order.[223] However, such orders, albeit binding, 'do not interfere with the responsibility of States to award reparations to victims under other treaties or national law'.[224] In deciding on the allocation, as mentioned above, the Presidency shall give priority to the reparations of victims.[225]

The Presidency shall also monitor the financial situation of the sentenced person, even post-imprisonment, in order to enforce fines, forfeiture, and reparation orders.[226] In case of 'continued wilful non-payment', the Presidency may, as a 'last resort', extend the term of imprisonment for a quarter of the term, or five years, 'whichever is less'.[227] The Presidency shall take this decision *in camera*, taking into account the views of the sentenced person, the Prosecutor, and the States in which enforcement was attempted and where the imprisonment

[215] Crit. Galvis Martínez, *JICJ*, 12 (2014), 208–9.

[216] Art. 93 (1)(k) ICCS.

[217] Crit. Galvis Martínez, *JICJ*, 12 (2014), 210–11.

[218] Art. 109 (3) ICCS.

[219] Rule 221 (1) RPE ICC; see also RegC 116 calling on the Presidency to make, with the assistance of the Registry, the necessary arrangements with regard to the fines (Art. 77 (2)(a) ICCS) and the property/proceeds (Art. 109 (3)) received, interest gained, and the transfer of money to the Trust Fund for Victims.

[220] cf. Galvis Martínez, *JICJ*, 12 (2014), 211–12.

[221] Art. 75 (5) ICCS; in more detail, see Chapter II, E.(6) in this volume. See also ICC, *Prosecutor v. Lubanga*, TC I, Decision Establishing the Principles and Procedures to be Applied to Reparations, ICC-01/04-01/06-2904, 7 August 2012, para. 256; ICC, *Prosecutor v. Lubanga*, AC, Amended Order for Reparations, ICC-01/04-01/06-3129-AnxA, 3 March 2015, para. 50; ICC, *Prosecutor v. Katanga*, TC II, Order for Reparations pursuant to Article 75 of the Statute, ICC-01/04-01/07-3728-tENG, 24 March 2017, paras. 323–4; ICC, *Prosecutor v. Ntaganda*, TC VI, Reparations Order, ICC-01/04-02/06-2659, 8 March 2021, para. 102; ICC, *Prosecutor v. Ongwen*, TC IX, Reparations Order, ICC-02/04-01/15-2074, 28 February 2024, para. 816. On the assessment of a reparations claim and on reparation orders, see also Ambach, in Ambach et al., *Protection of Non-Combatants* (2015), pp. 490–2, Cattin, 'Article 75', in Ambos, *Commentary* (2022), p. 2259; Langmack, *Reparation* (2023), pp. 143–93.

[222] Rule 217 RPE ICC.

[223] Rule 219 RPE ICC. On the contents of such an order, see Rule 218 (3), (4) RPE ICC. On the Court's discretion with regard to reparation orders, see Chapter II, E.(6) in this volume.

[224] cf. *Lubanga*, ICC-01/04-01/06-2904, para. 257; *Lubanga*, ICC-01/04-01/06-3129-AnxA, para. 50. See also Ambach, in Ambach et al., *Protection of Non-Combatants* (2015), p. 469. On the content of States' obligation to repair victims of international crimes, see Langmack, *Reparation* (2023), pp. 243–356. See also Pues, *EJIL: Talk!* 22 March 2024.

[225] Rule 221 (2) RPE ICC; cf. also Ambach, in Ambach et al., *Protection of Non-Combatants* (2015), pp. 476–7, and 500 ff., arguing in favour of further determining reparations 'on a collective basis' rather than in 'an individualized fashion' (519).

[226] cf. Reg. 117 RegC. cf. also Ambach, in Ambach et al., *Protection of Non-Combatants* (2015), p. 490, arguing on the basis of the different nature of fines (form of penalty) and reparations (benefit of victims) that when ordering reparations 'the Court is not obliged to take into account the convicted person's financial capacity'.

[227] Rule 146 (5) RPE ICC.

is served.[228] If, upon extension of imprisonment, the person concerned pays the respective fine in full or in part, the Presidency shall revoke or reduce the extension ordered.[229]

## D. National implementation: Some examples

Given the crucial role States play in the enforcement of ICC sanctions and orders, there is a strong need for the national implementation of the respective rules and provisions. A comparison of some jurisdictions shows that those States that issue implementing legislation are usually Court-friendly and thus try to make implementation as smooth as possible.

In *Germany*, the enforcement of custodial sentences, fines, forfeitures, and reparation orders is dealt with in §§ 40–6 IStGHG.[230] Given the ICC's recognition as an interstate organization in the sense of Article 24 of the German Constitution (*Grundgesetz*),[231] the ICC sanctions are directly applicable in the German domestic legal order, without the need of an *exequatur* procedure[232] otherwise required for the execution of foreign sanctions.[233] The responsible German authority is the public prosecutor of the Higher Regional Court ('*Oberlandesgericht*').[234] The necessary court orders/injunctions are to be made by the Higher Regional Court.[235]

In the *UK*, Part 4 of the 2001 ICC Act[236] deals with the enforcement of sentences and orders. The Secretary of State is responsible for making way for the enforcement of sentences and fines or forfeiture orders within England, Wales, or Northern Ireland.[237] According to Section 42 (2), the detention of an ICC prisoner in Scotland is only possible if the Scottish Ministers agree and issue a warrant authorizing the detention.

In the *Netherlands*, the enforcement of sentences of imprisonment is dealt with in § 3 of the 2002 ICC (Implementation) Act,[238] which, unlike the cooperation legislation with the ad hoc tribunals, also foregoes an *exequatur* procedure.[239] According to Section 66, the Act is applicable to requests of the ICC in accordance with Article 103 (1)(a) and (4) of the ICC Statute. In both cases, the Minister of Justice is the competent authority to enforce custodial sentences, based on the recommendation of the public prosecutor at The Hague District

[228] Reg. 118 (1) RegC.

[229] Ibid.

[230] Generally on the German enforcement assistance, see Wilkitzki, in Triffterer, *Gedächtnisschrift Vogler* (2004), pp. 263 ff.

[231] cf. Keller, in Ambos et al., *Rechtshilferecht* (2020), pp. 1486, 1509–10. See also Chapter VII, B. (2)(a)(i) in this volume.

[232] For an explanation, see above note 21.

[233] cf. MacLean, *ZRP*, 35 (2002), 260, 263; Meißner, *NJ*, 56 (2002), 347, 349; Nemitz et al., in Schomburg et al., *Internationale Rechtshilfe* (2012), p. 2545; Rochner, *Strafvollstreckung* (2014), p. 286; Keller, in Ambos et al., *Rechtshilferecht* (2020), pp. 1509–10. See also § 41 (2) IStGHG, which explicitly provides for the direct and unreserved enforcement of ICC sentences.

[234] § 46 (1), (2) IStGHG.

[235] § 46 (3) IStGHG.

[236] ICC Act 2001, <http://www.legislation.gov.uk/ukpga/2001/17/contents>.

[237] Sections 42 (3) and 49 (1) ICC Act 2001 respectively.

[238] UK Act of 20 June 2002 to Implement the Statute of the International Criminal Court in Relation to Cooperation with and the Provision of Assistance to the International Criminal Court and the Enforcement of its Decisions (International Criminal Court Implementation Act), <https://www.legal-tools.org/doc/015c1d/pdf/>.

[239] cf. Sluiter, *JICJ*, 2 (2004), 168–9, arguing that the main argument in favour of direct enforcement of sentences in the Netherlands is their residual duty as host State under Art. 103 (4) ICCS, pursuant to which 'the Netherlands may be obliged, as the host-state, to enforce sentences of imprisonment *unconditionally*' (emphasis in the original); Abels, *Prisoners* (2012), pp. 460–1. However, the *exequatur* procedure shall apply in the enforcement of other kind of sanctions, cf. Sluiter, *JICJ*, 2 (2004), 168–9 and Abels, *Prisoners* (2012), p. 460.

Court.[240] The enforcement of fines, forfeitures, and reparation orders is dealt with in § 4 of the Act, and depends on The Hague District Court's granting leave for enforcement,[241] upon application by the public prosecutor.[242]

Thus far, *Canada* does not have a law that specifically deals with the enforcement of ICC sentences, but it is regulated indirectly in Part 3 of the 1999 Extradition Act and in the 2004 International Transfer of Offenders Act.[243] Fines, forfeitures, and reparation orders are dealt with in the 1985 Mutual Legal Assistance Act.[244] Specifically, Section 9.2 of the latter Act proscribes that such requests are to be directed to the Minister of Justice, who 'may' then authorize the Attorney General of Canada to enforce the order by filing it with the superior court of criminal jurisdiction of the relevant province defined in sub-section (2), upon which the order is to be entered as a judgment of that court.

In *Australia*, Part 12 of the 2002 ICC Act[245] deals with the enforcement of ICC imprisonment sentences. Section 160 allows Australia to act as an enforcing State and Section 161 allows it to withdraw its agreement to act as such. Before accepting a request by the ICC, the Attorney-General of Australia must decide in which State the prisoner is to serve the sentence and seek permission from the Minister of that State.[246] The specific requirements for acceptance are listed in Section 164. The enforcement of fines and reparation orders by the ICC is dealt with in Part 10 of the ICC Act and forfeiture orders in Part 11 of that Act. The former must be executed by the Attorney-General if the ICC decision is final, by authorizing the DPP to register the order with the Federal or Supreme Court of a State (in Australia).[247] Forfeiture orders, on the other hand, may only be executed by the Attorney-General if he is satisfied that the ICC had the competence to make the order.[248] In this case, he is to authorize the proceeds of crime authority to apply for registration of the order in a court specified by the Attorney-General, which must be one with 'proceeds jurisdiction in a State or Territory in which the property... is reasonably suspected of being located'.[249]

In *Sweden*, the enforcement of penalty and forfeiture is dealt with in Sections 23–8 of the 2002 ICC Act.[250] Admission and enforcement of rulings for reparations to victims of crime are dealt with in Sections 29–31. According to Section 1, the Act is applicable to ICC requests. The Minister of Justice is the competent authority to receive such requests, followed by a decision of the government,[251] and based on the recommendation of the Prosecutor-General, and, in special situations, on the views of the Supreme Court.[252] In situations concerning early conditional release, Section 25 (3) of the Act allows the government to decide that such release takes place at a later date than prescribed by the domestic Penal Code.

In *Liechtenstein*, the 2004 ICC Cooperation Act deals with the enforcement of ICC imprisonment sentences in Part E. and with the acceptance of enforcement of fines, forfeiture

240 Sections 67 (4) and 68 (2) ICC (Implementation) Act respectively.

241 Section 79 ICC (Implementation) Act.

242 Section 73 ICC (Implementation) Act.

243 Extradition Act (S.C. 1999, c. 18) <http://laws-lois.justice.gc.ca/eng/acts/E-23.01/>; International Transfer of Offenders Act (S.C. 2004, c. 21) <http://laws-lois.justice.gc.ca/eng/acts/I-20.6/FullText.html>.

244 Mutual Legal Assistance in Criminal Matters Act (R.S.C., 1985, c. 30 (4th Supp.)), <http://laws-lois.justice.gc.ca/eng/acts/M-13.6/>.

245 ICC Act 2002, <http://www.comlaw.gov.au/Details/C2004A00992>.

246 Section 163 ICC Act 2002.

247 Sections 151 and 152 ICC Act 2002.

248 Section 155 (1)(b)(i) ICC Act 2002.

249 Section 155 (2) and (3) ICC Act 2002.

250 Cooperation with the International Criminal Court Act No. 2002.329 of 8 May 2002, <https://cjad.nottingham.ac.uk/en/legislation/70/>.

251 Sections 2 (1), 3 (1), and 23 ICC Act 2002.

252 Section 4 (2) ICC Act 2002.

measures, and orders for reparations or the return of property in Part F.[253] Enforcement requests are to be directed to the Ministry of Justice, which is also the competent authority to decide upon them.[254] As a general principle, Article 2 (1) of the Act states that all domestic authorities, and in particular the courts and the public prosecutor, are obliged to cooperate fully with the ICC and the international tribunals.[255] However, the Act only allows for the enforcement of a sentence of imprisonment if the sentenced person is either a Liechtenstein national or usually resides there, thus rendering any possible enforcement of sentences highly unlikely.[256]

[253] Law of 20 October 2004 on Cooperation with the International Criminal Court and other International Tribunals, No. 268, <https://iccdb.hrlc.net/documents/implementations/pdf/Liechtenstein_Cooperation_with_the_ICC_2004.pdf>.
[254] Art. 35 (1) of the ICC Act 2004.
[255] Art. 2 (2) of the ICC Act 2004 specifies in more detail the scope of this obligation, also entailing the enforcement of sentences as well as fines and forfeitures.
[256] Art. 34 (1) of the ICC Act 2004.

# IX
# Concluding Remarks

## A. Fragmentation and procedural models

Fragmentation is perhaps the most striking feature in international criminal procedure. The latter is characterized by a series of procedural models and systems, ranging from predominantly 'adversarial' (e.g. IMT, IMTFE, ICTY, ICTR, SCSL, and, to a more limited extent, KSC) to 'inquisitorial' (e.g. ECCC) ones, with different approaches as to the solution of recurrent procedural problems and mixed performances, and culminating in the ICC as the first permanent international criminal court with a rather mixed and flexible procedural framework.[1] Fragmentation demonstrates that there are always several competing procedural models, although this does not mean that the search for *the one* perfectly fitting model, while difficult,[2] should be abandoned. At any rate, it is high time to leave the rather unproductive debate on the one right procedural model, guided by the overstated inquisitorial–adversarial antagonism, behind.

Instead, a procedural model should be conceived just as a proposed general framework, leaving enough room for its operators,[3] especially the judges, to adjust the procedural rules to their daily procedural realities. This confirms the 'issue-oriented approach' advocated some time ago,[4] that is, an approach which looks at the concrete and real issues to be solved in a given procedural situation rather than being guided by abstract procedural models often detached from the day-to-day procedural business of a criminal investigator/prosecutor and a trial court. The solutions for the relevant issues or the paths to come to these solutions are to be found independently of their inquisitorial or adversarial origin. Instead one should focus on concrete performance, that is, ask for the effective contribution that a suggested solution can make to advance the quality and expeditiousness of proceedings and ultimately the mandate and cause of the respective tribunal.[5] It seems that the ICC has gone in that direction by creating a permanently updated *Practice Manual* and by regularly updating its Regulations. Several protocols such as witness familiarization and disclosure protocols, and especially the

[1] cf. in this volume Chapter IV, A.(3)(a) (regarding trial structure), B.(7)(b) (regarding recharacterization of facts), B.(8)(b)(ii) (regarding admission of guilt procedure), and Chapter V, A.(1)(b) (regarding submission of evidence).

[2] See also Vasiliev, in Sluiter et al., *International Criminal Procedure* (2013), p. 631 ('fragmentation of international criminal procedure . . . so significant as to make the detection of the common standards that could amount to principles and general rules particularly difficult').

[3] On parties and participants, see in detail Chapter II in this volume.

[4] Ambos, in Bohlander, *International Criminal Justice* (2007), p. 501; conc., Klamberg, *Evidence* (2013), pp. 501–2; more recently Heinze, in Bergsmo et al., *Power* (2020), pp. 155, 194 ff.

[5] In a similar vein, Byrne, *LJIL*, 26 (2013), 1006–7 ('Performance criteria should depart from the preferences of common-and civil-law approaches, and their respective takes on what constitutes good or bad judging and courtroom control. Instead, a template for a proactive trial process would require agency and adaptability as key characteristics of the presiding judge within these new sui generis proceedings.'). On the issue of 'performance indicators' to measure the ICC's efficiency in terms of the organs' activities, see Lindenmann, *ZIS*, 10 (2015), 530; see also ICC, *Report Performance Indicators* (2014); ICC, *Second Report Performance Indicators* (2016); ICC, *Report Key Performance Indicators* (2022).

conduct of the proceedings, serve similar purposes. At the same time this requires openness from all parties involved, especially the operators of the respective procedural system. They should not come to an international(ized) criminal tribunal with preconceived ideas derived from their domestic law and practice but rather be in a kind of 'learning mode', open to new approaches and ideas. After all, even though a judicial decision in an internationa(ized) criminal tribunal might impact the body of International Criminal Law itself, most tribunals' Statutes have a reservation clause, clarifying that decisions as to the interpretation of those Statutes shall not limit the development of ICL or even International Law.[6]

## B. Fairness and efficiency as guiding principles

Of course, a procedural 'framework model' needs some guiding principles and these are essentially two: namely, *fairness and efficiency/expediency*. Understood correctly, these principles do not contradict but complement each other, for it is also in the interest of the suspect/accused that his legal situation is clarified as expediently as possible as long as this does not entail an inacceptable curtailment of his fair trial rights. Indeed, on the one hand, the relevant fair trial framework, as presented in Chapter I of this volume,[7] has not only at its core the principle of equality of arms but also contains the temporal element of a speedy procedure/trial in several rights.[8]

### (1) Efficiency at the prosecutorial and administrative level

On the other hand, efficiency/expediency relates to speedy and well-managed investigations, prosecutions, and trials and thus speaks to the need—only touched upon *en passant* in this volume[9]—of pre-trial and trial management. In fact, efficiency has been at the core of reform efforts within and outside of the ICC.[10] In the time since the first edition of this volume in 2016, all organs of the ICC have evaluated their efficiency performance, for example the OTP with the *Policy on Situation Completion* as part of a 'trilogy' complementing the previous Policy Papers on Preliminary Examinations,[11] and the ICC (Presidency) with its response to the Independent Export Report.[12] Beyond the ICC, the KSC in particular has set a strong example of an effective court that dispenses justice in a fair and (cost)-efficient manner.[13] It is clear from all these efforts that the necessary reforms can be more easily and

[6] See e.g. Art. 10 ICCS.

[7] Chapter I, D in this volume.

[8] See e.g. the rights to prompt information about the nature and cause of the charge (Chapter I, D.(3)(c)) and to a trial without undue delay (Chapter I, D.(3)(h)).

[9] Chapter IV, A.(2)(a)(iv); Chapter V., A.(2)(a) (4)(c) *in fine* (on the 'E-Court').

[10] See, on the one hand, ICC, *Chambers Practice Manual* (2016) and (2023) as well as the various Reports of the Study Group on Governance (2011–2023), with consideration on efficiency most recently in ICC-ASP, *Report Study Group on Governance* (2023), p. 9; see, more specifically, the Report of the Working Group on Lessons Learnt in ICC-ASP, *Report Study Group on Governance* (2015), Annex II, pp. 29 ff.; for a comprehensive overview of this Court-led initiative since its inception, see Ambach, in Stahn, *Law and Practice of the ICC* (2015), pp. 1284 ff. On the other hand, see Mettraux et al., *Expert Initiative Effectiveness ICC* (2014) and the summary by Lindenmann, *ZIS*, 10 (2015), 529. All these documents have been extensively quoted throughout this volume.

[11] Chapter IV, B.(1) in this volume.

[12] Expert Group, *IER* (2020) and ICC, *IER Response* (2021), referred to throughout this volume.

[13] For concrete figures, see Chapter IV, A.(2)(b)(i) with note 296 in this volume. I make this statement in my academic capacity enriched by certain practical insights.

quickly achieved by changes in practice (via practice manuals like the already mentioned *Practice Manual*) than by—usually more cumbersome—normative reforms (via amendments of the RPE or even the Statute unless the former can be amended by the judges).[14] The ensuing management needs do not only concern the judges but—at least for the ICC—also the Prosecutor, who bears the main responsibility for the conduct of the—two-tiered[15]—investigation stage.[16] If we grant the Prosecutor a broad discretion at this procedural stage, especially during the preliminary examination, with virtually no judicial supervision[17] and unlimited freedom to select situations and cases,[18] a coherent and transparent prosecution strategy with the respective policies is required as a counterbalance.[19] Last but not least, the organ that is arguably the most important one to ensure efficiency at international(ized) criminal tribunals is the Registry and we have thus dedicated appropriate space to it in this volume.[20] At any rate, today managerial options are a necessary ingredient of any new tribunal or accountability mechanism.

### (2) Efficiency at the judicial level: trial management and judicial quality

It is also clear from the international experience so far that international criminal prosecutions and trials must be managed by experienced prosecutors and judges,[21] that is, persons with sufficient criminal trial experience to be able to organize such mega-trials and effectively structure the pre-trial and trial phase, for example, by limiting charges, setting fixed dates and deadlines (including getting the parties and participants to meet them),[22] joining cases, and holding status conferences.[23] Trial experience also has a strategic and personal aspect: strategically, international judges have to decide where a controversial legal or even factual question needs to be addressed and where it should be

[14] See already Lindenmann, *ZIS*, 10 (2015), 529; calling for 'changes of practice' (and only subsidiary for normative changes) also ICC-ASP, *Report Study Group Governance* (2015), p. 3 (para. 14).

[15] On the stages of 'preliminary examination' and 'formal investigation', see Chapter IV, A.(1) in this volume.

[16] For a crit. discussion of the management structures of the OTP, see Mettraux et al., *Expert Initiative Effectiveness ICC* (2014), pp. 51 ff. (paras. 4 ff.) (recommending, inter alia, a streamlining of the prosecutorial investigations, pp. 65–6 (para. 55)); more comprehensively now Expert Group, *IER* (2020), pp. 12 ff. (para. 26 ff.) and *passim* with regard to the different organs' reply in ICC, *IER Response* (2021), pp. 7 ff. (para. 15 ff.).

[17] cf. Chapter IV, B.(3) in this volume. From a policy perspective against judicial oversight during investigation, Mettraux et al., *Expert Initiative Effectiveness ICC* (2014), p. 8 (para. 8), 11 (para. 36).

[18] cf. Chapter IV, B.(1) in this volume.

[19] In this regard, see ICC-OTP, *Policy Case Selection* (2016), setting out some considerations on the general principles (paras. 16–23) and the legal criteria for the selection and prioritisation of cases (paras. 24–33), as well as the actual case selection (paras. 34–46) and prioritization criteria for selected cases (paras. 47–55). See also ICC-OTP, *Policy Situation Completion* (2021) and *Complementarity and Cooperation* (2024).

[20] Chapter II, B.(1), C.(1)(d), E.(3) and Chapter V, A.(7), B.(1)(c).

[21] See also Mettraux et al., *Expert Initiative Effectiveness ICC* (2014), pp. 8, 9 (paras. 10, 26), p. 72 (paras. 79–80) ('qualified', 'experienced' prosecutors) and p. 227 (para. 35) ('trial-management experience'); on the selection of judges in this regard, see Chapter II, A.(3) in this volume.

[22] For good examples, see ICC, *Prosecutor v. Abd-Al-Rahman*, PTC II, Order on disclosure and related matters, ICC-02/05-01/20-116, 17 August 2020, para. 17; previously *Prosecutor v. Bemba et al.*, TC VII, Decision on Defence Request to Postpone the Commencement of the Trial, No. ICC-01/05-01/13-1254, 15 September 2015, paras. 15 ff. (16: commencement date for trial binding and postponement 'exceptional measure'; *in casu* rejecting the defence postponement request).

[23] On status conferences see in this volume, Chapter IV, A.(2)(a)(iv), (3)(a) *in fine* and B.(3) (with regard to judicial control of the Prosecutor); Chapter V, A.(2)(a), (5)(b), B.(2)(c)(i) *in fine* (to organize disclosure); see also ICC, *Practice Manual* (2023), para. 19 (pre-trial status conferences).

ignored. The judicial toolkit is rich enough to allow for managerial efficiency decisions, for example by defining burdens and standards of proof and persuasion, requirements as to substantiation, and granting broad deference to trial decisions. There are of course limits to these tools once principled considerations, especially those related to fairness and rights, come into play. A good example in this regard is pre-trial detention and its review. Judges often face a serious rights dilemma when they feel compelled to uphold the detention of a suspect, having to balance the causes of detention (risk of flight and obstruction of justice, including by intimidating victim-witnesses) against the suspect's right to liberty reinforced by the presumption of innocence.[24] The personal aspect of judicial quality involves the ability to make compromises: international judges within a chamber need to strike a good balance between compromising and—where necessary—issuing a dissent in whatever form. Of course, judges should not try to impose their domestic procedural system but, as already said above, rather be open to new approaches and ideas.

### (3) Efficiency at the level of the mandate providers

The ICC's procedural framework is flexible enough to allow for the management practices referred to.[25] It is thus up to the State Parties to nominate the appropriate judicial candidates.[26] I note in passing that it is also the task and responsibility of the State Parties to protect the integrity and independence of the Court against attempts at undue interference (as witnessed at the 2015 ASP with regard to Rule 68 RPE ICC)[27] or, even worse, attacks by major powers.[28] States' support must include a robust budget,[29] to make the Court less dependent on additional and/or external funding mostly related to specific situations. Especially prosecutorial decisions are often resource (and feasibility) driven, be it with regard to proceedings *in absentia* (recently: *Kony*),[30] a (new) deprioritization policy,[31] or to the continuation of an investigation.[32]

[24] See my Separate Concurring Opinion in KSC, CoAP, *Decision on Hashim Thaçi's Appeal against Decision on Interim Release*, KSC-BC-2020-06/IA004/F00005/RED, 30 April 2021, annex (stressing the presumption of innocence and the right to liberty and criticizing the 'world-wide practice of prolonged pre-trial detention, including the practice of international criminal tribunals' [paras. 3–4]; arguing that the balancing exercise must take into account 'the actual (realistic) *possibility of re-arrest* of a released suspect or accused' [para. 5]).

[25] The ICC *Practice Manual* (2023) attempts to codify some of these management possibilities; see e.g. the considerations on temporal issues ('timing of the first appearance' (para. 7) and the 'date of the confirmation hearing' (paras. 12–14) and 'time limit for responses' under Reg. 24 RegC (para. 16)) and on the conduct of the confirmation hearing (paras. 40–54). See also Ambos, in Jackson and Summers, *Fairness* (2018), pp. 179, 182–3 with further references; Kuczynska, *Accusation Model ICC* (2015), p. 355 ('effective managerial judging system that led to adopting of a hybrid model between the adversarial and inquisitorial systems').

[26] Similarly Lindenmann, *ZIS*, 10 (2015), 530.

[27] cf. Chapter V, A.(4)(d) in this volume.

[28] On the (first) Trump government's assault on the ICC, see Ambos, *Treatise ICL I* (2021), p. 62; on the recent draft of an 'Illegitimate Court Counteraction Act (ICCA)' (as a reaction to the Prosecutor's application for arrest warrants against Prime Minister Netanyahu und Defence Minister Gallant) see Hamilton and Goodman, *Just Security* 24 September 2024. On Russian sanctions against the ICC, including criminal investigations against the Prosecutor and Judges, see HRW, 5 May 2023, < https://www.hrw.org/news/2023/05/05/russia-law-targets-international-criminal-court>.

[29] Chapter IV, B.(1) in this volume.

[30] Chapter IV, A.(2)(b)(ii) in this volume.

[31] Chapter IV, B.(1) in this volume.

[32] Chapter IV, B.(4)(c) in this volume.

### (4) Fairness and efficiency at the mandate level: The goals of international criminal justice

A procedural model informed by the guiding principles of fairness and expediency is fully in line with the (above analysed[33]) historical experience and the goals of international criminal justice.[34] In other words, a departure from one system and its replacement by another cannot be justified with the mere recourse to the goals of international criminal justice.[35] There is no 'superiority' of either system or model as such.[36] In fact, the two major models in criminal procedure can, perhaps with some reforms, be merged and adjusted to these goals.[37] Similarly, both systems, taking into account their peculiarities and local differences, have advantages and disadvantages. One can test this thesis by looking at some more concrete examples, mainly from the law and practice of evidence. In that sense, fairness is not a political frame but something that needs to be established in the daily work of an international(ized) criminal tribunal, where problems often lie in the nitty-gritty application of legal rules ('technicalities') which remain a black box for outside observers and policymakers. This has been shown by the IMT proceedings: the fairness-commitment by then US President Truman[38] could not prevent the fairness challenges levelled at the trials.[39]

## C. Expediency and fairness gains by the adversarial or inquisitorial mode?

Arguably, an investigation conducted as an official (judge-led) inquest may be better suited to produce an objective, historical record than a party-driven, necessarily selective adversarial procedure;[40] yet, we have argued that this is, at any event, not the task of a criminal trial and should be left to an interdisciplinary truth commission.[41] Alternative fact-finding mechanisms might also be suitable.[42] More importantly, a judge-led examination of witnesses may

[33] Chapter I, B. and C. in this volume.

[34] In a similar vein, Vasiliev, in Sluiter et al., *International Criminal Procedure* (2013), p. 642 ('The experience of improvising and reforming procedures in international and hybrid criminal courts accumulated in the past decades, may attest that neither a predominantly "adversarial" nor "inquisitorial" style of conducting a trial is per se incompatible with the fundamental objectives of the enterprise of international prosecutions. By and large, the teleological parameter cast no ready preference for one or the other set of fact-finding arrangements. Both the trial format in which the evidence is presented alternately by each party before an unengaged and impartial fact-finder and that in which the bench actively steers and takes part in the evidentiary process ... can effectively promote the broader institutional goals of international criminal justice')

[35] See also Vasiliev, in Sluiter et al., *International Criminal Procedure* (2013), p. 646 (considering it 'misleading ... to rely on any conceptual inadequacies of adversarial procedure with regard to the goals of international criminal justice in advocating a departure from it' and advocating more 'experimentation and empirical research and analysis, ideally resulting in "hard data" ... before even tentative conclusions can be reached on the best procedure to meet the goals of international criminal justice').

[36] See also Vasiliev, in Sluiter et al., *International Criminal Procedure* (2013), p. 648 ('there is no reliable and convincing empirical—as opposed to merely intuitive and speculative—basis on which to claim the "superiority" of either the inquisitorial or the adversarial model in terms of efficiency and expediency').

[37] Thereto Heinze, *ICLR*, 18 (2018), 929, 947 ff.

[38] Truman remarked at the start of the trials before the IMT: '[T]he world should be impressed by the fairness of the trial. These German murderers must be punished, but only upon proof of individual guilt at a trial.' Cited in Biddle, *In Brief Authority* (1962/1972), p. 372.

[39] Chapter I, B.(1)(d) in this volume.

[40] cf. de Meester, Pitcher, Rastan, and Sluiter, in Sluiter et al., *International Criminal Procedure* (2013), pp. 210, 211, 251 (but ultimately sceptical, leaving it open: 'no definite answer').

[41] Chapter IV, B.(8)(b)(ii) in this volume.

[42] Chapter I, B.(3) in this volume.

be preferred to a party-driven approach for basically two reasons. First, it is more inclusive (less selective) since the (inquisitorial) judge usually reviews all witness statements in the dossier first and then decides on this basis which witnesses should be ordered to appear for personal interrogation; there is no pre-selection by the parties.[43] Secondly, it may also be more respectful of witnesses than the party-driven, contest-like cross-examination, especially if practised in an aggressive manner by counsel of one side or the other. The latter may rather alienate witnesses instead of instilling confidence in the criminal process and thus lead them to conceal information instead of sharing it with the interrogators and the chamber.[44] However, from a broader perspective, it may be argued that the more dynamic features of the adversarial criminal process, especially the dialectical approach to truth-seeking, allows for a more communicative procedure which is more inclusive with regard to non-legally trained participants and the public in general. Such a procedure based on (horizontal) communication instead of a (vertical and hierarchical) inquest seems also to be more open to possible reforms.[45] In addition, one should not underestimate the burden for a judge to lead the evidentiary process throughout the trial phase in mega-trials with potentially hundreds of witnesses for either side.

Given the importance of orality for communication and outreach, a departure from this principle can only be admitted exceptionally, namely in the case of a witness who is no longer available—be it due to his passing or refusal to testify (again) due to pressure or for other reasons—that is, in the situation where there is only prior recorded testimony of a witness or no evidence at all.[46] Both prior recorded testimony and live testimony may and should be used by means of audio or video-link technology. Of course, such written evidence which cannot be verified in open court—given the absence of the relevant witness as its source—needs to be treated with utmost caution and it is up to each Chamber, depending on the concrete circumstances of the case, to refuse or admit it, and what weight to give it. It is a different question whether and to what extent written evidence, for example, in the form of well-prepared written witness statements[47] or as bar table evidence,[48] should be admitted in addition to the witness' potential oral testimony in order to have a broader and well-documented basis for judicially controlled cross-examination.[49] From a fair trial perspective this is acceptable as long as the other party, that is, normally the defence, has a fair chance to examine the respective evidence, especially to question the witness (which will be possible since this scenario is predicated on his presence). In addition, given the sheer amount of evidence in international criminal trials, the handling of evidence needs to be modernized: apart from the already mentioned used of video and audio technology, case

[43] See also Safferling, *International Criminal Procedure* (2012), pp. 279–80, 280–1.

[44] For a discussion, see Chapter V, A.(3)(a) in this volume, esp. with reference to Combs, *Fact-Finding* (2010), pp. 303 ff., who therefore proposes a *sui generis* mixed system which combines adversarial and non-adversarial presentation of evidence and questioning (pp. 319–21, 319: 'grafting initial judicial questioning onto a system of evidence presentation that is otherwise adversarial. Witnesses would be called by the parties, and, after the judges conducted their questioning, the lawyers would be expected to examine and cross-examine their respective witnesses').

[45] See also Safferling, *International Criminal Procedure* (2012), p. 461 (considering the ICC procedure conceptually as 'communication and cooperation in the search for the truth', thereby allowing for different trial structures).

[46] See in this regard Rule 68 RPE ICC and the discussion in Chapter V, A.(4)(d) in this volume.

[47] Chapter V, A.(4)(a) in this volume.

[48] Chapter V, A.(4)(e) in this volume.

[49] See, in this vein, Gaynor, in Sluiter et al., *International Criminal Procedure* (2013), pp. 1077–9, 1082 (proposing to 'generally dispense with oral direct examination' and rather rely on 'well-organized, comprehensive written witness statements' which would form the basis of a 'tightly controlled' cross-examination) and p. 1079 (advocating a rule regulating bar table evidence in order to encourage its use).

charts may be useful to order, systematize, and link evidence to the relevant facts and elements of crime; E-Court protocols should be used extensively; artificial intelligence can be used to save time and costs for translations and transcriptions.

In any case, one should not be too optimistic with regard to the expediency gains to be achieved by a shift to a predominantly judge-led and/or written procedure.[50] The ICTY experience shows that such reforms must be accepted by the operators, especially the judges.[51] They must be flexible and, I insist, open to new ideas and approaches—no matter whether these are brought about by practice regulations or proper normative changes. If the judges stick to their old (inquisitorial or adversarial) national habits, basically ignoring the new and unique international normative framework they are operating in, nothing will change. Matters may even get worse if operators continue to act as if the old legal regime were still in place. This way of thinking is certainly fuelled by the fact that ICL creates epistemic communities where judges, prosecutors, and staff members move from one tribunal to another.[52] Of course, an unreflective return to domestic or local procedures is no solution; it does not solve the particular fact-finding and evidence-gathering problems of international criminal proceedings.[53] The way forward is (critical) reflection, transparency, and rationality.

[50] Sceptical also Vasiliev, in Sluiter et al., *International Criminal Procedure* (2013), p. 648 ('It cannot be guaranteed that sacrificing the "adversarial" mode of presentation, with its convoluted rules governing the examination of witnesses, for the chance to implement a purely "inquisitorial" unitary scheme would result in significant time-saving and increased decisional rectitude, thus making reforms worth the cost.').

[51] See the study by Langer and Doherty, *YaleJIL*, 36 (2011), 252 ff. as summarized in Chapter IV, A.(2)(a)(iv) with note 261 in this volume.

[52] Chapter II, A.(3) in this volume.

[53] See also Combs, *Fact-Finding* (2010), pp. 297 ff. (while 'local procedures should be best suited to meet local needs and expectations', they 'are not necessarily better suited to eliciting clear, accurate testimony in *international* criminal trials, and, even if they were, other factors might counsel against their adoption' (p. 297 [emphasis in original]).

# General Literature


Ahlbrecht, H., et al., *Internationales Strafrecht in der Praxis* (Heidelberg: C. F. Müller, 2nd edn, 2018), quoted as: Author, in Ahlbrecht et al., *Internationales Strafrecht* (2018)

Ambos, K., *European Criminal Law* (Cambridge, New York, Port Melbourne, New Delhi, Singapore: CUP, 2018), quoted as: Ambos, *EuCrL* (2018)

Ambos, K., *Internationales Strafrecht. Strafanwendungsrecht, Völkerstrafrecht, Europäisches Strafrecht, Rechtshilfe* (Munich: C.H. Beck, 5th edn, 2018), quoted as: Ambos, *Internationales Strafrecht* (2018)

Ambos, K., ed., *The Rome Statute of the International Criminal Court. Article-by-Article- Commentary (Munich,* Oxford, Baden-Baden: C.H. Beck, Hart, Nomos, 4th edn 2022), quoted as: Author, 'Article X', in Ambos, *Commentary* (2022)

Ambos, K., *Treatise on International Criminal Law*, Vol. I: *Foundations and General Part* (Oxford: OUP, 2nd edn, 2021), quoted as: Ambos, *Treatise ICL I* (2021)

Ambos, K., *Treatise on International Criminal Law*, Vol. II: *The Crimes and Sentencing* (Oxford: OUP, 2nd edn, 2022), quoted as: Ambos, *Treatise ICL II* (2022)

Ambos, K. and Rackow, P., eds., *The Cambridge Companion to European Criminal Law* (Cambridge, New York, Port Melbourne, New Delhi, Singapore: CUP, 2023), quoted as: Author, in Ambos and Rackow, *European Criminal Law* (2023)

Ambos, K., König, S., and Rackow, P., eds., *Rechtshilferecht in Strafsachen* (Baden-Baden: Nomos, 2nd edn, 2020), quoted as: Author, in Ambos et al., *Rechtshilferecht* (2020)

Ambos, K., Large, J., and Wierda, M., eds., *Building a Future on Peace and Justice—Studies on Transitional Justice, Conflict Resolution and Development* (Berlin: Springer, 2009), quoted as: Author, in Ambos et al., *Building a Future* (2009)

Ambroise-Casterot, C. and Bonfils, P., *Procédure pénale* (Paris: Presses Universitaires de France, 4th edn, 2022), quoted as: Ambroise-Casterot and Bonfils, *Procédure pénale* (2022)

American Law Institute, *Restatement of the Law Third, The Foreign Relations Law of the United States*, i; §§ 1 to 488 (Saint Paul, Minnesota: American Law Institute Publications, 1987), quoted as: ALI, *Restatement* (1987)

American Law Institute, *Restatement of the Law, Fourth, The foreign relations law of the United States: selected topics in treaties, jurisdiction, and sovereign immunity*; as adopted and promulgated by the American Law Institute at Washington, D.C., May 22, 2017, §§ 301–313; 401–464; 481–490 (Saint Paul, Minnesota: American Law Institute Publications, 2018), quoted as: ALI, Restatement (2018)

Arbour, L., Eser, A., Ambos, K., and Sanders, A., eds., *The Prosecutor of a Permanent International Criminal Court—International Workshop in Co-operation with the Office of the Prosecutor of the International Criminal Tribunals (ICTY and ICTR) Freiburg im Breisgau, May 1998* (Freiburg im Breisgau: Max Planck-Institut für ausländisches und internationales Strafrecht, 2000), quoted as: Arbour et al., *Prosecutor* (2000)

Ashworth, A. and Horder, J., *Principles of Criminal Law* (Oxford: OUP, 7th edn, 2013), quoted as Ashworth and Horder, *Principles* (2013)

Bantekas, I., *International Criminal Law (Oxford, Portland: Hart,* 4th edn, 2010), quoted as: Bantekas, *ICL* (2010)

Bassiouni, M. C., *Introduction to International Criminal Law* (Leiden, Boston: Martinus Nijhoff, 2nd edn, 2013), quoted as: Bassiouni, *Introduction ICL* (2013)

Bassiouni, M. C. and Nanda, V. P., eds., *A Treatise on International Criminal Law*, Vol. II: *Jurisdiction and Cooperation* (Springfield/Illinois: Thomas, 1973), quoted as: Bassiouni and Nanda, *Treatise II* (1973)

Bergsmo, M., ed., *Criteria for Prioritizing and Selecting Core International Crime Cases* (Oslo: Torkel Opsahl Academic EPublisher and Peace Research Institute Oslo, 2nd edn, 2010), quoted as: Author, in Bergsmo, *Criteria for Prioritizing* (2010)

Bergsmo, M. and Stahn, C., eds., *Quality Control in Preliminary Examination, Volume 1* (Brussels, Torkel Opsahl 2018), quoted as: Author, in Bergsmo and Stahn, *Preliminary Examination I* (2018)

Bergsmo, M. and Stahn, C., eds., *Quality Control in Preliminary Examination, Volume 2* (Brussels, Torkel Opsahl 2018), quoted as: Author, in Bergsmo and Stahn, *Preliminary Examination II* (2018)

Boas, G., Bischoff, J. L., Reid, N. L., and Don Tayor III, B., *International Criminal Law Practitioner Library, Vol. III: International Criminal Procedure* (Cambridge, New York: CUP, 2011), quoted as: Boas et al., *Procedure* (2011)

Bock, S., *Das Opfer vor dem Internationalen Strafgerichtshof* (Berlin: Duncker and Humblot, 2010), quoted as: Bock, *Opfer* (2010)

Bohlander, M., ed., *International Criminal Justice—A Critical Analysis of Institutions and Procedures* (London: Cameron May, 2007), quoted as: Author, in Bohlander, *International Criminal Justice* (2007)

Bohlander, M., *Principles of German Criminal Procedure* (Oxford, Portland: Hart, 2nd edn, 2021), quoted as: Bohlander, *German Criminal Procedure* (2021)

Borsari, R., *Diritto punitivo sovranazionale come sistema* (Padova: CEDAM, 2007), quoted as: Borsari, *Diritto punitivo* (2007)

Bouloc, B., Stefani, G., and Levasseur, G., *Procédure pénale* (Paris: Dalloz, 28th edn, 2021), quoted as: Bouloc et al., *Procédure pénale* (2021)

Brown, B. S., ed., *Research Handbook on International Criminal Law* (Cheltenham, Northampton: Edward Elgar Publishing, 2011), quoted as: Author, in Brown, *Handbook ICL* (2011)

Brown, D. K., Turner, J. I., and Weißer, B., eds., *The Oxford Handbook of Criminal Process* (Oxford: OUP 2019), quoted as: Author, in Brown, Turner and Weißer, *OxfHb Criminal Process* (2019)

Calvo-Goller, K. N., *The Trial Proceedings of the International Criminal Court—ICTY and ICTR Precedents* (Leiden: Martinus Nijhoff, 2006), quoted as: Calvo-Goller, *Trial Proceedings* (2006)

Carter, L. and Pocar, F., *International Criminal Procedure—The Interface of Civil Law and Common Law Legal Systems* (Cheltenham, Northampton: Edward Elgar Publishing, 2013), Author, in Carter and Pocar, *Procedure* (2013)

Cassese, A., ed., *The Oxford Companion to International Criminal Justice* (Oxford, New York: OUP, 2009), quoted as: Author, in Cassese, *Companion* (2009)

Cassese, A. and Gaeta, P., *Cassese's International Criminal Law—Revised by: A. Cassese and P. Gaeta, L. Baig, M. Fan, C. Gosnell, and A. Whiting* (Oxford: OUP, 3rd edn, 2013), quoted as: Cassese and Gaeta, *ICL* (2013)

Cassese, A., Chiavario, M., and De Francesco, F., eds., *Problemi attuali della giustizia penale internazionale* (Torino: Gappichelli, 2005), quoted as: Cassese, Chiavario and De Francesco, *Problemi* (2005)

Cassese, A., Gaeta, P., and Jones, J. R. W. D., eds., *The Rome Statute of the International Criminal Court—A Commentary, 3 Volumes* (Oxford: OUP, 2002), quoted as: Author, in Cassese et al., *Rome Statute [volume]* (2002)

Cirener, G., Radtke, H., Rissing-van Saan, R., Rönnau, T., and Schluckebier, W., eds., *Leipziger Kommentar StGB*, 19 Volumes (Berlin: de Gruyter Recht, 13th edn, 2020 ff.), quoted as: Author, '§ XX', in [volume editor], *LK [volume]* (year)

Combs, N. A., *Fact-Finding without Facts: the Uncertain Evidentiary Foundations of International Criminal Convictions* (Cambridge: CUP, 2010)

Corstens, G. and Pradel, J., *European Criminal Law* (The Hague: Kluwer Law International, 2002), quoted as: Corstens and Pradel, *European Criminal Law* (2002)

Cryer, R., *Prosecuting International Crimes—Selectivity and the International Criminal Law Regime* (New York: CUP, 2005), quoted as: Cryer, *Prosecuting* (2005)

Cryer, R., Friman, H., Robinson, D., and Wilmshurst, E., *An Introduction to International Criminal Law and Procedure* (Cambridge: CUP, 1st edn, 2007), quoted ad: Author, in Cryer et al., *ICL* (2007)

Cryer, R., Friman, H., Robinson, D., and Wilmshurst, E., *An Introduction to International Criminal Law and Procedure* (Cambridge: CUP, 2nd edn, 2010), quoted as: Author, in Cryer et al., *ICL* (2010)

Cryer, R., Friman, H., Robinson, D., and Wilmshurst, E., *An Introduction to International Criminal Law and Procedure* (Cambridge: CUP, 3rd edn, 2014), quoted as: Author, in Cryer et al., *ICL* (2014)

Cryer, R., Robinson, D., and Vasiliev, S., *An Introduction to International Criminal Law and Procedure* (Cambridge: CUP, 4th edn, 2019), quoted as: Author, in Cryer et al., *ICL* (2019)

Damaška, M. R., *The Faces of Justice* (New Haven: Yale University Press, 1986), quoted as: Damaška, *Faces of Justice* (1986)

deGuzman, M. M. and Oosterveld, V., eds., *The Elgar Companion to the International Criminal Court* (Cheltenham, Northampton: Edward Elgar Publishing, 2020), quoted as: Author, in deGuzman and Oosterveld, *Elgar Companion ICC* (2020)

Dammer, H. R. and Albanese, J.S., *Comparative Criminal Justice Systems* (Belmont/CA: Wadsworth/ Thomson Learning, 5th edn, 2014), quoted as: Dammer and Albanese, *Criminal Justice Systems* (2014)

Del Carmen, R. V., *Criminal Procedure: Law and Practice* (Belmont: Thomson, 10th edn, 2016)

Delmas-Marty, M. and Spencer, J. R., eds., *European Criminal Procedures* (Cambridge: CUP, 2002), quoted as: Author, in Delmas-Marty and Spencer, *Criminal Procedures* (2002)

Desportes F. and Lazerges-Cousquer, L., *Traité de procédure pénale* (Paris: Economica, 4th edn, 2014), quoted as: Desportes and Lazerges-Cousquer, *Procédure pénale* (2014)

Dörr, O., Grote, R., and Marauhn, T., eds., *EMRK/GG—Konkordanzkommentar zum europäischen und deutschen Grundrechtsschutz,* Vol. I: *Kapitel 1–19 (Tübingen: Mohr Siebeck,* 3rd edn, 2022), quoted as: Author, in Dörr et al., *EMRK/GG—Kommentar* (2022)

Dworkin, R., *Law's Empire* (Cambridge/Massachusetts: Harvard University Press, 1986), quoted as: Dworkin, *Law's Empire* (1986)

Erb, V. and Schäfer, J., eds., *Münchener Kommentar zum Strafgesetzbuch*, 9 Volumes (Munich: C. H. Beck, 4th edn, 2020–2022), quoted as: Author, '§ XX', in [volume editor], *MüKo [volume]* (year)

Esser, R., *Auf dem Weg zu einem europäischen Strafverfahrensrecht—Die Grundlagen im Spiegel der Rechtsprechung des Europäischen Gerichtshofs für Menschenrechte (EGMR) in Strassburg* (Berlin: De Gruyter, 2002), quoted as: Esser, *Europäisches Strafverfahrensrecht* (2002)

Esser, R., *Europäisches und Internationales Strafrecht (Munich: Beck,* 3rd edn, 2022), quoted as: Esser, *Internationales Strafrecht* (2022)

Fawcett, J. E. S., *The Application of the European Convention on Human Rights (Oxford: Clarendon Press, 1987),* quoted as: Fawcett, *ECHR* (1987)

Fernandez, J. and Pacreau, X., eds., *Statut de Rome de la Cour pénale internationale—Commentaire article par article,* Vol. I or II (Paris: Editions A. Pedone, 2012), quoted as: Author, 'Article X', in Fernandez and Pacreau, *Commentaire CPI I or II* (2012)

Fernandez, J., Pacreau, X., and Ubéda-Saillard, M., eds., *Statut de Rome de la Cour pénale internationale—Commentaire article par article,* Vol. I or II (Paris: Editions A. Pedone, 2nd edn, 2019), quoted as: Author, 'Article X', in Fernandez et al., *Commentaire CPI I or II* (2019)

Findlay, M. and Ying, J. C. H., *Principled International Criminal Justice – Lessons from Tort Law* (London, New York: Routledge 2019), quoted as: Findlay and Ying, *Principled International Criminal Justice* (2019)

Fischer, H., Kreß, C., and Lüder, S. R., eds., *International and National Prosecution of Crimes under International Law—Current Developments* (Berlin: Arno Spitz, 2001), quoted as: Author, in Fischer et al., *Prosecution* (2001)

Fischer, T., *Strafgesetzbuch und Nebengesetze* (Munich: C. H. Beck, 71st edn, 2024), quoted as: Fischer, *StGB* (2024)

Fletcher, G. P., *The Grammar of Criminal Law,* Vol. I: *Foundations* (New York: OUP, 2007), quoted as: Fletcher, *Grammar I* (2007)

Frowein, J. A. and Peukert, W., *Europäische Menschenrechtskonvention—EMRK-Kommentar* (Kehl: N. P. Engel, 3rd edn, 2009), quoted as: Frowein and Peukert, *EMRK* (2009)

Gaede, K., *Fairness als Teilhabe—Das Recht auf konkrete und wirksame Teilhabe durch Verteidigung gemäß Art. 6 EMRK* (Berlin: Duncker and Humblot, 2007), quoted as: Gaede, *Fairness* (2007)

Garner, B. A., *Black's Law Dictionary* (Saint Paul/Minnesota: Thomson Reuters, 11th edn, 2019), quoted as: Garner, *Dictionary* (2019)

Glendon, M. A. et al., *Comparative Legal Traditions in a nutshell,* (St. Paul, Minnesota: West Publishing 1985), quoted as: Glendon, *Traditions* (1985)

Glendon, M. A. et al., *Comparative Legal Traditions in a nutshell*, (St. Paul, Minnesota: West Publishing, 2nd edn, 2016), quoted as: Glendon, *Traditions* (2016)

Gless, S., *Internationales Strafrecht—Grundriss für Studium und Praxis* (Basel: Helbing Lichtenhahn, 3rd edn, 2021), quoted as: Gless, *Internationales Strafrecht* (2021)

Gollwitzer, W., *Menschenrechte im Strafverfahren—MRK und IPBPR—Kommentar* (Berlin: De Gruyter Recht, 2005), quoted as: Gollwitzer, *Menschenrechte* (2005)

Gómez Colomer, J. L., González Cussac, J. L., and Cardona Lloréns, J., eds., *La Corte Penal Internacional—Un Estudio Interdisciplinar* (Valencia: Tirant lo Blanch, 2003), quoted as: Gómez Colomer et al., *Corte Penal Internacional* (2003)

Grabenwarter, C. and Pabel, K., *Europäische Menschenrechtskonvention (Munich, Basel Wien: C. H. Beck et al.*, 7th edn, 2021), quoted as: Grabenwarter and Pabel, *EMRK* (2021)

Grützner, H., Pötz, P. G., and Kreß, C., eds., *Internationaler Rechtshilfeverkehr in Strafsachen—Die für die Rechtsbeziehungen der Bundesrepublik Deutschland mit dem Ausland in Strafsachen maßgeblichen Bestimmungen*, IV A1 (Supplement 60, delivery 2003), III 27, (Supplement 55, delivery 2002) (Heidelberg: C. F. Müller, 2012), quoted as: Author, in Grützner et al., *Rechtshilfeverkehr* (year)

Guariglia, F., Batros, B., Gallmetzer, R., and Mugwanya, G., *The Appeals Chamber of the International Criminal Court—Commentary and Digest of Jurisprudence* (CUP 2018), quoted as: author, in Guariglia et al., *AC ICC Commentary* (2018)

Haefliger, A., *Die Europäische Menschenrechtskonvention und die Schweiz* (Bern: Stämpfli, 2008), quoted as: Haefliger, *EMRK* (2008)

Harris, D. J., O'Boyle, M., Bates, E., and Buckley, C., *Law of the European Convention on Human Rights* (New York: OUP, 4th edn, 2018), quoted as: Harris et al., *ECHR* (2018)

Harvard University, 'Draft Convention on Jurisdiction with Respect to Crimes ("Harvard Draft Convention")', *AJIL, 29* (1935) Suppl. 435, quoted as: Harvard University, *Draft Convention* (1935)

Heinrich, B., *Strafrecht—Allgemeiner Teil* (Stuttgart: W. Kohlhammer, 6th edn, 2019), quoted as: Heinrich, *Strafrecht AT I* (2019)

Heinze, A., *International Criminal Procedure and Disclosure—An Attempt to Better Understand and Regulate Disclosure and Communication at the ICC on the Basis of a Comprehensive and Comparative Theory of Criminal Procedure* (Berlin: Duncker and Humblot, 2014), quoted as: Heinze, *Disclosure* (2014)

Heinze, A. and Dittrich, V., eds., *The Past, Present and Future of the ICC*, (Brussels: Torkel Opsahl, 2021), quoted as: Author, in Heinze and Dittrich, *ICC* (2021)

Heller, K. J., Mégret, F., Nouwen, S., Ohlin, J., and Robinson, D., eds., *The Oxford Handbook of International Criminal Law* (OUP 2020), quoted as: Author, in Heller et al., *Oxford HB ICL* (2020)

Herdegen, M., *Völkerrecht* (Munich: C. H. Beck, 22nd edn, 2023), quoted as: Herdegen, *Völkerrecht* (2023)

Hernández, G., *International Law* (Oxford: OUP, 2nd edn, 2021), quoted as Hernández, *IL* (2021)

Ho, H. L., *A Philosophy of Evidence Law: Justice in the Search for Truth* (2008), quoted as: Ho, *Philosophy* (Oxford: OUP, 2008)

Horder, J., *Ashworth's Principles of Criminal Law* (Oxford: OUP, 10th edn, 2022), quoted as: Horder, *Principles* (2022)

Ingraham, B. L., *The Structure of Criminal Procedure—Laws and Practice of France, the Soviet Union, China, and the United States* (New York: Greenwood Press, 1987), quoted as: Ingraham, *Criminal Procedure* (1987)

Irving, E., *Multi-Actor Human Rights Protection at the International Criminal Court* (Cambridge: CUP, 2020), quoted as: Irving, *Human Rights Protection* (2020)

Jennings, R. and Watts, A., *Oppenheim's International Law* (Harlow: Longman, 9th edn, 1992), quoted as: Jennings and Watts, *Oppenheim's International Law* (1992)

Jescheck, H.-H., *Die Verantwortlichkeit der Staatsorgane nach Völkerstrafrecht: eine Studie zu den Nürnberger Prozessen* (Bonn: Röhrscheid, 1952), quoted as: Jescheck, *Verantwortlichkeit* (1952)

Jescheck, H.-H. and Weigend, T., *Lehrbuch des Strafrechts—Allgemeiner Teil* (Berlin: Duncker and Humblot, 5th edn, 1996), quoted as: Jescheck and Weigend, *Strafrecht AT* (1996)

Khan, K. A. A., Buisman, C., and Gosnell, C., eds., *Principles of Evidence in International Criminal Justice* (Oxford: OUP, 2010), quoted as: Khan et al., *Evidence Principles* (2010)

Khan, K. A. A., Dixon, R., and Fulford, A., eds., *Archbold International Criminal Courts—Practice, Procedure and Evidence* (London: Sweet & Maxwell, Thomson Reuters, 5th edn, 2018), quoted as: Khan et al., *International Criminal Courts* (2018)

Kindhäuser, U. and Hilgendorf, E., *Strafgesetzbuch—Lehr- und Praxiskommentar* (Baden-Baden: Nomos, 9th edn, 2022), quoted as: Kindhäuser and Hilgendorf, *StGB Kommentar* (2022)

Kindhäuser, U., Neumann, U., and Paeffgen, H.-U., eds., *Nomos Kommentar—Strafgesetzbuch*, Vol. I: *Allgemeiner Teil—§§1–79b* (Baden-Baden: Nomos, 6th edn, 2023), quoted as: Author, '§ XX', in Kindhäuser et al., *NK I* (2023), mn.

Kirsch, S., ed., *Internationale Strafgerichtshöfe* (Baden-Baden: Nomos, 2005), quoted as: Author, in Kirsch, *Internationale Strafgerichtshöfe* (2005)

Klamberg, M., *Evidence in International Criminal Trials—Confronting Legal Gaps and the Reconstruction of Disputed Events* (Leiden: Martinus Nijhoff, 2013), quoted as: Klamberg, *Evidence* (2013)

Klamberg, M., ed., *Commentary on the Law of the International Criminal Court* (Torkel Opsahl, 2017), <https://www.casematrixnetwork.org/cmn-knowledge-hub/icc-commentary-clicc/>, quoted as: Author, in Klamberg, *Commentary ICC* (2017), URL (if the online commentary is cited) or note XX (if the print version is cited)

Klamberg, M., Nilsson, J., and Angotti, A., eds., *Commentary on the Law of the International Criminal Court: The Statute.* Volume 1 (Torkel Opsahl 2nd edn, 2023), quoted as: Author, 'Article X', in Klamberg et al., *Commentary ICC I* (2023), p. XX

Klamberg, M., Nilsson, J., and Angotti, A., eds., *Commentary on the Law of the International Criminal Court: The Statute.* Volume 2 (Torkel Opsahl, 2nd edn, 2023), quoted as: Author, 'Article X', in Klamberg et al., *Commentary ICC II* (2023), p. XX

Klamberg, M., Nilsson, J., and Angotti, A., eds., *Commentary on the Law of the International Criminal Court: The Rules of Procedure and Evidence.* Volume 3 (Torkel Opsahl, 2nd edn, 2023), quoted as: Author, 'Article X', in Klamberg et al., *Commentary ICC RPE* (2023), p. XX

Knoops, G. J. A., *An Introduction to the Law of International Criminal Tribunals—A Comparative Study* (Leiden: Martinus Nijhoff, 2nd edn, 2014), quoted as: Knoops, *International Criminal Tribunals* (2014)

Kolb, R., *Droit International pénal* (Basel: Helbing Lichtenhahn, 2008), quoted as: Kolb, *Droit International Pénal* (2008)

Kolb, R. and Scalia, D., eds., *Droit International pénal; Précis* (Basel: Helbing Lichtenhahn, 2nd edn, 2012), quoted as: Author, in Kolb and Scalia, *DIP* (2012)

Krüßmann, T. M., *Transnationales Strafprozessrecht* (Baden-Baden: Nomos, 2009), quoted as: Krüßmann, *Transnationales Strafprozessrecht* (2009)

Kuczyńska, H., *The Accusation Model before the International Criminal Court—Study of Convergence of Criminal Justice Systems* (Cham: Springer, 2015), quoted as: Kuczynska, *Accusation Model* (2015)

Kühne, H.-H., *Strafprozessrecht—Eine systematische Darstellung des deutschen und europäischen Strafverfahrensrechts* (Heidelberg: C. F. Müller, 9th edn, 2015), quoted as: Kühne, *Strafprozessrecht* (2015)

Kühne, H.-H., Esser, R., and Gerding, M., eds., *Volkerstrafrecht* (Osnabrück: Jonscher, 2007), quoted as: Author, in Kühne et al., *Völkerstrafrecht* (2007)

LaFave, W. R., Israel, J. H., King, N. J., and Kerr, O. S.., *Criminal Procedure* (Saint Paul: West Academic Publishing, Thomson Reuters, 6th edn, 2017), quoted as: LaFave et al., *Criminal Procedure* (2017)

Lattanzi, F. and Schabas, W. A., eds., *Essays on the Rome Statute of the International Criminal Court*, Vol. I (Ripa Fagnano Alto: Il Sirente, 1999), quoted as: Author, in Lattanzi and Schabas, *Rome Statute I* (1999)

Lee, R. S., *The ICC—The Making of the Rome Statute—Issues, Negotiations, Results* (The Hague: Kluwer Law International, 1999), quoted as: Author, in Lee, *ICC* (1999)

Lee, R. S. K. and Friman, H., eds., *The ICC—Elements of Crimes and Rules of Procedure and Evidence* (New York: Transnational Publishers, 2001), quoted as: Author, in Lee and Friman, *ICC* (2001)

May, L. and Hoskins, Z., eds., *International Criminal Law and Philosophy* (New York: CUP, 2010), quoted as: May and Hoskins, *ICL* (2010)

McDonald, G. K. and Swaak-Goldman, O. Q., eds., *Substantive and Procedural Aspects of International Criminal Law—The Experience of International and National Courts, Vol. I: Commentary* (The Hague, London, Boston: Kluwer Law International, 2000), quoted as: Author, in McDonald and Swaak-Goldman, *ICL I* (2000)

Merle, R. and Vitu, A., *Traité de droit criminel,* Vol. II: *Procédure pénale* (Paris: Éditions Cujas, 5th edn, 2001), quoted as: Merle and Vitu, *Droit criminel II* (2001)

Merryman, J. and Pérez-Perdomo, R., *Civil Law Tradition* (Stanford, Calif: Stanford University Press, 4th edn, 2019), quoted as: Merryman and Pérez-Perdomo, *Civil Law* (2019)

Meyer-Ladewig, J. and Nettesheim, M., *EMRK—Europäische Menschenrechtskonvention—Handkommentar* (Baden-Baden, Basel: Nomos, Helbing Lichtenhahn, 4th edn, 2017), quoted as: Meyer-Ladewig and Nettesheim, *EMRK* (2017)

Mulgrew, R. and Abels, D., eds., *Research Handbook on the International Penal System* (Northampton: Elgar, 2016), quoted as: Mulgrew and Abels, *RH Penal System* (2016)

Nouwen, S. M. H., *Complementarity in the Line of Fire—The Catalysing Effect of the International Criminal Court in Uganda and Sudan* (Cambridge: CUP, 2013), quoted as: Nouwen, *Complementarity* (2013)

O'Keefe, R., *International Criminal Law* (Oxford: OUP, 2015), quoted as: O'Keefe, *ICL* (2015)

Olásolo, H., *International Criminal Law, Transnational Criminal Organizations and Transitional Justice* (Leiden, Boston: Brill Nijhoff, 2018)

Oppenheim, L. and Lauterpacht, H., *International Law—A Treatise,* Vol I: *Peace or* Vol II: *Disputes, War and Neutrality* (London, New York, Bombay: Longmans Green and Co, 1st edn, 1905, 8th edn, 1955 or 7th edn, 1955), quoted as: Oppenheim and Lauterpacht, *International Law I or II* (1955)

Pakes, F., *Comparative Criminal Justice* (Cullompton, Devon: Willan Publishing, 4th edn, 2019), quoted as: Pakes, *Criminal Justice* (2019)

Peters, K., *Strafprozeß—Ein Lehrbuch* (Heidelberg: C. F. Müller, 4th edn, 1985), quoted as: Peters, *Strafprozeß* (1985)

Powderly, J., Judges and the Making of International Criminal Law (Leiden, Boston: Brill, Nijhoff 2020), quoted as: Powderly, *Judges* (2020)

Pradel, J., *Procédure pénale* (Paris: Édition Cujas, 20th edn, 2019), quoted as: Pradel, *Procédure Pénale* (2019)

Radtke, H. and Hohmann, O., eds., *Strafprozessordnung—Kommentar* (Munich: Verlag Franz Vahlen, 2011), quoted as: Author, in Radtke and Hohmann, *StPO Kommentar* (2011)

Reydams, L., Wouters, J., and Ryngaert, C., eds., *International Prosecutors* (Oxford: OUP, 2012), quoted as: Author, in Reydams et al., *International Prosecutors* (2012)

Roberts, P., *Roberts and Zuckerman's Criminal Evidence* (Oxford: OUP, 3rd edn, 2022), quoted as: Roberts, *Evidence* (2022)

Rohan, C. and Zyberi, G., eds., *Defense Perspectives on International Criminal Justice* (CUP 2017), quoted as: Author, in Rohan and Zyberi, *Defense Perspectives* (2017)

Röling, B. V. and Rüter, C. F., eds., *The Tokyo Judgment—The International Military Tribunal for the Far East (I.M.T.F.E.) 29. Apr. 1946–12. Nov. 1948, Two Volumes* (Amsterdam: University Press Amsterdam, 1977), quoted as: Author, in Röling and Rüter, *Tokyo Judgment I or II* (1977)

Romano, C., Alter, K., and Shany, Y., eds., *The Oxford Handbook of International Adjudication* (OUP 2014), quoted as: Author, in Romano et al., *OxfHB IntAdjudication* (2014)

Roxin, C. and Greco, L., *Strafrecht—Allgemeiner Teil, I* (München: C. H. Beck, 5th edn, 2020); quoted as Roxin and Greco, *Strafrecht AT I* (2020)

Safferling, C. J. M., *Towards an International Criminal Procedure* (Oxford: OUP, 2003), quoted as: Safferling, *International Criminal Procedure* (2003)

Safferling, C. J. M., *International Criminal Procedure* (Oxford: OUP, 2012), quoted as: Safferling, *Criminal Procedure* (2012)

Sanders, A., Welsh, L., and Skinns, L., *Sanders and Young's Criminal Justice* (Oxford: OUP, 5th edn, 2021), quoted as: Sanders et al., *Criminal Justice* (2021)

Satzger, H., *International and European Criminal Law* (Munich, Oxford, Baden-Baden: C. H. Beck, Hart, Nomos, 2012, 2nd edn, 2018), quoted as: Satzger, *ICL* (2018)

Satzger, H., *Internationales und Europäisches Strafrecht—Strafanwendungsrecht, Europäisches Straf- und Strafverfahrensrecht, Völkerstrafrecht* (Baden-Baden: Nomos, 10th edn, 2022), quoted as: Satzger, *Internationales Strafrecht* (2022)

Schabas, W. A., *The UN International Criminal Tribunals—The Former Yugoslavia, Rwanda and Sierra Leone* (Cambridge, New York: CUP, 2006), quoted as: Schabas, *UN Tribunals* (2006)

Schabas, W. A., *The International Criminal Court—A Commentary on the Rome Statute* (Oxford: OUP, 2nd edn, 2016), quoted as: Schabas, *ICC Commentary* (2016)

Schabas, W. A., *Nowak's CCPR Commentary* (Kehl am Rhein: N. P. Engel, 3rd edn, 2019)

Schabas, W. A., *An Introduction to the International Criminal Court* (Cambridge: CUP, 6th edn, 2020), quoted as: Schabas, *Introduction ICC* (2020)

Schabas, W. A. and Bernaz, N., eds., *Routledge Handbook of International Criminal Law* (London: Routledge, 2011), quoted as: Author, in Schabas and Bernaz, *Handbook ICL* (2011)

Schabas, W. A., McDermott, Y., and Hayes, N., eds., *The Ashgate Research Companion to International Criminal Law—Critical Perspectives* (Farnham: Ashgate, 2013), quoted as: Author, in Schabas et al., *Research Companion ICL* (2013)

Schomburg, W., Lagodny, O., Gleß, S., and Hackner, T., *Internationale Rechtshilfe in Strafsachen* (Munich: Beck, 6th edn, 2020), quoted as: Schomburg et al., *Internationale Rechtshilfe* (2020)

Schönke, A., Schröder, H., and Eser, A., eds., *Strafgesetzbuch Kommentar* (Munich: C.H. Beck, 30th edn, 2019), quoted as: Author, in Schönke and Schröder, *Strafgesetzbuch* (2019)

Schuon, C., *International Criminal Procedure—A Clash of Legal Cultures* (The Hague: T.M.C. Asser Press, 2010), quoted as: Schuon, *International Criminal Procedure* (2010)

Sluiter, G. and Vasiliev, S., eds., *International Criminal Procedure—Towards a Coherent Body of Law* (London: Cameron May, 2009), quoted as: Sluiter and Vasiliev, *International Criminal Procedure* (2009)

Sluiter, G., Friman, H., Linton, S., Zappalá, S., and Vasiliev, S., eds., *International Criminal Procedure—Principles and Rules* (Oxford: OUP, 2013), quoted as: Author, in Sluiter et al., *International Criminal Procedure* (2013)

Stahn, C., ed., *The Law and Practice of the International Criminal Court* (Oxford: OUP, 2015), quoted as: Author, in Stahn, *Practice* (2015)

Stahn, C., *A Critical Introduction to International Criminal Law* (CUP, 2019), quoted as: Stahn, *Introduction ICL* (2019)

Stahn, C. and El Zeidy, M. M., eds., *The International Criminal Court and Complementarity—From Theory to Practice, 2 Volumes* (Cambridge: CUP, 2011), quoted as: Author, in Stahn and El Zeidy, *Complementarity* [volume] (2011)

Stahn, C. and Sluiter, G., eds., *The Emerging Practice of the International Criminal Court* (Leiden: Martinus Nijhoff, 2009), quoted as: Author, in Stahn and Sluiter, *ICC* (2009)

Stahn, C. and van den Herik, L., eds., *Future Perspectives on International Criminal Justice* (The Hague: T.M.C. Asser Press, 2010), quoted as: Author, in Stahn and van den Herik, *Perspectives* (2010)

Stegmiller, I., *The Pre-Investigation Stage of the ICC—Criteria for Situation Selection*, (Berlin: Duncker and Humblot, 2011), quoted as: Stegmiller, *Pre-Investigation* (2011)

Swoboda, S., *Verfahrens- und Beweisstrategien vor den UN-ad-hoc-Tribunalen—Mit Schwerpunkt auf dem vorbereitenden Verfahrensstadien* (Baden-Baden: Nomos, 2013), quoted as: Swoboda, *Verfahrens- und Beweisstrategien* (2013)

Tochilovsky, V., *The Law and Jurisprudence of the International Criminal Tribunals and Courts—Procedure and Human Rights Aspects* (Cambridge, Antwerp, Portland: Intersentia, 2nd edn, 2014), quoted as: Tochilovsky, *ICTs* (2014)

Triffterer, O., ed., *Commentary on the Rome Statute of the International Criminal Court* (Munich, Oxford: C. H. Beck, Hart, 2nd edn, 2008), quoted as: Author, 'Article X', in Triffterer, *Commentary ICC* (2008), mn. XX

Triffterer, O. and Ambos, K., eds., *The Rome Statute of the International Criminal Court—A Commentary* (Munich, Oxford, Baden-Baden: C. H. Beck, Hart, Nomos, 3rd edn, 2016), quoted as: Author, 'Article X', in Triffterer and Ambos, *Commentary* (2016)

Vagias, M., *The Territorial Jurisdiction of the ICC* (Cambridge: CUP, 2014), quoted as: Vagias, *Territorial Jurisdiction* (2014)

van Dijk, P., van Hoof, F., van Rijn, A., and Zwak, L., eds., *Theory and Practice of the European Convention on Human Rights* (Antwerpen, Oxford: Intersentia, 4th edn, 2006), quoted as: Author, in van Dijk et al., *ECHR* (2006)

Verbruggen, F. and Franssen, V., eds., *International Encyclopaedia of Laws—Criminal Law* (Alphen aan den Rijn: Kluwer Law International, Supplement 46, 2012), quoted as: Author, in Verbruggen and Franssen, *Encyclopedia* (2012)

Verdross, A. and Simma, B., *Universelles Völkerrecht: Theorie und Praxis* (Berlin: Duncker and Humblot, 3rd edn, 1984), quoted as: Verdross and Simma, *Völkerrecht* (1984)

Villiger, M. E., *Handbuch der Europäischen Menschenrechtskonvention (EMRK)—Mit besonderer Berücksichtigung der Rechtsprechung des Europäischen Gerichtshofs für Menschenrechte in Schweizer Fällen* (Baden-Baden, Wien, Zürich, Basel, Genf: Nomos, Verlag Österreich, Schulthess, 3rd edn, 2020), quoted as: Villiger, *Handbuch EMRK* (2020)

Vogler, R., *A World View of Criminal Justice* (Aldershot: Ashgate, 2005), quoted as: Vogler, *Criminal Justice* (2005)

Vogler, R. and Huber, B., eds., *Criminal Procedure in Europe* (Berlin: Duncker and Humblot, 2008), quoted as: Author, in Vogler and Huber, *Criminal Procedure* (2008)

Werle, G. and Jessberger, F., *Principles of International Criminal Law* (Oxford: OUP, 3rd edn, 2014), quoted as: Werle and Jessberger, *Principles ICL* (2014)

Werle, G. and Jessberger, F., *Principles of International Criminal Law* (Oxford: OUP, 4th edn, 2020), quoted as: Werle and Jessberger, *Principles ICL* (2020)

Wigmore, J. H., *A Treatise on the Anglo-American System of Evidence in Trials at Common Law*, Vol. I: (Boston: Little Brown, 3rd edn, 1940), quoted as: Wigmore, *Evidence* (1940)

Zahar, A. and Sluiter, G., *International Criminal Law—A Critical Introduction* (Oxford: OUP, 2008), quoted as: Zahar and Sluiter, *ICL* (2008)

Zappalà, S., *Human Rights in International Criminal Proceedings* (Oxford: OUP, 2005), quoted as: Zappalá, *Human Rights* (2005)

# Documents List


ASP,* *Independent Expert Review of the ICC and the Rome Statue System - Final Report*, ICC-ASP/18/Res.7 (30 September 2020)

Commission of the European Communities, *Green Paper on Criminal Law Protection of the Financial Interests of the Community and the Establishment of a European Prosecutor* (Brussels, 11 December 2001), <http://eur-lex.europa.eu/legal-content/EN/TXT/PDF/?uri=CELEX:52001DC0715&rid=1>, quoted as: Commission EC, *Green Paper Financial Interests* (2001)

Commission of the European Communities, *Green Paper from the Commission—Procedural Safeguards for Suspects and Defendants in Criminal Proceedings throughout the European Union* (Brussels, 19 February 2003), <http://eur-lex.europa.eu/legal-content/EN/TXT/PDF/?uri=CELEX:52003DC0075&rid=7>, quoted as: Commission EC, *Green Paper Procedural Safeguards* (2003)

Commission of the European Communities, *Green Paper on Conflicts of Jurisdiction and the Principle of ne bis in idem in Criminal Proceedings* (Brussels, 23 December 2005), <http://eur-lex.europa.eu/legal-content/EN/TXT/PDF/?uri=CELEX:52005DC0696&rid=3>, quoted as: Commission EC, *Green Paper Jurisdiction* (2005)

Eurojust, *Guidelines for Deciding 'Which Jurisdiction should Prosecute?* (The Hague, 2016), <https://www.eurojust.europa.eu/sites/default/files/assets/eurojust_jurisdiction_guidelines_2016_en.pdf>, quoted as Eurojust, *Guidelines* (2016)

European Parliament, *Workshop – Envisioning International Justice: what role for the ICC?* (Brussels, November 2021), <https://www.europarl.europa.eu/RegData/etudes/STUD/2021/653659/EXPO_STU(2021)653659_EN.pdf>, quoted as: EP, *ICC* (2021)

Expert Group (Guillou, N., Pinto, M., Smith, M., Bednarek, A., Bonomy, I., Othman, M. C., Goldstone, R., Jallow, H. and Schwansee Romano, C.), *Independent Expert Review of the International Criminal Court and the Rome Statute System—Final Report* (30 September 2020), <https://asp.icc-cpi.int/sites/asp/files/asp_docs/ASP19/IER-Final-Report-ENG.pdf>, quoted as: Expert Group, *IER* (2020)

Greenwood, F., Howarth, C., Escudero Poole, D., Raymond N.A., and Daniel P. Scarnecchia D.P., *The Signal Code: A Human Rights Approach to Information During Crisis*, (January 2017), <https://hhi.harvard.edu/files/humanitarianinitiative/files/signalcode_final.pdf?m=1607469621>, quoted as Greenwood et al., *Signal Code* (2017)

Human Rights Watch, *Policy Paper – The Meaning of 'the Interests of Justice' in Article 53 of the Rome Statute* (June 2005), <https://www.hrw.org/news/2005/06/01/meaning-interests-justice-article-53-rome-statute>, quoted as: HRW, *Interests of Justice* (2005)

ICC, *Booklet. Victims Before the International Criminal Court – A Guide for the Participation of Victims in the Proceedings of the Court* (undated), <https://www.


* This list only contains the most important documents referred to.

icc-cpi.int/sites/default/files/NR/rdonlyres/8FF91A2C-5274-4DCB-9CCE-37273C5E9AB4/282477/160910VPRSBookletEnglish.pdf>, quoted as: ICC, *Booklet* (undated)

ICC, *Chambers Practice Manual* (1 February 2016), <https://www.icc-cpi.int/sites/default/files/iccdocs/other/Chambers_practice_manual--FEBRUARY_2016.pdf>, quoted as: ICC, *Practice Manual* (2016)

ICC, *Chambers Practice Manual* (25 March 2022), <https://www.icc-cpi.int/sites/default/files/2022-06/20220323-chambers-practice-manual-fifth-edition-eng_2.pdf>, quoted as: ICC, *Practice Manual* (2022)

ICC, *Chambers Practice Manual* (13 July 2023), <https://www.icc-cpi.int/sites/default/files/2023-07/230707-chambers-manual-eng.pdf>, quoted as: ICC, *Practice Manual* (2023)

ICC, *Comprehensive Report on the Reorganisation of the Registry of the International Criminal Court* (August 2016), <https://www.icc-cpi.int/sites/default/files/itemsDocuments/ICC-Registry-CR.pdf>, quoted as: ICC, *Report Registry* (2016)

ICC, *Cooperation Agreements* (2023), < https://www.icc-cpi.int/sites/default/files/2024-01/2023-cooperation-agreements-v.3-rgb.pdf>, quoted as: ICC, *Cooperation Agreements* (2023)

ICC, *Guide for Applicants to the ICC - List of Counsel and Assistance to Counsel* (undated), <https://www.icc-cpi.int/sites/default/files/ICC_GuideForApplicants_ENG.pdf>, quoted as: ICC, *List of Counsel* (undated)

ICC, *Guidelines Governing the Relations between the Court and Intermediaries* (March 2014), <https://www.icc-cpi.int/sites/default/files/GRCI-Eng.pdf>, quoted as: ICC, *Guidelines Intermediaries* (2014)

ICC, *ICC Judges amend Code of Judicial Ethics,* Press Release (7 October 2022), <https://www.icc-cpi.int/news/icc-judges-amend-code-judicial-ethics-0>

ICC, *Information Sheet on the Defence* (undated), <https://www.icc-cpi.int/sites/default/files/Publications/DefenceENG.pdf>

ICC, *Overall Response of the International Criminal Court to the "Independent Expert review of the ICC and the Rome Statute System – Final Report". Preliminary Analysis of the Recommendations and information on relevant activities undertaken by the Court* (14 April 2021), <https://asp.icc-cpi.int/sites/asp/files/asp_docs/ASP20/Overall%20Response%20of%20the%20ICC%20to%20the%20IER%20Final%20Report%20-%20ENG%20-%2014April21.pdf>, quoted as: ICC, *IER Response* (2021)

ICC, *Registry's Single Policy Document on the Court's Legal Aid System* (4 June 2013), <https://asp.icc-cpi.int/sites/asp/files/asp_docs/ASP12/ICC-ASP-12-3-ENG.pdf>, quoted as: ICC, *Registry's Single Policy Document on the Court's Legal Aid System* (2013)

ICC, *Report of the Court on Key Performance Indicators* (2 June 2023), <https://www.icc-cpi.int/sites/default/files/2023-06/2022-Report-of-the-Court-on-KPIs.pdf>, quoted as: ICC, *Report Key Performance Indicators* (2022)

ICC, *Report of the Court on the development of performance indicators for the International Criminal Court* (12 November 2014), <https://www.icc-cpi.int/sites/default/files/itemsDocuments/Court_report-development_of_performance_indicators-ENG.pdf>, quoted as: ICC, *Report Performance Indicators* (2014)

ICC, *Report on the Adoption by the Judges of Provisional Amendments to Rule 165 of the Rules of Procedure and Evidence* (29 February 2016), <https://www.icc-cpi.int/iccd

ocs/PIDS/press/01-03-16_Report-Adoption-by-Judges-Provisional-Amendments_ENG.pdf>, quoted as: ICC, *Report Provisional Amendments Rules* (2016)

ICC, *Second Court's report on the development of performance indicators for the International Criminal Court* (11 November 2016), <https://www.icc-cpi.int/sites/default/files/itemsDocuments/ICC-Second-Court_report-on-indicators.pdf>, quoted as: ICC, *Second Report Performance Indicators* (2016)

ICC-ASP, *Consolidated Report of the Independent Oversight Mechanism on its Activities during 2013*, ICC-ASP/12/55 (6 November 2013), <https://asp.icc-cpi.int/sites/asp/files/asp_docs/ASP12/ICC-ASP-12-55-ENG.pdf>, quoted as: ICC-ASP, *Report IOM 2013* (2013)

ICC-ASP, *Proposed Programme Budget for 2006 of the International Criminal Court*, ICC ASP/4/5 (24 August 2005), <https://asp.icc-cpi.int/sites/asp/files/asp_docs/library/asp/ICC-ASP-4-5_English.pdf>, quoted as: ICC-ASP, *Budget* 2006

ICC-ASP, *Proposed Programme Budget for 2014 of the International Criminal Court*, ICC-ASP/12/10 (29 July 2013), <https://asp.icc-cpi.int/sites/asp/files/asp_docs/ASP12/ICC-ASP-12-10-ENG.pdf>, quoted as: ICC-ASP, *Budget* 2014

ICC-ASP, *Proposed Programme Budget for 2015 of the International Criminal Court*, ICC-ASP/13/10 (18 September 2014), <https://asp.icc-cpi.int/sites/asp/files/asp_docs/ASP13/ICC-ASP-13-10-ENG.pdf>, quoted as: ICC-ASP, *Budget* 2015

ICC-ASP, *Proposed Programme Budget for 2023 of the ICC*, ICC-ASP/21/10 (19 August 2022), <https://asp.icc-cpi.int/sites/asp/files/2022-08/ICC-ASP-21-10-ENG.pdf>, quoted as: ICC-ASP, *Budget 2023*

ICC-ASP, *Proposed Programme Budget for 2024 of the ICC*, ICC-ASP/22/10 (31 July 2023), <https://asp.icc-cpi.int/sites/default/files/asp_docs/ICC-ASP-22-10-ENG-PPB-2024-31jul23-1500.pdf>, quoted as: ICC-ASP, *Budget 2024*

ICC-ASP, *Proposed Programme Budget for 2025 of the ICC*, ICC-ASP/23/10 (24 July 2024), <https://asp.icc-cpi.int/sites/default/files/asp_docs/ICC-ASP-23-10-AV-ENG.pdf>, quoted as: ICC-ASP, *Budget 2025*

ICC-ASP, *Report of the Advisory Committee on Nominations of Judges on the work of its seventh session* (30 September 2020), ICC-ASP/19/11, <https://asp.icc-cpi.int/sites/asp/files/asp_docs/ASP19/ICC-ASP-19-11-ENG.pdf>, quoted as: ICC-ASP, *ACN Report* (2020)

ICC-ASP, *Report of the Advisory Committee on Nominations of Judges on the work of its ninth session* (31 July 2023), ICC-ASP/22/4, <https://asp.icc-cpi.int/sites/default/files/asp_docs/ICC-ASP-22-4-ACN9%20report-ENG-31Jul23.1800.pdf>, quoted as: ICC-ASP, *ACN Report* (2023)

ICC-ASP, *Report of the Bureau on Complementarity* (21 November 2022), ICC-ASP/21/19, <https://asp.icc-cpi.int/sites/asp/files/2022-12/ICC-ASP-21-19-ENG.pdf>, quoted as: ICC-ASP, *Report complementarity* (2022)

ICC-ASP, *Report of the Bureau on Cooperation* (21 November 2014), ICC-ASP/13/29, <https://asp.icc-cpi.int/sites/asp/files/asp_docs/ASP13/ICC-ASP-13-29-ENG.pdf>, quoted as: ICC-ASP, *Report Cooperation* (2014)

ICC-ASP, *Report of the Bureau on Cooperation* (7 December 2021), ICC-ASP/20/26, <https://asp.icc-cpi.int/sites/asp/files/asp_docs/ASP20/ICC-ASP-20-26-ENG.pdf>, quoted as: ICC-ASP, *Report Cooperation* (2021)

ICC-ASP, *Report of the Bureau on Cooperation* (2 December 2022), ICC-ASP/21/35, <https://asp.icc-cpi.int/sites/asp/files/2022-12/ICC-ASP-21-35-ENG.pdf>, quoted as: ICC-ASP, *Report Cooperation* (2022)

ICC-ASP, *Report of the Bureau on Cooperation* (13 December 2023), ICC-ASP/22/27, <https://asp.icc-cpi.int/sites/default/files/asp_docs/ICC-ASP-22-27-ENG.pdf>, quoted as: ICC-ASP, *Report Cooperation* (2023)

ICC-ASP, *Report of the Bureau on the Study Group on Governance* (22 November 2011), ICC-ASP/10/30, <https://www.icc-cpi.int/iccdocs/asp_docs/ASP10/ICC-ASP-10-30-ENG.pdf>, quoted as: ICC-ASP, *Report Governance* (2011)

ICC-ASP, *Report of the Bureau on the Study Group on Governance* (28 November 2014), ICC-ASP/13/28, <https://www.icc-cpi.int/iccdocs/asp_docs/ASP13/ICC-ASP-13-28-ENG.pdf>, quoted as: ICC-ASP, *Report Governance* (2014)

ICC-ASP, *Report of the Bureau on the Study Group on Governance* (16 November 2015), ICC-ASP/14/30, <https://www.icc-cpi.int/iccdocs/asp_docs/ASP14/ICC-ASP-14-30-ENG.pdf>, quoted as: ICC-ASP, *Report Governance* (2015)

ICC-ASP, *Report of the Bureau on the Study Group on Governance* (14 November 2016), ICC-ASP/15/21, <https://asp.icc-cpi.int/sites/asp/files/asp_docs/ASP15/ICC-ASP-15-21-ENG.pdf>, quoted as: ICC-ASP, *Report Governance* (2016)

ICC-ASP, *Report of the Bureau on the Study Group on Governance* (22 November 2017), ICC-ASP/16/19, <https://asp.icc-cpi.int/sites/asp/files/asp_docs/ASP16/ICC-ASP-16-19-ENG.pdf>, quoted as: ICC-ASP, *Report Governance* (2017)

ICC-ASP, *Report of the Bureau on the Study Group on Governance* (27 November 2018), ICC-ASP/17/30, <https://asp.icc-cpi.int/sites/asp/files/asp_docs/ASP17/ICC-ASP-17-30-ENG.pdf>, quoted as: ICC-ASP, *Report Governance* (2018)

ICC-ASP, *Report of the Bureau on the Study Group on Governance* (20 November 2019), ICC-ASP/18/27, <https://asp.icc-cpi.int/sites/asp/files/asp_docs/ASP18/ICC-ASP-18-27-ENG.pdf>, quoted as: ICC-ASP, *Report Governance* (2019)

ICC-ASP, *Report of the Bureau on the Study Group on Governance* (8 December 2020), ICC-ASP/19/21, <https://asp.icc-cpi.int/sites/asp/files/asp_docs/ASP19/ICC-ASP-19-21-ENG.pdf>, quoted as: ICC-ASP, *Report Governance* (2020)

ICC-ASP, *Report of the Bureau on the Study Group on Governance* (30 November 2021), ICC-ASP/20/21, <https://asp.icc-cpi.int/sites/asp/files/asp_docs/ASP20/ICC-ASP-20-21-ENG.pdf>, quoted as: ICC-ASP, *Report Governance* (2021)

ICC-ASP, *Report of the Bureau on the Study Group on Governance* (29 November 2022), ICC-ASP/21/18, <https://asp.icc-cpi.int/sites/asp/files/2022-11/ICC-ASP-21-18-ENG.pdf>, quoted as: ICC-ASP, *Report Governance* (2022)

ICC-ASP, *Report of the Bureau on the Study Group on Governance* (29 November 2023), ICC-ASP/22/7, <https://asp.icc-cpi.int/sites/default/files/asp_docs/ICC-ASP-22-7-ENG.pdf>, quoted as: ICC-ASP, *Report Governance* (2023)

ICC-ASP, *Report of the Committee on the Election of the Prosecutor* (30 June 2020), ICC-ASP/19/INF.2, <https://asp.icc-cpi.int/iccdocs/asp_docs/ASP19/ICC-ASP-19-INF2-ENG-CEP.pdf>, quoted as: ICC-ASP, *Election Prosecutor* (2020)

ICC-ASP, *Report of the Court on Cooperation* (23 October 2014), ICC-ASP/13/23, <https://asp.icc-cpi.int/sites/asp/files/asp_docs/ASP13/ICC-ASP-13-23-ENG.pdf>, quoted as: ICC-ASP, *Cooperation* (2014)

ICC-ASP, *Report of the Court on Principles Relating to Victims' Reparation*, ICC-ASP/12/39 (8 October 2013), <https://asp.icc-cpi.int/sites/asp/files/asp_docs/ASP12/ICC-ASP-12-39-ENG.pdf>, quoted as: ICC-ASP, *Report Victims' Reparation* (2013)

ICC-ASP, *Report of the Court on the Basic Size of the Office of the Prosecutor* (7 August 2015), ICC-ASP/14/21, <https://www.icc-cpi.int/iccdocs/asp_docs/ASP14/ICC-ASP-14-21-ENG.pdf>, quoted as: ICC-ASP, *Basic Size* (2015)

ICC-ASP, *Report of the Court on the Review of the System for Victims to Apply to Participate in Proceedings*, ICC-ASP/11/22 (5 November 2012), <https://asp.icc-cpi.int/sites/asp/files/asp_docs/ASP11/ICC-ASP-11-22-ENG.pdf>, quoted as: ICC-ASP, *Report Victims to Participate* (2012)

ICC-ASP, *Report of the Court on the Status* of Ongoing Cooperation between the ICC and the UN, Including in the Field (14 October 2013), ICC-ASP/12/42, *<https://asp.icc-cpi.int/sites/asp/files/asp_docs/ASP12/ICC-ASP-12-42-ENG.pdf>, quoted as: ICC-ASP, Ongoing* Cooperation (2013)

ICC-ASP, *Report of the Review Mechanism on the overall progress of its work* (30 June 2023), <https://asp.icc-cpi.int/sites/default/files/asp_docs/RM-report-overall-progress-2023.pdf>, quoted as: ICC-ASP, *Review* (2023)

ICC-ASP, *Report on the Conditions of Service and Compensation of the Prosecutor and the Deputy Prosecutors pursuant the Paragraph 26 of Resolution ICC-ASP/3/Res. 3*, ICC-ASP/4/11 (9 August 2005), <https://asp.icc-cpi.int/sites/asp/files/asp_docs/library/asp/ICC-ASP-4-11_English.pdf>, quoted as: ICC-ASP, *Conditions and Compensation* (2005)

ICC-ASP, *Resolution ICC–ASP/8/Res. 9* (25 March 2010), <https://asp.icc-cpi.int/sites/asp/files/asp_docs/Resolutions/ICC-ASP-8-Res.9-ENG.pdf>, quoted as: *Resolution ICC-ASP/8/Res.9*

ICC-ASP, *Resolution ICC–ASP/11/Res. 6* – Complementarity (21 November 2012), <https://asp.icc-cpi.int/sites/asp/files/asp_docs/Resolutions/ASP11/ICC-ASP-11-Res6-ENG.pdf>, quoted as: *Resolution ICC–ASP/11/Res. 6*

ICC-ASP, *Resolution ICC–ASP/12/Res. 4* – Complementarity (27 November 2013), <https://asp.icc-cpi.int/sites/asp/files/asp_docs/Resolutions/ASP12/ICC-ASP-12-Res4-ENG.pdf>, quoted as: *Resolution ICC–ASP/12/Res. 4*

ICC-ASP, *Second Report of the Court on the financial implications of the draft Guidelines governing the relations between the Court and Intermediaries*, ICC-ASP/12/53 (30 October 2013), <https://asp.icc-cpi.int/sites/asp/files/asp_docs/ASP12/ICC-ASP-12-53-ENG.pdf>, quoted as: ICC-ASP, *Report Court and Intermediaries* (2013)

ICC-ASP, *Second Session, New York, 8–12 September 2003, Official Records*

ICC-ASP, *Third Session, The Hague, 6–10 September 2004, Official Records*

ICC-ASP Secretariat, *The Hague Working Group, Complementarity* (1 October 2021), Summary, <https://asp.icc-cpi.int/sites/asp/files/asp_docs/ASP20/Compl.%204%20summary.pdf>, quoted as: ASP, *Complementarity* (2021)

ICC-ASP, *Study Group on Governance—Lessons Learnt—First Report of the Court to the Assembly of States Parties* (23 October 2012), ICC-ASP/11/31/Add.1, <https://www.icc-cpi.int/iccdocs/asp_docs/ASP11/ICC-ASP-11-31-Add1-ENG.pdf>, quoted as: ICC-ASP, *First Report* (2012)

ICC-ASP, *Study Group on Governance Working Group on Lessons Learnt—Second Report of the Court to the Assembly of States Parties* (31 October 2013), ICC-ASP/12/37/Add.1, <https://www.icc-cpi.int/iccdocs/asp_docs/ASP12/ICC-ASP-12-37-Add1-ENG.pdf>, quoted as: ICC-ASP, *Second Report* (2013)

ICC-OTP, *Draft Paper – Criteria* for *Selection of Situation and Cases* (June 2006), quoted as: ICC-OTP, *Draft Selection* (2006)

ICC-OTP, *First Public Hearing of the Office of the Prosecutor* (17 and 18 June 2003), <https://www.icc-cpi.int/news/public-hearings>, quoted as: ICC-OTP, *First Hearing* (2003)

ICC-OTP, *Guidelines for Agreements Regarding Admission of Guilt* (October 2020), <https://www.icc-cpi.int/sites/default/files/itemsDocuments/20201009-Guidelines-for-agreement-regarding-admission-of-guilt-eng.pdf>, quoted as: ICC-OTP, *Guidelines Admission of Guilt* (2020)

ICC-OTP, *Informal Expert Paper—Measures Available to the International Criminal Court to Reduce the Length of Proceedings* (2003), <https://www.icc-cpi.int/NR/rdonlyres/20BB4494-70F9-4698-8E30-907F631453ED/281982/length_of_proceedings.pdf>, quoted as: ICC-OTP, *Length of Proceedings* (2003)

ICC-OTP, *Informal expert paper: Fact-finding and investigative functions of the office of the Prosecutor, including international co-operation* (2003), < https://www.icc-cpi.int/sites/default/files/NR/rdonlyres/20BB4494-70F9-4698-8E30-907F631453ED/281983/state_cooperation.pdf>, quoted as: ICC-OTP, Fact-finding (2003)

ICC-OTP, *Informal Expert Paper—The Principle of Complementarity in Practice* (2003), <https://www.icc-cpi.int/sites/default/files/NR/rdonlyres/20BB4494-70F9-4698-8E30-907F631453ED/281984/complementarity.pdf>, quoted as: ICC-OTP, *Complementarity* (2003)

ICC-OTP, *Paper on Some Policy Issues before the Office of the Prosecutor* (September 2003), <https://www.icc-cpi.int/sites/default/files/NR/rdonlyres/1FA7C4C6-DE5F-42B7-8B25-60AA962ED8B6/143594/030905_Policy_Paper.pdf>, quoted as: ICC-OTP, *Policy Issues* (2003)

ICC-OTP, *Annex to the 'Paper on Some Policy Issues before the Office of the Prosecutor': Referrals and Communications* (2003), <https://www.icc-cpi.int/NR/rdonlyres/278614ED-A8CA-4835-B91D-DB7FA7639E02/143706/policy_annex_final_210404.pdf>, quoted as: ICC-OTP, *Referrals and Communications* (2003)

ICC-OTP, *Policy on Children* (15 November 2016), <https://www.icc-cpi.int/sites/default/files/20161115_OTP_ICC_Policy-on-Children_Eng.PDF>, quoted as: ICC-OTP, *Policy Children* (2016)

ICC-OTP, *Policy on Children* (1 December 2023), <https://www.icc-cpi.int/sites/default/files/2023-12/2023-policy-children-en-web.pdf>, quoted as: ICC-OTP, *Policy Children* (2023)

ICC-OTP, *Policy on Complementarity and Cooperation* (April 2024), <https://www.icc-cpi.int/news/policy-complementarity-and-cooperation-2024>, quoted as: ICC-OTP, *Complementarity and Cooperation* (2024)

ICC-OTP, *Policy on Cultural Heritage* (14 June 2021), <https://www.icc-cpi.int/sites/default/files/itemsDocuments/20210614-otp-policy-cultural-heritage-eng.pdf>, quoted as: ICC-OTP, *Policy Cultural Heritage* (2021)

ICC-OTP, *Policy on Situation Completion* (15 June 2021), <https://www.icc-cpi.int/sites/default/files/itemsDocuments/20210615-Situation-Completion-Policy-eng.pdf>, quoted as: ICC-OTP, *Policy Situation Completion* (2021)

ICC-OTP, *Policy on the Crime of Gender Persecution* (7 December 2022), <https://www.icc-cpi.int/sites/default/files/2022-12/2022-12-07-Policy-on-the-Crime-of-Gender-Persecution.pdf>, quoted as: ICC-OTP, *Policy Gender Persecution* (2022)

ICC-OTP, *Policy on Gender-Based Crimes* (1 December 2023), <https://www.icc-cpi.int/sites/default/files/2023-12/2023-policy-gender-en-web.pdf>, quoted as: ICC-OTP, *Policy Gender-Based Crimes* (2023)

ICC-OTP, *Policy Paper on the Interests of Justice* (September 2007), <http://www.icc-cpi.int/NR/rdonlyres/772C95C9-F54D-4321-BF09-73422BB23528/143640/ICCOTPInterestsOfJustice.pdf>, quoted as: ICC-OTP, *Interests of Justice* (2007)

ICC-OTP, *Policy Paper on Victims' Participation* (12 April 2010), <https://www.icc-cpi.int/iccdocs/asp_docs/RC2010/RC-ST-V-M.1-ENG.pdf>, quoted as: ICC-OTP, *Policy Victims' Participation* (2010)

ICC-OTP, *Policy Paper on Preliminary Examinations* (November 2013), <https://www.icc-cpi.int/sites/default/files/iccdocs/otp/OTP-Policy_Paper_Preliminary_Examinations_2013-ENG.pdf>, quoted as: ICC-OTP, *Policy Prelim. Examinations* (2013) [now 'under revision', <https://www.icc-cpi.int/news/policy-paper-preliminary-examinations-under-revision>]

ICC-OTP, *Policy Paper on Sexual and Gender Based Crimes* (February 2014), <https://www.icc-cpi.int/iccdocs/otp/OTP-draft-policy-paper-February2014-Eng.pdf>, quoted as: ICC-OTP, *Policy Sexual Crimes* (2014)

ICC-OTP, *Policy Paper on Case Selection and Prioritisation* (15 September 2016), <https://www.icc-cpi.int/sites/default/files/20160915_OTP-Policy_Case-Selection_Eng.pdf>, quoted as: ICC-OTP, *Policy Case Selection* (2016)

ICC-OTP, *Prosecutorial Strategy 2009–2012* (1 February 2010), <https://www.icc-cpi.int/NR/rdonlyres/66A8DCDC-3650-4514-AA62-D229D1128F65/281506/OTPProsecutorialStrategy20092013.pdf>, quoted as: ICC-OTP, *Prosecutorial Strategy* (2010)

ICC-OTP, *Report on the Activities Performed during the First Three Years (June 2003-June 2006)* (12 September 2006), <http://www.icc-cpi.int/NR/rdonlyres/70CB178C-15C7-4BDB-B09E-9E93CEF0E165/143610/3yearreport20060914_English.pdf>, quoted as: ICC-OTP, *Report Activities* (2006)

ICC-OTP, *Report on Prosecutorial Strategy* (14 September 2006), <https://www.icc-cpi.int/NR/rdonlyres/D673DD8C-D427-4547-BC69-2D363E07274B/143708/ProsecutorialStrategy20060914_English.pdf>, quoted as: ICC-OTP, *Prosecutorial Strategy* (2006)

ICC-OTP, *Report on Preliminary Examination Activities* (13 December 2011), <https://www.icc-cpi.int/NR/rdonlyres/63682F4E-49C8-445D-8C13-F310A4F3AEC2/284116/OTPReportonPreliminaryExaminations13December2011.pdf>, quoted as: ICC-OTP, *Prelim. Examination* (2011)

ICC-OTP, *Report on Preliminary Examination Activities 2012* (November 2012), <https://www.icc-cpi.int/NR/rdonlyres/C433C462-7C4E-4358-8A72-8D99FD00E8CD/285209/OTP2012ReportonPreliminaryExaminations22Nov2012.pdf>, quoted as: ICC-OTP, *Prelim. Examination* (2012)

ICC-OTP, *Report on Preliminary Examination Activities 2013* (November 2013), <https://www.icc-cpi.int/sites/default/files/itemsDocuments/OTP%20Preliminary%20Examinations/OTP%20-%20Report%20%20Preliminary%20Examination%20Activities%202013.PDF>, quoted as: ICC-OTP, *Prelim. Examinations* (2013)

ICC-OTP, *Report on Preliminary Examination Activities 2014* (2 December 2014), <https://www.icc-cpi.int/iccdocs/otp/OTP-Pre-Exam-2014.pdf>, quoted as: ICC-OTP, *Prelim. Examinations* (2014)

ICC-OTP, *Report on Preliminary Examination Activities (2015)* (12 November 2015), <https://www.icc-cpi.int/iccdocs/otp/OTP-PE-rep-2015-Eng.pdf>, quoted as: ICC-OTP, *Prelim. Examinations* (2015)

ICC-OTP, *Report on Preliminary Examination Activities (2016)* (14 November 2016), <https://www.icc-cpi.int/sites/default/files/iccdocs/otp/161114-otp-rep-PE_ENG.pdf>, quoted as: ICC-OTP, *Prelim. Examinations* (2016)

ICC-OTP, *Report on Preliminary Examination Activities (2017)* (4 December 2017), <https://www.icc-cpi.int/sites/default/files/itemsDocuments/2017-PE-rep/2017-otp-rep-PE_ENG.pdf>, quoted as: ICC-OTP, *Prelim. Examinations* (2017)

ICC-OTP, *Report on Preliminary Examination Activities (2018)* (5 December 2018), <https://www.icc-cpi.int/sites/default/files/itemsDocuments/181205-rep-otp-PE-ENG.pdf>, quoted as: ICC-OTP, *Prelim. Examinations* (2018)

ICC-OTP, *Report on Preliminary Examination Activities (2019)* (5 December 2019), <https://www.icc-cpi.int/sites/default/files/itemsDocuments/191205-rep-otp-PE.pdf>, quoted as: ICC-OTP, *Prelim. Examinations* (2019)

ICC-OTP, *Report on Preliminary Examination Activities (2020)* (14 December 2020), <https://www.icc-cpi.int/sites/default/files/itemsDocuments/2020-PE/2020-pe-report-eng.pdf>, quoted as: ICC-OTP, *Prelim. Examinations* (2020)

ICC-OTP, *Report on the Situation in Mali – Article 53 (1)* (16 January 2013) <https://www.icc-cpi.int/sites/default/files/itemsDocuments/SASMaliArticle53_1PublicReportENG16Jan2013.pdf>, quoted as: ICC-OTP, *Situation* in Mali (2013)

ICC-OTP, Report on the Situation in Nigeria: Article 5 Report (5 August 2013), <https://www.icc-cpi.int/sites/default/files/iccdocs/PIDS/docs/SAS%20-%20NGA%20-%20Public%20version%20Article%205%20Report%20-%2005%20August%202013.PDF>, quoted as: ICC-OTP, *Situation in Nigeria* (2013)

ICC-OTP, *Report on the Situation in the Central African Republic II – Article 53 (1)* (24 September 2014), <https://www.icc-cpi.int/sites/default/files/iccdocs/otp/Art_53_1_Report_CAR_II_24Sep14.pdf>, quoted as: ICC-OTP, *Situation in the Central African Republic II* (2014)

ICC-OTP, *Report on the Situation on Registered Vessels of Comoros, Greece and Cambodia – Article 53 (1)* (6 November 2014), <https://www.icc-cpi.int/sites/default/files/iccdocs/otp/OTP-COM-Article_53(1)-Report-06Nov2014Eng.pdf>, quoted as: ICC-OTP, *Situation on Registered Vessels of Comoros, Greece and Cambodia* (2014)

ICC-OTP, *Situation in Iraq/UK. Final Report* (9 December 2020), <https://www.icc-cpi.int/sites/default/files/itemsDocuments/201209-otp-final-report-iraq-uk-eng.pdf>, quoted as: ICC-OTP, *Iraq/UK Final Report* (2020)

ICC-OTP, *Report on the Situation in Colombia (2023)* (30 November 2023), <https://www.icc-cpi.int/sites/default/files/2023-11/2023-11-30-otp-report-colombia-eng.pdf>, quoted as: ICC-OTP, *Report on Colombia*, (2023)

ICC-OTP, *Second Public Hearing of the Office of the Prosecutor* (The Hague, 25/26 September 2006 and New York 17/18 October 2006), <https://www.icc-cpi.int/sites/default/files/iccdocs/otp/OTP_PH2_HGNGO.pdf>, quoted as: ICC-OTP, *Second Hearing* (2006)

ICC-OTP, *Eighth Report of the Prosecutor of the International Criminal Court of the UN Security Council pursuant to UNSCR 1593 (2005)* (3 December 2008), <https://www.icc-cpi.int/sites/default/files/iccdocs/otp/otp-report-UNSCR%201970-11-11-2014-Eng.pdf>, quoted as: ICC-OTP, *Eighth Report Prosecutor* (2008)

ICC-OTP, *Statement by Luis Moreno Ocampo – Informal Meeting of Legal Advisors of Ministries of Foreign Affairs* (24 October 2005), <https://www.icc-cpi.int/sites/default/files/NR/rdonlyres/9D70039E-4BEC-4F32-9D4A-CEA8B6799E37/143836/LMO_20051024_English.pdf>, quoted as: ICC-OTP, *Statement Moreno Ocampo* (2005)

ICC-OTP, *Statement of the Prosecutor of the ICC, Fatou Bensouda, on opening a new Preliminary Examination in Central African Republic* (7 February 2014), <https://www.icc-cpi.int/news/statement-prosecutor-international-criminal-court-fatou-bensouda-opening-new-preliminary>, quoted as: ICC-OTP, *Statement Bensouda CAR* (2014)

ICC-OTP, *Statement of the Prosecutor of the ICC, Fatou Bensouda, on the conclusion of the preliminary examination of the situation in Nigeria* (11 December 2020), <https://www.icc-cpi.int/news/statement-prosecutor-fatou-bensouda-conclusion-preliminary-examination-situation-nigeria>, quoted as: ICC-OTP, *Statement Bensouda Nigeria* (2020)

ICC-OTP, *Statement of the Prosecutor of the ICC, Fatou Bensouda, on the conclusion of the preliminary examination of the Situation in Palestine, and seeking a ruling on the scope of the Court's territorial jurisdiction* (20 December 2019), <https://www.icc-cpi.int/news/statement-icc-prosecutor-fatou-bensouda-conclusion-preliminary-examination-situation-palestine>, quoted as: ICC-OTP, *Statement Bensouda Palestine* (2019)

ICC-OTP, *Statement of the Prosecutor of the ICC, Karim A. A. Khan QC, following the application for an expedited order under article 18(2) seeking authorisation to resume investigations in the Situation in Afghanistan* (27 September 2021), <https://www.icc-cpi.int/news/statement-prosecutor-international-criminal-court-karim-khan-qc-following-application>, quoted as: ICC-OTP, *Statement Khan Afghanistan* (2021)

ICC-OTP, Statement of ICC Prosecutor, Karim A.A. Khan QC: Contributions and support from States Parties will accelerate action across our investigations, 28 March 2022, <https://www.icc-cpi.int/news/statement-icc-prosecutor-karim-aa-khan-qc-contributions-and-support-states-parties-will>, quoted as: ICC-OTP, *Statement Khan Ukraine* (March 2022)

ICC-OTP, Statement by ICC Prosecutor, Karim A.A. Khan QC: Office of the Prosecutor joins national authorities in Joint Investigation Team on international crimes committed in Ukraine, 25 April 2022, <https://www.icc-cpi.int/news/statement-icc-prosecutor-karim-aa-khan-qc-office-prosecutor-joins-national-authorities-joint>, quoted as: ICC-OTP, *Statement Khan JIT Ukraine* (April 2022)

ICC-OTP, ICC Prosecutor Karim A.A. Khan QC announces deployment of forensics and investigative team to Ukraine, welcomes strong cooperation with the Government of the Netherlands, 17 May 2022, <https://www.icc-cpi.int/news/icc-prosecutor-karim-aa-khan-qc-announces-deployment-forensics-and-investigative-team-ukraine>, quoted as: ICC-OTP, *Statement Khan Ukraine* (May 2022)

ICC OTP, Statement of ICC Prosecutor, Karim A. A. Khan KC, to the United Nations Security Council on the Situation in Darfur, pursuant to Resolution 1593 (2005), 26 January 2023, <https://www.icc-cpi.int/news/statement-icc-prosecutor-karim-khan-kc-united-nations-security-council-situation-darfur> quoted as: ICC-OTP, *Statement Khan Darfur* (2023)

ICC-OTP, *Strategic Plan June 2012–2015* (11 October 2013), <https://www.icc-cpi.int/sites/default/files/iccdocs/otp/OTP-Strategic-Plan-2013.pdf>, quoted as: ICC-OTP, *Strategic Plan* (2013)

ICC-OTP, *Strategic Plan 2016–2018* (6 November 2015), <https://www.icc-cpi.int/iccdocs/otp/070715-OTP_Strategic_Plan_2016-2018.pdf>, quoted as: ICC-OTP, *Strategic Plan* (2015)

ICC-OTP, *Strategic Plan 2016–2018* (6 July 2015), <https://www.icc-cpi.int/sites/default/files/iccdocs/otp/070715-OTP_Strategic_Plan_2016-2018.pdf>, quoted as: ICC-OTP, *Strategic Plan* (2015);

ICC-OTP, *Strategic Plan 2019–2021* (17 July 2019), <https://www.icc-cpi.int/sites/default/files/itemsDocuments/20190726-strategic-plan-eng.pdf>, quoted as: ICC-OTP, *Strategic Plan* (2019)

ICC-OTP, *Strategic Plan 2023–2025* (13 June 2023), <https://www.icc-cpi.int/sites/default/files/2023-08/2023-strategic-plan-otp-v.3.pdf>, quoted as: ICC-OTP, *Strategic Plan* (2023)

ICC-OTP, *Third Report of the Prosecutor of the International Criminal Court to the UN Security Council pursuant to UNSCR 1593 (2005)* (14 June 2006), <https://www.icc-cpi.int/sites/default/files/NR/rdonlyres/E61D7F34-7D21-44B9-8840-53B254172AF7/0/OTP_ReportUNSC_3Darfur_English.pdf>, quoted as: *Report Prosecutor UNSC* (2006)

ICC-OTP, *Towards a more just world every day. Annual Report of the Office of the Prosecutor – 2022* (1 December 2022), <https://www.icc-cpi.int/news/annual-report-office-prosecutor-2022>, quoted as: ICC-OTP, *Report 2022* (2022)

ICC-OTP, *Delivering better together. Annual Report of the Office of the Prosecutor – 2023* (6 December 2023), <https://www.icc-cpi.int/sites/default/files/2023-12/2023-otp-annual-report.pdf>, quoted as: ICC-OTP, *Report 2023* (2023)

ICTY, *Defence Counsel – Pre-Trial Legal Aid Policy* (1 May 2006), <https://www.icty.org/en/documents/defence> quoted as: ICTY, *Pre-Trial Legal Aid Policy* (2006)

ICTY, *Defence Counsel - Trial Legal Aid Policy* (1 November 2009), <https://www.icty.org/x/file/About/Defence/trial_legal_aid_policy_2009.pdf>, quoted as: ICTY, *Trial Legal Aid Policy* (2009)

ICTY, *Manual on Developed Practices* (Turin: UNICRI Publisher, 2009), <http://www.icty.org/x/file/About/Reports%20and%20Publications/manual_developed_practices/icty_manual_on_developed_practices.pdf>, quoted as: ICTY, *Manual Practices* (2009)

ILA (Committee on Complementarity), Complementarity in International Criminal Law, adopted at the Lisbon Conference as Resolution 4/2022 (June 2022), <https://www.ila-hq.org/en_GB/documents/re5558-1>, Report available at <https://www.ila-hq.org/en_GB/documents/ila-report-complementarity-lisbon-final-corrected-0223-1>, quoted as: ILA, *Positive Complementarity* (2022)

ILC, *Draft Code of Offences against the Peace and Security of Mankind*, in Yearbook of the International Law Commission, Vol. 2, Part 1 (46th Session, 1954), 21–96, <https://legal.un.org/ilc/texts/instruments/english/draft_articles/7_3_1954.pdf>, quoted as: ILC, *Draft Code 1954*

ILC, *The Obligation to Extradite or Prosecute (aut dedere aut iudicare)*, Final Report of the ILC (2014), <https://legal.un.org/ilc/texts/instruments/english/reports/7_6_2014.pdf>, quoted as: ILC, *Obligation to Extradite or Prosecute* (2014)

KSC, *Registry Practice Direction - Directive on Counsel* (22 February 2022, Rev. 2), <https://www.scp-ks.org/en/documents/directive-counsel>, quoted as: KSC, *Directive on Counsel*

KSC, *Registry Practice Direction - Legal Aid Regulations & KSC Annex C to Legal Aid Regulations (KSC-BD-25-Annex C)*, (20 September 2020), <https://www.scp-ks.org/sites/default/files/public/content/documents/ksc-bd-25-legalaidregulation-public.pdf>, quoted as: KSC, *Legal Aid Regulations*

Leiden Guidelines on Digitally Derived Evidence in International Criminal Courts and Tribunals (2022), <https://leiden-guidelines.com/guidelines/>, quoted as: Leiden Guidelines (2022)

Mettraux, G., Fisher, S. A., Groome, D., Whiting, A., McIntyre, G., De Hemptinne, J., and Sluiter, G., *Expert Initiative on Promoting Effectiveness at the International Criminal*

*Court* (December 2014), <https://papers.ssrn.com/sol3/papers.cfm?abstract_id=2659331>, quoted as: Mettraux et al., *Effectiveness ICC* (2014)

OHCHR and Human Rights Center at UC Berkeley School of Law, *Berkeley Protocol on Digital Open Source Investigations: A Practical Guide on the Effective Use of Digital Open Source and Information in Investigating Violations of International Criminal, Human Rights and Humanitarian Law* (2022), <https://www.ohchr.org/en/publications/policy-and-methodological-publications/berkeley-protocol-digital-open-source>, quoted as: OCHR and Human Rights Center, *Berkeley Protocol on Digital Open Source Investigations* (2022)

Princeton Project on Universal Jurisdiction, *The Princeton Principles on Universal Jurisdiction* (Princeton: Program in Law and Public Affairs Princeton University, 2001), <http://hrlibrary.umn.edu/instree/princeton.html>, quoted as: Princeton, *Universal Jurisdiction* (2001)

Trust Fund for Victims, *The impact of our programmes* (2024), <https://www.trustfundforvictims.org/en/about/our-impact/programme-impact>, quoted as; TFV, *Impact* (2024)

UN Human Rights Council, *Report of Independent International Fact-Finding Mission on Myanmar* (27 August 2018), <https://www.ohchr.org/en/hr-bodies/hrc/myanmar-ffm/reportofthe-myanmar-ffm>, quoted as: HRC, *Myanmar Report* (2018)

UN Security Council, *Report of the Secretary-General Pursuant to Paragraph 2 of Security Council Resolution 808* (1993), UN doc. S/25707 (3 May 1993), <http://www.icty.org/x/file/Legal%20Library/Statute/statute_re808_1993_en.pdf>, quoted as: UN Security Council, *Resolution 808* (1993)

UN Security Council, *Report of the Secretary-General pursuant to Paragraph 5 of Security Council Resolution 955* (1994), UN doc. S/1995/134 (13 February 1995), <http://www.un.org/en/ga/search/view_doc.asp?symbol=S/1995/134>, quoted as: UN Security Council, *Resolution 955* (1994)

# Index of Names

*For the benefit of digital users, indexed terms that span two pages (e.g., 52–53) may, on occasion, appear on only one of those pages.*

# Index of Subjects

*For the benefit of digital users, indexed terms that span two pages (e.g., 52–53) may, on occasion, appear on only one of those pages.*

Figures are indicated by an italic *f* following the page number.

ICC = International Criminal Court
ICTR = International Criminal Tribunal for Rwanda
ICTY = International Criminal Tribunal for the former Yugoslavia
SCSL = Special Court for Sierra Leone (SCSL)